A Dictionary
of Biblical Tradition
in
English Literature

A Dictionary
of Biblical Tradition
in
English Literature

David Lyle Jeffrey

GENERAL EDITOR

WILLIAM B. EERDMANS PUBLISHING COMPANY
GRAND RAPIDS, MICHIGAN

Distributed in Europe by Gracewing
2 Southern Avenue
Leominster HR6 0QF
England
Gracewing ISBN 0 85244 224 6

Printed in the United States of America

Library of Congress Cataloging-in-Publication Data

A Dictionary of biblical tradition in English literature /
general editor, David Lyle Jeffrey.
p.   cm.
Includes bibliographical references.
ISBN 0-8028-3634-8
1. English literature—Dictionaries.   2. Religion and
literature—Dictionaries.   3. Bible in literature—Dictionaries.
I. Jeffrey, David L., 1941-   .
PR149.B5D53   1992
820.9'382'03—dc20   92-30648
                                                    CIP

for Gideon and Joshua

‏. . . לְהוֹדִיעָם לִבְנֵיהֶם: לְמַעַן‎

‏יֵדְעוּ דּוֹר אַחֲרוֹן . . .‎

— Ps. 78:5-6

Contents

Acknowledgments

This volume would not have been possible without the participation of a large and diversified team of collaborating scholars. Among the more than 200 persons who contributed in one way or another to the *Dictionary of Biblical Tradition in English Literature,* the Associate Editor for Biblical Studies and hard-working board of editorial advisers each reviewed and offered editorial suggestions for entries. Their patience, good will, and perseverance were a repeated source of refurbishment, moreover, when my own energies were flagging. The contributors themselves, many of whom have waited as much as a decade to see their work appear in its final form, and have graciously consented to revisions suggested in the course of a complex and demanding editorial process, have provided the very fabric of this Dictionary, brick by brick and stone by stone.

In the earliest stages of planning, W. W. Gasque (then of Regent College) was an enthusiastic co-conspirator, boundless in his conviction that the work would prove worthwhile, and instrumental in obtaining the material cooperation of many others. Though in failing health, Samuel Sandmel provided valued early encouragement to the project; other early supporters include Sacvan Bercovitch, James Reaney, Roland Mushat Frye, Leo Damrosch, and Pierre Savard. I am grateful that the University of Ottawa, notably through the offices of Paul Hagen and Marcel Hamelin, supported the work in a variety of practical ways, as did also the Social Sciences and Humanities Research Council of Canada, which underwrote the cost of a full-time research assistant for three years (1983-86).

I have been blessed with a number of able graduate research assistants: among those who worked for me on the Dictionary at various times over the last twelve years I want to thank especially Gary Hauch, Linda Hauch, Jennifer Bradshaw, Marnie Parsons, Tobi Christensen, and Patricia Sunderland, to each of whom I owe a special debt for cheerfully performing a variety of tedious, even mind-numbing tasks. Individual scholars from many quarters generously offered practical assistance at various points: Ruth Dean, Catherine Brown Tkacz, and Sol Liptzin shared bibliographical resources. And among my own departmental colleagues, Cam La Bossière, John Hill, and Dominic Manganiello spiritedly dug in at the eleventh hour and helped with the weighty burden of defaulted entries — comradeship under pressure for which I am abidingly grateful.

In a project of this magnitude, editorial and production staff at the Press play a crucial role. Milton Essenburg and especially Charles Van Hof have, by their practical encouragement as well as patient and thoughtful labors, proved indispensable collaborators. What chaff here remains is not from any lack of effort on their part to sweep my threshing floor clean.

The DBTEL has been many years in the making — long enough that some of the people deserving to be acknowledged for their active support or participation have not lived to see the fruits of their labors. Among the editorial advisers, F. F. Bruce was a particular strength; Peter Craigie, J. G. Davies, Joseph E. Duncan, Herbert Giesbrecht, David Greenwood, Colin Hemer, Sarah Horrall, Mark S. Madoff, and Joseph McClatchey are among valued contributors who, I regret, have not been able to review their work in print.

* * *

Almost everyone who undertakes work of this kind reflects at some point with bittersweet whimsy on Dr. Samuel Johnson's definition of the dictionary-maker as a "harmless drudge." Yet for those upon whom life visits the experience, this quotable advertisement can seem self-deceived. It is the adjective which tells the lie; the dictionary-maker is far from harmless — especially to those most near and dear, from whom are stolen the thousands of hours which otherwise might go to family life. My wife Katherine has coped with the many and often ignominious ills of her situation by the ingenious (and

ACKNOWLEDGMENTS

costly) stratagem of working alongside me for the last ten years. In many ways, let it be plainly said, she is more to be credited with the completion of the *Dictionary of Biblical Tradition in English Literature* than I am myself. But our two young sons, unable to devise a comparable expedient at this stage of their lives, have deserved much better than they have gotten from their parents for too long a time. The dedication of this volume, at last, implies a commitment afresh to them, for whom we are so thankful, and to whom we would entrust all that matters, *dor le dor,* not only of the work we have been enabled to do, but of the love which kept us to it.

DLJ
Windhover Farm
Spencerville, Ontario
June 2, 1992

Preface

To understand something of the Bible, and of its transmission in and through English literature, is to reckon sympathetically with the development of English cultural consciousness in its richest and most coherent levels of expression. Matthew Arnold recognized this when, in *God and the Bible* and *Literature and Dogma* especially, he wrestled with the late-nineteenth-century "problem" of how to preserve the cultural richness and coherence of biblical tradition while somehow getting out from under the Bible's religious and ethical constraints. Though subsequently admired and imitated, Arnold's secularizing archivalism largely failed to achieve its stated objective. Yet it is no less widely recognized now than a century ago that for literature in the English-speaking world no text has continued to exert a more formative influence than the Bible, and, correspondingly, that the fading recognition of biblical narrative, especially in the second half of the twentieth century, has shadowed into nearly intractable obscurity many of the greatest secular texts in our literary heritage. Indeed, the need for recovery of biblical tradition is perhaps more urgent now than Arnold could have anticipated.

These factors have contributed to a recent dramatic increase of critical interest in the Bible *as* literature. At the same time, literally hundreds of books and articles have appeared which try to recover for modern readers an appreciation of the role of the Bible *in* literature. These studies are diffuse and widely targeted, with many of the most valuable known only to specialized literary scholars working on a given body of texts on which the articles or books are focused. Meanwhile, the few works of general reference which have been available to map this scholarly and critical effort at recovery often remain inadequate to the needs of students or serious general readers whose cultural memory comprises only a sketchy or fragmentary biblical literacy. It is in this context that *A Dictionary of Biblical Tradition in English Literature* was conceived. It has been designed to help meet the evident need for a general reference guide to an already compendious and still growing field of critical inquiry. In addition, it is intended to provide initial guidance for further, more focused particular study, and so offers extensive (if still select) bibliographies in basic biblical studies, in the history of biblical interpretation, and of the presence of the Bible in works of English literature.

The general plan of the *Dictionary* may be briefly described as follows:

Form of the Entries

Each of the more important alphabetically listed entries normally consists of three parts, sometimes written by more than one author but edited for continuity by the editors. The entry describes how the word or phrase has been understood and used: (a) in the Bible; (b) in exegetical tradition, including Jewish commentators, the church fathers, and exegetical writers by period, especially those whose influence has been well established (e.g., Aqiba, Rashi, St. Augustine, St. Jerome, St. Bernard, St. Thomas Aquinas, Nicholas of Lyra, Wyclif, Luther, Calvin, Beza, Lapide, Poole, Henry, etc.; and (c) in English literature — a basically chronological outline of literary adaptation. This section does not attempt to provide an exhaustive catalogue of specific references. Rather, it traces significant strands in literary development through exemplary representations from the Middle Ages to the twentieth century.

The entries are drawn from six general categories:

1. Biblical proper noun: e.g., BABEL, JACOB, GABRIEL
2. Common noun: e.g., HARP. Several types of common nouns occur in the *Dictionary*: distinctive biblical terms (e.g., MAMMON); ordinary nouns which have acquired iconic overtones in later tradi-

tion (e.g., APPLE); words which have specific allusive value because of association with a well-known biblical passage (e.g., MILLSTONE).

3. Concept: e.g., CONSCIENCE. Concept terms are not always biblical terms, since they occasionally derive from exegetical and theological formulations (e.g., TRINITY, OMNISCIENCE). These formulations themselves, of course, are part of established biblical tradition.

4. Common quotation or allusion: e.g., JUDGE NOT, FLESHPOTS OF EGYPT, I ONLY AM ESCAPED

5. Parable: e.g., PRODIGAL SON. There are individual entries for most of the parables of Jesus, as for a selection of Old Testament parables.

6. Familiar terms in Hebrew, Greek, and Latin, in the latter case drawn from the Vulgate text of the Bible or from liturgical adaptations of it (e.g., *AGNUS DEI, NOLI ME TANGERE, IN PRINCIPIO*)

The *Dictionary* also includes numerous short identification notes (e.g., to more commonly used terms from the Siddur and talmudic literature) and hundreds of cross-references directing readers to main entries.

Biblical Translation

Because the King James ("Authorized") Version has been the favorite text of the clear majority of post-Renaissance English authors, up to and including even modern authors such as D. H. Lawrence, James Joyce, Toni Morrison, and John Updike, it is the English Bible referred to in all quotations and references, unless otherwise noted. Other versions, including a variety of modern as well as historically important translations, are sometimes adduced for comparative or illustrative purposes, or where literary allusions or references clearly reflect a version other than the KJV. This is particularly the case in medieval references, for which the Vulgate Latin text is normative. (References to the Psalms are, however, silently corrected from Vulgate order to correspond to the numbering in the King James Version [the English norm], thus harmonizing medieval and post-Reformation references.)

References to Exegetical Sources

There remain such widely divergent practices in the citation of Jewish as well as Christian sources that no perfectly consistent rule could be achieved. The reader will discover evident norms, however. These include:

1. Sephardic rather than Ashkenazi transcription of Hebrew;

2. Anglo-American rather than German or continental form for chapter and section division, as well as titles (e.g., Genesis Rabba, not Bereshit Rabbah; Leviticus Rabba, not Wayyiqra Rabbah);

3. Latin titles and established conventions of chapter division for patristic and medieval commentaries (titles of Greek works are generally translated);

4. Where practicable, as in the case of Calvin (Torrance and Torrance), or the Mishnah (Danby), the reader has been directed to standard modern translations rather than to the text in the original language.

References to English Literary Texts

In general, the reader may assume that line references for poetry and drama are to conventionally accepted standard editions. Prose fiction presents enough controversy concerning standard editions and so much diversity in printing formats that citations of novels are generally limited to chapter references only.

Conventions of Nomenclature and Usage

This is a reference work focused on literature of the English-speaking world and the exegetical tradition most pertinent to it. Accordingly, and to maximize the utility of the entries for readers with no particular religious background or informed interest, nomenclature has been normalized to reflect English cultural standards. Thus, references are to the Old Testament rather than, as in other contexts they should be, to the Hebrew Scriptures; dates are given in the conventional B.C. and A.D. format rather than B.C.E. and C.E. Every effort has been made to arrive at a readable gender-inclusive prose. Texts from the Bible, biblical commentators, and English authors, nonetheless, have not been altered, but quoted, even in translation, consistently with the original.

Bibliographies

Most of the longer entries have pertinent bibliography items cited at their conclusion. The three detailed and annotated bibliographies at the back of the volume, however, are widely inclusive. They are organized according to the following scheme:

A. Biblical Studies
   A1. A Guide to Biblical Studies for the Student of Literature
   A2. Studies of the Bible as Literature: A Select List
   A3. The English Bible: A Brief History of Translation
B. The History of Biblical Interpretation
   B1. Historical Studies in Biblical Hermeneutics

The Bible is a book like no other book. It presents itself to those who read it as revelation, the enduring Word of God, not merely the ephemeral words of men and women. Yet, as a poem by Jorge-Luis Borges reminds us, it also declares itself to have been entrusted to *"un hombre cualquiera,"* a "common man" — with all the incomprehensible risks that necessarily entails ("Juan 1,14"). Men and women for more than three millennia have been "writing out" these hallowed words, soberly and sometimes foolishly, or "reading them in" to their own lives. And writers especially have interlineated the scriptural words again and again in verbal half-tones, echoes, quietly investing their own authorship with an authority human writers could not pretend otherwise to claim. To acknowledge that the Bible is foundational for Western literature is in part to admit an irony in typical quests for literary identity. Explicitly or not, writers tend to depend for personal authority on authority clearly not their own. But it can also seem — as it does to Borges — that divine authority itself persists in curious symbiotic dependency: the Word "condescends to the written word" only when mortal readers somehow again accept it as "entrusted" to them, and so renew it, from generation to generation, each time in a new vernacular.

If dependence upon unstable translation, upon "reading in" as well as "reading out," is clearly the paradoxical condition of each generation's reading of the Book, our recurrence to biblical tradition as foundation is unavoidably temporized and self-implicating. That it has always been so for English writers is precisely what makes a comparative historical analysis so interesting. Nor is this the only enriching complexity such a retrospect discloses. The Bible, for many of the English-speaking peoples of the world at least, is in some sense foundational for literacy as well as literature. By it many who spoke in the unlettered dialects of four continents learned the lineaments of their own language written, as well as the English many have come also to speak and write. All of this happened, at least initially, to enable access to a book written after all in Hebrew, then in Greek (and a little Aramaic), and for centuries known in the West only as mediated through Latin. Bede's famous story of Caedmon, the illiterate cowherd whose "Creation Hymn" is adduced as the earliest example of recorded English poetry, is indicative. With his new and biblical literacy came poetic free translation and the earliest identifiable tradition of Anglo-Saxon literature, marked by titles such as *Genesis, Exodus,* and *Daniel.* Cynewulf's adaptation of New Testament narrative further exemplified a tradition extending through Chaucer, Shakespeare, Milton, Bunyan, and Defoe, as through Hawthorne, Melville, Whitman, and Dickinson, to Eliot, Auden, MacLeish, and Nemerov. As a result, contemporary readers of English literature for whom the Bible itself remains a closed book, even a "dead" book, continue to "hear" it persistently, inter alia. Whether or not the Bible's literary presence comes to be reckoned with cogently is a question upon which, it seems, much else depends—even, perhaps, the probable shelf life of a substantial body of our most accomplished literature.

Abbreviations

1. GENERAL

a.	answer	Gk.	Greek
A.D.	after Christ	Heb.	Hebrew
Akk.	Akkadian	Hom.	Homily
Arab.	Arabic	ibid.	*ibidem*, the same
Aram.	Aramaic	i.e.	*id est*, that is
art.	article	IE	Indo-European
Assyr.	Assyrian	Intro.	Introduction
ASV	American Standard Version	JB	Jerusalem Bible
Bab.	Babylonian	KJV	(Authorized) King James Version
B.C.	before Christ	km.	kilometer
bk.	book	Lat.	Latin
ca.	circa	lit.	literally
cent(s).	century, -ies	l. (ll.)	line(s)
cf.	*confer,* compare	LXX	Septuagint
chap(s).	chapter(s)	m.	meter (prose)
Comm(s).	commentary, -ies	ME	Middle English
comp.	compiler	MT	Masoretic Text
d.	died	mod.	modern
dim.	diminutive	MSS	manuscripts
diss.	dissertation	n. (nn.)	note(s)
ed(s).	editor(s), edited by	NAB	New American Bible
e.g.	*exempli gratia,* for example	NJB	New Jerusalem Bible
Eng. trans.	English translation	NEB	New English Bible
Ep.	Epistle	no(s).	number(s)
e.s.	extra series	n.s.	new series
esp.	especially	NT	New Testament
et al.	*et alii,* and others	OE	Old English
etc.	*et cetera,* and so on	op.	opus
fasc.	fascicle	o.s.	old series
ff.	following	OT	Old Testament
fl.	flourished	p.	page
fig.	figure	par.	paragraph
Fr.	French	pl(s).	plate(s)
frg.	fragment	pr.	proem
ft.	feet	pref.	preface
Ger.	German	prob.	probably

Prol.	Prologue	s.s.	supplementary series
pt.	part	St.	Saint
publ.	published	st.	stanza
q.	question	Sum.	Sumerian
q.v.	*quae vide,* which see	sup.	*supra,* about, on
QL	Qumran literature	Supp.	Supplement
R.	Rabbi	s.v.	*sub vocibus,* under the words
Rab.	Rabbah, Rabba	Tg.	Targum
rev.	revised by, revision	trans.	translation, translated by
rpt.	reprinted	TEV	Today's English Version
RSV	Revised Standard Version	unpubl.	unpublished
RV	Revised Version	Vg	Vulgate
sc.	scene	viz.	namely
sect.	section	vol.	volume
ser.	series	vs.	versus
sig.	siglum	v(v).	verse(s)
sing.	singular		

2. BIBLICAL AND EXTRABIBLICAL LITERATURE

a. Old Testament

Gen.	Genesis
Exod.	Exodus
Lev.	Leviticus
Num.	Numbers
Deut.	Deuteronomy
Josh.	Joshua
Judg.	Judges
Ruth	Ruth
1-2 Sam.	1-2 Samuel
1-2 Kings	1-2 Kings
1-2 Chron.	1-2 Chronicles
Ezra	Ezra
Neh.	Nehemiah
Esth.	Esther
Job	Job
Ps. (pl. Pss.)	Psalms
Prov.	Proverbs
Eccl.	Ecclesiastes
Cant.	Canticles (Song of Songs)
Isa.	Isaiah
Jer.	Jeremiah
Lam.	Lamentations
Ezek.	Ezekiel
Dan.	Daniel
Hos.	Hosea
Joel	Joel
Amos	Amos
Obad.	Obadiah
Jonah	Jonah
Mic.	Micah
Nah.	Nahum
Hab.	Habakkuk
Zeph.	Zephaniah
Hag.	Haggai
Zech.	Zechariah
Mal.	Malachi

b. New Testament

Matt.	Matthew
Mark	Mark
Luke	Luke
John	John
Acts	Acts
Rom.	Romans
1-2 Cor.	1-2 Corinthians
Gal.	Galatians
Eph.	Ephesians
Phil.	Philippians
Col.	Colossians
1-2 Thess.	1-2 Thessalonians
1-2 Tim.	1-2 Timothy
Titus	Titus
Philem.	Philemon
Heb.	Hebrews
James	James
1-2 Pet.	1-2 Peter
1-2-3 John	1-2-3 John
Jude	Jude
Rev.	Revelation (Apocalypse)

c. Apocrypha

Bar.	Baruch
2 Esdr.	2 Esdras
4 Esdr.	4 Esdras
4 Ezra	4 Ezra

Jdt.	Judith
1 Macc.	1 Maccabees
2 Macc.	2 Maccabees
4 Macc.	4 Maccabees
Sir. (or Ecclus.)	Sirach (or Ecclesiasticus)
Tob.	Tobit
Wisd. of Sol.	Wisdom of Solomon

d. Pseudepigrapha and Early Christian Writings

Adam and Eve	Books of Adam and Eve
Apoc. Abr.	Apocalypse of Abraham
2 Apoc. Bar.	Slavonic Apocalypse of Baruch
3 Apoc. Bar.	Greek Apocalypse of Baruch
Apoc. Mos.	Apocalypse of Moses
Barn.	The Epistle of Barnabas
1 Clem.	1 Clement
Did.	Didache
Diogn.	Epistle to Diognetus
1 Enoch	Ethiopic Enoch
2 Enoch	Slavonic Enoch
Eph.	*Epistle to the Ephesians*
Gos. Thom.	Gospel of Thomas
Jub.	Jubilees
Magn.	Epistle to the Magnesians
Pss. Sol.	Psalms of Solomon
Sib. Or.	Sibylline Oracles
T. Abraham	Testament of Abraham
T. Issachar	Testament of Issachar
T. Levi	Testament of Levi
T. Naphtali	Testament of Naphtali

e. Orders and Tractates in Mishnaic and Related Literature

'Abot.	'Abot
'Abod. Zar.	'Aboda Zara
'Arak.	'Arakin
B. Bat.	Baba Batra
Bek.	Bekorot
Bera.	Berakot
B. Meṣ.	Baba Meṣi'a
B. Qam.	Baba Qamma
'Ed.	'Eduyyot
'Erub.	'Erubin
Giṭ.	Giṭṭin
Ḥag.	Ḥagiga
Ker.	Keritot
Ketub.	Ketubot

Meg.	Megilla
Menaḥ.	Menaḥot
Mid.	Middot
Nazir	Nazir
Nez.	Neziqin
Nid.	Niddah
Pesaḥ.	Pesaḥim
Qidd.	Qiddushin
Rosh Hash.	Rosh Ha-Shana
Sanh.	Sanhedrin
Shab.	Shabbat
Shebu'.	Shebu'ot
Soṭa	Soṭa
Sukk.	Sukka
Ta'an.	Ta'anit
Yebam.	Yebamot
Yoma	Yoma
Zebaḥ.	Zebaḥim

f. Other Rabbinic and Jewish Works

'Abot R. Nat.	'Abot de Rabbi Nathan
'Ag. Ber.	'Aggadah Bereshit
Bar.	Baraita
DR	Midrash D'varim Rabba
Exod. Rab.	Exodus Rabba
Gen. Rab.	Genesis Rabba
Lam. Rab.	Lamentations Rabba
Lev. Rab.	Leviticus Rabba
Num. Rab.	Numbers Rabba
Mek.	Mekilta
Midr.	Midrash
Pesiq. R.	Pesiqta Rabbati
Pesiq. Rab. Kah.	Pesiqta de Rab Kahana
Pirqe R. El.	Pirqe de Rabbi Eliezer
Sipra	Sipra
Sipre	Sipre
S. 'Olam Rab.	Seder 'Olam Rabba
Tan. Ber.	Tannaim Bereshit
Tan. Noah	Tannaim Noah
Tg. Onq.	Targum Onqelos
Tg. Ket.	Targum of the Writings
Tg. Neof.	Targum Neofiti
Tg. Ps.-J.	Targum of Pseudo-Jonathan
Tg. R. Bahya	Targum of Rabbi Bahya
Tg. Yer.	Targum Yerushalmi
Z.	Zebulun

3. PATRISTIC AND MEDIEVAL WRITERS

St. Thomas Aquinas

In. Lib. Sent.	*In Libros Sententiarum*	*Summa Theol.*	*Summa Theologica*

St. Augustine
Conf.   Confession(e)s
De civ. Dei   De civitate Dei
De Trin.   De Trinitate
Enarr. in Ps.   Enarrationes in Psalmos
In Joan. Ev.   In Joannis Evangelium Tractatus

The Venerable Bede
Hist. Eccl.   Historica Ecclesiastica Gentis
                         Anglorum

St. Bonaventure
In Lib. Sent.   In Libros Sententiarum

Calvin
Inst.   Institutes

Eusebius
Hist. eccl.   Historia ecclesiastica

St. Irenaeus
Adv. haer.   Adversus haereses

St. Jerome
Adv. Jov.   Adversus Jovinianum
Adv. Lucif.   Adversus Luciferianos
Comm. in Gen.   Commentarii in Genesim

Josephus
Ant.   Antiquities
J. W.   Jewish War

St. Justin Martyr
Apol.   Apology
Dial.   Dialogue with Trypho

Luther
WA   Weimarer Ausgabe

Tertullian
Adv. Jud.   Adversus Judaeos
Adv. Marc.   Adversus Marcionem

4. PUBLICATIONS

AAUP Bulletin   American Association of University
                    Professors Bulletin
AB   Anchor Bible
ABR   American Benedictine Review
ACW   Ancient Christian Writers
AF   Anglistische Forschungen
AGJU   Arbeiten zur Geschichte des antiken
                    Judentums und des Urchristentums
AH   American Heritage
AHDLMA   Archives d'histoire doctrinal et
                    littéraire du moyen âge
AJA   American Journal of Archaeology
AJSL   American Journal of Semitic
                    Languages and Literature
AL   American Literature
AnBib   Analecta biblica
ANEP   The Ancient Near East in Pictures
ANET   Ancient Near Eastern Texts
ANF   Ante-Nicene Fathers
AnM   Annuale Mediaevale
ANQ   Andover Newton Quarterly
APOT   Apocrypha and Pseudepigrapha of
                    the Old Testament
AQ   American Quarterly
ArQ   Arizona Quarterly
ARW   Archiv für Religionswissenschaft
ASE   Anglo-Saxon England

ASTI   Annual of the Swedish Theological
                    Institute
ATD   Das Alte Testament Deutsch
BA   Biblical Archaeologist
BeO   Bibbia e Oriente
BGDSL   Beiträge zur Geschichte der
                    Deutschen Sprache und Literatur
Bib   Biblica
BJRL   Bulletin of the John Rylands
                    Library
BKAT   Biblischer Kommentar: Altes
                    Testament
BSUF   Ball State University Forum
BZAW   Beihefte zur Zeitschrift für die
                    alttestamentliche Wissenschaft
CahiersE   Cahiers Elisabéthains
CBQ   Catholic Biblical Quarterly
CChr   Corpus Christianorum
CCSL   Corpus Christianum, Series Latina
CE   College English
CH   Church History
ChauR   Chaucer Review
CJT   Canadian Journal of Theology
CL   Comparative Literature
CLAJ   College Language Association
                    Journal
CompD   Comparative Drama
ComQ   Commonwealth Quarterly

ABBREVIATIONS

CP	Concerning Poetry	JPOS	Journal of the Palestine Oriental Society
CritQ	Critical Quarterly		
CSEL	Corpus scriptorum ecclesiasticorum latinorum	JQR	Jewish Quarterly Review
		JQRS	Jewish Quarterly Review Supplement
CSR	Christian Scholars Review		
DA	Dissertation Abstracts	JR	Journal of Religion
DACL	Dictionnaire d'archéologie chrétienne et de liturgie	JSS	Journal of Semitic Studies
		JTS	Journal of Theological Studies
DAI	Dissertation Abstracts International	JWCI	Journal of the Warburg and Courtauld Institutes
DBSup	Dictionnaire de la bible, Supplément	LCC	Library of Christian Classics
		LCL	Loeb Classical Library
DTC	Dictionnaire de théologie catholique	LJ	Legends of the Jews (Ginzberg)
		MAE	Medium AEvum
EAL	Early American Literature	M & H	Medievalia & Humanistica
EBib	Etudes bibliques	MD	Modern Drama
EETS	Early English Text Society	MiltonS	Milton Studies
EIC	Essays in Criticism	MLA	Modern Language Association
ELH	Journal of English Literary History	MLN	Modern Language Notes
ELit	Etudes Littéraires	MLQ	Modern Language Quarterly
ELN	English Language Notes	MLR	Modern Language Review
ELR	English Literary Renaissance	ModA	Modern Age
EncJud	Encyclopedia Judaica	MP	Modern Philology
EnlE	Enlightenment Essays	MS	Mediaeval Studies
ES	English Studies	MSEx	Melville Society Extracts
ESA	English Studies in Africa	MTJ	Mark Twain Journal
ESC	English Studies in Canada	N & Q	Notes and Queries
EvQ	Evangelical Quarterly	NCB	New Century Bible
Expl	Explicator	NCE	New Catholic Encyclopedia
ExpTim	Expository Times	NCF	Nineteenth-Century Fiction
FC	Fathers of the Church	Neophil	Neophilologus
FranS	Franciscan Studies	NEQ	New England Quarterly
FrSt	Franzikanische Studien	NICOT	New International Commentary on the Old Testament
HLQ	Huntington Library Quarterly		
HQ	Hopkins Quarterly	NIDNTT	New International Dictionary of New Testament Theology
HTR	Harvard Theological Review		
HTS	Harvard Theological Studies	NM	Neuphilologische Mitteilungen
HUCA	Hebrew Union College Annual	NOR	New Orleans Review
IB	Interpreter's Bible	NovT	Novum Testamentum
IDB	Interpreter's Dictionary of the Bible	NovTSup	Novum Testamentum, Supplements
IDBSup	Supplementary volume to IDB	NPNF	Nicene and Post-Nicene Fathers
Int.	Interpretation	NRT	Nouvelle revue théologique
IR	Iliff Review	NTS	New Testament Studies
ISBE	International Standard Bible Encyclopedia	NYFQ	New York Folklore Quarterly
		ODCC	Oxford Dictionary of the Christian Church
JBL	Journal of Biblical Literature		
JDJ	John Donne Journal	OED	Oxford English Dictionary
JEGP	Journal of English and Germanic Philology	OTL	Old Testament Library
		PAAS	Proceedings of the American Antiquarian Society
JHI	Journal of the History of Ideas		
JJQ	James Joyce Quarterly	PEGS	Publications of the English Goethe Society
JJS	Journal of Jewish Studies		
JMRS	Journal of Medieval and Renaissance Studies	PEQ	Palestine Exploration Quarterly
		PG (Migne)	Patrologia Graeca
JNES	Journal of Near Eastern Studies	PL (Migne)	Patrologia Latina
JNT	Journal of Narrative Technique	PLL	Papers on Language and Literature

PPMRC	Proceedings of the Patristic, Medieval and Renaissance Conference	SP	Studies in Philology
PMLA	Publications of the Modern Language Association of America	SQ	Shakespeare Quarterly
		SR	Studies in Religion
		SSF	Studies in Short Fiction
		ST	Studia Theologica
PQ	Philological Quarterly	SVT	Supplements to Vetus Testamentum
PR	Partisan Review	SWR	South West Review
RArch	Revue archéologique	SzEP	Studien zur Englischen Philologie
RB	Revue biblique	TDNT	Theological Dictionary of the New Testament
REA	Revue des études Augustiniennes		
RechA	Recherches Augustiniennes	TDOT	Theological Dictionary of the Old Testament
RenD	Renaissance Drama		
RES	Review of English Studies	TJ	Theatre Journal
RGG	Die Religion in Geschichte und Gegenwart	TS	Theological Studies
		TSL	Texas Studies in Literature
RHR	Revue de l'histoire des religions	TWA	Transactions of the Wisconsin Academy of Sciences, Arts, and Literature
RSR	Recherches de science religieuse		
SAV	Schweizerisches Archiv für Volkskunde		
		TZ	Theologische Zeitschrift
SBT	Studies in Biblical Theology	UAJ	Ural-Altaische Jahrbücher
SC	Sources chrétiennes	UDQ	University of Detroit Quarterly
SCL	Studies in Canadian Literature	USQR	Union Seminary Quarterly Review
SD	Studi Danteschi	UTQ	University of Toronto Quarterly
SEL	Studies in English Literature	VigC	Vigiliae Christianae
SFQ	Southern Folklore Quarterly	VP	Victorian Poetry
ShakS	Shakespeare Studies	VT	Vetus Testamentum
ShawR	Shaw: The Annual of Bernard Shaw Studies	WBC	Word Biblical Commentary
		WC	Wordsworth Circle
ShS	Shakespeare Survey	YES	Yearbook of English Studies
SJT	Scottish Journal of Theology	YSE	Yale Studies in English
SMC	Studies in Medieval Culture	ZAW	Zeitschrift für die alttestamentliche Wissenschaft
SN	Studia Neophilologica		
SoQ	Southern Quarterly	ZNW	Zeitschrift für die neutestamentliche Wissenschaft
SoR	Southern Review		

List of Entries

*This list includes all major entries as well as short identification entries,
but does not include headings that simply refer the reader to a cross reference.*

ENTRIES

ENTRIES

ENTRIES

ENTRIES

List of Contributors

General Editor
DAVID LYLE JEFFREY
University of Ottawa

Managing Editor
KATHERINE B. JEFFREY

Board of Editorial Advisers
LARRY W. HURTADO, ASSOCIATE EDITOR
University of Manitoba

ROY W. BATTENHOUSE
Indiana University

F. F. BRUCE (DECEASED)
University of Manchester

MICHAEL EDWARDS
University of Warwick

GILLIAN R. EVANS
Fitzwilliam College
Cambridge University

DAVID C. FOWLER
University of Washington

PATRICK GRANT
University of Victoria

KENNETH HAMILTON
University of Winnipeg

U. MILO KAUFMANN
University of Illinois

ARTHUR POLLARD
University of Hull

Contributors

STEPHEN G. W. ANDREWS
Corpus Christi College
Cambridge University

DAVID W. ATKINSON
University of Saskatchewan

WILLIAM BAIRD
Bright Divinity School
Texas Christian University

DAVID W. BAKER
Ashland Theological Seminary

JOYCE G. BALDWIN
Bristol, England

E. BEATRICE BATSON
Wheaton College

MURRAY BAUMGARTEN
Kresge College
University of California, Santa Cruz

LINDA BEAMER
Ryerson Polytechnic Institute
Toronto, Ontario

DAVID S. BERKELEY
Oklahoma State University

LAWRENCE BESSERMAN
Hebrew University of Jerusalem

ELIZABETH BIEMAN
University of Western Ontario

RONALD B. BOND
University of Calgary

CONTRIBUTORS

MADELEINE BOUCHER
Fordham University

JAMES F. BOUND
Greenfield Park, Quebec

GEOFFREY W. BROMILEY
Fuller Theological Seminary

F. F. BRUCE (DECEASED)
University of Manchester

H. DAVID BRUMBLE
University of Pittsburgh

CORBIN S. CARNELL
University of Florida, Gainesville

LARRY CARVER
University of Texas, Austin

RONALD E. CLEMENTS
Fitzwilliam College
Cambridge University

CAROLYN P. COLLETTE
Mount Holyoke College

SHARON COOLIDGE
Wheaton College

BRIAN P. COPENHAVER
University of California, Riverside

RAYMOND G. CORRIN
Ottawa, Ontario

JOHN D. COX
Hope College

PETER C. CRAIGIE (DECEASED)
University of Calgary

EDWIN D. CRAUN
Washington and Lee University

DENNIS DANIELSON
University of British Columbia

F. W. DANKER
Christ Seminary
St. Louis, Missouri

PETER H. DAVIDS
Langley, British Columbia

J. G. DAVIES (DECEASED)
University of Birmingham

JAMES M. DEAN
University of Delaware

FRANS DE BRUYN
University of Ottawa

JAMES DOELMAN
Center for Renaissance and Reformation Studies
University of Toronto

JOHN R. DONAHUE, S.J.
University of Notre Dame

DEANE E. D. DOWNEY
Trinity Western University

JOSEPH E. DUNCAN (DECEASED)
University of Minnesota

JAMES D. G. DUNN
University of Durham

BRUCE L. EDWARDS
Bowling Green State University

LAURENCE M. ELDREDGE
University of Ottawa

SAAD EL-GABALAWY
University of Calgary

RICHARD K. EMMERSON
Western Washington University

JOYCE Q. ERICKSON
Warner Pacific College

ROBERT FARRELL
Cornell University

MICHAEL FIXLER
Tufts University

JOHN V. FLEMING
Princeton University

JAMES F. FORREST
University of Alberta

DAVID C. FOWLER
University of Washington

R. T. FRANCE
Wycliffe Hall
Oxford, England

DAVID NOEL FREEDMAN
University of Michigan

RAYMOND-JEAN FRONTAIN
University of Central Arkansas

PAUL GARNET
Concordia University (Montreal)

HERBERT GIESBRECHT (DECEASED)
Mennonite Brethren Bible College

JERRY A. GLADSON
Psychological Studies Institute
Atlanta, Georgia

ALEXANDER GLOBE
University of British Columbia

PAUL GOETSCH
Freiburg Universität
Freiburg, Germany

MICHAEL GOLDBERG
University of British Columbia

BRYAN N. S. GOOCH
University of Victoria

PAUL W. GOOCH
University of Toronto

R. P. GORDON
The Divinity School
Cambridge University

JOHN GOTTCENT
University of Southern Indiana

PATRICK GRANT
University of Victoria

NORMA A. GRECO
Pittsburgh, Pennsylvania

LEONARD GREENSPOON
Clemson University

DAVID GREENWOOD (DECEASED)
University of Maryland

PETER GROTH
Universität Hamburg
Hamburg, Germany

LENORE GUSSIN
New York, New York

VICTOR YELVERTON HAINES
Dawson College

MARGARET HANNAY
Siena College

R. K. HARRISON
Wycliffe College
University of Toronto

GERHARD F. HASEL
Andrews University

DAVID STEN HERRSTROM
Roosevelt, New Jersey

COLIN HEMER (DECEASED)
Cambridge, England

JOHN SPENCER HILL
University of Ottawa

MORNA D. HOOKER
The Divinity School
Cambridge University

WM. DENNIS HORN
Clarkson College

SARAH HORRALL (DECEASED)
University of Ottawa

LARRY W. HURTADO
University of Manitoba

CHARLES A. HUTTAR
Hope College

ALAN JACOBS
Wheaton College

WALDEMAR JANZEN
Canadian Mennonite Bible College

KATHERINE B. JEFFREY
Spencerville, Ontario

CATHERINE KARKOV
Miami University of Ohio

U. MILO KAUFMANN
University of Illinois

ERNEST N. KAULBACH
University of Texas, Austin

WILLIAM KINSLEY
Université de Montréal

CAMILLE R. LA BOSSIÈRE
University of Ottawa

GEORGE M. LANDES
Union Theological Seminary

GEORGE P. LANDOW
Brown University

SOL LIPTZIN
Hebrew University of Jerusalem

JOSEPH MCCLATCHEY (DECEASED)
Wheaton College

DIANE MCCOLLEY
Rutgers University

WAYNE O. MCCREADY
University of Calgary

RODERICK MCGILLIS
University of Calgary

MARK S. MADOFF (DECEASED)
Royal Roads Military Academy
Victoria, British Columbia

DOMINIC MANGANIELLO
University of Ottawa

JOHN MARGESON
University of Toronto

I. HOWARD MARSHALL
University of Aberdeen

LAWRENCE T. MARTIN
University of Akron

MARTIN E. MARTY
University of Chicago

RONALD M. MELDRUM
Washington State University

ROBERT JAMES MERRETT
University of Alberta

LEON MORRIS
Ridley College (Melbourne)

VIRGINIA MOSELEY
University of Ottawa

MICHAEL MURPHY
Brooklyn College
City University of New York

JAMES I. PACKER
Regent College

DAVID J. PALMER
University of Manchester

MARNIE PARSONS
Wilfrid Laurier University

CONTRIBUTORS

DAVID F. PAYNE
London Bible College

RUSSELL A. PECK
University of Rochester

DWIGHT H. PURDY
University of Minnesota

ESTHER O. QUINN
New York, New York

KATHERINE QUINSEY
University of Windsor

MARJORIE REEVES
St. Anne's College
Oxford University

BRENDA E. RICHARDSON
University of Sussex

PHILLIP ROGERS
Queen's University (Kingston, Ontario)

ERWIN P. RUDOLPH
Wheaton College

JEFFREY BURTON RUSSELL
University of California, Santa Barbara

LELAND RYKEN
Wheaton College

RAYMOND ST-JACQUES
University of Ottawa

JOHN SANDYS-WUNSCH
Thorneloe College
Laurentian University
(Sudbury, Ontario)

RICHARD SCHELL
Laurentian University

GEORGE L. SCHEPER
Essex Community College and
Johns Hopkins University School
of Continuing Study

CHARLES H. H. SCOBIE
Mount Allison University

HERBERT SCHNEIDAU
University of Arizona

MANFRED SIEBALD
Johannes Gutenberg Universität
Mainz, Germany

KLYNE SNODGRASS
North Park Theological Seminary

WILLIAM M. SOLL
Aquinas Institute of Theology
St. Louis University

DONALD V. STUMP
Virginia Polytechnic Institute

HENRY SUMMERFIELD
University of Victoria

PATRICIA SUNDERLAND
University of Ottawa

KARL TAMBURR
Sweet Briar College

ANTHONY C. THISELTON
University of Sheffield

CATHERINE BROWN TKACZ
Spokane, Washington

A. A. TRITES
Acadia Divinity College
Acadia University

M. W. TWOMEY
Ithaca College

L. JOHN TOPEL, S.J.
Seattle University

NORMAN VANCE
University of Sussex

STEVEN C. WALKER
Brigham Young University

MARIE MICHELLE WALSH
College of Notre Dame of Maryland

RHONDA L. WAUHKONEN
University of Ottawa

G. J. WENHAM
Cheltenham and Gloucester
College of Higher Education

ANTHONY WESTENBROEK
Ottawa, Ontario

FAYE PAULI WHITAKER
Iowa State University

MURIEL WHITAKER
University of Alberta

W. ROGER WILLIAMS
Marianapolis College (Montreal)

BRUCE WILLOUGHBY
University of Michigan

ROBERT WILTENBURG
Washington University

ROBERT E. WRIGHT
National Humanities Center
North Carolina

ANTHONY D. YORK
University of Cincinnati

The author's name appears at the end of each entry. Unattributed entries were written by the general editor, David Lyle Jeffrey. In the case of coauthored entries, we have endeavored to list the authors' names in the order of the proportion of material contributed by each author, with the author who wrote the larger portion of the entry listed first.

A

AARON Although there is talmudic speculation to the effect that Aaron's name, reflecting Pharaoh's edict against the male Hebrew children, means "woe to this pregnancy" (Yashar Shemot 128a; T. Levi 17), its etymology is uncertain. The older brother of Moses, Aaron stayed in Egypt after Moses' flight to avoid prosecution for murder. Later, when at his call to service Moses pleaded a lack of eloquence (Exod. 4:10), God said that Aaron would be his spokesman; Aaron came out to meet Moses in the desert "at the mountain of God" as Moses was en route back to Egypt (4:27). In cooperation with his brother, Aaron was instrumental in the subjection of Pharaoh and the exodus of the children of Israel from bondage. In a later incident, he, with Hur, held up Moses' hands over the battle scene until the Israelites had defeated the forces of Amalek (17:10, 12). When Moses went up onto Mt. Sinai to receive the commandments, Aaron's career sank to its low point as he yielded to the clamor of the people for a tangible material god and allowed the building of the golden calf idol, which so angered Moses on his return that he smashed the two tablets of the Law (Exod. 32).

Chosen for the official priesthood, Aaron was anointed with the holy oil (Lev. 8:12), and with his sons served in the Tabernacle. Only he, however, could enter into the Holy of Holies, once a year on the Day of Atonement, there to make sacrifice for the sins of the people (Deut. 16:12-14).

Two further events are prominently associated with Aaron: the revolt of Korah and his confederates against Moses and Aaron, which was ended by the rebels being swallowed up in an earthquake and 14,700 of their allies dying of the plague, a number which would have been far greater, it is said, had not Aaron rushed into the midst of the dying with his smoking censer, standing between the living and the dead to offer atoning intercession (Num. 16). Immediately following, all dissent concerning the right to the priesthood was ended when God commanded that a "rod" (or staff) from each of the eleven tribes be laid with that of Aaron, as representative of the Levites, overnight near the Ark of the Covenant in the sanctuary. In the morning Aaron's rod blossomed, and put forth as well both leaves and ripe almonds (Num. 17).

Haggadic literature concentrates on these latter elements and on the famous priestly garments with which Aaron was invested (Exod. 28:4-39; Lev. 8:8). The eight garments are given symbolic association with the expiation of sins: his coat for murder, breeches for unchastity, miter for pride, girdle for theft, breastplate for prejudiced judgments, ephod for idolatry, bells on his robe for slander, and golden plate for effrontery (Yoma 9.44b-44c; cf. Philo, *De vita Mosis*, 2.2-14; Josephus, *Ant.* 3.7.7). The breastplate and ephod were set with precious stones, the ephod with two and the breastplate with twelve, one for each of the twelve tribes. The stones for each tribe were, according to later rabbinic literature (following medieval lapidaries): Reuben, ruby, for fecundity in marriage; Simeon, smaragd, which is said to have the property of "shattering as soon as looked at by an unchaste woman"; Levi, carbuncle, which beams like lightning, reflecting piety and erudition; Judah, emerald, which makes its wearer victorious in battle but also recalls Judah's shame over the Tamar incident; Issachar, sapphire, the stone out of which the tables of the Law were made; Zebulun, pearl, a remedy against insomnia; Dan, topaz, in which was visible the inverted face of human evil; Naphtali, turquoise, which gives its owner speed in riding, since Naphtali means speed "like a hind let loose"; Gad, crystal, which gives its owner courage in battle; Asher, chrysolite, which aids digestion and brings jovial health; Joseph, onyx, which endows its owner with grace; Benjamin, jasper, which varies its colors, since Benjamin was thought to be of volatile emotions (Tg. R. Bahya Exod. 28:17; Tg. Yer. Exod. 28:17).

The fate of Korah and his confederates is elaborated in grisly imaginative detail in a number of sources (see Ginzberg, *LJ* 3.298-300), and Aaron's blossoming rod is said to have remained in use by the kings of Judah until the time of the destruction, when it miraculously vanished; it will appear only in the last days, when it will be fetched forth by Elijah for presentation to the Messiah (Yelammenedu in Yalqut 1.763; 2.869 on Ps. 110; Midr. 'Aggadah Gen. 32:11). According to other sources (e.g., Pesiq. Rab. Kah. 42a) Aaron and his sons and Zadok were the only "anointed" priests; many sources (Ginzberg, *LJ* 6.72 gives a list) emphatically state that neither Aaron nor the Messiah will be anointed in the Day of the Lord, a point which Ginzberg suggests was probably directed against the Christian identification of Jesus as the Christ, "the anointed one."

Patristic reflection on the significance of Aaron's priesthood focuses on many of the same elements as the prominent targums, but almost entirely within the context provided by NT typology suggested in the Epistle to the Hebrews (5:4; 7:11; 9:4), in which the eternal vocation of Christ as "great high priest" is elaborated in connection with both Melchizedek and Aaron. This typology focuses on pastoral qualities, as in the Nisibene Hymns (no. 14) of St. Ephraim Syrus, in one of which the voice of Satan is made to say how the "censer of Aaron caused me to fear, for he stood between the dead and the living and conquered me" (39.6), an obvious reference to the event in Num. 16:48. This same incident was for St. Ambrose the high point in Aaron's priesthood (*De officiis ministrorum*, 2.4.11). While Aaron's priestly character is exemplary in many respects (*Ep.* 63.50), none of his qualities is more important than his courage in this incident (cf. St. Isidore, *Etymologiae*, 7.6.47, who says that his name means *mons fortitudinis*):

When a terrible death on account of the rebels was spreading over the people, he offered himself between the dead and the living, that he might arrest death, and that no person should perish. A man of truly priestly mind and soul, as a good shepherd with pious affection he offered himself for the Lord's flock. And so he broke the sting of death, restrained its violence, refused it further course. (63.51)

Aelfric reiterates the importance of Aaron's divine calling in his sermon *De Populo Israhel,* saying that if Korah had been able to usurp the priestly function it would have resulted in a view of the priesthood based on mere political power — "swylce hi mihton he sylfe gewyrcan" — but Aaron was shown in the events to be chosen by God himself, "and gesette him to bisceope / on þa ealdan wisan eafter Moyses áe" (237-45).

The rod of Aaron which bloomed is also the subject of extensive commentary. That it alone blossomed after God's intervention suggests that a priestly vocation derives from the grace of divine election rather than from the mere accretion of human merit, according to Ambrose (*Ep.* 63.58), a grace which flowers through many ages in a priest truly "called of God." The almond fruit on the rod is generally held to be a symbol of the *lex Dei* itself, "bitter in its rind, hard in its shell, [but] inside pleasant," which it is the duty of the priest to set fearlessly before his people (Ambrose, *Ep.* 41.3-4). Preeminently perhaps, at least in later medieval typologies, the budding rod is seen to prefigure the miraculous fecundity of the virgin birth of Jesus (e.g., St. Anthony of Padua, *In Nativitate Beatae Mariae Virginis*, 3.696a), partly because the divine pregnancy of Mary is heralded by Elisabeth the mother of John the Baptist (Luke 1:40-45), who is said to be of Aaron's lineage (1:5). Franciscan poet James Ryman makes frequent use of the typology: "O Aaron yerde moost of honoure, / O moder of oure Savioure" (R. Greene, *Early English Carols*, nos. 192, 193; cf. 190b, 182, etc.). In a verse like the following, one sees the typology of the Virgin serving exegesis of the passages from Hebrews about the "high priesthood" of Jesus:

As Aaron yerde withoute moistoure
Hath florisshed and borne a floure,
So hath she borne oure Savyoure
Withouten touch of dishonoure
Of mannes sede,
For God his self in her did brede. (Greene, no. 203)

Aaron's iconographic attributes from the Middle Ages through Renaissance and baroque art include his rod, censer, and priestly vestments, especially the twelve-jeweled breastplate — the latter of which is the subject of lapidarial symbology in writers from Ambrose (*De fide*, 2, intro. 1-10) to Pope Innocent III (in his famous letter to King John). Also depicted are his garment with bells on the lower fringe, Urim and Thummim, and, when he signifies the Christian priesthood, his miter. Occasionally he has a tiara, in which case he represents the Pope. In Protestant art after Calvin, especially in the Netherlands, his typical headdress becomes a turban, partly in reaction to Catholic ecclesiology and vestments. A rarer iconographic association is the *tau,* or a bishop's crosier topped with a *tau.* In the destruction of Jerusalem discussed in Ezek. 9:2-6, an unnamed figure with an inkhorn at his side marks a *tau,* the last letter of the Hebrew alphabet, on the foreheads of those to be spared. Franciscan exegesis related him to Aaron and the *tau* to the mark upon the lintels of houses to be spared in the Passover (St. Bonaventure, *Legenda Major,* 9.9ff.), and St. Francis himself used the *tau* in signature, identifying himself with a prophetic priesthood, like the man *"similis Aaron"* in Ezek. 9, setting out to save some souls from the general judgment upon his age.

The development of Aaronic typology after the Reformation reflects divergent ecclesiological concerns. In England, where Anglicanism preserved much if not all of the typology of the medieval Church, George Herbert can make one of his most powerful reflections on his own priesthood a contrast between the rich inward significance of Aaron's vestments and the poverty of his own spirit in the moments before divine service:

> Holinesse on the head,
> Light and perfections on the breast,
> Harmonious bells below, raising the dead
> To lead them unto life and rest:
> Thus are true Aarons drest.

But only when he can say "Christ is my onely head, / My alone onely heart and breast," is he able to put off the burdens of the "old man" and, his "doctrine tun'd by Christ," face his congregation: "Come people; Aaron's drest" ("Aaron").

In a contrasting assessment, Calvin comments on Heb. 5:4 that "it was clear that Aaron's priesthood had been temporary, and was due to cease." He continues, making it clear that he has in mind the traditional analogy between Aaron and his sons and the doctrine of apostolic succession in connection with the priesthood of Rome: "What then is to be said of Aaron and the rest of his successors? This, that they had as much right as was given to them by God, but not as much as men have given them according to their own thinking."

Aaron has thus little role in works by writers like Milton and Bunyan, although in *Pilgrim's Progress* Christian is warned about the "sins of Korah" by Hope. It may be coincidental, but Shakespeare's Aaron in *Titus Andronicus* is the agent and virtual personification of evil ministrations. In *Absalom and Achitophel,* Dryden calls the rebel Levites "Aaron's race," though six years later, in his Catholic phase, *The Hind and the Panther* satirizes Calvin ("In Israel some believe him whelp'd long since") as actually descended from Korah:

> When Corah with his brethren did conspire
> From Moyses hand the Sov'reign sway to wrest,
> And Aaron of his Ephod to divest:

> Till opening Earth made way for all to pass,
> And cou'd not bear the burden of a class. (185-89)

Most 18th-cent. allusions are casual, such as Pope's reference in the *Essay on Man* to the danger of obsession: "And hence one MASTER PASSION in the breast, / Like Aaron's serpent, swallows up the rest."

Relatively rarely, despite Dryden's imagination, does Aaron obtain the affection of the Protestant typologist. One exception in American literature is Cotton Mather, who describes an old pastor welcoming his successor in terms drawn from the divesture of Aaron from his priestly garments just before his death so that his son Eleazar could be invested (Num. 20:12-29): "The good Old Man like Old Aaron, as it were disrobed himself, with an unspeakable Satisfaction, when he beheld his Garments put upon a Son so dear to him" ("The Life of John Eliot"). This passage may also be in Joyce's mind, less charitably, when "Mulligan is stripped of his garments" in the "Telemachus" section of *Ulysses.* Melville, perhaps reflecting his rebellion against Calvinism, also identifies the Hebrews with Korah in an allusion to the fate of ships and crews likewise "swallowed up" by the elements (*Moby-Dick,* chap. 58). In *Democratic Vistas* Walt Whitman seems to be thinking of Aaron's rod when, in reference to capitalistic opportunities, he says that "the magician's serpent in the fable ate up all the other serpents; and money making is our magician's serpent, remaining sole master of the field." The episode of the golden calf is the one which may most provide an opportunity for psychological development of Aaron's character: it is tantalizingly seized upon by Arnold Schoenberg in his opera *Moses und Aron* (1930-32); the work remains, however, unfinished.

Aaron's rod rather than Aaron himself seems most to have endured in modern literary allusions. In D. H. Lawrence's novel *Aaron's Rod* (1922) the image is applied, with typical syncretism, to the ambiguous artistic and sexual liberation of the central character, Aaron Sisson. David Jones, however, in his *Sleeping Lord* sequence, recurs to "the budding rod" of Aaron in its larger christological context (64), the *historia humanae salvationis.* Howard Nemerov draws this whole context of relationships concerning Aaron's rod and *tau,* as well as the root of Jesse and the cross, together in the eleventh stanza of his poem "Runes":

> A holy man said to me, "Split the stick
> And there is Jesus." When I split the stick
> To the dark marrow and the splintery grain
> I saw nothing that was not wood, nothing
> That was not God, and I began to dream
> How from the tree that stood between the rivers
> Came Aaron's rod that crawled in front of Pharaoh,
> And came the rod of Jesse flowering
> In all the generations of the Kings,
> And came the timbers of the second tree,
> The sticks and yardarms of the holy three-

Masted vessel whereon the Son of Man
Hung between thieves, and came the crown of thorns,
The lance and ladder, when was shed that blood
Streamed in the grain of Adam's tainted seed.

See also TRIBES OF ISRAEL; URIM AND THUMMIM.
Bibliography. Fleming, J. V. "The Scribe of the Tau." In *From Bonaventure to Bellini* (1982); Needham, E. A. *Melchizedek and Aaron as Types of Christ* (1904); Steck, O. H. *Moses und Aron: Die Oper Arnold Schoenbergs und ihr biblischer Stoff* (1981); Valentin, H. *Aaron: Eine Studie zur vorpriesterschriftlichen Aaron-Ueberlieferung* (1978).

AARONIC BLESSING   Num. 6:24-26.
See also BENEDICTION.

ABADDON   The name of hell in Job (26:6; 28:22; 31:12) is Abaddon (Heb. *'abaddon,* "destruction"). It is paralleled with Sheol (Job 26:6; Prov. 15:11; 27:20), death (Job 28:22), and the grave (Ps. 88:11). In Rev. 9:11 it is the name of the angel who rules over "the place of destruction," the Greek equivalent being Apollyon. Milton uses Abaddon as a name for hell in *Paradise Regained* (4.624), while in *Pilgrim's Progress* Bunyan calls the field over which Christian triumphs Apollyon. The "great black bird, Apollyon's bosom friend" is one of the beasts encountered by the knight in Browning's "Childe Roland."

ABEDNEGO   *See* SHADRACH, MESHACH, AND ABEDNEGO.

ABEL   Abel, whose name may derive from the Hebrew word *hebel,* meaning "breath," was the brother of Cain and second son of Adam and Eve; his story is told in Gen. 4:1-10. Abel, a "keeper of sheep," and Cain, a "tiller of the ground," made offerings of their produce to God. When Abel's was accepted and Cain's rejected, Cain was furious and "rose up against Abel his brother, and slew him" (neither a motive nor a murder weapon is expressly mentioned). Subsequently, "the voice of [Abel's] blood" cried unto God from the ground.

In the NT, Abel appears in three contexts: (a) in Matt. 23:35 and Luke 11:51 he is named as the first martyr to have shed blood; (b) in Heb. 11:4 (cf. 1 John 3:12) his righteousness, manifest when God accepts his offering, leads to his enrollment as the earliest of those who acted "by faith"; and (c) in Heb. 12:24 he appears as a prefigurative type of Christ, although the latter's shedding of blood "speaketh better things than that of Abel."

The sparse biblical account is expanded and embellished by early commentators. Philo (*De sacrificiis Abelis et Caini,* 3) allegorized Abel — whose name, he says, means "one who refers [all things] to God" — as the "God-loving principle" in mankind, while Cain is said to symbolize the principle of self-love. Josephus (*Ant.* 1.2.1) says that the name Abel means "nothing" (cf. the LXX rendering of Isa. 49:4) and contrasts Abel's respect for

justice and virtue with Cain's depravity and rapacity; the reason, he maintains, that Abel's sacrifice was accepted is that God is honored by things that grow spontaneously and in accordance with natural laws (viz., sheep), and not by products "forced from nature [like Cain's agricultural produce] by the ingenuity of grasping man."

Later Jewish commentators were also inventive, suggesting, e.g., that a fight between the brothers was provoked when a sheep trampled Cain's field, that Abel proved the stronger and, when Cain begged for mercy, let him go — only to have Cain pick up a stone and strike him in the neck. Other additions — some ingenious, some touching — include theories about the murder weapon (a cane, a sword, a club, Cain's teeth) and speculation about Abel's burial (the body protected by his faithful dog, a raven's burying carrion giving Adam and Eve the idea of digging a grave, or, in one account, Adam and Abel interred together by angels in the precise spot in Paradise where Adam had been created by God); see Ginzberg, *LJ* 1.100, 107-13; 5.135-42. In the Testament of Abraham, Abel is seen in a vision seated on a mighty throne judging the righteous and wicked (chaps. 12 – 13). In cabalistic literature, Abel is said to return to the world in the persons of Jacob and Moses.

Early Christian reflection on Abel is largely concerned with his righteous nature and his symbolic significance in world history. J.-P. Migne (PL 219.274) gives a useful summary of the Fathers' emphasis on Abel's character: "*in vita innocens, in morte patiens, post mortem non silens, in martyrio primus, in obedientia summus*" ("innocent in his life, patient in death, afterward not silenced, first amongst martyrs, obedient unto the end"). St. John Chrysostom, who opposed allegorical exegesis, asserted the primacy of love in Abel's nature: "Whence was Abel slain, and did not slay? From his vehement love to his brother, he could not even admit such a thought" (*Hom.* 4, on 1 Thess. 3:5-8). The most persistent and well-developed patristic approach, however, is allegorical. St. Ambrose, e.g., in discussing God's declaration to Rebekah (pregnant with Esau and Jacob) that she would give birth to "two nations . . . and two manner of people" (Gen. 25:23), stresses the connection with Cain and Abel, who represent, respectively, the Old and New Covenants: "The two figura 'Synagogue' and 'Church' are anticipated by the two brothers, Cain and Abel. From Cain derives the people known as the Jews; from Abel those faithful to God known as Christians" (*De Cain et Abel,* 1.1.5). It was left to St. Augustine in *De civitate Dei* (15.1-8), however, to work out the fullest and most influential historical allegory, in which Cain founds an earthly city (Gen. 4:17) while Abel, a "pilgrim," is the type of those destined to people the New Jerusalem, the "City of the saints [which] is up above" (15.1). Augustine puts his position succinctly elsewhere: "Jerusalem received beginning through Abel, Babylon through Cain. . . . Two loves make up these two cities: love of God maketh Jerusalem, love of the world maketh Babylon" (*Enarr. in Ps.*

65). Like most early Christian exegetes, Augustine treats Cain as symbolic of the envious "Jews by whom Christ was slain," while Christ himself, "the shepherd of the flock of men, [is] prefigured in Abel, the shepherd of the flock of sheep" (*De civ. Dei* 15.7; cf. 15.18).

In contrast to his stature among theologians, Abel is decidedly a minor figure in English literature. There is little in OE; he appears very briefly in *Genesis A* (969, 1003), and the only other poetic reference (*Beowulf,* 108) cites him merely in a periphrasis for Cain: "þæs þe he Abel slog." References in ME literature are more substantial. In the 14th-cent. *Cursor Mundi* (1045-1118), Abel is presented as a "hali man . . . rightwis . . . and godds freind," who gladly makes offering to God, while Cain "gaf him wit iuel will." When the latter's offering is rejected, Cain, proud and envious, murders his brother "wiþ þe cheke bon of ane asse" (1073) — a detail which may have been imported from the Samson saga (Judg. 15:15-17) and is found only in English accounts of Abel's death (e.g., *Hamlet,* 5.1.76). Another detail, imported from Jewish legend, is that Cain is unable to hide Abel's body because the earth keeps throwing it up: "For vnder erth most it not rest, / þe clai ai vp þat bodi kest" (1079-80).

Popular tradition was reflected also in the miracle cycles, each of which (although the play in the York cycle is defective) contains a Cain and Abel play. These plays uniformly contrast Abel's humble righteousness with Cain's proud rebelliousness, and they stress that Abel makes offering willingly and gives his best lamb, while Cain grudgingly sacrifices his worst. The N-Town (Coventry) play is the only drama explicitly to see Abel as prefiguring Christ (73-78); two plays give the murder weapon as a jawbone: "chavel-bone" (N-Town, 149) and "cheke-bon" (Towneley, 324).

In Malory's *Morte Darthur* (17.5-6) Sir Galahad, a postfiguration of Christ, is told the story of how a white tree, planted by Eve from a branch of the forbidden apple tree, turns green when Abel is conceived under it, then red when he is murdered under it.

References to Abel in Renaissance literature develop aspects of the story often ignored or played down in medieval texts. In *Hamlet,* the king likens himself to Cain in a soliloquy which confesses: "My offense is rank, it smells to heaven; / It hath the primal eldest curse upon't, / A brother's murder" (3.3.36-38). In *Richard 2,* Henry Bolingbroke accuses Thomas Mowbray of having murdered the Duke of Gloucester, whose blood, "like sacrificing Abel's, cries . . . to me for justice" (1.1.104-06). By the end of this play, however, Henry is himself indirectly guilty of the murder of Richard and promises a pilgrimage to the Holy Land to wash the blood from *his* hand; at the same time he consigns Exton, the slayer, to "go wander" with Cain. The patristic tradition which has Damascus as the place of Abel's murder is reflected in *1 Henry 6* when the Bishop of Winchester, posing as an innocent Abel, says to his enemy the Duke of Gloucester: "Nay, stand thou back, I will not budge a foot; / This be Damascus, be thou cursed Cain, / To slay thy brother Abel, if thou wilt" (1.3.38-40).

Henry Vaughan's "Abel's Blood" in pt. 2 of *Silex Scintillans,* an ardent Royalist's meditation on lives lost in the Civil Wars, opens with Abel's blood crying to heaven and modulates to Christ's "milde blood" of atonement which, as John Diodati observes in a note on Heb. 12:24, "presents it selfe before God, not to desire vengeance of the murtherous Jews, as *Abels* did against Cain, *Gen.* 4.10, but to obtain favour and pardon for them" (*Pious Annotations upon the Holy Bible* [1681]). The same theme appears in two quatrains (203 and 204) in Herrick's *His Noble Numbers.*

Milton's treatment of the Cain and Abel story in *Paradise Lost* (11.429-47) is largely conventional, although the imagery subtly links Abel (who places his sacrifice "on the cleft Wood") with Christ, and Cain "the sweaty Reaper" with the infernal triad of Satan, Sin, and Death. The most original and perplexing use of Abel in Renaissance literature is in Donne's "The Progresse of the Soule" (1601), a fragmentary mock-epic poem tracing the history of a "deathlesse" soul through a series of incarnations from the forbidden apple plucked by Eve, through plants, birds, and fish, to a wolf (401-28) which seduces Abel's bitch in order to prey on the sheep until he is killed in one of Abel's traps, then to the offspring (428-50) of the wolf and Abel's bitch, a schizoid beast which both protects and eats the herd, and then finally passes into the body of Themech, "sister and wife to *Caine*" (510). Ben Jonson (*Works,* 1.136) says Donne's "generall purpose was to have brought in all the bodies of the Hereticks from the soule of Caine & at last left it in the body of Calvin."

References in the 18th cent. are few and uninteresting (Pope, *Essay on Man,* 4.118; Cowper, "Hope," 644), although Burns has an amusing stanza on an English antiquarian prepared to prove that "The knife that nicket Abel's craig . . . was a faulding jocteleg [= clasp-knife]" ("On the Late Captain Grose's Peregrinations Thro' Scotland," 44-48).

English translations of Salomon Gessner's prose-epic *Der Tod Abels* (1758), coupled with the general Romantic interest in the psychology of guilt and remorse, led to a revival of interest in the Cain and Abel story in the early 19th cent. The common feature of these versions is the secularization of the theme, the use of biblical event and language for psychological, aesthetic, even political, ends. In Coleridge's gothic fragment "The Wanderings of Cain" the ghost of Abel confronts Cain as an externalization of guilt-ridden conscience; in Byron's *Cain: A Mystery,* the pious Abel dies with Christ's words from the cross (Luke 23:34, 46) on his lips: "Oh, God! receive thy servant, and / Forgive his slayer, for he knew not what / He did" (3.318-20); in Shelley's political drama *Hellas,* the Turkish sultan Mahmud opines that the Spirit of fallen Greeks cries against him for vengeance "like the blood of

Abel from the dust" (355). In Blake's theophanic "Ghost of Abel," the visionary poet cries out, through Abel, in defense of the creative imagination.

Post-Romantic references to Abel tend to be conventional. In George Eliot's *Middlemarch*, the only thing Mr. Bulstrode can say about Abel, his shepherd-bailiff at Stone Court, is that he "has done well with the lambs this year" (chap. 69). More recently, John Updike has penned his own version of the Abel story in "The Invention of the Horse Collar" *(Museums and Women)*, where Abel (Ablatus) represents a personalized society destined to give in to the way of Cain (Canus) in technological revolution.

See also CAIN; MARK OF CAIN.

Bibliography. Aptowitzer, V. *Kain und Abel in der Aggada der Apokryphen, der hellenistischen, christlichen und mohammedanischen Literatur* (1922); Emerson, O. "Legends of Cain, Especially in Old and Middle English." *PMLA* 21 (1906), 831-929; Hooke, S. "Cain and Abel" (1937), rpt. in *The Siege Perilous* (1959), 66-73; Tannenbaum, L. "Lord Byron in the Wilderness: Biblical Tradition in Byron's *Cain* and Blake's *The Ghost of Abel*." *MP* 72 (1975), 350-64; Schapiro, M. *Late Antique, Early Christian and Medieval Art: Selected Papers* (1980), 249-65.   JOHN SPENCER HILL

ABIGAIL   The story in 1 Sam. 25:2-42 recounts how Abigail (Heb. *'abigayil*; prob. "My father rejoices") intervened to preserve her husband Nabal from sudden destruction at the hands of David and his men, only to become the handmaiden and bride of David after Nabal's death. Nabal and his flocks had been protected by David, but when David's messengers asked for hospitality from Nabal they were insulted and rebuffed; hence David's anger. Before David's avenging party could reach Nabal, Abigail met them on the road with gifts of food and a well-spoken apology for her churlish husband, who was on her account thus spared. Upon hearing of his narrow escape, Nabal became frightened, fell into a fit of despair (his "heart turned to stone"), and died.

Abigail is noted in early Jewish commentary as the most important of David's wives, "in whom beauty, wisdom and prophetical gifts were joined" (Ginzberg, *LJ* 4.117). She is reckoned with Sarah, Rahab, and Esther as one of the four most beautiful of all women (Meg. 15a; S. 'Olam Rab. 21), and is also celebrated for her piety and quick-wittedness. Yet in some of the same sources it is observed that her appeal to David to "remember thine handmaid" was really a form of coquetry and should not have been uttered to a man other than her husband (Meg. 14b; Sanh. 2.20b; 4.22b). In the "Paradise of Women" she joins the wives of the patriarchs in supervising one of the seven divisions.

Abigail is the subject of relatively little patristic commentary; her beauty is overlooked, though her sagacity in waiting until Nabal had slept off his drunkenness before telling him of his escape is praised by later biblical commentary (e.g., *Glossa Ordinaria* [PL 113.561]).

Prudence, in Chaucer's *Tale of Melibee*, intervening to temper her own husband's wrath, uses Abigail as perhaps a double-edged example to demonstrate the value of a virtuous wife's wit and prudent counsel (*Canterbury Tales*, 7.1099). In Dryden's *Absalom and Achitophel* (34) she becomes merely "the Charming Annabel" whom "God-like" David could not deny himself. Mark Van Doren's "Abigail" (*Collected and New Poems* [1963]) is a cunning and shrewd as well as beautiful envoy who, in a sense, condemns foolish Nabal even as she saves him from the retribution of another man with whom she has already fallen in love.

See also DAVID; NABAL.

ABINADAB   *See* ARK OF THE COVENANT.

ABISHAG   Abishag the Shunammite makes her appearance in 1 Kings 1:1-4 to "cherish" old King David and minister to him, "that my lord the king may get heat." David is presented as weakened and nearing death (1:1), as indicated both by his inability to be warmed by the "clothes" (better, "blankets") put on his bed and by his inability to be sexually aroused by the maiden. The episode of old king and young virgin serves as transition to the drama of succession and the establishment of the Davidic dynasty.

Rabbinic interpretations follow the biblical account, assigning Abishag a limited yet significant and even heroic role. In Jewish tradition, Abishag is ancillary to David, and when Adonijah wants to marry her after David's death, the rabbis approve of Solomon's decision to eliminate his half-brother's oblique claim to the Davidic role by denying him her hand (1 Kings 2:13-25). Solomon's action recognizes that marriage to his father's concubine would have legitimated Adonijah's claim to the throne; though yet a virgin, Abishag here has the status of kingly widow, who might thereby bestow the power of succession upon her husband. In the Talmud as well as the Haggadah she is linked to another woman of Shunem, whose hospitable welcome of the prophet Elisha brings her praise and succor when he revives her comatose son in 2 Kings 4:8-37 (see Pirqe R. El. 33; Sanh. 22a and Rashi's commentary, as well as 39b; Ginzberg, *LJ;* Y. Hasidah, *Ishei Ha Tanakh* [1954]).

Modern scholarship is reluctant to assign an etymological meaning to the name Abishag, and earlier attempts are not now favored. Through the association of Shunem, her home village, with Shulem, Abishag has been linked by some commentators to the "black but comely" Shulammite beloved by Solomon in Canticles (1:5; 6:13). Despite the wealth of material on King David, there are no classical or medieval midrashim in which the Abishag of 1 Kings 1:1-4 figures, and few literary references of any kind. Nevertheless, her paradoxical situation as virgin/wife and widow have fascinated 20th-cent. writers, who have produced remarkable work about her in Yiddish, German, French, Hebrew, and English. And it is just possible that there is an echo of Abishag's situation in that of Dickens's Miss Havisham, the virgin jilted bride of *Great Expectations* (1861).

In the 4th cent., Abishag is cited by St. Jerome in his allegorical reinterpretation of the relationship of sexuality and knowledge in his influential letter 52 to Nepotian on the education of clergy. He inverts the biblical usage first applied to Adam's knowledge of Eve: "Who then is this Shunamite, this wife and virgin, so fervid as to give heat to the cold, so holy as not to excite to lust the man she had warmed?" Jerome transforms her into an ideal figure of wisdom: "She shall give to thine head an ornament of grace: a crown of glory shall she deliver to them." In his "Confutation of Tyndale's Answer" of 1532, St. Thomas More remembers how "St. Jerome expowneth by an allegory the text of Scripture, that the holy prophet David, by the counsel of his physicians, when he waxed very cold for age, took to wife . . . the fairest young maid that could be founden in all the country about, to do him pleasure in his presence by day, and lie in his arms and keep him warm a nights."

With these exceptions, Abishag does not figure in patristic exegesis or the literature of Renaissance England. Nor does she have a significant role in other retellings of or references to the Davidic narrative until Dryden's 1681 *Absalom and Achitophel,* whose opening lines link David's political and sexual powers:

> Then *Israel's* Monarch, after Heaven's own heart,
> His vigorous warmth did, variously, impart
> To Wives and Slaves: and, wide as his Command,
> Scatter'd his Maker's Image through the Land.

Here Abishag's presence is only suggested as the terminus ad quem of David's procreative powers. An echo of these lines of Dryden's is added by Alexander Pope to his 1709 version of Chaucer's *Canterbury Tales,* "David, the Monarch after Heav'ns' own Mind, / Who lov'd our Sex, and honour'd all our Kind" (693-94). And there may be a similar hint of Abishag's role in Milton's *Paradise Lost* in the Archangel Michael's speech revealing the future to Adam in bk. 11:538-46.

In "The Shunnamite" the self-taught rural poet Stephen Duck produced what was acknowledged to be his best poem. In heroic couplets which echo Pope's diction and Dryden's choral structure, the woman of Shunem tells the story of how the prophet Elisha revived her son. After this Augustan compliment, more than seventy-five years elapsed before a poet was to refer to Abishag. She appears next in the first canto of Byron's *Don Juan* (1819), serving to fill out a stanza and cap a joke about the progress of young Don Juan's amorous education:

> Of his position I can give no notion:
> Physicians, leaving pill and notion,

> Prescribed, by way of blister, a young belle,
> When old King David's blood grew dull in motion,
> And that the medicine answer'd very well;
> Perhaps 'twas in a different way applied,
> For David lived, but Juan nearly died. (1.168)

While other Romantic writers and Victorians, for all their considerable interest in the Bible, do not refer to Abishag, some of the qualities of Byron's complex tone are present in Joseph Heller's 1984 novel *God Knows,* which begins with the demure and girlish Abishag ministering to David, who compares her to the worldly "widehipped" Bathsheba, in a brilliant, wise-alecky monologue. Similarly, Julius Leibert's witty 1962 play *The Wives of King David* takes the form of a dramatic monologue recited by Abishag. Some modern works emphasize Abishag's place in the folk imagination. Thus, Aldous Huxley's aging Earl of Hauberk in *After Many a Summer* (1939) records in his diary that "I have tried King David's remedy against old age and found it wanting," as if Abishag were part of the lore of folk-medicine; Robert Frost's poem "Provide Provide" makes her a Hollywood beauty queen and uses the biblical episode as a folk warning: "The witch that came (the withered hag) / To wash the steps with pail and rag / Was once the beauty Abishag." Neither invites reflection on the biblical account; the Abishag episode (and by extension the Bible) is considered hardly more than a warehouse of stock literary references. A more cynical view is offered by the debunking *David: The Biography of a King* (Eng. version, 1965), written by the scholar and politician Juan Bosch. By contrast, in Shirley Kaufman's recent poem Abishag takes back her identity as a woman despite her status as object in the folk imagination ("Abishag," *Claims* [1984]), and like Karen Gershon's lyric ("David and Abishag," *Coming Back from Babylon* [1979]) makes a complex Zionist statement which brings her readers to a deeper reading of the original biblical tale.

In much 20th-cent. Yiddish poetry, Abishag becomes King David's equal. The meeting of the two — great king and little woman at his service — marks out the area Yiddish literature made its own, focusing in particular on the encounter of the world-historical Jewish king and the *pintele yid,* the anonymous Jew, who makes up the substratum of Jewish life so often unreflected in its national consciousness. In the 1926 poem by Jacob Glatstein ("Abishag," Eng. version in *The Golden Peacock* [1939]), as well as in the cycle of four poems by Itsik Manger, their encounter is ironic and full of wit and feeling. Manger's Abishag knows — because she has read her story in the Bible — that for her deeds she will only receive

> A line in the bible,
> A line for her young flesh,
> the years of her youth.
> A line of ink on parchment
> for the whole long truth. ("Abishag Writes a Letter
> Home," Eng. trans. by Ruth Whitman, *An Anthology of*

Modern Yiddish Poetry [1966]; cf. his "Abishag," "Abishag's Last Night in the Village," and "King David and Abishag" [*Lied un Balade* (1952)])

As country girl meets city king, Manger rescues Abishag from her subservient position in the David chronicle and transforms her into a symbolic figure powerfully expressing the predicament of the modern Jewish immigrant to the metropolis. Rooted in the biblical tale, in these poems the figure of Abishag takes on the Chagallian hues of the shtetl faced with its disintegration before the force of the modern world.

These Abishag poems make reference to a famous literary topos of Western culture, that of the *senex amans*. In their silence on the subject, the rabbis suggest the extent of their embarrassment at what the biblical story includes in a matter-of-fact way as part of the history of the Davidic era. Both Manger's and Glatstein's poems echo the biblical account. Unlike Boccaccio's senescent males or Chaucer's January lusting after May, the Yiddish writers depict a *senex amans* despite himself. Old King David's impotence takes on a personal rather than social value, which enables them to focus on Abishag's role, and transforms her into his equal by allowing her the right to speech.

By contrast Abishag plays a mythic role in Rainer Maria Rilke's poem "Abisag" (Eng. trans. by J. B. Leishman, *Rainer Maria Rilke: New Poems* [1964]), developing his thematic concern with the relation of singing, poetry, and knowledge which draws on the rich history of biblical exegesis. She appears with the same lyric force in Gladys Schmitt's magisterial 1946 historical novel *David the King*. Alexandre Arnoux's 1925 fantasy novel *Abishag* has her come to life like Pygmalion (along with David and Solomon) from a carving in a medieval Church. A year later a translation of the play *The Shunamite*, by the important Yiddish and Hebrew writer Yehoash — the pen name of Solomon Bloomgarden, who was also a brilliant translator of the Hebrew Bible — was performed by the Menorah Societies of Harvard and Radcliffe in Cambridge. Here the fiery poet-warrior is forever young in Abishag's songs and woos her for the old King David. Like Bloomgarden's work, David Pinski's play *Abishag* (*King David and his Wives* [1923]) introduces Abishag as a mythic erotic figure by presenting her through the eyes of King David:

> My whole life I have been fire and motion, and I thought I was like that bush that burned and was not consumed. . . . You are my riddle. Desire for you will waken all my powers. . . . The yearning for you will be the sharp goad that will neither let me sleep nor freeze. But if you were to be my wife, then you would become a riddle solved. What would then keep King David warm?

Two Hebrew poems of the 1940s expand the brevity of the biblical account by dramatizing Abishag's thoughts about her situation. For Yaakov Fichman, Abishag serves

David the poet while ministering to the king; for Anda Finkerfeld-Amir, Abishag, who first rebels against her fate in warming a dying old man, is recalled to her king's service by her art. Both poems are monologues spoken by Abishag: Finkerfeld-Amir's free verse is stormy and dramatic, while Fichman's rhymed couplets are subtly restrained ("Abishag," trans. by Robert Friend, *Voices from the Ark* [1980]; see also "Abishag HaShunamit," *Lifnim Mishurat Hashir* [1975]).

In these Hebrew presentations of Abishag one encounters Abishag as contemporary. This is a strategy used by James Joyce in *Ulysses,* where in the middle of the Circe episode — Nightown, Joyce called it — Leopold Bloom remembers his father's dying moments and makes a bathetic comparison: "Near the end, remembering King David and the Sunamite, he shared his bed with Athos, faithful after death. . . ." Joyce's interest in Abishag depends upon the interpenetration of the contemporary and biblical worlds, thereby signaling the ways in which the strategies of midrashic retelling are once more available to the modern writer.

See also DAVID.

Bibliography. Arton, E. "Abishag." *EncJud* (1972), vol. 1; Baumgarten, M. "Abishag." *Biblical Patterns in Modern Literature* (1984); *City Scriptures: Modern Jewish Writing* (1982), chap. 4; Caspi, M. "The Figure of the Aged Lover in our Literature." *Bitzaron* 67 (1976); Liptzin, S. "Abishag the Shunammite." In *Biblical Themes in World Literature* (1985).

MURRAY BAUMGARTEN

ABNER Abner was commander of the Israelite army under Saul and Ishbosheth — perhaps Saul's cousin or uncle (1 Sam. 14:50; 1 Chron. 8:33; 9:39) — who introduced young David fresh from his conquest of Goliath to the king's court (1 Sam. 17:57). He also accompanied Saul in pursuit of David, and was rebuked by the latter for not more carefully guarding his liege (chap. 15). Abner took up the claim of Ishbosheth to the throne. In a formal battle against Joab and David's supporters, he lost and fled, suffering the further loss of 360 men in flight. Despite the fact that he made peace with David, Joab eventually slew Abner to avenge the murder of his brother; he "smote him there under the fifth rib" (2 Sam. 3:27). David sincerely mourned Abner's death, though in fact it sped his ascension to the throne.

In early Jewish commentary Abner is a figure of considerable interest. A giant of a man in size and strength, he is said to be not only the cousin of Saul but also a son of the Witch of Endor. Proud of his vast strength, he is said to have exclaimed, "If only I could seize the earth at some point, I should be able to shake it!" (Ginzberg, *LJ* 4.73). He is elsewhere credited with being a saint (Soṭa 176) and a "lion in the Torah" (Midr. Tehillim 7.67) whose name, signifying "father of light," was granted to him as head of the Sanhedrin (Ginzberg, *LJ* 6.240). He is of less interest to medieval Christian commentators, except as a dim foil to David, and appears too early in the David narrative to attract interest from John Dryden (*Absalom and Achitophel*). In Vittorio Alfieri's *Saul* (1784, trans. into Eng. 1815, 1821) Abner turns the king's heart against David with envious insinuations, whereas in Browning's *Saul* (1845; 1855) David favorably recalls Abner's calling upon him to solace the stricken Saul with music. Abner appears in Charles Heavysage's three-part drama *Saul* (1857) and in Mark Van Doren's "Michal" (1946), where Abner forces a separation between Michal and her husband Palatiel, ordering her back to the harem of David. *Under the Fifth Rib* (1932) is the title of a novel by C. E. M. Joad; the phrase is used cryptically by John Galsworthy in "Soames and the Flag" and Henry James in "The Death of the Lion."

    See also DAVID; SAUL; WITCH OF ENDOR.

ABOMINATION OF DESOLATION   The frequently occurring OT word *abomination* designates loathsome or repugnant violation of established religious custom: eating "unclean" foods, offering imperfect sacrifices, committing moral or sexual offenses, and, above all, indulging in idolatrous practices. The more specific "abomination of desolation" appears in the OT book of Daniel. The probable context is the reign of Antiochus Epiphanes (175-63 B.C.), which included religious suppression, a ban on the Torah, sale of the high-priestly office, and desecration of the Temple, including the placing of an image of Zeus of Olympus on the high altar, a sacrilege designated the "abomination that makes desolate" (Dan. 9:27; 11:31; 12:11; cf. 1 Macc. 1:54). The circumlocution was presumably designed to avoid voicing the dangerous proper name of the contaminating deity. The Hebrew word translated "make desolate" can mean "to be appalled or overwhelmed with astonishment and dread"; it can also mean "to be desolated in the sense of emptied of inhabitants" — in the case of the Temple, emptied of both worshipers and of the Lord. The term can also mean "to be mad" and may thus reflect a contemporary pun: Antiochus's self-designation, Epiphanes ("divine manifestation"), was echoed sarcastically in his unofficial nickname, Antiochus Epimanes ("madman").

    In the NT "abomination of desolation" (Matt. 24:15; Mark 13:14) seems to designate the Roman destruction of the Temple. (The Markan tag "let him that readeth understand" seems to suggest that a tacit code is being used.) In Revelation the exclusion from the holy city of anyone "who practices abomination or falsehood" (21:27, RSV) seems to be aimed at creating a vision of the rewards awaiting those who keep the faith.

    When used by the Church Fathers, *abomination* often has decidedly apocalyptic overtones. St. Hippolytus (in ANF 5.191) understands Daniel as speaking of two abominations, one the specific destructions of Antiochus, the other a more universal reference to the coming of the Antichrist. The *Clementine Recognitions* (see ANF 8.749)

discusses the abomination in connection with general moral judgment. St. Augustine's *Contra Faustum* takes Matt. 24:15 as referring to his own time as well as Christ's.

    The word *abomination* is ubiquitous in English literature. Although it frequently refers to sexual practices subject to varying degrees of social proscription, it more often refers to serious offenses of almost any kind against decency and decorum, religious or otherwise. Only a few references are sufficiently biblical in connotation to be noteworthy in this context.

    Milton's roll call of fallen angels pointedly identifies Satan's followers with those who placed abominations in the Temple (*Paradise Lost*, 1.389). Blake is more specific about the abomination of desolation: for him it designates what he sardonically calls "the Holy Reasoning Power" (*Jerusalem*, 10.15). He also identifies it with reason's offspring, state religion, and the comprehensive tyranny of codified morality which destroys imagination (*Milton*, 41.1.25).

    Melville in *Moby-Dick* (chap. 95) associates Ishmael's jet-black idol, Yojo, with an idol which belonged to Judah's Queen Maacah (a contemporary of Israel's King Ahab) and was burned by her son, King Asa, "for an abomination at the brook Kedron." Melville says that the matter is "darkly set forth" in 1 Kings 15, which tells (as Melville does not) that Asa also "put away the male cult prostitutes out of the land" (RSV).

    Bibliography. Frost, S. B. "Abomination That Makes Desolate." *IDB* 1.13-14.   RICHARD SCHELL

ABRAHAM   The biography of Abraham, first of the Hebrew patriarchs, is recorded in Gen. 11:26–25:18. Named Abram by his father, who was in the line of Shem, he was called by God to leave his homeland, Ur of the Chaldeans, with a promise that he would be the progenitor of a great people and that God would bless him and, through him, "all families of the earth" (Gen. 12:3). With his wife (and half-sister) Sarai, his nephew Lot and Lot's family, and his father, Abram began a journey first to Haran, then to Canaan and Egypt, and finally back to Canaan, where he remained — although he continued a nomad until the end of his life.

    In spite of Sarai's barrenness God repeatedly promised Abram innumerable offspring (e.g., Gen. 12:2, 7; 15:4-5, 18; 17:2, 4ff.; 18:18; 21:13; 22:17-18). When it seemed clear to 85-year-old Abram that he would have no children by Sarai, he took her Egyptian handmaid, Hagar, as a concubine, following the custom of several ancient Middle Eastern societies, and fathered his first son, Ishmael. When Abram was 99, however, God made a covenant with him, promising that Sarai would indeed bear a son who was to be named Isaac. The covenant was sealed by several symbolic actions: circumcision ("a token of the covenant") of all male members of Abram's household; and a change of name for both Sarai and Abram, who became Sarah and Abraham. The new names, like the rite of circumcision, manifested the exchange of an old state for a new. God further promised that although Ishmael would beget a "great nation" Sarah's son Isaac would be the bearer of the covenant (chap. 17). Abraham carried out the circumcision injunction but laughed at the thought of Sarah conceiving, as did Sarah herself when the promise was subsequently repeated by three angelic visitors (chap. 18).

After the birth of Isaac, at Sarah's insistence, Abraham banished Hagar and Ishmael. Later God tested Abraham's faith by asking him to sacrifice his long-promised son. When Abraham demonstrated his willingness to offer his child and raised his hand to slay him, the demand was withdrawn and a substitute offering provided — a ram caught in a thicket. Having found Abraham obedient to this degree, God renewed his covenant with him.

In the NT Abraham is recognized as the father of Israel and of the Levitical priesthood (Heb. 7), as the "legal" forebear of Jesus (i.e., ancestor of Joseph according to Matt. 1), and spiritual progenitor of all Christians (Rom. 4; Gal. 3:16, 29; cf. also the *Visio Pauli*). For St. Paul, Abraham is the chief OT type of Christian faith because he "believed God, and it was counted unto him for righteousness" (Rom. 4:3) — before the law of Moses, before the requirement of circumcision, before the establishment of any religious ritual.

Philo *(De Abrahamo)* relates Abraham's treatment by God to concepts of Stoic virtue, interpreting virtually all aspects of the narrative allegorically: Abraham symbolizes the Mind and Sarah Wisdom; Hagar the lowly handmaid represents the liberal arts. Abraham is accorded an important place in several extracanonical Jewish writings. In Jub. 11–22 he is treated as a great hero of monotheism and purity. The Apocalypse of Abraham begins with a legendary account of his Mesopotamian background and then recounts a divine revelation bestowed on him, in which he sees the future of the Jewish people. The Testament of Abraham is an elaborate account of God's attempts to get Abraham to agree to die. So righteous is he that Abraham must consent to this!

St. Augustine, following Paul, regards all Christians as children (or "seed") of Abraham by faith, although "born of strangers" (e.g., *In Joan. Ev.* 108). St. Ambrose likewise says that by means of their faith Christians possess the promises made to Abraham. Abraham's initial departure from his homeland is understood by St. Caesarius of Arles as a type of the Christian leaving the world of carnal habits to follow Christ. Later commentators as diverse as Luther and Kierkegaard recall Abraham as a paradigm of the man of faith.

Among the specific incidents in Abraham's life recorded in the OT, several have inspired considerable commentary. The angelic visitation is frequently cited as an early witness to the Trinity (e.g., Augustine, *De Trin.* 3.11.25; 2.10.17–2.11.21). Abraham's meeting with Mel-

chisedek (Gen. 14:18-20) is seen as an anticipation of the Eucharist. Thus Cranmer, reflecting the ancient witness of St. Cyprian among others, observes that the bread and wine given to Abraham "figured and signified" the "sacrifice of Christ upon the cross" *(A Defence of the True and Catholick Doctrine of the Sacrament).* Finally, the offering of Isaac is viewed almost universally as one of the most powerful OT types of the atonement, God's willing sacrifice of his only-begotten Son.

In English literary tradition, the Abraham narrative has a diverse and colorful history. More than one-third of the Caedmonian *Genesis* is devoted to the story of Abraham and his clan, with emphasis throughout on the various forms of God's covenant *(treowe).* The poem ends with an account of the sacrifice of Isaac. In early English literature the promises made to Abraham are exploited in complex ways in relation to the fulfillment of the promises in Christ. In the OE *Exodus,* stories of both Noah and Abraham appear in connection with the narrative of the crossing of the Red Sea because of the typological relationship of all three stories to the atonement. For Milton, Abraham's seed is the "great deliverer, who shall bruise / The Serpent's head" *(Paradise Lost,* 12.149-50; cf. Gen. 3:15). Marlowe's Barabas perverts the notion of God's promises to Abraham when he says that material goods are "the blessings promised to the Jews / And herein was old Abram's happiness" *(The Jew of Malta,* 1.1.106).

Piers Plowman accords Abraham a significant role as Faith in search of the Trinity and of Christ's Church (B.16ff.), and the dreamer there is given a somewhat confusing account of Abraham's life from the patriarch himself. In *Andreas,* as in its model, the apocryphal Acts of Andrew, Abraham is "resurrected" from the dead so that he can explain the nature of the Trinity to Jews. *Cleanness* devotes a lengthy passage to paraphrasing Abraham's meeting with the angelic visitors, primarily in order to contrast Abraham's goodness with the wickedness of the citizens of Sodom, but presenting also a noteworthy treatment of the triune God. A famous visual representation of the OT trinity is the early 15th-cent. icon by the Russian Andrei Rubler.

The offering of Isaac is a crucial subject in medieval religious drama. The incident is also dramatized in the French *mystères.* French Calvinist theologian Theodore Beza composed an influential play on the subject, *Abraham Sacrifiant* (1550), which was subsequently translated into English by Arthur Golding (1577) to teach "the mightie power of earnest faith / And what reward the true obedience payth." Henry Fielding treats the incident comically in *Joseph Andrews,* where Parson Abraham Adams (who, like his biblical namesake, spends much of his time wandering) is unable to accept the (erroneous) news of his son's death, even while he is lecturing on the subject of Abraham's willingness to sacrifice Isaac. Blake's *Book of Urizen* reflects the incident ironically in Los's willing sacrifice of Orc. In *Tess of the D'Urbervilles* Hardy compares the love of Mr. Clare for his son Angel to the love of Abraham for Isaac.

In his *Castle of Indolence* James Thompson presents an eccentric picture of Abraham's wanderings as a time of idyllic happiness. The nomadic life of Abraham and his large progeny form the basis of Faulkner's comparison to him of the character Flem Snopes (in *Sartoris*), although the likeness is ironic in view of Flem's impotence. *Father Abraham* was the title of an early version of some of the material of Faulkner's *The Hamlet*. One of the two occasions on which Abraham suppressed the information that Sarah was his wife (Gen. 12; 20) is used by Walter Scott to characterize the Countess of Leicester in *Kenilworth* (chap. 22). Margaret Laurence's *The Stone Angel* chronicles the life of Hagar Shipley and her husband Bram (from Abram) and explores many of the themes of the Genesis narrative in contemporary terms.

See also HAGAR; ISAAC; ISHMAEL; SARAH.

Bibliography. Ames, R. M. *The Fulfillment of the Scriptures: Abraham, Moses, and Piers* (1970); Bamberger, B. J. "Abraham." *IDB* 1.14-21; Scott, R. T. "Odysseus, Aeneas, and Abraham: Three Archetypes of Personal Identity in Western Thought." *DAI* 33 (1973), 3020A; Speiser, E. A. "The Wife-Sister Motif in the Patriarchal Narratives." *Biblical and Other Studies* (Brandeis University) 1 (1922), 15-28; Steinmetz, D. C. "Abraham and the Reformation: The Controversy over Pauline Interpretation in the Early Sixteenth Century." *Medieval and Renaissance Studies* 10 (1984), 94-114.
PHILLIP ROGERS

ABRAHAM'S BOSOM This expression denotes, in the parable of the rich man (Dives) and Lazarus, the place of repose to which Lazarus went after his death (Luke 16:22ff.). The Jewish character of the image arises from the custom in which an honored guest at a feast might recline against the chest of his neighbor, as John reclined on the breast of Jesus at the Last Supper (John 21:20). Though rabbinic thanatology divided Sheol into realms of the righteous and wicked, the words of Jesus do not precisely correspond — here "Abraham's bosom" is not identified with Sheol but distinguished from it. The image suggests to subsequent commentators a "paradise" where Abraham receives the covenant faithful to the intimacy of an eternal feast. Christian commentators relate Abraham's bosom to the "perfect health" of eternal felicity (e.g., St. Augustine, *Sermo,* 97.3; 101.3-4).

King Richard, the errant rich man of Shakespeare's *Richard 3,* rationalizes to himself following his murder of the young princes in the Tower that "the sons of Edward sleep in Abraham's bosom" (4.3.38); the allusion is parodied in *Henry 5* when the Hostess remarks on Falstaff's death, "Nay, sure, he's not in hell; he's in Arthur's bosom, if ever man went to Arthur's bosom" (2.3.9-11). A similarly parodic reference occurs in Alexander Pope's *Dunciad,* where "Shadwells' bosom" is a place of ignorant bliss.

In Matthew Henry's *Comm. on the Whole Bible* (1728) the parable is made the basis for an argument for immortality of the soul: the soul of the beggar "did not *die,* or *fall asleep,* with the body . . . but lived, and acted, and knew what it did, and what was done to it." Further, "his soul was *removed* to another world, to the world of spirits; it returned to God who gave it, to its native country." The carrying was by ministering angels who, as Henry puts it, were no more offended by the leprous sores on his body than was Abraham, "the *father of the faithful,*" in whose bosom he lay:

> and whither should the souls of the faithful be gathered but to him, who, as a tender father, lays them *in his bosom,* especially at their first coming, to bid them welcome, and to refresh them when newly come from the sorrows and fatigues of this world? (5.759)

In Wordsworth's sonnet, "It is a Beauteous Evening, Calm and Free," the poet addresses his illegitimate daughter Caroline in terms which do not mask, however gently phrased, his sense of the vast gulf which separates them: "If thou appear untouched by solemn thought, / Thy nature is not therefore less divine. / Thou liest in Abraham's bosom all the year." This sonnet is apparently a mediate influence upon Hardy's allusion in *Desperate Remedies,* where Cytherea discusses Springrove, whom she loves, with her rival. To her question, "Are you fond of him?" the "miserable Cytherea" obtains an ambiguous reply: " 'Yes, of course I am', her companion replied, but in the tone of one who 'lived in Abraham's bosom all the year', and was therefore untouched by solemn thought at the fact" (chap. 8). A more direct allusion (with a transference from Abraham to Jesus) comes in the guilty agony of the Chaplain of Shaw's *St. Joan,* after Joan has been condemned to be burned. He cries, "O Christ, deliver me from this fire that is consuming me! She cried to thee in the midst of it: Jesus! Jesus! Jesus! She is in Thy bosom; and I am in hell for evermore."

See also DIVES AND LAZARUS.

ABSALOM Absalom was the third son of King David. The account of his rebellion against his father (2 Sam. 13–18) is widely regarded as a masterpiece of OT prose narrative. The events of Absalom's life form the sequel to the preceding narrative of David's sin with Bathsheba (2 Sam. 11–12), bringing to fulfillment Nathan's prophecy that, as a consequence of that sin, the sword would never be lifted from his house (2 Sam. 12:10-11). David's transgressions of lust, treachery, and murder are mirrored in the conduct of his sons, whose willful repetition of their father's sins ironically becomes the instrument of divine retribution upon David's house.

The portrayal of Absalom's extraordinary beauty and luxurious hair (2 Sam. 14:25-26), which underscores his virility, power, and personal appeal, serves also to identify the nature of Absalom's hubris; the very qualities which favor his rebellion ultimately ensnare him and prove his undoing, a fact graphically dramatized in the ignominious manner of his death. According to the biblical text Absalom was caught by his head in the boughs of a tree, leaving him vulnerable to attack by Joab's men. Subsequent tradition (as early as Josephus) maintains that he was suspended by his hair, a significant alteration in the narrative which underscores the poetic justice of his humiliating end. "As he rode along at full speed, he was lifted up by the unsteady motion, and his hair became entangled in a rugged tree . . . and in this strange fashion he remained suspended" (*Ant.* 7.238-39). Andrew Willet, in his *Harmonie upon the Second Book of Samuel* (1614), points out that to be hanged aloft between heaven and earth is a death accursed by God (cf. Gal. 3:13), a curse Absalom shares with his co-conspirator Ahithophel who, Judas-like, takes his own life by hanging himself. Jewish tradition held that Absalom failed to cut himself down with his sword because he saw hell yawning beneath him, hence preferring to remain hanging (L. Ginzberg, *LJ* 4.106).

A wealth of Jewish lore has accumulated around the character of Absalom. His treachery against his father was considered a crime so heinous that he remains one of the few Jews who have no portion in the world to come. Yet, for the sake of his father, his punishment in hell is mitigated. In the story of Rabbi Joshua ben Levi's visit to the underworld a divine voice stays the hand of the avenging angels who intend to scourge Absalom: "Do not beat or burn him, for he is a Jew, the son of my servant David" (*Universal Jewish Encyclopedia* [1939], 56).

Christian writers joined in the prevailing chorus of moral condemnation. St. Augustine and others cite Absalom's rejection of Ahithophel's counsel (2 Sam. 15:31; 17:1-14) as an illustration of the paradoxical co-existence of human free will with an overruling Providence: "Was it not by Absalom's own will that he chose to follow advice that proved detrimental to him, though he only did so because the Lord had heard his father's prayer to this effect?" (*De gratia et libero arbitrio*, 41). In his poem *The Origin of Sin* Prudentius reads Absalom's dismal life and character as an emblem of humanity's unregenerate nature and need for divine grace (*Hamartigenia*, 562-80). But the circumstance that most frequently inspires commentary is David's grief over the death of his errant son, which is interpreted not as a final gesture of parental affection and indulgence but as a sign of David's renewed recognition of divine justice. Augustine expresses the prevailing view in *De doctrina Christiana*, 3.21.30:

He mourned over his son's death, not because of his own loss, but because he knew to what punishment so impious an adulterer and parricide had been hurried. For prior to this, in the case of another son who had been guilty of no crime [2 Sam. 12:15-23], though he was dreadfully af-

flicted for him while he was sick, yet he comforted himself after his death.

Literary response to the story of Absalom evidences three distinct, though by no means exclusive, phases. Poets of the Middle Ages were fascinated with Absalom as an ideal of physical beauty, though their treatment of this tradition was usually heavily didactic. This preoccupation gave way in Renaissance and Restoration literature to an almost exclusive emphasis on the political implications of the story. Finally, with the advent of the novel in the 18th cent., writers increasingly drew attention to the pathetic, human elements of the narrative, especially David's heart-rending lament upon the death of his son.

In medieval literature, Absalom's name appears frequently in the interminable lists of *Ubi sunt?* poems, a popular poetic form emphasizing the transitoriness of life and the fragility of beauty. One of the most famous of these, *De Mundi Vanitate,* variously attributed to St. Bernard, Walter Map, and Jacopone da Todi, and translated in ME under the title *Cur Mundus Militat?,* recalls the name of Absalom and his legendary beauty: "Telle me where is salamon, sumtyme a kinge riche? . . . Or þe fair man absolon, merueilous in chere. . . ?" Absalom also appears in the roll of biblical names cited in Lydgate's "As a Mydsomer Rose," so named from its refrain verse, "Al stant on chaung lyke a mydsomyr roose," and in Sir David Lyndsay's *Ane Dialog betuix Experience and ane Courteour.* The *Ubi sunt?* tradition (and Absalom's place in it) survives well into the Renaissance; indeed, *Cur Mundus Militat?* remains current well into the 17th cent., appearing in the most popular of all the Elizabethan poetic miscellanies, *The Paradise of Dainty Devices* (1576).

The most celebrated Absalom in medieval literature is Chaucer's "joly Absolon" in *The Miller's Tale.* Chaucer's description of the hapless parish clerk emphasizes his effeminacy and fastidiousness: "Crul was his heer, and as the gold it shoon, / And strouted as a fanne large and brode — / Ful streight and evene lay his joly shode" (1.3314-16). In portraying Absolon in this way Chaucer reflects a marked inclination among medieval poets to transmute the biblical Absalom into a type of feminine beauty. Peter Riga's use of the rhetorical device of the *effictio* in his description of Absalom in the *Aurora* or *Biblia Versificata* is the most prominent instance of this tendency, but Chaucer himself, with calculated irony, includes Absalom and his "gilte tresses clere" in the catalogue of beautiful women which inaugurates his "balade" in praise of Alceste (Prologue to *The Legend of Good Women*). The didactic impulse which underlies this emphasis on Absalom's beauty is underscored by Adam Scotus, who warns in his *De Triplici Genere Contemplationis,* "Woe unto you, O perfidious Absalom, weighed down by your hair — that is, by carnal excess, concupiscence of the eyes, and the pride of life!"

Writers of the Renaissance were more responsive than

ABSALOM

their medieval counterparts to the tragic dimensions of Absalom's history and frequently reflect these sympathies in the more than sixty 16th- and early 17th-cent. European plays deriving their inspiration from the David story. Though some of these dramas are now lost, two notable works have survived, Thomas Watson's Latin *Absalom* and George Peele's *The Love of King David and Fair Bethsabe: With the Tragedie of Absalon* (1594). The former work exploits elements in the narrative which readily adapt themselves to a Senecan formula: "the blood-feud which works itself out within a noble family, the exile who nourishes resentment, the hypocritical reconciliation masking revengeful purpose, the suicide of a highly placed personage, and the political ramifications of an emotional situation" (Blackburn, 82). Peele's treatment of the story differs from those of his contemporaries in its awareness of the moral ambiguity of the situation; his Absalom, rather than embracing David's concubines, vehemently denounces them as symbols of the king's lust, and the play ends not with the rebel's eternal damnation but with a vision of his participation in heavenly bliss.

Peele's tragedy is striking in its divergence from the received interpretation of the Absalom story. Tudor Royalist political doctrine predictably demanded that rebels be portrayed as coming to a bad end. Thus the 1574 "Homily against Disobedience and Wilful Rebellion" points to the example of Absalom to illustrate the moral that "neyther comelinesse of personage, neither nobilitie, nor fauour of the people, no nor the fauour of the king himselfe, can saue a rebell from due punishment." Numerous homilists and biblical commentators in the period, including Archbishop Cranmer, enforce this doctrine, as do John Marbecke in *Holie Historie of King David* (1579) and Anthony Munday in *The Mirrour of Mutabilitie*.

Renaissance writers also display a keen interest in Absalom's reputation for false eloquence (2 Sam. 15:1-6), a proverbial attribute of the political schemer. In Shakespeare's *1 Henry 4,* the king, himself a usurper of the throne, describes to his son Hal the manner in which he swayed public opinion: "And then I stole all courtesy from heaven, / And dress'd myself in such humility / That I did pluck allegiance from men's hearts" (3.2.50-52). His words echo the biblical report of Absalom's campaign for public support: "So Absalom stole the hearts of the men of Israel" (2 Sam. 15:6). Similarly, in bk. 6 of *The Faerie Queene,* Spenser describes Sir Calidore as a man of "comely guize," who through "gracious speach, did steale mens hearts away" (6.1.2).

Protestant polemicists found in David's trials and suffering at the hands of Absalom a powerful analogue to their own precarious state, a parallel which St. Thomas More detects in Tyndale's veiled reference to himself as Chusai in his *Answer unto More's Dialogue* (1531): "As though the princes that would repress heresies were as Absalon with his army, and Achitophel therein, that persecute King David" (*The Confutation of Tyndale's Answer*

[1973], 138). In the course of rejecting Tyndale's self-characterization More expounds Tyndale's implicit allegorization of Absalom's rebellion in a manner which anticipates Dryden's subsequent adaptation in *Absalom and Achitophel* (1681): "And then hath Tyndale a trust that some Chusy . . . shall by his high wisdom . . . beguile all the company, and so scatter them and make them to be taken and slain as Absolon was and his folk" (*Confutation,* 138). This allegorizing tendency grows more pronounced in the polemics arising out of the civil conflict of the 17th cent., as the title of one anonymous pamphlet (1645) indicates: "Absalom's Rebellion . . . with some Observations upon the Severall Passages Thereof. Too fit a Patterne for the present Times, whereinto we are Fallen."

Dryden, in fashioning his parallel history, found several models ready to hand. Nathaniel Carpenter's *Achitophel, or, the Picture of a Wicked Politician* (1627) lays out the general lines of characterization which Dryden was to adopt. Another pamphlet, *David's Troubles Remembred* (1638), describes Absalom in verses which directly anticipate those of Dryden: "In all the Kingdomes of the *East* not one / Was found, for *Beauty* like to Absolon" (cf. *Absalom and Achitophel,* 17-18). Other references likening Absalom's rebellion to contemporary political events occur in *Absalom's Conspiracy; or, The Tragedy of Treason* (1680), *Character of a Rebellion* (1681), and Francis Gifford's *The Wicked Petition* (1681).

With characteristic subtlety, Dryden adapts this long polemical tradition to his defense of Charles II against the attacks of his Whig opponents during the time of the Popish plot (1678-81). Unlike Carpenter, who introduces some of the more repugnant aspects of Absalom's conduct, such as his public rape of David's concubines, Dryden adopts a more conciliatory tone, portraying his hero as a fine young man misled by the consummate treachery of Ahithophel and dazzled, like Narcissus, by his own noble attributes. The portrayal required great tact because his original, Charles's illegitimate son, the Duke of Monmouth, still retained his father's affection. At the level of explicit statement Absalom emerges as an attractive person deceived by subtler men than he, but his own speeches reveal a mind only too willing to receive the blandishments of others. From a historical point of view, perhaps the most striking feature of Dryden's poem is its tone. The ironic and sardonic treatment of the Scriptures anticipates a new and increasingly secular attitude toward biblical narrative which places it alongside classical mythology as a kind of miscellany of allusions.

In Byron's passing reference to David's lament over his son in the poem "Oscar of Alva" ("Oscar! my son! — thou God of Heaven, / Restore the prop of sinking age!"), biblical allegory has dwindled into incidental metaphor; this is typical not only in Byron's canon (see also *Cain,* 3.1.381; *Two Foscari,* 3.1.340) but also in those of Melville, Longfellow, Whittier, and Crane. Byron's choice of

13

this episode underscores the increasing admiration which writers, particularly novelists, expressed for the poignant scene in which David mourns Absalom's death: "O my son Absalom, my son, my son Absalom! would God I had died for thee, O Absalom, my son, my son!" (2 Sam. 18:33). Thomas Hardy pronounced this chapter of the Bible the "finest example of [prose narrative] that I know, showing beyond its power and pathos the highest artistic cunning" (*Fortnightly Review,* Aug. 1887, 304-06). Sir Walter Scott, in *The Fair Maid of Perth* and in *Woodstock,* underscores moments of heightened emotion (such as the Duke of Rothesay's death) by alluding to David's lament. Hardy, by contrast, eschews such pathos; in *Desperate Remedies,* there is irony in his reference to Manston as an "unmoved David" for displaying no emotion at the news of his wife's death.

Faulkner's profound reenactment of the narrative in his novel *Absalom, Absalom!* (1936) is centered around the triad of Thomas Sutpen, his son Henry, and Henry's half-brother Charles Bon, a triangle reflecting the David/Absalom/Amnon relationship in 2 Sam. 13. Like Absalom, who murders his half-brother Amnon in revenge for the latter's drunken rape of Absalom's sister Tamar, Henry kills Charles to forestall his incestuous and miscegenational marriage to Henry's sister Judith. In killing Charles, Henry is more a victim than a murderer, and his act is motivated by love rather than anger or revenge. Nevertheless, Sutpen's house, like David's, is doomed to play out the consequences of the father's sin: "Who should do the paying if not his sons, his get, because wasn't it done that way in the old days?" In both families the failure of love ends in fratricide and civil war.

Another modern novelist powerfully attracted to this biblical chronicle of a house divided is Alan Paton, who shares Faulkner's reluctant inheritance of a society built upon racial enmity and division. Paton weaves an extended allusion to Absalom into the very structure of his novel *Cry, the Beloved Country* (1948). Like his biblical namesake, Stephen Kumalo's wayward son, Absalom, rejects his family and his tribe, commits a murder, and hangs for his crime. In the course of his quest to find and reclaim his son, Stephen Kumalo encounters another bereaved father, James Jarvis, whose son is the victim of Absalom's violence; though their sorrow seems irreconcilable, the two fathers find comfort and redemption in their mutual grief. When Kumalo finds his son in prison, he utters the words "My child, my child" in echo of David's lament, and during his mountain vigil on the morning of his son's execution he cries out, "My son, my son, my son." These anguished words at the end of the novel are a cry not only for his own son but also for Jarvis's, and ultimately blend with countless other voices lamenting all the sons of South Africa: "Cry, the beloved country, for the unborn child that is the inheritor of our fear."

Perhaps the most revisionist reading of the Absalom story in modern literature is Christopher Fry's play, *A Sleep of Prisoners.* In it four British soldiers captured by the Germans are confined in a church, where they reenact in their dreams the lives of various OT characters whose circumstances in some way mirror their own. Private Peter Able, a pacific young man, plays Abel to the belligerent David King's Cain in the opening dream sequence; King's own dream follows, in which he assumes the role of King David and Able becomes Absalom. But this Absalom is a Christ-like figure who responds to David's tyrannical efforts to "make a soldier of him" with words which echo the language of the Gospels: "You and your enemies! Everlastingly / Thinking of your enemies. Open up. / Your enemies are friends of mine."

See also AHITHOPHEL; DAVID; TAMAR.

Bibliography. Blackburn, R. H. *Biblical Drama under the Tudors* (1971); Coffee, J. M. *Faulkner's Un-Christlike Christians: Biblical Allusions in the Novels* (1983); Evett, D. "Types of King David in Shakespeare's Lancastrian Tetralogy." *ShakS* 14 (1981), 139-61; Frontain, R., and J. Wojcik, eds. *The David Myth in Western Literature* (1980); Kartiganer, D. M. "The Role of Myth in *Absalom, Absalom!*" *Modern Fiction Studies* 9 (1964), 357-69; Roston, M. *Biblical Drama in England from the Middle Ages to the Present Day* (1968).   FRANS DE BRUYN

ABYSS *See* DEEP CALLETH UNTO DEEP.

ACELDAMA *See* FIELD OF BLOOD.

ACHAN Josh. 7:16-25 records the story of Achan (Heb. *'akan;* from *'akar,* "troubler"). The root word from which his name comes denotes trouble of the most serious kind, often the result of disloyalty, greed, and wickedness. Achan stole sacred spoils which were under the "ban" (*ḥerem*) and so put all of Israel in jeopardy. For this act of betrayal he and his family were stoned to death in the valley of Achor (the name of which derives from the same root).

Jewish commentators describe Achan as a hardened criminal whose perfidy extended well back into the lifetime of Moses (Sanh. 43b; Yerushalmi 6.23b), most of which involved violation of ritual purity: unchastity with a betrothed woman, desecration of the Sabbath, and *epispasmos,* disguising his circumcision (Sanh. 44a). His crime of "taking the anathema" is thus seen as consistent with his whole life; his punishment accords, although his confession is seen as sparing him in the life to come. Josephus (*Ant.* 5.1.14) adds that he was buried at night in the disgraceful manner reserved for criminals.

The *Glossa Ordinaria* reflects a thin patristic commentary on all but the crime itself of Achan, which, following St. Isidore of Seville and Adam of St. Victor among others, is construed as the acquisition of "heretical teachings" of the world (Jericho) such as would contaminate the Church (the Tabernacle), while the theft against the ban is *anathemate* (PL 113.511). For Calvin, Joshua's address to Achan as "my son" is not ironic but indicates "sincere personal regard" such as ought to exemplify the decorum observed by contemporary judges, "that whilst merciful they should not be careless or remiss" (*On Joshua,* 7.19).

Robert Burton, in his *Anatomy of Melancholy,* criticizes authors who prostrate their talent to curry patronage for the sake of covetousness, "the root of all these mischiefs, which Achan-like compel them to commit sacriledge." Rochester, in Charlotte Brontë's *Jane Eyre,* describes Thornfield Hall as "this accursed place — this tent of Achan."

ADAM Curiously, *Adam* as a proper noun does not assuredly occur in the Hebrew text of Genesis until well after the Garden of Eden story. In 4:25 the word occurs as a proper name for the first time: "Adam lay with his wife again." Throughout the previous passage, the character is referred to simply as "the man," which of course is the definition of *Adam.* The problem arises in translation. The LXX (3rd cent. B.C.) began the tradition of rendering the common noun *'adam* as "Adam" in Gen. 2:16: "And the LORD God commanded Adam" (Heb.: "Thus Yahweh God commanded the man"). The Vg subsequently introduced "Adam" in 2:19, which in turn was reproduced in early Catholic English translations. The KJV read "Adam" in 2:19 and inconsistently thereafter (*ha'adam* is "Adam" in 2:19 and 2:20, but "the man" twice in 2:22 and "Adam" again in 2:23). This most popular of English Bibles set the standard for centuries to follow, and the character Adam, particularly in the Garden of Eden story, became firmly entrenched in English and American literature. Some modern English Bibles, seeking to be more faithful to the Hebrew text, are introducing the proper noun "Adam" much later in the story. Thus, the ASV and the RSV read "Adam" for the first time in 3:17. The NEB and TEV both wait until 3:21 to introduce the name; the modern Catholic Bibles, the NAB and the JB (including the NJB), do not read "Adam" until 4:25.

The etymology of the word is not certain. Josephus (*Ant.* 1.1.2) thought that it was formed from the Hebrew root *'adom,* "to be red." Comparative Semitic philology has suggested that the word is related to an Ethiopic word meaning "the fair one," or Arab. "creatures," or South Arab. "servant, slave," or Akk. "maker, producer." Now, even a Sumerian origin for the word, by way of the Hebrew word *dam,* "blood," is claimed (*Beth Miqra* 30 [1984-85], 510-13). The numerous possibilities indicate the difficulty of the matter. The Hebrew text (Gen. 2:7) relates the name to *'adamah,* "ground, soil," but this is but one of the many *jeu de mots* characteristic of this particular writer, who puns outrageously and delightfully, as in 2:24, *'arummim* ("naked"), and in the very next sentence, 3:1, *'arum* ("wise," referring to the snake), or as in 4:1, *qayin* ("Cain") and *qaniti* ("I have acquired"),

or as in 11:9, *Babel* and *balal* ("he confused"), and many other such passages.

The Adam story of Gen. 2 and 3 is most closely related to ancient Near Eastern stories like Adapa, sage of Eridu, who, although acquiring great wisdom, nevertheless lost an opportunity for immortality. Gilgamesh, too, great and wise though he was, lost immortality to a serpent. In the biblical account, the man and his wife "became like gods" (3:21) by eating of the tree of knowledge of good and evil and consequently were driven away from the tree of life lest they should also achieve immortality (3:21-22).

In the Hebrew Bible itself, the only unambiguous reference to Adam outside of Genesis is in the genealogy of 1 Chron. 1:1. Due to the consonantal nature of the Hebrew script, some passages, such as Job 31:33, Hos. 6:7, and Mic. 6:8, are sometimes cited as referring to Adam, but the common modern opinion, as reflected in most Bibles, is that the word in those passages is the common noun translated "human being, humankind." The Vg, interestingly, translated the Hebrew to include "Adam" in Josh. 14:15: *"Nomen Hebron ante vocabatur Cariath Arbe; Adam maximus ibe inter Enacim situs est"* (Rheims-Douai: "The name of Hebron before was called Cariath Arbe; Adam the greatest among the Enacim was laid there"). There was a Jewish tradition (Gen. Rab. 58), evidently known to St. Jerome, that "the Four" (*Arbe* of the Vg text) — Abraham, Isaac, Jacob, and Adam — were buried at Hebron; hence its name, "Village of the Four." A similar pattern is evident in Zech. 13:5 in the Vg: *"Sed dicet: Non sum propheta; homo agricola sum, quoniam Adam exemplum meum ab adolescentia mea"* (Rheims-Douai: "But he shall say: I am no prophet; I am a husbandman, for Adam is my example from my youth"). The meaning of the last clause is not clear.

Many of the familiar Adamic themes of later literature first make their appearance in the Jewish writings which separate the Hebrew Bible from the NT. In the Life of Adam and Eve, a pseudepigraphal work, parts of which are also known as The Apocalypse of Moses and different recensions of which reached the West through Christian mediation by way of the Gospel of Nicodemus and the Lat. *Vita Adae et Evae,* Satan says that it was because of Adam that he was banished from heaven and that his hatred and envy of Adam are justified on that account. Also, in this ancient book appears for the first time the tradition of Seth's search for the oil of life which will heal his dying father. Seth does not find the oil, and Adam dies, but not before revealing the future to Seth (see Josephus, *Ant.* 1.2.3; the Coptic Apocalypse of Adam 64:2-6; and the Armenian "Death of Adam," *HTR* 59 [1966], 283-91). In some accounts, Satan is jealous because Michael commands all angels to worship Adam; in others, he is jealous because the earth is to be subject to Adam (2 Enoch 31; Wisd. of Sol. 2:23-24; cf. Pirqe R. El. 13; see L. Ginzberg, *LJ,* "Adam").

According to some Jewish sources, Satan tempts man through the woman (2 Enoch 31:6); the man sins and so dies on that very day; nevertheless, inasmuch as a day to God is as 1,000 years, Adam lives to 930 years and allots the remaining 70 years to David, who would otherwise have died in infancy (Jub. 4:30; Gen. Rab. 19; Life of Adam and Eve). So death as a penalty for sin is passed on to the generations which follow Adam (2 Bar. 17:3; Sipra Vayyiqra 20; Sipre Deut. 32:32). But the literature stresses that death is a penalty for the sin of the individual, not the result of an inherited evil nature. 2 Baruch says explicitly, "Adam is, therefore, not the cause except only for himself, but each of us has become our own cause" (54:19). Jewish literature generally follows the teaching of Ezekiel that "It is the soul that sins, and no other, that shall die; a son shall not share his father's guilt, nor a father his son's" (18:20). When the souls who are about to enter Paradise begin to reprove Adam for causing their death, he replies, "I died with one sin only, but you have committed many; for this reason you have died, not on my account" (Tanḥuma to Num. 20:24).

Adam was formed from the "dust of the earth" (Gen. 2) — variously defined in Jewish literature as dust from the Holy Place (the later Temple) and the four parts of the earth, or simply dust from the whole world (Sanh. 38aff.; Tg. Yer. to Gen. 2:7; Gen. Rab. 8), or even as "mother earth," which Josephus terms "virgin soil" (Ant. 1.1.2; cf. 2 Esdr. 5:28; Ecclus. 40:1). Adam is thus the first man, the father of all human beings from all corners of the world. Jewish literature stresses this point in many ways. Even the name *Adam* in Greek is an acronym for the four directions, *A*natole (East), *D*ysis (West), *A*rktos (North), and *M*esembria (South) (Sib. Or. 3:24-26; 2 Enoch 30:13). The reasons for stressing the unity of all human beings is given in the Tosepta: (1) he who destroys one soul destroys the world; (2) no one race of humankind can claim a nobler ancestry than the rest; and (3) the God who could create the great diversity of human beings from one man is a great God (Sanh. 8:4ff.; Mishnah Sanh. 4:5; Talmud Sanh. 38aff.). It was on the basis of this unity that Simeon ben Azzai regarded Gen. 5:1, "This is the record of the descendants of Adam," as the fundamental principle of the Law, and not the Golden Rule of Lev. 19:18 (Sipra to Lev. 19:18; Gen. Rab. 24).

Various Jewish sources assert that Adam was created a "second angel" (2 Enoch 30:11). His body reached from earth to heaven (Sanh. 38b) or filled the whole world (Lev. Rab. 18). When he sinned, he began to sink and lost the "brightness of the sun" which clothed him and thus appeared naked (Gen. Rab. 11; B. Bat. 58a; Tg. Yer. to Gen. 2:7). According to one tradition, Adam was created as an androgynous creature with "two faces." God then sawed him in two and made two backs, one for each figure (Gen. Rab. 8; cf. Plato's *Symposium*, 189-90, where the expression "two faces" is also used). Philo saw two different Adams, a "heavenly Adam" of Gen. 1 and an "earthly Adam" of Gen. 2 (*Legum allegoriae*, 1.31-32; *De opificio mundi*, 46).

The most significant contribution of NT writers in the development of the Adam of Western literature is the Adam/Messiah typology, and for this St. Paul is chiefly responsible. Paul might well have learned in his Jewish education that Adam was the ideal man and that the Messiah would someday restore all that humanity lost in the Fall, but he is the first writer to see an explicit connection in the two concepts or, as he puts it, to see Adam as "a type of the one to come" (Rom. 5:14). Through the first Adam came sin and death; through the second came grace (Rom. 5:12-21); through the one came the death of the body; through the other came resurrection (1 Cor. 15:20-23); in the "first Adam" man became an animate being (this based on Paul's midrashic rendering of the LXX of Gen. 2:7); in the "last Adam" man will become a "spiritual body" in the resurrection (1 Cor. 15:44-49). Elsewhere in the NT Luke traces the genealogy of Jesus to Adam (chap. 3), whereas Matthew begins with Abraham. Mark's account of the temptation of Jesus, with its wild beasts and angels, is very suggestive of the Adam of the Midrash.

Adam is also recalled in the NT to justify the subordinate position of women in the church. The writer of 1 Timothy reasons that since (1) Adam was created first and (2) the woman, not Adam, was deceived by the serpent, a woman should not be permitted to be a teacher, nor should she be in a position superior to man (2:11-15). Paul is probably responsible for this teaching in the Christian community. He explicitly taught the Corinthians that "woman's head is man" and that "man did not originally spring from woman, but woman was made out of man; and man was not created for woman's sake, but woman for the sake of man" (1 Cor. 11). Elsewhere the Adam and Eve story is cited in support of monogamy (Mark 10:6-9 et al.) and the familiar Jewish theme of the unity of the human race (Acts 17:26).

Adam has a small but important place in the harrowing of hell narrative popularized by the spurious but extremely influential Gospel of Nicodemus. In this text, Seth's quest for the oil of life is recorded, as is the anointing of Adam by the "Second Adam," before Christ leads him by the hand out of hell.

Among apocryphal Coptic (probably gnostic, originally Greek) books now referred to as "the Nag Hammadi Library," Adam is treated as the creation of Yaldabaoth, also known as Saklas ("Fool"), the name reflecting this community's assessment of the creator God of Genesis, together with the other rulers of the lower earth (in accordance with Gen. 1:26, "Let *us* make man in *our* image"). Adam, however, is also in the image of the perfect Spirit who was mirrored in the water while Adam was being made from the earth. Thus, Adam (humanity) is imprisoned in a material body while his inner being yearns for its spiritual counterpart. It is this knowledge (*gnōsis*) which Adam imparts to his son Seth and his descendants, which in turn will lead humans to salvation,

16

i.e., to freeing themselves from the material and uniting with the spiritual. Christ, in this scheme of things, came to remind human beings of their heavenly origins (Apocryphon of John, Apocalypse of Adam, Hypostasis of the Archons, and others).

More specifically, Adam was an androgynous being whose separation from Eve was repaired in the coming of Christ (Apocalypse of Adam 64; Gospel of Philip 70). Adam also came "from the two virgins, from the Spirit and from the virgin earth." Therefore, the text continues, "Christ was born of a virgin" (Gospel of Philip 71). The text thus combines the Jewish (or at least Josephus's) notion of Adam's virginal mother with the Christian doctrine of the virgin birth. The Coptic Apocalypse of Adam is among the first of those books in a variety of languages — Syriac, Ethiopic, Armenian, Arabic, etc. — which portray Adam prophesying great mysteries which will eventually be syncretized in the well-known *Book of the Cave of Treasures.* In this text Adam predicts his own burial in a cave which will provide the treasures which the Magi will present to the Christ Child.

St. Irenaeus in the late 2nd cent. directly challenged the doctrines of these books, devoting his best-known work, usually cited as *Adversus haereses* but more descriptively as *The Detection and Overthrow of the False Gnosis,* to a refutation of these "false teachers" and in the process offered his view of the Genesis story: Adam was made in the image and moral likeness of God, Irenaeus wrote. In the Fall, the divine likeness was lost, but not the image. The likeness can be recovered by faith in Christ. Though only a child when he fell, Adam represented the human race, afflicted with error and sin in its infancy, but capable of growing to moral maturity (bks. 1 and 3 of *Adversus haereses*). Irenaeus's view of Adam as an infant (perhaps in a metaphorical sense) was questioned by later Church Fathers, who, noticing that Adam was able to "work the ground" and "consummate marriage," argued that he was created an adult (see St. Augustine, *De Genesi ad litteram,* 6.13). Irenaeus's view of the restorability of the moral likeness might seem to preclude the notion of original sin, but his first Adam/ second Adam model, taken from St. Paul, is couched in language which at least suggests original sin: "We have offended God in the First Adam by transgressing his command; but we have been reconciled with him in the Second Adam" (*Adv. haer.* 5.16). Augustine later cited Irenaeus as a like-minded believer in original sin (see M. Gaudel, *DTC* 12.326-27).

Also in the 2nd cent., Tatian raised the question of Adam's salvation, concluding that he was not saved (*Orations to the Greeks* [lines 803-88]). This question would engage writers for the next thousand years, the most notable writers in Christianity expressing their opinions. Augustine, e.g., expressed the view of many when he wrote that Adam "was loosed from that prison [hell]" at the *"descensus Christi,"* even though the

teaching did not have canonical support (*Epistle to Euodius,* chap. 3).

St. Theophilus of Antioch reiterated the most persistent question in Christian literature concerning Adam: what was the effect of his transgression on his descendants? Theophilus answered that Adam's descendants are capable of mortality or immortality according to the decisions of their free will (*Ad Autolycum,* 2.27). He was to be joined in this conclusion by St. Clement of Alexandria, most of the Greek Fathers (such as St. Athanasius, St. John Chrysostom, St. Gregory of Nazianzus, and St. Cyril of Jerusalem), and many others. Chrysostom addressed the specific issue of the relationship of Adam's descendants to their first parent's sin when he asked, "Must I perish on his account?" He answered, "First, it is not on his account for neither have you remained without sin, though it be not the same sin" (*Hom. on 1 Corinthians,* no. 17, sect. 4 on 6:12). The schismatic Athanasius, ironically referred to as "the Father of Orthodoxy" because of his stand against Arius, pointedly remarked that "as man can turn to things good, so he can turn away from the same" (*Contra Gentiles,* 4). Cyril of Jerusalem explicitly wrote, "We come sinless into this world; we sin now voluntarily" (*Catecheses,* 4.19; see also 21).

The other and dominant view, however, was the position associated with Augustine, who gave the idea its classic formulation: the sin of Adam, the cause of his fall, is imputed to his descendants, and they therefore are sinners by nature before they are sinners by deed (e.g., *De civ. Dei,* bks. 11-14). Adam's assertion of independence, his abuse of free will, was itself the root of sin and thus destroyed free will in humankind (*De civ. Dei* 13.14). The solidarity of the human race is the controlling principle in Augustine's system. Adam lived, and all humankind lived "in him." When Adam sinned, all humankind sinned "in him." "In him" is the operative phrase, according to Augustine in bk. 3 of *De peccatorum meritis et remissione,* written to refute Pelagius's exegesis of Rom. 5:12: "For as by one man that sin entered the world, and through sin death, and thus death pervaded the whole human race *'eph' hō pantes hēmarton.*" St. Jerome fatefully translated those last four words as *in quo omnes peccaverunt,* "in whom [so "Adam," according to Augustine] all have sinned." Augustine concluded, then, that through Adam all have sinned. The sense of the Greek words is practically the same in all modern Bibles, e.g., the NEB: "inasmuch as all have sinned." As G. F. Moore observed, "If the translator [Jerome] had used *eo quod,* it is possible that the Western church might have been as little afflicted with original sin as the Greeks or the Orientals" (*History of Religions,* 2.198, n.1). Moreover, Augustine himself first sets aside the possibility that the antecedent of *quo* is either "sin" or "death" and infers that it must refer to Adam (see G. P. Fisher, *History of Christian Doctrine* [1901], 186).

Augustine was not alone, however, in associating

original sin with Adam. Origen speaks of "the filth of sin that clings to every soul that is born in the flesh" (*Homily*, preserved in *Enchiridion patristicum,* 496). And Tertullian writes, "The poison of evil desire has invaded human nature through the sin of Adam" (*De anima*, 41). Tertullian generally speaks of Adam and humanity interchangeably (e.g., *De baptismo*, 5) to such an extent that he can say, "Man . . . transgressed the commandment of God, and on that account being given over unto death, has thenceforth made his whole race, that is infected of his seed, the transmitter of his condemnation also" (*De testimoni animae*, 3). St. Ambrose, a contemporary of Augustine, writes clearly of the sinful state which every man inherited from Adam and which renders him guilty before God (see B. Altaner, *Patrology* [1961], 453).

While the relationship of Adam to his descendants and the precise nature and consequences of his sin were the major concerns of these Christian writers, there were other questions about Adam, too. There was the question of Adam's knowledge. What did he know and how did he learn it? St. Cyril of Alexandria, in the 5th cent., explicitly said that Adam did not acquire his knowledge successively; rather, the Word of God infused in him at the moment of his creation a perfect knowledge. The *Pseudo-Clementine Homilies,* now dated to the 3rd cent., have Peter saying that, since Adam was created in the image of God, he must have possessed foreknowledge and therefore could not have sinned through ignorance. Eve was made the instrument of evil, following 1 Tim. 2:14, "It was not Adam who was deceived; it was the woman who, yielding to deception, fell into sin." Chrysostom graphically portrays corruption emerging from the side of Adam and life gushing from the side of Christ (*Hom.* 20, on Eph. 5:24-33). It was principally because Adam was viewed as a rational adult that various writers assigned an age to him, ranging from thirty to sixty years. Clement of Alexandria, on the other hand, like Irenaeus, thought that Adam had a childlike knowledge and therefore succumbed to the serpent's temptation.

This fascination with Adam as the newly minted man led many of these writers to ask very detailed questions. For example, was he circumcised? St. Justin Martyr and Tertullian asserted that he was not. What did he eat? Novatian, in the 3rd cent., reasoned that Adam ate not only vegetables but also the fruit of trees because he was "upright in stature." With his fall, however, he had to cultivate grain and eventually eat meat because now he had to labor by the sweat of his face and needed the energy those foods provide. Because Genesis says, "His eyes were opened," when he ate the fruit (*De civ. Dei* 14.17), some writers in Augustine's day apparently believed that Adam was created blind. Finally, these writers exhibited an intense interest in the burial place of Adam. Some followed the Apocalypse of Moses in believing that Adam was buried near Eden; others accepted the Jewish tradition that he was interred at Hebron (see above). Origen in his *Comm. on Matthew* introduced the tradition which

was to become very popular: Adam, he thought, was buried under Calvary so that the redemptive blood of Jesus would flow onto his grave.

Early English literature typically tends to objectify or externalize earlier abstract or metaphorical ideas. Thus, Genesis B, the oldest English text treating the subject of Adam's sin, repeatedly emphasizes his literal "uprightness," his physical standing in his prelapsarian state, and his literal "falling" to the ground upon eating of the forbidden fruit (see K. Cherewatuk, *NM* 87 [1986], 537-44). This text also explicitly refers to the "tree of knowledge" as the "tree of death."

This same tendency toward literalness underscores the popular medieval legends concerning the Holy Rood, in which the wood of the cross was believed to have been taken from the tree of knowledge. The early 14th-cent. poem *Cursor Mundi* includes the tradition that Seth, after journeying to the Garden of Eden for the oil of life for Adam, who was dying in Hebron, brought back instead three kernels of the tree of knowledge, which he planted in the mouth of his father upon his death. These trees in turn provide the wood for the cross. The fully christianized version of the Jewish Life of Adam and Eve comes to us through ME writers (see O. F. Emerson, ed., *A Middle English Reader* [1905], 64ff.). This tradition of the cross, of course, is an extension of Paul's Adam / Christ typology, which produced a whole complex of such symmetries: just as Eve listened to the serpent and brought death, so Mary attended the angel and brought forth life; just as Adam disobeyed in the Garden of Eden, so Christ obeyed in the Garden of Gethsemane, etc. Most of these parallels go back to the Fathers (see, e.g., Irenaeus, *Proof of the Apostolic Preaching*, chap. 34).

In the rich poetic tradition of the ME period Adam appears chiefly as the means by which sorrow afflicted the human race: "Adam alas and waylaway! / A luther dede dedest thou that day!" A "Doomsday" poem of the 13th cent. asserts, "From that adam was i-wrout that / comet domesday." Even children's songs and lullabies such as "Lollai little child, why weepest thou so sore?" locate the source of all grief in Adam's sin: "This woe Adam thee wrought / When he of the apple ate."

Yet this "woe" is to be gloriously redressed, according to countless lyrics:

Also Adam wyt lust and likynge
Broghte al his ken into wo and wepynge,
So schal a child of the kende springe,
That schal brynge hym and alle hyse
Into joye and blisse habbynge.

The Fall as a *"felix culpa"* — the paradoxical phrase comes from the Easter liturgy — is most clearly seen in the well-known 15th-cent. "Adam lay i-bowndyn," which leaves no doubt concerning the beneficent effect of the Fall: "Blyssid be the tyme that appil take was, / Therefore we mown syngyn *'Deo gracias!'* " But the theological formulation most formative of this relation, and still echoing in the 15th cent., is that of St. Anselm of Canterbury, whose 12th-cent. *Cur Deus Homo, si Adam non pecasset* is a groundbreaking theology of the Incarnation. Anselm's influence upon the sermon literature and lyrics of the Franciscans in particular is evident in English allusions to the subject after the 13th cent.

ME lyrics and drama rehearse the familiar harrowing of hell tradition, as do authors such as Chaucer, who also embraces, or at least echoes, the Augustinian doctrine of original sin:

> Loo Adam, in the feeld of Damyssene
> With Goddes owene fynger wroght was he,
> And nat bigeten of mannes sperme unclene.
> (*The Monk's Tale*, 7.207-09)

The matter is quite explicit in *The Parson's Tale:* "Of thilke Adam tooke we thilke synne original; for of hym flesshly descended be we alle, and engendered of vile and corrupt mateere."

By the end of the Middle Ages, the simple account of Adam's life given in Genesis had been overlaid with an elaborate mythology, detailing practically everything from the fall of the angels to the precise identification of the fruit of the tree of knowledge. All this became the subject of the mystery plays, which were chiefly associated with the Feast of Corpus Christi. The Fall of Adam was dramatically presented in the York, Chester, and N-Town (Coventry) cycles and probably in the incomplete Wakefield (Towneley) cycle, as well as in the sole survivor of some twelve plays performed in Norwich in the 15th and 16th cents., now known as the Norwich Grocers' Play. Although most of the material in these plays is familiar, occasionally a new twist on the subject appears, such as the dulling of Adam's and Eve's senses after eating of the fruit: "A lord for synne oure flourys do ffade / I here thi voys but I see the nought" (N-Town, 275-76). The second play of the Chester cycle contains the relatively novel idea of Adam's dream, which grew out of the simple statement that God put Adam to sleep when he took the rib to make woman. In this dream, which Adam later relates to Cain and Abel, the great Flood, the Incarnation, and the Last Judgment are prophesied. The early Syriac Testament of Adam contains a similar scheme: Creation, the Flood, Incarnation, and Judgment — communicated by Adam to Seth, not to Cain and Abel.

At the heart of these plays is a concern to dramatize the standard Adam / Christ typology. Thus, in the "Annunciation" play of the Wakefield cycle, e.g., God proclaims,

> I wyll that my son manhede take,
> ffor reson wyll that ther be thre,
> A man, a madyn, and a tre;
> Man for man, tre for tre,
> Madyn for madyn, thus shal it be. (30-34)

Edmund Spenser characteristically fuses Adam and the Adam tradition to classical culture in his *Faerie Queene.* Una's parents rule over "Eden" (1.12.26.1), "which Phison and Euphrates floweth by, / And Gehons golden waues doe wash continually" (1.7.43.8-9; cf. Gen. 2:11-14). After long exclusion from their native land, they are restored to it by holiness. The Redcrosse Knight and Una encounter Error, half serpent and half woman, in a forest-like setting, suggesting the Fall story. Yet, as E. Smith has pointed out,

> The historicity of a first fall is neither affirmed nor denied in any exclusive terms, and the state of the Red Cross Knight at the beginning is neither totally depraved nor totally paradisaic; Adam is not only the first man, but all men, of whom the Knight is one. (*Some Versions of the Fall*, 98-99)

If Spenser's self-consciously fictive epic treats its Adam figure somewhat ambiguously, a more straightforward rendering of the Fall story occurs in his "Hymne of Heavenly Love":

> But man forgetfull of his makers grace,
> No lesse then Angels, whom he did ensew,
> Fell from the hope of promist heavenly place,
> Into the mouth of death to sinner dew,
> And all his off-spring into thraldome threw. (120-24)

Sir Walter Raleigh, a correspondent of Spenser, was certainly not setting up straw men when he spoke out against the tendency to read the Adam and Eve story as allegory. In his *History of the World* Raleigh lamented the Vg's rendering of Gen. 2:8 (*"Plantauerat Dominus Deus Paradisum voluptatis a principio"*), in which "Eden" becomes *voluptatis* ("pleasure") and "eastward" becomes *a principio* ("at the beginning") as an allegorical reading of a geographical passage. Eden, he wrote, is as much a part of world geography as "that land west of Cuba that the Spaniards call Florida" and has similar meaning, "pleasure or flourishing" (1.3.3).

Shakespeare used the Adam tradition almost entirely for secular, even comical, purposes. In *Much Ado About Nothing,* Beatrice and Benedick take turns evoking the Genesis story in unusual and humorous ways. First Beatrice vows that she will never marry:

> Not till God made men of some other metal than earth.
> Would it not grieve a woman to be overmaster'd with
> a piece of valiant dust? to make an account of her life
> to a clod of wayward marl? No, uncle, I'll none.
> Adam's sons are my brethren, and truly I hold it a sin
> to match in my kindred. (2.1.50-55)

Benedick, for his part, swears, "I would not marry her though she were endowed with all that Adam had left before he transgressed" (2.1.218-20). In *Love's Labour's Lost* (5.2.323) Berowne observes of the witty and silver-tongued Boyet, "Had he been Adam, he had tempted Eve."

Elsewhere in Shakespeare the Adam image has more

serious implications, as in the Henry trilogy, where repeated references to the "old man" and "th' offending Adam" (*2 Henry 4; Henry 5,* 5.1.1.28-29) underscore Falstaff's comic and pathetic identification: "Dost thou hear, Hal? Thou knowest in the state of innocency Adam fell; and what should poor Jack Falstaff do in the days of villainy?" (*1 Henry 4,* 3.3.172-74).

Milton provides the most complete statement of the Adam tradition in world literature. *Paradise Lost,* according to its own declarations, is an epic *apologia* in the context of 17th-cent. culture. The poet invokes the Spirit to enable him "to justifie the wayes of God to men" (1.26). The long description of the Satanic rebellion, specifically placed before the introduction of Adam, is designed to indicate that Adam's disobedience does not have God as its source. So, too, the visit of Raphael to prelapsarian Adam (bks. 5-8), surely a major portion of the poem, functions chiefly in the poem as rendering Adam without excuse. Milton previously has the Deity ensure that he is not held responsible either for Satan's fall (3.95ff.) or for Adam's (3.111ff.).

For Milton, Adam was created by the Son with only a single restriction: "Not to taste that onely tree" (4.423). "The rest, we live / Law to our selves, our Reason is our Law" (9.653-54). Seduced by the serpent, the woman eats of the forbidden fruit, and Adam follows her, though he is not deceived (10.145). Having enjoyed pure physical love before the Fall (4.312, 506), they now, immediately afterward, engage in an orgiastic union which marks their fallen nature. The poet seems to have sifted carefully through the various theological traditions of European culture to recover every detail and tradition which might aid him in his specifically apologetic cause.

Milton was responding to the secular forces which were calling into question — or even ridiculing — the whole notion of a historical Adam and a geographical Eden. In the burlesque *Hudibras,* by Samuel Butler, Milton's contemporary, it is said of the titular hero that he knew

> . . . the seat of Paradise,
> Could tell in what degree it lies;
> And, as he was disposed, could prove it,
> Below the moon, or else above it:
> What Adam dreamt of when his bride
> Came from her closet in his side:
> Whether the devil tempted her
> By a High-Dutch interpreter;
> If either of them had a navel;
> Who first made music malleable;
> Whether the serpent, at the fall,
> Had cloven feet, or none at all. (1.173-84)

The satirical tone of Butler is all the more biting because his description reflects the actual concerns of his contemporary writers, such as Sir Thomas Browne, who alludes to the notion of original sin with the memorable words "The man without a navel yet lives in me" (*Religio*

Medici, 2.10) and in his *Pseudodoxia Epidemica* devotes a chapter to the "error" of artists such as Michelangelo who represent the first man with a navel (see J. Borges's essay on Adam's navel in his "The Creation and P. H. Gosse," rpt. in *Other Inquisitions (1937-1952),* trans. R. Simms [1964]).

Ironically, Milton's own use of the epic form contributed to the further decline of the Adam tradition. Increasingly, after Milton writers talk mythically of the Fall but not historically of Adam.

One of the most radical mythic departures from the biblical story is that of Blake, who inverted the vision of *Paradise Lost* to create his own version of the Fall in which

> The Combats of Good and Evil is Eating of the Tree of Knowledge. The Combats of Truth and Error is Eating of the Tree of Life. . . . There is not an Error but it has a Man for its Agent, that is, it is a Man. There is not Truth, but it has also a Man. *(A Vision of the Last Judgment)*

Lord Byron, too, employs the Fall story, but Adam is merely a minor character in his tragedy *Cain,* which centers on Adam's firstborn. Mary Shelley's classic *Frankenstein* echoes the biblical story with its implication that Frankenstein usurps the knowledge of God in the manner of Adam.

The protagonist of George Eliot's *Adam Bede* is a young carpenter who manages the woods of a great estate and whose character is torn between what he knows is moral on the one hand and what is attractive and immoral on the other. Robert Browning adopts the talmudic story of Lilith to present a very human Adam in a most unusual *ménage à trois,* in his "Adam, Lilith, and Eve."

In 20th-cent. literature, Adam is most often a completely mythical figure whom writers use to denote themes of societal conflict (e.g., Shaw's *Back to Methuselah* or Edwin Muir's "Adam's Dream," in which the traditional story is applied to the confusion in modern life), or the common plight of mankind (Yeats, "Adam's Curse" and "Why Should Old Men Be Mad?"), or some aspect of the perceived conflict between the sexes (as in John Fowles's several novels), or a nostalgic longing for a golden youth (Dylan Thomas, "Fern Hill"). The Adam figure has a more traditional role in G. K. Chesterton's "In Praise of Dust" and C. S. Lewis's *Perelandra.*

American literature from the colonial period on has been characterized by a persistent attraction to the character and the narrative of Adam. Hawthorne and Melville, as well as Walt Whitman, James Fenimore Cooper, and Montgomery Bird, contributed to the literary development of the American Adam. No American writer, however, made greater use of the Adam tradition than Mark Twain. Not only did he write the delightful and witty *Extracts from Adam's Diary* (1893), which was reprinted with *Eve's Diary* (1905) in 1931 as *The Private Lives of Adam and Eve,* but he also used many of the significant themes of the Adam tradition in some of his better-known works such as *Huckleberry Finn,* where the images of the innocence of Adam's Edenic world are central to Huck's experiences.

Much of William Faulkner's work is set against the background of the Adam tradition. Robert Penn Warren's *All the King's Men* evokes Adam by name and the idea of fallenness in its title, its images, and its events.

Of the many American poets who have used the Adam tradition, Archibald MacLeish generally interprets the story as involving the growth and maturation of humanity, not its decline. His "Eve's Exile" contrasts the primordial pair with the fish and hawk:

> They mirror but they may not see,
> When I had tasted fruit of tree
> Fish and hawk, they fled from me:
>
> "She has a watcher in her eyes,"
> The hawk screamed from the steep of skies,
> Fish from sea-deep where he lies.
>
> Our exile is our eyes that see.
> Hawk and fish have eyes but we
> Behold what they can only be.
>
> Space within its time revolves
> But Eve must spin as Adam delves
> Because our exile is ourselves.

See also APPLE; EDEN; EVE; FALL; *FELIX CULPA;* HARROWING OF HELL; LILITH; NAMING OF THE ANIMALS; ORIGINAL SIN; SECOND ADAM; TREE OF KNOWLEDGE; TREE OF LIFE.

Bibliography. Benz, E. *Adam; der Mythos vom Urmenschen* (1955); Boas, G. "Primitivism." *In Dictionary of the History of Ideas* (1973); Harty, K. J. "Adam's Dream and the First Three Chester Plays." *CahiersE* 21 (1982), 1-11; "The Norwich Grocers' Play and Its Three Cyclic Counterparts: From English Mystery Plays on the Fall of Man." *SN* 53 (1981), 77-89; Hort, F. J. A. "Adam (Books of)." *In A Dictionary of Christian Biography* (1967); Jeremias, J. "Adam." *TDNT* 1.141-43; Lee, A. A. *The Guest Hall of Eden: Four Essays on the Design of Old English Poetry* (1972); Lewis, R. W. B. *The American Adam: Innocence, Tragedy, and Tradition in the Nineteenth Century* (1951); Pirot, L. "Adam et la Bible." *DBSup* (1928); Robinson, S. E., trans. "Testament of Adam (Second to Fifth Century A.D.)." In *The Old Testament Pseudepigrapha* (1983).   ANTHONY D. YORK

ADAM'S ALE   Colloquial allusion to water. A beverage before the Flood and the advent of fermentation, discovered by Noah, it could contain no alcohol. In Matthew Prior's *The Wandering Pilgrim,* it is the only drink of poor Will, whose deprivation is hence that of a "Rechabite." "A cup of cold Adam from the next purling stream" (Tom Brown, *Works,* 4.11) came in frontier American literature to be a spartan tribute, preferring nature to culture.

ADONIJAH   One of the rebellious sons of David who, with the backing of Joab and Abiathar the priest, at-

tempted to overthrow him in his later years (1 Kings 1:5-10, 25). Solomon was hastily anointed King, Adonijah eventually put to death.

See also DAVID; SOLOMON.

ADONIS   Adonis was originally a Sumerian vegetation god, Tammuz. When his worship spread to Greece, the honorific title *'adonai* (lit. "my lord[s]") converted into a proper name. In the Sumerian pantheon Tammuz was *Dumu-zi,* meaning "true son." Still extant are a number of hymns in his honor written around 2,000 B.C. on inscribed Sumerian texts. In Babylonian religious literature, Tammuz was the youthful spouse or lover of Ishtar. Each year Tammuz was believed to die, passing from earth to the subterranean world, where Ishtar annually journeyed in quest of him. Despite resistance from Allatu, queen of the netherworld, Ishtar and Tammuz were allowed to return to the upper world so that nature, which had withered in their absence, might revive. The counterparts of the Babylonian story reappear in Greek mythology, Tammuz, Ishtar, and Allatu being replaced by Adonis, Aphrodite, and Persephone.

The cult of Adonis was known to the Greeks in the 7th cent. B.C. Sappho, Bion, Theocritus, Moschus, and Pausanias refer to mourning ceremonies for Adonis (cf. J. M. Edmonds, *The Greek Bucolic Poets* [1910], 387-95, 451, 177-95; Pausanias, *Description of Greece,* trans. J. G. Frazer [1965], 1.101; M. Bernard, *Sappho* [1958], poem 11). During the same period Ezek. 8:14 notes the presence of the cult in Jerusalem, where at the gates of the Lord's house "there sat women weeping for Tammuz." During their Babylonian exile, Jews named the fourth month of the Hebrew calendar Tammuz (June). The Semitic origins of the myth, the spread of its cultic rites, and Ezekiel's allusion to it are brought together by Milton in *Paradise Lost* (1.446-57):

> Thammuz came next behind,
> Whose annual wound in *Lebanon* allur'd
> The *Syrian* Damsels to lament his fate
> In amorous ditties all a Summer's day,
> While smooth *Adonis* from his native Rock
> Ran purple to the Sea, suppos'd with blood
> Of *Thammuz* yearly wounded: the Love-tale
> Infected *Sion's* daughters with like heat,
> Whose wanton passions in the sacred Porch
> *Ezekiel* saw, when by the Vision led
> His eye survey'd the dark Idolatries
> Of alienated *Judah.*

A funeral cult in honor of Adonis was widely observed throughout the ancient world. Its rites included the forced growth of unrooted plants in shallow vessels (cf. *Phaedrus,* 276b; Theocritus, *Idyll,* 15.113). The plants, which quickly died, were known as "gardens of Adonis." The phrase in Isa. 17:10 rendered in the KJV as "pleasant plants" and in the JB as "plants for Adonis," probably alludes to these miniature gardens, whose rapid decline was a symbol of the god or of the spring verdure which he personified. The prophet, in alluding to a custom at least similar to the gardens of Adonis, is denouncing the adoption of pagan rites and warning of their uncertainty.

The treatment of Adonis in classical mythology has been most influential in English literature. The garden imagery associated with him contributed to the long tradition of earthly paradises, including Homer's Garden of Alcinous (*Odyssey*, 7.112-34), Claudian's Garden of Venus (*Epithalamium of Honoris and Maria*, 49-96), the Eden of Dante (*Purgatorio*, 28), and Milton's Eden (*PL* 9.439-40). Spenser's Garden of Adonis, which offers an account of the life process in terms which center on the myth of Venus and Adonis, draws on a large variety of sources, including Plato, Arthur Golding's Elizabethan translation of Ovid, Natalis Comes's discussion of Adonis (*Mythologiae*, 5.16), and other titles previously noted.

The central concern of the myth, early death, has naturally associated it with the pastoral elegy. Milton's *Lycidas*, according to Northrop Frye, is concerned with the vegetable life which dies in autumn. In this aspect, "Lycidas is the Adonis or Tammuz whose 'annual wound,' as Milton calls it elsewhere, was the subject of a ritual lament in Mediterranean religion, and has been incorporated in the pastoral elegy since Theocritus . . ." (*Anatomy of Criticism*, 121). In *Adonais,* Shelley's pastoral elegy written to mark the premature death of John Keats, the name assigned the poet is derived from Adonis, and several aspects of the myth are apparent. The role of the wild boar which killed the mythic Adonis is assigned to John Wilson Croker, whose vituperative review of Keats's "Endymion" in the *Quarterly Review* was incorrectly believed by Shelley to be responsible for Keats's death. The death and revival of Adonis is recalled in Adonais-Keats's triumph over death in the poem. A key symbol in this is the identification of Keats with the planet Venus, which appears both as Lucifer, the morning star, and Hesperus, the evening star. In st. 46 the spirit of Keats assumes its place in the sphere of Hesperus, and in st. 55 it inspires the lamenting Shelley: "the soul of Adonais, like a star / Beacons from the abodes where the Eternal are."

Several variations on the myth have been introduced in English redactions. Shakespeare's *Venus and Adonis* takes the central figure and background of the myth from the tenth book of Ovid's *Metamorphoses* but introduces the conceit of a boar merely wanting to kiss, not to kill, Adonis. This same conceit had already appeared in the translation of Theocritus's *Six Idilia*, anonymously published at Oxford in 1588, and reappeared later in Milton's *On the Death of a Fair Infant* in the image of amorous Winter seeking to kiss but killing the child instead.

The story of Adonis has continued to exercise a hold on the literary imagination to the present day. In T. S. Eliot's *The Waste Land* (1922), Adonis, the slain vegetation god, is merged with the figure of Christ in the concluding section of the poem, although, as Douglas N. Bush remarks, Eliot's Adonis "has more to do with [Sir James] Frazer than with Venus" (*Mythology and the Romantic Tradition in English Poetry* [1963], 515). Noting similarities between Easter ceremonies and the rites for Adonis, Frazer had surmised that "the Easter celebration of the dead and risen Christ was grafted upon a similar celebration of the dead and risen Adonis" (*The Golden Bough*, 4.256).

Bibliography. Hamilton, A. C. "Venus and Adonis." *SEL* 1 (1961), 1-15; Hatto, A. T. "Venus and Adonis — and the Boar." *MLR* 41 (1946), 353-61; Jackson, R. S. "Narrative and Imagery in Shakespeare's Venus and Adonis." *Papers of the Michigan Academy of Science, Arts, and Letters* 43 (1958), 315-20; Langdon, S. *Tammuz and Ishtar* (1914); Price, H. T. "Function of Imagery in Venus and Adonis." *Papers of Michigan Academy of Science, Arts, and Letters* 31 (1945), 275-97; Rochette, R. "Mémoire sur les jardins d'Adonis." *RArch* 8 (1851), 97-123; Witzel, M. *Tammuz-Liturgen und Verwandtes* (1935); Zimmern, H. "Der babylonische Gott Tamuz." In *Abhandlungen der philologisch-historischen Klasse der Königlichen. Sächsischen Gesellschaft der Wissenschaften* 27.2 (1909).   MICHAEL GOLDBERG

ADULLAM   When young David was fleeing the wrath of Saul, he and his small group of men hid in the cave of Adullam (1 Sam. 22:1-2) in the lowlands of Judah, whereupon they were joined by "every one that was in distress, and every one that was in debt, and every one that was discontented." Though the text specifies only about 600 (23:13), legend has it that included in the number of malcontents were 1,400 scholars (see L. Ginzberg, *LJ* 6.254) and that this was the same cave in which Lot became drunk and slept with his daughters (Yashar Wa-Yera 39a; see Gen. 19:33-38). Patristic commentary sees David and his men as prefiguring Christ and those who first came to him from among the Jews in the days before the kingdom was revealed (e.g., *Glossa Ordinaria* [PL 113.559-60]).

In English literature the term *Adullam* is occasionally used as a kind of shorthand for a sanctuary for outcasts. Thus Thomas Hardy in *The Mayor of Casterbridge* refers to Mixen Lane in the lowest section of town as "the Adullam of all the surrounding villages. It was the hiding place of those who were in distress, and in debt, and trouble of every kind."

ADULTERY   In biblical tradition, adultery is regarded as a sin against God, society, and posterity. To uphold their theocratic identity, OT Jews viewed the willful sexual intercourse of a man with the wife of someone else as a great sin (Exod. 20:14); the law required adulterers to be put to death (Lev. 20:10; Deut. 22:22-27).

In a wider sense, adultery becomes a powerful figure for breach of covenant. Beginning perhaps with Hosea, OT prophets often portray ancient Israel's reverence of other gods as adultery against the Lord (e.g., Hos. 1:2; 2:1-23). Ezekiel's allegory of whorish sisters pictures Samaria and Jerusalem as sacrificing to idols the children

God has fathered on them (Ezek. 23:3-49), and he, the wronged husband, threatens to have the sisters stoned. Elsewhere Israel's idolatry is said to prompt God to divorce her (Jer. 3:8-9) and to lament that her adulteries have separated them as man and wife (Hos. 2:2); Jerusalem will be destroyed, he says, because of her idolatry (Jer. 13:27). But God is also depicted as a forgiving and longsuffering husband: indeed, he tells Hosea to imitate his forbearance toward the faithless Israelites by marrying an adulteress (Hos. 3:1-3).

Adultery is frequently condemned in the NT as well (e.g., 1 Thess. 4:1-8), as is consorting with prostitutes (1 Cor. 6:15-20), for all such sexual sins grieve the Holy Spirit, defile his "temple," and deny the redeeming work of Christ. In Revelation (e.g., 2:20-22), the metaphorical use of the charges of adultery and fornication reappears in describing the idolatry and false teaching of certain figures in the churches. Also noteworthy is the description of the Roman system as "the great whore," who fornicates with all the kings of the earth (17:1-18).

In the Gospels Jesus employs the OT metaphorical use of adultery to describe religious unfaithfulness (Matt. 12:39-40; Mark 8:38). In the Sermon on the Mount, adultery is not only a proscribable deed but also a default of spiritual discipline: he who lusts after a woman commits adultery (Matt. 5:27-28). Jesus modifies, too, the OT law that a man who divorces a wife must give her a certificate, insisting that he who does so on grounds other than fornication makes her and her new husband commit adultery (Matt. 5:31-32; 19:1-9; cf. Mark 10:1-12). Perhaps the most familiar episode concerning Jesus' view of adultery is that in which an adulterous woman is brought to him for condemnation by the religious authorities (John 8:3-11). Jesus turns the tables on the woman's accusers by inviting the one who is sinless to cast the first stone. He himself then (although sinless) also refrains from condemning her but urges her to sin no more.

Early Christian writers variously proscribe adultery. Tertullian suggests that the Church, in maintaining her own Virgin status, cannot forgive adultery but must exact punishment on adulterers. Furthermore, since all intercourse outside marriage is adultery, the Church must ban relations not professed and ordained openly. He opposes the notion that the NT changed the OT law against adultery (*De pudicitia,* 4.74-85). While insisting that bishops keep away from adulterers because, in violating matrimony or visiting brothels, the latter abuse free will and defile the sanctified body, God's temple, St. Cyprian nevertheless urges that adulterers be granted repentance. The Church's own continence, he reasons, cannot be devalued or compromised by forgiveness (*Ep.* 5.332-34). Increasingly complex views are expressed by other early writers. St. Augustine, holding both sexes responsible for adultery, claims that the woman who keeps faith with her adulterer is better than she who does not and proposes that the husband take back the repentant wife who pledges

herself to marital chastity (*De bono coniugali,* 3.400-401). St. John Chrysostom argues that adultery involves self-seduction, indicating how a lustful man habituates himself to shameful images and pointing out how mental adultery leads to actual adultery and murder (*Hom. on Matthew,* 10.117, 300). While St. Basil refines female responsibility by maintaining that it is worse for a virgin to commit adultery than a widow since the former is the bride of Christ, he is troubled that there is no canon against men who fornicate with unmarried women: he does not approve the custom which allows the husband to expect the polluted wife to leave his house, while the wife must take back the fornicator (*Ep.* 8.237). The Shepherd of Hermas says that, whereas a man ignorant of his wife's adultery is not guilty, he shares her crime if he knows of it and she does not repent. He must take her back if she repents, but, if she does not, he must divorce her and not remarry (FC 1.264). Athenagoras of Athens insists on the indissolubility of marriage: death does not dissolve it; a second marriage is no more than decent adultery. Since God in the beginning created one man and one woman, he who marries a second time is but a cloaked adulterer (*Patrology,* 1.235). Later commentators debate similar issues: whereas Erasmus thinks death preferable to adultery (*Colloquies,* 330), Luther stresses that the victim of sexual assault must not consider herself an adulteress (*Works,* 9.223-25), even as he supports the traditional view of legitimate sex (1.96) and holds that adultery is the worst of thefts since it takes a living body from the spouse, its rightful possessor (28.13).

Chaucer, like other ME authors, satirizes as well as defends the church's handling of adultery. In *The Friar's Tale,* he suggests that hypocritical church officers employ spies to exploit rather than reform adultery (*Canterbury Tales,* 3.1301-74). *The Parson's Tale* epitomizes arguments against adultery: marriage betokens that union of Christ and Church; desiring to commit adultery is as bad as doing so; it is the worst kind of theft for a woman to steal her body from her husband and let the adulterer defile it, since this is stealing her soul from Christ and giving it to the devil; it is worse than breaking into the church and stealing the chalice because it is breaking into the temple of the Lord and taking the vessel of grace. Adultery is placed between theft and murder among the sins proscribed by the Ten Commandments because it constitutes both the greatest theft and greatest murder: since it involves a theft of body and soul and a murder of the "one flesh" union of spouses, the severity of the OT penalty is justifiable. He cites the NT law represented in the story of the woman taken in adultery to stress that, unless adultery is overcome by penitence, its punishment is hellfire. (In *The Tale of Melibee* Chaucer uses the story to stress Christ's humane and scrupulous judgment [*CT* 7.2220-50].) The Parson also elaborates various species of adultery: it is regarded as having different degrees of seriousness for religious and lay people; the higher the religious office, the worse the sin; adultery includes husbands and wives who marry only for sexual pleasure (*CT* 10.870-90; the extension of adultery to unspiritual marriages is stressed also in Taylor's *Holy Living* and in Defoe's *Conjugal Lewdness*). In *The Merchant's Tale,* Chaucer amusingly punishes January for rationalizing his sensuality by saying that to marry an older woman would oblige him to commit adultery and suffer damnation (*CT* 4.1435). His immoral view that his wife is a sexual slave whom he cannot wrong is nicely exposed when his young bride, May, cuckolds him.

Tudor and Elizabethan writers reflect diverging attitudes toward adultery. In More's secular Utopia, operating according to natural reason rather than divine revelation, adultery ends a marriage, the guilty party is condemned to celibacy and penal servitude, and the injured party is allowed to remarry, but wronged spouses may stay married, if they share their mates' lot. Although such couples can be freed from legal penalties, a second offense merits capital punishment. (On a personal level, More, referring to Potiphar's wife's attempted adultery with Joseph, argues that it is better to flee than to face temptation [*Sadness of Christ,* 295; cf. *Joseph Andrews,* 1.5].) Both Spenser (*Faerie Queene,* 5.48) and Sidney (*Defense of Poesie,* 21) hold that adultery characteristically leads to worse crimes.

Shakespearean drama affords a variety of complex and theologically sophisticated explorations of adultery. In *The Comedy of Errors,* Adriana urges her husband to be faithful, unaware that she addresses his twin (2.1), by suggesting that, if she were unfaithful, he would divorce her! She declares that she is adulterate. Her blood is tainted with lust: since the two of them are one and he plays false, he strumpets her. Adriana's witty argument owes much to the Church Fathers' rule that husband and wife cannot condone one another's infidelity and to the view of adultery expounded by Jesus in the Gospels. Shakespeare's technical sense of adultery is evident when Isabella rightly calls Angelo an adulterous thief (*Measure for Measure,* 5.1.40): he breaks his betrothal to Mariana, thinking he is free to fornicate with Isabella; while actually lying with Mariana, in his mind he lies with Isabella. In his angry conviction that adultery explains family strife, Lear's voice is almost prophetic: Regan's unfilial conduct makes him threaten to disown his dead wife and conclude her an adulteress (*King Lear,* 2.4). When, on the heath, he changes his view about adultery and pardons the life of an imaginary adulterer in the belief that, since lechery is universal, adultery does not deserve death (4.6), he is the victim of a bitter irony: his evidence is that Edmund has been kinder to his father than his daughters have been to him. Yet Edmund and the two sisters are equally vicious and adulterous.

In "An Epistle to a Friend, to perswade him to the Warres," Jonson rages like a prophet against fashionable and famous people who flout their adulteries without reprimand. He complains that men take others' wives and let out their own and that he who will not let his wife become a whore is stigmatized. Donne, in "Elegy 18," offers a witty tongue-in-cheek argument that being a deluded and idealistic lover is more sinful than being an unfaithful one. Defoe insists that adultery leads to greater crimes (e.g., *Moll Flanders* [1976], 59; *Roxana* [1964], 38). Fielding stresses the material and legal reasons for avoiding adultery (*Amelia* [1983], 257). Observing that adultery is punished neither by state nor by church (375), he adopts the expedient view that it is better to make love to an unmarried rather than to a married woman (413-17). Like Congreve (*Old Batchelor,* 4.1.69) and Dryden (*Juvenal's Satires,* 1.87) before him, Fielding regards wives as their husbands' property. Cowper satirizes government for pardoning adultery. He hates the adulteress who glories in her abandonment, and loathes society matrons who regard adulteresses as virtuous (*The Task,* 3.63-64).

Romantic writers celebrate adultery as a means of challenging traditional theology. In *Jerusalem,* Blake makes Joseph accuse Mary of adultery, because he wants to stress that the reality of sin makes divine forgiveness real. Since adultery belongs to the old moral order which breeds sin, Mary does not deny the charge; she accepts it by way of getting to the greater truth (pl. 61). Byron redefines adultery as a social rather than a sexual sin: the flirtation of prudes and hypocrisy of society matrons are adulterous (*Don Juan,* 12.504). In *Jane Eyre* Charlotte Brontë punishes Rochester for his attempted adultery, but she lessens the stigma attached to it by having Jane marry him. Browning suggests that the Bible is inconsistent and that there is a conflict between the way the Bible and the Church deal with adultery (*The Ring and the Book,* 810). Ruskin lashes out at church-going adulterers who, having destroyed their own souls, remain religious conformers while their victims are outcasts. His OT equation of idolatry and adultery is fiercely social (*Works,* 34.199, 685).

Shaw, like other modern writers, is ambivalent about adultery: he both minimizes its status as "sin" and extends its meaning. He attacks the OT law from a social and cultural standpoint: stoning a woman for marrying a second time might be a kindness in the East but is an atrocity in the West. Shaw rejects adultery as the ground for divorce, complaining that the divorce laws uphold paternal rights rather than sexual companionship (*The Complete Prefaces,* 109, 419-20, 423, 430).

Hardy makes adultery central to the plots of *The Return of the Native* and *Jude the Obscure* in order to defy contemporary mores, but his sympathetic and tragic view of adulterers owes as much to his sense of cosmic forces as to his dislike of biblical rules. Joyce in *A Portrait of the Artist as a Young Man* records a fierce debate about whether Parnell is an adulterer and traitor to his country. Lawrence both reduces adultery to acceptable physical love (*Two Blue Birds*) and suggests that adultery is a spiritual crime which steals God's blessing from humankind ("Michael-Angelo"). Pound admits that adultery is a sin but suggests that it is not important as long as it is undetected ("The Patterns"). The narrator of John Updike's *A Month of Sundays* speaks for numerous characters in contemporary fiction when he proclaims in his first sermon that Jesus came to reveal "the sacrament of adultery." A more traditional examination of the moral and theological issues surrounding adultery is afforded by the novels of Graham Greene — notably *The Heart of the Matter* (1948) and *The End of the Affair* (1951).

See also AHOLAH AND AHOLIBAH; BRIDE, BRIDEGROOM; *DELECTATIO MOROSA;* MARRIAGE FEAST, APOCALYPTIC; SONG OF SONGS.

Bibliography. Armstrong, J. *The Novel of Adultery* (1976); Parten, A. "Masculine Adultery and Feminine Rejoinders in Shakespeare, Dekker and Sharpham." In *"For Better or Worse": Attitudes toward Marriage in Literature.* Ed. E. J. Hinz (1985); Stone, L. *The Family, Sex and Marriage in England, 1500-1800* (1977); Tanner, T. *Adultery in the Novel: Contract and Transgression* (1979).

ROBERT JAMES MERRETT

ADVENT   *Advent* (Lat. *adventus,* "coming") denotes the ecclesiastical season immediately preceding Christmas, which starts in the Western church on the Sunday nearest the feast of St. Andrew (Nov. 30). A period of anticipation of the birth of Christ, since the 9th cent. it has also been the beginning of the ecclesiastical year. In the ancient Church the words *adventus, epiphania,* and *natale* were used interchangeably to name the feast of the nativity; an early introit for Epiphany begins, *"Ecce Advenit Dominator Dominus."* Observance of Advent has been part of the liturgy of the church since at least the 6th cent., when the church in Gaul, where Epiphany was a baptismal feast, created an ascetical (not a liturgical) season of preparation parallel to the season of Lent and called it "St. Martin's Lent" because it began on that saint's feast day, November 11. Several sermons by St. Caesarius of Arles intended for delivery in the Advent season speak of the necessity of preparation for the Incarnation. From France the observance of Advent spread to England in the 7th and 8th cents., but only in the 9th cent. was a similar season introduced into the Roman rite. St. Gregory the Great is largely responsible for the structure of the Advent liturgy, but it was greatly enriched by existing collects, epistles, and gospels in the Gallican rite when the Roman rite was introduced in Gaul.

Advent is associated with the annunciation, the birth, and the preaching of John the Baptist, with the parable of the wise and foolish virgins, and with OT prophecies of a Messiah, all of which deal with anticipation of an important "coming" or "arrival." Advent is also associated with the Second Coming of Christ at the time of judgment

(this connection is primarily a contribution of the Gallican church).

The earliest use of Advent materials in English literature is in the so-called "Advent lyrics" in Old English, sometimes known as *Christ I,* based largely on some of the "O antiphons" of the season (seven "greater" antiphons — *O Sapientia, O Adonai, O Radix Jesse, O Clavis David, O Oriens, O Rex Gentium,* and *O Emmanuel* — and four "lesser" antiphons — *O Virgo Virginum, O Mundi Domina, O Rex Pacis,* and *O Hierusalem);* some of the poems have connections with other liturgical materials.

In *Sir Gawain and the Green Knight* the poet makes a comic allusion to Advent fasting when on Christmas Eve Gawain is served an elaborate feast comprising only fish and the servants promise "better fare" when the penitential season is over. Pope, in the *Dunciad,* makes a parodic allusion to Christ's first (and second?) Advent when Dulness's entrance is announced: "She comes! She comes" (4.629). There may be a veiled reference to Advent as a period of anticipation in George Eliot's *The Mill on the Floss* when Tom Tulliver puts 21 sticks into the ground three weeks before going home for Christmas (during the previous half-year he has learned an "epitomised history of the Jews"); though in this instance it is his own "homecoming" that is anticipated. T. S. Eliot's "Journey of the Magi" exploits the various implied connections between Advent and other liturgical seasons.

See also NATIVITY.

Bibliography. Campbell, J. J., ed. *The Advent Lyrics of the Exeter Book* (1959); Gueranger, D. P. *The Liturgical Year: Advent* (1867).

PHILLIP ROGERS

AGAG   Agag was an Amalekite king defeated by Saul. Though under the "ban" and ordered destroyed, Agag was brought home (along with the choicest spoil) in defiance of the divine command. Samuel the prophet rebuked Saul and executed Agag in judgment for earlier Amalekite atrocities (1 Sam. 15:8-33). In patristic and medieval commentary the focus is less on Agag himself than on the cupiditous motives of Saul in making him prisoner, the disobedience which led directly to Saul's loss of the crown (cf. *Glossa Ordinaria* [PL 113.555]). Samuel's reproach, "Behold, to obey is better than sacrifice" (v. 22), similarly anchors Protestant commentary. Samuel's bloody execution of Agag (vv. 32-33) is seen as a completion of God's judgment upon Agag who, Matthew Henry notes, "trod in the steps of his ancestors' cruelty" (*Comm. on the Whole Bible,* 2.364).

Medieval midrashim reflect that the execution was in fact a form of pagan rather than Jewish justice, since no witnesses of Agag's crime could be summoned before the court. As a result of Saul's not killing him in battle, according to some sources, injustice was added to disobedience, and a son conceived by Agag after his capture became ancestor to the terrible Haman (Alphabet of Ben Sira 11c; Tg. Sheni 4.13; cf. Pesiq. R. 12.52b; Pesiq. Rab.

Kah. 3.25a-26b; Shemuel 18.101). The question of whether Samuel, a Nazarite, could have done the deed himself or delegated it to others raises the possibility of further increments of iniquity.

The author of *Piers Plowman* offers a medieval reading strikingly responsive to the biblical narrative. In Passus 4 Lady Lucre's subversive effort to ingratiate herself at the palace are met with the objections of Conscience, who directs Lucre to the text in 1 Samuel. He recapitulates the passage at length, observing that because Saul

> coueited hyre catel and the kyng spared,
> For-bar hym and hus beste bestes as the byble
> witnesseth,
> Otherwise than god wolde by warnyng of the prophete,
> God seide to Samuel that Saul sholde deye,
> And al hus for that synne and shendfulliche ende.
> Thus was kyng Saul ouercome for couetyse of mede,
> That god hatid hym for euere and alle hus ayres after.
> (C.4.429-35)

Conscience concludes her condemnation with a prophetic extension of the parallel, observing that in the time when at last Reason (here the returned Messiah) shall rule over all nations, there will be many who "ryht as Agag hadde" yet then too,

> Samuel shal sle hym and Saul shal be blamed,
> And Dauid shal be diademyd and daunten alle oure
> enemyes,
> And on Cristene kyng kepen ows echone. (C.4.442-45)

The eschatological dimension found in *Piers Plowman* disappears after the Renaissance. In Dryden's *Absalom and Achitophel* (674-77) Agag may represent one of the Catholic peers executed in 1680 on the (false) testimony of Titus Oates, who figures in the poem as Corah:

> But Zeal peculiar priviledg affords;
> Indulging latitude to deeds and words.
> And *Corah* might for *Agag*'s murther call,
> In terms as coarse as *Samuel* us'd to *Saul*.

In Whittier's "The King's Missive" Governor Endicott is a zealous Puritan offended at the Quakers who sees himself in Samuel's stead:

> Shall I spare? Shall I pity them? God forbid!
> I will do as the prophet to Agag did:
> They come to poison the wells of the Word.
> I will hew them in pieces before the Lord.

The Agag incident has emerged to prominence in post-Holocaust Jewish literature. In Max Zweig's *Saul* (1949) the conflict is between a magnanimous Saul and the angry fundamentalist Samuel, whose view of God's justice precludes mercy. This theme, which involves a rehabilitation of Saul, is echoed in David Pinski's Yiddish play *Shaul* (1955), in which once again Saul is heralded as the champion of a God of mercy over and against Samuel's God of justice.

See also SAMUEL.
Bibliography. Liptzin, S. *Biblical Themes in World Literature* (1985), 135-43.

AGAR *See* HAGAR.

AGONY OF CHRIST *See* GETHSEMANE.

AGNUS DEI From John 1:29, the Baptist's announcement of Jesus as ultimate atonement sacrifice, in Latin it can signify the incipit to the prayer intoned just before the Communion (cf. Isa. 53:7). Repeated thrice, as a prayer for mercy ("O Lamb of God, which taketh away the sin of the world, have mercy upon us") since the 11th cent., it has been the recipient of numerous elegant musical settings.

See also ATONEMENT; EUCHARIST; LAMB OF GOD; LITURGY.

AHAB Ahab, whose Hebrew name suggests "God is a close relative," is notorious for behaving as though the opposite were true. Seventh king of Israel (ca. 874-852 B.C.), he entered into suspect alliances with neighbor states and even erstwhile enemies and, under the influence of his fanatical pagan queen Jezebel, came to worship Baal (1 Kings 16:31-33), to pursue political tyranny (1 Kings 21), and to engage in religious persecution (18:4) and human sacrifice (16:34). These actions put him in conflict with the prophets, notably Elijah and Micaiah; at Jezebel's request, he massacred Hebrew prophets and then installed prophets of Baal as counselors in his court (18:4, 19).

Jewish commentators note both the great power of Ahab and his almost unprecedented wickedness. At his order the gates of Samaria are said to have borne the inscription "Ahab denies the God of Israel" (Sanh. 102b, 103b; cf. Tan. Shemot 29). His miserable fate under divine judgment (1 Kings 22) is said to be occasioned above all by his murder of Naboth for his vineyard (Sanh. 48b; Tosefta 4.6). This occurred when Ahab, having decided to make war with the Arameans, asked his 400 prophets of Baal for advice and received unanimous encouragement — exactly what he wanted to hear (1 Kings 22:6, 11-13). Micaiah (a faithful prophet of God) then being sent for — someone whom Ahab hated, for, as he said, "he doth not prophesy good concerning me, but evil" (v. 8) — the judgment of God was rendered as a vision of the court of heaven deciding how Ahab should be "tricked" into his death. The device suggested by "the Spirit" (which Sanh. 89a identifies as that of murdered Naboth) was simple concurrence with the raving 400 prophets of Baal — to reiterate the promise of victory, and so encourage Ahab to attack at Ramoth-gilead. In a powerfully ironic conclusion the narrator records that though Ahab apprehensively disguised himself, one of the enemy archers, drawing his bow at random (KJV "at a venture" [v. 34]), struck the king in the tiny place between the joints of his armor. Despite his plea to be taken out of the battle, his officers strapped him into his chariot upright lest the troops (who knew his identity) be demoralized, and as the battle wore on, he bled to death. At the end of the day the army fled in disarray, Ahab's corpse was removed, "and one washed the chariot in the pool of Samaria, and the dogs licked up his blood" (22:38). The archer, nameless in the text, is identified by Josephus (*Ant.* 18.15.5; cf. Midr. Tehillim 78.50) with Naaman, the leprous Syrian commander who was healed by Elisha (2 Kings 5).

In patristic commentary Ahab is either an epitome of wickedness (e.g., St. Jerome, *Ep.* 77.4) or else his actions are divorced, in a sense, from his character so as to allow for topical allegorization (e.g., *Glossa Ordinaria* [PL 113.605-10]). Pseudo-Fulgentius characterizes him as an exemplum of one who, though he had been witness by day to Elijah's miracles and other clear signs of God's divine authority, "yet at night he drank in the poison of his wife Jezebel's vicious persuasion" (*Of the Ages of the World*, 8 [trans. Whitbread]) and so perished eternally.

In his fourth Latin elegy Milton compares his former tutor, then a chaplain to English merchants in Germany, to Elijah fleeing "from the hands of King Ahab" (99-100). Satan in Milton's *Paradise Regained* boasts of being the spirit who proposed to all God's angels "to draw the proud King Ahab into fraud / That he might fall at Ramoth" (1.372-77), a superposition of the Job contestation onto the Micaiah story, probably following Lavater's commentary *In Libros Paralipomenon sive Chronicorum* (which Milton annotated). On the random arrow, Merrick, in Montague's *Right off the Map,* alludes to biblical precedent sarcastically: "'Bow drawn at a venture', was it? Lots of first-class scientific fighting in the Bible" (16.2). While there are numerous incidental allusions to Ahab in modern literature (e.g., Stephen Dedalus is compared to Ahab in *Ulysses*), the most important characterization is undoubtedly Melville's Captain Ahab in *Moby-Dick,* who drinks in his own species of poison at night, rails against God, and goes to his death following a false rather than true prophecy. His fate is foreshadowed early in the narrative when one of the characters proclaims, "Ahab's above the common. . . . He's *Ahab,* boy; and Ahab of old, thou knowest, was a crowned King!" — only to receive the rejoinder, "And a very vile one. When that wicked King was slain, the dogs, did they not lick his blood?"

See also ELIJAH; ELISHA; JEZEBEL; NABOTH'S VINEYARD.

AHASUERUS *See* ESTHER.

AHAZ Ahaz was the thirteenth king of Judah (732-715 B.C.) whose name is an abbreviation from Jehoahaz (cf. *ANET,* 282). Due to his reluctance to join in an anti-Assyrian coalition with Israel and Syria, he was invaded by them (2 Kings 16:5). Isaiah encouraged the king to rely on God's deliverance (Isa. 7:1-16) but he decided instead to rely on Assyria, who put Judah under vassalage. These domestic problems are portrayed as results of profligate

apostasy (2 Kings 16:3-4, 10-16; 2 Chron. 28:2-7, 23-25; Isa. 7:17–10:4).

The rabbis saw Ahaz as an extremely wicked man (Lev. Rab. 30.3) who, among other things, seized schools and synagogues (11.7), and introduced the worship of Moloch. His place was secured in the world to come, however, through having been the son (Gen. Rab. 63.1; Lev. Rab. 36.3) and father (Eccl. Rab. 7; 15.1) of devout kings (Sanh. 104a). In Milton's *Paradise Lost* he is a devotee of one of the fallen angels, "against the house of God," Rimmon, the Syrian deity associated with Damascus (*PL* 1.467-75).

See also DAGON; MOLOCH.   DAVID W. BAKER

AHITHOPHEL Ahithophel (Achitophel in Vg) appears in the account of Absalom's rebellion against his father, King David (2 Sam. 15:12–17:13). For whatever motives — he may have been the grandfather of Bathsheba (see 2 Sam. 11:3; 23:34; and 1 Chron. 3:5) — Ahithophel, a counselor to David, betrayed the king and joined forces with the son. Sagacious, pragmatic, but unscrupulous, he advised Absalom to secure his position by taking David's concubines and by killing the king. As an exercise in realpolitik, Ahithophel's good advice. But when Absalom accepted instead the counsel of Hushai, David's spy, because "the LORD had appointed to defeat the good counsel of Ahithophel, to the intent that the LORD might bring evil upon Absalom" (2 Sam. 17:14), Ahithophel hanged himself.

Mentioned little in early Christian tradition, Ahithophel becomes in English literature a conventional tag for traitor, wicked politician, and suicide. In *The Canterbury Tales* Chaucer's Parson admonishes that "wikked conseil yeveth is a traytour. For he deceyveth hym that trusteth in hym, *ut Achitofel ad Absolonem*" (*The Parson's Tale*, 10.635-40). If he were to betray his love, says a character in *The Book of the Duchess,* he would be "wers than was Achitofel" (1118). In refuting Tyndale St. Thomas More alludes to Absalom's revolt, implicitly comparing Henry VIII to Absalom and his chancellor to Ahithophel. George Peale dramatizes Ahithophel's treachery in *The Love of King David and Fair Bethsabe. With the Tragedie of Absalom* (1599); Shakespeare's Falstaff calls a merchant who refuses him credit "A whoreson Achitophel" (*2 Henry 4*, 1.2.35).

Later in 17th-cent. England, as numerous writers drew parallels between the life of David and contemporary political affairs, Ahithophel became a commonplace. In tracts, sermons, and poetry, from Nathanael Carpenter's *Achitophel, or the Picture of a Wicked Politician* (1627) to Dryden's satire *Absalom and Achitophel,* the most skillful literary rendering of the story in the language, Ahithophel is a synonym for political machination and rebellion. A verb was even coined out of his name, one poet writing of a group of plotters being "out-Achitophel'd" by another (see R. F. Jones, "The Originality of *Absalom and Achitophel*," *MLN* 46 [1931], 211-18).

After the 17th cent., references to Ahithophel are few and scattered. Burns alludes to him as a suicide (*Letters,* ed. J. De Lancey Ferguson [1931], 1.120); Blake ranks him with Caiaphas, Pilate, and Judas: "Achitophel is also here with the cord in his hand" (*A Vision of the Last Judgment,* 608); Scott in *The Fair Maid of Perth* (chap. 13) writes of the "wisdom of Achitophel, crafty at once and cruel."

See also ABSALOM.   LARRY CARVER

AHOLAH AND AHOLIBAH The names of two harlots in an allegory of Ezek. 23:1-44 (sometimes transcribed Oholah and Oholibah) derive from Heb. *'ohel* ("tent") — perhaps signifying Israel's tent of worship, the Tabernacle, or, as is suggested in the recollection of Esau's wife, Oholibamah (Gen. 36:2), "tent of the high place," a pagan shrine. The harlots are said to be sisters; Aholah may mean "her tent," while Aholibah almost certainly means "my tent is [in] her," suggesting, despite the cultic associations, God's relation to the two Hebrew nations of Samaria and Jerusalem. In the allegory, God is married to both, yet they go "awhoring after the heathen" (v. 30) — engaging in pagan rites and political association with alien nations, principally Assyria and Egypt. The parable recounts in raw sexual terms the adulteries of Aholah and Aholibah and the inevitable abuse and destruction they suffer at the hands of their "lovers," which God allows as a judgment upon them (vv. 22-24).

Aphrahat construes Ezekiel to have "said concerning righteous men that they shall judge Ahola and Aholibah" (*Select Demonstrations,* 22.16); St. Gregory the Great allegorizes their "whoredoms in Egypt" (v. 3) as prostitution to carnal desire: "teats of virginity are bruised in Egypt when the natural senses, still whole in themselves, are vitiated by the corruption of assailing concupiscence" (*Liber regulae pastoralis,* 28.39). In the English *Homilies Appointed to Be Read in Churches* (1562), the second and longest sermon, "Against Peril of Idolatry," links this and other OT "whoredoms" to a thinly veiled attack on Roman Catholic liturgy and ecclesiastical art; Milton repeats this view of the "Romish liturgy" in *Apology for Smectymnuus:* "What was that which made the Jews, figured under the names Aholah and Aholibah, go a-whoring after all the heathen's inventions, but they saw a religion gorgeously attired and desirable to the eye?" (cf. vv. 14-16). Although later Protestant commentaries, including Matthew Poole's *Annotations upon the Holy Bible* (1685), refrained from such associations in favor of a more strictly historical reading, these connections persisted in some preaching of the dissenting tradition. The story was also eisegetically moralized: Thomas Hardy, perhaps reflecting the preaching of his own day, has Tess of the D'Urbervilles accept her rape passively, believing that "if she should have to burn for what she had done,

burn she must. . . . Like all village girls, she was well grounded in the Holy Scriptures, and had dutifully studied the histories of Aholah and Aholibah and knew the inferences to be drawn therefrom."

See also ADULTERY.

AJALON, VALE OF Ajalon is a valley northwest of Jerusalem (Heb. *'ayyalon,* "deer field") in which numerous historic battles were fought, including not only Saul's and Jonathan's victory over the Philistines (1 Sam. 14:31) and Joshua's army's defeat of the Amorites (Josh. 10:1-14) but in later times Judas Maccabeus's defeat of Gorgias in 166 B.C. (1 Macc. 3:40; 4:1-15). Vespasian marshaled his army here for the assault on Jerusalem in A.D. 70 (Josephus, *Ant.* 4.8), as later did the Crusaders, and in modern times the Israeli army fought to reach Jerusalem by the same route (1948). It is in connection with Joshua, however, that Ajalon is best remembered in literature, for it is here, when the battle was not yet decisive and the sun was setting, that Joshua called upon the Lord "and he said in the sight of Israel, 'Sun, stand thou still upon Gibeon; and thou Moon in the valley of Ajalon.' And the sun stood still, and the moon stayed, until the people had avenged themselves upon their enemies" (Josh. 10:12-13).

This event, one of the most remarkable in the accounts of the life of Joshua, is said by an unknown midrash quoted by Rashi (*on* Josh. 24:30) to have occasioned erection of a pillar over his grave. Early Christian commentators see it, with the casting down of the walls of Jericho (Josh. 3:17), as evidence of Joshua's exemplary faith (Aphrahat, *Select Demonstrations,* 1.16; St. Ambrose, *De officiis ministrorum,* 1.40.205) such as provides a model of Christian courage. St. Jerome relates the wonder to the virtue of prayer with fasting (*Adv. Jov.* 2.15). In *Paradise Lost* Milton has the angel Michael describe future battles of the world to Adam, including Joshua's "voice commanding, Sun in Gibeon stand, / And thou Moon in the vale of Aialon, / Till Israel overcome" (12.265-67); but at the conclusion of "To His Coy Mistress" Andrew Marvell uses the allusion to press his amorous opportunity: "Thus, though we cannot make our sun / Stand still, yet we will make him run."

It is Marvell who signals the advent of modern interpretations. Matthew Poole (1685) observes that though the event is referred to elsewhere in Scripture (Hab. 3:11; Sir. 46:5-6), "some take this to be but a Poetical Phrase and Relation of the Victory" (*Annotations upon the Holy Bible*). Peake (*Comm. on the Bible,* 253) two centuries later relates the incident to the figurative words of Deborah's song, "the stars in their courses fought against Sisera."

Mark Twain alludes to the story in *Innocents Abroad* (chap. 5), where the narrator describes the intensity of a recurring full moon as he and his party travel "in the same spot in the heavens at the same hour every night. . . . To us Joshuas it stood still in the same place, and remained always the same." Tennyson holds it "better men should perish one by one / Than that earth should stand at gaze like Joshua's moon in Ajalon!" (*Locksley Hall,* 179-80). Somerset Maugham has in mind making love rather than war in his story "Red," in which he describes ideally matched lovers as ones for whom the intensity of passion is as if "the sun stands still, as it stood when Joshua prayed to the God of Israel."

See also DEBORAH, SONG OF DEBORAH; JOSHUA.

ALL HELL BROKE LOOSE   Not a biblical phrase, but Milton's, in *Paradise Lost,* 4.918.

ALL THINGS TO ALL MEN   *See* PAUL.

ALL THINGS WORK TOGETHER FOR GOOD   In a verse frequently cited in relation to Christian responses to the adversities of fortune, St. Paul writes "And we know that all things work together for good to them that love God, to them who are called according to his purpose" (Rom. 8:28). In medieval texts it is sometimes cited in Latin: *omnium in bonum.* Joseph, the servant in Emily Brontë's *Wuthering Heights,* exclaims: "Thank Hivin for all! All warks togither for gooid tuh them as is chozzen, and piked aht froo' th' rubbidge! Yah knaw what t' Scripture ses" (chap. 9).

See also ELECTION.

ALLEGORY   Ancient Greeks, Romans, and medievals understood allegory (from Gk. *alles + agoreuein:* "other" + "speak openly, speak in the assembly or market") as to say one thing and mean another. Thus St. Paul in Gal. 4:24-27 labels "allegory" the birth of Isaac as the promise of free Jerusalem above and the birth of Ishmael as the bondage of the Old Law of Sinai, a configuration now plausibly regarded as typological. John, in equating God and *agapē* (1 John 4:16), employs what the ancients understood as allegory.

In *De principiis* Origen argues for the allegorical status of the Scriptures on the basis of the nature of the universe and God's relation to it, his emphasis being ethical and literalism per se being his aversion. Origen and other allegorizing Christian commentators are notably fond of 2 Cor. 3:6 — "the letter killeth, but the spirit giveth life" — which they regard as a license for preferring allegorical interpretations. St. Augustine, who embraces allegorizing as a settled principle in biblical interpretation, separates in bks. 11-13 of *The Confessiones* spiritual truths of the creation from their *visibilia,* assuming Moses to be a polysemous author: thus the "waters" in one place and the "dry land" in another figure two societies — one vexed by infidelity and steeped in natural bitterness, the other a society of the righteous, zealous for God's gifts.

Early Christian writers were aware that interpreters of Homer's epics — defenders of the profundity and moral usefulness of that author's apparent ascription of frivolity and indecency to the gods — anciently allegorized these poems. Pre-Socratic philosophers such as Heraclitus ("War is the father of all things, the king of all things," frg. 53[44]) and Parmenides exhibit allegory in non-literary contexts. Plato helped to bring forth allegory by replacing gods with divinized thought-images (cf. "Allegory of the Cave," *Republic* 7); and Philo of Alexandria hypostatized such powers between God and humankind, especially the Logos, God's rational power, his creative word. Lucretius in *De rerum natura* allegorizes the punishments of the classical Hades. Plutarch may have been the first critic to use the term *allegory,* and the first to use *allegorically* critically. But understandably, Christian allegorists have never entertained the debasing view that their primary text, the Bible, was filled with extravagant and immoral legends as Homeric scholiasts and ancient Greek and Roman (and later) philosophers did with the texts of Greek mythology.

A definition of allegory given in the Middle Ages by St. Isidore of Seville (in *Etymologiae,* 1.7) was *alieniloquium (aliud enim sonat, aliud intelligitur),* of which trope irony was a species. A medieval tag helpful for remembering the famous four senses — *"Littera gesta docet, quid credas allegoria / Moralis quid agas, que tendas anagogia"* — is given its perhaps most widely known medieval formulation in Dante's letter to Can Grande, which associates his *capolavero* with scriptural allegory: even today laypeople would maintain the ancient and medieval latitude, ignoring distinctions between *allegoria* and *figura,* and declare *The Divine Comedy* to be an allegory (to the consternation of critics who see typological configurations as also present therein). Thus read, Virgil is Reason only and not also himself.

Symbols (which are the *visibilia* into which allegory pours its meaning) and types do of course have a basic congruence in that they are meaningful only in terms of something else, symbols to their referents, types to their antitypes. But in many ways they differ, as Erich Auerbach has observed ("Figura," in *Scenes from the Drama of European Literature* [1959]). Symbols (if understood) attract or repel readers; types possess no such magic power. Symbols directly interpret life or nature and are not necessarily based upon texts; types are related to history and are based on texts. Symbols fuse the concrete and the spiritual, or may be abstract; types are always concrete. Symbols devalue sense experience whereas types attach value to history. A symbol and its referent are inseparable whereas an antitype makes its type unnecessary. Symbols represent what is immaterial in picturable terms; types represent the higher material by the lower material. Symbols imply power to transcend the immediate situation whereas types possess no such implication. Antitypes of course have transcending power over the typical situation by reason of lapse of time and fuller knowledge. Symbols do not necessarily imply a providential order of history whereas types are based on God-penetrated history. Symbols do not imply as types do a fuller knowledge with the passage of time: they are (if understood) at one moment all that they are. Symbols develop after a distinction is made between mind and body whereas types are invariably formed by persons unaware of the typological quality of their actions.

Modern critical usage also restricts allegory to developed and continued metaphors, usually narrative fictions in prose and verse. Fable and parable are seen as crudely allegorical. Allegorical procedures are both exegetical, as in interpreting the prime scriptural allegory, Canticles, and creative, as in the writing of *The Faerie Queene*. C. S. Lewis (*The Allegory of Love* [1936], 60-61) remarks that Christian allegory's natural theme is temptation. Its two fundamental patterns are the battle (sometimes verbal), made prominent in Prudentius *(Psychomachia),* and the questing journey, as in Bunyan's *The Pilgrim's Progress.* Some allegorists have been regarded as "purer" than others (e.g., Dante, Spenser, and Bunyan) because they often relate their visual images to examples and precepts; but Canticles is arguably purest allegory because it never explains the meaning of its images and incidents. Angus Fletcher (*Allegory: The Theory of a Symbolic Mode* [1964], 208) distinguishes between intentional allegories like *The Faerie Queene* and works like the *Odyssey* and the *Aeneid* in which scholiasts have found allegorical meaning. Indeed, some readers (e.g., Fletcher) find allegory in even the most mimetic fiction (and in all art forms), ordinarily an antithesis of allegorical art and a historical cause of the decline of allegory.

Prominent among the characteristics of allegory is: a kind of epideictic rhetoric, allegory by praise and ceremony which urges upon the reader a course of action and dissuades from other courses, thus violating the Kantian value of disinterestedness. It is governed by rigid destiny or inevitability, and it resists interpretation in solely rational terms. Yet it may be the simulacrum of a scientific theory, as in Phineas Fletcher's *The Purple Island,* and it may present a whole world in which all learning is connected, as in *The Divine Comedy.* It is concerned with power, for good or evil. Its plots turn not on probability but on thematic necessity, for allegory is a theme-charged genre. Consistent with its quasi-Platonic and referential character, it is tolerant of an order in which natural cause-and-effect is at times violated; holding hypostatized ideas under strong logical control, allegory (which readers understand as they gradually proceed with the fiction) does not necessarily aim at creating a mimetic world. Readers gather not only from this but from type-names like Everyman that the experience recorded in allegory is not unique but supposedly is "just representations of general nature," raising questions beyond the work such as "What shall I do to be saved?" (*The Pilgrim's Progress*) and "How can I attain a life of nobility and virtue?" (*The Faerie Queene*). Allegory, nevertheless, may be topical,

as in Dante and Spenser. It characteristically employs significant details and settings significant of states of mind (e.g., Bunyan's "Slough of Despond"). The heroes of allegory endure change, even transformation (e.g., Piers and the Dreamer in *Piers Plowman*); but characters totally derived from abstractions cannot change because they are ideas, though they may bring essences to view by reason of the action (e.g., Archimago, Mammon, Talus). Christian allegory may use sacred places, "symbols of the center," free from evil, such as Spenser's House of Holiness; and allegory of both Christian and secular provenance may use places of concentrated evil, such as the islands in Golding's *Lord of the Flies.* Allegories may or may not include authorial commentary and analysis. They may be deceptive, Puttenham labelling the genre "the figure of false semblant" (*The Arte of English Poesie* [1589], 3.18 — an allusion to the allegorized bad friar of the *Roman de la Rose*) — or instruments of accommodation and compromise, as in Augustine's famous willingness to accept Bishop Ambrose's allegorical explanation of parts of the OT, Augustine having been "killed" spiritually by taking them literally (*Conf.* 5.14). Allegory may achieve an ending by summoning a *deus ex machina* of supreme value, as in Christian's homecoming in *The Pilgrim's Progress* and the vision of the Harrowing of Hell in *Piers Plowman.* Bertrand Bronson ("Personification Reconsidered," *ELH* 14 [1947], 163-77) argues that allegory is more mature than mimetic fiction because it invests order apprehended in multiplicity with power and beauty, whereas naturalism is no more than a mimesis of the chaotic impressions and responses of the phenomenal world.

Modern critics may dislike allegory, Northrop Frye (*Anatomy of Criticism* [1957], 90) suggests, because it directs them to understand it rather than leaving them to their own interpretive devices. Critics may also experience distaste for its awareness of system and its imposition of hierarchical order upon its materials, for its unwillingness in older examples to accept sense data as the end-all and be-all of existence, for its dualism of absolute good and absolute evil, for its fondness for sudden overthrow, for its apparent determinisms, for its tendency to caricature, seeing human character in terms of signal traits, such as Malbecco-jealousy in *The Faerie Queene,* and for supposedly translating abstractions into images (instead of beginning with images). Allegory *qua* allegory is not presently fashionable; allegory regarded as myth, as archetype, or as language for psychoanalysis currently is. In the wake of Romanticism moderns have tended to be averse to the intellectuality, didacticism, universalized significance, a-temporality, and hierarchically conservative tendency of allegory (preferring multiple rather than unified hierarchies).

Of Judeo-Christian allegory Canticles, or the Song of Solomon, almost surely owes its canonicity to perceived allegorical intent: if not allegorical it would have failed "the analogy of the faith," harmony of divine teaching with that of other canonical books. Prudentius's *Psychomachia* has been regarded as the first allegory completely modern in form; it features the *bellum intestinum* (internal conflict) that Lewis held to be "the root of all allegory" (*Allegory of Love*, 68). In depicting such struggle Christian allegorists would of course avoid strict Manicheism in their concern for redemption from sin. Some notable older allegories are Boethius's *De Consolatione Philosophiae*, in which philosophy is personified; Dante's *The Divine Comedy;* the medieval debate poems, e.g., *The Owl and the Nightingale;* Langland's *Piers Plowman,* highly remarkable for personification allegory in the guise of a dream; *Pearl,* with many characteristically medieval analogies of the physical, moral, and spiritual worlds; *Everyman;* Spenser's *The Faerie Queene;* Bunyan's *The Pilgrim's Progress,* whose biblical tags, marginal notations, and emblem-like materials render this work most explicit allegory; and Milton's characterization on the basis of James 1:15 of Sin and Death, the only strictly allegorical figures in *Paradise Lost.*

Douglas Bush indicates that the medieval writer, accustomed to allegorical interpretation of Scripture, was not at all defensive about the use of secular allegory, both kinds constituting "the bone, muscle and nerves of serious medieval literature" (*Mythology and the Renaissance Tradition in English Poetry* [1932], 11). Spenser and Bunyan, however, already felt the need to offer justification for writing allegory. Both medieval and Renaissance authors could assume a readership accustomed to the energetic referential reading which allegory requires. Allegorists used traditional biblical symbols, such as Bunyan's Christian's armor (Eph. 6), assuming that their world and their transcription of it were thus legible. All earlier allegorists assume that their teachings are applicable to humankind without limit of time, however much *The Faerie Queene* makes use of past chivalry and *The Divine Comedy* of history. Older allegorists employ at the center of their fictions an image or an event which, although not completely susceptible to rational analysis, posits value: Dante's multifoliate Rose, Langland's Harrowing of Hell, Bunyan's entrance into the Heavenly City, Spenser's Destruction of the Dragon.

Modern allegories such as Capek's *R. U. R.,* Orwell's *1984,* Huxley's *Brave New World,* and Kafka's *The Trial* and *The Castle* (but not Golding's *Lord of the Flies*), because of materialism, individualism, fragmentation, internalization of value, and distrust of intellectual, political, artistic, and metaphysical systems of coherences (such as teleology and hierarchy in general), move away from objective meaning and toward significance limited to author, protagonist, and readers. But *reading* such works as allegory has biblical roots, even in writers so oblique as Kafka. The long Judeo-Christian tradition has prepared readers for allegorical reading, and has given them both respect for the literal text and expectation that external conflict in a narrative may well represent spiritual warfare, conflict within. Many works of the 19th and 20th cents. are in this fashion regarded as allegorical or quasi-allegorical (i.e., where allegory is one of many possible interpretations), such as Melville's *Moby-Dick,* Proust's *A la recherche du temps perdu,* or Joyce's *Ulysses.* In many modern allegories, however, unitary hierarchies especially are characteristically threatening and katagogic. Modern allegories accordingly tend to become personal odysseys devoid of the counsel, clarity, encyclopedism, and confident Christian morality of earlier literary allegory. *Gulliver's Travels* (1726) rests on the borderline and is historically close to the major shift in development away from allegory in the medieval tradition toward modern configurations.

On the modern interpretive side Freud's *Interpretation of Dreams* has encouraged reading literature as psychological allegory, with such allegory supplying clues to sexual motives in authors, characters, and readers. Frazer's *Golden Bough* has supplied an impulse to search for patterns in ancient myths as explanations of primitive rituals.

It is generally felt that inferior allegory is produced by using personification obtrusively and otherwise heavily signifying one's intentions, so that, as with Robert Grosseteste's 13th-cent. *Chasteau d'Amour* there is an assumption that the reader is unintelligent. Allegory is helped by removing accidental description, something that makes for greater concentration of symbolic force. Good allegory is nuanced, some shades of meaning being discerned by readers rather than being obtruded on their sensibilities. Thus the descent of Guyon (*The Faerie Queene,* bk. 2) draws upon the Christian Hell, the classical Hades (*Aeneid,* 6), and the underworlds of folklore. On the other hand, *Everyman* and *The Pilgrim's Progress* are one-for-one allegory whose force perhaps gains from lack of such a polysemous texture in the sense that the simpler the allegory, the more cogently the reader is confronted with allegorical meaning.

See also TYPOLOGY.

Bibliography. Clifford, G. *The Transformations of Allegory* (1974); Fletcher, A. *Allegory: The Theory of a Symbolic Mode* (1974); Green, R. H. "Dante's 'Allegory of Poets' and the Medieval Theory of Poetic Fiction." *CL* 9 (1957), 118-28; Honig, E. *Dark Conceit: The Making of Allegory* (1959); Lewis, C. S. *The Allegory of Love: A Study in Medieval Tradition* (1936); McClennen, J. *On the Meaning and Function of Allegory in the English Renaissance.* Ann Arbor, MI: The University of Michigan Contributions in Modern Philology 6 (1947), 1-38; MacQueen, J. *Allegory* (1970); Nuttall, A. D. *Two Concepts of Allegory* (1967); Pepin, J. *Myth et allégorie* (1958); Quilligan, M. *The Language of Allegory: Defining the Genre* (1979); Rollinson, P. *Classical Theories of Allegory and Christian Culture* (1981); Wimsatt, J. I. *Allegory and Mirror: Tradition and Structure in Middle English Literature* (1970).   DAVID S. BERKELEY

ALPHA AND OMEGA   Scriptural reference to *alpha* and *omega*, the first and last letters of the Greek alphabet, is confined to Revelation, in which God twice asserts, "I am Alpha and Omega, the beginning and the end" (1:8; 21:6), and Christ once declares, "I am Alpha and Omega, the beginning and the end, the first and the last" (22:13). (The KJV's use of the phrase again in Rev. 1:11 is not warranted by the MSS.) The use of alpha and omega to denote God's eternity and infinitude is rooted in such OT texts as Isa. 44:6 (cf. 41:4; 48:12), "I am the first, and I am the last; and beside me there is no God"; but it is probable that the Johannine locution itself is derived, by analogy, from rabbinic tradition, where *aleph* and *tau*, the first and last letters of the Hebrew alphabet, express a parallel symbolic sense: e.g., "My Saints . . . are the sons of men who have kept the whole Law from Aleph to Taw" (Shabbethai 55a on Ezek. 9:6). Most authorities also point out that the Hebrew word for "truth" (*'emet*) is composed of the first, middle, and last letters of the alphabet.

There is, it seems, no precedent for the application of alpha and omega to Christ in Rev. 22:13, although it is this text which becomes the mainstay of subsequent tradition. Both Greek and Latin Fathers draw attention to it as affirming the divinity of Christ. Thus, St. Clement of Alexandria, in *Stromateis*, 4.25, says that the Son "is called the Alpha and the Omega, of whom alone the end becomes the beginning, and ends again at the original beginning without any break" (cf. Tertullian, *De monogamia*, 5, and St. Ambrose, *In septem visiones*, 1.8). Prudentius paraphrases Rev. 22:13 in "Hymnus omnis horae" (*Cathemerinon*, 9.10-12):

> corde natus ex parentis ante mundi exordium,
> alpha et Ω cognominatus, ipse fons et clausula
> omnia quae sunt, fuerunt, quaeque post futura sunt.

("Born of the Father's love before the world's beginning, called Alpha and Omega, he is both source and end of all things that are or have been or hereafter shall be.") The phrase recurs in the Christmas hymn, *In Dulci Jubilo*.

Both in antiquity and the Middle Ages, alpha and omega occur more frequently in Christian art and inscriptions than in literature. With few exceptions, Christian iconography employs the letters on coins, vases, and monuments in connection with figures symbolic of Christ (rather than God the Father), the usual form being a monogram of Χριστός *(Christos)* flanked by alpha and omega.

An instance of liturgical use occurs in an early Irish eucharistic hymn,

> Alpha et omega
> Ipse Christus dominu
> Venit, venturus
> Judicare homines,

which probably alludes to the inscription of the letters A and Ω on the Host itself.

In English literature, from the Middle Ages to the end of the 18th cent., there are oblique allusions, as in *Paradise Lost*, 5.165, but no explicit references in any of the major poets. In the 19th cent., by contrast, allusions abound, although often cut adrift from traditional christological moorings. The sacred river Alph (= Alpha or Aleph) meanders though Coleridge's *Kubla Khan*, and Wordsworth in a pantheistic effusion in *The Prelude* (1805) construes Alpine scenery in imagery invoking Revelation, as

> Characters of the great Apocalypse,
> The types and symbols of Eternity,
> Of first, and last, and midst, and without end.
> (6.638-40)

In Charlotte Brontë's *Jane Eyre,* thorough secularization is evident in Rochester's confession that "the Alpha and Omega of my heart's wishes broke involuntarily from my lips in the words — 'Jane! Jane! Jane!'" (chap. 37).

In 20th-cent. literature, alpha and omega symbolize a variety of beginnings and endings, religious and secular, apocalyptic and mundane, serious and comic. In the "Proteus" episode of Joyce's *Ulysses,* Stephen Dedalus, cynical and dépaysé, imagines finding his roots by placing a call on the umbilical telephone network that connects him back to Mother Eve: "Hello. Kinch here. Put me on to Edenville. Aleph, alpha: nought, nought, one." In Wallace Stevens's private mythology in *An Ordinary Evening in New Haven* (canto 6, long version), "Naked Alpha" balances "the hierophant Omega" as antagonistic "interpreters of life" in the poet's exploration of "plain reality":

> But that's the difference: in the end and the way
> To the end. Alpha continues to begin.
> Omega is refreshed at every end.

In a lighter vein, W. H. Auden in "Victor" offers the ballad (to the tune of "Frankie and Johnny") of a mousy bank teller who murders his unfaithful wife and succumbs to messianic delusion as the ironic fulfillment of puritanical indoctrination in childhood:

> He stood there above the body,
>   He stood there holding the knife;
> And the blood ran down the stairs and sang:
>   "I'm the resurrection and the Life."
>
> They tapped Victor on the shoulder,
>   They took him away in a van;
> He sat as quiet as a lump of moss
>   Saying: "I am the Son of Man."
>
> Victor sat in a corner
>   Making a woman of clay,
> Saying: "I am Alpha and Omega, I shall come
>   To judge the earth one day."

In the Neoplatonic anthropology of Teilhard de Chardin, the Omega Point is the imagined moment in human evolution where biogenesis yields to nougenesis, where body yields to mind: "We reach the Omega Point when we attain to the Hyper-Personal" (*Phenomenon of Man,* 4.2). More pessimistically, the mutant human remnant of a nuclear holocaust in *Beneath the Planet of the Apes* (1970), first sequel to Pierre Boulle's *Planet of the Apes* (1967), worships an ICBM carrying a cobalt bomb, with A and Ω depicted on the rocket's fins.

    Bibliography. *DACL* (1924), 1.1-25; Hastings, J., ed. *Dictionary of the Bible.* Rev. by F. C. Grant and H. H. Rowley (1963); *The New Schaff-Herzog Encyclopedia of Religious Knowledge.* Ed. S. M. Jackson et al. (1966).

                                  JOHN SPENCER HILL

ALPHABET, HEBREW The Hebrew alphabet, which consists of twenty-two consonants and no true vowels, received little direct attention from biblical authors, though a variety of allusions to the alphabet or its individual letters may be found in both the OT and the NT. The best-known alphabetic poems in the OT are the acrostic Psalms (9–10; 25; 34; 37; 111; 112; 119; 145). Ps. 119, the longest poem in the collection, has twenty-two stanzas of eight verses, one for each letter of the alphabet, and the purpose of its acrostic structure has been variously interpreted as mnemonic, magical, or simply an expression of poetic craft. Similar suggestions have been made for the first chapter of Nahum and the first four chapters of Lamentations; the acrostic features of the latter will be visible to English readers in Ronald Knox's translation but not in the KJV.

    The unfamiliar term "Sheshach" in Jer. 25:26 (cf. 51:1 MT) is an alphabetic cipher for "Babel" or "Babylon"; it uses a substitution code called *atbash,* wherein the last letter of the alphabet replaces the first, and so on. In the MT of Isa. 28:10 the function of the repeated letters *ṣadeh, waw,* and *qop* is more obscure, as is the sense of the whole passage, though the alphabetic repetition may allude to the teaching of the ABC's. The meaning of Judg. 12:6, the source of the English word *shibboleth,* hinges on phonetic differences among the letters *samek, śin,* and *shin,* and Ezek. 9:4-6 (cf. Lev. 19:28) is clearer if one recognizes that the primitive form of the letter *tau,* whose name means "mark" or "sign," was a cross or an "X." (That all twenty-two letters acquired meaningful names as well as quantitative values was a great incentive to the eventual development of hermeneutic systems based on the alphabet.) The "jot" of Matt. 5:18 (cf. Luke 16:17) is clearly the Hebrew *yod,* the smallest letter of the alphabet, but of the "tittle" it is difficult to say more than that the evangelists had in mind some minor element or stroke in one or more of the written letters. If these passages of Mark and Luke insist on respect for the letter of the Mosaic Law, they may be contrasted to the anti-Jewish polemic of Rom. 2:27-29, where Paul opposes the *gramma* or letter to the heart and spirit.

    With their very literal interpretation of the first clause of Ps. 33:6, "By the word of the LORD were the heavens made," the early rabbis inaugurated a long tradition of talmudic and midrashic speculation on the creative and other properties of the twenty-two letters. *Bet,* e.g., which begins the first word of Genesis, was a powerfully creative letter because it also came first in *berakah,* the word for "blessing," and because its form (like an upright rectangle open on the left) was closed to all directions save the future. When the rabbis commented on the name changes of Abraham (Gen. 17:5) and the other patriarchs, they remarked on the role of the letters added to or subtracted from their names. In Gen. Rab. 47.1, e.g., the tiny *yod* taken from Sarah's original name (Gen. 17:15) and attached to Joshua's (Num. 13:16) acquires a personality of its own and complains of its fate to the Almighty. St. Jerome and other early Christian exegetes were aware of the rabbinic fascination with the Hebrew letters, but the alphabetic speculations of the *Seper yeṣirah* and kindred works of medieval Judaism remained more or less closed to Christian contemporaries. It was not until Johann Reuchlin and Pico della Mirandola developed a distinctly Christian Cabala in the late 15th cent. that Latin scholarship began to feel the impact of the various traditions of alphabetical exegesis which had grown up in medieval Judaism. Though Cabala was more attentive than Talmud or even Midrash to the several species of *gematria,* a hermeneutic procedure based on the manipulation of the numerical values of letters or on the substitution of letters for one another, Christian commentators were apt to exaggerate the importance of *gematria* at the cost of other features of Cabala. The Trinitarian and christological meanings attributed to the letter *shin* (e.g., by inserting a medial *shin* among the four letters of the Tetragrammaton, Reuchlin was able to certify the divinity of Jesus by deriving the Hebrew form of his name from Yahweh's) were especially important to the Christian Cabalists.

    Since Marlowe mentions "the Hebrew Psalter" in the company of works of Roger Bacon and Peter Abano in *Doctor Faustus* (1.1.148-49), he was probably aware of the magical powers attributed to Hebrew letters. Sixteenth- and 17th-cent. discussions of the privileged character of the Hebrew language as original and divinely instituted involved even the properties of the individual letters. Such speculations culminated in the strange but influential writings of Francis Mercury van Helmont, and they were of interest even to such figures as Henry More and Gottfried Leibniz. But Swift's promise to Sheridan that

"Philologers of Future Ages
. . . [will] help thee to be read with Points.
Or else, to shew their learned Labour, you
May backwards be perus'd, like Hebrew.
("George Nim-Dan-Dean, Esq., to Mr. Sheridan. . . ,"
37-44)

is less respectful of the properties of the alphabet, attending only to the mechanics of writing it. The learning of Don Juan's mother is similarly superficial since it is limited to the Latin of the Paternoster, the Greek of the alphabet, and a few vague notions:

> She liked the English and the Hebrew tongue,
> And said there was analogy between 'em;
> . . . this I heard her say . . .
> 'Tis strange — the Hebrew noun which means "I am"
> The English always use to govern d — n. (*Don Juan*, 1.13-14)

The joke, of course, depends on Exod. 3:13-16.

Joyce is more sensitive to traditional views on the powers of the alphabet, but he is still willing to make jokes with it. When (in *Ulysses*) Stephen telephones his first parents in Edenville, the number is "Aleph, alpha: nought, nought one"; and Bloom, to the accompaniment of rams' horns and with the aid of a translator, later recites the first four Hebrew letters in a nonsensical jumble of Hebrew terms. Somewhat more serious matters emerge when Jewgreek meets Greekjew. Bloom and Stephen exchange information, some of it alluding to *gematria*, on the significance of the Irish and Hebrew alphabets and "on the supernatural character of Judaic scripture," here meaning "writing" as well as "holy writ." The reader of *Finnegans Wake* (Viking ed. [1958], 18) is advised to "(Stoop) if you are abcedminded, what curios of signs (please stoop), in this allaphbed! Can you rede . . . its world?" The world of hermeneutic labor implied in that question reminds one of the cabalist view that the signs of the alphabet were so full of creative power that they literally encompassed the universe. Such "curios of signs" alluding to the alphabet are everywhere in *Finnegans Wake*. Babel, where language was confused, becomes "Lebab" (*Wake*, 258) when read backward as it would be in Hebrew. Shem is frequently (*Wake*, 148, 258, 513, 517, 595) called "Shin," the penultimate letter of the alphabet. When Joyce writes (*Wake*, 553), "I did learn my little ana countrymouse in alphabeater cameltemper, from alderbirk to tannenyou. . . ," the term "camel" is in the right sequence not only because it begins with "c" but also because the third Hebrew letter, *gimel*, resembles the word for camel; likewise, "tannen" makes the sequence the equivalent of the English "a to z" because *tau* is the last letter of the Hebrew alphabet.

See also CABALA; GEMATRIA.

Bibliography. Munk, R. M. L., *The Wisdom in the Hebrew Alphabet* (1979).   BRIAN P. COPENHAVER

ALTAR "The Altar" is an important penitential poem by George Herbert. An example of "shaped verse," it visually re-creates the approximate shape of the symbolic altar of the traditional Christian church, itself a recollection of the altars of the OT upon which sacrifice was made in atonement for human sin.

See also ATONEMENT, DAY OF; EUCHARIST; ISAAC; TEMPLE.

AMALEKITES Descendants of Esau through his son Eliphaz (Gen. 36:12, 16; Exod. 17:8; Num. 24:20; Judg. 3:13), the people generally designated in the OT as Amalekites are bedouins, mainly of the Negeb and Sinai regions.

See also AARON; AGAG.

AMAZIAH *See* AMOS.

AMEN Heb. *'amen,* "surely," is from the root "to be firm, trustworthy." It indicates acceptance of a curse or oath in a liturgical formula (Num. 5:22; Deut. 27:15ff.; Neh. 5:13; Jer. 11:5) as well as a response to blessing (1 Chron. 16:36; Neh. 8:6). In the NT, it is used as a response to prayer and is common in public worship (1 Cor. 14:16; St. Athanasius, *Apologia ad Constantinum,* 16). When it was prefaced by Jesus to his teachings (e.g., Matt. 6:2; John 8:34), his words were given special authority. This authority is also used of God's promises (2 Cor. 1:20) and is a title of God himself (Rev. 3:14).

In later Jewish practice, responding with "Amen" was regarded as equivalent to having said the blessing itself and came to be viewed as superior to the engendering prayer (Bera. 53b). Its use prolongs life (Bera. 47a) and opens the gates of Paradise (Shab. 119b), leading to the forgiveness of the respondent's sins.   DAVID W. BAKER

AMIDAH "Standing" Prayer.
See also HANNAH; PRAYER.

AMINADAB One of David's ancestors (Ruth 4:19ff.; 1 Chron. 2:10), great-grandson of Perez son of Judah by Tamar (Gen. 38:29; 46:12; cf. Matt. 1:4) and great-grandfather of Boaz. Aaron's wife Elisheba was the daughter of Aminadab (Exod. 6:23). Not of much importance in English literary allusion, he has, however, been connected to Hawthorne's story "The Birth-Mark."

Bibliography. Rees, J. O. "Aminadab in 'The Birth-Mark': the Name Again." *Names* 28 (1970), 171-82; Thompson, W. R. "Aminadab in Hawthorne's 'The Birth-mark.'" *MLN* 70 (1955), 413-15.

AMNON Firstborn son of King David, he fell in love with his half-sister Tamar, raped her, and then rejected her. Tamar's brother Absalom later had him murdered (2 Sam. 13:1-19), and fled, himself, into exile.

See also TAMAR.

AMORITES Sometimes referring to the inhabitants of Palestine generally (Gen. 15:16; Deut. 20:17; Judg. 6:10; 1 Sam. 7:14), sometimes the subgroup living in the mountains (Num. 13:29).

See also AJALON, VALE OF.

AMOS   Amos (not to be confused with Amoz, father of Isaiah) was a prophet of the 8th cent. B.C. and author of the third book of the Minor Prophets. Born in the shepherds' village of Tekoa, near Bethlehem, his name means either "burdensome" or "bearer of a burden" — i.e., bad news. Without special preparation he was called, he says, directly from his flocks to prophesy to the people of Israel (7:15). Though a rustic, he was broadly informed and politically aware. Because of a widening gap between the powerful rich and oppressed poor Amos saw no hope for the nation. His message was one of strong judgment which described the Day of the Lord not as a day of light and triumph but rather darkness and doom for Israel (5:18); the nation would be like one "who did flee from a lion and a bear met him" (7:19); only a remnant (9:8) would survive.

With the possible exception of Joel, Amos is the earliest biblical prophet whose utterances have been collected in writing. Among his best-known speeches, ironically, is his disclaimer of office: "I was no prophet; neither was I a prophet's son; but I was an herdman, and a gatherer of sycamore fruit" (7:14). Because his prognostications at Bethel included judgment on Ephraim itself, the priest Amaziah tried to have him exiled for treason. Nothing is known of his fate.

Amos has typically been characterized as the ragged prophet of doom; St. Jerome sees him "upon his crag blowing his shepherd's horn" (*Ep.* 46.13), yet in his famous oration to Paulinus on knowledge of the whole Scriptures (*Ep.* 53.7-8) he draws attention to the historical and metaphorical richness of Amos's writing. The prophet's iconography in Christian tradition reflects his rustic origin: typically he is shown with a shepherd's crook, occasionally with a basket of figs.

Although there has been a spate of minor modern plays based on the life of Amos (Fritchman [1923]; Overton [1927]; Raine [1927]) and a novel by Dorothy Clarke Wilson entitled *The Herdsman* (1946), literary interest has been intermittent. Medieval vernacular writers infrequently allude to Amos; exceptions include John Purvey, who, in his preface to the second version of the Wycliffite Bible, castigates Oxford in the oft-quoted words of Amos's prophecy concerning Damascus (1:3-5). And it may be, as D. Fowler has argued, that the author of *Piers Plowman* has Amos in mind in much of his own writing (*The Bible in Middle English Literature* [1984], 244-45; passim). Izaak Walton imagines Amos as a fisherman because, like Job, he mentions fishhooks (4:2); Bunyan in *Grace Abounding* parodies Amos 7:14 in saying of himself, "I am no poet, nor poet's son, but a mechanic" — a topos reiterated by the modern Israeli poet Bialik when he says, "What is my sin, what my strength? / I'm not a poet, not a prophet — I'm just a wood-cutter" ("My Soul Bends," *Selected Poems of Bialik* [1965]). John Greenleaf Whittier invokes the judgment of "the herdsman of Tekoah" upon those who would sell "the poor and

righteous again for silver and gold" ("Cassandra Southwick"). In Robert Nathan's ironic novel *The Son of Amittai; or Jonah* (1925), Amos figures as a saintly young mystic and visionary who eventually retreats to desert solitude.

ANAK, ANAKIM   *See* GIANTS IN THE EARTH.

ANAMNESIS   *Anamnēsis* is a Greek term meaning "commemoration" or "remembrance." In the LXX *anamnēsis* refers to rites of sacrifice performed as a remembrance of past sins (Wisd. of Sol. 6:16); the paschal feast is designed not simply to restore fading memories of the great events of the Exodus, but to renew the covenant relationship in worship. The OT here establishes a precedent: "liturgy is the privileged medium in which the covenant attains actuality" (Jungmann, in Rahner, 452). In the NT the Lord's Supper is a commemorative sacrifice of thanksgiving which Christ enjoined believers to perpetuate "in remembrance of me" (Luke 22:19; cf. 1 Cor. 11:24; Heb. 10:3). Remembrance here has the force of "re-actualize"; remembrance of Christ in this context means to seek fresh communion with him so that, as St. Paul puts it, "I may know him, and the power of his resurrection, and the fellowship of his sufferings, being made conformable unto his death; if by any means I might attain unto the resurrection of the dead" (Phil. 3:10-11). Anamnesis can also be understood in the sense of "memorial" before God (Acts 10:4; Mark 14:9), but in connection with the Eucharist it is more than that, related directly to the intercession the Church must make in its thankful response to God's grace in the sacrament. It is impossible, according to the model afforded by the Passover and deliverance of the Jews, that the Church should omit to pray at the Lord's table for the salvation of all persons.

The Anglican *Book of Common Prayer* order for the administration of the Lord's Supper translates anamnesis as "remembrance" ("Take and eat this in remembrance that Christ died for thee. . . ; Drink this in remembrance that Christ's blood was shed for thee . . ."), while the Roman Missal, following the Latin Vg, uses "commemoration." As St. Thomas's celebrated eucharistic hymn *"Adoro Te Devote"* has it (in G. M. Hopkins's translation) the liturgy is "our reminder of Christ crucified" (cf. his Breviary Lessons for the Feast of Corpus Christi); it both recollects and re-presents Christ's sacrifice (*Summa Theol.* 3a.75.1-5).

Christian anamnesis in this strict sense is to be distinguished from Platonic anamnesis (as represented in "Anamnestes" in Spenser's *Faerie Queene*, 2.58, the character who, according to the Platonic doctrine, knows by merely recalling). For St. Augustine, in whose thought the Platonic element is evident, ideas are not the recollection of past knowledge but the memory of a knowledge which is always available within the self, and is present to us inasmuch as we are present to ourselves. Thus, the soul's knowledge of God could also be called anamnesis, memory of him (*Conf.* 10.10-29). Augustine's consideration of these matters comes in a discussion of how the elements of art, images, and literature are "brought to birth" by memory (10.9.16), a discussion echoed in Dante's *Convivio* and *Vita Nuova,* and again in somewhat divergent fashion in Coleridge's *Biographia Literaria.*

Unsurprisingly, Christian anamnesis in the liturgical sense came into dramatic literature of the Middle Ages by way of the Canon of the Roman Mass. The Canon offered a commemorative re-presentation of all the mysteries of Christ's redemption, "proclaiming the Lord's death till he come" (1 Cor. 11:26). Liturgical plays such as the Passion Play or the *"Quem Quaeritis"* began as commemorative reenactments.

In the course of his disputation with Matthew Tyndale and others, St. Thomas More affirmed the traditional Thomist understanding: "He turned the bread into his own precious body, and the wine into his blessed blood, and commanded the same to be done for ever in his Church after, in remembrance of his passion" ("Confutation IV," 561H, quoted from Marc'hadour). Newman reiterates this same view: "And so he bids the commemoration of His Bloody Sacrifice to be made day by day over the earth, and He Himself is there in Person to quicken and sanctify it" ("The Infinitude of the Divine Attributes"). T. S. Eliot's wry sense of "Friday good" ("East Coker") demands a sacramental sense of "remembrance":

> The dripping blood our only drink,
> The bloody flesh our only food:
> In spite of which we like to think
> That we are sound, substantial flesh and blood —
> Again, in spite of that, we call this Friday good.

In the "Interlude" of *Murder in the Cathedral,* Eliot's archbishop speaks of the "re-enactment" of the "Passion and Death of Our Lord" (cf. Ezra Pound's "Ballad of the Goodly Fere," 13-14; 53-54). Anamnesis is a recurrent theme in the *Anathemata* of David Jones.

See also EUCHARIST; PASSOVER; SACRAMENT.

Bibliography. Cabrol, F. "Anamnèse." *DACL* (1907-53), 1.2.1880-88; Casel, O. "Das Mysteriengedächtnis der Messliturgie im Lichte der Tradition." *Jahrbuch für Liturgiewissenschaft* 6 (1926), 113-204; Cross, F., and E. Livingston. "Anamnesis." *ODCC,* 2nd ed. (1974); Dix, G. *The Shape of the Liturgy* (1945); Jungmann, J. *The Mass of the Roman Rite: Its Origins and Development (Missarum Sollemnia)* (1955), 2.218-26; "Eucharist." In *The Concise "Sacramentum Mundi."* Ed. K. Rahner (1975); Marc'hadour, G. *The Bible in the Works of Thomas More* (1969), 3.71.   ERNEST N. KAULBACH

ANANIAS AND SAPPHIRA   The early Christian community described in the Acts of the Apostles held all possessions "in common." When Ananias and his wife Sapphira sold a portion of land and secretly kept back part of the price, laying the balance "at the apostles' feet" (5:1-10), St. Peter accused Ananias of having defrauded God. Ananias fell down and died on the spot, a fate repeated by Sapphira three hours later when she also lied, claiming the land had been sold for exactly the amount surrendered to the community. (This Ananias, archetype of the liar, is not to be confused with the high priest who ordered St. Paul to be struck on the mouth [Acts 23:2].)

Patristic writers see the sin of Ananias and Sapphira as fraud and, inasmuch as it paid too much respect to material goods, as idolatry (e.g., St. Jerome, *Ep.* 14.5). It is also said to involve a failure to obey the divine injunction to holy poverty (Jerome, *Ep.* 130.14) and a resistance of stewardship in faith; St. Gregory the Great holds the crime of Ananias and Sapphira to be a form of turning back, having put one's hand to the plow (Luke 9:62) — effectively a denial of the salvation offered by grace (*Ep.* 34). As the *Glossa Ordinaria* puts it, "better never to have made a promise to the Holy Spirit at all than to have made one and not kept it" (PL 114.437; cf. Eccl. 5:5). The *Cursor Mundi,* in its retelling of the incident, says that Ananias withheld the money because of his commitment to "ese" (19236), and cautions its readers to consider that such an extreme judgment pertained chiefly to the fledgling church, for "yeit was it noght stablid þan" (19262); the penalty was intended as a warning to others.

Bunyan's pilgrim is shown a door in the side of a hill which is "a By-way to Hell, a way that Hypocrites go in at; namely, such as sell their birthright with Esau . . . and that lie and dissemble with Ananias and Sapphira his wife." Bunyan would not have been pleased to know that Ananias appears as a Puritan deacon in Ben Jonson's *The Alchemist,* "the valet that cozen'd the apostles!" Ruskin, in *Sesame and Lilies,* shifts the focus onto a commitment to life (in Pater's sense) and to community, observing that "most of us think not of what we are to do, but of what we are to get . . . the sin of Ananias. . . . We want to keep back part of the price" (135). When Melville's Billy Budd kills the scheming Claggart, Captain Vere calls it "the divine judgment of Ananias." The story from Acts has been dramatized by H. W. Githens (1929) and A. B. Knowles (1925).

Bibliography. Fallon, J. L. "Jonson's Ananias." *Expl* 43 (1984), 16-17; Williamson, L. "The Use of the Ananias and Sapphira Story (Acts 5:1-11) in the Patristic Period." Unpubl. Ph.D. diss., Yale, 1963.

ANASTASIS   See HARROWING OF HELL.

ANATHEMA   The Greek term *anathema* denotes something "placed on high" — set aside or consecrated: a votive offering hung on a temple wall was thus "anathema." The word is also used of a thing set apart because execrable, and so given over to destruction. Both uses are found in the Bible, though Christian usage, following St. Paul's example, has more to say on the negative sense than on the affirmative.

Judith 16:23 and Luke 21:5 provide examples of the affirmative anathema, and Deut. 7:26, Josh. 7:11-12, and Zech. 14:11 of the negative (curse or malediction), which in the OT is often severe, calling for extermination of the anathematized to protect Israel from idolatry. Conveyance of malediction is the chief sense of "anathema" in the Pauline letters (e.g., Rom. 9:3; Gal. 1:9; 1 Cor. 16:22), and the Church used the word to signify exclusion of a sinner, and especially to denounce heresy, the conciliar formula being: "If any one says . . . let him be anathema."

Among the Fathers anathema is predominantly a negative term, though its affirmative meaning is also recalled. St. John Chrysostom, commenting on Rom. 11:1, distinguishes between the two uses of the word (*Hom.* 16). St. Athanasius (*Epistola encyclica*, 1), St. Augustine (*Adv. Jud.* 5), and St. Cyril of Alexandria (*Anathemas*) use it negatively. Aquinas deals with it etymologically and historically ("*suspendebant illud in templo*"), and distinguishes between the two uses, though stressing that which sets people apart from Christ (*Ep. ad Rom.* 9.1).

The association of anathema and excommunication is direct but complex: the Roman Pontifical distinguishes three sorts of excommunication, the solemn pronouncement of anathema being a severe form. (Based on a misunderstanding of Paul's words in 1 Cor. 16:22, "Let him be anathema. Maranatha [= Our Lord, come!]," there is a further solemn office, Maranatha, which is an intensified anathema.)

Use of the term in English literature reflects special concern about anathema's entailing the delivery of a heretic to the secular arm (e.g., T. Erastus, *A Treatise of Excommunication* [1568]; George Gillespie, *A Late Dialogue* [1644]; William Prynne, *Foure Serious Questions* [1645]). Andrew Marvell catches the sense of Puritan distaste in *The Loyall Scot:* "A Bishop's self is an anathema" (111). The word here is held in contempt by the Presbyterian faction and indicates unjust usurpation of power. Similar uses occur in Marvell's *Historical Essay on General Councils, Creeds, and Imposition in Religion:* "Would you anathemise, banish, imprison, execute us, and burn our books?" (ed. Grosart, 4.132) and Francis Bacon's *Advancement of Learning:* "The elected saints of God have themselves anathematised" (2.20.7).

During the Renaissance the solemn force of negative anathema remained prevalent. This is the case with John Donne: "Which Anathema . . . was utter damnation" (*Biathanatos,* 192); Bacon: "He would wish to be anathema from Christ" (*Essays,* "Goodness"); John Foxe: "A solemne anathematization of all that woulde call an image an idol" (*Acts and Monuments,* 751-52). However, as the Church's authority waned in secular affairs, anathema increasingly indicated pompous but ineffective malediction, as, e.g., in Dickens's "venerable parent promptly resorts to anathematization, and turns him out" (*Our Mutual Friend,* 1.2) and Carlyle's "well may

mankind shriek, inarticularly anathematising as they can" (*French Revolution,* 2.3.1.6).

Affirmative use is less frequent, but occurs in incidental references: Edward Topsell (in his *The History of Serpents* [1608], 779) describes a spider's web as "the very pattern, index, and anathema of supernaturall wisdome." David Jones's *The Anathemata* (1952) restores the full affirmative sense in a major work inspired by the idea that the artist's "signs" are most valid when most fully laid aside, as nonutilitarian offerings of the human creative spirit.

See also MARANATHA.   PATRICK GRANT

ANCIENT OF DAYS   Daniel 7:7-22 describes an apocalyptic night-vision of Daniel in which "the books" are opened before the Ancient of Days, "whose garment was as white as snow, and the hair of his head like the pure wool: his throne was like the fiery flame, and his wheels as burning fire" (v. 9). This scene of judgment climaxes with an approach to the throne by "one like the Son of man" (v. 13), unto whom is then given "dominion, and glory, and a kingdom . . . which shall not pass away" (v. 14). The title "Ancient of Days" alternates in the passage with "Most High" (vv. 18-27) and seems to indicate God enthroned in judgment over world empires. In Aramaic ʿ*attiq yomin* means "advanced in days" and corresponds to a similar description of Zeus in hellenic art and literature. The term is cited throughout talmudic literature and becomes "the head of days" in 1 Enoch 46. Rashi identifies the figure with God, other sources with an angel. St. Augustine typifies patristic exegesis in seeing the Ancient of Days as God the Father, and adds that Daniel's vision provides a concrete example of the Father's appearing to the prophets in bodily form, so that "it is not, therefore, unsuitably believed that God the Father was also wont to appear in that manner to mortals" (*De Trin.* 18.33).

John Donne, in his "La Corona" sonnet, asks the "all changing unchang'd Antient of dayes" to receive his collection of sonnets as a "crown of prayer and praise." The most famous evocation of the Ancient of Days in English literary history, however, may well be Blake's frontispiece illustration for *Europe,* in which he is also a *deus pancreator,* constricted, as Blake would see it, by the limitations of mathematical form (rpt. M. Klonsky, *William Blake* [1977], 40). For Coleridge, "to contemplate the ancient of days and all his works with feelings as fresh as if all had then sprung forth at the first creative fiat characterizes the mind that feels the riddle of the world, and may help to unravel it" (*Biographia Literaria,* chap. 3; cf. Byron, *Childe Harold's Pilgrimage,* 2.2.1).

ANDREW   Andrew the apostle appears only briefly in the Synoptic Gospels: in lists of the Twelve (Matt. 10:2; Mark 3:14; Luke 6:13), at the healing of Peter's mother-in-law (Mark 1:29), at Christ's foretelling of the destruction of the Temple (Mark 13:1-2), and in Matthew's slight expansion on the calling of Simon and "Andrew his brother" (4:18-20). In John's Gospel Andrew's stature grows: he finds the boy whose loaves and fishes are multiplied (6:8-9) and he introduces "certain Greeks" to Jesus (12:20-22). The most important Johannine contribution lies in the chronology of apostolic selection: Andrew was the first of John the Baptist's disciples called by Jesus, and it was he who brought Simon (1:35-42).

According to Eusebius (*Hist. eccl.* 3.1), when the apostles drew lots after Pentecost, Andrew was sent to Scythia on the Black Sea. Later apocryphal "acts" center on his preaching and martyrdom in Achaia (Greece). Despite opposition of church leaders to such apocrypha, veneration of the apostle led to generic transformation of these extracanonical "acts" into a liturgically acceptable "passion" of a martyr (see *Acta Apostolorum Apocrypha,* eds. Richard A. Lipsius and Maximilian Bonnet [1898], 2.1.1-37). This in turn evolved into readings, antiphons, and responsories for his feastday office (Nov. 30). An Eastern version of the Achaian narrative established Andrew as the founder of the church in Byzantium; this tradition, linked to John's story of the first-called, helped Andrew's see to rival in importance the see of his brother Peter (see Dvornik).

Other apocrypha place Andrew among the *Anthropophagi,* or cannibals, of Mermedonia or among the *Cynocephali* (see J. Friedman, *The Monstrous Races in Medieval Art and Thought* [1981], 61, 70-71, 102). In the Mermedonian context, Andrew rescues Matthew (Matthias in some recensions), confronts Satan, and allows himself to be imprisoned and tortured. From his cell he produces a miraculous flood which converts the populace; after instructing and baptizing the former cannibals, he appoints a bishop and returns to Achaia, where he is martyred. An abbreviated 6th-cent. account by St. Gregory of Tours inserts the Mermedonian trip into the Achaian narrative (see *Liber de Miraculis Beati Andreae Apostoli,* ed. Max Bonnet, Monumenta Germaniae historica [1885; rpt. 1969]; cf. Mermedonian variants in Blatt).

Andrew's association with Scotland stems from a separate legend according to which St. Regulus, a 4th-cent. bishop of Achaia, brought relics of the saint to what later became the see of St. Andrews. The flag of Scotland has exhibited the x-shaped cross of St. Andrew since the 8th cent. when, according to another legend, Acaius and Hungus, kings of the Scots and the Picts, saw this cross in the heavens before their victorious battle against the Angles. The Scottish chivalric Order of the Thistle was dedicated to St. Andrew by James VII of Scotland (James II of England) in 1687. Swift, satirizing court honors, identifies this order by "the green ribbon of St. Andrew" ("Verses on the Revival of the Order of Bath"; cf. *Gulliver's Travels,* 1.3).

Like the Synoptics, literary writers link Andrew to his more famous brother. Milton, e.g., refers to only two of "the new-baptized" waiting for Christ's return from the desert: "Andrew and Simon, famous after" (*Paradise Regained,* 2.7). Edgar Lee Masters, paying tribute to Peter's courage in "Simon Surnamed Peter" (in *Songs and Satires* [1916]), names only the hero's brother among the non-courageous when he says, "Then Andrew and all of them fled, but you followed him . . ." (st. 3).

Despite Masters's slighting reference, Andrew's courage is etymologically his major attribute. The Gk. *Andreas* (Lat. *virilis*) means "manly," and it was in exercising his manliness that Andrew earned his fame. The most extended literary treatments of the apostle, the anonymous OE *Andreas* and a prose version of the story, follow the Mermedonian narrative (see *Andreas and the Fates of the Apostles,* ed. K. R. Brooks [1961]; cf. the OE homily version in *The Blickling Homilies,* ed. R. Morris, EETS 73, o.s. [1880; rpt. 1967], 229-49). The 9th-cent. poet referred frequently to Andrew as an *æðeling* ("hero"), describing him as *modig, mægene rof, beadu-rof* ("brave," "valiant in might," "valiant in battle"). When the poet Andrew returned to Achaia, "he sawulgedal, / beaducwealm gebad" ("he endured soul-separation, death in battle" [1701-02]). Cynewulf's fragmentary *Fates of the Apostles* (ed. Brookes) reduces the Achaian exploits to seven lines, omitting Mermedonia; the hero motif remains in Andrew's death scene: "æfter guðplegan gealgan þehte" ("after the battle-play he was stretched on the cross" [22]). As Cranmer stands on the scaffold in Tennyson's "Queen Mary," he is encouraged to remember "The triumph of St. Andrew on his cross" (4.2.94). It is the triumphant martyr apostle that both literature and liturgy honor.

Bibliography. Blatt, F., ed. *Die lateinischen Bearbeitungen der Acta Andreae et Matthiae apud Anthropophagos.* ZNW 12 (1930); Brooks, K. R., ed. *Andreas and the Fates of the Apostles* (1961); Dvornik, F. *The Idea of Apostolicity in Byzantium and the Legend of the Apostle Andrew* (1958); Flamion, J. *Les Actes apocryphes de l'apôtre André* (1911); Hennecke, E. *New Testament Apocrypha.* Ed. W. Schneemelcher. Trans. R. McL. Wilson et al. 2 vols. (1963-65); Peterson, P. *Andrew, Brother of Simon Peter, His History and His Legends.* NovTSup 1 (1958).   MARIE MICHELLE WALSH

ANGEL The word *angel* (Gk. *angelos*; Heb. *mal'ak*) means "messenger." Biblical angels not only bring tidings and commandments but also act as rescuers, ministrants, guardians, guides, stern admonishers and encouragers, interpreters of visions, warriors, destroyers, controllers of the forces of nature, and perpetual worshipers in the court of heaven. Angelic beings are sometimes referred to as "sons of God" (e.g., Job 1:16), and they are often pictured in art as God's courtiers.

Angels appear in a variety of memorable biblical visions: e.g., to Jacob, ascending and descending a ladder between heaven and earth (Gen. 28:12); to Isaiah as six-winged seraphim (Isa. 6:1-8); to Ezekiel in "the likeness of four living creatures" (Ezek. 1); to Daniel around God's flaming throne where "thousand thousands ministered unto him, and ten thousand times ten thousand stood before him" (Dan. 7:10); to Zechariah, as "a man riding upon a red horse . . ." (Zech. 1:8-11); and to John on Patmos, in many forms, including "four beasts full of eyes" (Rev. 4–5).

Angels interpret these last three visions as well as appearing in them. Obedient in all things, angels both "pour out the vials of the wrath of God" (Rev. 16) and bring comfort (e.g., Dan. 10:11-12).

Angels announce the births of Ishmael, Isaac, Samson, John the Baptist, and Jesus, and they interact in task and colloquy with patriarchs, prophets, apostles, and the family of Christ. Among notable instances, three dine with Abraham (Gen. 18), and two rescue the family of Lot from Sodom (Gen. 19); an angel or a celestial form succors Hagar and Ishmael in the wilderness (Gen. 21:17-19), intervenes in the sacrifice of Isaac (Gen. 22:10-12), wrestles with Jacob (Gen. 32:24-29), appears to Moses in a burning bush (Exod. 3:2), leads the Israelites out of Egypt and through the wilderness (Exod. 14:19; 23:20), exhorts Balaam (Num. 22:22-35), comes sword in hand as "captain of the LORD's host" to Joshua (Josh. 5:13-15), rebukes the Israelites (Judg. 2:1-2) and calls Gideon to deliver them (Judg. 6:11-23), brings pestilence (2 Sam. 24:15-17), feeds and instructs Elijah (1 Kings 19; 2 Kings 1), smites Assyrians (2 Kings 19:35; Isa. 37:36), and protects Daniel in the lions' den and his companions in the fiery furnace (Dan. 6:22; 3:25). Angels advise Joseph in dreams (Matt. 1:20; 2:13, 19), minister to Jesus after his temptation (Matt. 4:11) and during his agony in the garden (Luke 22:43), roll the stone from the mouth of his tomb and announce his resurrection to the women disciples (Matt. 28; Mark 16; Luke 24; John 20), comfort the apostles after his ascension (Acts 1:10-11), rescue Peter and others from prison (Acts 5:19; 12:7-10), instruct Philip (Acts 8:26) and Cornelius (Acts 10:3-7), destroy Herod (Acts 12:23), and stand by Paul in his shipwreck (Acts 27:23-24). They will accompany Christ at his second coming, execute judgment upon the wicked, and gather up the elect (Matt. 13:41 and 24:31; Jude 14).

When ministering to humankind, angels sometimes adopt human form; Abraham and Tobias both fail at first to recognize that their visitors are heavenly, and the writer of the Epistle to the Hebrews counsels: "Be not forgetful to entertain strangers; for thereby some have entertained angels unawares" (13:2). Sometimes they are "ministers of flaming fire" (Ps. 104:4) whose brightness lights the earth (Luke 2:9-10) and who must tell their quaking witnesses, "Fear not" (cf. Matt. 28:3-4; Judg. 6:22; Job 4:15; Dan. 10). Yet they are devoted to the welfare of the heirs of salvation (Heb. 1:7, 14), whose redemption is a mystery they desire to look into (1 Pet. 1:12), and they rejoice over each sinner who repents (Luke 15:10). Ps. 91:11 declares that God "shall give his angels charge over thee, to keep thee in all thy ways" (cf. Matt. 4:6; Luke

4:10-11), and Jesus speaks of children whose "angels do always behold the face of my Father which is in heaven" (Matt. 18:10). Though mighty, holy, and pure, angels are not to be worshiped; when John falls to his knees, the angel by whom God "sent and signified" the Revelation says, "See thou do it not; for I am thy fellow servant. . . ; worship God" (Rev. 22:9).

The description of angels, apart from their dealings with humankind, is scattered throughout Scripture and amplified in tradition. Though sometimes associated with Platonic Forms, Aristotelian Intelligences, polytheistic deities, or allegorical embodiments of natural and psychic forces, for most of English literature, especially before the mid-18th cent., angels are pure celestial spirits having individual consciousness and free will, made in God's image and present at the creation of the world "when the morning stars sang together, and all the sons of God shouted for joy" (Job 38:7). But the brightest of them, Lucifer, rebelled and fell from heaven with his followers, henceforth to harry humankind, while the obedient angels, confirmed in blessedness, lead lives of joyful praise, celeritous service, mutual love, and profound solicitude for their human charges. Angels are not sexual beings and do not propagate (Matt. 22:30; Luke 20:35-36); each is apparently a special creation. They can, however (according to Genesis Rabbah, Maimonides [*Guide* 1.49], and Milton [*Paradise Lost*, 1.423-24]), assume either sex for earthly appearances. Although the bliss of the obedient angels is immutable, Western art and literature see them as capable of choice and initiative, compassion and grief (especially at the Crucifixion), and continual growth in perfection and love.

Particular angels named in the Bible and Apocrypha are: Gabriel ("Man of God"), who appears to Daniel, Zacharias, and the Virgin Mary; Michael ("Who is like God?"), the guardian or prince of Israel (Dan. 12:1) who leads the good angels in the war in heaven (Rev. 12:7-8) and contends with Satan for the body of Moses (Jude 9); Uriel ("Fire of God"), named in 2 Esdr. 4:1; and Raphael ("Medicine of God"), who accompanies Tobias in the book of Tobit. Other angels are named in pseudepigraphal works such as 1 Enoch and The Testament of Solomon, in the Cabala, and in the Koran. Most angels have three-syllable names ending in "-el," a Semitic name of God.

During the Middle Ages, angelology was a normal branch of science, and its literature is vast. In both Judaism and Christianity, references to angels became more abundant the more the faith was established, though both traditions were careful early on to distinguish the doctrine of angels from the worship of polytheistic cultures around them. Much commentary and speculation may be found in the Talmud and Midrash; in the mystical writings on the Merkabah, the divine chariot seen by Ezekiel, and the Hekalot, or heavenly palaces; and in the work of hellenistic and medieval writers such as Philo and Maimonides, who related Jewish angelology to Greek philosophy.

Christian writers, whether Patristic, Scholastic, or Re-formed, have much to say about angels: major sources include Augustine's *De civ. Dei* 11.9 – 12.2; Aquinas's *Summa Theol.* 1.50-64 and 107-14; Luther's commentaries, "Fruteful Sermon," and *Table Talk,* 2829; and Calvin's *Inst.* 1.14.3-19, in which he affirms the reality of angels and devils and believes that the OT "angel of the LORD" is Christ. The ordering of angels into three hierarchies in nine choirs was the work of Dionysius the Pseudo-Areopagite (ca. A.D. 500); his ranks, in de-scending order, are the seraphim, cherubim, thrones, dominations, virtues, powers, principalities, archangels, and angels, their purpose being the transmission of the primal light by degrees to all the receptive parts of cre-ation. Dante gives poetic expression to his conceptions in the last six cantos of the *Paradiso.*

The golden age of angelology in Protestant England is the 17th cent. James I (who wrote a book about fallen angels) had an official angelologist, Jesuit-educated John Salkeld, author of *A Treatise of Angels;* other works in-clude Thomas Heywood's compendium of poems and commentary *The Hierarchie of the Blessed Angels,* and works by Isaac Ambrose, Richard Baxter, and Bishops Ussher and Hall. *An History of Angels* by Henry Lawrence, the "virtuous father" of Milton's sonnet and a member of parliament, teaches that "our communion is very great with the Angells, both good and bad"; since by "writing on our fancies" they "represent objects to our understandings, and our wills which often take and moove us," we should stock our memories with good images so that good angels "may have matter to work upon" (36-41). Richard Hooker says that angels are "unsatisfiable in their longing to doe by all meanes all maner of good unto all the creatures of God, but especially unto the children of men" (*Lawes,* 1.4), and Sir Thomas Browne that "many mysteries ascribed to our own inventions, have been the courteous revelations of Spirits; for those noble essences in heaven beare a friendly regard unto their fellow-natures on earth" (*Religio Medici* [1634/35], 71-72).

In both the Jewish and the Christian tradition those gathered on earth to worship God join their voices with the angelic choirs. Two of the most sacred texts of Chris-tian liturgy are angelic utterances: the Sanctus (Isa. 6:3) and the beginning of the Gloria (Luke 2:14). In the *Book of Common Prayer* the Sanctus is said or sung "with angels and archangels, and with all the company of heaven." The Anglican Church celebrates the Feast of St. Michael and All Angels (Sept. 29) and (in addition to the daily lectionary and psalter) mentions angels in the can-ticles for morning and evening prayer and in the propers of many holy days. Angels are thought to be present at all gatherings of the faithful (Hooker, *Lawes,* 5.25; Milton, *De Doctrina Christiana,* 1.9). "The house of prayer is a Court," Hooker says, "bewtified with the presence of celestiall powers."

Angels abound in psalmody and hymnody, especially annunciation and Christmas carols, as well as in epithala-mia, obsequies, medieval lyrics, and cycles of poems for the liturgical year (e.g., those by Thomas Ken, Chris-topher Smart, Christopher Wordsworth, Christina Rosset-ti, and John Greenleaf Whittier).

In medieval mystery plays angels are presented as speaking characters; indeed, if the *"Quem Quaeritis"* trope is the beginning of English drama, the angels at the tomb are its first voices. They appear in the Pearl Poet's *Cleanness* in dialogues with Abraham and Lot, and play musical instruments "that make hearts chastely glad" at the birth of Christ (1081-84). Chaucer depicts speaking angels in *The Second Nun's Tale* and, briefly, in the Sum-moner's Prologue, in which an angel guides a friar through a Bosch-like hell. In Malory's *Morte Darthur* guardian angels protect Sir Galahad, and fallen angels, disguised as fair ladies, priests, and hermits, tempt Sir Bors; Galahad and his companions see "a great fellowship of angels" with the Grail, and "a great multitude" bear it and his soul to heaven (17.22). Angels recur in the Ar-thurian poems of the 19th cent.

English Renaissance angels include Guyon's guardian in Spenser's *Faerie Queene* (2.8.1-8), the "triune triplici-ties" of *Fowre Hymns,* and the angels who surround the bride in *Epithalamion.* A Good and a Bad Angel (in addition to Mephistopheles) recurrently exhort Mar-lowe's Faustus. Shakespeare does not give angels major roles, but his characters often invoke them as guardians, especially in history plays, and they are nonfiguratively addressed in *Macbeth, Measure for Measure,* and espe-cially *Hamlet:* "Angels and ministers of grace defend us" (1.4.39); "I see a cherub that sees them" (4.3.50); "Help, angels! Make assay!" (3.3.69); and "flights of angels sing thee to thy rest" (5.2.371).

A detailed angelology could be gathered from the poems, sermons, and meditations of John Donne, who celebrates their multiple ministrations in Expostulation 7 of his *Devotions.* Milton joins his songs to angels' in his early poems, compares his calling to Isaiah's (*Reason and Church Government,* 2, pref.), and provides highly devel-oped angelic characters in *Paradise Lost.* Raphael recounts the war in heaven and the creation of the world to Adam and Eve in rich images accommodated to their understanding and gives Adam counsel on knowledge, nurture, and divine, human, and angelic love. Michael shows in vision and narrative the consequences of the Fall and the prophetic history of redemption. Abdiel furnishes the angelic model of heroic choice (5.803-906), and Gabriel, Uriel, Zephon, Ithuriel, and Zophiel take an ac-tive part. Among the fallen angels, Satan, Beelzebub, Moloch, Mammon, and Belial oppose hate, vandalism, and degeneracy to the joyful service and resplendent arts of dance and hymnody in which the unfallen fellowship delights.

The literary role of angels declines during the 18th cent., even where one might expect to find them: Cowper's *Olney Hymns* allude to OT messages and ministrations without mentioning their angelic bearers. However, angels do not entirely disappear from the many collections of hymns published during that rational age, especially Christmas carols (e.g., Nahum Tate's "While Shepherds Watched Their Flocks" and Charles Wesley's "Hark! The Herald Angels Sing"), and they make dramatic if heterodox appearances in the works of Christopher Smart (who speculated that angels *do* marry, in "A Song to David," 113-14), and of William Blake, in whose poems angels can be anything from whatever is seen to be divine in nature or human genius to spirits of orthodoxy who suppress revolution and delight.

In the late 18th cent. and much of the 19th, angels receive frequent mention, often figurative or allegorical, sometimes in their solemn, festive biblical identities, abundantly enough in Wordsworth, Coleridge, the Brownings, Meredith, Poe, and Hawthorne to merit study, and often enough as fellow artists or spirit muses to constitute an important theme. Wordsworth, steeped in Milton, describes the colloquy of humans with angels before the Fall, their compassion for humankind and joy at the Sabbath, their pure perceptions, and their welcoming of humans after death (*Excursions*, 4.631; 7.1; "In the Cathedral at Cologne," *Prelude*, 14.94-99), and in "On the Power of Sound," "flaming Seraphim" transmit the hymns of nature to heaven. Coleridge, too, renews this strain in "Religious Musings" and "On the Death of Chatterton." Keats hints at angel artists in "On Leaving Some Friends" and "Sleep and Poetry." Byron's dramatic *personae* include Lucifer and the Angel of the Lord in *Cain* and Raphael and two questionable angels from 1 Enoch named Azazel and Samiasa who carry off two of the "daughters of men" (Gen. 6:2) in *Heaven and Earth;* in his satirical *Vision of Judgment* Michael and Satan quarrel over the body of George III.

Both Robert and Elizabeth Barrett Browning write legions of angels into their poems. Elizabeth Barrett's first published works are dramatic renderings of Scripture: *The Seraphim* is primarily a dialogue of two angels at the time of the Crucifixion, and *A Dream of Exile* (on the expulsion from the Garden of Eden) includes Gabriel, Lucifer, and a chorus of innumerable angels. An angel speaks extensively in *A Vision of Poets,* and in "The Seraph and the Poet" angel and human sing — one of glory, the other of sorrow — equally. Robert Browning depicts an interlocutory angel Gabriel in "The Boy and the Angel" and in "The Guardian Angel" addresses the angel in Guercino's painting at Fuco; this is one of many instances in which 19th- and 20th-cent. writers describe angels at second hand by describing works of art (e.g., the "Annunciation" poems of D. G. Rossetti and Edwin Muir). In Tennyson's "St. Simeon Stylites" an angel "stood and watched me as I sang." Christina Rossetti writes often about angels, in "Are They Not All Ministering Spirits?"

and "The Watchers" as well as in *Some Feasts and Fasts.* Emerson's "Uriel" is an unorthodox questioner, and Poe's "Israfel" a spirit in the Islamic heaven whose music the poet compares with his own. Hopkins invokes a colorful spirit in "Il Mystico." George Macdonald's novel *At the Back of the North Wind* features an implacably beneficent female angel of death. In Newman's *Dream of Gerontius* a newly liberated soul converses with his guardian angel, who conducts him to judgment and purification.

Within the last hundred years, angels have appeared in dramatic works such as Yeats's *The Countess Cathleen* and *The Hour-Glass,* and J. B. Priestley's *An Inspector Calls.* Dorothy Sayers's *The Zeal of Thy House,* based on the life of the 12th-cent. architect of Canterbury Cathedral, gives major roles to Michael, Raphael, and a recording angel named Cassiel.

Among novels, Charles Williams's *The Place of the Lion* contains angels as Platonic Forms; C. S. Lewis's space trilogy *Out of the Silent Planet, Perelandra,* and *That Hideous Strength* is full of angels called *eldila;* and in his *Screwtape Letters* fallen angels plot to corrupt a soul. Marianne Moore's "By Disposition of Angels" speculates on the nature of angelic beings. Wallace Stevens's many angels are entirely metaphorical. In *Angels and Awakenings,* M. Cameron Grey gathers short stories that "spring from the intellectual skepticism and sense of spiritual dislocation" of the contemporary world, yet show a persistent interest in "a divine presence" (xv-xvii). Robertson Davies's *What's Bred in the Bone* has as a major character "the Lesser Zadkiel, Angel of Biography."

In popular media angels incline to be sentimental, comical, or even raffish, and angelology has largely been replaced by strictly secular allegorical, psychological, and anthropological explanations which drain them of spiritual power. Nevertheless, recent studies by Catholic, Protestant, and philosophical writers (Huber, Graham, and Adler respectively) reaffirm their scriptural identities, hymns continue to mention them, and students of literature — especially of Milton — keep their splendors and ardent songs before us.

See also ANNUNCIATION; DEVIL; GABRIEL; MICHAEL; RAPHAEL; SERAPH.

Bibliography. Bamberger, B. J. *Fallen Angels* (1952); Davidson, G. *A Dictionary of Angels* (1967); Ellrodt, R. "Angels and the Poetic Imagination from Donne to Traherne." In J. Cary, ed. *English Renaissance Studies Presented to Dame Helen Gardner in Honour of her Seventieth Birthday* (1980); Greene, T. *The Descent from Heaven: A Study in Epic Continuity* (1963); Jung, L. "Fallen Angels in Jewish, Christian, and Mohammedan Literature." *JQR* 15 (1924-25), 16 (1925-26); Moore, J. R. "Tradition of Angelic Singing in English Drama." *JEGP* 22 (1923), 89-99; Patrides, C. *Premises and Motifs in Renaissance Thought and Literature* (1982); Pollack, R. "Angelic Imagery in the English Mystery Cycles." *Theatre Notebook* 29 (1975), 124-39; Swaim, K. *Before and After the Fall: Contrasting Modes in "Paradise Lost"*

(1986); Ward, T. *Men and Angels* (1969); West, R. *Milton and the Angels* (1955); Wilson, P. *Angels* (1980).

DIANE MCCOLLEY

ANGEL OF LIGHT The archetypal angel of light is Lucifer, or Satan. When Paul wished to acknowledge the existence of false apostles who had tried to pass themselves off as true, he said that it was "no marvel; for Satan himself is transformed into an angel of light" (2 Cor. 11:14). The phrase prompts a large body of commentary in the patristic period concerning the devil's penchant for dissimulation and the need for the faithful to be on their guard against his wiles and disguises. In literary terms the "angel of light" becomes synonymous with the clever tempter (or temptress). In Shakespeare's *Comedy of Errors,* when a prostitute wishes to claim from the wrong Antipholus a promised gold chain, he tells his servant Dromio that she is the devil himself. "Nay," Dromio replies,

> she is worse, she is the Devil's dam; and here she comes in the habit of a light wench. And thereof comes that the wenches say, "God damn me." That's as much as to say, "God make me a light wench." It is written they appear to men like angels of light. Light is an effect of fire, and fire will burn; ergo, light wenches will burn. Come not near her. (4.3.50-56)

For William Cowper the false courtier "whose trade it is to smile, to crouch, to please; / In smooth dissimulation, skilled to grace / A devil's purpose with an angel's face" (*Table Talk,* 128-30) is such an "angel" (cf. Byron, *Cain,* 3.1.486). The term becomes clichéd before the end of the century, as when Jane Austen, misplacing the original pejorative association, writes in *Pride and Prejudice* (chap. 48) that "all Meryton seemed striving to blacken the man who, but three months before, had been almost an angel of light." In Samuel Butler's *The Way of All Flesh* Ernest reflects bitterly on the failure of his marriage to Ellen to preserve him from falling into sin: "It seemed to him that in his attempt to be moral he had been following a devil which had disguised itself as an angel of light" (chap. 75).

See also BELIAL; DEVIL.

Bibliography. Barry, J. M. "The Angel of Light Tradition in Biblical Commentary and English Literature of the Middle Ages and Renaissance." *DAI* 38 (1977), 252A.

ANGELS UNAWARES The writer of the Epistle to the Hebrews enjoins his readers to obedience and generosity in hospitality: "Be not forgetful to entertain strangers: for thereby some have entertained angels unawares" (Heb. 13:2). In Twain's *The Innocents Abroad* the gulled victims of a street huckster see the text in an ironic light: "We threw all the purchases away together this morning. They were coarse, unsubstantial, freckled all over with broad yellow splotches and could neither stand wear nor public exhibition. We had entertained an angel unawares, but we did not take her in. She did that for us" (chap. 7).

See also LOT.

ANNA An elderly prophetess who, with Simeon, was present when Jesus was presented as an infant at the Temple. Like Simeon she recognized Jesus as bringing "redemption in Israel" (Luke 2:38-39).

See also NUNC DIMITTIS.

ANNAS *See* CAIAPHAS AND ANNAS.

ANNE Anne and Joachim are the traditional names of the mother and father of the Virgin. The Bible makes no mention of Mary's parents, and most of the information about their lives comes from the apocryphal Protevangelium of James (ca. A.D. 170-180). A number of early Church Fathers, including St. John of Damascus and St. Sophronius, cited or commented on the story found in this ancient document.

There are three ME stanzaic versions of the *Life of St. Anne;* these rely on various other sources, including the apocryphal Gospel of Pseudo-Matthew and Jacobus de Voragine's *Legenda Aurea.* The poems relate the whole life of Anne after her marriage to Joachim as well as the life of Mary and of Jesus. The account centers on the married couple's childlessness for twenty years, at which point Joachim flees to the hills in shame and apparently abandons Anne. The couple's prayers are finally answered when an angel of the Lord appears to each spouse individually and promises a child who will be known throughout the world. Joachim and Anne thereafter meet at the golden gate (the subject of Dürer's painting) and are reunited. The story here, and especially as it is related in the Protevangelium of James, bears a strong resemblance to that of the conception and birth of Samuel; Samuel's mother's name, Hannah ("Anna" in the Douay version), is a variant of Anne (1 Sam. 1).

A number of English poems were written in honor of St. Anne between the end of the 13th cent. and beginning of the 16th cent. The most prominent are John Lydgate's "A Praise of St. Anne," his "An Invocation to Seynte Anne," John Audelay's "De Sancta Anna Matre Marie," and Osbern Bokenam's "Life of St. Anne." Anne deserves veneration, the poets claim, because whoever loves the daughter (Mary) must, out of courtesy, love the mother. Other poems, such as the anonymous "Thou Shalt Bear the Fruit of Life," make passing references to the mother of Mary. Chaucer has incidental references to Anne in *The Man of Law's Tale* (64), *The Friar's Tale* (1613), and *The Second Nun's Tale* (70).

From the Renaissance forward only scattered references to St. Anne are found. In *The Excursion* (4.910), Wordsworth imagines one of the products of re-sowing the "weeds of Romish phantasy" to be the reconsecration of English wells to "fair St. Anne." Perhaps the most interesting use of the narrative is in Pater's *The Renaissance.* Noting the resemblance between the smiles of "La Gioconda" and of St. Anne in Leonardo's "St. Anne, the Virgin and the Child," Pater describes the Mona Lisa as a reincarnation of Leda, Helen, and St. Anne. In the next century Yeats, who considered the description pure poetry, published it in verse form at the beginning of his *Oxford Book of Modern Verse 1891-1935,* under the title "Mona Lisa":

> . . . and, as Leda,
> Was the mother of Helen of Troy,
> And, as St. Anne,
> Was the mother of Mary. . . .

Pater's essay seems to provide the context for Yeats's own poem "Leda and the Swan." In *Finnegans Wake* Joyce recalls that Anna means "grace" in Hebrew and also links his heroine, Anna Livia Plurabelle, to St. Anne.

See also MARY, MOTHER OF JESUS.

Bibliography. Melchiori, G. *The Whole Mystery of Art* (1960), 137-39; Parker, R., ed. *The Life of St. Anne* (1928).

DOMINIC MANGANIELLO

ANNUNCIATION The angel Gabriel's announcement of the Incarnation to the Virgin Mary, specifically the announcement of her conception of Jesus by means of the Holy Ghost, forms part of the infancy narrative of the first chapter of Luke's Gospel. This appearance of Gabriel forms one part of the first of two narrative diptychs which begin the Gospel: that of the announcements and that of the births of John the Baptist and Jesus. (Doubling is a favorite Lucan device.) The Annunciation is commemorated today as one of five feast days devoted to Mary in the Roman rite of the church (May 25, "Lady Day"). The Annunciation is also celebrated as the first of the traditional "five joys" of the Virgin. The Vg rendering of the angel's greeting — *"Ave gratia plena; Dominus tecum; benedicta tu in mulieribus"* ("Hail, highly favored [traditionally: 'full of grace']; the Lord is with you; blessed are you among women") forms the basis for the prayer *Ave Maria,* first widely used in the 11th cent. but elaborated and given authority in the 16th.

Luke's accounts of the annunciations, one to Zacharias, the other to Mary, are related in both pattern and substance to various other angelic announcements in both the OT and NT. The nearest chronological instance is that recorded in Matthew of an unnamed angel's appearance to reassure Joseph, in a dream, about Mary's pregnancy, but its closest analogues are found in various OT angelic appearances, e.g., to the woman who would become the mother of Samson.

When Mary questioned whether she could conceive, "seeing I know not a man," the token given to her was the miraculous conception of John by her aged cousin Elisabeth.

Gabriel's greeting to Mary (probably recalling Zephaniah's "rejoice, O daughters of Jerusalem") and his attribution to her of the special favor of God puzzled her but did not frighten her, and Gabriel's use of the formula "Fear not" seems intended to introduce the reiterated assurance of special favor, which is elaborated in three verses concerning Jesus' conception and his attributes, couched in the language of OT treatments of God's redemptive presence, especially as found in Genesis, Psalms, and the prophetic books. Mary's response to Gabriel was a simple assertion of her obedience and humility.

For Christian commentators, the Annunciation is a pivotal point, for it marks a new start for humankind. Paul's explicit typological connection of Adam and Christ (Rom. 5:14, 19) is picked up by St. Justin Martyr, who first links Eve and Mary typologically, one as the cause of mankind's death and the other as the vessel of its salvation *(Dialogue with Trypho).* Jacobus de Voragine further develops the contrasting parallels of the Annunciation and events surrounding the Fall by noting the appropriateness of an angel as messenger for the Annunciation: "for in this wise the fall of the angels was repaired." St. Bernard of Clairvaux, noting that Gabriel's name means "God's fortitude," finds it appropriate that he was chosen for the Annunciation: the power of God announces the coming of Christ, "the angel's name is in harmony with his message" *(Hom.* 1). St. Ambrose calls Gabriel the herald of the Holy Spirit (in *De Spirito Sancto,* 1).

The Annunciation early became a popular subject in religious art. The scene quickly developed a standard iconography, sometimes drawn from apocryphal gospels or the *Legenda Aurea;* in addition to the Virgin, the angel, and the dove (the Holy Ghost), the scene frequently includes a flower, most commonly a lily; the Virgin is often pictured reading or sewing. Sometimes the dove is represented as speaking into the Virgin's ear or borne on golden rays which enter her ear (signifying conception by the Word). Certain of these details also found their way into literary representations of the Annunciation, such as the 14th-cent. *Meditations on the Life of Christ.* Part of the elaboration of one of the "lesser" O antiphons for Advent in the OE *Christ I,* "O Mistress of the World," concerns the Annunciation, when *"heht sigores fruma / his heahbodan hider gefleogan / of his maegen rymme"* ("the Lord of Victory commanded his messenger to fly hither from majesty"). The Annunciation is alluded or referred to in most Marian lyrics of the Middles Ages and in, e.g., Chaucer's *ABC* (translated freely from the French of Guillaume de Deguilleville), where the mystery of the Incarnation is described as when "the holy ghost thee sought / [And] Gabriel's voice came to thine ear." It forms a part of every mystery-play cycle, either as a discrete play or as part of a nativity or prophets sequence. In some cases it is attached (as in the Wakefield and Chester cycles) to a treatment of "Joseph's troubles about Mary," a development of materials from the 2nd-cent. Protevangelium of James, which are themselves elaborated from

Matt. 1:18-25. Chaucer presents an ironic parody of the Annunciation when the student Nicholas in *The Miller's Tale* sings *"Angelus ad Virginem"* in his room upstairs in the house of the aged but newly-wed carpenter John. In *Piers Plowman* the Annunciation is the speaking of *"Spiritus Sanctus* in Gabrielis mouthe / To a maide that highte Marie," and it seems to announce the conception of Piers himself (B.16).

The Annunciation forms one of the chaplet of poems in Donne's *La Corona* and provides a meditative subject in "Upon the Annunciation and Passion falling upon one day": "Th' abridgement of Christ's story; which makes one . . . of the Angel's Ave, and *Consummatum est."* Robert Southwell exploits the clichéd parallel of Eve and Mary in "The Virgin's Salutation": "Spell Eva backe and Ave shall you finde." Similarly, Milton has Raphael speak to Eve as Gabriel would speak "Long after to blest *Mary,* second *Eve."* Pope's parody of the Annunciation in *The Rape of the Lock,* canto I, casts Ariel in the role of Gabriel and Belinda in that of Mary (the allusion is made explicit in line 33: "Virgins visited by Angel powers"). Rossetti's "Ave," a "prayer-poem," uses allusion to the Annunciation as a structural element. In Tennyson's *Aylmer's Field* a dead child is said to have been fairer than Rachel or Ruth and "Fair as the Angel that said 'hail'. . . ." Yeats associates the Annunciation with terror ("The Mother of God"). Blake refers both to the angel's physical beauty and to the awe he inspires when, in *Samson,* he uses words from the NT Annunciation to Mary to describe the angel's appearance to the woman who would become the mother of Samson: "His form was manhood in the prime, and from his spacious brow shot terrors through the evening shade! But mild he hailed her, 'Hail, highly favored!'"

Many writers refer to the *Ave Maria* without more extensive allusion to the Annunciation itself. In his polemic against Roman Catholicism in the *Faerie Queene,* Spenser characterizes the villainous Archimago as one who strews *Ave Marys* wherever he goes, and Corcecca, the "blind-hearted," as one who says thrice nine hundred aves. Several writers refer to the prayer simply as an aspect of setting (Swift, *Description of an Irish Feast*; Tennyson, "Mariana in the South"); in Browning's *The Ring and the Book* it both contributes to the setting and, frequently, provides ironic counterpoint to the grim events of the plot.

See also ELISABETH; GABRIEL; MAGNIFICAT; MARY, MOTHER OF JESUS.

Bibliography. Alter, R. "How Convention Helps us Read: The Case of the Bible's Annunciation Type-Scene." *Proof* 3 (1983), 115-30; Audat, J.-P. "L'Announce à Marie." *RB* 63 (1956), 346-74; Brown, R. *The Birth of the Messiah* (1977).

PHILLIP ROGERS

ANTICHRIST In the Bible the word *Antichrist* appears only in the NT Johannine epistles (1 John 2:18-22; 4:3; 2 John 7), where it is used in the singular and the plural primarily to denote those who deny that "Jesus is the Christ" (1 John 2:22). However, these references connect with other more specifically apocalyptic passages in the NT, in particular: 2 Thess. 2:1-2; Rev. 11:7 and 13:11-18; and Mark 13:6-8, 21-22 (with parallels in Matt. 24:23-24; Luke 21:8-9). In these passages a figure variously identified as the "man of sin," the "son of perdition," the "wicked one," or as a "beast" takes on a distinct eschatological significance as Christ's principal opponent at the time of his Second Coming.

When it speaks of Antichrist, the NT undoubtedly draws on Jewish apocalyptic literature (cf. Ezek. 38 and 39; Dan. 7:7-28). In its most elaborate form, the Christian legend, which relies principally on Daniel, 2 Thessalonians, and Revelation, describes the appearance at the end of time of a powerful leader who will subdue the world's rulers, set himself up in the temple of God (2 Thess. 2:4), persecute the faithful, and, by performing "signs and lying wonders" (2 Thess. 2:9) through the power and authority of Satan, deceive many into believing that he is divine (cf. Mark 13:5-6, 21-23). He will subsequently reign for three and a half years (Rev. 13:5), destroying God's two "witnesses" (Rev. 11), usually identified as Elijah and Enoch, before being overthrown by the true Christ at his Second Coming.

Despite the implication throughout Revelation that Rome would be the last great anti-Christian power, the early Church Fathers, among them St. Irenaeus, St. Hippolytus, and especially Tertullian (*Apology,* 32), argued that Antichrist would appear only *after* the fall of the Roman Empire, thus equating Rome with the "he who now letteth" in 2 Thess. 2:7. This suggests either that the Johannine apocalypse (Revelation) was a departure from the most widely disseminated form of eschatological prediction or (more likely) that such commentators reflect a later, less hostile attitude toward Rome.

The early Church's belief in the imminence of Christ's return prompted many attempts to identify Antichrist with a specific historical figure. Such speculation is indirectly evidenced in Augustine's skeptical reference to an early and persistent *Nero redivivus* legend which said that Nero had not died or, as time elapsed, that he would be resurrected to return as Antichrist (*De civ. Dei* 20.19).

By the end of the patristic period, the early ferment of apocalyptic expectation and attempts to apply eschatological prophecy to actual historical events gave way to more generalized, conceptual commentary (cf. St. John of Damascus, *Exposition of the Orthodox Faith,* 26). Nonetheless, the substance of the Christian expectation concerning the coming of an Antichrist persisted, perpetuated in such works as the Venerable Bede's *Explanatio Apocalypsis* and the later, extremely influential *Libellus de Antichristo* of Adso. By the end of the first Christian millennium, the sense of an imminent apocalypse regained its momentum, emerging most forcefully in the works of Joachim of Fiore, who believed that Antichrist would appear as a pseudo-Pope. The popes of the crusading era had hoped to fire the Crusades by charging that "the Turk" was Antichrist, a charge which occasionally reappeared in eschatological predictions. But it was the Papacy itself and the institutional church as a whole which came to bear the brunt of the accusation. More and more groups, distressed by what they perceived to be widespread corruption and worldliness within the Roman Church, identified the church, and frequently the popes themselves, as the apocalyptic Antichrist. Among those who published such views were the anonymous author of the 12th-cent. Waldensian treatise *On Antichrist*, the Spiritual Franciscans, and the Bohemian reformer John Milic of Kromeriz. In England the charge against the Papacy was leveled by Wyclif and a number of his Lollard sympathizers, among them Sir John Oldcastle, whose views on Antichrist are described in Tennyson's ballad "Sir John Oldcastle." Identification of the Papacy with Antichrist was incorporated by Martin Luther in the Schmalkaldic Articles, and the association became a commonplace of early Protestantism. Luther and Calvin were both constant in their dogmatic assertion that "spiritual-minded people are right in their conviction that the pope is Antichrist" (Luther, "Table Talk," in *Works*, 54.346).

Not surprisingly, Antichrist figures prominently in the literature of this same period. Among the earliest and best-known instances is the 12th-cent. German *Ludus Antichristus*. In England an Antichrist play is included in the Chester miracle cycle. In the Northumbrian *Cursor Mundi* the "Seventh Age of the World" contains a section which treats "Of Antichrist," and Chaucer's Parson makes a fleeting reference in *The Parson's Tale* (10.788). But the most extensive consideration of Antichrist in this period is found in the B and C texts of Langland's *Piers Plowman*, the last *passus* of which describes "The Coming of Antichrist." Rather than restrict the figure to its eschatological context, Langland succeeds in adapting it to suit his hope for spiritual and social reform. Hence, the appearance of Antichrist signals not the end of time, but a necessary, temporary period of upheaval before society can be renewed. In this way Langland avoids the limitations imposed on the allusive value of Antichrist by its strong apocalyptic ties or by the demand for a specific historical correlative. With the Reformation, the Protestant insistence that the Pope was Antichrist restricted allusions almost exclusively to partisan literature and drama (cf. John Bale's *King Johan* and *The Three Laws*).

As Protestant sects proliferated, however, the label *Antichrist* was applied with increasing vigor and diminishing precision. In England, e.g., the Puritans were to include under that title the prelates of the English church (cf. Milton, *Of Reformation*, 2.440-41) and later the Royalist party in general. Indeed, as the Puritans splintered, the charge was even leveled at Cromwell himself. As early as 1610 Ben Jonson had recognized that a strident emphasis on things apocalyptic might be used to carica-

ture the self-righteous excesses of overzealous sectarians. In *The Alchemist*, confronted by Surley in the guise of a Spaniard, Ananias berates him for his appearance: "Thou look'st like *Antichrist*, in that leud hat" (4.7.55). And in *Bartholomew Fair*, Zeal-of-the-Land Busy dismisses Smithfield as "the seate of the Beast" (3.6.44-45). The old Protestant identification of Antichrist with the Papacy survives in such widely disparate sources as Sir Isaac Newton's *Observations upon the Prophecies of Daniel, and the Apocalypse of St. John* and in the American colonies in Benjamin Harris's popular *New England Primer,* the 1737 and pre-1737 editions of which included a detailed illustration of "The Pope, or Man of Sin."

The Counter-Reformation also took up the issue, though such apologists as Ribera and Bellarmine insisted on a nonhistoric interpretation, arguing for the appearance in the distant future of the apocalyptic Antichrist as a distinct individual, thus exonerating the institution of the Papacy. As the sense of an imminent historical apocalypse began to weaken once again, the "futurist" interpretation found favor even among many 18th- and 19th-cent. Protestant commentators. Meanwhile, literary references to Antichrist became increasingly limited to casual allusion. Swift, in "A Serious Poem upon William Wood," addresses Wood as "this Son of Perdition" (1.67), and Pope compares Colley Cibber to the Roman Camillo Querno, "Thron'd on sev'n hills, the Antichrist of wit" (*Dunciad* A, 2.12; *Dunciad* B, 2.16). Blake is predictably and provocatively idiosyncratic in arguing that "Jesus and his Apostles and Disciples were all Artists. Their works were destroy'd by the Seven Angels of the Seven Churches in Asia, Antichrist Science" (*The Laocoon*). Further Antichrist references are provided by historical pieces such as Browning's *The Ring and the Book* (2.127 and 3.95), Byron's *The Deformed Transformed* (2.3.242, 244), and Shaw's *Saint Joan* (sc. 4).

In the past two centuries, eschatological speculation has continued to flare in times of perceived or actual crisis. In the cataclysmic aftermath of the French Revolution, Napoleon was thought of by many as Antichrist; in the 20th cent. Hitler, Mussolini, Stalin, and a host of others have been so identified. Antichrist figures still make occasional appearances in popular fiction — especially fantasy and futuristic novels and the cinema — in which apocalyptic themes have had a continuing vogue.

See also BELIAL; DEVIL; MARK OF THE BEAST; SECOND COMING; TWO WITNESSES.

Bibliography. Bousset, W. *The Antichrist Legend: A Chapter in Christian and Jewish Folklore.* Trans. A. H. Keane (1896); Emmerson, R. K. *Antichrist in the Middle Ages: A Study of Medieval Apocalypicism, Art, and Literature* (1981); Hill, J. E. C. *"Antichrist" in Seventeenth Century England* (1971); Lucken, L. U. *Antichrist and the Prophets of Antichrist in the Chester Cycle* (1940); Macfarlane, J. E. "Antichrist in English Literature 1380-1680." *DAI* 41 (1980), 2615A; Marshall, M. H. "Antichrist in Medieval Drama and in the Drama of the Reformation in England." M.A. thesis,

Yale, 1928; Mellen, F. D. "The Antichrist Legend in Middle English." M.A. thesis, Chicago, 1928; Stein, S. J. "Cotton Mather and Jonathan Edwards on the Number of the Beast: Eighteenth-Century Speculation about the Antichrist." *PAAS* 84 (1974), 293-315; Wright, J., trans. and ed. *The Play of Antichrist* (1967).   W. ROGER WILLIAMS

ANTIOCHUS EPIPHANES *See* ABOMINATION OF DESOLATION; JUDAS MACCABEUS.

APAGE SATANA *See* GET THEE BEHIND ME.

APOCALYPSE Biblical scholarship is divided upon the precise definition of *apocalypse*, and the problem is complicated by the fact that most examples of the genre designated "apocalyptic" which flourished between the 2nd cent. B.C. and the 2nd cent. A.D. are noncanonical. It is scriptural apocalypse — principally as found in the books of Daniel and Revelation — however, which contribute most significantly to the literary tradition. Other noteworthy biblical texts include Isa. 2:9-19; 24:1–27:13; Jer. 4:18-28; Ezek. 38–39; Matt. 24–25; Mark 13:14-20; 24–27 (sometimes called the "little apocalypse"); Luke 21; 1 Cor. 15:42-55; 1 Thess. 4:13–5:11; 2 Thess. 2; 2 Pet. 3:1-13.

Etymologically, the word *apocalypse* means "uncovering" or "unveiling." It is the Greek title of the NT book of Revelation. Apocalyptic texts usually proceed by means of a series of visions which foretell God's destruction of social, political, and cosmic order as we know it, the punishment of the wicked, and the inauguration of a holy kingdom ruled by the righteous or directly by God himself. The visions usually include fantastic, obscure symbols and elaborate numerology. Apocalyptic thought has something in common with OT prophecy, especially messianic prophecy; the main difference is that classical OT prophecy usually sees God working through history to establish his kingdom, whereas in apocalyptic texts there is a radical break between history and the new kingdom. Apocalypse grows out of a conviction that most persons and institutions are irredeemably corrupt, fit only for destruction. To this extent it expresses pessimism or despair; but it is also inspired by unshakable faith that God will put everything right for the virtuous few.

The main apocalyptic events foretold in the book of Revelation may be summarized as follows: (a) calamities and cataclysms on earth and in the heavens (chaps. 6, 8–9, 15:5–16:21); (b) the dragon's attack on the woman clothed with the sun and his defeat by Michael (chap. 12); (c) two beasts rising from sea and land (chap. 13); (d) the harlot on her scarlet beast (chap. 17); (e) the destruction of Babylon, which stands for Rome, the persecutor (chap. 18); (f) the Marriage-feast of the Lamb (19:5-10); (g) the Second Coming of Christ and the great battle at Armageddon (19:11-21); (h) the binding of Satan and the Millennium, the thousand-year reign of the saints (20:1-6); (i)

the second loosing of Satan and the second great battle (20:7-10); (j) the resurrection of the dead and the Last Judgment (20:11-15); (k) the new heaven and new earth, and the heavenly Jerusalem (21:1–22:15).

Most early Christians expected that these events would occur in the near future. When they failed to, Revelation was reinterpreted figuratively and spiritually, a process which culminated in St. Augustine's *De civitate Dei* (20.7-9). For example, the Millennium became an image of the individual Christian's soul under the rule of Christ and of the Church Militant as City of God. This approach has predominated in many mainstream churches, although historic interpretation and a literal expectation of the catastrophic events of the end time have continued to exert a strong influence, particularly in evangelical circles — where prophetic timetables and forecasting of future events have enjoyed a continuing vogue.

Various individuals and groups have attempted to read their own immediate future in the visions of Revelation and other biblical apocalypses. In 17th-cent. England the Fifth Monarchists expected the imminent establishment of the "kingdom which shall never be destroyed" (Dan. 2:44), the successor to the kingdoms of Babylon, Persia, Greece, and Rome. Sir Isaac Newton labored tirelessly to correlate the prophecies of Daniel and Revelation with ancient and modern history. The American and French Revolutions revived a variety of apocalyptic speculations. In 19th-cent. America the Millerites and other groups fixed precise dates for the end of the world and made elaborate preparations for it. After World War II the establishment of a Jewish state in Israel provided a new point of departure for apocalyptists, and prompted a spate of popular works of prophetic speculation (e.g., H. Lindsey, *The Late Great Planet Earth* [1970], a national best-seller in the United States). Most apocalyptists await the end of the world passively; however, when others, like many medieval groups or like John of Leyden and his Anabaptists in Münster (1534-35) and several radical sects which flourished during the English Civil War, feel compelled to help destroy the old world, the apocalyptic outlook can become an important inspiration for violent revolution.

Apocalyptic (especially millennial) ideas have sometimes been reinterpreted to support a belief in human progress. Nineteenth- and 20th-cent. revolutionaries who proclaim that social justice can exist only if present corrupt institutions are totally destroyed are very close in spirit to the original writers of apocalypse.

The influence of apocalypse, and especially of the book of Revelation, on art and literature is profound, far-reaching, and diverse. In Northrop Frye's estimate, Revelation is "our grammar of apocalyptic imagery" (*Anatomy of Criticism* [1957], 141), combining and unifying the most potent symbols of the Western literary tradition. Milton, who followed Pareus and other Reformation commentators, concluded that Revelation embodied the structure of tragedy (*The Reason of Church Government*). The presence in apocalyptic writings of themes of both destruction and re-creation has always made *apocalypse* an ambiguous term. Some literary critics use it simply to mean "visionary"; others, like Frye, use it to refer to renewal and the imagery of heaven; for the majority it usually means catastrophic destruction of the earth or the whole universe, or, in increasingly figurative applications, of a society, a city, a family, or even an individual; for Dennis Costa its hallmark is its combination of violence and an emergent peace. Many critics would use the term *apocalyptic* for works as diverse as Blake's prophetic books, Robert Frost's "Once by the Pacific," and *Dr. Strangelove*. Some use the term in more extended senses: Morton Bloomfield has called Piers Plowman a "Fourteenth-Century Apocalypse"; Michael Wheeler called Dickens's *Hard Times* an apocalpyse for a mechanical age because of its allusions to Revelation and the sense of fiery doom which pervades it; Dennis Taylor in *Hardy's Poetry, 1860-1928* (1981) sees the "visionary grotesque" in Hardy's poetry as constituting a kind of apocalypse.

John's vision of the New Jerusalem is transcribed quite literally in Spenser's *Faerie Queene* (1.10.55-58) and at the conclusion of Bunyan's *Pilgrim's Progress*. A highly elaborate version occurs toward the end of the medieval *Pearl*. Less explicit versions appear in Wordsworth's *Excursion* (2.827-81) and at the end of Shelley's *Prometheus Unbound*, and of e. e. cummings's *The Enormous Room*. These are all positive images; but Hagar Shipley, the heroine of Margaret Laurence's *The Stone Angel*, has no use for St. John's "sequined heaven . . . how gimcrack a place . . . like a gigantic chunk of costume jewelry."

M. H. Abrams has demonstrated that much Romantic poetry can be seen as the result of a subjective reinterpretation of apocalyptic motifs: when the events of the French Revolution betrayed the hopes of millennial justice aroused by its early promise, the Millennium was retranslated into the individual psyche, and the unifying Marriage of the Lamb became the marriage of the mind to Nature. Meanwhile, as E. S. Shaffer has shown, the book of Revelation itself was being radically reinterpreted as poetry and mythology.

Images of apocalyptic destruction are probably more common in literature than those of renewal. In the 18th cent. odes on the end of the world enabled poets to express unbridled enthusiasm for sensational and sublime descriptions. Their imaginations were particularly fired by the collapse into chaos of Newton's version of the universe, so much vaster but also so much more precisely ordered than earlier versions. The most interesting poetic apocalypse of the period is Pope's *Dunciad*, whose presiding goddess, Dulness, creates bizarre new worlds of bad poetry and in the end annihilates language, reason, and art. The 19th cent. offers Byron's "Darkness," Poe's "Masque of the Red Death," the collapse of Camelot in

Tennyson's *Idylls of the King*, and John Martin's vast paintings of deluge and destruction.

Visions of destruction also dominate the 20th cent.; heavenly cities are rare. Some of the most memorable apocalyptic images occur in *The Wasteland* and *The Hollow Men* of T. S. Eliot; the novels of Wyndham Lewis, William Burroughs, Thomas Pynchon, and perhaps John Barth; and essays such as D. H. Lawrence's *Apocalypse* and James Baldwin's *The Fire Next Time*. Nathanael West's *The Day of the Locust* (cf. Rev. 9:3-7; also Joel) is a particularly clear example of modern literary apocalyptic: it ends with the hero, who is working on a vast painting called "The Burning of Los Angeles," barely escaping from a riotous mob awaiting a movie premiere. Some consider the "literature of silence and exhaustion" — such as that of Samuel Beckett — to be a form of apocalypse.

Apocalyptic themes have been treated in short poems in a diversity of ways: e.g., Donne's "At the Round Earth's Imagined Corners," with its worldwide death and resurrection; Henry Vaughan's joyous "Day of Judgement"; Swift's bitterly satirical "Day of Judgement," in which God declares that humankind is not even worth damning; Dryden's "Song for St. Cecilia's Day," in which divine music first creates and then "untunes" the universe; Blake's exhortation to build the New Jerusalem in England in "And Did Those Feet"; Tennyson's fusion of the beast from the sea with Scandinavian myth in "The Kraken"; Whittier's poem on Abraham Davenport, who, when the end of the world seemed imminent and his companions were panic-stricken, calmly declared that until the Lord *did* appear he would get on with his appointed task; Edith Sitwell's "Solo for Ear-Trumpet," about an old woman too deaf to hear Gabriel's horn; Leroi Jones's (Imamu Amiri Baraka's) "Babylon Revisited," where the godless city becomes a horrifying symbol of drug addiction; the cosmic nothingness of Archibald MacLeish's "The End of the World"; and the vision of total political disintegration in Yeats's "The Second Coming."

Apocalypse has had a scientific side at least since the enlarged edition of Thomas Burnet's *Sacred Theory of the Earth* (1689), which sought to apply the discoveries of the new science to the physical aspects of the end of the world. Speculation about the expansion of the sun, entropy, and the heat death of the universe carry on this tradition. In the 20th cent. science fiction has imagined many varieties of new heaven and new earth as well as many new ways of destroying the old ones, perhaps because the invention of the nuclear bomb and other weapons of mass destruction has made humanity capable of instigating its own apocalypse.

See also DRAGON OF THE APOCALYPSE; LAST JUDGMENT; THE MILLENNIUM; NEW JERUSALEM; REVELATION; SECOND COMING; WHORE OF BABYLON.

Bibliography. Abrams, M. H. *Natural Supernaturalism: Tradition and Revolution in Romantic Literature* (1973), chap. 1; Beasley-Murray, G. R. *Jesus and the Future* (1954); Boklund, G. "Time Must Have a Stop: Apocalyptic Thought and Expression in the Twentieth Century." *University of Detroit Quarterly* 2 (1967), 69-98; Charlesworth, J. H., ed. *The Old Testament Apocrypha and Pseudepigrapha*, vol. 1: *Apocalyptic Literature and Testaments* (1983); Costa, D. *Irenic Apocalypse: Some Uses of Apocalyptic in Dante, Petrarch, and Rabelais* (1981); Gannaway, S. S. "Secular Apocalyptic in the Novel Between the Wars." *DAI* 44 (1983), 746A; Kermode, F. *The Sense of an Ending* (1967); Ketterer, D. *New Worlds for Old: The Apocalyptic Imagination, Science Fiction, and American Literature* (1974); Lewalski, B. K. "*Samson Agonistes* and the 'Tragedy' of the Apocalypse." *PMLA* 85 (1970), 1050-62; Lewis, R. W. B. "Days of Wrath and Laughter." In *Trials of the Word* (1965), 184-235; Mani, L. "The Apocalypse in Cooper, Hawthorne, and Melville." *DAI* 34 (1973), 783A; May, J. R. *Toward a New Earth: Apocalypse in the American Novel* (1971); Morris, L. *Apocalyptic*, 2nd ed. (1973); Patrides, C. A., and J. Wittreich, eds. *The Apocalypse in English Renaissance Thought and Literature: Patterns, Antecedents, and Repercussions* (1984); Rowley, H. H. *The Relevance of Apocalyptic: A Study of Jewish and Christian Apocalypses* (1964); Shaffer, E. S. *"Kubla Khan" and The Fall of Jerusalem: The Mythological School in Biblical Criticism and Secular Literature 1770-1880* (1975); Wheeler, M. *The Art of Allusion in Victorian Fiction* (1979), chap. 5.   WILLIAM KINSLEY

APOCRYPHA AND PSEUDEPIGRAPHA   As typically employed, the term *Apocrypha* (or *Deuterocanonical Books*) denotes the collection of religious texts found in the LXX and Vulgate Bibles which are not included in the Jewish or Protestant canon. Many of the books are connected with the OT, having been written in Hebrew; some are NT apocrypha — extracanonical epistles and gospels. *Pseudepigraphal* writings are texts ascribed by their actual authors to ancient Jewish authorities (e.g., Enoch, Abraham, Moses) who evidently did not write the texts, but whose names were intended to lend the works authority. In Greek *apokryphos* denotes "things hidden," and in early Christian usage the term was used to classify Jewish and Christian apocalyptic writings. Later it came to refer more generally to books held to be of inferior authority to the canonical Scriptures of the OT and NT. Most of these works were late (e.g., latter 2nd cent. A.D.), and many associated with gnostic sects. Irenaeus and St. Jerome generally used the term to designate "untrustworthy" documents claiming authoritative status — both apocrypha and pseudepigrapha alike.

Apocryphal works known to the English from fairly early in the Anglo-Saxon period, and certainly by 1066, include: *Liber Enoch* (1 Enoch); 4 Ezra; *Esdras Propheta Secundus; Esdras Propheta* (Esdras 4); *Oratio Moysi* (a fragment of the Assumption of Moses); Acts of Andrew; Acts of Andrew and Matthias; Poenitentiam Jannis et Mambris; *Liber de Infantiae Salvatoris* (Pseudo-Matthew); Gospel of Nicodemus (many Latin versions); *Visio Pauli* (though disparaged by Aelfric and

Aldhelm, of considerable influence down into the later Middle Ages); *Passio SS. Apostolorum Petri et Pauli; Contradictio Salomonis; Acta S. Thomae; Passio S. Thomae.* By 1500 most, if not all, of the apocryphal and pseudepigraphal writings known on the Continent were also known and available in England.

See also JESUS CHRIST, CHILDHOOD OF.

Bibliography: Charlesworth, J. H., ed. *The Old Testament Pseudepigrapha* (1982–); Goodspeed, E. J. *The Apocrypha: An American Translation* (1938); Metzger, B. M. *Introduction to the Apocrypha* (1957); Oesterley, W. O. E. *Books of the Apocrypha* (1916).

APOKATASTASIS   Not a biblical term, *apokatastasis* is the doctrine of universal salvation, associated with Origen in the 3rd cent. in his *De principiis*, where he doubted a literal hell.

See also HELL.

APOLLYON   *See* ABADDON.

APOSTLE   The Greek word *apostolos* (from the verb *apostellō*, "to send out") is used several times in the NT to designate a messenger in general (John 13:16; 2 Cor. 8:23; Phil. 2:25) and a messenger from God in particular (Luke 11:49; Heb. 3:1 — here with reference to Christ as God's messenger). The word is used most frequently in a special sense to identify "the twelve," those commissioned by Jesus to "learn of him" and to preach the gospel: Simon Peter; James and John, sons of Zebedee; Andrew; Philip; Bartholomew; Matthew; Thomas; James, son of Alphaeus; Thaddaeus; Simon the Zealot; and Judas Iscariot. Having received from Jesus the simple call "Follow me," the apostles were subsequently empowered to act in his name and with his authority — in certain circumstances both to forgive sins (Matt. 18:18; John 20:23) and to work miracles (Mark 3:15; 6:7; Acts 2:43; 5:12). Conventionally, in medieval and later literature (e.g., Sholem Asch's novel *The Apostle* [1943]) "the Apostle" designates St. Paul, "apostle to the Gentiles" (cf. 2 Tim. 1:11).

In early Christian tradition, notably in the writings of St. Ignatius, St. Polycarp, and St. Clement of Rome, considerable emphasis fell upon the special character of apostolic vocation and, within the administrative hierarchy of the church, a succession of apostolic teaching. St. Augustine is typical in emphasizing the idea of the call itself as an action of the Holy Spirit (*Enarr. in Ps.* 133.6), transforming "common men" (*idiotas*) or "unlearned persons" (*rudibus*) into honored ambassadors whose words of witness and transmission of Scripture will, like the witness of creation to the glory of God (Ps. 19:3-4), go everywhere in the world ("Concerning Faith of Things Not Seen," 10; cf. *In Joan. Ev.* 7.17). Such persons, says Augustine, are not chosen because they are righteous but justified because they are willing to serve (*De patientia*, 14-17); where once they were "of the world," now they are drawn "out of the world." This notion of separation, along with the ideal of the brethren dwelling together in unity (*Enarr. in Ps.* 133.5), readily attaches apostolic vocation to the monastic life. Proceeding typically from an etymology (*monachos monos),* Augustine identifies the ideals of monastic community — many living as one — with apostolic labor (cf. *Opus monachorum,* 8-10); spiritual labor is given preference over physical work and seen to be deserving of the support of other Christians since, on scriptural authority, "the laborer is worthy of his hire" (Luke 10:1-7; 1 Cor. 9:7-10). For Augustine and subsequent medieval tradition the apostles obedient to their calling are "the means of our faith"; "as those who in Greek are called *angeli* and in Latin called *nunti* ['messengers'], so the Greek *apostoli* becomes the Latin *missi* ['persons sent']" (*In Joan. Ev.* 54.3).

This sense of commission is paramount in the OE poem *Andreas,* in which an apostle is spoken of as one to whom God has "assigned his lot" *(hylt geteode)* and whose duty it is to "suffer that fate." In the poem the apostolate of St. Andrew is characterized by God himself in terms of uncompromised commitment: "You may not weary in this wayfaring, nor waver in heart if you think to keep covenant, compact with God" (trans. Kennedy, 127). The natural connection between apostolic fealty and loyal service in the *comitatus* is suggested by presentation of the faithful apostle as one of the "twelve mighty heroes . . . thanes of God" *(twelfe under tunglum . . . eodnes egnas).* This description stands in contrast to the metaphor of Augustine which likens true apostles to the twelve hours which, in Mediterranean mythical representation, "follow the Day," the Son of Light. Using this figure, Augustine summarizes early expectations of apostolic service: "Let the hours then attend upon the Day, let them preach the Day, be made known and illuminated by the Day; and by the preaching of the hours may the world believe in the Day" (*In Joan. Ev.* 49.8).

In English literature, from early carols to Joyce's *Finnegans Wake,* reference is most often to "the twelve" (Donne's "The Apostles" is typical). Allusions to apostleship in the wider sense are scattered but significant. Chaucer's description of the Good Parson, who "Cristes gospel trewely wolde preche," prompted Blake, a few centuries later, to speak of "the Good Parson; an Apostle, a real Messenger of Heaven, sent in every age for its light and its warmth" ("Descriptive Catalogue," *Complete Writings,* ed. Keynes, 570). Dryden affirms that a good parson should "like a Primitive Apostle preach" and be "still cheerful; ever Constant to his Call" ("The Character of a Good Parson," 128-29). William Cowper likewise venerates the man "whose doctrine and whose life [are] coincident," but prays to be spared the false apostle who makes "God's work a sinecure; a slave / To his own pleasures and his patron's pride." "From such apostles," he implores, "oh, ye mitred heads, / Preserve the Church" (*The Task,* 2.373-74, 392-93). Wordsworth praises the

American Pilgrim fathers as "Patriots formed with Apostolic Light" (*Ecclesiastical Sonnets,* 3.15.1). Shelley, on the other hand, mocks "apostles" sent into the world for the cause of religion (*Queen Mab,* 6.136).

More recently, the term *apostle* has frequently been used to designate the advocate of a secular cause. Oscar Wilde was sometimes called the "apostle of beauty"; Byron called Rousseau the "apostle of affliction" (*Childe Harold's Pilgrimage,* 3.726). Members of the Cambridge Conversazione Society, an influential literary society formed in 1820 (including such eminent writers as Hallam, Tennyson, G. E. Moore, Leonard Woolf, and Bertrand Russell), took the name The Apostles. In a shift of definition made most memorable by Goethe *(Faust),* Joyce *(Portrait of the Artist as a Young Man),* and Wilde, apostleship came frequently to designate "aesthetic" vocation. Sensing this reorientation, Kierkegaard warned that if the sphere of religion is abolished

> or explained away in aesthetics, an Apostle becomes neither more nor less than a genius, and then —good night, Christianity! *Esprit* and the Spirit, revelation and originality, a call from God and genius, all end by meaning more or less the same thing. *(Of the Difference between a Genius and an Apostle)*

In the first chapter of D. H. Lawrence's *Sons and Lovers,* Gertrude Morel's father is described as being drawn in sympathy to one man, the apostle Paul. Gertrude's son, also named Paul, is sometimes called "'postle," and he understands his mission in part as being that of an evangelizer of love. This development takes a grotesque turn in the character of Keneally, or "Brother Twelve," the self-styled latter-day apostle and demonic con artist of Jack Hodgins's *The Invention of the World* (1979), and provides for a "post-Christian" exploration of the meaning of apostleship in the apocalyptic tale *The Thirteenth Apostle* by Eugene Vale (1959).

See also ANDREW; JOHN THE BELOVED DISCIPLE; JUDAS ISCARIOT; LUKE; MATTHEW; PAUL; PETER; PHILIP; THOMAS, DOUBTING.

Bibliography. Bainvel, J. "Apôtres." *DTC* (1909); Kirk, K. E., ed. *The Apostolic Ministry* (1957); Patrick, W. "Apostles." *Dictionary of the New Testament: Christ and His Gospels.* Ed. J. Hastings et al. (1973), 101-11.

DOMINIC MANGANIELLO

APOSTLE, THE In medieval and Renaissance texts in particular, this is almost invariably a reference to St. Paul.

APPLE KJV "apple" is used to translate Heb. *tappuaḥ,* which occurs in Prov. 25:11 and Cant. 2:5; 7:8. Modern biblical scholars continue to debate whether the fruit or tree designated by this term should indeed be identified as the apple *(pyrus malus),* which is not prominently associated with biblical lands, or some other fruit, such as the citron *(citrus medica),* the golden orange *(citrus sinensis),* the apricot *(prunus armeniaca),* or the quince *(cydonia oblonga)*. The latter two interpretations have been especially favored, the quince having the advantage of being a fruit indigenous to the area. The LXX *mēlon* and Vg *malum* — any tree-borne fruit — indicate ancient uncertainty in the matter of identification.

The "apple" of the OT is said to be fairest among trees, a good shade tree, bearing fruit of sweet savor (Cant. 2:3) and pleasant odor (Cant. 7:8). Of particular interest is the attribution of curative powers to the apple (still prevalent in the Near East), especially for sickness of heart or love-longing ("Stay me with flagons, comfort me with apples; for I am sick of love" [Cant. 2:5]).

The association of the apple, and other fruit trees, with love is an archetype attested widely in world mythology and folklore. Various ancient Near Eastern goddesses of love are identified with the apple or quince (S. N. Kramer, *The Sacred Marriage Rite* [1969], 100-101). The common hellenistic and Roman depictions of *Venus genetrix* show her holding such a fruit, where it has evident connotations of sexuality and fertility. (Mythologically, the fruit is also suggestive of the judgment of Paris and his awarding to Venus the "apple of Discord," inscribed "To the Fairest," which led to the abduction of Helen and the Trojan War.) The apple is also a prominent motif in Ovidian narratives.

The association of the apple with love and lovesickness in Canticles seems early to have led to the identification of the apple with sexual temptation, and thus with the "forbidden fruit" of the tree of the knowledge of good and evil — an association not made in the texts nor supported by modern biblical scholarship, but firmly entrenched by the confusion of the Vg *malum* (apple) with *malum* (evil), and reinforced by the designation of the deceptive fruit said to grow near the Dead Sea (Wisd. of Sol. 10:7; Josephus, *J.W.* 4.8.4) as the "apples of Sodom."

An alternate and more positive transference of the Canticles imagery occurred in ancient Jewish allegorization of Cant. 2:3, 5 and 8:5, which identified the "fair apple tree" as Israel, fairest among nations for its fruitful zeal for the Law (Shab. 88b; Tg. Ket. Cant. 2:3), or as the Lord, in whose shade Israel is protected (Midr. Rab. Cant. 2:3). Christian allegorists subsequently identified the apples with which the bride asks to be comforted (Cant. 2:5) with the fruits of Christ's sacrifice, particularly the Eucharist, and the tree under whose protection the bride sits and under which she (or the groom) is said to be raised up (Cant. 8:5) with the cross. The specific exegesis of this latter, textually difficult, verse varied greatly (R. F. Littledale, *Comm. on the Song of Songs from Ancient and Medieval Sources* [1869], 352-55), but the identification of the apple tree with the cross was constant and also inevitably involved an association with the tree of the original garden: as Anselm of Laon explained, the cross is called an apple tree to remind us specifically of "that other tree" (Littledale, 354). According to ancient liturgi-

cal typology, the second Adam on the cross is understood to have reversed the Fall suffered by the first Adam under the tree of knowledge: "for you ordained that the salvation of mankind should be accomplished upon the tree of the cross, in order that life might be restored through the very instrument which brought death, and that Satan, who conquered us through the tree, might also be overcome by it" (Preface of the Holy Cross for Masses of Holy Week). In medieval legend, the cross is said to have been composed of the actual wood of the tree of knowledge and erected on the same spot where the original tree stood (see Jacobus de Voragine, *Legenda Aurea*, May 3 [1969], 269; R. Morris, ed., *Legends of the Holy Rood* [EETS o.s. 46]; A. S. Napier, ed., *History of the Holy Roodtree* [EETS o.s. 103]; R. Norris, ed. *Cursor Mundi* [EETS o.s. 57, 59, 62, 63], passim; Donne, "Hymne to God my God, In My Sicknesse," 21-25; "The Progresse of the Soule," 71-90).

Against the backdrop of exegetical commentary, literary references to apples by early English authors follow predictable patterns. In OE, the well-established association of the apple with the forbidden fruit is reflected, e.g., in *Genesis* (636-41).

> Sum heo hire on handum bær, sum hire æt heortan læg,
> æppel unsælga, þone ær forbead
> drihtna drihten, deað beames ofet,
> and þæt word acwæð wuldres aldor,
> þæt þæt micle morð menn ne þorfton
> þegnas þolian. . . .

("Of the fatal apples some she carried in her hands and some lay on her breast, the fruit of the tree of death whereof the Lord of lords, the Prince of glory, had forbidden her to eat, saying His servants need not suffer death" [C. W. Kennedy, *The Caedmon Poems* (1916), 28].)

The same relationship appears in Aelfric's homily on the Passion:

> þurh treow us com deað, þaða Adam geæt þone forbodenan æppel, and ðurh treow us com eft líf and alysednyss, ðaða Crist hängode on róde for ure alysednysse.

("Through a tree death came to us, when Adam ate the forbidden apple, and through a tree life came again to us and redemption, when Christ hung on the rood for our redemption" [*Homilies of Aelfric*, ed. Thorpe, 2.240-41].)

ME literature is filled with references to the apple of Eden (see Kurath, *Middle English Dictionary*, 1.321-22). ME lyrics routinely allude to the apple as the fruit whereby Paradise was lost and for which Christ had to become man and suffer:

> Aȝenis my fadris wille i ches
> An appel with a reuful res;
> Werfore myn heritage i les,
> & nou þu wepist þer-fore. (C. Brown, *Religious Lyrics of the XIVth Century*, no. 59)

Many lyrics also emphasize the typological identification

of the apple tree with the cross, and the paradoxical joy resulting from man's transgression *(felix culpa):* "Blyssid be þe tyme þat appil take was, / þer-fore we mown syngyn, 'deo gracias!' " (C Brown, *Religious Lyrics of the XVth Century,* no. 83).

The apple appears in Chaucer's *Canterbury Tales* in a variety of contexts, including folk proverbs *(Cook's Tale,* 1.4406; *Canon's Yeoman's Tale,* 8.964), and occurs, often ironically, as an emblem of love — as in the description of the Garden of Love in the *Romaunt* (1374) or that of the fair Alison, which echoes the Vg of Cant. 7:8 *("et odor oris tui sicut malorum"):* "Hir mouth was sweete as bragot or the meeth, / Or hoord of apples leyd in hey or heeth" *(Miller's Tale,* 1.3261-62).

A more elaborate paraphrase of the Canticles (in which "merchants' daughters" take the place of the "daughters of Jerusalem"), with appropriate apple imagery, is found in Spenser's "Epithalamion," 167-73, and also, alongside references to the classical apples of Hercules and Atalanta, in *Amoretti,* no. 77. Both *in bono* and *in malo* significations of the apple are presented in the *Faerie Queene:* Redcrosse Knight finds the apple tree which is the tree of life (1.11.46.2), while Sir Guyon is tempted with a view of the golden apples of the underworld in the Garden of Proserpina (2.7.54-55).

The Edenic apple occurs as an image of deceiving beauty in one of Shakespeare's sonnets to the Dark Lady ("How like Eve's apple doth thy beauty grow, / If thy sweet virtue answer not thy show' " [93.13-14]), but other Shakespearean references are chiefly folkloric or proverbial, lacking any significant biblical associations.

In visual representations, the depiction of the forbidden fruit of Genesis as an apple had become all but standard by the late Middle Ages and early Renaissance; prominent examples are paintings by Lucas Cranach the Elder, Titian, Tintoretto, and Rubens (Moldenke, 286). Notable literary elaborations of the image appear in Donne's "Progresse of the Soule" (sts. 8-16) and in *Paradise Lost,* where Satan boasts: "Him by fraud I have seduc't / From his Creator, and the more to increase / Your wonder, with an Apple" (10.485-87) — although Milton generally avoids reference to the apocryphal identification of the fruit with the apple. In what is perhaps the best-known passage in Milton's prose, he refers to the intermixture of good and evil in the postlapsarian world by alluding to the fateful apple: "Good and evil we know in the field of this world grow up together almost inseparably. . . . It was from out the rind of one apple tasted, that the knowledge of good and evil, as two twins cleaving together, leaped forth into the world" *(Areopagitica).*

Apples appear as part of the general pastoral imagery of such works as Dryden's translations from Virgil's *Georgics* and *Eclogues,* Jonson's country-house poems "To Sir Robert Wroth" (43) and "To Penshurst" (52), and Keats's "Sleep and Poetry" (103, 361), *Endymion* (1.276; 3.147; 4.683), and "To Autumn" (1-6). Keats also makes

use of the erotic associations of apples in the sensuous description of the feast Porphyro lays out for the sleeping Madeline in her chamber ("The Eve of St. Agnes," st. 30.1-4). And in Tennyson's "The Lotos-Eaters," apples are part of the soporific autumnal atmosphere described in the Choric Song (77-79). These several allusions, nonetheless, like those in Tennyson's "The Hesperides," are indebted principally to classical myth. In Tennyson's "The Holy Grail," by contrast, Percival tells of his encounter with a brook and with apples, both of which turn to dust as soon as they are tasted (384-88), recalling the so-called "apples of Sodom," which Byron also alludes to in *Childe Harold's Pilgrimage:*

> but Life will suit
> Itself to Sorrow's most detested fruit,
> Like to the apples on the Dead Sea's shore,
> All ashes to the taste. (3.301-04)

Byron elsewhere reflects Lucifer's perverse interpretation of the apple as the gift of reason *(Cain,* 2.364, 529, 614, 664; cf. Gen. 3:5); in *Don Juan,* he alludes, humorously, to Eve's transgression ("Since Eve ate apples, much depends on dinner" [13.99.8]), and the reversal of the Fall effected not by Christ but Newton who, in "discovering" gravitation, proved himself the "sole mortal who could grapple, / Since Adam, with a fall or with an apple" (10.1.2).

Blake, another revisionist of biblical imagery, describes, in "A Poison Tree," the fruit of secretly nurtured wrath as "an apple bright" — a more truly evil fruit than that of Eden. The poison apple, familiar in other contexts (e.g., the tale of Snow White), recurs as the fruit of the Tree of Mystery in bk. 7 of *The Four Zoas* (228-306); the Tree of Mystery appears also in *America* and *Jerusalem,* under the names Urizen's Tree and Albion's Tree.

The apple of Eden makes a number of appearances in Browning's *The Ring and the Book* (3.169-73; 4.851-59; 7.761-66, 828-29; 9.448-52). There is also one clear allusion to Cant. 2:5, conflated in this instance with the signification of archetypal temptation: "lust of the flesh, lust of the eye" (2.446-52). In Browning's "A Bean-Stripe: Also Apple-Eating," the apple appears as an emblem of the natural world and occasions consideration of whether a personal Creator stands behind the forces of nature. Similar associations of the apple with the course of human life are strongly present in Frost's "After Apple-Picking," but in much modern usage the peculiar force of the biblical archetype has largely dissipated. Thus, the image is generalized, if prominent, in Yeats's poetry, both as the forbidden fruit (the "brigand apple" in "Solomon and the Witch") and as an emblem of love ("Baile and Aillinn" and "The Song of the Wandering Aengus," in the latter of which the Master of Love pursues "a glimmering girl / With apple blossom in her hair" and longs to "pluck till time and times are done / The silver apples of the moon, / The golden apples of the sun" [17-24]).

In the poetry of Dylan Thomas, apples are emblematic of the libidinous energy of youth, often innocent, as in the opening lines of "Fern Hill": "Now as I was young and easy under the apple boughs / About the lilting house and happy as the grass was green. . . . / And honoured among wagons I was prince of the apple towns." In "If I Were Tickled," the poetic persona imagines the fearless pleasure of erotic awakening: "If I were tickled with the rub of love . . . / I would not fear the apple nor the flood / Nor the bad blood of spring." Elsewhere, however, the poet contemplates "the boys of summer in their ruin," carelessly "setting no store by harvest," and sees how they "drown the cargoed apples in their tides" ("I See the Boys of Summer"). More traditional yet is the imagery of "Incarnate Devil," where the youthful sexuality symbolized by the apple is seen, by less innocent eyes, to be a "shape of sin":

> Incarnate devil in a talking snake,
> The central plains of Asia in his garden,
> In shaping-time the circle stung awake,
> In shapes of sin forked out the bearded apple,
> And God walked there who was a fiddling warden
> And played down pardon for the heavens' hill.

See also EDEN; FALL; *FELIX CULPA;* SONG OF SONGS; TREE OF KNOWLEDGE.

Bibliography. Buttrick, G. A., ed. *IDB* 1.175-76; Moldenke, H. N. and A. L. *Plants of the Bible* (1952); Pope, H. *Song of Songs: A New Translation with Introduction and Commentary.* AB (1977).   GEORGE L. SCHEPER

APPLE OF THE EYE   *Apple of the eye* is a figurative idiom meaning "pupil of the eye" in the traditional English translation of three different Hebrew expressions denoting the pupil. One of these (Deut. 32:10 and Prov. 7:2), lit. "little man" of the eye, refers to a person's reflected image in another's eye. Another (Lam. 2:18) means "daughter" of the eye, with the same implication. Both expressions are combined in Ps. 17:8. The third (Zech. 2:8) means "gate" of the eye.

In virtually all OT occurrences, the phrase is used to indicate something precious and needing careful protection. Thus, Deut. 32:10 tells how God found Israel in the desert and "he led him about, he instructed him, he kept him as the apple of his eye." The same sense occurs in Zech. 2:8 and Ps. 17:8 ("Keep me as the apple of the eye; hide me under the shadow of thy wings"), while in Prov. 7:2 the image is applied to the preciousness of the Law to a devout student.

The Vg translates these expressions simply with *pupilla,* or "pupil," but as early as the West-Saxon Psalter, the OE translation uses the apple metaphor: "Geheald mè, Drihten, and beorh mē, swā swā man byrhð þām aeplum on his éagum mid his bræwum" (*The West-Saxon Psalms,* eds. J. W. Bright and R. L. Ramsay [1907], 30-31). The idiom is also found in other OE prose passages, e.g.,

Alfred's translations of St. Gregory's *Regulae pastoralis* (11.4) and Boethius, *De Consolatione Philosophiae* (30.9.10), in the latter instance with the same force as the OT occurrences: "Hī scilde swā geornlīce swā swā man dēth ðone aepl on his eāgan" ("He protected them as carefully as a man does the apple of his eye").

As an expression simply denoting the pupil, "apple of the eye" is common in ME, occurring numerous times, e.g., in the early 15th-cent. translation of Guy de Chauliac's *Grande Chirurgie.* (It is used in this way also in Shakespeare [*A Midsummer Night's Dream,* 3.2.102-04; *Love's Labour's Lost,* 5.2.475-76].) The phrase is used in ME biblical translations of the relevant passages and subsequent English versions of Scripture, as well as poetic paraphrases, as in Sidney's translation of Ps. 17:8: "Then keepe me as the Aple of an ey: / In thy wings shade then lett me hidden ly."

In a wide variety of literary instances the image carries the OT significance of something held most precious. In this sense Browning uses it in "One Word More": "You and I will never read that volume. / Guido Reni, like his own eye's apple / Guarded long the treasure-book and loved it" (26-28) and *Strafford,* where Charles I says, ". . . Henceforth touching Strafford is / To touch the apple of my sight" (1.2.246-47). Similarly in *The Ring and the Book:*

> Pompilia will not have the old year end
> Without a present shall ring in the new —
> Bestows upon her parsimonious lord
> An infant for the apple of his eye. . . . (9.1313-16)

Other instances occur in Sir Walter Scott's *Old Mortality* ("Poor Richard was to me as an eldest son, the apple of my eye") and Henry Adams's *Mont-Saint-Michel and Chartres* (St. Bernard "was regarded as the apple of the Virgin's eye"). In James Joyce's *Portrait,* Dante exclaims angrily: "If we are a priestridden race we ought to be proud of it! They are the apple of God's eye. *Touch them not,* says Christ, *for they are the apple of My eye.*" In Dante's defense of the "priestridden" condition of Ireland, one encounters not only a novel piece of exegesis, but the growing tendency to shift the meaning of "apple of the eye" away from the original sense of something to be protected toward the sense of that which is most important or even fairest. This notion is evident in the citations from Walter Scott and Henry Adams, or the colloquial use of the expression today by those who take the idiom to mean "as fair as an apple in my sight."

Bibliography. Buttrick, G. A., ed. *IDB* 1.176; Hastings, J., et al. *Dictionary of the Bible* (rev. ed. 1963), 1.46.
                                                        GEORGE L. SCHEPER

'AQEDAH   See ISAAC.

ARAMAIC   The official language of the Persian (Chaldean) Empire, and chief *lingua franca* in Palestine until the time of Jesus, it is sometimes referred to among patristic writers (e.g., St. Jerome) and later medieval authors as "Chaldee."

ARARAT A mountainous district in Armenia near the borders of Turkey, Iran, and Russia, it is said to be the resting place for the ark of Noah after the Flood subsided (Gen. 8:4). P. K. Page's title poem in *Cry, Ararat!* (1967) is about the recovery of creativity: in it "the green twig the dove saw fit / to lift across a world of water" instances the power of creation's gift to obliterate as well as focus creative vision: "A single leaf can block a mountainside; / all Ararat be conjured by a leaf."

See also FLOOD; NOAH.

AREOPAGITE *See* DIONYSIUS THE AREOPAGITE.

AREOPAGUS This is the hill ("Mars Hill," KJV) northwest of the Acropolis in Athens where St. Paul debated Epicurean and Stoic philosophers, as reported in Acts 17. Most notably it gives rise in literature to the *Areopagitica: a speech of Mr. John Milton for the liberty of unlicenc'd printing, to the Parliament of England,* published by Milton in 1644. Milton's analogy between his unlicensed pamphlet, directed against Parliament's attempt to suppress his pamphlet on divorce, invokes the image of a marginalized but just apostle challenging the unexamined assumptions of the Athenian Upper Council.

ARIANISM *See* HERESY.

ARIEL The etymology of the name *Ariel* (Heb. *'ari'el*) is uncertain: it may mean "lion of God" or "great Lion"; "hearth (or altar) of God"; or (as a loanword from Akkadian), "mountain of God." In 2 Sam. 23:20 and 1 Chron. 11:22 the term is applied to two bold Moabite men slain by David's warrior Benaiah. The Vg follows the LXX in rendering the Chronicles passage "two ariels of Moab"; in the Samuel passage, however, it has "two lion-like men." The latter form is followed in the KJV for both passages.

The Hebrew word occurs also in Ezek. 43:15-16, where it is rendered by most translations, including the KJV, as "altar." In Isa. 29:1-2, 7, *Ariel* is used as a poetic and somewhat cryptic synonym for Jerusalem, perhaps in view of the fact that the main altar of God was present there. It has also been suggested that the designation is prophetic: Jerusalem will become like the altar, a place where the fire and furnace of God's wrath shall suddenly appear.

In rabbinical literature the name *Ariel* was applied not only to the altar (Tg. Isa. 29:1) but also to the Temple as such (Talmud Midr. 4:7). In early gnostic literature (e.g., "On the Origin of the World," *Nag Hammadi Library in English* [1977]) *Ariel* is an alternative name used by the more enlightened gnostic believers ("perfect ones") for

the figure Yaldabaoth, an arrogant demiurge involved in the creation of the world. In the Testament of Solomon Ariel appears as a "thwarting angel" who controls demons, and in other writings associated with magic, cabalistic demonology, and the occult, Ariel is variously represented as a lion-headed angel (*Greater Key of Solomon; Gand Ginoire*) or as one of the seven princes who rule the waters (e.g., Heywood's *The Hierarchy of the Blessed Angels* [1635]). Such texts may have influenced Milton's characterization of Ariel as one of the rebel angels cast out of heaven (*Paradise Lost,* 6.371).

Shakespeare has immortalized the name *Ariel* in his delicately nuanced portrayal of an airy sprite in *The Tempest.* Imprisoned by the witch Sycorax in a cloven pine, Ariel is released by Prospero to serve as the executor of his magical schemes; Ariel is entirely freed only after Prospero renounces all magic at the end of the play. Though Shakespeare was almost certainly indebted to Isa. 29 for his choice of the name *Ariel,* subsequent writers were generally not; their conscious debt is to *The Tempest.* Thus Alexander Pope applies the name to Belinda's guardian spirit in *The Rape of the Lock* (1712). Shelley refers to himself as Ariel in "Guitar Jane," a choice recollected in André Maurois's biography of Shelley, *Ariel* (1921; Eng. trans. 1935). Byron alludes to Ariel in *Don Juan* (canto 11), as does Wallace Stevens in his "The Planet on the Table." T. S. Eliot titles five of his Christmas poems *Ariel Poems* (1927-30), and Sylvia Plath's best-known collection of poetry, published posthumously in 1965, is entitled *Ariel.*

Bibliography. Charlesworth, J. H., ed. *The Old Testament Pseudepigrapha: vol. 1, Apocalyptic Literature and Testaments* (1983); Davidson, G. *A Dictionary of Angels Including the Fallen Angels* (1967); Johnson, W. S. "The Genesis of Ariel." *SQ* 2 (1951), 205-10; Slater, A. P. "Variations within a Source: From Isaiah XXIX to 'The Tempest.'" *ShS* 25 (1972), 125-35.
                                    HERBERT GIESBRECHT

ARK (NOAH'S) *See* FLOOD.

ARK OF THE COVENANT The *Ark of the Covenant* (Heb. *'aron habberit*) — so named because it contained the stone tablets on which the Ten Commandments were written (see Exod. 25:16, etc.) — is referred to variously in the Bible as "the ark of the covenant of the LORD," "the ark of the covenant of God," "the Testimony," and the "ark of God" (Num. 10:33; Exod. 16:34; 1 Sam. 3:3, etc.). It was a portable wooden chest built by the Israelites in compliance with a divine commandment received during their wanderings in the desert (Exod. 25:10-22). The ark originally stood in the Tabernacle in the desert, but it was also, by means of rings and poles, carried by the Israelites on their journeyings; and later it stood in the Holy of Holies of the Temple of Solomon (Exod. 25:12-14; 1 Kings 8:1-9).

There seems to have been early confusion over the

uses and history of the ark. According to Heb. 9:4, the ark contained "the golden pot that had manna, and Aaron's rod that budded, and the tables of the covenant," but according to 1 Kings 8:9, the ark contained only "the two tables of stone, which Moses put there at Horeb, when the LORD made a covenant with the children of Israel, when they came out of the land of Egypt" (for the original placement of the pot of manna and Aaron's rod *before* rather than *within* the ark, see Exod. 16:33-34 and Num. 17:25; and for the placement of the "book of the law" — apparently meaning a part or the whole of the book of Deuteronomy — "in the side of the ark of the covenant," see Deut. 31:26).

Made of acacia wood (KJV "shittim wood"), approximately four-feet-two-inches long and thirty inches wide and deep ("two cubits and a half . . . and a cubit and a half . . . and a cubit and a half" [Exod. 25:10; see Grintz, 460]), the ark was overlaid with gold inside and out, decorated with a golden rim or border, and equipped with four gold rings, one at each of its four feet, through which gilded poles of "shittim wood" were permanently kept in place (Exod. 25:10-15). The ark cover, or "mercy seat" (KJV; Heb. *kapporet*), was a slab of gold which sat atop the ark (Exod. 25:17). That the root of the Hebrew word *kapporet* means "atone" or "propitiate" as well as "cover" points to the ritual function of the mercy seat (see Lev. 16:2, 14), and this also explains why the *kapporet* is referred to as "the propitiatory" rather than "the mercy seat" in English Bibles before the KJV. Facing each other at opposite ends of the mercy seat were two winged cherubim. The mercy seat, or more specifically its surface between the cherubim, was the place of the manifestation of the Divine Presence and Divine Will (Exod. 25:22; 30:6; Lev. 16:2; Num. 7:89). Touching or even looking at or into the ark was generally prohibited, but in performing the ritual of the scapegoat and sin offering the high priest sprinkled the blood of the sacrificial bullock and goat upon it, "to make an atonement" (see Lev. 16).

After the settlement of the Israelites in the land of Canaan, the ark was initially lodged at Shiloh (Josh. 18:1; 1 Sam. 3:3). On one occasion when it was carried into battle by the Israelites (see 1 Sam. 4; for other evidence of the use of the ark in wartime, cf. Num. 10:35-36; 1 Sam. 14:18; 2 Sam. 11:11), it was captured by the Philistines and placed in the house of their god, Dagon, in Ashdod. When the image of Dagon was cast down mysteriously several mornings (1 Sam. 5:3-4), and when the Philistines of Ashdod were themselves smitten by God with tumors (KJV "emerods" [1 Sam. 5:6]), the ark was removed to Gath, where once again the people were afflicted. The ark was sent on to the Philistine city of Ekron, and death and plague again ensued (1 Sam. 5:10-12). The Philistines decided to return the ark to the Israelites, enclosing, at the advice of their priests and diviners, a most unusual "trespass offering": ". . . Five golden emerods, and five golden mice, according to the

number of the lords of the Philistines" (1 Sam. 6:4-5; cf. 6:17). The Philistines placed the ark and "a coffer with the mice of gold and the images of their emerods" on a cart drawn by "two milch kine" which headed for the Israelite city of Beth-shemesh, where "fifty thousand and threescore and ten men" were struck down "because they had looked into the ark of the LORD" (1 Sam. 6:7, 19). The men of Beth-shemesh then sent messengers to Kirjath-jearim, and the men of the latter city "fetched up the ark of the LORD, and brought it into the house of Abinadab in the hill, and sanctified Eleazar his son to keep the ark of the LORD" (1 Sam. 6:20 – 7:1).

In the time of King David the ark was brought up from Kirjath-jearim to Jerusalem, "and Uzzah and Ahio, the sons of Abinadab, drove the new cart" upon which it was carried (2 Sam. 6:3). But when the ark reached "Nachon's threshing floor," Uzzah "put forth his hand to the ark of God, and took hold of it; for the oxen shook it," and God became angry and struck Uzzah dead. The harsh punishment meted out to Uzzah for what appeared to have been an inadvertent act of desecration caused David to change the name of the place to "Perez-uzzah" (lit. "Uzzah's breach" but by popular etymology: "Yahweh has brought destruction [lit. 'broken through'] on Uzzah"; see JB, 391, n. g), and to leave the ark at the house of Obed-edom the Gittite for three months, where it brought blessings on Obed-edom and all his household (2 Sam. 6:6-11). David thereupon brought the ark joyfully up to Jerusalem "with shouting and with the sound of the trumpet . . . leaping and dancing before the LORD" (6:12-16), on account of which his wife Michal, daughter of Saul, "despised him in her heart" and rebuked him (6:16, 20); and with sacrifices, feasting, and celebration the ark was installed "in the midst of the tabernacle that David had pitched for it" (6:17).

In medieval and later Christian exegesis the ark was usually taken to be either an OT type of Christ or Christ's Incarnation, and hence of the Virgin Mary; or a symbol of the Church, of the New Testament, or of a true knowledge of the spiritual sense of Scripture, or of the Christian faith as a whole (see, respectively, the Venerable Bede, *De Tabernaculo*, 1.4 [PL 91.401]; Pseudo-Ambrose [Maximus of Turin], *Sermo*, 42 [PL 17.689]; Bruno of Asti, *Expositio in Exodum*, cap. 25 [PL 164.308]; St. Eucherius of Lyon, *Commentarii in Libros Regum*, 2.4 [PL 50.1084]; St. Gregory the Great, *In Primum Regum Expositionis*, 3.5.2 [PL 79.202]; and Rupert of Deutz, *Liber Unus inter Libros Regum Quartus*, cap. 5 [PL 167.1192]). Less typologically explicit and more philosophical are meditations on the mercy seat as a symbol of Christ-as-Logos and cosmic principle of mediation by such early Greek writers as Origen and St. Clement of Alexandria, and, in the Latin West, by St. Bonaventure, in his *Itinerarium Mentis in Deum* (for references and discussion see Budick, 25-26, 154-65 *et passim*). Both strands of medieval commentary are evident in Protestant exegesis. Thus John Diodati, a friend of the poet Milton, comments on the word *kapporet* in Exod. 25:17:

> the Hebr. word signifieth also a mercy-seat; and so the Apostle calls it, *Heb.* 9.5 *viz.* a means of purging and expiating sin; because that this cover signified Christ, who with his righteousness covereth all our sins, and containeth within himself all the Churches righteousness, as the tables of the Law were inclosed under the cover; and interposeth himself as Mediator, between the Law which accuseth us, and God our Judge, as the cover was between the said Tables, and the majestie of God, which shewed it self present over the Cherubims of this Cover, as sitting upon his throne. (*Pious and Learned Annotations Upon the Holy Bible* [1651], cited in Budick, 55)

Gervase Babington, another of Milton's contemporaries, provides a further instance of Protestant exegesis of the mercy seat as symbol of Christ as both mediator and cosmic separator or divide (see Budick, 55-56).

Milton, in both *Paradise Lost* and *Paradise Regained*, draws on the exegetical tradition (e.g., *PL* 11.1-17; *PR* 4.596-600; see Budick, 50-53, 68-69, etc.). But the description of the ark, occurring in the narrative of the angel Michael (*PL* 12,244-54), stays close to its biblical source.

In William Cowper's *The Task* (1785-1800), a compressed allusion to the ark and its later-Israelite history enables the poet to lament the decadence of his countrymen and at the same time to hint at the dire consequences which will ensue:

> How, in the name of soldiership and sense
> Should England prosper, when such things, as smooth
> And tender as a girl, all essenc'd o'er
> With odours, and as profligate as sweet;
> Who sell their laurel for a myrtle wreath
> And love when they should fight; when such as these
> Presume to lay their hand upon the ark
> Of her magnificent and awful cause? ("The
> Time-Piece," 2.225-32)

In Keats's fragmentary "The Eve of St. Mark" (1819), the heroine Bertha, "a maiden fair," reads (in "A curious volume patched and torn" which "Perplexed her with a thousand things") about: "The Covenantal Ark / With its many mysteries, / Cherubim and golden mice" (36-38).

In Charles Dickens's *David Copperfield* (1849-50), the minor character Barkis (famous for uttering the proverbial line "Barkis is willin'") is a carriage driver who, for all his amusing and seemingly benign eccentricity, is revealed to be "something of a miser" who keeps "a heap of money in a box under his bed. . . ." When David Copperfield pays a sick call, he finds Barkis lying in bed "face upward, and so covered, with that exception, that he seemed to be nothing but a face — like a conventional cherubim. . . ." Another character, Mr. Omer, tells David that he has observed Barkis driving his carriage along its route for "forty years" (the length of time the Israelites wandered in the desert); later one learns

that "For years and years, Mr. Barkis had carried this box, on all his journeys, every day." That the word *ark* is encoded in the character's name (Barkis) may thus be more than mere coincidence (see Vogel, 190-205).

Thomas Hardy's *Tess of the D'Urbervilles* includes a heavily ironic and allusively rich reference to the ark. Following upon the death of her father and the termination of the family's lease, the heroine, together with her mother and siblings (including a brother named for the peripatetic OT patriarch Abraham), joins the other farm laborers in a general seasonal exodus to new regions and new tenancies:

> The day being the sixth of April, the Durbeyfield wagon met many other wagons with families on the summit of the load, which was built on a well-nigh unvarying principle, as peculiar, probably, to the rural labourer as the hexagon to the bee. The groundwork of the arrangement was the family dresser, which, with its shiny handles, and finger-marks, and domestic evidences thick upon it, stood importantly in front, over the tails of the shaft horses, in its erect and natural position, like some Ark of the Covenant which they were bound to carry reverently.

Although these wandering Israelites are here shown revering their dresser / ark, a bit later Hardy tells us how the "cold sunlight . . . peered invidiously upon . . . the brass handles of the dresser" and all the rest of the Durbeyfields' possessions, which have been unloaded by their unsympathetic carter and left out in the open, where they "gave out the reproachful gleam of indoor articles abandoned to the vicissitudes of a roofless exposure for which they were never made." The biblical history of the ark — from the time of its construction in the desert to its capture, sacrilegious handling, and recovery from the Philistines — along with its exegetical association with redemption reverberates ominously at this point in the novel, as the pace at which Tess moves along the downward curve of her tragic fate begins to accelerate.

See also DAGON; MICHAL; SHILOH.

Bibliography. Budick, S. *The Dividing Muse: Images of Sacred Disjunction in Milton's Poetry* (1985); Grintz, Y. M., and H. Freedman. "Ark of the Covenant." *EncJud* (1972), 3.459-66; Souvay, C. L. "Ark." *Catholic Encyclopedia* (1907; rpt. 1913), 1.720b-24b; Springer, M. *Hardy's Use of Allusion* (1983); Vogel, J. *Allegory in Dickens* (1977).

LAWRENCE BESSERMAN

ARMAGEDDON   Rev. 16:16 says that the word *Armageddon* (Gk. *harmagedōn*) is Hebrew, although no occurrences in Hebrew writings are known. The meaning is obscure, most obviously suggesting the "Hill or Mountain (Heb. *har*) of Megiddo." (Another possible etymology is *har migdo*, "fruitful mountain," i.e., Mt. Zion.) Although no such geographical designation is known, the phrase aptly describes the almost ideal strategic site of the city of Megiddo on a spur of Mt. Carmel. There the city guards the Plain of Esdraelon (Vg: Plain of Megiddo) at the intersection of major trade routes, one linking Egypt with the Fertile Crescent, the other connecting Palestine with the Phoenician coast. The plain has been a frequent scene of battle throughout history, from the early Bronze Age to Allenby's victory in World War I. Ancient accounts of the conquest of the Promised Land tell how Deborah and Barak, with the stars fighting on their side, defeated Sisera and the Canaanite kings at Taanach and Megiddo (Judg. 5:19-20); Josiah (the great reformer and one of only two preexilic Hebrew kings to do "that which was right in the sight of the LORD") died at Megiddo at the hand of Pharaoh Neco (2 Kings 23:29), and Judah's final downfall and deportation followed quickly; other OT references to the city abound.

The 3rd- and 4th-cent.-B.C. messianic prophecies included in Zech. 9–14 tell of an apocalyptic purging of Jerusalem, with mourning reminiscent of that for the popular fertility god Hadad-rimmon, in the valley of Megiddon (12:11). Revelation's evocation of an end-of-time battle of "the kings of the east" (16:12) perhaps appropriates contemporary superstition that the Emperor Nero would return to life at the head of Parthian forces. Associating the encounter with the mountain rather than the plain is of course more appropriate to apocalyptic symbolism than to the realities of battle. Furthermore, the context suggests not a physical battle but an ideological confrontation in which the Word of God confronts its demonic antithesis. The account in Ezek. 38–39 of a final apocalyptic battle in which God symbolically defeats a grandiose version of Babylon in the mountains of Israel is probably of some significance.

Thomas Brightman's Lat. *Apocalypsis Apocalypseos* (1609, though written in the late 16th cent., followed by an English version, *A Revelation of the Revelation* [1615]) designates Geneva as the place of Armageddon. There Brightman expected imminent attack by and final defeat of the forces of Catholicism following a literal attack and destruction of Rome by Reformed forces. In the mid-19th cent., Samuel Baldwin engages in a similar kind of prophetic speculation in his *Armageddon; or the . . . existence of the United States Foretold in the Bible, its expansion into the millenial republic, and its dominion over the whole world* (1854).

References to Armageddon are rare in the classics of English literature. Supplements to the *Oxford English Dictionary* trace its first English occurrence to a Shelley letter and also quote Kipling's *England's Answer.* But even Blake, for whom the concept of a final apocalyptic battle figures significantly, does not use the term.

In the present century the word has become almost trite, suggesting any battle the user wishes to project as being decisively final or (more often) simply as being cataclysmic and highly consequential. Theodore Roosevelt called his last political fight an armageddon, and H. L. Mencken, in "Puritanism as a Literary Force," remarks wryly that "there has not been a presidential

election since Jackson's day without its Armageddon, its marching of Christian soldiers. . . ." In Joyce's *Ulysses* Armageddon appears among a series of miscellaneous religious images that symbolize the events of Bloom's day.

See also APOCALYPSE.

Bibliography. Christianson, P. *Reformers and Babylon: English Apocalyptic Visions from the Reformation to the Eve of the Civil War* (1978); Bowman, J. W. "Revelation, Book of." *IDB* 4.58-71.   RICHARD SCHELL

ARMOR AND WEAPONS   Isaiah looked forward to an "intercessor," one who would "put on righteousness as a breastplate, and an helmet of salvation upon his head" (59:16-17). St. Paul was later to recall and expand these metaphors:

> Put on the whole armour of God, that ye may be able to stand against the wiles of the devil. . . . Stand therefore, having your loins girt about with truth, and having the breastplate of righteousness; and your feet shod with the preparation of the gospel of peace; and above all, taking the shield of faith, wherewith ye shall be able to quench the fiery darts of the wicked. And take the helmet of salvation, and the sword of the Spirit, which is the word of God. (Eph. 6:11-17; see also Rom 13:12: "Let us therefore cast off the works of darkness, and let us put on the armour of light"; cf. 2 Cor. 6:7; 1 Thess. 5:8)

The Fathers take up this allegory, sometimes keeping strictly to Isaiah's and Paul's scheme, sometimes altering and expanding it. For Aphrahat, in *Demonstrations,* 6, the shield is baptism, the armor the gospel; for St. Augustine, in *Letters,* 75 (NPNF 1.333), the armor is Christ, and it was with such spiritual weapons only that "King David went forth in his day to battle" with Goliath. St. Gregory of Nazianzus (NPNF 7.222) also contrasts the weakness of David's physical arms with the might of his spiritual armor, this with reference to Ps. 18:39: "For thou hast girded me with strength unto the battle." Recalling Eph. 6:16 and Ps. 11:2, Gregory adds that it is the "Spirit, by which all the fiery darts of the wicked shall be quenched." St. Cyril assures believers that in their catechism they are "receiving armour against the adverse power, armour against heresies, against Jews, and Samaritans, and Gentiles. Thou hast many enemies; take to thee many darts, for thou hast many to hurl them at" ("Procatechesis"). Erasmus provides one of the most elaborate accounts of spiritual armor and Christian soldiering in his *Enchiridion Militis Christiani* ("A Handbook of the Christian Soldier"), even declaring that the *Enchiridion* itself was fashioned as "a kind of hand dagger . . . so that even if you must sojourn at times in the business of this world and find it cumbersome to carry around that whole armor. . . . At least it should not be inconvenient to keep with you this little blade" (trans. Himelick).

A much narrower tradition is that of the bootlessness of such apparently mighty armor as Goliath's (1 Sam.

17:4-7), the armor in which worldlings trust: "When a strong man armed keepeth his palace, his goods are at peace: But when a stronger than he shall come upon him, and overcome him, he taketh from him all his armour wherein he trusted, and divideth his spoils" (Luke 11:21-22). Augustine speaks of people trusting in the pleasures of this world, and of these pleasures becoming, then, "an armour" (*In Joan. Ev.* 15.16).

The allegory of spiritual armor was prominent in literature of the Middle Ages; indeed, one finds references to it in such popular drama as the Grocers of Norwich's "Creation of Eve." After the expulsion from the Garden of Eden, Adam and Eve are comforted by the Holy Ghost:

Theis armors are preparyd, yf thou wylt turne ageyne
To fyght wyth — take to the, and reach Woman the same:
The brest plate of rightousness Saynte Paule wyll the retayne.

The Holy Ghost goes on to offer the shield of faith, the helmet of salvation, and the sword of the spirit (137-43).

Spenser, in his letter to Sir Walter Raleigh, identifies the armor of the Redcrosse Knight as "the armour of a Christian man specified by Saint Paul v. Ephes." It is no surprise, then, that after he doffs his armor, the Redcrosse Knight dallies with Duessa — and so falls victim to Orgoglio, "Disarmd, disgrast, and inwardly dismayde" (*Faerie Queene,* 1.7.11.6); after his repentance and renewal, he "did himselfe to battell readie dight" before slaying the Satanic dragon (1.11.52.3. These associations are also vividly present in Bunyan's *Holy War*).

But if he explicitly associates the Redcrosse Knight with "the armour of a Christian man," inviting consideration of specific correspondences — it is appropriate, e.g., that Redcrosse slay the Demon Errour with the sword of truth (1.1.24) — elsewhere Spenser makes use of these traditions less strictly: in the Bower of Bliss one finds a man who has hung upon a tree "His warlike armes, the idle instruments / Of sleeping praise" (2.12.80.1-2), and Britomart, chaste warrior maiden that she is, pointedly refuses to lay aside her arms in the Castle of Joy (3.1.42). The doffing of armor, partly because of the story of Gideon (Judg. 7), comes to suggest simply a succumbing to temptation. Perhaps, then, when Shakespeare's temptress Cleopatra dresses Antony in her "tires and mantles," while she put on "his sword Phillipan," his audience might have judged that more was at stake than Antony's manhood (*Antony and Cleopatra,* 2.5.22-23). Similarly, when Donne's lusty lover urges his mistress to "Unpin that spangled brest-plate," the suggestion is that she must put off her spiritual defenses, just as she must put off her bodice, if he is to achieve his amorous ends ("To his Mistris Going to Bed").

Finally, in Hopkins's "The Windhover" —

Brute beauty and valour and act, oh, air, pride, plume, here

Buckle! AND the fire that breaks from thee then, a billion
Times told lovelier, more dangerous, O my chevalier!

— at least one of the several meanings possible for "Buckle!" is the buckling on of the spiritual armor so appropriate for the Christ-chevalier.

See also MILES CHRISTI; SHIELD; SWORD OF THE SPIRIT.

H. DAVID BRUMBLE

AS FOR ME AND MY HOUSE Joshua's farewell address to the people of Israel involves a representation of their choice to confirm or deny their covenant with God: "Choose you this day whom ye will serve; whether the gods which your fathers served that were on the other side of the flood, or the gods of the Amorites, in whose land ye dwell: but as for me and my house, we will serve the LORD" (Josh. 24:15).

This passage receives little or no commentary from either Jewish or early Christian exegetes and is conspicuously absent from early biblical paraphrases in Latin (e.g., Peter Riga's *Aurora*) and English *(Cursor Mundi).* When the Reformers comment on it, they tend to downplay the aspect of choice, apparently because it seems inconsistent with a covenantal theology emphasizing God's election and free grace. Matthew Poole's *Annotations upon the Holy Bible* reflects the general Calvinist reading: "Not that he gives them to their liberty, whether they would serve God or Idols; for Joshua had no such power, or liberty himself, nor could give it to any other." The Arminian tradition, by contrast, is reflected in the "Scripture Scales" or *Checks to Antinomianism* (1771) of John Fletcher, the putative successor to John Wesley, who arranges in extensive double columns the "weights of Free Grace" (i.e., the covenant, or Calvinist position) against the "weights of Free Will," under which he places this verse, relating it back to Deut. 30:19 and forward to "Mary hath chosen the good part" (Luke 10:42). The strength of the latter emphasis in North American evangelical preaching in the later 19th and 20th cents. is reflected in the title of the Canadian novel by Sinclair Ross, *As for Me and My House* (1941), which ironically recounts the failure of a minister who has at last himself chosen for the "Amorite" life of a small Saskatchewan town.

ASCENSION The ascension of Jesus marks the conclusion of his ministry on earth and his exaltation to power and glory at the right hand of the Father in heaven.

In the OT, Jesus' ascension is prefigured by the "translation" of Enoch (Gen. 5:24) and Elijah (2 Kings 2). The Church believed that several psalms also contained foreshadowings of Jesus' ascension (Pss. 68:18; 24:7; 47:5-9; 110). Psalm 110 was widely quoted in the NT (Matt. 22:44; Mark 12:46; Luke 20:42; Acts 2:34; 1 Cor. 15:25; Heb. 5:6; 6:20; 7:7, 21; 10:12-13).

The Gospels and Acts offer eyewitness accounts of the event. According to Mark's account the resurrected Christ appeared to his disciples, admonished those who had lacked faith in him, outlined the Church's future ministry, and was exalted "at the right hand of the Father" (16:19-20). In Luke's Gospel, the ascension took place in Bethany. As he ascended, Christ blessed the gathered disciples (24:51) and instructed them to remain in Jerusalem awaiting "the power from on high" (24:49), which he would send at Pentecost.

According to Acts 1:1-12 the ascension took place on Mt. Olivet forty days after the resurrection. The disciples beheld Jesus as "he was taken up; and a cloud received him out of their sight." The cloud conveying Jesus to heaven is associated with the Shekinah, the abode of the power and glory of God in the OT (Exod. 13:21; 40:34; 1 Kings 8:10-11).

By being "received up into glory" (1 Tim. 3:16) and exalted at the right hand of the Father (Acts 5:31; John 12:23; 17:15), Jesus Christ is said to extend his dominion over the entire creation. He led "captivity captive" in his ascension, a definitive victory over sin and death (Eph. 4:7-10) and Satan's dominion (1 Pet. 3:18-22). The presence of the Son of Man in heaven, there "seen of angels" (1 Tim. 3:16), ensures that mankind can never again be entirely separated from God (Eph. 2:4-6). The prospect of Christ's Second Coming in glory and the subsequent Last Judgment gives hope and enjoins vigilance (Mark 13).

The ascension has a central place in patristic literature, which emphasizes the exalted Christ's dominion over the angels, fallen and unfallen. St. Augustine's theology of the ascension is especially noteworthy for its synthesis of the salvation history revealed in the Scriptures and incorporated in the earliest creeds. In his ascension sermons Augustine links the Son of Man's elevation with the Incarnation and underscores that Christ not only redeems but also glorifies humanity.

The popularity of the ascension as a theme in Christian art since the 5th cent. corresponds to its theological importance. In the earliest representations, the apostles watch Christ from below as he nears the top of a hill, his hand grasping the Father's hand extended from a cloud. The rendering preferred later in the Middle Ages shows Christ suspended in or on a cloud, the signs of his Passion often prominently displayed, with Mary and the apostles watching below.

The presence of the mother of Jesus in the York Play of the Tailors has a similar effect of emphasizing the risen Lord's humanity. Mary keens at the departure of her son (210), whose feelings for his Father are not less tender: "Sende downe a clowde, fadir! for-thy / I come to thee, my fadir deere" (176-77). Mary plays an even larger role in the Wakefield "Ascension of the Lord," the role of a mother torn between heartbreak and joy (348-52) and a staunch advocate enjoining the apostles not to forget her son's instructions regarding the conversion of the Jews

(404-10). There is, by contrast, little familial sentiment in Langland's dream of the Conqueror who will return to punish and reward on the Day of Doom (*Piers Plowman,* B.19.165-95).

Many of the major Renaissance and Romantic poets drawn to the theme of the ascension see in it the exaltation and glorification of humanity. The last sonnet of Donne's *La Corona,* e.g., figures the rising Sun as the Ram which batters heaven for the poet, the Lamb, whose blood washes him clean, and the Torch which lights his way. In his "Ascension — Hymn," Vaughan makes no mention of Christ: he yearns for his own lifting out of the darkness into the clear light of heaven. A virtual transcription from the NT, the Miltonic account in *Paradise Lost* embraces larger concerns and a more comprehensive humanism (cf. 10.185-89 and Eph. 4:7-10). Twice Adam hears foretold the coming of the Redeemer, who "to the Heaven of Heavens . . . shall ascend / With victory, triumphing through the air" over the foes of God and man (*PL* 12.451-52; cf. 10.222-26). At the end of *Jerusalem,* Blake records his private heavenly dream of Albion's ascent into the clouds to join the Divine Friend. The Parson in holy transport atop a mountain in the last book of Wordsworth's *The Excursion* is heartened by the history of man's rise from barbarism and the vale of tears and envisions his restoration to a peaceful garden kingdom.

The ascension theme is absent from the expansive main body of Victorian literature on dying, death, and the dead. Tennyson's exemplary *In Memoriam A. H. H.,* which Queen Victoria set "next to the Bible" as a source of comfort (S. Day, *History of English Literature: 1837 to the Present* [1964], 24), includes several recollections of Christmas (sts. 28, 78) but no memory of either the resurrection or the ascension. The sole events recalled from the life of Christ in Tennyson's "Vastness" are his Crucifixion and death. For this most popular of the Victorian poets, the once and future king is Arthur, not risen, but lost from sight on the distant horizon. Belief in the ascension seems implicitly contested in Butler's *Erewhon Revisited,* a satire on human credulity: Higgs's departure in a gas-filled balloon at the end of his first visit has given rise to "Sunchildism" and rival schools of speculative theology. In *Erewhon,* Butler's earlier and sunnily wry dystopia, Higgs exploits the queen's eagerness to see "so strange a sight as the ascent of a human being into the sky" (chap. 28).

In the 20th cent., Robert Lowell's verse-epistle "After the Surprising Conversions" reconstructs how people two centuries ago responded to the ascension and the prospect of the Second Coming. Writing in a voice borrowed from Jonathan Edwards, Lowell recalls a suicide "hard on our Lord's Ascension": one gentleman's reflections and readings on the Last Judgment fill him with hope and fear, and, in terror, he slits his own throat. The effect of this event on other members of the congregation is to make them more attentive to the spiritual life even as it leads them to infer that "the breath of God had carried out a planned / And sensible withdrawal from this land." Dylan Thomas's "Vision and Prayer" chants the glory of a humanity lifted up with Christ in a "Spiral of ascension" (st. 3). The opening six lines of Thomas's "And Death shall have no dominion," which conceives of an afterlife when men "shall have stars at elbow and foot," provide the first epigraph of James Blish's tetralogy *Cities in Flight*, in which, having mastered the force of gravity and checked the process of aging, human beings conquer space and are conquered by endless cosmic time.

See also ELIJAH; ENOCH; RESURRECTION; SECOND COMING.

Bibliography. Knoepflmacher, U. C. *Religious Humanism and the Victorian Novel* (1965); Schillebeeckx, E. H. "Ascension and Pentecost." *Worship* 35 (May 1961), 336-63; Toon, P. *The Ascension of Our Lord* (1984).

CAMILLE R. LA BOSSIÈRE
LENORE GUSSIN

ASA *See* ABOMINATION OF DESOLATION.

ASENATH After Joseph had interpreted Pharaoh's dream, forewarning of the seven years of plenty followed by seven of famine, Pharaoh made him his chief minister and gave him Asenath, daughter of the Egyptian priest Potiphera, to be his bride (Gen. 41:45-50; 46:20). Having refused to succumb to the adulterous enticements of the wife of his employer Potiphar, Joseph was thus ultimately rewarded with a bride who was, as the priest's similar name *poti-phera'* ironically suggests, the "gift of the Sun-god." Subsequently she bore him two sons, Manasseh and Ephraim, during the seven years of plenty.

Her Egyptian name possibly means "she belongs to . . . the deity Neit." The Hebrew derivation of her name (Midr. 'Aggadah Gen. 41:45) takes the *aleph* in her name to stand for On, the place where Potiphera was priest; the *samek* for *setirah,* "hidden," referring to the protection of her extraordinary beauty; the *nun* for *nohemet,* the "weeping" of her entreaty to be delivered from the house of Potiphera; and the *tau* for *tammah,* "perfect," on account of her exemplary Jewish piety. For while the older midrashim take her to have been the actual daughter of Potiphera and hence Egyptian (Gen. Rab. 85.1), later targums and talmudic legends, unlike the Maccabean (apocryphal) Testament of Joseph, contrive to make her a Jewish foundling: R. Eliezer (8th cent.) has her brought to Egypt by an angel (Pirqe R. El. 38), while an elaborate Syriac legend makes the conductor an eagle. (The assumption of these later reflections is that, as priest, Potiphera would have been a eunuch; hence Asenath must either have been adopted or have been born before he was made a eunuch.)

Sometime between the end of the 1st cent. and middle of the 2nd cent. a Greek version of the legend gained wide circulation. In it the story was amplified and turned into a vibrant romance in which passion and purity overcome convention and its corruption, and in which Asenath's conversion and prayer of confession figure largely. By the 12th cent. an edition of the 2nd-cent. Greek original had been transcribed in the 11th-cent. MS Vaticanus Graecus 803 and a Latin version of the 12th cent., and a redaction of the 13th cent. by Vincent of Beauvais (included in his *Speculum Historiale,* 6.118-24) is based upon it. Sixteen MSS of the Greek version, along with Syriac, Armenian, Latin, Slavonic, Rumanian, Ethiopian, and modern Greek translations survive, and following the Latin text came versions in German, Dutch, Norse, Czech, Polish, and Middle English. In 16th-cent. France it was turned into a Corpus Christi play.

The ME version, *The Storie of Asneth* (Huntingdon MS Ellesmere 26 A 13), is a romance of 934 lines concluding in an epilogue on the death of Asenath (cf. C. Brown, *Religious Lyrics of the XVth Century,* 241-43). It follows closely the traditional legends in making her a romantic heroine of extraordinary loveliness, less the unbidden chattel awarded by Pharaoh than a courted beauty, herself already deeply smitten with Joseph. Philip von Zesen's *Assenet* (1670) novelizes her legend, as does Jakob Christoffel von Grimmelshausen's *Keuscher Joseph* (1667), and the story figures marginally in Hannah More's English dramatization (1782), as well as in numerous 19th-cent. Yiddish dramas *(Gdolas Yosef).* Thomas Mann's *Joseph und seine Bruder* (1933-42), by contrast, passes her over in a few pages in an account unremarkable except for his insistence on the biblical warrant for her Egyptian ancestry.

See also JOSEPH THE PATRIARCH; PHARAOH; POTIPHAR'S WIFE.

Bibliography. Aptowitzer, V. "Asenath, the Wife of Joseph — A Haggadic Literary-Historical Study." *HUCA* 1 (1924), 239-306; Batiffol, P. *Studia Patristica,* fasc. 1, *Le livre de la prière d'Asenath* (1899); Burchard, C. "Joseph and Asenath: A New Translation and Introduction." In *The Old Testament Pseudepigrapha.* Ed. J. H. Charlesworth (1985), 2.177-247; Dwyer, R. A. "Asenath of Egypt in Middle English." *MAE* 39 (1970), 118-22; Hamilton, G. L. "The Latin Historia Assenech." *JEGP* 11 (1912), 143ff.; Liptzin, S. *Biblical Themes in World Literature* (1985), 62-73; MacCracken, H. N., ed. "*The Storie of Asneth:* An Unknown Middle English Translation of a Lost Latin Version." *JEGP* 9 (1910), 224-64; Peck, R. A., ed. *Heroic Women from the Old Testament in Middle English Verse* (1991); Sarna, N. M. "Asenath." *EncJud* (1972), 3.693.

ASHDOD *See* ARK OF THE COVENANT.

ASHER One of the twelve sons of Jacob.
See also AARON; JACOB; TRIBES OF ISRAEL.

ASHES TO ASHES This phrase is from the "Burial of the Dead" liturgy in the *Book of Common Prayer:* ". . . earth to earth, ashes to ashes, dust to dust, in sure and certain hope of the resurrection to eternal life, through our Lord Jesus Christ." It echoes several biblical passages (e.g., Gen. 18:27; Job 30:19; 42:6), though it has no exact source. Cf. the "Hades" chapter in James Joyce's *Ulysses,* in which the reference is to the burial of Parnell.

ASHMEDAI *See* ASMODEUS.

ASHTORETH The most prominent pagan goddess in the Bible, *Ashtoreth* is presented as the consort of Baal. Her name derives from the deliberate conflation of the Phoenician *Ashtart* with the Hebrew word *boshet* ("shame"). The plural form of *Ashtoreth* is *Ashtaroth,* as in the term "the Baalim and the Ashtaroth" — gods and goddesses, or Baals and Ashtoreths (e.g., 1 Sam. 7:5-6). Ashtoreth was worshiped widely in the ancient world under many different names. In Phoenicia she was called Ashtarte; in Babylonia, Ishtar and also Mulitta or Mu'allidtu (given in Herodotus as Mylitta); in both Babylonia and Assyria she was also called Zarpanit and Nina, after whom Nineveh was named; Zarpanit was the spouse of Assur or of Marduk. In north Africa Ashtoreth was called Tanith and also Dido. Ishtar of Uruk (Erekh) is found in the Idzubar (Gilgamesh) legend. In the Greco-Roman world Ashtart was identified with the goddess of love and known variously as Venus, Aphrodite, and Astarte. A celestial being — the Queen of Heaven — she was associated both with the planet Venus and the moon.

Ashtoreth was frequently worshiped as a local goddess; hence her name became associated with particular temples and towns, as in Ashteroth Karnaim, Karnaim Ashtareth, and Ashtaroth in Bashan. Ethbaal (or Ithobal), king of the Sidonians, father of Jezebel, was a priest at the temple of Ashtart, built by Hiram. Saul's armor, after his death, was deposited by the Philistines in the temple of Ashtoreth at Beth-shan (1 Sam. 31:10).

As her appearance varied according to regional traditions, so too did the manner of worshiping her. She was sometimes revered as "the Queen of Heaven," as by the women of Judah, who, hoping thereby to increase fertility and plenty, made crescent-shaped cakes and burned incense for her (Jer. 44:17-20; 7:18). As the goddess of maternity and fertility, she was worshiped by those seeking motherhood. In Canaanite society, women from all ranks prostituted themselves at her temple, and the money obtained was used for offerings. The priestesses at the temples of Ashtoreth were themselves prostitutes. It is apparent that the worship of Ashtoreth was characterized by extreme licentiousness. Solomon seems to have succumbed to such worship in his old age.

Milton makes frequent reference to Ashtoreth. In *Paradise Lost* (1.419-24) he alludes to those

who from the bord'ring flood
of old *Euphrates* to the Brook that parts
Egypt from *Syrian* ground, had general Names

of *Baalim* and *Ashtaroth,* those male,
These Feminine. For Spirits when they please
Can either sex assume, or both. . . .

At 1.437-46 he adds,

With these in troop
came *Ashtoreth* whom the *Phoenicians* call'd
Astarte, Queen of Heav'n, with crescent Horns;
to whose bright Image by the Moon
Sidonian Virgins paid their Vows and Songs,
In *Sion* also not unsung, where . . . that uxorious King
[Solomon] . . . fell to Idols foul.

There are further references in *Paradise Regained* (3.414-17) and *Samson Agonistes* (1242-43). And in *On the Morning of Christ's Nativity* Ashtaroth is named among the pagan gods whose reign is superseded by the coming of Christ (197-201).

Swinburne in *Dolores,* dedicated to "Our Lady of Pain," asks, "Where are they, Cottytto or Venus, Astarte or Ashtaroth, where?" In *Ligeia* Ashtoreth may be implied in a reference to the "wan and the misty-winged Ashtophet." In Byron's *Manfred,* the hero cries out, "Astarte! my beloved! speak to me. . ." (2.4.117). Other references occur at 2.4.103 and 3.3.44-47. Poe alludes to "Astarte's bediamonded crescent" in his "Ulalume" (st. 4).

William Blake in *Milton* writes that "in Tyre and Sidon I saw Baal and Ashtaroth in Moab" and speaks further of "war woven in looms of Tyre and Sidon by beautiful Ashtaroth." Robert Browning in "Popularity" alludes to the intense blue of "Astarte's eyes." D. H. Lawrence makes passing reference to Ashtoreth in *England, My England* and in *In a Spanish Tram-car* speaks of a woman "half Madonna half Astarte."

See also BAAL; BABYLON; JEZEBEL; NINEVEH.

Bibliography. Albright, W. F. *Yahweh and the Gods of Canaan: An Historical Analysis of Two Contrasting Faiths* (1968); Cassuto, U. *The Goddess Anath: Canaanite Epics of the Patriarchal Age.* Trans. I. Abrahams (1971); Grigson, G. *The Goddess of Love: The Birth, Triumph, Death and Return of Aphrodite* (1976).   RONALD M. MELDRUM

ASMODEUS *Asmodeus* (possibly from *Aeshma-daeva,* "the furious demon," and one of the seven arch-demons of Zoroastrianism) is a demon in the apocryphal book of Tobit (3:8, 16; 8:3). He appears in the Babylonian Talmud (Pesaḥ. 110a; Giṭ. 68a-b) as Ashmedai, and his escapades are further elaborated in the Testament of Solomon, *Clavicula Salomonis,* and cabalistic literature from antiquity to the early Renaissance. In Tobit, Asmodeus torments Sarah by killing in turn seven bridegrooms before the couple are able to consummate their union. He is eventually exorcised on Raphael's instructions by the smell of burning fish.

The Talmud introduces traditions of Asmodeus as a demon of marital discord (reflected in Milton's *Paradise Regained,* 2.151) and a wily Mephistophelian spirit. Ashmedai helps build Solomon's Temple, offers magic books, and is ultimately lamed through his own mischief. Cornelius Agrippa (*De Occultate Philosophia,* 3.18) establishes a tradition followed by Burton (*Anatomy of Melancholy,* 1.2.1.2), Heywood (*Hierarchie of the Blessed Angels* [1635], sig. Oo2ᵛ), and Milton (*Paradise Lost,* 6.365) which has Asmodeus leading the fourth order of fallen angels, "malicious revenging devils." In *PL* 4.168 Satan, lingering in fragrant Eden, is contrasted with the infatuated Asmodeus repelled by the stench from Sarah's home, an image of unnatural hate set against one of tormented love.

Asmodeus as satirical commentator, a derivative of the Solomon legends, reaches England in *The Devil upon Two Sticks* (1708) — translated from Le Sage's *Le diable boiteux* (1707), which is in turn an adaptation of De Guevara's *El diablo cojuelo* (1641). Having achieved a level of popular currency thus, the name appears widely in titles of satirical works (including Bulwer Lytton's *Asmodeus at Large*) and in Carlyle's *French Revolution* ([1902], 2.342). Allusions by Byron (*Vision of Judgement,* 295-96; "The Waltz," 224) and Emerson ("Fragments on the Poet and the Poetic Gift," in *Poems* [1900], 277) reflect the trivialized magician Asmodeus of 19th-cent. pantomime (e.g., *Harlequin and Asmodeus* [1810]). Tennyson ("St. Simeon Stylites," 172) and Browning ("Faust and his Friends," 66), however, revert to the more dangerous demon of Agrippa.

In a 20th-cent. version, James Bridie's *Tobias and the Angel* (1930) has Sarah's maidservants insulting her by calling her "Madam Asmoday."

See also TOBIT AND TOBIAS.

Bibliography. Baring-Gould, S. *Curious Myths and Legends of the Middle Ages* (1872); Conway, M. *Solomon and Solomonic Literature* (1899); West, R. H. *Milton and the Angels* (1955).　　　　BRENDA E. RICHARDSON
NORMAN VANCE

ASP *See* COCKATRICE.

ASS The ass was an animal normally ridden by non-military personnel (cf. Num. 22:21; Judg. 10:4; 1 Sam. 25:20); Jesus' use of an ass to ride into Jerusalem (Matt. 21:1-7; John 12:14; cf. Zech. 9:9) rather than a horse thus graphically depicts him as Prince of Peace or, as St. John Chrysostom says, "not driving chariots, like the rest of the kings, not demanding tributes . . . but displaying his great meekness even hereby" (*Hom. on Matthew,* 46.3). Chrysostom sees the ass as signifying the Church, a "new people, which was once unclean, but which, after Jesus sat thereon, became clean"; he notes that although the animal is said to be not yet broken to ride, it nevertheless was instantly tamed and compliable — not the "wild ass" it might in the nature of things have been expected to be. Western exegetical tradition follows in the same track, seeing the previously untamed mount as the unredeemed people, *"liber et lascivus,"* who are made docile in penitence by Jesus; the *Glossa Ordinaria* thus observes that

the ass ought not so much to be understood literally as spiritually representing the hearts of the people (PL 114.152). The cloaks of the disciples thrown over its back as a makeshift saddle *("vestes apostolorum")* are divine precepts and grace which bring moral turpitude under control. In modern poetry the Palm Sunday procession has been invoked ironically; e.g., Anthony Hecht's reference to the "ass's back on which the lamb comes to Jerusalem" in his poem "Pig" (*Hard Hours,* 13; cf. David Jones, *Anathemata,* 5.157).

In conventional iconography Mary is pictured riding on an ass toward Bethlehem and the birth of Jesus, as she is later during the flight to Egypt; there is no actual canonical warrant for this, the reference coming, rather, from the apocryphal Protevangelium 12.5. In Western hagiography the ass appears as a faithful companion of St. Jerome, and in the *Legenda* of St. Anthony of Padua the saint causes an ass to kneel in the presence of the sacraments to convince an unbeliever.

The Torah prohibited the use of an ox and ass yoked together for plowing (Deut. 22:10), provoking the medieval commentary that such plowing figures receipt of the gospel harnessed to Old Law observances. While the ox in this allegory signifies good works, the ass is an emblem of foolish stubbornness, and the "harnessing" thus effectively a yoking of wisdom and folly (*Glossa Ordinaria* [PL 113.476]). The Towneley play "Cain and Abel" characterizes Cain's obdurate insensitivity to the spirit of grace (and graciousness) by introducing him plowing with animals recognizable by their names as oxen and asses (25-35). It was permissible under the Law, however, to use ox and ass in tandem to tread out (thrash) grain (cf. Isa. 32:20 [LXX]), prompting Jerome to observe that this text, like the verse stating that "the ox knoweth his owner, and the ass his master's crib" (Isa. 1:3), is a prophecy of the Bethlehem manger so regularly featured in medieval nativity painting; he alludes here to the reinterpretation of the Law as a separation of kernel and chaff.

In quite a different vein, it was predicted of Ishmael that he would be a "wild ass of a man" (Gen. 16:12), a prophecy which the *Glossa Ordinaria* suggests refers to the nomadic, desert-wandering life of his "Saracen" descendants (PL 113.122). Numerous OT passages (esp. Job 6:5; 39:5; Isa. 32:14) comment upon, allude to, or imply the eremitic self-sufficiency of the wild ass; beginning at least with the early scriptural dictionary of St. Eucherius of Lyons the beast was for this reason also commonly taken as an emblem of the ascetic religious. The elaboration of the idea in two famous books — the *Collationes* of St. John Cassian and the *Moralia in Iob* of St. Gregory the Great — guaranteed the image's currency. The wild ass thus appears frequently in medieval monastic texts and, in the Renaissance, in paintings dealing with ascetic scenes. *Piers Plowman* (B.15.311ff.) offers a dramatic example of the manner in which the Latin exegetical tradition could touch upon an English vernacular text.

Balaam's ass (Num. 22:1-35), seeing what the pagan prophet did not (an angel turning them back until the prophet should receive explicit instructions from the Lord concerning his mission), spoke aloud to Balaam when he tried to force her insensitively on the road (cf. the classical allusion, *pons assinorum*). This creature is also a popular source of allusions, as in Thomas Nashe's quip, "That which thou knowest not peraventure thy Asse can tell thee" (*Anatomie of Absurditie*, E.b), and Herrick's voyeur in "Upon Julia's Fall" becomes a "Nagge (like to the Prophet's Asse)" who "Began to speak, and would have been / A telling what rare sights h'ad seen."

The ass is the subject of many proverbial expressions which have their counterpart, though not necessarily their origin, in the Bible (e.g., the dumb ass speaking, 1 Pet. 2:16). One of these is memorable from Boethius's *De Consolatione Philosophiae* where Lady Philosophy questions Boethius's dullness, "Artow lyk an asse to the harpe?" (Chaucer's trans. [*Boece*], 1.4), an association sometimes reflected in allusions to Isa. 1:3 in medieval art and literature but which is loosened from those connections by the Renaissance and 18th cent. (cf. Erasmus's *Praise of Folly;* also Sheridan, *Persius,* 1.23: "As the world goes, who has not Asses' Ears?"). The notion is comically deployed in Bottom's famous dream speech in *A Midsummer Night's Dream,* when Shakespeare's rustic awakes sporting ass's ears and more, and commences to confuse (and parody) 1 Cor. 2:9-10: "The eye of man hath not heard, the ear of man hath not seen, man's hand is not able to taste . . . what my dream was" (4.1.216-19). Many such allusions involve a conflation of classical, biblical, and proverbial references, such as Anthony Hecht's "An ass may look at an angel" — a reference to Balaam's ass which appears nevertheless in his "Improvisations on Aesop" (*Hard Hours,* 61).

See also BALAAM; EYE HATH NOT SEEN; ISHMAEL.

Bibliography. Fleming, J. V. *From Bonaventure to Bellini* (1982), 35-40; Robertson, D. W., Jr., and B. F. Huppé. *Piers Plowman and Scriptural Tradition* (1951), 185-86; Steadman, J. M. "Una and the Clergy: The Ass Symbol in *The Faerie Queene." JWCI* 21 (1958), 134-37.   DAVID L. JEFFREY
JOHN V. FLEMING

ASSUMPTION OF THE VIRGIN   A tenet of Catholic teaching about Mary, based upon noncanonical writings of the 5th cent. A.D., this doctrine declares Mary to have ascended bodily into heaven in a manner analogous to her Son. It was formally defined as dogma in 1950 by Pope Pius XII.

See also MARY, MOTHER OF JESUS.

ASTARTE   Name for Ashtoreth, e.g., in Milton, *Samson Agonistes* (596), and a character in Byron's *Manfred.*
See also ASHTORETH; BAAL.

AT EASE IN ZION   The prophet Amos attacked his complacent and luxury-loving contemporaries, saying, "Woe to them that are at ease in Zion, and trust in the mountain of Samaria" (6:1). Such people are described by Matthew Henry in his *Commentary* as "vainly conceited of their own dignities, and [thinking] those would secure them from the judgments threatened and be their defense against the wrath both of God and man."

Somewhat mislocating his source, Matthew Arnold observes in *Culture and Anarchy*

a saying . . . which excellently marks the essential point in which Hebraism differs from Hellenism. "Socrates," this saying goes, "is terribly at ease in Zion." Hebraism, — and here is the source of its wonderful strength, — has always been severely preoccupied with an awful sense of the impossibility of being at ease in Zion. ("Hebraism and Hellenism")

A witty allusion appears in Chesterton's *George Bernard Shaw,* where in his chapter entitled "The Puritan" he observes, "You musn't 'be at ease in Zion' unless you are only paying it a flying visit."

ATONEMENT   In Jewish and Christian theology, *atonement* signifies the making of God and sinners "at one" by the offering of sacrifice. In the KJV the term *atonement* occurs most often in the translation of the Hebrew verb *kipper,* "to make atonement" (e.g., Exod. 30:10; Lev. 1:4), though it is also the rendering of the noun *kippur* (which for some reason is always in the plural), as in the expression "day of atonement" (Lev. 23:27-28). It is found often in Leviticus, less in Exodus and Numbers, and infrequently elsewhere.

The OT stresses the importance of the removal of human sin as a hindrance to relationship with God. It also points to the importance of reckoning with the wrath of God, as is suggested by the LXX translation of the Hebrew verb as *exilaskomai.* The English word *atonement* — suggesting the restored relationship itself — appears first in St. Thomas More's *History of King Richard III* (1513) with reference to political discord, although the idea had theological precedent in Wyclif's *onement* and Julian of Norwich's *onyng.* Tyndale used the word in his translation of the NT (1526), as did the KJV's translators throughout the OT; in the NT of the 1611 version, the native word appears only once (Rom. 5:11), the Latinate "reconciliation" being preferred.

The role of vicarious atoning sacrifice is central in the Bible from the story of Cain and Abel (Gen. 4:3-7). It reaches a dramatic climax in the Passover (Exod. 12:21-27) and full cultic development in the Mosaic law (Lev. 1–7), where the term sometimes designates a specific part of the sacrificial ritual — the laying of a hand on the head of the victim (Lev. 1:4), or the burning of the fat (Lev. 4:26) or the blood (Lev. 17:11) — but more typically refers to the whole offering. Thus one reads of "a bullock for a sin offering for atonement" (Exod. 29:36), and there is a recurring expression, "the priest shall make an atonement for him" (Lev. 14:20; "for his sin," Lev. 4:35; "for him for his sin," Lev. 5:10). Outside the cultus atonement resulted from the execution of a murderer (Num. 35:33), an adulterer (Num. 25:13), or the descendants of a sinning king (2 Sam. 21:1-9). Or it might involve payment of money (Exod. 30:11-16). As ritual atonement became increasingly mechanical, the prophets stressed the primacy of the spiritual dimension (Isa. 1:11-17), which was to become exclusive in rabbinic literature following the destruction of the Temple.

The NT's treatment focuses entirely upon the work of Jesus. NT writers draw upon the OT expiatory (John 1:29; Heb. 9:6-14) and substitutionary (Matt. 8:17) language of sacrifice, as well as metaphors of commerce (1 Cor. 6:20), ransom (Mark 10:45), redemption (Eph. 1:7), and propitiation (Rom 5:9). The variety and highly suggestive nature of these figures have allowed radically divergent understandings throughout Christian history. No dogma of the atonement was ever promulgated by the Church, and although broad "ideas" may be identified (cf. Gustaf Aulén, *Christus Victor* [1951], 157-58), these are not always clearly delineated.

Alternative versions of the early "ransom" theory interpret the sacrifice of Jesus as a transaction with the devil, or an "exchange" made possible only by God's identification with humankind in Christ (Origen, *Oratio catechetica magna,* chap. 26), a strategy luring the devil into forfeiting his rights (St. Augustine, *Sermo,* 263.1; cf. *De Trin.* 13.12ff.), or a military victory over him (Fortunatus's *"Vexilla Regis Prodeunt"*). St. Anselm's "satisfaction" theory, set forth in *Cur Deus Homo?* and later elaborated by St. Bernard of Clairvaux and St. Thomas Aquinas (*Summa Theol.* 3.48.1), rejected the implicit dualism of the patristic view and stressed reparation by the offending human party to the rightful Lord. Both Luther (*Romans,* 2.218) and Calvin (*Inst.* 2.12.1; 2.16.1; 4.14.21) stressed the juridical dimension of Jesus' role as humankind's representative, an emphasis taken up in the 20th cent. by Karl Barth (*Church Dogmatics,* 4.1-3). The subjective view, earlier espoused by Peter Abelard and dominating liberal Protestant thought from the Enlightenment to the present, rejects mythological and ontological perspectives and argues instead for the exemplary value of Jesus' sacrifice. "Liberation theology," developed in the context of late 20th-cent. revolutionary ideology, revives the military conception and applies it — at times literally — to social and political structures.

The poetic complementarity of differing theological views is represented in Sonnet 68 of Edmund Spenser's *Amoretti,* "Most glorious Lord of lyfe." The three quatrains treat in succession the military, the expiatory, and the commercial views, while the concluding couplet points to the example: "So let us love, deare love, lyke as we ought, / Love is the lesson which the Lord us taught."

At other times, a single idea of atonement may predominate. Christopher Marlowe's *Doctor Faustus* is a parodic exploration of the commercial and juridical aspects of the ransom theory, epitomized in the blood-sealed "deed of gift of body and of soul" made with Lucifer (2.1.90). In both *Paradise Lost* and *De Doctrina Christiana,* John Milton sets the problem in juridical terms (C. A. Patrides, *Milton and the Christian Tradition* [1966], 130-52), while he stresses the heroic and exemplary in *Paradise Regained,* a song of "Recoverd Paradise to all mankind, / By one mans firm obedience fully tri'd / Through all temptation" (1.3-5). Lyrical poetry often calls for an affective response to shared human suffering, with pathos coming to dominate in such 20th-cent. treatments as Wilfred Owen's depiction of Abram's slaying of "his son, / And half the seed of Europe, one by one" in "The Parable of the Old Man and the Young" or Edith Sitwell's evocation of the bombing of Britain in "Still Falls the Rain."

Affective considerations together with inherent drama may account for the prevalence, throughout the history of English literature, of the view depicting the Savior as a conquering warrior. Set in Germanic terms to describe the "young hero, who was God Almighty" in the *Dream of the Rood,* in the later Middle Ages the idea was translated into the chivalric ideal of the knight, as in *Piers Plowman:* "This Jesus of his gentries wol juste in Piers armes, / In his helm and in his haubergeon — *humana natura*" with "the fend and fals doom to deye" (B.18.21-36). Yet viewing him as the universal human representative against two thousand years of an unrealized ideal, David Gascoyne can still — and in distinctively modern terms — call upon the "Christ of Revolution and of Poetry" to "Redeem our sterile misery, . . . That man's long journey through the night / May not have been in vain" ("Ecce Homo").

See also BLOOD OF THE LAMB; INCARNATION; PASSOVER; REDEMPTION; SCAPEGOAT.

Bibliography. Aulén, G. *Christus Victor: An Historical Study of the Three Main Types of the Idea of the Atonement.* Trans. A. G. Hebert (1935); Bennett, J. A. W. *Poetry of the Passion: Studies in Twelve Centuries of English Verse* (1982); Bromiley, G. W. "Atone." *ISBE* 1.352-60; Brunner, E. *The Mediator* (Eng. trans. 1934); Dinsmore, C. A. *Atonement in Literature and Life* (1906); Grensted, L. W. *A Short History of the Doctrine of the Atonement* (1920); Harpole, R. O. "The Development of the Doctrine of the Atonement in American Thought from Jonathan Edwards to Horace Bushnell." *DA* 27 (1967), 4253A-54A; Kelly, J. N. D. *Early Christian Doctrines* (1958); Patrides, C. A. "Milton and the Protestant Theory of the Atonement." *PMLA* 74 (1959), 7-13; Rashdall, H. *The Idea of Atonement in Christian Theology* (1920); Rivière, J. *Le dogme de la rédemption au début du moyen âge.* Bibliothèque thomiste 19 (1934). ROBERT E. WRIGHT LEON MORRIS

ATONEMENT, DAY OF The fourth of the five annual feasts of pre-exilic Israel, Yom Kippur (Heb. *yom hakkipurim,* "day of the covering over") remains the most important religious festival in modern Judaism. It falls on the tenth day of the seventh month Tishri (Sept./Oct.), nine days after the ancient Feast of Trumpets and five days before the Feast of Tabernacles, or Ingathering, which also precedes it in its institution (Exod. 23:16; cf. 19:1). According to Lev. 25:9, the Year of Jubilee begins with the Day of Atonement, the institution of which, with Aaron as high priest, is described in Lev. 16. (According to rabbinic tradition, this is the same day Moses came down from Mt. Sinai with the second tablets of the Law and announced to the people divine pardon for the sin of the Golden Calf [B. Bat. 21a].)

Celebration of the Day of Atonement involves cessation from all work (it is the "sabbath of sabbaths"), fasting, and abstention from sexual intercourse. The priest was on this day alone to enter into the Holy of Holies — stripped of his golden vestments and attired only in a plain white robe — there to plead before God for the sins of the people. This annual representative confession of sin and the blood sacrifice accompanying it have ceased since the destruction of Jerusalem in A.D. 70, but a form of the Aaronic confession is still recited in the plural, "because of the mutual responsibility of all Jews" (Shebu'. 39a). According to Num. 15:30 the ritual of atonement, which in ancient times included departure of the sin-laden scapegoat (Lev. 16:8-10, 20-22), is ineffectual unless accompanied by sincere repentance (cf. Yoma 8-9). On the eve of Yom Kippur the modern liturgy commences with recitation, usually sung, of the *Kol Nidre,* a formula for the cancellation of unpaid vows and promises. It concludes with the *Neilah,* the service which ends with an invocation of the Shema and exhorting affirmation, "Next year in Jerusalem."

OT references to the celebration post-Torah are rare, though there is adequate testimony (Sir. 50:5ff.; 3 Macc. 1:11; Philo, *De specialibus legibus,* 2.32.193-223; Josephus, *Ant.* 14.4.3; Acts 27:9; Heb. 6:19; 9:7, 13ff.; 10:1ff.) that it had been in continuous observance since Mosaic times.

References to the feast abound in Jewish literature. Occasionally, as in Mordecai Richler's *Joshua Then and Now,* the entire liturgical season is referred to as the "Days of Awe." Howard Nemerov, in the fifth stanza of his poem "Runes," captures the reflection of a modern, restless penitent:

> The fat time of the year is also time
> Of the Atonement; birds to the berry bushes,
> Men to the harvest; a time to answer for
> Both present plenty and emptiness to come.
> When the slain legal deer is salted down,
> When apples smell like goodness, cold in the cellar,
> You hear the ram's horn sounded in the high
> Mount of the Lord, and you lift up your eyes
> As though by this observance you might hide
> The dry hash of an eaten heart which brings
> Nothing to offer rep, no sacrifice
> Acceptable but the cancelled out desires
> And satisfactions of another year's
> Abcess, whose zero in His winter's mercy
> Still hides the undecipherable seed.

"Black fast Yom Kippur" in the curious Jewish-Catholic syncretism of Joyce's Leopold Bloom in *Ulysses* ("Lestrygonians") is associated with the "Black Fasts" in Irish Catholic tradition, Ash Wednesday and Good Friday.

Bibliography. Cohen, H. *Judaism* 17 (1968), 352-57; 18 (1969), 86-90, 216-22; Lepon, E. *The Abarbanel on the Yom Kippur Service in the Beis Hamikdash* (1991); Payne, J. B. *Theology of the Older Testament* (1962).

See also SCAPEGOAT.   ROBERT E. WRIGHT
                                    LEON MORRIS

AZARIAH *See* SHADRACH, MESHACH, AND ABEDNEGO.

— B —

BAAL *Baal* ("Master") is the name or title of a deity found throughout Semitic literature. Originally there was no single god named Baal and the name was used in conjunction with those of a number of specific deities (e.g., Baal-Peor [Num. 25:3, 5]). When used alone, Baal referred usually to a particular, often local, deity. In Hebrew *ba'al* is commonly used to denote "lord" or "possessor," as in the *ba'al* of a house. It is also used in terms denoting a condition or particular attribute, as in *ba'al koah* ("man of strength") or *ba'al shalom* ("man of peace"). But the title was most commonly applied to "the fertility god *par excellence* of Canaan" (J. Gray, *IDB* 1.328), Hadad, about whom there was a large body of mythic lore, as evidenced in the Ras Shamra texts (ca. 1400 B.C.). Baal's consort was Astarte (referred to in the OT often in the plural form Ashtaroth (as in Judg. 2:13; 10:6), and the worship of these deities often involved orgiastic rites repugnant to the Israelite prophets and reformers. Jezebel, Ahab's queen, promoted Baalism in Israel. Ahab is said to have worshiped Baal and set up an altar to him in Samaria (1 Kings 16:31). During his reign the prophet Elijah challenged and defeated the priests of Baal in a contest of fire on Mt. Carmel (1 Kings 18:20-40).

References to Baal are frequent — if often incidental — in English literature. Milton alludes straightforwardly to Baal in connection with the apostasy of ancient Israel in *Paradise Regained* (3.414-17) and with reference to the defeat of pagan gods at the Incarnation in "On the Morning of Christ's Nativity" (197). Swift, in *Window Inns* (10), uses the conceit of someone being "like Baal, fast asleep" (recalling Elijah's satiric taunting on Mt. Carmel [1 Kings 18:27]).

Byron makes frequent reference to Baal, especially in the historical tragedy *Sardanapalus,* where such allusions lend exotic coloring to his sympathetic portrait of pagan culture. Sardanapalus, the king of Assyria, routinely swears oaths "by the god Baal" and speaks reverently of him as guardian of the empire (1.159-60). Baal is spoken of as "father" of Sardanapalus by his subjects (3.28) and by the officer Altada, who remarks that "Baal himself / Ne'er fought more fiercely to win empire, than / His silken son to save it" (3.312-14). Myrrha, a Greek slave and favorite of the king, confesses that she has become "almost a convert to your Baal" (5.48); at the end of the poem she and Sardanapalus immolate themselves on a pyre "before Baal's shrine" (5.421).

Political self-seekers are satirized in Nahum Tate's *Second Part of Absalom and Achitophel* with reference to the apostasy of ancient Israel:

Our *Jews* their Ark shall undisturb'd retain,
At least while their Religion is their Gain,
Who know by old Experience *Baal's* Commands,
Not onely claim'd Their Conscience, but their Lands.
(557-60)

65

Pope likewise attacks dunces, flatterers, pretenders, and tasteless admirers "who, false to Phoebus, bow the knee to Baal" (*The Dunciad*, 4.93; cf. Byron's contemptuous reference to his detractors in *English Bards and Scotch Reviewers:* "Each country book-club bows the knee to Baal").

Unsurprisingly, the priests of Baal are often recalled in the context of religious polemic. As Carlyle's Professor Teufelsdröckh suggests, "There are 'true priests' as well as Baal-priests in our own day" (*Sartor Resartus*, 2.9.154). The Puritan leader Governor Endicott in Hawthorne's *The Maypole of Merry Mount* denounces an Anglican priest, saying, "Stand off, priest of Baal." A different note is struck by Tennyson's Averill in *Aylmer's Field*, when he addresses the congregation on the theme of desolation and hopelessness; in despair he says, "Gash thyself, priest, and honour thy brute Baal" (644), but he is sustained by the thought that there is a "lord in no wise like to Baal" (647). In Tennyson's *Becket* Thomas à Becket complains to King Henry that the church has been slandered and plundered: "The priests of Baal tread her underfoot" (3.3.179).

Shaw recalls the contest on Mt. Carmel in the preface of *Back to Methuselah* when advocating confrontation; "Elijah . . . confuted the prophets of Baal in precisely that way." The notorious character of Baal-worship is alluded to by D. H. Lawrence in *England, My England;* a woman who has become alienated from her husband because of a growing distaste for his sensuality says that she has her "own gods to honour" and asks herself if she could betray them, submitting to "his Baal and Ashtaroth."

See also AHAB; ASHTORETH; JEZEBEL.

Bibliography. Albright, W. F. *Yahweh and the Gods of Canaan: An Historical Analysis of Two Contrasting Faiths* (1968); Habel, N. C. *Yahweh Versus Baal: A Conflict of Religious Cultures* (1964); Gray, J. *The Legacy of Canaan* (1965).   RONALD M. MELDRUM

BABEL Genesis 11:1-9 follows upon an onomastic genealogy (Gen. 10:1-32) of known language groups at the time of the text, tracing their ancestry to the sons of Noah. A sparse etiological narrative, it appears to have two evident purposes: (a) to interpret the name of an alien power, Babylon (Heb. *babel*), and (b) to explain the plurality of languages. It opens with a retrospective imagination of unilingual descendants of Noah moving into new territory. Underscoring their wish to establish their autonomy ("Let us make a name for ourselves," v. 4), it relates how in their pride the people build a monumental tower (*migdol*) and city (*'ir*) in the plain of Shinar. The story concludes with God confounding their language and scattering them over the whole earth.

Babel corresponds to Akk. *Babili/u*, "gate of the god(s)," but Gen. 11:9 explains it by a popular etymology with the Hebrew verb *balal*, "to confuse." The origin of the name itself, neither Sumerian nor Akkadian, is unknown. The tower is sometimes identified with the

great temple of Nabu in the city of Borsippa, now called Birs Nimrud (corruption of Birj Nimrud, "tower of Nimrod"), following early conflations with Nimrod, the descendant of Ham, whose kingdom is said to be Babel in Gen. 10:8-10 (*ISBE* 1.382; *TDOT* 1.466-67). Penultimate among the "primeval" narratives in Genesis, the Tower of Babel nonetheless marks the end of a road upon which humankind set out after Eden, eastward before the watchful angel with its flaming sword. In itself, the story "ends without grace" (cf. G. von Rad, *Old Testament Theology* [1962], 1.163-64), thus requiring a new beginning — the call of Abraham in Gen. 12:1-3.

Traditions of Jewish Haggadah, early and late, add new elements and motifs to the Babel story which depend upon the association with Nimrod, who is characterized both as a rebel (his name means "we will revolt" [Keil, C. F., and F. Delitzsch, *Comm. on the Old Testament*, 1.165] and a "hunter before the LORD" (Gen. 10:9: Sepher Hayyashar; Pirqe R. El., chap. 24; Sanh. 109a; A. Jellinek, *Beth-Hamidrash*, 3.46). He builds the tower because he fears another flood as well as the prospect of "scattering," but also because he wants vengeance. Here the idea of ascent into heaven is first introduced, with Nimrod desiring to open the firmament with axes so that it might never again build up a reservoir, to make war in vengeance against God and the angels, to set up his own idols in heaven, and to assure himself fame and permanent rule of the world. In various Jewish accounts the tower's height is given as 4 miles, 70 miles, and 10,000 miles. Ginzberg reports a certain whimsy in some of these accounts (*LJ*, 1.179; 7.202-03), following one Targum (Ecclus. 7:28): "When one considers the extraordinary dimensions, one marvels at the rapid progress of the building." It is less the issue of language which occupies this body of commentary than the consequences of disobedience. Josephus (*Ant.* 1.4.1) thinks that the sin of the people consisted in their disobeying God's repeated command to "fill the earth" in colonies. In another midrash, it is said that "whoever passes the tower forgets all he knows" (Ginzberg, *LJ* 1.179), an idea which may be reflected in the hermetic philosopher Robert Fludd's chapter on "spiritual memorizing" called *Ars Memoriae* (*Historia*, 2.2.48-49), in which the Tower of Babel is pictured as one of five memory loci (cf. F. Yates, *Art of Memory* [1966], 315). The story is regularly advanced as integral to post-Edenic diminishment of human glory and potential; the linguistic fragmentation acquires graphic physical analogues. Midr. 'Aggadah Gen. 11:8 says that when the tower fell some of the confounded were thrown into the water, some into the forest, others into the desert, becoming respectively water sprites, apes, and demons. This may be a precedent for St. Augustine, who adds a discourse on monstrous humanoids to his discussion of the tower (*De civ. Dei* 16.8). *Mandeville's Travels* (1.9.25-26) still has it that no one dares travel nearby for fear of the desert full of dragons and serpents.

Augustine's commentary (*De civ. Dei* 16.4-6) begins with a full citation of the Genesis passage, translating Babel / Babylon as "confusion." Furthering the connection to Nimrod, he also adheres to the adversary theory. Ambiguity in the LXX rendering *enantion* (both "before" and "against"), and a precedent in Job 15:13, lead him, like Jewish commentators earlier, to read Nimrod as a hunter "against" the Lord, whose hunting is a figure for "destruction of the animals," i.e., creation. In another influential passage (*De civ. Dei* 16.3), Augustine draws on a pre-Vg Latin text of Gen. 10:8-12 — which has *gigans* rather than *potens* in vv. 8-9; Nimrod becomes, thus, a "giant." Resisting St. Jerome's linguistic imagination that "Hebrew is the matrix of all languages" (Jerome, *Ep.* 46), Augustine locates the central value of the Babel story in the dialectic of pride and humility: it is fitting irony that "man, who would not understand God when he issued his commands, should be misunderstood when he himself gave orders" (16.6). Echoing the midrash that Nimrod's motive may have been unwarranted apprehension of another flood, Augustine, in his homilies on the Gospel of John, refers the fragmentation of the proud tower toward a recollection in Christ: "If pride caused diversities of tongues, Christ's humility has unified these diversities in one" (6.10). This idea is rooted in his view that Pentecost, with its reuniting of disparate communities in the hearing of the gospel, composes an answer to Babel's confusion — much as the subsequent story of Jacob at Bethel (Gen. 28:10-19) offers a response in the immediate narrative.

By the 9th cent., an additional tradition regarding Nimrod, Eastern in origin, was current in western Europe. It derived in part from the *Liber Nimrod,* the Latin translation of a Syriac mythological and astronomical handbook which was cast in the form of a dialogue between the astronomer Nimrod and his disciple Ioanton. The notion that Nimrod was an astronomer had already appeared in the West, notably in the *Itinerary of St. Clement,* which, despite condemnation by Eusebius and others, was used by St. Gregory the Great, St. Isidore of Seville, the Venerable Bede, Rabanus Maurus, Hugh of St. Victor, and Vincent of Beauvais. In this work Nimrod is said to have been of the seventeenth generation since Adam, a king of Babylon, who then moved to Persia, where he taught the natives to worship fire and signs in the heavens. (This idolatry helped bring about the judgment of the Flood.) Nimrod was also a magician who drew sparks from the stars in order to win esteem for himself, and obtained thus the name Zoroaster ("living star"). The 9th-cent. *Revelationes* spuriously attributed to St. Methodius make Nimrod's disciple Ioanton a fourth son of Noah. The important *Historia Scholastica* of Peter Comestor gathers in the Eastern as well as Western traditions, as later does Nicholas of Lyra's 14th-cent. *Postilla super Totam Bibliam,* 1.26-27.

In his *Etymologiae* (7.6.22; 15.1.4), Isidore of Seville reflected the more familiar Western tradition: "Nimrod is to be interpreted as a tyrant . . . opposing God," the original "giant of Babylon" lusting after fame; such views are commonly reiterated in works such as Bede's *Hexaemeron* or vernacular compendia such as the OE *Genesis* A (1649-1701) and *Cursor Mundi* (1.2199-2304 = *Southern Version*, 1.2199-2312). But in his commentary on Genesis, Isidore takes up the Babel folly itself and laments the consequence — a loss in language of an essential bond uniting a thing and its name since creation. The languages created at Babel are arbitrary; though the human species is still *homo loquens*, language has now become ambiguous. The language theme, uniting discussion of the seventy-two language groups apparently indicated in the genealogies of Gen. 10 with the tower narrative, developed especially in the 12th through 16th cents. an enormous literature (see Borst, *Der Turmbau von Babel*), most of which is concerned with the question of ur-languages and the relation of pride to confusion of tongues. In this tradition, Nimrod can be associated with *gigas super terram,* "giants in the earth" *(Glossa Ordinaria), gigas Sathanas,* Satan (P. Riga, *Aurora,* 1.691), or the Antichrist, and there is a general notion, reflected in works as apparently diverse as Aelfric's homilies (*Catholic Homilies,* 1.22; 1.318; 2.198; 2.472), Pope Innocent's *De Contemptu Mundi* (2.32), and Wolfram von Eschenbach's *Parzival* (K. Lachmann, 399.18-19) that the fragmentation of human speech signifies a deepening intellectual darkness in the fallen world (cf. Dante, *Paradiso,* 26.109-38). Humankind is no longer capable of maintaining a right relation between knowing subject and known object which the original gift of language made possible.

Dante begins his tour of Inferno in a cacophany of *diverse lingue* (3.22-30), seeking, with Virgil's aid, to bypass the babble of Nimrod (31.77) and transcend it. Virgil, however, mirroring Dante's teacher Brunetto Latini (*Tresor,* 1.24), resents Nimrod's forfeit of *un linguaggio.* Chaucer, in his "Former Age," links Nimrod, "desirous to regne," with Jupiter, the god who overthrew his monarch father and thus precipitated the demise of the Saturnian Golden Age.

St. Thomas took a more optimistic turn, reflecting St. Augustine in moving toward an antithesis in Pentecost and, with it, remedial transmission of the gospel to counter Babel's effects (*Summa Theol.* 1.24.1; 2.2.176; 3.7.7; 2.1.51.4). This is the spirit of Erasmus's reaction as well: he finds the plurality of language a mere fact of nature and not a theological problem. In Methodius's history (Trevisa, *Dialogus,* 96.2-10), the division of languages is not even discussed. St. Thomas More, like Luther, reverts to the issue of language; he suggests that Latin might now, as sanctified holy speech, become a universal language, while Luther, content with the plurality, is happy simply to identify *'ashkenaz* (Gen. 10:3) with his own German tongue. He dismisses the speculations concerning Nimrod and his motives as non-biblical, urging that the central point of the story is to prove that "unto Heaven Christ alone is the true builder" (*Works*, 14.208-17). Tyndale calls those who oppose translation of the Bible "stubborn Nimrods who fight God and strive against his Holy Spirit" (pref. to *Obedience of a Christian Man*), and this movement toward metonymy is also explicit in Calvin: Nimrod stands for tyranny; his tower is tyranny's monument. Josephus's notion that he built for fear of another flood is, according to Calvin, "unalloyed fantasy"; the story is a fable to describe "fragmentation in the history of humankind" (*Comm. on Genesis*, 11:1; *Acta Apostolorum*, 2.2-3). Thomas Elyot's *Boke named the Governour* (1531) ignores Nimrod altogether in using the Babel story to appeal for the study of language and improvement of English. By the middle of the next century, members of the Royal Society would inquire seriously after a "Universal Character," a language which would make amends to humankind for what their pride lost them in the Tower of Babel (R. Boyle, *Works*, 1.22).

The development of the tower narrative in English literature is erratic but colorful. It is altogether absent from the cycle plays, presumably because of its lack of liturgical import. Nimrod, however, is one of the imprisoned proud tyrants in Spenser's *Faerie Queene* (1.5.48.1; cf. Dante, *Inferno*, 31.77). John Donne has one clichéd reference to Nimrod's vain presumption in "The Second Anniversary" (417). But with an eye on the language motif he creates an eerily brilliant character, his Mephistophelian accuser of "Satire 4" who "speaks all tongues" yet "one language," insinuating: ". . . Nay, your apostles were / pretty linguists, and so Panurge was. . . ." Following this reference to Rabelais's babylonian mischief (*Works*, 2.9), the strange petitioner

> . . . such wonders told
> That I was fain to say, "If you had lived, Sir,
> Time enough to have been an interpreter
> To Babel's bricklayers, sure the Tower had stood."
> (26-29; 58-59; 62-65)

For Herbert, on the other hand, Babel recollects the old adversity of invention and creation, inviting penance for a shared folly ("Sin's Round").

Milton's Nimrod (*Paradise Lost*, 12.24-62) is a subverter of "fair equality, fraternal state," who arrogates "dominion undeserved over his brethren" — a hunter not of beasts but of people who refuse his domination. His tower, built at the "mouth of Hell" as a monument of fame, becomes an object of divine ridicule, aptly reduced to "Confusion." For Dryden, Babel images the schismatic dissenting churches (*The Hind and the Panther*, 2.470); in Swift's poetry it suggests confusion in politics and the state — "Confounded in that Babel of the Pit" ("To Congreve," 122; cf. "V's House," 66; "Death of Dr. Swift," 384). William Cowper's view of the calamity in *The Task*,

by contrast, is, like Herbert's, sympathetic and imaginative of grace:

> When Babel was confounded, and the great
> Confed'racy of projectors wild and fain
> Was split into a diversity of tongues,
> Then, as a shepherd separates his flock,
> God drave asunder . . .
> . . . Ample was the boon
> He gave them, in its distribution fair
> And equal. (5.193-200)

He notes that the peace did not last, and that the tradition of Cain and Tubal-cain, "first artificers of death," was to continue in invention and war (208-29).

Blake's Vala, in crucifixion imagery drawn from Ps. 22, describes being let down from the gates of Jerusalem (*Jerusalem*, 1.22.2-8) by Nimrod, "Jehovah's hunter." This arresting inversion finds analogues in the Romantics. The Byronic hero can shout, "Well done, old Babel! Ha, right nobly battled!" ("Deformed," 2.266; cf. 2.81; 1.677), and Byron himself fancies Nimrod as a romantic lover (*Don Juan*, 13.78). Keats's Otho will feast "nobly as Nimrod's masons" (2.1.132).

Wordsworth, typically, is more traditional: "Go back to antique ages" makes of the Tower of Babel what Chaucer did of Nimrod in his "Former Age"; in the *Prelude*, the young French Republic, "how Babel-like their task . . . by the recent deluge stupefied," promises its citizens "to build a tower / For their own safety" (11.35-40). Elizabeth Browning makes a sentimental allusion to the notion of Babel as a painful separation of friends ("Victoire," 5; cf. *Aurora Leigh*, 5.554), while her husband forges an almost despairing resignation in his tragedy *The Return of the Druses:* "All great works in this world spring from the ruins / Of greater projects — ever, on our earth, / Babels men block out, Babylons they build" (4.128-30).

In American literature of the period Melville's remembrance is merely cynical (*Piazza Tales*, 253), but Hawthorne is more subtly ironic when, in *The Marble Faun*, Miriam at the palace of the Virgin's Shrine in Rome begins "to mount flight after flight of a staircase, which, for the loftiness of its aspiration, was worthy to be Jacob's ladder or, at all events, the staircase of the Tower of Babel." Anna Hempstead Branch's *Nimrod* (1910) is a narrative poem based on the rebellion of Nimrod and his building of the tower in defiance of God.

James Joyce offers in *Finnegans Wake* "a tour of Bibel," the pun proposing an alternate Scripture even as it invokes the tower. But Robert Frost's less certain Jonah will later imagine an appropriate destruction for unrepentant New York:

> Babel: everyone developing
> A language of his own to write his book in,
> And one to cap the climax by combining

All language in a one-man tongue confusion. (*Masque of Mercy,* 620.13-16)

This sobriety, at once reflective and prophetic, quietly anticipates Orwell's *1984* as well as C. S. Lewis's coven of scientists at the fortress of Belbury, where "Babble about the *élan vital* and flirtations with panpsychism were . . . dragging up from its shallow and unquiet grave the old dream of Man as a God" (*That Hideous Strength,* chap. 9). Tolkien's dark towers, Minas Morgul and Orthanc, in *The Two Towers* echo a post–World War II uneasiness over the specter of technology unhinged from ethics which, for Tolkien, has also its linguistic dimension in the fragmentation and diminishment of poetic "elven" language. While the emphasis on pride and social fragmentation continues to be reflected in Morris West's *Tower of Babel* and William Golding's *The Spire,* it may be that the most profound echoes of Babel in the modern literary imagination, whether in nostalgia or apprehension about the future, have to do with a sense of diminished power of the word. Theodore Roethke puts an old question in contemporary accents:

Among us, who is holy?
What speech abides? . . .
For the world invades me again,
And once more the tongues begin babbling. ("Abyss,"
2.8-9, 14-15)

See also BABYLON; EAST, EAST OF EDEN; PENTECOST.

Bibliography. Borst, A. *Der Turmbau von Babel: Geschichte der Meinungen über Ursprung und Vielfaldt der Sprachen und Volker.* 3 vols. (1957-60); Céard, J. "De Babel à la Pentecôte: La transformation du mythe de la confusion de langues au XVIe siècle." *Bibliothèque d'Humanisme et Renaissance* 42 (1980), 577-94; Dean, J. "The World Grown Old and Genesis in Middle English Historical Writings." *Speculum* 57 (1982), 548-68; Lemay, R. "Le Nimrod de l'enfer de Dante et le *Liber Nemroth.*" *SD* 40 (1963), 57-128; Livesey, S. J., and R. H. House. "Nimrod the Astronomer." *Traditio* 37 (1981), 203-66; Rappoport, A. S. *Myth and Legend of Ancient Israel.* 2 vols. (1966).

BABYLON In the OT *Babylon* is a magnificent, sinful, pagan, and prideful city-state upon the Euphrates in the land of Chaldea (Shinar). Gen. 10:8-10 mentions the founding of Babylon, or Babel, by the "mighty hunter" Nimrod, and in Gen. 11:1-9 the proud Babylonians are building their "tower, whose top may reach the heavens." 2 Kings 24–25 chronicles the wars of Babylon's Nebuchadnezzar upon Israel, wars which resulted first in Jerusalem's subjugation and the exile to Babylon of its leading citizens (whence the so-called "Babylonian exile" of the popes to Avignon, 1307-77), and ultimately in Jerusalem's destruction.

The wars with mighty Babylon are at the heart of repeated condemnations of the city by Jeremiah, Isaiah, and Ezekiel, and of their prophecies of its catastrophic demise and Jerusalem's deliverance. Isaiah prophesies

that "Babylon, the glory of kingdoms . . . shall be as when God overthrew Sodom and Gomorrah" (Isa. 13:19; cf. 21:1-10). Jeremiah is equally vivid: Babylon "shall become heaps, a dwelling place for dragons, an astonishment and a hissing, without an inhabitant" (Jer. 51:37; cf. chaps. 50–51).

Where Babylon is mentioned in the NT, Rome, the "new Babylon," is usually intended. Certainly this interpretation was a commonplace from St. Victorinus to the marginal glosses of the Geneva Bible. Babylon could also be used to stand for earthly power and moral decadence in the last days. For John, Babylon is "the great whore" (Rev. 19:2), a city in which merchants peddle "gold, and silver . . . and chariots, and slaves, and souls of men" (Rev. 18:10-13). This Babylon will be cast down and utterly destroyed in the last days (Rev. 18).

For St. Augustine the Babylonian captivity is "our captivity," Israel's deliverance "our deliverance." Jerusalem and Babylon are to be contrasted, the "vision of peace" vs. "confusion." (For Augustine, this contrast was rooted in the etymology of their respective names; the popular meaning of Babel, and hence for Babylon — sanctioned in Gen. 11:9 — was accepted generally; cf. St. Isidore of Seville, *Etymologiae,* 15.1.4.) Augustine associates the two cities with two loves — the love of God, or charity, with Jerusalem and the love of the world, cupidity, with Babylon. Drawing on the experience of the captive Hebrews, he argues that one can be a true citizen of Jerusalem even while a captive sojourning in Babylon (cf. *De civ. Dei,* esp. bk. 14). Rabanus Maurus (PL 112.872) elaborates this typology, providing a whole set of allegorical equivalences: Babylon is the "evil city" and so Jer. 51:6 ("flee out of the midst of Babylon") can be taken to mean "condemn and forsake immorality"; Babylon can represent hell, the world, the impious, sin, and even, recalling 1 Pet. 5:13, the Gentile church. In his commentary on Ezek. 3:10-11, St. Gregory says that the journey from Jerusalem to Babylon is the soul's descent from righteousness to evil (*Homiliarum in Ezechielem* [PL 76.894]).

These traditions are carried over into English literature. In the ME poem *Cleanness* Babylon is an exemplum of pride and worldly grandeur brought low, while after the Reformation Babylon was an oft-hurled barb in sectarian debate: "By Babylon we understand the church of Rome," says Richard Hooker confidently (*Sermons,* 2.10), reflecting a well-established connection (cf. Luther's *Babylonian Captivity of the Church*). Had his allegiances been otherwise, he might, along with certain Puritans, have understood the Church of England. David Austin's *Downfall of Mystical Babylon* (1794) is an American variation, in which the author of *The Rod of Moses upon the Rock of Calvary* (1816) attempts to establish connections between Protestant typology and Masonic symbolism.

In less polemical contexts Babylon is frequently

recalled as a place of wealth (Chaucer, *Book of the Duchess,* 1061), worldly renown (Pope, "Temple of Fame," 64), and sin (Herbert, "Church Militant," 103). F. Scott Fitzgerald's "Babylon Revisited" makes use of a wide range of these traditions: his protagonist Charlie has left America, with its work ethic and related values, to go to Paris to live the gaudy life in the years before the stock market crash of '29. There he squanders his wealth, his wife, and his daughter. In remorseful memory, Charlie's return to Paris, now depression Paris, Babylon after its fall, is also a return to his Babylonian state of mind. The power of Babylon figuratively to entrap its habitual denizens is well illustrated by Jorge Luis Borges's short story "The Lottery in Babylon," a dispassionate narration of life in a Dantean hell of random fortune and terror.

See also BABEL; EXILE AND PILGRIMAGE; NEBUCHAD-NEZZAR; RIVERS OF BABYLON; WHORE OF BABYLON.

Bibliography. Christianson, P. *Reformers and Babylon* (1978).   H. DAVID BRUMBLE

BABYLONIAN EXILE / CAPTIVITY   Biblically, this term refers to the fall of Samaria, or the northern kingdom (722 B.C.), and of Jerusalem, or Judah (586 B.C.), and subsequent imprisonment and deportation, largely to Babylon, of a substantial proportion of the people. Extra-biblically, it is applied consistently with Christian spiritual readings of the OT to characterize spiritually analogous events in Christian history. The most famous medieval example is the exile of the Popes and Cardinals at Avignon from 1309 to 1377, referred to by Petrarch, Wyclif, and others as the "Babylonian Captivity" of their day.

See also BABYLON.

BACA, VALLEY OF   The Baca valley in Lebanon, evidently a route used by worshipers heading to Jerusalem, is referred to in one of the pilgrim Psalms of Ascent: "Blessed is the man whose strength is in thee; in whose heart are the ways of them. Who passing through the valley of Baca make it a well; the rain also filleth the pools" (Ps. 84:5-6). The Hebrew word apparently derives from a root which means "to weep," leading St. Jerome to translate the phrase "valley of Baca" as "vale of tears" (*Ep.* 22.10) or "vale of weeping" (*Ep.* 130.16). The origin of the name may in fact lie in the balsam tree which flourishes there, and the gum it exudes. Wyclif follows Jerome's translation, *in valle lacrymarum* (Vg); hence also the Wycliffite Bible: "In the vale of teris," which seems to yield up the conventional usage signifying "this present world of sorrow and want." (The KJV preserves "valley of Baca"; the RV makes it "of weeping" and refers to the balsam trees in a marginal note; the *Book of Common Prayer,* employing Coverdale's translation, has "vale of misery.")

Sir Walter Scott follows the KJV in *Ivanhoe,* where Rebecca's Norman abductor, lascivious designs all too apparent, taunts her: "But know, bright lily of the vale of Baca! that thy father is already in the hands of a powerful alchemist" (chap. 24); in *Kenilworth* Janet buys for the Countess a series of books whose titles are suggestively religious, including *A Draught of Water from the Valley of Baca* (chap. 22). Anthony Trollope's *Framley Parsonage* adopts the proverbial usage: "Henceforth let him take a lantern in his hand, and look warily to his path, and walk cautiously among the thorns and rocks — cautiously, yet boldly, with manly courage, but Christian meekness, as all men should walk on their pilgrimage through this vale of tears" (chap. 15). In "Hazel Blossoms" John Greenleaf Whittier reflects contemporary interest in the geography and archeology of biblical lands (large supplements of such material were printed in 19th-cent. American Bibles) in his suggestion that the valley was especially dry:

> O Love! the hazel wand may fail,
>   But thou canst lead the surer spell,
> That, passing over Baca's vale,
>   Repeats the old-time miracle,
> And makes the desert-land a well.

BALAAM   The oracles of the Amorite soothsayer Balaam, the son of Beor, date in their written form perhaps from the time of David and in their oral form from possibly even earlier. The later Balaam narrative (Num. 22:1–24:25), which has been praised for its "harmony of theological argument and narrative art" (R. Alter, *Art of Biblical Narrative* [1981], 107), incorporates the oracles in a story mixing history and folklore motifs. Summoned by Balak, king of Moab, to curse Israel, Balaam, while riding on an ass, was confronted by an armed angel whom he recognized only after being rebuked by his ass for ill treatment. Still intent on serving Balak, Balaam instead became the unwilling instrument of the Lord when, on three attempts to curse Israel, he pronounced blessings and prophesied Israel's future victories over Moab and Edom. Balaam, who was killed in Israel's war against Midian (Num. 31:8), is also mentioned in negative contexts in later OT references (Deut. 23:4-5; Josh. 13:22 and 24:9-10; Neh. 13:2; Mic. 6:5). In the NT, Balaam is seen as the prototype of those heretics in the early Church who practiced and advocated a permissive morality (2 Pet. 2:16; Jude 11; Rev. 2:14).

Although in some Haggadot Balaam is considered an important non-Jewish prophet (Num. Rab. 20.1), generally in Jewish tradition he is denounced as a sorcerer and condemned for advising the Midianite women to seduce the young men of Israel. Only briefly mentioned in the scriptural account (Num. 31:16), Balaam's role in the seduction of Israel is particularly developed by Josephus, who notes that although he was prevented from cursing Israel, Balaam gave advice that "well-nigh corrupted the whole multitude of the Hebrews . . ." (*Ant.* 4.6.13). Christian tradition similarly developed Balaam's responsibility for the seduction of Israel (OE *Genesis* and *Exodus*), and exegetes associated him with both Simon Magus and Antichrist (G. von Reichersberg, *De Investigatione Antichristi*, 1.4).

Since most Christian commentary also interpreted Balaam's oracle concerning the star to arise from Jacob (Num. 24:17) as a prophecy of Christ, the portrayal of Balaam in medieval literature is mixed. In the Old French *Mistère du Viel Testament*, e.g., he both calls on devils (26717) and prophesies the birth of Christ (27007-10). As a prophet of Christ he plays a crucial role in the Latin *Ordo Prophetarum* and the Benediktbeuern Christmas play, in which he appears on stage riding on his ass. The most developed account of Balaam in English literature is the fifth pageant of the Chester mystery cycle, which portrays Balak as a ranting tyrant and Balaam as both unwitting prophet and villain. The play links the OT pageants to the nativity story by providing both a type of Herod and a prophecy about the coming of Jesus. Sir Balaam, the main character in Pope's *Epistle to Bathhurst,* is a parodic Job figure tempted by the devil with riches rather than poverty, who at the end of his life "curses God, and dies." Although later literature alludes to the story of Balaam's ass, the only developed treatment of the Balaam story is Charles Davy's "Balaam: An Attempt Towards an Oratorio" (1769).

Bibliography. Albright, W. F. "The Oracles of Balaam." *JBL* 63 (1944), 207-33; Young, K. *The Drama of the Medieval Church.* 2 vols. (1933).   RICHARD K. EMMERSON

BALAAM'S ASS   *See* ASS; BALAAM.

BALAK, KING OF MOAB   *See* BALAAM.

BALM OF GILEAD   *Balm of Gilead* is popularly conceived as something which is healing or soothing, especially to the mind, temper, or spirit. Ṣori, the Hebrew word for "balm," is at one level simply a generic name for resins issuing from trees. Derived from an unused root meaning "to flow as a vein or wound with blood," it describes the process by which the gum is collected. However, read with John 19:24, this word also has christological implications which color later readings and uses of the term. *Gilead* is even more complicated etymologically. Descriptive of the terrain, *gil'adh* means simply "rocky" or "rugged." The significance of the word is compounded, though, by the folk etymology given in Gen. 31:47 where Jacob marks his treaty with Laban by a rock pile which he names *Galeed* or "heap of witnesses." This wordplay retains the radical letters of the original name, but slightly alters the pronunciation by joining *gal* ("heap") with *'ed* ("witnesses") to give the name a spiritual as well as a geographical value.

Such adaptability of designation is often demonstrated by the name *Gilead*. Given to a mountain (Gen. 31:25), a country (1 Kings 4:19), a city (Hos. 6:8), a person (Num. 26:29), and the personification of a community (Judg. 11:1-2), it is an accommodating term, referring generally to the central region east of the Jordan. Such flexibility is also seen in the area's moral signification. On the one hand, it is an area of valuable spices and rich pasturage (Num. 32:1), a place of promise (Mic. 7:14), and the home of a prophet (1 Kings 17:1); however, it is also a place of war (1 Kings 22; 2 Kings 10:32-33), iniquity (Hos. 12:11), and brutality (Amos 1:13). Though most literary references to Gilead emphasize its positive associations, in some works, such as Margaret Atwood's *The Handmaid's Tale,* which is set in Gilead, this negative aspect comes to the fore and inverts the conventional allusion, presenting a state which is anything but healthful or soothing.

Little is known about the actual "balm of Gilead." From the references to ṣori in the Bible, all that is certain is that it was valuable as a commodity, a gift, and a medicine, and that by the time of Jeremiah it had acquired a proverbial usage. Occurring twice in Genesis, balm first appears among the wares carried by the Ishmaelite traders to whom Joseph is sold. Listed with "spicery . . . and myrrh," it is taken from Gilead to Egypt for trade (Gen. 37:25). That Egypt had an active market for this substance is reinforced by the second appearance of ṣori when Jacob sends his sons into that country with a gift "of the best fruits in the land . . . a little balm, and a little honey, spices, and myrrh, nuts and almonds" (Gen. 43:11). Over a thousand years later, Ezekiel again mentions the value of this balm when, listing products traded in the markets of Tyre, he includes "wheat . . . and honey, and oil, and balm" (27:17). It is not until Jeremiah's repeated use of the phrase as a symbol for healing and relief from national and spiritual distress that its medicinal qualities are indicated in Scripture. He holds up the balm of Gilead as a possible solution which is not realized: "Is there no balm in Gilead? Is there no physician there? Why then is not the health of the daughter of my people recovered?" (cf. 46:11; 51:8-9). For Jeremiah, the balm itself, physical or symbolic, is insufficient for a cure; it must be willingly, actively, and spiritually received and applied to be effective.

Most scholars in the Jewish tradition are little concerned with a precise botanical identification of the balm. Frequently taking ṣori to be simply one of many names for balsam, they consider it with the biblical *bośem, beśem,* and *naṭap* and the rabbinical *kaṭap, appobalsamon* and *aparsemon*. Commenting on Gen. 37:25, Rashi defines balm as "a resin that exudes from the wood of the balsam tree" and equates it with the *naṭap* "that is enumerated among the ingredients of the incense used in the Tabernacle" (Exod. 30:34; cf. Ker. 6a). Drawing on Gen. Rab. 84.16, he links the balm with "the reward of the righteous." R. Tafon gives a similar reading to clarify Ps. 37:28. For him, the presence of the balm is comforting, for it argues that "If at a time that the righteous incur anger

71

they find compassion, how much more so when mercy is due" (Tanḥuma Yelammedenu Wayyesheb 14).

Commentary on the second Genesis passage incorporates other biblical texts and interprets Gen. 43:11 in terms of the sacred books of Judaism, equating the "balm in Gilead" with the Torah (Tanḥuma Yelammedenu Miqqetz 17). As substance and blessing, this same balm is to be the part of the reward of the righteous, for in the world to come they "will bathe in thirteen rivers of Balsam" ('Abod. Zar. 3.1, 42c).

The balm is understood morally in the explication of Prov. 3:34 in Yoma 38b-39a where

Resh Laqish said: What is the meaning of: If it concerneth the scorners He scorneth them, but unto the humble He giveth grace? i.e., if a man comes to defile himself, the doors are opened to him, but if he comes to purify himself, he is helped. In the school of R. Ishmael it was taught: It is as when a man sells naphtha and balm: If [a purchaser] comes to measure naphtha, he [the shopkeeper] says to him: Measure it out for yourself; but to one who would measure out balm he says: Wait, till I measure together with you, so that both you and I may become perfumed.

Other sources speak of pleasant-smelling balm being used perversely: Lamentations Rabbah records that a prostitute "would place the balsam between her and her shoe and, when she saw a band of young men, she pressed upon it so that the perfume seeped through them like snake poison" (4.18). Though containing this potential for corruption, "balm of Gilead" is customarily a positive image in Jewish tradition, being not only a type of mercy, spiritual blessing, and divine providence on this earth, but a part of the blessedness of 'olam haba, the world to come.

Balm of Gilead is a late entry into Christian typology. Little attention is given to it by the Church Fathers, and the Reformers deal with it in a cursory fashion. Calvin, e.g., notes the original Hebrew term and discusses its literal nature (Comm. on Jeremiah, 1.455). He then explicates Jer. 8:22 in terms of the historical situation. At no time, however, does he suggest a symbolic or christological value for the phrase. This connection is only made later, as in Matthew Henry's Comm. on the Whole Bible, where he provides an affirmative and definite response to the questions of Jer. 8:22: "Yes . . . God is able to help and heal them. . . . They had among themselves God's law and his prophets, with the help of which they might have been brought to repentance. . . ." That healing was not forthcoming, Henry explains: "This verse . . . lay[s] all the blame of the incurableness of their diseases upon themselves. . . . Gilead was a place in their own land, not far off. . . . The physician and physic were both ready, but the patient was wilful. . . ." He goes on to specify the spiritual nature of both the cure and the dilemma: "The blood of Christ is balm in Gilead, his Spirit is the Physician there, both sufficient, all-sufficient, so that they might have been healed, but would not." Similar spiritual value is given to the phrase by John Wesley, but with an added social dimension. In his sermon "Causes for the Inefficacy of Christianity," he declares: "Christianity . . . [is] the balm, the outward means, which the great Physician has given to men, to restore their spiritual health" (116.1). Lamenting the spiritual state of Methodists, he calls for a renewed joining of doctrine with discipline so that Christians might be an effectual "balm" to the world, practicing Christian self-denial and caring for the poor.

Anne Steele, in her hymn "Deep Are the Wounds Which Sin Has Made," offers as a cure to the sinner the "sovereign balm," "the Saviour's dying blood," in which "Life, health, and bliss abundant flow." Similar typology is evidenced in the African-American spiritual "There Is a Balm in Gilead," which speaks to both individual discouragement and personal mission, proclaiming a gracious deliverance from oppression and sufferings: through the "balm in Gilead," the soul can be revived, the gospel can be preached, the wounded can be made whole, and the "sin-sick soul" can be healed.

In British literature, the phrase is often suggested by the word balm alone. Stripped of its overtly biblical context, balm can convey something soothing to the mind by focusing largely on earthly remedies rather than spiritual cures. By far the most common balm put forth in the Renaissance is sleep:

Sleep that knits up the ravell'd sleave of care,
The death of each day's life, sore labour's bath,
Balm of hurt minds, great nature's second course,
Chief nourisher in life's feast — . (Macbeth, 2.2.36-39)

Sidney emphasizes the democratic nature of this "certain knot of peace," calling it "the balm of woe, / The poor man's wealth, the prisoner's release, / The indifferent judge between the high and low" ("Astrophel and Stella," 39.1-4). Shakespeare recalls the theological tradition with a conventional reference to regal benevolence: King Henry, speaking of his relationship with his underlings, declares: "My pity hath been balm to heal their wounds, / My mildness hath allay'd their swelling griefs, / My mercy dried their water-flowing tears" (3 Henry 6, 4.8.41-43). Donne, in The First Anniversary, adapts the same tradition less conventionally as an extravagant compliment to Elizabeth Drury:

. . . it be too late to succor thee,
Sick world, yea, dead, yea putrefied, since she,
Thy intrinsic balm and thy preservative,
Can never be renewed. . . . (55-58)

Later writers, particularly the Romantics, make much of "that delicious hour of balm, / Stillness, solitude, and calm" (Wordsworth, The Waggoner, 4.238) which comes with peace and the despair which exists without it. Closest to the biblical sources and later Christian exegesis is

Blake. In *Jerusalem,* he uses the image of Gilead to great advantage as he bewails judgment in the land:

> The mountain of blessing is itself a curse and an astonishment
> . . . I walk like a lost sheep
> Among precipices of despair: in Goshen I seek for light
> In vain: and in Gilead for a physician and a comforter
> . . . Gilead hath joined with Og! (79.7, 10-13)

Elsewhere, he gives a pithy summary of humanity's relationship with God as he understands it: "First God Almighty comes with a Thump on the Head. Then Jesus Christ comes with a balm to heal it" ("A Vision of the Last Judgment," 94). Coleridge also sees these two aspects of God: ". . . ere thy righteous vengeance strikes the wound, / Thy grace prepares the balm divine!" ("The Tears of a Grateful People," 87-88). As well, he knows "the renovating wells of love" which are "To sickly Nature more medicinal / Than what soft balm the weeping good man pours / Into the lone despoiled traveller's wounds" ("Religious Musings," 83, 85-87). Shelley speaks directly to the "Sacred Peace" to intervene and by "pitying shed / One drop of balm upon my withered soul" ("Queen Mab," 3.72-74). Keats rounds out the potential appeal of balm as an image by equating it with "Sweet Hope" ("To Hope," 5), the "sovereign power of love" ("Endymion," 2.1), and "truth" ("Hyperion," 2.243).

In American literature the complete phrase is often retained, and its biblical associations therefore remain evident, however ironically treated. In "Old King Cole," E. A. Robinson's use of the expression apparently conveys simple, poignant sorrow: the old King, lamenting his wayward sons, comments that "For grief like mine there is no balm / in Gilead, or in Tilbury Town" (67-68). This phrase is complicated, though, by an implied christological connection between the King and the "One whom you may forget . . . [who has] meat you know not of" (75-76). In Poe's "The Raven" a desperate speaker cries out for hope, but does so to a "thing of evil": "Desolate yet all undaunted — on this desert land enchanted — / Or this home by Horror haunted — tell me truly, I implore — / Is there — *is* there balm in Gilead? — tell me — tell me, I implore!" (87-89). Even when the phrase is used facetiously, it can have a double effect, being both insult and compliment. For instance, in Mark Twain's *Tom Sawyer,* Aunt Polly's interest in "patent medicines and all new-fangled methods of producing health or mending it" is mocked — but her intention and motivation are praised even as they are casually dismissed: "She was as simple-hearted and honest as the day was long, and so she was an easy victim . . . she never suspected that she was not an angel of healing and the balm of Gilead in disguise, to the suffering neighbours" (chap. 12).

Occasionally, *balm* alone is used with apparently conscious reference to its OT associations. In *The House of the Seven Gables,* Hawthorne presents Hepzibah in spiritual turmoil, trying "hard to send up a prayer through the dense gray pavement of clouds. . . . Her faith was too weak; the prayer too heavy to be thus uplifted. It fell back, a lump of lead, upon her heart. It smote her with the wretched conviction, that Providence intermeddled not in these petty wrongs of one individual to his fellow, nor had any balm for these little agonies of a solitary soul, but shed its justice, and its mercy, in a broad, sun-like sweep, over half the universe at once. Its vastness made it nothing" (chap. 16). Though Hawthorne provides the corrective for this view in the next sentence, the despair is powerfully conveyed through the image of a sickness without an effectual balm, an image which itself harkens back to Jeremiah's proverbial use of the term.

See also DISEASE AND HEALING.

RHONDA L. WAUHKONEN

BALTHASAR *See* MAGI.

BAPTISM The word *baptism* is derived from the Gk. *baptizō,* which means "to immerse" or "dip." In the NT it appears as a ritual washing of the body, signifying spiritual purification. OT forerunners of baptism are found mainly in the baths of ritual cleansing (e.g., Exod. 40:12; Lev. 11:32; Deut. 23:10-11; 2 Sam. 12:20) which were still in use at the time of Christ (Mark 7:2-4). NT writers and Church Fathers, however, found many types of baptism in the OT. Paul interprets the Exodus as one such foreshadowing (1 Cor. 10:2-11), and Peter understands the Flood as another (1 Pet. 3:20-21). Patristic writers saw further references to baptism in the bathing of Naaman in the Jordan (2 Kings 5), in the Spirit of God moving "upon the face of the waters" (Gen. 1:2), and in the rivers of Paradise (see Tertullian, *De baptismo,* 2.4, 5, 8, 9; St. Ambrose, *De mysteriis,* 73.94).

The ministry of John the Baptist introduced a "baptism of repentance for the remission of sins" (Mark 1:4; Luke 3:3) in preparation for the future kingdom of God (Matt. 3:2; Mark 1:15; Luke 3:4). His mission was not only to prepare people for the approaching judgment but to make way for one who would baptize "with the Holy Ghost, and with fire" (Matt. 3:11; cf. Mark 1:8; Luke 3:16; John 1:33; Acts 1:5; 11:16; 19:4-5).

Throughout the NT baptism is inseparably linked with the presence of the Holy Spirit. In Jesus' own baptism and especially in the "baptism of the Holy Spirit" upon his disciples, NT writers saw the fulfillment of the OT prophetic hope of the coming of God's Spirit (expressed, e.g., in Ezek. 36:25, 26, where there is mention of "clean water" and "a new spirit"). In the baptism of Jesus by John the Baptist, the rite is authenticated by the revelation of the Holy Spirit: "And, lo, the heavens were opened unto him, and he saw the Spirit of God descending like a dove, and lighting upon him: and lo a voice from heaven, saying, This is my beloved Son, in whom I am well pleased" (Matt. 3:16-17; cf. Mark 1:10-11; Luke 3:21-22;

John 1:32). And in John 3:5, Christ himself affirms the necessity of being born of "water" and "the Spirit" if one is to enter the kingdom of God.

In two other Johannine passages Jesus identifies water as the means to "everlasting life," the source of which is in himself: "But whosoever drinketh of the water that I shall give him shall never thirst; but the water that I shall give him shall be in him a well of water springing up into everlasting life" (John 4:14); "If any man thirst, let him come unto me, and drink. He that believeth on me, as the scripture hath said, out of his belly shall flow rivers of living water" (John 7:37-38). In a symbolic context that originates in the OT comparison of God's Spirit to the revivifying effects of water (Isa. 44:3), John then identifies the water of Christ as the Holy Spirit: "But this spake he of the Spirit which they that believe on him should receive" (John 7:39). A more cryptic reference, also identified by many early exegetes (e.g., St. Augustine, Ambrose) with the renewing water of baptism, is found in the description of the river of life in Rev. 22:1.

Whether Jesus himself ever administered baptism is uncertain (cf. John 3:22; 4:2), but after his resurrection he clearly invested his disciples with the power of the Holy Spirit and the form of baptism: "Go ye therefore, and teach all nations, baptizing them in the name of the Father, and of the Son, and of the Holy Ghost" (Matt. 28:19; cf. Luke 24:47; John 20:22-23; Acts 2:38, 41).

From the outset the practice of Christian baptism was firmly grounded in the life, death, and resurrection of Christ. Jesus himself alludes to his crucifixion as a "baptism" into a higher life (Luke 12:50). And Paul understands baptism as a ritual reenactment of Christ's death, burial, and resurrection through which one is reborn like the risen Christ: "Therefore we are buried with him by baptism into death: that like as Christ was raised up from the dead by the glory of the Father, even so we also should walk in newness of life" (Rom. 6:4). Indeed, participation in Christ's death and resurrection is more than symbolic for Paul; through faith the Christian becomes one with Christ by the same divine power that raised Christ from the dead: "Buried with him in baptism, wherein also ye are risen with him through the faith of the operation of God, who hath raised him from the dead" (Col. 2:12). Paul acknowledges the Holy Spirit as the operative power of God through which the baptized are incorporated into the Christian community, i.e., the "body of Christ" (1 Cor. 12:27): "For by one Spirit are we all baptized into one body, whether we be Jews or Gentiles" (1 Cor. 12:13; cf. 2 Cor. 1:22; Eph. 1:13; 4:30). Baptism is for him a spiritual "circumcision" through which in "putting off the body of the sins of the flesh" (Col. 2:11) one "puts on Christ" (Gal. 3:27), and the "old man [of sin] is crucified with him" (Rom. 6:6). Paul refers to baptism as a sacrament of eschatological fulfillment: the messianic expectations of the OT, realized in the Christian Gospels, are now attained in the seal or pledge of baptism, through

which one also secures a place in the future heavenly kingdom (2 Cor. 1:22; Gal. 3:29; Eph. 1:13; 4:30).

Other NT writers generally reinforce Pauline teachings. Baptism is a "washing of regeneration, and renewing of the Holy Ghost," according to Titus 3:5; the letter to the Hebrews stresses the necessity of baptismal faith (10:22; cf. 1 Pet. 3:21).

The Church Fathers likewise emphasized the Pauline connection between baptism and Christ's death and resurrection. Augustine says that Christians "should live by being born again from the font, as did Christ by rising again from the sepulchre" (*Enchiridion*, 42). Proclaiming that the Holy Spirit "sanctifies the nature of the water," St. John Chrysostom in his *Baptismal Instructions* describes baptism as a "burial and a resurrection" through which the "new man is resurrected . . . according to the image of his Creator." For Tertullian, the "efficacy of the font" is secured through the "Passion and Resurrection" (*De baptismo*). Recalling John 4:14 and 7:37, St. Cyprian likens baptism to "the drinking of the Lord's cup."

Along with the Eucharist, baptism was regarded from the NT period as one of the two central sacraments of the Church. By the 12th cent., with the elaboration by Peter Lombard of seven formal sacraments (*Sententiae*, 4.1ff.), baptism had been confirmed as a rite of initiation, although not typically of adult converts. By the time Europe had been largely Christianized, infant baptism of the newest members of nominally Christian families had become normative, though it is clear from Hugh of St. Victor's *De Sacramentis* (2.6.2) that adult baptism by immersion was still occasionally practiced, usually "on the Holy Sabbath of the paschal solemnity," as he puts it — Easter Sunday (2.6.7).

The argument for infant baptism from Hugh to Calvin is that "among those children who are born of the faithful . . . Mother church, provident with dispensation, does not wish them to be deprived of the sacrament of salvation meanwhile, lest perhaps by the very delay they become estranged from salvation, if without receiving the sacrament of salvation they should suddenly depart from this life" (*De Sacramentis*, 2.6.9). Calvin adds a stronger analogy with OT circumcision of infants as a *causa logicus*, the initiation here being thus into "covenant privilege," and baptism being "a seal of the promise of the covenant" (*Inst.* 4.16.4-6). Calvin defends "paedobaptism" against the Anabaptists, who argued for the exclusive practice of "believer's baptism," the baptism (often by immersion) of adult converts or of catechumens of an age of understanding.

The practice of proselyte baptism predates Christianity; it may have begun before the intertestamental period (Ker. 9a; Gerim 2; cf. Philo, *De decalogo*, 11; Yebam. 46a; Shab. 9.12a); later arguments for believer's baptism have usually made note of the fact that baptism in the context of Judaism was by total immersion, in the case of adult males, after healing of the circumcision was complete (Lightfoot, *Horae Hebraicae et Talmudicae*, Matt. 3:7). Immersion is practiced also in the Greek church, although sprinkling ("aspersion") was initiated in the 3rd cent. for sick or disabled persons. In the West, aspersion (which was already widely practiced by the 13th cent.) came into general Catholic usage after the Council of Trent (1547). The "pouring on of water" ("affusion"), which is mentioned as early as the Didache, was another early form of baptism in cases where immersion was not possible. In Calvinist tradition affusion — traditionally spoken of as offering "a vivid picture of the bestowal of the Holy Spirit" — has in some churches given way to aspersion.

In English literary tradition through the 17th cent., baptism commonly appears in its actual theological sense as a sign of spiritual rebirth in Christ. Typically, baptismal water is closely associated or even identified with the "well" or "fountain" of Christ and his everlasting water, the Holy Spirit. In the ME *Pearl* baptism thus occurs as a spiritual cleansing effected by Christ's death: Christ is a "welle," and the water from his wound is baptism, "þat wasche₃ away þe gulte₃ felle" (11.655). Langland refers to the three modes of baptism stressed in medieval thought — by water, fire (baptism of the Holy Spirit), and blood (martyrdom) — in relation to the question of the righteous heathen (*Piers Plowman*, B.12.282). In *St. Erkenwald* a bishop's tears fall on the disinterred body of a "virtuous pagan," creating a baptism which sends the pagan's soul to paradise. *Cleanness* likens confession to baptism (1109-40). In Spenser's *Faerie Queene*, Redcrosse Knight falls into a "well of life," from which he rises spiritually reborn in the image of Christ, as represented by his physical prowess against the Satan-like dragon: "his baptized hands now greater grew" (1.11.36). In "The Water-fall," Vaughan sees in the waters the "sacred wash and cleanser" of baptism and asks that his baptism be understood as a deliverance into the powers of Christ's everlasting water: "My first consigner unto those / Fountains of life, where the Lamb goes." Two of the most noteworthy English poems on "Holy Baptisme" are those of George Herbert, the first of which relates the cleansing waters of baptism typologically to the water which flowed from Christ's side on Calvary, and the second of which is a prayer beginning

> Since, Lord, to thee
> A narrow way and little gate
> Is all the passage, on my infancie
> Thou didst lay hold, and antedate
> My faith in me

and ending with a plea that he may remain childlike in faith.

For Blake, baptism is defined within the context of his unique interpretation of the Christian mythos. In its largest sense, baptism is a rejection of error (see *A Vision of the Last Judgment*), but in *Jerusalem* it is more specifi-

cally a "baptism of repentance" (*Jerusalem*, 28) that retains its traditional association with rebirth in Christ. Thus, Albion dies to the errors of this world by throwing himself into Los's "furnace of affliction," symbolic of fallen mortal life. The furnaces are transformed into baptismal fonts — "Fountains of living waters flowing from the Humanity Divine" (37) — from which Albion emerges in the image of Christ.

Charles Dickens has a memorable baptism scene in *Dombey and Son*, where the christening of Paul (chap. 5) is a satire on the "religion of Mammon" in which the infant is almost forgotten in the ceremonies of social jockeying for power and influence. As Janet Larson puts it, "To Dickens this innocent child, of course, does not need the washing of regeneration so much as Dombey himself" (*Dickens and the Broken Scripture* [1985], 88). The title of Hardy's *A Laodicean* (1881) refers to a young candidate for baptism by immersion, who draws back and decides not to go through with the ceremony. The arguments of the pastor of the chapel demonstrate that Hardy was well versed on both sides of the controversy between paedobaptists and advocates of "believer's baptism." Baptism occurs ironically — as a diabolical pact — in Melville's *Moby-Dick*, when the demonic Ahab baptizes his harpoon barbs in the name of the devil: " '*Ego non baptizo te in nomine patris, sed in nomine diaboli!*' " (chap. 113). In his polemic against "the modern education which Joan escaped," Shaw asks: "As to the new rites, which would be the saner Joan? the one who carried little children to be baptised of water and the spirit, or the one who sent the police to force their parents to have the most vicious racial poison we know thrust into their veins?" (*St. Joan*, pref.). And in Flannery O'Connor's "The River," baptism appears with strong ironic overtones: young Harry Ashfield's spiritual embrace of Christ is confirmed publicly when the preacher "baptizes" him in the "River of Life," but later, trying to "find the kingdom of Christ in the river" by baptizing himself, Ashfield drowns.

See also HOLY SPIRIT; JOHN THE BAPTIST; SACRAMENT.

Bibliography. Daniélou, J. *Bible et liturgie* (1951); "Déluge, baptême, jugement." *Dieu vivant* 8 (1947), 97-112; Green, B. "The Mode and Meaning of the Old English Exodus." *ESA* 24 (1981), 73-82; Lundberg, P. *La Typologie Baptismale dans l'ancienne Église* (1942); Mann, B. T. "Water Imagery and the Baptism Motif in Beowulf." *DAI* 38 (1978), 4149A-50A; Old, H. O. *The Shaping of the Reformed Baptismal Rite in the Sixteenth Century* (1992); Steinmetz, D. C. "The Baptism of John and the Baptism of Jesus in Zwingli, Hubmaier, and Late Medieval Theology." In *Continuity and Discontinuity in Church History.* Ed. F. F. Church and T. George (1979), 169-81.   NORMA GRECO
                                                                 DAVID L. JEFFREY

BAPTISM OF FIRE   In Matt. 3:11 John the Baptist says: "I indeed baptize you with water unto repentance, but he that cometh after me is mightier than I . . . : he shall baptize you with the Holy Ghost, and with fire" (cf. Luke 3:16). Two views of the second baptism are found in the history of Christian interpretation: that it signifies trial and tribulation for believers, and that it is to be associated with giving of the Holy Spirit. St. Augustine acknowledges both views, favoring the second (*Sermo,* 71.19); Calvin, noting the balance of the passages in Matthew and Luke, reads "fire" as an "epithet," suggesting a refining process, as with gold.

BARABBAS   When Pilate, wishing to observe the custom of freeing one person at the feast of Passover, and believing Jesus to be innocent, offered to let him go, the crowd called instead for the release of Barabbas, a notorious prisoner (Matt. 27:16-26; Mark 15:15; John 18:40). His name suggests that he may have been the son of a rabbi; Mark identifies him as a political rebel who had committed murder in a recent insurrection, a reasonable indication that he was a Zealot and resistance fighter against the Roman occupation. John calls him simply a robber or "brigand."

In early patristic commentary there is little interest in Barabbas himself — the request for his release is simply an evidence of the viciousness of the crowd calling for Jesus' crucifixion (e.g., St. John Chrysostom, *Hom. on Matthew,* 86.1-2). The *Glossa Ordinaria* reflects the tendency of later commentators to be horrified at the invidious comparison of Jesus' innocence and Barabbas the robber's "authorship of sedition and homicide," noting that the choice of the crowd guaranteed genuine disturbance of the public peace. The Gloss allegorizes Barabbas as "Antichrist, whom they preferred to Christ, of whom it is said, 'You are of your father the devil,' " and establishes Barabbas as a type of the Antichrist (PL 114.173-74).

This intensity of reprobation is not always followed closely in secular treatment. In the "Tyllemakers' Pageant," Play 33 of the York cycle, Pilate urges that Barabbas be released "with grace" and Barabbas makes a brief, gracious speech: "ȝe worthy men, þat I here wate, / God increce all your comely estate, / For ȝe grace þe haue graunt me vn-till" (447-49). Marlowe's protagonist Barabas in *The Jew of Malta* (1589) is an angry Machiavellian whose antagonists, ironically, are Christian rulers. George Herbert turns the instinct for judgment back on those who judge the robber:

> Thou who condemnest Jewish hate,
>   For choosing Barabbas a murderer
>   Before the Lord of glorie;
> Look back upon thine own estate,
> Call home thine eye (that busie wanderer):
>   That choice may be thy storie.
> ("Self-condemnation," 1-6)

There are incidental allusions to Barabbas in modern literature, such as when Tennyson's *Becket* blames Rome

for his exile from England, saying, "Why should this Rome, this Rome / still choose Barabbas rather than Christ." Barabbas also occurs in historical fiction such as Robert Graves's *I, Claudius.* His most memorable literary appearance, however, is in the psychological study of his life after the Crucifixion by Pär Lagerkvist (*Barabbas* [1949]), in which the notorious felon's fate is ironically intertwined with that of Christians whose lot is also to be martyrdom under the Romans.

See also PASSION, CROSS; PONTIUS PILATE.

BARAK   The military leader summoned by Deborah the prophetess to lead Israel to battle against the Canaanite army headed by Sisera (Judg. 4–5; cf. Heb. 11:32).

See also AJALON, VALE OF; DEBORAH, SONG OF DEBORAH; JAEL.

BARNABAS   Barnabas, a native of Cyprus, was commissioned by the Jerusalem church to go to Antioch (Acts 11:22) as a missionary, after which he became an apostle and companion to Paul. Along with Paul and John Mark, he was then sent by the Antioch church to Cyprus and the northern mainland. The team of Barnabas and Paul split after Barnabas insisted that John Mark accompany them on their second missionary journey, even though he had abandoned them on their first efforts. Also, Barnabas showed some wavering on the status of Gentiles in the early Church (Gal. 2:11).

The mid-2nd-cent. Epistle of Barnabas has sometimes been attributed to the apostle (e.g., Tertullian, St. Clement of Alexandria), but this opinion is not supported by contemporary scholarship. Barnabas does not play a significant role in the exegetical tradition of the Church, and he is usually discussed only in connection with the Pauline missionary journeys.

John Milton, in his *Considerations Touching the Likeliest Means to Remove Hirelings out of the Church,* recalls the sending out of Barnabas from Jerusalem to Antioch approvingly, as a model of wealthier congregations supporting ministry to surrounding villages. In his *De Doctrina Christiana* (1.29, "Of the Visible Church"), Milton supports his view of a class of "extraordinary ministers" within the Church by appealing to Barnabas and Saul (Paul). "Barnabas" is often used as a name for a loyal supporter of a more notable figure ("I played Barnabas to his Paul").   WAYNE O. McCREADY

BARTHOLOMEW   *See* APOSTLE.

BARTIMAEUS   The blind beggar healed by Jesus as he went out from Jericho to Jerusalem for the last time (Mark 10:46-52) is usually assumed to be the same one described by Luke (18:35-43; cf. Matt. 20:29-34) "as they went out of Jericho." The most notable poem on the subject in English is Longfellow's "Blind Bartimaeus," actually a macaronic Greek/English poem which casts the event as a dramatic paradigm for the condition of all persons who would be healed of spiritual blindness. Both John Newton (1779) and, later in the 19th cent., George Macdonald also wrote poems on the subject.

See also BLINDNESS.

BASHAN *See* OG OF BASHAN.

BASILISK *See* COCKATRICE.

BATHSHEBA 2 Samuel 11 tells the story of King David and the beautiful Bathsheba, daughter of Eliam and wife of Uriah the Hittite. Her name may derive from Heb. *bat-sheba'* ("daughter of fullness"; but cf. 1 Chron. 3:5: "Bath-shua"). David's seduction of Bathsheba while her husband was away at war left her pregnant, news of which prompted the king to recall Uriah in an attempt to conceal the adultery. The valiant Uriah refused to return home to his wife while his comrades in arms were doing battle; David then surreptitiously arranged for his death at the siege of Rabbah at the foremost point of attack. Once her mourning was over, Bathsheba was brought to David and taken as his wife. The prophet Nathan publicly denounced the king's secret sins, prophesying truly the early death of the child born of their adulterous union. With the help of this same prophet in later years (1 Kings 1), the politically astute Bathsheba was instrumental in the accession of Solomon, her second child by David, to the throne of Israel. According to 1 Chron. 3:5, she also bore other sons — Shimea, Shobab, and Nathan. Matt. 1:6 lists her in the genealogy of Jesus Christ, though not by name: "And David the king begat Solomon of her that had been the wife of Urias."

Because of their commitment to see David as an antetype of Christ, the typical strategy of early medieval commentators was either to evade the obvious import of the Bathsheba incident or to allegorize it elaborately. St. Augustine, whose David was "not lustfull, though he fell into adultery" (*De doctrina Christiana,* 3.21), was less engaging of Bathsheba's role than later commentary. The *Glossa Ordinaria* (PL 113.571-72) gives the meaning of her name as "well of fullness" or "seven-fold well," contributing thereby to the iconography of the bathing / temptation scene in medieval and Renaissance iconography; the Gloss also draws on St. Eucherius and the *Etymologiae* of St. Isidore of Seville to present Bathsheba as a type of the Law, needing to be liberated from the carnal letter of its identification with the Synagogue (Uriah) and married to the spirit of Christ. This association became conventional allegory, despite its disjunction with the literal level of the story, in such sources as the *Aurora* of Peter Riga, in which Bathsheba is presented to David as the bare *(nuda)* law, divested of legalizing accretions, because it is the *"candida scriptorum"* which "Christ loves" (ed. P. Beichner [1965], 1.278). In the

14th-cent. *Cursor Mundi,* Bathsheba is given considerable space as a sophisticated rhetorician whose advocacy, "sli knot . . . on skil knyt" (8411), ensures the ascendancy of her son Solomon to the throne. In the 14th-cent. Cornish biblical drama, the *Ordinalia,* Bathsheba urges David to kill Uriah, then weeps as Uriah unwittingly departs toward his doom and melodramatically threatens to kill herself. Surprisingly, the predictable tropological reading of the story (derived from St. Gregory the Great and others), in which Bathsheba represents the perils of carnal appetite, has more vogue in medieval art than in literature.

Bathsheba's place in subsequent English literature is small. George Peele's *The Love of King David and Fair Bethsabe,* which closely follows 2 Samuel, assigns her approximately one-twentieth of the play's lines (Uriah, who appears in but one scene, is given as many). Bathsheba is here a radiantly beautiful and chaste wife betrayed by her charms and obedience to her liege: "The Kings poore handmaid will obey my lord" (117). She disappears from the stage at the end of scene 6, but returns in the final scene to help secure with Nathan's assistance the succession of Solomon to his father's throne, finishing the play a wise counselor and supportive wife. It is in this role of *eminence grise* that Robert Cleaver remembers her in his *Bathshebaes instructions to her sonne Lemvel: containing a fruitful and plaine exposition of the last chapter of the Proverbs. Describing the duties of a greatman, and the vertues of a gracious woman* (1614). In accordance with the rabbinic tradition, which takes the name Lemuel ("belonging to God") to refer to Solomon (cf. Ginzberg, *LJ* 6.277), Cleaver identifies Bathsheba as the mother whose instructions concerning prudent kingship and the dangers of intemperance are recorded in Prov. 31. She does not appear at all in Cowley's unfinished epic *Davideis, a Sacred Poem of the Troubles of David.* Similarly, Herbert omits any mention of Bathsheba in his reflections on the ethical aspects of David's adultery (*Brief Notes on Valdesso's "Considerations,"* 62). She is mentioned by name in Dryden's *Absalom and Achitophel,* but only in passing and as a stand-in for the Duchess of Portsmouth, a mistress to the promiscuous Charles II: the king "Is grown in Bathsheba's embraces old" (710). Christopher Smart's *A Song to David* leaps directly from the Michal of David's youth to the Abishag of his old age without even a passing mention of Bathsheba.

Bathsheba does play a significant role, though again by association, in *Far from the Madding Crowd.* Hardy's heroine, the enticing Bathsheba Everdene (in a manner suggestive of her biblical namesake), grows through suffering and misfortune into a wise woman. In *Tess of the D'Urbervilles,* Angel Clare reflects belatedly on his desertion of Tess because of her past sexual relations with another man; remembering "the wife of Uriah being made a queen," he regrets having failed to judge Tess "by the will rather than by the deed." In *The Scarlet Letter,* the story of David and Bathsheba serves Hawthorne well: a good widow gives her brooding pastor Dimmesdale the sunniest room, hung all around with tapestries "representing the scriptural story of David and Bathsheba, and Nathan the Prophet, in colors still unfaded, but which made the fair woman of the scene almost as grimly picturesque as the woe-denouncing seer" (chap. 9).

A number of minor works of 20th-cent. literature — including Stephen Phillips's pseudo-Elizabethan verse drama *The Sin of David* — recall the wife of Uriah. Gladys Schmitt's *David the King,* a historical novel, develops Bathsheba's feelings of uncertainty as an obedient subject powerless before her king and as a woman made pregnant by someone other than her husband. David Robert Perry Marquis's *David and Bathsheba (As Interpreted by the Old Soak)* is democratic in the manner of Twain: "Oh, what the hell, it's Spring! / And just for the sake of argyment, / I'll show 'em who is king."

See also DAVID; NATHAN; SOLOMON.

Bibliography. Davidson, E. "Dimmesdale's Fall." *NEQ* 36 (1963), 358-70.   CAMILLE R. LA BOSSIÈRE

BE FRUITFUL, AND MULTIPLY God's words "Be fruitful, and multiply" (Gen. 1:28) constitute both a blessing and a commandment, the first *mitzvah* (precept) given to mankind (see Hertz on Gen. 1:28). They are associated throughout the OT with God's covenant with creation (in Gen. 1:22 and 8:17 they refer to the animals) and particularly with Israel, his chosen people.

When the natural bond between Creator and creation is broken by Adam and Eve's transgression, the blessing becomes a curse; God now tells Eve, "I will greatly multiply thy sorrow and thy conception" (Gen. 3:16). In his mercy, however, God establishes a formal covenant for the protection of the fallen creation, suggesting a new beginning with his echo, spoken to Noah and his sons (Gen. 9:1, 7), of the prelapsarian "Be fruitful, and multiply."

In the renewal of God's covenant with Abraham and with each successive generation of Hebrew patriarchs, emphasis is placed upon God's providence; it is he who multiplies and who makes fruitful (Gen. 17:2; 26:4; 28:3; 49:22-25). This message is recalled in the books of the Prophets, in which Israel is reminded that, despite her multitude of iniquity and increase of sins (Jer. 30:15), a remnant of the faithful will be made fruitful and be multiplied by God (Isa. 54:9; 61:9, 11; Jer. 30:19; Ezek. 36:10, 11).

In the NT, fruitfulness and multiplication are spoken of primarily in terms of their figurative meanings. St. Paul, invoking Christ's parable of the sower (Mark 4:20), refers to the multiplication of the seeds of the Word and the increase of the fruits of righteousness within the faithful (2 Cor. 9:10). The parable of the vine in the Gospel of

John emphasizes both the endurance of spiritual fruits and, in keeping with OT themes, the origin of those fruits in God (John 15:16; see also Gal. 5:22).

The Fathers of the Church provide a diversity of interpretations of the phrase "Be fruitful, and multiply." St. Ambrose infuses his many commentaries on Genesis with NT terminology, making reference to the multiplication of virtue (*De Noe,* 24.87) and characterizing the inheritance of Abraham as one of faith (*De Abraham 2,* 10.77; see also Heb. 6). St. Jerome, on the other hand, emphasizes the differences between the exigencies of the Old Law and the New Law, asking, "And if both before and after the deluge the maxim held good 'be fruitful and multiply and replenish the earth': what has that to do with us upon whom the ends of the ages are come. . . ?" (*Ep.* 123.13). He generally interprets the commandment as a literal call to marriage and procreation, which he rejects in favor of a higher calling, virginity (*Ep.* 48.2); nevertheless, he does recognize the need for marriage, since its offspring and fruit is virginity (*Adv. Jov.* 1.3).

St. Augustine views the command to increase and multiply as a blessing, inextricably linked to the blessed institution of marriage (*De civ. Dei* 14.22). While, because of humanity's fallen nature, marriage and procreation inevitably contain the potential for lustful activities, they do produce children, "something good out of the evil of lust" (*De bono coniugali,* 3.3). Marriage also promotes the order of charity through the subduing of that lust, a mastery which is figured in the command to rule the beasts of the earth (Gen. 1:28).

John of Salisbury, in his 12th-cent. *Policraticus,* tends toward a moral reading firmly based in the literal. He writes that "This is the order: to increase in themselves and, as it were, to multiply in their descendants; in themselves, for progress of merit; in their descendants, by a kind of propagation of virtues" (7.10). Martin Luther deals separately with the commandment to Adam and Eve and that to Noah, saying that while the first is a "marred blessing" because of the "leprosy of lust" (*Lectures on Genesis,* 1:28), yet the second "deals with the honorableness of marriage" (*Lectures,* 9.1). Like Augustine, he also calls children "a gift of God" *(ibid.),* given through the fulfillment of this commandment.

Chaucer's Wife of Bath is interested neither in the spiritual multiplication of virtues, nor in the goal of procreating children. Rather, her assertion that "God bad us for to wexe and multiplye" (*Wife of Bath's Prologue,* 28) is an attempt to give the stamp of authority to an activity which caters to her own carnal desires. Chaucer's Pardoner, Canon, and Canon's Yeoman also abuse the principle of multiplication, while St. Cecilia of *The Second Nun's Tale* is an emblem for fruitful multiplication of virtue (D. W. Robertson, 332, 376; R. Peck, esp. 34-35).

In *Paradise Lost,* Milton's Adam laments the consequences of his fall as follows:

All that I eat or drink, or shall beget,
Is propagated curse. O voice once heard
Delightfully, 'Increase and multiply,'
Now death to hear! For what can I increase
Or multiply, but curses on my head? (10.728-32)

The lines are ironic to the reader, who, unlike Adam, knows of the blessing and commandment which will be repeated to Noah and the other patriarchs, and of salvation which comes from Christ, the "second Adam." In Rose Macauley's 1923 work, *Told by an Idiot,* there is a similarly ill-founded reaction to the commandment "Be fruitful, and multiply." The central character, a woman by the name of Rome, criticizes "old Bibly clergymen" who "think it so important to produce more life" (2.9). While overly literal readings sometimes need correctives, Rome's critique stems not from a true understanding of the text, but rather from a miscontextualization of it within her own nihilistic view — one in which multiplication must necessarily be of curses rather than blessings.

See also CHARITY, CUPIDITY; COVENANT; EDEN; NOAH; VIRGINITY, CHASTITY.

Bibliography. Peck, R. "The Ideas of 'Entente' and Translation in Chaucer's *Second Nun's Tale." AnM* 8 (1967), 17-37; *The Pentateuch and Haftorahs.* Ed. J. H. Hertz (1938); Robertson, D. W., Jr. *A Preface to Chaucer* (1962); Yegerlehner, D. A. "'Be Fruitful and Multiply and Fill the Earth. . .' A History of the Interpretation of Genesis 1:28A and Related Texts in Selected Periods." Unpubl. Ph.D., Boston, 1975.

PATRICIA SUNDERLAND

BE NOT YE CALLED RABBI   Jesus so admonished the scribes and Pharisees, who loved to be greeted ceremonially in the marketplace by the title, which means "master" (cf. Lat. *magister*) or "teacher." To his disciples he added, "for one is your Master, even Christ; and all ye are brethren" (Matt. 23:7-8).

St. Francis of Assisi enjoined his followers to heed the passage carefully, and it is reflected in *The Rule* (1221). There is thus a double hypocrisy in the behavior of the Friar in Chaucer's *Summoner's Tale.* Having been gulled by Thomas into receiving an odorous "gift" for the "fundement" of his "covent" building fund, he rushes out to see a rich lord at whose table he has often dined. The lord addresses him as master, only to be ever-so-gently corrected by the Friar's false modesty:

No maister, sire, quod he, but servitour,
Thogh I have in scole that honour.
God liketh nat that "Raby" men us calle
Neither in market ne in youre large halle. (*Canterbury Tales,* 3.2185-88)

Arnold invokes the phrase ironically in the "Sweetness and Light" chapter of *Culture and Anarchy* to satirize anti-authoritarianism.

See also RABBI.

BEATITUDES   A beatitude (Lat. *beatitudo,* from Vg

Rom. 4:6-9) is a statement proclaiming the happiness, good fortune, or blessedness of certain types of people in the OT and NT; beatitudes are also called makarisms because the most important series, in the Sermon on the Mount (Matt. 5:3-11) and in the Sermon on the Plain (Luke 6:20-22), begin with Gk. *makarioi.* The many scattered OT beatitudes (e.g., in Pss. 2:12; 32:1; Prov. 8:34; Isa. 32:20; 56:1-2) and other NT beatitudes (e.g., Matt. 11:6; 13:16; Rom. 4:7; Rev. 1:3) will not be considered here.

Both the Matthean and Lucan series upend worldly values, redefining conditions such as poverty and suffering. The beatitudes of both series state the blessing in the first clause and the reason for the blessing in the second clause: "Blessed are . . . for. . . ." Otherwise the two series differ considerably. Luke's four blessings are followed by four exactly corresponding woes, all of which are in the second person. Focusing on external conditions such as poverty, the Lucan series stresses the vast social reversal which will occur through the coming of God's kingdom. Whereas Luke offers eschatological consolation, Matthew offers eschatological challenge, for in the Sermon on the Mount the blessed are those who live by certain spiritual values. Luke's poor are here the poor in spirit, and the hungry are those who hunger and thirst for righteousness. Matthew's eight beatitudes are addressed generally, in the third person, and are ethically conditional: only those who live by the specified spiritual values will be saved (*ISBE* 1.443-44). Of the two series, Matthew's has been more central to Christian doctrine because it begins the Sermon on the Mount; therefore, hereafter "Beatitudes" will refer to the Matthew passage unless otherwise noted.

In Roman Catholic exegesis, which follows St. Augustine (*De sermone Domini in Monte* [PL 34.1229-1308]) and St. Thomas Aquinas (*Summa Theol.* 1a2ae.69 [24.43-63]), the Beatitudes are sequential stages in temporal spiritual growth ending with the person's becoming perfected in the divine image; they are also adjunct to the gifts of the Holy Spirit and to the vices and virtues. As such, the Beatitudes often appear in septenary schemes (e.g., *The World of Piers Plowman,* eds. J. Krochalis and E. Peters [1975], 170-79). Thus, Dante's ascesis through Purgatory is marked by the Beatitudes, and in St. Thomas More's *Dialogue of Comfort against Tribulation,* 1.10 and 1.19, the Beatitudes are key reminders of radical Christian detachment from the world.

Modern Protestant theology tends to see the Beatitudes as "illustrative of a new set of mind and of the will, a disposition grounded on the consciousness that God is our all in all and that love, unlimited in its volition and free from all external constraints, is life's only good" (Windisch [1951], 45). The 19th-cent. theologian Johannes Weiss saw the Beatitudes as an "Interim-Ethik," binding only for the short period before the imminently expected Second Coming (*Matthew* [AB 26], 51). Earlier theologians such as Luther and Calvin were much closer in spirit to the Augustinian view of the Beatitudes as an ethic for all Christians to attempt to live by (Luther, *The Sermon on the Mount,* in *Luther's Works,* ed. J. Pelikan [1956], 21.3-4; Calvin, *Commentary on a Harmony of the Evangelists,* trans. W. Pringle, Calvin Translation Society [1845], 1.260). The same holds true for Anglican theologians (e.g., Lightfoot, *Harmony, Chronicle, and Order of the New Testament* [1655], 26; Poole, *Synopsis Criticorum Aliorumque Sacrae Scripturae Interpretum* [1674], 4.114-15). In both Catholic and Anglican liturgies, Matt. 5:1-12 is the gospel for the Feast of All Saints (Nov. 1).

Although the Beatitudes hold a central position in biblical commentary and in Christian theology, their occurrence in English literature is limited mainly to statements beginning "Blessed be . . ." which seldom contain the rhetorical and ethical qualities of the originals, and which seldom have much significance for the works in which they occur. Nevertheless, some authors have used the Beatitudes or the beatitude form with great learning and wit, and sometimes with great thematic import.

Matthew 5:3 is one of the central ideas of Pacience's speech to Haukyn in *Piers Plowman* (B.14.214) and one of the main ethical messages of the poem's *Dowel* section (see R. W. Frank, Jr., *Piers Plowman and the Scheme of Salvation,* YSE 136 [1957], 72-77). The homiletic, alliterative poems *Cleanness* and *Patience* both take Beatitudes as their themes (Matt. 5:8 and Matt. 5:3, 10 respectively). *Cleanness* discusses purity by contrasting it with profanation in the stories of the Flood, Sodom and Gomorrah, and the fall of Belshazzar; *Patience* focuses on the story of Jonah in such a way as to link patience with vocational obedience. Chaucer uses the beatitude form ironically in *The Miller's Tale,* where the carpenter's "Ye, blessed be alwey a lewed man / That noght but oonly his bileve kan!" (*Canterbury Tales,* 1.3455-56) proclaims his ignorance and gullibility before the student Nicholas, who dupes the carpenter precisely by preying on his *bileve.* The avaricious friar in *The Summoner's Tale* uses Matt. 5:3 to wheedle a donation from the flatulent Thomas (3.1923). In *Melibee,* Matt. 5:9 is one of Prudence's main themes in her efforts to get Melibeus to make peace with his enemies (7.1680), and thus one of the tale's central themes. *The Parson's Tale* concludes with a pastiche of Matt. 5:3, 5, 6.

In Spenser's *Faerie Queene* (4.10.8.8-9) the inscription "Blessed the man that well can use his blis: / Whose ever be the shield, faire Amoret be his" sends Scudamor on his quest. Throughout his works, Shakespeare adopts the beatitude form to express a blessing, although he alludes directly to only two of the Beatitudes per se. Matt. 5:9 is alluded to three times in the plays, but always ironically, since for various reasons the peacemakers are ineffectual and peace is impossible (*2 Henry 6,* 2.1.35; *Richard 3,* 2.1.50-53; *Coriolanus,* 5.3.138-40). The

Lucan beatitude form combined with a Lucan "woe to . . ." reveals Falstaff's vindictive selfishness as well as his vain hope for preferment in *2 Henry 4,* 5.3.133-34: "Blessed are they that have been my friends and woe to my Lord Chief Justice!" In *Eastward Ho,* by Chapman, Jonson, and Marston, Matt. 5:6 is applied by several characters in a humorously literal, appetitive sense; e.g., to express Gertrude's desire for sex with Sir Petronel (2.2.431-32; cf. 2.2.164 and 3.2.246-47).

After the Renaissance the Beatitudes are usually pressed into the service of secular values. Pope's "Ode on Solitude" makes a heaven of earth through two extended beatitudes celebrating rustic contentment and anonymity. Blake's letter to John Flaxman (19 Oct. 1801) saw peace with Napoleon as the inauguration of an artistic eschaton: "Blessed are those who are found studious of Literature and Humane and polite accomplishments. Such have their lamps burning and shall shine as the stars." Wordsworth's Wanderer (*Excursion,* 2.591-92) exclaims at the sight of a rustic funeral procession: "Oh! blest are they who live and die like these, / Loved with such love, and with such sorrow mourned!" although his optimism is soon challenged by the despairing Solitary. Thoreau pronounces the sixth Beatitude, in Transcendentalist fashion, on those who remain pure by avoiding knowledge of current events: "Blessed were the days before you read a president's message. Blessed are the young, for they do not read the president's message. Blessed are they who have never read a newspaper, for they shall see Nature, and through her, God" (Thoreau to Parker Pillsbury, 10 Apr. 1861).

The Beatitudes are central in Melville's *Confidence-Man* and *Billy Budd.* In *CM* (chaps. 3–7), the first three appearances of the confidence-man are "types from the Beatitudes: the Negro Black Guinea, who solicits alms, the poor in spirit; John Ringman, the man with the weed, those who mourn; the man with the grey coat, those who hunger and thirst after righteousness" (Wright [1949], 102). The Beatitudes are thus a vehicle for the confidence-man's manipulation of Christian virtues, which Elizabeth Foster saw as a "criticism of religion itself and [an] attack on optimistic philosophy" (ed. pref., *CM* [1954], xlvii). In *Billy Budd,* Billy's being called a peacemaker (" 'Well, blessed are the peacemakers, especially the fighting peacemakers,' " chap. 1) is ironically prophetic: by removing the evil Claggart, Billy is, in a way, a peacemaker, and by dying an innocent he remains a child of God. In Tennyson's "Aylmer's Field," 753-56, Averill's sermon on the suicides of Edith and Leolin laments Aylmer's destructive avarice by reinterpreting "poor in spirit" as vile.

See also SERMON ON THE MOUNT.

Bibliography. St. Augustine. *Commentary on the Lord's Sermon on the Mount.* Trans. D. J. Kavanaugh. FC, vol. 11 (1951); Dodd, C. H. "The Beatitudes: A Form-Critical Study." *More New Testament Studies* (1968), 1-10; Dupont, J. *Les béatitudes.* 2nd ed. *EBib.* 3 vols. (1969-73); *ISBE* 1.443-

44; Windisch, H. *The Meaning of the Sermon on the Mount.* Trans. S. MacLean Gilmour (1951).   M. W. TWOMEY

BEDLAM   *See* BETHLEHEM.

BEELZEBUB   The Greek name *Beelzebul* or *Beelzeboul* means "master of the heavenly dwelling," although in its Latin and Syriac version, *Beelzebub,* it can mean "lord of the flies" (Matt. 12:24, 27; Mark 3:22; Luke 11:15, 18). A relatively obscure name for Satan or the prince of demons, Beelzebub was claimed by some enemies of Jesus to be the "unclean spirit" (Mark 3:30) through which he performed miracles. The root of the etymology is both Aramaic and Hebrew: *beʿel* ("master; lord") is Aramaic, and *zebul* ("height, abode, dwelling") the only Hebrew word ascribed to Jesus in the NT. The compound appears to have been a pejorative nickname for Jesus coined by the scribes (cf. Matt. 10:25). In origin the name may have referred to a Canaanite god, represented as Baal-zebub (2 Kings 1:2ff.). Postbiblical Hebrew, like Syriac, used *zbl* to mean "dung, excrement," suggesting a further association to later writers. The accusation against Jesus is meant to imply demon possession, a charge which was laid also against John the Baptist (Matt. 11:18; Luke 7:33) and which suggests sorcery; it is paralleled by explicit charges that Jesus had a demon (John 7:20; 8:48-52; 10:20). The claim, based on these associations, that Jesus was merely a magician is found in pagan sources (see Origen, *Contra Celsum,* 1.6, 38, 49, 53, 68; Justin, *Apol.* 1.30; *Dial.* 69.7), in Jewish writings (e.g., Sanh. 43a), and in the Koran (5.113). Origen elsewhere observes that all "those who invoke Beelzebub are magicians" (*In Numeros homilia,* 13.5).

Jewish commentators apply the name to a variety of objects of pagan worship. Commenting on the lapse of the Israelites after the death of Gideon, Tg. Yerushalmi 9.11d, ʿAbod. Zar. 3.43a, and Shab. 83b refer to pocket-sized phallic images of Beelzebub which the people carried about with them and "every now and then were in the habit of bringing . . . forth and kissing . . . fervently" (Ginzberg, *LJ* 4.41; 6.201). In the legends of Solomon's perversion of wisdom the king is depicted as a magus who uses magical devices, among which is a magic ring inscribed with the tetragrammaton to call up the demons, including finally Beelzeboul. This "prince of all the demons," who says that he alone has survived of the fallen angels, and rules over all who are in Tartarus, calls on lesser spirits, including the demon Envy, all of whom are pressed into service, ironically, in building the Temple (Ginzberg, *LJ* 4.149-54; 6.291-92). The account ends with Solomon's drastic demise, wherein "he sank so low that to please his beloved he built temples to Baal."

Patristic commentary on the subject is slow to develop, but St. Ambrose (*De poenitentia,* 2.4.21-26) connects Matt. 10:25 to the narrative of Simon Magus (Acts 8:21ff.). St. Jerome regards the charge against Jesus to be

the ultimate blasphemy (*Ep.* 42.1-2), an injury to the Lord so severe that comparable injury to his followers must seem by comparison much more bearable (*Ep.* 38.5). The *Glossa Ordinaria* etymologized the name as "fly [or pest] of Baal" (PL 114.119), hence "Beelzebub is to say, the lord of the flies," on account of the way in which the flies are attracted to the bloody filth associated with sacrifices to him (PL 114.289). Calvin follows these sources in his commentary on Matt. 10:25, but opines from his northern perspective that the Philistines probably invoked their god Beel-zebub rather "to save them from the flies which infested the district" (*Harmony of the Gospels*).

Belsabub, as he is called in the York cycle, is a vigorous captain of the underworld, reporting only to Satan himself (37.109-19). Both here and in the Towneley cycle, as Christ knocks at the gates he endeavors in vain to marshal the forces of hell against Christ's deliverance of the elect (the harrowing of hell): "Harro! our yates begin to crak, / In sonder, I trow, they go" (Towneley, 25.194-95). Alluding to the Harrowing of Hell plays as much as to the Bible, Shakespeare has the porter in *Macbeth* respond to the imperious knocking at the gate with "Knock, knock, knock! Who's there, i' the name of Beelzebub?" (2.3.3-4; cf. 17-19). Marlowe's *Tragicall Historie of Doctor Faustus* (1604) bears striking resemblance to the talmudic legends of Solomon's demise. After the appearance of Mephistopheles, when Faustus is told that "the shortest cut for coniuring / Is stoutly to abiure the Trinitie, / And pray deuoutly to the prince of hell," the wise man-turned-magician replies: "So Faustus hath already done, & holds this principle / There is no chiefe but onely Belsibub" ([1604], ed. Greg, 1.3.297-302). Later he admonishes himself to "Despaire in God, and trust in Belsabub" (442), concluding:

> The good thou servest is thine owne appetite,
> Wherein is fixt the loue of Balsabub,
> To him Ile build an altar and a church,
> And offer luke warm blood of new borne babes.
> (448-51)

In Milton's *Paradise Lost* Beelzebub is still Satan's chief adviser, and Bunyan makes him captain of the strong castle near the Wicket-gate in *Pilgrim's Progress.* Melville's Ishmael refers to castaway whalers so queer that Beelzebub would pass unnoticed in their company, and later refers to the way he intends to deal with a potential mutineer: "I'll just take the nape of his neck and say — 'Look here, Beelzebub, you don't do it', and if he makes any fuss, by the Lord, I'll make a grab into his pocket for his tail" (*Moby-Dick,* chap. 73). In Shaw's *St. Joan* Bishop Cauchon appears to defend Joan, observing that "the names on that white banner were not the names of Satan and Beelzebub, but the blessed names of our Lord and His Holy Mother" (4.44). William Golding's title *Lord of the Flies* unambiguously invokes the malignancy associated with the oldest references to Beelzebub in a modern parable of a fall from false innocence to neo-pagan horrors.

See also BAAL; DEVIL; GRAVEN IMAGE; HARROWING OF HELL; SIMON MAGUS.

BEHEMOTH Hebrew *behemot* is the plural intensive form of *behemah*, "beast," "animal," or "cattle" (cf. the Arabic root *bhm*, "to be dumb") and is rendered "beasts" in a variety of OT passages (e.g., Deut. 28:26; 32:24: Isa. 18:6; Hab. 2:7). The term *behemoth* appears in the KJV in Job 40:15-24 only, where it is found in company with leviathan (41:34). Apparently referring to a large, marsh-dwelling animal in this context, it is traditionally glossed as "hippopotamus," and sometimes (as in the Geneva Bible notes) "elephant," or (in the NEB) "crocodile." Some have suggested an etymological conection with *bohu* (KJV, "void"), which is used always (Gen. 1:2; Isa. 34:11; Jer. 4:23) alongside *tohu* (KJV, "without form") and would seem to suggest something incalculable and threatening. In any case, Job 40:15 apparently refers to an identifiable existing animal which has here taken on mythic or supernatural proportions.

In 1 Enoch 60:8 behemoth dwells in the wilderness of Dundayin (i.e., the land of Nod [Gen. 4:16]), east of Eden. Elsewhere, in a fanciful interpretation of Ps. 50:10, it is said to dwell in a land of a thousand hills (2 Esdr. 6:49-52). In the Apocrypha and Pseudepigrapha, as in the Job passage, behemoth always occurs in company with the mythic Leviathan (cf. Rev. 13, where there is a sea beast and land beast). In Rev. 13:11 the "beast" which comes "up out of the earth" translates *thērion*, the LXX word for behemoth.

Jewish folklore asserts that there is but a single male and female of the species and that these are incapable of producing offspring — lest they should overrun the earth. Other legends have it that on the Day of Judgment the righteous will see a titanic struggle between the land monster behemoth and its watery counterpart, the leviathan, in which both creatures perish. The blessed will then be called to a banquet to feast on their flesh.

Exegetical commentary on behemoth is minimal. Origen sees behemoth as the prototype of those who bear "the image of the earthy" (*On Prayer,* 26.5). Luther, in his lectures on Hebrews, attributes evil or "beastly" propensities to the "belly" and "loins" of men and connects the latter with behemoth.

Thomas Hobbes's *Behemoth,* clearly so named to make it in some sense a companion to his *Leviathan,* is an inquiry into the causes of the English civil wars. Milton's behemoth (*Paradise Lost,* 7.471), a creature of the sixth day of creation (as in Jewish tradition), is significant as the biggest of the earth animals. In Thomson's *Summer* (710), behemoth is an invulnerable inhabitant of a verdant land of the poet's vision. The "earth-convulsing" behemoth of Shelley's *Prometheus Unbound* (4.1.310), formerly one of the "monarch beasts" said to be "abolished" with the deluge, is found in Penthea's vision of "the secrets of the Earth's deep heart." In Byron's *Deformed Transformed* (3.57) behemoth is the object of a hunt in a more heroic age. Browning alludes incidentally to behemoth in both "Christmas Eve and Easter Day" (578) and *Prince Hohenstiel-Schwangau* (677), as does Joyce in *Finnegans Wake.* The etymologically related *bohu* appears (in combination with *tohu*) in Robertson Davies's *The Rebel Angels,* as *tohubohu,* a kind of verbal talisman on the lips of the gypsy protagonist.

See also LEVIATHAN; MARRIAGE FEAST, APOCALYPTIC.

RICHARD SCHELL

BEL AND THE DRAGON Two separate and unrelated didactic stories not found in the Hebrew Bible, yet undoubtedly deriving from a Semitic legend, relate to episodes in Dan. 3 and 6; both are designed to expose and ridicule paganism. They appear with variations in the Apocrypha, a single 9th-cent. copy of the LXX, and Theodotion. In the story of Bel, King Cyrus asks Daniel why he does not worship Bel (the Babylonian deity Marduk); Daniel's response is to devise a plan exposing Bel worship by entrapping the priests who secretly remove offerings left in the temple for the god. Cyrus has the false priests put to death and the idols destroyed. In the story of The Dragon, the king worships a serpent; Daniel scorns it and feeds it pitch, fat, and hair, so that it bursts. The people are enraged and Daniel is thrown into the lions' den, where he languishes without food but remains unharmed for six or seven days. On the last day Habakkuk, bearing food, is taken by an angel to the lions' den; Daniel is rescued and his enemies are immediately devoured when they are put in the den.

Occurrences in English literature principally involve characterizations of fraud. In *Much Ado about Nothing,* Shakespeare's Borachio likens villainous misrepresentation to the deceptions of "god Bel's priests in the old church window" (3.3.143).

Tribulation Wholesome, A Pastor of Amsterdam, in Ben Jonson's *The Alchemist* (5.5.15), attacks Subtle the alchemist and his friends, calling them as "profane as Bel and the Dragon."

In an essay entitled *Shooting Niagara: And After?* (*Macmillan's Magazine,* Aug. 1867), Carlyle says that nine-tenths or three-fourths of the cost of rebuilding England every seventy years could be saved if men behaved "like sons of Adam, and not like scandalous esurient Phantasms and sons of Bel and the Dragon."

See also BABYLON; DANIEL; GRAVEN IMAGE.

Bibliography. Metzger, B. M. *An Introduction to the Apocrypha* (1957); Pfeiffer, R. H. *History of New Testament Times, with an Introduction to the Apocrypha* (1949).

RONALD M. MELDRUM

BELIAL Belial (Heb. *beliya'al,* "worthless, useless")

is used in the OT primarily to describe various categories of the "lawless," "wicked," and "ungodly." Thus "children of Belial" (Deut. 13:13; Judg. 20:13; 1 Sam. 10:27; 1 Kings 21:13; 2 Chron. 13:7), "sons [or daughters] of Belial" (Judg. 19:22; 1 Sam. 1:16; 2:12; 25:17; 2 Sam. 23:6; 1 Kings 21:10), "man [or men] of Belial" (1 Sam. 25:25; 30:22; 2 Sam. 16:7; 20:1; 1 Kings 21:13); also a (false) "witness of Belial" (Prov. 19:28), and an evil thought or "word of Belial" (Deut. 15:9; Ps. 101:3). Its use as a proper name synonymous with Satan and the Antichrist and associated particularly with lawlessness, violence, and deceit is developed in many apocryphal texts (e.g., Jub. 1:20; 15:33) and is reflected in St. Paul's "And what concord hath Christ with Belial? or what part hath he that believeth with an infidel?" (2 Cor. 6:15). Patristic and later commentators follow Paul in identifying Belial with Satan and stress his powers of deceit.

In English literature before Milton Belial is synonymous with Satan (see, e.g., Wyclif [*English Tracts,* 7.17.5], Langland [*Piers Plowman,* B.18.319]; Chaucer somewhat more pointedly describes corrupt priests as "sons of Belial" who imagine themselves to be "without a judge" [*Parson's Tale,* 10.895-900]). Milton elaborates the special character of Belial in *Paradise Lost* (1.490-505; 2.108-228) and *Paradise Regained* (2.150-91). In *PL* he appears last of the major fallen angels, "than whom a Spirit more lewd / Fell not from heaven, or more gross to love / Vice for itself." He has no definite temples or rites because he is worshiped in many places and in many ways: no other avatar of Satan is so universal, so irresistible in his easy familiarity and adaptability. His speech in council is remarkable for its eloquence, its acute diagnosis of the situation — and for drawing the wrong conclusion from the right premises, counseling "ignoble ease, and peaceful sloth / Not peace," hoping for improvement without repentance. As Luther observed, "Belial alone is the best devil, who can dispute himself as an angel of light . . . and can turn God's word into darkness in the hearts of men" (*Lectures on the Psalms,* 101:3). In *PR* Belial is similarly associated with lust and with deceitful eloquence, advising Satan, Jesus' tempter, to "Set women in his eye . . . [who, with their "enchanting tongues" and other arts] draw / Hearts after them tangl'd in Amorous Nets."

Blake writes of "Belial of Sodom and Gomorrha, obscure Demon of Bribes / And secret Assassinations, not worship'd nor ador'd, but / With the finger on the lips and the back turn'd to the light" (*Milton,* 30-33). Browning's soliloquist speaks of

> my scrofulous French novel
> On grey paper with blunt type!
> Simply glance at it, you grovel
> Hand and foot in Belial's gripe. ("Soliloquy of the
> Spanish Cloister," 8.1-4)

Dryden alludes to "sons of Belial" in *Absalom and Achit-*

ophel. Joyce, in *Finnegans Wake,* seems to assume the NT identification of Belial with Satan: "All Saints beat Belial! Mickil Goals to Nichil! Not possible! Already?"

See also ANTICHRIST; DEVIL.

Bibliography. Langton, E. *Satan, A Portrait* (1946); McHenry, R. "'The Sons of Belial' in *Absalom and Achitophel." ELN* 22 (1984), 27-36; Russell, J. B. *The Devil: Perceptions of Evil from Antiquity to Primitive Christianity* (1977); *Lucifer: The Devil in the Middle Ages* (1984); *Mephistopheles: The Devil in the Modern World* (1987).

ROBERT WILTENBURG

BELSHAZZAR   The son and co-regent of the Babylonian king Nabonidus (ca. 556-539 B.C.) during whose reign Babylonia fell to the Persians under Cyrus (12 Oct. 539 B.C.). According to Dan. 5 his "father" (most probably grandfather) was Nebuchadnezzar. Belshazzar is remembered for the great feast during which a message of doom was written by God on the palace wall. This was interpreted by Daniel (5:17-28). Belshazzar's death that very night (5:30) is unmentioned in Assyrian sources. Calvin proposed that even the queen chided Belshazzar for not turning to God (sup. *Daniel,* 457). Other forms of the name are Balthasar (Bar. 1:11-12) and Baltasar (LXX; Josephus, *Ant.* 10.245). Heinrich Heine's "Belshazzar" (1820), translated into English by C. G. Leland (1863), is one of many poems about his orgiastic feast whose central subject is the "handwriting on the wall."

See also HANDWRITING ON THE WALL.

Bibliography. Beaulieu, P. A. *The Reign of Nabonidus: King of Babylon 556-539 B.C.* (1989); Dougherty, R. P., *Nabonidus and Belshazzar* (1929); Grayson, A. K., *Assyrian and Babylonian Chronicles* (1975), 104-11.   DAVID W. BAKER

BENEDICTION   Despite its etymology (Lat. *benedictio, bene dicere*), to pronounce a benediction does not mean simply to speak well of or to express kindly wishes. It involves an actual transference of blessing from its source to a recipient. The ultimate source of benediction is God himself, and when persons bless it is often by prayer (Gen. 48:15); in the NT benediction frequently takes the form of a thanksgiving (Mark 14:22-23). God himself may be blessed in the sense of being praised (Luke 1:68). To speak of a person as blessed is to affirm that God is with him (2 Sam. 7:3). In the OT benediction was associated with worship (1 Kings 8:14), gradually becoming the prerogative of priests and expressed in fixed formulas (e.g., the Aaronic blessing of Num. 6:22-27). In Christian worship formulaic benedictions include those deriving from 2 Cor. 13:14, Phil. 4:7, and Heb. 13:20-21. Not only persons but places and objects, including churches, liturgical furniture, and items such as palms or wedding rings are also blessed (although the terms *consecration* and *dedication* may be used in such instances). In the Roman Catholic Church, a devotional rite in which the congregation is blessed with the sign of the cross made with the consecrated Host enclosed in an ostensorium or ciborium is properly called "The Benediction of the Blessed Sacrament" but often goes by the abbreviated name "the Benediction."

Benediction occurs in literature frequently as a synonym for "blessing," either at the level of casual epithet, such as the *"A benedicitee!"* of one of Chaucer's suspect clergy (*Friar's Tale*, 3.1456), or as a sincere invocation of the formal liturgical blessing. Malcolm, in Shakespeare's *Macbeth*, speaks of the royal touch of healing as a benediction (4.3.155-56), Kent in *King Lear*, of "the common saw, / Thou out of Heaven's benediction comest / To the warm sun!" (2.2.163-65). Later, Kent refers to Lear's having "stripped" Cordelia "from his benediction" (i.e., his blessing, as well as his will) (4.3.44-46). George Herbert observes a fluctuation in usage, that "in the time of Popery, the Priests *Benedicite,* and his holy water were overvalued; and now are we fallen to the clean contrary, even from superstition to coldnes" (*A Priest to the Temple*, 36.15-17). J. G. DAVIES

BENJAMIN One of the twelve tribes of Israel, named for the youngest son of Jacob.

See also AARON; JACOB; JOSEPH THE PATRIARCH; TRIBES OF ISRAEL.

BESETTING SINS *See* CLOUD OF WITNESSES.

BETHANY A village less than two miles (3 km.) from Jerusalem, home of Lazarus and his sisters, Mary and Martha.

See also ASCENSION; LAZARUS OF BETHANY; MARTHA; MARY MAGDALENE.

BETHEL *See* AMOS; JACOB; JACOB'S LADDER; SHILOH; WRESTLING JACOB.

BETHESDA The pool of Bethesda, near Jerusalem's Sheep Gate, is mentioned only in John 5:2, where it is described as the site of a miraculous healing (vv. 2-16). Owing to variants in the MSS, the name has assumed a number of forms and etymologies: "Betheder" ("sheepfold"), the form suggested by St. Jerome, has long been rejected. The KJV and others read "Bethesda" (probably from Aram. *bet-hisda'*, "house of mercy," or from Heb. *bet-'eshdah*, "place of outpouring," a reading which seems to be confirmed by the Copper Scroll from Qumran [3Q15], which, compounding the dual, calls it *bet-'eshdatayin*, "place of [two] outpourings"). The RSV and others read "Bethzatha" (the name of a northern suburb of Jerusalem). The pool was surrounded by five porticos in which the sick waited for an angel to stir the water (John 5:3-4) and provide healing for the first to step into it. Here Jesus healed a man who, during his thirty-eight years of sickness, had never been helped into the pool.

Since this healing took place on a Sabbath, the religious Jews sought to kill Jesus (v. 16).

In the early Church, the healing at Bethesda is often interpreted allegorically. For St. Augustine the pool signifies the Jewish people, the five porches being the Law, and Christ himself the one who troubles the water and rouses it "towards his own death" (*In Joan. Ev.* 17.7.3; he is anticipated here by Tertullian, *Adv. Jud.* 13). The corporeal healing in the pool is seen as a type of spiritual healing in general, and of baptism in particular (Chrysostom, *Hom. on John*, 36.1; see also Tertullian, *De baptismo*, 5; for a late Puritan echo, see Jonathan Edwards, *Efficacious Grace,* 95.1).

Some later exegetes suggest factual details concerning Bethesda which have mostly been refuted by modern scholarship. Tyndale takes the pools of Bethesda and Siloam to be identical (*Answer to Sir Thomas More's Dialogue,* 1.4). Calvin, in his commentary on John's Gospel, assumes that the sick around the pool were also beggars.

Early English literature appropriates the place name in various paraphrases of the Gospels, reflecting the variant spellings but generally preferring the form "Bethsaida" (*Rushworth Gospel, West Saxon Gospels, Lindisfarne*). In the *Cursor Mundi* the Antichrist, it is predicted, will be fostered in Bethesda (22101).

The typological interpretation of the Bethesda event was soon secularized and led to frequent figurative uses which usually focused on one part of the narrative such as the troubling of the water, its healing powers, or the sick man's coming too late. Thus the ending of Andrew Marvell's "The First Anniversary of the Government under His Highness the Lord Protector" calls Cromwell the "Angel of our Commonweal." He troubles the waters of parliament only to provide healing. American Puritan Cotton Mather titled his collection of medical lore *The Angel of Bethesda*. Wordsworth compares Bethesda to the human heart, describing the poet's words as

Words that can soothe, more than they agitate;
Whose spirit, like the angel that went down
Into Bethesda's pool, with healing virtue
Informs the fountain in the human breast
Which by the visitation was disturbed. ("Lines
Suggested by a Portrait from the Pencil of F. Stone,"
124-28)

A. H. Clough's poem "Bethesda: A Sequel" tells of a man who is sick of duty, of serving the world's desires. The poem ends in uncertainty about the nature of the pool's waters — "Of Lethe were they, or Philosophy" — and about the possibility of the sick man's being healed prematurely by "some more diviner stranger."

Ironic use is made of the Bethesda story by Charlotte Brontë in *Jane Eyre*. According to Mr. Brocklehurst, the hypocritical manager of Lowood Institution, young Jane has been sent there "even as the Jews of old sent their diseased to the troubled pool of Bethesda." He asks the teachers and superintendent "not to allow the waters to stagnate round her" (chap. 7). In George Eliot's *Felix Holt* the town of Treby is to be turned into a fashionable watering-place and given the name of "Bethesda Spa" — a name which is considered blasphemous by those who object to this plan (chap. 3).

The sick man's disappointment about always coming too late is echoed ironically by Samuel Butler, whose Theobald Pontifex feels "like the impotent man at the pool of Bethesda." He tries to meet young ladies but is "almost immediately cut out by someone less bashful than himself" (*The Way of All Flesh*, chap. 10). Similar references to the sick man's belatedness can be found in Thomas Hardy's *A Pair of Blue Eyes*, chap. 30, and in his *The Mayor of Casterbridge*, chap. 10.

A more serious handling of the story by Herman Melville combines social protest with a (certain) Christian hope. Wellingborough Redburn compares the dockwall beggars of Liverpool to the Jewish cripples and offers up a prayer "that some angel might descend, and turn the waters of the docks into an elixir, that would heal all their woes, and make them, man and woman, healthy and whole as their ancestors, Adam and Eve, in the garden" (*Redburn*, chap. 38). In *Villette* Charlotte Brontë makes the pool representative of both the world and history: "thousands lie round the pool, weeping and despairing, to see it, through slow years, stagnant. Long are the 'times' of Heaven: the orbits of angel messengers seem wide to mortal vision" (chap. 17).

A late example of allegorizing is Cardinal Newman's sermon on the text. Identifying sickness with sin, he sees Bethesda as the "waters of health," where a man who has been "taken with the goods of this world" lies, "unable to advance himself towards a cure, in consequence of his long habit." Others pass him by, who are perhaps unable to help one who "obstinately refuses to be comforted" (*Parochial Sermons*).

In 20th-cent. American literature Thornton Wilder, in *The Angel That Troubled the Waters*, dramatizes the urgent wish of the sick to be healed, and their feelings of envy and suspicion toward each other. When a physician arrives at Bethesda who wants only to be healed of his sin, he is denied the cure by the angel. The moral of the play is: "In Love's service only the wounded soldiers can serve." In "Nocturne at Bethesda," a poem by African-American poet Arna Bontemps, the sick man's waiting for healing serves as an image of unfulfilled hope for racial equality:

> This pool that once the angels troubled does not move.
> No angel stirs it now, no Savior comes
> With healing in His hands to raise the sick
> And bid the lame man leap upon the ground.

See also DISEASE AND HEALING.
Bibliography. Brown, R. *The Gospel According to John*

I-XII (1966), 205-11; Newman, J. H. *Parochial Sermons,* 5th ed. (1844), 1.376-88; Temple, W. *Readings in St. John's Gospel* (1939), 107-19.   MANFRED SIEBALD

BETHLEHEM   Two biblical places bear the name *Bethlehem* (probably meaning "house of bread") — Bethlehem of Zebulun (cf. Judg. 19:15) and Bethlehem Judah (also Bethlehem Ephratah), 7 km. south of Jerusalem. The latter is by far the better known. Bethlehem is the setting for most of the book of Ruth, and David's home (1 Sam. 17:12). The prophet Micah names it as the Messiah's birthplace (Mic. 5:2), and the Gospels record Christ's birth in a stable there (Matt. 2:1; Luke 2:4-7). It is also the place where the adoration of the shepherds (Luke 2:8-20) and the Magi (Matt. 2:1-12) occurred, and the site of Herod's slaying of the innocents (Matt. 2:16-18).

Bethlehem's place in Christian tradition owes mainly to its being the site of Christ's birth, but there are also allegorizations of the town. Luther concludes from its name that "without the Gospel there is nothing but desert on earth, no professing of God nor thanksgiving. But where the Gospel is, and Christ, there is Bethlehem, rich of grain, and Judea, the thankful" (*Kirchenpostille*, WA 10.1.1, p. 78). A similar allegorization by Roger Hutchinson ("Second Sermon on the Lord's Supper") draws a parallel to the sacramental bread.

In early English literature, Bethlehem is usually mentioned in paraphrases of the Christmas story. Laȝamon's *Brut* (1.386-87) alludes to it, as do the mystery plays of the Nativity. *Cursor Mundi* describes it as the dwelling place of Jesse (7348-49), as the burying place of David (8537) and Solomon (9137), and the birthplace of Christ (11177). The same work then describes the slaying of the innocents there (11559-94), an event which is referred to also in John Audelay's poem *"In Die Sanctorum Innocencium"* (EETS o.s. 184, 189-90). Almost all the details of Christ's birth were discussed by medieval writers — the time of year (Lydgate, *Fall of Princes*, 1405-08) and the type of house in which he was born (*Piers Plowman*, B.12.147-49; cf. also 17.122). *Piers Plowman*, in an expression of antifraternal polemic perhaps, claims that the birth of Christ was not in a stable or other relatively disreputable edifice, but in the best dwelling place in Bethlehem.

"Bethlehem" acquired a new meaning when, in the 14th cent., the priory of St. Mary of Bethlehem (founded in 1247 as the English residence of the titular bishop of Bethlehem — who is mentioned in *Piers Plowman*, B.15.538) became a hospital for lunatics. References to this "bedlam" can be found in Shakespeare (*2 Henry 6*, 5.1; *King Lear*, 3.4), in Dryden ("The Medal," 285), in Carlyle's *Sartor Resartus* (2.6), and in Dickens's *Uncommercial Traveller* (chap. 13). Often the reference is ironic, as in Dryden's "Art thou of Bethlehem's noble college free? / Stark, staring mad, that thou wouldst tempt the sea?" ("Fifth Satire of Perseus," 212-13). "Bethlehem" or

"Bedlam" soon came to refer to any insane asylum in both English and American literature (cf. Cotton Mather, *Magnalia Christi Americana,* 7.4: "A Bethlehem seems to have been fitter for them than a gallows"; Melville, *Redburn,* chap. 60; and Anne Sexton's poem "Lullaby"). The name has served as an equivalent of "crazy" (e.g., Shakespeare, *Henry 5,* 5.1, and Hart Crane, "To Brooklyn Bridge") and is also used in a figurative sense: Poe speaks (in "Ligeia") of the "Bedlam patterns of the carpets."

"Bethlehem" in its original sense serves as a symbol of Christ's birth in such poems as Henry Vaughan's "The Search" (and, later, Emily Dickinson's "They Have Not Chosen Me"). Milton refers to the star which guided the Magi when he describes how the "rayes of Bethlehem" blind the eyes of the heathen gods ("On the Morning of Christ's Nativity"). References to the "star of Bethlehem" are also found in Richard Crashaw, "Herod"; Shelley, "Hellas"; Emerson, "Fragments on the Poet and the Poetic Gift"; Emily Dickinson, "If He Dissolve"; and Hopkins, "Moonless Darkness." Milton's Satan has heard the "angelic song in Bethlehem field" but still doubts whether Christ is the Son of God (*Paradise Regained,* 4.505; Coleridge, "Religious Musings").

"Tom May's Death" by Andrew Marvell alludes to a legend according to which the house of the Virgin Mary was miraculously conveyed from Bethlehem (actually Nazareth) to Loreto. Wordsworth, in "The Council of Clermont," mentions Bethlehem as one of the places which the Pontiff wants to conquer by means of a crusade (*Ecclesiastical Sonnets,* 1.33). He also alludes to the flower known as "Star-of-Bethlehem" in "To a Lady" (cf. also Ruskin, *The Queen of the Air,* 2.81; and Robert Frost, *A Masque of Reason,* 12). William Blake exploits the meaning "house of bread" in *Jerusalem* (chap. 2, pl. 31, line 25); and Tennyson, in "Sir John Oldcastle," equates Lutterworth, where Wyclif lived, with Bethlehem, for in it "the word was born again."

Emerson's reference to "Bethlehem's heart" ("Monadnoc," 299) implies being touched by Christ's birth. John Ruskin, who mentions St. Jerome's stay at Bethlehem (*Valle Crucis,* 1.28; 2.6), elsewhere contrasts biblical and modern relationships between parents and children by referring to Matt. 2:18: ". . . as the Rachel of Bethlehem weeps for her children, and will not be comforted, because they are not, the Rachel of England weeps for her children, and will not be comforted — because they are" (*Fors Clavigera,* 4.46.11).

Bethlehem is the setting of an entire section of Melville's long poem *Clarel* (4.6). It is discussed as the site of Christ's birth but also as the destination for pilgrims of all denominations in the 19th cent. In Hopkins's "The Blessed Virgin compared to the Air We Breathe," Bethlehem becomes a place within human beings. The poem talks of the continuation of the mystery of incarnation: Christ makes "New Bethlems" in us, and he is born there, "evening, noon, and morn. . . ."

W. B. Yeats's poem "The Second Coming" proclaims the replacement of Christian civilization and ends on the image of an apocalyptic "rough beast," which "Slouches towards Bethlehem to be born." James Joyce, in *Ulysses,* twice mentions the slaughter of the innocents — once as an ironic indicator of the Christmas season (Vintage [1961], 172), and once as an equally ironic description of childless marriage (423). John Updike's town of Olinger in *The Centaur* becomes "yet one more Bethlehem," the unknowing site of a spiritual visitation by the "infant God."

Bibliography. Brown, R. *The Birth of the Messiah* (1977).　　　　　　　　　　　　　MANFRED SIEBALD

BETHUEL *See* REBEKAH.

BETRAYAL OF JESUS *See* JUDAS ISCARIOT.

BETTER TO MARRY THAN TO BURN　The apostle Paul, in 1 Cor. 7:7-9, expresses the wish that "all men" in pursuit of a religious life were, like himself, single. Nevertheless, if the "unmarried and widows" cannot cope with sexual frailty, "let them marry," he says, "for it is better to marry than to burn." The "burning" in question is typically associated by patristic commentators with "the devouring fire of lust" (e.g., St. Ambrose, *Libri duo de poenitentia,* 14.68-77). As St. Jerome has it, "it is better to take a husband than to commit fornication" (*Ep.* 48.17). Jerome's reading is subtended by an overriding case he makes for monogamous relationship; hence, "it is better that a woman should know one man (though he should be a second or third) than that she should know several" (48.8). Characteristically of patristic discussions, those of Ambrose, Jerome, and St. Augustine (*De bono viduetate*) concern themselves with women, chiefly widows, because the care of widows — many of whom lost their husbands while still young — was a significant burden of care in the Church.

Literary applications tend to see a humor in the lines not so apparent to earlier readers of St. Paul. When Chaucer's oft-widowed Wife of Bath expounds the verse, she also takes liberty with Jerome's well-known interpretation as a means of making her case for a sixth marriage:

> . . . th'apostle seith that I am free
> To wedde, a Goddes half, where it liketh me.
> He seith that to be wedded is no synne;
> Bet is to be wedded than to brynne. (*Canterbury Tales,* 3.49-52)

Her sense of the "burning" is as a consequence of promiscuity, which she later admits to knowing quite a bit about:

> Al were it good no womman for to touche —
> He mente as in his bed or in his couche —
> For peril is bothe fyr and tow t'assemble —
> Ye knowe what this ensaumple may resemble. (3.87-90)

If beneath the surface humor of Chaucer's characterization of the Wife's passion there is genuine pathos, there
is pathos without the humor in Howard Nemerov's poem
"Young Woman," a kind of introspective *carpe diem.* The
speaker, standing naked before a mirror, contemplates her
options:

> "One way or the other way," she said,
> "How shall I know the difference,
> When wrinkles come, to spinster or bride?
> Whether to marry or burn is bless–
> ed best, O stranger to my bed,
> There is no pity in flesh."

See also ADULTERY; BRIDE, BRIDEGROOM.

BEULAH   In Isa. 62:4 the name *Beulah* (Heb.; "married") is symbolically applied to Israel in its future state
of restoration; the etymology is given in the verse: "thy
land shall be married . . . so shall thy sons marry thee."
As the tranquil land where pilgrims pause before crossing
the River of Death in Bunyan's *Pilgrim's Progress* (pt. 2)
Beulah assumes a visibility unprecedented in either
Jewish or Christian commentary. Influenced by Bunyan,
William Blake sees Beulah, for all its paradisal qualities,
still the land of a fettered imagination from which Milton
is unable to cross the gulf into creative freedom (*Milton,*
21.4-10). Its eternal complement is Eden. Sexual love, for
Blake, can be a "Beulah" experience, an opening into
"Edenic" bliss — a place of flowers (*Four Zoas,* 133.10-
13) and beautiful maidens (*Jerusalem,* 79.73-77) — but
not to be mistaken for Eden itself (*Four Zoas,* 83.20-26).
As it had been for Bunyan, nonetheless, Blake's Beulah
still represents a state of spiritual marriage, in *Jerusalem*
symbolizing "not a union between male and female but
rather between mankind and the Savior" (Damrosch,
230). Robert Louis Stevenson parodies Bunyan in describing his young man on the verge of amatory success
as entering "that land of Beulah which is upon the borders
of Heaven and within sight of the City of Love" (*Virginibus Puerisque,* "On Falling in Love"; cf. his *Weir of
Harmiston,* 6, and "Walt Whitman"). Also on the strength
of Bunyan's influence, but modified by later Protestant
typology, Beulah figures in gospel songs and American
spirituals as a synonym for heaven itself.

See also HEAVEN.

Bibliography. Damrosch, L. *Symbol and Truth in Blake's
Myth* (1980).

BIBLE   The English word *Bible* is an equivalent of Gk.
biblia ("books"), the diminutive of which is *biblos,* the
inner bark of the papyrus. The expression "the books,"
referring to the Torah and perhaps other parts of the
Hebrew Scriptures, occurs in LXX Dan. 9:2, *ta biblia.* St.
Jerome, translating the Vg Latin Bible, called the canonical collection of books which make up the scriptural
anthology in his own time *biblioteca divina* ("the divine

library"). Change from this generally plural to the singular form is a 13th-cent. development, in which the
neuter plural came to be regarded as a feminine singular;
in Latin, *biblia* might thus mean not only "the books," but
"the book." *Biblia Sacra* (The Holy Book) then becomes
in English simply the "Bible" or "Bibel," the first English
uses of which are found more or less simultaneously in
Wycliffite sermons, in Chaucer's *Canterbury Tales,* and
in Langland's *Piers Plowman.* In English Christian Bibles
there are typically sixty-six canonical books, with up to
eight apocryphal books sometimes included, sometimes
appended, sometimes (as in the 1613 KJV edition) published as a supplementary volume. The Hebrew Bible, in
the arrangement of Josephus, has twenty-two sacred
books (one for each letter of the Hebrew alphabet) corresponding to the thirty-nine books of the Christian OT:
five of the Law, thirteen of the Prophets, and four poetic
books (Psalms, Proverbs, Song of Songs, and Ecclesiastes). The Talmud also admits of a division into twenty-
four books, separating Ruth from Judges and Lamentations from Jeremiah (B. Bat. 14b). A brief history of
English translations of the Bible may be found in the
bibliographical essays included in this volume.

Numerous English poets have written lyrical praise of
the Bible. Among the best known are George Herbert's
twin sonnets "The Holy Scriptures," the second of which
reads:

> Oh that I knew how all thy lights combine,
>   And the configurations of their glorie!
>   Seeing not onely how each verse doth shine,
> But all the constellations of the storie.
> This verse marks that, and both do make a motion
>   Unto a third, that ten leaves off doth lie:
>   Then as dispersed herbs do watch a potion,
> These three make up some Christians destinie:
> Such are thy secrets, which my life makes good,
>   And comments on thee: for in ev'rything
>   Thy words do finde me out, & parallels bring
> And in another make me understood.
>   Starres are poore books, & oftentimes do misse:
>   This book of starres lights to eternal blisse.

Other memorable examples include Isaac Watts's paraphrase of Ps. 19, "God's Word and Works," William
Cowper's "The Bible" ("The Spirit breathes upon the
word, / And brings the truth to sight"), and John Greenleaf Whittier's "The Book," which views the Bible as
foundational to literature and culture:

> Gallery of sacred pictures manifold
> A minister rich in holy effigies
> And bearing on entablature and frieze
> The hieroglyphic oracles of old . . .

The Bible is to Whittier what the whole *"Temple"* is to
George Herbert (cf. Whittier's "The Word").

Felicia Heman's "To a Family Bible" celebrates the role
of the English Bible in domestic life, even as Robert

Nicoll's "The Ha' Bible" celebrates the "Chief of the household gods / Which hallow Scotland's lowly cottage-homes." Wordsworth's "Translation of the Bible" is an historical poem recalling the embattled Reformers' success in getting English versions into print, evidently recollecting in particular Erasmus, and Tyndale's Preface to the NT:

> But, to outweigh all harm, the sacred Book
> In dusty sequestration wrapt too long,
> Assumes the accents of our native tongue;
> And to who guides the plough or wields the crook,
> With understanding spirit now may look
> Upon her records, listen to her song,
> And sift her laws. . . .

These are largely the sentiments of Ruskin, though like Whittier and Matthew Arnold *(God and the Bible)* the Victorian aesthetic writer is also keenly attuned to the Bible's value as cultural foundation:

> Only therefore, in days when the Cross was received with courage, the Scripture searched with honesty, and the Pastor heard in faith, can the pure word of God, and the bright sword of the Spirit, be recognised in the heart and hand of Christianity.
>
> The effect of Biblical poetry and legend on its intellect, must be traced farther, through decadent ages, and in unfenced fields; — producing 'Paradise Lost' for us, no less than the 'Divina Commedia'; — Goethe's 'Faust', and Byron's 'Cain', no less than the 'Imitatio Christi'. Much more, must the scholar, who would comprehend in any degree approaching to completeness, the influence of the Bible on mankind, be able to read the interpretations of it which rose into the great arts of Europe at their culmination. *(Our Fathers Have Told Us,* 3.37)

Emily Dickinson's lines are less sanguine:

> The Bible is an antique Volume —
> Written by faded Men
> At the suggestion of Holy Spectres —
> Subjects — Bethlehem —
> Eden — the ancient Homestead —
> Satan — the Brigadier —
> Judas — the Great Defaulter —
> David — the Troubadour —
> Sin — a distinguished Precipice
> Others must resist —
> Boys that "believe" are very lonesome —
> Other Boys are "lost" —
> Had but the Tale a warbling Teller —
> All the Boys would come —
> Orpheus' Sermon captivated —
> It did not condemn —

For Western Christians after the Reformation, there is a persistent tendency to link the "the Word made flesh" with the written word of the Bible. The first two stanzas of a 19th-cent. hymn by W. W. How (1867) typifies this important post-Renaissance connection:

> O Word of God incarnate,
> O Wisdom from on high,

> O Truth unchanged, unchanging
> O Light of our dark sky;
> We praise thee for the radiance
> That from the hallowed page,
> A lantern to our footsteps,
> Shines on from age to age.

> The Church from thee, her Master,
> Received the gift divine.
> And still that light she lifteth
> O'er all the earth to shine.
> It is the golden casket
> Where gems of truth are stored;
> It is the heaven-drawn picture
> Of thee, the living Word.

A noteworthy 20th-cent. capturing of some of the same ideas occurs in Margaret Avison's poem, "The Bible to be Believed" *(sunblue,* 56).

BILDAD *See* JOB'S COMFORTERS.

BILHAH Handmaiden of Rachel, the beloved wife of Jacob.
See also RACHEL.

BINDING OF ISAAC *See* ABRAHAM; ISAAC.

BIRDS The main classification of biblical birds is into those birds which were "clean" and could be eaten, as opposed to those which were "unclean" (Deut. 14:11-20; cf. Lev. 11:13-19). In general, birds of prey which took carrion in their claws were to be avoided for food. Birds were also the poor person's sacrificial offerings: pigeons were readily available because they were bred as domestic birds, and turtledoves, though they migrated south in winter, could be trapped in season (Lev. 1:14; 14:22; Num. 6:10; Luke 2:24; John 2:14-16).

In the account of creation (Gen. 1:21) birds are said to have been made on the fifth day. Man was to have dominion over them (v. 26) and to name them (2:20). Noah took birds into the ark at the time of the Flood and found the raven and the dove useful in determining when the waters had receded. In the Joseph story the baker, who dreamed he saw birds eating out of the basket on his head, ultimately became carrion for the birds (Gen. 40:17). God bore his people "on eagles' wings" and brought them safely out of Egypt (Exod. 19:4; Deut. 32:11). Elijah was fed by the ravens (1 Kings 17:6). In Canticles singing birds prompt human love songs (Cant. 2:12), and the Psalmist calls on them to praise the Lord (Ps. 148:10).

Though references to bird song are few in the Bible, its absence denotes desolation (Jer. 4:25; 9:10; 12:4; Zeph. 1:3). The Lord's protection is likened to the hovering wing of a parent bird over its nest (Pss. 17:8; 91:4; Isa. 31:5), which is a place of security (Pss. 84:3; 104:17; Prov. 27:8), and the return of migratory birds speaks of Israel's return from exile (Hos. 11:11).

Since owls and birds of prey haunt ruined buildings they indicate destruction (Isa. 34:11, 15; Zeph. 2:14); the melancholy moan of doves depicts remorse (Isa. 59:11; Ezek. 7:16), and birds in general can be harbingers of doom (Jer. 49:22). On the other hand, desolation can be signified by their absence: "all the birds of the air had fled" (Jer. 4:25; cf. Hos. 4:3). The thought of becoming carrion for the birds was so horrifying as to become a picture of ultimate doom (1 Sam. 17:44; 1 Kings 14:11; Jer. 7:33; Ezek. 29:5).

In the NT birds illustrate God's providential care: "Your heavenly Father feedeth them" (Matt. 6:26); though they are sold cheaply, "not one of them is forgotten before God" (Luke 12:6); "you are of more value than many sparrows" (Luke 12:7; cf. Pss. 50:11; 104:12, 17). They can also, however, have a sinister meaning. In the parable of the sower birds snatch away the good seed and represent the evil one who opposes the kingdom of God (Matt. 13:4, 19). In Revelation birds play a part in fulfilling God's final judgment. The massive carnage provides a feast for all the fowls which fly in the heavens (Rev. 19:17-18; cf. Ezek. 39:4, 17-20).

In early English the general term was "fowl," while "bird" meant a small or young fowl or a maiden. Only in the 16th cent. did "bird" begin to have its present connotation, and the KJV most often uses "fowl." In the ME poem *Gaude Maria, Christes moder* Maria is called "thou byrde so bryght," where "byrde" clearly means "maiden."

Chaucer, in his Prologue to *The Legend of Good Women,* pictures birds who have escaped the net of the fowler, reflecting traditional imagery drawn from texts such as Pss. 91:3; 124:7 (cf. the *Occupatio* of Odo of Cluny [3.837-41]).

The proverbial warning, "Curse not the king, no not in thy thought, . . . for a bird of the air shall carry the voice" (Eccl. 10:20), is echoed several times in English literature, perhaps most memorably by Shakespeare (*2 Henry 4*, 5.5.13) and Jonathan Swift ("Letter to Stella," May 23, 1711).

Henry Vaughan ("Man") makes clear reference to Matt. 6:26: "The birds nor sow nor reap, yet sup and dine," while J. G. Holland (alias Timothy Titcomb) comments shrewdly that "God gives every bird its food, but does not throw it into the nest" ("Gold Foil: Providence"). Tennyson, subtly altering Cant. 2:12, mourns that "The song of the bird shall no more be heard" ("All Things Will Die"). Wordsworth, in his *Ecclesiastical Sonnets*, pictures the Reformers as "Scattering, like birds escaped the fowler's net" ("English Reformers in Exile," 1), where the simile exactly follows OT usage. Thomas Hardy in *Tess of the D'Urbervilles* employs the same image to depict the fall of Tess, "a girl of simple life, . . . who had been caught . . . like a bird in a springe" or "like a bird caught in a clap net."

Bibliography. Brown, C. "Birds." *NIDNTT* 1.172-76; Cansdale, G. S. *Animals of Bible Lands* (1970), 140-93;

Driver, G. R. "Birds in the Old Testament: 1." *PEQ* 87 (1955), 5-20; "Birds in the Old Testament: 2." *PEQ* 87 (1955), 129ff.; "Once Again: Birds in the Bible." *PEQ* 90 (1958), 56ff.; McCullough, W. S. "Bird." *IDB* 1.439-40; Rowland, B. *Birds with Human Souls: A Guide to Bird Symbolism* (1978); Waltke, B. "Birds." *ISBE* 1.511-13.

JOYCE G. BALDWIN

BIRTHRIGHT When Jacob wrested the birthright from his elder brother Esau by means of trading it for a mess of red pottage, Esau was relinquishing his spiritual inheritance, the covenant God had made with their grandfather Abraham (Gen. 12:1-8; 13:14-17). This loss apparently meant little to Esau (cf. Pirqe R. El. 35; Tg. Yer. Gen. 25–29). However, when he later associated with it certain material benefits it became a matter of much graver concern, so that Jacob, with his mother Rebekah's help, had to deceive blind Isaac into mistaking Jacob for the firstborn of the twins (Gen. 25:24-26; 38:27-30; cf. Gen. Rab. 65–67).

Being the firstborn male in a Near Eastern society entitled one to numerous privileges, including a double portion of the material inheritance of the father (Deut. 21:15-17). Substitution of a younger son for the eldest, thus overturning the order of primogeniture, is a significant theme in the Bible, affecting not only the stories of Jacob and Esau (repeated later in Jacob's "adopting" of the two sons of favored Joseph and the "blessing" of the younger of these, Ephraim [Gen. 21:11; 48:5-19]), but also the story of David who, though the youngest son of Jesse, was made king, and of his own youngest son Solomon, who became king after him (1 Sam. 16:12; 1 Kings 1:28-30; 1 Chron. 21:3; cf. Gen. 37:3; 44:20). Later, talmudic law provided for the disposal of property prior to death in accordance with parental preference, rather than strict adherence to the law of primogeniture (Heb. *bekorah;* cf. the precedents usually cited, Gen. 21:10; Deut. 21:15ff.). In the NT one of Jesus' most memorable parables concerns the relationship between the firstborn son and his younger brother, the latter of whom squanders his inheritance yet is "favored" by his forgiving father over the elder son, who in some measure "despises" his own birthright by taking it for granted (Luke 15:11-32).

Allegorizations of the Jacob-Esau story, locus classicus for biblical tradition concerning the birthright, are common in patristic commentary. In extreme versions such as that of St. Hippolytus (quoted by St. Jerome, *Ep.* 36):

> Isaac conveys a figure of God the Father; Rebecca of the Holy Spirit; Esau of the first people and the devil; Jacob of the Church, or of Christ. That Isaac was old points to the end of the world; that his eyes were dim, denotes that faith had perished from the world. . . . That the elder son is called expresses the Jews' bondage to the law.

St. John Chrysostom reads the passage morally: "How

came Esau to be overcome? How came he to prefer the present pleasure to the future honor? . . . Esau through greediness abandoned his birthright, and was set upon fratricide" (*Hom.* 27 [Acts 12:18-19]). Jerome imagines that "the Jews go on weeping to this day. . . . They follow a foolish custom of the Pharisees, and eat lentils, it would seem, to show for what poor fare they have lost their birthright" (*Ep.* 39.4). In the relatively simple but sweeping typology of St. Augustine, the statement that "the elder shall serve the younger" applies to Jews and Christians; Jacob or "Israel" becomes typologically the Church (*Enarr. in Ps.* 47.4-5; 114.2-4). However, Augustine insists that the birthright is not conveyed automatically as a family inheritance. Rather, as he argues in *De baptismo* (5.16.21):

> it rests only in a holy conversation and good life, in which all of whom that Bride consists are to participate as members, so that the Bride may be without spot or wrinkle, and like a dove which groans amidst the wickedness of many crows. Otherwise we would be in the position of arguing that while Esau lost his birthright on account of his lust after a mess of pottage, we are entitled to imagine that it is now held by defrauders, thieves, usurers, envious persons, drunkards and the like.

These sentiments (reinforced by Boethius in his *De Consolatione Philosophiae*; cf. Wyclif's *De Domino Civilo*) are reflected in Chaucer's "Gentilesse," in which he observes:

> But ther may no man, as men may wel see,
> Bequethe his heir his vertuous noblesse
> (That is appropred unto no degree
> But to the firste fader in magestee,
> That maketh hem his heyres that him queme),
> Al were he mytre, croune, or diademe. (16-21)

Much the same view is expressed by the Countess of Rousillon in Shakespeare's *All's Well That Ends Well* (1.1.63-66), and in William Cowper's "Conversation" (763-66).

These ideas are stock-in-trade for Reformation commentators on the Jacob and Esau narrative. Thus Luther: "Esau has the name and the glory of being the firstborn, but meanwhile he falls suddenly and is deprived of all glory and honor. Therefore do not sleep; but be attentive to all opportunities, lest you lose your gifts and the kingdom of God because of your negligence. For this reason Scripture has set this example before us, not as a cold and dead story, but for our instruction and to remind us of the state of affairs and persons as it exists in all ages" (*Comm. on Genesis,* 25.29-30 [*WA* 43.417-18]). Esau is thus a type of "the wicked and hypocritical church" because "it is in the habit of glorying very much in the name of God and wants to be regarded as the [true] church. And as far as the world is concerned it *is* the church. Similarly, Esau has the primogeniture, but he despises it. His contempt causes him to lose it; accordingly he in turn becomes

despised, rejected and despoiled" (Gen. 25:31-34 [*WA* 43.427-28]). Esau is then identified by Luther with Rome and Jacob with the Reforming churches of northern Europe. Calvin devotes much of his commentary on the passage to arguing that the choice of Jacob over Esau had nothing to do with merit; God simply and freely chose to elect Jacob for no evident reason that reason might adduce (*Comm. on Genesis* [chap. 25]). He does observe, however, the "remarkable indifference" of Esau to the transaction, and says, "Thus are all profane persons accustomed to act: alienated from the celestial life, they do not perceive that they have lost anything till God thunders upon them out of heaven. As long as they enjoy their carnal wishes, they cast the anger of God behind them; and hence it happens that they go stupidly forward to their own destruction" (25:34). In his commentary on Hebrews, Calvin adds that the narrative "may be viewed as an exposition of the word 'profane'; for when Esau set more value on one meal than on his birthright, he lost his blessing" (12:16-17).

Lapide follows talmudic sources and Nicholas of Lyra in maintaining that Jacob did not sin by taking advantage of the birthright exchange, but that Esau sinned in selling it (*Comm. in Genesim,* 25.31-34). While this view is later adopted by Matthew Henry, the *Annotations* of Matthew Poole proclaim Jacob a sinner also, "because he tempted his Brother to an act of Profaneness and Folly, and so was guilty of his Sin. . . . He addeth another Sin, in hurrying his Brother into an Oath by precipitation, which neither his Brother should have taken, nor Jacob should have advised him to take, without mature Advice" (Gen. 25:31; 33). John Wesley focuses on Esau's offense, but is the first major commentator to consider at length his repentance and the possibility of his salvation (*Works,* 10.236-37). Like some of the later Catholic commentators (see also Lapide), he takes up in one of his sermons the connection of primogeniture with the rights of the priesthood (*Works,* 7.274). In his own treatment Wesley indicates a tendency among Protestant exegetes after Calvin to shift the typological foundation for authority and leadership within the Church in such a way that an OT type replaces the NT model of Peter and apostolic succession as the pattern for sacerdotal governance. A simpler paradigm is that of Matthew Poole, who says:

> the birthright then had divers privileges; as 1. Dignity and Authority over his Brethren, *Gen.* 4.7 and 27.29, 37 and 49.3.2. A double portion, *Deut.* 21.17. *1 Chron.* 5.1.3. A special blessing from his Father, *Gen.* 27.4. 4. The Priesthood and the chief Government of the Affairs of the Church in his Father's absense, or sickness, and after his death, *Numb.* 8.16, 17 &c. 5. The firstborn was a special type of Christ, who was to be a firstborn; and of the Church, which is called God's firstborn, as *Exod.* 4.22, and of the great privilege of the Church, particularly of Adoption and Eternal Life. See *Heb.* 12.23. (*Annotations*)

Renaissance authors found a classical analogue to the

biblical tale of usurped birthright in the story of Titan and Saturn, one invoked by Spenser in his "Mutability" Canto 6, and by Milton in the first book of *Paradise Lost,* where the classical and biblical contexts are in effect interwoven (510-13ff.). In bk. 3, God the Father tells Christ that while Adam's "crime makes guilty all his Sons, thy merit / Imputed shall absolve them who renounce / Thir own both righteous and unrighteous deeds," adding that he "has been found / By Merit more than Birthright Son of God" (290-92; 308-09). Donne makes a cosmological application in "The Storm," where "Darkness, light's elder brother, his birthright / Claims o'er this world, and to heaven hath chased light" (67-68). Robert Herrick takes up a NT reading in "Coheires":

> We are Coheires with *Christ,* nor shall his own
> *Heire-ship* be lesse, by our adoption:
> The number here of Heires, shall be from the state
> Of His great *Birth-right* nothing derogate.

Crashaw contrasts two world-orders when he welcomes the infant Jesus "to more than *Caesars* Birthright" ("Hymn on the Holy Nativity").

Swift offers a parody of the Jacob and Esau exchange in "Robin and Harry" (29-36), in which:

> Robin, who ne'er his mind could fix
> To live without a coach and six,
> To patch his broken fortunes, found
> A mistress worth five thousand pound;
> Swears he could get her in an hour,
> If Gaffer Harry would endow her;
> And sell, to pacify his wrath,
> A birth-right for a mess of broth.

The "birthright" recognized by some Romantic poets is a kind of original pastoral harmony with nature. Wordsworth is the chief among nostalgic celebrants of this lost inheritance: "With our pastures about us we could not be sad, / ... But the comfort, the blessings, and wealth that we had, / We slighted them all, — and our birth-right was lost" ("Repentance," 21-24). An allusion to Esau's folly is muted in "Vaudracour and Julia" (102-06; cf. "Liberty," 21-26; "Desultory Stanzas," 591-92). The theme is more extensively developed by Wordsworth in *The Prelude* (2.265-72; 10.209-21) and *The Excursion* (5.615-20; 8.276-82; 9.93-101). Ironic or parodic references to the mess of pottage are found in Byron's *Don Juan* (e.g., 5.351-52) and "The Age of Bronze" (628-35), in which the predicament is cast in more modern terms:

> And will they not repay the treasures lent?
> No: down with every thing, and up with rent!
> Their good, ill, health, wealth, joy, or discontent,
> Being, end, aim, religion — rent, rent, rent!
> Thou sold'st thy birthright, Esau! for a mess;
> Thou shouldst have gotten more, or eaten less;
> Now thou hast swill'd thy pottage, thy demands
> Are idle; Israel says the bargain stands.

In Browning's "Fifine at the Fair" a dilemma of the Prince is imagined as his being forced to "sell . . . / His birthright for a mess of pottage" (520-31); the birthright characterized in "Fillipo Baldinucci on the Privilege of Burial" (14.105-12) is akin to Wordsworth's (cf. "Halbert and Hob," 1-4). In his "The Flight of the Duchess," Browning's "Smooth Jacob still robs homely Esau: / Now up, now down, the world's one see-saw" (907-08); as in Elizabeth Browning's *Aurora Leigh* (8.777-83) the birthright is here universal entitlement to social justice. Kipling's "The Birthright" concerns the glory of the British Empire, while A. E. Housman's "Poem 17" *(Additional Poems)* expresses a nostalgic longing for an idealized birthright of the English common man (5-8); neither, however, develops a pertinent biblical allusion. A straightforward evocation of "Esau's Lament" by John Keble is directed against "any opinion as to the general efficacy of what is called 'a death-bed repentance,'" and cautions that

> We barter life for pottage; sell true bliss
> For wealth or power, for pleasure or renown;
> Thus, Esau-like, our Father's blessing miss,
> Then wash with fruitless tears our faded crown. (*The Christian Year,* "Second Sunday in Lent")

In American literature the Romantic legacy takes its characteristic form in Thoreau, who, in his essay "Life without Principle," declares his resistance to the common lot: "If I should sell both my forenoons and afternoons to society, as most appear to do, I am sure that for me there would be nothing left worth living for. I trust that I shall never thus sell my birthright for a mess of pottage." Hawthorne draws the analogy familiar from English romanticism between "the story of the fall of man" and "our lost birthright" in *The Marble Faun* (chap. 47). The "Fire and the Hearth" narrative in Faulkner's *Go Down Moses* (1940) involves a sold-out birthright and recollects the Jacob and Esau story. In Ezra Pound's *Cantos* the "birthright of every man here and at home" is once again a political right to social justice rather than a "blessing" or spiritual inheritance (64.56-58; 66.164-70). Something of both senses seems to be intended by Salman Rushdie in *Midnight's Children* in which the recurrent position of the narrator is Esau-like: "Once more exiled from my home, I was also exiled from the gift which was my truest birthright: the gift of the midnight children" (284). These echoes of Kipling as well as of biblical tradition (recorded also in the Koran) culminate in a burning question (430):

> Why did midnight's child betray the children of midnight and take me to my fate? For love of violence, and the legitimizing glitter of buttons on uniforms? For the sake of his ancient antipathy towards me? Or — I find this most plausible — in exchange for immunity from the penalties imposed on the rest of us . . . yes, that must be it; O birthright-denying war hero. O mess-of-pottage-corrupted rival. . . .

See also ELECTION; ESAU; JACOB; PRODIGAL SON.

BLASPHEMY The first biblical mention of blasphemy is in Lev. 24:10-16, where a man is stoned to death at God's command after the man "blasphemed the name of the LORD, and cursed." The LXX translation, "he named the Name and cursed," reflects the ancient Jewish view that unnecessary pronunciation of God's sacred name (Yahweh) was itself a great sacrilege. Indeed, the rabbinical view enshrined in the Mishnah (Sanh. 7.5) is that a person is punishable for the crime of blasphemy (a capital offense under Mosaic law) only if he pronounced the sacred Name itself. The English terms *blaspheme, blasphemy* come from the Gk. *blasphēmein* and *blasphēmia,* and, like their Greek equivalents, they render several Hebrew terms in the OT (e.g., *gadap, na'aṣ, ne'aṣah*). The OT passages where these terms appear describe a variety of cases where someone speaks against God, reviling him, making light of him, etc. (e.g., 2 Sam. 12:14; Pss. 44:16; 74:10, 18; 2 Kings 19:3, 6, 22; Ezek. 35:12-13), reflecting a wider conception of blasphemy than the technical definition of the crime in rabbinic tradition.

Blasphemy is referred to far more frequently in the NT than in the OT, and the Greek terms are often used in an extended and more general sense, following Greek usage, to convey abusive or slanderous talk about human beings or religious teaching (Titus 3:2 or 2 Pet. 2:12) — although ultimately such talk is always regarded as an offense against God. Still, in many significant instances the NT bears witness to a narrower concept of blasphemy. In the Gospels the Jews charge Jesus with blasphemy: "For a good work we stone thee not; but for blasphemy; and because that thou, being a man, makest thyself God" (John 10:33). In Mark 2:7 blasphemy clearly involves laying claim to divine authority or prerogative (e.g., to forgive sins), so violating God's unapproachable and infinite majesty (see Gerhard Kittel, ed., *TDNT* [1964], s.v. *blasphēmia*). This becomes the formal grounds on which the Sanhedrin condemns Jesus to death (Mark 14:64). The early Christian community quickly extended this sense of God's majesty to Jesus himself, considering any denial of his status as Messiah or any insult directed to him as blasphemy (1 Tim. 1:13 or Acts 13:45).

Patristic writers, who usually list blasphemy among the "sins unto death" (e.g., Tertullian, *Adv. Marc.* 4.9), define it generally as speaking anything false about God (St. Augustine, *Contra mendacium,* 19.39; it is often cited in the Middle Ages, especially in biblical glosses). As a result, opposing theological positions were commonly stigmatized as blasphemy during the doctrinal controversies of the 4th cent., and the term was sometimes interchangeable with heresy (see Levy, *Treason against God,* 63-100). All blasphemous utterances were attributed to vices "of the heart": pride (St. Isidore, *Quaestiones in Vetus Testamentum* [PL 83.366-67]), and, more often, anger (St. Gregory the Great, *Moralia,* 36.45), especially when misfortune prompts people to question God's jus-

tice (St. Jerome, *Comm. in Epistolam ad Ephesianos,* 3:14).

This patristic definition of blasphemy as falsehood and the various biblical instances of blasphemy "strictly speaking" were systematically conceptualized by St. Thomas Aquinas in a *quaestio* disseminated for over 300 years by catechetical and confessional manuals. For Aquinas blasphemy was language which unjustly insults God by radically misrepresenting his nature, either by asserting something which does not conform to his nature (also denying what does) or by attributing to a "creature" something which uniquely characterizes God (*Summa Theol.* 2-2.31.1; see also Wyclif, *De Blasphemia,* 1). In the Pearl Poet's *Cleanness,* Nebuchadnezzar is guilty of this sin when he claims, "I am god of þe grounde, to gye as me lykes" — a denial of God's power which the omnipotent God of the poem counters by demonstrating that very attribute when he condemns the king to madness and deposition (1657-1704). Yet such a misrepresentation of God's nature is only a mortal sin, according to Aquinas, when the speaker consciously and maliciously intends, usually in a fit of anger, to disparage God's goodness or power (*Summa Theol.* 2-2.31.1, 2, 3). It is therefore an act of vengeance (Albert the Great, *Summa Theol.* 2.18.119), like that of Robert Henryson's Cresseid, who angrily accuses her "awin gods," Venus and Cupid, of being false and blind when she is callously abandoned by the predatory Diomeid (*The Testament of Cresseid,* 120-40; 274-94). In much ME literature violent oaths, like "God's wounds," which tear "our blissed Lordes body," were branded as blasphemy of this kind because they irreverently denied God's transcendent nature, treating him as a mere human being (John Lydgate's *Fall of Princes,* 8.1681-87). (Later English writers often use the term far more loosely as a synonym for oaths of any kind; the "British 'Damme' " is "Platonic blasphemy, the soul of swearing," according to Byron [*Don Juan,* 11.337-44].)

This sharply defined concept of blasphemy is preserved by Renaissance poets who retell biblical story. So, Milton's Abdiel brands Satan's rebellious speech as blasphemous because it denies the "honour due" to the Son and the power and goodness of the Creator:

> Who can in reason then or right assume
> Monarchy over such as live by right
> His equals, if in power and splendor less,
> In freedom equal? (*Paradise Lost,* 5.794-97; cf.
> *Samson Agonistes,* 440-43; Herbert's "The Sacrifice,"
> 61-63)

This sense of blasphemy persists even into the 19th cent. among writers who use biblical language extensively, as Coleridge does ("Religious Musings," 187-92) when he condemns the claims of jingoists that "Accomplice Deity"

> In the fierce jealousy of wakened wrath
> Will go forth with our armies and our fleets
> To scatter the red ruin on their foes.

O blasphemy! to mingle fiendish deeds
With blessedness!

From the late Middle Ages into the 19th cent., British writers, also following biblical tradition, sometimes extend the object of blasphemy to anyone or anything holy, as when the importunate, meddling friar of Chaucer's *Summoner's Tale* accuses Thomas of blasphemy after the angry old man gives him a fart to enrich his convent (*Canterbury Tales*, 3.2183, 2213) or when Spenser's Malfont slanders the divinely sanctioned ruler Mercilla (a type of Queen Elizabeth in *Faerie Queene*, 5.9.25-26). They also use the term loosely, like many of the Fathers and the Reformers, to damn particularly offensive heresy. "Such stupid blasphemy and nonsense" is Jonathan Swift's reaction to a naturalistic account of Jesus' miracles ("A Dialogue between an Eminent Lawyer and Dr. Swift," 38; cf. William Blake's *Jerusalem*, 90.32-35).

From the Augustan period forward, the target of blasphemy was often extended from God, his agents in church and state, and religious truth to any human being (e.g., Shelley's *The Cenci*, 2.1.162, where blasphemy is simply a highly charged word for slander) or to some new sacral object — a development anticipated by Sir Francis Bacon when he writes in 1605 of Cato's "blasphemy against learning" (*The Advancement of Learning*, 1.2.9). Usually the new "gods" are poetry or poetic inspiration (e.g., Keats, "Sleep and Poetry," 202-03), although Pope writes mockingly of blaspheming quadrille (*The First Satire of the Second Book of Horace Imitated*, 38).

Extending the object of blasphemy to anything a writer judged holy inevitably led to a much more general sense of the term: irreverent, defiant language or gesture. Thus T. S. Eliot, commenting on Baudelaire's Satanism, writes of "romantic blasphemy" ("Baudelaire"), an irreverent, rebellious self-assertion notoriously exemplified by Byron's Cain. In Byron's iconoclastic "mystery play," Cain contemptuously refuses to join in the morning sacrifice and prayers of his family and, in words Adam calls blasphemy, expresses his defiance of God:

And wherefore pluck'd ye not the tree of life?
Ye might have then defied him. . . .
The snake spoke *truth:* it *was* the tree of knowledge;
It *was* the tree of life: knowledge is good,
And life is good. . . . (*Cain*, 33-34, 36-38)

Under the influence of this "Byronic" notion of blasphemy post-Romantic writers tended to stress the spirit in which blasphemy is uttered more than its object as it is misrepresented by words (see Foster, "Blasphemous Poets," 394-96). Thus Ruskin writes that "The real sin of blasphemy is not in the saying, nor even in the thinking; but in the wishing which is father to thought and word: and the nature of it is simply in wishing evil to anything" ("Fiction Fair and Foul—IV," par. 96). Here the concept of blasphemy is stretched to the utmost. Blasphemy may be directed against any morally innocent object; the

malice which prompts it, not the words themselves, is what matters. Herman Melville's Starbuck thinks of blasphemy in just this elastic manner when he denounces as blasphemous Captain Ahab's vengeful fury at Moby Dick, a "dumb brute" (*Moby-Dick*, chap. 36). Except in historical plays (W. B. Yeats's *Resurrection*, 120-22; G. B. Shaw's *Saint Joan*, 6) and in works with an anti-clerical bent (James Joyce's *Ulysses*, episode 1), modern writers generally conceive of blasphemy in these subjective terms, often wondering if such defiance of God (when God is its object) is itself a sign of belief. So, Eugene O'Neill's architect Dion Anthony boasts that his newly drawn cathedral will be "one vivid blasphemy from sidewalk to the tips of its spires," adding "Well, blasphemy is faith, isn't it?" (*The Great God Brown*, 2.3).

See also UNPARDONABLE SIN.

Bibliography. Craun, E. D. "*Inordinata Locutio:* Blasphemy in Pastoral Literature, 1200-1500." *Traditio* 39 (1983), 135-62; Foster, K. "Blasphemous Poets." *Blackfriars* 34, no. 402 (1953), 394-403; Levy, L. *Treason against God: A History of the Offence of Blasphemy* (1981).

EDWIN D. CRAUN

BLESSED ARE THE MEEK   "Blessed are the meek, for they shall inherit the earth" (Matt. 5:5).

See also BEATITUDES; THE MEEK SHALL INHERIT THE EARTH.

BLESSING   *See* BENEDICTION.

BLIND LEAD THE BLIND   When the disciples intimated to Jesus that he was apparently "scandalizing" rather than persuading the Pharisees, he replied, "Let them alone: they be blind leaders of the blind. And if the blind lead the blind, both shall fall into the ditch" (Matt. 15:14; Luke 6:39). This statement has become proverbial; Bunyan's pilgrim is one of many literary travelers who have looked into "that ditch . . . into which the blind have led the blind in all ages." Carlyle uses the phrase with reference to "the Clergy of the Neighbourhood" who advise Carlyle's pilgrim to "drink beer and dance with the girls" (*Sartor Resartus*, 3.1); elsewhere Professor Teufelsdröckh applies the figure knowingly to the typical progress of a university education. Both Wilkie Collins (*Moonstone*, 1.10) and G. K. Chesterton (*The Poet and the Lunatics*, 4) seem to have Carlyle as well as Matthew in mind in their citations. Anthony Hecht ironically characterizes "Sloth" in his poem "The Seven Deadly Sins" as blind discipleship (*The Hard Hours*, 52).

See also BLINDNESS.

BLINDNESS   In the OT blindness is a stigma, sent by God (Deut. 28:28) and revoked by God (Ps. 146:8; Isa. 35:5; 42:7, 16-19). According to Jewish law, the blind were forbidden to take priestly office (Lev. 21:17-23; 2 Sam. 5:8), though they were not to be maltreated (Deut.

27:18; Job 29:15). Samson suffered blindness at the hands of the Philistines (Judg. 16:21), and Zedekiah at the hands of Nebuchadnezzar (2 Kings 25:7; Jer. 39:7; 52:11). As a metaphor, blindness is associated with faulty understanding (Isa. 6:9-10) and with the intellect held captive in darkness (Isa. 42:7, 16-19).

Among Christ's miracles, those which involve healing of the blind are prominent (Matt. 9:27-31; 20:30-34; Mark 8:22-36; 10:46-52; John 9:1-41). Although Elymas was punished with blindness (Acts 13:11), Christ specifically denies that blindness is necessarily a penalty for sin (John 9:2-3). Jesus calls the Pharisees "blind leaders of the blind" (Matt. 15:14; Luke 6:39), and this metaphor for unbelievers is repeated in John 12:40; 2 Cor. 3:4, 4:4; and Eph. 4:18. When Christ proclaims that he is the light of the world (John 9:5), he speaks in the context of his ability to restore sight. In four instances the KJV misconstrues the Greek as "blinded" (Rom. 11:7; 2 Cor. 3:14) or "blindness" (Rom. 11:25; Eph. 4:18); the more accurate translations "hardened" and "hardness" are found in the RSV. But just as Christ mollifies the hardened heart, he regenerates sight in benighted humankind. As B. Lewalski points out (*Protestant Poetics and the Seventeenth-Century Religious Lyric* [1979]), the whole series of NT texts which contrast light and darkness enlarges the associations which blindness has with sin in the Scriptures (89-90).

Nonetheless, several passages in the NT set corporal sight over against spiritual insight. The thrust of these is that "lust of the eyes" (1 John 2:16) can lead to irreligious fascination with temporal *visibilia*. Pauline faith is predicated on seeing heavenly things through (in) a glass darkly (1 Cor. 13:12), walking not by sight (2 Cor. 5:7) but by the "evidence of things not seen" (Heb. 11:1).

In medieval exegesis, human existence is often described in terms of blindness. Thus, St. Gregory the Great comments on Job 9:25:

> Man was created for this end, that he might see "good" which is God; but because he would not stand in the light, in flying therefrom he lost his eyes; for in the same degree that by sin he began to let himself run out to things below, he subjected himself to blindness, that he should not see the interior light. (*Moralia in Iob*, 1.530-31)

Similarly, St. Augustine says that the interior eye is "bruised and wounded" through the transgression of Adam, who "began to dread the Divine light" and "fled back into darkness," "anxious for the shade" (*Sermons on New Testament Lessons* [Matt. 20:30]). Luther glosses Gen. 3:5: " 'Your eyes will be opened,' that is, they will become blind. Before their eyes were closed, but after the Fall, they were opened" (*Luther's Works*, 51.38). These paradoxes are further complicated by the pseudo-Dionysian description of three eyes, to which Hugh of St. Victor was indebted. "By the fall the eye of flesh was left unimpaired, the eye of reason and self-knowledge

bleared, and the eye of contemplation [which focused on God] blinded" (*The Didascalion*, trans. Jerome Taylor [1961], 14). All the commentators would concur, however, with St. Jerome's statement that it is better to have "spiritual than carnal vision and to possess eyes into which the mote of sin [Luke 6:42] cannot fall" (*Ep.* 68, to Castrutius [a blind man of Pannonia]) and with Augustine's ringing affirmation that the blind "killed the Light, but the Light Crucified enlightened the blind" (*Sermons on New Testament Lessons* [John 9]).

It became customary in the Middle Ages to associate blindness particularly with the Jews (cf. John 9:40-41; 2 Cor. 3:14-16). Augustine suggests that spiritual obduracy caused them to read even their own Scriptures blindly (*De civ. Dei* 17.46; cf. Boethius, *De Consolatione Philosophiae*, 4, par. 4). Thus "Old Testament" and "Synagogue" were often preceded by the epithet "blind" (see E. Mâle, *The Gothic Image* [1958], 189). D. W. Robertson notes (*A Preface to Chaucer* [1963], 189) that blindness became a metaphor for "flesh, old Law, the 'letter,' " all aspects of the Mosaic dispensation. In Chaucer's *Merchant's Tale*, January, the Old Man who is blindly cupidinous, is hoodwinked by May, the externalization of his own carnality. It is spiritual blindness, according to Erasmus's *Enchiridion* (9), which "clouds the mind's judgment with the fog of ignorance" (cf. John of Salisbury's remark to the same effect in *Policraticus*, 24.8). In Spenser's *Faerie Queene*, Corcecca is a character whose name means "blind heart," though the Argument to 1.3.10 refers to her as "blind devotion." She dwells in "eternal night" (12.4) and in a "darkesome corner" (13.5). Although she has affinities with sinaic legalism through her association with the "mountain hore" (10.6), the names of her daughter (Abessa) and her colleague (Kirkrapine) link her with the deprivations Spenser assigns to Roman Catholicism, a kind of "blind faith." A modern instance of "flesh, old Law, the 'letter' " as related to blindness occurs in the Canadian novel *The Stone Angel* (1964), where Margaret Laurence depicts Hagar Shipley's hardened heart and dulled vision with the symbol of the stone angel who presides sightlessly over the action of the book.

Some of the most compelling treatments of biblically conceived blindness occur in the 17th cent. In Bunyan's *Pilgrim's Progress*, failure to respond to the inner light is a token of the faithlessness of Atheist, who is "blinded by the god of this world," and of Mr. Blindman and Mr. Hate-light, who are among the jurors who condemn Faithful at Vanity Fair in a travesty of the Law. As S. Fish points out (*Self-Consuming Artifacts* [1972], 240), throughout the book there is an "inverse relationship between visibility and reliability." The episode in which Christian passes through the Valley of the Shadow of Death best exemplifies how harrowing it can be to live in darkness. Christian walks on a narrow path bounded by the quagmire into which David fell, on one side, and by the ditch into which the blind lead the blind, on the other (Matt.

15:14; Luke 6:39). Only when the Sun shines at break of day is Christian able to see clearly the "hazards he had gone through in the dark." The ditch here is clearly a type of death and hell. More intricate presentations of blindness appear in the works of the devotional poets. The whole of Traherne's canon, e.g., though tinged with hermetic thought, relies also on Christian exegetical tradition, to pose against the eye which sin astigmatizes the "Infant-eye" of prelapsarian innocence. God's ability to restore sight is acknowledged by Herbert, who says in "Submission," "Thou hast both my eyes." Vaughan ends "Easter-day" with a passage which celebrates the victory of Light over Darkness:

> Arise, arise
> And with his healing bloud anoint thine Eys,
> Thy inward Eys; his bloud will cure thy mind
> Whose spittle only could restore the blind.

(In patristic commentary on John 9:6-7 Christ's spittle was taken by St. Ambrose and others for a figure of baptism or of the Grace which Christ mixed with the clay-like Law in order to illumine the blind.) In Vaughan's "Cock-crowing," God, the "full-ey'd" "Father of lights," must "close the eye" of the sinner distracted by mundane *visibilia* lest it gaze only on "a dark Egyptian border" of death and disorder.

Milton, the blind "Homeric" poet, adopts two quite different attitudes to blindness. In the sonnet on his blindness (no. 17), the *Second Defence,* and the eulogy of light in the Invocation to the third book of *Paradise Lost,* he spiritualizes blindness and proposes that in darkness "the light of the divine countenance does but the more brightly shine." *Samson Agonistes* is more equivocal on the subject. The beginning of the dramatic poem challenges the Apostle's assurance (Luke 11:33-36) that vision is not restricted just to the eye (85, 93-94), an assurance which was liturgically coupled with the Samson story. (See M. Radzinowicz, *Toward "Samson Agonistes"* [1978], 19.) At the end the Chorus indicates, however, that Samson is "with inward eyes illuminated" (1689) and uses the image of the dragon (1192; lit. "seeing one") to suggest that he observes what the spiritually blind Philistines do not. That Samson's suffering epitomizes spiritual awareness in some measure accounts for the allusions to him in Charlotte Brontë's *Jane Eyre* (chaps. 24, 27, 37). Rochester's blindness, though germane also to his adultery and to the quasi-Freudian and quasi-Oedipal correlation between blinding and sexual sin (cf. Matt. 5:27-32), is a prelude to his spiritual convalescence. The theme of physical blindness as an aid to spiritual blessing reappears in Updike's characterization of Elizabeth Heineman in *The Poorhouse Fair;* it is typically twisted by Samuel Beckett in *All That Fall,* where the blindness of Mr. Rooney is a kind of blessing — a stage en route to total oblivion. Theodore Roethke's "Prayer," in consideration of Milton's sonnet, asks God that he be spared the "blessing";

if all other losses of senses might befall him, he would have his vision at all costs.

An ironic variation on the semantics of blindness is J. M. Synge's *The Well of the Saints,* a play originally called *When the Blind See.* Martin and Mary Doul are given their sight by a saint who uses water from a sacred well to cure the blindness which, according to him, sin has brought into the world. The water's influence lasts only long enough to convince the Douls to spurn the saint's second attempt to cure them after their blindness has returned, for they realize that possessed of sight they had become preoccupied with appearances. Like Gloucester in *King Lear* (4.1.19), their sight deluded them; they stumbled when they saw.

See also BLIND LEAD THE BLIND; DISEASE AND HEALING; *ECCLESIA, SYNAGOGA.*

Bibliography. Monbeck, M. E. *The Meaning of Blindness* (1973); Sandbank, S. "Henry Vaughan's Apology for Darkness." *SEL* 7 (1967), 141-52.   RONALD B. BOND

BLOOD   Since "the life of the flesh is in the blood" (Lev. 17:11; cf. Gen. 9:4), blood comes in the Bible to be a figure for life and, frequently, of human frailty and mortality. "Flesh" and "blood" are regularly associated, often in contrastive reference to things spiritual (e.g., Matt. 16:17; cf. 1 Cor. 15:50; Gal. 1:16; Eph. 6:12). Murder is spoken of as the shedding of blood; to commit murder is to have blood upon one's hands (e.g., 2 Sam. 1:16). Thus Pilate washed his hands to suggest his innocence of the death of Christ, while the crowd shouted, "His blood be on us, and on our children" (Matt. 27:24-25). Among English writers, the association of "flesh and blood" with human frailty is commonplace, as is the image of "blood-guiltiness" with unclean hands: Macbeth is only the most memorable of protagonists in English literary tradition to wonder, "Will all great Neptune's ocean wash this blood / Clean from my hand?" (*Macbeth,* 2.2.59-60).

The "sprinkling of the blood of Jesus Christ" (1 Pet. 1:2) which sanctifies the faithful in the NT was the typological equivalent of the blood sprinkled upon the altar in the OT to make "an atonement for the soul" (Lev. 17:11). The same typological relationship pertained between the sprinkling of blood to seal the OT covenant (Exod. 24:8) and the sprinkling of Christ's blood to seal the NT covenant (Heb. 9:12-23). Thus Christ's own words at the Last Supper, "This cup is the new testament in my blood, which is shed for you" (Luke 22:20; cf. 1 Cor. 11:23-29), simultaneously recollect the old dispensation and inaugurate the new. In 1 Cor. 5:7, Paul likens the death of Christ to the slaughter of the paschal lamb of deliverance, a theme elaborated by the writer to the Hebrews, who describes Christ as both High Priest and sacrificial offering for sin.

The Fathers elaborated these notions in a variety of ways. St. Augustine is representative in seeing the water which flowed from the rock in Horeb as a type for the blood from Christ's side (*Contra Faustum*, 16.15). A strikingly different symbology is suggested by Jewish commentary (e.g., Tg. Yer. Num. 20.11; Midr. Tehillim 78.344) in which blood precedes the water from the rock when Moses strikes it in anger, portending his death as a judgment and embittering the waters of Meribah.

St. Ambrose argues that the drinking of Jesus' sacred blood (in the sacrament) will quench one's thirst for things of this world (*De Spirito Sancto*, 1.184). Typologically, Christ is considered the fruit of Noah's vine, pressed in the bitter agony of the Passion to make out of the old dispensation the sweet wine of the new, which becomes a saving drink to all nations (e.g., *Glossa Ordinaria* [PL 113.112]). This motif appears in many medieval church windows and in some vignettes of the *Biblia Pauperum* and *Speculum Humanae Salvationis*. It is also used extensively in the liturgical poetry of Adam of St. Victor. There are striking examples of the blood-grape-wine symbol in such poems as William Alabaster's "Sonnet 32," Herbert's "The Bunch of Grapes," Henry Vaughan's "The Passion," Francis Quarles's *Divine Fancies* (2.76), and Hopkins's "New Readings." A related image, that of the apocalyptic cup of judgment to be drunk by those who oppose God in the last days (Rev. 14:8-10; 16:19), is memorably alluded to in Julia Ward Howe's "Battle Hymn of the Republic" and Steinbeck's *The Grapes of Wrath*.

Medieval tradition abounds with texts devoted to the blood of the Crucifixion as the supreme emblem of divine love. Such symbology occurs in Franciscan-inspired religious lyrics on the Passion and in works such as the ME translation of the *Stimulus Amoris* ascribed to Walter Hilton, *The Goad of Love*. The sacrificial blood becomes a unifying theme in George Herbert's *The Temple*, acting as a constant reminder of the self-sacrificing love of God which establishes the joyful covenant of grace.

Christ's blood is also connected to the typology of baptism. In the medieval *Pearl* (11.5) and in Herbert's "H. Baptisme I," the water of baptism is identified with the blood which flowed from the side of the crucified Christ. In his "Love unknown," Herbert describes the painful cleansing of the heart "in a font, wherein did fall / A stream of bloud, which issu'd from the side / Of a great rock." Likewise, Robert Southwell refers in "The Burning Babe" to the "wounding thornes" and the "bath" of "bloud." Such images have parallels in contemporary emblem books, as in Georgette de Montenay's Emblem 3 (*Emblèmes* [1571]), where Christ is portrayed as a fountain at which a crowd of people are drinking avidly of his blood, or in the memorable hymn by William Cowper, "There is a fountain fill'd with blood, drawn from Emmanuel's veins. . . ."

See also ATONEMENT; ATONEMENT, DAY OF; EUCHARIST.

Bibliography. Gatto, L. C. "The Blood Theology of Medieval English Literature." *SMC* 2 (1966), 84-92; Gilsdorf,

R. W. "Rabbinic Blood Theology: Partial Background to the Eucharistic Cup Formula." Ph.D. diss., St. Louis University, 1973; Rohling, J. H. "The Blood of Christ in Christian Latin Literature Before the Year 1000." Ph.D. diss., Catholic University, 1932.   H. DAVID BRUMBLE
                                                                            SAAD EL-GABALAWY

BLOOD CRIETH FROM THE GROUND   In Gen. 4:10 God addresses Cain, who has just murdered Abel out of jealousy: "The voice of thy brother's blood crieth unto me from the ground." The blood of the victim, regarded in most exegesis as a symbol of innocence and purity, calls to its rightful Lord for vengeance and retribution. The murder of Abel makes him the first righteous martyr (Matt. 23:35; Luke 11:51; 1 John 3:12), so that he is generally considered a prototype of Christ (Heb. 12:24; cf. *Glossa Ordinaria* [PL 113.98-99]). The writers of the medieval mystery plays, reflecting this typological tradition, see Abel's murder and the ensuing curse on Cain as an intensification of the penalties of the Fall (e.g., York "Sacrificium Cayme and Abel," 99-116), and sometimes suggest a relationship betweeen Abel's blood and the Crucifixion (e.g., Wakefield "Mactacio Abel," 328-29 350-54; cf. *Cursor Mundi*, 1132-36, 1347-62).

The concept of vengeance is stressed by Milton, who dwells at length on the first crime of fratricide (*Paradise Lost*, 11.432-60), closely following the commentary of St. Augustine in *De civitate Dei* (15.7 *et passim*). In *The Faerie Queene*, Spenser associates Gen. 4:10 with Rev. 6:9-10, noting that the "blessed sprites" of the "holy Martyrs" to God "for vengeance cryde continually" (1.8.36). Many of Shakespeare's plays include textual and topical allusions to the innocent victim's blood crying for vindication at the gates of heaven (e.g., *1 Henry 6*, 5.4.52-53). In *Richard 2* (1.1.102-06), Shakespeare echoes the scriptural text when he applies Abel's story to Gloucester's death, innocence sacrificed being protested here by the cry of the victim's blood "from the tongueless caverns of the earth," demanding "justice and rough chastisement."

In *Cain* (3.1.469-74), Byron scrupulously poetizes the biblical verse about the cry of the "slain brother's blood," putting the words of the Lord into the mouth of the "Angel." But, like Coleridge and other Romantics of his era, Byron betrays an iconoclastic intent in his play, diminishing the value of divine justice in his portrayal of Cain as a heroic figure who challenges the "Omnipotent tyrant." Implicit in Byron's reinterpretation of the first murder is a condemnation of divine dispensation.

See also ABEL; CAIN.   SAAD EL-GABALAWY

BLOOD FOR BLOOD   *See LEX TALIONIS.*

BLOOD OF THE LAMB   On the night of the final plague in Egypt, before the release of the children of Israel, Moses called for every Jewish family to slay a lamb and sprinkle its blood on the doorposts and lintel of the house so that the Lord, seeing the blood, would "pass over the door" and not suffer the angel of death to enter and slay the firstborn of the house (Exod. 12:21-23). This action instituted the Passover feast, which Israel was to celebrate annually thereafter as a memorial of God's deliverance of the people (vv. 24-27), a focusing of the earlier provisions for blood sacrifice, and a reminder, according to the recurrent phrase in the *Hadar,* that "there is no atonement without blood" (e.g., Sipra 1.4; Yoma 5a).

Patristic commentary invariably subordinates the Exodus narrative to typology of Christ as the Paschal Lamb (e.g., St. Jerome, *Ep.* 108-10), citing the presentation of Jesus in John's narrative (1:29) as "the Lamb of God who takes away the sins of the world" (e.g., St. Ambrose, *De mysteriis,* 7.34) and John's vision, in Rev. 7:14, of the glorified martyrs who "came out of great tribulation, and have washed their robes, and made them white in the blood of the Lamb." Tertullian, commenting on the passage in Revelation, emphasizes the idea of baptism in blood; the stains of the flesh "are changed into dazzling whiteness by martyrdom," an idea reflected by Ambrose (*De mysteriis,* 7.34-35). In the medieval poem *Pearl,* the maiden tells the dreamer that she is a Bride of the Lamb of God, who "washed in his blood these robes I wear, / And clad me in pearls immaculate" (13.4).

Donne, reflecting on Rev. 7:14, expounds the symbolic distinction between "red" and "white," suggesting that the "rednesse" in man comes from Adam's sin and that "the more that rednesse is washed off, the more we return to our first whitenesse." He continues: "Some Grammarians have noted, the word *Washing* here, to be derived from a word, that signifies a Lambe; we must be washed in the blood of the Lambe, and we must be brought to the whitenesse, the candor, the simplicity of the Lambe" (*Sermons,* eds. Potter and Simpson, 5.313-14; cf. 9.64-65). Similarly, in a poetic meditation on redemption *(Charitas Nimia),* Richard Crashaw asks:

What did the Lamb that He should die?
What did the Lamb that He should need,
When the wolf sins, Himself to bleed?

. . . Why should the white
Lamb's bosome write
The purple name
Of my sin's shame?

The notion of purification acquires a more homely aspect in T. S. Eliot's "The Hippopotamus," in which the titular animal, presumably representing the lowest creatures, ascends to heaven, washed clean by the "Blood of the Lamb."

In a spirit of cynical profanity, Shelley subverts the religious implications of the biblical motif. In his *Defense of Poetry,* he argues that if the sins of great poets " 'were as scarlet, they are now white as snow' " (citing Isa. 1:18); "they have been washed in the blood of the mediator and

the redeemer Time." In his revisionist *Apocalypse* D. H. Lawrence typically rejects orthodox interpretations, associating the "Lamb" of Revelation with pagan mysteries: "A Lamb it has to be: or with Mithras, a bull: and the blood drenches over the initiate from the cut throat of the bull . . . and makes him a new man." The refrain of Vachel Lindsay's "General William Booth Enters into Heaven" is drawn from the popular American hymn by Elisha Hoffman, "Are You Washed in the Blood of the Lamb?"

See also ATONEMENT; ATONEMENT, DAY OF; EXODUS; REDEMPTION.   SAAD EL-GABALAWY

BOANERGES   *See* SONS OF THUNDER.

BONE OF MY BONE   Related to *'aṣam,* a primary root meaning "to bind fast" or, causatively, "to make strong," the Hebrew word *'eṣem,* "bone," is suggestive of unity and strength. As used in the genitive superlative in Gen. 2:23, it signifies quintessentially positive community and relationship. Accordingly, Adam's exclamation upon seeing Eve is not merely an exaltation in his newly formed mate, but it is the first statement of personal intimacy. Paralleled by "flesh of my flesh," "bone of my bone" not only refers, therefore, to the physical circumstances of Eve's creation but, through the Hebraic idiom which equates "bone" with the totality of one's being (Ps. 35:10; Prov. 15:30), it indicates the fundamental parity and complementarity of nature shared by the two sexes. In this way, the wife is a "help" — not a shadow or subordinate, but man's other self as no other creature can be. As one "meet for him" (Heb. *kenegdo*), she is "at his side" as well as "over against or opposite to him," suggesting a composite unit with woman corresponding to, yet being distinct from, man. In its first appearance, then, this phrase suggests nearness of relationship, sameness of nature, and a wholehearted embracing of the other as part of the self. In later occurrences, the phrase is debased as it moves into popular speech. Becoming suggestive of political and social maneuvering, variants are thus used by Laban, Abimelech, the tribes of Israel, and even David (Gen. 29:14; Judg. 9:2; 2 Sam. 5:1; 19:12-13; 2 Chron. 11:1). Not until the NT does this locution lose such insidious coloring. In Eph. 5, through Jesus the New Adam, humankind is brought again into a composite union: "we are members of his body, of his flesh, of his bones" (v. 30). Connected to the original by Paul's quotation of Gen. 2:24, this passage reinterprets Gen. 2:23 to speak of "a great mystery . . . concerning Christ and the church" (5:32). By doing so, it frames the community of God in unity and strength from fellowship in the garden to fellowship in Christ.

Jewish tradition expounds the phrase in various ways — some theoretical, others practical. Concern with the manner of Eve's creation tends to focus on her suitability as true companion for Adam in light of the Lilith myth and the possibility of a first, androgynous Adam. Eve is formed when and as she is, the argument goes, to forestall a Lilith-like challenge based on simultaneous and similar creation as well as to grant man precedence and prerogative in matters of authority. Moreover, that Eve comes from Adam betokens the organic and lasting bond which ought to exist between man and woman since "when like is joined unto like the union is indissoluble" (Midr. Hagadol 1.83). The second matter is also theoretical in that it attempts to reconcile the two accounts of humankind's creation (Gen. 1:27; 2:2, 21-22). In the Zohar, speculation centers on the ambiguous meaning of ṣela' ("rib" or "side") and a case is made for a "two faced . . . dual sex . . . hermaphrodite" Adam (3.44), from whose side Eve is separated to create two sexes. More Platonically, others postulate an initial, ideal, and incorporeal creation in which humankind is spirit and without gender; later, a second, material creation completes the process and brings man down to earth in the physical forms of male and female (Philo, *De opificio mundi,* 134).

Eve's creation is also studied to explain the distinctive nature and role of woman in relation to man. As distinct from man, woman — created from "a modest part" — is to be humble, modest, and restrained in speech, conduct, and manner (Gen. Rab. 18). Created from bone, she is "less easily pacified," needs to adorn herself, and has a higher voice (Nid. 31b). And, though the point is disputed, her intellect is thought to mature more quickly for, having been "built" (*wayyiben*) by the Lord, she is endowed with more understanding (*binah*) than the man (Nid. 45b). Ultimately, her creation even sets the pattern for male-female relationships, from courtship to intercourse: the man is to court the woman, for "he who lost the thing [the rib] goes in search of what he lost"; and, in the most intimate of relations, both are to face the material of their creation, "he [faces the elements] from which he was created and she [faces the man] from whom she was created" (Nid. 31b). Though much of the attention given to the phrase concentrates on the physical, some readings are closer to the metaphysical interpretation given it in Ephesians and in Christian tradition. For example, in the Zohar, an explication of the *samek* in *wayyisgor* ("and he closed," Gen. 2:21) leads to an understanding of mutual dependence, not only of man and woman but, by analogy, of the upper and lower worlds, which, like husband and wife, sustain and delight each other, becoming whole and complete only when they are separated so that they can face one another. In this way, "bone of my bone" has not only natural but cosmic significance in the Jewish tradition.

Throughout church history, "bone of my bone" has been read literally (St. Jerome, *Ep.* 51.5), figuratively (St. Methodius, *Convivium decem virginum,* 3.1), and typologically (St. Augustine, *De civ. Dei* 22.17), and has been used to discuss hermeneutical principles, to explain the nature of the soul (Augustine, *De anima,* 1.29-30; 2.20),

and to establish the corporeal nature of the resurrection (Tertullian, *De resurrectione carnis,* 7). Most often, though, it pertains to marriage, earthly and heavenly, as Paul presents it in Eph. 5.

Commentary on Eve's creation develops in two directions in the early Church. The first, represented by St. John Chrysostom, puts forth the historical sense, emphasizing the mutual dependence of man and woman (*Hom.* 15, on Gen. 12–13) and the equality of nature suggested by Eve's formation from Adam's rib. Unlike those who appeal to chronological precedence as the basis for Adam's authority, Chrysostom, holding to the literal-historical sense of the text, insists that Eve "was not subjected as soon as she was made; nor, when he brought her to the man, did she hear any such thing from God, nor did the man say any such word to her; . . . of rule or subjection he no where made mention unto her" (*Hom.* 26, on 1 Cor. 2). The other tradition, seen in Augustine, is figurative and presents Eve as a type of the Church. Drawn from the wound in Adam's side as he slept, even as the Church grew from the sacraments symbolized by the blood and water which flowed from Christ's side after his death (John 19:34), Eve is considered an ideal figure for the Church (*Enarr. in Ps.* 127.4). Like Chrysostom, Augustine emphasizes that Eve is not inferior by nature to Adam (*De Genesi ad litteram,* 9.15.26), and that she becomes a figure for concupiscent flesh only after the Fall. Therefore, his discussion of her creation is positive, depicting it as "a prophecy of Christ and his Church" (*De civ. Dei* 22.17). He extends this consideration of Eve to include the paradox of bone, rather than flesh, being the source of woman: "it was the weaker sex that was being made, and weakness ought to have been made of flesh rather than of bone." Whereas the rabbis discuss this in terms of woman's nature, Augustine glosses with it the idea that "it is the weakness of Christ that makes us strong": "Woman was made . . . strong from the rib; Adam was made . . . weak from the flesh. It is Christ and his Church; His weakness is our strength" (*In Joan. Ev.* 15.8). And, in accordance with Eph. 5, it is suggested that Christ, Adam, the man, and the spirit ought to rule the Church, Eve, the woman, and the flesh with tender, compassionate, and self-sacrificing love (ibid., 2.14; Eph. 5:21-25). In this way, Augustine underscores the original as well as the NT form of unity, community, and relationship expressed in "bone of my bone."

These same themes are picked up by later exegetes. Luther, e.g., explicates Gen. 2:23 as revealed wisdom concerning both marriage and the holy, passionate love which causes Adam's celebration of Eve (*Lectures on Genesis 1–5*). More casually, in acknowledgment of a friend's wife, he closes a letter with "Greet your flesh and rib" ("To John Agricola," May 12, 1521). Calvin also discusses the verse, at times distinguishing "between the rule of marriage and the spiritual union of Christ and the Church" (*Inst.* 2.12.7), and at other times reinforcing the type of relationship suggested by the phrase (2.12.1). Glossing texts from Isaiah to Hebrews, he refers the phrase to the Mediator and also uses it "to show married men with what singular love they ought to embrace their wives" (4.19.35), thus presenting "bone of my bone" as determinative for both earthly and heavenly relations.

From the 12th-cent. Anglo-Norman play *Jeu d'Adam* to Susan Wilkinson's novel *Bone of My Bones* (1982), the mode and significance of Eve's creation have also been recurrent themes in English literary tradition. Early presentations, such as those of the mystery plays, give — with varying degrees of extrapolation — the basic biblical account. Some accounts are pithy and direct: "Fflesch of þi fflesch • And bon of þi bon / Adam here is þi wyf . . ." (Coventry, "The Creation of the World and the Man," 100-101). Others make reasonable additions to the original: "take hyr unto the, that you both be as one / To comfort one th'other when from you I am gone" (Norwich B, "Creation and the Fall," 15-16). Still others, none better than *Jeu d'Adam*, move from the story into detailed and spiritual instructions for marriage:

Ce est ta femme e tun pareil:
Tu le devey estre ben fiel.
Tu aime lui, e ele ame tei,
Si serey ben ambedui de moi.
. . . De tei eissit, non pas de fors.
Tu la governe par raison.
N'ait entre vus ja tencon.
Mais grant amor, grant conservage:
Tel soit la lei de marriage.

("She is your wife and your partner;
You ought to be entirely faithful to her.
Love her, and let her love you,
If you would both be mine.
. . . From you she issued, not from outside.
Govern her by reason.
Let no dissension come between you
But great love and mutual obedience:
Such is the law of marriage.") (11-14; 20-24)

Chaucer, in *The Canterbury Tales*, develops this instruction in an Augustinian fashion, having his Parson say not only that "mariage is figured bitwixe Crist and holy chirche" (*Parson's Tale*, 10.921), but that "a man sholde bere hym with his wif, and namely in two thynges; . . . in suffrance and reverence, as shewed Crist whan he made first womman" (10.924). He further glosses the passage by noting that "God made womman of the rib of Adam, for womman sholde be felawe unto man. / Man sholde bere hym to his wif in feith, in trouthe, and in love, as seith Seint Paul . . ." (10.929).

Since Chaucer's time, most literary allusions to "bone of my bone" deal with relationship, with the responsibility that comes from intimacy, and with the natural and spiritual manifestations of it. Conventionally, they refer to man and wife as in *Paradise Lost,* where Adam reflects upon Eve's creation and its natural implications:

. . . to give thee being I lent
Out of my side to thee, nearest my heart
Substantial Life, to have thee by my side
Henceforth an individual solace dear;
Part of my Soul I seek thee, and thee claim
My other half. . . . (4.483-88)

Later, he vows eternal fidelity to Eve on that same basis, assuming unto himself not only the earthly blessings, but the spiritual consequences of his role in her creation:

Should God create another *Eve,* and I
Another Rib afford, yet loss of thee
Would never from my heart; no no, I feel the Link of
Nature draw me: Flesh of Flesh,
Bone of my Bone thou art, and from Thy state
Mine never shall be parted, bliss or woe. (9.911-16)

In later literature, both natural and spiritual aspects recur — though not necessarily in the same work. Charlotte Brontë, e.g., presents marital relations through a developing, rather than an inherent, closeness with the result that Jane Eyre, married to Rochester, becomes "ever more absolutely bone of his bone, flesh of his flesh" (*Jane Eyre,* chap. 38). Faulkner takes the innate relationship further, extending a shared oneness to the psychological: "Bone of my bone, blood and flesh and even memory of my blood and flesh and memory . . ." (*Wild Palms,* 217). Browning, who in *The Ring and the Book* refers to an Augustinian reading in which ". . . the bride [is] / To groom as is the Church and Spouse to Christ" (11.1300-1301), also keeps the greater significance natural, linking "bone of his bone" not with a higher spiritual relation but with the post-Fall curse of Gen. 3:16: "Thy desire / Shall be to thy husband, o'er thee shall he rule!" (1300, 1302-03).

Such earthbound readings lead to application of the phrase to parent-child relationships, for after the original marriage only one's offspring can literally be "bone of one's bone." Thus, Congreve's Lady Wishfort bewails Mrs. Fainall's status as "my child, bone of my bone, and flesh of my flesh . . . another me" who, despite such auspicious origins, "lean[s] aside to iniquity" (5.1.130). Tennyson, in "Rizpah," plays on this physical connection and has the mother lament the ignominious death and decay of her son's corporeal being as she goes out to steal his mortal remains and inter them in holy ground:

Flesh of my flesh was gone, but bone of my bone was left —
I stole them all . . . My baby, the bones that had suck'd me,
The bones that had laughed and had cried —
Theirs? O no! They are mine — not theirs — they had moved in my side. (51-56)

This same sense of relationship may also have social rather than, or in addition to, physical connotations. Thus, in Wilkinson's *Bildungsroman,* questions of race relations, of modern history, and of faith and doubt are subsumed under a general consideration of a child's "bone of my bone" relationship to her mother and family. Individual and state may be referred to as well, as in Shakespeare's *Troilus and Cressida,* where Ulysses outlines the metonymic importance of Agamemnon as

> nerves and bone of Greece,
> Heart of our numbers, soul and only spirit,
> In whom the tempers and minds of all
> Should be shut up. (1.3.55-58)

Social obligations may also be suggested. They may be specific or general, acted upon or not, and pertain to an individual, to society, or to an idea. Cowper, e.g., calls for active intervention on behalf of those "Bone of my bone, kindred souls to mine" who die en masse because of social neglect (*The Task,* 3.1783). Pound, on the other hand, in "Canto 64" repudiates any such commitment to one Hutchinson, who, though "Bone of our bone, educated among us" (255), is politically incorrect and is therefore cut off from society. This responsibility to others may even be historical, as when ideas — "All that we sucked in with our mother's milk, / Grew up with, got inside of us at last, / Till it's found bone of bone and flesh of flesh" (Browning, "Mr. Sludge, 'The Medium,' " 836-38) — affect "the mode of intercourse / Between us men here, and those once-men there" (834-35).

For more spiritually oriented writers, the phrase betokens origins — the birth or renewal of an individual in relation to an Other. This may be understood in traditional terms, as when Hopkins writes of Christ

> Of her flesh he took flesh:
> He does take fresh and fresh,
> Though much the mystery how,
> Not flesh but spirit now
> And makes, O marvellous! ("The Blessed Virgin compared to the Air we Breathe," 55-59)

Or, as in Blake, it may be more metaphysical:

> . . . brooding over me the Enormous worlds
> Reorganize me shooting forth in bones & flesh & blood
> I am regenerated to fall or rise at will or remain
> A labourer of ages. . . . (*The Four Zoas,* 6.223-26)

As used by Roethke, the phrase tells of a dying man's desire to "undo all dying by my death":

> I love the world; I want more than the world,
> Or after image of the inner eye.
> Flesh cries to flesh; and bone cries out to bone;
> I die unto this life, alone yet not alone. ("The Dying Man," 77, 56-59)

Always, however, from its original occurrence in Genesis to its function as title and epigraph for Wilkinson's novel, "bone of my bone" connotes relationship and intimacy.

See also BRIDE, BRIDEGROOM; EVE.

Bibliography. Bevington, D. *Medieval Drama* (1975); Epstein, I., ed. *The Babylonian Talmud* (1935-52); Hertz, J. H. *The Pentateuch and Haftorahs with Commentary* (1872-1946); Kasher, M. M. *Encyclopedia of Biblical Interpretation: A Millennial Anthology.* Trans. Harry Freedman (1953-79).   RHONDA L. WAUHKONEN

BOOK In physical format, all the books mentioned in the Bible are scrolls. Whether "book" appears in a given passage or not depends considerably upon the translator, and recent versions often use other terms where the KJV has "book."

In the Bible, the main purpose of the book is to serve as a permanent record: of historical events (Exod. 17:14), of the Law (Deut. 17:18), of "constitutional" matters (1 Sam. 10:25), of a financial transaction (Jer. 32:12), or of the sayings of a prophet (Jer. 30:2). The book can thus be used as a metaphor for God's memory (Ps. 56:8) or for his foreknowledge (Ps. 139:16), and in Daniel and Revelation as a register of the just. Isaiah uses a sealed book as a metaphor for the people's spiritual blindness (29:11-12); an angelic interpreter reads to Daniel from the heavenly book, "the book of truth" (Dan. 10:21), an outline of future events (Dan. 11:2–12:5); and the gradual opening of the book with seven seals is a striking feature of Revelation (5–6, 8).

Books play a prominent part in the symbolic actions of the prophets. Jeremiah tells Seraiah to read to the Babylonians a book prophesying their destruction and then to "bind a stone to it, and cast it into the midst of Euphrates" (51:60-64), thus showing how Babylon will sink into oblivion. Ezekiel is given a book of "lamentations, and mourning, and woe." This book is written "within and without," an unusual and impractical way of treating a scroll, to show how the woes of Israel surpass normal limits. He is told to eat the book — to make its message an integral part of himself (2:8–3:3). Both of these motifs recur in Revelation, though here two separate books are involved (5:1; 10:8-10).

Once the Jews, and later the Christians, had established their canons of divinely inspired writings, the Bible obviously became the Book, the medium through which God reveals himself to humanity. But according to a metaphor which exerted a profound influence on medieval and Renaissance thought, the Bible is not God's only means of self-revelation. He reveals himself also in the whole of his creation, which is seen as another "book" analogous to the book of Scripture: the Book of Nature or Book of the Creatures. As with Scripture, a proper reading of the Book of Nature can lead one to God, for God is the author of both books. Underlying this metaphor of the two books is the belief that the created world has value and meaning, and this attitude provided a rationale for studying it. St. Augustine provides a concise early reference to the Book of Creatures when, after citing Rom. 1:18-20, he declares:

> The very form of creation is a great book: behold it, examine it, read it from top to bottom. God did not make

letters of ink by which you might know him; he set before your eyes the very things that he made. Why do you seek greater testimony? Heaven and earth cry out to you: "God made me!" (*Sermo* sup. Matt. 11:25-26)

Its best-known formulation is probably that of Hugh of St. Victor (12th cent.):

This whole visible world is like a book written by the finger of God — that is, created by divine power; and individual creatures are figures . . . established by the divine will to show forth the wisdom of the invisible things of God. (*De Tribus Diebus,* 4; printed by Migne as bk. 7 of the *Didascalicon* [PL 176.814B]; for a translation of the whole passage, see Josipovici, 29)

St. Bonaventure mentions the Book of Nature several times: *Breviloquium,* 2.5; 2.11; 2.12; *Collationes in Hexaemeron,* 12.14-17. At the climax of the *Paradiso,* Dante unites the two books as his ultimate symbol of their divine author: "I saw ingathered, bound by love in one single volume, that which is dispersed in leaves throughout the universe: substances and accidents and their relations, as though fused together in such a way that what I tell is but a single light" (33.85-90; trans. C. S. Singleton [1975], 1.376-77).

The main biblical sources for the idea of the Book of Nature are St. Paul's declaration that "ever since the creation of the world [God's] invisible nature, namely, his eternal power and deity, has been clearly perceived in the things that have been made" (Rom. 1:20, RSV) and the famous words of Ps. 19, which speak of the whole cosmos as an eloquent, though silent, witness of God's glory (cf. also Wisd. 13:1-9). Praise of God based on his works, as in Job 38–41 and Sir. 42:15–43:33, also contributed to the development of the idea. Apart from the existence of the Bible itself as a book, the image probably goes back to the way God spoke the world into being in Genesis and to the idea of creation as full of object lessons of God's power and of his purpose for his creatures (see, e.g., Prov. 30:18-31).

Sir Thomas Browne's use of the two books is characteristic of a great many during the Renaissance:

Thus there are two bookes from whence I collect my Divinity; besides that written one of God, another of his servant Nature, that universall and publik Manuscript, that lies expans'd unto the eyes of all; those that never saw him in the one, have discovered him in the other. (*Religio Medici,* 1.16; cf. 12.12)

Other examples may be found in Joshua Sylvester's translation of Du Bartas's *Divine Weeks and Works* (1.1.173-200); Bacon, *Advancement of Learning* (3.268, 301); Donne, *Essays in Divinity* (ed. E. M. Simpson [1952], 7-8); and Milton, *Paradise Lost* (8.66-69).

During the 18th cent. John Ray, William Whiston, and others used the Book of Nature as part of their demonstrations of the wisdom of God from the works of creation. In the introduction to his *Physico-Theology* (10th

ed. [1742], 2), William Derham approvingly quotes St. Bernard: "the world is God's book, and we must read in it continually." Like Bacon, these writers believed that a better reading of the Book of Nature would improve their reading of Scripture, as well as the converse. Such conceptions lie behind satires like Swift's *Tale of a Tub* and Pope's *Dunciad,* which are mock-books, books of anti-nature and revelations of mindlessness. Later in the century, in pt. 3 of David Hume's *Dialogues concerning Natural Religion,* Demea denies the validity of the analogy between book and nature, but Coleridge makes use of it in his *Lectures on Revealed Religion,* and it survives into the 20th cent. (see Peacocke).

Other metaphors grew out of this main one, or, arising from other sources, were influenced by it. The memory and the soul can be seen as divinely written books. A less explicitly religious use of the Book of Nature, already common in the 14th cent. (see Curtius, 321), contrasts it to human books as a superior source of knowledge about Nature. Thus Abraham Cowley praises William Harvey, who discovered the circulation of the blood, because he "sought for Truth in Truth's own Book / The Creatures, which by God himself was writ" ("Ode upon Dr. Harvey," st. 4). Galileo declares that the Book of Nature is written in mathematical language (*Discoveries and Opinions,* ed. S. Drake [1957], 237-38). A more esthetically-oriented metaphor equates nature and books of human poetry, as in the discovery which Pope attributes to Virgil: "Nature and Homer were, he found, the same" (*Essay on Criticism,* 135). Joyce makes striking use of the Book of Creation in the early pages of *Finnegans Wake:* "(Stoop) if you are abcdminded, to this claybook, what curios of signs (please stoop), in this alephbed! Can you rede . . . its world?" For Stéphane Mallarmé, the artist becomes God and the world disappears into his book: "tout, au monde, existe pour aboutir à un livre" ("Le livre, instrument spirituel," *Oeuvres* [Pléiade ed.], 378). Jorge Luis Borges's story, "The Library of Babel," begins: "The Universe (which others call the Library). . . . "

See also BOOK OF LIFE; SEVEN SEALS.

Bibliography. Curtius, E. R. *European Literature and the Latin Middle Ages.* Trans. W. R. Trask (1953), chap. 16, "The Book as Symbol"; Jeffrey, D. L. "The Self and the Book: Reference and Recognition in Medieval Thought." *By Things Seen.* Ed. D. L. Jeffrey (1979); Jones, W. P. *The Rhetoric of Science . . . in Eighteenth-Century English Poetry* (1966); Josipovici, G. *The World and the Book,* 2nd ed. (1979), chap. 2; Kinsley, W. "The *Dunciad* as Mock-Book," *HLQ* 35 (1971), esp. 32-38; Patrides, C. A. *Milton and the Christian Tradition* (1966), 68-71; Peacocke, A. R. *Creation and the World of Science* (1979), esp. 3-7, 11.   WILLIAM KINSLEY

BOOK OF LIFE   In the Revelation to St. John on Patmos are found three references to the book of life (Gk. *hē biblos tēs zōēs; to biblion . . .*), where it refers to a great ledger read out on the Day of Judgment from the throne of God:

And I saw the dead, small and great, stand before God; and the books were opened: and another book was opened, which is the book of life: and the dead were judged out of those things which were written in the books, according to their works. And the sea gave up the dead which were in it; and death and hell delivered up the dead that were in them: and they were judged every man according to their works. And death and hell were cast into the lake of fire. This is the second death. And whosoever was not found written in the book of life was cast into the lake of fire. (Rev. 20:12-15)

Also called "the Lamb's book of life" (21:7), the single volume contains the names only of those who persevere in the gift of their redemption. Christ, as Son of Man, declares in his dictation to the church at Sardis that those who "have not defiled their garments . . . shall walk with me in white: for they are worthy. He that overcometh, the same shall be clothed in white raiment; and I will not blot out his name out of the book of life, but I will confess his name before my Father, and before his angels" (3:5; cf. Phil. 4:3). Only the Lamb of God is counted fit to open the book: the four beasts (evangelists) and twenty-four elders greet the "lion of Judah," now figured as the Lamb, singing "a new song, saying, 'Thou art worthy to take the book, and to open the seals thereof: for thou wast slain, and hast redeemed us to God by thy blood out of every kindred, and tongue, and nation' " (Rev. 5:9).

The only OT use of the complete expression (Heb. *seper hayyim*) is found in Ps. 69:28, but God's book in Exod. 32:32ff. is clearly antecedent, as are similar "books" referred to in Ps. 139:16, Isa. 4:3, and Mal. 3:16. It is in Daniel that the idea of a book (or books) as the basis upon which final judgment is to be made is most thoroughly developed (Dan. 7:10, 12); the same notion recurs in other apocalyptic writing (e.g., 1 Enoch 47:3; 108:3; Jub. 30:20-22; 36:10; 39:6). Midr. Tannaim regards the book of God referred to by Moses in Exod. 32 as the book of eternal life in which are enrolled all the faithful (cf. Ber. 32a; Soṭa 14a). In cabalist legend Abel is the one before whom every soul must one day appear to be judged, according to books of account similar to those referred to in Rev. 20:12-15; these later writings suggest, however, that for each person an individual book is kept (T. Abraham 13.11).

St. Augustine's commentary on Rev. 20 in *De civitate Dei* (20.14) considers the distinction (v. 12) between "the books" and the single "book of life," identifying them respectively as "the sacred books old and new, that out of them it might be shown what commandments God has enjoined, and that book of life of each man . . . to show what commandments each one has done or omitted to do." But since, if materially considered, "such a volume would be beyond fathoming in its size and length it should be understood as a

certain divine power, by which every one shall recall to memory all his own works, whether good or evil, and shall [be obliged] mentally to survey them with a marvellous rapidity, so that this knowledge will either accuse or excuse conscience, and thus all and each shall be simultaneously judged. And this divine power is called a "book," because in it we shall "read," so to speak, all that it causes us to remember. (20.14)

In later medieval tradition Augustine is typically followed, except that the "book of life" is sometimes viewed either as Christ himself, who reveals himself before all as indeed the gift of life, or the *praescientia Dei,* since when it is opened it will reveal instantly to each person whether or not he or she was one of those predestined by God to eternal life (*Glossa Ordinaria* [PL 114.745]). This latter sense especially is followed in the covenant theology of Calvin, who comments upon Phil. 4:3 that "the book of life is the roll of those who are foreordained to life, as in Moses, Exod. 32:32. God has this roll laid up with himself. Hence the book is nothing but his eternal counsel, determined in his own breast" (*New Testament Commentaries,* 11.286). Calvin applies this context of final judgment, however, to the "books" of the present church: "The same thought comes in Ps. 69:28, 'Let them be blotted out of the book of the living, and let them not be written among the righteous'; that is, let them not be numbered among the elect of God, whom he receives within the borders of his Church and Kingdom" (ibid.).

Perhaps the most remarkable English poem on this subject, *The Last Judgment (Christ III),* creates a powerful scene (drawn on Matt. 24, Isa. 13, and Mark 13) in which each sinner is revealed to himself by the light of the Cross: Christ crucified for the sins of the world is raised up to tower over the whole of the universe and the implicit call to remembrance in each life is by way of a question about one's response to Calvary. But the trace of the "book of life" is then introduced in phrases which speak of how the damned "shall find reward / Befitting their record of words and works" (1363-64), and Augustine's notion that the "books" of Rev. 20:12 are the OT and NT construed as Divine Word is echoed in the summary reflection of the poet on the damned: "They broke God's word, / The Books' bright bidding" (1628-29). In Aelfric's Sermon for Ascension Eve he quotes Rev. 3:5, observing that the names of "all those persons who are to come into the kingdom of God are written in the book of life *(liflican bec)* and we shall with zeal *(geornfulness)* and with good works find that our names too are written there" (ed. Pope, *Homilies of Aelfric,* 25.757.15-19). In the Towneley "Judgment" pageant (no. 30) it is the devils who, on hearing the last "trumpet" sound, hasten to gather books of reckoning, "rentals" (134) which record the sins of all mankind; in the N-Town cycle the psychological force of the trope is rendered by *Primus diabolus,* who is the first of the devils to observe that each sinner is a book — in effect a book of death — in that "on here fforehed wyttness I take / Ffor þer is wretyn with letteris blake / Opynly all here synne" ("Doomsday,"

74-77). *The Book of Margery Kempe* records her vision of an angel who, despite the traditional reservation expressed in Rev. 5:9, shows her the "Book of Life," in which she discovers her own name written. There follows the record of a revelation in which Jesus speaks to her, confirming that her name is "written at the Trinity's foot" in the Book, for which reason she is entitled to be "right merry" (chap. 85). Dante, in his final apocalyptic vision in the *Paradiso,* speaks of an "Eternal Light" in whose depth he sees ingathered "bound by love in a single volume, that which is dispersed in leaves throughout the universe" *(legato con amore in un volume, / ciò che per l'universo si squaderna)* — image clearly related to the book of life (33.85-87).

Exod. 32:32 evidently lies behind the reference in *Richard 2,* where Shakespeare has Mowbray say to his colleague in exile, Bolingbroke, "If ever I were traitor, / My name be blotted from the book of life, / And I from Heaven banished as from hence!" (1.3.201-03). The books and book, singular and plural, are set in relation to one another by John Donne in his *Meditation 17,* in a passage reminiscent of Dante:

> All mankind is of one author and is one volume; when one man dies, one chapter is not torn out of the book, but translated into a better language; and every chapter must be so translated. God employs several translators; some pieces are translated by age, some by sickness, some by war, some by justice; but God's hand is in every translation, and his hand shall bind up all our scattered leaves again for that library where every book shall lie open to one another.

Byron's Manfred, weighed down with his sense of responsibility to a final reckoning, exclaims, "My days are numbered, and my deeds recorded" *(Manfred,* 3.4.314). But the weighty force of the biblical image in medieval and Renaissance literature is unmatched in usage after the Enlightenment generally speaking. Typically the book of life is invoked in analogy with something of less moment, or psychologized. In Thomas de Quincey's *Suspina de Profundis* those like the Pariah, the Jew, and the English criminal are "blotted out from the books of remembrance in sweet far-off England," and in the same writer's *Confessions of an Opium Eater* the drug prompts *la recherche du temps perdus,* suggesting to de Quincey that "the dread book of account which the Scriptures speak of is, in fact, the mind of each individual." A similar allusion may be found in Dickens's *David Copperfield* (chap. 38); in Conrad's *Outcast of the Islands* drowned sailors go to their watery grave "without needing to open the book of life, because they could look at eternity reflected on the element that gave the life and dealt the death" (1.2). In Tennyson's "Sea Dreams" books of financial accounting are connected to ultimate accountability. A young man who has been defrauded asks to see the records of his oppressor and, when unsuccessful,

reflects wistfully that "When the great Books — see Daniel seven and ten — / Were opened, I should find he meant me well." In *Sesame and the Lilies* Ruskin observes that while some in his generation no longer believe in immortality, others anticipate that "within these five, or ten, or twenty years, for every one of us the judgment will be set, and the books opened" ("The Mystery of Life and its Arts").

See also BOOK; LAST JUDGMENT; SEVEN SEALS.

Bibliography. Charles, R. H. *APOT* 2.216; Josipovici, G. *The World and the Book* (1971); Koep, L. *Das himmlische Buch in Antike und Christentum* (1952).

BOOK OF THE COVENANT   *See* COVENANT.

BORN AGAIN   John 3:3-8.
See also CONVERSION.

BOTTOMLESS PIT   *See* ABADDON; HELL; LAKE OF FIRE AND BRIMSTONE; WORM THAT DIETH NOT.

BOW THE KNEE TO BAAL   *See* BAAL; ELIJAH.

BOWELS OF MERCY   1 John 3:17 is exemplary of numerous biblical locutions employing this figurative expression, here as rendered by the KJV translation to signify compassion, or as later idiom would have it, "heartfelt compassion."

BRAND PLUCKED FROM THE BURNING   In Amos 4:11 the prophet declares God's summary of his judgments upon sin as they were well known to most listeners, saying to Israel: "I have overthrown some of you, as God overthrew Sodom and Gomorrah, and ye were as a firebrand plucked out of the burning: yet have ye not returned unto me, saith the LORD" (cf. Zech. 3:2). This image for being saved just in the last possible instant provides the title for Cotton Mather's *A Brand Plucked out of the Burning* (1693), a study of demonology, and was used by John Wesley to describe his having been rescued as a child from his family's burning home. Charlotte Brontë employs the phrase in *Jane Eyre* (chap. 35) in a context which suggests the mediating influence of the "Litany" from the *Book of Common Prayer:* "He supplicated . . . a return . . . for those whom the temptations of the world and the flesh were luring from the narrow path. He asked, he urged, he claimed the boon of a brand snatched from the burning."

See also DEMONS, DEMON POSSESSION; STRAIT AND NARROW; WORLD, FLESH, AND DEVIL.

BRAZEN SERPENT   En route from Mt. Hor, the Israelites "spake against God" and were punished by a plague of poisonous serpents. When they repented, Moses followed God's orders to set up a serpent of brass on a pole. Looking at the serpent cured anyone who had been bitten (Num. 21:4-9). Much later, King Hezekiah destroyed the image because the Israelites were worshiping it as an idol (2 Kings 18:3-4). Wisd. of Sol. 16:5-8 distinguishes the serpent's function as a "sign of salvation" from the idolatry practiced by Israel's enemies. Jesus himself inaugurated its typological interpretation: "As Moses lifted up the serpent in the wilderness, even so must the Son of man be lifted up" (John 3:14). That the Hebrew term for *pole* means more precisely "standard-bearer" and can just as well be translated "sign" (as in the Vg) also encouraged typological readings.

Because it draws on several texts (see also 1 Cor. 10:9) and a divinely authorized interpretation, the exegetical tradition is rich and complex. The dominant themes are the parallel between the brazen serpent as remedy for physical illness and the Crucifixion as remedy for spiritual illness, the seeming inappropriateness of both remedies, the necessity of faith in appropriating both remedies, and the parallel between the serpent without venom which provided healing for venomous bites and a sinless sacrifice who provides healing for sin. St. Augustine speaks of

> the deadly serpents' bites, sent in just punishment of sin, but healed by looking at the lifted brazen serpent, so that not only were the tormented people healed, but a symbol of the crucifixion of death set before them in this destruction of death by death. (*De civ. Dei* 10.8; cf. *In Joan. Ev.* 12.11)

St. Justin Martyr, among others, assumed that the brazen serpent must have formed the shape of a cross. Medieval illustrations of the Crucifixion, especially in pedagogical contexts such as the *Biblia Pauperum,* are frequently accompanied by a picture of the brazen serpent. Later commentators, including Samuel Mather (*The Figures and Types of the Old Testament*), Edward Taylor (*Preparatory Meditations,* 2nd ser., no. 61 on John 3:14), and Simon Patrick (*A Commentary on the Historical Books of the Old Testament* [1732], 1.648-51; 2.502-03) rehearse the same themes.

As an object of idolatrous worship, the brazen serpent was sometimes regarded as a metaphor for things good in themselves but valued too highly. Milton uses it in this way in referring to the memory of martyrs (*Of Reformation*) and Coleridge for the historical evidence of Christianity (*The Statesman's Manual,* Appendix A).

Dryden and Carlyle exploit the serpent texts and parts of the traditional exegesis of them for complex ironic satire. In *Absalom and Achitophel* (632-34) Dryden combines them with Horace's "monument more lasting than brass" (*Odes,* 3.30.1), the brass memorials of Korah's rebellion (Num. 16:36-40), and "brass" in the sense of "impudence," for his portrait of Titus Oates as false witness and false prophet:

> Yet, *Corah,* thou shalt from Oblivion pass;
> Erect thy self thou Monumental Brass:
> High as the Serpent of thy mettall made. . . .

Carlyle applies the texts to two events which embody excessive faith in illusory modern ideas: the revolutionary States-General (*The French Revolution,* 5.1) and a campaign to erect a statue of an unscrupulous railway magnate ("Hudson's Statute").

See also HEZEKIAH; MOSES; TYPOLOGY.

Bibliography. Brinsley, J. *The Mystical Brasen Serpent* (1653); Landow, G. P. *Victorian Types, Victorian Shadows* (1980); Pickering, F. P. *Literature and Art in the Middle Ages* (1970); Rowley, H. H. "Zadok and Nehushtan." *JBL* 58 (1939), 113ff.   WILLIAM KINSLEY

BREAD OF LIFE   Bread is an extraordinarily rich symbol in the Bible, appearing as a figure for providential gifts — both physical and spiritual — as well as gifts of human hospitality. The word can be metonymic for solid food of any kind, but when referring to baking generally means wheat bread. In the OT sanctuary it is only in connection with the jealousy offering that barley is even mentioned (Num. 5:15). According to Num. 6:15 it was the duty of a Nazarite after expiration of his vow to make a presentation at the sanctuary of a (wheat) bread offering. In the NT, however, it was barley loaves from a little boy's lunch which Jesus used to feed the multitudes (John 6:9); barley was less desirable, hence cheaper and more often used by peasants. St. Augustine establishes a medieval convention based upon the distinction when he allegorizes the loaves as the five books of Moses, saying "rightly are they not wheaten but barley loaves, because they belong to the Old Testament" (*In Joan. Ev.* 24.5), the letter of which, he goes on to say, is "invested in a covering of carnal sacraments; but yet, if we get at its pith, it feeds and satisfies us." St. Jerome presses a further allegory on the distinction in his famous letters on marriage and virginity: "I call virginity fine corn, wed-lock barley, and fornication cow dung" (*Adv. Jov.* 1.7; *Ep.* 48.14). Chaucer's Wife of Bath, who "nyl envye no virginitee. / Lat hem be breed of pure whete-seed, / And lat us wyves hoten barly-breed" (*The Wife of Bath's Tale,* Prol. 3.142-44), is aware of Jerome, but might take more comfort from Augustine's typology.

The locus classicus for NT iconography of bread is John 6, in which Jesus remonstrates with those who pursue him the day after the miracle of the loaves and fishes, hoping for another free meal, some alluding to the "manna in the desert," the "bread from heaven" which they attribute to Moses. Jesus says rather, "My Father giveth you the true bread from heaven. For the bread of God is he which cometh down from heaven, and giveth life unto the world." Still confused, they ask for "this bread," imagining corporeal food, but Jesus startles them by saying, "I am the bread of life; he that cometh to me shall never hunger; and he that believeth on me shall never thirst" (John 6:31-35). St. Augustine's commentary *In Joannis Evangelium* sets the tone for Western tradition, which depends on an opposition of the corporeal bread of the Old Covenant and the spiritual bread of the New: "They considered therefore the things promised by Moses, and they considered the things promised by Christ. The former promised a full belly on earth, but of the meat which perished; the latter promised not the meat which perishes but that which endures unto eternal life" (25.12). To hunger after the bread which Christ offers — himself — is to express "the hunger of the inner man," and "consequently, he that hungers after this bread, hungers after righteousness — that righteousness which comes down, however, from heaven, the righteousness that God gives, not that which one works for on his own" (26.1). This notion appears to underlie the double irony of Herbert's narrator Jesus in "The Sacrifice," who says of his adversaries, "They do wish me dead, / Who cannot wish, except I give them bread" (6-7).

Augustine had been led to make an analogy of the Incarnation — the Word made flesh (26.10) — and the bread of the Eucharist. Concerning the bread "which comes down from heaven," he says: "Manna signified this bread; God's altar signified this bread. Those were sacraments. In the sign they were diverse; in the thing which they signified they were alike" (26.12-20). The incarnational reference is echoed in numerous medieval lyrics which, inspired also by an Antonian iconography of the Virgin, makes her womb the oven in which the bread of life was baked (e.g., a eucharistic hymn by James Ryman [R. Greene, *The Early English Carols*, no. 318]: "In virgyne Mary this brede was bake, / Whenne Criste of her manhoode did take"). Herbert develops the same idea in a different fashion: "I could believe an Impanation / At the rate of an Incarnation, / If thou hadst died for Bread" ("H. Communion," 25-28). Herbert's "Prayer for after the Sermon" in *A Priest to the Temple* may reflect a tendency after the Reformation to identify eucharistic nourishment with the nourishment of expounded Scriptures: "Lord, thou hast fed us with the bread of life" (290; cf. Matthew Poole, *Annotations upon the Holy Bible* [John 6:35ff.]). A general conflation of all the spiritual senses as opposed to the simple literal "staff of life" or "daily bread" of the *paternoster* (Matt. 6:11) is common after the 19th cent. Carlyle, in *Sartor Resartus,* says: "A second man I honour, and still more highly: Him who is seen toiling for the spiritually indispensable; not daily bread, but the bread of life" (3.4).

See also BY BREAD ALONE; EUCHARIST; INCARNATION; MANNA; NAZARITE.

BREAD UPON THE WATERS

One of the many proverbs bequeathed by the book of Ecclesiastes to English literary usage is "Cast thy bread upon the waters, for thou shalt find it after many days" (11:1). The injunction is to disinterested benevolence; as the *Glossa Ordinaria* cryptically notes, "*aptos fructificationi*" (PL 113.1125). This is the sense employed by Mark Twain in *The Man That Corrupted Hadleyburg,* where Mrs. Richards learns of the reward left for whoever had played Good Samaritan to the stranger, calling it "a fortune for that kind man who set his bread afloat upon the waters!" In 20th-cent. literature the expression more often has ironic overtones, as when Shaw in *Village Wooing* uses it as a pretext for extravagant spending. O. Henry's card shark reflects on the returns of what he "had cast upon the waters" — the deck he has marked in code ("The Man Higher Up"). And Somerset Maugham's narrator adverts to

> the philanthropist who with altruistic motives builds model dwellings for the poor and finds he has made a lucrative investment. He cannot prevent the satisfaction he feels in the ten per cent which rewards the bread he has cast upon the waters, but he has an awkward feeling that he detracts somewhat from the savor of his virtue. ("The Fall of Edward Barnard")

BREAKING OF BREAD   *See* EUCHARIST.

BREASTPLATE OF RIGHTEOUSNESS   *See* ARMOR AND WEAPONS; *MILES CHRISTI.*

BRICKS WITHOUT STRAW

Exodus 5:6-19 recounts how when Moses and Aaron requested a respite for the Israelite prisoners from their brickmaking to celebrate a religious festival, Pharaoh ordered them to make as many bricks as before, but to be deprived of straw while doing so. In Egyptian brickmaking straw was added to claymud in quantities appropriate to modify the rate of drying; if bricks did not have enough straw, many would crumble.

In English literature this incident acquires proverbial status. One of Dekker's *Villanies Discovered* is "to compell thy Vassall to make more Bricke when straw and stuffe is taken from him." Burton, in *The Anatomie of Melancholie,* is scornful of patrons who behave like Pharaoh (1.2; 3.15). In *Sartor Resartus* Carlyle's Teufelsdröckh speaks of "the poor Hebrew, in this Egypt of an Auscultatorship, [who] painfully toiled, baking bricks without stubble" (2.5); and in a similarly academic vein, Lytton Strachey describes Cowper's poetry as "the art of making bricks without straw" ("Gray and Cowper," in *Characters and Commentaries*). Marlowe finds the manager's secretary at the Central Station in *Heart of Darkness* to be so engaged because he had been a failure in an earlier dubious enterprise, the "making of bricks." "It seems," says Marlowe, that "he could not make bricks without something — straw maybe." Somerset Maugham, in the opening pages of his book on the *Theatre,* claims that this impossible task is the lot of actors in an age of poor dramatists; Phillpott (*The Marleybone Miser,* 16), and Malcolm Muggeridge silently quoting him (*The Thirties in Great Britain,* 6.7), "know only too well how a newspaperman can make bricks without straw."

See also EXODUS; MOSES; PHARAOH.

BRIDE, BRIDEGROOM The one-flesh nuptial union of man and woman and the command to be fruitful and multiply, presented as the primordial divine injunction in Gen. 1:28, are reflected throughout the OT, which is as much a story of marriages and begettings as of any other human activity. Weddings were a principal festal occasion in the Hebrew, as in other Near Eastern cultures, notably the "wedding-week" celebrations in which the bride and groom were feted as symbolic "king" and "queen" with the singing of *wasfs* or lyric songs of praise (see N. Snaith, "The Song of Songs: the Dances of the Virgins," *AJSL* 50 [1934], 129-43). A mishnaic passage describes ritual folk dances of courtship performed by "the daughters of Jerusalem" in connection with the annual festivals of summer harvest and autumnal vintage (Ta'an. 4:8), and associates the joy of this "day of espousals" with Israel's joy in the giving of the Law and the building of the Temple. The "voice of the bridegroom and the bride" in fact became paradigmatic of joy in the land (Jer. 33:11), as, conversely, its absence was emblematic of desolation (Jer. 7:34; 16:9; 25:10; cf. Rev. 18:3). The rising of the sun in the east was compared to a bridegroom emerging joyfully from the bridechamber (Ps. 19:4-5). This tradition is reflected in nuptial poetry from Canticles through the epithalamia of the Renaissance, and in descriptive re-creations of traditional Jewish weddings as in the stories of Sholem Aleichem or Chaim Potok's *The Chosen*.

Figurative uses of nuptial imagery from the Bible are many and varied. The image of Israel as bride in her covenant relationship to God, and the period of her Exodus deliverance and the giving of the Law as the time of her espousals, undoubtedly goes back to the period of conflict with Baal worship and the widespread mythos in surrounding cultures of sacred marriage of god and goddess, and the institution of sacred prostitution (see S. N. Kramer, *The Sacred Marriage Rite* [1969]). Hebrew theology substituted for such symbolism the image of Israel herself as corporate bride. Most frequently, the image is encountered in a negative context: Israel has proven to be a faithless bride and has gone "whoring" after alien gods (e.g., Exod. 34:12; Lev. 17:17; 20:7; Deut. 31:16; 1 Chron. 5:25; Jer. 2:32; Ezek. 16:15); but God is not only a "jealous" God, he is also a superabundantly loving husband, who will be true to his covenant despite the bride's unfaithfulness, take her back (Hos. 1–2), and establish with her a renewed nuptial bond (Isa. 54:5; 62:5).

In light of this symbolism, Ps. 45, a royal epithalamium, was interpreted by the rabbis as an allegory of God's betrothal to Israel, exactly as was Canticles. This allegorization runs through the entire history of Jewish exegesis, from the Targum on Canticles, through the Mishnah and Talmud, the Midrash Rabbah, and all the great Jewish commentators of the Middle Ages and Renaissance; it lies at the heart of the Zohar and other classics of the Cabala, such as Leon Hebraeus's *Dialogues of Love*. In popular devotional literature of Judaism, the symbolism is most familiar in the image of the Sabbath as Bride of God, as in the Sabbath hymns of Judah Halevi and other religious poets (see *Daily Prayer Book / Ha-Siddur Ha-Shalem*, ed. P. Birnbaum [1949]).

In the Gospels the metaphor reappears with a new emphasis on the Messiah as bridegroom. John the Baptist describes himself in relation to the mission of Jesus as "friend of the bridegroom" (John 3:29). In the Synoptics, Jesus himself, answering questions about why his own disciples do not fast, says, "Can the children of the bridechamber fast, while the bridegroom is with them? As long as they have the bridegroom with them, they cannot fast. But the days will come when the bridegroom shall be taken away from them, and then shall they fast in those days" (Mark 2:19-20; cf. Matt. 9:14-15; Luke 5:33-35). In these Gospel references one finds the symbolism of the messianic bridegroom and the messianic wedding, but no explicit mention of the bride. The same is true of the parable of the wise and foolish virgins: the bridegroom tarries, and when at midnight the cry is heard, "Behold, the bridegroom cometh; go ye out to meet him," the five foolish virgin-attendants find that they are unprepared and the door to the wedding is shut against them (Matt. 25:1-13). The parable seems to assume a familiarity with the analogy of the Parousia to a wedding banquet, implied in another Matthean parable, the invitation to the wedding banquet (22:1-14; cf. St. John Chrysostom, *Hom. on Matthew*, 69), and is explicit in the symbolism of the marriage of the Lamb in Rev. 19:9. Thus, in the NT we find a fusion of two eschatological images of late biblical and intertestamental Judaism: the messianic banquet and the messianic marriage.

The Apocalypse presents a composite version of the foregoing biblical nuptial imagery in the context of the climactic eschatological battle between good and evil built around three contrasting pairs of characters: God, Christ, and the Bride on one side, and Satan, the Antichrist, and the Harlot on the other. Early Christian commentators regularly identified the Bride of chaps. 19–22 (and the Lady of chap. 12) as the Church, while medieval and subsequent Catholic expositors (e.g., William of Newburgh) often favored a more specifically Marian reading. Especially influential in Christian symbolism was the description of the heavenly Jerusalem as the Bride of Christ (Rev. 21:2, 9), and the concluding words of the book, and of the NT, in which "the Spirit and the bride say, Come," and the evangelist echoes with the prayer, "Even so, come, Lord Jesus." Commentators frequently paralleled these words with the love-invitation of Canticles — and indeed, taken together, Canticles and the Apocalypse have been the key texts for the subsequent elaboration of Christian bride / bridegroom symbolism.

The most fully worked out nuptial symbolism in the NT occurs in the Pauline corpus. Galatians uses the image of the community as a woman and the covenant as a marriage bond in an elaborate allegorization of the marriages of Abraham: the marriage to Hagar symbolizes the covenant of Sinai and the marriage to Sarah the dispensation of the gospel, bringing forth, respectively, "children unto bondage" and "children of promise" (Gal. 4:28-31). In another allegorization, in Romans Paul expresses the Christian community's freedom from the Law under the image of a woman whose former husband, the Law, has died, and who has remarried in freedom: "Wherefore, my brethren, ye also are become dead to the law by the body of Christ; that ye should be married to another, even to him who is raised from the dead" (Rom. 7:1-6). The marriage image here is made to reinforce the soteriology of Rom. 4, which teaches that in baptism all are baptized into death with Christ and are also resurrected with him into newness of life — a life which Paul here defines as everlasting marriage with Christ. (These connections underlie the nuptial imagery associated with the early rites of Christian initiation.)

Even more important are those passages in 1 and 2 Corinthians and Ephesians in which the nuptial image is inextricably bound up with the central Pauline images of the mystical Body of Christ and the conjugal one-flesh union. In 2 Cor. 11:2-3, Paul expresses his solicitude for the Church under the image of himself as the *paranymphos* ("friend of the bridegroom"), presenting the Church as a fit bride for Christ, simple and chaste in contrast to Eve, who was beguiled by the subtlety of the serpent. In 1 Cor. 11:3 Paul constructs an analogy that implies the nuptial metaphor: "the head of every man is Christ; and the head of the woman is the man; and the head of Christ is God"; but as Chrysostom pointed out, the image properly implies no domestic subordination, but rather perfect union and equality *(Hom. on 1 Corinthians)*. This implication of the metaphor is best worked out in a crucial passage in Ephesians dealing with the relations of husbands and wives but grounding the teaching in ecclesiology: wives should be "subject" to their husbands, and husbands should "love" their wives, "even as Christ also loved the church, and gave himself for it; that he might sanctify and cleanse it with the washing of water by the word, that he might present it to himself a glorious church, not having spot, or wrinkle, or any such thing; but that it should be holy and without blemish" (5:25-27). So men ought to love their wives, the text continues, as their own bodies, "even as the Lord the church; for we are members of his body" (vv. 29-30). For husband and wife are "one flesh" — and, the apostle concludes, "This is a great mystery; but I speak concerning Christ and the church" (vv. 31-32). The passage shows that the central Pauline doctrine of the mystical Body of Christ is actually a concomitant of the metaphor of the spiritual marriage: for we are members of the Body of Christ precisely because in our nuptial relation with him we become "one flesh" with him, that itself being symbolic of being "one spirit"

with him in conformity of will (see, e.g., St. Bernard, *Sermones super Cantica,* 71).

Given this biblical imagery, it is not surprising that the Church Fathers could view the life of Christ as a whole, from Incarnation to Resurrection, in terms of the nuptial allegory, as St. Augustine expresses in a single sentence: "If a man should give his own blood for his bride, he would not live to take her for his wife. But our Lord, dying without fear, gave his blood for her (the Church) whom he was to obtain at His resurrection, and whom He had united to Himself in the Virgin's womb" *(In Joan. Ev.* 8 [PL 35.1452]). Even more prominent was the elaboration of the image of the Church as Bride of Christ, as in such early Christian writings as St. Methodius's *Symposium* (see esp. "Thecla's Hymn") and the *Shepherd of Hermas* and, above all, in Christian allegorizations of Canticles beginning with the earliest commentators, St. Hippolytus and Origen in the 3rd cent., and extending through hundreds of commentaries and poetic paraphrases from medieval to modern times, especially in monastic circles, notable examples including the commentaries of St. Gregory of Nyssa, St. Gregory the Great, St. Bernard, William of St. Thierry, Gilbert of Hoyland, St. John of the Cross, and, among Reformers, Beza, Luther, and John Cotton, and such influential poetic paraphrases as the Cantica section of Peter Riga's *Aurora,* William's *Expositio in Cantica Canticorum* with its Old High German gloss, and the Canticles section of Macé de la Charité's French versification of the Bible or the 12th-cent. French paraphrase in Le Mans MS 173 (ed. Pickford [1974]). Dante uses the imagery when in the Earthly Paradise Beatrice is called to heaven with the words of Cant. 4:8, *"Veni sponsa, de Libano"* (*Purgatorio,* 30.11), and Dante calls Paradise itself a wedding (*Paradiso,* 30.135) and the Church Triumphant Christ's spouse: "In form, then, of a white rose displayed itself to me that sacred soldiery which in his blood Christ made his spouse" (*Paradiso,* 31.1-3).

The application of this nuptial imagery to the life of the Church had from earliest times special reference to the liturgy and the sacraments. The early ritual for the dedication of a Church, for instance, emphasized the Bride of Christ figure, as is reflected in the 6th-cent. hymn *"Urbi Beate Hierusalem"* and later adaptations such as the sequences of Adam of St. Victor. More centrally, the sacraments of Eucharist and baptism, especially in the context of the Paschal liturgy of the Easter Vigil (traditional setting in the West for the ritual of Christian Initiation for adults) are given nuptial overtones in the basic early Christian texts. About the Eucharist Theodoret says, "In eating the elements of the Bridegroom and drinking His Blood, we accomplish a marriage union" (PG 81.1285), an image incorporated into various Eastern liturgies. Similarly, the important catechetical addresses by St. Cyril of Jerusalem (*Procatechesis* and *Catechesis*) and St. Ambrose (*De mysteriis* and *De sacramentis*), directed to candidates for baptism and the newly baptized, explicate the baptism ritual as a "nuptial bath" and the Eucharist as a "wedding banquet." This symbolic imagery is reflected in liturgical poetry and hymnody from St. Ephraim Syrus and Adam of St. Victor to modern times; one sees it in a ME poem on the Mass in the Balliol MS:

> The chirche is callid þe spowse of Jhesu Criste,
> þe cavse of þis mariage is þe holy messe,
> Wher dayly at þe auter offreth vp þe priste
> The son to þe fader, þat is no lesse.
> (EETS e.s. 101, p. 69)

It becomes a prominent motif in Edward Taylor's "Preparatory Meditations" in 17th-cent. New England, as in Keble's *The Christian Year* in Victorian England. A familiar example in interdenominational hymnals is S. J. Stone's well-known Protestant hymn "The Church's One Foundation":

> From heaven He came and sought her
> To be His holy bride;
> With His own blood He bought her,
> And for her life He died.

In traditional Catholic doctrine the symbolic images applied to the Church generally *(generaliter)* applied with special force *(specialiter)* to the Virgin Mary, as paradigm of the Church; thus the Mother of God became also, paradoxically, the Bride of Christ. Evidence from early liturgies (Mozarabic, Gallican) indicates that the original Marian feast included celebration of her role as Queen of heaven's King, through application of the epithalamial Ps. 44. By the 7th cent. the Roman rite recognized four Marian feasts (Purification, Annunciation, Assumption, and Nativity of Mary), and in the 13th and 14th cents. the number of Marian feasts multiplied greatly and with regional variants; the Masses for these feasts, especially for the Assumption, all contained lections, such as selections from Canticles, which imply the nuptial metaphor. This symbolism is more fully developed in the monastic offices for these same feasts, as can be seen in such examples from the medieval English Church as the Durham Collectar, the Leofric Collectar, the York Breviary, or a Sarum Missal from about 1300 (ed. Legg [1916], 308-09). A particularly rich example is the office developed by nuns of the Brigittine order at Isleworth, who also produced an English translation and commentary, *The Myroure of oure Ladye,* printed in 1530 (EETS e.s. 19). The hymns and prayers of the hours for each day of the week in *The Myroure* consistently make use of nuptial symbolism, as in the Thursday compline hymn "Sponsa Iungende," and its commentary, which claims that St. Bridget herself was told by God the Father to tell "that preste my louer that he make that hympne . . . to stande as hathe sette yt. For whyle holy cherche calleth all sowles the spouses of my sonne, moche more maye the sowle of Mary be called hys spowse" (p. 238). It is above all in the office for Saturday, Mary's day, devoted to her life from

the Passion to the Assumption, that this symbolism is most elaborated.

Further evidence of the Marian application of nuptial symbolism occurs in the homiletic literature and hymnody associated with the Marian feasts, especially the Assumption, in the Middle Ages. A good example is the collection of eight Marian homilies of Amedeus of Lausanne, especially the third (on the Assumption) and sixth (on Mary's joy in the Resurrection), in which the nuptial symbol supplies the central motif and concluding peroration. Similarly, the Blickling homily for the Annunciation speaks of Gabriel as announcing a wedding ("Gabriel waes þissa bryd inga serenwreca"), and Mary's womb as a bridechamber ("brydbur") in which the spiritual marriage between Christ and humanity is accomplished — though, once again, Mary herself is also the bride (EETS o.s. 58, pp. 2-13). Another OE example is Aelfric's first Assumption homily (based on the Pseudo-Jerome *Ep. 9,* *"Cogitis Me"* [PL 30.130]), which applies the praises of the bride of Canticles to Mary in her glorification (ed. Thorpe [1844], 1.436-54), as also does a ME homily on the Assumption following the Sarum rite (EETS o.s. 209, p. 366).

Marian liturgical poetry makes similar use of such nuptial symbolism, as evidenced by Ephraim Syrus's Nativity Hymns and Adam of St. Victor's sequences for Epiphany, such as *"De Beate Virgine,"* and the Nativity of Mary, such as *"Lux Advenit Veneranda"* (ed. Wrangham [1881], nos. 90, 95). Numerous similar examples may be garnered from among the poems collected in *Lateinische Hymnen des Mittelalters* (ed. F. J. Mone [1964], 3 vols.) and *Analecta Hymnica Medii Aevi* (eds. Dreves and Blume [1886], 55 vols.), such as *"Psalterium Beate Mariae Virgine,"* attributed to Edmund of Canterbury, in which Mary is repeatedly addressed, *"Ave, sponsa. . ."* (Dreves and Blume, vol. 35, no. 10; cf. vol. 9, nos. 58, 60, and 61; and Mone, nos. 326, 336, 371, 373, 447, 450, 469, 471, 473, 505, 510, 511, 515, 531, 555, and 600). The same motifs are discernible in medieval vernacular religious poetry — as in the use of the "bryd" image in the Advent lyrics of the Exeter Book (ed. Campbell [1959], 49, 67), the early ME "On god ureisun of ure lefdi" (C. Brown, *English Lyrics of the XIIIth Century,* no. 3), the Lambeth MS poem *"Gaude, Flore Virginali,"* whose second stanza begins, "Gaude, goddys spouse so deere!" (EETS o.s. 15, pp. 174-75), or the well-known *"Quia Amore Langueo,"* ending with Mary's invitation to the soul to participate with her in the spiritual marriage (Brown, *Religious Lyrics of the XIVth Century,* no. 132). The 15th cent. was the golden age of ME poetry of this sort, much of it modeled on the rhetoric of secular love lyrics, again using the precedent of Canticles, as in the Assumption poem, *"Surge Mea Sponsa, So Swete in Syȝte"* (Brown, *Religious Lyrics of the XIVth Century,* no. 37), or the various versions of hymns on the Seven Heavenly Joys of the Virgin Mary, the second of which is her spousehood (ibid., nos. 33-36; cf. nos. 6, 14, 23, and 72). So exalted is this title, spouse of God, that one lyric (no. 69) does not shrink from naming her "goddes," being of "One spyrte and will with cryst."

Comparable to these ME productions, and with even more elaboration of this nuptial imagery, are the Marian poems of Heinrich von Frauenlob (d. 1317), notably his impassioned "Unser Frauen Lied" (see P. Wackernagel, ed., *Das Deutsche Kirchenlied von der altesten Zeit bis zu Anfang des XVII. Jahrhunderts* [1867], 2.216-20). Here Mary's life is described allegorically under various images relating to the figure of Wisdom, the Lady of the Apocalypse, and the Bride of Canticles; in the second half she speaks in her own voice as the Bride, telling how her divine Lover came to her by night, kissed her, lay between her breasts, and entered — as an infant — her maiden womb, making her at once bride and mother (6-18, citing Cant. 1:13), bringing about her nuptial "deification" or interidentification with Christ:

> er got, si got, ich got: daz ich vor niemen spar.
> ich vater muter, er min muter vater zwar,
> wan daz ist war. (12.27-29)

The love-lyric analogy culminates in st. 15, in which Mary portrays Christ and herself as a pair of lovers discovered by the Swain's angry Father, who "punishes" him and casts him out of the kingdom; but by patiently bearing his suffering, the lover wins back the kingdom, to which he brings his spouse. This daring allegory is in fact comparable to other mystical representations of the spiritual marriage as a passionate love story, as in Thomas of Hales's "Love Rune" (C. Brown, *English Lyrics of the XIIIth Century*, no. 43), the kingly wooer parable in *The Ancrene Riwle* (pt. 7), or St. John of the Cross's poem "Madrigal a lo divino," in which the young lover, Christ, despised by his beloved, goes off to fight in foreign wars, until eventually he "swarmed a tall tree and arms balancing wide / beautifully grappled the tree till he died / of the love in his heart like a ruinous wound" (trans. Nims [1959], 41), or as in late medieval iconographic depictions of the Crucifixion showing Christ stabbed in the heart not by a Roman centurion but by the Sponsa herself (see Schiller, *Iconography of Christian Art*, vol. 2 [1972], 447, 452, 453).

As these latter references indicate, whatever is said of Mary *specialiter* becomes true of the Church *generaliter* and of every faithful soul *individualiter* — and first of all in the case of certain female saints to whom the nuptial symbolism became particularly attached, notably Mary Magdalene and Katherine of Alexandria. The Mass and office of Mary Magdalene (July 22) is filled with nuptial references, especially to the bride's nocturnal search for her lover, which is applied to the Magdalene's Easter morning vigil, and the image appears in vernacular literary treatments, such as Robinson's *Life and Death of Mary Magdalene* (1620). But the saint most consistently identified as spouse of Christ is Katherine of Alexandria,

the highborn patron of philosophy and learning who refused to take any husband other than Christ; the story of her martyrdom is highlighted by the account of her mystical marriage to Christ and at her death she is called by her divine Spouse to join him in heaven, in the words which conclude the Apocalypse: "Come thou, my much beloved, come my bride!" The imagery occurs in the liturgy for Katherine (Nov. 25) and in the associated hymnody, such as Konrad von Heimburg's *"Ave Candens Lilium"* or Albert von Prag's *"Salve, Virgo Floriosa"* (Dreves and Blume, *Analecta Hymnica Medii Aevi*, vol. 3, nos. 56 and 20; cf. Mone, *Latinische Hymnen des Mittelalters*, nos. 987, 989, 995, 997, 1000, and 1001), and in narrative accounts such as the late OE *Life of St. Katherine* (EETS o.s. 80) or John Capgrave's monumental poetic version of the 15th cent. (EETS o.s. 100). Capgrave's bk. 3 describes Katherine's conversion (baptism is her nuptial bath [1069-73]) and mystical marriage to Christ (1268-1309); subsequently, rejecting any repudiation of Christ, she dies a martyr for her spouse: "I wil neuere chaunge, whil I haue lyf, / I shal been euere to hym truwe spouse and wyf" (4.1049-50). Subsequently, Katherine's mystical marriage became a favorite theme of Renaissance painters, such as Fra Angelico, Correggio, Luini, Raphael, Titian, Veronese, Tintoretto, and Murillo.

Just as mystical nuptial symbolism attached to certain specific saints (others include Catherine of Siena, Cecelia, Margaret, and Bridget), so it attached itself to female mystics and holy women generally in the late Middle Ages (see H. Taylor, *The Mediaeval Mind*, 2 vols. [1966], 2.465-76; and P. Pourrat, *Christian Spirituality*, 4 vols. [1953], 2.82-92), and is reflected in the ritual for the investiture of nuns and in the rite for the Consecration of a Virgin. The background for these rites is found in early Christian texts dealing with the concept of virginity as dedication to spiritual marriage with Christ, such as Methodius's *Symposium*, Ambrose's treatises *De Virginitate, Exhortatio ad Virgines,* and *De Virginibus,* and Jerome's *Ep. 22* ("To Eustochium") and the influential *Adversus Jovinianum* (cited, e.g., by Chaucer's Wife of Bath — as an antifeminist diatribe), and such later medieval texts as *The Ancrene Riwle* (EETS o.s. 225, 249) and *Hali Meidenhad* (EETS o.s. 18). The theme is developed in the liturgies and offices for holy women (Common for a Virgin, Common for a Virgin Martyr, Common for a Holy Woman), especially in the repeated use of the Ambrosian hymn *"Jesu, Corona Virginum."* The investiture of a nun and the rite for the Consecration of a Virgin are the liturgical culmination of the theme, being conceived according to the imagery of a wedding ceremony, including the donning of wedding garb and veil, bestowal of a ring, and the exchange of vows: "My Lord Jesus Christ has espoused me with his ring and as a bride has adorned me with a crown" (P. Botz, *"Sponsa Regis Aeterni," Benedictine Review* 9 [1954], 10; cf. K. Sullivan, "The Ceremony of the Consecration of Religious

Women," *Liturgical Week Proceedings* [1958], 58-60). A richly detailed explication of the Consecration Rite occurs in the third exercise of Gertrude the Great's *Exercises:* "Espousals and Consecration of the Anniversary of Holy Profession" (trans. Gertrude Jaren Lewis and Jack Lewis [1989]). As the opening rubric explains: "This is the way in which thou shalt solemnize the spiritual wedlock, the marriage of love, the betrothal, and the nuptials of thy chaste soul with Jesus the heavenly Bridegroom in the deathless bond of thy heart's affection," for Christ is an impassioned Lover who "loveth thee immoderately."

While having special force in the context of female saints and the rituals of nuns and holy women, the nuptial metaphor was always understood to be applicable to every individual devout soul (as is evident in tropological commentaries on Canticles); consequently, it is a frequent image in the writings of the mystics, for whom it had great appeal. A striking instance is the lyrical treatise *The Flowing Light of Godhead* by St. Mechthild of Magdeburg, an associate of Gertrude the Great. Mechthild's book, widely circulated and translated (a 15th-cent. Eng. version was entitled "The Book of St. Maud or Book of Ghostly Grace"), tells in loosely connected lyric sections the story of a divine Youth and the maiden he woos in a flowery meadow, their festive wedding, her apparent abandonment and inconsolable longing, and his reaffirmation and promise of everlasting union in the heavenly Garden of Love (*Revelations of Mechthild*, trans. Menzies [1953]). Her inconsolable sense of loss in this world is the inevitable condition of souls spiritually advanced, for nothing else can satisfy her — not the Church, not the communion of saints, not even the adoration of the Christ-Child — for "That is a childish love, to quiet children with. I am a full-grown bride and will have my Bridegroom." The final mysteries of love are unutterable, as Soul explains to Understanding: "No bride may tell what happens to her!" At last, she can only pray (in lines akin to those of Donne's "Batter My Heart") to be vanquished by God.

A whole tradition of mystical literature similarly reflects this nuptial allegory, from Latin and vernacular poems such as Konrad's *"Epithalamium Christi Virginum Alternantium"* (Dreves and Blume, *Analecta Hymnica Medii Aevi*, vol. 50, no. 343), or the many variants of Bernard's *"Dulcis Jesu Memoria"* (Dreves and Blume, *Ein Jahrtausend Lateinischer Hymnendichtung* [1909], 2.35), or Ger. *Geistliche minne*, such as the monumental "nuptial epic," *Christus und die Minnende Seele* (ed. Banz [1908]; cf. Wackernagle, 2.262-63, 290ff.), to the classic works of systematic mysticism, such as Richard of St. Victor's *Benjamin Minor* (bk. 5) and *The Four Degrees of Passionate Charity*, Hugh of St. Victor's *The Soul's Betrothal-Gift*, Suso's *Love-Book* and *Little Book of Wisdom*, Lull's *Book of the Lover and the Beloved*, and the treatises on spiritual marriage by Gerson *(Spiritualibus Nuptiis)* and Ruysbroek (*The Adornment of the*

Spiritual Marriage, ed. Underhill [1916]). Important examples in ME literature include the ascetic/contemplative treatise *The Wohunge of Ure Lauerd* and the poetic and prose pieces associated with it (EETS o.s. 241), and above all the works of Richard Rolle, especially *Incendium Amoris* and the various poems of love-longing and heart-wounding of the "school of Rolle," such as those of the Vernon MS (EETS o.s. 98) or Camb. MS Dd. 5.64.III. In *The Pearl* the visionary maiden describes herself as a bride of the Lamb (757-59), one of those arrayed for the wedding in the heavenly Jerusalem (781-92), and she goes on to teach that "Forþy vche saule þat hade neuer teche / Is to þat lombe a worthyly wyf" (845-46).

The undisputed classics of nuptial spirituality are the poems and commentaries of the 16th-cent. Spanish mystics, especially John of the Cross's *Dark Night of the Soul*, *Spiritual Canticle*, and *Living Flame of Love* (each work taking the form of a commentary on a love poem of the same name), and St. Teresa's *Interior Castle* (the sixth Mansion concerns Spiritual Betrothal, and the seventh Spiritual Marriage) and *Conceptions of the Love of God*. Other examples include Luis de Leon's commentary on Canticles, and passages relating to the spiritual marriage theme in his *Names of Christ* ([1921 ed.], 2.217-19, 228-30, 236-38), as well as the Canticles commentaries of Juan de los Angeles, Jeronimo Gracien, and Luis de la Puente. While most prominent in Catholic milieux, the theme also appears among radical and Anabaptist writers of the Reformation (e.g., Melchior Hofmann's "The Ordinances of God" or the Letters of Samuel Rutherford) and also in mainstream Protestant literature, but usually with an emphasis on the corporate Church rather than on the contemplative soul as Bride of Christ — as in the Canticles commentaries of Beza, Luther, John Cotton, James Durham, and Joseph Hall or the biblical annotations of the Geneva Bible, the Synod of Dort, or the Westminster Assembly (1645), or in such occasional references as John Winthrop's use of the Bride / Church metaphor in his 1645 "Speech to the General Court" (Miller, *The American Puritans* [1982], 93).

In English poetry other than the ME religious lyrics discussed above, bride / bridegroom symbolism occurs in a diversity of contexts. Chaucer's Parson alludes to the image of a chaste virgin as a "spouse to Jhesu Crist" (*Parson's Tale*, 10.947), but Chaucer's other references are in the vein of moral satire. Whereas the significance of the erotic imagery derived from Canticles in goliardic Latin love lyrics remains a matter of critical dispute (i.e., whether such poems as *"Iam Dulcis Amica"* or *"Veni Delectissime"* of the Cambridge MS, or the love songs of the *Carmina Burana*, are composed in the spirit of romantic elevation of carnal love or of irreverent bawdy parody or yet again of moral satire), it is clear that the parodies of Canticles in the mouths of Absolon (*Miller's Tale*, 1.3698-3707) and January (*Merchant's Tale*, 4.2138-48) are ironic devices used to heighten the moral disparity between Chaucer's lewd and grotesque pairs of lovers, on the one hand, and Christ and Mary, his spouse, on the other. Similarly, in the *Roman de la Rose* echoes of Canticles reinforce a pattern of moral satire in which the *hortus deliciarum* of Amant contrasts with the Garden of the Good Shepherd, and Genius's advice to men to labor assiduously at copulation and Amant's final rape of the Rose serve as a brutal satiric parody of the idea of spiritual marriage. In the *Book of the Duchess,* on the other hand, the description of Blanche in terms of the Bride of Canticles (895-984) seems to be part of a "Boethian" awakening on the part of the sorrowful knight as he comes to recognize that what he really loves in the Duchess is beyond death and time.

In a similar vein Renaissance epithalamia and other love poems could use biblical imagery to elevate their praise of a maiden through implied comparison to the heavenly Bride and Groom, as in Spenser's "Epithalamium" (167-84) and *Amoretti* (nos. 15, 64, 77) or the descriptions of noble women in the *Faerie Queene* (1.12.21-22) [Una]; 2.3.22-29 [Belphoebe]; 6.8.42 [Serena]), whose heavenly archetype appears in Spenser's description of Sapience in "An Hymne of Heavenly Beautie" (183ff.). In the emblem book tradition, bks. 4 and 5 of Quarles's *Emblems* (1635) contain love lyrics of the soul enamored of the Divine Lover, Van Veen's *Amoris Divini Emblemata* (1660) features engravings of a winged Amor Divinis and the beloved Anima, along with verses in Dutch and French, while Hugo's *Pia Desideria,* Englished by Arwaker (1686), similarly presents images of the allegorical pair of lovers. Related to these are the numerous poetic paraphrases of Canticles in Renaissance poetry, such as Drayton's *Harmonie of the Church* (1591), Wither's *Hymns and Songs of the Church* (1623), Quarles's *Sions Sonnets* (1625), or Isaac Watts's *Hymns and Spiritual Songs* (1707-48 [nos. 67-68]).

Donne refers to the Church / Bride figure in "Upon the Annunciation and Passion falling upon one day," noting that, as God has joined creation and judgment, death and conception, so the liturgical calendar of the Church, "his imitating Spouse," occasionally celebrates Annunciation and Passion simultaneously. Donne devotes Holy Sonnet 18 ("Show me, dear Christ, thy Spouse") to the Church / Spouse metaphor, but adding the apparently paradoxical petition that Christ share his spouse with all —

> Betray kind husband thy spouse to our sights,
> And let myne amorous soule court thy mild Dove,
> Who is most trew, and pleasing to thee, then
> When she's embrac'd and open to most men,

thus putting the soul in the unusual role of husband of the Church. More conventionally, in the *Second Anniversary,* Donne speaks of the deceased Elizabeth as she who "was here / Betroth'd to God, and now is married there" (462). The individual as spouse of God is implicit also in the more violent erotic paradoxes of the concluding sestet of Holy Sonnet 14, "Batter My Heart." Herbert calls the Church Christ's Spouse in "The Church Militant" (9-13), and in "Sunday" describes the Sundays of a person's life, threaded on time's string, as bracelets that "adorn the wife / Of the eternall glorious King." Additionally, "Longing" is a love poem addressed to God in the manner of Rolle's songs of love-longing. Vaughan frequently alludes to the nuptial metaphor in *Silex Scintillans,* e.g., in "The Search" (64), "Faith" (5), "The Dawning" (2), "The World" (5, 59), "The Constellation" (57), "The Knot" (1), and "L'Envoy" (33).

In Crashaw's poetry the spousal imagery is associated primarily with poems about female saints or addressed to religious women. "The Hymn in the Assumption" makes the conventional association of Mary with the Bride of Canticles; the "Third elegie" of the Alexias series ends with an account of the life of St. Cecilia as a bride of Christ; and, most dramatically, "A Hymn to Sainte Teresa" hails her as a spouse of Christ, especially in the image of the transverberation or piercing of her heart by a seraphic angel with "a Dart thrice dip't in that rich flame / Which writes the spouse's radiant Name" (81-82), and the final movement of "The Flaming Heart" (69-108), which is wholly premised on the image of Teresa as Christ's enraptured bride. Crashaw also applies the image in a series of poems urging religious women to take Christ as their spiritual husband: "A Letter to the Countess of Denbigh," "To [Mrs. M. R.] Councel concerning her Choice," and especially "Ode on a Prayer-Book," the second half of which is an unrestrained panegyric on the

> Amorous languishments, luminous trances . . .
> Delicious Deaths, soft exhalations
> Of soul; dear and divine annihilations . . .
>   Which the divine embraces
> Of the deare spouse of spirits with them will bring.
> (70-84)

concluding

> Happy proof! she shall discover,
>   What joy, what bliss,
>   How many heavens at once it is,
> To have a God become her Lover! (121-24)

After the 17th cent., the biblical metaphor of spiritual marriage becomes less common outside strictly church-related literature. Variants of the symbolism appear among the Romantic poets, as in Blake's image of *The Marriage of Heaven and Hell* as a mystical "coincidential oppositorum." Jung, in *Mysterium Coniunctionis,* traces the whole history of such mystical marriage symbolism in gnostic, hermetic, and alchemical texts, and relates it to his anima / animus theory of the psyche; and much Romantic poetry, such as Shelley's "Epipsychidion," his spousal song to his divine anima, could be read in this context. In a different vein, Coleridge in "Dejection" speaks of the wedding of nature and the imagination:

"And in our life alone does Nature live: / Ours is her wedding garment, ours her shroud!" (49-50). Wordsworth, in "Home at Grasmere," similarly posits the wedding of "the discerning intellect of Man . . . to this goodly universe," and tells how in a prophetic mode he "Would chant, in lonely peace, the spousal verse / Of this great consummation" (52-58), symbolism fulfilled in the climactic Mt. Snowdon episode in bk. 14 of *The Prelude.*

The more conventional Church as spouse symbol does continue to appear, as in some passing references in Browning's *The Ring and the Book* (6.961-65; 7.446-49; 8.694-96; 10.1484-86; 11.1297-1300), where the reference is used variously to refer to the archetypal standard of either marriage or the priesthood, or in some passages of dialogue in Tennyson's plays, e.g., *Queen Mary* (3.3.205; 4.199) and *Becket* (5.2.22 and 3.3.174-75, where Becket uses the image to proclaim the plight of the English church: "Ay, King! for in thy kingdom, as thou knowest, / The spouse of the Great King, thy King, hath fallen"). In "St. Agnes' Eve" Tennyson recounts the prayer of a nun longing to be drawn up to the heavens to be reunited with her heavenly spouse, ending with her vision of an eternal Sabbath, "A light upon the shining sea— / The Bridegroom with his bride!" Conventional nuptial imagery is used in Keble's *The Christian Year* in the hymns for the Second Sunday after Epiphany, Sexagesima Sunday, S. Matthias Day, Holy Communion, the Visitation and Communion of the Sick, Commination, and for the Gunpowder Treason (in which he speaks of "The Widow'd Church . . . the lonely Spouse"). In "The Starlight Night" Gerard Manley Hopkins concludes his sacramental meditation with the words, "This piece-bright paling shuts the spouse / Christ home, Christ and his mother and all his hallows," and his "Habit of Perfection" incorporates the Franciscan-inspired image of holy Poverty as a bride.

Other writers have approached the spiritual marriage symbolism in a satirical or ironic mode, as in the many gothic novels utilizing a monastic setting in a lurid manner such as M. G. Lewis's *The Monk,* or Huxley's *The Devils of Verdun;* or they have approached it with ambiguity, as in the case of Pielmeier's *Agnes of God;* or from the point of view of neocabalistic symbolism, as in the case of Nathaniel Tarn's epic poem *Lyrics for the Bride of God* (1970). Finally among contemporary writers, several poems by William Everson (Brother Antoninus) in *The Veritable Years* revive the imagery of spiritual eroticism, as in "The Encounter" or "The Song the Body Dreamed in the Spirit's Mad Behest," which begins, "Call Him the Lover and call me the Bride," and goes on to recount a violent ravishing of Flesh by Spirit:

Folding Him in the chaos of my loins
I pierce through armies tossed upon my breast,
Envelop in love's tidal dredge of faith
His huge unrest.

Everson's "River-Root / A Syzygy" parallels the rising of a river and a married couple's sexual conjunction as an incarnational participation in the cosmic mystery of union. Another example of erotic nature-mysticism is the opening passage of Annie Dillard's *Holy the Firm,* in which the author describes her moment of waking as a spiritual betrothal:

I wake in a god. I wake in arms holding my quilt, holding me as best they can inside my quilt
Someone is kissing me — already. I wake, I cry "Oh," I rise from the pillow. Why should I open my eyes?
I open my eyes. The god lifts from the water. . . .
Today's god rises, his long eyes flecked in clouds. He flings his arms, spreading colors; he arches, cupping sky in his belly; he vaults, vaulting and spread, holding all and spread on me like skin.

See also ADULTERY; BE FRUITFUL, AND MULTIPLY; FRIEND OF THE BRIDEGROOM; MARRIAGE FEAST, PARABLE OF; MARY, MOTHER OF JESUS; SONG OF SONGS.

Bibliography. Batey, R. "The Church, the Bride of Christ." Ph.D. diss., Vanderbilt, 1961; "Paul's Bride Image." *Int.* 17 (1963), 176-82; Chavasse, C. *The Bride of Christ* (1940); Daniélou, J. *The Bible and the Liturgy* (1956); Edwards, C. "Bridegroom-Bride Imagery for Christ and the Church in the New Testament." Ph.D. diss., Northwestern, 1964; Klimisch, M. *The One Bride* (1965); Robitaille, L. "L'Église, épouse du Christ dans l'interprétation patristique du Psaume 44 (45)." *Laval théologique et philosophique,* 27.1 (1971), 41-65; Scheper, G. "The Spiritual Marriage." Ph.D. diss., Princeton, 1971; "Reformation Attitudes Toward Allegory and the Song of Songs." *PMLA* 89 (1974), 551-62.

GEORGE L. SCHEPER

BROAD WAY, THE   *See* STRAIT AND NARROW.

BROKEN AND CONTRITE HEART   *See* CONTRITION.

BRUISE THY HEAD, BRUISE HIS HEEL   In Gen. 3:14-15 God pronounces a curse on the serpent for beguiling the woman to eat of the fruit of the tree of knowledge in the Garden of Eden: "Because thou hast done this, thou art cursed above all cattle, and above every beast of the field; upon thy belly shalt thou go, and dust shalt thou eat all the days of thy life. And I will put enmity between thee and the woman, and between thy seed and her seed; it shall bruise thy head, and thou shalt bruise his heel."

The passage is often interpreted as conveying an etiological explanation for the hostility commonly felt between humans and snakes. On a theological level Gen. 3:15 expresses humanity's unceasing struggle with sin, symbolized by a continuing conflict with the serpent. Moreover, in the expression of this enmity, it is unclear whether either side will gain a decisive victory. On the one hand, humanity's trampling foot will be able to "bruise" the serpent's head, while on the other, the serpent will in turn be able to "bruise" a human's heel.

Elsewhere in the OT, there appear occasional faint hints of the cancellation of this enmity (cf. Isa. 11:8; 65:25). A messianic interpretation is placed upon the verse by Tg. Jonathan and Tg. Yerushalmi, which see the bruising or crushing of the head of the serpent as a mortal blow inflicted by the Anointed One. And in the NT this same expectation of ultimate triumph over the "serpent" (Satan, the devil) is rendered explicit. Thus, in Rom. 16:20, Paul asserts that "the God of peace shall bruise Satan under your feet shortly." Rev. 12:11-17 describes the apocalyptic climax of the conflict between the serpent and the seed of the woman.

In the early Church the Genesis passage comes thus to be seen as the first OT foreshadowing of Christ, the so-called protevangelium. St. Irenaeus speaks of Christ "both taking up the battle against our enemy, and crushing him who at the beginning had led us captive in Adam" (*Adv. haer.* 5.21). Origen brings Luke 10:19 to bear on the passage: "Since Jesus journeys with you to paradise, scorn the serpent vanquished and bruised by Jesus's feet, and through him by yours as well" (*Exhortation to Martyrdom,* 36). St. Jerome, recalling Rom. 16:20 as well as the Genesis passage, sees the bruising as a moral allegory for the present world: "And may the God of Peace, according to his mercy, grant to us that Satan may be bruised under the feet of Christians, and every occasion of evil may be shunned." For St. Ambrose Christ's divine nature is revealed in the fact that "He exposed his heel to [the serpent] but did not experience its poisons" (*De interpellatione Job et David* [FC 65.392]). In the Middle Ages, Marian interpretation of the passage gains currency, drawing on Jerome's rendering in the Vg that "she" *(ipse)* — i.e., the woman, rather than the "seed" of the woman — shall wound the serpent's head; the passage is still thus taken as the first biblical prophecy referring to the Virgin.

Erasmus uses Gen. 3:15 with reference to the *miles Christi* in his *Enchiridion:* "Against him (i.e., Satan) put yourself in quiet readiness, that you may immediately and shortly repulse his onslaught, and hiss him away, crushing straightway the head of the plague-bearing serpent" (LCC 14.363). Luther sounds a similar note, writing to offer advice in time of epidemic and famine: "Christ . . . will triumph in us over that old serpent, murderer and author of sin, however much he may bruise Christ's heel" (*Letter to Spalatin* [19 Aug. 1527]). In commenting directly on Gen. 3:15 he criticizes as idolatrous applications of the passage to the Virgin but gives it, with reference to Christ, its widest possible interpretation:

This statement includes the redemption from the law, from sin, and from death; and it points out the clear hope of a certain resurrection and of renewal in the other life after this life. . . . These treasures we possess in Christ, but in hope. . . . Accordingly, we now find Adam and Eve restored, not indeed to the life which they had lost but to hope of that life; through this hope they escaped, not the first fruits of death, but its tithes. (*Works,* 1.196-97)

The Geneva Bible commentator sums up: "Satan shall sting Christ & his members, but not overcome them."

Most of these themes are recapitulated in Calvin's *Institutes:* the foreshadowing of the redemption (". . . at the beginning when the first promise of salvation was given to Adam it glowed like a feeble spark" [2.10.20]); confidence concerning the ability of believers to withstand Satan ("But because that promise to crush Satan's head pertains to Christ and all his members in common, I deny that believers can ever be conquered or overwhelmed by him. Often indeed, they are distressed, but not so much as not to recover" [1.14.18]); continuing conflict until Satan's ultimate downfall ("Paul shows that the promise . . . begins to have effect in this life, wherein we must struggle; and that after the struggle it is fulfilled" [1.14.18]).

John Donne sees in the passage a prophecy of Christ's death — "His *Father* calls it *a bruise* . . . and yet that was, that the serpent should *practise* and *compasse* his death" (*Sermons,* eds. Potter and Simpson, 10.244) — but also his victory: "That the Messias should bruise the Serpent's head for us, included our redemption. . ." (10.165). Believers, too, share in this triumph: "*In Christ we can doe all things,* and therefore, in him, we can *bruise the serpents* head. . ." (3.136). Donne speaks of the "semen contract" (3.259), the "assurance of a Messias and Redeemer to man [which] was the first promise made to him in Adam" (2.365).

In *Paradise Lost* Gen. 3:15 is recalled seven times in a series designed to illustrate the spiritual education of Adam and Eve. The Genesis curse and prophecy is simply recounted in 10.181ff. It is later used to allow Satan to quibble arrogantly while making himself the butt of savage irony:

His seed, when is not set, shall bruise my head:
A world who would not purchase with a bruise
Or much more prievous pain? (10.449-51)

Initially Adam sees what is promised as mere revenge (10.1031), but soon with almost Christian precognition he regards the prophecy as assurance that "the bitterness of death / Is past and we shall live" (11.157-58). Later Michael recurs to the passage to define the "great deliverer" whose achievement is anticipated in Jewish ritual law "by types / And shadows" (12.149, 232-33). Finally, when Adam's joy in the promise shows too much gleeful bloodthirstiness, Michael explains that Satan's works must be destroyed by Christ's defeat of death and by human participation in that achievement "by faith not void of works" (12.427).

Later allusions, diverse in tone and import, play off in various ways the mainstream theological tradition. Cowper in *Charity* (584) sees the bruising of the serpent's head as an aspect of God's defeat of the infernal powers in the human form of Christ. Blake's Adam in "The Ghost of Abel" taunts Jehovah for allowing Abel's slaying: "Is this the promise that the woman's seed / Should bruise the serpent's head?" In Browning's *Inn Album* the lady advises that revenge will come inevitably to the abuser:

> Safe let him slink hence till some subtler Eve
> Than I, anticipate the snake — bruise head
> Ere he bruise heel.

For the early 20th-cent. editors of the Scofield Reference Bible (1909) Gen. 3:15 still provides "the first promise of a Redeemer." Its notes suggest that

> Here begins the "highway of the Seed," Abel, Seth, Noah (Gen. 6:8-10), Shem (Gen. 9:26, 27), Abraham (Gen. 12:1-4), Isaac (Gen. 17:19-21), Jacob (Gen. 28:10-14), Judah (Gen. 49:10), David (2 Sam. 7:5-17), Immanuel-Christ (Isa. 7:9-14; Matt. 1:1, 20-23; 1 John 3:8; John 12:31).

The protevangelium has been popularized for contemporary audiences in the "Festival of Nine Lessons and Carols" for Christmas by Eric Milner-White of King's College, Cambridge, for which Gen. 3:15 is the first reading. Literary references to Gen. 3:15 in this century are nonetheless for the most part insubstantial — as in Aldous Huxley's examination of "Advertisement," which, he says, "begins abjectly, crawling on its belly like the serpent after the primal curse" — and ignore the bruising of head and heel altogether.

See also FALL; SERPENT.

RICHARD SCHELL
GEORGE M. LANDES

BRUISED (BROKEN) REED   King Hezekiah had been warned not to trust Egypt, "the staff of this bruised reed . . . on which if a man lean," it will break and pierce his hand (2 Kings 18:21; Isa. 36:6); but of the Lord's chosen Isaiah later wrote, "A bruised reed shall he not break, and the smoking flax shall he not quench: he shall bring forth judgment unto truth" (42:3). This latter verse was quoted by Jesus (Matt. 12:20).

The expression is developed especially in Protestant commentary as an encouragement to perseverance in faith and repentant hope. Matthew Poole's *Annotations upon the Holy Bible* (Matt. 12:20) interprets the passage as saying that "He will not discourage those that are weak in Faith, or weak in Hope," and sees the smoking flax as an "apt Metaphor to express such as believe, but are full of Doubts and Fears, or such as have a Truth of Grace, but yet much Corruption."

George Herbert makes a graceful liturgical use of the allusion in "The Banquet":

> But as Pomanders and wood
>   Still are good,
> Yet being bruis'd are better sented:
> God, to show how farre his love
>   Could improve,
> Here, as broken, is presented. (25-30)

In Shakespeare's *2 Henry 6* (1.2.1; 24–27) Duke Humphrey's wife describes him in his dispirited state: "Why droops my lord, like overripened corn, / hanging the head. . . ," and he answers concerning his troubling dream, "Methought this staff, mine office badge in Court / Was broke in twain" — as he imagines, by the Cardinal. Edward Young, in his *Night Thoughts,* urges his reader to "Lean not on Earth, 'twill pierce thee to the heart; / a broken reed at best"; Longfellow, in his sonnet to Keats, would rewrite the dead poet's epitaph: "The smoking flax before it burst to flame / Was quenched by death, and broken the bruised reed." In commending "The Eternal Goodness" Whittier writes "The bruised reed he will not break / But strengthen and sustain," but the phrase is often applied to strictly human relationships, as when Holmes says to Watson in A. C. Doyle's "The Adventure of the Three Gables" *(The Case-Book of Sherlock Holmes),* "I made a mistake, I fear, in not asking you to spend the night on guard. This fellow has clearly proved a broken reed." In Dickens's *Little Dorrit* old Dorrit says of poor Nandy: "I do — ha — extend as much protection and kindness to the — hum — bruised reed — I trust I may call him so without impropriety — as in my circumstances, I can," a satiric and intentionally damning use of the allusion.

See also CONTRITION.

BURNING AND SHINING LIGHT   Jesus said of John the Baptist: "He was a burning and a shining light: and ye were willing for a season to rejoice in his light" (John 5:35; cf. Prov. 4:18). St. Augustine relates this passage to Ps. 132:17, seeing John's forerunner ministry as designed to confuse enemies of God who were waiting to deny Jesus *(Sermo,* 128.2). The passage is read more straightforwardly by Calvin and other Reformers as a commendation of one whose vocation was to prepare the way of the gospel by preaching repentance. It is in this sense that the phrase is applied by Izaak Walton in his *Life of John Donne,* where he says that after Donne's conversion "his life was as a shining light among all his old friends" of the Law Courts at Lincoln's Inn. This figural use of John the Baptist (called the "day starre" by Jonathan Edwards [Works, ed. S. E. Dwight, 8.555]) is characteristic among the New England Puritans as well. In the sermons of Increase Mather, if "John the Baptist arose like a bright and shining light," a light like unto it shone at the "dawning" of the Reformation, the fullness of which was for Mather "the end of our coming hither" to America *(Morning Star,* appended to *The Righteous Man* [1702], 71, 75-76).

In the 18th cent. the phrase was an idiom of praise among figures in the great Evangelical Revival, appearing frequently in the writings of the Wesleys, George Whitefield, Thomas Howeis, and Charles Simeon to refer to preachers such as Howell Harris and Lady Selina, Countess of Huntingdon, a protector of many of the evangelical preachers. It may be Simeon's reputation and memory which lies behind the reference in Samuel Butler's *The Way of All Flesh*, where Butler says that Theobald had known the imperious headmaster Dr. Skinner of Cambridge as "a burning and a shining light in every position he had filled from his boyhood upwards."

See also JOHN THE BAPTIST.

Bibliography. Bercovitch, S. *The American Jeremiad* (1978), 14-15; Jeffrey, D. L. *A Burning and A Shining Light: English Spirituality in the Age of Wesley* (1987).

BURNING BUSH The burning bush was the shrub which burst into flame yet was not consumed at the theophany on Mt. Horeb where Moses heard the call to take up his vocation as a deliverer of his people (Exod. 3:2-22; cf. Deut. 33:16). After the voice called and Moses answered, he was commanded, "put off thy shoes from off thy feet, for the place whereon thou standest is holy ground" (v. 5); the voice was that of God, who identified himself: "I AM THAT I AM" (v. 14).

Jewish commentary sees the shrub as a thornbush, a type of Israel because it bears both blooms and thorns ("pious and impious members)," because it suffers injury but is not destroyed, and because its Hebrew name, *Hasseneh*, has numerical values adding up to 120, the number of years Moses was to live and the number of days that the Shekinah glory would rest on Mt. Horeb (Pirqe R. El. 40; Shaba Shemot 66d, 67a; Midr. Tehillim 37.223). The latter point is picked up by Philo as well (*De vita Mosis*, 1.2). These commentaries also include a legend that the theophany precipitated a visitation by Moses to each of the seven heavens, paradise, and hell (see Ginzberg, *LJ* 2.304-16; this narrative anticipates in several respects the 3rd-cent. Greek *Vision of St. Paul* and Dante's *Commedia*).

Early Christian commentary focuses principally on two aspects of the biblical account not developed in the midrashim: the command that Moses remove his shoes and, above all, God's declaration of his name. As to the latter, St. Augustine argues that the significance of the name is in declaring God's unchangeableness as distinct from the mutability of everything he has created — adding that Plato may not have been ignorant of the Pentateuch, since he is the only other writer "so zealously to command this truth" (*De civ. Dei* 8.11; cf. *De fide et symbolo*, 4.6). Augustine also stresses (*De Trin.* 2.13) that a chief importance of the passage lies in the use of the word *angel* (meaning "minister") in association with the voice, suggesting that the Spirit or the Son might as easily be speaking, and that the theophany in this sense is an analogue of the Incarnation, an enfleshment of the Divine Logos (2.7). St. Ambrose notes that the encounter above all "places" Moses as a servant of God: "Moses was not the Bridegroom, for to him comes the word 'Loose thy shoe from off thy foot,' [indicating] that he must give place to his Lord" (*De fide*, 3.7), and he connects the incident to Ruth's "loosening the shoe" of

the kinsman of Boaz (Ruth 4:4-7) and John the Baptist's disclaimer concerning Jesus, "I am not worthy to loose the latchet of his shoe" (John 1:27). Hence, he says, the words spoken to Moses teach our own need for repentance before the absolute holiness of God (*De poenitentia*, 2.107). If one is repentant and obediently waits upon the word of God, then he "stands" upon holy ground; forgiven, he is enabled to stand "firm in his heart by faith" (*Ep.* 63.4).

St. Gregory of Nyssa in his 4th-cent. *Vita Mosis* draws parallels between the bush burning and not being consumed and the two natures of Christ (2.26), and likens the bush also to the Virgin Birth (2.21). The latter connection becomes a source of popular medieval imagery of the Virgin Mary. St. Anthony of Padua, who collated an extensive iconography of the Virgin, writes that the bush may be understood as the Virgin who gave birth to the Son of God without losing her maidenhead (*In Domenica XIII post Pentecosten*, 2.400a); this view is reflected in a host of allusions in medieval verse of which a stanza from one of the carols of James Ryman is typical:

> O flamed bushe in all stature
> Of Moyses, of whom nature
> Ihesus hath take, o Mary mylde
> For vs thou pray vnto thy childe. (R. Greene, *Early English Carols*, no. 192; cf. Chaucer, *The Prioress's Tale*, Prol. 7.467-69)

The *Glossa Ordinaria* seems to echo Jewish tradition in seeing the bush as an image of the Church, suffering under persecution but not consumed, "since the voice of God can not be destroyed by fire" (PL 113.191; cf. Judg. 9:15 *et comm.*).

Of the saintly lady to whom he dedicated his "Death" elegy, Donne wrote that "Her heart was that strange bush, where, sacred fire, / Religion, did not consume, but inspire" (45-46). Elizabeth Barrett Browning, for whom in *Aurora Leigh*, "Nature comes sometimes / And says, 'I am ambassador for God'" (7.493), "Earth's crammed with heaven, / And every common bush afire with God, / But only he who sees takes off his shoes" (*Aurora Leigh*, 7.499; cf. Whittier's "Miracle of Autumn" for a similar sentiment). Ralph Waldo Emerson in his "Good-Bye" laughs

> . . . at the love and pride of man,
> At the sophist schools and the learned clan;
> For what are they all in their high conceit,
> When man in the bush with God may meet. ·

Although Flannery O'Connor makes an amusing but biblically significant allusion to the incident in "Parker's Back," naturalism continues to characterize most 20th-cent. allusions. Willa Cather's prairie in the August sun is like "the bush that burned with fire and was not consumed" (*My Antonia*, chap. 1); for Aldous Huxley nature is "proof of God's goodness," shining "from every burning bush of incandescent blossom" (*Eyeless in Gaza*, 16). In the writing of D. H. Lawrence, where theophany is often reduced to sexual initiation, *The Lovely Lady* "could not trust herself so near the Burning Bush, dared not go near for transfiguration, afraid of herself" ("The Overtone"). And in Joyce's *Portrait of the Artist*, Stephen recalls his near apprehension of vocation, and of communion with God, recalling how once "he had lifted up his arms and spoken in ecstasy to the sombre nave of trees, knowing that he stood on holy ground and in a holy hour" (chap. 5).

See also I AM THAT I AM; MOSES.

BY BREAD ALONE   When Jesus had fasted forty days and forty nights in the wilderness, he was tempted by the devil. The first of three temptations was directed to his physical need: "If thou be the Son of God, command that these stones be made bread" (Matt. 4:3). Jesus answered, quoting Deut. 8:3, "It is written, Man shall not live by bread alone, but by every word that proceedeth out of the mouth of God" (Matt. 4:4; cf. Luke 4:4). While the passage is occasionally adduced by patristic writers in support of the virtues of fasting as a preparation for spiritual struggle (e.g., St. Ambrose, *Ep.* 63.15), the *Glossa Ordinaria* summarizes what will become the conventional application when it says: "No other power but the authority of Scripture suffices for such combat" (PL 114.84), then goes on to identify the Word of God as essential sustenance for the human spirit, adding that all the words (plural) which proceed from Scripture constitute "one word, that is the wisdom of God" (114.85). Later exegetes largely concur.

Milton's *Paradise Regained* provides a poetic elaboration of the passage (1.342-51). In later literature the traditional reading is loosely adapted, even trivialized. Ruskin makes the necessary bread natural beauty, "the wild flower by the wayside" (*Unto this Last*, chap. 4). Trollope uses the passage to describe excessively functional architecture of a rectory (*The Warden*, chap. 8). Stevenson observes drily that "Man is a creature who lives not upon bread alone, but principally by catch words" (*Virginibus Puerisque*, chap. 2), and Aldous Huxley, in his "Guatemala City" essay in *Beyond the Mexique Bay*, conflates two orders of proverb to offer cynical wisdom: "Men cannot live by bread alone. But neither can they live only by circuses. To some extent, however, a shortage of bread can be made up for by a surfeit of circuses."

See also BREAD OF LIFE; TEMPTATION OF CHRIST.

BY THEIR FRUITS   In the Sermon on the Mount Jesus warned his hearers about false prophets who come "in sheep's clothing, but inwardly are ravening wolves" (Matt. 7:15). A discerning eye will identify them, he indicated: "Ye shall know them by their fruits. Do men gather grapes of thorns, or figs of thistles? Even so, every good tree bringeth forth good fruit; but a corrupt tree bringeth forth evil fruit. . . . Wherefore by their fruits ye shall know them" (Matt. 7:16-20; cf. Luke 6:43-45). A variant of the figure was employed by Jesus on a later occasion when he said that "the tree is known by his fruit" (Matt. 12:33).

In exegetical tradition from the writings of the early Church through medieval glosses (e.g., *Glossa Ordinaria* [PL 114.110-11]) to Reformation commentary (e.g., Calvin, in his *Harmony of the Gospels*) the false prophets identified by Jesus can be construed as heretics, but are most often seen as self-promoters or hypocrites.

This latter sense, linked closely to Jesus' denunciation of the Pharisees for their hypocrisy and religious pride, determines the typical force of literary allusion. William Cowper thus offers a scathing 18th-cent. portrait of a self-aggrandizing religious ascetic in his poem *Truth*: "Such are the fruits of sanctimonious pride, / Of malice fed while flesh is mortified" (165-66). Although typically confounding Pharisaism with Puritanism and hypocrisy with prudery, D. H. Lawrence's *Lady Chatterley's Lover* invites a similar judgment: "there's something wrong with the mental life, radically. It's rooted in spite and envy, envy and spite. Ye shall know the tree by its fruits" (chap. 3). Aldous Huxley is still thinking of pharisaical self-arrogation when he writes in *The Olive Tree:*

> It is difficult for people whose main preoccupation is sensual enjoyment to do harm on a very large scale. But where the cravings to be justified are cravings for power, glory and the like, the case is different. *The tree is known by its fruits.* Judged by this standard, sympneumatism, for example, is a joke; nationalism, which is a theory intrinsically almost as preposterous as poor Oliphant's, is a tragedy and a menace. ("Justifications")

T. S. Eliot instances a further tendency in 20th-cent. humanism to associate science and technology with sanctimoniousness and fraudulent claims to moral authority, especially the scientists' habit of proclaiming successive hypothetical accounts of natural process as fact: "Until science can teach us to reproduce such phenomena at will," he notes, "science cannot claim to have explained them; and they can be judged only by their fruits" (Intro. to *Pensée*).

In the Victorian period and in 20th-cent. usage, the phrase has been degraded to cliché, yet even ironic and jesting invocation tends to depend for its effect upon some recognition of the original association with hypocrisy and sanctimony. "By the cigars they smoke," writes John Galsworthy, "and the composers they love, ye shall know the texture of men's souls" (*Indian Summer of a Forsythe*, chap. 1). And in his notable early 20th-cent. essay on the study of literature Louis Cazamian complains of a self-righteous hardening of the categories, presumably, when he concludes that "when all is said, and if the tree is to be judged by its fruit, the technique of literary studies seems in some danger of being hardened and fossilized" ("The Aims and Methods of Higher Literary Studies"). Finally, reflecting on the way in which poets ritually invoke what Boccaccio called "the myths of the pagan gods" *(De gesta deorum gentilium)* to prompt or accredit their own musings, Howard Nemerov writes mockingly (in "Cloud Seeding"):

Poets, in their majestic wigs,
Pen canzonetti on these themes,
And by the fruits ye know the trees:
By sour grapes, by withered figs,
These Minotaurs and Semeles
Are raddled through all modern dreams. . . .

See also CHARITY, CUPIDITY; TREE; VINE, VINEYARD.

C

CABALA The fundamental object of Cabala is greater apprehension of the Torah; it is basically a system of exegesis which has also acquired mystical, theosophical, magical, cosmological, cultic, and even political elements. Cabala has no direct expression in the OT text or in early biblical commentary; it was invented in the High Middle Ages. The "Jewish Gnosticism" of late antiquity as well as early medieval texts like the *Seper yeṣirah* contributed to the growth of cabalist ideas, but the beginnings of Cabala as such awaited the 12th cent. and the *Seper ha-Bahir.* In the 13th cent., Moses ben Shem Tov de Leon wrote most of the *Zohar,* the best-known work of medieval Cabala. Isaac Luria (1534-72) and his disciples substantively transformed the Cabala of the *Zohar,* and it was Lurianic Cabala which provided the foundations for the remarkable messianic movement led by Shabbatai Zevi (1626-76).

Cabala was closed to the Christian West until the late 15th cent. when Pico della Mirandola and Johann Reuchlin established a tradition of Christian Cabala which borrowed some of its ideas and techniques (e.g., *gematria*) from Hebrew sources but rarely touched more than the surface of Zoharic thought. Consequently, any claims for cabalist influence on Spenser or Shakespeare and their contemporaries must be limited to that of the Latin works of Christian Cabalists or to their vernacular imitators. Hebrew learning made sufficient progress in Cambridge and Oxford by the middle of the 17th cent. to have

allowed — at least in principle — persons as learned as Milton a greater access to genuine cabalist texts, though claims for the influence of Cabala on Milton's poetry are no better established now than they were fifty years ago in the works of Denis Saurat. Genuine Cabala became widely available to European, Latin-reading Christians only with the publication of Christian Knorr von Rosenroth's *Kabbala Denudata* between 1677 and 1684.

In 1887 parts of Knorr's miscellany of texts and polemics were translated into English by S. L. MacGregor Mathers, an associate of William Butler Yeats in the Order of the Golden Dawn; thus, Mathers and Knorr were the main source of Yeats's acquaintance with Cabala, which made no significant mark on his more important poetry and drama. Moreover, the "Cabala" frequently mentioned by Yeats's theosophical companions rarely has anything to do with the *Zohar* or Isaac Luria. Adam Kadmon, a genuine Lurianic figure of cosmic and primal humanity, had already made an indirect appearance in Blake (*Milton,* 2.6.26), and later appeared more explicitly in Joyce (*Finnegans Wake* [Viking ed., 1958], 18); *Ulysses* (Penguin ed., 1968, 43) speaks of "Heva, naked Eve" as "spouse and helpmate of Adam Kadmon." Joyce seems to have known as much about Cabala as any major English author. He also mentions such Lurianic themes as *Ṣimṣum,* the process of contraction away from a center whereby the Creator left room for the universe of space and time, and *'en sop,* the divine

119

Infinite which transcends human comprehension or description (*Finnegans Wake,* 48, 261, 500-501). Such allusions to Cabala seem superficial, however, even in Joyce.

Until the recent work of Gershom Scholem, Cabala remained an enigma to most readers and writers of English: either part of the linguistically and culturally inaccessible tradition of Jewish *esoterica;* or, worse, part of the panoply of *exotica* assembled by Mathers, A. E. Waite, Mme. Blavatsky, Aleister Crowley, and other modern occultists.

While not typical of his own learning, Coleridge's facile allusion to Cabala in "The Rash Conjuror" (48-51) as a mere instance of the incomprehensible is normal for writers of English:

> Cabbalists! Conjurors! great and small,
> Johva Mitzoveh Evohaen and all.
> Had I never uttered your jaw-breaking words,
> I might now have been sloshing down Junket and Curds,
> > Like a Devonshire Christian:
> > But now a Philistine!

Chaim Potok's novel *The Book of Lights* (1981) offers a more engaged modern response. The protagonist, Gershon Loran, is a young rabbi disillusioned following World War II and its horrors, who is attracted to the representation of Cabala by his old professor in which it is "the heart of Judaism, the soul, the core. Talmud tells us how the Jew acts; Kabbalah tells us how Judaism feels." In this work the structure of the narrative hinges on the cabalistic principles of *Ṣimṣum, Shebirath Ha-Kelim* ("break of the vessels") and *Tikkun* ("restoration") — which for Loran involves going to Jerusalem to study with his old teacher, a character clearly modeled after Gershom Scholem.

See also GEMATRIA.

Bibliography. Bloom, H. *Kabbalah and Criticism* (1975); Handelman, S. A. *Fragments of Redemption: Jewish Thought and Literary Theory in Benjamin, Scholem, and Levinas* (1991); Secret, F. *Les kabbalistes chrétiens de la renaissance* (1964); Scholem, G. *Kabbalah* (1974); Werblowsky, R. J. Z. "Milton and the *Conjectura Cabbalistica.*" *JWCI* 18 (1955), 90-113; Yates, F. *The Occult Philosophy in the Elizabethan Age* (1979).   BRIAN P. COPENHAVER

CAIAPHAS AND ANNAS Annas and his son-in-law Caiaphas were high priests of the Jerusalem Temple in the time of Jesus (John 18; Luke 3:2; cf. Josephus, *Ant.* 20.9.1). The family of Annas was evidently notorious for corruption, the chief source of its wealth coming apparently from the sale of requisites for sacrifice in four booths on the Mount of Olives; hence the talmudic curse, "Woe to the family of Annas!" (Pesaḥ. 57a) and, most likely, the occasion of Jesus' anger with what he called "a den of robbers" (Mark 11:15-19). While Caiaphas seems to have been titular head of the Sanhedrin which condemned Jesus,

Annas was the real power. Jesus was brought to him first (John 18:19-23), then sent bound to Caiaphas (v. 24). Annas was present at the defense of Peter and John before the Sanhedrin after Pentecost (Acts 4:6).

Caiaphas and Annas attract surprisingly little attention in patristic exegesis. As actors in the Passion story, especially in medieval plays and semidramatic representations, they offer a means of dramatizing the Old Law which cannot see Jesus except as a threat: in the Towneley "Coliphizacio" they incite the torturers and prove astonishingly literal-minded — incapable of discerning the metaphorical language in Jesus' replies (73-78). Farcically overdrawn, they exhibit a commitment to law rather than service or stewardship (160-62, 204-05, 211, 229, 244). "Anna" is represented as the elder here, having to check the more extravagant ire of Caiaphas lest it cause a loss of privilege with the Romans or indeed disrespect for the Old Law itself. A 13th-cent. Franciscan dramatic sermon for the Palm Sunday procession, probably at Wells, is entirely enunciated by the preacher in the person of "Cayface, bisshop of þe olde lawe" (MS Sloan 2478), who uses the emphasis on Old Law justice to make clear the need for New Law mercy to his hearers.

Subsequently Caiaphas becomes a type: Milton refers to his opponent in *An Apology for Smectymnuus* as "as perfect a hypocrite as Caiaphas," and in the *Tetrachordon* complains that modern interpreters are on the verge of turning St. Paul into a prophet like Caiaphas, one who speaks the word without thinking. In Blake's wry *The Everlasting Gospel,* such reflexive self-assurance is to be expected:

> . . . Caiaphas was in his own Mind
> A benefactor to Mankind:
> Both read the Bible day and night.
> But thou read'st black where I read white. (2a)

David Jones still refers to "bishop" Caiaphas (*Anathemata,* 5.157). Caiaphas is credited with the counsel that "it was expedient that one man should die for the people" (John 18:14), a position echoed by the "bullnecked English chaplain" in G. B. Shaw's *St. Joan:* "Let her not infect the whole flock. It is expedient that one woman die for the people" (4.53); a 19th-cent. variant is in Tennyson's *Queen Mary,* where Father Cole applies the same phrase as a justification before the burning of Archbishop Cranmer. In E. A. Robinson's "Nicodemus," Caiaphas is the Machiavellian superior to whom the almost-persuaded Nicodemus is obliged to report after his visit with Jesus.

Bibliography. Brown, C. "Caiaphas as a Palm Sunday Prophet." *Anniversary Papers Presented to G. L. Kittredge* (1913), 105-17; Jeffrey, D. L. "St. Francis and Medieval Theatre." *FranS* 43 (1983), 321-46.

CAIN Cain, whose name in Hebrew means "smith," was the eldest son of Adam and Eve. His story, related in Gen. 4:1-17, immediately follows the Fall, God's curses on the serpent, humankind, and the earth, and the expulsion of Adam and Eve from Eden (Gen. 3). The Cain narrative divides into two parts, murder and exile. The first part is a tale of sibling rivalry and fratricide, as Cain, "tiller of the ground," slays his younger brother Abel, a shepherd, after the Lord accepts Abel's sacrificial offering but spurns Cain's. Following this murder Cain disavows his brother ("Am I my brother's keeper?" v. 9). The narrative is thematically related to the Fall and God's curses on Adam, Eve, and the earth, since God explains to Cain that he shall be "cursed from the earth" (v. 11), and that when he tills the ground, "it shall not henceforth yield unto thee her strength." In the second part of the Cain story, God orders that Cain become "a fugitive and a vagabond in the earth" (v. 12). When Cain fears that he will be slain in his wanderings, God proclaims that he shall be avenged "sevenfold" if anyone should kill him and places on him a "mark" (v. 15). Finally, Cain wanders to the land of Nod, "on the east of Eden" (v. 16), builds the world's first city, and names it Enoch after his son. The remainder of Gen. 4 chronicles Cain's descendants, including Lamech and his sons and daughter, who make various discoveries. The Cain narrative, then, represents a moralized tale of the continuing descent from Eden, the original garden, to the city and its luxuries. Passages in the NT connect Cain with Satan (1 John 3:12) and present him as an evil example (Jude 11).

Jewish commentary and legends elaborate the laconic biblical text. Philo and Josephus fostered, respectively, the allegorical and literal-historical traditions of Cain for the Judeo-Christian Middle Ages and beyond. Philo, in writing on Cain, maintains that he symbolically represents an evil tendency in humankind to turn away from God and toward the self, a tendency embodied even in Cain's name ("acquisition," according to folk etymology; see *De sacrificiis*, 2). His mind was unstable, and to achieve continuity in his life he made a "city" of his thoughts by erecting false dogma (*De posteritate Caini*, 14-15). Others after Philo stress Cain's evil nature — that the devil spawned him (Pirqe R. El. 21) or that he was associated with the "impure side," an "unclean spirit," or the "angel of death" (Zohar: Bereshit 54a). Josephus highlights Cain's rapacity and his passion for order and security. He interprets the building of Enoch as an expression of Cain's desire to tyrannize his neighbors. Cain introduced measures and weights, and boundaries to fields; he resorted to violence and robbery; and he brought cunning and deceit into the world (*Ant.* 1.2.2).

Later Jewish commentary suggests a sharp division between Cain and Abel (Adam kept the brothers apart by establishing separate dwellings for them), an erotic side to Cain's nature not found in Scripture (he was said to fall passionately in love with his twin sister), and an apocryphal legend concerning his death (Lamech killed him accidentally; see, e.g., the late medieval Cornish drama "The Creation of the World"). Some commentaries point out that when Cain murdered Abel he slew as well his brother's potential children, a people, and hence God said, according to the Talmud, "the voice of thy brother's blood ["bloods" in Hebrew] crieth unto me from the ground" (4:10; see 'Abot R. Nat. 31.2). Yet Cain blamed God for instilling in him the evil impulses; he lied concerning the murder; he only feigned contrition; and he complained that his punishments were unendurable (Gen. Rab. 22.10-11; Ginzberg, *LJ* 1.110-11). God agreed to alleviate the punishment somewhat, allowing Cain to rest from his wanderings and protecting him by a "mark," a letter or a name on his forehead or arm (Tg. Ps.-J. 133; Pirqe R. El. 21).

Early gnostic sects and Christian commentators emphasized Cain's significance in world history. St. Irenaeus tells of the Cainites, 2nd-cent. gnostic heretics, who worshiped Cain, Esau, and other opponents of the Lord, whom they regarded as the evil principle (*Adv. haer.* 1.31). Following St. Ambrose, St. Augustine adopted Philo's allegorization of Cain, establishing as the historiographical thesis of *De civitate Dei* the struggle between Cain the evil one and Abel the just, sinners versus saints, the city of man versus the city of God (see esp. 15.5). Augustine's concept of Cain as czar of the secular city became standard in later chronicle histories such as Ranulf Higden's *Polychronicon* (2.5) and Raleigh's *History of the World* (1.5.2).

Literary writings from the earliest periods of English and continental literatures identify a "spirit of Cain" which has persisted from primeval biblical times to the present. The *Beowulf* narrator, perhaps via St. Isidore of Seville (*Etymologiae*, 11.3.12), traces Grendel, and the origins of monsters, to Cain's *cyn,* or lineage (102-14). The story of Cain's fratricide appears at key moments in the epic; just before Beowulf's fight with Grendel's mother the narrator characterizes Cain as the "swordslayer" *(ecg-bana)* of Abel (1262). Dante names the outermost region of Cocytus, lowest part of hell, after the original fratricide: those in Caina are punished for treachery to kindred (*Inferno*, 32). Cain also assumes a prominent role in medieval antifraternal writings. One political lyric of 1382 attacks the friars for various abuses suggesting "þat þat caytyfe cursed cayme / first þis ordre fonde" (*Historical Poems of the XIVth and XVth Centuries* [1959], no. 65, lines 107-08). In *Piers Plowman* Langland explains the mystical Antichrist as the *spiritus Cain* unleashed upon the world, a collocation of spiritual evils, when "Caym shal awake" (B.10.326) to spur on "Beliales children" (B.20.79). Mandeville identifies the "field" where Cain slew Abel (Gen. 4:8) as the Damascus field, where God formed Adam before "translating" him to Paradise (*Travels,* chaps. 14, 9). He also mentions the legend, reported in *The Book of Adam and Eve* and transmitted by Peter Comestor (*Historia Scholastica: Liber Genesis*, 29), that blind Lamech, seventh from Adam in Cain's line, accidentally shot Cain through the eyes while Cain stumbled restlessly through "breres and busshes as a wylde best" (chap. 13). From this same legend arose the tradition, to which both Dante (*Inferno*, 20.126) and Chaucer (*Troilus and Criseyde*, 1.1024) allude, that Cain became the man in the moon with a thornbush, an emblem of his adversarial relationship with the earth. The Cain story echoes through the Arthurian cycle, in the stories of Balin and Balan, of Modred, and of Launcelot, who kills his best friend Gareth and his sworn brother Gawain.

English writers from the Renaissance through the 18th cent. invoked Cain's name especially as a curse. Marlowe's Barabas in *The Jew of Malta,* e.g., characterizes Lodowicke as "This offspring of Cain, this Jebusite" (2.3.301), while the newly crowned Henry IV, in Shakespeare's *Richard 2,* banishes Exton, slayer of Richard, with the words: "with Cain go wander through the shades of night" (5.6.43). Moreover, Claudius confesses that his "offense is rank": "It hath the primal eldest curse upon it, / A brother's murder" (*Hamlet*, 3.3.36-38). If medieval writers were fascinated by Cain as a historical figure of biblical primitivism, these later writers saw him rather as a byword, as the figural progenitor of a "cursed" race (Donne's *Progresse of the Soule,* 516). Milton speaks of Cain as the "sweaty Reaper" (*Paradise Lost*, 11.434) and reiterates the common view that his sacrifice was rejected because it was half-hearted; he likens Cain to Judas, who also despaired of God's grace (*De Doctrina Christiana,* 2.3). For Dryden, Cain is the archetype of violence and murder, a spirit "latent" in Adam's seed which would lead ultimately to the religious divisions of Dryden's times (*The Hind and the Panther,* 1.279).

In the later 18th and early 19th cent., writers began to reassess Cain's significance. If Christ brought about the possibility of salvation for all sinners, does this include the hardest cases such as Cain, or Judas the despised suicide? Are these traitors to humankind and deity damned from the beginning? Influenced by Arminianism, particularly after translations of Salomon Gessner's sentimental *Der Tod Abels* (1758), English and American writers inquired as to Cain's state of mind and discovered a brother who came to hate his more successful sibling, a soul to be pitied, even a scapegoat or a human being in distress.

In Coleridge's *The Wanderings of Cain* (1798) Abel's ghost returns to torment Cain while he and his young son wander by moonlight in the wilderness. Enos pathetically asks his father why the squirrels refuse to play with him. A man of poetic imagination, Cain replies: "The Mighty One that persecuteth me is on this side and on that; / he pursueth my soul like the wind, like the sand-blast he passeth through me; / he is around me even as the air!" (31-33).

Byron, in his drama *Cain: A Mystery* (1821), exploits the moral and psychological complexities of Cain's dilemma. A man who "thirst[s] for good" (2.2.238) but who is preoccupied with death, Cain recognizes the world's beauty and sadness, but from the play's opening he feels

cut off from his family, even from his sister-wife Adah. When Lucifer observes that the world before the Fall was lovely, Cain realizes that his quarrel is not with the still beautiful earth but with his own restless unhappiness:

> It is not with the earth, though I must till it,
> I feel at war, but that I may not profit
> By what it bears of beautiful, untoiling,
> Nor gratify my thousand swelling thoughts
> With knowledge, nor allay my thousand fears
> Of death and life. (2.2.124-30)

Cain bitterly criticizes his parents for depriving him of his inheritance, Eden, and for preferring Abel to him, a resentment Lucifer manipulates. Lucifer imparts to Cain Faustian knowledge, including a vision of Hades and the "mighty Pre-Adamites"; and Cain, like some primeval Wordsworth, equates his son's infancy with lost innocence (3.1.18-34). After the murder Eve delivers a terrible curse on her firstborn, banishing him from the Adamic fellowship.

William Blake answered Coleridge and Byron in *The Ghost of Abel* (1822), in which Abel returns to denounce the Lord and stir up revenge: "My desire is unto Cain," says the Ghost, "And He doth rule over Me" (31-32). In this poetic drama Blake challenges the implicit Byronic equation of criminality and the visionary imagination. Cain has typically been romanticized in the modern period; he becomes the visionary wanderer, estranged from ordinary society, both cursed and privileged with a terrible burden of guilt. Here is the informing principle of not only the Wandering Jew, the Ancient Mariner, and Shelley's Adonais, but also Melville's Ishmael, Twain's Huck Finn, Conrad's Lord Jim, Steinbeck's Cal *(East of Eden),* Kerouac's Dean Moriarty *(On the Road),* and John Gardner's *Grendel.* In J. W. Thompson's *Cain* (1926), the original fratricide is a heroic figure who has "something of the character of Prometheus, something of that of Milton's Satan" (p. 6).

See also ABEL; MARK OF CAIN.

Bibliography. Aptowitzer, V. *Kain und Abel in der Aggada der Apokryphen, der hellenistischen, christlichen und mohammedanischen Literatur* (1922); Bandy, S. C. "Caines Cynn: A Study of Beowulf and the Legend of Cain." *DA* 28 (1967), 1780A; Bayle, P. *The Dictionary Historical and Critical.* 2nd ed. 5 vols. (1734-38), s.v. "Cain, Cainites"; Davis, M. "Cain since Lord Byron: A Study of the Sympathetic Treatment of the Character of Cain in the Nineteenth and Twentieth Centuries." *DAI* 36 (1975), 3647A; Emerson, O. F. "Legends of Cain, Especially in Old and Middle English." *PMLA* 21 (1906), 831-929; Harney, M. C. "The Characterization of Cain and Abel in the English Mystery Plays." M.A. thesis, Catholic University, 1940; Reisner, T. A. "Cain: Two Romantic Interpretations." *Culture* 31 (1970), 124-43; Tennenbaum, L. "Lord Byron in the Wilderness: Biblical Tradition in Byron's *Cain* and Blake's *The Ghost of Abel.*" *MP* 72 (1975), 350-64; Williams, D. *Cain and Beowulf: A Study in Secular Allegory* (1982).   JAMES M. DEAN

CALEB   The Kenizzite chosen by Moses to go, along with Joshua and others, to "spy out the land" of Canaan (Num. 13:6; 32:12). Only he and Joshua of the original twelve returned with an encouraging report; hence only they survived to enter "the promised land" (14:38; 32:12; Josh. 14:9). By driving out the Anakim forty years later, he received Hebron as his inheritance. His name is closely tied to the word for "dog," as in a "faithful dog."

See also JOSHUA.

CALVARY   The site of Jesus' crucifixion.

See also PASSION, CROSS.

CAMEL THROUGH A NEEDLE'S EYE   The story of the encounter between Jesus and the rich man seeking "eternal life" appears in Matt. 19:16-30; Mark 10:17-31; Luke 18:18-30 and the noncanonical Gospel of the Nazarenes, cited by Origen. In Mark and Luke, Jesus rejects the title "Good Teacher." Similarly in Matthew, he refuses to point to the "good deed" which will win salvation (19:16). In all three Gospels, the rich man is instead referred to God as the source of goodness (Matt. 19:17; Mark 10:18; Luke 18:19) and to the commandments as the traditional guides to right conduct (Matt. 19:18-19; Mark 10:19; Luke 18:20).

The rich man asserts his faithful observance of "all these" commandments. In response, Jesus adds a new list of radical demands which exceed traditional piety. The rich man is told to sell his possessions, donate the proceeds to the poor, and undertake a life as Jesus' disciple. With sadness, the man declines to comply and leaves. His great wealth is cited as the reason for his refusal and consequent inability to gain "treasure in heaven" (Matt. 19:22; Mark 10:22; Luke 18:23).

A dialogue continues between Jesus and his disciples. Jesus stresses the barrier wealth represents for those who seek to enter the kingdom of God with an oft-repeated maxim: "It is easier for a camel to enter the eye of a needle than for a rich man to enter heaven." To the amazement of those who doubt that anyone can then be saved, Jesus responds that although the situation is impossible by human effort alone, it is "possible with God."

The apostle Peter then asks what reward the disciples will receive, having "left everything" and "followed him" in sharp contrast to the reluctant rich man. Jesus not only promises the eternal life the rich man sought in vain but also rulership in Israel, judging the twelve tribes (Matt. 19:28). Furthermore, the sacrifices of disciples will be repaid abundantly, a "hundredfold" in Matthew (19:29) and "manifold" times in Luke (18:30). Mark adds more soberly that discipleship will also bring "persecutions" (10:30). To stress that the disciples' reward is a matter of God's grace and not earned by human merit, the episode concludes with the admonition that many of those who are seemingly "last" will be "first" in the kingdom of God (Matt. 19:30; Mark 10:31; Luke 18:30).

In medieval exegesis the young man's riches were usually allegorized as works and honors obtained on his own merit, and Christ's call to radical divestment as an invitation to imitate him in his Passion. In the light of the version in Mark 10:23-27, Jesus was not seen as prohibiting the rich but speaking of the difficulties for those who place their confidence in riches (e.g., *Glossa Ordinaria* [PL 114.151]; St. Jerome, *Ep.* 145; *Adversus Pelagianos,* 1.10); in one of his best-known letters, Jerome is at pains to emphasize the metaphorical character of Jesus' utterance. Calvin nonetheless observes that Satan holds the very affluent "bound in chains," in that "they bury and constrict themselves and enslave themselves completely to this world," but adds that "the simile of the camel" refers rather to "a ship's rope than the animal" (*Harmony of the Gospels,* Matt. 19:23-26).

In Shakespeare's *Richard 2,* the imprisoned king struggles with his soul's lack of elected peace: "I have been studying how I may compare / This prison where I live unto the world" (5.5.1-2); he finds that those in religious doubt

> do set the word itself
> Against the word; as thus, "Come little ones,"
> And then again,
> "It is as hard to come as for a camel
> To thread the postern of a small needle's eye."
> (5.5.13-17)

Anthony Trollope reflects the conventional interpretation: "How hard it is for a rich man not to lean upon his riches! harder, indeed, than for a camel to go through the eye of a needle" (*Framley Parsonage,* chap. 8), while Charles Dickens incorporates the allusion as a satire on riches as poverty in *Little Dorrit:* its Antichrist figure, Mr. Merdle, is an imperial tycoon of unknown and unquestioned sources of vast income, for "it was the last new polite reading of the camel and the needle's eye to accept without enquiry" his riches (1.33; cf. *Martin Chuzzlewit,* chap. 25). Aldous Huxley takes up the Dickensian application in *After Many a Summer,* where he observes that "Poverty and suffering ennoble only when they are voluntary. By involuntary poverty and suffering men are made worse. It is easier for a camel to pass through the eye of the needle than for an involuntarily poor man to enter the kingdom of heaven" (1.8), while in his essay "On Grace" he adds that it is "almost as difficult for the spiritually rich to enter the kingdom of heaven as it is for the materially rich" (*Music at Night*).

American literature often engages the phrase less soberly. Twain's antinomian humor leads to typical parody: "It is easier for a cannibal to enter the Kingdom of Heaven through the eye of a rich man's needle than it is for any other foreigner to read the terrible German script" (*Notebook,* chap. 31). Rhett Butler executes an antebellum slur on Southern decorum in Mitchell's *Gone with the Wind,* turning the original point about riches inside out. Responding to Scarlett's assurances concerning his prospects ("If you've got money, people always like you") he retorts, "Not Southerners. It's harder for speculators' money to get into the best parlours than for the camel to go through the needle's eye" (chap. 48).

LENORE GUSSIN
DAVID L. JEFFREY

CANA WINE Only the Gospel of John (2:1-11) reports the incident of Jesus' miraculous turning of water into wine at a wedding feast in the Galilean town of Cana. John locates the episode at the beginning of Christ's ministry, just after the baptism and temptation and the calling of the disciples, and just before the cleansing of the Temple (which John alone of the evangelists places at the beginning of the ministry). John notes at the end of the episode that this was the first of the miracles or signs wrought by Jesus (one of the seven mentioned in this Gospel) and that he thereby "manifested forth his glory; and his disciples believed on him." This helps to explain why the incident at Cana, along with the visit of the Magi and the baptism of Jesus, was originally associated with the ancient feast of Epiphany (Jan. 6); in the Middle Ages Cana came to be celebrated by itself on the Second Sunday after Epiphany.

Critical commentary has always focused on the implications of Jesus' attendance at the wedding, the import of the exchange between Jesus and his mother prior to the working of the miracle, and the purpose and significance of the miracle itself. While there are no explicit OT allusions in the account, the miracle at Cana has been variously associated with several acts of Moses — procuring water from a rock (Exod. 17:1-7), making bitter water sweet (15:23-25), and turning water to blood (7:17-25) — and of Elisha and Elijah (1 Kings 17:1-16; 2 Kings 2:19-22; 4:1-7).

The Cana episode accords with much which is known about Near Eastern wedding customs, especially the importance ascribed to the provision of wine for the wedding feast; commonly the wine was diluted with water. The Christian liturgies, Eastern and Western both, have always placed special significance on the mingling of water and wine in the chalice for consecration, as a symbol of the unity of divine and human natures in the person of Jesus Christ (for examples from the Eastern liturgies see E. S. Drower, *Water into Wine* [1956], chaps. 4–5).

In early Christian and medieval exegesis Christ's attendance at the wedding is said to have sanctified the institution of matrimony (see St. Gaudentius, *Sermo,* 8 [PL 20] and St. Cyril [PG 73.223] — both trans. in Toal, *The Sunday Sermons of the Great Fathers* [1957], 1.269, 276; also St. Augustine, *Hom.* 9, on John). More importantly, his presence was seen as symbolic of the spiritual marriage, the union of the spirit of Christ with human flesh, and the union of Christ the Bridegroom with his spouse the Church. (Cf. Augustine, *Hom.* 8, on John, and

Gaudentius, Cyril, and St. Bernard in Toal, 1.271, 277, 282.)

With respect to the actual transformation, the commentators all emphasize the mystical significance of the miracle; indeed, its physical aspect is seen as only an extension or heightening of the perpetual miracle of the natural order of creation (Augustine, *Hom.* 8, on John, and St. John Chrysostom, *Hom.* 22, on John [trans. in Toal, 1.263]). The six water pots, associated in the text with the Jewish ritual of purification, are commonly allegorized as standing for the six ages of the world (e.g., Augustine), or the six stages of purification, in which the water of the fear of the Lord becomes the wine of spiritual joy (e.g., Bernard, cited in Toal, 1.278-80). The miraculous change of water into wine is seen as symbolizing the transformation of the water of the Old Law into the wine of grace or the Holy Spirit (e.g., Gaudentius and Cyril, cited in Toal, 1.272, 277); the transformation of flat, literal understanding into the inebriating wine of the spiritual sense, such as Christ brought to the disciples on the road to Emmaus (Augustine, *Hom.* 9, on John); or the transformation of a cold and inconstant human will into a sturdy and fortifying redeemed will which is a joy to others (Chrysostom, cited in Toal, 1.265). Chrysostom also aims to allay skepticism centering on naturalistic interpretations of the miracle. Against the accusation that the alleged miracle was reported only by drunkards, Chrysostom replies that the chief witness was the steward, not the guests (Toal, 1.264); and against the suggestion that the water had been poured into jars with a residue of wine, which would thus have created the effect of "a very diluted wine," he points to the detail that these are specified to be jars of purification, "showing that there never had been wine in these vessels" (Toal, 1.263).

The miracle at Cana appears very early in Christian art, undoubtedly because of symbolic associations with the miraculous feeding and the Last Supper. A 2nd- or 3rd-cent. catacomb in Alexandria conjoins the Cana incident with the multiplication of loaves, and similar associations occur in a number of sarcophagi and early Christian ivories as well as the 4th-cent. wooden doors of S. Sabina in Rome (see Schiller, *Iconography of Christian Art,* 1.163). The earliest images show only Christ (sometimes with a thaumaturgical wand) and the water pots, and sometimes a witness. Later examples present more of the imagery of the wedding feast itself, often in the manner of a Last Supper (especially in late medieval art), but increasingly in the manner of a realistic wedding festival, as in Giotto's Arena Chapel painting at Padua (1305) or Bosch's 16th-cent. version (see Schiller, *Iconography,* 1.164). The bridegroom is often made to resemble the beloved disciple John, for according to a tradition found in St. Jerome, the *Golden Legend,* and other sources, the wedding celebrated at Cana was none other than that of John himself; the bride was sometimes identified as Mary Magdalene — who, however, renounced marriage to follow Jesus. (In a modern variant, in Kazantzakis's *Last Temptation of Christ,* the Cana wedding becomes Jesus' abortive nuptials with Mary Magdalene.)

This tradition occasions Aelfric's reference to the Cana wedding in his homily for the feast of the Assumption of St. John the Apostle (*Homilies of the Anglo-Saxon Church,* ed. Thorpe [1844], 1.59), emphasizing a dramatic choice of celibacy. Otherwise, the major treatment of the Cana episode in OE literature occurs in Aelfric's homily for the Second Sunday after Epiphany. He begins with a citation from Bede and in the homily closely follows the traditional explications of the allegory of the spiritual marriage, the transformation of the Old Law into the wine of the New, and the allegorization of the six water pots as the six ages of the world. Later medieval English sermons continue to reflect the same interpretations.

The first appearance of the Cana story in English poetry occurs in the ME verse paraphrases of Scripture, as in the *English Metrical Homilies* (199.1-121.16), the *Stanzaic Life of Christ* (1525-28, 1577-84), and, most elaborately, in the *Cursor Mundi* (13.360-13.451). The passage ends with reference to the apocryphal tradition that this was indeed the wedding of John, who "there laft the bridegome his bride & followed ihesu fra that tide."

A few references to Cana occur in ME lyrical poetry, as in a 13th-cent. antiphon dedicated to St. Thomas of Canterbury, which refers to the Cana miracle in relation to a prayer to St. Thomas for help: "Selcuth dude vre dryhtin, / that he water wende to win; / thu ert help in engelaunde / vre stephne vnderstonde" (C. Brown, *English Lyrics of the XIIIth Century* [1932], no. 42). In a more familiar context is a 15th-cent. carol on the Epiphany premised on the tradition that the visit of the Magi, the baptism of Jesus, and the Cana wedding occurred on the same day of the year (R. Greene, *Early English Carols* [1977], no. 130; cf. Mirk's *Festial* [EETS e.s. 96], 48).

In *The Canterbury Tales,* Chaucer's Parson gives the usual exposition, that by his presence at the wedding Christ hallowed the institution of marriage, and he goes on to allegorize the miracle of the wine as Christ's transformation of the mortal sin of sexual intercourse into the merely venial sin it is in marriage (*The Parson's Tale,* 10.915-20). This reading is in marked contrast to the famous reference by the Wife of Bath, who indeed acknowledges that she was told:

> That sith that Crist ne wente evere but onis
> To weddyng, in the Cane of Galilee,
> That by the same ensample taughte he me
> That I ne sholde wedded be but ones. (*Wife of Bath's Tale,* Prol. 3.10-13)

She draws a connection with Jesus' message to the Samaritan woman at the well — but quickly demonstrates her inability to fathom these teachings ("What that he mente therby, I kan nat seyn").

In later English literature references to the Cana miracle occur frequently in religious contexts, but one also finds proverbial allusions to water changed to wine or saving the good wine until last." A more direct allusion, by Herbert, occurs in "Divinite," in which the association of the transformation of water into wine with the imparting of spiritual insight contrasts with theological speculation which only clouds such insight:

> Could not that Wisdome, which first broacht the wine,
>   Have thicken'd it with definitions?
> And jagg'd his seamlesse coat, had that been fine,
>   With curious questions and divisions? (9-12)

A baroque, quite secular allusion occurs in Herrick's "To the Water Nymphs, drinking at the Fountain," in which the speaker bids the nymphs but touch the cup to their lips "And I shall see by that one kisse, / The Water turn'd to Wine" (7-8). This playful image is reminiscent of a similar line in one of Crashaw's Latin Epigrams: "Nympha pudica Deum vidit, & erubuit" ("The chaste nymph has seen [her] God *and blushed*"). Crashaw echoes the line in his translation "Out of Grotius his Tragedy of Christes sufferinges":

> What would they more? th'ave seene when at my nod
> Great Natures selfe hath shrunke and spike mee god.
> Drinke fayling there where I a guest did shine
> The Water blush'd, and started into Wine. (49-52)

Curiously, the image is anticipated, almost exactly, by Caelius Sedulius (5th cent.): "Now Cana sees in wonder new — / the water blushes at his view" (trans. H. Henry). A second Divine Epigram by Crashaw is based on the conceit that Christ's sinful enemy reverses the miracle by abusing wine and bringing on quarrels and tears:

> Thou water turn'st to Wine (faire friend of Life);
>   Thy foe to crosse the sweet Arts of thy Reigne
> Distills from thence the Teares of wrath and strife,
>   And so turnes wine to Water backe againe.

Several 19th-cent. poets make use of water-and-wine imagery in a romantic context in such a way as to leave uncertain whether any allusion to Cana is intended. In *Don Juan* Byron compares the sequence of love and marriage to the turning of wine to vinegar (3.5.5) and, with reference to drinking and drowning, speaks of a "wine and watery grave" (2.57.5). Tennyson, following the now proverbial expression of saving the best wine till last, makes reference in "The Grail" to Lancelot's being the last of Arthur's knights (757-60). A similar allusion occurs in Browning's "Popularity" (st. 4), with reference to the recognition of a poet. In G. M. Hopkins's "Easter" the allusion retains its explicit religious context:

> Build His church and deck His shrine,
>   Empty though it be on earth;

Ye have kept your choicest wine —
Let it flow for heavenly mirth.

In Browning's *The Ring and the Book,* Pompilia bitterly recalls how the cynical priest who conspired to marry her off to his brother Guido preached the doctrine of Cana to her:

Read here and there, made me say that and this,
And after, told me I was now a wife,
Honoured indeed, since Christ thus weds the Church,
And therefore turned he water into wine,
To show I should obey my spouse like Christ.
(7.445-49)

But her experience quickly teaches her that things are otherwise: "Nothing is changed however, wine is wine / And water only water in our house" (7.474-75).

Treatments of and references to Cana continue to occur in modern religious poetry, e.g., in Edgar Lee Masters's "The Wedding Feast," which builds strongly on the exegetical tradition, with references to Moses' striking water from a rock (st. 7), Elisha's provision of oil for a widow (st. 8), and the supplanting of OT signs with new spiritual doctrine (*Selected Poems* [1925], 238-40). Sister Mary Edwin's collection of verse *Water into Wine* (1928) utilizes the Cana theme not only in the Proem and title poem but also in the poem "Marriage in Galilee."

The Cana miracle is also dealt with in Dorothy Sayers's radio play "A Certain Nobleman," one of the series *The Man Born to Be King* (1943). Another pious modern paraphase is Agnes Turnbull's short story "The Miracle of Cana" (from the collection *Far Above Rubies,* rpt. in Cynthia Maus, *Christ and the Fine Arts* [1938], 269-76). In Emil Ludwig's *Son of Man* (1928), the miracle is treated as an illusion effected by Jesus' hypnotic powers. Douglas's *The Robe* (1942) illustrates the struggle of modern piety with the idea of miracles, introducing every conceivable rationalistic explanation for Jesus' miracles through the reflections of Marcellus, the Roman centurion. Regarding the miracle at Cana, Marcellus at first explores the explanation that the water had been poured into jars which had been used for storing wine, but eventually rationalization shifts into allegorization reminiscent of Chrysostom, as Marcellus comes to see that transformation of attitude and personality is even more of a miracle than the changing of water into wine. Robert Graves's novel *King Jesus* (1946) presents the incident at Cana as a moral demonstration by Jesus which has subsequently come to be distorted and interpreted precisely contrary to Jesus' intent. What Jesus did, as Graves tells it, was to command that the jars of purification be filled with water, which he then drank, declaring that to be the true wine Adam drank in Eden: "The master of ceremonies followed his example and swore that never had he tasted such good wine. He meant that he approved Jesus' message: Cleanliness, that is to say 'holiness before the Lord,' is better than excessive drinking." In substitut-

ing lustral water for wine, Jesus was also saying "that Adam and Eve in the days of innocency abstained from carnal love — of which the emblem in the Canticles is wine" (293). More orthodox treatments of the Cana miracle abound in the host of modern novelizations of the life of Christ.

See also BRIDE, BRIDEGROOM; EUCHARIST; MARRIAGE FEAST, APOCALYPTIC.

Bibliography. Drower, E. *Water into Wine: A Study of Ritual Idiom in the Middle East* (1956); Schiller, G. *Iconography of Christian Art.* Trans. J. Seligman. Vol. 1 (1971); Toal, M., trans. and ed. *The Sunday Sermons of the Great Fathers.* Vol. 1 (1957).   GEORGE L. SCHEPER

CANAAN *See* EXODUS; JOSHUA; LAND FLOWING WITH MILK AND HONEY.

CANDLE The candle is part of the complex pattern of light imagery in the Bible and its meaning depends on its context. The candle can suggest knowledge or comfort derived from God's guidance (Job 29:3; Rev. 22:5) or a gift not to be hidden under a bushel (Matt. 5:15; Mark 4:21; Luke 8:16). Another sense arises out of Rev. 22:5 (and St. Bridget of Sweden's comparison of Joseph's earthly candle to the magnificence of the light radiating from the child Christ [*Revelations,* 1]). Thus Francis Quarles's candle is but "a dying sparke" as compared to the "promis'd light" (*Emblemes* [1635], 57). Candles can also signify grace (following Job 29:3, "His candle shined upon my head"), as in St. Hippolytus's *Canons* and Vaughan's "To . . . Jesus Christ."

The principal reference, however, is Prov. 20:27: "The spirit of man is the candle of the Lord." The soul is a light placed by God in individuals to inform and direct their activities and thoughts. St. Augustine relates this enlightenment of every person to the baptism of infants: the human mind "is internally besprinkled with that light which remains for ever, and which shines even in darkness." The light is "reason herself, which causes the human soul to be called rational," and it "is made when the soul is created" (*De baptismo,* 38). Later commentators sometimes quibble over whether God lights the candle, as in Ps. 18:28, or is himself the lamp, as the parallel passage in 2 Sam. 22:29 suggests. St. Augustine finds the passages entirely reconcilable (*Sermo,* 18.8). In the 17th cent. the Cambridge Platonists became famous for their use of Prov. 20:27 as the expression of *recta ratio.* For example, the argument between Benjamin Whichcote and Anthony Tuckney revolves around Whichcote's analogy between the spiritual candle and reason which allows him to know God.

Augustine makes the point that "that which can be lighted can be extinguished also" (*Sermo,* 68.9), drawing on numerous biblical texts which warn of the candle's being put out (Job 18:6; 21:17; Prov. 24:20; Rev. 18:23). John Donne's sermon on Matt. 5:15-16 (*Sermons,* 10.3)

accords with the sense expressed by Henry Vaughan that his sins remove "that candle given from above ("The Agreement"). Macbeth's sigh, "Out, out, brief candle!" (*Macbeth*, 5.5.23), signals not only death but also the extent of his spiritual darkness; the light of his spirit flickers out with his bodily life. (Lighted candles were a part of the burial ceremony for Christians during the Middle Ages, while heretics and excommunicates, who had snuffed the light within and could not hope for any resurrection of that light, were buried with candles extinguished.)

As a metaphor for the perceiving mind, the candle becomes the "auxiliar light" of Romantic poetics. Knowledge of biblical antecedents lends force to a minor verse like Coleridge's "To my Candle," in which the poet, while ostensibly saying farewell to his evening light, comments on perception and his own vitality.

In the 20th cent. Joyce alludes to the ritual significance of candles in *Ulysses,* and in Lawrence's "The Witch A La Mode" candles represent Winifred's refusal to "go by instinct," her reliance on "speech, symbols and so forth" to protect her from relationships. Her candles represent rationalism which has lost its light.

See also LIGHT; LIGHT UNDER A BUSHEL.

Bibliography. Farley, R. *Lynchnocausia* (1638); Whichcote, B. *Select Sermons* (1689), and *Several Discourses,* ed. J. Jeffrey (1701). RODERICK MCGILLIS
H. DAVID BRUMBLE

CANON The Greek word *kanōn* refers to a "rod," "measuring rod," or "rule." Used metaphorically to refer to an authoritative catalogue of books, it was adopted in Western Christianity to signify the list of biblical books the Church regarded as inspired and therefore authoritative, containing the "rule of faith." The word, first found in Origen, was general by the 4th cent. in Christian writers.

The idea, however, was firmly established in Judaism of the 2nd cent. B.C. where, according to the apocryphal 4 Ezra (cf. Pirqe 'Abot), the canon of the Hebrew Scriptures was "closed" by the Great Synagogue following the return from exile under Ezra. Diaspora Jews regarded several Greek works as equally authoritative, including most of the Apocrypha as printed in the original KJV and subsequent RV, Douai, and JB translations. When the authority of these books was challenged in the patristic period, notably by St. Jerome (contra St. Ambrose and St. Augustine), they persisted in moderate use in the lectionary, but their influence was subordinated theologically to that of the Hebrew texts which, alone, Jerome felt to be properly "canonical." Reformation theologians followed Jerome, but the Council of Trent (1546) required the acceptance of apocryphal books as "deutero-canonical," relevant in matters of faith for all Roman Catholics, a position confirmed by Vatican I (1870).

By the 2nd cent. A.D. the four Gospels and 13 Pauline epistles were regarded by the Church as inspired. Hebrews, Jude, 2 Peter, 2 and 3 John, and Revelation were more slowly accepted; the present NT canon appears as a list *de fide,* as the "rule of faith" in the Festal Epistle of St. Athanasius for A.D. 367. The list of OT and NT books confirmed at Rome in 382, and again under Gelasius (495, in the "Gelasian Decree"), is identical with that of the Council of Trent. Because of the dominant influence of the Reformation upon English literary use of the Bible, allusions to apocryphal (deuterocanonical) OT and NT books tend largely to be confined to OE and ME literary texts. There are, however, numerous exceptions persisting into the Renaissance and even 18th cent., and even in the sermons of English Reformation leaders (e.g., Latimer, Ridley, Coverdale) they continue to flourish, providing illustrious "holy examples."

See also APOCRYPHA AND PSEUDEPIGRAPHA; BIBLE; INSPIRATION.

Bibliography. Filson, F. V. *Which Books Belong to the Bible? A Study of Canon* (1957); Howarth, H. W. "The Influence of St. Jerome on the Canon of the Western Church." *JTS* 10 (1908-09), 481-96; 11 (1909-10), 321-47; 13 (1911-12), 1-18; Kermode, F. "The Canon." In *The Literary Guide to the Bible.* Ed. F. Kermode and R. Alter (1987), 600-610.

CANTICLES *See* SONG OF SONGS.

CAPTAIN OF THE LORD'S HOST The book of Joshua (5:13-15) narrates an encounter between Joshua, leader of the Israelite forces, and the armed "captain of the LORD's host," an angelic figure at the head of the divine army. This encounter comes just after the Israelites have crossed the Jordan River into the Promised Land, reinstituting the rite of circumcision and celebration of the Passover, and just before their first battle against a Canaanite foe, the inhabitants of Jericho.

In several respects, including the command to Joshua to remove the shoe from his foot, this narrative is reminiscent of the earlier account of Moses at the burning bush (Exod. 3:1–4:17, see esp. 3:1-5), one of many parallels between the careers of Moses and Joshua. Somewhat more distantly, this passage looks forward to David's encounter with a similar figure in 1 Chron. 21:16-17. But it has other analogues (Judg. 6:11-24; 13:2-5) and may be what Robert Alter (*The Art of Biblical Narrative*) has called a "type-scene."

While to some scholars the very brevity of the narrative in Joshua is evidence of incompleteness, it nevertheless functions well as an assurance to Joshua that the Lord would be fighting alongside Israel, that this was in effect a Holy War. (Textually the interpretation of this story remains somewhat unclear, owing to the enigmatic reply, "Nay. . . ," offered by the angelic figure to Joshua's question: "Art thou for us, or for our adversaries?" Attempts to emend the Hebrew text or to provide a less puzzling translation for this reply are unconvincing.)

This narrative, as well as similar stories, stimulated a wealth of exegetical comment on the part of Jewish scholars throughout the ages. Thus, Maimonides holds that all references to humans' seeing an angel refer to a prophetic vision or dream. According to Rashi, the unnamed angel encountered by Joshua was Michael (on whom, see Dan. 10:13, 21; Rev. 12:7).

Christian commentary focuses on the character of the scene as theophany (e.g., St. Jerome, *Ep.* 22.19; *Adv. Jov.* 1.21), as well as on the order of command: in Matthew Henry's *Commentary* (1728): "Joshua was in his post as a general when God came and made himself known as Generalissimo" (2.27).

William Cowper's account of the post-Exodus guidance of Israel by God, with its litany of blessings, ("the favours pour'd upon the Jewish name") includes preeminently, in reference to Joshua's divine appointment, that he was:

> Their leader arm'd with meekness, zeal, and love,
> And grac'd with clear credentials from above;
> Themselves secur'd beneath th'Almighty wing
> Their God their captain, lawgiver and king.
> ("Expostulation," 187-90)

Cowper provides a marginal note, "Vide Joshua v.14." Also following this passage is the characterization of "de Lawd" in "The Stratagem of Joshua," part of Roark Bradford's *Ol' Man Adam an His Chillun,* where the Lord appears as commander of an army (Bradford's text is the source for the musical "Green Pastures").

See also JOSHUA; MICHAEL.

Bibliography. Boling, R. G., and G. E. Wright. *Joshua.* AB (1982), 195-99; Bratcher, R. G., and B. M. Newman. *A Translator's Handbook on the Book of Joshua* (1983), 65-67; Butler, T. C. *Joshua.* WBC 7 (1983), 53-63; Drucker, R. *Yehoshua: The Book of Joshua.* ArtScroll Tanach Series (1982), 170-75; Soggin, J. A. *Joshua: A Commentary.* OTL (1972), 76-78; "La 'negazione' in Gios. 5.14." *BeO* 7 (1965), 75-76; Woudstra, M. H. *The Book of Joshua.* NICOT (1981), 103-06.　　　　　　　　　　　　　　LEONARD GREENSPOON

CARMEL, MOUNT　*See* BAAL; ELIJAH.

CASPER　*See* MAGI.

CAST THE FIRST STONE　*See* WOMAN TAKEN IN ADULTERY.

CASTLE　The most distinctive figurative use of castle arises from a bizarre elaboration of the Vg version of Luke 10:38, in which St. Jerome employs *castellum* (dim. of *castrum,* "fort") to signify "village." Military connotations of the word apparently combined with mention in the following verse of Mary (ironically, if commonly and mistakenly, held in medieval times to be the sinful Magdalene) and with a peculiar interpretation of Cant. 4:4 to produce the notion of the immaculate Virgin as a castle

protecting the Savior. Thus Rabanus Maurus (d. 856) comments: "*Castelum* est Virgo Maria, ut in Evangelio, 'Intravit Jesus in quoddam castellum,' quod Christus in singularis virginis venit uterum" (*Allegoriae in Universam Sacram Scripturam* [PL 1.2.885]).

More readily understandable, perhaps, is the conception of the body as a castle with the guardians of the five gates (the senses) assigned to shelter the soul as the stronghold's inhabitants. The allegory appears in the enormously popular poem of the early 14th cent., *The Pricke of Conscience* ("Ilka man's body may be cald, / As a castell here" [ed. R. Morris (1973), 5.11.5280-81]), in the morality play *The Castell of Perseverance,* and in the Castle of Anima in Langland's *Piers Plowman* (B.9.1-63). In the Digby play of *Mary Magdalen,* Mary's "castell" proves insufficient protection from the assaults of (the kings of) the World, the Flesh and the Devil, who with the Seven Deadly Sins besiege it, Luxuria finally prevailing against it (1.7-8). Spenser's Castle of Alma is similarly represented, and here the inviolable nature of the castle's occupant, when properly protected, appears in the description of Alma as "a virgin bright" and "full of grace" (*Faerie Queene,* 2.9.19). Persisting well into the 17th cent., the castle motif is the foundation upon which Bunyan erects his most ambitious allegory *The Holy War,* conceiving of the beautiful town of Mansoul as a fastness besieged by the contending forces of Shaddai and Diabolus, salvation and damnation depending upon control of the town's five gates and the castle at the heart of it. Within the same moral tradition is a quite different allegory presented in James Thomson's poem "The Castle of Indolence" (1748), wherein pilgrims are enticed into the keep of the wizard Indolence and left to languish there until the castle is destroyed by the Knight of Arms and Industry. With the virtual demise of allegory following Romantic antipathy to it, the tradition has faded in English.

Bibliography. Cornelius, R. *The Figurative Castle* (1930); Owst, G. W. *Literature and Pulpit in Medieval England* (1933), 77-85.　　　　　　　　JAMES F. FORREST

CELIBACY　*See* BETTER TO MARRY THAN TO BURN; MARY, MOTHER OF JESUS; VIRGINITY, CHASTITY.

CEPHAS　*See* PETER.

CHAFF　*See* LETTER AND SPIRIT.

CHALDEA, CHALDEANS　The term *Chaldea* refers to a geographical area in southern Babylonia found in Assyrian sources from the 9th cent. B.C. on. The name later was used for the last, neo-Babylonian dynasty (626-539 B.C.). The Bible depicts the Chaldeans as seminomads (Job 1:17) who settled in this area (Gen. 11:28; Acts 7:4). By Daniel's time the name was used of all Babylonia (Dan. 3:8; 9:1). The "tongue of the Chaldeans" (Dan. 1:4), possibly a Babylonian dialect, led to the erroneous identification of "Chaldee" with Aramaic, a virtual equivalent in the usage of St. Jerome and, later, many medieval writers.

The "Chaldeans" became associated with magic (St. Athanasius, *De incarnatione,* 48-51), especially astrology (Dan. 2:5, 10; Herodotus 1.181.5; Strabo 739), as well as physical strength (Esth. Rab. 1:17). For scholastic and Reformation commentators they were symbolic of idolatry (Luther, *Works,* 2.248-49), though they were later seen as masters of science as well as the arcane arts (Calvin, *Comms.,* 12.92; Luther, *Works,* 2.305).

Bibliography. Millard, A. R., *EvQ* 49 (1977), 69-71; Wiseman, D. J., ed. *Peoples of Old Testament Times* (1973), 179-96.   DAVID W. BAKER

CHAM *See* HAM.

CHARIOT OF FIRE   The OT recounts that when Elijah the Tishbite was walking in conversation with Elisha "there appeared a chariot of fire, and horses of fire, and parted them both asunder; and Elijah went up by a whirlwind into heaven" (2 Kings 2:11; see also 2 Kings 6:16-17, where Elisha, Elijah's successor, is granted a vision of God's army surrounding and protecting Israel: "the mountain was full of horses and chariots of fire round about Elisha"). A promise of Elijah's return is referred to in Mal. 4:5-6; in Jewish tradition Elijah is expected to prepare for the coming of the Messiah (Pirqe R. El. 43, 47; Mishnah and Tosepta at the conclusion of 'Eduyyot; Menaḥ. 45a). Another OT figure frequently associated with a chariot of fire (though without biblical warrant) is Enoch, who "walked with God: and he was not, for God took him" (Gen. 5:24); some sources attribute his translation also to provision of a fiery chariot (e.g., Yashar Bereshit 11a-13a).

In Christian exegetical tradition, as with talmudic commentary, the fiery chariot translation is associated with extreme piety and ascetical purity: St. Ambrose credits Elijah's virginity with his being "carried by a chariot into heaven" (*De virginibus,* 1.3.12). St. Augustine sees Elijah's ascension in the fiery chariot as an apt prefiguration of things to come for the persevering elect (*De civ. Dei* 20.29). In later medieval typological tradition the *Biblia Pauperum* pictures the ascensions of Enoch, Elijah, and Christ together: Elijah in his fiery chariot is both antitype of Enoch and type of Christ (pl. 34). Franciscan hagiography borrows the motif, with Thomas of Celano's *Vita Prima* recording an appearance of the spirit of St. Francis to the brothers at Rivo Torto, an event carefully analyzed by St. Bonaventure so that Francis is seen as an antitype of Elijah (*Legenda Major,* 4.4; *Legendae,* 573), an application clearly influenced by the apocalyptic "third age" spirituality of Joachim of Fiore. There is evidence of a lost 14th-cent. English saints' play on the life of St. Francis incorporating the fiery chariot vision. It

powerfully offended a Wycliffite opponent of saints' plays, who savagely wishes for (to him) a fitting theatrical mishap and general conflagration of friars:

> A cart was made al of fyre as it shuld be,
> A Gray frere I saw ther inne that best lyked me.
> Wele I wote thai shal be brent by my leaute,
> God graunte me that grace that I may it se.
> (*Monumenta Franciscana,* 1.606)

In Milton's *Paradise Regained* the disciples, considering Jesus' long absence in the wilderness, think that he might be "for a time caught up to God, as once / . . . the great Thisbite who on fiery wheels / Rode up to Heaven, yet once again to come" (2.16-19). God's chariot of fire also forms part of the mystic vision of the prophet Ezekiel (Ezek. 1:16) which is the source for Milton's description in *Paradise Lost:*

> Forth rushed with whirlwind sound
> The chariot of Paternal Deity,
> Flashing thick flames, wheel within wheel indrawn,
> Itself instinct with spirit, but convoyed
> By four cherubic Shapes. (6.749-53)

Paralleling the biblical chariot of fire as a source of literary imagery is the classical chariot of the sun ridden by Phaeton or Phoebus. The special circumstances of Elijah's translation to heaven, however, have spawned a variety of distinct allusions in English literature. Robert Southey in his *Life of Nelson* comments that "if the chariot and the horses of fire had been vouchsafed for Nelson's translation, he could scarcely have departed in a brighter blaze of glory" (chap. 9). Blake's reference to a "chariot of fire" in the preface to his poem *Milton* alludes to the vision of the earlier poet in Gray's *The Progress of Poesy* (3.2.95-104) as well as to 2 Kings 2:11. In Blake's version the chariot is not a death car but one of the flaming instruments by means of which the apocalyptic renewal of England is to take place. The famous hymn setting for Church of England use ("Jerusalem") by Sir C. Hubert H. Parry (1916) has made this the best-known literary use of the image:

> Bring me my Bow of burning gold:
> Bring me my Arrows of desire!
> Bring me my Spear! O clouds, unfold!
> Bring me my Chariot of fire!
>
> I will not cease from Mental Fight,
> Nor shall my Sword sleep in my hand,
> Till we have built Jerusalem
> In England's green & pleasant Land.

References to "Elijah's firey charet" (Traherne, *Thoughts,* 4) abound in English and Commonwealth literature from the medieval Land of Cokayne to Patrick White's contemporary reworking of medieval Jewish, Christian, and primitive traditions in *Riders of the Chariot* (1961). The image provides the title of a film about Olympic sprinters Harry Abrams and Eric Liddell, later a missionary to China. A notable modern recollection of Elijah's translation to heaven occurs in the vision offered by Marchbanks in Shaw's *Candida* where he speaks of "a tiny shallop to sail away in . . . or a chariot to carry us up into the sky, where the lamps are stars, & don't need to be filled with paraffin oil every day" (2.114). American literature affords a whimsical moment in Emily Dickinson's lines:

Elijah's wagon knew no thill
Was innocent of wheel,
Elijah's horses as unique
As was his vehicle.

But as these later examples suggest, the fire in the chariot has noticeably abated in modern literary allusion.

See also ELIJAH; ELISHA; ENOCH; WHEELS WITHIN WHEELS.

Bibliography. Spicer, H. O. "The Chariot of Fire: A Study of William Blake's Use of Biblical Typology in the Minor Prophecies." *DA* 33 (1962), 2142A. MICHAEL GOLDBERG

CHARITY, CUPIDITY The opposition *caritas / cupiditas,* while reflecting a basic moral distinction in the Bible, owes its particular formulation in Western tradition to difficulties encountered by St. Jerome in rendering several biblical words for love accurately in available Latin equivalents. The OT Hebrew word *'ahab,* while generally referring to spontaneous desire, applies to a range of human and divine expressions of affection. Another word, *hesed,* is used to connote deliberately chosen affection, loyalty, and kindness, typically translated by the KJV as "mercy" (cf. *raham,* "to have compassion" [Deut. 30:3]). Any of these terms may be involved in connection with sexual love, fraternal love, or God's love for his people. In Greek literature before the NT *erōs* is the most common word for love; it suggests spontaneity (like *'ahab)* and yet is almost always sexual in connotation, even when, as in the erotic narratives of classical mythology (e.g., Leda and the swan), it refers to the love of the gods for human persons. In Platonic discourse, "noble *erōs*" can refer to the human quest for "God" (cf. Plato, *Symposium*). When the LXX translators tried to find Greek equivalents for the familiar Hebrew words for love they rejected *erōs* because of its overwhelming cultural associations with libidinous activity, choosing instead the obscure *agapē* to translate *'ahab; erōs* appears only once in the LXX, in a prostitute's invitation to sexual promiscuity (Prov. 7:18). The NT eschews *erōs* altogether. It makes limited use of *philia* ("love," "affection, as for a spouse") to describe parental love (Matt. 10:37), the disciples' love for Jesus (John 21:15-17; 1 Cor. 16:22), and Jesus' love for Lazarus (John 11:3, 36), as well as God's love for Jesus (John 5:50) and for his people (John 16:27; Rev. 3:19). It is never used, however, to describe human love for God. The principal NT word is *agapē, agapaō* (in English Bibles usually translated "love," though 29 times in the KJV as "charity"). In St. Paul's First Epistle to the Corinthians (13:4-8), *agapē*

(Vg *caritas;* KJV "charity") is succinctly described in negative as well as positive terms. Charity is not jealousy, conceit, ostentation, arrogance, self-centeredness, and resentment (various expressions of self-love); it is rather expressed in patience, kindness, truth, righteousness, hope, benevolence, and endurance (self-transcending love).

The KJV "charity" derives from Lat. *caritas* (and its 13th-cent. French equivalent *charité*). St. Jerome chose *caritas* ("love," "esteem," "affection") and *dilectio* ("delight," "love," "high esteem") to translate Gk. *agapē,* knowing that they were imprecise Latin equivalents, themselves overlapping in Roman usage. He then chose *cupiditas* ("lust," "desire," "passion," "ambition") to translate *agapaō* in cases where the object of the affection or desire was of a carnal order — e.g., "Demas, in love with this present world" (2 Tim. 4:10). In 1 Tim. 6:10 (KJV "the love of money is the root of all evil") Jerome renders Gk. *philargyria* in the same way: *"radix malorum cupiditas est."* *Caritas* and *cupiditas* thus become, in the Vg NT and early commentary upon it, divergent, even polar, words for love, the neutral Latin word for which was usually *amor* (cf. *erōs,* "desire"). What determines whether the *amor* is *caritas* or *cupiditas* is its object, or, in St. Augustine's more precise formulation, the intention the "lover" bears toward the object. The Vg translator's attempt to characterize the "sense," as Jerome was wont to say, rather than the semantic "letter" in translating the Bible, is basic to subsequent Western usage. Developing the distinction in a passage of enormous influence, Augustine writes:

I call "charity" the motion of the soul toward the enjoyment of God for His own sake, and the enjoyment of one's self and of one's neighbor for the sake of God; but "cupidity" is a motion of the soul toward the enjoyment of one's self, one's neighbor, or any corporal thing for the sake of something other than God. (*De doctrina Christiana,* 3.10.16)

In other words, desire *(amor)* never remains neutral, but is sharply defined by intention and object. Moreover, the intentions and objects of *caritas* and *cupiditas* are not compatible, so that "the more the reign of cupidity is destroyed, the more charity is increased" (ibid.). For Augustine this is the fundamental spiritual conflict figured in every ethical choice, internally or externally. Vice and virtue, depredation and beneficence, wounding and healing — all manner of opposites are a relative function of choice between cupiditous and charitable promptings of the will. Augustine is thus able to reduce the pedagogical strategy of the Bible to a single governing precept: "Scripture teaches nothing but charity, nor condemns anything except cupidity, and in this way shapes the minds of men" (3.10.15). If this scriptural pedagogy is not immediately apparent at the literal level of a specific biblical text, one seeks it "beneath the veil" of the letter. The literary theory of the *De doctrina* is founded upon this principle: searching for the charitable spirit beneath the letter of the text will prove both spiritually and aesthetically rewarding (2.8.6).

Elaborations in medieval iconography follow directly from this principle of the "two loves." The distination of the pilgrim (*viator*) prompted by charity is the peace and communion of celestial Jerusalem; the destination of the wanderer drawn on by cupidity is the chaos and alienation of Babylon. The two cities spring from the two loves (*De civ. Dei* 24.28). They are the dwelling place of the spiritual "lineage" of Abel and Cain respectively (cf. Peter Lombard, sup. Ps. 97 [PL 191.581]). These and similar analogies illustrate that cupidity is the source of all sin and strife, making "a Babylon of the individual mind, a Babylon of society, and leads to an ultimate Babylon in eternal damnation" (Robertson, 27). Charity is, however, the occasion of love and peace — in the individual mind, in society, and finally in the celestial Jerusalem forever. While cupidity is haunted by the fear of misfortune, charity is conditioned by the fear of God which leads to wisdom, by which in turn the human spirit rises above the happenstance of fortune and its temporal effects (e.g., Lombard [PL 191.766]).

Numerous positive studies of the "virtues" of *caritas* in the 12th cent., notably including two by the Cistercians St. Bernard of Clairvaux (*De Diligendo Deo*) and Aelred of Riveaulx (*Speculum Caritatis*), are effectively what we should today style "psychological" treatments of their subject. Bernard related both to inward promptings, saying: "Only Charity can convert the soul, freeing it from unworthy motives" (*De Diligendo*, 12). Aelred's *Speculum Caritatis* theologically anticipates St. Thomas Aquinas; psychologically it recapitulates Augustine. One of its major themes is the inner peace which derives from charity, and the role charitable affection can play in overcoming the disordering psychic effects of cupidity. The condition of charity is "Sabbath rest," enjoyed in this life as a prefiguration of the life to come. He argues further that practical charity is illuminated by the order of priorities established in the Great Commandment (Deut. 6:5; Matt. 22:37-40): love of God ought to be uppermost, followed by love of one's neighbor, with self occupying the humblest rung in one's ladder of affection. If this hierarchy of the "law of love" is inverted, cupidity reigns, and with it inevitably idolatry (3.2-6). "Choice," Aelred says, "is the beginning of love, whether it be *caritas* or *cupiditas*." In practice, then,

> Charity means that in the first place we have chosen something we are permitted to have; that we have gone about attaining it in the right way, and that having attained it we enjoy it in the way that God meant it to be enjoyed. Charity implies a wise choice and an enjoyment that will benefit us. It begins as a choice, it develops as the pursuit of something good, and comes to its term in enjoyment. But if we choose unwisely, and seek what we have chosen in a wrongful manner, and end by abusing what we have acquired, this is greed, and the root of all evil. But charity is the root of all that is good. (3.8)

Although cupidity usually signifies in the Middle Ages the entire range of self-directed desires, it was typically figured (as the connection with "Cupid" suggests) in carnal passion. In St. Bonaventure's prologue to his commentary on Ecclesiastes, perhaps because he is thinking of its author as Solomon (the Wise Man destroyed by his lust) he uses the word *libido* in place of cupidity to describe the passions which enmesh the soul, typologically, in Babylon (*Opera* [Quarrachi], 6.4). The ambiguous possibilities of Lat. *amor* also opened up a range of wordplay for medieval writers (e.g., Andreas Capallanus, *De Amore*, or *Art of Courtly Love;* Jean de Meun's *Amant* in *Le Roman de la Rose;* Chaucer, in his *General Prologue* description of the Prioress's brooch, inscribed *"Amor vincit omnia"*). Some were inclined to extended witty discourse on the principle that, as Aquinas puts it, echoing Aelred (3.7), if "Charity is love, not all love is charity" (*Summa Theol.* 1a-2ae.62.2-3).

For Aquinas, "Charity is driven out, not because sin is strong, but because the human will subjects itself to sin." Conversely, "Charity brings to life again those who are spiritually dead" (*De Caritate,* 1.24). It is capable of overcoming cupidity's sorry effects, if chosen in repentance by the errant soul (*Summa Theol.* 2a-2ae.23.2). In its requirement of responsibility, charity is ennobling (cf. Richard of St. Victor, *De Trinitate,* 3.2), it has the character of human friendship with God (Aquinas, *De Potentia,* 9; *De Caritate,* 1.3), and it is the basis of perfection in all the other virtues (*Summa Theol.* 1a-2ae.114.4; *De Virtutibus Cardinalibus,* 2). Accordingly, Aquinas concludes, "we must look for the perfection of the Christian life in charity" (*Summa Theol.* 2a-2ae.184.1-2; *De Perfectione Vitae Spiritualis,* 5). For mystical writers like pseudo-Dionysius, Richard of St. Victor, or the author of *The Cloud of Unknowing,* the ultimate perfection of *caritas* is achieved in the mystical union of the soul with God.

Just as *cupiditas* was frequently associated with carnal lust, so *caritas* was often identified by Aquinas and others with *castitas,* chaste affection. Aquinas observes that "chastity" has both and literal and metaphorical sense:

> By a figure of speech, accordingly, spiritual chastity is engaged when our spirit enjoys God, with whom it should be joined, and refrains from enjoying things God does not mean us to mingle with: *I have espoused you one husband, that I may present you a chaste virgin to Christ.* So also may we speak of spiritual fornication, when our spirit delights in embracing things against God's fair order: *thou hast played the harlot with many lovers.* Chastity in this sense is a characteristic of every virtue, each of which holds us back from contracting illicit unions. Yet charity is at the centre of every virtue, and so also are the other theological virtues, which unite us immediately with God. (*Summa Theol.* 2a-2ae.151.2)

The persistence of this association means that in medieval and Renaissance literature especially, a cupiditous abuse of chastity can serve as an exemplum prompting to charity. This appears to be the case in Chaucer's *Merchant's Tale,* where the distinctly selfish and uncharitable motivation of old Januarie in acquiring his young bride May in the marketplace is debated in terms of its consequences for "peace" or "discord" by Justinus and Placebo. When Januarie chooses, for reasons expressly cupiditous, to eschew "chastitee" (4.1455) and acquire a convenient sexual partner, he makes a private enclosed garden to consummate his amours. The garden is associated by the narrator with Priapus and the *Romance of the Rose* —i.e., with unchaste love. Yet when Januarie wishes to call May to a liaison "in his gardyn, and no wight but they tweye," he does so in words which derive from the Songs of Songs:

> Rys up, my wyf, my love, my lady free;
> The turtles voys is herd, my dowve sweete;
> The wynter is goon with alle his reynes weete.
> Com forth now, with thyne eyen columbyn.
> How fairer been thy brestes than is wyn!
> The gardyn is enclosed al aboute;
> Com forth, my white spouse! Out of doute
> Thou hast me wounded in myn herte, O wyf.
> No spot of thee ne knew I al my lyf.
> Com forth and lat us taken oure disport;
> I chees thee for my wyf and my confort.
> (*Canterbury Tales,* 4.2138-48)

Here the biblical garden of chaste love (read allegorically in connection with *caritas;* e.g., St. Bernard, *Super Canticum*) is parodied. But by juxtaposing the unchaste discord of Januarie's garden with the call of the eternal Bridegroom to his Bride, Chaucer highlights the profound contrast between self-deceiving cupidity and divine charity.

Chaucer typically stresses a hierarchical aspect to the relation of *cupiditas* and *caritas.* The lower love, either through bitter experience of its imperfections in fact or through the virtues of vicariously apprehended sorrow, can be instrumental in a lover's progress to higher love (cf. Gower's *Confessio Amantis*). In Dante's *Vita Nuova,* e.g., the narrator pictures himself as loving Beatrice first in an erotic, carnal way (Sonnets 1-7), then gradually for the character in her which the "God of love himself" admires (7), and finally (16.1) for the sake of Love himself to whom her virtues, he sees at last, are to be referred. Chaucer's *Knight's Tale* juxtaposes the concord of a chaste married love (Theseus and Hippolyta) with unchaste, discordant passions (Palamon's and Arcite's feelings for Emilye), yet only so as to show how charitable judgment and chaste marriage can in the end restore what Theseus calls "the fair cheyne of love," that order of Divine Providence by which God established the creation (1.2987-3074; cf. Dunbar's "Of Luve Erdly and Divine," a similar "progress" poem).

Connection of charity with the Law of Love is the subject of a treatise by 14th-cent. spiritual writer Richard Rolle, in which sin, especially mortal sin, is made the "enemy of love" at each level — self, neighbor, and God (Jeffrey, 155-61). A similar theme runs through Langland's *Piers Plowman,* where the Tree of Charity has roots of Mercy and Pity for its trunk (B.16.3-5). By the same token, *Caritas* in *The Castle of Perseverance* tells Humanum Genus that she informs other virtues and is the enemy of vice, particularly *invidia:*

> To Charite, Man, have an eye,
> In al thinge, Man, I rede.
> Al thy doinge as dros is drye,
> But in charite thou dyth thy dede.
> I distroye alwey Envye. . . . (1602-06)

The communion into which Humanum Genus is invited is the Eucharistic "Love Feast," in which sacrament, as 15th-cent. preacher John Mirk puts it, the Christian should understand charity to be "enfleshed" each time it is offered at the altar (*De Solemnitate Corporis Christi,* ed. Erbe, 168-69). A Wycliffite treatise of the same period, *Of Servants and Lords,* advises its hearers that "whoever is most incharity will be most readily heard by God, whether he be a shepherd or a common laborer, whether he be in the church or out in the field." To summarize: medieval texts typically emphasize the crucial nature of choice (intention or *animus* of heart); the ordinate hierarchy of affections (the Law of Love, or Great Commandment); and the foundational relationship of *caritas* and *cupiditas* to all the other vices and virtues respectively.

Renaissance texts of the 16th cent. innovate materially upon the medieval paradigm. Calvin, e.g., discusses charity as pertaining to the Ten Commandments in detail (rather than the summarizing Law of Love). The two tables of the Decalogue, he assumes, are divided into injunctions concerning the "cultivation of piety" and "how we are to conduct ourselves toward our fellow men." Worship is what we owe to God, "charity . . . he enjoins us to have toward our fellow men" (*Inst.* 2.8.11-12). The parable of the Good Samaritan (Luke 10:36) illustrates the principle in its widest sense for Calvin (*Inst.* 2.8.55), which is to say that charity for him is less to be understood as a matter of intentions of the heart, or their object, than in terms of external social "works" — a point which characterizes his later argument against Sadoleto that faith rather than charity is the first cause of salvation (since charity is a matter of works [*Inst.* 3.18.8]). Though St. Paul actually contrasts benevolence, or "bestowing one's goods to feed the poor" (1 Cor. 13:3), with *agapē* (KJV "charity"), Calvin's emphasis is basic to a shift in English usage after the Reformation, in which "charity" becomes an outward action in relief of one's neighbor, or even political toleration, while "love" denotes the inward feeling or prompting of the heart. "Cupidity" largely retains its established meaning — self-love in its cruder forms — though it ceases to be prominent. "Hate" begins to emerge as the usual opposite to "love," while when "charity" is used in its new social sense, its opposites include "greed" and "selfishness."

Already in the 17th cent. this semantic shift can be observed in even a moderate Calvinist like George Herbert, in whose poetry "charitie" appears but three times — twice with but a residue of the medieval sense ("Love-joy"; "Trinitie Sunday"). In the third instance ("The Church-floore") it is paired with "love" in such a way as to suggest that he uses one word for the inward, the other for a complementary outward action: "But the sweet cement, which in one sure band / Ties the whole frame, is *Love* / And *Charitie*" (10-12). Confirmation comes in his prose, where Herbert uses "charity" thirty times to signify the parson's duty: "a debt of Charity to the poor" (*A Priest to the Temple,* 11.6); "any present good deed of charity" (10.6) is proper to the faithful parson, "exposing the obligation of Charity, and Neighbour-hood" (19.34), "so is his charity in effect a Sermon" (12.17). The entire second book of Sir Thomas Browne's *Religio Medici* (1642) is devoted to charity in Herbert's sense of the word — sensitivity and response to the need and miseries of others, and, above all, toleration of their various differences of religious and political opinion. Indeed, after this period, "charity" becomes synonymous with toleration for many writers (e.g., Norris, Locke, Tillotson).

For Puritan writers this was not so, yet the emphasis upon love as a duty was, if anything, stronger. In John Winthrop's famous mid-Atlantic lay sermon aboard the *Arabella* ("A Model of Christian Charity") he tied charity to the "double law," the "law of nature and the law of grace, or the moral law and the law of the Gospel." Charity is above all an exemplary witness of Christian obedience to these laws:

> Whatsoever we did or ought to have done when we lived in England, the same must we do, and more also where we go. That which the most in their churches maintain as a truth in profession only, we must bring into familiar and constant practice: as in this duty of love we must love brotherly without dissimulation, we must love one another with a pure heart fervently, we must bear one another's burdens, we must not look only on our own things but also on the things of our brethren.

Charity is here a covenant obligation; the Lord has "ratified this covenant and sealed our Commission, [and] will expect a strict performance of the articles contained in it" (ed. Miller, 82).

The old usage of *caritas* did, however, continue side by side with the new usage for a time — even self-consciously so. One element which continued to attract Renaissance poets was the old connection of *caritas* and *castitas,* charity and chastity, though in Protestant poets especially this likely owes as much to the Neoplatonic notion that to move toward God was to renounce the flesh, as to the formulations of Aquinas or Aelred (Grant, 82-83). In Spenser's *Faerie Queene,* e.g., Charity (Charissa) is a daughter of Dame Coelia of the House of Holiness. Her characterization as a paragon of chastity may seem at first glance at odds with her description:

> She was a woman in her freshest age,
> Of wondrous beauty, and of bounty rare,
> With goodly grace and comely personage,
> That was on earth not easie to compare;
> Full of great love; but Cupids wanton snare
> As hell she hated; chaste in worke and will;
> Her necke and brests were ever open bare,
> That ay thereof her babes might sucke their fill;
> The rest was all in yellow robes arayed still.

Charity here is allied to "married Chastity," rather than virginity. Later in the poem Britomart is the representative heroine of the Book of Chastity. Her "charity" is an active virtue: she subdues the forces of lust, then marries Artegall in an alliance of Justice and Mercy to reproduce Spenser's model for married chastity. Britomart's opposite in this connection is Malecasta ("corrupted chastity"), the wanton and lustful lady of the night who entertains in Castle Joyous, and who corresponds exactly to medieval figurations of *cupiditas* as *luxuria* (e.g., *Roman de la Rose;* cf. *Sir Gawain and the Green Knight*).

Shakespeare reflects these associations in his *The Tempest,* where Miranda, who represents the "wonder" of *caritas,* is strongly identified with chastity. In *King Lear* Cordelia, whose love is "nothing," or no-thing, and which knows "no cause," functions also as a representation of charity and married chastity to counter the *cupiditas* and *luxuria* of her sisters. Milton's *Comus* cannot be well understood apart from the tradition which would read the Lady's chastity as a prima facie manifestation of Christian charity (Grant, 82; Tuve, 130ff., 154). Chastity in this light still figures in the valiant struggle of the *miles Christi* to overcome sin in the world — a figuration particularly transparent in Bunyan's *Pilgrim's Progress,* where Charity is one of the virgins who (with Discretion, Prudence, and Piety) arm Christian with the sword and shield of faith.

Other lineaments of biblical and medieval tradition are apparent throughout Renaissance literature. In Henry More's "Charity and Humility," the linkage clearly pertains to self-effacing love for God and then others, a love which for More may never be self-generated because of pride's inevitable complicity. Catholic convert Richard Crashaw's "*Caritas Nimia,* Or the Dear Bargain" is a poem about *agapē,* God's unparalleled and almost incomprehensible love expressed at Calvary. The poet can scarcely reckon with "the bargain":

> If my base lust
> Bargain'd with death and well-beseeming dust,
>   Why should the white
>   Lamb's bosom write
>   The purple name
>   Of my sin's shame?

Crashaw's "On a Treatise of Charity" provides an interesting counter-Reformation reprise of the Reformers' derogation of charity (construed as "works" or "merit") in contrast with "justifying faith." What can happen in such a scorning, says Crashaw, is that all sense of *caritas* love for God as a "sacrifice of the heart" in worship gets lost and love grows cold. He yearns for a spiritual renewal in which the hypocrite will no longer be regarded as "upright . . . / Because he's stiff, and will confess no knee," but rather the altar and its representative sacrifice will once more, even as in biblical times, be central. Then,

> . . . for two turtle-doves, it shall suffice
> To bring a pair of meek and humble eyes;
> This shall from henceforth be the masculine theme
> Pulpits and pens shall sweat in; to redeem
> Virtue to action; that life-feeding flame
> That keeps religion warm; not swell a name
> Of faith, a mountain-word, made up of air,
> With those dear spoils that want to dress the fair
> And fruitful charity's full breasts, of old,
> Turning her out to tremble in the cold.
> What can the poor hope from us? when we be
> Uncharitable even to Charity.

Restoration and 18th-cent. literature tends either to codify the Calvinist and Puritan emphasis, or to define charity against such codifications by appeal to classical and rationalist authors. Matthew Prior's poem "Charity" is a verse paraphrase of 1 Cor. 13, a dialogue in Hudibrastic couplets written, he says, with ideal rational readers like Socrates or Montaigne in mind (*Poems*, 252). On his view, Paul's "charity" is the practice of a temperate balance and mean enjoined by the knowledge that in this world all things are equivocal. Swift's "Letter to a Young Gentleman," advising him on his desire to enter the ministry, adduces Socrates as authoritative on the greatest of the theological virtues, "charity" (his own definition proves indeed to be a blending of Socratic and Pauline wisdom). In his *Sermon on the Trinity* charity is a "duty," as, he says, Socrates teaches (*Sermons*, ed. Landa, 159). In his sermon on "Brotherly Love" charity is prudential temperance, standing firm in the Anglican middle of the road between two enemies, "the Papists and Fanaticks" (Landa, 172). Even John Wesley, whose Methodist "Love Feasts," system-disturbing works of mercy and emotional spirituality, identify him with Swift's "fanaticks," could stress the priority of Love as Christian duty. Advising a correspondent to steer clear of mystics like Boehme, he counsels him to "keep in the plain, open Bible way. Aim at nothing higher, nothing deeper, than the religion described in our Lord's Sermon upon the Mount, and briefly summed up by St. Paul in the 13th chapter to the Corinthians" (*Letters*, 5.342).

For all this apparently unarguable similarity, and the Methodists' intensive involvement in ministries of relief to prisons, mental hospitals, orphanages, and the like, they were keenly disliked by latitudinarian churchmen and their sympathizers both for an apparent Spartan severity and their insistence that faith, not accrued "charity," was the redemptive agent in human salvation. For example, in his sermon "The Nature and Necessity of Self-Denial" (1737), the "Calvinist-Methodist" George Whitefield opposes what a medieval preacher would have called *cupiditas, luxuria,* and *superbia* to "denying our self-will," denying "the pleasurable indulgence and self-enjoyment of riches," and denying "pride of the understanding." What he calls "the medicine of self-denial" is based upon imitation of the self-sacrificing love of Christ, the apostles, and martyrs — their *agapē* or *caritas*. In his homiletic description of "The Almost Christian" (1738) he says of such a person that even his apparently charitable actions proceed "not from any love to God or regard to man, but only out of a principle of self-love — because he knows dishonesty will spoil his reputation and consequently hinder his prosperity in the world." In a style reminiscent of William Law (a major influence upon Whitefield) he adds that the nominal Christian "is no enemy to charitable contributions, if not too frequently requested. But then he is quite unacquainted with the kind offices of 'visiting the sick and inprison'd, clothing the naked, and relieving the hungry' " (ed. Jeffrey, 302).

Latitudinarian preachers such as Isaac Barrow, Archbishop John Tillotson, Bishop Benjamin Hoadley, and Samuel Clark countered such preaching with their own more relaxed doctrines. On their modified Pelagian view, human nature is essentially, not accidentally, benevolent. Salvation is dependent upon active charity, which is "natural to mankind" (although, in a world corrupted and confused by bad custom and miseducation, an inducement of future rewards and punishments seems to be required). Comprehensive and energetic charity is a specific manifestation of "good nature"; such charity is not mere almsgiving but rather "universal love of all mankind, embracing friend and enemy, and limited only by the opportunity, position, or political power of the individual" (i.e., the latitudinarians set off their view also from the proto-positivistic "politic charity" of Hobbes and Mandeville). Like Whitefield they censured self-love (esp. avarice, ambition, vanity, and hypocrisy), but unlike him they stressed the priority of the Epistle of James ("Faith, if it hath not works, is dead" [James 2:17]) over Paul's Epistle to the Ephesians ("For by grace are ye saved through faith; and that not of yourselves: it is the gift of God: Not of works, lest any man should boast" [Eph. 2:8-9]). The "hero of faith" is here a "hero of works," so to speak. The truly heroic individual is not the powerful, wealthy, or prestigious person but the "good man," whose moral superiority is typically described in terms of benevolence (e.g., R. Steele's *The Christian Hero* [2701], *Spectator*, no. 248; Henry Fielding's "Of True Greatness"). Isaac Barrow's sermon "On Being Imitators of Christ" provides a pattern in terms of which one may understand Fielding's preface and opening chapters in *Joseph Andrews* (1742). The historian's task, says Barrow, is to provide examples of the "good man" which emphasize his *chastity* with respect to himself (control of reason over the passions), the biblical model for which is Joseph resisting the advances of Potiphar's wife, and his *charity* with respect to society, the biblical model for which is Abraham, the epitome of faith revealed in works and hence of active charity. But the good historians will depict, says Barrow, human imperfections as well as virtues because a flawless model of righteousness would induce only despair. In *Joseph Andrews* (1.11-13) treatment of the theme of charity is characterized by Parson Abraham Adams, whose recasting of the parable of the Good Samaritan stresses good works rather than faith. Fielding's *Tom Jones* (1749), a "man of good feeling," is less plausibly a representative of chastity. Rather, "no better than he should be," in Fielding's phrase, he progresses from wanton amours toward wisdom ("Sophie" Western), union with whom entails a presumably chaste marriage and a return to Paradise Hall. But for Fielding, as for the latitudinarian divines, a little cupidity is infinitely to be preferred to the slightest whiff of "hypocrisy" or "affectation," which Fielding (in *Shamela* and *Tom Jones*) calls the source of the "truly ridiculous," the laughable but pitiable morality of self-love.

William Cowper's long poem *Charity* (1782) is on the side of Whitefield (whom he admired). Like Hannah More's "Ode to Charity" of the same period, it associates charity less with outward actions of benevolence — though these are discussed in detail — than in terms of an inward peace of relationship with God which overflows into loving actions toward humanity. But if More's pragmatic view of charity is barely tacit in her poem (she was in fact energetic in founding and funding charity schools for children), in the palpably Calvinist Cowper (a virtual recluse) it gets top billing. Like More, Cowper invokes Charity as a muse by whose guidance he will write her praise, lest a writer's vanities should obscure the subject, "whether we name thee Charity or Love." Cowper takes up the theme of the *socius* first: "God, working ever on a social plan, / By various ties attaches man to man" (15-16). His "hero" of charity is the explorer Cook, who

> . . . lamented, and with tears as just
> As ever mingled with heroic dust —
> Steer'd Britain's oak into a world unknown,
> And in his country's glory sought his own,
> Wherever he found man, to nature true,
> The rights of man were sacred in his view.
> He sooth'd with gifts, and greeted with a smile,
> The simple native of the new-found isle. . . .

Cook's antithesis, for Cowper an icon for *cupiditas,* is Cortez, "odious for a world enslav'd." "Mammon makes the world his legatee," he continues: the ugly slave trade is "most degrading of all ills, that wait / On man" (155-56) and an epitome of all that defiles charity and a Christian

name" (179-217). For Calvinist Cowper this is the effect of innate depravity, which revelation (if not reason) shows to be the true opponent of charity (337-44); Socrates therefore must be corrected by Scripture:

> Philosophy, without his heave'nly guide,
> May blow up self-conceit, and nourish pride;
> But, while his province is the reas'ning part,
> Has still a veil of midnight on his heart;
> 'Tis truth divine, exhibited on earth,
> Gives Charity her being and her birth. (373-78)

Here he means *agapē*, charity in the older sense, which is then celebrated in an extended paraphrase of 1 Cor. 13 (412-34). True charity must thus be distinguished from alms (447-68); indeed, the motivation for "subscription" from wealthy donors is suspect (469-84), and even what sum is collected "the office clips as it goes." For what is commonly called "charity" to be meritorious, and not merely affectation, vanity, and hypocrisy, it must be an overflowing of *caritas:*

> No works shall find acceptance, in that day
> When all disguises shall be rent away,
> That square not truly with the scripture plan,
> Nor spring from love to God, or love to man. . . .
> True charity, a plant divinely nurs'd,
> Fed by the love from which it rose at first,
> Thrives against hope; and, in the rudest scene,
> Storms but enliven its unfading green;
> Exub'rant is the shadow it supplies;
> Its fruit on earth, its growth above the skies. (557-60; 573-78)

What Cowper wishes to do, in effect, is to affirm Whitefield's "charity" against that of the Latitudinarians, rooting the meaning of charity in the primary relationship between the individual and God rather than between the individual and his neighbor. In this he was consistent with the raison d'être of "charitable" social reforms among the 18th-cent. Methodists and even with the usage of closet-Catholic Christopher Smart, in whose (most charitable) poetry charity is an axiom of gratitude, the root of all virtues (cf. Aquinas):

> Thus in high heaven charity is great,
> Faith, hope, devotion hold a lower place;
> On her the cherubs and the seraphs wait,
> Her, every virtue courts, and every grace;
> See! on the right, close by th' Almighty's throne,
> In him she shines confest, who came to make her known.
>
> Deep-rooted in my heart then let her grow,
> That for the past the future may atone;
> That I may act what thou hast giv'n to know,
> That I may live for THEE and THEE alone,
> And justify those sweetest words from heav'n,
> "THAT HE SHALL LOVE THEE MOST TO WHOM THOU'ST MOST FORGIVEN."

Smart said elsewhere, in more medieval fashion than

perhaps he knew: "For I have translated in the charity, which makes things / better & I shall be translated myself at the last" (*Jubilate Agno*). But desire to achieve the goals of charity as benevolence without the encumbrance of religious characterizations of social responsibility were growing stronger. Jeremy Bentham, with his plan to reform the British Poor Law (1795) and plans to create a modern welfare state, finds "charity" *ab initio* a distasteful and even demeaning term. For Bentham, the function of a "national charity company" is not to dispense kindness or generosity, but to accord basic human rights (Bahmueller).

For the most part, Romantic poetry lacks interest in charity defined as benevolence or alms. On the other hand, love is a primary subject, both in its divine and human modes of expression. Wordsworth's very conception of the poet, in his preface to *Lyrical Ballads* (1802), is "the rock of defence of human nature; an upholder and preserver, carrying everywhere with him relationship and love" (ed. Zall, 52). But the "love" of Romantic poetry is hard to identify with the *agapē* or *caritas* of Christian tradition; even when it draws upon mystical Christian writers like Jacob Boehme, Romantic "love" is rather the integrative force binding the disparities of individual and community experience together in a comprehension, however vaguely formulated, of the divine purpose in Creation. To this ideal of love, narrow *Selbheit* (Boehme) or *Ichheit* (Schelling) is still, like self-centeredness, the technical opposite to unitive love (Abrams, 294-97). But the means by which the Romantic poet transcends his ego is not worship; it is what Shelley calls "the expression of the imagination." In his *Defence of Poetry* (1821),

> The great secret of morals is love, or a going out of our own nature and an identification of ourselves with the beautiful which exists in thought, action, or person, not our own. A man, to be greatly good, must imagine intensely and comprehensively; he must put himself in the place of another and of many others; the pains and pleasures of his species must become his own. The great instrument of moral good is the imagination. . . . Poetry enlarges the circumference of the imagination. (Ed. Clark, 277, 282-83)

In other words, the "good" and hence heroic person manifests love not in active works of benevolence or alms, but rather — in a curious but perhaps predictable sentimentalizing of the Latitudinarians and Methodists both — by vicarious imagination of the plight of the less fortunate. But in the usage of Romantic poets, Shelley and Byron in particular, "love" covers "a multitude of sins," often by becoming a name for many of them. If Coleridge takes *philia*, friendship, to be the paradigm for "love," Shelley is more visceral. As he puts it,

> That profound and complicated sentiment which we call love . . . is rather the universal thirst for a communion not merely of the senses but of our whole nature, intellectual,

imaginative, and sensitive. . . . This want grows more powerful in proportion to the development which our nature receives from civilization, for man never ceases to be a social being. The sexual impulse, which is only one and often a small part of these claims, serves from its obvious and external nature as a kind of type or expression of the rest, as common basis, an acknowledged and visible link. ("On the Manners of the Ancient Greeks")

Thus, according to M. H. Abrams,

> In the broad Romantic application of the term love . . . all modes of human attraction are conceived as one in kind, different only in object and degree, in a range which includes the relations of lover to beloved, children to parents, brother to sister, friend to friend, and individual to humanity. The orbit of love was often enlarged to include the relationship of man to nature as well. (*Natural Supernaturalism*, 297)

Here one returns to Gk. *erōs*. Augustine's basic distinction *caritas / cupiditas* is accordingly by this point not only blurred but in some instances reversed. Further, the laissez-faire morality of Shelley or Byron comes to have its counterpart in broader social terms, leading writers such as Carlyle (in *Past and Present*) to lament "our present system of individual Mammonism" in which "cash payment is . . . the sole nexus of man with man." None of this has to do with love, Carlyle insists, only with the lust of meaner desires (*Works*, 10.257, 272-74). Each of these developments complicates thought about "charity" for Victorian Christians, without doing much to clarify cupidity or another contrastive vice. Charity thus becomes what Matthew Arnold would call a "problem"; preoccupation with the virtues of vicarious identification often produces ethically evasive exegesis. An example is provided by Ruskin, who writes:

> You know how often it is difficult to be wisely charitable, to do good without multiplying the sources of evil. You know that to give alms is nothing unless you give thought also; and that therefore it is written, not "blessed is he that *feedeth* the poor," but "blessed is he that *considereth* the poor." And you know that a little thought and a little kindness are often worth more than a great deal of money. Now this charity of thought is not to be exercised toward all men. There is assuredly no action of our social life, however unimportant, which, by kindly thought, may not be made to have a beneficial influence upon others; and it is impossible to spend the smallest sum of money, for any not absolutely necessary purpose, without a grave responsibility attaching to the manner of spending it.

Ruskin goes on to talk about consumer "ethics," about whether "the sum we are going to spend will do as much good spent in this way as it would if spent in any other way" (*Lectures on Architecture and Painting*, 44). But Ruskin is also able to indicate succinctly the self-serving rationalizations (quite well) anticipated by Bentham:

> We have heard only too much lately of "indiscriminate charity," with implied reproval, not of the Indiscrimina-

tion merely, but of the Charity also. We have partly succeeded in enforcing on the minds of the poor the idea that
it is disgraceful to receive; and are likely, without too
much difficulty, to succeed in persuading not a few of the
rich that it is disgraceful to give. (*Munera Pulveris,* Appendix 6)

Charles Dickens, in his *A Christmas Carol* (1843), set
out to contrast cupidity and charity in terms practical
enough that the dangerous ephemerality of this debate
should become clear, but had only limited success. In such
an environment, "charity" soon gave *caritas* a bad name.
George Bernard Shaw, a Fabian Socialist, was among
those who later rejected the concept as misnomer, exploring as alternative values the grand idealism of a Christian
socialist clergyman in *Candida* (1898), and a naive but
well-motivated Salvation Army charity in *Major Barbara*
(1907) — a play which not only satirizes the disguising
of self-interest as "duty," but teaches that "poverty is the
worst of crimes" and that the *lack* of money is the root of
all evil. Shaw's impatience with traditional Christian notions of charity surfaces again in *The Intelligent Woman's
Guide to Capitalism and Socialism* (1928). (G. K. Chesterton's book-length study of his friend continues a debate
over the subject which had been at the core of their testy
friendship for many years.)

The Romantics' strong desire to find in idealized love
(amor/erōs) the unifying and integrating of all experience
had been notoriously sidetracked into erotic confusions
of that purpose. Yet their idealism persists in a significant
strain of religious as well as secular poetry. The erotic
mysticism of Christina Rosetti, with its theme of the
spectre bride or bridegroom *(The Hour and the Ghost;
The Ghost's Petition),* and her sublimation of sexual
desire as the pilgrim's longing for "a better country" (cf.
Heb. 11:13-16) in *Marvel of Marvels* and *Passing away,
saith the World* lend to the traditional medieval language
of *caritas* eerily erotic overtones precisely inverse in their
function to the de-eroticizing allegories of the Song of
Songs by St. Bernard of Clairvaux. Patmore's postconversion poetry (he became a Catholic in 1864) similarly blurs *agapē* and *erōs* (e.g., *The Unknown Eros* [1877]),
to the point where his spiritual advisers asked him to
destroy a long MS, his *Sponsa Dei,* in which the confusion
had apparently become identification.

The orthodox English poet of the modern period has
thus had two misprisions to answer. These are the Enlightenment tendency to split charity as benevolence to
the neighbor off from its roots in *caritas* as love directed
toward God above all things, and the Romantic and post-
Romantic tendency to dissolve the distinction in a cosmic
love so ambiguous that *erōs* or *cupiditas* can be its most
apparent vital expression (cf. D. H. Lawrence's *Apocalypse*). In strikingly diverse poets the strategy has been
similar: to try to re-establish the vertical or hierarchical
relation of the precepts of the Great Commandment so
that, in typical Augustinian fashion, *caritas* in the com-

munity of men and women is comprehensible only in
terms of its referential governance by each person's prior
love for God. Thus John Keble's "Charity the Life of
Faith" (*The Christian Year* [1827]) takes as its epigraph
1 John 3:13-14: "We know that we have passed from
death unto life, because we love the brethren." The test of
regeneration, the presence of supreme love for God and
not self, is love for those who love him also. To do this
is, in effect, to love Christ both in his divine and human
nature:

> Wouldst thou the life of souls discern?
> Nor human wisdom nor divine
> Helps thee by aught beside to learn:
> Love is life's only sign.
> The spring of the regenerate heart,
> The pulse, the glow of every part,
> Is the true love of Christ our Lord,
> As man embrac'd, as God ador'd.

But this is what T. S. Eliot also says in *The Four Quartets.*
The "liberation" from cupiditous "attachment to self and
to things and to persons," he writes, lies in a type of love
which is "not less of love but expanding / Of love beyond
desire, and so liberation / From the future as well as the
past." When this love is shared abroad, then, all people,
even Englishmen like those who fought bloody (religious) civil wars, will be "folded in a single party," and
"All manner of thing shall be well / By the purification
of our motive / In the ground of our beseeching" ("Little
Gidding," 3). In other words, desire itself shall be
redeemed.

See also GOOD SAMARITAN; GREAT COMMANDMENT;
HORTUS CONCLUSUS; VIRGINITY, CHASTITY.

Bibliography. Abrams, M. H. *Natural Supernaturalism:
Tradition and Revolution in Romantic Literature* (1971);
Bahmueller, C. F. *The National Charity Company: Jeremy
Bentham's Silent Revolution* (1981); Graham, G. *The Idea of
Christian Charity: A Critique of Some Contemporary Con-
ceptions* (1990); Grant, P. *Images and Ideas of the English
Renaissance* (1979); Jayne, S. "The Subject of Milton's Lud-
low *Mask*." In *A Maske at Ludlow,* ed. J. S. Diekhoff; Jeffrey,
D. L., ed. *A Burning and a Shining Light: English Spirituality
in the Age of Wesley* (1987); Jeffrey, D. L., ed. *The Law of
Love: English Spirituality in the Age of Wyclif* (1988);
Miller, P., ed. *The American Puritans* (1956); Moffatt, J.
Love in the New Testament (1929); Nygren, A. *Agape and
Eros* (trans. 1953); Quinsey, K. M. "'Am'rous Charity': *Eros*
and *Agape* in *Eloisa to Abeland.*" *Renascence: Essays on
Value in Literature* 39 (1987), 407-20; Robertson, D. W., Jr.
"The Doctrine of Charity in Medieval Literary Gardens."
Essays in Medieval Culture (1980), 22-50; Smith, B. H., Jr.
Traditional Imagery of Charity in Piers Plowman (1966);
Spicq, C. *Agape.* 2 vols. (1958); Tuve, R. *Images and
Themes in Five Poems by Milton* (1957); *Allegorical Im-
agery: Some Medieval Poets and their Posterity* (1966).

CHASTITY *See* VIRGINITY, CHASTITY; CHARITY, CUPID-
ITY.

CHILDREN The relationship between God and his chosen people, often described in the Bible as a marriage, is also figured in terms of a parent-child relationship (e.g., Deut. 14:1; see also Pss. 73:15; 103:13). Occasionally in the OT Gentiles are also referred to as children of God (e.g., Isa. 45:11). In the NT what the Israelites were by birthright Gentile Christians, according to the apostle Paul, could hope to be by adoption: "He hath chosen us. . . . Having predestinated us unto the adoption of children by Jesus Christ to himself" (Eph. 1:4-5; see also Rom. 8:15-23; Gal. 4:5). Just as there are children of the flesh, then, so there are also "children of the promise," and these may be as Isaac was to Ishmael — "not children of the bondwoman, but of the free" (Gal. 4:22-31).

The injunction to "honour thy father and thy mother" is prominent among the Ten Commandments and the first commandment with a promise attached. Dependence, trust, and humility are taken as normative in a child's relationship to his or her parents and, indeed, in that of the children of God to their heavenly Father: "LORD my heart is not haughty, nor mine eyes lofty . . . as a child that is weaned of his mother: my soul is even as a weaned child" (Ps. 131:2). Thus, when Jeremiah was called by God, he pleaded inadequacy in terms of childlike dependence: "Ah, Lord GOD! behold, I cannot speak: for I am a child." Exemplary obedience and trust are likewise emphasized in the story of the child Samuel, as well as in canonical accounts of Jesus' childhood. (Extrabiblical childhood narratives, by contrast, are concerned to demonstrate that Jesus' divine powers were already present in his early years.) Such qualities are also assumed in Christ's words, "Suffer the little children to come unto me, and forbid them not: for of such is the kingdom of God" (Mark 10:13-16; cf. Matt. 11:25; 18:3). It was a child whom St. Augustine heard in his garden, saying, *"Tolle, lege; tolle, lege"* ("Take it up, read; take it up, read") (*Conf.,* bk. 8). Since Augustine was struggling at this time against (among other things) his Manichaean desires for special knowledge, the child seems to recall not only humility like Jeremiah's but also the biblical tradition of divine wisdom which is often seen as foolishness in the eyes of the world (1 Cor. 1:18-27).

In English literary tradition Vaughan, Traherne, Herbert, Herrick, and Crashaw among others adopt a posture of comparable humility: each writes poems using a child, or a childlike persona (see, e.g., Herrick's "To his Saviour, a Child; a Present, by a Child" and Herbert's "H. Baptisme II"). Chaucer's Prioress, too, wants to be seen as a participant in this tradition. She realizes that God can be praised "by the mouth of children" as well as "by men of dignitee" (Prologue to the *Prioress's Tale*) and so hopes that, like the child in her tale, she might sing a song of praise. But since she neglects her adult and spiritual responsibilities, the apostle Paul probably provides the aptest gloss: "In malice be ye children, but in understanding be ye men" (1 Cor. 14:20; cf. Matt. 10:16). Paul is expressing his displeasure that the Corinthians are still spiritual children at a time when they ought to have developed in the faith. As Augustine puts it, "Let your old age be childlike, and your childhood like old age; that is, that neither may your wisdom be with pride, nor your humility without wisdom" (*Enarr. in Ps.* 113.2 [NPNF 8.548]; see also *Enarr. in Ps.* 131.5 [NPNF 8.615]).

The Bible has little to say about the innocence of children. Even Christ's "Except you be converted, and become as little children" (Matt. 18:3) has more to do with humility and obedience than innocence per se. In traditional Christian thought, innocence is attached to infancy but not to childhood. The infant, although guilty of original sin, has not the capacity to turn the inclination to sin into actual sin; hence the phrase "the slaughter of the innocents" used of Herod's murder of infants (cf. Augustine's comment that "the infant's innocence lies in the weakness of his body and not in the infant mind" (*Conf.,* bk. 1).

The notion of childhood innocence arose in connection with the Enlightenment's rejection of the doctrine of original sin and belief in naturally good human nature being perverted by evil social customs. Rousseau's *Emile* is the key statement of this view, although Locke's philosophy of education had already shifted the understanding of human nature away from original sin to human potentialities and so made the education of children more important — because more promising — than hitherto. Wordsworth's "Intimations of Immortality from Recollections of Early Childhood" is an important Romantic expression of the Enlightenment view of childhood, as are Blake's "Songs of Innocence" and "Songs of Experience," which together reflect the author's gnostic belief that good has to encompass evil but that innocence can be recovered on a higher level of inclusive gnosis.

Victorian literature is characterized by a sentimental view of children. Many of Dickens's child protagonists, embodying a kind of Edenic innocence, act as parents to their elders, protecting adults who have become victims of an evil environment. Thus Little Nell in *The Old Curiosity Shop* embodies both the tradition of the innocence of the child — being contrasted with the evil Quilp and with all the ancient instruments of war which surround her in the Shop — and the tradition of the wisdom of the child — as in her reversing roles with her grandfather (chaps. 15 and 16).

By the end of the 19th cent., reaction to Victorian sentimentality gave rise to a more realistic (and sometimes Christian) portrayal of children as by nature inclined to evil rather than good and deserving to be made accountable for their actions. Literary examples of this changed attitude include Harry Graham's *Ruthless Rhymes for Heartless Homes,* Hilaire Belloc's *Bad Child's Book of Beasts* and *More Beasts for Worse Children,* and the stories of P. G. Wodehouse. Wodehouse's early school stories show children as displaying the same good and evil characteristics found in adults. Increasingly, though, his fiction portrays children as consistently adult in their capacity for evil but lacking in adult social conscience. Wodehouse's spirited female adults encourage girl children to act on their antisocial impulses. His male adults view with dismay the destructive deeds of their boy counterparts, often expressing sympathy for Herod's solution to the problem of their continued existence.

Freud's theories of sexuality in infants support the new antisentimental view of childhood innocence which is reflected in such books as Richard Hughes's *High Wind in Jamaica*. William Golding's *Lord of the Flies* is in the same tradition, having been written, the author says, as a deliberate refutation of the view of boyhood projected in R. M. Ballantyne's popular adventure story, *Coral Island* (1858).

See also JESUS CHRIST, CHILDHOOD OF; OUT OF THE MOUTH OF BABES.

Bibliography. d'Ariès, P. *Centuries of Childhood* (1962); Marcus, L. S. *Childhood and Cultural Despair: A Theme and Variations in Seventeenth Century Literature* (1978); Stone, H. *Dickens and the Invisible World* (1979); Walquist, D. J. "The Best Copy of Adam: Seventeenth-Century Attitudes Toward Childhood and the Poetry of Donne, Herbert, Vaughan, and Traherne." *DAI* 39 (1979), 6785A.   H. DAVID BRUMBLE

CHILDREN OF LIGHT The phrase "children of light" appears notably four times in the NT, each time to denote those who follow Jesus, having thus been "enlightened" by the light which has come into the world (cf. John 1:4-5). In each of these passages (Luke 16:8; John 12:35-36; Eph. 5:8; 1 Thess. 5:5) the "children of light" are contrasted with the "children of this world" (Luke 16:8), "children of disobedience" (Eph. 5:8), or those who "walk in darkness" (John 12:35), and the context is such as to exhort believers to distinguish themselves by a seriousness of commitment to their future hope in Christ. This contrast parallels the rabbinic distinction between "sons of the age to come" and "sons of this age" or generation (*TDNT* 1.206), though the phrase "sons of light" as such is not used by the rabbis, but is Palestinian (H. Braun, *Qumran und das Neue Testament* [1966], 1.90-91).

Among these passages the one which has acquired the most controversial status is the parable of the unjust steward (Luke 16:1-13). Here a lazy and wasteful steward is called to account by his overseer. Seeing that he is about to lose his employment, the unjust steward craftily calls in all the debts owed to his master, quickly discharging them for a fraction of the amount owing. Astoundingly, the overseer "commended the unjust steward, because he had done wisely: for the children of this world are in their generation wiser than the children of light" (v. 8).

For most patristic commentators the parable proved awkward and the phrase received strikingly little early commentary. Traditional medieval interpretation is sum-

marized by the *Glossa Ordinaria,* which says that the overseer in the story praises the unjust steward for his prudence in looking out for his future, not for the fraud which has characterized his past and present actions; further, it illustrates that Christ is more prone to mercy than to the judgment which sin so obviously merits. Nonetheless the *filii huius saeculi* are clearly the children of darkness *(tenebrarum)* whereas the *filii lucis* are destined to eternal life (PL 114.314). The "light" is typically identified by medieval commentary with belief, so that "children of light" becomes a synonym for credal believers, both in commentary (e.g., on John 12:36) and in baptismal liturgy (cf. *Glossa* [PL 114.403]). Calvin dismisses the fragmentary allegorizing of details by some patristic commentators and essentially follows the general path established in later medieval commentary, but with an added dimension which harkens back to the "summary of the law" (Deut. 6:5). "The sum of this parable is that we must treat our neighbors humanely and kindly, so that when we come before God's judgment seat, we may receive the fruit of our liberality" (*New Testament Commentaries,* trans. T. Parker [1972], 2.111). In treating Luke 16:8 he confronts the apparent ethical conflict in the overseer's commendation by intensifying his focus on the overseer's intention (rather than adopting the Gloss's inference about Christ's mercy):

> There is nothing laudable in giving away other men's goods; and who would put up with a dishonest rascal robbing him and letting off his debtors at will? It would be too crass altogether for a man to see part of his possessions embezzled and the rest given away by the thief, and then approve of it. But all Christ meant was, as He adds just after, that heathen and worldly men are more industrious and clever in taking care of the ways and means of this fleeting world than God's children are in caring for the heavenly and eternal life, or making it their study and exercise. By this comparison He reproves our worse than spineless laziness that we do not at least have the same eye to the future that heathen men have to feathering their nests in this world. How wicked it is that the children of light, on whom God shines by his spirit and his Word, should sleep and neglect the hope of everlasting bliss offered to them, when greedy, worldly men are so devoted to their own interests, so far-sighted and shrewd!

The shift in Protestant commentary away from seeing the parable as an allegory about the extent of God's mercy is completed in Matthew Henry's early 18th-cent. reading, in which the parable is taken to be principally concerned with the duties of all Christians as "stewards of the manifold grace of God." Henry's opening remarks (*Comm. on the Whole Bible,* 5.752) anticipate his entire (extensive) reading:

> We mistake if we imagine that the design of Christ's doctrine and holy religion was either to amuse us with notions of divine mysteries or to entertain us with notions

of divine mercies. No, the divine revelation of both these in the gospel is intended to engage and quicken us to the practice of Christian duties, and, as much as any one thing, to the duty of beneficence and doing good to those who stand in need of any thing that either we have or can do for them.

Henry goes on to make the management of money the application or moral for the children of light, taking his cue from v. 9: "Make to yourselves friends of the mammon of unrighteousness, as the steward with his lord's goods made his lord's tenants his friends." He regards the intent of the parable to be pecunious:

It is the wisdom of the men of this world so to manage their money as that they may have the benefit of it hereafter, and not for the present only; therefore they put it out to interest, buy land with it, put it into this or the other fund. Now we should learn of them to make use of our money so as that we may be the better for it hereafter in another world, as they do in hopes to be the better for it hereafter in this world. (5.754)

Ideally, sound practical stewardship of one's money, says Henry, will result in an estate passed on "for the honour of God and the good of our brethren, that thus we may with them *lay up in store a good bond,* a good security, a good foundation *for the time to come,* for an eternity to come. See 1 Tim. VI.17-19, which explains this here."

The potential of the parable thus construed to lead to preaching of confused distinction seems to have been realized more than once by the 19th cent., at which time literary allusions commence in earnest. In his *Castles in Spain* Galsworthy seems to ponder the matter: "One could not help wondering," he writes, "wherein lay the superiority of ourselves, Children of Light, over those old Sons of Darkness." A different sort of imperialism (and more likely the reference in John 12:36) prompts Arnold in *Culture and Anarchy* to an ironic dismissal: "The characteristic . . . proper to aristocracies . . . points to our extending to this class also the designation of Philistines; the Philistine being, as is well known, the enemy of the children of light or servant of the idea" ("Barbarians, Philistines, Populace"). In the *Letters of Henry Adams* the Philistines are "capitalists" who "protect themselves . . . and are wiser than these children of light" (1.304). For Yeats, in his essay "The Irish Dramatic Movement," it is "the great realists [who] seem to the lovers of beautiful art to be wise in this generation, and for the next generation, perhaps, but not for all generations that are to come" — an apposite situating of the "children of light" which is curiously contrasted by G. K. Chesterton's critical observations on the social realism of Dickens: "In no dishonorable sense, but still in a definite sense, he might, in early life, be called worldly; and the children of this world are in their generation infinitely more sensitive than the children of light" (*Charles Dickens,* chap. 2). Somerset Maugham's attribution to the "wise in their genera-

tion" of the discovery that "intellectual pleasure is the most satisfying and most enduring" (*Books and You,* chap. 1), if hardly consistent with the chief distinctions of the parable or Chesterton's compliment to Dickens, anticipates the self-congratulatory identification of Edwin Arlington Robinson's poem "The Children of the Night," in which an odyssey of religious doubt is held to be distinctly preferable to piety or credulous belief. Robinson concludes his exhortation with an apparent allusion (cf. 1 Thess. 5:5):

Let us, the Children of the Night,
Put off the cloak that hides the scar!
Let us be Children of the Light
And tell the ages what we are.

A more palpable indebtedness to the parable in Luke 16 is explicit in Joyce's story "Grace" *(Dubliners).* The Jesuit priest sees his text (vv. 8-9) as ideally "adapted for the guidance" of "business men and professional men," before whom he would set "as exemplars in the religious life those very worshippers of Mammon who were of all men the least solicitous in matters religious." His theme, it turns out, is stewardship, his purpose to call his "commercial" hearers to a spiritual accounting, so that "with God's grace" they may be implored to "set right" their accounts. Dorothy Sayers's *The Nine Tailors* offers, it seems, the one modern literary interpretation in which the simple distinction between blameworthy stewardship and praiseworthy prudence is vividly maintained:

But quickness in the 'ed don't mean a good 'eart. There's many evil men is as quick as monkeys. Didn't the good Lord say as much? *The children o' this world is wiser in their generation than the children o' the light.* He commended the *unjust steward,* no doubt, but he give the fellow the sack just the same, none the more for that.

See also UNPROFITABLE SERVANT, PARABLE OF.

CHILDREN OF THE NIGHT   *See* CHILDREN OF LIGHT.

CHRISTMAS   The Feast of the Nativity of Christ was called in OE *Cristes Maesse,* the Mass of Christ; the first appearance of this term in extant writing dates to the 11th cent., and parallels Dutch *Kerst-misse.* (The Latin term *Dies natalis* lies behind Ital. *Il natale* and possibly Fr. *Noel,* though Ger. *Weihnachtsfest* is named for the preceding "eve," or "vigil." Yule may derive simply from OE *geola,* a feast — though this is by no means certain.)

However surprising to modern perspectives, Christmas was not celebrated in the early Church. Probably in reaction to the discreditable "birthday" feasts *(natalitia)* of Roman emperors, Origen asserts that in the Bible only the unregenerate celebrate such festivals (*Hom.* on Leviticus, 8). St. Irenaeus and Tertullian do not show a Feast of the Nativity on their lists of Christian celebrations. Interest in assigning a date for the birth of Jesus grew slowly after the 3rd cent., though it was still being opposed by

St. Jerome after 410 (*Comm. in Ezechielem* [PL 25.18]). By 386 St. John Chrysostom had urged the church in Antioch to agree upon Dec. 25 as a day for celebrating the Nativity, and in Rome the Philocalian calendar (A.D. 354) includes under Dec. 25, opposite the pagan *Natalis invicti*, or "birth of the unconquered (sun)," the phrase *"VIII kaali ian natus Christus in Bethleem Iudea."* Thus, without any warrant in the Gospels for it, by the time of St. Augustine the date of the Feast of the Nativity had been established, over the opposition of those like Jerome who denigrated the celebration on principle. Augustine himself omits it from his list of important Christian observances (PL 33.200). The role of the competing solar cult, with its feast of *Natalis invicti,* had presumably a foundational relationship to the date; Chrysostom, acknowledging the coincidence, writes: "But our Lord, too, is born in the month of December . . . the eighth before the Kalends of January [i.e., Dec. 25]. . . . But they [the Romans] call it the 'Birthday of the Unconquered'. Who indeed is so unconquered as our Lord? . . . Or, if they say that it is the birthday of the Sun, [we may say] He is the Sun of Justice" (*Of Solstices and the Equinox,* 2.118). Though later *Sol iustitia* would become a synonym for Christ. Tertullian (*Apologia,* 16), Origen (*Contra Celsum,* 8.67), and St. Augustine (*In Joan. Ev.* 34) all denounced identification of Christ with the pagan Sol as heretical, and Pope Leo I reproved customs which he understood to be syncretistic, such as turning toward the rising sun before entering church (*Sermo in Natalis Domini,* 27.7.4; cf. 22.2.6).

Christmas, as it has come to be known in the English-speaking world, owes much of its biblical tradition at least to St. Francis and the influence of Franciscan spirituality on later medieval popular literature, notably the lyric (including the medieval carol) and drama. Francis in 1223 obtained permission for the first *crèche* and nativity pageant in church. Before this time only liturgical tropes (e.g., the *Quem Quaeritis*) and two or three early hymns on the Incarnation by Prudentius (4th cent.) and Sedulius (5th cent.) could be called "Christmas literature." The earliest noels are 11th cent., and the earliest *Weihnachtslieder,* 11th- and 12th-cent. Franciscan friar Jacoponi's influential *"Stabat Mater Speciosa,"* recounting the joy of Mary at the birth of Jesus, is late 13th cent., with its ME imitations a century later.

These developments were not without their own additional syncretism: boar's head carols, yule songs, the ME "Holly and Ivy" song, the legend of Joseph of Arimathea's rod flowering at Glastonbury, mistletoe, the putting out of a sheaf of grain on Christmas eve to be imbued with fertility from the dew of Holy Night — all these customs are evident carryovers from druidical lore and legend. The 15th and 16th cents., as the annals of the English carol illustrate, are the high-water mark of such blendings of observance, and the boisterousness of the resulting popular celebrations as much as the influence of Calvin's

sympathy for Jerome led the English Puritans to forbid celebration of Christmas by an Act of Parliament in 1647. The day was to be a fast, not a feast; shops and businesses were required to be open; and the selling of traditional plum puddings and mince pies was condemned as a heathen and even blasphemous indulgence.

The Christmas tree, associated with Luther and in general use in Strassburg by the 17th cent., was not introduced into England until the 1840s, via the Prince Consort. It is in this period especially that romanticization and secularizing of Christmas — perhaps best exemplified in works such as Charles Dickens's *A Christmas Carol* and later Dylan Thomas's "A Child's Christmas in Wales" — produced both in England and America a profuse and sentimental literature of Christmas. Little of this literature is connected in more than superficial fashion with the Feast of the Nativity. Nevertheless, continuing celebration of Christmas on Dec. 25 has ensured the popularity of a much larger body of poetry, drama, fiction, and hymnody to which the events surrounding Christ's birth are central.

See also ADVENT; ANNUNCIATION; INCARNATION; JOSEPH THE CARPENTER; MAGI; MARY, MOTHER OF JESUS; NATIVITY.

CIRCUMCISION Circumcision is an operation in which part or all of the foreskin covering the glans penis is removed. It dates to prehistoric times and was practiced among various peoples. In biblical tradition, circumcision as a Jewish religious ritual of initiation (Heb. *berit milah*) began with Abraham, who, at the age of ninety-nine, circumcised himself in fulfillment of a divine commandment which also propounded a general law:

> And God said unto Abraham, Thou shalt keep my covenant therefore, thou, and thy seed after thee in their generations. This is my covenant, which ye shall keep, between me and you and thy seed after thee; Every man child among you shall be circumcised. And ye shall circumcise the flesh of your foreskin; and it shall be a token of the covenant betwixt me and you. And he that is eight days old shall be circumcised among you, every man child in your generations. (Gen. 17:9-12)

In later haggadic legend, the birth of a patriarch or other remarkable male person already "circumcised" in the womb becomes a common theme. Adam, Seth, Enoch, Noah, Melchizedek, Shem, Terah, Joseph, Moses, Balaam, Samuel, David, Isaiah, and Jeremiah are among those to whom this natal condition is ascribed ('Abot R. Nat. 1.12; 2.2; Gen. Rab. 11.6; 46.3, etc.). The most memorable of such births is that of Jacob, since while he is said to have been born circumcised, his twin brother Esau was not (Midr. Tehillim 9.84; Tan. Ber. 32; Tan. Noah 5).

In keeping with Jewish law, Christ was circumcised and named when he was eight days old (Luke 2:21; cf.

1:31). The traditional date of Christ's circumcision is held to have been January 1, which is marked in the Roman liturgical calendar by the celebration of the Feast of Circumcision. In the early Christian Church circumcision ceased to be a sign of election, as St. Paul explains: "For in Jesus Christ neither circumcision availeth any thing, nor uncircumcision; but faith which worketh by love" (Gal. 5:6; cf. Rom. 3:28-29). Here, as elsewhere in the NT, the OT commonplace discriminating between Jews and Gentiles as "the circumcised" versus "the uncircumcised" (i.e., the godly versus the ungodly) has been transcended (see Judg. 14:3; 1 Sam. 14:6, etc.; cf. Rom. 3:1, 9, 30). This development is partially anticipated in the OT, which refers to "uncircumcised hearts" (e.g., Lev. 26:41; Deut. 10:16; 30:6); and by the OT prophets, who use the term "uncircumcised" figuratively, in reference to the "heart" or "ear" of the unrighteous, Jew or Gentile (e.g., Jer. 6:10; Ezek. 44:1, 9; etc.).

St. Augustine states that circumcision was instituted as a material and visible sign of spiritual regeneration (*De civ. Dei* 15.16), and then develops the view, in line with the teaching of Paul, that after the Atonement the redemptive and regenerating force of circumcision has been superseded (16.27). Faith in God and God's grace obviate circumcision, and Augustine maintains that even under the Old Law "Abraham believed and his faith was reputed to him 'as justice'" before he was circumcised (16.23). Of the rite's sacramental and typological symbolism, Augustine writes (16.26):

> . . . what circumcision symbolizes is that something old is put off in order that nature may be renewed. What the eighth day means is that Christ rose from the dead when the week was over, that is to say, on the day after the Sabbath. . . . It is the new covenant being foreshadowed in the old.

Similarly, St. Jerome in his homilies refers to the "spiritual circumcision" which obtains "among the Gentiles," while Rabanus Maurus explains that the rite of circumcision prefigured the sacrament of baptism which replaced it (*Comm. in Genesim*, 3.1 [PL 107.561-62]). The view that circumcision was meant to restrain carnal desire and was also a figure of, and ultimately replaced by, the sacrament of baptism is found in Aquinas: "For just as circumcision removed a carnal pelicule, so Baptism despoils a man of carnal behaviour" (*Summa Theol.* 3.70.1).

For Luther, the rite of circumcision was one of those "certain accidental, physical, external temporal matters, which it is right to consider worldly, not comparable with the articles of faith, and not to be kept as a permanent law, for they have passed and fallen out of use" ("On the Councils and the Church"). Calvin's view of the matter is similar, but more reminiscent of earlier formulations:

> . . . whatever belongs to circumcision pertains likewise to baptism. . . . For circumcision was for the Jews their first

entry into the church. . . . In like manner we are consecrated to God through baptism. . . . By this it appears incontrovertible that baptism has taken the place of circumcision to fulfill the same office among us. (*Inst.* 4.16.3)

In English literature, references to circumcision are relatively few and overt uses of the theme of circumcision are even fewer. A possible exception, oblique but significant, occurs in the ME verse romance of *Sir Gawain and the Green Knight* (ca. 1375), in which the hero undergoes a series of tests that culminates when — on January 1, the Feast of the Circumcision — he is "nicked on the neck" by the blade of an axe wielded by a supernatural "Green Knight." It has often been suggested that *Sir Gawain and the Green Knight* is best understood as a kind of ritual of initiation. If this is indeed the case, it is more than likely that the setting of its opening and closing key events on two January firsts contains an implicit reference to the circumcision ritual and its symbolic significance.

A more explicit allusion to circumcision occurs in Shakespeare's *Othello* (1603-04), where Othello reverses the cliché of the Saracen who curses a Christian as an "uncircumcised dog." Just before taking his own life, the protagonist says:

> . . . set you down this,
> And say besides, that in Aleppo once,
> Where a malignant and a turban'd Turk
> Beat a Venetian, and traduc'd the state,
> I took by the throat the circumcised dog,
> And smote him thus. (5.2.354-56)

Milton's poem "Upon the Circumcision" is held to have been written in 1633, on or about January 1, the day commemorating the event in the church's calendar which it treats. Using the stanza from Petrarch's *canzone* to the Blessed Virgin, it celebrates Christ's circumcision, looking back to the Nativity and forward to the Passion. Milton feels and tries to convey the pain which Christ felt: "He who with all Heav'ns heraldry whilere / Enter'd the world, now bleeds to give us ease" (10-11). Using the historical present tense, Milton draws the connection between circumcision and the Passion explicitly when he says that in submitting to the rite Jesus thereby

> . . . seals obedience first with wounding smart
> This day, but O ere long
> Huge pangs and strong
> Will peirce [*sic*] more neer his heart. (25-28)

An interesting parallel occurs in a poem on the circumcision, published in 1640, by Christopher Harvey, a disciple of George Herbert. Relying on the same figural interpretation of the circumcision as Milton, who asserts that Jesus, when circumcised, "bleeds to give us ease," Harvey maintains that the circumcision served "to asswage / The wrath of heaven" (24-25). Robert Herrick, likewise, has several poems on the circumcision of Jesus, including "The New-yeeres Gift, or Circumcision Song . . ." and "another New-yeeres Gift, or Song for the Circumcision," which speak of the child's spilt blood, which anticipates the Passion, as "the best New-yeeres Gift to all."

The theme of circumcision in George Eliot's *Daniel Deronda* (1876) has elicited some intriguing commentary (see Newton, with references to studies by Marcus, Chase, et al.). Even though circumcision is not explicitly mentioned in chap. 16 of the novel, Deronda's fears that he is illegitimate are expressed repeatedly through images of wounding, maiming, and the like — all of which indirectly allude to it (Newton, 323-25). Circumcision, it has been claimed, can be seen to function implicitly in the novel as a crucially mysterious, if ambiguous, sign.

Bibliography. Newton, K. M. "Daniel Deronda and Circumcision." *EIC* 31 (1981), 313-27; Snowman, L. V. "Circumcision." *EncJud* (1971), 5.567-76; Tierney, J. J. "Circumcision." *Catholic Encyclopedia* (1908; rpt. 1913), 3.777a-79b.
LAWRENCE BESSERMAN

CIRCUMCISION OF THE HEART *See* CIRCUMCISION; CONSCIENCE.

CITY The chief words in the Bible translated by "city" are the Heb. *'ir,* meaning a fortified place, and the Gk. *polis,* meaning a walled or enclosed space for human habitation. These words have no specific political content, but often, when referring to the holy city of Jerusalem, carry the theological significance of holiness and eschatological hope (Pss. 46:4; 48:2; Isa. 48:2; Heb. 12:22-24).

In the OT, the city may be viewed morally. Cain, the first homicide, builds the first city (Gen. 4:17); Babel is built by proud men intending to exalt themselves against God, who halts its construction by confusing their language (Gen. 11); and Sodom and Gomorrah, steeped in sin beyond redemption, are ripe for divine judgment (Gen. 13:13; 18:16–19:29). Yet the place of Jacob's vision of the ladder and angels is called "Bethel," the house of God (Gen. 28:16-19); and Zion, the city of David, is God's choice for establishing his name (2 Chron. 6:38). Babylon, the city of confusion and captivity, contrasts most sharply with Jerusalem, for which her exiles yearn as their spiritual home (Ps. 137). Nineveh, a wicked city warned of coming calamity, repents in sackcloth and ashes (Jonah 3).

It is probably significant that no great Hebrew hero founded a city; even Jerusalem was a city of aliens, the Jebusites. The Israelite entry into the Promised Land was effected by the destruction of one of the world's oldest cities, Jericho, which was besieged by the Hebrews in a fashion similar to the Greek assault upon Troy. Yet Jericho was not for its conquerors a prize to be plundered: its riches were considered unclean (Josh. 6:24-26).

In the NT, the city is variously interpreted. Jesus weeps over Jerusalem because he knows it will be totally destroyed for killing the prophets and rejecting his messiahship (Matt. 23:37; Luke 41:44). But Jesus also pronounces judgment on numerous cities — Chorazin, Bethsaida, and Capernaum (Matt. 11:21-23). Paul speaks of two Jerusalems, the present and the heavenly city, relating them allegorically to Sarah and Hagar, symbols of the covenants of spiritual bondage and freedom (Gal. 4:22-26). In his apocalyptic vision of the new order, John sees the new Jerusalem descending out of heaven, adorned like a bride, to be God's dwelling place among his people (Rev. 21:2-4).

In the patristic period, the city became a prominent image for the church. St. Augustine, developing Ticonius's idea of two cities — one of God and one of the devil, wrote *De civitate Dei* (*The City of God*) to delineate their nature and history. Whereas Plato had seen the city as the tangible earthly state dispensing justice, and Aristotle had called it a unity of unlike persons who come together in order to live the good life, Augustine says that it is an assemblage of rational beings united by their unanimous love of some object: "the better the love, the better the people; the lower the love, the lower the people" (19.24). Those whose sole concern is worldly happiness — and who make the earth their final home — form the city of man. All whose end is God and home is heaven make up the City of God. The distinguishing difference between the two cities is the humility of the City of God and the pride of the city of man. "The humble City is the society of holy men and good angels; the proud city is the society of wicked men and evil angels. The one City began with the love of God; the other had its beginnings in the love of self" (14.13). Christ is the founder and king of the Heavenly City, which can be traced all the way back to Adam's son Seth and which today is the church, or people of Christ, spread over all the earth. Its two major symbols, Noah's ark and the Israelite people, suggest its historical durability and single-minded aim of righteousness. Its citizens are pilgrims, alien to this world. Their City crosses all cultural boundaries and welcomes likeminded persons of every tongue and nation (19.17). Its chief and worthiest preoccupation is calling upon God, its *summum bonum* the perfect peace of eternal life. "The peace of the heavenly City lies in a perfectly ordered and harmonious communion of those who find their joy in God and in one another in God" (19.13). Its most honored citizens are the martyrs.

The city of man, by contrast, was founded by the fratricide Cain, who slew Abel, the first prophetic symbol of citizenship in the City of God (cf. Heb. 11). However good and peaceful the earthly city's aims may appear, it compulsively attempts to achieve them by war. Its citizens seek possessions and the domination of others through the exercise of power. Babylon is its symbolic name, and its king is the devil. The city of this world is doomed to die and its members to suffer endless torment, but the people of the City of God will live in everlasting beatitude.

By the 12th cent. Augustine's view, so disparaging of the earthly city for its ephemerality to the Christian *viator,* had begun to be modified in various quarters. Otto von Freising, bishop of that city and uncle to Frederick Barbarossa, authored the view that Augustine's "two cities" might be seen as now united in the Catholic Church as a continuation of the Roman Empire (*Chronicon seu Historia de Duabus Civitatibus,* 1143-46). In the following century came St. Thomas Aquinas, who, influenced by Aristotle, said that the city (or state) is a good and worthy end of human reason and endeavor. Dante, influenced in turn by Thomas, describes two cities of the world to come in *The Divine Comedy,* infernal Dis, full of flames and demons to punish the damned; and the White Rose, the celestial gathering of all the holy angels and the saved around God, singing his praises with perfect joy and peace in his will.

In ME literature, the city can figuratively signify the community of the saved, as in *Pearl,* where "Jerusalem" is both the city in which the soul was made serene by Christ's sacrifice and the city in which it will receive everlasting peace (949-56). In *Cleanness,* the poet describes the destruction of the four cities of the plain, including Sodom and Gomorrah, but in *Patience* he pictures Nineveh repenting at Jonah's preaching (353). Chaucer's London and Canterbury, as city of the world and City of God, begin and end an analogous pilgrimage and reordering of affections which the Parson identifies finally as the pilgrimage "that highte Jerusalem celestial" (*CT* 10.51).

In the Renaissance, the image of the city often carries political as well as spiritual content. Spenser has the Redcrosse Knight see the New Jerusalem — "The Citie of the great king hight it well, / Wherein eternall peace and happinesse doth dwell" — in an eschatological vision; but he still has praise for Cleopolis, where the "fairest *Faerie Queene* [Elizabeth I] doth dwell" (*FQ,* 1.10.53-61). Shakespeare's best image of the city is Rome in *Julius Caesar,* the scene of political intrigue.

In the 17th cent., the city is still a forceful moral image, but it begins to be used satirically also. Thus, for Donne, cities are sepulchers or anthills; the nearest thing to a suburb of heaven is the churchyard. Milton's Pandemonium is a city of political demons who, while suffering spiritual anguish alienated from heaven, plot to overthrow or mar God's new kingdom, earth and its human race. For both metaphysical and cavalier poets, the city is usually a foil for wit; but by the Restoration, it has become synonymous with court and theater, scandal, seduction, and dissolute living. Bunyan, however, returns to the pilgrimage motif, and offers three spiritually significant images: the City of Destruction, Vanity Fair, and the Celestial City. His achievement in *Pilgrim's Progress*

was to relate them to the individual Christian in his private, inward life.

In the 18th cent., Boswell quotes Dr. Johnson as saying that "A great city is, to be sure, the school for studying life" (3.253), and that "when a man is tired of London he is tired of life; for there is in London all that life can afford" (3.178). But this view differs sharply from that of some other writers of his time. For Pope, the city is the center of corruption; its vices threaten order, morality, reason, and personal integrity at every turn. Fielding finds it the place where the ambitious and unscrupulous vie for eminence while only the poor tend to be charitable (*Joseph Andrews*). In *Tom Jones* the city is typically a Babylonian counterfoil to the pastoral delights of Squire Alworthy's Paradise Hall. Swift underlines humanity's fallen state in *Gulliver's Travels* in his portrayals of city and court.

In the Romantic period, Blake gives us three notable images of the city: London, Jerusalem, and Golgonooza, each in some way informed by biblical tradition. London, once the Albion of nations, harmonious and peaceful, has become a place of degradation and woe. "I behold Babylon in the opening Streets of London: I behold / Jerusalem in ruins wandering about from house to house" (*Jerusalem,* 74.15-16). In every face appear marks of weakness, in every voice "mind-forged manacles" ("London"). Here are the miserable poor of England, neglected by the church: chimney sweeps, dying soldiers, and harlots. "The Cry of the Poor Man" loudly accuses the unresponsive (*Milton,* 42.34). Jerusalem is Blake's ideal city of Liberty, the "Divine Vision," "Jerusalem in every Man" (*Jerusalem,* 54.2-3), which someday will be realized over the whole earth (*Milton,* 6.18; 25:55), signifying peace among human beings and communion with God for everyone. Golgonooza is the city of art, built by Los, the creative imagination in humankind, who is also Jerusalem's architect. Golgonooza gives form to imagined things (*Milton,* 24-50; *Four Zoas,* 5.7.8). Shelley, in his mock-epic satire *Peter Bell the Third,* jokes:

Hell is a city much like London —
A populous and a smoky city;
There are all sorts of people undone,
And there is little or no fun done. (3.1)

This negative English view contrasts with the German romanticism of Goethe, in whose *Faust* the hero builds his city of human brotherhood on a swamp (the created universe).

In the Victorian period, the city continues to have largely negative connotations. For Carlyle it is a "spectral Necropolis, or rather City both of the Dead and of the Unborn," awaiting the Communion of Saints (*Sartor Resartus,* 3.7). The novels of Charles Dickens leave one with memorable and mostly negative images of the city, although he seems to envision the city as capable of being transformed spiritually: it is also the setting for conversion and the rewriting of history in his *A Christmas Carol*. In Thackeray, all is Vanity Fair, without one redeeming quality or admirable character to be found, and Morris likewise recommends forgetting the reality for a "dream of London, small, and white and clean" (*The Earthly Paradise*). But the severest and most uncompromisingly negative picture of the worldly city is James Thomson's infernal vision (*The City of Dreadful Night*). Its final word is its theme throughout: "despair." The poets of the '90s concentrated for the most part on the individual's loneliness in the city, often using the figure of the street prostitute. But standing in contrast to all this darkness is the poetry of several Christians, including Hopkins and Francis Thompson, who, looking at the same city, see Christ in its streets, ministering peace and comfort (Hopkins's "The Lantern out of Doors"; Thompson's "The Kingdom of God").

In the modern period, the Dublin of James Joyce is the city as image of humankind in time, specifically a disquieted Everyman in a single 24-hour day, unwittingly repeating or rehearsing the mythical movements of an ever-hopeful but always defeated, all-too-human hero (*Ulysses*). No escape from the daily rounds appears, except that described by Yeats, a holy city of timeless art, safely beyond reach of despicable and rootless humans ("Byzantium"; "Sailing to Byzantium").

T. S. Eliot presents the city of man in the modern sense of place, not idea ("The Love Song of J. Alfred Prufrock"). Unlike secular man in Augustine, the speaker has no citizenship in the earthly city; he is out of place, for he is a man of ideas. He has "measured out [his] life with coffee spoons," trying to be a real member of the city (cf. the "unreal city" of *The Waste Land*), but his very act of self-analysis, which is the poem's content, ironically frustrates his purpose and will. Even more ironically, he himself is the image of the city in which he will never feel at home. But Eliot's clearest statements on the city are a plea for a complete reversal of the modern way (*Choruses from "The Rock"*). London, "the timekept City," has become far too secular, having no time or place for its most vital feature, the church. Like Nehemiah, the speaker grieves over the God-denying, "broken city," hoping to rebuild it, like Jerusalem. His solution is that life must be lived in community and the praise of God. But it must begin in humility and purity, which, if they "be not in the heart, they are not in the home: and if they are not in the home, they are not in the City."

In the novels, plays, and poems of Charles Williams one meets the most striking Christian image of the city since Augustine (*All Hallows' Eve, Descent into Hell, Taliessin through Logres, The House of the Octopus*). Williams bases his image of the city on the patristic conception of coinherence, the unity of the Trinity and the union of the Trinity with the church. Its operation is exchange, and its mode of exchange is substitution: "Bear ye one another's burdens, and so fulfill the law of Christ"

(Gal. 6:2). Williams says that the City's name is Union and its exchanges "range from childbirth to the Eucharist — the two primal activities of the earth and the Church" ("The Redeemed City"). "There is no final idea for us but the glory of God in the redeemed and universal union — call it Man or the Church or the City."

W. H. Auden refers to modernity as "the Trivial Unhappy Unjust City," but his Enlightenment view that the "just" city can be humanly constructed (cf. Blake's "And Did Those Feet . . ."), a view shared by Marxist and Social Gospel Christians, is in stark contrast to the preindustrial Revolution and essentially Augustinian pessimism concerning any celestial Jerusalems in the here and now. A bias away from the city may be observed still among Christian writers and critics as diverse as the prophets of New Criticism, the "Southern Agrarians" (Cleanth Brooks, Robert Penn Warren, and Allen Tate), and J. R. R. Tolkien in his *Lord of the Rings* trilogy. No comparable aversion to the city (or mistrust of it) exists in modern Jewish fiction. Here, as in the novels of Saul Bellow (e.g., *Herzog*), Bernard Malamud (e.g., *The Fixer*), or Mordechai Richler (*St. Urbain's Horseman*), only the city affords imaginable cultural and religious life. In some Jewish fiction since World War II, nonetheless, there is implicit or explicit contrasting of European and American cities of exile ("Babylon") with Jerusalem next year — or perhaps, as in Chaim Potok's *The Chosen* or Leon Uris's *Exodus,* Jerusalem tomorrow.

See also BABYLON; SODOM AND GOMORRAH.

Bibliography. Dyos, H. J., and M. Wolff, eds. *The Victorian City: Images and Realities* (1973); Ellul, J. *The Meaning of the City* (1970); Hittinger, R. "The Two Cities and the Modern World: A Dawsonian Assessment." *Modern Age* (1984), 192ff.; Miller, S. "Studies in the Idea of the City in Western Literature." *DAI* 31 (1970), 6018A; Moorman, C. *The Precincts of Felicity: The Augustinian City of the Oxford Christians* (1966); Rosenau, H. *The Ideal City* (1953); Stout, J. "Sodoms in Eden: The City in American Fiction Before 1860." *DAI* 34 (1973), 1257A; Tonsor, S. J. "The Iconography of Disorder: The Ruined Garden and the Devastated City." *ModA* 17 (1972), 358-67; Weimer, D. R. *The City as Metaphor* (1966); Williams, C. *The Image of the City and Other Essays.* Ed. Anne Ridler (1958).   JOSEPH McCLATCHEY

CITY OF REFUGE Num. 35:11 states that Moses was instructed by the Lord to appoint cities of refuge for those who committed unintentional homicide; the intent was to provide sanctuary until a judgment could be made. Of the forty cities designated for the use of the Levites before the entry into Canaan, six were to be cities of refuge: "Ye shall give three cities on this side Jordan, and three cities shall ye give in the land of Canaan" (Num. 35:14). Moses designated three of the cities — Bezer, Ramoth, and Golan (Deut. 4:43) — and Joshua the other three — Kedesh, Shechem, and Hebron (Josh. 20:7). Asylum or sanctuary was not granted in cases of intentional homicide. Once granted asylum, a fugitive was protected from his avengers as long as he stayed within the boundaries of the city of refuge; the local sanctuary of a temple was also an asylum since killing in a holy place was considered a sacrilege. Joab, hoping to escape the wrath of Solomon, fled to the sanctuary and "caught hold on the horns of the altar"; however, Benaiah slew him at the order of Solomon (1 Kings 2:28-34).

Kate, the heroine of De Quincey's picaresque tale *The Spanish Military Nun*, is rescued after a duel in which she kills her adversary: "Every convent and altar had the right of asylum for a short period. According to the custom, the monks carried Kate . . . to the sanctuary of their chapel." Later in her travels, Kate descends from the Andes in a state of exhaustion:

> Staggering, fainting, reeling, she entered beneath the canopy of umbrageous trees. But, as oftentimes the Hebrew fugitive to a city of refuge, flying for his life before the avenger of blood, was pressed so hotly that . . . as he kneeled in deep thankfulness . . . he could not rise again . . . so sank . . . the martial nun.

Still later after another incident in which Kate is badly wounded, she is granted asylum by a bishop who "pitied her, and had her attended in his palace; then removed to a convent; then to a second convent at Lima." In the essay "Swedenborg; or, the Mystic," Emerson says, "If we tire of the saints, Shakespeare is our city of refuge." In Stevenson's *Dr. Jekyll and Mr. Hyde,* the protagonist, contemplating his perilous situation, says, "Jekyll was now my city of refuge; let Hyde peep out an instant, and the hands of all men would be raised to take and slay him." John Keble's poem for the first Sunday in Lent is devoted to this subject (*The Christian Year* [1827], 72-74).

See also MARY, MOTHER OF JESUS; TEMPLE.

Bibliography. Albright, W. F. "The List of Levitic Cities." *American Academy for Jewish Research. Louis Ginzberg Jubilee Volume* (1945), 49-73; Greenberg, M. "The Biblical Conception of Asylum." *JBL* 78 (1959), 125-32; Smith, R. *Lectures on the Religions of the Semites: The Fundamental Institutions* (1889; rpt. 1927).   RONALD M. MELDRUM

CLAUDIA PROCLA   *See* PILATE'S WIFE.

CLAVIS DAVIDICA   *See* FREEDOM, BONDAGE.

CLEAN AND UNCLEAN   The theme of ritual purity or defilement, of being clean (Heb. *tahor* and other terms) or unclean (Heb. *tame'* and other terms), pervades the OT, the intertestamental literature, and especially the sources of rabbinic Judaism. "Cleanness" is also prominent in both testaments as a metaphor for ethical behavior.

J. Neusner (*The Idea of Purity in Ancient Judaism* [1973], 18-22) lists seven main sources of uncleanness: eating forbidden animals (Lev. 11:1-47; 17:15-16; Deut. 14:3-21); childbirth (Lev. 12:1-8); swellings, eruptions, or spots on the skin, loosely translated as "leprosy" (Lev. 13:1–14:57); a "disease" or mildew on the walls of a house (Lev. 14:33-57); bodily discharges (Lev. 15:1-33; Deut. 23:10; 2 Sam. 11:4); sexual misdeeds (Lev. 18:6-24; Num. 35:34); and contact with a corpse (Lev. 21:1-24; Num. 19:11-16; 31:19-20). In a metaphorical sense, all sin defiles (Isa. 1:15-16; 6:5; Ps. 51:1-2, 7, 10), especially the sin of idolatry (Ps. 106:34-40; Ezek. 22:3). The foreign idolatrous nations and their lands are sometimes called unclean (Isa. 52:1; Amos 7:17).

Defilement disqualifies one from entering the Temple or participating in cultic functions, including holy war (Lev. 22:1-9; 12:4; Num. 9:6). Purification is achieved through the passing of time (Lev. 11:25, 28, 40; Num. 19:8, 10, 22), by washings (Lev. 11:40; 14:8; 15:16-18; Num. 19:7, 10, 17-22; 2 Sam. 11:4), by bringing a sin offering (Lev. 4–5; 12:6-8; 14:19-20), or by a combination of these. In certain cases, separation from the community is necessary (Lev. 13:45-46; Num. 5:2-3).

The OT provides few clues to an interpretation of the meaning and function of clean and unclean, leaving room for several theories. Perhaps the most comprehensive of these is that of M. Douglas (*Purity and Danger* [1966]), who relates clean and unclean to cosmic order. Clean and unclean serve to draw a line between order, the state of wholeness (*shalom*), conferred through divine blessing, and disorder, literally "dirt," symbolically expressive of confusion and chaos. Thus an animal clearly belonging to a certain group, e.g., those which part the hoof and chew their cud, such as a cow, is clean, whereas one which shares characteristics of two groups, such as the pig, which parts the hoof but does not chew its cud, or a hare, which chews the cud but does not part the hoof, is unclean (Lev. 11:1-8; Deut. 14:3-8; cf. also Lev. 11:9-12, 20-23; Deut. 14:9-10).

Philo allegorizes the purity laws into moral precepts. Jesus subordinates their observance to moral demands (Matt. 23:25-26; Luke 11:37-41), and the NT church absolves Gentile converts from almost all purity laws (Acts 15:28-29). For St. Paul, practices engaged in with a guilty conscience or without loving concern for others make one unclean (Rom. 14; cf. 1 Cor. 8; Titus 1:15). The vocabulary of purity and impurity also continues in the NT to provide metaphors for ethical behavior (Matt. 5:8; Acts 18:6; 1 Tim. 1:5; Heb. 10:22).

Clean and unclean animals receive prominent attention in postbiblical tradition and literature. Jewish legends speak of clean animals having "suckled the male children of the Hebrews" during the time of Pharaoh's oppression, and they recount that 700 species of clean fish, 800 of clean beasts, and many fowl left the Holy Land to settle in Babylon at the time of the Babylonian Exile, later returning (with the single exception of the turbot) with the restored captives (see L. Ginzberg, *LJ* 6.12; 6.390). In early Christian writings, moral allegorization of the clean and unclean animals is common. In *The Testament of Asher Concerning Two Faces of Vice and Virtue,* certain people are said to be like the hare, "half clean, but in very deed . . . unclean," in that they combine virtue and vice in their actions (ANF 8.31; cf. 5.647). The *Glossa Ordinaria* allegorizes Deut. 14:7 along similar lines and also puns upon *ruminare:* "The Jews ruminate upon the word of the law but they do not divide the hoof; that is, they do not believe in the Father *and* the Son, neither do they accept the two testaments" (PL 113.464). St. Thomas Aquinas works out the implications of the pun more explicitly: chewing the cud signifies "meditation" (*Summa Theol.* 2.102.6; cf. Bede, *Hist. Eccl.* 4.24).

Such exegesis lies behind Dante's reference in *Purgatorio,* 16.98-99; evidently, spiritual authority is identified by him with chewing the cud — ruminating, or meditating — and temporal authority with dividing the hoof — making distinctions (see C. Singleton edn., *Commentary*, 363-64). In the 17th cent. Vaughan enlists the commonplace of the "clean" animal to urge his readers to ruminate on their sins: "That done we shall be safe, and good, / Those beasts were cleane, which chew'd the cud." Hopkins refers ironically to "the godless flock" which "chew'd the cud . . . rolled into the bitterness of sin" ("Glimmer'd along the square-cut steep").

The most extensive literary treatment of the general biblical theme of clean and unclean is the ME poem *Cleanness,* in which three biblical narratives of profanation and God's judgment upon it — the narratives of the Flood, Sodom and Gomorrah, and Belshazzar's feast — are paraphrased.

Bibliography. Douglas, M. *Purity and Danger: An Analysis of Concepts of Pollution and Taboo* (1966); Feldman, E. *Biblical and Post-Biblical Defilement and Mourning: Law as Theology* (1977); Neusner, J. *The Idea of Purity in Ancient Judaism* (1973); Toombs, L. E. "Clean and Unclean." *IDB* 1.641-48; Wenham, G. "The Theology of Unclean Food." *EvQ* 53 (1981), 6-15.   WALDEMAR JANZEN
                                                      H. DAVID BRUMBLE

CLEANSING OF THE TEMPLE   The account of the *purgatio templi,* or "cleansing of the temple" by Jesus, is given in each of the Synoptic Gospels (Matt. 21:12-13; Mark 11:15-17; Luke 19:45-46):

> And Jesus went into the temple of God, and cast out all them that sold and bought in the temple, and overthrew the tables of the money changers, and the seats of them that sold doves. And said unto them, It is written, My house shall be called [of all the nations; Mark 11:17] the house of prayer; but ye have made it a den of thieves. (Matt. 21:12-13; cf. John 2:13-17, where Jesus is said to have used a "scourge of cords")

It appears that Jesus may have been reacting against unscrupulous and predatory merchandising in the "Court of the Gentiles" in the Temple precinct, the one place Gentiles were permitted to worship.

The passage is typically applied by the Fathers to clerical misappropriation of moneys intended as tithes and offerings. St. Jerome holds up to a young priest the

worthy example of St. Exuperius, Bishop of Toulouse, as one who resists every temptation to enrich himself at the expense of God's house:

> Like his Master he has banished greed out of the Temple; and without either scourge of cords or wounds of chiding he has overthrown the chairs of them that sell doves, that is, the gifts of the Holy Spirit. He has upset the tables of Mammon and scattered the money of the money-changers; zealous that the house of God may be called a house of prayer and not a den of robbers. (*Ep.* 125.20)

St. Gregory the Great uses the passage to condemn the purchase of sacred orders — or bribery to gain consideration — as a species of simony: "For 'to sell doves' is to receive a temporal consideration for the Holy Spirit, whom, being consubstantial with Himself, Almighty God gives to men through imposition of hands" (*Ep.* 57). In his famous letter to Eustochium about the vocation of a nun, St. Jerome allegorizes the passage, applying it to compromise concerning the principle of spiritual virginity: "Where money is to be counted, where doves are sold, where simplicity is stifled — where, that is, a virgin's breast glows with the cares of this world — straightaway the veil of the temple is rent, the bridegroom rises in anger. . ." (*Ep.* 22.24).

These two themes, the condemnation of any form of simony and the call to spiritual purity, persist in medieval tradition (cf. *Glossa Ordinaria* [PL 114.153; 222]) and prove attractive to Franciscan writers, who find their own contemporary analogy to Christ's driving corruption out of the Church with knotted cords (e.g., *Meditations on the Life of Christ,* 42.229), a scene powerfully depicted by Giotto di Bondone for the Scrovegni Chapel in Padua. Calvin's commentary on the narrative urges temperance among his Reformed readers: "If foul stains have spread over the Church of God, then all God's children must burn with grief, but God has not put weapons in the hands of all," even though "the audacity of those hypocrites when they are covered with false piety increases almost to the point of believing that God is mocked. Seeing that the metaphor of a den takes in all forms of vice, Christ well takes this phrase of the Prophet [Jer. 7:11] for the present case" (*Harmony of the Gospels,* Matt. 21:12-14).

Ben Jonson's *The Alchemist* presents a deacon, Ananias, and pastor, Tribulation Wholesome, who, when disillusioned with the alchemist, try to retrieve the metals of widows and orphans which they had earlier brought to be turned into gold, "the portion of the righteous / Out of the den of thieves" — playing on the traditional theme of corruption of the priesthood. Smollet recurs to the same theme in *Humphrey Clinker:* "Degenerate rascal! You have made my father's house a den of thieves. . . ." Similarly, Robert Burns's sarcastic narrator in "Address to the Unco Guid" is "wae to think upon yon den," even for the sake of "Nickie-ben." The reference tends to literal application in the 19th cent., as in *Sartor Resartus,* where

Carlyle speaks of walking through Monmouth Street "but with little feeling of 'Devotion': probably in part because the contemplative process is so fatally broken in upon by the brood of moneychangers who nestle in that Church" (3.6). Ruskin describes "St. Marks" (in his chapter of that title in *Stones of Venice*) as having its porches degraded by a modern version of the old corruption, "not 'of them that sell doves' for sacrifice, but of the vendors of toys and caricatures." In Joyce's *Portrait of the Artist,* however, the idea of personal, spiritual poverty returns, as Stephen contemplates his decision to give up the priesthood for a life in which he would transmute the elements of that vocation into secular artistry: watching a flight of birds by the library steps, "circling about a temple of air," he muses: "But was it for this folly he was about to leave from this house of prayer and prudence into which he had been born and the orders of life out of which he had come?" (chap. 5).

See also PURIFICATION; SIMON MAGUS.

CLOSED GATE OF EZEKIEL   *See* MARY, MOTHER OF JESUS.

CLOUD LIKE A MAN'S HAND   After his servant ran seven times to a point on Mt. Carmel to look for signs of rain in answer to Elijah's prayer, he at last reported "a little cloud out of the sea, like a man's hand" (1 Kings 18:44-45) which presaged a swift and mighty torment of rain to end a long drought.

The expression is often used simply to portend the imminence of greater things. It is of little moment in medieval and Renaissance literature, but emerges to prominence in Protestant preaching of the Puritan tradition in connection with meditations on prayer "in faith believing" (see Matthew Poole's commentary in his *Annotations upon the Holy Bible;* also on James 5:7), and in Sunday sermons on Elijah and Elisha such as Cytherea reflects on sorrowfully as she ponders being forced into marriage in Hardy's *Desperate Remedies.*

The image (which lends Joyce the title of one of his short stories in *Dubliners*) could, however, readily be naturalized: John Greenleaf Whittier speaks of

> A cloud, like that old-time Hebrew saw
> On Carmel prophesying rain, began
> To lift itself o'er wooded Cardigan,
> Growing and blackening. ("Storm on Lake Asquam")

Conrad's dark weather reverses the image: "not a break in the clouds, no — not the size of a man's hand" ("Youth"). Sherwood Anderson's would-be-credible narrator in "A Man of Ideas" sets the stage for his tale describing a cloudless sky — then ominously retracts to admit, "Yes there was a cloud. I don't want to keep back any facts. There was a cloud in the west down near the horizon, a cloud no bigger than a man's hand" (*Winesburg, Ohio).* D. H. Lawrence, speaking of personal

doldrums, says he looks "like Elijah, or Elisha, whichever it was, for a cloud as big as a man's hand — but see[s] nothing" (*Letters,* 385). For John Updike, the image presages an approaching "Great Scarf of Birds" in autumn, "As if out of the Bible / or science fiction, / a cloud appeared, a cloud of dots . . ." (*Telephone Poles,* 82).

CLOUD OF WITNESSES   The writer of the Epistle to the Hebrews urges his readers on in their faith in a time of great persecution and martyrdom: "Wherefore, seeing we also are compassed about with so great a cloud of witnesses, let us lay aside every weight, and the sin which does so easily beset us, and let us run with patience the race that is set before us, looking unto Jesus, the author and finisher of our faith . . ." (12:1-2a).

While the *Glossa Ordinaria* lays most stress in its commentary on the Christian's acquisition of patience (PL 114.666), Calvin anticipates the main line of Protestant commentary in his emphasis on the encouragement and example which ought to be taken from the "heroes of faith" described in chap. 11. Drawing upon St. Augustine, who referred to his "wretched weights" as a propensity to be "sucked in by my old habits" (*Conf.* 10.40.65), Calvin warns against the "weights" or "burdens" with which Satan "binds" and "entangles" the would-be Christian athlete; these are described as "the love of this present life, the pleasures of the world, the desires of the flesh, earthly cares, riches and honours" — much the same sort of baggage as Bunyan's pilgrim was overjoyed finally to be rid of. Calvin interprets the "patience" spoken of in the text as Christian perseverance (*Comm. on Hebrews,* 12:1).

Robert Louis Stevenson says of crisis points in life that "a man should stop his ears against paralysing terror, and run the race that is set before him with a single mind" (*Virginibus Puerisque,* "Æs triplex"). e. e. cummings describes being abandoned to "a cloud of angry witnesses" in *The Enormous Room* (chap. 11), and in Sinclair Lewis's classic novel about a charlatan American evangelist, *Elmer Gantry,* "Sharon had spoken vaguely of brothers and high-nosed aunts and cousins, of a cloud of Falconer witnesses" (chap. 12).

From this same text comes also the proverbial phrase "besetting sins." Thomas de Quincey, in *Confessions of an English Opium Eater,* says, "I confess it to be a besetting infirmity of mine, that I am too much of an Eudaemonist" ("Introduction to the Pains of Opium"). In *Father and Son,* Edmund Gosse describes Ann as "a very worthy woman, but masterful and passionate, suffering from an ungovernable temper, which, at calmer moments, she used to refer to, not without complacency, as 'the sin which does so easily beset me' " (chap. 6). In the Oxen of the Sun episode of *Ulysses,* James Joyce cobbles in more of the phrase: "Prince Edward easily beset us, and let us run with patience the race that is set before us."

See also MILES CHRISTI.

CLOVEN HOOF *See* CLEAN AND UNCLEAN.

CLOVEN TONGUES OF FIRE *See* PENTECOST; TONGUES, GIFT OF.

COALS OF FIRE The injunction ascribed to Solomon, "If thine enemy be hungry, give him bread to eat; and if he be thirsty, give him water to drink: For thou shalt heap coals of fire upon his head, and the LORD shall reward thee" (Prov. 25:21-22), is quoted by St. Paul (Rom. 12:20) in urging Christians to eschew vengeance and to "overcome evil with good" (v. 21). Human nature being what it is, there has been a tendency to miss the point.

St. Jerome reminds his readers that the heaping of coals is "not by way of curse and condemnation, as most people think, but to chasten and bring him to repentance, so that, overcome by kindness and melted by the warmth of love, he may no longer be an enemy" (*Dialogus adversus Pelagianos,* 1.30). Calvin still strives for the same emphasis in his *Commentary on Romans.* Something of this is lost in the tone of Puritan commentator Matthew Poole, who interprets the passage to say, "Either make him relent, or bring down the greater Vengeance from God upon him" (*Annotations,* Rom. 12:20).

Dame Prudence, in Chaucer's pilgrim *Tale of Melibee,* actually quotes only the context provided by Rom. 12:19 (*Canterbury Tales,* 7.1459-60), but her whole discourse is in the spirit of the text and Jerome's commentary. In the same vein, Trollope describes the chagrin of lax servants: "Now their aged faces were covered with shame, and every kind word from their master was a coal of fire burning on their heads" (*The Warden,* chap. 20). In the 19th cent. the text comes to be applied as an encouragement to "increase the burden of guilt, or conscience," a point anticipated in Poole. Henry James lightly refers in his correspondence to the receipt of a letter from one of his neglected correspondents as "a heaping, on my unworthy head, of coals of fire" (*Letters* [ed. Lubbock], 2.107): shades of Dickens's Uriah Heep. Dickens himself uses the phrase frequently, both in this mild sense of increasing guilt when in *Our Mutual Friend* Fledgeby "proceeded to heap coals of fire on [Twemlow's] sensitive head" (3.13) and in the sense of deliberately exacting a kind of unanswerable revenge when in *Dombey and Son* Florence's apparently self-sacrificing love causes her father bitter discomfort: "How few of those who suffered in her father's freezing atmosphere suspected what a heap of fiery coals were piled upon his head!" (chap. 24). It is the emphasis on punishing by adding to a burden of guilt which dominates 20th-cent. usage (see E. M. Forster, *A Passage to India,* chap. 20; Aldous Huxley, *After Many a Summer,* 1.10).

COAT OF MANY COLORS A gift out of Jacob's favoritism to Joseph (Gen. 37:3), occasioning his brothers' envy and enmity. It gives rise to the title of a novel by Herbert Read, *A Coat of Many Colors* (1945).

See also JOSEPH THE PATRIARCH.

COCK Most of the biblical references to the cock find their place in the four Gospel accounts of Peter's denial of Jesus. After the Last Supper Jesus said to Peter, "The cock shall not crow, till thou hast denied me thrice" (John 13:38). Despite his protests of loyalty, before the night was over Peter did indeed deny Christ three times, each time more emphatically than before. "And immediately the cock crew. And Peter remembered the word of Jesus. . . . And he went out, and wept bitterly" (Matt. 26:74-75; see also Matt. 26:34; Mark 14:30, 68, 72; Luke 22:34, 60, 61; John 18:27). Elsewhere there are but two references: Job 38:36 (Vg): "Who placed wisdom in the heart of man, or who gave the cock understanding?"; and Mark 13:35, where Jesus warns of the Last Judgment: "Watch ye therefore: for ye know not when the master of the house cometh, at even, or at midnight, or at the cock crowing."

The Job reference occasioned a talmudic *berakah,* "Blessed art thou, O Lord! Our God, King of the world, who gives the cock intelligence to distinguish between day and night." The *berakah* is not whimsical; in Palestine the cock typically crowed during the third watch, i.e., between midnight and 3 a.m. (M. J. Harris, *NIDNTT* 3.114). It is thus the cock's predictive discrimination which is being noted. A midrash on Job 38:36 observes that the cock is called in Arabic a far-seer, closely related to the Arabic word for prophet (Yalqut 905; cf. Lev. Rab. c.1). In classical tradition the cock was typically associated with the sun, as the bird of dawn (see Ovid, *Fasti,* 1.455-56; *Metamorphoses,* 11.597).

The earliest patristic source for the allegory of the cock may be a hymn by St. Ambrose, traditionally chanted at Sunday Lauds (PL 14.255), but the most elaborate treatment among the Fathers is Prudentius's "Hymn for Cock-Crow":

> The winged messenger of the day
> Sings loud, foretelling dawn's approach,
> And Christ in stirring accents calls
> Our slumbering souls to life with Him. . . .
> The cock's loud voice . . .
> A symbol is of our high Judge. . . .
> In night's dark shadows, it is said,
> The evil spirits in joy may roam,
> But at the crowing of the cock
> In sudden fear they take to flight. . . .
> The Savior once to Peter showed
> What hidden power this bird may have . . .
> Hence all now hold in firm belief
> That in the stillness of the night
> When loudly crows the joyful cock
> Our Lord came back from Hell's dim shore. . . .

The ancient notion that witches and demons flee at

cock crow was still widespread through the Middle Ages and Renaissance (and cf. John Masefield, "Enslaved," 835). But the cock was also a figure for the effective priest, notably identified as such in the *Regulae pastoralis* of St. Gregory the Great, the best-known treatise on pastoral care down to the Reformation. Here Gregory makes an elaborate allegory of priestly vestments and the plumage and coloration of the common rooster, and relates the cock to the preacher principally in terms of the Job reference: "For a holy preacher, crying aloud in time of darkness, is as the cock crowing in the night, saying 'It is even now the hour for us to arise from sleep' (Rom. 13:11), and again, 'Awake ye righteous and sin not' (1 Cor. 15:34)." Gregory goes on to say of the cock / preacher analogy: "He who preaches aright cries aloud plainly to hearts that are still in the dark, but shows them nothing of hidden mysteries, that they may then hearken to more subtle teaching concerning heavenly things as they draw nigh to the light of truth" (*Regulae pastoralis,* 3.39-40). The analogy became a commonplace, figuring prominently in the treatment of the cock in medieval bestiaries (e.g., *De Bestiis et Alius Rebus* [PL 177]) and later emblem books, and in the widespread symbol of the weathercock atop church steeples. The cock is the vigilant preacher calling the sleeping sinners, announcing the resurrection of the sun, and foretelling the light which is Christ. (The cock is also, though less widely, known as a figure for the apostles [Rabanus, PL 112.939].)

In Chaucer the "cokkes crowe" is often used ironically to underscore the denial of Christ embodied in a cleric's sinful behavior: Absalom the Oxford "parissh clerk" in *The Miller's Tale* sets out to declare his "love-longynge" for the old carpenter's wife "at cokkes crowe" (*CT* 1.3675; 3687). In the following tale of the Reeve the two predatory clerks-in-training from Cambridge fornicate with the Miller's wife and daughter "til that the thridde cok bigan to synge" (1.4233), and in *The Nun's Priest's Tale* Chaunticleer is an evident figure for the teller of the tale — or any priest who might succumb to sloth or flattery and thus become a prey to the "colfox ful of sly iniquitee." Of Chaunticleer Chaucer writes that "his voys was murier than the murie organ / On messe-days that in the chirche gon" (7.2851-52).

In Alexander Barclay's version of *The Ship of Fools* a similar complaint is taken up when the poet chastises "clerks" who bear the academic accreditation of the University into their parish work but do not live holy lives. Drawing upon Gregory's *Regulae pastoralis,* 40, he writes:

Ye clerks that on your shoulders bear the shield
Unto you granted by the University,
How dare ye aventure to fight in Christes field
Against sin without ye clear and guiltless be?

Consider the cock and in him shall ye see
A great example, for with his wings thrice

He betides himself to wake his own body
Before he crow to cause others wake or rise.

In Shakespeare's *Hamlet* the Ghost disappears at cock crow, and so Horatio and Marcellus understand it to be of demonic origin (1.1.149-56). Marcellus then observes:

Some say that ever 'gainst that season comes
Wherein Our Saviour's birth is celebrated,
The bird of dawning singeth all night long.
And then, they say, no spirit dare stir abroad,
The nights are wholesome, then no planets strike,
No fairy takes nor witch hath power to charm,
So hallowed and so gracious is the time.

Vaughan's "Cock-Crowing" may be the most elaborate working out of the allegory of the cock in English literature:

Father of lights! What Sunnie seed,
What glance of day hast thou confin'd
Into this bird? . . .

Vaughan's poem develops the familiar association of the cock awaiting the dawn and the Christian awaiting Christ's coming, and the association of dark with evil, to a final plea that God be with him until the dawn.

Tales of the cock and the fox on the pattern of *The Nun's Priest's Tale* persist in folktale literature and are alluded to in Masefield's "The Passing Strange":

But in the darkest hour of night
When even the foxes peer for sight
The byre-cock crows; he feels the light.
So, in this water mixed with dust,
The byre-cock spirit crows from trust
That death will change because it must.

Thoreau, in his epigram to *Walden,* employs the cock/ clergy image, casting himself in the role of Transcendental preacher: "I do not propose to write an ode to dejection, but to brag as lustily as Chanticleer in the morning, standing on his roost, if only to wake my neighbors up." Melville's deflating short story "Cock-A-Doodle-Doo!" offers an antidotal perspective to such a self-proclamation. In a 20th-cent. poem "Cock-crow: Woodstock," Henry Morton Robinson draws on Mark 13:35 and Christ's warning of the Last Judgment to make of the cock's crow a warning of apocalypse and final reckoning:

The cock that crew when Peter lied
Crows now, and in his throat
Lugubrious and solemn pride
Strains with a warning note.

More melancholy than the owl
This chantecleer of death;
This tragi-comic barnyard fowl
Whose triple-taken breath

Reminds us that another morn
In beauty riding high
Will scarcely echo his vain horn
Before we shall deny

Thrice and three times thrice His name;
(How cunning art Thou, Lord
To herald our perpetual shame
By this perennial bird.)

See also PETER.

Bibliography. Fehrle, E. "Der Hahn in Aberglauben."
SAV 16 (1912), 65ff.; Friedman, H. *A Bestiary for Saint
Jerome* (1980); Owst, G. R. *Preaching in Medieval England*
(1926).   H. DAVID BRUMBLE

COCKATRICE   In Isaiah's prophecy of the messianic
age to come, among the symbols of reconciled nature,
along with the wolf which dwells peaceably with the
lamb, he predicts that "the suckling child shall play on the
hole of the asp, and the weaned child shall put his hand
on the cockatrice's den" (Isa. 11:8). In Jer. 8:17 the cockatrice is a symbol of judgment which comes from "the
serpent's root," and its "fruit shall be a fiery flying serpent." The Heb. *ṣepaʿ* (cockatrice, adder, viper, asp) is
sometimes called a "basilisk." A legendary beast in
medieval times, it was believed to be hatched by a serpent
from a cock's egg; it had the head, legs, and wings of a
cock but a serpent's tail, an arrow-headed tongue,
poisonous breath, and eyes which could slay at a glance.
It is this creature, the "basilisk" rather than the biblical
ṣepaʿ which is implicated in Shakespeare's *Twelfth Night*
when Sir Toby Belch plans to set Sir Andrew and Cesario
(Viola in disguise) against each other: "This," says Sir
Toby, "will so fright them both that they will kill one
another by the look, like cockatrices" (3.4.199-201; cf.
Richard 3, 4.1.54-55; *Romeo and Juliet,* 3.2.45-47). The
same creature, and not any specific biblical allusion, is
intended by Donne in "Elegie IV," where he describes his
lover's disapproving father searching "with glazed eyes,
/ As though he came to kill a Cockatrice." The Jeremiah
reference is evidently in the mind of George Herbert,
however, in "Sinnes round," in which the poet repents
("Sorrie I am, my God, sorrie I am") a vagrant imagination:

My thoughts are working like a busie flame,
Untill their cockatrice they hatch and bring:
And when they once have perfected their draughts,
My words take fire from my inflamed thoughts.

See also LION LIES DOWN WITH THE LAMB; MILLENNIUM.

COMFORTER, THE   *See* HOLY SPIRIT.

COMMUNION   *See* EUCHARIST.

CONFESSION   The Greek verbs *homologeō* and *exho-
mologeō* denote both confession of sin and confession of
faith (e.g., Matt. 10:33 and 1 John 1:9 for the former;
Matt. 3:6 and James 5:16 for the latter). The noun
homologeō, however, is employed only once in the NT
with reference to confession of faith.

In the OT confessions of faith in God can be found on
the lips of psalmists and prophets (e.g., Pss. 7:1; 48:14;
Isa. 12:2; 61:10). In the NT confessions of faith in the
person of Jesus as Christ abound. Such a confession by
Jews could result in their expulsion from the synagogue
(John 9:22), as indeed happened to a blind man cured by
Jesus (John 9:34). The fear of excommunication, therefore, kept many of the chief rulers who believed in Jesus
from professing their faith openly (John 12:42). In the
Epistles of John a twofold confession, that "Jesus Christ
is come in the flesh" (1 John 4:2-3; 2 John 7) and that
"Jesus is the Son of God" (1 John 4:13), is deemed essential to a true and saving faith. Similarly, St. Paul makes it
clear that believing with the heart must be accompanied
by confession with the mouth (Rom. 10:9-10). In the
Epistle to the Hebrews Jesus is described as "the Apostle
and High Priest of our confession" (3:1).

Confession of sin, as the expression of true penitence
and the condition of divine forgiveness, figures prominently in the OT. The idea is found in the provisions of
the Mosaic ritual (Lev. 5:3ff.), in the utterances of the
penitential and other psalms (e.g., 32:5; 51:3ff.), and in
prayers such as those of Ezra (10:1) and Nehemiah (1:6-
7). Perhaps surprisingly, actual confession of sin is
recorded on only one occasion in the NT, and that with
reference to the ministry of John the Baptist (*ex-
homologoumenoi tas hamartias autōn* [confessing their
sins], Matt. 3:6; Mark 1:5). The idea is nevertheless
prominent. Jesus begins his ministry with a call to repentance (Matt. 4:17; Mark 1:15), and a humble acknowledgment of sin as a condition of divine forgiveness is the
focus of a number of parables (e.g., the prodigal son [Luke
15:17-21], and the Pharisee and the Publican [Luke
18:10-14]), as well as other Gospel narratives. The believer, moreover, is encouraged by John that "if we confess our sins, he is faithful and just to forgive us our sins,
and to cleanse us from all unrighteousness" (1 John 1:9).

Four classes of confession of sin are found in the
Bible: to God alone (Ps. 32:3-6; Dan. 9:19); to one's
neighbor, when he has been wronged (Luke 17:4; James
5:16: "Confess your sins to one another"); to a spiritual
adviser (Matt. 3:6; Acts 19:18); to the entire church
(1 Cor. 5:3ff.; 2 Cor. 2:6ff.). St. Augustine, who makes
confession to God, in both senses of the word (*Conf.*
5.1.1), and urges confession to "the Priest whom we have
in the heavens" (*De virginitate,* 50), urges also confession
to one another (*In Joan. Ev.* 59.5), as well as confession
of "even minute" sins to a priest of the church (*In Joan.
Ev.* 13.13-14). Hugh of St. Victor, in his 12th-cent. *De
Sacramentis,* interprets James 5:16 to mean "sheep to
shepherds, subjects to prelates" (2.14.1) — though he allows confession of "daily and slight sins to equals . . . in
order that we may in turn be saved by prayers," thus
combining the second and third class of confession. He
then merges these with the first, suggesting that confession to God is "inseparable, effectively, from confessing

to man." The ME lyric "Swete ihesu crist, to þe, / copable wrecche ich ȝelde me, / of sennes þat ich habbe ydo" (e.g., C. Brown, *Religious Lyrics of the XIVth Century,* no. 87) is a form of direct confession to Christ.

From the 8th cent. onward the term *confession* tended to designate the entire sacrament of penance, which is made up of three acts on the part of the penitent — contrition, confession, and satisfaction or reparation for sins committed (the matter) — and the words of the priest "I absolve thee, etc." (the form). Both public confession and private, or secret, confession (called auricular since it is spoken to the priest alone) were practiced. In the case of the latter the priest was under strict obligation to treat as inviolably secret everything revealed by the penitent in confession. This is the "confession's seal" to which the surveyor in Shakespeare's *Henry 8* refers (1.2.165).

Luther's confessional doctrine was in most respects traditional; he argued that "As for secret [auricular] confession as practiced today, though it cannot be proved from Scripture, yet it seems a highly satisfactory practice to me; it is useful and even necessary" (*The Pagan Servitude of the Church,* chap. 3). Calvin insisted that confession must be made to God alone, arguing that auricular confession was a "tyrannical imposition" and that James 5:16 read in context clearly justified "confession mutually" and, in extraordinary cases, group or "public confession" (*Inst.* 3.4).

Responding to resistance to auricular confession by various Reformation theologians, the Catholic Church formalized confessional doctrine in the definition of the Council of Trent, "a sacramental accusation of one's sins, made to obtain pardon by virtue of the keys." This sacrament, instituted to forgive sins after baptism, was considered by the Church Fathers to be of divine origin and necessary for salvation, a view based on the words of Jesus to his apostles after the Resurrection: "Receive ye the Holy Ghost: whose soever sins ye remit, they are remitted unto them; and whose soever sins ye retain, they are retained" (John 20:22-23). The power to forgive sins or the "power of the keys" was understood to refer to the promise Christ made to Peter under the formula of binding and loosing (Matt. 16:19). The power of the keys constituted priests as judges who, without a detailed statement of sins by the penitent, could not authoritatively loose or bind. Thus the Council of Trent draws upon St. Basil (*Regulae brevius tractatae,* 229), who refers to the priests as the only proper recipients of the avowal of penitents.

In *The Parson's Tale* Chaucer seems to have made use of some of the many penitential manuals which appeared as a result of the decree on penance issued by the Fourth Lateran Council in 1215. The Parson enumerates the three things necessary to receive the sacrament worthily: "Contricioun of herte, Confession of Mouth, and Satisfactioun" (*Canterbury Tales,* 10.105-10). He also mentions four conditions necessary to make a true and profitable confession (10.980ff.). Gower's *Confessio Amantis* tells how the poet, a lover weary of life, appeals to Venus, who requires him to make a full confession to Genius, her priest. Like the Parson, Genius instructs the poet on each of the seven deadly sins and its remedy. Similarly, in Passus V of *Piers Plowman* Langland describes how the seven deadly sins make confession to the figure of Repentance.

Gawain is able to resist the allurements of his scheming hostess with the aid of the Blessed Virgin Mary only after he has been "confessed so clene beknowen of thy mysses" (*Sir Gawain and the Green Knight,* 2391). In Malory's *Morte Darthur* Sir Lancelot, at the end of his days, goes to confession to the Bishop of Canterbury and asks to be absolved of his adultery with Guinevere. As a result of being pardoned, Lancelot decides to become a priest himself. The course of Redcrosse Knight's penance when he visits the House of Holiness in *The Faerie Queene* (1-11) is the same, generally, as that advocated by medieval writers. "To tell his grief" or make his confession (1.25) remains necessary for salvation. Ultimate confession, as in Shakespeare's *Measure for Measure* (2.1.33-36; 3.1.165-69), is of particular importance.

This point is dramatically reinforced in *Everyman,* where the protagonist hastens to the House of Salvation in a deathbed confession. Lucretia in Shelley's *The Cenci* (42.12) ponders the horror of dying without confession and contrition; Marlowe's *Doctor Faustus* experiences it and is eternally damned. Similarly, in Byron's play *Manfred* the abbot proposes to Manfred that "there is still time / For penitence and pity: reconcile thee / With the true church, and through the church to heaven" (3.1.49-51), but the hero prefers "remorse without the fear of hell" (71) instead, and dies presumably without being saved or damned.

In Swift's satiric fable the King of Brutes declares that all subjects "Should to the priest confess their Sins" ("The Beasts' Confession to the Priest," 11). Confession is the theme through which Swift renounces the corruption of reason in humankind. In another unorthodox use of the sacrament, Coleridge's Ancient Mariner wants to be absolved of his crime against the animal world and hopes that when the Hermit will "shrieve my soul, he'll wash away / The Albatross's blood" (512-13). For Wordsworth Nature provides "an apt confessional for One" (*Trosachs,* 2; cf. *Excursion,* 3.473).

In the modern period Yeats heralds the power of the imagination to forgive sins. On looking back at his past life, the poet is thereby enabled to "forgive myself the lot" ("A Dialogue of Self and Soul," 67). He claims, with Blake, "that the sympathy with all living things, sinful and righteous alike, which the imaginative arts awaken, is that forgiveness of sins commanded by Christ" (*Essays and Introductions* [1968], 112). He insists that "Great literature is . . . the Forgiveness of Sin," but complains that in George Eliot "we find it becoming the Accusation of Sin"

(*Essays and Introductions*, 102). Joyce presents the act of writing as a confessional. He has Bloom mock the sacrament as a masochistic exercise in the "Lotus Eaters" episode of *Ulysses*, and in *A Portrait of the Artist* has Stephen complain that his lover "would unveil her soul's shy nakedness, to one who was but schooled in the discharging of a formal rite rather than to him, a priest of eternal imagination." In a less lyrical account in *Stephen Hero*, Stephen asks Emma, much to her chagrin, if she would go to confession to him (chap. 22). Dorian Gray exhibits the same prurience: "He used to look with wonder at the black confessionals and long to sit in the dim shadow of one of them and listen to men and women whispering through the worn grating the true story of their lives" (chap. 11). In *De Profundis* Wilde observes that Christ was the supreme Artist because of his forgiveness of aberrant behavior. Joyce, however, says that Stephen's poetry allowed him to combine the offices of penitent and confessor (*Stephen Hero*, chap. 16). Flann O'Brien parodies these ambitions in *The Dalkey Archive* by having Joyce combine the offices of priest and barman. The whiskey priest's desire for sacramental confession in Graham Greene's *The Power and the Glory*, on the other hand, leads him to a sober reconversion and is a prominent structural motif in the novel.

C. G. Jung has claimed that the beginnings of psychiatry "are to be found in its prototype, the confessional" (*Modern Man in Search of a Soul* [1933], 31). In Eliot's *The Cocktail Party* O'Reilly acts as psychotherapist for some of the characters and as priest for Celia in helping her to discover a sense of sin in her previous life.

As several of these examples make clear, confession has entered literature not only as a major theme, but also as a dominant mode of writing. Augustine established the autobiographical form which deals with matters ordinarily hidden or private in the 5th cent. with his *Confessiones*. Sir Thomas Browne's *Religio Medici* and John Bunyan's *Grace Abounding* are 17th-cent. English confessions. Byron mocks Augustine's confession of sin in *Don Juan* (1.57.375-76): "Saint Augustine in his fine Confessions, / make(s) the reader envy his fine transgressions." Rousseau's *Confessions* in the 18th cent. are a deliberate counterpoint to Augustine, offering to provide the individual with a forum and form for self-justification. Wilde said in *The Critic as Artist* that "Humanity will always love Rousseau for having confessed his sins, not to a priest, but to the world" (pt. 1). Blake, however, branded him as a "pharisee" and a "hypocrite": "Rousseau thought Men good by Nature: he found them Evil & found no friend. Friendship cannot exist without Forgiveness of Sins continually. The Book written by Rousseau call'd his Confessions, is an apology and cloke for his sins & not a confession" (*Jerusalem*, pl. 52). Rousseau's work led to the publication of other nonfictional confessional autobiographies in the 19th cent., such as De Quincey's *Confessions of an English Opium Eater*, Coleridge's *Con-*

fessions of an Inquiring Spirit, and Wilde's *De Profundis*, as well as fictional works such as James Hogg's *The Private Memoirs and Confessions of a Justified Sinner*. A mixture of the confessional and the novel helped to produce the fictional autobiography, the *Bildungsroman* and *Künstlerroman* and kindred types. In this sense Defoe's *Moll Flanders*, Carlyle's *Sartor Resartus*, Wordsworth's *The Prelude*, George Moore's *Confessions of a Young Man*, and Joyce's *A Portrait of the Artist as a Young Man* all derive from the confessional mode. The compulsion "to confess in ink," as Robert Frost put it (*Quandary*, 19), persists in its most degraded and insincere form in the fiction of the "true confessions" pulp magazines.

Bibliography. Forman, J. S. "The Literature of Confession." *DAI* 40 (1980), 6263A; Hastings, J., et al. *Encyclopedia of Religion and Ethics*, 9.714-15; McNeill, J. J., and H. M. Gower. *Medieval Handbooks of Penance* (1938); *New Catholic Encyclopedia* (1967), 4.131-33; 11.73-78; Lambert, J. C. "Confession (of Christ)." In *Dictionary of the New Testament: Christ and His Gospels*. Ed. J. Hastings et al. (1973), 1.358-60; Peterson, D. L. "John Donne's *Holy Sonnets* and the Anglican Doctrine of Contrition." *SP* 56 (1959), 504-18; Spender, S. "Confessions and Autobiography." In *Autobiography: Essays Theoretical and Critical*. Ed. J. Olney (1980), 115-22; Spengemann, W. C. *The Forms of Autobiography* (1980); Starr, G. A. *Defoe and Spiritual Autobiography* (1965); Tentler, T. *Sin and Confession on the Eve of the Reformation* (1977); Watkins, O. D. *A History of Penance* (1920), 2 vols.   DOMINIC MANGANIELLO

CONSCIENCE The noun *conscience* appears thirty times in the KJV NT (in the RSV it occurs 28 times in the NT, and once to translate the much broader Heb. *leb* [KJV "heart"] in 1 Sam. 25:31). In all cases but one (John 8:9) the KJV is translating Gk. *syneidēsis* (e.g., Rom. 2:15; 9:1; 13:5; 2 Cor. 1:12; 4:2; 1 Tim. 4:2; Heb. 10:2; 1 Pet. 3:16, 21).

Most NT terms acquire their content from OT precedent (equivalent or near equivalent), but not so this word; not only the term but the concept appears to owe to a particularly Greek ethos. Moreover, the noun is to some degree an intellectual or "literate" term; including two instances (Acts 23:1; 24:16) where St. Paul's dialogue is being reported, twenty-one of its biblical occurrences are attributable to Pauline theological discourse. The related verb, *synoida*, is found earlier (from the 6th cent. B.C.) and is colloquial, meaning "to know in common with," or perhaps "to be conscious of" or "aware"; the reflexive form *synoida emautō*, "I know with myself," begins to approximate, in classical writings, the sense of the later NT noun derived from it — *syneidēsis* — a neologism first appearing in Greek only in the century before Christ.

Philologists regard such a development as instanced here with utmost interest. Following the shift from a verb (*synoida* [*emautō*]) to a noun, *syneidēsis* signifies not merely another action performed *by* the self; it is now an agent within the self, lit. "the self that knows with itself." The development of the noun form of the word thus signals "the recognition of an alter ego, another self within the self that observes the self and then testifies as to what it sees" (Opperwall).

The prehistory of *syneidēsis* for the NT — i.e., the use of the reflexive form of the verb *synoida emautō* — is pertinently illustrated in the trial of Socrates as recorded by Plato and Xenophon. Socrates explains that the probing questioning which so disturbs his follow citizens is simply a reflex of his being "aware within myself," as he says, of his own utter lack of knowledge. Alcibiades claims the same "inner awareness" that he is helpless to resist Socrates's dialectical persuasion as long as he is listening to him (Plato, *Apology*). In Xenophon's account (24) Socrates uses the term in another way, to signify the "bad conscience" of those who have testified against him. This association of moral response with *synoida emautō* pertains also to Orestes's claim that conscience is a kind of sickness which has destroyed him (Euripides, *Orestes*, 396). Plutarch characterizes a conscience which reminds people of their sins and evokes the torments of Hades (*De tranquillitate animi*, 476-77a). The Stoic philosopher Epictetus is credited with an analogy whereby just as wealthy parents entrust the care of their children after a certain point to a "nursery slave," so God entrusts souls to "the conscience implanted in us." To reject or evade the protection which the conscience provides, Epictetus is reputed to have said, is self-destructive, since it is "ill-pleasing to God" and makes "our own conscience an enemy" (Pierce, 41). Here the conscience is clearly a voice of constraint, *in loco parentis*. For Socrates in Plato's *Apology*, the check of self-consciousness is likewise defined in largely negative fashion: "This sign," he says, "which is a kind of voice, first began to come to me when I was a child; it always forbids, but never commands me to do anything which I am going to do" (trans. B. Jowett). In all these examples we may perceive in the hellenic imagination the well-developed self-awareness of a true "guilt culture," something quite absent from either the "shame culture" of Homer's *Iliad* or even, it might be argued, the Mosaic patriarchal narratives.

The new noun *syneidēsis* does not occur in any of the four Gospels (KJV "conscience" in John 8:9 translates the reflexive verb), where Hebraic orientation is strong. In the writings of Paul, however, educated in Greek literature and culture, the noun occurs repeatedly. Since "conscience" is nowhere defined by Paul, we must assume that he expected his readers to be able to gather the sense he intends, partly by contrasting hellenic and Judaic thinking. Writing to the Romans, he indicates certain differences between the perspective of Jews, who possess the external constraint of the law, and Gentiles, who do not: "For when the Gentiles, which have not the law, do by nature the things contained in the law, these, having not

the law, are a law unto themselves: Which shew the work of the law written in their hearts, their conscience also bearing witness, and their thoughts the mean while accusing or else excusing one another" (Rom. 2:14-15). Paul then uses this distinction to sharpen another, that between the Jew who "rests in the law" (v. 17) and his circumcision (v. 25) merely in the sense of outward observance, and one who has internalized the law, having written it in the heart, where it can best bear its witness (cf. Acts 23:1; Rom. 9:1; 2 Cor. 1:12). This person will be a better Jew, the one of "conscience," so to speak: "he is a Jew, which is one inwardly; and circumcision is that of the heart, in the spirit, and not in the letter; whose praise is not of men, but of God" (Rom. 2:29). "Circumcision of the heart" (cf. Lev. 26:41; Deut. 10:16; 30:6; Jer. 6:10) here is tropic, congruent with OT language; it adds specific biblical content to a novel Greek tropic noun, derivative rather of hellenic philosophical language.

The Latin translation of NT *syneidēsis* is *conscientia*, a compound of *con*, "together," and *scire*, "to know" (paralleling the original Greek compound). If in classical Latin *conscientia* typically means something like "consciousness" or "knowledge," not typically of an ethically charged nature, in Christianized usage already in the 4th cent. and widely by the 13th cent. it has acquired the fuller, spiritualized sense found in the NT. St. Thomas Aquinas (*De Veritate*, 17.5) illuminates a general medieval application of Paul when he says:

Spiritual and inward ties are stronger than bodily and outward ones. Our duty to a human superior is material and external, for legal authority works by managing temporalities. All that will be changed at the last trump, when Christ shall have put down all rule and all authority and power. Therefore conscience is more to be obeyed than authority imposed from outside. For conscience obliges in virtue of divine command, whether written down in a code or instilled by Natural Law. To weigh conscience in the scales against obedience to legal authority is to compare the weight of divine and of human decrees. The first obliges more than the second, and sometimes against the second.

The notion of self-consciousness as we know it is a further development. It arises later, after the Renaissance and Reformation, when writers like Descartes and Montaigne could begin to distinguish between a "true" self, the inner and self-conscious identity (e.g. Descartes's *cogito ergo sum*) and an artificial or outer self (Montaigne's "artifice"). When Locke (in 1632) adopts the new word *consciousness*, he distinguishes it from *conscience*, defining it as "perception of what passes in a man's own mind"; as in classical Lat. *conscientia* perception is separated from evaluation.

One difficulty which presents itself to study of the concept of conscience in English literature, even where it is an apparent function of biblical tradition, is that *conscience* and *consciousness* (Lat. *conscius*, "knowing something with others," "being privy to") could be used almost interchangeably up to the 19th cent. The possible doubleness of some usages becomes apparent in *Sir Gawain and the Green Knight,* e.g., where the hero is said to search his "conscience" to try to understand the meaning of his hostess's entry into his bedroom (1197).

In Langland's personification of Conscience (*Piers Plowman* B.19), as in the debates of Good and Bad Angels contesting for the soul of Everyman, Mary Magdalene, or Doctor Faustus, or in Bunyan's characterization of Mr. Conscience in *The Holy War,* conscience acts as an external witness; the internal sense, as when Paul uses "conscience" (1 Cor. 4:4) to say that he knows nothing against himself, is by the Renaissance capable of ironic and more complex assignation. Milton has Eve withdraw at first from Adam's courting, so impelled by "her virtue and the conscience of her worth" (*PL* 8.102).

Conscience in these examples clearly bears witness to personal history — one's own past actions — as measured against divine standards. Some passages in the NT have contributed greatly to this sense. In 1 Cor. 8:7-12 and 10:25-29 Paul speaks of the duty of Christians to respect the conscience of a "weak brother" whose faith might be destroyed by careless actions of those with less tender conscience. As C. S. Lewis suggests, *syneidēsis* here means not simply shared knowledge but "judgment as to what is right or wrong." In Rom. 13:5 Paul joins this meaning of conscience with the Jewish notion of the wrath of God, the internal pain of conscience gnawing at a person for his sins becoming parallel to the punishment of the wicked which God administers in the world. But what is at stake is the potential of the conscience to be educated — sensitized or desensitized — not merely by knowledge of the law but also by the accretion of experience. 1 Tim. 4:2 and Titus 1:15 teach that the scar of sin weakens the conscience and upsets the mind or the power of choice in matters of future conduct. A "defiled conscience," or what St. Thomas Aquinas (in *De Veritate,* 17.5) calls an "erring conscience," is a result of bad moral education, so to speak. In Shakespeare's *Henry 8* the possibility that a conscience may become corrupted through persistent error is suggested in Lord Chamberlain's remark concerning Henry's despondency and aggravation: "It seems the marriage with his brother's wife has crept too near his conscience." Suffolk then replies, "No, his conscience has crept too near another lady" (2.2.17-18). Excusing morally or politically dubious actions on the grounds of "reasons of conscience" (esp. by public officials) came to be regarded as a scandalous abuse of the NT term. Bishop Jeremy Taylor takes up Aquinas in his *Ductor Dubitantium* (1660) when he writes:

> Nothing is more usual, than to pretend *Conscience* to all the actions of men which are publick, and whose nature cannot be concealed. If arms be taken up in a violent warre; inquire of both sides, why they ingage on that part respectively? they answer, because of their Conscience. Ask a Schismatick why he refuses to joyn in the Communion of the Church? he tels you, it is against his Conscience: and the disobedient refuse to submit to Laws; and they also in many cases pretend Conscience. Nay, some men suspect their brother of a crime, and are perswaded (as they say) in Conscience that he did it: and their Conscience tels them that *Titius* did steal their goods, or that *Caia* is an adulteress. And so Suspicion; and Jealousie, and Disobedience, and Rebellion are become *Conscience;* in which there is neither knowledge, nor revelation, nor truth, nor charity, nor reason, nor religion. (1.26)

Taylor's admonition is directed against abuse of "good conscience" (Heb. 9:9; 10:2, 22; 13:18), which inculcates abstinence from reproach or reproachability; the result of such corruption is "bad conscience" (cf. Milton, *Areopagitica*).

In the general Christian frame of reference "the conscience" becomes in popular discourse a kind of storehouse of moral principles or knowledge of good and evil. This omnibus sense of the term with its Pauline overtones reverberates throughout literature. Chaucer's use of the word to describe the tears the Prioress sheds because of her "conscience and tendre herte" at the sight of a mouse in a trap (*General Prologue,* 150) appears to be ironically loaded, but the irony is dependent upon a normative expectation that *conscience* means the ability to judge between right and wrong in one's actions (rather than mere "sensibility" or tenderness). Thus Shakespeare talks of deeds "done in the testimony of a good conscience" (*Love's Labour's Lost,* 4.2.2). In ME *conscience* took the place of the earlier term *inwit,* as in the *Ancrene Riwle* (ca. 1230): "Inwið us seluen ure ahne conscience" (16). (The title of a 14th-cent. work called *Ayenbite of Inwyt, or Pricke of Conscience* [1340] by Dan Michel of Northgate becomes a central motif in James Joyce's *Ulysses.*) We also have Spenser's "grieved conscience" (*FQ* 1.10.23), and Shelley's "accuser conscience" (*Cenci,* 2.2.120) and "hounds of Conscience" (5.1.9). George Herbert calls conscience in his poem of that title an insidious "pratler," a carping adversary he can only silence by purging himself in the Eucharist.

In the LXX Wisd. 17:11 reads: "Wickedness condemned by an internal witness is a cowardly thing and expects the worst, being hardpressed by conscience [*syneidēsis*]" (cf. Wisd. 2:15). Subtle and ironic variations on this theme are common in English literature. Thus, the murderer in Shakespeare's *Richard 3* says that this knowledge or conscience "makes a man a coward" (1.4.132), and Richard himself apostrophizes "Coward Conscience" (5.3.180). Lord Henry in Wilde's *The Picture of Dorian Gray* argues that: "Conscience and cowardice are really the same things. Conscience is the tradename of the firm" (chap. 1).

A "bad conscience" is in the Christian context usually associated with fear of God's ultimate judgment. The writer in tune with biblical language sees conscience bearing witness against him on Judgment Day in terms of external standards to which all persons are held accountable by God. Robert Herrick, a 17th-cent. Cavalier poet whose amatory verse suggests that he may have had as much reason to feel the "prick of conscience" as anyone, makes the relation explicit ("To his Conscience"):

> Can I not sin, but thou wilt be
> My private *Protonotarie?*
> Can I not wooe thee to passe by
> A short and sweet iniquity?
> I'le cast a mist and cloud, upon
> My delicate transgression,
> So utter dark, as that no eye
> Shall see the hug'd impietie:
> *Gifts blind the wise,* and bribes do please,
> And winde all other witnesses:
> And wilt not thou, with gold, be ti'd
> To lay thy pen and ink aside?
> That in the mirk and tonguelesse night,
> Wanton I may, and thou not write?
> It will not be: And, therefore, now,
> For times to come, I'le make this Vow,
> From aberrations to live free;
> So I'le not feare the Judge, or thee.

The "norm" from which he has been aberrant, he owns, is not subjective or relativistic, despite his natural inclination to wish it so. This is the apprehension Coleridge describes in "Lines suggested by the last words of Berengarius":

> No more 'twixt conscience staggering and the Pope
> Soon shall I now before my God appear,
> By him to be acquitted, as I hope;
> By him to be condemned, as I fear. (1-4)

Belief that the normative standard in terms of which conscience speaks is indeed objective, eternal, and expressed in the law as rooted in the holiness of God is basic to dramatic conflict in Marlowe's *The Tragicall Historie of Doctor Faustus.* It helps to explain why Faustus, stung by his conscience and fretting over the fact that he has denied God, succumbs to despair. (Marlowe's play has been linked to another, *The Conflict of Conscience,* by his contemporary Nathaniel Wood.) Goethe's Faust has less difficulty with conscience, partly because, like the *Übermensch* of Nietzsche's *Also Sprach Zarathustra* or the manly hero of his *Genealogy of Morals* (pt. 2), he is true to the instinct to mastery, especially self-mastery, an "autonomous and supra-moral man" who may with impunity shun the "bad conscience" which arises from "the will to mistreat oneself" (*Antichrist,* 55).

Some of the Church Fathers understood conscience to be a divine faculty in humans (e.g., St. Augustine, *De utilitate credendi,* 34). Similarly, Oscar Wilde's Dorian Gray claims that conscience is the image of God in mankind: "It is the divinest thing in us" (chap. 8). Antonio in *The Tempest* scoffs at the idea — "I feel not this deity in my bosom" (2.1.278) — but Milton's God says, "I will place within them as a guide My umpire conscience" (*PL* 2.194-95). Marvell describes conscience as "that Heaven-nursed plant," the reward of whose tilling in the earthly garden is sanctity in heaven ("Upon Appleton House," 353-60). Yet Milton's famous cry in his *Areopagitica* could be readily adapted to libertarian as well as evangelical purposes: "Give me the liberty to know, to utter, and to argue freely according to conscience, above all liberties." Browning later defines conscience as "the great beacon-light God sets in all" (*Stafford,* 4.2.178).

The claim that conscience was itself a divine lawgiver led to the troublesome conclusion that different persons acknowledge different inner laws. Consequently, we have the notion of "Liberty of Consciences" which appears in Butler's *Hudibras* (1.1.765) or Robinson Crusoe's self-congratulatory boast just before departing from the island that he had "allowed liberty of conscience throughout my dominions" to a Protestant, a Catholic, and a pagan. Shakespeare's *Henry 8* focuses on the battle between the primacy of "private conscience" (5.2.178-80) and the authority of the Church, and Launcelot Gobbo's humorous dialogue with his conscience in *The Merchant of Venice* (2.1.1-32) echoes the explicit discussion of Aquinas on this question (*De Veritate,* 17.5; cf. *2 Sententiae,* 44.2.2). Robert Bolt's *A Man for All Seasons* presents the other side of the coin, yet Sir Thomas More is made to argue from the same premise: "I believe when statesmen forsake their own private conscience for the sake of their public duties . . . they lead their countries by a short route to chaos" (Act 1). These plays seem to pit a Catholic or "foundational" point of view, which tends to find the ultimate guide to personal conscience in an external authority and tradition, against a post-Reformation disposition to find guidance by letting conscience itself interpret and apply the gospel. The *Sermons* and *Analogy of Religion* (1736) of the Anglican Bishop Butler, e.g., anticipate a more general post-Enlightenment or Latitudinarian view (cf. Tillotson's sermons): individual conscience is made the pivot of ethics — perhaps not precisely what the apostle Paul had in mind. A generation earlier Dryden's *The Hind and the Panther* had joined the debate against such views by investigating the consequence of letting "private conscience" be the guide against "her claim to church auctority" (1.478-80). A harbinger of 19th- and 20th-cent. developments is Wordsworth's *Excursion,* where the author insists that the aesthetic awareness of nature leads inevitably to the ethical imperatives of conscience and that victory in life is "entire submission to the law / Of conscience — conscience reverenced and obeyed" (4.224-25).

The older idea of conscience as witness to God's law came under direct attack in the Victorian period. Matthew Arnold, in a celebrated chapter in *Culture and Anarchy,* decried as repressive the "Hebraic impulse" which had inculcated "strictness of conscience" or a sense of sin in mankind throughout history, advocating in its place a new Hellenism which would sponsor a "spontaneity of consciousness" free yet not anarchic. What Arnold really argues for, in effect, is the relativity of conscience, its independence from biblical law or revelation. (Arnold's aversion to a "guilty" conscience may seem to parallel that of Freud, though for Freud the negative element in self-consciousness is associated also with Pauline and hence "hellenistic" internalization.) It is here that the seeds of the radical separation of conscience as a term for ethics and "consciousness" as one for psychology were first planted. James Joyce widened this split even further. In *A Portrait of the Artist as a Young Man* Stephen Dedalus leaves behind both the priesthood and Ireland "to forge in the smithy of his soul the uncreated conscience of his race." Stephen dismisses the traditional "ache of conscience" he feels as a result of his sins earlier in the book in order to become both internal and external lawgiver, the standard himself by which to judge the acts of his countrymen. Ultimately, he substitutes a personal aesthetic conscience for an ethical one. Wilde's *The Picture of Dorian Gray,* on the other hand, where the portrait of the hero acts as "a visible emblem of conscience," apprehends a profound psychic disturbance in the unresolved modern split between psychology / aesthetics and theology / ethics. *A Case of Conscience,* by James Blish (1958), is a space-age fantasy whose protagonist, a Jesuit priest and scientist Fr. Ruiz-Sanchez, attempts to resolve a crisis among a race of reptilian aliens so totally reliant upon reason that they have become incapable of faith or belief, and hence socially paralyzed.

Bibliography. Barfield, O. *History in English Words* (1967), 133, 169-72; Brown, C., and H. C. Hahn. "Conscience." *NIDNTT* 1.348-53; Burke, C. *Conscience and Freedom* (1978); Campbell, L. B. *"Doctor Faustus:* A Case of Conscience." *PMLA* 67 (1952), 219-39; *Catholic Dictionary of Theology* (1962), 2.99-105; Delumeau, J. *Sin and Fear: The Emergence of a Western Guilt Culture* (13th-18th Centuries). Trans. E. Nicholson (1989); *Dictionnaire de spiritualité* (1932), 2.1547-75; Engelberg, E. *The Unknown Distance: From Consciousness to Conscience* (1972); Hastings, J., et al. *Encyclopedia of Religion and Ethics,* 4.30-47; Lewis, C. S. *Studies in Words* (1960), 181-213; Opperwall, R. "Conscience." *ISBE* 1.761-65; Pierce, C. A. *Conscience in the New Testament* (1955); Slights, C. W. *The Casuistical Tradition* (1981); Vitz, P. C. *Sigmund Freud's Christian Unconscious* (1988); Young, A. R. "Shakespeare's *Henry VIII* and the Theme of Conscience." *ESC* 8 (1981), 38-53.   DOMINIC MANGANIELLO

CONTRITION   *Contrition* is perhaps most succinctly defined in English literature by Chaucer's Parson, who says that "contricioun is the verray sorwe that a man receyveth in his herte for his synnes, with sad purpose to shryve hym, and to do penaunce, and nevermoore to do synne" (*Parson's Tale,* 10.128). The idea is rooted in the

biblical notion of a "broken and contrite heart" (Ps. 51:17), which, rather than burnt offerings, is the precondition of spirit which the Psalmist, repenting of his litany of sins involving Bathsheba, is comforted to know that God "will not despise."

The Hebrew word here used, *dakah,* literally means "bruised" (cf. Isa. 57:15), as does the Lat. *contritus* (also used in Vg to translate Heb. *nekeh,* from *naka',* "broken" or "distressed," in Isa. 66:2). This was a pre–18th-cent. literal meaning in English as well; hence the sometime association with "bruised" and "broken" reed (e.g., Jeremy Taylor, "strengths . . . no greater than a contrite reed," in *Sermons for the Yeare,* 1.27.345).

For the Fathers, contrition was fundamental to a biblical view of divine and human relations. As St. Augustine observed in his *Confessiones,* it is a chief feature distinguishing the ethical thought of ancient Greece and Rome from that of the Bible. Referring especially to his erstwhile favorite, he says that Plato's "pages contain not the expression of this piety — the tears of confession, thy sacrifice, a troubled spirit, 'a broken and a contrite heart', the salvation of thy people . . . the cup of redemption" (7.21.27). St. Gregory the Great stresses the psychopharmical foundation:

> For it is not as if God were fed by our torments but that he heals the diseases of our transgressions by medicines opposed to them, in order that we, who have departed from him delighted by pleasures, may return to him embittered by tears . . . and that the heart which a demented joy had flooded may be burnt clean by wholesome sadness, that what the elation of pride had wounded might be cured by the dejection of a humble heart. . . . Hence it is said "A bruised and a humbled heart God does not despise." (*Regulae pastoralis,* 30.31)

Strictly speaking, in Catholic doctrine contrition is but one aspect of the Sacrament of Penance. The others are confession and satisfaction. Drawing on Augustine and St. John Chrysostom, St. Thomas Aquinas begins his treatment of the process with an etymological grounding: "Since it is requisite for the remission of sin that one break away entirely from that habitual taste for sin which implies a sort of ongoing and hardened cast of mind, the act which obtains forgiveness is termed by a figure of speech, *contrition* [the breaking of something which has hardened]" (*In Lib. Sent.* 4, dist. 17; cf. Supp. 3, q.1.a.1). The "spirituality of the broken heart" was particularly developed in the later Middle Ages, however, by the Franciscans. With their emphasis on identification with the Passion of Christ as the font of all sacramental grace, and in the precedence they gave to affectual over intellectual response (to some degree anticipated by St. Bernard of Clairvaux), contrition came to be the central aspect of penance. For Alexander of Hales it is "that action proceeding out of charity and justice" which places a heart in the way of God's grace: as a person annihilates self in contrition, God then annihilates his or her guilt in the remission of sin (*Glossa Ordinaria*, 4.22.382). In contrition, typically, "guilt is remitted," whereas "in confession and satisfaction the penalty is remitted, yet at times both are remitted through contrition alone" (*Glossa*, 4.14.210). The influence of the Franciscans on medieval vernacular lyrics, from the *Stabat Mater* poems of Jacopone da Todi to the proliferation of affectual Passion lyrics in ME such as "Behold to þe lord, man, where he hangiþ on rode, / And weep, if þou miȝt, teris al of blode" (MS Harley 913), is characterized by this emphasis:

> Hi sike, al wan hi singe,
> for sorue þat hi se
> wan hic wit wepinge
> bi-holde a-pon þe tre. (C. Brown, *English Lyrics of the XIIIth Century,* no. 64)

Sorrow, as well as hatred for sin, is seen as involved in contrition — but in attempting to correct somewhat the affectual emphasis of his earlier *confrères,* St. Bonaventure makes the former really a function of the latter; the commitment of the will against sin is what produces sorrow for sin's presence (cf. *In Lib. Sent.* 4, dist. 16.1.1). This contrition, he says elsewhere, is essential for conversion, since "no one can begin a new life who does not lay down the old" (ibid. 2.1.2; 1.1.3; cf. Council of Trent 14.4, *"De Contritione"*). Nevertheless he sees contrition as not entirely self-willed, but prompted and effected by "grace that disposes to forgiveness" (*In Lib. Sent.* 4, dist. 14.1.2.3; 17.1.1.3). When Langland in *Piers Plowman* (B.14.89) speaks of the necessity of being "inliche contrit," he reflects his disposition to emphasize the affectual as, alluding to Ps. 51:17, Cranmer does later in the *Book of Common Prayer* (1549): "Create and make in vs new and contrite heartes"; in the Prayer of General Confession (1564) one is *"heartily* sorry for these our misdoings," while the Absolution is pronounced as "forgiveness of sins to all them that with *hearty* repentance and true faith turn unto him."

Calvin resists the Catholic division of penance into three actions as a manipulation of dialectics: "No doubt, they talk much of contrition . . . torment of soul with many scruples, and involve it in great trouble and anxiety; but when they seem to have deeply wounded the heart, they cure all its bitterness by a slight sprinking of ceremonies" (*Inst.* 3.4.1). Calvin's own emphasis falls, characteristically, on divine mercy rather than individual sincerity: "Our doctrine was, that the soul looked not to its own compunction or its own tears, but fixed both eyes on the mercy of God alone . . ." since the sinner is, in Calvin's view, in any case incapable of "a full and complete contrition" (*Inst.* 3.4.3). The relegation of contrition as simply an effect or by-product of God's electing grace in Calvinism is somewhat more severe than its correspondence in Lutheran thought, which falls between the Catholic and Calvinist positions: the Augsburg Confession has repentance divided into two more or less balanced parts,

"contrition and faith," the one the fruit of the preaching of the Law, the other of the Gospel (art. 12).

Milton's Adam, perhaps following Calvin's emphasis, puts contrition in sequence after confession. Trying to comfort his spouse and fellow sinner, he says:

> What better can we do, than . . . prostrate fall
> Before him reverent, and there confess
> Humbly our faults, and pardon beg, with tears
> Watering the ground, and with our sighs the Air
> Frequenting, sent from hearts contrite, in sign
> Of sorrow unfeigned, and humiliation meek. (*Paradise Lost*, 10.1086-92)

The narrator adds that their confession and contrition had been made possible by "prevenient Grace descending" (11.3). Looking at Calvin (or Beza) from a more oblique angle, Donne's attention was captured by the "inconstancy" of will in contrition, forcing him to confess

> . . . that when I would not
> I change in vowes, and in devotione.
> As humorous is my contritione
> As my prophane Love, and as soon forgott. ("Holy Sonnet 19")

Here, influenced by the *Spiritual Exercises* of St. Ignatius of Loyola, he signals a strongly affective emphasis on the action of contrition in "Holy Sonnet 3," as well as a sense that God's grace must for him precede true sorrow for sin in the concluding lines of "Holy Sonnet 7" and "8."

The word *contrition* came only slowly to be used in a general way as simply an equivalent for self-effacement or regret. It still has its biblical force in Shakespeare's *Henry 5,* where Henry prays for mercy before battle, asking God to observe that despite his father's sins, in his own reburying the body of Richard, he bestowed upon it "more contrite tears / than from it issued forced drops of blood" (4.2.313-14). In its close assocation with humility, as, e.g., in Thackeray's *Vanity Fair,* one sees a secularization: "Sedley was very contrite and humbled though the fact is, that William Dobbin had told a great falsehood to the old gentleman" (chap. 38). Part of the shift toward the secularized synonymity with "humility" is attributable to the neoclassical spirit of the 18th cent. in which many, like Dr. Johnson, were "no friend to those who make religion too hard" (Boswell, *Life,* 5.316) and in which contrition became (in all but Methodist and non-Juror circles) an unpopular concomitant to "rational religion." In this vein the Rev. Dean Jonathan Swift will allow only a hypocritical contrition to the swine in "The Beasts' Confession to a Priest" (1745) who, "with contrite heart allowed his shape and beauty made him proud." Christopher Smart, however, felt the original meaning more deeply than most, and wrote:

> God's best offering is contrition
> From a man divinely meek;
> Thou reject'st not the condition
> Of a heart at point to break. (*Psalms of David*, 51)

A second influence upon the conflation with humility is probably *The Book of Common Prayer* itself, in which the last and increasingly most cited preface for the popular service of evensong or Evening Prayer is Isa. 57:15: "I dwell in the high and holy place, with him also that is of a contrite and humble spirit." One senses the echo of this passage, as well as of Ps. 51:17, in Kipling's "Recessional":

> The tumult and the shouting dies —
> The Captain and the Kings depart —
> Still stands Thine ancient sacrifice,
> An humble and a contrite heart.

Walter Scott's Rebecca had given earlier evidence of a blending of the similar passages in her hymn:

> But thou hast said, The blood of goat,
> The flesh of rams I will not prize.
> A contrite heart, a humble thought,
> Are mine accepted sacrifice, (*Ivanhoe*, chap. 40)

while Isa. 57:15 by itself, mediated by the liturgy for Evening Prayer, surely informs Aldous Huxley's description of Mr. Hutton in Act 3 of his *The Gioconda Smile*, who "went to bed humble and contrite, but with a sense that grace had entered into him."

In literature after Freud contrition remains a remarkably vigorous concept. Though occasionally invoked in parody, as by Hardy: "Ah well! let me take the name of drunkard humbly — let me be a man of contrite knees" (*Far from the Madding Crowd*, chap. 42), or bemusedly, as by Dickens's narrator in *Pickwick Papers* (chap. 6), it offers a powerful foil to the modernist ideal of moral and psychological self-sufficiency (cf. Richard Wilbur's poem "The Water Walker"). James Joyce instances a traditional reflection on contrition in the poignant vocational musings of Stephen Dedalus: "Their piety would be like their names, like their faces, like their clothes, and it was idle for him to tell himself that their humble and contrite hearts, it might be, paid a far richer tribute of devotion than his had ever been, a gift ten-fold more acceptable than his elaborate adoration" (*Portrait of the Artist*, chap. 4).

See also BRUISED REED; CONFESSION; CONVERSION; REPENTANCE; SACRAMENT.

Bibliography. Denzinger, H., and A. Schönmetzer. *Enchiridion Symbolorum* (1965); Jeffrey, D. L. *The Early English Lyric and Franciscan Spirituality* (1975); McNeill, J. J., and H. M. Gower. *Medieval Handbooks of Penance* (1938); Peterson, D. L. "John Donne's Holy Sonnets and the Anglican Doctrine of Contrition." *SP* 56 (1959), 504-18.

CONVERSION Despite the nominal Christianization of Europe by the 12th cent., conversion has remained an important feature of religious experience in the West, and figures importantly as a center of interest in English poetry, fiction, and drama.

The term appears in the OT *(shub;* also *panah; hapak;*

sabab), in later prophetic writings to refer to the return from captivity (Isa. 1:27; Jer. 29:14; Ezek. 16:53), and in other places figuratively meaning to turn back to God (1 Sam. 7:3; 1 Kings 8:33; Isa. 19:22; Hos. 6:1; 7:10). Gentile conversion to Judaism, a relatively rare phenomenon in the OT, involved circumcision; this is how Josephus reads the "turning" in Esth. 8:17 (*Ant.* 11.6.13); in later times such converts were not considered "perfect" Jews because their conversion was "not above suspicion" (Yebam. 24b).

The term as it appears in the LXX and NT is typically *strephō, epistrephō,* or a cognate, used figuratively to signify a turning from wrongdoing to right (Matt. 13:15; Mark 4:12; Luke 22:32; Acts 9:35; 11:21; 14:15; 15:19; 26:18; 2 Cor. 3:16; 1 Thess. 1:9; James 5:19ff.). The word *hypostrephō,* meaning to turn away from right to wrong, is used in 2 Pet. 2:21.

In the Bible, conversion has both a divine and human aspect. In the OT, it is God who "turns back" Israel, or "turns his people to himself," and while this is less explicit in the NT, the action of the Holy Spirit seems always to be implied in conversion. The human side of conversion involves repentance and faith. When the "call" to repentance is heard in a NT context, the individual first turns from idolatry, Satan, or worship of the "dead letter" in an authentic repentance which involves renunciation of past sins. But "the call is not simply a command to fulfill particular moral obligations to 'amend one's life'" (K. Rahner, *Concise "Sacramentum Mundi,"* 292); the individual completes his or her "revolution" by turning to God in true faith and heartfelt commitment. In most NT instances this is the process whereby unbelievers become followers of Christ (e.g., Acts 3:19; 1 Thess. 1:9), but a renewal of believers can also be signified (Luke 22:32). Such acts of conversion may be sudden, as in the cases of Paul (Acts 9) and the Philippian jailer (Acts 16), or gradual, with a period of preparation, as in the cases of the Ethiopian eunuch (Acts 8) and the centurion Cornelius (Acts 10).

By the 3rd cent. baptism of new converts from paganism, often involving exorcism, took place on the eve of Easter or Pentecost. In a dramatic ceremony, candidates renounced evil, professed faith in Christ, and promised obedience to him, then were given new garments and sometimes gifts of milk and honey, symbolizing their beginning of the "new life" (*ISBE* 1.769). In one of his Antioch homilies, St. John Chrysostom comments in reference to 1 Cor. 1:26-27 "that not many wise men after the flesh, not many mighty, not many noble" are called, that the impediments of pride of intellect, like pride of power, harden the heart. "Not unlearned persons only, but needy also, and contemptible and obscure he has called, that he might humble those in high places," he observes, since they are more open to response and more likely to be willing to bring their hearts into conformity with the will of God (*Hom.* 5, on 1 Cor. 1–3).

St. Augustine writes in the *Confessiones* of the effect upon himself and others of the dramatic conversion of Victorinus, the great Roman orator, who, like St. Ambrose, was led to the church to make his profession by St. Simplicianus (8.2.3-5). He then recounts his own struggles with carnal appetite, spiritual pride, and professional vanity (8.8-11), before yielding at last to the tears of contrition. In reflection on an account of the conversion of St. Anthony (whose "call" was the text in Matt. 19:21), and having heard the prompting of the Spirit in the form of children's singing over the wall *tolle lege,* "pick it up and read it," he grasped his copy of St. Paul's epistle and his eyes fell on Rom. 13:13-14: "Not in rioting and drunkenness, not in chambering and wantonness, not in strife and envying. But put ye on the Lord Jesus Christ, and make not provision for the flesh, to fulfil the lusts thereof" (8.12.29). The apropos of Augustine's "call" to conversion is abundantly evident from the account *(confessio)* of his life to this point; the denouement is a swift release into tranquility: "for instantly, as the sentence ended — by a light, as it were, of security infused into my heart — all the gloom of doubt vanished away."

Augustine's account of his own conversion proved seminal for subsequent Christian literature and has influenced, in a variety of ways, the conversion accounts of Luther, St. Ignatius Loyola, Pascal, Kierkegaard, and others.

Although the rapid nominal Christianization of Europe made adult conversion gradually less frequent, so that the term came at last to be applied to the taking of holy orders by St. Gregory the Great and others, referring especially to monastic profession (e.g., *Ep.* 48; 50), it was used also of notable incidents which combine the two senses — as in the conversions of St. Francis and St. Dominic. That of St. Francis in particular, with his dramatic casting away of his father's clothes to step naked into the protective enfolding of the bishop's surplice in front of the whole village, recalls in extravagant form early Christian baptismal liturgy described by Augustine and St. John Chrysostom (Thomas of Celano, *Vita*, 1.3; 1.6.14-15).

The best known of early English conversion stories is that of King Edwin of Northumbria, recorded by the Venerable Bede. In it two pagan counselors give their opinion in favor of such a conversion, the one on materialist grounds, for greater benefits, the other out of a yearning for greater certainty about what lies beyond mortal life, which he likens to the flight of a sparrow out of the stormy winter night for a fleeting moment through the warm, lighted hall, then again into the darkness (*Hist. Eccl.* 2.13). The *Emendatio Vitae* of Richard Rolle (ca. 1340) begins with a chapter *"De Conversio,"* which he describes as a "turning away from the world and sin, the devil and flesh" and a "turning to God . . . from changeable to unchangeable good"; Rolle is here reflecting Gregory's sense of "conversion" to the contemplative life,

although the text admits of a more general application. In Chaucer's *Canterbury Tales, The Second Nun's Tale* of St. Cecelia, coming near the end of the pilgrimage, is about the sanctity of an early Christian who proved an instrument of grace in the conversion of Romans all around her, including even her tormentors. This classic hagiographical theme, reflected also in *The Clerk's Tale,* is moved from "historical" setting (in the 2nd cent.) to contemporary "autobiography" in the next tale. Here the Canon's Yeoman confesses his erstwhile allegiance to the "false chanoun," a predatory alchemical magus; in the process of confessing he also "turns" away from his old master, joining the pilgrimage to Canterbury and a new profession. *The Parson's Tale* sums up the meaning of turning away from sins (in repentance) and turning toward God (in acceptance of Christ's grace through faith informed by love).

Medieval lyrics often put the appeal to conversion in still more urgent terms, sometimes reflecting a Franciscan spiritual emphasis on the need for an affectual, not merely intellectual response to God's offer of grace in Christ. The language, however, from the lyric "Lord, thou clepedest me" (C. Brown, *Religious Lyrics of the XIVth Century,* no. 5) to Friar James Ryman's "Revert, revert" (Jeffrey, *Law of Love,* 121) is often Augustinian; the former poem is based on a passage in *The Confessiones* (8.5), the latter on Augustine's *vertere, revertere, convertere* wordplay (8.7.16). Ryman's verses conclude with Jesus speaking to the sinner: "I axe namore, man, but thyne herte. Revert, revert, revert, revert." The Augustinian model also lies behind Dante's *Vita Nuova,* an allegorical essay with love poems to Beatrice in which he describes his conversion from carnal to spiritual love.

In the drama, it might be argued, morality plays like *Everyman* are essentially conversion plays; some saints' plays certainly are — including the Digby *Mary Magdalen* and *The Conversion of St. Paul.* In the Paul play biblical language and incident directly inform the play; in *Mary Magdalen* the biblical narrative is extensively augmented by use of the *legenda.* In Shakespeare's *2 Henry 4,* there is a vestige of this pattern when Prince Hal recognizes that he must rise from folly to pursue his regal duty; he puts off his former counselor, his "old man," characterized by Falstaff, saying:

> Presume not that I am the thing I was,
> For God doth know, so shall the world perceive,
> That I have turned away my former self,
> So will I those that kept me company. (5.5.60-63)

The Reformation introduced new views of the nature and necessity of conversion. The most significant of these is the terse view of Calvin, in which the penitent's response to the Word in contrition is downplayed and conversion seen as the work of God alone: "If it is like turning a stone into flesh when God turns us to the study of rectitude, everything proper to our own will is abolished, and that which succeeds in its place is wholly of God" (*Inst.* 2.3.6). Otherwise, he argues, "if any, even the minutest, ability were in ourselves, then would also be some merit." Accordingly, Calvin has little else to say on the subject except notably that conversion involves not only justification but also sanctification. Luther links conversion to repentance and faith. Pietist writers, including especially those influenced by Arminian theology like some of the dissenters and later Wesley in England, gave the element of "personal decision" a greater prominence. The Anglican *Homilies Appointed to Be Read in Churches* subsumes these matters under sermons on "Salvation," "The True and Lively Faith," and "Repentance," tending to follow a middle way between Luther and Catholic thought on the one hand and Calvin on the other.

John Donne offers a classic Augustinian example of conversion as repentance of a nominal believer in "Good Friday, 1613, Riding Westward," which moves from "forraigne motions" to a paradox in which, in response to Calvary, the speaker says, "I turne my backe to thee, but to receive, / Corrections," and then pleads that the divine image will be restored in him by grace: "That thou may'st know mee, and I'll turne my face." Bunyan's *Grace Abounding to the Chief of Sinners* (1666) describes his own conversion as a gradual awakening following the reading of two devotional books belonging to his wife, Dent's *Plain Man's Pathway to Heaven* and Bayly's *Practice of Piety*. Defoe's *Robinson Crusoe* presents the marooned hero who discovers a Bible in the ship's wreckage, begins to read it, and "not long after" is moved to repentance and conversion, something he later enjoins also upon his servant Friday. As is characteristic of Puritan treatments of conversion, the focus falls upon the individual encounter with Scripture, followed by a prompting by the Holy Spirit to repentance and resolution to declare faith in Christ and "confess him before men" — the latter "confession" providing much of the substance of Defoe's conversion narrative.

John Dryden, whose conversion to Roman Catholicism is reflected in the skeptical fideism of his *Religio Laici* and *The Hind and the Panther,* represents the conversion of a heathen philosopher Apollonius to the essentially rationalist arguments of St. Catherine in his play *Tyrannic Love* (1670). Swift suspects Presbyterians, Anabaptists, Independents, and Quakers of being "emissaries" of the Jesuits, presumably because they each preached a species of radical adult conversion *(The Abolishing of Christianity in England)*. The growth of pietism in the 18th cent., often derided under the name "enthusiasm," has much to do with the development of which Swift was apprehensive. John Wesley's High Church revivalism was substantially altered by his contact with the Moravians, who aspired to the life of the primitive Church and stressed the all-importance of conversion. The Arminian bias in subsequent Wesleyan thought split the Methodist movement; George Whitefield remained Calvinist, and, with other evangelicals of moderate Calvinist persuasion, emphasized "predestination unto salvation" although retaining more of a conversionist theology than is found in Calvin. Augustus Toplady, author of "Rock of Ages" ("Nothing in my hand I bring. . . .") wrote that "'Tis true that none can come except as they are *drawn* by God's Spirit. But 'tis also no less true that those are drawn who come, and that all who come shall be graciously received" (quoted in Wright, *Toplady and Contemporary Hymn-Writers,* 242). Conversion is thus proof of election. "Rock of Ages" was explicitly anti-Wesleyan, addressed to "The Holiest Sinner in the World," and pleading "Save me from its [sin's] guilt and power" — where Wesley taught that conversion saves from the guilt of sin but not its power. Toplady thus accords with Calvinist contemporaries in believing conversion to include sanctification as well as justification.

Dickens's *A Christmas Carol* is perhaps his clearest secularized version of the evangelical conversion experience. As with Calvin himself, or Bunyan, conviction of sin (accompanied by terror over the prospect of damnation) is the first stage in the conversion process. The "time-spirits" of past, present, and future take the place of the Holy Spirit in producing conviction in Scrooge, following whose repentance "Christ" is reborn in him as charity, or kindliness. With Wesley's followers as well as those of Whitefield, Doddridge, and others preaching in public places about repentance and conversion, anonymous satiric pamphlets soon sprang up with titles such as *Fanatical Conversion* (1779) and *The Temple of Imposture* (1778), in which Mahomet the arch-imposter declares:

In servile Imitation of my Plan,
Priests now in Tabernacles fish for Man.
There, to thy Honour, Goddess, thou canst see
M[ada]n, R[omai]ne, and W[esle]y, mimic *me.*

Other 18th-cent. treatments of conversion vary from *Tom Jones*'s gentle transformation in the fashion of Augustine and Dante in Fielding's great novel (1749) to John Newton's extremely popular *Authentic Narrative* (1764), a spiritual autobiography which may in part have influenced that of his friend and protégé, William Cowper. Cowper's *Memoir,* containing the account of his conversion, is influenced also by Augustine's *Confessiones.* His *Conversation* is a poetic plea against vain and idle talk (including religious talk of those who vainly rely on baptismal regeneration) and for the transformed "conversation in the Spirit" of those who have experienced the "new birth."

The 19th cent. offers a variety of literary treatments of conversion. Wordsworth, whose naturalism excluded much of Christian supernaturalism, writes in *Peter Bell* (1798; rev. 1819, 1827, 1832) of a moral rather than religious conversion, effected through a chain of natural events. The Oxford Movement, which saw figures of evangelical persuasion such as J. H. Newman move toward Rome while sons of High Churchmen, like Pusey and Keble, stayed, is indicative of a growing emphasis on Augustinian or Pauline conversion in 19th-cent. English Catholicism. A reaction to Romanticism and to various forms of romanticized faith, it helps in part to account for the appeal of the Catholic Church to the sons of notable evangelical statesman William Wilberforce, three of whom, with both his daughters and their husbands, became Catholics. While Keble's *Christian Year* upholds paedobaptism instead of conversion, Newman writes of the transforming "voice, speaking so clearly in my conscience and in my heart" (*Apologia pro Vita Sua,* 219). Francis Thompson's "The Hound of Heaven," rich with echoes of the Psalms, records how "I fled Him, down the nights and down the days," but moves to a point of recollection where "ever and anon a trumpet sounds," and Christ the trumpeter, "him who summoneth," turns him to himself at last.

In Protestant circles the emphasis on conversion was being expressed in strikingly similar terms, as in C. H. Spurgeon's sermon "Regeneration" (Sermon 14 on John 3:3). A novel like Dickens's *Little Dorrit,* with its metaphors of birth and rebirth, is closer in many respects to Spurgeon than to the apocalyptic romanticism of Carlyle. Carlyle's Teufelsdröckh experiences a conversion of *Weltanschauung* momentous enough that he wakes to visions of "a new Heaven and a new Earth," the product of a "Spiritual Newbirth" occasioned by his assertion of his personal freedom. Most religious conversions in the 19th-cent. novel, however, are after the pattern of Dostoevski's *Crime and Punishment,* conducted offstage.

In the 20th cent., G. B. Shaw's *Major Barbara* is a Fabian socialist's skeptical look at the Christian "socialism" and conversion theology of the Salvation Army of William Booth. Shaw's stated opinion was that conversion is impossible, so that a savage converted to Christianity means Christianity converted to savagery (cf. *Androcles and the Lion; The Shewing-Up of Blanco Posnet*). A conversion to Anglo-Catholicism was to redirect and subsequently recharacterize the major poetry of T. S. Eliot, who reflects on the new birth in his "Journey of the Magi." Eliot's conversion was not well received by critics (e.g., Edmund Wilson, *Axel's Castle*) at the time; subsequently it has become a major source of interest in defining his poetics. Margaret Avison's *The Dumbfounding* (1966) is a more recent poetic diary of conversion in which are found echoes of Eliot and Donne, as well as of Augustine and Paul. In it the familiar tension between personal freedom and death to self for the sake of "new life" in Christ marks a strong continuity with ancient as well as modern explorations of the "psychology" of conversion.

See also OLD AND NEW.

Bibliography. Bredvold, L. *The Intellectual Milieu of John Dryden* (1934; 1956); Bromiley, G. W. "Conversion." *ISBE* 1.768-70; Caldwell, P. *The Puritan Conversion Narrative* (1983); Freccero, J. *Dante: The Poetics of Conversion.* Ed. R. Jacoff (1986); Fredricksen, P. "Paul and Augustine: Conversion Narratives, Orthodox Traditions, and the Retrospective Self." *JTS* n.s. 37 (1986); Jeffrey, D. L. *A Burning and a Shining Light: English Spirituality in the Age of Wesley* (1987); *The Law of Love: English Spirituality in the Age of Wyclif* (1988); Kuder, S. R. "The Literature of Conversion: Religious Background and Literary Achievement in Dante Alighieri, John Bunyan, and James Joyce." *DAI* 36 (1975), 3655A; Larson, J. *Dickens and the Broken Scripture* (1985); Meulman-Young, S. "Coleridge and Conversion: A Reading of *The Rime* as a Poetic Confession." *DAI* 47 (1987), 3763A; Poland, L. M. "Augustine, Allegory, and Conversion." *Journal of Literature and Theology* 2 (1988), 37-48; Rahner, K. "Conversion." *Concise "Sacramentum Mundi"* (1975).

CORINTHIANS   The city of Corinth was a prosperous trading center, built by Julius Caesar in 46 B.C. as a Roman colony with Latin as its official language. Corinth was famous also for its temple of Aphrodite where a thousand prostitutes reputedly served, contributing thereby to the city's general reputation for immorality. Throughout the Mediterranean world "Corinthian girl" *(Korinthia kore)* became a euphemism for prostitute. As St. John Chrysostom notes in the preface to his *Homilies on 1 and 2 Corinthians,* these facts help to explain the principal concerns expressed in the two major epistles sent by the apostle Paul to the fledgling church in Corinth; it was a place of excessive self-indulgence of every kind. St. Isidore of Seville connects Corinth with Orestes and the troubled lineage of Thebes (*Sententiarum,* 15.1.45-46). Paul's two epistles are generally held to provide central Christian teaching on the transcendence of material preoccupation (e.g., 1 Cor. 2:9; 13:12; 2 Cor. 3:6) because of the Resurrection of Christ (1 Cor. 15:32, 52-56).

In Shakespeare's *A Midsummer Night's Dream,* Bottom recalls his encounter with Titania as "a most rare vision" and makes a comically garbled allusion to 1 Cor. 2:9. Shakespeare is probably indebted to Erasmus's *Praise of Folly,* which concludes by considering the deranged ecstasy of lovers as a foretaste of heavenly bliss. Erasmus adduces the text from Corinthians ("Eye hath not seen, nor ear heard . . .") to reinforce the Neoplatonic transcendentalism of his argument: spiritual experience seems merely foolish or inexplicable to limited human reason. The opening chapters of 1 Corinthians develop an antithesis between worldly and divine evaluations of folly and wisdom, and following Erasmus Shakespeare's comedy playfully allows his fool and his foolish lovers suprasensory experience. The Renaissance tradition of wise folly is indebted to St. Paul without deriving exclusively from him; hence "The fool doth think he is wise, but the wise man knows himself to be a fool" (*As You Like It,* 5.1.34-35) recalls the advice of Paul that "If any man among you seemeth to be wise in this world, let him become a fool, that he may be wise" (1 Cor. 3:18).

In *A Winter's Tale*, Paulina may owe her name to her dramatic function in restoring the supposedly dead Hermione to life (1 Cor. 15:51-52). A phrase used in these verses, "in the twinkling of an eye," is echoed in the report of a witness to the multiple and amazing reunions which take place before the "miracle" of Hermione's restoration: "Every wink of an eye some new grace will be born" (5.2.112-13). Throughout the play the recurrent word "grace" carries theological as well as courtly and humanist significance. But the restoration of Hermione, as a statue seemingly coming to life in the play's final scene, is pointedly not the "incorruptible" resurrection spoken of by Paul (the play draws poignant attention to the wrinkled appearance of Hermione after her sixteen years' seclusion) but a secular analogue to the scriptural assurance.

See also EYE HATH NOT SEEN; FOOL, FOLLY; THEOLOGICAL VIRTUES.

Bibliography. Kaiser, W. *Praisers of Folly* (1963).

DAVID J. PALMER

CORNERSTONE *See* STONE.

CORPUS CHRISTI The term *corpus Christi* ("body of Christ") derives from the NT accounts where the bread of the Eucharist is linked with the body of Christ sacrificed on the cross. In Matt. 26:26-28, Mark 14:22-24, Luke 22:19-20, and 1 Cor. 11:24-26, the NT attributes the origin of this association of the eucharistic bread with Christ's death to Jesus himself at the Last Supper.

In 1264 the annual feast of Corpus Christi was proclaimed by Pope Urban IV. Whereas Maundy Thursday, commemorating the historical institution of the Eucharist, is closely associated with the sorrowful events of Christ's Passion, Corpus Christi is marked by devotion to the consecrated elements themselves and by an unqualified joyful character, reflected in the proper Office and Mass traditionally attributed to St. Thomas Aquinas. The liturgical date of the feast, the Thursday after Trinity Sunday, may specifically reflect the sacrament's significance as a "memorial" of Christ's presence following the Ascension (*Speculum Sacerdotale,* 43). While proponents attributed pedagogical and moral as well as expiatory value to contemplation of the sacrament, critics from Wyclif (*De Eucharistia,* 9) to the Reformers objected to its association with the doctrine of transubstantiation.

Medieval vernacular preaching (e.g., *Mirk's Festial,* 41) promoted the feast of Corpus Christi by the use of *exempla* — the most popular being the Mass of St. Gregory — which dramatically depicted eucharistic miracles and influenced narrative literature of the period, including the unique Croxton *Play of the Sacrament.* ME mystery plays took the generic title "the plaie called Corpus Christi" from their performance at the time of the feast. Whether the association was incidental, as Rosemary Woolf believes (*English Mystery Plays,* 68-73), is a

matter of dispute. V. A. Kolve argues that the relationship between drama and feast was integral, that in celebrating the gift of the Eucharist, Corpus Christi also celebrates the mystical body of Christ and therefore entails the history of salvation from creation to the eschaton (Kolve, 44-49; see also Hardison, 286-87).

Devotional poetry of the Middle Ages and Counter-Reformation regularly links the Eucharist with the Incarnation and the mystery of faith. In his "Meditations on the Supper of our Lord" Robert Manning of Brunne emphasizes that sight of the sacrament implies perception of the Lord himself (205-18). A 15th-cent. lyric ("Ihū, my lord, welcome þu be!" in C. Brown, *Religious Lyrics of the XVth Century,* no. 115), which proclaims of the sacrament, "In flesch & blode I þe see, / Bath god and man veraly . . ." (2-3), rehearses the articles of the Creed pertaining to the Second Person of the Godhead. It also displays a liturgical intent, echoing the *Ave verum corpus* in its opening stanzas and commending (in an introductory rubric) its own recitation between the Agnus Dei and the elevation. The "Corpus Christi Carol" — which survives in British and American oral tradition into the 20th cent. — imaginatively links the Nativity and Passion and treats the mystery in chivalric terms (R. Greene, *Early English Carols,* 322).

Liturgical and theological treatments of the Host continue after the debates of the Reformation. In "Of the Blessed Sacrament of the Altar," Robert Southwell paraphrases the *Pange, Lingua* and appends several stanzas which expound Tridentine teaching and stress the Eucharist's paradoxical nature in metaphysical conceits: "The god of hoastes in slender hoste doth dwell" (61).

Post-17th-cent. literature often moves beyond doctrinal issues to suggest broader symbolic implications. In *Marius the Epicurean,* Walter Pater treats the Mass as the apex of cultural evolution — "the greatest act of worship the world has seen" — and quotes the *Tantum Ergo* in evidence of Christianity's having surpassed more primitive cults: "ET ANTIQUUM DOCUMENTUM / NOVO CEDAT RITUI." In contrast, the violent imagery of Dylan Thomas's "This Bread I Break" portrays nature as the sacrificial victim of humanity, reversing an earlier, positive view (e.g., "Of alle the spyces that I knowe, / Blyssid be the qwete flour" [Greene, *Early English Carols,* 320]). The Host in James Joyce's *Portrait of the Artist* manifests God's presence "burning with love for mankind, ready to comfort the afflicted" — as opposed to the fiery punishments of the damned — and serves for the newly shriven Stephen Dedalus as a symbol of new life through incorporation: "he would hold upon his tongue the host and God would enter his purified body." The motifs of the *Tantum Ergo* are central to Flannery O'Connor's "A Temple of the Holy Ghost," where they direct attention to the image of God in all human beings and, in a dramatic concluding statement, suggest the sacrament as a focal point for creation's primal role in conveying grace: "The sun was a huge red ball like an elevated Host drenched in blood and when it sank out of sight, it left a line in the sky like a red clay road hanging over the trees."

See also EUCHARIST; TRANSUBSTANTIATION.

Bibliography. Dix, E. *The Shape of the Liturgy* (1945); Hardison, O. B., Jr. *Christian Rite and Christian Drama in the Middle Ages: Essays in the Origin and Early History of Modern Drama* (1965); Jungmann, J. A. *The Mass of the Roman Rite: Its Origins and Development (Missa Sollemnia).* Trans. F. A. Brunner (1951); Kolve, V. A. *The Play Called Corpus Christi* (1966); Woolf, R. *The English Mystery Plays* (1972). ROBERT E. WRIGHT

CORRUPTIBLE AND INCORRUPTIBLE *See* TREASURES UPON EARTH.

COVENANT Covenant (Heb. *berit;* Gk. *diathēkē;* Lat. *feodus; pactum*) is a governing concept in biblical literature and one of the most pervasive motifs in biblical tradition. Covenant theology in various forms of Jewish and Christian elaboration is also one of the most complex and vexatious of subjects, with versions too prolix to be summarized in detail. Some of the foundational biblical narratives and a selection of historical literary responses may, however, be usefully identified.

In the OT, as in much of the ancient world, one of the earliest uses for written text was as a means of recording contractual agreements between individuals or groups. Indeed, "suzerainty" or lord-vassal treaties, established by the Hittite kings and recorded in surviving clay tablets, provided formal literary models for patterns observed in key biblical narratives; in one important case, it appears that the entire book of Deuteronomy closely adheres to the form of such treaties — preamble identifying parties, historical prologue, stipulations, list of divine witnesses, and a concluding statement of curses and blessings consequent upon performance of the terms (see Kline). In the case of Deuteronomy the covenant is a renewal document, gathering up and restating the substance of the covenants already iterated and reiterated in key patriarchal narratives. Among these are God's covenant with Noah not to destroy the earth again by flood, its "sign" being the rainbow (Gen. 9:9-17); his covenant with aged Abraham to provide offspring, a race from which deliverance would ensue, the sign of which is the rite of circumcision (Gen. 15:8-18; 17:1-14); God's covenant with the nation at Sinai (Horeb) in which refugee Israel is constituted as a "holy nation" and "kingdom of priests," the sign of which is not only the external sacrifice and sprinkling of blood (Exod. 14:4-8) but a text, the Decalogue (Exod. 20:1-17). Preeminently implicated, as many talmudic writings suggest, is the encapsulated Torah, sometimes identified with the "book of the covenant" from which Moses read (Exod. 24:7), containing, it seems, Exod. 20:22–23:33. Various other covenant renewals include that on the plains of Moab (Deut. 19), at Shechem with Joshua as leader of the people (Josh. 24), and in the "Davidic covenant," where God gave a promise to David that his descendants would have an "everlasting kingdom" (2 Sam. 7:12-17).

At such renewals typically a sacrifice was made to seal (or, as later Christian commentators would say, "sacramentalize") the agreement. Among Israel's neighbors such as the Hittites, the sacrificial animal was an ass; hence the expression "to kill an ass together" was among them figurative for making a covenant. The lamb typically sacrificed in Israel could also become a shared meal; hence the Jewish expression "a covenant of salt"; i.e., the parties eat together, indicating loyal friendship (Num. 18:19; cf. the Arabic expression, "there is salt between us"). Another Jewish expression arising from the sacrifice is "to cut a covenant" *(karat berit)* — i.e., to make a covenant; *berit* itself may derive from *barah,* "to eat bread with."

An important element in the biblical idea of covenant is the typically enduring nature of the commitments made: God's commitment to the seed of Abraham is said to be eternal; at the personal level, agreements between individuals were binding upon their successors, often for generations. An example is the pact sworn between Abraham and his servant that the latter should carry out his explicit directions in finding a wife for Isaac — not from among the Canaanites but from his own kindred. As the oath is sworn, Abraham directs the servant to place "thy hand under my thigh" (Gen. 24:1-4). In this ancient Near Eastern practice, making a promise with one's hand touching the testicles of the man to whom the promise is made is equivalent to binding performance of the vow on his successors as well, his "seed after him." The practice gives rise to a specialized form of "covenant," the "testament" (from Lat. *testes*), which in turn provides the English word for the Jewish and Christian scriptures.

Covenantal relationship with God provides both narrative structure and a basic historiography to OT literature and subsequent commentary upon it. The ethical opposition of obedience / disobedience is basic in both cases. When the "covenant people" transgress upon their covenantal obligations and fail to repent, disaster (the stipulated curse) falls upon them. In such a case God's mercy is still available if his people repent and seek him, but returning to obedience is the only path to salvation and renewed blessings. This theology of history is transparent in the books of Kings, Chronicles, and all of the prophets. In one prophetic book, Hosea, the covenant between God and his people is figured metaphorically in a marriage, the relationship between Hosea and his wayward wife.

In both theology and literature it is necessary to take cognizance of the term *new covenant,* which, despite its similarity to *New Testament,* occurs initially in the Hebrew Scriptures. Several passages in the prophets, but most notably in Jeremiah and Ezekiel, refer to a future new covenant to come in the time of the Messiah (Jer.

31:31-33; Ezek. 16:60-62; 34:25; 37:26; cf. Isa. 42:6; 49:6-8; 55:3; 59:21; Hos. 2:18). This is to be effectively a covenant renewal, except that it is to follow upon a long period of suffering and exile. It promises peace not only for Jews but for all the world (Jer. 32:37-40; Ezek. 34:23; 37:25ff.), a purification of worship (Ezek. 40–48), and true theocratic government. In the NT, when Gk. *diathēkē* ("testament" or "covenant") is adapted to convey the idea of *berit* in this sense of renewal and redemption, the most important context is the use Jesus makes of the term, according to St. Paul's summary (1 Cor. 11:25) at the Last Supper. The implicit analogy evoked by Jesus' words "this cup is the new testament in my blood" is with Moses sprinkling sacrificial blood, the "blood of the covenant which the LORD has made with you in accordance with all these words" (Exod. 24:8) as a ratification of the "book of the covenant." This blood is explicitly associated by the NT writers with forgiveness, reconciliation, and renewal (e.g., Matt. 26:28; Luke 22:20). For the Epistle to the Hebrews (9:11-23) Christ functions both as high priest or mediator in the covenant renewal — a second Moses — and also as the sacrificial lamb (vv. 14-15). St. Paul contrasts the New Covenant with the Old Covenant in 2 Cor. 3, a passage crucial, for different reasons, to both medieval and Reformation thought: "our sufficiency is of God; Who also hath made us able ministers of the new testament; not of the letter, but of the spirit: for the letter killeth, but the spirit giveth life" (vv. 5-6). Paul goes on to contrast the "letter" of the Old Covenant "engraven in stones" and glorious in its own right, with the "ministrations of the spirit" in the New Covenant sealed by the blood of Christ, whereby the abiding significance of the Old Covenant is more gloriously "unveiled."

This Pauline passage, and others like it (cf. Gal. 4:22-27), provides the key to understanding the dialectic of Old and New Covenant established in medieval Christian typology and historiography. Considering the unfulfilled (messianic) promises of covenant renewal heralded by the prophetic writings and the Psalms, St. Augustine recognizes the "ancient people of Jacob, the people of Israel, born of Abraham's seed in the promise to become one day the heir of God. That was indeed a real people, to which the Old Testament was given." But on Paul's authority he adds that "in the Old Testament the New was figured: that was the figure, this the truth expressed" (*Enarr. in Ps.* 84.2). He goes on to explain the relation of the Old Covenant globally considered as a "kind of foretelling of the future" revealed in the New, in which the promised "turning away" of the "captivity of Jacob" is fulfilled in the atonement. The covenant made with Abraham is indeed an "everlasting covenant," but not in "the old which is abolished, but the new which is hidden even in the old." Hence, after the New Covenant has been declared (the events and record of the NT), and with the aid of "searching in the Prophets," one sees "the Old Testament revealed in the New, the New veiled in the Old" (*Enarr.*

in Ps. 105.32-32). This leads Augustine to speak of all the Scriptures, OT and NT taken together, as "a kind of bond [*pactum*] of God's, which all who pass by might read, and might keep to the path of its promise." God has already done "great things" in accordance with his *pactum,* but more is to follow. It is as if God has said to humanity: "There in my bond read all that I have promised, reckon with me: verily even by counting up what I have already paid, you can well believe that I shall pay what I still owe" (*Enarr. in Ps.* 144.12). On this typological reckoning, then, the Bible is a binding record of the global covenant established and renewed with Israel, now in Christ extended to "spiritual" or "new" Israel. In essence, it is the Christian's "Book of the Covenant," in which OT and NT will always be found in agreement, when spiritually read (*Sermo,* 82.8). These formulations became normative to Christian use of the Bible.

This way of reading the text was, of course, troubling to many Jewish writers of the Middle Ages. A considerable portion of later rabbinic commentary is devoted, in fact, to disengaging Christian typological engrafting from passages in the Hebrew Scriptures which bind their covenant promises to the literal seed and lineage of Jacob. Of this considerable literature one example must suffice — Joseph Kimchi's *Seper ha-Berit,* or *The Book of the Covenant* (ca. 1160). The book is in Hebrew and is directed against apostates from Judaism who, following their conversion to Christianity, were endeavoring to evangelize Jews. The treatise is set forth as a dialogue between one who is faithful, a *ma'amin,* and a convert to Christianity, a *min;* in it the position of the *ma'amin* is represented as one of "reason," opposing the "foolishness" of an argument which would seem to suggest that God had annuled his original election of the Jews. The Mosaic covenant remains the normative covenant, Kimchi argues, and the Synagogue is still the "true Israel," despite rival Christian claims to that title.

One principal use of the covenant idea in the Middle Ages is unambiguously political: the analogy of OT covenants to the relations of kings to their peoples and lords to their vassals. The whole feudal order involved a system of analogous covenants, based upon biblical precedent, which provided for the form of legally binding covenant attestations for homage, marriage vows, and even for vows (poverty, chastity, obedience) made by priests to their bishop upon ordination (M. Bloch, *Feudal Society* [1964]). Echoes of these covenantal arrangements or pacts show up in medieval romance (Chrétien, Malory) and in Chaucer's *Troilus and Criseyde,* where Antigone's song, ostensibly composed by Helen of Troy, parodies covenant language (2.827-75).

Another more philosophical application has to do with a distinction made by nominalist theologians in the later Middle Ages between two "powers" of God, his eternal and absolute omnipotence by which anything is possible for him, and the covenantally limited powers in terms of which he allows to human persons free will to exercise moral responsibility in their lives. The "necessitee condicionel" of which Chaucer's Nun's Priest speaks in his *Tale* (7.3243-50) is conditioned by God's concessions in the covenant not to force compliance; his covenant is, as 14th-cent. theologian Robert Holcot puts it, *ex promisso suo et pacto sive lege statuta,* "an unfailing necessity appropriate to God because of his promise, that is his covenant, or established law" (*Super Libros Sapientiae,* 145.B).

The covenant theology of John Calvin differs in emphasis from the typical medieval Christian understanding in reading the New Covenant back into the Old in such a way that the Jews are included in both: "Who, then, will presume to represent the Jews as destitute of Christ, when we know that they were parties to the Gospel covenant, which has its only foundation in Christ?" (*Inst.* 2.10.4). The Israelites are here the Christians' "equals" before God, "not only in the grace of the covenant, but also in the signification of the Sacraments" (5). Speaking of the Jews of pre-New Testament times in particular, he says further: "Now when God, in ancient times, bound the Jews to him by this sacred bond [the *berit*], there cannot be a doubt that he separated them unto the hope of eternal life" (7). Calvin lays great emphasis on God's promise to extend his covenant blessings to Israel's seed and posterity (in 2.10.8-11, citing Gen. 17:7; Exod. 20:6, etc.); it is a generational "testament." Even as the patriarchs actually "had Christ as the pledge of their covenant" (2.10.23), so do Christians; hence their portion is to be the same in relation to their obedience. The "inheritance" is still that, passed on "from generation to generation of them that are called according to his word" (sup. Exod. 20:5-6). The "calling of the Gentiles" was a surprise to the apostles, being Jews (2.11.12), but they accepted it on account of Christ's commandment.

For Calvin, however, the OT is still the "literal" covenant, while the NT is "spiritual" (*Inst.* 2.11.7); hence as with Augustine and Paul, the Old belongs to "bondage," the New to "liberty" (2.11.9). Calvin and his followers distinguish also between a "covenant of works" (*Comm. on Genesis,* 1.117, sup. Gen. 2:3), basically the condition of Adam before the Fall and reiterated at Sinai, in which humanity was simply bound to obedience, and a "covenant of grace," the lineation of OT and NT covenants which together form the tradition of "salvation history" to which the "generations of the elect" are heir (cf. the *Westminster Confession of Faith,* 7.2; also Wollebius, *Compendium Theologiae Christianae,* 64). The covenant of works is also sometimes called in Calvinist and Puritan writings the "Covenant of Nature."

English literature in the Anglican tradition makes use of the relevant typologies but mitigates somewhat the Old Covenant / New Covenant vocabulary of Calvinist theology. The "implicite Covenant" to which George Herbert's Country Parson is bound (*A Priest to the Temple,* 2) is at one level his ordination vow, at another the Covenant of Grace; his duty is to declare the Law of God and the means of salvation. The "covenant 'twixt All and One" in Henry Vaughan's "The Rain-bow" is related by him in a footnote to "the everlasting covenant between God and every living creature" (cf. Gen. 9:16), explicitly the Covenant of Nature but implicitly a type of the Covenant of Grace. The litany of human disobedience he cites shows that "God doth keep / His promise still, but we break ours and sleep." The rest of the poem indicates that the sin which the Flood of the OT was not sufficient to wash away is washed away by "God's own blood," the seal of the NT and Covenant of Grace. English Puritan writers, however, echo Calvin's formulations on every page, and such concepts as the Covenant of Nature lie behind even Milton's *Tetrachordon* (*Works,* 4.74). Later, however, in his *De Doctrina Christiana* Milton argues that pre-fallen Adam was not required to perform any works, and that like the regenerate Christian he enjoyed freedom to fulfill the "inward law" (i.e., Covenant of Grace) through love (*Works,* 15.115). In *Paradise Lost* the conditions under which Adam is to live in Paradise are spelled out by God (8.317-33), but without any suggestion of covenant provisions (cf. 4.411-39).

The association of pre-fallen or paradisal conditions with regenerate sanctity is a strong feature of the Puritan covenant theology of New England, where the American "New Canaan" or "Promised Land" of the pilgrims is at once a paradise-like venue for new beginnings and also an unparalleled opportunity for the Puritans' long dreamed-of perfect theocracy. For their historiography, Jeremiah's prophecy of a New Covenant (31:31-33; 50:5) was central: this covenant was not for the Israel of Jeremiah's day but a new and "spiritual" Israel. In Peter Bulkeley's famous *The Gospel-Covenant* (1651), a developmental view of the covenant established six dispensations: "from Adam to Noah, from Noah to Abraham, from Abraham to Moses, from Moses to David, from David to CHRIST, from CHRIST to the end of the world" (113). But in Bulkeley's scheme, after Adam failed to keep the Covenant of Works, God voluntarily condescended to negotiate with humanity a new covenant for salvation by which, laying aside his omnipotent freedom, he would also abide. This Covenant of Grace applied to the elect only, of course, and to them "for the most part," but for practical purposes it guarantees God's perseverance in preserving the election of his "true Israel" from "Abraham to Boston" (Miller, 144). In Thomas Shepherd's preface to Bulkeley's sermons, he marks the sense of assurance New Englanders had in their special election:

And therefore when we break our Covenant, and that will not hold us, He takes a faster bond and makes a sure and everlasting Covenant, according to Grace, not according to Works; and that shall hold his people firm unto Himself, and hold Himself close and fast unto them, that He may never depart from us.

A disconcerting effect of this unbounded confidence is that it might make human responsibility — or obedience to God's law — somewhat less imposing a concern. Yet the New Englanders' concept of their "errand in the wilderness," a form of covenant stewardship, substantially countered this, allowing them simultaneously to herald the sovereignty of God and to encourage human initiative.

Covenant theology in 18th-cent. England had a significant poet in the person of William Cowper, an Anglican Calvinist. Like Vaughan, he sees the covenant with Noah as the birth of hope for a Covenant of Grace (*Hope,* 127-52), even while the culture of his own time is torn between this covenant and "a covenant of shame, / A dark confed'racy against the laws / Of virtue, and religion's glorious cause" (*Conversation,* 679-86). One of his *Olney Hymns* is titled "The Covenant," and cites Ezek. 36:25-28 as its inspirational text:

> The Lord proclaims his grace abroad!
> Behold, I change your hearts of stone;
> Each shall renounce his idol god,
> And serve, henceforth, the Lord alone.
>
> My grace, a flowing stream, proceeds
> To wash your filthiness away;
> Ye shall abhor your former deeds,
> And learn my statutes to obey.
>
> My truth the great design insures,
> I give myself away to you;
> You shall be mine, I will be yours,
> Your GOD unalterably true.
>
> Yet not unsought, or unimplor'd
> The plenteous grace shall I confer;
> No — your whole hearts shall seek the LORD,
> I'll put a praying spirit there.
>
> From the first breath of life divine,
> Down to the last expiring hour;
> The gracious work shall all be mine,
> Begun and ended in my pow'r.

Evangelical writing in the 18th cent. is full of references to Christians as the "true Israel," even in the sermons and poems of Methodists such as John and Charles Wesley and John Fletcher, but in such cases the references are an effect of their use of conventional biblical typology — not necessarily their assent to Calvinist "covenant" theology.

The Scottish "Covenanters," subjects in two important early 19th-cent. historical novels, were part of the Puritan tradition of covenant theology. Their name, however, derives from the national covenant (1638) binding Scottish Presbyterians in opposition to imposition of the Church of England's *Book of Common Prayer,* and the Solemn League and Covenant (1643) which made theoretical allies of the two Puritan churches and realms but was also a pact of mutual defense and a covenant of penitent Christians to live in obedience to God's law. While Scotland valued the spiritual element in this Covenant, the English Puritans were motivated more strongly by their desire for allies in their opposition to Royalists. With Cromwell's later rise to power the English Puritans lost interest in Scotland. Yet the "covenant" remained an important part of national spiritual identity there, and even Charles II, however reluctantly, subscribed to it in 1650 and 1651. Walter Scott's *Old Mortality* (1816) concerns itself (critically) with the uprising of the Covenanters in 1685; his *The Heart of Midlothian* (1818) presents in Jeanie Deans a much more sympathetic portrait of the Covenanters and their theology.

In modern literature in the Christian tradition express use of the covenant as a theme or motif is conspicuous for its absence, even from American literature. It appears parodically in Margaret Atwood's *Handmaid's Tale* (1985), a dystopic novel about a despotic America of the future in which covenant theology, literalized on the Puritan model, has produced a terrifying "theocracy." Earlier, Edwin Arlington Robinson's poem *Nicodemus* puts Nicodemus and Caiaphas in post-midnight dialogue after the protagonist has visited Jesus and been apparently profoundly affected by him. Caiaphas reasons with him against the "madness" of Jesus in the manner of Kimchi's medieval *ma'amin,* saying, "There is a covenant that has not changed, and cannot change" (*Nicodemus: A Book of Poems* [1932], 11). A. M. Klein's *The Second Scroll* (1951), a novel of Jewish covenant history, is a double tale composed of five books named for those of the Torah, with five modern *midrashim.* Within the Jewish community differences of opinion concerning fulfillment of the covenant promise in Jeremiah and Ezekiel, characterized as the voices of Zionism and conservative orthodoxy respectively, figure centrally in Chaim Potok's *The Chosen* (1967), as well as his *The Promise* (1969).

See also ECCLESIA, SYNAGOGA; ELECTION; EUCHARIST; MOSES; OLD AND NEW; TEN COMMANDMENTS.

Bibliography. Bercovitch, S. *The American Jeremiad* (1978); Bishop, J. *The Covenant: A Reading* (1983); Courteney, W. J. "Covenant and Causality in Pierre d'Ailly." *Speculum* 46 (1971), 94-119; Herford, R. T. *Christianity in Talmud and Midrash* (1907); Hillers, D. R. *Covenant: The History of a Biblical Idea* (1969); Johnson, J. T. "The Covenant Idea and the Puritan View of Marriage." *JHI* 32 (1971), 107-18; Kimchi, J. *The Book of the Covenant.* Trans. F. Talmage (1972); Kline, M. G. *Treaty of the Great King* (1963); Liao, P. S. "The Place of Covenant in the Theology of the Apostle Paul." Unpubl. Ph.D. diss., Hartford Seminary, 1973; MacCallum, H. *Milton and the Sons of God* (1986); McGiffert, M. "The Problem of the Covenant in Puritan Thought: Peter Bulkley's *Gospel-Covenant.*" *New England Historical and Genealogical Register* 130 (1976), 122ff.; Miller, P., ed. *The American Puritans: Their Prose and Poetry* (1956); Murray, J. *Covenant of Grace* (1954); Oakley, F. *Omnipotence, Covenant, and Order: An Excursion in the History of Ideas from Abelard to Leibniz* (1984); Simon, M. *Verus Israel* (1964); Sommerville, C. J. "Conversion versus the Early Puritan Covenant of Grace." *Journal of the Presbyterian Historical Society* 44 (1966), 180ff.;

Thundyil, Z. *Covenant in Anglo-Saxon Thought: The Influence of the Bible, Church Fathers and Germanic Tradition . . .* (1972); Zarilli, P. "From Destruction to Consecration: Covenant in the Chester *Noah* Play." *TJ* 2 (1979), 198-209.

CREATION The OT creation narrative (Gen. 1–3) is today commonly thought to be composed of two traditions. Gen. 1:1–2:3, known as the "priestly" account, describes a process extending over six days which transforms a dark watery chaos through the creation of light, then provides an overarching heaven, dry land producing vegetation, the constellations, living creatures, and finally humankind, both male and female, created in the image of God. On the seventh day, according to Gen. 2:1-3, having completed the work of creation, God rested.

Gen. 2:4-23, generally thought to derive from an older, "Jahwistic" tradition, begins with the creation of man from dust and the infused breath of life on the same (unspecified) day as the creation of heaven and earth — but before vegetation and animal life were made. God then planted a garden in Eden watered by four rivers, placed Adam in it, made animals for Adam to name, and finally made woman as Adam's companion out of a rib taken from him in sleep.

The two accounts can be regarded as complementary — the one establishing humankind's place in the scale of nature, the other his social role in a divinely arranged environment.

The creative power of God witnessed to in the book of nature is often celebrated in the OT (e.g., Pss. 8:3; 19:1-3; 24:2; Jer. 27:3) and linked with the divine shaping of history (Isa. 43:7, 15, 21; 44:2, 21, 24) and the divine wisdom (Ps. 104:24; Jer. 10:12). The NT stresses that creation was through the Son or Word of God (John 1:3; Col. 1:15-18; Heb. 1:2; 11:3) and links fallen humanity's hope for a renewed, transformed creation (Isa. 65:17; 66:22) with the prospect of Christian redemption (Rom. 8:19-25; 2 Cor. 5:17).

Initially Jewish tradition discouraged detailed speculation about the six-day work of creation as an esoteric matter (Ḥag. 11a; cf. St. Jerome, *Ep. 53* to Paulinus). But from early times commentators supplemented the Genesis account with other scriptural and apocryphal material and, more controversially, with classical matter, particularly from Plato, Aristotle, and the Epicurean tradition. Most Christian writers assume a single created world, as does Plato (*Timaeus*, 31a and b), but Leucippus and the Epicureans posit many worlds (see Cicero, *De natura deorum*, 1.24.66-67), a possibility entertained by Origen (*De principiis*, 2.3.4) and taken up by 17th-cent. astronomers as well as by Milton in *Paradise Lost* (3.565-66; 7.623). It is firmly rejected, however, by orthodox commentators from St. Augustine (*De civ. Dei* 11.5) to Joshua Sylvester's influential translation of Du Bartas's *Divine Weeks and Works* (1640) (1.1.340).

Plato's account of the creation of the cosmos from the four elements (*Timaeus*, 32) and Aristotle's doctrine of the eternity of the universe (*De caelo*, 1.10-12) encouraged St. Justin Martyr (*Apol.* 1.10) and St. Clement of Alexandria (*Stromateis*, 5.14) to read into Genesis a theory of creation out of formless matter, supported by Wisd. of Sol. 11:17. But the contrary doctrine of creation out of nothing (*creatio ex nihilo*), formulated to refute dualist theories, was supported by 2 Macc. 7:28, emphasized against Platonist ideas in Philo (*De somniis*, 1.13.76) and Jewish commentary (Gen. Rab. 1.9; b. Ḥag. 12a) and developed in 2nd-cent. Christian apologetic (St. Theophilus of Antioch, *Apologia ad Autolycum*, 2.4; St. Irenaeus, *Adv. haer.* 2.10.2). This view was widely accepted from the end of the 2nd cent. and was constantly reasserted against Plato and Aristotle (e.g., St. Ambrose, *Hexameron*, 1.1.1.1-2) and Epicureanism (Peter Comestor, *Historia Scholastica: Genesis* 1). The First Vatican Council of 1870 reaffirmed the doctrine, and it is alluded to in Joyce's *Ulysses* as a test of orthodoxy.

Ex nihilo creation is regularly asserted in mystery plays where the creation is treated only briefly through divine monologue (e.g., Chester, *Fall of Lucifer*, 277; cf. ME *Genesis*, 39), but it is less easily maintained in extended imaginative or dramatic treatments. The imaginative gap between an original nothing and finished creation was often supplied by adaptations of Ovid's depiction of primal chaos (*Metamorphoses*, 1.5-20), a source acknowledged by Peter Comestor (*Historia Scholastica: Genesis* 1). Poets such as Gower were attracted by the Aristotelian doctrine of preexistent matter: Gower uses the word *Ylem* (from Aristotle's Gk. *hylē*, "matter") for what was there "To fore the creacion / Of any worldes stacion" (*Confessio Amantis*, 7.203-22). Sylvester, in translating *The Divine Weeks* of Du Bartas (1640), is anxiously orthodox, insisting that God had "Nothing, but nothing" from which to build. He directly challenges Plato's notion of a paradigm or model of creation (e.g., *Timaeus*, 31a) by insisting the Almighty cannot be compared to an architect with a "fore-conceited Plot," yet he leaves it ambiguous whether original chaos is divinely conjured out of nothing or is equivalent to the nothing out of which God creates matter and form (*Divine Weeks*, 1.1.212-97).

Milton is more rigorous. Intellectually and imaginatively he rejects arguments based on creation out of nothing, proposing instead that in a sense the world was created out of an omnipresent God (*De Doctrina Christiana*, 1.7). In *Paradise Lost*, 7.170, God is omnipresent from eternity though not corporeally so, and when he wills creation he withdraws his full potency of will from the void. The Son, in the full panoply of divine power, carries God's creating word to the chaotic abyss and with God's golden compasses creates matter "unformed and void" (7.233). The Spirit, since orthodoxy involves the Trinity in creation (e.g., Irenaeus, *Adv. haer.* 4.38.3), infuses this with "vital virtue" and elemental order (7.234-42). The six-day work of creation by a disposing wisdom ensues. This distinction between the work of power and of wisdom is spelled out in Bacon's *Advancement of Learning* (1.6.2) and reflects a two-stage model of creation favored from Tertullian (*Adversus Hermogenem*, 29-30, 33) and Augustine (*De vera religione*, 18.36) to the mid-17th cent. (e.g., James Ussher, *A Body of Divinity* [1645], 98-100).

The warring elements of Milton's chaos owe something to Neoplatonic creation doctrine as embodied in Spenser's *Four Hymns*. In the "Hymn of Love," "Air hated earth, and water hated fire / Till love relented their rebellious ire" (83-84). Then all things were created according to a "pattern" of "perfect beauty" ("Hymn of Beauty," 36-42). In the later and more specifically Christian "Hymn of Heavenly Love" and "Hymn of Heavenly Beauty" Spenser is concerned with the creation of sentient beings, and with the creation itself as a reflection of divine glory. He avoids discussion of the origin of the world. Spenser remains satisfied with the Platonic notion that the significant mark of the divine hand was the imparting not of being itself but of order and beauty. In *The Faerie Queene*, 3.6, Spenser describes a Garden of Adonis where forms are joined to matter and beings are sent out into the world of time. Spenser seems to envisage a great reservoir of formless pre-created matter, perhaps drawing on the ancient belief alluded to by Augustine (*De Genesi ad litteram*, 1.1-3; 4.33.51) in *rationes seminales,* the seeds of all things which would not spring into immediate being divinely created at the beginning.

Platonism rather than the Bible underlies most incidental literary allusions to creation. Human love appears repeatedly in Donne as analogous to the divine love which creates and upholds the world (e.g., "The Canonization," "Song: Sweetest Love I do not go," "The Good Morrow"), but in the most extended treatment ("Nocturnal upon St. Lucy's Day") the analogy is inverted: if love gives form and vitality to existence, its withdrawal allows a collapse into chaos and death (cf. Jer. 4:23-27), as the world will collapse at the end of divinely appointed time, a return to the "Elixir" or the "first nothing" from which creation stemmed. Rochester's later poem "Upon Nothing" wittily develops this idea: if the divine creator had no antagonist from eternity, did Nothing exist, and if so, was it then Something? The round zero of nothing from which divine creation officially originated becomes a salacious and ironic image for the physical, sexual source of life created through love or lust, life which like the divine creation will at last return to nothing.

In the Renaissance it was asserted that poetic art also is analogous to the divine act of creation. Ben Jonson mingles creative love and creative art when he calls his dead son his "best piece of poetrie" ("On my first Sonne," 9), and Marvell in "The Garden" speaks of the mind's creations. Sidney's *Apology for Poetry* treats extensively

the Neoplatonic concept of the brazen world of created reality opposed to the golden world created in art. In parts of *Arcadia,* giving a new twist to the long-standing fusion of classical pastoral and Golden Age poetry and the Christian Paradise (see Evans [1968], 114-21), Sidney attempts to follow out his own precepts about the moral force of re-creating in detail an exemplary pristine world of ideal innocence. The world of art and the actual, human world may both dissolve into nothing, however, for Shakespeare's Prospero reminds us "We are such stuff / As dreams are made on" (*Tempest*, 4.1.156-57). Human art is more kindly treated when Perdita and Polixenes agree that "great creating nature" may be improved by a human art which is itself created by nature (*Winter's Tale*, 4.4.86-97). Much later the Romantics deliberately mingled poetic perception and creativity with the natural creation so that for Wordsworth nature is both what the senses "half create / And what perceive" ("Tintern Abbey," 106-07) and Shelley laments a departed Keats as now "a portion of the loveliness / Which once he made more lovely" ("Adonaïs," 388-89).

It was a traditional belief, stemming from God's observation that what he created was good (e.g., Gen. 1:4, 12), that at creation each created thing had its appointed nature and purpose and that noxious beasts and herbs became so only after the Fall (e.g., St. Basil, *Hexameron*, 5.6; Luther, *Table Talk* [trans. T. G. Tappert (1967)], 316). For Renaissance authors this meant that creation was a perfect work of art: according to Sir Thomas Browne creatures at worst were grotesques but not deformed, for nature was the art of God and there was beauty in the works of God "being created in those outward forms which best express the actions of their inward forms" in the approved Platonist manner (*Religio Medici*, 1.15-16). In the later Renaissance, metaphysical poets such as Marvell ("Upon Appleton House"), Vaughan ("The Recluse"), and Herbert ("Decay") pointed to traces of the divine Creator in the natural world, faint glimmerings of the original message of the goodness and glory of the Creator first written large in creation.

The work of creation as the inauguration of world history attracted both theological and historical discussion. Influenced by Plato's view that time itself was created with the world (*Timaeus*, 37d, e), Philo (*Legum allegoriae*, 1.2.2), St. Hilary (*De Trinitate*, 12.40), and Augustine (*De Genesi ad litteram*, 4.33) suggest simultaneous creation of the world to be apprehended as taking place over six days so that God's complex work can be properly understood, a view reflected in Raphael's description of creation in *Paradise Lost*, bk. 7, and accepted by the Platonist Thomas Browne (*Religio Medici*, 1.45), though rejected by more biblicist commentators such as Luther (*Lectures on Genesis 1–5*, 1.4).

The divine creation as historical event is assumed by early universal historians (Eusebius, *Hist. eccl.* 1.2; Orosius, *History*, 1.3). Later, in the Renaissance, the indivisibility of history, theology, and natural science leads Sir Walter Raleigh (*History of the World* [1614]) to begin with the creation, influentially dated by James Ussher as commencing at night on 22 October 4004 B.C. (*Annals of Creation* [trans. 1662], 1). At the end of *Paradise Lost* human history has just begun and for Adam and Eve "the world was all before them" (12.646). Creation associated with human history is central to Spenser's *Faerie Queene,* especially bk. 1: Archimago makes the false Una in parody of the OT creation of Eve (1.1.45) and Redcrosse has a vision of the New Jerusalem (1.10.57), representing the other end of history. Una herself, good, beautiful, and true, the bride of Christ, represents an ideal of creation in the divine image such as the world has never seen since Adam fell, alluding to the NT vision of redeemed creation (cf. Rom. 8:19-25).

The eclipse of traditional literal and historical readings of the biblical creation accounts can be linked with a gradual discrediting of so-called "natural religion" after Hume's *Dialogues concerning Natural Religion* (1779). The majestic order of creation in the OT, emphasized in Longinus's ascription of sublimity to the *fiat lux* of Gen. 1:2 (*On the Sublime,* 9.9) and in Calvin's account of God's wonderful power in ordering and sustaining the universe (*Inst.* 1.14.21), fostered a traditional belief in nature as the book of God, "the Scripture and Theology of the Heathens" (Browne, *Religio Medici,* 1.16). Addison's ode "The Spacious Firmament on High" (*Spectator*, 465, 23 Aug. 1712) is an expansion of Ps. 19:1-3 arguing that the glories of creation demonstrate the existence of a creator, a view he attributes to Aristotle, though it is also Augustinian (*De civ. Dei* 11.6). This rationalist perspective leads Pope to link Newtonian science with the language of Gen. 1:2: "Nature and Nature's law lay veiled in night: / God said: Let Newton be, and all was light!" ("Epitaph. Intended for Sir Isaac Newton") and to describe the spread of dullness in the *Dunciad* (4.652-56) as a return to primal Chaos, an undoing of the divine creation embodying light and reason. William Paley's equation of creation with a watch bespeaking a watchmaker God (*Natural Theology* [1802]) sums up this tradition, but already Blake, reacting against Newton and 18th-cent. rationalism, had identified it with tyranny and limitation, and in his *First Book of Urizen* (recalling "The first book of Moses," a subtitle of Genesis) he describes enslaved humanity as reversing the expanding creation: "Six days they shrunk up from existence" (486).

The historicity of the biblical creation and Ussher's date of 4004 B.C. were increasingly challenged in the 19th cent. in the face of geological evidence of the earth's immense antiquity and gradual formation and the associated development of evolutionary biology, a conflict described in retrospect in Edmund Gosse's autobiographical *Father and Son* (1907). Charles Kingsley's *Water Babies* contains an attempt to reconcile evolutionary theory with Christian beliefs. The new interest in

scientific rather than divine origins was accompanied by a nightmare vision of the ultimate fate of the creation: Kelvin's second law of thermodynamics seemed to imply a cooling sun and chilly annihilation, a prospect entertained in Conrad's *Heart of Darkness* (1902) and visualized at the end of H. G. Wells's *The Time Machine* (1895).

Post-Darwinian theologians such as Karl Barth and Emil Brunner have stressed the moral and theological rather than historical dimensions of creation, and from the Romantics onward imaginative writers have developed ahistorical readings of the creation idea. In *The Four Zoas* Blake fused ideas of creation and fall in a myth of humanity created in a state of division but with the possibility of wholeness. Characteristically these later literary treatments involve adaptation of heretical sources or doctrines. The doctrine of the distinctiveness of God from his creation, regularly affirmed against emanationist or pantheist theories (see, e.g., Lactantius, *Divinae institutiones*, 3.28), was emphasized by the First Vatican Council of 1870, but both Wordsworth's sense of "something far more deeply interfused / Whose dwelling is the light of setting suns" ("Tintern Abbey," 96-97) and Shelley's quasi-divine Power inhabiting the splendors of Mont Blanc indicate a pantheist tendency in the Romantic celebration of nature. For W. H. Carruths, "Some call it evolution / And others call it God" (*Each in his Own Tongue and Other Poems* [1908]). A post-Christian regenerated creation is envisaged at the end of D. H. Lawrence's *The Rainbow:* God's symbol guaranteeing the continuity of divine creation (Gen. 9:15-17) is transformed into a portent of "the world built up in a living fabric of Truth." William Golding's *Pincher Martin,* which is structured upon the six days of creation, shows an anticreation attempted by a wholly self-centered spirit deifying itself. And the gnostic view of the Demiurge as the evil source of creation, with affinities to Blake's Urizen, appears again as the "sporting God" of Beckett's *Unnameable.*

The godlike creative role of the artist and his involvement in his creation are proclaimed with a new defiance in Lawrence's "I was the God and the Creation at once" ("New Heaven and Earth," *Complete Poems* [1964], 257). To the same end the Jewish Cabala which had influenced Milton and the Cambridge Platonists is exploited by Joyce: Stephen Dedalus broods on physical and imaginative creation and alludes in *Ulysses* to the cabalistic Adam Kadmon, an emanation of the creator God and himself a creator of worlds to come, a type of the artist for Joyce and for the boastful H. C. Earwicker in *Finnegans Wake.* More diffidently Wallace Stevens proposes the linguistic structures of the imagination as necessary fictions which create afresh the mental world which is our nearest approach to reality (see D. M. La Guardia, *Advance on Chaos* [1983]).

See also EX NIHILO; FIAT LUX.

Bibliography. Corcoran, M. I. *Milton's Paradise Lost with reference to the Hexaemeral Background* (1945); Evans, J. M. *Paradise Lost and the Genesis Tradition* (1968); Gallagher, P. J. "Creation in Genesis and in *Paradise Lost.*" *MiltonS* 20 (1984), 163-204; Stevenson, S. W. "The Creation Motif in Romantic Poetry and Theory with Particular Reference to the Myth of Blake and the Poetic Theory of Blake and Coleridge." *DA* 19 (1958), 1368; Williams, A. *The Common Expositor. An Account of the Commentaries on Genesis 1527-1633* (1948).   BRENDA E. RICHARDSON
                                   NORMAN VANCE

CREED The word *creed,* denoting a summary of Christian belief, is not itself biblical. It derives, however, from Lat. *credo (in),* which corresponds to *pisteuō (eis)* in the NT. It is sometimes referred to in Latin writings as *symbolum,* meaning either a "sign" or a system of signs.

Already in the OT a creedlike statement exists in the Shema, which combines Deut. 6:4-9; 11:13-21; and Num. 15:37-41. The NT uses equivalents to creed in such concepts as the faith (Col. 2:7; 1 Tim. 1:18), the confession (Heb. 3:1), good or sound doctrine (1 Tim. 4:6; Titus 1:9), the pattern of sound words (2 Tim. 1:13), the gospel (Gal. 2:2), the preaching (Rom. 16:25), the word of God (1 Thess. 1:6; Phil. 1:14), and the traditions (2 Thess. 2:15). Terms and slogans which reflect primitive Christian tradition also contain something of the content of later creeds, e.g., Christ (John 1:41), Son of God (Acts 8:37), Lord (Rom. 10:9), and Jesus is Lord (1 Cor. 10:3). More fully St. Paul refers to the received account of Christ's death, burial, and resurrection (1 Cor. 15:3ff.) and to his Davidic descent and resurrection (Rom. 1:3-4; cf. 2 Tim. 2:8). Another group of statements supplies the structure for the creeds. Thus 1 Cor. 8:6 stresses faith in the one God and the one Christ, and 1 Tim. 2:5-6 and 6:13-14 not only relate God and Christ similarly but also anticipate the content of the second article with references to Christ's mediation and coming again. A more developed Trinitarian form occurs in Matt. 28:19, which by way of Christian baptism has a decisive impact on credal formation. Parallel statements are made in 2 Cor. 13:14, 1 Thess. 5:18-19, and 1 Pet. 1:2. Although it contains no creed in the later sense, the NT provides, thus, the material, structure, and terminology for the statements which catechetical, liturgical, and doctrinal forces finally fashioned into the Apostles' and Nicene Creeds.

These two creeds, each of which grew up anonymously in the practice of the Church and only later was "confirmed" for liturgical use, are the principal creeds of the Catholic and Anglican communions. The most widely used translations into English are those provided by Cranmer in *The Book of Common Prayer* (1549). Reformed Protestant groups have been more prolific in the production of creeds, about sixty of which have been influential (J. H. Leith, *Creeds of the Churches* [1982], 127). Among Calvinist and Lutheran groups these tend to function in

catechism more prominently than in liturgy, and that largely because, as with the creeds of the early Church, they were developed as a means of defining the particular manner in which individual communities read and received Scripture. In this way creeds or "confessions," as they are sometimes called (e.g., the Westminster Confession, worked out by the Puritan-dominated Westminster Assembly in 1643), composed at significant historical moments in various cultural contexts, became for their community the "record of the Church's interpretation of the Bible in the past and the authoritative guide to hermeneutics in the present" (Leith, *Creeds,* 9). In the history of the Catholic Church it has also been deemed necessary at various points to reemphasize the lay understanding of the "creed" in the larger sense of "received body of beliefs." In England, Archbishop John Pecham's Lambeth Constitutions (1273) ordered such a renewed emphasis on credal education, encouraging the proliferation of vernacular ME and Anglo-Norman catechetical lyrics and translations of "The articles of the fayth, The ten commaundementes, The two preceptys of the gospel, The seuen works of pyte, The seuen dedly synnes wyth ther braunches, The seuen principal vertuse, and The seuen sacraments of grace" (Holmstedt, *Speculum Christiani,* 6).

There was a tradition — probably originated in a pseudo-Augustinian sermon of the 6th cent. — that the Apostles' Creed was composed on the day of Pentecost when the eleven met together to choose a successor to Judas; each, including the newly elected Matthias, composed one clause. An Anglo-Norman versified creed similarly gives one tenet to each of the twelve apostles accordingly as they were held to have contributed it (Jeffrey and Levy, *The Anglo-Norman Lyric* [1989], 16). The York "Creed" play (1446), now lost, may have elaborated this schema. Last performed in 1535, it was a lengthy play, and seems to have had twelve individual pageants, one for each apostle.

For the Anglican tradition expanded credal statements are found in the first five of the *Certain Sermons, or Homilies, Appointed to Be Read in Churches,* probably authored by Cranmer himself and first issued in the reign of Edward VI, in 1547. Of Prayer Book creeds alluded to in English literature the Athanasian Creed, which Benjamin Disraeli described as "the most splendid ecclesiastical lyric ever poured forth by the genius of man" (*Endymion,* chap. 52), appears with considerable frequency. This is the *Credo* which Langland quotes in the words of the Parson in the *visio* of *Piers Plowman* (B.19.177ff.; cf. 190-93), and which George Herbert in *A Priest to the Temple* (21.256) expects to be the basis of sound catechism. When Herbert speaks of the creed which he expects ordinary parishioners to be able to recite from memory along with the Ten Commandments, he probably means the Apostles' Creed, which was most frequently used in the service of Morning Prayer as well as in the interrogation of candidates in the baptismal liturgy. The Nicene Creed, essentially an elaboration of the Apostles' Creed, has been normative to the Anglican and Roman Catholic eucharistic rite as well as Eastern Orthodox liturgy.

Largely because of the ecclesiastical turmoil of the 17th cent., the theological base of the Anglican Church broadened to include some (though by no means all) elements associated with challenges from the Calvinist and Puritan left, while at the same time uncomfortably harboring an evangelical revival associated with figures such as the "Methodists" John and Charles Wesley, George Whitefield, John Fletcher, and William Cowper's erratic cousin Martin Madan. Thus, though England had an Established Church, theologically its "creed" in the widest sense was being pulled in a diversity of ways, leading Pitt the Elder to utter his frustrated but not entirely misplaced exclamation in the House of Lords: "We have a Calvinistic creed, a Popish liturgy, and an Arminian clergy" (May 19, 1772). This practical heterodoxy helped induce in turn a general skepticism. Although Sterne in *Tristram Shandy* wants to reassure his readers that "Whenever a man talks loudly against religion, — always suspect that it is not his reason, but his passions that have got the better of his creed" (2.17), the fact is that even so patently faithful a poet as Cowper reflects exasperation with the proliferation of credal debate:

> My creed (whatever some creed-makers mean
> By Athanasian nonsense, or Nicene)
> My creed is — he is safe that does his best,
> And death's a doom sufficient for the rest. ("Hope," 393-96)

Emily Brontë is more emphatic: "Vain are the thousand creeds / That move men's heart: unutterably vain" ("Lost Lines").

These sentiments on the part of many fatigued members of the Established Church, coupled to some extent with the side effects of evangelical iconoclasm and emphasis on the Bible alone as the rule of faith, have prompted many negative comments about creeds in English literature. Wordsworth would "rather be / A Pagan suckled in a creed outworn" if he could only have a vision or two of pagan deities ("The World Is Too Much with Us"; cf. Shelley, *Prometheus Unbound*, 1.697). George Meredith complains of those who would make of the creed "a straight-jacket for humanity" (*Beauchamp's Career*, chap. 29), and Tennyson, in oft-quoted lines, concludes that "There lives more faith in honest doubt, / Believe me, than in half the creeds" (*In Memoriam*, 96). F. H. C. Doyle celebrates a late 19th-cent. ideal in "The Unobtrusive Christian":

> His creed no person ever knew
> "For this was still his simpler plan,"
> To have with clergymen to do
> As little as a Christian can.

Ella Wheeler Wilcox (d. 1919) sums up the exhaustion with doctrinal discord felt by many:

> So many gods, so many creeds,
> So many paths that wind and wind,
> While just the art of being kind
> Is all the sad world needs. ("The World's Need")

These lines echo Longfellow's "Thinking the deed, and not the creed, / Would help us in our utmost need" ("Tales of a Wayside Inn").

The generalized anticredalism of the Romantic movement is still evident in many of these statements, even late in the century. Tennyson formulates it affirmatively:

> And so the Word had breath, and wrought
> With human hands the creed of creeds
> In loveliness of perfect deeds,
> More strong than all poetic thought. (*In Memoriam*, 36)

Arnold idolizes "The Scholar Gypsy" in similar terms: "Thou waitest for the spark from Heaven: and we / Vague half-believers in our casual creeds . . . hesitate and falter life away." But Swinburne, for whom "a creed is a rod" ("Hertha"), rages against the interposition of Christian creeds between modern humanity and the unfettered liberty of his imagined paganism:

> What ailed us, O gods, to desert you
> For creeds that refuse and restrain?
> Come down and redeem us from virtue,
> Our Lady of Pain. ("Dolores," 35)

Emerson illustrates an anticredal response at least as sharp in American letters: "As men's prayers are a disease of the will, so are their creeds a disease of the intellect" (*Self-Reliance*, chap. 2). Pearl Buck's *Advice to Unborn Novelists* plays with the view that creeds are somehow the antithesis of Arnold's "spark from Heaven," warning her embryonic audience: "do not be born under the shadow of a great creed, nor under the burden of original sin."

There are few 20th-cent. reflections on the creed in English literature, with even poets of overtly Christian sensibility, such as Henry Van Dyke, praying to God to be set free from those who have "built temple walls to shut thee in, / And framed their iron creeds to shut thee out" ("God of the Open Air"). In his poetry G. K. Chesterton affirms a generalized notion of creed as an all-pervasive structure of belief informing the whole creative order: "There is one creed: 'neath no world-terror's wing / Apples forgot to grow on apple trees" ("Ecclesiastes"), leaving particular references to his theological writings.

Bibliography. Badcock, S. J. *History of the Creeds* (1930); Cochrane, A. C. *Reformed Confessions of the Sixteenth Century* (1966); Curtis, W. A. *History of the Creeds and Confessions of Faith* (1911); Griffith Thomas, W. H. *Principles of Theology: An Introduction to the Thirty-Nine Articles* (1930); Kelly, J. N. D. *Early Christian Creeds* (1950; 3rd ed. 1972); Pannenberg, W. *The Apostles' Creed* (1972); Pearson, J. *An*

Exposition of the Creed (1662); Schaff, P. *Creeds of Christendom.* 3 vols. (1877); Watson, J. R. "Wordsworth and the Credo." In *The Interpretation of Belief: Coleridge, Schleiermacher, and Romanticism.* Ed. D. Jasper (1986), 158-75.

DAVID L. JEFFREY
GEOFFREY W. BROMILEY

CROWN OF THORNS   Three of the four evangelists mention the oxymoronic *akanthinos stephanos* with which the Roman soldiers mocked Jesus (Matt. 27:29; Mark 15:17; John 19:2). Similar to the Roman poet's laurel diadem (cf. Ovid, Petrarch), the typical *stephanos* was a crown of exaltation, usually of flowers, for victors of games, and for military and festive honors; the same word is used to describe the crown of exaltation Christ will receive in the final "day of the Lord" (Heb. 2:9; Rev. 6:2; 14:14). That the Savior's crown is in this context made of thorns is thus bitterly ironic.

As one of the "instruments of the Passion," the crown of thorns is often featured heraldically; in the 13th cent. it was associated with St. Louis of France, who in 1248 built La Sainte-Chapelle in Paris to house the relic.

The crown's thorny pricks are associated by exegetical tradition with the pain Christ experiences on account of the multitude of human sins (e.g., *Glossa Ordinaria* [PL 114.420]). Yet because the suffering and sacrifice of Christ obtains remission of these sins, the crown is associated also with the thornlike holly and its berries in Celtic Christmas lore (hence the modern carol in which "of all the green trees in the wood, the Holly bears the crown)." In ME Passion lyrics the voice of Christ from the cross often invites the sinner to "loke to is heued wiþ þornis al bewende" (MS Harley 913 [ed. Heuser], *Die Kildare Gedichte,* 128-29), and the "crowning" scenes figure gruesomely in the Corpus Christi plays (e.g., York, "Christ Before Pilate"). Conscious of the symbolic irony, John Donne in "La Corona" *(Holy Sonnets)* prays not for the poet laureate's "vile crowne of frail bayes," "But what thy thorny crowne gain'd, that give mee, / A crowne of Glory, which doth flower alwayes" (5; 7-8).

Milton rejected allusions to King Charles I as a martyr who had chosen "to wear a crown of thorns with our Saviour," saying in "Eikonoklastes" that the king's thorns were rather of his "own gathering" and "twisting." Identifying innocent suffering as the central feature of "our highest religion" in his "The Worship of Sorrow," Carlyle observes that even for the Son of Man "there is no noble crown, well worn or even ill worn, but there is a crown of thorns!" (*Past and Present,* 3.4). In Wilde's *Salome* the sultry dancer, rebuffed, says that Jokanaan's unkempt prophet's hair is "like a crown of thorns which they have placed on thy forehead," thus foreshadowing his proleptic martyrdom as a reward for her dancing. Tennyson makes of his grief in *In Memoriam* a martyr's suffering, saying:

I took the thorns to bind my brows,
I wore them like a civic crown;
I met with scoffs, I met with scorns . . .
The fool that wears a crown of thorns.

Hopkins "read[s] the story rather / How soldiers platting thorns around CHRIST'S Head / Grapes grew and drops of wine were shed" ("New Readings"), anticipating the joyously ironic reversal and liberation from self celebrated in the Eucharist. A. M. Klein sees a fading image of "the thorns, the ready bier / Of leaves, the stains of blood . . ." in "Autumn Crucified" ("Calvary"), an enigmatic reference which recalls another more syncretistic, Howard Nemerov's "Deep Woods," a trove of myth and legend in which may be found "Glastonbury thorns to make December / Bleed for the Saviour."

See also ECCE HOMO; MAN OF SORROWS.

CRUEL AS THE GRAVE   *See* LOVE STRONG AS DEATH.

CRUSE OF OIL   Elijah the prophet, after his sojourn in the desert, came to the house of a poor widow about to die of starvation with her son (1 Kings 17:10-17). He asked, as instructed by God, for a "morsel of bread." She indicated her poor estate, that she had only "a handful of meal" and "a little oil in a cruse," and that she was in fact gathering two sticks to make a fire and prepare a last meal for her son. Elijah told her that if she would bake for him, then for herself and her son, neither meal nor oil would run out "until the day that the LORD sendeth rain upon the earth" (v. 14). She did as he asked, and the foodstuff continued to last, so that "she and her house did eat many days. And the barrel of meal wasted not, neither did the cruse of oil fail, according to the word of the LORD" (vv. 15-16).

In a typical allegorization, Peter Riga sees the two sticks as an antetype of the wood of the cross, the widow's generous gift as the wisdom of the Church, the elements of meal and oil a prefiguration of the Eucharist, and the cake the perdurable bread of faith which never gives out (*Aurora,* 1.302). This typology recurs in graphic art, as in the pedagogical illustrations of the *Biblia Pauperum.* In the official *Homilies Appointed to Be Read in Churches* (1562) of the Church of England the heroic generosity of the widow is made an admonition to those of better means to act charitably, trusting that God will honor unselfishness by supplying all their needs; there follows a warning to "merciless misers" that "as certainly as God nourished the poor widow in the time of famine, and increased her little store, so that she had enough . . . so certainly shall God plague you with poverty in the midst of plenty" ("Of Alms Deeds," 3).

In modern literature, "cruse of oil" or "widow's cruse" is proverbial, and used to signify a small but apparently inexhaustible supply — generally of food or money. Thackeray describes a predator as one who "had dipped ungenerously into a generous mother's purse; basely and recklessly spilt her little cruse" (*Pendennis,* chap. 20). Margaret Avison responds to the text directly in her poem "Dryness and Scorch of Ahab's Evil Rule," drawing upon its eucharistic associations:

the unfailing meal and oil a sign
to last through centuries.
It consecrates a time
of bony men and doom
lit toward the bread and drink of Him
whose is the final kingdom.

See also ELIJAH.

CUP The term *cup* (Heb. *kos*; Gk. *potērion*) refers to a vessel used ordinarily to drink from, occasionally for divination (Gen. 44:5), and figuratively of various experiences which life brings. It is used of blessings or disasters, and of the rewards or punishments meted out by God to the righteous and the wicked. The "cup of salvation" (Ps. 116:13) stands in contrast with the cup "in the name of the LORD" which is proffered to "all the wicked of the earth" for drinking, dregs and all (Ps. 75:8). The righteous person can call God "the portion of mine inheritance and of my cup" (Ps. 16:5). The role of Babylon as a temptation to debauchery or an instrument of judgment is vividly portrayed in Jer. 51:7, where she is called "a golden cup in the LORD's hand, that made all the earth drunken." The picture is changed in Rev. 17:4, where Babylon the Great, the scarlet woman, holds "a golden cup in her hand full of abominations and filthiness of her fornication." The reference here is to the corruption which found a congenial home in imperial Rome. By way of reprisal God makes her drain "the cup of the wine of the fierceness of his wrath" (Rev. 16:19); "in the cup which she hath filled fill to her double" (Rev. 18:6; cf. Shakespeare, *King Lear,* 5.3: "All friends shall taste / The wages of their virtue, and all foes / The cup of their deservings").

Jesus spoke of his death as the cup which he would have to drink, and told James and John that they would drink it too (Mark 10:38-39). In Gethsemane he prayed that this cup might be taken away (Mark 14:36), but submitted himself to God's will: "the cup which my Father hath given me, shall I not drink it?" (John 18:11).

The provision of "a cup of cold water," costing little but greatly appreciated in a thirsty land, is highly commended by Jesus (Matt. 10:42).

The eucharistic cup or chalice which Jesus gave his disciples at the Last Supper (Mark 14:23) acquired a special symbolism: "The cup of blessing which we bless, is it not the communion of the blood of Christ?" (1 Cor. 10:16). The cup stands by metonymy for the blood of Christ symbolized by the wine.

In calling it "the cup of blessing" Paul may have used a technical expression. The eucharistic bread and cup were given by Christ in the context of a Passover meal.

Traditionally four cups of red wine stood on the Passover table; the third of these was called "the cup of blessing" because it was over it that the "blessing" — the thanksgiving after the meal or the "grace after meat" — was said. The first cup accompanied the thanksgiving with which the meal was begun; the second accompanied the recitation of the traditional Passover story (in response to the question asked by the youngest participant: "Why is this night different from every other night?"); the fourth was drunk at the completion of the psalm sung when the meal was over (cf. Mark 14:26, "when they had sung an hymn, they went out . . .").

In the Christianized form of the legend of the Holy Grail, the Grail (med. Lat. *gradalis,* "cup" or "platter") was sometimes identified with the chalice used at the Last Supper. The medieval French poem by Robert de Boron, *Joseph d'Arimathie,* tells how the *vesseil* in which Christ initiated the eucharistic sacrament was given by a Jew to Pilate, who then gave it to Joseph of Arimathea. Joseph used it when Christ was being taken down from the cross to catch the last drops of his blood. This poem suggests that the "sangreal" would eventually be taken to the "vaus d'Avaron," presumably the flat marshlands surrounding Glastonbury, which came to be known as the "Vale of Avalon." Other poems such as the *Suite du Merlin* describe how Joseph brought the grail to England and Glastonbury, where it was later lost. In the *Morte Darthur* of Malory, as in other Arthurian romances, the quest for the lost grail becomes a central theme.

In Boron's poem, it is not Joseph but a faithful delegate Bron (or Hebron) who makes the journey. Because he has caught a special fish for an anniversary *pasch* with the grail, he is called the "Rich Fisher"; Chrétien de Troyes, in a different version, describes how Percival meets with the Fisher King and the grail procession. Spenser also alludes to the story in *Faerie Queene,* 2.10.34.

Reformation iconoclasm was unfriendly to the grail legend, and Milton may intend an allusion to it in a disparaging remark in *Of Reformation in England,* where he says of riches in the Roman church after Constantine that "former times had wooden chalices and golden priests, but they golden chalices and wooden priests." He might, however, have approved of the allusion of Lanier, who in "Psalms of the West" (1876) praised "Godly Hearts that, Grails of Gold, / Still the blood of faith do hold" (505).

Tennyson's "The Holy Grail," reflecting medieval sources, tells the story of "the cup, the cup itself, from which our Lord / Drank at the last sad supper with his own." The grail figures also in "Sir Galahad," in which at one point "Three angels bear the holy Grail" (42). A distant allusion appears in Robert Frost's "Directive," which tells of a stolen drinking cup hidden in an old tree, "A broken drinking goblet like the Grail / Under a spell so the wrong ones can't find it." Drawing upon Jessie L. Weston's book on the grail legend, *From Ritual to*

Romance, T. S. Eliot in *The Waste Land* (1922) appropriates the grail as a primitive female sexual symbol associated with the bleeding spear.

The "cup of abominations" (Rev. 17:4) seems to be in the prophet Jokanaan's mind in Oscar Wilde's *Salome,* when he asks, "Where is he whose cup of abominations is now full? Where is he who in a robe of silver shall one day die in the face of all the people?" But the cup of "Edom's daughter" in Donne's "The Lamentations of Jeremy" draws on Jer. 51:7: "This cup shall passe, and thou with drunkennesse / Shalt fill thy selfe, and shew thy nakednesse" (4.341-44). The cup filled with "the marks of future bane" in Herbert's "The Church Militant" (239) is probably that of Ps. 75:8 or Rev. 16:19.

See also HOLY GRAIL; JOSEPH OF ARIMATHEA.

Bibliography. Magennis, H. "The Cup as Symbol and Metaphor in Old English Literature." *Speculum* 60.3 (1985), 517-36.   F. F. BRUCE

CUP OF ABOMINATION   *See* CUP.

CUP RUNNETH OVER   "My cup runneth over" (Ps. 23:5) signifies that the speaker enjoys an abundance of good fortune. He recounts the blessings he has received from God and sums them up in these words. Their influence appears repeatedly in English literature; e.g., "the cup of his [Jeremy's] joy was full" (H. Walpole, *Jeremy and Hamlet,* 11.1). But perhaps even more often the figure denotes an excess of sorrow or anger; e.g., "the cup of her indignation ran over" (A. Trollope, *Barchester Towers,* chap. 11); "This was all that was wanted to make poor Tom's cup of bitterness run over" (W. M. Thackeray, *The Newcomes,* chap. 2).   F. F. BRUCE

CUR DEUS HOMO?   *See* ATONEMENT; *FELIX CULPA;* INCARNATION.

CURSE GOD AND DIE   This classic counsel of despair is uttered by Job's wife in the wake of all the evils which befall him (Job 2:9). It is preceded by the question, "Dost thou still retain thine integrity?" Her words may have been motivated by bitterness over what she and Job had endured (the LXX and the apocryphal Testament of Job both give her a lengthy speech in which she catalogues their degradation). Possibly she felt that blasphemy would have sudden death as a consequence, and that this would put Job out of his misery. In any case, the import of her words is to question the value of "righteousness" (cf. Tob. 2:11-14).

Rabbinic commentary contrasts Job and Adam, the latter of whom, unlike Job, heeded his wife's bad counsel, with disastrous consequences (cf. Midr. Rab. Gen. 19:12).

As Marvin Pope observes, Job's wife was called *diaboli adjutrix* by St. Augustine, and *organum Satanae*

by Calvin. St. John Chrysostom regarded her a scourge by which to plague Job more acutely than by any other means (*Job,* 21-22; AB).

Sir Balaam, the main character in Pope's *Epistle to Bathurst* — a parody of Job whom the devil tempts with riches rather than poverty — ultimately "curses God, and dies."

See also JOB.   WILLIAM SOLL

CYRUS   Cyrus the Great, son of Cambyses I and founder of the extensive Persian Empire (ca. 559-530 B.C.), was the conqueror of Babylon in the time of Nabonidus's self-indulgent son, Belshazzar (cf. Dan. 5). His early life history, as recorded by Herodotus (1.108-22) and Xenophon (*Cyropaedeia,* 7.5.7-34), describes his exile as an infant because of a prophecy that he would slay his father, surreptitious delivery by the father's lieutenant to a shepherd for rearing, and adult return to fulfill the prophecy and become king in his father's stead — events which parallel part of Sophocles's *Oedipus.* In Jewish history Cyrus is most important for repatriating the victims of the Babylonian captivity, an event recorded in the biblical book of Ezra. Although Cyrus was probably a Zoroastrian, in Ezra 1:2 he is said to claim: "The LORD God in heaven hath given me all the kingdoms of the earth; and he hath charged me to build him a house at Jerusalem, which is in Judah." In an expression of the religious tolerance and diplomacy which made him famous, he provided money and materials to the exiles for this purpose. The edict concerning rebuilding the Temple is repeated in Ezra 6:2-5 in Aramaic, the official language of the Persian (or Chaldean) Empire.

In Isa. 40–55, Cyrus is alluded to numerous times as a divine instrument, chosen by God (although an alien dictator) to deliver Israel by subduing her oppressors: "He is my shepherd, and shall perform all my pleasure" (44:28); he is called God's "anointed" and "elect" (45:1-4) and the man of God's "counsel from a far country" (46:11). He figures thus in providential history for Christian writers, especially those with a covenant theology such as strongly identifies the present Christian pilgrimage with OT antitypes. Milton's Satan, commencing his temptation of Christ, enjoys reflecting on the triumphs of "Babylon the wonder of all tongues" which "Led captive [the Jews], and Jerusalem laid waste, / Til Cyrus set them free" (*Paradise Regained,* 3.280-84). Another poem influenced by a Calvinist reading of the OT, William Cowper's "Expostulation," in an analogy between England and Israel, describes how

Long time Assyria had bound them in her chain;
Till penitence had purg'd the public stain,
And Cyrus, with relenting pity mov'd,
Return'd them happy to the land they lov'd. (74-77)

D

DAGON Dagon was a merman, a Philistine fertility god who was in the upper half of his body a man, the lower half a fish. St. Jerome's speculation that the etymology of his name was from Heb. *dag* ("fish") or *dagan* ("grain") is unsubstantiated. Samson (Judg. 16:23-24) pulled down the pillars in the temple of Dagon in Gaza, an event which Matthew Henry, in his *Exposition of the Old and New Testaments,* interprets as a type of Christ's destruction of the devil's kingdom (2.103).

1 Sam. 5:1-5 records that when the Philistines put the captured Ark of the Covenant on the threshold of Dagon's temple the idol of Dagon had in the morning mysteriously fallen over facedown, knocking off both head and hands. This story was very popular in books of "historical wonders" such as Sir Walter Raleigh's *History of the World* and George Sandys's *Relation of a Journey,* which reinforced the biblical account among readers in the Renaissance. Another successful adjunct to the biblical account was made by Milton's friend John Selden, in his book *De Dis Syris* ("On the Syrian gods"), which includes an anthropological elaboration of the story.

Milton accordingly makes Dagon one of the fallen angels, describing him expressly in biblical terms and drawing on Selden's commentary (*Paradise Lost,* 1.457-66). William Cowper describes how when the "light" of Christian faith reached Britain, the gods Woden and Thor, "each tottering in his shrine, / Fell, broken and defac'd, at their own door, / As Dagon in Philistia long before" ("Expostulation," 504-06). Edward Young, in his *Night Thoughts,* deals with the story of Samson at Gaza, and uses Samson's tearing down the temple of Dagon as an image of the apocalyptic destruction of time. Blake cut out this passage as a prompt to illustration no. 537 in his watercolor designs for Young's poem, then adapted the story of Dagon, fusing it with the story of Gideon's destruction of the altar of Baal as well as the Vulcan myth, in his *Book of Los.*

Charles Lamb, in "Grace Before Meat," whimsically remarks that "A man should be sure . . . that while he is pretending his devotions otherwise, he is not secretly kissing his hand to some great fish — his Dagon — with a special consecration of no ark but the fat tureen before him." In *Moby-Dick,* Melville was thinking of another fish when he dryly observed that the story that St. George killed a dragon, not a whale, "will fare like that fish, flesh, and fowl idol of the Philistines, Dagon by name," and then recounts the calamitous fall to pieces before the ark.

DAN One of the twelve sons of Jacob.
See also AARON; JACOB; TRIBES OF ISRAEL.

DANCING *See* SALOME; DAVID.

DANIEL The twelve chapters of the book of Daniel in the Hebrew canon represent two quite distinct literary genres. The first six chapters are narrative, presenting a

177

series of popular edifying stories about Daniel, his three companions, and their trials and accomplishments at the courts of various foreign rulers. The last six contain four apocalypses or visions of this same Daniel. In addition there are several deuterocanonical sections lacking in the Hebrew but found in the Greek text: (a) two hymns, the Prayer of Azariah (LXX 3:24-45) and the Song of the Three Young Men (LXX 3:51-90), together with a short narrative passage connecting them (LXX 3:46-50); (b) the story of Susanna (chap. 13); (c) the stories of Bel and the Dragon (14:1-30), and (d) a second story of Daniel in the lions' den, perhaps a doublet of the narrative in chap. 6 (14:31-42).

Josephus devotes more attention to Daniel than to any other prophet, giving a detailed picture of his life (*Ant.* 10.10-11). The earliest patristic commentary on Daniel is that of St. Hippolytus (d. 235), which emphasizes apocalyptic themes (SC 14; ANF 5.177-94). By far the most important patristic commentary is that of St. Jerome (PL 25.491-584 = CChr 75A). It was composed in 407, partly in response to Porphyry, a Neoplatonist who had denied that the book of Daniel was written by the biblical figure Daniel during the Exile and had argued instead that it was composed by someone living in Judea at the time of Antiochus Epiphanes, so that the book did not so much foretell the future as relate the past. Since Porphyry's work has not survived, we are indebted to Jerome for Porphyry's position, which is essentially that of most modern critics. Jerome's commentary also cites earlier Christian writers whose works are now lost and, in addition, offers valuable testimony concerning early Jewish interpretations of specific passages in Daniel (cf. J. Braverman, *Jerome's Commentary on Daniel* [1978]). Important medieval commentaries are those of St. Albert the Great and Nicholas of Lyra, and the section on Daniel in Peter Comestor's *Historia Scholastica;* Calvin later devoted important lectures to Daniel, and S. Münster exercised considerable influence on the early English versions of the text (cf. Montgomery, *A Critical and Exegetical Commentary on the Book of Daniel* [1950], 108).

The OE *Daniel* treats the episodes in the first five chapters as found in the Vg, presenting them as part of a struggle waged by Daniel and his friends against Nebuchadnezzar and his line. This poem is much more than a mere paraphrase of the biblical narrative, making important changes in emphasis in order to further the thematic concerns of the OE poet. The ME poem variously titled *Purity* or *Cleanness* has a long section (1143-1804) imaginatively retelling the story of Belshazzar's Feast (Dan. 5) and making several references to other episodes in Daniel as well.

Chaucer's *Monk's Tale* (7.2151-54) reiterates a rabbinic tradition (cf. Braverman, 53-71) based on Dan. 1:3-4 and mentioned by Jerome (PL 25.496 = CChr 75A.779.51-59) that Daniel was a eunuch of royal descent. Christian tradition generally, however, has em-

phasized instead the theme of Daniel's chastity. For St. Augustine, Daniel represents the celibate state in the Church (PL 37.1731 = CChr 40.1929.1-1930.15), and in the ME *Vices and Virtues* this theme is related to Daniel's renunciation of fine food (Dan. 1:8-16), which is taken as representative of all fleshly pleasures (EETS o.s. 89 [1888], 43). Daniel's diet of pulse is often mentioned in relation to fasting and moderation in eating, as, e.g., by Milton (*Comus,* 720-23), Sir Thomas Browne (*Works* [1964], 3.10-11), Cowper ("The Progress of Error," 215-16), and Longfellow (Samuel Longfellow, *The Life of Henry Wadsworth Longfellow* [1886], 1.36).

According to rabbinic tradition, Daniel's wisdom outweighed that of all the wise men of the heathen world (Yoma 77a; cf. Ezek. 14:14, 20; 28:3), and Daniel's wisdom is often alluded to in Christian literature. Commenting on the question "Who is wiser than Daniel?" (Vg Ezek. 28:3), St. Ambrose writes glowingly of him as uniquely blending a prophet's calling with the offices of a teacher of wisdom (*De officio clericorum,* 2.11.57-58). In the ME *Purity* the queen recommends Daniel to Belshazzar because of "his depe divinite and his dere sawes" ("his profound learning and his excellent advice"), and his knowledge of "derne coninges" ("secret branches of knowledge") (1609-11). Shakespeare, in *The Merchant of Venice,* 4.1.333-34, makes ironic reference to "a Daniel come to judgment" — a proverb based on Daniel's judicial acumen in the history of Susanna where he demonstrates Susanna's innocence and exposes the wickedness of her accusers. In Hawthorne's *Scarlet Letter* a townsman reflects upon the question of who may be the father of Hester Prynne's child: "Of a truth, friend, that matter remaineth a riddle; and the Daniel who shall expound it is yet a-wanting" (chap. 3). Many allusions to Daniel's wisdom refer to the story in Dan. 5 of the handwriting on the wall or to the stories in the deuterocanonical additions (chaps. 13 and 14) of Susanna and Bel and the Dragon.

Because of his wisdom in interpreting two dreams of Nebuchadnezzar (chaps. 2 and 4), Daniel is often mentioned in literary discussions of dreams and their significance, as in Chaucer's *Nun's Priest's Tale* (7.3127-28), *Piers Plowman* (A.8.137-44; B.7.151-58; C.10.304-07), *Handlyng Synne* (EETS o.s. 119 [1901], 443-60). There is even an alphabetical dream interpretation manual, the *Somniale Danielis,* which purported to give Daniel's authoritative interpretations of the dreams of the people of Babylon. This work probably originated in Greek; Latin versions are numerous throughout the Middle Ages and beyond. There are also versions in OE and ME, including one in ME verse (cf. L. Martin, ed., *Somniale Danielis* [1981]). In later literature Daniel continues to be mentioned as a wise interpreter of dreams, as in Charlotte Brontë's novel *Shirley* (chap. 1) and Emerson's poem "The Miracle" (25-30). In E. L. Doctorow's novel *The Book of Daniel,* however, Daniel Lewin reflects upon his biblical namesake: "Daniel seems to be a modest man, brave, and more faithful to God than wise, for it is by means of prayer and piety that he learns from God the dream interpretations he must make to the King in order to survive" ([1971], 11).

In Dan. 6 Daniel appears as a courtier whose success is envied by subordinates; they trap Daniel by exploiting his piety, and cause him to face the ordeal of the lions' den. Their intended victim miraculously escapes, and they must then suffer the fate they had planned for him. The intrigue, suspense, and irony of this story have naturally appealed to many writers. King Darius's capricious action is used as a humorous motif in Vachel Lindsay's poem "Daniel Jazz," where the motivation for Daniel's being put into the lions' den is stated by the king to Daniel's mother and sweetheart: "Your Daniel is a dead little pigeon. / He's a good hard worker, but he talks religion" (32-33). More serious approaches to this story emphasize the qualities of Daniel's character for which he was persecuted, as, e.g., in Jerome's commentary (PL 25.526 = CChr 75A.836.394-402) and in Aelfric's sermon "On the Memory of the Saints" (EETS o.s. 82 [1885], 78-82). In both Jewish and Christian tradition, Daniel's actions in this episode make him the model of a man of prayer (Midr. Tehillim 66; Josippon 3.8b; Jerome, *Comm. in Danielem* [PL 25.524 = CChr 75A.832.296-303]), while in a more secular context Thomas Hardy takes Daniel as representative of the refusal to conform as he "persisted in kneeling eastward when reason and common sense said that he might just as well follow suit with the rest" (*Far from the Madding Crowd*, chap. 13). Other writers have focused on Daniel's miraculous escape as exemplifying the justification and survival of the just person. Mrs. Mary Rowlandson, in her account of being carried off by Indians in 1675, reflects on her survival: "God showed his Power over the Heathen in this, as he did over the hungry Lyons when Daniel was cast into the Den" (R. Pearce, ed., *Colonial American Writing* [1950], 126). In two poems Whittier compares the escape of Quakers from Puritan persecution to Daniel's miraculous escape from the lions ("The King's Missive," 65-68; "Cassandra Southwick," 4 and 148).

Several treatments of the lions' den episode amplify the biblical account. In one of the deuterocanonical sections of the book of Daniel (14:31-42), God transports the prophet Habakkuk from Judea to Babylon, having an angel carry him by the hair, so that he can bring food to Daniel in the lions' den. Allusion is made to this story in the ME *Life of St. Katherine* (EETS o.s. 80 [1884], 1845-48), and Longfellow introduces his collection of verse dramas *Christus: A Mystery* with a dialogue between Habakkuk and the angel who is carrying him through the air (*Works* [1886], 5.21-24). In Jewish legend the lions receive Daniel like loyal dogs, wagging their tails and licking him or allowing him to ride upon their backs (Josippon 3.8b). Similar romantic touches are found in a

homily of the Syrian church father Aphrahat (cf. Hartman and Di Lella, AB 23 [1978], 22), and the behavior of the lion toward Una in Spenser's *Faerie Queene* perhaps suggests the influence of this tradition (1.3.6.1-3), particularly in view of Una's "wronged innocence" (cf. Dan. 6:22). In Saul Bellow's novel *Henderson the Rain King* King Dahfu frolics with a lion in its den, and numerous allusions to the book of Daniel throughout the novel suggest that this, too, may reflect a romantic tradition concerning Daniel's experience in the lions' den (chap. 16).

Jerome regards Daniel as a preeminent prophet of the Incarnation of Christ, "for not only did he assert that He would come, a prediction common to the other prophets as well, but also he set forth the very time at which He would come" (PL 25.491 = CChr 75A.772.16-18). In the Latin liturgical drama *The Procession of the Prophets* the speech given to Daniel is: "When the holy of holies shall come, your anointing shall cease" (K. Young, *The Drama of the Medieval Church* [1933], 2.134, 140, 147, 158). This statement is not clearly derived from any specific passage — Dan. 9:24 is the closest parallel — but from a pseudo-Augustinian sermon (cf. Young, 2.126-27). In the ME Towneley play "The Prophets" (EETS e.s. 71 [1897], 217-34), Daniel expands upon this same prophecy, which is also cited by Anima in *Piers Plowman* (B.15.589; cf. B.18.108-09). One of Donne's sermons deals with the related image of the seventy weeks in Dan. 9:24 as a prophecy of the time of Christ's birth (cf. G. Carrithers, *Donne at Sermons* [1972], 227). The "stone cut without hands" which smote the feet of the great image in Nebuchadnezzar's dream (Dan. 2:34) represents, according to Porphyry, the people of Israel, but Jerome interprets this passage as a prophecy of the virgin birth: "A rock (namely, the Lord and Savior) was cut off without hands, that is, without copulation or human seed and by birth from a virgin's womb" (PL 25.504 = CChr 75A.795.406-10). The Ambrosian hymn *"A Solis Ortus Cardine,"* on the birth of Christ, devotes a stanza to this theme (F. A. March, *Latin Hymns* [1883], no. 43, 25-28), and it occurs in several ME lyrics, some of which simply address Mary as "þe hel / Of wan spellede danyel" ("the hill of one spelled Daniel") (C. Brown, *Religious Lyrics of the XIVth Century* [1924], no. 32, 55-56), or as the "plentevous mounte of Daniel" (R. Greene, *Early English Carols* [1977], no. 192, 4). For Milton the stone of Dan. 2:34 represented not Christ's birth of a virgin, but rather his kingdom (*Paradise Regained*, 4.146-53), an idea known also to Anne Bradstreet (*Complete Works* [1981], 135) and to Keats (*Poetical Works and Other Writings* [1939], 7.220).

Daniel has been regarded as a prophet not only of the birth of Christ, but also of the end of the world and the advent of Antichrist and the millennium which precedes the final judgment. The prophecies of the second half of the book of Daniel, along with the dream of the composite statue in chap. 2, exercise considerable influence on NT authors (cf. N. Perrin, *The New Testament, An Introduction* [1974], 65-72, 76-79, 84), and on the whole tradition of apocalyptic prophecy. While the name Antichrist does not appear in Daniel, the figure of such a false messiah gradually came to be associated with texts on Daniel (B. McGinn, *Visions of the End* [1979], 22, 51-55, 82-87), and in "The Prophets of Antichrist" play in the ME Chester cycle Daniel appears to recount his vision of chap. 7, emphasizing the fourth beast and the little horn. The Expositor then appears to tell the audience that the little horn stands for Antichrist (EETS e.s. 115 [1916], 125-72).

The four empires motif, based on Dan. 2 and 7, and the theme of the millennial kingdom, based on the numerological prophecies in the later chapters, have been used frequently to uphold or challenge the existing social order (cf. McGinn, 66-73 and passim). Gower applies Daniel's interpretation of Nebuchadnezzar's dream of the composite statue to the state of the empire and the Papacy and the general situation of wars and dissension in the 14th cent. (*Confessio Amantis*, Prol. 585-909). Wordsworth (*Prose Works* [1974], 1.334) and Byron ("Ode to Napoleon Buonaparte," 19-27) apply the image of the composite statue to the career of Napoleon, and apocalyptic imagery from Daniel is used in reference to the Irish troubles by Byron ("The Irish Aviator," 53-60), Coleridge (*Collected Works* [1978], 3.1.263), and later by Joyce (*Ulysses* [1946], 616, 620, 634, 638). Some writers have seen America as a "fifth empire" (alluding to Dan. 7:13-14, 27) destined by God to succeed the four empires described in symbolic terms in Daniel — a notion familiar also to Samuel Johnson, who quotes some verses of Berkeley on the subject (*Works* [1977], 10.200). Jonathan Edwards's *Apocalyptic Writings* are full of references to Daniel, although Edwards does not favor using the numbers in Daniel to arrive at an exact date for the millennium ([1977], 331, 337, 343, 349-50, 395-98, 404-07). Isaac Newton devoted much of his later life to the study of biblical chronology and the dating of the millennium, and he made much use of the allegorical arithmetic in Daniel (cf. F. Manuel, *Isaac Newton, Historian* [1963]). Bernard Shaw was fascinated by this aspect of the career of the great scientist, and he refers to it at length in the prefaces to *Saint Joan* (*Works* [1930], 17.12) and *Buoyant Billions* ([1951], 5-6). Shaw's play *In Good King Charles' Golden Days* portrays a meeting of King Charles II, Newton, and George Fox, the founder of the Quakers. Newton here talks a great deal about the later chapters in Daniel, and he justifies his concern with such matters as being of great importance to the world ([1947], 179, 187-89). A different attitude toward Daniel in relation to the apocalyptic tradition is found in George Eliot's satirical portrayal of an evangelical preacher (*Essays* [1963], 160), and in Thoreau's *Journal,* where Thoreau rhapsodizes on watching milkweed pods bursting and releasing their seeds. He sees them as "a prophecy not only of the fall but of future springs. Who could believe in prophecies of Daniel or of Miller that the world would end this summer, while one milkweed with faith matured its seeds" (*Writings* [1906], 9.18).

See also BEL AND THE DRAGON; HANDWRITING ON THE WALL; NEBUCHADNEZZAR; SHADRACH, MESHACH, AND ABEDNEGO; SUSANNA; TORMENT, TORMENTOR.

Bibliography. Braverman, J. *Jerome's Commentary on Daniel: A Study of Comparative Jewish and Christian Interpretations of the Hebrew Bible* (1978); Colletta, J. P. "The Prophet Daniel in Old French Literature and Art." *DAI* 42 (1982), 3591A; Ginsberg, H. L. "Daniel, Book of." In *EncJud* 5.1277-89; Hartman, L. F., and A. A. di Lella, *The Book of Daniel.* AB 23 (1978); Jerome. *Commentary on Daniel.* PL 25. Ed. F. Glorie. CChr 75A (1964); McGinn, B. *Visions of the End: Apocalyptic Traditions in the Middle Ages* (1979); Moffatt, J. *Literary Illustrations of the Bible,* vol. 2, *The Book of Daniel* (1905); Montgomery, J. A. *A Critical and Exegetical Commentary on the Book of Daniel* (1950); Roston, M. *Biblical Drama in England: From the Middle Ages to the Present Day* (1968). LAWRENCE T. MARTIN

DAVID The basic source for David's life is found in the books of 1 and 2 Samuel and 1 Kings. The first part of this account (1 Sam. 16:1–2 Sam. 2:11) is a fairly continuous narrative covering David's first thirty years. The second part (2 Sam. 2:12–1 Kings 2:46), more thematically selected and arranged, relates certain highlights of his forty-year reign.

David first appears as the youngest son of Jesse the Bethlehemite, good-looking but scarcely noticed alongside his more accomplished brothers, yet chosen by God to be Saul's successor and already identified by God as "a man after his own heart" (1 Sam. 13:14). Samuel anoints him, and the Spirit of the Lord, having "departed from Saul," comes upon him (16:13-14). David is a shepherd, already tried in adventures against wild animals and possessing an air of confidence which combines self-assurance with trust in God (17:34-37). His reputation as a harpist, as well as for valor and prudence, reaches the court, and when the king is stricken with melancholy David is summoned to minister to him with music. Strongly drawn to the young man, Saul appoints him an armorbearer. When, later, he is moved by the shame of Israel's failure to respond to the Philistine champion's challenge, he persuades Saul to let him confront Goliath, unarmed save for his stones and sling and a firm trust in God. In an account emphasizing how hubris and blasphemy are punished, David fells the boaster with a single shot and carries off his head in triumph.

David is now firmly established as part of the king's retinue, captain and prospective son-in-law of the king and covenanted friend of the prince Jonathan, but a powerful ambivalence governs Saul's attitude toward him. He sees the popular young man as both a support and a threat; at some level he is aware that the divine favor has been transferred from himself to David. When oppressed again by "the evil spirit from God" (18:10), he calls the harpist to soothe him but twice tries to pierce him with a javelin. He advances David to the captaincy of 1,000 troops but is only made the more afraid by the youth's mature handling of his responsibility and growing popularity. After reneging once on a marriage offer, he allows David to have his second daughter, Michal, only upon performance of a formidable task designed to cost David his life (18:25); yet David and his men killed not 100 Philistines as required, but 200. Despite Saul's oath to the contrary (19:6), there follow other attempts on David's life, all of them frustrated by David's own watch-fulness (19:10) or with the aid of Michal (19:11-17), of Jonathan (19:1-7; 20:31-42), or directly of God (19:19-24). Finally David quits the court for good and assumes the life of an outlaw.

The years of exile are the proving ground for the qualities of leadership which will make David a great king. The narrative reveals in David exquisite honor and sensitivity toward his own people. He feels personally responsible for the tragic fate of the Nobites (22:22-23); he insists on equal shares in booty for camp guards who are prevented from the actual fighting (30:21-25); when his fury against Nabal is mollified by Abigail's con-ciliatory behavior, he blesses her for averting bloodshed (25:32-33); when Saul falls into his power he will not let anyone harm him (chaps. 24 and 26); he is loyal in friendship to the king's son (23:18); and, when Saul and Jonathan are killed in battle, he laments them eloquently and acts to avenge them (2 Sam. 1).

Prominence is also given to David's reverence for the sacred; e.g., "who can stretch forth his hand against the LORD's anointed, and be guiltless?" (1 Sam. 26:9; cf. v. 23; 24:6-12; 2 Sam. 1:14). David's close relationship to God and his enjoyment of divine favor (1 Sam. 25:26-31) are recognized by Abigail, among others. In warfare David has God's aid (23:14, 19-26; 24:4) and even a direct line of counsel from the Almighty (23:1-5, 9-13; 30:7-8).

In the succeeding chapters — part two of the narrative — are interwoven two main themes. The first involves the consolidation and expansion of David's power after Saul's death. The second concerns the establishment of the Davidic dynasty, with a strong admixture of domestic and personal tragedy which have proven an especially fruitful field for subsequent creative artists.

Prominent features of this narrative are the emphasis on David's devotion to cultic observances (2 Sam. 5:19, 21, 23-24; 8:11-12; 24:18-25) and the repeated attribution of his success to the Lord's being with him (5:10, 12, 19, 23-25; 7:1; 8:14; 23:1; cf. 6:12). In establishing Jerusalem as his capital David aims to make it the center of religious as well as political life and to this end he erects a taber-nacle for the Ark of the Covenant, which he brings up to Jerusalem from Kirjath-jearim (6:1-19) with music and dancing. David intends to house it in a permanent struc-ture as elegant as his own palace instead of a tent (7:2).

The prophet Nathan first endorses the plan but then is instructed by the Lord to veto it. The Israelites, their wanderings over, will "dwell in a place of their own" (7:10), but God's house can wait. Instead, "the LORD . . . will make [David] an house" — i.e., a dynastic line: "thy throne shall be established for ever" (7:11, 16). It will be left to David's son to build the Temple. If the ruler sins, he will be chastened, "but my mercy shall not depart away from him, as I took it from Saul" (7:15).

Despite this divine promise, however, the question of succession becomes central in the later episodes, especially as David is no longer able to control affairs so firmly as he had done. His adultery with Bathsheba, followed by his arranging the death of her husband Uriah (chap. 11), brings Nathan's sharp rebuke. The prophet first asks the king to judge a legal case involving the theft of a lamb — thus alluding to both David's former and present occupations in what is actually a parable concerning the abuse of power. After David passes judgment, in effect, on himself, Nathan speaks directly: "Thou art the man" (12:7). David's prompt repentance cancels his own death sentence, but the other consequences of his wrongdoing remain: David himself will be dishonored by the open defilement of his wives, the child Bathsheba conceived adulterously will not live, and "the sword shall never depart from thine house" (12:10-14). Thus the king's taking of Bathsheba is seen as the root of the troubles which follow. These begin with the death of the young boy (12:15-23) — after which, however, Bathsheba has other children, including Solomon, whose destined succession is indirectly confirmed at once by Nathan (12:24-25) and at some point directly promised by David (1 Kings 1:17, 30).

Solomon has many older brothers, however, of whom three in particular are obstacles to his succession: Amnon the firstborn (2 Sam. 3:2), Absalom, and Adonijah — none of them, as the narrative reveals, having the character proper to a king. Amnon rapes and then ruthlessly casts off his half-sister Tamar, and is murdered for his crime two years later by Absalom. Absalom himself, angry at his father for failing to intervene on Tamar's behalf, conceives an ambitious plot to overthrow him. His rebellion, which precipitates civil war, is eventually put down and Absalom killed, against David's express orders, by Joab, David's military commander. Upon hearing the news, David weeps for his son, "Would God I had died for thee," and thus "the victory that day was turned into mourning" (18:33; 19:2).

With David "old and stricken in years" (1 Kings 1:1), even beyond arousal by the young, beautiful Abishag, who is brought to "minister" to him, the struggle for succession breaks out openly. Adonijah, backed by Joab and Abiathar the priest, attempts a coup (1:5-10, 25), but Nathan and Bathsheba appeal directly to David to honor his promise to Solomon, who as a result is immediately anointed and proclaimed king. Adonijah, initially granted a probationary pardon, is later executed (2 Sam. 2:17, 22-25; cf. Deut. 22:30).

These accounts contain a great wealth of narrative, but what the name of David signified for many centuries thereafter, so far as the records we have indicate, consisted of just a few key theological and ideological points. For instance, the remaining sections of the books of Kings emphasize continuity: of Jerusalem, regularly designated "city of David"; of the Temple, which finally comes to fulfillment under Solomon (1 Kings 8:14-20); and of the dynasty. Subsequent events in the descent of kings are connected with God's promise to David, who is repeatedly cited as the model of the ideal ruler. Thus the summary of David's life (1 Kings 15:5) is that he did "right in the eyes of the LORD, and turned not aside . . . all the days of his life, save only in the matter of Uriah the Hittite." Similarly, the account in 1 Chron. 10–29 omits everything up to Saul's death and all the stories of David's and Solomon's rivals, to concentrate on the greatness of David's reign, his victories, his enjoyment of divine favor, and — greatly expanded — his devotion to cultic activities and facilities. Several references in 2 Chronicles reflect a continuing association of David with the liturgical side of worship, particularly the singing.

The same theological and ideological points dominate the treatment of David elsewhere in the OT, including the Apocrypha, and in rabbinical tradition. David as poet, musician, and liturgical reformer is mentioned by Amos (6:5), eulogized by Jesus ben Sirach (47:8-10), and of course most fully memorialized in the Psalms, nearly half of which have the ambiguous heading "of David," which has frequently been taken as an ascription of authorship. Fourteen psalm headings associate their poems with specific occasions in David's life. Apocryphal writings include psalms attributed to David after his anointing (Pseudo-Philo 59:4), in exorcising Saul (60:2-3), and after his victory over Goliath (Ps. 151, LXX).

The celebration of God's special favor to David, his chosen "servant" (Pss. 78:70; 89:3, 20), in establishing his throne dominates Pss. 132 and 89. In the latter, however, references to later events (89:38ff.; cf. 78:69) show that the Davidic covenant is being cited as an event in national history on which, in more dismal times, hope for a renewal of God's favor may be based. The age of David, when the nation was united, powerful, and prosperous, had come to represent a longed-for ideal. Such is the way the prophets use the name of David (Isa. 9:7; Jer. 33:17; Amos 9:11; Hos. 3:5); he is a byword for the faithfulness of God (Isa. 55:3, "the sure mercies of David"; Jer. 33:20-21). When the prophetic vision came to focus on an individual expected deliverer, his connection with the line of David was stressed (Isa. 11:1; Jer. 23:5; Mic. 5:2; 4 Ezra 12:32), and he was even designated by the name "David" (Jer. 30:9) and further identified as a king-shepherd after the Davidic tradition (Jer. 23:4-5; Ezek. 34:23-24; 37:24-25; cf. 2 Sam. 7:8; Ps. 78:70-71). Psalms used in coronation ritual became interpreted as referring to the coming Anointed; in fact, many psalms were given

messianic interpretations in rabbinic teaching. By ca. 50 B.C. the use of the term *Messiah* and description of the expected deliverance by reference to David's conquest were explicit (Pss. Sol. 17). David had progressed from being a type of the ideal king (both in goodness and in greatness) to being a type of the Messiah.

David symbolized a conquest which was spiritual and moral as well as military and political. His victory over Saul's evil spirit was a forecast of the subduing of Satan (Pseudo-Philo 60.3). He was an exemplum not only of confidence in God's power (Zech. 12:8; 1 Macc. 4:30; Sir. 47:5; Scroll of the War of the Sons of Light against the Sons of Darkness 11.1-3) but also of mercy (1 Macc. 2:57), care for his subjects, devotion to the study of Torah, ascetic discipline (4 Macc. 3:6-18), thankfulness (Sir. 47:8), and prayer (4 Ezra 7:108). So much was made of his superior virtue (Sir. 47:2; cf. 1 Kings 15:5 and the eulogy by Josephus, *Ant.* 7.15) that attempts were even made to excuse his adultery and homicide, and he was honored alongside the three great patriarchs by the phrase "the God of David" (Isa. 38:5).

The figure of David also took on a miscellany of embellishments over the centuries in rabbinic commentary, usually by way of adding details not given in the biblical text (cf. Ginzberg, *LJ* 4.79-121; 6.245-76). Sometimes their purpose is to explain difficulties or obscurities, sometimes to connect different stories together, often simply to give added information or introduce frankly fictional details having a heuristic function. Exaggeration, miracle, and the fantastic are prominent in these legends, as are the activities of angels and detailed knowledge of the decrees and purposes of God.

For the writers of the NT, however, it was the canonical David that mattered: an example of the faithful life (Heb. 11:32; cf. Acts 13:22), one whose behavior could in itself provide a strong ethical argument (Matt. 12:3-4 and parallels), a divinely inspired poet (Rom. 4:6; Heb. 4:7), but above all, one who was intimately associated in various ways with the messianic hope. Essential marks identifying Jesus as the Anointed, the Christ, included his Davidic birthplace (Matt. 2:4-6; Luke 2:4; John 7:42) and ancestry (Matt. 1:1-16; Luke 1:27, 69; Rom. 1:3; 2 Tim. 2:8; cf. Rev. 5:5; 22:16). It was in those terms, and thus as heir to the throne promised to David, that he was acclaimed upon entering Jerusalem (Matt. 20:30-31; 21:9-15 and parallels, esp. Mark 11:10). "The son of David" was in fact a popular designation for the Messiah (Matt. 12:23). So firmly established was the Davidic pattern of the messianic hope (Luke 1:32-33; Acts 1:6; 15:16) that Jesus found it necessary to assert unequivocally the superiority of the fulfillment over the type (Matt. 22:42-45 and parallels). By a similar argument in his Pentecost sermon Peter traced in Christ the fulfillment of Pss. 16:8-10 and 110 (Acts 2:24-35; cf. 13:35-37). David was considered not only a type but also a prophet (Luke 24:44; Acts 2:30; cf. 2 Sam. 23:2). Drawing in some cases on messianic interpretations already established in rabbinic teaching, Jesus and his followers applied at least fifteen of the Psalms to himself and the circumstances of his life and death (cf. John 2:17; 15:25; 19:36; Matt. 21:9, 16, 42; 27:35, 39, 46, 48; Luke 23:46; Acts 1:16-20; 4:11, 25-28; 13:33; Rom. 15:3; Heb. 1:5-13; 2:6-9; 5:5-6; 10:5-7; 1 Pet. 2:7).

Such views were perpetuated (and elaborated) in subsequent Christian tradition. David's designation as prophet is regularly assumed by the Fathers and in medieval literature — as in the *Ordo Prophetarum* plays or in various versions of the "harrowing of hell" narrative, where David identifies Christ as the light penetrating the darkness of Limbo. Chaucer, in *The Canterbury Tales,* refers to David both as "the psalmist" and "the prophet," as do a host of other medieval writers.

David is one of the most important OT types of Christ for St. Athanasius, Origen, St. Augustine, and other early Fathers; the details of his life are frequently seen as prefiguring specific aspects of the earthly life of Jesus. A convenient summary of some of the main points of comparison may be had in Henry Vertue's 17th-cent. *Christ and the Church; or, Parallels* (1659):

> *David* was a Shepherd, and Christ a Shepherd; but *David* of Sheep, Christ of Souls. *Samuel,* a Priest, anointed *David* to be a King; and *John,* as a Priest, baptized our Saviour. *David,* being anointed to be a King, came not presently to the Kingdom, but was content for a long time to serve *Saul:* and so our Saviour, though he was begotten a King from all Eternity, was yet content to serve. . . . *Saul* persecuted David, and Herod persecuted Christ. . . . *Absalon, Davids* Son, rose up against his Father: and *Judas* rose up against Christ. . . . *David* was anointed by man, but Christ by his Almighty Father.

Similarly, Rupert of Deutz (d. 1135), after enumerating various attacks on David, explains that

> by those seven persecutions of David are signified the whole sum of those persecutions which the devil stirred up against Christ and His Church. . . . Moreover there were also seven persecutions which Christ endured in his own person. (PL 167.1104-05; trans. T. D. Hill)

Such typologizing continues in the New World. According to Jonathan Edwards (*A History of the Work of Redemption*), "David . . . the ancestor of Christ . . . was the greatest personal type of Christ of all under the Old Testament." He goes on to explain:

> The types of Christ were of three sorts: instituted, providential, and personal. The ordinance of sacrificing was the greatest of the *instituted* types; the redemption out of Egypt was the greatest of the *providential;* and David the greatest of the *personal* ones. Hence Christ is often called David in the prophecies of Scripture. (*Works* [1820], 3.227)

David's notorious sins of adultery with Bathsheba and the murder of her husband Uriah could hardly be accommodated to this straightforward prefigurative scheme and needed to be handled in a different way. A commentary on the books of Kings attributed to St. Eucherius treats "The Adultery of David" as a complex allegory of the Messiah (David), the Law (Bathsheba), and the Jewish people (Uriah). St. Isidore of Seville chooses rather to follow St. Augustine (*Contra Faustum,* 22.87) in interpreting Bathsheba as the Church, Uriah as Lucifer, and David as the beloved Redeemer "who has liberated us from the Devil through his mercy" (PL 83.411-12, trans. J. Wojcik, in *The David Myth,* 34).

On another level, David is also, despite these crimes (temporary, though flagrant, lapses, according to Augustine, and not indicative of a continuing disposition of heart), seen as a moral exemplum, a man of faith, or in Nicholas of Lyra's term, a *viator* who has set a standard for Christian conduct. He is perhaps most important in this regard as a model of penitence and a guide in spiritual reformation. (His "penitential psalms," identified by the 6th cent. [cf. Cassiodorus, PL 70.371-72], were prominent in medieval liturgy and private devotion. They were subsequently translated by Pietro Aretino, Sir Thomas Wyatt, and others and imitated by Petrarch.) Medieval preachers repeated over and over that if David, who sinned so ignobly, could be forgiven, then no one should be without hope. Thus, Gottfried of Admont, in his *Homiliae Dominicales Aestivales* (PL 174.476), avows that:

> David, king and prophet, was a frail stalk of grass when he saw Bathsheba, and took her, and killed Uriah by the sword of the children of Ammon, committing at the same time two wicked sins, adultery and homicide. Then was David frail grass. But afterward he was made a firm tree, when Nathan came to him, rebuking him out of the mouth of the Lord, by whose words he was inflamed with so great a fire of penitence that he lay on the ground for seven days, not eating bread or drinking water. Look, he who was a frail stalk, to how great a treelike strength has he come through penitence!

David's patience, humility, and faith in God when confronting adversity combine with his penitential qualities to make his spiritual experience a model for every Christian's own. "*David* was not onely a cleare Prophet of Christ himselfe, but a Prophet of every particular Christian; He foretels what I, what any shall doe, and suffer, and say," John Donne advances (*Sermons,* ed. Potter and Simpson [1954], 7.51), assimilating in his *Devotions upon Emergent Occasions* his own spiritual experience to the Psalmist's, as Augustine had in his *Confessiones.* The Reformers found in David's life a reflection of their own experience, Calvin commenting (in his Pref. to *Comm. on the Psalms,* trans. J. Dillenberger) that it was "of very great advantage" to him to find in David

> as in a mirror, both the commencement of my calling, and the continued course of my functions; so that I know the more assuredly, that whatever the most illustrious king and prophet suffered, was exhibited to me by God as an example for imitation.

David's sin, punishment, and repentance form the center of dramatic interest for a host of early playwrights: it is this part of his story which governs his treatment in the Cornish *Ordinale de Origine Mundi,* John Bale's *Chief Promises of God unto Man,* a "new interlude of the ij synnes of kynge DAVYD," Thomas Watson's *Absalom,* and George Peele's *Love of King David and Fair Bethsabe.* Interest in David's complex personality and varied experience effects his gradual translation from theology and devotional literature to imaginative literature, in which he is assigned four principal roles: king, epic hero, lover, and poet-musician.

With the institution of the Holy Roman Empire David was studied as a model of the divinely appointed king, a ruler whose religious duties were concomitant with political ones. The ideals of Davidic kingship, as well as David's personal and domestic tragedy, have a formative influence on much of Britain's Arthurian literature. David's refusal to slay Saul, the Lord's anointed, and his character under persecution by Absalom became arguments for both sides in the 17th-cent. Puritan-Royalist debates. Marvell attempted to legitimize Cromwell politically by investing him with qualities of the Davidic king (see J. Mazzeo), while Dryden argued, in *Absalom and Achitophel,* for Stuart right to rule.

For those attempting to accommodate pagan heroic themes to Christian subjects, David proved an especially viable subject. John Marbecke offers *The Holie Historie of King David* (1579) as a substitute to "lewd" works, while Thomas Fuller makes an epic of David's spiritual development in *David's Heinous Sin, Hearty Repentance, and Heavy Punishment* (1631). David's encounter with Goliath receives epic treatment in Drayton's *David and Goliah,* and provides a model for the Samson-Harapha episode in Milton's *Samson Agonistes* (see Steadman). Abraham Cowley's *Davideis* (1656), of which only four books of the projected twelve were completed, was to be a classical epic "after the pattern of our master Virgil"; according to his Preface, one of its principal themes is the relationship between David and Jonathan, here seen in the light of classical ideals of friendship.

For some writers, the story of David's adultery provided a pretext for writing erotic poetry, such as Francis Sabie's epyllion "David and Beersheba" (1596) or engaging in risqué dramaturgy: George Peele opens his play *David and Fair Bethsabe* (1599) with Bathsheba naked in her bath. So great were David's sensual excesses considered to be that Dryden could achieve sly comic effect in opening *Absalom and Achitophel* with a comparison of libertine Charles II to him. Throughout the early 18th cent. a controversy raged as to the propriety of including David in Sacred Writ at all.

Modern writers have sometimes characterized David's relationship with Jonathan and/or Saul as having an explicit or implicit homosexual character. Herman Melville defines the nature of Claggart's feeling for Billy Budd by referring to Saul's obsession with the comely shepherd boy (cf. André Gide's *Saul*). D. H. Lawrence used David and Jonathan as a model for homosexual relations in several of his novels.

David's skill as a musician and poet were celebrated early by St. Jerome, who explained that "David, who is our Simonides, Pindar, and Alcaeus, our Horace, our Catullus, and our Sirenus all in one, sings of Christ to his lyre." David was indeed, throughout the Middle Ages, the quintessential Christian poet. In Renaissance debates on the morality and usefulness of poetry, David is cited by Sidney and Lodge; and in the movement to create a body of religious poetry, David's name is consistently invoked (see B. Lewalski, *Protestant Poetics* [1979], 231-50). Ralph Knevet alludes to the psalmist/musician in expressing his praise for "Pious Herbert": "For it was Hee who rightly knew to touch Davids Harpe." For many poets, David is a conscious model as well as subject; thus, Thomas Traherne delights in celebrating David's own delight in creation, and Christopher Smart praises the "Blessed light" which David brought into the world.

The power of David's harp-playing to cure Saul's melancholy and madness was often emphasized. Lydgate follows an old tradition when he couples David with Orpheus in their power to produce a melody "so heuenly and celestiall" (*Reason and Sensuality,* 5599-5612). Cowley makes a long digression on "The mystick pow'rs that in blest *Numbers* dwell" when he narrates David's playing to Saul in *Davideis.* While Byron treats David's libertinism humorously in *Don Juan* (1.168), he also poignantly praises "The Harp the Monarch Minstrel Swept" in his *Hebrew Melodies.* Following Byron's depiction of melancholic Saul as a spiritually troubled man, Browning, in *Saul,* uses David to speak of the poet's ability to express "the new law."

The human experience of David has attracted, finally, a number of inferior dramatists in addition to J. M. Barrie *(The Boy David),* D. H. Lawrence *(David),* and Christopher Fry *(A Sleep of Prisoners),* as well as such diverse novelists as Charles Dickens *(David Copperfield),* Thomas Hardy *(Far from the Madding Crowd; The Mayor of Casterbridge),* William Faulkner *(Absalom, Absalom!),* and Joseph Heller *(God Knows).* Such emphasis on his complex humanity, however, has never obscured his religious dimension: for Smart and his contemporaries David represents the "intense and personal overflowing of religious emotion" praised by Bishop Lowth in *The Sacred Poetry of the Hebrews* (1753); for Byron and Browning he is still the man of faith capable of rousing others from the black slough of despair.

See also ABISHAG; ABSALOM; BATHSHEBA; GOLIATH; HARP; JONATHAN; SOLOMON.

Bibliography. Evett, D. "Types of King David in Shakespeare's Lancastrian Tetralogy." *ShakS* 14 (1981), 139-61; Ewbank, I.-S. "The House of David in Renaissance Drama: A Comparative Study." *RenD* 8 (1965), 3-40; Frontain, R.-J.,

and J. Wojcik. *The David Myth in Western Literature* (1980); Gedalof, A. J. "The Rise and Fall of Smart's David." *PQ* 60 (1981), 369-86; Gosselin, E. A. *The King's Progress to Jerusalem: Some Interpretations of David during the Reformation Period and their Patristic and Medieval Background* (1976); Gros Louis, K. R. R. "The Difficulty of Ruling Well: King David of Israel." *Semeia* 8 (1977), 15-33; Hill, T. D. "Davidic Typology and the Characterization of Christ: *Piers Plowman* B. XIX, 95-103." *N&Q* 23 (1976), 291-94; Jacobson, D. C. *Modern Midrash: The Retelling of Traditional Jewish Narratives by Twentieth-Century Hebrew Writers* (1987), 161-73; Jones, R. F. "The Originality of *Absalom and Achittophel*." *MLN* 46 (1931), 211-18; Lerner, A. L. *Passing the Love of Women: A Study of Gide's Saul and its Biblical Roots* (1982); Loomis, L. H. "Sir Thopas and David and Goliath." *MLN* 51 (1936), 311-13; Mazzeo, J. "Cromwell as Davidic King." *Renaissance and Seventeenth-Century Studies* (1964); McBryde, M. "A Study of Cowley's *Davideis*." *JEGP* 2 (1899), 469-76; Moynahan, J. "*The Mayor of Casterbridge* and the Old Testament's First Book of Samuel." *PMLA* 71 (1956), 118-30; Roston, M. *Biblical Drama in England* (1968); Shoaf, R. A. "The Alliterative Morte Arthure: The Story of Britain's David." *JEGP* 81 (1982), 204-26; Steadman, J. M. *Milton's Epic Characters* (1968), 185-93; Vogel, J. *Allegory in Dickens* (1977), chap. 1; Wiersma, S. M. *More than the Ear Discovers: God in the Plays of Christopher Fry* (1983), chap. 7.   CHARLES A. HUTTAR
                                      RAYMOND-JEAN FRONTAIN

DAY OF THE LORD

DAY OF THE LORD (Heb. *yom YHWH;* Gk. *hē hēmera tou Kyriou*) References in the OT are generally to the future glorious establishment of the kingdom of God (Isa. 2:12; 34:8; Ezek. 13:5; 30:30; Zeph. 1:14; Zech. 14:1). In the NT it generally refers to Christ's Second Advent (Rev. 6:17; Jude 6; 2 Pet. 3:12).

Added dimensions accrue to other references in the Hebrew Scriptures, where the present day ("this day," *hayyom hazzeh;* e.g., Josh. 24:15), the opportunity for present decision or enactment of the will in choosing to obey (cf. Deut. 30:19), is contrasted with "that day" (*bayyom hahu*, e.g., Exod. 14:30 — a past moment of confirmation; or, e.g., Deut. 31:17; Isa. 2:11-17 — a future day of confirmation, "the LORD alone will be exalted in that day").

See also SECOND COMING.

Bibliography. Cullmann, O. *Christ and Time* (Eng. trans. 1964); De Vries, S. J. *Yesterday, Today, and Tomorrow* (1975).

DAYS OF AWE

DAYS OF AWE *See* ATONEMENT, DAY OF.

DE PROFUNDIS

DE PROFUNDIS The opening words of Vg Ps. 129:1 are *"De profundis clamavi, ad te, Domine."* In the corresponding Ps. 130, the KJV reads, "Out of the depths have I cried unto thee, O LORD." Sometimes related to this text is Lam. 3:55, *"Invocavi nomen tuum Domine, de lacu novissimo"* (KJV, "I called upon thy name, O LORD, out of the low dungeon"; Douai, "I have called upon thy name, O Lord, out of the lowest pit"). And Jonah utters something like the Psalmist's cry from the "fish's belly" (Jonah 2:2-3), in repentance for his disobedience. Liturgically, the *De profundis* came to be associated with the seven penitential psalms (6, 32, 38, 51, 130, and 143), which were recited after the hour of lauds on Fridays in Lent in medieval Christendom.

In Roman Catholic practice, the *De profundis* was recited as a penitential psalm among the prayers for the ill; it was chanted in funeral processions for the dead on the day of burial, and at Lauds and Vespers in the Office for the Dead. It accompanies also the blessing of a new bell in a church or chapel, perhaps because the tolling of a church bell connotes a transition through death to life beyond (*Rituale Romanum*). In the English *Book of Common Prayer,* Ps. 130 is recited as a penitential psalm at Evensong on Ash Wednesday, and throughout the year on the twenty-seventh day of the month.

The 12th-cent. *Ancrene Riwle* dictates that *"de profundis"* be one of the psalms said for the souls of the faithful departed:

> ʒe doþ ʒet betere. & her also sig-geð
> deprofundis. bivore þe pater noster.

Various effective medieval English translations notwithstanding, the text receives some of its richest adaptation in the Renaissance. John Skelton uses the text of Ps. 130:1 paradoxically, together with its proper antiphon, found in the Office of the Dead ("Phyllyp Sparowe"):

> "Si in i qui ta tes,
> Alas, I was evyll at ease!
> De profun dis cla ma vi,
> Whan I sawe my sparowe dye!"

Thomas Campion's elegant air is perhaps unsurpassed in poetic translation in the period. It begins:

> Out of my soules deapth to thee my cryes haue sounded
> Let thine eares my plaints receiue, on iust feare grounded
> Lord, should'st thou weigh our faults, who's not confounded?

But the long poem of George Gascoigne (ca. 1575) is almost equal to it in vigor. Entitled *"De Profundis,"* it renders in colorful 16th-cent. language the whole of Ps. 130, affirming the covenant promise of God to Israel, here typologically also the Christian elect:

> From depth of dole wherein my soul doth dwell,
> From heavy heart which harbours in my breast,
> From troubled sprite which seldom taketh rest,
> From hope of heaven, from dread of darksome hell,
> O gracious God, to thee I cry and yell,
> My God, my Lord, my lovely Lord alone,
> To thee I call, to thee I make my moan. . . .

John Donne, whose meditations and psalms resonate the *de profundis* theme, employs in his "Lamentations of

Jeremy" translations a collation of Ps. 130:1 with Lam. 3:55: "I called Lord, upon thy name, / Out of the pit. . . ."

Robert Browning uses the traditional context of Ps. 130 in the *Ring and the Book* (1.1318-19). Count Guido Franceschini, having confessed to the murder of his wife, is about to be executed when the "black fellowship" (of chaplains) "intone the lamentable psalm, 'Out of the deeps, Lord, have I cried to thee!' " It is invoked in a similar context by Melville in *Clarel* (2.25.190): "Her God her deprofundis roll."

In Søren Kierkegaard's *Journals*, the theme becomes to some extent a preoccupation. Speaking of the sufferings which each person has to endure to improve the lot of all mankind, Kierkegaard claims that individuals must be sacrificed to be a "little dash of cinnamon" in God's recipe for divine Providence. "Painful it is to be sacrificed in this manner — to be a little dash of cinnamon!" Each person so sacrificed learns to sing a

> *deprofundis* — that God is love. . .
> Underneath, supporting, as it were,
> all these sopranos as the bass part
> does, [and] sounds the *deprofundis* from
> the sacrificed ones: God is love.

Following Kierkegaard, Lev Shestov takes the "*de profundis*" into philosophic-theological inquiry in his essay entitled "*De Profundis.*"

The title given to Oscar Wilde's "*Epistola: in Carcere et Vinculis*" by his editor Robert Ross, *De Profundis*, does not reflect a penitential intent. Wilde seems rather to have created his own religion from a hell within himself, reflected in the external geography of the place where he was imprisoned. To be released, he has to deliver himself from bitter feelings much, as he imagines, like those of Dante in the *Inferno*. In the midst of a threatening flood, the parishioners in Dorothy Sayers's *The Nine Tailors* (3.3) cry for help in the *Book of Common Prayer* version, "Out of the deep, O Lord, out of the deep" as the sluice begins to give way.

Bibliography. Booty, J. E., ed. *The Book of Common Prayer, 1159: The Elizabethan Prayer Book* (1976), 24; *Rituale Romanum Pauli V Pontificis Maximi* (1917).

ERNEST N. KAULBACH

DEAF ADDER Ps. 58:4-5 describes the incorrigibility of the wicked as "like the deaf adder that stoppeth her ear." Though Rabbi Solomon (Rashi) offers a quasi-literal explanation of this expression in the fabulous biology of a viper which puts its "ear" to the ground to hear approaching prey, stopping the other with its tail, the referent here remains obscure. But not without charm. Dickens says of Ralph in *Nicholas Nickelby* that "To all entreaties, protestations, and offers of compromise. . . [he] was 'deaf as an adder' " (chap. 2). And Nellie, in Willa Cather's *My Mortal Enemy*, is warned not to approach her potential antagonist: "She'd turn a deaf ear to you. You

know the Bible says the wicked are deaf like the adder. And, Nellie, she has the wrinkled, white throat of an adder, that woman, and the hard eyes of one. Don't go near her!" (2.2)

DEATH In the OT death comes into the world as a result of the disobedience of Adam and Eve (Gen. 3:16-19; Ps. 90:7-10) and functions as a final sign of humanity's separation from God (Prov. 2:18; 7:27; 21:16; 22:23; Isa. 5:14). While death involves the loss of God's gift of continuing physical life, the more important implication of Gen. 3 is that the penalty of transgression is spiritual death: humanity is driven from Paradise and from the presence of God. Death is the common fate of all humanity, but can be lightened by a long life, which is a reward for righteousness (Deut. 30:15-20; 32:47; Prov. 10:2; 11:4). Conversely people bring an early death upon themselves by committing sin (Job 15:32; 22:16; Ps. 55:23). Through extraordinary providential intervention, Enoch and Elijah were spared from death; a widow's son was raised by Elijah (1 Kings 17:17-24), and the son of a Shunammite woman by Elisha (2 Kings 4:32-37). And there are hints in the OT that death will ultimately be overcome. In Daniel (and in the apocryphal books of Wisdom and 2 Maccabees), death becomes a period of sleep prior to a general resurrection of body and soul: "And many of them that sleep in the dust of the earth shall awake, some to everlasting life, and some to shame and everlasting contempt. . ." (Dan. 12:2).

In the NT, death is the fruit and wages of sin (James 1:15; Rom. 6:23), and the expression of divine wrath (Rom. 2:5-8). Jesus himself suffered death, although sinless, bearing the sins and suffering the judgment of all humanity. Through his death and resurrection he "abolished death" (2 Tim. 1:10), making it possible for those who are "dead in trespasses and sins" (Eph. 2:1; Col. 2:13) to be reborn, and made "alive to God" (Rom. 6:11). At the graveside of Lazarus, prior to his own crucifixion, Jesus reassured grieving Martha, "I am the resurrection, and the life: he that believeth in me, though he were dead, yet shall he live: And whosoever liveth and believeth in me shall never die" (John 11:25-26; cf. 1 Cor. 15:51-57). Having thus spoken, he called Lazarus forth from the grave. Those who refuse the grace of God in Christ become subject to the "second death," the final loss of opportunity to repent, which confirms their eternal separation from God (Rev. 2:11; 20:6, 14; 21:8).

Of early Christian commentaries, St. Augustine's *De civitate Dei* contains the most extensive exegesis of the major OT teachings on death: that Adam, in disobeying God, became subject to the death of the body and the soul (13.12), that the punishment of death inflicted on our "first parents" is passed on to all humanity (13.3), and that Adam and Eve, if they had obeyed God, would have passed to blessed eternity without the intervention of temporal death (13.1). These same teachings receive attention from St.

Thomas Aquinas (*Summa Theol.* 1a2ae.81.3), and are reaffirmed by the Synod of Carthage (A.D. 418) and again by the Council of Trent (1545). Augustine also stresses the central NT teaching that those who die in Adam are reborn spiritually in Christ (13.23); this rebirth does not imply an escape from temporal death, which is still a sign of humanity's fallen condition, but gives it new meaning and robs it of its "sting" (1 Cor. 15:54-57). Many early Church writers view death as a blessing; it becomes a test of faith and a gateway to eternal life. This is the case in St. Athanasius (*De incarnatione verbi Dei,* 21) as well as in St. John Chrysostom (*Homilies concerning the Statues,* 5.6), St. Gregory (*Panegyric on His Brother,* 18-20), St. Cyprian (*De mortalitate,* 2-3), and even Augustine himself (*De civ. Dei* 13.20). This emphasis persists among Reformation writers, for, in the context of Calvinist predestination, those who maintain faith in the face of death receive a further sign of their election (*Inst.* 2.10.14).

The preachers and moralists of the Middle Ages were, by modern standards, morbidly preoccupied with death: at great length they exhorted their listeners to remember death, calling upon the age-old themes of the *Ubi sunt?* and *memento mori.* In homiletic exhortations the exegesis of the Church Fathers is often obscured by a primitive psychology of the macabre. For John Bromyard in his *Summa Predecantium* (ca. 1300), physical death involves worms, toads, and decomposing corpses, while spiritual death means the horrors of the pit. Other works, such as the anonymous *Pricke of Conscience* (ca. 1340), a translation of the German mystic Suso's *Orologium Sapientiae* (1328), and Hoccleve's *How to Learne to Die* (ca. 1400), are less ghoulish and emphasize the need for spiritual preparation for death. These works anticipate the *Tractatus Artis Bene Moriendi* (1414). When translated by Caxton as *The Boke of the Craft of Dying* (1491), this small tract initiated in England the important tradition of the *ars moriendi,* which, over the next two hundred years, flowered with Thomas Lupset's *Waye of Dyenge Well* (1534), Thomas Becon's *Sycke Mans Salue* (1591), and Jeremy Taylor's *Holy Dying* (1651).

Biblical concepts of death are diffused throughout Renaissance literature, and especially Elizabethan and Jacobean drama. Death is a punishment for sin in Ford's *'Tis a Pity She's a Whore* (1633), when the friar tells Giovanni that "death waits on my lust" (1.1), although death also leads to heavenly reward, as Delio so nobly sums up at the end (5.5.123-24) of Webster's *Duchess of Malfi* (1623). Also common is the OT notion that life can be extended through righteous living; good deeds, Hippolito says in Dekker's *The Honest Whore* (1604), "keepe men sweet, long aboue ground" (4.1.75). Much, of course, has been reduced to the commonplace — the image of death as sleep is typical — although the commonplace is memorably rendered in Hamlet's "To die, to sleep, / To sleep — perchance to dream" (3.1.65). Not surprisingly, preparation for death is also prominent; the protagonist in the late medieval *Everyman* is actually caught unprepared, and Marlowe clearly plays on the same idea in *Doctor Faustus* (1604), where there is a perverse reversal of the idea of spiritual preparation. Shakespeare's plays, too, contain a myriad of references to preparing for death (e.g., *Richard 3,* 1.4.256; *Henry 5,* 4.2.56; *Measure for Measure,* 2.2.84-86). But it is Hamlet's soliloquy (3.1.56-89) and Claudio's lament (3.1.118-32) in *Measure for Measure* which capture the essential anxiety of a humanist age: the grave, despite the promises of heaven, seems a poor ending for a creature as noble as mankind.

Numerous 17th-cent. poets echo biblical teachings on death. John Donne, whose own preoccupation with death is perhaps best expressed in the prose works *Biathanatos* (1624) and *Devotions Upon Emergent Occasions* (1624), speaks of death as "one short sleepe past" from which "wee wake eternally" (*Holy Sonnets,* 10.13 [1635]). George Herbert explains how death, which "wast once an uncouth hideous thing," is now "grown fair and full of grace" ("Death," 14). Henry Vaughan expresses similar sentiments, although his most revealing statements, like Donne's, are not in poetry but in prose, particularly his *Of Life and of Death* (1654), where he argues, "For life, if thou livest not well, is the greatest evill; and Death, if thou dyest not ill, is the greatest good." Milton, in *Paradise Lost,* portrays Death as the son of Satan — child of his incestuous liaison with his daughter Sin. Much of the poem, because of its central preoccupation with the consequences of the Fall, is concerned with death in both its physical and spiritual aspects. Indeed, nowhere is the notion of death as life apart from God portrayed more dramatically than in Milton's epic, or expressed so simply as in the uncomprehending Adam's statement, "Death is to mee as Life" (9.954).

In his short essay *Of Death* (1597), Francis Bacon, in divorcing death from religion, anticipates the more objective rational theism of the 18th cent. When he writes that death is no "terrible Enemie" because "it is as Natural to die, as to be borne," his sentiments are not unlike those of Pope, who in *An Essay on Man* sees the "great teacher Death" (92) as part of the natural order of things. For Samuel Johnson death is still a source of great spiritual anxiety: in his tragedy *Irene* (1749), the heroine, awaiting execution, expresses all the typical fears of the deathbed, and cries out for "peaceful death, and Happiness eternal" (9.47). Samuel Richardson, in *Clarissa* (1747), provides his heroine with books on preparing to die, including Lewis Bayly's popular *Practice of Piety.*

In the middle of the 18th cent. the "graveyard school," represented by poets such as Edward Young, Robert Blair, and Thomas Gray, engaged in somber, melancholy philosophizing on death and immortality: this literature reflects a series of biblical commonplaces concerning death. Typical is Young's "Night Thoughts," where he talks of death as the "great proprietor of all" (104), the "deliverer" (511), the "rewarder" (512), and the "crown of life" (525). Vestiges of a biblical view may also be found in Wordsworth's Ecclesiastical Sonnet (3.31) on 1 Cor. 15:55 ("O death, where is thy sting") and his reference to "the faith that looks through death" (185) in "Intimations of Immortality," as well as less obvious allusions in Blake's *Songs of Innocence* and *Songs of Experience,* Coleridge's *The Rime of the Ancient Mariner,* and Shelley's elegy on the death of Keats, *Adonaïs.*

Among the most significant 19th-cent. treatments of death is Tennyson's *In Memoriam.* Written in memory of his close friend Henry Hallam, Tennyson's long elegy traces his struggle to accept physical death as a necessary good, subject to "that God, which ever lives and loves" (131.141). Despite its rationalistic bent, Browning's long philosophical poem "La Saisiaz," also expresses an essentially Christian viewpoint on death: "I affirm and re-affirm it . . . / As that man now lives, that, after dying, man will live again" (449-50). A similar message is implicit in "The Bishop Orders His Tomb," where, as in *Faustus,* and Matthew Lewis's late 18th-cent. Gothic thriller *The Monk* (1796), the central character is depicted as perversely refusing to die well. The Bishop would have done well to read Hopkins's sermon *On Death,* which deals with the terrors and comforts of death, as well as preparation for death, drawing upon the biblical teachings central to the *ars moriendi* of several hundred years earlier. Not all Victorians, of course, possessed Hopkins's deep-seated faith. Thomas Hardy, believing in a First Cause which was either unaware of or disinterested in humanity, found no comfort in death and, in novels such as *Tess of the D'Urbervilles* (1891) and *Jude the Obscure* (1895), portrays death as a moment of desolating loneliness, the end of a life which itself makes no sense.

In the 20th cent., such despair becomes ever more acute. It is a time of concern with spiritual death, of a fallen world, in which, as Eliot says in *The Waste Land,* one hears only the "rattle of bones." Such a view lies at the base of Samuel Beckett's plays, which depict humanity's loss of spirituality and the hopelessness of ever finding God; as one of the tramps in *Waiting for Godot* says, "Nothing happens, no one comes, no one goes, it's awful." Even more acute, however, is the nihilism of the existentialists, who regard physical death as absolute darkness and a return to meaningless chaos. For Frederic Henry in Hemingway's *Farewell to Arms* (1929) the death of Catherine is an event about which nothing can be said. Death is, as William Empson says, something "that most people should be prepared to be blank upon" ("Ignorance of Death").

Avowedly Christian writers such as C. S. Lewis still write of death in traditional biblical terms, that it is at once "the triumph of Satan, the punishment of the Fall, and the last enemy," as well as "the means of redemption from sin, God's medicine for Man, and His weapon against Satan" (*Miracles*). The fiction of Flannery O'Connor —

which bespeaks the author's own preparation for death in the face of incurable disease — explores the nature and meaning of death in powerfully contemporary yet Christian terms (see, e.g., "The Enduring Chill," "Everything that Rises Must Converge").

See also DEATH, WHERE IS THY STING?; HEAVEN; HELL; LAZARUS OF BETHANY; RESURRECTION.

Bibliography. Alger, W. R. *The Destiny of the Soul: A Critical History of a Future Life* (1878; rpt. 1968), vol. 1; Beaty, N. L. *The Craft of Dying: A Study in the Literary Tradition of the "Ars Moriendi" in England.* YSE 175 (1970); Boase, T. *Death in the Middle Ages: Mortality, Judgement, and Remembrance* (1972); d'Ariès, P. *The Hour of Our Death* (1981); Enright, D. J., ed. *The Oxford Book of Death* (1983); Fairman, M. *Biblical Patterns in Modern Literature* (1972); Glicksberg, C. I. *Literature and Religion: A Study in Conflict* (1960); O'Connor, M. C. *The Art of Dying: The Development of the Ars Moriendi* (1942); Pelikan, J. *The Shape of Death: Life, Death, and Immortality in the Early Fathers* (1962); Spencer, T. *Death and Elizabethan Tragedy* (1936).
                                                    DAVID W. ATKINSON

DEATH, WHERE IS THY STING?   After readings from Psalms, the *Book of Common Prayer* designates as the Lesson for the Burial of the Dead 1 Cor. 15:20-58, where St. Paul, triumphant, asks, "O death, where is thy sting? O grave, where is thy victory?" (v. 55). Its place in the Anglican liturgy is no doubt responsible for its rich literary tradition in English.

Paul himself is engaging in the rhetoric of allusion, combining Isa. 25:8 and Hos. 13:14. Conzelmann has examined the complex textual tradition of these verses (292-93), and he remarks that the "sting," derived from the LXX rendering of Hosea, refers variously to "the drover's goad, [to any] instrument of chastisement, . . . [or to] the sting of an animal," especially a scorpion (see also Grosheide, 394). Whatever its metaphorical origin, the sting becomes in the LXX "the symbol of tyranny and force." Conzelmann also notes that Paul's meaning is consistent with the customary Jewish understanding of the two prophetic verses, "the expectation that death will cease."

St. Athanasius, in his *De incarnatione verbi Dei,* uses these words in discussing how death is "brought to nought by the death of Christ" (chap. 21). St. Cyril in his *Catechetical Lectures* stresses that it is the "sting of death" which is "drawn by baptism" (3.2). For St. Augustine, the Pauline passage epitomizes the spiritual man's ultimate release from the tensions of existence under the Law. The text signifies freedom: "For who shall hinder us, when shall be brought to pass the saying that is written, Death is swallowed up in victory" (*Conf.* 9.4). It signifies emancipation from "all manner of concupiscence" (*De spiritu et littera,* chap. 56). It signifies, as against the Manicheans, the harmony of the NT with the OT (*De moribus ecclesiae catholicae,* chap. 30). It indicates "the fulness of peace" (*Conf.* 10.30), the end of the intolerable pain of humanity's alienation from God (*De civ. Dei* 20.17), and God's loving omnipotence (*De natura et gratia,* chaps. 8 and 16; *De civ. Dei* 22.23).

Augustine's influence is apparent in the commentaries of Protestant theologians. For Luther, only faith in Christ can take away the agonizing sense of sin which is death; one is saved not by merit but by God's forgiveness (*Epistle to the Hebrews,* 62; *On the Bondage of the Will,* 268). Calvin, on the contrary, argues that the text says that God will save only those who allow him to (*Commentary,* 62). Coverdale quotes this passage in his *Treatise on Death* (1553) to reveal the mercy and lovingkindness of Christ (chap. 28), as do the Calvinist Thomas Becon in his *New Catechism* (1564) and the 17th-cent. Anglican divine Christopher Sutton in his *Disce Mori: Learne to Die* (1600). But Barth accepts Luther's meaning, that Christ's victory signifies how absolute is one's dependence upon God. Moreover, according to Barth, Paul's verse implies that the whole truth of Christianity depends upon God's "reversal," consuming death (*The Resurrection,* 219-21).

Chaucer exploits death's sting in *The Pardoner's Tale.* The rioters of the Pardoner's exemplum seek to slay the body's death, but their quest leads them to "the real spiritual death found under the oak tree" (Miller, 65). The ambiguous Pardoner conveys the irony of the rioters' quest when he has them shout as they leave the tavern, "Death shal be deed, if that they may hem hente!" (*Canterbury Tales,* 6.710).

Chaucer's allusion looks forward to the ultimate line of Donne's "Holy Sonnet 10," "And death shall be no more; death, thou shalt die." So, too, Shelley, commemorating Keats: "He lives, he wakes — 'tis Death is dead, not he" (*Adonaïs,* 41.1). Wordsworth ends his Ecclesiastical Sonnet "The Funeral Service" and Pope his "A Dying Christian to his Soul" in Donne's fashion. Paul's text becomes a cliché of closure. But Swift is somewhat more inventive, using the text to praise the late Archbishop of Canterbury, Sancroft, who had been ejected from Lambeth for refusing allegiance to William and Mary ("Ode to Dr. William Sancroft," 201). Byron, more inventive still, thoroughly secularizes the text so as to invert its meaning. In Canto 9 (st. 11) of *Don Juan,* Byron is describing war as it actually is, unglorified. Napolean and Waterloo inspire this meditation:

> Death laughs at all you weep for: — look upon
> This hourly dread of all, whose *threaten'd sting*
> Turns life to terror, even though in its sheath!
> Mark! how its lipless mouth grins without breath!
> (85-88)

The italics are Byron's, perhaps betraying some anxiety that his allusion could be missed.

The warrant for secularizing, though not inverting, may be found in Shakespeare. When Hamlet rails at Gertrude, "O shame, where is thy blush," over the corpse of Polonius, one is reminded of Paul's idea of the duality of death, of the body and of the soul. Gertrude seems to catch the allusion, for Hamlet's words turn her eyes into her soul, where she sees "such black and grained spots / As will not leave their tinct" (3.4.81-91).

Allusions in Melville and Conrad follow the Byronic mode. In Melville's story of an impoverished laborer, Merrymusk, the man's prize rooster, crows so lustily as to give "stuff against despair." Its crowing sustains Merrymusk's family of invalids, who nonetheless die one by one. When the last expires, so does the ironically named Trumpet, who gives his last prodigious crow. The narrator finds that Merrymusk had made a tombstone for the bird, on it inscribed, "O death, where is thy sting? / O grave, where is thy victory?" Melville's supernaturalism in the tale makes these into genuine rather than rhetorical questions.

Along somewhat different lines, Thoreau's *Walden* quotes 1 Cor. 15:55-56 to stress his belief that the light of an early spring morning is a telling sign of immortality. Less direct references occur in Emily Dickinson's "Love is that later thing than Death" and Christina Rossetti's "Maundy Thursday" and "Thread of Life 3."

The title of one of Conrad's late novels, *Victory,* is derived from St. Paul, and the work is a meditation upon the text. Its climax comes when the deluded heroine, Lena, seeks to save her beloved by disarming a villain who threatens them. She means to get "the very sting of death in her hands," to "carry off the terrible spoil, the sting of vanquished death." But Lena, accidentally shot in a scuffle, dies instead, "as if fatigued only by the exertions of her tremendous victory, capturing the very sting of death in the service of love."

Bibliography. Conzelmann, H. *1 Corinthians: A Commentary on the First Epistle to the Corinthians.* Trans. J. W. Leitch (1975); Grosheide, F. W. *Commentary on the First Epistle to the Corinthians* (1953); Miller, R. P. "Chaucer's Pardoner, The Scriptural Eunuch, and *The Pardoner's Tale.*" In *Twentieth-Century Interpretations of "The Pardoner's Tale."* Ed. D. R. Faulkner (1973).   DWIGHT H. PURDY
DAVID W. ATKINSON

DEBORAH, SONG OF DEBORAH The victory ode in Judg. 5, ascribed to Deborah, a prophetess, celebrates the northern Israelite triumph over a powerful Canaanite coalition as early as 1150 B.C. (D. N. Freedman, "Early Israelite History," 13) or 1200 B.C. (A. Globe, "Muster"). Vv. 1-11 praise the covenant God of Sinai for the deliverance when Deborah "arose, a mother in Israel." In vv. 12-18, Deborah summons the warriors whom Barak leads to battle; six loyal tribes are praised, and four absentees are taunted. In vv. 19-31, after the Canaanite defeat, the non-Israelite Jael harbors the escaping general, Sisera. Lulling him to sleep, she violates the hospitality code, hammering a tent peg through his skull. At the ironic conclusion, Sisera's mother, anxious about his delay, is silenced by the deluded princesses' dreams of booty. The poem contains many features of great antiquity, including archaic words, repetitious parallelism, paratactic syntax, conventions found in Near Eastern odes from 1300-1150 B.C., and motifs from Canaanite mythology (A. Globe, "Literary Structure"; A. J. Hauser, "Judges 5"; J. G. Taylor, "The Song of Deborah").

The rabbis discover references to the Messiah and to the world to come in the last verse of the Song (Gen. Rab. 12.6; Num. Rab. 13.12; Midr. Ps. 49.1), but Deborah remains an ambiguous figure. One of the seven prophetesses, her praises to God are unequaled by men's (Meg. 14a; Zohar Lev. 19b). Still, her hateful name — "hornet" — suits her arrogance in sending for Barak rather than going to him (Meg. 14b). St. Augustine stigmatizes the Song as too obscure for comment (*De civ. Dei* 18.15). The allegorical interpretation sketched by Origen (*In Librum Iudicum homilium V* [PG 12.974-78]), developed by St. Jerome, St. Isidore of Seville, and the Venerable Bede (*In Hiezechielem*, 4.16.13; *Quaestiones in Veterum Testamentum, In Lib. Judicum*, 2 [PL 83.380-81]; *Quaestiones super Librum Judicum* 2 [PL 93.423-24]), and reflected in the notes of the English Catholic Douai-Rheims Bible (1610) sees Deborah, the "bee," as inspired with honey-sweet prophecies. Barak's initial unwillingness to accompany the prophetic Deborah represents the inability of Israel to triumph over the devil (Sisera) until the deliverance of mankind through the cross. Jael, the church gathered from the Gentiles, helps save believers by destroying the devil. Sometimes Jael appears as a duplicitous double of Delilah, as in Chaucer's Wife of Bath's prologue (*Canterbury Tales*, 3.769-70).

Sidney judges the song to be one of the best antique imitations of "the inconceivable excellencies of God" (*An Apologie for Poetrie*). Spenser makes Britomart more stout-hearted than "*Debora* [who] strake / Proud *Sisera*" (*Faerie Queene*, 3.4.2-3). In Shakespeare's *1 Henry 6* (1.2.105), the Dauphin Charles cries out that his female victor fights "with the sword of Deborah." Donne's sermon of September 15, 1622, embroiders the medieval allegorical interpretation to defend James I's religious settlement against Papists and Puritans (*Sermons*, ed. Potter and Simpson [1959], 4.178-209). In Milton's *Samson Agonistes* (982-94), Dalila, failing to ensnare Samson anew, storms off with the prophecy that she, like Jael, will be praised for saving her country from a deadly enemy. Robert Lowth glosses over the Song's violence in favor of its "striking picture of maternal solicitude" and praise of Israelite liberty (*Lectures on the Sacred Poetry of the Hebrews* [1753], chaps. 13, 28). In Browning's *The Ring and the Book* (10.663-64) the stars of Judg. 5:20 condemn the drawing together of a priest and a married woman; Tennyson's *The Princess* (5.500-501) places Ida ominously "Between a cymballed Miriam and a Jael." Mark Twain, critical of violence in the Bible, sets Deborah and Jael in Satan's "history of the progress of the human race" as it moves from the murder of Abel to the mass exterminations of modern warfare (*Mysterious Stranger*, chap. 8).

Victorian and Edwardian feminist pageants, such as Alfred Ford's *Jael and Sisera: A Woman's Rights Drama* (in his *Scenes and Sonnets* [1872], 1-14), celebrate the Song's heroines uncritically. *Daughters of Dawn,* by Bliss Carman and Mary Perry King (1913), chooses Deborah, who rouses an oppressed nation, as one of a dozen characters "typical chiefly of the liberal and beneficent power of woman's nature in her leadership and ascendancy in the life of the spirit and the destiny of the world" (vii).

See also JAEL.

Bibliography. Alter, R. *The Art of Biblical Poetry* (1985), 43-50; Coogan, M. D. "A Structural and Literary Analysis of the Song of Deborah." *CBQ* 40 (1978), 143-66; Freedman, D. N. "Early Israelite History in the Light of Early Israelite Poetry." In *Unity and Diversity.* Ed. H. Goedicke (1976), 3-35; Globe, A. "The Literary Structure and Unity of the Song of Deborah." *JBL* 93 (1974), 493-512; "The Muster of the Tribes in Judges 5.11e-18." *ZAW* 87 (1975), 169-84; Hauser, A. J. "Judges 5: Parataxis in Hebrew Poetry." *JBL* 99 (1980), 23-41; Liver, J. "Deborah." *EncJud* (1971); Taylor, J. G. "The Song of Deborah and Two Canaanite Goddesses." *JSOT* 23 (1982), 99-108.   ALEXANDER GLOBE

DEEP CALLETH UNTO DEEP   Etymologically and mythologically this deep (Ps. 42:7) has affinities with a symbolically related set of primordial sea monsters, and some connection is intended also with the deep upon the face of which darkness lay at the creation (Gen. 1:2) and the deep which God will bring upon wicked Tyre (Ezek. 26:19). KJV's "waterspouts" is improved upon by RSV's "cataracts," which give the watery ferment a clearer context. St. Augustine explains that the first "deep" is the human heart, "For what is more profound than that abyss? . . . 'Deep calls to deep,' then, is, 'man calls to man.' Thus is it wisdom is learnt, and thus faith, when 'man calls to man' " (*Enarr. in Ps.* 42). Elsewhere he sees an allegory of carnal humanity:

> But even so, we still live by faith and not by sight, for we are saved by hope; but hope that is seen is not hope. Thus far deep calls unto deep, but now in "the noise of the waterfalls. . . ." And he calleth to this lower deep. . . . for him he is jealous, not for himself, but because not in his own voice but in the voice of the water falls he calls on that other deep, of which he is jealous and in fear. (*Conf.* 13:13)

Luther extends this reading, adding a psychological dimension to it:

> . . . the "deep" is in every man. . . . It applies in a personal way to human nature seeking and hoping to be saved in Christ. . . . Therefore the whole psalm is a sigh of human nature seeking to enter the church of God. . . . But human nature is unable to say when it is outside the church. . . . Therefore this psalm is ascribed to Christ speaking for mankind, and the context of this psalm is taken from the story of the exodus from Egypt and the entrance unto the land of promise. (*Comm.* on Ps. 42:7)

Calvin's *Commentary* sees the deep as a metaphor for misery, and the Geneva Bible commentator moralizes and simplifies: "Afflictions come so thicke upon me, that I felt my self as overwhelmed: whereby he showeth there is no end to our miserie, til God be pacified & send remedie."

A mythologized "deep" (often again in combination with "dark") is in *Paradise Lost* the abode of the fallen angels, meant to reflect both the abysses of their own nothingness and the hoary unreality which God's creativity has not touched. Biblical resonances of this deep help to damn the devils, and in Pope's *Dunciad* a metamorphosed version of it gives weight to the dunces' self-damnation. In Traherne the unfulfilled heart can be "a deep profound Abyss" ("Desire," 22).

In Vaughan's "Abels Blood" the blood of Abel which cries out in Gen. 4:10 leads up to the blood of all those murdered by their fellow humans, a

> deep, wide sea of blood?
> A sea, whose lowd wave cannot sleep,
> But *Deep* still calleth unto *deep*. . . .

And in Hopkins's "Nondum" Nondum likens mankind's searching for God (to which "not yet" is the answer) to an abyss where "Deep calls to deep and blackest night / Giddies the soul with blinding daze. . . ."

Whittier, in "Massachusetts to Virginia," characterizes the moral outrage over the re-taking of an escaped Southern slave in Boston as

> The voice of Massachusetts! Of her free sons and
>   daughters
> Deep calling unto deep aloud, the sound of many
>   waters!
> Against the burden of that voice what tyrant power
>   shall stand?
> No fetters in the Bay State! No slave upon her land!

Emerson's *Nature* (sect. 8), on the other hand, uses the deep calling as a metaphor for his notion of transcendental integration with self and nature:

> The reason why the world lacks unity . . . is, because man
> is disunited with himself. . . . In the uttermost meaning of
> the words, thought is devout, and devotion thought. Deep
> calleth to deep.
> RICHARD SCHELL

DEFORMITY The Hebrew term *mum,* "deformity" or "blemish," occurs primarily in Levitical ordinances, where it is used to describe not only the types of growths and malformations usually associated with the English terms, but also such infirmities as blindness, lameness, and castration (Lev. 21:18-20). The deformed are forbidden to perform sacrificial rites, and deformed animals are considered to be unsatisfactory offerings; both priest and sacrificial victim must be "without blemish" (Lev. 22:19-24). These ordinances emphasize the holiness of God, whose sanctuaries are not to be profaned (Lev. 21:23), and

also provide for an expression of the wholeness or holiness to which humanity aspires (see Lev. 11:44).

While a deformed person is not permitted "to offer the bread of his God," yet "he shall eat the bread of his God" (Lev. 21:21-22); exclusion from priestly office is not exclusion from the saving justice of the Lord. In Isaiah it is promised that "the eyes of the blind shall be opened, and the ears of the deaf shall be unstopped. Then shall the lame man leap up as an hart, and the tongue of the dumb sing" (Isa. 35:5-6). In the meantime, the deformed are not to be abused (Lev. 19:14; Deut. 27:18); rather, the faithful are exhorted to "Strengthen ye the weak hands, and confirm the feeble knees" (Isa. 35:3). David's "kindness of God" toward lame Mephibosheth (2 Sam. 9:3) is an example of enduring charity which provides both present sustenance and future hope.

In the NT, Christ is characterized as the ideal High Priest who "offered himself without spot to God" (Heb. 9:14) and whose blood is "as of a lamb without blemish" (1 Pet. 1:19). The Greek term *amōmos* is used both here and in the LXX to translate Heb. *tamim,* "without blemish" (see *ISBE* 1.522-23). In the Vg, Hebrew *mum* is translated as *macula,* with Christ in the NT being called *"immaculatus."*

According to St. Paul, Christ's bride, the Church, has no "spot, or wrinkle, or any such thing," having been made "holy and without blemish" by Christ's love (Eph. 5:25, 27). The messianic wedding of Rev. 19 and 21 is, however, prefigured in the parable of the feast in the Gospel of Luke, a banquet offered to "the poor, and the maimed, and the halt, and the blind" (Luke 14:21). As in Isa. 35, both the deformed and those who treat them well shall "be recompensed at the resurrection of the just" (Luke 14:14; cf. Rev. 19:9).

The image of Christians as members of Christ's body (1 Cor. 12:12-27; Eph. 5:30) stresses that the harmony of those members is necessary in order to prevent the deformity of any constituent part, and of the whole. Charity, humility, and respect for the diversity of creation are requisite individual contributions to this harmony and soundness, while sins such as the proud seeking of preeminence among the members are spiritual deformities which cause deformity and imbalance in the whole.

St. Augustine, in his *De civitate Dei,* uses the concept of deformity in order to discuss the problem of humanity's limited perspective. He warns against attributing bodily imperfections such as extra digits on a hand or a foot to God's error:

> This is a comparatively trivial abnormality; and yet it
> would be utterly wrong for anyone to be fool enough to
> imagine that the Creator made a mistake in the number of
> human fingers, although he may not know why the Creator so acted. So, even if a greater divergence from the
> norm should appear, he whose operations no one has the
> right to criticize knows what he is about. (16.8)

He develops the paradigm, explaining that God's divine purpose also accounts for "all those races which are reported to have deviated, as it were, by their divergence in bodily structure, from the normal course of nature followed by the majority, or practically the whole of mankind" (ibid.). Later in the same work, Augustine notes that, while deformities in one's body or mind are debilitating to a certain extent, to view them as a Supreme Evil is a wrongful identification of a sound body and mind with the Supreme Good, that which properly is attributed to God alone (*De civ. Dei* 19.4).

It is in the later Middle Ages that the biblical concept of deformity is given its fullest tropic expressions through both typology and allegory. The *Glossa Ordinaria,* in its commentary on 1 Pet. 1:19, refers to Christ as the uncontaminated and immaculate lamb of Levitical rites, adding that this "signifies, however, the spirit [made] clean through justice which is offered to God" (PL 114.681). The glosses on Lev. 21:18-23 give a moral figurative value to each of the enumerated deformities. Blindness, e.g., is interpreted as an emblem for one who is suppressed by the darkness of this present life, ignorant of the light of contemplation. Lameness is seen as an inability to follow the way of God, and a deformed nose is said to signify a lack of discretion or discernment (PL 113.358-59).

English literature of the Middle Ages and the Renaissance seizes upon the figurative value of the idea of deformity. The ME poem *Pearl* (841-46), e.g., explores the allegorical, tropological, and anagogical implications of biblical images of blemish and spotlessness:

Thys Jerusalem Lombe hade neuer pechche
Of oþer huee bot quyt jolyf
þat mot ne masklle moȝt on streche,
For wolle quyte so ronk and ryf.
Forþy vche saule þat hade neuer teche
Is to þat Lombe a worthyly wyf.

(This Jerusalem Lamb had never a mark
Of another hue but fairest white.
No blot or blemish made Him dark,
But all was white wool, rich and bright.
Therefore each soul without a mark
is to the Lamb His spouse by right.)

Spenser, in bk. 1 of *The Faerie Queene,* embodies impediments to the Redcrosse Knight's holiness in such allegorical figures as Errour, a "monster vile" (1.13.7), half serpent, half woman, whose offspring are "deformèd monsters" (1.22.7).

In John Donne's "Good Friday 1613. Riding Westward," the persona's "deformity" is internalized; it is a loss of the *imago Dei* within the self which may be restored through the combination of the surrender of the individual's will and the grace of God; not the burnt offerings of the Old Law, but the purifying fire of charity is what is required. The poem concludes as follows:

I turn my back to Thee but to receive
Corrections, till Thy mercies bid Thee leave.
O think me worth Thine anger; punish me;
Burn off my rusts and my deformity;
Restore Thine image so much, by Thy grace,
That Thou may'st know me, and I'll turn my face.
(37-42)

Several later writers make use of the sociocultural force of biblical attitudes toward the deformed. Two notable examples, Longfellow's *Song of Hiawatha* and Matthew Arnold's *Culture and Anarchy,* draw upon Isa. 35:3. Longfellow alludes to the passage when he cautions against a European view that Native Americans are somehow less than human, saying that

. . . the feeble hands and helpless,
Groping blindly in the darkness
Touch God's right hand in that darkness
And are lifted up and strengthened. (*Hiawatha,* Intro. 90-93)

Arnold makes a somewhat weaker appropriation of the text, recalling England's aristocratic and middle classes to their respective duties:

But we, beholding in the State no expression of our ordinary self, but even already, as it were, the appointed frame and prepared vessel of our best self . . . we are willing and resolved, even now, to strengthen against anarchy the trembling hands of our Barbarian Home Secretaries and the feeble knees of our Philistine Aldermen-Colonels. (*Culture and Anarchy,* "Conclusion")

It is rather Isa. 35:6 that Flannery O'Connor has in mind in her story "Revelation," in which the proper and self-righteous "good woman," Mrs. Turpin, has a horrific apocalyptic vision from her hog pen, of a path of light leading up into the sunset:

Upon it a vast horde of souls were rumbling toward heaven. There were whole companies of white-trash, clean for the first time in their lives, and bands of black niggers in white robes, and battalions of freaks and lunatics shouting and clapping and leaping like frogs. And bringing up the end of the procession was a tribe of people whom she recognized at once as those who, like herself and Claud, had always had a little of everything and the God-given wit to use it right. She leaned forward to observe them closer. They were marching behind the others with great dignity, accountable as they had always been for good order and common sense and respectable behaviour. They alone were on key. Yet she could see by their shocked and altered faces that even their virtues were being burned away.

The ironic message is similar to that in another of O'Connor's stories, "The Lame Shall Enter First," in which a self-righteous sociologist, Sheppard, is determined to reform a club-footed young delinquent. As the boy, Rufus, points out, however, it is Sheppard who is the more deformed of the two. Sheppard's pride, selfishness, and short-sightedness make him a "moral leper." To his assertion that he is going to save Rufus, the boy replies, "Save yourself. . . . Nobody can save me but Jesus."

Bernard Pomerance's 1979 play *The Elephant Man*, based upon the last years of the life of John Merrick, a severely deformed Englishman who died in 1890, is infused with allusions to Scripture. From Merrick's simple faith in the Bible's promise that "in heaven the crooked shall be made straight" (*Elephant Man*, 16; cf. Luke 3:5; Isa. 42:16) to Pomerance's description of the surgeon Treves as one whose "mouth, deformed by satisfaction at being at the hub of the best of existent worlds, was rendered therefore utterly incapable of self-critical speech, thus of the ability to change" and whose "back was horribly stiff from being kept against a wall to face the discontent of a world ordered for his convenience" (18), this play reflects the diversity of connotations of the term *deformity* which is representative of the concept's treatment in the Bible.

See also BLINDNESS; DISEASE AND HEALING; LEPROSY.
Bibliography. Moyer, J. C. "Blemish." *ISBE* 1.522-23; *The Pentateuch and Haftorahs.* Ed. J. H. Hertz (1938).
PATRICIA SUNDERLAND

DELECTATIO MOROSA   In considering the ethics of thought, moral theologians have normally paid heed to the role of the will. Perceiving significance in the precision of Christ's remark, "whosoever looketh on a woman to lust after her hath committed adultery with her already in his heart" (Matt. 5:28), the Fathers focus on the sin of intent and proceed to elaborate a casuistical tradition which finds responsibility not so much in the existence of corrupting thoughts (by no means always sexual) as in the mind's harboring of them. Hence St. Thomas Aquinas, following St. Augustine and others, defines the evil thought as a "sin of lingering delectation" (*peccatum morosae delectationis*) and holds this description as valid, not from the length of time involved, but from the fact that it is a deliberating reason which lingers, "holding to and revolving with pleasure what ought to have been thrust out as soon as it reached the mind, as Augustine says, *XII de Trin.*" (*Summa Theol.* 1a-2ae.74.6.ad 3). The term *morose delectation* (from Lat. *mora*, "delay"), thus established early, is later picked up by Protestant divines who find it particularly helpful in making their own moral discriminations (e.g., Henry Hammond, *Practical Catechism* [1646], 77-78; Jeremy Taylor, *Holy Dying* [1674], 144).

The tradition is commonly portrayed in medieval drama in *psychomachia* and assaults of the seven deadly sins (cf. *Castell of Perseverance* [ca. 1425]). Situations embodying it abound in Shakespearean drama: a controversial scene in *Othello* (2.1), e.g., not only comically shows how nasty thoughts can legitimately invade the mind and leave it blameless, but also points to a grander cognate theme tragically realized in the drama as a whole.

The notion is often dramatized directly, as in Spenser's depiction of Guyon's temptation in the Bower of Bliss (*Faerie Queene,* 2.12.53, 65-69) or in Milton's narration of Eve's dream and Adam's reassuring comments thereon ("Evil into the mind of god or man / May come and go, so unapproved, and leave / No spot or blame behind" [*Paradise Lost,* 5.28-93, 117-19]), which ironically anticipate the display of morose delectation in Adam's fall (9.896-959). Authors of didactic works, moreover, like Bunyan (see esp. the "Author's Apology" to *Pilgrim's Progress*), frequently exploit the concept as a means to the reader's total involvement by contriving his exposure to certain suggestions and situations to which his will must respond and thus to bring him to a saving self-knowledge.

See also SEVEN DEADLY SINS.
Bibliography. Snoeck, A. "De delectatione morosa uti est peccatum internum." In *Periodica de Re Morali Canonica Liturgica* 40 (1951), 167-209; Forrest, J. F. "The Fathers on Milton's Evil Thought in Blameless Mind." *CJT* 15 (1969), 247-67.
JAMES F. FORREST

DELILAH   In Judg. 16, Delilah (Vg and Milton "Dalila"; LXX "Dalida") is the last in a series of women amorously involved with Samson. She is not, explicitly, either his wife or a harlot, although in the 1st cent. both Josephus (*Ant.* 5.8.11) and Pseudo-Philo (43.5) view her as a harlot, and in Pseudo-Philo she becomes Samson's wife. At the instigation of the Philistine lords Delilah sets herself to find out from Samson the secret of his great strength. Three times he deceives her; finally he tells her the truth, that his strength is in his hair, uncut because of his Nazarite vow. She accepts money from the Philistines, lulls her lover to sleep in her lap, and calls for a man to shave off his "seven locks." The enfeebled Samson cannot resist capture by the Philistines and is blinded by them.

In literature and art Samson and Delilah are often associated with other biblical lovers (e.g., Solomon and Sheba, David and Bathsheba). St. Philaster (*Liber de haeresibus* 8 [PL 12.1122]) and St. Augustine (*De civ. Dei* 18.19 [PL 41.576]) identified Samson with Hercules, and 19th-cent. scholarship connected the stories as solar myths and associated Delilah with Omphale, who humiliated Hercules, or (more frequently) with Dejanira, who caused his death. Some scholars argued that Delilah and Dejanira are actually the same name (see Moore [1895], 364); Robert Graves compared Delilah's shearing of Samson with ritual shearing of the sun-god, associated with Hercules, by women (*The Greek Myths* [1960], 145.4).

In Jewish tradition the name Delilah is linked with Heb. *dalal* ("weaken" or "impoverish") (Soṭa 9b; Midr. Num. 9:24) and specifically connected with the sapping of Samson's strength. From St. Jerome (*Liber interpretationis Hebraicorum nominum*, 32 [PL 23.853]) to St. Isidore of Seville (*Etymologiae*, 7.56 [PL 82.279]), however, this doubtful etymology is invoked by Christian commentators in a somewhat different fashion; they gloss Delilah as "impoverished little woman" *(paupercula)*. Her clinging to Samson can thus be made to typify the Church in the world clinging to Christ (e.g., Jerome, *Comm. in Epistolam ad Ephesianos*, 1.1 [PL 26.484]). Chiefly, though, the Fathers view Delilah as a sexual temptress and as a type of the treacherous, avaricious, inconstant woman (St. Cyril of Alexandria, *De sanctissima trinitate dialogi*, 7.641 [PG 75.1094]; St. Ambrose, *Apologia altera prophetae David*, 3.16 [PL 14.892]). Peter Comestor pithily sums up this view in his widely read *Historia Scholastica* (PL 198.1290); it is reflected also in the *Speculum Historiale* of Vincent of Beauvais (2.67), and becomes a commonplace of medieval homiletic literature (see G. R. Owst, *Literature and Pulpit in Medieval England* [1961], 385).

Delilah the betrayer was easily allegorized. Since Samson was viewed as a type of Christ (e.g., Augustine, *Sermo*, 364 [PL 39.1639]), Delilah could be seen as the synagogue which connives at the Crucifixion (Rabanus Maurus, *De Universo*, 3.1 [PL 111.57]). Isidore of Seville makes her an emblem of the (feminine) flesh betraying the (masculine) rational sense in mankind (*Quaestiones in Vetus Testamentum*, Judg. 8 [PL 83.389-90]), a reading reflected in Lydgate's *Pilgrimage of the Life of Man* (9533-58), which makes Delilah the flesh luring the pilgrim soul away from salvation.

But literal readings were also common. *Cursor Mundi* (7187-7262) stresses Samson's stupidity in succumbing to his wife Delilah after so much experience of women's wiles. It goes on to recount how she leaves him, engages to remarry, and then has Samson brought in to the wedding feast as "entertainment," whereupon he pulls down the pillars; his revenge, in this version, is thus directed more at Delilah than Dagon. Abelard (*Planctus Israel super Samson* [PL 178.1820-21]), the *Roman de la Rose* (9165-76), Gower (*Confessio Amantis*, 8.2703) and Chaucer's *Monk's Tale* develop the theme of Delilah as a domestic traitor who brings about disaster through love. Chaucer has the Wife of Bath's husband read her the tales both of Samson and Delilah and Hercules and Dejanira to illustrate how women ensnare brave men (*Wife of Bath's Tale*, Prol. 3.721-26).

By natural extension the name Dalila was given to an unruly daughter easily seduced by Iniquity in the Tudor interlude *Nice Wanton*. From the 16th to the 19th cent., the name was used both in literature and homiletics of treacherous harlots, especially those luring men from religious or patriotic duty (see *OED Supp.*, s.v. "Delilah"; C. Hill, *Milton and the English Revolution* [1977], 429-30). Thackeray's Becky Sharp is dubbed Delilah in her ambivalent relations with her enormous soldier-husband (*Vanity Fair*, chaps. 16, 45). Kipling's poem "Delilah" concerns the betrayal of a Viceregal confidence imparted to a highly placed gossiping wife. In Browning's *The Ring*

and the Book (11.2200) Guido calumniates his wife as being a Delilah to his Samson. Scott's references to beguiling books as "Delilahs" (*Heart of Midlothian*, chap. 1; *Letters*, 8.127) are in the same tradition.

Only in the 16th and 17th cents. did the dramatic and erotic possibilities of the story attract close attention. Lost to us now are several English Samson plays, evidently following continental precedent (see F. M. Krouse, *Milton's Samson* [1949], 85-87; Middleton's *Family of Love*, 1.3.299; Henslowe's *Diary*, 29 July 1602), in which Delilah must have appeared. A famous painting by Rubens emphasizes Delilah's harlotry by incorporating a statuette of Venus and an aged procuress. Here, as in Milton's *Samson Agonistes* (711-22) and in Blake's "Samson" (*Poetical Sketches 1769-1778*), she is voluptuously and immodestly dressed. In Titian's painting she wields the shears herself, as she does in Quarles's *Historie of Samson* (*Meditation*, 19.22) and in Milton, although in the biblical narrative she calls in a barber.

Milton's is the only sustained and imaginative treatment of the story and forms, in turn, the basis of Handel's oratorio *Samson*. In an episode original to the Miltonic version, Dalila, exotic, perfumed, and enticing, visits Samson in prison in Gaza seeking both to salve her conscience and to prove once again that she can dominate Samson by female guile. Dramatically, her visit allows Samson to demonstrate, before renouncing his role as God's champion, that despite past colorful sexual exploits he can now resist the lures of the flesh. Though Samson calls Dalila "concubine" (537), Milton depicts her as his wife (227). This enables him to stress the traditional theme of domestic treachery while bringing in the hedonistic associations of the splendid courtesan.

The modern adventures of Delilah in opera (Saint-Saëns, op. 47, 1877), ballet (Ruth Page, 1946; Marcia Graham, 1961), and film (Cecil B. de Mille, 1949) seem to owe more to the sexual and dramatic interest of the story and its opulent visual dimension than to literary or exegetical tradition.

See also PHILISTINE; SAMSON.

Bibliography. Krouse, F. M. *Milton's Samson* (1947); Moore, G. F. *A Critical and Exegetical Commentary on Judges* (1895).   BRENDA E. RICHARDSON
                                                                                        NORMAN VANCE

DEMONS, DEMON POSSESSION The sole OT term translated "demon" is Heb. *shed* (Deut. 32:17; Ps. 106:37), possibly related to Assyr. *shedu*, "protecting spirit." Heb. *śaʿir*, "satyr" (lit. "hairy one"), found only in the plural (Lev. 17:7; 2 Chron. 11:15), is also translated "devils" (KJV) or "demons" (NEB). Two specific demons, Azazel (Lev. 16:8, 10, 26 [KJV "scapegoat"]) and Lilith (Isa. 34:14; "night hag" [KJV "screech owl"]), are named; most others are identified with terms meaning "plague" or "pestilence." The term *ʿaluqah*, "leech" (or, as in KJV Prov. 30:15, "horseleech"), may relate to *ʿaulaq*, the Arabic name for a vampire. Most of these were thought to be creatures of the wilderness or desert; the "night hag" or Lilith of Isa. 34:14 inhabits ruins.

In the NT *daimonion* ("demon") is the most common term; *daimōn* is found only once (Matt. 8:31). *Daimonizomai*, "to be possessed by a demon" or "to be a demoniac," is used frequently (Matt. 4:24; 8:16, 28, 33; 9:32; 12:22; 15:22; Mark 1:32; 5:15ff.). In the letters of St. Paul *pneumata plana* is used to designate "deceitful spirits" (1 Tim. 4:1 [KJV "seducing spirits"]; cf. the related phrases *to pneuma tēs planēs* [1 John 4:6], meaning "the spirit of error," and *ho theos tou aiōnos toutou*, "the god of this world" [2 Cor. 4:4]).

According to later mishnaic tradition God created the evil spirits *(mazziqim)* on Friday of Creation Week ('Abot 6). These were either "fallen angels" (1 Enoch 69:1-5; cf. Philo, *De gigantibus*, 6, 16, which divides demons into good and bad angels) or the offspring of the fallen angels and mortal women (1 Enoch 69:4; 106:13-17; 2 Apoc. Bar. 56:12), the "giants" of Gen. 1:4 who are said ever after to oppress mankind, "to work destruction on the earth, and cause trouble" (1 Enoch 15:11).

In the OT demons are sometimes implicated in the transmission of disease. In the NT Luke speaks of a "spirit of infirmity" (Luke 8:2; 13:11); a crippled woman who had this spirit for eighteen years before being healed was described by Jesus as having been "bound by Satan" during this time (Luke 13:11-17). Not all disease was thought, however, to be associated with demonic influence. Jesus described his ministry as involving both the calling out of demons and the healing of illness (Luke 13:32; cf. Matt. 8:16; Mark 1:32-34).

Exorcism was a familiar practice in the ancient world, as is known from a wide range of nonbiblical as well as biblical references (e.g., Matt. 12:27; Mark 9:38; Acts 19:13-17). While the only OT exorcist would seem to have been David (1 Sam. 16:13-23), in later writings Solomon is said to have ruled over demons and been a practiced exorcist as well (Pesiq. R. 69a; Josephus, *Ant.* 8.2.5). Exorcism was generally understood as a means of expelling a demon or evil spirit which had possessed an individual and afflicted him or her in some way. It involved several regular features: the attempt to ascertain the demon's name in order to gain power over it; the invoking of a higher, more powerful authority in a formula of expulsion ("I adjure you in the name of X to leave this person"); and often some kind of physical manipulation.

Exorcism was a regular feature of Jesus' ministry in Galilee (Mark 1:23-27; 3:11; 5:1-20, etc.). His practice, although similar in some respects to that of other exorcists, was distinctive in that he expelled demons on his own authority and apparently without physical contact. His critics attributed his success to black magic, but Jesus spoke of his exorcisms as divine deliverance from Satan's power and as evidence of the inbreaking of the final rule of God (Matt. 12:24-28; Mark 3:22-29).

The early Fathers, no less than the NT writers, took the world of spirits for granted. St. Jerome, the scholarly translator of the Vg Bible, in his biography of St. Hilarion recounts straightforwardly that the fasting cenobite was alarmed at night in the desert by strange sounds, that naked women appeared to him and sumptuous feasts were laid out before him, and that on one occasion a tormenting demon leapt on his back and beat him with a horsewhip (*Vita S. Hilarion*, 6-8). This type of "temptation" is a commonplace of later saints' lives (e.g., the *Vita S. Benedict*).

There was already a substantial body of Greek, Roman, and Egyptian writing on the subject of demons when Christianity came to the Mediterranean world and Europe. Summarizing Apuleius of Madaura and other Platonists, St. Augustine observes that these writers posit "a threefold division of all animals endowed with a rational soul, namely into gods, men, and demons. The gods occupy the loftiest region, men the lowest, the demons the middle region. For the abode of the gods is heaven, that of men the earth, that of the demons the air" (*De civ. Dei* 8.14). According to this view, demons were seen as sharing immortality of body with the gods but "the passions of the mind" with human beings. Accordingly, "they are delighted with the obscenities of the theatre, and the fictions of poets, since they too are subject to human passions, from which the gods are far removed and altogether strangers." After an extensive discussion of Roman authors such as Varro and Ovid as well as biblical sources reflecting the subject, Augustine says that Christians ought to shun the delusions wrought by demons: "Flee out of the city of this world, which is altogether a society of ungodly angels and men. Indeed, the greater we see the power of demons to be . . . so much the more tenaciously must we lay hold upon the Mediator through whom we ascend from these lowest to the highest places" (18.18).

Because the evil of original sin, like some physical diseases, was seen to be inherited, the early Church took infants about to be baptized and first exorcised them with exsufflation (blowing upon them), which was "intended to show that they were not removed into the kingdom of Christ without first being delivered from the power of darkness" (Augustine, *De nuptiis et concupiscentia*, 2.50). In the case of lapsed believers or heretics, baptism was regularly preceded by exorcism (Augustine, *De baptismo, contra Donatistas*, 6.9.12; cf. 6.38.73-74; 44.85).

Such views were not soon to disappear. Incidents ascribed to demonic influence were always greater near the frontiers of expanding European evangelization, but the activity of demons was still regarded as widely prevalent in the late Middle Ages. St. Thomas Aquinas puts it matter-of-factly: "By experience, we know that a great deal is done by demons" (*Summa Theol.* q.115.a.5). While Calvin felt that inquiry into the nature of the fall of the angels was idle and unprofitable, he nevertheless shared the conviction that the number of these demonic "enemies with which we have to war is almost infinite"

(Inst. 1.14.14-18); he entirely opposed any attempts to psychologize either angels and demons or demonic "possession" as mere "affections or perturbations suggested by our carnal nature" (1.14.19). Luther, as is well known, retained a folk belief in elves, gnomes, fairies, sprites, and witches, and fearfully believed that "many regions are inhabited by devils. Prussia is full of them, and Lapland of witches. In my native country on the top of a high mountain called the Pubelsberg is a lake into which, if a stone be thrown, a tempest will arise over the whole region because the waters are the abode of captive demons" (quoted in R. Bainton, *Here I Stand* [1950]).

Fascination with the occult sciences and widespread belief in demonic influence persisted at all levels of society through the Renaissance and well into the Enlightenment. Even the regal sponsor of the King James Bible wrote a *Daemonologia* (1597). Sir Thomas Browne argued for the existence of demons on what he considered rational and empirical grounds; he also upheld the traditional view that disbelief in spirits was tantamount to atheism.

Against this background, it is easy to see that the demons and monsters in *Beowulf,* and the good angels, bad angels, and demons of medieval drama and of Marlowe's *Doctor Faustus* are likely to have been engaged by their audiences as more than an artificial convention of fiction; rather, they would have been seen as dramatizing palpable dangers and genuine spiritual warfare. The "fall" of Mary Magdalene in the Digby play bearing her name is presented as having been occasioned by demon possession; Jesus exorcises the "vij dyllys" after observing her contrition and, commending her faith, bids her *"vade in pace"* ("depart in peace"). The devils then come out of her and "enter into hell with thondyr" (1.14). In Shakespeare's *Macbeth* the diabolical pact into which Macbeth enters in yielding to the promptings of the witches is heightened by Lady Macbeth's invocation of the powers of evil, the "murdering minsters" and "sightless substances" that "wait on nature's mischief" (1.5.49-54).

The association of demonic possession with witchcraft, familiar from northern Europe in the Midddle Ages, had an unfortunate continuation in 17th-cent. Massachusetts, where those with perceived mental disorders were often branded as witches. Cotton Mather's demonology, which includes an extensive discussion of the nature and character of possession, is found in *The Wonders of the Invisible World* (1693) and *A Brand Pluck'd out of the Burning* (1693). Literature about the Salem witchcraft trials includes John Neal's *Rachel Dyer* (1828), Cornelius Matthew's blank-verse tragedy *The Martyrs of Salem* (1846; 1852), Longfellow's "New England Tragedies," and Arthur Miller's play *The Crucible* (1953), all of which look back on the hysteria of the witchcraft trials with horror and, at the same time, with a sense of modern clinical detachment.

A less serious evocation of the subject is apparent in Sir Walter Scott's *Kenilworth,* where an "exorcism" is attempted: "With thy will. . . , Amy, thou canst not choose this state of slavery and dishonour — thou hast been bound by some spell. . . . But thus I break the charm — Amy, in the name of thine excellent, thy broken-hearted father, I command thee to follow me!" (chap. 4). The folk motif of the demon-lover enjoyed considerable vogue in the 19th cent., but most literary references to biblical passages concerning demons and possession from this period are trivial or whimsical. In Scott's *Ivanhoe,* Front-de Boeuf asks the jester priest how many bandits there are, and is answered, with an allusion to the most memorable of NT demoniacs (Mark 5:9; Luke 8:30), *"nomen illis legio* — their name is legion" (chap. 26). Dickens refers to the host of mediocre journals being published in the United States with the same allusion (*American Notes,* chap. 18). T. S. Eliot strikes a similar note in *The Use of Poetry and the Use of Criticism,* where he remarks that "In reviewing English poetry, Mr. Read seems to charge himself with the task of casting out devils — though less drastically than Mr. Pound" (chap. 4).

More sober treatments of demon possession in modern literature include George Macdonald's *Lilith* (1895), George Bernard Shaw's reflections on *St. Joan* (1924), and Charles Williams's *Descent into Hell* (1937), in the latter of which the historian Wentworth is gradually taken over by a demon lover, or succubus, and the heroine, threatened also with possession, is nearly lured to destruction by the apparently innocuous Mrs. Lily Sammile (cf. Sammael, the chief devil and accuser of Israel in the Mishnah). In the latter years of the 20th cent. the subject has featured largely in popular fiction, cinema, and sensationalist tabloids.

See also BEELZEBUB; DEVIL; DEVIL'S PACT; GADARENE SWINE; LILITH; MADNESS; SCAPEGOAT; WITCH OF ENDOR; WITCHCRAFT.

Bibliography. Grudin, P. D. *The Demon-Lover: The Theme of Demoniality in English and Continental Fiction of the Late Eighteenth and Early Nineteenth Centuries* (1987); Reed, T. *Demon-Lovers and Their Victims in British Fiction* (1988); Shumaker, W. *The Occult Sciences in the Renaissance* (1972); Stock, R. D. *The Holy and the Daemonic from Sir Thomas Browne to William Blake* (1982).

DAVID L. JEFFREY
JAMES D. G. DUNN

DEPART IN PEACE   *See* NUNC DIMITTIS.

DESCENT OF THE HOLY SPIRIT   *See* BAPTISM; PENTECOST.

DESPAIR   The term *despair* appears only four times in the KJV (1 Sam. 27:1; Eccl. 2:20; 2 Cor. 1:8; 4:8), but the concept of religious despair as it formed through patristic literature and into the Renaissance was understood to have its roots in a wide range of biblical texts, including texts other than those in which the word itself appears.

Central to the concept of despair in Christian tradition is the Pauline distinction between "godly" sorrow, prompted by a recognition of one's sinfulness, which leads to repentance, and "worldly" sorrow, which is self-preoccupied and does not seek a remedy of grace: "For godly sorrow worketh repentance to salvation . . . but the sorrow of the world worketh death" (2 Cor. 7:10). The distinction is crucial to the early Fathers, who see worldly sorrow as a sin rather than merely a pitiable malady, and as the instrument of Satan. They define despair in terms of its spiritual opposite, presumption — despair evidencing a lack of confidence in Christ's mercy, and presumption an overconfidence in such mercy (e.g., St. Augustine [PL 38.778]; St. John Chrysostom [PG 61.75; 62.447-48]).

The sin of despair has been traditionally associated with a variety of biblical figures, including most prominently Judas, whose suicide evidenced the magnitude of his unrelieved and ineffectual sense of guilt over the betrayal of Jesus. (Origen asserts, as do other later commentators, that even his crime was not so great that it might not have been forgiven had he completely repented [PG 13]. A gloss in the Geneva Bible (1560) comments that "Although he abhorre his sinnes, yet is he not displeased there with, but dispaireth in Gods mercies and seketh his own destruction" [Matt. 27:5]) The other prominent biblical suicide, Saul, is also seen by some as acting out of despair; thus the Geneva Bible notes that "his cruel life hathe a desparate end, as is commonly seene in them, that persecute the children of God" (1 Sam. 31:4).

The logic of despair is alluded to in *De anima liber quartus* (PL 177.185-88), attributed to Hugh of St. Victor, in which a future of judgment and hell is threatened by Memoria Mortis, who argues that life and sin are inexorably intertwined. This argument is put to rest by Disiderium Vitae Aeternae, who proposes a transformation of worldly grief into godly and redemptive repentance. An early English version of Hugh's narrative is found in the 13th-cent. homily *Sawles Warde* (ed. Wilson [1938]).

Chaucer, in *The Parson's Tale,* examines despair in the context of his discussion of Sloth, a vice dominated by loss of hope and inability to do good works. "This horrible synne is so perilous that he that is despeired, ther nys no felonye ne no synne that he douteth for to do, as sheweth wel by Judas" (*Canterbury Tales,* 10.695). In Sackville's "Induction" in *Mirrour for Magistrates* (1563), Sorrow guides the persona/narrator to the depths of Hell where, passing by personifications of Revenge, Maladie, and Warre, he meditates despairingly on the defects of the world. The stories of tyrannical princes which follow reveal the errors of arrogance and presumption.

In early English drama, especially in the morality tradition, despair is portrayed in the protagonist's sinful absorption with his depravity. In *Mankind* (ca. 1465) the central character expresses suicidal desperation: "A rope, a rope! I am not worthy." Despair first appears as a personified figure in John Skelton's allegorical examination of princely morality, *Magnificence* (1515; ed. Scattergood [1983]):

In tyme of dystresse I am redy at hande;
I make hevy hertys, with eyen full holowe.
Of farvent charyte I quenche out the bronde;
Faythe and good hope I make asyde to stonde.
In Goddys Mercy, I tell them, is but foly to truste. . . .
(2285-89)

Mischief offers a choice of a knife or a rope, but rescue comes in the form of Good Hope. The rope and dagger subsequently appear frequently in the iconography of Despair.

Dispayre appears among the temptations to Wastefulness, the protagonist of George Wapull's morality play *The Tyde Tarryeth No Man* (1576) — using rhetoric and logic to bring Wastefulness to believe that his sins are outrageous and his soul beyond repair. Wastefulness bids the world and his wife farewell and announces that he will end his "life with cord or knyfe." He is rescued by Faithful-Few and through prayer "that wicked Monster of Dispayre" is banished. Wastefulness learns that God's Justice (the Old Dispensation) has been overridden by God's Mercy (the New Dispensation).

Edmund Spenser's allegorical portrait of Despair (*Faerie Queene,* 1.9.33-54) is probably the best known in English literature. A gaunt, hollow-eyed, and ragged cave-dweller, he assails Redcrosse Knight with accusations of his sinfulness, arguing that the longer he lives the greater will be his guilt, and counsels that suicide is the most reasonable remedy. Redcrosse, moved by Despair's rhetoric, lifts a dagger and prepares to take his life; but Una, snatching the weapon away, reprimands him and bids him to "arise, and leave this cursed place." She immediately leads him to the house of Holiness where he is instructed in repentance. Despair is left behind, condemned to an eternity of unsuccessful suicide attempts.

Giles Fletcher, in his *Christs Victorie and Triumph* (1610), patterns his personification of Despair on Spenser's reclusive deceiver Archimago, including the clerical disguise which satirizes the false comforts offered by the Roman Church. Despair, the agent of Satan, is the first of the three tempters introduced to Christ. Fletcher's association of Despair with the initial temptation faced by Christ in the wilderness (Matt. 4:3-4) borrows from expositors such as Lancelot Andrewes, who called the first temptation the temptation to "murmur against God" (*The Wonderfull Combate betweene Christ and Satan* [1592]). The second tempter in Fletcher's scheme is the traditional opposite of Despair, the tyrant Presumption.

Phineas Fletcher, Giles's brother, uses a female allegorical figure for Despair, "a sad ghastly Spright" who wishes for death but cannot die (*Apollyonists* [1627], 1.15). Another Spenserian imitator, William Browne, brings his protagonist to a fork in a road where he must choose between Repentance and Despair. He is given direction by a heavenly choir just as he is about to make the wrong choice (*Britannia's Pastorals* [1613-16], 1.5). In Anthony Copley's *A Fig for Fortune* (1596) the protagonist is advised to kill himself by Cato's ghost, "a spirit of Despair and self-Misdoom," which combines the classical image of suicide with Christian allegory. This protagonist is able, through his own powers of recognition, to reject Despair.

John Donne, in his "Biathanatos" (ca. 1607), engages in a lengthy and erudite consideration of suicide — distinguishing between suicide and martyrdom on the basis of intention. His two *Anniversary* poems, marking the untimely death of the daughter of his patron, portray a decayed world on the brink of despair which regains its sense of worth from the memory of Elizabeth Drury. George Herbert, in "The Bag," casts off despair by recounting the extraordinary grace of Christ — especially his unstinting forgiveness of grievous sin and injury to himself in the Passion. The poet, having recited the "strange story" of Jesus' love, is able to defy his adversary, "Harke, Despair away."

In his "Definition of Love," Andrew Marvell adapts the theological understanding of despair to amorous verse, suggesting that his love was "begotten by Despair / Upon Impossibility." Borrowing from the tradition that sees despair leading to godly sorrow and thus inaugurating the spiritual journey, Marvell asserts that "magnanimous Despaire alone / Could show me so divine a thing" as Love.

Burton's *Anatomy of Melancholy* bases its learned paramedical discussion of despair on traditional sources, defining it as the malady of those who cannot believe in divine mercy and the prospect of their salvation, and naming Satan as the principal agent and procurer of this mischief. The symptoms of despair, says Burton, are sleeplessness, a trembling heart, and a sorrowful mind. And many (including such biblical characters as Cain, Saul, and Judas) "make away themselves." Those afflicted with despair, he argues, should consider the sins of such as Job, David, Peter, and Paul, and learn that no crime is so great that it cannot be pardoned.

A memorable dramatic treatment of despair is afforded by Marlowe's *Doctor Faustus* in which the protagonist, at the end of his twenty-four-year pact with Mephistopheles, rejects the Old Man's counsel to repent and the Scholar's reminder of the infinity of God's mercy and chooses his own damnation, dying with cries of despair on his lips: "See, see, where Christ's blood streams in the firmament! One drop would save my soul, half a drop. Ah, my Christ!" Many of Shakespeare's characters are beset by despair. Richard III, the presumptive tyrant, hears the ghosts of his victims taunt him with the refrain, "Despair and die" (*Richard 3*, 5.3). Hamlet contemplates whether suicide is to be preferred to bearing the ills of life. King Lear confronts despair in Gloucester's view of the universe bereft of purpose and his own experience of the absence of justice.

In *Paradise Lost* Milton associates despair directly with Satan, whose unresolved despair informs his daring attack on Adam and Eve. Eve, after the Fall, loses hope and proposes that she and Adam "seek Death" (*PL* 10.989-1007), but Adam counsels repentance, the first step in their regeneration and their emergence from crippling sorrow. In Bunyan's *Pilgrim's Progress* the giant Despair imprisons Hopeful and Christian in Doubting Castle, urging them to commit suicide. Christian, like Spenser's Redcrosse Knight, is susceptible to the arguments of Despair, but Hopeful urges patience; discovering a key called Promise, the pair eventually escape. (In pt. 2, the giant Despair is slain and Doubting Castle is leveled.)

Since the 17th cent. the allegory of Despair has all but disappeared from English literary tradition. Prominent biblical figures who fell into despair have, however, continued to attract literary interest (e.g., Swift's "Judas"; Byron's *Cain*). Lady Gregory, in "The Story Brought by Brigit" (1924), combines an Irish folk story with the material of a Passion play. Her characterization of Judas shows him overtaken by despair: "Dogs tearing, hounds hunting, a rock frozen in the waves. A wave of ice and a wave of fire — that is the wages of the betrayal of the King!"

Religious despair is a prominent theme in the writings of William Cowper, whose preoccupation with his own sinfulness prompted several suicide attempts and much mental distress. Despite having collaborated with John Newton on a considerable body of hymns celebrating confidence in God's grace and his own salvation, his last original poem, "The Castaway," expressed again the despair he once referred to as "a sentence of irrevocable doom in my heart":

> No voice divine the storm allayed,
> No light propitious shone,
> When, snatched from all effectual aid,
> We perished, each alone;
> But I beneath a rougher sea,
> And whelmed in deeper gulfs than he.

In Emily Dickinson's poem "It was not Death, for I Stood Up" (no. 510) a form of desperate meaninglessness is mistaken for death:

> But, most, like Chaos — Stopless — cool
> Without a Chance, or Spar —
> Or even a Report of Land —
> To justify — Despair. (20-23)

Twentieth-century literature is replete with characters caught in purposeless and despairing lives. Theodore Roethke, in "In a Dark Time," portrays agony and isolation: "I know the purity of pure despair, / My shadow pinned against the sweating wall." John Barth's *The Floating Opera* (1956) traces the suicidal steps of its protagonist, and in Arthur Miller's *Death of a Salesman* (1949) Willie Loman responds with suicide to the futility of his life. The traditional resolution of despair through a Christian acceptance of the power of grace is seldom portrayed: even in a work with an implied biblical subject matter such as Archibald MacLeish's *J.B.* (1956) Jobian despair is resolved by the power of human love to overcome the crippling inaction engendered by unresolved guilt.

See also HOPE; JUDAS ISCARIOT; SAUL; SEVEN DEADLY SINS; UNPARDONABLE SIN.

Bibliography. Bowe, E. "Doctrines and Images of Despair in Christopher Marlowe's *Doctor Faustus* and Edmund Spenser's *The Faerie Queene.*" *DA* 29 (1969), 2206; Brashear, W. *The Gorgon's Head: A Study in Tragedy: Despair* (1977); Britain, K. "The Sin of Despair in English Renaissance Literature." *DA* 24 (1964), 281; Chew, S. *The Virtues Reconciled: An Iconographic Study* (1947); McCloskey, J. "The Theme of Despair in Marlowe's *Faustus.*" *CE* 4 (1942), 110-13; Sachs, A. "The Religious Despair of Doctor Faustus." *JEGP* 63 (1964), 625-47; Sawyer, D. "The Theme of Despair in the Poetry of John Donne." *DA* 31 (1971), 4134; Seamans, A. "The Phenomenon of Religious Distress in Cowper and Johnson and Its Relationship to their Theological Milieu." *DA* 24 (1964), 5417; Snyder, S. "The Paradox of the Despair Theme in Medieval and Renaissance Literature." *DA* 25 (1964), 1201; "The Left Hand of God: Despair in Medieval and Renaissance Tradition." *Studies in the Renaissance* 12 (1965), 18-59; Wymer, R. *Suicide and Despair in Jacobean Drama* (1986).

FAYE PAULI WHITAKER

DEUTEROCANONICAL BOOKS A term referring to the "second-order of canon," those apocryphal and pseudepigraphal books, largely as included in the LXX version of the OT, which though rejected as authoritative *de fide* by St. Jerome and subsequently the Reformation theologians, were so designated by the Council of Trent (1546).

See also APOCRYPHA AND PSEUDEPIGRAPHA.

DEVIL The English word *devil* derives through OE *deofol* and Lat. *diabolus* from Gk. *diabolos,* meaning "slanderer" or "false accuser." The Greek term is the LXX translation of Heb. *śatan,* "adversary" or "obstructer." The devil is to be distinguished from the demons, identified in Christian tradition with the angels who followed Lucifer in his fall, and from other lesser evil spirits. The devil has been given a number of names by tradition. Most commonly he is called Satan or Lucifer, but he sometimes takes the name Beelzeboul or Beelzebub, Belial, Azazel, Mastema, Satanail, Sammael, or Semyaza, all of which names derive from the OT and Intertestamental literature. In modern times he also bears the name Mephistopheles. Legend and literature sometimes assign these names to different characters, usually for dramatic purposes; thus frequently in medieval and modern literature, Satan, Lucifer, Belial, and others play different parts.

In the OT, *śatan* was originally a common noun (e.g., 2 Sam. 19:22), but gradually it became the title of a particular being. Early biblical references picture a creature of God who prompts evil (1 Chron. 21:1), accuses the righteous (Job 1–2), or even opposes God's will

(Zech. 3:1-2). From these passages there developed the more fully defined rebellious angel of later tradition. Two key OT passages which were not originally intended to apply to the Evil One came to be associated with Satan. The serpent of Eden was not identified with the devil until the Intertestamental period (see Rom. 16:20). Isa. 14:12-15, which relates the fall of "Lucifer, son of the morning," refers explicitly to the king of Babylon, but this passage also (and the name Lucifer) became associated with the devil during the Intertestamental period. The Isaiah passage is attached to the devil in 2 Enoch 29:4-5 in the apocalyptic Life of Adam 14.16 and apparently in Luke 10:18, but the identification was not clear and definite before the writings of Origen (A.D. 185-251). On the whole, the OT devil is still a shadowy and inchoate figure.

In the postexilic period, the suffering of the Jews under Greek and Roman rule prompted an intense concern with the problem of evil and the powers of evil. In 1 Enoch, 2 Enoch, Jubilees, and the Testaments of the Twelve Patriarchs, a portrait of the devil began to emerge in which he is the head of a band of evil angels in rebellion against God and enmity against humanity. The Qumran community, with its intense dualism, envisioned scenarios in which Satan led an army of evil angels and evil humans against the divine host, and the NT reflects similar Jewish traditions.

The temptation of Christ in the desert by Satan (Matt. 4 and Luke 4:1-13) is the most dramatic NT episode involving the devil, but his sinister power is referred to frequently (e.g., 1 Cor. 7:5; Eph. 5:10-16; 1 Pet. 5:8). The essential function of the NT Satan is to obstruct the kingdom of God; one of his strategies is possession. Christ's exorcisms and cures are blows struck against the devil's power and signs of the imminent victory of God's kingdom over Satan (Matt. 12:22-32). The devil is "god of this world" (2 Cor. 4:4) but his lordship is being broken by Christ (1 Cor. 15:20-28), a process culminating in the eschatological triumph of Christ and his elect (Rom. 16:20; Rev. 12:7-12).

Patristic diabology can be best understood in the context of the struggle against Gnosticism and, later, Manicheism. The Gnostic-Manichean view combined apocalyptic diabology, Iranian dualism, and Greek Orphism to produce a mythology which posited a cosmic struggle between a good God of spirit and an evil god of matter, the latter being equated with Satan. In its strongest and most coherent forms, this dualism denied monotheism and was therefore unacceptable to Judaism and the Christian community. Early patristic writings such as The Epistle of Barnabas, and works by Didymus, Hermas, and St. Ignatius of Antioch, show both a reaction against gnostic dualism and some influence from it, the influence manifesting itself in a doctrine of a strong dichotomy between the followers of good (often identified with the Christian community) and the followers of the devil (often identified with pagans and heretics). The power of gnostic dualism was evident still in the writings of Lactantius (ca. 245-325).

The classic elements of Christian diabology, however, were established by Origen and St. Augustine (354-430) and were popularized in the West by St. Gregory the Great, especially in his *Moralia in Iob*. In Gregory's account, God created the angels good and gave them free will. Lucifer, one of the highest angels, sinned through pride and envy, choosing his own will over God's, and he led many of the other angels after him (these became the demons). Envious of God's love for humanity, Satan used the serpent to tempt Adam and Eve to transgress his divine ordinance. God punished fallen humanity by leaving it in the devil's power, though this power was ultimately limited by God's sovereignty. In his mercy, however, God the Father sent God the Son to liberate humanity from this slavery to Satan. The Incarnation and especially the Passion of Christ restored human freedom. Those who accept Christ form the community of the saved, "the city of God." Those who do not accept Christ are cut off from salvation and form "the city of this world." From the Incarnation until the end of the world, some will be continually added to the kingdom of God through faith in Christ; Satan continues to attempt, however vainly, to block that saving work. In the last days, Satan and the Antichrist will make a last pitched battle against the Christian community but will be foiled by the Second Coming of Christ, who will bring his kingdom to fulfillment and utterly destroy the power of Satan (cf. St. Ephraim Syrus, *Nisibene Hymns; Hymns of the Nativity*).

Through the influence of Gregory the Great and the other Fathers, such views were firmly imprinted on OE literature, most clearly in the homilies of Aelfric and the poems *Genesis B, Christ and Satan,* and in the "harrowing of hell" narrative. These works offer a powerful extrabiblical rendering of the history of the struggle between Christ and the devil, to which further details were gradually added by folklore. Medieval theology reduced the patristic emphasis on the devil by tending to replace the ransom theory (which saw the act of salvation as God's payment of a ransom for mankind to Satan) with Anselm's satisfaction theory in *Cur Deus Homo?* (which made it a sacrifice offered by the incarnate Son to the Father and put Satan in the background), but literature on the whole preferred the more dramatic ransom theory.

The devil is a powerful figure in Langland's *Piers Plowman,* usually behind the scenes but sometimes overtly, as in his attack on the Tree of Charity in C.16 and in the harrowing of hell (B.18; C.20). Chaucer, for the most part, prefers to present the devil satirically (*Monk's Tale; Friar's Tale* and *Prologue*), an approach taken also frequently in the morality plays. His most dramatic appearances in ME literature are in the York, N-Town, Towneley, and Chester mystery plays, especially in the plays centered on his fall, the temptation of Adam and Eve, the Annunciation, and the harrowing of hell. Sometimes frightening in these plays, he is more often a fool, as the playwrights exploit the audience's knowledge that

all of his posturings against the kingdom of God will be foiled. By the 14th cent., then, the devil had, in literary treatments at least, become more often comic than fearsome. This trend was reversed, however, during the 15th through 17th cents., the period during which Satan's power was perceived to be at its height.

The leading Protestant Reformers, especially Luther (who came to the subject with strong Germanic convictions about the existence and power of demons), returning to what they saw as a biblical emphasis upon the power of Satan, added to the new fear of the devil. The legend of Faust, homocentric, pessimistic, and individualistic, reflected this view; it also produced, in the German Faustbook of 1587, the first use of the name Mephistopheles. Marlowe's adaptation of the legend in *Doctor Faustus* (1588 or 1589) produced the first major diabolical portrait in modern English literature in the character of Mephistopheles, here Satan's agent, rather than the devil himself. Spenser shows the devil in human guise (e.g., Archimago, Orgoglio) and in the form of a dragon. Shakespeare presents humans demonized by their sin (Aaron in *Titus Andronicus,* Richard in *3 Henry 6* and *Richard 3,* Angelo in *Measure for Measure,* Edmund in *King Lear,* and Iago in *Othello*), though in both *Hamlet* and *Macbeth* the devil's evil, destructive power can also be felt more directly.

Although belief in the devil's power was almost universal among both the elite and the uneducated during the early 17th cent., English philosophers such as Francis Bacon (1561-1628) and John Locke (1632-1704) laid the basis for skepticism regarding both witchcraft and the devil. English writers, as a result, were divided over whether to treat the devil seriously (as in Barnabe Barnes, *The Devil's Charter* [1607]), or satirically. The comic Satan of Ben Jonson's *The Devil Is an Ass* (1616) clearly indicates Jonson's skepticism; John Webster's *The White Devil* (1608) and Thomas Middleton's *The Changeling* (1623) emphasize the evil in humanity. Sir Thomas Browne argues in *Religio Medici* (1.30, 31, 37; cf. *Pseudodoxia Epidemica,* 1.10, 11) that the denial of supernatural evil is tantamount to atheism, that the devil, being the father of lies, often seduces people into a skepticism concerning his own existence in order to pursue his diabolical ends.

John Bunyan, in his characterization of Apollyon in *The Pilgrim's Progress* (1678) and Diabolus in *The Holy War,* presents a potent Satanic presence. But the most vivid (and influential) portrait of the devil in English literature is unquestionably that of Milton in *Paradise Lost* (1667; rev. 1674) and *Paradise Regained* (1671). Milton added a wealth of detail, color, and texture to the traditional story, but the two most important effects of his poems on diabology were first to set the story in language so powerful and memorable that it was henceforth fixed in the literary imagination in Milton's terms even more than in the Bible's, and second to portray the devil's character in a "heroic" vein. Critics still argue whether Milton made Satan more heroic than he intended; whatever one's critical position, it is undeniable that Satan, "High on a Throne of Royal State, which far / Outshone the wealth of Ormus and of Ind," can be seen as a figure of immense majesty (*PL* 2.1-2).

The deism and skepticism of the 18th cent. undermined belief in the existence of the devil, the key philosophical text being David Hume's "Essay on Miracles," the tenth chapter of *An Enquiry concerning Human Understanding* (1748). Daniel Defoe's *The Political History of the Devil* (1726) affirms orthodox belief in the devil's existence, but his interest in the subject is not apologetic but "aesthetic": stories about diabolical encounters are intrinsically fascinating. By the end of the century, traditional beliefs had eroded to the point that Satan could scarcely be taken even as a credible metaphor. "Gothic" writings degraded the "sublime" to produce horrors and thrills by portraying the grotesque, the decadent, the wild, and the monstrous. Matthew Lewis's *The Monk* (1796), Robert Maturin's *Melmoth the Wanderer* (1820), and Walter Scott's *Letters on Demonology and Witchcraft* (1830; 1884) exemplified this attitude, using demons alongside ghosts, corpses, and witches for the purpose of inducing horror.

The French Revolution acted as a catalyst for a radical revision of the concept of the devil. English writers perceiving the Revolution as a just rebellion against a tyrant king recharacterized Satan as heroic rebel against the tradition and authority of the evil tyrant, God. Thus William Blake (1757-1827) reinterprets Milton's devil as a hero in the struggle against tyranny, church, and convention. Satan is good, and Jesus is Satanic because he acts from feelings rather than rules and breaks the commandments out of mercy. But Blake's Satan is also evil, representing hardness of heart, insensitivity, lack of love, and obstruction of the creative processes of art. The evil of both God and Satan are underscored in *The Book of Urizen* (1794), where Urizen represents Jehovah, the blind tyrant of rules and laws; Orc struggles for liberation from Urizen's tyranny, but Orc's violence and hostility make him evil as well. On the whole Blake tends to perceive God and devil, heaven and hell, good and evil as elements of a shattered whole which seeks reunion, centering, and integration. Real evil lies in anything which obstructs that process of integration.

The Romantics perpetuate Blake's ambivalence toward the devil. Lord Byron's *Cain* (1821) asks who is the more evil, Lucifer, who gave Adam and Eve knowledge, or Jehovah, who drove them out of the Garden to exile and death? But Lucifer also is blind and self-absorbed, rejecting the only possible creative road, his integration with Jehovah. In his treatise *On the Devil and Devils* (1821), Shelley argues that Manichean dualism affords a valid insight into the divided state of the human soul. For Shelley, Milton's great insight lay in his making his God no better than his devil. In *Prometheus Unbound* (1820) Shelley recognizes the difficulty in making Satan a hero and so shifts the qualities of heroic rebellion to Prometheus, who is free of the aggressive, stingy, unloving elements which make Satan an inappropriate hero for the Romantic ethos. Meanwhile Mary Shelley's *Frankenstein; or, The Modern Prometheus* (1818) took a great step in shifting the focus of terror from the demon to the monster and from the supernatural to science fiction, presenting a character who was made a monster by a humanity which first created and then abused him. The early Romantic experiment with making the devil a symbol of good was gradually replaced with the tendency to divorce the devil from serious discussions of good and evil. He is frequently made the subject of light or humorous stories such as Thackeray's "The Devil's Wager" (1833) and "The Painter's Bargain" (1834), reviving an earlier folklore motif concerning battles of wits between the devil and humans over a bargain which had been struck between them (cf. Max Beerbohm's "Enoch Soames" [1917], Stephen V. Benét's "The Devil and Daniel Webster" [1937], and more recent stories, some collected in Basil Davenport's *Deals with the Devil* [1958]).

In 19th-cent. America the tendency to center evil in humanity rather than in the supernatural was even more pronounced than in England. For example, in stories of real horror Poe always eschewed Satan; his devil stories, such as "The Devil in the Belfry" (1839) and "Never Bet the Devil Your Head" (1841), are humorous. The devil appears incidentally, however, in Hawthorne's "Young Goodman Brown" (1835) and his presence is evident in Melville's *Moby-Dick* (1851) and *The Confidence-Man* (1857), the latter of which presents a demonic trickster who makes fools of the passengers on the riverboat Fidèle.

The revival of the occult at the end of the 19th cent. produced some late Romantic sympathy for the devil (Marie Corelli, *The Sorrows of Satan* [1895]) and the explicit Satanism of Aleister Crowley (1875-1947), but ironic treatment remained the norm, as in the "Don Juan in Hell" section of Shaw's *Man and Superman* (1903). The attack on traditional views by Darwin, Marx, Nietzsche, and Freud had demolished the old concept and opened the door to a nihilism seen at its bleakest in Mark Twain's work on "The Mysterious Stranger," which appeared in three main versions, the latest of which was *No. 44, The Mysterious Stranger* (1982). At its conclusion the devil announces that there "is no God, no universe, no human race, no earthly life, no heaven, no hell. It is all a Dream, a grotesque and foolish dream."

The horrors of the mid and late 20th cent., which have contradicted liberal optimism about the essential goodness of human nature, have prompted the revival of serious treatments of the traditional devil, as in C. S. Lewis's *Screwtape Letters* (1942) and *Perelandra* (1944),

Dorothy Sayers's *The Devil to Pay* (1939), and Flannery O'Connor's *The Violent Bear It Away* (1960). John Updike's *The Witches of Eastwick* affords a recent noteworthy devil-portrait, one which has also found its way into film, alongside *The Omen, The Exorcist,* and other "popular" tales of diabolical horror.

See also BEELZEBUB; DEMONS, DEMON POSSESSION; DEVIL'S PACT; TEMPTATION OF CHRIST; WITCHCRAFT; WORLD, FLESH, AND DEVIL.

Bibliography. Baine, M. R. "Satan and the Satan Figure in the Poetry of William Blake." *DAI* 35 (1974), 5335A-36A; Bercovitch, S. "Diabolus in Salem: Bunyan and Hawthorne," *ELN* 6 (1969), 280-85; de Bruyn, L. *Woman and the Devil in Sixteenth Century Literature* (1979); Cuddon, J. A. B. "The Transition from the Late Medieval to the Renaissance Conceptions of Satan in English Literature with Especial Reference to the Drama." Unpubl. B. Litt., Oxford, 1958; Cushman, L. W. "The Devil and the Vice in the English Dramatic Literature Before Shakespeare." *SzEP* 6 (1900), 1-148; Dunaway, R. K. "The Formative Impact of the Devil Upon Selected Renaissance Dramas," *DAI* 36 (1975), 1480A; Dustoor, P. E. "Legends of Lucifer in Early English and in Milton." *Anglia* 54 (1930), 213-68; Gardner, H. *Milton's Satan and the Theme of Damnation in Elizabethan Tragedy* (1948); Gokey, F. X. *The Terminology for the Devil and Evil Spirits in the Apostolic Fathers* (1961); Kubis, P. L. "The Archetype of the Devil in Twentieth Century Literature." *DAI* (1976), 3604A; Levenson, G. B. "That Reverend Vice: A Study of the Comic-Demonic Figure in English Drama and Fiction." *DAI* 38 (1977), 283A; Lynch, J. J. "The Devil in the Writings of Irving, Hawthorne, and Poe." *New York Folklore Quarterly* 9 (1952), 111-31; Marx, C. W. D. "The Devil's Rights and the Deception of the Devil: Theological Background and Presentations in Middle English Literature." *DAI* European Abstracts 44 (1983), 22C; Mallory, T. O. "The Devil and Thomas Hardy: A Study of the Manifestation of Supernatural Evil in Hardy's Fiction." *DA* 27 (1966), 2012-13; Rudwin, M. *The Devil in Legend and Literature* (1931); Russell, J. B. *The Devil: Perceptions of Evil from Antiquity to Early Christianity* (1977); *Satan: The Early Christian Tradition* (1981); *Lucifer: The Devil in the Middle Ages* (1984); *Mephistopheles: The Devil in the Modern World* (1986); Steadman, J. M. "Archangel to Devil: The Background of Satan's Metamorphosis." *MLQ* 21 (1960), 321-35; Stein, W. B. *Hawthorne's Faust, A Study of the Devil Archetype* (1953); Stock, R. D. *The Holy and the Daemonic from Sir Thomas Browne to William Blake* (1982); Trefz, E. K. "Satan as the Prince of Evil: The Preaching of New England Puritans." *Boston Public Library Quarterly* 7 (1955), 3-22; "Satan in Puritan Preaching." *Boston Public Library Quarterly* 8 (1956), 71-84, 148-57; Williams, P. N. "Satan and His Corpus: Cultural Symbolism in the English Mystery Plays." *DAI* 37 (1977), 5813A; Woolf, R. "The Devil in Old English Poetry." *RES* 4 (1953), 1-12.   JEFFREY BURTON RUSSELL

DEVILS BELIEVE AND TREMBLE   The Epistle of St. James puts intellectual assent to religious doctrine in ironic perspective: "Thou believest that there is one God; thou doest well: the devils also believe and tremble" (2:19). This principle, well illustrated by Mephistopheles

in Marlowe's *Dr. Faustus,* becomes a proverbial phrase by the 19th cent. In Melville's *Billy Budd,* the narrator observes that even the evil Claggart has a conscience, "for though consciences are unlike as foreheads, every intelligence, not including the Scriptural devils who 'believe and tremble', has one."

DEVIL'S PACT   The motif of a devil's pact is broadly founded on two biblical episodes of temptation. In Gen. 3:5, the serpent entices Eve to eat of the forbidden fruit, assuring her that if she does so, "ye shall be as gods." In yielding, Eve binds herself and humanity to "an implicit pact" with the tempter (see Diamico, 1). The NT narrative of Satan's temptation of Christ in the wilderness is a countertype to this first disobedience. Here, the devil prompts Christ to trade in inappropriate ways upon his messianic status ("If you are the Son of God") — by commanding that "stones be made bread" to satisfy his hunger; by performing stunts to force God's hand ("Cast thyself down [from the pinnacle of the Temple]"); or by embracing the devil's own power ("All these things will I give thee, if thou wilt fall down and worship me"). All three temptations are resisted and the diabolical pact refused (Matt. 4:1-11; Luke 4:1-13). The tempter's basic appeal is to pride; he offers power in exchange for a renunciation of the true God. Jesus, unlike Eve, recurs to the authority of the Father and the Word: "It is written." (Interestingly, one of the charges later brought against Jesus by his opponents [e.g., Mark 3:22-30] was that he was indeed in league with the devil, a charge Jesus rejected in memorable imagery.)

Among the early Fathers of the Church, possession of unnatural power suggests a knowledge which is forbidden and therefore of unholy provenance. St. Justin Martyr generally associates divination with demonic witchcraft, while Origen avers that diviners and augurs are in league with the devil. St. Augustine's *De doctrina Christiana* is specific, speaking of the "endeavors of the magical arts" as "things instituted concerning consultations and pacts involving prognostications with demons who have been placated or contracted with" (2.20 [Robertson trans.]). This passage, which is repeated in the 12th-cent. *Decretum Gratiani*, comes to figure prominently in canon law touching on diabolical commerce.

Legends of the devil's pact were popular in the Middle Ages. Frequently retold is the story of St. Cyprian, a *magus-philosophus* who strikes a bargain with the devil to learn the secrets of the universe. As a result of the example of the virtuous Juliana, however, Cyprian repents and ends his days in holiness. In the even more popular legend of Theophilus of Adana, a Jewish sorcerer serves as intermediary between Satan and the ambitious cleric. The pact is formally set down in writing, but the devil and his agent are foiled by the intercession of the Virgin, as prefigured in Genesis (3:15). Among works which recount the lapse and conversion of Theophilus are

Latin poems by Hrostvitha of Gandersheim and Marbod of Rennes, narrative poems in the vernacular by Gautier de Coinci and Gonzalo de Berceo, and a play by Rutebeuf. The *Gesta Romanorum* contains a number of stories involving a diabolical pact. In "Of Extreme Fear," e.g., the devil promises to perform the task Celestinus has been set by his master, of writing correct verses on an apparently intractable theme, if the young man will serve him. The poem written, Celestinus subsequently confesses all to his teacher and renounces "this fearful confederacy" (*Gesta Romanorum* [1876], 311-13). "De la charte du diable fet a coveytous," an Anglo-Norman poem by Peter Pecham (eds. D. Jeffrey and B. Levy, *The Anglo-Norman Lyric* [1988], no. 28), offers a full legal document deeding the souls of rich consignors to the devil and his party forever in exchange for "freedom to act as they desire," especially in exploitation of the poor.

Chaucer's *Friar's Tale* is an amusing, though serious, exemplum of the diabolical pact. It tells how an insatiably avaricious summoner, sworn to brotherhood with a hell-fiend who explains his purposes, methods, limitations, and powers, is damned when a poor widow's curse means what it says. *The Canon's Yeoman's Tale* deals with alchemy, greed, and false clerics, and has a moral tag warning against the lust for secret knowledge and wealth: the seeker after the philosopher's stone makes God his adversary.

The principal figure of Renaissance legend to enter into a formal bargain with the devil is the German magician and charlatan Faustus. In Marlowe's *Tragical History of the Life and Death of Doctor Faustus,* the protagonist, swollen with conceit, signs a blood pact with Lucifer, exchanging his soul for the services of Mephistopheles, who agrees to be Faustus's slave for twenty-four years. The overreacher's subsequent magical exploits are more madcap and ribald than constructive and enlightening; Faustus dies a terrible death, his presumption ending in pusillanimity: "I'll burn my books! Ah, Mephistopheles!" There is in Marlowe none of the romantic self-actualization of Goethe's *Faust.* In Shakespeare's *The Merchant of Venice,* the notarized bond between Shylock and Antonio invites comparison with the devil's pact. Proposed by Shylock as "a merry sport" (1.3.136), the bond is actually meant in earnest. Portia takes it literally and proceeds to foil the lender's deadly intent. In *Paradise Regained,* the offer of all the kingdoms of this world in exchange for Christ's worship of the tempter (cf. Matt. 4:9) is described by Milton as an "abhorred pact" (4.191).

Blake proposes, in *The Marriage of Heaven and Hell,* that diabolical commerce is the necessary condition of free and energetic poetical activity: "The reason Milton wrote in fetters when he wrote of Angels & God, and at liberty when of Devils & Hell, is because he was a true Poet and of the Devil's party without knowing it" ("The Voice of the Devil"). Shelley's *Defense of Poetry* gives

an account of poetic energy which approaches the Blakean view (see Praz, 56-57). Similarly, the Byronic hero's pursuit of power and immortality in *Manfred* and his embracing of apostasy in *Cain* ally the suffering solitary man with the dark powers. Kin to Prometheus, Satan, and Faust, Matthew Lewis's proud and luxurious Ambrosio in *The Monk* finally enters into a "compact with the infernal spirits" and dies unrepentant (3.5). Mary Shelley's "modern Prometheus," Doctor Frankenstein, binds himself by oath to "the fiend" of his own creation to provide him with a mate (chap. 17). Smitten with curiosity to learn "the secrets of heaven and earth" (chap. 2), the scientist eventually breaks that agreement for the good of humanity. In George Eliot's *The Lifted Veil,* a protagonist of poetical sensibility but cursed with the power of divination sees that his beloved is evil and yet he enters into marriage with her: "It is an old story, that men sell themselves to the tempter, and sign a bond with their blood, because it is only to take effect at a distant day" (chap. 1). Seven years later the marriage ends in catastrophe. Eliot explicitly links poetical activity with tormenting illness and solitude: "There is no religion possible, no worship but a worship of devils" for those who continually suffer (chap. 2). In Wilde's *The Picture of Dorian Gray,* Lord Harry, the Mephistophelian esthete and voluptuary who becomes Dorian's tempter, plays a role like that of the biblical devil.

American literature of the 19th cent. is rich in devilish commerce. Irving's "The Legend of Sleepy Hollow" tells of a schoolmaster versed in the lore of Cotton Mather's *History of Witchcraft* who comes to experience firsthand "the Devil and all his works." Ichabod's dreams of the lavish Katrina, endless suppers, and fabulous wealth lead, however, to his comeuppance: "He that runs races with goblin troopers is likely to have rough riding of it." In contrast to the folksy wisdom of Irving is the blunt rationalism of J. N. Barker's *Superstition,* a blank-verse tragedy set in early New England. Here the Unknown, initially taken for a diabolical agent summoned by Isabella, is revealed to be the very human regicide Goffe, who is pardoned for his deed. In Hawthorne, the devil's pact is often rendered as psychodrama. The protagonist's intercourse with the devil in "Young Goodman Brown," e.g., narrates a loss of faith, while in "Egotism; or, The Bosom Serpent," Roderick Elliston bonds himself to the evil within by his "diseased self-contemplation." In "The Birthmark," the wondrously learned Aylmer, aided by his servant Aminadab (Badanima), would make his wife Georgiana perfect by removing the red hand-shaped mark on her cheek. He succeeds and she dies, to Aminadab's delight. Poe's "Never Bet the Devil Your Head" tells a macabre joke: a swearer of oaths is taken at his word, with grim results. Part 1 of Longfellow's dramatic poem *The Divine Tragedy* retells Christ's colloquy with Lucifer in the wilderness. Twain is more businesslike in handling the contest of metaphysical allegiances. His Connecticut

Yankee reckons himself a champion of unsentimental common sense against the frivolous black arts. And *Huckleberry Finn* continues the serio-comic meeting of these two forces: in "Our Gang's Dark Oath" (chap. 2), where the superstitious Jim poses as a sorcerer in league with the devil, Tom and his gang sign a blood pact binding them to murder, mayhem, and secrecy in the authentic manner prescribed by pirate books.

More recently, Conrad in *Heart of Darkness* has Marlowe say that "no fool ever made a bargain for his soul with the Devil." The irony is that in the Conradian universe all things are double or infernally ambiguous. As a consequence, the artist who would tell the truth of that world must himself speak in a diabolical tongue and so enter into a bargain with the devil.

The Devil and Daniel Webster, a one-act folk opera by Stephen Vincent Benét and Douglas Moore, tells of a New Hampshire farmer who sells his soul for ten years of plenty, then goes scot-free thanks to his eloquent lawyer. In Elizabeth Bowen's "The Demon Lover," a horrific retelling of the traditional popular ballad "James Harris," Kathleen plights a most "sinister troth" with an unfeeling and faceless lover. The pact, sealed with a mark on her palm, is redeemed twenty-five years later as the demon returns from the dead and whisks her away, screaming, into desolation.

See also DEVIL; TEMPTATION OF CHRIST.

Bibliography. Diamico, E. "The Diabolical Pact in Literature: Its Transition from Legend to Literary Theme." *DAI* 40 (1979), 2650A; Gardner, H. "Milton's 'Satan' and the Theme of Damnation in Elizabethan Tragedy." *ES* 1 (1948), 46-66; Praz, M. *The Romantic Agony* (1956); Sayers, D. "The Faust Legend and the Idea of the Devil." *PEGS* 15 (1946), 1-20; Spivey, R. "Damnation and Salvation in *The Picture of Dorian Gray.*" *Boston University Studies in English* 4 (1960), 162-70; Vandenbroucke, F. "Démon: en occident." *Dictionnaire de spiritualité* (1957), 3.231-34.

CAMILLE R. LA BOSSIÈRE

DIANA OF THE EPHESIANS   Artemis, the Greek goddess of wild animals, wild nature, chastity, and childbirth, appears also as the Ephesian goddess of fertility, having little but the name in common. In the *Hippolytus* of Euripides Artemis was a virgin huntress; on Crete, as in Ephesus, she was a Mother Goddess, and her worship involved phallic dances and symbols. Homer may be partly responsible for channeling a tradition which made her the patron of maidens of marriageable age. To the Romans, who kept this tradition, Artemis was known by the Latinization "Diana," but even in Ovid she retains features of both origins, so that St. Ambrose, writing in defense of virginity, feels compelled to observe ironically that it was said by Diana's advocates that "she was a virgin, and (of which even harlots would be ashamed) yet could love one who did not love her," and that she was "a most excellent huntress, no doubt, not of wild beasts,

but of lust: yet also of wild beasts, so that she was worshipped naked" (*De virginibus,* 3.2.6-7).

The only biblical reference to Diana is in Acts 19:23-41, where St. Paul, in Ephesus, encountered intense opposition from silversmiths and trinket makers whose trade depended on the fertility cult of Diana as well as pilgrims to her shrine and who saw Christianization as a threat. A spokesman for the tradesmen argued publicly that if Paul's ministry were allowed to continue, "not only this our craft is in danger to be set at nought; but also . . . the temple of the great goddess Diana should be despised, and her magnificence should be destroyed, whom all Asia and the world worshippeth" — to which the assembled crowd shouted indignantly, "Great is Diana of the Ephesians" (vv. 28, 34).

The ambivalent connotations of Diana's role as fertility goddess prompt discussion of the perceived Puritan notion that sex is sin in Henry Adams's *The Dynamo and the Virgin,* where the overheated Adams exclaims that in other ages sex was a source of cultural vitality: "Everyone, even among Puritans, knew that . . . Diana of Ephesus . . . was goddess because of her force; she was the animated dynamo; she was reproduction — the greatest and most mysterious of all energies; all she needed was to be fecund." Matthew Arnold is by comparison tepid: discussing the "unsound majority" in his *Discourses in America,* he compares the Ephesian adulation of Diana to the Frenchman who is "a worshipper of the great goddess Lubricity." Thomas Paine, in *The Age of Reason,* argues that Christianity "sprung out of the tail of heathen mythology," and adduces as evidence his notion that "the statue of Mary succeeded the statue of Diana of Ephesus."

Perhaps the most interesting use of Diana in English literature is by Chaucer in *The Knight's Tale.* Duke Theseus, married to Ypolita after his conquest of her Amazon kingdom (associated by medieval commentators with unchecked lust), goes out on a hunt under the influence of "Dyane." This hunt for the hart, following Ovid in part, is a medieval type of the "virtuous pursuit." But later in the tale, before the tourney of Palamon and Arcite for the hand of Emilye, the temple of Diana into which Emilye goes to pray is of a more ambivalent character. Emilye strips, bathes, then prays — to the "chaste goddesse of the wodes grene" (1.2297) and "goddesse of maydens" (1.2299), but also to "Queen of the regne of Pluto derk and lowe" (1.2298). She asks to remain a maiden, not to wed either suitor, but in ambiguous language declares her love of "venerye, / And for to walken in the wodes wilde, / And noght to ben a wyf and be with childe" (1.2307-10). Yet if she is to wed she wants the one who, in "al hir hoote love and hir desire" (1.2319), most wants her. Diana appears, and tells her that indeed she will marry after all.

DIASPORA   After the close of the First Temple period and the Babylonian Exile and defeat of Judah (6th cent.

B.C.), a majority of those Jews exiled from their homeland did not return to Palestine but dispersed over the world — not only throughout the Persian Empire (as is attested to in the book of Esther) but also Asia Minor, Greece, and Rome, and subsequently northward into Europe, thence to America and Australasia as well. The term is Greek, meaning "dispersion."

DIDO   *See* ASHTORETH.

DIES IRAE   The "day of wrath" of Zeph. 1:15, a prophesied time of "trouble and distress," is associated in medieval exegesis with the Last Judgment. These are the opening words of a famous Latin hymn by 13th-cent. Franciscan Thomas of Celano, used to begin the sequence proper to funeral and requiem Masses in the Catholic Church. It is also said or sung on All Souls' Day. Allusions in English are typically to the hymn, important poetic translations of which have been penned by Crashaw, Charles Wesley, and Sir Walter Scott, whose "Lay of the Last Minstrel" includes a partial translation.
See also LAST JUDGMENT.

DINAH   The only named sister of the twelve sons of Jacob, Dinah figures briefly in Gen. 34, which records that she was first ravished and then sought in marriage by a certain man named Shechem. Two of her brothers (Simeon and Levi) determined to avenge her, and subsequently treacherously killed not only the culprit but all the males of his city, which also bore the name Shechem. Modern scholarship tends to interpret the story in tribal rather than individual terms, in which case Dinah herself could be taken as a personification of Israelite womanhood in a Canaanite environment. In the story itself she is a victim rather than an actor.

According to the Tg. Jonathan, an Aramaic translation and commentary on Genesis of the 7th cent., and the 8th-cent. Pirqe R. El., Asenath (wife of Joseph) was actually the daughter of Dinah and Shechem. Here Dinah's story includes her being sent away by Jacob to protect her from her brothers' anger, whereupon, in the manner of Hagar and Ishmael, she and her child are cared for by an angel and brought to Egypt and the house of Poti-phera, priest of On. This haggadic tale is preserved in the Yiddish *Gdolas Yosef* plays of the 19th cent. (trans. from the Hebrew drama of the 18th cent. by Eliezer Favir [1801]), including *Mekhiras Yosef* by Eliakum Zunser (1874). Zachary Boyd's "Dinah ravished by Shechem" is a dramatic poem (*Zion's Flowers* [1855]), as is Edwin T. Whiffen's "Dinah" in *Jephthah Sacrificing, and Dinah* (1908).

Bibliography. Caspi, M. M. "The Story of Dinah — Scripture, Reader, and Midrash." *Beth Miqra* 28 (1982/83), 236-55; Liptzin, S. *Biblical Themes in World Literature* (1985).   DAVID F. PAYNE

DINNER OF HERBS   One of the domestic maxims in Proverbs reads: "Better is a dinner of herbs where love is, than a stalled ox and hatred therewith" (Prov. 15:17). This is the telling verse which lies behind Thackeray's advertisement in *The Newcomes*: "This . . . is to be a story . . . in which there will be dinners of herbs with contentment and without, and banquets of stalled oxen where there is care and hatred — aye, and kindness and friendship too" (chap. 1).

DIONYSIUS THE AREOPAGITE   Acts 17:34 mentions a convert of St. Paul named Dionysius the Areopagite, of whom nothing else is said in the Bible. A Syrian writer of the early 6th cent., heavily influenced by Neoplatonism, took the name in order to lend authority to his mystical writings, the most significant of which is his *On the Divine Names*. Another treatise, *The Celestial Hierarchy*, is noteworthy for its division of the angels standing nearest to God into two classes: the seraphs, "aflame with perfect love" and "all wings," and the cherubs, "filled with perfect knowledge" and "all eyes" — suggesting to later mystics the two most intense aspirations of the human soul and the two chief conditions of the beatific vision (6.2; cf. 7.1). In his *De Mystica Theologica* Pseudo-Dionysius observes that "the highest and most divine things which it is given us to see and to know are but the symbolic language of things subordinate to him who himself transcends them all. Through these things his incomprehensible Presence is shown, walking on those heights of his holy places which are perceived by the mind" (1.3).

The impact of this Eastern mystical writer was felt directly in the writing of John Scotus Erigena, the 9th-cent. monastic author of *De Divisione Naturae,* who translated Pseudo-Dionysius as well as other Neoplatonists into Latin. He also wrote a commentary, the *De Caelesti Ierarchia*, which, with the other principal works of the "Areopagite," was influential on later medieval mystics. Among these the author of the ME *Cloud of Unknowing* (ca. 1370), a chief English exponent of the "negative way," is eminent. The same writer's *Book of Privy Counselling,* a highly speculative work, and *Deonise Hid Diuinite,* a translation of Pseudo-Dionysius, are among the high points of ME spiritual literature.

Bibliography. Hodgson, P., ed. *The Cloud of Unknowing* and *The Book of Privy Counselling.* EETS o.s. 218 (1944); *Deonise Hid Diuinite and Other Treatises on Contemplative Prayer.* EETS o.s. 231 (1955); Underhill, E. *Mysticism* (1955).

DIRGE   *See* DIRIGE.

DIRIGE   The term *Dirige* is derived from Vg Ps. 5:9 and Ps. 5:8 (*"Dirige, Domine Deus meus, in conspectu tuo viam meam"* ["Direct, O Lord my God, my way in your sight"]). In Christian liturgy, Ps. 5:8 was used as the first antiphon in the first Nocturn of Matins in the Office of the Dead. The first word, *Dirige,* came to signify the recitation of Matins for the souls of the dead and ultimately the recitation of the entire Office of the Dead. It was also used to signify one's obligation to pray for the dead, as in the C-text of *Piers Plowman* (4.467-68): "Prestes and persons . *placebo* and *dirige,* / Here sauter and here seuene psalmis . for alle synful preyen" ("Priests and parsons pray *placebo* and *dirige* / Their psalter and their seven psalms for all the sinful").

With the loss of a syllable, *Dirige* became *dirge,* as in Sydney's "'Love is Dead'": "Let Dirge be sung, / and trentals rightly read."

The refrain at the end of each stanza, "Good Lord, deliver us," imitates the Litany in the *Book of Common Prayer,* and parallels the Latin Litany ("*Libera nos, Domine*") said over the grave of the deceased in the liturgical ceremonies of graveside burial. The later poetry of Alexander Pope conserves the liturgical sense of the word ("Nor hollow'd dirge be muttered o'er thy tomb" ["Elegy," 67]; cf. "Chaucer: January and May," 146-47, 221). Spenser, satirizing Roman Catholic practices, refers to "their dirges, their trentals, / and their shrifts" ("Prosopopoia: or Mother Hubbard's Tale," 452).

For the transferred sense of a song sung at the burial or commemoration of the dead, see Shelley's "Ode to the West Wind" ("Thou dirge / Of the dying year"); Thomas Gray's "Elegy Written in a Country Churchyard" ("The next with dirges due in sad array / Slow through the church-way path we saw him borne"); Melville's *Clare* ("with litany or dirge they wend"); and Eliot's note to line 74 of *The Waste Land.*

Bibliography. "Officium Defunctorum (Office of the Dead)," *Pars Verna: Breviarium Romanum,* 3rd ed. (1957), 4 vols.   ERNEST N. KAULBACH

DISEASE AND HEALING   In the KJV, the words "illness," "infirmity," "disease," and "sickness" usually represent Heb. *ḥoli* or one of its derivatives in the OT and Gk. *astheneia* or *nosos* in the NT. "Pestilence" and "plague" translate a number of Hebrew and Greek words, often with the root sense of "stroke" or "blow." "Health" (from Heb. *rapa';* Gk. *therapeuō*) encompasses spiritual and physical soundness.

Human disease and suffering first occur in the Bible when Eve and then Adam partake of the forbidden fruit (Gen. 3:6). God curses the guilty couple with pain in childbirth and discomfort associated with corruption and rebellion against the created order (Gen. 3:16-19). Exiled from Eden because of their sin, Adam and Eve become progenitors of a race imperfect in body and spirit. The tree of life is denied them; they shall "surely die" (Gen. 2:17).

In general, obedience to God's commands is said to afford freedom from disease: "If thou wilt diligently hearken . . . I will put none of these diseases upon thee, which I have brought upon the Egyptians, for I am the

LORD that healeth thee" (Exod. 15:26). The opposite is also asserted: disobedience of God's law violates a moral ecology of which created physical nature is also an expression, and the consequence is disease (cf. Isa. 1:5-7; Acts 12:23). God may heal such self-induced sickness, or sickness brought on as punishment, where repentance is shown; such healing is then a signal of God's redemption and forgiveness (e.g., Isa. 35:5-6, a passage read and expounded by Jesus at the beginning of his ministry [Luke 4:17-21]). In the Mosaic covenant God's sovereignty in judgment and mercy is asserted: "I kill, and I make alive; I wound, and I heal; neither is there any that can deliver out of my hand" (Deut. 32:29).

Deliverance from many "natural" ills was given to Israel through OT food laws and purification rites. The OT laws may reflect ancient practices of "public health" (esp. in the prohibitions of blood and fat, regulations with respect to the burial of the dead and disposal of excreta, and in the extraordinary appearance of the notions of contagion and quarantine).

Pestilence appears repeatedly as one of three "sore judgments" (sword, famine, and pestilence [Jer. 38:2; 42:17]) visited upon both disobedient Israel and the surrounding nations who attempt to thwart the divine purpose. But the image of God as healer is preeminent, especially in such passages as the brazen serpent (Num. 21:5-9, cited in the Gospel of John [3:14-15; 12:32-36] as prefiguring Christ's cross) and the Servant Song of Isa. 53 ("and with his stripes we are healed" — which, in its reference to vicarious suffering and atonement, is applied to Christ in Matt. 8:16-17 and 1 Pet. 2:24).

Descriptions of specific diseases in the Bible are vague and phenomenal (e.g., "And it came to pass that . . . after the end of two years, his [Jehoram's] bowels fell out by reason of his sickness; so he died of sore diseases [2 Chron. 21:19]). A spiritual dimension to such description, implying that the illness is a punishment, is sometimes patently obvious (e.g., in the plagues of Egypt in Exod. 7–12) but not always: Hezekiah's nebulous illness is unattributed (2 Kings 20:1-11) and Job's afflictions are explicitly dissociated from any notion of punishment. In the NT the emphasis is on Jesus' power to perform miracles and cures as a sign that the kingdom of God has arrived (Luke 11:20). When asked for specific reasons for human suffering (e.g., the man born blind in John 9 or the Galileans murdered by Pilate in Luke 13), Jesus sometimes deflects the queries and engages the immediate issues of repentance and belief. On other occasions he juxtaposes the two issues (Mark 2:9-11).

The phrase "signs and wonders," widely used in the OT (esp. in the miraculous events surrounding the Exodus), is taken over by NT writers recounting healing activities of Jesus and his followers. Distinctly absent from these narratives is anything which could correctly be labelled as magical. St. Paul describes the creation as "subject to vanity" but nonetheless hoping for deliverance from the "bondage of corruption," even as believers wait for "the adoption, that is, the redemption of our body" (Rom. 8:20-23).

Jesus' teaching and his healing ministry reflect his compassionate acknowledgment that sickness and death in human experience are real and terrible (see his response to Lazarus's death [John 11]), as well as his authoritative declaration that they are not final. His own agony at Gethsemane and on the cross are subsumed in the triumph of the Resurrection and the glorious eschatological promise that the leaves of the tree of life will be at last "for the healing of the nations. And there shall be no more curse" (Rev. 22:2-3).

Early Christians, combating prevalent magic and occult practices, combined medicine and prayer for the sick (James 5:14-15: "and let them pray over him, anointing him with oil"). A suspicion of the practice of medicine persisted, though, perhaps due to the apparent low regard for physicians reflected in several biblical passages (e.g., 2 Chron. 16:12; Mark 5:26; cf. Ecclus. 38:1-8; Tobit, passim). By contrast, the talmudic period in Judaism exhibited considerable interest in medical therapies, though surgery (except for circumcision) and dissection remained forbidden. Some early Christian writers, especially those influenced by Gnosticism, regarded the body as impure and of little value, if not despicable. St. Augustine was skeptical of anatomists rummaging at people's insides (*De anima,* 4.3), yet he was fascinated with accounts of human freaks of nature (*De civ. Dei* 16.8.1). His teacher St. Ambrose, in his *De interpellatione Job et David,* devotes considerable attention to the real physical and moral ills from which humanity suffers.

The Church began to invoke the assistance of saints, particularly St. Sebastian, after the time of the plague of Justinian in the 6th cent. Relic cults were symptomatic of an increasing syncretism with pagan magic, an ever appealing option to the orthodox disciplines of prayer and penitence. Ambivalence toward medicine thus is characteristic of medieval Christianity. Bede, who displays considerable scientific acumen and an interest in medicine, nevertheless is more interested still in recording miraculous healings in response to intercessory prayer. The Council of Clermont in 1130 forbade the practice of medicine for monks. Yet in 1181 the Order of Saint John first incorporated what could be called medical practice into its hospital in Jerusalem. By this time disease was still often regarded as sin's just due, but the appropriateness of human intervention was increasingly asserted. In the penitential theology of the later Middle Ages, the confessor, as a soul's physician, is seen as Christ's minister: absolution and healing are interdependent (cf. Archbishop John Pecham's *Lambeth Constitutions; Speculum Sacerdotale*). Boethius's *De Consolatione Philosophiae* and its commentaries had an influential role here, evident in one of Chaucer's psychopharmical poems, *The Book of the Duchess. The Tale of Melibee,* which makes

Prudence the "confessor" of Melibeus, draws on a treatise by the Italian physician and canon lawyer Albertanus of Brescia to show the relationship of physical health to a spirit of forgiveness.

In English literature the perspective on disease and healing was strongly influenced from the beginning by pagan Greek medical tradition. Thus the "four humours" of Hippocrates and Galen (later related to the movements of the planets) and the "natural and vital spirits" (roughly corresponding to venous and arterial blood) make appearances up to and even after William Harvey's discovery of the circulation of blood in 1628. Chaucer's Doctour of Phisyk was "grounded in astronomye" (i.e., astrology) and knew his humors well (*General Prologue,* 413-23). Shakespeare, Milton, and Burton often allude to phlegms, cholers, and astrological portents. (Such references decrease sharply after 1800.)

The fact that classical modes of interpreting human physiology and pathology continued to be attractive derives from their convenience as tools for explanation and manipulation. The Bible, as has been noted, is thin on explanation, offering bare phenomena only. It knows no system but the "finger of God" (Exod. 8:19; cf. Luke 11:20). Yet under the influence of Robert Grosseteste, 13th-cent. Chancellor at Oxford, study of the physical sciences was encouraged not merely for its practical benefits (as in St. Albertus Magnus and Roger Bacon) but as an aid to better understanding of the Scriptures. The *De Proprietatibus Rerum* of Bartholomaeus Anglicus, translated in the 14th cent. by John Trevisa as *The Nature of Things,* sees knowledge in the natural and spiritual realms as complementary (bks. 6–7). (That Chaucer describes his Doctour of Phisyk as one whose "studie was but litel on the Bible" [*General Prologue,* 438] is in this light a material criticism of his balance as a physician.) Sir Thomas Browne's *Religio Medici* represents an attempt to explore that complementarity as well as some of the tensions which remain between Christian faith and the physician's practice.

Suspicion of the physician and of medical arts carries over from medieval Christianity into much of later literature. Writing in a time of gloom and social enervation following the Black Death (1347-50), Chaucer and Langland regarded medicine and surgery as powerless against illness and death. Physicians were especially vulnerable in such times to charges of malpractice (*Piers Plowman* A.7.261; cf. B.20.174-78), and were often accused of loving gold. This jaundiced view continues through the Renaissance in Marlowe ("the end of Physicke is our bodies health / Why, Faustus, has thou not attain'd that end?" [*Doctor Faustus,* 1.1.45-46]) and on to modern times (cf. G. B. Shaw, *The Doctor's Dilemma;* Walker Percy, *Love in the Ruins*).

Disease as divine retribution remains a popular theme for writers in the Middle Ages and Renaissance. Dante, e.g., has the Alchemists who sinned against nature tormented by her appropriate diseases *(Inferno,* 22.72-84; but cf. also Burton's *Anatomy of Melancholy).* Popular, too, is the theme of psychic or spiritual healing (e.g., Cordelia's cure of her father's madness in *King Lear,* 4.7; cf. *Macbeth,* 4.3.140-52), and of the instructive benefits of sickness. Thus John Donne's appeal to the divine Healer ("Hymn to God, my God, in my Sickness") concludes: "Therefore that he may raise the Lord throws down."

In different periods one finds various prominent "symbolic" diseases. In the Middle Ages the popular view of plague as divine judgment was perhaps inevitable when no other explanation was available. During the Renaissance, syphilis ("the pox") supplanted plague as the literary malady — a more personal disease for a more individualist era, and obviously befalling only those who had had moral lapses (cf. John Donne's humorous "Why Doth the Pox So Much Affect to Undermine the Nose?"). By the 18th cent. Daniel Defoe is still wrestling with the divine vengeance issue, but he suspects a naturalistic explanation and promotes public health precautions reminiscent of Jewish law *(Journal of the Plague Year).* The Romantics' morbid infatuation with the pale creative grace of tuberculosis is well known (e.g., Keats's wistful "I have been half in love with easeful Death" ["Ode to a Nightingale," 52]). This complete inversion evidences a post-Enlightenment estrangement of literature from biblical norms, presaging the Victorians' indulgent fascination with the sickness and death of the young (e.g., Dickens's Paul Dombey and Little Nell). The prominent "symbolic" diseases of 20th-cent. literature would seem to be cancer and psychological disorder (though at the end of the century at least one further candidate is apparent).

There is an important skeptical literature, particularly after the 19th cent. with its legacy of creative antirealists like Emerson (who once said, "Never name sickness"). One of the wittiest, and yet most ferocious, rejections of any purported connection between physical health and spiritual well-being is Mark Twain's long essay *(Christian Science* [1907]) on Mary Baker Eddy, author of *Science and Health: A Key to the Scriptures* (1875). Twain's attack is directed not only at the form of possibility thinking expressed by Eddy, but at Transcendentalist thought in general.

It has remained for the 20th cent. to reassert the perfidious nature of disease and to despair of its ravages as "absurdity" in such dark works as Mann's *Magic Mountain,* Camus's *The Plague,* and Kafka's *Metamorphosis.* Yet this is not the whole story for the 20th cent. either. Writers such as T. S. Eliot, C. S. Lewis, Flannery O'Connor, Walker Percy, and Aleksandr Solzhenitsyn still link repentance and healing by the "wounded surgeon," so "resolving the enigma of the fever chart" (Eliot, "East Coker," 147-51).

See also BLINDNESS; LEPROSY; NAAMAN; PHYSICIAN; PLAGUES OF EGYPT.

Bibliography. Ackerknecht, E. H. *A Short History of Medicine* (1955); Harrison, R. K. "Disease." *IDB* 1.847-54; Curry, W. C. *Chaucer and the Medieval Sciences* (1960); Kee, H. C. *Medicine, Miracle and Magic in New Testament Times* (1986); Myers, J. *Disease and the Novel, 1880-1960* (1985); Rubin, S. *Medieval English Medicine* (1974); Sigerist, H. E. *Civilization and Disease* (1943); Trautman, J., and C. Pollard. *Literature and Medicine: an annotated bibliography* (1982); Ziegler, P. *The Black Death* (1969). RAYMOND G. CORRIN

DIVES AND LAZARUS Jesus' parable of Dives and Lazarus (Luke 16:19-31) has two parts. In the first, the beggar Lazarus lies at the gate of a rich man (Lat. *dives,* whence the traditional name), hungry and suffering from sores, while the rich man fares "sumptuously every day" (v. 19). In the second, both have died, and the situation is completely reversed. Lazarus now rests in "Abraham's bosom," whereas the rich man is tormented in the flames of the underworld. The rich man tries to persuade Abraham to send Lazarus with a drop of water. When Abraham refuses, because "between us and you there is a great gulf fixed" (v. 26), the rich man asks for Lazarus to call his five brothers to repentance, "lest they also come into this place of torment" (v. 28). Abraham refuses again, because they "have Moses and the prophets" (v. 29).

The context of the parable suggests a comment on the divergence of earthly appearance and spiritual reality (cf. v. 15), but many interpreters have either used it as a source of information about life after death, or have emphasized its practical illumination of earthly life. Both interpretations were introduced by the Fathers. That the climactic statement has to do with one who "rose from the dead," an evident allusion to the resurrection of Jesus, suggests that the story is also a polemic directed against those who refuse the gospel, failing to heed "Moses and the prophets."

Because of the rich man's fate, St. John Chrysostom (in his *Hom. on Ephesians,* 24) and others denied the possibility of repentance after death. St. Augustine drew upon the text to prove the immateriality of the soul (e.g., *De anima et ejus origine,* 2.8 and 4.29) and concluded from the parable that part of the happiness of the blessed consists in contemplating the torments of the damned — a thought which later was taken up by St. Thomas Aquinas *(Summa Theol.,* Supp. q. 94.1).

Augustine also asks his listeners to rely on the heart and not on the eyes when judging human beings and concludes, "Have respect unto the poor, do good works" *(Sermons on New Testament Lessons,* 52); cf. Chrysostom *(Hom. on Thessalonians,* 9), who draws a parallel to Luke 14:12-14. Luther considers the parable "a picture that is terribly and seriously against avarice, which makes people merciless; avarice is full of injustice and hinders every fruit of the gospel" (Sermon of June 6, 1535), and sees it as restricting the notion of personal property: "But God's word suppresses this natural and civil right. . . .

Yes, a Christian owes help to everybody" (Sermon of June 7, 1523).

Lazarus is a Greek derivation of the common Jewish name *Eleazar* ("God helps") — the only proper name to occur in any of the parables. It entered the English language as *lazar,* meaning "a poor and diseased person, usually with a loathsome disease; esp. a leper" *(OED).*

The parable of Dives and Lazarus was paraphrased in various ME poems *(The Pricke of Conscience,* 84.3062-66; *Handlyng Synne,* 214.6635-6720), but truly literary treatment began with John Gower, who exploited its practical consequences. In his *Confessio Amantis* (6.975-1150), he retells the parable as an example of one of the seven deadly sins — gluttony. The parable shows that "bodili delicacie / Of him which yeveth non almesse / Schal after falle in gret destresse." The other exegetical strand is also found in ME literature. In Langland's *Piers Plowman* (B.16.252-71; A.11.38-57; C.11.279-90), William meets Abraham and sees the leper in his lap, "amonges patriarkes and profetes pleyande togyderes." Since the devil has claimed both Abraham and Lazarus, they wait for Christ to deliver them. This emphasis developed from the belief of the early Church in Christ's descent into hell (cf. 1 Pet. 3:19; 4:6), reflected in apocryphal books such as the Gospel of Nicodemus; the belief in a *limbus patrum* was given doctrinal status by Aquinas *(Summa Theol.,* Supp. q. 69, 4 , 5). The begging friar in Chaucer's *Summoner's Tale* hypocritically alludes to the parable when advising man to "fatte his soule and make his body lene."

Shakespeare's allusions to the parable are either ornaments or parodies. In *1 Henry 4* (3.3) Falstaff is reminded of "hell-fire, and Dives that lived in purple" when looking at Bardolph's face. His charge of soldiers consists of "slaves as ragged as Lazarus in the painted cloth, where the Glutton's dogs licked his sores" (4.2). In *2 Henry 4* (1.2) Falstaff refers to the rich man — "Let him be damn'd, like the Glutton; pray God his tongue be hotter!"

Sir Thomas Browne denied the proximity of heaven and hell on the sole grounds of the "discourse" *[sic]* between Dives and Lazarus, because that would mean an underestimation of the faculties of the glorified *(Religio Medici,* 1.49). A further reference to Lazarus accompanies a broad definition of charity: "It is no greater Charity to cloath his body, than apparell the nakednesse of his Soule" (2.3).

Milton, in his *De Doctrina Christiana,* uses the parable to argue that miracles cannot produce belief (1.29). He distinguishes the luxury of the rich from Aristotelian "elegance," a "discriminating enjoyment of food, clothing and all the civilized refinements of life, purchased with our honest earnings" (2.9 — "of the first kind of special virtues, connected with a Man's Duty Toward Himself"). In *Paradise Lost,* Milton uses the parable to depict the torments of Satan (1.56) and to refer to the "gulf" which separates hell from heaven (e.g., 2.1027; 3.69-70; 10.253-54). Other contemporary references to

Dives and Lazarus are found in poems by Richard Crashaw ("Upon Lazarus his Teares") and Thomas Traherne ("The World"). John Bunyan's Interpreter in *Pilgrim's Progress* quotes v. 25 in characterizing the figures of "Passion, of the men of this world; and Patience, of the men of that which is to come."

The question raised by the parable concerning the state of the soul after death is dealt with in one of Boswell's conversations with Samuel Johnson. The latter supposes the parable either to be metaphorical or to support the Purgatorians, but does not want to make it an article of faith "that departed souls do not all at once arrive at the utmost perfection of which they are capable" *(Life of Samuel Johnson,* Saturday, 28 Mar. 1772). Laurence Sterne, in a "Charity Sermon" (no. 23 of *The Sermons of Mr. Yorick),* calls the parable "one of the most remarkable in the gospel" and uses it to elaborate the wrong use of riches.

Tennyson alludes to the parable in "To Mary Boyle," and it is one of the more frequent NT references in Lord Byron's poems (e.g., *Don Juan,* 2.683-88). There is a short reference to Lazarus as the patron saint of the lepers in Thomas Hardy's *The Return of the Native* (4.3), and a specific use of the parable in Charlotte Brontë's *Jane Eyre*: St. John Rivers, the stern and exacting missionary, in one of his last attempts at persuading her to marry him, exhorts Jane to remember the fate of Dives, citing Luke 10:42 (chap. 9).

The parable's social implication made it a welcome source of illustrations for writers depicting social conflicts of the mid-19th cent. A prominent example is Elizabeth Gaskell's *Mary Barton: A Tale of Manchester Life* (1848), in which Chartist and union man John Barton uses the parable as an illustration of the slavelike condition of the poor (chap. 1), and as a threat for the rich (chap. 9). John Ruskin makes a passionate appeal to the "Judasian Dives" of his time to learn what alms mean, "while Lazarus yet lies among the dogs" *(Fors Clavigera,* 7.82.24-25; cf. also "The Crown of Wild Olive," 1).

The 19th cent. also provides whimsical treatments such as Charles Lamb's definition of a poor relative ("Poor Relations") as "a Lazarus at your door." Hilaire Belloc's poem "To Dives" is a playful comparison of the lot of the poet and of the rich man, soon moving away from Scripture toward Greek mythology: Charon will transport the light burdens of poets, "the vain imaginaries," but not Dives's "weighty things."

American literature reflects similar adaptations. Poe briefly alludes to the crumbs which fell from the rich man's table ("Hop-Frog"), but Melville refers to the parable repeatedly. His Wellingborough Redburn, witnessing the death of a mother and two children, cries, "Tell me, oh Bible, that story of Lazarus again, that I may find comfort in my heart for the poor and forlorn" *(Redburn,* chap. 37). Ishmael, the narrator of *Moby-Dick,* ironically weaves the elements of the parable into his whimsical description of the Spouter Inn (chap. 2). The result is a curious combination of social criticism and attack against a divine world-order which permits and even creates vast social differences. Melville's famous reference to the parable in Sketch First of *The Encantadas* is also more than a narrative adornment in that it introduces the metaphysical pessimism which pervades the sketches: " 'Have mercy upon me,' the wailing spirit of the Encantadas seems to cry, 'and send Lazarus that he may dip the tip of his finger in water and cool my tongue, for I am tormented in this flame.' "

The skeptical modern attitude toward God's providence and love which Melville introduced can also be felt in Canadian poet W. W. Campbell's poem "Lazarus." It shows a humanistic pauper unable to rest in Abraham's bosom; he follows Dives's call for help, and then, "Christ-urged, love-driven," floats toward hell. Another modernist response emerges in T. S. Eliot's "Love Song of J. Alfred Prufrock." Whether its allusion is to Luke 16 or John 11 is not clear; it is connected with the Dantean motto (". . . but because no one ever returned alive from this depth . . .") and warns against asking "overwhelming questions."

In Walker Percy's *Love in the Ruins,* Monsignor Schleifkopf, preaching a sermon on "Property Rights Sunday," deliberately changes Lazarus from a poor man to one who "lived comfortably in a home that he owned."

Bibliography. Hunter, A. *The Parables Then and Now* (1971); Jeremias, J. *Die Gleichnisse Jesu,* 10th ed. (1984); Lindstrom, B. "Two Descriptions of the Signs before the Last Judgment." *SN* 48 (1975), 307-11; Linnemann, E. *Gleichnisse Jesu: Einführung und Auslegung* (1975); Marshall, I. *The Gospel of Luke* (1978), 632-39.   MANFRED SIEBALD

DIVIDE THE CHILD IN TWO   *See* SOLOMON.

DOCETISM   *See* HERESY.

DOG RETURNETH TO HIS VOMIT   According to one of the common ancient Near Eastern proverbs recorded in the book of Proverbs, "As a dog returneth to his vomit, so a fool returneth to his folly" (Prov. 26:11; cf. 2 Pet. 2:22). The classical application of this *mashal* appears in Bunyan's *Pilgrim's Progress,* as Hope explains the failure of Temporary to go along with Christian on his journey:

> When the power of guilt weareth away, that which provoked them to be religious ceaseth. Wherefore they naturally turn to their own course again, even as we see a Dog that is sick of what he has eaten: he vomits and casts up all . . . but now when his sickness is over . . . he turns him about and licks up all; and so it is true which is written, The Dog is turned to his own vomit again.

Jonathan Edwards, in a similar echo of Puritan exegesis, tells how as a boy he lost his love for Christian faith and observance, and "returned like a dog to his vomit, and

went on in the ways of sin" *(Personal Narrative).* In spiritual autobiography and sermon literature of the 17th–19th cents. this trope is commonly paired with "backsliding."

DOGS LICKED UP HIS BLOOD   *See* AHAB; JEZEBEL.

DONATISM   *See* HERESY.

DOOMSDAY   *See* LAST JUDGMENT.

DOVE   The dove in biblical literature and tradition is a "clean" creature, symbolizing purity, and was used in sacrifice. It is commonly identified with baptism, via its association with Noah's ark typologically and the baptism of Jesus by John historically; and hence with the Holy Spirit. Because of its return to Noah's ark with the olive branch, signaling the end of the Flood, it is a symbol of peace and reconciliation; near an apostle or saint in artistic representation it signifies the inspiration of the Holy Spirit.

See also ANNUNCIATION; BAPTISM; FLOOD; HOLY SPIRIT; NOAH.

DOXOLOGY   (Gk. *doxologia,* from *doxa,* "praise," and *logos,* "utterance"). Brief expressions of praise to God or, in Christian usage, to Christ and the Holy Spirit as well, were used at the conclusion of prayers, psalms, or hymns from earliest records of worship. As basic as "Blessed be the Lord. . . ." (Heb. *baruk* — Gen. 24:27; Exod. 18:10; 1 Chron. 16:36), or the imperative variants such as "ascribe" or "give unto the LORD glory and strength" (Heb. *yahab* — Pss. 29:1ff.; 68:34) or simply "praise the LORD" (Heb. *halal* — Ps. 150), they are familiar as editorial additions marking the conclusion of each of the five sections of the Psalter. In addition to the exclamatory "Blessed is he who comes in the name of the Lord" (Matt. 21:9; 23:39), popular NT doxologies include 1 Tim. 6:15ff.; 2 Pet. 3:18; Heb. 13:20ff.; Jude 24ff. In Church of England hymnaries, the most popular is "Praise God from whom all blessings flow," a stanza penned by Bishop Thomas Ken (1637-1711). Christopher Smart *Jubilate Agno* is replete with doxological formulations, beginning "Rejoice in God, O ye Tongues; give glory to the Lord, and the Lamb."

DRAGON OF THE APOCALYPSE   In Rev. 12:3 there appears in the heavens "a great red dragon, having seven heads and ten horns and seven crowns upon his heads." All the ancient mythologies (e.g., that of BelMarduk) contain such a dragon creature — usually serpentine in body, hydra-headed, and winged — which embodies the wild forces of chaos and destruction against which a cosmic conflict must be fought. The slaying of the dragon restores order and brings blessedness.

In the prophetic literature of the OT the "dragon"

(KJV, from *tannin,* "sea monster") represents all hostile and arrogant powers which rise up against the Lord and are subdued by him (Isa. 27:1; 51:9-10; Jer. 51:34; Ezek. 29:3; 32:2). In Bel and the Dragon, an apocryphal addition to the book of Daniel which appears in the LXX text (chap. 14), the dragon worshiped by the Babylonians is fed balls of hair mixed with tar and fat, a concoction which demonstrates the dragon's mere mortality.

Later rabbinical commentators incorporated the supernatural monsters Behemoth and Leviathan of Job 40–41 into this tradition (B. Bat. 75a; Alphabetot 98; Pirqe Mashiah 76). In the Jewish messianic program these monsters are to be released to wreak havoc on the human race until finally slain by the will of God (Apoc. Bar. 29.4); thereafter they are to be consumed in the messianic banquet (Tehillim 18.153; 23.202).

The Apocalypse is the only NT book which takes up the dragon motif. In two passages (Rev. 12:9; 20:2) the dragon is explicitly identified with "the ancient serpent, he who is called the devil and Satan," and so takes its place in the gallery of Christian images as the source and personification of all evil as well as the monster of darkness and chaos. In chap. 12 the author of the Apocalypse describes a vision which incorporates the ancient tale of enmity between the serpent/dragon and the woman (see Gen. 3:15) in new terms. It may also reflect an ancient astronomical pattern of the conflict between Scorpio and Virgo (cf. Virgil, *Georgics,* 1.32) and the myth of a prince whom the usurper tries to kill at birth but who is providentially snatched away and hidden until in maturity he kills the usurper and takes the throne. In biblical terms the sun-clothed woman gives birth to the Messiah, who is exposed to Satanic dangers until he is taken up into heaven, whence he will return in triumph.

Immediately after this cosmic battle with the dragon, two beasts appear, one from the sea and one from the land; both exercise the power of the dragon (Rev. 13:1-18). They have affinities with the four beasts of Dan. 7, the first beast combining characteristics of all four. A generally accepted interpretation is that these two beasts represent Roman imperial power, which — for the province of Asia — came up annually "out of the sea" with the arrival of the proconsul at Ephesus and the local *Commune Asiae,* which managed the imperial cult and exercised the delegated power of Rome in local government (see Rev. 13:12-16). In chap. 17 the first monster returns in the form of the scarlet beast, once more with seven heads and ten horns, being ridden by the Whore of Babylon. Here its identification with imperial power is made clear by the reference to the seven hills of Rome (v. 9).

While many commentators, e.g., Tyconius in the 4th cent., have seen the dragon image as embodying the cosmic force of evil to be fought in all ages, others have identified the dragon and the two beasts with historical forces or persons. Many examples of the first interpreta-

tion are to be found in medieval art, where either Christ or St. Michael is represented trampling the dragon. Ps. 91:13 — "the dragon shalt thou trample under feet" — gave rise to numerous allied legends of the slaying of dragons by saints (cf. *Glossa Ordinaria* [PL 113.1000]). The most widely known version of this conflict is enacted in the legend of St. George of Cappadocia (named patron saint of England after 1222) and his victory over the dragon, echoes of which are found both in the 14th-cent. alliterative *Morte d'Arthur* and Malory's version of the following century.

From the beginning, however, interpretive imagination has been focused on the identification of the dragon's seven heads and, most famous of all biblical puzzles, the solution to "the number of the beast," as propounded in Rev. 13:18: "Here is wisdom. Let him that hath understanding count the number of the beast: for it is the number of a man; and his number is Six hundred threescore and six." The seven heads were at an early stage identified with Roman emperors, and the expected eighth head (Rev. 17:11), with a Nero *redivivus.* As for the number 666, it is generally agreed that the author was here using the method of *gematria,* i.e., equating letters of an alphabet with numerals. Using the Hebrew alphabet, one can get Nero out of the puzzle, and this may well be the intended solution, but at a more fundamental level of symbolism, 666 persistently falls short of 7, the number of completeness, and parodies 888, the perfect number of Jesus; 666 is also "triangular," in contrast to the "square" of the elect — 144,000 — and of the New Jerusalem (see Rev. 7:4; 21:16).

A typical early medieval interpretation of the dragon and the beasts is that of Beatus of Liebana (8th cent.). All these figures, he argues, are limbs of Antichrist. The seven heads and ten horns symbolized Roman emperors, but they also, by extension, suggest all evil political powers. Nero, in particular, prefigures Antichrist, who now reigns secretly but will someday be manifest (*In Apocalypsim Libri Duodecim,* ed. H. A. Sanders [1930], 23, 133, 456-98). Although Beatus wrote in Spain under the scourge of Islamic invasions, he did not specifically identify Mahomet or the Saracens with one of these symbols of evil. In the next century, however, Alvarus of Cordoba saw Mahomet as the precursor of Antichrist and calculated the date of his death as 666 (PL 121.535). Much later Pope Innocent III again equated Mahomet with the number of the beast (PL 216.818), as did Alexander of Bremen in the 13th cent. in his *Expositio in Apocalypsim.*

A new stimulus to the interpretation of the apocalyptic beasts in historical terms was given by Joachim of Fiore in the later 12th cent. He identified the heads of the dragon as the seven chief tyrants persecuting the Church from its beginning: Herod; Nero; Cosdroe, King of Persia (representing Mahomet); Constantius Arrianus; Melsemutus (a Saracen tyrant) or sometimes the Emperor Henry IV; Saladin, a contemporary of Joachim; and the Antichrist still to come. By this pattern he accounted for the seven heads of the beast from the sea and for the scarlet beast of chap. 17. But he also interpreted the beast from the sea as the menace of the Saracens and the beast from the land as a pseudo-Pope, the two being prefigured in Nero and Simon Magus. Joachim drew a dragon figure and labeled its heads. This drawing may well have been in front of them when at Messina in 1190-91 Richard Coeur de Lion and his courtiers eagerly discussed Antichrist and the dragon with Joachim himself. This figure was circulated, imitated, and discussed in the following century — e.g., by the Franciscans Thomas of Pavia and Salimbene di Adam.

Joachim set the medieval precedent for a radical reinterpretation of the conflict with the forces of evil. In the pseudo-Joachimist works of the 13th cent., the sixth or seventh head of the dragon was identified with the Hohenstaufen Emperor Frederick II or one of his brood, and later the expected political tyrant was variously interpreted as a contemporary ruler. Joachim's interpretation that the beast from the land would be a false religious Antichrist — an idea derived directly from the Apocalypse — was seized upon and developed into a program in which false Pope and political tyrant combine their evil forces against the Church. This view characterized several of the radical Franciscans, including Peter John of Olivi (see D. Burr, *Transactions of the American Philosophical Society* n.s. 66 [1976], 21-22). Ubertino da Casale in the early 14th cent. actually identified the two beasts as Popes Boniface VIII and Benedict XI, whose "number" he read as 666 (P. E. B. Allo, *Saint Jean*, 202-03), and although such an extreme interpretaion was rare at that time, the idea of a pseudo-Pope personifying one of the limbs of Antichrist became widespread even among orthodox commentators. An echo of this radical interpretation can be seen in Dante's use of the seven-headed monstrosity and the whore in *Purgatorio,* 32, and it became part of antipapal rhetoric in the era of the Great Schism (1378-1417), for English tradition most notably in the later writings of John Wyclif and the Lollards.

When after the fall of Constantinople in 1453 western Europe was shocked into awareness of the Turkish threat, the dragon figure returned with an Eastern face to haunt the imagination. William Aytinger, reviving in 1498 a timely edition of the so-called *Revelations of Methodius,* drew a lurid picture of the beast from the sea as the total force of Mahomet, including the seven kingdoms of the Turks and their ten provinces (chap. 2). These supposed revelations went into a number of editions.

For Protestants the powers of the dragon were focused in the Papacy at Rome. An early Protestant commentator on the Apocalypse, Francis Lambert (*Exegesis in Sanctam Divi Ioannis Apocalypsim Libri VII* [1539], 416-63), first interpreted the seven heads in terms of the whole of history and then as the persecutors of the true Church: (1) Jews; (2) idolaters; (3) heretics; (4) hypocritical churchmen and Mahomet; (5) false sects; (6) the abomination in the Papacy and the Mohammedan menace again; and (7) the Antichrist. To his own generation belonged the sixth tribulation — a tribulation of the two beasts, one from land and one from sea: the Papists and the Turks. The Swiss divine Bullinger, in his *A Hundred Sermons upon the Apocalips of Jesu Christe* (1561), saw the Papacy, the beast from the land, as having succeeded the power of the Roman Empire, the beast from the sea. Various Protestant writers fastened on the episode of Joachim and Richard I at Messina. John Foxe, e.g., in *Actes and Monuments* (1563) related how Joachim expounded the seven heads down to the final one, Antichrist:

> And this Antichrist (he sayde) was already borne in the citie of Rome, and should be there exalted in the Apostolicall see. . . . And then shall the wicked man be revealed, whom the Lord shall consume with the spirits of his mouth, and shall destroye with the brightness of his coming.

Such associations govern the apocalypticism of Spenser in *The Faerie Queene.* From his vision of the New Jerusalem, Redcrosse Knight is imbued with new strength to go forth and slay the Great Dragon (1.9) — a dragon Spenser's audience is clearly expected to associate with the Papacy (or even Catholic Spain, the archenemy, threatening to devour the "woman's issue" of Rev. 12, the new Protestant dynasty).

The whore on the scarlet beast was universally taken by Protestant commentators to represent the Pope at Rome. Thus John Napier identified the whore as the "verie presente City of Rome" and the "great horned beast" as the "whole bodie of the Latine Empire, whereof the antichrist is a part" (*A Plaine Discovery of the Whole Revelation of St. John* [1593], 34, 36). Thomas Brightman interpreted the dragon and the first beast as Roman emperors and later the Turks, while the second beast and the whore on the scarlet beast stood for the popes and papal Rome (*A Revelation of the Revelation* [1615], 552-53, 571-88). The hopes of many expectant prophets in England in the 1640s and 1650s hung on the belief that the dominion of the beast was nearing its end. E. Burroughs, in *A Measure of the Times* (1657), is optimistic:

> And now after the long night of Apostacy and darknesse which hath been upon the face of the earth, is the Lord approaching and his day dawning, and his light breaking forth as the glory of the morning, and the Kingdome of God is revealed, and his dominion is setting up, after the long reigne of the Beast.

Despite such apparent optimism about the unfolding of apocalyptic events, new and varied interpretations for the dragon-beasts continued to emerge; to the Fifth Monarchists, splitting off from the government in the Barebones Parliament of 1653, Oliver Cromwell looked less like St. George than like the "little horn" or the dragon himself. In Milton's *Reason of Church Government urg'd against Prelaty* (1642) the Anglican prelates are associated with the dragon, the Presbyterians in Parliament with "our old patron St. George." In *Paradise Lost* Milton allots the final victory, however, not to Michael the archangel or to St. George but (on the authority of Rev. 12:11) to the Son of God himself.

Writers in the 18th cent. seem in general to have lost interest in the dragon of the Apocalypse. Even Blake passes over what might have seemed an irresistible opportunity for expansion of his repertoire of apocalyptic symbolism — although his protean serpent occasionally appears where one might expect a dragon (L. Damrosch, *Symbol and Truth in Blake's Myth* [1980], 106). Imagery drawn from the defeat of the dragon by Michael recurs in the 19th cent. Coleridge in his sonnet to Sheridan laments "the apostate by the brainless rout adored, / As erst the elder Fiend beneath great Michael's sword." And George Eliot in *The Spanish Gypsy* speaks of ridding the earth — much in the manner of Michael — of "human fiends / who carry hell for pattern in their souls":

> The great avenging angel does not crawl
> To kill the serpent with mimic fang;
> He stands erect, with sword of keenest edge
> That slays like lightning.

In the 20th cent., various versions of the apocalyptic dragon persist in science fiction and fantasy literature. Notable examples in which the biblical associations are apparent are Tolkien's *The Lord of the Rings* and W. H. Reddy's *The Worm Ourobouros*.

See also ANTICHRIST; BEHEMOTH; BEL AND THE DRAGON; DEVIL; LEVIATHAN; MARK OF THE BEAST; WOMAN CLOTHED WITH THE SUN.

Bibliography. Allo, P. E. B. *Saint Jean. L'Apocalypse* (1921); Bousset, W. *The Antichrist Legend: A Chapter in Christian and Jewish Folklore.* Trans. A. H. Keane (1896); Caird, G. B. *A Commentary on the Revelation of St. John the Divine* (1966); Emmerson, R. K. *Antichrist in the Middle Ages: A Study of Medieval Apocalypticism, Art, and Literature* (1981); Farrer, A. *A Rebirth of Images* (1949); *The Revelation of St. John the Divine* (1964); McGinn, B. *Visions of the End: Apocalyptic Traditions in the Middle Ages* (1979); Patrides, C. A., and J. Wittreich, eds. *The Apocalypse in English Renaissance Thought and Literature* (1984); Reeves, M. *The Influence of Prophecy in the Later Middle Ages* (1969); Reeves, M., and B. Hirsch-Reich. *The Figurae of Joachim of Fiore* (1972).   MARJORIE REEVES

DREAMS, VISIONS In the Bible, as in contemporary usage, dreams could figure the ephemeral, evanescent stirrings of wistful (or slothful) imagination (Heb. *shenah,* "sleep" [Ps. 90:5]; *halom,* "dreams" [Job 20:8; Ps. 73:20; 90:5; Isa. 29:7]), even the empty words of a fool (Eccl. 5:3, 7; Jude 8). But they could also signal the nature of a higher reality (Ps. 126:1; Isa. 29:8), and God could choose dreams as a means of revealing his purposes to select individuals. Thus, prophets received revelation in dreams

(Num. 12:6; 1 Sam. 28:6, 15; Joel 2:28), and though false prophets might "dream up" antithetical schemes, there was a reliable test: dreams which were truly revelation from God would prove consistent with his Word, or Torah (Deut. 13:1-5; Jer. 23:25-32). The self-authored "revelation" of imposters would then prove to be dreaming in the most derogatory and damnable sense: in Isa. 56:10 such blind "watchmen" (the Heb. term is *hozim,* "raving," a play on *hozeh,* "seer") are "blind," "ignorant," "dumb dogs" who cannot bark, "sleeping, lying down, loving to slumber."

Truly revelatory dreams tend to appear in the biblical text in clusters, three of which have had a notable impact upon literary tradition: the dreams of the patriarchs Abraham, Jacob, and Joseph (Gen. 20–41), the apocalyptic dreams of Nebuchadnezzar and Daniel (Dan. 1–7), and dreams associated with the birth of Christ (Matt. 1:20; 2:12-22). Additionally, the last book of the NT, the Revelation of St. John upon Patmos, is the unique example of an entire biblical book written in the form of a dream-vision. Of lesser importance among dream narratives are those involving the dreams of Gideon (Judg. 7:13-15), Solomon (1 Kings 3:5, 15), and the wife of Pilate (Matt. 27:19). Some revelatory dreams in the Bible are "message" dreams with specific verbal content (Gen. 31:24; Matt. 1:20; 2:12-22), but symbolic, imagistic dreams predominate, as in the cases of Jacob (Gen. 28:12; 31:10ff.), Joseph (Gen. 37:5-9); Pharaoh's butler and baker (Gen. 40:9-19), Pharaoh (Gen. 41:1-24); Nebuchadnezzar (Dan. 2:31-36; 4:9-24), and Daniel (7:1-28; 8:1-27). In some of these cases a dream may be called a "night vision" (e.g., Dan. 7:2, 7); the term is probably related to that used in Acts 2:17 in which dream *(enypion)* and vision *(horasis)* are effectively variants of the same prophetic phenomena. A common feature of symbolic dreams is that they leave the dreamer psychologically troubled and yearning for clarity of interpretation, especially since symbolic dreams tend to be predictive of future events. Occasionally revelatory dreams may occur in pairs (Gen. 37:5-9; 41:1-24), which is taken in the latter case to indicate both the reliability of the warning and its imminence (41:32). In the case of St. Peter's vision of the clean and unclean animals the shocking and counterintuitive character of the vision necessitates a triple repetition (Acts 10:10ff.).

In the antique Mediterranean world a tradition of "dream vision" literature and commentary upon it was in existence before NT times. But the prominence of dreams in biblical literature gave rise to a rapid growth of dream vision texts in the Roman–Judeo-Christian world, both as a form of biblical commentary and as a kind of parallel wisdom writing in which the dream-vision as genre or structural motif might signal the type of authority a text was claiming for itself (which could indeed include status as a kind of "revelation"; e.g., apocryphal writing such as The Book of the Secrets of Enoch, 4 Ezra, or the hermetic

Poimandres). The *Visio Pauli,* an apocalypse describing what the apostle Paul saw when he was taken up into the "third heaven" (2 Cor. 13:2), was very popular in its time (late 4th cent.) and, through the mediation of chap. 12 of St. Augustine's *De Genesi ad litteram,* enjoyed continued influence down through the Middle Ages (Dante, e.g., quotes from it in *Inferno,* 2.28). The most important early Christian treatise on dream theory, however, was Tertullian's *De anima* (ca. A.D. 210). For Tertullian the soul did not sleep, but continued to participate in the transtemporal order of eternity, unfettered by the body's constraints within time. The potentially prophetic character of dreams owed to an ambience of eternity, the soul being lifted above the order of mundane causality.

Macrobius's *Commentary on the Dream of Scipio* (ca. A.D. 390), though accessory to a classical Roman text (the closing section of Cicero's *De re publica*), became an important influence on medieval dream theory as developed by Christian writers. Macrobius's fivefold classification of dreams helped establish terms of reference for a medieval sense of genre: the *visum,* or apparition, in which the dreamer thinks himself awake while imagining specters, and the *insomnium,* or nightmare related to evident physical or mental stress, required little or no interpretation. But the enigmatic *somnium* "conceals with strange shapes, and veils with ambiguity the true meaning of the information offered, and requires an interpretation for its understanding." More declaratively, the prophetic *visio* is a dream which "comes true," and the *oraculum* is a dream in which a parent or other revered figure reveals the future and gives advice. While medieval authors could appeal to Macrobius directly, as, e.g., Chaucer seems to in his *Book of the Duchess, Parliament of Fowls, House of Fame,* and *Nun's Priest's Tale,* medieval thinking about dream-vision literature was substantially a blending of Macrobius with the commentary of theologians upon biblical texts. Chief among these intermediary sources is Augustine in chaps. 24 and 25 of his *De spiritu et anima* (cf. his *Liber de divinatione daemonum,* chap. 5). Augustine follows the general classification of Macrobius, but because of the weight given to scriptural literary example, *visio* is the subgenre upon which he and his successors tend to concentrate their effort. Augustine further divides this category into *visio corporale* (a sensory and realistic presentation of natural images), *visio spirituale* (resulting from spiritual powers shaping the imagination by the use of sensory images), and *visio intellectuale* (a revelation of divine *mysterium* without the mediation of images, appealing directly to the intellect). While John of Salisbury *(Policraticus)* accepts the classification of Macrobius, as later does Alexander of Hales in his *Summa Universae Theologiae,* their 12th-cent. contemporary Vincent of Beauvais in his *Speculum Naturale* (26.41) argues (after Augustine) that there can in fact be no dreams *(visio, somnium),* properly speaking, without images or *simulacra,* thus strengthening the bias toward

models such as are provided by dreams in the Joseph narrative in Genesis or in the book of Daniel. In Vincent, Augustine's third subclass, *intellectuale,* becomes then the sphere of direct apprehension of the divine will, as in the appearance of God to Isaiah, Jeremiah, and Ezekiel, in which they are directed to specific revelatory proclamations, or prophecy. Augustine's *corporale* and *spirituale* are reduced to a single class, generically "revelation." Revelatory dreams are seen to be influenced, however, by malignant as well as holy angelic influence: the *spiritus malus,* such as troubled Saul, produces not revelation but illusion, so that "discerning the spirits" becomes a pivotal question in dream interpretation (26.56; 61.74-96; cf. Deut. 13:1-5).

Successive efforts by theologians down through the Middle Ages to refine understanding of the biblical subgenres enhanced the literary as well as theological status of dream narrative in Scripture and made the question of genre a crucial ancillus to the fundamental issues of authority and revelation. The *visio intellectuale,* yielding up authoritative specific revelation as in the prophecy of Ezekiel, becomes a model for authentic delegation even for retailers of "classical" revelation. The *Mitilogiae* of Fulgentius, one of the standard compendia of classical knowledge in the Middle Ages, is described by its author as an old story which came to him in a dream, and Boethius's *De Consolatione Philosophiae,* though not formally a dream vision, by virtue of Lady Philosophy's appearance to the persona was often thought of by later writers as allied to the genre. King James of Scotland's free translation of Boethius in his *Kingis Quair,* e.g., presents the narrative as a dream-vision. William of Conches's *Moralium Dogma Philosophorum,* Alain of Lille's *De Planctu Naturae,* and Matthew of Vendome's *Ars Versificatoria* are 12th-cent. examples of the use of a dream-vision "frame" as a means of establishing authority for a general educational treatise. The legendary vision of St. Patrick, variously narrated as *St. Patrick's Purgatory,* is in the form of a *visio spirituale,* and though offering a medieval vision of Paradise and Hell, draws upon Virgil as well as upon biblical sources. The most important medieval poem in this "mixed" use of dream-vision is undoubtedly Dante's pilgrim dream "in the middle of the road of this life," his *Divina Commedia,* an extended and comprehensive vision which leads at last to conversion of the dreamer.

One of the most powerful uses of dream-vision in English literature is found early in the Anglo-Saxon period, the 8th-cent. *Dream of the Rood,* in which the dream comes to the poem's speaker at midnight. Here the Cross itself, suspended in the air and surrounded by angels, narrates the events of Christ's Passion, owning itself the dumb sign of terrible shame, whose "story," by the irony of grace, now dawns upon the hearer as one of unspeakable glory. Here the *visio* is revelatory in the formal sense; the poem is translated *evangelium.*

In Dante's *Commedia*, or Guillaume de Guillville's 13th-cent. *Pèlerinage de la vie humaine*, the dream-vision framework is a means of conveying associative authority in which the *speculum humanae salvationis*, or revealed scriptural history of redemption, is made formally analogous to the representative spiritual journey of the "dreaming" poet. These continental precedents, and the satiric dream-vision *Roman de la Rose* (which cites Macrobius), bear mediately upon the flourishing of dream vision literature in 14th-cent. England. Not only the Chaucer poems previously noted, but *Piers Plowman*, *Pearl*, the *Parliament of the Three Ages*, and *Wynnere and Waster* are all self-consciously constructed as dream-vision texts, with variously "prophetic" and (or) para-evangelical purposes evidently in their authors' minds. Chaucer's pose at the beginning of his *House of Fame* (ca. 1378) that he has had a great deal of difficulty himself trying to sort out the various classifications and subgenres of dreams — naming as he discourses Macrobius's five categories though leaving to others to determine the proper significance of the "gendres" — is an effective way of forcing upon the reader responsibility for observing that his dream-poem is in the species of the "avisioun," a prophetic vision with its attendant issue of authority, an issue to be raised for the reader again at the ("broken") closure of the poem. That this poem involves a prophetic dimension, however, is suggested by the putative dream's repeated Dec. 10 date (from Ezek. 40:1-2) and its general eschatological surmise. By contrast, the debates over the significance and genre of dreams as "texts" to be interpreted in the private moral life between Pandarus and Troilus (*Troilus and Criseyde*, 5.295-378) and the parallel debate between the rooster Chaunticleer and his favorite Pertelote in the *Nun's Priest's Tale* (*CT* 7.2892-3156), by offering dismissive relegation of fateful dreams to the category of insignificant *insomnia*, again force the reader to consider the question of genre. Chaunticleer's defensive citation of the "olde Testament of Daniel / . . . eek of Joseph," and "Pharao, / His bakere and his butiller also" (7.3128-34), alerts the reader to anticipate that as with Nebuchadnezzar or the Egyptian Pharaoh, or indeed the butler and baker who confided in Joseph, self-revelatory *insomnia* can prove accurate foreshadowing, a *visio* for one whose prospect for interpretation is God's universal view of history rather than the singular and time-locked prospect of the addled dreamer himself. But his warning dream, with its victim sleeping in a stable in an "ox's stall," clearly evokes the NT nativity dreams of forewarning, suggesting that if Chaunticleer were better attuned to divine than temporal affairs he might have little trouble grasping the genre and purpose of his *visio*. "Reading the text" of such a dream in Scripture, as Joseph and Daniel put it, is in fact only fully possible from such a divinely ordained vantage point: "interpretations belong to God" (Gen. 40:8; cf. Dan. 2:28, 45 and Augustine, *De Genesi ad litteram;* cf.

also Bartholomaeus Anglicus, *De Proprietatibus Rerum,* trans. Trevisa, 6.24-27).

Chaucer's contemporary, the poet of *The Pearl*, crafts an allegory of the soul's struggle with the frustration and unanswerable questions of an earth-locked perspective, urging its "dreamer" to trust that in the fullness of time God's providence will be revealed and that in this life, "the grace of God is great enough." This dream-vision draws heavily on the book of Revelation for its vision of Paradise and heavenly reward, and the dreamer's personal vision is formally analogous to that of the apostle: its purpose is prophetic instruction for the persona and, through him, the reader. Similarly prophetic, but a jeremiad focusing on the evils of the present day, is the great dream-vision poem ascribed to Langland, *Piers Plowman*. Here a succession of eight dreams, called explicitly *visio*, both decry present evil and portend the advent of divine judgment. Yet their subject is authority. The first dream comes "on a May mornynge," as does the warning dream to Chaunticleer in the *Nun's Priest's Tale,* apparently following the notion of Augustine (*De Genesi ad litteram,* 12.12.27; seq. St. Thomas Aquinas, *De Veritate,* q.8, a.12, ad 3) that true dreams come after midnight and false or doubtful dreams before (cf. St. Albertus Magnus, *De Apprehensione,* 3.9). Thus, when in the York Cycle play "The Dream of Pilate's Wife" Satan appears in a dream to the procurator's spouse endeavoring to frustrate Jesus' crucifixion, so thwarting the Atonement, the dream is appropriately pre-midnight (195-96).

Renaissance writers remain sensitive to the possibility that demonic as well as angelic forces might inspire a dream, and that demonic illusion, such as Archimago's projection of the dream-phantasm Duessa in Spenser's *Faerie Queene* (1.2), ought to be reckoned as a powerful enemy of true vision. Cowley's Saul is tempted to kill David by a pleasant phantasm (*Davideis,* 1), and Eve is tempted in a dream in Milton's *Paradise Lost* (4.776-809). Shakespeare's Leontes is similarly tempted in a dream in *A Winter's Tale,* and classic dreams of forewarning resembling in structure and function those in the NT nativity narratives are found in Calpurnias's dream of forewarning in *Julius Caesar* and Hastings's dream in *Richard 3.* The dream of Posthumus in *Cymbeline* (5.4.92ff.), with Jupiter's descent and benediction, parallels the benediction dream of Jacob at Bethel (Gen. 28:11-16). But with the notable exception of Bunyan's *Pilgrim's Progress,* in which the plight and pilgrimage of Christian are said to appear to the narrator as a prison dream, the genre of dream-vision fades notably in prominence during this period, and allusions to biblical dreams become more irregular and often parodic, as when Dryden has Achitophel flatter Absalom that he is to be a messianic deliverer whose birth "exercised the Sacred Prophets rage . . . / The Young-mens Vision, and the Old mens Dream!" (*Absalom and Achitophel,* 237-39; cf. Joel 2:28; Acts 2:17). Addison's "The Vision of Mirzah" (*Spectator,* no. 159) is a Bunyanesque adaptation, focusing on the question of life after death.

Eighteenth-century suspicions of religious "enthusiasm" tended to downgrade the traditional associations with revelation and authority: Swift's *Tale of a Tub* is representative of an extensive literary critique of pretensions to spiritual dream and vision as merely the result of overeating — *insomnia* which each fool wants to regard as a *visio*. Swift would have been troubled by the Romantic characterization of the poet as a visionary and prophet, perhaps particularly by Blake, who saw his work as revelation and deserving comparable authority: "Now I a fourfold vision see / And a fourfold vision is given to me," Blake writes, and his *Visions of the Daughters of Albion* (1793) borrows biblical language and allusion to effect a revolt against authority. But Blake's use of dream and vision, however personalized, is consistent with the biblical emphasis on prophetic declaration and a forewarning of ultimate judgment, the eschatological and apocalyptic character of his *Marriage of Heaven and Hell* and *A Vision of the Last Judgment* typifying his thorough absorption of biblical dream and vision narrative. Robert Southey's *A Vision of Judgment* (1821) is parodic, focusing on the postmortem fate of King George III, which because of its attack on Byron as a "Satanic" poet invites the latter's satire, *The Vision of Judgment* (1822), a kind of pilgrim's regress for George III in which the real purpose is to preview Southey's fall into the infernal abyss. Here too, in both cases, Bunyan is an evident mediator for biblical style and even allusion. John Henry Newman's *Dream of Gerontius* (1865) is a more Dantesque pilgrimage of the soul to God at the hour of death, built formally upon the Requiem Office, and rich in allusion to biblical dreams. In 1886-87 appeared William Morris's socialist eschatology, *A Dream of John Ball,* which draws upon the visions of St. John in Revelation as well as upon *Piers Plowman* and events of the 1381 Peasants' Revolt to project a political Last Judgment in which Englishmen "shall see things as they verily are," throw off their chains, and fashion "Jerusalem in England's green and pleasant land," much as Blake had hoped.

American literature of the 19th cent. has little to add to the development of dream-vision as a genre, but James Russell Lowell's long poem *The Vision of Sir Launfal* (1848) allied itself with British 19th-cent. medievalism in using the grail legend for social-ethical commentary. Lowell has his protagonist Sir Launfal's vision of Christ become a prophetic revelation to America of its vocation to achieve a Sermon-on-the-Mount democracy. Historical novels, retellings of scriptural narrative such as Henry K. Sienkiewicz's *Quo Vadis?* (1896) and Lloyd C. Douglas's *The Big Fisherman* (1949), offer interesting "realistic" treatment of NT dream revelation. In John Updike's *Of the Farm,* Joey Robinson is a "constant dreamer" portrayed as a "little Joseph" unable to interpret his own dreams. Updike's tale suggests a post-Freudian perspec-

tive on the biblical tradition which, along with postmodern suspicion of literary devices which imply authority, undermines the appeal of biblical dream-vision. Dream-vision still thrives, however, in fantasy and science fiction, and as Flannery O'Connor's brilliant short story "Revelation" indicates, the form may yet have great potency even in realist writing.

See also OLD MEN DREAM DREAMS.

Bibliography. Doob, P. *Nebuchadnezzar's Children* (1974); Hieatt, C. *The Realism of Dream Visions* (1967); Lewis, C. S. *The Discarded Image* (1964); Newman, F. X. "*Somnium:* Medieval Theories of Dreaming and the Form of Vision Poetry." *DA* 24 (1963); Nolan, B. *The Gothic Visionary Perspective* (1977); Spearing, A. C. *Medieval Dream Poetry* (1976); Stahl, W. H., ed. and trans. *Macrobius: Commentary on the Dream of Scipio* (1953); Weidhorn, M. *Dreams in Seventeenth-Century English Literature* (1970); Whitman, F. H. "Exegesis and Chaucer's Dream Visions." *ChauR* 3 (1969), 229-338.

DRY BONES, VALLEY OF   In Ezek. 37 the prophet describes being "carried out in the spirit of the LORD" and set down "in the midst of the valley which was full of [human] bones" (v. 1), which were very dry. The Spirit asked him, "Son of man, can these bones live?" to which Ezekiel replied, "O Lord GOD, thou knowest." Ezekiel was then instructed to prophesy upon the bones, commanding them to "hear the word of the LORD" (v. 4). God declared that he would cause the bones to be reknit, sinews and flesh laid upon them, and their skin to return, by his "breath" *(ruah);* immediately the earth shook and the bones were enfleshed. Ezekiel was then told to say, "Come from the four winds, O breath, and breathe upon these slain, that they may live" (v. 9). When the four winds came rushing together into the valley the corpses arose and came to life as "an exceeding great army" (v. 10). In the text itself the vision is interpreted as an allegory of the restoration of defeated Israel and its return to its own land (vv. 11-14).

With the exception of Ezekiel's initial vision of the Shekinah glory of God in its mystical chariot, "wheels within wheels," this is the most influential passage in Ezekiel's prophecy. The liturgical use of Ezek. 37:1-14 is ancient, providing the *hapthard* for Passover and its Sabbath, corresponding there to the Sidroth (Exod. 33:12–34:26 and Num. 28:19-25). It appears in early temple art on the lower frieze of the north wall at the Synagogue of Dura-Europos (3rd cent. A.D.), which interprets the resurrection of the dead in literal terms as an eschatological promise, not as an image for the restoration of Israel. The resurrected souls appear here with wings. This interpretation is not, however, shared by many other Jewish sources. R. Eliezer says that one should understand that immediately after the resurrected individuals stood up, they died (Sanh. 92b). Other targums say the dead were Ephraimites, or that they went up to Palestine, married, and had children (e.g., Diéz-Macho, *Targum Pales-*

tinense, 201). In a lighter vein, the Talmud tells how Nebuchadnezzar learned of the resurrection of the dry bones: he had a drinking cup made of the skull and bones of a slain Jew. When he lifted it to drink, the bones came swiftly to life and then punched the Babylonian king in the face as a voice declared: "A friend of this man is at this moment reviving the dead!" (Sanh. 93a). Another midrash tells how the resurrected men wept because they feared that, having been once resurrected, they would lose their share in the life to come: Ezekiel is said to have reassured them on this count (Pirqe R. El. 33).

In Christian tradition the Fathers (e.g., St. Irenaeus, Tertullian, St. Justin Martyr, St. Cyprian, St. Cyril of Jerusalem, and St. John of Damascus) tended to see the episode as a prefiguration of the final resurrection. St. Ambrose writes: "Great is the loving kindness of the Lord, that the prophet is taken as a witness of the future resurrection, that we, too, might see it with his eyes" (*De excessu fratris satyri*, 2.73; cf. *De Spiritu Sancto*, 3.19.149). In the services of the Church the passage was associated with Lent and Easter, and in all Latin rites it formed one of the lections for the baptism of catechumens on Easter Eve; as St. Jerome says, it was *in omnium ecclesiarum Christi lectione celebrata*.

Perhaps the most whimsical use in English literature, saving Du Bose Heyward's "Roll dem bones," is Izaak Walton's record of John Donne's melodramatically preaching his own funeral sermon, so ill that "many did secretly ask that question in Ezekiel: 'Do these bones live?'" (*Life of Dr. John Donne*). Dryden, following the early tradition, connects the whole passage to the Resurrection and Last Judgment:

> When in mid-aire, the Golden Trump shall sound,
> To raise the Nations under ground;
> When in the Valley of Jehosaphat,
> The Judging God shall close the Book of Fate . . .
> When rattling Bones together fly,
> From the four Corners of the Skie,
> When Sinews o'er the Skeletons are spread . . .
> The Sacred Poets first shall hear the Sound,
> And foremost from the Tomb shall bound. ("To the Pious Memory of . . . Anne Kiligrew," 178-89)

In *Benito Cereno* Melville describes a neglected whaleboat as looking like it must have been "launched, from Ezekiel's Valley of Dry Bones." Whittier, in "Howard at Atlanta," describes a group of slaves reading the Bible together, in a scene perhaps proleptic of the famous spiritual:

> Behold! — the dumb lips speaking,
> The blind eyes seeing!
> Bones of the Prophet's vision
> Warmed into being!

Daniel Sargent's "The Last Day" calls up the army of bones for a battle to end all battles, seeing the ghostly army as set for Armageddon.

See also EZEKIEL; WHEELS WITHIN WHEELS.

Bibliography. Cross, J. E. "The Dry Bones Speak — A Theme in Some Old English Homilies." *JEGP* 56 (1957), 434-39; Neuss, W. *Das Buch Ezekiel in Theologie und Kunst bis zum Ende des XII. Jahrhunderts* (1912); Watkins, F. C. "'De Dry Bones in de Valley'." *SFQ* 20: 136-40; Wischnitzer-Bernstein, R. "The Conception of the Resurrection in the Ezekiel Panel of the Dura Synagogue." *JBL* 60 (1941), 43-55; Zimmerli, W. *A Commentary on the Book of the Prophet Ezekiel* (1969; Eng. trans. 1983). 2 vols.

DULCIS JESU MEMORIA   Derived from allegorical commentary on the Song of Songs, and not any biblical text itself, this phrase becomes the title of one of the best-known hymns of St. Bernard of Clairvaux (ca. 1150). The hymn was translated twice in the 19th cent., both by James W. Alexander (1859) and later Edward Caswall ("Jesu! The very thought of thee / With sweetness fills my breast"). *See also JESU, DULCIS MEMORIA.*

DUST AND ASHES   *Dust and ashes* is a metonymic term for the human condition as conceived humbly by Abraham (Gen. 18:27) and also by Job who, in lamenting his lot, said, "I am become like dust and ashes" (Job 30:19), and later, when he finally was able to answer the voice of God speaking out the whirlwind, said, "I abhor myself, and repent in dust and ashes" (42:6).

In Christian tradition these passages are associated with discussion of repentance and the need for humility before God (e.g., St. Ambrose, *De poenitentia*, 2.1.3-4). The image also has a place in the liturgy for burial of the dead, where it is conflated with Gen. 3:19, "for dust thou art, and unto dust thou shalt return." In this context it is cited by Washington Irving in "The Pride of the Village" and Thomas Wolfe in *Look Homeward, Angel*, where, as Eugene's mind "fumbled at little things" despite the nasal drone of the Presbyterian minister, "Horse Hines bent ceremoniously, with a starched crackle of shirt, to throw his handful of dirt into the grave. 'Ashes to ashes — '" (chap. 37). In the Anglican (and Episcopalian) liturgy the phrase which immediately follows is "in sure and certain hope of the Resurrection to eternal life, through our Lord Jesus Christ," prompting Longfellow's rejoinder: "'Dust thou art, to dust returnest', / Was not spoken of the soul" ("A Psalm of Life," 2). Reflecting on the grave of his father, Dickens's narrator in *David Copperfield* considers "the mound above the ashes and dust that once was he, without whom I had never been" (chap. 1). Hardy uses the phrase as a kind of shorthand for death (*Desperate Remedies*, chap. 21) as well as "living death": in *Tess of the D'Urbervilles*, after Tess has been raped by Alec, Hardy says of her feelings that "he was dust and ashes to her," and later, after her husband has left her, Tess feels that in her "was the record of a pulsing life which had learnt too well, for its years, the dust and ashes of things."

By natural extension the phrase was adopted for the imposition of ashes on Ash Wednesday in Anglican and

Catholic Lenten liturgies. It is likely this connection which Dickens has in mind in *A Tale of Two Cities*, where his attention is turned toward the lot of one of the ordinary laborers: "For, in these times, as the mender of roads worked, solitary, in the dust, not often troubling himself to reflect that dust he was and to dust he must return, being for the most part too much occupied in thinking how little he had for supper and how much more he would eat if he had it" (2.23). Farrell's Studs Lonigan, in *Judgment Day*, is crudely reminded of his mortality: "Remember, O Lonigan, that thou art dirty dust, and like a dirty dog thou shalt return to dirtier dust" (chap. 17). A variant of the penitential formulation forms the title — "Wash, this Sand and Ashes" — of the eleventh chapter in Rudy Wiebe's saga of the Mennonite diaspora, *The Blue Mountains of China*.

E

EARS TO HEAR Frequently coupled with "Eyes that see not," this phrase and its biblical variants (e.g., Deut. 29:4; Ps. 115:6; Isa. 48:8; Jer. 5:21; Ezek. 11:15; 12:2; Mark 4:9-12; Luke 14:35) derives its power from the typical Semitic reference to the organ as metonym for all its functions understood in their widest sense. Accordingly, the ear is regularly used as a synonym for "heart" or "mind" (Prov. 2:2; 18:15); in idiomatic use "to incline" the ear means to be favorably disposed to a speaker (Ps. 31:2; Isa. 1:10), whereas obtuseness may be expressed as having "uncircumcised," "heavy," or "deaf" ears (Jer. 6:10; cf. Isa. 6:10; 43:8; Acts 7:51). In the writings of the prophets the ear is given privilege over the eye (Isa. 22:14; 50:4ff.), and the most important invocation of the Jewish faith is *shēma Ysrael,* "Hear, O Israel" (Deut. 5:1; 6:3; Jer. 2:4).

The *Glossa Ordinaria* notes that "uncircumcision" of the ears (Jer. 6:10), like circumcision, is spoken of in reference not only to the *praeputium* but to the heart and the ear in a wider spiritual sense (PL 114.19). God himself is spoken of as having ears that hear (Isa. 59:1; James 5:4); he may, however, "close" his ears to sinful and arrogant petitioners (Ezek. 8:18). In Ps. 135:16-17, divine obtuseness is attributed in a mocking sense to gold and silver idols, leading St. Augustine to say that "having ears to hear and hearing not" is a symptom of idolatry, worship of the material at the expense of meaning (*Enarr. in Ps.* 135:13). This connection leads in the later Middle Ages

to an iconography of the senses in which literary deafness is taken, as by Berchorius in his dictionary *(Reportorium Moralii),* as a figure for "obtuseness to the spirit" of a text; Chaucer's Wife of Bath, who is "somdel deef" according to her physiognomic General Prologue description (1.446), may perhaps be perverse, accordingly, as an exegete of scriptural texts in her own Prologue. Such an association prevails in Theodore Beza (*Novum Testamentum,* 39) and is reflected in John Donne's "Litany," in which the speaker prays "That our eares sicknesse we may cure," then, in typical fashion, still consistent with biblical precedent, "That we may locke our eares, Lord, open thine."

In his "Ode to a Nightingale" Keats describes his frustrated "darkling" inability to attune himself to the nightingale's inspiring melody: "Still wouldst thou sing, and I have ears in vain — / To thy high requiem become a sod." Emily Brontë speaks of the challenge unavoidably entailed in profound understanding: "Oh! dreadful is the check — intense the agony — / When the ear begins to hear, and the eye begins to see" ("The Prisoner"), a problem eschewed, according to Coleridge, by numbers of Wordsworth's readers who, obtuse to his call to natural-supernatural awakening because of the "lethargy of custom," have "eyes, yet see not, ears that hear not, and hearts that neither feel nor understand" (*Biographia Literaria,* chap. 4). In Samuel Butler's narrative attacking the stiffness, exaggerated piety, and hypocrisy of Victorian life, he describes distraught

Ernest as one who "had learnt nothing by experience: he was an Esau — one of those wretches whose hearts the Lord had hardened, who, having ears, heard not, having eyes, saw not, and who should find no place for repentance though they sought it even with their tears" (*The Way of All Flesh,* chap. 75). Also speaking of a "hardening" of the heart, Melech Davidson, in A. M. Klein's *The Second Scroll,* alludes to Isa. 6:9 to describe the alienation from faith of his fellow Jews.

EAST, EAST OF EDEN   When Cain was sent out as a perpetual fugitive he "went out from the presence of the LORD, and dwelt in the land of Nod, on the east of Eden" (Gen. 4:16). Since "Nod" in Hebrew means "wandering" — an irony noted by St. Jerome — there is a double edge to Cain's condemnation. He wanders in the land of wanderings; as Jerome puts it, there is in fact no "Land of Nod." Strictly speaking, it is a "no man's land," in which Cain is said (v. 17) to build a city called *Ḥanok* or "Enoch" (Jerome, *Ep.* 46.7; cf. *Glossa Ordinaria* [PL 113.100]). To "drop into the Land of Nod" has come to mean to have wandering thoughts or daydreams, or to fall asleep; Melville's Ishmael uses the phrase in this way in *Moby-Dick* to describe his nearly unfortunate nap in the Spouter Inn, and Charles Reade's narrator uses it of his "lady" in this sense in *Hard Cash* (chap. 17). Talmudic lore assigns to the area east of Eden the abode of Adam also after the Fall (Konen 29), the view that Paradise itself was in the East being based upon Gen. 1:8 (although some rabbinic authorities understood that there was a preexisting Paradise situated in the West, or Northwest [Bera. 55b; 1 Enoch 32]).

Early English literary references are typically to the monstrous or reprobate descendants of Cain, as in Sir Walter Raleigh's *The History of the World,* where the Henochii, citizens of Cain's city Enoch, are said to dwell "towards the east side of Eden, where Cain dwelt." Sir John Mandeville reflects the tradition that one of Noah's sons, Ham, inherited the East after the Flood, seizing it by cruelty, and that his son was Nimrod the giant, who built the "tower of Babylon." The people of Ham were said to have sexual commerce with demons, producing monstrosities of all kinds, the ultimate incarnation of which was "the Emperor" or Ghengis Khan, with his "Lordes from the East" (*Travels,* chap. 24).

Dryden, in his essay "Virgil and the Aeneid," calls Cain the first traveler, who "went into the land of Nod" before either Ulysses or Aeneas was born. But the less pleasant associations with Cain persist, both whimsically — as in the case of O. Henry's loquacious interlocutor's wife in "Municipal Report," who though she "traced her descent back to Eve" felt it necessary to deny "any possible rumor" that she may have had her beginnings "in the land of Nod" — and somberly, as in John Steinbeck's novel *East of Eden* (1952). In this dark and loosely biblical saga the protagonist Adam Trask marries and moves west to California with his twin sons Caleb and Aron, only to be abandoned there by his sinister wife, who becomes a brothel madam in Salinas after murdering its previous owner.

All these allusions belie other associations of the east with wisdom, magnificence, and spiritual knowledge, such as are reflected in the story of the Magi, "wise men from the east" who came to Jerusalem asking for the king of the Jews, saying that they had "seen his star in the east, and [were] come to worship him" (Matt. 2:1-2, 9). The East in this sense has often been connected, as have the Wise Men, with magic, astrology, and such Eastern religions as Zoroastrianism. Rose Macaulay describes a modern wanderer in the land of Nod who "was in travail with a new set of ideas, and their pressure rent him cruelly. Then one day, 'I have seen his star in the east,' cried papa, and became a Theosophist" (*Told by an Idiot,* 2.20).

See also BABEL; CAIN; MAGI.

EAT, DRINK, AND BE MERRY   *See* RICH FOOL, PARABLE OF.

EBENEZER   Ebenezer (Heb. for "stone of help") is both a geographical location and a monument of Israel's victory. Ebenezer was the place where Israel was defeated by the Philistines (1 Sam. 4:1ff.), and likely the site at which the Ark of the Covenant was captured (1 Sam. 5:1). Later in the narrative (1 Sam. 7:12) Samuel commemorated a God-given victory over the Philistines there: "Then Samuel took a stone, and set it between Mizpeh and Shen, and called the name of it Ebenezer, saying, Hitherto hath the LORD helped us."

Josephus mentions Samuel's erecting of the emblematic stone (*Ant.* 6.2.2), calling attention to the symbolism of victory at a location he identifies as "Corrhoea" (Heb. *Beth-Car*). St. Jerome (*Onomasticon,* s.v. Abenezer) refers to Ebenezer, placing it between Jerusalem and Ashkelon. There is little or no reference to Ebenezer in later theological literature.

Ebenezer is occasionally alluded to in English hymnody (e.g., the 18th-cent. hymn "Come, Thou Fount of Every Blessing," by Robert Robinson, in which st. 3 reads, "Here I raise my Ebenezer; / Hither, by thine help, I'm come; / And I hope, by thy good pleasure, / Safely to arrive at home"), but the word has little presence in English literature, occurring only occasionally, as a character name. Ebenezer is associated with one major work, Dickens's *A Christmas Carol,* a 19th-cent. novel whose protagonist, Ebenezer Scrooge, is an embittered, miserly soul whose particular disaffection is with Christmas and the season of giving. An encounter with three ghosts causes him to repent, and stony-hearted Scrooge is reborn as a selfless, caring individual. He thus exemplifies both senses of the term *Ebenezer* in the OT: a picture of early defeat and later triumph through supernatural "help."

See also ROCK.   BRUCE L. EDWARDS

ECCE HOMO "*Idou ho anthrōpos*" (Lat. *Ecce homo*, "Behold the man") are the words used by Pilate in presenting Jesus to the Jews, bound, scourged, crowned with thorns, and wearing a purple robe (John 19:15). Most interpreters of Pilate's laconic statement have taken *Ecce homo* to mean, "Here is the poor fellow!" the speaker's rhetoric having the purpose of eliciting pity from the spectators, or contemptuously ridiculing the Jews for taking such a lowly and risible figure's claim to kingship over them so seriously, or provoking them into demanding Christ's release. Among those exegetes interested in drawing out the theological implications of Pilate's pronouncement, some suggest that John here emphasizes the Incarnation ("the man" reflects the messianic title "Son of Man"), while others equate the "man of sorrows" (Isa. 53:3) with Jesus in his humanity (*The Gospel According to John, xiii-xxi* [AB, 1970], 876).

Only with the gradual proliferation of meditational and devotional writings in the Middle Ages, from Anselm of Canterbury's contemplations of Christ's sufferings and death in his Prayer to the Cross and *Cur Deus Homo?* in the 11th cent. to Thomas à Kempis's *Imitatio Christi* in the 15th, does the *Ecce homo* theme and its iconography become a marked feature in artistic expressions of Christian culture (see A. Feuillet, *L'agonie de Gethsémani* [1977], 8).

In the York "Christ before Pilate: the Judgement," Pilate's "Ecc*e homo*" introduces a "fool-king" (434); the anonymous playwright effectively develops the drama built into the Johannine account of Christ's response to Pilate's "Whence art thou?": "But he gave him no answer" (19:9). Representations of the *ecce homo* scene by Bosch and Dürer set precedents for treatments of the subject by Titian, Correggio, Tintoretto, Rubens, and Rembrandt, among many others. The frequency of these renderings has made a virtual genre of the subject, adding *Ecce homo* to the English lexicon, as a substantive for a picture of Christ wearing the crown of thorns.

The marked interest in the Passion which emerged during the later Middle Ages continues among major writers of the English Renaissance, though their meditations tend to be more autobiographical. Donne's "Spit in my face, yee Jewes," seventh of his *Holy Sonnets* of 1633, shows a characteristic double movement: the poetic divine identifies himself both with the reviled Christ and with those who continue to crucify him by their sinning. The closing couplet speaks of the Son of God's humility in taking on "vile mans flesh," a theme Donne takes up again in *A Litanie*:

> Through thy submitting all, to blowes,
> Thy face, thy clothes to spoile; thy fame to scorne,
> All waies, which rage, or Justice knowes,
> And by which thou could'st shew, that thou wast
> born. . . . (172-75)

In "Out of Grotius his tragedy of Christes sufferinges,"

Crashaw calls up the image of Christ mocked at his trial, while in *Steps to the Temple* and *Carmen Deo Nostro,* he enters into sympathetic union with the suffering Christ even as he tearfully confesses his responsibility for the Passion. The Miltonic *Ecce homo* adds a political dimension to autobiographical reflection. Milton's Samson, a type of Christ as the Man of Sorrows and the Savior, is pictured in the dual role of fool and champion: he is an object of pity to his people and of derision to the infidel. The Chorus in *Samson Agonistes,* at a loss to understand the inscrutable workings of Providence, appeals to God to deliver the champion brought low: "Behold him in this state calamitous" (708). God has pity in the end; the blind man in Gaza and theocracy prevail.

Like Milton's Samson, Blake's Christ is the great agent of revolution against Caesarism and all its works. In his annotations to Dr. Thornton's "New Translation of the Lord's Prayer," e.g., Blake identifies Pilate with Caesar, the "Learned," or the man of natural reason; and Christ with the "Illiterate" man of the spirit or imagination who serves the "Kingdom of Heaven." Though Jesus does "suffer himself to be Mock'd by Caesar's Soldiers Willingly," his proud silence pronounces the free spirit's anathema against the agents of science and rational ethics and the secular state these uphold. In the words of *Jerusalem,* the agonized Christ "in weak & mortal clay" no less shows the "Form Divine," "the Divine Vision" (st. 18): Blake's Jesus is his fully realized visionary man. As Alfred Kazin remarks, Blake heralds something of the "heroic vitalism" which impels the writings of Nietzsche and D. H. Lawrence (Introduction to *The Portable Blake* [1946], 23). Nietzsche's autobiography, *Ecce Homo,* pictures the self-reliant divine man scornful of rational ethics and received values, while Lawrence's novella *The Man Who Died* imagines a Christ more vital if less heroic: "the man" is grateful to "Pilate and the high priests" for reminding him of his humanity.

Sir John Seeley's mid-Victorian *Ecce Homo: A Survey of the Life and Work of Jesus Christ* presents "the man" as the greatest exemplar of moral virtue, whose teachings have been made insipid by the materialism of a church wed to the state. Seeley's *Ecce Homo* neither affirms nor denies Christ's divinity, but calls on the people of England to imitate Christ and thereby establish a republic of charity in which Christians will be governed solely by the moral imperatives dictated by the soul to each citizen. Having found "little in it but what was questionable or fanciful," Newman is persuaded to write a mildly favorable review of the book for the *Month* (Wilfrid Ward, *The Life of John Henry Cardinal Newman* [1912], 2.118). On the other hand, Lord Shaftesbury, the philanthropist, denounced it as "the most pestilential volume ever vomited forth from the jaws of hell." The problematic conjunction of church and state is also at issue, though indirectly, in Matthew Arnold's "The Sick King in Bokhara," which seems to make use of the biblical *Ecce homo:* "In the King's path, behold, the man" (94). Caught between the law and the spirit, duty and mercy, Arnold's king reluctantly condemns "the man," a self-confessed lawbreaker, and gives him an opportunity to save himself, which the man refuses. The sick monarch himself buries the conscientious lawbreaker.

Browning's *The Ring and the Book* incorporates an extended and ingenious treatment of the *Ecce homo* theme. In bk. 8, Count Guido Franceschini's lawyer figures his guilty client before the papal civil court as the mocked Christ suffering in silence (657-59) and casts him in the role of "Samson in Gaza ... the antetype / Of Guido at Rome" (638-39). Guido's testimony in bk. 5 shows him assuming that posture for himself. Similarly and ironically, the prosecutor likens his method of presenting Guido's wife and innocent victim to that of a painter of sacred subjects. In "Behold Pompilia" (9.162), Juris Doctor Johannes-Baptista Bottinius sees himself unveiling her Madonna-like portrait before the court. Pope Innocent implicitly confirms the verisimilitude of the prosecutor's rendering when he likens Guido to Barabbas and so casts the convicted murderer in the role of an Antichrist (10.2175-78). The Pope finally resists the temptation to unjust clemency: both Christian charity and civil law call for Guido's execution.

Other 19th-cent. references to Christ's trial are found in the appendix to Frederick Douglass's *Narrative of the Life of an American Slave,* where the autobiographer pictures his people as whipped and reviled drudges at the mercy of Pilate and Herod, who represent an unholy alliance of church and state; and in Hall Caine's novel *The Christian,* where the protagonist, unjustly accused of sedition and manslaughter, is likened to the mocked Christ (4.7) who maintains a calm and dignified silence before a court which serves Caesar more than God (4.12).

More recently, Conrad's *Nostromo* sardonically rewrites the biblical *Ecce homo.* "He made no answer," records Hirsch's response to Sotillo's demand that the prisoner reveal the location of the hidden silver (3.9). And when the Jewish merchant suffering the strappado receives a blow from the frustrated Sotillo's riding whip, he spits in the face of his inquisitor, who shoots him without thinking and so loses the informant innocent in fact of any knowledge of the silver. Sotillo's pronouncement to the soldiers who respond to the gunfire, "Behold a man who will never speak again," obliquely points to Nostromo, "the man of the people" fully apprised of the silver's location and whose unintentional death by gunfire will keep the secret safe. In Faulkner's *A Fable,* a parable set in World War I, and pitting against each other the powers of life and death, love and hate, a corporal and his twelve companions are judged by a military court to be the ringleaders of a mutiny by an entire regiment. The generals are mistaken. The entire fable pictures not *the* man before Pilate, but humanity itself.

See also MAN OF SORROWS; PASSION, CROSS.

Bibliography. Blinzler, J. "Passion of Christ." In *Encyclopedia of Theology: The Concise "Sacramentum Mundi."* Ed. Karl Rahner (1975), 1163-66; "Ecce Homo." In Larousse, *Grand dictionnaire universel du XIXe siècle* (1870), 7.54-55; Matczak, S. "God before Man." In *Karl Barth on God* (1962), 51-96; Pelikan, J. *Jesus through the Centuries: His Place in the History of Culture* (1985).

CAMILLE R. LA BOSSIÈRE

ECCLESIA, SYNAGOGA *Ecclesia,* the Latin form of Gk. *ekklēsia* ("gathering," "assembly"), associated in the ancient Greek world with the calling by a herald of a public assembly (*ek + kalein,* "to call out"; cf. Acts 19:32, 39ff.), was used in the LXX to translate Heb. *qahal,* the congregation of the people of Israel before God. The term, as it was used in the NT first by Jesus ("On this rock will I build my church"), is evidently indicative of a specifically Christian congregation. However, in his only other use of the term ("Tell it to the church" [Matt. 18:17]), Jesus' reference seems to be to the Jewish synagogue. The implicit continuity between synagogue and church suggested in the Gospels is blurred somewhat in Acts, where *ekklēsia,* "church," is regularly used to signify the small but growing company of believers whose apostolic task was to preach the kingdom. The reference here is to local assemblies (Acts 5:11; 13:1; 18:22), a usage also occurring in the Revelation of St. John on Patmos, a letter to the "seven churches." It has in the Pauline Epistles also a general sense, comprehensive of all local assemblies (e.g., 1 Cor. 10:32; 12:28). In Paul's doctrine of the church, the *ekklēsia* is identified with the "Israel of God" (Eph. 2:12; cf. 1 Pet. 2:10) as a covenant-bearing congregation, the Body of Christ (Eph. 4:15ff.), the Bride of Christ (Eph. 5:25).

Gk. *synagōgē* (derived from *syn* and *agō,* "to bring/come together") was originally used for any assembly. The LXX uses it to translate Heb. *'edah,* "congregation," usually meaning by *synagogue* the whole congregation of Israel assembled for religious or judicial purposes. Only in apocryphal texts does *hē synagōgē* (e.g., Ecclus. 4:7) come to mean a local congregation. In rabbinic writings it is identified with Heb. *bet keneset* (e.g., 'Abot 1.1, "gathering"), often used in preference to *'edah* or *qahal,* where it can mean the building in which the assembly occurs. It is generally believed that synagogues grew up in the time of Babylonian Exile or later in place of Temple worship, which was no longer possible. In the NT *synagoga* typically refers to the place of Jewish worship (cf. Josephus, *Ant.* 19.6.3), but it can also be applied to a Christian assembly (e.g., James 2:2). In subsequent tradition the synagogue is above all a *bet hammidrash,* a house of instruction or exposition (Midrash). Philo is among the first to call synagogues "schools" (*De specialibus legibus,* 2.15.62); Yiddish *shul* is a term still used by orthodox congregations to identify the house of prayer. Like Christian churches, synagogues are typically built on high ground and oriented toward Jerusalem.

In medieval Christian tradition the intimate connection and evident parallel between the church and the synagogue were frequently commented upon in ways which highlight both continuity and discontinuity. *Ecclesia/synagoga* could, at the most elementary typological level, be fitted into the binary structure suggested by Old Law/New Law, Letter/Spirit, Law/Grace (e.g., the Preface to Peter Lombard's *Libri IV Sententiarum*). St. Ambrose typifies the generalizing nomenclature whereby *ecclesia* symbolizes "all those of whom Christ is the head," whereas *synagoga* is effectively a forerunner, that which precedes and "introduces" the more fulsome *ecclesia* (*Expositio in Psalmum,* 118 [PL 114-15; 1560-61]). The OT is often represented as *synagoga,* and *ecclesia* represents the NT; as the NT "unveils" the OT by making its obscure passages clear in relation to messianic fulfillment in Jesus, so *synagoga* is redeemed by *ecclesia* even as it is surpassed and made, *sui generis,* obsolescent.

This antinomy is figured in numerous examples of ecclesiastical iconography from the high Middle Ages, such as a medallion from the French cathedral of St. Denis in which Christ crowns the church with one hand and unveils the synagogue with the other (E. Mâle, *The Gothic Image* [1958], 170). In allegorical exegesis of the Canticles and of Jer. 2:13, the "daughter of Jerusalem" is often understood to be Synagoga, and Ecclesia becomes the "New Jerusalem" (Lactantius, *Divinae institutiones* [PL 6.542]). In a copy of *De Originibus Rerum* by Rabanus Maurus (ca. 1023) is an illustration in which on the left an OT priest teaches three adherents from a book, pointing at them with one finger. On the right, a nimbed priest teaches three persons also, but points two fingers toward them: Synagoga offers the OT; Ecclesia, both testaments. The OT is necessary to an understanding of the NT, yet, by implication, the latter interprets the former so as to relegate its status to that of a "handmaiden." Synagoga, according to the *Glossa Ordinaria,* can actually be thought of as the Mother of Christ (PL 113.756).

Both Solomon's Song and his Temple are rich sources for the Ecclesia/Synagoga allegory. In the 12th-cent. poetry of Adam of St. Victor *(Dedicationes Ecclesiae)* Ecclesia becomes "Jerusalem, daughter of Zion," *sponsa* of Solomon's Song, and Mary, the mother of Jesus: in this instance Synagoga is thus transformed into Ecclesia. Occasionally both are shown in Crucifixion scenes, the crowned Ecclesia to the right and veiled, downcast Synagoga to the left of the crucified Christ, with Mary standing between them. In some of these depictions Synagoga carries a circumcision knife (MS Codex Latinus 9838, Bibliothèque Nationale, Paris); in one 14th-cent. Florentine fresco (Santa Croce) she is seen circumcising a child beside a lamb and a pictorial representation of Abraham about to sacrifice Isaac — a type of the Crucifixion.

Sometimes such pairing suggests an altercation, however, as in the Passion play *Passion de Semur,* in which Ecclesia predicts the Nativity and debates with Synagoga on Christmas Eve after Mary and Joseph have been led to the stable. A further development of the altercation motif, one with evident Augustinian roots, is exemplified over the northwest portal of Erfurt Cathedral, in which Ecclesia is pictured with the five wise virgins, Synagoga with the five foolish (Matt. 25:1-13).

In medieval liturgical drama Ecclesia and Synagoga appear on stage as dramatis personae, notably in Philippe de Mézières's dramatic representation of the Presentation of the Blessed Virgin Mary in the Temple (ca. 1372). In this work Synagoga, standing for Moses and the OT, carries the tables of the Decalogue. When Mary ascends the Temple steps, it is to meet the seated Ecclesia and Synagoga, who receive her jointly. The 14th-cent. Frankfurt *Ordo sive Registrarum* is a director's guide for an elaborate German play which begins with the prophets and has St. Augustine as its "narrator." Here, after scenes involving the Nativity, Ministry of Jesus, Passion, Resurrection, Revelation to St. Thomas, and Ascension, there is finally a "disputation" between Ecclesia and Synagoga, in which the former triumphs. It is the *disputatio* motif which colors Chaucer's *Prioress's Tale.*

With the Reformation, the typological emphasis shifted, and the motif almost disappeared. In the 18th cent. William Cowper illustrates a tendency for Protestant writers to incorporate the Ecclesia/Synagoga disputation into anti-Catholic polemical writing — often with reference to Jesus' parable of the publican and the Pharisee (Luke 18:9-14). For Cowper, the graceful garments and veil of Synagoga are replaced by the religious "fine trappings, for a show" of the Pharisee, "A praying, synagogue-frequenting, beau." Ecclesia's role is subsumed in the self-reproaching publican, who, "christian-like, retreats with modest mien" ("Truth," 44-78).

See also OLD AND NEW.

Bibliography. Calisch, E.N. *The Jew in English Literature* (1909); Figueroa, G. F. *The Church and Synagogue in St. Ambrose* (1949); Mâle, E. *The Gothic Image* (1958); Modder, M. F. *The Jew in the Literature of England* (1939); Parkes, J. W. *The Conflict of the Church and Synagogue: A Study in the Origins of Antisemitism* (1934; 1969); Seiferth, W. *Synagoge und Kirche im Mittelalter* (1964); Wrangham, D. B., ed. *The Liturgical Poetry of Adam of St. Victor* (1881).

ECCLESIASTES *See* QOHELETH; VANITY OF VANITIES.

EDEN The Hebrew word *'eden* (possibly derived from Sum.-Akk. *edinu* ["plain, steppe"]) refers to the location of a garden planted by God for the habitation of humanity (Gen. 2:8, 10; 4:16). The term comes by association also to indicate the garden itself (Gen. 2:15; 3:23-24; Ezek. 36:35; Joel 2:3), which is elsewhere called the "garden of God" (Ezek. 28:13) or "garden of the LORD" (Isa. 51:3).

The LXX and Vg translate the name from a homophonous Hebrew root *(adanim)* meaning "delight" (i.e., LXX *paradeisos tēs tryphēs;* Vg *paradesus deliciarum* = "paradise of delight" [Gen. 2:15]), leading to the traditional interpretation of the garden as Paradise.

God planted varied vegetation in the garden (Gen. 2:5-9), including the tree of life and the tree of the knowledge of good and evil, the latter of which was expressly forbidden for food (2:17; 3:3). There were also animals in the garden, which God brought to Adam to name (Gen. 2:19-20). Adam and Eve enjoyed perfect communion with God and each other in Eden, without fear of death and without guilt or shame. When they partook of the forbidden fruit of the tree of knowledge, their communion was destroyed and both alienation and expulsion ensued (Gen. 3).

Josephus identifies the four rivers referred to in Gen. 2:10-14 as the Tigris, Euphrates, Ganges, and Nile (*Ant.* 1.1.3), thus helping to fix a literal geographic site for Eden. Philo, in his *Allegorical Interpretation of Genesis* (1.14.43-46), finds in *paradeisos* a symbol for the rational soul and its virtues. In *T. Levi* 18:10-14 the patriarchs are said to await resurrection in the garden. Eden is envisioned as the abode of the pious after death (cf. Midr. Ps. 90:12; 31:6 and 'Abot 5.20); it is, according to some sources, especially reserved for scholars of the Law (Lev. Rab. 25.2). Other Jewish sources claim that Eden alone was unaffected by the Flood (Gen. Rab. 11.9).

Christian writers developed a variety of historical and figurative interpretations of Eden (e.g., St. Basil, *Hom. on Paradise;* St. Isidore of Seville, *Etymologiae,* 14.3.2-7; *Quaestiones in Vetus Testamentum,* 3.2.5; the Venerable Bede, *Hexaemeron,* bk. 1). St. Augustine's description, in *De civitate Dei,* is typical in its emphasis on the spiritual, rather than natural, landscape:

> In Paradise, then, man lived as he desired so long as he desired what God had commanded. He lived in the enjoyment of God, and was good by God's goodness; he lived without any want, and had it in his power so to live eternally. He had food that he might not hunger, drink that he might not thirst, the tree of life that old age might not waste him. There was in his body no corruption, nor seed of corruption, which could produce in him any unpleasant sensation. He feared no inward disease, no outward accident. Soundest health blessed his body, absolute tranquility his soul. As in Paradise there was no excessive heat or cold, so its inhabitants were exempt from the vicissitudes of fear and desire. No sadness of any kind was there, nor any foolish joy; true gladness ceaselessly flowed from the presence of God, who was loved "out of a pure heart, and a good conscience, and faith unfeigned." The honest love of husband and wife made a sure harmony between them. Body and spirit worked harmoniously together, and the commandment was kept without labor. No languor made their leisure wearisome; no sleepiness interrupted their desire to labor. (14.26)

> Their love to God was unclouded, and their mutual affection was that of faithful and sincere marriage; and from this love flowed a wonderful delight, because they always enjoyed what was loved. Their avoidance of sin was tranquil; and, so long as it was maintained, no other ill at all could invade them and bring sorrow. (14.10)

An influential tropological reading of the Fall narrative — most clearly elaborated in John Scotus Erigena's *De divisione naturae* — gives form to the conventional "garden of the soul" motif in medieval literature. In Scotus's analysis the "garden" of human nature has two regions. The inner garden is indwelt by the spiritual Adam, both husband and husbandman of the soul. It contains the tree of life and *fons vitae,* which is the source of cardinal virtues. The outer garden, the arena of temptation, is conversely "feminine," subject to fantasy and the wiles of the serpent. Morally understood, the Fall is an inversion of internal hierarchies, an offense against the proper marriage of wisdom and knowledge through the insidious adulteration of the "serpent" of sensuality.

Medieval descriptions of Paradise, such as Dante's "ancient holy wood" atop the Mount of Purgatory, refer preeminently to a spiritual habitation (*Purgatorio,* 28.1-21). But speculation about a literal Eden and its exact geographical location in or near Mesopotamia, a popular topic in late medieval travel lore (e.g., *Mandeville's Travels,* chap. 33), flourished in the Reformation and Renaissance (see Calvin, *Comm. on Genesis,* trans. J. King [1847], 1.119-52). In the 19th and 20th cents. scholarship has generally regarded the Edenic Paradise as a pious fiction, emblematic of human temptation and loss of innocence.

In English literature Eden is usually alluded to as a lost Paradise (historical, mythic, or figurative). The traditional association of Paradise with marital bliss is given ironic treatment in Chaucer's *Merchant's Tale* (e.g., 4.1264-65, 1331-32); the walled garden, with its deception, suggests an Edenic "fall." In Spenser's *Faerie Queene* the Redcrosse Knight seeks to protect Eden, a land of uncorrupted human nature, from the dragon Satan (1.10.46; 1.12.26). (A more ambiguous Spenserian garden, though with some Edenic qualities, is the "Joyous Paradise" [3.6.29.1] of the Garden of Adonis [3.6.29-40].) One of the best-known false paradises in English literature — comparable to the Garden of Deduit in the *Romance of the Rose* — is Spenser's Bower of Bliss, which is compared ironically with Eden (*FQ* 3.13.52).

England is described as "other Eden, demi-paradise" by the dying John of Gaunt in Shakespeare's *Richard 2* (2.1.42); later in the same play, however, the prelapsarian image is undercut when England is likened to a weed-infested garden (3.3.55-57; similar images recur in the Henriad [e.g., *2 Henry 4,* 4.1.203ff.; 4.4.54-56; *Henry 5,* 5.2.37ff.]). Andrew Marvell offers no such qualification in hailing Britain as "Thou Paradise of the four seas" ("Upon Appleton House," 323). Dryden praises Charles II as the "royal husbandman" who has rid his paradise of "rank Geneva weeds" (*Threnodia Augustalis,* 354-63). For many, however, nostalgic longing for a pristine garden of new beginnings was redirected from England to the New World. Thus Michael Drayton envisions Virginia as "Earths onely paradise" ("To the Virginian Voyage," 23-24; cf. Marvell's "Bermudas"), while Thomas Morton is typical of many colonists in finding New England "Paradise . . . Natures Masterpeece" (*New England Canaan* [1637; rpt. 1883], 180).

The most influential literary depiction of Eden in English is in Milton's *Paradise Lost,* which, while providing a rich examination of the psychological and spiritual habitation (it is a place of "Truth, wisdom, and sanctitude" [4.293] and knowledge [8.272-73]), affords also an unprecedented wealth of elaborate descriptive detail frankly borrowed from classical texts:

> Thus was this place,
> A happy rural seat of various view:
> Groves whose rich Trees wept odorous Gums and
>   Balm,
> Others whose fruit burnisht with Golden Rind
> Hung amiable, *Hesperian* Fables true,
> If true, here only, and of delicious taste:
> Betwixt them Lawns, or level Downs, and Flocks
> Grazing the tender herb, were interpos'd
> Of palmy hillock, or the flow'ry lap
> Of some irriguous Valley spread her store,
> Flow'rs of all hue, and without Thorn the Rose:
> Another side, umbrageous Grots and Caves
> Of cool recess, o'er which the mantling Vine
> Lays forth her purple Grape, and gently creeps
> Luxuriant; meanwhile murmuring waters fall
> Down the slope hills, disperst, or in a Lake,
> That to the fringed Bank with Myrtle crown'd,
> Her crystal mirror holds, unite thir streams.
> The Birds thir choir apply; airs, vernal airs,
> Breathing the smell of field and grove attune
> The trembling leaves, while Universal *Pan*
> Knit with the *Graces* and the *Hours* in dance
> Led on th'Eternal Spring. . . . (*PL* 4.246-68)

Milton's version of the Edenic landscape had a lasting impact on the popular imagination. The wealthy began to trim their estate gardens in "miltonic" style because of its pleasing sublimity, and estate poetry, already popularized by Jonson, Carew and Marvell, became highly fashionable, with elevated, often spurious, comparisons being drawn between the horticultural details of the garden in question and that of the earthly Paradise. Inscribed in one of the alcoves of the Welwyn garden of Edward Young was the phrase: *"Ambulantes in horto audiverunt vocem Dei"* — a mere stylish fancy, for as Alexander Pope, himself a master gardener, acknowledged: "The Groves of Eden, vanished now so long, / Live in description, and look green in song" ("Windsor Forest").

In Blake's prophetic books, Eden is consistently a higher spiritual paradise, a realm of life, generation, and harmony, while Beulah, a lower paradise, is closer to the Garden of Gen. 2 (cf. esp. *Milton,* sect. 30; *Jerusalem,* pl. 28; and *Descriptive Catalogue,* no. 578A). The natural world is seen as Edenic by Thomas Traherne (*Centuries,* 3.3), William Cowper ("Retirement," 28; *The Task,* 3:296-99), and preeminently by William Wordsworth, who in *The Prelude* (3.108-09) speaks of "Earth nowhere unembellished by some trace / Of that first Paradise whence man was driven." A similar perception occurs in *The Excursion* (9.714-19).

The self-conscious skepticism of the 19th and 20th cents. is frequently highlighted in literature. Shelley in *Queen Mab* refers to "fabled Eden" (4.89), and Robert Browning's Sordello (4.304) and Mr. Sludge (1431-32) disparage the "Eden tale." Emily Dickinson's whimsical wit toys with "Eden — a legend dimly told" (no. 502; cf. nos. 215, 1545), while Matthew Arnold simply asserts "the story is not true" (*Complete Prose Works* [1960-77], 7.383). Satiric works set in Eden include Mark Twain's *Diary of Adam* and *Diary of Eve* and Act 1 of G. B. Shaw's *Back to Methuselah.*

Even in an age of skepticism, however, the Eden story has continuing power for such writers as George Eliot (e.g., chap. 49 of *Felix Holt*). It provides a mythological or symbolic framework for Charles Dickens's *Martin Chuzzlewit* (chaps. 21, 23) and *Great Expectations* (chap. 19), Nathaniel Hawthorne's *The Marble Faun* (chaps. 27, 31), William Faulkner's "The Bear" (long version, sect. 4), and a predictable series of punning allusions in James Joyce's *Finnegans Wake.* In his space thriller *Perelandra* C. S. Lewis re-creates an Edenic landscape, temptation, and fall on the planet Venus, inviting serious theological reflection on the biblical story.

See also ADAM; CREATION; EVE; FALL; HEAVEN; *HORTUS CONCLUSUS;* NAMING OF THE ANIMALS.

Bibliography. Comito, T. *The Idea of the Garden in the Renaissance* (1978); Corcoran, M. I. *Milton's Paradise with Reference to the Hexameral Background* (1945); Duncan, J. *Milton's Earthly Paradise: A Historical Study of Eden* (1972); Freedman, W. "The Garden of Eden in *The Rape of the Lock.*" *Renascence* 34 (1981), 34-40; Giamatti, A. B. *The Earthly Paradise and the Renaissance Epic* (1966); Hardt, J. S. "The Darkening Garden: Paradisal Skepticism in American Fiction, Brown Through Melville." *DAI* 45 (1984), 521A; Ledbetter, R. R. "The Idea of the Earthly Paradise in Wordsworth's Poetry." *DAI* 44 (1983), 1800A; Marx, L. *The Machine in the Garden: Technology and the Pastoral Ideal in America* (1964); Miller, P. "The Garden of Eden and the Deacon's Meadow." *AH* 7 (1955), 54-61; Patch, H. R. *The Other World According to Accounts in Medieval Literature* (1950); Pearsall, D., and E. Salter. *Landscapes and Seasons of the Medieval World* (1973); Pradhan, N. S. "Edenic Themes in Modern American Drama." *DAI* 33 (1972), 1178A; Prince, R. J. "To Arrive Where We Started: Archetypes of the American Eden in Popular Culture." *DAI* 39 (1978), 288A; Robertson, D. W., Jr. "The Doctrine of Charity in Medieval Literary Gardens: A Topical Approach through Symbolism and Allegory." *Speculum* 26 (1951), 24-49; Vital,

A. P. "Pirates in Eden: Byron's Transformations of a Personal Myth." *DAI* 43 (1983), 3607A; Williams, G. *Wilderness and Paradise in Christian Thought* (1962).　　JOSEPH DUNCAN
DAVID W. BAKER

EDOM　Edom (Heb. = "red") was the land of the Edomites descended from red and hirsute Esau, and was typologically regarded as the foe of Jacob's descendants (Israel) — the enemy who would at last be overcome when the Messiah came. The wrath of God to be poured out on Edom in the last days (Isa. 34–35) precedes the restoration of Zion (cf. Isa. 63:1-3). These passages were read by Christian commentators in the Middle Ages in the light of certain typologically construed Psalms (e.g., Ps. 24) to refer to the Second Coming of Christ; the rhetorical question *"Quis est iste qui uenit de Edom?"* ("Who is this that cometh from Edom?") (Isa. 63:1) thus introduces a lection for Wednesday of Holy Week (Isa. 63:1-7). The 14th-cent. lyric of that title, collected by Bishop Sheppey, develops the answer in such a way that the conquering Christ is revealed red-stained from the last battle with "Edom," the Crucifixion thus juxtaposed with the last battle and victory (C. Brown, *Religious Lyrics of the XIVth Century,* no. 25). Later adaptations of the Edom theme in literature, especially those by William Blake, are more directly connected with the Jacob/Esau narrative and its traditional as well as nontraditional interpretation.
　See also ESAU.

EGG　The biblical references are as follows: Deut. 22:6, where "thou shalt not take the dam" when gathering eggs; Job 6:6: "is there any taste in the white of an egg?"; Job 39:13-17, where the ostrich "leaveth her eggs in the earth . . . and forgetteth that the foot may crush them"; Isa. 10:14, where God's hand of judgment sweeps the earth "as one gathereth eggs that are left"; Isa. 59:5, where evil-doers are spoken of as hatching "cockatrice's [i.e., adder's] eggs"; Jer. 17:11, where partridges are said to sit on eggs without hatching them; and Luke 11:11-12: "If a son . . . shall ask an egg, will he offer him a scorpion?"
　In the face of this allegorically parsimonious legacy, St. Augustine, in his commentary on Luke 11:12 (*Sermo,* 105 [PL 38.621]), established the egg as a figure for hope, especially the hope of resurrection: the egg, like the hope of resurrection, is a thing which has not yet come to fruition. Augustine was probably influenced by the egg cosmogony and fertility lore of the pagans. Certainly this lore was known to Augustine's contemporaries (e.g., Pseudo-Clement, *Recognitions,* 10.17.30; Macrobius, *Saturnalia,* 7.16.8; Martianus Cappella, *The Marriage of Mercury and Philology,* 2.139).
　Of course the egg was a symbol of the renewal of life for the vulgar as well as for the learned pagans. Shortly after their respective conversions the Christians, especially of northern Europe and Russia, appropriated the egg for their Easter celebrations. In England Edward I (1307)

had Easter eggs boiled and colored for the royal household (cf. F. X. Weiser, *Handbook of Christian Feasts and Customs* [1958], 234). And so the Easter egg became and has remained the most widely known repository of egg symbolism in the West. Indeed, the egg was so obviously a figure for the promise of renewed life that Bosch and Brueghel could allow broken or empty eggs to suggest spiritual death — the promise of renewal blasted by sin (see esp. Bosch, "Hell" panel of "The Garden of Earthly Delights," and Brueghel, *"Dulle Griet"*). For Filippo Picinelli, in *Mundus Symbolicus* (1681), the egg was also a symbol of the Virgin Mary — although this connection seems not to have occurred in England.
　In the English tradition Herbert prays:

> Listen sweet Dove unto my song,
> And spread thy golden wings in me,
> Hatching my tender heart so long,
> Till it get wing, and flie away with thee.
> ("Whitsunday," 1-4)

Herbert thus hopes that the Holy Ghost will brood over his heart-egg until it is hatched and ready to soar in communion. For Hopkins "the Holy Ghost over the bent / World broods" ("God's Grandeur"); and in "Spring," he associates eggs with spring, renewal, and prelapsarian innocence.
　In the 20th cent. the speaker in Robert Frost's "The Egg and the Machine" arms himself to fight a steam engine (a figure here for the threat of mechanization) with an egg and its promise of continued natural life. And Sherwood Anderson, in "The Egg" — in the collection of stories Anderson entitled *The Triumph of the Egg,* after the original title of the short story — allows the egg to stand as a figure for the whole process of life.
　Bibliography. Dimler, G. R. "The Egg as Emblem: Genesis and Structure of a Jesuit Emblem Book." *Studies in Iconography* (1976), 2.85-106; *Reallexikon zur deutschen Kunstgeschichte,* 4.893-903; West, M. D. "Sherwood Anderson's Triumph: 'The Egg'." *AQ* 20 (1968), 675-93.
H. DAVID BRUMBLE

EGYPT　*See* AARON; ABRAHAM; EGYPTIAN GOLD; EXILE AND PILGRIMAGE; EXODUS; MOSES; PHARAOH.

EGYPTIAN GOLD　When the children of Israel were told by Moses that the Lord had prepared for their exodus from Egypt, the injunction was added that they "borrow" from their Egyptian neighbors jewels and vessels of gold and silver to take with them on the journey, thus "spoiling" their former masters (Exod. 3:22; 11:2; 12:35). For the Fathers of the Church, including Origen, St. Jerome (*Ep.* 70), and St. Ambrose, these verses came to provide a key to the cultural mandate of Christianity, not to reject pagan culture wholesale but to take from it whatever things seemed of value so as to put them to a Christian purpose. Origen was concerned lest the borrowed gold become transformed into a golden calf (*Ep. ad Gregor*

226

1.30), but the opinion of St. Justin Martyr that "whatever things were rightly said among all peoples are the property of us Christians" (*Apol.* 2.13) set the generally more optimistic tone. As Ambrose formulates the spirit of inquiry in his commentary on 1 Cor. 1:24, 30, "all truth which is Truth is of Christ"; elsewhere he says Moses' appropriation of the "wisdom of the Egyptians" (cf. Acts 7:22) was not naïve or uncritical but rather undertaken in the spirit of searching for the Lord's truth wherever it might be found (*De officiis ministrorum,* 1.26.122-24). Above all this principle was applied to the preservation and reading of classical literature, especially Greek and Roman authors of note, in the new light afforded to their understanding by the Bible.

The best-known disquisition on the literary principle comes in the most influential work on Christian education between the Epistles of St. Paul and the Renaissance, St. Augustine's treatise *De doctrina Christiana.* With reference to the Egyptian borrowings of the Exodus Augustine says:

> In the same way all the teachings of the pagans contain not only simulated and superstitious imaginings and grave burdens of unnecessary labor, which each one of us leaving pagan society under the leadership of Christ ought to abominate and avoid, but also liberal disciplines more suited to the uses of truth, and some most useful precepts concerning morals. . . . These are, as it were, their gold and silver, which they did not institute themselves, but dug up from certain mines of divine Providence, which is everywhere infused, and perversely and injuriously abused in the worship of demons. When the Christian separates himself in spirit from their miserable society, he should take this treasure with him for the just use of the teaching of the Gospel. (2.40.60; cf. 2.28)

Augustine continues by observing that many of the Christian leaders of the previous generations were substantially enriched in their work as theologians by their classical learning: "Do we not see with what a quantity of gold and silver and garnets Cyprian . . . was loaded when he came out of Egypt? How much Lactantius brought with him! And Victorinus, and Optatus, and Hilary. . . ! And prior to all these . . . Moses had done the same thing." So, speaking of his own studies in his *Confessiones,* he says, "And I had come unto Thee from among the Gentiles, and I strained after that gold which you willed that your people should take out of Egypt, seeing that wheresoever it was, it belonged to you" (7.9.15).

This argument was taken up repeatedly throughout the Middle Ages, notably by John Scotus Erigena (*De Divisione Naturae* [PL 122.723-24]), Rabanus Maurus (*De Institutione Clericorum* [PL 107.404]), Alain of Lille (*Ars Praedicandi* [PL 210.180]), John of Salisbury (*Policraticus,* 7.2), and Jacques de Vitry (*Sermo ad Scholares,* 2.366). To this reiterated commitment we probably owe the preservation of the large part of extant classical texts, even manuscripts of Ovid, which have come down to us from monastic libraries. Pierre Bersuire (Berchorius) writes in the 14th cent. that it is in fact scripturally appropriate "to erect and fabricate the Tabernacle of the Law with the treasures of the Egyptians" (cf. Exod. 35:21–39:43), something which in his *Ovidus Moralizatus* he attempts to do, allegorizing each aspect of the Roman author's poetry so as to refer its "inner sense" to Scripture. In this way, like the authors of the vernacular *Ovide moralisée,* he takes up the fundamentally ironic view of Ovid's purpose in texts like the *Amores* and *Ars amatoria,* seeing the poems as a corrective satire against carnal excess — a position repeated in the later Renaissance by Salutati (*De Laboribus Herculis,* 1.68) and others. The weight of opinion in favor of studying pagan classics was so strong that not even the reservations of St. Thomas Aquinas (*Summa Theol.* 1.1.9.1; 1-2.101.2.2) were sufficient to deter it from becoming a foundation stone for Renaissance Christian humanism. The attachment of these ideas to the study of literature particularly helps clarify why it is that Boccaccio should write his defense of poetry as the 14th chap. of a book entitled *De Genealogia Deorum Gentilium,* "About the Genealogy of the Pagan Gods." Erasmus writes in his *Enchiridion* (chaps. 2–3) that cultivation of a delight in reading pagan literature is indeed most profitable "if everything is referred to Christ," observing to his audience of young "soldiers of Christ" that "You love learning properly if you do so for the sake of Christ; and if you are confident of yourself and hope for a good reward in Christ, travel like a bold merchant, journey for a long while among pagan letters, and convert Egyptian wealth for the ornament of the Temple of the Lord" (chap. 25). Thomas Traherne, in his poem "The Author to the Critical Peruser," alludes to this spirit of appropriation and reference, urging it upon his readers.

In the 18th cent. an apologetic for classical literature was no longer needed and the image of Egyptian gold is to be found most frequently in discussions of the figurative language of Scripture itself. *The Divine Legation of Moses* (1738) by William Warburton was particularly influential. In it Warburton argues that pictorial language was employed by the Egyptians in the "vessels" of their hieroglyphic alphabet, and that while God encouraged the Hebrews to metaphorical speech he gave them the second commandment as an injunction against hieroglyphics, the original form of pictorial understanding, since idolatry would result from mistaking the signifier for the thing signified. The Hebrews were rather to transform their understanding of language and symbol in the light of God's direct revelation to them of his prophetic purpose, a revelation in which meaning was not to reside in the word or symbol itself but in the person of God.

Sir Walter Scott invokes the context (Exod. 3:22) if not the medieval content of this interpretative tradition when Locksley (Robin Hood) defends his trade as a "lawful spoiling of the Egyptians" (*Ivanhoe,* chap. 33).

See also EXODUS.

Bibliography. de Lubac, H. *Exégèse médiévale* (1959), 1.5; Robertson, D. W., Jr. *A Preface to Chaucer* (1962); Seznec, J. *Survival of the Pagan Gods* (1940; 1953).

EIGHTEEN BENEDICTIONS *See* PRAYER.

ELAM Elam refers to the ancient geographical area including modern southwest Iran and southeast Iraq, with its capital at Susa, for which classical sources called it Susiana. It is identified with the Parthians by Calvin (*Comms.* 11.114) and with the Persians by Luther (*Works,* 2.205). Inclusion in the Table of Nations (Gen. 10:22) indicates its antiquity, as has archeology, which has traced it back to the fourth millennium, from which time it had military and economic contacts with its neighbors. Able to raise a military force in the time of Abram (Gen. 14:1), Elam was conquered by Ashurbanipal (ca. 645 B.C.) as foreseen by the Hebrew prophets (Isa. 21:2; Jer. 49:34-39). Elamites were found in the Palestine area during Ezra's time (Ezra 4:9) as well as at the birth of the Church at Pentecost (Acts 2:9). The latter passage, with its reference to "Parthians, and Medes, and Elamites," is made use of by Lamb in his essay "The Two Races of Men."

Bibliography. Hinz, W. *The Lost World of Elam* (1972).

DAVID W. BAKER

ELEAZAR 1. Third son of Aaron by Elisheba (Exod. 6:23; Num. 3:2) and father of Phinehas, he also was consecrated a priest, succeeding Aaron on his death (Num. 20:25ff.) and becoming priest and advisor to Joshua (Num. 27:19; 31:12ff.).

See also AARON.

2. Son of Abinadab.

See also ARK OF THE COVENANT.

3. Priest who came back from Babylon with Ezra, son of another Phinehas (Ezra 8:33; Neh. 12:42).

4. An ancestor of Jesus, three generations preceding Joseph (Matt. 1:15).

ELECTION Discussions of divine election, with its subheadings of predestination and divine foreknowledge, provide the millstones by which countless theological efforts in Western Christendom have been ground. Yet in its rudiments, election means simply the act of choice whereby God in love picks an individual or group out of a larger company for a purpose or destiny of his own appointment. The main OT verb is *bahar,* which expresses the concept of deliberate selection after weighing alternatives. In the LXX and NT the corresponding verb is *eklegomai,* the middle voice of *eklegō,* with reflexive overtones; its meaning is "choose out for oneself." The cognate adjectives are *bahir* and *eklektos,* translated "elect" or "chosen," and the NT also uses the noun *eklogē,* "election." The Hebrew verb *yada',* "know," which is used of various acts of knowing that imply the expression of affection (e.g., relations between the sexes, and the

believer's acknowledgment of God) is used to denote God's electing — i.e., his taking cognizance of persons with love — in Gen. 18:19; Amos 3:2; Hos. 13:5. The Greek verb *proginōskō,* "foreknow," is similarly used in Rom. 8:29; 11:2 to mean "forelove." The biblical link between election and affection is recurrent and powerful.

OT faith rested on the belief that Israel was God's chosen and beloved people, chosen through two complementary acts. First, God chose Abraham and his seed, taking Abraham from Ur to Canaan, making there an everlasting covenant with him and his descendants, and promising him that his seed would be a blessing to all the earth (Gen. 11:31–12:7; 15; 17; 22:15-18; Neh. 9:7; Isa. 41:8). Second, God chose Abraham's family, redeeming them from Egyptian slavery, renewing the Abrahamic covenant with them in an amplified form at Sinai, and setting them in the Promised Land as their national home (Exod. 3:6-10; Deut. 6:21-23; Ps. 105). The covenant relation, whereby God totally and permanently commits himself to love and bless people and requires that they similarly commit themselves to love and serve him, is a bond of fidelity expressing affection. Each of these two acts of divine choice is also described as God's call, i.e., his sovereign utterance of words and disposal of events which summoned first Abraham and then his offspring to acknowledge God the Creator as their God and live before him as his people (Isa. 51:2; Hos. 11:1). Israelite faith looked back to these two acts as having created the nation.

The meaning of Israel's election may be understood under five aspects. First, its source was God's free, omnipotent love. God "set his love on" Israel although Israel was neither impressively numerous nor admirably righteous, but was instead feeble, small, and rebellious (Deut. 7:7; 9:4-6). Some talmudic sources make a claim for a basis in merit, that more than other nations Israel had maintained family purity (Esfah in Yalqut I, 683; cf. Midr. 'Aggadah Num. 13:4); the emphasis in the Torah itself is that God's love was the spontaneous expression of a generous purpose which had no source or cause in anyone's virtue but, as in the case of Noah's generation, was a choice out of God's good pleasure, highlighted by choices made against that goodness by people bent on their own pleasure (cf. Deut. 9:46).

Second, the goal of Israel's election was, proximately, the welfare of the people through God's separating them for himself (Ps. 33:12), and ultimately God's own glory through Israel's showing forth his praise to the world and bearing witness of the great things he had done (Isa. 43:10-12, 20-21; 44:8; cf. Pss. 79:13; 96:1-10). Election involved separation from irreligious and immoral ways for a life of communion with God, fulfillment of the unique life-style he commanded, and enjoyment of the protection and prosperity he promised. Election was thus the basic act of blessing (the name of the tribe Asher is said, in the Talmud, to signify the "good fortune" of Israel to be God's chosen), and fount of all other blessings;

hence the prophets express their hopes of postexilic restoration by saying that God will again "choose" Israel and Jerusalem (Isa. 14:1; Zech. 1:17; 2:12; cf. 3:2).

Third, far-reaching religious and ethical obligations were involved in Israel's election: grateful praise (Ps. 147:19-20), loyal law-keeping (Lev. 18:4-5), and resolute nonconformity to the idolatry and sin of the unelected world around (Lev. 18:2-3; 20:22-23; Deut. 14:1-2; Ezek. 20:5-7). Irreligious Israelites imagined that they could always rely on God for protection and preferential treatment no matter what their lives were like, and in the days before the Exile false prophets assiduously fostered their delusion and assured them that Jerusalem, as the city of God, was inviolable (Jer. 5:12; 7:1-15; 23:9-15; Ezek. 13; Mic. 3:11). But national election implied strict judgment for national sins (Lev. 26:14-39; Deut. 28:15-68; Amos 3:2), as the Exile finally showed.

Fourth, within the chosen people, God chose individuals for special tasks to further the purpose of national election — i.e., Israel's enjoyment of God's blessing and, ultimately, mediation of it to the world. Such "callings" to personal vocation came to Moses (Ps. 106:23), Aaron (Ps. 105:26), the priests (Deut. 18:5), the prophets (Jer. 1:5), the kings (1 Sam. 10:24; 2 Sam. 6:21; 1 Chron. 28:5), and the Messiah or Servant-Savior of Isaiah's prophecy (Isa. 42:1; cf. 49:1, 5) who suffers persecutions (50:5-9), dies for sins (chap. 53), and brings the Gentiles light (42:1-7; 49:6).

Fifth, the blessings of election are forfeited through unbelief and disobedience. God rejects the ungodly among his people (Jer. 6:30; 7:29); only a faithful remnant will live to enjoy the golden age which follows judgment for sins (Isa. 10:20-22; 27:6; 37:31-32). In a time of judgment prophets looked for a day when God would regenerate such of his people as he had spared, ensuring their future faithfulness by giving them a new heart (Jer. 31:31-37; 32:39-41; Ezek. 11:19-20; 36:25-27).

In the NT the divine election of Israel is put into crisis by the rejection of the gospel by a majority of Jews. This is treated most explicitly in St. Paul's letters, especially Romans and Galatians. Basically two points are emphasized: first, through Christ both Jews and Gentiles can now inherit the divine promise of electing love and become "children of Abraham" (e.g., Gal. 3:1-29); second, the present "hardening" of Israel against the gospel is not the last word, for God will overcome this unbelief and "all Israel shall be saved" (e.g., Rom. 11:25-36). The outworking of election to those to whom God owed only wrath (Rom. 1:18-32) thus highlights the gratuitousness of grace, as mercy contrary to merit.

In the NT, as in the OT, election is a sovereign choice, prompted by God's good pleasure alone (Eph. 1:5, 9), not by any works accomplished or foreseen (Rom. 9:11) or any human efforts to win God's favor (vv. 15-18). For Paul, such efforts would in any case be vain, for however high sinners aspire and however fast they run, they still

only sin (Rom. 8:7-8). God in sovereignty treats some sinners as they deserve, hardening (Rom. 9:18; 11:7-10; cf. 1:24, 26, 28; 1 Thess. 1:15-16) and destroying them (Rom. 9:21-22), but he selects others to be "vessels of mercy," receiving "the riches of his glory" (v. 23). This discrimination involves no injustice, for the Creator owes mercy to none, and has a right to do as he pleases with his rebellious creatures (vv. 14-21). The wonder for Paul is not that he withholds mercy from some but that he is gracious to any when sin and unbelief are natural to all. Election explains why, when the gospel is preached, some do in fact respond to it. God by his Spirit leads the elect to believe, so that when people manifest a true and active faith in Christ it proves their election to be a reality (1 Thess. 1:4-10; Titus 1:1; cf. Acts 13:48).

Election is also seen as an eternal choice, made "before the foundation of the world" (Eph. 1:4; 2 Thess. 2:13; 2 Tim. 1:9), an act of predestination (Eph. 1:5, 11; cf. Rom. 8:29-30; 1 Pet. 1:2). Where the OT, dealing with national election to privilege, equated God's choosing with his calling, Paul, dealing with personal election to salvation, distinguishes the choice from the call, and speaks of calling as a stage in the temporal execution of God's eternal purpose of love (Rom. 8:30; 9:23-24; 2 Thess. 2:13-14; 2 Tim. 1:9). Paul's purpose in stressing that election is eternal is to assure his readers that it is immutable, so that nothing which happens in time can shake God's resolve to save them.

Election is the means by which God's chosen are enabled to bear the moral image of Christ and share his glory (Rom. 8:29-30; cf. v. 17; 2 Cor. 3:18; Phil. 3:21). The blessings of election are bestowed through union with Christ — his union with them representatively, as the last Adam, and vitally, as the life-giver, and their union with him by faith (Rom. 5:14b; 6:2-11; 1 Cor. 15:45b; Gal. 2:20).

Paul finds in the believer's knowledge of being personally elected a threefold religious significance. First, it assures him that his salvation is all of God, a fruit of sovereign discriminating mercy. So he glories in God only (1 Cor. 1:30) with incessant thanksgiving and doxology (Rom. 11:33-36; Eph. 1:3-14; 1 Thess. 1:3-10; 2:13). Second, it assures him of his eternal security and removes all ground for fear and despondency (Rom. 8:28-39). If he is in grace now he is in grace forever; nothing can affect his justified status (vv. 33-34); nothing can cut him off from God's love in Christ (vv. 35-39). Third, it prompts ethical endeavor. So far from sanctioning license (cf. Eph. 5:5-6) or presumption (cf. Rom. 11:19-22), this knowledge is the supreme spur to humble, thankful, joyful love, the mainspring of the holy practice which pleases God (Col. 3:12-17).

St. Augustine was the first Christian thinker to celebrate election as a tenet basic to piety because it inculcates humble dependence and confident hope as the right temper, and grateful love as the right motivation, in the

Christian life (*De praedestinatione sanctorum*, 5-6). Seeing election as the source of the grace which changes sinners from self-deifying unbelievers into lovers of God in Christ (ibid., 17-18), Augustinian thinking is characteristically conversionist, in antithesis to all forms of "once-born" Christianity which limit the work of grace to helping nature. Later "semi-Pelagian" projection (St. John Cassian and others) of God as strengthening the weak to work successfully for eternal life damped down emphasis on Augustine's formulations, although Augustinian elements are still evident in the influential *Moralia in Iob* of St. Gregory the Great.

Later medieval emphasis on the doctrine of predestination is indebted to a 13th-cent. revival of interest in prophecy, partly because of Joachim of Fiore (d. 1202). Successful prophecy implies that the Holy Spirit has spoken God's intention to the prophet and that God's will inescapably realizes its purpose; the sign is proved true in the event. The discussion of contingent and necessary futurity occasioned much scholastic debate, reawakening the Pelagian controversy. Speaking to these issues in the context of their relevance to saving grace for individual persons, St. Thomas Aquinas formulates the dominant emphasis of the later Middle Ages in this way: "Christ's merit stands equally for all human beings as regards its sufficiency, not its efficacy, for this last comes partly from human freewill, partly from divine election" (*De Veritate*, 29.7.4). Later, Aquinas puts it differently: "Providence supplies the plan, and directs all human beings to happiness. Predestination, however, relates to the success of the plan, and applies only to those who will actually reach heaven" (ibid., 6.1). He uses Scripture to confound the Pelagian view, citing Rom. 9:13 ("As it is written, Jacob have I loved, Esau have I hated"), taking a position which lines up with Augustine: "No one is silly enough to suppose that divine activity is prompted by our deserving" (*Summa Theol.* 1a.23.5). Citing Augustine as well as the parable of the vineyard (Matt. 20:1-16), he argues that it is a human vanity to question why it is that God chooses some and not others: "His will is the sole reason" (ibid., 1a.23.5.3).

The ME poem *Pearl* makes central use of the vineyard parable of unequal merit for equal reward to explain the salvation of innocents, who obviously can have acquired no merit, using the "obtuse" materialism of the "gentyl jueler" to prompt answers concerning God's free grace which are essentially Augustinian, but which show familiarity with semi-Pelagian positions represented by Occam and Holcot on the one hand and the Augustinianism of Bradwardine, Fitzralph, and Wyclif on the other (cf. 13.757-60; 15.889-912).

The impact of later medieval semi-Pelagianism as represented by Gabriel Biel and others was to maintain the debate well into the Reformation. Here Luther and Calvin revived certain aspects of Augustinian thought, including the conviction that holiness is a consequence of

election and can only proceed from it (e.g., Calvin, *Inst.* 3.22.3); so, as he says, "Wherever this good pleasure of God reigns, no good works are taken into account." Calvin's rigorous denigration of merit strongly influenced the main branches of Reformation theology and emerged unchanged in the Puritans. In Anglican tradition, with its indebtedness to Roman Catholic spirituality and the formulations of the doctrine of justification wrought by Colet and Erasmus rather than Luther, some notions of cooperation of the human will crept back in the 17th cent. to balance the more extreme position of Calvin, which the Anglican reformers had earlier endorsed in full (see Articles 10, 12, and 17 of the 39 Articles). In the *Homilies Appointed to Be Read in Churches* (1562), of the doing of works of mercy it is said that "nothing can be more thankfully taken or accepted of God" ("Of Alms Deeds") than charity to the poor, who are described as "chosen to be the heirs of his kingdom" (cf. James 2:5); yet in the second part of the sermon Cranmer speaks against the notion that "our work and charitable deed is the original cause of our acceptation before God." Rather, works of mercy (see Augustine; cf. Calvin) "declare openly" that those persons who do them "are the sons of God, and elect of him unto salvation. For as the good fruit is not the cause that the tree is good, but the tree must first be good before it can bring forth good fruit; so the good deeds of man are not the cause that maketh man good, but he is first made good by the spirit and grace of God, that effectually worketh in him, and afterward he bringeth forth good fruits." Article 17, however, takes a less ambiguously Calvinist stance.

These elements of the Reformation debate lie behind Marlowe's *The Tragicall History of Doctor Faustus,* the Wittenberg theologian's predicament being here viewed from the Anglican and Catholic as well as a continental reformationist perspective. In George Herbert's *A Priest to the Temple,* the "Prayer after Sermon" reflects Herbert's Augustinian "conversionist" view of the relation of election to preaching and justification: "Thou hast elected us, thou hast called us, thou hast justified us, sanctified and glorified us," asking that "the bread of life" nourish and strengthen its hearers "untill our obedience reach the measure of thy love, who hast done for us as much as may be." John Donne, in a whimsical celebration of the "merits" of a lady ("To the Countesse of Bedford"), evokes "the Catholique voice" to say, "I study you first in your Saints, / Those friends, whom your election glorifies, / Then in your deeds. . . ."

In 18th-cent. England, where after the Restoration "conformity" had become the political evidence of election, the doctrine was in less dispute until the rapid growth of Methodism. In Wesley's preaching, with its Arminian emphasis on the doctrine that "Christ died for all" (2 Cor. 5:14), as in the dissenting tradition represented by Isaac Watts's *The Ruin and Recovery of Mankind* (cited by Wesley in "Predestination Calmly Considered"), a passive Calvinism with respect to the "reprobate" was challenged by the insistence that "Our Lord does indisputably command and invite 'all men everywhere to repent'" (Acts 17:30). What struck Wesley as offensive was Calvin's doctrine that even as there are those elected to salvation so, deterministically, many more are appointed to damnation or "reprobation," a view sometimes expressed with a certain degree of smugness — as in

> Ah Lord, we know thy chosen few
> Are fed with heavenly fare;
> But these, the wretched husks they chew,
> Proclaim them what they are. (Cowper, *Olney Hymns,* no. 61)

Wesley's characterization of strict Geneva Calvinism was, if not in principle a misrepresentation, as inflammatory: "One in twenty of mankind is elected; nineteen in twenty are reprobated. The elect shall be saved, do what they will; the reprobate shall be damned, do what they can." This anti-Calvinism generated much controversy.

Wesley's colleague, John Fletcher of Madeley, in his widely circulated *Five Checks to Antinomianism,* charges Calvinists like Richard Hill and Dr. Crisp with a pharisaical self-congratulation and disregard for "sinners," especially the poor and needy. That is, Calvinists are thought readily to become antinomian in that once election is imagined as being conferred by baptism, and since it ostensibly owes nothing to good actions in an individual's life, there is little incentive to personal virtue, especially of a self-sacrificing kind. The Wesleyans found it hard, e.g., to reconcile the words of Jesus in Matt. 25:14-46 with a notion that God would not judge according to the way in which a life was lived. On the other hand, Fletcher distinguishes the Wesleyan position from a view of election based simply on God's foreknowledge that some persons will eventually turn out to live virtuously, saying, "We believe that out of mere mercy, and rich free grace in Jesus Christ, without any respect to forseen repentance, faith, or goodness, God places all men in a state of initial salvation; electing them to that state according to the mysterious counsel of his distinguishing love" (*The Fictitious Creed,* art. 7). For Methodists there are thus two aspects of the doctrine. In the first, described here, the initial purpose of God that we be made holy, the election "has nothing to do with prescience; it depends entirely on free grace. . .'"; but in the second "we are chosen to receive the rewards of perfected holiness and persevering obedience, in proportion both to the talents which free distinguishing grace has afforded us, and to the manner in which our assisted free will has improved those talents" (Fletcher, *Works,* 1.414-15). The Calvinism of evangelicals like George Whitefield, John Newton, and Lady Huntingdon served to keep them in the Church of England, while non-Calvinist evangelicals like Fletcher and Rowland often left the Anglican Church to become

Methodists or, like the sons of Charles Wesley and later of William Wilberforce, to convert to Catholicism.

In Puritanism, as in moderate Calvinism in the Church of England, the quest for assurance of one's election became a major pastoral concern. Such assurance was sought either through satisfactorily discerning objective evidence in oneself of personal calling and regeneration or through receiving a direct witness from the Holy Spirit. Much subsequent Calvinist hymnody enshrines this anxious introspection. John Newton's lines,

> 'Tis a point I long to know —
> Oft it causes anxious thought:
> Do I love the Lord or no?
> Am I his, or am I not?

find echo in the poetry of his still more Calvinist parishioner William Cowper. Never sure whether he was one of "the sacramental host of God's elect" (*The Task,* 2.349) or, "having preached to others," become, like St. Paul says (1 Cor. 9:27), a "castaway," Cowper experienced notorious agonized doubt about whether he could detect in himself the evidences of his election. Even in his *Olney Hymns,* coauthored with Newton, are many poems of doubt along with "songs of assurance" (cf. also his "The Castaway"). This is in notable contrast to another famous poet-hymnist of Calvinist persuasion, Augustus Toplady, whose "How Vast the Benefits Divine" (1774) expresses the more characteristic confidence: "not one of all the chosen race / But shall to heaven attain."

Resistance to Calvinist formulations of the doctrine of divine election spread well beyond the Methodists, and radically antinomian figures such as William Blake, who warmly commends Wesley and Whitefield by name for their practical social gospel and recovery of "the Book of God . . . trodden underfoot," join Wesley in resisting every kind of deterministic rendering of human existence. Blake makes of Wesley and Whitefield the two witnesses of Rev. 11, "signs and miracles" who champion liberty of the human spirit over a cold rationalism, and sees this as crucial to their evangelical social concern (*Milton,* 22.52-62; 23:1-2). Elements of Arminian reaction to the doctrine of election enter thus indirectly into the general individualism of the Romantic period. Shelley's atheism is in rebellion against the idea of personal election in "Queen Mab" when he has Ahasuerus portray a sadistic god, whose servants were "cold-blooded slaves, who did the work / Of tyrannous omnipotence." This "omnipotent fiend," bent on destruction, is made to say of those not elect who "shall curse their reprobation endlessly,"

> What then avail their virtuous deeds, their thoughts,
> Of purity, with radiant genius bright,
> Or lit with human reason's earthly ray?
> Many are called but few will I elect.
> Do thou my bidding Moses! (7.153-57)

If the NT emphasis on personal election is the focus of much of the British literary response in the 18th and early 19th cents., in America it was rather the OT idea of a "chosen people" which captured the literary imagination. In *White Jacket* Herman Melville echoes a conviction, to be found in Cotton Mather's *Magnalia Christi Americana* (1702) and Timothy Dwight's *The Conquest of Canaan* (1785), that the OT history of Israel, God's chosen people, is the prefiguration of a divine plan to be realized in the history of the American people, the "new elect." In American texts from Thomas Shepard's *The Covenant of Grace* (1651) and Edward Johnson's *Wonder-Working Providence of Sion's Saviour* (1654) to Michael Wigglesworth's *Day of Doom* (1662) it is suggested that just as God had in the past delivered his chosen people by means of the Exodus from Egypt into the Promised Land of Canaan, so now he was delivering his "elect from every tribe and nation" (cf. Matt. 24:31) into the land of milk and honey across the Atlantic. Melville writes to prepared readers when he says, "We Americans are the peculiar, chosen people — the Israel of our time; we bear the ark of the liberties of the world" (*White Jacket*, 189; cf. 1 Pet. 2:9). Melville's own religious background in the Reformed Dutch Protestant Church well fitted him to take up the Calvinist theme, since it was integral to the "family history" of his own denomination as the "elect" or "covenant people," a connection he would have celebrated many times a year as a boy when, after a baptism in the Sunday morning service, the congregation sang from the denominational hymnbook (1847; 1860) the 1562 Geneva setting for Ps. 105 by "Maitre Pierre," the tune for which was also denominated "PIERRE" in the hymnal, "Unto the Lord Lift Thankful Voices." It includes the words:

Ye seed from Abraham descended,
To whom his favors were extended,
And Jacob's children, whom the Lord
Has chosen, hearken to his word.

This hymn, which, with its emphasis on the precedence of family ties throughout the generations over any worldly affections, may bear relationship to Melville's troubled autobiographical novel *Pierre, or the Ambiguities* (1852), concludes:

The Lord his covenant people planted
In lands of nations which he granted,
That they his statutes might observe,
Nor from his laws might ever swerve.

The American literary penchant for biblical typology, so strongly developed in writers of Calvinist background such as Melville, Hawthorne, and Edward Taylor, is itself rooted in this application of OT covenant to a present in which America is seen as Israel, as Dwight's poem puts it, now finding itself on "new Canaan's promised shores" (*Conquest of Canaan*, 10.1.484). American literary typology thus depends to some degree upon a doctrine of election as premise. When in the 19th cent. the premise

is subtly eroded by, among other things, Romantic individualism and residues of Methodist and evangelical conversionism, then, as in James Russell Lowell's famous Harvard "Oration Ode" (1810), the old Puritan vision of American as "the Promised Land / That flows with freedom's honey and milk" is not always attributed to divine election but often to individual faith: "'Tis not the grapes of Canaan that repay, / But the high faith that failed not by the way."

In England, despite Galsworthy's gentle jibe (*Talking at Large*, 153) that he supposed Americans and Britons "both . . . consider our respective nations the chosen people of the earth," the doctrine of election was made most conspicuous in literature by providing a focus for attacks on self-righteousness. In Charles Dickens's *Little Dorrit*, in which people of all sorts subscribe to formulas "sacred and salutary" while living moral lives of grotesque impropriety, Mrs. Clennam's assumption that she is one of the chosen, full of the "grace and favour to be elected," justifies to her own mind obsessive vengefulness. In her jealous hatred of an old rival for Mr. Clennam's love she asserts: "it was appointed to me to lay the hand of punishment upon that creature of perdition." In exhibiting a self-appointed religious woman who is anything but humbled by the doctrine, Dickens caricatures what he takes to be a rigid and oppressive view of personal election, one still satirized by John Betjeman in "Calvinistic Evensong" a century later. Betjeman countenances a view of poetic inspiration, however, which owes something to the history of the doctrine in England (see his poem *Olney Hymns*).

John Galsworthy's story (1915) turned into a play, *The First and the Last* (1921), deals, however ironically, with a central element in the doctrine of election frequently better grasped, as G. K. Chesterton observed, by its opponents than its adherents: the NT idea of election ought above all to produce humility in the "elect," since they have and can do nothing to merit it; in practice, many who consider themselves "elect" are unduly "puffed up" (cf. 1 Cor. 4:6). In writing of George Bernard Shaw, who had an ardent distaste for the doctrine, Chesterton suggests that Shaw nevertheless grasps the NT principle well enough in his distinction of true from false virtue: "*that* reversal is the whole idea of virtue; that the last shall be first and the first last" ("The Dramatist"; cf. Matt. 20:16).

The great 20th-cent. novel on the theme of election is undoubtedly Chaim Potok's *The Chosen* (1967), an American Jewish tale of the search for both individual and national identity in which election as personal calling to rabbinic vocation contests with an appeal to fulfillment of the biblical covenant and promise to Israel of a return from diaspora and captivity to the Promised Land in Palestine. Resistance to the American appropriation of the "chosen" mythos in political life reaches its zenith in Margaret Atwood's *The Handmaid's Tale* (1985), a dystopia in which American fundamentalists have erected a society based upon rigid implementation of OT law and social custom. Atwood's anti-jeremiad deplores the possibility of a biblicist America declaring itself the only "chosen" and judging the rest of the world "reprobate."

See also PREDESTINATION; VOCATION.

Bibliography. Armour, L. "Newman, Arnold, and the Problem of Particular Providence." *Religious Studies* 24 (1988), 173-87; Bercovitch, S. *Biblical Typology in Early American Literature* (1972); Brumm, U. *American Thought and Religious Typology* (1970); Jeffrey, D. *A Burning and a Shining Light: English Spirituality in the Age of Wesley* (1987); "The Influence of the Bible on North American Literature." *The Oxford Companion to the Bible* (1992); Oberman, H. *The Harvest of Medieval Theology* 1963; 1967).

DAVID L. JEFFREY
JAMES I. PACKER

ELEVENTH HOUR   *See* LABORERS IN THE VINEYARD.

ELI   *See* HOPHI AND PHINEHAS; SAMUEL.

ELI, ELI, LAMA SABACHTHANI?   Aramaic for "My God, my God, why hast thou forsaken me?" this is Jesus' cry from the cross (Matt. 27:46; Mark 15:34).

See also SEVEN LAST WORDS.

ELIHU   *See* JOB.

ELIJAH   The varied and colorful career of Elijah the Tishbite may be divided into seven distinctive episodes: his sudden appearance on the national scene of Israel, as he announces to King Ahab the forthcoming drought and immediately flees (on God's command) to the brook Cherith, where he is fed by ravens (1 Kings 17:1-7); his reviving of the son of the widow of Zarephath (1 Kings 17:8-24); his successful contest with the prophets of Baal at Mt. Carmel (1 Kings 18:20-40); his flight from the wrath of Ahab's wife Jezebel, in the course of which he despairs, falls asleep under a broom (KJV "juniper") tree, is awakened and fed by an angel, and then fasts for forty days and forty nights at Mt. Horeb (1 Kings 19:1-18); his judgment upon Ahab and Jezebel in the matter of Naboth's vineyard (1 Kings 21:1-29); his intervention in Ahaziah's attempted embassy to Baal-zebub (2 Kings 1:1-18); and his translation into heaven in a fiery chariot (2 Kings 2:1-12).

There are scores of legendary embellishments of these events in Jewish tradition. According to one, the son of the widow of Zarephath was to become the prophet Jonah; another has it that in the contest with the prophets of Baal, the water which filled the trench around the altar to God sprang from Elijah's own fingers (see Ginzberg, *LJ,* vol. 4). But it was Elijah's translation into heaven which most sparked the imagination of later generations; this incident, together with the prophecy of

Malachi (4:5-6) that God will send Elijah before "the great and terrible day of the LORD" to "turn the heart of the fathers to the children, and the heart of the children to their fathers," generated a veritable torrent of speculation. According to Zohar Haddah Ruth (1–2), Elijah had to fight with and vanquish the Angel of Death before (as a living man) he could gain entrance to heaven; once admitted, he took on the responsibility of ordering and directing the blessed. He has, according to some sources, protected and instructed the great talmudic scholars, lesser rabbis, and the poor and destitute; he rewards the just and punishes the unjust; and in the last days he will bring peace to Israel and order the tribes for Messiah's coming (Ecclus. 48:10-11; 'Ed. 8.7; cf. S. Liptzin, "Elijah in Yiddish Literature." Many of these legends and beliefs have also been adopted and modified by Muslim commentators).

In Christian tradition, the Gospels' association of Elijah with John the Baptist (Matt. 11:14; Luke 1:17; 9:8; 9:19; John 1:21) complicates the understanding of his role. In Christian pictorial iconography his appearance usually follows NT descriptions of John — a tendency justified in part by Elijah's habit of living (by choice or necessity) in the wilderness. The Desert Fathers and other ascetics trace their lineage not only to Christ's sojourn in the wilderness, but back through John to Elijah. (A 3rd-cent. Apocalypse of Elijah strongly resembles the book of Revelation.)

In general, however, the attention the Fathers give to Elijah is slight. He is typically seen as exemplifying absolute devotion to God in the face of enmity and persecution — a position modified by Luther, who in a polemical vein compares the Reformers to Elijah and the Roman church to the prophets of Baal (*Works,* ed. T. Bachmann [1960], 35.200-201) — or, through his dealings with the prophets of Baal, as providing justification for the slaying of God's enemies. For St. Clement of Rome, Elijah is a type of the simplicity and poverty to which Christians are called (1 Clem. 17:1). Many Christian commentators have identified Elijah and Enoch, the other biblical character who did not experience a natural death, as the two witnesses of Rev. 11 who will appear in the last days.

Many of the theological uses of the Elijah narrative are repeated in literature. In Chaucer's *Summoner's Tale,* the prophet is cited as an example of the virtue of fasting (3.1890-93). The same tale's friar asserts that both Elijah and Elisha were friars (3.2116-18), an allusion to the traditional identification of Elijah as the founder of the Carmelites. Milton, in his *Apology for Smectymnuus,* sees Elijah's mockery of the prophets of Baal as an example of humor used properly for instruction — in response to Bacon, who had called such tactics into question. Swinburne, however, turns Elijah's mockery of the prophets of Baal against Christians in his "Hymn of Man":

Is he drunk or asleep, that the rod of his wrath is unfelt
and unseen? . . .
Cry aloud till his godhead awaken; what doth he to
sleep and to dream?
Cry, cut yourselves, gash you with knives and scourges,
heap on to you dust;
Is his life but as other gods' lives? Is not this the Lord
God of your trust?
. . . O fools, he was God, and is dead.

Hardy, in *Tess of the D'Urbervilles,* is similarly skeptical,
implicitly comparing the silence of the Christian God with
that of Baal: after Tess is raped, his narrator asks, "Where
was Tess's guardian angel? where was the Providence of
her simple faith? Perhaps, like that other god of whom the
ironical Tishbite spoke, he was talking, or he was pursuing, or he was on a journey, or he was sleeping and not
to be awaked." Howard Nemerov recalls the contest on
Carmel to make a different kind of point:

. . . when Elijah on Mount Carmel brought the rain
Where the prophets of Baal could not bring rain,
Some of the people said that the rituals of the prophets
of Baal
Were aesthetically significant, while Elijah's were very
plain. ("On Certain Wits")

Milton makes significant use of Elijah in *Paradise
Regained,* where he cites Elijah's sojourns in the wilderness as types and patterns for Christ's own desert fast.
Christ himself, addressing Satan disguised as an inquiring
stranger, calls attention to Elijah's example (1.351-55).
Andrew and Simon, unable to find Jesus, fear that he has
been "caught up to God . . . like the great Tishbite," and
seek him "as those young Prophets then with care / Sought
lost Elijah" (1.1-20). This connection is further explored
when Christ dreams that he sees Elijah fed by the ravens,
then fed by the angel under the juniper (2.260-78). This
incident comes in for ironic treatment in Butler's *The Way
of All Flesh,* where it becomes a concern of Ernest Pontifex, thanks to a painting of "Elijah or Elisha (whichever
it was) being fed by ravens in the desert" which hung in
the dining room.

When Ernest was a very small boy it had been a constant
matter of regret to him that the food which the ravens
carried never actually reached the prophet. . . . One day
. . . he had clambered up to the picture and with a piece
of bread and butter traced a greasy line right across it from
the ravens to Elisha's mouth, after which he had felt more
comfortable.

Later Ernest, as a young priest, angered his Bishop by
preaching a sermon on "what kind of little cake it was that
the widow of Zarephath had intended making when Elijah
found her gathering a few sticks. He demonstrated that it
was a seed cake."

Although the notion of inheriting another's mantle
(from 2 Kings 2:1-12) has become common enough to
lose the force of allusion, some English writers have

recalled the source. Robert Burns, in his prefatory
"Dedication" of his *Poems* ("to the Noblemen and
Gentlemen of the Caledonian Hunt"), writes that "The
poetic genius of my country found me, as the prophetic
bard Elijah did Elisha — at the plow; and threw her inspiring mantle over me." In *Billy Budd,* Melville describes
the dawn of the day on which Billy was hanged: "Like
the prophet in the chariot disappearing in heaven and
dropping his mantle to Elisha, the withdrawing night
transferred its pale robe to the peeping day." Dryden
produces an ironic reversal of the story. As his Elijah
(Flecknoe, the dullest of poets) sinks, the mantle rises up
to Mac Flecknoe:

Sinking he left his drugget robe behind,
Borne upwards by a subterranean wind.
The mantle fell to the young prophet's part,
With double portion of his father's art. (*Mac Flecknoe,*
214-17)

Another common phrase deriving from the Elijah narrative is the "still small voice" of 1 Kings 19:9-12 —
modified in Wordsworth's "Tintern Abbey" to "the still,
sad music of humanity," and in Tennyson's "Break,
Break, Break" to "the sound of a voice that is still."

William Blake refers to Elijah more generally as a
great exemplar of uncompromising prophetic power. In
Milton

Los is by mortals nam'd Time. . . .
But they depict him bald & aged who is in eternal youth
All powerful and his locks flourish like the brows of
morning
He is the Spirit of Prophecy the ever apparent Elias.
(pl. 24, 68-71)

In *The Marriage of Heaven and Hell* (pls. 22-24), Blake
creates "A Memorable Fancy" in which an angel — convinced by a devil that "no virtue can exist without breaking
[the] ten commandments," and that "Jesus was all virtue,
and acted from impulse, not from rules" — embraces the
"flame of fire" out of which the devil speaks, and thus "[is]
consumed and [arises] as Elijah."

Melville's *Moby-Dick,* in which Ahab is so prominent,
is not without an Elijah, although his appearance is brief
(chap. 19, "The Prophet"). Just before he boards the
Pequod, Ishmael is confronted by an apparently crazy old
man, an ambiguous prophet — "wants to be, will be, and
then again, perhaps it won't be, after all" — who warns
vaguely of disaster to come. On finding that the man's
name is Elijah, Ishmael is worried, but soon shrugs off his
concern. This Ahab will be spared nothing — perhaps
because his Elijah is so peripheral to his story.

See also CHARIOT OF FIRE; ELISHA; JEZEBEL; NABOTH'S
VINEYARD; TWO WITNESSES.

Bibliography. Liptzin, S. "Elijah in Yiddish Literature."
Biblical Themes in World Literature (1985), 228-35.

ALAN JACOBS

ELIPHAZ   *See* JOB'S COMFORTERS.

ELISABETH   Elisabeth is remembered in Christian tradition because of her relationships to others who are more significant in the story of salvation: she was the mother of John the Baptist and cousin to Mary the mother of Jesus (Luke 1:5-18). Elisabeth and her husband Zechariah were given a child in their old age, a miraculous event foretold (Luke 1:11-22) by the angel Gabriel. In the tradition of barren women in the OT, Elisabeth attributed her pregnancy to God's care for and pity on her: "to take away my reproach among men" (Luke 1:25).

News of Elisabeth's pregnancy was also part of the angels' annunciation to Mary (Luke 1:26-37). When Mary arrived for a visit with her cousin, the child in Elisabeth's womb lept, prompting her to utter the words which became part of the liturgy venerating Mary: "Blessed art thou among women, and blessed is the fruit of thy womb . . ." (Luke 1:42). Some commentaries have compared John's leap in Elisabeth's womb to David's dancing before the ark because her words of greeting to Mary ("And whence is this to me, that the mother of my Lord should come to me?" [Luke 1:43]) echo those of David ("How shall the ark of the LORD come to me?" [2 Sam. 6:9]). According to tradition, Elisabeth protected John from the slaughter of the innocents by fleeing with him to Ui-Desert, where a rock opened up to conceal them until danger had passed.

Elisabeth and Zacharias are celebrated as saints, their feast day being November 5. Elisabeth is more prominent in the visual than in the literary arts, particularly in mosaics and paintings depicting the visitation of Mary or in scenes of the two mothers with their sons. She is included in a list of notable biblical women in the Anglo-Saxon "Journey Charm"; and she is routinely mentioned as part of Gabriel's message to Mary in annunciation carols (e.g., R. Greene, *Early English Carols* [1977], nos. 233-57). She is featured in the "Visitation" or "Salutation" plays of the medieval mystery cycles.

Later references to Elisabeth are scanty. William Blake mentions her in a description of an illustration in *The Vision of the Last Judgment:* "The Holy Family consisting of Mary Joseph John the Baptist Zacharias & Elisabeth receiving the Bread & Wine among other Spirits of [the] Just made perfect." In James Joyce's *Portrait of the Artist*, Stephen Dedalus compares his friend Cranly to John the Baptist: "the child of exhausted loins . . . those of Elisabeth and Zachary."

See also MAGNIFICAT; MARY, MOTHER OF JESUS.

Bibliography. McIver, M. "Elizabeth, St."; "Visitation." In *New Catholic Encyclopedia* (1967).   JOYCE Q. ERICKSON

ELISHA   The career of Elisha, although intimately connected with that of the prophet Elijah, has a distinctive history to which both commentators and writers have attended. His independent prophetic vocation begins at 2 Kings 2:13, as he picks up the mantle of the departed Elijah; his story continues (with occasional interruptions) through 2 Kings 13:21, which describes how a dead man, tossed into Elisha's tomb, was restored to life upon coming into contact with the prophet's bones. This final miracle is alluded to in Ecclus. 48:12-14, where it is said of Elisha, "No word could overcome him, and after his death his body prophesied. He did wonders in his life, and at his death were his works marvellous."

Theological commentators, both Jewish and Christian, tend to focus on two special problems arising from the biblical account. The first revolves around the proper interpretation of Elisha's claim to "a double portion of [Elijah's] spirit" (2 Kings 2:9). The events related in the text hardly seem to support the conclusion that Elisha was twice as great a prophet as Elijah (the Hebrew phrase itself, meaning literally "a mouth of two" or a double mouthful, is ambiguous); yet St. Jerome, Martin Luther, and many other translators and interpreters have tried to save the "plain sense." Rabbinical commentators argue that Elisha performed twice as many miracles as Elijah, sixteen to eight (Baraita of 32 Middot, 1); the medieval Christian theologian Peter Damian uses the same argument, but attributes twenty-four miracles to Elisha, twelve to Elijah (*Acta sanctorum*, July 20). The second issue which has prompted extensive commentary is the incident in which Elisha called bears down upon a group of boys who taunted him (2 Kings 2:23-25): was the prophet following the will of God? Here the rabbis are particularly inventive: the Haggadah argues that those who mocked Elisha were not boys, but men behaving like boys; other commentators say that Elisha saw, with his prophetic gifts, that the boys were the sons of evil parents and would grow up to be evil themselves, and furthermore argue that God punished him for yielding to his anger by visiting him with a serious illness (Soṭa 46b-47a).

The morbid humor associated with this incident is not lost on Charles Lamb, who writes of one Thomas Coventry that he "made a solitude of children wherever he came, for they fled his insufferable presence, as they would have shunned an Elisha bear" ("The Old Benchers of the Inner Temple"). Joyce provides a modification of the Vg rendering of the taunt of the boys in *Ulysses* ("Proteus" episode): "*Descende, calve, ut ne nimium decalveris*" ("Come down, bald one, lest you become even balder"). In his poem "Baldhead Elisha," A. M. Klein comments on "the horrible / Vengeance that bears / Wreaked for the honour / Of forty-two hairs!"

Elisha's miracle of making "iron swim" (2 Kings 6:5-7) is alluded to by Milton in his "Animadversions," when he says that his opponent needs a better foundation for argument than the trivial one he has provided, "which you may now deplore as the axehead that fell into the water and say, 'Alas, master, for it was borrowed,'" unless you have as good a faculty to make iron swim, as you had to make light froth sink." Of all Elisha's miracles, however, his revival of the dead son of the Shunammite woman (2 Kings 4:8-37) is the most thoroughly detailed, and has produced some of the most intriguing echoes. A sermon of John Donne (eds. Potter and Simpson [1953-62], 2.300) is particularly striking:

> And as *Elisha* in raysing the *Shunamits* dead child, put his mouth upon the childs mouth, his eyes, and his hands, upon the hands, and the eyes of the child; so when my crosses have carried me up to my Saviours Crosse, I put my hands into his hands, and hang upon his nailes, I put mine eyes upon his, and wash off all my former unchast looks, and receive a soveraigne tincture, and a lively verdure, and a new life into my dead teares, from his teares. I put my mouth upon his mouth, and it is I that say, *My God, My God, why hast thou forsaken me?* and it is I that recover againe, and say, *Into thy hands, O Lord, I commend my spirit.*   ALAN JACOBS

ELKANAH *See* HANNAH.

EMMANUEL *See* IMMANUEL.

EMMAUS The precise identification of Emmaus, a village 60 furlongs (11 km.) from Jerusalem according to Luke 24:13, is disputed. The traditional site is Amwas, 32 km. northwest of Jerusalem, where remains of a basilica have been found, but a case has been made also for a Roman colony at ancient Ammaous, some 6 km. west of Jerusalem. St. Jerome thought it the village called Nicopolis in his time (*Ep.* 108.8). The lone biblical reference concerns the appearance of the risen Jesus to two travelers, one of whom is named Cleopas, within the vicinity of Jerusalem (the locus of all resurrection appearances in Luke-Acts). The travelers were joined as they walked toward Emmaus by an apparent stranger who spoke with him about recent happenings involving the prophet whom they had hoped would be the redeemer of Israel. Stories that his grave had been discovered empty were circulating, but merely tantalized their hopes. Jesus, whose identity was concealed to them, demonstrated from the Scriptures that the Messiah had to suffer and then, joining them for a meal, broke bread in such a way that "their eyes were opened, and they knew him." Realizing retrospectively how their "hearts had burned within them" during the previous conversation, the two companions rushed to Jerusalem to describe what had happened.

This account, which shares some features with that of the conversion of the Ethiopian eunuch (Acts 8) and also with those of the feeding miracles, is primarily concerned to provide evidence for the identification of Jesus as the Messiah and for the historicity of the Resurrection. At a secondary level it also suggests that in the exposition of the Scriptures and the breaking of bread the risen Lord, though unseen, still makes himself present and real to his Church.

The verse which prompts most commentary is Luke 24:32: "Did not our hearts burn within us, while he talked with us by the way, and while he opened to us the Scriptures?" St. Jerome cites this verse in a letter to Pope Damasus, saying that it is the Spirit's ministration that "warms" the heart when Scripture is opened (*Ep.* 18). In his famous letter to Eustochium on the pilgrimage of a Christian contemplative he urges the novitiate to "keep close to the footsteps of Christ, and, intent upon his words, you will come to say 'Did not our heart burn within us by the way while Jesus opened to us the Scriptures?'" (*Ep.* 22.17). St. Augustine refers to the Emmaus incident in a discussion of figurative vs. literal language in Scripture, using the phrase spoken of Jesus — "and he made as if he would have gone further" (v. 28) — showing how the gesture was not intended as deception but its opposite, prompting an invitation such as would reveal Truth himself to his companions (*Sermo,* 89.4). Others, including St. Gregory the Great, add that it is the opened word of Scripture which allows the Spirit to free the "heart grown cold and fearful in the torpor of unbelief" (cf. *Glossa Ordinaria* [PL 114.353]). The *Gloss* allegorizes the passage to say that Christ is not known to his followers except in the breaking of the bread, by which we are to understand the Eucharist; the incident thus prefigures the life of the Church (PL 114.353). The appearance of Christ to the two wayfarers is similarly seen (351) as an exemplum of the promise given by Jesus that "where two or three are gathered together in my name, there am I in the midst of them" (Matt. 18:20).

The story was popular in the later Middle Ages. Following Cistercian precedents, the pseudo-Bonaventuran *Meditations on the Life of Christ* emphasizes the "hidden communion" of Christ's lovers and the Beloved; the *consolatum* offered by Jesus is understood in terms of the Eucharist. In the 19th play of the Chester cycle Luke the Evangelist appears, following traditional conjecture, as the companion pilgrim to Cleopas. As in the York play (no. 40), in which the two travelers are simply unnamed pilgrims, the play affords a brief recapitulation of the Passion sequence. The pilgrims have been thrown into doubtful confusion, Chester's "Lucas" actually saying he had always found it hard to believe that Jesus would rise again after three days (25-28) just as Jesus approaches; in the York play, Jesus subtly indicates his knowledge of the way in which doubt has deflected the two companions' spiritual journey so that they are "walkyng þus . . . by þes wayes" (69). In Chester Jesus, attired as a pilgrim, is informed by his fellow travelers that "Bishopps" have taken their innocent Master, "damned him and nailed him on a Tree" (51). Isa. 66:13 is cited from the Vg by Jesus in his "consoling" of them and, as in York play, the three stop at a "castell" for the night. When the bread is broken, and Jesus disappears, Luke then says

> A burning hart is vs he masse;
> for whyle that he with vs here was,
> to know him we might haue no grace,
> for all his luxom lore. (133-36)

The powerful simplicity of the narrative as a whole was frequently overlooked in later commentary, emphasis being shaped according to the theological persuasions of various commentators. Calvin fastens on Luke 24:27 ("And beginning at Moses and all the prophets he expounded unto them . . .") and comments that an understanding of Christ "comes from the light of the Law and the Prophets," and that "Readers must be warned not to lend their ear to fanatics who, by suppressing the Law and the Prophets, wickedly mutilate the Gospel" (*Harmony of the Gospels*, 3.235). John Wesley makes allusion to the Emmaus journey in the account of his own conversion, "The Aldersgate Experience," in which he is a pilgrim joined on the road by Peter Bohler, leading him, his "heart strangely warmed," to a declaration of his faith at Gerrard's Cross. Charles Wesley's hymn "Talk with us, Lord, thyself reveal, / While here o'er earth we roam" sees the pilgrim's ideal walk of faith as one subtended by the Emmaus experience. The experience of "Christ-in-the-midst" of faithful worshipers, powerfully developed in Methodist tradition, is reflected in the prayer recounted in George Eliot's *Adam Bede:* "Thou art with thy people still: they see Thee in the night-watches, and their hearts burn within them as thou talkest with them by the way" (chap. 2).

Sir Walter Scott, in his *Lay of the Last Minstrel*, adapts the incident to secular purposes, asking,

> Breathes there the man, with soul so dead, . . .
> Whose heart hath n'er within him burn'd
> As home his footsteps he hath turn'd,
>   from wandring. . . . (6.1)

The fainter echo here is reminiscent in the context also of Ps. 39:3. A. H. Clough cites the story as a question for contemporary doubting believers in "Easter Day," and Butler's Althea, "as nearly a free thinker as anyone could be," calls the narrator's attention to the story, emphasizing the verse, " 'O fools and slow of heart to believe ALL that the prophets have spoken.' " Lucetta, in Hardy's *Mayor of Casterbridge*, is made to be "the third and haloed figure" when she has her uncomfortable tea with Michael Henchard and Donald Farfrae. In Margaret Avison's "To Emmaus" it is the haunting simplicity of the story which still appeals, as "the Risen One . . . simply came when asked at evening / and broke bread there, a third, with them" (*sunblue*, 53).

See also CASTLE; EUCHARIST.

Bibliography. Marshall, I. H. *The Gospel of Luke* (1978), 889-900.

DAVID L. JEFFREY
I. HOWARD MARSHALL

EMPRESS OF HELL   A traditional (medieval) title sometimes applied to the Virgin Mary.

See also MARY, MOTHER OF JESUS.

ENCLOSED GARDEN   *See HORTUS CONCLUSUS.*

ENOCH   There are two biblical Enochs. The first is the eldest son of Cain (Gen. 4:17; *ḥanok,* "initiate" or "initiation"; Gk. *Henoch*), who was father of the Henochii of later legend, the rapacious denizens of the land east of Eden. This is the Enoch who appears in Byron's *Cain*.

The second Enoch is the father of Methuselah, who himself lived to be 365 years of age (Gen. 5:23), was seventh in descent from Adam in the line of Seth (1 Chron. 1:3; Jude 14), and is said not to have died in the natural way but to have been translated: "Enoch walked with God; and he was not, for God took him" (Gen. 5:24). The Hebrew expression "walked with God" denotes a devout life; the allusion to prefallen Adam and Eve with whom God walked in the cool of the day (Gen. 3:8) points to Enoch as one who maintained something like the original communion with God planned for humankind. Hence, for the writer to the Hebrews, he is one of the great symbols for the "walk" or pilgrimage of faith (Heb. 11:5); this is the force of the allusion in the title of Mrs. Felicia Heman's poem *He Walketh with God* (ca. 1830). Enoch is typically identified by later exegetes (e.g., the *Glossa Ordinaria* [PL 114.730]) as one of the "two witnesses" of Rev. 11:3 (the other being Elijah) who are resurrected in the last days to prophesy and are then slain by the forces of the Beast, after which they rise again and ascend into heaven.

The name of the Enoch of Gen. 5 is also attached to three apocryphal apocalypses: 1 Enoch, an Ethiopian text; 2 Enoch, a Slavonic text; and a late Hebrew pseudepigrapha, 3 Enoch. These books concern the "Secrets of Enoch," which he is said to have acquired on his heavenly journey, and include astrological information as well as lore about the fallen angels and the genesis of the problem of evil. In the second book of 1 Enoch, called the "Parables or Similitudes," the Son of Man (cf. Dan. 7 and the Gospel of Mark) is characterized as a superman, a preexistent heavenly being also called "the Elect One."

Milton may have known of this book, especially its angel lore, through rabbinic commentaries, though he did not likely know the book itself firsthand. 1 Enoch was translated into English by Richard Laurence (1821) and became influential for William Blake, John Flaxman, and Thomas Moore among English authors. Blake makes use of it in his *Africa*, in which he retails the notion that the fallen angels or "watchers" landed in the Sahara (4.20), there to intermarry with "the daughters of men" and propagate the race of giants, an early stage in the fall of humankind into the world of "Generation." Blake did sketches for the published translation of *The Book of Enoch*.

The Enoch of Gen. 5 became for Christian exegetes a symbol for *dedicatio* (*Glossa Ordinaria* [PL 113.103]), and the fact that he was seventh from Adam was allegorized by St. Isidore of Seville and others as a sign of perfection in things human and temporal; hence, as for Alcuin, Enoch suggests how little death would affect us if we lived without sin, like Christ. Because of his translation, Enoch prefigures the raptured elect who are alive on the Last Day (e.g., St. Ambrose, *De excessu*, 2.94).

Tennyson's *Enoch Arden* (1864) is the tale of a fisherman who disappears at sea after seven years of happy marriage with his wife Annie. When, finally, she consults the Bible to learn his fate, letting it fall open at random, her finger rests on the line "under a palm tree" (Judg. 4:5), which she takes to mean "in heaven." She remarries; Enoch comes home, is stricken with anguish, and dies. Carlyle likens Cromwell to Enoch in *Heroes and Hero-Worship*, where his superiority to Napoleon is said to derive from "silent walking, through long years, with the Awful Unnamable of this Universe, 'walking with God' as he called it."

The association of the phrase with a deeper spiritual life, especially in pastoral vocation, is strong in 17th-cent. Puritan and Reformed writings (e.g., Richard Baxter, *Saints' Everlasting Rest*, chaps. 10–13; Matthew Poole, *Annotations*, Heb. 11:5), and leads to subsequent anticlerical satire in Hawthorne's *Scarlet Letter*, in which Chillingworth tells the ailing Rev. Dimmesdale that "saintly men, who walk with God on earth, would fain be away, to walk with him on the golden pavements of the New Jerusalem" (chap. 9). Later, when the fallen Dimmesdale longs to confess his sin, he wishes for courage to say from the pulpit: "I, in whose daily life you discern the sanctity of Enoch, — I, whose footsteps, as you suppose, leave a gleam along my earthly track . . . I, your pastor . . . am utterly a pollution and a lie!"

In G. B. Shaw's play *Back to Methuselah* Enoch is a blend of both biblical Enochs. At first he is a young intellectual who develops a theoretical pretext to justify Cain's rapacity. Although he lives long enough to begin to hear "the Voice" and so learn to repudiate Cain, Shaw suggests that modern intellectuals are seldom so long-lived. In act 2 of Shaw's play *The Gospel of the Brothers Barnabas*, Franklyn Barnabas says to a younger clergyman: "I was not shoved into the church, Mr. Haslam: I felt it to be my vocation to walk with God, like Enoch. After twenty years I realized that I was walking with my own ignorance and self-conceit." Enoch also appears in the "biblical" genealogy of Leopold Bloom in Joyce's *Ulysses*, after Moses and Noah, but his name is here twisted to "Eunuch" ("Circe" episode). In John Barth's *Giles Goat-Boy* (1966), Eros Enoch is the "Shepherd Emeritus" of the university, a parodic Christ figure.

See also GIANTS IN THE EARTH; SONS OF GOD; TWO WITNESSES.

Bibliography. Bentley, G. E., Jr. "A Jewel in an Ethiop's Ear: The Book of Enoch as Inspiration for William Blake, John Flaxman, Thomas Moore, and Richard Westall." In *Blake in His Time*. Eds. R. Essick and D. Pearce (1978), 213-15; Brown, A. "Blake's Drawings for the Book of Enoch." In *The Visionary Hand*. Ed. R. Essick (1973), 104-15; Greenfield, J. C., and M. E. Stone. "The Books of Enoch and the Traditions of Enoch." *Numen* 26 (1979), 89-103; Gregory, D. "Enoch Emery and His Biblical Namesake in [O'Connor's] *Wise Blood*." *SSF* 10 (1973), 417-19; West, R. H. *Milton and the Angels* (1955); Peters, U. *Wie der biblische Prophet Henoch zum Buddha wurde* (1989).

ENTER INTO THY CLOSET   In the Sermon on the Mount Jesus said that prayer should not be ostentatiously public: "but . . . when thou prayest, enter into thy closet, and when thou hast shut thy door, pray to thy Father which is in secret; and thy Father which seeth in secret shall reward thee openly" (Matt. 6:6). Ruskin, in his *Grown of Wild Olives*, uses the passage to argue that one may worship anywhere, at any time — there is no requirement to be in church. Emerson psychologizes the point in his "The Over-Soul": "The sources of nature are in his own mind, if the sentiment of duty is there. But if he would know what the great God speaketh, he must 'go into his closet and shut the door,' as Jesus said. God will not make himself manifest to crowds."

See also PRAYER.

ENTHUSIASM   An 18th-cent. term of opprobrium for demonstrative piety. Not a biblical term.

See also CONVERSION; FAITH; HOLY SPIRIT.

EPHESIANS   An important seaport of the Roman province of Asia, Ephesus was the nominal address of one of the most famous epistles ascribed to St. Paul. Ephesus was a commercial and banking center which boasted a great stadium, a Roman theater (Acts 19:29), and the famed Temple of Diana (Artemis) whose cult was a significant source of local income (Acts 19:24-28). The city's main street, the Arkadiane, was paved with marble. Early legends associated Ephesus with the Amazons, who were said to have built it because of its proximity to the birthplace of the earth goddess. About 1044 B.C. the Athenian King Adroclus conquered the Asians (cf. Strabo, *Geographia*, 14.1.4; 1.21).

The legendary history of Ephesus is referred to in Chaucer's *Knight's Tale*, in which Duke Theseus, "of Atthenes . . . lord and governour" (1.861), is represented as having "conquered al the regne of Femenye, / That whilom was ycleped Scithia, / and weddede the queene Ypolita." Ypolita is then described as the "hardy queene" of the Amazons (*Canterbury Tales*, 1.866-68, 875-84).

Several of Shakespeare's plays make more than incidental reference to Ephesus and to St. Paul's letter. *Pericles* reaches its culmination in the Temple of Diana at Ephesus. *The Comedy of Errors*, by changing the location of its Plautine source, Epidamnum, to Ephesus, evokes for the purposes of comic confusion the scriptural associations of the city with evil spirits, "curious arts," exorcism, and public riot, while the cult of Diana is perhaps recalled in the baptized form of the Abbess-mother (see her final speech in 5.1). The exhortations of the Epistle concerning proper domestic relationships between husbands and wives, parents and children, masters and servants (chaps. 5 and 6) are germane to the whole play; Adriana's reproach to her supposed husband specifically draws upon Eph. 5:31 ("and they two shall be one flesh"), a conception particularly appropriate to a play of twin identities lost and found.

In the two parts of *1 Henry 4*, Hal's progress from the irresponsibilities of a scapegrace youth to the assumption of kingship makes witty allusion to Ephesians in its concern with spiritual renewal. The Prince's soliloquy promising an eventual reformation concludes with a reference to Eph. 5:16: "I'll so offend to make offense a skill, / Redeeming time when men think least I will" (*1 Henry 4*, 1.2.213-14). When Hal later asks in which tavern Falstaff may be found, and in what (lewd) company, Falstaff's page replies that his master is with "Ephesians, my lord, of the old church" (*2 Henry 4*, 2.2.149), meaning "libertines" or "rascals." (Falstaff's host in dubious lodgings in *Merry Wives of Windsor* similarly refers to himself as Falstaff's "Ephesian" [4.5.16].) The Apostle's metaphoric expression for spiritual regeneration, putting off the old man and putting on the new (Eph. 4:22-24), is given dramatic actualization at the end of *2 Henry 4* when the new king in his coronation robes publicly renounces his elderly and reprobate former companion.

When Swift wishes to attack the institution of Bishop Rundle, he recalls another biblical reference to the Ephesian Christians (Acts 19:2), claiming in regard to Rundle's supporters that

> there are but four at most,
> Who know there is a Holy Ghost;
> The rest, who boast they have conferred it,
> Like Paul's Ephesians never heard it. ("On Dr. Rundle, Bishop of Derry")

See also DIANA OF THE EPHESIANS.

Bibliography. Jorgensen, P. A. *Redeeming Shakespeare's Words* (1962); Palmer, D. J. "Casting off the Old Man: History and St. Paul in *Henry IV*." *CritQ* 12 (1970), 267-83.

DAVID J. PALMER

EPHOD *See* AARON.

EPHRAIM The son of Joseph by Asenath (Gen. 41:52), Ephraim was later adopted by his grandfather Jacob (Gen. 48:5-6, 12-22). Accordingly, he was father of a tribe in Israel, in fact the dominant tribe of the northern kingdom.

See also AARON; ASENATH; JACOB; JOSEPH THE PATRIARCH; TRIBES OF ISRAEL.

EPIPHANY From the Greek word meaning "manifestation," it is the name of a feast of the Christian church originating in the East and celebrated January 6 from the 3rd cent. A.D. In the 4th cent. it was, with Easter and Pentecost, one of the three chief festivals of the Christian

year. In the West it became firmly associated with the visit of the Magi in the next century, partly on account of a series of homilies on the adoration of the Wise Men by Pope Leo I. In an English poem of the early 17th cent. closely reflecting the office for Epiphany, Sir John Beaumont ("Of the Epiphany") writes of the surpriseful manifestation to the Magi after their gifts have been presented:

> The crib becomes an altar: therefore dies
> No ox nor sheep; for in their fodder lies
> The Prince of Peace, who, thankful for his bed,
> Destroys those rites in which their blood was shed.

See also MAGI.

EPITHALAMIUM *See* BRIDE, BRIDEGROOM; SONG OF SONGS.

ESAU The narrative concerning Esau (Gen. 25–28) is inseparable from that of his twin brother Jacob and the story of the lost birthright. The salient features of Esau's characterization for later literary development are that he was a hunter (25:27), was red and hirsute (27:11), and sold his birthright as eldest son to his twin for a mess of red pottage (25:30). He was thus named Edom (red), and he became father of the Edomites (cf. Gen. 36:1).

In the extensive talmudic lore about Esau he is said to be a hunter of people as well as beasts, and the murderer of Nimrod (Yashar Toledot 51b-52a) among others. One of the means by which Isaac suspected that a disguised Jacob and not Esau had come to him for his blessing was that Jacob inadvertently mentioned the name of God, something Esau would not have done (Tan. Ber. 1.131; Gen. Rab. 65.18). Esau is said, for his sins, to have "no share in the world to come"; his blessing is rather the "goods of this world" (Meg. 6a; Pirqe R. El. 39; Midr. Tehillim 10.39). A legend that Esau had unusually long teeth seems to be an adaptation of the Og story (Ber. 54b), and symbolically reinforces another legend that Esau disguised the evidence of his circumcision by an operation (Tan. Ber. 1.158; 127; Pirqe R. El. 29; Sanh. 44a). His descendants are said to be nomadic desert peoples who refuse the Torah because they wish to live by the sword, and therefore cannot accept the sixth commandment, "Thou shalt not kill" (Tg. Yer. Gen. 30:8). The Gentiles, particularly Christians, are held to be the descendants of Esau, having received "dominion over the things of this world" (Midr. ha Ne'elam 36d; Hasidim 341), and a late work, *Shibhe Israel*, says that when the Messiah comes he will go with the "sons of Moses" to Mt. Seir to judge the sons of Esau (218) for their choices.

For patristic writers like St. Augustine, Esau is memorable principally for having foolishly bartered away his birthright (e.g., *Contra mendacium*, 24; *De civ. Dei* 16.37) and is regarded as a type of the proud and carnal man (*Enarr. in Ps.* 47.4-5) who, although "firstborn," gives way to the "last," just as in divine election "the last shall be first." Descendants of Esau, "the children of Edom," are said to be bent on "the lust of the flesh," and to war against the spiritual good of Jerusalem (*Enarr. in Ps.* 137.10). The words of St. Paul, "Jacob have I loved, but Esau have I hated" (Rom. 9:13), receive a great deal of commentary in this connection, since election and reprobation are here linked to the Genesis narrative. Esau is for Augustine in every sense a radical foil to Jacob (*De civ. Dei* 5.4), all the more appropriately an illustration of what God has rejected in those he did not choose (*De praedestinatione sanctorum*, 3). This leads to a reversal of talmudic associations: in the *Glossa Ordinaria* Esau is still a representative of "those who do not believe," but a figure also for the *"populum Synagogae"* as Jacob is for the *"populus Ecclesiae"* (PL 113.146). This point is developed in prophetic contexts with reference to Edom, the land of Esau's descendants. In Isa. 34 and 35 the prophet describes the pouring forth of God's wrath upon Idumea (Edom), and the restoration of Zion to come. Edom here, as in Isa. 63:1-3, is symbolic of all the foes of Israel, or, as the story is typologized by Christian commentators such as Matthew Henry (*Exposition of the Old and New Testaments*, 4.135) and Matthew Poole (*Annotations upon the Holy Bible*, 2.477), all enemies of the true Church, even Antichrist. The ancient feud between Jacob and Esau thus has its prophetic analogue in the "last days," and traditional readings of Isa. 34 and 35 see the passage as figuring the crushing of reprobate Edom and glorification of the chosen Israel.

Swedenborg, however, interpreted Isaac's blessing of Esau as the restoration of the birthright Jacob had stolen from him and saw the "dominion of Edom" as the "New Heaven." William Blake seized upon this reading to reverse the prophets' anathema upon Edom (cf. Obad. 10-14; Ezek. 25:12-14; 35:1-15; Amos 1:11-12; Joel 3:19) and with it the mythologization of OT history around the Jacob-Esau story. In his *The Marriage of Heaven and Hell* (pl. 3; pls. 5-6), he presents an infernal reading of Isa. 34–35, according to which the hosts of heaven fall upon Edom not to punish but to revitalize it; Edom is not cast out, but rather her enemy, as the roles of damned and chosen are inverted. This interpretation of Edom is expanded in *America*, where Orc is identified with Esau or Edom (as also in *The Song of Liberty*), a red and hairy rebel from France who inspires the American Revolution.

Esau has otherwise been much overshadowed in literature by his brother, the relative richness of theological reflection and symbol notwithstanding. Milton, in "Eikonoklastes," allows him to be a figure for the Presbyterians (Jacob stands for the independent Puritans); Melville refers to the rarity of twin births in whales with an allusion to the story in *Moby-Dick.* A more favorable reference comes in a letter to John Hamilton Reynolds by Keats, who wonders why modern poets should be so limited as Wordsworth and Hunt "when we can wander

with Esau." "Wandering about in the East" is made by Galsworthy to reflect "the curse of Esau" (*Flowering Wilderness,* chap. 1), however, and in *The Way of all Flesh* Butler writes that Ernest's marriage to Ellen, his mother's maid, was worse than his "marriage" to the Church: "He was an Esau — one of those wretches whose hearts the Lord has hardened." In Rudy Wiebe's chapter "Sons and Heirs" in *The Blue Mountains of China* Escha is a redhaired Russian serf whom his putative Mennonite half-brother Jacob kills after a drunken sexual initiation in the ruins of Jacob's Gnadenfeld *hof.*

Ironically empathetic is A. M. Klein, who, in a reflection on the persecution of the Jews in his "Childe Harold's Pilgrimage," parodies a sympathy of Byron's when he makes "Esau, my kinsman" a man who would "devise a different answer for the foe; / And let the argumentative bullet dent / The heart of the tyrant, let the steel blade show" — an option not so morally available to the son of Jacob who receives the Torah: "Alas for me that in my ears there sounds / Always the sixth thunder of Sinai."

See also BIRTHRIGHT; JACOB.

ESCHATOLOGY Eschatology concerns those beliefs which have to do with the end of time. The word derives from Gk. *eschatos,* the last or furthest thing, as used, e.g., in 1 Cor. 15:26, 52, where St. Paul speaks about the resurrection at the last day. In the 19th cent. the term came into doctrinal use for belief in both the afterlife and the final resurrection. Now it applies to biblical materials touching on the end times and, more loosely, to religious or secular end-of-world thinking and expression.

OT eschatology conforms to the covenantal pattern in which God's relationship to Israel is framed as blessings and curses, threats and rewards. The earliest kind of prophetic eschatology (e.g., Amos 5:18ff., 9:1-15) turns the anticipation of a Day of the Lord judgment upon Israel's enemies reflexively upon Israel itself, yet couples doom with the promise of renewal. In the Intertestamental period eschatological thought flourished so that by the time of Jesus end-of-world thinking animated many groups such as the Qumran community (G. Vermes, "Dead Sea Scrolls," *IDBSup* [1976], 8, 9). After the Easter events of the Gospels, early Christians expected the imminent return of Jesus Christ to judge the world, destroy the wicked, and resurrect and glorify the saints. Then, as elaborated in the Revelation to St. John of Patmos, all things would be made new in an eternal beatitude wherein earth would be indistinguishable from heaven.

Through Christianity this eschatological expectation of renewal out of destruction passed into world consciousness. Yet when the anticipated Second Advent of Jesus did not come in the first several generations after the Ascension, Christianity itself to some degree spiritualized eschatology, turning it inward as an immediate experience of renewal in those who believe in Christ. Such "realized" eschatology has been typically the interpretation of the established Church. A characteristic expression of it can be seen in John Donne's Holy Sonnets, nos. 7, 10, and 13 (1609-17), those beginning respectively with the lines, "At the round earth's imagined corners blow," "Death be not proud, though some have called thee," and "What if this present were the world's last night?" Realized eschatology typically includes as well the assurances of the world's end (howsoever deferred), of an afterlife of rewards and punishments, and of the ultimate resurrection of the dead. The expression of these assurances, particularly as they are elicited by thoughts of death or the transitoriness of life, are among the most common forms of Christian writing, as in the conclusions to Edmund Spenser's "Mutabilitie Cantos" appended to *The Faerie Queene* (1596), to John Milton's "Lycidas" (1637), and to Alfred Lord Tennyson's *In Memoriam* (1850).

Yet temporal eschatological expectations remained endemic within Christianity, often reviving in times of great dislocation. Historically the Church has always had to contain within bounds what Norman Cohn has called "the central fantasy of revolutionary eschatology" (*The Pursuit of the Millennium* [1957], 4), wherein the saints militant saw the world dominated by an oppressive demonic power shortly to be destroyed by the coming of Jesus Christ to avenge them and renew creation. The Protestant Reformation both encouraged such views and tried to restrain them, as rebellious reformers became in turn the guardians of established churches and settled order (T. F. Torrance, "The Eschatology of the Reformation," in *Eschatology, SJT* Occasional Papers, no. 2 [1952]). No important English writer expresses with such eschatological exuberance his faith in the imminent coming of Jesus Christ to transform creation as does Milton in his *Of Reformation* (1641). At the outset of the Puritan Revolution he threw himself into its polemical war against Antichrist. As the Revolution became a reality he came to suspect and ultimately deny the validity of such expectations (M. Fixler, *Milton and the Kingdoms of God* [1964]).

With the transvaluation of religious thought after the Enlightenment eschatology entered into the ferment of revolutionary Romanticism. But anyone then moved by such excitement had to create, as it were, a new system to contain his ideas of catastrophic change and renewal, as William Blake did in his prophetic writings, particularly in *The French Revolution* (1791) and in *America, A Prophecy* (1793). William Wordsworth, who had been touched with a kind of eschatological expectation at the outset of the French Revolution, transmuted his hope into a Romantic form of "realized" eschatology by spiritualizing his sense of the possibilities of human self-renewal in a Nature perpetually renewing itself (*The Prelude, Book Sixth* [1850], 624-40). But by the end of the 19th cent. there emerged in France and elsewhere a curious cultural identification of the "fin de siècle" with a "fin du monde" (M. Nordau, *Degeneration* [1895]). It was in the context of such ideas that William Butler Yeats, who called himself one of

the last Romantics, wrote his eschatological Rosicrucian stories of 1897, "The Tables of the Law" and "The Visit of the Magi," the second of which touched on the theme he later developed in his poem "The Second Coming" (1921), an ambiguous vision of an imminent demonic apocalypse destroying one age and ushering in a new one.

After World War II explicit eschatological thinking seems to have focused on the implications of The Bomb, which, coupled with ecological anxieties, seems capable of producing an unending flow of popular doomsday writings. Additionally, the creation of Israel and related events in the Middle East have prompted a renewal of popular interest in biblical prophecy concerning the end times. Hal Lindsey's *Late Great Planet Earth*, an American best-seller, is only one of hundreds of speculative tracts produced in the last several decades. But more subtle and pervasive in serious literature has been what Frank Kermode has described (in *The Sense of an Ending* [1967]) as the eschatology of modernism, reflected in the writings of Ezra Pound, T. S. Eliot, D. H. Lawrence, and others as a rigid preoccupation with destroying what is decadent by means of an art whose moral, or even political, powers of renewal extend into culture. There is a tendency to parody modernist eschatological thinking in such writers as Thomas Pynchon (*V* [1961], *Gravity's Rainbow* [1972]) and Samuel Beckett (*Endgame* [1957]), where an evident winding down of the world disjoins renewal from the old eschatological pattern, leaving only a movement from decadence to an ending resolutely devoid of meaning.

See also APOCALYPSE; ARMAGEDDON; REVELATION; SECOND COMING.

Bibliography. Bloom, H. *The Visionary Company* (1971); Davies, W. D., and D. Daube, eds. *The Background of the New Testament and Its Eschatology* (1956); Hanson, P. D. *The Dawn of Apocalyptic* (1975); Mannheim, K. *Ideology and Utopia.* Trans. L. Wirth and E. Shils (1936); Plöger, O. *Theocracy and Eschatology.* Trans. S. Rudman (1968).

MICHAEL FIXLER

ESDRAS In the Vg, as in the older Latin version of the Bible used by St. Ambrose, there are four books of Esdras. The first and second of these alone were finally accorded canonical status, and correspond to KJV Ezra and Nehemiah. Esdr. 3 and 4 came to be regarded as apocryphal, but are still quoted as canonical by St. Ambrose, St. Augustine, and the Third Council of Carthage.

ESTHER The heroine of the book of Esther recalls, even in her name, the plight of Jews in exile. First named Hadassah (Heb. for "myrtle"), she later took the Persian name Esther (from "star" or possibly from the goddess Ishtar). An orphan or foundling Jewess raised by her cousin Mordecai, she was chosen to succeed Vashti as consort to King Ahasuerus. As queen she prevailed on Ahasuerus to save her people from the treacherous designs of Haman, a prominent court official.

The historicity of the book of Esther is problematic. Its composition followed Persian hegemony and is probably to be placed during the 2nd cent. B.C. Numerous additions to the core narrative are found in the LXX, Targum, Talmud, Midrash, and Josephus. While Queen Esther does not match any known Persian consort, King Ahasuerus has been tentatively identified with Xerxes I (486- 485 B.C.), partly on account of there being a notable courtier, Marduka (Mordecai?), in Xerxes's court. Esther is a late addition to the canon, unnoted in Sirach, the NT, and the Qumran scrolls or the Pirqe 'Abot (ca. 180 B.C.). In the Midrash, however, it is called Megillah, "the Scroll," chief among the Megilloth of five scrolls appropriated to chief festivals (Ruth, Song of Songs, Ecclesiastes, Lamentations, and Esther), Esther being read at Purim. Maimonides valued the book next after the Pentateuch, signaling its growing importance in medieval Jewish community life.

The story is mainly didactic and etiological, accounting for the Festival of Purim (Esth. 9:20-32), which celebrates the ultimate failure and demise of Haman the Agagite, Ahasuerus's favorite, who conspired to eliminate the Jewish exiles. When Haman sent instructions throughout the kingdom "to destroy, to kill, and to cause to perish, all Jews, both young and old, little children and women, in one day . . . and to take the spoil of them for a prey," Esther courageously broached court decorum to appeal for her people before the king. Haman was hanged on the gallows he had erected for Mordecai, and Mordecai was elevated to prominence in the court, whereby the Jews gained continuing advocacy for their cause.

Esther's fabled loyalty and courage are not depicted as being especially religious; there is no mention of God in the account, and the concluding theme of vengeance is handled in a way which has raised doubts among canonists from the rabbis at Jamnia (ca. A.D. 80) to Martin Luther. Greek apocryphal additions to Esther spiritualize the narrative by introducing divine agency and prophecy through dream interpretation. Copious midrashic commentary subsequently synthesizes the secular and religious aspects of Esther's history: her concern for her endangered people exemplified the Jews' relationship with God, while Haman's perfidy not only tested divine providence but foreshadowed Seleucid and Roman oppression (Pesaḥ. 117a; Yoma 29a; Meg. 6b-7a, 10b-11a, 12a n.1, 13a-b, 15a-b, 16a-b, 19a; Yebam. 24b; Sanh. 74b, 93a). Esther entered Jewish legend as a figure of female virtue, piety, resolve, and national resistance, akin to Deborah, Judith, and Hannah; occasionally she is also regarded as a prophetess. Talmudists and midrashic commentators also stress her extraordinary beauty, making her one of the four most beautiful women in the world (along with Rahab, Sarah, and Abigail).

The Fathers of the Christian Church and later commentators built upon this Jewish legendary foundation. St. Ambrose regards Esther as an exemplar of virtuous and courageous action in the face of danger (*De officis ministrorum*, 3.21.123). St. Jerome (*Ep.* 53.8) regards her as a type of the Church defending the faithful against iniquity and persecution (typified by Haman). She is seen also to prefigure the Virgin Mary, similar to her in chaste beauty and in intercessional efficacy.

Numerous medieval lyrics make the connection between Esther and the Virgin:

> þou ert hester, þat swete þynge,
> And asseuer þe ryche kynge
> þe heþ ychose to hys weddynge
>   And quene he heþ a-uonge;
> For mardocheus, þy derlynge,
>   Syre aman was y-honge.
> (C. Brown, *Religious Lyrics of the XIVth Century,* no. 32)

Franciscan lyricists typically were indebted in such typology to St. Anthony's famous treatise *In Annuntiatione Sanctae Mariae* (3.836b); in another medieval lyric Esther becomes *mater misericordi* (R. Greene, ed., *The Early English Carols* [1977], no. 210; cf. no. 194).

Geoffrey Chaucer refers to Esther *ad sensus literalis* four times: predictably, in *The Book of the Duchess* and *Legend of Good Women* she is a model of womanly and saintly virtue. Prudence advances her as an example of woman's good counsel in *The Tale of Melibee*. And in *The Merchant's Tale* the beautiful, loyal Esther of medieval legend is contrasted with January's treacherous bride. In a rare application of the Esther story as political parody, the anonymous *New Enterlude of Godly Queene Hester* (1560/61) coyly invites the audience to identify Ahasuerus with King Henry VIII, Haman with Cardinal Wolsey, and Esther with Catherine Parr, emphasizing the conspiratorial features of the narrative (cf. the contemporary 16th-cent. play *Queen Esther and Proud Haman*). Racine, in 1689, composed a dramatic versification of Esther for the Sisters of St. Cyr to read or chant, finding Esther an ideal subject for such a community, because the heroine exemplifies *"de détachement du monde au milieu du monde même"* (pref.).

Post-Reformation references to Esther, such as Milton's in *Reason of Church Government* (3.1.188) or Gray's in his "Extempore on Dr. Keene, Bishop of Chester," conventionally allude either to Esther's extraordinary beauty or to her virtue, themes which persist in the few Joycean references to her (e.g., *Finnegans Wake*). An exception to the pattern of casual allusion is Browning's reversion in *The Ring and the Book* to the climactic moment of the biblical narrative. Browning cites the Queen's defiance of royal courtly protocol, at risk of her own life, in order to treat it ironically in terms of masculine dreams of power over women. The relationship between the orphaned Esther Summerson of Dickens's *Bleak House* and her guardian-wooer John Jarndyce, is suggestive of the somewhat mysterious connection between the biblical Esther and Mordecai. Esther's memory is romanticized by a variety of 19th-cent. authors (e.g., Tennyson's "The Princess"; cf. also Melville's "The Bell Tower") as well as in a modern and more cynical vein by the poet A. M. Klein in "Five Characters." Klein's Esther, like a "new star's sudden naissance," walks moonlit in the palace garden, her pardon the sequestered token of her gratifying the "Persian-hot passion" of Ahasuerus.

See also HAMAN; MORDECAI; VASHTI.

Bibliography. Berg, S. B. *The Book of Esther* (1979); "Esther." *EncJud* (1903), 5.232-41; Harty, K. J. "The Reputation of Queen Esther in the Middle Ages: The Merchant's Tale, IV [E]. 1742-45." *BSUF* 19 (1978), 65-68; Harvey, D., and E. W. Saunders. "Esther, Book of," "Esther (Apocryphal)." *IDB* 2.149-52; Sassoon, J. M. "Esther." In *The Literary Guide to the Bible.* Ed. R. Alter and F. Kermode (1987), 335-42; Shaked, S. "Iranian Influence on Judaism." In *The Cambridge History of Judaism* (1984), 1.308-25.   MARK S. MADOFF

ETERNITY   The word *eternity* appears only once in the KJV (Isa. 57:15). The concept, for which there is no word in biblical Hebrew or Greek, derives from formulas translated "everlasting" (e.g., Gen. 17:8; Isa. 40:28), "for ever" (e.g., Ps. 110:4; John 6:51), or "eternal life" (e.g., Matt. 19:16; John 4:14). Such terms in the OT indicate (usually as an attribute of God) infinite duration (Gen. 21:33; Deut. 5:23; Jer. 10:10) or existence unbounded by time (Ps. 89:2; Isa. 40:28). In the NT the same terms are extended to Christ (Heb. 13:8; Rev. 5:14). Both the NT and rabbinic Judaism speak of the destiny of the righteous in terms of "everlasting" life or life in the "age to come."

The terms *eternal* and *eternity* are sometimes used hyperbolically in English literature, but the traditions of biblical understanding of the concept also persist. The idea of infinite extension is often rhetorically contrasted with finite time, as in Bede's story comparing life to a sparrow's flight through a hall (*Hist. Eccl.* 2.13). This is a common theme in the writings of Calvin, and the idea sharpens the despair of Marlowe's Faustus when he realizes that he has traded eternal joy for the vain pleasures of twenty-four years (*Doctor Faustus*, 1860). This kind of eternity attracts the concern of Milton's fallen Adam (*Paradise Lost*, 12.556) and of Marvell's impatient lover dreading "Desarts of vast Eternity" ("To his Coy Mistress"). It is partly secularized in the Renaissance under Horace's influence (*Odes*, 3.30.1, 6) to describe the survival of one's name in the world through fame or progeny (e.g., Spenser, *Amoretti*, 69.9-10), a notion Milton seeks to reconcile with an otherworldly eternity in "Lycidas" (76-84). More modern romantic associations of eternity with the moral survival of the ego, influenced by Kant (see B. Lytton, "Posthumous Reputation," in *Caxtoniana* [1863]), are graphically denounced in William Golding's *Pincher Martin,* which presents both the physical and spiritual death of a grasping egotist.

Another tradition, associated with a variety of early Christian commentators, involves an adaptation of Plato's doctrine of time as the moving image of an eternity in which there is neither past nor future (*Timaeus,* 37d.e). This eternal present, beyond time and change, is ascribed to God by Philo (*Quod Deus immutabilis sit*, 32), by St. Augustine (*De civ. Dei* 11.6), and by Boethius (*De Trinitate*, 4). Such a view reinforces the climax of Spenser's "Mutabilitie Cantos," resting all upon "the pillars of Eternity / That is contrayr to Mutabilitie" (*Faerie Queene*, 7.8.2). For Augustine (*De Trin.* 15.26) God's eternal present, transcending temporal sequence, resolves the paradox of coeternal Father and Son — a view which may have influenced Milton's "Hail holy light, offspring of Heav'n, firstborn, / Or of th'Eternal Coeternal beam" (*PL* 3.1-2). The light of God's eternity may be apprehended in this life, Augustine argues, in visionary release from the "tumult of the flesh" (*Conf.* 9.10.2, 3, 25). Such mystical awareness is represented by Vaughan's glimpse of eternity as a "ring of pure and endless light" ("The World"). Eternity as light or ring (a common 17th-cent. emblem; see R. Freeman, *English Emblem Books* [1948], 75, 96, 210) contrasts with more pedestrian linear notions of eternity as extension, a distinction Milton exploits in *Paradise Lost* by attributing the former to God (3.5) and the latter to Satan (2.148, 247-48). Donne wittily plays off the conventional Platonic eternity of love against a linear eternity of duration in "The Legacy." Melville sharpens metaphysical unease into tension between the two eternities, particularly in *Mardi* (the first notion being expressed in chaps. 2 and 78, the second in chaps. 71, 81, and 91). The Romantics were attracted by the idea — easily secularized — of eternity as transcendent mystery, apprehended as moral intuition in Wordsworth (*Prelude,* 3.122; 6.639) and as a Platonic rationale of art and beauty in Shelley (*Adonaïs,* 52.4; "Hymn to Intellectual Beauty," st. 2) and Keats ("Ode on a Grecian Urn," st. 5), culminating in Yeats's "artifice of eternity" in "Sailing to Byzantium" (st. 3).

The emphasis on eternal life as independence from time, reformulated for the Victorians in F. D. Maurice's controversial *Theological Essays,* is dramatized in the dream sequence of Thomas Hughes's *Tom Brown's Schooldays* and in Charles Kingsley's *The Water-Babies* and is presented in nonreligious form in D. H. Lawrence's celebration of sexual fulfillment in *The Rainbow* (chap. 6). T. S. Eliot in the *Four Quartets* ("Little Gidding") provides the most famous modern evocation of the notion of all time being "eternally present."

See also ALPHA AND OMEGA.

Bibliography. Baillie, J. *And the Life Everlasting* (1933); Hügel, F. von. *Eternal Life,* 2nd ed. (1913); Patrides, C. A. *The Grand Design of God: The Literary Form of the Christian View of History* (1972).   BRENDA E. RICHARDSON
                                          NORMAN VANCE

EUCHARIST   The apostle Paul gives the earliest written citation of the tradition of the last meal held by Jesus with his disciples before his betrayal and death (1 Cor. 11:23-26), and all four Gospels describe the event. While a Passover meal is indicated in the Synoptics, John places the meal before the official Passover and replaces the account of the significant eucharistic features of the meal with the story of how Jesus washed the disciples' feet after it; the differences may be due to the use of different calendars and a desire to place the eucharistic teaching of Jesus in a broader context (John 6:51-58). Within the context of the Passover meal Jesus gave new significance to the bread and cup as symbols of his body and blood. Drawing on language from Exod. 24, Isa. 53, and Jer. 33, he spoke of giving himself in sacrifice on behalf of all people in order to inaugurate the New Covenant through which sins are forgiven. The token meal was to be celebrated as a foretaste of the messianic banquet. In obedience to the Lord's intention the early Church adopted the pattern of the meal for its own regular "Lord's Supper" at which it proclaimed the Lord's death, enjoyed fellowship with him, and looked forward to his future coming.

The accounts of the meal, although clearly based on actual reports of the event, are liturgically shaped in that they present those features of the Supper which became significant for the pattern of the Church's meal. The precise wording of the accounts differs, suggesting two lines of transmission (Lucan/Pauline and Marcan). The Passover setting emphasized in St. Mark's narrative provides the atmosphere for the meal with its remembrance of God's act of redemption under the Old Covenant and its eager anticipation of his future, final act of redemption. The disciples, reflecting anew on the significance for their people of the exodus from Egypt, would have interpreted Jesus' words "This do in remembrance of me" in light of the Passover, and recalled how he had previously spoken of the "exodus" which he, as one "greater than Moses," would accomplish for all humankind through his death.

The meal table expresses the motifs of table fellowship with Jesus (seen in the post-Resurrection context in the Emmaus story) and also of spiritual nourishment for those who partake of the elements. Notably, it is the cup rather than the wine which is specifically mentioned; attention should be directed to OT cup imagery rather than simply to vine and wine imagery (e.g., Pss. 16:5; 23:5; 116:13; cf. Jer. 16:7). Above all, the contrast between the Old and New Covenants is decisive for interpreting the Supper. The narratives show an increasing interest (from Mark via Luke to John) in the teaching given by Jesus at the meal, suggesting the principle that Word and Sacrament belong together. Finally, the Supper demonstrates how Jesus turned the fate which he suffered as a result of opposition to his message of the kingdom of God into the means of reconciliation and salvation for others through his vicarious, sacrificial death, and how he called his disciples, who shared in the Supper, to be ready to tread the same path of suffering and service.

The Greek term *eucharistia,* which appeared in the 1st cent. in connection with the Lord's Supper, and which has predominated since, derives from the word for "gratefulness," reflecting the thanksgiving of Jesus at the Last Supper (Matt. 26:27; Mark 14:23; Luke 22:19; 1 Cor. 11:24) and signifying not only an attitude of thankfulness but also its outward evidence. The concept traces to the Hebrew equivalent of "blessing" the Lord, a form of praise which, as in the Psalms, specifically recounts God's generosity and mercy. It is the action of thanksgiving which actualizes, in this sense, God's gift of grace, allowing it to be real and present to the recipient.

For the early Church the Eucharist was the central point of life and worship. St. Justin Martyr, St. Ignatius, and St. Irenaeus likened it to the feeding of the five thousand (John 6). Artistic representations of the Eucharist in early 2nd-cent. catacomb art show a basket of bread containing a cup of wine resting upon a fish (W. Lowrie, *Art in the Early Church* [1947], pl. 13b, c, 15). For Ignatius it was "the elixir of immortality, the antidote that we should not die but live in Christ Jesus forever" (*Eph.* 20:2); for Justin, "The food which is blessed by the prayer of his Word, and by which our blood and flesh by transmutation are nourished . . . the flesh and blood of that Jesus which was made flesh" (*Apol.* 1.66-67; cf. St. Augustine, *Sermo,* 57.7, "On the Lord's Prayer"). Such language, when reported to hostile Roman authorities, was enough to arouse the convenient charge of cannibalism (e.g., Pliny the Younger).

It was customary in the life of the early Church to recite or sing the prologue to John's Gospel (1:1-14) as the last element in the service; i.e., the transmutation was understood in a spiritual sense, such as later is reflected in Augustine's phrase, "Believe and thou hast eaten" (cf. Hugh of St. Victor, *De Sacramentis*, 2.8.5); for Augustine the incarnational union of Christ with human flesh continues in every generation as the Church continues to celebrate the Eucharist (*Sermo,* 131, sup. John 6:53; cf. *Sermo,* 112.4-5). The vigor of this idea can still be felt (ca. 1100) in St. Anselm of Canterbury's eucharistic hymn "To Our Lord in the Sacrament," which begins, "Hail! Christ's pure body — born of the Holy Virgin — / Living flesh, and true Man, and perfect Godhead!"

From the 3rd cent., careful attention was paid to Christ's words in the institution. Accordingly, Tertullian and St. Cyprian identify the bread and wine with the body and blood of Christ, Cyprian developing the idea of the Eucharist as a sacrifice. Tertullian, however, also calls the bread a *figura* of the body, and Origen elaborates an extensive allegory of the Lord's Supper. St. Ambrose (*De mysteriis,* 9.50-55), along with Fathers of the Greek church such as St. John Chrysostom and St. Cyril of Jerusalem, alludes to a transformation of the elements themselves on an analogy with the transformation of water into wine at the marriage feast in Cana and the transformation of Moses' rod into a serpent (Exod. 4). These ideas are foundational to the doctrine of transubstantiation, although the doctrine was not fully developed until the 12th cent. nor systematically defined until the analysis of St. Thomas Aquinas in the 13th cent. and the declaration of the doctrine in the decrees of the Fourth Lateran Council (1215). Much of the difficulty and controversy surrounding the doctrine may relate, ironically, to semantic difficulties: *substantia* meant "spiritual" substance to writers of the 12th cent. — i.e., they understood it in the sense in which it is used in the Creed, where Christ is said to be "one substance with the Father" before his Incarnation; from the 16th cent., popular usage began to apply the term largely to material substance (our modern usage), which character it bears almost exclusively from the empiricists (e.g., John Locke) forward.

The oldest Christian communities celebrated the sacrament much as Jesus had — in connection with a meal of friends and in the order which Jesus himself observed: breaking of bread, meal proper, cup "after the meal" (Luke 22:20; 1 Cor. 11:25). By the 2nd cent. (Did. 10:1; Justin Martyr, *Apol.* 1.67) the "elements" had been combined at the end of the meal; they were then moved to the conclusion of the morning liturgy of the Word, the pattern which has survived. At first the Eucharist was celebrated on Sunday (Acts 20:7; Did. 14:1; Justin, *Apol.* 1.67); by the 4th cent. it was observed also on Wednesday and Friday, and from that period on, daily. Participants brought the bread and wine, and offered them up as gifts at the altar in thanksgiving to God (this was the original "offertory"; only later was money brought as "offering" to the altar).

The emphasis on offering and thanksgiving dictates the first words of the early liturgy, of which the text of St. Hippolytus serves as example: the "bishop" or presiding elder lifted up his hands over the gifts of bread and wine on the altar and said, "The Lord be with you." The people answered, "And with thy spirit." "Lift up your hearts," the bishop then enjoined the people. "We lift them up unto the Lord." Then, "Let us give thanks to our Lord," to which the people responded, "It is meet and right so to do." The bishop then began his prayer of thanksgiving, "We give thee thanks, O God, through thy beloved servant Jesus Christ, whom thou didst send to us in these last days to be our deliverance and our Redeemer and to make known thy counsel. He is thy inseparable Word . . ." (trans. Jungman). Thus, the relationship between an offering of the gifts and of the self to God in thanksgiving *(eucharistia)* for his gift is made explicit at the beginning of this part of the service.

Also rendered explicit is the inseparability of Jesus from his Word, or Christ from the Scriptures. With the "Lord's Prayer" or Paternoster as preparatory transition, the eucharistic meal follows immediately after readings and exposition of passages from the Bible. Whereas in the synagogue, on which the pattern of readings is based, the lections come from the Law and the Prophets, in the Church they are from the Law and Prophets, Gospels, and Epistles. At first the ancient Church read the books of the Bible more or less sequentially, but later individual texts began to be appropriated to various feasts or seasons of the Christian year; in Lent the books of Moses; in Holy Week, Job; from Easter to Pentecost, the Acts of the Apostles; in Advent, the Prophets; and a distribution of the Gospels throughout the year in such a way that a portion was read at every Eucharist, preceded by at least one other part of the Bible, usually typologically or thematically related to the Gospel passage on which the sermon would be based. This organization of the Scripture readings so as to bear relevantly upon feasts and seasons also reflects the custom of the synagogue.

Besides "the Lord's Supper" (1 Cor. 11:20) and "the breaking of bread" (Acts 2:42, 46; 20:7), and, after the 1st cent., "Eucharist," the words *sacrificium* (Augustine, Cyprian) and *oblatio* (Ambrose) were used to designate the liturgy. Later, still other terms, *collecta* ("collect" or "assembly"), *processio* (for the "gathering" of the people), *officium* ("office" or divine service), and *dominicum* ("the Lord's" celebration), are used. The term *Mass,* which probably derives from *missa* (cf. *missio / dismissio*), seems to be shorthand for the blessing and "sending out" into the world at the conclusion of the liturgy (Hugh of St. Victor, *De Sacramentis,* 2.8.14). This term, related in popular usage to the rather abrupt medieval dismissal after Mass, *Ite missa est* ("Go, you are dismissed"), came into general currency in the 5th cent. and has persisted in the Roman rite ever since.

In the early Church the Eucharist was the focus of fellowship and community, as well as of worship. The Eucharist was above all corporate worship, an expression of unity in Christ of all local members of his body, in which the very meaning of community coinhered in the notion of communion with Christ. The offering, as the old Celtic church called it (cf. mod. Irish "aifreann"), was thus of one's heart: an anonymous communion hymn of the ancient Irish church reads:

> May the sweet name of Jesus
> Be lovingly graven
> On my heart's inmost haven.
> O Mary, sweet mother,
> Be Jesus my brother,
> And I Jesus' lover.
> A binding of love
> That no distance can sever
> Be between us forever;
> Yea, O my Saviour, for ever and ever. (ca. A.D. 650)

Precisely the same spirit characterizes St. Bernard of Clairvaux's *Jesu, Dulcedo Cordium,* "Jesu, thou Joy of loving hearts" (trans. R. Palmer [1858]).

Early forms of the liturgy all stressed participation: the various chants of the Mass — the *Kyrie, Gloria, Credo, Sanctus,* and *Agnus Dei* — were sung by the congregation. Later they were allotted to the clergy and choirs. In the 12th cent. the practice of giving the cup to the laity was discontinued, out of concern that consecrated wine might be spilled. These developments, the retention of Latin long after the development of vernacular languages had put the old Roman language beyond most parishioners' comprehension, the adoption of regal ceremonial presentation arising from the stronger ties of the Church to political power, and the development (after the 6th cent.) of the "private Mass" in which only the priest was present, all tended to have the effect by the late Middle Ages of significantly reducing participation (Jungman, 467).

One effect of such changes was drastically reduced attendance. The Fourth Lateran Council issued injunctions to try to reverse the trend, and in England Franciscan Archbishop John Pecham in his Lambeth Constitutions (1273) urged intensified catechesis, vernacular instruction, and regular preaching for the same reasons. This attempt by the English Church to reinvigorate liturgical life may well be responsible for a large number of extant ME lyrics, a number of them by Franciscans such as William Herebert and John Grimestone in the 14th cent. and James Ryman in the 15th. Particularly striking examples of lyrics on the Eucharist include Grimestone's "Gold and al þis werdis wyn" (C. Brown, *Religious Lyrics of the XIVth Century,* no. 71) and Ryman's more pedestrian and frankly catechetical "Ete ye this brede," in which the "brede fro hevene" is said to be baked in the oven-womb of the Virgin Mary:

> In virgyne Mary this brede was bake,
> Whenne Criste of her manhoode did take
> Fre of all synne mankeynde to make:
> Ete it so, ye be not dede. (Jeffrey, *Early English Lyric,* 237-38)

The image comes from the pseudo-Bonaventuran *Meditations on the Life of Christ,* a popular treatise which emphasized the importance to effective communion in the sacrament of a deep emotional response to Christ's atoning Passion — an idea theologically formulated by Franciscan theologian Alexander of Hales, who said, "For as much as is experienced from the love of the Passion, so much the greater becomes the union through love of the members of the mystical body to the Head" (*Glossa,* 4.8.132). The large number of 13th- to 15th-cent. vernacular meditations on the Passion, both lyric and prose, owes heavily to this invitation to emotional identification as a means of validating the experience of the sacrament. This in turn brought about opposition from those who felt that lay participation and even prayers in English were dangerous innovations (e.g., the author of *The Chastizing of God's Children,* ca. 1382).

Perhaps the most significant vernacular catechism in the 14th and 15th cents. was the Corpus Christi drama. The full cycle of plays on the biblical history of salvation included, centrally, a play on the Last Supper (see especially the Coventry and York plays), and in York at least the plays were performed just before the eucharistic feast of Corpus Christi (Thursday after Trinity Sunday) in which the history of salvation was recapitulated in a Mass dedicated to the subject of the Eucharist itself. The Coventry play extends the analogy with the Passover feast, attributing the detailed connections to Jesus in a gathering of NT typology from the Exodus: "And as þe paschal Lomb etyn Haue we / In þe old lawe was vsyd for a sacryfyce / So þe newe lomb þat xal be sacryfyced be me" (690-92). The analogy is extended explicitly, teaching the Real Presence of Christ's body and blood in the sacrament (703-13) and the use of the "chalys of þe newe testament" as defense against the devil (807-10). The Croxton Play of the Sacrament is a 15th-cent. miracle play of anti-Semitic character about a Jew who disbelieves in the doctrine of the Real Presence, obtains a Host, tries to destroy it, is then confronted by a vision of Christ, whereupon he repents and is converted. Tales designed to reinforce the doctrine spread widely in this period, usually involving miracles attributed to the Host (cf. John Myrc, *Festial,* "Corpus Christi"; Robert Mannyng, *Handlyng Synne;* and the conclusion of Nicholas Love, *Mirrour of the Blessed Lyf of Jesu Christ,* a trans. of the *Meditations on the Life of Christ*). In *The Pearl* the dreamer is invited to consummate his instruction at the end of the poem by reintegration into the life of the Blessed on earth by participation in the Eucharist.

The blasphemous feast of Belshazzar (Dan. 5), in which the liturgical vessels of the Temple were profaned, is starkly contrasted by the Pearl Poet to the purity which ought to attend the Eucharist, in his poem *Cleanness.* He then goes on to argue that priests who administer the elements of communion should be examples of spiritual purity. The same point is made implicitly by Chaucer, in whose *Canterbury Tales* a broad spectrum of the community is heading, under the directions of a thoroughly secular "Host," Harry Bailly, toward an encounter with the Sacred Host in the Eucharist at Canterbury, and whose final guidance and preparation is happily at the hands of a model priest, for "Wel oghte a preest ensample for to yive, / By his clennesse, how that his sheep sholde lyve" (*General Prologue,* 1.505-06). The value of such a priest is highlighted by Chaucer's previous presentation of a number of corrupted clerics, especially the Pardoner, whose own sermon presents a dark and deathly repast of bread and wine under a tree up a "croked wey" in which community is horribly destroyed through cupidity — a kind of demonic Eucharist like that of Belshazzar's orgiastic profanation, and with similar consequences.

Along with concerns for purity of the priesthood and administration of the Church, a concern for the renewal of informed congregational participation had much to do with developments in the Reformation. The Reformers typically rejected the notion that the Eucharist is primarily a sacrifice offered to God, the efficacy of which is in any sense automatic. Rather, in Luther's view, the grace of the sacrament could be actualized only in the heart of the person in an active relationship of faith in God through Christ; the blessed sacrament was above all, as for the disciples and early adherents, a joyful communion with Christ within the fellowship of his Church. Luther rejected allegorization of John 6 as a basis for eucharistic doctrine and like other Reformers restored communion in both kinds on the biblical model (*The Babylonian Captivity of the Church,* "On the Lord's Supper"; *Sermons on the Catechism,* "The Lord's Supper"). He developed Augustine's argument that in the Lord's Supper a miracle takes place comparable to the Incarnation yet, following the lead of Pierre d'Ailly, suggested that while there was not a physical change in the elements (transubstantiation), there was certainly a radical objective presence ("This is my body") of Christ in the sacrament, a position which has come to be called "consubstantiation."

For Calvin the mystical union of Christ with the members of his body in the Church is also analogous to the union of the Word from the beginning with human nature in the Incarnation. He retains the model of John 6, but adds a supporting exegesis of John 15 ("I am the vine; ye are the branches"). Calvin insists, no less than Luther or the Roman Church, that Christ is "truly given and received" in the sacrament, and that the elements "are received not by the imagination or intellect merely but are enjoyed in reality as the food of eternal life" (*Inst.* 4.17.19). His spiritual view of the sacrament was thus, like Luther's, far closer to the Roman view than later disputants have sometimes imagined. Calvin also stressed church members' communion with one another in sharing one loaf: in becoming one with the body of Christ (bread) participants thus become one with the Body of Christ (his Church). While leaving more freedom in the liturgy for prayer, he also strove for a reflection of early Church practice and maintenance of a liturgy of the Word before celebration of the Last Supper "at least once a week" (*Inst.* 4.17.43). Like Luther, he quickly moved toward vernacular translation of Scripture, prayers, and hymns. The eucharistic doctrine expressed in the definitive Edwardian formulation of the Anglican Church in the same period is a blend of Calvinistic theology with historic Roman liturgical form, albeit in vernacular translation. The Prayer Book of 1549, issued by Cranmer, retains more of the old Roman rite; the revisions obtained by those of more Calvinistic sympathies (1552) led to the Prayer Book of 1662, which has been in general use until the late 20th-cent. Anglican theologians, like Wyclif and Fitzralph before them, and like Calvin, stressed the relationship of the Eucharist to the Incarnation. Nicholas Ridley's *A Brief Declaration of the Lord's Supper* claims, in Ridley's anti-realist approach to the doctrine, to be following the 9th-cent. monk Ratramnus, but the argument was perceived as Calvinist. The Puritans' Westminster Confession of Faith and Directory of Public Worship also developed a doctrine with a notable Calvinist flavor, but with a more material and strictly "historical" notion of "remembrance." Counter-Reformation theology, reacting to these developments in the Council of Trent and elsewhere, reaffirmed the doctrine of transubstantiation (in a somewhat less graceful fashion than had Aquinas), and unified all Roman eucharistic liturgy under one rite.

In England, Catholic poets such as the Jesuit priest Robert Southwell (1561-95) and Henry Constable (1562-1613) wrote poems on the Blessed Sacrament expressing the Tridentine view (see esp. Southwell's "The God of hoastes in slender host doth dwell"). Richard Crashaw (1612-49), a Catholic convert whose father was a Puritan minister, translated the celebrated eucharistic hymn of Aquinas, the *"Adoro Te,"* beginning:

> With all the powers my poor soul hath,
> Of humble love and loyal faith,
> Thus low (my hidden life!) I bow to thee,
> Whom too much love hath bow'd more low for me.
> Down, down, proud sense! discourses die!
> Keep close, my soul's enquiring eye!

The "mystery of faith" in the Eucharist is thus said to be beyond theological explanation or rational reduction; that Christ makes himself present is simply to be accepted by faith. These were not auspicious times for Catholic views of the sacrament, however; Southwell was arrested going to Mass, repeatedly tortured, and executed; Constable was arrested and put in the Tower in 1604 and after his release fled to France, where he died in exile. Crashaw similarly was forced to flee to the Continent after his conversion. One of the most beautiful poems of the 16th cent., the famous "Corpus Christi Carol," encodes, in the form of a lullaby, a profound sense of the mysterious reciprocity of flowing tears of the penitent, grateful Church and the flowing blood of her sacrificial champion Knight, experienced in a hidden *sanctum* where "stondith a ston, / *Corpus Christi* wretyn theron" (R. Greene, *Early English Carols,* no. 322); the poem is very likely an expression of secret but loyal Catholic devotion to the Eucharist.

It is the Anglican tradition, therefore, which chiefly characterizes poetry on the Eucharist in the 17th cent. Among the finest of these meditative poems are Henry Vaughan's "The Feast" from the second part of his *Silex Scintillans,* which contains the stanza:

> Spring up, O wine,
> And springing shine
>   With some glad message from his heart,
> Who did, when slain,
> These means ordain
>   For me to have in him a part.

These lines reflect both the Anglican liturgical practice of receiving the two elements and the strengthened meditative emphasis on direct relationship between the participant and Christ in his sacrifice. John Donne, who left the Catholic Church to become an Anglican divine, wrote a number of powerful poems relating to Christ's sacrifice (e.g., "Good Friday, 1613") but has little to say about the Eucharist directly (cf. "The Crosse"). For George Herbert, another priest-poet of the Anglican Church, a deep devotion to the Eucharist is coupled with a fideist's skepticism concerning the possibility of adequately describing or even intellectually apprehending the mystery of Christ's presence in the sacrament. Accordingly, he follows in his poems the advice he gives to theologically uncertain country parsons in *A Priest to the Temple,* saying of the faithful parson that "Neither finds he any issue in this, but to throw himself down at the throne of grace, saying, Lord, thou knowest what thou didst, when thou appointedst to be done thus; therefore doe thou fulfill what thou didst appoint; for thou art not only the feast, but the way to it" (chap. 22). The apparent dichotomy between the appearance of bread and the reality of the flesh of Christ offered in sacrifice is, in the brilliant dialectic of his second poem on "H. Communion," resolved in rerooting and expanding the reader's sense of substance:

I could beleeue an Impanation
At the rate of an Incarnation,
  If thou hadst dyde for Bread. . . . (25-27ff.)

Here, as in his first poem on "H. Communion,"

Onely thy grace, which with these elements comes,
  Knoweth the ready way,
  And hath the privie key,
Op'ning the soul's most subtile rooms. (19-22)

As in "An Offering" and "The Banquet," an attitude of thankfulness is the best preparation for the sacrament in which, as he says in "The Elixir" (echoing Irenaeus), "all may of thee partake." Herbert then compares the sacrament to the philosopher's stone:

This is the famous stone
That turneth all to gold:
For that which God doth touch and own
  Cannot for lesse be told. (Cf. Chaucer, *The Canon's Yeoman's Tale*, 8.1428-71)

Herbert's sentiments accord with the general line of theological argument reflected by Jeremy Taylor a generation later in his *The Real Presence and Spirituall of Christ in the Blessed Sacrament* (1654) and also *The Worthy Communicant* (1660) in which the lyrical Bishop argues that there is danger on all sides in trying to reduce *mysterium,* like metaphor, to material analytics. From a Puritan perspective the danger was primarily that of making religion mystical; the American Calvinist Edward Taylor's celebrated verse in *Preparatory Meditations before my Approach to the Lord's Supper* (1682; 1693-1725), eschewing that path, ironically makes instead all the real world symbolic of scriptural theme and doctrine, and composes thereby one of the most useful compendia of American biblical typology from the period.

The 18th cent., with its tendency toward rationalism in both theology and poetry, is not rich in eucharistic themes in literature. As a fresh convert to Catholicism, Dryden in *The Hind and the Panther* (1687) had expressed a weariness with eucharistic controversy now felt by many:

Could he his god-head veil with flesh and bloud
And not veil these again to be our food?
His grace in both is equal in extent,
The first affords us life, the second nourishment.
And if he can, why all this frantick pain
To construe what his clearest words contain,
And make a riddle what he made so plain?
To take up half on trust, and half to try,
Name it not faith, but bungling biggottry. (1.134-42)

Poems and hymns by Isaac Watts ("When I Survey the Wondrous Cross") and Philip Doddridge ("My God, and Is Thy Table Spread") refer to the elements as "sacred pledges" of the actual sacrifice on Calvary, a theme still found in Reformed hymnody in the 19th cent., as in Horatio Bonar's "For the bread and for the wine, / For the pledge that seals him mine" ("The Supper of Thanksgiving" [1870]). Other hymns, expressions of the evangelical revival, hearken back to a Catholic formulation such as is found in the longer version of John Wesley's "Author of Life Divine" (1745) and Charles Wesley's "The Eucharistic Mystery" and "Jesu, my Lord and God Bestow" (1745). The former of these hymns takes up the incomprehensibility of the eucharistic mystery in terms which recall Herbert; the latter specifically recollects a Catholic understanding of the sacrament:

And make the real sign
a sure and effectual means of grace. . . .
Only do thou my heart prepare
To find thy real presence there,
And all thy fullness gain.

It is in the Calvinist *Olney Hymns,* especially those of William Cowper (which draw their imagery largely from the OT), that the most arresting depiction of the sacramental trope occurs:

There is a fountain filled with blood
Drawn from Emmanuel's veins;
And sinners, plunged beneath that flood,
Lose all their guilty stains. ("Praise for the Fountain Opened" [Zech. 13:1]; cf. "Welcome to the Table")

In one of the many ironies of ecclesiastical history in the 18th cent., this was to become a popular eucharistic hymn among those Reformed, Baptist, and Congregational churches and chapels most keen to disavow Catholic doctrine of the Real Presence because it was felt to provoke a ghoulish imagination. Yet the idea of the Eucharist as a sacrament of thanksgiving, reemphasized in the 17th cent. by Richard Hooker (*Ecclesiastical Polity*) and Jeremy Taylor (*The Worthy Communicant*), survived intact in virtually all English Christian traditions, validating the succinct definition of Dr. Johnson in his

Dictionary: "the sacramental act in which the death of our Redeemer is commemorated with a thankful remembrance; the sacrament of the Lord's Supper."

The Eucharist has, of course, provided inspiration for great music of every era, from the Gregorian chant to the recent *Requiem* of Andrew Lloyd Weber. On the Continent, the 18th cent. was a particularly fruitful period for musical settings for the Mass, such as Bach's "B-Minor Mass," his cantatas, and "St. Matthew's Passion," and shorter meditations on the sacrament such as Mozart's *"Ave Verum Corpus."* In Protestant England, however, all of Handel's oratorios are on OT subjects; it was a thin period for church music on the grand scale, with only Samuel Wesley (1766-1837), the son of Charles Wesley, composing notable settings for the texts of Holy Communion.

In the early part of the 19th cent., especially in American literature, the sacrament had a less than prominent literary history. In part this owed to the decreased importance it occupied in the worship life of Reformed, Congregational, and Baptist churches, which, following Zwingli and some of the early radical reformers among the Anabaptists, variously reduced observance of the Eucharist to four times a year (adopted by Reformed churches) or, at most, to one Sunday each month (among some of the Baptists). Further, formal religious consciousness was becoming more and more subtended by an empiricist and, in the modern linear sense of the word, "historical" self-consciousness, even as popular spirituality was tending toward subjectivism. In poetry, the "Communion Hymn" of William Cullen Bryant is characterized by misty, romantic sentiment:

> In tender memory of his grave
> The mystic bread we take,
> And muse upon the life he gave
> So freely for our sake.

The more profound communion in Bryant's verse, as in much poetry of the period, is with Nature (e.g., "Thanatopsis"). Longfellow's "Midnight Mass for the Dying Year" is charged with the "real presence" of Nature rather than of God; his "The Children of the Lord's Supper," presented as a translation from a Swedish tale by Bishop Tegner, concerns the sense of awe and reverie felt by children preparing for their first communion — here presented as a bit of anthropological exotica. Whittier's *Snow-Bound* takes a more macabre turn, with a ship's captain offering to feed his starving sailors on his own body; when at the last minute a school of porpoises arrive, " 'Take, eat,' he said, 'and be content. / These fishes in my stead are sent. . . .' " Such uneasiness with the sacrament could prompt a more openly hostile view such as D. H. Lawrence expresses in his essay on Melville in *Studies in Classic American Literature,* where he observes that there is an odd inconsistency in Melville's horror at the cannibalism of the Typees:

He might have spared himself his shudder. . . . If the savages like to partake of their sacrament . . . and to say, directly: "This is thy body, which I take from thee and eat. This is thy blood, which I sip in annihilation of thee," why surely their sacred ceremony was as awe inspiring as the one Jesus substituted.

In England during this period, the Oxford (or Tractarian) movement, under Keble, J. H. Newman, Froude, and others, concerned with "national apostasy" (see Keble's 1833 sermon of that title), set out to reform prevalent Erastian and latitudinarian tendencies in the Church of England. They launched a series of *Tracts for the Times* which attracted the support of still others, including Edward B. Pusey, and urged a movement in liturgy, worship, and theology toward the Roman rite. Pusey, after Newman's departure as the Tractarian leader, preached his famous sermon "The Holy Eucharist, a Comfort to the Penitent" in 1843. It was quickly condemned by the Oxford Chancellor and six doctors of divinity for its advocacy of the doctrine of the Real Presence, but this merely had the effect of guaranteeing its publication and wide circulation. While only Newman among the most prominent members became a Catholic (later Cardinal), the movement did much to revive medieval views of the Church and its sacraments such as influenced Tennyson, William Morris, Christina Rossetti, and the Pre-Raphaelites, among others. It also prompted the translation for Anglican use of a number of medieval eucharistic hymns, including the *"Adoro Te," "Pange Lingua Gloriosi,"* and *"Lauda Sion Salvatorem"* of St. Thomas Aquinas (trans. John Mason Neale). While Tennyson's *Holy Grail,* like much of the flowery romanticism of Morris and cloudy religiosity of the Pre-Raphaelites generally, applies eucharistic language to the creation of a symbolic mystical iconography, the poetry of Gerard Manley Hopkins makes sacramental language the font of all understanding which may be called "poetic." In "The Bugler's First Communion," he deflects the Tennysonian theme in regarding the "housel," as it was called in the Middle Ages, of "an our day's God's own Galahad" from the priest's point of view. As a priest, he is attracted to the diversity and oddity of all those whose "pure fasted faces draw unto this feast," whose bent and feeble knees "God shall strengthen" ("Easter Communion"); the deep sense of communion within the multifaceted Body of Christ receiving the sacrament causes him to write:

> The dappled die-away
> Cheek and the wimpled lip,
> The gold wisp, the airy-grey
> Eye, all in fellowship —
> This, all this beauty blooming,
> This, all this freshness fuming,
> Give God while worth consuming. ("Morning, Midday, and Evening Sacrifice")

The impact of the Oxford Movement expresses itself in the 20th cent. in a variety of ways. One of these is the conversion to Anglo-Catholic faith and practice of T. S. Eliot, whose historical understanding of the Eucharist lies behind the reverent irony of these lines from "East Coker":

> The dripping blood our only drink,
> The bloody flesh our only food;
> In spite of which we like to think
> That we are sound, substantial flesh and blood.

Within the tradition of Hopkins as well as Eliot is David Jones, whose *Anathemata* is woven through with eucharistic motifs, especially those of anamnesis and the Real Presence (e.g., 8.227-29, 241, etc.). These themes are explored psychologically by Graham Greene in his novels *The Power and the Glory* (1940), *The Heart of the Matter* (1948), and *Brighton Rock* (1938). Greene's fiction is one of the prominent influences on Canadian Mennonite novelist Rudy Wiebe, whose *Blue Mountains of China* (1970) contains a chapter, "Drink Ye All of It," in which David Epp, who led his own small community in a successful "exodus" from Russia into China in the oppressions of 1927, then goes back, sacrificing himself, so that the authorities will not take vengeance upon those families who have chosen not to flee.

For J. R. R. Tolkien, the whole character of the happy ending in Western Christian narrative, especially of the type we call "fairy story," is charged with a *consolatum* which evokes the symbolic significance of the Eucharist; hence he calls its special sense of joy and release to life a "euchatastrophe," a "far-off gleam or echo of *evangelium* in the real world" ("On Fairy Stories"). If Tolkien is right, the persistence of eucharistic imagery in literature may owe in some measure to its power as an integrator of biblical narrative and symbol, not only of the Last Supper and Atonement directly but all of the narrative and typology leading up to it. The sacrifice to which the believing person appeals invokes participation in the catastrophes of human experience which render it necessary: as Margaret Avison's "For the Murderous: The Beginning of Time" suggests, it is also stories like that of the self-willed and failed sacrifice of Cain, with its aftermath in the spilling of Abel's innocent blood, which still speak (cf. Heb. 11:4) in the Eucharist, leading as they do to a point where

> In time the paschal lamb
> before the slaying did
> what has made new the wine
> and broken bread. (*sunblue*, 49)

so that blood for blood no more need be required.

See also ANAMNESIS; BREAD OF LIFE; *CORPUS CHRISTI;* CUP; EMMAUS; MANNA; MARRIAGE FEAST, APOCALYPTIC; SACRAMENT; TRANSUBSTANTIATION.

Bibliography. Bahr, G. J. "The Seder of Passover and the Eucharistic Words." *NovT* 22 (1970), 181-202; Bridgett, T. E. *History of the Holy Eucharistic in Great Britain* (1881). 2 vols.; de Lubac, H. *Corpus Mysticum: L'Euchariste et l'Église au Moyen Âge, étude historique* (1944); Denzinger, H., and A. Schönmetzer. *Enchiridion Symbolorum* (1965); Gollnick, J. *Flesh as Transformation Symbol in the Theology of Anselm of Canterbury* (1985); Jeffrey, D. L. *The Early English Lyric and Franciscan Spirituality* (1975); Jungman, J. A. *The Mass of the Roman Rite* (Eng. trans. 1959); Kolve, V. A. *The Play Called Corpus Christi* (1966); Leenhardt, F. J., and O. Cullmann. *Essays on the Lord's Supper* (Eng. trans. 1958); Lepow, L. E. "Eucharistic Reference in the Towneley Cycle." *DAI* 41 (1981), 3571A; Martz, L. *The Poetry of Meditation* (1962); Owst, G. W. *Literature and Pulpit in Medieval England* (1966); Priscardaro, M. T. "Middle English Eucharistic Verse: Its Imagery, Symbolism and Typology." *DAI* 36 (1975), 5275A; Ross, M. M. *Poetry and Dogma: The Transfiguration of Eucharistic Symbols in Seventeenth Century English Poetry* (1954); Terrien, S. L. "Demons also Believe: the Parody of the Eucharist in Contemporary Theater." *Christian Century* 87/49 (1970), 481-86; Tolkien, J. R. R. "On Fairy Stories." In *Essays Presented to Charles Williams* (1947); Vloberg, M. *L'euchariste dans l'art* (1946). 2 vols.; Wallace, R. S. "Eucharist." *ISBE* 3.164-70; *Calvin's Doctrine of the Word and Sacrament* (1953).

DAVID L. JEFFREY
I. HOWARD MARSHALL

EUNUCH The initiation of the ancient practice of castration is ascribed by the Byzantine historian Ammianus Marcellinus to the legendary Assyrian Queen Semiramis, known to readers of English literature through her role as prototype for the evil "Sowdanesse" mother-in-law in Chaucer's *Man of Law's Tale* (2.358-64); Dante had earlier made her an archetypal Whore of Babylon (*Inferno*, 5.52-60). The origins of human castration may well be Mesopotamian, but they certainly predate Semiramis (ca. 810-805 B.C.) by many centuries. Xenophon reports that it was the belief of the Persian king Cyrus that emasculation yielded more docile and easily managed slaves who, undistracted by family obligations, tended to be loyal and also reliable in the harem. Accordingly, says Xenophon of Cyrus, "he selected eunuchs for every post of personal service to him, from the doorkeeper up" (*Cyropaedeia*, 7.5.65). While Greek and European culture generally abhorred the practice, in hellenized Asia Minor, particularly in the cults of Cybele, Attis, and Artemis, ritual castration of the priesthood flourished.

In ancient Israel, by contrast, castration was prohibited. Deut. 23:1 excludes eunuchs from temple service. The rationale for this exclusion seems to have been a conviction that emasculation violates divine creational order and that it represents syncretistic accommodation to foreign barbarisms. The sexually maimed are thus accounted unsuitable for divine service (cf. Lev. 21:20); further, the practice undermines patriarchal succession in the priesthood. Despite the Deuteronomist prohibition, a eunuch is later considered admissible to the worship assembly (Isa. 56:3-5). This expression of wider latitude was made particularly necessary by the lot of many young Israelites under Assyrian and Babylonian captivity (likely including, e.g., Daniel and his companions Shadrach, Meshach, and Abednego [Dan. 1]). Isaiah suggests that although an individual may be a "dry tree," physically unable to produce heirs, his most important requirement before God is to keep the covenant. So, "Blessed is the eunuch, if he has never done anything against the law," according to Wisd. of Sol. 3:14, the reference here being to those born eunuchs or castrated involuntarily (cf. Midr. Megillot 176; cf. Shab. 4.8d); such a person "will find a place in the Lord's Temple." A distinction was made, however, for some purposes, between the *seris 'adam* ("manmade eunuch") and the *seris ḥammah* ("eunuch by nature") (Yebam. 8.4-6).

The Hebrew term by which a eunuch is designated, *saris,* is also used frequently to render "civil servant," "bureaucrat," or "courtier" (e.g., Dan. 1; Esth. 1–2; Sir. 30:20; Isa. 56:3-5; 2 Chron. 18:8; 2 Kings 8:6); rarely, a *saris* might even be a military commander (2 Kings 25:19; Jer. 52:25). The LXX renders the term most often as *eunouchos* but also as *spadōn* (Isa. 39:7).

Jesus' teaching concerning eunuchs distinguishes three types: congenital, the involuntarily castrated, and those who "have made themselves eunuchs for the sake of the kingdom of heaven" (Matt. 19:12). Normative interpretation of the latter is figurative, seeing a reference to those who abstain from sexual life for the sake of religious service, such as the Essenes at Qumran, with whose vows of celibacy Jesus' hearers would have been familiar. Nonetheless, literal interpretations were not lacking in the life of the early Church, nor were self-mutilations. By the 4th cent. canons were adopted which admitted congenital and involuntarily castrated eunuchs to ministry, but denied it to those who, like Origen, had castrated themselves (J. Hastings, *Encyclopaedia of Religion and Ethics,* 5.583). Later, Isa. 56:3-5 was connected by patristic commentators with the passage in Matt. 19:12 so as to understand "spiritual eunuchs" as those called to service as priests, and who, like the Essenes, led a life of chastity for the sake of the kingdom of heaven (e.g., Rupertus Tuitiensis, *De Trinitate et Operibus Ejus: In Deut.* 1.22 [PL 147.941-42]). By following the usual method of interpreting the "Old Law" in the light of the New, a triple distinction like that of Matt. 19:12 is read into the OT passages, yielding a second figurative or spiritual type, not laudable voluntary chastity but "detestable" refusal to serve or to be fruitful in good works. Such a person is idle, silent (not presenting the gospel to his neighbor), refusing grace, presumptuously committing the unpardonable sin despite his knowledge of the kingdom of heaven (PL 147.947). This person is an *eunuchus non Dei,* a perverted clergyman, the polar opposite of the *eunuchus Dei,* a faithful cleric who, as St. Augustine observes, understands Gen. 1:28, "Be fruitful and multiply," as a spiritual injunction to multiply virtue in the life of the community (*Enarr. in Ps.* 128:6; cf. Rabanus Maurus, *Comm. in Genesim,* 19:12 [PL 107.1019; 458-62; 468]).

In this light, the description of Chaucer's Pardoner in the *General Prologue* to the *Canterbury Tales* is likely to have as much figurative as literal sense:

Swiche glarynge eyen hadde he as an hare . . .
A voys he hadde as smal as hath a goot.
No berd hadde he, ne nevere sholde have;
As smothe it was as if it were late shave.
I trowe he were a geldyng or a mare. (684-91)

Symbols of lechery (hare, goat, horse) do not override the fact that the Pardoner is here judged a eunuch. While it seems evident from his remarks to the Wife of Bath that he has carnal experience and appetite, his sorry perversion of office, even in his tale-telling charade, with its "relics" and racketeering, makes it clear that his "eunuchry" is *non Dei* and to be understood as above all a spiritual condition, the emblem of religious fraud.

After the Renaissance, such associations virtually disappear. Ben Jonson's *Volpone* keeps a retinue of freaks, including one Castrone; Shakespeare's Cleopatra keeps a court servant Mardian whom she taunts about his lost manhood; and in *Twelfth Night* Viola postures as a eunuch to gain a position of service to the Duke, but none of these plays upon biblical allusion so much as a fascination and horror with "Turkish" or "Moorish" customs. The typos of the "unfruitful" clergyman as unmanly, familiar in 18th- and 19th-cent. fiction, may arise in part from medieval associations. The Rev. Laurence Sterne, certainly familiar with these traditions, creates a humorously ineffectual clergyman, Parson Yorick, in his novel *Tristram Shandy* (1759), a text which makes much of the theme of congenital and "accidental" castration. Not only is Tristram genitally mutilated while endeavoring to urinate out a window, but Uncle Toby proves one of the *eunuchii quae facti sunt* by virtue of his war wound. The education of Tristram, curiously modeled on Xenophon's *Cyropaedeia,* contains its own suggestions concerning the uses of this condition.

Bibliography. Burke, D. "Eunuch." *ISBE* 2.200-202; Miller, R. "Chaucer's Pardoner, the Spiritual Eunuch, and the Pardoner's Tale." *Speculum* 30 (1955), 180-99.

EVE   The Bible says that while Adam slept, God created Eve from one of Adam's ribs to be a "help meet for him"; at first the text refers to her simply as "woman" (Gen. 2:20-22), thereby establishing her generic relationship to all women as well as her genetic relationship to man: "Adam said . . . she shall be called Woman, because she was taken out of Man" (2:23). The author then states her normative marital relationship to the man — "they shall be one flesh" (2:24) — and outlines her encounter with the serpent (involving, first, credulity [3:1-6], but afterwards, according to the so-called "protevangelium" of

3:15, enmity). It is only after this account of humankind's creation, disobedience, and judgment that Adam is said to call his wife by a proper name: "Adam called his wife's name Eve; because she was the mother of all living" — *mater viventium* (Vg, Gen. 3:20). Her name (Heb. *Haw-wah*) thus bespeaks her role as life-giver, a role emphasized by the OT's second and last mention of her name: "Adam knew Eve his wife; and she conceived, and bare Cain" (Gen. 4:1).

Eve, then, both participates in the sin of disobeying God and signifies the gift of continuing generational life. One of the two NT references to her reinforces these negative and positive functions. St. Paul comments, "Adam was first formed, then Eve. And Adam was not deceived, but the woman being deceived was in the transgression. Notwithstanding she [i.e., a woman] shall be saved in childbearing" (1 Tim. 2:13-15). The other NT reference to her, also by Paul, presents her, beguiled by the serpent, as one whose example the church ought not to follow (2 Cor. 11:3). Yet here too the negative associations pertaining to Eve exist side by side with the positive, for Paul also implicitly compares her to the Corinthian church, which he wishes to present "as a chaste virgin to Christ" (2 Cor. 11:2; cf. Eph. 5:22-27).

The NT's depiction of the Church as the bride of Christ, together with Paul's parallel between "the first man Adam" and Christ "the last Adam" (1 Cor. 15:45), led to an explicit association in the writings of the Church Fathers between Eve, *mother of the living,* and "mother" church, *mater ecclesia.* Zeno of Verona declared that just as Eve was created from the side of Adam, so the Church was created from the side of Christ, from which flowed blood and water, figuring the martyrdom and baptism wherein the Church actually took its beginning. In this way, says Zeno, "Adam is restored through Christ, and Eve through the church" (PL 11.352). The same idea is expressed by St. Augustine: *"Eva de latere dormientis, Ecclesia de latere patientis"* (PL 37.1785) — "Eve from the side of the sleeping one, the Church from the side of the suffering one." This parallel became commonplace in the Middle Ages and was endorsed, e.g., by St. Thomas Aquinas (*Summa Theol.* 1a.92.3) and by St. Bonaventure, who saw Eve as representing not only the Church in relation to Christ, but also the soul in its relationship to God (*2 Sententiae,* d.18,a.1,q.1; cf. *Biblia Pauperum*).

The second major parallel developed by the Fathers is that between Eve and the Virgin Mary. Most believed that Eve remained a virgin until the Fall, and this similarity between the two women served to set off the contrast between them. St. Justin Martyr says that

Eve, who was a virgin and undefiled, having conceived the word of the serpent, brought forth disobedience and death. But the Virgin Mary received faith and joy, when the angel Gabriel announced the good tidings to her that the Spirit of the Lord would come upon her. (ANF 1.249)

St. Irenaeus draws the same parallel, adding that in this way "the Virgin Mary [became] the patroness *[advocata]* of the virgin Eve" (ANF 1.547; cf. 1.455). Augmenting this analogy, Tertullian expresses the view that Adam's being formed from the virginal earth, "with no seed as yet cast into its furrows," prefigures the virgin birth of Christ (ANF 3.536), and his comments serve to point out a further extension of the complex analogy/disanalogy between mothers earth, Eve, Mary, and church. Moreover, just as Eve the virgin *manquée* has her true role fulfilled by the Virgin Mary, so Mary, like Ecclesia, inherits Eve's title *mater viventium.* St. Peter Chrysologus points out the symmetry of the curse of Eve — "in sorrow thou shalt bring forth children" (Gen. 3:16) — and the blessing of Mary, spoken by Elisabeth — "blessed art thou among women" (Luke 1:42). Thus by grace Mary became indeed the mother of the living (PL 52.576). Or, as another early Christian writer puts it,

Mary is filled by grace, and Eve is emptied *[vacuata]* of guilt. The curse of Eve is transformed into the blessing of Mary. . . . Eve is the authoress of sin, Mary the authoress of merit. . . . [But] this offspring of Mary prevailed over that of Eve, and the lamentation of Eve was drowned out by the song of Mary. (Pseudo-Augustine [PL 39.2105])

In rabbinic tradition Eve's name, *Havvah,* is linked with the Aram. *hewyah,* "serpent," and this connection is particularly a feature of allegorical interpretation of the story of the Fall, much of which identifies the first sin with the acquisition of sexual knowledge. One such Jewish allegorization sees "the fruit of the tree which is in the midst of the garden" (Gen. 3:3) as "merely a euphemism" for that which is in the middle of the woman and receives "whatever is sown therein." According to this view, Sammael (i.e., Satan) "riding on the serpent," came to Eve and seduced her, so that her firstborn, Cain, the first murderer, was literally the son of the devil (Pirqe R. El. 21).

A more influential Jewish allegorization of the story of the Fall was that provided by Philo: Adam is the mind (Gk. *nous*), Eve is sense perception *(aisthēsis),* and the serpent is pleasure; and mind falls away from God when drawn by the senses operating under the influence of pleasure (*Legum allegoriae,* 2.12; *De opificio mundi,* 56). Such a view clearly has profoundly negative implications for the roles of woman and of sexuality in a spiritual scheme of things, though it does not go so far as the dualistic teaching of Manichaeism, according to which Satan and his devils actually created Adam and Eve, "imparting to her [Eve] of their own lust, with a view to the deceiving of Adam" (ANF 6.185). The Church Fathers rejected the open dualism of the Manichaeans; however, Philo's psychological reading of Adam, Eve, and the serpent was explicitly endorsed by St. Ambrose (PL 14.295) and continued to hold sway throughout the Middle Ages. Augustine typically spoke against an allegorical and sexual interpretation of the Fall, for God

EVE

himself bid unfallen Adam and Eve to "be fruitful, and multiply" (Gen. 1:28). And yet elsewhere, reflecting Philo's paradigm, Augustine warns that "our flesh is an Eve within us" (NPNF, 1st ser. 1.278-79; 8.170).

These positive and negative associations provided a rich source of material for medieval and Renaissance art. To generalize, medieval art favored typological representations such as those connecting Eve and Mary. Renaissance art, while not eschewing typology, depicted Eve with greater dramatic immediacy, often either tempting Adam or being tempted by the serpent. (For examples, see Guldan and Frye.)

The typological symmetry characteristic of many pictorial treatments of Eve finds its most concise analogue in medieval wordplay on Eve's name, notably the 9th-cent. hymn *"Ave Maris Stella"* and its ME versions. The "AVE" of Gabriel's greeting to Mary (Luke 1:28) is seen to encapsulate the way in which the obedience of Mary reverses the disobedience of EVA (see E. Guldan, *Eva und Maria,* 45, 58-59, 121, 135, and *Religious Lyrics of the XIVth Century,* ed. C. Brown, nos. 41, 45, 131). Yet that contrast also implies similarity between Eve and Mary, the "second Eve," as Milton calls her (*Paradise Lost,* 5.387; 10.183); and the two women are frequently presented as facially and physically identical. The serpent, too, often appears to have features identical to Eve's, as in Raphael's ceiling fresco of the temptation scene (Stanza della Segnatura, Vatican). Consequently, Eve's physical beauty can be taken as a diabolical snare, as it seems to be in Jean Cousin's sensual *"Eva Prima Pandora"* (ca. 1549 [Louvre, Paris]). Here again, though, the similarity can simultaneously suggest a contrast, as it does in Milton's exaltation of Eve's unfallen

> naked beauty more adorned,
> More lovely than *Pandora,* whom the Gods
> Endowed with all their gifts, and O too like
> In sad event. (*PL* 4.713-16)

In the OE *Genesis B,* Eve's beauty is likewise presented as being very great, though by no means diabolical: she is "wifa wlitegost . . . handweorc godes" — "most beautiful of women . . . the handiwork of God" (820-22). What renders her susceptible to the devil's corruption is "wifes wac gethoht" — "woman's weak mind" (648). Yet in fact this commonplace serves, in the context of *Genesis B,* to mitigate Eve's culpability in the Fall, for she takes the word of the serpent and offers the fruit to Adam in good faith, and "thurh holdne hyge" — "with loyal intent" (707).

In the later Middle Ages the theme of Eve's credulity is repeated in the temptation scenes of the mystery plays. But in *Cursor Mundi* (14th cent.) there is no longer any trace of her good faith or loyalty to her husband:

> Bitwene sathan & his wif
> Adam is sett in mychel strif
> Bothe thei be on o party
> To ouercom man with tricchery. (Trinity MS 725-28)

In Chaucer's Wife of Bath's Prologue, Eve is the first to appear in Jankyn's misogynist catalog, for "that woman was the los of al mankynde" (*Canterbury Tales,* 3.715-20). Chaucer's self-serving merchant, however, blithely recalls Eve's role as a "help meet": "That wyf is mannes helpe and his confort, / His paradys terrestre, and his disport" (4.1331-32).

In the Renaissance, Spenser's Una, who represents the true church (or simply Truth) and within the narrative is literally the daughter of Eve, becomes unequivocally the helpmeet of the questing Redcrosse Knight (see *Faerie Queene,* 1.1.5; 1.11.1; 1.12.16-41). But the traditional ambivalence toward the woman reappears in Guillaume du Bartas's *La Sepmaine* (1578; trans. Joshua Sylvester, 1605). Although du Bartas praises Eve and her marriage union with Adam — "Source of all ioyes! sweet *Hee-Shee*-Coupled-One" — he goes on to underline the tradition that Satan first approached the woman because she was "wavering, weake, and vnwise" (W. Kirkconnell, *The Celestial Cycle,* 226, 310; cf. Hugo Grotius, *Adamus Exul* [1601], 191-201, in Kirkconnell, 108-09). Sir Walter Raleigh, in his *History of the World* (1614), provides a similar explanation for Satan's approaching Eve, though he emphasizes not so much her mental weakness as her "vnquiet vanity" (p. 70). Thomas Peyton represents yet another strand of the same tradition: although he declares that God made Eve "the Tipe our senses all to rouse, / Of Christ himselfe, and of the Church his spouse," he goes on to imply that she was sought out by Satan and susceptible to his wiles because, like other women, she delighted in "much idle prattle" (*The Glasse of Time* [1620, 1623], 65, 72; Kirkconnell, 268-69).

The richest and fullest treatment of Eve in English is Milton's. Within the context of the theodicy of *Paradise Lost* (1667), Milton recognizes that an "unfallen" Eve actually possessing the faults ascribed to her by Raleigh, Peyton, and others would stand as an indictment of the justice and providence of her Creator. Thus Milton takes pains to depict her as both conspicuously fallible — for how else could human free agency meaningfully have operated? — and yet decidedly unfallen. And her unfallen marriage with Adam involves full intercourse, both sexual and intellectual, in accordance with Milton's conviction that the blessings of marriage are not to be viewed as either entailing or resulting from the Fall and that "there is a peculiar comfort in the married state besides the genial bed, which no other society affords" (*Tetrachordon* [1645], in *Complete Prose Works* [1953-82], 2.596). As Diane McColley puts it, "while retaining some degree of subordination for Eve, [Milton in *Paradise Lost*] purges that state of all suggestion of weakness or wickedness, inferiority or limitation, carnal precedence or unequal responsibility, and avoids the radically false dichotomy of opposing freedom and service" (*Milton's Eve,* 35).

Paradise Lost forms the principal backdrop for many subsequent treatments of Eve in English. Dryden's Eve, like Milton's, has full sexual relations with Adam before the Fall, though Dryden trivializes that aspect of their marriage: in Act 2, Scene 1 of *The State of Innocence and Fall of Man* (1712), the supposedly prelapsarian Eve, sounding a little like Chaucer's Wife of Bath, implies a connection between the withholding or granting of sexual favors and the maintenance or loss of her "much lov'd Soveraignty." Eve appears in Blake's late vision *The Ghost of Abel* (1822) as well as in Byron's drama *Cain* (1821), in which she utters a long and vehement curse against her Byronic firstborn. Elsewhere, Byron frequently alludes to the sexual associations of Eve, though he assumes, unlike Dryden and Milton, that life before the Fall was sexless and boring (e.g., *Don Juan*, 1.18), an opinion which has increasingly taken hold in thought and literature since the Romantic period. Visual depictions of Eve are discussed in Robert Browning's "Parleyings with Francis Furini," in which one of the issues is the interrelationship of art and lust (157, 180). And Eve's relationship to her offspring is a main theme of Elizabeth Barrett Browning's *A Drama of Exile*. This play, focusing on the postlapsarian scene, develops Milton's portrayal of the magnanimous and penitent Eve. Christ himself, whom Eve addresses as "Seed" (1754), appears and commands Adam to "bless the woman"; and Adam, obeying, honors Eve as "First woman, wife, and mother! . . . / And also the sole bearer of the Seed / Whereby sin dieth" (1837-39). The maternal and loving characteristics of Eve receive further emphasis in Christina Rossetti's "Eve" (1865), a lament Eve utters after the murder of Abel, though in this poem, as the occasion would suggest, the tone of the reference to Eve as *mater viventium* is much more somber than it is in E. B. Browning's exploration of the protevangelium: Rossetti's Eve exclaims, "I, Eve, sad mother / Of all who must live" (26-27).

In the 20th cent. the theme of Eve as *mater viventium* is given a new twist by the Irish writer James Stephens. In his poem "Eve" (in *The Hill of Vision* [1912], 100-103), Eve precedes Adam; indeed, she gives birth to him, after she has felt "Immensity's caress" and the "primal kiss." In this way Eve is removed from her traditional narrative context and made to embody a primal and eternal feminine principle. G. B. Shaw similarly removes Eve from the bounds of time. In *Back to Methuselah,* Eve does appear at the beginning of history but reappears far on in time, in A.D. 31,920, and together with Adam and Cain has an opportunity to evaluate history, once (in Cain's words) "the strong have slain one another; and the weak live forever." And although Adam can make "nothing of it," it is Eve who declares, "All's well."

In 20th-cent. American writing, Eve's presence is the subject of Robert Frost's beautiful sonnet "Never Again Would Birds' Song Be the Same," which portrays Adam's wonder at how the voice of the newly created Eve has somehow infused nature itself with a new richness. By contrast, Archibald MacLeish, in *Songs for Eve* (1954, in

New and Collected Poems, 1917-1976 [1976]), glorifies Eve's sin as a kind of Byronic rebellion, seeing the unfallen state as tedious and insipid and, hence, disobedience to God as an act of transcendence: "But for [Eve's] fault the wine / Were sweet as water is" ("What the Vine Said to Eve"). Similarly, for MacLeish, the savor of sex required the consciousness which came with the Fall; as Eve puts it, Adam "touched me never till he took / The apple from my hand" ("Eve in Dawn"). *The Book of Eve* (1973), a novel by Canadian writer Constance Beresford-Howe, suggests too that Eve's "fall" was guiltless and liberating. Its protagonist, Eva, a modern though aging woman, leaves her home and her husband to make a fresh start in life.

See also ADAM; FALL; LILITH; MARY, MOTHER OF JESUS.

Bibliography. Evans, J. M. *Paradise Lost and the Genesis Tradition* (1968); Fresch, C. H. "Milton's Eve and the Theological Tradition." *DAI* 37 (1977), 5846A; Frye, R. *Milton's Imagery and the Visual Arts: Iconographic Tradition in the Epic Poems* (1978); Guldan, E. *Eva und Maria: Eine Antithese als Bildmotiv* (1966); Kirkconnell, W. *The Celestial Cycle: The Theme of Paradise Lost in World Literature with Translations of the Major Analogues* (1952); McColley, D. K. *Milton's Eve* (1983); Motherway, T. J. "The Creation of Eve in Catholic Tradition." *TS* 1 (1940), 97-116; Peczenik, F. "Adam's Other Self: A Reading of Milton's Eve." *DAI* 41 (1981), 5110A; Phillips, J. *Eve: The History of an Idea* (1984).   DENNIS DANIELSON

EX NIHILO *Ex nihilo* (Lat., "out of nothing") is not a canonical term but comes from 2 Macc. 7:28. It refers to the doctrine of creation generated from the creation account in Gen. 1–2, in which God is said to bring the world into being from primal chaos: "the earth was without form and void" (Vg *inana et vacua*). This doctrine typically stresses two points: that the universe is not eternal, but finite, having a definite point of beginning, and that only God can create *ex nihilo*; all human creation is necessarily derivative, "subcreation," as J. R. R. Tolkien puts it ("On Fairy Stories"), and therefore, as David Jones suggests (*Anathemata*, 1.79), an inherently "ironic" activity.

See also CREATION.

EXILE AND PILGRIMAGE The motif of the faithful servant of God as a pilgrim for whom this world is not his final home is deeply rooted in the exilic narratives of Genesis (the calling of Abraham) and Exodus. It also finds reflection in numerous psalms, where the motif of the "way" or "path of righteousness" predominates. Noteworthy among these are the Songs of Ascent — Pss. 120–134 — which may be named for the fifteen steps leading upward to the Court of Men in worship (Mid. 2.5; cf. Sukk. 51b). Early patristic commentary associates these psalms with songs of the returning exiles, taking a cue from Ezra 7:9, where the return is called "the going-up *(hamma'alah)* from Babylon." These psalms were likely sung by pilgrims on their way to Jerusalem for Passover and Yom Kippur, since the pilgrim journey to Jerusalem was always referred to as a "going-up." But the pilgrimage motif is also found elsewhere, permeating, e.g., Ps. 119, where the Word of God is said by the Psalmist to be a light to the pilgrim's path (v. 105) and his "statutes . . . my song in the house of my pilgrimage" (v. 54). The Hebrew term for pilgrimage, *magur,* derives from *gur,* "to sojourn"; hence pilgrims are by definition "sojourners," a people en route.

The necessity of pilgrimage for God's chosen is rooted in two senses of alienation: the first results from sin and the Fall, in which estrangement all persons share (cf. Ps. 39:13); the second arises from the terms of the covenant, in which Israel is commanded to have no "strange gods" (Exod. 20:3) and so to eschew settlement among "an alien people clutching their gods," as the magus in T. S. Eliot's "Journey of the Magi" puts it. Under the terms of the New Covenant the imperative is as fundamental: St. Peter addresses the early Christian community, "Dearly beloved, I beseech you as strangers and pilgrims, abstain from fleshly lusts, which war against the soul" (1 Pet. 2:11). The writer to the Hebrews describes those who were faithful to the first covenant as having seen the promises of God for a spiritual promised land "afar off, and were persuaded of them, and embraced them, and confessed that they were strangers and pilgrims on the earth" (11:13), and enjoins those to whom he writes to take up the same pilgrim calling and "run with patience the race that is set before . . ." (12:1).

These concepts were quickly elaborated by the early Church. Indeed, Peregrinus and Viator became common early Christian baptismal names. The Epistle to Diognetus says of the earthly lot of Christians that

> they reside in their own fatherlands, but as if they were non-citizens; they take part in all things as if they were citizens and suffer all things as if they were strangers. Every foreign country is [thus] a fatherland to them, and every fatherland a foreign country. . . . They sojourn on earth, but they are citizens in heaven. (Diogn. 5:5, 9)

These phrases are echoed by Origen in *Contra Celsum* (8.75). Later, St. Augustine wrote of the *civitas Dei peregrinans,* drawing on NT passages (*De civ. Dei* 1, pref.) and establishing a powerful metaphor for conceiving of the meaning in history. For Augustine, the Christian is a wayfarer, a *viator* who seeks in the world only that temporary comfort which travelers find in a roadside inn (e.g., *Sermo,* 14.4.6; 70.7; *In Joan. Ev.* 40.10). Augustine's intention was in part to minimize Christian preoccupation with political calamity; St. Gregory the Great, a monk and later Pope, takes up the figure with religious vocation in mind. In his *Moralia in Iob* he says that the elect are those who do not settle for any of the goods of this world but, realizing that they are here only pilgrims and guests, desire to press on to the place in which they may be fully happy (*Moralia,* 8.54.92; cf. *Ep.* 2.204).

Either application implies a hierarchy of values. "Thus," says Augustine,

> in this mortal life, wandering from God, if we wish to return to our native country where we can be blessed we should use this world and not enjoy it [i.e., for itself], so that the "invisible things" of God "being understood by the things that are made" may be seen, that is, so that by means of corporal and temporal things we may comprehend the eternal and spiritual. (*De doctrina Christiana,* 1.4.4; cf. 2 Cor. 5:6; Rom. 1:20)

The alienation from the present world which a pilgrim life presupposes is rooted in the Fall; indeed, for Gregory the fallen angel is the archetypal *alienus* (*Moralia,* 12.36.41), and the *alieni* or strangers to wisdom against whom the author of Proverbs warns the young man are seen by Gregory as *spiritus maligni,* demons (*Regulae pastoralis,* 3.12.36). Alienation is defined, first, as a failure to love God, and second, a refusal to adhere to his *regula,* his lawful order. Human alienation is then a result of imitating demonic rebellion, as in the estrangement of humankind from God and persons from each other in the Fall in Eden and the Tower of Babel, both of which narratives concern the destruction of communion and community by the sins of human presumption. Babel begets Babylon, and the "city of confusion" generates the sterile mind of those who refuse to accept God's given order for the good life (*Moralia,* 6.16.24; cf. Augustine, *De catechizandibus rudibus,* 20.37).

These texts influenced conceptions of the ascetic or contemplative life (e.g., St. Benedict, *Regula,* 4.20ff.). Adamnan's *Vita* of St. Columba (ca. 700) describes the 6th-cent. Irish monk of Iona as *"pro Christi peregrinari volens,"* and argues that God's calling of Abraham and his descendants to desert exile and pilgrimage applies to all who desire to be faithful. In a vein familiar in medieval texts, Adamnan suggests that there are three ways "to leave the fatherland and go into pilgrimage": in body only, with the mind not severed from habitual vices, for which there is no reward; in heart and mind, but *not* in body, as with contemplatives, which obtains reward; and in both species, spirit and flesh, as exemplified in the lives of the twelve apostles and St. Columba (674).

The exile motif exerted a powerful hold on the Anglo-Saxon mind, since one who became *ut-lagu,* literally an "outlaw" to the received social order of Anglo-Saxon culture, had long been subject to the terrible penalty of permanent exile. Adam's "exile" in *Genesis B* is thus cast in relevant social terms (925-64), and *Christ and Satan I* pictures Satan's lamenting his exile from his "native home."

While the exilic experience as a result of Adam's Fall was seen to bedevil all mortal sojourners (Aelfric, *Homily for Shrove Sunday*), the penitent person could move beyond exile (*Blickling Homily,* 2) to return to his true "ancestral home," as Alcuin puts it in his poem *De Rerum*

Humanorum Vicissitudine. The exile was a "man lost," but the obedient servant of God thus became, as St. Boniface said of Archbishop Cuthbert, "a pilgrim through this world for love of the eternal land." The OE poem *The Wanderer* describes an "aimless exile," hallucinating about reunion with the lord from whom he is estranged; its companion poem *The Seafarer,* developing a pilgrim motif found in Augustine, depicts in its first part the despair of one exiled at sea and then moves in the second half of the poem to describe a desire for journey out of exile into heavenly joys such as transcend earth's mutable happiness. Whereas in this poem, as in several Old Irish pilgrim lyrics, there is a penitential aspect, a monastic, almost mystical longing characterizes *The Dream of the Rood.* This famous Anglo-Saxon poem ends with the dreamer describing himself as an exile from this present world, deprived of friends, and longing for a new patron, the Lord himself who "us onlysed, us lif forȝeaf, / heofonlicne ham" (147-48). When the pilgrimage motif is coupled with the sea voyage metaphor, as in *Christ II* and *Andreas,* the "heavenly home" to which humankind is released from exile becomes the "harbor of salvation"; the "ship," as the Venerable Bede, Augustine, and others point out, figures the Church, or Faith, while the invisible pilot is Christ. The sea voyage elaboration may well owe something to patristic exegesis of the voyages of Ulysses as a type of the Christian's journey (Rahner, 328ff.); to the audience of Anglo-Saxon Christian poetry, however, the invitation to *forðferan* ("fare forth") suggested not only life's immediate pilgrim journey but the death and faring forth from this world of the *peregrinus.*

In the later Middle Ages, the idea of pilgrimage as a figure for the penitent life of a Christian *viator* was a commonplace, and took objective as well as literary form. Pilgrimages to such places as S. Iago da Compostella (St. Jaques de Grand), Rome, Walsingham, or Canterbury were regularly assigned as penances, especially to those whose sins involved a significant breach of the social fabric of the Christian community. This is the context for Chaucer's *Canterbury Tales,* whose enclosing frame is a pilgrimage from a London suburb to Canterbury, from roadside inn to divine sanctuary, and, as the Parson in the Prologue to his sermon on repentance makes clear, it figures forth "in this viage," as he puts it, "thilke parfit glorious pilgrymage / That highte Jerusalem celestial" (*CT* 10.49-51). The Parson's quoted text, "to knytte up al this feeste" (10.47) is Jer. 6:16: "Stand ye in the ways, and see, and ask for the old paths, where is the good way, and walk therein, and ye shall find rest for your souls." The "ful noble way" which the Parson then elaborates "is cleped Penitence" (10.81). It is typical of such texts to move from confusion and alienation, as from Dante's *selva oscura* (dark wood) or Langland's chaotic field of folk in *Piers Plowman* through a clarification and reordering toward a truth outside the self, a sense of reconciliation and "true home" in which alone "verray

felicitee" or true blessedness ("Beatrice") can be known and possessed. This movement is always to restore an order lost by losing one's path — *nel mezzo del cammin di nostra vita,* as Dante puts it, or, in Chaucer's terms, "wandryng by the weye" — and to reinstate communion and community.

The tale of two cities suggested in Chaucer's *Canterbury Tales,* on the model established by Augustine in *The City of God,* might be represented figurally as a voyage from Babylon to the New Jerusalem or, as in Dante, from *Inferno* to *Paradiso;* it is the social or civic form of this most important narrative structure in Western literature. Its personal form, as a quest for salvation or Truth (with psychic as well as social implications attendant upon success or failure) is represented by a series of psychomachic allegorical texts including Guillaume de Guilleville's mid-14th-cent. *Pèlerinage de la vie humaine, Pèlerinage de l'âme,* and *Le pèlerinage Jhesu-crist.* The first two were translated into English more than a generation later, in a free version ascribed to John Lydgate, along with a second, more precise ME translation of the first poem, *The Pilgrimage of the Lyfe of the Manhode.* In this text, although pilgrimage per se is less the structure of the work than a context for discussion of the perils of sin and its sacramental remedies, the poet commences his dreamvision by saying: "Me thowte as I slepte þat I was a pilgrime / and þat I was stired to go to þe citee of Jerusalem in a mirour" (19-20); his decision to become a pilgrim causes him to "dream" his birth, or to "wake" himself into spiritual life, an experience of journey "to Jerusalem in a mirour" which he shares with the tutored dreamer of *The Pearl.*

Chivalric literature of the later Middle Ages owes directly to the *peregrinatio* theme, partly because of monastic popularization of the trope *militia Christi* but also because of the establishment of military orders with vows reminiscent of monastic vocation for the purposes of pilgrimages of arms to recapture Jerusalem. After interest in the Crusades waned, from the late 12th cent. there developed the literary image of the solitary knight errant who must seek out and triumph over hostile forces in *aventure* by which means he may then hope to realize his true identity. That these hostile forces come from sin within as much as without is central to Chrétien de Troyes's *Yvain* and *Erec et Enide,* as also to Laȝamon's version (derived from Wace) of Arthur's demise in his *Brut.* The *chevalier errant,* Yvain, is a spiritual pilgrim in search of *le sentier tot droit;* the anonymous *Sir Gawain and the Green Knight* of 200 years later seeks the same, though in the internalization of the quest its destination had become somewhat more ambiguous. Only the purest of knights, Percival, can hope to find the castle in the wilderness where the Holy Grail is kept; yet when in Chrétien's *Le roman de Perceval* he finds the castle of the Grail King it is only to discover that the King's own faithlessness has turned the country into a "waste land."

Early medieval romances were typically adaptations from Roman epics, *romans,* such as *Eneas* (1155) or *Le roman de Troie* (1160); later Anglo-Norman ancestral romances such as *Gui de Warewic* and *Boeve de Haumtone* and their ME successors, *King Horn, Havelok, Sir Orfeo,* and others, reflect a more thorough Christianization. The pilgrimage or quest still involves a typical exile, occasionally wanderings over the sea, exotic places, and signs and wonders, and features a struggle with the forces of evil, sometimes a fight with a dragon, or, as in the case of *Orfeo,* a descent into hell, there to contest for his captured bride. The consummation of these quests by the Christian institution of marriage (or reaffirmation of marriage) symbolizes the representative character of the hero's quest, which ultimately is to found a Christian family and *societas.* To this end, e.g., *Sir Orfeo* is a juxtaposition of biblical optimism concerning the pilgrimage of the human soul in Christ over the usual "lesson" of the classical story of Orpheus and Euridice, which is that death cannot be cheated. In the medieval English tale a Christlike Orfeo does not look back.

The chivalric development of the pilgrimage motif, familiar also in Renaissance art (e.g., Dürer's "Ritter, Tod, und Teufel"), did not cease with the meandering versions of Malory's *Morte Darthur.* Reinforced by Tasso's *Gerusalemme Liberata* (1580-81; Eng. trans. by R. Carew [1594] and Edward Fairfax [1600]), it also directly influenced Spenser's *Faerie Queene* (1590-96). Here the pilgrimage of the Redcrosse Knight of Holiness (the Church of England) becomes a quest for national purpose and ecclesiastical identity in an allegory designed to flatter the court of Queen Elizabeth I. In Shakespeare's *Pericles* the motif of virtuous knight errant survives in another mutation, drawing on both medieval romance and saints' lives for its characterization of faithful pilgrimage rewarded. In *Romeo and Juliet,* Romeo, whose very name suggests pilgrimage, is called "good pilgrim" by Juliet (1.5.95-104), a term which he himself invites; the language in this case derives at least in part from medieval parody of the pilgrimage motif found in such texts as *Le Roman de la Rose,* in which the "pilgrimage" of the lover is intended to find its consummation in an amorous rather than spiritual union.

Exile and pilgrimage are Bolingbroke's themes in *Richard 2* (1.3.49; 229; 263-64). In *All's Well That Ends Well* Helena's letter presents her as "Saint Jacques pilgrim, thither gone" (3.4.4), a disguise she maintains in Florence (3.5.33ff.). But the term "pilgrimage" was already, by Shakespeare's time, something of a cliché, meaning "life story," as when Othello describes his wooing of Desdemona (*Othello,* 1.3.152) or simply "life," and as when arrogant Angelo commands that Claudio be readied for execution: "Bring him his confessor, let him be prepared, / For that's the utmost of his pilgrimage" (*Measure for Measure,* 2.1.35-36).

In meditative verse of the 17th cent. the figure of life as a pilgrimage was accordingly a literary commonplace, with poets recording the experience of having defaulted by turning back, as in Donne's "Holy Sonnet 4," or come by grace and perseverance to the penultimate station: "This is my playes last scene, here heavens appoint / My pilgrimages last mile . . ." ("Holy Sonnet 6"). The goal of the pilgrimage to the New Jerusalem becomes identified with Mt. Zion, the "city set on a hill" (Matt. 5:14), as in Herbert's "The Pilgrimage," which begins "I travell'd on, seeing the hill, where lay my expectation," and goes on to characterize a spiritual journey in allegorical terms which anticipate Bunyan. Henry Vaughan's poem of the same title talks about the traveler's wayside rest in terms recalling St. Gregory:

> Then Jacob-like I lodge in a place
> (A place, and no more, is set down), . . .
> So for this night I linger here,
> And full of tossings to and fro,
> Expect still when thou wilt appear
> That I may get me up, and go.

Vaughan concludes his poem by appealing to Christ for the sustenance of the Eucharist as he travels: "So strengthen me, Lord, all the way, / That I may travel to thy Mount" (cf. his "Looking Back" and "Righteousness").

The psychomachic pilgrim allegory reaches its apogee, perhaps, in John Bunyan's *Pilgrim's Progress from This World to That Which is to Come* (1678-84), a Reformation version of the late medieval pilgrimage of the soul. Drawing on Puritan spiritual writings indebted to Augustine, but more directly on the Bible itself, Bunyan traces the pilgrim journey of Christian from the City of Destruction to the Celestial City, and vigorously enriches the elements of wayfaring *aventure* with direct biblical allegory.

This form of pilgrimage narrative fared poorly in the Enlightenment (except perhaps in the case of adaptation of classical analogues such as the *Telemache* and in interlinear interpretations or revisions of Homer such as those by Pope and Cowper). Two other forms, however, flourished. The first of these was the spiritual autobiography of Puritan tradition in which, following both OT biblical typology and models such as provided by Augustine's *Confessiones,* individual "pilgrimages" of life in the modern sense became a Protestant realist version of the medieval saints' life. These narratives, of which Bunyan's *Grace Abounding to the Chief of Sinners* (1666) and John Newton's *An Authentic Narrative* (1764) are notable examples, were given fictionalized form by Daniel Defoe in such works as *Robinson Crusoe* (1719) with its classic sea voyage, island exile, conversion, rescue by grace (in the form of suffering servant Friday), and return home; less plausibly it may be observed in his *Moll Flanders* (1722), a tale of "wandering by the way" which somehow obtains a similar destination. The second novel is a forerunner of the widely popular picaresque novel of the mid-century, such as Tobias Smollet's *Peregrine Pickle* (1751), which, despite its dependence on Tasso and Bunyan, is rather a parody of the pilgrimage of biblical tradition. An example which develops the tradition more positively is Henry Fielding's *Joseph Andrews* (1742), which parallels the stories of the biblical Joseph, incorporates the parable of the wayfaring Good Samaritan, and in Parson Abraham Adams offers a pilgrim's guide en route to Joseph's eventual marriage and a happy ending.

Meanwhile, Puritan development of the pilgrimage motif had gone with the "Mayflower" pilgrims and their successors to America, who carried with them a "covenant-people's" typology of community exodus from the European City of Destruction, their bondage in Egypt or "Babylonian Captivity," into the New Canaan, the Promised Land. The Old World had "forfeited its national covenant"; as Ainesworth, Winthrop, and others phrased it, since Truth had been driven out of England, the Lord "had chosen New England as her residence," a literalization of biblical typology which shocked conscientious Calvinists like Roger Williams with the presumptuousness of American claims to be the earthly paradise or even "the Type of the . . . Kingdom of Christ Jesus" (*Complete Writings*, 4.403; 1.76; 3.322). Over the next century American literature produced numerous secular elaborations of biblical pilgrimage, among them two of Melville's novels: the first-person narrative *Mardi* (1849) in which the narrator searches the seas of the world for his sweetheart Yillah, a symbolic quest to discover goodness and purity in the present world; and *Israel Potter* (1855), an uneven satire on the "Americanization" of biblical typology in what came to be called "manifest destiny." The motif, still more secularized, reappears in narratives of westward migration, from Willa Cather's *O Pioneers!* (1913) to John Steinbeck's *Grapes of Wrath* (1939), an agnostic pilgrimage not merely to the promising land of California but toward a socialist America.

Romanticism chose to idealize the chivalric pilgrimage as personal spiritual quest in works as diverse as Byron's *Childe Harold's Pilgrimage* (1812-18), a romanticization of alienation, Scott's *Ivanhoe* (1820), a romanticization of medieval chivalry, and, on the Continent, Goethe's *Wilhelm Meister's Travels* (1821-29), which is as much influenced by Cervantes's parody of chivalric romances, *Don Quixote* (1605-15), as by the biblical tradition from which Goethe draws his pilgrim Joseph, Mary, and child and a Sophia figure, Makaria. Alfred Lord Tennyson's *The Holy Grail* (1869) concentrates on the ideal of purity and its sad destiny; Charles Reade, on the other hand, fictionalizes a biography of the parents of Erasmus of Rotterdam in his *The Cloister and the Hearth* (1861) to suggest that the goal of a Christian pilgrim may lie beyond the reach of one life, the faithful pilgrimage achieving even its temporal consummation in the subsequent generation. John Keble's poem "And Wilt Thou Hear the Fevered Heart?" suggests that a sense of Christ's

presence is all that is needed in our pilgrim "darkness" (*The Christian Year,* "Second Sunday After Christmas"), "To bless / Our trial hour of woes," however exacting. *Quo Vadis?,* a historical novel about the life of the early Christian community in Rome by Henryk. Sienkiewicz (1895), makes the same point with reference to the life of St. Peter. After most of his flock have been killed by Nero, Peter decides to backtrack from his earlier pilgrimage to Rome and seek refuge elsewhere. On the road he sees a vision of Jesus, and asks him, "*Quo vadis, Domine?*" ("Where are you going, Lord?") and Jesus replies, "As thou art deserting my people I go to Rome to be crucified for the second time." Hearing these words, Peter comes to his senses and returns to his pastoral calling, caring for his flock as best he can until he too is arrested and crucified, upside down.

Twentieth-century pilgrimage narratives generally depart from romantic externalization of the personal spiritual quest and, in the era of Freud, internalize the quest as a voyage through consciousness and memory. The central example in modern poetry is provided by T. S. Eliot, who develops the theme of desert exile and frustrated search for symbols of healing in *The Waste Land* (1933); after his own "Ash Wednesday" of repentance and "Journey of the Magi," his pilgrimage unfolds as an internal voyage of spiritual self-discovery relating "time past and time present" through the processes of memory and enactment of the will in *The Four Quartets* (1936-43). In prose fiction the famous example is Joyce's *Ulysses* (1922), in which Stephen relentlessly scrutinizes all aspects of his existence in a fruitless search for the nature and meaning of life. For this modern Telemachus neither patriotism nor piety provides an answer, nor does discovery of his symbolic "father Ulysses," the wandering Jewish salesman Bloom; not even his profession as a purveyor of learning can give him fulfillment. Like the tentative and estranged survivors of Joyce's *Exiles,* Stephen is finally unable to accept the moral responsibility of an enduring commitment to a goal outside the self. Even more internalized is the twelve-volume odyssey through conscious and subconscious memory of Miriam Henderson, in Dorothy M. Richardson's *Pilgrimage* (1915-38), an often brilliant, often meandering exercise in stream-of-consciousness writing whose title belies its self-conscious avoidance of any ultimate sense of direction. Joyce Cary's *To Be a Pilgrim* (1942), taking its title from the refrain of John Bunyan's hymn of 1684 ("He who would valiant be, 'gainst all disaster"), concerns Tom Wilcher, a man who has sacrificed a religious vocation to handle family affairs, become a liberal, and then begun to have deep nostalgia for the old religious values of the past. But these fail him in the end, and the consummating marriage and new beginning he has planned with Sara Monday is denied him.

More optimistic is a series of works which deal with community destiny and a realization of the goals of personal pilgrimage through participation in a social progress modeled on biblical and medieval typologies. Often these come from subcultural experience, such as Rudy Wiebe's multifaceted novel of Mennonite persecution and exodus from Russia via China and South America to the Canadian prairies in *The Blue Mountains of China* (1970). Alex Haley's *Roots* (1975), a novel of exile from Africa, slavery in America, emancipation, and social pilgrimage, adapts metaphors familiar from African-American spirituals and echoed in the preaching of Martin Luther King to create a story of pilgrimage toward full citizenship in the American "promised land." Also drawing on exodus narrative and symbol, Australian novelist Patrick White's *The Tree of Man* (1955) and *Voss* (1957) offer two sides of the secular coin of modern pilgrimage typology; the first consummates in a terrestrial peaceful kingdom, the second, frustrated of that realization, nevertheless liberates a sense of transpersonal historical destiny.

The fate of the biblical pilgrimage motif in 20th-cent. literature has become interwoven with the rise and popularity of fantasy literature. These include allegorical works such as C. S. Lewis's *Pilgrim's Regress* (1933), which, in nostalgia for the past as "home," inverts Bunyan to describe a process of loss of faith, and semiallegorical mythologizing of the present such as J. R. R. Tolkien's trilogy *The Lord of the Rings* (1954-55). Tolkien utilizes biblical and Augustinian typology as well as adaptations of medieval romance to create a parable about the dependence of personal meaning upon identification with a company, however small, of those who will set out through the wilderness way as pilgrims "fighting the good fight" against besetting evil. An example of the motif applied to futuristic imagination is Stephen Donaldson's *The Chronicles of Thomas Covenant, The Unbeliever* (1977). Covenant's pilgrimage is harried by the freight of a modern gnosticism; to avoid mere wandering and ultimate destruction he has to consider the destiny embedded in his own name. Like Margaret Laurence's errant pilgrim Hagar Shipley in *The Stone Angel*, he must decide whether in fact he can accept direction and believe, as Christopher Smart's translation of Ps. 121:8 phrases it, that:

The Lord shall for thy ways provide
Thro' every sea and shore;
Thy travel and return to guide
From henceforth evermore. (*Psalms of David*, no. 121)

See also EXODUS.

Bibliography. Greenfield, S. B. "The Formulaic Expression of the Theme of Exile in Anglo-Saxon Poetry." *Speculum* 30 (1955), 200-206; Guillet, J. "La thème de la marche au désert dans l'Ancien et le Nouveau Testament." *RSR* 36 (1949), 164ff.; Henry, P. L. *The Early English and Celtic Lyric* (1966); Knauer, G. N. "Peregrinatio Animae." *Hermes* 85 (1957), 216ff.; Ladner, G. B. "Homo Viator: Medieval Ideas on Alienation and Order." *Speculum* 42 (1967), 233-59; Loxton, H. *Pilgrimage to Canterbury* (1978); Mazzotta, G. *Dante: Poet of the Desert* (1979); Rahner, H., S.J. *Greek Myths and Christian* Mystery (1963); Rondet, H., S.J. "Le symbolisme de la mer chez St. Augustin." *Augustinius Magister* 2 (1954), 691-701; Smithers, C. V. "The Meaning of 'The Seafarer' and 'The Wanderer.'" *MAE* 26 (1957), 137-53; 28 (1959), 1-22; Williams, G. H. *Wilderness and Paradise in Christian Thought* (1962).

EXODUS Exodus is the name given by the Vg and English translations of the Bible to the book which describes the bondage in Egypt of Jacob's and Joseph's descendants (1:1– 6:27) and the subsequent departure from Egypt of the captive people under the leadership of Moses and Aaron (chaps. 13–19); it narrates also the journey to Sinai, the giving of the Decalogue (20:1-17) and Covenant Law (20:22–23:33; 34:1-35), as well as directions for the erection of the Tabernacle. Its Hebrew name is *we'ellah shemot,* taken from the opening words "and these are the names." The events contained in this eponymous narrative are the most dramatic in the epic saga of the Jewish pilgrimage; from them spring fundamental biblical conceptions of law, justice, freedom, covenant, and worship, including the most important of Jewish feasts, the Passover. It is also the single most important biblical sourcebook for Jewish and Christian typology as well as hymnody. It provides plot and theme to countless narratives, a list of which would occupy a volume in itself.

Possibly the first Jewish drama ever written is a play entitled *The Exodus,* attributed to an Alexandrian poet of the 2nd cent. B.C. whose nom de plume was Ezekiel. Preserved in fragments by Eusebius from the lost work of Alexander Polyhistor, its remaining characters are Moses, Zipporah, Chum, Jethro, God, and a messenger. The first English treatment of the material, also preserved in a fragmentary copy, is the OE *Exodus,* a Caedmonian poem of the 8th cent. which adds a great deal of elaboration to its biblical source (itself limited essentially to Exod. 13:17 through chap. 14). Beginning with praise of Moses the lawgiver, emphasizing the *sapientia et fortitudo* which is said to have characterized his leadership, within barely fifty lines it reaches the tenth plague and Pharaoh's agreement to release the Israelites. The pillars of cloud and fire, the Egyptian pursuit, and the Red Sea deliverance are major features in the OE poem, along with a disquisition on the covenant from Noah through Abraham.

The *Exodus* may have been intended for use in the Holy Saturday liturgy of the Anglo-Saxon church in connection with baptism. Passover and Easter were linked, and the Red Sea crossing was traditionally associated in Western Christianity with baptism (e.g., Tertullian, *De baptismo*, 9; St. Ambrose, *De mysteriis*, 3.14); the extent of Christian typologizing beginning with the prophets and NT writers is, however, much more elaborate and thoroughgoing than this suggests. Israel's post-diaspora deliverance from captivity is presented by Isaiah as the antitype of the deliverance from Egypt (43:16-20; 48:21-22; 49:10). Building on the typology of the prophets, Palestinian Judaism at the time of Christ saw Moses the deliverer as a type of the Messiah, and looked for their own messianic deliverance to come in the spring, at the time of Passover (Bonsirven, *Judaïsme palestinien*, 1.416). Jean Daniélou has shown that Matthew's Gospel is permeated with allusions to Exodus, with Christ's life presented in the framework of the "New Exodus, foretold by the Prophets" (157). Hence, immediately after his baptism, Jesus is "led by the Spirit into the desert" (Matt. 4:1), where he spends forty days (cf. Israel's forty-year sojourn in the desert and Moses' forty-day fast). When Satan tempts Christ on the mountaintop he is rebuked with the first commandment given on Sinai, and in his Sermon on the Mount Jesus assumes the role of lawgiver of the New Covenant. As Moses took the people over the waters into the "land of promise," Jesus walks on the waters (Matt. 8:23-27); as through Moses' intercession manna was given to the twelve tribes, so Jesus gives bread miraculously to feed his twelve disciples and the multitude (Matt. 14:4). These parallels unfold not only in the first Gospel but throughout the NT, a notable example coming in John 3:14, where the incident of Moses elevating the brazen serpent (Num. 21) is seen as predictive of Jesus' Crucifixion.

Typology based upon Exodus became fundamental to Christian catechism from St. Augustine through to Calvin and the American Puritans. The journey out of "Egypt" through the "waters of baptism" and through the desert toward the "Promised Land" becomes a type of the Christian's pilgrimage out of a place of spiritual exile through testing in this world toward a life of faithful obedience to God's law and eventual entrance into the "New Canaan."

In early medieval allegorizations the essential features are largely consistent: Egypt is the world, Pharaoh the devil, and the Egyptian army "besetting sins." The desert sojourn is a figure for exile and pilgrimage, and the cloudy or fiery pillar a type of Christ who leads in the journey. This scheme is evident in the writings of St. John Chrysostom, St. Hilary, and Eusebius, among others, and is rehearsed by Aelfric in a series of Lenten sermons on the pilgrimage theme (e.g., *Catholic Homilies*, 2.12). In his *De Populo Israhel*, Aelfric also details and allegorizes seven occasions on which the people grumbled or actively rebelled against God and the leadership of Moses and Aaron, and incurred the divine wrath (*Homilies* [ed. Pope], 2.20).

The York "Departure" (no. 11), "Towneley Pharaoh" (no. 11), N-Town "Moses and the Two Tables" (no. 6), and Stonyhurst "Eight Pagean of Moyses" all reflect both the biblical material from Exodus and the typological tradition it generated, especially with regard to liturgical presentation of the *humanae salvationis historia*. (The Towneley play has been modernized, with the christological conclusion omitted, by Abram Lipsky,

An Old English Haggada [1907].) The exodus motif itself becomes central to the development of the pilgrimage theme in medieval and Renaissance literature from *Piers Plowman* to *Pilgrim's Progress,* but it also generates models for a typologizing of history and future events which are of considerable importance for Protestant — especially Puritan — tradition. Calvinist typology and covenant theology were drawn to view this world from the perspective of "a stranger in a strange land" (Exod. 2:22). Calvin (*Inst.* 2.8.15) observes that:

> We again, instead of supposing that the matter has no reference to us, should reflect that the bondage of Israel in Egypt was a type of that spiritual bondage, in the fetters of which we are all bound, until the heavenly avenger delivers us by the power of his own arm, and transports us into his free kingdom. Therefore, as in old times, when he would gather together the scattered Israelites to the worship of his name, he rescued them from the intolerable tyranny of Pharaoh, so all who profess him now are delivered from the fatal tyranny of the devil, of which that of Egypt was only a type.

By a curious hermeneutical inversion, the "spiritual" reading afforded by Calvin was often "literalized" by subsequent writers, so that the Exodus story came to be seen as predictive of postbiblical national destinies. Thus, the type of national allegory found in Spenser's *Faerie Queene* is metamorphosed by the use of exodus typology in William Leigh's *Queen Elizabeth Paraleld* (1612) and *Israel and England Paralleled* (1648) by Paul Knell; it takes on particularly Calvinist flavoring in John Welles's *The Soules Progress to the Celestiall Canaan* (1639) and Faithfull Teate's *A Scripture Map of the Wilderness of Sin, and Way to Canaan* (1655). In New England Samuel Mather's *Figures and Types of the Old Testament* (1673), Cotton Mather's *Magnalia Christi Americana* (1702), and Jeremiah Romayne's *The American Israel* (1795) all illustrate the power of the Exodus story in the formation of American national identity. In this context a leader of the Plymouth pilgrims, William Bradford, is seen by Cotton Mather as Moses leading Israel away from the European "fleshpots of Egypt" into the American wilderness (*Magnalia*, 1.104); John Winthrop is also a second Moses (1.109), and the expedition against Canada under Phips is described as a pushing out of Philistines from "the skirts of Goshen" (1.167-68). In a later period, the experience of African slaves in America was often expressed in terms — borrowed, ironically, from their masters — of longing for release from Pharaoh's oppression and for access to the Promised Land. Nor has the exodus motif disappeared from contemporary American literature: Steinbeck's *The Grapes of Wrath* presents the Joads as modern Israelites fleeing through the desert from persecution toward the promised land of milk and honey in California, with Tom as their Moses. Leon Uris uses the re-establishment of Jews in Israel after the holocaust as the subject and theme of his modern *Exodus,* a novel which attempts to return the motif, without much of its attendant Western typology, to its original Canaan.

See also EXILE AND PILGRIMAGE; MOSES; PILLAR OF CLOUD AND FIRE; PLAGUES OF EGYPT.

Bibliography. Bercovitch, S. *Typology and Early American Literature* (1972); Bloch, J. "The Exodus of Ezekielos." *Jewish Tribunal* 94 (1929), 18-19, 60; Cross, J., and S. I. Tucker. "Allegorical Tradition and the Old English Exodus." *Neophil* 44 (1960), 122-27; Daniélou, J. *From Shadows to Reality*. Trans. Dom W. Hibbard (1960); Daube, D. *The Exodus Pattern in the Bible* (1963); Ferguson, P. "The Old English Exodus and Patristic Tradition." *DAI* 38 (1978), 7317A; Goppelt, L. *Typos: The Typological Interpretation of the Old Testament in the New* (1939; Eng. trans. 1982); Hauer, S. "A Commentary on the Old English Exodus." *DAI* 39 (1979), 4958A; Lucas, P. J., ed. *[The Old English] Exodus* (1977); Mazzotta, G. *Dante, Poet of the Desert: History and Allegory in the Divine Comedy* (1979); Shockley, M. "Christian Symbolism in *The Grapes of Wrath*." *CE* 18 (1956), 87-90; Wilson, J. *Christian Typology and Old English Poetry* (1974).

EXPEDIENT THAT ONE MAN SHOULD DIE *See* CAIAPHAS AND ANNAS.

EYE HATH NOT SEEN 1 Corinthians 2:9-10 falls in the midst of St. Paul's discussion of the *mystērion* of Christ crucified (1 Cor. 2:6-16), providing an introduction to his admonishment of the carnal Corinthians. The wisdom of God manifest in the Crucifixion, he says, cannot be grasped by those who are "material" or spiritually "immature." It is, however, revealed to the "spiritual" or "perfect," for whom it is experienced in "the totality of sensual and spiritual perception," comprehended by the heart (*TDNT* 5.341; 3.612).

The quotation in v. 9 ("But as it is written, Eye hath not seen, nor ear heard, neither have entered into the heart of man, the things which God hath prepared for them that love him") was attributed by Origen and others to a lost Apocalypse of Elijah or to the Ascension of Isaiah. It more likely derives directly from Isa. 64:4 — an attribution preferred by St. Jerome and supported by rabbinical exposition — with possible echoes of Isa. 52:15 and 65:17 and Jer. 3:16, sources cited by the Fathers and confirmed by modern critics (*TDNT* 1.756; 2.929; 3.988-99; 5.557). Despite the esoteric nature of the Pauline passage and its occasional heterodox use in the early Christian centuries, its clear affiliation with scriptural sources renders the influence of pre-Christian gnosticism unlikely (*TDNT* 5.378; 3.988-99).

The passage's immediate import, like that of its sources, is eschatological. Exegesis commonly stresses both anagogical and tropological aspects, as when Origen associates participation in eternal glory with Platonic purification and the development of the "spiritual body" (*De principiis*, 3.6.4). For mystical writers, "those unspeakable joys, which [God has] prepared for them that

unfeignedly love [him]" (Collect for All Saints' Day, *Book of Common Prayer* [1662]), may be glimpsed now in contemplation as, e.g., by St. Augustine in his vision at Ostia (*Conf.* 9.10). Exegetes from St. Leo the Great (*Tract* 65.3 [*De Passione Domini*]) to Cornelius à Lapide (*Great Commentary*, 1 Cor. 2:9) interpret the passage with direct reference to the mystery of the Incarnation. Its allegorical significance is extended in eucharistic interpretations, which appear as early as the 1st cent. (1 Clem. 34:7-8) and reach full theological and literary development in the 13th-cent. *Queste del saint graal* (cf. Ambrose Autpert, *In Apocalypsin*, 2 [2:17a]; 8 [19:9a]). Luther argues that the Pauline passage "applies to all cases of faith" (*Lectures on Isaiah*, 64:4; cf. John Wesley, *Letter to the Bishop of Gloucester*, 2.11), while Calvin directs attention to "the favours of God, which are daily bestowed on believers," signifying God's spiritual beneficence (*Comm. on 1 Corinthians*, 2:9; cf. Matthew Poole, *Annotations,* Isa. 64:4).

The richness of the exegetical tradition is paralleled in literature. With reference to the joys of heaven, quotations of the Pauline passage appear regularly in ME devotional works, often making explicit the corollary, "ne mannes tonge [may] telle" (*Ayenbite of Inwyt*, 261-62). Anagogical uses appear also in later poetry, as in a 15th-cent. lyrical description of celestial music ("The Seven Joys of the Virgin in Heaven" [III], 35-42 [C. Brown, *Religious Lyrics of the XVth Century*, 36]), Spenser's depiction of the "fairness" of heaven in "An Hymne of Heavenly Beautie" (78-105), or Crashaw's baroque portrayal of "Words which are not heard with eares, . . . Sights which are not seen with eyes . . ." ("Ode on a prayer booke sent to Mrs. M. R.," 59, 64). Giles Fletcher in "Christ's Triumph after Death" hails the heavenly Jerusalem where the saints "things unseen do see, and things unheard do hear."

The Wakefield Master's "Prima Pastorum" provides an incarnational context for Paul's words, recounting the uniqueness of Christ's Nativity (332-40, 364-68), while numerous works recall the text in describing the unimaginable sufferings of Christ (Julian of Norwich, *Showings,* Short Text 11.11-15) and his mother ("Mary so myelde alone," st. 5 [R. Greene, *Early English Carols,* no. 160]) at the Crucifixion. Drawing descriptive elements from Canticles, Edward Taylor develops incarnational and sacramental connotations of the text in his *Preparatory Meditations* (Second Series 56, sts. 2-3; 119, sts. 1-2).

Chaucer parodies the text's eucharistic associations in describing Sarpedoun's orgiastic feast (*Troilus and Criseyde,* 5.442-50). In Shakespeare's *A Midsummer Night's Dream,* Bottom's garbling of the Pauline passage is rhetorical and comic: "The eye of man hath not heard, the ear of man hath not seen, man's hand is not able to taste, his tongue to conceive, nor his heart to report what my dream was" (4.1.208-11). In more serious contexts, the allusion may be referred to the sufferings of hell, itself a parody of heaven: "Ne miȝte no tunge tellen þat euer wes iboren / þe stronge pine of helle" ("The Latemest Day," 29-30 [C. Brown, *English Lyrics of the XIIIth Century*, 29B]).

A similar reversal informs the description of Mammon's cave in the *Faerie Queene* (2.7.19, 31, 38; cf. the New Jerusalem, *FQ* 1.10.55), as well as Macduff's reaction to the murder of Duncan: "O horror, horror, horror! Tongue nor heart / Cannot conceive nor name thee!" (*Macbeth*, 2.3.60-61).

The text is used occasionally with reference to the Virgin Mary's bounty ("On God Ureisun of Ure Lefdi," 47-50 [C. Brown, *English Lyrics of the XIIIth Century*, 3]) and appears also in poetic treatments of romantic love. Early instances, often echoing Canticles, are ironic, as in the lyric description of a mistress's unparalleled beauty ("The Beauty of His Mistress" [II], 49-56 [R. H. Robbins, *Secular Lyrics of the XIVth and XVth Centuries*, 129]), Troilus's declaration of boundless devotion to Criseyde (Chaucer, *Troilus and Criseyde*, 5.1317-23), or the satiric description of the bliss of marriage in *The Merchant's Tale* (*Canterbury Tales,* 4.1338-41; cf. 4.1263-65). Yet from the Renaissance forward, poets recall the text when idealizing love. Shelley uses it in describing *The Daemon of the World* — "Human eye hath ne'er beheld / A shape so wild, so bright, so beautiful" (1.70-71) — as does Byron in a hymn to love: "But never yet hath seen, nor e'er shall see / The naked eye, thy form, as it should be . . ." (*Childe Harold's Pilgrimage,* 4.121).

Such Neoplatonic treatment of the allusion has dominated its literary use since the Renaissance. From Raphael's narrative of the world's creation in *Paradise Lost* (". . . to recount almighty works / What words or tongue of Seraph can suffice, / Or heart of man suffice to comprehend?" [7.122-24]) Pope proceeds to describe, in the terms of 18th-cent. rationalism, the

> Vast chain of being, which from God began,
> Natures aethereal, human, angel, man,
> Beast, bird, fish, insect! what no eye can see,
> No glass can reach! (*Essay on Man*, 237-40)

Keats, reflecting the Romantics' secularized view of nature, incorporates the allusion in describing the phenomenon of poetic contemplation ("To My Brother George," 19-46). Elizabeth Barrett Browning joins poetic sentiment to traditional religious reference in expressing the enduring desire for that which transcends human experience: "There is a land of rest deferr'd: / Nor eye hath seen, nor ear hath heard . . ." ("Weariness," 17-18).

See also HEAVEN.

Bibliography. Bruce, F. F. *Jesus and Christian Origins outside the New Testament* (1984), 120-21; Fee, G. *The First Epistle to the Corinthians* (1987), 107-10.

ROBERT E. WRIGHT

EYE FOR EYE, TOOTH FOR TOOTH   *See LEX TALIONIS.*

EZEKIEL   Ezekiel was a prophet at the time of the Babylonian Exile. His book, the last of the three major prophets, has become a particularly rich mine for artists and poets. Not only Milton's *Paradise Lost* and Blake's *Jerusalem,* but also American short stories such as Poe's "The City in the Sea" and O'Connor's "The Lame Shall Enter First" are indebted to the vivid narrative of Ezekiel.

Ezekiel's calling, like many aspects of his prophetic witness, is highly dramatic, commencing with his stunning, surreal vision of the Divine Presence enthroned on a chariot supported by four tetramorphic creatures moving, "wheels within wheels" (chap. 1). The prophet describes how "a voice of one that spake" (1:28) commanded him, "Son of man, stand upon thy feet, and I will speak unto thee" (2:1). He then received his divine calling to prophesy to a "rebellious" and "stiff-hearted" nation, his own fellow citizens in exile, who, he was assured, would reject virtually everything he said. He was nonetheless to speak the word God gave him, whether they would hear or not (2:7). Ezekiel was then commanded to open his mouth and eat "a roll of a book . . . written within and without" on which was written "lamentations, and mourning, and woe" (2:8-10) yet of which Ezekiel says, having consumed it, that "it was in my mouth as honey for sweetness" (3:3). This incident is seen by the Fathers as an analogy with the "Word made flesh" in the prepared heart of one with religious vocation (e.g., St. Gregory, *Hom. in Ezechielem,* 1), where the word is only "sweet" (cf. Pss. 19:11; 119:103) when the bitterness of its truth is swallowed whole. In Rev. 10:10 John the Divine is commanded, like Ezekiel, to "eat" a book which, he says, quoting Ezek. 3:3, "was in my mouth sweet as honey" — but adds that "when I ate it my belly was made bitter." This irony concerning the swallowing of truth is alluded to by Dante (*Purgatorio,* 32.44ff.) but adopted directly by Flannery O'Connor, whose club-footed fourteen-year-old prophet Rufus Johnson eats pages of the Bible before his sociologist would-be mentor and exclaims, "I've eaten it like Ezekiel and it was honey to my mouth!" ("The Lame Shall Enter First"; cf. Vg Ezek. 3:3).

The book of Ezekiel records other visions which likewise receive considerable literary development — notably his vision of the resurrection of the army of dry bones (chap. 37) and of the rebuilding of the Temple (chap. 40), the latter of which is reflected in Chaucer's *House of Fame.* Like Ezekiel, St. John the Divine in Rev. 21:10 was "carried away to a great, high mountain" where he saw "the holy city Jerusalem," but with this striking difference, that Ezekiel saw the New Temple (40-47) whereas John's New Jerusalem had no Temple in it, "for its temple is the Lord God Almighty and the Lamb" (Rev. 21:22). In this respect the "holy city" of Revelation is exactly like the millennial capital of Israel (Ezek. 45:7; 48:15-22), which, although it will have no temple, will be called *Yahweh Shammah,* "The LORD is there" (48:30-35). The geographic description of Ezekiel (47:13–48:29) places the New Temple, however, some distance south of the sanctuary, perhaps even at Bethlehem. Extensive medieval commentary on the temple vision in the time of the Middot commentary by Moses Maimonides (ca. 1180) includes Richard of St. Victor's *In Visionem Ezekielis* (1175), a reconstruction based, unlike Maimonides's, on Ezekiel's text, and the *Postillae* of Nicholas of Lyra in the 14th cent., the latter of which was known to John Wyclif and possibly, given the "courts" of Rumor and Fame in his *House of Fame,* by Chaucer.

Ezekiel is significant also for his insistence that the proverb "The fathers have eaten sour grapes, and the children's teeth are set on edge" (18:2) will no longer apply; i.e., it must no longer be assumed that virtuous obedience to the covenant on the part of a parent guarantees anything for a disobedient generation which follows (chap. 18). Each person is responsible before God for his own sins (18:19-22). Yet Ezekiel himself as a "watchman to the house of Israel" bears eternal responsibility for everyone to whom he is called to speak; if he fails to proclaim God's word, making clear that each person bear responsibility for his or her conduct, their blood will be upon his head (3:17-21). In this vein, Emily Brontë, in *Wuthering Heights,* writes that

It gave Joseph satisfaction . . . to watch [Hareton] go to the worst lengths; he allowed . . . that his soul was abandoned to perdition; but then, he reflected that Heathcliffe must answer for it. Hareton's blood would be required at his hands; and there lay immense consolation in that thought. (Chap. 18)

There is much talk in Ezekiel about images, as well as their creation. God speaks to the prophet about the fantasizing elders of his people: "Son of man, hast thou seen what the ancients of the house of Israel do in the dark, every man in the chambers of his imagery?" (8:12). Browning applies this passage in retrospect to Shelley, asking: "Or did some sunken and darkened chamber of imagery witness, in the artificial illumination of every storied compartment we are permitted to contemplate, how rare and precious were the outlooks through here and there, an embrasure upon a world beyond?" ("An Essay on P. B. Shelley"). T. S. Eliot's persona in *The Waste Land* finds the chambers of imagery in ruins:

What are the roots that clutch, what branches grow
Out of this stony rubbish? Son of man,
You cannot say, or guess, for you know only
A heap of broken images. . . .

Ezekiel's prophecies concerning the great battle (chaps. 38–39; cf. "Armageddon" in Rev. 16:16) have generally been of more interest to theologians and biblical scholars than they have to writers of poetry and fiction. They have, however, helped to characterize Ezekiel as an apocalyptic prophet, a quality Thackeray seems to have in mind in *The Newcomes,* where the Irish priest Dr. McGuffog is said to be "called in his native country the Ezekiel of Clackmannan" (chap. 7). In American literature John Woolman writes in his journal about feeling impelled to speak out against "drinking and vain sports" in a tavern, "while reading what the Almighty said to Ezekiel, respecting his duty as a watchman." In the 20th cent. A. M. Klein takes a disenchanted view concerning the apropos of the prophet's message in "Ezekiel the Simple Opines," doubting that fasting, litanies of worship, charity to the poor, and sackcloth and ashes repentance can prevent the recurrence of Jewish captivity and suffering.

See also DRY BONES, VALLEY OF; WHEELS WITHIN WHEELS.

Bibliography. Eichrodt, W. *Ezekiel: A Commentary* (1970); Widengren, G. *Literary and Psychological Aspects of the Hebrew Prophets* (1948).

EZRA   In Jewish tradition the most luminous character of this name is the ascribed author of the memoirs in Ezra 7–10 and Neh. 8–10. He traced his genealogy to Aaron (Ezra 7:1-6) and is regarded as a scribe especially learned in the Torah. After holding a high position in the court of Artaxerxes, he was allowed to return with other expatriates to rebuild Jerusalem in either 458 B.C. (Artaxerxes I) or 397 B.C. (Artaxerxes II). At the Feast of Tabernacles (Neh. 7:73–8:12) he read and expounded the "book of the law of Moses" to the people, encouraging their return to faithful observance. Some later writers identify him with Malachi (Meg. 15a; Tg. Mal. 1:1).

F

FACE TO THE WALL *See* HEZEKIAH.

FAITH The most concise biblical definition of faith is found in the Epistle to the Hebrews: "Faith is the substance of things hoped for, the evidence of things not seen" (11:1). In this chapter faith is exemplified by memorable figures from salvation history who, having heard the call of God, obeyed at once. By faith they became heirs of the covenant and pilgrims on earth searching for a better heavenly country (11:13, 16).

The writer explains that "through faith we understand that the worlds were framed by the word of God" (11:3); i.e., faith grants the possibility of understanding things one can never know with evidential certitude. Faith also prompted the parents of Moses to hide him in the bullrushes despite Pharaoh's edict: i.e., faith gives courage to choose the good, or life itself, without fear of the consequences (11:23). Faith also sees one through persecution because of loyalty to the word of God (vv. 24-28, 35-39), even though receipt of God's promises is not complete in mortal life (cf. St. Augustine, *Enchiridion,* 6-8).

The cornerstone of NT faith is the Resurrection: "If Christ be not raised, your faith is vain" (1 Cor. 15:17). Because miracles (especially the Resurrection) are central to the meaning of faith, the commitment of faith is intrinsically resistant to purely rational analysis. Nor does it depend upon a consensus of human judgment (Rom. 3:3; cf. 14:22-23). For the writer to the Hebrews, faith is at bottom simply an acknowledgment of Jesus as "author and finisher of our faith" (Heb. 12:2); hence, "without faith it is impossible to please him" (Heb. 11:6).

The term *faith* is used in a variety of ways in English literature, most derived, through centuries of tradition, from the Bible itself. First, in the OT, the Heb. noun *'emunah* has the basic sense of trustworthiness and corresponds to the verb "to believe," *'emun* (e.g., Deut. 7:9; Ps. 89:1-33). It normally refers to the "faithfulness" of God rather than the "faith" of persons (cf. Rom. 3:3; Gal. 5:22). The substantial development of this term, however, is in the NT (cf. John 3:1-5). Jesus refers to faith strong enough to work miracles (Matt. 17:20; 9:28); the sense here is of absolute trust (cf. Lat. *fiducia*) or reliance upon the preexisting faithfulness of God; to believe God is to rely on his word (e.g., Gen. 15:1-6; Exod. 4:15, 28-30). The degree to which individuals trust God, as the story of St. Peter's attempt to walk out to meet Christ on the water suggests, is the degree to which they can overcome the typical limitations of their human nature (Matt. 14:23-33). Here the word of God which must be trusted is Jesus himself.

Second, St. Paul says that faith is a product of the word written and the word preached: "Faith cometh by hearing, and hearing by the word of God" (Rom. 10:17). While faith thus defined must have an intellectual content, mere assent to facts or truths does not count as "saving" faith: as the characterization of Mephistopheles in Marlowe's

Doctor Faustus makes clear (e.g., 1.3.320-27), "the devils also believe, and tremble" (James 2:19). Faith does not merely "accept the Gospel"; it accepts it as God's irrefragible word (2 Thess. 2:13).

Third, "faith without works is dead" (James 2:17-26), not proscriptively but evidentially. For the "faith which comes by hearing" is also acceptance of the truth about one's self; hence repentance and faith which "justifies" are intimately connected (Acts 2:38-44; 17:30, 34; 26:20). St. Thomas Aquinas insists that the person must be primary in the act of faith; just as an individual's word is believed, so also the formal aspect of faith consists in the fact that God is believed (*Summa Theol.* 2.2.q.11,a.1; q.2,a.2). In the "act of faith," says Aquinas, a person enters into a personal relationship with the God who speaks to him.

Finally, the term "the Faith" signifies the whole body of Christian doctrine and precept; this use of the term has its origin in the letters of Paul, where Gk. *pistis* is used as such a metonym (Gal. 1:23; 1 Tim. 4:1, 6; cf. Rom. 1:5). It is in this latter sense that the Epistle of Jude exhorts its readers "that ye should earnestly contend for the faith which was once delivered unto the saints" (v. 3). *Fides* so defined is unitive (the word is cognate with Sanskrit *bhidh,* "unite" or "bind together"); and in the NT the goal of faith is said to be unity (Eph. 4:5, 13).

The burden of early patristic commentary falls on the second and fourth aspects of faith, what Tertullian called the "rule of faith" — the core of credal and catechetical doctrine necessary to salvation (or membership in the church). St. Augustine illustrates the chief reason for this focus in his *Enchiridion* — protection of the fledgling church from rampant syncretism and heresy. He is also at pains to say that persons are not saved "through the merit of their own works" or by the determination of their own free will, but are dependent upon grace. He quotes Paul, "By grace are ye saved through faith; and that not of yourselves: it is the gift of God: Not of works, lest any man should boast" (Eph. 2:8-9). But that his readers may understand good works are not wanting "in those who believe" Augustine is careful to quote also the following verse, "For we are his workmanship, created in Christ Jesus unto good works, which God hath before ordained that we should walk in them" (v. 10; *Enchiridion,* 30-31).

Despite concern for the "rule of faith," matters of faith soon grew too theologically complex for simple and untutored laypeople. The *praeambula fidei* or *antecedens fidem,* as 13th-cent. scholastics called them, were "antecedent" philosophical questions concerning the nature of humanity, the character of God, the demonstrability of moral law, the problem of knowledge, and the relationship of nature and grace (to name a few). This corpus was elaborated with such dense and labored prolixity that matters of reason and faith could seem almost at odds. One of Aquinas's major efforts was to resolve this problem: reason, he said, enables us to perceive the

"divine signs"; however, it is grace which makes us to see *in* them a call to personal faith (*Summa Theol.* 2.2.q.1,a.5 ad 1). But an unfortunate effect of the sheer industry as well as method of the scholastics was that the rational element proved more amenable to philosophical analysis. The questions of grace operating at a personal level to create faith or of God's faithfulness being the foundation of faith's possibility, clear in both Augustine and Aquinas, tended to slip into the background. *Fides quaerens intellectum,* faith seeking understanding, was the privilege of a few: for the majority all that was held necessary (or possible) was *fides in ecclesiam* or "implicit faith."

Partly for this reason, faith is often opposed to heresy or apostasy in medieval poetry; in *Cleanness* one learns of "folke in her fayth waȝt founden vntrue," who "forloyne her fayth and folȝed other goddes" (1161-65). In *St. Erkenwald* the first Roman missionary to Britain, St. Augustine of Canterbury, is praised for having "preched he here the pure fayth and plantyd the trouthe" (13). The term "god fayth" (good faith) is found dozens of times in works of the Pearl Poet, Langland, and Chaucer with much the same value as in modern usage, except that on occasions it bears a residue of its origins in the notion of "God's faithfulness" as the model for trustable intent, usually reinforcing the natural pun: "In god fayth quoth the godman with a goud wille" (*Sir Gawain and the Green Knight,* 1969); "In goud faythe quoth Gawayn God yow forȝelde" (1535; cf. 1264).

The Augustinian monk Martin Luther found implicit faith unsatisfactory. Studying Paul's letter to the Romans, he discovered anew the Pauline doctrine of justification by faith, in the initial sense above, and also as declared in Eph. 2:8-9. His resulting opposition to any evidence of justification by works or merit (the sale of indulgences, quantified penances, etc.) put him on his collision course with the authority of Rome, and at the same time, inadvertently perhaps, established the modern notion of faith as essentially a personal and hence subjective matter: *Hier steht ich.* "Every man is responsible for his own faith, and he must see to it for himself that he believes rightly. As little as another can go to hell or heaven for me, so little can he believe or disbelieve for me; and as little as he can open or shut heaven or hell for me, so little can he drive me to faith or unbelief " (*Secular Authority,* 211). That is, no sacrament of the church, be it baptism or penance, can, for Luther, give "justifying faith." Accordingly, the scholastic's "faith informed by love" was not sufficiently articulate for Luther: sacrifice did not for him "grant" faith; sacrifice only became meaningful where faith was already established in the heart. "What justified Abel was by no means his sacrifice, but his faith; for by this he gave himself up to God, and of this his sacrifice was only the outward figure." Luther was not fond of the Epistle of James and felt it should possibly be dropped from the canon because of its emphasis on works. His rejection of natural theology in favor of the Reformation formula *sola fide, sola scriptura, solus Christus* set him sharply at odds with the orthodox Catholic definition of "faith" in its sense of *fides in ecclesiam.*

Calvin, who disputes Augustine and Erasmus that Heb. 11:1 provides a definition of faith, nevertheless offers an Erasmian modification of Luther's emphasis: "It is faith alone which justifies, but the faith which justifies is not alone" (*Comm. on James,* 2:14-25; cf. *Comm. on Hebrews,* 11:1; for his own definition of faith see *Inst.* 3.2.7, 14). On the dispute concerning faith and works, or, as it was styled, between Paul and James, Calvin observes: "When Paul says we are justified by faith, he means precisely that we have won a verdict of righteousness in the sight of God. James has quite another intention, that the man who professes himself to be faithful should demonstrate the truth of his fidelity by works" (*Comm. on James,* 2:21). Thus Calvin sees the arguments of Paul and James as distinct but complementary.

The 16th cent. in England was characterized by a collapsing of all previous *distinctiones* of discussion concerning faith into matters of catechism and conformity. The 1562 *Articles of Religion* of the Church of England and the *Official Homilies Appointed to Be Read in Churches* of the same year, although largely drafted by Cranmer, were an imposition of "consensus" in the form of an itemized "test of faith." St. Thomas More had suggested in his *Utopia* that this was not a proper definition of the Christian state, and he is famous for reminding his accusers (in the spirit of Rom. 3:3; 14:22-23) that faith does not depend upon a consensus to be valid (see Roper's *Life*). Protestant poetics, as developed in Sidney's *Defense of Poetry* (1579-80), argues that poetry is to be preferred to philosophy as a means of teaching virtue because, in effect, it naturally engages the mystery of faith — meaning here something not unlike "the suspension of disbelief." In Spenser's *Faerie Queene* the personification of faith is not in the minor character Fidessa but in the Redcrosse Knight himself and in Una, who comprise faith in its institutional and unitive senses.

Seventeenth-century treatments tend to deal with a broader spectrum of the theological and psychological aspects of faith. Donne, whose language about faith in his poems is often applied to courteous or amorous analogy, reflects in his "1613 Ecologue" that "As, for divine things, faith comes from above, / So, for best civil use, all tinctures move / From higher powers" (65-67); in his verse letter to the Lady Carey he wishes "to speake things which by faith alone I see" (12), not the hidden things of God, of course, but such as he imagines of the lady in question. Similarly, in "To the Countesse of Bedford," he parodies a theological commonplace: "Reason is our Soules left hand, Faith her right, / By these we reach divinity, that's you." Faith is here again a synonym for innocence of experience which nonetheless imagines it. In another theological allusion,

Then back again to implicit faith I fall,
And rest on what the Catholique voice doth teach.
That you are good: and not one Heretique
Denies it. (15-18)

On a higher plane, when he wishes to compliment George Herbert's mother in "To the Lady Magdalene Herbert," he compares her to her namesake, saying that in Mrs. Herbert "An active faith so highly did advance, / That she once knew, more than the Church did know, / The Resurrection." As a priest and student of theology, however, Donne was keenly aware of the tendency of rationalism to kill personal faith and prays in his "Litanie," "Let not my mind be blinded by more light / Nor Faith, by Reason added, lose her sight."

Herbert's poem on faith celebrates its power to transform vision and understanding:

> Faith makes me any thing, or all
> That I beleeve is in the sacred storie:
> And where sinne placeth me in Adam's fall,
> Faith sets me higher in his glorie. ("Faith," 16-20)

In a passage later much admired by John Wesley, Jeremy Taylor warns against equating faith with mere belief. He writes that

> though a great part of mankind pretend to be sav'd by Faith, yet they know not what it is, or else wilfully mistake it, and place their hopes upon sand or the more Unstable water [i.e., their baptism as an infant]. Believing is the least thing in a justifying Faith. For Faith is a conjunction of many Ingredients; and Faith is a Covenant, and Faith is a law, and Faith is Obedience, and Faith is a work, and indeed is a sincere cleaving to and a closing with the termes of the Gospel in every instance, in every particular. (*Righteousness Evangelical* [1663], 205)

While neither Henry Vaughan nor Herbert would in the end disagree with Taylor, Vaughan's conversion poems in *Silex Scintillans* (1650) include one on "Faith" which stresses the centrality of belief. Observing how "when the Sun of righteousness / Did once appear" the limitations of natural revelation as well as the Law and its liturgy ceased to have spiritual power in themselves, he describes how in their stead:

> So are now *Faith, Hope, Charity*
> Through him Compleat;
> Faith spans up blisse; what sin, and death
> Put us quite from,
> Lest we should run for't out of breath,
> Faith brings us home;
> So that I reed no more, but say
> *I do believe,*
> And my most loving Lord straitway
> Doth answer, *Live.* (35-44)

Vaughan, converted in part through the poetry of Herbert, in this respect joins with him in anticipating the mainstream of evangelical piety in the 18th cent.

At the same time a skeptical fideism influenced by

developments among French Catholic writers was gaining ground in England. Its roots trace to earlier writers such as Pico della Mirandola, who published (1520) a six-book argument, itself indebted to Sextus Empiricus, dedicated to showing the insufficiency of human reason for certitude. Dividing all philosophers into three groups — the dogmatists who claim certitude, the academics who deny, and the skeptics (or Pyrrhoists) who do neither but rather doubt, Mirandola placed himself in the last category.

This line of thinking influenced Montaigne's *Apology for Raymond Sebond* (1580), which argues that human learning may be dangerous and quite often useless, whereas "only humilitie and submission is able to make a perfect honest man. Every one must not have the knowledge of his dutie referred to his own judgment, but ought rather to have it prescribed unto him, and not be allowed to chuse it at his pleasure and free will" (*Essays* [trans. Florio], 2.189). Montaigne applies this argument for the necessity of "higher authority" to "the lawes of religion and Politik decrees."

Montaigne's disciple Pascal, of Jansenist (French Augustinian) sympathies, and a near contemporary of Jeremy Taylor, applied Montaigne's argument more directly to matters of faith: "If we submit everything to reason, our religion will have no mysterious and supernatural element. If we offend the principles of reason, our religion will be absurd and ridiculous" (*Pensées* [trans. Trottier], 78). In effect, it is more rational to submit to authority in religion, says Pascal, than not: "There is nothing so conformable to reason as the disavowal of reason."

In the Church of England, whose officially "rationalist" position was still closely reflected in Richard Hooker's *The Laws of Ecclesiastical Polity* (1593-97), Montaigne and Pascal were nearly anathema, and in the 18th cent. the influence of "Port-Royal" mystical fideism was roundly repudiated in pulpit and treatise alike. The appeal of Catholic fideism of this stripe to figures as diverse as John Wesley, John Fletcher, Elizabeth Rowe, and William Cowper made the evangelical and Methodist adherents susceptible to hysterical charges of Jesuitical subterfuge, a "secret Catholicism."

Ironically, this association was made possible by Catholic apologetic strategies for undermining Calvinist and Anglican "rational religion," including such famous and controversial works as Father Simon's *Critical History of the Old Testament* (trans. 1682) — which called into question the reliability of the text of the Bible itself. Skeptical fideism had not since Aquinas been welcomed by Catholic theologians as a means of "defending the faith" *inside* the Church. (Montaigne and Thomas Browne were alike put on the Index.) Hence the Jesuits opposed Jansenism in France with passionate intensity, even as they and others used parallel arguments in England to achieve apologetic objectives. *Fiat Lux* (1661) by the Franciscan John Canes begins by establishing a case for skepticism concerning the

powers of reason and ends by leading the reader to fideist submission to the authority of the Church. Although this was "answered" by John Owen's *Animadversions* (1662), in which the Independent pastor and spiritual writer analyzed Canes's strategy, pointing out that it steers "poor unstable souls . . . to the Borders of Atheism, under a pretense of leading them to the Church" (156), in fact the tactic was quite effective in a number of cases.

Despite the efforts of Chillingworth (*Religion of Protestants* [1638]), Stillingfleet (*Rational Account of the Protestant Religion* [1665]), and Tillotson (*The Rule of Faith* [1666]), Anglican theology during this period may have, in fact, proved weakest in the point it most wished to defend — a rationally grounded faith, with the more rational buttressing for faith arguably coming from Dissenters such as Richard Baxter, John Owen, and literary apologists such as John Milton, whose prose works as well as poetry show he was not shy of attempting a rational justification of faith.

The popular mind in this period was, however, quite evidently open to such a skeptical fideism, as is well evidenced by the remarkable popularity of Sir Thomas Browne's *Religio Medici* (1642) through the 17th and early 18th cents. Browne suggests, in ways which also recall Donne's "Litany 7," that it is better to remain in ignorance and believe than to strive for that knowledge which seems to make belief unnecessary. Browne comments that it is the devil's stratagem to persuade us to "raise the structures of . . . Reason," while using the resulting overbalance "to undermine the edifice of . . . Faith" (*Works*, 1.31-32). The task of an intelligent person of science and learning is also then to teach "haggard and unclaimed reason to stoop to the lure of Faith. . . . And this I think is no vulgar part of Faith, to believe a thing not only above, but contrary to Reason, and against the arguments of our proper Senses" (17-18). (Here Browne almost precisely anticipates Kierkegaard, who also drew on Pascal.)

Browne's *Religio Medici* was one of the most important books in the life of John Dryden; Father Simons's *Critical History* was another. Together they led Dryden to reject the rationalist apologetic of the Church of England and to conclude with Burnet that "there was no certain proof of the Christian religion, unless we took it from the authority of the church as infallible" (Burnet, *History*, 1.1.335). The choice for one convinced of the skeptical argument was thus between atheism and submission to the authority of Rome, and for Dryden, as Louis Bredvold has observed, "skepticism became a high road leading from Anglicanism to Rome" (Bredvold, 86). His own *Religio Laici* (1682), its title drawn from Browne, and his *The Hind and the Panther* (1687) reflect this movement to a Catholic definition of faith. In the first poem, that reason which "pale grows . . . at Religion's sight" leads him to cry out for dependable authority: "Such an *Omniscient* Church we wish indeed; / 'Twere worth *Both Testaments,* and cast in the *Creed . . .*" (282-83). In the second poem Dryden urges: "Let reason then Her own quarry fly . . . how can finite grasp Infinity?" (104-05; cf. *Religio Laici,* 39-40, 114).

The real issue defining faith grew out of what might have been seen in earlier times as a lack of faith; a profound need for certitude made the central question in this period one of authority. For most Protestants authority remained in the Bible itself and was mediated through individual reason and judgment; Catholics, seeing the apparent undependability of this process, found certitude in the infallible authority of Rome. For a Protestant, faith was to be grasped and integrated in personal terms; for a Catholic, faith was more pronouncedly implicit and an institutional matter.

Accordingly, literary discussions of faith in the 18th cent. tend to confuse faith as personal belief and subscription to ecclesiastical authority more readily even than their 16th- and 17th-cent. precedents. Subjectively asserted personal belief, a central feature in the spirituality of Quakers (the "inner light"), Baptists, Congregationalists, and a variety of Dissenters, was dismissed by rationalist latitudinarians such as Archbishop John Tillotson and philosopher John Locke (*Discourse Concerning Human Understanding,* chap. 19) as lamentable "enthusiasm." Against the appeal to personal experience of "enthusiasts" Tillotson typically argues for the rational ethical principles of "Christian religion," effectively a reduction of the content of faith to "observable duty" and moral principles (Sermon 1 [1695]: "Of the great Duties of Natural Religion, with the Ways and Means of Knowing them") which are to be derived by observation from general human practice.

The question of authority, of its origin and relation to institutional faith, is explored in Swift's ecclesiastical satire *A Tale of a Tub* (1704), in which Martin (i.e., Luther, but here identified with the Anglican Church), Jack (Calvin and the Dissenters), and Peter (Roman Catholicism) adulterate their inherited vestments of faith. (Although Martin comes off least scathed, he is not entirely spared.) An implicit purpose of Swift's work is to ask the question, "What has happened to original faith?" For a Catholic like Alexander Pope, whose "Messiah" (1712) parallels Isaiah and the *Pollio* of Virgil, answering the question could lead to a different conclusion altogether from Dryden's, one in which the Deist's universalism seems a way out of the impasse. In a poem which he later affixed to his *Essay on Man* (1734), Pope pledges his faith to the

Father of All! In every Age,
In every Clime ador'd,
By Saint, by Savage, and by Sage,
Jehovah, Jove, or Lord! ("The Universal Prayer")

In some respects the evangelical revival under Wesley accented the confusion, even in its own attempt to revitalize personal faith. Among the Dissenters, Isaac Watts — a

rigorous Cartesian, author of a student textbook on *Logick* (1725), and a Calvinist — laid strong emphasis upon rational grounding for faith. However, one of his own parishioners, Elizabeth Rowe, wrote her popular poems and *Devout Exercises* (1737) almost completely under the influence of the Port Royal mystics. John Wesley, despite his strong rationalist tendencies, articulated a doctrine of salvation which, like Luther's, depended on personal faith alone ("The Scripture Way of Salvation" [1765]), stressing the subjective element of personal experience as the measure of faith. For the evangelical Anglican writer Hannah More, the rational foundation of faith suggested in Calvinist theology toughened her early neo-Gothic Romanticism and made her later work outward, analytical, and apologetically directed; for the Calvinist evangelical Cowper, whose emotional instability eventually predominated in his work, the question of personal faith was increasingly entangled in subjective uncertainty. His poetry emphasizes hope ("Hope," "Lively Hope, and Gracious Fear") rather than certitude, and when addressing faith he takes refuge in the Augustinian-Calvinist doctrine that faith cannot be self-generated and must be given by God ("Praise for Faith," in *Olney Hymns,* 65).

The subjective element in faith, even the self-generation of faith, is a bridge leading to the Romantics. The faith in "divine Nature" and in himself which Wordsworth works out in "The Prelude" is derived, like the self-generated "system" of Blake's theology, from earlier Christian epistemologies, and faith as a means of knowing for Wordsworth is, as for Wesley, a matter of "inner light." In "Resolution and Independence" "Genial faith, still rich in genial good" (38) is a threatened tranquility, one supported only by the resolve which gives "human strength" (112). When he reflects, however, on institutional faith, Wordsworth finds it in decay ("Decay of Piety"), and in his "Ecclesiastical Sonnets" he wonders about an earlier age in which "faith thus sanctified the warrior's crest / While from the Papal Unity there came, / What feebler means had failed to give, one aim / Diffused thro' all the regions of the West" (no. 9). Now, in another age, that Unity is attested "By works of Art, that shed, on the outward frame / Or worship, glory, and grace, which who shall blame / That ever looked to heaven for final rest?"

It was not the ardent atheism of Shelley and Byron, nor Coleridge's laborious journey from Unitarianism to Trinitarian faith, nor Coleridge's influence through *Aids to Reflection* (1825) on Sterling, Kingsley, and the young Christian socialists which most accurately anticipated the balance of the 19th cent. Rather, it was Wordsworth's idealization of art as a means of faith. Aestheticism, variously developed by the Morrises, Christina Rossetti, the Pre-Raphaelites, and even Oscar Wilde, is fundamentally a movement from identifying the shape of faith with its expression in art and architecture to a substitute faith in art itself, or "faith in the sublime." As such, like the Christian socialism of Kingsley, Fabian socialism of

G. B. Shaw, or Marxism of William Morris, faith is no longer faith in the biblical sense, but rather an optimism and even reverence concerning human achievement.

Matthew Arnold, an ardent opponent of faith in the biblical sense in *Literature and Dogma* (1873), *God and the Bible* (1887), and *St. Paul and Protestantism* (1870), could, while placing his faith in the same liberal sphere, nevertheless mourn a loss of religious faith of the sort that gives a kind of quiet certitude. His famous "Dover Beach" is, among other things, a lament for an age which has used up all its mythologies.

From the perspective of the 17th cent., at least, the romanticized fideism of Tennyson would have seemed ill-formed and substantially without biblical content; the poetry of Robert Browning seems as tantalized by the power of faith *(Saul)* as, in earlier times, its perversion (a theme in the dramatic monologues), but nonetheless it lacks any substantial positive address to personal faith. Despite some apparent similarities in the subject matter of religious poetry, the underlying *pietas* had been radically altered. The theme of the loss of faith, or rejection of faith, so vivid in the fiction of Hardy (see esp. *Jude the Obscure*) and the poetry of Swinburne (e.g., "Hymn of Man"), overshadowed the theme of "faith given," as in Francis Thompson's "Hound of Heaven," or "faith experienced," as in the poems of Hopkins.

Much of the same was true in America. Earlier Calvinist and Puritan poets wrote confidently of a faith they securely possessed because it had been granted by God and passed on in the covenant of grace, but they had relatively little to say about the personal struggle to find faith. Faith, too, could become a matter of "manifest destiny." James Russell Lowell celebrates the rewards of public faith in his famous Harvard "Oration Ode" (1810) when he writes "'Tis not the grapes of Canaan that repay, / But the high faith that failed not by the way." The content of the faith Lowell has in mind is surely biblically derived, but tends to be literarily directed to a revelation of the divine in nature, in a manner distinct from Wordsworth only to the degree that it maintains more of the familiar language of institutional piety. William Cullen Bryant's "Forest Hymn" represents a more widespread aspiration:

Be it ours to meditate
In those calm shades thy milder majesty,
And to the beautiful order of thy works,
Learn to confirm the order of our lives." (cf. "I Cannot
Forget with what Fervid Devotion")

For the Calvinist rebel Melville such sentiments as Bryant (or Transcendentalists like Thoreau) expressed and the ideals of public faith of a "covenant America" were two sides of the same coin, and alike repulsive. In *The Confidence-Man* (1857) he has Satan himself come on board the American ship of faith, *Fidele,* and by taking up the arguments of skepticism familiar from Father

Simon's *Critical History* and Montaigne, demonstrate that there are in fact no biblical Christians on board.

In the 20th cent. public or institutional faith has largely ceased to be a vital issue. James Joyce's *Portrait of the Artist as a Young Man* is one of the last major treatments of the theme of loss of faith familiar from the 19th cent. The modern era, perhaps more than any previous, emphasizes individual personal identity and has produced some literarily significant individual pursuits (and affirmations) of biblical faith. The classic case is T. S. Eliot, whose Dryden-like progress grows through a dark and weary skepticism ("Mr. Eliot's Sunday Morning Service," *The Waste Land,* and "The Hollow Men") to a revelation of personal faith ("Journey of the Magi") and finally an affirmation of public faith (e.g., *Four Quartets*). In one of the choruses from *The Rock,* heavily influenced by medieval and 17th-cent. spiritual writers, Eliot asks his readers to

Remember the faith that took men from home
At the call of a wandering preacher. Our age is an age
Of moderate virtue
And of moderate vice
When men will not lay down the Cross
Because they will never assume it.
Yet nothing is impossible, nothing,
To men of faith and conviction.
Let us therefore make perfect our will.
God, help us. (8)

Novelist and Catholic convert Graham Greene views the age as one of frankly immoderate vice. *Brighton Rock* (1938) introduces his notion of the only plausible ground of faith, not a rational theology but a realization of the "otherness," "the appalling strangeness of the mercy of God." *The End of the Affair* (1951) is designed to suggest, from a Catholic perspective, the modern need for personal faith; his earlier novel *The Power and the Glory* (1940) in its penultimate scene offers a back-porch analysis of the divergence between a subjective Lutheran and rigorously objective Catholic definition of faith.

Attempts at a traditionalist theology of faith have been made from the Catholic perspective by G. K. Chesterton *(Orthodoxy; The Everlasting Man)* and from the Anglican by C. S. Lewis *(Surprised by Joy; Mere Christianity),* both writers enjoying wide popularity as Christian apologists, lay theologians, and writers of fiction. In these authors, as in the poets David Jones *(Anathemata; The Sleeping Lord)* and R. S. Thomas *(Pieta; Laboratories of the Spirit),* there is evident nostalgia for the clearer definitions of an earlier age, but also a principled working out of a biblical tradition of faith in the secular modern context.

While American literature of the later 20th cent. offers fewer notable examples of such declarative addresses to faith, a similar recrudescence is discernible. Sometimes, as in the case of John Updike, it comes in the voice of

American antinomianism, and hence, as in Updike's "Seven Stanzas at Easter," surprises:

Make no mistake: if He rose at all
it was as His body;
if the cell's dissolution did not reverse, the molecules
reknit, the amino acids rekindle,
the Church will fall.

The stark "either/or," on reflection not so surprising in a Lutheran and American writer, leads Updike to impatient rebuke of 19th- and 20th-cent. poetry about faith:

Let us not mock God with metaphor,
analogy, sidestepping, transcendence;
making of the event a parable, a sign painted in the
faded credulity of earlier ages:
let us walk through the door. (*Telephone Poles and Other Poems*, 72-73; cf. 1 Cor. 15:17; Acts 14:27)

In another fashion, Flannery O'Connor makes much the same point in her short story "The Enduring Chill." In it a skeptical young student, embarrassed by what he imagines to be intellectually lowbrow origins, aspires to affect a Catholic prospect on faith partly because he imagines it to be much more "rational" and partly because he hopes it will offend his Baptist mother. The humor of the story lies in the young man's outrage and defeat when the garrulous Irish Jesuit priest who comes to give him last rites insists that the "faith which comes by hearing" can only be obtained by his first accepting the truth about himself: "How can the Holy Ghost fill your soul when it's full of trash?" the priest roars. "The Holy Ghost will not come until you see yourself as you are — a lazy, ignorant, conceited youth!" (*The Complete Stories*, 377; cf. 2 Tim. 1:6-14).

See also THEOLOGICAL VIRTUES.

Bibliography. Brantley, R. *Locke, Wesley, and the Method of English Romanticism* (1984); Bredvold, L. *The Intellectual Milieu of John Dryden* (1934; rpt. 1962); Cragg, G. R. *From Puritanism to Romanticism* (1984); Grant, P. *Six Modern Authors and Problems of Belief* (1979); Lewalski, B. *Protestant Poetics* (1979); Ridenour, G. M. "Justification by Faith in Two Romantic Poems." *WC* 10 (1979), 351-52; Vos, A. *Aquinas, Calvin, and Contemporary Protestant Thought* (1985).

FAITH WITHOUT WORKS A famous passage in the Epistle of St. James reads: "Yea, a man may say, Thou hast faith, and I have works: shew me thy faith without thy works, and I will show thee my faith by my works. . . . But wilt thou know, O vain man, that faith without works is dead?" (2:14-26). Seen by early commentators as a practical qualification to St. Paul's emphasis on faith alone as the entitlement to salvation, among some of the Reformers (especially Luther) this passage seemed to undermine the canonicity of the Epistle.

See also FAITH; GRACE, WORKS.

FALL The Fall traditionally refers to the first human transgression of the divine command. The biblical narrative gives an account of this transgression, including the events leading up to it and its immediate consequences. Doctrinally the narrative is usually interpreted as describing the cause and nature of humanity's wickedness, suffering, and estrangement from God. In turn, the doctrine influences how the narrative is read or rewritten. But stories of the Fall and doctrines of the Fall are not necessarily interdependent, and should be distinguished.

The story of the Fall is told in Gen. 2–3: the Lord God, having created man (Adam), placed him in the Garden of Eden and commanded him not to eat of the tree of the knowledge of good and evil: "for in the day that thou eatest thereof thou shalt surely die" (Gen. 2:17). After woman was created, the serpent spoke to her, contradicting God's warning about the consequences of eating the forbidden fruit and ascribing to God a jealous motive for his interdiction: "God doth know that in the day ye eat thereof, then your eyes shall be opened, and ye shall be as gods" (Gen. 3:5). The woman then tasted the fruit and gave some to her husband, who likewise ate. Immediately they knew themselves to be naked (Gen. 3:7), and hid themselves. God responded to their transgression by pronouncing a threefold curse: the serpent will crawl on its belly and eat dust; the woman will experience sorrow in bearing children and be dominated by her husband; and the man will sorrow and sweat to obtain food from the ground (Gen. 3:14-19).

Some critics have viewed this story "as a straightforward aetiological myth, designed to explain why a man cleaves to his wife and why he is the senior partner in the union, why he has to labor in the fields and she in childbirth, why we wear clothes, why we dislike snakes, and why they crawl on their bellies" (Evans, 9). The Fall also, notably, affords an explanation of human mortality.

The rest of the OT makes no clear mention of the story of Adam and Eve (but cf. Job 31:33; Ezek. 28:12-15; see also 4 Ezra 3:5-8; 7:11-13). According to various apocrypha and pseudepigrapha, such as 2 Enoch, Satan (Sotona, or Satomail) attacks humanity by means of an actual seduction of Eve: "He conceived thought against Adam, in such form he entered and seduced Eve, but did not touch Adam" (31:6; cf. also The Life of Adam and Eve; see Williams, 118-22; Evans, 28-34). But the familiar biblical interpretation of the Fall is given in the NT by St. Paul (Rom. 5:12-21; 1 Cor. 15:21-22), who treats the story as authoritative and archetypal. Paul focuses principally on the sin of Adam as being, in its nature and consequences, significant for the entire human race, and symmetrical with the sinlessness and life-giving acts of Jesus Christ, whom he calls "the last Adam" (1 Cor. 15:45): "For since by man came death, by man came also the resurrection of the dead. For as in Adam all die, even so in Christ shall all be made alive" (1 Cor. 15:21-22). Similarly in Romans, Paul declares, "For as by one man's disobedience many were made sinners, so by the obedience of one shall many be made righteous" (5:19). In this way, he amplifies and universalizes the significance of Adam and of his transgression by making them the backdrop against which Christ's redeeming acts are to be read. (References such as 4 Ezra [2 Esdr.] 3:5-8, 21; 7:11-13 suggest that the idea that Adam's sin had universally baleful effects was held in ancient Jewish circles as well as in early Christianity.)

Typological interpretation also links the serpent in the Fall-story to Satan himself. For if the second Adam was tempted by Satan (Mark 1:13), must it not also have been Satan who tempted the first Adam? In Revelation, John makes the identification explicit, referring to the overthrow of "that old serpent, called the Devil, and Satan" (Rev. 12:9). The same identification is supported by the words of Jesus: "I beheld Satan as lightning fall from heaven. Behold, I give unto you power to tread on serpents and scorpions, and over all the power of the enemy" (Luke 10:18-19; see also Rom. 16:20).

The Bible nowhere uses the term *Fall* in connection with the story of Adam and Eve. Once the story is read as involving the agency of Satan, however, the first transgression of Adam is plausibly paralleled with the first transgression of Satan. The latter is suggestively described in terms of a "fall from heaven" by Christ in Luke 10, and traditional interpretation of Isa. 14 sees the fall of the proud king of Babylon as post-figuring that of Satan: "How art thou fallen from heaven, O Lucifer, son of the morning! . . . For thou hast said in thine heart, I will ascend into heaven . . . I will be like the most High. Yet thou shalt be brought down to hell" (14:12-15).

How one conceives the Fall theologically depends on what humanity is thought to have fallen *from* and *to*. N. P. Williams thus distinguishes the early Church Fathers according to whether their Fall-teachings are "minimizing" or "maximizing" (Williams, 189-91), the latter typified by St. Augustine, the former by St. Irenaeus. Augustine's tendency to exalt Adam's original perfection and righteousness in Eden (see *De civ. Dei* 14.26) maximizes the physical and spiritual consequences of Adam's sin. Furthermore, Augustine extends the Pauline teaching that all die in Adam (1 Cor. 15:22), claiming that all sin in Adam. Hence Augustine's maximizing doctrine of original sin, which is based on Rom. 5:12 — "and so death passed upon all men, for that all have sinned" — but which mistranslates Gk. ἐφ ὁ by Lat. "*in quo*," thus construing the text as saying "*in whom* [i.e., in Adam] all sin" (*Contra duas epistolas Pelagianorum*, 4.7 [NPNF 5.419]; see also Williams, 307-10).

By contrast, Irenaeus, writing much earlier and in a hellenistic rather than a Latin milieu, teaches that God made Adam and Eve in a childlike state, as yet "unaccustomed to, and unexercised in, perfect discipline" (ANF 1.455, 521). Irenaeus's Fall-teaching accordingly "minimizes" the guilt of Adam and Eve and also renders more narratively explicable how they might have succumbed

to the temptations of the serpent (see Williams, 189-99). He even suggests that experience of "both the good of obedience and the evil of disobedience" may be a necessary component of humanity's "instruction in that which is good" (ANF 1.522; cf. Lactantius, ANF 7.142).

Maximizing and minimizing versions of the Fall should, however, be seen as diverging tendencies rather than as antithetical. Irenaeus, e.g., in no way denies the seriousness of the Fall and makes much of the Pauline doctrine of the two Adams, explicitly asserting that Adam, "who was so deeply injured by the enemy," was also "rescued by Him who conquered the enemy" (ANF 1.456), and underlining the symmetry of Adam's transgression and Christ's sinlessness. In Christ's resisting the devil's temptation to turn stones into bread, "the corruption of man . . . which occurred in paradise by both [our first parents] eating, was done away with by [the Lord's] want of food" (ANF 1.549). And yet the Augustinian tendency, magnifying original righteousness and original sin, predominated in orthodoxy from Augustine's time on, whether manifested in literal or in allegorical psychological readings.

In English literature the Fall-story is sometimes retold or treated thematically in analogues and echoes of that story, and doctrinally in literary interpretations of evil and of the human condition. Milton's *Paradise Lost,* which is the most influential treatment of the Fall in English, comprehends both the story of Adam and Eve and its main predecessor and analogue, the fall of Satan, and has much to say also about the condition of fallen humanity — "death . . . and all our woe" (*PL* 1.3). Milton combines maximizing and minimizing interpretations, emphasizing Adam and Eve's prelapsarian glories and the profound consequences of their sin, but also depicting the prelapsarian conditions for their further sinless growth and development, including work, storytelling, instruction, mutual deliberation and understanding, and what Milton refers to as "the triall of vertue" (*Areopagitica,* 1644; in *Complete Prose Works* [1953-82], 2.528; see also Evans, 242-71; Lewalski passim; Danielson, 164-201).

Other notable English treaments of the Fall-story are found in the OE *Genesis B,* in the ME mystery plays, and in *Cursor Mundi.* Spenser's *Faerie Queene* (bk. 1) recounts how Una's parents, Adam and Eve, after long exclusion from their native land (Eden) by a dragon (Satan), are restored to it by the Redcrosse Knight (Holiness). Other notable Renaissance retellings, in addition to Milton's, include those of Du Bartas, Grotius, and Vondel (for English translations of these and other versions and analogues, see Kirkconnell). Sidney incorporates "the accursed fall of Adam" into his poetics early in the *Apology.* Dryden's *The State of Innocence and Fall of Man* (1712), based on *Paradise Lost,* begins to blur, perhaps unintentionally, the distinction between pre- and postlapsarian existence. In *An Essay on Man,* Alexander Pope presents a naturalistic version of the prelapsarian "state of Nature," which becomes undermined by a general outbreak of unenlightened self-love (3.147-282).

In America, Nathaniel Hawthorne memorably explores the nature of fallen humanity and the mystery of sin in *The Marble Faun* and *The House of the Seven Gables* and in his short stories "Rappaccini's Daughter" and "Young Goodman Brown." Still other writers, such as Archibald MacLeish (*Songs for Eve*), revise the story altogether in order to portray the Fall as actually desirable for the evolution of human consciousness, a view with antecedents in 1st- and 2nd-cent. gnostic writings.

Such diverse poets as Thomas Traherne and William Wordsworth present pictures of the paradise of childhood followed by a "fall" into adulthood, Traherne in fact recurring to the minimizing views of Irenaeus (see Grant, 170-97; and on the Romantic poets, Smith, 137-62; cf. also Gerard Manley Hopkins's "Spring and Fall," Dylan Thomas's "Fern Hill," and e. e. cummings's "in Just spring").

Different writers use the Fall-story for very different doctrinal ends. Godfrey Goodwin in *The Fall of Man* (1616) paints a pessimistic view of human nature and history based on a thoroughly maximizing view of the Fall; but George Hakewill, in *An Apologie for the Power and Providence of God* (1627), without at all rejecting the story of the Fall, opposes Goodman's gloomy conclusions regarding its consequences by postulating a correspondingly high view of the grace and power of God in mitigating those consequences. Or, again, a writer like Thomas Hobbes, who does not use the Fall narrative at all, in fact creates his own etiological myth of the "natural condition of mankind" against the backdrop of the orthodox Fall-story and raises parallel questions concerning human nature, human misery, and the relief of human misery (see *Leviathan,* 1.13).

In thought and literature since the Romantic period, as suggested in the example of MacLeish, the tendency increasingly has been to revise both the story and the doctrine of the Fall. For centuries Christian interpreters have wondered whether the Fall, if it occasioned the advent and work of Christ, could ultimately be regretted; hence the paradoxical view of the "felix culpa" (see Danielson, 202-27). But Shelley openly assumed a view of the fall of Satan as Promethean and progressive (see the preface to *Prometheus Unbound*). What Shelley did for Satan, the evolutionism of the later 19th cent. did for humankind, so that "Fall" was radically reinterpreted as "Progress."

And yet modern literature by no means sustains an optimistic view of human nature or the trajectory of civilization. The story of the Fall, what Terry Otten has called "this most elemental of myths," thus appears "woven into the texture" of modern literature (Otten, 7). It can be seen as either undergirding or background, e.g., in the fiction of William Golding (*The Inheritors, Free Fall, Lord of the Flies*), Joseph Conrad (*Heart of Dark-*

ness), and Albert Camus (*La Chute*); in the fantasy of Lewis Carroll (*Alice in Wonderland, Through the Looking Glass*), C. S. Lewis (*Perelandra*), J. R. R. Tolkien (*Lord of the Rings*), and Stanley Kubrick and Arthur C. Clarke (*2001: A Space Odyssey*); and in the drama of Edward Albee (*Who's Afraid of Virginia Woolf?*). For even in its most basic form, in Gen. 2–3, the story of the Fall not only speaks of the first man and the first woman naked before each other and God, thus engaging the reader's sense of entanglement in the complex web of progenitor and progeny, of genesis and generation. It also faces the mystery of the perverse will that listens to the voice of the beast rather than the voice of God, and chooses death rather than life.

See also ADAM; EDEN; EVE; *FELIX CULPA;* ORIGINAL SIN; SECOND ADAM.

Bibliography. Brandes, R. P. "The Myth of the Fall in the Poetry of D. H. Lawrence and Ted Hughes." *DAI* 46 (1986), 2697A; Canfield, D. "The Fate of the Fall in Pope's Essay on Man." *In The Eighteenth Century: Theory and Interpretation* 23 (1982), 134-50; Danielson, D. R. *Milton's Good God: A Study in Literary Theodicy* (1982); Evans, J. M. *Paradise Lost and the Genesis Tradition* (1968); Grant, P. *The Transformation of Sin: Studies in Donne, Herbert, Vaughan, and Traherne* (1974); Kirkconnell, W. *The Celestial Cycle: The Theme of Paradise Lost in World Literature with Translations of the Major Analogues* (1952); Lewalski, B. K. "Innocence and Experience in Milton's Eden." *In New Essays on Paradise Lost.* Ed. T. Kranidas (1974); Murdoch, O. *The Fall of Man in the Early Middle High German Biblical Epic* (1972); *The Recapitulated Fall: A Comparative Study in Medieval Literature* (1974); Otten, T. *After Innocence: Versions of the Fall in Modern Literature* (1982); Smith, E. *Some Versions of the Fall: The Myth of the Fall of Man in English Literature* (1973); Tennant, F. R. *The Sources of the Doctrines of the Fall and Original Sin* (1903); Werge, T. "Mark Twain and the Fall of Adam." *Mark Twain Journal* 15 (1970), 5-13; Williams, N. P. *The Ideas of the Fall and of Original Sin* (1927).

DENNIS DANIELSON

FAT OF THE LAND Despite their maltreatment of their brother Joseph, at the time of his self-disclosure and their consequent apprehension that he would seek revenge, Joseph promised his siblings "the good of the land of Egypt, and ye shall eat the fat of the land" (Gen. 45:18). The phrase in Hebrew signifies fruitfulness and easy prosperity — the sense captured in the KJV translation and reflected in Melville's *Redburn,* where the life of American sailors on shore leave in Liverpool is described as "an exceedingly easy one, and abounding in leisure. They live ashore on the fat of the land" (chap. 30). The irony occasioned by the transformation of this condition to one of oppressive captivity in Egypt seems to be reflected in Mitchell's *Gone with the Wind,* where a Civil War soldier says, "I was captured after first Manassas and exchanged later and when I was in prison, they fed me off the fat of the land, fried chicken and hot biscuits" (chap. 28). But while the phrase is generally used as a conscious biblical allusion, it is typically without reference to the Joseph-story (e.g., Faulkner, *The Sound and the Fury*, chap. 2; Steinbeck, *In Dubious Battle*, chap. 14). Maugham's short story "The Unconquered," in *Creatures of Circumstance*, reflects some sense of the narrative from which the allusion is drawn.

FATHER, FORGIVE THEM   "Father, forgive them, for they know not what they do" (Luke 23:34): Jesus' prayer for his executioners.

See also LOVE YOUR ENEMIES; SEVEN LAST WORDS.

FATHER OF LIES   See BEELZEBUB; DEVIL.

FATTED CALF   See PRODIGAL SON.

FEAR NOT   See ANGEL; ANNUNCIATION.

FEAR OF THE LORD IS THE BEGINNING OF WISDOM   This is a fundamental precept of the sapiential tradition of the Bible (Ps. 111:10; Prov. 9:10). Bunyan's Christian in *Pilgrim's Progress* discusses with Hope the "good use of fear" which makes people "right at their beginning to go on Pilgrimage," as Hope says. "Without doubt," Christian replies, ". . . if it be right; for so says the Word, The fear of the Lord is the beginning of wisdom" (cf. Calvin, who distinguishes between servile "fear of unbelief" and "reverence mingled with honour and fear" in the believer, *Inst.* 3.2.26-27). In *God and the Bible* Matthew Arnold argues that secular liberalism cannot replace religion as an effective social force: ". . . however poorly men may have got on when their governing idea was: *The fear of the Lord is the beginning of wisdom*, they can get on even less by the governing idea that *all men are born naturally free and equal.*"

See also WISDOM.

FEET OF CLAY   One of the dreams of Nebuchadnezzar recorded in the book of Daniel is of a great composite giant, gold, silver, and bronze from head through torso but with legs of iron and "his feet part of iron and part of clay" (Dan. 2:33). The insubstantial support is shattered by a stone and the giant falls with a crash, reduced to powder. This description has given rise to the English expression "feet of clay" — meaning to be vulnerable out of proportion to superficial appearances. In Tennyson's "Merlin and Vivien" the magician condemns Vivien for, "harlot"-like, slandering Arthur's knights, judging "all nature from her feet of clay." Oscar Wilde's *An Ideal Husband* makes a generic complaint: "Why do you place us on monstrous pedestals? We have all feet of clay, women as well as men" (chap. 2). In the same vein, Dolly, in Somerset Maugham's *Theatre*, is determined not to grant her admirer "a peep at her feet of clay" (chap. 22). In his *Studies in Classic American Literature* D. H.

Lawrence laments Melville's homecoming from South Sea island adventures to "a wife: a thing with clay feet." The association in modern literature is thus typically with sexual frailty, something not implicit in the biblical source.

See also DANIEL; NEBUCHADNEZZAR.

FELIX CULPA   The paradoxical doctrine of the *felix culpa* teaches that the Fall of Adam was from one point of view fortunate, since without it humankind could not have experienced the unsurpassable joy of redemption. The finally comic history of the world is brought about by salvation through Calvary and the Atonement wrought on the cross. These acts of redemption in love and self-sacrifice inspire the believer with such joys as hopeful penance, patient suffering, acceptance of forgiveness, reconciliation, thanksgiving for conquered sin, and resurrection from penal death, none of which would have been possible (or, of course, necessary) without the Fall. Redemption is thus not the mere restoration of prelapsarian innocence with no memory of sin or guilt; the record of human sin, according to the doctrine of the *felix culpa*, is to be redeemed, not wiped out or changed.

The phrase "*felix culpa*" appears in the Easter Vigil of the Roman liturgy as part of the *Exultet*, a hymn composed in the 4th cent., probably by St. Ambrose, and sung in connection with the lighting of the paschal candle: the first light of the risen Christ breaks the darkness of human sin: "*O certe necessarium Adae peccatum, quod Christi morte deletum est! O felix culpa, quae talem ac tantum meruit habere Redemptorem!*" ("O assuredly necessary sin of Adam, which has been blotted out by the death of Christ! O fortunate fault, which has merited such and so great a Redeemer!"). Early Jewish Christians were keenly aware that the joyous feast of Passover is celebrated with the bread of affliction (*'ny*); St. Paul's reflection on the dialectic of broken law and grace, Fall and redemption, was extended by the Church Fathers to a series of binary images: first and second Adam; virgin Eve and the Virgin Mary; the wood of the tree of knowledge and the wood of the cross; the fruit of knowledge and the fruit of Mary's womb as the fruit of the tree of life in the Host. The dialectic became focused in the oxymorons of the *Exultet* and later hymns such as the *"Pange Lingua"* and *"Ave Maris Stella."* In medieval narrative, the juxtaposition of images from the Fall and redemption was used with similar effect in stories such as the "Legende" of Seth and the Holy Cross, *Le pèlerinage de l'âme* by Guillaume de Deguilleville, the end of Dante's *Purgatorio*, and the prologue and epilogue of *Sir Gawain and the Green Knight*.

In addition to the implicit allusion to the doctrine in the frequent technique of image juxtaposition, more explicit reference may be found in the writings of theologians such as Pope Leo I (PL 54.396) and Gregory the Great (PL 79.222). In the 12th cent. St. Anselm of

Canterbury's great theological treatise *Cur Deus Homo?* places the doctrine squarely under the primary doctrine of the Incarnation, and in the following century Franciscan theologians in particular use it to strengthen their emphasis on the "joys" of contemplating the Passion of Christ (e.g., St. Bonaventure, *Tractatus de Preparatione ad Missam*, 1.10). The question "*Cur Deus homo si Adam non pecasset?*" ("Why would God become man if Adam had not sinned?") is central in the works of other Franciscans such as Alexander of Hales, and receives dramatic if not hyperbolic expression in the writings of Duns Scotus. St. Thomas Aquinas refers directly to the doctrine (*Summa Theol.* 3a.1.3) in order to refute Scotus's claim that the Incarnation had to happen as part of a benevolent God's plan for the human race even if it did not fall. Devotion to Mary in the later Middle Ages extended the doctrine to a Marian *felix culpa*, expressed in the well-known ME song, "Adam lay I-bowndyn . . . Ne hadde the appil take ben, the appil taken ben, / ne hade never our lady a ben heuene qwen" (R. D. Stevick, *One Hundred Middle English Lyrics* [1964], no. 53). For those who saw the Virgin Mary as Queen of Heaven only because of the Incarnation, the Marian *felix culpa* would completely refute Scotus, although a more orthodox view of the Marian *felix culpa* would have to see her reign as also a result of her unique part in the Savior's work of redemption. The Marian *felix culpa* is referred to in poems by John Lydgate and in various late medieval salutations to the Virgin. A variation on it is found in the "*Dies Irae*" of the *Missa pro Defunctis* when the sinner implies that an incarnation could not have taken place in an unfallen race and pleads with Jesus that he is the "*causa*" of Jesus' life (efficient as well as final cause).

The doctrine also appears in the difficult context of theodicy in sermons by John Wyclif and in *Piers Plowman* (B.5.491) when Repentance vindicates God's permission of sin. In the Renaissance, John Donne preached that a great sin may in fact finally bring a sinner to repentance. John Milton, drawing upon parallels in Fletcher in England and Du Bartas in France, as well, perhaps, as Calvin (*Inst.* 3.23.7), has Adam refer to the doctrine in the twelfth book of *Paradise Lost*, a reference made famous in the 20th cent. by Lovejoy's essay "Milton and the Paradox of the Fortunate Fall." But even Milton has God elsewhere deny the *felix culpa*: "Happier had it sufficed him [Adam] to have known / Good by itself, and evil not at all" (11.88-89). The desuetude of the *Exultet* in Protestant churches and the future-oriented worldview of the Renaissance combined to submerge the *felix culpa* in the general doctrine of the Fall. Not until the World Wars and nuclear eschatology of the 20th cent. did the notion become current in English culture again. Lovejoy noted in 1937 that the doctrine would surprise his readers; standard encyclopedias of religion have not included a separate entry for *felix culpa* or Fortunate Fall. A more simplistic fascination, however, has been noted in such authors as James Joyce, Graham Greene, and Sheila Watson, and the *felix culpa* has even been seen, however dubiously, as a cross-cultural motif or archetype.

See also FALL; INCARNATION.

Bibliography. Danielson, D. R. *Milton's Good God: A Study in Literary Theodicy* (1982); Godard, B. "Between One Cliché and Another." *SCL* 3 (1978), 149-65; Haines, V. Y. *The Fortunate Fall of Sir Gawain: The Typology of Sir Gawain and the Green Knight* (1982); "The Iconography of the felix culpa." *Florilegium* 1 (1979), 151-85; Lovejoy, A. O. "Milton and the Paradox of the Fortunate Fall." *ELH* 4 (1937); rpt. *Essays in the History of Ideas* (1948), 277-95; Lukken, G. M. *Original Sin in the Roman Liturgy* (1973); Quinn, E. C. *The Quest of Seth for the Oil of Life* (1962); Tolomeo, D. "Leopold Bloom and the Law of Falling Bodies: Joyce's Use of the Fall in *Ulysses*." *ESC* 5 (1970), 301-10; Waugh, E. "Felix Culpa? Evelyn Waugh Reviews Graham Greene's New Novel [*The Heart of the Matter*]." *Commonweal* 48 (1948), 322-27; Weisinger, H. *Tragedy and the Paradox of the Fortunate Fall* (1953).

VICTOR YELVERTON HAINES

FELL AMONG THIEVES   *See* GOOD SAMARITAN.

FIAT LUX   The divine fiat of Gen. 1:3 by which God called light into being—"Let there be light: and there was light" (Vg: "*Dixitque Deus: Fiat lux. Et facta est lux*") — was the first in a series of commands or fiats which successively brought forth the created universe. This text, with its potent conception of a God who calls the entire cosmos into existence through a single, simple utterance, has exerted a powerful influence on the English poetic tradition, which has found in the "ordering efficacy of the divine Word" a paradigm or analogy for the act of artistic creation (Battestin, 79).

The earliest commentaries on this passage underscore the aesthetic dimensions of creation. In his treatise on the six days of creation, e.g., St. Ambrose remarks, " 'Let light be made,' [God] said. . . . But the good Author uttered the word 'light' so that He might reveal the world by infusing brightness therein and thus make its aspect beautiful" (*Hexaemeron*, 1.9.33). St. Basil speaks of the "sweet and gracious aspect" conveyed by the divine fiat (*In Hexaemeron*, Hom. 2.7). In his *Comms. on Genesis* Calvin returns to this theme, affirming that the *fiat lux* preceded all other divine commands because God intended that "the world was to be adorned with . . . excellent beauty." Calvin argues further that with this utterance God begins to manifest his wisdom, for light makes possible the act of "distinguishing" — the establishment and perception of differences — which is an attribute of wisdom.

Most patristic citations reflect homiletic concerns. Both Basil's and Ambrose's hexaemeral works were composed as a series of homilies, directed particularly against the doctrines of Manicheanism. In refuting the Manicheans, who maintained that the cosmos is divided between the forces of light and darkness, good and evil, St. Augustine asserts the absolute priority of God over all other existence. He argues that the Manicheans, in interpreting Gen. 1:2 to mean that God was enveloped in darkness before the creation of the world, fail to distinguish between the light which *is* God and the light which God has made; and he cites the *fiat lux* in support of his contention (*Contra Faustum Manichaeum*, 22.8).

On the question of the Trinity, Tertullian identifies Gen. 1:3 as one of the important biblical texts bearing on the issue (*Adversus Praxeam,* pars. 7, 12). Later defenders of Trinitarian orthodoxy, such as St. Gregory of Nyssa and St. Athanasius, argue that Gen. 1:3 affirms the Son's consubstantiality with the Father because it reveals a perfect union in the intention and execution of the divine will: the *fiat lux* is not to be understood as the command of a Creator to his creature but as the expression of an immediate and natural, rather than an instrumental, agency. As Athanasius puts it in his *Four Discourses against the Arians,* chap. 18: "And [God] spoke, not that, as in the case of men, some under-worker might hear, and learning the will of Him who spoke might go away and do it; for this is what is proper to creatures, but it is unseemly so to think or speak of the Word. For the Word of God is Framer and Maker, and He is the Father's Will."

Luther and Calvin, while reaffirming and amplifying the views of the early Fathers, frown on some of their allegorical readings of the Genesis fiat. Augustine, e.g., had suggested that Gen. 1 is an allegorical account of the origin of the Church and its worship. The earth, before it received the "form of doctrine," was formless and void, and into this emptiness the *fiat lux* comes as a call to repentance: "Repent ye, let there be light . . . and upon our being displeased with our darkness, we turned unto Thee, 'and there was light' " (*Conf.* 13.12). St. John of the Cross, in his late 16th-cent. *Commentary* on *The Living Flame of Love,* extends Augustine's allegory with his own mystical reading of the opening verses of Genesis: "Until the Lord said, *fiat lux,* darkness was over the face of the abyss of the caverns of the soul's feeling." Luther in his *Comm. on Genesis* indignantly rejects such allegorical interpretations, exclaiming that "Moses is here historically recording facts." The Reformers feared that an allegorical approach to the creation account would reduce it to the status of philosophical discourse or, worse yet, a species of myth (C. A. Patrides, *Milton and the Christian Tradition* [1966], 26-28).

The OE *Genesis,* strongly influenced by patristic hexaemeral tradition, offers a poetically embellished rendering of the *fiat lux:*

Metod engla heht,
lifes brytta, leoht forð cuman
ofer rumne grund. Raþe waes gefylled
heahcininges haes; him waes halig leoht
ofer westenne, swa se wyrhta bebead.

("The creator of angels, the Giver of Life, commanded light to come forth over the spacious ground. Quickly fulfilled was the command of the knight king; a holy light spread over the wilderness, as the Maker ordered.")

Most of the early references to Gen. 1:3 occur in similar paraphrases. An OE homilist refers to the text in a sermon on the subject of the Lord's day: "On Sunday was seen the first light on earth, for our Lord said this day . . . *beo liht and hit wes liht.* Of this day took all others their beginning" (*Old English Homilies and Homiletic Treatises*, ed. R. Morris [EETS o.s. 34], 138).

Writers of the English Renaissance show scant interest in the *fiat lux* motif. Spenser alludes to it briefly in *The Faerie Queene* (1.7.23), and in Donne's verse letter *The Storm,* 71-72, a poem describing an ocean tempest, the narrator declares that only a divine fiat can preserve his ship from foundering. But with the publication of Nicolas Boileau-Despréaux's translation of the late classical, pseudo-Longinian treatise *Peri Hupsous (On the Sublime)* in 1674, this attitude of relative indifference changed dramatically. The author of *Peri Hupsous* sets out to analyze the sources of an elevated style in writing, the first of which, grandeur of thought or conception, he illustrates by way of the biblical example of Gen. 1: "So likewise the Jewish legislator [Moses], no ordinary person, having conceived a just idea of the power of God, has nobly expressed it in the beginning of his law. 'And God said,— *What?*— Let there be light, and there was light. Let the earth be, and the earth was' " (*Dionysius Longinus on the Sublime,* trans. William Smith [1739], sect. 9). In the preface to his translation of *Peri Hupsous,* Boileau seizes upon the example of the *fiat lux* to illustrate a distinction between true sublimity and the sublime style (elaborate and elevated diction). Boileau's distinction was to become a critical commonplace in the 18th cent., as Hugh Blair's comments in his *Lectures on Rhetoric and Belles Lettres* (1783) testify:

> As for what is called the Sublime style, it is, for the most part, a very bad one; and has no relation whatever to the real Sublime. . . . "God said, Let there be light, and there was light." This is striking and Sublime. But put it into what is commonly called the Sublime style: "The Sovereign Arbiter of nature, by the potent energy of a single word, commanded the light to exist"; and, as Boileau has well observed, the style indeed is raised, but the thought is fallen. (95-96)

Thanks to Boileau, the *fiat lux* passage became the locus classicus of 18th-cent. sublimity. With the conspicuous exception of Edmund Burke, almost every critic of the sublime in the period — Joseph Addison, John Baillie, William Smith, Richard Hurd, Hugh Blair, Laurence Sterne, Lord Kames, James Beattie, Robert Lowth, and Dugald Stewart, among others — devotes space to this text in his analysis of the sublime. As Martin Battestin observes,

The divine Word supplied the premiss for the Augustan ethos; in Newton and the divines, in Milton and Dennis and the aestheticians, it remained the ultimate authority for assertions about the nature of reality. For by God's fiat, anarchy was dispelled, the jarring elements harmonized, due bounds prescribed, and all things given form. (79-80)

Thus, e.g., Sir Isaac Newton's scientific discoveries, by elucidating the laws of nature that the divine fiat had established at the beginning of time, were seen to confirm the "design" argument for the existence of God — the argument that the harmony of the creation bespeaks a divine artificer. Not surprisingly, Alexander Pope's witty epitaph for Newton celebrates this triumphant conjunction of faith and reason by recalling Gen. 1:3: "Nature, and Nature's Laws lay hid in Night. / God said, *Let Newton Be!* and All was *Light*."

The fiat of Genesis is, in fact, one of the controlling motifs of Pope's poetry, revealing itself in numerous guises and contexts, both serious and ironic. In *The Rape of the Lock,* he invokes it ironically in Belinda's command at the game of Ombre — "*Let Spades be Trumps!* she said, and Trumps they were" (3.46) — to suggest the disproportion between the elegant little world presided over by this goddess of the coffee table and the great cosmos called into being by the creating Word. The same compliment, when addressed to Queen Anne, assumes a vastly different significance: "At length great ANNA said — Let discord cease! / She said, the World obey'd, and all was *Peace*!" These lines, taken from *Windsor Forest,* draw on a panegyric tradition, influenced by 17th-cent. theories of divine right and royal absolutism, which approaches monarchy through the metaphor of divinity. Thus Dryden, in the Epilogue to *Albion and Albanius* (33-34), compares the royal command to the divine fiat: "*Thus* Britain's Basis on a Word is laid, / As by a word the World itself was made." Similarly, in a sermon commemorating the restoration of Charles II, John Garnett turns to Gen. 1 to describe the act which re-established order after the civil war: "May the same blessed spirit which pronounced the words, 'let there be light and there was light'; which brought order at last, out of all this confusion . . . continue to bless both our church and our state, with its influence, and our governors with its direction . . ." ("A Sermon Preached before the University of Cambridge," in *A Dissertation on the Book of Job* [1751], 342).

Numerous hymns and odes of the 17th and 18th cents. take as their subject the praise of order and creation, beginning with Milton's celebration in *Paradise Lost* of the "Omnific Word" who bids an end to discord and calls into being "Light / Ethereal, first of things, quintessence pure" (7.216-49). James Thomson's *The Seasons* carried forward the theme of a providential order in creation with his concluding apocalyptic vision of "the second birth / Of heaven and earth," summoned forth by "the new-creating word" ("Winter," 1042-44). Other poets who allude to Gen. 1:3 in treating this subject include Thomas Yalden ("Hymn to the Morning: In Praise of Light"), John Taylor ("Ode on Light"), and Thomas Blacklock ("Hymn to the Supreme Being"). Perhaps the apotheosis of this faith in the rationality and intelligibility of the divine fiat is Haydn's setting of the *fiat lux* passage in his oratorio *The Creation,* a work which owes its inspiration to Milton. As an ironic counterpoint to this prevailing strain of optimism stands the conclusion of Pope's *Dunciad,* which prophesies the return of night and chaos in a demonic reversal of the ordering fiat of Genesis:

Lo! thy dread empire, CHAOS! is restor'd;
Light dies before thy uncreating word:
Thy hand, great Anarch! lets the curtain fall;
And Universal Darkness buries All.

The original ending to the 1728 *Dunciad* makes the allusion to Gen. 1:3 even more explicit: "Let there be darkness! (the dread pow'r shall say)."

Another element in the period's interpretation of the *fiat lux* passage recognizes that the divine command is an expression of power which inspires terror and awe. These responses, which were to become the basis of the 18th-cent. understanding of the sublime, were identified as early as the 1670s by the great latitudinarian preachers of the Restoration. Isaac Barrow describes in one of his sermons our response to the divine fiat: "What a power must that be (how unconceivably great, both intensively and extensively, must it be!) which could so expeditiously and easily rear such a stupendously vast frame! vast beyond the reach of our sense, of our imagination, of any rational recollection that we can make!" (Sermon 12, *The Maker of Heaven and Earth*). John Baillie's observation in his *Essay on the Sublime* (1747) that the sublimity of Gen. 1:3 "consists in the Idea it gives of the *Power* of the Almighty" expresses the critical consensus which emerged from the period's exploration of the sublime.

With the advent of Romanticism, the prevailing interpretations of the *fiat lux* passage are restated in new and often radical ways. The analogy between God's creating word and the human artist is carried much further than in previous poetic theory, which had acknowledged that "God's art (nature) always transcends the poet's ability to imitate it." Whereas, in his *Essay on Criticism,* Pope had lamented the gap between the artist's power of conception and the imperfection of artistic execution by ironically invoking Gen. 1:3 (484-93), a typical expression of the Romantic and post-Romantic understanding of the creative process is A. M. Klein's celebration of the poet's naming power in *Portrait of the Poet as Landscape:*

. . . Look, he is
the nth Adam taking a green inventory
in world but scarcely uttered, naming, praising,
the flowering fiats in the meadow. . . .

Though aestheticians continue to cite Gen. 1:3 in their

treatises on the sublime, they begin to erect on this foundation much more elaborate theoretical edifices. In his *Oxford Lectures on Poetry,* A. C. Bradley emphasizes the Romantic preoccupation with the absolute transcendence of the sublime experience:

> The idea of the first and instantaneous appearance of light, and that the whole light of the world, is already sublime; and its primary appeal is to sense. The further idea that this transcendently glorious apparition is due to mere words, to a breath — our symbol of tenuity, evanescence, impotence to influence material bulk — heightens enormously the impression of absolutely immeasurable power. ("The Sublime," 57)

Though writers of the 19th and 20th cent. frequently allude to the fiat of Genesis, their references are usually local and passing, serving merely as a species of incidental metaphor. In *Don Juan,* 7.321-22, Byron observes ironically: " 'Let there be light!' said God, and there was light / 'Let there be blood!' says man, and there's a sea!" Other 19th-cent. poets who make use of the *fiat lux* in their poetry include Tennyson (*The Princess,* 3.306); Browning (*The Ring and the Book,* 12.588); Whittier ("Freedom in Brazil"); and Christina Rossetti (*Christmas Carols,* 2). In the 20th cent., Faulkner invokes the passage almost lyrically in his early novel *Mosquitos* to describe the mist which envelopes the yacht *Nausikaa.*

Bibliography. Battestin, M. *The Providence of Wit: Aspects of Form in Augustan Literature and the Arts* (1974), 79-91; Monk, S. *The Sublime: A Study of Critical Theories in XVIII-Century England* (1935), 31-35; Morris, D. *The Religious Sublime: Christian Poetry and Critical Tradition in 18th-Century England* (1972), 36-39; Rawson, C. *Order from Confusion Sprung: Studies in Eighteenth-Century Literature from Swift to Cowper* (1985), 383-89.

FRANS DE BRUYN

FIELD OF BLOOD   (Aceldama) After receiving his reward of thirty pieces of silver for betraying Jesus, Judas returned it to the Temple and went and hanged himself. The chief priests took the money and purchased a field (the "potters' field") in which to bury strangers (Matt. 27:7-10), events which, according to Matthew, fulfilled a prophecy of Jeremiah. (Peter later ascribes the purchase to Judas himself [Acts 1:19].) The evangelist observes that because of the source of its purchase money it is called "Aceldama . . . the field of blood" to this day.

The text itself caused St. Jerome problems sufficient to deflect exegesis: he observes that Matthew either misquotes Jeremiah, mistakes the passage for one in Zechariah (11:12-13), or has access to a text by Jeremiah now lost (*Ep.* 57.7). Following Jerome, textual matters alone still preoccupy the *Glossa Ordinaria* (PL 114.173), in part because most patristic commentators had on these accounts avoided the passage. The medieval Corpus Christi plays (e.g., *Ludus Coventriae*) are for the most part content to be done with Judas as soon as he has hanged

himself, and omit to feature the field of blood. An exception is the York "Remorse of Judas," where it is Pilate who suggests that the abandoned thirty pieces of silver be used: "A spotte of erthe for to by, wayte now I will, / To berie in pilgrimes þat by þe wey dies" (332-33). Similarly uninterested in pursuing exegesis, Calvin, in his *Harmony of the Gospels,* opined that Jeremiah's name had simply been put in error for Zechariah (*Harmony of the Gospels,* 3.177) and treats the passage sketchily, as in the 18th cent. does Matthew Poole (*Annotations upon the Holy Bible*), who feels the remembrance of prophetic reference may involve a conflation with Jer. 32:6-9.

The emergence of numerous 19th-cent. literary references to Aceldama are thus not evidently indebted to exegetical or liturgical tradition. Yet the narrative is familiar enough from the NT and perhaps also the Prayer Book lection for the Sixth Sunday of Advent that Thomas de Quincey can refer to a battlefield disaster as "one bloody aceldama" (*The English Mail Coach*), and John Ruskin (*Unto this Last,* chap. 2) can speak of material wealth as "the purchase-pieces of potter's fields, wherein shall be buried together the citizen and the stranger" with reasonable assurance of being understood. Francis Thompson's "Whereto Art Thou Come?" makes of a traitor to truth an analogue of Judas: "the Haceldama of a plot of days / He buys, to consummate his Judasry."

See also JUDAS ISCARIOT; THIRTY PIECES OF SILVER.

FIERY FURNACE   *See* SHADRACH, MESHACH, AND ABEDNEGO.

FIG LEAVES   What Adam and Eve used to cover their nakedness after the birth of shame (Gen. 3:7).
See also FALL.

FILIOQUE **CLAUSE**   *See* CREED; HOLY SPIRIT.

FILTHY LUCRE   One of the qualifications of bishops and deacons, according to the apostle Paul, is that they must not be "greedy of filthy lucre" (1 Tim. 3:3, 8). According to the *Rule of St. Francis,* which enjoins poverty on the friars, money ought to be understood in the light of the Pauline injunction as "excrement," from a spiritual point of view. In Chaucer's *Summoner's Tale,* the Friar's evident greed for monetary gain is thus a betrayal of his vocation; when groping for the gold "ferthyng" Thomas says that he has hid in his breeches he gets instead a thunderous "ferthyng" (fart), Chaucer's pun suggesting that in terms of the Rule to which he is bound the iniquitous Friar gets exactly what he is "looking for." Robert Burton's criticism of literary patronage in his *Anatomy of Melancholy* similarly associates the phrase with having "sold out" on first-order values: "Some out of that insatiable desire of filthy lucre, to be enriched, care not how they come by it *per fas et negas,* hook and crook, so they have it." In short, the phrase is attached not to money itself so much as to corrupt motives in acquiring it. A similar understanding attaches to Hawthorne's description of the panhandler in *The House of Seven Gables* (chap. 11), and is explicit in Anthony Trollope's shrewd observation about appearance of the phrase in Victorian idiom: "When we talk of sordid gain and filthy lucre, we are generally hypocrites" (*Thackeray,* chap. 1).

See also CHARITY, CUPIDITY; MAMMON; *RADIX MALORUM;* SIMON MAGUS.

FINGER OF GOD   The finger of God is an OT metaphor for God's power and authority as inscriber of the Law (Exod. 31:18; Deut. 9:10), as scourge of Egypt (Exod. 8:19), and — in the plural — as creator (Ps. 8:13) and source of dire warning (Dan. 5:5). In the NT the finger of God denotes Christ's power to expel devils (Luke 11:20; the Matt. 12:28 parallel substitutes "the Spirit of God").

Jewish commentary (Philo, *De vita Mosis,* 1.19; Ginzberg, *LJ* 1.53; 6.7, 62) often linked God's finger with vengeful and destructive action, a common emphasis in Blake ("I behold the finger of God in terrors," *Jerusalem,* pl. 12, 1.5) and Melville (*Moby-Dick,* chap. 119; *Pierre,* chaps. 7, 8). The image of God's finger in the act of writing (cf. Dan. 5:5) becomes an effectively pagan image of destiny in Byron's "Vision of Belshazzar" (9-16) and in Fitzgerald's "translation" of Omar Khayyam (st. 51), where the writing of the "moving finger" is actually unprecedented in the sources.

St. Augustine (*De civ. Dei* 16.43) and his successors linked OT and NT references in such a way as to stress the continuity and range of divine power, a theme reiterated in English preaching from the time of Aelfric (*Catholic Homilies,* 2nd ser. [EETS s.s. 5], no. 12).

The finger, pointed, could also symbolize divine guidance — sometimes, as in Sir Thomas Browne (*Christian Morals,* 3.5), in natural association with the hand of God, itself a common Renaissance emblem (see Rosemary Freeman, *English Emblem Books* [1948], 62-63). In Hopkins's "Wreck of the Deutschland" the symbolism of guidance and terror coalesce:

> Thou hast bound bones and veins in me, fastened me
>   flesh,
> And after it almost unmade, what with dread,
> Thy doing: and dost thou touch me afresh?
> Over again I feel thy finger and find thee. (st. 1)

God's finger as creative instrument, stressed by early commentators (e.g., Tertullian, *Adv. Marc.* 4.26.11; St. Clement of Alexandria, *Stromata,* 6.16) and in Chaucer's account of Adam's creation (*Monk's Tale,* 7.2008), is prominent in Michelangelo's portrayal of Adam's creation and is a common image for disclosure of benign creative energy, especially in poems by Browning ("Abt Vogler," 49; "Halbert and Hob," 50) and D. H. Lawrence ("Michael-Angelo," 21). This same image is deliberately

inverted by Tennyson in describing Hallam's death (*In Memoriam,* 85.20) to establish tragic irony.

Bibliography. Kittel, G., and G. Friedrich. *"daktylos."* *TDNT* 2.20f.

BRENDA E. RICHARDSON
NORMAN VANCE

FIRE AND BRIMSTONE   Associated in the Bible with the extremity of God's judgment upon sin, the rain of fire and brimstone upon Sodom and Gomorrah (Gen. 19:24) becomes a figure for apocalyptic judgment in the last days, both upon the world (Luke 17:29) and in eternity upon those who have rejected God (Ezek. 38:22; Rev. 9:17; 14:10; 21:8; cf. Ps. 11:6). Both rabbinic and Christian exegetes regarded these passages as explicit enough to require no commentary. Rev. 14:10 and 21:8 served to characterize hell for poets such as Dante *(Inferno),* Raoul d'Houdene *(Songe d'Enfer),* and the authors of medieval dramas such as the Anglo-Norman *Jeu d'Adam* and ME Corpus Christi plays. The vivid infernos of Hieronymus Bosch in *"Sicut Erat in Diebus Noe"* (popularly and ironically known as "The Garden of Earthly Delights") and the "Haywain Triptych" have this same unattractive "climate," as Milton's "lost Archangel" calls the heated and sulphurous environment in which he and his fallen cohorts find themselves floating: "the Lake with liquid fire . . . sublim'd with Mineral fury . . . all involved with stench and smoke" (*Paradise Lost,* 1.225-45; cf. 1.61-69; 670-74).

The striking force of the image, focused in Rev. 21:8, finds its way into countless English sermons from the Middle Ages to the present. Chaucer's good Parson is in the company of Jonathan Edwards ("Sinners in the Hands of an Angry God") and Sinclair Lewis's evil evangelist Elmer Gantry in at least this respect. The reason for the literary persistence of the scene is obviously, as Cardinal Manning suggested in his *Journal,* its power to *"confixit carnem timore."* Many readers have likewise been cautioned by the images retailed vividly by poet Francis Quarles (1592-1664) in his *Emblems:*

> I see a brimstone sea of boiling fire,
> And fiends with knotted whips of flaming wire,
> Torturing poor souls, That gnash their teeth in vain,
> And gnaw their flame-tormented tongues for pain. (no. 14)

Bunyan's Christian in *Pilgrim's Progress* warns Obstinate and Pliable that if they stay in the City of Destruction they too will "sink lower than the grave, into a place that burns with Fire and Brimstone."

In the 18th cent. the phrase "fire and brimstone" was used to describe certain kinds of Methodist and evangelical preaching which emphasized "the wages of sin"; by the early 19th cent. the theme was the butt of parody, as in Coleridge's "The Devil's Thoughts" in which

> From his brimstone bed at break of day
> A walking the Devil is gone,

To visit his snug little farm the earth,
And see how his stock goes on. (cf. Southey, "The Devil's Walk")

The stiff and judgmental Rev. Mr. Brocklehurst in Charlotte Brontë's *Jane Eyre* darkly observes that deceitful children will "have their portion in the lake burning with fire and brimstone" (chap. 4), and another of his kind, the "Walsall gentleman" who preaches that Catholics will all have this same destination by virtue of participation in the Mass, is held up by Matthew Arnold as an example of religious bigotry in *Culture and Anarchy* ("Doing as One Likes").

The image is commonly trivialized in the 19th cent., as when Melville's Ishmael, upon tripping over an ash box and stirring up ashes, laughs, "Are these the ashes from that destroyed city, Gomorrah?" (*Moby-Dick*, chap. 2). In the 20th cent. "fire and brimstone" becomes metonymic for hell, often the "hell" of war (e.g., Stephen Crane, *The Red Badge of Courage*) and, having lost its literal biblical power, still retains its post-Enlightenment association with a falsely smug preaching of gloom and doom. Such a case is found in Somerset Maugham's *Of Human Bondage:* "Now all he had anticipated was come to pass: the Vicar felt the satisfaction of the prophet who saw fire and brimstone consume the city which would not mend its way to his warning" (chap. 5).

See also HELL; SODOM AND GOMORRAH.

FIRST SHALL BE LAST   *See* LAST SHALL BE FIRST.

FIRSTBORN OF EGYPT   In the final and most severe of the ten plagues by which hard-hearted Pharaoh was afflicted in order to move him to release the Hebrew slaves, "at midnight the LORD smote all the firstborn in the land of Egypt, from the firstborn of Pharaoh that sat on his throne to the firstborn of the captive that was in the dungeon; and all the firstborn of the cattle" (Exod. 11:4-6; 12:29-33).

Charlotte Brontë's *Jane Eyre,* about to marry Rochester, suddenly learns of the existence of his mad wife. "My hopes were all dead," she says, " — struck with a subtle doom, such as, in one night, fell on all the first-born in the land of Egypt" (chap. 26; cf. Exod. 12:33). The recollection has sinister overtones in Samuel Butler's *The Way of All Flesh,* where the Bible-quoting but devilish Theobald Pontifex is angered by his son Ernest's disappointing performance at Dr. Skinner's school: "Then his thought turned to Egypt and the tenth plague. It seemed to him that if the little Egyptians had been anything like Ernest, the plague must have been something very like a blessing in disguise. If the Israelites were to come to England now he should be greatly tempted not to let them go." Howard Nemerov's pensive Pharaoh in "Moses," in his hard-hearted state, is similarly bereft of human feeling for his offspring: "My first-born

son is dead, the first-born sons / Of all Egypt are dead, but that's no matter. I am astounded, but I do not weep."

See also PHARAOH; PLAGUES OF EGYPT.

FISH   A product of divine creative activity on the fifth day of creation (Gen. 1:21), fish constituted a distinct component of the living creatures over which Adam and Eve (Gen. 1:26, 28), Noah (Gen. 9:2), and humanity in general (Ps. 8:8) were given dominion. No single species of fish is named in Scripture. The only biblical classification of fish occurs in the Mosaic dietary laws, which distinguish clean (i.e., those with fins and scales) from unclean fish (Lev. 11:9-12; cf. Deut. 14:9, 10).

Jesus considered fish one of the "good gifts" illustrating God's response to requests from his children (Matt. 7:10). Fish were directly involved in several miracles of Christ: the feeding of the multitudes (Matt. 14:19; 15:36), the tribute coin found by Peter in a fish's mouth (Matt. 17:27), and the great draughts of fish (Luke 5:4-7; John 21:6). In the incident recorded in the final chapter of John's Gospel, it is said that "one hundred and fifty and three" fish were found in the net which Peter drew to land, "yet was not the net broken" (21:11) — to the narrator an evident marvel worthy of recording in precise detail.

It was "a great fish" which delivered reluctant Jonah to his mission in Nineveh. On two occasions in the OT the folly of humanity is compared to the actions of fish. Qoheleth draws an analogy between those who succumb suddenly to evil and "the fishes that are taken in an evil net" (Eccl. 9:12). The writer of Habakkuk, wondering why the Lord chooses to use the wicked to punish unrighteousness, asks whether he makes "men as the fishes of the sea, as the creeping things, that have no ruler over them" (Hab. 1:14).

Talmudic and rabbinic commentators, as well as later theologians, speculated about whether fish, like other creatures, fell under the curse of the Flood. (In the 14th cent. Nicholas of Lyra questions one rabbinic tradition describing the waters of the Flood as boiling hot, requiring that fish be preserved aboard the ark.) Alfonso Tostado suggests that since mankind had not yet "sinned upon the waters," aquatic life continued in a kind of creational purity (Allen, 76). But association of the fish with uncontaminated purity clearly long predates medieval attempts at this rationalistic apologetic.

Since before the end of the 2nd cent. the fish had come to symbolize Christ and the Christian believer. One of the most famous references to this symbol occurs in bk. 8 of the *Sibylline Oracles* where, in a 27-line passage written in Greek hexameters, the first letter of each line spells out *'Iēsous Christos theou huios sōtēr* (Jesus Christ Son of God Savior). The first letters of each of these words spell *ichthus,* the Greek word for "fish." This collection of prophecies and religious teachings, partly heathen and partly Jewish-Christian in origin, the product of the assumed inspiration of a sibyl or prophetess, was referred to on several occasions by various Church Fathers. St. Augustine, e.g., in *De civitate Dei* draws attention to it, adding that the *ichthus* symbol applied very appropriately to Christ "because he was able to live . . . without sin in the abyss of this mortality as in the depth of waters" (18.23). In this connection, the fish became an important trope in Christian commentary on the Atonement (Battenhouse, 1040-42).

Tertullian draws perhaps the most explicit analogy between fish and the believer. Speaking about newly baptized neophytes in his *De baptismo,* he refers to them as "little fishes" who, after the example of "our *ICHTHYS* Jesus Christ," are born in water and thrive only by continuing in the water. Similar references occur in the writings of the Shepherd of Hermas, St. Gregory the Great, St. Clement of Alexandria, Lactantius, and Eusebius.

As persecution of Christians became more intense, the use of the fish symbol as a kind of password increased, both in written and iconographical form. In much of the catacomb art in which this symbol appears, it is explicitly associated with the Eucharist: in some pictures the mysterious fish is shown "swimming in the water with a plate of bread and a cup on wine on his back, with evident allusion to the Lord's Supper" (P. Schaff, *Ante-Nicene Christianity: A.D. 100-324* [1910], 279). Inscriptions containing fish symbols appeared on early sepulchral monuments and the fish image was also widely employed as a mezuzah at the doors of Christian homes and as an amulet on gems, medals, and rings.

Patristic writers often interpreted scriptural references to fish in symbolic terms, completely independent of the acrostic significance of *ichthus.* The writer of Barn. 10 sees the Mosaic stipulations in Lev. 11 and Deut. 14 regarding clean and unclean fish as being primarily a spiritual analogue, for the latter tended to swim in the deep part of the sea and "make their abode in the mud which lies at the bottom," rather than swimming nearer the surface like their scaled and finned counterparts. Similarly Origen, in his *Comm. on Matthew,* interprets the kingdom parable of the net (Matt. 13) in symbolic terms, the net typifying the Bible, with some of the fish therein caught in the prophetic net of Isaiah, Jeremiah, and Daniel, others in the net of the Law, and still others in the gospel net or the apostolic net. In his commentary on the feeding of the 5,000, Origen draws an analogy between the nourishment of the loaves and the fish and the impact of the Scriptures on the minds and hearts of those who feed on them (bk. 11). Augustine interprets the miraculous draught of fish in John 21 allegorically, suggesting that the 153 fish signify the elect redeemed at the last day, and drawn to Jesus and the Father by the Holy Spirit. The unspecified draught recorded in Luke 5 is thought, by contrast, to suggest the present "visible" church, in which good and bad, like the wheat and tares of Jesus' parable (Matt. 13:24-30), are commingled together (*In Joan. Ev.* 122.5-9).

The eating of fish rather than flesh in conjunction with religious observances, particularly during Lent, was an established tradition by the 4th cent. Exemplary literary references to this practice are to be found in *Sir Gawain and the Green Knight,* Shakespeare's *King Lear* (1.4.18) and *Pericles* (2.1.86), and Swift's "Holyhead, Sept. 25, 1727" and "Cadenus and Vanessa."

Comparing someone in an alien environment to a fish out of water need have no religious overtones, but in light of the context, Chaucer's comment in the *General Prologue* to *The Canterbury Tales* about the monk out of his cloister being like "a fissh that is waterlees" recalls Tertullian's comments in *De baptismo* about the significance of the water of grace as an appropriate environment for believers. Choosing to forsake the environment is commonly figured as rejection of baptism or of vocation (*Vitae Patrum* [PL 73.858]). John Gower, in *Vox Clamantis,* reiterates Chaucer's specific application to the monk, adding: "If there were a fish that forsook the waters of the sea to seek its food on land, it would be highly inappropriate to give it the name of fish; I should rather give it the name of monster. Such shall I call the monk who yearns for worldly delights and deserts his cloister for them" (4.5). Gower concludes by calling such a monk a "monster of the Church," a spiritual grotesque.

Milton on several occasions in *Paradise Lost* refers to God's extension of human dominion to the fish of the sea (*PL* 7.521, 533; 8.341, 346; 12.67). The image of the fish as a symbol of Christ or his followers is, however, infrequent. Browning's *The Ring and the Book* contains an incidental reference to the symbol in a passage from the account of the desecration and eventual reinstatement of Pope Formosus, whose body had been exhumed and cast into the Tiber River by Pope Stephen, in order that, in the latter's words, "my Christian fish may sup!" (10.88). The medieval chronicler relating the incident goes on to explain:

> Either because of *ICHTHYS* which means Fish
> And very aptly symbolizes Christ,
> Or else because the Pope is Fisherman,
> And seals with Fisher's-signet.

Another reference, less certainly biblical, is made in the "Gareth and Lynette" section of Tennyson's *Idylls of the King* where Gareth, seeing the Lady of the Lake, perceives that "o'er her breast floated the sacred fish. . . ."

Samuel Beckett's "Dante and the Lobster" (in *More Pricks than Kicks*) compares the boiling alive of a lobster to Christ's crucifixion. The lobster is called fish, Beckett writes mischievously, because "Fish had been good enough for Jesus Christ, Son of God, Saviour." Beckett's hero Belaqua sees the boiling of the lobster as part of the continual suffering which is existence. In Beckett's *How It Is,* the mud-immersed narrator carries a sack containing a tin of sardines and a can opener. The sardines represent Christian doctrine or ideology, but it is the can opener which the narrator uses to produce words, suggesting that language (or art) is more important than religion. The title story of W. D. Valgardson's *God Is Not a Fish Inspector* presents the overlooking of illegal fishing by the inspector as an image for the operation of divine grace.

See also EUCHARIST; FISHERS OF MEN; JONAH; LEVIATHAN; LOAVES AND FISHES.

Bibliography. Allen, D. C. *The Legend of Noah* (1963); Battenhouse, R. W. *"Measure for Measure* and the Christian Doctrine of the Atonement." *PMLA* 61 (1946); Quasten, J. "Fish, Symbolism of." *NCE* 5.943-46.   DEANE E. D. DOWNEY

FISHERS OF MEN   Perhaps the most famous call to discipleship in the NT occurred when Jesus, walking by the Sea of Galilee, saw Simon Peter and his brother Andrew casting a net into the water. He spoke to them, saying, "Follow me, and I will make you fishers of men" (Matt. 4:18-19; cf. Mark 1:16-17). The association of this episode with the future "rock" upon which the new Church was to be built, and with the evangelistic Andrew, led to the phrase acquiring wide early association with the activity of soul-winning. Jesus subsequently called two other fishermen from their task, the sons of Zebedee, James and John (Luke 5:1-11), Peter's fishing partners, who, with him, obtained a miraculous draught of fish. In response to their astonishment Jesus said, "Fear not; from henceforth thou shalt catch men" (v. 10).

Since the analogy in these passages suggested the fish as a symbol for the soul, it is not surprising that the fish became an important element in early Christian iconography. Souls, according to St. Augustine, are fished away by the apostles and their successors, from waters in which they are unwittingly captive to God's enemy (*De civ. Dei* 20.30). Because of the widespread use of the symbol and the special association of the NT trope with St. Peter and his apostolic vocation, it became natural to think of Peter's successors as occupying the chair of "the great fisherman," so that "the fisherman" became in time a nickname for the Pope. In later Protestant commentaries, such as that of Matthew Henry, the emphasis falls upon the apostolic activity of all Christians in evangelism as a response to Christ's "Follow me," drawing people into "the gospel net" (*Comm. on the Whole Bible*, 5.632; cf. 5.42-44).

The renegade Friar in Chaucer's *Summoner's Tale*, who regards himself as superior in prelatical efficacy to the parish priest, protests his apostolic vocation in terms which draw upon the traditional exegesis:

> I walke, and fisshe Cristen mennes soules
> To yelden Jhesu Crist his propre rente;
> To sprede his word is set al myn entente. (*Canterbury Tales*, 3.1820-22)

The pirate Lambro, in Byron's *Don Juan* (2.1001-03) is yet more obviously a parody:

> A fisher, therefore, was he — though of men,
> Like Peter the Apostle, — and he fished
> For wandering merchant-vessels, now and then.

Later in the poem Byron pictures the devil as a fisherman, baiting his hook with "lies / Which Satan angles with for souls, like flies" (8.687-88). This infernal reading is echoed in Tennyson's *Harold,* in which the shipwrecked crew accuse their rescuer of having lured them with lights to their destruction. The fisherman replies, "Nay then, we be liker [more like] the blessed apostles; / they were fishers of men, Father Jean says." When a Provincetown clerk in Thoreau's *Cape Cod* lists a town representative as "Master Mariner" rather than "Fisherman," Thoreau reports himself as "reminding" the clerk that "Fisherman had been a title of honor with a large party ever since the Christian era at least." When the Jesuit rector in James Joyce's *Portrait of the Artist as a Young Man* is endeavoring to lure Stephen Dedalus into a career in the Church he appeals to the shining example of St. Francis Xavier:

> He had the faith in him that moves mountains [cf. 1 Cor. 13:2]. Ten thousand souls won for God in a single month! That is a true conqueror, true to the motto of our order: *ad majorem Dei gloriam!* . . . A great saint, saint Francis Xavier! A great fisher of souls! (chap. 3)

More modestly, G. K. Chesterton's Father Brown gently distinguishes the spiritual servanthood involved in following the call of Christ into prelatical life, when the priest says to his sometimes mercenary associates: "You are The Twelve True Fishers, and these are all your silver fish. But He has made me a fisher of men" ("The Queer Feet," in *The Innocence of Father Brown*). Morris West's *The Shoes of the Fisherman* is a novel based upon the life of Pope John XXIII.

See also FISH.

FIVE WOUNDS   *See* STIGMATA.

FLAMING SWORD   A "flaming sword which turned every way" is wielded by cherubim at the east gate of the Garden of Eden to prevent exiled Adam and Eve from returning (Gen. 3:24). The one holding the sword is typically identified in both Jewish and Christian commentary as Michael. In Milton's *Paradise Lost,* however, the "brandisht Sword of God before them blaz'd" unhanded (*PL* 12.632-36). The Paradise to which the flaming sword bars entrance in literary contexts often has sexual overtones: Carlyle, in *Sartor Resartus,* conjectures that "in every well-conditioned stripling . . . there already blooms a prospective Paradise, cheered by some fairest Eve. . . . Perhaps too the whole is but the lovelier, if Cherubim and a Flaming Sword divide it from all footsteps of men; and grant him, the imaginative stripling, only the view, not the entrance" (2.5). In Shaw's *Candida,* Marchbanks the poet tells Candida's husband that on the previous evening spent with Candida he "approached the gate of Heaven. . . . Then she became an angel; and there was a flaming sword that turned every way, so that I couldn't go in; for I saw that the gate was really the gate of Hell." James

Joyce's Stephen hears concerning the expulsion from Eden in Father Arnall's sermon that it is "Michael, prince of the heavenly host, with a sword of flame in his hand" who drives out "the guilty pair"; later, sexually tempted, Stephen prays to his own "guardian angel to drive away with the sword the demon that was whispering to his brain" (*A Portrait of the Artist as a Young Man,* chap. 3).

See also FALL; MICHAEL.

FLEA There are two references to a flea (Heb. *par'osh*) in the KJV, at 1 Sam. 24:14 and 26:20. David, having spared Saul's life, compares himself to a flea to stress his own insignificance and the unnecessary vehemence of Saul's persecution: "After whom dost thou pursue? after a dead dog, after a flea?" The use of "flea" in 1 Sam. 26:20 is disputed and may be a corrupt reading in the Hebrew OT. (See the RSV and the JB for alternate readings.)

Early commentary on the 1 Sam. 24 passage tends to stress David's meekness (e.g., St. John Cassian, *Conferences,* 17.19; St. Augustine, *Contra Faustum Manichaeum,* 22.66; St. Athanasius, *Apologia contra Arianos,* 1.2). Milton (*Tenure of Kings*) praises David's restraint and "sanctified prudence."

The flea's insignificance with respect to God's design is reinforced by a false etymology in St. Isidore of Seville: *"Pulices vero vocati sunt quod ex pulvere magis nutriantur"* ("indeed, fleas *pulices* are so called because they derive their being from dust *pulvere*") (*Etymologiae,* 5.15). Small physical stature and humble origins, however, provide material for ironic commentary in the 18th cent., when Van Leeuwenhoek's microscopes (known as "flea glasses") helped to stress the relativity of size. "So, naturalists observe," writes Swift,

> a flea
> Hath smaller fleas that on him prey;
> And these have smaller yet to bite 'em
> And so proceed *ad infinitum.* ("On Poetry," 353-56)

This Hobbes-inspired vision of nature at war with itself all the way to "Parnassus" bears no direct relation to 1 Sam. 24:14, but is relevant to larger issues concerning divine providence and humanity's place in creation. This is the case also with the implication of Pope's line, "When Man's whole frame is obvious to a *Flea*" (*Dunciad,* 4.238) and, more clearly, with Shaw's preface to *Back to Methuselah,* which deals with natural selection. Reference to the "almighty Celestial Flea," creating food for ordinary fleas, is used ironically to stress the affinity of all living things.

Another tradition, linking fleas with Satan, may derive from the popular association of fleas with lust, both being sources of irritation, difficult to get rid of, and infesting the body's private parts. There is a history of allusions to fleas in erotic poetry, reaching back at least to Catullus. The late medieval *Carmen de Pulice,* attributed to Ovid, provided a model for the poet imagining himself to be a flea on his mistress's person, a motif which gave rise to a widespread fashion of mock encomia. (See, e.g., Caspar Dornavius, *Amphitheatrum Sapientiae Socraticae Joco-Seriae* [1619].) John Donne's "The Flea" is the best-known English example, and extends the tradition to contain a comment on the sacrament of marriage (the flea sucks the blood of both, and so they are two in one), as well as the Eucharist. The blood-sucking flea is here perversely antisacramental.

Demonic associations occur also in the writings of Erasmus, who complains about an infestation of fleas which prevents him from sleeping or writing: *"Soleo per iocum amicis dicere, non esse pulices sed daemones. Non erat ille jocus sed divinato"* ("I am accustomed to say to friends as a joke that these are not fleas but devils. That was no joke, but a prophetic intuition") (To Peter Richardt, Freiburg, 19 Nov. 1533). Although fleas do not entirely cease to be amusing, they nevertheless *are* really demonic; Erasmus goes on to suggest that such infestations can be due to witchcraft.

The infernal characteristics of fleas can be traced also in Dante, who likens their torment to punishment in the seventh circle of hell (*Inferno,* 17, 51), and in Shakespeare: "A saw a flea stick upon Bardolph's nose, and a said it was a black soul burning in hell-fire" (*Henry 5,* 2.3.42). Blake's "Ghost of a Flea" is overtly Satanic and (perhaps as a further consequence of the "flea-glass") also monstrous.

An interesting conflation of the tradition of devilish fleas with 1 Sam. 24:14 occurs in Andrew Willet's *Harmonie upon the first booke of Samuel* (1607), where Willet commends David's humility (266) and patience (267) and, in a strange inversion of the text's ostensible meaning, compares Saul's "temeritie and meanes" to "a dead dogge, or a flie." In itself, the attribution of flea-likeness to Saul rather than David is inexplicable, but Willet's substitution of "flie" for "flea" suggests a deliberate allusion to necromancy (a sin to which Saul was particularly subject, and for which he was harshly condemned). "Fly" was a common Renaissance term for a conjurer's familiar (in Ben Jonson's *The Alchemist,* e.g., the conjurers pretend to provide the duped clerk with a "fly"), and a lengthy discussion of the Satanic practices of conjurers follows closely upon this passage.

Although *The Alchemist* provides grounds for linking the conjurer's "fly" metaphorically with plague, the actual association between fleas and bubonic plague was not confirmed until early in this century. For modern readers, with the knowledge that fleas have been history's most effective mass-murderers, the monstrosity of Blake's flea seems all the more horrific. In Albert Camus's *The Plague,* where the priest examines his theories of divine retribution in the face of horrible disease, the two traditions coalesce: the very insignificance of fleas in relation to their effectiveness as transmitters of deathly sickness is at the heart of their destructive potency.

Bibliography. Francon, M. "Un motif de la poésie amoreuse au XVI^c siècle." *PMLA* 56 (1941), 307-36; Lehane, B. *The Compleat Flea* (1969).   PATRICK GRANT

FLESH IS GRASS The opening passage of the second part of the book of Isaiah, "Comfort ye my people," made memorable to millions in the English-speaking world through Handel's *Messiah,* continues with the reminder: "All flesh is grass, and all the goodliness thereof is as the flower of the field: The grass withereth, the flower fadeth: because the spirit of the LORD bloweth upon it: surely the people is grass. The grass withereth, the flower fadeth: but the word of our God shall stand forever" (Isa. 40:6-8). The image of human life as grass, eventually to be mowed down for hay, is found throughout the Psalms (e.g., 37:2; 102:4, 11; 103:15), in Job (5:25), and in 1 Peter (2:24-25, where the apostle is citing the Isaiah passage).

The text receives straightforward commentary from the Fathers. St. Augustine is representative when he observes, reflecting on Ps. 103: "The whole splendor of the human race; honor, powers, riches, pride, threats — is the flower of the grass. That house flourishes, this family is great, that family prospers, but how many years do they live? Many years to you are but a short season to God. God does not count as you do" (*Enarr. in Ps.* 103.19, sup. v. 15). Death is a kind of harvest, as of hay, or a winnowing of the grain from the chaff, the chaff then being "for the fire" (*Enarr. in Ps.* 52.8, sup. v. 6; cf. 60.2). In this sense, he says, even "grass bearing fruit, as is that of wheat . . . is called 'grass' in Holy Scripture" (72.18). The contrast between perishable grass and the durable Word of God is, for Augustine, another reason to marvel at the Incarnation:

> Inasmuch then as he knows as a father our forming, that we are but grass, and can only flourish for a time, he sent unto us his Word, and his Word, which abides for evermore, he has made a brother unto the grass which does not last long. Do not wonder that you shall be a sharer in his eternity then; he became first himself a sharer in your condition as grass. . . . How great then is the hope of the grass, since the Word has been made flesh? That which lives forever has not disdained to assume the lot of grass, that grass might not despair of itself. (*Enarr. in Ps.* 103.19-20; sup. vv. 15-16).

Because of its recurrence in the Psalms and Job as well as Isaiah, the phrase was well worked in medieval preaching and in spiritual literature. An interesting reflection of the image in painting of the 16th cent. is provided by the "Haywain Triptych" of Hieronymus Bosch, an altarpiece which, when folded, shows a harried pilgrim; when the panels are opened the story of Creation and Fall is represented on the left, while in the center a host of secular and ecclesiastical persons frantically pursue a large wagon-load of hay (or chaff, really — straw) into the fiery hell depicted on the right. The connection of the phrase with life's pilgrimage persists in poetry as well. Donne

writes ("To Sr. Henry Wotton"): "But I should wither in one day, and passe / To 'a bottle' of Hay, that am a locke of Grasse. / Life is a voyage. . . ." In Herbert's "Miserie," the poet observes, "Man is but grasse, / He knows it, fill the glasse." In his poem "Frailtie" he builds upon Augustine's commentary (*Enarr. in Ps.* 103.21), as well as the text:

> Lord, in my silence how do I despise
> What upon trust
> Is styled *honour, riches,* or *fair eyes;*
> But is *fair dust!*
> I surname them *guilded clay,*
> *Dear earth, fine grasse,* or *hay.*

In later literature the phrase is a cliché whose biblical origin is nevertheless usually recognized. Byron deals in *Don Juan* with the inevitability of death as Cheops's mummy is confronted, but to a different conclusion: "And 'flesh' (which Death mows down to hay) 'is grass'; / You've passed your youth not so unpleasantly" (1.1756-57). Elizabeth Gaskell illustrates one type of 19th-cent. adaptation in "The Old Nurse's Story": " 'Flesh is grass,' they do say; but who would have thought that Miss Furnivall had been such an out-and-out beauty, to see her now?" Similarly, in Shaw's *Back to Methuselah* the phrase signifies merely the fading potency of elderly life. When Zoo reproaches the Elderly Gentleman for being apparently proud of his age, he says, "What does it matter to you whether anything is true or not? Your flesh is as grass: you come up like a flower, and wither in your second childhood. A lie will last your time: it will not last mine" (4.1; cf. Job 14:2). P. G. Wodehouse makes light-hearted use of the phrase in several of his novels and stories: "We are all sorry that the Reverend Whatever-he-was-called should be dying of adenoids, but after all, here today, gone tomorrow, and all flesh is grass, and what not. . ." (*Right Ho, Jeeves,* chap. 17; cf. *The Adventures of Sally,* 8.3; "Romance at Droitgate Spa").

FLESH IS WEAK When Jesus in Gethsemane returned to find his disciples not praying but asleep he chided Peter, "What, could ye not watch with me one hour? Watch and pray, that ye enter not into temptation: the spirit indeed is willing, but the flesh is weak" (Matt. 26:41; cf. Luke 22:45-46). The flesh is often said to be in conflict with the spirit in this way in the NT (e.g., Rom. 8:13; Gal. 4:23, 29; 5:17; 1 Pet. 2:11) — not that the physical nature per se is sinful but that it is frail and subject to temptation and sin.

The Fathers, reacting against preoccupation with the flesh and its appetites in decadent Roman culture, tended to make the weakness of the flesh equivalent to sin *sui generis.* Hence, for St. Jerome, Christians are those who "by abstinence subjugate our refractory flesh, [which is] eager to follow the allurements of lust. The eating of flesh, the drinking of wine, and fulness of stomach, is the seed-plot of lust. And so the comic poet [Terence, in *Eunuch*, 4.5-6] says, 'Venus shivers unless Ceres and Bacchus be with her' " (*Adv. Jov.* 2.7). So great is Jerome's concern about the propensity of fleshly appetites to undermine spiritual health that he gathers a host of classical authors to support an argument (despite "the liberty of the Gospel") for vegetarianism as a preventative against carnal arousal (2.14). Similar sentiments abound in the writings of St. Augustine, for whom, as he writes in his *Confessiones,* weakness of the flesh in sexual matters especially had been a major impediment to spiritual development. For the author of the 12th-cent. *De Fructibus Carnis et Spiritus* (ascribed to Hugh of St. Victor [PL 176.997-98]), the fruits of the flesh, from the "forbidden" fruit tasted in Eden on, are by nature corruptible, while the fruits of the spirit, love, joy, peace, etc., are not. In later theological writers and in Reformation theologians (e.g., Calvin, *Comm.* sup. Matt. 26.41), the weakness ascribed to the flesh is broadened to include general human limitations and frailty.

Both biblical and patristic notions of the frailty of the flesh became proverbial in medieval literature; one has only to reflect on Chaucer's Wife of Bath, for whom both the biblical text and Jerome's *Adversus Jovinianum* are authorities to be challenged, and whose motto is "Freletee clepe I." Much the same philosophy is claimed by another vivid personification of the weakness of the flesh, Shakespeare's Falstaff in *1 Henry 4.* When Prince Hal chides him for his behavior with Mistress Quickly, Falstaff rejoins: "Dost thou hear, Hal? Thou knowest in the state of innocency Adam fell, and what should poor Jack Falstaff do in the days of villainy? Thou see'st I have more flesh than another man, and therefore more frailty" (3.3.172-76; cf. *Richard 2*, 1.3.195). Byron's *Don Juan,* which offers a considerable catalogue of the temptations to which flesh is vulnerable, includes the observation that in warm Mediterranean climes,

> howsoever people fast and pray,
> The flesh is frail, and so the soul undone;
> What men call gallantry, the gods adultery,
> Is much more common where the climate's sultry.
> (1.501-04)

Later in the same poem he inverts the relation in parody (5.878-80). Hardy's *Jude the Obscure* is a kind of fictive treatise on the frailty of the flesh. In *The Mayor of Casterbridge* Hardy applies the phrase to an incident of deception, as a rationale (chap. 13). In one of his *Letters* D. H. Lawrence uses the text to mask his lack of resolve to visit a sometime friend (385). Aldous Huxley offers a modernist rewriting of the biblical text which nevertheless constitutes a plausible psychological insight into the original remark of Jesus: "It wasn't a case, he reflected ruefully, of the spirit being willing and the flesh weak. That was altogether the wrong antithesis. The spirit is always willing; but the person, who is a mind as well as a body, is always unwilling — and the person, incidentally, is not weak but extremely strong" (*After Many a Summer*, 1.8).

FLESH POTS OF EGYPT   The phrase "flesh pots of Egypt" is based on Exod. 16:3, where the Israelites, hungry in the wilderness, expressed a longing to be back in Egypt with its "flesh pots," or pots of meat. Meat was not a poor man's dish, and this wish amounted to a desire for luxuries. The term "flesh pots" (which dates from Coverdale's 1535 translation of the Bible) came to symbolize high living and self-indulgence. St. Jerome observes of such appetites that they lead to spiritual dullness: "In short, the people ate and their hearts grew thick, lest they should see with their eyes, and hear with their ears, and understand with their heart" (*Adv. Jov.* 2.15). Subsequent interpretation focused also on the tendency for affluent living to produce obtuseness to the Spirit and neglect of spiritual food (i.e., the Eucharist). A visual representation of the theme is found in Peter Breughel's "Kermis Flamande" ("Flemish Fair"), in which a whole village is preoccupied with flesh pots and related indulgences while only one woman with a small child enters the church for Mass.

The fierce anti-Puritan Thomas Nashe felt the essence of a decline in fortunes was to fare "from the flesh-pots of Egipt, to the Prouant of the Lowe countreyes" (*Pierce Penniless, His Supplication to the Divell* [*Works*, 2.74]). Swift, in a letter to Sterne (17), talks about expecting "to hear . . . two ladies lamenting the flesh-pots of Cavan Street." Benjamin Franklin in his *Autobiography* observes of his friend Keimer's agonized perseverance with their experiment in vegetarianism that he "long'd for the flesh-pots of Egypt, and ordered a roast pig." Emerson, in *Nature*, opines that "some theosophists have arrived at a certain hostility . . . towards matter, as the Manichean and Plotinus. They distrusted in themselves any looking back to these flesh-pots of Egypt. Plotinus was ashamed of his body." Thackeray's characters in *The Newcomes* have no such qualms; as the narrator says of an unusually abstemious denizen, "Nor was he a supping man (in which case he would have found the parties pleasanter, for in Egypt itself there were not more savory flesh-pots than at Clapham" (chap. 2). In a variety of 19th- and 20th-cent. English texts other place names or locations (e.g., a Pacific island [*Spectator*, 12 May 1939]) have been substituted for "Egypt" in the phrase. George Meredith coined the nonce word "flesh-pottery" (*Beauchamp's Career,* chap. 29).

See also LEEKS, ONIONS, AND GARLIC.

DAVID F. PAYNE

FLOOD   Gen. 6–9 describes the flood by which God punished sinful humanity, sparing only Noah and his family, along with representatives of all the animals, in an ark constructed according to divine directions. The waters came from forty days of rain (Gen. 7:4, 12) heightened by primeval waters erupting from the "fountains of the great deep" and pouring through "the windows of heaven" (7:11).

The Genesis story resembles the flood narrative in the Gilgamesh epic and shares some characteristics with many other flood stories from all over the world. The Greek parallel, in which Jove punishes the evil world, sparing upright Deucalion and his wife, is found in Ovid's *Metamorphoses* and given English form in the late 17th cent. by Dryden in his translation (*The First Book of Ovid's Metamorphoses,* 193-606).

The basic structure of the Genesis version is simple: God decides to destroy his creation but to save some of his creatures; after the catastrophe he establishes a covenant with Noah, promises never again to send a Flood, and thus makes life on earth possible again. In Isa. 54:9 the Lord repeats his promise never to send another Flood (Gen. 9:9-11). In the NT the Flood and the ark are taken as examples of divine judgment and salvation (Matt. 24:37-39; 1 Pet. 3:20-21; 2 Pet. 2:5), and Noah as an example of faith in God (Heb. 11:7).

Rabbinic commentary focuses on reasons for God's wish to destroy his creation as well as details concerning the construction of the ark and the nature of life aboard ship during the Flood. Philo allegorizes the narrative, seeing the ark as the body and Noah as the righteous mind. The story as a whole is taken by him to signify the cleansing of the soul.

Early Christian commentary emphasizes the universality of the Deluge and defends the credibility of the story. Typological interpretation, which begins in the NT comparison of the Flood to "the waters of baptism" (1 Pet. 3:21) or the end of the world (2 Pet. 3:6), becomes prominent in medieval treatment of the story.

Lewis distinguishes four major typological approaches. First, in the spiritual approach, St. Augustine and others follow Philo, comparing the ark to the body, using it to signify matters of the soul. Second is the christological approach, typified by St. Justin's belief that "the water and the wood which saved Noah, along with his faith, prefigure baptism, the cross, and the faith of the Christians" (Lewis, 114). For others the ark represents the sepulcher of Christ, its door the Savior's wounds (cf. Augustine, *De civ. Dei* 15.26). Third, in the apocalyptic approach, the general wickedness of people before the Deluge prefigures the beast of Revelation while the Flood itself anticipates the fire of judgment (cf. Augustine, *De civ. Dei* 20.18, 24). Fourth, in ecclesiastical interpretation, the ark is taken to be the Church. Every detail of the narrative is then read allegorically (e.g., Hugh of St. Victor, *De Arca Noe Morali:* the ark's height expresses the hierarchy, its squared beams the learned members of the Church, its rooms the many mansions in heaven, the dove the Holy Spirit, and so on.

Some early literary redactions follow Scripture closely

and without significant elaboration: in the OE *Genesis* (1270-2542) God repents for having created sinners, communicates with Noah in biblical fashion, and sends waters from above and below, maintaining the *"drenceflod"* until waters flow fifteen ells above the mountains; the ark eventually settles on a mountain in Armenia. But typological readings are also influential in literary transmission of the story. The flood mentioned in the OE *Andreas* is linked in traditional ways to baptism — the death of the old and the birth of a new creation. *Judgment Day I,* and *Christ II* and *III* recall the connection between the destructive waters of the Flood and the fire of the apocalypse.

In the ME *Cursor Mundi* the biblical account is embellished by realistic detail and the satiric observation that for the victims of the Flood social rank is irrelevant (cf. *Piers Plowman* B.10.405-13). *Cleanness* gives a more affecting description of the victims. The medieval Noah plays make the events meaningful in contemporary terms by showing Noah as a craftsman who might belong to one of the local guilds, and as a husband who has difficulty establishing authority in his own household. Comedy pervades Chaucer's *Miller's Tale,* where a gullible carpenter prepares to save himself, his wife, and a pseudo-prophet from anticipated rain "so wilde and wood, / That half so greet was nevere Noes flood" (*CT* 1.3517-18).

In the 16th and much of the 17th cent. the Flood story is treated in unremarkable ways, drawing on the biblical account and its commentaries for detail. Following the example of Du Bartas's *Divine Weekes,* some writers, including William Hunnis and Francis Sabie, retell the biblical narrative in verse. Michael Drayton, in *Noah's Flood,* is especially interested in the loading of the ark, the nature and consequences of the Deluge, and the joy of the animals at the end of the Flood. He takes up a number of controversial points and insists on the veracity of the story. So also does Milton in *Paradise Lost* (11.556-900). Skillfully alternating between Michael's account and Adam's reactions to it, he emphasizes the wickedness of the antediluvian generations, Adam's sorrow about the destruction of creation, and his joy concerning Noah for whose sake God raises another world.

In Shakespeare's *Comedy of Errors* (3.2.105-07) references to the Flood and the apocalypse are combined in a witty dialogue between Dromio and Antipholus (cf. *As You Like It,* 5.4.35-38). In Donne's *The First Anniversary* the ark's dimensions are said to parallel the proportions of a human body and the vessel thus typifies the individual Christian (cf. "To Sir Edward Herbert at Julyers"). In "A Hymne to Christ" Donne adopts conventional baptism-salvation typology, which appears also in Crashaw's "Upon the Bleeding Crucifix." Herbert expresses grief in connection with the first return of Noah's dove ("The Church"). Elsewhere he identifies the ark with the Church ("Affliction") and speculates that the place where Noah landed was the starting point of Abraham's journey toward Egypt with the Ark of the Covenant ("The Church Militant"). Vaughan connects the ark with the pillar of Jacob's vision, the Temple, and the individual soul ("Jacob's Pillow and Pillar") and recalls God's covenant with Noah ("The Rainbow"). Marvell draws on traditional typology in "Upon Appleton House," but in other instances provides a political application, associating Cromwell's son with the rainbow after the Deluge ("A Poem upon the Death of His Late Highness the Lord Protector"). The Royalists employed a similar strategy. Dryden begins his poem "To His Sacred Majesty" by comparing Charles's landing in England with Noah's on Mt. Ararat, a reading perhaps influenced by R. Filmer's *Patriarcha,* which Locke attacked in "An Essay Concerning False Principles" (G. Reedy, *The Bible and Reason* [1985], 70).

Sir Thomas Browne, in *Pseudodoxia Epidemica* and *Religio Medici,* defends the notion that the biblical Flood was universal but raises a number of questions about the credibility of certain details of the story. Thomas Burnet, in his influential and controversial *Sacred Theory of the Earth* (1684), also argues that the Flood was a worldwide phenomenon and provides an elaborate "scientific" hypothesis to account for the mechanics of the Deluge. His physico-theology made it possible to explain misproportioned aspects of landscape (cf. James Thomson, "Spring," 309-18) but his rational defense of the story was seen by many to promote skepticism concerning the historical accuracy of the biblical account. It also spawned a series of countertheories and "explanations" of the Flood (see Allen, 96-112).

As the literal accuracy of the story began to be questioned more openly, satiric and trivial treatment of the Flood in literature became increasingly common. Edward Ecclestone's drama *Noah's Flood* (ca. 1679) toys with biblical material and Miltonic themes. Swift makes a series of satiric allusions in "Ode to the Athenian Society," "An Answer to Dr. Delany's Fable of the Pheasant and the Lark," and "A City Shower." Hardy, in *Under the Greenwood Tree,* pokes fun at Mrs. Day, who, when furnishing the house, follows the principle established by Noah of having two articles of every sort. In *Far from the Madding Crowd* he compares Oak's shepherd's hut and its environment to a small Noah's ark on a small Ararat.

For Wordsworth the story provides a backdrop for meditation on the natural world: the dove is the happiest bird of the ark ("A Morning Exercise") and a symbol of hope ("The Waggoner," 1.53). In his sonnet "Skyprospect" Wordsworth imagines seeing Ararat and the ark in the west, but then reassures himself that "all is harmless" — the vista innocent of any hint of destruction.

For Carlyle, heroic man finds himself adrift and clutches at literature, "wonderful Ark of the Deluge, where so much that is precious, nay priceless to mankind, floats carelessly onwards through the Chaos of distracted times." Emerson, likewise, in "The Poet" likens the poet's mind to a Noah's ark. In Tennyson's "Two Voices" the pessimistic voice seems to wreck the poet's "mortal ark,"

but then a hidden hope, like a rainbow, breaks out of the speaker's sullen heart (cf. *In Memoriam,* 12).

Byron alludes to the Flood several times in *Don Juan,* and in *Childe Harold's Pilgrimage* (4.826-28) he associates the Napoleonic era with a universal deluge for which there is no ark. Like West, Turner, Danby, and Doré in their Deluge paintings (see Landow, *Images,* 140-44), Byron sides with the victims of the Flood: his uncompleted play *Heaven and Earth* draws more on the apocryphal book of Enoch than Genesis, expanding references to a liaison between "the sons of God and the daughters of men," which in the Bible is condemned as one of the evils which prompted God's wrath before the Flood (Gen. 6:2-4; 1 Enoch 6–9, 54–55): two angels fall in love with the daughters of Cain, and, rejecting God's warnings, escape with them from the earth, which is about to be deluged.

In James Thomson's "The City of Dreadful Night" a preacher tells his melancholy brothers who are "battling in black floods without an ark" that there is no God. George Eliot, in *The Mill on the Floss,* describes young Tom's dream of building a Noah's ark in case of a flood: ironically, years later Maggie tries in vain to save Tom and herself from drowning. Hardy shows God repenting, as in Noah's time, that he "made Earth, and life, and man" ("By the Earth's Corpse") and satirizes the bourgeois who have learned to "hold the flood a local scare" and on Sundays read Voltaire ("The Respectable Burgher on 'The Higher Criticism'"). Kipling, in "The Legend of Evil," is indebted to folk legends in suggesting that the salvation of Noah and his family was ineffective because the devil got into the ark when Noah cursed the stubborn donkey.

Melville was fascinated with the Flood-story, and the continuing impact of the Flood is a central preoccupation of the characters in *Moby-Dick.* Nantucketers' boats are said to be their arks. Ahab sees waters the same as Noah's; after Moby-Dick's victory, "the great shroud of the sea rolled on as it rolled five thousand years ago" in Noah's days. Ishmael remarks that "Noah's flood is not yet subsided," but the sea in this instance is controlled by no mercy and no power but its own. Mark Twain describes what he perceives as the absurdity of the biblical story and comments bitterly on the victims of the Deluge ("Adam's Soliloquy").

Modern skepticism concerning the narrative is summarized by Dickinson in "The Winters Are So Short": "But Ararat's a legend — now — / And no one credits Noah — ." In his preface to *Back to Methuselah* G. B. Shaw asserts that "The feeling against the Bible has become so strong at last that educated people . . . refuse to outrage their intellectual consciences by reading the legend of Noah's Ark. . . ." Nevertheless, the vitality of the story in the 20th cent. is remarkable. Yeats deals with the Flood in *The Player Queen;* Connelly devotes three scenes of *The Green Pastures* to the Noah story. For

C. Day Lewis in *Noah and the Waters* the Deluge serves as a convenient political symbol for breaking with bourgeois liberalism. In *The Skin of Our Teeth* Wilder associates details from the biblical source with a series of different catastrophes, asserting that his archetypal family will begin life again after each one. Odets's *The Flowering Peach* is less optimistic, transforming the narrative into a realistic family drama in which Japheth temporarily rebels against the building of the ark and the brutality of God, and Noah learns that humanity itself can make or destroy the world.

Following Jules Verne's *L'eternel Adam,* some novelists rewrote the biblical story as science fiction, often casting Noah as a scientist and the ark as a spaceship (e.g., Serviss, *The Second Deluge;* Wylie and Balmer, *After Worlds Collide;* and A. C. Clarke, *Rendezvous with Rama* and *The Songs of Distant Earth).* H. G. Wells, in *All Aboard for Ararat,* focuses on a utopian writer who, refusing to act like the biblical Noah, attempts to improve upon God's work by designing blueprints for the New Ark, the reconstruction of society after World War II. Anthony Burgess's *The End of the World News,* a montage of the biographies of Freud and Trotsky, and a parody of Serviss's *The Second Deluge,* makes the point that all designs for the new world will ultimately be mocked. In Vonnegut's satire *Galapagos* a few human beings escape the general ruin of the world to become the ancestors of a smaller-brained and happier race.

Apart from such modernizations of the basic story, some imaginative retellings are noteworthy. David Garnett relates in *Two by Two* how two young girls hide in the ark as stowaways and, after the Flood, begin life with two of Noah's renegade grandsons. Timothy Findley's *Not Wanted on the Voyage* deals with the sexual and other tensions in Noah's family, everyday life aboard the ark, the rebellion of Noah's wife, Ham's wife Lucy (Lucifer) and others, and Noah's manipulation of the rainbow miracle after God has failed to answer his prayers.

James Joyce alludes to the Deluge and calls attention to associated baptismal symbolism in connection with Father Arnall's sermon and Stephen's wading in the sea in his *Portrait of the Artist as a Young Man.* More idiosyncratic references occur in *Ulysses* and *Finnegans Wake.* In D. H. Lawrence's *The Rainbow* imagery of the Flood and new beginning describes the maturation process of Ursula and illuminates Lawrence's attitude toward industrial civilization. Like R. P. Warren in "Blackberry Winter," Faulkner uses the Flood-story to characterize the religious sensibility of his African-American characters. Social injustice is the theme of Sillitoe's story "Noah's Ark," in which two poor boys steal a ride on a Noah's ark roundabout and are chased away by the owner. For Thomas Pynchon the apocalypse in *Gravity's Rainbow* is man-made and the rainbow no longer functions as a covenantal or providential sign.

An actual flood reminds Charles Tomlinson *(The*

Flood) of the biblical one, but the nightmare of the end of the world which he and his partner face "with elate despair" turns out to be a dream after all. Beauty characterizes Rumer Godden's post-Flood vision in *In Noah's Ark* (1949): the world lies "washed and sparkling in the newborn day." Renewal also climaxes Lorenz Graham's Flood-story for children: *God Wash the World and Start Again* (1946).

See also NOAH; RAINBOW.

Bibliography. Abrams, M. H. *Natural Supernaturalism* (1971); Allen, D. C. *The Legend of Noah: Renaissance Rationalism in Art, Science and Letters* (1949; rpt. 1963); Beck, C. A. "Waters over the Earth: The Flood in Modern Drama." *DAI* 42 (1982), 5112A; Daniélou, J. "Déluge, baptême, jugement." *Dieu vivant* 8 (1947), 95-112; Goetsch, P. "Die Sintfluterzählung in der modernen englisch-sprachigen Literatur." In F. Link, ed., *Paradeigmata: Literarische Typologie des Alten Testaments* (1989), 651-84; Heidel, A. *The Gilgamesh Epic and Old Testament Parallels* (1946); Hornback, B. G. *"Noah's Arkitecture": A Study of Dickens's Mythology* (1972); Lamberts, J. J. "The Noah Story in *Cursor Mundi.*" *MS* 24 (1962), 217-32; Landow, G. P. *Images of Crisis: Literary Iconology, 1750 to the Present* (1982); Lewis, J. L. "Noah and the Flood in Jewish, Christian, and Muslim Tradition." *BA* 47 (1984), 224-39; Lewis, J. P. *A Study of the Interpretation of Noah and the Flood in Jewish and Christian Literature* (1968); Marks, J. H. "Flood (Genesis)." *IDB* 2.278-84; Utley, F. L., D. Noy, and R. Patai, eds. *Studies in Biblical and Jewish Folklore* (1960); Walsh, M. M. "The Baptismal Flood in the Old English 'Andreas': Liturgical and Typological Depths." *Traditio* 33 (1977), 137-58.

PAUL GOETSCH
MARIE MICHELLE WALSH

FOOL, FOLLY Most uses of the word *fool* in the English Bible refer not to the literal fool, i.e., the mentally incompetent, but to the moral or willful fool whose choices identify him as one rejecting the counsel of God. In the OT these include the boaster (Heb. *halal;* Ps. 75:4); the egocentric (Heb. *kesil;* Ps. 92:6-8), the arrogant (Heb. *'ewil;* Prov. 12:15); and the fool par excellence (Heb. *nabal),* who believes there is no God (Ps. 14:1). In the NT, "fools" include the thoughtless (Gk. *anoētos;* Luke 24:25), the witless (Gk. *aphrōn;* Luke 12:20); and those who persistently choose an unworthy path (Gk. *mōron;* Matt. 23:17).

The classic biblical opposition between folly and wisdom is found in the book of Proverbs, where Wisdom *(hokmah)* is personified as a woman desirable above all forms of worldly wealth or pleasure; the harlot who lurks in alleys to lead the gullible young man of the text astray, and who would seduce him to idolatry and wastefulness, is a personification of "Folly." Dame Wisdom's function in much literature is to teach the character of folly by opposing virtue to vice and wise precept to wanton action: an important medieval example, making heavy use of the "Proverbs of Solomon," is Chaucer's *Tale of Melibee.* This text is further influenced by Boethius's *De Consolatione Philo-*

sophiae, also translated by Chaucer, in which Lady Philosophy is a physician who ministers to the narrator's "folly," into which he has been led by "strumpet muses." Erasmus's *Praise of Folly* is an influential Renaissance satire with much the same tactic and purpose.

The fool was a kind of *personnage régnant* of the Renaissance, much as the pilgrim and wayfarer had been for the Middle Ages. Yet this role for the fool had actually developed in the Middle Ages; in Jakop van Oestvoren's poem *Blauwe Scuut* (1413) and in Sebastian Brant's *Ship of Fools* (1494; trans. 1509), the description of the passenger/crew constitutes a satire against true spiritual pilgrimage, teaching by negative example (with considerable indebtedness to the book of Proverbs). Proverbs is also a significant influence in John Lydgate's *Ordre of Folys.* Many of the writings of Jonathan Swift, including *Gulliver's Travels,* are similarly "wisdom literature," by virtue of their satire of folly, although in his case (as in that of Erasmus) classical literature has begun to eclipse biblical literature as a source of allusion.

The character of folly, from a biblical point of view, is that it consistently mistakes the tangible goods of this world for ultimate value, and runs the risk of the rich man whose entire goal in life is summarized in his fuller and bigger barns. The voice of God makes a contrary evaluation: "Thou fool, this night thy soul shall be required of thee: then whose shall those things be, which thou hast provided?" (Luke 12:20). Such a person, observes St. Augustine, invariably seems "wise in his own eyes" (*Sermo,* 107.5; cf. Prov. 3:7; Rom. 1:20-22), but the measure of his actual foolishness is his failure to distinguish between tangible and intelligible goods — a distinction reflected on in several places by Erasmus and by St. Thomas More in his defense (Roper's *Life*). John Wesley records in his *Journals* a preacher's example:

> We rode by a fine seat: the owner of which (not much above fourscore years old) says he desires only to live thirty years longer; ten to hunt, ten to get money (having at present but twenty thousand pounds a year) and ten years to repent. O that God may not say unto him, "Thou fool, this night shall thy soul be required of thee."

In 1 Cor. 1:18–4:21, St. Paul develops an extended contrast between the wisdom of the world and the wisdom of God. The latter is as foolish to the world as the former is to God. In 1 Cor. 3:18 Paul exhorts the Corinthians to become "wise toward God," even as they appear as fools to the world. In 1 Cor. 4:10 the apostle then ironically compares the precarious state of his apostolic ministry to the standing of the Corinthians who, though Christians, were apparently known for a kind of easy arrogance about their superior knowledge: "We are fools for Christ's sake, but you are wise in Christ," he quips (cf. 1:5; 3:1-4). The fool for Christ, according to Paul, risks the derision of the world in order to be pleasing to God. So too, presumably, does the addressee of Donne's "To Mr. Tilman, after he

had taken orders," about whose calling the poet asks, "Why doth the foolish world scorn that profession, / Whose joys passe speech?"

The wise fool, who appears foolish but is in fact wiser than his companions, is a familiar character in English literature, beginning well before Shakespeare's professional fool in *King Lear,* who stands by the faltering king when all others speak lies and treachery. This kind of fool, kept in court to counsel the "wise," may be seen as a secular counterpart to the "fool for Christ's sake." For Jacopone da Todi madness for the sake of Christ was the only true way to him (*Laudi,* 84.11ff. [ed. Ageno]; cf. 33.37). The same image is developed by Dostoyevsky in Prince Myshkin in his *The Idiot.* The self-possession of the *fol sage,* familiar in Montaigne, is whimsically deployed by Donne in the concluding line of his "the triple Foole," where he observes that those "who are a little wise, the best fooles be." This development, unless perhaps as anticipated by David's playing the fool in the court of Achish (1 Sam. 21:13-15), is not a truly biblical conception.

In Arnold's *Culture and Anarchy* a reference to 1 Cor. 1:20 is apparent, however, in his remark that "It is justly said of the Jewish people . . . that they were 'entrusted with the oracles of God,' as it is justly said of Christianity . . . that the wisdom of the old Pagan world was foolishness, compared to it" ("Hebraism and Hellenism"). A secular descendant of the fool who is wise toward God is found in P. G. Wodehouse's Berty Wooster, whose folly (as contrasted to the worldly wisdom of Jeeves) lies in his resolute adherence to an ideal "code." Kingsley Amis's *Lucky Jim* reveals a similar hero — a fool who seems unprincipled but is superior in morality to the ostensibly moral persons around him.

In contemporary literature, Harold Fickett has used the image of the "fool for Christ's sake" in his *The Holy Fool* (1983), a comic novel which depicts one week in the life of a Los Angeles pastor undergoing a crisis in his ministry. Fickett's "fool" must risk the alienation and bitterness of his church in order to be true to himself and his convictions.

See also WISDOM.

Bibliography. Beverly, N. *The Fool Hath Said* (1936); Blank, S. H. "Folly." *IDB* 2.303-04; Foucault, M. *Folie et déraison: Histoire de la folie à l'âge classique* (1961); Gifford, D. J. "Iconographic Notes toward a Definition of the Medieval Fool." *JWCI* 37 (1974), 336-42; Goldsmith, R. H. "Wise Men in Motley: the Fool in Elizabethan Drama." *DA* 12 (1952), 618; La Bossière, C. R. *The Victorian Fol Sage* (1989); Ladner, G. B. *"Homo Viator:* Medieval Ideas on Alienation and Order." *Speculum* 42 (1967), 256-59; Swain, B. *Fools and Folly During the Middle Ages and Renaissance* (1932); Welsford, E. *The Fool: His Social and Literary History* (1935); Wenzel, S. "The Wisdom of the Fool." In *The Wisdom of Poetry: Essays in Early English Literature in Honor of Morton Bloomfield.* Ed. L. Benson (1982), 225-40.

DAVID L. JEFFREY
BRUCE L. EDWARDS

FORBIDDEN FRUIT *See* APPLE; FALL; TREE OF KNOWLEDGE.

FOR THINE IS THE KINGDOM *See* PATER NOSTER.

FOUGHT A GOOD FIGHT Anticipating his death, St. Paul wrote to Timothy of his contentedness and peace of mind: "I have fought a good fight, I have finished my course, I have kept the faith" (2 Tim. 4:7). In Chaucer's *Second Nun's Tale* Cecilia tells the about-to-be-martyred Maximus and others, "Ye han forsothe ydoon a greet bataille, / Youre cours is doon, youre feith han ye conserved . . ." (8.386-90), quoting the entire verse. (Cf. 1 Tim. 6:12.)

 See also ARMOR AND WEAPONS; *MILES CHRISTI;* PAUL.

FOUNTAIN *See* FOUR RIVERS OF PARADISE; LIVING WATER; RIVER OF LIFE.

FOUR BEASTS In a vision of Daniel (7:3-8), "four great beasts came up from the sea. . . . The first was like a lion, and had eagle's wings." The second was "like to a bear," the third "like a leopard" — with four wings and four heads — the fourth was "dreadful and terrible, and strong exceedingly; and it had great iron teeth . . . and it had ten horns." It is generally agreed that these beasts symbolized four kingdoms, each of which ruled Israel in its turn, although which of the kingdoms corresponds to which of the beasts has long been a subject of debate. For St. Jerome (*Comm. in Danielem*) and St. Augustine (*De civ. Dei* 20.23), Assyria, Persia, Macedonia, and Rome were the appropriate designates. The beast of Rev. 13:1-10, which John saw "rise up out of the sea . . . like unto a leopard, [with] . . . the feet of a bear . . . the mouth of a lion," and the power of a "dragon," is apparently a composite of Daniel's four beasts and seems for John to have stood for worldly government in general and/or Roman government in particular. The *Glossa Ordinaria* interprets it synthetically as "Antichristus, *vel generaliter tota collectio malorum*" (PL 114.733).

 In medieval and Renaissance English literature the beasts come to be more simply associated with the devil and evil — especially in apocalyptic contexts — as in Spenser's borrowing of "Three ranckes of yron teeth" with which the Redcrosse Knight's dragon is endowed (*Faerie Queene*, 1.11.13), although the two-horned composite creature of Rev. 13:11-18 is adopted as "the Ram" by David Jones in a parodic passage in his *The Sleeping Lord* sequence, with "the Ram's wife," probably here a reference to the city of Rome, a counterpart of "the Lamb's wife," or New Jerusalem, in St. John's Apocalypse (Rev. 21:9). A lighthearted reference to some of the many attempts in apocalyptically-oriented preaching to find modern historical allegory in every aspect of biblical apocalyptic is afforded by Coleridge, who comments on a "true lover of liberty" who had "proved to the satisfac-tion of many that Mr. Pitt was one of the horns of the second beast in The Revelation, that spoke as a dragon" (*Biographia Literaria,* chap. 10).

 See also DRAGON OF THE APOCALYPSE.

 Bibliography. Heaton, E. W., *The Book of Daniel* (1964), 169-90; Rowley, H. H., *Darius the Mede and the Four World Empires in the Book of Daniel* (1964), 174-82.

H. DAVID BRUMBLE

FOUR DAUGHTERS OF GOD The Daughters or Graces of God are said to be Truth, Righteousness (Justice), Mercy, and Peace — allegorical characters whose origin is in the words of Ps. 85:10, "Mercy and truth are met together; righteousness and peace have kissed each other." In Jewish tradition these virtues were seen as the four standards of the throne of God (see L. Ginzberg, *LJ* 6.82). Christian development of the motif owes largely to the commentaries of Hugh of St. Victor and the sermons of St. Bernard of Clairvaux.

 In later medieval literature the narrative of the four daughters has many variations. In general, it consists of debate (sometimes in the presence of God in heaven) about the wisdom of creating humanity and about the propriety of strict justice or mercy for the fallen human race. Justice and Truth appear for the prosecution, representing the old Law, while Mercy speaks for the defense, and Peace presides over their reconciliation when Mercy prevails.

 In many English texts the scene is set at some point well after the creation, e.g., just before the Annunciation (as in the *Ludus Coventriae* and most other literary and iconographic occurrences) or immediately after the death of Christ (as in *Piers Plowman*). In *The Castle of Perseverance* the debate occurs after the death of Humanum Genus, who is then admitted to heaven. In a version known as *Processus Belial (The Devil's Lawsuit)*, Belial summons Justice and Truth to his aid, and the Virgin calls on Mercy and Peace. In the late 16th-cent. fragment *Processus Satanae*, God himself calls Mercy and Peace to plead against Justice and Verite.

 The virtues appear with some frequency in books of hours, generally in the Annunciation section. The colors of their clothes are specified in the map to *The Castle of Perseverance:* Mercy wears white, Justice red, Truth "sad green," and Peace black.

 Other iconographic conventions appear with some frequency. Justice is generally represented with scales or a sword; Peace with a palm, inverted torch, or truncated sword; Truth with a carpenter's square or tables of the Law; and Mercy with a box of ointment. The virtues are not always represented as female: in *Mankind* Mercy and Truth are male.

 The debate of the Four Daughters occurs in a variety of ME texts, including *Cursor Mundi* (1.9517-52); *Gesta Romanorum* (no. 55); Grosseteste's *Castel of Love*, a translation of *Chasteau D'Amour* (1275); *The Court of*

Sapience (bk. 1); *Piers Plowman* (B.18; C.21); *Castel of Perseverance* (3130); *Mankind* (832-82); *Ludus Coventriae* (97-103).

The allegory persisted through the Renaissance and even into minor Stuart poetry. There are possible echoes in the court scene in the *Merchant of Venice* (4.1) and in Milton's *Paradise Lost* (3.132-34). But while the relationship of Justice to Mercy continues to have currency in literary tradition well after the 17th cent., the elaborated allegory of the four virtues does not.

See also HARROWING OF HELL.

Bibliography. Chew S. *The Virtues Reconciled* (1947); Gleckner, R. J. "Blake and the Four Daughters of God." *ELN* 15 (1977), 110-15; Houle, P. *The English Morality and Related Drama* (1972); Proudfoot, R. "The Virtue of Perseverance." In *Aspects of Early English Drama*. Ed. P. Neuss (1983), 92-109; Traver, H. *The Four Daughters of God* (1907); "The Four Daughters of God: A Mirror of Changing Doctrine." *PMLA* 40 (1925), 44-92.   MICHAEL MURPHY

FOUR LEVELS OF ALLEGORY   *See* ALLEGORY; HERMENEUTICS; LETTER AND SPIRIT.

FOUR RIVERS OF PARADISE   Gen. 2:10-14 describes a river watering the paradisal garden which split into four rivers: "The name of the first is Pison: that is it which compasseth the whole land of Havilah, where there is gold. . . . And the name of the second river is Gihon: the same is it that compasseth the whole land of Ethiopia. And the name of the third river is Hiddekel: that is it which goeth toward the east of Assyria. And the fourth river is Euphrates."

Various attempts to offer literal identification of the four rivers exist in contradiction with one another; ancient geographers (e.g., Strabo) were less certain of their maps than we are. Pison has been associated with the Ganges (Josephus, St. Augustine) but also with the western branches of the Nile, Gihon with the Nile or its eastern branches, and Hiddekel with the Tigris. Alternatively, John Scotus Erigena (9th cent.) takes "Paradise" as a figurative expression signifying "nothing other than human nature made in the image of God," so that the "Fountain of Life" or Divine Wisdom in Paradise issues forth as the four cardinal virtues, prudence, temperance, fortitude, and justice — an interpretation deriving ultimately from Augustine (*De divisione naturae*, 4.16). The ME *Cursor Mundi* returns to patristic geography, but adds that the fountain in Paradise from which the rivers issue was set so high above the earth that it remained undisturbed by the Flood. Milton, in *Paradise Lost,* follows tradition in describing the "four main streams" (4.222-46), and has Satan enter Eden by an underground channel of the Tigris which "Rose up a Fountain by the Tree of Life" (9.71-86).

See also EDEN.

FOWLER   *See* TRAP.

FOX   The Hebrew word *shu'al* is used for any type of fox, jackal, or member of the wild dog family (in the Geneva Bible occasionally "hyaena"). In OT Semitic contexts, the fox was a creature of low cunning, generally considered to be a nuisance and undesirable (cf. Neh. 4:3). Ezekiel compares the ideal prophets of Israel in his time to denned up foxes (Ezek. 13:4ff.); foxes are the inhabitants of wasted ruins of Zion (Lam. 5:18). In one of the many vivid narratives of the book of Judges, Samson trapped 300 foxes and attached burning brands to their tails to lay waste the crops of the Philistines (Judg. 15). The love poet of the Song of Songs allusively warns of "the little foxes that spoil the vines" (Cant. 2:15), and in Luke 13:32 Herod is uncomplimentarily referred to as a fox. Finally, Jesus refers to his choice for a life of poverty and mendicancy by observing that even "the foxes have holes and the birds of the air have nests, but the Son of man hath not where to lay his head" (Matt. 8:20; Luke 9:58).

The slyness of the fox has earned him a devilish role in almost all folk literature within his habitat, much of which is so bound up in biblical allusion to the fox that it becomes nearly indistinguishable from it. Accordingly legends such as those of Reynart, Reinhard, or Reinart de Vos color the reception of patristic commentary which sees the fox as a symbol for *seductor* of the faithful (e.g., St. Gregory, *Comm. in Cant.*, sup. 2.15 [PL 79.500]; *Glossa Ordinaria* [PL 114.283]). In medieval art the fox sometimes appears with a miter, signifying not only a false prelate but probably also the Antichrist who, if possible, "would deceive even the very elect" (Matt. 24:24). In the 14th cent. the fox is represented on carved misericords as a Franciscan friar, preaching to geese and other barnyard fowl or occasionally a rooster, the former symbolizing the flock of the faithful, the latter typically a parish priest. Chaucer's Chaunticleer in *The Nun's Priest's Tale,* who only narrowly escapes the devilish "coal-fox" Russell, is thus likely providing a warning to clergy and others against suspect friars. Heywood's adage, "For though this appeare a proper pulpet peece, / yet whan the fox preacheth, then beware your geese" (*Proverbs* [1546], 2.7.67), still echoes in Jonson's *Volpone,* where the devilish "Fox fares ever best, when he is cursed" (5.3.119). After Dryden's conversion to the Catholic faith he styles Protestantism as tending toward the Socinian heresy, and characterizes it in his *The Hind and the Panther* as "False Reynard."

References to devilish foxes have become a literary cliché and relatively few of them require biblical contextualization. Among the exceptions is Keats's social criticism of those "who lord it o'er their fellow men" in *Endymion.* Such persons, he says (in reference to Judg. 15:4), "through an idiot blink, will see unpack'd / Firebranded foxes to sear up and singe / Our gold and ripe-ear'd hopes" (3.6-8). A context of social concern also motivates Oliver Goldsmith's use of Matt. 8:20 in his Vicar's discussion of Christian hospitality in *The Vicar of Wakefield* (chap. 4). Thoreau's discussion of the "Economy" in *Walden* quotes Matt. 8:20 to highlight his argument that "in modern civilized society not more than one-half the families own a shelter." Ruskin quotes the same passage (as well as Cant. 2:15) to take up a similar issue: "Oh — you queens — you queens; among the hills and happy greenwood of this land of yours, shall the foxes have holes, and the birds of the air have nests; and in your cities shall the stones cry out against you, that they are the only pillows where the Son of Man can lay His head?" (*Sesame and Lilies*, "Of Queen's Gardens").

Jewish and medieval Christian associations of the fox with surreptitious devilish activity have metamorphosed in modern times to express sexual double entendre. Arrestingly, e.g., one of D. H. Lawrence's lovers attempts to seduce with an uprooted quotation of Matt. 8:20: "Foxes have their holes. They even have their mates, Lady Daphne, that they bark to and are answered. And an adder finds his female" ("The Ladybird").

Bibliography. Anderson, M. D. *Misericordes* (1954); Dahlberg, C. "Chaucer's Cock and Fox." *JEGP* 53 (1954), 277-90; Fleming, J. V. *The Roman de la Rose: Allegory and Iconography* (1969).

FREEDOM, BONDAGE The interrelated motifs of freedom and bondage serve as major organizing principles in the Bible and biblical tradition. In the creation story (Gen. 1), God gives each creature freedom to live and multiply in a good world, and to humanity the added freedom of ruling over the lower creation. In Gen. 2, God decrees: "Of every tree . . . thou mayest freely eat: But of the tree of the knowledge of good and evil, thou shalt not eat . . ." (Gen. 2:16-17), thereby establishing the boundary which when trangressed will determine humanity's subsequent loss of freedom, its bondage on earth to sin and death.

The book of Exodus, most pointedly in the Song of Miriam (Exod. 15:21), celebrates God's liberation of the Israelites from slavery in Egypt: the Lord "hath triumphed gloriously," Pharaoh's "horse and his rider hath he thrown into the sea." A stern reminder of the debt God's people owe for their liberation from Egypt prefaces the Ten Commandments (Exod. 20:2-17): grateful obedience to the Lord is the condition of freedom.

The history recorded in Judg. 2–16 shows the people in the Promised Land oscillating between freedom and self-generated bondage. Each time they "do evil in the sight of the LORD" by "whoring after" the false fertility gods of the neighboring nations, they fall into enslavement to their enemies; when, tutored by adversity, they are ready again to be led to freedom, God raises up another judge for the purpose.

With the decline of the monarchy after David and

Solomon, and subsequent captivity under Assyria and Babylon, the antithesis of freedom and bondage becomes a major prophetic theme. Here the issues are presented in personal and social, as well as nationalistic, terms. Amos thunders against the rich oppressors of the poor: the Lord will scourge them before he restores his people in their land (Amos 4:2; 9:4, 15). Jeremiah and Ezekiel preach redemptive warnings from various positions of undeserved personal affliction and bondage (Jer. 7; 16; 26; 27; Ezek. 4; 24:16).

In the NT the earthly life of Jesus begins in a humble stable in the symbolic bondage of swaddling wraps for the Word made flesh (Luke 2:7; John 1:14); it ends in humiliating submission to the bondage of death on the cross and entombment in linen burial cloths. Though sought after as a political messiah, Jesus repeatedly declares his kingdom and the liberty of its citizens in spiritual terms. He proclaims his role as liberator from the letter of the old law (Mark 2:27) and imposes the more difficult demand of an inner righteousness which will fulfill the spirit of the old (Matt. 5:17-48). He promises, by bearing the burden of the new law with his followers, to make it light (Matt. 11:29-30). In his Resurrection, he leads captivity captive (Eph. 4:8) and robs death of its sting (1 Cor. 15:55-56).

St. Paul constantly and paradoxically emphasizes the continuing sense of bondage to sin in the flesh, and joy in freedom from that sin in Christ (Rom. 6:14-23; Gal. 5:1; etc.); St. Peter who, like Paul, was imprisoned more than once for the sake of the gospel, uses "prison" as a metaphor for the bondage suffered by sinners in hell (1 Pet. 3:19-20). St. John, writing to churches helpless before the bondage of political and military occupation, devotes much of his Apocalypse to visions of God's wrathful justice against those who oppress the poor and faithful, and affords a vision of blissful freedom in the New Jerusalem after these oppressors have been overcome. The Bible thus begins, climaxes, and ends in acute consciousness of the tension between freedom and bondage.

In subsequent times the modes of freedom proclaimed or sought have been influenced by biblical precedent. Some early Christians sought deliverance from this world in a martyr's death. Like John, others awaited the realization of apocalyptic hopes. Midrashic literature shows that Jews, too, continued to hope for deliverance in the day of the Lord as prophesied in Isa. 2, Zech. 14, and elsewhere; in the meantime they could see each Sabbath as a limited respite figuring the future time of deliverance (*Midrash on Psalms*, trans. W. G. Braude, 786).

Origen came to believe, under the influence of pagan thought, that the doctrine of eternal bondage for sinners in hell was inconsistent with a belief in genuine human freedom and God's justice and goodness. His complex solution, involving a curative hell and a doctrine of rebirth, had lasting influence, although it was judged heretical (D. P. Walker, *The Decline of Hell* [1964], 11-

13). St. Augustine follows Paul in stressing the bondage of fallen humanity to sin: he argues that the will is free in terms of its responsibility for choices made but is bound to make evil choices unless delivered through the goodness and mercy of God in Christ. He advances a doctrine of predestination rooted in Rom. 8:29: some persons are apparently incapable of responding to God's liberating initiative. Boethius wrote his influential *De Consolatione Philosophiae* in response to his actual bondage in prison. Like Augustine, he takes up the thorny questions of fate and providence, foreknowledge, predestination, and free will, finally confessing that inferior human reason cannot of itself attain the mode of divine knowledge in which these issues resolve themselves. True freedom for Boethius is freedom of the will to choose intelligible or higher good, and it may not be diminished by physical bondage. To choose such freedom is indeed the only way to preserve rationality.

It is in this sense that medieval English writers understood the promise of Jesus concerning belief in his word, "And ye shall know the truth, and the truth shall make you free" (John 8:32). The phrase concludes each line of Chaucer's "Balade de Bon Conseil," which suggests that fortune's adversity, an inevitable condition of "wrastling for this world," may be overcome by appeal to God's mercy and "godeness" for spiritual deliverance: "Unto the world leve now to be thral," he concludes, "And trouthe the shal delivere, it is no drede." Among his numerous treatments of this theme, Chaucer offers in his Knight of *The Canterbury Tales* a concise insight into medieval understanding of the relation between freedom and bondage. In response to Harry Bailey's terms for a story contest en route to Canterbury, the Knight forgoes his privilege of station and draws straws with the company to see who shall have the less desirable lot of initial narrator. As fortune would have it, the lot falls to him,

> And whan this goode man saugh that it was so,
> As he that wys was and obedient
> To kepe his foreward by his free assent,
> He seyde, "Syn I shal bigynne the game
> What, welcome be the cut, a Goddes name!" (*General Prologue*, 1.850-54)

Having bound himself by his "foreward" (promise), he now assents in freedom to that condition. He "freely obeys." His tale, unsurprisingly, contrasts the infelicity and unreason of those who make physical bondage their "reality" with those who know the rational felicity of preserving inward, spiritual freedom.

Medieval lyrics and carols, as well as "Harrowing of Hell" plays, make use of patristic typology in which Christ is the "key of David."

> *O clauis David inclita,*
> *Dans viam in portis,*
> *Educ nos de carcere*
> *Et de umbra mortis*

is the incipit to both a Latin hymn and the 16th-cent. English carol which "translates" it:

> O David, thow nobell key,
> Cepter of the howse of Isreall,
> Thow opyn the gate and geff us way . . .
> And saue vs fro owre fendys felle.

> We be in prison; vn vs haue mynde,
> And lose vs fro the bonde of synne,
> For that thou losest no man may bynde. (R. Greene, *The Early English Carols*, no. 2)

Optimism concerning the potentiality of human freedom in this life re-emerged for a time in the Renaissance. Pico della Mirandola's "Oration on the Dignity of Man" (ca. 1486) rests its hopes under God in "moral philosophy and dialectic" as a means to "set us free" so that "Gabriel, the 'strength of God', shall abide in us, leading us through the miracles of nature and showing us on every side the merit and the might of God." But English writers of the 16th cent. remained more aware of the tension. Spenser, working within the patterns of Christian redemption in the first book of his *Faerie Queene*, characterizes the strict limits to earthly freedom: Redcrosse can freely imitate Christ in liberating Una's parents and their lands from the Satanic dragon, but he is not free to enjoy full union with his heavenly bride until his earthly quest is done.

John Donne's sense of the paradoxical relationship between freedom and bondage is reflected amply in his poetry as well as his sermons, perhaps most memorably in the appeal of "Holy Sonnet 14":

> Take me to you, imprison me, for I
> Except you enthral me, never shall be free
> Nor ever chaste, except you ravish me.

George Herbert's poetry is replete with analogous reflections on the paradoxical relationship between apparent bondage (which comes as a result of obedience to God) and true inner freedom (e.g., "The Collar"; "Obedience"). This theme is central to Bunyan's *Pilgrim's Progress* (another work written in prison), and it is prominent in Milton's relation of obedience and love in *Paradise Lost*.

Milton takes an affirmative view of the potential for good in human freedom of choice without minimizing the difficulties and pains involved: "I cannot praise a fugitive and cloistered virtue," he writes, "that never . . . sees her adversary, but slinks out of the race" (*Areopagitica* [ed. Hughes], 728). Milton's writings demonstrate repeatedly the power of the individual to exercise obedient freedom, standing firm in testing circumstances (*Comus*; *Paradise Lost*, esp. bk. 12; *Samson Agonistes*). Such freedom is perhaps most notably dramatized in Christ's reasoned and scripturally obedient refusal of Satan's temptation in *Paradise Regained*.

The theme is amplified in numerous 18th-cent. poems (e.g., Christopher Smart's *Jubilate Agno*) and hymns, perhaps most memorably in Charles Wesley's "And Can it Be," which relates Christ's free sacrifice to human liberty, in terms echoing (perhaps unconsciously) medieval Latin hymns on the harrowing of hell:

> Long my imprisoned spirit lay,
> Fast bound in sin and nature's night.
> Thine eye diffused a quick'ning ray;
> I woke; the dungeon flamed with light.
> My chains fell off, my heart was free,
> I rose, went forth, and followed thee.

Spiritual deliverance is also a major theme in the fifth book of William Cowper's *The Task,* where Cowper argues (cf. John 8:32) that "Grace makes the slave a freeman":

> He is the freeman whom the truth makes free
> And all are slaves beside. There's not a chain
> That hellish foes, confed'rate for his harm,
> Can wind around him, but he casts it off
> With as much ease as Samson his green wyths. . . .
> His freedom is the same in ev'ry state;
> And no condition of this changeful life,
> So manifold in cares, whose ev'ry day
> Brings its own evil with it, makes it less:
> For he has wings that neither sickness, pain,
> Nor penury, can cripple or confine.
> No nook so narrow but he spreads them there
> With ease, and is at large. Th'oppressor holds
> His body bound; but knows not what a range
> His spirit takes, unconscious of a chain;
> And that to bind him is a vain attempt
> Whom God delights in, and in whom he dwells.
> (5.598, 733-34, 767-78)

With the Enlightenment, however, and the Romantic period, important changes in dominant use of the word *freedom* affect the way in which the biblical opposition is understood and applied. Use of the words *free* and *freedom* to mean simply independence or escape from restraint — in Herbert's "The Collar" still a mere counterfeit of true freedom — begins to assert itself even in contexts where biblical allusion is involved, as the primary understanding. Partly this is a result of chiliastic attachments to national identity — in Britain and in America — of the biblical concepts of election and covenant: political liberty under present regimes becomes identified with exodus freedom, liberty from Egyptian bondage (or Babylonian captivity), so that biblical deliverances formally allegorized or spiritualized in prevalent exegesis, commentary, and allusion now become typologized as analogues, effectively, for modern state polity or privilege. Such a tendency is evident, e.g., in Cowper's *Expostulation* (1782), where England is the object of praise:

> Freedom, in other lands scarce known to shine,
> Pours out a flood of splendour upon thine;
> Thou hast as bright an int'rest in her rays
> As ever Roman had in Rome's best days.

> True freedom is where no restraint is known
> That scripture, justice, and good sense, disown,
> Where only vice and injury are tied,
> And all from shore to shore is free beside. (588-95)

This is also the dominant usage of Thomas Paine, and of Rousseau and Voltaire. Hence it figures largely in the rhetoric of poetry admiring the French and American Revolutions. In American romanticism, with Whitman, or in English romanticism, with Blake, emphasis on the individual's personal liberty is opposed to the restraint of social conventions or the curb of kings and priests (cf. Wordsworth, Byron, Shelley). Thus, whereas the medieval emphasis in understanding the relationship between truth and freedom is inward and spiritually directed, the post-revolutionary understanding is chiefly libertarian or political. In Julia Ward Howe's "Battle Hymn of the Republic" (1862) the last stanza effectively makes an analogy of what formerly would have been distinguished — spiritual and political freedom: "As he [Christ] died to make men holy let us die to make men free / — His truth is marching on." This understanding proves surprisingly amenable to Marxism and modern "liberation theology."

In American literature at the popular level, Emerson's luminous essay "Self-Reliance," with its insistence that "No law can be sacred to me but that of my nature," follows Rousseau and Montaigne in making the psychology of individual liberty — even to the point of anarchy — the essence of freedom's meaning. In historical perspective Emerson may appear somewhat confused: he commences with an apparent acknowledgment of biblical and Boethian wisdom which actually asserts the contrary of his own thesis. Wordsworth's similar concern in the *Prelude* with "genuine freedom" is also largely divested of biblical associations. Freedom becomes more or less the prerogative of the absolute ego of Fichte's *Wissenschaftslehre,* despite Coleridge's criticism that such self-assertion is "a crude egoismus, a boastful and hyperstoic hostility to NATURE as lifeless, godless, and altogether unholy" (*Biographia Literaria,* 1.101-02). Wordsworth's "bondage" in *The Prelude* (1805) is still to be understood as spiritual bondage, though his "liberation" is won by the advent of self-mastery, including especially mastery of consciousness, rather than by Milton's or Chaucer's obedience to biblical precept:

> A captive greets thee, coming from a house
> Of bondage, from yon City's walls set free,
> A prison where he hath been long immured.
> Now I am free, enfrancis'd and at large.
>   . . . With a heart
> Joyous, nor scar'd at its own liberty,
> I look about. . . .
> Enough that I am free. (1.6-33)

As a result, though biblical allusion may lurk in the shadows, the tension in much Romantic and post-Romantic poetry between freedom and bondage is characterized by a strikingly postbiblical definition of the term *freedom:* whereas for Chaucer the word is largely other-directed and bespeaks a benefit of obedience (ME *fredom* is glossed in medieval French by *largesse*), for Wordsworth its meaning is largely self-directed and signifies a triumph of self-mastery. For Chaucer's Knight to love "trouthe, honour, fredom and curtesye" is thus to cherish a different sort of character than is admired by Wordsworth, despite the latter's allusively Pauline phrasing:

> Oh! who is he that hath his whole life long
> Preserved, enlarged this freedom in himself?
> For this alone is genuine Liberty. (*Prelude,* 13.120-23)

Most subsequent literary use of the binary opposition has only vestigial connection to the biblical concepts.

Bibliography. Abrams, M. H. *Natural Supernaturalism: Tradition and Revolution in Romantic Literature* (1971); Anderson, B. W. *Understanding the Old Testament* (1957); Cassirer, E., P. O. Kristeller, and J. H. Randall, Jr., eds. *The Renaissance Philosophy of Man* (1948); Rist, J. M. "Augustine on Free Will and Predestination." In *Augustine, A Collection of Critical Essays.* Ed. R. A. Markus (1972); Sanders, E. B. *Jewish and Christian Self-Definition,* vol. 1 (1980).

ELIZABETH BIEMAN

FRIEND OF THE BRIDEGROOM This expression (*philos tou nymphiou,* "best man," chief of the groom's party) appears in John 3:29 on the lips of John the Baptist, as a self-designation, in what is generally regarded as a parable, perhaps in wide use, the import of which was to designate the more important or prestigious (the bridegroom) of two persons. In John 3:29, the term signifies the Baptist's role as the one whose task it is to act as the representative of "the Christ" (Messiah) in securing the "bride" (likely here the elect) for the "bridegroom" (here, Jesus "the Christ"), and whose joy is in the rejoicing of the groom over his bride. St. Paul seems to imply a similar role for himself in 2 Cor. 11:2, for in ancient Jewish culture the bridegroom's "friend" (Heb. *shoshbin,* a special term for the office) acted in arranging the wedding, and, as implied in the John 3:29 passage, superintended the consummation of the marriage. Compare Judg. 14:10–15:6, where Samson's "friend" is given Samson's wife, this constituting a serious breach of custom, bringing on Samson's revenge (15:1-5) and the wrath of the Philistines as well (15:6). The wedding images used in John 3:29 may allude to the OT custom of Israel as God's wife (e.g., Hos. 1–2), but, contrary to rabbinic tradition, the Messiah (here Jesus) instead of God is the groom (cf. Rev. 21:2, 9). In rabbinic tradition Moses is sometimes described as playing the role of "friend of the bridegroom" for God, in leading Israel to the covenant at Sinai, viewed as the "marriage" ceremony. (For other references to parties to weddings, cf. Matt. 9:15; Mark 2:19; Luke 5:34; 1 Macc. 9:39; Ps. 45:11; Cant. 3:11.)

The "friend of the Bridegroom" becomes a topos in the spiritual literature of the Middle Ages, where the writer, often a male contemplative writing to nuns, presents himself as a friend of the Bridegroom wooing his reader to full relationship with Christ. Richard Rolle opens his *Ego Dormio,* addressed to a woman who may later have joined a contemplative order, with language borrowed, like his title, from the Song of Songs, and then adds: "For þi þat I lufe, I wow þe, þat I myght have þe als I walde, noght to me, bot to my Lorde. I will become þat messanger to bryng þe to hys bed, þat hase made þe and boght þe, Criste, þe keyng sonn of heven" (6-10).

Shakespeare adapts the topos in his comedy *Twelfth Night,* where the shipwrecked heroine Viola dresses in male clothes to find employment as a page (pseudonymously called "Cesario") with Orsino, Duke of Illyria. The Duke sends her to press his suit for the hand of Countess Olivia, with whom he is in love. Viola, having fallen in love with the Duke herself, nevertheless makes a splendid effort to woo Olivia on his behalf. The plot, further complicated when Olivia falls in love with "Cesario," is only resolved by Shakespearean magic in the last act.

The term recurs in writings of the 18th-cent. Methodist leaders such as John Wesley, John Fletcher, and George Whitefield, where it is made to apply to the task of the evangelist, as well as, in some cases (especially in the letters of Wesley), to urge a spiritual calling upon correspondents.

Bibliography. Jeremias, J. *"nymphē, nymphios," TDNT* 4.1099-1106; van Selms, A. "The Best Man and the Bride — From Sumer to St. John." *JNES* 9 (1950), 65-75.

LARRY W. HURTADO

FRUIT OF THE SPIRIT *See* GIFTS OF THE SPIRIT.

FULNESS OF TIME St. Paul speaks of the Incarnation as occurring after a divinely planned elapse of human history: "But when the fulness of the time was come, God sent forth his Son, made of a woman, made under the law, to redeem them that were under the law" (Gal. 4:4-5). This happened, he says, "that in the dispensation of the fulness of times he might gather together in one all things in Christ" (Eph. 1:10). The sense of the phrase in these verses for Christian exegetes has always been to underline divine control in history, especially with respect to the *historia humanae salvationis* (e.g., *Glossa Ordinaria* [PL 114.578]). The singular "time" of Gal. 4 is seen to refer to the Incarnation of Christ, the plural reference in Ephesians to the final consummation of the work of redemption and closing of the "age of grace" which was ushered in by Christ's life and atonement (PL 114.589). As Matthew Poole puts it, the interval between the "fulness of time" and "fulness of times" is the dispensation of grace, "the time of the promulgation of the Gospel" (*Annotations upon the Holy Bible,* sup. Eph. 1:10).

The phrase "fulness of time" has been used in an

apocalyptic sense by generations of Independent preachers, and even when secularized it often maintains its association with the culmination of history. One of Aldous Huxley's characters in *Chrome Yellow* writes in his diary: "If God is good . . . the name of Lapith will be preserved and our rarer and more delicate race transmitted through the generations until in the fulness of time the world shall recognize the superiority of those beings whom now it uses to make mock of" (chap. 13). H. G. Wells, in *The Time Machine,* writes that "Man had been content to live in ease and delight upon the labors of his fellow-man, had taken Necessity as his watchword and excuse, and in the fulness of time Necessity had come home to him" (chap. 7). Margaret Avison's "The Dumbfounding," a conversion poem about the Incarnation, sees Christ as "the all lovely, all-men's way / to that far country" in an age of restoration and healing to last "until / time be full."

Bibliography. Barr, J. *Biblical Words for Time* (SBT 1/33 [1962]); Cullmann, O. *Christ and Time* (Eng. trans. 1964); Marsh, J. *The Fulness of Time* (1952).

G

GABRIEL Gabriel, whose Hebrew name may mean "God is powerful" *(gabriel)* or possibly "man of God," is mentioned four times in the Bible. In Dan. 8:16 he comes in human form to clarify the eschatological significance of Daniel's vision; later (Dan. 9:21) he grants Daniel special wisdom and understanding. In the NT he appears to Zacharias the priest "on the right side of the altar of incense" in the Temple, announcing the coming birth of a son (John the Baptist) to Zacharias and his wife Elisabeth (Luke 1:11). Gabriel is also the angel of the Annunciation, informing Mary that she will become the mother of Jesus (Luke 1:31). Each of these appearances, in both the OT and NT, is connected in some way with the promise of Immanuel, the coming Messiah.

In pseudepigraphic texts, Gabriel is an archangel. He is one of the "glorious ones" who look down upon all mankind (1 Enoch 40:3); he is one of four angels who lift up to God's presence the prayers of the martyrs as they appeal for an end to anarchy and violence upon the earth (9:1-11); and, as an agent of God's supreme power, he is seated at his right hand (2 Enoch 24:1). His duties include casting the wicked into the fiery furnace after the Last Judgment (1 Enoch 54:6). Various Targums extend to him, among other things, agency in guiding Joseph to his brothers (sup. Gen. 37:5), in the burial of Moses (sup. Deut. 34:6), and even in gathering dust for the creation of mankind (Hag. 12a; Pirqe R. El. 3). Indeed, his role expands so dramatically in later midrash that he dominates all angels, although often he is accompanied by Michael, Uriel, and others in marvelous exploits. In Islam Gabriel is revered for having dictated the Koran to Mohammed.

Among the Fathers, and down to the later Middle Ages, Gabriel acquires significance principally from his role in the Nativity story (including his calling Jesus "Lord," according to St. Ephraim Syrus, *Hymns on the Nativity*, 14.23). The *Glossa Ordinaria,* citing Bede, says Gabriel is named in the Annunciation scene only in order to indicate that it is the "fortitude of God" which here declares itself to be coming into the territory of the devil to claim victory (PL 114.246; the point is later amplified by Calvin in his commentary on Luke 1:9). For St. Ambrose Gabriel's power is to be distinguished from that of Christ. That Christ, unlike Gabriel, experienced death for the redemption of humankind should not be taken to suggest that the sovereignty of God was not far more powerfully displayed in Christ than in his *nuncio* (*De fide,* 3.21). Peter Abelard's hymn "To Gabriel of the Annunciation" begins "On with your embassy! / Say AVE! Say ALL HAIL!"

Gabriel's "embassy" is often featured in early English literature: it becomes, e.g., a prominent subject in the *Advent Lyrics of the Exeter Book,* where he is the "bearer of grace" to Mary; hence the poet's prayer: "Iowa us nu þa are þe se engel þe, / godes spelboda, gabriel brohte" (9.61-62; cf. 7.37-38). Numerous ME Annunciation lyrics are direct translations or paraphrases of the Latin sequence *"Angelus ad Virginem"* (Dreves, *Analecta,* 8.49), and many were set to music (e.g., "Gabriel, fram evene-king," in C. Brown, *English Lyrics of the XIIIth Century,* no. 44). The Latin original is parodied in Chaucer's *Miller's Tale,* where "hende Nicholas," a "false clerk" and far from angelic, descends from his loft to commence an unsubtle wooing of his landlord's wife after announcing himself by playing "a gay sautrie" and singing *Angelus ad Virginem* (1.3213-16). In many Annunciation carols and poems on the "Five Joys of the Virgin" (e.g., R. Greene, *The Early English Carols,* nos. 229-56), the "archaungell shynyng full bright" (nos. 248, 252) is represented as kneeling to the Virgin ("In the most demuere and goodly wys he ded to hyre omag" [Greene, no. 239; cf. 237]), although occasionally, in a variation of earlier iconography, he stands or hovers and Mary "was full sort abashyd, iwis, / And wened that sche had don amysse" (no. 238; cf. the "Annunciation" of Simone Martini). Other features of the iconography represented in the poems include a figuration of the conception "as the sonne beame goth thurgh the glass" (Greene, no. 246); Gabriel's bearing of a lily (Brown, *Religious Lyrics of the XIVth Century,* no. 112); and his utterance of the *"Ave Maria, gratia plena, Dominus tecum,"* the Vg text of Luke 1:28 — often rendered in Latin in English poems much as it often appears in art in a phylactery or scroll issuing from Gabriel's mouth. Typically, as in Van Eyck's altarpiece, Mary indicates her submission to her unique calling by placing her hand over a copy of the opened Scriptures (cf. Luke 1:38):

> "Goddes handemayde behold," seide she
>   To Gabriell, that archaungell;
> "Thy worde in me fulfilled be,"
>   *Vt pariem Emanuel.*" (Green, no. 245)

In literature after the Reformation Gabriel is much less prominent, largely because of Protestant de-emphasis not only of the Virgin (and hence, the Annunciation) but of angel lore as well. In Tasso's *Gerusalemme Liberata* Gabriel is sent by God to urge the Crusaders after seven years to march on Jerusalem. In Donne's "The Annunciation and Passion," he links the two events: "At once a Sonne is promis'd her, and gone, / Gabriell gives Christ to her, He her to John." Milton is the great angelologist of this period, however, and Gabriel plays an important role in *Paradise Lost,* where he is the "chief of the Angelic Guards" who fights against Moloch until the blasphemous foe of heaven "down cloven to the wàist . . . fled bellowing" (6.354-62). He returns in *Paradise Regained* as the angel chosen to hear the divine plan of redemption and to bear the news to Mary. Cowper finds an odd place for him in his apostrophe to free trade and international shipping in "Charity," in which he well wishes a ship "That flies, like Gabriel on his Lord's commands, / An herald of God's love to pagan lands" (135-36), a dubious evocation of the missionary spirit.

Hardy seems to have the biblical angel in mind in the character of Gabriel Oak, the rejected suitor of Bathsheba Everdene, who watches over her farm as she marries someone else in *Far from the Madding Crowd.* In George Eliot's narrative poem *The Death of Moses,* based on haggadic Jewish sources, Gabriel does not have the heart to carry the soul of Moses to God when commanded to do so. In Melville's *Moby-Dick* a "scaramouch" is hired on as seaman, "but straightaway upon the ship's getting out of sight of land, his insanity broke out in a freshet. He announced himself as the archangel Gabriel, and commanded the captain to jump overboard" (chap. 71). Emily Dickinson's two robins in her apple tree are "Two Gabriels"; more retiring than the scaramouch, they "have that modest way / To screen them from renown" ("Forever Cherished Be the Tree"). Joyce paraphrases Luke 1:38 in the litany section of the "Nausicaa" episode of *Ulysses,* while in *A Portrait of the Artist as a Young Man* Stephen co-opts the Annunciation scene to describe the birth of a poem: "O! in the virgin womb of the imagination the word was made flesh. Gabriel the seraph had come to the virgin's chamber." He is parodied as an ineffectual suitor in Katherine Anne Porter's *Old Mortality,* where Amy has kept her second cousin, Gabriel, waiting for five years.

See also ANGEL; ANNUNCIATION; MARY, MOTHER OF JESUS.

GAD   One of the twelve tribes of Jacob.
See also AARON; JACOB; TRIBES OF ISRAEL.

GADARENE SWINE   In an incident recorded in the Synoptic Gospels (Matt. 8:28-32; Mark 5:1-20; Luke 8:26-32) the Gadarene swine, possessed by the devils Christ had expelled from a demoniac, rushed to their death in a lake. Swine were regarded as unclean by the Jews, a fact underscored in Shakespeare's reference to the incident in *The Merchant of Venice.* Responding to Bassanio's invitation to dine with him, Shylock retorts, "Yes, to smell pork; to eat of the habitation which your prophet the Nazarite [sic] conjured the devil into" (1.3.33-35).

Christian commentators from St. John Chrysostom (*Sermons on Matthew,* 28 [PG 57.355]) to Calvin (*Harmony of the Gospels*) moralized the story by seeing the "unclean" pigs as types of humanity's bestial lower nature through which the devil seeks the destruction of humankind. This general interpretation supplied English literature with a metaphor, satiric or moral, for degraded humanity, ranging from the directors of the South Sea Bubble in Swift ("The Bubble," 213-16) to modern humanity engaged in the arms race in Shaw (Pref. to *St. Joan*). Shelley's *Swellfoot the Tyrant* (1.1.55-59) ironically transfers the iniquity from degraded swine to tyrannical master (George III).

Christ's power to defeat evil spirits, stressed by St. Jerome (*Comm. in Matt.* 8:31) and Tertullian (*Adv. Marc.*

4.20), is emphasized in Milton's association of the Gadarene swine with Satan's defeated legions (*Paradise Regained*, 4.626-32).

From Spenser (*Faerie Queene*, 2.12) to Joyce (the Circe episode of *Ulysses*), the biblical narrative is often conflated with the moralized legend of Circe (see Horace, *Epistles*, 1.2.23-26), in which men are transformed into brutes by unclean desires.

See also DEMONS, DEMON POSSESSION.

BRENDA E. RICHARDSON
NORMAN VANCE

GAMALIEL   When St. Paul was arrested in the Temple in Jerusalem on charges of being a seditionist, he gave, among his credentials as a proper Jew, that he had been "brought up in this city at the feet of Gamaliel, and taught according to the perfect manner of the law of the fathers, and was zealous toward God, as ye all are this day" (Acts 22:3). Gamaliel, a grandson of the famous Pharisee Hillel, was a liberal social legislator who, among other achievements, drafted regulations aimed at the improvement of the lot of women. Until his time (according to Meg. 21a) it was customary for both master and disciple to study the Torah standing (cf. Sanh. 17a). Gamaliel enters English literature as an archetype of the teacher, and "to sit at the feet" of someone means to be a devoted student or disciple.

In Trollope's *Barchester Towers* the newly-minted Rev. Mr. Slope stirs up controversy in the community to such a degree that parties form, with the "polite" ladies on his side and the men opposed: "No man — that is, no gentleman — could possibly be attracted to Mr. Slope, or consent to sit at the feet of so abhorrent a Gamaliel" (chap. 7). Emerson, in "The American Scholar," inverts the association further, saying, "I ask not for the great, the remote, the romantic. . . . I embrace the common, I explore and sit at the feet of the familar, the low."

GARDEN   *See* EDEN; *HORTUS CONCLUSUS*.

GATE OF HEAVEN   *See* BABEL; JACOB'S LADDER.

GATES OF HELL   In his naming Simon Barjona, Jesus said to him, "Thou art Peter, and upon this rock will I build my church; and the gates of hell shall not prevail against it" (Matt. 16:18). The "gates of hell" are recollected in connection with the harrowing of hell, especially in medieval hymns, poems, and plays upon the subject, in which the crucified Christ descends into hell, breaks down its gates, and delivers its imprisoned OT faithful to the covenant, so "leading captivity captive."

See also HARROWING OF HELL.

GATH   *See* ARK OF THE COVENANT; GOLIATH.

GAZA   A strategic town on the vital highway connect-

ing Egypt with Syria and Mesopotamia, Gaza was the southernmost limit of the land of Canaan (Gen. 10:19) and northernmost limit of the Negeb desert. In the division of the land among Israel's twelve tribes (Josh. 15:47), Gaza is mentioned: according to the MT it is assigned to Judah, though the LXX for a variety of textual reasons translates Judg. 1:18 to say that "Judah did *not* take Gaza with its territory" (cf. Josh. 13:2ff.; Judg. 3:3). Associated in biblical times with the Philistines, this is the city of Samson. After one of his amorous trysts the residents of Gaza tried to surprise and capture Samson, but he wrenched off the gates of the city, put them on his back, and "carried them up to the top of an hill that is before Hebron" (Judg. 16:1-3). When he was finally captured by his Philistine enemies, Samson was blinded and taken to Gaza, where he was forced to grind at the prison mill; here he pulled down the temple of Dagon by dislodging its pillars (16:23-31), killing himself along with the Philistines inside.

The incident of the wrested gates is important in early medieval typology, which sometimes sees it as prefiguring the rolling away of the stone at the Resurrection of Jesus (e.g., *Biblia Pauperum*). In Chaucer's *Monk's Tale* it is simply cited as one of the wondrous incidents in a great but tragic life (*Canterbury Tales*, 7.2047-54). Milton's *Samson Agonistes* has the hero memorably soliloquize in his final imprisonment:

> O glorious strength
> Put to the labor of a Beast, debas't
> Lower than bondslave! Promise was that I
> Should *Israel* from *Philistian* yoke deliver;
> Ask for this great Deliverer now, and find him
> Eyeless in *Gaza* at the Mill with slaves,
> Himself in bonds under Philistian yoke.

In the first chapter of *Desperate Remedies* Hardy says of Aneas Manston that "after passing through three weeks of sweet experience, he had arrived at the last stage — a kind of moral Gaza before plunging into an emotional desert." Aldous Huxley's *Eyeless in Gaza* (1936), a semi-autobiographical novel, charts the dyspeptic career of Anthony Beavis.

See also DAGON; SAMSON.

GEHAZI   Gehazi was the confidential servant of Elisha (2 Kings 4:8-37; 5:25; 8:16). He intercedes on behalf of the Shunammite woman for the raising of her son, is confounded when Elisha refuses the gifts of wealthy Naaman, and his deceptions incur for him the punishment of leprosy. The former story attracted attention particularly in the 19th cent., an example of which is John Keble's "Gehazi Reproved" (*On the Christian Year* [1827], 165-67).

See also ELISHA; NAAMAN.

GEHENNA *See* HELL; LAKE OF FIRE AND BRIMSTONE; TOPHET; WORM THAT DIETH NOT.

GEMATRIA Gematria, the substitution of numbers for letters to discover hidden meaning in words through numerological analogies, is primarily associated with cabalistic scriptural exegesis in Jewish mysticism dating from 12th-cent. Languedoc and flourishing throughout Europe into the 17th cent. Although *gematria,* along with its related cabalistic arts of *notaricon* (acrostics) and *temura* (substitution of letters according to code), is an occult method of explication, it had, as did other principles of scriptural exegesis, some bearing on literary arts apart from Scripture. In the 15th cent., the Italian humanist Pico della Mirandola made extensive use of Cabala in his *Apologia* and *Heptaplus.* His interest was shared by subsequent Christian commentators, including such distinguished humanists and occultists as Anton Reuchlin (1494), Paul Ricci (1510), John Colet (1517), Jean Thenaud (1519), John Fisher (1521), Francesco Giorgio (1525), Henry Cornelius Agrippa (1532), Peter Bongo (1585), Giordino Bruno (1590), Robert Fludd (1629), Francis Bacon (1631), Thomas Vaughan (1650), John Dee (1659), Henry Moore (1662), and Bishop Burnet (1692). To some extent study of Cabala was looked on as a means of resurrecting Pythagorean study, because of its emphasis on number lore in general. Peter Bongo's *Mysticae Numerorum Significationis* (1585) placed a wealth of numerology at the disposal of Renaissance authors.

But *gematria* is much more ancient than Cabala. The name is first recorded ca. A.D. 200; its beginnings may be traced several hundred years earlier, however, to Pythagorean as well as midrashic practices, where letters in Greek as well as Hebrew alphabets were used for numbers (*alpha* = 1; *beth, beta* = 2; *gimel, gamma* = 3, and so on, 1-9, 10-90, 100-900, with diacritical marks to indicate multiples of thousands). The influence of *gematria* as an exegetical tool is well established by NT times and appears in John 2:17-22, where Jesus says that he will raise in three days the Temple, which was forty-six years in building; the temple of which he speaks is to be understood as his body. St. Augustine explains the riddle, noting that forty-six is a gematric sign for ADAM (1 + 4 + 1 + 40 = 46), from whom Jesus takes his body, which will be resurrected on the third day (*In Joan. Ev.* 10.12). It also appears in Rev. 13:18, where the number of the beast is said to represent a man's name with numerical value of 666. A further example may be seen in scriptural glosses on Gideon's 300 fighting men, represented by T *(tau),* which gematrists in the *Glossa Ordinaria* explain as a symbol anticipating the cross. In the hands of Christian cabalists in the Renaissance, *gematria* reveals such mysteries as the analogy between Gen. 49:10, "Shiloh shall come" (YBA ShILH = 358), where the number prefigures "Messiah" (MShYCh = 358) and also the ser-

pent *Nachash* (NChSh = 358) which Moses lifted in the desert (Num. 21.9) and which Jesus mentions as a prefiguration of his own Crucifixion in John 3:14. That the name of Jesus, which in its Greek spelling equals 888, should be congruent in its iteration of eights with other scriptural eights associated with Jesus in addition to the 358 — circumcision, baptism, and Resurrection — confirmed the mysteries of *gematria* with mystery upon mystery.

Fourteenth-century curricula at Oxford devoted several hours a week to the study of *gematria.* Evidences of its influence on vernacular literature may be seen in riddles such as

> In 8 is alle my loue
> & 9 be y-sette byfore
> So 8 be y-closyd aboue
> Thane 3 is good therefore,

which works out in the English alphabet to the anagram for Jesus Christ: IHC. Some of the complex dating of the old judge's life in the ME poem *St. Erkenwald* may entail gematric cruxes. Medieval authors sometimes built their names into their "anonymous" works by means of *notaricon* (cf. Thomas Usk's signature THSKNVI="Thin Usk" in *Testament of Love* [1385] and Ethel Seaton's claims of acrostics in 15th-cent. poetry in her study of *Sir Richard Ros*). In the Renaissance one encounters number riddles like John Skelton's "17.4.7.2.17.5.18/18.19.17.1.19.8.5.12" in *The Garland of Laurel,* which, through his special variant on *gematria,* spells the name Rogerus Stratham. Sometimes the riddles are based on syllable count. But *gematria* and cabalistic arts are so obscure that it is difficult to detect their presence, let alone explicate the riddles. Nonetheless, in view of the love of enigma in the coterie poetry of medieval and Renaissance secular and religious courts, there are probably more of such clever obscurities than modern readers suspect or would care to investigate.

See also CABALA; MARK OF THE BEAST; *TAU.*

Bibliography. Blau, J. L. *The Christian Interpretation of the Cabala in the Renaissance* (1944); Hopper, V. *Medieval Number Symbolism* (1937), 62-68; Karpinski, C. C. "Greek Arithmetic Notation." In *Introduction to Arithmetic by Nicomachus of Gerasa.* Trans. D'Ooge (1926), 66-70; Peck, R. A. "Number Structure in *St. Erkenwald.*" AnM 14 (1973), 9-21; "Number as Cosmic Language." In *Essays in the Numerical Analysis of Medieval Literature.* Ed. C. D. Eckhardt (1979); Scholem, G. *On the Kabbalah and Its Symbolism.* Trans. R. Manheim (1965); Westcott, W. W. *Numbers: Their Occult Power and Mystic Virtue* (1890); Yates, F. A. *Giordanō Bruno and the Hermetic Tradition* (1964).

RUSSELL A. PECK

GENERATION OF VIPERS The phrase *gennēmata echidnōn* (lit., "offspring of vipers," the archaic meaning of "generation," explains the KJV) appears in Matt. 3:7

and Luke 3:7, on the lips of John the Baptist, and in Matt. 12:34 and 23:33, spoken by Jesus. Although Luke 3:7 has John addressing the crowds this way, in all the Matthean references the Pharisees (with the Sadducees in 3:7) are in view. The phrase seems to refer to the venomous hostility of those addressed. In the apocryphal 3 Corinthians (3:38), the term describes those who turn from the teaching of the gospel. The term's imagery may derive from such passages as Pss. 58:4; 140:3; Deut. 32:33, where the wicked are likened to poisonous serpents (cf. Rom. 3:13). All this suggests strongly that the image is one of cruelty, and danger, especially for the innocent and righteous.

The *Glossa Ordinaria* relates the image in these contexts to the "vipers that had slain their fathers," i.e., the plague of serpents visited upon the children of Israel in the wilderness (Num. 21), and allegorizes the phrase in Matt. 12:34 as "the fruit of the tree of evil, issuing forth in blasphemy" (PL 114.80, 127). The phrase "generation of vipers" is used widely in polemical contexts, as, e.g., in Wycliffite pamphlets attacking clerical abuse, and in religious controversy generally through to the 19th cent. wherever a charge of "Pharisaism" could be leveled.

Shakespeare is concerned with a different kind of Pharisaism in *Troilus and Cressida*, where he has Paris jibe at Pandaras for his preoccupation in wartime with "doves" and the "hot deeds" of sexual encounter. Pandaras, the go-between, replies, "Is this the generation of love — hot blood, hot thoughts and hot deeds? Why they are vipers. Is love a generation of vipers?" (3.1.139-47). In Trollope's *Barchester Towers* "this generation of unregenerated vipers . . . still perverse, stiffnecked, and hardened in their iniquity" is the judgment, ironically, of a woman who is herself a *pharisienne* (chap. 43). François Mauriac's novel *Le noeud de viperes* (1933) deals similarly with a "pharisaical" judgmentalism more damnable than the hypocrisy it believes it sees in the next generation, although in this case the story ends in regeneration for the old "Pharisee." Somerset Maugham uses the phrase against self-appointed guardians of religion who arrest a girl they take to be a witch in *Catalina* (chap. 19). It may be Aldous Huxley, however, who most succinctly grasps the force of the criticism of both Jesus and John the Baptist when he writes: "Who are the Scribes and Pharisees? Simply the best citizens; the pillars of society; all right-thinking men. In spite of which, or rather because of which, Jesus calls them a generation of vipers" (*After Many a Summer*, 2.7).

See also PHARISEE.

Bibliography. Hill, D. *The Gospel of Matthew* (1972); Schweizer, E. *The Good News According to Matthew* (1975).
LARRY W. HURTADO

GENTILES Heb. *goy,* plural *goyim* ("heathen," or, in the plural, "the nations"; cf. Gk. *ethnos;* Lat. *gentiles*): in the Bible the term generally refers to non-Jews (though not always; see, e.g., Gen. 12:2; Deut. 32:28; Josh. 3:17; Isa. 1:4; Zeph. 2:9).

GENTLENESS In Scripture several allied concepts are referred to by the word *gentleness*. First, there is the idea of being moderate, good, or kind, as a ruler who does not exercise strict justice but shows leniency toward enemies (2 Cor. 10:1, 6; Phil. 4:5; Tit. 3:2; James 3:17). This concept expands to include God's own graciousness and love, which Christians pass on because of his Spirit in them (Gal. 5:22; 2 Cor. 6:6; Col. 3:12; Rom. 2:4). The term may also include the idea of kindness, such as that of a parent toward a child, which Christians are expected to demonstrate in leadership (1 Thess. 2:7; 2 Tim. 2:24).

The English word *gentle* (IE *gnasci,* "nature"), like *kind* (ME *kynde,* "nature") is associated both with character and behavior. Because the word, by derivation from Lat. *gens,* "genteel" ("noble"), became associated with the class or status of persons of privilege, rank, or birth, explictly Christian usage is often at pains to distinguish between gentleness of character and "gentility" of title. Chaucer's poem "Gentilesse" draws on St. Paul as well as Boethius (*De Consolatione Philosophiae,* 3, pr. 4) to reflect the view, shared by his contemporary Wyclif (*De Domino Civilo; Sermones,* 4.317), that only the ruler who imitates the gentleness of Christ is entitled to be called "gentle" in the sense of noble. "For unto vertu longeth dignitee, / And noght the reverse, saufly there I deme, / Al were he mytre, croune, or diademe" ("Gentilesse"). This argument is expanded upon to telling effect by the loathly lady in *The Wife of Bath's Tale* (3.1109-76) in response to the ill-mannered Knight's attempt to evade his promise of marriage because she is "comen of so lough a kynde" (3.1101).
PETER H. DAVIDS

GERSHOM Firstborn son of Moses and Zipporah (Exod. 2:22), his name derives from *gur,* "be a sojourner." A second Gershom was a son of Levi (1 Chron. 6:1); a third was descended from Phinehas, and a companion of Ezra in his journey from Babylon to Jerusalem during the reign of Artaxerxes (Ezra 8:2; 1 Esdr. 8:29).

GET THEE BEHIND ME When the devil tempted Jesus in the wilderness (Matt. 4:10; Luke 4:1-8), the condition of his promise of wealth and power was that Jesus should worship him. But "Jesus answered and said unto him, Get thee behind me, Satan: for it is written, Thou shalt worship the Lord thy God, and him only shalt thou serve." The same expression was used by Jesus in rebuking Peter when he resisted Jesus' resignation to his own imminent suffering, death, and resurrection: "Get thee behind me, Satan . . . for thou savorest not the things that be of God, but those that be of men" (Matt. 16:21-23; cf. Mark 8:31-33).

The second instance, coming as it does immediately after the apostolic commission, "Thou art Peter, and upon this rock I will build my church; and the gates of hell shall not prevail against it" (Matt. 16:18), is arresting, and has attracted considerable commentary. St. Augustine takes the matter up directly:

> The very same Peter a little while before blessed, afterwards Satan, in a moment, within a few words! You may wonder at the discrepancy in these names; consider the divergent reasons for them. . . . Mark the reason why he is blessed: "Because flesh and blood hath not revealed it unto thee, but my Father which is in heaven"; therefore blessed. . . . For if flesh and blood revealed this to you, it be your own insight. . . . Now you have heard why he is "blessed." . . . But why was he also the very thing we shudder to think of, or even to repeat — why else but because [his protest] was self-generated: "For thou savorest not the things which be of God, but those that be of men." (*Sermo,* 76.3)

Augustine goes on to apply the lesson of Peter to members of the Church, urging self-examination to "distinguish what is of God and what of ourselves." How much, he asks, is Peter like the whole Church, composed of both strength and terrible weakness: "Yet see this Peter, who was then our figure; now he trusts, and now he totters; now he confesses the Undying, and now he fears lest he should die." In another application to the life of the Church Augustine connects this passage to Matt. 18:8-9, making the case that if loved ones or friends entice us to evil, however precious, the Christian must cut them off or "put them behind" in order that, as in the case of Bunyan's Christian in *Pilgrim's Progress,* those following Christ will not be impeded (*Sermo,* 81.4).

Calvin sees Peter's outburst as "thoughtless enthusiasm," and the passage as teaching "how much what are thought to be good intentions avail before God." Accordingly, "in the person of one man [Jesus] wanted everyone to restrain themselves and not give way to their enthusiasm" (*Comm.* sup. Matt. 16:20-28). Theodore Beza says the intensity of Jesus' rebuke is attributable to the fact that Peter's sin is really the archetypal pride of Satan, a desire to have God do things his way, which makes Peter for the moment nothing less than the threat of Antichrist (*Comm. on the New Testament,* 58).

The temptation incident is repeated in Milton's *Paradise Regained* and is recollected by Carlyle in *Sartor Resartus:* "Was 'that high moment in the *Rue de l'Enfer'*, then, properly the turning-point of the battle; when the Fiend said, Worship me, or be torn in shreds, and was answered valiantly with an *Apage Satana?*" (2.9; cf. Vg Matt. 4:9-10). In Sir Walter Scott's *Ivanhoe* Garth urges Wamba to restraint of passion, saying, "It may all be as thou doest guess; but were the horned devil to rise and proffer me his assistance to set at liberty Cedric and the Lady Rowena, I fear I should hardly have religion enough to refuse the foul fiend's offer, and bid him get behind me" (chap. 20). In Thackeray's *The Newcomes* the temptation to sell tableware to pay debts is called "the suggestion of *Satanas;* but I say to him *Vade retro*" (chap.

28; cf. Vg Matt. 16:23). One of Joyce's characters in *Dubliners,* recalling also the baptismal liturgy, says, " 'We'll all renounce the devil . . . together, not forgetting his works and pomps.' 'Get behind me, Satan!', said Mr. Fogarty, laughing" ("Grace"). G. B. Shaw, in his preface to *Back to Methuselah,* opines that "A body of schoolmasters inciting their pupils to infinitesimal peccadilloes with the object of provoking them to exclaim, 'Get thee behind me, Satan,' or telling them white lies about history . . . would certainly do less harm than our present educational allopaths do."

See also TEMPTATION OF CHRIST.

GETHSEMANE After the Last Supper, Jesus retired with his disciples to a quiet place "called Gethsemane" (Matt. 26:36; Mark 14:32; in John 18:1 Gethsemane is identified as "a garden") on the Mount of Olives to pray and prepare himself for the suffering and death he knew to be imminent. Here he instructed his disciples to "pray that ye enter not into temptation" while he went apart to agonize in prayer himself over the "cup" of sufferings he was to be presented: "Father, if thou be willing, remove this cup from me: nevertheless not my will, but thine, be done" (Luke 22:42; cf. Matt. 26:39, 42, 44; Mark 14:35-36, 39). The intensity of his prayer was such that "his sweat was as it were great drops of blood," and an angel came to strengthen him. The disciples, enjoined repeatedly to "watch and pray," were nevertheless overcome with exhaustion and despondency, and slept until Judas arrived with a "multitude with swords and staves" to arrest Jesus.

This episode, often known as the Agony of Christ, is typically set within the context of the whole passion narrative in both exegetical and literary recollection. The early Fathers, often in contention with heretics, wrestled with the nature and meaning of Jesus' agony, seeing it as a clear demonstration of the Incarnation — that Jesus, though divine, faced and endured his sufferings utterly as a man. "Though he were a Son, yet learned he obedience by the things which he suffered" (Heb. 5:7-8), becoming thus the perfect priestly mediator. St. John Chrysostom asserts that by saying "If it be possible . . ." Jesus "showed us his humanity"; in the second part of the prayer, "Nevertheless not as I will, but as thou wilt," he demonstrates his "virtue and self-command, teaching us even when nature pulls us back, to follow God" (*Hom. on Matthew,* 83). St. Athanasius, in his *Four Discourses against the Arians,* 3.29, emphasizes Jesus' willing submission: "He let his own body suffer, for therefore did He come . . . that in the flesh He might suffer, and thenceforth the flesh might be made impassible and immortal" (Discourse 3). St. Augustine, likewise, asserts Christ's voluntary laying down of his life, his acquiescence to the fear and suffering which he could, by a word, have dismissed. The Fathers argue that it was not death or physical pain which Jesus feared but the awesome mystery of judgment and redemption inherent in the Cross, the cataclysmic collision of human sin with divine wrath which he was to experience as an act of loving obedience. The language of Jesus' warning to his disciples, as well as the formulation of his own prayer, suggests that he regarded the event as a temptation to evade the very meaning of his coming; early commentators often saw in his garden temptation the "remedy" for that which occurred in Eden — willing submission providing the counter to willful rebellion.

The temptation motif underlies the discussion of the Agony in the medieval *Meditationes Vitae Christi*, where the episode receives dramatic embellishment for didactic ends. The angel, identified as Michael, converses with Jesus — not only comforting him but offering him options:

> I have taken your prayer and sweat of blood to your Father before the whole supernal court, and, all kneeling, we have prayed humbly that this chalice be lifted from you. The Father replied, "My most beloved Son knows that the redemption of mankind . . . cannot be accomplished properly without the shedding of His blood; consequently, if He wishes the salvation of souls, He must die for them." Therefore I would know what you have decided to do. Then the Lord Jesus replied to the angel, "I wish above all and finally the salvation of souls; and therefore I choose rather to die, that the souls of those whom my Father created in his image may be saved, than that I do not die and the souls not be redeemed. Therefore let the will of my Father be done." ("Meditation on the Passion of Christ before the Morning," trans. Isa Ragusa [1961], 323)

Richard Rolle's consideration of Gethsemane, part of his prayerful "Meditation on the Passion of Christ," asks that God will likewise sustain him: "be my help through my own anguish and temptation, and send me, Lord, your angel of counsel and comfort in all my needs. . . ." Both the York and Coventry mystery cycles provide dramatic re-enactments of Jesus' sojourn in Gethsemane (York no. 28, "The Agony and the Betrayal"; Coventry no. 28, "The Betrayal of Christ").

George Herbert, in "The Sacrifice," recalls the failure of Jesus' disciples to sustain him in his darkest hours: "Yet my Disciples sleep: I cannot gain / One houre of watching; but their drowsie brain / Comforts not me, and doth my doctrine stain: Was ever grief like mine?" Notable poetic reflections on the agony of Jesus include those of Giles Fletcher ("In Gethsemane") and German poet Annette von Drost-Hulshoff ("Gethsemane"), each of which emphasizes the incomprehensible depth of Jesus' suffering. Emily Dickinson, less plausibly, sees a Gethsemane-like "transporting anguish" in Charlotte Brontë's return to Haworth from her travels abroad ("All Overgrown by Cunning Moss").

Allusions to Gethsemane occur in a wide range of English novels. An apparent extended analogue underlies chap. 48 of Dickens's *Bleak House,* which climaxes in the mysterious murder of Lady Dedlock's enemy Tulkinghorn (see J. Larson, *Dickens and the Broken Scripture* [1985], 22-23). In Hardy's *Jude the Obscure* Phillotson, hearing of the death of the children of Jude and Sue, muses in the manner of Christ in the garden: "Their cup of sorrow is now full." In Conrad's *The Secret Agent* Jones refers jestingly to Jesus' rebuke of the sleeping disciples when addressing Ricardo, " 'Watch, eh? Why not pray a little, too?' " But as Dwight Purdy observes, "The joke is on Jones, for Ricardo has already entered into temptation" (*Joseph Conrad's Bible* [1984], 101). In Graham Greene's *The Power and the Glory* the disciple-less whiskey priest re-enacts the agonies of Gethsemane, as does the corporal in Faulkner's *A Fable* when, in "a Gethsemane-like scene above the city . . . [he] is momentarily tempted to let the cup pass from him" (T. Ziolkowski, *Fictional Transfigurations of Jesus* [1972], 289). D. H. Lawrence, speaking of the weariness of Melville's Ahab before his last confrontation with Moby-Dick, sees it as "the Gethsemane of Ahab, before the last fight: the Gethsemane of the human soul seeking the last self-conquest, the last attachment of extended consciousness" (*Studies in Classic American Literature*) — thereby expressing a view of the garden agony in which it is merely a concomitant of obsessive and self-destructive passion.

See also JESUS CHRIST; JUDAS ISCARIOT; PASSION, CROSS.

Bibliography. Miller, C. H. "The Heart of the Final Struggle: More's Commentary on the Agony in the Garden." In *Quincentennial Essays on St. Thomas More.* Ed. M. J. Moore (1978), 108-23; Stanley, D. M. *Jesus in Gethesemane* (1980).   KATHERINE B. JEFFREY

GIANTS IN THE EARTH   Gen. 6:1-4 speaks of the era before the Flood, noting that "there were giants in the earth in those days." The word here (as in Num. 13:33) is Heb. *nepilim,* the etymology of which has been the subject of extensive and inconclusive scholarly debate. Some assume that the word derives from *napal,* "fall," in the sense of morally fallen humans or "fallen ones" ejected from heaven with Satan. The suggestion in Num. 13:33 (the report of the fearful spies sent by Moses to reconnoiter the Promised Land) is that the offspring of Anak in Canaan were descended from the notorious Nephilim of Gen. 6:4, evidently having somehow escaped or survived the Flood. Hellenistic Jewish commentary connects Nimrod with this race (e.g., Philo, *De confusione linguarum*); St. Clement's *Homilies* (9.4-6) continue this tradition, but identify the gigantic tower builder also with Zoroaster. Both Josephus (*Ant.* 5.23) and R. Johanan ben Zakkai (Tan. Ber. 5.6) attempt to prove on the basis of uncovered Palestinian skeletal remains the extraordinary size of the giants. According to other sources they are to be regarded ultimately as descendants of Cain ('Ag. Ber. 38-39; Zohar 1.37; cf. Ḥasidim 455).

St. Augustine's famous discussion of the Genesis passage in *De civitate Dei* (15.23; cf. 16.8) helped channel some of these ideas into medieval Christian commentary and legendary speculation. Augustine allows that the existence of the giants affords moral instruction:

> And it pleased the Creator to produce them, that it might thus be demonstrated that neither beauty, nor yet size and strength, are of much moment to the wise man, whose blessedness lies in spiritual and immortal blessings, in far better and more enduring gifts, in the good things that are the peculiar property of the good, and are not shared by good and bad alike. It is this that another prophet confirms when he says, "These were the giants, famous from the beginning, that were of so great stature, and so expert in war. Those did not the Lord choose, neither gave he the way of knowledge unto them; but they were destroyed because they had no wisdom, and perished through their own foolishness."

Augustine's "prophet" here is Baruch; medieval exegesis of the relevant passage (3:26-28) typically follows Augustine's tropological reading (cf. St. Jerome, *Ep.* 10.1). Orosius's history, translated into OE by Alfred the Great in the 9th cent., takes considerable interest in giants and monsters as "lessons" of the past. In the 10th and 11th cents. a book called by its modern editor *Marvels of the East* appeared, copiously illustrated and depicting gigantic man-eating *þyrs* and *eoten,* rough, hairy, and gorilla-like giants. The same sort of creature emerges in the OE heroic poem *Beowulf*—the monster Grendel and his dam, cannibalistic giants who stalk the hall of Hrothgar to devour his people. They are called by the poem *Caines cynne,* descendants of the first murderer, from whom, it is said, "all evil broods were born, ogres and elves and evil spirits — the giants also, who for a long time fought with God" (107, 111-14). The sword Hrunting, with which Beowulf goes to battle against these monsters, has on its hilt an account of a battle "long ago, when a flood, a rushing sea, slew the race of giants . . . [which] was estranged from the eternal Lord."

The Middle High German *Genesis* (12th cent.) fuses Germanic traditions of outcast and malevolent monsters with the talmudic and patristic tradition; in fact, the Cain connection, not found in the scriptural passages or Augustine, must be imagined either to have arisen independently in the recently Christianized Germanic context or to owe, perhaps, to some transmission of views represented in medieval haggadic commentary. The 14th-cent. pseudo-geographer Mandeville asks how Cain's race could have survived the Flood and answers that the "Cam" involved is, in effect, "Cham," the errant son of Noah, one of whose offspring was "Membroth [i.e., Nimrod], the geaunt þat was the firste kyng þat euer was in the world & he began the fundacioun of the tour of Babylone." This confusion and conflation of Cain and Ham (*Travels,* chap. 25) persists in much popular medieval literature.

It is typical of late medieval moral iconography that significant figures have both good and bad manifestations. Thus, set off against malevolent giants such as those of Gen. 6:4 and the Philistine Goliath, one finds the legendary St. Christopher, the benevolent giant who is said to have carried the Christ Child across a swift-flowing river. In the legend he announces himself as a converted Canaanite. Puns on this name *(canancus/canineus)* undoubtedly lie behind occasional representations of him as one of the *cynocoephali* (cf. Augustine, *De civ. Dei* 16.8), a dog-headed giant. One of the fourteen "auxiliary saints," Christopher is traditionally said to have suffered martyrdom in Asia Minor early in the 3rd cent. (*Analecta Bollandiana,* 1 [1882], 122-48; 10 [1891], 393-405).

The original giants in the earth, however, with specifically negative associations, continued to have a role in Renaissance and post-Reformation literature. Milton's Satan, floating on his back in the Lake of Fire, is "as huge / As whom the Fables name of monstrous size, / *Titanian,* or *Earth-born,* that warr'd on Jove" (*PL* 1.196-98). In bk. 11 of *Paradise Lost* (683-99) Michael draws a contrast between saintly Enoch and the prediluvian "Giants, men of high renown," whose sole fame rests in brutal acts of oppression. And in *Samson Agonistes* Milton makes Samson's Canaanite tormentors the sons of Gath, principally Harapha (cf. Heb. *rapa',* "giant"), whose five sons include Goliath (cf. 2 Sam. 21). Samson is unperturbed: "I dread him not, nor all his Giant-brood, / Though Fame divulge him Father of five Sons / All of Gigantic size, Goliath chief" (1247-49).

A generation later Dryden could write out of precisely the reverse understanding when comparing the Elizabethan poets — "Conqu'ring with force of arms, and dint of wit" — to "the giant race, before the flood" ("To My Dear Friend Mr. Congreve"). This is perhaps an ironic recollection, but it soon becomes proverbial praise for heroes of a bygone era, as in the humor of Mark Twain: "There were nabobs in those days — in the 'flesh times' I mean. Every rich strike in the mines created one or two" (*Innocents at Home,* chap. 1). O. E. Rölvaag's epic novel about Scandinavian pioneer life in the American Midwest, *Giants in the Earth* (1927), characterizes Beret, the beautiful and pious yet superstitious wife of the protagonist, Peder Holm, as one whose struggle with the untamed frontier is akin to holding off the trolls and giants of a dark wild, a contest expressed in language evocative of early Norse and Germanic conflations of Gen. 6:4 with Nordic *skogs-ra, þyrs,* and *eoten.*

See also BABEL; GOLIATH; SONS OF GOD.

Bibliography. Friedman, J. B. *The Monstrous Races in Medieval Art and Thought* (1981); James, M. R. *Marvels of the East* (1929); Jeffrey, D. L. "Medieval Monsters." In *Manlike Monsters.* Ed. M. Halpin and M. Ames (1980), 47-64; Steadman, J. M. " 'Men of Renown': Heroic Virtue and the Giants of Gen. 6:4 (*PL* xi, 638-99)." *PQ* 40 (1960), 580-86; Williams, D. *Cain and Beowulf: A Study in Secular Allegory* (1982); Wittkower, R. "Marvels of the East: A Study in the History of Monsters." *JWCI* 5 (1942), 159-97.

GIBEON   *See* ABNER; AJALON, VALE OF; SOLOMON.

GIBEONITES   *See* HEWERS OF WOOD.

GIDEON   Gideon, son of Joash, described himself as a lesser scion of an obscure family: "poor in Manasseh and . . . least in [his] father's house" (Judg. 6:15). His name means "wood-cutter" or "feller of trees" (Heb. *gid'on*). Nevertheless, he became one of the great heroes of Israel and its fifth judge.

While Gideon was secretly threshing grain for his family to save it from the rapacious Midianites, a celestial visitor appeared to him and enjoined him to take up arms on behalf of his people: "Go in this thy might and thou shalt save Israel. . . . have I not sent thee?" (Judg. 6:14). Gideon, wanting assurance that the origin of the call was divine, asked for a sign and was answered when the food he offered to the angel was consumed by fire at the touch of his staff (6:17-22). Gideon's mission was inaugurated later that night when the Lord commanded him to cut down the grove dedicated to the pagan deity Baal on his father's land and burn the wood on the altar. When the people discovered what Gideon had done, they demanded his death. His father, however, defended him, saying, "If [Baal] be a god, let him plead for himself" (6:31). This incident earned Gideon the nickname "Jerub-baal," indicating that he was a fighter against the pagan god.

Seeking further confirmation of his divine office, Gideon asked yet another sign —that God should cause the evening dew to fall upon a lamb's fleece while all the ground around it should remain dry. The next morning, discovering that this had indeed happened, he dared to ask for an alternate version of the miracle; the following morning the fleece was dry while all around the earth was soaked (Judg. 6:36-40). Finally confident both of the origin and nature of his calling, he assembled his forces for battle. The Lord asked him to reduce his army by offering release from duty to any who were fearful. Twenty-two thousand gladly went home, leaving only ten thousand. The Lord then commanded that all the would-be soldiers be sent by Gideon to the spring at Harod. Those who scooped up water to drink with one hand, still alert and able to hold their spears, were separated from those who knelt down on hands and knees to drink. A drastically reduced army of 300 men remained (7:1-9). Dividing his forces into three groups of 100 each, Gideon gave every soldier a trumpet and a pitcher to hold over a lamp. They surrounded the enemy and simultaneously blew their trumpets, shattered their pitchers, revealed the lamps, and cried, "The sword of the LORD, and of Gideon." At this the startled enemy forces were put to rout. The princes of Succoth and Penuel, both of whom had refused assistance to Gideon's men (8:5-17), were punished by Gideon; the first was beaten with thorns, and the second had his military tower destroyed.

When the delivered people wished to make him king

(Judg. 8:22-23), Gideon refused. He did, however, take the gold earrings captured from slain enemies and make an ephod — probably a surrogate for an "ark" or sacral box — which he then placed in the house of the Lord at Ophrah. This became an object of idolatry and "a snare unto Gideon and his house" (8:27).

Haggadic sources are restrained in their praise of Gideon, saying that in making use of an altar dedicated to an idol and of sacrifices which would have been intended for idolatrous purposes, he transgressed the law — even though he was obeying a special command from God (Meg. 1.72c; Shemuel 13.83). The Haggadah offers a novel reading of the water test (Judg. 7:5), suggesting that a prevailing sin of this generation of Jews was self-worship, practiced by Narcissus-like admiration of their reflection in the water. Those who bent down to the water thus betrayed themselves as idolaters (Yalqut 2.62; Ps.-Philo 38; 36.1-2; cf. Josephus, *Ant.* 5.6.3, which takes a more deprecatory view of the 300).

The emblem of Manasseh, symbolizing the achievement of Gideon, is said in some Jewish sources to be a unicorn on a black flag (Num. Rab. 2.7; Midr. 'Ag. Num. 2.2). Christian additions to the iconography of Gideon derive from a generally much higher valuation and include his depiction in armor as an antetype of Christ (*Glossa Ordinaria* [PL 113.526]) and as an example of the *miles Christi*. A broken pitcher typically recalls the successful battle strategy, a fleece the confirmation of his divine appointment; a tau cross (the Greek numerical sign for 300 is T) proleptically signifies the victory of the cross over paganism (cf. St. Augustine, *Enarr. in Ps.* 68.29). Among the incidents most frequently depicted in art is the punishment by beating with thorns inflicted on the seventy-seven elders of Succoth, sometimes treated as an antetype for torments of the damned in hell.

In the NT Gideon appears in Heb. 11, where, in recounting the exemplary OT heroes of faith, the writer includes him with David, Samuel, and others among those "who through faith subdued kingdoms, wrought righteousness, obtained promises . . . [and] out of weakness were made strong" (vv. 32-34).

Patristic commentary focuses both on the tests of Gideon and on the parallel test of the would-be warriors. Gideon's caution in dealing with the angel is regarded as an evidence of spiritual discernment; the *Glossa Ordinaria* observes that he wanted to be sure that it was an angel of light and not a posturing angel of darkness he was speaking to, adding, "He examined the spirit, to see whether it was of God —as indeed the spiritual person ought always so to do" (PL 113.526). The meal he prepared for the angel, sacrificing a kid, is proleptic of the sacrament of the Eucharist, according to St. Ambrose; the rock on which the meal is laid to be consumed by fire is said also to be a figure for Christ (*De Spiritu Sancto*, 1.1.2; cf. Augustine, *De doctrina Christiana*, 4.21.46; St. Gregory the Great, *Moralia*, 1.17). Ambrose speaks of the mystery of the old history where Gideon, the warrior of the mystic conflict, receiving the pledge of future victory, recognized the spiritual sacrament in the vision of his mind, that that rain was the dew of the Divine Word, which first came down on the fleece. (*De viduis*, 3.18)

For Augustine, "the mystery of the New Testament appeared not in the nation of the Jews. What there was the fleece, is here the veil, for in the fleece was veiled the mystery" (*Enarr. in Ps.* 46.9); it was also "the grace of the sacraments, not indeed openly manifested [in the OT] but hidden . . ." (*Enarr. in Ps.* 138.7). Elsewhere the dew becomes a symbol for the Church of God permeating the world (PL 113.527) or, following from Origen (*Hom.* 8) and Augustine (*Enarr. in Ps.* 72.9), the dew is Christ himself, who comes down for the sake of the lost sheep of Israel to "a Mother" chosen by him, "by whom to receive the form of a servant"; the miracle of the fleece comes thus to be seen as a type of Mary's virginal conception (e.g., St. Anthony of Padua, *Sermo in Purificatione Sanctae Mariae*, 3.722b), a connection frequently reiterated in medieval lyric poetry. For Ephraim Syrus the waters to which Gideon sent the men to drink, thereby separating the faithful from the unfaithful, typify baptism; the lamps the 300 carried anticipate the lamps or candles of the newly baptized and symbolize the Spirit's presence (*Hymns for the Feast of the Epiphany*, 7.8-9). For Dante, the Hebrews "who at the drinking showed themselves soft" afford an exemplum of failed perseverance (*Purgatorio*, 24.124-26).

Calvin's commentary on Heb. 11, concerned to demonstrate that "in every saint there is always to be found something reprehensible," concentrates on faults in the hero. Calvin argues that Gideon was "slower than he need have been to take up arms." George Herbert, seeing that "the world grows old," looks back fondly upon the days when biblical characters could find themselves in the presence of God, times when God would directly "struggle with Jacob, sit with Gideon" ("Decay"). In Milton's *Paradise Regained* Jesus rejects Satan's offer of wealth, declaring that without "Virtue, Valor, Wisdom," they are empty: "But men endu'd with these have oft attain'd / In lowest poverty to highest deeds." Gideon is the first example Jesus gives of such a person (2.430-39). In *Samson Agonistes* the Chorus remembers "the matchless Gideon" as Israel's "great Deliverer" of his generation (277-81). In Bunyan's *Pilgrim's Progress*, when Christian reaches The House Beautiful, he is taken to the celestial Armory and shown some of the instruments by which the Lord's servants of yore "had done wonderful things. They shewed him . . . the Pitchers, Trumpets and Lamps too, with which Gideon put to flight the Armies of Midian." Cromwell in his fourth speech to Parliament (1655) bitterly denounced Anabaptists as "levelers," referring to their fate with an allusion to the fate of the Midianite confederates Zebah and Zalmunna at Gideon's hand (Judg. 8:20-22). Andrew Marvell's poem in praise of

Cromwell of a year earlier alludes to the same score-settling events, "when Gideon so did from the war retreat," but draws a further conclusion: "No king might ever such a force have done, / Yet would not he be lord, nor yet his son" —a reference to Cromwell's refusal, on biblical principles drawn in part from the book of Judges, to perpetuate the English monarchy. Abraham Cowley, apostrophizing his muse, refers to the miraculous sign of the fleece to complain that he has been neglected since the Restoration of Charles II:

> But then, alas! to thee alone,
> One of old Gideon's miracles was shown.
> For every tree and every herb around,
> With pearly dew was crowned,
> And all upon the quickened ground
> The fruitful seed of Heaven did brooding lie,
> And nothing but the Muse's fleece was dry.

Characterization of Gideon in the 18th cent. reflects the tension between Calvin's rigorous qualification of his heroism and a strong affection in Independent and Calvinist preaching for the results of that heroism. Both elements are visible in the poetry of William Cowper. In "Table Talk" he is at pains to ascribe all human achievement to the will of Providence: "So Gideon earn'd a victr'y not his own; / Subserviency his praise, and that alone" (360-61), a point he returns to in describing a postconversion letdown in "The New Convert." In *Olney Hymns* 4, "Jehovah-Nissi," he ascribes Gideon's triumph to God yet laments his own "unbelief, self will / Self-righteousness and pride" which prevent him from spiritual victory, concluding with a hopeful assertion: "Yet David's Lord, and Gideon's friend, / Will help his servant to the end." The miracle of the fleece is adduced by Cowper as comfort to "A Protestant Lady in France" (49-50), but according to the same premise, "to give the creature her Creator's due / Were sin in me, and an offense to you" (3-4).

The 19th cent. tends to plant virtue more firmly in the human and to secularize or make humor of miraculous events. In one of his essays Charles Lamb compares two teachers, the more secure of whose "thunders rolled innocuous for us; his storms came near, but never touched us; contrary to Gideon's miracle, while all around were drenched, our fleece was dry" ("Christ's Hospital Five and Thirty Years Ago"). A. H. Clough aspires "to bleed for others' wrongs / In vindication of a cause, to draw / The sword of the Lord and of Gideon —oh, that seems / The flower and top of life." Tennyson uses Gideon's chastisement of the men of Succoth as an analogue for the English victory over Napoleon at Trafalgar: "late he learned humility / Perforce, like those whom Gideon school'd with briers" ("Napolean"). Carlyle's appropriation of the narrative in *Past and Present* makes the case that if one has courage, patience, and faith, one's work will be rewarded: "Thy heart and life purpose shall be as a miraculous Gideon's fleece, spread out in silent appeal to heaven; and from the kind Immensities [will come] blessed dew-moisture." "Peace may be sought in two ways," declares Ruskin in *The Two Paths;* "One way is as Gideon sought it, when he built his altar . . . naming it, 'God send peace,' yet sought this peace that he loved, as he was ordered to seek it, and the peace was sent in God's way."

Hardy's uses of the story are, like those of Joyce, erudite but disaffirming. In *The Woodlanders* one of the characters declares that an abused tree will fall "and cleave us, like the sword of the Lord and of Gideon" (chap. 14). A less apt borrowing is his favorable comparison of Tess ("despite her not inviolate past") with her still sexually innocent peers: "Was not the gleaning of the grapes of Ephraim better than the vintage of Abi-ezer?" (*Tess of the D'Urbervilles,* chap. 49). In the "Oxen of the Sun" passage in *Ulysses,* Joyce subverts the common medieval association between Gideon's fleece and virginity, especially that of Mary, when he makes sexual double entendre of the phrase "thy fleece is drenched."

Paddy Chayefsky's Broadway play *Gideon* (1961), adapted also for television, is a humorously ironic story of man's refusal to acknowledge God even after a series of miracles. Chayefsky's modern Gideon is a comic antihero but made so out of the playwright's poignant reflection that part of what it means to be resignedly "modern" is the knowledge that heroism and faith are inextricable; when faith disappears, heroic self-transcendence disappears soon after.

GIFTS OF THE HOLY SPIRIT   Isaiah prophesied that the Spirit of God would bestow upon the coming Messiah "the spirit of wisdom and understanding, the spirit of counsel and might, the spirit of knowledge and of fear of the LORD" (Isa. 11:2); to these "six gifts," the Vg adds a seventh (i.e., piety) from the opening phrase of v. 3. These gifts, often represented in art by seven doves, lamps, or flames, are listed in medieval commentaries as *Sapientia, Intellectus, Consilium, Fortitudo, Scientia, Pietas,* and *Timor Domini.* They represent a *scala* of the good life in St. Augustine and St. Ambrose, and are attached by Augustine to two similar lists, the seven petitions of the Lord's Prayer and seven Beatitudes, a tradition amplified by later commentators, including Hugh of St. Victor and St. Bonaventure. Frère Lorens in his *Somme le roi* refers to the commonplace that the Holy Spirit "by the seven gifts," "doth away and destroieth the seven deadly sins" in individual hearts.

These gifts are supported and in some respects paralleled by the NT gifts of the Spirit, chiefly (though not exclusively) associated with 1 Cor. 12. In this passage St. Paul describes the possession of gifts in the Church as partial and corporate ("diversities of gifts but the same Spirit"): "For to one is given by the Spirit the word of wisdom; to another the word of knowledge by the same Spirit; to another faith . . . to another the gifts of healing . . . to another the working of miracles; to another prophecy; to another discerning of spirits; to another divers kinds of tongues; to another the interpretation of tongues." Paul concludes by underscoring the "organic" nature of the gifts and their function in the Church: "For as the body is one, and hath many members, and all the members of that one body, being many, are one body: so also is Christ" (vv. 4-12). (Related to these, but not precisely parallel, are the "fruits of the Spirit" spoken of in Gal. 5:22-23: "love, joy, peace, longsuffering, gentleness, goodness, faith, meekness, temperance.") The tendency toward conflation of the OT and NT lists is reflected in at least one ME carol:

> God hath yeuen, of myghtis most,
> The vii yiftis of the Hole Gost.
> Mynd, resun, vertu, and grace,
> Humelete, chast, and charete,
> These vii yiftis God yeuen has
> Be the vertu of the Hole Gost to man onle;
> Ellis were we lost. (R. Greene, *The Early English Carols,* no. 327)

Friar William Herebert's "Com, shuppere, Holy Gost" appeals to the Holy Spirit as himself the essential "ȝyft vrom god y-send, / Welle of lyf, vur, charite and gostlych oynement. / þou ȝyfst þe seueue ȝyftes, þou vinger of godes honde" (C. Brown, *Religious Lyrics of the XIVth Century,* no. 18). Both poems reflect versions of the hymns "*Veni, Sancte Spiritus*" and "*Veni, Creator Spiritus.*" The question of the nature and number of gifts was not precisely defined in Catholic tradition until the 19th cent., at which time the explanation of St. Thomas Aquinas (*Summa Theol.* 2.2.q.8) was accepted.

In Cranmer's *Homilies Appointed to Be Read in Churches* (1562) the 16th sermon, for Whitsunday, is entitled "The coming Down of the Holy Ghost, and the manifold Gifts of the same." Its concern is with the "fruit" (Gal. 5) as well as the "gifts" listed in 1 Cor. 12 as a test for the presence of the Spirit in an individual life; as is typical in Reformation commentary, the list from Isa. 11 is not mentioned. George Herbert discusses the gifts of the Spirit in a general way in *A Priest to the Temple* (chap. 2), but with reference to Rom. 12 rather than the traditionally more popular passages. Along with other favorite medieval lists and hierarchies the "seven gifts" faded from prominence in English literary texts after the Renaissance. Bunyan may intend an obverse of the Isaiah list in his retinue of dissuaders of Christian in the "Mr. Worldly Wiseman" episode of *Pilgrim's Progress:* Simple, Sloth, Presumption, Formalist, Hypocrisy, Timorous, and Mistrust.

Stephen Dedalus reflects in traditional ways on the traditional list in Joyce's *Portrait of the Artist as a Young Man* — but in such a way as to make Joyce's own skepticism apparent:

On each of the seven days of the week he prayed that one of the seven gifts of the Holy Ghost might descend upon his soul and drive out of it day by day the seven deadly sins which had defiled it in the past; and he prayed for each gift upon its appointed day, confident that it would descend upon him, though it seemed strange that wisdom and understanding and knowledge were so distinct in their nature that each should be prayed for apart from the others. (chap. 4)

See also HOLY SPIRIT; TEMPLE OF THE HOLY GHOST.

GILEAD   An area east of the Jordan River.
See also BALM OF GILEAD.

GIRD UP THY LOINS   When the Lord speaks out of the whirlwind in answer to Job's importunate questioning, he does so with a challenge, as if to a wrestling match (cf. Gen. 32): "Gird up now thy loins like a man; for I will demand of thee, and answer thou me" (Job 38:3; cf. 40:7). This is a customary metaphoric reference to the practice of wrapping up loose-fitting Near Eastern garments in order to be able to run, to do serious physical work, or, indeed, to fight (cf. Exod. 12:11, referring to the symbolic state of preparedness for flight during the Passover meal; cf. also 1 Kings 18:46; 2 Kings 4:29; 9:1). As used in the NT, the expression bears the same value metaphorically. Jesus uses it in encouraging his followers to divest themselves of worldly encumbrance so as to be ready for service: "Let your loins be girded about, and your lights burning" (Luke 12:35). St. Paul's injunction to put on "the whole armor of God" commences with the admonition to "stand therefore, having on your loins girt about with truth, and having the breastplate of righteousness" (Eph. 6:13-14). St. Peter recollects the sense of Jesus' words in Luke 12: "Wherefore gird up the loins of your mind, be sober, and hope to the end for the grace that is to be brought unto you at the revelation of Jesus Christ" (1 Pet. 1:13).

In Bunyan's *Pilgrim's Progress,* after Christian has fallen into indecisive doldrums ("musing in the midst of my dumps") at the Strait Gait, he is comforted and encouraged by Good-will: "Then *Christian* began to gird up his loins, and to address himself to his Journey." The phrase becomes a byword among 19th-cent. proponents of "muscular Christianity" in England. In Butler's *The Way of All Flesh* Mr. Hawke, an evangelical Charles Simeon-like preacher, exhorts a group of Cambridge students including Ernest Pontifex to "turn, turn, turn, now while it is called today . . . stay not even to gird up your loins; look not behind you for a second, but fly into the bosom of Christ." Thoreau offers an American formulation of the injunction in *Civil Disobedience,* suggesting that those who reverse the truth of "the Bible and the Constitution . . . where it comes into this lake or that pool [of cultural life], gird up their loins once more, and continue their pilgrimage toward its fountainhead." One of

the most memorable and informed invocations of the metaphor in a secular context is that of Walter Pater in the Preface to his *The Renaissance,* where he writes,

> The Renaissance, in truth, put forth in France an aftermath, a wonderful later growth, the products of which have to the full that subtle and delicate sweetness which belongs to a refined and comely decadence, just as its earliest phases have the freshness which belongs to all periods of growth in art, the charm of *ascesis,* of the austere and serious girding of the loins in youth.

GLASS, MIRROR   The Bible as a whole is complex in its uses of the mirror image. "Hast thou with him spread out the sky, which is . . . as a molten looking-glass?" Elihu asks Job (Job 37:18). The sage in Sirach says of a false friend, "Rub him as one polishes a brazen mirror, and you will find that there is still corrosion" (12:11). St. James likens the person who hears but does not follow God's Word to a man who looks at himself in a mirror and then leaves and forgets what kind of man he really is (1:23-25). In St. Paul's second letter to the Corinthians, those from whom the veil of darkness and unbelief has been removed are said to behold "as in a glass the glory of the Lord" and to be "changed into the same image from glory to glory" (3:18). In 1 Corinthians Paul uses the shimmering imperfections of the primitive metal mirror to express the difference between a person's indirect and therefore partial knowledge of God in the present life and the fullness of vision in the final time of eschatological revelation: "For now we see through a glass darkly; but then face to face; now I know in part; but then shall I know even as also I am known" (13:12).

The mirror figures which draw the early Church Fathers most strongly are those of the Pauline Epistles. For Origen the potential of humankind to reflect the glory of God shows a "power to be transformed from being serpents, swine, and dogs" (*Dialogue with Heraclides,* 151). St. Augustine, in *De Trinitate* (15.14), links the mirror image with the notion of the *imago Dei:* ". . . in a mirror what is seen is no more than an image. What we have tried to do is to gain through this image which is ourselves some vision, as through a mirror, of him who made us."

Elsewhere, Augustine speaks of the divine clarity with which the 1 Corinthians passage is principally concerned, noting that "By it the righteous lives in his pilgrimage here, and by it he is led on from mirror and dark saying, and all that was in part, to the region of sight, that he may know face to face, as also he has been known" (*De spiritu et littera,* sect. 49).

Later in the same work (sect. 64) 1 Cor. 13:12 is used to illustrate "the imperfection in this life of both our knowledge of God's will and of our love for him." In *The Confessiones* the movement to a deeper faith is frequently illustrated with reference to the dark glass of 1 Corinthians:

Thus, for the time being I understand that "heaven of heavens" to mean the intelligible heaven, where to understand is to know all at once —not "in part," not "darkly," not "through a glass" —but as a simultaneous whole, in full sight, "face to face." (12.13; cf. 8.1; 10.5)

Many subsequent spiritual and mystical writers in the Middle Ages take up the same theme (e.g., St. Bonaventure, *Itinerarium Mentis ad Deum*).

Erasmus, in his *Enchiridion,* uses 1 Cor. 13:12 to contrast the visible world with a higher world which is intelligible and angelic (LCC 14.335). Luther, writing to Myconius (Jan. 9, 1541), speaks of his friend's sickness unto death as in reality a sickness unto life, for "the veil and dark glass will be removed." In his *Institutes,* Calvin cites Augustine to show that the imperfection of man's love for God necessarily follows from the inadequacy of man's knowledge of him in a life where "we see in a mirror dimly." The image is ubiquitous in the *Institutes* (see 1.15.4; 3.2.20; 3.25.11; 4.8.5; 4.18.20; etc.). Zwingli's *On the Clarity and Certainty or Power of the Word of God* uses the dark glass of 1 Cor. 13:12 to argue that as

> we have never seen God as he is in himself, therefore we can never know in what respect our soul is like him in its substance and essence. For the soul does not even know itself.... And in the last analysis we can only conclude that the activities and faculties of the soul, will, intellect and memory, are merely the signs of that essential likeness which we shall never see until we see God as he is in himself, and ourselves in him.

For John Donne, the inadequacy of present knowledge underscores the need for the "true glas of [God's] word explicated in the Church" (*Sermons,* ed. Potter and Simpson, 1.3.189). Elsewhere he reiterates that if this "glass" does not allow us to see the truth fully, it nevertheless permits us to see truly:

> Our blessed Saviour thus mingles his Kingdomes ... that if we see him *In hoc speculo, in this his glasse,* in this Ordinance in his kingdome of Grace, we have already begun to see him *facie ad faciem, face to face* in his Kingdome of Glory. (4.3.73)

More than a century later, American divine Jonathan Edwards effectively reduces the distance between the two kingdoms in his sermon "A Divine and Supernatural Light" by pulling up short before the end of the Pauline text: "The Gospel is a glass, by which this light is conveyed to us.... 'now we see through a glass' " (pt. 2).

Milton alludes to 1 Cor. 13:12 in *Areopagitica* in order to argue the cause of change and reform against established secular and ecclesiastical authority (2.549) and in *An Apology against a Pamphlet* refers sarcastically to dogmatists and would-be seers as those who see through "the dim glass of ... affection" (1.909). In *Reason of Church Government,* however, Milton avers that God has made his plan for humanity plainly manifest in the gospel,

which "architecture" shall soon be realized: "we shall see with open eyes, not under a vaile" (1.758).

That the true love of Spenser's "Hymne of Love" (196) is the "mirrour of so heavenly light" depends upon an exquisitely complementary extension of 2 Cor. 3:18. The "Envoy" to Vaughan's *Silex Scintillans* sees the image transformed at the end of time into a "cloudless glass, / Transparent as the purest day." In his syncretistic "Resurrection and Immortality," intimations of the divine within the cosmos are the shadowy truths seen "darkly in a glasse" to reflect the world of "eternall light." For Traherne mirror imagery is a unifying element in the poet's visionary transcendentalism. Sometimes the imagery is recognizably biblical, as in "Thoughts 4" (95-96): "O give me Grace to see thy face, and be / A constant Mirror of Eternitie" (echoing 2 Cor. 3:18).

In Shaftesbury's *Characteristics* the 1 Corinthians passage is enlisted in aid of the thesis that "the most dangerous" state of mind is "the dogmatical" and "the safest ... the skeptical" (6.2.3). Melville's *Mardi,* which pictures all signs as images "darkly reflected ... in glassy water" (2.25), similarly observes that "St. Paul ... argues ... the doubts of Montaigne" (2.54). In *Moby-Dick,* in an extended burlesque of 1 Cor. 13:12, Melville underscores his skepticism: "Here ye strike but splintered hearts together —there ye shall strike unsplinterable glasses!" — so the sub-sub-librarian's commentator, in a company with "full eyes and empty glasses," proposes a toast to launch a bookish enterprise not to be taken "for veritable gospel cetology." Outlandish punning establishes the iconoclasm of *Moby-Dick,* where the glass of 1 Corinthians is translated as a Narcissus mirror (1.3-4; 2.190-91). Such doubting and solipsism reach their *terminus ad quem* with *The Confidence-Man:* the book opens with a deaf-mute copying out verses from 1 Cor. 13 and ends in complete darkness.

Browning's "The Pope" in *The Ring and the Book* (10.1312-13) contrasts the two lives of "Here" and "There" as the poem reflects on the constraints which partial knowledge imposes on judgment, language, and, consequently, on earthly authority: "Man's mind —what is it but a convex glass" (10.1306). The mirror of mist or smoke in the opening chapter of Carroll's *Through the Looking-Glass,* a medium for entry into a world where "the written word is *rather* hard to understand," broadly suggests an allusion to the Pauline text. Twain comes straight to the point in "Fenimore Cooper's Literary Offenses": "Cooper's eye was splendidly inaccurate.... he saw nearly all things through a glass eye, darkly."

The title of J. S. Le Fanu's volume of five ghostly tales, *In a Glass Darkly* [1872], conveys not much more than a general sense of mystification. Joyce uses 1 Cor. 13:12, however, to advance the aesthete's creed: the certain truth of doubt and relativity makes dogmatism untenable. His *Ulysses,* e.g., jokingly tells of a person who, though still "in the flesh," claims that unambiguous and direct sight of "the heavenworld" is available only to those "in the spirit." When the authenticity of his heavenly vision is challenged, the enraptured visionary replies "that previously he had seen as in a glass darkly." D. H. Lawrence's "So There!" teases a "dear little girly-wirly" whose hairstyle is not what she thinks it is: "see yourself in a glass, darkly." Although the echo is biblical, the meaning is clearly not so, the passage serving only to suggest something mildly sacrilegious about youthful feminine vanities.

Through a Glass Darkly, a well-known Ingmar Bergman film, uses the image as a metaphor for the complex failures of human communications. More recently, the Benedictine monk narrating the prologue of Umberto Eco's *The Name of the Rose* opens with the initial verse of the Gospel of John —concerning the Word from the beginning —and then, taking 1 Cor. 13:12 for his text, immediately moves to the obscure world of human language, of traducing or mistranslating, of error, sin, and crime. In the world of *The Name of the Rose,* the semiotician's and the detective's problems in decoding dark signs are not easily solved.

See also IMAGO DEI.

Bibliography. Behm, J. "Das Bildworth vom Spiegel I Korinther 13,12." In *Reinhold Seeberg Festschrift.* Ed. W. Koepp (1929), 1.315-42; Bradley, R. "Backgrounds of the Title *Speculum* in Medieval Literature." *Speculum* 29 (1954), 110-15; Dupont, J. "Le chrétien, miroir de la gloire divine." *RB* 56 (1949), 393-411; Grabes, H. *The Mutable Glass: Mirror Imagery in Titles and Texts of the Middle Ages and the English Renaissance.* Trans. G. Collier (1983); Hugede, N. *La métaphore du miroir dans les Epîtres de saint Paul aux Corinthiens* (1957); Schmidt, M. "Miroir." *Dictionnaire de spiritualité* (1980).　　　　　　　　　　　　　CAMILLE R. LA BOSSIÈRE
　　　　　　　　　　　　　　　　　　　　　　RICHARD SCHELL

GLORIA　*Gloria in excelsis deo,* "Glory to God in the highest" (Luke 2:14 [Vg]), were the opening words of the angelic annunciation of Christ's birth to the shepherds. Incorporated into a hymn of praise used in the Mass, in the early and medieval Church it was sung by the whole congregation. Later, especially after the 17th cent., increasing complexity of the music causes the *Gloria,* or "Greater Doxology," to be appropriated by the choir, though in revised and contemporary liturgies it is often sung by the congregation once again. Sung on all feast days and Sundays except during Advent and Lent, in the English *Book of Common Prayer* (1549) it followed the *Kyrie* but later was moved to the conclusion of the liturgy, before the benediction. It is distinct from the *Gloria Patri,* the "Lesser Doxology" (deriving from Rom. 16:27; Phil. 4:20; Rev. 5:13): "Glory be to the Father and to the Son and to the Holy Spirit," which has been used since the 4th cent. A.D. at the end of the Psalms and hymns in the offices. English Puritans forbade it as "unscriptural" during the Commonwealth period, but it was reinstated at the Restoration (*Book of Common Prayer,* 1662). George Herbert uses the incipit to the *Gloria* (Luke 2:14) as a final coda to his collection of poems *The Church* (cf. David Jones, *Anathemata,* 7.215).

GLORIA PATRI　*See* GLORIA.

GLORY　Heb. *kabod,* from the root *kbd* ("be heavy"), can mean "wealth" (Gen. 31:1) or "impressiveness," whether of human presence (Gen. 45:13) or of God's (e.g., Exod. 16:10). The glory manifested in the local presence of God, often spoken of as a light (e.g., Ezek. 1:28) or a fire (e.g., Exod. 24:17), was called the Shekinah ("that which dwells") in the Targums, from where it is possible that certain NT uses of "glory" originated (esp. Rom. 9:4). Gk. *doxa,* because of its use in the LXX to translate *kabod,* has in the NT a very similar range of meanings.

In both testaments the noun *glory* can often helpfully be paraphrased "manifest character," especially in Isaiah, Ezekiel, the Gospel of John, and the Pauline Epistles. The corresponding verb, *glorify,* sometimes means "vindicate," although often it can simply mean "honor," as can also the noun; *kabod/doxa* cognates are often rendered "honor" in the KJV. Scripture abounds in doxologies "glorifying" God in this sense.

In the OT God insists on being glorified (Lev. 10:3; Hag. 1:8), for his character must be recognized for what it is ("they shall know that I am the LORD"), whether in his acts of judgment (Ezek. 28:22; 39:13, 21-22) or of salvation (Isa. 26:15 and, through the Servant of the Lord, 49:3-6). Israel, too, is to be glorified in the last days (Jer. 30:19), even with God's own glory (Isa. 60). The Qumran literature speaks of the "glory of Adam" belonging to the righteous in the last days (1QS 4:23; CD 3:20), perhaps an allusion to Adam's creation in the image of God, a glory subsequently forfeited through sin, according to Rom. 3:23. The sayings of Jesus often connect the glory of the last days with that of the Son of Man; throughout the NT it is asserted that the glory of God is supremely manifested in Jesus Christ and communicated through him to the believer (John 17:1, 4-6, 10, 22, 24; 2 Cor. 4:3-6). KJV "glory" also occasionally renders words meaning "rejoice" or "boast" (Jer. 9:23f.; Gal. 6:14).

The term *glory* is used in a surprising variety of ways in English literature, many of which derive from biblical precedent. Though *glory* is not originally dependent upon the notion of popular acclaim, the term may be frequently understood in the sense of honorable fame or renown. Jeremy Taylor, in one of his sermons, sets out to define a term already somewhat unwieldy in the mid-17th cent.:

> God is the eternal fountain of honour, and the spring of glory; in him it dwells essentially, from him it derives originally; and when an action is glorious, or a man honourable, it is because the action is pleasing to God, in the relation of obedience or imitation, and because the man is honoured by God. (*28 Sermons Preached at Golden Grove* [1651], 8)

The term *glory* retains its biblical sense where, as in much of the literature of the Middle Ages and Renaissance, a distinction between "fame in the eyes of persons" and "fame in the eyes of God" is readily grasped, the latter being seen as true fame. Self-glorification is understood by writers from Dante and Langland through the Renaissance to amount to vainglory or idolatry.

For Taylor, Christ is the perfect exemplar of God's glory in himself, as well as the exemplar of the human *imago Dei* achieving his "highest perfection" in that he "glorified God by the instrument of obedience"; a person who imitates Christ's holiness in obedience, whether "by remaining innocent, *or becoming penitent,* also is GIVING GLORY TO THE LORD OUR GOD." These are notions which charge George Herbert's extensive use of the term in his poetry. Before the Fall, he says, humanity was a kind of glory,

> . . . a garden in Paradise:
> Glorie and grace
> Did crown his heart and face.
> But sinne hath fool'd him. ("Miserie," 70-72)

Humankind's opportunity for recovery of its lost glory is rooted in the redemption, in which "Love and Grace took Glorie by the hand, and built a braver Palace than before" ("The World"). On a personal level, Herbert's dedication of his poetry to divine ends is noted in a letter to his mother from Cambridge, where he vows "that my poor Abilities in *Poetry,* shall be all, and ever consecrated to God's glory" (New Year, 1609/10). Defoe (*The Family Instructor*, 1.1) argues for the advisability of a similar consecration: "You are to live here to the glory of Him that made you": indeed, he argues, the individual only realizes his identity in the process of "giving glory to Him that made him" (1.3). The use of *glory* to describe human achievements not necessarily possessed of such worshipful purpose is of course also common in this period — reinforced by classical precedent — as evidenced in Donne's typical use of the term (e.g., "The Anniversarie," "A Valediction: of the Booke").

A further use of the term common in English literature came to prominence in the 17th cent., especially in the writing of the Puritans, who, following the language of the *Shorter Catechism of the Westminster Assembly*, used *glory* as a synonym for *heaven* or *Paradise*: "The soules of Beleevers are at their death made perfect in holiness, & do immediately pass into glory" (A. 37). There is no clear biblical warrant for this use of the term, although KJV Ps. 73:24 (the translation of which is suspect) is generally understood as a precedent. In America, this use of the term became common in popular preaching and so found its way into literature at every level — from Harriet Beecher Stowe's *Uncle Tom's Cabin* ("Tell her ye found me going into glory" [chap. 41]) to popular hymnody and spirituals.

The term *glory* may also refer to the halo or nimbus surrounding the head of a saint (or Christ) in sacred painting.

The halo itself is an iconographic device intended to symbolize reflected divine glory, the "glorification" of the saints. Sir Thomas Browne believed this sense of *glory* had been imported from France (*Pseudodoxia Epidemica*, 5.9.247); a century later the *Gentleman's Magazine* (1745.197) discussed it as an art-historical term, and it was just recherché enough to appeal to Henry Kingsley, who uses it in *Ravenshoe* (1862), where he describes a "saintly" young beauty's "own glorious hair, which hung round her lovely face like a glory" (1.21.246). *Sic transit gloria mundi* ("thus passes away the glory of this world") are words addressed to each successive Pope at his investiture, while an object symbolizing worldly glory is burned before him; it has also become a popular saying to indicate the transience of worldly prosperity or reputation.

PAUL GARNET
DAVID L. JEFFREY

GNOSTICISM   *See* HERESY.

GO AND SIN NO MORE   *See* WOMAN TAKEN IN ADULTERY.

GO TO THE ANT, THOU SLUGGARD   The verse continues, ". . . consider her ways and be wise: Which having no guide, overseer, or ruler, provideth her meat in the summer and gathereth her food in the harvest. How long wilt thou sleep, O sluggard?" (Prov. 6:6-9). This verse, generally adduced by patristic writers in condemnations of sloth, is what awakens Bunyan's Christian, asleep in his "pleasant Arbour" on the "Hill called Difficulty." Milton uses it to argue against monarchical rule in *A Free Commonwealth,* modifying the translation to read "having no prince, ruler, or lord."

GOD IS LIGHT   *See* LIGHT.

GOG AND MAGOG   Magog is listed among the sons of Japheth (Gen. 10:2), and Gog of the land of Magog appears in Ezekiel's vision of the last days as the enemy of Israel against whom God will rain fire and brimstone (Ezek. 38–39). In the LXX of Amos 7:1, Gog is the name of the leader of the locust horde (symbolizing foreign invaders). The most influential biblical reference to Gog and Magog, however, is Rev. 20:7-8. In the final apocalyptic battle between good and evil, Satan, released from his thousand-year imprisonment (Rev. 20:2), will lead Gog and Magog against the New Jerusalem.

Both Jewish and Christian commentators have identified Gog and Magog with ferocious barbaric peoples ultimately defeated by God (Jub. 8:25; Sib. Or. 3.319; Sanh. 17a). St. Ambrose established an early precedent by attempting a historical identification. For him Gog and Magog were the Goths (*De fide,* 2.16.138). St. Augustine was more reticent about identifying them with any specific peoples. Arguing that they symbolize the universal city of the devil, he developed St. Jerome's influential etymological interpretation in which Gog represents "a roof" from under which Magog — the devil and his supporters — rush out to attack the Christian Church (*De civ. Dei* 20.11).

Later exegetes associate Gog and Magog with Antichrist's followers and his terrible armies, often specifically connecting them with Islam (an identification influenced by the popular Pseudo-Methodius *Revelations*), the lost tribes of Israel, or the Turks. In the Reformation, Gog and Magog were variously identified with the Turks or the Roman papacy. For David Pareus "The Gogish warre . . . is the Turkish warre against Christendome" (*Commentary on Revelation* [1644], 558). John Napier, manipulating Augustine's etymological interpretation, argues that Gog signifies a "covered" enemy, the hypocritical pope, whereas Magog signifies a "discovered" enemy, such as Islam (*Plaine Discovery of the Whole Revelation* [1593], 59-60).

Another tradition, dating at least to the 1st cent. A.D., identified Gog and Magog with the Scythians (Josephus, *Ant.* 1.6.1). Since the Scythians were among the barbaric peoples whom Alexander the Great enclosed behind iron gates in the Caucasus, Gog and Magog became a part of the Alexander legend (see the 5th-cent. metrical homily of the Syrian Jacob of Serugh, 427-664).

Early literary references sometimes combine both traditions. The 14th-cent. English romance *Kyng Alisaunder,* e.g., discusses Gog and Magog at some length (5932-6287), and describes how Antichrist will destroy the work of the great emperor. In didactic works such as the *Pricke of Conscience,* Gog and Magog are simply the armies of Antichrist. *Mandeville's Travels* links Gog and Magog with the lost tribes of Israel and develops the apocalyptic legend to play on popular fears concerning the evils of the Jews. Describing the mountains of "caspye" where Gog and Magog are imprisoned, the text predicts that they will escape in the time of Antichrist to destroy all Christians. John Foxe alludes to Gog and Magog to describe how Satan, recently released from prison, stirs up the Turks against Palestine and eastern Europe (*Christus Triumphans,* 4.4).

Many later authors refer to such specific identifications with contempt. In a summary of disasters during the decline of the Carolingian Empire, Macaulay cites the ravages of the Huns, "in whom the trembling monks fancied that they recognized the Gog or Magog of prophecy" (*Historical Essays,* "Lord Clive," Jan. 1840). Blake maintains the eschatological significance of Gog and Magog yet reverses their traditional role as the armies of Satan. He visualizes Gog and Magog as Satan's hellish guardians and describes their binding the Great Red Dragon: "He is bound in chains by Two strong demons; they are Gog & Magog, who have been compell'd to subdue their Master . . . with their Hammer & Tongs, about to new-Create the Seven-Headed Kingdoms" (*A Vision of the Last Judgment,* K 609).

The notion that Gog and Magog represent barbarous and gigantic peoples may have influenced the peculiar British legend of Gogmagog in Geoffrey of Monmouth's *History of the Britons.* In his conquest of Britain, Brutus is said to have fought Gogmagog, a giant whom he spared but who was subsequently thrown to his death in the sea. This Gogmagog is referred to by Spenser (*Faerie Queene*, 2.10.10), Milton *(History of Britain),* and Blake (*Jerusalem*, 98.52). H. Leivick's futuristic play, *Comedy of Salvation* (ca. 1932), concentrates on an eschatological conflict between Gog, Magog, and an unholy pretender Messiah of the House of Joseph on one hand and the pure suffering servant, the holy Messiah of the house of David. Gog, Magog, and Messiah ben Joseph prevail for a time, but the true Messiah suffers through to victory, comforted by the blind old beggar Elijah.

Bibliography. Anderson, A. R. *Alexander's Gate, Gog and Magog, and the Inclosed Nations* (1932); Emmerson, R. K. *Antichrist in the Middle Ages: A Study of Medieval Apocalypticism, Art, and Literature* (1981).

RICHARD K. EMMERSON

GOLD Mentioned more than any other metal in the Bible (385 times), gold was highly prized and hence associated with worship. It was collected for the Tabernacle and construction of the Ark as well as the priestly vestments (Exod. 25:11; 39:2-30). It was also associated with idolatrous worship and materialism, however, from the golden calf episode (Exod. 32:2-24) to Belshazzar's feast (Dan. 5). In wisdom literature gold is said to be of less value than wisdom (Job 28:15, 17; Prov. 3:14; 8:10, 19; 16:16). Elsewhere in the OT the Law is seen as better than gold (Ps. 19:10), as is faith in the NT (1 Pet. 1:7). It usually retains symbolic value as "spiritual wealth" (Rev. 3:8): the Magi brought gold to the infant Jesus (Matt. 2:11); the Holy City will consist of "pure gold, as it were transparent glass" (Rev. 21:21). As in the OT, however, it may symbolize idolatry of wealth: the Great Whore of the Apocalypse is dressed in gold (Rev. 17:4; 18:16; the flaunting of gold was expressly forbidden by Peter and Paul [1 Tim. 2:9; 1 Pet. 3:3]).

In the Middle Ages gold thus developed a twofold spiritual distinction. In his *Dictionari sev Repertorii Moralis* Berchorius distinguishes *in bono* significations, such as wisdom and eternal felicity, and those *in malo,* such as cupidity and idolatry, following closely upon biblical usage as developed in St. Augustine (*Enarr. in Ps.* 19) and St. Gregory (*Moralia in Iob*). These are the conventional associations employed throughout the ME *Cleanness* and in the same poet's *Pearl,* where in heaven "the strete3 of gold as glasse al bare" are among the wonders the dreamer awaits (1025). In John Grimestone's ME lyric, "Gold & al þis werdis wyn / Is nouth but cristis rode," "Gold and all the wine of this world" — or, in a pun, "Gold and all the joy of words" — "is nothing by comparison with the cross of Christ" (C. Brown, *Reli-*

gious Lyrics of the XIVth Century, no. 71). The gold tried in the refining fire of God's judgment (Zech. 13:9; cf. Prov. 17:3; Mal. 3:3; 1 Cor. 3:12-16), a kind of residue of virtue in the believer, is alluded to by Donne in praise of autumnal beauty in "Elegy 9" and in "To the Lady Bedford"; it is applied directly by Herbert in "Valdesso" (22); for Herbert Christ himself is the mine from which spiritual gold is drawn ("To All Angels and Saints"), and in "Easter" he assures the believer that "as his death calcined there to dust, / His life may make thee gold, and much more, just." In Donne's "The Lamentations of Jeremy," the versification in chap. 4 adapts the gold of the Temple and of "Sion" to his biblical text-paraphrase of Lamentations. In Hawthorne's *Scarlet Letter* Rev. Dimmesdale preaches that "Saintly men who walk with God on earth, would fain be away to walk with him on the golden pavements of the New Jerusalem" (chap. 9), pavements the next generation of immigrants would come looking for in America.

See also BELSHAZZAR; GOLDEN CALF.

GOLDEN BOWL   The poem of the wise man in Eccl. 12, "Remember now thy Creator in the days of thy youth," pictures approaching death: ". . . or ever the silver cord be loosed, or the golden bowl broken, or the pitcher be broken at the fountain" (v. 6; cf. Zech. 4:2-6).

In English literature the three images are used for the most part straightforwardly. In Washington Irving's "The Pride of the Village," the deserted heroine "felt a conviction that she was hastening to the tomb, but looked forward to it as a place of rest. The silver cord that had bound her to her existence was loosed." Lytton Strachey writes of "Sarah Bernhardt" in his *Characters and Commentaries* that since her death "The pitcher is broken at the fountain; the voice is silent now forever."

Most allusions refer specifically to the golden bowl. Thoreau makes much of little when he writes: "His pipe lay broken on the hearth, instead of a bowl broken at the fountain" (*Walden,* "Former Inhabitants"), a sentimentalism Melville whimsically eschews in "I and My Chimney," which recounts how his wife campaigned against both: "I live in continual dread," quips Melville, "lest, like the golden bowl, the pipes of me and my chimney shall yet be broken." Oliver Wendell Holmes in "The Iron Gate" writes of the heavy impact of "Ecclesiastes, or the Preacher" upon his declining "sighs o'er the loosened cord, the broken bowl." Poe's "Lenore" begins "Ah, broken is the golden bowl! — the spirit flown forever!" J. B. Priestley applies the image of the broken golden bowl to loss of the writer's inspiration: "That's done with. What do we do now? I can't go back to that beastly little room of mine and try to write. The mood, Miss Callander, the precious mood, is shattered; the golden bowl, Felton, is broken" (*The Good Companions,* 1.3.1). Whether *The Golden Bowl* (1904) of Henry James is broken in the

sense intended by Ecclesiastes or merely broken to save appearances is one of the novel's teasing questions.

GOLDEN CALF   Exod. 32 records how, while Moses was gone up Mt. Sinai to receive the tablets of the Law, Aaron succumbed to pressure from the people to provide for them an idol-god like the fertility god Apis of the Egyptians — perhaps (as is suggested in Exod. 32:1) as a surrogate for the absent mediator Moses. Collecting golden earrings from the Israelites, Aaron melted them down to fashion the calf, the offense of which to Moses was so great that on his return he smashed the tablets of the Ten Commandments in his rage, then destroyed the idol. Jeroboam's calf worship (1 Kings 12:28-33) echoes, in some respects, the Exodus narrative.

Worship of the golden calf came to signify not merely cultic idolatry but also the idolatry of wealth. Matthew Henry, e.g., echoes medieval and Reformation commentators in seeing the Exodus narrative as centering especially on the Israelites' impatience for material well-being (*Comm. on the Whole Bible,* 1.408-09); the Jeroboam story, by contrast, he sees as principally concerned with the rejection of monotheism in favor of fertility cult religion (2.642-43).

Sir Epicure Mammon in Ben Jonson's *The Alchemist* promises to make Surly so rich that no more "the Sons of Hazard fall before / The golden calf." In A. H. Clough's "The New Sinai," the "gilded beast" is the golden calf of atheism. "Profit" is the idol in Charles Dickens's *Martin Chuzzlewit,* in which Mr. Pecksniff exclaims, "The profit of dissimulation! To worship the golden calf of Baal, for eighteen shillings a week!" (chap. 10). Wealth is what O. Henry has in mind when, in his story "The Enchanted Profile," an affluent character is said to be "mighty popular down in the part of town where they worship the golden calf."

See also AARON; GRAVEN IMAGE; TEN COMMANDMENTS.

GOLDEN RULE   The term *golden rule* is not biblical but has been applied to the injunction of Jesus: "Whatsoever ye would that men should do to you, do ye even so to them" (Matt. 7:12; cf. Luke 6:31). "This is the law and the prophets," Jesus adds; in effect, his "rule" is a broad summary of the Sermon on the Mount with respect to conduct, loosely paralleling the Great Commandment or summary of the Law (Matt. 22:37-40). It may be compared with the words of R. Hillel: "That which displeases you do not do to another. This is the whole law; the rest is commentary" (Shab. 31a). In the *Book of Common Prayer* "Catechism," the phrase becomes part of one's answer to the question "What is thy duty towards thy Neighbour?" According to Isaac Watts's *Improvement of the Mind* the verse speaks of "that golden principle of morality which our blessed Lord has given us" (1.14). In the 17th cent. the "rule" is occasionally referred to as the "Golden Law."

The phrase from Matthew, along with slight variants from the Gospel of Luke, the *Prayer Book*, and elsewhere (i.e., "Do unto others as you would have them do unto you"), is ubiquitous in English literature. Illustrating something of the range of adaptation (and frequent trivialization) during the Enlightenment are Pope and Blake. In Pope's "Essay on Dedications" he observes, "These, when they flatter most, do but as they would be done unto." In Blake's *Miscellaneous Epigrams* he scorns Cromek: "He has observed the Golden Rule / Till he's become the Golden Fool." Thoreau reflects that "The law to do as you would be done by fell with less persuasiveness on the ears of those, who, for their part, did not care how they were done by" (*Walden,* "Economy"), a point Melville modifies in *Moby-Dick:* " 'I will not go,' said the stranger, 'till you say *aye* to me. Do to me as you would have me do to you in the like case. For you too have a boy, Captain Ahab' " (chap. 128). A commercial twist is on Dickens's mind in his *American Notes,* where he observes that "the merits of a broken speculation, or bankruptcy, or of a successful scoundrel, are not gauged by his or its observance of the golden rule, 'Do unto others as you would be done by,' but are considered with reference to their smartness" (chap. 18).

A weakened form of the rule as modern creed is expressed in Somerset Maugham's *Of Human Bondage:* " '. . . But what do you suppose you are in the world for?' . . . 'Oh, I don't know: I suppose to do one's duty, and make the best use of one's faculties, and avoid hurting other people.' 'In short, to do unto others as you would they should do unto you?' 'I suppose so' " (chap. 45). G. B. Shaw takes a calculatedly negative view of such a "creed," saying in the Afterword to *Man and Superman:* "Do not do unto others as you would they should do unto you. Their tastes may not be the same." Later he adds cryptically, "The golden rule is that there are no golden rules" (*Maxims for Revolutionists,* 227, 228).

See also GREAT COMMANDMENT; SERMON ON THE MOUNT.

GOLEM The *golem* (Heb. "shapeless mass"; cf. Ps. 139:16 [KJV: "members . . . when as yet there was none of them"]) is a creature from Jewish folklore, called up by magical means, with no precedent in the Bible (cf. Sanh. 65b). After the 15th cent., under the influence of alchemical beliefs, the *golem* became a kind of beserker genie; one could impose tasks upon it, but as in Leivick's play *The Golem* (ca. 1920) the creature could without warning wreak havoc upon its supposed "master." A. M. Klein's "golem" is a wooden puppet, like the Gibeonites "a hewer of wood — to keep their Sabbath hot; / A drawer of water — to fill his master's crock" ("The Golem"), and draws upon the 16th-cent. story of R. Judah Low ben Bezalel of Prague. Jorge Luis Borges's "El Golem" develops the notion that the demonic creature is called up by a perverse incantation of holy names, drawing on the

writings of Sephir Yetzirah as well. The fate of the rabbi parallels, in some respects, that of Marlowe's *Doctor Faustus* in his own (similar) conjuring. When J. R. R. Tolkien has his sometime Hobbit Gollum devolve into a treacherous shapeshifter under the malign influence of the Ring, he may have these legends in mind. In modern Yiddish a *golem* is simply a stupid person; the term is used in this way in the writings of Bernard Malamud and Mordecai Richler, although Richler's Horseman in *St. Urbain's Horseman* transposes the "beserker" golem of R. Judah from the Prague ghetto to Montreal.

GOLGOTHA A skull-shaped mount called accordingly in Aramaic by this name, of which the Latin derivation, *calvaria,* is Calvary (see Matt. 27:33; Luke 23:33), the site of Jesus' crucifixion. In Margaret Avison's "He couldn't be safe":

> He went down the road
> to the Place of the Skull.
> The soldier was there, and the criminal,
> and the ones who thought if he didn't have pull
> they wouldn't be safe to know him. (*sunblue,* 52)

The term sometimes signifies simply a graveyard, as when De Quincey says that he would rather be buried in a "green churchyard, amongst the ancient and solitary hills" than in any of the "hideous Golgothas of London" (*Confessions of an Opium Eater,* "Appendix").

See also PASSION, CROSS.

GOLIATH Goliath was the giant of Gath and champion of the Philistines who was eventually defeated and killed by the boy David (1 Sam. 17:4-23; 21:9; 22:10; 2 Sam. 21:19; 1 Chron. 20:5ff.). Scholars speculate that he was not, strictly speaking, a Canaanite but was perhaps of aboriginal stock such as the Anakim, some of whom were still to be found near Gath in the reign of Saul (2 Sam. 21:22; 1 Chron. 20:8). According to the usual reckoning of a cubit as 45 centimeters, Goliath would have been almost 3 meters (9 ft.) tall ("six cubits and a span").

Haggadic commentary suggests that Goliath was descended from Samson, the enemy of giants (Tg. 1 Sam. 17:4); he wore into his battle with David the insignia of the Canaanite deity Dagon, whose temple was in Gaza (Tehillim 18.160; 144.533; Shemuel 21.109). Patristic and later Christian commentary typically allegorizes him as a type of Satan, contesting against Christ: *"Goliath vero superbiam diaboli significat: quam David, id est Christus . . ."* (*Glossa Ordinaria* [PL 113.556]).

Because of the popularity of the David-Goliath narrative, Goliath's name has become in modern literature a byword for prodigious strength and size. The lance of Ivanhoe is compared by Isaac in Scott's *Ivanhoe* to "that of Goliath the Philistine, which might vie with a weaver's beam" (chap. 10). Huck Finn compares the burly Hines to "Goliar" (*Huckleberry Finn,* chap. 29). American poet Anthony Hecht pictures Goliath lying "on his back in Hell," a Miltonic conflation (cf. *PL* 1.196-98), in *"La Masseur de ma Soeur."* A. M. Klein's "Sling for Goliath" in "Five Weapons against Death" uses the giant as an image for the reversal of fortune, the victory of death over life; and in Margaret Avison's *Winter Sun* poems Goliath acquires mythic attributes from yet another source, notably a "purple beard" (92).

    See also DAVID; GAZA; GIANTS IN THE EARTH; PHILISTINE.

GOMER   An ally of Gog and Magog in Ezek. 38:6. Also the name of the prostitute who was wife to Hosea.

    See also GOG AND MAGOG; HOSEA.

GOOD SAMARITAN   The parable of the good Samaritan is told in Luke 10:30-35 in response to a lawyer's request for a definition of "neighbor" in the second of the great commandments: "thou shalt love thy neighbor as thyself." Jesus tells the story to make evident that a good neighbor comes sometimes from the least expected quarter and that true charity transcends the limits of community. A traveler is set upon by thieves, robbed, beaten, and left for dead. Two subsequent travelers, a priest and a Levite, observe his tattered body, but hasten on their way. A third, who would have been considered both an alien and a moral inferior, stops to give aid, then carries the man to a hospice where he undertakes for his recuperation expenses. The Samaritan was far from a *socius* to the Jew, and Jesus' story would have shocked his hearers, whose expectation would have been that such a "reprobate" would more likely have finished off what the muggers had begun. The parable is intended to chasten self-righteousness.

    The earliest allegorization of the parable is provided by Origen (*Hom.* 34 [PG 13.1886]), who may well be reflecting the exegesis of apostolic times. He writes:

> . . . the man *who went down* is Adam; *Jerusalem* means Paradise; *Jericho,* the world; the *robbers,* the enemy powers; the *Priest* stands for the Law; the *Levite* for the Prophets; the *Samaritan* for Christ. The *wounds* stand for our disobedience; the *beast,* the body of the Lord. The common house, that is the *inn,* which receives all who wish to enter it, is interpreted as the Church. Furthermore, the *two denarii* are understood to mean the Father and the Son; the *innkeeper,* the Head of the Church, to whom the plan of redemption and its means have been entrusted. And concerning that which the Samaritan promises at his return, this was a figure of the Second Coming of the Saviour.

    This teaching reached the West in St. Jerome's Latin translation of Origen and is faithfully transmitted by St. Ambrose (*Expositio Evangelii secundum Lucam* [PL 15.1806], St. Augustine (*Quaestiones Evangeliorum* [PL 35.1340]), and the Venerable Bede (*In Lucae Evangelium Expositio* [PL 92.469]) among the most noteworthy.

    As the Samaritan pericope came to be employed in the liturgy, its exegesis became even more widely known; portions of Bede's commentary on this passage were, e.g., used in several lessons at Matins in the Roman and Sarum rites. Liturgical commentators such as Rupert of Deutz (*De Divinis Officiis* [PL 170.322], Sicard of Cremona (*Mitrale* [PL 213.396]), and especially Guillaume Durandus (*Rationale Divinorum Officiorum,* 6.127), using the other scriptural texts of the proper of the Mass, explain the Samaritan's remedies in terms of the sacraments of baptism, penance, and the Eucharist.

    It is in liturgical homilies rather than the poetry of the OE period that one encounters the Samaritan parable and its traditional exegesis. Two homilies (ed. R. Morris, EETS o.s. 29 and 34 [1868]) for Christmas Day use the Samaritan parable in a discussion of the Incarnation and its place in salvation history. Striking use of the parable and its biblical and liturgical exegesis in ME occurs in Langland's *Piers Plowman* where Will, after meeting with Faith and Hope, encounters Charity in the person of the Samaritan. Passus 17 of the B text employs the Samaritan episode to sum up preceding developments in Will's quest for firsthand knowledge of Christ and salvation and to point the way to the poem's climax in Passus 18. There, Christ "semblable to the Samaritan and somedel to Piers the Plowman" jousts with Death in Langland's depiction of the Passion and harrowing of hell.

    Although Spenser makes no extended use of the parable in the *Faerie Queene,* his wounded characters are generally treated in a manner sufficiently resembling the Samaritan's to lead critics to believe that he had Luke's text in mind (e.g. 1.5.17; 6.2.4.8; 3.28).

    Fielding puts the parable to excellent satirical use in the twelfth chapter of *Joseph Andrews.* The cries of Joseph, lying wounded and bloody by the roadside, are heard by the passengers in a passing coach. A lawyer, a "man of wit," a haughty lady, and several other characters are all anxious to pass by. When after much debate among the passengers Joseph is rescued, it is because the passengers fear some legal action if Joseph dies. A further debate follows about clothing the naked Joseph, and it is a postillion, "a lad who hath been since transported for robbing a hensroost," who gives Joseph "his only garment, at the same time swearing a great oath (for which he was rebuked by the passengers) that he would rather ride in his shirt all his life than suffer a fellow-creature to be in so miserable a condition."

    Brief sarcastic allusions to Samaritan-like behavior or lack of it in certain characters are found in Byron's *Don Juan* (5.955-58) and the "Age of Bronze" (690-91), as well as Browning's "Inn Album" (946-47). As is indicated in the full title of Thackeray's novel *The Adventures of Philip on His Way Through the World; Shewing Who Robbed Him, Who Helped Him, and Who Passed Him By,* the Samaritan parable acts as the novel's framework for the various trials of Philip Firmin and as a model to test the charity and loyalty of those around him. In *The Way of All Flesh* (chap. 57), Samuel Butler describes Ernest Pontifex as having fallen "among a gang of spiritual thieves," and Ernest himself feels "as though if he was to be saved, a good Samaritan must hurry up from somewhere — he knew not whence."

Bibliography. Gerhardsson, B. *The Good Samaritan — The Good Shepherd?* (1958); Manson, T. *The Sayings of Jesus* (1949), 259-63; Marshall, I. H. *The Gospel of Luke* (1978), 440-50.   RAYMOND ST-JACQUES

GOOD SHEPHERD   *See* LOST SHEEP, PARABLE OF.

GORGIAS   *See* AJALON, VALE OF; JUDAS MACCABEUS.

GOSPEL   *Gospel* (Gk. *euangelion*) derives from the noun *angelos* ("messenger") and the verb *angellō* ("announce," "proclaim," or "publish news"). The *eu-* prefix conveys the sense of "good." At its most basic level the gospel is "good news" with respect to its content, and the activity of its proclamation (Gk. *euangelizomai;* e.g., Gal. 3:8) is "spreading or declaring the good news."

In the NT the term refers to the spoken word, and not writing. Reference to the initial four texts of the NT (Matthew, Mark, Luke, and John) as "gospels" occurs for the first time in a description of worship by Justin Martyr, where there is reference to "memoirs of the apostles . . . called gospels." While after the 3rd cent. the term is associated in general with the content of the kerygma or events crucial to the Atonement, it came gradually to be reserved for the writings of the four "evangelists" mentioned, in which the kerygma was transmitted — the three "synoptic Gospels," which closely harmonize with one another to form an integrated view, and "the fourth Gospel," John, which organizes its material rather differently. In Western liturgy at least one reading in every Eucharist is from "the Gospel" — i.e., one of the four Gospels.

Among the Reformers there grew up a custom — anticipated in Wyclif — of referring to the whole of canonical Scripture as "the Gospel." References to the "Gospel side" (i.e., to the congregation's right of the altar) of the church for the place from which it is traditionally read, and the "epistle side" (left) for the place of reading lections usually from the balance of the NT, are found occasionally in English poetry, e.g., in Robert Browning's "The Bishop orders his Tomb at St. Praxed's" and in David Jones's *Anathemata* (1.64).

GOY, GOYIM   *See* GENTILES.

GRACE, WORKS   "For by grace are ye saved through faith; and that not of yourselves. It is the gift of God: not of works, lest any man should boast. For we are his workmanship, created in Christ Jesus unto good works, which God hath before ordained that we should walk in them" (Eph. 2:8-10). These words of St. Paul situate theological grace in its traditional relationship to salvation, faith, personal freedom, and merit.

Although *charis* is substantially a NT concept (by which Paul in particular sought to distinguish salvation through the substitutionary atonement of Christ from salvation by adherence to the Law, a hermeneutic recontextualization of the concept of grace in terms of the OT patterns of covenant faithfulness to the Law substantially affects development of the term in Christian thought. Heb. *hen* ("favor" [Esth. 2:17; Ps. 45:2]) and *no'am* ("kindness" [Zech. 11:7, 10]) are translated by the KJV as "grace"; Heb. *hesed* ("tender love" [Esth. 2:9, 17; Ecclus. 7:33]) is typically rendered "loving-kindness," "goodness," or "mercy." The LXX uses *charis* for *hesed* only rarely; the Vg, however, regularly gives *gratia* for Heb. *hesed,* the love which is exhibited by both partners to the covenant (e.g., Exod. 20:6; Deut. 7:12; Hos. 6:4; 2:19). This divergence in translation of Hebrew terms between the precedent of St. Jerome and later direct address to the Hebrew (KJV, RSV, JB) accounts for some of the divergences of theological emphasis within Christian tradition.

In secular Greek *charis* had been used with aesthetic and social connotations, and could suggest that which is "gracious," "artful," "charming," or even, as in the case of a superb wine, "exquisite." The gracious acts of a host prompt gratitude: the word for "thanks" is also *charis.* And it is a kind of noble generosity which grants favor to suppliants. It is the last context which most closely approximates the usage of Paul, who uses the word almost twice as often as all other biblical writers together. Paul's essential message is that "saving" grace is uniquely God's to give (Rom. 5:15; Eph. 2:5); justification is clearly an act of God and cannot be claimed as a right by anyone; hence it must be received as a gift (Gal. 2:17-21). This excludes the possibility of the recipient taking credit for it, "boasting" (1 Cor. 1:29, 31), or "glorying" (Gal. 6:14), except in the cross of Christ. In this sense, the term can imply the whole impact of Christ's Incarnation and ministry (Tit. 2:11). Grace is not an entity which God dispenses, but the quality of forgiveness and the thanksgiving in freedom which it invites; to experience that reciprocity is a matter of relationship rather than possession — a typically Pauline definition of what it means to live in a "state of grace." (The later definition of the Council of Trent uses this phrase in a narrower sense, to mean sanctification by grace [e.g., of absolution] for receipt of the Blessed Sacrament.)

In Paul's Epistles justifying or saving grace is thus set against not only the Law but also human works or moral effort. There are at least two theological meanings of the term *works* in Scripture, both of which are taken up in later literature. First, there are what Paul calls "the works of the law," obedience to covenant requirements (Torah) which focuses especially on the ceremonial commands, or Halakah. These had been adduced by some of Paul's contemporaries as the proper means of achieving a right relationship with God. Paul emphatically denies that for followers of Jesus these suppositions are appropriate (Rom. 3–4; cf. 9:31-33; 11:6; Gal. 2:14–5:14). Attempting to earn one's own way to God does not produce or add to salvation, he argues. Rather, it detracts from Christ's work on the cross and is thus a type of apostasy. There are, however, "good works" (as opposed to "dead works" [Heb. 9:14]; "works of the flesh" [Gal. 5:19], or "works of darkness" [Rom. 13:12]), and they are a necessary expression of a person committed to God, the fruit of every true conversion. So St. James (2:14-26) argues that an intellectual conversion to orthodoxy without practical works is useless and unredemptive. Jesus points to his works as evidence of his relationship with the Father (John 14:10-11) and expects the same from his followers (Matt. 5:16). Repeatedly the NT calls Christians to such "works," which are mainly charitable actions (2 Cor. 9:8; Eph. 2:10; Col. 1:20; 2 Thess. 2:17; 1 Tim. 6:18; Heb. 10:24). These will be the basis of future judgment (1 Cor. 3:13-15; 1 Tim. 5:25; 1 Pet. 1:17; Rev. 20:11-15; 22:12; cf. Matt. 25), and even now they are being examined and judged in this world by Christ, who knows all (Rev. 2–3).

A related issue in subsequent interpretation of the Pauline definition of grace concerns whether grace is given to an individual because of his or her faith, or whether personal faith is itself the effect of God's grace. Paul himself does not appear to notice a problem here, nor does he try to set grace and faith in any causal relationship (Eph. 2:8-9; Rom. 4:16) — faith is simply the manner of receiving the gift and acknowledging that it is free and unmerited (Rom. 3:21-31). In his Epistle to the Galatians, accordingly, Paul takes up the traditional contention of Judaism that persons may gain favor with God by moral and religious achievement, countering with an insistence that one has status with God only through faith — which is to say, in effect, only through accepting one's salvation as an unearned "gracious" gift from God. Paul argues in Romans that Israel's own divine election should be understood in this way: Israel was chosen by grace (11:5) and not because "of works, but of him that calleth" (9:11). What Scripture shows to be most remarkable about God's grace toward humankind is its sheer extravagance, a "grace abounding" — always exceeding expectations as much as deserts (Rom. 5:15, 18; 2 Cor. 4:15; Eph. 1:7, 23; 2:7).

St. Augustine's extensive treatment of grace, which forms the first of the three great Western reflections on Paul, follows the Pauline corpus closely in all respects except that in response to Pelagian antinomianism he observes that "the law is good to edify, if a man use it lawfully (cf. 1 Tim. 1:8), for the end of it is 'charity out of a pure heart, and of faith unfeigned'. And so did our Master acknowledge, when upon these two commandments he hung all the Law and the Prophets" (*Conf.* 12.18.27). Commenting on John 1:17, Augustine says

further, "The law itself by being fulfilled becomes grace and truth. Grace is the fulfilment of love" (*Contra Faustum,* 17.6). In fact,

> from the word "I came not to destroy the law but to fulfill it," we are not to understand that Christ by his precepts remedied lacunae in the law, but that what the literal command failed to accomplish due to the pride and disobedience of men is accomplished by grace . . . so that Apostle says, "faith worketh by love." (19.27)

It is in this sense that for Augustine "love is the perfection of the Law" (*Sermo,* 125), and that he writes to St. Jerome of the "royal law" as being "the law of liberty, which is the law of love" (*Ep.* 167.19).

St. Thomas Aquinas, like Augustine, adheres strongly to the Pauline notion of unmerited divine grace. This he calls "actual grace . . . God's help moving the soul to good," and says that free will itself, in motion toward grace, is a motion prompted by God (*Summa Theol.* 1a-2ae.112.2.c *ad* 1, 2). Yet he adds another category, one much more evidently rooted in human volition and efforts. While fully appreciating the emphasis of Augustine upon unmerited grace in his opposition to the Pelagian heresy especially, Aquinas characterizes obedient life as the "habit" of being in a state of grace: "A man needs grace, not only for good works, but also to prepare himself for grace, yet differently. For by good deeds well done he merits; these require habits of virtue, and therefore habitual grace" (*1 Quodlibets,* 4.7.c *ad* 1, 2). This leads Aquinas to say that "Virtues and Gifts are not in themselves contrasting terms, since the former are defined as good habits while the latter are defined by reference to their cause" (*Summa Theol.* 1a-2ae.68.1). Further, while "grace is not a habit in the strict sense of the term, because it is not immediately directed toward activity, as the virtues are . . . it causes a spiritual condition of being in the soul: it is a disposition to glory, which is consummate grace" (*De Veritate,* 2, ad 7). Habitual grace is thus what later scholastic writers call an "entitative habit" like beauty or good health, not an "operative habit" like faith, justice, or study — or in Aquinas's own tidier formulation: "Grace is a glow of soul, a real quality, like beauty of body" (*Summa Theol.* 1a-2ae.110.2). The element of "preparation" for habitual grace which subsequently received much elaboration with the Tridentine and post-Tridentine theology of the sacraments and penance especially tended to suppose an "inward new creation of man by habitual grace" as the means of salvation. This in turn prompted the view that habitual grace is the grace conveyed in the sacraments, thus consolidating and, from the point of view of the Reformation, complicating and even confounding the distinction between grace and works (or merit). The related question, "how to reconcile human freedom with the divinely efficacious power of grace," remains undecided in Catholic theology (Rahner, *Concise "Sacramentum Mundi,"* 598, 601).

John Calvin (like the Catholic Jansenius) was seen by the Council of Trent as opposing the notion of universality in God's will to grace. For Calvin common grace is the source of all that is good in humankind. But as far as any particular invocation of grace is concerned, "the will is abolished." Redeeming grace is visited only upon the elect; the reprobate are "void" of grace (*Inst.* 2.1.4-5). Yet in the elect, God begins "a work of grace, by exciting in our hearts a desire, a love, and a study of righteousness . . . turning, training and guiding our hearts . . . and he completes this good work by confirming us unto perseverance" (*Inst.* 2.3.6). Calvin goes on to resist the notion (contra Peter Lombard and St. John Chrysostom, as well as Aquinas) that the will can in any way effectively cooperate with grace; he thus sees habitual obedience to the Law as only an "evidence" of grace proceeding from its presence in the life of the elect (2.3.8-9). Calvin and his Protestant successors thus differ from Catholic and Arminian (Methodist) traditions in effectively limiting the availability of grace as experience and making it causally independent of human effort, even while stressing, like Augustine, the continual importance of obedience to the Law.

OE poetry with its emphasis on the OT develops the notions of "glory," "power," and salvation from the experience of uncertain exile in places where later poetry will talk of the experience of an "inward" grace. OE *are,* as in the opening lines of "The Wanderer" *("Oft him anhaga are gebide . . ."),* can mean "mercy" but also "honor," "glory," or, in the social sense, "grace." In Cynewulf's *Christ* the condition of the sinner before salvation is described in terms of spiritual exile: *". . . þaet we, tires wone, / a butan ende   sculon ermþu dreogan, / butan þu usic þon ofostlicor,   ece dryhten, / . . . hreddan wille"* ("that we, deprived of glory, must endure misery without end unless You, eternal Lord . . . save us in all haste" [1.270-74]). This passage owes to the liturgy, the *"O Rex Pacifice,"* and reflects a subordination of the elaborate theology of grace to the fundamental matter of salvation itself. The strong Nordic idea of perseverance in hardship may seem to color some OE poetry with a slight Pelagian tint, but grace is more often simply displaced as a principal subject because of the stronger appeal of OT heroism and the motifs of exile and pilgrimage.

ME poetry tends, by reason of later catechetical formulation and a parallel social concern for grace as "courtesy," to see Christ's action on the cross less in terms of its raw heroism (cf. "The Dream of the Rood") and more as a gracious and divine noblesse oblige. This pattern is still clear in the Anglo-Norman poem "Christ's Chivalry" (D. Jeffrey and B. Levy, *The Anglo-Norman Lyric* [1989], no. 29). Grace in this period is closely connected to mercy: "Mercy and grace moste hem then stere," writes the Pearl poet (*Pearl,* 623), speaking of "enabling" grace. The Pearl poet consciously opposes any idea of salvation by works, not only in *The Pearl* itself but in *Cleanness,*

where all guilt is said to be forgiven only through grace (731). But grace is universal: "alle called on that cortesye and claymed his grace" (1097). The great theme of *Pearl* is that "the grace of God is gret inogh" (612, 624, 625, 636, 648, 660) for any who are brought into the kingdom by the water of baptism which flowed from the wound of Christ on the cross (649-53): "Grace innogh þe mon may haue / þat synneȝ þenne new, ȝif hym repente" (661-62). The idea that the font of every grace is the Passion of Christ is Bonaventuran as well as Augustinian, but *Pearl* is particularly an ally of 14th-cent. English theologians such as Bradwardine, Fitzralph, and Wyclif against resurgent neo-Pelagian and semi-Pelagian notions of "merited grace." For Chaucer's Parson, repentance is crucial to the operation of grace; without it no one may see God.

After the Reformation grace is treated in English literature from a diversity of theological perspectives. The contrast of grace and works is not so evident in Renaissance literature, in part because of the position taken in the *Official Homilies* (1562) of the Church of England. The three-part sermon "Of Good Works annexed unto Faith" (1.5), construing the connection in terms of the apparent split between the apostle Paul and the Epistle of James, concludes that good works are indeed necessary and profitable, though only if performed in faith (cf. also "Of good Works; and first of fasting" [2.4]). Shakespeare's *Measure for Measure* sets itself a "straw man" (Angelo) who embodies a Calvinist Puritan notion of grace by election, then uses the Puritans' favorite texts from Romans to make the point that mercy is to be preferred to justice; indeed, that mercy is a function of grace. The gracious Duke ("your Grace") motivates reconciliation wherever he obtains the cooperation of human will in his kingdom. His arch rival, the strife-making Lucio, knows well enough the biblical doctrine of grace, and Shakespeare uses him comically to highlight his point that the role of God's grace in human affairs is simpler and more to be valued than the theological warfare with which it was burdened in the 16th cent. Speaking to a bewildered pair of "gentlemen," ostensibly about the subject of a "grace" before meals, Lucio says mischievously, "Grace is grace, despite of all controversy. As, for example, thou thyself art a wicked villain, despite of all grace" (1.2.25-27) — a statement concerning the sinner's absolute need of grace with which no theological party could disagree.

John Donne, raised a Catholic but later an Anglican priest, knew both principal traditions: in his poetry "sinne insinuates twixt just men and grace" ("Elegie on Mrs. Boulstred"); grace, however, keeps the soul from sin ("Death," 36). A person may fall into mortal sin, but contrary to the conclusion of Marlowe's Faustus, "Yet grace, if thou repent, thou canst not lacke" ("Holy Sonnet 4"). It is God, nonetheless, who gives the grace necessary for repentance and conversion (cf. Aquinas, *De Veritate,* 28.2). In "Goodfriday 1613," Donne concludes by praying, "Restore thine Image, so much, by thy grace, / That thou may'st know mee, and I'll turne my face" — lines which recall the notion of Chrysostom and Aquinas that what God recognizes in persons, by the presence of grace, is his own handiwork or "reflection," and that there is thus, in Aquinas's words, "no conversion to God unless God turn us" (*Summa Theol.* 1a-2ae.109.6; cf. John 6:44). The principle, if not the phrasing, is here conformable to Calvin as well. George Herbert's "Grace" is a poem about the powerlessness of the best-intended Christian endeavor without grace; Herbert's good preacher will, accordingly, follow the model of Jesus in his teaching, by bringing "out of his treasure things new and old; the old things of Philosophy, and the new of Grace" (*A Priest to the Temple,* 23). Herbert implies by this contrast, here and elsewhere, that grace cannot be reduced to precept or analysis; the Parson like anyone else must in the face of his own sin and inadequacy "creep to the throne of grace" ("Discipline") and "throw" himself there in recognition of his own inability to understand and unworthiness to administer the mysteries of faith and the sacraments (*A Priest to the Temple,* 22). In his "Prayer before Sermon" he comes there again:

> O brand it in our foreheads forever: for an apple once we lost our God, and still lose him for no more; for money, for meat, for diet: But thou Lord . . . hast exalted thy mercy above all things; and hast made our salvation, not our punishment, thy glory: so that then where sin abounded, not death, but grace superabounded. . . .

Here the throne of mercy, clearly, is the font of grace.

Grace Abounding to the Chief of Sinners, or the brief Relation of the exceeding Mercy of God in Christ to his poor servant John Bunyan (1666), drawing its title from Paul (Rom. 5:15-20; cf. 6:1), is a homiletic spiritual autobiography focusing on the unmerited as well as the "abounding" character of grace. Bunyan's discussion of grace is more intense and "enthusiast" than Jeremy Taylor's eloquent description of grace in "daily experience" (*Via Intelligentia,* 31ff.), but the underlying understanding is Calvinist in both cases, to the degree that Taylor's comments (1662) may serve as an introduction to Bunyan's text.

The Enlightenment tended to highlight other objects of admiration. One effect of this was to deflect poets from religious subjects altogether. Alexander Pope began his prodigious career with paraphrases, one of which, "done by the author at 12 years old," is of Thomas à Kempis: "Speak, Gracious Lord, oh speak; thy Servant hears," and asks for "grace to hear" and "grace afford" to receive the word of God. Fifteen years later, attuned to a time in which Nature and Reason were seen by the Deists (as well as some Anglicans and Catholics) as prompting human virtue more often than grace, Pope understands grace as, in effect, a backstop to reason: "If I am wrong, Thy Grace impart / To find that better Way" ("The Universal

Prayer"). At the height of his career, in his *Essay on Man* (1730-32), he proclaims that "The gen'ral ORDER, since the whole began, / Is kept in Nature, and is kept in Man" (1.5.171-72), and that "Whatever is, is right" (1.10.294). Here Pope illustrates the degree to which a doctrine of grace is sustainable in its strong form only where there is a correspondingly strong sense of a fallen and disjointed world. Pope resists Catholic as well as Protestant theological efforts to split Grace and Nature, Grace and Works (or "Virtue") (12.2.80-92).

Two poets of the next generation, one Catholic and one Anglican (and Calvinist), each in his own way distressed by Reason's evident fallibility and Nature's corruptibility by human sin, give grace a more central place. Christopher Smart sees himself as a beneficiary of particular saving grace, comparing himself to the healed King Hezekiah in "Hymn to the Supreme Being," while in *Jubilate Agno* he reiterates the theme that human history and nature are alike redeemed by grace, and their beauty and health hence made known in grace or, to put it another way, recognized in the act of thanksgiving. Hence: "the Sin against the HOLY GHOST is INGRATITUDE." It is grace which helps one see redemption's work, grace which makes one grateful:

> 'Tis the story of the Graces,
> Mercies without end or sum;
> And the sketches and the traces
> Of ten thousand more to come.
>
> Lift, my children, lift within you,
> Dread not ye the tempter's rod;
> Christ our gratitude shall win you,
> Wean'd from earth, and led to God. (*Hymn* 22, "Gratitude")

William Cowper views grace in a strict Calvinist light, "grace undeserv'd — yet surely not for all!" ("Truth," 483) — i.e., grace is made available independently of human volition and effort, or even in spite of it. Human choices are not, however, entirely irrelevant for Cowper, since though the will may not choose grace, it can refuse it once offered:

> Grace leads the right way: if you choose the wrong,
> Take it, and perish; but restrain your tongue.
> Charge not, with light sufficient, and left free,
> Your wilful suicide on God's decree. ("Truth," 17-20)

Cowper's priest at Olney, John Newton, less rigidly Calvinist than his parishioner and always mindful of his own radical conversion from sordid profiteering in the slave trade (*Authentic Narrative* [1764]), composed the hymn "Amazing Grace." Its celebration of grace is written in the spirit of Smart's gratitude and ties its experience in Pauline and Augustinian fashion to the inception of faith, "the hour I first believed."

In the 19th and 20th cents. grace at least as a subject in poetry is either almost entirely diffused in Nature (as in the Romantics and Tennyson) or else subsumed in the matter of salvation (as in Francis Thompson's "The Hound of Heaven," in which the persistent love and grace of Christ rescues the narrator despite his utter lack of desert: "How hast thou merited — of all men's clotted clay the dingiest clot?"). If it is "saving grace" which characterizes the poetry of Catholic converts such as Thompson and Belloc, "habitual grace" is celebrated by Hopkins:

> the just man justices;
> Keeps grace: that keeps all his goings graces;
> Acts in God's eye what in God's eye he is —
> Christ. ("As Kingfishers")

but each in such a way as to reveal the imprint not only of post-Tridentine but the medieval theology of grace. For Hopkins, as for the Romantics, nature, too, reveals grace in its beauty, though it must yield at last to "God's better beauty, grace" ("To What Serves Mortal Beauty").

T. S. Eliot conjures in *Ash Wednesday* with the face of Christ looking down from the cross and reflects that there is "no place of grace for those who avoid the face" (5.18), ending his poem with the plea: "And let my cry come unto Thee." In the American poet Richard Wilbur's "Grace," a poetic reflection on Hopkins, there is a consideration of the degree to which grace in nature, habitual grace, and human freedom expressed in choice come together; perfect grace is then perfect freedom, even where "piety makes for awkwardness."

See also CONTRITION; REPENTANCE; THRONE OF GRACE.

Bibliography. Glueck, N. *Ḥesed in the Bible* (trans. 1967); Henson, G. "A Holy Dispensation: The Literary Quest for Grace in the Reformed English Tradition from John Bale to John Bunyan." Ph.D. diss., University of Louisville, 1981; Moffatt, J. *Grace in the New Testament* (1932); Rahner, K. "Grace." *The Concise "Sacramentum Mundi"* (1975); Torrance, T. F. *The Doctrine of Grace in the Apostolic Fathers* (1948).

DAVID L. JEFFREY
PETER H. DAVIDS

GRAIL *See* HOLY GRAIL.

GRAPES OF ESCOL The fabulous cluster of grapes which it took Joshua and Caleb together to bring back "between two upon a staff" from their mission to "spy out the land" of Canaan is associated with the "land flowing with milk and honey" (Num. 13:17-27). William Bradford compares the fruit of this biblical expedition with that bringing back Indian "corn" (maize) to the Cape Cod Pilgrims. In Whittier's "The Fruit-Gift," he reflects on his pleasure:

> Thrilled with a glad surprise, me thought I knew
> The pleasure of the homeward turning Jew
> When Eschol clusters on his shoulders lay,
> Dropping their sweetness on his desert way.

See also JOSHUA; LAND FLOWING WITH MILK AND HONEY.

GRAVEN IMAGE The term *graven image* is used in the KJV to translate Heb. *pesel,* literally a carved figure of a god. *Pesel* is often linked with *massekah,* an image cast from metal, to describe all possible types of idols (e.g., Deut. 27:15). *Pesel* can also have the extended meaning of idol in general, as in Jer. 51:47.

In the Ten Commandments (Exod. 20:4; Deut. 5:8) it is forbidden to make for the purposes of worship a graven image or likeness of any being of any kind (cf. Ps. 97:7). No explanation is given for this prohibition in the commandment itself, though in Deut. 4:12-31 it is emphasized that Israel did not see God's form at Sinai and should not presume, therefore, to make any image or "likeness" of him. Some modern interpreters suggest that the reason for the prohibition of images is to be found in the ancient understanding of idols. An idol was seen not as a mere representation of a god but in some sense as its corporeal presence. Thus gods could be controlled by withholding gifts from their idols, or even on one recorded occasion by flogging the idol. In apparent contradistinction to these practices, images of any sort were prohibited in Israel lest worshipers should imagine that their God could be controlled or manipulated.

In the OT there are several narratives about Israelite graven images — the episode of the golden calf (Exod. 32–33); Jeroboam's images (1 Kings 12:28ff.), the theft of Micah's graven and molten image (Judg. 17–18), and Manasseh's setting up of a graven image of the goddess Asherah (2 Kings 21:7; not an "image of a grove," as in the KJV). These and other examples of the use of images are condemned by the biblical writers as apostasy.

In the early Church and the patristic era a theological debate developed concerning whether the use of icons was a violation of the commandment against graven images. The iconoclasts associated icons with idol worship and pagan practices forbidden in the OT (e.g., Origen, *Contra Celsum,* 4.31; 6.14; 7.44, 62-67; 8.17-19). Those defending icons argued for the value icons had both for instruction of the faithful and as extensions of the principle of the Incarnation, and pointed to biblical precedents in which God had actually commanded images to be made for inclusion in the furniture of worship (Exod. 25; Ezek. 41). Final settlement of the Iconoclastic Controversy of the 8th cent. (stirred up by Emperor Leo's having mandated the destruction of images throughout the Byzantine Empire) came in the Council of Nicaea (A.D. 787). This Council declared that images might lawfully be displayed in churches because they called up memories of their archetypes and so aroused contemplation of God and his gracious condescension to human estate, his love, his providence, and his mercy. The Council distinguished between true worship (belonging to God alone) and veneration or reverence which might properly be accorded images. The honor paid to an image, it was argued, is in reality directed to its archetype.

In the later Middle Ages, evidence of confusion of

"signifier and signified" among uneducated persons especially led to a need for clarification and restatement. St. Bernard of Clairvaux, fearful lest the veneration of images might lead to idolatry among his fellow Cistercians, wrote to William of St. Thierry in 1124 to urge their removal from Cistercian houses. The defense of images in the 13th cent. by St. Thomas Aquinas rests on the Pauline relation of "things seen" to the "unseen things of God" (Rom. 1:20). (His argument is paralleled in principle by that of St. Bonaventure in his *De Reductione Artium ad Theologiam.*) The principle of reference for understanding is crucial to such an argument:

> We must say that no reverence is shown to Christ's image, as a thing — for instance, carved or painted wood: because reverence is not due save to a rational creature. It follows, therefore, that reverence should be shown to it, in so far only as it is an image. Consequently the same reverence should be shown to Christ's image as to Christ Himself. Since, therefore, Christ is adored with adoration of *latria,* it follows that his image should be adored with the adoration of *latria.* (*Summa Theol.* 3.25; cf. 2.2.84; 1.1.1.9)

Latria —full worship of God — is here distinguished from *idōlolatria* —worship of something in place of God — but also from *dulia* —"service," or the honor and respect which may legitimately be paid to the saints. (Mary the mother of Jesus is, in later Catholic theology, accorded *hyperdulia,* extreme honor or veneration). Aquinas defines *dulia* as the adoration of recognized saints through images which reflect the perfection of the gift of grace. This hallmark distinction was, for Aquinas himself at least, pertinent to a differentiation between iconolatry and actual idolatry.

By the 14th and 15th cents in England the veneration of images had become an issue again, largely because of concern that intellectual distinctions of this sort were lost on the vulgar imagination of simple piety. On the one side were contemporaries of Chaucer like Wyclif, Purvey, and the poet Deschamps, the latter of whom proposed in one of his *ballades* that no graven images should be allowed in the churches (save only the Crucifix and the Virgin), "for fear of idolatry" (*Oeuvres,* 8.201). The unknown author of the influential ME *Dives and Pauper* sees abuses as partly the fault of the institutionalized language of worship itself, in which the sign may seem to be addressed as if it were the thing itself:

> This blyndeth much peple in their redyng [understanding]. For they meane [assume] that all the prayers that Holy church maketh to the Cross, that she maketh them to the tre that Christ died on, or else to the cross in the church, as in that anthem, *O crux splendidor.* And so for lewdness [vulgar misunderstanding] they be deceived, and worship creatures as God hymself. (1.4)

For the Franciscan Matthew Paris (ca. 1370) such confusion is of utmost seriousness, in that it threatens to undermine orthodox understanding of the sacraments, even that of the Body of Christ, the Eucharist (*Opera,* 2.53). Yet few medieval writers oppose images altogether; their purpose is rather to inculcate in the actual practice of worshipers a proper referential understanding. The author of *Dives and Pauper* thus goes on in his second chapter to urge contemplation of the Crucifix as a means of identification with the Passion of Christ, even while cautioning, "kneel if thou wilt before the ymage, but not to the ymage," and "make thy prayere before the ymage, but not to the ymage. For it seeth thee not, heareth thee not, understandith thee not. . . ." To pray or kneel *to* an image, he says, amounts to "ydolatry." But images have always been permitted as aids to devotion because (1) they stire up "mannys mynde to thynke on cristes incarnacion" as also his virtuous life and that of the apostles and other saints; (2) they function to "styre mannys affection and his herte to deuocion" because visual representation is often a more powerful stimulus than aural; and (3) they are a "token & a boke to the leude peple," the illiterate masses, who by this means may "rede in ymagery & painture" what educated persons "rede in the boke" (1.1). A similar argument is found in Walter Hilton's *Ladder of Perfection.* The approach is still basic to John Mirk's defense of images against the iconoclasm of the later Lollards: "just as a person may do worschip to the kyngis sele, not for loue of the sele, but for reuerence of þe man þat owet hit," so might the worshiper reverence the "roode" or Cross as the seal of the King of Heaven (*Festial,* 41.171). Attacks by the Lollards and their sympathizers, however, in tracts and in broadside poems, continued to plague both plastic and literary representation of Gospel personages and narratives. Particularly offensive to them was any embellishment of biblical elements with what they construed to be spurious iconography. One poem expresses its objections to dramatic representation of the Passion in which the cross has become a "tree of life":

> First þai gabben on god þat all men may se,
> When þai hangen him on hegh on a grene tre,
> With leues & with blossemes þat bright are of ble,
> þat was neuer goddes son by my leute. (R. H. Robbins, *Historical Poems of the XIVth and XVth Centuries,* 163)

It seems clear that this sort of objection was instrumental in obtaining curtailment of the Corpus Christi plays by early in the 16th cent. One surviving saints' play, the Digby *Conversion of St. Paul* (1502), includes many explicit assurances by the narrator (*Poeta*) that every element of the play is biblically derived:

> . . . we may, under your correccion,
> [represent] the conuersion of Seynt Paule, as the
>   Bible gif experiens.
> Whoso list to rede the booke *Actum Apostolorum,*
> Ther shall he have the very noticion. (10-12; cf.
> 158-60, 350-52, 653)

This play illustrates the pressure of iconoclasm being felt before and after the Reformation, even in what would become Counter-Reformation circles. The Council of Trent proscribed a substantial body of medieval iconography, and spartan disaffection for gothic extravagance is at least as common among Roman Catholics of the 17th cent. as among the adherents of high Anglicanism such as Bishops Lancelot Andrews and Jeremy Taylor, and far more so than among the circle of Archbishop Laud.

Calvin, who believed that following the Reformation the unlettered would soon learn to read, viewed images in churches in a generally hostile light; he calls them "idols," and though recognizing that what makes for idolatry is not the image but its use, he finds everywhere that "papist" practice is in contravention of the Second Commandment. Part of the problem is human depravity itself: "we may infer [from Scripture]," he writes, "that the human mind is, so to speak, a perpetual forger of idols" (*Inst.* 1.11.8). Far from guiding the mind from tangible, physical reality to the spiritual reality it signifies, a kind of crass sensuality takes over:

> what are the pictures or statues to which they append the names of saints, but exhibitions of the most shameless luxury or obscenity? . . . indeed, brothels exhibit their inmates more chastely and modestly dressed than churches do images intended to represent virgins . . . [and] martyrs. (1.11.7)

So at their least offensive, he argues, the "books of unlettered folk" display bad pedagogy. Taking up the Thomist distinction *dulia / latria,* he maintains that in logic and in practice it dissolves (1.11.11). Yet Calvin does not go so far as to ban artistic representation altogether:

> I am not, however, so superstitious as to think that all visible representations of every kind are unlawful. But as sculpture and painting are gifts of God, what I insist for is, that both shall be used purely and lawfully, — that gifts which the Lord has bestowed upon us, for his glory and our good, shall not be preposterously abused, nay, shall not be perverted to our destruction. We think it unlawful to give a visible shape to God, because God himself has forbidden it, and because it cannot be done without, in some degree, tarnishing his glory. . . . The only things, therefore, which ought to be painted or sculptured, are things which can be presented to the eye; the majesty of God, which is far beyond the reach of any eye, must not be dishonored by unbecoming representations. Visible representations are of two classes — viz. historical, which give a representation of events, and pictorial, which merely exhibit bodily shapes and figures. The former are of some use for instruction or admonition. The latter, as far as I can see, are only fitted for amusement. And yet it is certain, that the latter are almost the only kind which have hitherto been exhibited in churches. (*Inst.* 1.11.12)

The emphasis on history — by which Calvin means biblical history — tends to favor those portions of the Bible most vividly narrative, but since representation of God is proscribed, the events of the Passion and Resurrection are not to be included. The effect of these constraints is to validate OT narrative in particular for representation. With Calvin's correlative emphasis on covenant history and typology, a radical new form of OT iconography arose among Protestants of Calvinist persuasion after the Reformation. Luther, similarly, had stopped short of total iconoclasm, but permitted more of the traditional iconography than Calvin — including the Crucifix. He was more chastening, also, of iconoclasm and actually encouraged church walls to be painted with biblical narrative. (He also urged that wealthy householders do the same in their houses.)

It is Calvin's legacy, however, which particularly affected English arts and letters. The controversy between William Tyndale and St. Thomas More involves a recapitulation of Calvin against Aquinas: Tyndale champions what he takes to be the exemplary restraint of the early Church (*An Answer to Sir Thomas More's Dialogue* [1531], 56-57, 64, 80) against More's reiteration of Aquinas that the biblical prohibition against graven images does not intend destruction of images but only their proper use (*Dialogue concerning Tyndale,* 20, 60-63, 163-64). Latimer took Tyndale's side in 1536, attempting to persuade Convocation to abolish images from English churches. Article 6 of the Convocation nevertheless hedges, prohibiting the idolatrous worship of images but allowing their correct use "as laymen's books to remind us of heavenly things." Archbishop Cranmer's *Bishops' Book* allowed, against his own profound misgivings, the provision of images for instruction as well as provocation to faith and virtue:

> The image of our Saviour, as an open book, hangeth on the cross in the rood, or is painted in cloths, walls or windows, to the intent that beside the examples of virtues which we may learn at Christ, we may be also many ways provoked to remember his painful and cruel passion, and also to consider ourselves, when we behold the said image, and to condemn and abhor our sin, which was the cause of his so cruel death, and thereby to profess that we will no more sin. (*Miscellaneous Writings,* 101)

Despite the secularizing (or regalizing) of iconography under Elizabeth I and partial restoration of medieval tradition under Archbishop Laud, iconoclasm was to return in force in the 17th cent. With the Puritans a yet stricter Calvinism pertained and, in addition to the systematic destruction of images during the reign of Edward VI (d. 1553), the Long Parliament (Jan. 1641) sent out an order "to demolish and remove out of churches and chapels all images, altars, or tables turned altarwise, crucifixes, superstitious pictures, and other monuments and relics of idolatry," including "all images of the Virgin Mary" (*Journal of the House of Commons,* 2.279). The *Autobiography* of the Puritan spiritual writer Richard

Baxter describes how these orders were carried out despite the spirited attempt of "poor journeymen and servants . . . to defend the crucifix and the church images" (ed. J. Thomas, 38). Iconoclasm became a crusade for orthodoxy. John Milton wrote:

> He that will clothe the gospel now, intimates plainly that the gospel is naked, uncomely, that I may not say reproachful. Do not, ye church maskers, while Christ is clothing upon our barrenness with his righteous garment to make us acceptable in his Father's sight; do not, as ye do, cover and hide his righteous verity with the polluted clothing of your ceremonies, to make it seem more decent in your eyes. (*Reason of Church Government*, 2.2)

Milton here silently incorporates a biblical trope familiar to his readers: "all our righteousnesses are as filthy rags" (Isa. 64:6), his point being that God's Word alone is perfect, and the accretions of human invention, even religiously prompted invention, are a blasphemous offense (cf. Rev. 22:18).

When such an attitude was applied to the arts more generally, of course, it had the effect of undermining the whole system of medieval and Renaissance iconography (and its attendant or implied allegories). Oliver Cromwell is reported by Horace Walpole *(Anecdotes of Painting in England)* to have imposed consistent strictures on the artist commissioned to paint his portrait, Sir Peter Lely: "Mr. Lely, I desire you would use all your skill to paint my picture truly like me, and not flatter me at all; but remark all these roughnesses, pimples, and warts, and everything as you see me, otherwise I never will pay a farthing for it." In this way, iconoclasm is connected to Enlightenment rationalism and ultimately the growth of "realism" in art generally. That the result might not be a victory over idolatry, but merely a shift from graven to grave images is suggested by Thoreau in his encomium on an American abolitionist hero. In a time when too many Christians were hypocritical about slavery, John Brown stood out: "The curse is the worship of idols . . . and the New Englander is just as much an idolator as the Hindoo. John Brown was an exception, for he did not set up even a political graven image between him and his God" ("A Plea for Captain John Brown").

A. H. Clough saw the Second Commandment rewritten by Victorian imperialism to read "No graven images should be / Worshipped except the currency" ("The New Decalogue"). If Matthew Arnold's equation of iconoclasm with Puritanism *(Culture and Anarchy*, 129-64) is not quite historically adequate, it is undeniable that the Puritans played a large role in characterizing English response to the Second Commandment, even among writers who lived their life in reaction to it. Arnold himself has evidently shaped the modern tradition, however. In the play *Moses* (1924) by Lawrence Langner the conflict between Moses and Miriam over graven images is essentially a conflict between law and beauty. Adher-

ence to the commandment is, ironically enough, reduced to "philistinism."

See also IMAGO DEI; TEN COMMANDMENTS.

Bibliography. Baynes, N. H. "The Icons before Iconoclasm." *HTR* 44 (1951), 93-106; Bevan, E. *Holy Images* (1940); Davies, H. *Worship and Theology in England from Cranmer to Hooker: 1534-1603* (1970); Jeffrey, D. L. "Franciscan Spirituality and the Rise of English Drama." *Mosaic* 8 (1975), 17-46; Kitzinger, E. "The Cult of Images in the Age before Iconoclasm." *Dumbarton Oaks Papers* 8 (1954), 83-150; Ladner, G. B. *Ad Imagem Dei* (1965); "The Concept of the Image in the Greek Fathers and the Byzantine Iconoclastic Controversy." *Dumbarton Oaks Papers* 7 (1953), 1-34; Phillips, J. *The Reformation of Images: Destruction of Art in England, 1535-1660* (1973); Seznec, J. *Survival of the Pagan Gods* (1940; trans. 1953); Stamm, J. J., and M. E. Andrew. *The Ten Commandments in Recent Research* (1969); Thomson, J. A. F. *The Later Lollards* (1965); Van der Leeuw, G. *Sacred and Profane Beauty* (1963). DAVID L. JEFFREY
JOHN SANDYS-WUNSCH

GRAVES WERE OPENED *See* RESURRECTION.

GREAT COMMANDMENT The Great Commandment, or "Summary of the Law," as it is sometimes referred to in Western Christian liturgies, is found in the renewal document of the Torah, Deut. 6:4-5. It reads: "Hear, O Israel: the LORD our God is one LORD; and thou shalt love the LORD thy God with all thine heart, and with all thy soul, and with all thy might." The *Shema*, as it is called in Jewish liturgy, is above all a call of the chosen to obedience: *shama* conveys the sense of the imperative "obey" (cf. Num. 27:20; Josh. 1:17; 1 Kings 2:42); hence the call to "hear" this commandment and obey it implies obedience to the whole of the Law. Recited each morning and evening as a call to prayer, on a pattern ascribed to the angels themselves (Tan. Ber. 4.144-45; Liqqutim 4.70a-70b; Bera. 5a), the *Shema* is uttered also on joyous occasions. Talmudic midrashic sources regard it rather than the Ten Commandments as containing the substance of the entire Torah (e.g., Bera. 1.3c).

In the NT, when Jesus is asked "which is the greatest commandment in the law?" he quotes the Deuteronomy passage, intensifying the last phrase by adding "with all thy *mind,*" and linking the *Shema* to a "second" commandment in Lev. 19:18: "And the second is like unto it, Thou shalt love thy neighbor as thyself. On these two commandments hang all the law and the prophets" (Matt. 22:36-40; Mark 12:28-34; cf. Luke 10:25-37). The Great Commandment thus becomes foundational to Christian ethical life since, according to St. Augustine, it is clearly a summary of both law and prophets as well as of Christian wisdom *(De sermone Domini in Monte,* 2.22.74-75; cf. *De consensu Evangelistarum,* 2.73.141-42). St. Thomas Aquinas refers to this "Law of Love" as the basis of "perfection in the Christian life," observing in a famous passage that "Christian perfection lies directly and essentially in charity, primarily in the love of God, secondarily in the love of our neighbour." He continues: "No measure is demanded in our loving, the reason being that 'the end of the commandment is charity'" (1 Tim. 1:5), so that "while nobody in this life may fully achieve this perfection" it is perfectly appropriate to our life's proper goal that the command should be given and obeyed (*Summa Theol.* 2a-2ae.184.3). In this vein Richard Rolle speaks of obedience to the Great Commandment as a willed motion of the heart toward God ("a wilful stiryng of owre thoght intil God"), so that it accepts nothing which opposes the love of Jesus Christ ("The Commandment").

The Ten Commandments themselves were often divided on the pattern of the twofold commandment of love, so that the first three were said to pertain to the love of God, the balance to the love of one's neighbors (e.g., Wyclif, *De Decem Precepta*). The Lollard Knight, Sir John Clanvowe, says in his devotional treatise *The Two Ways* that the Great Commandment thus simplifies one's approach to the Ten: "Sithen þat we mown with the lovyng of God and of oure neighebour keepen all the Commaundementȝ of god, we aughten not þanne hoolde it heuy for to keepen his hestes ne we shulden not grucchen to keepen hem on þat wise" (670-74). To Chaucer's Parson, similarly, "soothly the lawe of God is the love of God" (*The Parson's Tale*, 10.127) and "the love of God principal, and lovyng of his neighebor as hymself" is the "remedie agayns this foule synne of Envye" (10.514-30), but also intrinsic to the remedy, he adds, for each of the other Seven Deadly Sins. It is this fact which makes the poor Parson's brother the Plowman an ideal of the perfect Christian (*General Prologue*, 1.529-38).

The Great Commandment is a familiar element in Catholic, Anglican, and Calvinist catechisms but became less prominent in literary allusion after the Reformation. In the 19th cent. the second precept tended to predominate in theological and philosophical reflection and, where present, the "first and great" commandment was often subsumed under duties to one's "higher self," so that, for Carlyle, the personalized first commandment assumes its importance in terms of the second ("Characteristics"). During his debate over vocation in *A Portrait of the Artist as a Young Man*, Joyce has Stephen Dedalus reflect that it would be for him "Idle and embittering, finally, to argue, against his own dispassionate certitude, that the commandment of love bade us not to love our neighbour as ourselves with the same amount and intensity of love but to love him as ourselves with the same kind of love" (chap. 4).

See also SHEMA; TEN COMMANDMENTS.

Bibliography. Craigie, P. C. *The Book of Deuteronomy* (1976); France, R. T. *Jesus and the Old Testament* (1971); Jeffrey, D. L. *The Law of Love: English Spirituality in the Age of Wyclif* (1988).   PETER CRAIGIE

GREATER LOVE HATH NO MAN   Jesus said, "Greater love hath no man than this, that a man lay down his life for his friends" (John 15:13).

See also CHARITY, CUPIDITY.

GREEN PASTURES   "He maketh me to lie down in green pastures" (Ps. 23:2) is one of the best-known pastoral images of God's provident care for his people. As such it is often used ironically, as in Shakespeare's *Henry 5*, when at the reporting of Falstaff's death the tavern hostess, who would believe him gathered into "Arthur's bosom," says of his last words that "'a babbled of green fields" (2.3.17). In Coleridge's *The Wanderings of Cain* the ghost of Abel cries out to Cain in bitterness that he has been bereft of the delights of feeding his "flocks in green pastures by the side of quiet rivers." In an incidental allusion to the Psalm John Galsworthy describes the habitat of the Forsythes as "green pastures" (*In Chancery*, 3.10). Menken, in similar fashion, argues that a college degree "lifts [a young person] over a definite fence, and maketh him to lie down in greener pastures" (*A Menken Crestomathy*, 314). Marc Connelly's *The Green Pastures* (1929) is a slapstick comedy based on Roark Bradford's stories of African-American interpretation of biblical lore.

GROVES   *See HORTUS CONCLUSUS.*

H

HADES *See* HELL.

HAGAR Hagar was the handmaiden of Sarah (Gen. 16–17; 21) who, when Sarah proved unable to bear children for her husband Abraham, was presented to him in order that Sarah might have a child by a surrogate. The resulting male child was named Ishmael. Some years afterward came an extraordinary promise to Abraham, the beginning of the covenant, whereby Abraham was promised an heir, through Sarah, in his old age. After Sarah's son Isaac was born, rivalry between the two women grew so intense that Abraham was persuaded to exile Hagar and Ishmael into the desert. The Genesis story is concerned with God's preservation of Hagar and her offspring, while making it clear that his covenantal blessing resided with the second son, the offspring of Sarah.

In Scripture, Hagar's descendants (Gen. 25:12-17; 1 Chron. 5:10; 19-22) are said to go a separate way; ultimately the "Hagarenes" are, with the "Ishmaelites," enemies of Israel (Ps. 83:6). The midrash on Genesis (which makes Hagar "Pharaoh's daughter" [1.380]) identifies her as "the one who had sat by the well and besought Him who is the life of all worlds, saying 'Look upon my misery'" (2.537; cf. the NT account of the Samaritan woman by the well [John 4:6-13]).

Christian typological reading of the story begins in Gal. 4:22-27. Here St. Paul describes the Genesis account as *allēgoria,* which he reads as follows: "for these are the two covenants; the one from the mount Sinai, which gendereth to bondage, which is Agar. For this Agar is mount Sinai in Arabia, and answereth to Jerusalem which now is, and is in bondage with her children. But Jerusalem which is above is free, which is the mother of us all" (24b-26). In early and medieval patristic exegesis this distinction modeled the relationship not only of the two covenants of law and grace, but also of the Old and New Testaments, and of Ecclesia's ascendency over Synagoga (e.g., the Portal carvings at Chartres). St. Augustine describes the divided course of human spiritual history by placing Hagar's story immediately after that of Cain, calling Hagar the "image of an image," which prefigures another tradition or "city," that of Sarah and Isaac, after which the prefigurement can, as a shadow, pass away as the full light appears.

> In the earthly city (symbolized by Hagar) . . . we find two things — its own obvious presence, and its symbolic presentation of the heavenly city. New citizens are begotten to the earthly city by nature vitiated by sin, but to the heavenly city by grace freeing nature from sin; whence the former are called "vessels of wrath," the latter "vessels of mercy." (*De civ. Dei* 15.2)

This passage was later to become indicative for medieval exegetical theory, teaching the distinction between the literal, or historical, level of a text, and its hidden relationship to the text of the New Covenant, the spiritual meaning. Even so strict an advocate of the primacy of historical sense as Wyclif follows Aquinas in using this passage as the basis for teaching the "inherent gospel principle" of spiritual understanding, which in Scripture is found to have four senses: (1) historical; (2) allegorical; (3) tropological; (4) anagogical, all of which receive an elaborate exegesis. For Wyclif, the central idea of Scripture is that Abraham's children, through Sarah, being spiritual and obedient through faith, are God's people and true pilgrims, while Hagar's offspring are carnal by nature and mere exiles (*Sermons*, 2.33-36). In the 17th cent., Matthew Poole (*Annotations upon the Holy Bible*) identifies Hagar still more pejoratively with spiritual bondage to the Law.

In literary characterization within the Christian tradition of the Middle Ages and the Renaissance, Hagar figures only indirectly, usually as an image of the outcast and rebel. In Shakespeare's *Merchant of Venice* ("What says that fool of Hagar's offspring, ha?" [2.5.44]), the perspective is "old law" and the allusion is therefore culturally reversed, to a Gentile. Milton's Satan implies, as he commences his temptation of Christ, that the latter's desert condition is like that of Hagar and Ishmael (*Paradise Regained*, 2.308). In an essay of Daniel Defoe in *The Review* (no. 3, Sept. 15, 1711), he develops the theme of Hagar's prayer, "give me not poverty, lest I steal," to make the point that economic "distress removes from the soul . . . all obligations moral or religious." *Moll Flanders, Roxanna,* and *Captain Jack* among his outcast protagonists all claim Hagar's predicament and excuse. But even with inversions, the covenantal connection remains: Coleridge's Zapolya will comfort herself and her child, saying, "Thou art no Hagar's offspring: thou art the rightful heir to an appointed king" (*Zapolya*, 1.1.439), appealing in her case to the Pauline identification. Blake anticipates modern feeling, however, and puts Hagar and Ishmael back with Abraham, Sarah, and Isaac in his *The Last Judgement*.

In the modern period Hagar herself figures more directly in English literature. Aside from her use in incidental allusion, she becomes heroine to a spate of quasi-historical fictions written in America during the 19th and 20th cent., which for the most part concern either the ironies of divine judgment or the romance of rejection. *Hagar,* by Pearl Rivers (Mrs. Elizabeth Poitrevant), *Hagar in the Wilderness* by Nathaniel Parker Willis, and *Hagar's Farewell* by Augusta Moore are exemplary of the wide appeal of the outcast handmaiden in the United States during the 1920s and 1930s.

The Stone Angel (1964), a novel by Canadian author Margaret Laurence, takes the modern tradition a step further. Here, the heroine is called Hagar and her husband Bram, but the novel seeks to explore the psychology of the Pauline exegesis from the outcast side, in a characterization of the rebellious spirit facing death, utterly defiant of repentance.

See also ABRAHAM; ISHMAEL; SARAH.

Bibliography. de Lubac, H., *Exégèse médiévale* (1959), 1.373-83; Shute, J. *Sarah and Hagar.* Ed. E. Sparke (1649).

HAGGADAH   Heb. *haggadah* signifies originally "narration," specifically that of the story of the Exodus related by a father to his children on the first evening of Passover. In the context of its role in talmudic writings, specifically the authoritative tradition known as the Babylonian Talmud, it refers to "lore" or legends. The Babylonian talmudists applied a process of systematic exposition similar to that used for the Mishnah to Scripture itself, so that an almost formal analogy was constituted between *halakah* and *haggadah. Midrash haggadah* is then the interpretation of a biblical story, which may in practice consist of an amplification of that story. Most "legendary" amplification of scriptural narrative derives from the Babylonian Talmud, the principal source for many elements of commentary in the present dictionary. A. M. Klein's poem "Haggadah" is a Passover litany (*Collected Poems* [1974], 143-46).

See also HALAKAH.

Bibliography. Ginzberg, L., ed. *The Legends of the Jews.* 7 vols. (1909-38); Ginzberg, L. *Die Haggada bei den Kirchenvatern . . .* (1900); Heinemann, J., and S. Werses, eds. *Studies in Hebrew Narrative Art through the Ages* (1978); Neusner, J. *Invitation to the Talmud* (1973; 1984); Rappoport, A. S. *Myth and Legend of Ancient Israel.* 2 vols. (1966); Sandmel, S. "The Haggadah within Scripture." *JBL* 80 (1961), 105-22.

HALAKAH   The legal portion of talmudic and later Jewish literature (Heb. *halak,* "to follow"), as distinct from Haggadah (the narrative literature and its midrash), is especially associated with the "oral law," established traditions of interpretation of written Torah which were only gradually reduced to written form in the Mishnah (2nd cent. A.D.). The most eminent compilation was that of R. Akiba and his disciples; it forms the basis of the codification of the Mishnah by R. Judah Ha-Nasi. The Mishnah became, as a kind of philosophical law code, the primary text in the Jewish schools of both Palestine and Babylonia.

See also MIDRASH.

Bibliography. Danby, H., trans. *The Mishnah* (1933; rpt. 1991).

HAM (CHAM)   Ham was the third of Noah's sons and father of Canaan. When Noah fell asleep drunk and lay uncovered in his tent, Ham saw him in that condition and reported it to his two brothers. Shem and Japheth, averting their eyes and backing into the tent, covered their father with a garment. When Noah awoke, he reprimanded the voyeur severely, pronouncing a curse upon his progeny: "Cursed be Canaan; a servant of servants shall he be to his brethren" (Gen. 9:18-27).

Older talmudic sources relate Ham's punishment to immoral sexual behavior on the ark and make him the ancestor of the African peoples (e.g., Sanh. 108b; Ta'an. 1.64d). His immorality during the deluge was imitated, reportedly, by the dog and raven. This legendary elaboration of the biblical narrative is followed by Philo (*Quaestiones*, 2.49; the pseudepigraphal Book of Adam and Eve 3.11 and Evangel of Seth 40) and Origen. According to another tradition Ham committed sodomy (Sanh. 70a), while in yet another he is said to have castrated his father to prevent him from having more children (Tg. Yer. Gen. 9.24-25; Gen. Rab. 36.4-5, 7; Tan. Ber. 1.49; cf. Midr. Haserot 50). Canaan, Ham's son, said to be equally base in character (Philo, *De ebrietati*, 2, 7, 10; *Quaestiones*, 2, 65, 70, 77), was father of the Canaanites and ultimately the Philistines. Ham, like Nimrod, is occasionally linked with magic; in the Clementine *Recognitiones* (1.30; 4:28-29) he is said to be the first sorcerer, who tried to draw sparks from a fire with the aid of a demon and was burned up in the process. The crowd who observed this, instead of seeing the catastrophe as God's judgment, began to worship him as a living star, or, in the case of the Persians, as the celestial fire Zoroaster. Another of Ham's sons, Cush, was said to have fathered Nimrod, the giant who built the Tower of Babel (Gen. 10:6-9). In later Christian commentary, the genealogies are etymologized in such a way that Ham is seen as the father of the Egyptians. The voyeuristic sin of Ham is seen as having been amplified by his call to his brothers to participate in the ridicule. Ham, or "Cham" as his name is rendered in Latin texts, is made by commentaries from St. Augustine indistinguishable in culpability from his son Canaan, who is variously assigned a participatory role. Of Cham himself the judgment is made that instead of being a "son of wisdom" he became "father of sinners" (*Glossa Ordinaria* [PL 113.112]).

In the post-deluge epoch, "Cham" is made, by an etymological connection and in the light of his moral character, the representative of Cain's fallen people, or "Canes cynne," as the monstrous beings of *Beowulf* are called (107-14). This lineage extended, according to Sir John Mandeville, to "the great Chane," Ghengis Khan, who is made to descend from "Cham" via Nimrod, along with various monsters and "the Paynemes" (*Travels*, 25.263).

Sir Walter Raleigh, in *The History of the World*, argues that Egyptian knowledge of early human history descended orally from Noah via Ham and his sons. In Washington Irving's *History of New York* the author opines that America was discovered late because Noah had only three sons among whom to divide the earth, and that after Shem had gone to Asia, Japheth to Europe, and Ham to Africa, there was no one left to travel westward over the sea. In later literature the putative connection of Ham to Egypt, Ethiopia, and northeastern African peoples was used to justify Negro slavery and segregation. Whittier's "rough river boatmen" in his "Letter from a Missionary of the Methodist Episcopal South" are depicted as cursing blacks, imagining they were "fulfilling the word of prophecy, 'Cursed be Canaan.' " In the same vein, the slave trader

in Stephen Vincent Benét's *John Brown's Body* justifies his evil traffic:

> I got my sailing orders from the Lord.
> . . . It's down there [in the Bible], Mister,
> Down there in black and white — the sons of Ham —
> Bond-servants — sweat of their brows.

Thomas Nelson Page's Civil War novel *Marse Chan* (1887) has for its protagonist a young Virginia gentleman named Channing, who is called "Marse Chan" by his loyal black servant and boyhood playmate Sam, in a prototypical and romanticized slave-master relationship. Ham Fisher, a black carriage driver in the same novel, is rescued from burning by the father of "Marse Chan." Zora Neale Hurston's one-act play *The First One* (1927) deals with Noah's cursing Ham with blackness (ed. C. S. Johnson, *Ebony and Topaz: A Collectanea*, 53-57). In the "Lestrygonians" sequence of *Ulysses*, Bloom puns, "Ham and his descendents mustered and bred there," following it with a limerick beginning "there was a right royal old nigger. . . ." Samuel Beckett may have intended his character Ham to reflect the son of Noah; in *Endgame*, Ham refers to his father Nagg as his "accursed progenitor."

See also BABEL; CAIN; NOAH.

Bibliography. Peterson, T. V. "The Myth of Ham among White Antebellum Southerners." *DAI* 36 (1975), 6157A.

HAMAN   The wicked Haman was a vizier of the Persian Empire under Xerxes (Ahasuerus) and mortal enemy to Mordecai, cousin of Esther. His history is recorded in the book of Esther. Enraged that Mordecai, a devout Jew, would not bow down and reverence him, Haman plotted to achieve the destruction of the whole Jewish nation. Esther interceded with Ahasuerus, and Haman was himself hanged on the gallows he had prepared for Mordecai.

In Jewish legend Haman is an Iago-like figure, whose hostility toward the king's first consort Vashti precipitated her downfall (Abba Gorion 17; Esth. Rab. 1.16), even as he intended to eradicate Esther and her people. In Haman's lengthy iteration of charges against the Jews he gives a précis of their observance of the Torah, including its principal ritual laws and festal observances, at the conclusion of which God is said to remark: "You did well to enumerate the holidays of the Jews, yet you forgot two — Purim and Shushan-Purim — which Jews will henceforth celebrate to commence your downfall" (2 Targum 3:8; cf. Meg. 13b; 'Aggadat Esth. 30.34; Tg. Esth. 3.8-9).

Patristic commentary makes the first of Haman's sins his desire to be worshiped (Esth. 3:1-2; *Glossa Ordinaria* [PL 113.743]). The reversal of the plot and Haman's ultimate condemnation (7:8-10) is cited by the *Glossa* as an example of "the oppressor oppressed" or "tormentor tormented" (113.745), a reading accorded prominence in many literary treatments of the narrative.

In ME lyrics, where the Virgin Mary is often compared to Esther, Haman is a type of Satan, the serpent whose head is struck off by the "Second Eve" (e.g., R. Greene, *The Early English Carols*, no. 194). As one who was rightfully executed on a "tree" (gallows), he is occasionally contrasted with Christ, in a typological juxtaposition of two victories over evil:

Aman alsoo, the fende, oure foo,
   Thou hast hangyd vppon a tre;
Thus thou hast brought mankynd fro woo,
   Mater misericordie. (Greene, no. 210)

Several Renaissance plays *(Queen Esther and Proud Haman, Godly Queen Hester)* as well as the 19th-cent. *The Death of Haman* consider Haman's fate. A. M. Klein, in his "Five Characters," a poetic analysis of the book of Esther, invites a consideration of the ironic final elevation of the ambitious Haman to the gallows he intended for another, and in his "Song of Sweet Dishes":

Foul Haman swung from a gallows-tree!
May all such end in similar fashion.
Therefore in Israel, jubilee;
We munch our *haman-taschen.*

See also ESTHER; MORDECAI; TORMENT, TORMENTOR.

HANANIAH *See* SHADRACH, MESHACH, AND ABED-NEGO.

HAND TO THE PLOW In Luke 9:62 Jesus comments on the half-hearted commitment of those who say they would like to follow him after they have tended first to other duties: "No man, having put his hand to the plow, and looking back, is fit for the kingdom of God." The passage is widely referred by Christian commentators both to conversion and to spiritual vocation (e.g., St. Jerome, *Ep.* 22.1; 71.1; 118.4; St. Augustine, *Sermo,* 50.3).

Later Protestant commentary is reflected in Matthew Poole's *Annotations* (1635), which observes that the point of the figure is to compare a minister of the word or one who has a special calling to the

Plough-man [who] is obliged to look forward to his Work, or he will never draw his furrows either strait enough, or of a just depth; so must a Minister of the Gospel, if he be once called out of secular imployments to the service of God in the Ministry, he is bound to mind and attend that; that is enough, to take up the whole Man.

Walter Scott, in *Old Mortality,* has this connection in mind in his characterization of the theological polity of the Covenanters: "When I put my hand to the plough, I entered into a covenant with my worldly affections that I should not look back on things I left behind me" (chap. 6). In Sinclair Lewis's *Dodsworth,* the titular character is lectured: "I tell you Dodsworth, to me work is a religion. 'Turn not thy hand from the plough.' Do big things!" (chap. 3). In Hardy's *Tess of the D'Urbervilles,* Alec jokes about abandoning his preaching to court Tess again: "I believe that if the bachelor-apostle, whose deputy I

thought I was, had been tempted by such a pretty face, he would have let go the plough for her sake as I do" — apparently associating the phrase with St. Paul rather than Jesus. The injunction is central to C. H. Spurgeon's popular *John Ploughman's Talk,* and maintains its connection to the idea of religious or spiritual vocation also in Shaw's *St. Joan,* where Joan asks that a message be taken to the king: "Tell him that it is not God's will that he should take his hand from the plough" (5.60).

See also PLOWMAN.

HANDMAID In ancient Hebrew culture, female slaves were of two types: the *shiphah* was perhaps originally an indentured but sexually untouched girl (1 Sam. 28:21-22; 2 Sam. 14:6-19), corresponding to Gk. *doulē* (Luke 1:38); the *'amah* was either a concubine or the wife of a slave (1 Sam. 25:24-41). Heb. *ben-'amah* ("the son of thy handmaid") is a term of humility spoken by a man (e.g., Pss. 86:16; 116:16). In Luke 1:38, 48, the Virgin Mary speaks of herself as *doulē* — a conventional term signifying humility or obeisance before God. In the patriarchal period it was customary for an infertile wife, after several years of barrenness, to present her handmaid to her husband so that she might have a child by her; notable OT examples include the narratives of Sarah, Hagar, and Abraham (Gen. 16:1-4) and Rachel, Leah, Bilhah, Zilpah, and Jacob (Gen. 30:1-13).

The Virgin's expression of submission to the divine will in the Incarnation of Jesus is the most important source of the term in literature, occurring mainly in its strict NT context in numerous ME lyrics, narratives of the life of the Virgin, and Corpus Christi plays. Male as well as female medieval spiritual writers use the term of themselves in relation to God (e.g., Richard Rolle, *Stimulis Amoris*). In the 19th cent. this conventional motif is still reflected in literature and in art (e.g., D. G. Rossetti's Annunciation painting *Ecce Ancilla Domini* [Vg Luke 1:38]). More recently, reflecting contemporary feminist response to the biblical "handmaid" motif, Margaret Atwood's dystopian novel *The Handmaid's Tale* (1985) imagines a future America in which fundamentalists have erected a society based upon rigid implementation of OT law and social custom. Focusing on the life of Ofred, a literal handmaid, the *Tale* is an anti-jeremiad directed against the myth of America as the Promised Land.

See also HAGAR; *MAGNIFICAT.*

HANDWRITING ON THE WALL The handwriting (or hand writing) on the wall (Dan. 5:5) is one of five incidents in the narrative section (chaps. 1–6) of Daniel in which the power of God is proved to an unbelieving king. Of these incidents — Nebuchadnezzar's dream, the men in the furnace, Nebuchadnezzar's metamorphosis, Belshazzar's feast, Daniel in the lions' den — this is the only one in which the unbeliever is destroyed rather than reproved, because only Belshazzar practices idolatry and desecrates the temple vessels (Dan. 5:3-4).

The inscription in Dan. 5:25, *mene', mene', teqel, upharsin* (KJV, MT; cf. LXX, Vg, Josephus, *Ant.* 10.11.3 *mane, thekel/tekel, phares*), describes the diminishing worthiness of the Babylonian kings from Nebuchadnezzar by means of a monetary metaphor. Debates too involved to be recounted here have arisen over the meaning of the inscription and the question of why in the MT (and hence in the KJV) it differs from the interpretation given by Daniel *(mene, tekel, peres)* in Dan. 5:26-28. The inscription has been deciphered to read, "a mina, a mina, a shekel, and half-minas (or half-shekels)." The saying may be proverbial, and answer the riddling question, "What is the worth of the kings of Babylon?" *Mene* may be repeated rhetorically, as in "Babylon is fallen, is fallen" (Isa. 21:9); or perhaps the first Aram. *mn'* here means *menah*, "he was weighed." The MT for Dan. 5:26-28 may represent the inscription differently from Dan. 5:25 because Daniel, in interpreting the inscription, altered it after the practice of eisegesis, a midrashic adaptive interpretation of texts, according to O. Eissfeldt, "Die Mene-Tekel Inschrift und ihre Deutung," *ZAW* 63 (1951), 105-14. Daniel's interpretation of the inscription is built on a paronomastic reworking of the Aram. *mene', teqel,* and *upharsin*: "MENE: God hath numbered *[menah]* thy kingdom and finished it. TEKEL: Thou art weighed *[teqiltah]* in the balances, and art found wanting. PERES: Thy kingdom is divided *[perisat]*, and given to the Medes and Persians *[paras]*." (See *IDB* 3.348-49; *NCE* 9.650.)

St. Jerome's influential *Commentarius in Danielem* (PL 25.519-21) sees Belshazzar's idolatry and sacrilege as instances of pride; Dan. 5 foreshadows typologically the downfall of Antichrist and the subsequent reign of the saints. This view was adjusted only slightly in the later Middle Ages; e.g., Rupert of Deutz held that Belshazzar's punishment was a type of the destruction of Babylon the Great in Rev. 18:2-3 (*De Trinitate; In Danielem,* 9 [PL 167.1510]). To Rupert, the hand which did the writing was that of Christ, the right hand of God (col. 1509). To Protestant commentators, however, the hand itself was incidental — perhaps only the "appearance" of a hand (Calvin, *Commentaries on . . . Daniel,* trans. T. Myers [1852], 322), or possibly that of the angel Gabriel (Matthew Poole, *Synopsis Criticorum Aliorumque Sacrae Scripturae Interpretum* [1673], 3.1454).

If the story of Belshazzar's feast is excellent literary material, its earliest literary adapters were just as interested in its theological value as in its narrative strengths. The incomplete OE *Daniel* stops before Daniel interprets the handwriting, but it provides enough of Dan. 5 directly and through foreshadowing (675-94) to bring out a clear parallel between Belshazzar's feast and the sins of the Jews before the Captivity. This parallel suggests that the theme of *translatio imperii,* God's handing over imperial rule from a just to an unjust people (see W. Goez, *Trans-*

latio Imperii [1958]), may lie behind the poet's reworking of his source. Two 12th-cent. Latin Daniel plays (see K. Young in *Drama of the Medieval Church* [1933], 2.276-301) are noteworthy examples of the literary tradition already well established by the Middle Ages. ME *Cleanness* includes a full and vivid retelling of Dan. 5 as the last of three OT examples of sin which brought about God's angry retribution (1529-1804). Belshazzar's feast is one of Chaucer's Monk's illustrations of tragedy, but the moral the Monk draws from it reveals only his own spiritual blindness, since he sees the story simply as a warning that misfortune may strike anyone at any time (7.2239-46).

Interest in the narrative and dramatic aspects of Dan. 5 prompted the creation of verse dramas by Hannah More ("Belshazzar," in *Sacred Dramas* [1782]) and the Oxford historian Henry Hart Milman, whose *Belshazzar* recounts Babylon's last day before the Persian conquest. Perhaps seeking to outdo Milman, Robert Eyres Landor, in *The Impious Feast* (1828), set the beginning of his exotic poetic epic two days earlier.

Belshazzar appealed to the Byronic imagination: Byron retells Dan. 5 in "The Vision of Belshazzar," and in "To Belshazzar" he places himself at the feast, where he urges Belshazzar to reform even as he recognizes that Belshazzar is "unfit to govern, live, or die" (24). The fall of Napoleon prompted him to observe, in "Ode to Napoleon Buonaparte," that "weigh'd in the balance, hero dust / Is vile as vulgar clay" (109-10). Describing the destruction of the Suez city Ismael by Russian troops, Byron ironically compared the victory message of Catherine the Great's general Suvarov to the handwriting on the wall (*Don Juan,* 8.133-34).

Colloquially, "the handwriting on the wall" can refer simply to a warning of approaching (but not necessarily inevitable or divinely sent) disaster, and so it is often used in literature. Among the more original uses of the phrase are Milton's (*Paradise Lost,* 4.977-1015), where the Homeric golden scales in the heavens which Satan beholds after being chased from Eden by angels suggest not only that he is like Achilles, Hector, and Turnus, but that he is like Belshazzar. Swift's broadside, "The Run upon the Bankers," resurrects the economic metaphor in Dan. 5:26-28 and applies it to bankers who lend their banks into bankruptcy; at Judgment

> Other Hands the Scales shall hold,
> And They in Men and Angels Sight
> Produc'd with all their Bills and Gold.
> Weigh'd in the Balance, and found Light. (61-64)

The Romantic period brought further adaptation of the handwriting motif. Keats's castle builder entertains guests lavishly in his apartment, in which he keeps a mirror inscribed with the handwriting; thus, he is both Belshazzar and Daniel to himself ("The Castle Builder," 54). Shelley inverted the balance image so that vice, not virtue, was found wanting, in *Defence of Poetry:* "[the great poets' moral] errors have been weighed and found to have been dust in the balance" (*Shelley's Poetry and Prose,* eds. D. Reiman and S. Powers [1977], 506). The handwriting is the image of a past injury of crime in Dickens's *David Copperfield* and Hawthorne's *The Scarlet Letter.* In Dickens, the scar from the hammer wound on Rosa Dartle's lips becomes as pronounced as the handwriting during an argument between Rosa and Steerforth, a harsh judge (chap. 20; see J. Vogel, *Allegory in Dickens* [1977], 179). In Hawthorne, Hester Prynne's offense is as mysterious to her neighbors as the handwriting (chap. 3). In *Moby-Dick* (chap. 119), Ishmael prophetically calls the fire in the *Pequod's* masts God's handwriting, whereas Ahab sees it only as a guiding light to the white whale. The narrator in Browning's "Too Late," 92-94, attributes a supernatural power to the dead woman who rejected him in life, and imagines his heart inscribed with "her mark, / *Tekel,* found wanting, set aside / Scorned!" (see L. Perrine, "Browning's 'Too Late'; A Reinterpretation," *VP* 7 [1969], 339-45).

The handwriting is a symbol of guilt in Emily Dickinson's "Belshazzar Had a Letter" (no. 1459). In Hardy's *Return of the Native* (1.6), the "small human hand, in the act of lifting pieces of fuel into the fire" with which Eustacia Vye signals Wildeve appears dismembered, "like that which troubled Belshazzar." The allusion adds to the larger symbolism which makes Egdon Heath an agent of fate.

Robert Louis Stevenson makes a poignant allusion to the handwriting in *The Strange Case of Dr. Jekyll and Mr. Hyde*; in Jekyll's letter to his friend Utterson, he recalls the discovery that he had, asleep, transformed unwillingly into Hyde. "This inexplicable incident, this reversal of my previous experience, seemed, like the Babylonian finger on the wall, to be spelling out the letters of my judgment." Lawrence's short story "Things" transmutes Emma Lazarus's poem at the base of the Statue of Liberty into both the handwriting and the first commandment in the American work ethic for a young American couple returning from years wasted gathering possessions abroad: "Erasmus, of course, ought to get a job. This was what was written on the wall, . . . the strange, vague threat that the Statue of Liberty had always held over them: 'Thou shalt get a job!' " (*Complete Short Stories* [1961], 850).

Bibliography. Bentzen, A. *Daniel.* 2nd ed. Handbuch zum Alten Testament, 1.19 (1952); Frost, S. B. "Mene, Mene, Tekel and Parsin." *IDB* 3.348-49; Lacocque, A. *The Book of Daniel.* Trans. D. Pellauer (1979); McNamara, M. "Mene-Tekel-Peres." *NCE* 9.650; Roston, M. *Biblical Drama in English* (1968). M. W. TWOMEY

HANNAH One of the two wives of Elkanah, Hannah devoutly visited the sanctuary at Shiloh annually with her husband to offer sacrifice. On one such occasion, distressed at her persistent barrenness and the scorn of Penin-

nah, Elkanah's other wife, she prayed for a son, whom she promised to dedicate to the Lord from his birth. Eli the priest, hearing her prayer and her vow, assured her of God's blessing. She conceived and gave birth to Samuel, then subsequently had five other children (1 Sam. 1:1-2:21).

Hannah is regarded in Jewish tradition as a prophetess (Tg. 1 Sam. 2:1-11). Her prayer is said in haggadic sources to have been a model for the 'Amidah, which ought to be uttered in a low voice, and some sources credit her with being the first to call God "the Lord of Hosts" (Shemuel 9.75; Ber. 13b). Because Eli, observing her lips moving but hearing no words, thought she was drunk (1 Sam. 1:12-15), some medieval Christian commentators, in the light of Acts 2:1-15, suggest that she was "praying in the Spirit" (e.g., Richard Rolle, "The Song of Hannah"). Her exultant song celebrating God's answer to her prayer, which has been translated and commented upon by both Jewish and Christian writers (Tg. 1 Sam. 2:1-11; Shemuel 4-6, 55-65; Batte Midrashot 4.6-9; Pseudo-Philo 51.3-8; Yelammedenu in Yalqut 2.80; St. Augustine, *De civ. Dei* 17.4), is in structure and content foundational to the *Magnificat* (Luke 1:46-55).

Augustine, observing that her name means "[His] grace," sees her actions and gratitude as an example of "true Christian religion, and the true city of God"; she is also an exemplary "pious mother" (*De civ. Dei* 17.4), and thus associated by later writers such as St. Bernard of Clairvaux with the Virgin Mary. For the *Glossa Ordinaria,* accordingly, she is a type of the true Church, "which is always sterile spiritually until redeemed by the grace of Christ." Hannah (or Anna, as she appears in Latin and medieval orthography) signifies grace while the other wife, Peninnah, signifies *synagoga,* which generated its fruits according to the Law (PL 113.539). Hannah rarely appears in English literature after the Middle Ages, though George Herbert cites her as an example of the ministration of the Spirit in the blessing of the priest (*A Priest to the Temple,* chap. 36, "The Parson's Blessing").

See also HOPE; *MAGNIFICAT;* SAMUEL.

HARAN *See* ABRAHAM; LOT.

THE HARLOT *See* WHORE OF BABYLON.

HARLOTRY *See* ADULTERY; AHOLAH AND AHOLIBAH.

HARP Among the principal biblical references to the harp are Ps. 57 and Ps. 137:2, in the latter of which the harp is symbolically hung on the willows by the captive Jews. David plays his harp before Saul in 1 Kings 16; it figures as an instrument of worship, particularly in the Psalms, both for songs of praise and of penitence (Pss. 149; 150; 71:22, etc.). The harp is an instrument of the music of heaven in St. John's apocalyptic vision (Rev. 5:8; 14:2; 15:2).

The *Midrash on Psalms* (trans. Braude) notes that David woke himself at midnight to play the harp: "when the sages of Israel heard him, they found his vigilant occupation with the Torah and praises exemplary," so that "it turned out that because of David all the children of Israel sat down and occupied themselves with the Torah" (1.305). The *Midrash* observes that the psaltery is often confused or equated with the harp (2.65). St. Augustine's distinction between the two instruments may have been suggested by Job 30:31 ("My harp is also turned to mourning"): in his reading, the psaltery represents Christ as Son of God and the harp the man Jesus in his suffering (PL 36.671-72). Augustine's further distinction between *psalterium* and *cithara* — the first the instrument of heavenly, the second of temporal good works — dominated the medieval exegetical history of the harp.

Throughout the Middle Ages the music of the harp was considered above all to be spiritual music and accorded power to overcome evil and to heal the mind, the usual reference being to David's calming of the *spiritus malus* of Saul (1 Kings 16:16-23); the *Glossa Ordinaria* (PL 113.555-56) comments on the sweetness of the harp of speech *(cithara locutionis)* whereby our tranquility, like Saul's, is restored. For St. Bruno the harp represents the humanity of Christ but also ordinary humanity; the tempering of one's tones to Christ's sweetness enables one to awake from spiritual torpor (PL 152.898). Pierre Bersuire (14th cent.) compares David to Orpheus and his harp to Christ, so that the harp becomes the *verba singula singulis,* both the poet's word and the Word Incarnate. This comparison undergirds a transformation of classical narrative by biblical tradition in the medieval poem *Sir Orfeo.*

An important figurative use of the harp (drawing on Pss. 22 and 57) connects it with the Crucifixion. The first seven verses of Ps. 57 were understood as the prayer of the Son as he awaits deliverance from the cross: appealing to his Father's mercy he expresses confidence that God will set him free. Verse 8 was seen to mark a change of speakers, with the Father now addressing the Son: "Awake up, my glory; awake, psaltery and harp," in reference to Christ's divine and human natures. As a text for the Easter liturgy this psalm celebrated the escape of Christ from the bonds of death. In the exegesis of Cassiodorus "the harp means the glorious Passion which with stretched sinews and counted bones [cf. Ps. 22:14, 17] sounded forth his bitter suffering as in a spiritual song" (PL 70.404).

Use of the crucifixion harp metaphor is largely confined to the medieval period. The cross in the OE *Dream of the Rood* says that it was wounded with arrows, echoing the *sagittae* of Ps. 57:4. Alcuin views the harp as the Passion of Christ and in his commentary on the Apocalypse (PL 100.1122) understands the "new song" harped by the redeemed to be their "imitation of the Passion of Christ in themselves, as the divine members are made one in concord." For St. Bernard of Clairvaux Christ on the cross is like the strings stretched over the wood of a harp, which, if we learn to play and sing to it, will move ourselves and others to a knowledge of our redemption (PL 184.655). St. Anthony of Padua, reflecting on Isa. 23:16, makes of the harp in this reference confession (*In Festo S. Stephani,* 3.757a); and Wyclif, treating Ps. 71:22, identifies it with "confessioun of mouth, and sorow of hert" as the theme of the penitential psalms (*English Works,* 340). A 12th-cent. Psalter depicts David as a harpist, with the Crucifixion simultaneously shown as musical prefiguration; a related illustration, ironically employed, is the figure crucified on a harp in Hieronymus Bosch's *Sicut Erat in Diebus Noe.* In medieval drama the emphasis on the stretching of Christ's body by the torturers and the boring of holes for the (peg) nails may have been initially suggested by the harp image. Reference to the crucifixion harp in ME often treats it as a commonplace, as in *Handlyng Synne* (4753-56), Lydgate's *The Virtues of the Mass* (121-24), and the *Orologium Sapientiae (Anglia,* 10.352).

An important 17th-cent. variation occurs in George Herbert's devotional poem "Easter." A possible case of secularization of the crucifixion harp image occurs in "The Two Sisters," an international ballad first recorded in the 17th cent., which describes the construction of a harp from the body of a girl drowned by her sister. When played by a minstrel, the harp reveals the murderess; when the instrument is shattered, the drowned girl springs back to life.

The aeolian harp, a favorite metaphor for poetic inspiration, has, by contrast, no scriptural warrant or history. Invented in the 17th cent. by Athanasius Kircher, it was an automatic harmony instrument which played itself when the wind swept over its strings. Christened *Aeolium instrumentum* (in honor of Aeolus, Greek god of the winds) by J. J. Hofmann in his encyclopedic *Lexicon universale,* the harp of Aeolus first appears in English literature in 1748, in James Thomson's *Castle of Indolence* (1.60-61). Thereafter it occurs frequently over the next seventy years, often as a symbol of poetic afflatus (e.g., Smart, *Jubilate Agno,* 10.29-33; Gray, *Progress of Poesy,* 1; Wordsworth, *The Prelude,* 1.94-99; Keats, *Endymion,* 2.866, and *Lamia,* 1.386-87; Shelley, *Prometheus Unbound,* 2.1.25-27; 4.186-88). The most powerful sustained use of the image, however, occurs in two poems by Coleridge, *The Eolian Harp* (1796) and *Dejection: An Ode* (1802), especially in the latter where the poet explores the loss of his "shaping Spirit of Imagination."

See also DAVID; MUSIC AND MUSICAL INSTRUMENTS.

Bibliography. Andersson, O. *The Bowed Harp* (1930); Bauer, V. H. *Das Antonian-Feuer in Kunst und Medizin* (1973); Brewster, P. G. *The Two Sisters* (1953); Brody, A. *The English Mummers and their Plays* (1970), esp. Appendix B, 137-44; Grigson, G. "The Harp of Aeolus." *In The Harp of Aeolus and Other Essays on Art, Literature and Nature* (1948), 24-46; Jeffrey, D. L. "Sir Orfeo's Harp and the Second Death of Eurydice." *Mosaic* 9 (1976), 45-60; Rondet, H. "Notes d'exégèse augustinienne: psalterium et cithara." *RSR* 46 (1958), 408-09; Steger, H. *Philologia Musica, Sprachlicher, Bild und Sache in Literarisch-musikalischen Leben dis Mittelalters: Lire, Harfe, Rotte, und Fidel* (1971).

DAVID C. FOWLER
JOHN SPENCER HILL

HARROWING OF HELL The harrowing of hell is the English expression for Christ's descent into Hades, a belief held by early Christians that between Jesus' death and resurrection, while his body lay sealed in the tomb, his spirit visited the world of the dead and brought the souls of the righteous into paradise. The idea is not found in the Bible but was associated with certain key biblical passages. Christian writers from the 2nd cent. interpreted various OT texts as referring prophetically to Christ's triumph over Sheol and its guardians: esp. Ps. 16:10 ("For thou wilt not leave my soul in hell; neither wilt thou suffer thine Holy One to see corruption") and Ps. 24:7-10 ("Lift up your heads, O ye gates; and be ye lifted up, ye everlasting doors; and the King of glory shall come in . . ."). These were reinforced by John 5:25, Eph. 4:8-10, and an enigmatic reference in 1 Pet. 3:18-22, which speaks of Christ, "put to death in the flesh, but quickened by the Spirit," having gone to preach "unto the spirits in prison; which sometime were disobedient, when once the longsuffering of God waited in the days of Noah, while the ark was a preparing. . . ." Although this text refers to "disobedient spirits," the early Christian descent motif stressed Christ's deliverance of those righteous OT saints who had to wait in Hades for the messianic atonement before being admitted into paradise.

While the motif was a commonplace among early Christian writers, a theological dispute developed concerning whether Christ thereby opened the door of salvation to souls who then acknowledged him (the interpretation favored by Alexandrian theologians such as St. Clement, St. Cyril, and Origen) or whether he drew forth only those whose righteous lives and prophetic faith had already saved them (the position favored by Augustine and the Latin Church generally). Although the phrase "he descended into hell" was added to the Apostles' Creed, Protestant theology has generally minimized the concept of the Descent.

The descent motif found its most important embodiment in Christian literature in the apocryphal Gospel of Nicodemus (5th cent., although the actual "harrowing" section probably dates from the 2nd cent.). The story of the descent is narrated by two sons of Simeon, who were raised from the dead after the Crucifixion. They tell how a bright light intruded into the darkness of hell, terrifying the evil spirits but rejoicing the righteous who had been imprisoned there; the Prince of Hell fears the advent of this new soul and blames Satan for having contrived Jesus' death. As the words of Ps. 24 thunder out — "Lift up your heads, O ye gates. . . ." — Christ breaks down the doors of hell, binds and tramples upon the foul spirits, and, taking Adam by the hand, conducts the saints to paradise. This text had an enormous influence on the art and literature of the Middle Ages. There were at least three prose translations in OE; it was subsequently translated into ME, both in prose (of which at least 9 MSS are known) and verse. A rendition of the whole story into ME occurs also in verse as one 1300-line section of the monumental poem *Cursor Mundi* (ca. 1300 [EETS o.s. 57, 59, 62, 63]).

In Byzantine art the descent motif provided a chief mode for representing the Resurrection: the scene, called the Anastasis, shows Christ reaching out to the crowd of OT saints while trampling the devil underfoot and planting the standard of the cross in hell. In Western art, from the 10th through the 16th cents., the theme is pervasive; Christ is shown storming or invading Hades, the entrance to which is commonly depicted as a monstrous yawning hell-mouth. The motif is prominent in Carolingian, Ottonian, Anglo-Saxon, and Anglo-Norman manuscript illumination as well as in works by Cranach the Elder, Dürer, Jac. Bellini, Donatello, Fra Angelico, and Tintoretto.

Perhaps because the theme lent itself to the distinctive integration of heroic Germanic ideals and Christian doctrine in Anglo-Saxon culture, the harrowing of hell was particularly prominent in OE literature ("harrowing" derives from OE *hergian,* "to harry or despoil"). The theme of the harrowing occurs in a number of OE homilies, notably the homily for Easter Sunday in the 10th-cent. Blickling collection, which emphasizes the triumphal aspect of Christ's invasion of hell and the dramatic responses of Adam and Eve. (Based on some linguistic parallels between that Blickling homily and the description of Beowulf's descent into Grendel's Mere, some critics have suggested that the *Beowulf* poet was deliberately constructing an analogy between that episode and Christ's harrowing of hell.) In OE poetry references to the harrowing appear in the Bestiary ("Panther," 55-64), "The Phoenix" (417-23), *Guthlac* (1074-77), and *Elene* (900-915), the latter embodying an interesting complaint by Satan that Christ has unfairly deprived him of guilty souls, an allusion to the theological controversy over who was saved at the descent. There are also several references to the harrowing in the Exeter book *Christ,* including the passage (derived from St. Gregory) on the six "leaps" of Christ, from the Incarnation to the Ascension, the fifth being the descent into hell (728-30). The two major poetic treatments of the theme in OE, however, are the second section of *Christ and Satan* and the poem in the Exeter book called "The Harrowing of Hell."

Part 2 of *Christ and Satan* opens with Christ's forceful entry into hell and Eve's repentance. After the elect are led apart from the damned, Christ recounts to the saints the story of the fall of man and of redemption through his own Incarnation and Passion. The poet then describes the Resurrection and Ascension and concludes this section of the poem with a description of the Last Judgment, which thus is seen as a completion or fulfillment of the action of the harrowing of hell. The Exeter "Harrowing" focuses almost entirely on two figures: Christ the triumphant, and John the Baptist, his herald in hell as he had been on earth.

The emergence of the harrowing as an element of liturgical drama began as early as the 11th cent. in the ritual of the *Elevatio crucis,* the taking of the consecrated host from the tabernacle or "sepulchre" just before or after Matins on Easter Sunday. Thus the *Elevatio* from the 11th-cent. breviary of St. Gall concludes with the verse, "This is the propitious day in which hell is plundered" *(Haec est alma dies in qua spoliatur avernus).* Of particular interest are a 14th-cent. version from the Church of St. John the Divine, Dublin, and a 14th-cent. Benedictine Ordinal of Barking Nunnery, a text which gives specific dramatic directions for the representation of the harrowing of hell.

Unlike other motifs of medieval liturgical drama, the development of the Latin dramatic form may have been preceded by its evolution in the vernacular. W. Hulme notes that "specimens of Harrowing plays have been preserved in all those European literatures in which any serious effort was made to develop a religious drama in the Middle Ages. . . . But in no other literature do we find the dramatic Harrowing of Hell so extensively and artistically described as in Middle-English" (EETS e.s. 100, lxvi-vii). It occurs in the Chester, Coventry, York, Wakefield, and Cornish cycles. The York play offers a highly inventive rendering, particularly in the heightening of the dramatic conflicts. The devils interact directly in dialogue with the OT saints, and Satan and Jesus enter into direct verbal confrontation. The second half of the play includes an extended debate over the justice of releasing the souls which had been bound over to Satan because of original sin.

Even older than these mystery plays, and apparently the earliest version of the descent motif in ME, is a dramatic poem called "The Harrowing of Hell," dating from the mid-13th cent. As in the York play, the poem is marked by a rather legalistic debate between Christ and Satan over the possession of human souls: Satan argues that the eating of the apple bound humankind over to him, but Christ replies that as the apple belonged to Christ and not Satan, whatever was won with the apple belongs to God! Following the debate Christ breaks down the doors of hell and rescues the OT saints who, led by Adam and Eve, welcome him joyfully.

Langland, near the conclusion of *Piers Plowman,* Passus B, tells the story of the Passion (seen as Christ's chivalrous combat, as a true knight, against man's enemies, Death and the Devil) and the harrowing of hell. Langland's version is noteworthy for combining the harrowing theme with another medieval legend, the story of

the "four daughters of God." Here the "daughters" debate the propriety of the harrowing: Justice and Truth at first disapprove of it, until Peace and Mercy show how Jesus was able to "stand bail" for sinful mankind and satisfy divine justice.

Briefer references to the harrowing of hell occur in other ME poetry, including the *Northern Passion* (1811-27), and in Chaucer's *Miller's Tale* (1.3512) and *Summoner's Tale* (3.2107). Other occurrences of the theme are found in the religious lyric poetry of the 13th through 15th cents. as in the well-known dialogue between Mary and Christ on the cross:

> Moder, merci, let me deye
> And adam out of helle beye. . . .
> Moder, I ne may no lengore dwelle,
> The time is comen I go to helle. (C. Brown, *English Lyrics of the XIIIth Century,* no. 49)

or the brief 14th-cent. lyric from the Bishop Sheppey collection:

> The uendus of helle beth sorwuel & mad,
> Whanne the kyng godus sone
> The strengthe of the deth hadde ouercome:
> Helle dore he brak with his fot,
> & out of pyne vs wreches he tok. (Brown, *Religious Lyrics of the XIVth Century,* no. 37)

A 15th-cent. Nativity carol alludes to the harrowing in terms of Jesus fetching his bride, the church, from hell — perhaps a deliberate Christianizing of the Orpheus theme:

> Be hys powste he his emprys
> Schal take fro helle at hys vprys,
> And saue mankende vp-on thys wys. Nowel, nowel
> Thus tellth vs the prophecys,
>   That he is kyng of heuen & helle. (Brown, *Religious Lyrics of the XVth Century,* no. 76)

Since the Reformation and the Council of Trent (which prohibited devout use of the Gospel of Nicodemus), the harrowing of hell ceased to be a major motif in art and literature. Brief allusions occur in Spenser *(Amoretti,* 68.3; *Faerie Queene,* 1.10.40) and Donne ("Resurrection, Imperfect" — which combines the harrowing with the alchemical conceit that Christ, like tincture of gold, transmuted to gold those who lay in the underworld), or, much later, in Keble's *The Christian Year* ("Wednesday before Easter," 5.9). One highly original use of the motif occurs in Blake's *Milton,* 1.10, where, in a complex and confusing allegory, Satan usurps the harrow of the Almighty and causes havoc in the universe; his daughter and coconspirator Leutha offers to atone and so Satan is forgiven, not judged, and Orc, the spirit of human liberty, who had been bound by Los or Time, is loosed.

In modern English literature perhaps the most direct allusion to the harrowing of hell appears in Charles Williams's novel *Descent into Hell* (1937). The commonly understood reference of the title is to damnation, particularly the spiritual descent of the self-deluded Lawrence Wentworth into the solipsistic hell of his own "Unreal City." But the title also refers to the redemptive acts of the saintly Peter Stanhope and his disciple Pauline Anstruther, who both reach down into the Unreal City to rescue souls from limbo — thus participating in Christ's archetypal harrowing of hell.

See also FOUR DAUGHTERS OF GOD; FREEDOM, BONDAGE; HELL; PURGATORY.

Bibliography. Cabaniss, J. "The Harrowing of Hell." *VigC* 7 (1953), 65-74; Crotty, G. "The Exeter *Harrowing of Hell:* A Re-Interpretation." *PMLA* 54 (1939), 349-58; Finnegan, R. E. *Christ and Satan/A Critical Edition* (1977); Hieatt, C. "The Harrowing of Mermedonia/Typological Patterns in the Old English 'Andreas.'" *NM* 77 (1976), 49-62; Hulme, W. "The Old English Gospel of Nicodemus." *MP* 1 (1903-04), 598-614; "The Old English Version of the Gospel of Nicodemus." *PMLA* 13 o.s. (1898), 457-71; *The Middle English Harrowing of Hell and Gospel of Nicodemus.* EETS e.s. 100 (1907); Kirkland, J. *A Study of the Anglo-Saxon Poem, The Harrowing of Hell* (1885); MacColloch, J. *The Harrowing of Hell: A Comparative Study of an Early Christian Doctrine* (1930); Monnier, J. *La descente aux enfers* (1905); Rand, E. K. *"Sermo de confusione diaboli." MP* 2 (1904-05), 261-78; Schiller, G. *Ikonographie der Christlichen Kunst.* Bd. 3 (1971); Tamburr, K. "The *Harrowing of Hell* in the English Mystery Cycles: Perspectives on the Corpus Christi Drama." *DAI* 35 (1975), 5367A; Tillyard, E. M. W. *Some Mythical Elements in English Literature* (1961); Trask, R. *"The Descent into Hell* of the Exeter Book." *NM* 72 (1971), 419-35; Turmel, J. *La descente du Christ aux enfers* (1905); Turner, R. "Descendit ad Infernos: Medieval Views on Christ's Descent into Hell and the Salvation of the Ancient Just." *JHI* 27 (1966), 173-94; White, W. D. "The Descent of Christ into Hell: A Study in Old English Literature." *DA* 20 (1960), 2814-15; Wülker, R. *Das Evangelium Nicodemi in der Abendländischen Literatur* (1872); Young, K. *The Drama of the Medieval Church* (1933); "The Harrowing of Hell in Liturgical Drama." *TWA* 16 (1909), 889-947.

GEORGE L. SCHEPER

HART "As the hart panteth after the water brooks, so panteth my soul after thee, O God" (Ps. 42:1). The hart (Heb. *'ayyal*) is the male (the hind or doe being the female) of this species of "clean" animals (Deut. 12:15). Its name is occasionally connected in rabbinic tradition with *'eyal* ("strength" or "help"), and it was generally thought to be the swiftest of the animals (Ketub. 112a; cf. the description of Napthali as "a hind let loose" in Gen. 49:21). In the Yalqut annotation of Ps. 42:2 the hart is designated as the most pious of all animals, since it digs in the earth for water with its antlers, praying to God, and is rewarded with springs of living water rising from the desert sands, enough for itself and other creatures.

In patristic commentary the hart symbolizes the Christian who thirsts after the water of eternal life (e.g., St. Augustine, *Enarr. in Ps.* 42; St. Jerome, *Ep.* 122.1). Augustine allegorizes the pool of water as the baptismal

font. Indeed, Ps. 42 was customarily chanted at the Easter baptism of adult catechumens; hence, the *Glossa Ordinaria* makes the "voice" of the Psalm that of the singing catechumens coming to baptism (PL 113.905).

In *Beowulf* the pool where the hero's successful conflict with Grendel's dam takes place is said to be so full of serpents that a hart would rather face the hunters' dogs than leap in — a possibly ironic allusion to another tradition concerning the hart. According to medieval bestiaries, the hart is able to smell out a snake in its den and then stamp it to death; as such it is likened to Christ, who hunts out the Serpent, Satan, to destroy him (e.g., *De Bestiis et Aliis Rebus* [PL 176]). Typically, however, the hart is symbolic of the human soul, as in Chaucer's *Book of the Duchess,* where the Emperor Octavyen's harthunting concludes simultaneously with the successful "heart-hunt" of the psychopharmical dialogue between the grieving Black Knight and Chaucer's persona. In his adaptation of "the Lamentations of Jeremy" Donne speaks of the desolate state of Jerusalem in words close to his text (Lam. 1:6):

> From Sion's daughter all beauty gone,
> Like Harts, which seek for Pasture, and find none,
> Her Princes are, and now before the foe
> Which still pursues them, without strength they go.
> (21-24)

These associations are compounded in romance literature by Celtic borrowings, in which, however, the hart may still be symbolic of the soul (e.g., *Erec et Enide, Mabinogion*).

In later literature allusions to the well-known *incipit* to Ps. 42 take a wide variety of verbal forms. The image of the exhausted soul "Like as the hart desires the brook / In summer heat's extream degree" (Christopher Smart's translation) appealed to the psychologically distressed William Cowper, among whose best-known lines are:

> I was a stricken deer, that left the herd
> Long since; with many an arrow deep infixt
> My panting side was charged when I withdrew
> To seek a tranquil death in distant shades.
> There was I found by one who had himself
> Been hurt by the archers. (*The Task*, 3.108-13)

This type of loose association of the two conventional symbols — the hart as the soul and the hart as Christ — is reduced to a reference to the exhausted human soul alone with itself in Byron's *Manfred:*

> We can number
> How few, how less than few, wherein the soul
> Forbears to "pant for death" and yet draws back
> As from a stream in winter. (2.2.266-69)

In Dickens's *Dombey and Son* Cuttle confusedly misremembers the text of Ps. 42: "The wery planks she walked on was as high esteemed by Wal'r as the waterbrooks is by the hart which never rejoices."

Bibliography. Toperoff, S. P. "The Hart and Hind in Bible and Midrash." *Dor le Dor* 16 (1988), 216, 271-72.

HASENAH *See* BURNING BUSH.

HE MAY RUN THAT READETH The Lord ordered the prophet Habakkuk to "write the vision" given him, and "to make it plain upon the tables, that he may run that readeth it" (Hab. 2:2) — i.e., that it might be read "on the run." Cowper invokes the phrase in his "Tirocinium; or a Review of Schools," as does Tennyson, whose "The Flower" concludes with the *envoi,* "Read my little fable; / He that runs may read." Carlyle refers to "sham Metaphors, which overhanging that same Thought's-Body (best naked) . . . may be called its false stuffings. . . : whereof he that runs and reads may gather whole hampers, — and burn them" (*Sartor Resartus,* 1.11). John Keble's "Who Runs May Read" uses the phrase to suggest the Book of God's Works:

> There is a book, who runs may read,
> Which heavenly truth imparts,
> And all the lore its scholars need,
> Pure eyes and Christian hearts.

For T. H. Huxley the phrase calls to mind graffiti ("On a Piece of Chalk"). Macaulay, reflecting on the Puritans, "the most remarkable body of men, perhaps, that the world has ever produced," observes that their true worth is often obscured by obvious extravagances: "The odious and ridiculous parts of their character lie on the surface. He that runs may read them" *(Milton).*

HE THAT DIGGETH A PIT Six times in the OT and once in the book of Sirach the belief in a just recoil upon the wicked is expressed as the evildoer's falling into the very pit he had dug to destroy another; often this image is paired with that of a net set to snare another and, in Proverbs, Ecclesiastes, and Sirach, of a stone set or thrown to harm him, but harming the evildoer instead (Pss. 7:14-16; 9:15-16; 35:7-8; 57:6; Prov. 26:27; Eccl. 10:8-9; and Sir. 27:28-30).

St. Jerome glosses the evildoer in Ps. 7 as the devil: the image of the stone demonstrates how *diabolus occiditur sua superbia* ("the devil is killed by his own pride") (*Tractatus de Psalmo,* 7.196-208; cf. *Tractatus in Psalmo,* 9.28-52). Such an interpretation apparently influenced the ME cleric who translates Ps. 7 into the vernacular, rendering pit as "helle" (*The Complete Prose Psalter. . . ,* ed. K. D. Bülbring [EETS o.s. 97], 6).

Cassiodorus explicates Ps. 7:15 as a reference to Judas's betrayal of Christ, which caused Judas's own damnation (*Expositio in Psalmo,* 7.310-22). In Ps. 9:15, he sees retribution against sinners in general, *quia propria unusquisque iniquitate torquetur* ("because everyone is tormented by his own wickedness"), and specifically, the lot of those who crucified Christ (*Expositio in Psalmo,*

9.256-74). Ps. 56/57, with the same imagery, is used in the Easter liturgy, clearly with the same interpretation (F. P. Pickering, *Literature and Art in the Middle Ages* [1970], 288-89).

St. Augustine uses the pit in his *Confessiones* (9.3.6) and elsewhere glosses the imagery as fraud, exampled by the financial deceiver who seeks to harm another but who deals himself the wound of avarice (*Enarr. in Ps.* 7.17). Augustine's interpretation may have influenced Prudentius's description of Fraud's pit, dug to catch Humility, but causing the death of her cohort Pride; in any case, *Psychomachia,* 255-58, uses the vocabulary of Ps. 7. The B text of *Piers Plowman* includes the pit image by quoting Ps. 7:16 in Latin in the midst of 150 lines on the *gylourbigiled* (Trickster Tricked) theory of the Atonement (see P. B. R. Doob, *Nebuchadnezzar's Children,* 199-200), clearly using the patristic associations.

The late 16th-cent. biblical "comedy" *Queen Esther and Proud Haman* concludes with Haman's being dragged off to the gallows and with Ahasuerus's allusion to evildoers who, having dug a pit for others, fall into it themselves. Marlowe uses the same pit image twice. In *The Massacre at Paris,* King Henry III, knowing that the Duke of Guise intends his overthrow and death, hires three murderers, then urges: "Come, Guise, and see thy traitorous guile outreached, / And perish in the pit thou mad'st for me" (20.32-33). The association of this image with the traitor Judas and the other Jews who participated in the Crucifixion, and with financial fraud, may have recommended this means for the demise of the traitor and usurer in *The Jew of Malta.* Barabas plans to betray his allies so that their leader will fall "into a deep pit past recovery" where he will burn to death in a cauldron. Instead, the trap is sprung on Barabas himself so that he perishes in a "Cauldron placed in a pit."

George Herbert sets Ps. 7 into verse (as had Sidney) and alludes to related stone images three times in other pieces. Twice he refers to the cast stone of Sir. 27:28. In "Charms and Knots" he notes: "Who by aspersions throw a stone / At th' head of others, hit their own" (9-10). In *A Priest to the Temple,* Herbert describes the parson as immune to others' scorn, either ignoring it, "shewing that reproaches touch him no more, than a stone thrown against heaven," or reminding the "contemner, Alas, why do you thus? you hurt your selfe, not me; he that throws a stone at another, hits himselfe" (chap. 28). Once, in "Outlandish Proverbs," Herbert uses the other stone image associated with the pit, e.g., in Eccl. 10:9: "Whoso removeth stones shall be hurt therewith." Herbert writes: "Who remove stones, bruise their fingers" (no. 40).

Stevenson invokes the image of pit and snare twice in his *New Arabian Nights,* to adumbrate and to clarify the climax. The diabolical, nameless President of the Suicide Club is the villain of the first, three-installment tale. In the second installment, he frames a young man for murder; the pit and snare allusions occur in a friend's words of sympathy for the youth. In the third installment, the President plans to murder the Prince of Bohemia and digs a secret grave for him. Prince Florizel, however, surprises his plot; before slaying him in a duel, the prince declares, "[Y]ou have laid your last snare and your own feet are taken in it . . . . And the grave you had dug for me this afternoon shall serve, in God's almighty providence, to hide your own just doom."

When Sherlock Holmes discovers the corpse of the murderer Grimesby Roylott, killed by the swamp adder he had meant to kill his stepdaughter, Doyle has his detective observe, "Violence does, in truth, recoil upon the violent, and the schemer falls into the pit which he digs for another" ("The Case of the Speckled Band").

At least three 20th-cent. novels use the pit image. In Dorothy Sayers's *The Documents in the Case* (1930), the adulterous Margaret Harrison writes to her lover, pretending that her husband's death was the accidental result of his experimenting with mushrooms, which she compares to "digging a pit for himself to fall into, like the wicked man in the Bible" (Document 46). Her own correspondence with her lover, however, is the pit she dug for herself, for it is the evidence of her inciting him to murder. Patricia Wentworth's *Lonesome Road* (1939) is informed by the image, for two attempts at murder recall the pit, the second sustaining the image through three chapters. Chap. 35 concludes with the first half of the verse echoing in the main character's thoughts; at the end of chap. 38 the would-be murderer backs into the well which he had uncovered in order to kill someone else, and the chapter concludes, "The verse which Rachel had not been able to finish finished itself: They have digged a pit and fallen into it themselves."

The final book of J. R. R. Tolkien's Middle-Earth trilogy features literal pits: the orcs besieging Gondor dig deep trenches which they fill with fire; then, however, the Roherrim surprise the orcs from behind, "hewing, slaying, driving their foes into the fire-pits" (*The Return of the King,* chap. 6).

See also TORMENT, TORMENTOR.

Bibliography. Doob, P. B. R. *Nebuchadezzar's Children: Conventions of Madness in Middle English Literature* (1974); Pickering, F. P. *Literature and Art in the Middle Ages* (1970); Tkacz, C. B. "*The Jew of Malta* and the Pit." *South Atlantic Review* 52 (1988), 47-57; "The Topos of the Tormentor Tormented in Selected Works of Old English Hagiography." *DAI* 43 (1983), 749A.   CATHERINE BROWN TKACZ

HEAD   The word *head* occurs more than 350 times in the OT (KJV), almost invariably translating Heb. *ro'sh* (or Aram. *re'sh* in Daniel), and 72 times in the NT, where it represents Gk. *kephalē.* "Head" is normally used in a literal sense, though it can also refer to those occupying positions of superiority (e.g., Exod. 18:25; Deut. 33:5; Judg. 10:18); this leads to the imagery in Daniel, where

rulers are represented by heads (Dan. 2:32, 38; possibly 7:6; cf. Rev. 17:7, 10).

The head expresses moods — it can be shaved (Job 1:20), strewn with dust (Josh. 7:6) or ashes (2 Sam. 13:19), or simply covered (Jer. 14:3), all such gestures symbolizing sorrow, penitence, or shame. It can also be left unshaved and uncut, as a sign of dedication to God (Num. 6:5). Anointing the head is a sign of prosperity and well-being (Ps. 23:5; Eccl. 9:8); to lift up someone's head is to cause him to prosper (Gen. 40:13). The head represents the whole person: blessings are invoked upon it (Prov. 10:6), but so is retribution (2 Sam. 1:16; Prov. 25:22; Acts 18:6; Rom. 12:20). The worshiper identifies the offering as his by laying hands on its head (Lev. 3:2).

The word is used metaphorically of the chief cornerstone of a building in Ps. 118:22, and this verse became a key text in the NT (Matt. 21:42; Mark 12:10; Luke 20:17; Acts 4:11; 1 Pet. 2:7). Paul plays on the word's double meaning in 1 Cor. 11, where he states that because Christ is the head of the man, and the man is the head of the woman, a man must bare his head during worship, but a woman must keep hers covered; his point seems to be that the bare head reflects the glory of the metaphorical head, and in worship Christ, not man, should be glorified (cf. also Eph. 5:23). In Colossians and Ephesians the metaphor of Christ as head is developed in relation to the Church — already described as Christ's body in Rom. 12 and 1 Cor. 12: Christ is described not only as the head of the body (Col. 1:18; 2:19; Eph. 4:15; 5:23) but as head over all things (Eph. 1:22; Col. 2:10). A combination of these senses governs the opening lines of the hymn (P. Gerhardt), "O Sacred Head! Sore Wounded."

A political usage based upon the Pauline figure developed in the Middle Ages (e.g., John of Salisbury, *Policraticus*) and flourished in the Renaissance, whereby the king was seen as "head" of the "body politic." Laertes has this derivative usage in mind when he speaks of the political limitation of Hamlet's actions: "And therefore must his choice by circumscribed / Unto the voice and yielding of that body / Whereof he is the head" (*Hamlet,* 1.3.22-24).

The verses pertaining to Christ's headship are occasionally alluded to in English literature. John Donne reflects in "Holy Sonnet 17" on his departed spouse, saying his admiration of her, "my mind did whett / To seeke thee God; so streams do shew their head. . . ." In "The Annunciation and Passion" he speaks more directly of "the church, God's Court of faculties" in its celebration of "Th'Abridgement of Christ's story": "Her Maker put to making, and the head / Of life, at once, not yet alive, yet dead." George Herbert's poem "Aaron" offers a better-known synthesis, beginning, "Holiness on the head," referring to the priest's anointing, which has to deal in Herbert's case with "Profanenesse in my head." "Onely another head," he says ("Christ is my onely head") can fit him for priestly headship: "So holy in my head . . . / My doctrine tun'd by Christ, (who is not dead, / But lives in me while I do rest) / Come people; Aaron's drest."

In modern literature, Somerset Maugham's Domingo Perez in *Catalina* pleads with Father Antonio to be let in, saying that he has a message of great importance: "the stone which the builders rejected is become the head of the corner" (chap. 13). A grisly parody of the Pauline imagery concerning Christ as head of the body of his faithful is found in the third volume of C. S. Lewis's science fiction trilogy, *That Hideous Strength*. In it a group of scientists who desire control over the world obtain the guillotined head of a notorious criminal, Alcasan, and purportedly keep it alive in a laboratory *sanctum sanctorum* from whence it directs their demonic activities in subverting the order of creation and salvation alike. Here Alcasan is an Antichrist, whose "body" is the membership of the academic and political cabal which goes by the acronym NICE.   MORNA D. HOOKER

HEART In the OT the Hebrew substantives *leb* and *lebab* ("heart") occur about 850 times; *nephesh* ("soul") occurs only 11 times in instances where the translation "heart" seems warranted in English. It can signify compassionate feelings, desires, mind (Ps. 7:9), and the concept rendered in the NT not only by Gk. *kardia* but by *psychē*, "soul" (e.g., Eph. 6:6; Col. 3:23; cf. Acts 4:32). The heart is clearly in Hebrew thought a "psychological organ" as well as a physical one — in fact, only rarely does *leb* mean the physical organ (e.g., 1 Sam. 25:37; 2 Kings 9:24). Josephus typically uses *dianoia*, "mind," or *psychē* where the OT has *leb*. The heart is also the center of the will or purpose (Deut. 8:2; 1 Kings 8:17; Jer. 23:20); to "incline the heart" (Josh. 24:23; Ps. 117:36) is to express intention to comply or accord. As the seat of the intellect, the heart is the mediatory and integrative center, the place associated with *hokmah*, "wisdom," and with *da'at*, "knowledge" (Prov. 2:2; Deut. 29:4). Accordingly, it is at the core of religious life, the "conscience" which speaks (2 Sam. 24:5; cf. 1 John 3:20ff.).

The tendency of English poetry until the Enlightenment to use "heart" in this integrative way for all the faculties we call "human" is thus a Hebraism, or biblicism — sometimes contextualized as such, often not. When Donne says, "As man is of the world, the heart of man, / is an epitome of God's great booke of creatures, and man need no farther looke" ("1613 Eclogue"), he invokes a metonym widely used by biblical commentators such as Beza, Lapide, etc. and theologians such as Aquinas. Herbert makes his heart "a broken altar" — both the place of sacrifice and the sacrifice itself — in describing submission of the will to God ("The Altar"): his question, "My God, what is a heart?" is analogous to Ps. 8:4: "What is man, that thou art mindful of him?" ("Mattens"). A "hard heart" or a "stony heart" (cf. Dante's "Rime Pietrose") is an obstinate will, akin to Pharaoh's "hardened heart" in

Exodus; yet, Herbert observes, when convicted of sin, "stonie hearts will bleed" ("Discipline"). For Herbert, whose comfort is that "Jesu is in my heart, the sacred name / Is deeply carved there" ("Jesu"), prayer is the "soul in paraphrase, the heart in pilgrimage" to a full measure of Christ's presence ("Prayer 1").

The heart may also be spoken of as the seat of memory: "Thy word have I hid in my heart, that I might not sin against Thee" (Ps. 119:11), or, as Sir Philip Sidney and the Countess of Pembroke translate it: "Thy speeches have I hidd / close locked up in the Caskett of my heart" (*The Psalms* [ed. Rathmell], 277; cf. Christopher Smart, "Thy wholesome dictates are imprest, / And treasured up within my breast"). Accordingly, the hidden word is a healer of memory, and clarifies: William Cowper writes,

> But if his word once teach us, shoot a ray
> Through all the heart's dark chambers, and reveal
> Truths undiscerned but by that holy light,
> Then all is plain. Philosophy, baptized
> In the pure fountain of eternal love,
> Has eyes indeed. (*The Task*, 3.240-45)

HEAVEN The primary meaning of *heaven* in the Bible is "that which is above the earth." Although it can refer (in either singular or plural) to the sky or heavenly bodies, its important religious meaning is the transcendent "other" world, the abode of God. Throughout the OT God is called the Lord of heaven and is pictured as dwelling in a transcendent heaven (e.g., Gen. 14:19; Exod. 20:22; Deut. 4:36; Ps. 103:19; Eccl. 5:2). The epithet "God of heaven" is recurrent in the OT (e.g., 2 Chron. 36:23; Neh. 2:4; Dan. 2:18, 19).

Throughout the Bible the term *heaven* appears as a synonym and metonym for God (Gen. 49:25; Luke 15:18, 21; John 3:27). Heaven is also the abode of angels, as in the OT vision of Jacob — in which angels were seen ascending and descending a ladder which reached from earth to heaven (Gen. 28:12-13) — and numerous NT passages (Matt. 18:10; Mark 12:25; Luke 2:15).

Two aspects of heaven are distinctive to the NT. Heaven is said to be the place from which Christ came and to which he returned (John 3:13; 6:33, 38, 50, 51, 58; Luke 24:51; Acts 1:11). In the Epistles the ascended Christ is pictured as one "who is gone into heaven, and is on the right hand of God" (1 Pet. 3:22; cf. Eph. 6:9; Col. 4:1). The NT also pictures heaven as the place where believers are glorified and eternally present with God (Col. 1:12; 1 Pet. 1:4). The greatest repository of passages picturing heaven as the abode of God and glorified believers is the Apocalypse, where the word appears more than fifty times and where chaps. 4, 7, 19, 21, and 22 contain the most extensive descriptions of heaven in the Bible. In Rev. 21–22, heaven and earth are pictured as joined in the New Jerusalem, the antitype of Eden. Like the paradisal garden, the heavenly city has a tree of life and fountain of pure water issuing from its center (from under the throne of God, a detail also foreshadowed in Zech. 14:8).

In rhetorical terms, heaven is generally described in one of five ways: (1) contrast, in which the qualities of heaven are set over against those of earth or hell; (2) negation, in which imperfections are denied to heaven; (3) analogy, in which heaven is likened to some feature of earthly reality; (4) distancing, in which the mystery of heaven is preserved by picturing it as remote from ordinary human experience; and (5) conceptual imagery, in which terms such as bliss, joy, and peace are used to suggest a realm which transcends physical reality.

The greatest medieval vision of heaven, Dante's *Paradiso*, is Italian, but it had a profound impact upon English and other literatures. The English work most similar to it is *Pearl*, a dream vision which pictures heaven as a city of jewels and light, inhabited by glorified saints and distanced from earth by a river. The OE *Doomsday* poem concludes with a detailed picture of the glory of those who will dwell in heaven. For morality plays like *Everyman*, heaven is the acknowledged destination of every Christian soul after this life; *contemptus mundi* literature takes for granted the contrast between the eternal heavenly realm and the transience of earthly things.

In the Renaissance, Spenser pictures heaven at the end of the November eclogue of *The Shepheardes Calender*, in *An Hymne of Heavenly Love* and *An Hymne of Heavenly Beauty*, and in *The Faerie Queene*, 1.10.55-58. Marlowe's *Doctor Faustus* repeatedly alludes to the Christian concept of heaven as a place of transcendent glory and reward. Giles Fletcher's *Christ's Victorie and Triumph* is an exalted poetic description of heaven, while Bunyan's *Pilgrim's Progress* makes the Celestial City the goal of his protagonist's quest. Heaven is, for Bunyan, the joyous end, God's place, which renders worthwhile all the perils and rigors of earthly wayfaring. Milton picks up an idiom familiar in Shakespeare (e.g., *A Midsummer Night's Dream*, 1.1.207; 2.1.243), to "make a heaven of hell" or "hell of heaven," to characterize the rejection of an objective paradise by the self which insists on its autonomy. Satan's thesis, that "The mind is its own place, and in itself / Can make a Heav'n of Hell, a Hell of Heav'n" (*Paradise Lost*, 1.254-55), while a harbinger of modernist epistemologies, is here his attempt to rationalize away his eternal loss of heaven's joys.

Milton's elaborate treatment of heaven reflects the Reformers' (especially Calvin's) emphasis upon a carefully imaged heaven as the goal of Christian pilgrimage. Heaven appears as a major part of Milton's imaginative world even in his early poetry (e.g., "On Time," "At a Solemn Music," "Lycidas," and Sonnets 9, 14, 19, 23). The heaven presented in *Paradise Lost*, especially bks. 3, 5, and 6, is a transcendent reality accommodated to human eyes and shaped to a surprising degree by free

creaturely action. A revolt of the angels leads to war in heaven, a mining of heaven's floor, the invention of cannons, and a short-term transformation of the landscape. Such a heaven appears to be a realm of process and contingency, though Milton's God says emphatically that he is approached by neither necessity nor chance.

Heaven is also one of the most important subjects of 17th-cent. lyric poets such as Vaughan ("Peace," "They Are All Gone into the World of Light"), Crashaw ("A Hymn to . . . Saint Teresa"), Traherne ("Shadows in the Water," "Felicity"), Herbert ("Heaven"), and Herrick ("The White Islands: or Place of the Blest"). Descriptive pictures of heaven are most predictable in poetic elegies; examples include Donne's *Second Anniversarie* and Dryden's "Ode on the Death of Mrs. Anne Killigrew."

The Saints' Everlasting Rest (1650), the most popular treatise on heaven in the 17th cent., presents at great length the felicity of the blessed, a felicity which includes all the activities appropriate to and delighted in by the rational soul. The fourth part of the work is a manual on heavenly meditation. This devotional method, preached also by the popular Puritan divine Richard Sibbes, represented within Reformed tradition the strategy of the affirmative way evidenced much earlier in Dante's *Paradiso*: earth is seen as the pilgrim way to heaven.

In the Enlightenment, English letters saw an abundance of casual references to heaven, but virtually all of these alluded either to the natural domains of sky and stars or, in a religious context, to a vague transcendent realm which admits of no detailing.

Bolder treatments are evident again with the 19th-cent. poets. In *The Excursion*, Wordsworth presents a heavenly afterlife as the only suitable context for human affections "else betrayed and lost." In bk. 14 of *The Prelude* he traces out the course of spiritual love, necessarily ending in "Eternity, and God." Tennyson, in his eclectic poem celebrating Arthur Hallam, *In Memoriam* (1850), presents his conviction that heaven must involve a continuation of personal and self-conscious life along with the recognition of and reunion with loved ones; moreover, it must allow for growth and service. These sentiments are echoed by Robert Browning, through a variety of dramatic spokesmen, in *The Ring and the Book*. In "Paracelsus" Browning argues that heaven must also involve the opportunity to correct earthly error. Heaven makes notable appearances, also, in the poetry of Francis Thompson ("The Kingdom of God"), Gerard Manley Hopkins ("The Starlight Night"), and Emily Dickinson ("I Never Saw a Moor," "Heaven has Different Signs to Me"), and in T. S. Eliot's play *Murder in the Cathedral*.

The fullest fictional exposition of the Christian heaven in the 20th cent. has come from C. S. Lewis. While the Edenic paradise is vividly detailed in *Perelandra*, a fantasy set upon an unfallen Venus, the more strictly heavenly paradise is set forth in the dream-allegory *The Great*

Divorce (a work which disjoins what Blake had put together in *The Marriage of Heaven and Hell*). Lewis's contemporary, J. R. R. Tolkien, has written his own artful allegory of the heavenly afterlife in the story "Leaf by Niggle."

In the poetry of Theodore Roethke heaven is a framing concept. "All finite things reveal infinitude," Roethke says, in a vein reminiscent of Wordsworth. His verses explore in a variety of ways the imagery of the edge, where finite and infinite meet. Heaven is left without specified content, however, and in this reticence Roethke allies himself with all those moderns who, cautious about the possibility of revelation, remain silent on the question of transcendence.

See also ANGEL; EDEN; HELL; NEW JERUSALEM.

Bibliography. Kaufmann, U. M. *Paradise in the Age of Milton* (1978); Lawes, R. W. "The Heaven of Fourteenth-Century English Poets: An Examination of Paradisal References in the English Works of Chaucer, Gower, Langland, and the Pearl Poet." *DAI* 45 (1984), 1111A; Patch, H. R. *The Other World According to Descriptions in Medieval Literature* (1950); Simon, U. *Heaven in the Christian Tradition* (1958); Tristram, H. "Stock Descriptions of Heaven and Hell in Old English Prose and Poetry." *NM* 79 (1978), 102-13; Whitehead, L. D. *The After-World of the Poets* (1929).

LELAND RYKEN
U. MILO KAUFMANN

HEBREW POETRY Hebrew poetry is characterized by certain rhythmical patterns which can to a large extent be reproduced in translation. There is rhythm of sound, which is mainly based on a regular sequence of stressed syllables; there is rhythm of sense, which takes the form of "parallelism." That is to say, what is essentially the same idea is expressed twice over in parallel clauses; the idea is the same, but the words are different.

There are three main varieties of parallelism: complete parallelism, incomplete parallelism, and step parallelism.

Complete parallelism. Here each significant word in one line has its counterpart in another. The parallelism may be synonymous:

"Adah and Zillah, hear my voice;
ye wives of Lamech, hearken unto my speech." (Gen. 4:23)

It may be antithetic:

They are brought down and fallen:
but we are risen, and stand upright." (Ps. 20:8)

Or it may be emblematic, where the situation in one line is compared to the situation in the adjoining line:

Like as a father pitieth his children,
so the LORD pitieth them that fear him. (Ps. 103:13)

Sometimes the parallelism is more elaborate, and consists in the balancing of groups of lines rather than of single lines. A good example is provided by Ps. 27:1:

The LORD is my light and my salvation;
whom shall I fear?
the LORD is the strength of my life;
of whom shall I be afraid?

This pattern, in which lines of three and two stressed syllables alternate, is often called the "dirge" rhythm because it is so characteristic of the book of Lamentations, but the example just quoted shows that it can also serve as the vehicle of joyful praise.

Incomplete parallelism. Sometimes one word in a line has no counterpart in the parallel line. Consider, e.g., Ps. 40:2:

He brought me up out of an horrible pit,
out of the miry clay.

Here there is no verb in the second line; it is understood from the first line. The result is again an alternation of three and two stressed syllables. But sometimes an additional stressed syllable will be provided in the second line to preserve the same rhythm as in the first line. Where no additional stressed syllable is supplied, we have incomplete parallelism *without compensation;* where one is supplied, we have incomplete parallelism *with compensation.* Thus Ps. 1:5 runs:

Therefore the godly shall not stand in the judgment,
nor sinners in the congregation of the righteous.

Here, as in Ps. 40:2, the verb is lacking in the second line, but now the number of stressed syllables is made up by the use of a heavier phrase, "the congregation of the righteous," in the second line as the counterpart of "the judgment" in the preceding line. Sometimes there is even less parallelism of meaning and correspondingly more compensation in the supply of stressed syllables, until the point is reached where we have all compensation and no real parallelism. An example of this formal parallelism, as it has been called, comes in Ps. 27:6:

And now shall mine head be lifted up
above mine enemies round about me.

There are three stressed syllables in each line, but no single word in the one line has a sense counterpart in the other.

Step parallelism. Occasionally part of one line is repeated in the next, and becomes the starting point for a further step; this process may be repeated from line to line. Ps. 29:1, 2 presents a good example of this:

Give unto the LORD. O ye mighty,
give unto the LORD glory and strength.
Give unto the LORD the glory due unto his name;
worship the LORD in the beauty of his holiness.

Here the step parallelism is seen in the repeated "give unto the LORD" of the first three lines; lines 3 and 4 stand in complete synonymous parallelism the one to the other. Another example is Ps. 92:9:

For, lo, thine enemies, O LORD,
for, lo, thine enemies shall perish;
all the workers of iniquity shall be scattered.

Lines 1 and 2 show step parallelism; lines 2 and 3 show complete synonymous parallelism.

Hebrew poetry sometimes exhibits strophic structure. One sign of this is the recurrence of a refrain. The recurring refrain of Pss. 42 and 43 (originally a single psalm) marks the end of three strophes, at vv. 5 and 11 of Ps. 42 and v. 5 of Ps. 43. A strophic arrangement is indicated in Ps. 46:7, 11 by the refrain:

The LORD of hosts is with us;
the God of Jacob is our refuge —

but vv. 1-7 probably comprised two strophes, with their dividing point marked by "Selah" at the end of v. 3 (where the refrain was originally sung too). Ps. 80 is divided into four strophes by the refrain "Turn us again, O God . . ." (or "Return. . . , O God . . .") in vv. 3, 7, 14, and 19. The second part of Ps. 24 shows a more involved strophic pattern, with the repeated command "Lift up your heads, O ye gates!" and the question "Who is this King of glory?" (with response).

Strophic arrangement is also involved in certain acrostic poems. The most outstanding acrostic scheme is that of Ps. 119, whose twenty-two sections are formal strophes, corresponding to the twenty-two letters of the Hebrew alphabet, each of the eight sentences in the first section beginning with the first letter, and so on to the eight sentences of the last section, each of which begins with the twenty-second letter.

Numerous attempts have been made in English to capture the "Hebraic" quality of biblical poetry. Most have been as unsuccessful in this respect as the translation of the Psalms (1586; 1599) by Sir Philip Sidney and the Countess of Pembroke. Despite the fact that John Donne labeled the "Sydnean Psalmes" an important achievement, the best rendering was much closer to hand. The influence of Hebrew poetry first enters English literary tradition in a significant way with the 1611 "Authorized" translation. The forty-seven translators working under the auspices of King James may have had less intention to capture in English the prose rhythms and parallelism of Hebrew poetry with which they are credited; however, subsequent understanding of Hebrew verse (Alter [1985]) has suggested that certain corresponding features of Renaissance English prosody and a stong intuitive feeling for the Hebrew of the Psalms particularly combined to make the KJV a remarkable access into the character of Hebrew verse. A similar poetic intuition is reflected in the canon of George Herbert, whose "Antiphon" not only conflates lines from a number of Psalms, but in its "focusing parallelism" can be seen as a direct response to "the dynamics of biblical poetry and its relation to the life of the Spirit" (Alter, 210).

In the 18th cent. when the KJV had already wrought an enormous influence on English prosody generally, Bishop Robert Lowth did an extended analysis of Hebrew poetry in his *Lectures on the Sacred Poetry of the Hebrews (De Sacra Poesi Hebraeorum),* published in 1753. This volume had an immediate impact on Christopher Smart, among others, whose brilliant, structurally and conceptually intricate *Song to David* (1763) and often powerfully rhythmic exercise in the Hebrew "Let" / "For" sequence (discussed by Lowth), the *Jubilate Agno* (1759-63), are among the most innovative 18th-cent. responses to the Bible. Lowth had noted that the crowding of metaphors, while a violation of Aristotle's edicts about perspicuity, was a natural expression of oriental style, in which "the language of poetry . . . [is] wholly distinct from that of common life." Lowth also established that prophetic poetry consisted of the accumulation of individual distichs and in this respect his work may have had a significant influence on William Blake's early prophecies.

Byron's collection of short poems, *Hebrew Melodies* (1815), are on scriptural subjects (e.g., "The Destruction of Sennacherib"), and some were arranged to traditional Hebrew melodies by I. Nathan. Later in the 19th cent. Robert Browning was interested enough in Hebrew poetry to pursue rabbinical literature for analysis of biblical tradition and expression. His "Rabbi Ben Ezra" and "Jochanan Hakkadosh" are efforts to create the feel of Hebrew prose rhythms, however, rather than the actual qualities of Hebrew poetry.

Despite Arnold's having cast aspersions on "Hebraism" in culture generally and literature particularly (*Culture and Anarchy* [1869]), interest in the qualities of Hebrew biblical poetry persisted into the 20th cent., influencing not only Israeli poets such as Tavia Rubner but also Jewish poets writing in English such as A. M. Klein, whose *Hitleriad* and *Psalter of Avram Hakni* (1944) capture much of the flavor of the poetry of wisdom literature, favoring especially incomplete or verb–carry-over parallelisms.

Bibliography. Alter, R. *The Art of Biblical Poetry* (1985); ApRoberts, R. "Old Testament Poetry: The Translatable Structure." *PMLA* 92 (1977), 987-1004; Berlin, A. *Biblical Poetry Through Medieval Jewish Eyes* (1991); Carmi, T., ed. *The Penguin Book of Hebrew Verse* (1981); Fisch, H. *Poetry with a Purpose: Biblical Poetics and Interpretation* (1988); Greenstein, E. "How Does Parallelism Mean?" *JQRS* (1982), 41-70; Hrushovski, B. "Prosody, Hebrew." *EncJud* (1971), 13.1200-1202; Kugel, J. L. *The Idea of Biblical Poetry: Parallelism and its History* (1981); Prickett, S. *Words and the Word: Language, Poetics and Biblical Interpretation* (1986); Watson, W. G. E. *Classical Hebrew Poetry: A Guide to Its Techniques* (1984).   F. F. BRUCE

HELL   The word *hell* derives from the Anglo-Saxon root *hel* or *hol,* meaning "to conceal" or "hide." In Old Norse mythology, Niflheim was an underground world ruled by Hel or Hela, "the queen of death." The most common Hebrew word in the OT for the place of the dead is *She'ol,* which was not, at first, a place of punishment. In the time of the Pharisees, Sheol came to include a place of retribution called *Ge-Hinnom* (Gk. *Gehenna*), a name derived from the valley outside Jerusalem where municipal waste was incinerated by continual fires.

In its earliest conception Sheol shared certain general features with Semitic heathenism, especially the view that the departed retained a degree of knowledge of and power over the living. In contrast, Ps. 88:12 depicts Sheol as a place of forgetfulness, in which there is "no work, or thought, or knowledge, or wisdom" (Eccl. 9:10); all "love, hatred, and envy has perished" for the dead, who no longer have "a portion for ever in any thing that is done under the sun" (Eccl. 9:5-6). The overall impression of the OT hell is of a pallid state of monotonous tranquility (Job 3:17-19) not unlike the classical Hades, a gloomy abode of the dead. In the NT the abode of the dead is called "Hades" and retains the same force as OT "Sheol." Tartarus, a dark abyss below Hades, and reserved as a place of punishment, is the Greek equivalent of Gehenna.

Despite minor variations, including disagreement over whether Sheol is located underground (Num. 16:30), under water (Jonah 2:7), or under mountains (Job 26:5), Sheol is at first seen as an ethically neutral place inhabited by both the righteous and the evil. Judgment of the dead is a feature of later OT writing, as in the book of Daniel ("Many of those who sleep in the dust of the earth shall awake, some to everlasting life, and some to shame and everlasting contempt" [12:2]). Daniel, along with apocalyptic books written between Maccabean and NT times, develops the idea of resurrection which came to exercise a profound influence on early Christianity and affected a transition from the neutral Sheol to the retributive Gehenna.

In talmudic literature, Gehenna takes the place of the biblical Sheol as the place of the dead. The punishments of Gehenna reflect hellenic elements: the punishment of the offender's tongue hanging out to lap at water which constantly recedes beyond reach (Hag.) recalls the fate of Tantalus in Hades (*Odyssey,* 2.582-85; Ovid, *Metamorphoses,* bk. 10), while the rivers of fire (Hag. 13b) recall the classical *Phlegethon.* The general characteristics of Gehenna are fire (B. Mes. 85a; B. Bat. 74a) and darkness (1 Enoch 10:4). According to Josephus (*J.W.* 2.155) the Essenes believed it to be a "murky and tempestuous dungeon, big with never-ending punishments."

Post-talmudic writings, though offering longer and more elaborate descriptions of Gehinnom, substantially agree with the briefer accounts in the Talmud and classical Midrashim.

Essential NT teaching on hell is contained in Matt. 25:41, 46, where Jesus is depicted at the Last Judgment separating the sheep from the goats and dismissing the damned "into everlasting fire, prepared for the devil and his angels." The sins leading to eternal punishment are

failures of love, especially in this instance the refusal of charity and hospitality to the disadvantaged. St. Paul also specifies that fornicators, idolaters, adulterers, the effeminate, abusers of themselves, drunkards, revilers, and extortioners (1 Cor. 6:9-10) and those who practice witchcraft, variance, emulations, sedition, and heresy (Gal. 5:20) shall not inherit the kingdom of God.

Each of the Synoptic Gospels mentions Gehenna, describing it as a place of unquenchable fire (Matt. 5:22; Mark 9:43), of torture (Matt. 5:25-26), of darkness, weeping, and gnashing of teeth (Matt. 8:12; 13:42; Luke 13:28), and of never ending corruption (Mark 9:48). Revelation foresees a general judgment at the end of the millennial period when death and hell deliver up their dead for judgment "according to their works," whereafter death and hell are to be cast into the lake of fire (Rev. 20:13, 14).

Some of the early Fathers propounded vivid materialistic descriptions of hell (e.g., St. Basil of Caesarea [*De Spiritu Sancto,* 40]; St. John Chrysostom [*Ad Theodorum lapsum,* 1.9-10]). Most assumed it to be a place of literal fiery torment. In the 3rd cent., however, Origen questioned the literal nature of hellfire, identifying hell rather as a spiritual state of separation from God, and in *De principiis* he advanced the doctrine of *apokatastasis* or universal salvation. His view was judged heretical at the council of Alexandria in 400, which upheld the opinion of St. Augustine in *De civ. Dei* 21.2-10; 22.19 that the damned, while suffering spiritually, are also embodied and burn everlastingly in literal flames. St. Thomas Aquinas reiterated this view, arguing that the punishments of hell are twofold: pain of loss of the vision of God and pains of sense — both in proportion to the gravity of willful, unrepented sin. Among the Reformers, Luther rejected the graphic medieval representations of hell and regarded Jesus' "descent into hell" as the anguish of his separation from God. Calvin, following Luther, disputed a biblical basis for a literal place called hell, treating the corporeal images of hell in Scripture as figurative for the terrors occasioned by willful sinfulness.

Anglo-Saxon poetry reflects a popular belief in a connection between hell and morasses, as, e.g., in *Beowulf,* where the home of Grendel, a "feond on helle," is located in the fen districts. Later medieval thought was dominated by Plato's geocentric theory of the sun and planets, according to which each sphere grew more sublime with its distance from the earth up to the final Empyrean or realm of pure essences. Since reality became coarser as it approached the earth's center, it was logical to think that hell, as the most grotesque of realities, should be located there. Copernican theory challenged the basis on which such ideas were founded and led to attempts to site hell elsewhere. In 1714, e.g., Tobias Swinden (*An Enquiry into the Nature and Place of Hell*) suggested the center of the sun as more plausible because it was both hotter and roomier. Nevertheless the idea of a subterranean hell continued to dominate Christian imagination as it had that of the OT and classical antiquity. Several possible entrances to hell have been proposed. Rabbinic literature often mentions the notorious valley of Hinnom. Lake Avernus was favored by Virgil, Lucretius, and Livy and echoed by Spenser: "deepe Avernus hole, / . . . descends to hell" (*FQ* 1.5.31). Equally celebrated is Taenarus in the southern Peloponnese, described by Apuleius as one of the "ventilation holes of the underworld." In medieval literature and iconography the entrance to hell is often depicted as a mouth, a view deriving from Isa. 5:14 and recurring in the Psalter of St. Swithin's Priory, the famous York Minster Mouth of Hell, and adapted metaphorically in Tennyson's *Charge of the Light Brigade:* "Into the mouth of hell / Rode the six hundred" (25-26). The ladder, bridge, and dark wood (cf. Spenser, *FQ* 1.1.13; Dante, *Inferno,* canto 1) were also considered avenues or pathways to hell.

The signal description of hell and its inhabitants in the Western literary tradition is that of Dante, in his *Inferno,* which provides a stock of graphic images to later writers (and artists). Homiletical literature, particularly that which has a penitential focus, also affords a store of images. Chaucer's Parson, outlining the "thridde cause that oghte moeve a man to contricioun," provides a harrowing account of the "Day of Doome" and of "the horrible peynes of helle." In so doing he provides a rich compendium of patristic and medieval commentary on the subject (*CT* 10.157-230). Penitential tracts in subsequent periods almost invariably include similar materials. Among the most celebrated and influential postmedieval accounts of hell in English literature are those of Spenser's *Faerie Queene* and Milton's *Paradise Lost.* Spenser's treatment of hell's torments (1.5.34-35) are largely derived from Ovid's *Metamorphoses* (bks. 4 and 10), the *Odyssey* (bk. 11), and the *Aeneid* (bk. 6). In depicting the physical features of hell in *Paradise Lost,* Milton also borrows from classical sources. Five infernal rivers, Styx, Acheron, Cocytus, Lethe, and Phlegethon, feed into the burning lake; the climate is sulphurous, a "darkness visible"; hell's portals are ninefold gates guarded by gorgons, hydras, and chimeras where Satan meets Sin and Death. The damned are exposed by turns to "fierce extremes" of fire and ice, just as Claudio in *Measure for Measure* fears that his soul will "bathe in fiery floods" or "reside / in thrilling region of thick-ribbed ice" (3.1.121-22), a torment reflected in Dante (*Inferno,* 32.29-30), categorically confirmed by St. Thomas Aquinas (*Summa Theol.,* supp. 3.2.97), and mentioned in a variety of medieval lyrics (e.g., C. Brown, *English Lyrics of the XIIIth Century,* no. 296 [line 71]).

Milton's imagination, however, was most keenly engaged by the notion of an inner hell, expressed in Satan's cry "Myself am Hell" (*PL* 4.75). The idea was not original to Milton but had its root in Virgil (*Aeneid,* 6.743)

and in patristic commentaries. Among Milton's more immediate literary precedents are Marlowe's *Doctor Faustus,* where Mephistopheles asserts, "Why, this is hell, nor am I out of it," and Sir Thomas Browne's more prosaic "I feel sometimes a hell within myself" (*Religio Medici,* 1.51). Nevertheless, Milton's treatment of hell as an inward condition rather than an external location was profoundly influential, especially among the English Romantics. Satan's *non-serviam* speech in bk. 1 of *Paradise Lost* and his view that "the mind is its own place" lie behind the statement of Byron's *Manfred:* "The mind . . . makes itself / . . . Is its own origin of ill and end — / And its own place and time" (3.4.129-32). It is also the inspiration for Wordsworth's *Prospectus to the Recluse,* in which he argues that traditional views of heaven and hell can not breed such "fear and awe" as when "we look / Into our Minds, into the Mind of Man — / My haunt, and the main region of my song" (38-41), an idea dramatically reworked in Hopkins's sonnet, the "mind has mountains; cliffs of fall / Frightful, sheer, no-man-fathomed . . ." (9-10) and echoed in T. S. Eliot's *The Cocktail Party* ("What is hell? Hell is oneself") and in Robert Lowell's *Skunk Hour* ("I myself am hell").

For writers from the 19th cent. onwards hell has often become a metaphor for the city. Blake's *London* is darkly Satanic, for Shelley "Hell is a city much like London / A populous and smoky city" (*Peter Bell,* 3.1), while Wordsworth places the "monstrous anthill" London at the center of the *Prelude,* the point at which in classical epics the hero usually descends into the underworld. A major precedent for the association of the city and hell is *Paradise Lost* (bk. 9), where Satan issues from hell as one "in populous city pent" and breaks into the bucolic landscape of Eden. Just as Edenic imagery was assimilated by the tradition of pastoral poetry, the city has in modern writing absorbed the imagery of hell. To the "modern imagination the city becomes increasingly something hideous and nightmarish," as Northrop Frye observes (*The Modern Century* [1967], 37), citing the "fourmillante cité" of Baudelaire, the "unreal city" of Eliot's Waste Land, and the "ville tentaculaire" of Verhaeren.

Contemporary literature also reflects the continuing debate concerning the dogma of eternal punishment and the existence of a literal hell. Since the 17th cent. skepticism concerning hell has been increasingly widespread while at the same time such thinking has been condemned as subversive for undermining the bulwarks of society. Thus William Dodwell concludes that "since men have learned to ward off the Apprehensions of Eternal Punishment, Progress of Impiety and Immorality among us has been very considerable" (*The Eternity of Future Punishment Asserted and Vindicated* [1743], 85). Notwithstanding Dr. Johnson's firm response to Dr. Adams on the meaning of "damned": "Sent to Hell, Sir, and punished everlastingly!" (Boswell's *Life of Johnson* [1960], 1296) the debate has continued. The dismissal of F. D. Maurice from King's College, London, in 1853 for his unorthodox views on eternal punishment, and the rebuttal of such opinions by Joseph Cottle, arguing that they had extinguished "hell with a Trope" and confuted "Heaven with a syllogism" (Cottle, *Essays on Socinianism* [1850], 114, 149) are items in the ongoing controversy.

Stephen Dedalus reflects on the terrors of hell in response to Father Arnall's vivid fire and brimstone sermon in *A Portrait of the Artist as a Young Man* (chap. 3), but his agonies of conviction and spiritual apprehension are short-lived. George Orwell observes, sarcastically, that "Most Christians profess to believe in Hell. Yet have you ever met a Christian who seemed as afraid of Hell as he was of cancer? . . . I say that such belief has no reality. It is a sham currency like the money in Samuel Butler's Musical Banks" (*The Collected Essays*, 3.147-48). Yet modern literary pictures of hell are common, from Shaw's depiction of it as culture without pain to Golding's *Pincher Martin*, where hell is viewed as egoism attempting self-creation. In Graham Greene's *Brighton Rock*, the value of positive belief in hell is set against the spiritual emptiness of modern life. Vivid modern reifications of personal damnation occur in works as diverse as Oscar Wilde's *Picture of Dorian Gray* (1890) and Charles Williams's *Descent into Hell* (1937).

See also HARROWING OF HELL; HEAVEN; PURGATORY.

Bibliography. Bromiley, G. W. "Hell, History of the Doctrine of." *ISBE* 2.677-79; Charles, R. H. *A Critical History of the Doctrine of a Future Life* (1913); Davidson, C., and T. Seiler, ed. *The Iconography of Hell* (1992); Furia, P. "Pound and Blake on Hell." *Paideuma* 10 (1981), 599-601; Hick, J. *Death and Eternal Life* (1976); Hotberry, M. *An Enquiry into the Scripture—Doctrine concerning the Duration of Future Punishment* (1744); McLachlan. *The Religious Opinions of Milton, Locke & Newton* (1941); *Socinianism in Seventeenth Century England* (1951); Patrides, C. A. "Renaissance and Modern Views on Hell." *HTR* 57 (1964), 217-36; Richmond, I. A. *Archaeology and the After Life in Pagan and Christian Imagery* (1958); Rowell, G. *Hell and the Victorians* (1974); Sutcliffe, E. F. *The Old Testament and the Future Life* (1946); Sutherland, R. C., Jr. "Medieval English Conceptions of Hell as Developed from Biblical, Patristic, and Native German Influences." *DA* 20 (1960), 4115-16; Walker, D. P. *The Decline of Hell: Seventeenth Century Discussions of Eternal Torment* (1964).   MICHAEL GOLDBERG

HELMET OF SALVATION   *See* ARMOR AND WEAPONS; *MILES CHRISTI.*

HEM OF HIS GARMENT   When Jesus walked among the people of Gennesaret all manner of the sick and infirm were brought to him "and besought him that they might only touch the hem of his garment: and as many as touched were made perfectly whole" (Matt. 14:34-36). In another incident, a woman afflicted for twelve years with "an issue of blood" touched the hem of Jesus' garment surreptitiously and was healed. When Jesus

realized what had happened, he addressed her, "Daughter, be of good comfort; thy faith hath made thee whole" (Matt. 9:20-22).

Francis Thompson's "The Kingdom of God" concludes with a reference combining elements from both episodes:

Yea in the night, my Soul, my daughter,
Cry, — clinging Heaven by the hems;
And lo, Christ walking on the water
Not of Gennesareth, but Thames!

In Twain's *The Man that Corrupted Hadleyburg,* a mysterious stranger who exposes the hypocrisy of the town's genteel society sends a letter to one family which escapes his judgment, saying that "This town is not worthy to touch the hem of your garment" (echoing also John the Baptist's words [John 1:27; Mark 1:7; Luke 3:16]). There are numerous parodies of the phrase: Byron's *Don Juan* offers two: "Dearest father [Lambro], . . . I 'kiss / Thy garment's hem' with transport" (4.300-302); "She signed to Baba, who first 'kiss'd the hem' / Of her deep purple robe, and speaking low, / Pointed to Juan who remained below" (5.766-68). Oliver Wendell Holmes denigrates the learning of James Russell Lowell in *The Autocrat of the Breakfast Table,* saying that "all men are afraid of books who have not handled them. Do you suppose that our dear *didascalos* over there ever read *Poli Synopsis* or consulted *Castelli Lexicon,* while he was growing up to their stature? Not he; but virtue passed through the hem of their parchment and leather garments whenever he touched them."

HERESY   When illustrating the definition of *heresy* as "a heretical opinion or doctrine" held to be "contrary to the 'catholic' or orthodox doctrine of the Christian Church," the *Oxford English Dictionary* cites the *Translators' Preface* to the *1611 Bible:* "The Scripture is . . . a Physionsshop . . . of preseruatiues against poisoned heresies." This line is a legitimate extension of one or two NT uses of the word *heresy* to translate the Greek cognate which originally implied nothing more than "choice."

The LXX does use the Greek word in rare instances, but the KJV translators and most of their successors have not chosen to render this as "heresy" in English. In most NT cases there it refers to parties, factions, or sects of "choice," which is not at all what the translators of 1611 had in mind when speaking of poisons.

When the Greek uses the word behind "heresy" to refer to Sadducees and Pharisees in Acts 15:5, 24:5, 26:5, and 28:22, the translators employ "sect." Only in 24:14, where the shoe is on the other foot and Jews speak of Christianity as "the way which they call heresy" do they use that word in English.

The beginning of a tendency toward a broader definition shows up not in the book of Acts but in the Pauline writings, particularly in passages such as 1 Cor. 11:19. In this instance heresy is a sign of the times, an eschatological note: "For there must also be heresies among you, that they which are approved may be made manifest among you." Yet one learns nothing specific of the reference: what were these heresies? Similarly, a moral as opposed to intellectual tone enters in Gal. 5:20 where "heresies" are listed with "works of the flesh" such as lasciviousness and witchcraft.

In all these respects, the Bible had not anticipated the situation for which KJV translators in their time felt they had to speak up: the preservation of the orthodox or catholic body of doctrine over against poisonously errant opinions or counterdoctrines. That usage begins to slip in in the very late writing, 2 Pet. 2:1, which reports that "there were false prophets . . . even as there shall be false teachers among you, who privily shall bring in damnable heresies. . . ." (The RSV also uses "heresies" here, uniquely.) Such a verse is a reflection of a church in need of boundaries, a body of believers, the *ecclesia*, which has intruded itself into a complex world. Seeking identity and faithfulness, it cannot tolerate surreptitious or damnable erosion of those boundaries by evil agents who deny that "the Lord bought them."

From a postmedieval Catholic point of view, heresy is a formal denial or doubt of any defined doctrine of the Catholic Church. When contumacious — willful and persistent adherence to doctrinal error by a baptized Catholic — it is "formal" heresy, and subject to the full weight of penalties provided by canon law, including excommunication and, in certain cases, death. "Material" heresy, on the other hand, is the error of one in ignorance of Catholic doctrine, which is not in canon law therefore a punishable offense. St. Thomas Aquinas observes that after two admonitions (cf. Titus 3:10), if the heretic "be found still stubborn, the Church gives up hope of his conversion and takes thought for the safety of others, by separating him from the Church by sentence of excommunication. Further, it leaves him to the secular court, to be exterminated from the world by death" (*Summa Theol.* 2.q.11.art.3). This was the classic argument later used to justify the Inquisition.

The early Fathers of the Christian Church had spent a large percentage of their literary and hortatory efforts combating heresy; major doctrinal works of Western Christendom include the *Contra Celsum* of Origen; St. Jerome's *Adversus Jovinianum*, and St. Augustine's *De gestis Pelagii; De gratia Christi et de peccato originali, contra Pelagium; De correctione Donatistae; De baptismo contra Donatistas; De duabus animabus, contra Manichaeos; De natura boni, contra Manichaeos;* and *De civitate Dei*, which is *contra paganos*. Many of the Fathers' opponents were pious Christians, and Augustine, e.g., acknowledges this. To be a heretic was not necessarily to be a "sinner" in the licentious sense: St. Gregory the Great says of the "righteous" friends of Job that they were exemplary of the character of heretics — well inten-

tioned, almost right, but nonetheless perverting divine truth (*Moralia in Iob*, 1.1.11, 15). In Western literature, from Dante's *Inferno* to modern American poetry, references are made to recurrences or similitudes of several of the major heresies with which these early writers struggled. Among the most important are the following.

Arianism. Arius was a Libyan, and priest in Alexandria from the latter half of the 3rd cent. to his death (ca. 336). His was a christological heresy, claiming that Jesus the Son of God was not eternal but created by the Father, the name being bestowed upon him because God foresaw his righteous life. Arius was opposed by St. Athanasius and condemned at the Council of Nicaea (A.D. 325); the careful elaboration of the Apostles' Creed in the Nicene Creed was a specific attempt to correct the Arian error: "God of God, Light of Light, true God of true God, begotten not made, being of one substance with the Father. . . ." Arianism was an influential heresy, tempting even Constantine, although fragmentation of its adherent communities in the 4th cent. led to its surviving largely in the north. Theodoric the Ostragoth, under whom Boethius served as consul, was an Arian, and Milton, because of the character of his dramatized relationship of God the Father to Christ the Son in *Paradise Lost,* has been charged with being a 17th-cent. Arian. Swift accuses Bishop Rundle of being an Arian ("On Dr. Rundle, Bishop of Derry"). "Arius, warring his life long upon the consubstantiality" is one of the heretics featured by James Joyce in *Ulysses,* where he appears in the "Telemachus" and "Proteus" as well as "Circe" chapters, not least because of his ignominious death "in a Greek watercloset."

Monarchianism. Also know as the "Modalist" heresy, monarchianism was propounded by "the subtle African Heresiarch Sabellius," as Joyce calls him in *Ulysses* ("Telemachus"), a North African who was teaching in Rome ca. 215. In an attempt to counter gnostic dualism, he overreacted, propounding a view of the Trinity in which the three persons are simply diverse modes of a single substance. In his discussion of the Trinity, St. Thomas Aquinas says that "we must beware of two opposite errors, and proceed cautiously between them — namely, the error of Arius . . . and the error of Sabellius" (*Summa Theol.* 1.q.22.art.2). Dante pairs them in *Paradiso*, 13.127-30.

Nestorianism. Nestorius was bishop of Constantinople (d. ca. 451). He objected to the Platonism of the Alexandrian theologians, who stressed the divinity of Jesus almost to the exclusion of his humanity. The Alexandrians had also referred to Mary not as the "mother of Jesus," but as a vehicle, the *theotokos* ("God-bearer"), a usage followed by Origen and others. Nestorius objected to the apparent avoidance of the humanity of Jesus, but so extremely as to assert two separate persons in the incarnate Christ. He was condemned at the Synod of Rome (430).

Monophysitism. Eutyches (ca. 378-454) was abbot of a monastery in Constantinople and an opponent of Nestorius who hewed to the opposite extreme, so confusing the two natures of Christ that they became indistinguishable; hence the term *monophysite* (from *mono* ["one"] and *physis* ["nature"]). Boethius wrote a treatise against both Eutyches and Nestorius.

Montanism. Named for Montanus of Phrygia, a 2nd-cent. apocalyptic prophet, Montanism was essentially a charismatic and eschatological movement. Montanus believed that the heavenly Jerusalem would descend, imminently, near Pepuza in Phrygia. His sect enjoined asceticism and abstention from marriage, and forbade flight in the face of persecution. Tertullian, by the time of his *De anima,* had become a Montanist. Derivatively montanist sects of more modern times, refurbished with elements of 19th-cent. utopian socialism, are found in the pages of Tolstoy. As Emerson wrote to Carlyle in 1940, hundreds of such communities were being founded in America in the 19th cent.: "We are all a little wild here with numberless projects of social reform. Not a reading man but has a draft of a new community in his waistcoat pocket." Jack Hodgins's *The Invention of the World* (1979) is a novel about a modern "montanist" community, with all the typical features gone badly sour.

Donatism. The Donatists, who share many characteristics and views of the Montanists, were a group of African schismatics who refused to accept one Caecillian as Bishop of Carthage (311) because he was consecrated by a *traditor,* someone who later recanted his own faith under persecution. The Africans consecrated their own bishop, and in developments parallel to some of those in Montanism, refused to accept ordinations or baptisms by *traditores,* depending rather on "direct witness of the Spirit" to assure divine sanction. With their emphasis on charismatic and personal revelation, they tended to be iconoclastic. Catholic apologists and Calvinists alike tended to see some Protestant groups (e.g., Anabaptists) at the time of the Reformation as Donatists or Montanists; the charge was later repeated against Methodists. Unsurprisingly, the movement's antinomianism found strong support in American literature, in which Walt Whitman's *Song of Myself* may be the classic example of secular donatism. Whitman disparages "the old cautious hucksters," including Jehovah, Zeus, and Allah, who "did the work of their days, but are now an impediment to the spirit."

Docetism. Some members of the early Church tended to see Christ's human body as illusory, a semblance or *dokēsis,* and his sufferings and death as merely dramatic "appearance": "If he suffered he was not God; if he was God he did not suffer." Docetism was popular among Greeks since its dismissal of Christ's body helped remove the scandal hellenic thinkers found in the Incarnation. The response of the early Fathers was to insist, as had St. Paul, on the historicity of Christ's life, death, and resurrection. St. Ignatius, Bishop of Antioch, asked, "If . . . he suffered in mere appearance . . . why am I in bonds?" (*Trallians,* 9.10).

Gnosticism. Gnosticism is notoriously protean and difficult to define. Gnostic sects, often hellenist, spread at the same time as Christianity and frequently attached themselves parasitically to Christian as well as other traditions. Gnostics had two central preoccupations: belief in a dualistic world in which good and evil contested; and belief in the existence of a secret code of true knowledge passed on from one master "knower" to the next, in a succession of oral or written tradition reaching back (in Christian contexts) to Jesus or (in Jewish contexts) to Moses. This emphasis on an inner circle of those possessing secret knowledge persists in modern literature in W. B. Yeats, Charles Williams, and other members of the Order of the Golden Dawn. In Yeats's "Sailing to Byzantium" the human spirit is "sick with desire / And fastened to a dying animal," longing for release from a dying material world and for spiritual rebirth through secret knowledge. *Gnōsis* means "knowledge" and abstracted and elevated knowledge typically becomes the supreme object of "worship," tending therefore to cast Christianity or Judaism off from their historical origins. This "Hellenizing" process had particularly the effect of cutting Christianity off from its Judaic roots, a feature popular in Hellenized communities where there was latent or open anti-Semitism.

Ethical systems among Gnostics were similarly protean; they could be ascetic or orgiastic. Antinomianism was strong in some groups. "Mythologizing" of the life of Jesus, which Paul found to his dismay among the Christians in Corinth, or worship of intermediate spirits, demons, or angels, which he found among the Colossians, exemplified a post-Platonist tendency among the gnostics, which was to abstract into systems of knowledge and principles what had been before merely the reporting of gospel history. The "remythologizing" of Judeo-Christian history by William Blake is not a novel phenomenon in literary tradition but the expression of a fairly consistent gnostic impulse. Some early groups were willing to accept the Christian notion of redemption, but not with Christ as redeemer. The Samaritans preferred Simon Magus, others Hercules. Competing groups attested to their purity and authority by elaborating genealogies of succession, in which gnostics listed their teachers and those preceding them all the way back to Jesus, all faithfully transmitting the "true tradition" of knowledge. The idea of establishing authority through a magisterial chain of secret *gnōsis* proved more durable institutionally than the idea of Tertullian and other charismatics that it came personally by direct witness of the Spirit, and may even have led, directly and indirectly, to the orthodox Catholic doctrine of apostolic succession.

Manicheanism. Manes (ca. 215-275) was a Persian who founded a religious sect which viewed the world as struggling in a primeval conflict between light and darkness. For Manes the task of religion was to release the particles of light which Satan stole from the realm of light and imprisoned in the human brain. Jesus, Moses, Buddha, and Manes were divinely appointed assistants to this task. Since the body was seen as a vehicle of Satan's work, the cult was severely ascetic, considering it a crime to conceive children, who would simply become more vile bodies imprisoning light to Satan's purpose. This analogue to gnostic views of the body spread vigorously in North Africa, where St. Augustine came to be an adherent for a time. As Albert Camus observed in his Algiers M.A. thesis (1939), Augustine's own extreme asceticism (like that of St. Jerome and the "desert fathers"), as well as his metaphysic of light and darkness, owes more to Manes than is generally acknowledged. Later writers associate the god of the Manicheans with tyranny; as Cowper puts it, "Ador'd through fear, strong only to destroy" (*The Task*, 5.444-45).

Pelagianism. Pelagius was an early British theologian (360-420), probably Irish, and described unflatteringly by St. Jerome as being large and ponderous of body and mind. In response to the Augustinian doctrine of the total depravity of humankind and of the consequent bondage of the will, Pelagius and his followers argued that the acceptance of such a doctrine threw blame on God which really belonged to the individual. His motto was "If I ought, I can": in short, he believed that holiness could be achieved by simple exercise of human free will and a rigorous discipline. This idea had the effect of undermining the traditional notion of original sin and also tended to downplay the role of divine grace. The other side of his position is then that ability limits obligation, that there can be no sin where the will is not absolutely free — able to choose good or evil. The favorite Pelagian formula, *"Si necessitas est, peccatum non est; si voluntatis, vitari potest"* (if it is a function of necessity, it is not sin; if of the will choosing, it may be), had a ring of finality about it which, according to Jerome, impressed superficial minds. In the 14th cent. the Pelagianism of some theological writers promoted the Augustinian counterattack of Bishop Bradwardine, who figures in Chaucer's *Nun's Priest's Tale.* James Joyce hints with a pun in *Finnegans Wake* that he writes with "Pelagiarist pen."

The proliferation of heresies in both ancient and modern times has produced varieties too numerous to be fully listed, even though many have had a role to play in literature. Among the more important of these are: the "Albigensian" or "Catharist" heresy, which influenced Provençal troubadour poetry, including that of Guido Calvacanti, thence becoming an interest to Dante and still later to Ezra Pound; the "Jansenist" heresy, a kind of Calvinism among Catholics, which claimed François Mauriac among its sympathizers; the "Socinian" heresy of Lelio and Fausto Sozzini that Jesus was not God but merely a prophet, and that the sacraments had no supernatural quality, was an influence on Unitarianism and a code word for Protestantism generally among Catholic writers of the Enlightenment such as Dryden in *The Hind*

and the Panther. This merely parallels the nomenclature of Calvinist apologists for Catholics or Arminian Methodists who are thought to emphasize free will more than foreordination and "electing grace" in discussions of salvation: these were (and still often are) called by such writers "semi-Pelagian."

While formal heresy is for obvious reasons of less interest to modern writers, it is not entirely absent. R. Ellman, in his biography of James Joyce, may be overstating a point when he says Joyce is Manichean "because he thinks the sex act is dirty," but the American writer and poet Wendell Berry is probably within the mark in suggesting that modern intellectual life is prone to a kind of gnosticism. In his essay "The Loss of the University," Berry questions the attempt of literary theory to study language in detachment from the real historical world of objects and human actions, a concern apparently shared by novelist Walker Percy (in *Lost in the Cosmos*). Both see deconstructionist theory, e.g., as a kind of literary gnosticism. Whether or not the practice of modern literary theory and poetics involves the cultivation of a high-priestly elite with a secret knowledge and language, the general abstractionism of modern thought — its rejection of the world as it has been created — may, as Richard Wilbur suggests, constitute an invitation to secular gnosticism which poets have seen their perennial duty as resisting. In Wilbur's "Love Calls Us to the Things of this World," "The soul descends once more in bitter love / To accept the waking body . . ." (cf. "A World Without Objects is a Sensible Emptiness"); however, if Donne was right, that "Arguing is heretiques game, and Exercise / As wrastlers, perfects them" ("The Progress of the Soul," 12.118-20), then literary theory may well be a new battleground for competing gnostic (structuralism and post-structuralist deconstruction, Freudianism) and Montanist movements (new criticism, Marxism, feminism) whose ostensible root texts are secular as well as sacred scripture. Insofar as this may be true, however, it is not a unique phenomenon. Since the Enlightenment gnostic heresies in particular have been refurbished, welcomed, opposed, and extensively analyzed. Among theologians and intellectual and cultural historians, for many of whom, since the 20th-cent. prominence of Hegel and Heidegger, *gnōsis* has become more attractive than the biblical insistence upon historical revelation, it can have the effect of desymbolizing or resymbolizing many of the chief narrative elements in biblical tradition.

Bibliography. Barth, K. *Protestant Thought: from Rousseau to Ritschl* (1969); Berger, P. *The Heretical Imperative* (1979); Hamilton, K. *Earthly Good: the Churches and the Betterment of Human Existence* (1990); Lundin, R. "Grace in the Given: Gnosis and Enlightenment." *Reformed Journal* 39 (1989), 16-24; Rahner, K. "Heresy." In *The Concise "Sacramentum Mundi"* (1975).   DAVID L. JEFFREY
MARTIN E. MARTY

HERMENEUTICS Hermeneutics inquires into the conditions under which the interpretation of texts or symbols is valid, productive, or simply possible. Traditionally, biblical hermeneutics formulated principles which would facilitate responsible, appropriate, and controlled interpretations of biblical passages. In recent years, however, hermeneutics has broadened considerably in scope. The focus is no longer simply on technical interpretative procedures, but on the very process of understanding itself. Attention is given not only to the text, but also to the purposes and horizons of the reader.

The term *hermeneutics* probably first featured as the name for a subject-area in J. C. Dannhauer's work *Hermeneutica Sacra* (1654). But conscious reflection on problems of interpretation began in the ancient world. Probably the earliest hermeneutical issue to be raised was the status of allegorical interpretation. Since at least the 5th or 6th cent. B.C. the narratives of Homer were interpreted allegorically by those who wished to appropriate the Homeric tradition while rejecting the face-value meaning of Homer's stories of the exploits of the gods (including Hermes, the god who came to be associated not only with interpretation, but with thievery). Allegorical interpretation of the Jewish Scriptures was used extensively by Philo of Alexandria (ca. 30 B.C.–A.D. 40) in order to commend a radically reinterpreted Bible to his educated Greek readers. This kind of interpretation characteristically occurs when interpreters wish to appeal to the authority of a sacred or classical text while modifying its meaning.

There are traces of allegorical interpretation in the NT itself (cf. 1 Cor. 10:1-6; Gal. 4:21-31). Some prefer, however, to think of such instances as more usually examples of typology. While allegory depends on correspondence between ideas, typology more strictly presupposes patterns or correspondences between events or personal histories. Both the NT writers and Jewish 1st-cent. exegesis reflect a similar concern to apply the OT to their own situations; in the case of the Church, to the coming of Christ. This interpretative tradition of concern for contemporary application has sometimes been called *pesher* exegesis.

The early Church had both positive and negative attitudes toward allegorical interpretation. The School of Antioch and especially St. John Chrysostom (ca. 347-407) opposed it. But it was favored by the School of Alexandria, and many of the Church Fathers used it. Origen (ca. 185-254) argued explicitly for a threefold interpretation of Scripture: the literal or outward, the moral, and the spiritual. This led essentially to the four senses of medieval interpretation. The hermeneutical reflection of the early Church was also decisively influenced by controversy with Marcion in the 2nd cent., as a result of which the theological unity of the OT and NT was firmly asserted. One further issue concerned the role of tradition or church doctrine. As against the rival biblical interpretations of the gnostics, St. Irenaeus and others insisted on the importance of the rule of faith as a necessary interpretive framework for understanding the Bible. The Bible, in Tertullian's view, was the Church's book.

The Reformers did not reject the importance of faith or even of tradition. But they did insist that the Bible could stand, as it were, on its own feet, in such a way as to correct tradition where this might be necessary. But the Bible, Luther insisted, was not a nose of wax to be pushed into any shape fancied by the reader. Thus hermeneutics in the Reformation tradition has most commonly been seen as offering ground rules for "correct" interpretation. The rise of historical criticism facilitated the task of viewing biblical passages in terms of their own historical situation and context. However, historical inquiry in some circles tended to become almost an end in itself as if textual interpretation were simply an aid for the historian of religion.

After the mid-20th cent. hermeneutics achieved new significance. Fresh attention was paid to the earliest claims of Schleiermacher (1768-1834) and Dilthey (1833-1911) that hermeneutics concerns not just methodological procedures, but the very nature of the process of understanding. The decisive philosophical influence in the present century has been Hans-Georg Gadamer, whose point of departure was Heidegger. Once again attention is given to the tradition within which the interpreter makes his or her judgments. How does the reader's situation and prior world of understanding engage with that of the text? Rudolf Bultmann's proposals about demythologizing the NT had already raised questions about the readiness of the reader to be challenged, rather than merely informed, by the biblical text, even though his posing of an either / or alternative gave his work a severely reductionist aspect. The so-called new hermeneutic of E. Fuchs and G. Ebeling inquired not only about how the reader interpreted the text, but also about how the biblical text interpreted the reader. In recent years biblical hermeneutics has become sensitive to a wider range of intellectual and cultural traditions.

English literary tradition is rich with engagement of these historical developments in biblical hermeneutics, and while no detailed summary can be offered, something of the main outline and most prominent questions can be indicated. To begin with, questions about interpretation — as well as about the establishment of valid or generically appropriate guidelines for individual acts of interpretation — are an abiding preoccupation of patristic, scholastic, and Reformation literature. St. Augustine's *De doctrina Christiana* is the foundational text, and John Wyclif's *De Veritate Sacrae Scripturae,* Hugh of St. Victor's *Didascalion,* Luther's *Commentary on Romans,* and Milton's *De Doctrina Christiana* are each in their own way exemplary of Western Christian preoccupation with the establishment of a right basis for interpretation of the Bible. St. Jerome's letter to Paulinus, Bishop of Nola (A.D. 394) may be taken as articulating one of the poles of opinion against which biblical exposition theory has historically measured its task: "The art of interpreting the scriptures," writes Jerome, "is the only one of which all men everywhere claim to be masters. To quote Horace . . . 'Taught or untaught, we all write poetry' [Horace, *Ep.* 2.1.115-16]." Among the worst, he implies, are those who, like himself,

> have been familiar with secular literature before they have come to the study of the Holy Scriptures. Such men, when they charm the popular ear by the finish of their style, suppose every word *they* say to be a law of God. They do not deign to notice what the prophets and apostles have intended, but construe conflicting passages to suit their own meaning. (*Ep.* 53.7)

Jerome then goes on to point out that one of the most egregious offenses of the interpreter who ignores authorial intention is refusal to pay attention to questions of genre and internal logic; in fact, obtuseness to such formal questions obliterates the recovery of intention in many cases. Linkage of irresponsible interpretation to questions of genre and authorial intention in particular is a recurring theme in Western tradition: it is the preoccupation of John Wyclif's first book of *De Veritate*, e.g., and Chaucer makes variations upon these themes in his great, symphonic excursus into theory and practice of interpretation, *The Canterbury Tales.* Wyclif's central argument is that the divine authorial intention is not discernible until the reader corresponds to that intention by a willed commitment to affirmation in the heart. Thus, for Wyclif, echoing Augustine in *De doctrina Christiana,* the first requisite of hermeneutics is a "Christ-like moral life." Anything less than that will introduce ulterior motives in the interpreter. Such motives can, wittingly or not, turn interpretation toward an exercise in self-justification or, in a more extreme instance, transform what purports to be interpretation into the devil's rhetoric, calling God's Word at its obvious commonsensical level into question (cf. Gen. 3:1, where Satan says to Eve, "Yea, hath God said. . . ?"). Distinguishing intention — in the characters of a narrative pericope, in the actual author, and finally in the ultimate Author — are thus crucial for Wyclif in the establishment of the full meaning (and hence *auctoritas*) of a text. Supporting his hermeneutic, Wyclif defines his position as in the tradition of Augustine, St. John Chrysostom, St. Gregory, St. Bonaventure, and his near-contemporary, Bishop Bradwardine — an Augustinian consensus to which he was prepared to submit his own synthesis for an appropriate test of correspondence.

The essential difference between Wyclif's still arguably Catholic view (despite his surprisingly modern reflections on intrinsic genre, narrative logic, linguistic matters, and intention in the reader, or what might be called "reader response") and that of many of the 16th-cent. Reformers lies in the Reformers' more general disavowal of reasoned analysis and comparative assessment of previous or other readings in a perceived "community" of interpretation. Zwingli represents this view when he writes that one may only approach Scripture properly when he,

> despairyinge of hys owne witte and reason, wholly, doth altogether submit and humble hym selfe, & confesseth that he knoweth nothinge but hanging wholly upon God, doth geve a diligent eare, to his inspiratyon. . . . But he is sayde to have nothyng, whiche doth ingerate and bryng to the scriptures his owne carnall and fleshly sense. . . . The wordes of the spirite, are manifeste and cleare, the doctryne of god, is lightsome, illuminatyng teaching, and certifiyng mans heart and mynde, of his salvation, without any patchyng of humayne reason. . . . Wherfor we do see that the symple wyttes of ye disciples, were taughte of God, to thys ende, that wee myghte learne too seeke all the knowledge of heavenly things in God onely. (*A Short Pathway. . .* , trans. J. Veron)

In the Baptist Samuel How's *The Sufficiencie of the Spirits Teaching without Humane Learning* (1640) the point is put still more forcefully:

> I doe acknowledge it [learning] in it selfe to be a good thing, and good in its proper place, which is for the repayring of that *decay which came upon man for sin* . . . but bring it once to be a *help to understand the mind of God in the holy Scriptures,* and there it is *detestable filth, drosse, and dung* in that respect, and so good for nothing, but [to] *destroy, and cause men to erre.*

While this position appears not far from that of Jerome, for the Protestant interpreter, no hermeneutic tainted with the medieval and Catholic notion that philosophy was to be the handmaid of theology, especially in matters of exegesis, could be acceptable. Milton's Christ seems to say much the same thing in *Paradise Regained,* in debating with Satan:

> Think not but that I know these things; or think
> I know them not; not therefore am I short
> Of knowing what I ought: he who receives
> Light from above, from the fountain of light,
> No other doctrine needs. (4.286-90)

In his tract *The Likeliest Means to Remove Hirelings out of the Church* (1659) Milton had already argued this subtler position, not that a classical education is in any respect superfluous for one who would minister God's Word to his parishioners, but rather that above and beyond learning, what "makes fit a minister, the scripture can best informe us to be only from above" (*Works,* ed. Patterson, 6.93). But Milton indicates in his *De Doctrina* that he considers "requisites for the public interpretation of Scripture" to properly include "knowledge of languages; inspection of the originals; examination of the context; care in distinguishing between literal and figurative expressions; consideration of cause and circumstance, of antecedents and consequents; mutual comparison of texts; and regard to the analogy of faith" (*Works,* 16.263, 265). That is, as Barbara Lewalski has shown, on Milton's view a broad learning in the classical disciplines fits the minister for *exposition,* while for the *apprehension* of spiritual truth it remains irrelevant (*Milton's Brief Epic,* 282-88).

Interpreter is a positive character in Bunyan's *Pilgrim's Progress,* instructing Christian in the principles of faith. But he is more in the tradition of Samuel How than of Milton, showing Christian a picture of a figure with "eyes lift up to Heaven, the best of Books in His hand, the Law of Truth . . . written upon its lips, the World . . . behind its back" which "stood as if it pleaded with men." Interpreter tells Christian that this is "the only Man, whom the Lord of the Place whither thou art going, hath Authorized, to be thy Guide." Subsequently subordinate hermeneutic principles are adduced: the ascendency of Grace over Law, Patience over Passion; and desire for an understanding of eternal verities rather than merely temporal knowledge (citing 2 Cor. 4:18; cf. Rom. 1:20). The Man of Despair in the Iron Cage is shown as one who has lost the good of interpretation in much the same fashion as some of the damned souls in Dante's *Inferno* lost "the good of intellect"; intention in the interpreter (reader) having been perverted to obduracy by "the Lusts, Pleasures, and Profits of this World; in the injoyment of which," says the caged man, "I did then promise my self much delight: but now even every one of those things also bite me, and gnaw me like a burning worm." Interpreter's final revelation to Christian is a vision of the Last Judgment, in which he sees "the Man that sat upon the Cloud, open the Book; and bid the World draw near" — i.e., he discovers that the only fully reliable reader (interpreter) of the text is the divine Author of that text. It is this Author / Reader who will one day give the text of each person's life its ultimate "reading," effectively an evaluation of one's lifelong interpretation of Scripture as that has ensued in ethical life.

Such a version of Christian hermeneutic principles as Bunyan proposes echoes formulations like that of Luther in his *Commentary on Romans* and How's *Sufficiencie;* his is a general Protestant persuasion to respect the efficacy of individual interpretation under the guidance of the Holy Spirit. For a Catholic convert like John Dryden, however, it was precisely this individualistic and subjective basis, where "each may be his own Intepreter" (*The Hind and the Panther,* 1.463; cf. 2.470-73), which had led to the destructive factionalism of the 16th and 17th cents. Hence, Dryden opts in later life for a Catholic grounding in venerable consensus, or tradition in the Church, as necessary arbiter:

> The church alone can certainly explain,
> That following ages, leaning on the past,
> May rest upon the Primitive at last.
> Nor wou'd I thence the word no rule infer,
> But none without the church interpreter. . . .
> But what th'Apostles their successours taught,

They to the next, from them to us is brought,
Th'undoubted sense which is in scripture sought. (*The Hind and the Panther,* 2.354-63)

Reformed hermeneutics in the 18th cent. distinguished itself from latitudinarian practice (e.g., Tillotson, Butler) largely in respect of this issue. One Church of England poet, William Cowper, declares his leanings in the controversy in the final stanza of his *Olney Hymns* ("God moves in a mysterious way, / His wonders to perform") where, against the prevalence of skeptical relativism in interpretation, he writes:

> Blind unbelief is sure to err,
> And scan his work in vain;
> God is his own interpreter,
> And he will make it plain.

And in *The Progress of Error* Cowper inveighs against the extremes of "philosophers astray" and the "wild enthusiast" alike, offering no hermeneutic principle more profound than the Augustinian tests of spiritual maturity and moral life:

> A critic on the sacred book should be
> Candid and learn'd, dispassionate and free;
> Free from the wayward bias bigots feel,
> From fancy's influence, and intemp'rate zeal:
> But, above all, (or let the wretch refrain,
> Nor touch the page he cannot but profane)
> Free from the domineering pow'r of lust;
> A lewd interpreter is never just. (452-59)

This becomes almost a topos in Englsh literature. As Carlyle suggests in *Latter Day Pamphlets,* the *sine qua non* of irresponsible interpretation will invariably prove to be the improper motives of an unjust life ("Hudson's Statue"). This topos, familiar from 18th-cent. satirists to 20th-cent. biblical and literary scholars alike, is residually present in the Southern Agrarians and New Critics. It has been fiercely resented and rejected in the formulations of several structuralist and poststructuralist theorists, however, who on this account as much as any other have desired to depose once and for all the question of authorial intention (e.g., Roland Barthes, *S/Z*), if not intention in the reader. As for the vexed post-Reformation question about the relation of divine light and reasoned textual analysis in ferreting out the message of the gospel, modern poet Margaret Avison holds sagely against a false dichotomy:

> Interpreters and spoilers since the four
> rivers flowed out of Eden,
> men have nonetheless
> learned that the Pure can bless
> on earth *and* from on high
> ineradicably. ("Light [III]")

See also ALLEGORY; TYPOLOGY.

Bibliography: Allen, J. B. *The Ethical Poetic of the Later Middle Ages* (1982); Barr, J. *The Bible in the Modern World* (1973); Blackman, E. C. *Biblical Interpretation* (1957); Caird, G. B. *The Language and Imagery of the Bible* (1981);

de Lubac, H. *Exégèse médiéval: Les quatre sens de l'Ecriture.* 4 vols. (1959-64); Ebeling, G. "Hermeneutik." In *RGG,* 3rd ed. (1959), 3.242-62; Frei, H. W. *The Eclipse of Biblical Narrative: A Study in Eighteenth and Nineteenth Century Hermeneutics* (1974); Funk, R. W. *Language, Hermeneutic and Word of God* (1966); Gadamer, H.-G. *Truth and Method* (trans. 1975); Hirsch, D. *Validity in Interpretation* (1967); Jeffrey, D. L. "John Wyclif and the Hermeneutics of Reader Intention." *Int.* 99 (1985), 272-87; Lewalski, B. *Milton's Brief Epic* (1966); Longenecker, R. *Biblical Exegesis in the Apostolic Period* (1975); Marshall, I. H. *New Testament Interpretation* (1977); Palmer, R. E. *Hermeneutics. Interpretation Theory in Schleiermacher, Dilthey, Heidegger, and Gadamer* (1969); Prickett, S. "Words and the Word: Language." In *Poetics and Biblical Interpretation* (1986); Smart, J. D. *The Interpretation of Scripture* (1961); Stuhlmacher, P. *Historical Criticism and Theological Interpretation of Scripture* (1977); *Vom Verstehen des neuen Testaments. Eine Hermeneutik* (1979); Thiselton, A. C. *The Two Horizons. New Testament Hermeneutics and Philosophical Description with Special Reference to Heidegger, Bultmann, Gadamer, and Wittgenstein* (1980).   DAVID L. JEFFREY
ANTHONY C. THISELTON

HERMON   Assumed by some to be the mount of the transfiguration of Jesus.

HEROD ANTIPAS   Herod Antipas, son of Herod the Great by his Samaritan wife Malthrace, was Tetrarch of Galilee from 4 B.C. to A.D. 39. He is mentioned in the Synoptics chiefly for his execution of John the Baptist (Matt. 14:1-12; Mark 6:17-28) and because Jesus was sent to him by Pilate shortly before the Crucifixion (Luke 23:7-12; Acts 4:27). In later years, Caligula's elevation of his brother-in-law Agrippa as King of Traconitis, while he remained only a tetrarch, led Herod to seek redress in person. While conferring with the emperor at the resort of Baiae, a message arrived accusing Antipas of making common cause against Rome with the Parthians, in consequence of which he was banished to Gaul in 39, where he died (Josephus, *Ant.* 18.7.2; *J. W.* 2.9.6).

Described by Jesus as "that fox" (Luke 13:32) and condemned for various evils by John, Herod is presented in the Gospels as a weak man prevailed upon by Herodias. Both Matthew and Mark describe him as reluctant to execute the Baptist and "exceeding sorry" after he had ordered it. By the 2nd cent., however, in the apocryphal literature of the NT, he is treated more harshly, as, e.g., the Gospel According to Peter, in which it is Herod rather than Pilate who gives the order for the execution of Jesus. Though contrary to the evidence of the Synoptics and of Tacitus (*Annales,* 15.44), this view recurs in the 8th-cent. OE *Andreas,* attributed to the school of Cynewulf:

> þone Herodes ealdre besnyðede,
> forcom aet campe cyning Iudea,
> rices beraedde, ond hine rode befealg,
> þaet heon gealgan his gast onsende. (1324-27)

("Herod deprived Him of life, the king of the Jews vanquished Him in battle, reft Him of His realm, and committed Him to the cross, so that He sent forth His spirit on the gallows.")

The Greek recension of *Andreas* also claims that Christ was put to death by Herod. Thus, while the primary reference in the outburst of Chaucer's Prioress against the "cursed folk of Herodes al newe" (7.574) is, in the context of child murder and on the analogy of Matt. 2 a reference to Herod the Great, considering the examples above there may be an oblique allusion to Herod Antipas in his assumed role as Christ killer. In the OE *Juliana,* a demon confesses to having prompted Judas's betrayal, urging the Roman soldier to wound Jesus, and inciting Herod to kill John the Baptist, all of which amplifies the Vita in *Acta Sanctorum* which has only *"ego sum qui feci ab Herodes Joannem decapitari."*

In *De Doctrina Christiana,* Milton argues that the oath given by Herod to Salome was, on analogy with 1 Sam. 25:22, not binding, and he suggests that "the breach of such oaths is better than the performance." Milton also agrees with Chaucer's Pardoner (6.488-91) that liquor was influential in Herod's decision: "It may also be thought that Herod had well bedew'd himself with wine," which "made him grant the easier to his wives *[sic]* daughter."

In his annotations to Dr. Thornton's translation of the Lord's Prayer, Blake takes issue with Dr. Johnson's claim that the Bible cannot be understood by the unlearned, "except through the aid of critical and explanatory notes," countering: "Christ & his Apostles were Illiterate Men; Caiphas *[sic],* Pilate & Herod were Learned." In the Preface to *St. Joan,* Shaw contrasts the coventional superiority of "Herod and Pilate" with the mysterious superiority of Christ, Socrates, and Joan.

See also HEROD THE GREAT; JOHN THE BAPTIST; SALOME.
Bibliography. Buchler, A. *Types of Jewish Palestinian Piety from 70 B.C.E. to 70 C.E.* (1926); Busch, F.-O. *The Five Herods* (1958); Ginsburg, M. S. *Rome et la Judée* (1928); Jones, A. H. M. *The Herods of Judaea* (1967); Josephus. *The Jewish War.* Trans. H. St.-J. Thackeray. 9 vols. (1928); Perowne, S. *The Later Herods* (1958); Radin, M. *The Jews among the Greeks and Romans* (1915); Stauffer, E. *Jerusalem und Rom im Zeitalter Jesu Christi* (1957); Tacitus. *The Histories.* Trans. K. Wellesley (1964); Willrich, H. *Das Haus des Herodes zwischen Jerusalem und Rom* (1929).
MICHAEL GOLDBERG

HEROD THE GREAT   The son of Antipater, Herod was born ca. 73 B.C., appointed Tetrarch of Galilee in 41 B.C., and named King of Judea the following year. As related in Matt. 2:1-8, 15-19, he reigned at the birth of Jesus and died shortly afterward (ca. 4 B.C.). Upon being informed by the Wise Men of the birth of the "King of the Jews," Herod sent them to find the child, claiming that he too desired to worship him. When they eluded Herod by returning to their country another way, he "was exceeding wroth, and sent forth, and slew all the children that were in Bethlehem, and in all the coasts thereof, from two years old and under," his Slaughter of the Innocents paralleling the murder of Jewish infants at the behest of an equally tyrannical Pharaoh (Exod. 1). This action prompts Christian commentators such as St. Isidore of Seville to see Herod as a type of the devil and of pagans who wish to destroy the name of Christ: *"Herodes . . . diaboli formam expressit, vel gentium, qui, cupientes exstinguere nomen Christi de mundo, in caede martyrum saevierunt"* (*Allegoriae quaedam Scripturae Sacrae* [PL 83.118]).

Herod was celebrated by 1st-cent. historian Josephus for his creation of a magnificent seaport of Caesarea as a monument to his own fame (Josephus, *J.W.* 1.21). Josephus's assessment of Herod is that he was "fortunate" in nearly all respects, "since from a private man, he obtained the kingdom," but that in his domestic affairs he was "a most unfortunate man" (*J.W.* 1.33). He was notorious for his rages and for impulsive acts of violence, including the murder of his own sons. Augustus is credited with the quip: "I had rather be Herod's pig than Herod's son."

This aspect of Herod's character lost nothing in the long centuries of Christian commentary on biblical events. Herod became renowned as a cruel tyrant — indeed, as a personification of Anger and Pride — to English writers from Aelfric (homily for "The Nativity of the Innocents" [*Homilies of the Anglo-Saxon Church*, ed. Benjamin Thorpe (1844), 1.76-91]) to Yeats *(The Cat and the Moon)*. His violent temper and ranting became part of his stock characterization in medieval drama, as indicated, e.g., in his opening speeches in the Towneley "Offering of the Magi" and "Herod the Great." Similarly, in the Coventry "Pageant of the Shearmen and Tailors" Herod "rages in the pageant and in the street also" (rubric following line 783). Such behavior is in these plays typically treated as both mad and ridiculous; like many of the vain and ambitious opponents of God, including Satan himself, he ultimately becomes the brunt of divine comedy.

The histrionic qualities associated with the Herod of medieval drama appeal to Chaucer's egotistical Absolon, who "somtyme, to shewe his lightnesse and maistrye, / . . . pleyeth Herodes upon a scaffold hye" (*Miller's Tale*, 1.3383-84), and are alluded to in Hamlet's famous rebuke to amateur actors — "I would have such a fellow whipped for o'erdoing Termagant. It out-herods Herod. Pray you avoid it" (3.2.12-13). The view of Herod as a foolish ranter who would "tear a passion to tatters . . . to split the ears of the groundlings" survived well past the Renaissance.

There is another less comic side to Herod's literary characterization. The demonic violence attributed to him is often referred to in describing excessive cruelty of any kind: for Chaucer, that of the Jews who murder the child in *The Prioress's Tale* (7.572-75); for Shakespeare, *Henry 5*'s proposed destruction of Harfleur (3.3.38-41) and

Cleopatra's ferocity at a messenger (*Ant.* 3.3.3-4); for Burns, the Earl of Breadalbane's tyranny against the Highlanders, for which the devil assigns the nobleman a place in hell "'Tween Herod's hip, an' Polycrate" ("Address of Beelzebub," 58); for Browning, the cruelty of the murder in *The Ring and the Book* (9.128, 136); for Shaw, the indiscriminate slaughter of a terrorist attack (pref. to *Major Barbara*). In *Moby-Dick* the watchmen of the *Pequod* are "startled by a cry . . . plaintively wild and unearthly — like half-articulated wailings of the ghosts of all Herod's murdered Innocents." This eerie event presages the meeting with the *Rachel*, whose captain, like the ship's biblical namesake, is weeping for a lost child.

The contrast between Herod's assumed authority as King of Judea and the divine authority of Jesus, emphasized in the events of Matt. 2, is central to many literary presentations. Medieval dramatists draw attention to the contrast in their juxtaposition of court and Nativity scenes, as does Milton in *Paradise Regained* (2.76; 4.422-24) and Crashaw in *Sospetto d'Herode* (250-53). The ultimate triumph of Christ the King is demonstrated by having Herod cut down by death in the midst of his earthly pomp, as in the N-Town cycle. Elsewhere his demise is slow and horrible; *Cursor mundi* shows him dying the most disgusting of deaths, a fearful combination of palsy, itch, leprosy, dropsy, and other ailments. In the *Fall of Princes* (211ff.) he dies, body black and swollen, eaten by worms, and giving off a violent stench (see also Longfellow's "The Birds of Killingworth," in *Tales of a Wayside Inn*). Such descriptions evidence a conflation of Herod's own demise with the excruciating death that his grandson, Herod Agrippa I, suffered as a judgment on his pride (Acts 12:21-23).

Herod has predictable appearances in modern fictional "biographies" of Jesus, as well as biblical plays, but elsewhere his place is often reduced to comic allusion; the characters of P. G. Wodehouse frequently express their sympathy with Herod when they have to deal with objectionable small boys.

See also RACHEL; RAMAH; SLAUGHTER OF THE INNOCENTS.

KARL TAMBURR
MICHAEL MURPHY

HEWERS OF WOOD   When Joshua had razed Ai and Jericho, the western tribes of Canaan banded together to fight the invaders — all save the Gibeonites, who "worked wilily" instead. They disguised themselves as travelers from afar come to "make a league" with Israel. Joshua and the "princes of the congregation," failing to ask "counsel at the mouth of the LORD," swore peace with the Gibeonites. The ruse was quickly discovered, but the oath could not be undone. To appease his people, Joshua condemned the Gibeonites to perpetual servitude, to be "hewers of wood and drawers of water for the congregation, and for the altar of the LORD" (Josh. 9).

That a treaty was made with the Gibeonites seems

certain (Fensham, ad loc.), and this treaty, succeeding as it does that on Mt. Ebal (Josh. 8:30), indicates a special relationship between the invading Hebrews and the Hivite peoples inhabiting the region (Boling and Wright, 270-71); the relationship was such that Saul suffered for violating it (2 Sam. 21:1-3).

Interpreters have stressed the notion of justice implied in the tale. St. Jerome (*Adv. Jov.* 2) uses the text to exemplify and justify differences among the righteous about degrees of worth in God's eyes. St. Ambrose emphasizes the Gibeonites' punishment, using the text to illustrate the moral that fraud must be avoided: Scripture validates civil law (*De officiis ministrorum*, 3.10). Calvin (*Comms. on the Book of Joshua*) interprets the tale as a lesson in justice and free will. Joshua finds a "middle course" which will keep the oath yet punish trickery. The punishment is indeed hard, but just because the Gibeonites were "cursed of their own accord, or by their own fault." The Gibeonites, so Calvin argues, are aware that they have erred and have been fairly dealt with.

Allusions in English literature to the euphonious phrase "hewers of wood and drawers of water" usually invoke its primary meaning, an epitome of taking on a lowly occupation (see also Deut. 29:11). Thus Chaucer, in *The Knight's Tale,* relates how Arcite, like the Gibeonites, disguises himself "poorly" as a servant to be near his beloved Emelye. The disguise prospers, for "Well koude he hewen wode, and water bere" (1.1355-1422). Similarly, Tennyson — perhaps alluding both to Chaucer and Joshua — describes how Gareth in laborer's guise is set to "draw water or hew wood" by the spiteful Sir Kay (*Idylls,* "Gareth and Lynette," 486). Less certain because no explicit verbal allusion is made but more developed than either Chaucer's or Tennyson's allusions are the spectacular demotions in *The Tempest* of Caliban, who fetches wood, and Ferdinand, who piles logs. Caliban's wiliness and perpetual servitude are in fact more in keeping with the biblical source than are the characterizations of Arcite and Gareth. A delightfully witty allusion is Swift's in "A Serious Poem Upon William Wood," who had received from Parliament a much debated order to mint copper coins for Ireland:

> When Foes are o'ercome, we preserve them from
>   Slaughter,
> To be *Hewers of Wood* and *Drawers of Water,*
> Now, although to *Draw Water* is not very good,
> Yet we all should Rejoyce to be Hewers of *Wood.*

The Gibeonites are thus the original of the "harmless drudge," as Dr. Johnson calls the maker of dictionaries, an association Carlyle was only too happy to return to Johnson in its biblical context in his essay "Boswell's Life of Johnson": "With giant's force he toils . . . were it but at hewing of wood and drawing of water" (cf. *Sartor Resartus*, 3.1). But Conrad, in an essay on John Galsworthy,

considers the metaphor to refer to the novelist's necessary commitment to earth and reality (*Last Essays,* 126).

See also JOSHUA.

Bibliography. Boling, R., and G. Wright. *Joshua: A New Translation with Introduction and Commentary* (1982); Calvin, J. *Commentaries on the Book of Joshua.* Trans. H. Beveridge (1854); Fensham, C. "The Treaty Between Israel and the Gibeonites." *BA* 27 (1964), 96-100.   DWIGHT H. PURDY

HEZEKIAH Hezekiah, son of Ahaz, was king of Judah in the time of the prophet Isaiah. His notable deeds are recorded in 2 Kings 18:1–20:21; 2 Chron. 29:1–32:33; Isa. 36–39; Sir. 48:17-25. He reigned from ca. 616 to 687 B.C., during a time of fairly constant military threat from the Assyrians, of whose empire Judah under Hezekiah had become a vassal state. A pious king, he is celebrated for opposing idolatry and destroying the "high places" of pagan worship as well as cleansing and opening the Temple. After a "sickness unto death," he was instructed by the prophet Isaiah to "set [his] house in order" in preparation for his death. Hezekiah "turned his face to the wall" and appealed to God to extend his life. He received a promise that the Lord would indeed grant him fifteen more years and, as a sign of assurance, a reversing of the sun's shadow on "the sun dial of Ahaz" by 10 degrees. When, after his recovery, Hezekiah foolishly showed the Babylonians the royal treasury and armor, Isaiah predicted disaster — plunder and destruction at the hands of his enemies and his own sons made eunuchs in the palace of the Babylonian king. Instead of anguish Hezekiah expressed relief, saying, "For there shall be peace and truth in my [own] days" (Isa. 39:1-8).

Rabbinic legends esteem Hezekiah as steeping the nation in the Law (Sanh. 94b) as well as fulfilling the whole Law himself (Lam. Rab. 25). He was seen by some as the Messiah (Gen. Rab. 97; Lev. Rab. 36.6; Ruth Rab. 7.2; cf. St. Cyril, *Lectures,* 12.22), and one tradition credits him and his disciples with the composition of Isaiah, Proverbs, Canticles, and Ecclesiastes (B. Bat. 15a).

Hezekiah is chiefly remembered in Christian tradition for his piety and for the extraordinary answer to his prayer for a stay of death (e.g., Cyril, *Lectures,* 2.15; 12.22). In New England Puritanism he was sometimes adduced as a type of Christ (e.g., Thomas Frink, *A King Reigning in Righteousness* [1758]) and as a moral example for temporal magistrates.

Christopher Smart's poem of gratitude on recovering from spiritual depression in 1756 is drawn from the story of Hezekiah's recovery, expressing for Smart his "second birth . . . a birth of joy" ("Hymn to the Supreme Being"). However, with the exception of biblical dramas, such as William Allen's *Hezekiah, King of Judah: or, Invasion Repulsed* (1798) and W. H. T. Gairdner's *King Hezekiah: A Tragical Drama* (1923), Hezekiah has a minimal place in English literature.

Several phrases drawn from the story have become commonplace. In Henry James's *The Wings of the Dove*, it is twice said of Milly that "she turned her face to the wall" (cf. 2 Kings 20:2) in a Hezekiah-like gesture of resignation and acceptance of death (the same expression is used in James's "The Abasement of the Northmores" and "The Beldonald Holbein"). While A. W. Pinero's *His House in Order* (1906) makes conscious reference to the Hezekiah narrative (as does Kierkegaard's *Sickness Unto Death*), such phrases are most often used in a merely proverbial way, with no recollection of their biblical source.   DAVID W. BAKER

HIGH PRIEST   Chief minister of the Tabernacle or Temple.

See also AARON; CAIAPHAS AND ANNAS; HOLY OF HOLIES.

HISTORIA SALVATIONIS   The *historia humanae salvationis,* or history of human salvation, is a term given to the biblical overview or scheme which focuses on the genealogy of redemption culminating in the Passion. It is this schema which determines the selection of narrative elements for representation, typically, in the Corpus Christi drama of medieval England.

See also ATONEMENT.

HITTITE   Two apparently distinct groups with this name appear in the OT. One was a great nation which arose in northern Syria and eastern Asia Minor (Josh. 1:4). It had contacts with David (2 Sam. 24:6; cf. 8:9ff. where the Neo-Hittite capital Hamath is mentioned) and was active during subsequent reigns (1 Kings 10:28-29; 11:1; 2 Kings 7:6). Finally Hamath fell to the Assyrians (cf. 2 Kings 18:34; 19:13; Isa. 10:9).

The second was an ethnic group in Canaan during the patriarchal age and until the monarchy. From one member Abraham bought a cave as a burial ground (Gen. 23). Occasionally there was intermarriage with the Israelites (Gen. 27:46; cf. Ezek. 16:3, 45).

Bibliography. Wiseman, D. J., ed. *Peoples of Old Testament Times* (1973), 197-228.   DAVID W. BAKER

HOLINESS   *Holiness (qodesh), holy (qadosh),* and *sanctify (qiddesh)* all derive from the same Hebrew root *qdsh.* Occurring over 600 times in the OT, most often in Leviticus, Numbers, Isaiah, and Ezekiel, it represents one of the most significant concepts of biblical theology.

The most fundamental and comprehensive description of God is that he is holy. "Be holy, for I am holy" (Lev. 11:45) is the slogan of Leviticus reiterated by 1 Pet. 1:16. "Holy, holy, holy is the LORD of hosts," the angelic cry in Isaiah's call-vision (6:3), expresses the keynote to his understanding of God, whom he likes to call "the holy one of Israel." So central is the idea of holiness to the biblical view of God that it might almost be paraphrased by "divinity," and holy as "divine" or "godly." Holiness,

intrinsic to God's character, is not an elevated morality, but constitutes the essence and substance of the Godhead — its purity and otherness.

If holiness primarily describes God's character, it can secondarily be applied to Israel, its religious leaders, the sanctuary, and objects used in divine service. But in these cases the holiness is clearly derivative. Creatures have no intrinsic holiness of their own: their holiness is acquired by accepting a divine call and submitting to the appropriate sanctification ritual. Israel became a holy nation because she was called by God, promised to obey the Law, and was sprinkled with sacrificial blood (Exod. 19–24). The priests, the holiest men within the nation, were chosen by God through Moses for their office and then were ordained according to the procedures described in Lev. 8–9. The Tabernacle and its furniture were holy because they were built according to heavenly design and then dedicated with appropriate forms (Exod. 25–40; Num. 7).

Biblically, holiness stands in contrast to three other important terms, "common, or secular," cleanness, and uncleanness. Everything that is not holy is "common." The "common" divides into two categories, clean and unclean. Cleanness is the state of normal healthy creatures, but uncleanness results from sin, bodily discharges, skin diseases, and death. Of these pollutants death is the most potent, so the holiest men of Israel, the priests and Nazarites, had to keep away from corpses, which would destroy their sanctity (Lev. 21:1, 11; Num. 6:6-12). That death is the most potent destroyer of human holiness suggests as a corollary the close association of holiness with life, since God who is the preeminently holy is also the creator of life.

That sin can also destroy human holiness draws attention to its moral aspect. "The Holy God shows himself holy in righteousness" (Isa 5:16 [RSV]). It is because God is holy that Israel is repeatedly reminded to keep the Law. Infractions of the Law provoke divine wrath, itself an expression of God's holiness when confronted by sin. The holier the person the more strictly he was expected to obey the Law. Thus the apparently minor infringements of the priests in Lev. 10:1-3 and later of Moses and Aaron (Num. 20:7-12) led to their death. Indeed, contact between the holy and the unclean is always dangerous. Thus when God appeared on Mt. Sinai it was fenced off lest unholy people or animals approached too close (Exod. 19). The ark and sacred furniture were kept in a tent to prevent unholy people from dying by looking at them (Num. 4:15; 1 Sam. 5; 6:19). For an unclean person to eat holy, i.e., sacrificial meat could also be lethal. He would be "cut off" (Lev. 7:20).

Holiness thus expresses the dynamic, intensely moral life of God, characteristics which the people chosen by God, especially its leaders, are expected to reproduce and imitate.

In English literature the subject of holiness is treated extensively, especially in the literature of spirituality. The ME poem *Cleanness* paraphrases three biblical narratives

— the Flood (Gen. 6–8), the destruction of Sodom and Gomorrah (Gen. 19), and Belshazzar's feast (Dan. 5) — in such a way as to strike a contrast between holiness and profanation. The cultivation of personal holiness is a strong theme in the writings of Richard Rolle, Walter Hilton, and Sir John Clanvowe (*The Two Ways*). Their contemporary Chaucer is at pains to distinguish those among his Canterbury pilgrims who, like the Parson, are noted for "hooly thoght and werk" and exemplary "clennesse" (*General Prologue*, 1.479; 504) and those who, professing holy orders, nonetheless exhibit only profane disposition.

In Spenser's *Faerie Queene* the Redcrosse Knight is a personification of "Holiness" — a holiness specifically imagined in terms of the institutional purity of the Anglican Church. George Herbert's *A Priest to the Temple* is concerned above all with the holiness of the priest's life and preaching, and speaks of ambition and "curiosity in . . . unprofitable questions" as a "great stumbling block to the holinesse of Scholars." In a rich evocation of Levitical sources, Herbert's "Aaron" describes his desire for the "Holinesse on the head" of a "true Aaron" or priest, which must, by the grace of Christ alone, overcome "profanenesse in my head, / Defects and darknesse in my breast." This same contrast is highlighted in Thomas Fuller's *The Holy State and the Profane State* (1642), a collection of character essays ("The Good Widow," "The True Gentleman," etc.) offered as examples of practical holiness. Jeremy Taylor's *The Rule and Exercise of Holy Living* (1650) is perhaps the best written of 17th-cent. meditations on the subject, though nearly as popular and more influential were Richard Baxter's *Saints' Everlasting Rest* (1650) and Bunyan's allegory of the struggle between Diabolus and King Shaddai for possession of the human city of Mansoul, *The Holy War* (1682). Each of these texts deals with the quest for practical holiness in a profane world.

The 18th cent. is marked by a renewal of the call to personal holiness in the sermons and hymns of John and Charles Wesley and their followers, though in the Calvinist mainstream of the Church of England where personal holiness was less emphasized than divine grace, it is spoken of by Cowper in the context of Sabbath observance: "Let that day be blest / With holiness and consecrated rest" ("Progress of Error," 157-58), by which Cowper means "abstention from secular endeavor." Robert Burns's "Holy Willie's Prayer" is a profane attack on profanation, a vivid parody of so-called "holiness." Wordsworth transposes the spiritual solitude of the medieval mystic into that of the nature mystic, whose "holiness" and "inner light" are obtained by communion with the purity of nature and avoidance of the polluted city: in "Tintern Abbey" he describes how he,

> so long
> A worshipper of Nature, hither came
> Unwearied in that service: rather say
> With warmer love — oh! with far deeper zeal
> Of holier love. (151-55)

Later in the 19th cent., holiness is often defined in subjective terms: "Holiness consists in the subjection of the whole being . . . to the authority of conscience" (F. Temple, *The Relationship of Religion and Science* [1885]). G. M. Hopkins has a different starting point: "Myself unholy, from myself unholy. . . ," and can find no adequate benchmark for holiness even in his most admirable friends. He turns, therefore, *ad fontes:* "No *better* serves me now, save *best;* no other / Save Christ: to Christ I look, on Christ I call." Life as *imitatio Christi* is also for Thomas Merton the route to holiness; hence, it is not an achievement of personal discipline or "Christian perfection" but "seems to imply something of communion and solidarity in a 'holy People of God.' . . . A 'holy' person is one who is sanctified by the presence and action of God in him" ("Life and Holiness").

See also CLEAN AND UNCLEAN; PERFECTION.

Bibliography. Eichrodt, W. *Theology of the Old Testament* (1961), 270-82; von Rad, G. *Old Testament Theology* (1962), 204-07; Wenham, J. *The Book of Leviticus* (1979), 18-25.

DAVID L. JEFFREY
G. J. WENHAM

HOLOFERNES   *See* JUDITH.

HOLY GHOST   *See* HOLY SPIRIT.

HOLY GRAIL   Whether or not the Grail was originally a Celtic bowl of plenty, the vessel of a ritual meal associated with the worship of Adonis, or the female symbol of a vegetation myth, Christian legend has identified it with the chalice of the Last Supper, the platter of the Paschal Lamb, and the vessel in which Joseph of Arimathea caught Christ's blood. Similarly, the spear, which may be analogous to the weapon of the Celtic sun god Lugh, is identified as the one used by the Roman soldier ("Longinus") to pierce Christ's side. Subsequently, in romance this was also the weapon used to strike the Dolorous Stroke that wounded the King and created the Waste Land. The relevant biblical references are concerned with the Last Supper (Matt. 26:26-29; Mark 14:22-25; Luke 22:14-20), the piercing of Christ's side (John 19:34-37), Joseph of Arimathea's presence at the Crucifixion and his provision of the tomb (Matt. 27:57-60; Mark 15:43-46; Luke 23:50-53; John 19:38-42), and Christ's words about evangelization (Matt. 28:19-20; Mark 16:15). The biblical account was expanded by the legend of Longinus and by a myth which represented Joseph as acquiring the Hallows and bringing them to England where he established the Christian Church at Glastonbury.

The union of Christian myth with Arthurian romance was effected by the French. In the earliest extant work of this type, Chrétien de Troyes's *Perceval* (ca. 1191), there is a procession in which the luminous, life-giving Grail appears. In *Parzival* (ca. 1200-1212) the German poet

Wolfram von Eschenbach transforms Chrétien's romance into a masterpiece which exalts constancy and chastity, makes love the key to spiritual perfection, and harmoniously combines the ideals of chivalry and Christianity. Robert de Boron's *Joseph d'Arimathie* (ca. 1200) describes the Grail as a eucharistic vessel filled with the Holy Blood; the history of its wanderings from Israel to Britain adumbrates the foundation of a worldwide Christian Church under the New Covenant. The didactic and aesthetic culmination of this tradition is achieved in the *Queste del Saint Graal,* part of the Old French *Vulgate Prose Cycle* (1215-30), apparently written by Cistercian monks to illustrate the superiority of *la chevalerie celestienne* (represented by Galahad, who is a type of Christ) over *la chevalierie terrienne* (represented by Lancelot). Sir Thomas Malory's "The Tale of the Sankgreal" in *Le Morte Darthur* (1470) follows this French source closely.

The Grail quest (an allegory of Christian life) proceeds from Camelot, the center of the secular world, to Corbenic, the castle which exists to enshrine the Grail and to permit the celebration of a Christian mass combining three contemporary theological concepts — the Divine Liturgy, the Apostolic Communion, and the miracle of Transubstantiation (a dogma promulgated by the Fourth Lateran Council in 1215). Under the probable influence of St. Bernard's *De Gratio et Libero Arbitrio,* the authors of *La Queste* view the Grail as a symbol of grace. It appears at Pentecost in conditions which suggest that descent of the Holy Spirit on the apostles. It covers the table with food and drink suited to each taste. It sustains the sick and wounded. And it is available to any quester who through chastity, humility, prayer, and abstinence seeks to achieve it. Only Galahad, Perceval, Bors, and in a limited way Lancelot are successful. Because Arthur's kingdom is doomed, the Grail is carried back to the Holy Land (Sarras) and finally borne to heaven by a divine hand.

Malory's *Morte Darthur* contains the most complete and influential version of the Grail legends in English literature. In the wake of Protestant rejection of the doctrine of transubstantiation, the theme vanished from literature for more than 300 years. When it surfaced again in the 19th cent. it was Malorian with a difference. In William Morris's "Sir Galahad" (1858) and in Thomas Westwood's *The Quest of the Sancgreall* (1868) the fallible hero is subject to temptation. R. S. Hawker's *Quest of the Sangraal* (1863) begins vigorously — "Ho! for the Sangraal! Vanished vase of heaven!" but gets no further than Arthur's vision of Galahad holding the Grail. J. R. Lowell's "The Vision of Sir Launfal" (1848) exalts the humanitarian ideal more extensively developed in Tennyson's *Idylls of the King.* In the idyll entitled "The Holy Grail" Percival is restored to his original preeminence, humility rather than chastity is the paramount virtue, the Grail appears and disappears erratically and seemingly without meaning, and the quest, far from

representing a way of life open to every Christian, is reserved for the chosen few.

While the Grail legends produced some uneasiness in the 19th cent., they have been a "bowl of plenty" for 20th-cent. writers. In Victor Canning's Arthurian trilogy *The Crimson Chalice* (1976), *The Circle of the Gods* (1977), and *The Immortal Wound* (1978) the Grail is treated historically as a real vessel found in the disintegrating Britain of the 5th cent. T. H. White's *The Once and Future King* (1958) is preoccupied with political and ethical concerns: the spiritual quest is narrated at second hand by unsuccessful knights and the reader is referred to Malory for a complete version. Closer to medieval didacticism is Jim Hunter's *Percival and the Presence of God* (1979). A number of authors have imagined what might happen if the Grail were to reappear in modern times and become a weapon in a contemporary struggle between good and evil. The idea, which seems to have originated with Arthur Machen's short story "Great Return" (1915) and his novel *The Secret Glory* (1922), is pursued in Charles Williams's *War in Heaven* (1930), J. Cowper Powys's *A Glastonbury Romance,* C. S. Lewis's *That Hideous Strength,* Susan Cooper's series for younger readers, *The Dark is Rising,* and Anthony Powell's *The Fisher King* (1986), which reincarnates Grail Quest characters — Amfortas, Perceval, and the Loathly Lady — using the metaphor of a cruise ship. The discovery of the Grail is the unlikely basis of the plot of Margery Allingham's detective story *Look to the Lady.* Several modern poets have found in the Grail legends metaphors for moral and spiritual experience. Notable examples are T. S. Eliot's *The Waste Land,* Charles Williams's *Taliessin Through Logres* and *The Region of the Summer Stars,* and David Jones's *Anathemata.*

Bibliography. Bennett, J. A. W., ed. *Essays on Malory* (1963); Locke, F. W. *The Quest for the Holy Grail, A Literary Study of a Thirteenth Century French Romance* (1960); Loomis, R. S., ed. *Arthurian Literature in the Middle Ages: A Collaborative History* (1959); Matthews J. *The Grail: Quest for the Eternal* (1981); Moorman, C. *Arthurian Triptych: Mythic Materials in Charles Williams, C. S. Lewis, and T. S. Eliot* (1960); Pauphilet, A. *Études sur la Queste del Saint Graal* (1921); Taylor, B., and E. Brewer. *The Return of King Arthur* (1983); Thompson, R. H. *The Return from Avalon: A Study of the Arthurian Legend in Modern Fiction* (1985); Whitaker, M. *Arthur's Kingdom of Adventure: The World of Malory's Morte Darthur* (1984); *The Legends of King Arthur in Art* (1990).   MURIEL WHITAKER

HOLY GROUND   See BURNING BUSH.

HOLY OF HOLIES   The "most holy place" (Exod. 26:31-34) of the inner sanctuary of the Tabernacle, or later, the Temple, was a room of about 10 cubits (or 15 ft.) to each side in the Tabernacle, twice that in Solomon's Temple. Its only furniture was the Ark of the Covenant, which held the two tablets of the Law, and was surmounted by the "mercy seat." The room was veiled or curtained off. Access to the inner sanctuary was forbidden to all save the High Priest, who came there once annually, on the Day of Atonement, to bring sacrificial blood and pray on behalf of the people. The Hebrew genitive superlative is translated literally in the LXX and Vg, *sanctum sanctorum,* whence the rendering "holi of Halowes" (Wyclif) and "holy of holies" (KJV).

Since the ark was lost when the Babylonians destroyed Jerusalem in 587 B.C., the most holy place in the rebuilt Temple had no furniture at all. In the NT, both Matthew (27:51) and Luke (23:45) record that the veil of the Temple was rent at the moment of Jesus' death, an event whose theological import is elaborated by the writer to the Hebrews. He views the death of Jesus as rending the veil or partition which separates a holy God from humankind: "Now where remission of [sin] is, there is no more offering for sin. Having therefore, brethren, boldness to enter into the holiest by the blood of Jesus, by a new and living way, which he hath consecrated for us, through the veil, that is to say, his flesh; and having an high priest over the house of God; let us draw near . . ." (Heb. 10:18-22; cf. 9:1-12).

The enormous theological significance of the "holy of holies" is largely undeveloped in earlier English literature, possibly because of its high sacredness. By the 19th cent., the "holy of holies" had become a secularized term for any inner chamber of refuge, such as a person's study where one sought to be free from intrusion. Thus, in Dickens's *A Tale of Two Cities,* "Monseigneur was in his inner room, his sanctuary of sanctuaries, the Holiest of Holiests to the crowd of worshippers in the suite of rooms without" (2.7). Carlyle's Professor Teufelsdröckh, describing the profound influence made upon him by his mother, says "such things . . . reach inwards to the very core of your being; mysteriously does a Holy of Holies build itself into visibility in the mysterious deeps." In Melville's *Moby-Dick,* after the harpooner Tashtego falls into the whale's head, the narrator observes, "Now had Tashtego perished in that head, it had been a very precious perishing; smothered in the very whitest and daintiest of fragrant spermaceti; coffined, hearsed, and tombed in the secret inner chamber and *sanctum sanctorum* of the whale" (chap. 78). Perhaps recalling this passage as well as the biblical source, Lawrence suggests in *The Lovely Lady* that "Melville never turned and looked at his sixteenth century Venetian bookcase, with its two or three dozen of choice books, without feeling his marrow stir in his bones. The holy of holies!" ("Things").

See also HOLINESS; TEMPLE; THRONE OF GRACE.

HOLY SPIRIT In the Bible, *spirit* originally denoted the mysterious life force of creation, evident in the wind, in breath, and in experiences of ecstatic or charismatic endowment. The overlap of meaning is most clearly seen in Ezek. 37:9 and John 3:8 and 20:22. Although the early

concept was dynamistic in character, Israel's monotheism ensured that this cosmic force was always seen within the OT as God's. The term "Holy Spirit" itself appears in only two OT passages (Ps. 51:13; Isa. 63:10-11), and indicates that this mysterious and invisible power partakes of God's awesome purity and splendor. The more common term is "Spirit of God" (e.g., Gen. 1:2; Job 12:10; Ezek. 37:7-10); this spirit holds sway in history (Exod. 33:14-17) and is imparted to chosen individuals (e.g., Abraham, Moses, Gideon), especially to the prophets (e.g., Isaiah, Jeremiah, Ezekiel).

Rabbinic commentary and various Targums identify the Spirit of God principally with prophecy and the pledge of a bodily resurrection of the dead. The Talmud prefers to read *ruah* in the Creation account as "wind," probably in opposition to early Christian identification of it with Christ (Hag. 12a); earlier Jewish sources, however, identify this "Spirit" with the Messiah (Midr. Tehillim 139.529; Sanh. 38a). Still other sources equate *ruah* with God's mercy (Tg. Yerushalmi; Tan. Ber. 1.36-37; Philo, *Quaestiones,* 2.28; cf. Tg. Ps. 29:10). In the OT the Spirit of God is praised as the instrument of Israel's salvation (Pss. 51:11-12; 143:10) and the announcer of the coming Messiah in whose "age" salvation will finally be accomplished by an outpouring of the Spirit upon all persons (Joel 3:1-5; cf. Isa. 11:1ff.; 32:15-18; 41:1–42:9). Moreover, God's fidelity to his covenant is guaranteed by the promise of his Spirit (Isa. 59:21).

In the NT Jesus' Incarnation is attributed to this Spirit (Luke 1:35; John 1:1-14, 32-33), and his ministry was launched by further endowment following the descent of the dove at his baptism in the Jordan (Mark 1:10; John 1:33-34; Acts 10:38); he was subsequently sent by the Spirit into the desert to be tempted (Matt. 4:1; cf. Milton, *Paradise Regained,* 1.189-95). These events were understood by the early Christians as a fulfillment of Isa. 61:1-2 (see Luke 4:18), and Jesus himself understood his ministry thus empowered as evidence of the inbreaking of God's final rule (Matt. 12:28). He promised that his disciples would experience the same inspiration in their own ministry (Mark 13:11; cf. Acts 1:8), a promise elaborated in John's Gospel in terms of the Spirit as the Paraclete or Comforter (John 14:16-17, 26; 15:26-27; 16:5-15).

Christianity traces its beginning to such an experience of empowering and charismatic endowment by the Spirit at Pentecost (Acts 2:1-4), and the NT writers attributed its early expansion to the initiative of the same Spirit acting upon and through various individuals (Acts 6:8-10; 8:9-17; 10:19-20, etc.). The apostles Paul and John in particular present the work of the Spirit in personal renewal as the beginning of the Christian life (John 3:3-8; 7:37-39; Rom. 8:9; Gal. 3:2-3), and as the beginning of a transformation which will end in the resurrection of the body (Rom. 8:11, 23; 2 Cor. 1:22; 3:18; 4:16–5:5). The Holy Spirit was experienced as coming to expression in a variety of ways (e.g., Rom. 5:5; 1 Cor. 1:4-7; 6:9-11;

Gal. 3:5; 5:22-23), and daily life was expected to reflect the Spirit's presence and direction (e.g., Acts 9:31; Rom. 8:4-6, 14; 1 John 3:24). This common participation "in the Spirit" was seen as the basis of the common life of the early believers (1 Cor. 12:13; Eph. 4:3-4; Phil. 2:1), and Paul especially expected the worship of the Church to be guided by the Spirit (Rom. 12:3-8; 1 Cor. 12:4-11). Both Paul and John were nevertheless conscious of the need to maintain a critical attitude toward individual claims of inspiration (1 Cor. 2:12-16; 14:29; 1 Thess. 5:19-22; 1 John 4:1-3), one principal criterion being that the Holy Spirit was now also understood as the Spirit of Christ (John 14:26; 16:12-15; Rom. 8:9-17; 2 Cor. 3:17–4:6).

The formal doctrine of the Church concerning the Holy Spirit developed much more slowly than did Christology, and in the early period was largely subsumed under it in connection with invocation or discussion of the Trinity, as in the baptismal formulary and catechesis (e.g., St. Irenaeus, *Adv. haer.* 2.6.4 and "Proof of the Apostolic Preaching," 1.1, 6ff.). Sometimes identified by heterodox thinkers with the Word (e.g., Theophilus, *Ad Autolycum*, 2.10; 2.15), or said to have been created by the Son (as in Arianism), the Spirit was recognized as having full divine status with the Father and Son by the Council of Constantinople (A.D. 381). The Nicene Creed asserted that the Holy Spirit "proceedeth from the Father." To this statement, in the 6th-cent. Synod of Braga, was added the *filioque* clause ("and from the Son"), an addition rejected by the Greek Church. Though Pope Leo III declared the *filioque* unnecessary to the Creed, it was included again by Pope Benedict VIII (1014).

Anglo-Saxon poetry reflects this early concern for Trinitarian theology: references are brief and tend to locate or praise the power of the *halig gaest* as an agency of the Godhead. In the tenth Advent Lyric of the *Exeter Book* (10-11), Father and Son are addressed directly, with the comment added: *"Baem inc is gemaene / heahgaest hleofaest"* ("Common to you both is the protecting Holy Spirit"). The closing lines of the OE *Christ III* refer to the expectation that at the Last Judgment, *Ðonne halig gaest helle biluceð* " ("Then will the Holy Ghost lock up hell").

St. Augustine's *De Trinitate* provided another basis for the development of Western doctrine, defining the Holy Spirit as the love which binds the Father and the Son. Peter Lombard's *Sententiae* later identified grace with the action of the Holy Spirit, building on St. Ambrose's identification of the water of grace as a "pouring out of the Holy Spirit" (*De Spiritu Sancto*, 1, intro. 15-18). Ambrose, in turn indebted to Greek writers (ironically including both St. Basil the Great and St. Athanasius from the other side of the *filioque* controversy), takes issue with heretical interpretations of Amos (esp. 4:13) which would make the Spirit "created" and essentially the "Spirit of Nature" (2.6.48-55). The identification of the Holy Spirit with grace was contested in the 13th and 14th cents., with the Scholastics maintaining that the indwelling of the

Spirit in individuals spoken of in Scripture is only an "appropriation." St. Thomas appears to hew a line closer to Augustine than most. Although he identifies the Holy Spirit with the "gifts of the Holy Spirit" (*1 Sententiae*, 14.2.1), he says that *"Love . . . is the proper name of the Holy Spirit, as Word is the proper name of the Son"* (*Summa Theol.* 1a.37.1). He adds, however, that it is of the essence of love to be indivisibly a gift: "A gift is freely given, and expects no return. Its reason is love. What is first given is love; that is the first gift. The Holy Ghost comes forth as the substance of love, and *Gift* is his proper name" (*Summa Theol.* 1a.38.2).

In ME poetry references to the Holy Spirit are often associated with the "gifts" of the Holy Spirit (e.g., "Com, shuppere, Holy Gost" by William Herebert, translating the Latin hymn *Veni Creator Spiritus;* cf. R. Greene, *The Early English Carols*, no. 327). This theme is evident also in *Cleanness*, where Belshazzar observes to Daniel: "Goddes gost in þe geuen, þat gyes alle þynges, / and þou vnhyles vch hidde þat Heuenkyng myntes" (1627-28). Invocations of the Trinity are also common in the ME lyric; sometimes these add a prayer for protection to the Holy Spirit. In one such poem occurs an extensive catalogue of symbols of late medieval pneumatology:

> To whome is approched, the holy gost by name,
> The third person, one god in trinite,
> Of parfite loue thow art the gostly flame.
> Emperour of mekeness, pease & tranquyllite,
> My coumford, my counsell, my parfite charite,
> O water of life, O well of consolacion,
> Agaynst all stormes of hard aduersite. . . .
> (C. Brown, *Religious Lyrics of the XVth Century*, no. 51)

The association of the Holy Spirit with the Incarnation is persistent in Annunciation lyrics and carols (e.g., Brown, *Religious Lyrics of the XIVth Century*, no. 16 [*"Mater Salutaris"*]; 18 ["Prayer of the Five Joys"]; 60 ["A Song to the Queen of Heaven"]; also R. Greene, *The Early English Carols*, nos. 31, 96, 236), as is, more rarely, the descent of the Holy Spirit in the form of a dove at Christ's baptism as a sign of God's authentication:

> When Jhesus Criste baptyzed was
> The Holy Gost descended with grace;
> The Fader voys was herde in the place:
> *"Hic est Filius meus; ipsum audite."* (Greene, no. 131)

The Corpus Christi plays include Christ's words from John's Gospel about the Comforter (e.g., Chester 15.241-48; 23.194-200) and project a parallel between the life of the Bride of Christ (his Church) and the life of the Virgin Mary his mother. These plays also recall that the Spirit had been given to the prophets in anticipation of the Incarnation and New Covenant which they announced (e.g., Chester 8.318-24). In *St. Erkenwald*, the miracle of restored life occurs because the Holy Spirit is invoked in prayer: "And so longe he grette after grace, þat he graunte hade, / An ansuare of þe Holy Goste and afterward, hit dawid" (126-27). In Chaucer's *Second Nun's Tale,* Cecile assures her brother, in terms from the Apostles' Creed, that those who receive Christ obtain eternal salvation, as "The Goost, that fro the Fader gan procede, / Hath sowled hem, withouten any drede" (8.328-29).

The Reformation brought few modifications to the doctrine of the Holy Spirit except an increased emphasis on his prompting of the preaching of the gospel. For Luther, "the Holy Spirit comes and preaches, that is, the Holy Spirit leads you to the Lord, who redeems you" and "it is the Holy Spirit who sanctifies us" (*Sermon on the Catechism,* 1 [*Werke,* 51.164-66]). For Calvin it is the "Communion of the Holy Spirit" which guarantees participation in the covenant; the Spirit not only "adopts" individuals into the family of God but assures them of their salvation and pours out upon them the water of "quickening grace" which "irrigates" their lives for fruitful service (*Inst.* 3.1.2-3).

Concern for perseverance in the state of grace is, however, a strong theme in Reformation theology. Calvin modifies Augustine's definition of the unpardonable sin — obstinate distrust of forgiveness persisted in until death — saying, "he sins against the Holy Spirit who, while so constrained by the power of divine truth that he cannot plead ignorance, yet deliberately resists and that merely for the sake of resisting." He continues: "Those who are convinced in conscience that what they repudiate and impugn is the word of God, and yet cease not to impugn it, are said to blaspheme against the Spirit [cf. Matt. 12:31], inasmuch as they struggle against the illumination which is the work of the Spirit," and concludes, "You will perceive that the Apostle speaks not of one particular lapse or two, but of the universal revolt by which the reprobate renounce salvation" (*Inst.* 3.3.22-23).

When in England Bishop Latimer takes up the question (ca. 1562), he has a less defined sense of what the specific "sin against the Holy Ghost" might be, and reduces the problem to its crux: a refusal to cry out for God's mercy. Latimer is skeptical that anyone can judge whether another has committed this sin (it is not de facto in evidence when one is abstinent from worship or resistant to catechism) and counsels against preoccupation with any imagined "unpardonable" offense: "Despair not of the mercy of God, for it is immeasurable . . . for though a man be wicked at this time, yet he may repent, and leave his wickedness tomorrow, and so not commit that sin against the Holy Ghost" (*Sermon* 25). The predicament of Marlowe's *Doctor Faustus* invited from its original audience reflection on such definitions. Offense against the Spirit is considered in quite different terms by George Herbert in his poem on Eph. 4:30, "Grieve not the Holy Spirit." Here, the poet marvels that God's Holy Spirit might "grieve" when he lapses from the purity of his own commitment ("when I am swore / And crosse thy love"); such knowledge prompts in him tears of contrition.

In Cranmer's *Homilies Appointed to Be Read in Churches* (1562) prayer for help in adversity is to be directed to the Holy Spirit especially ("Concerning Prayer"; cf. Robert Herrick's "His Letanie, to the Holy Spirit"), as is prayer for "illumination" or insight (cf. Calvin, *Inst.* 3.1.4). For many Protestant poets, the Holy Spirit was in fact invoked as "muse." Whereas in the Middle Ages the third person of the Trinity had often been pictured as a dove of inspiration coming into the ear of theological writers and biblical translators, writers in a more secular context most often called upon the Virgin Mary to inspire their verse, especially from the time of St. Bernard of Clairvaux; she is memorably invoked on a number of occasions by Chaucer. Spenser, however, as a Protestant poet, seeks what he regards as a more appropriate source of inspiration in "An Hymne of Heavenly Love":

> Yet, O most blessed Spirit, pure lampe of light,
> Eternall spring of grace and wisedom trew,
> Vouchsafe to shed into my barren spright
> Some little drop of thy celestial dew,
> That may my rhymes with sweet infuse embrew,
> And give me words equall unto my thought,
> To tell the marveiles by thy mercie wrought. (43-49)

Milton's muse, invoked at the beginning of *Paradise Lost,* recollects Spenser's "most gentle sprite breathed from above," the spirit of creation. Yet in saying that he intends the Spirit who "on the secret top / of *Oreb,* or of *Sinai,* didst inspire / That Shepherd, who first taught the chosen Seed" (1.6-8), he suggests a view of the Holy Spirit compatible with both rabbinic and Calvinist formulations. Donne's "Ascension" concludes: "And if thy holy Spirit, my Muse did raise, / Deigne at my hands this crown of prayer and praise": only the Holy Spirit can render human words fit homage to Christ. Ben Jonson's "The Sinner's Sacrifice" makes use of the *filioque* clause for a wider sense of "inspiration":

> Eternal Spirit, God from both proceedings,
> Father and Son; the comforter, inbreeding
> Pure thoughts in man: with fiery zeal them feeding
> For acts of grace. (25-28)

In the later 17th and 18th cents., an increasing popular emphasis on the Holy Spirit, either in inspiration or as a bestower of charismatic "gifts of the Spirit," brought about from proponents of "rational religion" the charges of "enthusiasm," or ungoverned subjectivity and emotionalism. Dryden's *Religio Laici* (404-16) sees charismatic spirituality as anti-intellectual and in vulgar disrespect of even biblical authority:

> The tender Page with horney Fists was gaul'd;
> And he was gifted most that loudest baul'd:
> The *Spirit* gave the *Doctoral Degree:*
> And every member of a *Company*
> Was of *his Trade,* and of the *Bible free,*
> Plain *Truths* enough for needfull *use* they found;
> But men wou'd still be itching to *expound:*

Each was ambitious of th'obscurest place,
No measure ta'n from *Knowledge,* all from GRACE
Study and *Pains* were now no more their Care;
Texts were explain'd by *Fasting,* and by *Prayer:*
This was the Fruit the *private Spirit* brought;
Occasion'd by *great Zeal,* and *little Thought.*

Dean Jonathan Swift, who would have concurred with these sentiments, felt that the Holy Spirit was to be imagined as conferred on prelates episcopally, and not much spoken of otherwise ("On Dr. Rundle, Bishop of Derry"). Exacerbating these feelings among conservative Anglicans was the rapid rise in popularity of the evangelicals and especially Methodists after 1730. John and Charles Wesley in particular preached the "Indwelling of the Holy Spirit in Believers" and their meetings were often attended by "charismatic manifestations," leading in turn to much literary and even artistic satire (e.g., Kenrick's "On the Investigation of Truth"; Hogarth's "Enthusiasm Delineated"). Though the emotional William Cowper might be suspected of "enthusiasm," his poetry exhibits a typical Calvinist reserve concerning the Holy Spirit, who is invoked only as the "spirit of instruction" ("Bill of Mortality" [1790]).

In literature the tradition of the Holy Spirit as a source of personal inspiration was taken over by the Romantic movement and psychologized in a fashion anticipated to some degree even in Blake. In Blake's *Jerusalem: The Emanation of the Giant Albion,* the prophetic admonition is:

Go, tell them that the worship of God is honouring his
    gifts
In other men & loving the greatest men best, each
    according
To his Genius which is the Holy Ghost in man; there is
    no other
God than that God who is the intellectual foundation of
    Humanity. (4.91.8-11)

Blake criticizes the abstraction of Milton's Trinity, and especially the thinness of his treatment of the Holy Spirit: "in Milton, the Father is Destiny, the Son a Ratio of the five senses, & the Holy Ghost a vacuum!" ("The Marriage of Heaven and Hell"). While he himself prays in orthodox fashion, "Teach me, O Holy Spirit, the Testimony of Jesus!" (*Jerusalem,* 3.74.14), he fashions his myth of prophetic inspiration for a world in which rationalism has almost displaced spirituality:

For thus the Gospel Sir Isaac [Newton] confutes:
"God can only be known by his Attributes;
And as for the Indwelling of the Holy Ghost
Or of Christ & his Father, it's all a boast
And Pride and Vanity of the imagination,
That disdains to follow this World's Fashion."
("The Everlasting Gospel," 43-48)

In American letters the Romantic sublimation of the Holy Spirit to artistic genius is reflected in the writings of Ralph Waldo Emerson, where it is the brooding Spirit of Nature, the "Worldsoul" or "Passive Master" Emerson finds in every religious and artistic high moment:

In groves of oak . . .
Still floats upon the morning wind
Still whispers to the willing mind,
One accent of the Holy Ghost
The heedless world hath never lost. ("Problem," 58-62)

Nineteenth-century texts often reveal a cynicism concerning claims made for the operation of the Holy Spirit in personal affairs. Emily Dickinson, who "would run away / From Him — and Holy Ghost — and all . . ." (*Poems,* no. 413), is metaphysically apprehensive about what it might mean to be "Bride of the Holy Ghost" (no. 817). Charlotte Brontë's Jane Eyre is on the one hand repulsed by her rejected suitor St. John Rivers's affected invocations of "the help of the Holy Spirit to subdue the anger I have roused in him," but says later:

I mounted to my chamber; locked myself in; fell on my knees; and prayed in my way — a different way to St. John's, but effective in its own fashion. I seemed to penetrate very near a Mighty Spirit; and my soul rushed out in gratitude at His feet.

G. M. Hopkins effectively resublimates the Romantic apotheosis of the Spirit of Nature to Creation and the action of the third person of the Trinity in its renewal:

And for all this, nature is never spent;
There lives the dearest freshness deep down things;
And though the last lights of the black West went
Oh, morning, at the brown brink eastward, springs —
Because the Holy Ghost over the bent
World broods with warm breasts and with ah! bright
    wings. ("God's Grandeur")

By contrast, "Father, Word, and Holy Breath" *(Ulysses)* are alike abstracted from nature for Joyce, whose Stephen Dedalus wonders only briefly if he has "found the true church all of a sudden in winding up to the end like a reel of cotton some finespun line of reasoning upon insufflation or the imposition of hands or the procession of the Holy Ghost" (*Portrait of the Artist as a Young Man,* chap. 5). Though more self-consciously antagonistic, Joyce bespeaks an affinity with Emerson when he writes of the Irish housewife in his story "Grace" that "her faith was bounded by her kitchen, but, if she was put to it, she could believe also in the banshee and in the Holy Ghost."

Margaret Avison's poem ". . . Person or a Hymn on and to the Holy Ghost," in the vein of Herbert, sees the Holy Spirit as "the self-effacing / whose other self was seen / alone by the only one," and prays,

to lead *my* self, effaced
in the known light,
to be in him released
from facelessness,
so that where you

(unseen, unguessed, liable
to grievous hurt) would go
I may show him visible.

An evocation of the Spirit's role in revealing the second person of the Trinity is also found in Larry Woiwode's *Even Tide*, where the Holy Spirit is presented typologically as "Second Adam's Eve . . . within the Word walking" (44).

See also GIFTS OF THE HOLY SPIRIT; HOPE; INSPIRATION; TEMPLE OF THE HOLY GHOST; UNPARDONABLE SIN.

DAVID L. JEFFREY
JAMES D. G. DUNN

HOLY WAR *See MILES CHRISTI.*

HOPE Hope respecting the future (Heb. *baṭaḥ* ["trust"], *yaḥal* ["wait for"], *qawah* ["expect"]) was not a characteristic of the ancient worldview generally. It became a significant feature of Hebrew and subsequently Christian religious outlook largely because of the promises embodied in the covenant and the doctrine of bodily resurrection and heavenly reward. Though developed strongly in the future orientation of classic Hebrew narrative (both pentateuch and chronicle), it features significantly also in Hebrew wisdom literature. A classic OT text is Job, where despair ("My days are swifter than a weaver's shuttle, and are spent without hope" [7:6]) gives way to its opposite ("For I know that my Redeemer liveth, and that he shall stand at the latter day upon the earth: And though after my skin worms destroy this body, yet in my flesh I shall see God" [19:25-26]), the hope of eternal life.

In the NT the resurrection of Jesus is presented as the ground both for optimism concerning present experience (despite trials) and expectation concerning one's inheritance in heaven (1 Pet. 1:3). This "lively hope" (Gk. *elpizō; elpis*) was expected to form the Christian character (Col. 1:27; Rom. 5:2; Heb. 7:19). The quintessential object of Christian hope is the Second Coming (Titus 2:13), and also involves the anticipation of seeing and enjoying the fellowship once again of loved ones who have died in the faith — including the saints of bygone ages (1 Thess. 4:17; cf. Phil. 1:21). As well, one may look forward to a "reward" for faithfulness (2 Tim. 4:8; 1 Cor. 9:24-27). By contrast, Paul speaks of those without a saving faith in Jesus as being "without hope" (Eph. 2:12; 1 Thess. 4:13).

The NT yields up the most common iconography of hope: the "anchor of the soul" (Heb. 6:19), a symbol commonly painted in the catacombs of ancient Rome, and the "helmet of the hope of salvation" (1 Thess. 5:8; cf. Eph. 6:17). Hope is also regarded in Christian tradition as one of the three "theological virtues," the others being faith and charity (1 Cor. 13:13).

The biblical emphases are treated straightforwardly by the Fathers. Representatively, St. Augustine speaks of hope particularly in the context of the Resurrection, which he sees as having "strengthened our faith by adding a great buttress of hope" (*De doctrina Christiana*, 1.15.14), providing assurance of the resurrection of believers (*De civ. Dei* 19.4), and the sense of peace concerning ultimate destination which characterizes believing pilgrims in the world (*De civ. Dei* 19.20). Yet hope does not develop as an untested virtue. St. Gregory the Great, commenting on Job 11:18 ("And thou shalt have confidence, because hope is set before thee"), says, "For hope lifts itself up to the degree that it is firmly rooted in God, is built up to the degree that one has suffered hard things for his sake, since the joy of the recompensing is never gathered in eternity which is not first sown here below in religious sorrowing" (*Moralia in Iob*, 2.10.36). Gregory cites Ps. 126:6 ("He that goeth forth and weepeth, bearing precious seed, shall doubtless come again with rejoicing, bringing his sheaves with him") and concludes: "Therefore because we now sow in tribulation that we may afterward reap the fruit of joy, the heart is strengthened with the larger measure of confidence in proportion as it is pressed with the heavier weight of affliction for the Truth's sake."

This sensibility is powerfully reflected in the closing imagery of the OE *Christ*, in which the temporal lot of the Christ-bearer awaiting the Parousia is likened to a perilous sea journey. The Holy Spirit tells him where an anchor (*ancrum faeste*) may be found, and the poet concludes: "Utan us to þaere hyðe hyht staþelian, / ða us gerymde rodera waldend / halge on heahþu, þa he heofenum astag" ("Let us fix our hope to this haven which the Master of the skies opened to us, holiness on high when he rose into heaven").

In the ME poem *Cleanness*, "hope in the Lord" is a virtue of purity of heart: "For of the hyȝest he had a hope in his hert" (1653). Yet in medieval English literature hope is often defined in terms of its contrary. *Wanhope* or despair was considered a sin against the Holy Spirit — according to St. Thomas "more dangerous than sins against faith or charity, for when hope dies we lose heart and flounder in wickedness" (*Summa Theol.* 21-2ae.20.3). In Chaucer's *Book of the Duchess* the seriousness of the Black Knight's melancholia is defined by the degree to which it is *wanhope;* despair annihilates the very raison d'être of the Christian knight (598-619) to the point where he has "lost suffisance" (703). The essence of Christian serenity is the confidence, as Dame Julian of Norwich puts it in her *Showings*, that "all shall be well."

Chaucer's Parson, in describing despair or *wanhope*, the last dread enemy, identifies it as having "two maneres": the first wanhope, he says,

> is in the mercy of christ; that oother is that they thinken that they myghte nat longe persevere in goodnesse. / The firste wanhope cometh of that he demeth that he hath sinned so greetly and so ofte, and so longe leyn in sinne, that he shal nat be saved. / Certes, agayns that cursed wanhope sholde he thynke that the passion of Jhesu Crist is moore strong for to unbynde than synne is strong for

to bynde. / Agayns the second wanhope he shal thynke that as ofte as he falleth he may rise agayn by penitence. And though he never so longe have leyn in synne, the mercy of Crist is alwey redy to receiven hym to mercy. / Agayns the wanhope that he demeth that he sholde nat longe persevered in goodnesse, he shal thynke that the feblenesse of the devel may nothyng doon, but if men wol suffren hym; / and eek he shal han strengthe of the help of God, and of al hoolychirche, and of the protection of aungels, if hym list. (*Canterbury Tales*, 10.1.1068-75)

In Spenser's *Faerie Queene,* Speranza ("Hope") figures as one of the daughters of Dame Coelia living in the House of Holiness. Despair is an emaciated creature who drives knights to suicide with his insinuating recitals of their sins. In Shakespeare's *Henry 8,* Cardinal Wolsey finds himself over his head in intrigue, prompting a self-damning view of the "state of man": "when he falls, he falls like Lucifer, / Never to hope again" (3.2.371-72). In Marlowe's *Doctor Faustus* the fallen theologian's damnation consists in his commitment to despair: "Away with such vaine fancies, / Despaire in God, and trust in Belsabub" (1.4.393-94). When at his last resort Faustus believes "nothing can rescue me" (5.2.1977) his condition is evident to Mephistopheles: "Faustus, now thou hast no hope of heaven / Therefore despaire, think onely vpon hell" (5.2.1983-84).

Later in the 17th cent. Abraham Cowley's poem "Hope" disparages it as a virtue "whose weak being ruin'd is, / Alike if it succeed and if it miss," concluding sardonically, "If things from their end we happy call, / 'Tis Hope is the most hopeless thing of all." Dr. Johnson, a century later, retorted (in his *Life of Cowley*) that of "the learned puerilities of Cowley there is no doubt," and that "what Cowley has written upon Hope shows an unequalled fertility of invention." Richard Crashaw answered the poem stanza for stanza in its own time, drawing upon biblical precept to do so: "Dear Hope! earth's dowry, and heaven's debt, / The entity of things that are not yet, / Subtlest, but surest being!" He goes on to describe hope as "love's legacy under lock / Of faith: the steward of our growing stock" ("On Hope"). George Herbert's "Hope" is a playful dialectic between worrisome carefulness and simple trust and confident expectation of God's goodness: "I gave to Hope a watch of mine: but he / An anchor gave to me." In Bunyan's *Pilgrim's Progress* the quintessential pilgrim virtue is personified in Hopeful, who joins Christian in Vanity Fair and alone persists with him to the end of his journey toward the Celestial City. In Bunyan's characterization, hope is strongly identified with perseverance in faith, praying for salvation and believing it will eventually be granted: "*And withall, this came into my mind, If it tarry, wait for it, because it will surely come, and will not tarry.* So I continued Praying until the Father shewed me his Son" (ed. Sharrock, 142). The connection of hope with the perseverance of the saints in their mortal pilgrimage had also been stressed by Calvin (*Inst.* 3.25.1), who argues for the inseparability of hope

from faith: "Whenever this living faith exists, it must have the hope of eternal life as its inseparable companion, or rather must of itself beget and manifest it" (*Inst.* 3.2.42).

In a long poem recollecting the antithesis between Cowley and Crashaw, William Cowper sets out a view of Christian hope substantially informed by Calvinism, in which

Hope sets the stamp of vanity on all
That men have deem'd substantial since the fall
Yet has the wondrous virtue to educe
From emptiness itself a real use. ("Hope," 153-56)

It is in this Calvinist sense of hope fully grounded in an intellectable faith that "Hope, as an anchor firm and sure, holds fast / The Christian vessel, and defies the blast" (167-68). Nevertheless, hope is also the experience and acknowledgment of the reborn heart: "Hope, sweet hope, has set me free" (536). The second of Christopher Smart's *Hymns for the Amusement of Children* styles aged and barren Hannah, in her supplication for the child who was to be Samuel, as a heroine of the virtue of hope.

In the 19th cent. hope was somewhat displaced as a celebrated theological virtue, in time acquiring a sense of uncertainty rather than the assurance it conveyed to earlier writers and readers. Tennyson captures this usage when he says, in *In Memoriam* (45), "I . . . call / To what I feel is Lord of all, / And faintly trust the larger hope."

"Hope deferred maketh the heart sick" (Prov. 13:12) speaks of temporal rather than eternal hope. In Samuel Butler's *The Way of All Flesh,* as Ernest's friend is on his way to tell Theobald and Christina of Ernest's imprisonment, he recalls "Christina's long years of hope deferred that maketh the heart sick, before she was married." Hardy quotes the same lines in "Alicia's Diary" (June 21) as, in a similarly romantic context, does Hudson in *Green Mansions* (chap. 10). Hope and despair are often paired by T. S. Eliot, almost as if equally vain (*The Waste Land*); in *Little Gidding,* however, Eliot comes to a traditional affirmation of hope for life's pilgrimage in his famous citation of Julian of Norwich ("And all shall be well and / All manner of things shall be well").

See also DESPAIR; THEOLOGICAL VIRTUES.

Bibliography. Caspar, R. " 'All Shall be Well': Prototypical Symbols of Hope." *JHI* 42 (1981), 139-50; Hartman, G. "Marvell, St. Paul, and the Body of Hope." *ELH* 31 (1965), 175-94; Lynch, W. F. *Images of Hope* (1964).

HOPHNI AND PHINEHAS Hophni and Phinehas were the two sons of Eli, the priest in charge of the Shiloh sanctuary in the immediate premonarchical period. Their names are Egyptian in origin, and may reflect that period when the ancestral Israelites (or, according to some, the tribe of Levi) were in Egypt. They were unprincipled men, whose misdemeanors are blamed for both the demise of the Elide priestly house and the Israelite defeats by the Philistines at Ebenezer (1 Sam. 2:27-36; 3:11-14; 4:4,

11). They are the priests of Ps. 78:64. In 1 Sam. 2–3 the writer achieves a notable chiaroscuro effect by interleaving material on the acolyte Samuel, who progresses under divine auspices (2:11, 18-21, 26; 3:1-10; 3:19–4:1a), with the narrative of Eli's sons, who head for divine judgment (2:12-17, 22-25, 27-36; 3:11-18).

William Cowper, in his "Expostulation," says that the priestly brotherhood should

> fly the world's contaminating touch,
> Holy and unpolluted . . .
> Except a few with Eli's spirit blest,
> Hophni and Phineas may describe the rest. (446-49)

R. P. GORDON

HOREB The name *Horeb* (Heb. *ḥoreb*, lit. "desert, desolation, dryness") refers to the "mountain of God" (Exod. 3:1; 1 Kings 19:8) and is once designated as "mount Horeb" (Exod. 33:6). It is the location where Moses received his divine call (Exod. 3:1), and where God appeared in a theophany (Deut. 1:6; 4:10, 15), made a covenant with Israel (Deut. 5:2; 9:1; 1 Kings 8:9), and gave them his laws (Mal. 4:4). It is also the scene of experiences of rebellion (Deut. 9:8) and idolatry (Ps. 106:19). In Exod. 17:6 "the rock in Horeb" is struck for water. Here Horeb is a location where the Israelites arrive before proceeding to Mt. Sinai (cf. Exod. 19:1, 2) by way of Rephidim (Exod. 17:8). In the Bible Horeb is never identified with a particular mountain peak or summit, so that the phrase "the rock in Horeb" is believed to refer to "the rock in [the region of] Horeb." Accordingly it is suggested that "Horeb" may be the name of an entire mountain area in the Sinai desert, and that Mt. Sinai is a specific peak in the Horeb mountains (so M.-J. Lagrange, *RB* 8 [1899], 369-92, with others following him). All references to Horeb refer to the time of Moses, except one in which the prophet Elijah undertakes a journey or pilgrimage to "Horeb, the mountain of God" (1 Kings 19:8).

The exact location of Horeb remains disputed. Among the various hypotheses is the tradition going back to Eusebius (4th cent. A.D.) that *Jebel Serbal* (6,791 ft.) in the Sinai peninsula is the mountain of law-giving. The traditional identification of Byzantine and Christian provenance holds that *Jebel Musa* (7,363 ft.), the southeast crest of a two-peaked granite mountain, is Mt. Sinai, while others hold that it is the northwest peak called *Ras es-Ṣafṣafeh* (6,540 ft.) in front of which is a wide plain suitable for the large-sized Israelite encampment (Exod. 19:2). It is well to keep in mind that Horeb is the general designation within which Mt. Sinai, the specific peak, was located.

See also BURNING BUSH; SMITTEN ROCK; TEN COMMANDMENTS.

Bibliography. Abel, F.-M. *Géographie de la Palestine* (1933), 1.391-96; Aharoni, Y. *The Land of the Bible. A Historical Geography* (1967), 182-83; Clifford, R. J. *The Cosmic Mountain in Canaan and the Old Testament* (1972), 121-22; Craigie, P. C. *The Book of Deuteronomy* (1976), 91; Lagrange, M.-J. "Le Sinai biblique," *RB* 8 (1899), 369-92; Perlitt, L. "Sinai und Horeb." In *Festschrift für W. Zimmerli zum 70. Geburtstag* (1977), 302-22; M. H. Segal. *The Pentateuch. Its Composition and its Authorship* (1967), 17-18;

GERHARD F. HASEL

HORNS OF THE ALTAR Altar tops in the OT normally had horns protruding from each corner. Their significance is not known, unless they were simply to facilitate the binding of the sacrificial animal to the altar (Exod. 27:2). The horns were smeared with sacrificial blood on certain occasions, as part of an atonement rite (cf. Exod. 29:12; 30:10); this gives point to Jeremiah's charge that Judah's sin was engraved upon the horns of her altars, i.e., the horns symbolized exposure rather than expiation (Jer. 17:1). Altar horns had a further significance, in that an unintentional homicide could seek sanctuary at God's house by taking hold of them (Exod. 21:13-14; 1 Kings 1:50-53). When, therefore, Amos announces the destruction of the horns of the Bethel altar, he is warning that even the possibility of suppliancy will be denied Israel (Amos 3:14). Suppliants could, for that matter, be dragged away from the altar, if their guilt was provable (Exod. 21:14; cf. 1 Kings 2:28-34). It is, perhaps, in the awareness of this friability of the OT altar-suppliant's hope that the writer of Hebrews refers to those "who have fled for refuge to lay hold upon the hope set before us" (Heb. 6:18). For this hope is not attached to an altar in a sanctuary court, but goes right into "that within the veil" (v. 19); it is thus inviolable.

In De Quincey's "Dream Fugue" (*The English Mail Coach*), "There, suddenly, within that crimson radiance, rose the apparition of a woman's head, and then of a woman's figure. The child it was — grown up to a woman's height. Clinging to the horns of the altar, voiceless she stood — sinking, rising, raving, despairing." In Scott's *Ivanhoe*, "Vows are the knots which tie us to Heaven — they are the cords which bind the sacrifice to the horns of the altar — and are therefore . . . to be unloosed and discharged" (chap. 4). Whittier makes reference to the horns of the altar in reinforcing his protest over the men of Massachusetts being asked to help recapture Virginia's fugitive slaves:

> We hunt your bondmen, flying from slavery's fateful
>   hell;
> Our voices, at your bidding, take up the bloodhound's
>   yell;
> We gather, at your summons, above our fathers' graves,
> From Freedom's holy altar-horns to tear your
>   wretched slaves. ("Massachusetts to Virginia")

See also CITY OF REFUGE; TEMPLE.   R. P. GORDON

HORSELEECH   *See* DEMONS, DEMON POSSESSION.

HORSEMEN OF THE APOCALYPSE   In the Apocalypse of St. John the Divine, John sees God seated upon a throne and holding in his right hand a scroll, sealed with seven seals. When the first four of these are opened, four horses and riders appear — white, red, black, and dun or piebald (Rev. 6:1-8). These horsemen are typically taken to symbolize conquest, slaughter, famine, and death, all of which are to ravage the earth "before the end shall come," and which indicate elements of judgment in which the devil is permitted to be an agent of God's wrath (*Glossa Ordinaria* [PL 114.721-22]). Following the ME lyric "Ihesu, þat al þis world haþ wroȝt, / haue merci on me!" in Merton Coll. Oxford MS 248 (ed. C. Brown, *Religious Lyrics of the XIVth Century,* no. 35) are lines based upon the vision of the horsemen, allegorizing the rider of all four horses as Christ; the horses are taken to represent his Incarnation (white), Crucifixion (red), conquest of Satan (black), and Ascension (dun) (Brown, 258). Allusion in later English literature is infrequent. In Byron's *Manfred* an amalgamation under the figure of a single "Pale horse of Death" is apparent: "And to and fro, like the pale courser's tail, / The Giant steed, to be bestrode by Death, / As told in the Apocalypse" (2.2.100-102).

HORTUS CONCLUSUS   The only direct biblical reference, albeit a metaphorical one, to a *hortus conclusus* or enclosed garden is Song of Songs 4:12: "my spouse is an enclosed garden." However, the orchards of Song 4:13 and Eccl. 2:5 and the "King's forest" of Neh. 2:8 also denote enclosed parks or pleasure gardens similar to Cyrus's garden at Ceaenae (Xenophon, *Anabasis,* 1.2.7), Solomon's garden (Josephus, *Ant.* 8.7), the king's garden near Siloam (Neh. 3:15), or the vivaria described by Aulus Gellius (*Noctes Atticae,* 2.20.4). Designated by the Hebrew word *pardes,* which occurs in the OT in only the three instances cited above, such grounds are perhaps related to the Old Persian *pairidaeza,* meaning an enclosed park, and should be distinguished etymologically from the Garden of Eden, the *gan 'Eden* of Gen. 2:8. In the LXX translation of the Pentateuch, the Greek term *paradeisos* is used to refer not only to the Garden of Eden but also to render the Hebrew word *pardes.* Thus through Greek translation all gardens are semantically linked to the Garden of Eden.

The primal Paradise of the OT is a distinct geographical location, but in the NT its meaning is extended to the celestial paradise, as in Luke 23:43. A merging of the concepts of earthly and heavenly paradise occurs frequently in later apocalyptic and rabbinic commentaries, especially after the Hebrew word *pardes* had been influenced by its Greek cognate *paradeisos.*

Some midrashic interpretation of the allusion to the bride as an enclosed garden has construed it as a reference to the confinement of the Hebrews in Egypt, thus treating it as part of the commentary on Exodus. Comparable Christian interpretation holds that the enclosed garden signifies the Church, which contains only the faithful. (Such a view persists until after the Reformation, as in Isaac Watts's hymn "We are a Garden Walled Around.") The lines of Song 5:4-5 ("My beloved put in his hand by the hole of the door, and my bowels were moved for him. I arose up to open to my beloved; and my hands dropped with myrrh, and my fingers with sweet smelling myrrh, upon the handles of the lock") were interpreted as a chaste allegory of Christ knocking at the door of the world and appealing to the faithful. Similarly, 7:7-8 ("This thy stature is like to a palm tree, and thy breasts to clusters of grapes. I said, I will go up to the palm tree, I will take hold of the boughs thereof") was taken to mean that Christ would cling to his Church and prevent its branches from being shaken by winds of heresy. In developing Christian exegesis of the Canticles, the bride came also to represent both the individual soul wooed by God and the Virgin Mary.

In medieval literature the image of the virgin as a locked garden became intermingled with the motif of classical gardens of love, a factor in the tradition of courtly love in which the lover had to undergo certain trials before he could win the chaste love of his lady. Such a pattern is exemplified in *Roman de la Rose* and in Chaucer's *Parliament of Fowls;* it is memorably parodied in Chaucer's *Merchant's Tale.* Claudian's *Epithalamion for Honorius Augustus* offers perhaps the most elaborate description of the classical *hortus conclusus* as the abode of Venus, and his legacy to the Middle Ages was, according to Giamatti (*The Earthly Paradise and the Renaissance Epic,* 252), "to fix firmly the conventions of a natural bower or grove or enclosure dedicated to Venus and her pastimes." Once Claudian's garden of Venus was transferred into a Christian context, it was fused with allegorized treatments of the enclosed garden of Canticles to produce the religious symbol of the Virgin Mary in her *hortus conclusus.* A complicated iconographical scheme for representing the Incarnation in this way appears in many paintings and tapestries, e.g., the Dame à la Licorne in the Cluny Museum or the Annunciation of Domenico Veneziano.

The enclosed garden acquired its most potent connotations from its association with Eden and hence its connection with visions of earthly paradise. Such visions, particularly in the Renaissance, were nourished by myths of the Golden Age, Elysium, and the Isles of the Blest found in Hesiod, Homer, Ovid, Pindar, and Virgil. For Christian commentators such pagan fables were understood to be dim, sometimes distorted versions of the true paradise of Eden, a link made by Thomas Burnet in his *Sacred Theory of the World.* Milton ransacked classical legends to adumbrate the qualities of the true Paradise in *Paradise Lost.* His Eden is more delightful than the "feigned" gardens of Adonis or Alcinous, or even the actual garden of Canticles, where Solomon, the "sapient king," dallied with his "fair Egyptian spouse" (9.440-43). Milton's Eden also recalls the Golden Age sites of antiquity where there is perpetual spring and the Christian Latin paradises whose atmosphere is laden with fragrant breezes. Following Horace's *Epode 16,* it is also a peaceable kingdom, a "Heaven on earth," and a *hortus conclusus,* an "enclosure wild," a "narrow room wherein Nature's whole wealth" is confined (4.207), surrounded by a "verdurous wall" (4.143) from whose eastern gate Adam and Eve are expelled. Spenser's Garden of Adonis also belongs in the literary tradition of earthly paradises which include Homer's Garden of Alcinous (*Odyssey,* 7.112-34), Claudian's Cyprus garden in his Epithalamion, Dante's Eden in *Purgatorio* (28.138-40), and the Garden of Nature in Chaucer's *Parliament of Fowls* (120-308). It is linked with Eden, and in describing its weather as a "continuall spring," Spenser follows medieval and Renaissance literary models in offering the garden as a metaphor for the ideal world.

Certain common features of the earthly paradise emerged from the conflation of classical and biblical sources. Menelaus (*Odyssey,* bk. 4) learns of the "Elysian plain at the world's end . . . where living is made easiest for mankind, where no snow falls, no strong winds, or rain." This eternally balmy weather recurs in Ovid's *Metamorphoses* (bk. 1) in Claudian's garden of Venus, in the Christian paradise in *De ave phoenice* attributed to Lactantius, in *De judicio Domini* ascribed to Tertullian, and in the OE *Phoenix* of Cynewulf. The unchanging, innocent, and protected state of these paradises reappears in the latter-day Edens of Dickens's Dingley Dell and the gardens of P. G. Wodehouse's Blandings Castle.

For certain 17th-cent. writers such as Henry Hawkins in *Partheneia sacra* the enclosed garden remained a specific religious emblem to be distinguished from the Hesperides, the garden of Tempe, the Elysian fields, and the earthly Paradise. Gradually during the 17th cent. the "analogic reading of nature" surrendered "to more empirical appreciation"; thus Ralph Austen's *A Treatise of Fruit Trees* contains not only an emblem in which Solomon's praise of his bride as a *hortus conclusus* encircles a garden, but a geometrical plan for planting and a collection of tools for grafting and pruning.

In the 18th cent., the image of Eden as a specific place devolved into mere literary allusion. In *Windsor Forest,* Pope writes: "The Groves of Eden, vanished now so long, / Live in description, and look green in song" (7-8). And in his *Essay on Man,* he appeals to a more suitable source of inspiration, projecting the image of his Twickenham estate onto the universe: "A mighty maze! but not without a plan; / A wild, where weeds and flowers promiscuous shoot, / Or garden tempting with forbidden fruit. . . ." Despite Romantic enthusiasm for nature, "Paradise, and groves / Elysian" were for Wordsworth "a history of departed things"; in the

Prospectus to the Recluse, he relocates paradise as a property of the human intellect.

See also BRIDE, BRIDEGROOM; EDEN; SONG OF SONGS.

Bibliography. Abrams, M. H. *Natural Supernaturalism* (1973); Giamatti, A. B. *The Earthly Paradise and the Renaissance Epic* (1966); Greene, T. M. *The Descent from Heaven: A Study in Epic Continuity* (1963); Hunt, J. D. *The Figure in the Landscape* (1976); Kermode, F. *English Pastoral Poetry* (1952); Mack, M. *The Garden and the City* (1969); Stewart, S. *The Enclosed Garden: The Tradition and the Image in Seventeenth Century Poetry* (1966).   MICHAEL GOLDBERG

HOSEA   The prophet Hosea shares his name with one of the kings of Israel (2 Kings 15:30) who is usually assigned the form Hoshea; etymologically the name, which means "savior" or "salvation," is the same as Joshua and Jesus (in Joshua / Jesus the root is compounded with the divine name).

Hosea's prophecy concerning the unfaithfulness of Israel to God is made particularly vivid by the circumstances of his own life: commanded by God to marry Gomer, a prostitute, he finds a mirror of Israel's turning from God in his wife's unfaithfulness.

The text of Hosea is in some respects obscure. Nonetheless, two common traditions of interpretation emerge. First, St. Paul (Rom. 9:25-26) cites Hosea's observation that true faith passed from Israel to Judah as a precedent for the "new covenant" to be made with the Gentiles (cf. 1 Pet. 2:10). Second, St. Jerome stresses the relation between Hosea and his wife and that between God and Israel as types of the later "marriage" between God and the Church *(Comm. in Osee Prophetum).* Both views dominate subsequent commentary.

As with talmudic and rabbinic writings (e.g., Pesaḥ. 87a-87b; Maimonides, *Guide of the Perplexed,* 2.46), Christian commentators have sometimes been embarrassed by the nature of Hosea's marriage, despite the fact that God commanded it. The embarrassment does not stem from the imagery of the marriage and subsequent adultery per se, for such imagery is used countless times in the OT and NT as a symbol of the mercurial relations between God and his people. That Hosea alone, however, experiences the imagery concretely in his own life has caused a number of commentators from Jerome (*Ep.* 123:13) and Maimonides onward, to want to see the marriage as fictional on the grounds that God would not have condoned such immorality. Many modern commentators, on the other hand, believe that the marriage was actual and that Hosea's courageous grappling with his own personal history led to his deeper understanding of the public history of God's painful relationship with his people. Medieval commentary focuses largely on the connection between Gomer's adultery and Israel's idolatry, seeing the main force of the book contained in Hosea's warnings against idols and false gods (e.g., 4:17), a theme associated with Hosea by John Gower in his *Mirour de l'omme.* In a morality play of the late 16th cent., *A Looking Glass for London and England,* by Thomas Lodge and Robert Greene, scenes of social and moral abuse alternate with warnings against sin by a prophetic character called Hosea.

Numerous individual sayings of Hosea are recalled in literary contexts, as when Whittier, writing against capital punishment in "The Human Sacrifice," asks that God may cause a change of heart in the authorities responsible for hanging, adapting to his purpose Hos. 6:6:

> Soften his hard, cold heart, and show
> The power which in forbearance lies,
> And let him feel that mercy now
> Is better than old sacrifice!

Hardy's Alec d'Urberville, having betrayed Tess earlier, proposes a second time: "You say you have a husband who is not I," he postures:

> However, even if you have one I think I am nearer to you than he is. . . . The words of the stern prophet Hosea come back to me. Don't you know them, Tess? — "And she shall follow after her lover, but she shall not overtake him; and she shall seek him, but shall not find him; then shall she say, I will go and return to my first husband: for then it was better with me than now!" (chap. 47)

The prophet's name, if not his life, is remembered in Elias Hoseason, the captain of the brig *Covenant* in R. L. Stevenson's *Kidnapped.* At the end of Marc Connelly's *Green Pastures* Hezdrel, facing death in his fight with Herod, tells God that he is not afraid because he believes in the God of Hosea. God inquires if he doesn't mean the God of Moses. "No," replies the disdainful Hezdrel, "Dat ol God of wrath and vengeance? We have de God dat Hosea preached to us. . . . De God of Mercy . . . he ain't a fearsome God no mo." When God asks how it was that Hosea discovered that mercy, Hezdrel's philosophical answer is, "De only way he could find it. . . . Through sufferin'." Suffering is a major theme of a (1929) three-act play *The Marriage of Hosea,* published pseudonymously in New York under the name Izachak, and which is described with double entendre in the subtitle as "A passion play." The book of Hosea has been seen as a narrative influence in Isaac Bashevis Singer's "Gimpel the Fool."

See also ADULTERY; BRIDE, BRIDEGROOM.

Bibliography. Chavasse, C. *The Bride of Christ* (1939); Hennings, T. "Singer's 'Gimpel the Fool' and the Book of Hosea." *JNT* 13 (1983), 11-19; Mays, J. L. *Hosea* (1969).

LAURENCE ELDREDGE

HOST *See* EUCHARIST.

HOUSE DIVIDED AGAINST ITSELF When the aggrieved Pharisees suggested among themselves that Jesus cast out devils "by Beelzebub, the prince of devils," Jesus perceived their thoughts and spoke to them directly, saying, "Every kingdom divided against itself is brought to desolation; and every city or house divided against itself shall not stand" (Matt. 12:22-25). These words have become a watchword of political wisdom. In Shakespeare's *Richard 2* the Bishop of Carlisle uses them in describing the looming Wars of the Roses (5.5.23-31). Thoreau speaks apprehensively about the division among Northerners over the slavery question, saying of his fellow citizens, "There is hardly a house but is divided against itself, for our foe is all but the universal woodenness of both head and heart." *A House Divided* (1935) is the title of a novel by Pearl Buck, and allusion to the text is pivotal to the action in chap. 18 of Thomas Wolfe's *Look Homeward, Angel.*

HOUSE NOT MADE WITH HANDS St. Paul's contrast of the body as "tabernacle" of the spirit on earth with "a building of God, an house not made with hands, eternal in the heavens" (2 Cor. 5:1) leads Macaulay in his famous essay "Milton" to praise the Puritans for living in the knowledge that "Their palaces were houses not made with hands." Robert Browning wonders, however, what his happy marriage will seem like in heaven, "in the house not made with hands" ("By the Fire-Side").

HOUSEL *See* EUCHARIST.

HOW ARE THE MIGHTY FALLEN! When David mourned the deaths of Saul and Jonathan he cried out, "The beauty of Israel is slain upon thy high places: how are the mighty fallen!" This refrain accorded itself well to a major theme in OE homiletics and, subsequently, Anglo-Saxon poetry. In both cases the thematic *Ubi sunt?* can have eschatological overtones (e.g., Bede, *De Temporum Ratione;* Wulfstan, *Hom.* 49; "The Ruin"; "The Fortunes of Men") but is also consistent with the meditation of Boethius on the subject (*De Consolatione Philosophiae,* 2.7; see the trans. of King Alfred) in emphasizing the ephemerality of all merely human greatness. Later medieval poems such as "Ubi Sount Qui Ante Nos Fuerount?" (from the trilingual MS Digby 86 [ed. C. Brown, *English Lyrics of the XIIIth Century,* no. 48] may treat the subject in general terms:

> Were beþ þey biforen vs weren
> Houndes ladden and haukes beren
> And hadden feld and wode?
> þe riche leuedies in hoere bour
> þat wereden gold in hoere tressour.

Some, however, such as Dunbar's "Of Manis Mortalitie," list among the fallen mighty both classical (Hector, Hercules, Achilles, Alexander) and biblical heroes. In the 14th-cent. preaching lyric *"Cur Mundus Militat sub Vana Gloria":*

> Telle me where is salamon, sumtyme a kinge riche?
> or sampson in his strenkeþe, to whom was no man
> liche?

Or þe fair man absolon, merueilous in chere,
or þe duke ionatas, a weel biloued fere?

Where is bicome cesar, þat lord was of al?
or þe riche man cloiþd in purpur and in pal?

Telle me where is tullius in eloquence so swete?
or aristotil þe filisofre wiþ his witt so grete?

Where ben þese woriþi þat weren here to-foren —
boiþe kingis & bischopis, her power is al loren.

All þese grete princis, wiþ her power so hiȝe,
ben wanischid a-way in twinkeling of an iȝe.

Specific allusions recur in English literature, but by
the 19th cent. the theme had become much less important.
When the poor father of Hardy's Tess learns that he is
actually descended from an ancient and once great family,
he asks the parson what he should make of his discovery,
obtaining this laconic reply: "Oh — nothing, nothing; except chasten yourself with the thought of 'how are the
mighty fallen'. It is a fact of some interest to the local
historian and genealogist, nothing more" (*Tess of the
d'Urbervilles*, 1.1). Twentieth-cent. allusions tend to be
less elegiac than humorously fatalistic, as in Somerset
Maugham's *Of Human Bondage*, where the context is
likewise genealogical. When Philip comments on Mr.
Athelny's unusual name, the latter replies: "It's a very old
Yorkshire name. Once it took the head of my family a
hard day's riding to make the circuit of his estates, but the
mighty are fallen. Fast women and slow horses" (chap.
86).

HOW LONG, O LORD, HOW LONG?   This is the
cry of the martyrs (Vg *"Quousque Domini?"*) who were
"slain for the word of God, and for the testimony which
they held," heard coming out from under the altar in St.
John's apocalyptic vision (Rev. 6:9-10). Associated in
traditional exegesis with reflection on "the last days," the
passage is referred to explicitly by Spenser, who, in *The
Faerie Queene*, describes:

An Altare, carv'd with cunning ymagery,
On which trew Christians blood was often spilt,
And holy Martyres often doen to dye
With cruell malice and strong tyranny:
Whose blessed sprites, from underneath the stone,
To God for vengeance cryde continually;
And with great griefe were often hearde to grone,
That hardest heart would bleede to hear their piteous
        mone.

Sir Thomas Browne, referring to "that general opinion
that the world grows near its end," says that "souls that
now depart cannot escape that lingering expostulation of
saints under the altar, *Quousque Domini?* and groan in
the expectation of the great jubilee" (*Religio Medici*, pt.
2). Rev. 6:9-10 provides the theme for Dante Gabriel
Rossetti's *"Vox Ecclesiae Vox Christi,"* and the last words

of St. Joan in Shaw's play of that name, after Joan has
been condemned to death.

HOWLING WILDERNESS   Where the Lord found
Jacob, then led and protected him (Deut. 32:10). In 19th-
cent. England the "howling wilderness" was a fashionable
location for the unfashionable, as in Thackeray's *Vanity Fair*
(chap. 51); curiously, in Carlyle's *Sartor Resartus*, the ideal
plan for "our young Ishmael" to "acquire for himself the
highest of all possessions, that of self-help" (2.3). In North
America, where numerous young Ishmaels were sent, it
became part of frontier hyperbole; e.g., James Fenimore
Cooper: "In the old war, when I was out under Sir William,
I travelled seventy miles alone in the howling wilderness,
with a rifle bullet in my thigh, then cut it out with my own
jack-knife" (*The Pioneers*, chap. 1). Thoreau's sage observation is better acclimatized: "Generally speaking, a howling wilderness does not howl; it is the imagination of the
traveller that does the howling" (*The Maine Woods*).

HUMILITY   In contrast to classical Greek literature,
which denigrates humility (or meekness) as weakness,
Scripture celebrates humility as a cardinal virtue. Both the
OT and NT commend (and indeed command) humility as
the only appropriate response to God's authority. To exalt
oneself in pride against God or without regard to God is
not only sinful but also foolish. God frequently pledges
to exalt the humble and to humble those who exalt themselves (e.g., Prov. 3:34; 2 Kings 19), and both testaments
abound in examples of just such reversals; notable among
those "brought low" after asserting themselves against
God are pagan rulers: Nebuchadnezzar, Pharaoh, and
Herod the Great. The first creature of God to fall through
pride was Satan. The subsequent Fall of the human race
resulted largely from a failure of appropriate creaturely
humility on the part of Eve and Adam.

To humble oneself before God is to admit one's weakness and dependence, God's power and goodness, and
one's trust and hope in God. This disposition (described
in Mic. 6:8 as one of the principal requirements of a
"good" life) is expressed in obedience and repentance
(James 4:6-10). Such humility is a chief characteristic of
the OT heroes of faith (e.g., Gideon, Hannah, David, and
Solomon) and a virtue celebrated repeatedly in wisdom
literature (e.g., Pss. 10:17; 25:18; 31:7; 34:18; 51:17;
etc.). It is exemplified most vividly in the NT by Mary,
the mother of Jesus, and by John the Baptist, the former
of whom characterizes herself as a "handmaid of the
Lord" (Luke 1:38), the latter as an "attendant" or grooms-
man to the Bridegroom (John 3:28-30).

Jesus taught and modeled humility. Although "being
in the form of God," he condescended to a humble birth,
"made himself of no reputation," lived and ministered
among the poor and dispossessed, consciously enacted a
servant's role (e.g., Matt. 20:28; Mark 10:45; Luke
22:27), enjoined his disciples to do the same (John 13:4-

17), and finally submitted to an ignoble and unjust execution (Phil. 2:6-11). Many of his parables and discourses stress the paradoxical greatness of the lowly (e.g., Luke 9:48; 18:9-14); the meek and the poor in spirit are singled out as "blessed" in the Beatitudes.

St. Paul emphasizes the need for a similar pattern of humility in the life of the Christian. As one shares in Christ's humiliation and death through conscious imitation of him, so will one share in his exaltation; humility flows out of identification with Christ and concomitant rejection of the world, its status, and standards. Willingly suffering abuse, imprisonment, and hardship for the sake of the gospel, Paul instructs his readers to do the same, condescending to those of low estate (Rom. 12:16) and "glorying" in weaknesses rather than in perceived strengths — because through them the power of God is made most evident. Other NT writers reiterate these themes: St. Peter, in urging mutual submission, enjoins believers to "Be clothed with humility: for God resisteth the proud, and giveth grace to the humble. Humble yourselves therefore under the mighty hand of God, that he may exalt you in due time" (1 Pet. 5:5-6).

In the writings of the Western Fathers humility is a chief virtue, opposing the chief vice, pride. In the *Psychomachia* of Prudentius (early 5th cent.), Superbia (Pride) is the principal enemy of Mens Humilis and Spes (Hope). In the 12th-cent. *De Fructibus Carnis et Spiritus,* sometimes mistakenly ascribed to Hugh of St. Victor, Humility is found with the three theological virtues (Faith, Hope, and Charity) and the four cardinal virtues, opposing the tyranny of Superbia and her followers, the other deadly sins. Humility is the preeminent virtue in monastic writings about the Christian life, from the Rule of St. Benedict (6th cent.) to the *Ladder of Perfection* by Walter Hilton (14th cent.), in which Hilton observes that humility, or meekness, consists not in self-abasement to the point of misvaluation or misrepresentation; rather, "he is truly meek who truthfully knows and is conscious of himself as he actually is." Humility in this sense is the essence of the character of Chaucer's Parson, who, while his speech was "discreet and benygne," yet was not afraid of correcting persons "of heigh or low estat," who "waited after no pompe and reverence, / Ne maked him a spiced conscience" (*Canterbury Tales,* 1.515-26). In the Parson's sermon, the "remedie agayns the synne of Pride . . . is humylitee, or meekness" (10.476), qualities displayed in the characterization of the Knight and the Clerk as well. When personified in ME texts, humility may become Dame Mekenesse, as in the alliterative poem *Patience,* or Humilitas, as in *The Castle of Perseverance.*

To be self-conscious of humility, as is Gloucester in Shakespeare's *Richard 3* ("I thank God for my humility"), is to destroy it, perverting the virtue to its opposite vice. Donne says, "So may a selfe-dispising, get selfe-love. . . . / So is pride, issued from humility" ("The Crosse"). In "The Litanie" Donne therefore prays,

> From tempting Satan to tempt us,
> By our connivence . . .
> From indiscreet humilitie,
> Which might be scandalous,
> And cast reproach on Christianitie . . .
> From thirst, or scorne of fame, deliver us.

For Herbert, "profound humility" is accordingly "the exact temperance of our Lord" (*A Priest to the Temple,* 9.33). In his poem "Humilitie" he sees in a beast-fable vision that Humility sits lowest among the virtues gathered together with the animals who will be paired with their appropriate virtues; in the fracas over place which ensues, Humilitie's tears despoil the peacock vanity of pride. An 18th-cent. version of the caution against false humility is found in William Cowper's "Conversation" (373-78):

> True modesty is a discerning grace,
> And only blushes in the proper place;
> But counterfeit is blind, and skulks through fear,
> Where 'tis a shame to be ashamed t'appear:
> Humility the parent of the first;
> The last by vanity produc'd and nurst.

Because "humility is gentle, apt to learn," it is for Cowper the indispensable attribute of the seeker after truth ("Expostulation," 450-67).

In later literature biblical humility proves harder to characterize plausibly, although Wordsworth attempts it in *The Excursion* when he says of "The Pastor," "He sought not praise, and praise did overlook / His unobtrusive merit" (5.44-45). Dickens's famous characterization of false modesty in the fawning clerk Uriah Heep of *David Copperfield* (like Gilbert and Sullivan's Poobah in *The Mikado*) affords a memorable parody of the biblical virtue.

See also LAST SHALL BE FIRST; MEEK SHALL INHERIT THE EARTH; SEVEN DEADLY SINS.   DAVID L. JEFFREY
                                                                                            PETER H. DAVIDS

HUNGER   Biblical hunger or famine often resulted from draught, blight, or war (e.g., Gen. 41:53-57; Amos 4:9; 2 Kings 25:3); at times it was God's punishment for evil (Deut. 28:48; Job 18:12; Isa. 65:13; Jer. 42:16). Alleviating hunger could show God's mercy, e.g., by manna given to the wandering Israelites and loaves and fish multiplied by Christ. When Milton's Satan tempts Christ, he refers to OT people fed miraculously (*Paradise Regained,* 2.306-36). Like his scriptural counterpart (Matt. 4:2-4; Luke 4:2-4), Milton's Christ tells Satan: "Man lives not by Bread only, but each Word / Proceeding from the mouth of God" (1.349-50; cf. Deut. 8:3). Christ's hunger was part of his preparation for preaching this word.

Patristic exegesis explains spiritual hunger as desire to hear God's word. St. Gregory, e.g., in *Moralia in Iob* (6.27.44; 14.15.17), quotes Amos 8:11, where the Lord foretells "not a famine of bread, nor a thirst for water, but of hearing the words of the Lord" (cf. St. Jerome's *Comm. in Isa.* 2.3.1; 2.5.13). Flannery O'Connor's reluctant young prophet Tarwater reverses the hunger symbol: because he rejects his call to preach about the bread of life, his body rejects physical food despite a gnawing inner emptiness (*The Violent Bear It Away* [1960]).

Extreme hunger sometimes leads to cannibalism (e.g., Lev. 26:29; 2 Kings 6:27-29; Jer. 19:9; Ezek. 5:10). John Donne's "The Lamentations of Jeremy" describes starvation which brought women to "eate their children of a spanne," "children drest with their owne hands for meat" (translating Lam. 2:20; 4:10). Blake, too, notes the plight of "starv'd children," children "born for Sacrifice, for the meat & drink / Offering" (*Jerusalem*, 2.28, 64-65). In the OE *Andreas* spiritual starvation, symbolized by lack of bread and water (19-25), becomes physical when Andrew rescues the cannibals' prisoners; both hungers are satisfied when Andrew's preaching replaces their old "symbeldæge" ("banquet," 1527). Even devils are punished by hunger in Milton's *Paradise Lost* (10.547-77): desire plagues them with famine when they reach for fruit that turns to "soot and cinders." The resurrected pagan in "St. Erkenwald" contrasts souls "Hungrie inwith hellehole" with those "richely . . . refetyd" in heaven (304-07), reflecting the promise in Rev. 7:16 that the righteous "shall hunger no more."

See also BREAD OF LIFE; LOAVES AND FISHES; MANNA.

Bibliography. Brière, J. "Hunger & Thirst." Trans. A. F. McGovern. *Dictionary of Biblical Theology*. Ed. X. Leon-Dufour (1973); Casteen, J. "*Andreas*: Mermedonian Cannibalism and Figural Narration." *NM* 75 (1974), 74-78; Scott, R. B. Y. "Famine." *IDB* 2.241; Walsh, M. M. "Physical and Spiritual Sustenance: Food and Drink as a Structural Image." In "Ecclesiastical Backgrounds of Imagery in the Old English *Andreas*." *DA* 36 (1975), 1492A. MARIE MICHELLE WALSH

HUNGER . . . AFTER RIGHTEOUSNESS The phrase "hunger and thirst after righteousness" appears only in the fourth beatitude (Matt. 5:6). The object of this desire has been sometimes imagined as ultimate world salvation, God's ushering in of a truly righteous order (Isa. 51:1-3). But, as commentators from St. Augustine (*De sermone*

Domini in Monte, 1.3.6) to D. Hill (*Greek Words and Hebrew Meanings* [1967], 127ff.) have observed, it more likely means behavior consistent with God's law and will. Many, as a result of such an uncompromising pursuit of holiness, will suffer or be martyred (Matt. 5:10, 12; cf. 6:1, 33). Yet they are "blessed" on account of being "lovers of a true and indestructible good" (Augustine).

Ruskin observes in *The Crown of Wild Olive* that "the entire object of true education is to make people not merely do the right things, but enjoy the right things . . . not merely just, but to hunger and thirst after justice" ("Traffic"). Shaw, in his preface to *Back to Methuselah,* is skeptical about the possibility of realizing such beatitude:

> But if Man is really incapable of organizing a big civilization . . . what is the use of giving him a religion? A religion may make him hunger and thirst after righteousness; but will it endow him with the practical capacity to satisfy that appetite?

See also BEATITUDES.   PETER H. DAVIDS

HUR There are several men named Hur in the Bible. Of these the most important is the leader in Israel who, during the battle against the Amalekites, joined with Aaron to hold up Moses' hands (Exod. 17:10-12 — see Aaron). Josephus (*Ant.* 3.2.4; 6.1) identifies him with the husband of Miriam and grandfather of Bezalel (Exod. 31:2; 35:20; 38:22). But in 1 Kings 4:8 the father of one of Solomon's personal officers was Hur, or Ben-Hur of Ephraim. And another Hur, father of Rephaiah, was one of the builders of the wall of Jerusalem working under Nehemiah (Neh. 3:9). It is thus a distinguished name in Judaic tradition, and when Lew Wallace borrowed it for his *Ben Hur: a Tale of the Christ* (1880), it was to denominate a protagonist who is the son of one honored among his own people as by Rome.

HUSHAI *See* AHITOPHEL.

HYPOCRISY *See* JUDGE NOT; MOTE AND BEAM; WHITED SEPULCHRE.

I

I AM THAT I AM When God spoke to Moses from the burning bush, he said, *'ehyeh- 'asher-'ehyeh,* "I AM THAT I AM," and enjoined Moses to tell the children of Israel, "I AM hath sent me unto you" (Exod. 3:14). Although it is widely agreed that *'ehyeh* is derived from the root *hayah,* "to be," and that that name hints at "Yahweh," the meaning has never been satisfactorily explained. The inherent ambiguities of the text and radical inadequacies of subsequent translations have prompted scores of attempts to explain the precise significance of the name. The LXX *egō eimi ho ōn* ("I am the one who is" or "I am the existent one") and Vg *Ego sum qui sum* ("I am who I am") suggest a definition of God's Person in terms of "essential being," whereas the original Hebrew suggests a definition "in terms of active presence" (J. Plasteras, *The God of Exodus,* 94-95). Various English translations have been tried. In addition to the KJV rendering, *The Interpreter's Bible* offers "I am who I am," "I am what I am," "I am because I am," and "I will be what I will be." (The last rendering was suggested as early as Nicholas of Lyra in his *Postilla* on Exodus.)

Underlying all patristic commentary is the implicit assumption that at the heart of the name is God's self-revelation as pure or essential Being — a notion which has had profound philosophical as well as theological repercussions in Western Christendom (cf. St. Thomas Aquinas, *On Being and Essence*). In his *Enarrationes in Psalmos,* St. Augustine distinguishes his own "self" and that which "rather seems to be than really is" from "what has a true being" — the one "who said 'I AM HE THAT IS.'" He goes on to say that "that which I now am is nothing in comparison to that which truly 'IS'" (39.7, 9). In his *Confessiones,* he refers to this passage in recalling the climax of his search for God. At that moment he hears "in the heart" the words "I AM THAT I AM" (7.10). Elsewhere, Augustine sees in the name proof of God's immutable eternality (*De naturi boni contra Manichaeos,* chap. 19; *De Trin.* 1.8), as does St. Jerome (*Eps.* 15 and 48). St. Gregory of Nyssa regards it as proclaiming God's absolute immanence (*The Great Catechism,* chap. 35; *Contra Eunomius,* 2.4). St. Ambrose dwells upon the text's insights into the nature of the Son (*De fide,* 1.13; 1.19; 5.1).

English literary allusions frequently occur in parodic contexts. One of Spenser's deceitful villains says of herself: "I, that do seeme not I, Duessa ame" (1.5.26). Shakespeare's devilish Iago likewise admits (*Othello,* 1.1.65), "I am not what I am." Elsewhere in the Shakespeare canon Richard III utters the blasphemously egotistical "I am I" (5.3.182).

In *Religio Medici* (1.11), Sir Thomas Browne gives a reductive solution to the problem of explanation, saying of God's self-definition "'twas a short one, to confound mortalitie, that durst question God, or aske him what hee was." Browne's near contemporary, the Catholic poet Henry Constable, alludes to Exod. 3:14 in the first quatrain of his "Sonnet 1, To God the Father":

Greate God! within whose symple essence wee
Nothyng but that, which ys thyself can fynde:
When on thyself thou did'st reflect thy mynde,
Thy thought was God, which tooke the forme of
Thee.

The 19th cent. provides a range of less devout allusions. In his crucial chapter "On the Imagination"
(*Biographia Literaria,* chap. 13), Coleridge defines the
"primary Imagination" as "the living power and prime
agent of all human perception" and as "a repetition in the
finite mind of the eternal act of creation in the infinite I
AM." Byron's Manfred gives an exemplary definition of
the romantic hero when he says, "Then wonder not that
'I / Am what I am,' but that I ever was" (3.1.151-52).
Manfred finds the fact of his own existence more as-
tonishing than God's. Tennyson, querulous in "The
Higher Pantheism," asks his darkling soul if God "is . . .
not all but that which has the power to feel 'I am I'?" In
contrast, Swinburne, bursting with pagan enthusiasm, has
the Germanic earth goddess Hertha declare, "before God
was, I am" ("Hertha"; cf. John 8:58).

More recent allusions may be found in two of
Conrad's novels. The villain of *Victory,* Mr. Jones, is an
inebriate of theology. Having explained that he has been
spending his days as "a rebel now, and was coming and
going up and down the earth," Jones twice adds, as though
consulting Douay as well as KJV, "I am he who is" and
"I am he that is." Jones imagines himself both Job's
adversary (Job 1:7; 2:2) and the voice from the burning
bush. Conrad turns to the text again in his next novel *The
Rescue,* where the vainglorious protagonist Tom Lingard
declares that his temper could "burn you all up" because
"I am what I am."

See also BURNING BUSH.

Bibliography. Gilson, E. "Notes sur le vocabulaire de
l'Être." *MS* 8 (1946), 150-58; Noth, M. *Exodus: A Commentary* (1962); Plasteras, J. *The God of Exodus: The Theology
of the Exodus Narratives* (1966).   DWIGHT H. PURDY

I KNOW THAT MY REDEEMER LIVETH   Job's
statement of faith *in extremis* is "For I know that my
redeemer liveth, and that he shall stand at the latter day
upon the earth: And though after my skin worms destroy
this body, yet in my flesh shall I see God" (Job 19:25-26).
The conjectural uncertainty of the KJV rendering for v. 26
has not been completely solved by subsequent translations. (The translation "skin worms destroy this body"
may arise in part from a later medieval notion that one's
living flesh already harbors the eggs of worms set to hatch
at death and do their grisly work.)

In one of the most influential English commentaries
on the passage Matthew Henry (1728) draws attention to
the Hebrew word *go'el,* translated Redeemer, showing
that it properly indicates a "next of kin," as in the kins-
man-redeemer of the book of Ruth. He thus reads the
passage as prefigurative of Christ, the "son of Man" as

"near of kind to us, the next kinsman that is able to
redeem; he has paid our debt" (*Comm. on the Whole
Bible,* 3.109). These words are among the best known in
the Bible, not only because of their use in funeral oration
but also through their magnificent setting in Handel's
Messiah. Hence, for a character in Mulock's *John
Halifax,* as soon as the first musical phrase falls upon the
ear, "That is Handel — 'I know that my Redeemer liveth'.
Exquisitely she played it, the clear treble notes seeming
to utter like a human voice the very words. . . ," at which
the entire passage comes back, word by word, note by
note (chap. 27). It is the triumphal christological note that
Shaw's St. Joan sounds: "My sword shall conquer yet:
The sword that never struck a blow. Though men destroyed my body, yet in my soul have I seen God" (*St.
Joan,* Epilogue).

See also RESURRECTION.

I ONLY AM ESCAPED   In Job 1, after God had per-
mitted Satan to test Job's faith (v. 12), a series of catastrophes
befell Job: his oxen and asses were stolen and their keepers
slain by Arabs (vv. 14-15); his sheep and shepherds were
consumed by lightning (v. 16); his camels were stolen and
the servants tending them killed by Chaldeans (v. 17); and,
finally, in a terrible climax, his seven sons and three
daughters died when the house in which they were feasting
collapsed in a storm (vv. 18-19). All of these calamities,
alternately caused by human violence and natural phenomena, were reported to Job by four sole survivors in rapid
succession ("While he was yet speaking, there came also
another . . . "), each concluding his item of "news" with the
words "and I only am escaped alone to tell thee" (vv. 15-17,
19). The parallel structure of these reports gives this concluding sentence the function of a refrain and heightens the
impression of "cruel irony" (Weiser) in the shattering sequence of events.

The Fathers suggest allegorical meanings for each of
the dire messages. St. Jerome sees the house (Job 1:18) as
representing the Church and the Chaldeans as symbolizing
demons (*Comm. in Job,* 1). In St. Gregory the Great's view,
the messengers are Satan's tools, whose words are meant
to make Job believe that God is hurting him (*Moralia in
Iob,* 2.14; cf. also Didymos the Blind, *Comm. in Job*).

In English literature the messengers' refrain frequently
serves to establish a narrative frame. William Blake's *The
Four Zoas* (3.103) and *Jerusalem* (chap. 2, pl. 29, lines
29, 82) offer examples. Herman Melville cites the refrain
for the same rhetorical purpose in *Moby-Dick* (having
made an earlier allusion to it in *Redburn,* chap. 59). As a
motto for the novel's epilogue, the sentence finally identifies Ishmael, the narrator, as the fate-ordained sole survivor of the wreck of the *Pequod.* At the same time, it
reinforces many previous allusions to the book of Job and
once again takes up Ahab's notion that the evil in the
world is wrought, or at least tolerated, by God.

In Archibald MacLeish's *J. B.,* two messengers announce the deaths of J. B.'s children. The Second Messenger repeatedly asserts, "I only am escaped alone to tell thee" (sc. 3, 4, and 6). He transcends his traditional role as "Job's post" (as Carlyle termed the carriers of bad news in *The French Revolution,* 3.3.4) and emerges as a complex and reluctant witness:

> Someone chosen by the chance of seeing,
> By the accident of sight,
> By stumbling on the moment of it,
> Unprepared, unwarned, unready,
> Thinking of nothing, of his drink, his bed,
> Caught in that inextricable net,
> His belly, and it happens, and he sees it . . .
> Caught in that inextricable net
> Of having witnessed, having seen . . .
> He alone!

Howard Nemerov's poem "I Only Am Escaped to Tell Thee" suggests that a Victorian lady's whalebone corset is a violation of nature. Its title alludes to Melville's use of the sentence at the end of *Moby-Dick,* but in its new context it also exploits the sinister overtones of the words from the original source, Job, to convey feelings of impending catastrophe.

Bibliography. Pope, M. H. *Job.* AB (1973); Weiser, A. *Das Buch Hiob.* ATD 13, 4th ed. (1963).

MANFRED SIEBALD

ICHABOD After the Philistines defeated Israel and captured the Ark of the Covenant (which was taken onto the battlefield by the sons of Eli, Hophni and Phinehas, as a talisman for victory), Eli fell down dead at the news. His sons also had been killed, and when the pregnant wife of Phinehas heard of the defeat and her husband's death, she went into early labor and delivered a son. As she lay dying, refusing to look at her infant, she gave it the name Ichabod ("inglorious"), saying "the glory (*kabod*) is departed from Israel: for the ark of God is taken" (1 Sam. 4:1-22).

Among important theological reflections on Ichabod is the American Puritan Increase Mather's *Ichabod, or the Glory Departing* (1701). The best-known Ichabod in English literature is Washington Irving's ungainly protagonist in "The Legend of Sleepy Hollow," of whom Irving says, "the cognomen of Crane was not inapplicable to his person." Whittier's poem "Ichabod," attacking Daniel Webster for favoring the Fugitive Slave Law, begins,

> So fallen! so lost! the light withdrawn
> Which once he wore!
> The glory from his grey hairs gone
> Forevermore.

T. H. Huxley comments on the fear that a debilitated educational system will result in commercial decline: "And then, Ichabod! Ichabod! the glory will be departed from us" ("A Liberal Education"). The phrase is most often used in this latter sense of moral or cultural decline,

as by the narrator in P. G. Wodehouse's *Ukridge:* "Ichabod! I murmured surely to myself as I passed on down Oxford Street. Ichabod!" (chap. 1). The genealogy of Leopold Bloom in Joyce's *Ulysses* ("Circe") includes one Ichabudonosor, combining Ichabod with Nebuchadnezzar (Vg Nabuchodonosor).

ICHTHUS *See* FISH.

ICON, ICONOGRAPHY Not found in the Bible, these terms are nonetheless significant in biblical tradition. An icon (*eikōn*) is literally a similitude, likeness, or image of something; as typically applied in the study of graphic, plastic, and literary art, iconography is a systematic discipline or vocabulary for such representation. In ancient, medieval, or Renaissance art, certain abstractions (vices, virtues, qualities of character) may be conventionally represented by figures of animals (e.g., the goat or rabbit for lechery, or the turtledove for faithful love). These conventional associations extend to color, number, and structural relationship in composition.

Although infrequently found in Western tradition, *icon* (*ikon*) may also be used to denote representation of a sacred personage, which art object is then accorded relative status as an object of devotion.

See GRAVEN IMAGE.

IDOLATRY *See* GRAVEN IMAGE.

IF THY RIGHT EYE OFFEND THEE The context of Jesus' remark in the Sermon on the Mount is a consideration of the seventh commandment and of general human disposition to lusts of the flesh (Matt. 5:27-28). He then says, "And if thy right eye offend thee, pluck it out, and cast it from thee: for it is profitable for thee that one of thy members should perish, and not that thy whole body should be cast into hell. And if thy right hand offend thee, cut if off . . ." (vv. 29-30; cf. Job 31:1).

Exegetes have always understood the injunction symbolically. St. Augustine comments, "For whatever it is that is meant by the 'eye,' undoubtedly it is such a thing as he ardently loved. For those who wish to express their affection strongly are wont to speak thus: 'I love him as my own eyes. . . .' Then, when the word 'right' is added, it is meant perhaps to intensify the strength of the affection." Augustine opines that the "right hand" could stand similarly for a close friend or counselor, especially when relationship with such a person might prove a stumbling block to spiritual purity (*De sermone Domini in Monte,* 1.13.37-38). "This is not meant of outward members," Tyndale echoes, more than a millennium later: "It is a phrase of speech of the Hebrew tongue, and wills that we cut off occasions of dancing, kissing, riotous eating and drinking, and the lust of the heart, and filthy imaginations, that move a man to concupiscence" (*Exposition upon the Fifth, Sixth, and Seventh Chapters of Matthew,* sup. 5.29-

30). As Calvin puts it in his commentary on Matthew (sup. 5:29-30), "Christ in hyperbole bids us prune back anything that stops us offering God obedient service, as He demands in His law."

A. E. Housman makes allusion to the passage in "A Shropshire Lad," first urging stoical resolution in the face of adversity and then, somewhat inconsistently, suicide in the case of despair:

> If it chance your eye offend you,
>   Pluck it out, lad, and be sound:
> 'Twill hurt, but here are salves to friend you,
>   And many a balsam grows on ground!
>
> And if your hand or foot offend you,
>   Cut it off, lad, and be whole;
> But play the man, stand up and end you,
>   When your sickness is in your soul.

A bitterly ironic twist on the Augustinian reading of the text is provided by Margaret Mitchell in *Gone with the Wind:* "Everyone admired him tremendously for having cut me off and counted me as dead. 'If thy right eye offend thee, pluck it out'! I was his right eye, his oldest son, and he plucked me out with a vengeance" (chap. 43).

See also SERMON ON THE MOUNT.

IMAGO DEI   God's final work on the sixth day of creation was humanity: "And God said, Let us make man in our image *[ṣelem]*, after our likeness *[demut]*. . . . So God created man in his own image, in the image of God created he him" (Gen. 1:20-27). Some form of physical as well as spiritual "likeness" may be implied in this expression; similar terms are used in Gen. 5 with reference to human procreation: "Adam begat a son in his own likeness *[demut]*, after his image *[ṣelem]*." In the NT, the divine image is understood spiritually. St. Paul writes that "the Lord is spirit. . . . But we all, with open face beholding as in a glass the glory of the Lord, are changed into the same image from glory to glory" (2 Cor. 3:17-18). Once believers have "put off the old," he says elsewhere, they "put on the new man, which is renewed in knowledge after the image of him that created him" (Col. 3:9-10).

The Genesis passage is at the heart of St. Augustine's *De Trinitate,* where he attempts to discover what he can about God by examining the *imago Dei.* The most important way in which humanity images the triune God, argues Augustine, is in his mind. Since mind, for Augustine, is made up of memory, understanding, and will, and since these three faculties interpenetrate and act upon one another, and since "all are mutually comprehended by each, and . . . each as a whole is equal to each as a whole. . . . these three are one . . . one mind, one essence," like the Trinity itself (*De Trin.,* trans. Haddan [1873], 10.11). This three-facultied mind, then, is "an image of the Trinity in its own memory, and understanding, and will" (10.12). Augustine's analysis came to be important for many later writers. St. Bonaventure, e.g., plays with the notion of

trinities of faculties (*Itinerarium Mentis ad Deum,* 3), as does Sir Thomas Browne (*Religio Medici,* 1.12). Donne carries it into his "Second Sermon on Genesis 1:26," arguing that

> the Understanding, stands in the image of the first Person, the Father. . . . The second faculty which is the Will, is the Image . . . of the second person, the Sonne. . . . And then, in the third faculty of the soule, the Memory, is the Image of the third person, the Holy Ghost. (*Sermons,* ed. Potter and Simpson, 9.84-85)

An 18th-cent. secularization of this idea is found in Pope's *Essay on Man,* where enlightened self-interest "if not God's image, yet his shadow drew" (3.288), while a modern recapitulation of the more traditional view is reflected in Dorothy Sayers's *The Mind of the Maker* (1941).

In a more mundane literary application of the *imago Dei,* moral excellence is frequently said to be reflected in the outward beauty of a character. This tradition is not uniquely Christian: Ficino's *Commentary on Plato's Symposium,* e.g., exemplifies the marriage of classical and Christian ideas about beauty and virtue, ideas which Spenser, among others, adopted. Una is a "Louely Ladie" (*Faerie Queene,* 1.1.3), her outward beauty mirroring her inward spiritual state; or, as Spenser puts it in his "Hymne of Beautie,"

> . . . euery spirit, as it is most pure,
> And hath in it the more of heauenly light,
> So it the fairer bodie doth procure
> To habit in.

The Duke-friar's response to the beauty of Isabella in Shakespeare's *Measure for Measure* is more specifically Christian: "The hand that hath made you fair hath made you good. . . . grace, being the soul of your complexion, shall keep the body of it ever fair" (3.1.183ff.).

Donne sums up these attitudes — and introduces a corollary — in his Holy Sonnet "What if this Present": "To wicked spirits are horrid shapes assign'd, / This beauteous forme [Christ crucified] assures a piteous mind." When a person sins, his or her spirit comes to resemble the "horrid shapes" of Donne's "wicked spirits." The image of God is thus defaced and, as Augustine argues, "while his honor is like the likeness of God . . . his dishonor is the likeness of the beast," so that one who sins "arrives in the end at the likeness of beasts" (*De Trin.* 12.11; see also St. Ambrose [FC 42.91]; St. John Chrysostom [NPNF 12.53). This figure becomes a commonplace. John of Salisbury, in the *Policraticus* (trans. J. B. Pike) writes that when "the light of reason is extinguished [by vice] the creature of reason becomes a brute; thus the image of the creator is transformed into a beast by virtue of a sort of similarity in character." This kind of thinking underlies the literary tradition of assigning ugliness to immoral characters: the outward form is a mirror of the inward spiritual state. Insofar as characters are ugly or bestial, they have lost the image of God. Indeed, much of what we think of as evidence of the rise of realism in medieval art and literature is due to the search for the kinds of details which will signify the moral ugliness of such a character as Chaucer's Summoner, with his "fyr-reed cherubynnes face.... With scalled browes blake and piles berd" (*Canterbury Tales,* 1.624-27).

When Spenser's Redcrosse Knight is able to see clearly with the eye of the spirit, he recognizes that Duessa, who had recently seemed to him so beautiful, is in fact "a loathly, wrinckled hag, ill fauoured, old, / Whose secret filth good manner biddeth not be told" (*Faerie Queene,* 1.8.46). In *The Tempest* Caliban is ugly and misshapen — an "ab-horred slave, / Which any print of goodness wil not take" (1.2.353-54). Like the half-men half-beasts of Bosch and Pieter Brueghel, he is distorted by passion and sin to resemble the lower animals, unable to exercise that reason or spirit which alone could separate him essentially from the beasts. He may be contrasted with Blake's "red Orc" in *America,* whom the Daughter of Urthona calls "the image of God who dwells in darkness of Africa" (Preludium, 28), a Caliban reversed. By the 19th cent., ugly characters can often be morally good, but the older tradition continues to flourish, too. One recalls the red and otherwise unfortunate physiognomy of Trollope's Mr. Slope in *Barchester Towers* — and perhaps especially Dickens's cruel dwarf Quilp, in *The Old Curiosity Shop,* whose misshapen body mirrors a spirit capable of lusting after one as pure (and lovely) as Little Nell. Wilde's *Picture of Dorian Gray* and Steven-son's *Dr. Jekyll and Mr. Hyde* are variations on this same theme: Dorian's picture is the outward manifestation of his spiritual ugliness, just as Hyde is Jekyll's.

As Augustine argued, however, reformation of the divine image is possible. Citing Rom. 12:2 ("Be not conformed to this world: but be ye transformed by the renewing of your mind"), he attests that "that image may begin to be formed again by Him by whom it had been formed at first," explaining that even when the image of God has become "defaced and tarnished," it can be "formed again and renewed" (*De Trin.* 14.16; cf. *De civ. Dei* 22.16). These ideas lie behind the second book of Walter Hilton's *Ladder of Perfection,* where he discusses the loss of the original prelapsarian image of God by Adam and Eve and its restoration by Christ (2.1, 4, 5); he builds upon a reading of the parable of the lost coin (Luke 15:8-9) in which the image on a coin is darkened by misuse, and its restoration made to illuminate the relation-ship between self-discovery and the image of God (1.49-55). The same notion is at work in a general way in the changes in appearance which Redcrosse Knight under-goes from the time of his imprisonment — with "his sad dull eyes deepe sunck in hollow pits . . . / His bare thin cheekes . . . his rawbone armes . . . and all his vitall powres / Decayd, and all his flesh shronk up like withered flowres" (*FQ* 1.8.41) — to the renewing of his spirit in the House of Holiness. Here he becomes, once again, a "Faire Knight" (1.10.57). So it is that Donne prays, in "Goodfriday, 1613, Riding Westward": "Burne off my rusts, and my deformity, / Restore thine Image, so much, by thy grace, / That thou may'st know mee, and I'll turn my face."

Elizabeth Barrett Browning's "The Image of God" takes two epigraphs from the Bible, the first from Isaiah, "I am God, and there is none like me" (46:9), and the second from 2 Corinthians, in which St. Paul speaks of "Christ, who is the image of God" (4:4). For Browning, nothing is "like" God — neither sun nor earth nor the human soul — except only Christ: "Thou, who didst bear the sin, and shame, and woe. . . . / none, save only Thou, — below, above, — / O God, is like to God!" For Hop-kins, whose "As Kingfishers catch fire" is a meditation upon the dynamic imaging of God in the human, "Christ plays in ten thousand places, / Lovely in limbs, and lovely in eyes not his / To the Father through the features of men's faces."

See also DEFORMITY; GLASS, MIRROR; OLD AND NEW.

Bibliography. Hill, E. "St. Augustine on the Divine Im-age in Man." Appendix 4 of St. Thomas Aquinas, *Summa Theologica,* vol. 13 (Blackfriars ed. [1963]), 209-12; Martz, L. *The Poetry of Meditation* (1969), 32-58; Sulli-van, J. *The Image of God: The Doctrine of St. Augustine and Its Influence* (1963); Tuve, R. *Allegorical Imagery* (1966), 189-93.   H. DAVID BRUMBLE

IMMACULATE CONCEPTION   In a doctrine of the Catholic Church, based upon the apocryphal Protevan-gelium or Gospel of St. James, the Immaculate Concep-tion is that of the Virgin Mary, not of Jesus her Son. It was confirmed as dogma by Pope Pius IX in 1854.

See also MARY, MOTHER OF JESUS.

IMMANUEL   In Isa. 7:14 the prophet announces that "a virgin shall conceive, and bear a son, and shall call his name Immanuel." The name is glossed in Matt. 1:23 (where it is given as "Emmanuel") to mean "God with us." From early times, Isa. 7:14 was incorporated into the divine office as one of the so-called "O Antiphons," short prose passages inserted at the beginning of the *Mag-nificat,* the canticle of the Virgin Mary sung at Vespers in the Western church. From the 8th cent., these antiphons were sung at each *Magnificat* of the octave before Christmas (i.e., from Dec. 16-23). The antiphon based on Isa. 7:14 is recited on Dec. 23: "*O Immanuel, Rex et legifer noster, expectatio gentium, et Salvator earum; veni ad salvandum nos, Domine Deus noster.*" ("O Immanuel, King and our lawgiver, expectation of the nations, and Saviour of them: come to save us, Lord our God.")

In the OE *Christ,* Isa. 7:14 is separated into two "O antiphons." The first half of the verse, "Behold a virgin shall conceive," is paraphrased in lines 71-77. The second half, "And he shall be called Emmanuel," is then rendered (130-35):

Eala gasta god, hu þu gleawlice
mid noman ryhte nemned wære
Emmanuhel, swa hit engel gecwæð
ærest on Ebresc! þæt is eft gereft

("O god of spirits, how wisely were
you named with the right name
Emmanuel, as the angel spoke it
first in Hebrew: 'Now is the ruler of
the spheres, God Himself with us.'")

By the Middle Ages, the "O antiphon" had found its way into the drama. In the Towneley play "Herod the Great," Herod tries to discover the identity of the king who competes with his power. One of the counselors has said that "a madyn shuld bere anothere to be kyng" (200), and Herod has the others search for the "expectation of the nations" in the books of Virgil. His first counselor speaks (210-17):

We rede thus by Isay
he shal be so kynde,
that a madyn, sothely which neuer synde,
    Shall hym bere:
"virgo concipiet,
Natumque pariet";
"Emanuell" is hete,
    his name for to lere
"God is with vs," that is forto say.

Virgil is invoked because of analogous expression in his "Fourth Eclogue" (4-8):

Now has come to last age of the Sybil's song
A great order is born from all the ages.
Now has the virgin returned . . .
Now a new progeny has been sent from high heaven
Lucina, smile upon the boy being born.

The play "Processus Prophetarum," in the same cycle, has the (Cumaean) sibyl recite the significance of the "expectation of the nations" in the first three lines of her Sibylline Oracle (163-65): *"Iudicii signum / tellus sudore madescit, / E celo rex adveniet per secla futurus, / Scilicet in carne presens vt iudicet orbem."* ("A sign of judgment: the earth will be wet with sweat, From heaven a once and future king will come, Present in the flesh to judge the world.") The *expectatio gentium* is also encoded in the first letter of each of the twenty-seven lines of her oracle, which together spell out in Greek letters IESVCS CREISTOS TES DNTOS SEOTED — approximating "Jesus Christ, Son of God, Savior." The inspiration for the play came from Augustine's *De civitate Dei* (18.23) and a sermon of Quodvultdeus printed among the works of St. Augustine.

Milton's "Nativity Ode" incorporates many of these elements in its own celebration of the coming of Immanuel to silence the oracles and triumph over pagan deities. The most familiar musical setting of the "O Antiphon" based on Isa. 7:14 may be the popular carol "O Come, O Come, Emmanuel."

See also FISH; JOSEPH THE CARPENTER; MESSIAH.

ERNEST N. KAULBACH

IMPANATION A doctrine of the Eucharist, first articulated in the 11th and 12th cents., in explanation of the Real Presence of Christ's body and blood in the elements of the Eucharistic meal, that they are "hidden" in the apparently unchanged bread (and wine), "impanated." In the later Middle Ages and Reformation periods it came into general use (e.g., George Herbert's "H. Communion," 25-28).

See also BREAD OF LIFE; EUCHARIST; TRANSUBSTANTIATION.

IN THE BEGINNING *See IN PRINCIPIO.*

IN PRINCIPIO The first words of Genesis, "In the beginning," are mirrored in the first verse of the Gospel of John, from whence they are cited in Latin by Chaucer's Friar (*Canterbury Tales,* 1.254) as part of his means of impressing vulnerable widows. John 1:1-14 ("In the beginning was the Word . . .") was sometimes quoted from memory by medieval friars as a form of exalted salutation or blessing or even as a charm. In Goethe's *Faust* the perverse Wittenberg theologian is found (1.3) trying to translate the first verse of John's Gospel into German, rejecting *Wort* and, after a series of alternatives, writing, "In the beginning was the Act" *(Tat)* — a redefining formulation which signals his dark rebellion. The narrator of Umberto Eco's *The Name of the Rose,* considering the strange history he is about to relate (and the semioticians' questions it poses), commences his portentous "re-creation" with a sonorous *in principio,* announcing thereby a nominalist rather than Johannine logocentrism.

See also INCARNATION; LOGOS.

INCARNATION The term *Incarnation* refers to the unique union of divinity and humanity in Jesus Christ, the study of which is known as Christology. Although variously construed, the doctrine is central to all Christian theological traditions and germane to broader understanding of the relationship between God and creation (cf. Col. 1:14-20). The NT's treatment is declarative rather than explanatory. The prologue to the Gospel according to John asserts that "the Word was made flesh" (1:14) — the Gk. *sarx* denoting not merely the physical body but humanity in its fullness (*TDNT* 7.139) — as the climax to the creation of the cosmos and the epitome of God's self-revelation. Other passages, notably Phil. 2:5-11, develop implicit themes of descent and ascent and establish the doctrine's paradoxical force.

The NT does provide evidence of early disputes with Gnosticism over the question of Jesus' human nature (1 John 4:1-3). Such controversy within Christianity, together with the need to respond to Jewish and pagan refutations, led to doctrinal elaboration during the patristic era. Two distinct and opposing views emerged: one, associated with Alexandria, stressed the divinity of Christ;

and the other, associated with Antioch, his humanity — each assailing the inadequacy of the other. Thus St. Cyril of Alexandria guarded Christ's divinity by championing the term *theotokos* — "God-bearer" — for the Virgin Mary, whereas St. Gregory of Nazianzus advocated Jesus' humanity, physical body and human soul: "For that which he has not assumed, he has not healed; but that which is united to his Godhead, is also saved" (*Ep.* 101).

In 451 the Council of Chalcedon endorsed the "Tome" (*Ep.* 28) of Leo I, who argued that by the principle of *communicatio idiomatum* the properties of both the divine and the human natures could be attributed to the single person of Jesus. In its definition, which for a millennium would be accepted almost universally as the basis for further discussion, the council decreed that Jesus be confessed as having "two natures, without mingling, without change, indivisibly, undividedly [united], the distinction of the natures nowhere removed on account of the union but rather the peculiarity of each nature being kept, and uniting in one person and substance. . . ."

In the centuries following, western European writers turned increasing attention to Jesus' human nature as they grew concerned with matters of soteriology and sacramental theology. St. Anselm's argument for the logical necessity of the Incarnation (*Cur Deus Homo?*) was followed by scholastic disputes on whether the Incarnation would have taken place at all if not for the Fall. Meanwhile, affective devotion to Jesus' humanity was incorporated into the theological schemes of such influential monastic writers as St. Bernard of Clairvaux, adopted by mystical writers of the *via positiva*, and promoted in the vernacular by the Franciscans.

With the Reformation,

> the controversy between the two major parties of Protestantism . . . over the real presence of the body and blood of Christ in the Lord's Supper . . . was responsible for the most detailed Western preoccupation with the intricacies of christology since the ancient church. (J. Pelikan, *The Christian Tradition,* 4 [1984], 158)

The Reformed party stressed the distinction between the two natures of Christ, as in John Calvin's explication of the Apostles' Creed (*Inst.* 2.2). Lutherans emphasized the unity of his person (Augsburg Confession, art. 3), with Luther himself prescribing adherence to the *"Deus incarnatus et humanus Deus"* (*In Epistola S. Pauli ad Galatas Commentarius,* 1.3) and declaring that "to seek God outside of Jesus is the devil" (*"extra Iesum quaerere Deum est diabolus," In XV Psalmos Graduum* [Ps. 130:1]). Reflecting an alternative tradition, more radical Protestants would avoid the intellectual problem altogether, as in the Mennonite Dordrecht Confession (1632): "But how, or in what manner, this worthy body was prepared, or how the Word became flesh, and He Himself man, we content ourselves with the declaration which the worthy evangelists have given and left in their description thereof . . ." (art. 4).

Modern developments — being heavily influenced by a philosophical aversion to metaphysics and by the rise of the historical method — have tended to focus on existential, psychological, and moral dimensions of the Incarnation. In *The Essence of Christianity* (1841), the German positivist Ludwig Feuerbach claimed,

> The Incarnation, the mystery of the "God-man," is . . . no mysterious composition of contraries, no synthetic fact . . . it is an analytic fact, — a human word with a human meaning. . . . And the Incarnation has no other significance, no other effect, than the indubitable certitude of the love of God to man. (Trans. George Eliot, 56-57)

In a similar vein, Emerson declared in his Divinity School Address (1838) that Jesus' authority lay in his proclamation of the universal incarnation of God in humanity. The new developments in biblical criticism were notably represented in Schweitzer's *The Quest for the Historical Jesus* (1906; trans. 1910) and radically epitomized in Bultmann's "demythologizing": "For what God has done in Jesus Christ is not an historical fact which is capable of historical proof" (*Jesus Christ and Mythology* [1958], 80). Reflecting 20th-cent. developments while contending with tradition, recent treatments — from the Second Vatican Council's Pastoral Constitution on the Church in the Modern World (1.1.22) to *The Myth of God Incarnate* (ed. John Hick [1977]) — have focused on the cultural significance of the doctrine.

Christological concerns appear throughout the history of English literature. The *Dream of the Rood* depicts the *communicatio idiomatum* graphically and dramatically: "I saw the journey-ready beacon / shift in robes and colors; now it was reddened with wet / drenched with the shedding of blood, now it was sheathed with treasure" (21b-23 [trans. B. Huppél]). Reflecting the rise in affective devotion, medieval lyric poetry on the Passion often employs detailed description and the language of romantic love:

> Quanne hic se on rode
> ihesu mi lemman, . . .
> And his rig i-suongen,
> and his side i-stungen,
> for þe luue of man,
> Wel ou hic to wepen
> and sinnes for-leten,
> yif hic of luue kan. . . .
> (C. Brown, *English Lyrics of the XIIIth Century,* no. 35B)

In contrast, the 15th-cent. "A God and yet a man?" cedes both "witt" and affection, preferring a simple faith — "Beleeve and leave to wonder!" (C. Brown, *Religious Lyrics of the XVth Century,* no. 120). Julian of Norwich integrates affective response and theological rigor in her *Showings,* arguing for the essential unity of her mystical experience on the basis of the Incarnation: "For I saw full suerly that oure substance is in god, and also I saw that in oure sensualyte god is . . ." (Long Text 55 [eds. Colledge and Walsh, 2.566-67.23-25]). Whereas medieval mystery plays featured Jesus' humanity, often in realistic detail (see esp. the York Crucifixion play of the Pinners and Painters), post-Reformation concern to avoid idolatry and sacrilege led to a ban on the onstage representation first of God the Father and then of Jesus — a prohibition which survived in Britain until the 20th cent.

The paradox of the Incarnation provided apt subject matter for the metaphysical poets, as in Richard Crashaw's "Hymn on the Holy Nativity" (1652):

> Wellcome all WONDERS in one sight!
> AEternity shutt in a span.
> Sommer in Winter. Day in Night.
> Heaven in earth, and GOD in MAN. (79-82)

While devotion to Jesus' humanity continued, lyrical treatments took a sentimental turn: John Milton's "Ode on the Morning of Christ's Nativity" — its hymn "a present to the infant God" — has its direct progeny in Christina Rossetti's "A Christmas Carol" ("In the bleak midwinter"), and for Robert Browning the Incarnation becomes a symbol of "archetypal Love" (E. L. Lawson, *Very Sure of God* [1974], 77-78). Paralleling scholarly debate on the historical Jesus, 20th.-cent. literature has often stressed Jesus' humanity: D. H. Lawrence depicts him in sheerly physical, sensual terms in *The Man Who Died,* whereas Dorothy Sayers — offering an orthodox corrective to the other extreme — presents *The Man Born to Be King* "realistically and historically," as the one in whom "the prophecies of the poets had become furnished with a name, a date, and an address."

In the face of intractable doctrinal dissent, poets of the past two centuries have often turned to broader considerations, particularly those of a literary nature. While Shelley sees "Imagination" as "the immortal God which should assume flesh for the redemption of mortal passion" (Pref. to *The Cenci*) and Jesus as the supreme poet who "divulged the sacred and eternal truths [of Platonism] . . . to mankind" (*A Defence of Poetry*), Auden views the Incarnation as "redeeming" the poetic function: "Because in Him the Flesh is united to the Word without magical transformation, Imagination is redeemed from promiscuous fornication with her own images" ("The Meditation of Simeon," *For the Time Being*). Addressing matters comprehensively in his own epic meditation, Eliot presents the Incarnation as the key to the mysteries of time, eternity, and art: "The hint half guessed, the gift half understood . . ." in which "the impossible union / Of spheres of existence is actual" ("The Dry Salvages").

See also SON OF GOD; SON OF MAN.

Bibliography. Auerbach, E. *Mimesis: The Representation of Reality in Western Literature* (1946). Trans. W. R. Trask (1953); Bennet, J. A. W. *Poetry of the Passion: Studies in Twelve Centuries of English Verse* (1982); Hunter, W. B. "Milton on the Incarnation." *JHI* 21 (1960), 349-69; Kean, P. M. "Langland on the Incarnation." *RES* 26 (1964), 349-63; Nichols, A. *The Art of God Incarnate: Theology and Image in Christian Tradition* (1980); Pelikan, J. *Jesus through the Ages: His Place in the History of Culture* (1985; rpt. 1987); Welch, D. M. "'Cloth'd with Human Beauty': Milton and Blake's Incarnational Aesthetic." *Religion and Literature* 18 (1986), 1-15; Whitla, W. *The Central Truth: The Incarnation in Robert Browning's Poetry* (1963); Woolf, R. "Doctrinal Influences on *The Dream of the Rood.*" *MAE* 27 (1958), 137-53.   ROBERT E. WRIGHT

INCEST In common with other societies the OT proscribed sexual relations between close relatives. Lev. 18:6-18 gives a detailed list of forbidden unions from the man's side. A man is barred from marrying a female relative who is genetically consanguineous to the first or second degree. First-degree consanguines include sister, mother, and daughter. Second-degree consanguines include aunt and granddaughter. Furthermore, this bar extends to the former wives of male consanguines, e.g., stepmother, daughter-in-law, and normally sister-in-law.

In marriage a woman became part of her husband's family and thus related to his relatives. It was wrong, therefore, for one of the husband's close male relatives to marry her should her first marriage end in divorce or widowhood. The levirate was an exception to this rule (see Deut. 25:5-10); in the case of a woman being left a widow, she was to be wedded to the oldest available brother to "raise up seed" to the dead man (Gen. 38:8). The story of Judah and his daughter-in-law Tamar illustrates a shameful flight from levirate responsibility.

In patriarchal times (i.e., at least 500 years before the pentateuchal laws just cited) some of these regulations seem to have been unknown, or at least were disregarded. Abraham married his half-sister, and Jacob his wife's sister (Gen. 20:12; 29:21-30). The way Lot's daughters arranged to have intercourse with their father, however, was obviously regarded as shameful, and the story underlines Israel's contempt for her neighbors Ammon and Moab, whose origin is traced to this incestuous relationship (Gen. 19:30-38). In the reign of David Amnon's passion for another Tamar, his half-sister, triggered the disastrous train of events recorded in 2 Sam. 13–19. John the Baptist's criticism of the marriage of Herodias to Herod Antipas after divorce from his brother Herod Philip led to the dance of Salome and loss of the prophet's head (Matt. 14:3-11; Mark 6:17-28; cf. Josephus, *Ant.* 18.5.4).

Though marriage with one's closest relative was forbidden, the OT does favor unions with those of common blood. Law and custom dictated that a man ought to marry an Israelite, not a foreigner (Deut. 7:3; Judg. 14:3; Ezra 10). In some circumstances marriage within the same tribe was insisted on (Num. 36:6), and the Genesis narratives imply that the ideal marriage partners are parallel cousins, i.e., that a man should marry his uncle's daughter.

Subsequent Christian tradition, especially following St. Augustine and St. Gregory the Great, added several degrees of consanguinity to guidelines for marriage eligibility, these being codified by the 12th cent. to prohibit union of persons within six degrees of relationship (e.g., Hugh of St. Victor, *De Sacramentis*, 2.11.14-19). The Church of England reduced the degrees of prohibition along biblical guidelines after 1562 (e.g., *Book of Common Prayer*, "Table of Kindred and Affinity").

"Incest scare" motifs abound in folk literature, and surface in major works from *Oedipus Rex* to Henry Fielding's *Tom Jones* and *Joseph Andrews,* but few texts in English or American literature develop explicitly biblical perspectives on the subject. In Oscar Wilde's *Salome,* however, the incestuous activities of Herodias are implicated in the perversity of Salome, an aspect highlighted in Richard Strauss's one-act opera based on Wilde's play. Robinson Jeffers's narrative poem *Tamar* is loosely based on the account in 2 Sam. 13, but deals with a modern California Tamar who seduces her brother, a neighbor, and her father; communicates with the dead; and eventually achieves the destruction of her entire family. It turns out that this destruction is in some sense the result of an earlier incestuous relationship between her father and his own sister.

See also LOT; TAMAR.

Bibliography. Dalke, A. F. "Had I Known Her to be My Sister, My Love Would Have Been More Regular: Incest in Nineteenth-Century American Fiction." Ph.D. diss., Pennsylvania, 1982; Wilson, J. D. "Incest and American Romantic Fiction." *Studies in the Literary Imagination* 7 (1974), 31-50.
G. J. WENHAM

INFANCY OF CHRIST   *See* JESUS CHRIST, CHILDHOOD OF.

INHERITANCE   The Hebrew and Greek words translated "inheritance" in the KJV have the primary meaning of what is allotted to one. Only secondarily do they denote a patrimony. Associated words in the KJV are "lot," "portion," and "heir."

God's promise to Abraham entailed descendants, territory, fame, and blessing for himself and for the world (Gen. 12:1-3, 7). All these were involved in the inheritance contested within the patriarchal families (21:9-13) and eventually settled upon Jacob (Israel) and his sons (25:19-34; 27:1-40; 28:10-15).

When the Israelites finally entered the Promised Land, it was understood that both Israel itself and its new territory were ultimately the Lord's portion (1 Sam. 26:19; Deut. 9:26-29; 32:9). Israel inherited the land only on the condition that it kept the covenant. The land was divided into tribal territories and subdivided into family lots, which could not be permanently alienated (Lev. 25:8-17). Owners held it on trust (1 Kings 21:2-3). The Levites did not receive a tribal territory; the Lord was their portion and they were supported from offerings (Num. 18:20, 24).

Because of Israel's persistent sin, it lost the inherited territory and went into exile (Deut. 30:15-20), but the prophets promised a restoration. Although some Jews returned in 538 B.C., the general feeling was that the inheritance had not been restored, for foreigners still ruled over them (Neh. 9:36-37). The expectation of a national restoration forms the background to the message of Jesus, "Blessed are the meek, for they shall inherit the land" (Gk. *gēn* [Matt. 5:5]). The parable of the wicked husbandmen (Mark 12:1-12) emphasizes that Christ is the true heir, a message reinforced by St. Paul, for whom Christ is the heir and believers fellow heirs of the promise made to Abraham (Rom. 4:13-16; 8:15-17; Gal. 3:6-18; 4:1-7).

The idea of national inheritance, reinforced by biblical typologies developed especially in Puritan texts such as Foxe's *Book of Martyrs,* remains strong in colonial and Third World literature in English. The idea of the "Promised Land," an "inheritance forever," is fundamental to American writing in the colonial period (e.g., Samuel Danforth's *Brief Recognition of New England's Errand into the Wilderness* [1670], John Cotton's *God's Promises to His Plantations* [1630], and John Norton's *Sion the Outcast* [1664]). It is also a powerful metaphor in more recent Commonwealth literature, such as Chinua Achebe's *No Longer at Ease* (1960), Ngugi Wa Thiong'o's *The River Between,* and Salman Rushdie's *Midnight's Children* (1981), the latter of which draws its application of the Jacob/Esau narrative from its treatment in the Koran. The biblical notion of a national inheritance or restored Israel has more than metaphoric value in modern American novels such as Leon Uris's *Exodus* and Chaim Potok's *The Chosen* and *The Promise,* in each of which Zionist aspirations for a return of the state of Israel as a divinely appointed inheritance is vigorously presented and debated.

See also BIRTHRIGHT; ELECTION; TRIBES OF ISRAEL.

Bibliography. Baritz, L. *City on a Hill: History of Ideas and Myths in America* (1964); Brumm, U. *American Thought and Religious Typology* (1970); Haller, W. *The Elect Nation: The Meaning and Relevance of Foxe's Book of Martyrs* (1963); Sanford, C. *The Quest for Paradise: Europe and the American Moral Imagination* (1961).   PAUL GARNET

INSPIRATION   In biblical usage, inspiration is of divine origin. The breath of God which created life (Gen. 2:7) also inspires the minds of the prophets, "flooding" them, as Tertullian puts it, with the Holy Spirit. The English verb *to inspire* does not translate any single word in Hebrew or Greek but derives from the Vg *inspiro* (as in Gen. 2:7; 2 Tim. 3:16; 2 Pet. 1:21) and the noun *inspiratio* (Job 32:8; Ps. 18:15; Acts 17:25).

The belief in divine inspiration extends also to Scripture. The Pentateuch, the five books of Moses, was held to be the result of the Sinaitic revelation, but the Hebrew Scriptures as a whole were thought to have been inspired. Josephus (*Contra Apion,* 1.8) uses the word *inspiration* to describe the books Jews consider divine, and states that the closing of the canon coincides with the cessation of prophecy, an argument followed by R. Aqiba in excluding

Ecclesiasticus as having been written "since the days of the prophets."

The NT emphatically reaffirms the inspired nature of the Hebrew Scriptures, most clearly in 2 Tim. 3:16: "All scripture is given by the inspiration of God" (Gk. *pasa graphē theopneustos;* Vg *divinitus inspirata*). This view was taken for granted by all the major Fathers of the Church, including St. Irenaeus (*Adv. haer.* 3.1.1), Tertullian (*Apology,* 18), Origen (*De principiis,* 4.9), St. Hippolytus (*Contra Noetum,* 2), and Eusebius (*Hist. eccl.* 3.4.7), among others. Patristic writers assume, indeed, not merely general inspiration but a "God-breathed" aspect in details and phraseology. Thus St. Clement of Alexandria (*Protrepticus,* 9.82.1) argues that not a jot or tittle can be disregarded, since all Scripture is spoken by the word of the Lord. In accepting the basic Judaic premise of the inspired nature of the OT Scripture, the Church assumed that the Spirit responsible for inspiring it was there as in the NT principally concerned to bear witness to Jesus Christ. This entailed an interpretation of the OT as speaking in types and figures about Christ, prophetically anticipating the events of the gospel. Such interpretation begins in the NT itself, which regularly speaks of events in the life and Passion of Christ as "fulfilling" the OT Scriptures (e.g., Matt. 1:22; 2:15, 17, 23; 4:14; 8:17; 12:17; 13:14, 35; 21:4; 26:54, 56; 27:9, 35, etc.).

Thus, according to St. Ignatius the OT prophets "were disciples in the Spirit" (Magn. 9:1-2) while Origen, in his preface to *De principiis* (1-2), argues that Moses and the prophets "spoke and performed all they did by being filled with the Spirit of Christ." There were, said St. Justin Martyr, Christians before Christ. However, if God had once spoken through the prophets but more recently "by a Son" (Heb. 1:1-2), the new word was not discontinuous with the earlier language of prophecy; on the contrary, the validity of the Gospels rested in part upon their prophetic anticipation by the prophets of Israel (1 Pet. 1:10-12). Overzealous application of such a method of reading the OT provoked resistance from, among others, St. Isidore of Pelusium, who condemned as an encouragement to skeptics the attempt to see the figure of Christ everywhere in the OT.

The view of the NT as "fulfillment" was extended also to some degree to Greek philosophy. One tendency was to see, as did Justin, the seeds of Logos in Greek philosophical writings or with Clement that Greek philosophy was a gift of divine providence. However, on the manner in which inspiration manifested itself, the OT, the NT, and the early patristic writers were generally eager to separate their own concept of inspiration from those familiar to the pagan world.

In the OT, prophetic inspiration was sometimes accompanied by trance or ecstasy, an example being Num. 24:4, where Balaam fell prostrate with the inrushing of divine afflatus. External signs of spirit possession such as the *enthousiazon* or *theia mania* attributed by Socrates to

the oracles of Delphi were, however, not taken as an assurance of genuine prophecy (Deut. 13:1-5; 1 Kings 22:19-28). In Saul's time a sharp distinction was drawn between accredited prophets and mere ecstatics or false prophets such as appear in Jer. 29:26 and 2 Kings 9:11. The test of prophetic inspiration lay in both the consistency of its message with the Law and in the effects of the prophetic message: the manner of its delivery was not enough to validate it (Jer. 7:25; 25:4; Hos. 6:5; Amos 3:7).

The same distinctions were applied in the NT and reinforced by the early Church, which, acknowledging the authenticity of ecstatic experience and gifts, nonetheless required that all such phenomena be submitted to interpretation and corroboration by the witness of the Word. Such a view accounts for the profound resistance to the Montanists and their extravagant claims to direct inspiration, as expressed, e.g., in Miltiades's treatise *That a Prophet Should Not Speak in Ecstacy*. Similar views may be seen in a letter ascribed to Clement (ca. A.D. 96) to the ascetics of Corinth who boasted of "gnosis" or secret knowledge of the faith revealed only to the elite, and in the 2nd-cent. Didache, which cautions that "not everybody making ecstatic utterances is a prophet, but only if he behaves like the Lord" (*Early Christian Fathers,* ed. C. Richardson [1953], 177). In general, the early Fathers were at pains to disengage scriptural from pagan prophecy and to contrast the teaching of the prophets inspired by the Holy Ghost with the foolishness of pagan religion.

Subsequent theological debate which assumed the inspiration and authority of Scripture focused on the nature of the inspiration — whether it was verbal, dictating every word; plenary, covering all subjects treated; or moral, restricted to moral and religious teaching.

The iconography of inspiration takes several forms. It is often represented by a flame (Acts 2:3) or the hot coal applied to Isaiah's mouth by a seraph which gave him the power of prophetic speech (Isa. 6:7; this image recurs in Shakespeare's "muse of fire" and in Hopkins's "blow pipe flame" of inspiration in "To R.B."). Inspiration is also figured by the dove (representative of the Holy Spirit; see, e.g., Gen. 1:2; Matt. 3:16), as in Hopkins's "God's Grandeur" (13-14) and in *Paradise Lost* (1.20-21); in paintings the dove is sometimes shown entering the ear of a prophet or apostle, signifying his direct inspiring presence. The most important metaphor for inspiration is wind or breath. God's breath inspires creation, revivifies the dead in Ezek. 37:9, and produces spiritual revival in John 3:7; "a mighty wind," like that at Pentecost (Acts 2:2), is the external accompaniment to St. Augustine's conversion (*Conf.* 8.11-12).

Such an association finds a parallel in classical mythology in the inspiriting power of the west wind. Thus, the initial impetus for the spiritual pilgrimage in the *Canterbury Tales* occurs when "Zephirus with his sweete breeth / Inspired hath in every holt and heeth / the tendre croppes" (*General Prologue,* 5-7). Apollo was said to have founded the Delphic oracle over a chasm which exhaled "a wind that spoke," and the Pythian priestess was said to be inspired by inhaling this pneuma or *anima mundi* (Lucan, *Civil War,* 5.82-85), a belief recalled in Shelley's *Epipsychidion* as "A Pythian exhalation." Joannes Lodovicus Vives in his 1523 commentary on Augustine's *De civitate Dei* (4.11) also cites the inspiring vapors at the Delphic shrine. A goat feeding there by chance was reported to leap and dance as a result of inspiration. The shepherd coming to the mouth of the cave "grew rapt himself and began to prophesy."

The drawing of such parallels between these classical and biblical treatments of inspiration was encouraged in the Renaissance by Christian humanism. The vision vouchsafed the knight in Spenser's *Faerie Queene,* 1.10.53-54, is on a mountaintop analogous with Sinai, the Mount of Olives and Parnassus, as places of former inspiration, while E. K.'s argument in the *Shepherd's Calendar* (October) that poetry is not "arte, but a divine gift ... poured into the witte by a certaine enthousiasmos, and celestiall inspiration" makes the familiar connection between poetic and prophetic inspiration which recurs in Shelley's claim in the *Defence,* that in former times poets were called prophets (the Roman *vates*). The fusing of the classical invocation to the muses with the idea of biblical prophecy is nowhere more effectively combined than in *Paradise Lost.* Though Milton follows epic tradition in seeking superhuman inspiration, the "Heav'nly Muse" whose aid he invokes is identified with the Hebrew God who inspired Moses on Sinai. The inspiration Milton courts is analogous to that given the prophet: "Instruct me. . . . What in me is dark / Illumin; what is low raise and support" (1.19-23). By suggesting that his Muse may prefer to dwell on Mt. Zion near Siloah's brook, Milton invites comparison with the Greek muses who had inhabited Olympus, Parnassus, and Helicon and the nearby Hippocrene and Castalian springs. However, the comparison also implies Milton's recognition that classical mythology was a shadow of the truth of Scripture. Thus, as Woodhouse points out, the invocation "finds its precedent and point of departure in the classical tradition," for here as elsewhere in the poem there is a contrast between classical form and Christian content (*The Heavenly Muse* [1972], 182). In bk. 7, Milton invokes his muse by the name Urania, the patroness of astronomy borrowed by tradition to furnish poets with a muse for specifically Christian verse; she is later recalled by Wordsworth in his Prospectus to *The Recluse* (24-27): "So prayed, more gaining than he asked, the Bard — / In holiest mood. Urania, I shall need: Thy guidance, or a greater Muse, if such / Descend to earth or dwell in highest heaven!"

The "blessing in this gentle breeze" to which Wordsworth refers at the opening of the *Prelude,* and which produces a "correspondent breeze" of inspiration within him, is equated with the inspiration of the prophets when touched by the Holy Spirit. An important new element is Wordsworth's attempt to "naturalise" the concept of inspiration while retaining its links with older conventions, for as he says later in the poem, "Nature's self" is "the breath of God" (*Prelude,* 5.221).

This correspondence between wind and poetic inspiration occurs in a wide range of Romantic poems including Coleridge's *Dejection: An Ode* and Shelley's *Ode to the West Wind* and constitutes, according to M. H. Abrams, "a distinctively Romantic image or icon" (*English Romantic Poets,* 50-51). The sense of being used as a mouthpiece by supernatural power is not confined to religious experience but is an aspect of the creative process, frequently attested to. Sidney Dobell when writing always had the strong feeling "of being a receiver, an instrument, a mouthpiece" (*Life and Letters* [1878], 1.105). Both Blake and Shelley cite Milton's claim in *Paradise Lost* (9.21-24) that the muse "dictated" to him while "slumbering," and Blake contended that some of his own poetry was the result of "immediate Dictation," he being no more than the "Secretary" of the work, the "Authors being in Eternity" (ed. Keynes [1932], 1076). "What," said Thackeray, "if there is an *afflated* style, — when a writer is like a Pythoness on her oracle tripod and mighty words, words he cannot help, come blowing, and bellowing, and whistling, and moaning through the speaking pipes of his bodily organ?" (*Roundabout Papers,* 374-75).

John Oldham, however, likens "mere fanatics, and enthusiasts in poetry" to religious schismatics "Who make't all revelation, trance and dream," despising the rules and forms of art (*Upon the Works of Ben Jonson,* 3-6). This tension between inspiration and the ordering skill of poetry recurs in Marianne Moore's line: "Ecstacy affords the occasion and expediency determines the form" (*The Past Is Present,* 10-11). In acknowledging the inspirational aspect of the creative process, poets have ascribed it to many sources including God, the muses, imagination and intuition. Poetry cannot be produced by the will, writes Shelley, but the mind "in creation is as a fading coal which some invisible influence, like an inconstant wind, awakens to transitory brightness" (*Defence of Poetry*).

In secular literature from the Romantic to the modern period inspiration is increasingly identified as having a psychological rather than a divine origin, as in the "epiphanies" of James Joyce or the more mysterious "duende" in Lorca.

See also ALLEGORY; HERMENEUTICS; HOLY SPIRIT; TYPOLOGY.

Bibliography. Camfield, F. W. *Revelation and the Holy Spirit* (1945); Harding, R. *An Anatomy of Inspiration* (1967); Levie, J. S. J. *The Bible, Word of God in Words of Men* (1958); Pieper, J. *Enthusiasm and Divine Madness.* Trans. R. and C. Winston (1964); Robinson, H. W. *Inspiration and Revelation in the Old Testament* (1913); Sanday, W. *The Oracles of God* (1892); *Inspiration* (1894).

MICHAEL GOLDBERG

INTERPRETER, INTERPRETATION *See* HERME-
NEUTICS.

IPHIS *See* JEPHTHAH AND HIS DAUGHTER.

ISAAC Isaac (Heb. *yiṣḥaq,* "he laughs") was the
second of the patriarchs of Israel, the only son of Abraham
and Sarah, husband of Rebekah, and the father of Esau
and Jacob. His name is connected with Sarah's immediate
response to the divine promise that she would bear a son
though long past childbearing age — she found the notion
risible (Gen. 18:12-15) — and with the laughter at once
comic and joyful which followed the realization of that
promise (Gen. 21:6). Gen. 22 relates what became for
posterity the most significant episode in the life of Isaac,
Abraham's offering of his obedient son at God's command. Isaac's resignation is praised in 4 Macc. 16:20; but
in 13:12 and 14:20, the triumph is Abraham's. The same
two currents are discernible in the Jewish *'akedah* legends
(*'aqedah* = "binding," from Gen. 22:9): according to one,
Isaac is the hero, while in the other Abraham is glorified
(Ginzberg, *LJ* 5.249). As he approaches his death, old and
blind, Isaac is victim again, though of a different kind, in
his deception at the hands of Rebekah and Jacob, who
conspire to strip Esau of his birthright (Gen. 27). The NT
recalls Abraham's offering of Isaac as an example of faith
(Heb. 11:17) and obedience (James 2:21). For Philo,
Isaac's name signifies that exultation and benediction
which come with the practice of virtue or obedience to
God's will (see Gribomont, 7.1990).

The Fathers of the Church read in Abraham's offering
of Isaac a type of the Crucifixion and a prefiguration of the
Eucharist: the sacrifice of the son by the father foreshadowed God's willingness to offer his only begotten son
for the redemption of mankind. Structured in accordance
with this typology, medieval plays of Abraham and Isaac
are comedies centered not on the father but on the son: "It
is he [the son] whose feelings are emphasized, and it is his
confession of obedience to his father and to his death, which
is the dramatic peak in all but one [i.e., Towneley] of the
plays" (Woolf, 806). The typology which generates the
medieval comedies of Abraham and Isaac is altogether
absent from Theodore Beza's *Abraham Sacrifiant* (*A
Tragedie of Abrahams Sacrifice,* trans. Arthur Golding
[1577]). In this Protestant classical tragedy, the protagonist,
a man and no more, is confronted with the awesome choice
between two horrifying alternatives — killing his son or
disobeying his God. A "witty comedy or interlude" in five
acts, the anonymous *History of Jacob and Esau* (1568)
casts Isaac in the role of a pious and kindly father who
accepts God's will in all things. He comes to love Esau all
the more for having forgiven Jacob his trickery and having
accepted the lot accorded him by heaven's king.

Henry Vaughan considers Isaac's marriage in his poem
of that title, which takes as its text Gen. 24:63 ("And Isaac
went out to pray [KJV "meditate"] in the field at even-

tide"). This verse was frequently alluded to in Renaissance discussions of meditation (cf. *Pilgrim's Progress,*
which opens with Christian walking "solitarily in the
fields, sometimes reading, and sometimes praying: and
thus . . . he spent his time"). George Herbert infers from
the case of Abraham and Isaac that "the godly are exempt
from Law," but not from obeying God's will (*Briefe Notes
on Valdesso's Considerations,* 62). For Richard Crashaw
in *"Lauda Sion Salvatorem,"* both Isaac and the ram
sacrificed in his stead prefigure Christ in the Eucharist (st.
12). Abraham Cowley's *Davideis* is more domestic, imagining the feelings of "the sad old Man" and "the
inn'ocent Boy" as they approach the moment of sacrifice,
then picturing the child's exuberant response to his release
(300-328). For Sir Thomas Browne in *Religio Medici,* the
appearance of the ram at just the right moment illustrates
how mysterious the ways of Providence really are (1.15).

Walter Scott's Isaac of York in *Ivanhoe* suggests something of his biblical namesake: the sound of a bugle
rescues him at the last moment from death by fire. In the
"Genesis" chapter of *Sartor Resartus,* Carlyle seems to
parody the Bible's account of Isaac's miraculous entry
into the world (2.1). The reference in Thomas Hardy's
Tess of the D'Urbervilles, by contrast, is direct and
charged with pathos: Mr. Clare mourns over his son Angel
"as Abraham might have mourned over the doomed Isaac
while they went up the hill together" (chap. 49).

James Joyce's *Finnegans Wake* plays with the second
patriarch of Israel, his name and life. "A bland old Isaac"
who is "buttended" by a "kidscad" on the first page is
subsequently victimized by a running joke on butting,
ramming, and asses. In the short story "England, My England," D. H. Lawrence is earnest: the Catholic patriarch
Godfrey Marshall "was a man who kept alive the old red
flame of fatherhood, fatherhood that had even the right to
sacrifice the child to God, like Isaac."

See also ABRAHAM; JACOB.

Bibliography. Daniélou, J. "La typologie d'Isaac dans le
Christianisme primitif." *Bib* 28 (1947), 363-93; Elliott, J., Jr.
"The Sacrifice of Isaac as Comedy and Tragedy." *SP* 66
(1969), 36-59; Gribomont, J. "Isaac." In *Dictionnaire de
spiritualité* (1971), 7.1987-2005; Lancashire, A. "Chaucer
and the Sacrifice of Isaac." *ChauR* 9 (1974), 320-26; Moule,
C. F. D. "The Sacrifice of Isaac in Paul's Theology." *JBL* 65
(1946), 385-92; Smith, A. M. "The Iconography of the Sacri-
fice of Isaac in Early Christian Art." *AJA* 26 (1922), 159-73;
Spiegel, S. *The Last Trial: On the Legends and Lore of the
Command to Abraham to Offer Isaac as a Sacrifice.* Trans.
J. Goldin (1967); Woolf, R. "The Effect of Typology on the
English Mediaeval Plays of Abraham and Isaac." *Speculum*
32 (1957), 805-25.   CAMILLE R. LA BOSSIÈRE

ISAIAH The greatest among Israel's prophets, and the
one most quoted in connection with messianic prophecies,
Isaiah lived in 8th-cent.-B.C. Judah. The book which bears
his name was composed under the reigns of Uzziah,
Jotham, Ahaz, and Hezekiah. The prophet is thought to

have met his death at the hands of King Manasseh for making unflattering speeches (Ta'an. 26b; Yerushalmi 4.68d; Tosepta Tg. Isa. 66:1); according to the Mishnah, he was sawn in half (cf. Ascension of Isaiah; Sanh. 10.28c; Pesiq. R. 4.14; Midr. 'Aggadah Num. 30:15). This tradition entered into Christian literature via Justin Martyr's *Dialogue with Trypho* and the 2nd-cent.-A.D. Jewish apocalypse the Ascension of Isaiah, and is reflected in St. Isidore of Seville and the anonymous *De ortu et obitu patrum.*

Isaiah is celebrated for the brilliance of his style and metaphorical language — a brilliance not entirely lost in translation. His vocabulary is one of the richest among Hebrew writers. In the greatest of early Christian commentaries (PL 24.17-678), St. Jerome compares him to Demosthenes as an orator and poet, an opinion which has stood the test of time. Because of the strong note of messianic expectation and an attendant sense of hope and consolation — particularly in the latter half of Isaiah's prophecy — Christian commentators have often followed Jerome's lead in referring to his book as an OT "Gospel." Thus, according to the Prologue to Isaiah in *The Wycliffe Bible* (eds. Forshall and Madden [1850], 3.225):

> Isaye is worthi to be seid not oneli a profete, but more, a gospellere, for he declaireth so opynli ether priutees of Crist and of Hooli chirche, that thou gesse hym not oneli to ordeyne a profess of thing to comynge, but to ordeyne a stori of thynges passid.

Isaiah's call to office was attended by an angel (the Mishnah identifies the archangel Michael), who placed a live coal upon his lips to purge him from the condition he raised in pleading his own inadequacy: "Woe is me! For I am undone; because I am a man of unclean lips, and I do dwell among a people of unclean lips" (Isa. 6:5). In medieval and Renaissance painting and in block books such as the *Biblia pauperum,* Isaiah is typically pictured holding a scroll with the words of one of the celebrated passages of his prophecy: Isa. 7:14 ("Behold, a virgin shall conceive, and bear a son, and shall call his name Immanuel"); 9:6 ("For unto us a child is born, unto us a son is given: and the government shall be upon his shoulder"); 11:1 ("And there shall come forth a rod out of the stem of Jesse"); 11:6-9 ("The wolf shall dwell with the lamb . . . and a little child shall lead them"); 40:1-3 ("Comfort ye . . . my people"). Isaiah's iconography includes a branch (cf. 11:1) and a saw.

Although Isaiah is frequently cited in English literature, he seldom appears as a character. When he does, as in the various "Prophets" plays of the medieval Corpus Christi cycle, his role is typically limited to a recitation of his messianic prophecies:

> I am þe prophete callyd Isaye
>   Replett with godys grett influens
> And sey pleynly þe spyryte of prophecie
>   þat a clene mayde thourgh meke obedyens
> Shall bere a childe. . . . (N-Town, 7.1-5)

Isaiah's irradiations of phrasing commend themselves to Herbert's preacher (*A Priest to the Temple*, 7, 34). Milton recollects the prophet's calling and the lips seared with a coal in "On the Morning of Christ's Nativity," and makes extensive use of the messianic prophecies in *Paradise Lost* and *Paradise Regained.*

In the late 18th cent. the writings of Isaiah came to the forefront of literary interest in the Bible with Robert Lowth's *Isaiah: A New Translation* (5th ed. 1778), a widely read text as much valued for Lowth's introductory comments on the relation of prophetic and poetic language as for the translation itself. Lowth sees the book of Isaiah as chiefly messianic and regards the debate among commentators concerning the literary and mystical sense as a misconstrual: "The mystical or spiritual sense," he observes, "is very often the most literal sense of all." Lowth's *Lectures on the Sacred Poetry of the Hebrews* (1753; trans. G. Gregory, 1787) helped to ensure Isaiah's role as a master versifier and to establish a firm connection between biblical lyricism and the prophetic mode. Coleridge employed Lowth's translation in his 1795 Lectures (cf. *Biographia Literaria*, 2.11); Hugh Blair's account of Lowth's remarks on Isaiah in his *Lectures on Rhetoric and Belles Letters* (1783) influenced Wordsworth in *The Prelude*. In Blake's *The Marriage of Heaven and Hell* (1790), in which he directs his readers to Isaiah 34 and 35, he reveals his own familiarity with Lowth's discussion of Isaiah. His connection of "poetic genius" with "the Spirit of Prophecy" emerges as a "memorable fancy" in which Isaiah and Ezekiel dine with him. The poet asks his guests "how they dared so roundly to assert that God spoke to them." Isaiah's reply makes him a spokesman for Romantic views of the poet-as-prophet which are the inverse of Lowth's observations:

> Isaiah answer'd: "I saw no God, nor heard any, in a finite organical perception; but my senses discover'd the infinite in everything, and as I was then perswaded, & remain confirm'd, that the voice of honest indignation is the voice of God, I cared not for consequences, but wrote."
>
> Then I asked: "Does a firm perswasion that a thing is so, make it so?"
>
> He replied: "All poets believe that it does, & in ages of imagination this firm perswasion removed mountains; but many are not capable of a firm perswasion of any thing." ("A Memorable Fancy")

Bibliography. George, D. H. "Reading Isaiah and Ezekiel through Blake." *NOR* 13 (1986), 12-21; Roston, M. *Poet and Prophet: The Bible and the Growth of Romanticism* (1965); Prickett, S. *Words and the Word: Language, Poetics, and Biblical Interpretation* (1986).

ISH-BOSHETH   Saul's son, he was initially acclaimed as Saul's successor by the northern tribes. After he was assassinated, David became king of the united kingdom. *See also* ABNER; DAVID.

ISHMAEL Ishmael was the natural son of Abraham and Hagar, the handmaiden of Abraham's wife Sarah. He was conceived after Sarah had herself proved unable to produce a child. After Ishmael's conception Hagar became contemptuous of her mistress, and consequently fled into the wilderness. There an angel of the Lord appeared to comfort her (Gen. 16:11) and directed her to return and submit to Sarah.

In the Gen. 21 account Hagar and her son were sent into the desert by Sarah, who saw Ishmael as a threat to her own son Isaac, more recently born to her after many years of barrenness. The angel of God told both Abraham and Hagar (21:12-13, 17-18) that Ishmael would be the founder of a mighty nation; the Ishmaelites subsequently became the enemy of God's chosen people (Ps. 83:6).

The Jewish Haggadah identifies Ishmael as one of the six men who were "given a name by God before their birth" (Ginzberg, *LJ* 1.239). Another Jewish legend elaborates Ishmael's domestic life, describing how his first wife was disrespectful and inhospitable toward Abraham while his second wife was a perfect hostess to the aging patriarch (*LJ* 1.266).

In Gal. 4:22-31, St. Paul discusses the story of Ishmael and Hagar as an "allegory" (v. 24) which differentiates between the two covenants: "the one from the mount Sinai, which gendereth to bondage, which is Agar. . . . But Jerusalem which is above is free, which is the mother of us all. . . . Now we, brethren, as Isaac was, are the children of promise. . . . We are not children of the bondwoman, but of the free."

According to Origen, St. Paul's allegorical treatment of Ishmael and Isaac is designed so "that we might learn how to treat other passages, and especially these in which the historical narrative appears to reveal nothing worthy of the divine Law" (Origen, *Hom.* 7 on Genesis). For Origen the opposition of Hagar and her offspring and Sarah and her children is a type of the interior conflict between carnality and spirituality which goes on in each individual Christian (see Daniélou, *From Shadows to Reality,* 140-41).

This same juxtaposition is reflected also in St. John Chrysostom's commentary on Galatians: "Ishmael . . . who was born according to the flesh, was not only a bondman, but was cast out of his father's house; but Isaac, who was born according to the promise, being a true son and free, was lord of all."

Similarly, St. Augustine, in *De civitate Dei* (15.2), equates Ishmael "born in the course of nature," with the flesh and Isaac, "born in fulfillment of a promise," with the spirit. For Augustine, Ishmael exists outside the realm of God's grace; for this reason, and because of their enforced wanderings in the desert, he associates Ishmael and Hagar with Cain.

The ME *Cursor Mundi* recounts the Genesis story of Ishmael without elaboration. In *Mandeville's Travels*

(1357), Ishmael is referred to as the father of the Saracens and the prophet Mohammed is called one "of the generacioun of ysmael" (chap. 16). Luther, in his lectures on Genesis, draws the same connection, describing the Arabs and Saracens as Ishmael's descendants. Commenting on Gen. 16:12 Luther argues that

> Ishmael's manners and disposition are really at variance with everybody else's; for other people remain in definite cities or districts, but Ishmael is fond of wildernesses and is wild and roaming: Today he lives with his family under one tree, tomorrow under another, just as the Arabs and cave dwellers do today.

In his lecture on Gal. 4:22-23, Luther echoes Augustine, observing that "Ishmael was born according to the flesh, that is, apart from the promise and the Word of God, while Isaac was born in accordance with a promise." Calvin mentions Ishmael in relation to Abraham's faith, which was tested when he had to expel Ishmael and Hagar (Gen. 21:14) and when he was ordered to sacrifice Isaac (Gen. 22:1-18) (*Inst.* 2.10.11).

References to Ishmael in English literature are diverse. Spenser's *Faerie Queene* (3.3.6.7) refers to "the Africk Ismaell," evoking Ishmael's associations with the Arabs and Saracens. In Shakespeare's *The Merchant of Venice,* Shylock, one of God's chosen people, finds himself ironically in the position of Ishmael, an outcast in a society which is largely composed of "Hagar's offspring" (2.5.44), or Gentiles. In *Paradise Regained* (2.306-10), Satan tempts Jesus, hungry after his long fast, with a reference to the son of the "Fugitive Bondwoman," who would have perished in the desert had he not "found . . . relief by a providing Angel" (cf. Gen. 31:17-19).

Henry Vaughan in some of his poems reflects an interpretation of the story in which Ishmael becomes a type of the Gentiles, latter-day heirs of the promise; God's providential preservation of him foreshadows his grace bestowed on suppliant believers: "If pious griefs Heavens joys awake / O fill his bottle! Thy childe weeps!" ("The Seed Growing Secretly"; cf. "Providence," "Begging," "The Timber").

William Blake, in *A Vision of the Last Judgment,* includes Ishmael along with Abraham, Sarah, and Isaac in part of the community of the Just. But Coleridge, in *Zapolya,* uses the image of Hagar and Ishmael to denote exile and alienation. Ironically, Zapolya and her child, "the rightful heir" (*Zapolya,* 1.1.440), are treated in much the way Hagar and Ishmael were treated in the biblical account (Gen. 21). Byron's *The Island* compares Christian, the leader of the mutiny on the *H.M.S. Bounty,* to Ishmael (2.182), transforming both Christian and Ishmael into outcasts of heroic stature.

James Baird has argued (*Ishmael: A Study of the Symbolic Mode in Primitivism*) that, as the archetypal outcast, "Ishmael is the overseer of every major work in [Melville's] literary record":

When he is not the protagonist, he is at least the attendant genius, as the narrator in *Moby-Dick.* He is Tom in *Typee;* Paul in *Omoo;* Taji in *Mardi;* the young sailor-heroes of *Redburn* and *White-Jacket;* the Ishmael of *Moby-Dick;* the tragic hero of *Pierre* in his early life; the veteran fugitive Israel R. Potter; the narrator of the *Confidence Man;* the youth of *Clarel;* the handsome sailor of *Billy Budd.* He is Ishmael, the outcast, condemned to wander. (92-93)

In Longfellow's *Evangeline* (2.4), North American Indians, like the Arabs and Saracens in *Mandeville's Travels,* are called "Ishmael's children." Emily Dickinson associates Ishmael with the lunar phases and the physical changes which occur, over time, in a human face (*Complete Poems,* ed. T. Johnson, no. 504). In Thomas Hardy's *The Return of the Native,* Egdon Heath is described as an "Ishmaelitish thing" (chap. 1) and thus a fitting foil to both Eustacia and Clym (*Hardy's Use of Allusion* [1983], 100).

A picture of "Hagar and Ishmael in the Wilderness" hangs in the parlor of the Templeton home, in Willa Cather's "Old Mrs. Harris," underscoring the theme of exile in the story. The aristocratic Reggie Salmon, in Ernest Hebert's novel *Whisper My Name,* uses the name Ishmael to identify himself to a prostitute called the Witch. In Hebert's novel, Ishmael is associated with activities "in which duty, honour, family and land played no role."

See also HAGAR; ISAAC.

Bibliography. Baird, J. *Ishmael: A Study of the Symbolic Mode in Primitivism* (1956); Daniélou, J. *From Shadows to Reality: Studies in the Biblical Typology of the Fathers.* Trans. W. Hilberd (1960); Hirsch, D. H. "Melville's Ishmaelite." *American Notes and Queries* 5 (1967), 115-16; Lewalski, B. "Typological Symbolism and 'The Progress of the Soul' in Seventeenth-Century Literature." In *Literary Uses of Typology.* Ed. E. Miner (1977); Liptzin, S. *Biblical Themes in World Literature* (1985).

ANTHONY WESTENBROEK

ISHTAR   Ancient northeast goddess of love, parallel to the Roman Venus. See David Jones, *Anathemata* (8.233).
See also ASHTORETH.

ISLAND   The KJV translates Lat. *insulae* (Heb. *'iyyim;* Gk. *nēsoi*) as "islands," a word frequently changed in the RSV to "coastlands." The OE *ealand* literally means "water land," i.e., land reached by, bordered by, or surrounded by water. The word *islands* (or *isles*) as it is used in the KJV usually refers to both the islands and the coasts of the Mediterranean or the Aegean (the "isles of the sea" or "of the Gentiles," as in Gen. 10:5). To the early inhabitants of Britain, as to the Hebrews, these places were characterized by cultural and geographical remoteness.

In Isaiah, islands are often Gentile or heathen places perceived as waiting for the Lord in some way (e.g., for his law in 42:4; for his message or call in 11:11; 49:1; 51:5; 66:19). The Psalmist rejoices that the "isles" have responded to the call and accepted the Lord's dominion (72:10; 97:1). Instead of their joyful conversion, Jer. 25:22 sees the Lord's cup of fury given to "the isles which are beyond the sea" (cf. Ezek. 39:6; Zeph. 2:11). The isles share in the Lord's punishment of the wicked merchant cities of Tyre and Tarshish in Isa. 23:1-6 (cf. Ezek. 26:15, 18; 27:3-8, 15, 35). Milton alludes to the wicked merchandising of these cities in his description of Dalila as "a stately Ship / Of Tarsus [Tarshish], bound for th' Isles" (*Samson Agonistes,* 1.714-15).

In the eschatological imagery of Rev. 6:14 and 16:20, islands are moved at the opening of the sixth seal and the emptying of the seventh vial. The mad seaman of Melville's *Moby-Dick,* who proclaims himself the Archangel Gabriel, exploits this belief and maintains his influence over credulous whalers by threatening to open the seventh vial, which he controls as "the deliverer of the isles of the sea and vicar-general of all Oceanica."

Although there is no scriptural foundation for the theory, some exegetes attributed the creation of islands to the cataclysmic Flood in Noah's day, which, they say, changed the form of the earth's surface (see D. Allen, *The Legend of Noah* [1949], p. 191). Sir Thomas Browne in *Pseudodoxia Epidemica* (6.6) supports the "probability" that there were no islands before the Flood. Milton's Michael explained to Adam how Paradise itself would be "push'd by the horned Flood" into a gulf, where it would "take root an Island salt and bare" (*PL* 2.828-34).

The desert island as an earthly paradise — both innocent and fallen — is an important theme in English literary tradition. R. H. Ballantyne's *Coral Island* (1858), a classic Victorian adventure novel about three shipwrecked boys, is reworked in William Golding's *Lord of the Flies* (1954) into an allegory of human depravity. H. G. Wells's *Mr. Blertsworthy on Rampole Island* (1928) and Aldous Huxley's *Island* (1962) both grapple in different ways with the utopian/dystopian possibilities of island life.

Bibliography. Bosworth, J. *An Anglo-Saxon Dictionary.* Ed. T. N. Toller (1898; rpt. 1973); Grollenberg, L. H. *Atlas of the Bible.* Trans. and ed. J. M. H. Reid and H. H. Rowley (1956); Nicol, T. "Island, Isle." *A Dictionary of the Bible.* Ed. J. Hastings (1899); Reed, W. L. "Island." *IDB* 2.750.

MARIE MICHELLE WALSH

ISSACHAR   One of the twelve sons of Jacob.
See also AARON; JACOB; TRIBES OF ISRAEL.

J

JACOB Jacob is the most colorful of the Hebrew patriarchs, with his name and eponymous narrative alike declaring the core and structure of biblical history and presaging its penchant for irony. His name has been variously etymologized. The root *ʿqb*, "heel," is common to Arabic and Assyrian as well as Hebrew, yielding a verb meaning to "follow closely" or "guard." *Yaʿaqub-il*, a name found in numerous West Semitic records, seems to mean something like "May God protect." "Jacob" is its abbreviated form. Among the events in Jacob's life most developed in literary tradition are his twin birth, at which he grasped the heel *(ʿqb)* of his brother Esau in what is presented as an attempt to be the firstborn (Gen. 25:24-26); his cunning "purchase" of his elder brother Esau's birthright with a "mess of pottage" (25:27-34); his deception of his aged father Isaac and procuring of the blessing due the firstborn (27:1-41); his pilgrim dream of the ladder with angels ascending and descending (28:10-22); his double service to Laban for his intended wife Rachel (29:1-28); his successful dubious husbandry in the matter of the rods and spotted sheep (30:28-43); his wrestling with the angel and ironic "victory" at the ford of the river Jabbok (32:22-32); and his inverting of his hands at the last minute in blessing his grandsons, thus frustrating the intention of their father Joseph and mirroring the supplanting of his own brother Esau (48:8-22). Only four NT passages recall events in the life of Jacob: the conversation of Jesus with the Samaritan woman at Jacob's well (John 4:5, 6, 12); St. Stephen's recollection of the journey to Egypt (Acts 7:8-16); St. Paul's identification of Jacob as exemplifying the predestination of the elect (Rom. 9:10-13); and the writer to the Hebrews' inclusion of him as an example of vital and pragmatic faith (Heb. 11:9, 20-22).

Talmudic legend concerning Jacob is more colorful even than the biblical record. It makes the guardian angel of Jacob Michael, while Esau, identified with Rome, has for his the demonic Sammael (Abir in Yalqut 1.110; Jub. 25:17). Jacob comes to occupy a role of messianic proportions in later Jewish legend, in which he "supplants" all other patriarchs, including Abraham. According to Sanh. 19b, Abraham was to have been the father of the twelve tribes himself, but Jacob took his place to spare him the bother of raising children. Other sources state that all of humankind, including Abraham, was created for the merits of Jacob (Lev. Rab. 36.4). It is because of the merits of Jacob that the Jordan dried up to allow Israel to enter the Promised Land (Gen. Rab. 76.5). For Jacob's sake Israel was redeemed from Egyptian bondage; for his sake the nation will again be redeemed by the Messiah (Haberot 2B; Gen. Rab. 75.13). Other haggadic sources add that God loves Israel "on account of Jacob," and it is for Jacob's sake that he makes his Shekinah glory dwell in Israel (Lekah, Exod. 20:19; Shir 7.6). Moreover, it is claimed that the Torah would have been revealed to Jacob rather than Moses, except that at the time the Jews were

385

not numerous enough to make it necessary (Shemini 'Azaret 126b; Yitro 32b). When Israel sins or strays, it is Jacob who feels it most deeply (Midr. Tehillim 14.115; Pesiq. R. 41.174b). In the Cabala and elsewhere (e.g., Kanah 10b), the man in the moon has Jacob's face; rabbinic literature often says that Jacob's face is to be perceived in the *merqabah* (Gen. Rab. 73.12-14; Tan. Ber. 1.149-50; Midr. Tehillim 78.347; Gen. Rab. 78.3; 82.2; Alphabet of R. Akiba 40, etc.). While older haggadah accord preeminence to Abraham, later sources, self-consciously confronting Christianity and developing a more nationalistic character, make Jacob the "ideal man" (Tan. Ber. 3.72-73; 'Ag. Ber. 61.126). Jacob is said to be among the few males born circumcised (Midr. Tehillim 9.84; Tan. Ber. 1.32), and although he was born after his twin Esau, he was conceived first (Gen. Rab. 63.8). Late Haggadah rejects the possibility that Jacob would have uttered an unqualified lie (Tan. Ber. 1.131; Gen. Rab. 65.18; Sanh. 92a); Gen. 27:19 (Jacob's declaration, "I am Esau thy firstborn," spoken in response to blind Isaac's "Who art thou, my son?") is explained as an ironic ambiguity (cf. Jub. 26:13).

For early Christian tradition Jacob has great importance as a type of "redeemed Israel" and of Christ. In *Adversus haereses* (21.3), St. Irenaeus comments on the verse "Jacob have I loved, but Esau have I hated" (Mal. 1:2; Rom. 9:13), seeing not only Israel's election but the history of human salvation foreshadowed:

> If any one . . . will look into Jacob's actions, he shall find them . . . full of import with regard to the dispensations. Thus, in the first place, at his birth, since he laid hold on his brother's heel, he was called "Jacob," that is, the "supplanter" — one who holds but is not held . . . striving and conquering. . . . For to this end was the Lord born, the type of whose birth he set forth before hand. . . . In the next place he received the rights of the firstborn, when his brother looked on them with contempt; even as also the younger nation received Him, Christ, the first-begotten, when the elder nation rejected Him, saying, "We have no king but Caesar." In Christ every blessing is summed up, and therefore the latter people has snatched away the blessings of the former from the Father, just as Jacob took away the blessing of his brother Esau. . . . In a foreign country were the twelve tribes born, the race of Israel, inasmuch as Christ also was to generate, in a strange country, the twelve-pillared foundation [the twelve disciples] of the Church. Various colored sheep were allotted to Jacob as his wages; and the wages of Christ are human beings, who from various and diverse nations come together in one fold of faith.

Irenaeus goes on to say that as Jacob begat sons from two sisters, so did Christ from "two laws of one and the same Father" (the OT and NT), as well as from their handmaids (Christian tradition). Rachel prefigures the Church, even as Jacob's wanderings prefigure the pilgrimage of the Christian *viator.* This typology is extended by St. Augus-

tine, for whom the statement "The elder shall serve the younger" signifies that the Jews will serve their younger sibling, the Christians (*De civ. Dei* 16.35). "The blessing of Jacob is a proclamation of Christ to all nations" (16.37); the angel who wrestles with him is a type of Christ, and when Jacob "prevails," the irony is akin to that in what it prefigures, Christ's Passion, "in which the Jews are seen overcoming him" but only, as it were, in order that God's will and purpose should triumph (16.39; cf. *De catechizandibus rudibus*, 3.6). Augustine is also willing to see Jacob's deception of his father as nonmendacious: "That which he did at his mother's bidding, so as to seem to deceive his father, if with diligence and faith it be attended to, is no lie, but a mystery" (*Contra mendacium*, 24). On the other hand, his own experience of being deceived by Laban and then his sons tends to earn him sympathetic treatment. St. John Chrysostom asks, "And this very Jacob, served he not for wages with his kinsman twice seven years? Was he not together with his bondage subject to mockery in that trick? What then? Did he feel the mockery?" (*Hom.* sup. 1 Corinthians, 33).

The typology associated with Jacob has in Christian tradition also a tropological dimension: St. Ambrose can urge his reader, "In Jacob, too, let us imitate the type of Christ," citing Jacob's obedience to his mother, service to his father-in-law, and so on (*De excessu*, 2.22; cf. *Ep.* 63.99). For Aphrahat Jacob is a type of the shepherd of souls, a pastor (*Select Demonstrations*, 24). Even for Luther, who sees Jacob's being preferred to Esau primarily as a matter of God's unpredictably free election, choosing the younger over the elder and choosing an apparently unreliable "supplanter" to father his people (*Comm.* sup. Gen. 25:21), Jacob's conduct is morally exemplary in a number of respects (*WA* 63.576-78). This view is shared by Calvin (*Inst.* 2.10.12). For the Counter-Reformation commentator Cornelius à Lapide, who observes that the declaration that "the elder shall serve the younger" obviously did not apply precisely to Jacob and Esau in their own lifetime but in that of their progeny, the two brothers are still interpreted allegorically: Christians shall be served by the Jews. This view nevertheless becomes the basis for a tropological reading in which the good person shall be served by the malefactor (*Comm. in Scripturam Sacram*, 1.267). Picinelli's *Mundus Symbolicus* (1694) sums up Jacob's typology in the words "*vide:* Christ was made sin for our sake" (125.216).

The most commonly referred to events in the Jacob narrative — the winning of the birthright, the dream of a ladder of angels, the rods and spotted sheep, and the night spent wrestling with an angel — are all treated elsewhere. The main lines of Jacob's typological development in literature are otherwise clarified in terms of his relationship to other characters; his typological connection with Christ remains a commonplace. Chaucer's Wife of Bath, in the Prologue to her *Tale,* uses the story of Jacob as an excuse for serial marriage (*Canterbury Tales*, 3.55-58), but he is cited elsewhere by Chaucer as exemplary in wisdom: "Loo, Jacob, by good conseil of his mooder Rebekka, wan the benysoun of Ysaak his fader, and the lordshipe over alle his brethren" (*The Tale of Melibee*, 7.2285-87; *The Merchant's Tale,* however, seems to acknowledge that this was deceitful counsel). The staff of Jacob becomes a pilgrim's badge and sometimes a conjuring rod, even to the time of Spenser (e.g., *Faerie Queene*, 1.6.35-44; "Daphnaides," 37-42) and Marlowe (*Tamburlaine the Great*, 3.3.49-53). Shylock, in Shakespeare's *Merchant of Venice,* sees Jacob as a role model in enterprise, and swears "by Jacob's staff " (2.5.36; cf. 1.3.68-97). According to the exegesis of Cranmer, Coverdale, and others, however, Jacob's staff is in Gen. 32:10 a sign of his own mortal limitations. As Henry Ainsworth comments, it emblemizes his pilgrim status, "on foot, in poor estate" (*Annotations upon the Five Books of Moses* [1627]). John Donne reflects this view in his "Sermon Preached at Whitehall, April 12, 1618" when he observes (following St. Jerome, *Ep.* 22.32) that his prayer to God at the fording of the Jabbok ("For with my staff I passed over the Jordan and now I am become two bands") is tantamount to a confession and "the establishment of all true prayers, a disclaiming of Merit" (ed. Potter and Simpson, 1.7.269); "He came over it but with a staffe, in a poor and ill provided manner; and with his staffe, no assistance but his own" (1.7.270). Hence Jacob discovered that it was God's electing grace and not his own strength that he must lean on.

Jacob's typological association with Christ is seen in its ironic aspect by Donne in "Holy Sonnet 11":

And *Jacob* came cloth'd in vile harsh attire
But to supplant, and with gainfull intent;
God cloth'd himself in vile man's flesh, that so
Hee might be weake enough to suffer woe.

Herrick sees Jacob as exemplary in his importunity: "Jacob God's Beggar was; and so we wait / (Though ne're so rich) all beggars at his gate" ("Beggars"). In Vaughan's "Jacob's Pillow, and Pillar" the stone pillow is a type of the Church and Jacob's struggles with Esau are compared to the English Civil War. Yet there is comfort for "Jacob":

But blessed *Jacob,* though thy sad distress
Was just the same with ours, and nothing less,
For thou a brother, and blood-thirsty too
Didst flye, whose children wrought thy childrens wo:
Yet thou in all thy solitude and grief,
On stones didst sleep and found'st but cold relief;
Thou from the Day-star a long way didst stand
And all that distance was Law and command.
But we a healing Sun by day and night,
Have our sure Guardian, and our leading light;
What thou didst hope for and believe, we finde
And feel a friend most ready, sure and kinde.
Thy pillow was but type and shade at best,
But we the substance have, and on him rest.

Enlightenment poetry is on the whole less favorable to Jacob. Dryden's political allegorizing of "Jacob's seed . . . chosen to rebel" (*Absalom and Achitophel*, 2.6) concentrates on his descendants, finding in many of them Jacob's vices (1.977-84; cf. "To Sir Godfrey Kneller," 93-96). In "Sandys' Ghost" Pope hears "the Beat of Jacob's Drums. / Poor Ovid finds no Quarter!" a reference to what Pope sees as overuse of OT allusion in literature. While William Blake's admiration for stories of usurpation is extensive, Jacob becomes an analogue of fallen Adam, with Esau or Edom a type of Adam in innocence and restored: "Now is the dominion of Edom, & the return of Adam into Paradise" ("The Marriage of Heaven and Hell," pl. 3). For Robert Browning, "Smooth Jacob still robs homely Esau: / Now up, now down, the world's one see-saw" ("The Flight of the Duchess," 907-08), yet like homilists in the evangelical tradition he avers in "Holy-Cross Day" (73-78) that:

The Lord will have mercy on Jacob yet,
And again in his border see Israel set.
When Judah beholds Jerusalem,
The stranger-seed shall be joined to them:
To Jacob's house shall the Gentiles cleave
So the Prophet saith and his sons believe.

Ernest Hemingway substituted the name "Jacob" for Ernest in the published versions of *The Sun Also Rises* (1926), in which the protagonist is told "You've a hell of a biblical name, Jake." With his wounded groin or thigh, the "devout cynic" is compared to Jacob in his struggling, combative nature. A quasi-typological development is to be found in Sholem Asch's *The Apostle,* in which Reb Jacob, a strict Jew who is a son of Joseph and younger brother of Jeshua, leads the messianic cult in Jerusalem after Yeshua's disappearance. Marianne Moore reflects on Jacob's blessing the sons of Joseph in "The Hero," and in her "The Jereboa" compares Jacob to the pestiferous but admirably clever "sand-brown jumping rat-free born":

Part terrestrial,
and part celestial,
Jacob saw, cudgel staff
in claw hand — steps of air and angels; his
friends were the desert stones. The translucent mistake
of the desert, does not make
hardship for one who
can rest and then do
the opposite.

See also BIRTHRIGHT; JACOB'S LADDER; JACOB'S RODS; JACOB'S STAFF; WRESTLING JACOB.

Bibliography. Colley, J. S. "Launcelot, Jacob, and Esau: Old and New Law in *The Merchant of Venice*." *YES* 10 (1980), 181-89; Crozier, R. D., "Home James: Hemingway's Jacob." *Papers on Language and Literature* 11 (1975), 292-301; Kerzer, G. "George Herbert and the Tradition of Jacob." *Cithara* 18 (1978), 18-26; Liptzin, S. *Biblical Themes in World Literature* (1985); Schonhorn, M. "The Sun Also Rises: I. The Jacob Allusion. II. Parody as Meaning." *BSUF*

16 (1975), 49-55; Tannenbaum, L. *Biblical Tradition in Blake's Early Prophecies* (1982).

JACOB'S LADDER After his deception of Esau made it necessary for him to flee his home, Jacob stopped for the night on the way to Padan-aram, gathering stones around him for pillows, and lay down to sleep. "And he dreamed, and behold a ladder set up on the earth, and the top of it reached to heaven: and behold the angels of God ascending and descending on it. And, behold, the LORD stood above it, and said, I am the LORD God of Abraham thy father, and the God of Isaac: the land whereon thou liest, to thee will I give it, and to thy seed" (Gen. 28:12-13). What followed was a confirmation that God's covenant with Abraham had indeed passed to Jacob. When he awoke Jacob declared, "this is none other but the house of God, and this is the gate of heaven"; although the place had been known as Luz, Jacob renamed it Bethel ("House of God").

The ladder vision has been given a host of interpretations in subsequent literature, many of the more expansive of these appearing in haggadic commentary. One version has it that Jacob saw on the ladder the same two angels who were sent to Sodom; these called all the other angels to come down to look at him (Gen. Rab. 73.12-14; Midr. Tehillim 78.347; cf. *Monumenta Germaniae Historicae*, ed. T. Mommsen et al., 1.449-51), admiring the face which they recognized as graven in the merqabah, the divine Throne. Jacob is also said to have seen on the ladder the guardian angels of the four kingdoms — Babylon, Media, Greece, and Edom (or Rome) (Tg. Yerushalmi and Yalqut Reubeni on Gen. 28:12).

In Christian commentary the stone pillow is allegorized by St. Augustine as "Christ, the head of man." Augustine also relates the incident to Christ's words spoken at the confession of Nathanael (John 1:47-51): "Ye shall see heaven open, and the angels of God ascending and descending upon the Son of Man." Thus, "Christ is the ladder reaching from earth to heaven, or from the carnal to the spiritual," or "He is the ladder, for he says, 'I am the way'" (*Contra Faustum*, 12.25; cf. *Sermo*, 89.5; 122.2). In another commentary (*In Joan. Ev.* 23) Augustine establishes a comparison between the ladder dream and the vision of St. Paul (2 Cor. 12:2-4), with Paul's "ascending" signifying his mystical vision of God, his "descending" being his condescension to utter in "child's language" the plain truths of the gospel. St. Jerome connects the "ascending and descending" tropologically to the worship life of Bethel, the house of God, or the Church (*Ep.* 118.7). St. Hilary of Poitiers sees the incident as a foreshadowing of the Incarnation (*De Trinitate*, 5.20). These views are held to be compatible with the anagogical interpretation of St. Ambrose, for whom "that sign [was not] without a purpose, the ladder from earth to heaven, wherein was seen the future fellowship between men and angels through the cross of Christ. . . ." (*De excessu,*

2.100). St. Gregory the Great develops a point made by Augustine and others in seeing the ladder as an image of mystical contemplation and the whole narrative as signifying the relationship of meditation to active proclamation of the word in the life of the good preacher (*Regulae pastoralis,* chap. 5). For Rabanus Maurus the ladder signifies charity (*Allegoriae in Scripturam Sacram* [PL 112.1043]), for Zeno, the two Testaments (PL 11.428). For the *Glossa Ordinaria* the angels ascending minister to God, while those descending minister to humanity (PL 113.154). For Nicholas of Lyra the rungs of the ladder are the patriarchs in the Matthean genealogy of Christ and the ascent is the devotion of saints when they pray (*Postilla ad Gen.* 28:12-14).

In the spiritual literature of the Middle Ages Jacob's ladder becomes an analogue for spiritual growth and progress. Perhaps the most famous application of the image to religious life is that found in the Benedictine Rule, which governed the life of the earliest monastic communities in Britain. Commenting on Luke 14:11 (cf. Ps. 131:1-2), "whosoever exalteth himself shall be abased, and he that humbleth himself shall be exalted," the author of the Rule argues that the way to heavenly heights is along the steps of humility, beginning with the fear of God and moving through obedience and perseverance in humility to the twelfth degree, in which outward comportment is consonant with inward humility, and to the "top, the charity which is perfect and casts out all fear." The way up is the way down. In the preface to his *Ars Praedicandi,* a handbook for preachers, Alain of Lille develops the allusion in Pope Gregory's *Regulae pastoralis* to say that "the ladder represents the progress of the catholic man in his ascent from the beginning of faith to the full development of the perfect man." In this tradition the emphasis (as in the familiar camp-meeting song "We Are Climbing Jacob's Ladder") is upon ascent alone. Alan associates each of the rungs with a stage in spiritual progress: confession, prayer, thanksgiving, the careful study of Scriptures, the pursuit of sound instruction in scriptural exegesis, the expounding of Scripture, and, finally, preaching. St. Bonaventure's *Itinerarium Mentis in Deum* describes the "mind's journey to God," using Jacob's ladder to figure the mystical progress of the soul toward union with God, dividing the ascent into "six stages of the soul's powers by which we mount from the depths to the heights, from the external to the internal, from the temporal to the eternal" (pref.). The final moment in such an ascent is utter self-transcendence, in which all fetters of the world fall away and, in Bonaventure's words, "another Jacob is changed into Israel, so through him all truly spiritual persons have been invited by God to passage of this kind. . . ." The English title of Walter Hilton's vernacular classic *The Ladder of Perfection* draws upon these same associations.

The chief voices of Reformation commentary follow a basically Augustinian line of interpretation. For Luther, who reviews a substantial body of the medieval commentary from Gregory to Nicholas of Lyra's *Postilla,* the ladder is above all a symbol of the Incarnation (*Lectures on Genesis,* 26-30 [*WA* 43.576-80]); he draws heavily on the traditional juxtaposition of the Jacob narrative with the Nathanael incident (John 1:47-51). For Calvin "it is Christ alone . . . who connects heaven and earth: he is the only Mediator who reaches from heaven down to earth: he is the medium through which the fulness of all celestial blessings flows down to us, and through which we, in turn, ascend to God" (*Comm. on Genesis,* 2.28). Cornelius à Lapide cites Theodoret and Ibn Ezra, sources Calvin rejects, to say that the ladder is first of all a symbol for divine providence, with the angels as ministers of providence; allegorically, he says (following Augustine, *Sermo,* 79) the ladder is the cross of Christ and a sign of the Incarnation of the Word, while tropologically it is the human spirit, with the descending angels signifying carnal appetite and those ascending representing intellectual and spiritual aspiration. The rungs are virtues in the "ladder of perfection." Anagogically, the angels signify the various levels of achievement and orders of the blessed (*Comm. in Genesim,* 28.286-89).

In one of John Donne's sermons (eds. Potter and Simpson, 3.58), he draws on Lapide to say that God holds his ladder up to heaven "and all those good works which are put upon the lowest step . . . that is, that are done in contemplation of him, they ascend to him, and descend to us" (cf. 2.186; 5.264). In *Paradise Lost* (3.510-15) Milton describes what Satan sees at the portal of heaven:

> The Stairs were such as whereon Jacob saw
> Angels ascending and descending, bands
> Of Guardians bright, when he from *Esau* fled
> To *Padan-Aram* in the field of *Luz,*
> Dreaming by night under the open Sky,
> And waking cri'd, *This is the Gate of Heav'n.*

In his essay *The Means to Remove Hirelings* Milton cites Jacob's vow following his dream (Gen. 28:22) as the formal biblical proclamation of tithing as part of service to God, though "not to any priest."

Ben Jonson, in celebrating Lady Digby ("LXXXIV Eupheme"), speaks of her

> getting up
> By Jacob's ladder, to the top
> Of that eternal port kept ope
> For such as she.

Dryden sees the ladder as a symbol of the progress of culture,

> Where ev'ry age do's on another move,
> And trusts no farther than the next above;
> Where all the rounds like *Jacob's* ladder rise,
> The lowest hid in earth, the topmost in the skyes

— a latitudinarian sentiment, although it appears in his Catholic *The Hind and the Panther* (2.218-21). An intentionally humorous reference is found in Thomas Gray's

"The Characters of Christ-Cross Row," in which the reader is obliged to imagine the corporal bulk of "his hugeness H . . . / Henry the Eighth's most monstrous majesty" ascending and descending the ladder in place of angels (21-28). Charles Wesley's hymn,

> What doth the ladder mean
> Sent down from the Most High?
> Fasten'd to earth its foot is seen,
> Its summit to the sky,

while seeming to echo Dryden, is actually indebted to Augustine, Luther, and Calvin:

> Jesus that ladder is,
> Th'incarnate Deity,
> Partaker of celestial bliss,
> And human misery;
> Sent from His high abode,
> To sleeping mortals given,
> He stands, and man unites to God,
> And earth connects to heaven.

Wordsworth's angels are expressions of human aspiration remarkably akin to Dryden's: "Glorious is the blending / Of right affections climbing or descending / Along a scale of light and life." The Lake poet's Jacob, however, while sleeping, was also himself "treading the pendent stairs" ("Humanity," 27-40). Thomas de Quincey argues in his essay "Literature of Knowledge and Literature of Power" that Milton's is the latter category, promoting the "exercise and expansion of your own latent capacity of sympathy with the infinite, where every pulse is . . . a step upwards, a step ascending as upon Jacob's ladder from earth to mysterious altitudes above." In Robert Browning's "Fefine at the Fair," the cure's sermon on Jacob's dream of the ladder sets out to

> put in proof,
> When we have scaled the sky, we well may let alone
> What raised us from the ground, and — paying to the
>   stone
> Proper respect, of course — take staff and go our way.
> (2108-11)

In a nice juxtaposition, Hawthorne's Miriam in *The Marble Faun* mounts a serial staircase to the palace which seems to her "for the loftiness of its aspiration . . . worthy to be Jacob's ladder, or, at all events, the staircase of the Tower of Babel."

An analogous scene occurs in Melville's "The Two Temples," in which the fifty stone steps ascended by the protagonist (reminiscent of the ascent to Solomon's temple) are surmounted by "another Jacob's ladder" — a figure which in Melville's mind is associated with charity. But while in "Temple First" the narrator mounts a Jacob's ladder, in "Temple Second" Richelieu asserts that one sees the ladder only in dreams. The "lamb-like" man sleeping at the foot of the ship's ladder in *The Confidence-Man* is, presumably in this second sense, likened by

Melville to Jacob "dreaming at Luz." In Longfellow's *Evangeline* (2.2) the vision is reduced to a rope ladder hanging from a cedar tree, with hovering hummingbirds as angels.

Carlyle has modern, rather than ancient, interpretations of the passage in mind when he writes in *Sartor Resartus:* "To our young Friend all women were holy, were heavenly. . . . All of air they were, all Soul and Form; so lovely, like mysterious priestesses, in whose hand was the invisible Jacob's ladder, whereby man might mount into very heaven" (2.5). And if ascent of one kind or another had been the aspiration expressed in allusions from the medieval mystics to 18th- and 19th-cent. liberal and Romantic humanism, Shaw's *Back to Methuselah* returns full circle to a crashing descent. The ex-curate Franklyn Barnabas, proclaiming the "Gospel of the Brothers Barnabas," includes in his crypto-theology of the fall from Adam and Eve's vegetarian socialism to meat-eating mayhem the following invitation: "I ask you to contemplate our fathers as they came crashing down all the steps of this Jacob's ladder that reached from paradise to a hell on earth in which they multiplied the chances of death from violence, accident, and disease until they could hardly count on three score and ten years of life, much less the thousand that Adam had been ready to face!"

See also JACOB.

Bibliography. Anderson, J. *Five Themes from Genesis* (1972); Ginsberg, W. "Dante's Dream of the Eagle and Jacob's Ladder." *Dante Studies* 100 (1982), 41-69; Rowland, B. "Melville Answers the Theologians: The Ladder of Charity in 'The Two Temples.'" *Mosaic* 7 (1974), 1-14; Steinmetz, D. C. "Luther and the Ascent of Jacob's Ladder." *CH* 55 (1986), 179-92.

JACOB'S RODS   In the appointing of Jacob's wages for his service to Laban, the two agreed that Jacob's share would be the spotted offspring of the flocks (Gen. 30:28-36). Jacob, to increase his portion, placed partially peeled green rods of poplar, almond, and plane trees by the watering troughs of the animals so that they would look on them while they drank and copulated, thus conceiving lambs and kids of speckled and diverse colors (vv. 37-43).

St. Augustine uses the story to illustrate how things "diverse in nature are tempered together into a kind of unity" (*De Trin.* 11.2.5). Rabanus Maurus comments: "What does it mean to place green rods of almond and plane before the eyes of the flock except to offer as example to the people the lives and lessons of the ancient patriarchs as they appear throughout the Scriptures? . . . And when from these the bark [cortex] of the letter is taken away, the interior whiteness is shown allegorically" (PL 107.603). John Gower follows Peter Riga's *Aurora* (ed. Beichner, 1080-94) in using the passage to exemplify the behavior of a good preacher who should place before the eyes of his congregation Holy Scripture from which the bark (the letter) has been partly, but not entirely,

removed so that the whiteness of true doctrine might glisten forth and the congregation conceive profitably (*Vox Clamantis*, 3.13.1118-24). In Shakespeare's *Merchant of Venice* Shylock adduces the incident in defending to Antonia his practice of lending at high rates, arguing that in effect his profit is, like Jacob's, "indirect" interest (1.3.68-97).

The trick later acquires more clearly negative literary associations. Swift quips in his "Epigrams against Carthy" (no. 18), "Your works are like old Jacob's speckled goats, / Known by the Verse, yet better by the Notes." In a related reference Keats chastises slavish adherents of neoclassical poetry like Boileau, who, he finds,

> were closely wed
> To musty laws lined out with wretched rule
> And compass vile: so that ye taught a school
> Of dolts to smooth, inlay, and clip, and fit,
> Till, like the certain wands of Jacob's wit,
> Their verses tallied. ("Sleep and Poetry," 194-99)

The incident still signifies the repression or control of spontaneous nature to Elizabeth Barrett Browning, who, in *Aurora Leigh* (5.237-42), observes:

> 'Tis true the stage requires obsequiousness
> To this or that convention; "exit" here
> And "enter" there; the points for clapping, fixed,
> Like Jacob's white-peeled rods before the rams,
> And all the close-curled imagery clipped
> In manner of their fleece at shearing-time.

See also JACOB.   RUSSELL A. PECK

JACOB'S STAFF   According to Yashar Shemot 141a, in the quarrel of remonstrance after Jacob's usurping the birthright from Esau, Jacob is supposed to have wrested the rod, or staff, from Esau. This became the staff with which he traveled to Haran, and he is said to have used it later magically to divide the waters of the Jordan in escaping from the wrath of Esau (Tan. Ber. 1.145; 'Ag. Ber. 45, 93). According to some sources, he then bequeathed it to Joseph, from whom it was passed down to Aaron; this was the same rod with which Aaron performed miracles before Pharaoh (Exod. 7:9ff.; Midr. 'Aggada sup. Gen. 32:11 adds that Moses used it to divide the Red Sea). Among jugglers, a "Jacob's staff" (Fr. *bâton de Jacob*) refers to a conjuring rod — an association reflected in Spenser's *Faerie Queene* (1.6.35), when Archimago, disguised as a pilgrim, bears "a Jacob's staff, to stay / His weary limbs upon." Shakespeare's Shylock swears "by Jacob's staff" (*Merchant of Venice*, 2.5.36). Browning's "Doctor — " speaks of "the mystic Jacob's staff" as having talismanic powers, yet "scarce would Jacobs-Staff rescind / Fate's firm decree!" (217-19; 232-34).

See also JACOB.

JAEL   Jael (Heb. = "wild goat") was the wife of Heber the Kenite. After Deborah and Barak had defeated the

Canaanite army of Sisera, the general fled to the tent of Jael (Judg. 4:17), where she pretended hospitality, gave him warm milk, and covered him with a blanket to rest. After he had fallen asleep she took a tent-peg and with a hammer pounded it through his temples into the ground. Her deed was praised in song by Deborah as the culmination of the Hebrew victory (Judg. 5:24-31).

In the Prologue of Chaucer's *Wife of Bath's Tale* Jankyn's litany of treacherous wives oddly includes Jael: "And somme han dryve nayles in hir brayne, / While that they slepte, and thus they had hem slayne" (*Canterbury Tales*, 3.769-70). Caliban, in urging Stephano to usurp Prospero, offers to put the magician asleep "where thou mayst knock a nail into his head" (Shakespeare, *The Tempest*, 3.2.64). In Milton's *Samson Agonistes,* Delilah declares that she wants someday to become famous like Jael (988-90). In Christopher Smart's *Hymns for the Amusement of Children* the story offers a moral:

Sleep not — but watch the chamber well,
By sleeping Holofernes fell;
And Jael's memorable nail
Did o'er a sleeping king prevail. (20.17-20)

In Sir Walter Scott's *Old Mortality* the incident is recalled in conversation between Morton and Mistress Maclure, the kindly covenanting widow. When she tells of harboring one of the covenanters' enemies in flight for his life, she adds that "I gat ill-will about it among some o' our ain folk. They said I should hae bin to him what Jael was to Sisera. But weel I wot I had nae divine command to shed blood, and to save it was baith like a woman and a Christian." Charlotte Brontë's narrator in *Vilette* speaks of certain longings which she felt obliged "to knock on the head," which she says she did, "figuratively, after the manner of Jael to Sisera, driving a nail through their temples. Unlike Sisera, they did not die: they were but transiently skinned, and at intervals would turn on the nail with a rebellious wrench: then did the temples bleed, and the brain thrill to its core." J. B. L. Warren (Baron de Tabley) published in *Poems, Dramatic and Lyrical* (1893-95) a poem on "Jael," which sees her as a sinister violator of universal hospitality codes:

She stood, the mother-snake, before her tent,
She feigned a piteous dew in her false eyes, . . .
Slid like a snake across the tent — struck twice —
And stung him dead.

Hardy describes Anne's suspicion of Manston in *Desperate Remedies* as Jael's sizing up Sisera for the "thin tent nail," an allusion which recurs in reference to the betrayal of Stephen in his *A Pair of Blue Eyes.* Lamb, in his essay "Imperfect Sympathies," claims to be at once attracted to and intimidated by Jewish women: ". . . Jael had those dark, inscrutable eyes." John Halifax, in Mrs. Dinah (Mulock) Craik's novel of that name (1856), can think of no higher praise for a woman than to say, "Bravo,

Jael! The wife of Heber the Kenite was no braver woman than you!" (chap. 8). Margaret Avison's poem "Jael's Part," like Byron's "The Giaour," tells the story from the vantage point of "the mother of Sisera in late afternoon" (cf. Judg. 5:28) as she watches the empty chariot return and awaits the terrible news of the defeat and her son's death.

See also DEBORAH, SONG OF DEBORAH.

Bibliography. Bal, M. *Death and Dissymmetry: the Politics of Coherence in the Book of Judges* (1988).

JAMES *See* APOSTLE.

JAPHETH One of the three sons of Noah preserved with their wives on the ark, Japheth (usually held by rabbinic sources to be the oldest) is made in the genealogy of Gen. 10 to be father of northern and European peoples. Medieval Christian glosses typically make him *"minoris filii,"* of whom *"European sortitus est"* (*Glossa Ordinaria* [PL 113.113]), with Gomer, following Josephus, ancestor of the peoples of Galatia, *"qui Latine Gallograeci dicuntur,"* Tubal being regarded as father of the Iberian peoples, etc. Speculation into the origin and development of languages in the 18th cent. sparked numerous attempts to trace a linguistic genealogy, among which James Parson's *The Remains of Japhet* (1767) is noteworthy. Fredrick Marryat's *Japhet in Search of a Father* (1836) is a dark-humored riddling novel which explores European cultural roots and identity.

JEALOUSY *See* CHARITY, CUPIDITY; LOVE STRONG AS DEATH.

JEBUSITES Ethnic Canaanitic peoples, associated with "Jebus," a city denominated by a scribal gloss (Josh. 18:28; Judg. 19:10) as the site of Jerusalem before Israelite times. A disparaging reference in Zech. 9:7, glossed in some patristic and later commentaries as "superstitious pagans," seems to lie behind polemical use of the term in Protestant Reformation writers to designate Catholic opponents. Gen. 10:16 makes them descendants of Cain: hence Marlowe's Barabas in *The Jew of Malta* characterizes Lodowicke as "this offspring of Cain, this Jebusite" (2.3.301). In 17th-cent. English poetry they can designate the Jesuits, or, as in Dryden's *Absalom and Achitophel,* the Jacobites (33-40) who threaten Protestant supremacy.

JEHONADAB *See* RECHABITES.

JEHOSHAPHAT, VALLEY OF In Joel 3:2, 12 the scene given for the final judgment of the nations is the "valley of Jehoshaphat." The name does not refer to the fourth king of Judah (see 1 Kings 22:41-50) but, in accordance with Heb. *yehoshaphat,* means "The LORD (Yahweh) shall judge." Although the name was later applied to the vale of Kidron near Jerusalem and to the location of the future battle of Armageddon, Joel's reference to it as "the valley of decision" (3:14) makes it clear that the name is to be associated with the final judgment itself.

In York's medieval Corpus Christi play presenting the apocryphal "Appearance of our Lady to Thomas" (no. 46), St. Thomas, on his way from India, is transported to "þe Vale of Josaphat, in Jury so gente," where he falls asleep and has his vision of Mary. This play immediately precedes "The Judgement Day" in the York pageant. Edith Wharton's *The Valley of Decision* (1902) takes its title from Joel 3:14. Whittier's "What of the Day" applies the term to the battle for liberty of Fremont: "Behold the burden of the prophet's vision; / The gathering hosts, — the Valley of Decision." In contrast, in *Culture and Anarchy* Matthew Arnold advises young Liberals not to oppose the Philistine Parliament with extremism: "For our part, we rejoice to see our dear old friends, the Hebraizing Philistines, gathered in force in the Valley of Jehoshaphat previous to their final conversion, which will certainly come." There is no comparable assurance of universal salvation, political or religious, in Stephen Dedalus's mind in Joyce's *Portrait of the Artist as a Young Man.* After hearing a powerful sermon on sin and judgment, Stephen reflects on the Day of Judgment: "The last day had come. The doomsday was at hand. . . . The three blasts of the angel filled the universe. Time is, time was, but time shall be no more. At the last blast the souls of universal humanity throng towards the valley of Jehoshaphat, rich and poor, gentle and simple, wise and foolish, good and wicked" (chap. 3).

See also ARMAGEDDON.

JEHOVAH   *See* NAMES OF GOD.

JEHU   Jehu became the tenth king of the northern nation of Israel (ca. 842-815 B.C.) and established its fourth dynasty by killing the Judaean king Ahaziah and the Israelite Jehoram. The latter had continued the apostasy of his father Ahab, which Jehu attempted to eradicate by ending the line, including Ahab's wife Jezebel (2 Kings 9–10). Jehu himself became apostate by worshiping the calves at Bethel and Dan, for which punishment was brought by Syrian invasion (2 Kings 10:29-33).

Jehu, or a representative, is depicted in an attitude of obeisance to his overlord on the Black Obelisk of Shalmaneser III (*ANEP,* 351, 353). Regarded by St. Augustine as an example of lying (*Consentius,* 3), in Wesley he is credited with the positive characteristic of being open in his opinions (*Sermons,* 2.83).

The most alluded to portion of the narrative is 2 Kings 9:20, in which a watchman for Ahaziah announces Jehu's approach from a distance, saying "and the driving is like the driving of Jehu the son of Nimshi; for he driveth furiously." Milton accused Charles II of having "forced the parliament to drive like Jehu" (*Eikonoklastes*), and

Dryden more aptly draws an analogy with the Earl of Shaftesbury as a rebel against the crown:

> But this new Jehu spurs the hot-mouth'd horse;
> Instructs the beast to know his native force,
> To take the bit between his teeth and fly
> To the next headlong step of anarchy.

In O. Henry's "A Municipal Report" the analogy is with a hack driver who provides the narrator with a breathtaking ride (cf. Galsworthy, *Over the River,* chap. 18).

DAVID W. BAKER

JEPHTHAH AND HIS DAUGHTER   The source of the story of Jephthah and his daughter is Judg. 11:30-40. Jephthah, at war with the Ammonites, vowed that, if he was victorious, he would upon his return from battle offer up to the Lord whatever first came from his house to meet him. When he returned home triumphant, the first to emerge was his daughter, his only child. Regretting his vow but unable to go back on it, he allowed her, upon her request, two months to bewail her lot, and then he sacrificed her.

This tale of Jephthah's rash vow, regret, grief, and remorse and of his daughter's acceptance of her fate has inspired a variety of artistic treatments, including more than a hundred musical interpretations, and numerous paintings and etchings (including those by Lucas van Leyden, William Blake, Edgar Degas, Gustave Doré, J. E. Millais, and Benjamin West), and sculptures ranging from that of 15th-cent. Florentine Lorenzo Ghiberti to 20th-cent. Naum Aronson and Enrico Glicenstein.

The earliest literary treatment dates from the 1st cent. A.D., in a document known as *The Biblical Antiquities of Pseudo-Philo* (see J. Charlesworth, *Old Testament Pseudepigrapha,* 2.351-54), where the daughter's name is given as "Seila." Seila is only one of more than forty names given by subsequent writers to this girl, who is unnamed in the biblical story.

Talmudists and early midrashic writers condemn Jephthah for having offered a human sacrifice. A few medieval Jewish interpreters, however, suggest that the biblical text may not actually imply a sacrifice, that in fulfilling his vow Jephthah might rather have made his daughter live in perpetual seclusion, dead to society, devoting herself entirely to the service of God.

Patristic writers found the Jephthah story provocative and treated it in a variety of ways. The *Glossa Ordinaria* cites several allegorical readings of the narrative, including one which sees in Jephthah, who gives up his dearly beloved offspring, a figure for God the Father and in his daughter, because of her perpetual virginity, a figure for the Church. St. Isidore is cited as seeing in Jephthah a figure for Christ, who turned away from his daughter Israel in order to offer salvation to the Gentiles. St. Jerome, bypassing allegory, nonetheless offers Jephthah as a pertinent moral example: in a consolatory and exhortative letter to a nobleman concerning his grief at the loss of his wife and two daughters (*Ep.* 118), he discusses the story in the context of extravagant sacrifice: "Jephthah . . . offered up his virgin daughter, and for this is placed by the apostle in the roll of the saints" (cf. Heb. 11:32). But some Church Fathers wrestled more directly with what St. Augustine calls "the great question" raised by the story — whether indeed such incidents should be understood as happening according to divine ordinance. St. Ambrose (*De officiis ministrorum,* bk. 1) is unequivocal in his castigation of Jephthah: "It is sometimes contrary to duty to fulfill a promise, or to keep an oath," he reasons, citing Herod's impetuous promise to the daughter of Herodias, which cost the life of John the Baptist (Matt. 14:6ff.), as well as Jephthah's rash vow. Of the latter, he observes, "It would have been better to make no promise at all than to fulfill it in the death of his daughter." St. John Chrysostom likewise judges that Jephthah, through his lack of wisdom, fell into the heinous sin of child murder. By "allowing" this vow to be fulfilled, he argues, God actually put a stop to such vows being repeated by others — as may be understood by the (apparently divinely sanctioned) annual lamentation of the daughters of Israel ("Concerning the Statues," *Hom.* 14).

Chaucer refers to the story of Jephthah's daughter in *The Physician's Tale* (*Canterbury Tales,* 6.238-44), and his contemporary John Gower, in the *Confessio Amantis* (4.505-1595), elaborates the narrative in great detail. English ballads about Jephthah survive from the 16th cent. Shakespeare includes verses of the ballad "Jephthah, Judge of Israel" in *Hamlet* (2.2.410-25), here referring satirically to Polonius as an old Jephthah who had "one fair daughter and no more, / The which he loved passing well."

The popularity of the theme in this period may owe largely to the Scottish humanist George Buchanan, who rendered the Jephthah story as a tragedy in the mid-16th cent. His Lat. drama *Jephthes,* written in 1540, and printed in 1554, was translated at least six times into English and exerted great influence throughout Europe, especially upon Christian Weise's German drama (1670) and Joost van den Vondel's Dutch play (1659). Humanists likened the Jephthah story to that of Iphigenia as treated by Euripides in his *Iphigenia in Aulis.* Erasmus translated the play in 1506, and his version influenced English humanist John Christopherson, who composed a Jephthah drama in Greek in 1544. Christopherson, who also rendered his play into Latin, explained that he had chosen the theme because of its similarity to the Euripidean play: Jephthah, like Agamemnon, father of Iphigenia, was caught in a conflict between his duty to God and his fatherly love. More than fifty dramas on this theme are recorded between the 16th and the 18th cents. throughout Europe. An English *Jephthah* drama was written by Thomas Dekker and Anthony Munday in 1602, but the text has not survived.

Among 17th-cent. poets, Francis Quarles includes a

lyric of eighteen lines, "On Jeptha's Vow," in his *Divine Fancies* (2.4). Robert Herrick's "The Dirge of Jephthah's Daughter" (1647) recounts the annual lament of the young women of Israel over the plight of Jephthah's daughter.

In the 18th cent. the story was often treated in oratorios, the most popular being Handel's of 1751, for which Thomas Morell wrote the text. Though Iphis (Handel's name for Jephthah's daugher) is prepared, like Iphigenia, to go stoically to her death, Morell has an angel appear and announce that God is a loving, forgiving deity who does not want bloody sacrifice but rather that Iphis serve him as a priestess.

Byron's Jephthah poem of 1815, included in his *Hebrew Melodies,* emphasizes the daughter's nobility of soul, her filial obedience, her acquiescence in sacrificing herself for her country and her God. There follow poems by James Campbell, "Jeptha's Rash Vow" (1826), and by Hartley Coleridge, "On a Picture of Jephthah and His Daughter" (1851). Tennyson includes Jephthah's daughter in his long poem *A Dream of Fair Women* (1833) and in "Aylmer's Field" and "The Flight." Among American poets, N. P. Willis includes "Jephthah's Daughter" in his *Poetical Works* (1888), and Mark Van Doren has a poem of the same title in his *Collected New Poems* (1963).

The theme has also been popular among American Yiddish writers such as Yehoash and I. I. Schwartz. The Yiddish dramatist Sholem Asch, in his Jephthah play of 1915, introduces not the Jewish God but Moloch, the god of Jephthah's mother, as the deity who grants the victory and to whom the daughter is to be sacrificed. This daughter rejoices in her father's vow and is glad to answer the wild call of Moloch, the savage sun-god, whose fiery darts warm her longing limbs.

Another noteworthy recasting of the tale is that by Lion Feuchtwanger in his last novel *Jephthah and his Daughter* (1957). Though the father fulfills his rash vow and sacrifices his pure and innocent daughter, his heart is a desert thereafter. Revered in Gilead and ruling his people justly, he nevertheless feels that his life's blood has been drained away. In the character of Jephthah, the novelist voices his own loss of faith in his earlier ideals and his disillusionment with his German countrymen, who drove him into exile and brought his Jewish kin as burnt-offerings to Auschwitz. The poem "Jephthah's Daughter" by the British lyricist Karen Gershon appeared in the volume *Coming Back to Babylon* in 1979, after she had settled in Israel, and Naomi Ragen's novel *Jepthe's Daughter* appeared in 1989.

See also MOLOCH.

Bibliography. Bal, M. "The Rape of Narrative and the Narrative of Rape: Speech Acts and Body Language in Judges." In *Literature and the Body* (1988), 1-32; *Death and Dissymmetry: the Politics of Coherence in the Book of Judges* (1988); Boling, R. *Judges.* AB (1975); Charlesworth, J., ed. *The Old Testament Pseudepigrapha.* 2 vols. (1983, 1985);

Feinberg, N. P. "Jephthah's Daughter: The Parts Ophelia Plays." In *Old Testament Women in English Literature.* Ed. R.-J. Frontain (1991); Liptzin, S. *Biblical Themes in World Literature* (1985); Porwig, J. *Der Jephthahstoff in der deutschen Literatur* (1932); Sypherd, W. O. *Jephthah and His Daughter: A Study in Comparative Literature* (1947).

SOL LIPTZIN

JEREMIAH Jeremiah was one of the major prophets of the period of the Babylonian captivity, and the nominal author of the book which bears his name and most probably the book of Lamentations which follows. Jeremiah's name is linked by talmudic sources to the roots for *God* and the verb *to raise up against* (2 Alphabet of Ben Sira 17b), with later rabbinic sources offering an etymology from the Gk. *erēmia* ("desert") (Pesiq. Rab. Kah. 13, 115a; Qohelet 1.1). As is typical of illustrious prophets, he is said in the *legenda* to have been born circumcised (Tehillim 9.84) and immediately upon birth to have begun the wailing which earned him in adult life the name of "the weeping prophet" ('Abot. R. Nat. 2.12). He also is said to have begun almost at once to speak with an adult voice and to possess numerous other attributes conspicuously paralleling those ascribed to Moses, with whom he has in haggadic sources an almost typological relationship (Ginzberg, *LJ* 6.385-86).

The principal subject of the book of Jeremiah is the threat to Judah and Jerusalem posed by the Babylonian campaigns in Judah at the close of the 6th cent. B.C., culminating in the destruction of Jerusalem and its Temple in 587 B.C. This latter action also removed the Davidic kingship from Jerusalem and brought an effective end to Judah's political identity as a separate state. In spite of these catastrophic events, the message contained in the book is one of hope, showing that God had forewarned of such adversities, which were a punishment for national apostasy, and had promised a restoration of all Israel in the future.

The book falls into four clear sections. The first of these, chaps. 1–25, is comprised of a collection of prophecies, mainly in poetic form, some of which, however, are in an elevated prose style. A sequence of narratives in chaps. 26–29, 32, 34–45 forms a second section, which narrates incidents in Jeremiah's life, centering upon the destruction of Jerusalem by the Babylonians in 587 B.C. In the midst of this material a group of prophecies expressing hope and assurance of the nation's restoration from ruin and exile is to be found in chaps. 30–31, 33, clearly filling out the narrative expressing such a hope contained in chap. 32. A fourth section, chaps. 46–51, contains prophecies directed against foreign nations, including Babylon. A concluding narrative epilogue (chap. 52) brings the entire book to a close.

This unusual structure evidently reflects in large measure the process of collecting and preserving materials having to do with Jeremiah's preaching and sufferings, and it is only within these large sections that any semblance of chronological order or thematic association is to be found. Narrative incidents appear in a loosely chronological order, though no clear dates are attached to most of the prophecies.

Jeremiah's call to become a prophet has been traditionally dated to 626 B.C. (Jer. 1:2). A scroll containing prophecies from Jeremiah was made in 605-604 B.C. (Jer. 36), and the narrative reports do not start before the beginning of Jehoiakim's reign in 609 B.C. (Jer. 26:1). All the indications are that the preservation of Jeremiah's prophecies and the records of his actions have been dictated by the concern to recall and illuminate the events concerning the downfall of Judah at the hands of the Babylonian conquerors in the years 605-583 B.C. These political catastrophes, with their strong religious implications, form the central point of interest for the book, which both interprets them as divine judgments and provides assurance of God's persistent purpose for Israel.

St. Ambrose, who calls Jeremiah approvingly the "Peasant Prophet," comments upon Jeremiah's having bewailed his birth (15:10), urging, "If then, holy men shrink from life whose life, though profitable to us, is esteemed unprofitable to themselves; what ought we to do who are not able to profit others, and who feel that it, like money borrowed at interest, grows more heavily weighted each day with an increasing mass of sins?" (*De excessu,* 2.34; *De fide,* 1.3.30).

Jeremiah does not figure significantly as a character in English literature, but his writings are a popular source, from the *"O Vos Omnes"* hymn of the liturgy and ME lyric (e.g., C. Brown, *Religious Lyrics of the XIVth Century,* no. 74) to the jeremiad, a type of declamatory lamentation which looks to the past for causes of a present calamity and promises better times in the future if appropriate reforms are made. George Herbert refers typically to "Jeremy, Chapt. 10," where "after he had complained of the desolation of *Israel,* [he] turns to God suddenly, *Oh Lord, I know that the way of man is not in himself*" (*A Priest to the Temple,* 7), indicating both the dual focus of the prophet and what came to be thought of as his almost mercurial rhetoric. John Donne composed a series of poetic imitations, following Tremelius, on "The Lamentations of Jeremy." Hannah More observed that "it has long been the fashion to make the most lamentable *Jeremiades* on the badness of the times" (quoted in Roberts's *Memoirs of Hannah More,* 1.186); the jeremiad had already become an important literary form in Puritan America. Matthew Arnold complains in *Culture and Anarchy* that preachers of culture like himself have "a hard time of it, and they will much oftener be regarded . . . as elegant or spurious Jeremiahs than as friends or benefactors" ("Sweetness and Light"). In modern poetry it is still the "tears of Jeremiah" (A. M. Klein, "To the Jewish Poet") which characterize the memory of his oratory. Some, like Klein, criticize Jeremiah's florid prolixity from the perspective of a hard-bitten cynicism:

Omit your adjectives, sad Jeremiah,
Spare you your adverbs; let your phrases house
No too-protesting tenant of despair;
And if the meagre tale brings no Messiah,
Messiah is a short conspiracy of throat and air.
("Greeting on this Day")

Bibliography. Bercovitch, S. *The American Jeremiad*
(1978).   RONALD CLEMENTS

JERICHO   The city which, after being circled for seven
days by Joshua's forces carrying the Ark of the Covenant,
had its walls fall down at the blast of the trumpet and "a
great shout" (Josh. 6). In the Preface to Shaw's *Saint Joan,*
he observes that Joan "did not expect besieged cities to
fall Jerichowise at the sound of her trumpet, but, like
Wellington, adapted her methods of attack to the
peculiarities of the defense" (25).

See also GOOD SAMARITAN; JOSHUA; RAHAB.

JERUSALEM   *See* NEW JERUSALEM.

JESU, DULCIS MEMORIA   A celebrated late 12th-
cent. poem (wrongly) attributed to St. Bernard of Clairvaux, it has been translated in part in English by E. Caswall ("Jesus the very thought of Thee / With sweetness
fills my breast") and J. M. Neale ("Jesu! The very thought
is sweet"). The phrase is not biblical, though often cited
as if it were. Used as an office-hymn for the Feast of the
Holy Name, it is sometimes known as the "Rosy Sequence." A 14th-cent. ME version has been printed by
C. Brown, *Religious Hymns of the XIV Century,* no. 89.

JESUS CHRIST   The name *Jesus* comes from the Gk.
Iēsous, the adaptation of the Hebrew name *Yehoshuaʿ*
(Aram. *Yeshuaʿ*), the name of the great hero of the conquest of Canaan, familiar to OT readers as Joshua. The
term *Christ* is adapted from the Gk. *Christos,* which
translates the Heb. *mashiah* (from which the term *Messiah* is derived), meaning "anointed." *Christ* is thus originally not a name but a title reflecting the early Christian
conviction that Jesus is the Messiah, the "anointed one,"
who fulfills the hope for a God-sent savior.

The four Gospels of the NT are our major source of
information about Jesus of Nazareth and the primary basis
for the picture of him which is accepted by traditional
Christianity. Commonly dated by scholars between A.D.
65 and 95, they are also recognized as embodying the
Jesus tradition of much earlier years. With the rise of
modern historicism, especially in the 19th cent., many
strove to construct a somewhat detailed, chronologically
arranged life of Jesus from the Gospels. A. Schweitzer's
classic *The Quest of the Historical Jesus* traces the failure
of this enterprise, and NT scholars today recognize that
the Gospels (like all ancient biographical literature) were
not written to provide a chronological or developmental
account of their subject but were intended as collections

of Jesus tradition and interpretations of him for the religious needs of 1st-cent. churches. Nevertheless, nearly all
NT scholars today are persuaded that, although a detailed
life of Jesus cannot be written, the Gospels do provide a
basis for a more modest historical description of Jesus'
ministry and message which accords with the standards
of modern historical criticism.

The traditional picture of Jesus was formed by a har-
monistic reading of the Gospels, the following elements
of which are most important for the literary tradition.
Jesus was miraculously conceived in Mary without a
human father, born in Bethlehem of Judah in the time of
Herod the Great (37-4 B.C.; see Matt. 1-2; Luke 1-2), and
grew up in Nazareth of Galilee. In his young adult years
he was baptized by John the Baptist (who preached a
message of radical religious reform among the Jews), on
which occasion he was acclaimed by God as his "beloved
Son" (e.g., Mark 1:1-11).

Shortly after his baptism and a period of testing in the
wilderness, Jesus began his own ministry. His message
focused upon the approach of the kingdom of God (e.g.,
Mark 1:14-15) and was often conveyed by means of
parables (Matt. 13; Mark 4). He collected disciples and
with them traveled about, preaching his message, which
was accompanied by healings, exorcisms, and other
miraculous works (Mark 1:34, 39). He clashed with
Jewish scribes over matters of religious practice, such as
Sabbath observance and his fellowship with "sinners"
(e.g., Mark 2:1–3:6), and defended his positions with
assertions of special, divinely authorized authority.

Jesus' ministry began in Galilee and eventually took
him to the holy city, Jerusalem, where his conflict with
Jewish religious authorities intensified over such matters
as his condemnation of the priestly leadership and claims
to direct authority from God (e.g., Mark 11:15–12:44). As
a result, these leaders sought to do away with him. With
help from Judas Iscariot, a disciple of Jesus who betrayed
him, the Jewish authorities arrested Jesus during Passover
celebrations (Mark 14:26-50). After a hearing by the high
priest (e.g., Mark 14:53-65), Jesus was condemned for
blasphemy, taken to the Roman governor, Pontius Pilate,
and accused of making himself King of the Jews, which
constituted rebellion against Caesar (e.g., Mark 15:1-26).
Jesus was executed by the Romans, with the full encouragement of the Jewish leaders, and was forsaken by
his disciples, including Simon Peter, who publicly denied
being Jesus' disciple (e.g., Mark 14:50, 66-72).

On the third day after his execution, however, Jesus
was seen by his disciples alive and glorified, having been
raised from death by God (e.g., Matt. 28:1-10, 16-20;
John 20:19-29). He restored the disciples who had forsaken him and charged them to preach the gospel message
to all nations.

The Gospels present Jesus as the true Messiah of Israel
(e.g., John 1:40-41, 45, 49), the fulfillment of all God's
promises of salvation. He is also called "the Son of God"

(e.g., Matt. 27:45) and is acknowledged as such by God himself (e.g., Mark 1:11; 9:7). According to the Gospels, Jesus foresaw his rejection and execution (e.g., Mark 10:33-34), viewed his death as redemptive (Mark 10:45; 14:22-25), and endured his bitter fate as the will of God (Mark 14:32-36; John 12:27). Jesus was therefore not a victim, and his suffering and death were his greatest acts of love for his own (e.g., John 15:13).

Even in ancient times readers of the Gospels noticed that the four books varied in their emphases, arrangement, and style. Thus, Matthew was seen as the Gospel of the royal Messiah of Israel, Mark as the Gospel of the obedient Son of God, Luke as the Gospel of the ideal Son of Man and noble martyr, and John as the Gospel of the divine Son of heavenly origin. The picture of Jesus in John's Gospel is particularly distinctive. Jesus here speaks of himself much more explicitly as the divine Son who knows himself to have been preexistent with God (e.g., 5:19-25; 6:51; 8:23, 56-58; 9:39), and he demonstrates a kind of divine insight into things (1:47-48; 2:24-25; 13:1, 3). John's Gospel was sometimes called "the spiritual Gospel," because Christians recognized in it the much more overt emphasis upon Jesus as the redeemer of heavenly origin.

Other noteworthy presentations of Christ in the NT include Hebrews' theme of Jesus as the new high priest who replaces and supersedes the OT priesthood and its sacrificial system and Revelation's theophanic imagery in 1:12-20, its triumphant Lamb who executes the divine book of redemption in 5:1-14, and its heavenly warrior of final judgment in 19:11-16.

The development of the Christian doctrines of the Trinity and the "two natures" of Christ (divine and human) took several centuries, but already in the NT the essential steps are taken. Here Jesus is presented as genuinely human (e.g., Heb. 2:14-18) — the reality of his death is powerfully insisted upon — but he is also understood to be of heavenly origin (e.g., John 1:1-18) and worthy or worship (e.g., Phil. 2:9-11). All things were created through the preexistent Christ (e.g., Col. 1:15-20), and in Jesus of Nazareth, now glorified at God's "right hand," God was (and is) genuinely manifested (e.g., Col. 2:9). In Paul's words, "God was in Christ reconciling the world" (2 Cor. 5:19). Christ is now the divinely appointed savior of all (e.g., Acts 4:10-12), and through him the entire plan of redemption is to be executed to rescue humankind from the effects of Adams's Fall (e.g., 1 Cor. 15:20-28).

This dual affirmation of Jesus as genuinely human and yet also truly divine continues on and is sharpened by such early Christian theologians as St. Ignatius of Antioch (1st and early 2nd cent.). The logical difficulties involved in such a view of Christ are illustrated by the various heresies of the early centuries, which can be seen as attempts to simplify matters by minimizing either the human or the divine in Jesus. The development of the doctrine of Christ is marked by two events of special importance. The Council of Nicaea in A.D. 325 stated the full divinity of Christ against attempts (e.g., those of the Arians) to define Christ as a lesser divinity. The Council of Chalcedon in A.D. 451 produced a statement which emphasized both Christ's human and divine natures over against various interpretations which were viewed as failing to do justice to the unique union of divine and human in Jesus. These two early Christian councils attempted to state as precisely as possible the traditional Christian belief that Jesus is the unique incarnation of God; the position statements they arrived at have endured as major touchstones of orthodox Christian doctrine to the present time.

A quite different type of Christian thought on the subject of Jesus is to be found in the tradition of literary apocrypha. The silence of the Gospels on so much of the life and activities of Jesus and his family soon led to pious curiosity, which gradually produced a corpus of largely imaginative stories. Among the earliest examples of these are the pseudepigraphal Protevangelium of James, whose author indicates, e.g., that it was Mary who wove the veil of the Temple which was rent in twain at her Son's death; the Infancy Gospel of Thomas, in which the boy Jesus claims to possess an occult knowledge of the meaning underlying the letters of the Greek alphabet; and the Acts of Pilate, with its touching picture of the Roman standards of the imperial ensigns bowing to Jesus against the wishes of the pagans who hold them.

Among the early poetical lives of Jesus were the *Historiae Evangelicae Libri Quattuor,* written about 300 by the Spanish priest Juvencus, and the anonymous Old Saxon alliterative epic *Heliand,* i.e., *Savior,* of about 825-840, which presented Jesus to contemporary Low Germans in the guise of a prototypical warrior leader, the "might-wielding Christ." These verse accounts were followed later in the Middle Ages by several prose lives in Latin, including the *Meditationes Vitae Christi,* sometimes attributed to St. Bonaventure and translated with adaptations into English by Nicholas Love under the title *Mirrour of the Blessed Lyf of Jesu Christ*; Simon Fidati's *De Gestis Domini Salvatoris*; and Ludolph of Saxony's *Vita Jesu Christi.* In 1602 the Jesuit Hieronymus Xavier completed a life of Jesus in Portuguese, which was subsequently translated into Persian and Latin: it depicts a somewhat triumphalist religious leader, many of whose achievements depend only on the authority of the Apocrypha of the 1st and 2nd cents. In 1649 Jeremy Taylor published what may have been the first original life of Christ to be written in English, *The Great Exemplar.* A classic of English devotional literature, it was followed by Abraham Woodhead's *Historical Narrative of Our Lord* (1685), Edmund Law's *Discourse on the Character of Christ* (1749), George Benson's *History of the Life of Jesus Christ* (1764), and John Fleetwood's *Life of Our Lord* (1767).

The earliest example of a biographer of Jesus writing for strictly secular motives was Karl Friedrich Bahrdt, who in several publications written toward the end of the 18th cent. maintained that Jesus was a hellenistically trained member of the Essenes. This conception of Jesus was further developed by Karl Heinrich Venturini in his *Natürliche Geschichte des grossen Propheten von Nazareth* (1800-1802). Perhaps the most popular of the 19th-cent. lives of Jesus was Ernest Renan's *Vie de Jésus* (1863), which is in some respects a historical novel rather than a work of scriptural scholarship. Religiously more orthodox was the life of Christ written by Henri Didon and published in 1890, which was also widely read. Many lives of Jesus were written in English during the Victorian period, including the anonymously published *Ecce Homo* (1865), actually the work of John Seeley; William Hanna's *The Life of Our Lord upon Earth* (1869), F. W. Farrar's *The Life of Christ* (1874), and J. Cunningham Geikie's *Life and Words of Christ* (1877).

Among the examples of what can properly be termed modern apocrypha, two of the best known are Robert Graves's *King Jesus* (1946) and Nikos Kazantzakis's *The Last Temptation of Christ* (1953). Both involve a considerable degree of learned fiction: the Jesus of Graves is presented as the child of a secret wedding between the second Antipater and Mary before she was betrothed to Joseph; the Jesus of Kazantzakis is faced with a final temptation before his death: a vision of life in which he enjoys romantic love, marriage, children, and longevity. Such examples of imaginative christological fiction should be distinguished from the academic lives of Jesus which have appeared in the last century or so, e.g., those of Alfred Edersheim, Joseph Klausner, and Everett Harrison, and the more popular biographies of recent years, e.g., Giovanni Papini's *Story of Christ* (1921), John Erskine's *The Human Life of Jesus* (1945), Frank Slaughter's *The Crown and the Cross* (1959), and Robert Payne's *The Shepherd* (1959).

In a general sense the person and doctrines of Jesus Christ underlie most English religious literature (e.g., hymnody, meditative poetry and prose, and sermons) of both Christian and non-Christian writers. In the OE period some of the best pieces of Jesus literature are poems, including *Christ and Satan* (anonymous, ca. 790-830), *Christ* (in three parts, the second definitely by Cynewulf, 9th cent.), and *The Dream of the Rood* (anonymous, early 9th cent.). An East Midland poem in dialogue, *The Harrowing of Hell,* constitutes a precursor to the later miracle plays, in several of which Jesus has a central role. The life of Christ —especially his Incarnation and Passion —is the principal subject of many medieval lyrics, as well as of devotional verse in the Renaissance and 17th cent. (e.g., John Donne, "La Corona"). In 1610 Giles Fletcher the Younger published *Christ's Victorie, and Triumph in Heaven, on Earth, over, and after Death,* an important anticipation of Milton's *Paradise Regained.*

John Milton (1608-74) is perhaps the most important English contributor to the literature about Jesus Christ. In *Paradise Lost* (published 1667) Milton assigns a significant part of the process of creation to God the Son. God the Father in effect withdraws, and the Word, God the Son, shapes the universe from the unformed matter which had originated with the Father. Underlying this Christian interpretation of the Genesis creation account is the Johannine conception of Jesus as the *Logos,* who existed from all eternity. Jesus as savior and redeemer is the hero of *Paradise Regained* (published 1671). Milton concentrates on the Gospel accounts of Jesus' Baptism, the proclamation that he is the Son of God, and his heroic overcoming of the temptations of Satan.

The first significant 18th-cent. contributor to the literature of Jesus was Sir Richard Steele, who proposed in his literary manual of ethics entitled *The Christian Hero* (1701) that the best preceptor of conscience was Christ rather than any of the classical philosophers. Alexander Pope's *Messiah* (1712), a sacred eclogue on the messianic prophecies of Isaiah, is a noteworthy presentation of OT prophetic expectations, understood as having their fulfillment in Christ.

It was not until the 19th cent. that Jesus and Jesus-like heroes became incorporated in the novel. This development was partly an offshoot of Christian socialism. Its first two exemplars were Elizabeth Linton's *The True History of Joshua Davidson* (1872) and Elizabeth Phelps's *A Singular Life* (1895). Both present a socialistic hero. Linton's Joshua Davidson, the son of a carpenter in a small Cornish village, comes to London and there meets Félix Pyat, clearly meant to represent Karl Marx. A prostitute whom Joshua helps, Mary Prinsep, is the counterpart of Mary Magdalene. Joshua is eventually trampled to death by a London crowd when he vainly attempts to convince them that Christ and his apostles were communists. The implication of this rather awkwardly written novel is that, if Jesus were alive today, he would be an egalitarian working man with a provincial accent and a home in the slums of London who would vituperate against capitalists, landlords, Sabbatarians, bishops, and residents of the West End. Less extreme in her views, the American author Elizabeth Phelps proposes as her Jesus hero in *A Singular Life* a young clergyman, Emanuel Bayard, whose late father, Joseph, a clergyman and carpenter, had married his wife, Mary, in the New England village of Bethlehem. Emanuel's theology is not impeccably orthodox, so his application for the pastorate of the wealthy church of Windover is turned down by the congregation. Instead, he remains to minister to the poor fisher folk of the town. He practices Christian socialism for the rest of his brief life, advocates teetotalism, and causes a scandal by befriending a local prostitute named Lena. By the age of 33, having alienated the town fathers and the local liquor interests beyond reconciliation, he dies as the result of being struck by a stone hurled at him by a grog-shop owner nicknamed Judas. Both of these novels are characterized by rigorous attention to the chronological sequence in the Gospels, by their undisguised moral earnestness, and by their obvious highlighting of the biblical parallels.

Writers of this genre in the 20th cent. have been generally more sophisticated. John Steinbeck's *The Grapes of Wrath* (1939) recounts the exodus-like wanderings of the poverty-stricken Joad family, who leave the Oklahoma dust bowl with a horde of others like them and set out for California in an old, dilapidated car. Set against this OT pattern is a secondary motif derived from the NT, involving a leader with the same initials as Jesus Christ —Jim Casy —and his twelve fellow migrants, the Joad family. Casy is a former preacher who gradually moves from being an orthodox revivalist Christian to being a believer in the essential sanctity of man. While his religious thinking is slowly changing, Casy goes to prison to protect Tom Joad. Shortly after his release, he is killed by one of a group of antiunion men who hate his intentions. His attitude toward his attackers is epitomized in the words "You don't know what you're a-doin," words which echo Jesus' appeal on the cross, "Forgive them, Father, they know not what they do."

Graham Greene's *The Power and the Glory* (1940) has as its hero a nameless whiskey priest. Shifty and alcoholic, he lives in the virtually Marxist state of Tabasco in Mexico. His antagonist, the police lieutenant, is a fanatical atheist; he has all the fervor about his beliefs which the priest should have but lacks. The priest is ultimately executed by the state; he gives up his life for the sake of the criminal James Calver, a bank robber and murderer whose name suggests Calvary. Peter's denial of Jesus is symbolized by Padre José, who refuses to hear the whiskey priest's confession, and Judas is represented by the mestizo, who in effect causes the hero's arrest.

The Jesus hero of Harold Kampf's *When He Shall Appear* (1953) is Janek Lazar, a Russian Jew living in London, who practices faith healing, gains disciples, and preaches a religion of simplicity. He is convinced that Christianity has become too dogmatic and has ceased to be a way of life. The clergy of all denominations unite against him, and he is subsequently arrested on a Thursday in the gardens of Leicester Square. Though the judge dismisses the charges, the clergy plot to have him banished. They are eventually successful, and Lazar is deported to Russia.

The Christ motif appears in a number of William Faulkner's works but nowhere more directly than in *A Fable* (1954). The Jesus figure here is the corporal, whose name, Stephan, is mentioned only once, after his death. Born at Christmas in a Middle Eastern stable, he associates himself with twelve men of his squadron and is executed at the age of 33. Parallels with the Gospel accounts are ubiquitous: they include a Judas figure, Polchek, who commits suicide by hanging himself, and two women who claim the corporal's body after his death, Marthe and Marya.

Gore Vidal's novel *Messiah* (1954; somewhat revised in later editions) is to a considerable degree a parodic reflection on the spread of 1st-cent. Christianity. The central character, John Cave, is a mortician from the state of Washington who comes south to California at the age of 30 and preaches that life on this earth is not worth living and that it is good to die. Suicide thus becomes a supremely virtuous act, provided that this "better way" is chosen for the proper reasons. Cave quickly develops a huge following, and millions express their belief in Cavesword or Cavesway, the new religion, created largely by publicity agents, which soon displaces Christianity. Cave himself writes nothing, but his brilliant follower, Paul Himmell, publicizes Cave's oral teachings. Three years after Cave's arrival in California Himmell arranges to have him murdered and cremated and his ashes spread over the United States from a jet plane. Subsequently a special Congressional hearing proclaims Cavesword as the national religion.

John Barth's *Giles Goat-Boy or, The Revised New Syllabus* (1966) is also a parodic novel. The long and complicated plot evolves in a hypothetical university world controlled by the heartless computer WESCAC. The Shepherd Emeritus, Enos Enoch, is analogous to Jesus, and George Giles, by imitating him, constitutes a secondary Jesus figure, whose mission in life is to redeem the university. The Virgin Mary, John the Baptist, Pontius Pilate, Mary Magdalene, and other biblical figures are represented by roughly comparable characters. This protracted and irreverent work constitutes in effect an undisguised literary caricature of Jesus and his followers.

An entirely different category of Jesus literature is devoted to stories of imaginary appearances of Jesus in modern times: early examples include an interpolated episode in Archibald McCowan's novel *Christ, the Socialist* (1894), William Stead's *If Christ Came to Chicago* (1894), and Edward Everett Hale's response to Stead, *If Christ Came to Boston* (1895). Jerome K. Jerome's play *The Passing of the Third Floor Back* (1907) presents a Jesus who lives in a London boardinghouse and works miracles for the benefit of his fellow lodgers. Perhaps the most meritorious contribution of this kind is Upton Sinclair's novel *They Call Me Carpenter* (1922), in which the narrator, having fallen unconscious in a church in Western City, dreams that Jesus steps down from a stained-glass window and enters public life under the name of Mr. Carpenter. He supports a strike by the local tailor's union and is befriended by a film star named Mary Magna. Later he is betrayed by an agent of the American Legion posing as one of his disciples and is ordered to appear in the court of Judge Ponty. Before the trial takes place, the narrator's dream comes to an end.

A few inspirational novels in English present heroes who deliberately attempt to pattern their lives on what they believe Jesus would have done had he been in their place. The two best-known examples of this genre are Mary Augusta Ward's *Robert Elsmere* (1888), the tale of an English vicar who leaves his parish to form a "New Brotherhood" of working men in the slums of London, and Charles Sheldon's *In His Steps, or What Would Jesus Do?* (1896), which tells of an American Congregationalist minister's campaign to persuade his followers not to do anything without first asking themselves "What would Jesus do?" Glenn Clark's sequel to this novel, entitled *What Would Jesus Do?* (1950), incorporates a similar moral ideal for readers living in the post–World War II era.

Jesus has also been the subject of a number of 20th-cent. radio plays, films, and television series. These generally make no pretense to literary worth, but among the exceptions are Dorothy Sayers's *The Man Born to Be King* (1943) for radio and Anthony Burgess's *Jesus of Nazareth* (1977) for television.

See also JESUS CHRIST, CHILDHOOD OF; PASSION, CROSS; SECOND ADAM; SON OF GOD; SON OF MAN; TEMPTATION OF CHRIST.

Bibliography. Birney, A. *The Literary Lives of Jesus: An International Bibliography* (1989); Brumm, U. "The Figure of Christ in American Literature." *PR* 24 (1957), 404-13; Cary, N. R. "*Christus Mundi:* The Jesus Figure in Post-colonial Literature." *Christianity and Literature* 41.1 (1991), 39-60; Detweiler, R. "Christ and the Christ Figure in American Fiction." *The Christian Scholar* 47 (1964), 111-24; Eastman, F. *Christ in the Drama: A Study of the Influence of Christ on the Drama of England and America* (1947); Erskine, J. *The Human Life of Jesus* (1945); Funk, R. W. *Jesus as Precursor* (1975); Goodspeed, E. J. *Modern Apocrypha* (1956); Grillmeier, A. *Christ in Christian Tradition* (1965); Johnston, A. F. "The Christ Figure in the Ministry Plays of the Four English Cycles." *DA* 28 (1967), 632-633A; Kee, H. C. *Jesus in History* (1970); Kissinger, W. *The Lives of Jesus: A Bibliography* (1985); Locke, W. R. "Novels on the Life of Jesus." *JBL* 18 (1950), 226-29; Mims, E. *The Christ of the Poets* (1969); Moseley, E. M. *Pseudonyms of Christ in the Modern Novel* (1962); Pals, D. L. *The Victorian "Lives" of Jesus* (1982); Pelikan, J. *Jesus Through the Centuries: His Place in the History of Culture* (1985); Wagenknecht, E., ed. *The Story of Jesus in the World's Literature* (1946); Ziolkowski, T. *Fictional Transfigurations of Jesus* (1972).

DAVID GREENWOOD
LARRY W. HURTADO

JESUS CHRIST, CHILDHOOD OF The Gospel of Luke contains the only canonical story of the childhood of Christ (Luke 2:41-52). The story of the twelve-year-old Jesus in the Temple establishes the spiritual and intellectual precocity of the child and asserts his physical and spiritual separation from his human parents. The immediate literary ancestry of this story may be found in ancient Jewish stories of Moses' youth, which portray him as exceptionally learned (Josephus, *Ant.* 2.9.6; Philo, *De vita Mosis,* 1.5) and the canonical story of the call of

Samuel (1 Sam. 3:1-18). The absence of additional stories about Jesus' childhood in the canonical literature allowed for the growth of legends which either support a particular Christology or reflect some forms of popular Christianity which delighted in wonders and portrayed the child Jesus wholly as a supernatural being and as a miniature thaumaturge.

Legendary expansions are found in the apocryphal gospels, some dating from as early as the 2nd cent. The Infancy Gospel of Thomas (E. Hennecke, *New Testament Apocrypha,* 1.388-401) narrates several childhood stories and culminates with Luke's Temple story. Its episodes show a playful boy who creates sparrows from clay and enlivens them, a magician who displays authority over natural laws by stretching a piece of wood miscut in Joseph's carpentry shop, an iconoclast who violates the Sabbath, and a capricious rascal who is responsible for the death of a teasing child whom he then miraculously restores to life. He taunts adults, especially teachers, into revealing the limits of their knowledge and leaves them in awe at his superior wisdom. Other apocryphal gospels, of gnostic origin, report miracles performed en route to Egypt as well as miracles performed in Egypt in which Mary's role is significant. A pseudo-Matthean collection of legends written to venerate the Virgin dates from the 8th-9th cent. (Hennecke, 1.406-13). It includes such miracle stories as the fall of the idols. The child often exasperates Joseph, but Mary unfailingly understands Christ's special mission (M. R. James, *The New Testament Apocrypha,* 73-79).

The early Church Fathers relied upon the four canonical Gospels for their understanding of Jesus' childhood. To accommodate Luke's emphasis that Jesus "grew in wisdom," Origen describes the humiliation of Christ in the flesh as analogous to that of an adult who willfully adopts baby tal': in order to communicate with a child.

Perhaps the most influential and elaborate medieval writing on the childhood of Christ is the *Meditationes Vitae Christi,* a work of 13th-cent. Franciscan piety attributed for some time to St. Bonaventure (Ragusa and Green, ed. and trans. [1961]). Like pseudo-Matthew, these meditations depict many of the childhood episodes in an Egyptian setting where the holy family spent seven years living in poverty. Though the *Meditations* includes the story of the fall of the idols, miracle stories do not dominate as they did in the early legends. During the stay in Egypt, Mary works at sewing and spinning, and Jesus, who serves as her messenger, is abused by quarrelsome women who engage Mary's services. Joseph works as a carpenter but plays a secondary role. After the holy family departs from Egypt, their saintly poverty is rewarded by gifts of money and a donkey for their journey. At home in Galilee, Jesus dutifully brings water to his mother from the well.

Nicholas Love's translation of the *Meditations, The Mirrour of the Blessed Lyf of Jesu Christ* (1410), is more properly thought of as an abridgment and paraphrase. Though his version of the sojourn in Egypt is told in less detail than the original, Love retains the story of the obedient child doing errands: "Christ was in all his deeds showing buxomnesse, lowenesse, and mekeness."

Several medieval carols include legendary narratives based on themes from Jesus' childhood: the scene with the doctors in the Temple (*Oxford Book of Carols* [1928], no. 72) and the picture of Jesus as a hard-working apprentice carpenter (no. 167). Others offer domestic legends: in one (no. 197), Jesus has a garden in which he grows roses, which he gives to the scornful children (the thorns he keeps for a crown), and in another, children taunt him and bring him to tears because he was born "in an ox's stall" (no. 56). A 15th-cent. carol (no. 39) includes a dialogue between the child Jesus and his mother in which he explains why he was laid in a manger and how she should rear him.

The 14th-cent. *Stanzaic Life of Christ* (EETS o.s. 166) details the story of Herod's tyranny and death but says little about the childhood of Christ. However, it preserves the notion that the childhood years were spent in Egypt and includes a stanza demonstrating Jesus' wisdom in the Temple.

The English mystery cycles rely on the dispute with the doctors in the Temple to develop the narrative from the Slaughter of the Innocents to the Baptism (e.g., York and Towneley cycles). Mary and Joseph are portrayed as bewildered, even ignorant. When they return to the Temple to retrieve Jesus, Joseph is reluctant to intrude, and Mary takes the lead, though she possesses no special gifts of understanding. There is nothing in the characterization of Jesus which suggests youthfulness. His youth is conveyed by the reception he receives from the doctors, who see him first as insubordinate and then as a prodigy.

Though the mystery plays do not include episodes relating the early childhood of Christ, the child Christ as sacrifice is implied typologically in plays portraying the sacrifice of Isaac (e.g., *The Chester Cycle*, EETS e.s. 115). The child-sacrifice motif is evidently linked to a tradition of miracles in which the Eucharist is transformed into the child Christ in flesh and blood. Examples of the host/child miracle are found in such homiletic writings as *Gesta Romanorum* (EETS e.s. 33), where a blaspheming judge receives a vision of the mutilated child Jesus bleeding from wounds inflicted by his false oaths, and in Corpus Christi poems such as "The Legend of the Sacrament" (*Vernon Manuscript*, EETS o.s. 98).

Though stories of Mary's miracles usually exclude the Christ child, "The Mary Miracles" of *The Vernon Manuscript* include a poem, "The Harlot's Prayer," in which the Christ child's harsh judgment of the harlot is turned to forgiveness after Mary's pleading. The same manuscript includes a paraphrase of Luke 2:41-52: "Disputison Bitween child Ihesu & the Maisters of Pe Law of Jewus." It borrows from the apocryphal stories which show the

child's knowledge of the spiritual meaning of the alphabet, and it includes pseudo-Matthew's story of the rescue of the boy in the tower found in the apocryphal Gospel of Thomas (James, 69).

The English humanists, who emphasize the development of the individual through education, celebrate Christ's humanity in his intellectual triumph in the Temple. His is the perfect example of a studious childhood, according to Erasmus ("The Whole Duty of Youth," *Colloquies* [1965], 32-34).

For John Donne, the Temple episode provides a focus for meditative consideration of Christ's childhood. Readers, like Joseph, register surprise that "a shallow seeming child should deeply know" ("La Corona," 4). Donne defines the episode in the Temple as the "morning" of Christ's divine work. Richard Crashaw's approach to meditation has its roots in St. Bernard's devotion to the humanity of the Christ child. He follows apocryphal tradition by associating the childhood stories closely with Mary. In a series of Latin poems based on Luke 2:41-50, Crashaw reflects on Mary's fear that her child will not return to her.

In "To his Saviour, a Child; a Present, by a Child," Robert Herrick creates a scene in which a child presents a flower and a whistle to the little savior. In return the child anticipates receiving a kiss. The gift of a whistle introduces a touch of childhood realism into a poem otherwise governed by adult sentiments (cf. Christina Rossetti, "In the Bleak Mid-Winter"). Henry Vaughan does not invoke the Christ child of legend. In "The Search" he looks for Jesus everywhere, even in the Temple among the doctors. His unsuccessful inquiries are answered by the singing voice of Christ, a spiritual, cherubic presence like that of the popular *scola cordis* emblem books.

Francis Quarles joins his poems to emblems by Hugo Hermannus; together they portray Christ as a childlike cherub (*Emblemata* [1658]). Addressing the Virgin Mother, Quarles imagines her joy in seeing the child grow, watching "him nuzzle at thy Virgin brest. . . . To see him diddle up and downe the roome!" (221). In this poem based on Cant. 8:1, Quarles envisions himself caring for Christ, his younger brother, in a nursery appointed with a go-cart and a cradle. Recusant emblem books which develop the idea of the child Christ portray him in various allegorical roles — searching with a lantern for a lost soul, knocking at the door of a heart, singing from a songbook, and bleeding as a fountain to provide sustenance for a sinner. They evidence little interest in either legendary stories of Jesus' childhood or canonical accounts of his infancy (e.g., *Vis Amoris Jesu* [1624] and *The Devout Hart* [H. Hawkins, 1634]).

In *The Great Exemplar* Jeremy Taylor imagines the Christ child employed by his "supposed father" in carpentry, an example of humility and poverty. Taylor appreciates "the smallness, improbability and indifference of His first beginnings," which in no way diminish the grandeur of his full divinity (*Works* [1847-54], 2.159).

Jesus speaks of his childhood in the opening section of John Milton's *Paradise Regained* (1671). He recalls how "no childish play / To me was pleasing" (1.203) because he was "born to promote all truth." He tells how at age 12 he went to the Temple and was "admir'd by all" at the same time that he felt his growing desire to take on his enemy, Satan. Knowledgeable of his mission and the epitome of good sense, Mary subdues his emerging passions. "High are thy thoughts / O Son, but nourish them and let them soar" (1.229).

Christopher Smart is unusual among 18th-cent. imaginative writers, who as a group show little enthusiasm for the childhood of Christ. The *Parables of Our Lord and Savior Jesus Christ* (1768) includes a verse paraphrase, *"Christ* disputing among the Doctors," which interprets this childhood event as the beginning of the revelation of Christ's commission. Smart emphasizes Christ's separation from his family and the ignorance of his parents and does not attribute special qualities to the child Jesus.

Among William Blake's illustrations of biblical subjects, a small watercolor titled *Christ in the Carpenter Shop: The Humiliation of the Savior* has been preserved. The youthful Christ holds a pair of compasses, perhaps a symbol of creative imagination, as he watches Joseph. Two of Blake's tempera paintings associated with the childhood of Christ have been lost: *The Christ Child Taught by the Virgin to Read* and *Christ with the Doctors in the Temple*. The latter subject is taken up in *The Everlasting Gospel* (1818), where Jesus emphatically renounces his mundane human parents:

No earthly parents I confess
My heavenly Father's business!
Ye understand not what I say,
And angry, force me to obey.

Emily Dickinson considers the puzzle of the early life of Christ in "Dust is the open Secret" (ed. Johnson, no. 153), in which she associates the mysteries of his childhood with the ultimate mysteries of time and death:

Nobody knew "His Father" —
Never was a Boy —
Hadn't any playmates,
Or, "Early history" —

The question of when the Virgin Mary understood her son's sacrificial mission informs Dante Gabriel Rossetti's poem "Ave." He imagines the Christ child as "He tottered round thy knee," as they enjoyed Passover together in his boyhood years, and as he left the household toward independence. Rossetti concludes that Mary, because of her great sensitivity, understood the meanings in these prefiguring events.

Sara Teasdale's "In the Carpenter's Shop" (*Rivers to the Sea* [1935]) depicts Jesus and Joseph working together at carpentry while Mary doubts that the angel's words of promise to her will ever be realized. Carl Sandburg in "Child" recognizes the humanity of Christ, whose childhood innocence allows him to understand the "questions / Found under running water for all children" (*Chicago Poems* [1916]).

In "A Journey to Jerusalem" (1940), a short play in three acts, Maxwell Anderson uses the setting of 1st-cent. Palestine to represent Hitler's occupation of Poland. He parallels the 20th-cent. Holocaust with the Slaughter of the Innocents, the most significant political event of Jesus' childhood. Anderson casts Jesus as a busy childhood reader tutored by his father, a contrast with the traditional view that Mary was his teacher and confidant.

Fictionalized biographies of Jesus in the 20th cent. often include childhood material. Robert Graves in *King Jesus* (1946) dramatizes the childhood of Christ as taking place in Egypt, the return to Galilee occurring in Jesus' twelfth year. Graves fleshes out the childhood years with selected stories derived from the apocryphal gospels, which emphasize precocity and playfulness, and he recasts the miracle stories to emphasize the humanity of Christ. The Temple story is expanded to take into account rumors of his illegitimate birth.

The Gospel According to Joe (1974), a somewhat whimsical novella by A. R. Gurney, presents the childhood of Jesus from the point of view of Joseph, a 20th-cent. hippy-style craftsman. Jesus is known at school as a dreamer upset by violence and injustice but also as a fair ball player with a "good crouch and a good peg to second." He brings to his father's pedestrian talents as a carpenter an artistry which distinguishes their collaborative work.

Bibliography. Brown, R. E. *The Birth of the Messiah* (1979); Hennecke, E. *New Testament Apocrypha.* Ed. W. Schneemelcher. Trans. R. M. Wilson et al. (1963); James, M. R., trans. *The Apocryphal New Testament* (1924); Marcus, L. S. *Childhood and Cultural Despair: A Theme and Variations in Seventeenth-Century Literature* (1978); "The Christ Child as Sacrifice: A Medieval Tradition and the Corpus Christi Plays." *Speculum* 48 (1973), 491-509.

FAYE PAULI WHITAKER

JEZEBEL Jezebel, wife of Israel's wicked King Ahab, initially appears as sponsor of a powerful political alliance entered into by the ruling families of Israel and Sidon (1 Kings 16:29-33). Their connivance in the worship of the Canaanite god Baal forms the backdrop to the Elijah cycle of stories. Jezebel herself reappears in 1 Kings 18–19 as the persecutor of the Hebrew prophets and the deadly opponent of Elijah the Tishbite. The most notorious evidence of her wickedness is the "contrived" murder of Naboth, which she orchestrates in order to acquire his vineyard for Ahab (1 Kings 21:1-16). This ruthless crime, which elicits Elijah's pronouncement of a divine curse upon Jezebel and Ahab (1 Kings 21:17-24), is seen as the worst of Jezebel's atrocities, receiving more attention than her slaying of the prophets or her reinstitution of paganism.

Elijah's gruesome prophecy that "dogs [shall] eat the flesh of Jezebel: And the carcass of Jezebel shall be as dung upon the face of the field" (2 Kings 9:36-37) is realized in Jehu's assassination of her. Arriving in Jezreel, years after Ahab's death at Ramoth-gilead (1 Kings 22:29-38), Jehu is taunted by a painted and adorned Jezebel. He solicits aid from the eunuchs attending her, two or three of whom quickly obey his command to throw her out of a window to her death. While Jehu feasts, Jezebel's deserted corpse is trampled by horses and eaten by dogs, until only her skull, the palms of her hands, and the soles of her feet remain (2 Kings 9:30-37).

Ginzberg (*LJ* 4.189) records the tradition that despite her sinfulness, Jezebel showed sympathy for the joy or sorrow of those in marriage or funeral processions. The parts of her body used in these occasions — head, hands, and feet — were preserved thus as testaments to her capacity for kindness. "Jezebel" appears in the NT (Rev. 2:20-23), the name given to a "prophetess" who teaches false doctrine and encourages immorality.

Many aspects of Jezebel's character are highlighted by the Church Fathers. St. Methodius, in his "Banquet of the Ten Virgins," represents her as lust incarnate and suggests that it was Jezebel's desire, rather than political persecution, from which Elijah fled. St. Jerome (*Ep.* 122) notes Jezebel's refusal to repent: "Ahab's sin and Jezebel's were the same; yet because Ahab repented, his punishment was postponed so as to fall upon his sons, while Jezebel persisting in her wickedness met her doom then and there." Both St. Ambrose and Aphrahat see Jezebel as prefiguring the "Synagogue" which would persecute Christ. In the Nisibene Hymns, St. Ephraim Syrus equates Jezebel with hell: "Sheol was not indeed Sheol, but its semblance: Jezebel was the true Sheol, who devoured the just" (no. 67). St. Augustine, in his letter "To Vincentius," contrasts Jezebel's murder of the Hebrew prophets with Elijah's slaying of the prophets of Baal (1 Kings 18): "They were not alike in the motive of regard to the people's welfare, — the one being inflated by the lust of power, the other inflamed by love."

St. Isidore of Seville and many subsequent commentators focus on Jezebel's fateful reduction to dung. This aspect of her history is expanded in the Renaissance writings of Picinelli and Lapide, who see in Jezebel's story a reminder of human mortality and of the precarious nature of fame. Both note also a similarity between Jezebel's demise and that of Isabella of Spain, whose decaying remains were viewed with horror by Franciscus Borgia (Picinelli, *Mundus Symbolicus* [1694; 1976], 1.208; Lapide, *Comm. in Scripturam Sacram* [1868], 4.43).

When Andrew Aguecheek, in Shakespeare's *Twelfth Night,* refers to Malvolio as "Jezebel" (2.5.42), the con-

notation is as much one of political aspiration and intrigue as it is of lust; Congreve's mention of Jezebel in "The Old Batchelour" (4.4.161-66) has similar implications. Crashaw, in "Sospetto d'Herode," associates Jezebel with such wicked and bloodthirsty women as Medea and Circe (43.337-39), while Shelley, in "Charles the First" (1.66-70), uses Jezebel in a slighting reference to "the papist queen." One of the most noteworthy Jezebel figures in English literature is Charlotte Brontë's Bertha Mason Rochester, who incarnates the notorious lust and promiscuity of Ahab's consort.

For Browning's "Pietro of Abano" Jezebel is a painted, immoral woman (213-16). G. K. Chesterton notes his contemporaries' tendency to equate "the Modern Girl" who wears makeup with lascivious Jezebel (*Sidelights on New London and Newer York; and Other Essays* [1932], 28). The name has in fact become a term of derision, denoting a wicked, lascivious, or "painted" woman. Thus, James Joyce in *Finnegans Wake* refers to a "jezebel" or an immoral girl, and Faulkner, in *Light in August,* makes repeated use of the name as a term of abuse delivered by religiously fanatical men. The biblical Jezebel's political machinations have largely escaped notice in contemporary literature.

See also AHAB; ELIJAH.

Bibliography. Gray, J. *I and II Kings: A Commentary* (1964); Johnston, E. B. "Jezebel." *ISBE,* rev. ed. vol. 2 (1982), 1057-59.   MARNIE PARSONS

JOAB *See* ABNER; ABSALOM; DAVID.

JOACHIM *See* ANNE.

JOASH Two OT figures bear the name Joash. The first of these was the eighth king of Judah (ca. 837-800 B.C.), who was hidden by his aunt when his grandmother Athaliah sought to annihilate the royal line upon the death of her son Ahaziah (2 Kings 11:1-2; 2 Chron. 22:10-12). When acclaimed king at the age of seven, Joash had Athaliah executed (2 Kings 11:7-20; 2 Chron. 23:12-15). Although he rebuilt the Temple (2 Kings 12:5-16; 2 Chron. 24:4-14), he let pagan practices intrude, for which he was reprimanded by the prophet Zechariah (2 Chron. 24:20-22), whom he had executed. After trying to fend off the invading Syrians by offering a bribe from the Temple funds (2 Kings 12:18-19), he was assassinated by his own officers (2 Kings 12:20-21; 2 Chron. 24:25-26). A rabbinical tradition saw this evil as befalling him because of his claiming deity (Exod. Rab. 8.2).

The second Joash (also called Jehoash) was the twelfth king of Israel (ca. 801-786 B.C.; 2 Kings 13:10), who had to pay tribute to Assyria (S. Page, *Iraq* 30 [1968], 139ff.). He was challenged by Syria (2 Kings 13:22-25) and Judah under Amaziah, but was able to sack Jerusalem (2 Kings 14:8-14; 2 Chron. 25:17-24).   DAVID W. BAKER

JOB The book of Job (one of the OT wisdom books, placed in the Vg and KJV after the book of Esther and before Psalms) recounts how Job, a perfectly righteous and extraordinarily prosperous man, is afflicted by Satan, who instigates a wager with God about how Job would behave if he were to suffer material losses. God allows Satan to kill Job's ten children and take away all his wealth, but Job remains firm in his devotion to God. Next God allows Satan to smite Job "with sore boils from the sole of his foot unto his crown" (2:8). Despite his wife's advice to "curse God and die" (2:9), Job accepts his lot without disowning God. Three friends — Eliphaz, Bildad, and Zophar — come from afar to comfort him. He enters into a debate with them, for the most part lamenting his fate and protesting against God's injustice, while they advise him that his suffering and misfortune must be attributed to some sin on his part (3:1-31:37). A fourth comforter, Elihu, subsequently appears and rebukes the other three, offering his own answer to the mystery of Job's suffering. God then speaks to Job "out of the whirlwind" (38:1), first rebuking and then vindicating him, and chiding the three comforters. Neither Elihu nor Satan is mentioned again. Job is rewarded with "twice as much as he had before" (42:10).

Within the Bible, Job is remembered and commended principally for his righteousness (Ezek. 14:12-14) and patience (Tob. 2:10-23; James 5:11). The latter virtue is stressed more in the LXX than in the original Hebrew; Job's wife's role in the story is also expanded (2:7-9, 11), and other minor details of the plot are modified. The pseudepigraphal Testament of Job, a Greek work of the 1st cent. B.C., alters the plot even more drastically, adding characters (serving women, physicians) and greatly expanding the roles of Satan, Job's wife, and his daughters.

In medieval Christian exegesis Job figures as a paragon of patience, an *athleticus Dei* or *miles Christi* figure, and an antitype of Christ. He appears in all these roles in St. Gregory the Great's influential *Moralia in Iob,* a work heavily indebted to St. Jerome (*Commentarii in librum Job* [PL 26.655-850]), St. Ambrose (*De interpellatione Job et David* [PL 14.797-850]), and St. Augustine (*De patientia* [PL 40.615-16]). Gregory's *Moralia* dominates almost all subsequent medieval treatment of the book of Job, including those of St. Thomas Aquinas and Nicholas of Lyra. In light of Job 19:25-27 ("For I know that my redeemer liveth . . .") Gregory is typical of medieval commentators in regarding Job as a prophet of the general resurrection of the dead. Jerome, Gregory, and others discuss the verse structure of the book of Job (most think it to be in hexameters); some go further and classify it as epic or drama. Protestant exegetical tradition, as represented in Calvin (*Sermons on the Book of Job* [1563]) and Beza (*Iobus . . . Illustratus* [1589]), is largely consistent with that of the Middle Ages.

In the matins of the Office of the Dead (the *"Dirige"*) of the High Middle Ages, nine lessons from the book of Job alternate with readings from the Psalms. Job himself has a place in medieval liturgy as patron saint of sufferers from worms, leprosy, various skin diseases, venereal disease, and melancholy.

Literary representations draw upon all of these biblical, apocryphal, and ecclesiastical sources, as well as Prudentius's influential portrait of Job in the *Psychomachia.* Job appears briefly in Cynewulf's *Ascension (Christ II),* in the OE *Phoenix,* and in a homily by Aelfric. In the 12th cent., Peter Riga's *Aurora* treats the story of Job in 576 Latin hexameters, mainly a précis of passages from the *Moralia.* Peter of Blois's prose *Compendium in Iob* (1173), also indebted to the *Moralia,* was translated into French in the late 13th cent. as *L'hystore Job.* In ME there are three different versions of a 15th-cent. work called *Pety Iob* (also known as *Lessons of the Dirige*), a paraphrase and elaboration of the verses from Job in the matins of the Office of the Dead. Other ME treatments of the Job legend include an early-15th-cent. verse paraphrase of the biblical narrative (indebted in places to the *Pety Iob*), and a brief late-15th-cent. "Life of Job" in rhymeroyal (with affinities to the Testament of Job). In addition there are medieval Portuguese and Middle High German paraphrases of Job, a poem in Italian (ca. 1495) by Giuliano Dati of Florence, and a popular 15th-cent. French play, *La pacience de Job,* which freely combines elements from earlier tradition.

Chaucer's Clerk (*Canterbury Tales,* 4.932-34) and Wife of Bath (3.433-36) both make reference to Job in novel, ironic contexts. Marlowe, Shakespeare, and other Elizabethans refer to Job's proverbial patience and there are, in the 17th cent., a number of verse reworkings of the book of Job. The first major English author to use the narrative in an extensive way is Milton, whose *Paradise Regained* (1671) not only contains unmistakable echoes of the book of Job but is also, as Lewalski's landmark study (1966) has shown, self-consciously modeled upon it. *Samson Agonistes* also has strong affinities with the Job story.

Blake's *Illustrations of the Book of Job* (1825) occupies a pivotal place in the history of the Job story and its influence on English literature. Stressing the propriety of Job's rebellious questioning of God's justice, Blake refashioned the patient Job of earlier tradition into a romantic rebel. Shelley, who at one time apparently intended to compose a "lyrical drama" based on the book of Job, expresses his own somewhat Blakean view of the narrative in *Prometheus Unbound* (1820). Tennyson actually learned Hebrew in order to translate the book of Job, though he never achieved his goal.

Of the many plays based on the Job story which have appeared in the 20th cent., Archibald MacLeish's *J.B.* (1958) is the best known and most significant. In it Job has become a modern businessman who suffers a series of catastrophes and who finds redemption in the love of his wife and of God. Robert Frost's *Masque of Reason* (1945) is a wry dramatic poem in which the theological paradoxes of the book of Job are held up to Voltairean ridicule. I. A. Richards's *Job's Comforting* (1970) is a bitterly ironic play in verse made up of passages from the biblical narrative "re-arranged, and with a single sentence added." In the spirit of Blake, Richards rejects the easy reconciliation of God and man at the end of the biblical story.

Since 1970 numerous short poems based on various facets of the Job story have appeared (favorite topics being the relationship between Job and his wife and his wife's point of view on the story). Some critics find deep connections between the book of Job and absurdist drama, in particular the plays of Ionesco, Adamov, and Beckett, but the relationship may be one of analogy rather than of a source to its immediate derivatives. In either case, whether directly or indirectly, the book of Job — which Tennyson called "the greatest poem of ancient and modern times" — continues to exert a profound influence on the literary culture of our time.

See also JOB'S COMFORTERS.

Bibliography. Allen, M. J. "The Book of Job in Middle English Literature (1100-1500)." Ph.D., King's College, London, 1971; Besserman, L. *The Legend of Job in the Middle Ages* (1979); Datz, G. *Die Gestalt Hiobs in der kirchlichen Exegese und der 'Arme Heinrich' Hartmanns von Aue* (1973); Fulton, P. R. "Milton's Use of the Book of Job in *Paradise Regained* and *Samson Agonistes.*" *DAI* 44 (1983), 1092A; Greenberg, M. "Job." In Alter, R., and F. Kermode, *The Literary Guide to the Bible* (1987), 283-304; Jung, C. *Answer to Job*. Trans. R. F. C. Hull (1954); Labin, L. L. "The Whale and the Ash-Heap: Transfigurations of Jonah and Job in Modern American Fiction — Frost, MacLeish, and Vonnegut." *DAI* 41 (1981), 4713A; Levenson, J. D. *The Book of Job in Its Time and in the Twentieth Century* (1972); Lewalski, B. *Milton's Brief Epic: The Genre, Meaning, and Art of Paradise Regained* (1966); May, J. E. "Early Eighteenth-Century Paraphrases of the Book of Job." In *Man, God, and Nature in the Enlightenment*. Ed. D. C. Mell, Jr., T. E. D. Braun, and L. M. Palmer (1988), 151-61; Neher, A. "The Theme of Job in Modern Jewish and World Literature." *Ariel* 42 (1975), 66-76; Siger, L. "The Image of Job in the Renaissance." Unpubl. diss. (1960); Stock, E. "'Masque of Reason' and 'J. B.': Two Treatments of the Book of Job." *MD* 3 (1961), 378-86; Stout, J. "Melville's Use of the Book of Job." *NCF* 25 (1970), 69-83; Vogler, T. A. "Eighteenth-Century Logology and the Book of Job." *Religion and Literature* 20 (1988), 25-47; Whedbee, J. W. "The Comedy of Job." *Semeia* 7 (1977), 1-39.   LAWRENCE BESSERMAN

JOB'S COMFORTERS   In the second chapter of Job, after Job has lost all his belongings, his family, and his health, three friends come "to mourn with him and to comfort him." After sitting silent with him for seven days and seven nights, they try to convince Job, in three rounds

of discussion (Job 3–31), that he has deserved his misfortunes. Job's judgment in 16:2, "miserable comforters are ye all" (lit. "comforters of trouble"), sets the tone for subsequent interpretation of them.

The eldest of the friends, Eliphaz of Teman, emphasizes man's iniquity; Bildad the Shuhite stresses God's justice, and Zophar from Naamah enlarges on God's inscrutability. In the end, after they have given up talking to Job and after a fourth man, Elihu, has continued the discussion, the friends are reproached by God for not having "spoken the thing which is right" (42:7, 8). They are told to make a burnt offering, and God accepts Job's prayer on their behalf (42:9, 10).

Talmudic legend (Ginzberg, *LJ* 2.236-37; 3.356) makes the three comforters cousins of Job; all four cousins are said to be kings of lands 300 miles apart from one another and descendants of Nahor, the brother of Abraham. They each wear crowns adorned with pictures of the other three, and when adversity or misfortune comes upon one of them, the others immediately perceive alteration in the picture of that cousin.

Medieval commentary is typically less interested in the three comforters than in Job's response to them and his discussion with God. Standard medieval views on the comforters were heavily influenced by St. Gregory's *Moralia in Iob*, 2.13, which presents the comforters as well intended but lacking in restraint, guilty of the reproach, "Cursed be he that does the work of the Lord negligently" (Jer. 48:10). Commenting on Job 16:2, Gregory applies the point especially to the counseling of fellow Christians, observing that "elect persons, even when they are bereft of temporal glory, do not lose the forcibleness of interior judgment," and adding that the "windy words" of the comforters (v. 3) serve only "the end of temporal inflating, rather than the end of righteousness."

For Calvin, in his *Sermons on Job*, the comforters are "like devils," torturing Job "worse than he has been tortured before." Though they have good intentions, they lack love and so, according to 1 Cor. 13, all their efforts are in vain. St. Thomas More's Anthony suggests that the alternative to the behavior of the "burdenouse & hevy comfortours" is to tell an afflicted person "to stand & percever still in the confession of his faith," so that "all his hole payne shall tourne all into glorye" (*Dialogue of Comfort*, 1.10).

Burton, in his *Anatomy of Melancholy* (3.4.1.1), compares the comforters to the "Schismaticks" and "Hereticks" of his day: "they speak not, they think not, they write not well of God, and as they ought." Shakespeare's allusion to the comforters in *Othello* 4.2.48-57 is indirect. Othello suggests that his lot is harder than Job's. He could bear becoming "the fixed figure for the time of scorn / To point his slow unmoving finger at!" — but he could not bear Desdemona's faithlessness. Sir Thomas Browne echoes Calvin's verdict when he calls the "oblique expostulations" of Job's friends "a deeper injury than the downe-right blows of the Devill" (*Religio Medici*, 2.5; cf. *Pseudodoxia Epidemica*, 7.8).

Dryden speculates on the comforters' later actions: "The friends of Job, who rail'd at him before, / Came cap in hand when he had three times more" ("Prologue to His Royal Highness," 24-25). One of the few positive evaluations of their behavior occurs at the beginning of Defoe's *Roxana*. The heroine, left by her husband and facing destitution, is visited by two women: "They sat down like *Job's* three Comforters, and said not one Word to me for a great while, but both of them cry'd as fast, and as heartily as I did." Swift's allusion (in *Ingenious Conversation*, 3) is disparaging, as is Fielding's in *Tom Jones*. Tom receives a letter from Sophia that asks him not to visit her again: "This Letter administered the same Kind of Consolation to poor *Jones,* which *Job* formerly received from his Friends" (14.3).

Cowper, in his poem "Retirement," characterizes Job's comforters and those of his own time as

> Blest, rather curst, with hearts that never feel,
> Kept snug in caskets of close-hammer'd steel,
> With mouths made only to grin wide and eat,
> And minds that deem derided pain a treat. (307-10)

In a curiously mistaken reference, Byron's *Don Juan* mentions Job's "two friends." The misanthropic lesson Byron offers is that they are "but bad pilots when the weather's rough" (14.48). Blake's *Illustrations of the Book of Job* depict the development of genuinely sympathetic friends into accusers.

A man named Bildad is half-owner of Captain Ahab's ship *Pequod* in Melville's *Moby-Dick*. As N. Wright (1949) has observed, "He seems to practice piety and to aim at the conversion of all his sailors in order to insure a prosperous voyage for the *Pequod*." The ironic depiction of his pragmatism recalls the utilitarianism of his biblical counterpart (cf. Melville's comparison of the ambiguous characters Old Plain Talk and Old Prudence to Eliphaz and Bildad in China Aster's story, chap. 40 of *The Confidence-Man*). The economic implications of the friends' speeches are also recognized by John Ruskin. In his introduction to *The Bible of Amiens,* he calls Zophar's second speech the "leading piece of political economy."

In Anthony Trollope's *Barchester Towers* (2.17), Mary Bold is praised for not being triumphant when her sister-in-law describes her involvement in all the intrigues she had already been warned against: " 'I told you so, I told you so!' is the croak of a true Job's comforter. But Mary, when she found her friend lying in her sorrow and scraping herself with potsherds, forbore to argue and to exult." Fulkerson, in W. D. Howells's *A Hazard of New Fortunes*, feels he is not treated so kindly. He reacts to the irony of Beaton by saying: "Go on, Bildad. Like to sprinkle a few ashes over my boils?" (4.9). Hardy's poem "In the Seventies" has as a motto the Vg version of Job

12:4: *"Qui deridetur ab amico suo sicut ego."* The poem thus identifies as Job's comforters those friends of the poet's who did not take his literary ambitions seriously.

Frost's Job, in *A Masque of Reason,* contemptuously calls his comforters "that committee"; God continues in a jocular tone:

> I saw you had no fondness for committees.
> Next time you find yourself pressed onto one
> For the revision of the Book of Prayer
> Put that in if it isn't in already:
> Deliver us from committees. 'Twill remind me.
> (368-73)

Equally humorous is the reference to Bildad in a riddle in Carl Sandburg's *The People, Yes* (46): his cognomen "Shuhite" ("shoe-height") marks him as one of the shortest people in the Bible.

Samuel Beckett compares the appearance of his character Murphy, who is "on the jobpath" (an obvious pun), to Blake's picture of Bildad. The narrator remarks that Bildad is "but a fragment of Job, as Zophar and the others are fragments of Job. The only thing Murphy was seeking was what he had not ceased to seek from the moment of his being strangled into a state of respiration — the best of himself " (*Murphy,* chap. 5). If such psychologizing reflects 20th-cent. thinking, Archibald MacLeish's *J.B.* may be said to do so even more systematically. It attempts to show how the role of modern comforters differs from that of the biblical ones: "Where Job's comforters undertook to persuade him, against the evidence of his own inner conviction, that he WAS guilty, ours attempts to persuade us that we are not . . ." (MacLeish). *J.B.*'s Eliphaz is a modern scientist (he wears an intern's jacket) who tries to explain guilt away as an illusion. Bildad, in turn, a leftist park-bench orator, calls it a "sociological accident," and Zophar, who wears "the wreck of a clerical collar" and seems to represent theology, puts the blame for mankind's sin on the Creator. All three fail to understand the Distant Voice of God when it speaks to J.B.

Harvey Gotham, the stricken hero of Muriel Spark's *The Only Problem,* considers the comforters "very patient and considerate" in their trying to relieve Job's suffering: They keep him talking like an analyst's patient on the couch (chap. 3). On the other hand, Gotham sees the Job narrative as teaching "the futility of friendship in times of trouble. That is perhaps not a reflection on friends but on friendship. Friends mean well, or make as if they do. But friendship itself is made for happiness, not trouble" (chap. 9).

See also CURSE GOD AND DIE; JOB.

Bibliography. Ellison, H. *From Tragedy to Triumph* (1958); MacLeish, A. "About a Trespass on a Monument," *New York Times* (Dec. 7, 1958), 2.5, 7; Robinson, T. *Job and His Friends* (1954).   MANFRED SIEBALD

JOEL About the prophet Joel, the son of Pethuel and the second of the minor OT prophets, virtually nothing is known, either from the book which bears his name or from the rest of the Bible. The book of Joel, apparently written after the fall of Judah in the 6th cent. B.C., is a forceful statement of hope and aspiration out of disaster and despair, a story about the destruction and restoration of God's people to be told to future generations (1:3). In the common prophetic imagery of a locust plague, the author paints a terrible picture of the "day of the LORD" (1:1–2:11). This vivid account is followed by a call to repentance and a promise of restored abundance of the land (2:12-27). In typical prophetic fashion, Joel follows the punishment and restoration of God's people with the judgment of God upon the nations and his blessing upon Israel "in the last days" (2:28–3:21). This section contains the most familiar passage in the book, that concerning a pouring out of God's Spirit "upon all flesh" so that "your sons and your daughters shall prophesy, your old men shall dream dreams, your young men shall see visions" (2:28). The passage itself conveys images of despair and disaster as well as those of hope and happiness. The dreams and visions of fire, blood, smoke, and darkness (vv. 30-31) portend destruction for those who do not call upon the Lord. To those who do call upon him, however, the visions promise prosperity and everlasting blessing.

Joel 2:28-32 is quoted by the apostle Peter in his Pentecostal sermon (Acts 2:17-21) as part of a call to repentance. It serves in this context both to refer to the Crucifixion of Christ and the inauguration of the last days and to anticipate the imminent universal judgment. The predicted "pouring out of the Spirit" is realized in the disciples' glossolalia, a sign that the "day of the Lord" has come and evidence that the end of the world is near.

In Dryden's *Absalom and Achitophel* Achitophel urges Absalom to rebel against his father, David, by (anachronistically) applying Joel's words to his surrogate, calling him "the young men's vision, and the old men's dream." Washington Irving writes of his legendary valley in "The Legend of Sleepy Hollow" which anyone who lingers long in that place, "however wide awake they may have been before . . . they are sure, in a little time, to inhale the witching influence of the air, and begin to grow imaginative, to dream dreams and see apparitions."

Joel's prophecy is redolent with eschatological phraseology (e.g., "the day of the LORD") and apocalyptic imagery showing forth the judgment at the end of the world. But its immediate purpose, reflecting a local manifestation of God's judgment in the form of a locust plague, is to call the nation to repentance and so to reverse the fortunes of Judah and Israel. Another of the book's most memorable and frequently cited passages concerns God's promise of restoration: "And I will restore unto you the years that the locust hath eaten, the cankerworm, and the caterpillar, and the palmerworm, my great army which I sent among you" (2:25). Besides giving rise to A. E.

Holdworth's *The Years That the Locust Hath Eaten* (1897), the phrase has become proverbial. Referring to survivors of the Great War, J. B. Priestley asks, "And who shall restore to them the years that the locust hath eaten?" (*English Journey,* chap. 6). In *The Web and the Rock,* Thomas Wolfe writes of a "heart, as the heart of the king, inscrutable, and in it was all the knowledge of countless obscure lives and forty thousand days, and of all the years that the locust hath eaten" (chap. 38).

See also OLD MEN DREAM DREAMS; PENTECOST.

DAVID NOEL FREEDMAN
BRUCE WILLOUGHBY

JOHN THE BAPTIST The appearance of John the Baptist in the wilderness signals "the beginning of the gospel" (Mark 1:1, 4; Acts 1:22; 10:37). Luke is unique in furnishing an account of John's birth which parallels that of Jesus (Luke 1, 2). John was of priestly descent, son of the aged Zacharias and Elisabeth (Luke 1:5-7). When the angel Gabriel's annunciation was questioned by Zacharias, he was afflicted with dumbness (Luke 1:8-23), which did not depart until after the birth of John, an event which Zacharias was inspired to hail in the words of the Benedictus (Luke 1:57-79). Mary's visit to her cousin Elisabeth ties the two stories together (Luke 1:39-56). A single verse alludes to John's infancy and youth (Luke 1:80).

In the Synoptics John is an ascetic figure whose dress recalls the ancient prophets (Matt. 3:4; Mark 1:6). He preaches the coming judgment (Matt. 3:7-10, 12; Luke 3:7-9, 17) and summons the people to a "baptism of repentance for the remission of sins" (Mark 1:4), hence his title "the Baptist." A short summary of John's ethical teaching is peculiar to Luke (3:10-14). John proclaims the coming one, mightier than he, the agent of God's judgment who will baptize "with the Holy Ghost and with fire" (Matt. 3:11, 12; Luke 3:15-18; Mark 1:7, 8 omits "with fire").

Jesus is baptized by John in the Jordan. Mark simply states this as a fact (1:9); Luke glosses over it (3:21); in Matthew Jesus assures John that "it becometh us to fulfil all righteousness" (Matt. 3:13-15); the Fourth Gospel has John refer to the incident indirectly (John 1:32, 33).

The NT presents John as the forerunner of Jesus and identifies Jesus with the coming one prophesied by John, although in the Synoptics and especially in Mark this is implied rather than stated. Matthew and Luke depict John near the end of his life as unsure of Jesus' identity and sending disciples to ask, "Art thou he that should come, or do we look for another?" (Matt. 11:2-6; Luke 7:18-23). In the Fourth Gospel, on the other hand, John explicitly hails Jesus as "the Lamb of God, which taketh away the sin of the world" (1:29, 36), the one who baptizes with the Holy Spirit (1:33), and "the Son of God" (1:34). John is repeatedly subordinated to Jesus, who is the "true Light" to whom John merely bears witness (John 1:6-8), the Bridegroom, to whom he is merely an attendant (John 3:29), the one who "is preferred before me: for he was before me" (John 1:15, 30), and who must increase while John decreases (John 3:29, 30).

Several sayings indicate Jesus' high opinion of John (Matt. 11:7-19; 21:23-27, 32; Mark 11:27-33; Luke 7:24-35; 16:16; 20:1-8; cf. John 5:35). Mark (1:2; 9:13) suggests the identification of John with the returning Elijah who is to "prepare the way" (see Mal. 3:1; 4:5, 6; Sir. 48:9, 10); Luke asserts this in guarded fashion (1:17); Matthew makes it quite explicit (11:14; 17:13); but in the Fourth Gospel John denies that he is Elijah (1:21) and claims only to be the voice crying in the wilderness (cf. Matt. 3:3; Mark 1:3; Luke 3:4; and see Isa. 40:3).

Only the Fourth Gospel mentions a period when Jesus' and John's ministries overlap (John 3:23, 24). John's arrest by Herod Antipas, his imprisonment and death are narrated in Mark 6:17-29 (cf. Matt. 14:3-12). John attracted a circle of disciples (Matt. 11:2; Luke 7:18; John 3:25; 4:1) who practiced prayer (Luke 11:1) and fasting (Matt. 9:14; Mark 2:18; Luke 5:33). The Fourth Gospel stresses the transfer of allegiance of such disciples from John to Jesus (John 1:35-40), but Acts 19:1-7 suggests the continuance of a "Baptist" sect after John's death.

For writers in the Middle Ages as for the Fathers of the Church, John is the model ascetic whose words and example rebuke the worldly. His life of temperance provides a standard by which Dante's repentant gluttons can measure their sin (*Purgatorio*, 22.151-54), and his desert hermitage is not the place for the self-indulgent False-Seeming in the *Romance of the Rose* (6998-7000). The denunciation of the varieties of "luxury" which opens *The Pardoner's Tale* recalls the execution of the "ful giltelees" Baptist John at the command of a drunken Herod (6.488-91). John Gower in *Vox Clamantis* appropriates the Baptist's voice to denounce the materialism of his time and call people to repentance. In *Piers Plowman*, John is imagined with the other souls in Limbo, where he is reported as announcing that the time of their release and the kingdom of Christ are near at hand (B.16.82, 249-52). Late medieval and early Renaissance drama contrasts the virtue of John with the vices of Herod, Herodias, and Salome, the wantons instrumental in his beheading.

John's ministry and his poverty are a standing rebuke to worldly prelates for Milton. John is also "the great Proclaimer" of the Son of God's coming and a hero of the Spirit whose baptizing and anointing of the previously unknown son of Joseph launches the action of *Paradise Regained* (1.18-38). By contrast, the role of Blake's John is largely limited to that of the polemicist arguing in "All Religions Are One" that "the true Man is the source [of all Religions], he being the Poetic Genius." The Scripture which heads the seven Blakean theses set out here — "The Voice of one crying out in the Wilderness" — more than suggests their author's adoption of the Proclaimer's *persona*. In "Nehemias Americanus," Cotton Mather's

tribute to John Winthrop in the *Magnalia Christi Americana,* the recollection of the early Massachusetts governor brings the Baptist to mind: as humble as he was firm, he wore rude clothing and ate plain fare.

As exemplary ascetic and heroic proclaimer of the heavenly kingdom, the figure of John in Dryden's *Mac Flecknoe* provides an inverted image of the fools targeted by the mock-epic writer. The bloated and licentious prince of unreason Flecknoe defers to the "thoughtless majesty" of his successor: "I . . . / Was sent before but to prepare thy way" (26, 32). Flecknoe is an anti-Baptist, and the one he announces an anti-Christ who will "reign, and wage immortal war with wit" (12). Allusion to the Baptist and his ministry serves a similar purpose in Pope's *Dunciad,* where the Goddess of Folly anoints with "the sacred Opium" a new monarch in the empire of Dulness: "All hail! and hail again! / My son! the promised land expects thy reign" (1.288, 291-92). When addressed typologically in Pope's earlier "Messiah: A Sacred Eclogue," the theme of John's proclaiming and baptizing of Christ is given neo-classical dress: "Hark! a glad voice the lonely desert cheers" (29). In poems such as Thomas Parnell's *The Hermit* and James Beattie's *The Minstrel,* the figure of John as the fearless critic of vice is displaced by the shepherd-swain living frugally in a mossy seat far from the noise and corruption of urban existence. Sterne's robustly unsentimental *Tristram Shandy* names John once: "May . . . the praecursor, and . . . the Baptist," Dr. Slop reads from his interminable litany of curses (3.11).

Carlyle, in a manner which invites comparison with Blake, assumes the dual role of Baptist and Jeremiah to his age. The "wild Seer" of *Sartor Resartus* is pictured not altogether seriously as "shaggy, unkempt, like a Baptist living on locusts and wild honey." Teufelsdröckh's power of insight allows him to penetrate the most profound mysteries in "the Life of Man," and so qualifies him to serve as teacher of the true way (1.4). That volcanic seer partially anticipates his author, who comes with increasing earnestness to clamor against and lament the evils of Mammonism in his self-proclaimed role as latter-day prophet. The narrator of Melville's *The Piazza* makes plain his estimate of the biblical prophet's efficacy as teacher: the sight of "Jacks-in-the-pulpit" brings to mind "their Baptist namesake," who "preached but to the wilderness." Longfellow's "Vox Clamantis" dramatizes the impact of John's preaching repentance upon the Priest, Scribes, and Pharisees who suspect him of making himself a Messiah.

With the growth of a literature of sensuality in the second half of the 19th cent., Edward FitzGerald's *Rubáiyát of Omar Khayyám* renounces the gospel of "Repentance" proclaimed by "foolish Prophets" (sts. 7, 26), and the agents and circumstances of John's execution come to draw close attention. The picturing of the Baptist's severed head and Salome's white breasts creates a sensation in *Fra Lippo Lippi,* Browning's ironic treatment of carnality in religious art and, implicitly, of Victorian prudery, while Wilde's *Salomé* dramatizes something of the complex dynamics of love and hatred, sex and death, the flesh and the spirit.

References to John are frequent in Conrad — e.g., in *Heart of Darkness* (pt. 2), *Nostromo* (1.3), and *The Secret Agent* (3.13). Purdy has argued that "the ferocious Gospel figure" provides Conrad and his reader with "a model of perfect fidelity" against which to measure shams (92). It is likely as well that the association of John with false prophets and treacherous leaders, as in the "Gian' Battista Fidanza" of *Nostromo* (3.11), does not leave the Conradian biblical figure untouched. T. S. Eliot's dramatic monologue "The Love Song of J. Alfred Prufrock" also sets a modern John against the biblical character and in a tone which suggests impotent nostalgia: "But though I have wept and fasted, wept and prayed, / Though I have seen my head (grown slightly bald) brought in upon a platter, / I am no prophet . . ." (81-83). A "plump and pink" minister is imagined falling into a swoon at the sight and sound of the Baptist in Margaret Laurence's *The Stone Angel* (chap. 1), and in Updike's *Rabbit, Run,* the Episcopal minister, Eccles, appears to Harry Angstrom as John the Baptist reminding him of repentance. The most complete John the Baptist figure in modern literature, however, is probably Jean-Baptiste Clamence, the narrator in Albert Camus's *The Fall,* who discourses at length on "my career as a false prophet crying in the wilderness and refusing to come forth."

See also REPENTANCE.

Bibliography. Johnson, L. S. "St. John the Baptist and Medieval English Ideology." *ABR* 27 (1976), 105-25; Purdy, H. *Joseph Conrad's Bible* (1984); Scobie, C. H. H. *John the Baptist* (1964); Wink, W. *John the Baptist in the Gospel Tradition* (1968). CAMILLE R. LA BOSSIÈRE
CHARLES H. H. SCOBIE

JOHN THE BELOVED DISCIPLE John the "beloved disciple" (John 13:23), also called by later writers "St. John the Divine," was one of the sons of Zebedee and probably the younger brother of James. James and John, early followers of Jesus, were by him named "Boanerges" ("sons of thunder"). Along with St. Peter they accompanied Jesus on three important occasions: the raising of Jairus's daughter (Mark 5:37), the Transfiguration (Matt. 17:1), and the night of prayer in the Garden of Gethsemane (Mark 14:32-33). John was, after the Resurrection and Ascension, one of the leaders of the Christian community in Jerusalem. St. Irenaeus reports that he lived to be an old age, composing his Gospel in Ephesus. It has been conjectured that he incurred banishment under Emperor Domitian or Trajan, to Patmos, where he composed the Apocalypse attributed to him sometime between A.D. 95 and 98 St. Jerome records a tradition identifying John as the bridegroom of the marriage at Cana; in medieval *legenda* the bride is sometimes said to be Mary Magdalene. John's iconographic attributes

include a scroll with the words *In principio erat Verbum* (from the Vg rendering of the first verse of his Gospel) and an eagle. He is normally depicted with a long beard, although in representations emphasizing his friendship with Jesus he can appear also as a handsome youth. Because of his association with *amicitia spiritualis,* perhaps, he becomes the "addressee" of the elegant *"Verbum Dei, Deo Natum,"* a poem by an anonymous writer of the circle of Adam of St. Victor, in which he is associated with "Ezekiel's eagle," sent to the Bride of Christ to bear "of him whom thou didst loue so well, / Glad tidings" (trans. E. H. Plumptre). These associations may lie behind some of the imagery in Chaucer's *The House of Fame.*

On the cross Jesus, near death, commended John to his mother: "Woman, behold thy son!" and then addressed his disciple, saying, "Behold thy mother!" "And from that hour that disciple took her unto his own home" (John 19:26-27). In his *De Amicitia Spirituali,* Aelred of Rievaulx contrasts the personalities of John and Peter, suggesting that the characteristic strengths of each were revealed in the fact that "to Peter he gave the keys of his kingdom; to John he revealed the secrets of his heart. Peter, therefore, was the more exalted; John, the more secure. . . . Peter . . . was exposed to action, John was reserved for love" (3.117). The force of the contrast, like that commonly made between Martha and Mary or Leah and Rachel, is to associate "the Beloved Disciple" with the contemplative life. The intimate friendship of Jesus and John is also compared to that of David and Jonathan, as is still evident in Herbert's "The Church-Porch" (271-76), where advice for Christ-like conduct is given:

> Thy friend put in thy bosome: wear his eies
> Still in thy heart, that he may see what's there.
> If cause require, thou art his sacrifice;
> Thy drops of bloud must pay down all his fear:
>   But love is lost, the way of friendship's gone,
>   Though *David* had his *Jonathan, Christ* his *John.*

These and other elements of John's character and role are developed in medieval *legenda,* notably in the Franciscan *Meditations on the Life of Christ,* of which Nicholas Love's *Mirrour of the Blessed Lyf of Jesu Christ* (ca. 1400) was a popular ME translation. The Calvary scene lies behind Jacopone da Todi's widely adapted poem *Stabat Mater,* the commendation of Mary to John being popularized in ME lyrics such as "Maiden & moder, cum & se" (C. Brown, *Religious Lyrics of the XIV Century,* no. 67; cf. no. 128): "Ion, þis womman for my sake, / Womman, to Ion, I þe be-take." This scene is dramatized in the ME Corpus Christi plays (e.g., Towneley 33.463-68) and N-Town, where it is amplified considerably as a three-way conversation between Jesus, Mary, and John (891-962).

In Dante's *Commedia* Peter, James, and John are representatives of Faith, Hope, and Charity respectively, and examine the pilgrim Dante to assure that he understands the importance of these qualities (*Paradiso*, 24-26).

The literary power of John's Apocalypse ensured lasting association of him with its myriad visions of the New Jerusalem and "white lamb celestial," of which, as Chaucer's Prioress reflects, "the grete evaungelist, Seint John, / In Pathmost wroot" (*Canterbury Tales*, 7.581-83). Though Burns's model of a good Christian father in "The Cotter's Saturday Night" reads from Revelation "How he, who lone in Patmos banished, / Saw in the sun a mighty angel stand," not everyone in later ages was so taken with John's last composition. Charles Lamb called it "a disappointing book" ("A Chapter on Ears") and, despite occasional appearances (e.g., David Jones, *Anathemata*, 5.136), subsequent literary interest in "the seer of Patmos gazing, / On the glory downward blazing" (Whittier, "The Curse of the Charter Breakers") has not been equivalent to that expressed in Peter or Paul.

See also CANA WINE; PETER; REVELATION; SONS OF THUNDER.

Bibliography. Bauckman, R. "The Figure of John of Patmos." In A. Williams, ed. *Prophecy and Millenarianism: Essays in Honour of Marjorie Reeves* (1980), 107-26.

JOHN THE DIVINE   *See* JOHN THE BELOVED DISCIPLE.

JONADAB   *See* RECHABITES.

JONAH   Jonah, the son of Amittai, was the fifth of the twelve minor prophets of the OT. Rejecting God's command to preach to the Gentiles of Nineveh, capital of Assyria, he fled in a ship bound for Tarshish, but the sailors, harassed by a storm, reluctantly cast him into the waves. Immediately "a great fish" (often assumed to be a whale) swallowed him; after three days in its belly, he prayed and was regurgitated. Proceeding at last to Nineveh, he prophesied its destruction within forty days, and the terrified Ninevites repented. When God granted them a reprieve, however, Jonah callously resented that his prophecy of destruction was not fulfilled. To teach him the virtue of compassion for living creatures, God raised a gourd to shelter him from the sun and a day later sent a worm to kill it.

The brief (forty-eight verses) OT book of Jonah proves an exception to the prophetic rule by not reporting the substance of Jonah's prophecy but rather the tale of his mission: his initial flight (chap. 1:1-16), his three-day sojourn in the belly of the fish (1:17–2:10), his successful ministry in Nineveh (chap. 3), and his petulant response to God's mercy extended to the repentant Ninevites (chap. 4). The disobedient prophet himself becomes the object of satiric attack in the book because he embodies the type of nationalism and religious ethnocentrism which regards God as the exclusive property of the Israelites. Jonah's bigotry is contrasted to the character of God, whose mercy extends beyond national bounds; this emphasis accounts

for the reading of the book of Jonah on the Day of Atonement in the Jewish liturgical calendar.

Jewish sources provide extensive commentary, both serious and fanciful, on the book of Jonah. Early interpretations from the Targums link Jonah with Moses in that Moses ascended to the heights of Mt. Sinai and Jonah descended to the depths of the sea. Midr. Rabbah equates the fleeing Jonah with the fallen Adam, who shunned God's presence (Gen. 21:5). Other Jewish sources include fantastic descriptions of the whale's belly and its contents, together with the legend that Jonah used the whale's eyes as windows into the depths.

In Matt. 12:41 and Luke 11:29-32 Jesus uses the repentance of the Ninevites as a standard by which to condemn the unbelief of his listeners. In Matt. 12:38-41 he foretells that, like Jonah in the whale's belly, he will remain for three days "in the heart of the earth" (cf. Matt. 16:1-4; Luke 11:29-32). These prophetic words establish Jonah as a type of Christ, especially the resurrected Christ, and he figures as an emblem of the Resurrection in nearly sixty early Christian paintings in the catacombs. Here he appears in company with other OT figures who escaped certain death: Daniel in the lions' den (Dan. 6:16-24) and the three children in the fiery furnace (Dan. 3).

Jonah's history is frequently cited by the Church Fathers, who see it as a lesson on the efficacy of repentance and the greatness of God's mercy (e.g., St. Clement of Rome, *Epistle to the Corinthians,* 7; Tertullian, *Adv. Marc.* 2.17; 5.4; St. John Chrysostom, *Ep.* 1.15). Following Matt. 12:38-41, many refer to Jonah as a type of Christ (St. Justin Martyr, *Dialogue with Trypho*, 107-08; St. Augustine, *De civ. Dei* 18.44). St. Cyril of Jerusalem draws a detailed parallel between the lives of Jonah and Jesus and regards the whale's belly as an analogue of hell, which Christ harrowed (*Catechetical Lectures*, 14.17-20). Noting that the literal meaning of *Jonah* is "dove," St. Jerome associates the prophet with the Holy Spirit (*In Jonam,* 391). He further emphasizes that the conversion of the Ninevites, a non-Jewish people, typifies the transfer of faith from the Jews to the Gentiles. In line with midrashic exegesis, some of the Fathers regard Jonah's flight as emblematic of Adam's fall (e.g., St. Irenaeus, *Adv. haer.* 3.20.1; St. Methodius, *On the History of Jonah*). Augustine (*Ep.* 102), Jerome (*In Jonam,* 422), and St. Gregory of Nazianzus (*Orationes,* 2.107-08) interpret Jonah's sorrow as grief for the passing of God's favor from Jews to Gentiles, while Origen (*Contra Celsum,* 7.53, 57), Augustine (*Ep.* 102), and Jerome (*In Jonam,* 406) counter the arguments of pagan scoffers at the miracle of the fish.

Although interest in Jonah is less marked in the Middle Ages, commentators follow the Fathers in observing his role as a type of Christ and the etymology of his name (e.g., *Glossa Ordinaria* [PL 114.128], and Haymo of Halberstadt [PL 117.128]). Rupert of Deutz recalls St. Cyril of Alexandria in his search for minute parallels between Jesus' life and that of Jonah (PL 168.399-440). The Jewish Zohar (Exod. 199a-b) expounds Jonah's story as an allegory of the soul's experience in the mortal body (the ship), its descent into a grave (the whale), and its resurrection (regurgitation).

One persistent early tradition has it that Jonah was swallowed fully clothed by the whale and was vomited forth both naked and bald. A naked Jonah occurs on an early Christian sarcophagus from Arles. A bald Jonah appears in the 9th cent., when he is mentioned in both the Midrash and the *De Cena Cypriani* by John the Deacon; the 12th-cent. goliardic Archpoet, in his poem *"Fama Tuba Dante Sonum,"* mentions, likewise, that Jonah emerged bald from the whale.

Disdaining such fanciful speculation and distrusting allegorical hermeneutics, the Reformers emphasize the inner struggles of Jonah, whom they see as a fallible human being saved by grace, a man whose example should dispel spiritual despair. Calvin lays especial stress on Jonah's sin of disobedience (*Comm. on the Prophet Jonah* [1559]; cf. Luther, *Lectures on Jonah* [1525, 1526]; Tyndale, *Prologue to the Prophet Jonah* [1531]). In the Enlightenment, skeptics revive the pagan incredulity over the miracle of the great fish (e.g., Voltaire, "Jonas," *La Bible enfin expliquée* [1776]; Paine, "The Best Way to Serve God," *The Age of Reason*, pt. 1 [1794]). Today the book of Jonah is widely regarded as didactic fiction.

In English literature Jonah serves as both a type and an exemplum. In a number of OE sermons for Rogationtide he illustrates the power of prayer and the efficacy of fasting and good deeds. His emergence from the whale's belly in the fifth of the Chester mystery plays illustrates God's mercy and prefigures the Resurrection. A variation on the traditional moral interpretation appears in *Patience*, a 14th-cent. alliterative poem, which rebukes the prophet for repining at the lot God had decreed for him and uses the story as the occasion to teach by the negative example of Jonah's impatience the virtue announced in the title. In Jonah's fear of being "on rode rwly to-rent with rybaudes mony" ("on a cross pitifully torn to pieces by many ruffians" [96]) and his ordeal "in saym and in sorwe [grease and filth] that savoured as helle" (275), the poet also glances at the prophet's role as a type of Christ.

Dramatizing Jonah's story in *A Looking Glasse for London and England* (ca. 1590), Thomas Lodge and Robert Greene soften it by letting him announce to the Ninevites God's change of heart, but the main purpose of their play is to accuse England of the sins of Nineveh. In Francis Quarles's *A Feast for Wormes* (1620), a verse paraphrase of the biblical book, the emphasis is on God's mercy, the efficacy of repentance, and the saving power of faith, although the poem mentions that Jonah is "the blessed Type of him, that di'de for us" (1.7). Blake, in *The Four Zoas*, turns Jonah into a type of fallen man oppressed by a Satanic spirit who boasts, echoing Jonah 2:3, "I roll my floods over his body, my billows & waves pass

over him, / The sea encompasses him" (ed. Keynes, 4.133-34; cf. 9.95-96 with Jonah 2:5). In chap. 9 of Melville's *Moby-Dick* the devout Father Mapple sees in Jonah's story a lesson on the wickedness of disobeying God and on the importance of true faith to the penitent. In Mapple's sermon the motivation for Jonah's flight is not, as in the Bible, dismay over God's universal mercy, but fear of being an alien in the hostile pagan city of Nineveh, and the final application of the sermon is a warning against becoming what Jonah became, the archetypal outcast.

James Bridie's satirical comedy *Jonah and the Whale* (1932) presents Jonah as the killjoy tyrant of his village and undermines his claim to divine inspiration. Laurence Housman's short play *The Burden of Nineveh* (1942) explains away the miracles (replacing the fish, e.g., with timber) to throw the whole emphasis on obedience to God's promptings and the fullness of his mercy. Free of marvels, likewise, is Robert Frost's *A Masque of Mercy* (1947), in which a modern American Jonah, a contemporary Paul, and an egalitarian discuss whether God can be both just and merciful. In a lighter vein, Aldous Huxley's and A. M. Klein's fanciful lyrics, both entitled "Jonah" (1917 and 1933 respectively), follow Jewish midrashic lore in romanticizing the wondrous innards of the fish: for Klein's prophet, indeed, the return to land ironically becomes an expulsion from a paradise. Wolf Mankowitz's *It Should Happen to a Dog* (1956) casts Jonah as a kind of traveling salesman who is timid to announce the prophecy and resentful of his lot (constantly complaining that what happens to him "should happen to a dog"). Other modern versions of the story appear in David Compton's *Jonah*, a modern psychological drama with a priggish and unpleasant hero, and Gordon Bennett's *So Why Does That Weirdo Prophet Keep Watching the Water?*

There are numerous passing references to Jonah in English literature. His name is given to one who brings trouble on his companions (e.g., Milton, *Eikonoklastes*, bk. 5; Defoe, *Robinson Crusoe;* Emily Brontë, *Wuthering Heights*, chap. 9; Byron, *The Two Foscari*, act 4; Kipling, *Captains Courageous*, chap. 4). A transient good is referred to as a Jonah's gourd (Tennyson, *The Princess*, 4.292; Hardy, *Far from the Madding Crowd*, chap. 33). And the great fish is recognized as a stumbling block to faith (Browning, "Easter-day" [1850], 180; Shaw, "The All or Nothing Complex," Preface to *Farfetched Fables* [1948]).

Bibliography. Bowers, R. H. *The Legend of Jonah* (1971); Dahl, C. "Jonah Improved: Sea-Sermons on Jonah." *MSEx* 19 (1974), 6-9; Duval, Y. *Le livre de Jonas, dans la littérature chrétienne grecque et latine: sources et influences du commentaire sur Jonas de saint Jerome.* 2 vols. (1973); Faj, A. "The Jonah Theme in World Literature." *UAJ* 50 (1978), 53-59; Holstein, J. A. "Melville's Inversion of Jonah in *Moby-Dick." IR* 42 (1985), 13-20; Labin, L. L. "The

Whale and the Ash-Heap: Transfigurations of Jonah and Job in Modern American Literature — Frost, Macleish, and Vonnegut." *DAI* 41 (1981), 4713A; Park, J. M. "Patience: The Story of Jonah in a Middle English Poem." *DA* 33 (1973), 3599A; Schatt, S. "The Whale and the Cross: Vonnegut's Jonah and Christ Figures." *SWR* 56 (1971), 29-42; Strack, H., and P. Billerbeck. *Kommentar zum neuen Testament aus Talmud und Midrasch.* 6 vols. (1922-61); Szarmach, P. E. "The Versions of the Jonah Story: An Investigation of Narrative Technique in Old English Homilies." *ASE* 1 (1972), 183-92.

HENRY SUMMERFIELD
LELAND RYKEN
LAURENCE ELDREDGE

JONATHAN   Jonathan was King Saul's oldest son and David's closest friend. He is portrayed as gentle, brave, pure-hearted, kind, swift as an eagle and strong as a lion, devoted to his father despite disagreements, true to his friend even at the cost of his own claim to the throne, resourceful in snatching victory out of the jaws of defeat, and courageous in facing death at the side of his father.

Jonathan first appears in 1 Sam. 14, when he wins an important victory over the Philistines but finds himself condemned to die for disobedience to a parental order. But because the people plead for him he is spared. He reappears in chap. 18, when he makes a covenant of friendship with David, and in chaps. 19 and 20, when he keeps this covenant, even risking his life to defend his friend against his father's wrath. David's lament for Jonathan in 2 Sam. 1 ranks among the world's great dirges.

St. John Chrysostom cites Jonathan as a preeminent example of charity in his *Homilies on First Corinthians* (*Hom.* 33, on 1 Cor. 13:4), a view reflected by the Fathers and medieval exegetes. Aelred of Rievaulx in his *De Spirituali Amicitia* observes that "the sacred bond of friendship between David and Jonathan . . . was consecrated not through hope of future advantage, but from contemplation of virtue" (2.63). "Jonathan was found a victor over nature, a despiser of glory and of power, one who preferred the honor of his friend to his own" (3.95) (*On Spiritual Friendship,* trans. M. E. Laker [1974]).

In English literature, it is Jonathan's friendship for David which receives most attention. Edmund Spenser includes, among the great friendships which inspired brave thoughts and deeds, the friendship of "true Jonathan and David who were trusty and tried" (*Faerie Queene,* 4.10.27). George Herbert compares the relationship of David and Jonathan to that of Christ and the beloved disciple John (*The Church Porch,* st. 46).

In Lord Byron's "Song of Saul Before His Last Battle" (included in his *Hebrew Melodies* of 1816), the doomed monarch, foreseeing his end, bids farewell to his warriors and chiefs but not to Jonathan. In the last stanza, he expresses his affection for his son from whom he has become estranged and with whom he will now share death in battle:

Farewell to others, but never we part,
Heir to my royalty, son of my heart!
Bright is the diadem, boundless the sway,
Or kingly the death, which awaits us today!

Jonathan plays an important role in Abraham Cowley's *Davideis* (1656), a sacred epic in four books. In bk. 1, Lucifer's emissary characterizes him as an unnatural fool cheated by friendship. Book 2 deals with Jonathan's relationship to David, depicting Jonathan as gentle and innocent. He endures patiently his father's invective when accused of being a spy and agent of David. In bk. 4, Jonathan is idealized as a person of fine judgment, and a praiseworthy husband, master, father, son, friend.

Charles Jennens, who wrote the libretto for Handel's oratorio *Saul,* acknowledged his indebtedness to Cowley's epic. In Jennen's text Jonathan frustrates Saul's designs against David and risks his life by refusing to carry out the orders of his envious father to execute vengeance upon David.

In D. H. Lawrence's *David* (1926), Jonathan is torn between his father, the king, and his friend, the king-to-be. He concludes that his life belongs to his father but that his soul is David's. The last scene depicts the final parting of the two friends. Jonathan acknowledges that the hope of Israel is with David, but he himself will remain with his father. "I would not see thy new day, David. For thy wisdom is the wisdom of the subtle and behind thy passion lies prudence. Thy virtue is in thy wit and thy shrewdness. But in Saul have I known the magnanimity of a man."

J. M. Barrie's play *The Boy David* (1936) presents Jonathan as a boy of about 12, cultured, handsome, honest, intelligent, but unimaginative. His dejection is contrasted with David's lightheartedness. The play ends with a covenant between the two boys ever to remain friends.

See also DAVID; SAUL.

Bibliography. Liptzin, S. "Noble Jonathan." *Biblical Themes in World Literature* (1985), 164-69.   SOL LIPTZIN

JORDAN   The Jordan River is the most important watercourse in Palestine, dividing it from north to south and flowing from above the Sea of Galilee to the Dead Sea. In the Bible the fertile plains of the Jordan were Lot's choice of settlement (Gen. 13:11); Israel was commanded to "pass over Jordan" into the Promised Land (Deut. 9:1; 11:31). When Joshua directed the Ark of the Covenant to be brought across it, the waters were held back (Josh. 3:8-15), an event reminiscent of the Red Sea crossing in Exodus. The Jordan is also famous as the river in which Naaman the leper washed himself at Elisha's bidding (2 Kings 5:1-27) and where John the Baptist baptized Jesus (Matt. 3:6; Mark 1:5-9).

For typological reasons medieval writers such as the Franciscan author of the *Meditationes Vitae Christi* imagined that on returning from their flight to Egypt, Mary, Joseph, and the Christ child passed over Jordan at the very spot where Jesus was later to be baptized. And this was "the same place where the children of Israel crossed when they came from Egypt through the desert" (chap. 13).

Such typology figures in baptismal liturgy throughout the Christian Church and in English hymnody and spirituals. It also lies behind George Herbert's two "Jordan" poems, both of which are concerned with poetic vocation. Here the poet commits himself to pass beyond the "quaint words, and trim invention" of contemporary style, "Curling with metaphors a plain intention," in order to achieve "in love a sweetnesse readie penn'd" and "plainly say, *My God, My King.*" William Cowper lauds the wisdom of Christ, which "drawn from the deep well of life, / Tastes of its healthful origin, and flows / A Jordan for th'ablution of our woes" ("Conversation," 561-66). Not all literary references focus on the "healing stream" and NT baptismal imagery; as the story of Naaman makes clear, the literal Jordan, tepid and often muddy, can also symbolize the self-abasement of penance.

See also BAPTISM; JOHN THE BAPTIST; LOT; NAAMAN.

JOSEPH OF ARIMATHEA The biblical Joseph of Arimathea was a secret disciple of Jesus, a wealthy member of the Sanhedrin who obtained Pilate's consent to remove the body of Jesus from the cross and place it in his own new tomb (Matt. 27:57-60; Mark 15:43-46; Luke 23:50-53; John 19:38-42). The 4th-cent. apocryphal Acts of Pilate (or the Gospel of Nicodemus) adds to this NT information Joseph's imprisonment, his miraculous rescue, and his testimony to Christ's ascension. The story of Christ's descent into hell is also developed through Joseph. In subsequent medieval literature Joseph is said to have traveled to Britain and to be the guardian of the Holy Grail.

Geoffrey of Monmouth's *Historia Regum Britanniae* (ca. 1139) and earlier British histories are silent about Joseph, but Robert de Boron's *Joseph d'Arimathie* and the Arthurian *L'estoire del Saint Graal* testify to a 12th-cent. French tradition. By ca. 1250 the monks of Glastonbury had interpolated into William of Malmsbury's earlier *De Antiquitate Glastoniensis Ecclesiae* an account of Philip the apostle, who sent Joseph and companions to Britain; at Ynyswitrin (Glass Isle) they settled and built a church of wattles dedicated to Mary. About a hundred years later John of Glastonbury's *Chronica* blended the Acts of Pilate, the *Estoire,* and the interpolated *De Antiquitate.* In an appendix John traced Arthur's descent from Joseph's nephew and referred to the quest for the "Sanctum Graal"; John did not associate Joseph with this grail, however, but with two cruets "filled with the blood and sweat of the prophet Jesus," buried in Joseph's hidden sarcophagus near the old wattle shrine. These cruets figure in the 15th-cent. Glastonbury coat of arms and in the stained glass portrait of Joseph in Langport church, near Glastonbury.

The 14th-cent. alliterative *Joseph of Arimathie* incorporates more fabulous elements of Joseph's care of the vessel containing Christ's blood and his conversion of Emperor Vespasian and of Evelak(e), King of Sarras. Here and in early printed "lives" of Joseph miracles associated with Evelake's shield and with the grail remain slight. Thomas Malory's *Le morte Darthur* (ca. 1470; printed by Caxton in 1485), following the anonymous French *Queste del saint Graol,* develops Joseph's role as grail bearer, traces Galahad's lineage to him, expands miracles concerning Evelake's shield, and portrays Joseph's son, Bishop Josephé, appearing to special knights in visions of the grail. Malory alludes to Joseph frequently in "The Tale of the Sankgreal" and fleetingly elsewhere.

Spenser's *Faerie Queene* and Tennyson's *Idylls of the King* preserve Joseph's role in Arthurian legends. Spenser's Arthur reads that "Ioseph of Arimathy / ... brought with him the holy grayle" and preached Christianity (2.10.53). Tennyson's Pellam descends from "Arimathean Joseph" and enshrines relics of the passion "brought / By holy Joseph hither" ("Balin and Balan," 98-111); Percivale identifies the "cup" of the quest as Christ's chalice brought by Joseph to Glastonbury ("The Holy Grail," 46-52, 731-32). Tennyson also incorporates Glastonbury legends ignored by Malory: "the winter thorn" that "blossoms at Christmas" (supposedly growing from Joseph's rooted thorn staff), the church of wattles, and a monk who can say, like monks of Glastonbury, "these books of ours . . . seem / Mute of this miracle," i.e., the miracle of the "holy cup" which disappears in evil times ("Grail," 52-66). A decorated goblet in "Balin" (357-62) depicts Joseph's sea voyage and his wattled church. Wordsworth, too, praised "Arimathean Joseph's wattled cells," displaced by the "high pomp" of "Proud Glastonbury" ("Dissolution of the Monasteries," 11-14).

William Blake's Joseph reflects Gospel traditions when, in *The Four Zoas* (8.338-40), Los, representing Joseph, takes the body of the "Lamb of God" from the cross and buries it. Beneath an engraving entitled "Joseph of Arimathea among The Rocks of Albion," Blake wrote: "This is one of the Gothic Artists who Built the Cathedrals in what we call the Dark Ages," fit tribute to one whose story rose from rocklike simplicity to cathedral complexity during the Dark Ages.

See also HOLY GRAIL.

Bibliography. "Gospel of Nicodemus. Acts of Pilate and Christ's Descent into Hell." In Hennecke, E. *New Testament Apocrypha.* Ed. W. Schneemelcher. Trans. R. M. Wilson et al. (1963), 1.444-81; Lagoria, V. M. "The Legend of Joseph of Arimathea in Middle English Literature." *DA* 27 (1967), 3431A; Loomis, R. S. *The Grail: From Celtic Myth to Christian Symbol* (1963); Robinson, J. A. *Two Glastonbury Legends* (1926); Skeat, W. W., ed. *Joseph of Arimathie: Otherwise Called the Romance of the Seint Graal, or Holy Grail.* EETS o.s. 44 (1871).   MARIE MICHELLE WALSH

JOSEPH THE CARPENTER Most of the NT information about Joseph, the husband of the Virgin Mary and father of Jesus by right of marriage and by legal ties, is given in the first two chapters of Matthew and of Luke. Both evangelists record that Joseph came from the line of David and Solomon, kings of Israel. Although the details of his ancestry are not clear, the genealogical lists support the claim of Jesus, as legal son of Joseph, to be the "Son of David" (Matt. 15:23), a recognized title of the Messiah (Matt. 22:42). As the legal father of Jesus, Joseph had the right to name his child (Matt. 1:21). Chaucer's Parson quotes the relevant scriptural text: "And therefore seyde the aungel to Joseph, 'Thou shalt clepen his name Jhesus, that shall saven his peple of hir synnes'" (*Canterbury Tales,* 10.285).

In Matt. 13:55 Jesus is called "the son of the τέκτων." The Greek word, like the corresponding Latin word *faber,* means "craftsman." Some Church Fathers assumed that Joseph was a carpenter. St. Justin argued that Joseph made plows and yokes; St. Isidore of Seville concluded that he was a blacksmith. In actual usage the Greek word most often designated a woodworker —i.e., either a carpenter or a cabinetmaker —and this meaning has prevailed both in biblical exegesis and in literary tradition. Blake, e.g., elaborates in two paintings his sense of the relationship between Joseph and Jesus as coworkers. In *The Christ Child Asleep on a Cross Laid on the Ground,* he depicts Joseph holding a compass, while the L-square with which he measures the cross-shaped coffin lies on the ground. In *Christ in the House of the Carpenter* the Christ child himself holds the compass and the L-square. Similarly, in his poem "Wisdom" Yeats depicts the child who is to become a "working-carpenter" like his father Joseph, while his "majestic Mother" sits stitching in the workshop of Nazareth.

Matthew (1:19) praises Joseph as a "just" man, one who is very conscientious in the observance of the Law and of God's will. When Joseph learned of Mary's pregnancy during their betrothal (a frequent subject in medieval and subsequent literature), he was thus confronted with a serious moral dilemma. St. Augustine suggests that Joseph actually suspected Mary of adultery; St. Bernard argues that Joseph actually surmised she was the mother of the Messiah and wished to withdraw in humility. The third and most commonly accepted interpretation of Joseph's actions is that he felt bound to obey the law concerning adulterous wives but that his strong conviction of Mary's virtue led him "to put her away privately" without revealing why he did so, thereby protecting Mary from public humiliation and punishment by stoning. This view is held by Milton, e.g., in his *Tetrachordon (Complete Prose Works,* ed. Sirluck, 2.2.673.10). Joseph's promptness in obeying the divine will is manifested elsewhere in his response to the angel's command to flee from Herod and to take refuge in Egypt (Matt. 2:13). The last time Joseph is mentioned in the Gospels is when he and Mary discover the child Jesus talking with the teachers of Israel in the Temple (Luke 2:46). This is the setting of John Donne's poem "The Temple," in which the poet urges Joseph to "turne backe: see where your childe doth sit."

The early English carols refer to some of the events in Joseph's life as recounted in the Gospels. Joseph's spirit of service at the birth of Jesus, e.g., is commended (R. Greene, *The Early English Carols,* no. 125). A number of carols treat the troubles which beset Joseph on learning that Mary was pregnant. Thus, in James Ryman's carol (no. 258), the angel informs Joseph that Mary's child is God's son, and Joseph himself comes to recognize Mary's "grete vertue." In other carols Joseph is implored in the familiar refrain to "mervele noght" on these events: "Mervell nothyng, Joseph, that Mary be with child; / She hath conceyved *vere* God *and* man *and* yet she undefiled" (no. 260).

In their depiction of Joseph, the English mystery plays mix details from the canonical Gospels with those from noncanonical texts, including the traditional Catholic identification of Joseph as an aged man rather than peer to his young wife.

The Protevangelium of James, e.g., narrates how the priests of Jerusalem chose a spouse for Mary. Joseph was selected because a dove emerged from his staff and flew onto his head. Joseph, however, excused himself as a candidate on account of his old age. Likewise, the apocryphal History of Joseph the Carpenter (ca. A.D. 400) describes Joseph as an "old man" (cf. the Franciscan *Meditationes Vitae Christi*). Accordingly, the author of the *Ludus Coventriae* stresses Joseph's old age and his reluctance to marry: "I am old and also cold, walkyng doth me wo"; "I am so Agyd and so olde / . . . both myn leggys gyn to folde." Joseph eventually accepts marriage in a reverent and obedient spirit, but his initial reticence paves the way for his later suspicions. The plays all begin with Joseph's return after several months' absence and his discovery of Mary's pregnancy. The dramatic action revolves around Joseph's spirited incredulity in the explanations given him. For instance, when Mary reveals the child is God's son, Joseph protests that, "God dede nevyr jape so with may," thereby distinguishing the Christian God from Jove. When one of Mary's attendants refers to the angel's visit at the Annunciation, Joseph replies, as in the Gospel of pseudo-Matthew, that it was rather some boy in disguise who gave himself "an Aungel name." It is clear from the speeches, in which the phrase "I am begiled" reverberates, that Joseph pictures himself in these plays as standing in the long tradition of men who have been deceived by women, an "olde cokwold," who sees the story of Adam repeated in his situation. Despite the apparent irreverence, Joseph's suspicions are ironically turned against him. As Mary says in the York play, "yhe ar begiled." Joseph, in Rosemary Woolf's words, "thinks that he is married to the first Eve, whereas in fact he is married to the second" (172). In Towneley and in the *Ludus Coventriae* the episode of Joseph's doubts concludes with Mary's brief but solemn act of forgiveness. The reconciliation is complete when Mary permits Joseph to kiss her on the mouth; in this way the symbol of their chaste marriage is restored.

Sustained literary treatment of the relationship between Joseph and Mary is not witnessed again until the 19th cent. In *Jerusalem,* pl. 61, Blake reverses the roles of Mary and Joseph in the reconciliation scene from the mystery plays and transvaluates its significance. In his reading of Matt. 1:18-25, Blake has Mary admit her guilt but justify herself: "if I were pure, never could I taste the sweets / Of the Forgive[ne]ss of Sins" (11-12). Then Joseph, like Hosea, forgives his wife:

> There is none that liveth & Sinneth not! And this is the
> Covenant
> Of Jehovah: If you Forgive one-another, so shall
> Jehovah Forgive You,
> That He Himself may Dwell among You. Fear not then
> to take
> To thee Mary thy Wife, for she is with Child by the
> Holy Ghost. (24-27)

By making Joseph the great exemplar of forgiveness, Blake at the same time attacks the symbol of female chastity, or what he calls the "Virgin Eve" (*Jerusalem,* pl. 90), the ancient and traditional commonplace of Mary as the second Eve.

Later writers, like Blake, often treat Joseph as the stereotypical old cuckold, but, unlike Blake, they fail to attach the edifying conclusions drawn from the English mystery plays. Half-Rome in Browning's *The Ring and the Book,* e.g., deliberately exaggerates the protestations of innocence made by the priest, Giuseppe Caponsacchi, after his inn encounter with Pompilia by alluding ironically to Joseph's doubts:

> Together for a minute, perfect pure.
> Difficult to believe, yet possible,
> As witness Joseph, the friend's patron-saint. (2.113-15)

Joyce also refers to Joseph's suspicions as dramatized in the scandalously anticlerical *Vie de Jésus* (1884) by Léo Taxil (pseudonym of Gabriel Jogand-Pages). Mary's gross reply in this text, "C'est le pigeon, Joseph!" sounds one refrain for the paternity theme in *Ulysses.* This view of fatherhood differs radically from the one proposed by St. Augustine: "How was Joseph father? All the more effectively, the more chaste the paternity" (*Sermo,* 51.20). Modern texts are also far removed from the commentary of the Church Fathers on Matt. 1:25 ("Joseph knew her not, until she had brought her firstborn") against those who disputed the virginity of Mary (cited by Herbert in his *Briefe Notes on Valdesso's Considerations*). In Yeats's "A Stick of Incense" St. Joseph rejects what he considers emphasis on abstract passion and longs for the sexuality of earlier religions: "Saint Joseph thought the world

would melt / But liked the way his finger smelt." E. M. Forster likewise presented a pagan-visioned Joseph and Mary in his short story "The Story of the Siren," where the principal character, Giuseppe, who has seen the siren, marries Maria because she, too, has beheld the wonder. Joseph's "Mervele noght" has finally been reversed.

Dear Mili, an unknown tale by Wilhelm Grimm discovered in 1983 (trans. R. Manheim, 1988), marks a faithful return to the traditional portrait of Saint Joseph as model of the good worker and patron of the "happy death." A young girl, sent by her mother into the forest to save her from a terrible war, comes upon the hut of an old man, who gives her shelter just as he had protected the Christ child long ago. Saint Joseph has the girl repay his kindness by sending her out to work for what she thinks are three days but are actually thirty years "because he didn't want her to be idle." The girl's whole life seems but "one joyful moment," and when she is finally reunited with her mother one evening, they fall "happily asleep," their peaceful death symbolized by Saint Joseph's rose in full bloom.

Bibliography. Deasy, C. P. *Saint Joseph in the English Mystery Plays* (1937); Faverly, F. E. "Legends of Joseph in Old and Middle English." *PMLA* 43 (1928), 79-104; Gibson, G. M. "The Images of Doubt and Belief: Visual Symbolism in the Middle English Plays of Joseph's Troubles about Mary." *DAI* 36 (1976), 5315A-16A; Hennecke, E. *New Testament Apocrypha.* Ed. W. Schneemelcher. Trans. R. H. Wilson et al. (1963); James, M. R. *The Apocryphal New Testament* (1953); *NCE* 7.1106-08; Suarez, F. *Joseph of Nazareth* (1985); Woolf, R. *The English Mystery Plays* (1972).   DOMINIC MANGANIELLO

JOSEPH THE PATRIARCH The story of Joseph, Jacob's favorite son, who was sold into slavery by his jealous brothers and ultimately rose to a position of prestige and prominence in Egypt, constitutes the entire final section of the book of Genesis. It is a masterpiece of biblical narrative, not only in its subtle characterization but also in its remarkable structural integrity. Joseph's first experiences with his family in Canaan and his later adventures and misadventures in Egypt —notably the attempted seduction by Potiphar's wife and his several demonstrations of remarkable skill as an interpreter of dreams —are woven together into a "romance" plot which plays a pivotal role in the larger epic of Israel. The relocation of Joseph's father and brothers to Egypt, with which the narrative concludes, provides a sense of closure to Joseph's own quest for familial reunion and restoration and sets the stage for the great events of the Mosaic era: exile, exodus, wandering, and the receiving of the Law.

The Joseph story also draws to a close the colorful and sometimes infamous story of Jacob, the wily patriarch who wrested a birthright from his brother (Gen. 25), a benediction from his father (Gen. 27), and a blessing from the angel of the Lord (Gen. 32). There are many ironies in the final chapters of his life: Jacob the deceiver is, in his old age, deceived by his own sons (Gen. 37:31-35). He who had, as the younger of two sons, claimed the firstborn's privilege now "accidentally" blesses Joseph's younger son, Ephraim, rather than the elder, Manesseh (Gen. 48:8-20). As Robert Alter has noted, God's determination that the "young" nation of Israel take precedence over the older cultures which surrounded it apparently found symbolic enactment in each patriarchal generation.

Surprisingly, the story of Joseph goes virtually unmentioned in the rest of the Bible. "The tribe of Joseph" (i.e., the half-tribes of Ephraim and Manasseh) is referred to frequently in the OT (and twice in the NT), but Joseph himself is spoken of only in the covenantal history of Ps. 105 (vv. 16-23). The Apocrypha is only slightly more attentive, with a few scattered references: Wisd. of Sol. 10:13-14 argues that Wisdom preserved Joseph in his Egyptian trials, and in 1 Macc. 2:53 the dying Mattathias holds Joseph up to his sons as an example of one who kept the commandments of God under great duress. There is extensive treatment of Joseph in an ancient noncanonical romance now known as Joseph and Asenath, in which Joseph is portrayed in heroic terms and credited with angelic beauty. Joseph and his story are not mentioned at all in the NT.

Rabbinic commentators tend to emphasize Joseph's exemplary status as the ideal of humanity. Josephus, expanding on the text's terse comment that Joseph was "a goodly person, and well favored" (Gen. 39:6), argues that Joseph's moral excellence was matched by his extraordinary physical beauty (*Ant.* 2.2-8). Other commentators sometimes carry this emphasis to fanciful extremes: the Talmudists report that the odor emanating from Joseph's body was so fragrant as to overwhelm the exotic spices carried by the Midianites who bought him from his brothers (Midr. Shir 3a; 'Ag. Shir 1.12; see L. Ginzberg, *LJ* 2.19).

Patristic commentators continue the emphasis on Joseph's moral stature, presenting him as a model of Christian virtue. Some writers, notably St. Athanasius (*Apologia ad Constantium* [PG 25.609]) and St. Cyprian (*Ad Fortunatum de martyrio* [PL 4.693]), take Joseph as a model of constancy to God in the face of enemies, temptations, and trials. More common, though, is an emphasis on Joseph's perfect chastity, e.g., St. Gregory of Nyssa (*Contra fornicarios* [PG 46.493-94]) and St. Basil (*De temperantia et incontinentia* [PG 32.1348]), among many others.

Also important for the literary tradition is the persistent identification of Joseph as a type of Christ. St. Justin Martyr treats him in this way, as do Tertullian and St. Irenaeus. Of special note also are the references scattered throughout the writings of St. John Chrysostom (see esp. his homily on Gen. 37 [PG 54.528]) and the complete book devoted to Joseph by St. Ambrose *(De Joseph patriarchia).* In the latter text, Ambrose provides point-by-point correspondences between the lives of Joseph and

Christ: Joseph suffered at the hands of his brothers; Jesus, at the hands of his people; Judah sold Joseph; Judas sold Jesus; Joseph, after revealing himself to his brothers, told them not to grieve (Gen. 45:5); and Jesus, after his Resurrection, told his disciples not to fear (Matt. 28:10); Joseph's wife Asenath prefigured the Church, the bride of Christ (PL 14.646).

Typological patterns established by the Fathers find their way into all forms of medieval art: thus, e.g., stained-glass windows at King's College, Cambridge, juxtapose Joseph's being cast into a well by his brothers with Christ's entombment and Reuben's seeking Joseph with the women's seeking the resurrected Christ. The same consistency may be found in the history of interpretation of individual episodes. An early tradition that Joseph's "coat of many colors" (KJV; the RSV reads "a long robe with sleeves") represents the humanity (and the mortal suffering) which Christ "put on" in the Incarnation may be found in the OE poem *Physiologus.* This identification —as R. Tuve explains (*A Reading of George Herbert* [1952], 176-80) —is reflected in medieval glossed Bibles (the *Glossa Ordinaria* and the *Bibles moralisées*) and in poems such as George Herbert's "Joseph's Coat." Herbert's poem makes no mention of Joseph except in the title, instead describing the identification of a believer's sufferings with those of Christ; the author assumes that the typological connections will be evident to the educated reader. In a transmuted form, that typology survives even in Blake, who has Joseph sold into slavery as an infant —in order to emphasize continuity with Moses in the bulrushes and the flight of the Holy Family into Egypt —and suggests that the coat was a kind of swaddling-cloth complete with hieroglyphic stitching; he refers to Joseph "stolen from his nurses cradle wrapd in needle-work / Of emblematic texture" (*Milton,* pl. 24, lines 18-19). In *Jerusalem* the reference to "Josephs beautiful integument" (pl. 81, line 11) is given precisely the same typological context.

The identification of Joseph with Christ is sometimes so close that the two stories become entangled. In Melville's *Billy Budd,* the title character is evidently and persistently portrayed as a Christ figure, yet it is said of Claggart, when he has falsely accused Billy, that he surveys Captain Vere's face with "a look that might have been that of the spokesman of the envious children of Jacob deceptively imposing on the troubled patriarch the blood-dyed coat of young Joseph."

Full-scale retellings of the Joseph story frequently draw upon nonbiblical sources to elaborate (or alter) details. Thus, the ME *Iacob and Ioseph* makes use of Tertullian, whose *Ad nationes* excises Potiphar from the story, sending Joseph directly into Pharaoh's service and making his temptress the sovereign's wife, the Queen of Egypt herself. Another anonymous retelling, *Genesis and Exodus* (ca. 1250), relies heavily on the amplified *Historia Scholastica* of Peter Comestor.

Joseph was a popular subject of Renaissance drama, both in England and abroad. English plays share with their continental counterparts an emphasis on the Egyptian scenes, as the titles of such plays as *Pharaoh's Favorite* (Robert Aylet [1623]) and *Egypt's Favorite* (Sir Francis Hubert [1631]) indicate. The Puritan ban on drama put an end to such entertainments, and Joseph's story did not find a significant place on the English stage again until the 18th cent., with the production of Handel's highly operatic oratorio *Joseph* (1743). One year earlier, Henry Fielding created in Joseph Andrews, the titular character of one of his most popular novels, a chaste hero modeled to a considerable extent on his biblical namesake.

There have been few modern retellings in English of the Joseph narrative apart from minor sacred dramas and Webber and Rice's rock cantata *Joseph and the Amazing Technicolor Dreamcoat.* The definitive modern rendering of the Joseph story is Thomas Mann's magisterial four-volume series *Joseph and His Brothers,* published in Germany from 1933 to 1944 and translated into English in 1949. Mann's tetralogy —which finds its germ in Goethe's remark (in his autobiography *Dichtung und Wahrheit* [*Poetry and Truth*]) that the Joseph story is fascinating but "thin" —reflects profound study of the whole range of Jewish and Christian interpretation, as well as an intimate knowledge of cultural anthropology and ancient history. It constitutes perhaps the greatest single commentary on the life of the biblical Joseph.

Allusions to individual episodes of the story are numerous in English literature. Joseph's famous chastity is earnestly invoked by Chaucer's Parson, who argues that the adulterous behavior of Potiphar's wife exemplifies "the fouleste thefte that may be, whan a womman steleth hir body from hir housbonde" and that the wise Joseph "of this thefte douted gretly" (*Parson's Tale,* 10.877-79). By the 19th cent., that chastity could become a source of irony —as in Byron's *Don Juan* (1.187), when Juan is discovered in his lover Julia's closet by her husband, Alfonso:

> At last, as they more faintly wrestling lay,
> Juan contrived to give an awkward blow,
> And then his only garment quite gave way;
> He fled, like Joseph, leaving it; but there,
> I doubt, all likeness ends between the pair.

The same episode is sometimes invoked metaphorically, as in Emerson's "Self-Reliance," where he urges his readers to "leave your theory, as Joseph his coat in the hand of the harlot, and flee" (265).

Many writers recall Joseph's success in interpreting dreams; in Chaucer's *The Nun's Priest's Tale,* Chauntecleer cites Joseph's experience as proof that dreams do betoken truth; and in *The Book of the Duchess,* when the insomniac narrator finally falls asleep, he dreams a dream which, he asserts, even Joseph could not interpret (274-83). Even specific dreams recorded in the Genesis ac-

count have enriched our language and literature; thus Falstaff replies to Hal, who has just called him a "stuffed cloak-bag of guts," by saying, "If fat is to be hated, then Pharaoh's lean kine are to be loved" (*1 Henry 4,* 2.4.414; cf. Gen. 41).

See also ASENATH; DREAMS, VISIONS; POTIPHAR'S WIFE.

Bibliography. Alter, R. *The Art of Biblical Narrative* (1981); Arbab-Shirani, Saʿīd. "Shapes of a Myth: Literary Transformations of the Joseph Figure." *DAI* 37 (1977), 5099A; Argyle, A. W. "Joseph the Patriarch in Patristic Teaching." *ExpTim* 67 (1955-56), 199-201; Budd, L. J. "Mark Twain and Joseph the Patriarch." *AQ* 16 (1964), 577-86; Faverty, F. E. "Legends of Joseph in Old and Middle English." *PMLA* 42 (1928), 79-104; Fiedler, L. A. "Master of Dreams." *PR* 34: 339-56; "Joseph and Asenath." In *The Apocryphal Old Testament.* Ed. H. F. D. Sparks (1984), 465-503; King, J. R. "Thomas Mann's *Joseph and His Brothers:* Religious Themes and Modern Humanism." *Thought* 53 (1978), 416-32; Yohannan, J. D., ed. *Joseph and Potiphar's Wife: An International Anthology of the Story of the Chaste Youth and the Lustful Stepmother* (1968).   ALAN JACOBS

JOSHUA Joshua, son of Nun, is the military leader par excellence in the OT. He appeared suddenly in Exod. 17:9 to lead the Hebrew people in their first armed struggle after the Exodus from Egypt, against the Amalekites, a prelude to the series of battles in which he commanded his forces in the conquest of the land of Canaan. This conquest is one of the major themes in the book of Joshua, the other being the subsequent division of land among the tribes of Israel.

In the Pentateuch, Joshua is associated closely with Moses, whose assistant, not equal, he is said to be (Exod. 24:13; 33:11, etc.). He won high praise after he and Caleb remained loyal to God when the other spies sent to reconnoiter the land of Canaan proved faithless (Num. 13–14). For this act of faithfulness Joshua and Caleb, unlike Moses, were allowed to enter the Promised Land (Num. 14; 26:65; 32:12). Joshua's piety and obedience are prime assets in military engagements as well, for the conquest of the land of Israel is portrayed as a holy war, in which Hebrew success is impossible apart from close adherence to the requirements of the covenant (e.g., Josh. 6–8).

When Joshua led the people in a ceremony of covenant renewal (Josh. 24), he once more demonstrated steadfastness of purpose and qualities of leadership appropriate to the individual whom Moses, at God's command, had appointed as his successor (Num. 27:12-33; 34:17; Deut. 1:38; 3:3-15, 23; 34:9).

Jewish legends hold that Joshua was designated first of conquerors at the world's creation (Esth. Rab., pr. 10). In other Jewish sources the respective glory of Moses and Joshua is compared to that of the sun and the moon (e.g., Deut. Rab. 9.11). This metaphoric identification of Joshua with the moon may lie behind the folkloric association of Joshua with the man in the moon (see Ginzberg, *LJ* 6.170, n. 6). Yet another Jewish tradition (at variance with the

NT [Matt. 1:5]) has it that Joshua became the husband of Rahab the (rehabilitated) harlot, whom he and Caleb encountered on their initial foray into Jericho.

As successor to Moses, the quintessential representative of the the Law, and as conqueror of the Promised Land, Joshua was readily viewed by early Christian writers as a type of Christ. This identification was reinforced by the fact that *Iēsous* is the Greek form of *Joshua*, leading the LXX translators to render *Joshua* as "Jesus" throughout the saga of the conquest of Canaan (cf. Heb. 4:8, where the KJV transliterates Joshua's name as "Jesus"). Joshua-Jesus typology was already well established in the early Church (cf. Heb. 3) and elaborated extensively in the patristic period. (Centuries later, Milton, reflecting the ancient commonplace, can refer to "Joshua, whom the Gentiles Jesus call" [*PL* 12.310].) In his working out of the typology, St. Jerome is emphatic that Joshua remained chaste throughout his life, unlike Moses, "the Law," who was married *(Adv. Jov.)*.

Joshua's military prowess won for him a place among the nine worthies, as attested, among other places, in Shakespeare's *Love's Labour's Lost* (5.1.123). William Wordsworth speaks of "righteous" Joshua as warrior in *The Excursion* (7.813), and Joshua was pressed into service as a patriotic hero in such works as Thomas Morell's *Joshua, A Sacred Drama* (1748) and Timothy Dwight's epic poem *The Conqueror of Canaan* (1785). The violent nature of the conquest, pointedly described by Blake (in his annotations to *An Apology for the Bible* by R. Watson [1796]), is taken up in such works as the anonymous American ballad *The Battles of Joshua* (1843). Joshua is notably absent from both medieval and Renaissance drama — apart from one lost play by Samuel Rowley (1602).

Individual episodes in the life of Joshua merit occasional reference in English literature. The courage of Joshua and Caleb in the wilderness is alluded to in Blake's *Jerusalem* (43.37; 49.58-59), and the capture of Jericho recorded in Josh. 6 is recalled in such works as Patrick Dickinson's poem "The Seven Days of Jericho" and the well-known spiritual "Joshua Fit the Battle of Jericho." The most popular single incident, however, is Joshua's stilling of the sun and moon at the valley of Ajalon (Josh. 10:12-13), which is remembered in various contexts by writers as diverse as Milton, Dryden, Tennyson, and Somerset Maugham. A witty allusion to Joshua's parentage is afforded in Emily Dickinson's "Son of None" (see P. Anderson, "Dickinson's 'Son of None'." *Expl* 41 [1982], 32-33).

See also AJALON, VALE OF; MOSES; RAHAB.

Bibliography. Aharoni, Y., et al. "Joshua." *EncJud* (1972); Boling, R., and C. Wright. *Joshua*. AB (1982); Greenspoon, L. "The Warrior God, or God, the Divine Warrior." In *Religion and Politics in the Modern World*. Eds. P. Mirkl and N. Smart (1983), 205-31; Porter, J. "The Succession of Joshua." In *Proclamation and Presence*. Eds. J. Durham and J. Porter (1970), 102-32.

LEONARD GREENSPOON

JOT AND TITTLE It is a strong emphasis of Jesus' teaching, explicated in his Sermon on the Mount, that he came not to destroy the Law, but to fulfill it: "For verily I say unto you, Till heaven and earth pass, one jot or one tittle shall in no wise pass from the law, till all be fulfilled" (Matt. 5:18; Luke 16:17). The *yod* (y) is the smallest letter in the Hebrew alphabet (Gk. *iota* [i]). The tittle is a diacritical mark, very small, distinguishing letters. Bunyan's Faithful in *Pilgrim's Progress* gives Hope "a Book of Jesus" in which "every jot and tittle thereof stood firmer than Heaven and Earth." Edmund Gosse says as soberly of the Father in his *Father and Son* that in his increasing disappointment with his son "He abated no jot or tittle of his demands upon human frailty" ("Epilogue").

JUBAL According to Gen. 4:21, Jubal, brother to Tubal-cain and son of Lamech, "was the father of all such as handle the harp and organ." In medieval literature Jubal (often mistakenly called Tubal) is treated as a kind of Hebrew Orpheus. The Black Knight in Chaucer's *Book of the Duchess* says that he

> koude not make so wel
> Songes, ne knewe the art al,
> As koude Lamekes sone Tubal,
> That found out first the art of songe. (1160-63)

Dryden takes up the Genesis reference in "A Song for St. Cecelia's Day":

> What passion cannot music raise and quell!
>   When Jubal struck the chorded shell,
> His listening brethren stood around,
>   And, wondering, in their faces fell
> To worship that celestial sound.

George Eliot, likewise, in her long poem "The Legend of Jubal," celebrates the first musician's gift of song to humanity:

> Thy limbs shall lie dark, tombless on this sod,
> Because thou shinest in man's soul, a god,
> Who found and gave new passion and new joy
> That naught by Earth's destruction can destroy.

Charles Lamb implies that "since Jubal stumbled upon the gamut" there have been few so tone-deaf and deficient in the appreciation of music as he ("A Chapter on Ears").

JUBILEE, YEAR OF According to Lev. 25:9-46, after seven successive Sabbaths of years (forty-nine years) a blast from the ram's horn trumpet was to proclaim "liberty throughout Israel" on the tenth day of the seventh month, Yom Kippur, or the Day of Atonement. In the fiftieth year sabbatical injunctions were to apply, allowing the land thus to rest uncultivated for two years successively (Lev. 25:11, 22). Also, land purchased during the previous fifty years reverted to its original settlers/owners (25:10, 13), and those who had been compelled by poverty or bankruptcy to sell themselves into indentured service were to gain their release (25:39). Thus, God's redemption of the people from Egypt (as also his creational provision from the beginning) was to receive special and practical commemoration in a "proclamation of liberty to all the inhabitants of the land." Except for the era immediately following Joshua's governorship (Num. 36:4; Judg. 3:11), keeping of the Jubilee provisions is not mentioned in the Bible, and according to the Halakah, the commandments of the Jubilee Year are to be considered valid only when all Jews are resident in the land, each tribe in its original territory. Ultraorthodox Jews in Israel, however, still observe the constitutive Sabbatical Year cycle (e.g., 5747, or 1986-87).

In Ezek. 46:17 there is an apocalyptic anticipation of an eschatological Jubilee in the time of the Messiah, dependent upon restoration of the actual land to the original tribes and owners as part of the messianic blessing (cf. Isa. 61:1-3). On this eschatological (and typological) reading, the Year of Jubilee foreshadows the final restoration of all that has become lost or alienated through human sin and the ultimate deliverance into liberty of all creation as well as the individual people of God. This messianic sense is invoked by Jesus in his reading of Isa. in the Nazareth synagogue (Luke 4:16-21), and it seems to be further alluded to by St. Paul in his Epistle to the Romans (8:18-23).

The eschatological import of the Year of Jubilee has continued to dominate its recollection in the Western Christian tradition. The seven sabbatical periods of seven years were generally read as the Seven Ages of the World before the Advent (or Second Advent) of Christ and the consummation of creation and history (*Glossa Ordinaria* [PL 113.368]). Calvin does not reject the possibility of an allusion to the Year of Jubilee in Jesus' synagogue discourse but prefers to deemphasize it, as does his disciple Theodore Beza, who nonetheless cites the great medieval rabbi David Kimchi with respect to the Leviticus passage in expounding Luke 4:18. In English Protestant apocalyptic writing the eschatological connection was likewise to predominate. It is this which undergirds Spenser's allusion to Lev. 25:10 (probably from the Bishops' Bible translation) to indicate the restoration of the kingdom following the Redcrosse Knight's vanquishing of the Great Dragon: the "aged syre, the Lord al all that land," on hearing the "tydings" of release, "Proclaymed ioy and peace through all his state" to the blast of "triumphant trompets sownd on hye" (*Faerie Queene,* 1.12.3-4). Milton makes the formal connection of Levitical Jubilee with the millenarian Sabbath of sabbaths following Christ's Second Advent in his *De Doctrina Christiana* (2.7).

Reinforcement of these eschatological associations in Reformation theology surfaces regularly in sabbatarian literature, as, e.g., in Thomas Shepherd's *The Doctrine of the Sabbath* (1649) and Thomas Bromley's *The Way to the Sabbath of Rest* (1759). In literature after the Enlightenment, references to a "jubilee reign" are typically millenarian or, as when invoked in a secular setting like that of Byron's play *Sardanapalus,* allusively so: "All hearts are happy, and all voices bless / The king of peace, who holds a world in jubilee" (3.1.17-18).

See also ATONEMENT, DAY OF; SABBATH REST.

JUDAH 1. The southern portion of the kingdom from the time of Solomon's death to the Babylonian Exile.

2. One of the twelve sons of Jacob.

See also AARON; JACOB; LION OF JUDAH; TAMAR; TRIBES OF ISRAEL.

JUDAS ISCARIOT Judas Iscariot (perhaps "Judah from the city of Keriyot" [in Judea; see Josh. 15:25]) is first mentioned in the Synoptic Gospels; in each instance he is identified as the betrayer of Jesus, his name coming at the end of a list of the apostles (Matt. 10:4; Mark 3:19; Luke 6:16). In the Gospel of John Judas is identified by Jesus himself as "a devil" among the apostles (6:70-71). John also records that Judas was in charge of the common purse, from which he pilfered money (12:1-6; 13:29). All four Gospels tell how Judas led a band of Roman soldiers to arrest Jesus. In the Synoptic accounts (Matt. 26:49; Mark 14:45; Luke 22:47) he identifies Jesus for the authorities by kissing him; in John's Gospel Jesus declares himself (18:5). Only Matthew mentions the thirty pieces of silver paid to Judas by the chief priests for betraying his master (26:15), and he alone recounts Judas's "repentance" and suicide by hanging (27:1-8). According to Acts 1:16-20 Judas died, apparently unrepentant, having bought a plot of land called "Aceldama, that is to say, the field of blood" with his thirty pieces of silver, where "falling headlong, he burst asunder in the midst, and all his bowels gushed out."

There are references by St. Irenaeus, Tertullian, and St. Epiphanius to a no-longer-extant apocryphal Gospel of Judas in which Judas was portrayed as the enlightened secret agent of the Redeemer who by his "treachery" foiled the evil designs of demonic powers ("the Archons") to prevent the salvation of mankind. According to the Fathers and later medieval exegetes, however, Judas was driven by avarice and betrayed Christ of his own free will. In spite of his heinous crime he might still have been saved were it not for his desperate act of suicide. St. Jerome, e.g., argues that "Judas offended the Lord more by hanging himself than by betraying Him" (Ps. 108 [109]; cf. also St. Ambrose, *De poenitentia,* 2.4.27; St. Augustine, *De civ. Dei* 1.17; St. Gregory the Great, *Moralia in Iob,* 11.12; and the Venerable Bede, *In Lucam,* 6.16). The association of the name and character of the avaricious and traitorous "Judas" with the name and qualities of the "Jew" is a medieval commonplace which has explicit patristic authority. According to Jerome, "The Jews take their name, not from that Judah who was a holy man, but from the betrayer. From the former, we [i.e., Christians] are spiritual Jews; from the traitor come the carnal Jews" (*Hom.* on Ps. 108).

Protestant exegesis of the Judas narrative is for the most part continuous with medieval tradition. Judas becomes a focus, however, of the theological debate concerning free will. Erasmus believed that Judas was free to change his intention (*De Libero Arbitrio*, 2), but Luther argued in rebuttal that Judas's will was immutable (*De Servo Arbitrio* [1931, 1943], 1:323, 238; 5:200). Calvin states unequivocally that Judas was predestined to damnation (*Inst.* 3.24.9), but writes on the question of Judas's guilt: ". . . surely in Judas's betrayal it will be no more right, because God himself both willed that his son be delivered up and delivered him up to death, to ascribe the guilt of the crime to God than to transfer the credit for redemption to Judas." Concerning Judas's repentance he says, ". . . because [he] conceived of God only as Avenger and Judge . . . [his] repentance was nothing but a sort of entryway of hell" (*Inst.* 1.18.4 and 3.3.4).

In the OE *Elene,* Cynewulf's poetic retelling of the *inventio crucis* legend, the leader of the Jews and arch-antagonist of Helena, mother of Constantine, is named Judas. At first he misleads Helena but then "betrays" his people by revealing the whereabouts of the True Cross and is converted. In a 13th-cent. variant of this story in the ME metrical biblical narrative *Cursor Mundi* Judas appears as a prototype of Shylock, demanding a pound of flesh from a goldsmith in Helena's circle who owes him money (see D. Fowler, *The Bible in Early English Literature* [1976], 112-14, 189).

The Anglo-Norman *Voyage of St. Brendan* (ca. 1121) includes an elaborate account of the meeting between the saint and Judas. The biblical traitor describes in detail his torments in hell and explains that he is granted respite on certain Sundays of the year as a reward for small acts of charity he had performed. Judas's piteous laments, Brendan's grief, and the terrible torments which Judas describes are additions to the earlier Celtic and Latin versions of the Judas-episode in the Brendan legend; the poet (Benedict of Gloucester?) has added these and other details to evoke sympathy for Judas, or at least to convey a terrifying object lesson by heightening the pathos of Judas's plight. This glimpse of the afterlife of Judas is repeated in the ME Brendan legend. The legendary life of Judas — from his birth and *enfance* to his eventual suicide, including the pseudo-Oedipal story of how he came to be an honored member of Pilate's court, unwittingly murdered his father and married his mother, sought out Jesus to seek pardon for his sins, and became an apostle — is recounted in the popular late-13th.-cent. *Legenda Aurea* by Jacobus de Voragine (trans. in the 15th cent. by Caxton).

The 13th-cent. ballad of *Judas* depicts the biblical traitor as a tortured, pathetic figure who is manipulated by his sister and the Jew *(sic)* Pilate. On Holy Thursday Jesus gives Judas thirty pieces of silver and sends him off to buy food for the Passover feast. The red-bearded Judas meets his sister, who berates him for following Jesus,

enchants him into falling asleep in her lap, and steals the money which Jesus entrusted to him. To recover the sum Judas perversely agrees to betray his master to Pilate (*Fourteenth Century Verse & Prose*, ed. K. Sisam [1921; rpt. 1970], 168-69).

In the ninth circle of Dante's *Inferno* Judas has pride of place in a triumvirate of traitors which also includes Brutus and Cassius. Judas's feet dangle while his head and upper torso are chewed eternally by the front mouth of Lucifer's three faces. The subdivision of the ninth circle of hell where this takes place is called *la Giudecca,* after Judas, a name which was also subsequently used for the Jewish ghettos of Europe. The linking of Judas and the Jews at large (as by Jerome, cited above) is also frequent in medieval art, by way of stereotypical details: red hair and beard, ruddy skin, yellow robe and money bag, large, hooked nose, big lips, and bleary eyes. In the early ME Peterborough Chronicle Judas and the Jews are linked in the annal for the year 1137, which states that "Iudeus of Noruuic" crucified a Christian child (St. William of Norwich). Langland in *Piers Plowman* (C.2.64) also stresses the Judas-Jews connection, alluding at the same time to the popular tradition that Judas hanged himself upon an elder tree. Similar references occur in Mandeville's *Travels,* Shakespeare's *Love's Labour's Lost,* 5.2.610, and Jonson's *Every Man Out of His Humour,* 4.4: "He shall be your *Judas,* and you shall be his *elder-tree* to hang on."

In *The Friar's Tale* (3.350) Chaucer refers to Judas as a "theef " with "little money bags" who kept back half of his master's due; and elsewhere in the *Canterbury Tales* Chaucer names Judas as the proverbial hypocrite and traitor (e.g., 7.3227; 8.1001-03), while in *The Parson's Tale* (10.502) Judas is adduced as an example of *grucching* brought on by avarice — a reference to John 12:4-6. Other references to Judas as the archetypal traitor and hypocrite, by writers from the Middle Ages to the present day, are far too numerous to list. This constitutes the predominant — and least interesting — significance assigned to the figure of Judas in the English tradition (e.g., in Emily Brontë's *Wuthering Heights,* the Bible-thumping Nelly Dean shouts down from the kitchen window at Heathcliff, who has just embraced Isabella Linton: "Judas! traitor! . . . You are a hypocrite, too, are you? A deliberate deceiver"; and in Robert Penn Warren's *All the King's Men* (1946) the hero, Willie Stark, turns on two corrupt associates, the politician Duffy and the contractor Gummy Larson, accusing them of being like "Judas Iscariot").

In medieval English drama Judas is regularly portrayed as an exemplary case of avarice and treason followed by despair. Three of the four English cycles — Wakefield, Chester, and York — show how Judas was driven by greed to betray Jesus. The suicide of Judas figures in the York and N-Town cycles, both of which follow the account in Matthew fairly closely. According to the popular homiletic view reflected in the latter two plays, as well as in the Wakefield play on the harrowing of hell and the *Southern Passion,* it was Judas's suicide rather than his betrayal which led to his eternal damnation (Kolve, p. 225). The Wakefield cycle also includes an incomplete play on Judas's suicide, *The Hanging of Judas,* of which all that survives is a monologue of about 100 lines in which Judas recounts a fantastic case-history, consisting of the same stock romance motifs from the Oedipus and Moses stories that appear in the *Legenda Aurea.* In addition to its slight but lurid narrative interest the fragment includes a lament of Judas which vividly conveys the pathos of his fate.

The medieval Judas legend continued to circulate in England well into the 18th cent., when it was widely distributed in five distinct versions in several editions of chapbooks and in ballads. Jonathan Swift's poem "Judas" is a satire on Irish clergy of the Church of England (ed. H. Williams [1958], 3.806-07). The major development in the history of Judas in the 19th cent. is the emergence of a sympathetic treatment of him, based not on the sentimentalities of the apocryphal tradition but on a critical, rationalist reading of his NT role, most notably in David Friedrich Strauss's *Das Leben Jesu* (1835), trans. by George Eliot (1846). This may be the spirit which informs Matthew Arnold's portrayal of Judas in "St. Brendan" (1860), a poem which reverts to the medieval legend but eschews its sentimentality. St. Brendan, sailing near the north pole on Christmas Eve, comes upon a red-haired Judas with "furtive mien" and "scowling eye" atop an iceberg, who relates how every Christmas he is granted an hour's respite from the flames of hell because he once gave his cloak to a leper. Arnold reduces the amount of relief granted Judas and highlights the traditional saints' life motif of the cloak and the leper. Richard Henry Horne's *Judas Iscariot* is a 19th-cent. miracle play. Robert Buchanan's *Judas Iscariot* is a powerful dramatization which adheres more closely than many to the NT narrative; Thomas Sturge Moore's dramatic effort of fifty years later, *Judas* (1923), is as powerful, but more textually dense and obscure.

George Russell (AE), in his poem "Germinal," suggests a Freudian perspective on Judas's childhood: "In the lost boyhood of Judas / Christ was betrayed." In a variety of modern revisionist versions of the Gospel narrative — e.g., Anthony Burgess's *Jesus of Nazareth;* George Moore's *The Brook Kerith;* Robert Graves's *King Jesus;* and Nicos Kazantzakis's *The Greek Passion* and *The Last Temptation of Christ* — Judas is absolved of the guilt associated with Christ's betrayal and passion, and accorded semi-heroic status. In Norman Mailer's *The Executioner's Song* (1980), the old gnostic view of Judas finds a fitting exponent in Gary Gilmore, the confessed murderer. When one of his lawyers says "I feel like Judas helping you get executed," the text continues:

"Judas," said Gary, "was the most bum-beefed man in history." Judas knew what was going down, Gilmore said. Judas was there to help Jesus tune into prophecy.

See also FIELD OF BLOOD; THIRTY PIECES OF SILVER.

Bibliography. Baum, P. F. "The Mediaeval Legend of Judas Iscariot." *PMLA* 31 (1916), 481-632; "Judas's Red Hair," *JEGP* 2 (1922), 520-27; Kahn, J. "Judas Iscariot: A Vehicle of Medieval Didacticism." *DAI* 37 (1976), 2919A; Kolve, V. A. *The Play Called Corpus Christi* (1966); Luthi, K. *Judas Iskarioth in der Geschichte der Auslegung von der Reformation bis zur Gegenwart* (1955); Mellinkoff, R. "Judas's Red Hair and the Jews." *Journal of Jewish Art* 9 (1982), 31-46; Schueler, D. G. "The Middle English *Judas*: An Interpretation." *PMLA* 91 (1976), 840-45; Stouck, M. "A Reading of the Middle English *Judas.*" *JEGP* 80 (1981), 188-98.   LAWRENCE BESSERMAN

JUDAS MACCABEUS   The heroic deeds and piety of Judas Maccabeus (Heb. *Yehudah Hammaqqabi*), leader of the Jewish revolt against the Greco-Syrian king Antiochus IV Epiphanes (ruled 175-164 B.C.), are recounted in 1 Macc. 2–9; 2 Macc. 2–15, and by Josephus (*J.W.* 1.1.3-6 and *Ant.* 12.6.4-12.11.2).

The title (or possibly family name) "Hasmonean" is applied to Judas, his Maccabean relatives, and their descendants by Josephus (*Ant.* 12.263), the Mishnah (Mid. 1.6), and the Talmud (*Shab.* 21b), but does not appear in 1 or 2 Maccabees. It may have been either a patronymic or a place-name epithet (*EncJud* 7.1455). The name *Maccabeus* (1 Macc. 2:4) may derive from Heb. *maqqebet,* "hammer," or *maqqab-yahu* (cf. *naqab,* "to mark, designate") — thus: "Judas the Hammer, or Hammerer," or "Judas the one designated by Yahweh."

Outnumbered and ill-equipped, Judas together with his brothers and their guerrilla forces inflicted a series of defeats on various Syrian commanders: Apollonius, Seron, Gorgias, Lysias, and — in a climactic encounter — Nicanor. After defeating Lysias in 164 B.C. Judas purified the Temple (where idolatrous sacrifices had been offered under the edicts of Antiochus) and instituted an eight-day festival "of the dedication of the altar" (1 Macc. 4:59), beginning on the twenty-fifth day of the Hebrew month Kislev. The festival was known in early rabbinic literature, and is still celebrated, as Hanukkah. Judas fell in battle in 160 B.C.

In medieval exegesis Judas and the Maccabees are often taken to be prototypical of the Christian martyrs (e.g., St. Jerome, *Comm. in Ecclesiasten* [PL 23.1066]; St. Augustine, *Contra Gaudentium* [PL 43.729]; *Sermo in solemnitate martyrum Machabaeorum* [PL 38.1376-80]). Judas was also taken to be a type of Christ, because he defeated Antiochus, who was considered a type of Antichrist; and because his cleansing of the Temple was seen to be a prefiguration of Christ's chasing of the money changers out of the Temple (e.g., Jerome, *Comm. in Danielem* [PL 25.569-70]; the Venerable Bede, *In Marci Evangelium Expositio,* 1.2.9). Rabanus Maurus, in his influential *Comm. in Libros Machabaeorum* (ca. 840), saw in Judas an OT type of militant Christian evangelism, a view which became especially popular in the time of the Crusades (PL 109.1142).

Protestant exegetes concurred in regarding him as a type of Christ (e.g., Luther, *Preface to 1 Maccabees*; Diodati, *Pious and Learned Annotations upon the Holy Bible* [1648]). Like Rabanus Maurus, Luther took Judas to be a type of militant evangelist, interpreting the sword of the Maccabees as the "good Holy Gospel . . . wherewith God's servants faithfully come to grips with the contemporary Anti-Christ." But some Protestant writers also cited the Maccabees' union of priestly and royal power as a negative example to the Christian Church (e.g., Calvin, *Comms. . . . upon . . . Daniel*; Milton, *Defensio*).

The first extended notice of Judas in English occurs in Aelfric's late-10th-cent. homily for August 1, the *Passio Sanctorum Machabaeorum,* an epitome highlighting the battle scenes of 1 Maccabees and portions of 2 Maccabees. This work was clearly intended to encourage the English in the face of Viking attacks by adducing a happy biblical precedent. Aelfric's Judas is as fearless and pious as the Judas of the Apocrypha, if not more so (cf. Judas's speech before the battle in which he loses his life [2.110-11]: "Ne ge-wurðe hit na on life þut we alecgan ure wuldor mid earh-licum fleame . . ." ["Let it never happen in our lives, that we lay aside our glory with slothful flight . . ."] and 1 Macc. 9:10). Aelfric seems almost embarrassed by his own martial tone, as he concludes his account of Judas by distinguishing four kinds of war: *justum, injustum, civile,* and *plusquam civile*. Judas's *justum bellum*, Aelfric says, was undertaken "his folce to gebeorge" ("to defend his people"); an equally *justum bellum*, Aelfric asserts, is the English struggle against the *flot-menn* ("Vikings") (2:112-13).

Throughout the High and Later Middle Ages Judas retained his status as a model of valor and piety, and was frequently rendered a chivalric warrior battling against the Saracens or Turks. The Picard soldier-poet Gautier de Belleperche composed a *Roman de Judas Macabee* (ca. 1250) of almost 24,000 octosyllabic couplets based on 1 Macc. 1–13 but with the addition of nonbiblical episodes in which the hero fights bears, leopards, and tigers, as well as "li sarrazin." Pierre du Riés extended Gautier's poem by 1,680 verses and in addition composed his own epic account of the biblical hero, *La chevalerie de Judas Macabé* (1285), an almost 8,000-line poem even more sharply focused on Judas's prowess (Pierre spends 300 lines describing Judas as a lion). These and other French narratives of Judas were intended as exhortations to, and celebrations of, the Crusades.

Judas appears briefly in ME poetry as a brave and pious biblical warrior: "Goddes knyght" in Chaucer's *Tale of Melibee* (7.1657-62); a "conquerour kydde" ("renowned conqueror") in *The Parlement of the Thre Ages*

(454-58); and "a jouster full noble" in the alliterative *Morte Arthure* (3412-13). In the latter two instances he is listed among the "nine worthies" (i.e., according to the traditional grouping of three triads of pagan, Jewish, and Christian warriors — Hector, Alexander, Julius Caesar; Joshua, David, Judas Maccabeus; Arthur, Charlemagne, Godfrey of Bouillon — a grouping first found in the early 14th-cent. Alexander romance by Jacques de Longuyon entitled *Voeux de Paon*, lines 7537-46; cf. the eight warrior-saints, including Judas, in Dante's *Paradiso*, 18.37-48).

Many 15th- and 16th-cent. verses on Judas and the other "worthies" survive (see Loomis and Roberts); Shakespeare adopted the presumably overworked commonplace for comic purposes in *Love's Labour's Lost*, 5.1-2, where the pedantic schoolmaster Holofernes plays Judas in a pageant of the "nine worthies" and is baited by the lords attending on King Ferdinand, who willfully mistake him for Judas "who was hanged on an elder" (i.e., Judas Iscariot).

In Milton's *Paradise Regained* there is a sharp turn away from the tradition of the brave and pious biblical warrior, as Satan tempts Christ to cast off heathen oppressors and to covet kingship by adducing the example of Judas:

> . . . and think'st thou to regain
> Thy right by sitting still or thus retiring?
> So did not *Machabeus:* he indeed
> Retir'd unto the Desert, but with arms;
> And o'er a mighty King so oft prevail'd,
> That by strong hand his Family obtain'd
> Though Priests, the Crown, and *David's* Throne usurp'd,
> With *Modin* and her Suburbs once content. (3.163-70)

Here for the first time in the English literary tradition the later Maccabean dynasty which was made possible by Judas's bold deeds is implicitly regarded as morally suspect.

Judas's unblemished heroic stature was restored in Thomas Morell's libretto for Handel's patriotic oratio *Judas Maccabeus* (London premiere, 1747), composed to celebrate the Duke of Cumberland's victory at Culloden (1746) over the Scottish Jacobite rebels. In three acts, the oratorio covers the period from the death of Mattathias through Judas's purification of the Temple (1 Macc. 3–4). The patriotic thrust of Handel and Morell's work is set forth in Judas's first aria, one of the best-known passages in the work:

> Call forth thy pow'rs, my soul, and dare
> The conflict of unequal war.
> Great is the glory of the conquering sword,
> That triumphs in sweet liberty restor'd. . . .

Similar in his tone and motivation to Morell's Judas is the titular hero of Henry Wadsworth Longfellow's five-act blank verse tragedy, *Judas Maccabeus* (3.3):

What is peace?
Is it to bow in silence to our victors?
Is it to see our cities sacked and pillaged,
Our people slain, or sold as slaves, or fleeing
At night-time by the blaze of burning towns;
Jerusalem laid waste; the Holy Temple
Polluted with strange Gods? Are these things peace?

British novelist C. E. Vulliamy (pen name: Anthony Rolls), in his *Judas Maccabaeus* (1934), subtitled: "A Study based upon Dr. Quarto Karadyne's Translation of the Ararat Codex," spoofs scholarly editions, the British government and army, and the heroic tradition of Judas Maccabeus — all at once. When Mattathias cuts off the head of Antiochus's officer, Vulliamy's Judas says: "Well, father . . . now you have done it properly, and there is nothing for us to do but to leave our houses and our goods and run up into the hills and raise the people." Judas is portrayed as a bloodthirsty and Samson-like dolt, who falls in love with "Hotta-Shimmi, the lady who played the part of Judah in the revival of *Punsho [and Judah]*."

In Howard Fast's *My Glorious Brothers* (1948) — a novel in the form of a memoir written by Simon, last of the Maccabees — the reversion to a fully heroic Judas is complete. Fast explains in his Preface that he chose his subject because "it was the first modern struggle for freedom, and it laid a pattern for many movements that followed." The heroic and pious tone of Judas is familiar from Longfellow, Morell, and ultimately, of course, from the apocryphal books of Maccabees; but Fast also attributes to Judas a mid-century American liberal's faith in the indomitable march of freedom: "Because we were slaves in Egypt, I think, it is held among us that resistance to tyrants is the first obedience to God. . . . If I am slain, the people will find a new Maccabee for themselves."

Bibliography. Bickerman, E. *The God of the Maccabees.* Trans. H. R. Moehring (1979); Loomis, R. S. "Verses on the Nine Worthies," *MP* 15 (1917), 19-27; McGrath, R. L. *The Romance of the Maccabees in Mediaeval Art and Literature.* Ph.D. diss. (1963), *DA* 24 (1964), 462D; Roberts, J. H. "The Nine Worthies," *MP* 19 (1922), 297-305.

LAWRENCE BESSERMAN

JUDE Jude, said to be a brother of James, authored a brief NT epistle warning of heresy and the danger of perversions of "the faith once delivered unto the saints" (v. 3). Such perverters of Christian faith, he says, "have gone in the way of Cain, and run greedily after the error of Balaam for reward, and perished in the gainsaying of Core [Korah])" (v. 11). Jude is concerned to warn against libertine "false teachers," "mockers in the last time, who should walk after their own ungodly lusts. These be they who separate themselves, sensual, having not the Spirit" (vv. 18-19). The final two verses of the epistle are the best-known doxology in dissenting tradition churches (vv. 24-25).

Jude himself, as scholars repeatedly observe, remains shrouded in obscurity. The text may be pseudepigraphic, but in view of the signal lack of prominence accorded Jude this seems unlikely (see Eusebius, *Hist. eccl.* 3.19; 20.1-7; 32.5). Among canonical NT books, 2 Peter is indebted to Jude; Jude itself makes heavy use of apocryphal writings such as the Assumption of Moses. This fact raised early doubts about the book's canonical status which were not resolved until the 4th cent. (e.g., Athanasius's festal letter of A.D. 367).

The relative obscurity of Jude among canonical writers and his absence from significant lections in the liturgy has meant that he has had little role in English literature. The notable exception is, of course, Thomas Hardy's novel *Jude the Obscure,* in which the title character is caught in a "deadly war waged between flesh and spirit," living and dying in the misery of failed aspirations. Springer observes that "Jude's name has proved to be his destiny: in the New Testament he is the writer who asks that the Christians remember the old laws, and apply them with compassion. He is also the patron saint of craftsmen and lost causes" (*Hardy's Use of Allusion* [1983], 171).

JUDGE NOT Matt. 7:1-5, taken as whole, provides one of the most trenchant of biblical admonitions against hasty or ill-considered judgment: "Judge not, that ye be not judged. For with what judgment ye judge, ye shall be judged: and with what measure ye mete, it shall be measured to you again. And why beholdest thou the mote that is in thy brother's eye, but considerest not the beam that is in thine own eye? . . ." This passage, like its parallel in Luke 6:36-38, points to the fact that all are culpable before God and as such should not be eager to condemn others. In short, it is a warning against self-righteousness. The conditional nature of the expression (which is elaborated in the Lucan passage) finds numerous analogues elsewhere in Jesus' teaching, one noteworthy example being the petition "Forgive us our debts, as we forgive our debtors," from the Lord's Prayer (Matt. 6:12).

St. Augustine, in his treatise *De sermone Domini in Monte,* interprets the injunction typically, arguing that it is not intended to enjoin against all judgment, since Scripture elsewhere clearly advocates discriminating judgment. He sees it rather as a command against rash, pretentious, or uncharitable judgment, when the judge himself may be guilty of comparable offenses. This interpretation, followed closely by later commentators (including Calvin in his *Gospel Harmony*) becomes important for Chaucer, who employs it as the explicit theme of *The Reeve's Tale* and makes it part of Prudence's counsel in *The Tale of Melibee* (7.2648-50); it is indeed an underlying concern of the *Canterbury Tales* as a whole.

By Shakespeare's day the phrase "measure for measure" (or "meed for meed") had acquired proverbial status and was applied in a variety of contexts with different meanings. As noted by M. P. Tilley, "measure for measure" often carried the sense of a violent, exactly matching revenge: in *3 Henry 6,* "measure for measure must be answered" refers to an order that Clifford's head be set up on the gates of York in reprisal for Clifford's having placed the Duke of York's head there (2.6.55). Similarly, at the end of *Titus Andronicus,* Lucio cries out, "Can the son's eye behold his father bleed? / There's meed for meed, death for a deadly deed," as he kills Saturninus, who has just killed Titus (5.3.65-66). The proverb used in this sense is close to the OT "eye for eye, tooth for tooth" (Lev. 24:20), bearing little relation to the Matthean injunction.

When the NT passage is quoted most directly, the phrase suggests not immediate revenge but a more general providential justice which brings eventual reward or punishment according to the individual's behavior to others. Thus, when the expression "measure for measure" is used by Shakespeare as a title of one of his major plays, the Matthew passage is central; integrated with a traditional Catholic exegesis of St. Paul's Epistle to the Romans, it provides a lucid commentary on extravagant legal mindedness of the "old Law" sort, such as was evidently associated with certain Puritans in Shakespeare's day. (Seventeenth-cent. Puritan exegesis could indeed seem almost to reverse the sense of Matt. 7:1-2; see, e.g., Matthew Poole's *Annotations.*)

In *Measure for Measure* the words of the title occur in the dialogue during the last act (5.1.405-09), at a point where the Duke is pronouncing judgment on his corrupted deputy, Angelo:

The very mercy of the law cries out
Most audible, even from his proper tongue:
"An Angelo for Claudio; death for death.
Haste still pays haste, and leisure answers leisure;
Like doth quit like, and Measure still for Measure."

The Duke's comment at this climactic moment has two functions: first to emphasize the exact justice which he apparently intends to exercise in the punishment of his deputy, an expected letter-of-the-law justice, which Angelo, now completely exposed, willingly embraces; and second to provide a trial or test for the attitudes of Mariana and Isabella: Is this the kind of justice they desire? Earlier in the play Shakespeare has Isabella remind Angelo of each individual's need for something more than mere judgment — indeed, for mercy: "How would you be, if He, which is the top of judgment, should but judge you as you are?" (2.2.77). It is this larger and more merciful concept of justice, dependent not upon equally weighted retribution but upon recognition, self-awareness, and forgiveness, which prevails in the conclusion to the play.

In later literature the text devolves toward commonplace morality. For Donne, such human judgment as the text implies is invalid simply because it cannot be more than "mere opinion" ("Progresse of the Soule," 520). Pope, who makes no explicit citation of the text, may perhaps intend an allusion in certain barbs at critics (e.g., *Essay on*

Criticism, 18) or in warnings concerning the limited perspective in any human judgment: "In Man, the judgment shoots at flying game" (*Essay on Man,* 1.96). Byron provides a representative instance of the encoded sentiment in *The Island:* "And they / Who doom to hell, themselves are on the way" (4.353-54). In Aldous Huxley's *Eyeless in Gaza,* "Mrs. Foxe found herself suddenly thinking that there were also cripples of the spirit. . . . John Beavis perhaps was one of them. But how unfair she was being! How presumptuous too! Judge not that ye be not judged. And anyhow, if it were true, that would only be another reason for feeling sorry for him" (chap. 9).

See also MOTE AND BEAM; TORMENT, TORMENTOR.

Bibliography. Battenhouse, R. *Measure for Measure* and Christian Doctrine of the Atonement." *PMLA* 61 (1946), 1029-59; Pope, E. "The Renaissance Background of *Measure for Measure.*" *ShS* 2 (1949), 66-82; Tilley, M. P. *The Proverbs in England in the Sixteenth and Seventeenth Centuries* (1950).   JOHN MARGESON

JUDGES   The book following Joshua in the Hebrew canon, seventh in the English Bible and second book of the Former Prophets, concerns itself with the settlement in Canaan following its conquest. This was a period of great temptation to syncretism, and sporadic further contestation with more numerous and powerful neighbors. In place of Moses and Joshua as national leaders, a series of governing arbitrators administered such government as existed, sporadically, from the death of Joshua to the time of Samuel, the last judge in Israel. Among the most prominent of these premonarchical rulers were Deborah and Barak, Gideon, Jephthah, and Samson.

JUDITH   Judith, the pious and beautiful heroine of the apocryphal book of Judith, relieved the siege of Bethulia on the eve of the city's capitulation. Armed only with faith, she went with her handmaid to the Assyrian camp where, using her beauty to entice Holofernes, leader of the Assyrian army, she was invited into his tent for a private interview. There in two strokes she beheaded the drunken Holofernes, and, concealing his head in her handmaid's sack, fled to Bethulia where the bloody trophy became a symbol of God's deliverance of his people. Thus heartened, the Israelites attacked and routed the Assyrians the next morning.

The Hebrew original of this story, from which all surviving versions are thought to derive, was probably composed during the Hellenistic period; by the 1st cent. A.D., however, this version had evidently disappeared. During the early Christian era the story existed in three Greek versions, an Old Latin version, and in an Aramaic version which Jerome translated into the Vg Judith. Although Judith was never accepted into the Hebrew canon, by the early Middle Ages several abridged versions of the story found their way into midrashic literature; over a dozen medieval midrashim are known to exist. Some of the events of the story were in this period also incorporated into the liturgy for Hanukkah.

Early Christian writers cited Judith to define and exemplify chaste widowhood and to symbolize God's power at work in the weak and humble. St. Clement of Rome describes Judith as an example of one who (like Esther) was "strengthened through the grace of God to perform a manly deed" (*First Epistle to the Corinthians*, 55.3). *The Constitutions of the Holy Apostles* (3rd cent. A.D.) praises Judith for her wisdom, modesty, and devout faith, and upholds her as a model for widows. St. Jerome's Letter to Furia, a widowed Roman, cites Judith as an exemplary widow, praiseworthy for her fasting and for wearing the somber garb of a mourner and a penitent looking forward to the "coming of the Bridegroom." In the latter connection Jerome sees her also as a type of the Church overcoming the devil. Allegorical elaboration of the story continues throughout the Middle Ages (see Rabanus Maurus's *Expositio in Librum Judith* [PL 104]). When Protestant commentators such as Hugh Latimer (in his Second and Fourth Sermons on the Lord's Prayer) refer to the text, it is to praise Judith's devout life and courage and to commend her for sanctifying God's name and doing his will. (She is likened to Susannah and Esther.)

Judith was a figure of significant appeal to Anglo-Saxon writers. The OE *Judith*, an anonymous fragment of the late 9th or early 10th cent., focuses on Judith's beauty and forethought; she is *gleaw onȝeþance, ides aelf-scienu* (prudent in thought, a radiant woman, bright as a fairy). Aelfric refers to *Judith* in his "On the Old and New Testament" where, apparently referring to the Danish invasions, he says, *þeo is eac on Englisc on ure wisan iset eow monnum to bisne, þet ge eower eard mid waepnum beweriaen wið onwinnende here*: "This is translated into English as a model to you men, that you defend your country with weapons against an attacking army" (EETS o.s. 160, 48). Aldhelm's *De Virginitate* praises Judith's chastity as the second degree of virginity.

In ME literature both Chaucer and Gower associate Judith with strength, probity, and chastity. Chaucer refers to her in *The Tale of Melibee*, where she is an example of womanly *conseil*. Elsewhere, in *The Man of Law's Tale* (2.939-40), *The Merchant's Tale* (4.1365-66), and *The Monk's Tale* (7.2551-52) references to Judith recall especially her bravery and prudence. Gower incorporates the story of Judith into the *Mirour de l'omme*, where Judith represents steadfastness and modesty (12037-48) and faith (11113-24), and is held as an example of a good woman (17461-72). The version contained in the ME *Metrical Paraphrase of the OT* (ed. H. Kalén [1923]) stresses her ingenuity in preserving her "maidenhead" whilst Olofernes loses his head, first in the metaphorical, then in the literal sense.

Renaissance writers stressed the story of Judith primarily as a story of resistance to idolatry and tyranny. Martin Luther's *Preface to the Book of Judith* in his 1534 translation of the Bible described the story as a witness to God's protection of his faithful: ". . . Judith is the Jewish people, represented as a chaste and holy widow, which is always the character of God's people. . . ." Judith appears as a symbol of resistance to ungodliness and to tyranny in 16th-cent. ballads such as the 1586 *A godlie Dittie to be song for the Preservation of the Queene's most Excellent Majestie's Raigne,* where Elizabeth is "A Judith just." In Thomas Hudson's *Historie of Judith* (1584) the story, coming by way of du Bartas and the French Huguenot tradition, affirms that God sanctions violence directed against idolatry and tyranny, for Judith was "peculiarly chosen" of God to "unlose the chaines, and breake the bands which retainde the Hebrewe people in more than Aegyptian Seruitude, and expresly called to kill those tyrants with a death as shamefull as their lives were wicked and abhominable." A second theme, that of exemplary morality, was developed in works by and about women (Thomas Bentley, *The Monument of Matrons* [1582], 41-46 and the address "To the Vertuous Reader" of Amelia Lanier's *Salve Deus Rex Iudaeorum* [1611]). In the *Homilies of the Church of England* (1547 and 1563) Judith is cited as exemplary for moderation in eating and for prayer, and in illustration of the evils of sumptuous clothing ("Against Excess of Apparel"; cf. Jdt. 12:15).

During the 19th cent. the sexual dimensions of the story began to attract interest. This emphasis is prominent in Friedrich Hebbel's tragedy *Judith* (1840), as well as in her treatment in paintings by Vernet — already well anticipated in the canvasses of Michelangelo, Caravaggio, and Gentileschi, as well as in Donatello's sculpture of "Judith and Holofernes." Ruskin, in an August 1874 letter to Thomas Carlyle, alludes to the popular interpretation of Salome and Judith as ". . . two pretty girls carrying two bloody heads." In *Mornings in Florence,* he writes of the artistic portrayal of Judith as a "double show of an execution and a pretty woman — especially with the added pleasure of hinting at previously ignoble sin. . . ." The late 19th and early 20th cents. produced several theatrical versions of *Judith,* including Thomas Bailey Aldrich's *Judith of Bethulia,* first performed in 1904, and Arnold Bennett's *Judith* (1919). In both instances the apocryphal account is embellished with a romantic subplot.

Bibliography. Chance, J. *Woman and Hero in Old English Literature* (1986); Craven, T. *Artistry and Faith in the Book of Judith* (1983); Dubarle, A. M. *Judith: Formes et sens des diverses traditions.* 2 vols. AnBib 24 (1966); Jacobus, M. "Judith, Holofernes and the Phallic Woman." In *Reading Woman: Essays in Feminist Criticism* (1986), 110-36; Magennis, H. "Adaptation of Biblical Detail in the Old English Judith: The Feast Scene." *NM* 84 (1983), 331-37; Metzger, B. M. *An Introduction to the Apocrypha* (1957); Pentin, H. *Judith, The Apocrypha in English Literature* (1908); Purdie, E. *The Story of Judith in German and English Literature* (1927).   CAROLYN COLLETTE

K

KABBALAH *See* CABALA.

KEPT THE FAITH *See* ARMOR AND WEAPONS; *MILES CHRISTI;* FOUGHT A GOOD FIGHT.

KEY OF DAVID The *clavis David* of medieval lyrics and carols is typological nomenclature for Christ, who unlocks the "prison" of hell, death, and sin by the power of his Atonement and Resurrection. See R. L. Greene, *Early English Carols* (1935; 1977), no. 2.

See also FREEDOM, BONDAGE.

KEYS OF THE KINGDOM This figure, from Matt. 16:19, signifies the authority Jesus Christ confers on Peter as the foundation-rock of his future community of the faithful: "I will give unto thee the keys of the kingdom of heaven: and whatsoever thou shalt bind on earth shall be bound in heaven: and whatsoever thou shalt loose on earth shall be loosed in heaven." Behind this saying lies "the key of the house of David" (Isa. 22:22), which denotes the authority over the royal household vested by the king in his chief steward.

Matt. 16:19 has a history of interpretation and application long marked by far-reaching differences as to the nature, agent, and scope of the power of the keys. Among the Fathers of the Church, Tertullian and St. Augustine broadly locate the power to loose and to bind — i.e., to forgive and retain sin, to accept into the communion and to excommunicate — in the body of the faithful, which acts efficaciously as an intercessor only when it is at one with the Spirit of God from whom all forgiveness comes. St. Cyprian and Pope Leo the Great, on the other hand, emphasize that the episcopate is the sole heir to the apostolic authority and is empowered to loose and to bind of its own accord. Of the efforts to integrate these readings in the late Middle Ages, the most sustained and influential is that of St. Thomas Aquinas, according to whom priestly absolution is not simply an expression of the forgiveness granted by God, but a judicial act sacramental in nature. The teaching that solely the priest can absolve, and not only *in foro ecclesiae* but also *in foro Dei,* was officially proclaimed by the Council of Trent. For Luther, however, the keys of the kingdom mean "nothing else than the authority or office by which the word is practiced and propagated"; there is no distinction between the absolution of a layman and that of a priest (M'Clintock and Strong, 5.66-67).

In ME literature, the matter of the keys is understandably charged with a sense of urgency or foreboding. Langland's *Piers Plowman* (B-text) repeatedly protests the abuses of apostolic power by an unworthy hierarchy, and ends with a nightmare of the coming Antichrist. Gower's *Confessio Amantis,* e.g., responds to the ills of the Great Schism (1378-1417) with a plea for a return to genuine spirituality, to a time when "the Church Key" did not stand in doubt ("Prologue," 211).

Later, after the breakup of European Christendom, Milton sounds a similar note in his pastoral elegy *Lycidas:* "the Pilot of the Galilean Lake," bearing "two massy keys" — "the golden opes, the iron shuts amain" — answers a question about the fate of the shepherd who betrays his flock — i.e., of an episcopacy which has become worldly. The reading privileged by dissenters is abridged in Bunyan's *Grace Abounding to the Chief of Sinners:* "the keys of the kingdom of heaven" are "the truth and verity" of Holy Writ; whom the Scriptures favor "must inherit bliss," whom they oppose "must perish" (sect. 245). Both Dryden in *Religio Laici* (379) and Wordsworth in his *Ecclesiastical Sonnets* (1.39) criticize as tyranny and arrogation the Church of Rome's reading of its authority to loose and to bind. Later, in *The Hind and the Panther* (1687), Dryden tactfully relegates the question of the keys to a subtext; and Wordsworth, writing of the age of Fisher and More, subsequently refers to Roman Catholicism as the "keystone" of Christendom, its "supremacy from Heaven transmitted pure, / As many hold" (*Ecclesiastical Sonnets*, 2.26).

With Olympian assurance Gibbon declares in *The Decline and Fall of the Roman Empire* that the "ecclesiastical governors" of the early Church, to whom "the Deity had committed the keys of Hell and Paradise" (a conflation of Matt. 16:19 with Rev. 1:18), used that authority to keep their subjects in line and expand their political power (chap. 8). For Macaulay, it is "a happy circumstance for the Protestant religion" that the conflict between Louis XIV and Innocent XI over "secular rights" and "the spiritual power of the keys" coincided with the moment of James II's accession to the throne of England (*History of England*, 1.4.463-64).

The several ironies intended by the reference to "Trade's master-keys . . . / To lock or loose" in Newman's "England" are absent from Henley's figure of the "mailed hand [that] keeps the keys / Of . . . teeming destinies" in "England, My England." By contrast, Tennyson's reference to "the Shadow cloak'd from head to foot, / Who keeps the keys of all the creeds" (*In Memoriam*, 23.4-5) conveys a lack of any assurance. The popular conception of Peter as *janitor coeli* is reworked in Kipling's cheerfully earnest "Tomlinson." There is a serious side as well to Joyce's running joke on "the house of keys" in *Ulysses*. The figure of the "two crossed keys" representing the house of Alexander Keyes, spirit merchant, has the "innuendo of home rule" (122). In T. S. Eliot's *Murder in the Cathedral,* Thomas à Becket is tempted to presume upon the power of the keys conferred on him by the Pope (1.378, 510).

See also FREEDOM, BONDAGE; PETER.

Bibliography. de Vaux, R. *Ancient Israel.* Trans. J. McHugh (1961); Houghton, W. E. *The Victorian Frame of Mind* (1957); M'Clintock, J., and J. Strong. "Power of the Keys." In *Cyclopaedia of Biblical, Theological, and Ecclesiastical Literature* (1873), 5.60-69.   CAMILLE R. LA BOSSIÈRE

KICK AGAINST THE PRICKS When Saul on the road to Damascus was struck off his horse and blinded by a great light, he heard a voice saying to him, "Saul, Saul, why persecutest thou me?" To Saul's query, "Who art thou, Lord?" the reply came: "I am Jesus whom thou persecutest: it is hard for thee to kick against the pricks" (Acts 9:4-5; cf. 28:14). This kicking against the goads or spurs is figurative for an unruly horse or beast of burden doomed to painfully unsuccessful rebellion. St. Augustine says that such "kicking" is the mark of preexisting inward conviction of actual guilt (*Conf.* 3.8.16).

In his poem of counsel to Phillip de la Vache, like Chaucer himself the dispossessed victim of a change of political order, Chaucer urges him to self-possession: "Gret reste stant in lytel bisynesse; / Be war also to sporne ayeyns an al" ("Truth"). To "spurn at the spur," as Matthew Henry translates it, is to attempt to "stifle and smother the convictions of conscience," to "rebel aainst God's truths and laws" as well as to persecute and oppose his ministers (*Comm. on the Whole Bible,* 6.112). This is still the sense intended by Hardy's narrator in *Desperate Remedies* when he says of someone's eyes: "By collecting the round of expressions they gave forth, a person who theorized in such matters would have imbibed the notion that their owner was of a nature to kick against the pricks" (chap. 8). Changes in English idiom somewhat obscure, however, Keats's unfavorable comparison of contemporary poets with earlier giants like Milton: "I will have no more of Wordsworth or Hunt in particular," he writes to J. H. Reynolds, "Why should we kick against the pricks, when we can walk on roses?" By D. H. Lawrence's allusion in *Sons and Lovers,* the phrase is idiomatic for a fatalistic pragmatism: "Paul was laid up with an attack of bronchitis. He did not mind much. What happened happened, and it was no good kicking against the pricks" (chap. 4).

See also PAUL.

KINGDOM OF GOD The Zealots and others of Jesus' time expected a messianic political deliverance from the tyranny of Roman occupation. When such persons asked Jesus when the "kingdom of God" should come, they were therefore discomposed by his answer: "The kingdom of God cometh not with observation: Neither shall they say, Lo here! or lo there! For, behold, the kingdom of God is within you" (Luke 17:20-22). On another occasion, when Pilate put a similarly political question to Jesus ("Art thou King of the Jews?"), Jesus answered, "My kingdom is not of this world: if my kingdom were of this world, then would my servants fight" (John 18:36).

This central idea of Jesus makes spiritual self-governance rather than political power the goal of moral and ethical endeavor. It provided Tolstoy with his criticism of mistaken materializations of Christianity in *The Kingdom of God Is within You* (1893), a book of essays on nonviolent resistance to oppression. Francis Thompson's poem "The Kingdom of God" begins with a series of paradoxes such as are central also to Jesus' so-called "kingdom parables":

> O world invisible, we view thee,
> O world intangible, we touch thee,
> O world unknowable, we know thee,
> Inapprehensible, we clutch thee!

Part of the object of Matthew Arnold's criticism of institutional Christianity in *Essays in Criticism, Final Series* is its tendency to materialize, to offer external reward when it should be saying, "The kingdom of God is within you." In *Culture and Anarchy* he comments further, "Religion says: *the kingdom of God is within you,* and culture, in like manner, places human perfection in an internal condition, in the growth and predominance of our humanity proper" ("Sweetness and Light"). In Tennyson's *Becket,* when the Archbishop is warned by John of Salisbury that his return to England has occasioned angry political opinion against him, Becket responds with Jesus' words: "Why John, my kingdom is not of this world." Salisbury replies with the worldly wisdom suitable to one who authored the *Policraticus* and a history of the Popes: "If it were more of this world, it might be / More of the next. A policy of wise pardon / Wins here as well as there." When Mr. Pontifex goes "the way of all flesh" in Butler's novel of that title, Butler observes that some persons find their happiness in having a higher moral standard than others: "If they go in for this, however, they must be content with virtue as her own reward, and not grumble if they find lofty Quixotism an expensive luxury, whose rewards belong to a kingdom that is not of this world" (chap. 19).

KOL NIDRE *See* ATONEMENT, DAY OF.

KORAH *See* AARON.

KYRIE ELEISON The supplication "Lord, have mercy" has been used in Christian worship since at least the 4th cent. In ancient Greek usage, the title *Kyrios,* suggesting authority within a particular domain, was applied to the gods as well as to human rulers regarded in their divine capacity, and the supplication *Kyrie eleison* appears in non-Christian prayer (Epictetus, *Dissertationes,* 2.7.12). Christian use of the prayer owes primarily to scriptural language, which defines both the *Kyrios* and the supplication itself in terms of monotheistic faith. Invocations of God's mercy appear throughout the OT, particularly in the Psalms (e.g., Ps. 51, *Miserere mei, Deus*), and in the LXX the Hebrew Tetragrammaton is translated *Kyrios,* with the supplication itself occurring in Isa. 33:2. NT writers ascribe to Jesus lordship which — unlike that of the classical gods — is unique (1 Cor. 8:5-6) and universal (Phil. 2:9-11). Throughout the NT, appeals for divine mercy are directed to Christ (e.g., Mark 10:47),

with variations on the formula *Kyrie eleison* occurring three times in the Gospel of Matthew (Matt. 16:22; 17:15; 20:30).

In Christian liturgical tradition, the supplication first appears in 4th-cent. Eastern usage as the people's response to the diaconal petitions of a litany described in the *Apostolic Constitutions* (8.6, 9). This practice was probably introduced to the West by pilgrims such as Egeria, who reports observing the custom in Jerusalem (*Travels,* 24.5-6). The earliest extant Western version of such a litany — with the Greek response — is attributed to Pope Gelasius (492-96), who promulgated its use in the "universal church." During the following century, the *kyrie* assumes its familiar position and form. In Rome the litany occurs as part of the entrance rite of the Mass, whereas in other provinces a threefold *kyrie* without the petitions appears in the same position. The Council of Vaison (529) directs the use of the *kyrie* in the daily office, as does the Rule of St. Benedict (9 and 17). At the end of the century (598), St. Gregory the Great describes the Roman addition of the response *Christe eleison* and the custom of omitting the petitions on nonfestal occasions, thus reducing the litany to the familiar threefold supplication for mercy.

By the 9th cent., the *kyrie* had expanded into a ninefold repetition, which the *Golden Legend* ("The Dedication of a Church") interprets as signifying the entrance of the faithful into the company of the nine orders of angels. Early forms of the *kyrie* regularly address its three divisions to the three Persons of the Trinity. The *kyrie* has appeared, translated, in the *Book of Common Prayer* since its composition, whether in the conventional threefold form as in the daily office or in a more penitential version as in the Trinitarian invocation of the Litany and introductory to the Order of Holy Communion in the recitation of the Ten Commandments. The more ancient use of the *kyrie* — in its original Greek or in translation — in the entrance rite of the Eucharist was revived in the 19th cent. and has become widespread in the liturgical renewal of the later 20th cent.

In English literature the *kyrie* sometimes appears in its proper form as a direct address to God, as when Adam welcomes Christ in the 14th-cent. *Harrowing of Hell* (Harley MS 161): "haue merci of vs, godes sone." Specific liturgical connotations of the supplication receive emphasis from Shakespeare in the dying words of Salisbury and Gargrave (*1 Henry 6,* 1.4.70-71), an occurrence which echoes the *kyrie*'s penitential use in the litany while also recalling its appearance in the burial office. Eliot uses the threefold supplication to conclude the final prayer in *Murder in the Cathedral,* integrating the penitential aspect of the Chorus's confession and the festive, expectant note of the *Te Deum.*

Less direct allusions to the *kyrie* appear in a number of forms. In Chaucer's *The Knight's Tale,* the Theban women's appeal to Thesus — "Haue mercy on oure wo and oure distresse!" (*Canterbury Tales,* 1.919) — may recall ironically the greeting of Christ in hell. At the opening of the vision of *Piers Plowman,* the narrator translates the supplication into the feminine gender in addressing the figure of Holy Church: "mercy, Madame, what is this to mene?" (B.1.11). One of the most frequent forms of reference to the *kyrie* is exclamatory, with or without religious significance. The *Cursor Mundi,* e.g., invests the supplication with theological implication — "Merci, lauerd! strang wickedhed / Broght adam to suilk a ded" (841-42) — while *Havelok's* use is mundane: "Louerd, haue merci of me! / To-day i wile fro denemark fle" (491). In its expletive usage, the *kyrie* is often colloquialized, appearing in such forms as "lord-a-mercy" and, as a complaint, "Kerry-Elison."

Perhaps the cleverest literary use of the *kyrie* is one which is overtly parodic, combining aspects both liturgical and profane. In the early 14th.-cent. lyric "Bytuene Mersh ant Aueril," the narrator expresses his love-longing in the name of his beloved "Alisoun"; the clerk Jankin, in the more explicit 15th-cent. lyric "As I went on Yol Day," sings the refrain "Kyrieleison" and in the course of the narrative, which follows the liturgy of the Mass, impregnates one of the faithful. It is to such popular usage that Chaucer alludes in *The Miller's Tale* when Nicholas — himself a clerk and singer — begs Alison for carnal mercy (*CT* 1.3288).

Modern echoes of the *kyrie* may be found in William Camden's *Epitaph* ("Betwixt the stirrup and the ground / Mercy I asked, mercy I found") and in John Updike's *Bech: A Book,* in which the religiously estranged Jewish writer throws himself on the ground begging "Someone, something, for mercy" ("Bech Panics").

Bibliography. Dix, G. *The Shape of the Liturgy* (1945); Jungmann, J. A. *The Mass of the Roman Rite: Its Origins and Development (Missa Sollemnia).* Trans. R. Brunner (1951); Lockton, W. "Kyrie eleison." *JTS* 6 (1915), 548-50; "Miserable Sinners." *JTS* 6 (1915), 550-52.   ROBERT E. WRIGHT

L

LABAN *See* JACOB; RACHEL.

LABOR OF LOVE The familiar expression "labor of love" derives from the KJV translation of 1 Thess. 1:3, where St. Paul commends the Thessalonian church for its "work of faith, and labour of love, and patience of hope in our Lord Jesus Christ." The phrase, which recurs in Heb. 6:10 (Gk. *tou kopou tēs agapēs*), may have been a Pauline coinage. It attracts little exegetical commentary.

The notion of a task prompted and sustained by love (generally human love) is ubiquitous in medieval and Renaissance literature (e.g., chivalric romances), and parodic treatment of sexual love as "labor" appears, e.g., in Chaucer's *Merchant's Tale* of old January and his nubile May-bride (*Canterbury Tales,* 4.1830-65). The biblical phrase "labour of love" (which precedes the KJV translation; cf. the Geneva [1557] rendering of Heb. 6:10) may lie behind the title of Shakespeare's *Love's Labour's Lost* as well as Milton's reference to "the night-warbling Bird, that now awake / Tunes sweetest his love-labor'd song" (*Paradise Lost,* 5.40-41).

Among later English poets who use the expression, Alexander Pope ("The First Epistle of the First Book of Horace Imitated," 1-2) has a poetic "labor" or achievement inspired by the "love" of a friend (patron) specifically in view. Cowper's reference to the "labours of his love" (*The Task,* 5.570) concerns divine rather than human initiative — God's loving labor for the sake of humanity.

Carlyle and Browning both accord the notion of labor, as prompted and nourished by love, considerable attention. Within the context of Carlyle's romantic idealism, the "noble chivalry of work" is activated by a love which arises in the human soul apart from divine assistance in the traditional Christian sense (*Sartor Resartus; Past and Present,* chaps. 1–2). In Browning's poetry the notion of human endeavor inspired by love acquires a more obviously Christian aspect: allusions to the biblical phrase itself appear in "Mary Wollstonecraft and Fuseli" (25-29) and "Red Cotton Night-cap Country or Turf and Towers" (3935).

In Trollope's *Barchester Towers* Mrs. Proudie muses about the potentially disastrous consequences of Obadiah Slope's intended marriage, and takes on the task of preventing it with a kind of vocational seriousness; "with her it would be a labour of love to rob Mr. Slope of his wife" (chap. 38). Longfellow, in *Evangeline* (2.1), may be recalling the wording of the Thessalonians passage, with its commendation of faith, love, and patience, when he enjoins Patience to "accomplish thy labour; accomplish thy work of affection! / Sorrow and silence are strong, and patient endurance is godlike. / Therefore accomplish thy labour of love, till the heart is made godlike." For most modern writers who employ it, however (including Benjamin Franklin, Hawthorne, Thoreau, and

Emerson, among others), the expression is merely prover-bial, with little or no recollection of its biblical source.

HERBERT GIESBRECHT

LABORERS IN THE VINEYARD In Matt. 20:1-16, Jesus tells a parable concerning a householder who hires five groups of laborers — at the first, third, sixth, ninth, and eleventh hours — to work in his vineyard. When at the end of the day everyone receives the same wages of one denarius (KJV "a penny"), the first group accuse the proprietor of unfair treatment. Although they agreed to work for a denarius, they feel that by bearing the burden and heat of the day they have earned more than the latecomers. The householder maintains that he may freely dispose of his property and that what seems an injustice done them actually is a sign of his goodness toward the others. The parable ends with the words, "So the last shall be first, and the first last: for many be called, but few chosen" (v. 16; cf. Matt. 19:30; Mark 10:31; Luke 13:30). Most modern interpreters see the parable as a defense of Jesus' welcome of sinners into the kingdom of God.

In the early Church, the text was understood allegori-cally. St. Irenaeus (*Adv. haer.* 4.36.7) interprets the vari-ous hours at which the workers are called as periods of history: morning: Adam — Noah; third hour: Noah — Abraham; sixth hour: Abraham — Moses; ninth hour: Moses — Jesus; eleventh hour: Jesus — world's end. Origen, by contrast, took the hours to signify the stages of human life: childhood, youth, adulthood, old age, ex-treme old age *(In Matthaeum)*. These renderings were repeated and sometimes combined by later exegetes (e.g., St. Jerome, *In Matthaeum;* St. Gregory, *Hom. in Evan-gelia,* 19; the Venerable Bede, *In Matthaei Evangelium Expositio;* St. Thomas Aquinas, *Summa contra Gentiles,* 58.8). The workers were often understood as representing the clergy, and the vineyard the Church (e.g., Gregory, Bede), while the denarius, paid equally to all, was generally thought to signify eternal life (Tertullian, *De monogamia*; St. Augustine, *De sancta virginitate* and *Sermons on New Testament Lessons*) or the contemplation and enjoyment of God (Aquinas). The "burden and heat of the day" (v. 12) in such readings was sometimes seen as the knowledge that divine retribution at the end of the world is still far away (Aquinas, *In Matthaeum*), or the heat of the flesh during the greater part of one's life (Gregory).

Wyclif (*In Omnes Novi Testamenti Libros,* 36c-37a) still holds to Irenaeus's reading, while Luther dismisses it as "idle talk." For the latter, the first workers signify those who want to go to heaven proudly on account of their good works (the Jews and the clergy of Luther's time), whereas those who are humble and do not look for pay may rejoice about God's mercy (*Fastenpostille,* 1525 [*WA* 17.2]). Calvin concludes from the text that "men are created in order to do something" and that "according to the decree of God everybody is placed in his special

province so that he sit not around idle" (*Harmony of the Gospels*).

For Latimer, the parable teaches "that all christian people are equal in all things appertaining to the kingdom of Christ" (Sermon 43). American Puritan Jonathan Ed-wards, on the other hand, used the text to argue that the Great Awakening signaled God's purpose to begin his renewal of the earth in America, the "utmost, meanest, youngest and weakest part of it" (*Some Thoughts Con-cerning the Present Revival of Religion,* 2.2).

Early English literature faithfully follows the domi-nant lines of patristic commentary. The laborers are iden-tified as "prechoures" by Langland in *Piers Plowman* (B.15.491; cf. also 10.474). In the anonymous poem *Pearl,* the poet's daughter, who died as an infant, appears to her father in a dream. When he wonders why she is made a queen in heaven, she retells the parable (501-76) and comments:

> Wheþer welnygh now I con bygynne —
> In euentyde into þe vyne I come —
> Fyrst of my hyre my Lorde con mynne:
> I watȝ payed anon of al and sum.

The poem, for which this vineyard parable is a thematic crux, argues that blessedness in heaven is not quantified or calculated according to people's meritorious actions, but that the "peny" of eternal life is given freely by God's grace (cf. the ME play *Wisdom* [EETS o.s. 262], 127).

St. Thomas More's Anthony in *A Dialogue of Comfort against Tribulation* (2.5) warns those who procrastinate in turning to God: "Now he that in hope to be callid toward night, will slepe out the mornyng, & drinke out the day, ys full likely to pass at night vnspoken to / & than shall he with shrewid rest go souperlesse to bedd." Shakespeare makes a more veiled reference to the parable by having Guiderius say in his dirge for the dead Cloten:

> Fear no more the heat o' the sun
> Nor the furious winter's rages;
> Thou thy worldly task hast done,
> Home art gone, and ta'en thy wages. (*Cymbeline,* 4.2.259-62)

In the 17th cent., the parable was often alluded to in discussions of predestination. Robert Burton quotes v. 16 in his *Anatomy of Melancholy* (3.4.2.6), where he warns against a fatalistic understanding of predestination and reminds the reader: "Thou mayest in the Lord's good time be converted; some are called at the eleventh hour." In Michael Wigglesworth's apocalyptic poem *The Day of Doom,* God uses Matt. 20:15 to justify his unconditional election. The phrase "the chosen few" came to acquire proverbial status, evidenced by Lord Byron's "Answer to Some Elegant Verses" (37), which applies it to those sensible lovers of his poetry who are "to feeling and to nature true" (for a similar reference cf. Wordsworth, "Written in a Blank Leaf of MacPherson's 'Ossian' "). In Charlotte Brontë's *Jane Eyre* (chap. 38), St. John Rivers, the stern missionary, is finally vindicated as one of those "who are called, and chosen, and faithful" (a description which also echoes Matt. 25:21).

While Christina Rossetti follows Origen's exegesis in her poem "How long?" John Ruskin makes the "penny" a symbol of any wages and suggests it be convertible into bread, cloth, etc. (*Fors Clavigera*, 8.86.8; cf. also his use of vv. 13 and 14 as a motto for his essays on political economy, *Unto This Last*).

The traditional equation of laborers and clergy occurs in Mark Twain's satire "Important Correspondence." An avaricious and ambitious bishop, hungry for money and fame, calls himself one of the "poor laborers in the vineyard" and refers to San Francisco as a "pleasant field for the honest to toil in." Similar ironic (and often incidental) applications can be found in modern works such as Thornton Wilder's *Heaven's My Destination* (chap. 7), where the obnoxious evangelist Dr. Bigelow has been "in the vineyard" for twenty-five years, does not belong to any church, but tries to help his "laboring brothers." In *Go Tell It on the Mountain* James Baldwin applies the parable repeatedly to the situation in the "Temple of the Fire Baptized," as when Gabriel and the elders are dining upstairs, and "the less-specialized workers in Christ's vineyard" are being fed at a table downstairs.

Emily Dickinson (in poem 1720) draws a somewhat hedonistic conclusion from v. 16:

> Had I known that the first was the last
> I should have kept it longer.
> Had I known that the last was the first
> I should have drunk it stronger.

Edwin A. Robinson uses "Many Are Called" as a title for a poem on the inscrutability and the arbitrary ways of the "Lord Apollo." The last group of laborers becomes the Unemployed in T. S. Eliot's choruses from *The Rock*. In having them complain: "In this land / No man has hired us," Eliot expresses the plight of the jobless of Britain. At the same time he seems to give an answer in the chant of the workmen building a church: "Each man to his work."

See also LAST SHALL BE FIRST.   MANFRED SIEBALD

LADDER OF HEAVEN   *See* JACOB'S LADDER; MARY, MOTHER OF JESUS.

LAKE OF FIRE AND BRIMSTONE   Not only the beast and the devil (Rev. 19:20; 20:10), but also "the fearful and unbelieving, and the abominable, and murderers, and whoremongers, and sorcerers, and idolaters, and all liars, shall have their part in the lake which burneth with fire and brimstone: which is the second death" (Rev. 21:8). This lake is where, at the outset of Milton's *Paradise Lost*, one finds downcast Satan and his cohorts "floating" — "Satan talking to his nearest Mate / With Head up-lift above the wave, and Eyes / That sparkling blaz'd, his other parts besides . . ." (1.192-94). It is here,

"chain'd on the burning Lake" (1.210), with "Sulphurous Hail" (1.171) falling and volcanic "combustible / And fuell'd entrails" (1.233-34) rising about him, that Satan offers what appears to be the most heroic, if not the earliest, demonstration of the power of positive thinking: "The mind is its own place, and in itself / Can make a Heav'n of Hell, a Hell of Heav'n" (1.254-55).

See also HELL.

LAMB OF GOD   Lamb of God is one of the messianic titles of Jesus, used of him by John the Baptist (John 1:29-30). Throughout the book of Revelation, Jesus is pictured as the Lamb (Rev. 5:6; 12:11; 13:8; 22:1). And in 1 Pet. 1:19, the sacrifice of Jesus is likened to that of a lamb "without spot or blemish." The key OT materials lying behind this NT application are the slaughtered lamb of the Exodus, whose blood smeared on the doorpost spared the Israelites from the judgment inflicted upon the Egyptians (Exod. 12:3-13), the sacrificial lambs used in OT worship, and also the lamb symbolism in Isa. 53:6-7, where the "suffering servant" of the Lord is likened to a lamb prepared for slaughter, whose vicarious sacrifice atones for the sins of wayward "sheep."

Identification of Jesus as both the Lamb of God and Suffering Servant receives frequent mention in the early Church (see, e.g., 1 Clem. 16:7; Barn. 5:2). In early Christian iconography the lamb pictured on the shoulders of Christ the Good Shepherd symbolizes the lost and found soul, but can also signify Christ himself as sacrificial victim. In the first quarter of the 8th cent. the image of the lamb as a *figura* of Christ achieved even greater prominence when Pope Sergius made the *Agnus Dei* a part of the ordinary of the Mass: "Lamb of God, who takes away the sin of the world, have mercy upon us." Anglo-Saxon homiletics are suffused with the image of the lamb, reflecting either direct quotations or paraphrases of the relevant biblical passages, or more often of the *Agnus Dei*. References to the Lamb of God are also common in ME. The *Second Shepherd's Play* can be viewed as an extended and daring verbal and visual paronomasia on the lamb, the shepherd, and Christ as both. Part of its message concerns the vocation of faithful *pastores*, who forsake their common calling to be shepherds of the Lamb of God.

Traditional scriptural interpretation of the Lamb is reflected in the writings of St. Thomas More (*Confutation*, 5.617G; *Passion*, 1.1296, where the reference is to Rev. 5:1, 13) and in Spenser's *Faerie Queene* (1.1.5; 1.10.42; 1.10.57). The sacrificial character of the Lamb of God is noted in Henry Constable's "O Gracious Shepherd," where the blood of Christ on Calvary is "lamb-like, offered to the butcher's block." Richard Crashaw's "In the Holy Nativity of Our Lord God" ends with a chorus "To thee, dread Lamb! whose love must keep / The Shepherds, more than they, the sheep."

The lamb is a crucial image in the poetry of Blake. His *Songs of Innocence* is introduced by a poem centering on "a song about a Lamb" which makes its hearers "weep with joy" ("Piping down the valleys wild"). In Blake's famous "Little Lamb, who made thee?" the answer given in his second stanza is:

> Little Lamb I'll tell thee,
> Little Lamb I'll tell thee!
> He is calléd by thy name,
> For he calls himself a Lamb:
> He is meek & he is mild,
> He became a little child:
> I a child & thou a lamb,
> We are calléd by his name.
> Little Lamb God bless thee.
> Little Lamb God bless thee.

Though apparently redolent with traditional biblical associations, the Lamb is here a figure for childhood innocence rather than atoning sacrifice (the same shift is evident in the writings of Laurence Sterne).

The identification of the Lamb of God with the Passion still governs Melville's allusion in *Billy Budd*, where

> the vapoury fleece hanging in the east, was shot through with a soft glory as of the fleece of the Lamb of God seen in mystical vision, and simultaneously therewith, watched by the wedged mass of upturned faces, Billy ascended, and ascending took the full rose of the dawn.

Frequent, though often idiosyncratic, references to the biblical Lamb of God have continued to appear in the 20th cent. Virginia Moseley (*Joyce and the Bible*, 91) has drawn attention to Bloom's identification of himself with the *Agnus Dei* in the Lestrygonians section of *Ulysses*:

> With minor changes the Dubliners of the twentieth century parallel the Israel of Ahab's and Jezebel's time. References are juxtaposed at the beginning of the chapter to "His Majesty the King," the evangelical movement in the church (Torry and Alexander), and the preaching of the Second Coming to the accompaniment of the famous Salvation Army song, "Are you washed in the blood of the Lamb?" When Bloom sees the words of this hymn, he thinks "Bloo . . . me? No. Blood of the lamb," at once forging a link between himself and the sacrificial lamb and dissociating himself from the lamb.

In "Mary's Song," Sylvia Plath draws on OT sacrificial imagery, setting the symbol of a roasting lamb against images of the Holocaust. Harley Ellison, in "Ernest and the Machine God," unites the image of the sheep being led to the slaughter with humanity in service of the Machine God; the biblical God is here replaced by "A New Testament of deities for the computerized age" and humanity becomes the lamb to be devoured or sacrificed upon the new altars. The Ghent altarpiece "The Adoration of the Lamb" provides a unifying symbol in Albert Camus's *La Chute (The Fall)*.

See also BLOOD OF THE LAMB; LOST SHEEP, PARABLE OF; MAN OF SORROWS; SHEEP; SHEPHERD.

Bibliography. Brown, D. *The Enduring Legacy: Biblical Dimensions in Modern Literature* (1975); Grabar, A. *Christian Iconography: A Study of its Origins* (1968); Moseley, V. *Joyce and the Bible* (1967); Wright, N. *Melville's Use of the Bible* (1949).   ROBERT FARRELL
CATHERINE KARKOV

LAMB TO THE SLAUGHTER   (Isa. 53:7; Jer. 11:19; Acts 8:32)
See also LAMB OF GOD; MAN OF SORROWS.

LAMECH   Gen. 4:19-24 tells the brief story of Lamech and his two wives: Adah, the mother of Jabal and Jubal, and Zillah, mother of Tubal-cain. The "Song of Lamech" is a primitive song of boasting after a revenge killing (vv. 23-24). In various haggadic sources Lamech's lineage is traced to Cain and the song is made to celebrate Lamech's slaying of his ancestor. He is also said in one genealogy to be the father of Noah, and to have been a prophet, receiving his knowledge of the future from Methuselah (Sabba, Bereshit 9b; Ephraim 1.47; cf. Josephus, *Ant.* 1.22). To him also is ascribed a pseudepigraphic work (Schürer, *Geschichte*, 3.358). The *Glossa Ordinaria* sees Lamech as a figure for *voluptas carnis,* sexual appetite which resists the Spirit, and as the archetypal bigamist. The *Gloss* follows, as did St. Jerome, the Haggadah which makes him the slayer of Cain, saying that the murder was an act of revenge for a humiliation Lamech was made to feel by Cain for his rampant libido (PL 113.101-02).

Chaucer follows the tradition in thinking of Lamech as above all a bigamist. In "Anelida and Arcite," when King Arcite is false to Queen Anelida, the narrator observes:

> . . . gret wonder was hit noon
> Thogh he were fals, for hit is kynde of man,
> Sith Lamek was, that is so longe agoon,
> To ben in love as fals as ever he can;
> He was the firste fader that began
> To loven two, and was in bigamye. (148-53)

Elsewhere, the Wife of Bath is only too glad to defend her own string of five husbands by citing the example of patriarchs who had more than one wife: "What rekketh me, though folk seye vileynge / Of shrewd Lameth and his bigamye?" (*Canterbury Tales*, 3.53-54). In Tennyson's *Maud,* it is the "song of Lamech" and its revenge motif which appears; the man who killed Maud's brother in a duel flees to the Continent,

> sick of a nameless fear.
> Looking, thinking of all I have lost;
> An old song vexes my ear;
> But that of Lamech is mine.

The most imaginative 19th-cent. treatment may be that by A. H. Clough. In his "The Song of Lamech," Lamech narrates the story of Adam going to exiled but repentant Cain after many years and, on the bidding of Abel in a dream, laying his hand upon Cain's head. The act of blessing releases Cain's spirit to go before the gates of Paradise, there to stand "with Abel, hand in hand." The "Song" ends with Lamech projecting a hopeful imagination of his own fate: "If unto Cain was safety given, and rest / Shall Lamech surely and his people die?"

Bibliography. Reiss, E. "The Story of Lamech and its Place in Medieval Drama." *JMRS* 2 (1972), 35-48.

LAMENTATIONS The dirge or lament was an ancient Near Eastern literary form used to memorialize disasters of various kinds. The Elamite destruction of Ur was commemorated vividly in a lengthy composition (cf. *ANET,* 455-63) bewailing the end of a once great culture. The Hebrew Scriptures contain similar laments regarding people (e.g., 2 Sam. 1:17-27; 3:33-34; Ps. 44:9-19), with Lamentations, traditionally ascribed to Jeremiah, comprising five dirge poems making up one large lament.

Four of the poems are acrostics, in which the twenty-two consonants of the Hebrew alphabet occur successively as the first letter of the word beginning each strophe. A slightly irregular order resulted in the second, third, and fourth dirges from the consonants *pe* and *ayin* being reversed. The first three dirges have three lines per strophe except for two four-line stanzas (Lam. 1:7; 2:19), while the fourth has only two lines per strophe. The third acrostic poem is particularly elaborate, since each of the three verses of the stanza begins with the same letter. The final dirge is not acrostic, but contains twenty-two verses to match the number of Hebrew alphabetic consonants, leading St. Jerome to say of the author that "he goes through the alphabet four times in different metres" (*Ep.* 53.8).

All Hebrew poetry is characterized by stress and rhythm, and Lamentations has a three-stress *stichos* or half-line separated by a caesura from a parallel two-stress *stichos* to complete the line of poetry. This 3:2 rhythm was named *qinah* or "dirge meter," and is typical of Hebrew elegiac poetry. Its sharp, pulsating form was admirably suited for expressing grief, confession of sin, and formal penitential declarations, furnishing a contrived and artificial literary form with a dramatic character compatible with deep emotional expression.

Something of this expression survives, despite the considerable vagaries of translation, in the Vg, and inspired more than usually dramatic treatment of the texts typologically associated, as *planctus,* with the Passion of Christ. Most important was the text from Lam. 1:12, *"O vos omnes, qui transitis per viam . . ."* (KJV "Is it nothing to you, all ye that pass by? behold, and see if there be any sorrow like unto my sorrow, which is done unto me, wherewith the LORD hath afflicted me. . . ."). This text inspired the Latin hymn, *"Vos Qui Transitis, Si Crimina Flere Uelitis,"* a rubric from which heads the MS version of the ME cross-lyric which begins: "Abyde, gud men, & hald yhour pays, / And here what god him-seluen says, / Hyngand on þe rode" (C. Brown, *Religious Lyrics of the XIVth Century,* no. 46). The poem continues in words ascribed to the Crucified, inviting the "passerby" to "behold" his sufferings, consider how sins such as he or she commits put him there, and then to repent and ask for God's mercy and grace. This poem is complemented by John Grimestone's likewise typically Franciscan cross-poem, "ȝe þat passen be þe weyȝe, Abidet a litel stounde!" asking for meditation upon Christ's suffering.

John Donne's poetic adaptation, "The Lamentations of Jeremy, for the most part according to Tremelius," uses the improved Latin text of the converted Jewish scholar John Immanuel Tremelius, who had been, following Cranmer's invitation to come to England, made King's Reader of Hebrew at Cambridge (1549). Donne drops the typology, and makes of his free translation a faithful lamentation of and for a captive and desolate Jerusalem, bereft of her people:

> Emptie are the gates of Sion, and her waies
> Mourne, because none come to her solemne dayes.
> Her Priests doe groane, her maides are comfortlesse,
> And shee's unto her selfe a bitternesse. . . .
>
> Now in her daies of Teares, Jerusalem
> (Her men slaine by the foe, none succouring them)
> Remembers what of old, shee esteemed most,
> Whilest her foes laugh at her, for what she hath lost.

In a dark hour recalling too well the time of Jeremiah's composition, Leonard Bernstein composed his "Jeremiah" symphony (his first, written in 1942 and performed in 1944). It is in three movements, "Prophecy," "Profanation," and "Lamentation," in the last of which a mezzo-soprano sings the Hebrew text of Lam. 1:1-3, 8; 4:14-15; 5:20-21 much in the style of a synagogue chant, said by Bernstein to be derived from the liturgy for Tisha B'Ab, the festival of mourning for the destruction of Jerusalem.

A proverbial phrase particularly associated with Lamentations is "gall and wormwood," which derives from Lam. 3:19: "Remembering mine affliction and my misery, the wormwood and the gall" (cf. 3:15; Jer. 9:15; 23:15). This phrase, which acquires typological significance among medieval commentators (e.g., *Glossa Ordinaria* [PL 113]), comes to stand for extremes of bitterness, as in Dickens's *Martin Chuzzlewit:* "I have summoned you here to witness your own work . . . because I know it will be gall and wormwood to you" (chap. 52).

See also HEBREW POETRY; JEREMIAH.

Bibliography. Alter, R. *The Art of Hebrew Poetry* (1985); Good, E. M. "The Bible and American Music." In *The Bible in American Arts and Letters.* Ed. G. Gunn (1983), 131-58.

R. K. HARRISON

LAND FLOWING WITH MILK AND HONEY
Speaking to Moses out of the burning bush, God describes the land to which he would have his people brought from Egypt as "a land flowing with milk and honey" (Exod. 3:8; 13:5), Canaan or Palestine.

English literary allusions tend to be indirect or parodic.

In *Don Juan,* e.g., Byron describes the carnal appeal of a sumptuous banquet, saying

> . . . all human history attests
> That happiness for man — the hungry sinner! —
> Since Eve ate apples, much depends on dinner.
>
> Witness the lands which 'flowed with milk and honey',
> Held out to the hungry Israelites:
> To this we have added since the love of money,
> The only sort of pleasure which requites. (13.797-803)

In Tennyson's "The Lover's Tale" the lovers fantasize upon their mountain view — "a land of promise, land of memory / A land of promise flowing with milk / And honey, of delicious memories." American usage often corresponds with or counters the typological use of the phrase in Puritan colonial myth about the "New Canaan" (e.g., Cotton Mather's *Magnalia Christi Americana*). Bonn's *The American Experiment* captures this tradition when it observes:

> The people of the United States may themselves not always have known where they were going; they have ever been willing to act as leaders to the rest of the world, and to guide it from the land of bondage, when it suffers from political oppression, or from want of economic opportunity . . . into the land of freedom where milk and honey flow. (Intro.)

This cliché about America (see also Frances Trollope's *Domestic Manners of the Americans,* chap. 34) is not, as the Puritan usage would suggest, without British analogies (e.g., Anthony Trollope, *Barchester Towers,* chap. 32) or British parody (e.g., Byron's comment that Britain was no longer rich "in mines, / or peace, or plenty, corn or oil, or wines; / No land of Canaan, full of milk and honey, / Nor (save in paper shekels) ready money," *Age of Bronze,* 688-71). In American literature, however, it achieves the stature almost of a type (or perhaps antitype). Melville's Ishmael in *Moby-Dick* says of New Bedford that it is "a land of oil, true enough: but not like Canaan; a land also of corn and wine. The streets do not run with milk; nor in the spring-time do they pave them with fresh eggs" (lines which are the basis, in turn, for a parodic passage in O. Henry's story "Telemachus, Friend"). The disenchanted Depression pilgrims in Steinbeck's *The Grapes of Wrath* are similarly disabused of the old typology: " 'Look', he said, 'this ain't no lan' of milk an' honey like the preachers say. . .' " (chap. 20).

See also EXILE AND PILGRIMAGE.

LAPIDARY *See* AARON.

LAST BATTLE *See* ARMAGEDDON.

LAST JUDGMENT Warnings of God's judgment on the wickedness of Israel and Israel's enemies abound in the OT and are particularly developed in the prophetic descriptions of the Day of the Lord (Amos 1:2–6:14) and

the vengeance of God (Nah. 1:2-8). In general this judgment is collective, on the nation or on all sinners, and does not necessarily result in the end of human history. A destruction of the world, symbolized by the universal Flood (Gen. 7) and the rain of fire on Sodom and Gomorrah (Gen. 19), is threatened in the later prophets and in apocalyptic works (Dan. 2:31-45), as well as in the NT, which compares the evil of the last days with the time of Noah (Matt. 24:37). These later writings also conceive of judgment as individual, on each person "according to his works" (Ezek. 7:8) and revealing "the secrets of the heart" (Rom. 2:16), a judgment from which the evil will try to hide by calling mountains upon their heads (Rev. 6:16). The judge will be the Ancient of Days, whose assessor is the Son of Man (Dan. 7:9-13), a figure which the NT associates with Jesus Christ (Matt. 24:30).

Preceded by signs and wonders (Joel 2:30-32; Matt. 24:29-30; Rev. 6:12-14), the release of Gog and Magog (Rev. 20:8), the battle of Armageddon (Rev. 16:16), the resurrection of the dead (Isa. 26:19; Dan. 12:2; Rev. 11:11), and the Second Coming of Christ (Rev. 1:7), the time of judgment is known only to God the Father (Matt. 24:36) and will surprise many as a thief in the night (Matt. 24:43). At the blast of a trumpet (Isa. 27:13; Matt. 24:31; Rev. 11:15), Jesus Christ will send his angels to gather mankind at the great white throne (Rev. 20:11-15). For the evildoers it will be worse than it was for Sodom and Gomorrah (Matt. 10:15), resulting in a fate of everlasting fire amid weeping and wailing and gnashing of teeth (Matt. 24:51). In the presence of the archangel Michael (Dan. 12:1), and reading from the opened books, God will judge each individual, meting out justice measure for measure (Isa. 27:8) by rewarding the righteous with eternal life in the New Jerusalem (Rev. 21) and damning those whose names are not found in the Book of Life (Rev. 20:15) to fire and brimstone (Rev. 21:8). Sinful creation will be destroyed and replaced by a new heaven and new earth (Rev. 21:1).

The Last Judgment was established early as a central expectation of Christian eschatology. Included in the Apostles' Creed and discussed at length by Augustine in his *De civitate Dei* (bk. 20), it was distinguished from the judgment occurring at each person's death since it is universal and apocalyptic (1 Thess. 4:15-16), like a final great harvest (Rev. 14:14-20). Literary treatments of the Judgment or "Doomsday" depend particularly on a series of parables and figures attributed to Jesus in Matt. 25. Warning his listeners to be prepared, Jesus told of the Wise and Foolish Virgins who awaited the bridegroom (Matt. 25:1-13), a parable dramatized in an early Latin play, the *Sponsus.* Each person will be called to account to his master for his talents, according to another parable (Matt. 25:14-30), cited by Milton in his sonnet "On His Blindness." Jesus also compared the judgment to a shepherd separating the sheep to the right from the goats to the left (Matt. 25:31-33), a common literary allusion and a key source for the iconography of the Last Judgment. Finally, he promised that charity for the most humble and needy in this life would be considered at the judgment to have been directed toward him and would therefore be rewarded, whereas disregard for suffering implied rejection of him and would be suitably punished (Matt. 25:34-46). This promise is the basis of Jesus' eloquent speeches in the "Last Judgment" plays of the medieval mystery cycles.

Portrayals of the Last Judgment in medieval art and literature emphasize the wretchedness of mankind when beyond mercy and facing a wrathful and strict judge. Even the saved are striken by terror under his scrutiny. Among OE poems describing the cataclysmic events of the "Last Days" and the punishments of hell are the anonymous *Doomsday* and *Christ III.* Cynewulf composes vivid descriptions of judgment, the most elaborate being the conclusion of *Elene,* where at the judgment seat mankind is divided into the saved, the damned, and those needing purification. In *Christ II* the poet weaves his runic signature into a description of doomsday's destructive fire, in what Daniel Calder has called "a striking participation in the terror of judgment on Cynewulf's part" (*Cynewulf* [1981], 71). Warnings of the Last Judgment support calls for repentance in the sermons of Aelfric and Wulfstan, conclude the surveys of Christian history and doctrine in ME moral works such as the *Cursor Mundi* and the *Pricke of Conscience,* and permeate short didactic lyrics, such as the carol refrain, "Gay, gay, gay, gay, / Think on drydful domisday" (R. Greene, *Early English Carols* [rev. 1977], no. 329; cf. "How Christ Shall Come," in C. Brown, *Religious Lyrics of the XIVth Century,* no. 36). Other works which do not explicitly describe the Last Judgment nevertheless allude to this central eschatological expectation in establishing the significance of the actions they portray. For example, at the conclusion of *The Canterbury Tales,* the Parson calls the pilgrims to contrition by reminding them of the certainty of Doomsday. Chaucer thus juxtaposes the end of the pilgrimage with suggestions of a final judgment at the end of life and the world. In *Cleanness* the Pearl Poet concentrates on commonplace typology of judgment, describing, e.g., the universal Deluge and the destruction of Sodom to prefigure the terrible wrath of God and final punishment of evil.

The Last Judgment is especially prominent in early drama. In the Chester cycle "Prophets of Antichrist," OT and NT prophets prophesy the general resurrection, Antichrist, the Fifteen Signs of Doomsday, and Judgment Day. Since they treat the entire course of salvation history from creation to the end of the world, all four major Middle English mystery cycles conclude with a "Last Judgment." Although sharing in common the basic doctrinal features outlined in Christian eschatology, including Christ's condemnation of the wicked, the cycle plays vary remarkably in developing their dramatic possibilities, so that the ef-

fect of the Last Judgment plays ranges from the highly formal pageantry of the Chester cycle to the comic escapades of Tutivillus in the Towneley cycle. Universal judgment is less prominent in the morality plays since they deal with the experience of the individual rather than with salvation history. Nevertheless, the "Castle of Perseverance" dramatizes the Four Daughters of God debating the relative demands of mercy and justice in judgment, with Peace concluding:

> We schal devoutly pray
> At dredful domysday,
> And I schal for us say
> That Mankind schal have grace. (3544-47)

The play ends at the judgment throne. The Bad Angel is sent to hell, Mankind is welcomed to the right hand of God, and the audience is warned that "Whanne Mihel his horn blowith at my dred dom" a reckoning will be demanded "At my gret jugement" (3617-22).

Renaissance drama does not stage the Last Judgment, although in Marlowe's *Doctor Faustus* Faustus, nearing the end of this life, calls on "Mountaines and hilles, come, come, and fall on me, / And hide me from the heavy wrath of God" (1436-39; cf. Rev. 6:15-16). Several other Renaissance plays, including Shakespeare's *Measure for Measure* and Tourneur's *The Atheist's Tragedy,* develop patterns common in earlier dramatic treatments of doomsday.

In Robert Herrick's "In the Hour of My Distress," allusions to Doomsday support petitions for mercy or divine comfort at the time "When the Judgment is revealed, / And that opened which was sealed." In some instances "Doomsday" is used as a word of shorthand to signify the end of history, as when Macbeth, reacting to the phantasmagoric eight kings produced by the witches, asks, "What, will the line stretch out to th' crack of doom?" (*Macbeth,* 4.1.117). Milton refers to the coming of Christ in judgment as a gift of the Father (*De Doctrina Christiana,* 1.5). Longer descriptions of Judgment Day are less frequent. They include the divine prophecy of the Last Judgment in *Paradise Lost* (3.323-43) and two short yet powerful poems by George Herbert: "Doomsday," which concentrates on the Resurrection and creates an overwhelming sense of urgency; and "Judgement," which notes the despair of "poore wretches" and calls on Christ's promises to argue that "my faults are thine."

More recent poets have both amplified and transformed the literary treatment of the Last Judgment. Pope composes an extravagant parody in bk. 4 of *The Dunciad,* a judgment enacted by the Goddess Dulness as she seeks to establish a new kingdom of Dull on earth (the object of Pope's poem is a satiric attack on contemporary poets of whom he disapproved; cf. Byron's *Vision of Judgment,* which uses apocalyptic imagery in satirizing the poetry of Southey). Most self-consciously idiosyncratic is Blake, who, commenting on his "A Vision of the Last Judgment," explains that the Last Judgment is "when all those are Cast away who trouble Religion with Questions concerning Good & Evil." Throughout his poetry Blake interfuses traditional expectations with his own prophetic visions. In *Milton* he beholds "the Twenty-four Cities of Albion / Arise upon their Thrones to Judge the Nations of the Earth" (42.16-17). *The Four Zoas*, Night 9, visualizes the Last Judgment in what Harold Bloom has called "Blake's most exuberant and inventive poetry" (*Blake's Apocalypse*, 266). The dream concludes with a new peace: "The war of swords departed now / The dark Religions are departed & sweet Science reigns" (139.9-10).

Other noteworthy reworkings of this eschatological theme include Browning's "Easter Day" (546-734), which is conceived as an intense inner dialogue on Judgment Day describing Christ the Judge in awful majesty; William Lisle Bowles's *St. John in Patmos* (3.228-63), which explicates the prophet's vision of the end; and James Westfall Thompson's *The Lost Oracles*, a masque which in its fourth act stages a Last Judgment.

See also APOCALYPSE; ARMAGEDDON; FIRE AND BRIMSTONE; HELL; MILLENNIUM; THIEF IN THE NIGHT; WISE AND FOOLISH VIRGINS.

Bibliography. Bevington, D., ed. *"Homo, Memento Finis": The Iconography of Just Judgment in Medieval Art and Drama* (1985); Bloom, H. *Blake's Apocalypse: A Study in Poetic Argument* (1963); Brandon, S. G. F. *The Judgment of the Dead* (1967); Charles, R. H. *Eschatology: The Doctrine of a Future Life in Israel, Judaism and Christianity* (2nd ed. 1913; rpt. 1963); Leigh, D. J. "The Doomsday Mystery Play: An Eschatological Morality." *In Medieval English Drama*. Eds. J. Taylor and A. H. Nelson (1972); Lochrie, K. D. "Judgement and Spiritual Apocalypse in Old English Poetry." *DAI* 42 (1982), 4008A; Martin, J. P. *The Last Judgment in Protestant Theology from Orthodoxy to Ritschl* (1963); Michaels, R. "The Judgment Day in Old and Middle English Literature: A Study of Continuity and Change." *DAI* 41 (1981), 3594A; Morris, L. *The Biblical Doctrine of Judgment* (1960); Whitbread, L. "The Doomsday Theme in Old English Poetry." *Beitrage zur Geschichte der Deutschen Sprache und Literatur* 89 (1967), 452-81.

RICHARD K. EMMERSON

LAST SHALL BE FIRST   In the parable of the vineyard told in Matt. 20:1-16, even the workers hired at the "eleventh hour" are paid the stipulated wages which those who labored from daybreak received. To the grumbling of those first hired the lord of the vineyard replies, "I will give unto this last, even as unto thee" (v. 14). Jesus then adds, "So the last shall be first, and the first last: for many be called, but few chosen" (v. 16). When the disciples dispute among themselves concerning "who should be greatest" in the kingdom of heaven, Jesus rebukes them, saying, "If any man desire to be first, the same shall be last of all, and servant of all" (Mark 9:33-37; cf. Mark 10:31; Matt. 19:30). This principle is stressed again in reminding the disciples that the order of preeminence in

the kingdom of God will respect divine judgment concerning due reward, not any contemporary sense of who is eminent in religious life: "there are last which shall be first, and there are first which shall be last" (Luke 13:30). This principle of divine preference echoes the theme of the younger son being "preferred" over the elder in OT narrative, Abel and Seth over Cain, Jacob rather than Esau, Ephraim rather than Manasseh, David rather than any of his older brothers — a feature notably reflected in the genealogy of Jesus appearing in Matt. 1 and Luke 3.

The dominant emphasis placed upon this theme in early Christian and medieval exegesis regards it as expressing a principle of humility to be observed in the kingdom of God in the present, since it will be a certain principle in heaven. St. Jerome illustrates this admirably in his memorable letter to Marcella (A.D. 386) on behalf of Paula and Estochium, inviting her to join them in Bethlehem, which was by now to be Jerome's home for the remainder of his life. After describing the beauties of the city, past and present, the letter goes on to celebrate the strikingly diverse and harmonious character of Christian community assembled there:

> In speaking thus we do not mean to deny that the kingdom of God is within us, or to say that there are no holy persons elsewhere; we merely assert in the strongest manner that those who stand first throughout the world are here gathered side by side. We ourselves are among the last, not the first; yet we have come hither to see the first of all nations. . . . Yet amid this great concourse there is no arrogance, no disdain of self-restraint; all strive after humility, that greatest of Christian virtues. Whosoever is last is here rewarded as first.

Calvin, in a contrast of both tone and application, sees the words (Matt. 19:30; 20:16) as "added to take away the laziness of the flesh," and Christ's purpose as exhortation to run the race of spiritual life effectively: "He tells them that to have begun the race fast will do no good if they break down in the middle. . . . Therefore," he concludes, "so often as we think of the heavenly crown, it should prick us with ever new incitements so that we should be less slack in future" (*New Testament Comms.* 2.263-64; 266).

Bunyan's Christian, in *Pilgrim's Progress*, echoes a Calvinist appropriation when he, after Faithful refuses to heed his call to wait until he could catch up with him, "putting to all his strength, he quickly got up with Faithful, and did also overrun him, so the last was first." In the first of Donne's Holy Sonnets, "La Corona," the biblical theme is central to both content and design. A song of prayer and praise in seven stanzas, it owns that "The ends crown our workes, but thou crown'st our ends, / For, at our end begins our endlesse rest; / The first last end, now zealously possest." The last line of each stanza is repeated as the first line of the stanza following, as the poem traces the life and ministry of Christ as prime model — the King of Glory in an ox's stall, the child in the Temple confounding the scholars, God on the cross, the dead raised to life

— all instancing the divine principle in both aspects. So instructed, the poet can see that he now need have no "Feare of first or last death," and may by grace "Salute the last and everlasting day."

In Sterne's *Tristram Shandy* (1760), the theme is stated on the first and last pages. In Tennyson's *Rizpah,* a despondent recollection is made by the mother of a young man hanged on the gallows. When she picks up his bones and secretly buries them she thinks of God's forgiveness, and in that context tells herself: "He'll never put on the black cap except for the worst of the worst, / And the first may be last — I have heard it in church — and the last may be first." G. K. Chesterton, in his *George Bernard Shaw,* reflects the texts more closely: "That reversal is the whole idea of virtue; that the last shall be first and the first last" ("The Dramatist"). Last but not least, John Galsworthy wrote a story entitled "The First and the Last" (1915), which he then adapted as a play (1921).

See also ALPHA AND OMEGA; LABORERS IN THE VINEYARD.

LAST SUPPER   *See* EUCHARIST; PASSION, CROSS.

LAST TRUMP   Of the Hebrew words translated "trumpet" in English Bibles, *haṣoṣerah* (Hos. 5:8) and *shopar* or *shofar* (e.g., Exod. 19:13; Josh. 6:4-5) are the most common. Of these, the *shofar* or "horn" is the most frequently named instrument in the OT and the only one to have survived prominently in Jewish religious observance, where it is still used to announce Rosh Hashanah and Yom Kippur. Among the ancient Hebrews the *shofar* was prominently a signaling device in battle, or a call to arms (Judg. 3:27; 5:34; Neh. 4:18-20), and it came to be used as a symbol of war itself (Jer. 4:19-21). Accordingly it is to herald destruction on the Day of Judgment (Zeph. 1:16) and the ultimate *aliyah,* or return to Zion (Isa. 28:13).

In this vein, NT references to the trumpet are primarily eschatological. Jesus tells his hearers in the Olivet discourse that "immediately after the tribulation of those days" the angels "with a great sound of a trumpet" will gather the elect of God (Matt. 24:29-31); that the "trump of God" will be sounded when the Messiah returns is reiterated by St. Paul (1 Thess. 4:16-17). In the Revelation to St. John the voice of God itself is like a trumpet (Rev. 1:10; 4:11; cf. 1 Thess. 4:16). But it is only in 1 Cor. 15 that the phrase "last trump" actually occurs, in a memorable Pauline passage on the Resurrection: "Behold, I shew you a mystery; We shall not all sleep, but we shall all be changed, In a moment, in the twinkling of an eye, at the last trump: for the trumpet shall sound, and the dead shall be raised incorruptible, and we shall be changed" (51-52). The trumpet's last blast is thus a declaration of final victory ("O death, where is thy sting?" O grave, where is thy victory?" [v. 55]; cf. 1 Thess. 2:1-8).

Christian commentary on the passage in 1 Cor. 15 is understandably rich and complex. Some of the main lineaments are represented (if not established) in the second book of the *De excessu fratris Satyri* ("On Belief in the Resurrection"), composed by St. Ambrose on the occasion of his brother's death. Ambrose identifies the last trump, and the trumpets of Scripture generally, with the word of God (2.105). For Ambrose, the meaning of the *last* trumpet is only apparent in light of its numerous predecessors in Scripture, from the blast which is to move the Hebrew pilgrims forward on their journey to each festival remembrance of the Lord's providence for them (2.107; cf. Num. 10:1-10) to the trumpet of the Jubilee, which proclaims liberty to captives and sabbath rest (2.108; cf. Rev. 8:2). The trumpets in Scripture generally announce the progress of divine redemption; the response of the individual of heart belief and confession of the mouth (Rom. 10:10) is a "twofold trumpet" echo by which the Christian arrives at the gate of "that holy land, namely the grace of the resurrection" (2.112; cf. Bunyan's Christian's reception crossing into the Celestial City). If the trumpet is in this sense everywhere in Scripture a proclamation of salvation, then the "last trump" will simply announce the completion of what has been won in Christ for all mankind. St. Augustine relates the last trump to the "cry . . . made at midnight" in the parable of the wise and foolish virgins (*Sermo,* 93), where the oil in the wise virgins' vessels when they "arose" at the cry is the gift of grace in a transformed heart (9-10). The medieval *Glossa Ordinaria* follows Augustine in seeing the last trump as preeminently the announcement of the Bridegroom's approach *(Ecce sponsus venit),* with the trump itself, "whether understood as the voice of the archangel or the trumpet of God," as the voice of the gospel announcing to those dead in their trespasses and sins the victory of the Resurrection (PL 114.550).

In the *Chanson de Roland* the trumpet bears the weight of its association with the *shofar* announcing God's will (cf. *Glossa* on Exod. 19) and divine power (cf. Rev. 1; 11–12), and the horn evokes an evidently apocalyptic context in lines 1434-35. The commentary of Ambrose and Augustine lies behind the 13th-cent. ME lyric "Doomsday" (C. Brown, *Religious Lyrics of the XIVth Century,* no. 28), which adds that "Foure engels in þe dairet blouit here bemen" ("Four angels at dawn shall blow their trumpets" / þenne comit ihesus crist his domes for to demen" (9-10).

In Reformation commentary on the last trump, Calvin prefers to "regard it as a metaphor" (*New Testament Comms.* 9.343). Less so Matthew Henry, for whom "the trumpet must sound . . . the loud summons of all the living and all the dead, to come and appear at the tribunal of Christ" (*Comm.* 6.596). In Renaissance literary imagination the last trump is securely associated with the Last Judgment: on hearing that both Romeo and Tybalt no longer live, Shakespeare's Juliet exclaims: "Then dreadful trumpet sound the general doom! / For who is living if these two are gone?" (3.2.67-68). John Donne begins his Holy Sonnet 7 on resurrection and repentance with the lines:

> At the round earths imagin'd corners, blow
> Your trumpets, Angells, and arise, arise
> From death you numberless infinities
> Of soules, and to your scattred bodies goe. . . .

Herbert, whose "Dooms-day" is in the form of an address to the last trumpeter, implores:

> Come away,
> Make this the day.
> Dust, alas, no musick feels,
> But thy trumpet: then it kneels. . . .

And in his poetic prayer for the restoration of "The Jews" he prays: "that some Angel might a trumpet sound; / At which the Church falling upon her face / Should crie so loud, untill the trump were drown'd" — so obtaining of the Lord a plea that at last Israel's spiritual vitality, her "sweet say" of grace, might flow once more.

William Cowper's representative 18th-cent. English Calvinism makes polemical (or homiletical) grist of the figure:

> Hark! universal nature shook and groan'd,
> 'Twas the last trumpet — see the Judge enthron'd:
> Rouse all your courage at your utmost need;
> Now summon ev'ry virtue — stand, and plead.
> What! silent? Is your boasting heard no more?
> ("Truth," 563-67; cf. "Retirement," 651-60)

A gloomy invocation is afforded also by Sir Walter Scott, whose narrator in Kenilworth ominously observes that "As, at the blast of that last trumpet, the guilty shall call upon the mountains to cover them, Leicester's inward thoughts invoked the stately arch which he had built in his pride, to burst its strong conjunction, and overwhelm them in its ruins" (chap. 34). Byron invokes the 1 Cor. 15 passage more hopefully in his "To Caroline: When I hear": "Our breasts, which alive with such sympathy glow, / Will sleep in the grave till the blast shall awake us, / When calling the dead, in earth's bosom laid low" (27-29).

When the house in Hawthorne's "Ambitious Guest" shakes it is "as if this awful sound were the peel of the last trump." And Emerson, as willing as Cowper's rhetorical straw man to rely upon himself rather than God, imagines no such terrifying assize in which one will be called one day to give an account of one's life. Rather, he says, "Speak your latent conviction, and it shall be the universal sense . . . our first thought rendered back to us by the trumpets of the Last Judgment." Whittier's "Abraham Davenport" portrays a society suddenly arrested in its daily round, as

> all ears drew sharp
> To hear the doom-blast of the trumpet shatter
> The black sky, that the dreadful face of Christ
> Might look from the rent clouds. . . .

In the 20th cent., H. G. Wells has two short stories featuring the last trump. His "A Vision of Judgment" begins with the sound of the Last Trump and proceeds to God's judging all people in alphabetical order, concluding with everyone being given a fresh chance on a new planet (God forgives all because evil is ridiculous rather than important). Wells's "The Story of the Last Trump" pictures the trumpet itself falling to earth and sounding briefly (having been fixed to an air compressor) before being snatched back up into heaven. For an instant, then, people see things exactly as they are, and one character actually sees God. But everyone soon forgets the vision and each returns to his or her typically petty existence. Such, Wells moralizes, is the inability of the human race to face the truth that, having seen it, no one is willing to be changed by it.

See also DEATH, WHERE IS THY STING?; RESURRECTION.

Bibliography. Farrer, A. *A Rebirth of Images: The Making of St. John's Apocalypse* (1949), 36-51; Nichols, S. G. *Romanesque Signs: Early Medieval Narrative and Iconography* (1983).

LATCHET OF WHOSE SHOES As the forerunner of Christ, John the Baptist said, "There comes one mightier than I after me, the latchet of whose shoes I am not worthy to stoop down and unloose" (Mark 1:7; Luke 3:16). The nature of this attribution forbids all but straightforward quotation in much early literature in English. An exception is the parodic allusion in Chaucer's humorous *The Squire's Tale,* in which the hysterical falcon says of her faithless tereted lover that not Jason, Paris, or even Lamech the bigamist could match him,

> Ne koude man by twenty thousand part
> Countrefete the sophymes of his art,
> Ne were worthy unbrokelen his galoche
> Ther doublenesse or feyning sholde approche.
> (5.553-56)

Positive analogy is intended, however, by Carlyle, in whose "Boswell's Life of Johnson" Hume and Johnson, though "half-men" for Carlyle, if combined would make a "whole man," the stature of whom would be almost of messianic proportions: "Till such a whole man arrive for us. . . . might the Heavens but bless poor England with half-men worthy to tie the shoe-latchets of these. . . ."

See also JOHN THE BAPTIST; FRIEND OF THE BRIDE-GROOM.

LAW OF LOVE *See* CHARITY, CUPIDITY; GRACE, WORKS; GREAT COMMANDMENT.

LAZARUS OF BETHANY Lazarus, brother of Martha and Mary and friend of Jesus, lived at Bethany in Judea and was resurrected by Jesus after having been dead for four days (John 11:1-44). When the sisters notified Jesus of Lazarus's sickness, Jesus waited two days, so that

God might be glorified by the miracle to happen (v. 40) and so that people's belief in his divine mission might be strengthened (vv. 15, 42). At the tomb, Jesus wept, and then, after praying, called Lazarus forth from death. This miracle, seen by many scholars as the seventh and concluding "sign" in the Johannine "book of signs" (chaps. 1–12; see 12:37), also marked the beginning of Christ's passion. Because many Jews came to believe in Jesus as a result of the miracle (11:45; 12:11), the chief priests conspired to put him (as well as Lazarus) to death.

The Fathers saw the raising of Lazarus as a foreshadowing of Christ's own resurrection (St. Augustine, *Ad Consentius: Contra mendacium*, 27) and of the final resurrection of the "dead in Christ" (Chrysostom, *Hom. on Thessalonians*, 8); the stone at the tomb was interpreted by some as a symbol of hard-heartedness (St. Peter Chrysologus, *Sermo*, 65:3). But most prominent in early exegetical tradition is the parallel Augustine repeatedly draws between Lazarus and the habitual sinner: ". . . the sinner is dead, especially he whom the load of sinful habit presseth down, who is buried as it were like Lazarus" (*Sermons on New Testament Lessons*, 17). Lazarus can therefore be called a type of the awakened sinner (cf. *In Joan. Ev.* 22, 7).

The life that Lazarus lived after his resurrection has been a perennial subject of speculation. The most popular legend, repeated in the 17th cent. by Sir Thomas Browne, was that "hee lived thirtie yeares after, and, being pursued by the Jewes, came by sea into Provence, by Marseilles, with Marie Magdalen, Maximinus, and others: where remarkable places carry their names or memories unto this day" (Browne, "A Letter to a Friend"). This legend, dating to at least the 11th cent., also made Lazarus the first bishop of Marseilles (probably in error for the 5th-cent. Bishop Lazarus of Aix).

Luther followed Augustine's typology (Sermon of March 19, 1518), but with reference to John 11:35 he also emphasized the depth of Jesus' sorrow over his friend's death: "Christ's gestures are so human that a man might never have thought that he was God" (Sermon of March 29, 1539; also March 14, 1540). For Calvin, Christ's groaning (vv. 33, 38) reflects the nature of his struggle against death: he comes to the sepulcher "like a wrestler preparing for the contest" (*Comm. on the Gospel of John*).

In early English literature, Lazarus is featured in various lives of Christ (e.g., *The Stanzaic Life of Christ* [MS BM Add 39996], 1586-1763). The anonymous *Meditations on the Life and Passion of Christ* (EETS o.s. 158, 209-52) contain an impressive rendering of the raising as a battle between Christ and Satan. Christ's command "Come out" is repeated over and over as a "word of batayle." Lazarus is mentioned also in the apocryphal Gospel of Nicodemus where, in its account of Christ's descent into hell, Satan calls Christ the one "þat called Lazar vs fra" (1306).

The miracle was dramatized in Latin by Hilarius — possibly an Englishman — in the 12th-cent. Later versions, usually in connection with the "Conversion of St. Mary Magdalen" (generally assumed, in the Middle Ages, to be one and the same with Mary of Bethany), are found in the Latin playbook of Fleury, France, and in the *Carmina Burana* of Benediktbeuren, Germany (in both Latin and Middle High German). English versions begin with the closely scriptural rendering of the miracle in the Chester cycle (1328), and thereafter in the York, Wakefield, and Coventry cycles, all of which adhere to the scriptural account. The Digby Play of *Mary Magdalen* (1402), which includes a "Resuscitation of Lazarus," reflects the growth of extracanonical legend surrounding the persons of Lazarus and Mary Magdalen (as does the *Golden Legend*).

In the 17th cent. Francis Quarles recurs to traditional typology in his poem "Why dost thou shade thy lovely face?" The poet asks God to redeem him like Lazarus: "If I am dead, Lord, set death's prisoner free." Milton, in his comments on bodily death, used John 11:13 to argue for the unorthodox view that in death the human soul is not separated from one's body, but sleeps the sleep of death (*De Doctrina Christiana*, 1.13). Blake makes symbolic use of the miracle in his poem *Milton* (1.24.26-33), where, according to S. Damon (A *Blake Dictionary* [1965], 224), Lazarus "represents the physical bodies of all mankind" and the resurrection becomes "part of the false doctrine of the church" because it is understood to happen to the physical (not spiritual) body.

The question "Where wert thou, brother, those four days?" is asked by Mary and the neighbors in Alfred Lord Tennyson's "In Memoriam A. H. H." (sect. 23). "There lives no record of reply," and the question is submerged in the disciples' joy. Christ's humanity, as demonstrated by his weeping, is one of the topics of Elizabeth Barrett Browning's sonnet "The Two Sayings," and of John Keble's poem "Fill High the Bowl," which meditates on Christ's agony.

Increasing theological skepticism in the 19th cent. prompted a variety of revisionist readings of the miracle. In Robert Browning's "An Epistle Containing the Strange Medical Experience of Karshish, the Arab Physician," the raising of Lazarus and his state of mind at the age of 50, years after Christ's death, is the object of skeptical scrutiny. For Karshish "'Tis but a case of mania — subinduced / By epilepsy, at the turning point / Of trance prolonged unduly some three days," and he sees Lazarus as divided between eternal and temporal existence. Doubts about the authenticity of the miracle are expressed indirectly by a bible-versed messenger boy in Dickens's *Our Mutual Friend*. He takes up the traditional high evaluation of the miracle in his report about the state of a drowned man: "If Lazarus was only half as far gone, that was the greatest of all the miracles" (chap. 3). In *David Copperfield* the protagonist's mother reads to him the story of Lazarus being raised, which frightens him so that his mother and the servant are afterwards "obliged to take me out of bed, and show me the quiet churchyard out of the bedroom window, with the dead all lying in their graves at rest, below the solemn moon" (chap. 2).

In "Lady Lazarus" Sylvia Plath fuses the experience of her earlier attempt at suicide with a criticism of the public's sensationalistic, dehumanized interest in the disclosures after the Nazi holocaust. *Lazarus was a Lady,* a drama by John Ford Noonan, is about a young woman who uses her terminal illness as a means of manipulation. Thom Gunn's poem "Lazarus Not Raised" describes the futility of merely human efforts to conquer death.

In Melville's *Moby-Dick,* Ishmael, making his will, observes that his future days will be "as good as the days that Lazarus lived after his resurrection; a supplementary clean gain of so many months or weeks as the case might be." This businesslike assessment of the value of life is consistent with the whole chapter (49) — if not the whole book — in which the universe is taken to be a "vast practical joke." The same detachment can be found in Mark Twain, who refers ironically to the legal implications of Lazarus's resurrection. In "The Second Advent" and "The Holy Children," he ridicules "special providences" and claims that a modern-day resurrection would raise disputes over the dead man's property.

"Lazarus," by Edwin Arlington Robinson, is a modern psychological study of the reactions of the sisters and Lazarus after Christ has left Bethany. The sisters want to have "all as it was before," but having lost the security of the tomb, Lazarus has become a homeless, brooding man who wonders why he has been resurrected and asserts that "there is worse than death." Other modern renderings take up the same theme: e.g., Alain Absire's *Lazarus* (Eng. trans. Barbara Bray), in which the protagonist, reeking of "damp earth and rancid oils," longs for the death which has been denied to him. The Lazarus in W. B. Yeats's one-act play *Calvary* is a death-hungry character who accuses Christ of having resurrected him against his will, of having dragged him to the light "as boys drag out / A rabbit when they have dug its hole away." He cannot find a tomb again and demands Christ's own death: "You took my death, give me your death instead."

In Eugene O'Neill's drama *Lazarus Laughed,* the protagonist, after having been raised by Jesus, begins to laugh "in the laughter of God" and answers "There is no death" when he is asked the familiar question about his experiences beyond death. His house becomes known as the "House of Laughter," and laughter is Lazarus's final comment on all adversities — even when members of his family are slain by Roman soldiers in a Jewish uproar against the new sect of his followers. Lazarus and his wife Miriam are taken to Athens, where he is hailed as a reincarnation of the god Dionysus, and then on to Rome. Here, too, his doctrines fascinate people, but also entangle them in a maze of love, hate, frenzy, and killing. Finally, Lazarus (who has become a young man again whereas

Miriam has grown old) is executed at the stake; his last words are, "There is no death!" The drama is less concerned with the proclamation of Christ's power over death than with a portrayal of Nietzsche's ideas of the Dionysian mode of life, of the Superman, and of the eternal return. In the end, Lazarus's soul flies "back into the womb of Infinity" (4.2). A different and more cynical kind of laughter is reflected in Joyce's debunking reference in *Ulysses,* where Leopold Bloom, pondering the resurrection of the dead, puns on John 11:43: "Come forth, Lazarus! And he came fifth and lost the job."

See also MARY MAGDALENE; RESURRECTION.

Bibliography. Frantzen, A. J. "St. Erkenwald and the Raising of Lazarus." *Mediaevalia* 7 (1981), 157-71; Kremer, J. *Lazarus: Die Geschichte einer Auferstehung* (1985); Wilkens, W. "Die Erweckung des Lazarus." *TZ* 15 (1959), 22-39; Pottet, E. *Histoire de Saint-Lazare 1127-1912* (1912); Thompson, L. "The Multiple Uses of the Lazarus Motif in Modern Literature." *CSR* 7 (1977), 306-29; Törnquist, E. "O'Neill's Lazarus: Dionysus and Christ." *AL* 41 (1970), 543-54.
MANFRED SIEBALD

LEAH Leah was the first wife of Jacob who, with his second wife Rachel, is remembered in Israelite history as "one of two who did build the house of Israel" (Ruth 4:11ff.; Gen. 29:15–30:25). She was given to Jacob by her father Laban in an act of deception; Jacob had worked seven years for Rachel, whom he loved "more than Leah" (Gen. 29:30), but Laban claimed that custom prevented the marriage of the younger daughter first. However, because Leah was not preferred by Jacob, the Lord consoled her with children; she bore six sons to Jacob (Reuben, Simeon, Levi, Judah, Issachar, Zebulun) and a daughter (Dinah), and her handmaiden Zilpah bore for her two more sons. Descendants of these eight sons became known as the Leah tribes. Leah, like Sarah before her and Hannah after her, is typical of those Israelite women whose plight God sees and comforts with children.

The comparison of Leah with Rachel in Gen. 29:16-17 is frequently alluded to in exegetical tradition: "Leah was tender eyed; but Rachel was beautiful and well-favored." The word (Heb. *rakkot*) rendered in the KJV as "tender eyed" has also been variously translated as "dull eyed" and "weak eyed." Jewish legend attributes the weakness of Leah's eyes to copious weeping, caused by her expectation that she was to be given as a bride to Esau, Jacob's brother. Yet the legends also attribute to her determination and strength of character; when Jacob reproaches her for deceiving him on their wedding night, she chides him for his own deception of his father Isaac. Her prayers, offered not only for herself but also for Rachel, were considered extremely efficacious (L. Ginzberg, *LJ* 1.358-69).

In patristic and later in mystical writings Leah is understood as a type of the active life (an OT equivalent of Martha) while Rachel represents the contemplative life, as in the NT does Martha's sister Mary. This distinction is reflected in Chaucer's *Second Nun's Tale* (*Canterbury Tales,* 8.96-98). In Arthur Hugh Clough's *The Bothie of Tober-na-Vuolich* (1848) the allegory is somewhat different: Rachel stands for "the heavenly-ideal" of marriage and Leah for "the other vulgar and earthy" (9.170). "Rachel we dream-of at night: in the morning, behold it is Leah" (9.179; cf. his later narrative poem about Leah and Rachel, "Jacob's Wives").

The triangle of love and deception among Leah, Rachel, and Jacob prompts a variety of literary responses. The "bed trick" substitution of one woman for another becomes a significant feature of Shakespearean drama — specifically in *Measure for Measure* and *All's Well That Ends Well.* "Rejected like Leah, wronged like Tamar, Shakespeare's Helena and Mariana imitate their desired rivals, tolerate more or less consciously the degradation of being loved for someone else and work a kind of salvation out of an ambiguous sexual encounter" (Jagendorf, 56). Thomas Wyatt recalls Jacob's chagrin at the discovery of his deception: "For Rachell have I servid, / For Lya caried I never" ("Perdye I said it not," 45-46). A character in Robert Browning's *The Ring and the Book* suggests that a divorce might be possible if the listener, "taking thought to wed / Rachel of the blue eye and golden hair, / Found swarth-skinned Leah cumber couch next day" (5.1304-06). William Blake's prophetic poem *Jerusalem* ascribes the evils of war to children "born in contentions of Chastity & in / Deadly Hate between Leah & Rachel, Daughters of Deceit & Fraud" (pl. 69, lines 10-11). Leah as the less desirable provides Angel Clare in Thomas Hardy's *Tess of the D'Urbervilles* an analogy for courting Tess. After having carried the other dairymaids across a flooded lane, he whispers to Tess in his arms: "Three Leahs to get one Rachel" (chap. 23).

See also JACOB; RACHEL.

Bibliography. Jagendorf, Z. "In the Morning Behold, It Was Leah: Genesis and the Reversal of Sexual Knowledge." In D. H. Hirsch and N. A. Schkenasy, eds. *Biblical Patterns in Modern Literature* (1984); Simonds, P. M. "Overlooked Sources of the Bed Trick." *SQ* 34 (1983), 433-34.

JOYCE Q. ERICKSON

LEAN, FAT KINE Gen. 41:1-14 describes how the Pharoah of Egypt dreamt of seven fat cattle, grazing in a meadow, suddenly set upon by seven lean and ravenous counterparts who devoured them. Unable to interpret his dream, he called for Joseph, who "read" the dream as a divine forewarning that seven years of bountiful harvests would be followed by seven years of devastating famine.

See also JOSEPH THE PATRIARCH; PHARAOH.

LEAVEN "Your boasting is not good. Do you not know that a little leaven leavens the whole lump?" (1 Cor. 5:6). This verse comes within the context of St. Paul's discussion of moral laxness in the Corinthian church. The church was tolerating a situation in which a member was

known to be living with his father's wife —a kind of immorality, says Paul, "not found even among pagans." Paul decreed that the man was to be excommunicated from the community and that the church should check any such moral irregularities lest they spread and infect the whole fellowship.

There are two main OT practices behind Paul's use of the leaven image in this passage. First, the OT forbids the use of leaven in sacrifices to God (e.g., Exod. 23:18; 34:25; Lev. 2:11; 6:17). Second, Israelites were forbidden to eat leavened bread, or even to have leaven in the household, during the Passover season (Exod. 12:15, 18-20; 13:7). These practices probably reflect an ancient view of leaven as a symbol of corruption. From this symbolic association there apparently developed the sort of proverb which Paul quotes in 1 Cor. 5:6 and Gal. 5:9: "a little leaven leavens the whole lump."

Leaven is used as a negative symbol in Jesus' saying in Matt. 16:6 (cf. Mark 8:15; Luke 12:1). Elsewhere it becomes a simile for the power of the kingdom of God growing silently (Matt. 13:33; Luke 13:20-22). Exegetical and literary usage reflects both associations: either leaven can refer to a former unregenerate or corrupt condition which has since been purged or abandoned, or, less commonly, it can signify a subtle (generally benign) but potent transforming influence.

The negative sense of the term is common in polemical religious literature from St. Clement of Alexandria (*Stromateis,* 3.18.105-06) to John Milton (*De Doctrina Christiana,* 1.28). An anonymous Wycliffite tract of the late 14th cent., "The Leaven of the Pharisees," castigates friars for traducing their vows.

English literary occurrences of the Pauline proverb or, indeed, of the image of leaven, are scarce and often insubstantial. Coleridge in *Biographia Literaria* speaks of those whose "faults were at least a remnant of the former leaven." And Arnold in *Culture and Anarchy* refers to the "subtle Hellenic leaven of the Renascence [which] found its way into the Reformation" ("Hebraism and Hellenism").

The title of Robertson Davies's *Leaven of Malice* (1952) derives from 1 Cor. 5:8: "Therefore let us keep the feast, not with old leaven, neither with the leaven of malice and wickedness; but with the unleavened bread of sincerity and truth."

Bibliography. Allis, O. "The Parable of the Leaven." *EvQ* 19 (1947), 254-73; Mitton, C. "Leaven." *ExpTim* 84 (1972/73), 339-42.

WAYNE O. MCCREADY

LED CAPTIVITY CAPTIVE (Ps. 68:18; Eph. 4:8)

See also ASCENSION; FREEDOM, BONDAGE; HARROWING OF HELL.

LEEKS, ONIONS, AND GARLIC In their desert journey the Israelites complained about the manna which God provided them to eat, saying, "We remember the fish, which we did eat in Egypt freely; the cucumbers, and the melons, and the leeks, and the onions, and the garlic" (Num. 11:5). Their grumbling "afflicted" Moses sufficiently that he in turn complained about having to lead the people (vv. 11-15). They were then given the "meat" they asked for in the form of quails — almost a plague of them (vv. 16-23).

Traditional commentary (e.g., St. Augustine, *De Genesi ad litteram; Glossa Ordinaria*) suggests, as does John Gower in his *Vox Clamantis,* that "Such are the people the bosom of the Church now nourishes — people who seek after earthly vanities instead of things divine" (*Major Latin Works,* ed. E. W. Stockton [1962], 119). Since the manna the people despised was readily identified by such commentary with the "bread of life," figuratively understood as spiritual sustenance, it became possible to equate the appetite for the sensual delights of Egyptian leeks, onions, and garlics with carnality inappropriate to the Christian *viator.* This is the force of the allusion in Chaucer's description of the Summoner, a supposedly vocational religious man whose fondness for spicy foods figures the unseemly appetites of a reprobate pilgrim, lusting after the fleshpots of Egypt: "Wel loved he garleek, onyons, and eek lekes, / And for to drynken strong wyn, reed as blood" (*Canterbury Tales,* 1.634-35).

See also BREAD OF LIFE; EXODUS; FLESH POTS OF EGYPT; MANNA.

Bibliography. Kaske, R. E. "The Summoner's Garleek, Onyons, and eek Lekes." *MLN* 74 (1959), 481-84; Wood, C. "The Sources of Chaucer's Summoner's 'Garleek, Onyons, and eek Lekes'." *ChauR* (1971), 240-44.

LEFT HAND, RIGHT HAND Biblical phrases referring to the right hand reflect a widespread human cultural attitude, namely the recognition that for most people the right hand is both stronger and more adept than the left, and is the hand with which many tasks are instinctively undertaken. The corollary has often been that left-handedness is regarded as odd, undesirable, and even antisocial; hence the view embodied in the word *sinister* (Latin for "left hand"). No such hostile attitude to left-handedness can be found in Scripture; there are stories of left-handed heroes, such as Ehud in Judg. 3:15-30 (cf. the left-handed soldiers of Benjamin in Judg. 20:16 and David's Benjamite warriors in 1 Chron. 12:2; interestingly, "Benjamin" in Hebrew means "son of my right hand"!).

A general disposition to prefer the right hand is nonetheless evident and persists in subsequent tradition. Eccl. 10:2 links "a wise man's heart" with his right hand, and "a fool's heart" with his left. When the Son of Man separates the sheep from the goats at the Last Judgment, it is to the damned "on the left hand" that he says, "Depart from me, ye cursed, into everlasting fire" (Matt. 25:41). (A classical parallel may be found in Plato's myth of Er [*Republic,* bk. 10], where at death the just souls take the righthand upward path while the unjust must take the

downward path on the left.) Rabbinic tradition also establishes hell to the left of God, and heaven on his right side (Midr. Ps. 90:12).

The right hand is often mentioned as a symbol of strength, both for human beings and anthropomorphically for God (e.g., Job 40:14; Isa. 48:13). This metaphor for God's power is used chiefly in connection with creation or the deliverance of God's people. For George Herbert, in "Providence," the right and left hand of God signify two aspects of the divine will:

> For either thy command or thy permission
> Lay hands on all: they are thy right and left.
> The first puts on with speed and expedition;
> The other curbs sinnes stealing pace and theft.

Another symbolism concerns the place at the right hand of a person or God, i.e., the place of preeminent dignity and favor (cf. 1 Kings 2:19; Ps. 110:1). Christ being enthroned at the right hand of the Father signifies his being God's agent in salvation.

In patristic writings scriptural distinctions between right and left are often ingeniously allegorized. Thus, in St. Augustine's discussion of the miraculous draught of fishes (John 21), the multitude of fish caught when, as Jesus directed, the disciples cast their net "on the right side of the ship" represent "those who stand on the right hand, the good alone." Augustine contrasts this incident with an earlier miracle recorded in Luke 5:3-7:

> On that occasion the nets are not let down on the right side, that the good alone might not be signified, nor on the left, lest the application should be limited to the bad; but without any reference to either side, He [Jesus] says, "Let down your nets for a draught," that we may understand the good and bad as mingled together. . . . He showed thereby in the former case that the capture of fishes signified the good and bad presently existing in the Church; but in the latter, the good only, whom it will contain everlastingly, when the resurrection of the dead shall have been completed in the end of this world. (*In Joan. Ev.* 122.6)

This broad tradition is evident in the conventions of visual and literary iconography. In medieval drama, such as the *Jeu d'Adam,* hellmouth is typically located to the left of God (i.e., on the audience's right). In medieval illustration left / right symmetries are common: the *Biblia Pauperum,* e.g., following patristic precedent, shows Eve created from the left side of Adam, whereas blood and water issue from the pierced right side of Jesus, the Second Adam — the first anticipates the Fall and signals human mortality, the second bespeaks redemption and the gift of eternal life. Milton in *Paradise Lost* (2.755-58) has Sin born out of the left side of Satan's head. Later, in Blake's *Vision of the Last Judgement* "the right hand of the Design is appropriated to the Resurrection of the Just; the left hand . . . to the Resurrection of the Wicked." The traditional bias is recalled also by Vladimir Nabokov in

Laughter in the Dark (1938) when Margot's two lovers, the one favored, the other unwelcome, touch her on each knee, "as though Paradise had been on her right hand and Hell on her left" (chap. 17).

Other literary allusions (e.g., Carlyle, *Sartor Resartus,* 1.8; 3.3) derive from Jonah 4:11, where God explains to hard-hearted Jonah his compassion toward Nineveh, in which live "more than sixscore thousand persons that cannot discern between their right hand and their left" (i.e., young children), or from Jesus' injunctions concerning secrecy in almsgiving: "Let not thy left hand know what thy right hand doeth" (Matt. 6:3). The latter text is the subject of frequent parodic adaptation, as in P. G. Wodehouse, *Meet Mr. Mulliner* ("He was a man who never let his left hip know what his right hip was doing"). In Christopher Isherwood's *Mr. Norris Changes Trains,* Mr. Norris introduces Herr Schmidt as "my secretary and my right hand. Only in this case, Mr. Norris tittered nervously, 'I can assure you that the right hand knows perfectly well what the left hand doeth'" (chap. 2).

Bibliography. Brown, M. *Left-handed, Right-handed* (1979); Lloyd, G. "Right and Left in Greek Philosophy." In *Right and Left: Essays on Dual Symbolic Classification.* Ed. R. Needham (1973); Silverstein, A. *The Left-hander's World* (1977). MICHAEL GOLDBERG
DAVID F. PAYNE

LEGION "My name is Legion," says the demon in the demoniac when Jesus asks his name (Matt. 8:28; Mark 5:9; Luke 8:30). In Shakespeare's *Twelfth Night,* Sir Toby describes Malvolio's antics as a kind of madness or possession: "If all the devils of hell be drawn in a little, and Legion himself possessed him, yet I'll speak to him" (3.4.94-95). Legion" is sometimes taken in late medieval and Renaissance popular literature to be the name of a compound, or hydra-headed devil.

See also DEVIL; GADARENE SWINE.

LEMUEL The addressee of the poem in praise of "The Good Woman," *Mulier fortis* (Lady Wisdom) in Prov. 31:10-30, whose name means "belonging to God." In some patristic commentary the name was held to be a pseudonym for Solomon.

See also BATHSHEBA; *MULIER FORTIS;* SOLOMON.

LEOPARD CHANGE HIS SPOTS In Jer. 13 the prophet is told by the Lord to condemn Judah for its habitual miscreance, castigating with a rhetorical question: "Can the Ethiopian change his skin, or the leopard his spots? then may ye also do good that are accustomed to do evil" (13:23). In early Christian exegesis these tropes are taken as signifying the natural condition of fallen humanity, "spotted" with sin in the case of the leopard and naturally without remedy (e.g., St. Jerome, *Ep.* 97.2). But still more frequently the figures are used to demonstrate a positive answer to Jeremiah's rhetorical query, asserting that by

grace just such radical transformations are possible. With reference to the story of the conversion of the Ethiopian eunuch (Acts 8:27-38) Jerome observes: "Though it is against nature the Ethiopian does change his skin and the leopard his spots" (*Ep.* 49.6). The Ethiopian eunuch is for him "a type of the Gentile, who in spite of the prophet changed his skin, and whilst he read the Old Testament found the fountain of the Gospel" (*Ep.* 108.11). The force of these allusions is accordingly not, as might at first be imagined, to characterize the incorrigibility of human nature without God, but to demonstrate that what alone can transform it is, as implied in Jeremiah's haranguing interrogation, an obedient response to God.

In medieval MS illustrations of the Fall of Adam and Eve a leopard is sometimes placed at their feet, iconographically indicating the state of sinful nature into which they have descended; this motif is replicated in a woodcut on the frontispiece of a 15th-cent. French Bible. In Chrétien de Troyes's *Erec et Enide,* after Erec has been at last humiliated by Enide into rising from overindulgence in their marriage bed at Carnant, he arms himself for his pilgrimage-quest while standing on a rug which is prominently decorated with a leopard. When in Shakespeare's *Richard 3* the King hears Bolingbroke accuse Mowbray of treachery and murder he tries to interpose, saying, "Give me his gage. Lions make leopards tame." Mowbray hotly retorts: "Yea, but not change his spots" (1.1.173-75). Robert Southey offers a similarly prejudicial determination in "Ode on Negociations with Bonaparte in 1814," warning against unwise diplomacy: "For sooner shall the Ethiopian change his skin, / Or from the Leopard shall her spots depart, / Than this man change his old flatigious heart." In Sir Walter Scott's *Talisman,* however, the force of the image to highlight an extraordinary transformation is preserved, when Richard Coeur de Lion praises the "brave knight of the Leopard," saying, "thou hast shown that the Ethiopian may change his skin, and the leopard his spots, though clerks quote Scripture for the impossibility." Scott's reading here implicates the potential for misconstruing Jeremiah's words by overlooking their original subjunctive and optative irony in order to make a merely indicative judgment.

LEPROSY The Bible's discussion of "leprosy" is concentrated in Lev. 13–14, where the laws for the ritualistic treatment of "unclean" conditions are found. The conditions described here and some instances elsewhere in the Bible are probably not true leprosy ("Hansen's disease") but are rather various milder skin diseases such as psoriasis. The disease is often said to be a result of sin, specifically, according to postbiblical Jewish tradition (Lev. Rab.), a punishment for the offenses mentioned in Prov. 6:16: "These six things does the LORD hate: yea, seven are an abomination unto him." The sins in question range from "haughty eyes" and "a lying tongue" to sowing discord among brethren. (Cf. also the punishment of Miriam [Num. 12], Uzziah [2 Chron. 26:16-23], and Gehazi [2 Kings 5:20-27] for their sins.) Once afflicted, the person is "unclean" *(tame')* and must either be sequestered from the clean *(tahor),* or healed. Accounts of lepers' healings are rare in the OT, Naaman's cleansing in the River Jordan (2 Kings 5) being unusual (Luke 4:27). In this respect, the contrast with the NT is remarkable, for the power of *Christus medicus* over sin is revealed repeatedly in the curing of lepers (Matt. 8:2-4; Mark 1:40-42; Luke 5:12-13 and 17:11-19). Naaman himself, although not called a "sinner" in the OT but a "just man," honorable, and valiant (2 Kings 5:1), nevertheless serves as a type of sinful man "made clean" in baptism for exegetes such as St. Ambrose (*De sacramentis*) and writers such as Donne (Sermon on Ps. 51:7).

Although the causal connections between generic sin and leprosy frequently obtain in literature, the malady sometimes symbolizes particular vices. A bond between envy and leprosy is established by the plight of Miriam, Moses' murmuring sister, whom God plagues with leprosy for her sin (Num. 12); her story is rehearsed in Gower's *Mirour de l'omme* (2553-2664) and in the 14th-cent. *The Book of the Knight of La Tour-Landry.* Connections between heresy and leprosy are evident in the case of Constantine, the Roman emperor whose apostasy makes him a leper. Subsequently converted by Saint Sylvester, Constantine appears in *The Golden Legend,* in Gower's *Confessio Amantis* (2.3187-3496), and in Dante (*Inferno,* 27.94-97). As putrefaction of the flesh, leprosy is usually reserved, however, as a just punishment for carnality. In *Amis and Amiloun,* a 13th-cent. romance which Pater invokes in *The Renaissance,* Amiloun engages in a deceptive cover-up of his friend Amis's adulterous liaison with the Duke's daughter and is smitten with leprosy as God had forewarned. In some versions of the Tristan and Isolde legend, the heroine's adulterous love eventuates in her confinement in a leper colony. Preeminently, Henryson's Cresseid epitomizes the lustful lover: her spotted condition (*maculait*) contrasts implicitly with that of the Virgin Unspotted, the Immaculate Lady. Swinburne parodies this tradition subtly in "The Leper," where God's curse isolates a leprous lady for the lover's private enjoyment.

Most modern literary treatments of lepers tend to invest their seclusion and alienation with heroic purposes. This tendency may draw upon biblical heroes such as Job, patron saint of lepers, the "suffering servant" whom the Vg describes as *"quasi leprosum"* (Isa. 53:4), and the Lazarus of Jesus' parable who, though full of sores, was transported from Dives's gate to Abraham's bosom (Luke 16:22-25). Several of the frequent references in Romantic and neo-Romantic poetry to leprosy promote disgust (Coleridge, "Rime of the Ancient Mariner," 192; Browning, "Childe Roland," 74). But others reveal the status of the leper as an archetypally sanctified outcast. Blake, in

a manner consistent with his inversion of biblical symbolism, conceives of Jehovah as leprous (*Four Zoas,* 8.405; *Milton,* 13.24); and Robert Graves depicts his white goddess, who is reviled by saints and sober men, as one "whose broad high brow was white as any leper's." Tennyson, in "Happy: The Leper's Bride," uses information about medieval rites for ostracizing lepers as the foundation for a poem about the victory of defiantly faithful love over defiled flesh (cf. François Mauriac's *A Kiss for the Leper*). Jack Hodgins's short story "The Leper's Squint" refers to the special cubicle in an Irish church from which the infected and quarantined person might observe (though not participate) in the sacrament — a figure for his writer's sense of alienated or marginalized perspective (*Barclay Family Theatre*). In Alden Nowlan's "The Last Leper in Canada," irony counterpoints the mundane townspeople against the outcast they try annually to propitiate with prayer and sacrifices. And in Yeats's play *The King's Threshold,* Seanchan the poet is a Lazarus-figure who has Blakean visions of the infected moon whose leprous curse confers a blessing in disguise.

Conceivably under the influence of Robert L. Stevenson's notorious open letter on Father Damien's work in the *lazarettos* of Hawaii, Graham Greene's *A Burnt-Out Case* combines the physical and spiritual senses of leprosy. On his quest for God and self-abnegation in the Congo, Querry, a "spiritual" leper, resists canonization. Yet he unwittingly achieves grace when he saves his servant, a leper called Deo Gratias. John Updike's "From the Journal of a Leper" (*Problems*) puts a new twist on the theme of the "leper" achieving sanctity through isolation in a story of a self-diagnosed leper being "cured" by the devil and thus rejoining American society, which values only the skin-deep appearance of health. In this instance the cure is equated with loss of sanctity.

See also DISEASE AND HEALING; MIRIAM; NAAMAN.

Bibliography. Brody, S. N. *The Disease of the Soul: Leprosy in Medieval Literature* (1974); Cochrane, R. G. *Biblical Leprosy: A Suggested Interpretation* (2nd ed. 1963); Harrison, R. K. "Leprosy." *IDB* 3.111-13; *ISBE* 3.103-06; Hirsch, R. S. M. "A Note on the Use of Leprosy in Henryson's *Testament of Crisseid* and Claudel's L'annonce faite à Marie." *Actaeus* (1970), 17-19; Weymouth, A. *Through the Leper-Squint: A Study of Leprosy from pre-Christian times to Present-Day* (1930).   RONALD B. BOND

LET THE DEAD BURY THEIR DEAD One of Jesus' disciples (identified by St. Clement of Alexandria as Philip), wishing perhaps to withdraw for a season, asked: "Lord, suffer me first to go and bury my father. But Jesus said unto him, Follow me; and let the dead bury their dead" (Matt. 8:21-22; Luke 9:60). This verse has occasioned divergent commentary, but the usual sense in patristic and medieval exegesis has to do with the soul rather than the body. In his discussion of Christian belief in the Resurrection St. Ambrose speaks of the first death as "when we die to sin but live to God." The second is "departure from this life," in which "the soul is set free from the fetters of the body."

> The third death is that of which it is said: Leave the dead to bury their own dead. In that death not only the flesh but also the soul dies . . . through the weakness not of nature, but of guilt. This death is not then a discharge from this life, but a fall through error. Spiritual death [i.e., to the "old man"], then, is one thing, natural death another, a third is the death of punishment. (*De excessu fratris Satyri*, 2.36-37)

For St. Augustine the "dead" who are to bury their own are those "dead in the soul" (*Sermo*, 88.3), as "all who are under sin are dead, dead servants, dead in their service, servants in their own death," only seeming to be alive (*Sermo*, 134.3). For such, the only means of Resurrection is the Word of God; hence Jesus' admonition to the disciple, about to leave the presence of the Word in which alone, Augustine says, "is the resurrection of hearts, the resurrection of the inner man, the resurrection of the soul" (*Sermo*, 127.7). Matthew Henry reads the passage in terms of a pattern of challenges to vocational single-mindedness in which purity of heart is to will one thing: "The meaning of *Non vacat* is, *Non placet — The want of leisure is the want of inclination*," he observes, whereas the principal obligation of discipleship is almost self-evident:

> Piety to God must be preferred before piety to parents, though that is a great and needful part of our religion. The Nazarites, under the law, were not to mourn for their own parents, because they were *holy to the Lord* (Numb. vi.6-8); nor was the high priest to *defile himself for the dead*, no, not for *his own father*, Lev. xxi.11, 12. And Christ requires of those who would follow him, that they *hate father and mother* (Luke xiv.26); love them less than God; we must comparatively neglect and disesteem our nearest relations, when they come in competition with Christ, and either our doing for him, or our suffering for him. (*Comm. on the Whole Bible*, 5.109)

Calvin's *New Testament Comms.* (1.255) had already suggested that Jesus' intent was to encourage focus on the future rather than the dead past. This notion seems to have been broadly adapted by the 19th cent., enough to be reflected in Longfellow's "A Psalm of Life," which contains the injunction "Trust no Future, howe'er pleasant! / Let the dead Past bury its dead." In Thoreau's "A Plea for Captain John Brown" he says that Harper's Ferry confronted him with the cold fact of death, yet he concludes that there was in some sense really "no death in the case, because there had been no life; they merely rotted or sloughed off. . . . Let the dead bury their dead" — an attitude which bears disturbing resemblance to that expressed by Lord Henry to Dorian after the suicide of Sibyl Vane in Oscar Wilde's *The Picture of Dorian Gray* (1891). Exemplifying the proverbial sense, Somerset Maugham's Kitty, in *The Painted Veil*, resists depression

after defeat in love, saying, "I have hope and courage. The past is finished; let the dead bury their dead. It's all uncertain, whatever is to come to me, but I enter upon it with a light and buoyant heart" (chap. 80). The older Catholic sense seems ironically present, however, in Joyce's *Portrait of the Artist as a Young Man*, even where it is being most obviously contested. Writing about his rejection of faith and apostolic vocation, Stephen writes in his journal: "*March 21, night*. Free. Soul free and fancy free. Let the dead bury the dead. Ay. And let the dead marry the dead" (chap. 5).

See also LILIES OF THE FIELD.

LET THERE BE LIGHT   *See FIAT LUX; LIGHT.*

LETTER AND SPIRIT   Contrasting the self-conscious legalism of their past understanding of religion with the new faith of the Corinthians, St. Paul describes his hearers as themselves a "living epistle of Christ . . . written not with ink, but with the Spirit of the living God; not in tables of stone, but in fleshy tables of the heart" (2 Cor. 3:3). He then reminds them that the "sufficiency" of such a proclamation is not human but "of God; who also hath made us able ministers of the new testament; not of the letter, but of the spirit: for the letter killeth, but the spirit giveth life" (v. 6). (The Greek word here translated "letter" is *gramma*, "character.")

In the most famous patristic exegesis of the passage, St. Augustine argues that the phrase

> prescribes that we should not take in the literal sense any figurative phrase which in the proper meaning of its words would produce only nonsense, but should consider what else it signifies, nourishing the inner man by our spiritual intelligence, since "being carnally minded is death, whilst to be spiritually minded is life and peace" [Rom. 8:6]. If, for instance, a man were to take in a literal and carnal sense much that is written in the Song of Solomon, he would minister not to the fruit of a luminous charity, but to the feeling of a libidinous desire. (*De spiritu et littera*, 4)

Augustine relates to this passage Paul's statements to the effect that the function of the Law is diagnostic, identifying sin and producing conviction, but at the same time unavoidably imparting knowledge of guilt and a loss of innocence (Rom. 7:7, 11). Theologically this leads to a necessary emphasis on grace as against law, providing in Christ the healing from sin (*De spiritu et littera*, 6-12) so that "the law of deeds" having proved too much for human nature to obey, "the law of faith" becomes available to overcome despair (v. 13). Indeed, the Decalogue "kills," if grace is not present to reformulate one's approach to it (v. 14). Hermeneutically the contrast between letter and spirit lays down an imperative for referential (or "allegorical") reading of much of Scripture, in which "everything that is said or done is to be understood either in its literal signification, or else it contains something figuratively; or at least contains both of these at once, both its own literal interpretation and a figurative signification as well" (*Sermo*, 89.4, 5-7).

Augustine (in *De doctrina Christiana*, 3.5.9) and other major Christian literary theorists after him made this verse central to their strategy for reading the Bible. St. Gregory the Great writes in his commentary on the Song of Songs (PL 79.472-73) that:

> the sacred Scripture with its words and senses is like a picture with its colors and things pictured. A man would be extremely stupid to confine his attention to the colors and to ignore the things that are depicted. And we, if we embrace only what the words say on the surface and ignore the other senses, are like those who ignore the things depicted and see only the colors. "The letter kills," as it is written, "but the spirit gives life"; thus the letter covers the spirit as the chaff covers the grain. But to eat the chaff is to be a beast of burden; to eat the grain is to be human. He who uses human reason, therefore, will cast aside the chaff and hasten to eat the grain of the spirit. For this reason it is useful that the mystery be covered in the wrapping of the letter.

Discriminating between the chaff and the wheat, letter and spirit, sense and meaning was regarded as the hallmark of morally responsible reading. "What is the chaff to the wheat? saith the Lord" (Jer. 23:28) resounds as a rhetorical question through most discussions of interpretation and textual theory from Augustine to Erasmus. The good man, as St. Ambrose observes of Gideon before the angel had called him to his task, will be found threshing, "beating out wheat": "In the predestined mystery of the Incarnation, he [Gideon] was bringing forth the visible grains of the fruitful corn from their hiding places and [prefiguratively] separating the elect of the saints from the empty chaff " (*De Spiritu Sancto*, 1.1). (For Ambrose, it was this that fitted Gideon for being "a judge in Israel" [cf. Judg. 6:11-21].) Bad reading, or perverse interpretation, is called by the *Glossa Ordinaria* "the doctrine of heretics — chaff — for chaff has no pith, nor does it nourish" (PL 114.39).

When applied to secular literature, as it was almost uniformly in the Middle Ages, the distinction between letter and spirit was enjoined upon readers who did not want to be "obtuse," as Boccaccio put it. Dante explains that interpretation of his poetry ought to proceed from the literal to spiritual understanding, and while he elaborates three levels of "spiritual" interpretation — allegorical, moral (or tropological), and anagogical (concerning "the supernal things of eternal glory") — all three are effectively subdivisions of the "spiritual sense" (*Convivio*, 2.1; *Epistola ad Can Grande*). The same may be said of the "foure wittes" spoken of in the prologue to the Wycliffite Bible.

The essentially moral imperative in medieval literary theory arises directly from the scriptural distinction between letter and spirit. Alan of Lille says in the preface to his 12th-cent. poem *De Planctu Naturae* that if one reads

rightly, the sweetness of the literal sense will caress the puerile ear, the moral sense will instruct those who are bent on perfecting their habit of life, and the allegory will sharpen spiritual understanding in the hearts of those "nearing perfection" (PL 210.445). Boccaccio makes similar (though less plausible) claims for his own poetry in the fourteenth book of his *De Genealogia Deorum Gentilium*.

It was of course possible to apply the principle perversely. In Chaucer's *Summoner's Tale* the hypocritical friar tells a doubting Thomas that he has preached a sermon

> nat al after the text of hooly writ
> For it is hard to yow, as I suppose,
> And therfore wol I teche yow al the glose.
> Glosynge is a glorious thyng, certeyn,
> For lettre sleeth, so as we clerkes seyn. (*CT* 3.1790-94)

Chaucer is here reflecting a view commonly expressed in anti-fraternal satire of the 14th cent. that a great deal of exegesis and commentary by friars and their ilk involved, under the guise of "spiritual" interpretation, gross distortion of the biblical text (cf. the Wycliffite tract *The Leaven of the Pharisees*).

Chaucer's Nun's Priest, by contrast, calls his audience of Canterbury pilgrims to an appropriate ethical and "spiritual" reading of a secular tale, modeled on biblical principles (*The Nun's Priest's Tale*, 7.3439-43):

> But ye that holden this tale a folye,
> As of a fox, or of a cok and hen,
> Taketh the moralitee, good men.
> For Seint Paul seith that al that writen is,
> To oure doctrine it is ywritte, ywis;
> Taketh the fruyt, and lat the chaff be stille.

It is the intention of the Parson, likewise, to preempt any literal-minded evasion of the clear spiritual sense of his sermon: "Why sholde I sowen draf out of my fest, / When I may sowen whete, if that me lest?" (10.35-36). The implied analogy in Chaucer's writings between the hermeneutic purpose of theology and the hermeneutic value of even a secular text — that both ought to engage "allegory" so as to achieve reference to spiritual nourishment — is basic to the Christocentrist theories of reference still found in Petrarch (see *Familiari*, 6.2.4) and Erasmus (*Enchiridion*, 2-3, 25). Petrarch observes in a letter to his brother that "theology is [in this sense] poetry concerning God" — to be valued not merely for its literal level but its spiritual point of reference, as Scripture language itself suggests:

> To speak of Christ as a lion, as a lamb, as a worm [Ps. 21:7] — what is this if not poetry? A thousand such things you would find in the Sacred Scriptures. . . . Indeed, how else do the parables of the Savior in the Gospels operate except, if I may express it in one word, by *alieniloquium*, which we are accustomed to call "allegory"? And with words of this kind the whole realm of poetry is clothed. (*Familiari*, 10.4)

His example from Ps. 21:7 is probably drawn from Augustine's use of it to discuss scriptural literary theory (*In Joan. Ev.* 47.5-6), a passage also influential in the textual theory of Wyclif (*De Veritate Sacrae Scripturae*, 1.2). The relation of letter and spirit in interpretation down to the Renaissance thus remains heavily charged with the reading Augustine gave to 2 Cor. 3:6 and related passages.

In the 17th cent. theological rather than hermeneutic concerns began again to predominate. Donne's "Holy Sonnet 16" takes up the Pauline principle (cf. Rom. 7:7-11) to observe:

> . . . men argue yet
> Whether a man those statutes can fulfill;
> None doth; but all healing grace and spirit
> Revive again what law and letter kill.

Herbert's "Sepulchre" returns to the argument of 2 Cor. 3:3-6 to reprove stony-heartedness in the Church:

> And as of old the Law by heav'nly art
> Was writ in stone; so thou, which also art
> The letter of the word, find'st no fit heart
> To hold thee.

Elsewhere he recalls the exegetical metaphor, only to comprise with it another (cf. Deut. 32:13; Ps. 81:16); the opening lines of his first "The H. Scriptures" poem read: "O Book! infinite sweetnesse! let my heart / Suck ev'ry letter, and a hony gain." (Ps. 81:16 may here be recollected from the liturgy for Corpus Christi, where it is an *introitus:* "He fed them with the finest wheat, alleluia! Not the chaff but the wheat. . . .")

William Cowper reflects a Calvinist reading of 2 Cor. 3:3-6 and Rom. 7:7-11 when he writes in his "Expostulation" that "the sons of Israel were; / Stiff in the letter, lax in the design / And import, of their oracles divine," but the sentiment parallels that of Chaucer's *Summoner's Tale* from another age, even as his opening line in "Pairing Time Anticipated" parallels the closing lines of Chaucer's *Nun's Priest's Tale* on the perils of literal-mindedness. In his *Studies in Classic American Literature,* D. H. Lawrence sympathizes with James Fenimore Cooper's Natty Bumppo who, when he was imprisoned at the age of seventy for violating the new game laws, observed: "The letter killeth. . . . The old hunter disappears . . . severed away from his race. In the new epoch that is coming, there will be no Letter of the Law." This secularization has its counterpart in theology, as is reflected in Butler's *The Way of All Flesh,* where Ernest is presented as discovering that "the spirit behind the Church is true, though her letter — true once — is now true no longer." On the other hand, "the spirit behind the High Priests of Science is as lying as its letter." Christina Rossetti's *Letter and Spirit* (1883) is a meditative, devotional prose reflection on the Ten Commandments. Its theme is echoed in E. A. Robinson's

short poem "The Spirit Speaking" (1929), the first stanza of which takes up the will to abuse or misread the gospel:

> As you are still pursuing it
> As blindly as you can,
> You have deformed and tortured it
> Since ignorance began;
> And even as you have mangled it,
> The Letter has killed man.

In Wolfe's *Look Homeward, Angel* the text is ironically turned against literature too: " 'Literature, literature, Dick,' he returned portentously, 'It's been the ruin of many a good surgeon. You read too much, Dick. Yon Cassius hath a lean and hungry look. You know too much. The letter killeth the spirit, you know' " (chap. 14). Wolfe's view seems to be that a principle which once placed the discriminating reading of important texts at the center of Western educational theory has now been turned on its head to become, in the blind irony of its decontextualization, the educational theory of an age in flight from literacy.

Bibliography. Allen, J. B. *The Ethical Poetic of the Later Middle Ages* (1982); Green, R. H. "Dante's 'Allegory of the Poets' and the Medieval Theory of Poetic Fiction." *CL* 9 (1957), 118-28; Haller, R. S. *The Literary Criticism of Dante Alighieri* (1973); Huppé, B. F., and D. W. Robertson, Jr. *Fruyt and Chaf: Studies in Chaucer's Allegories* (1963); Jeffrey, D. L., ed. *By Things Seen: Reference and Recognition in Medieval Thought* (1979); Lewalski, B. *Protestant Poetics and the Seventeenth Century Religious Lyric* (1979); Pépin, J. *Myth et allégorie: les origines grecques et les contestations judeo-chrétiennes* (1958); Robertson, D. W., Jr. *A Preface to Chaucer* (1962); Tuve, R. *Allegorical Imagery: Some Medieval Books and Their Posterity* (1966).

LEVI One of the twelve sons of Jacob.

See also AARON; JACOB; TRIBES OF ISRAEL.

LEVIATHAN Heb. *liweyatan* (possibly "coiled one") is from the root *lwh* (cf. Arab. *lwy,* "twist," "turn," or "wind"). A probable source is *Lotan* in the Ras Shamra texts (*ANET,* 137-38), defeated by Baal and his consort Anath and, like leviathan (in Isa. 27:1), "piercing" and "crooked" and (as in Ps. 74:14) with many heads.

While some details in Job 41 support the traditional glossing as "crocodile," an animal of mythic proportions is clearly intended. To God leviathan is but a plaything; the realization that God's perspective is not mankind's brings about Job's change of attitude (and of fortune). In Ps. 104:26 leviathan is associated with a primal sea-world. Job 3:8 (KJV, with rabbinic precedent, mistranslates leviathan as "the mourning") alludes to magicians summoning eclipses, seen as caused by a sun-consuming primordial monster disturbed from age-old sleep. Ps. 74:13-14 makes the division of the (Red) sea reiterative of a primordial cosmic combat and victory which established the creation. In Isa. 27:1 the apocalypse is seen to feature leviathan's final breaking of his bonds at the end of this age, followed by a final repetition of the defeat it suffered at the beginning of time. In Ezek. 29:1-4 a leviathan-like dragon to be fished out with a hook is symbolically identified as "Pharaoh king of Egypt."

Hebrew poetic parallelism and apposition make leviathan virtually identical with other named sea-monsters: *tannin,* KJV "whale" or "dragon" (Ps. 74:13; Isa. 27:1); *nahash,* KJV "serpent," such as the Eden serpent in Gen. 3:1 (Isa. 27:1); *rahab* (Isa. 51:9); and *yam,* KJV "sea," often personified (Job 7:12; 26:1; Ps. 74:13-14; Isa. 51:9). Also noteworthy is the background presence of the sea-monster Tiamat, which in *Enuma Elish* (*ANET,* 60-69) is defeated by Marduk, split in two to make earth and firmament, and has a watch or bound set on her, as God does on the sea (in Job 7:12). Tiamat appears as the deeps, *tehomot,* associated with dragons, in Ps. 148:7, and in the singular form *tehom,* KJV "deep" (Gen. 1:3), where the related *tohu,* KJV "without form" (1:2), also appears. In the LXX Gk. *drakōn* usually translates Heb. *liweyatan, tannin,* and *nahash.* In the Apocrypha and Pseudepigrapha leviathan (always, as in Job 40–41, in company with behemoth) replaces all of these and the imagery is deliberately systematized: leviathan is female and associated with the "abysses of the sea"; behemoth is male and of the "dry land of the wilderness" (1 Enoch 60:7-10). Tg. Jonathan on Gen. 1:21 identifies the whales of the fifth day of creation as leviathan, and 2 Bar. 29:1-8 and 4 Ezra 6:47-52 follow suit, the former adding that at the end of time the monsters will be food at an apocalyptic banquet for the faithful.

Rev. 12:9 identifies *drakōn* with *ophis* (the LXX word for the Eden serpent) as being cast out, and the disappearance of the sea (Rev. 21:1) is clearly another metaphor for apocalyptic reiteration of the victory of God over the cosmic antagonism that leviathan personifies. Corrupt worldly power is often identified with the primal chaos monster: the crocodile is sometimes symbolic of Egyptian monarchy, and leviathan's defeat is connected with Egypt's (Ps. 74:13-14). The connection of Rahab with Egypt is even more explicit. Egypt is OT Israel's archetypal political bogey, just as Rome is NT Christianity's.

A variety of Jewish sources, principally talmudic, provide amplification: God sports with leviathan for the last three hours of each day ('Abod. Zar. 3b); Jordan flows into its mouth; it mates with (or fights with) behemoth (B. Bat. 74b); it appears as the zodiac; its skin is used variously to clothe Adam and Eve, to make a tabernacle for the righteous, or is spread on the walls of Jerusalem, where "its splendour shall shine from one end of the world to the other" (B. Bat. 75a; there are rather fanciful summaries and elaborate references in Graves and Patai, 34-39, 47-53).

Origen extends the tendency toward coherent myth by making leviathan the "great fish" of Jonah, and by making

its final identity that of the devil himself (*Hom.* sup. Leviticus, 8.2). *On Prayer* describes the disobedient as being in "the belly of the fish" (13.4). Leviathan thus becomes a metaphor for the whole of the fallen world and for fallen humanity in it: "Does it not follow that he who has escaped from the belly of the great fish worsted by Jesus our Saviour, which swallows every fugitive from God, becomes a Jonah capable as a saint of receiving the Holy Spirit" (*On Prayer,* 16.3).

St. Cyril of Jerusalem, while discussing baptism in his *Catechetical Letters,* makes leviathan symbolically equivalent to the water world he inhabits:

> The dragon of the waters, according to Job, trusteth that he can draw up Jordan in his mouth. When then Jesus must break "the heads of dragons," he went down and bound the mighty one of the waters, so that we might receive "the power to tread upon serpents and scorpions." (LCC 4.95)

The Vg restores "leviathan" where the LXX used *drakōn.* St. Jerome's *Hom.* 30 (on Ps. 104) identifies leviathan as "the dragon that was cast out of Paradise, that beguiled Adam and Eve, and is permitted in this world to make sport of us."

For St. Augustine in *De civitate Dei* leviathan and behemoth are interchangeable symbols for the devil (11.15). So also for Luther, in whose writings is developed Origen's notion that fallen humanity is contained in leviathan's belly: his letters tell of "Satan's formidable teeth round about," alluding to the portrait of leviathan in Job 41, and describe mankind's estate "amid these ragings of Satan so that you may . . . not speak timidly or softly in the teeth of behemoth, as if you were overcome by him and feared the arrogance of Satan." In his commentary on Hebrews the destruction of leviathan is equivalent to the destruction of death. For Calvin (in his commentary on Isa. 27:1) leviathan denotes Pharaoh as well as enemies of the Church. According to the Geneva Bible commentators, Isa. 27:1 is said to prophesy "the destruction of Satan and his kingdome under the name of Leviathan, Asshur and Egypt"; in Ps. 74:14 leviathan is taken to refer to Pharaoh.

In Spenser's *Faerie Queene* a body of leviathan allusions accompanies description of the principal monsters. Duessa's beast is likened to leviathan (1.7.17) and Duessa herself is like a crafty crocodile (1.5.18). The beast which ravages the kingdom of Una's parents is a water monster (1.7.44) with numerous minor qualities reminiscent of leviathan. Mutabilitie's power to molest the moon is reminiscent of the power to rouse leviathan in Job 3:8 (see Nohrnberg, 182-83, 740).

Allusions to leviathan in Shakespeare reduce it to folklore: in *A Midsummer Night's Dream* (2.1.174) it suggests speed in Oberon's instruction to Puck; in *Henry 5* (3.3.26) the task of taming it is an illustration of the monumentally futile; in *Two Gentlemen of Verona*

(3.2.79) Orpheus's power is such that it could charm even leviathan. In Webster's *Devil's Law Case*, giving the name "Leviathan" to a ship is judged an ill omen. In Marvell's "Anniversary of the Government under O.C." (361) a "wood-leviathan" is simply a formidably large ship. So Thomas Campbell in "Battle of the Baltic" (st. 2) says of the Danish fleet: "Like leviathan afloat / Lay their bulwarks on the brine." Similarly in Milton: the leviathan of the fifth day of creation (*Paradise Lost*, 7.412) suggests only bigness. Leviathan's being confused with an island (*PL* 1.201) attracts interesting notes in the Hughes (1957) and Fowler (1968) editions.

The title of Hobbes's *Leviathan* designates the commonwealth, brought into being by the covenant through which man surrenders his sovereignty and becomes part of a social unity in "one and the same person." This is "the Generation of that great Leviathan or rather (to speak more reverently) of that Mortall God, to which we owe, under the Immortall God, our peace and defense" (2.17). The original (1651) frontispiece is suggestive: the minuscule bodies of numerous subjects are superimposed on the huge body of the king. Northrop Frye notes (*Fearful Symmetry,* 137) the symbolic appropriateness of naming a defense of tyranny after the mythic personification of Egypt. In *The Pilgrim's Progress,* Leviathan is symbolic of ultimate evil and can be defeated only with the shield of faith.

In Blake's *Marriage of Heaven and Hell,* Leviathan appears as a tempestuous sea in the void and is a consequence of the mortal views of an angel who represents the mental constrictions of conventional religion; as such it is part of an ultimately illusory world which suddenly vanishes. In *America: A Prophecy,* Albion's wrathful prince, more or less George III, stands in dragon form, characterized by leviathanic "scales." Leviathan and Behemoth are identified in *Jerusalem* (pl. 91) as "war by Sea" and "war by Land." (War is consequent upon the limitations of conventional morality and the two monsters are forms of fallen human selfhood.) In *Descriptive Catalogue* (nos. 1, 2) they are shown as guided by the spiritual forms of Nelson and Pitt respectively (see Erdman, 448-55, 521-22; Blunt, 97-103). Blunt further identifies leviathan with Los (spirit) and behemoth with Tharmas (senses). The two also appear in illustrations to the book of Job, where they symbolize the powers of the subconscious.

In Keats's *Endymion* the hero encounters in the waterworld of his lovelorn soul the skeletons of leviathan and behemoth. In Byron's *Marino Faliero,* leviathan is Hobbes's state, a personification of its tyrant, ironically viewed: it is a "never-gorged leviathan" because misery, slavery, and death merely whet its demonic appetite. In *Cain* leviathan is identified with the Eden serpent as part of Cain's vision of Hades. In *Heaven and Earth* leviathan's reconquest of the land world is an image of the end of time. In "The Holy Office" (*Pomes Penyeach*) Joyce sees himself as a subversive "Leviathan" conduct-

ing merciless satiric war on eminent and literary contemporaries who are seen as "servitors" of Mammon.

Leviathan has a lively presence in North American literature where undiluted Romanticism lasts much later. Melville's *Moby-Dick* routinely calls whales leviathans in the development of a personal mythic universe held together by syncretism and ambiguity. Thus the great whale suggests the mysteries of the biblical leviathan and a great many other kinds of mystery as well. D. H. Lawrence's fanciful interpretation in *Studies in Classic American Literature* (1915; publ. 1922) goes well beyond the book: Moby-Dick is "The last phallic being of the white man. . . . Our blood-self subjected to our will. . . . Jesus, the Redeemer, was Cetus, Leviathan. And all the Christians are his little fishes."

In Canadian literature the wilderness is often leviathanic. In E. J. Pratt's *Towards the Last Spike* (1952), epic railway building is a contest with an awakened reptilian monster of primordial malice and obviously leviathanic characteristics. In Margaret Atwood's "Progressive Insanities of a Pioneer" (1968) the settler loses all hold on reality as "the green / vision, the unarmed / whale invaded." In the work of Jay Macpherson, whose poetry is full of undersea imagery and the problem of raising the real world from the waters, "Leviathan" (1957) looks back to a playful prelapsarian world where the monster was not yet God's antagonist.

See also BEHEMOTH.

Bibliography. Blunt, A. *The Art of William Blake* (1959); Erdman, D. V. *Blake: Prophet Against Empire* (1977); Graves, R., and R. Patai. *Hebrew Myths: The Book of Genesis* (1966); Nohrnberg, J. C. *The Analogy of "The Faerie Queene"* (1976); Wallace, H. "Leviathan and the Beast in Revelation." *BA* 11 (1948), 3, 61-68; Young W. A. "Leviathan in the Book of Job and *Moby-Dick.*" *Sound* 65 (1982), 388-401.
RICHARD SCHELL

LEVITES Although the Levites constituted one of the twelve tribes of Israel, their duties and privileges were unique. Having no land holdings of their own, they were scattered throughout the land and depended on the generosity of the other tribes for their income (Josh. 21). Their function was the maintenance and protection of the national sanctuary (Num. 18), in return for which they were entitled to a tithe of the agricultural produce of the other tribes. One clan within the Levites constituted the priesthood, from whom came the high priest, the supreme religious leader.

The priestly Levites were responsible for administering the sacrifices and the other rituals described in the law. The other Levites had to undertake more menial chores. In the pre-monarchy period they were responsible for transporting, guarding, and erecting the national tent shrine called the Tabernacle (Num. 4). When Solomon built the Temple other duties were found for them, as temple doorkeepers, singers, accompanists on musical instruments, and preachers (1 Chron. 23–26).

Given the theocratic nature of ancient Israel it is evident that the Levites were among the most influential groups within the nation. The biblical account asserts that at first the Levites were a secular tribe like the others and descended from Levi, one of Jacob's sons. Moses and Aaron were Levites. When in the course of the journey from Egypt to Canaan the nation threatened to forsake the worship of the Lord promulgated by Moses, the Levites rallied to him and were consequently rewarded by being made the priestly tribe dedicated to the maintenance of covenant religion and its sanctuary (Exod. 32). This would later be seen (e.g., by Cornelius à Lapide, *Comm. in Gen.* 25:31) as making them the spiritual "firstborn" of Israel. The special calling of the family of Aaron to the priesthood, subsequently extended to the families of Eli and Zadok (Ezek. 40:46; 43:19), meant that all other Levites occupied a secondary role.

In the time of the Second Temple the officiating priests outnumbered the Levites and apparently shared their tithes. Halakic writings speak of the ordinary Levite as secondary to the priest, a position ceremonially indicated at the reading of the Law and when the Levite washes the hands of the priest before the priest blesses the congregation.

St. Ambrose sees the Levites and regulations pertaining to their lives as prefiguring the Christian priesthood (e.g., *De officiis ministrorum*, 1.50). Later medieval Christian commentary sees the Levites as a kind of lay-diaconate, or acolytes assisting with administering the elements in the Sacrament (e.g., *Glossa Ordinaria* [PL 113.379-82]).

William Cowper is thinking of the original Levites in "Expostulation" when he laments the loss of Israel's former glory:

> Thy services, once holy without spot,
> Mere shadows now, their ancient pomp forgot;
> Thy Levites, once a consecrated host,
> No longer Levites, and their lineage lost. . . . (261-64)

T. H. Huxley has another archaic tradition in mind when he complains that advocates of a scientific education "have been excommunicated by the classical scholars, in their capacity of Levites in charge of the ark of culture and monopolists of liberal education" ("Science and Culture").

See also TRIBES OF ISRAEL.

Bibliography. Cody, A. *A History of Old Testament Priesthood* (1969); Hubbard, D. A. *The Illustrated Bible Dictionary* (1980), 1266-73.   G. J. WENHAM

LEX TALIONIS   For a number of specified offenses the Mosaic law, like other Near Eastern codes (e.g., that of Hammurabi), provided for symmetrical retribution. The *lex talionis* or "tit for tat" formula is amplified as "life for life, eye for eye, tooth for tooth, hand for hand, foot for foot, burning for burning, wound for wound, stripe for stripe" (Exod. 21:23-25; cf. Lev. 24:20; Deut. 19:21). The intention of this law, as St. Augustine among many others

has observed, is actually to signify a measure of restraint in retribution, "so that vengeance should not exceed the injury" (*De sermone Domini in Monte*, 1.19.56). Augustine's comments come in the context of discussion of Matt. 5:38, in which Jesus urges his hearers to go beyond this principle in extending mercy and to "turn the other cheek." He goes on to observe that the person "who pays back just as much as he has received already forgives something: for the party who injures does not deserve merely just so much punishment as the one who was injured by him has innocently suffered" (1.19.57). Later commentators such as Matthew Poole argue that the "Law of Retaliation," though it "might sometimes be practiced in the letter, yet it was not necessarily to be understood and executed so; as may appear . . . by the impossibility of just execution of it in many cases. . . . Punishment may be less, but never should be greater than the Fault. And how could a Wound be made neither bigger nor less than that which he inflicted?" (*Annotations*, sup. Exod. 21:24).

This reflection, reminiscent of Portia's judgment concerning Shylock's bond in Shakespeare's *Merchant of Venice*, is directed against the "civilized" barbarity of ruthless legalism. In Tennyson's *Beckett,* King Henry is impatient with the bishops for their failure to act with the cruder civil justice, having brought to their own ecclesiastical courts a cleric who had

> violated
> The daughter of his host and murdered him
> . . . But since your canon will not let you take
> Life for a life, ye but degraded him
> When I had hang'd him.

From King Henry's point of view there is hypocrisy in the use of *lex talionis* for the one offense and not the other. In Emily Brontë's *Wuthering Heights,* Isabella says of Heathcliff that she will forgive him his ill-treatment of her only on the condition that she "may take an eye for an eye, a tooth for a tooth; for every wrench of agony return a wrench: reduce him to my level." Hardy's Bathsheba in *Far from the Madding Crowd* is driven by a similar confusion of justice with revenge: "In Bathsheba's heated fancy the innocent white countenance expressed a dim triumphant consciousness of the pain she was retaliating for her pain with all the merciless rigour of the Mosaic law: 'Burning for burning; wound for wound; strife for strife' [sic]" (chap. 43). Emerson, in "Compensation," construes a symmetrical recension of both OT and NT concepts, uniting allusions to Exod. 31:24 and the Sermon on the Mount when he observes: "All things are double, one against the other — Tit for tat; an eye for an eye; a tooth for a tooth; blood for blood; measure for measure; love for love."

See also JUDGE NOT; TEN COMMANDMENTS.

Bibliography. Daube, D. *Studies in Biblical Law* (1947); Falk, Z. *Hebrew Law in Biblical Times* (1964); Noth, M. *Laws in the Pentateuch and Other Studies* (Eng. trans. 1966).

LIGHT   Light, the first creation of God ("Let there be light" [Gen. 1:3]), is also one of the most important and complex symbols in the Bible. Five principal uses of the symbol may be discerned from both OT and NT texts.

First, light is frequently used to symbolize God himself (Pss. 4:6; 27:1; James 1:17; 1 John 1:5), and, by extension, his heavenly dwelling (Col. 1:12; 1 Tim. 6:16; Rev. 22:5). God covers himself with light as with a garment (Ps. 104:2), and his "dwelling" or Shekinah (cf. 1 Chron. 3:21ff.) is said to be in splendored light (cf. Sanh. 39a; Ber. 7a; Shab. 22b; Num. Rab. 7.8).

Second, light can suggest moral goodness or holiness, in contrast to moral darkness (Matt. 5:14; John 3:19-20; 12:36; Eph. 5:8). To "walk in the light" is to obey God's Word (1 Sam. 2:5); his "commandments enlighten the eyes" (Ps. 19:8). In talmudic teaching, whenever and wherever God's law is closely observed, a refulgence of the Shekinah spills over into the lives of his people (Menaḥ. 43b; B. Bat. 10a; Shab. 92a).

Third, light pictures salvation (Ps. 27:1) and is linked especially with the redemptive activity of Christ, "the light of the world" (Matt. 5:16; Luke 2:32; John 1:1-9; 8:12; 9:5). This light is not achieved through human wisdom or special knowledge (or, in Plato's analogy, by an ascent out of the cave of human ignorance) but descends into human darkness, unbidden, and radically transforms it.

Light also symbolizes truth and understanding, as opposed to error, ignorance, or folly (Ps. 119:105, 130; 2 Cor. 4:6). In eschatological contexts, it is related to justice (Ps. 37:6; Mic. 7:9; Zech. 3:5).

Finally, light represents joy, God's favor, and life, in contrast to sorrow and death (Ps. 112:4; Prov. 18–19; Isa. 58:8). To "see the light" can thus mean simply "to live" (Job 3:10; 33:29; cf. Ps. 58:9).

In the Middle Ages and Renaissance the biblical symbol of light sometimes became fused with extrabiblical traditions. The Jewish Zohar elaborated upon God as light and created reality as a series of emanations, in decreasing purity, of that light. Belief among the early gnostics in a higher God of Light and a lower God of Darkness (who ruled the created world) was regarded as a serious confusion of the biblical representation (1 John has been read as an antignostic polemic). The gnostics nonetheless influenced Christian representations of God as light. In the Middle Ages, the pseudo-Dionysian work *On The Celestial Hierarchy,* translated into ME by the author of the *Cloud of Unknowing,* had a direct influence on the preoccupation with light in gothic architecture (O. Von Simpson, 91-141) and on the light symbolism in a variety of mystical writings. Neoplatonism, as represented by Ficino, similarly developed the idea of a ladder of light emanating from God. The emanation of light from an originating source was also used as a symbol for the relationship of the Son to the Father within the Trinity (see W. B. Hunter, *MLN* 74 [1959], 589-92). Throughout

the Renaissance it became standard for scientists and poets to distinguish three forms of light: God, who is uncreated, essential light; natural light, a creation of God and frequent symbol for him; and the inner light of reason or understanding.

Works of English literature which made indisputable use of the biblical images of light cluster in the Middle Ages and Renaissance and occur chiefly in poetry which depicts God and heaven. Among major medieval examples are Dante's *Divine Comedy,* the ME *Pearl,* and the anonymous *Cloud of Unknowing.* Light is a chief symbol of moral goodness in Spenser (the image appears over 300 times in *The Faerie Queene*), and it permeates the 17th-cent. devotional poetry of Henry Vaughan ("They are all gone into the world of light"), Richard Crashaw, and Thomas Traherne.

No poet made more extensive use of light in its full range of biblical meanings than Milton, especially in *Paradise Lost* (where the invocation to bk. 3 is an encomium addressed to light). Milton's use of light imagery, doubtless affected by his own blindness, was so influential in English poetry that he is the pivotal figure in the development traced by Josephine Miles: whereas before Milton such epithets as "good," "great," and "true" were the dominant words denoting moral goodness, after Milton words such as "bright" and "light" became dominant.

A clear departure from the biblical perspective on light, however, is occasioned by emphasis on the "light of reason" as supreme during the 18th-cent. "Enlightenment." In Locke's psychology, Archbishop Tillotson's sermons, or Pope's *Essay on Man,* reason is no longer regarded as a divine gift enabling the rational creature to perceive and act upon God's laws written in Scripture and the obedient heart. Rather, as Whichcote's phrase has it, "the spirit of man is the candle of the Lord": the light of the awakening human spirit creates the new world of human freedom as envisaged, e.g., in Goethe's *Faust.* Light is no longer, as in Gen. 1, the condition of Creation, but of human consciousness. Its full glory lies in the future, in a Utopia to be achieved by human effort — in England, Blake thought, by the unification of Albion. In such contexts light as a literary symbol often appears as physical sight in conflict or tension with inner vision. Hence the frequent appearance of blind characters who, Tiresias-like, alone "see the light." (An ironic treatment of this theme occurs in Kipling's *The Light that Failed.*)

In numerous modern works a loss of belief in illumination through God's law (Ps. 119:105) or Christ (John 1:4-5; 2 Cor. 4:6; Eph. 5:14) occasions a felt need for alternative "light" for human vision (e.g., Virginia Woolf, *To the Lighthouse*). With postmodern loss of confidence in the Enlightenment era's supreme standard of reason, both gnostic notions of higher light and neopagan attractions to darkness tend to displace or syncretize biblical notions of the "light of the world" (cf. John 8:12; 9:5).

The biblical tradition extends, however, well beyond

the Enlightenment, sometimes self-consciously opposing rationalist or gnostic usage. In the 18th cent. William Cowper's "The Shining Light," "The Light and Glory of the Word," "Sometimes a light surprizes," and "Light Shining out of Darkness" all bear witness to familiar biblical images; the latter hymn is in an answer to those who think that human reason is sufficient light for the proper understanding of nature, concluding:

> Blind unbelief is sure to err
> And scan his work in vain;
> God is his own interpreter
> And he will make it plain.

For Cowper the rationalist's "light" is itself clearly a gift of God, though unrecognized as such:

> Their fortitude and wisdom were a flame
> Celestial, though they knew not whence it came,
> Deriv'd from the same source of light and grace
> That guides the Christian in his swifter race. ("Truth," 531-34)

The Christian's advantage is "the blaze of scripture light" (*Hope,* 298); he or she knows that in nature as well as Scripture, "the just Creator condescends to write, / In beams of inextinguishable light" (*Hope,* 133-34).

The 19th cent. affords similar examples. John Henry (Cardinal) Newman's "The Pillar of the Cloud" (better known as "Lead, Kindly Light") blends reference to Ps. 119:105 with the Exodus motif. A stronger use of OT imagery from the same period is that of W. Chalmers Smith (1867):

> Immortal, invisible, God only wise,
> In light inaccessible, hid from our eyes,
> Most blessed, most glorious, the Ancient of Days
> Almighty, victorious, thy great Name we praise.

> Great Father of Glory, pure Father of Light,
> Thine angels adore thee, all veiling their sight;
> All laud we would render: O help us to see
> 'Tis only the splendour of light hideth thee.

For 20th-cent. poet Margaret Avison (*sunblue* [1978]) the biblical image of light captures in metaphor the relationship not merely of God to the world but of human consciousness to its Creator ("Light I" — "the light has looked on Light"). God the Father's relationship to his Son is also expressed as more than mere reflection, but a closed circuit of reciprocal light:

> The circuit of the Son
> in glory falling
> not short
> and without clutching after
> His Being-in-Light. . . .

Yet, to bring light into darkness Christ puts on "the altar-animal form / and livery of Man / to serve men under orders"; then, returning with souls won from darkness, in freedom to God:

> this circuit celebrates the Father of Lights
> who glorifies this Son and all that He
> in glory sows
> of Light. ("The Circuit")

David Jones's reference in his *Anathemata* to those "that have the Lord for your light" (1.75) is an evocation of Ps. 27:1, especially its Latin hymn setting *(Dominus illuminatio mea)* but more widely familiar in the KJV English of Handel's anthem, "The Lord is my light."

See also BLINDNESS; CHILDREN OF LIGHT; *FIAT LUX;* LIGHT UNDER A BUSHEL.

Bibliography. Hughes, M. Y. "Milton and the Symbol of Light." *Ten Perspectives on Milton* (1965), 63-103; Miles, J. "From Good to Bright: A Note in Poetic History." *PMLA* 60 (1945), 766-74; *Major Adjectives in English Poetry from Wyatt to Auden* (1946), 408-21; Von Simpson, O. *The Gothic Cathedral* (1956), 21-58, 91-141; Williams, G. W. *Image and Symbol in the Sacred Poetry of Richard Crashaw* (1963), chap. 4.

LELAND RYKEN
DAVID L. JEFFREY

LIGHT OF THE WORLD   *See* LIGHT.

LIGHT UNDER A BUSHEL   In the Sermon on the Mount (Matt. 5:14-16; cf. Mark 4:21; Luke 11:33) Jesus said to his followers: "Ye are the light of the world. A city that is set on a hill cannot be hid. Neither do men light a candle and put it under a bushel, but on a candlestick; and it giveth light to all those that are in the house. Let your light so shine before men, that they may see your good works, and glorify your Father which is in heaven." This passage has been a keynote for Christian discussions of vocation and practical obedience. St. Jerome comments that "God's motive for lighting the fire of his knowledge in the bishop is that he may shine not for himself only but for the common benefit" (*Adv. Lucif.* 5). St. Augustine relates the passage to the commendation of John the Baptist, that "he was a burning and shining light" (John 5:35; *De consensu Evangelistarum,* 4.10.17), and to the vocation of every follower of Christ, which is "to be fervent and shine in good works, that is, to have our lights burning" (*Sermo,* 108.1).

The passage was important also in Puritan writing: hence the bite in Shakespeare's *Measure for Measure* (1.1.33-36), where the Duke ironically admonishes the Puritan Angelo for not showing his virtue in community life:

> Heaven doth with us as we with torches do.
> Not light them for themselves; for if our virtues
> Did not go forth of us, 'twere all alike
> As if we had them not.

By the same token, the traditional companion phrase from John 5:35 becomes widely applied in the 18th cent., especially by figures in the Methodist movement, to those exemplary in the practice of the virtues mentioned in Matt. 5:14-16. George Whitefield and others thus speak of Lady Selina Hastings, Countess of Huntingdon and guiding spirit of the Great Revival, as "a burning and a shining light." The same phrase comes also to be related to the image of the virtuous Christian life as a beacon or lighthouse (cf. the hymn, "Let the Lower Lights Be Burning"). Thoreau, speaking of the lighthouse at Provincetown *(Cape Cod),* says, "What avails it though a light be placed on top of a hill, if you spend all your life directly under the hill? It might as well be under a bushel."

Nineteenth-century liberal theology readily transferred the light imagery of the Bible, following 18th-cent. precedents, to the sphere of reason and knowledge. In James Fenimore Cooper's *The Pioneers,* "knowledge is not to be concealed, like a candle under a bushel" (chap. 29). In Hardy's *Far from the Madding Crowd* the covered candle is identified with personal gifts: when Joseph Poorgrass is praised he reluctantly owns to hidden virtues, and is chided: "But under your bushel, Joseph! Under your bushel with 'ee! A strange desire, neighbours, this desire to hide, and no praise due" (chap. 33). Joyce uses the familiar conjunction of Matt. 5:15 and John 5:35 in *A Portrait of the Artist as a Young Man:* "Is he the shining light now? Well I discovered him. . . . Shining quietly under a bushel of Wicklow bran" (chap. 5). A more obverse inflection is found in Gissing's "A Poor Gentleman": "It had come to be understood that he made it a matter of principle to hide his light under a bushel, so he seldom had to take a new step in positive falsehood." In an unusual allusion in Aldous Huxley's *The Olive Tree,* modern translations of Scripture are contrasted with the Codex Sinaiticus: "the five-shilling Bible is comprehensive and available; whereas the Codex is kept locked up in a box and can be read only by experts. Its light is permanently under a bushel" ("Modern Fetishism").

See also BURNING AND SHINING LIGHT; CANDLE; LIGHT.

LILIES OF THE FIELD In the Sermon on the Mount Jesus stressed the relative impropriety of worry over material things, including food, personal appearance, and clothing: "And why take ye thought for raiment? Consider the lilies of the field, how they grow; they toil not, neither do they spin: And yet I say unto you, that even Solomon in all his glory was not arrayed like one of these. Wherefore, if God so clothe the grass of the field, which today is and tomorrow is cast into the oven, shall he not much more clothe you, O ye of little faith?" (Matt. 6:28-30; cf. Luke 12:27-31).

St. Augustine insists that the plain character of the comparison be taken at face value and not allegorized; the meaning, he says, is simply stated by Jesus himself: "Seek ye first the kingdom of God and his righteousness, and all these things shall be added unto you" (v. 33). Most commentators have heeded his advice.

George Herbert alludes to the passage as one of a number which illustrate the correspondences of natural to special revelation. "God's generall providence extended

even to lillyes" makes the book of Nature mnemonic of Scripture so that "labouring people (whom he chiefly considered) might have everywhere monuments of his Doctrine, remembering in gardens, his mustard-seed, and lillyes; in the field his seed-corn, and tares; and so not be drowned altogether in the works of their vocation, but sometimes lift up their minds to better things, even in the midst of their pains" (*A Priest to the Temple*, 15, 23). The passage comes gradually to be a byword for perspective on overwork: the motto for Keats's "Ode on Indolence" is "They toil not, neither do they spin." Felicia Hemans in her reflection on the passage concludes: "The great ocean hath no tone of power / Mightier to reach the soul, in thought's hushed hour, / Than yours, ye lilies! chosen thus and graced" ("The Lilies of the Field"). For John Keble they are "Sweet nurslings of the vernal skies," but he laments that

> Alas! of thousand bosoms kind,
> That daily court you, and caress,
> How few the happy secret find
> Of your calm loveliness!
> "Live for today!" tomorrow's light
> Tomorrow's cares shall bring to sight. ("Consider the Lilies")

In Aldous Huxley's *Point Counter Point* the rejection of preoccupation with "tomorrow's cares" is also expressed: "I can't tell you how much I enjoy not being respectable. It's the Atavismus coming out. You bother too much, Mark. Consider the lilies of the field" (chap. 9). For Somerset Maugham the "lilies of the field" are idealists who "took it as a right that others should perform for them these menial offices" (*The Narrow Corner,* chap. 19). For P. G. Wodehouse they are aristocrats, as in his *Indiscretions of Archie:* " 'I always looked on you as one of our leading lilies of the field,' he said, 'Why this anxiety to toil and spin?' " to which comes the answer, "Well, my wife, you know, seems to think it might put me up with the jolly old dad if I did something" (chap. 4; cf. *Uncle Fred in the Springtime,* chap. 11). In his essay on "Providence and the Guitar," Robert Louis Stevenson quips that while a "commercial traveller is received" and may even "command the fatted calf " (cf. Luke 15:23), "an artist, had he the manners of an Almaviva, were he dressed like Solomon in all his glory, is received like a dog and served like a timid lady travelling alone." Ruskin alludes to the passage in a similar context in his essay "Grass," and a delayed performance occasions from the hard-pressed impresario in Henry James's "The Madonna of the Future" a brusque retort: "O ye of little faith!"

Among the more subtle allusions in American literature is that found in Edith Wharton's *The Custom of the Country* (1913), a novel about the decline of New York culture: "If Undine, like the lilies of the field, took no care, it was not because her wants were as few but because she assumed that care would be taken for her by those whose privilege it was to enable her to unite floral insouciance with Sheban elegance" (chap. 11; cf. 1 Kings 10:1-13). A. M. Klein's "Of the Lily Which Toils Not" is a satire on the rich, beginning

> You, Tillie the Toiler and Winnie the Worker, consider
> This fabulous lily — and her milk-fed pride, —
> She toils not, no, and neither does she spin!
> O not like yours her most egregious skin,
> Her epidermis gilt-edged, bonded hide!

Anthony Hecht's "Behold the Lilies of the Field" is a horrifying narration of a delirious torture victim being admonished to "take it easy. Look at the flowers there in the glass bowl," while in his poem "Envy" he refers to "the holy sloth of the lily." In Rudy Wiebe's *The Blue Mountains of China* the horrors of a Stalinist labor camp in Siberia are thrown into stark relief for some of its victims by a night spent waiting out a blizzard in the ruins of a cloister; on the wall is a fresco of a vase of lilies — symbol of the Virgin Mary as well as a reminder of the pre-revolutionary peacefulness of the convent. To Jacob Friesen the whole passage, "Think of the lilies. . . . Take therefore no thought for the morrow" filters through his fatigue and misery in cruel parody of the prisoners' situation ("Cloister of the Lilies").

Allusion to the "lilies" often implies or directly incorporates reference also to the subsequent verses in Matthew: "But seek ye first the kingdom of God and his righteousness; and all these things shall be added unto you. Take no thought for the morrow: for the morrow shall take thought for the things of itself. Sufficient unto the day is the evil thereof " (vv. 33-34). In Butler's *The Way of All Flesh* v. 33 is quoted in an ironic context in a sermon (chap. 24), but v. 34 has typically prompted a more varied pattern of allusion. Galsworthy's *The Patrician* "was a man who did not go to meet disturbance. . . . He temperamentally regarded the evil of the day as quite sufficient to it" (1.1). In Trollope's *Barchester Towers* the phrase "sufficient unto the day" is quoted by Bertie in facing up to the prospect of her deprivation (chap. 15). D. H. Lawrence turns the same phrase in *Lady Chatterley's Lover:* "Where should there be anything in them, why should they last? Sufficient unto the day is the evil thereof. Sufficient unto the moment is the appearance of reality" (chap. 2). Aldous Huxley applies the verse in sobering fashion in *Eyeless in Gaza,* where he opines that, in the wake of 19th-cent. secularized reading, the whole passage is an injunction simply to take life as it comes without much reflection: "Like Jesus's ideal personality, the total, unexpurgated, now canalized man is . . . like a little child, in his acceptance of the immediate datum of experience for its own sake, in his refusal to take thought for tomorrow, in his readiness to let the dead bury their dead" (chap. 11; cf. Matt. 8:22).

LILITH Lilith derives from Sum. *lil,* "wind" or "spirit," and has in folk etymology been inventively connected with Heb. *laylah,* "night." Lilith is Akk. *lilitu,* female counterpart to *lilu,* one of a large family of fiendish demons. In Mesopotamian texts she is a succuba, sporting with men in sexual dreams. This role is later combined with that of a child-stealing or child-killing hag, as found on an 8th-cent. Canaanite amulet perhaps used to facilitate childbirth and to protect the newborn infant. Aramaic incantation bowls of the 6th cent. show her with disheveled hair and tell how she can be bound with iron.

Hebrew *lilith* appears only once in the OT, in Isa. 34:14, where she is a female demon associated with night and storm, one of a host of unclean and ghoulish creatures inhabiting the ruins and waste places to which Edom will be reduced by God's vengeance. The KJV translates "screech owl" (as had the Geneva Bible); the NEB reads "nightjar." The Vg uses "lamia," linking Lilith to Roman sorceresses and vampires: Gk. *lamia* is a bogey to frighten children (cf. Keats's *Lamia,* a retelling of an anecdote from Philostratus [*De vita Apollonii*] concerning Lycius and his demon lover and bride).

The Talmud gives Lilith long hair and wings ('Erub. 100b; Nid. 24b), and a reputation for seizing men who sleep in a house alone (Shab. 151b). Midrashim elaborate a legend that, after parting from Eve, Adam fathered many demons by Lilith, whose offspring fill the world. In the Alphabet of Ben Sira she is identified as the "first Eve," created from the earth at the same time as Adam and before the creation of Eve, and is merged with the demon child-harmer of earlier legend. There are parallel developments in Christian and Arabic demonology, sometimes with varying names. The Cabala gives fixed form to many of these ancient traditions: charms against Lilith are to be deployed before intercourse (Zohar 3.19a); Lilith sports with men sexually in their dreams (1.54b); the period of Adam's intercourse with her is put at 130 years (1.19b); his separation from Eve dates from Cain's murder of Abel (1:54b). She is identified as the animator of the idols fashioned by the builders of Babel (Zohar, Ra'aya Meheimna 3.227b). Zohar elsewhere (3.19a) expands on Isa. 34:14: "She is still in cities of the sea coast trying to snare mankind. And when the Almighty will destroy the wicked Rome, He will settle Lilith among the ruins, since she is the ruin of the world." She is one of four mothers of demons. Other cabalistic writings provide an older Lilith (wife to Sammael) and a younger (wife to Asmodeus). She is identified as one of the harlots brought before Solomon for judgment (1 Kings 3:16) and also, frequently, with the Queen of Sheba, whose riddles to Solomon (1 Kings 10:1) are seen to duplicate her words of seduction to Adam.

St. Jerome (in *Adversus Vigilantus*) links Lilith with leviathan and behemoth and various classical monsters (cf. his *Comm.* on Isa. 34). Luther in his translation of Isa. 34:14 renders *Lilith* as *Kobold,* a gnomish creature from

German folklore who inhabits mines and mischievously contaminates silver. Calvin's commentary on Isaiah advises against inquisitively detailed interpretation and sees the horrific images as an indication of "the punishment threatened against the cruelty of a wicked nation" and of the "various delusions . . . practised by Satan."

The dissolution of Verulamium in Spenser's *Ruines of Time* shows consistency with biblical symbolism in being inhabited by the "Shriche-owle" (cf. *Teares of the Muse*, 282). In Shakespeare, likewise, there are frequent appearances of screech owls which are entirely consistent in symbolism with the Isaiah passage but which again betray no specific awareness of the Lilith tradition for which that passage is the only biblical reference. They appear, appropriately enough, in references to the fall and destruction of Troy (*2 Henry 6*, 1.4.18, and *Troilus and Cressida*, 5.10.16), in more generalized forebodings of death and doom (*2 Henry 6*, 3.2.326, and *3 Henry 6*, 2.6.56), and in Puck's closing speech which marks the reclaiming of the evening by the dark and sinister energies of midnight (*A Midsummer Night's Dream*, 5.1.362; cf. *Phoenix*, 5-9). Milton refers to a night hag, presumably a Lilith variant, in *Paradise Lost*, 2.662-66. Burton's *Anatomy of Melancholy* (1.2.1.2) raises the question of whether spirits and devils can cause melancholy and borrows from Pererius's commentary on Genesis words about "Lilis" (which are in turn cribbed by Carlyle to indicate the dilettantish range of Professor Teufelsdröckh's arcane learning in *Sartor Resartus* [chap. 5]).

The Romantic period created a flourishing career for Lilith. She appears in Goethe's *Faust* (pt. 1, 1.21.286) and in Shelley's translation fragment, *Scenes from Goethe's Faust*. Dante Gabriel Rossetti considers Lilith in both a poem of her name (1864) and in his "Eden Bower" ballad of 1869, giving full sway to typical Romantic ambivalence concerning her attractions and her destructiveness. She appears in Browning's "Adam, Lilith and Eve," "Two Camels," and *The Return of the Druses* (act 2).

The climax of Lilith's literary career in English comes with George Macdonald's *Lilith* (1895) in which Mr. Vane, palpably a version of Macdonald himself, and whose name echoes the vanity of vanities of Ecclesiastes, enters through a mirror in his family library into a fantasy world which is in essence another version of the ordinary world, a world where dream and waking consciousness are ambivalently mixed. There his intermittent guide and instructor is a librarian named Raven whose real identity is Adam, Lilith's former husband. Macdonald's Lilith is a personification of evil who regards the birth of children as the death of the parents, and every new generation as automatic enemy to the last. She succeeds in "killing" her own daughter Lona. But Lona is not irreversibly lost to death, and as she develops from child to adult in a trance-like state between dream and waking, a final imprecisely specified reunion with Vane is awaited. In such a world

even Lilith cannot be irredeemably lost, her ultimate redemption coming through the peculiarly biblical exercise of cutting off the offending hand.

In Shaw's *Back to Methuselah* (1921) the Serpent tells Eve of a Lilith who is a pre-sexual first creature who through a strenuous exertion of the imagination regenerates herself as Adam and Eve. Primal parent of humankind, she embodies creative evolution from matter to spirit. In Joyce's *Ulysses* Lilith is referred to as the patron of abortions; she is "patroness of plants" in Anthony Hecht's poem "La condition botanique" (*The Hard Hours*, 72-75). She is the sister of Satan in Victor Hugo's *La fin de Satan* (see "Le Gibet," 10, and "Hors de la terre," 3.6). Anatole France's *La fille de Lilith* tells the story of Leila, one of her daughters. The White Witch in C. S. Lewis's *The Lion, the Witch, and the Wardrobe* is briefly identified as one of Lilith's offspring and is said not to have a drop of human blood in her. The Lilith in Anais Nin's *Delta of Venus* is a figure of psychological interest, a sexually cold woman aroused to heights of passion in fanciful and near-hysterical belief that she has been administered an aphrodisiac. Lilith is the titular character of a dramatic poem by George Sterling, an untraditional fictionalization in a medieval setting, and a French quasi-biblical dramatization by Remy de Gourmont in which Lilith has an elaborately detailed relationship with Satan.

Lilith has become a prominent figure in recent feminist literature, a new archetype for the liberated woman and a staple of contemporary "goddess religion." Two recent scholarly books (Hurwitz and Bril) explore at length the interrelations of the religious, mythological, and psychological aspects of the Lilith theme.

See also BEHEMOTH; EVE; LEVIATHAN.

Bibliography. Briggs, K. M. "The Legends of Lilith and of the Wandering Jew in Nineteenth-Century Literature." *Folklore* 92 (1981), 132-40; Bril, J. *Lilith: ou la mère obscure* (1981); Graves, R., and R. Patai. *Hebrew Myths: the Book of Genesis* (1966), 65-69; Hurwitz, S. *Lilith die erste Eva: Eine Studie über dunkle Aspekte des Weiblichen* (1983); Liptzin, S. "Rehabilitation of Lilith." In *Biblical Themes in World Literature* (1985), 1-12; McGillis, R. F. "George Macdonald and the Lilith Legend in the XIXth Century." *Mythlore* 6 (Winter 1979), 3-11; Plastow, J. "The Coming of Lilith: Toward a Feminist Theology." In *Womanspirit Rising: A Feminist Reader in Religion*. Ed. C. P. Christ and J. Plastow (1979); Scholem, G. "Lilith." *EncJud*. Rpt. in his *Kabbalah* (1974; 1978).   RICHARD SCHELL

LILY OF THE VALLEY   An appellation of the bride in the Song of Songs (2:1), this term is typologically applied during the Middle Ages to the Virgin Mary, who becomes the *flos campi et lilium convallium* of the typological Bridegroom, Christ.

See also MARY, MOTHER OF JESUS.

LION IN THE WAY . . . IN THE STREET   Prov. 26:13 notes as one of the marks of the slothful man his paranoia:

"The slothful man saith, There is a lion in the way; a lion is in the streets." In Samuel Butler's *The Way of All Flesh,* after Ernest Pontifex was released from prison he prowled the streets for several nights, trying to reconstruct his confidence: ". . . he had been scared, and now saw lions when there were none, and was shocked and frightened" (chap. 71).

LION LIES DOWN WITH THE LAMB   One of the characteristics of the messianic kingdom of the future described by Isaiah is a return to prelapsarian innocence, in which "the wolf also shall dwell with the kid; and the calf and the young lion and the fatling together; and a little child shall lead them. . . . And the lion shall eat straw like the ox" (Isa. 11:6-7). The passage is frequently rendered as saying "the lion shall lie down with the lamb"; the text is quoted or alluded to by a number of major English poets, usually in the context of a utopian or millenarian imagination. In Shelley's *Queen Mab* (124-28), e.g., the Queen looks forward to such a future, when:

> The lion now forgets to thirst for blood:
> There might you see him sporting in the sun
> Beside the dreadless kid; his claws are sheathed,
> His teeth are harmless, custom's force had made
> His nature as the nature of a lamb.

Henry James, in "The Death of the Lion," depicts the soirées of socially predatory Mrs. Weeks Wimbush, "proprietress of the universal menagerie," as times in which "the animals rub shoulders freely with the spectators and the lions sit down for whole evenings with the lambs." In Margaret Avison's "Then,"

> The leopard and the kid
> are smoothness (fierce)
> and softness (gentle)
> and will lie down together. (*sunblue,* 98)

The phrase "The lion shall eat straw like the ox" acquires in Blake an antimillenarian response: "One Law for the Lion & Ox is Oppression" ("A Memorable Fancy"; cf. "Marginalia on Reynold's Discourses"; "Tiriel," 7.33). The relationship between the "kingdom of God within" and the messianic millennium is questioned in Anthony Hecht's "Pig," where also the iconographic association of the lion with St. Mark the Evangelist and St. Jerome the translator is recalled:

> And all things be redeemed — the suckling babe
> Lie safe in the serpent's home
> And the lion eat straw like the ox and roar its love
> to Mark and to Jerome. (*Hard Hours,* 13)

LION OF JUDAH   In A. M. Klein's poem "Reb Levi Yitschok Talks to God" the old rabbi expresses the modesty of his condition, saying, "The lion of Judah! no such parable is on my lips. . . ." In Gen. 49:9, when Jacob is blessing his sons, he praises Judah and predicts his future

prominence, saying, "Judah is a lion's whelp." Talmudic legend identifies Judah as bravest of the sons of Jacob, and credits him with a lion's countenance and teeth, and a terrible earthshaking voice (Gen. Rab. 93.7; Yalqut 2.897 on Job 4:10; Tan. Ber. 1.406). The standard of the tribe of Judah is said to bear a lion in its upper part (Tg. Yer. Num. 2:3ff.; cf. Midr. 'Aggada Num. 2:2ff.).

In the lineage of Jesus Judah has a privileged place. In Rev. 5:5 St. John the Divine is addressed by one of the "elders" in Paradise, who says to him, "Weep not: behold the Lion of the tribe of Judah, the root of David, hath prevailed to open the book, and to loose the seven seals thereof." This reference, and allegorizations of Gen. 49:9 to accord with it, led to the "lion of Judah" being a synonym for Christ in medieval writings; in the *Physiologus* and other medieval bestiaries the supposed biology of the lion is made a *symbolum* of Christ's role as redemptor and victor over Satan, who is also sometimes described as "a roaring lion" (1 Pet. 5:8).

See also TRIBES OF ISRAEL.

LITTLE CHILD SHALL LEAD THEM   *See* LION LIES DOWN WITH THE LAMB.

LITTLE EWE LAMB   *See* NATHAN.

LITTLE LOWER THAN THE ANGELS   Ps. 8 is a much quoted celebration of the peculiar honor accorded humanity as the centerpiece of God's creation, and having "dominion" (v. 6) over it: "Out of the mouth of babes and sucklings," he writes, "hast thou ordained strength. . . . What is man, that thou art mindful of him, and the son of man, that thou visitest him? For thou hast made him a little lower than the angels, and hast crowned him with glory and honor" (vv. 2, 4-5). For St. Augustine the "babes and sucklings" are those children who responded to Jesus openly (Matt. 21:16) and though young in the faith, having begun "by belief in the Scriptures . . . arrive at the knowledge of thy glory" (*Enarr. in Ps.* 8.5-7). The "son of man" who visits man is "the very Lord of Man, born of the Virgin Mary" (11); "a little lower than the angels" is to say just beneath the glory of the heavenly realm. This Psalm is invoked by Chaucer's Prioress in the Prologue to her tale, though only v. 2 is cited. Hamlet's speech to Rosencrantz and Guildenstern responds directly to vv. 4-5: "What a piece of work is man! How noble in reason! How infinite in faculty! In form and moving how express and admirable! In action how like an angel!" (2.2.315-18). Mark Twain applies the hierarchy to humanity's moral sense in his essay "The Damned Human Race," where in his view "there is only one possible stage below the Moral Sense: that is the Immoral Sense. The Frenchman has it. Man is but little lower than the angels. This definitely locates him. He is between the angels and the French."

See also OUT OF THE MOUTH OF BABES; SON OF MAN.

LITURGY The word *liturgy* does not appear in any English version of the Bible, but Gk. *leitourgia*, of which it is a transliteration, is not infrequent in the LXX, being translated as "work" or "service" (e.g., Exod. 38:21). It was applied especially to the duties of the Levites, and so designated cultic tasks (Num. 4:24) which embraced their ministry in the Temple (Exod. 40:46). In NT vocabulary the word has not such a confined cultic reference (Phil. 2:30), but later it was applied to all the services of the Church, e.g., the baptismal liturgy, and in particular to the Eucharist, being commonly so used among the Eastern Churches.

See also EUCHARIST; PRAYER; TEMPLE; WORSHIP.

Bibliography. Baumstark, A. *Liturgie comparée* (1939; Eng. trans. 1958); Daniélou, J. *The Bible and the Liturgy* (Eng. trans. 1956); Davies, H. *Worship and Theology in England from Watts and Wesley to Maurice, 1690-1850* (1961); Gibson, G. M. *The Story of the Christian Year* (1945); Harris, C., and W. K. Lowther Clarke, eds. *Liturgy and Worship: A Companion to the Prayer Books of the Anglican Communion* (1932); Hurlbut, S. A. *The Liturgy of the Church of England Before and After the Reformation* (1941); Michell, G. A. *Landmarks in Liturgy: The Primitive Rite, A Medieval Mass, The English Rite to 1662* (1961); Micklem, N., ed. *Christian Worship: Studies in its History and Meaning* (1936); Posner, R., et al. *Jewish Liturgy: Prayer and Synagogue Service through the Ages* (1975); Zundel, M. *The Splendour of the Liturgy* (Eng. trans. 1939).   J. G. DAVIES

LIVING DOG IS BETTER THAN A DEAD LION Death is the great leveler, according to Qoheleth. Hence, only for "him that is joined to all the living there is hope: for a living dog is better than a dead lion" (Eccl. 9:4). Thoreau says in his "Conclusion" to *Walden* that grating protests that "Americans, and moderns generally, are intellectual dwarfs compared to the ancients, or even the Elizabethan[s]," have little point: "A living dog is better than a dead lion." This Americanized version of Solomonic wisdom seems to be recognized by one of the characters in Somerset Maugham's *Cakes and Ale:* "'You don't know America as well as I do,' he said, 'they always prefer a live mouse to a dead lion. That's one of the reasons why I like America" (chap. 24).

LIVING WATER As might be expected from a land-locked people wresting a precarious living out of a desert environment, water imagery is prevalent in the Bible. On the demonic side, the (salt) water of the Dead (and life-destroying) Sea symbolizes the undifferentiated primordial chaos from which the creation emerges. The Exodus from Egypt through the rolled-back Red Sea reiterates that first creation out of watery chaos, and Israel's tyrant overlords (there and elsewhere) are symbolically linked to the demonic sea and its mythic monsters. Into that sea the timid disciples would sink in their unbelief, as Jesus does not, and at the end of time, with the New Jerusalem,

that sea disappears forever: ". . . and there was no more sea" (Rev. 21:1).

The closely parallel water of life also has recurrent symbolic meaning, derived obviously from water's essential role in the preservation of life itself, and celebrating precisely the opposite of the dead water which impinges so unrelentingly on a desert people. This water is associated with wells and fountains, like the one placed in Eden at creation (Gen. 2:6; KJV "mist," LXX "fountain") whence the fresh water of an underground sea-source went out through four great symbolic rivers to water the whole of the known world.

Loss of Eden symbolically entails loss of this water of life along with the tree of life, and the whole of the Bible is concerned to enunciate the shape of a myth of reconciliation through salvation from demonic waters (and the tyrant powers identified with them) and restoration of the water of life: the Israelites wandering in the wilderness are sustained by water from a "spiritual Rock that followed them," alluded to by St. Paul (1 Cor. 10:4); when the people turn away from God, it is described as refusing "the waters of Shiloah that go softly," the consequence of which is that God will bring "up upon them the waters of the river, strong and many, even the king of Assyria, and all his glory: and he shall come up over all his channels, and go over all his banks" (Isa. 8:6-7). Isaiah 35 presents an apocalyptic restoration of Zion, in which "in the wilderness shall waters break out, and streams in the desert. And the parched ground shall become a pool, and the thirsty land springs of water" (vv. 6-7). Ezekiel's prophecies (chap. 47) from exile equate the restoration of the Temple in Jerusalem with the return of clearly symbolic life-giving waters (identical with the four rivers of Genesis, according to St. Jerome [*Ep.* 69]), which flow out from under the altar and, though initially only a stream, become without tributary an unfordable river 4,000 cubits downstream, eventually flowing into the (Dead?) sea and thus healing it. Zech. 14:8-9 tells how "living waters shall go out from Jerusalem. . . . and the LORD shall be King over all the earth," a theme reiterated in the "water of life, clear as crystal, proceeding out of the throne of God and of the Lamb" (Rev. 22:1) of the celestial Zion. But for the Psalmist (Ps. 1:3) the man whose life is grounded in the Torah even in this life is "like a tree planted by the rivers of water," ever fruitful.

In Christian typology Christ is the fulfillment which absorbs all this symbolism: the water-giving rock in the desert, the temple of God, the fountain of living waters as God had been for Jeremiah (2:13; 17:13). The bride in the Song of Songs is also a well of living waters (4:15), and her marriage prefigures the apocalyptic marriage of the Church to Christ, the lamb who "shall lead them unto living fountains of water" (Rev. 7:17).

In short, the living waters become symbolic of all that biblical history strives toward. When Isaiah says (49:10), "They shall not hunger nor thirst; neither shall the heat nor sun smite them," he is envisioning the restoration of Jerusalem. But in the end the Bible absorbs that nationalistic vision into a symbolic universal New Jerusalem which replaces the sea world of earthly tyranny with an invitation to the redeemed to "take the water of life freely" (Rev. 22:17).

The Fathers usually equate living water with (1) faith: Origen contrasts "rivers of water springing up unto eternal life" as weapons against "the fiery darts of the evil one" (*On Prayer,* 30); (2) the gospel: St. Cyprian sees this as the possession of the true Church, over against the false claims of the heretics to possess it (*Letters,* 73.11; *Unity of the Catholic Church,* 11). St. Augustine's *Contra Faustum* goes further, making the Church itself the well of living water (NPNF 4.307); (3) the Holy Spirit: St. Augustine makes the identification in *De Trin.* 15.33 and *In Joan. Ev.* 11. For St. Ambrose, on the other hand, the waters are more ambiguously suggestive of the "nurture of a mystical kind" which humans receive from God (*De interpellatione Job et David,* 2.3).

The symbolism is much the same with later medieval writers and the Reformers. Thomas Münzer contrasts the "stagnant waters" which are all that presumptuous natural reason can gain access to (*Sermon before the Princes* [LCC 25.58]). Luther's *Commentaries* (on Zech. 14:8-9) equate water of life with the Holy Spirit: "This is the spiritual Jerusalem, from which the Holy Spirit flows through the Gospel." Zwingli quotes John 7:38 to deny the efficacy of water (in *Of Baptism*) since Christ himself is the living water "which quickens the soul" (LCC 24.154). Bullinger cites the same passage (as Augustine had earlier) connecting the living waters flowing out of Christ's body with the Holy Spirit (*Of the Holy Catholic Church* [LCC 24.305]). For Calvin living waters are variously faith (*Inst.* 3.2.8), the Holy Spirit in Scripture (3.1.3), or the gospel: "Whenever the prophets foretell the renewal of the Church or its extension over the whole globe, they always assign the first place to the word. For they say that from Jerusalem will issue forth living waters, which being divided into four rivers will inundate the whole earth" (*Reply to Sadoleto* [LCC 22.230]). On a more suggestive level they can be a metaphor for the certainty that God's grace will "flow continually" (*Comm.* on Zech. 14:8) or for the restorative effects of all his blessings on the "dry and barren soil" of mankind (*Comm.* on John 4:10).

The water of life described in Rev. 22:1 is clearly invoked by the 14th-cent. *Pearl,* which identifies it both with baptism (653) and with the heavenly fountain which eternally renews the paradisal garden (1977ff.). The cleansing waters "to wasch alle the world" are typologically the "water of schryfte" in the same poet's *Cleanness* (323, 1133). Spenser's Redcrosse Knight fights a symbolic three-day battle with "that old Dragon," identified in Rev. 20:2 as the devil and Satan, in a contest meant to reiterate and extend the Bible's apocalyptic closure of

history. The well of life in which he is baptismally "drenched" provides strength to continue after the first day (*Faerie Queene,* 2.11.arg., 29-34).

Donne's baptismal sermon (on Rev. 17:7) is broadly suggestive: "He shall lead them to the lively fountain of waters; give them outward and visible means of sanctification. . . . even in this life he shall settle and establish a heavenly joy in the faithful apprehension of the joyes of heaven here" (*Sermons* [ed. Potter and Simpson], 4.98). For Vaughan, living water is part of the symbolism of apocalyptic vision in "Tears," and in "Jesus Weeping" is equated with the tears which Jesus weeps for Jerusalem and which, rain-like, should revitalize dead hearts. Such baroque sentiment also occurs in Crashaw's "On the bleeding wounds of our crucified Lord": Christ was never "So sadly true, / The well of living Waters, Lord, till now." He recapitulates the reality of which all other rivers, however grand and impressive, are but ephemeral reflections. In "The Silence" Traherne uses the "Living Springs" as a symbol of oneness with God in a transcendentally immediate prelapsarian world: "My Bosom was an Ocean into which / They all did run." In "The Fullnesse" they connect the vitality of the imagination with that visionary world. In the apocalyptic vision of Cowper's *The Task* (6.763-65):

> Rivers of gladness water all the earth,
> And clothe all climes with beauty; the reproach
> Of barrenness is past.

In Byron's "Condolatory Address," by contrast, the garden is pointedly less than paradisal, without a rose and having "a fount that only wants its living stream" (25-27); while in Blake's "Night" the lion watching over the fold can speak of the baptismal waters of the everlasting river in almost Heraclitan terms:

> And now beside thee, bleating lamb,
> I can lie down and sleep;
> Or think on Him who bore thy name,
> Graze after thee, and weep.
> For, washed in life's river,
> My bright mane for ever
> Shall shine like the gold
> As I guard o'er the fold.

Ruskin somewhat dismally transforms the living water to a trope for money and wealth, saying, "No human laws can understand its flow. They can only guide it: but this . . . [it] can do so thoroughly, that it shall become the water of life — the riches of the hand of wisdom" (*Unto this Last,* 3). And speaking of Ann Whitefield's appeal to Octavius, Shaw writes in the stage direction of *Man and Superman* that

> She is to him the reality of romance, the inner good sense of nonsense, the unveiling of his eyes, the freeing of his soul, the abolition of time, place and circumstance, the etherialization of his blood into rapturous rivers of the

very water of life itself, the revelation of all the mysteries and sanctification of all the dogmas.

Many other post-Renaissance occurrences are merely decorative. Herrick invokes living waters as an instrument of blessing in "To the Genius of this House"; later Hazlitt (in "On Going on a Journey") and Hardy (in *Tess of the D'Urbervilles*) compare the clarity of the Rivers Dee and Froom to the biblical "living waters." Regenerative waters only somewhat less overtly biblical are central to themes of reconciliation in Shakespeare's *The Tempest* and T. S. Eliot's *The Waste Land*.

See also BAPTISM; MARAH; ROCK; THIRST; WATER.
Bibliography. Daniélou, J. *Primitive Christian Symbols* (1964); Frye, N. *The Great Code* (1 982); *T. S. Eliot* (1963), 64-71; ed. *The Tempest* (1959), "Introduction."
RICHARD SCHELL

LOAVES AND FISHES   After Jesus fed the hungry multitude of more than 5,000 who had followed him into the desert with a miraculous multiplication of the lunch of a small boy — five little barley loaves and two fishes (Matt. 14:15-21; John 6:5-27) — the crowds increased in size. Jesus observed that they seemed to be pursuing him merely for the sake of a "free lunch" and not out of concern for their spiritual welfare (John 6:26).

St. Augustine allegorizes the five loaves as "the five books of Moses; and rightly are they not wheaten but barley loaves, because they belong to the Old Testament" (*In Joan. Ev.* 24.1.5). The two fishes

> appear . . . to signify those two sublime persons in the Old Testament of priest and of ruler, who were anointed for the sanctifying and the governing of the people. And at length himself in the mystery came . . . who was pointed out by the pith of the barley, but concealed by its husk.

The 5,000 people are taken by Augustine to signify those who were

> under the law, which is unfolded in the five books of Moses. . . . Moreover they sat down upon the grass; therefore understood carnally, and rested in the carnal: 'for all flesh is grass' [Isa. 40:6]. . . . Why were twelve baskets filled? This was done both marvellously, because a great thing was done; and it was done profitably, because a spiritual thing was done. (6)

Commenting in the following tractate concerning Jesus' words — "Ye seek me, not because ye saw the miracles [Vg *signo*] but because ye did eat of the loaves and were filled" — Augustine reads, "Ye seek me for the sake of the flesh, not for the sake of the spirit. How many seek Jesus for no other object but that he may bestow on them a temporal benefit!" (25.10).

Cash-benefit Christianity is what appeals to Chaucer's Man of Law in his narration of his tale of Custance; in his solicitousness for attention to matters of comfort he asks how she was fed while adrift in her rudderless ship. As in the case of St. Mary the Egyptian, it was by

> no wight but Crist, sanz faille.
> Five thousand folk it was as greet mervaille
> With loves five and fisshes two to feede.
> God sent his foyson at hir grete neede. (*Canterbury Tales*, 2.501-04)

In Trollope's *Barchester Towers* the allusion is to ecclesiastical polity: "One or two of the neighbouring clergy . . . thought it not quite safe to neglect the baskets in which for the nonce were stored the loaves and fishes of the diocese of Barchester. They, and they only, came to call on Mr. Slope after his performance in the cathedral pulpit" (chap. 7). Van Wyck Brooks depicts Walt Whitman as grieving that "so many young men were hungry for loaves and fishes and fat berths that they seemed always ready to obey" (*The Times of Melville and Whitman*, chap. 15). Somerset Maugham published his own *Loaves and Fishes* in 1924.

LOCUSTS AND WILD HONEY   The diet of John the Baptist in his wilderness austerity (Matt. 3:4; Mark 1:6). In attributing prophetic character to Professor Teufelsdröckh of *Sartor Resartus*, Carlyle writes: "In our wild Seer, shaggy, unkempt, like a Baptist living on locusts and wild honey, there is an untutored energy, a silent, as it were, unconscious strength" (1.4). Although Lev. 11:22 represents insects of the locust family as "clean" and acceptable as food, some modern commentators have suggested that a type of bean may have been thus signified. Whatever the case, James Joyce's Stephen reflects on his friend Cranly, "the child of exhausted lions," like the child of "Elizabeth and Zachary . . . is the precursor. Item: he eats chiefly belly bacon and dried figs. Read locusts and wild honey" (*A Portrait of the Artist as a Young Man*, chap. 5).

See also JOHN THE BAPTIST.

LOGOS   *Logos* is the ordinary Greek word for "word"; there is nothing special about most of its biblical uses. But sometimes in Greek it has a meaning different from that of its English equivalent. The Greeks distinguished between the *logos prophorikos* (the word uttered) and the *logos endiathetos* (the word remaining within); the Stoics also spoke of the *logos spermatikos*, the "seminal" word, which is not so important for biblical tradition but figures importantly in the writings of Neoplatonists.

The *logos endiathetos*, the word which remains within a person, is something like reason. Some of the Greek philosophers, notably Heraclitus and the Stoics, thought of a logos in the universe, something like a world soul — a rational principle which runs through all that is. They did not conceive of it as personal, but rather as an ordering principle which accounts for the rationality they perceived in nature; a suggestion of agency, however, is discernible in Heraclitus: "Regarded as the Logos, God is the omnipresent Wisdom by which all things are steered" (cited in J. Adam, *The Religious Teachers of Greece* [1909], 233).

Jewish writers did not use "word" in quite the same way as the Greeks. They employed the term, along with other concepts like "Wisdom" and "the Law," in semipersonalizations, such as the association of Wisdom with God in the creation process (Prov. 8:22-31). The Word could mean much the same thing as the Law, as the parallelism in Isa. 2:3 (cf. Mic. 4:2) shows. The writer of the Wisdom of Solomon speaks of "thy all-powerful word" as leaping "from heaven, from the royal throne . . . a stern warrior . . . [which] touched heaven while standing on the earth" (Wisd. 18:15). The Alexandrian Philo uses the concept of the logos frequently, and can even speak of the logos as "God" or his agency (though guarding the concept that there is only one true God) in terms recalling the demiurge of Plato's *Timaeus*. In some Targums the Aramaic term *Memra* is used as a periphrasis for God. While this is not identical with the Heraclitan logos or that of Philo, it also associates "Word" with deity.

All these terms form the background for St. John's use of Logos as a designation of Christ (John 1:1, 14; cf. Rev. 19:13). John's Logos goes beyond anything else in the NT, though there are approximations in other NT writers. Thus St. Luke makes little distinction between preaching the word and preaching Jesus (e.g., Acts 8:4; 11:20) and in his reference to "eyewitnesses, and ministers of the word" (Luke 1:2) he is certainly speaking of the person as well as the words and actions of Jesus. St. Paul speaks of "the word of God" as "the mystery" and of "this mystery" as "Christ in you" (Col. 1:25-27). John thus makes explicit in a powerful trope what is suggested elsewhere in the NT, that Christ must be seen as not less close to God than his very thought or utterance (John 1:1-14).

The amenability of this idea (esp. as formulated in John's Gospel, but see also Col. 1:12-19) to the language of Philo, the *Timaeus*, and also some of the Neoplatonists has undoubtedly had an impact on Western representations of the Logos. In his commentary on Ps. 45 St. Augustine talks about the eternal unity of the Logos *(verbum)* comprising all that is creation, past, present, and to come, yet fully to be identified with "the Word from the beginning" as uttered in Christ. "In the Word itself are all the works of God [*nec esset in rebus, nisi esset in verbo*]," he writes:

> For whatever God designed to make in the creation already existed in "the Word"; and would not exist in the reality, had it not existed in the Word, just as with you the thing would not exist in the building, had it not existed in your design: even as it is said in the Gospel: "That which was made in Him was life." That which was made then was in existence; but it had its existence in the Word: and all the works of God existed there, and yet were not as yet "works." "The Word" however already WAS, as this "Word was God, and was with God": and was the Son of

God, and One God with the Father. "I speak of the things I have made unto the King." Let him hear Him "speaking," who apprehends "the Word": and let him see together with the Father the Everlasting Word; in whom exist even those things that are yet to come: in whom even those things that are past have not passed away. These "works" of God are in "the Word," as in the Word, as in the Only-Begotten, as in the "Word of God." (*Enarr. in Ps.* 45.5)

St. Jerome is likewise aware of the changing status of the word *logos,* including its tendency among later Stoics and Neoplatonists to acquire associations from Plato's demiurge in the *Timaeus* which make it function more like a gerund, or verbal, than a noun. Jerome says, however, that failure to identify the Logos with Christ as the active utterance of God in Christ is the signal inadequacy in Greek philosophy:

> *Logos* in Greek has many meanings. It signifies word and reason and reckoning and the cause of individual things by which those which are subsist. All of which things we rightly predicate of Christ. This truth Plato with all his learning did not know, of this Demosthenes with all his eloquence was ignorant. (*Ep.* 53, "To Paulinus")

Early translators from the Greek, like Jerome, are frustrated by the inadequacy of any single Latin word to convey the complexity and transitive, dynamic power they feel to be expressed in the Johannine Logos. The Vg *"In principium erat verbum"* (John 1:1) is constrained to use, however, the inadequate noun *(verbum)* for "word." Later romance language translations are advantaged by the development (from their Gallic component) of non-Latin words for "noun" (e.g., Fr. *le môt*), freeing the distinctive sense of Logos to be associated with Lat. *verbum. Verbum* then typically enters those languages in the Middle Ages to signify, as in English, the "verb" (e.g., Fr. *verbe;* Span. *verba*).

Reformation translators took another approach: Luther's German NT rejects *Zeitwort* ("verb") for the more static noun: *"Im Anfang war das Wort"* (though commentators in the Reformation tradition have repeatedly turned to expressions such as "the living Word" to try to recapture something of the dynamic, transitive sense of Logos in John 1:1-14 felt by Augustine, Jerome, and others.

The Neoplatonic *logos spermatikos* returns to complicate matters in Renaissance Neoplatonism. In Cudworth's *The Intellectual System of the Universe* (1678), the famous Cambridge Neoplatonist takes up the nonbiblical *logos spermatikos* or *rationes seminales,* anticipating in so doing the "plastic nature" concept of Romantic thinkers, including the German idealists. Coleridge, who began his intellectual life under the influence of such thinkers, expresses a rather woolly notion of the Johannine *Logos* in his *"Consciones ad Populam"* (1796). By 1803, endeavoring to articulate a clearer theory of the Logos, he proposed to write a *Logosophia,* a "history of logic." By

1814, when he had moved away from Unitarianism toward Christian orthodoxy, his working title was *Christianity, the one true Philosophy — Five Treatises on the Logos, or Communicative Intelligence, Natural, Human, and Divine.* Of these, the third "treatise," *Logos Theanthropos,* was to be a systematic commentary on the Gospel of John (*Collected Letters,* 3.533; 4.687).

Coleridge's manuscript was still in disarray at his death, though it is soon, at last, to be published. It would appear that his later efforts, to which he says he saw his whole corpus of poetry as a propaedeutic, were to "re-Christianize" an "idealized" or neoplatonized logos, returning it to communication of the orthodox NT usage (*Collected Works, The Friend,* 1.316n.). In his *Biographia Literaria* (1817), however, he still speaks of the Logos as the "communicative intellect in man and the deity" (chap. 13; cf. 12.9) — a formulation with which neither Augustine nor Luther would likely have been comfortable.

Association of the Logos with the Second Person of the Trinity, as is met with, e.g., in David Jones's *Anathemata* (7.221), John Donne's Holy Sonnet, "Temple," or in Milton's *Paradise Lost,* is normative to Western Christian usage. The choice of Goethe's Faust when translating John 1:1 (he rejects in turn *das Wort, der Sinn* [mind], *die Kraft* [power], before choosing the depersonalized *die Tat* ["the Act"]) is self-consciously a rejection of the orthodox connection. It accurately anticipates, however, developments in Romantic and post-Romantic literary theory. (Byron's free citation of John 1:1-3 at the beginning of his bizarre poem *Morgante Maggiore* is harder to categorize.) The "logo-centrism" characterized by Derrida and other poststructuralists as a nominal Christian "worship of the word" is defined by them in terms which trace in fact to post-Romantic rather than biblical or particularly Christian lineage.

See also WORD OF GOD.

Bibliography. Arnold, M. "The Logos Metaphor in Milton's Epics." *DAI* 34 (1974), 2546A; Barfield, O. *What Coleridge Thought* (1971); *Saving the Appearances: A Study in Idolatry* (1965); Blodgett, E. D., and H. G. Coward. *Science, the Word, and the Sacred* (1989); Freccero, J. "Dante's Medusa: Allegory and Autobiography." In *By Things Seen: Reference and Recognition in Medieval Thought.* Ed. D. L. Jeffrey (1979), 33-46; Jeffrey, D. L. "Breaking Up the Synthesis: From Plato's Academy to the 'School of Athens'." In *By Things Seen,* 227-52; "Mistakenly Logocentric: Centering Poetic Language in a Scriptural Tradition." *Religion and Literature* 22 (1990), 33-46.　　　　DAVID L. JEFFREY
LEON MORRIS

LONGINUS　St. John records in his account of the Crucifixion that after Jesus had died, "one of the soldiers with a spear pierced his side, and forthwith came there out blood and water" (John 19:34). The name of the soldier is not given in the text and arises only in the late 6th cent. (ca. 586) when it appears in a miniature or illumination in a Syriac manuscript (now held in the

Laurentian Library in Florence) over the head of a soldier piercing Christ. In later legends, most notably in *The Memorials of Nicodemus* (A.D. 600), later known as the Gospel of Nicodemus, it was asserted that when the spear pierced Christ's side Longinus was cured of his blindness by a drop of the blood. In subsequent elaborations he tended to be confused with the centurion spoken of in the Matthean Passion narrative who said, after Christ had expired, "Truly, this was the Son of God" (Matt. 27:54).

Longinus appears in the ME Corpus Christi drama, where the piercing of Christ's side and the miraculous healing from blindness occurs, e.g., in the Towneley "Crucifixion" (33.593-606). In the York "Mortificatio Cristi" (36.291-312), the centurion Longinus is ordered by Pilate to pierce Christ; his miraculous recovery of sight is followed immediately by a total darkening of the sky, which prompts his exclamation of belief. The lance of Longinus forms part of the legend of the Fisher-King, in which it accompanies the Holy Grail to his chamber. This legendary development may have been influenced by an elaborate Byzantine ritual described in the 7th- or 8th-cent. "Mass of Chrysostom," which includes a symbolic representation of the spear or lance of Longinus as a "relic" of the Crucifixion (see also Chrétien de Troyes's *Percival, ou le conte du Graal* [1312-1698; 2974-3592]). The lance in the Grail legend is identified by Malory (*Works,* ed. E. Vinaver, 54) as Longinus's spear.

See also HOLY GRAIL.

Bibliography. Peebles, R. J. *The Legend of Longinus and its Connection with the Grail* (1911).

LORD OF THE FLIES　*See* BEELZEBUB.

LORD'S ANOINTED　*See* MESSIAH.

LORD'S PRAYER　*See* PATER NOSTER.

LORD'S SUPPER　*See* EUCHARIST.

LOST SHEEP, PARABLE OF　Jesus' parable of the lost sheep is recorded in two different forms in Matt. 18:12-14 and Luke 15:4-7. J. Jeremias sees Matthew's version as secondary, reflecting a change of emphasis from Jesus' original *apologia* for his association with sinners to an exhortation to Christian leaders to seek out apostates. In both forms the parable derives its power from the basic human experience of being lost and found, especially as this is symbolized by the plight of a gregarious animal cut off from the herd which gives it identity and life.

Matthew 18 as a whole concerns the community's care for its members, who are not to be offended against in their weakness (18:1-9) and should be corrected and forgiven when they have erred (18:15-35). The parable of the lost sheep serves as conclusion and example of the former theme as well as introduction to the latter. The value of "little ones," already stated in the introduction (v. 10), is exemplified by the actions of the shepherd seeking the lost and forcefully reiterated as the "lesson" of the parable: "It is not the will of your Father . . . that one of these little ones should perish" (v. 14).

In Luke's version the author does not "introduce" the meaning of the parable but allows readers to discover it in their own experience. The Pharisees complain about Jesus' practice of receiving and eating with sinners. Abruptly Jesus confronts them with a parable which traps them in their own expectations. The parable's power resides in the imaginative shock of a shepherd abandoning his whole flock in the steppes to seek out the one lost sheep "until he finds it" (v. 4). (A Palestinian shepherd would ordinarily drive his remaining flock into a pen or natural enclosure, or turn it over to a neighboring shepherd lest it scatter or be ravaged.) This figure, then, illustrates the extravagant action of God himself, who rejoices more over one sinner who repents than over ninety-nine who need no repentance (v. 7). Jesus not only reveals the value of sinners but challenges his hearers to re-evaluate their conception of their own "righteousness." This two-pronged truth is repeated in the three subsequent parables of the lost coin (15:8-10), the prodigal son (15:11-32), and the unjust steward (16:1-13).

According to St. Irenaeus the gnostics connected the straying of the sheep with the enfleshment of the aeons. Within the Church the parable was used sparingly, to vindicate reconciliation of Christians who had sinned (*Apostolic Constitutions,* 2.13-14) and reception of those lapsed in the Decian persecution (St. Cyprian, *Ep.* 46, 51). Tertullian, in his *De poenitentia* (chap. 8), uses Luke 15:4-7 to vindicate the Church's practice of a second repentance for Christians; later, however, in his Montanist treatise *De pudicitia* (chap. 7), he denies this practice, there taking the wandering sheep to represent the heathen.

St. John Chrysostom, the first to treat the parable exegetically, notes (with reference to Luke 15:7) that the righteous are imperiled for the sake of the lost (*Hom.* 59, on Matthew). St. Augustine interprets the parable as manifesting the Lord's extravagant zeal in seeking the lost, whom he identifies as all of humanity implicated in original sin (*De peccatorum meritis et remissione,* 1.40). For St. Thomas Aquinas (following St. Gregory, *Hom. 34 on the Gospels*), the flock represents all rational creatures and (following St. Hilary's commentary on Matthew) the lost sheep the human race, strayed through Adam and redeemed by Christ, the Good Shepherd (*Super Evangelium Sancti Mattaei Lectura,* 1509-13).

The Reformers also used the parable rarely (Luther refers to it only twice). Calvin explains the angels' greater joy as caused by God's mercy shining more brightly in the liberation of a sinner (*Harmony of the Gospels*).

An extended literary parody occurs in the opening scene of Shakespeare's *Two Gentlemen of Verona,* where Speed and Proteus trade witticisms about Speed's relationship with his absent master Valentine. Speed responds to Proteus's calling him a sheep by countering: "The shepherd seeks the sheep, and not the sheep the shepherd; but I seek my master, and my master seeks not me. Therefore I am no sheep." Proteus replies: "The sheep for fodder follow the shepherd; the shepherd for food follows not the sheep. Thou for wages followest thy master; thy master for wages follows not thee. Therefore thou art a sheep." "Such another proof will make me cry 'baa'," exclaims Speed, who then identifies himself as "a lost mutton" (1.1.69-110).

Byron, who makes a comic allusion to Luke 15:7 in the dedication to *Don Juan* (41-43), elsewhere refers to the same passage straightforwardly, observing: "He who repents . . . occasions more rejoicing in the skies / Than ninety-nine of the celestial list" (*Morgante Maggiore,* 466-67). Ira D. Sankey, while touring Scotland with American evangelist Dwight L. Moody, composed a musical setting for an obscure, posthumously published poem by Elizabeth Clephane, "The Ninety and Nine" (1874). In this well-known hymn the shepherd's suffering in seeking the lost is implicitly connected to the Passion:

"Lord, whence are those blood drops all the way
That mark out the mountain's track?"
"They were shed for one who had gone astray
Ere the Shepherd could bring him back."
"Lord, whence are thy hands so rent and torn?"
"They are pierced tonight by many a thorn,
They are pierced tonight by many a thorn."

George Eliot, in her *Scenes from Clerical Life,* observes that for one who "has learned pity through suffering,"

the old, old saying about the joy of angels over the repentant sinner outweighing their joy over the ninety-nine just, has a meaning which does not jar with the language of his own heart. It only tells him . . . that for angels too the misery of one casts so tremendous a shadow as to eclipse the bliss of ninety-nine. ("Janet's Repentance")

In Galsworthy's *Flowering Wilderness,* the misery of the penitent somewhat outweighs any attendant joy: "There was no rejoicing as over a sinner that repenteth. All were too sorry for her, with a sorrow nigh unto dismay" (chap. 31). Allusion to the parable takes a sinister twist in Shaw's *Saint Joan* when Ladvenue, handing Joan's recantation to Cauchon, exults: "Praise be to God, my brothers, the lamb has returned to the flock; and the shepherd rejoices in her more than in ninety and nine just persons." Luke 15:7 provides the title for Morley Callaghan's novel *More Joy in Heaven* (1937).

See also SHEEP; SHEPHERD.   L. JOHN TOPEL, S. J.
KATHERINE B. JEFFREY

LOST TRIBES The tribes of Reuben, Simeon, Gad, Dan, Issachar, Asher, Naphtali, Zebulun, Ephraim, and Manasseh did not return from the Assyrian-Babylonian captivity of the people of the Northern Kingdom of Israel (2 Kings 15:29; 17:6; 18:11) with the remnants of Judah, Benjamin, and the Levites (Ezra 1:5; 4:1). The copious literature prophesying a return of Israel to its land (Jer. 30–31; Ezek. 37:19-28) poses a problem, especially for literalists, if the account in Ezra is correct: what is the fate of the ten lost tribes during the pre-*aliyah* [= return] period. (Moreover, NT references to twelve actual tribes of Israel [Acts 26:7] continue generations after the return from Babylon.) Extrabiblical commentary and haggadah are full of speculations and claims about the lost ten tribes (cf. Sanh. 94b, 110b; Shab. 147b; Pesaḥ. 51a n. 4; Meg. 14b; Yebam. 16b). Rabbis Aqiba and Eliezer, e.g., debate the exclusion of the generation of the ten tribes which went into Assyrian captivity from a "share in the world to come" (Sanh. 10.3). The haggadic tradition of the lost tribes divided by the legendary River Sambation (*Jewish Encyclopedia,* ed. I. Singer [1905], 12.249; cf. Lam. Rab. 2:9) comes from Tg. Pseudo-Jonathan to Exod. 34:10 and remains the core of most subsequent speculations and alleged discoveries. These have identified the lost tribes with everyone from the North American aboriginal peoples to the Mormons to the Japanese Shindai to the English. Peter Comestor, in his *Historia Scholastica* (PL 198.1498), reports that Alexander sealed up the ten tribes in the Caspian Mountains, whence they will escape at the end of the world. The extent, variety, and implausibility of all such researches have influenced the modern English literary uses of the tradition of the lost tribes as much as the idea of the loss itself.

When Marlowe's Barabas declares "I am a Jew, and therefore am I lost" (*The Jew of Malta,* 4.1.57), he evokes equivocally the main literary senses of the lost tribes — physical and spiritual loss. In Milton's *Paradise Regained* (3.378-79) the Tempter offers to secure the freedom of the lost tribes and thus the Savior's temporal power, likening their fate to their ancestors' servitude in Egypt. Cowper's "Expostulation" calls Israel, "o'er ev'ry country sown," "of all nations most undone," and refers to the "lineage lost" of the Levites. Blake's *Jerusalem* (pl. 16) claims the British Isles as the place of exile for all twelve tribes. Both Browning ("Jochanan Hakkadosh," 30-31) and Arnold ("Rachel," 168) allude to the scattering of Israel; in Arnold's poem Jewish exile becomes a metaphor for a more general alienation. Joyce in *Ulysses* likens the depopulation of Ireland to the exile of the lost tribes. Shaw deepens the analogy between the lost tribes and wandering Irish (*Back to Methuselah,* 5.509-10), in order to illustrate the perversity (hence the value) of the latter. In his Preface to *The Millionairess* he employs the legend of the lost tribes in order to mock the absurdities of Hitler's theories of racial superiority: "the lost tribes of Israel expose us all to the suspicion (sometimes, as in Abyssinia, to the boast) that we are the lost tribes, or at least that we must have absorbed them."

See also TRIBES OF ISRAEL.

Bibliography. Goudge, H. L. *The British Israel Theory* (1922); "Lost Ten Tribes." *The Jewish Encyclopedia.* Ed. I. Singer. 12 vols. (1905), 12.249-54; Rabinowitz, L. A. "Ten Lost Tribes." *EncJud* (1971), 15.1003-06; "Ten Tribes." *Universal Jewish Encyclopedia.* Ed. I. Landman (1969), 10.304-05.

MARK S. MADOFF

LOT   The son of Abraham's brother Haran, Lot traveled with Abraham until prosperity and quarrels among their servants forced them to set up separate establishments (Gen. 11:27–13:13). Lot chose to live on the plain of the Jordan and pitched his tent near the wicked city of Sodom, while Abraham remained in the land of Canaan. Nevertheless, when Lot was kidnapped by an invading army, Abraham rescued him (Gen. 14). Later, when angels were sent to destroy the inhabitants of the cities of the plain, Abraham again intervened on his nephew's behalf (Gen. 18:23-33); Lot and his family were given advance warning of the coming destruction and an opportunity to escape. Lot's wife, disobeying the angels' injunction not to look back as fire and brimstone rained down on Sodom, was turned into a pillar of salt, but Lot and his two daughters escaped to the hills. There the daughters, thinking that they were the last people on earth, plied their father with drink, and each conceived a child by him. Their children were the ancestors of the Moabites and Ammonites (Gen. 19:37-38; Deut. 2:9, 19; Ps. 83:6-7).

Lot is commended in the NT for his hospitality in that he "entertained angels unawares" (Heb. 13:2). Along with Noah, he also became a type of the just man who will be saved when God destroys the world at the Last Judgment (Luke 17:26-33; 2 Pet. 2:5-7).

Early Jewish tradition tends to focus on the less elevating aspects of Lot's history, suggesting that the quarrel with Abraham was his fault and that he behaved badly in Sodom (see Ginzberg, *LJ* 1.227-28).

Most Christian commentators, however, taking their cue from Luke 17, see Lot as numbered among the righteous. His flight from the wicked cities becomes an example to the Christian pilgrim to flee the temptations of the world and seek salvation (e.g., St. Augustine, *De civ. Dei* 10.8). Lot's example is often cited to encourage those who live under religious vows to forsake the world and keep themselves pure (e.g., Eugippius, *Life of St. Severin,* 9.4; St. Athanasius, *Life of St. Anthony,* chap. 20, etc.), and the same interpretation persists into Renaissance preaching (see J. W. Blench, *Preaching in England* [1964], 9). Lot's incest with his daughters is, however, neither celebrated nor spiritualized; rather, the incident is regularly cited to condemn drunkenness and the lack of self-control it induces.

Lot's story is told at length in OE *Genesis,* where the events take on a typically heroic and epic cast, and in ME *Cleanness,* where the escape from Sodom is seen as an illustration of God's punishment of sin and preservation of the faithful.

Lot also appears incidentally in the ME Chester play. Although, according to Henslowe's Diary (no. 34), an Elizabethan play called *Abraham and Lot* was performed three times in January 1593/94, no text survives. Milton apparently planned a tragedy on the subject of Sodom but managed no more than an outline (*Works* [Columbia], 18.233-34).

Generally in English literature, writers tend to use the story of Lot's escape from Sodom quite predictably —as an inducement to abandon the sinful world. Both Chaucer and Langland also refer to Lot's incest as an admonitory example of the perils of drunkenness (*The Pardoner's Tale,* 6.485; *Piers Plowman,* B.1.27-33; C.11.176-79; 2.25, 31). Milton, who generally praises Lot, uses the incest story in the same way (*De Doctrina Christiana,* 2.9). Mark Twain, in *Mysterious Stranger,* makes ironic reference to it as an example of "the progress of the human race," in which every act of divine favor —Eden, Noah's ark, Lot's escape—is followed by human betrayal —Cain's murder, Noah's drunkenness, Lot's incest. *Poor Richard's Almanac* includes a reference to Lot's story in a witty aphorism about the relative benefits of solitude: "Retirement does not always secure virtue; Lot was upright in the city, wicked in the mountain."

George Herbert and Henry Vaughan look back almost wistfully to the time of Lot, when God was closer to mankind than he is now ("Decay," 1-3; "The Rainbow," 1-5). A very different mood prevails in John Updike's fictive recasting of the story in *Couples,* the hero of which is identified with Lot living in the cities of the plain (the coast near Boston) and fleeing Sodom with his two daughters.

Perhaps the strangest appearance of Lot in English literature is in Milton's *Tetrachordon.* Whereas St. Thomas More cited Abraham's parting from Lot as a source of grief to Abraham (*A Dialogue of Comfort agaynst Trybulation,* 1.16), Milton uses it as an argument for divorce.

See also LOT'S WIFE; SODOM AND GOMORRAH.

Bibliography. Kliewer, W. "The Daughters of Lot: Legend and Fabliau." *IR* 25 (1968), 13-27.   SARAH HORRALL

LOT'S WIFE Lot's wife appears briefly in the OT narrative of Lot's deliverance from the evil city of Sodom (Gen. 19). Having been warned by angelic visitors that Sodom was about to be destroyed for its wickedness, Lot and his family were instructed to leave in haste without a backward glance. Lot's wife disobediently turned back and was transformed into a pillar of salt. In the NT, Jesus cites Lot's wife as an example of those who fail to heed God's warning and who, by attempting to save their life, lose it (Luke 17:31ff.).

Whether they regard her sin as simple disobedience or as a longing for the fleshly pleasures she was leaving behind, biblical commentators have characteristically treated Lot's wife as a type of those who turn away from salvation and refuse to abandon the world. St. Augustine

expresses the idea wittily: "Lot's wife, indeed, when she looked back, remained, and, being turned into salt, furnished to believing men a condiment by which to savor somewhat the warning to be drawn from that example" (*De civ. Dei* 16.30).

Many noncanonical legends about Lot's wife have embellished her story in subsequent literature, and some have attributed to her a name —Melusade or Edith. Early Jewish legends tend to paint a very human portrait of her. Some say that she quarreled with Lot over his hospitality to the angels, and several stories involve her misuse of salt —borrowing it, cooking with it, or failing to cook with it (see Ginzberg, *LJ* 1.254). The ME poem *Cleanness* incorporates some of these elements in its own retelling of the story; Lot's wife grumbles and quarrels with her husband when he brings home unexpected guests. Her shrewishness is the reason for her turning back —she *never* did as she was told. At least one early writer suggests that it was maternal love which made Lot's wife turn back; she wanted to see if her children were following her away from the burning cities.

Legends about the salt pillar are also common. According to many Jewish and early Christian sources the salt, although rained upon and licked by animals, did not dissolve and was still to be seen by travelers in Palestine "to this day" (e.g., Josephus, *Ant.* 1.11.4; Mandeville, *Travels,* chap. 12; Bunyan, *Pilgrim's Progress*). Some sources say that the statue grew and shrank with the phases of the moon. An early Latin poem speaks of the woman's flesh imprisoned in salt rather than transformed into it; she became her own tomb, and the statue continued to menstruate (Pseudo-Tertullian, *Sodoma*).

In English literature, Lot's wife appears occasionally as a simile for a statue (e.g., Byron, *Don Juan,* 6.68; Tennyson, *Princess,* 6; D. H. Lawrence, "Fanny and Annie"). Many writers, however, use her as a type of the disobedient, weak, or timid follower, always looking back to something either renounced or forbidden. Milton condemns her curiosity (*De Doctrina Christiana,* 2.2), as does Joyce (*Ulysses,* "Lestrygonians" episode). Marvell uses her as a metaphor for hesitating, backward-looking clergy ("The Loyall Scot," 120-25), and in *Jane Eyre* St. John Rivers uses a similar argument to urge Jane not to give up her teaching (chap. 31; cf. James Moffatt, *The Bible in Scots Literature* [1924], 137, 177). Blake is impressed by her change from one substance into another without losing her identity (*A Vision of the Last Judgment* [ed. Keynes], 607).

D. H. Lawrence makes Lot's wife the central image in his poem "She Looks Back." Here, as in the Jewish legend, mother love causes the protagonist to cast a backward, yearning glance toward her children in England — rather than "escaping" —into the arms of a Bavarian poet. Saline imagery is prominent, from the "bitter kiss" and "salt tear" to "Dry, sterile, sharp, corrosive salt." Finally, the poem's narrator feels himself imprisoned:

Ah, Lot's Wife, Lot's Wife!
The pillar of salt, the whirling, horrible column of salt,
    like a waterspout
That has enveloped me! (55-57)

See also LOT; SODOM AND GOMORRAH.

                            SARAH HORRALL

LOVE PASSING THE LOVE OF WOMEN *See*
DAVID.

LOVE STRONG AS DEATH Song of Songs 8:6 reads:
"For love is strong as death; jealousy is as cruel as the
grave: the coals thereof are coals of fire; which had a most
vehement flame." In English literary tradition the phrase
is often conjured up ironically in connection with
Shakespeare's *Romeo and Juliet* (e.g., Lynd, "It's a Fine
World"). In Christina Rossetti's *An End*, "Love, strong as
Death, is dead. / Come, let us make his bed / Among the
dying flowers." The symbiosis of love and death undergirds Oscar Wilde's "The Canterville Ghost," in which it
is said, "You can open for me the portals of Death's house,
for Love is always with you, and Love is stronger than
Death is." Dorothy Sayers's Miss Chimpson, in *Unnatural Death*, opines: "The longer I live, my dear, the
more certain I become that jealousy is the most fatal of
feelings. The Bible calls it 'cruel as the grave', and I'm
sure that it is so. Absolute loyalty, without jealousy, is the
essential thing" (chap. 16).

LOVE THY NEIGHBOR *See* GOOD SAMARITAN; GREAT
COMMANDMENT.

LOVE YOUR ENEMIES One of the most striking injunctions in Jesus' Sermon on the Mount is his challenge
to normal definitions of love: "Ye have heard that it hath
been said, Thou shalt love thy neighbor, and hate thine
enemy. But I say unto you, Love your enemies, bless them
that curse you, do good to them that hate you, and pray
for them which despitefully use you, and persecute you"
(Matt. 5:44). This commandment of Jesus, recollected by
many Christians of the early centuries in times of dire
persecution, was stressed as central to Christian obedience by bishops such as St. Ambrose (e.g., *De officiis
clericorum*, 1.48), who says that it is characteristic of
divine justice that it asks of us charity and not vengeance
(*Ep.* 63.84). A popular Yorkshire tract of the 14th cent.,
incorporated by Walter Hilton into his *Ladder of Perfection*, cites St. Stephen praying for those who stoned him
to death even as he was dying (an analogy with Jesus'
"Father, forgive them, for they know not what they do"
[Luke 23:34]) as one example of what such love in practice means. The other he adduces in Jesus' treatment of
Judas who, even though known by Jesus to be a betrayer,
was given all the intimacy and privilege accorded the
other disciples. This, says the English writer, can be

regarded as a corollary of Jesus' commandment to his
disciples, "that ye love one another, as I have loved you"
(John 15:12). It thus marks the extent of "love of neighbor" enjoined in the Great Commandment. The tract concludes, "He þat es meke suthfastly or wald be meke, can
luf his euen-cristene, & nan bot he" (ed. Horstmann,
Yorkshire Writers [1895], 1.104-05).

    American literary examples often serve to show how
this commandment is more honored in the breach than the
observance. Thoreau, e.g., comments on the irony in stoical Indians being burned at the stake by "missionaries":
"the law to do as you would be done by fell with less
persuasiveness on the ears of those . . . who loved their
enemies after a new fashion" (*Walden*, "Economy").
Mark Twain writes in *Innocents Abroad*, in a more
humorous vein, of the challenge of the standard: "I know
it is my duty to 'pray for them that despitefully use me',
and therefore, hard as it is, I shall still try to pray for these
fumigating, macaroni-stuffing organ grinders" (chap. 20).

    See also CHARITY; CUPIDITY; GOOD SAMARITAN; MEEK
SHALL INHERIT THE EARTH; TURN THE OTHER CHEEK.

LUCIFER *See* ANGEL; ANGEL OF LIGHT; DEVIL.

LUKE The Gospel ascribed to St. Luke is anonymous,
but early church tradition, such as the Muratorian Canon
(ca. A.D. 170-180) and St. Irenaeus (*Adv. haer.* 3.1.1;
3.14.1), identifies its author as the Luke who was associated with St. Paul (Philem. 24; Col. 4:14; 2 Tim.
4:11). Patristic tradition assumed him also to be the
physician mentioned in Col. 4:14. Luke is still popularly
referred to as "the Beloved Physician," although modern
scholarship has been inconclusive on the subject of his
professional vocation (J. Freind [*The History of Physick*,
1 (1725), 221-25] and W. K. Hobart [*The Medical Language of St. Luke* (1882)] argue in the affirmative; H. J.
Cadbury [*The Style and Literary Method of Luke* (1920)]
is more skeptical).

    Luke is thought by many early writers to have been
the unnamed companion of Cleopas to whom Christ appeared on the road to Emmaus (Luke 24; cf. Mark 16:12-
13), and thus one of the earliest witnesses to the Resurrection. This identification is assumed in several medieval
biblical play cycles (e.g., Chester). According to another
early tradition, one which claims no biblical warrant,
Luke, who became in the 13th cent. the patron saint of
painters, was himself thought to be a master of the brush.
The notion that he did a portrait of the Blessed Virgin first
surfaced in the *Historia Ecclesiastica* of Theodoros Anag-
nostes (fl. 6th cent. [PG 86.1.165]) and is repeated by
Nikephoros Kallistos in the 14th cent. (PG 146.1061).
Master Rypon of Durham refers to the legend (G. Owst,
Literature and Pulpit in Medieval England [1961], 140),
as does R. Steele in *The Spectator* (Saturday, Dec. 6,
1712).

    Luke's symbol in iconographic tradition is the ox (that

of the other four evangelists being a man for St. Matthew, a lion for St. Mark, and an eagle for St. John; all are derived from allegorical interpretation of Ezek. 1:10).

More than any other writer in the NT, Luke reveals in-depth acquaintance with contemporary political and economic realities. Using the Greco-Roman benefactor-philanthropist as an interpretive model — an approach which he shares with Paul — Luke emphasizes upright-ness as adjunct to piety, stresses proper use of wealth, and encourages a broad societal outreach which embraces women, the afflicted, and other marginal people.

Coleridge was impressed with the literary quality of Luke's Gospel, comparing it favorably to that of Matthew. After observing that "the Gospels, the three first at least & more especially, were written not as Evidence for Unbelievers and *Convertendis* but for those who had received the Faith" (*Notebooks,* ed. K. Coburn [1973], 3.4255.22.38), he passes, a few years later, the following judgment:

> The Genealogy and Evang. Infantiae [of Matthew] could have had no interest but for Palestine Jews. Compared with those prefixed to Luke's Gospel, it is like a rude tale in an old chronicle compared with the same taken up by a Southey or Scott & worked up into a splendid Poem. (*Notebooks,* 3.4402.22.78)

Characteristic of Luke's style is his indulgence in expression of duality and triplicity. The former is strik-ingly apparent in the relationship between Luke's Gospel and the book of Acts, which comprise a two-volume work, with Acts frequently echoing the Gospel (e.g., the lame man healed [Luke 5:17-26/Acts 3:1-10]; the popular centurion [Luke 7:1-10/Acts 10]). Within the Gospel it-self, the first and second chapters offer related stories of unusual conceptions. At 6:20-26 a set of four woes bal-ances a set of four blessings. Interest in a threefold em-phasis is displayed in 9:57-62 and chap. 15.

Some scholars have argued that Luke purchases Roman political innocence at the expense of Jewish guilt. But this view is not sustainable: Israelites are pardoned for their participation in the death of Jesus; Gentiles, who share responsibility for a travesty of justice (Acts 4:27), share on equal terms with Jews the privileges of the people of God (Luke 24:47; Acts 2:37-39). According to Luke, the Resurrection of Jesus is the primary attestation of God's goodwill toward all humanity (Acts 17:31).

Luke's collection of "forgiveness parables" (14:1–16:14) have earned him an association with the healing touch or "therapy" of the good news, so that despite George Herbert's proverb, "St. Luke was a Saint and a Physician, yet is dead" (*Proverbs,* 1008), he is a mysteri-ously enlivening "fifth business" in Maxim Gorky's *The Lower Depths* (1902) and, as a compassionate Greek physician, minister, and scholar, accompanies and writes the life of Yeshua in Sholem Asch's *The Apostle* (1943).

See also APOSTLE; EMMAUS.

Bibliography. Danker, F. W. *Jesus and the New Age Ac-cording to St. Luke* (1980); Emminghaus, J. H. "Lukas." In *Lexikon für Theologie und Kirche,* 3.1203-06; Fitzmyer, J. A. *The Gospel According to Luke (I–IX): Introduction, Transla-tion, and Notes.* AB (1981); Talbert, C. H. *Literary Patterns, Theological Themes and the Genre of Luke-Acts* (1974); *Reading Luke: A Literary and Theological Commentary on the Third Gospel* (1982).   F. W. DANKER

LUKEWARM LAODICEA   In the Revelation of St. John the Divine the aged disciple of Jesus hears the Spirit pronounce judgment upon the "seven churches which are in Asia." One of these is "the church of the Laodiceans," unto whom John is to write the Spirit's words: "I know thy works, that thou art neither cold nor hot: I would thou wert cold or hot. So then because thou art lukewarm, and neither cold nor hot, I will spew thee out of my mouth" (3:14-16).

St. Jerome, attributing the words to Jesus, observes that "the Saviour likes nothing that is half and half, and, while he welcomes the hot and does not shun the cold, he tells us in the Apocalypse that he will spew the lukewarm out of his mouth" (*Ep.* 31.3). Elsewhere he comments that "while he does not wish the death of a sinner, but only that he should be converted and live, he hates the lukewarm and they quickly cause him loathing" (*Ep.* 54.8). St. Augustine applies the passage to irresponsible or glib citation of Scripture:

> These persons who are quick to quote Scripture, and yet do not understand the usages of its language, would be better to recognize that not only what is consubstantial and of God's nature "proceeds" from his mouth. Let them hear or read what God says: "So then, because thou art lukewarm, and neither cold nor hot, I will spue thee out of my mouth." (*De civ. Dei* 13.24)

The emphasis of St. Jerome is substantially maintained in evangelical commentary after the Reformation. Matthew Poole is representative when he refers the passage to Titus 2:12, "Thou hast a form of Godliness, but denyest the Life and Power thereof," adding, "We must not think Christ wisheth any Persons cold absolutely, but comparatively, intimating to us, that the condition of a down-right *Atheist,* or *profane Person,* is more hopeful, than that of a close formal Hypocrite. The latter is on the road to Hell as well as the other, and no more pleaseth God, than the other" (*Annotations* 2, sup. Rev. 3:15), notwithstanding he is "a Christian, a Protestant, a Minister, or Member of the Reformed Church."

In John Bunyan's *Grace Abounding,* the narrator re-ports how the Tempter tried to discourage him from perseverance by saying, "You are very hot for mercy, but I will always cool you; this frame [of mind] shall not last always: Many have been as hot as you . . . but I have quenched their zeal. . . . I will cool you insensibly, by degrees, by little and little." Thomas Hardy, raised in the precincts of such a warning, writes of Gabriel in *Far from the Madding Crowd* that "On Sundays he was . . . one who felt himself to occupy morally that vast middle space of Laodicean neutrality which lay between the Communion people of the parish and the drunken section" (chap. 1); Manston of *Desperate Remedies* is similarly said to be "Laodicean" of religion. (Hardy's *A Laodicean* [1881] borrows from a theologian's article on Rev. 3:14-16, that of Charles Apperly in the 1833 *Quarterly Review*.) Sinclair Lewis's preacher turns a familiar term against his hearers when he cants, "Oh, woe to the Congregationalists for that you are all weak, wabbly, halfway-covenanting Laodiceans" (*The God-Seeker,* chap. 15). An ancient vice is sometimes heralded as a modern virtue: Ernest, in Samuel Butler's *The Way of All Flesh*, writes an essay in which he argues that a modern person should not "feel very strongly upon any subject. . . . We should be . . . somewhat lukewarm churchmen. . . . The Church herself should approach as

nearly to that of Laodicea as was compatible with her continuing to be a Church at all, and each individual member should only be hot in striving to be as lukewarm as possible." G. B. Shaw comments: "Thus the world is kept sane less by the saints than by the vast mass of the indifferent, who neither act nor react in the matter. Butler's preaching of the gospel of Laodicea was a piece of common sense founded on his observation of this" (*Back to Methuselah,* pref.).

See also SEVEN CHURCHES.

LUST OF THE FLESH   See 1 John 2:16. In George El-iot's *Adam Bede* Mr. Roe describes the Rev. Mr. Irvine "in a general statement concerning the Church clergy in the surrounding district, whom he described as men giving up to the lusts of the flesh and the pride of life" (chap. 5).

See also WORLD, FLESH, AND DEVIL.

M

MACCABEUS *See* JUDAS MACCABEUS.

MADNESS In the OT, God's anger at human sin and pride leads him to afflict people with madness: he frustrates sinners, forcing the godless lover to watch another lie with his beloved and the impious farmer to lose his harvest (Deut. 28:28-34); he humiliates wise men, driving diviners mad (Isa. 44:25). When he punishes Nebuchadnezzar by making him crop the fields like an ox, God also uses madness to lead the king to true religion (Dan. 4; cf. Doob [1974], 54-94); when God favors David and withdraws his spirit from Saul, the latter becomes mad (1 Sam. 16:14). God also punishes faithless nations with madness (Jer. 51:7; cf. Milton, *Samson Agonistes,* 1677).

The prophets serve divine wrath by scourging the Jews with madness: Jeremiah must drive the nations mad with fear of divine vengeance (Jer. 25:16), and Zechariah declares that, in purging Jerusalem, God will strike every horse with astonishment and every rider with madness (Zech. 12:4; cf. the spiritual perception of Balaam's ass, which contrasts with its master's mad refusal to accept his prophetic mission [Num. 22:21-31; 2 Pet. 2:16]). The prophets, being divinely inspired, have a reputation for dancing ecstatically and being mad (1 Sam. 10:6), and a sinful Israel dismisses their inspiration as mere madness (Hos. 9:7). Jeremiah is falsely arraigned as willfully mad for advising the exiles to aid Babylon (Jer. 29:26).

Prophets challenge their reputation for insanity: when Elisha foments Jehu's revolution by sending a prophet to anoint him, Jehu's followers accept his kingship only after recognizing that the prophet is not mad (2 Kings 9:11).

Madness is an effective guise for David when he wishes to evade Achish of Gath against whom he had fought successfully: David scrabbles on the town gate and drops spittle in his beard to escape the palace (1 Sam. 21:13). In the OT, madness is also simply godless conduct: David's enemies are madly hostile to him (Ps. 102:8), the Babylonians are mad about their idols (Jer. 50:38), and the deceiver of his neighbor is a self-destructive madman (Prov. 26:18). The preacher of Ecclesiastes uses a philosophical sense of madness to belittle human achievement: distinctions between wisdom and madness are sometimes tenuous, because knowledge is sorrow and grief (Eccl. 1:17; 7:25). Wisdom may be superior to madness, but the same fate befalls wise man and fool (2:12). If laughter is mad (2:2) and the fool mischievously mad in his talk (10:13), the wise man is driven mad by "oppression": he is no better off than the fool since madness and evil lurk in the hearts of all people (7:7; 9:3).

In the Apocrypha, opponents of God are mad yet attribute madness to the faithful: idolaters rave (Wisd. of Sol. 14:28); the lord promises salvation to the faithful who are destroyed by madmen (2 Esdr. 16:71; cf. 2 Macc. 15:33); the ungodly who think the righteous person mad will be grieved at his salvation (Wisd. of Sol. 5:4).

In the NT, the omniscience of Jesus frustrates his enemies. The Pharisees who plan to trap him about his conduct on the Sabbath are driven mad when he sees through them (Luke 6:11). Yet Jesus' enemies think him mad: when he explains his unity with God, Jews in the audience judge him possessed by the devil (John 10:20). Those who accuse others of madness are sometimes proved to be faithless. When Rhoda reports Peter's escape from prison, the other Christians call her mad because they are incredulous (Acts 12:15). Paul admits that he was mad when he persecuted Christians (Acts 26:11). He dissociates madness and Christianity: accused by Festus of being as mad as a Christian, he denies the charge and professes to speak the sober truth (26:24-25). To prevent unbelievers thinking Christians mad, he subordinates speaking in tongues to prophecy (1 Cor. 14:23; cf. Cornelius à Lapide, *Comm. in Scripturam Sacram*, 7.355 and Bacon, "Unity in Religion").

Since the Bible contains several discrete notions of madness, namely distraction and inspiration by God, possession by evil spirits, self-destructive and self-protective worldliness, hostility to God, individual godless conduct, social and ecclesiastical anarchy, and existential pessimism, Christian commentators often contrast its senses, creating paradoxes from them. To St. John Chrysostom, people impose madness on themselves by letting anger govern them (*Concerning the Statues*, 9.474) and by corrupting their souls with material desires: clinging to perishable instead of eternal things is less forgivable than being possessed by devils (*Hom. on 2 Corinthians*, 12.416). Luther claims that God preserves madmen to show normal people who lose their sense of identity in sleep that they are not themselves far removed from madness, an affinity proving that God cannot be approached by human reason. Luther defies the rational view of faith as madness: faith is rather a legitimate form of inebriation (*Works*, 8.317, 250). In *The Praise of Folly*, Folly separates poetic and other mad obsessions the Furies visit on people from the pleasing dotages with which she relieves their minds, holding that madmen are happy and that those who laugh at them are happy because they, too, are mad. Through Folly's bland version of Ecclesiastes's madness, Erasmus ironically defends spiritual values. While rejecting charges that his preaching drives people mad, Wesley voices the prophetic wish to drive the world mad by filling it with an inward religion which makes people despise material reality. Despising the world is true sanity: fear of God may seem madness, but real madness occurs when the soul seeking God is frustrated (*Works*, 2.123-24, 196; Smollett, typically of many 18th-cent. opponents of Wesley and Whitefield, associates madness and methodism [*Humphry Clinker*, 171]. By contrast, see Locke's *Essay concerning Human Understanding*, 3.27, and Johnson's *Rasselas*, chap. 44, for 18th-cent. views about the existential reality of madness).

Various biblical ideas of madness inform English literature. Caedmon, in describing Lucifer's revolt, equates disobedience to God with madness. Following St. Gregory the Great, he concludes that the builders of the tower of Babel are also mad; they aim for heaven without God's aid (*Metrical Paraphrase . . . of the Holy Scriptures*, 22.100-101). Grendel's disavowal of weapons is a madness stemming from his fiendishness (*Beowulf*, 434). In *The Canterbury Tales*, Emelye's fear at not understanding the vision of Diane's altar (*Knight's Tale*, 1.2342), John's lust for the Miller's wife (*Reeve's Tale*, 1.4231), Melibee's grief for his murdered daughter (*Melibee*, 7.2160-65), and the Canon's Yeoman's self-destructive and criminal pursuit of gold and alchemy (*Canon's Yeoman's Tale*, 8:742) reflect Chaucer's sense of how madness derives from spiritual frustration and materialism, or a lack of ordinate, charitable, "reasonable" love. Among medieval theologians, terms such as "irrational" or "inordinate" are often used interchangeably for "sin." In medieval lyrics, madness often serves rhetorical purposes: those who know that sin hurts Christ and yet continue to sin are mad ("How Sinners Crucify Christ Each Day"); God's love alone heals the madness caused by grief ("Ever more Thank God of All" [C. Brown, *Religious Lyrics of the XIVth Century*, no. 105]). Besides defining madness as a preference for the transitory world over heavenly permanence, *Pearl* sees it as the refusal to heed the Lord's call (267, 359). In *Utopia*, More views false pleasure and self-sacrifice without moral benefit as equally madness (97, 92). Besides using madness to expose both moral blindness and zeal, More relates it to casting oneself into hell for ephemeral pleasures (*A Dialogue of Comfort against Tribulation*, 243) and to Judas's delusion that he could deceive Christ's omniscience (*The Sadness of Christ*, 258). Madness abounds in the works of Gower, Spenser, Sidney, and Marlowe, often springing from unrequited love, bereavement, lust, drink, the Furies, and vengeance. Specific biblical ideas occur when Spenser views suicide as madness (*Faerie Queene*, 5.11), when Sidney equates madness with refusal to recognize God's wisdom ("Psalm 14"), and when Marlowe's Barabas, who thinks obedience to his gods madness and prides himself on driving others mad with his monetary policies, is utterly defeated (*The Jew of Malta*).

Biblical concepts of madness help Shakespeare heighten dramatic sense. In *The Comedy of Errors*, Pinch's invocation of the saints to exorcise Antipholus of Ephesus is offset by the abbess's claim that Antipholus is less possessed than frustrated by his wife's nagging (4.1). But her explanation is displaced because mistaken identity and accident explain the alleged madness. Madness recoils upon irreligious characters: Lady Macbeth chides her husband for being possessed by spiritual scruples (*Macbeth*, 2.2) yet she goes mad; and Angelo, the religious hypocrite, after calling the Duke mad (*Measure for Measure*, 4.4.4), is exposed by the Duke's reversal of his judgment of Isabella's insanity (5.1.60-63). Theseus, in *A*

Midsummer Night's Dream, when comparing the madman, lover, and poet for allowing imagination to dominate reason, forgets his own susceptibility to illusion (5.1.7-8; cf. Coleridge, "Reproof and Reply," 45). In his tragedies, Shakespeare employs multiple concepts of madness. Hence, Hamlet feigns madness for strategic reasons (*Hamlet,* 2.1) but cannot always control his acting because of his actual psychic distress. Whereas madness leads Ophelia to suicide, it leads Hamlet to occasional loss of identity (5.2). Lear is mad to give away his throne (*King Lear,* 1.1.148); and when on the heath he falls into madness, Cordelia's charitable, loving ministrations restore him to "fair daylight." Critics differ on whether or not he lapses again into madness when Cordelia dies; some interpret his exclamation, "Look there!" as indicating his final perception of a higher reality. Edgar feigns madness to look after his father and the king.

From the 17th cent. on, writers increasingly link madness and literary inspiration. If Marvell holds that madness results from excessive grief and joy ("A Dialogue between the Soul and Body") and from recalcitrance to providence ("An Horatian Ode") and if Traherne traces it to people creating a life independent of God ("Apostacy") and sees it causing social anarchy ("Ethicks V"), Dryden suggests that poets daringly bid their muses run mad since rashness, not sense, is the route to excellence ("Prologue to Tyrannick Love"). Dryden still connects madness to false religion, but his insistence that wit and madness are "allied" develops epigrammatic force (*Absalom and Achitophel,* 163; cf. Emerson, *Inspiration,* 264; Joyce, "Grace," *Dubliners*). In "A Digression concerning Madness," Swift applies madness to a satirizing of political, philosophical, and religious systems (cf. Burton, *The Anatomy of Melancholy,* 1.52-54, and Green, "The Spleen"). Yet, because his mad narrator ironically defends traditional moral values, Swift gives literary and spiritual purpose to madness. Pope more straightforwardly upholds biblical tradition when he claims that the worst madman is an overzealous saint while the worst madness is seeking worldly things rather than heaven (*Imitations of Horace,* 6.27, 68). In his annotations to *The Laocoon* and Reynolds's *Discourses on Art,* Blake undermines humanist views, dismissing Greece and Rome for judging visionaries madmen and insisting that the Bible is mad if inspiration is a lie: real madness is to restrict desires by convention (*Visions of Daughters of Albion,* pl. 5.25). Finding poetic sensibility in the maniac's anxiety, Wordsworth bases his poetry on dreams and mad images (*Prelude,* 5.152-60). Rejecting normalcy and depreciating popular views of poetic madness, he endows the world with moral life, convinced that his methods are prophetic, not mad (*Prelude,* 3.149-58). Byron takes madness as a proper discontent with normal achievements and a desire for heroism ("Childe Harold," 3.43), Shelley attacks the notion that it is madness to be unlike the rest of the world ("The Sunset"), and Emerson, who allies genius with

madness, argues that inspiration entails superiority to common humanity ("Fate," 533).

The trend relating madness to prophecy and literary inspiration is clear among 19th- and 20th-cent. writers, although conflict between the biblical concepts remains essential. While Austen treats madness as emotional excess which disrupts sociable life (e.g., *Love and Friendship;* cf. *Emma*), Dickens uses mad characters who are inherently virtuous to satirize society (cf. *Barnaby Rudge, David Copperfield, Bleak House,* and *Dombey and Son*). For Austen, real madness is self-induced; for Dickens, it is caused by society. While Browning details corrupt prophetic madness in "Bishop Blougram's Apology" (462.49), Ruskin thinks that his immoral contemporaries are plagued by infectious insanities. Although criticizing religious madness in terms of egotism and lack of social imagination, Ruskin accepts Hosea's view that community sins of necessity drive those who are spiritual mad. For Ruskin, truth cannot save a person from madness if he has to isolate himself from society (*Works,* 28.488, 312).

In *Moby-Dick,* Melville explores how social isolation turns moral indignation into madness. Ahab, in his monomania, views the white whale as evil incarnate; bent on supernatural revenge, he is an ungodly old man. Yet Pip, the idiot cabin boy who has a vision of the depths when lost overboard, achieves an almost divine perspective. Shaw disclaims interest in monomania but sympathizes with heroines like Ophelia; they are superior to men in their capacity for love: Ophelia's madness betokens her emotional superiority to Hamlet. Convinced that artists are madmen, Shaw laments their being locked up rather than reverenced. Yet in his defense of Joan of Arc's visionary habits, he denies that she was mad: fashions in belief lead to such charges of madness. Through her voices, Joan served evolutionary forces. Paradoxes about madness affect Shaw's view of social reform: the marriage laws need to be reformed because, if people are mad in their pursuit of sex, they are also mad in persecuting it. Hence, sane schemes for reform have to be made mad to secure popular endorsement. Yet he despises the fact that artistically ignorant priests are revered as reformers. They are unhappy lunatics because they do not regard the Bible as a high form of literature: the artistry of the Bible drives readers, whom lower kinds of reading would leave sane, mad. Shaw praises Shakespeare for transforming the madman into a serious figure of inspiration who has more brains than the crowd thinks (*The Complete Prefaces,* 331.155-57.609-10.584.86–101.115-16).

Of modern writers, Conrad is among the most concerned to explore the humanity of madness. In *Heart of Darkness* and other works, he shows people adoring ferocious deities and illustrates how the religion of undying hope resembles the mad cult of despair and annihilation. Because he believes that the motives of believers make a crucial difference, he rejects the philosophic madness of

Ecclesiastes. For Conrad, all is vanity only to those who are vain; all is deception only to those who have never been sincere with themselves (*Tale of Hearsay,* 136-37). Working against the public's inability to deal with madness, Conrad maintains that revelation is to be found in the incomprehensible self-destructiveness of his heroes: madness, though close to evil, reveals essential spiritual truths. This prophetic notion of madness is evident in various other modern writers (e.g., Yeats, "Ben Bulben"; Pound, "La Fraisne" and "Canto 70"; Roethke, "In a Dark Time"). Among the most powerful recent treatments of madness explicitly informed by or foiled against biblical tradition are Walker Percy's *The Second Coming* and Guy Vanderhaeghe's *My Present Age.* These late 20th-cent. novels portray madness, both cultural and personal, as the result of what vestigial Christian voices in each work call "sin," and draw on Søren Kierkegaard's influential analysis of madness as sin in shaping their narratives (*The Present Age; For Self-Examination; The Concept of Anxiety*).

See also DEMONS, DEMON POSSESSION; DESPAIR; FOOL, FOLLY; UNPARDONABLE SIN.

Bibliography. De Porte, M. V. *Nightmares and Hobbyhorses: Swift, Sterne, and Augustan Ideas of Madness* (1974); Doob, P. B. R. *Nebuchadnezzar's Children: Conventions of Madness in Middle English Literature* (1974); Feder, L. *Madness in Literature* (1980); Foucault, M. *Madness and Civilization* (1967); Gilbert, S., and S. Gubar. *The Madwoman in the Attic* (1979); Harrison, R. K. "Madness." *IDB* 3.220-21; La Bossière, C. R. *The Victorian Fol Sage* (1989); Love, J. O. *Virginia Woolf: Sources of Madness and Art* (1977); Rigney, B. H. *Madness and Sexual Politics in the Feminist Novel: Studies in Brontë, Woolf, Lessing and Atwood* (1978); Sugerman, S. *Sin and Madness: Studies in Narcissism* (1976).

ROBERT JAMES MERRETT

MAGI   The *Magi,* or "wise men," described in Matt. 2:1-12 came to Jerusalem and thence to Bethlehem from the East, being led by a star to the birthplace of Jesus. Later tradition added to the Gospel account that they were three in number, that their names were Casper (or Gaspar), Melchior, and Balthasar *(Excerpta Latina Barbari),* and that they represented different branches of the human family. The idea that they were kings (evidently based on Ps. 72:10 and Isa. 60:3: "Gentiles shall come to thy light, and kings to the brightness of thy rising") first appears in Tertullian, who reports that in the East magi are considered *fere reges* ("almost kings").

A rudimentary description of the Wise Men, which came to be influential for artistic depiction of them, appears in the treatise *Excerpta et Collectanea* (PL 94.541), sometimes attributed to Bede. In it Melchior is said to be old, white-haired, and bearded; Casper, young, ruddy, and beardless; and Balthasar, black-skinned and thickly bearded. The same treatise offers the ancient commonplace association of the three (biblically identified) gifts with specific attributes of the Christ child — gold signifying his kingship, incense representing his divinity,

and myrrh suggesting his humanity and portending his death (cf. Irenaeus, *Adv. haer.* 3.9.2). A later evocation of this tradition may be found in the popular 19th-cent. carol "We Three Kings," which devotes three verses to elaborating the meaning of the gifts.

Historically, magi were members of a religious caste numerous enough to be considered one of the six tribes of Media. They retained their power after the conquest of the Medes by the Persians. They are said to have worshiped the sun, moon, earth, fire, water, and winds (Herodotus, *History,* 1.132). Magi interpreted dreams and omens and claimed the gift of prophecy (Herodotus 1.107). (The Greeks later bestowed the epithet *"magos"* on any sorcerer who employed the enchantments of the East. Bar-Jesus [Acts 13:6] and Simon Magus of Samaria [Acts 8:9] were magi in this sense.)

Some scholars have found in Matthew's account of the Magi following the star a homiletical illustration of Balaam's words in Num. 24:17 — "There shall come a star out of Jacob" — a passage which was interpreted by the ancient Church as prophesying Christ. In the medieval *Ordo Prophetarum,* or prophet plays, a frequently inserted Balaam scene was regarded as paralleling typologically the offering of the Magi. In one of the Canterbury windows Balaam can be seen urging his ass forward as he points to the star, while the Magi, depicted in the central medallion, also point toward it:

> Balaam was not only the prophet of the Star, but his journey was the accepted antetype of that of the magi, and thus formed the natural prelude of the *Ordo Stellae,* the name often applied to the Christmas cycle in liturgical drama. (Anderson, 23)

The encounter of the Magi with Herod in Jerusalem and their subsequent thwarting of his intention to kill the infant Messiah feature prominently in a variety of medieval mystery plays.

Milton, in "The Morning of Christ's Nativity," speaks of the "star-led wizards," and Donne in his "Nativitie" recalls that "from the Orient, Starres, and wisemen . . . travell to prevent / Th'effect of Herod's jealous generall doome." In his verse letter to the Countess of Huntingdon Donne neatly turns the star into a complimentary analogue of the lady's virtue:

> As such a starre, the Magi led to view
> The manger-cradled infant, God below:
> By vertues beames by fame deriv'd from you,
> May apt soules, and the worst may, vertue know.

The personal need to follow metaphorically in the steps of the Magi was a popular theme of 17th-cent. sermons and poetry. "Thy Star," writes Vaughan,

> runs page, and brings
> Thy tributary Eastern kings.
> Lord grant some Light to us, that we
> May with them find the way to thee. ("The Nativity")

A similar theme forms part of the sermon preached by Lancelot Andrewes at Whitehall on Christmas Day 1622. "It is," he writes, "not commended to stand 'gazing up into heaven' too long; not on Christ Himself ascending, much less on his star. For they [the Magi] sat not still gazing on the star. Their *vidimus* begat *venimus;* their seeing made them come."

The opening lines of T. S. Eliot's "The Journey of the Magi" adapt part of Andrewes's sermon, but the modern poem focuses exclusively on one of the Magi who in old age recalls the original experience and its meaning. The poem deals with the alteration wrought in the thinking of the Magi by their encounter with Christ and how it cuts them off from their former religious beliefs. Yeats represents the Magi as "pale unsatisfied ones" no longer content with "Calvary's turbulence" but longing to experience once again the intensity of their first revelation, "hoping to find once more, / . . . The uncontrollable mystery on the bestial floor" ("The Magi").

The Magi are notably absent from most of the revisionist Jesus novels and "fifth gospels" of the last century. They appear with greater frequency in popular literature connected with the Christmas season. Henry Van Dyke's *The Other Wise Man* tells the story of "Artaban the Magician," who was delayed from joining the caravan of Casper, Melchior, and Balthasar by an act of mercy but ultimately found the King he sought on Good Friday. In "The Gifts of the Magi" by O. Henry (William Sidney Porter), the sacrificial gifts of a young couple to each other are implicitly likened to the adoration of the biblical Wise Men.

See also HEROD THE GREAT; NATIVITY; SIMON MAGUS.

Bibliography. Anderson, M. D. *Drama and Imagery* (1963); Brown, R. E. *The Birth of the Messiah* (1977); Elissagaray, M. *La légende des rois mages* (1965); Hindsley, L. "The Three Holy Kings in German Literature." *DAI* 40 (1980), 6298-A; Screech, M. A. "The Magi and the Star (Matthew 2)." In *Histoire de l'exégèse au XVIe siècle.* Eds. O. Fatio and P. Fraenkel (1978), 385-409; Shea, J. "Religious-Imaginative Encounters with Scriptural Stories." In *Art/Literature/Religion: Life on the Borders.* Ed. R. Detweiler (1983), 173-80.   MICHAEL GOLDBERG

MAGNIFICAT *Magnificat* (from the first word in the Vg. *Magnificat anima mea dominum,* "My soul doth magnify the Lord"), the song of the Virgin Mary, is one of two canticles in the first chapter of Luke's Gospel (vv. 46-55). Largely a compilation of traditional OT phrases, especially from the Psalms but also from the prophetic books and 1 Samuel, it may be an adaptation of a pre-Christian psalm, fitted to the present context by the addition, e.g., of v. 48. The canticle's structure and general conceptual frame closely parallel the song of Hannah in 1 Sam. 2:1-10, and some verbal parallels are also apparent. Sung on the occasion of the visit of Mary to her cousin in response to Elisabeth's greeting, the *Magnificat*

is a song of praise emphasizing God's strength in contrast to Mary's weakness and humility. Some early commentators (Origen, Nicetas, St. Irenaeus) and a few old Latin manuscripts of Luke assign the song to Elisabeth, but modern scholars generally do not favor the attribution.

The *Magnificat* is paired with the song of Zacharias, father of John the Baptist (vv. 68-79, commonly called the *Benedictus*), which also refers to the covenant of God and Abraham and gives thanks for the promise of salvation for Israel. But whereas Zacharias's song is public and triumphant, Mary's is private and joyful. The *Benedictus,* furthermore, suggests what is to come (fitting for the song sung by the father of the forerunner of Christ); the *Magnificat* gives a sense as of fulfillment and of events already accomplished. Such pairing is typical of Luke and appears several times in both the Gospel and Acts. These two songs are matched by the *Gloria* and *Nunc Dimittis* in 2:14, 29-32, and Simeon and Anna form a pair there, as do Ananias and Sapphira in Acts.

Bipartite in structure, Mary's song first praises God for the conception of Jesus (vv. 46-50) and then enumerates God's actions in the salvation of the poor, the oppressed, and the weak (vv. 51-55). Mary speaks as the voice of the Hebrews, as the descendant of the once-powerful line of David, and as the vehicle of the promise of salvation to Israel; she also represents the ark of the new covenant, i.e., the Church. Her song calls attention, thus, to Abraham, the earlier vehicle of the promise. Mary's status as one of the poor (Heb. 'anawim: the lowly, humble, poor) is emphasized in the Greek word of which "handmaiden" is the KJV translation: *doulē,* a bondservant, is the feminine form of the word Simeon uses of himself in 2:29, where Mary's poverty is again stressed in her purification sacrifice of a pair of pigeons instead of the lamb which would have been expected of a wealthy woman.

The *Magnificat* has been part of the liturgy of the Church since at least the time of St. Benedict and St. Caesarius (5th-6th cents.). In the Eastern Church it is often used in the morning office, but in the West it has always been a hymn for vespers. Aelfric refers to "þone lofsang þe we singað on Godes cyrcan aet aelcum aefensange." Thus it formed, and forms, part of the service of Evening Prayer in the *Book of Common Prayer.* Along with the *Nunc Dimittis* it was set to music by most English composers from the Reformation to the early 20th cent., as well as by numerous European composers (e.g., Pergolesi, Bach). The *Myrour of Oure Ladye* (15th-cent.) offers elaborate semi-allegorical reasons for this canticle's being sung in the evening office.

Patristic, medieval, and modern commentators have tended to concentrate on the two evident themes: the humility of Mary and the magnificence and power of God. Luther, in a letter to his patron, the Duke of Saxony, regarding his exposition of the *Magnificat,* found special importance in the transition verses, 50 and 51: "I commend the 'Magnificat' to your Grace, particularly the fifth and sixth verses, in which its chief content is gathered up." Zwingli refers to the *Magnificat* in commenting on the "nature and property of the Word to humble the high and mighty and to exalt the lowly." Minor variations on this general approach may be found in Bede (*Homilia*, 1, 4; *In Adventu*; *In Lucae Evangelium Expositio*) and in Hugh of St. Victor (*Explanatio in Canticum Beatae Mariae*), who contrasts the humility of Mary, by which life is brought into the world, with the pride of Adam and Eve, which brought death. Almost all commentators identify "his arm" (Luke 1:51) as Jesus, the terrestrial manifestation of God's power. Medieval commentary sometimes identifies the proud (in *dispersit superbos*) with the Jews, but most commentators equate the proud with Satan.

The *Magnificat* usually appears in ME cycle plays of the Visitation, as in the Wakefield "Salutation of Elizabeth." In *Ludus Coventriae* each sentence of the psalm, spoken by Mary in Latin, is followed by a two-line paraphrase or translation spoken in English by Elizabeth. Langland twice quotes bits of the *Magnificat* in Latin in *Piers Plowman:* once *Deposuit potentes* . . . ("He hath put down the mighty") as part of a warning to the Church against the holding of material possessions and once *Quam olim Abrahe* . . . near the end of the speech by Abraham himself (as Faith) in Passus 16.

The concluding allusion to Abraham in the *Magnificat* may lie behind some of the numerous references to Abraham and his seed in *Paradise Lost*. The suggestion is very strong in 12.346, where God's covenant with David is invoked (Ps. 89:29), but the wording is that of the *Book of Common Prayer* rendering of Luke 1:54. Similarly, Beelzebub's mention of God's "potent arm" (2.318) may recall the Latin phrase *Fecit potentiam in brachio suo* of v. 52. Newton, in Blake's *Everlasting Gospel*, "confutes" the gospel with words which echo Luke 1:51b. "The May Magnificat" of Gerard Manley Hopkins associates Mary with the earth's fecundity and links a sense of wonder at the glory of nature with Mary's exultation in God "who was her salvation."

See also ELISABETH; MARY, MOTHER OF JESUS.

Bibliography. Brown, R. E. *The Birth of the Messiah* (1977); Forestall, J. T. "The Old Testament Background of the Magnificat." *Marian Studies* 12 (1961), 205-44; Jones, D. "The Background and Character of the Lukan Psalms." *JTS* n.s. 19 (1968), 19-55; McHugh, J. *The Mother of Jesus in the New Testament* (1975); Warner, M. *Alone of All Her Sex* (1976). PHILLIP ROGERS

MAIMED, THE HALT, AND THE BLIND When you make a feast, Jesus said to certain lawyers and Pharisees, invite "the poor, the maimed, the lame, the blind" rather than well-off friends and neighbors. He then told a parable to illustrate such charity, in which "a certain man . . ." made a great supper, then sent out his servant to "bring hither the poor, and the maimed, and the halt,

and the blind" (Luke 14:13-21). The phrase is invoked in a parallel setting in Goldsmith's *The Vicar of Wakefield* (chap. 1).

See also MARRIAGE FEAST, PARABLE OF.

MALCHUS Malchus was a servant of the High Priest Caiaphas and a member of the party which arrested Jesus in Gethsemane. A disciple cut off his ear and was rebuked by Jesus. He is named only in John's Gospel (18:10), in the others being identified merely by his office. John identifies the disciple responsible for the injury as Peter and adds the detail that it was a kinsman of Malchus who prompted Peter's third denial of Jesus. (Only Luke explicitly notes that Jesus healed the ear [22:51].) Malchus is almost invariably present in visual representations of the betrayal and arrest of Jesus, where typically Judas kisses Jesus at the same moment that Jesus restores Malchus's ear.

The name *Malchus*, which may be Arabic (it occurs in Arabic inscriptions and is the name of an Arab in Josephus [*Ant.* 13.131]), reflects the Semitic root meaning "king." St. Augustine thus calls him "one destined to reign" and interprets the incident as the pruning away of the old hearing of the letter and the renewal of hearing in the spirit: Malchus will come to reign with Christ (*In Joan. Ev.* 112.18.5). Bede (*In Lucae Evangelium Expositio*) and Alcuin (*Comm. in Joannem*) both adopt this interpretation. Because Malchus was early associated with the unnamed high priest's servant who struck Jesus in John 18:22 (e.g., St. John Chrysostom, *Hom. on John*, 83), he provides the stimulus for one stream of the legend of the Wandering Jew (often called Malc, Marcus, Malco, Marco, but most often Buttedieu or some variant thereof).

In early English literature Malchus appears in the cycle plays dealing with the Passion, where he sometimes has no significant part (his only words in *Ludus Coventriae* are in a stage direction) and sometimes is a fully realized character (as in the Towneley "Conspiracy"). *The Southern Passion*, like some other medieval works, recounts the confrontation of Peter and Malchus's kinsman, and in *The Northern Passion* Malchus himself speaks to Peter in the high priest's house. Aside from such biblical paraphrase, Malchus occurs infrequently in English literature. But Browning, in *The Ring and the Book*, uses his name ironically in the speech of Count Guido Franceschini, who likens his wife, Pompeia, to Malchus by suggesting that, since it did Malchus no great harm to have his ear cut off and since he behaved himself afterward, Guido might have kept his wife under control by cutting off one finger joint as a warning against infidelity. He thus associates himself with Peter as a defender of justice and truth and perhaps even with Jesus as one who is betrayed.

Bibliography. Anderson, G. *The Legend of the Wandering Jew* (1965). PHILLIP ROGERS

MAMMON *Mammon* appears in Matt. 6:24 and Luke 16:9-13, where it is a transliteration of a Semitic word meaning "wealth," "riches," "property." The term was untranslated in the Greek text of these two Gospels, suggesting that it was familiar enough to require no explanation for the original readers. There are other occurrences of the term in ancient Jewish and Christian writings (Sir. 31:8 [Heb.]; 1 Enoch 63:10; 'Abot 2.12; 2 Clem. 6:1). In the Gospels mammon is personified as a master, service to whom is incompatible with service to God (Matt. 6:24; Luke 16:13). In Luke 16:9-11, mammon is described as "unrighteous," reflecting a view of wealth as obtained by injustice, coercion, trickery, and similar measures. These passages warn against preoccupation with obtaining wealth and pose the same stark alternative between hoarding riches and service to God that is reflected in other Gospel passages (e.g., Mark 10:17-27).

In subsequent tradition mammon came to be taken as the name of the demon of covetousness. Robert Burton observes in *The Anatomy of Melancholy*, "Yet thus much I find, that our School-men and other Divines make nine kinds of bad spirits, as Dionysius hath done of Angels. . . . The ninth are those tempters in several kinds, and their Prince is Mammon (1.2.1.2)." Mammon does not appear among the devils or vices in medieval morality plays, though there are many personified characters of a similar nature: Lucre, Avarice, Mundus, and Money.

There are three notable Renaissance examples of Mammon as a personification of avarice and worldliness. In *The Faerie Queene* (2.7), Spenser describes Guyon's encounter with Mammon as the first great temptation of his career. Wandering through a forest, Guyon stumbles upon "an uncouth salvage, an uncivil wight" counting his gold in a dark glade, the traditional medieval figure of Avarice. But as Mammon announces his rank as "greatest god below the sky" and leads Guyon to the underworld, he takes on a certain fearsome majesty. He leads Guyon to the very gate of Hell, where lies the "House of Richesse." Guyon's three-day ordeal is linked with Christ's temptation in the wilderness, Mammon taking the place of Satan as prince of this world and offering Guyon unlimited wealth and power if he will but serve him. Like Christ, Guyon is tempted three times and returns to the ordinary world sinless but in a state of exhaustion.

Milton's version of Mammon appears in the first two books of *Paradise Lost*. His description of Mammon as one of the fallen angels derives from the medieval tradition. From Spenser's vivid account of the fiends mining and smelting gold under Mammon's direction, Milton may have drawn his similar picture of Mammon and a crew of fallen angels digging out gold from a mountain in Hell for the building of Pandemonium. Original with Milton is the comic account of Mammon before the Fall as

> . . . the least erected spirit that fell
> From Heav'n, for even in Heav'n his looks and
>   thoughts
> Were always downward bent, admiring more
> The riches of Heav'n's pavement, trodd'n gold,
> Than aught divine. . . . (1.679-84)

In the diabolical council in bk. 2, Mammon speaks after Belial, advising that the devils accept their lot, "preferring / Hard liberty before the easy yoke / Of servile pomp."

In Ben Jonson's satiric comedy *The Alchemist* (1610), the most important of the clients who come to Subtle, the alchemist, is Sir Epicure Mammon. The play presents a realistic view of contemporary London, and yet the morality tradition survives in that the three rogues — Face, Dol Common, and Subtle — suggest that unholy trio, the World, the Flesh, and the Devil. Their clients make up a kind of corporate Mankind. Sir Epicure Mammon represents not only the lust for wealth implied by his surname but also all the appetites. Jonson pictures him as exuberant in his desires and extravagant in his projects. He becomes bloated with expectation, and the pricking of the balloon as alchemical apparatus explodes is one of the great comic moments in Jacobean drama.

Jack Drum's Entertainment (1601), a weakly plotted romantic comedy attributed to John Marston, presents a character called Mammon, a "yeallow toothd snuck-eyde, gowtie shankt Vsurer." He attempts to win Katherine, the daughter of Sir Edward Fortune, as his bride, turns villain, and is eventually discomfited by Katherine's lover, Pasquil.

In the late 19th and early 20th cents., Mammon becomes a symbol of commercial, materialist society, as in E. F. Benson's novel *Mammon & Co.* (1899) and in essays by Upton Sinclair (*Mammon Art: An Essay in Economic Interpretation* [1925]) and Robert Graves (*Mammon and the Black Goddess* [1965]). However, John Davidson (1857-1909) presents a Mammon of a very different kind in his two blank-verse dramas, *The Triumph of Mammon* (1907) and *Mammon and His Message* (1908), two parts of a projected trilogy. This Mammon is an allegorical character on a large scale engaged in a struggle against traditional moral and religious codes and proclaiming a society based on science and human will. Though denying the influence of Nietzsche and disapproving of Darwin's theory of natural selection, Davidson creates a worldview owing much to their ideas. Traditional concepts of good and evil are transcended by a dictator-like leader for whom: ". . . our watchword shall be still, / 'Get thee behind me, God; I follow Mammon.'" Davidson's Mammon is a version of Milton's Satan transformed into a prophet and leader of the coming age.

See also CHARITY, CUPIDITY; *RADIX MALORUM;* WORLD, FLESH, AND DEVIL.

Bibliography. Kermode, F. "The Cave of Mammon." In *Shakespeare, Spenser, Donne: Renaissance Essays* (1971), 60-83.   JOHN MARGESON

A MAN AFTER HIS OWN HEART (1 Sam. 13:14)
See also DAVID.

MAN OF SORROWS The "man of sorrows" of Isa.
53:5 is identified also (in the so-called "servant songs" of
Isaiah [42:1-4; 49:1-6; 50:4-9; 52:13–53:12]) as the "servant of the LORD." In exegetical tradition the same figure
is commonly referred to as the "suffering servant." The
character and mission of the servant is described in his
own words, in the words of the Lord, and in the words of
those to whom he has been sent (the "we" of Isa. 53:2-6).
The servant has been chosen by God to "bring forth
judgment to the nations" (Isa. 42:1); he will work patiently, confident that the Lord will in time vindicate the shame
and violent scorn which he must endure. The climax of
his story comes in the final poem, where those to whom
the servant has been sent recognize that this man of
sorrows, who is "despised and rejected" by them (53:3)
and apparently judged and afflicted by God, is nevertheless God's instrument to atone for their sins. He is
"wounded for . . . [their] transgressions" and, despite his
own innocence, condemned to die on their behalf. The
poem concludes with the reaffirmation that the servant
will not suffer in vain and that his mission will succeed.

The identity of the servant has long been the subject
of controversy. He has been identified as a historical
individual: the prophetic author himself, an anonymous
contemporary of the prophet, Moses, Jeremiah, Hezekiah,
and Zerubbabel, among others. Early rabbinic commentary was unanimous in seeing the description of the servant as a portrait of the Messiah. (A similar messianic
reference occurs in a talmudic legend in which Elijah tells
a rabbi seeking the Messiah, "A man of sorrows himself,
he ministers lovingly to those who suffer, and binds up
their wounds.") But the concept of a suffering Messiah
was generally problematic for later Jewish commentators
who, following Rashi in the 11th cent., chose rather to see
the servant as the embodiment of Israel.

Andrew of St. Victor incorporates in his (12th-cent.)
commentary on Isaiah Jewish exegetical identification of
the suffering servant with the Jews of captivity, or possibly Isaiah himself, not even mentioning a messianic or
typological reading (Smalley, 164). For other Christian
exegetes, however, the suffering servant was readily identified as Jesus Christ. Christ himself understood his mission in the light of the servant's atonement through suffering and patient endurance, and the early Church
reinforced the connection. The description of the Passion
and death of Jesus recorded in all four Gospels is colored
by references to the "servant songs" (e.g., Matt. 8:17;
Mark 15:28; John 19:9). From the patristic era to the 18th
cent. Christian interpreters were unanimous in seeing the
last of the "servant songs" especially as a prophetic witness to the death of a sinless Christ for the sins of
humankind. Martin Luther in his commentary on Isaiah
indicates the familiar view of Isa. 53:3 as a predictive

description of Christ's "physical, open and extremely
shameful suffering" (*Works*, 17.220). Calvin, in his commentary on Isaiah, posits the sorrow and suffering as itself
the motivation for humanity's rejection of Christ (4.114).
In his sermon of 1 July 1627 John Donne refers to Christ
as the type of all sorrow: "who fulfil'd in himselfe alone,
all *Types,* and *Images,* and *Prophecies* of sorrowes, who
was, (as the *Prophet* calls him) *Vir dolorum,* a man
compos'd, and elemented of sorrowes." In another sermon (25 Aug. 1622) Donne asks that he himself be allowed to "be *vir dolorum,* a man of affliction, a vessell
baked in that furnace, fitted by God's proportion, and
dosis of his corrections, to make a right use of his corrections." In "Palm Sunday," Henry Vaughan writes of "the
man of sorrow / Weeping still, like the wet morrow," who
"comes to borrow" the "shades and freshness" of palm
branches on his entrance into Jerusalem.

Melville takes quite a different approach when referring to the suffering servant in *Moby-Dick:* Ishmael suggests "that mortal man who hath more of joy than sorrow
in him, that mortal man cannot be true — not true, or
undeveloped. . . . The truest of all men was the Man of
Sorrows." Yeats's "The Sad Shepherd" contains echoes
of, if not direct references to, the man of sorrows in its
description of "a man whom Sorrow named his friend"
and who, because he was not listened to, could not be rid
of the "ancient burden" of his "heavy story." Joyce, in *A
Portrait of the Artist as a Young Man* (chap. 3), makes
more traditional use of the image, as Stephen considers
the contrast between the humiliation of the first advent
and the glory of the Second Coming.

Other echoes from the "servant songs" occur in a variety
of English texts. Wordsworth, in "Maternal Grief," speaks
of a small boy whose twin sister has died as suddenly
"acquainted with distress and grief " (Isa. 53:3). In his
"Stanzas to Augusta [B]" Byron echoes the same passage:
"Thy soul with my grief was acquainted. . . ." Perhaps the
most influential use of the man of sorrows motif, however,
is Handel's magnificent setting of the final servant song in
his *Messiah*.

See also ECCE HOMO; MARTYR.

Bibliography. Emmet, C. W. "Sorrow, Man of Sorrows."
In *A Dictionary of Christ and the Gospels*. Ed. J. Hastings
(1908), 2.665-68; McKenzie, J. L., ed. *Second Isaiah*. AB 20
(1968); North, C. R. *The Suffering Servant in Deutero-Isaiah*
(1956); Smalley, B. *The Study of the Bible in the Middle Ages*
(1952; rpt. 1964).   MARNIE PARSONS
                                                   W. ROGER WILLIAMS

MANASSEH Son of Joseph by Asenath (Gen. 41:51),
later adopted by his grandfather Jacob (Gen. 48:5-6, 15-
22). He became accordingly father of a tribe in Israel,
often associated with Manasseh and Benjamin.

See also AARON; ASENATH; JACOB; JOSEPH THE PATRI-
ARCH; TRIBES OF ISRAEL.

MANDRAKE When Leah's son Reuben found mandrakes in a field he gave them to his mother. She in turn, believing in the reputed powers of the plant to induce fertility, offered them to her barren sister Rachel in exchange for a night with Jacob, their mutual husband. The mandrake, or *duda'im,* thus becomes in talmudic legend the symbol of the tribe of Reuben.

Folkloric association of the mandrake with fertility and the occult goes back to pre-biblical culture in the Near East. Arabic sources (e.g., Ibn Beithar) call it the plant of the idol, because its root has the shape of a man. It is seen by such writers as talismanic as well as medicinal — a cure for maladies caused by jinn, demons, and Satan: among Arabs it is known as the "apple of the jinns." Belief that it is an antidote against spells and enchantments, or that it expels demons, is recorded by Theophrastus. Josephus, in his *Jewish War* (7.6.3), offers further an elaborate description of how, by moonlight, it may be procured without incurring death, since it is reputed to utter a lethal scream when pulled from the earth. In Greek literature, as in the comic plays of Alexis, the plant is called *mandragoras* and thought to be an aphrodisiac; Aphrodite, goddess of love, is sometimes called "Our Lady of the Mandrake" (Gaster, 200).

These associations dominate the mandrake's second biblical appearance in the Song of Songs (7:13), where the maiden entices her lover to her bed, saying that she has stored up for him fragrant mandrakes. Placing mandrakes under the bridal bed persisted into European culture of the time of Luther, who comments on the custom in his *Lectures on the Song of Solomon* (7.13) and *Lectures on Genesis* (26-30). Like St. Augustine, Luther finds the behavior of Rachel and Leah puerile and somewhat embarrassing. Augustine gets around the difficulty with an allegory in which Rachel stands for the contemplative life dedicated to study and communion with God, while Leah represents the secular and active life. The sweet-smelling mandrake stands for "good fame" (*Contra Faustum,* 22.56-58). St. Gregory the Great, following Cassiodorus, develops the medicinal associations by saying the mandrake denotes those saints not only fruitful in good works themselves, but able to heal others with the "wholesome odor of their good example," a point reminiscent of Philo's notion that the buried roots of the mandrake represent the buried saints and patriarchs (of the OT) awaiting the resurrection but in the meantime emitting a "sweet savor" of sanctity or good fame (cf. *Glossa Ordinaria* [PL 113.156-57; 1164]).

Calvin, unable to allegorize the incident with Leah and Rachel, comments only that such a story, which seems "light and puerile," underscores the mean and abject origins of God's chosen people (*Comm.* sup. Genesis, 1.146-47). Lapide sums up most of the established allegorical values and provides additional sources, referring the mandrakes in the Genesis account finally to the "fruitfulness of the Church." With respect to the mandrake's fragrance he repeats once again *"mandragora odorata symbolum est bonae famae"* (*Comm. in Scripturam Sacram,* 1.298-99; cf. Filippo Picinelli, *Mundus symbolicus* [1694], 28.147, which connects the plant also with the seductions of Circe, however, and the odor of bad fame). In treating the passage in the Song of Songs Lapide offers a more extensive allegory: the fragrant mandrake refers at the first level to the relation between Christ and the Church. Following St. Ambrose (*Expositio in Psalmos,* 118.19.4), he adds that the female plant, which has not a pleasant but a bad odor, can also be a symbol for the "body of the unfaithful" whose missing head is Antichrist. On another level, with respect to its narcotic and medicinal properties, the mandrake can be a symbol of contemplation and the mystical life (8.202-04).

The mandrake receives a great deal of attention in Renaissance literature, much of it deriving from the elaborations of commentary rather than from either of the biblical passages themselves. Machiavelli's comedy *Mandragola* hinges on the power of the plant to make barren women fruitful, and alludes to the Rachel/Leah story. In Marlowe's *The Jew of Malta* Barabas describes an escape made possible by the plant's narcotic properties:

> I drank of poppy and cold mandrake juice,
> And being asleep, belike they thought me dead,
> And threw me o'er the walls. So, or how else,
> The Jew is here.... (5.1.79-83)

Similar folkloric traditions, many of them obtained in scriptural commentaries, determine the allusions in Ben Jonson's *Sejanus* (3.595-601), Shakespeare's *2 Henry 4* (1.2.14-18; 3.2.318-20), *Romeo and Juliet* (4.3.45-48), *Othello* (3.3.326-29), and *Antony and Cleopatra* (1.5.3-5). Donne's famous reference in "Song" — "Goe, and catch a falling starre, / Get with child a mandrake roote" — is folkloric, although the reference in "Twick'nam Garden" may owe to Song 7:13:

> . . . Love, let mee
> Some sensless peece of this place bee;
> Make me a mandrake, so I may groane here,
> Or a stone fountaine weeping out my yeare. (15-19)

The Genesis passage is evoked contrastively in "Metempsychosis" (151-80).

In Blake's *Jerusalem,* "Scofield is bound in iron armour, / He is like a mandrake in the earth before Reuben's gate, / He shoots beneath Jerusalem's walls to undermine her foundations" (1.11.20-23; cf. 4.93.7-10; "Of the Gates," 1-6). An occult ambience colors Coleridge's "Limbo," in which "Moles (Nature's mute monks, live mandrakes of the ground) / Creep back from Light — " (cf. Shelley's *The Sensitive Plant,* 3.72.114-17). A similar context, echoing Philo perhaps, undergirds Browning's *Sordello:* "Call him no flower — a mandrake of the earth, / Thwarted and dwarfed and blasted in its birth, / Rather,

— a fruit of suffering's excess" (5.173-75; cf. "With Bernard de Mandeville," *Parleying*, 5.111-31). A Celtic version of the folklore tradition fosters Dylan Thomas's "mandrake music from the marrowroot" ("Faster the Light," 18; cf. "Altarwise by Owl-Light," 1-6). In *Finnegans Wake* "if a mandrake shrieked to convultures at last surviving his birth the weibduck will wail bitternly over the rotter's resurrection"; Joyce's homunculus, later in the book, is "the little fellow in my eye, Minucius Mandrake." In A. M. Klein's "Legend of Lebanon," heavily influenced by the Song of Songs, "Mandrakes did he give her which stir / Up love and tender passion, mandrakes torn / In moonlight to a murmuring of prayer." Jay MacPherson's "Mandrake" follows Blake's "Of the Gates" as well as Frazer (*Folklore in the Old Testament*, 2.372-97) in juxtaposing the Fall with the imagery from Song of Songs:

> The fall from man engenders me,
> Rooted beneath the deadly tree.
> My certain origin I show,
> Single above and forked below.
> Man grubs me from my peaceful sink
> To aid his horrid loves, and link
> My fate more strongly with his own;
> Foreknowledge racks me, and I groan.

See also LEAH; RACHEL.

Bibliography. Gaster, T. H. *Myth, Legend, and Custom in the Old Testament* (1969); Gibson, J. C. L. *Canaanite Myths and Legends* (1978).

MANICHEANISM *See* HERESY.

MANNA Manna, the name given in the LXX to the food which was miraculously provided to the Hebrews during their forty-year sojourn in the desert, is described in Exod. 16:15-35, where it is said to look like white coriander seed and to taste like honey wafers; in Num. 11:7-8 it is said to be the color of bdellium and to taste like fresh oil. Found on the ground each morning, it was gathered and made into bread. Manna has been thought by some modern interpreters to be an excretion produced by two different insects on the tamarisk tree (thus now *Tamarix mannifera);* it is similar to the honeydew produced by many plant lice and is still used by the Sinai bedouins as a sweetener. The OT account of manna, however, clearly emphasizes its miraculous nature, as do various other accounts. Josephus, e.g., several times notes that it had never been seen before and was provided by God for the special purpose of sustaining his people (*Ant.* 3.26-32, 86; 4.45).

Moses ruled that manna was not to be kept overnight, and some who disobeyed found that the retained manna stank and bred worms; on the eve of the Sabbath, however, the people were instructed to gather twofold, for no manna was provided on the Sabbath. In this instance it remained fresh. Later, when the people complained about the manna and wanted flesh, God provided them with a surfeit of quails and a "very great plague" (Num. 11:33). They continued, therefore, to eat manna until they arrived in Jericho, where Joshua performed the circumcision covenant a second time (it had been neglected during the desert wanderings) and the people ate "the old corn of the land" (Josh. 5:11), after which the manna disappeared.

Manna is allegorized by Moses, who says that God provided it to show that man does not live by bread alone but "by every word that proceedeth out of the mouth of the LORD" (Deut. 8:3). In the Psalms it is called "angel's food" (78:25) and "bread of heaven" (105:40). The latter term is used in the NT in John's account of the sequel to the feeding of the 5,000 (chap. 6), when Jesus calls himself the "living bread." Of the other NT uses of the word, one (Heb. 9:4) refers to literal manna set aside in a special urn as a memorial of God's salvation of Israel (see Exod. 16:32-34), and the other (Rev. 2:17), in the message to the church at Pergamum, refers to the "hidden manna" which will be given to "him that overcometh" (the Wycliffite translation glosses "manna hid" with "angel's mete"). In Hebrew tradition manna is associated with God as sustainer and protector (cf. Josephus's statement that the manna was sent "for salvation and sustenance"). Thus it is said to have been created at twilight on the sixth day of creation, along with nine other items of protective and utilitarian value (the mouth of the earth [Num. 16:32], the mouth of the well [Num. 21:16-18], the mouth of the she-ass [Num. 22:28], the rainbow, the rod [Exod. 4:17], the shamir, and the letters, writing, and tables of the Law ['Abot 5.6]). In Torah Shelemah manna is said to be white because it whitened (purified) the sins of Israel (Yoma 75a); this identification is related to the Haggadah tradition which says that receiving a new supply of manna daily made the Israelites always turn their hearts to God. In the *Wisdom of Solomon* manna is said to taste like whatever the eater most likes and to declare God's "sweetness unto thy children" as well as to bring "strength against the unrighteous" (16:20-21, 24). (Thus the Haggadah tradition that manna is called "bread of angels" because those who eat it become as strong as angels.)

St. Justin Martyr in his *Dialogue with Trypho* uses the appellation "angel food" for manna in support of his argument for the corporeality of angels. Other early commentators develop the "living bread" passage in John; thus in St. Ambrose the sacrament of the Eucharist is said to be both older (because first administered by Melchisedek to Abraham) and more potent than the manna (*The Mysteries,* trans. Deferrari [FC 44]) and to be "heavenly wisdom" which is "the unfailing food of the soul" (Letter to Justus). St. Caesarius of Arles develops an elaborate allegorical treatment of manna as the word of God, which is always given to Christians on the Sabbath, although the original manna was withheld from the Jews on that day. Manna is small and fine, white and sweet, for nothing is more shining or splendid than divine knowledge and nothing sweeter or more pleasant than the Lord's words. Finally, the analogy is extended even to the formation of worms, for if we sin after receiving the word, it will become a worm to gnaw at our hearts (Sermon 102, trans. Sr. Mueller, O.S.F., in FC 47). In the 17th cent. Jeremy Taylor similarly develops manna as "the word of God, the most honorable and eldest of things" *(Real Presence)*.

Aelfric's *Sermo de Sacrificio in die Pascae,* which owes much to the twenty-second homily of St. Gregory the Great (PL 76.1174-81), carries on the tradition, associating manna, "heofenlican hlaf" ("heavenly bread"), with the Eucharist. In George Herbert's "The Sacrifice" the Psalm term "angel's food" creates a two-layered metaphor in which manna is at once the Eucharist and Christ, the "living bread," who is the speaker of the poem and the "sacrifice." Southwell's "A Holy Hymn," also based on metaphorical treatment of the Eucharist, calls manna "Angel's bread made *Pilgrimes* feeding." In *Paradise Regained* Christ responds to Satan's temptation to turn stones into bread by referring to manna and quoting Moses' words from Deut. 8:3. Marvell closes "A Drop of Dew" with an image of manna and its property of melting in the sun, just as the dew, which is likened to the human soul, evaporates and "returns" to heaven. Thoreau uses the property of melting metaphorically when, in *Walden,* he says he waited at evening for "something, though I never caught much, and that, manna-wise would dissolve again in the sun."

Malory's Lancelot, aboard a strange ship for a month, is fed by the grace of God as the Hebrews were fed by God's manna (*The Castle of Corbenic* in *Works,* ed. Vinaver, 3.1011.28). And when the Holy Grail at last enters the hall, "every knight had such metes and drynken as he best loved in thys worlde" —a reference to the description of manna in Wisd. of Sol. 16:20 (*The Departure,* in *Works,* ed. Vinaver, 2.865.30-31). Defoe's Robinson Crusoe alludes to the manna when, having unwittingly discarded grain which later sprouted and produced fruit, he "thought these the pure productions of Providence for my support." In Blake's *Book of Thel* (1.23), "morning manna" is a gratuitous gift of God. The idea of manna as a gratuitous gift, without particular religious significance, is developed relatively early in English; thus in Shakespeare's *Merchant of Venice* when Portia and Nerissa reveal their trick, Lorenzo says, "Fair ladies, you drop manna in the way / Of starved people" (5.1). Donne contrasts the sweetness of manna with the bitter gall it may be transformed into by love in "Twick'nam Garden," and Keats several times includes manna in lists of delicacies, simply as something sweet (*Endymion,* "The Eve of St. Agnes," "La Belle Dame sans Merci").

In Otway's *The Atheist,* an allusion to manna concerns wishing for more than one already has (as the Israelites wanted flesh as well as manna) when the womanizing Courtine, who neglects his wife, is asked, "Do you despise your own Manna indeed, and long after Quails?" Similarly, in *The Ring and the Book*, Browning's Count Guido Franceschini refers contemptuously to a hypothetical monk "Who fancied Francis' manna meant roast quails." The speaker of Hopkins's "Soliloquy of One of the Spies Left in the Wilderness" grows tired of the manna and wishes for the comforts of Egypt.

C. Day Lewis's version of Virgil's fourth *Georgic* no doubt refers to European "manna" (produced on different trees in the same way as Middle Eastern "manna" and giving rise to the ancient belief that honey dropped like dew from heaven), appropriately if reconditely: "Next I come to the manna, the heavenly gift of honey" (1.1, translating *"aerii mellis celestia dona"*).

See also BREAD OF LIFE; EUCHARIST.

Bibliography. Bodenheimer, F. S. "The Manna of Sinai." *BA* 10 (1947), 2-6; Carr, G. L. "Manna." *ISBE* 3.239-40; Kennedy, R. B. "Anete-Nicene Greek and Latin Patristic Uses of the Biblical Manna Motif." *DA* 29 (1969), 668A.

MANY ARE CALLED At the conclusion of his parable about the laborers in the vineyard (Matt. 20:1-16), Jesus observes concerning the character of their summoning to work and the uniformity of their pay, "So the last shall be first, and the first last: for many be called, but few chosen," a phrase echoed two chapters later in connection with the parable of the wedding feast (22:14). Shelley's formulation in *Queen Mab* is in bitter sympathy with the offended laborers, but he connects the phrase with the OT doctrine of election:

> What then avail their virtuous deeds, their thoughts
> Of purity, with radiant genius bright,
> Or lit with human reason's earthly ray?
> Many are called, but few will I elect,
> Do thou my bidding, Moses! (8.153-57)

See also ELECTION; LABORERS IN THE VINEYARD; LAST SHALL BE FIRST; MARRIAGE FEAST, PARABLE OF; VOCATION.

MANY MANSIONS Jesus comforted his disciples with the assurance of reunion in heaven: "In my Father's house are many mansions: if it were not so, I would have told you. I go to prepare a place for you" (John 14:2). This description of heaven prompts Matthew Henry to note, as medieval commentators had before him, that the eternal relation of the One and his many faithful is such that neither dissolution of individuality nor rigid conformism pertains. As to the "distinct dwellings, and apartment for each," Henry conjectures an allusion to "the priests' chambers that were about the temple": "In heaven there are accommodations for particular saints; though all shall be swallowed up in God, yet our individuality shall not be lost there; every Israelite had his lot in Canaan, and every elder a seat, Rev. IV.4." He goes on to stress the perpetual lease: "Here we are as in an inn; in heaven we shall gain a settlement" (*Comm. on the Whole Bible,*

5.1108). Echoing Matthew Henry's commentary, though not the context of Jesus' words in the Gospel, Edmund Gosse reports of his father that "his one and only anxiety was to be at the end of his spiritual journey safe with me in the house where there are many mansions. The incidents of human life upon the road to glory were less than nothing to him" (*Father and Son,* Epilogue). In Samuel Butler's *The Way of All Flesh* it is weakly conjectured that "In the event of a Resurrection and Day of Judgment" those who have been happy in this world "will be most likely to be deemed worthy of a heavenly mansion" (chap. 26). Forster, in *Anonymity,* applies the phrase to what in more recent critical parlance has come to be known as "the prison house of language." He writes that words "have two functions, and the combination of those functions is infinite. If there is on earth a house with many mansions, it is the house of words."

See also HEAVEN.

MANY WATERS CANNOT QUENCH LOVE   Song of Songs 8:7 reads "Many waters cannot quench love, neither can the floods drown it." Thomas Hardy borrows these words to describe a love more complete than mere erotic attraction in *Far from the Madding Crowd:* "Where, however, happy circumstances permit its development, the compounded feeling proves itself to be the only love which is as strong as death — that love which many waters cannot quench, nor the floods drown, beside which the passion usually called by the name is evanescent as steam" (chap. 56).

See also CHARITY, CUPIDITY; LOVE STRONG AS DEATH.

MARAH   After the Israelites crossed the Red Sea (Exod. 15:23), they stopped in the wilderness of Shur at a place where the only water was bitter (Heb. *marah*). The people complained in their thirst, and at the Lord's bidding Moses threw a tree into the water, "and the waters were made sweet" (v. 25). In the book of Ruth, Naomi took Mara as her name on returning from Moab, feeling it was more appropriate in her bereaved state than her given name, which means "pleasant" (Ruth 1:20).

In talmudic literature the tree cast into the water is interpreted sometimes naturalistically (with a suggestion that it was possibly a laurel) but more often allegorically — as Torah, the "tree of life" (Mek. Wa-Yassa 1.45b). A minor thread in talmudic commentary suggests that parts of the Law were revealed already at Marah, including Sabbath rest (Sipre Zebulun 6b; cf. Tehillim 92.402).

In Protestant exegesis Marah is often contrasted to Elim, the place of twelve pure wells and seventy fruitful trees, to which the Israelites next came (Exod. 15:27), with the suggestion that sometimes one must be led through bitterness to appreciate God's blessing (e.g., Matthew Henry's *Comm. on the Whole Bible*). But primarily it is a figure for bitterness, even bitterness of heart. In Tennyson's *Becket,* Rosamund leaves her nunnery in the habit of a monk, determined to plead with Becket that mercy be shown to the king. When she reveals herself to the Archbishop, Becket exclaims, "Breaking again from thy novitiate / To plunge into this bitter world again — / These wells of Marah!" Ruskin argues in *Unto This Last* that laissez-faire economics has made affluence the last and most deadly of England's national plagues: "water of Marah — the water which feeds the roots of evil" (chap. 3). Longfellow returns the term somewhat more directly to its origin in his reflective poem "The Jewish Cemetery at Newport," where he empathizes with the diaspora suffering of the Jews:

> All their lives long, with the unleavened bread
>   And bitter herbs of exile and its fears,
> The wasting famine of the heart they fed,
>   And slaked its thirst with Marah of their tears.

In George Macdonald's novel *Lilith*, Mara is a bitter and deadly daughter of Adam whose bitterness is rooted in her intensive will to resist a passage through death to ultimate salvation.

MARANATHA   *Marana' tha'* ("Our Lord, come!"; cf. Rev. 22:20) is an Aramaic phrase, transliterated as a single Greek word in 1 Cor. 16:22. The phrase gained liturgical status at a very early date (as is evidenced also by Did. 10:5), and hence penetrated NT Greek.

As an Aramaic expression, *marana' tha'* makes a complete sentence; but Greek readers of the NT unfamiliar with the original language tended to attach the single transliterated word to the preceding sentence. This is demonstrated by many later Greek MSS (early MSS were not punctuated at all); the usage carried over into early English versions. Hence the KJV rendering of 1 Cor. 16:22, "If any man love not the Lord Jesus Christ, let him be Anathema Maranatha." More recent versions insert punctuation (e.g., RV ". . . let him be anathema. Maran atha") and clarify the meaning (e.g., NIV ". . . a curse be on him. Come, O Lord!").

Misunderstanding of the verse led to the earlier supposition that the word *maranatha* intensified the curse implied by the word *anathema*; and at times the word *maranatha* was even substituted for *anathema*. The idea of the double curse is contained in Macaulay's essay on Milton; he says that after the death of Cromwell "the principles of liberty were the scoff of every grinning courtier, and the Anathema Maranatha of every fawning dean." Longfellow's depiction of anti-Semitic persecution in "The Jewish Cemetery at Newport" includes the lines:

> Anathema Maranatha! was the cry
>   That rang from every town, from street to street;
> At every fate the accursed Mordecai
>   Was mocked and jeered, and spurned by Christian feet.

A related context for the allusion is found in Harriet

Beecher Stowe's *Dred: A Tale of the Great Dismal Swamp* (2.2.23).

See also ANATHEMA.   DAVID F. PAYNE

MARDUK   Also known as Merodach (Jer. 50:2), he was chief god of the Babylonian pantheon and specially venerated by Hammurabi (1750 B.C.) in his Code, and celebrated also in the Babylonian Creation Epic. His temple was guarded by a dragon with serpent's head, lion's body, and eagle's clawed hind feet.

See also BEL AND THE DRAGON.

MARK   St. Mark the Evangelist was the author of one of the three Synoptic Gospels. He is sometimes thought to be John Mark, cousin of Barnabas who accompanied him and St. Paul on their mission to Cyprus. Eusebius quotes a tradition that Mark was St. Peter's interpreter and that his account of the life and ministry of Jesus is based upon Peter's reminiscences (*Hist. eccl.* 3.39). Irenaeus's likening of the four evangelists to the four cherubim of Ezekiel and four living creatures of Rev. 4 vacillates concerning whether Mark should be associated with eagle, lion, man, or ox. Later tradition fixed on the winged lion, possibly because he concludes his Gospel with the Resurrection, for which the lion is sometimes a symbol (e.g., *De Bestis et Aliis Rebus* [PL 177]). First bishop of Alexandria, Mark's later legendary life associates him with Venice, of which he is patron saint. The cathedral of which he is patron, San Marco, is the environs of Galuppi's music in Browning's "A Toccata of Galuppi's."

MARK OF CAIN   After Cain murdered Abel, God placed a "mark" on him "lest any finding him should kill him" (Gen. 4:15). This was a token of protection, in part, since God had promised vengeance "sevenfold" on "whosoever slayeth Cain."

Early and medieval exegetes tended to imagine Cain's mark as a physical stigma of some kind. Early Jewish commentary, perhaps influenced by descriptions of other divine signs such as the mark of Tau (Ezek. 9:4, 6), postulated a letter from the tetragrammaton (Tg. Pseudo-Jonathan) or the alphabet (Pirqe R. El. 21) placed either on Cain's forehead or his arm (Ginzberg, *LJ* 1.111-12). Some Christian writers, following the LXX of Gen. 4:14, which reads "trembling and grieving" where the Vg has "vagus et profugus" ("a fugitive and a vagabond," KJV), understand the mark as an involuntary shaking of the head (Peter Comestor, *Historia Scholastica: Liber Genesis* [PL 198.27]; Peter Riga, *Aurora,* 418). As *þe lyff of Adam and Eue* puts it: "And þo sette Crist a mark upon him, þat he waggede alway forþ wiþ his heved" (*Sammlung altenglischer Legenden* [1878], 224). In *Cursor Mundi* the Lord places writing on Cain so that others may "read" it "als clerk" (1178), and in the Cornish Creation, God makes the sign of omega (ω) on Cain's forehead (1179), a mark which could resemble horns. But when Lamech, Cain's

great-grandson twice removed, accidentally kills Cain with a misdirected arrow as Cain stumbles through the forest, he does so not because of the horn-shaped mark but because Cain has grown shaggy and beastlike in the wilderness. From Cain's curse, according to medieval tradition, arose the monstrous races — the Grendels, Calibans, anthropophagi, and Apeneck Sweeneys — thought to exist in inhospitable terrestrial regions (Friedman [1981], 89).

Some have interpreted the mark as a psychological punishment (Philo) or an unspecified "sign of perdition" (Hugh of St. Victor, *De Vanitate Mundi,* 3). Both St. Ambrose (*De Cain,* 2.9.34-37) and St. Augustine (*Contra Faustum,* 12.13) allegorically equate Cain with the Jewish people and with the race which killed Christ. In *Beowulf* (1264) Cain is said to have been "marked by [or for his] murder" *(morþre gemearacod)*. From such interpretations derived the notion that the mark of Cain was his twisted personality, his despair, as Chaucer's Parson says, "of the mercy of Jhesu Crist" — in which he was likened to Judas (*Parson's Tale,* 10.1015). Byron's Cain cries out that his brow "burns" with the mark, "but naught to that which is within it" (*Cain,* 3.1.500-501).

One persistent theme, first advanced in Jewish writings, was that Cain's mark is reflected in black skin and negroid features (Mellinkoff, 76-80). Medieval and later writers regularly explained Ham, traditional patriarch of the Africans, as a descendant of Cain. By such means Cain's mark became something akin to a tribal curse, an explanation of deviance, a deep physical and moral stain.

Melville's narrator in Omoo alleges that Lem Hardy's tattoo is "far worse than Cain's." Cain's mark might have been obliterated with cosmetics, he says archly, "but the blue shark was a mark indelible, which all the waters of Abana and Pharpar, rivers of Damascus, could never wash out."

See also CAIN; GIANTS IN THE EARTH.

Bibliography. Emerson, O. F. "Legends of Cain, Especially in Old and Middle English." *PMLA* 21 (1906), 831-929; Friedman, J. B. *The Monstrous Races in Medieval Art and Thought* (1981); Mellinkoff, R. *The Mark of Cain* (1981).   JAMES M. DEAN

MARK OF THE BEAST   According to an apocalyptic vision described in Rev. 13:11-18, a creature rises from the earth and directs the worship of a seven-headed sea beast, the latter of which is likened to a leopard, a bear, and a lion and bears the name of blasphemy upon his heads (Rev. 13:1). Both beasts are identified as savage creatures *(thēria),* and the passage shows the influence of Dan. 7:1-18, in which the Gentile empires—Babylon, Persia, Greece, and Rome—are described as a series of four animal-like monsters. According to Revelation all mankind is to be marked on the right hand or forehead with the name or number of the beast (Rev. 13:16-18), which is 666. Here and later in the Apocalypse (14:9, 11;

16:2; 19:20) this mark identifies those who worship the beast in opposition to the Lamb, whose own faithful followers are also marked and sealed (Rev. 7:2-3; 9:4). The fact that those lacking the mark of the beast are unable to buy or sell has led scholars to identify this apocalyptic event with the enforcement of Caesar worship upon the early Christians. The exact meaning of the number and name of the beast is uncertain; it has been thought by some to be a cryptogram for Nero.

St. Augustine interprets the mark as designating those who pretend to be Christians but remain members of the godless city (*De civ. Dei* 20.9). Other patristic exegetes identify the number of the beast with Teitan (the pagan gods), Lateinos (the Roman Empire or church), Genseric (the Goths), Mohammed (Islam), the Turks, or simply Antichrist.

The latter interpretation prevails in medieval literature. Thus, in the Latin play *Ludus de Antichristo* and in the Perugia *Doomsday,* it is Antichrist who marks his followers on their foreheads and hands. More subtle variations are developed in the Old French *Jour du jugement* —in which Antichrist mints a coin stamped with his image, perhaps an allusion to the buying and selling spoken of in Rev. 13:17 —and in the *Tournoiement de l'Antecrist* —in which the wounded narrator is tagged with a letter marked by the names of Antichrist. Traditional accounts of Antichrist in didactic works such as the ME *Cursor Mundi* also include references to the mark of the beast, as do such polemical works as the Lollard *Lanterne of Li3t* and *Plowman's Tale.* By condemning contemporary preaching licenses as "a token of Antichrist," these works both allude to the mark and identify the licensed priesthood with followers of Antichrist.

During the Reformation the mark of the beast becomes a prominent tool of religious polemic: both the Papacy and the Reformers are identified with the beast and its mark. Thus Robert Bellarmine, a Roman Catholic theologian and apologist, identifies the beast as "one who came from Saxony," referring to Martin Luther. Thomas Goodwin, in his *Exposition upon the Revelation,* assumes the number to signify the fall of the Papacy in 1666. George Wither, in his "Campo-Musae" (collected in *Fragmenta Prophetica* [1669], 50), reiterates the prophetic connection with the fall of the Roman Church:

> Her date is near, if I aright have hit
> The meaning of the Number, left to be
> A trial and probation of their Wit
> Who seek the fall of Antichrist to see.

An influential treatise published by English rector Francis Potter in 1642, *An Interpretation of the Number 666 . . . ,* offers an ingenious numerical calculation of the mark of the beast: Just as the significance of the apocalyptic number 144 can be discerned in terms of its square root, 12, he reasoned, so also ought one to discern the significance of 666 in terms of its square root, calculated at 25 by

Potter (with further ingenious explanation of the fractional "remainder"). Potter's interpretation was adopted by many of his contemporaries and held great sway into subsequent generations both in England and abroad. Thus Cotton Mather, in his *Biblia Americana,* notes that just as 12, the square root of 144, is the "sacred number" of the true Church and of the New Jerusalem, "so 25, which is the square root of 666, is a sacred number in the Antichristian church." Following Potter, he identifies the number 25 exclusively with Rome and the Papacy, citing various traditions attributing 25 gates and 25 churches, 25 cardinals, 25 parishes, and 25 curates to the city of Rome, and noting that St. Peter's cathedral has 25 altars, etc.

In *The Alchemist* Ben Jonson parodies all such contemporary religious speculation and polemic when Subtle, who has earlier referred to the Puritan hope of "rooting out the bishops / Or th'Anti-Christian hierarchy" (2.2.82-83), is described by the deacon, Ananias, as bearing "the visible mark of the beast in his forehead" (3.1.8).

Swift may be alluding to the mark of the beast when he suggests that the imminent distribution of copper money in Ireland by William Wood has apocalyptic significance and urges the reader "when the *evil Day* is come" to "mark and observe those who presume to offer these Half-pence in Payment" *(The Drapier Letters).* Ernest Pontifex in Butler's *The Way of All Flesh* makes a trivial comparison between the editors of his articles and "the people who bought and sold in the book of Revelation; there is not one but has the mark of the beast upon him." Symbolic use of the image is developed in "The Mark of the Beast," the ninth story in Kipling's *Life's Handicap.* Fleete, who desecrates a temple, is touched by a leper and falls ill with leprosy and hydrophobia, bearing a physical mark which signifies his disrespect for the sacred.

See also ANTICHRIST; DRAGON OF THE APOCALYPSE.

Bibliography. Emmerson, R. K. *Antichrist in the Middle Ages: A Study of Medieval Apocalypticism, Art, and Literature* (1981); Hill, C. *Antichrist in Seventeenth-Century England* (1971); Macfarlane, J. "Antichrist in English Literature, 1380-1680." *DAI* 41 (1980), 2515A; Marshall, M. "Antichrist in Medieval Drama and in the Drama of the Reformation in England." M.A. thesis, Yale, 1928; Misner, P. "Newman and the Tradition concerning the Papal Antichrist." *CH* 40 (1973), 377-95; Sanders, H. A. "The Number of the Beast in Revelation 13, 18." *JBL* 37 (1918), 95-99; Stein, S. "Cotton Mather and Jonathan Edwards on the Number of the Beast: Eighteenth Century Speculation about the Antichrist." *PAAS* 84 (1974), 293-315.   RICHARD K. EMMERSON

MARRIAGE   *See* BRIDE, BRIDEGROOM; CANA WINE.

MARRIAGE FEAST, APOCALYPTIC   One of the most memorable and influential images of the book of Revelation is the apocalyptic banquet which celebrates the marriage of Christ (here figured as the Lamb) and his bride (the Church, the heavenly city) and inaugurates the new heaven and new earth: "And he saith unto me, Write, Blessed are they which are called unto the marriage supper of the Lamb" (Rev. 19:9; cf. Rev. 21:2, 9-10; 22:17). The OT background of this image is twofold. The first influence is the persistent metaphor of the covenant as a marriage between God and his people (e.g., Isa. 54:1-8; 62:4; Ezek. 16; Hos. 2–6). The second is the notion of a banquet prepared for the redeemed at the end of time.

An apocalyptic banquet for all peoples, held when the Lord has vanquished death, figures in Isa. 25:6-8, and ritual eating is sometimes associated with the sacrificial slaughter of enemies on the day of triumph (e.g., Ezek. 39:17-20; Zeph. 1:7-9). Leviathan, an archetypal enemy, becomes a sacrifice and food for the people in Ps. 74:12-17. A messianic banquet is a commonplace feature of Jewish apocalyptic thought. In Apoc. Bar. 29:4-8 Leviathan and Behemoth "shall be food for all that are left." A midrash on Ps. 23:5 identifies them as the feast laid out when God "preparest a table before me in the presence of mine enemies." According to 1 Enoch 62:14, the righteous shall eat with the son of man. The Apocalypse of Elijah tells of a forty-year interregnum with supernatural abundance of food which the righteous eat with the Messiah.

In the NT the marriage supper figures as a general motif both in the parables of the marriage feast (Matt. 22:1-14; Luke 14:15-24) and of the wise and foolish virgins (Matt. 25:1-13) and in the recurrent narratives of miraculous feeding. Jesus refers both to himself as the Bridegroom and to celebratory feasting in the Gospels (Matt. 9:15; Mark 2:19-20; Luke 5:34-35; cf. John 3:29), and alludes to an apocalyptic banquet at which "Many shall come from the east and west and shall sit down with Abraham, and Isaac, and Jacob, at the feast in the kingdom of heaven" (Matt. 8:11; cf. Luke 14:15). Those who have proven faithful can expect to dine at Jesus' table with him as the host (Luke 22:28-30). The apocalyptic banquet is also explicitly anticipated by the last supper of Christ, and commemorated in the Eucharist (1 Cor. 11:23-26).

"Blessed are they which are called unto the marriage supper of the Lamb" (Rev. 19:9) subsumes all earlier biblical marriage-feast imagery in a vision of a people redeemed through a symbolic marriage to the true king, at which they are both guests and marriage partner. (The promise in Rev. 2:7 suggests the persecuted and martyrs as special participants.) This apocalyptic marriage requires the annihilation of the bride's demonic parody, the scarlet whore of Babylon, symbolic of all tyrannies, physical and spiritual, from which redemption is needed (as in Rev. 17–18).

As M. H. Abrams observes, these and related passages proved fertile ground for patristic elaboration:

A number of Church Fathers established a tradition of coherent symbolism which viewed the apocalyptic marriage as initiated by the creation of Adam and Eve; predicted by the prophets; prefigured by a number of historical events in the Old Testament; detailedly imaged forth in Canticles; achieved in the Incarnation; consummated by the Passion; celebrated in the ritual sacraments . . . and awaiting its fulfillment and fruition in the marriage of the lamb at the end of the world. (*Natural Supernaturalism* [1971], 487 n. 59)

Most of these typological connections persist well after the Reformation.

Herbert's "Love (3)," with evident reference to Jesus' parable of the wedding feast (Luke 14:15-24), pictures a banquet to which "Love bade me welcome." The speaker, guilt-ridden, protests his unworthiness but is ultimately compelled by love to "sit and eat." Vaughan's "The Feast" deals principally with the sacramental communion of the Lamb "in the next world"; by comparison, to "toil and sow, / That wealth may flow" in this world is to pursue unreality. Milton's dead Lycidas "hears the unexpressive nuptial Song, / In the blest Kingdoms meek of joy and love" (176-77), while his Damon, who "did not taste the delight of the marriage bed, . . . shall enact [his] part eternally in the immortal marriage where song and the sound of the lyre are mingled in ecstasy with blessed dances, and where the festal orgies rage under the heavenly thyrsus" ("Epitaphium Damonis," 214-19; trans. Bush).

In Blake's *Milton* "the supper of the Lamb & his bride" features centrally in Los's grand vision of the awakening of Albion. Coleridge's *Rime of the Ancient Mariner* begins with the Mariner detaining one of three guests bidden to a wedding feast. Although protesting that the "Bridegroom's doors are opened wide" and that he is not only invited but obligated to attend, the Wedding Guest nonetheless stays to hear the tale and to be instructed in the meaning of love and communion. In Emily Dickinson's "There came a day. . ." a friendship (about to suffer separation) is a rehearsal "Lest we too awkward show / At Supper of the Lamb." E. J. Pratt, in "The Depression Ends," speaks of using the magic of Prospero to "usher in the golden era / With an apocalyptic dinner."

See also BRIDE, BRIDEGROOM; MARRIAGE FEAST, PARABLE OF; SONG OF SONGS; WISE AND FOOLISH VIRGINS.

Bibliography. Abrams, M. H. *Natural Supernaturalism* (1971), 37-46; Daniélou, J. *The Bible and the Liturgy* (1956), 191-220.

RICHARD SCHELL

MARRIAGE FEAST, PARABLE OF The parable of the marriage feast (Matt. 22:1-14) contains one of Christ's principal statements about the kingdom of God. Its main features are the king's two sets of invitations, each refused; the murder of the king's messengers and subsequent punishment of the murderers; the invitation to strangers from the highways; and the arrival and expulsion of the guest who is not in his wedding garment. The moral of the parable, that "many are called, but few are chosen," may apply to the parable as a whole or specifically to the expulsion of the improperly attired guest. Luke 14:15-24 gives what may be another version of the same parable, in which a man sponsoring a great supper invites guests who turn him down with various excuses. He then extends an invitation to the poor, maimed, halt, and blind; and when still there is room at the banquet he invites — indeed compels — people from the highways and hedges with the words, "for I say unto you, that none of those men which were bidden shall taste of my supper" (Luke 14:24). The two parables are treated interchangeably.

Throughout Christian history, and with greater or lesser elaboration, the version in Matthew is interpreted as an allegory of the Church Militant. The kingdom of heaven is the Church; the king is God, who invites the Jews to celebrate the coming of Christ. When they refuse, killing his prophets and apostles, God sends the Romans to conquer the Jews, and invites the Gentiles. But some approach him lacking works of charity, and these are cast into hell. (See, e.g., St. Jerome, *Comm. in Matthaeum,* 3.22 [PL 26.165-68]; Cornelius à Lapide, *Comm. in Scripturam Sacram,* ed. A. Crampon [1872], 15.474-75; Calvin, *Harmony of the Gospels,* trans. W. Pringle [1845], 2.168-69; Matthew Poole, *Synopsis Criticorum Aliorumque Sacrae Scripturae Interpretum* [1674], 4.521-24.) The Lucan version is considered an allegory of the Church Triumphant. God offers eternal life to all; the worldly scorn God's invitation, while those scorned by the world accept it. (See, e.g., Bede, *In Lucam Expositio,* 4.14 [PL 92.514-16]; Cornelius à Lapide, 16.196-200; Poole, 4.1036-38. On the currency of these interpretations, see C. H. Dodd, *Parables of the Kingdom* [1936], 122.) The image of the wedding garment is related to the image of the soul's clothing, which has penitential and baptismal significance in sermon literature (e.g., *Mirk's Festial,* EETS e.s. 96 [1905], 130; *Middle English Sermons,* EETS o.s. 209 [1940], 167). The condition of the soul's clothing generally marks the distinction between the old and new man.

Some of the few literary adaptations of the parables follow the allegorical and homiletic traditions as well as the biblical text. In such works, the image of the soiled garment of the soul is prominent, and the message is to cleanse one's soul while there is still time. The garment of the soul is a recurring image in *Piers Plowman,* culminating in Haukyn the Active Man, whose coat is stained with sin:

'I haue but oon hool hater [garment]', quod haukyn,
  'I am þe lasse to blame
Thouȝ it be soiled and selde clene: I slepe þerInne
  o nyȝtes;
And also I haue an houswif, hewen [servants] and
  children —
Uxorem duxi et ideo non possum venire [I have wedded
  a wife and therefore I cannot come; Vg Luke
  14:20]
That wollen bymolen it many tyme maugree my chekes

[despite all I can do]'. (B.14.1-4; cf. B.11.111-14; B.13.273-77; B.15.452-58; eds. G. Kane and E. T. Donaldson [1975])

A similar integration of the two parables is achieved in *Cleanness,* in which the parable serves as the introduction for the theme from Matt. 5:8 ("Blessed are the pure in heart: for they shall see God"). Like Langland, the *Cleanness*-poet freely combines both parables and changes the guest's inappropriate clothing into tattered, dirty clothing which represents the sinful soul. Unlike Langland, the *Cleanness*-poet provides a full retelling of the parable plus a moralizing gloss (25-192). The same image for the soul occurs in Francis Quarles's "My Glass Is Half Unspent," in which the poet begs God for more time to prepare for the heavenly banquet: "Behold these rags; am I a fitting guest / To taste the dainties of thy royal feast, / With hands and feet unwash'd, ungirt, unblest?"

Other uses are diverse. Browning's churlish narrator in *Christmas-Eve,* apparently remembering the exhortations to communion in the *Book of Common Prayer,* thinks to himself as he returns the suspicious stares of a poor congregation entering a chapel for services:

I prefer, if you please, for my expounder
Of the laws of the feast, the feast's own Founder;
Mine's the same right with your poorest and sickliest
  Supposing I don the marriage vestment:
  So, shut your mouth and open your Testament,
And carve me my portion at your quickliest! (117-22)

Instead of being cast into outer darkness, the speaker falls asleep during the service and dreams a vision of divine love which provides him his figurative marriage garment. Tennyson's Becket acquires a Christlike dimension by deliberately reenacting the Lucan parable (*Becket,* 1.4); when the beggars arrive from the streets, Becket waits on them himself. In the Sirens episode of Joyce's *Ulysses,* Ben Dollard recounts his efforts at finding a pair of trousers for his first concert with Molly Bloom, saying that he had "no wedding garment"; the allusion invites a significant comparison to Bloom, who must, if he is ever to collaborate successfully with Molly, put on what Virginia Moseley has called "the proper garment of faithfulness" (*Joyce and the Bible* [1967], 103).

See also MARRIAGE FEAST, APOCALYPTIC.

Bibliography. Dodd, C. H. *The Parables of the Kingdom.* Rev. ed. (1936); Lubac, H. de. "Le rencontre de *superadditum* et *supernaturale* dans la théologie médiévale." *Revue de Moyen Âge Latin* 1 (1945), 27-34.   M. W. TWOMEY

MARTHA Martha of Bethany was sister to the Mary who anointed the feet of Jesus (John 11:2; 12:3; cf. Matt. 26:6ff.; i.e., the Mary traditionally identified with Mary Magdalene) and brother to Lazarus, whom Jesus raised from the dead (John 11:38-44). It was Martha who met and conversed with Jesus as he approached their home after Lazarus's death. On this occasion she was first to declare openly her faith in Jesus' power to heal and her belief that he was the Son of God and the Messiah (John 11:21-27). Elsewhere, however, the Gospel accounts (cf. Luke 10:39-42) contrast the response of Martha and her sister Mary when in the presence of Jesus: Martha busied herself with the practical matters of hospitality, irritated that Mary devoted herself exclusively to his teaching. Her complaint led to Jesus' gentle reprimand of her for being "careful and troubled about many things." "One thing is needful," he counseled, "and Mary hath chosen that good part, which shall not be taken away from her." The "good part" involves a wordplay associating, and in the context contrasting, food and spiritual nourishment. Jesus' words parallel an injunction in the Mishnah: "Let thy house be a meeting-house for the Sages and sit amid the dust of their feet and drink in their words with thirst" ('Abot 1.4).

Western traditions concerning Martha are heavily influenced by the contrast between her and her sister, as is clear in St. Augustine's sermons on the passage. "Both occupations were good," he observes, "but yet as to which was the better, what shall we say?" He then goes on to suggest that the form of Jesus' words, and the repetition of Martha's name (Luke 10:41), indicate both his deep affection for her and his desire to teach her.

> Yes, Martha, you are blessed in your good serving . . . but even you seek this reward for your good labor — quiet. Now you are occupied with much serving, and have pleasure in feeding bodies which are mortal, though they be the bodies of saints; but when you shall have arrived in that country, will you find there any stranger which you may invite into your house? . . . None of all these will be there, but what will be there? What Mary hath chosen. (*Sermo*, 103.3, 6)

In another homily he observes that "Martha was intent on how she might feed the Lord; Mary intent how she might be fed by the Lord" (*Sermo*, 104.1), and

> that in these two women the two lives are figured, the life present, and the life to come, the life of labor, and the life of quiet, the life of sorrow, and the life of blessedness, the life temporal, and the life eternal. . . . What Martha was doing, that we are now; what Mary was doing, that we hope for. Let us do the first well, that we may have the second fully. (104.4)

The contrast between the two sisters led patristic and later writers, on a parallel with their similar contrasting of Rachel and Leah, to identify Mary with the reclusive or contemplative life and Martha with the active life of service in the world (Augustine, *In Joan. Ev.* 124.5; St. Gregory, *Hom. in Ezek.* 2.2.9; St. Bernard of Clairvaux, *De Institutione Inclusarum*, 2.28ff., and the ME trans. in the Vernon MS; William of St. Thierry, *Meditationes*, 11.9). While among the Cistercians and other *inclusarae* the exaltation of Mary's choice tends to predominate, in Walter Hilton's ME *Epistle on the Medled Life*, the "mixed" life combining the dedications of both Martha

and Mary is praised as especially suitable to those with leadership responsibility. Martha is on the whole portrayed very favorably in the Corpus Christi drama, as in the York "Raising of Lazarus," where she shows more readily than her sister a confidence that Jesus can do something about their brother's fate (159-70). In the Digby play *Mary Magdalen* Martha is more stable in temperament than her sister; in her pragmatism, she cannot help but understand the relationship of Lazarus's death to Jesus' power in rigidly causal terms (and as a lost opportunity therefore). This prompts Jesus to call her "Martha, docctor!" — suggesting perhaps that she thinks too much like a theologian (1.877).

In later literature a "Martha" is typically a reliable, good-natured drudge, such as Matty's faithful maid in Mrs. Elizabeth Gaskell's *Cranford* (1853). In Aldous Huxley's *Brief Candles,* the old idea of the "mixed life," combining Mary's "one thing needful" with the good servanthood of Martha, is given modern advocacy: "Jesus had said that the way of Mary was better than the way of Martha. 'But I'm a Martha', said Martha Claxton, 'who tries her best to be a Mary too. Martha *and* Mary — that's the best way of all' " ("The Claxtons"). As an allusion in David Jones's *Anathemata* suggests, a "Martha" can be simply any woman engaged in domestic duties (7.192). But it may be that Dorothy Sayers's characterization in "The Light and the Life" section of her *Man Born to Be King* cycle (1943) is the most trenchant modern rendering: "Martha is not a subtle character. 'House-proud' would sum her up, except that she is capable of a good, sturdy honesty about herself, when she has time to think about it" (7.183).

See also LAZARUS OF BETHANY; MARY MAGDALENE.

MARTYR Gk. *martys,* "witness," is used in the book of Acts (e.g., 1:8, 22) to signify the apostles who bore witness to Christ's life, death, and resurrection. Later the term came to be used of those Christians who suffered persecution for their faith; by the 2nd and 3rd cents. it usually identified those who had died for their faith. Martyrs are central among those saints whose exemplary lives are recorded in medieval and modern hagiographies; the most famous English examples are those of the Venerable Bede (ca. 730) and, in the 16th cent., John Foxe's *Acts and Monuments of matters happening in the Church,* more popularly known as *Foxe's Book of Martyrs,* which, though a general history, concentrates on the Protestant martyrs of Mary's reign. Lionel Johnson's poem *"Te Martyrum Candidatus"* modernizes an ancient hymn. Ignazio Silone's *Bread and Wine* (1936) takes up the theme of martyrdom in modern fiction, as does T. S. Eliot's *Murder in the Cathedral,* whose protagonist is the notable English martyr, St. Thomas à Becket. Melech Davidson, in A. M. Klein's *The Second Scroll,* seeks the role of "suffering servant" and provides an example in Jewish tradition of the exhaustion of the theme, where

Davidson's friend Kronghold says of him at last: "he is infatuated with suffering. And I, I am sick of martyrdom, sick of the passive role, sick of the equation, I suffer: therefore I exist" (54-55).

See also STEPHEN; WITNESS.

Bibliography. Fleenor, T. R. "The Martyr in the Dramatic Literature of the West, Preceded by an Essay on the Evolution of the Word Martyr." *DAI* 34 (1973), 271A-72A.

MARY MAGDALENE   Mary Magdalene, mentioned by Luke (8:2) as "a certain woman which had been healed of evil spirits and infirmities . . . out of whom went seven devils," is listed (Mark 15:40-41) among the women who followed Jesus and ministered to him. She was at the cross (Matt. 27:56; Mark 15:40; John 19:25) and watched Joseph of Arimathea bury Jesus (Mark 15:42-47). On Easter morning she came with other women to anoint Christ's body at the tomb; they were met by angels and sent to tell the apostles of the Resurrection (Matt. 27:61; 28:1-10; Mark 16:1-8; Luke 23:55–24:11; John 20:1-2). Mark mentions that the risen Christ "appeared to Mary Magdalene" (16:9-11), an account amplified by John (20:11-18).

Scripture gives no further details about this woman. Because early pagans and Jews commonly accused Jesus' mother of adultery, they often conflated Mary Magdalene and the Virgin Mary (e.g., Celsus, A.D. 178, quoted by Origen in *Refutation,* 1.28, who said that Mary was cast off by her husband, a carpenter, and bore a son to a Roman soldier). *M'gadd'la* (hairdresser) was a common euphemism for prostitute. Thus in the Babylonian Talmud, Mary Magdalene is represented as both a prostitute and as Jesus' mother (Shab. 104b, late 3rd cent.; see Dalman).

The Latin Fathers followed Tertullian (*De pudicitia,* 11.2) in combining the account of Mary Magdalene with that of the sinner who washed Christ's feet with her tears and wiped them with her hair (Luke 7:37-50). Because there is another Gospel account of an anointing, this time of Christ's head by Mary of Bethany (Matt. 26:6-13; Mark 14:3-9; John 12:1-8), the identities of Mary of Bethany and Mary Magdalene could be readily merged, as they were by St. Gregory the Great (*Hom.* 25.1.10). This provided Mary Magdalene with a sister and a brother (Martha and Lazarus), made Jesus a frequent visitor in her home, connected her with the contemplative life because of Jesus' comment that she had chosen "the better part" (Luke 10:38-42), and involved her in the story of the raising of Lazarus (John 11).

Origen (in his commentary on Matthew) and the Greek Fathers who followed him insisted on three separate Marys. Origen, however, inadvertently promoted Magdalene as a symbol of erotic asceticism by comparing the perfume of the anointing of Christ to the perfume of the bride in his commentaries on the Song of Songs (1:12-13). St. Bernard of Clairvaux, e.g., preached eighty-six sermons on the Song, allegorically identifying the Bride with the Church, the soul, the Virgin Mary, and Mary Magdalene (Sermon, 7:6).

The controversy over the identification of the three Marys is exceedingly complex (see esp. Faillon), but the identification of Mary Magdalene with Mary of Bethany and with the sinful woman of Luke 7 is the basis of Western iconographical representation of Mary in literature and art, and it was never seriously challenged until Jacques Lefèvre attacked the Magdalene cult in 1516.

Mary Magdalene, often called Marihamme, was given a prominent place in the apocryphal writings of the first four centuries after Christ. Because she is identified with the contemplative life and because Jesus sent her to tell the disciples he was risen, she is seen as fit to receive and communicate the *gnōsis.* In the Gospel of Mary (2nd cent.) Peter asks her, "Tell us the words of the Savior which you have in mind since you know them, and we do not, nor have we heard them." In addition to this Gospel, two other books of the 2nd cent. are attributed to Mary by the Fathers, The Great Questions and The Little Questions; in the Pistis Sophia (2nd cent.) Mary Magdalene asks 39 of the 46 questions as the disciples seek answers from the risen Christ. Although these documents and others such as The Gospel of Peter, The Gospel of Nicodemus (or The Acts of Pilate), and The Gospel of Bartholomew emphasize Mary Magdalene's role as disciple and preacher, the tradition includes a strong element of misogyny. In The Gospel of Thomas (2nd cent.) Peter asks that she be sent away, "for women are not worthy of the life." Jesus does not disagree with the premise, but makes an exception for her: "Behold, I shall lead her, that I may make her male."

According to Byzantine tradition, Mary Magdalene went to Ephesus to preach with Lazarus; both are said to be buried there. About the 11th cent., a rival tradition developed which asserted that Mary Magdalene came to Marseilles with Lazarus, Martha, and St. Maximin and that she is buried in the Monastery of Saint-Maximin. Sometime in the 12th cent. a long episode about the desert penance of Mary of Egypt was added to her story, localizing her penance at Saint Baume, thus providing another site for pilgrimage. For this Provençal story of Mary Magdalene, English literature is indebted primarily to *The Golden Legend of the Lives of the Saints* by Jacobus de Voragine. The child of noble parents, Mary is said in this account to have received her name from her castle at Magdalo; her brother, Lazarus, a knight, possesses Jerusalem, and her sister, Martha, owns the town of Bethany. After her debauchery, conversion, and commission to tell of the Resurrection, she is persecuted with the disciples. Fourteen years after the Passion, she is set adrift in a rudderless boat to be drowned with Martha, Lazarus, and St. Maximin, but God brings them safely to Marseilles, where Mary astonishes the populace by her beauty and her elegant preaching and where she eventually causes a miraculous conception and raises the queen from death. She then retires to the desert for thirty years of penance, fed only by the songs of angels. She dies at Aix; the legend concludes with a series of miracles performed at her tomb and with a note about her possible marriage to St. John.

Based on the *Legenda,* the *Early South English Legendary* gives essentially the same story; Osbern Brokenham, in the *Legendys of Hooly Wummen,* adds a comparison of the active and the contemplative life, prayers to the "gloryous apostolesse" Mary Magdalene, and her sermons in Marseilles. Both the *Northern Passion* and the *Southern Passion* stay close to the biblical account. The *Old English Martyrology* briefly summarizes the anointing and the Resurrection appearance and then, completely skipping the Marseilles account, proceeds to her desert penance; by contrast, Aelfric's *Lives of Saints* includes the penance of Mary of Egypt but does not attach it to Mary Magdalene.

Christians were frequently admonished to follow Mary Magdalene's example of penitence: *Jacob's Well* says that the hearers should weep, confessing their sins like Mary; *Old English Homilies* (EETS o.s. 53) includes a sermon titled "Mary Magdalene" (24), which says that Jesus forgave her sins because she hated them and loved him — "so be forgevn all ouers"; Will in *Piers Plowman* (A.11.279) cites Mary as one who was saved by grace despite her evil works.

In the 14th cent. the cult of the Magdalene was at its height. Petrarch made a pilgrimage to her shrine at Saint Baume and wrote several Latin hymns to her. Boccaccio, at the end of *The Decameron,* suggests that the levity of his work be balanced by serious pieces such as "The Complaint of the Magdalene." Because Chaucer listed among his writings *Origens upon the Maudeleyne,* Thynne published the so-called "Lamentatyon of Mary Magdaleyne" with the works of Chaucer. (Now believed to be of much later date, this text consisted of over 700 lines of poetic lamentation by Mary Magdalene at the empty tomb, very similar to the lamentations entitled "Marie Magdalens lamentations for the losse of her master Jesus," published in 1604.) Chaucer may have been referring not to a poetic lamentation, but to Pseudo-Origen's *De Maria Magdalena,* a Latin homily on John 20, which is almost a dramatization of the text, with a moral appended. Especially popular, the text survives in 130 Latin manuscripts and many translations, including a 1565 translation entitled "An Homilie of Marye Magdalene . . . written by that famous clerke Origin." Chaucer does mention Mary Magdalene several times, particularly in *The Parson's Tale.*

As her cult grew, Mary Magdalene was included in calendars and martyrologies and was the subject of innumerable homilies, legendaries, carols, and ballads. In addition, she became central to medieval drama, first appearing as one of the holy women who come to the tomb in the *Quem Quaeritis.* On the Continent three plays

dealt specifically with her: *Ludus de Maria Magdalena in Gaudio* (a German entertainment) and the Italian plays *Della Conversione di S. Maria Maddalena* and *Di un Miraculo di Santa Maria Maddalena.*

In England, each of the four extant cycles emphasizes the role of Mary Magdalene at the Resurrection, incorporating elements of the *Quem Quaeritis;* Towneley, York, and Chester also include her in the raising of Lazarus scene. In *Ludus Coventriae,* after Mary mourns her sins, Jesus releases her from seven devils (usually interpreted as the seven deadly sins), and then she anoints him.

By far the most important English dramas concerning Mary Magdalene are the Digby plays. *Christ's Burial and Resurrection* adds to her biblical role a long lament for Jesus at the Deposition, a theological discussion of the Crucifixion with Joseph of Arimathea, and laments at the tomb. The Digby *Mary Magdalen* play explains her debauchery as the result of grief over her father's death. She is besieged by the World, the Flesh, and the Devil and by their followers, the seven deadly sins. Seduced in a tavern scene, she sings a lyric to her "valentynes" but is quickly converted when an angel appears. The rest of the play follows Scripture and the Provençal legend.

The Reformation effectively ended the cult of the Magdalene when Calvin separated the three Marys, devaluing Mary Magdalene as a symbol of the contemplative life. Stripped of the Provençal accretions, her story was Protestantized: Lewis Wager turns her story into a play about justification by faith in *The Life and Repentaunce of Marie Magdalene* (1567); a 1595 sermon by Nicholas Breton on John 20 uses Mary as an example of divine love, proper humility, and repentance ("Marie Magdalen's Love, upon the Twentieth Chapter of John"; in *Good News for the Vilest of Men* John Bunyan cites Mary Magdalene as proof that true repentance brings forgiveness; Lancelot Andrewes, in his 1620 Easter sermon on John 20, quotes Pseudo-Origen and Augustine on her significance as an example of faith.

Mary remained a favorite saint of Catholics during the Counter-Reformation. Robert Southwell wrote "Mary Magdalen's Blush" about her shame for her sins and "Mary Magdalen's Complaint at Christes Death" (see also his prose treatise, *Marie Magdalen's Funeral Teares* [1591]). The most famous English poem about her is Richard Crashaw's "Saint Mary Magdalene; or, the Weeper," full of extended conceits, capturing the entire story of the anointing in the phrase "What prince's wanton'est pride e'er could / Wash with silver, wipe with gold?" Andrew Marvell is heavily influenced by Crashaw in his "Eyes and Tears," adding the striking simile of Magdalene's tears as "liquid chaines" which flowed "to fetter her Redeemer's feet." Thomas Robinson, in *The Life and Death of Mary Magdalene* (ca. 1620), emphasizes a lush, sensuous description of the lovers in the garden and of the palace of pleasure; after Mary's repentance he uses descriptions from the Song of Solomon to describe Christ. *St. Marie Magdalen's Conversion* (anon. 1603) uses the form of the epyllion to show the conquest of divine love over base passion as she seeks forgiveness.

Mary Magdalene was not totally rejected by Protestant poets in the early 17th cent. Robert Herrick in the quatrain "Upon Woman and Mary" concludes that Christ first called her "Woman" when her faith was small, "Mary" when she believed. George Herbert in "Marie Magdalene" focuses on a paradox of the anointing: "She being stain'd her self, why did she strive / To make him clean, who could not be defil'd?" John Donne compliments a patron in "To the Lady Magdalen Herbert, of St. Mary Magdalen," mentioning her holdings in Bethina and Magdalo, the Resurrection appearance, and the controversy over the number of Marys, concluding with an admonition to the lady to copy the latter half of Mary's life.

By the late 17th cent. the Magdalene is frequently referred to in jest. In Richard Brome's play *The Damoiselle* a comic character named Mrs. Magdalen is drunk: "She's in her Mawdlin fit; all her wine / Showres out in tears." She is rarely mentioned in the 18th cent., save in such ironic allusions as Alexander Pope's Epistle 2, "To a Lady: On the Character of Women," where a reference to "Magdalen's loose hair and lifted eye" serves as a transition between "naked Leda" and "sweet St. Cecilia."

Magdalene as a prostitute reenters English literature with William Blake, who suggests in "The Everlasting Gospel" that if Jesus wanted to take on the sins of the world, his mother should have been "an Harlot . . . Just such a one as Magdalen with seven devils." A character in Shaw's play *Good King Charles' Golden Days* who claims, "Nell is no worse than Mary Magdalene," is told by a proper matron, "I hope Mary Magdalen made a good end and was forgiven. . . . But I should not have asked her into my house" (act 1). The name Magdalene becomes a noun, indicating a repentant prostitute or an unwed mother. In *Man and Superman* Shaw argues that morality makes "a weeping Magdalen and an innocent child branded with shame" (act 1), exactly the situation portrayed by Wordsworth in *The Excursion* when the wanderer finds "a weeping Magdalene" by her baby's grave (6.814). Both Dylan Thomas ("The Countryman's Return," 85) and James Joyce *(Finnegans Wake)* later use the name in this sense, as does Hugh Blunt in his compilation of lives of reformed prostitutes, *The Great Magdalens* (1928). Paintings of the Magdalene are sometimes the subject of poetry; Wordsworth describes "the painted Magdalen of Le Brun . . . pale and bedropped with everflowing tears" (*The Prelude*, 3.76-80), Byron compares a sorrowful woman to "The Magdalen of Guido," and Browning writes about "Bold Castelfranco's Magdalen," penitent in her rock den.

The 20th cent. has seen a resurgence of dramatic interest in Mary Magdalene. In Paul Heyse's German drama *Mary of Magdala* she is placed in the dilemma of being able to save Jesus by giving herself to a Roman; Maurice Maeterlinck's *Mary Magdalene* is heavily indebted to Heyse. She is the focus of John Peale Bishop's *The Funeral of St. Mary Magdalene*, Florence Evans's *Mary Magdalen*, John Nicholson's *The Sainted Courtezan*, and Fernando Mota's *Maria de Magdala*, as well as of numerous plays written for religious instruction. Dorothy L. Sayers's radio dramas *The Man Born to Be King* follow medieval precedents in equating the three Marys, in giving Mary poetical lamentations, and in citing Mary's desire to kiss Jesus' feet as his body is being anointed. More recently, Mary Magdalene has played a role almost as important as Jesus in the American musicals *Jesus Christ Superstar* and *Godspell*.

Mary appears more often as a symbol of eroticism than asceticism in modern fiction. In *The Last Temptation of Christ* by Nikos Kazantzakis, she constitutes Christ's final test, symbolizing erotic love as "the sweetest the world can offer," an offer which Christ ultimately rejects. In *Report to Greco* Mary possesses life-giving power, resurrecting the Christ; however, in "The Man Who Died" D. H. Lawrence reverses that role when Jesus specifically rejects Mary and all others who want him to be God. Leopold Bruckberger has written a "biography" of her life, *Marie Madeleine: soror mea sponsa*, emphasizing the erotic asceticism with references to the Song of Solomon, and William E. Phipps, in his book *Was Jesus Married?*, concludes that Jesus married Mary Magdalene.

American poets have stressed her symbolic value. In Hart Crane's *The Bridge* the woman is asked, "Eve! Magdalene! or Mary, you?" ("Southern Cross") and is later addressed as "O Magdalene" ("National Winter Garden"); promiscuity and forgiveness are the themes of Louis Simpson's poem "The Man Who Married Magdalen." The erotic penitent reappears in Brother Antoninus's "A Savagery of Love," a canticle for the feast of St. Mary Magdalene, demonstrating the unresolved tension between the sacred and the profane which is at the heart of the legend of Magdalene, "the Venus in sackcloth."

See also JOHN THE BELOVED DISCIPLE; MARTHA; MARY, MOTHER OF JESUS.

Bibliography. Chauvin, M. J. *The Role of Mary Magdalene in Medieval Drama* (1951); Dalman, G. *Jesus Christ in the Talmud, Midrash, Zohar, and the Liturgy of the Synagogue* (1893; rpt. 1973); Davidson, C. "The Digby *Mary Magdalene* and the Magdalene Cult of the Middle Ages." *AnM* 13 (1972), 70-87; Faillon, M. *Monuments inédits sur l'Apostolat de Saint Marie-Madeleine en Provence, et sur les autres apôtres de cette contrée* (1848); Fowler, D. *The Bible in Middle English Literature* (1984), 102-21; Garth, M. *Saint Mary Magdalene in Medieval Literature* (1950); Jeffrey, D. L. "English Saints Plays." In *Medieval Drama*. Ed. N. Denny (1973); Malvern, M. *Venus in Sackcloth: The Magdalen's Origin and Metamorphoses* (1975); McCall, J. "Chaucer and the Pseudo-Origen *De Maria Magdalen:* A Preliminary Study." *Speculum* 46 (1971), 491-509; McDermott, J. "Mary Magdalene in English Literature from 1500-1650." *DA* 25 (1965), 5260.   MARGARET HANNAY

MARY, MOTHER OF JESUS Although Mary the mother of Jesus is of almost unrivaled importance in historic Christianity and her role in relation to salvation history is evidently central, she has a comparatively modest role in the Bible itself. Relationship between pertinent NT narratives and later elaborate growth of the cultus of the Virgin, a rich and complex study, may be but scantly apprehended in a sketch of literary developments alone (see R. E. Brown; A. J. Maas; M. Schmaus). The actual appearances of Mary in the NT narrative include Gabriel's Annunciation of her election as mother of the Messiah (Luke 1:26-38), Mary's visit to her cousin Elisabeth (Luke 1:39-56), the journey to Bethlehem and the Nativity (Luke 2:1-20), the presentation of Jesus at the Temple to Simeon and Anna (Luke 2:21-39), Mary's anxious discovery (with Joseph) of twelve-year-old Jesus discoursing with the elders (Luke 2:40-52), her intervention with Jesus on behalf of the wine stewards at the marriage of Cana (John 2:1-11), her visit to Jesus with his "brothers" (Matt. 12:46; Mark 3:31-35; Luke 8:19-21), her place at the foot of the cross with John, there to hear her son's last words to her (John 19:26-27), and her presence with the apostles at Pentecost (Acts 1:14). Yet in many of these narrative pericopes her appearances are cameo, and in several she is not accorded speech. The evangelists' reasons for seemingly spartan restraint in the treatment of Mary have prompted considerable theological reflection. Moreover, the silence in the biblical texts has invited manifold speculation, including apocryphal writings. Out of these, too, have evolved certain teachings of the Roman Catholic Church, which in their turn have become also the subject of literary allusion.

The central importance of Mary in Christian tradition and literature, however, is strictly biblical — her role as "mother of Jesus" or, in Elisabeth's words, "mother of my Lord" (Luke 1:43). Related to this is Mary's reference to herself in Luke's Gospel as "handmaiden of the Lord" (Luke 1:38, 48). In this regard Mary is presented in the NT as the instrument of divine grace whereby the awesome and unapproachable holiness of God condescends to be conjoined to the frailty and impermanence of fallen humanity: the centrality of the Incarnation to all Christian teaching about Jesus makes Mary, as the chosen vessel, the immediate focus of God's redeeming love for the world. Much in the manner of OT figures like Enoch (Gen. 5:22) and Noah (who "found grace in the eyes of the LORD" [Gen. 6:8]), Mary is "highly favoured" with God (Luke 1:28, 30) and particularly "blessed . . . among women" (28, 42), a blessing Mary herself recognizes explicitly in her *Magnificat* (Luke 1:46-55) as a fulfillment of God's covenant love and promise. It is evident that early associations of Jesus' conception and birth with OT messianic prophecies include notably Mary's un-

precedented virgin conception (cf. Luke 1:34). The promise in Isaiah — "Behold, a virgin shall conceive, and bear a son, and shall call his name Immanuel" (7:14) — is explicitly brought to bear in Matthew's nativity narrative (1:22-23). In this way, the virginity of Mary became one of the crucial tokens for early believers that Jesus was "the Christ" long expected, and thus a central tenet of basic Christology.

References to Mary are in other respects slight in the first centuries of the Church. It has been suggested that the first traces of special veneration for Mary as an intercessor possibly came by way of analogy to a (pre-Christian) cult of the angels, a thesis which is difficult to corroborate. What is unarguably apparent is that from the time of St. Irenaeus (d. A.D. 200) a necessity for clarifying the biblical case for Christ's human as well as divine nature, notably in combat with gnostic heresies, caused Christian apologists to draw attention to the significant place of Mary in salvation history (Irenaeus, *Adv. omnes haer.* 3.18.6-7; cf. St. Athanasius, *Contra Arianos,* 2.7.8). The formula offered by Irenaeus, that Mary is a "second Eve" (Eve being her *anti*-type, not ante-type), becomes a standard figuration in Marian literary typology:

> as the former [Eve] was led astray by an angel's discourse to fly from God after transgressing his word, so the latter [Mary] by an angel's discourse had the Gospel preached unto her that she might bear God, in obedience to his Word. And if the former was disobedient to God, yet the other was persuaded to obey God, that the Virgin Mary might become an advocate for the virgin Eve. And as mankind was bound unto death through a virgin, it is saved through a virgin; by the obedience of the one virgin the disobedience of that other is compensated. (*Adv. omnes haer.* 5.19.1)

Irenaeus, the first great theologian of the Church, is not here making a case for Mary as herself the cause of human redemption. Rather, as the chosen vessel, hers is a cooperating agency. The key to this typological reading is the opposition disobedience / obedience; consistently in Irenaeus's treatise (e.g., in his discussion of Christ as a "second Adam," 3.18.7) the crucial obedience is that of Mary's son. Typological identification with the "virgin" of Isa. 7:14 informs representations of Mary in 2nd-cent. catacomb frescoes in Rome; here, too, such representations form a credal statement about the two natures of Christ and the purity of his birth. These elements are stressed in the Apostles' Creed, Chalcedonian Council, Old Roman Baptismal Creed (St. Hippolytus), and Niceno-Constantinopolitan Creed (A.D. 381).

The apocryphal Protevangelium (known before the 16th cent. as The Gospel of St. James) is basic to many of the most important medieval legends, iconography, and ultimately theological characterization of Mary in the Middle Ages. A Jewish-Christian work of the 2nd cent., it is an infancy narrative with extensive elaborations attesting to the sanctity and special powers of Mary. It is here that the names of Mary's parents, Joachim and Anna, occur for the first time in a narrative of her conception and birth (closely paralleling that of Isaac) as well as the suggestion that Joseph was an old man, a widower with grown children, at the time of her espousal (chap. 8).

By the 4th cent., apocryphal Mary narratives had become popular among sects such as the Collyridians, whom St. Epiphanius denounced for offering sacrifices of cakes to Mary, saying: "Let Mary be held in honor. Let the Father, Son, and Holy Spirit be adored, but let no one adore Mary" (Lehner, 197-201). This position is reiterated by St. Ambrose as a matter of ordinate perspective. He first observes that it is proper for Christians to worship Christ in full appreciation of his Incarnation: "for Christ is not divided but is one; nor, when he is adored as the Son of God is he denied to have been born of the Virgin." The Incarnation is "the work of the Spirit," however; hence "the Holy Spirit also is to be adored." But, he adds emphatically, "let no one divert this [adoration] to the Virgin Mary; Mary was the temple of God, not the God of the temple. And therefore he alone is to be worshipped who is working in his temple" (*De Spiritu Sancto*, 3.11.79-80).

Continuing controversy concerning Mary's role led to various attempts by the Fathers to clarify her specific virtues. Virginity was already a high ascetic ideal for St. Jerome, St. Ambrose, and St. Augustine, each of whom readily celebrates Mary as the premiere example of virginity as a spiritual vocation (Ambrose, *De virginitate*, 2.2.6-17; Jerome, *Ep.* 39; Augustine, *De natura et gratia*, 36; *De sacra virginitate*, 4.4). Jerome wrote his influential *De perpetua virginitate Beatae Mariae adversus Helvidium* (A.D. 383) as a reply to Helvidius, who maintained (with Tertullian and Victorinus) that mention in the Gospels of the "sisters" and "brethren" of Jesus, as well as the statement that Joseph "knew her not until she had brought forth her firstborn son" (Matt. 1:25), suggests that the virginity associated with Jesus' conception and birth had evidently given way subsequently to a normal marriage relationship between Mary and Joseph. Concerned that such a view would rank virginity lower than matrimony, for Jerome an impossible hierarchy for Christians and a reversion to patriarchal Hebraism (20), he argues three positions which subsequently became central to Marian literature: (1) that Joseph was only putatively, not actually, the husband of Mary; that he was elderly and remained a virgin (3-8; 21-22); (2) that the "brethren" of the Lord were actually his cousins, children of another Mary, the wife of Cleophas (9-17); (3) that virginity is spiritually preferable to wedlock, which entails many hindrances to prayer, and that Scripture teaches the preferability of virginity and continence (19-22).

The perpetual virginity of Mary, *ante partum, in partu, et post partum*, was thus established doctrine after the 4th cent. and with it the literary characterization of Mary's relationship with Joseph determined. Augustine puts it succinctly, "as she was a mother without carnal desire, so was he a father without carnal intercourse" (*Sermo*, 51.30). For Augustine sexual sin tends to typify all forms of sin *(cupiditas);* Mary, free of sexual experience even in procreation, becomes for him uniquely free of sin among mortals (*De natura et gratia*, 36.42). An assertion of Mary's exemption from actual sin (which appears for the first time in the writings of Pelagius) was resisted in the exegesis of St. Basil (Letter 260 [PG 32.965-68]) and St. John Chrysostom (*Hom.* 4, sup. Matthew; also *Hom.* 44), among others, but was confirmed by the Council of Trent (6.23) in the 16th cent. A popular 19th-cent. summation of Catholic doctrine on this subject is found in John Henry (Cardinal) Newman's *Anglican Difficulties* (2.128-52).

Christological controversy led to Mary's most important theological title. The heretic Nestorius denied to Mary the locally popular title "Mother of God" (*Sermo*, 1.6-7 [PG 48.760-61]). This led to the Council of Ephesus (A.D. 325) proclaiming her *theotokos* (cf. Lat. *Deipara*) formally, a nomenclature which quickly spread in both Eastern and Western churches.

The *Ave Maria,* a liturgical prayer in echo of Elisabeth's greeting (Luke 1:42), entered formal worship in the Western church only gradually. It is missing in the Ambrosian fragments of the Canon of the Mass preserved in his *De sacramentis* and in early medieval canons generally. It seems first to have been used as an antiphon in the Little Office of the Blessed Virgin, and to have come into general use in the 12th cent — about the same time as the popular Marian hymn *"Salve Regina."* From this period tales of Mary's miracles became a notable feature of popular piety, as did the recitation of five psalms (the initials of which make up MARIA) and five salutations beginning *Gaude Maria Virgo* (cf. "the Five Joys of the Virgin") and use of the hymn *"Ave Maris Stella"* ("Hail, Star of the Sea").

Other doctrines, including many which are basic to Roman Catholic teaching about Mary, grew slowly in the later Middle Ages, some remaining in dispute or not officially promulgated until a later date. The idea that Mary was free of original sin (as well as actual sin) began to be considered after A.D. 1000 (it is countered in the *Catholic Homilies* of Aelfric, ca. A.D. 900). Although Marians as ardent as St. Bernard of Clairvaux, St. Albert the Great, St. Thomas Aquinas, and St. Bonaventure doubted the merit of such an assertion, the support of William of Ware and Duns Scotus Erigena (ca. 1300) laid foundations for the doctrine later encouraged by the Franciscan Pope Sixtus IV (1476) and approved as dogma by Pope Pius IX in 1854 *("Ineffabilis Deus")*. For its supporters, this doctrine, which came to be known as the Immaculate Conception of Mary, had already been anticipated in celebrations of the feast of her conception in Naples and Ireland in the 9th cent., and in England by the late 11th cent. In the 13th and 14th cents. teaching about Mary's immaculate conception was prominent among Franciscans in England, but bitterly opposed by the Dominicans; by the 17th cent., with additional support from the Jesuits and Carmelites, the Feast of the Immaculate Conception (Dec. 8) and its general belief had become normative among Catholics.

The apocryphal *Transitus Mariae* (late 5th cent.), condemned by Pope Gelasius (d. 496), provides the first narrative attestation of the Assumption of the Virgin, a parallel to the biblical Ascension of Christ. Supported in the Middle Ages by the pseudo-Augustinian *De Assumptione Virginis*, it became formal doctrine only in 1950 (Pope Pius XII: DS 3900-3904). The *Transitus* also contains an account of numerous miracles of the Virgin, forerunners to those which feature in late medieval legendaries and by then an important expression of Marian devotion. The doctrine that Mary is "Redemptrix" — a title for her which appears sporadically after the 9th cent. in Italy, is found in 10th-cent. MS prayers from Salisbury; replaced by "Co-Redemptrix" in the 15th cent., it is not (except incidentally) of significance in postmedieval literary allusion. Her title "Queen of Heaven," though borrowed from non-Christian mythology, appears from the 15th cent. on in poems and hymns, and was formally recognized by Pope Pius XII in 1954 (*Ad Caeli Reginam*, DS 3913-17).

Mary appears regularly in OE literature. A poem ascribed to Cynewulf accords her an elaborate dialogue with Joseph concerning the surpriseful pregnancy, and hails her in an apostrophe as "glory of this middle world," "the purest woman to be found on earth," and "bride / Of him that rules the celestial sphere" (*Christ II*, 274-80). In the seventh of the *Advent Lyrics* of the Exeter Book a similar dialogue is elaborated, in which Mary carries most of the poem's 49 lines. The fourth *Advent* lyric is in the form of an answer Mary gives to a question about the mystery of the Virgin Birth, and Mary's perpetual virginity *("efne unwemme a gehealdan")* is heralded in lyric no. 9. St. Aldhelm, the Venerable Bede, and Alcuin exhibit similar praises.

Yet is is not until the 13th cent. that literary tributes in English to Mary really begin to flourish. Franciscan devotion to Mary in particular was expressed in scores of lyrics and carols. Latin hymns such as the *"Stabat Iuxta Christi Crucem"* (Dreves, *Analecta Hymnica*, 8.55) and the *"Mater Salutaris"* (cf. Dreves, 31.207-08) were translated into the vernacular ("þat leueli leor wid spald ischent" [C. Brown, *English Lyrics of the XIIIth Century*, no. 4; "Seinte mari, moder milde" [Brown, no. 16]) and numerous poems began to appear on Marian subjects, e.g., "For on þat is so feir and brist" ("For one that is so fair and bright"), a *"Stella Maris"* poem (Brown, no. 17), and "A Prayer of the Five Joys" (Brown, no. 18). While on the Continent Marian devotion could enumerate from seven to as many as fifteen "joys" of the Virgin, among

the Franciscans in England the traditional number was five: the Annunciation, Nativity, Resurrection, Ascension, and her own Assumption (cf. Brown, no. 41; cf. Brown, *Religious Lyrics of the XIVth Century*, nos. 11, 26, 31). General devotional poems to the Virgin abound in this period, both in Anglo-Norman French (see Jeffrey and Levy) and in English (Brown, *XIIIth Century*, nos. 31, 61; *XIVth Century*, nos. 32, 58, 112). Notable are the poetic prayers to her, usually as intercessor with her son (*XIIIth Century*, no. 55; *XIVth Century*, no. 16). She is the subject of several surviving poetic prayers of repentance (*XIIIth Century*, nos. 32, 65), appeals for aid in the hour of death (*XIIIth Century*, no. 68), and in one extended adoration she is addressed as "heuene quene" (*XIIIth Century*, no. 60).

Complementary narratives flourish in the same period. The *Cursor Mundi*, a combined universal history and metrical Bible, treats her legendary as well as canonical life at length, dividing it according to the five feast days devoted to her in the *sanctorale:* Conception (Dec. 8), *CM* 10.123-574; Nativity (Sept. 8), *CM* 10.575-782; Annunciation (Apr. 7), *CM* 10.783-94; Purification (Feb. 2), *CM* 11.287-372; Assumption (Aug. 15), *CM* 20.11-848. Visible in the *Cursor Mundi* treatment is an extensive typology for Mary built directly upon OT antetypes. Some elements in this go back to 4th-cent. exegesis, e.g., the connection which Ambrose makes between the Hebrew form of her name, "Miriam," and her role as a "second Miriam," leading the heavenly choirs of virgins in songs of praise for the salvation of humankind (*De virginitate*, 2.2.17).

A great deal of medieval Marian iconography was codified in the early 13th cent. by St. Anthony of Padua, who sees Mary as the natural human channel for devotion to the Passion of Christ. In the first place she is a symbol for the Church, the *Sponsa* of Christ; hence she can be seen as the *flos campi*, the "flower of the field" or "lily of the valley" (Song 2:1), the *hortus conclusus* or "garden enclosed" (Song 4:12) by walls of humility and poverty, and the Temple not of Solomon but of the Messiah (*In Domenica XV post Pentecosten*, 2.453; *Sermo in Purificatione Sanctae Mariae*, 722). She is the Tower of David, the Refuge of Sinners foreshadowed by the cities of refuge which God commanded to be built (Num. 35:13); and she is a second Esther as Jesus is a second King Ahasuerus, who for her loyalty, intercession on behalf of her people, and devotion to her king will be crowned by her triumphant Lord as Queen of Heaven (*Sermo Domenica 2 in Quadragesima*, 1.91); *In Assumptione Sanctae Mariae Virginis*, 3.732). Her perpetual virginity is, in Anthony's exegesis, anticipated in the burning bush of Moses which burned without being consumed (Exod. 3:2), the fleece of Gideon which, as a sign of God's election, remained untouched by the nighttime dew (Judg. 6:37-38), and the "closed gate" of Ezek. 44:2, which after being entered by "the LORD God of

Israel" was never again to be used. Other symbols relating to her virginity include the mountain from which, without hands, is hewn the little stone which destroys the empires of this world (Dan. 2:34), the "rod out of the root of Jesse" (Isa. 11:1) which, like Aaron's, miraculously blooms (*Sermo in Purificatione Sanctae Mariae,* 3.722; *In Domenica XXII post Pentecosten,* 2.545, 800; *In Nativitate Beatae Mariae Virginis,* 3.696; *In Annunciatione Sanctae Mariae Virginis,* 3.836; *In Assumptione Sanctae Mariae Virginis,* 3.732). Other figures were constantly added to this list: Bonaventure's *"dulce lumen"* ("sweet light") because, he says, she is like the rising sun without which we could not apprehend the Incarnate Word (*De Nativitate Beatae Virginis Mariae,* Sermo, 2.708-09); her comparison with Lady Wisdom (Prov. 8:22-31), as in the fourth lesson for her Office (Dec. 10), and by Pope Pius IX (*"Ineffabilis Deus"*); Sarah, Deborah, and "strong Judith," as well as the Ark of the Covenant and throne of Solomon, are all used as antetypes of the Virgin in late medieval literature. (In the Irish litany of the 9th cent. where Jesus appears consistently as "Jesus macMary" she is also, courtesy of St. Bernard *[Super Missus Est],* the "Ladder of Heaven.") Also drawing on Song of Songs, St. Bernard of Clairvaux's *"rosa sine spina,"* rose without thorns, becomes as frequent a symbol for her loveliness as the lily is for her purity (e.g., R. Greene, *Early English Carols,* no. 174, "A roose hath borne a lilly white"; cf. nos. 175, 176), and even the prophecy of Balaam to Balak is seen as prefiguration (Greene, nos. 182, 190). Dante's address in the *Paradiso,* borrowed from Bernard, is *Figlia del tuo figlio,* "daughter of thy son" (a term borrowed again by T. S. Eliot in "Dry Salvages," 4.9). Finally, in one of the most important papal announcements of the Middle Ages, the *"Unam Sanctam"* of Pope Boniface VIII (1302), Boniface makes the *Sponsa* of Song of Songs 6:8 to stand officially for Mary as representative of the Church, thus coloring and amplifying much of the other typology.

By the late 15th cent., when the carol was becoming a prominent form, most of these antetypes occur regularly in the carols of poets such as the Franciscan James Ryman (see Greene, nos. 192, 193, and 194). Ryman amplifies the full litany of antetypes with analogies or similes such as:

> As the sonne beame goth thurgh the glas,
> Thurgh thy bodie so he did pas
> Taking nature as his wille was
> *Dei genetrix pia.*

Ryman illustrates the way in which the messianic focus of an elaborate list of typologies could shift toward Mary. In his next stanzas:

> In the is complete the prophecye
> Of alle the prophetes, by and by,

> That seide a mayde shulde bere Messye,
> *Dei genetrix pia.*

> O lady free, O quene of blis,
> Of thy conforte lete vs not mys,
> For why thy name nowe called is
> *Dei genetrix pia.*

> Lete thy mercy bothe springe and sprede;
> Forsake vs not for oure mysdede,
> But oute of drede to blis vs lede,
> *Dei genetrix pia.*

Prayer to the Virgin is in fact the prime reason for a large percentage of vernacular English lyrics and carols, and even so strict a biblicist as John Wyclif thought it "impossible that we should obtain the reward of heaven without the help of Mary. There is no sex or age," he continues, "no rank or position of anyone in the human race which has no need to call upon the help of the Holy Virgin" (*Sermones,* 1.200, ed. Lechler). Chaucer accords to his Second Nun's prologue her eloquent devotion to the Virgin, and his "Prière a Nostre Dame" (or "ABC of Our Lady") is an alphabetic 84-line penitential appeal, incorporating much of the traditional typology (as also does Lydgate's "Queen of Heaven, of Hell eke Empresse"). Like Wyclif, however, Chaucer steers clear of the more extravagant noncanonical legends. In Chaucer's *Prioress's Tale,* a sentimental and anti-Semitic melodrama in which the putative child-martyr sings the *alma redemptoris mater* (cf. Brown, *Religious Lyrics of the XIVth Century,* no. 19) even after his murder, Chaucer seems to satirize misfocused piety.

Typical of the large legendary literature are many tales of the *Gesta Romanorum, Speculum Laicorum,* and *Alphabetum Narrationum* —compilations of narrative designed to provide materials for preachers. In a representative tale from the *Alphabetum,* Mary is said to have come along just as a thief, who "had a grete devocion to our Ladie," was being hanged for his crimes. She "held hym up iij dayes, hur awn handis, so þat he felid no sare." When the justices came by they apparently perceived that "he had not been wele hanged." As they prepared to amend their handiwork with a sword, "our Lady putt it away with hur hand, so þat þai noyed hym noght." The thief then recounts how Mary saved him because of his devotion to her, and they let him go to live in an abbey happily ever after, there to serve "our Ladie ewhils he liffid" (ed. M. M. Banks, no. 464).

The Corpus Christi drama is more conservative. It offers nothing comparable even to Philippe de Mézières's pageant, the *Presentation of the Virgin* (ed. W. Coleman), based on the *Protevangelium* and subsequent legendary, let alone the more venturesome apocrypha of Rutebeuf's *Le miracle de Theophile* (ca. 1275) or the famous 14th-cent. collection of forty dramatic *Miracles de Nostre Dame par personnages* (e.g., G. Paris and V. Robert). In the English cycle plays Mary is found in scenes predicated for the most part upon canonical narrative — Annunciation, Nativity, Jesus at the Temple, Cana, and the Cross. All of these are found in the four major cycles — Towneley, York, N-Town, and Chester. N-Town, which has the most expansive treatment of Marian narrative, evidently once contained a play of St. Anne, and records at Lincoln indicate that a whole Marian cycle, now lost, was performed there on St. Anne's day (July 26). (Topics included "The Barrenness of Anna," "Mary in the Temple," and "Mary's Betrothal" — all tracing ultimately to the Protevangelium.) N-Town includes in its plays "St. Thomas of India," which involves an analogous "doubting" of Thomas as he watches Mary's ascension; this text is based upon the apocryphal Gospel of Nicodemus.) And though the prophet plays typically subordinate Marian messianic prophecy to that referring to Jesus himself (e.g., Chester), the N-Town cycle, which bears considerable evidence of Franciscan interpolations, has thirteen prophets and thirteen kings from a "genealogy of Mary," all who speak prophetically of the coming of the Virgin ("Jesse Root"). N-Town's "Assumption of the Virgin," immediately preceding the final "Domesday" play, includes both her Ascension and Coronation. The concluding speeches of Dominus ("the Lord") declare a full-orbed mariology:

Dominus:
arys now my dowe . my nehebour and my swete frende
tabernacle of Joye . vessel of lyf . hefnely temple to
    reyn
ye schal haue the blysse wyth me moder . that hath
    none end
Ffor as ye were clene in erthe . of alle synnys greyn
so schul ye reyne in hefne clennest in mend. . . .
A-bouen hefnys moder assende than we
In endles blysse for to be.

Michael:
Hefne and erthe now injoye may ye
Ffor god throw mary is mad manny frend
(Et hic assendent in celum cantantibus organis.)
Assumpta es maria in celum.

Dominus:
Yow to worchepe moder . it likyth the hol trinyte
Wherfore I crowne you here . in this kyndam of glory
of alle my chosyn . thus schul ye clepyd be
qwen of hefne . and moder of mercy.

Michael:
Now blysid be youre namys we cry
ffor this holy assumpcyon . alle hefne makyth melody.

If Marian devotion in England crested in the 15th cent., the wave was still being felt in Scotland half a century later. Dunbar's "Ros Mary: Ane Ballat of Our Lady" and "Ane Ballat of Our Lady" are the fulsome concordances of typology one might expect from a Franciscan poet; Henryson's "O Lady leal and lovesomest" is a simpler poem anticipating the lyricism of Henry

Constable's late 16th-cent. sonnet, "In that (O Queen of Queens) thy birth was free." Catholic convert Richard Crashaw, a "canon of Loretto," wrote several poems to the Virgin, including one "On the Glorious Assumption of the Blessed Virgin," a free translation of the hymn *"O Gloriosa Domina"* and a Latin poem for the Feast of the Immaculate Conception, *"Natalis Principis Mariae."*

Perhaps if England had been more influenced by Wyclif and Luther than by Calvin and Cromwell, even Reformation poets might have shied away less sharply from Mary as a subject for poetry. Calvin's central contention that Mary's "virtues and all her excellences are nothing other than the generosity of God" (*New Testament Comms.* 1.22) leads him to insist that it "is quite absurd to teach that we are to seek from her anything which she receives otherwise than we do ourselves" (cf. a similar formulation in St. Thomas Aquinas, *Summa Theol.* 3.2.2.3). Calvin consistently resists the parallel veneration of Mary "which has resulted in Christ being shoved down the bench, so to say, while Mary is given the place of honor" (*New Testament Comms.* 1.32-33). Yet he adds: "To this day we cannot enjoy the blessing brought to us in Christ without thinking at the same time of that which God gave as adornment and honor to Mary, in willing her to be the mother of his only-begotten Son" (32). The iconoclasm which denigrated Mary and largely banished her from English literature after the 1540s especially is more extreme (Phillips, 36, 81). Crowning the general iconoclasm was secularizing appropriation by Elizabeth I, the "Virgin Queen," of many traditional Marian symbols (Rose, Star, Moon, etc.). Thus, though in Anglican worship Mary was not excluded (the *Magnificat* continued be recited each day at Evensong), Protestant poets of the 16th and 17th cents. have less to say about Mary. In all the religious poetry of George Herbert, e.g., she is mentioned only in a two-line anagram "Mary / Army": "How well her name an *Army* doth present / In whom the Lord of Hosts did pitch his tent!" Milton's Mary is that of the canonical Bible. In *Paradise Regained* Milton builds up a sense of her role in the narrative by having her recount the chief events of her (canonical) life since the Annunciation, giving content to the scriptural notation "And Mary kept all these things and pondered them in her heart" (*PR* 2.60-108). But postbiblical doctrines of the Catholic Church are all absent from his text.

The 18th cent., with its tension-filled religious controversy and general hostility to any suspicion of "Papism" (Jesuit spirituality in particular) made little in the way of additional contribution to the literature. Even Catholic poets (e.g., Alexander Pope) eschew the subject. If by the beginning of the 19th cent. there is a sea-change, it owes in part to the same spirit of liberalism which agitated for the Roman Catholic Relief Act of 1829. Sir Walter Scott's *"Ave Maria!* Maiden mild!" in Canto 3 of his *Lady of the Lake,* and William Wordsworth's "The Virgin" (*Ecclesiastical Sonnets,* 2.25) are celebrations of ideal human nature, though each makes an explicit effort to recognize traditional Catholic teaching. In Wordsworth's poem the Immaculate Conception is suggested:

> Mother! Whose virgin bosom was uncrost
> With the least shade of thought to sin allied;
> Woman! Above all women glorified,
> Our tainted nature's solitary boast. . . .

Coleridge's younger cousin Mary Coleridge (1861-1907) treats Mary's representative role in such a way as to create a more radical political statement:

> Mother of God! no lady thou:
> Common woman of common earth!
> Our Lady ladies call thee now,
> But Christ was never of gentle birth;
> A common man of the common earth.
>
> For God's ways are not as our ways.
> The noblest lady in the land
> Would have given up half her days,
> Would have cut off her right hand
> To bear the Child that was God of the land.
>
> Never a lady did He choose,
> Only a maid of low degree,
> So humble she might not refuse
> The carpenter of Galilee.
> A daughter of the people, she.
>
> Out she sang the song of her heart.
> Never a lady so had sung.
> She knew no letters, had no art;
> To all mankind, in woman' tongue
> Hath Israelitish Mary sung.
>
> And still for men to come she sings,
> Nor shall her singing pass away.
> *"He hath filled the hungry with good things"* —
> O listen, lords and ladies gay! —
> *"And the rich He hath sent empty away."*

After the conversion of John Henry (Cardinal) Newman in 1845, the effect of the Oxford Movement among Anglicans and in English culture generally produced a signal recrudescence of interest in Mary. Much of this, and some of the best writing, came from new converts (e.g., Eric Gill, Lionel Johnson, G. K. Chesterton, and Gerard Manley Hopkins). Newman's close friend (and fellow priest of the Church of England) Edward Caswall translated Marian hymns and produced also a volume of poetry entitled *The Masque of Mary and Other Poems* shortly after his conversion to Catholicism in 1847. Catholic-born Oscar Wilde, though not religious in practice through much of his life, wrote traditional orisons to Mary ("San Miniato"; *"Ave Maria Gratia Plena"*). And from the pre-Raphaelite movement issued romanticized evocations of Mary's "ponderings" such as Dante Gabriel Rossetti's "Mary's Girlhood" (cf. his *"Ave"*):

> This is the blessèd Mary, pre-elect
>   God's virgin. Gone is a great while, and she
>   Dwelt young in Nazareth of Galilee.

> Unto God's will she brought devout respect
> Profound simplicity of intellect.
>   And supreme patience. From her mother's knee
>   Faithful and hopeful; wise in charity;
> Strong in grave peace; in pity circumspect.
>
> So held she through her girlhood; as it were
>   An angel-watered lily, that near God
>   Grows and is quiet. Till, one day at home
> She woke in her white bed, and had no fear
>   At all — yet wept till sunshine, and felt awed:
>   Because the fulness of the time was come.

Sublimation of Mary in 19th-cent. fiction would seem to account for female figures such as the Madonna figure in George Eliot's novel *Romola* (cf. Dickens's Ada in *Bleak House* and Amy in *Little Dorrit*). More telling, perhaps, is the explanation Ruskin gives to romantic nostalgia for her former place in the European mythos. Writing in his *Fors Clavigera* (Letter 41; cf. *Stones of Venice*, 2.3.39-40) Ruskin says:

> To the common Protestant mind the dignities ascribed to the Madonna have been always a violent offence; they are one of the parts of the Catholic faith which are openest to reasonable dispute, and least comprehensible by the average realistic and materialist temper of the Reformation.
>
> But after the most careful examination, neither as adversary nor as friend, of the influences of Catholicism for good and evil, I am persuaded that the worship of the Madonna has been one of its noblest and most vital graces, and has never been otherwise than productive of true holiness of life and purity of character. I do not enter into any question as to the truth or fallacy of the idea; I no more wish to defend the historical or theological position of the Madonna than that of St. Michael or St. Christopher; but I am certain that to the habit of reverent belief in, and contemplation of, the character ascribed to the heavenly hierarchies, we must ascribe the highest results yet achieved in human nature.

In the 20th cent. the theme of a modern Mary bearing a divine child, or one believed by the mother and others to have been miraculously conceived, is almost tediously common. A prominent example is John Barth's *Giles Goat-Boy, or, The Revised New Syllabus* (1966) in which the hero's mother, Miss Virginia Hector, who repeatedly assures people that she has never "gone all the way" with anyone, is seduced and raped by a giant computer. To escape the persecution of the Chancellor of the University, who, Herod-like, wishes the child destroyed, Virginia takes him away to raise him, disguised as a goat, on the college agricultural station (the goat is a parody of the Lamb of God). Those modern retellings of Gospel narrative that follow the Gospel fairly closely do least with their Mary figures (e.g., B. P. Galdos, *Nazarin* [1895], Antonio Fogazzaro, *The Saint* [1905], Elizabeth S. Phelps Ward, *A Singular Life* [1895], Elizabeth Linton, *Joshua Davidson* [1872]). It has been noted that for modern fiction writers Mary "is an awkward figure to deal with.

If she is present in a modern transfiguration, then realism will not permit her to be a virgin; but if she is not a virgin then she is no longer the venerated object of cultic adoration. It is much simpler to ignore her. In the Marxist-oriented novels there is no mother figure at all" (T. Ziolkowski, *Fictional Transfiguration of Jesus* [1972], 283). Yet faded memory, if not nostalgia, is a prerequisite for popular diabolical parallels such as the cinematic *Rosemary's Baby.*

Perhaps the best traditional poem on Mary published in the 20th cent. (1918; written in the 1870s) remains Hopkins's *"Rosa Mystica."* A poem expressing at once both evident devotion and great restraint, it probes the mystery of a traditional element in her typology and iconography (the "Rose" of the Song of Songs) as a way of re-establishing the meaning of the biblical Mary and her role in the divine plan of salvation:

> Is Mary the rose, then? Mary the tree?
> But the blossom,the blossom there, who can it be? —
> Who can her rose be? It could be but one:
> Christ Jesus, our Lord, her God and her son.
> *In the gardens of God, in the daylight divine*
> *Shew me thy son, mother, mother of mine.*

Among the most important modern collections of poems centered on Mary is *Pieta* (1966) by R. S. Thomas, a rector in the Church of Wales, also of a strikingly traditional character.

See also ANNUNCIATION; BRIDE, BRIDEGROOM; INCARNATION; JOSEPH THE CARPENTER; *MAGNIFICAT;* NATIVITY.

Bibliography. Balic, K. *Duns Scoti Theologiae Marianae elementa* (1933); Boyd, B. M. "Middle English Miracles of the Virgin: Independent Tales in Verse." *DA* 16 (1956), 334; Brady, I. "The Development of the Doctrine of the Immaculate Conception in the 14th century after Aureoli." *FranS* 15 (1955), 175ff.; Brown, R. E., et al., eds. *Mary in the New Testament* (1978); Coletti, T. "Devotional Iconography in the N-Town Marian Plays." *CompD* 11 (1975), 22-44; Crowne, J. V. "Middle English Poems on the Joys and on the Compassion of the Blessed Virgin Mary." *Catholic University Bulletin* 8 (1902), 304-14; Cunningham, F. L. B. "The Relationship between Mary and the Church in Medieval Thought." *Marian Studies* 9 (1958), 52-78; Ebel, U. *Das altromanische Mirakel* (1965); Emmen, A. "Einführung in die Mariologie der Oxforder Franziskanerschule." *FrSt* 39 (1957), 99ff.; Gnerro, M. L. "Marian Typology and Milton's Heavenly Muse." *PPMRC* 2 (1977), 39-48; Harlow, C. G. "The Old English Advent VII and the 'Doubting of Mary' Tradition." *Leeds Studies in English* 16 (1985), 101-17; Heider, A. B. *The Blessed Virgin Mary in Early Christian Latin Poetry* (1918); Heller, S. R. "The Characterization of the Virgin Mary in Four 13th Century Narrative Collections. . ." *DAI* 36 (1975), 2190A; Horan, T. J. "The Figure of Mary in *Finnegans Wake.*" *DAI* 37 (1976), 2174A; Jeffrey, D. L. *The Early English Lyric and Franciscan Spirituality* (1975); Jeffrey, D. L., and B. Levy, eds. *The Anglo-Norman Lyric* (1990); Lehner, R. *Die Marienverehrung in den ersten Jahrhunderten* (1866); Lennerz, H. *De Beata Virgine Tractatus Dogmaticus* (1957); Levi d'Anacona, M. *The Iconography of the Immaculate Conception in the Middle Ages and Early Renaissance* (1957); Luke, C. *The Role of the Virgin Mary in the Coventry, York, Chester and Towneley Cycles* (1933); Maas, A. J. "Virgin Mary." *The Catholic Encyclopedia* (1912), 15.464-72; Nesbitt, J. "Mary in the Literature of the Anglo-Saxon Period." *American Ecclesiastical Review* 40 (1909), 513-24; Neumann, C. W. *The Virgin Mary in the Works of Saint Ambrose* (1962); Newman, J. H. *Essay on the Development of Christian Doctrine* (1845); Oberman, H. *The Harvest of Medieval Theology* (1963; 1967), 281-322; Pecheux, M. C. "The Concept of the Second Eve in *Paradise Lost.*" *PMLA* 75 (1960), 359-66; Phillips, J. *The Reformation of Images: Destruction of Art in England 1535-1660* (1973); Sabine, M. "Crashaw and the Feminine Animus: Patterns of Self-Sacrifice in Two of His Devotional Poems." *JDJ* 4 (1985), 69-94; Schmaus, M. "Mariology." In *Concise "Sacramentum Mundi."* Ed. K. Rahner (1975), 893-901; Seaton, H. J. Q. "Marian Imagery in the Old English Writings." *DA* 24 (1964), 2910-12; Vriend, J. *The Blessed Virgin Mary in the Medieval Drama of England, with Additional Studies in Middle English Literature* (1928); Wade, C. L. "The Middle English Marian Lyric." *DAI* 43 (1982), 1143A.

MASHAL In Hebrew a *mashal* is almost any tropic utterance or writing. Hence epigram, apothegm, simile, metaphor, proverb, fable, and parable are forms of *mashal;* the term can even signify something like the Eng. *byword,* as when Israel is said, metonymically, to be a byword to the nations of the world (Deut. 28:37; 1 Kings 9:7). Etiological and onomastic narratives, such as the story of Jacob's wrestling with the angel at the ford of the Jabbok (Gen. 32:24-32), take the form of *mashal.* In modern colloquial use the term is often attached to apothegm or proverb, appearing as Yiddish *maschil* or *mosh'l* —not to be confused with *mazel,* "luck" (cf. A. M. Klein, *The Psalter of Avram Haktani* [*Collected Poems*, 1974], 210).

See also PARABLE.

Bibliography. Von Rad, G. *Wisdom in Israel* (1972).

MASS *See* EUCHARIST.

MATTHEW Matthew was one of the original disciples of Jesus, a Galilean tax collector who left everything to follow Jesus (Matt. 9:9). Elsewhere in the NT he is called Levi (Mark 2:14; Luke 5:27-29), and in subsequent Christian tradition he is sometimes referred to as "Matthew the Levite."

The first Gospel is traditionally attributed to Matthew. It has been suggested that, as a tax collector, he would have been not only literate but familiar with the use of shorthand and thus able to preserve Jesus' teaching in considerable detail (R. H. Gundry, *The Use of the Old Testament in St. Matthew's Gospel* [1967], 181-85). His name is linked spuriously to a Latin pseudo-gospel of the 3rd or 4th cent. (which contains such popular apocryphal legends as that of the attendant midwives in the Nativity story).

Most scholars believe that Matthew based his work on

the Gospel of Mark together with other traditions of the life and teaching of Jesus. He usually reduces Mark's vivid narratives to economical summaries in order to focus attention on their theological significance. The book is carefully structured, and demonstrates a liking for balanced groups of narratives, often in threes. The teaching material is far more extensive than in Mark, much of it grouped into five long discourses, each with a consistent theme, concluded by a stereotyped formula: thus, the Sermon on the Mount, in chaps. 5–7, is a discourse on discipleship, with its concluding formula in 7:28; the other discourses are found in chaps. 10, 13, 18, and 24–25.

Matthew's is above all the Gospel of fulfillment. He delights in introducing OT texts with the formula, "that it might be fulfilled which was spoken by the prophet, saying. . . ." He weaves OT allusions into much of his narrative to draw out typological connections between Jesus and the life and hopes of Israel. He presents Jesus as the true Israel and his Church as the chosen people of God, drawn from all nations. Thus an intensely Jewish Gospel is at the same time remarkable for its universal sympathies. Eusebius is representative among early commentators in observing of Matthew that he preached first to the "Hebrews," and then to the world (*Hist. eccl.* 3.24.6).

Of the traditional symbols routinely ascribed to the four evangelists (lion, ox, man, and eagle [cf. Ezek. 1:4-13]), Matthew's is normally the man (e.g., Picinelli, *Mundus Symbolicus*). Since he is a publican (Matt. 9:10) or tax collector, one of Matthew's iconographic attributes is a money bag. He is sometimes depicted with a scroll reading *Sanctam ecclesiam catholicam, sanctorum communionem* ("the holy catholic church, the communion of saints"), the phrase assigned him in dramatized Apostles' Creeds. Like most of the disciples he has cameo appearances in the ME Corpus Christi drama; in N-Town's "Prologue of the Doctors" his conversion is celebrated:

mathew the Apostel and Also evangelyst
that was clep y to þe fflok of gostly conuersacioun
From thyrknes of concyens þat ȝe were in ffest
. . . that ffled all carnell temptacion. (28.B.25-28)

But though Matthew's Gospel is of all four the most quoted by English authors, the evangelist himself appears infrequently in lists of *dramatis personae*.

In the fourth radio play of Dorothy Sayers's *The Man Born to Be King* (1943), however, Matthew the Tax Collector has a significant role. Sayers describes him, in her Introduction to the published text, as "a contemptible little quisling official, fleecing his own countrymen in the service of the occupying power and enriching himself in the process, until something came to change his heart." For the purposes of her dramatic reenactment ("Heirs to the Kingdom") of his role in the Gospel story, she describes him as having:

oily black hair and rapacious little hands, and though his common little soul has been converted as thoroughly as that of any Salvation Army penitent, his common little wits are in full working order. He has been swept off his feet by a heavenly kindness and beauty of mind which had never dawned, even as a possibility, on his sordid experience. He has no opinion of himself — he never had — but he is expanding and revelling in the sheer ecstasy of not being trodden upon. He has gleefully thrown away all his worldly goods — but, all the same, his professional instincts are shocked by financial stupidity and appealed to by financial astuteness. He thinks the Parable of the Unjust Steward is a frightfully funny story. He gives the account of his own conversion with the utmost sincerity and without any sort of self-consciousness. He is having a wonderful time and Jesus is wonderful, and he wants everybody to know it. Jesus likes Matthew very much.

A comparably vivid portrait of Matthew is afforded in Mikhail Bulghakov's *The Master and Margarita,* in which as a Palestinian historian and newsgatherer as well as "interpreter" of current events, Matthew the Levite has a central role, contributing significantly to Bulghakov's satire on the writing of "history" in Stalinist Russia.

See also APOSTLE.   R. T. FRANCE

MEASURE FOR MEASURE   *See* JUDGE NOT.

MEEK AS MOSES   An expression derived from the description of Moses at Num. 12:30.
  See also MEEK SHALL INHERIT THE EARTH; MOSES.

MEEK SHALL INHERIT THE EARTH   The phrase "the meek shall inherit the earth" is found in Ps. 37:11 and Matt. 5:5. In both cases the passage ties into the themes of poverty and oppression and God's eventual vindication.

Meekness in Scripture is the quality of humility, self-effacement, or gentleness which accepts personal abuse without retaliation or harshness. In this Moses in Num. 12:3 is the archetypal example in that he remains silent in the face of Aaron's and Miriam's accusations. Such non-retaliation may be due to inner restraint (as with Moses) or it may be due to external weakness, for the meek are the oppressed, the poor sufferers who are the victims of others' exploitation (Job 24:4; Ps. 37:14; Isa. 32:7). Since the meek cannot defend themselves, God will defend them (Exod. 22:21-24; Deut. 24:14-15; Pss. 25:9; 34:2; 149:4; Prov. 31:9, 20; Amos 2:7). This declared readiness of God to stand up for the meek (so evident in Moses' case) meant that those pious people in trouble or suffering who humbly hoped in God's deliverance appropriated this title for themselves as a favorite self-designation and claim upon God (Pss. 40:17; 102 [title]; Isa. 41:17; Zeph. 2:3). The basis of all this behavior is a confident expectation that *God* will bring salvation; thus it is not a product of human violence and scheming.

There is one direction in which this concept expands, namely the meekness of Christ. In Zech. 9:9 the messianic king is seen as a person of peace and gentleness rather than violence and war. This was picked up in the NT as a characteristic of Jesus, whose kingdom comes through peace, not violence (Matt. 11:29; 21:5; 2 Cor. 10:1), and thus a virtue to be imitated by his followers, who should likewise be characterized by gentleness and nonretaliation (Gal. 5:23; 1 Tim. 3:3; James 3:13, 17; 1 Pet. 3:4, 16).

The meek, then, are those who are oppressed or despised, the dispossessed physically or socially. They have only God to trust in, and they look to him for vindication as they live humbly and gently in the world. These "shall inherit the earth." The image is that of possessing the land of Israel (as in Deut. 4:1; 16:20; Ps. 68:36), but now the old image of God's giving Palestine to Israel has been transformed into a gift of the messianic kingdom (in Ps. 37) or the kingdom of God (Matt. 5). The message to the sufferer is that his or her humble dependence on God and obedience to God's commands (which is the message of the Sermon on the Mount) will not go unrewarded. God will deliver them from their oppression and reward their gentle nonretaliation, for theirs is his coming kingdom.

Patristic tradition for the most part simply confirms the obvious sense of the biblical writers. St. Augustine is typical: "The meek are those who yield to acts of wickedness, and do not resist evil, but overcome evil with good. Let those, then, who are not meek quarrel and fight for earthly and temporal things; but 'blessed are the meek, for they shall by inheritance possess the earth', from which they cannot be driven out" (*De sermone Domini in Monte*, 2.4). Fourteenth-cent. English spiritual writer Walter Hilton devotes a substantial portion of his *Ladder of Perfection* to defining meekness as the opposite of pride. Essentially, meekness is neither extreme, abject humility nor ostentation, but candid reflection on the truth about oneself (pt. 1). Hilton then distinguishes two types of meekness: one is obtained by the "operation of intellect" in examination of conscience, the other as "a special gift of love." It is the latter which is ultimately to be preferred, arising not merely from the necessity of an honest self-assessment, but from a true "self-forgetfulness," that higher Wisdom which comes when the mind is fully preoccupied with God's magnificence and eternal glory. Meekness is, in effect, the good sense of those who know that this world is not their home. In this respect, Hilton's "inheritance" is more spiritualized than that of Augustine. Chaucer's Knight in the *General Prologue* to *The Canterbury Tales* is described as a valiant warrior who, "though that he were worthy, he was wys, / And of his port as meeke as is a mayde" (*CT* 1.68-69). His chaste meekness is an attribute or function of his wisdom, and similarly declares his ultimate love and pilgrim spirit.

Matthew Henry, in his *Comm. on the Whole Bible* (5.50), defines the "meek" as those who are truly obedient to God, and

gentle towards all men (Titus 3:2); who can bear provocation without being inflamed by it; are either silent, or return a soft answer; and who can show their displeasure when there is occasion for it, without being transported into any indecencies; who can be cool when others are hot; and in their patience keep possession of their own souls when they can hardly keep possession of anything else.

Henry argues that the meek are blessed even in this world, for like Jesus himself they have learned to bear a mild yoke (Matt. 11:29). As to their inheriting the earth, which Henry notes is an echo of Ps. 37:11 and "the only express temporal promise in all the New Testament," he observes: "Meekness, however ridiculed and run down, has a real tendency to promote our health, wealth, comfort, and safety, even in this world. The meek and quiet are observed to live the most easy lives, compared with the froward and turbulent" (ibid.) Few biblical precepts, nonetheless, have gone down less well with modern intellectuals from Blake to Joyce, among whom Nietzsche and his admirers have been notably prominent.

Among American writers Theodore Dreiser articulates the objection succinctly: "Unless one acted for oneself, upon some stern conclusion nurtured within, one might rot and die spiritually. Nature did not care. 'Blessed be the meek' — yes. Blessed be the strong, rather, for they made their own happiness" ("Free"). G. B. Shaw's Eve (echoing parodically Homer's Athena) in *Back to Methuselah* remarks sardonically: "The clever ones were always my favorites. The diggers and the fighters have dug themselves in with the worms. My clever ones have inherited the earth. All's well." J. B. Priestley, however, in *Midnight on the Desert,* attempts to recover the meaning of the virtue for a modern context: "Rationalist critics have always seemed to me to miss the profound psychological truth of such observations as 'The meek shall inherit the earth', for the meek, that is, those who are modest but hopeful in heart and mind, continually inherit the earth, for it is theirs to enjoy" (chap. 14). Arnold Bennet offers a variation upon the sentiment in his novel about a miser's daughter, *Anna of the Five Towns:* "Blessed are the meek, blessed are the failures, blessed are the stupid, for they, unknown to themselves, have a grace which is denied to the haughty, the successful, and the wise" (chap. 6).

                                                            PETER H. DAVIDS

MELCHIOR *See* MAGI.

MELCHIZEDEK Melchizedek (Heb. *malki-ṣedeq,* "my righteous king," or "king of righteousness"; cf. Heb. 7:2) was the king of Salem (generally regarded as ancient Jerusalem; cf. Ps. 76:2) and the priest of "the most high God" (*'el 'elyon*) who came with bread and wine to meet Abram after his victorious encounter with Chedorlaomer the king of Elam, pronounced a benediction upon him in the name of the most high God, and received a tithe from him (Gen. 14:18-20).

In Ps. 110:4, which is probably an enthronement psalm, a Davidic king is declared to be "a priest for ever after the order of Melchizedek." This psalm may have been a victory song composed upon David's conquest of Jerusalem, thereby making him an "heir" of Melchizedek's priest-kingship. In the Intertestamental corpus of literature Melchizedek is variously interpreted as a historical person (Josephus, *J.W.* 6.438; *Ant.* 1.179-81), a representation of the Logos (Philo, *Legum allegoriae,* 3.79-82; *De congressu . . . gratia,* 99; *De Abrahamo,* 235), and an angelic, eschatological figure (11QMelch; see also 1QapGen). Representing Jesus as the Davidic Messiah, the writer to the Hebrews pronounces him "a priest for ever after the order of Melchizedek" (Ps. 110:4) and elucidates this identification in light of Gen. 14:18-20 where nothing is said of Melchizedek's birth, death, or ancestry, thus establishing the superiority of Melchizedek's (and so Christ's) priesthood over the Aaronic priesthood (Heb. 5:6-11; 6:20–7:28).

Melchizedek (Melchisedek) shows up in early Christian, Jewish, and gnostic sources in the context of Jewish-Christian debate (St. Justin Martyr, *Dial.* 33.1; 83.2-3), in references to a Melchizedekian heresy (St. Hippolytus, *Refutation of All Heresies,* 7.35-36; 10.23-24) and regarding the Eucharist (St. Clement of Alexandria, *Stromateis,* 4.161) — a tradition still attested in the canon of the Roman Catholic Mass in a feast celebrated April 25. According to early Christian tradition his priesthood is that of the Church of the Gentiles, or the cosmic pagan religion which preceded scriptural revelation. Mention of the Mass is intended to signify that the well-intentioned sacrifices of the pagan world are taken up and included in the sacrifice of the eternal high priest. Many of these sources also speculate on his origin or nature: that he was Shem, son of Noah (Tg. Neof. I and other Palestinian targums), an angel (Origen, *Dialektos,* 4.25), or the Holy Ghost (a view held by Hiercas the Egyptian, according to St. Epiphanius, *Refutation of All the Heresies,* 55).

The association of Christ with Melchizedek is left largely undeveloped by medieval and Renaissance literary typology, though it finds its way into ecclesiastical polemic: *Melchizedichs Antitype: Or, the Eternal Priesthood and All-Sufficient Sacrifice of Christ* (1624) by John Lewis is a typological anti-Catholic tract. After the 18th cent., however, there are a number of allusions in English literature. In Carlyle's *Sartor Resartus,* e.g., it is said of the mysterious origins of Professor Teufelsdröckh that

> Wits spoke of him secretly as if he were a kind of Melchizedek, without father or mother of any kind; sometimes, with reference to his great historic and statistic knowledge, and the vivid way he had of expressing himself like an eyewitness of distant transactions and scenes,

they called him the *Ewige Jude,* Everlasting, or as we say, Wandering Jew. (1.3)

In Butler's novel *The Way of All Flesh,* after receiving a letter from his father which he does not want to answer, Ernest Pontifex, longing to be free of his family, "brooded over the bliss of Melchisedek who had been born an orphan, without father, without mother, and without descent." More straightforwardly, John Keble's "Our Sacrifice of Praise and Thanksgiving" links the Gospel antitype of sacrifice to the encounter of Abram and Melchizedek, and Holman Hunt's painting *Melchizedek* (1825) reflects, in the vein of Heb. 7:2, similar eucharistic associations.

In contemporary literature James Joyce is the only major author to make significant use of Melchizedek. In a comment disparaging ecclesiastical societies Stephen is urged to join the priesthood: "He would hold his secret knowledge and secret power, being as sinless as the innocent: and he would be a priest forever according to the order of Melchisedec" (*A Portrait of the Artist as a Young Man,* chap. 4). Joyce again refers to Melchizedek in *Ulysses,* where Bloom is described as fulfilling the offices of Christ.

See also AARON.

Bibliography. Bardy, G. "Melchisédech dans la tradition patristique." *RB* (1926), 496ff.; (1927), 25ff.; Crehan, J. "Melchisedec." *A Catholic Dictionary of Theology.* Eds. H. F. Davis, I. Thomas, and J. Crehan (1971), 3.267-69; Daniélou, J. *The Pagans of the Old Testament* (1957); Horton, F. L., Jr. *The Melchizedek Tradition* (1976); Needham, E. A. *Melchizedek and Aaron as Types of Christ* (1904); Wuttke, G. *Melchisedech der Priesterkönig von Salem: Eine Studie zur Geschichte der Exegese* (1927).

STEPHEN G. W. ANDREWS

MELUSADE *See* LOT'S WIFE.

MENE, MENE, TEKEL, UPHARSIN *See* BELSHAZZAR; DANIEL; HANDWRITING ON THE WALL.

MEPHIBOSHETH The lame son of Jonathan who, upon Jonathan's death, is taken into David's household (2 Sam. 4:4; 9:1-13; cf. 1 Sam. 24:21-22).

See also DAVID; JONATHAN.

MERCY, JUSTICE In English translations of the Bible, *mercy* reflects a variety of Hebrew and Greek expressions, which can be translated by "favor," "[loving]kindness," "grace," "pity," and "compassion." The most frequent OT term *raham,* "to have compassion" (cf. *rahamim,* plural, yielding the expression "tender mercies"), represents the most basic affection which those related by birth have for one another (cf. "kindness"). Thus God's love for his people is familial: he is Israel's father (Ps. 103:13; Isa. 63:15-16; Hos. 11) or mother (Isa. 49:14-15) and, as such, extends to his frequently wayward child unchanging compassion and forgiveness. But God's mercy is, particularly, an attribute of covenant love (often typified as a marriage; cf. Isa. 54:4-8) and based upon his faithfulness to the terms of the covenant which he established with his chosen people (Exod. 33:19; Isa. 63:9; etc.). The idea of covenant love is emphasized by the OT word *hesed* ("tenderness," "steadfast love"), which contains the elements of loyalty, devotion, and faithfulness. A third important OT term is *hen* ("favour," "success," "acceptance," or "good fortune"), e.g., "find favour in the eyes of. . . ." In the NT the meanings of *hesed* and *hen* are largely combined in Gk. *charis*, "grace."

In the OT God's mercy to his people is always set in the context of his justice, and is manifested in various ways: he forgives the sinful rebellion of individuals and the nation (2 Sam. 24:14; Pss. 40:11; 51:1; Isa. 55:7); keeps the promises he has made (Deut. 13:17); gathers exiles to himself and restores them to their land (Jer. 33:25-26; Ezek. 39:25). God's deeds thus demonstrate his faithfulness to the covenant: he is "the LORD God, merciful and gracious, long-suffering, and abundant in goodness and truth, keeping mercy for thousands, forgiving iniquity and transgression and sin . . ." (Exod. 34:6-7a).

In the NT Jesus is said to be "a merciful and faithful high priest," interpreting the divine mercy to humanity by means of his actions, the friend of the "poor" (Luke 4:18; 7:22) and "sinners" (Luke 5:27, 30; 7:34; chap. 15; 19:7; etc.). Since Jesus demonstrates God's compassion for humanity, the response of the afflicted is often to address him in words appropriate to God himself: *Kyrie eleison!* (Matt. 15:22; 17:15; 20:30-31). As Jesus represents a God who is a merciful Father to his children, so he demands the same of his disciples: "Be ye therefore merciful, as your Father also is merciful" (Luke 6:36). Mercy is therefore an essential condition for entering the kingdom of God (Matt. 5:7), an essential attribute of the *imitatio Dei* which is to lead the followers of Jesus to be good neighbors (cf. the parable of the Good Samaritan, Luke 10:30-37), even to enemies, because God has shown mercy to all humanity (Matt. 6:12; 18:23-35). "For God hath concluded them all in unbelief, that he might have mercy upon all" (Rom. 11:32). Each is therefore to be judged according to the way he has shown mercy to other people, or, in this sense, to Christ himself (Matt. 25:31-46).

Mercy is regarded in early Christian tradition as the gift of the Incarnation. In the Nativity Hymns of Ephraim Syrus, Christ is personified as Mercy (15.20, 36), and St. Augustine uses the term virtually as another name for God (*Conf.* 3.1). In the writings of Augustine, St. Isidore of Seville (*Etymologiae*), and later Scholastic theologians, mercy is intimately associated with justice and the reciprocity of forgiveness. "Blessed are the merciful, for they shall obtain mercy" (Matt. 5:7) is related by Augustine to the conditional nature of forgiveness and the need for one's own perseverance in a forgiving spirit: the ideal

is "justice tempered with mercy to those who are penitent" (e.g., *De sermone Domini in Monte*, 1.2.7). Patristic writers observe that mercy, like justice, is fundamentally relational, that human mercy properly reflects the covenant, as in the terms of the Great Commandment. Mercy is expressed toward us by God; we should extend it likewise to our neighbor (Augustine, *Sermons on New Testament Lessons*, 56.4). An act of mercy on the part of the individual even toward animals (Prov. 12:10) can be expressive of gratitude for God's mercy.

A verbal similarity between *misery* and mercy in Latin (*miserere*) allows Augustine to reinforce these points (*Conf.* 10.38, 39) as prolegomena to the doctrines of the corporal and spiritual works of mercy. The corporal works are (1) to feed the hungry; (2) give drink to the thirsty; (3) clothe the naked; (4) house the homeless; (5) visit the sick; (6) ransom the captive; and (7) bury the dead (cf. Matt. 25:34-46). The spiritual works are usually defined as (1) to instruct the ignorant; (2) counsel the doubtful; (3) admonish sinners; (4) bear wrongs patiently; (5) forgive offenses willingly; (6) comfort the afflicted; and (7) pray for others' need. The obligation to perform the first six of the corporal works of mercy is set forth unequivocally by Christ — failure to comply invokes eternal damnation at the Last Judgment (Matt. 25:41). This theme is picked up by patristic writers down to Wyclif, and is to be found everywhere in late medieval homiletics.

In Chaucer the term *mercy* is employed with great frequency to refer both to the mercy of God (*Parson's Tale*) and to its reflection as a noble human quality (*Knight's Tale*, 1.1774, 3089): Prudence, in *The Tale of Melibee*, stresses the interdependence of divine and human mercy, "Wherefore I pray you, lat mercy been in youre herte, / to th' effect and entente that God Almighty have mercy on yow in his last juggement. / For Seint Jame seith in his Epistle: 'Juggement withouten mercy shal be doon to hym that hath no mercy of another wight' " (7.1867-71). But mercy can also apply, in an ironic and lighter vein, to the goal of amorous desires in "courtly" lovers: "And but I have hir mercy and hir grace . . ." (*Knight's Tale*, 1.1120). Spenser personifies the matron of the corporal works of Mercy (*Faerie Queene*, 1.34.4; cf. Mercilla, *FQ*, bk. 5) and reflects the transmission from Latin into English of the wordplay: "Mercy craves rather mercy than repriefe" (*FQ* 3.45.2). In the 17th cent. the concept receives, perhaps, its richest development in Shakespeare and Milton. The famous speech of Portia (*Merchant of Venice*, 4.1.184-205) emphasizing the relational aspect of mercy, and its connection with justice and judgment (borrowing from Ecclus. 35:25; Deut. 32:2; Isa. 55:1-10; Acts 20:35; Pss. 143:2; 145:8-9), is in fact foundational to the continuing biblical tradition of the concept; the same principles anchor the theme of *Measure for Measure*. Milton similarly has "Mercie colleague with Justice" (*PL* 10.59), reflecting both the Epistle of James (2:3) and the Hebrew Scriptures in referring mercy to the covenant (*PL* 12.346; 3.132-34). Jeremy Taylor's famous sermon on the text "God's mercy is above all his works" stresses that the "mercies of God" extend to all of the bountiful provisions of creation (*28 Sermons* [1651], 324-29); elsewhere he speaks of the surplus and interconnectedness of mercy in the lives of persons far removed from each other in time: ". . . so is Gods mercy; when it looked upon *Moses* it relieved *S. Paul,* and it pardoned *David,* and gave hope to *Manasses,* and might have restored *Judas,* if he would have had hope and used himself accordingly" (*Holy Dying,* 297).

By the 18th cent. mercy begins to tend toward abstraction as a principally human quality: "And Mercy here exalts her Throne" (Swift, "Young's Satire," 18). Dr. Johnson (in his *Dictionary*) traces the etymology to Lat. *misericordia* and gives as primary meanings "tenderness," "pity," "willingness to save," secondarily "legal pardon," but then "Discretion; power of acting at pleasure," citing Swift, "and when the lady ceases to be cruel, she is . . . at his mercy." So Swift's "Thus I look down with mercy on the age" ("To Congreve," 49), Pope's "But honouring age, in mercy I refrain" (*Odyssey,* 18.17.167), and Congreve's "at your mercy" (*Double Dealer,* 3.1.255) carry the secularized sense, centered on interpersonal advantage, which can also be found much earlier (e.g., Shakespeare, *The Rape of Lucrece,* 364: "She . . . lies at the mercie of his mortall sting"). This nontheological sense begins to dominate early modern usage of the word. Wordsworth's "Your life is at my mercy" (*The Borderers,* 146) and Browning's "At his mercy, at his malice . . ." ("Clive," 209) are in the secular tradition, in which mercy can mean, most positively, as in Shelley, simply clemency or pity of a human sort, or, elsewhere, something as negative as "malicious or perverse control." In this century Dylan Thomas illustrates a representative ironic engagement of both possibilities, when he says of Time's supervision of his childhood gamboling: "Time let me play and be / Golden in the mercy of his means. . ."; "oh I was young and easy in the mercy of his means, / Time held me green and dying / Though I sang in my chains like the sea" ("Fern Hill," 13-14, 52-54).

The biblical concept does not disappear from post-Enlightenment literature with the emergence of the secularized reference. Blake's "Mercy, Pitie, Peace and Love" still reflects biblical tradition, and in Fielding's *Tom Jones,* Squire Allworthy's modeling of judgment tempered with mercy is as thematically central as it is in Shakespeare's *The Merchant of Venice* or *Measure for Measure.* Cowper still defines mercy as the gift of the Incarnation (*Task,* 5.743) and the complement of justice in God's judgment ("Mercy's grand apocalypse displayed" [*Hope,* 448]).

During the 19th cent. the term itself begins to face away from secular literary usage: it is almost nonexistent, e.g., in the works of Emerson, Whitman, and Twain.

Dickens nonetheless uses it to provide a humorous characterization in a secular context: of his *Uncommercial Traveller's* childhood nurse, a sadistic narrator of wonderfully gruesome tales, he observes — "Her name was Mercy, though she had none on me." But by the 20th cent. two distinct usages have emerged, one of which may be said to invoke the biblical concept and one of which evidently does not. Whereas Chaucer's comic use of mercy to describe the amorous goal of an infatuated lover actually depends for its humor on a lively sense of (incongruous) reference to the biblical concept, the play in the lines of Dylan Thomas involves no comparable indebtedness.

See also COVENANT; FOUR DAUGHTERS OF GOD; GRACE, WORKS; JUDGE NOT.

Bibliography. De Smet, I. L. "A Study of the Roles of Mercy and Justice in the Morality Plays *Everyman, The Castle of Perseverance,* and *Mankind.*" *DAI* 32 (1971), 915A; Knight, W. N. "Equity and Mercy in English Law and Drama (1405-1641)." *CompD* 6 (1972), 51-67; Male, D. A. "The Concept of Christian Mercy: A Theme in English Literature and Drama from the Early Middle Ages to the Beginning of the Seventeenth Century." M. Litt., Bristol, 1968.

MERCY SEAT *See* HOLY OF HOLIES; THRONE OF GRACE.

MERIBAH The name of two different places visited by the Israelites during their wilderness journey — Rephidim (Exod. 17:17; cf. Deut. 33:8) and Kadesh-barnea (Num. 20:1-13; cf. Deut. 32:51). At both places the people complained over the lack of water (hence the name *meribah,* "strife"). The Psalmist castigates his hearers with the memory in Ps. 95:8: "Harden not your heart, as in the provocation, and as in the day of temptation in the wilderness."

See also SMITTEN ROCK.

MESHACH *See* SHADRACH, MESHACH, AND ABEDNEGO.

MESOPOTAMIA Greek Mesopotamia ("between the rivers") renders the Heb. *'aram naharayim,* which describes the fertile area between the Tigris and Euphrates in eastern Syria and northern Iraq. Abram lived here for a period (Gen. 11:31-32) and sent his servant back to find a wife for his son Isaac (Gen. 24:10). During the judges period, Mesopotamians were among Israel's oppressors (Judg. 3:8-10).

Usage was extended by later Roman and Greek authors to include all of the Tigris-Euphrates area. St. Stephen thus places Abram's original home here (Acts 7:2). Mesopotamians heard St. Peter's sermon at Pentecost (Acts 7:2).

Later interpreters viewed Mesopotamia with disfavor, as a place of darkness (Gen. Rab. 60.1) and martyrdom (Eusebius, *Hist. eccl.* 8.12.1). DAVID W. BAKER

MESS OF POTTAGE "A mess of pottage" refers to the meal for which a hungry Esau relinquished his birthright to his wily younger brother Jacob. The phrase itself is not from the KJV but appeared in a chapter heading in English Bibles of 1537 and 1539, and the Geneva Bible of 1560.

See also BIRTHRIGHT; ESAU; JACOB.

MESSIAH "Messiah" is a transliteration of Heb. *mashiah,* an adjective which means "anointed," and so can refer to anyone with a divinely appointed mission — kings (e.g., 1 Sam. 24:6; Lam. 4:20), high priests (Lev. 4:3, 5, 16; 6:22), priests (Exod. 28:41; Lev. 10:7; Num. 3:3), and even the Gentile king Cyrus (Isa. 54:1). The term *mashiah* is not, in fact, ever used in the OT as a reference to Messiah. The KJV twice mentions "the Messiah" in the OT, but it is now recognized that "the anointed one" is a more apt translation, since KJV's "the Messiah the Prince" (Dan. 9:25, "the anointed prince") probably refers to Cyrus (see Isa. 45:1), and "the Messiah" (KJV Dan. 9:26, "anointed one") to Onias III.

The OT does, of course, give voice to messianic longings and expectation. Gen. 49:10 is a very early messianic prophecy: "The sceptre shall not depart from Judah, nor a lawgiver from between his feet, until Shiloh come; and unto him shall the gathering of the people be." Moses promised that "The LORD thy God will raise up unto thee a Prophet . . . like unto me" (Deut. 18:15). Often such prophecies look forward to a time when Israel would again be united as it had been in the time of David: "Then shall the children of Judah and the children of Israel be gathered together, and appoint themselves one head" (Hos. 1:11), and at this time "shall the children of Israel return, and seek the LORD their God, and David their king" (Hos. 3:5; see also Amos 9:11-15). This leader, this new David, will be a scourge to the foes of Israel, such a one as had been prophesied in Num. 24:17: "there shall come a Star out of Jacob, and a Sceptre shall rise out of Israel, and shall smite the corners of Moab, and destroy all the children of Sheth." For the Psalmist this all-powerful, all-conquering king of Israel is "a priest for ever after the order of Melchizedek" (110:4), a spiritual leader, then, as well as political — and eternal in his rule.

Sometimes this idea of the messianic reunification of Israel is expanded to envision all the peoples of the world coming to Zion. Isaiah gives the most powerful and the most extended expression to such hopes: "And it shall come to pass in the last days, that the mountain of the LORD's house shall be established in the top of the mountains . . . and all nations shall flow into it . . . and they shall beat their swords into plowshares" (Isa. 2:2-4; Mic. 4:1-4); and for a ruler "there shall come forth a rod out of the stem of Jesse, and a Branch shall grow out of his roots" (Isa. 11:1-2; Isaiah is recalling the anointing of David, son of Jesse [1 Sam. 16:1-13]). Another image is provided by the "suffering servant" of Isa. 40–55, who

has "no beauty that we should desire him" (Isa. 53:2), one who labors for a time in vain, who suffers at the hands of the wicked, and who dies for his people, a "Redeemer of Israel" (Isa. 49:7). Yet this Redeemer will also be "a light to the Gentiles" and "salvation unto the end of the earth." He will "say to the prisoners, Go forth; to them that are in darkness, Show yourselves" (Isa. 49:1-9):

> For he shall grow up before him as a tender plant, and as a root out of dry ground. . . . He is despised and rejected of men; a man of sorrows, and acquainted with grief . . . and we esteemed him not. . . . But he was wounded for our transgressions . . . and with his stripes we are healed. . . . he is brought as a lamb to the slaughter. . . . his soul an offering for sin. (Isa. 53:1-10; see also 35:4; 40:10; 42:1-9; 52:13-15; 59:20)

For Daniel the mysterious and awesome figure associated with the triumph of the elect is at once human *and* divine: "behold, one like the Son of man came with the clouds of heaven, and came to the Ancient of days" (7:13-14).

In the NT, where Jewish hopes for a Messiah are seen as fulfilled in Jesus, the evangelists portray Jesus drawing all these — and other — strands together into a single thread of prophecy: "the Son of man came not to be ministered unto, but to minister, and to give his life up as a ransom for many" (Mark 10:45). In this one passage, Jesus casts himself as "the Son of man" of Dan. 7:13, as the "servant" of Isa. 49:3, and as the suffering Redeemer of Isa. 53:4-9. Jesus makes explicit his messianic role in John 4:25-26: the Samaritan woman "saith unto him, I know that Messias cometh, which is called Christ. . . . Jesus saith unto her, I that speak unto thee am he." And in John 1:41 Andrew says, "We have found the Messias, which is, being interpreted, the Christ"; indeed, since Christ was the Greek equivalent of Heb. *mashiah,* "the anointed one," every reference in the NT to Jesus as "the Christ" is a reference to Jesus as "the messiah" (see, e.g., Matt. 16:16; Mark 8:29; Luke 2:11; John 10:24; Acts 18:5).

Ps. 110 was given a messianic interpretation at least as early as the time of Jesus, and so was the most widely quoted Psalm in the NT: "Jesus saith unto him . . . Hereafter shall ye see the Son of man sitting on the right hand of power, and coming in the clouds of heaven" (Matt. 26:64; there is also a reference here to Dan. 7:13; for other NT references to Ps. 110, see, e.g., Matt. 22:41-46; Acts 2:34-35; 5:31; 7:55; Rom. 8:34; 1 Cor. 15:25; Eph. 1:20; Heb. 1:13; 5:6, 10; 8:1; 10:12-13; Rev. 3:21).

For patristic writers, of course, there was no question that many passages in the OT referred directly to Christ. St. Ambrose, e.g., writes that Gen. 49:8-12 only "appears" to refer to Judah, while "indeed . . . that later Juda is meant" — Christ (FC 65.251). Ambrose goes on to gloss Isa. 11:1: "The root is the household of the Jews, the rod is Mary, the flower of Mary is Christ" (65.252); this interpretation originated with Tertullian, *De carne Christi*, 251.5). St. Augustine understands Ps. 1:3 as referring to Christ: "That 'tree' then, that is, our Lord, from 'the running streams of water,' that is from the sinful people's drawing them by the way into the roots of discipline, will 'bring forth fruit,' that is, after He hath been glorified" (*Enarr. in Ps.* [NPNF 8.1]). The Vg sometimes even translates OT "anointed one" with *Christus* (e.g., Ps. 2:2; Dan. 9:25-26). Indeed, this christological reading of the OT encouraged the Fathers to find references to Christ in a very wide range of OT events; Eve's issuing from a wound in the side of Adam, e.g., was seen as a type for the blood issuing from the side of Christ (St. John Chrysostom, ACW 31.62).

The assumption of such passages is that God so arranged the events of history that they would be meaningful, functioning as a broad and detailed prophecy of the Messiah and his mission. History leads up to and is granted retrospective significance in terms of the birth, life, death, and resurrection of Jesus. Subsequent history likewise is adequated to the predicted eschaton: Christian historiography in the Middle Ages is charged with messianic expectation, and numerous attempts were made to correlate proximate historical events to biblical prophecy so as to arrive at a probable date for what Christians anticipated as the Second Coming of Christ. Favored dates (in their various periods) were A.D. 1000, 1233, 1260, 1300, 1333, 1360, and 1400. But Jewish speculation on the coming of the Messiah and the corresponding millennial reign was comparable: the year 1358 was the favorite Jewish date in the 14th cent., though the *De Jure Belli* of Giovanni da Legnano, written in 1360, refers to 1365 as a likely date (ed. T. E. Holland [1917], 77-78).

The first advent of the Messiah, in a Christian perspective, and expectation of his final coming and judgment, determine the structuring (or restructuring) of biblical narrative in numerous works of medieval English literature. In the 14th cent., e.g., one typically finds in the cycle plays not only a Prophets' Play, wherein the coming of the Messiah is explicitly foretold, but also such detailed prefigurations as the child-lamb being born to Gil in "The Second Shepherds' Play." In bk. 1 of *The Faerie Queene* one finds not only the messianic structure, with the dragon-devil waiting to be defeated at the coming of the Christ-like Redcrosse Knight, but also such typological details as the child playing with the dragon-serpent (*FQ* 1.12.11) in fulfillment of Isa. 11:8, "And the sucking child shall play on the hole of the asp, and the weaned child shall put his hand on the cockatrice's den" (see J. C. Nohrnberg, *The Analogy of the Faerie Queene*).

Eighteenth-cent. interest in the Eclogues of Virgil and the Sibylline prophecies, thought then to be parallel in many respects to OT prophecies concerning the coming Messiah, encouraged imaginative treatment of some of the chief "messianic" portions of Isaiah. Alexander Pope freely blends elements from Virgil's *Pollio* eclogue (*Eclogues,* 4, esp. 6-46) and Isaiah (7:14; 11:1; 40:1-4; 45:8, etc.) to create his "Messiah," first published in the *Spectator* (1712). Pope's stirring phrases reveal, however, a dominance of scriptural idiom:

> The SAVIOR comes! by ancient Bards foretold:
> Hear him ye Deaf, and all ye Blind behold!
> He from thick Films shall purge the visual Ray,
> And on the sightless Eye-ball pour the Day.
> 'Tis he th'obstructed Paths of Sound shall clear,
> And bid new Musick charm th'unfolding Ear.
> The Dumb shall sing, the Lame his Crutch foregoe,
> And leap exulting like the bounding Roe. (37-44)

Pope's triumphant concluding lines are consistent with the whole poem in their indebtedness to Isaiah (esp. 51:6; 54:10; 60:19-20):

> One Tyde of Glory, one unclouded Blaze,
> O'erflow thy Courts: The LIGHT HIMSELF shall shine
> Reveal'd; and *God's* eternal Day be thine!
> The Seas shall waste; the Skies in Smoke decay;
> Rocks fall to Dust, and Mountains melt away;
> But fix'd *His* Word, *His* saving Pow'r remains:
> Thy Realm for ever lasts! thy own *Messiah* reigns!

The most celebrated *Messiah* of the 18th cent. is undoubtedly that of G. F. Handel (1742). The oratorio is atypical in Handel's canon in that it tells no story; rather, it sets forth a series of scriptural texts arranged as a litany of meditations on redemption, commencing with a series of OT prophecies (notably centering on Isaiah again) and moving through the ministry of Jesus to the Cross and Resurrection. It was a peculiar accomplishment of Handel's composition that, as William Cowper put it ironically, thousands of auditors with no interest in the Messiah (or, he implies, in redemption) thus heard a fair précis of scriptural salvation history for the sake of Handel's great music. In Cowper's wry reflection:

> Man praises man. Desert in arts or arms
> Wins public honour; and ten thousand sit
> Patiently present at a sacred song,
> Commemoration-mad; content to hear
> (Oh wonderful effect of music's pow'r!)
> Messiah's eulogy for Handel's sake! (*The Task,*
> 6.632-37)

Cowper's priest, fellow hymn writer *(Olney Hymns),* and mentor at Olney, John Newton, having later become rector at St. Mary Woolnoth in London, was happy to take advantage of an extremely successful rerun of Handel's *Messiah* at Westminster Abbey during 1784-85 to preach a remarkable series of fifty sermons. These were published with considerable success as *Messiah: Or, the Scriptural Passages which Form the Subject of the Celebrated Oratorio of Handel* (1786). Handel thus has come to figure largely in English allusions, literary and otherwise, to "the Messiah." Interestingly parallel, however, is Friedrich Gottlieb Klopstock's religious epic *Messias,* inspired by Milton's *Paradise Lost.* After appearing in Germany in 1748 and 1773 it became well known also in England and America.

A contrasting deemphasis of the subject, or redefinition of it, becomes apparent in later literature. For Blake, who in *The Marriage of Heaven and Hell* wants to exalt the Subconscious (or hell) at the expense of Good and Reason, the Messiah becomes simply Desire: "the Messiah fell, & formed a heaven of what he stole from the abyss" (*Complete Writings* [1966], 149, pl. 5). In a related vein, Coleridge sees the integrated consciousness or "whole one Self" as "the Messiah's destined victory!" ("Religious Musings"). The American poet Robert Lowell, in "The Quaker Graveyard in Nantucket," asks his readers to see in the killing of a sperm whale a reenactment of the Crucifixion and so calls the whale "Jonas Messiah" — with a typological pun on Jonah (see also Lowell's "No Messiah" and "Once to Every Man and Nation"). Gore Vidal's *Messiah* (1954) is a parodic "fifth gospel," recounting the life and cult of John Cave, an unlikely savior and founder of Caveway, a new religion promising solace through death.

The term Messiah or "new Messiah" occasionally occurs in literature either as a term of derogation or in a purely secularizing sense. Dryden, e.g., disparages the motives of the refugee French Huguenots coming to England, suggesting in his Catholic poem *The Hind and the Panther* (1687) that since their motives are really materialist, it is British affluence which is their "new Messiah by the star" (3.173-78). Similarly, there are references to other "Christs," such as Oscar Wilde's "These Christs that die upon the barricades" ("Sonnet to Liberty"). A. M. Klein's acerbic "Ballad of the Days of the Messiah," from the section "A Voice was Heard in Ramah," in his *Collected Poems* (1944), bitterly heralds "Messiah in an armour-metalled tank," the liberation soldier arrived too late to redeem six million Jews. Klein's World War II poetry has many such references to the failure of Messiah to appear in the darkest hours:

> Where is the trumpeted Messiah? Where
> The wine long-soured into vinegar?
> Have cobwebs stifled his mighty shofar? ("Reb Levi
> Yitschok talks to God")

This poem, a troubled rabbi's series of unanswered Job-like questions, complains of a protracted historical silence of God and with it of the emptying out of meaning in messianic promises. Representative of a fair portion of Jewish poetry written through and after the Holocaust, both poems are at a far remove from Klein's early *(ashkenaz)* alphabetic "Messiah" (1927), a joyous, whimsical children's song about the golden messianic age which might have been written in the age of Maimonides.

See also ESCHATOLOGY; IMMANUEL; JESUS CHRIST; SECOND COMING.

Bibliography. Ames, C. R. "False Advertising: The Influence of Virgil and Isaiah on Pope's Messiah." *Studies in English Literature, 1500-1900* 28 (1988), 401-26; Axelrod, S. G. *Robert Lowell: Life and Art* (1978), 54-64; Brown, R. E. *The Birth of the Messiah* (1977); Greenstone, J. H. *The Messianic Idea in Jewish History* (1906), 21-80; Scholem, G. *The Messianic Idea in Judaism* (1971); Werblowsky, R. J. Z. "Messianism in Jewish History." *Journal of World History* 11 (1968), 30-445. H. DAVID BRUMBLE

DAVID L. JEFFREY

METATRON *See* MICHAEL.

METHUSELAH According to Gen. 5:21-27 Methuselah was the oldest of the ten sons of Enoch. He was the father of Lamech and the grandfather of Noah. He lived 969 years, thus making him the oldest of the descendants of Adam mentioned in the Bible. The meaning of the Hebrew name has been interpreted variously as "a man of the javelin," "a man of Selah or Sin (the god of Ur Casdim)," or as a corruption of the Bab. *Mutu-sa-ili* into *Mutu-sa-ilati*, meaning "husband of the goddess." Later commentary (Yerhameel 23.1-4; *Sifte Kohen,* Bereshit, and Noah 4d) relates the name to a knife or sword by which he is to have done battle with descendants of Lilith, principally female demons. In Yashar Bereshit (13a) he is a figure of great righteousness, and in some commentaries is said to have studied 900 orders of the Mishnah. Nevertheless, he lived in fear of sorceresses until his death (Midr. 'Aggada, Gen. 5:25, etc.).

According to the chronology of the MT Methuselah's life overlapped that of Adam by 243 years and he died in the year of the Flood. The LXX translation diverges in part of the chronology of his life; since the divergence was well known in the early Church, disputes occasioned by the discrepancy were, as St. Jerome puts it, "famous in all the churches" *(Hebraicae questiones in libro Geneseos).* St. Augustine took up the issue in his *De civitate Dei* (15.11), resolving it in favor of the MT, considering that the principal issue was establishing that people of that epoch "had lives so long as to make it possible that, during the lifetime of the first-born of two sole parents then on earth, the human race multiplied sufficiently to form a community." (He holds the variance in the LXX to be "a mere copyist's error.") Augustine also takes up and defends the literal nature of the ages given for the earliest patriarchs, against those who maintained that a different form of annual calculation must have obtained in archaic times. Methuselah subsequently is exclusively associated with the wondrous longevity of antediluvian humanity.

Spenser in *The Faerie Queene* thus describes an old man "of infinite rememberaunce," saying hyperbolically that "the yeares of *Nestor* nothing were to his, / Ne yet *Mathusalem,* though longest liv'd; / For he remembred both their infancies" (2.9.57.1-3). Herbert in "Affliction (2)" strikes a different note: "Kill me not every day . . . / Though I in broken pay / Die over each houre of Methusalems stay" (cf. Donne's *The First Anniversary,* 128). Sir Thomas Browne offers pragmatic grounds for not wishing such a long life, writing in the first book of his *Religio Medici* (1642) that "were there any hopes to outlive vice, or a point to be superannuated from sin, it were worthy our knees to implore the days of Methuselah. But age doth not rectify, but incurvate, our natures, turning bad dispositions into worser habits, and (like diseases) brings on incurable vices; for every day as we grow weaker in age, we grow stronger in sin, and the number of our days doth but make our sins innumerable. . . ."

In a poem affirming his love, Swift invokes the aid of Apollo, his muse, who replies, "Though you should live like old *Methusalem,* / I furnish Hints, and you should use all 'em" (*Upon Stella's Birth-Day,* 37-38). In the guise of "Honest Jo" Swift writes *An Excellent New Song Upon His Grace Our good Lord Archbishop of Dublin,* in which, after a lengthy complaint about hard times, Jo offers a tongue-in-cheek benediction: "God Preserve his Lordship's Grace, and make him live as long / As did *Methusalem* of old, and so I end my song" (47-48).

Burns, in a witty eulogy for one of his publishers, pleads, "May never wicked Fortune touzle him, / May never wicked men bamboozle him, / Until a pow as auld's Methusalem He canty claw!" (*Lament for William Creech,* 12-14). Blake in both *Milton* (41.34) and *Jerusalem* (12) connects Methuselah and Lamech: "these are Giants mighty Hermaphroditic," identifying them with the "giants in the earth" of Gen. 6:4. In Browning's introspective dramatic idyl *Martin Relph* the narrator suggests wryly, "If I last as long as Methuselah I shall never forgive myself" (4); *The Flight of the Duchess* poses the preposterous question: "What age had Methuselah when he begat Saul?" (884). Tennyson's Eva Steer in *The Promise of May* wishes her father "many happy returns of the day" on his eightieth birthday. Farmer Steer replies, "if I could ha' gone on wi' the plowin' nobbut the smell o' th mou'd 'ud ha' maade ma live as long as Jerusalem." Eva corrects him, saying, "[You mean] Methuselah, father" (1.375-79).

American literature generally follows in this clichéd usage. In his "Spring" chapter in *Walden,* Thoreau recounts the story of a man from Sudbury who marveled at the events of nature: "One old man, who has been a close observer of Nature . . . can hardly acquire more of natural lore if he should live to the age of Methuselah." Melville's *Moby-Dick* employs the patriarch more imaginatively, however, when Ishmael asks, "Who can show a pedigree like Leviathan? Ahab's harpoon had shed older blood than the Pharaohs. Methuselah seems a schoolboy." In *A Fable for Critics* James Russell Lowell writes of himself, "His lyre has some chords that would ring pretty well, / He'd rather by half make a drum of the shell, / And rattle away till he's old as Methuselah."

There are two allusions to Methuselah in Joyce's *Ulys-*

ses, the first apparently referring to Bloom's father, "Old Methusalem Bloom, the robbing bagman, that poisoned himself with the prussic acid"; elsewhere Bloom's age is compared to that of Methuselah: he "would have surpassed by 221 years the maximum antediluvian age, that of Methuselah."

Aside from John Kendrick Bangs's *Autobiography of Methusaleh* (1909), a burlesque which describes the patriarch's reaction to Noah's building of the ark, the most extensive literary use of the biblical figure and his tradition is that of George Bernard Shaw. In his *Back to Methuselah* Shaw envisages an English society which has evolved to the point that some persons are beginning to overcome previous limits to mortality. They form a progressive political party, committed to (among other things) the extension of life. The Play has five parts, the first being a revisionist look at the time of creation and the first patriarchs. Part 2 is "The Gospel of the Brothers Barnabas: AD 1920" in which Conrad, a biologist, and his brother Franklyn, a former cleric, hatch a plan by which human life is to be extended to 300 years. Franklyn tells Haslam, the boyish rector, that he himself was once in the Church but after twenty years realized that he was unsuited for it. Haslam replies that "old Methuselah must have had to think twice before he took on anything for life. If I thought I was going to live nine hundred and sixty years, I don't think I should stay in the Church." In the middle of a discussion on politics, Savvy, Franklyn's barbarously mannered 18-year-old daughter, says to the assemblage, "Our election cry is 'Back to Methuselah!'" Burge, a former Labour Prime Minister, adds playfully that they shall "become the Longevity Party" and later, asked about his political platform, replies, "haven't you taken in the revelation that has been vouchsafed to us? The line I am going to take is Back to Methuselah." According to the play's Elderly Gentleman the "greatest miracle in history" occurred in the British Isles, that "the first man to live three hundred years was an Englishman. The first, that is, since the contemporaries of Methuselah." The ancient patriarch, at least in light of his representation in haggadic narrative, provides the inspiration for the title story of Isaac Bashevis Singer's collection of short stories, *The Death of Methuselah* (1990).

RONALD M. MELDRUM

MICAIAH See AHAB.

MICHAEL Michael, usually listed as first of the archangels, appears to Daniel in a vision as "one of the chief princes" (Dan. 10:13), by implication a kind of special guardian angel to Israel (v. 21) who shall again come to Israel's aid in the last days, in the time of the Great Tribulation (12:1; cf. Rev. 12:7-9). His name is said to mean "Who is like God?" according to some targums (e.g., Tg. Yer. Num. 2:10) from utterances to that effect made at the crossing of the Red Sea and the handing down of the Torah to Moses, and talmudic legend makes him one of the four archangels who stand around the throne of God in heaven (the others being Gabriel, Uriel, and Raphael). In some sources he succeeds Shammiel (or Sammael) as leader of the heavenly choir following the excommunication of Lucifer and his cohorts (Seder Rabba di-Bereshit 28-30; 3 Hekalot 161-63; Gen. Rab. 78.2); he is sometimes given the name Metatron, and said to be the angel who wrestled with Jacob at the Jabbok (Abkir in Yalqut 1.132; Zerubbabel 5.5), from which event he had to return before daybreak so as to lead the choir in morning song (Gen. Rab. 78.1-2; Tan. Ber. 1.165). The appearance of Michael, and sometimes of Gabriel, was thought to indicate the presence of the Shekinah (Gen. Rab. 97.3; cf. Justin, *Dial.* 20, 128), and he is associated by various sources with the ascension of Enoch and Moses. In a rarer midrash the seraph which touched Isaiah's lips with a live coal is identified as Michael (Bera. 4b). The NT Epistle of Jude (v. 9) recollects a talmudic legend that Michael preserved the body of Moses from Sammael, the devil who had claimed it on account of Moses having murdered the Egyptian (cf. 2 Petirat Mosheh 381-82; Midr. D'varim Raba 11.10; also Origen, *On First Principles*, 3.2.1).

Michael's role in Dan. 12:1 and Rev. 12:7-9 largely defines his role in medieval Christian commentary and legend, where he becomes the angel who rescues souls from Limbo and Hell. In representations of the Last Judgment he is shown armed as a warrior, holding the scales which balance good deeds against bad (Picinelli, *Mundus Symbolicus*). His feast day, Sept. 29, is the quarter day Michelmas; on the Isle of Skye there was a Michelmas procession and feast-day cake called "St. Michael's Bannock." In Philippe de Mézières's office and pageant for "The Presentation of the Blessed Virgin" (1372) Michael, along with Raphael, Gabriel, and nine other angels, plays a part. In the ME Corpus Christi drama, the Chester *"Antichristus,"* the Archangel Michael strikes down the Antichrist as Enoch and Elijah rise from the dead. Michael then carries the patriarchs to heaven while the responsory *Gaudete, Justi, in Domino* is being sung. He also figures in the *"Judicium"* play which follows. As a patron saint and protector of high places (replacing the Germanic Wotan) Michael gives rise to names such as Mont-Saint-Michel, events surrounding which (as in the alliterative *Morte Arthure*) are connected with his medieval *legenda*. He was in the time of Constantine also styled a "heavenly physician," and became patron saint also of healing hot-springs in many locations.

In Milton's *Paradise Lost* Michael and Gabriel lead the war in heaven against Satan, where he is called by God "of Celestial Armies Prince" (6.44). It is something of a comedown when Byron in his "Vision of Judgment" has Michael receive the soul of King George III into heaven, and thus illustrates his point:

> 'Twas the archangel Michael; all men know
> The make of angels and archangels, since
> There's scarce a scribbler has not one to show,
> From the fiends' leader to the angels' prince. (st. 29)

In Joyce's *Portrait of the Artist,* there is a reference to "Michael, prince of the heavenly host," who "with a sword of flame in his hand, appeared before the guilty pair [Adam and Eve] and drove them forth [from Eden]," drawing upon a tradition reflected in bk. 10 of Milton's *Paradise Lost,* in which also is found reference to the expectation that it will be Michael who blows the trumpet in the last day, announcing the Final Judgment (10.73-75).

See also ANGEL; GABRIEL; RAPHAEL.

MICHAL   Michal, the beautiful younger daughter of King Saul (cf. Meg. 15a), was given in marriage to David as his first wife (1 Sam. 14:49; 18:20ff.). Saul attempted to use his daughter's love for David as a means to rid himself of a popular rival: he therefore set the *mohar* (bridal price) for Michal at one hundred Philistine foreskins (1 Sam. 18:20-30). When David presented double that number, "Saul saw and knew that the LORD was with David . . . and was yet more afraid . . . and became David's enemy continually" (vv. 27-29). When the jealous king subsequently tried to ambush David in his house, Michal helped him escape, and then lied about her assistance, saying that David had threatened her. Saul therefore gave her to Phalti (or Phaltiel) in marriage (1 Sam. 25:44; cf. Sanh. 19b-20a). Because there was no divorce, David demanded her back for his harem fourteen years later (2 Sam. 3:14ff.) in order to legitimate his succession to the throne. An embarrassed Michal rebuked David for dancing before the ark when it was brought to Jerusalem (2 Sam. 6), and was apparently bitter about his succeeding her father in God's favor — a rejection of God's ordinance to which her barrenness was attributed (2 Sam. 6:22ff.).

In D. H. Lawrence's play *David* Michal is presented as a passionate lover resentful of the religious motivation in David that seems to interfere with her total possession of him. Morris Raphael Cohen sees Michal as a tragic heroine in his *King Saul's Daughter* (1938), a five-act closet drama. Mark Van Doren's "Michal," a poem from his "The People of the Word" cycle, concentrates on the tragic moment of her separation from the weeping husband Palatiel, who follows her on her enforced route back to David's harem as far as he dare. Gladys Schmitt's novel *David the King* (1946) conjectures that Michal was originally intended to be the wife of Agag, hacked to pieces by Samuel, and presents her as a perpetual victim of unrequited love. Stefan Heym's *The King David Report* (1972) allows an aged Michal to tell her side of the story, a narration which characterizes David in extremely negative terms and undercuts the official "state history" being composed for posterity by the historian Ethan. Like Dryden's *Absalom and Achitophel,* the novel is a political allegory about the writer's own contemporary Europe.

See also DAVID.

Bibliography. Frontain, R.-J., and J. Wojcik, eds. *The David Myth in Western Literature* (1980); Liptzin, S. *Biblical Themes in World Literature* (1985).

MIDIAN, MIDIANITE   Gen. 25:2 identifies the Midianites as descendants of Abraham and Keturah. Jethro, a Midianite priest, was father-in-law to Moses (Exod. 2:15-21), though he is also called a Kenite (Judg. 1:16; 4:11), and joined Moses in worship on one occasion (Exod. 18). But the Midianites were later allies of Moab in attempts to subvert the Israelites (Num. 22:47; 25:1-9), and still later were pillaging raiders against Israel, especially at harvesttime (Judg. 6:1-6), until finally routed by Gideon (Judg. 7–8).

See also BALAAM; GIDEON; MOSES.

MIDRASH   *Midrash* signifies exegesis or interpretation either of the Mishnah or of Scripture, usually heuristic in motive. Midr. halakah typically derives a rule or law from a verse of Scripture, demonstrating in the process the pertinence to the passage of a rule of the Mishnah, thus establishing the accordance of oral and written Torah. Important examples are the Sipra to Leviticus and the Sipre to Numbers and to Deuteronomy. Midr. Haggadah (or 'Aggadah) consists of interpretation or amplification of a specifically biblical story, such as characterizes especially the narrative exposition of Genesis Rabbah. A. M. Klein's Hasidic "Preacher" in the poem of that name impresses his hearers because of the fluency with which he "quoted *midrash* and the psalms." The midrashic process as both literary and critical activity has become of special interest to literary theorists in the last part of the 20th cent., but this development is well anticipated in literary theory from the Middle Ages onward.

See also HAGGADAH; HALAKAH.

Bibliography. Fletcher, H. F. *Milton's Rabbinical Readings* (1930); Gaster, M. "Jewish Sources of, and Parallels to, the Early English Metrical Romance of King Arthur and Merlin." In *Papers Read at the Anglo Jewish Historical Exhibition . . . , 1887* (1888), 231-52; Handelman, S. *The Slayers of Moses: The Emergence of Rabbinic Interpretation in Modern Literary Theory* (1982); *Fragments of Redemption: Jewish Thought and Literary Theory in Benjamin, Scholem, and Levinas* (1991); Hartman, G. H., and S. Budick. *Midrash and Literature* (1986); Mendelsohn, L. R. "Milton and the Rabbis: A Later Inquiry." *SEL* 18 (1978), 125-35; Neusner, J. *Invitation to Midrash: The Workings of Rabbinic Bible Interpretation* (1989); Stollman, S. S. "Milton's Rabbinical Readings and Fletcher." *MiltonS* 4 (1972), 195-215.

MIGHTY RUSHING WIND   *See* PENTECOST.

MILES CHRISTI   In Eph. 6 St. Paul articulates a metaphor which became one of the most pervasive in Christian literary tradition: "Put on the whole armour of God," he urges, including "the breastplate of righteousness," "the shield of faith," "the helmet of salvation," and "the sword of the Spirit, which is the word of God" (see also Rom. 13:12 and 2 Cor. 6:7). Paul here adapts a metaphor from the OT: the armor of the Lord of Hosts ("god of battle"), alluded to in Isa. 11:4-5; 59:16-18 and Wisd. of Sol. 5:17-23. For ancient Israel, the central image of salvation was the exodus from Egypt, when God acted miraculously to deliver his people from slavery and at the same time gave them military victory over their oppressors (Exod. 14). Premonarchal Israel's military leader was therefore the Lord himself, and its wars were "holy"; indeed, the so-called "Day of the Lord" originated in the conception of God's literal military vindication of his people. One of the oldest images of God in the OT is "a man of war" (Exod. 15:3).

Two further developments lie between Israel's holy war and Paul's Christian armor. The first of these is the prophets' redefinition of the Day of the Lord. Amos, e.g., challenges the complacency of Israel's monarchy by interpreting the Day of the Lord as a day of judgment against Israel herself: "Woe unto you that desire the day of the LORD! to what end is it for you? the day of the LORD is darkness, and not light" (5:18). Amos's interpretation of defeat as providential distinguishes between military and spiritual success: there can on occasion be an inverse relation between the two. A second development in redefining the holy war can be seen in the mission and ministry of Jesus. In keeping with the ancient Hebrew concept of peace as *shalom* (wholeness, equilibrium, health), Jesus embodies the struggle against Satan, the adversary of God and the prime disrupter of *shalom.* Both Jesus' teaching about the kingdom (or kingship) of God and his actions as healer, judge, sufferer, and resurrected savior are to be understood in light of this struggle, whose outcome is indeed victory — but victory for *shalom,* not for one human party at the expense of another. Paul's use of military metaphors, then, is consistent with the conflict Jesus enacted, in which Paul sees every Christian as engaged: this is what it means to be a "soldier of Christ" (Lat. *miles Christi*) — even as every Christian participates in the victory won by Christ over Satan and death (1 Cor. 15:55-57; 2 Tim. 2:3). That Eph. 6 makes the enemies "the devil" and allied forces of evil (11–12) instead of foreign nations is probably also a reflection of postexilic Jewish thought in which demonic forces are seen as the deeper explanation of evil in the world.

For later literary tradition, two patristic treatments of the *miles Christi* are important. The first is Prudentius's (ca. 482) *Psychomachia,* a massive quasi-epic development of the Pauline metaphor in Eph. 6. Prudentius redefines the heroic values of Virgilian epic in a personification allegory of the struggle between Christian virtues and their detracting vices. The enemy here is not literal "principalities and powers" (Eph. 6:12) but habits in the human spirit itself (e.g., Worship-of-the-Old-Gods, Lust, Wrath) which militate against virtue. Prudentius thus combines the classical tradition (Platonic and Stoic) of the soul's moral struggle to become good with the Christian tradition of spiritual holy war. A second tradition reflects upon Christ's Passion as a literal battle with Satan (e.g., St. John Chrysostom, *Hom.* 6, on Col. 2:6-7); this homiletic trope came to be extensively elaborated in the later Middle Ages.

A third development should also be noted. The Church's nominal identification with political power—under Constantine encouraged a more literal response to "Christian" warfare which parallels ancient Israel's understanding of God's holy war. This response reached its apogee in the Crusades, which in turn fostered a literary tradition which supplements the tradition of the spiritual holy war advocated in Eph. 6. In 1128 St. Bernard of Clairvaux wrote a tract "In Praise of the New Knighthood" to encourage the Knights Templars, a military monastic order founded by the Council of Troyes. Adapting to his purpose St. Augustine's identification of monastic vocation with the call to be "soldiers of Christ" (*De opere monachorum,* 36), Bernard argues that Christ's soldier can fight in moral safety, for if he dies he finds Christ, and if he triumphs he glorifies Christ: "when he kills a malefactor, he is not a slayer of men, but a slayer of evil, and plainly an avenger of Christ against those who do amiss." While the effect of such reasoning on the Crusades was considerable, its literary impact was relatively slight. Chaucer contrasts the virtuous knight in the *The Canterbury Tales* with the frivolous squire on the basis of comparative campaigns: the knight has been a crusader (*General Prologue,* 1.51-66, 85-88). The major literary development in this vein awaited the Counter-Reformation and Tasso's *Jerusalem Delivered,* an epic about the First Crusade which is heavy with nostalgia for Christian unity.

The theme of Christ's battle with Satan figures prominently in Anglo-Saxon poetry. The 8th-cent. *Dream of the Rood,* a Passion poem, is replete with the language of such a battle, as is *Christ and Satan,* in which the fallen angels "must wage vain war on the might of God," knowing that the "Prince, / the Lord of hosts" will defeat them in the Last Battle as on the cross at Calvary. Christ's followers are his men at arms, fighting the good fight; the fallen angels are thanes of Satan. In this vein, the principal medieval literary tradition of the *miles Christi* remains spiritual and allegorical. The Pearl Poet's hero, in *Gawain and the Green Knight,* is a paragon of virtue and courtesy, who goes to confront the Green Knight with an extraordinary Shield of Faith (619-65). Yet Gawain's fear of the ordeal diverts his faith from what the shield symbolizes to a literal and seemingly life-preserving girdle, and for this lapse Gawain suffers: loving his own life, he very

nearly loses it, whereas he should have been prepared to lose it in the first place for Christ's sake (cf. John 12:24-25). *Gawain* is the most notable example in English of Arthurian legend being used as a vehicle of prophetic judgment on contemporary Christian society. As such, it bears comparison with the *Quest for the Holy Grail,* or with the French prose *Lancelot* (the source of Malory's *Sangreal* in the late 15th cent.), where the impeccable Christian knight is Sir Galahad.

Franciscan interest in this theme in the 13th cent. probably served to popularize it. In the *Speculum Perfeccionis* (chap. 7) St. Francis is said to have referred to his followers as *"fratres me milites tabulae rotundae,"* and the chivalric associations for Franciscan theologian Alexander of Hales link Christ as champion knight "struggling for us bravely on the cross against his enemies" with individual "soldiers of Christ," those who have through contrition, penitence, and identification with the cross become "conformed to him in his struggle" (*Introitus,* 7.31.55ff.; also *Quaestiones Disputatae Antequam Esset Frater* [Quaracchi 20.851]). Words ascribed to Christ, such as "I haue þe wonnen in fith," the last lines of a poem by Franciscan John Grimestone (C. Brown, *Religious Lyrics of the XIVth Century,* no. 66) are a commonplace in English Franciscan lyrics, and may be answered by poems such as one long lyric in which the *miles Christi* declares his willingness to join in the battle against Satan: ". . . swete ihesu, y am þi knyȝt, / aȝenus hym [þe fend] y take þe fiȝt" (Brown, no. 125). In this lyric the arming of the knight is a Pauline spiritual inventory, and the forces of the enemy include not only the devil but the other two "foes of man," the world and the flesh. In this tradition, Franciscan poet James Ryman (1492) refers to the members of his order as "oure knyghthoode" (Jeffrey, 250). And the beautiful 16th-cent. lullaby carol, "Lully, lullay" (R. Greene, *The Early English Carols* [2nd ed. 1977], no. 322A), still presents Christ as the archetypal *miles,* a knight with ever-flowing wounds from his redemptive battle.

If Galahad as the Christ-knight is derivative from patristic interpretation of the Passion as a battle, it may be that the Anglo-Norman poem by Franciscan friar Nicholas Bozon, *Coment le fiz Deu fu armé en la croyz* (D. Jeffrey and B. Levy, *The Anglo-Norman Lyric* [1990], no. 36), has influenced some nonfraternal ME treatments of this image. It still appears in some of John Lydgate's lyrics on the Passion more than a century later, and in Langland's *Piers Plowman,* where Christ "toke the bataille" on Calvary (Passus 16) and "of his gentrice wole juste in piers armes, In his helme & in his haberjoun *humana natura*" (Passus 18). In medieval drama the image is used by the York and Towneley playwrights: Christ's "armoure riche and goode" is elaborated at length in the York Cycle, while in the Towneley "Crucifixion" Christ's torturers use the language of chivalric contest when they mock him for his claim to kingship.

Yet the most influential tradition of the *miles Christi* in medieval drama is the personification allegory of Prudentius's *Psychomachia.* All medieval religious drama turns on a struggle between God and the devil for the destiny of humankind, and this struggle frequently includes representations of the seven deadly sins, the three Christian virtues (Faith, Hope, Charity), the three enemies of the soul (World, Flesh, Devil), and other personifications which take their inspiration from Prudentius. The morality play is generically identifiable as a contest for the soul between personified abstractions — from the late-14th-cent. *Pride of Life* through the ambitious *Castle of Perseverance* to the so-called "hybrid morality" of the late 16th cent. and its fruition in Marlowe's *Doctor Faustus.* Semidramatic courtly forms, such as the triumph, the masque, and the tournament, nearly always used personification as well, and sometimes the specific allegory of soul struggle, as in John Lydgate's *Triumphal Entry for Henry VI,* where variations of the Pauline "armour of God" are bestowed on the king.

With the flourishing of Christian humanism in the late 15th cent., a new emphasis is discernible in literary treatments of the *miles Christi.* Erasmus's *Enchiridion Militis Christiani* ("A Handbook for the Christian Soldier") is an early example of this emphasis. For Erasmus (who wrote polemically against literal war), the two chief weapons of the Christian are prayer and knowledge, including knowledge of the ancient pagans because it promotes practical piety. Erasmus thus stresses the life of Christian action in the world, and his little book anticipates a characteristic Renaissance application of the soldier of Christ. In Spenser's *Faerie Queene,* e.g., a succession of wandering knights is engaged in allegorical quests of virtue; the first of them is the Knight of Holiness, wearing "the armor of a Christian man specified by St. Paul" (according to Spenser's letter to Raleigh). Yet even this knight has a civic responsibility, for in addition to holiness, he also represents St. George, the patron saint of England, and the queen he serves is Gloriana, or Elizabeth I. Despite his ardor to reach the New Jerusalem and marry Truth, he is obliged to postpone these goals in order to serve Gloriana, and the fact that we never see him complete his quest suggests that the temporal quest is essentially open-ended: his victory over the dragon recalls the Passion of Christ and anticipates the eschatological conquest of Satan (Rev. 12:7-9; 20:7-10), but in the world of history the task goes on.

Shakespeare's adaptation of the morality play takes the emphasis on the life of action a step further. Henry V, "the mirror of all Christian kings," begins his dramatic life in *1 Henry 4* as an impressionable young prince caught between the indolent temptations of Falstaff and the stern demands of the king his father, a dilemma recalling morality play protagonists faced with competing personified loyalties. But the stakes in Prince Hal's struggle involve a temporal kingdom, not the salvation of his soul,

and the wars he makes as the paragon of Christian princes seem rather more designed to preserve his own political stability (e.g., *2 Henry 4,* 4.5.212-15) than to promote the kingdom of God on earth. Moreover, Henry V's temporal quest, like the Redcrosse Knight's, is open-ended: though we see him happily married and bravely predicting that his son will mount a crusade against the Turks, the final Chorus reminds us that Henry VI in fact lost everything that his heroic father had gained (*Henry 5,* Epilogue 6-14).

Milton's works culminate the Christian humanist interpretation of the *miles Christi.* In *Areopagitica,* Milton's forthright advocacy of the good use of "bad books" is in the spirit of Erasmus's *Enchiridion* (also Boccaccio, *De Genealogia Deorum Gentilium,* 14-15), and his praise of the "true, warfaring Christian" is reserved for one who "can apprehend and consider vice with all her baits and seeming pleasures, and yet abstain, and yet distinguish, and yet prefer that which is truly better." Milton's involvement in the tract wars of the mid-17th cent. and his willingness to serve as Secretary of State for Foreign Tongues in Cromwell's government indicate how seriously he took the humanist mandate to reform church and society: in effect, the struggle was a Protestant crusade, as it had been for Spenser. Yet by the time Milton wrote *Paradise Lost* after the restoration of the monarchy he had bitterly opposed, he portrayed the Christian soldier much less stridently. Literal warfare, in fact, now means nothing: if all military forces ever assembled, "baptized or infidel," were convened together, they would compare with Satan's forces as pygmies compare to cranes in Homer's simile (*PL* 1.573-87). Recalling the patristic and medieval tradition of heroic suffering, epitomized in Christ's Passion, Milton celebrates "the better fortitude / Of patience and heroic martyrdom" (9.31-32), and his portrait of the epic voice in the invocation which opens bk. 7 suggests that he aspires to the same spiritual perseverance. "Let Truth and Falsehood grapple," Milton had urged in *Areopagitica,* "Whoever knew Truth put to the worse, in a free and open encounter?" Now he portrays Truth's champion in defeat, "In darkness, and with dangers compast round / And solitude" (7.27-28), sustained only by the mysterious grace of the muse.

The other major Puritan treatment of the *miles Christi* in the 17th cent. is in the popular prose allegories of John Bunyan. In *Pilgrim's Progress,* Christian is armed by Piety, Prudence, and Charity with "all manner of Furniture, which their Lord had provided for Pilgrims, as Sword, Shield, Helmet, Brest plate" — in short, with the Pauline "armour of God." Christian quickly puts his armor to good use in his fight with Apollyon, who includes flaming darts among his arsenal (cf. Eph. 6:16). While the metaphor of Christian conflict is incidental in *Pilgrim's Progress,* Bunyan made it his central motif in *The Holy War,* which employs the allegorical device of the body as a castle for the soul, a device Bunyan may have learned from Richard Bernard's *Isle of Man,* though its literary ancestry included Phineas Fletcher's *Purple Island,* Spenser's Castle of Alma (*FQ* 2.9), the medieval *Castle of Perseverance,* and ultimately Prudentius's *Psychomachia.* A comic variation of the Pauline armor in *The Holy War* is Diabolus's description of his armor: the helmet of "hope of doing well at last what lives soever you live," the breastplate of "an hard heart," the sword of "a Tongue that is set on fire of Hell," the shield of unbelief, and the general body armor of "a dumb and prayerless Spirit."

Probably because of its association with religious "enthusiasm" and dissent in Bunyan, the *miles Christi* almost disappears from serious literature in the 18th cent. Exceptions include Charles Wesley's "Soldiers of Christ arise and put your armour on," and William Cowper's lines in bk. 6 of *The Task,* but William Blake foreshadows a growing tendency to politicize the *miles* by the end of the century. His familiar lyric in the Preface to *Milton,* "And did those feet," with its memorable call to arms ("Bring me my Bow of burning gold: / Bring me my Arrows of desire: / Bring me my Spear: O clouds unfold! / Bring me my Chariot of fire! . . .") invokes revolution in Romantic terms; set to Perry's music the poem became a virtual anthem for the British trade-union movement, a kind of secularized *miles Christi* hymn. The triumphalism of such church hymns as "Onward, Christian Soldiers," "The Son of Man Goes Forth to War," and "Stand Up, Stand Up, for Jesus" coincides with the heyday of British imperialism and the rapid development of the foreign missionary movement. These hymns therefore have an affinity with the Song of Moses and Miriam in Exod. 15 and with literature inspired by the Crusades and the Puritan Revolution of the 17th cent.: all identify militant religion with political success. But in the 19th cent. the voice of dissent is also heard, as it had been earlier. Kipling's short story "The Man Who Would Be King," e.g., takes "The Son of Man Goes Forth to War" as its central motif in a moral challenge to British imperialism. In 20th-cent. literature the *miles Christi* image has been invoked in order to be denounced, though for David Jones it can still call up traditional positive associations (*Sleeping Lords,* 26).

See also ARMOR AND WEAPONS; DEVIL; SEVEN DEADLY SINS; SHIELD; SWORD OF THE SPIRIT; WORLD, FLESH, AND DEVIL.

Bibliography. Chew, S. *The Pilgrimage of Life* (1962); Fleming, J. V. "'The Dream of the Rood' and Anglo-Saxon Monasticism," *Traditio* 22 (1966), 43-72; Jeffrey, D. L. *The Early English Lyric and Franciscan Spirituality* (1975); Leclerq, J. "Le sermon sur la royauté du Christ au moyen âge," *AHDLMA* 18 (1943-45), 143-80; Von Rad, G. *Der heilige Krieg im alten Testament* (1958); Wang, A. *Der "Miles Christianus" im 15. und 17. Jahrhundert und seine mittelalterliche Tradition* (1975); Woolf, R. "The Theme of Christ the Lover-Knight in Medieval English Literature." *RES* 13 (1962), 1-16.   JOHN D. COX

MILLENNIUM   Probably no biblical text has sparked off more prophetic expectations than the verses in the Apocalypse:

> And I saw an angel come down from heaven, having the key of the bottomless pit and a great chain his hand. And he laid hold on the dragon, that old serpent, which is the Devil, and Satan, and bound him a thousand years. And cast him into the bottomless pit, and shut him up, and set a seal upon him, that he should deceive the nations no more, till the thousand years should be fulfilled: and after that he must be loosed a little season. (Rev. 20:1-3)

The idea of the millennium (the thousand years during which Satan will be bound) may depend upon an interpretation of the days of Creation as forecasting a cosmic World Week of history in which each day represents one thousand years (see, e.g., Pseudo-Philo 28.8-9; 2 Enoch 33). This scheme culminates in the seventh, the Sabbath Age, a concept which became assimilated to the Jewish prophetic hope of a messianic kingdom in this world. The earthly character of this blessed age originated in a time when Jews did not expect an afterlife. When in later thought a state beyond time was expected, Jewish commentators interpreted the millennium as an intermediate reign of fruitfulness and peace upon earth before the conclusion of history (4 Ezra 7:28-35).

In the NT no writer explicitly took up the theme of the millennium except the author of the Apocalypse. The way he depicts it implies an earthly messianic regime which will have a definite end when Satan is loosed for a little while. He is here following Jewish tradition: the millennium will be Christ's reign on earth as God's Messiah. As G. B. Caird writes: "John wants the best of both worlds: the ultimate destiny of the redeemed is in the heavenly city, but he retains the earthly paradise, the millennium. . . . God has a purpose for the whole Creation and his purpose must be vindicated in history" (*A Commentary on the Revelation of St. John the Divine,* 254).

St. John's use of the Jewish millennium opened the door to Christian expectations of a blessed future age. Papias (early 2nd cent.), whose vision of an era of prodigious natural fecundity also shows Jewish influence, was followed by St. Irenaeus (late 2nd cent.), Tertullian and Commodian (3rd cent.), and Lactantius (4th cent.), who expected a glorious reign of Christ and his saints for a thousand years on earth (P. E. B. Allo, *Saint Jean. L'Apocalypse,* 294). But the dangers of millenarianism (Gk., chiliasm) were soon apparent to some, at least, of the early Church Fathers. Tyconius (late 4th cent.) supplies an alternative interpretation, that the thousand years means the spiritual victory of Christ which extends from the First to the Second Advent (Allo, 221). St. Jerome rejects a literal millennium as mere fable, while his contemporary St. Augustine, although at first attracted by the idea, later dismisses it as ridiculous (Allo, 221). From the 5th cent. onward literal millennial dreams would seem to have been stamped out by the weight of such authoritative exegesis.

But the idea continued to haunt a troubled and war-ridden Europe. Thus the crusading movement was in part the pursuit of a millennium focused on the earthly Jerusalem which, to the poor who flocked in such numbers to the "People's Crusade" in 1095, appeared as the dream city "flowing with milk and honey" (N. Cohn, *The Pursuit of the Millennium*, 61-68). A fresh impetus to such expectation was given by Joachim of Fiore (12th cent.), who supplied a Trinitarian basis to this hope by assimilating the idea of the Sabbath Age of history to his concept of the third "age" of the Holy Spirit (M. Reeves, *The Influence of Prophecy in the Later Middle Ages*, 302-05). This future third age would follow the main victory over the forces of Antichrist but, because this would still be an age within history, Satan would be loosed at its end and the final scourge of Gog and Magog would immediately precede the conclusion of history at the Last Judgment.

The belief in a Sabbath Age of history, or Millennium, or Age of the Spirit, can be traced through a number of medieval and Renaissance commentaries on the Apocalypse. It inspired the 15th-cent. sect of the Taborites in Bohemia, who established their communist society on the mountain they called Mt. Tabor (E. Werener, *Comparative Studies in Society and History*, 2, 344-63). A strong defense of millenarianism in a Renaissance context was made by the Dominican Giovanni Annio of Viterbo in a work written in 1481 which proclaimed his belief that a future pope and prince would together destroy the Saracens, unite all Christians, and inaugurate a final state of beatitude in the Church (Reeves, *Influence*, 463-64). Again, at the end of the century, the prophetic vision of Savonarola and his disciples designated Florence as the New Jerusalem (D. Weinstein, *Savonarola and Florence . . .* [1970], 30-66, 132-84). An early 17th-cent. commentator on the Apocalypse, Bartholomew Holzhauser, places against a black background of present wars and calamities a coming millennium when Emperor and Pope would break the Turkish power and give peace and justice to the world (*Interpretatio in Apocalypsim* [1850], 69-75). In the same period certain Franciscan and Jesuit visionaries were focusing their millennial dreams on missions in the New World (J. L. Phelan, *The Millennial Kingdom of the Franciscan in the New World;* M. Reeves, *Joachim of Fiore and the Prophetic Future*, 128-35).

It would seem natural for Protestants to be tempted into a heady millenarianism. By no means all were. For example, Henry Bullinger, the influential pastor of Zurich, in his *A Hundred Sermons upon the Apocalips of Jesu Christe* [1561], 593-99), writes expressly against the heresy of "the Chiliastes or Millenaries," interpreting the thousand years as from the beginning of the gospel preaching to the mid-11th cent., the point at which Bullinger saw the Papacy as entering upon its most fully Satanic course.

There was, however, a strong current of millennial

expectation flowing among radical Protestants on the Continent (e.g., Sebastian Franck; see G. Williams and A. Mergal, *Spiritual and Anabaptist Writers* [1957], 149-60), and equivalent aspirations were evident in England. John Bale's play *A comedy concerning three laws* (ca. 1531) elaborates the usual seven ages of world history, after the various infidelities of which will come a new heaven of renewed faith and a new earth of faith's practical application. John Foxe, author of the famous *Book of Martyrs* (1563), wrote a commentary on the Apocalypse in which the seven ages are successive millennia, the first six of which are to give way to the final millennial kingdom sometime before A.D. 2000 (*Eicasmi seu Meditationes in Sacram Apocalypsin* [1587], 60). Sir Walter Raleigh's *History of the World* describes three great periods of world history, before the law, under the law, and under grace (2.4.11). While the last era begins with the birth of Christ, it contains within it "the promise of an everlasting kingdom." Raleigh may have been influenced by Robert Pont's *A newe treatise of the right reckoning of the yeares, and ages of the world;* Pont, however, reckons the penultimate age from 1056 to an imminent date, ca. 1600, at which point the millennium will begin. Thomas Brightman's chronology reiterates his belief in a period when Christ will reign with his saints on earth, as distinct from in heaven (*A Revelation of the Revelation* [1615], Pref., 121-22, 199, 256, 559, 851-73). The greatest outburst of millennial expectations occurred in the Civil War and Commonwealth period when radical thinkers saw the political revolution as the prelude to the descent of the New Jerusalem to earth. At that time Christ's saints would be raised in a "first resurrection" (which they distinguished from the general resurrection at the end of time) and the whole world would be converted and brought under Christ's rule. Joseph Mede's *Clavis Apocalyptica* (1627) sees the millennium coming after the world has endured 6,000 years, or not later than the 19th cent. A.D. The "seventh thousand," the "glorious Sabbath of the reign of Christ," he believed to be probably much closer at hand. John Archer argues for *The Personall Reigne of Christ upon Earth* in 1642. Jeremy Burroughs, in *An Exposition of the Prophesie of Hosea* ([1643], 183-91), recalls Lactantius's dreams of a gloriously fruitful earth. Robert Maton emphasizes the conversion of the Jews and the conquest by Christ of the kingdoms of this world (*Israel's Redemption or the Prophetical History of our Saviour's Kingdome on Earth . . .* [1642]). Writing in 1653, in the midst of "these wars and wranglings," William Erbery affirms his belief in the Millennium:

> when God alone shall reign in Men and Men reign in Righteousness, and Righteousness arise in truth, then shall the Royal Law and Rule of Christ in love be followed: That Men and Magistrates shall do to all as they would be done unto, or rather, do to Men as God would. (*The Reign of Christ and the Saints with him, on Earth, A thousand years . . .* [1653], 192)

Milton's angel Michael in *Paradise Lost* (1.2585-87) prophesies to fallen Adam a millennial restoration and more,

> . . . for then the Earth
> Shall all be Paradise, far happier place
> Than this of *Eden,* and far happier days.

Milton was familiar with Reformation millenarian controversy through his tutor at Christ's College, Joseph Mede. Both in his essays "Of Reformation" (1641) and "Animadversions" (1642), influenced by Tyndale, Foxe, Brightman, and Mede, Milton sees his task in part as a preparation of English Puritans for the approaching millennium. He believed that England would be the seat of Christ's millennial empire ("Of Reformation," in *Works,* 1.525, 614) — unlike Foxe and Bale, who had explicitly denied that God had elected one nation above another, or that a reformed England would prove either a Utopia or a millennial kingdom.

Other millenarian thinkers, however, subscribed, like Milton, to nationalistic chiliasm. Gerrard Winstanley (1648), a radical Puritan, argued that the English Puritan Revolution itself marked the onset of the millennium, and if the revolutionary spirit of the 1790s failed to follow the Puritan eschatological schema, many were happy to extend millennial expectation to national prophecy. Blake's preface to *Milton* yields up the now famous lines ("And did those Feet"), set to music by Sir C. H. H. Parry (1916), a "working class" hymn envisioning the millennium brought on by social progress — a major theme in 19th-cent. literature. Blake's *Europe: A Prophecy* (1794), like Coleridge's "Religious Musings" of the same year, are modeled on Milton's "On the Morning of Christ's Nativity," except that each undertakes to adapt Milton's celebration of the First and Second Advent of Christ to contemporary revolution and its expected consequences, a "renovated Earth," a communist utopia in which, in Coleridge's phrase, "the vast family of Love / Raised from the common earth by common toil / Enjoy the equal produce" (340-43; cf. 356-66).

M. H. Abrams has shown that "at the formative period of their lives, major romantic poets" (including Wordsworth, Blake, Southey, Coleridge, and Shelley) shared a "hope in the French Revolution as the portent of universal felicity" (*Natural Supernaturalism,* 64), anticipating in this way the post-Marxian idealists of the next century, from Romantic medievalists like William Morris to Fabian socialists such as G. B. Shaw. After the French Revolution proved not, after all, to usher in a glorious, peaceable kingdom, some of the Romantics tended, like Wordsworth in his Prospectus, to shift their millennial aspirations to a perfection of the powers of human consciousness. Byron's several allusions to the millennium (esp. Rev. 20:1-3) also imply such a secularized understanding (e.g., *Don Juan,* 8.1081-84; *Marino Faliero,* 4.2.504-05; *The Prophecy of Dante,* 3.9-12).

In America, the development of literary references to the biblical millennium ran a slightly different course. Here nationalistic chiliasm was the dominant mode for more than two centuries, and it is reflected in a wide range of Puritan and later literature. In a sermon to passengers of the *Arabella* in 1630, John Cotton proclaimed America as the new promised land, reserved by God for his elect people as the actual site for a new heaven and a new earth. John Winthrop's *A Model of Christian Charity,* likewise a sermon delivered on the deck of the flagship *Arabella,* sees all history converging upon the new settlement. Though afflictions were to be endured, for Increase Mather, "This is Immanuels Land. Christ by a wonderful Providence hath dispossessed Satan, who reigned securely in these Ends of the Earth, for Ages the Lord knoweth how many, and here the Lord has caused as it were *New Jerusalem* to come down from Heaven" *(The Day of Trouble Is Near).* In *Magnalia Christi Americana* Cotton Mather claims prophetic vocation as "Herald of the Lord's Kingdome now approaching," and through his work on biblical chronology he assures his readers of an imminent "Sabbatism . . . just going to lay its arrest upon us." He views the American pioneer struggle as "the last conflict with anti-christ" before the millennium begins.

Though far more theocratic than any vision of England after Milton, the American millennial myth nonetheless parallels its trans-Atlantic counterpart to a considerable degree. As Bercovitch suggests of the American Puritans, "Far from being nostalgic or primitivistic, their paradise was to be the result of a series of reformations in history, and therefore a fulfillment of social as well as spiritual norms" (*American Jeremiad,* 111). Thus, for Thomas Frink, Nehemiah's rebuilding of Jerusalem is an apt "figure" for the task, and America is "Type of the Blessed Millenium expressed by the *new Heavens* and a *new Earth*" (*A Sermon Preached Before His Excellency* [1758], 30). The poet Philip Freneau teamed with Hugh Henry Brackenridge to write "A Poem, on the Rising Glory of America" in which it could still be affirmed that

> Here the pure Church, descending from her God,
> Shall fix on earth her long and last abode;
> Zion arise, in radiant splendors dress'd.

Later, the American Revolution made 1776 the apocalyptic moment (Samuel Sherwood, *The Church's Flight into the Wilderness* [1776]). Timothy Dwight, sometime president of Yale and signer of the Declaration of Independence, reflected on that moment when he wrote, "This great continent is soon to be filled with the praise and piety of the Millenium; *here,* is the stem of that wonderful tree whose topmost boughs will reach the heavens" (*A Discourse on the National Fast* [1812]). In his epic poem *The Conquest of Canaan,* he reiterates the theme.

These formative works of American literature and spirituality chart a tradition of American millenarianism which includes elements as diverse as the visionary poetry of Walt Whitman and the formation of radical religious communities such as the Millerites and Campbellites. The same tradition informs the literature of Christian socialism and Social Gospelism, a force affecting Canadian as well as American literary uses of the millennial theme.

As even a cursory overview will show, interest in the "thousand years" of Rev. 20:3 has been immense, controversial, and as curiously applied in the New World as in the Old. The added burden incumbent upon moderns of bringing it about themselves evokes an understandable weariness of the subject in G. K. Chesterton, who quips: "We are to remove mountains and bring the millennium, because then we can have a quiet moment to discuss whether the millennium is at all desirable" (*Charles Dickens*, chap. 11).

See also APOCALYPSE; DRAGON OF THE APOCALYPSE; GOG AND MAGOG; SECOND COMING.

Bibliography. Abrams, M. H. *Natural Supernaturalism: Tradition and Revolution in Romantic Literature* (1971); Allo, P. E. B. *Saint Jean. L'Apocalypse* (1921); Beasley-Murray, G. R. *The Book of Revelation* (1974), 287-92; Bercovitch, S. *The American Jeremiad* (1978); Bietenhard, H. "The Millennial Hope in the Early Church" *SJT* 6 (1955), 12-30; Boettner, L. *The Millennium* (1957); Caird, G. B. *A Commentary on the Revelation of St. John the Divine* (1966); Charles, R. H. *A Critical History of the Doctrine of a Future Life* (1913); Cohn, N. *The Pursuit of the Millennium* (1972); Fixler, M. *Milton and the Kingdoms of God* (1964); Firth, K. *The Apocalyptic Tradition in Reformation Britain, 1530-1645* (1979); Gilmore, M. T. "Melville's Apocalypse: American Millennialism and *Moby-Dick.*" *ESQ: A Journal of the American Renaissance* 21 (1975), 154-61; Kitson, P. "Coleridge, Milton, and the Millennium." *WC* 18 (1987), 61-66; Nydahl, J. "From Millennium to Utopia Americana." In *America as Utopia*. Ed. K. M. Roemer (1981); Phelan, J. L. *The Millennial Kingdom of the Franciscans in the New World* (1956); Popkin, R. H. *Millenarianism and Messianism in English Literature and Thought 1650-1800* (1988); Reeves, M. *The Influence of Prophecy in the Later Middle Ages* (1969); *Joachim of Fiore and the Prophetic Future* (1976); Toon, P., ed. *Puritans, the Millennium and the Future of Israel: Puritan Eschatology 1600-1660* (1970).

MARJORIE REEVES
DAVID L. JEFFREY

MILLSTONE ABOUT HIS NECK   When Jesus' disciples wanted to know "who is the greatest in the kingdom of heaven" Jesus called a little child to him, and set him in the midst of them. He then said, "Except ye be converted, and become as little children, ye shall not enter into the kingdom of heaven. Whosoever therefore shall humble himself as this little child, the same is greatest in the kingdom of heaven" (Matt. 18:1-4). Having thus disposed of the implicit question of personal merit or, as St. Augustine puts it, their "agitated dissension about preeminence" (*Sermo*, 145.6), Jesus continued, "And whoso shall receive one such little child in my name receiveth me. But whoso shall offend one of these little ones which believe in me, it were better for him that a millstone were hanged about his neck, and that he were drowned in the depth of the sea" (Matt. 18:5-6; cf. Mark 9:42; Luke 17:2). Jesus' condemnation is aimed not only at child abuse per se (Vg *Qui autem scandalizaveret*) but at the dissuasion of children from faith.

Patristic commentary generally passes over Jesus' assertion of the simplicity of children, and even neglects his equation of caring for a little child with receiving him, preferring instead to universalize "little ones" as any of the humble faithful. This bias is evident also in Calvin's *Commentary* on the passage, where he argues (the actual child in the incident notwithstanding) that the word "children" ought here to be understood metaphorically. The passage is thus read strictly as an injunction to humility. According to Matthew Poole (*Annotations*, sup. Matt. 18:4), Christ is not enjoining his followers to become "as little Children in all things (which was the *Anabaptists* dream in *Germany*, upon which they would run about the streets, playing with Rattles, etc.)." He nevertheless goes on to observe that children are, in their characteristic disposition, worthy of imitation:

> 1. Little Children know not what dominion means, and therefore affect it not, are not Ambitious. 2. They are not given to Boast and Glory, and to prefer themselves before others. 3. They are ready to be taught and instructed. 4. They live upon their Father's Providence, and are not over Sollicitous. 5. They are not Malitious, and Vindictive.

Poole's view of little children, echoed in countless post-Reformation sermons on this passage, might seem to such as William Golding (*Lord of the Flies*) to evidence a striking lack of familiarity with the young of the species, which Christopher Smart, for one, cannot suppose Jesus to have shared. Smart's "children" are, like their medieval predecessors, still adult *in potentis*. Hence, in his *Hymns for the Amusement of Children*, he appeals to the child's simplicity in accepting the gospel at face value, even while his children's hymns make clear his expectation that the actual behavior of children is proleptic of adult sinfulness. The interpretation he offers in "Parable 36: The Kingdom of Christ compared to a Little Child" —

> The man, who e'er shall not receive;
> (In strict attention to believe)
> Christ's kingdom, as 'tis preach'd by me,
> With all a child's simplicity,
> Shall in that kingdom find no place

— in this sense accords with the children's prayer in his "Charity":

> Make me, O Christ, tho' yet a child,
> To virtue zealous, errors mild,
> Profess the feeling of a man,
> And be the Lord's Samaritan.

Keble's somewhat more misty view of "child-like hearts"

(e.g., "Palm Sunday") applies the passage to a defense of the authenticity of children's response to faith in the fourth stanza of his "Catechism," a poem which begins,

Oh! say not, dream not, heavenly notes
To childish ears are vain
That the young mind at random floats,
And cannot reach the strain.

In the 19th cent. the millstone itself was frequently lifted from its context to become a term for any impediment or noxious burden. Thackeray's allusion in *The Newcombes* is typical: "He was anxious to break the connexion: he owned it had hung like a millstone round his neck and caused him a great deal of remorse" (chap. 30). In Melville's *White-Jacket* there is a trivialized reference with respect to the unfortunate reception of a pudding: "They beat down my excuses with a storm of criminations. One present proposed that the fatal pudding should be tied round my neck, like a millstone, and myself pushed overboard" (chap. 15). In a singularly apt (though ironic) borrowing, Ernest Pontifex in Butler's *The Way of All Flesh* thinks his readiest access to Mr. Holt to effect his conversion might be by way of first winning over his children: "Ernest felt that it would indeed be almost better for him that a millstone should be hanged about his neck, and he cast into the sea, than that he should offend one of the little Holts." D. H. Lawrence affords an ironically perverse allusion in one of his *Letters,* where he opines that "the old Moses wouldn't have valued the famous tablets if they hadn't been ponderous, and millstones around everybody's neck" (615). In Joyce's *Portrait of the Artist as a Young Man,* in the famous Christmas dinner scene, Dante charges that the credibility of Parnell has been undermined by his being a "public sinner." When Parnell is defended by Mr. Casey, Mrs. Riordan takes up Dante's point (quoting the Vg translation of Matt. 18:6): "'Woe be to the man by whom the scandal cometh! It would be better for him that a millstone were tied about his neck and he were cast into the depth of the sea rather than he should scandalise one of these, my dear little ones.' That is the language of the Holy Ghost" (chap. 1).

See also CHILDREN.

MIND In the Bible, no single concept corresponds to our idea of *mind;* no specific aspect of the human personality is designated the seat of intellectual activity. Instead, the Bible reflects a complex anthropology and psychology wherein thinking, feeling, and willing are functions of the whole personality. In the OT, human life is expressed by the term *nepesh* ("soul"). Describing the inner life as the locus of intellectual endeavor, it can be translated "mind." *Nepesh* is the seat of willing (Gen. 23:8; 2 Kings 9:15) or feeling (Deut. 18:6; 2 Sam. 17:8). Closest to "mind" is the term *leb* (or *lebab;* "heart") — the center of human personality. The heart can be the instrument of thought: "as he thinketh in his heart, so is

he" (Prov. 23:7; see also 1 Sam. 27:1). The heart seeks knowledge (Prov. 15:14), remembers (Isa. 46:8), decides (Deut. 6:5; Isa. 10:7), and feels (Ps. 21:2). The inner life is also expressed by *ruah* ("spirit"), which can be translated "mind" (Gen. 26:35; Ezek. 11:5).

In the NT, mental activity is expressed by the term *nous* ("mind"). To pray with the mind ("understanding") is to pray rationally and with intelligibility (1 Cor. 14:15). With the mind, a person can make decisions (Rom. 14:5) and serve the law of God (Rom. 7:25). The mind can be corrupted (Rom. 1:28), but also renewed (Rom. 12:2). Other terms from the same root have similar meanings: *dianoia* ("understanding"; Matt. 22:37) and *noēma* ("mind"; 2 Cor. 3:14). In the text "Let this mind be in you" (Phil. 2:5), the verb *phroneō* is used, meaning "to have this attitude." OT concepts are apparent in texts where "mind" and "heart" are parallel (Phil. 4:7; Heb. 8:10; 10:16). The heart understands (John 12:40), believes (Rom. 10:10), and desires (Rom. 1:24). Like *nepesh, psychē* ("life") can be used with intellectual meaning (Acts 14:2; Phil. 1:27). Like *ruah, pneuma* ("spirit") can describe the mind (2 Cor. 2:13; Gal. 6:1).

In general, Western biblical interpretation regards the mind as *imago Dei;* for St. Augustine in his *De Trinitate* (bk. 12) the faculties of memory, intellect, and will are a hierarchical dynamic reflecting the distinct but unified persons of the Christian Trinity in their mode of relation. Analogously, in his *De sermone Domini in Monte* (1.12) he speaks of the process of perception as passage of stimuli from the senses to the *scientia,* or knowledge of temporal relations, and then to the *sapientia,* for discernment between tangible and intelligible values. Mind remains the seat of understanding, but also the source of integrative focus and willed response. Augustine follows apostolic usage in emphasizing that an obedient follower of Christ is to eschew being "puffed up by his fleshly mind" (Col. 2:18) and rather to "serve with humility of mind" (Acts 20:19); the goal of Christian discipleship is to acquire "the mind of Christ" (1 Cor. 2:16; Phil. 2:5).

St. Thomas Aquinas follows Augustine in seeing mind as the respect in which "God made man unquenchable, the image of his own endless life" (Wisd. 2:25). In relating the *imago Dei* strongly to immortality in this way, and proceeding according to an Aristotelian distinction between form and matter, he emphasizes the relation of mind and body as an analogue of the relation of soul and body. Mind and soul are interchangeable terms (*De anima,* 14); the mind learns, nonetheless, via the instrumentation of bodily senses and thus carries the identity formed by its earthly experience and choices with it into eternity (15). Discussion of mind, therefore, is never finally separable from a consideration of spiritual and ethical questions of the most practical nature. These ideas are developed in largely consistent fashion by Calvin (*Inst.* 1.1-3), although he shows some reluctance to accept every relation of mind and heart in Scripture as consonant, and, drawing upon Hebrews and Philippians, tends to separate reason and emotion.

If it is in the mind that humanity is most *imago Dei,* and if, as Calvin formulates it, some aspect of the knowledge of God is already implanted in one's mind at birth, then the mind is for spiritual purposes a realm preferable in its wealth of potential to all the kingdoms of this world. Hence, too, it is in the mind, as St. Paul's confession suggests ("I have learned, in whatsoever state I am, therewith to be content" [Phil. 4:11]), not in the world, that the "peace of God which passes all understanding" (Phil. 4:7) is known — not in the body. The passage in Philippians anticipates Sir Edmund Dyer's "My Minde to Me a Kingdom Is" (adapted by William Byrd [1588]), which begins:

> My minde to me a kingdom is;
> Such perfect joy therein I finde
> As farre exceeds all earthly blisse
> That God or nature hath assignde;
> Though much I want that most would have,
> Yet still my minde forbids to crave.
>
> Content I live; this is my stay, —
> I seek no more than may suffice.
> I presse to beare no haughtie sway;
> Look, what I lack my mind supplies.
> Loe, thus I triumph like a king
> Content with that my minde doth bring.

John Donne reflects in "Holy Sonnet 17" how it is that the mind's affections in this world, when rightly ordered as to ultimate value, can draw him to mindfulness of a higher love:

> Since she whom I lov'd hath payd her last debt
> To Nature, and to hers, and my good is dead,
> And her Soule early into heaven ravished,
> Wholly on heavenly things my mind is sett.
> Here the admyring her my mind did whett
> To seeke thee God; so streames do shew their head. . . .
> (Cf. *The Second Anniversary,* 501-06)

Herbert's advice to *The Country Parson* is to distinguish between mind and mere emotion in the matter of repentance, where sincerity is not measurable in terms of the flow of tears; rather, "repentance is an act of the mind, not of the Body, even as the Originall signifies; and that the chiefest thing, which God in Scriptures requires, is the heart, and the spirit, to worship him in truth, and spirit" (chap. 33). In his poem "Dulness" he prays for intellectual "quickness," the better to praise God in his writing. Then, on reflection, he realizes his liability to the peril of confusing cleverness with the proper function of mind: cleverness, he admits, is too often carnality masking as intellect:

> But I am lost in flesh, whose sugred lyes
>   Still mock me, and grow bold:
> Sure thou didst put a minde there, if I could
>   Find where it lies.

> Lord, cleare thy gift, that with a constant wit
>   I may but look towards thee:
> *Look* onely; for to *love* thee, who can be,
>   What angel fit?

Milton's least fit angel in *Paradise Lost,* lying on his back in the lake of fire with his cohorts, encourages them to harden their hearts in the cosmic struggle against God. Satan describes himself as ". . . One who brings / A mind not to be chang'd by Place or Time," and argues that "The mind is its own place, and in itself / Can make a Heav'n of Hell, a Hell of Heav'n" (1.252-55).

Stewardship of the mind is a major theme among Puritan writers, evangelicals, and Dissenters in the 18th cent. (e.g., John Owen, Isaac Watts, Philip Doddridge, Joseph Priestly, Hannah More). So also is a distinction between that "peace of mind" resulting from stupefaction (most typically the anaesthetic effects of indolent pleasures) and the perdurable peace of a rightly ordered and godly mind. So William Cowper's satiric lines in *Hope:*

> Peace be to those (such peace as earth can give)
> Who live in pleasure, dead ev'n while they live;
> Born capable, indeed, of heav'nly truth;
> But down to latest age, from earliest youth,
> Their mind a wilderness, through want of care,
> The plough of wisdom never ent'ring there.

In *Truth* Cowper rejects post-Renaissance intellectual triumphalism as a species of delusory hubris in which the self-styled "Enlightened" take sentiments like those in Dyer's poem, marry them to the Cartesian *cogito ergo sum,* and make individual mind the center of the universe — "quite a God!" — "His mind his kingdom, and his will his law" (406, 413-14).

In the Romantic period, the highest faculty of mind is the individual imagination, and even in a poet like Blake, who uses biblical allusions and tropes to figure the mind's divine creativity, the hubristic development Cowper seems to have anticipated is vividly realized. Modern psychology and neurology, as well as philosophy, in turn, have entirely reorganized the way in which mind in all its manifestations and faculties is discussed. Literary allusions based in the biblical tradition, however, largely rely upon the older tropic values.

See also WISDOM.

Bibliography. Baumgärtel, F. "*leb, lebab* in the OT." *TDNT* 3.606-07; Behm, J. "*noeō, nous.*" *TDNT* 4.948-61; Blamires, H. *The Christian Mind* (1978); Bultmann, R. *Theology of the New Testament* (1951), 1.191-227; Dentan, R. C. "Mind." *IDB* 3.383-84; Jacob, E. "The Anthropology of the Old Testament" *TDNT* 9.617-31; Jewett, R. *Paul's Anthropological Terms.* AGJU 10 (1971); Plantinga, A. *God and Other Minds* (1967); Wolff, H. W. *Anthropology of the Old Testament* (1974).

DAVID L. JEFFREY
WILLIAM BAIRD

MIRACLES *See* CANA WINE; JESUS CHRIST; LAZARUS OF BETHANY.

MIRIAM Miriam was sister to Aaron and Moses, probably the unnamed sister who kept watch over the infant Moses and suggested to Pharaoh's daughter that she find a nurse "from among the Hebrew women" to care for the baby drawn from the bullrushes (Exod. 2:1-10). For her sagacity in thus preserving Moses from death she is regarded as one of the great women of Israel. Miriam was also a prophetess who composed a song of victory and led the women in singing it after the children of Israel crossed the Red Sea on their flight from Egypt (Exod. 15:20-21). Later, when she objected to the ordained interracial marriage of her brother Moses to an Ethiopian woman, she was afflicted with leprosy and turned completely white; after a week of exile and as a result of Moses' intercession on her behalf she was healed (Num. 12:1-15).

Miriam's name is said by talmudic sources to mean "bitterness" (Yashar Shemot 128a; S. ʿOlam. Rab. 3; Pesiq. R. 5.50a), although it may have an Egyptian component, in which case it could mean "loved of Yahweh" *(mr + yw/m).* St. Jerome interpreted the name as *stella maris,* "star of the sea," which became one of the appellations of the Virgin Mary. Miriam is linked with Mary in popular celebrations of the Virgin; for St. Ambrose, in his *De virginibus* (2.2.17), Miriam's song of victory is seen to anticipate Mary, and "choirs of virgins" are pictured in heaven as "singing to the Lord because they have passed through the sea of this world without suffering from its waves." A. M. Klein picks up these lineaments in his poem "Christian Poet and Hebrew Maid," where he contemplates how:

> The cross and double-triangle
>   Are morticed; rosary and thin
> Pendule are twined; the shield weds ball;
>   The vulgate and the scroll are twin;
> The spire and dome advance their call;
>   Mary and Miriam are kin.

See also AARON; MOSES; *STELLA MARIS.*

MIRROR WITHOUT STAIN Capable of the purest reception and rendering of light, the mirror appears in late medieval conception as a metaphor of one of the Virgin's attributes, based upon Wisd. of Sol. 7:26: "For she [Wisdom] is an effulgence from everlasting light, and an unspotted mirror of the working of God, and an image of his goodness." Hence the unstained mirror, *speculum sine macula,* is a token of the Virgin's purity. The comparison of the Savior's entering Mary's womb to the divine impregnating beams of the sun shining through glass is common in medieval literature, as in the lyric "The Poet's Repentance":

> In hire lyht on ledeþ lyf,
> and shon þourh hire semly syde.
> þourh hyre side he shon

ase sonne doþ þourh þe glas. (*The Harley Lyrics, the Middle English Lyrics of MS Harley 2253,* ed. G. L. Brook [1948], 35)

The immaculacy of the unblemished mirror naturally associates it with truth, whence in iconography it often signifies *Veritas;* rendering actuality without distortion, it is employed, early and late, both as an analogue of the art form itself (cf. *Hamlet,* 3.2: "a mirror up to nature") and as a specific literary genre known as the *speculum.*

Among Puritan and other popular divines of the 17th cent. scriptural use of the mirror is accepted as a metaphor of God's Word (as in James 1:23; 1 Cor. 13:12; 2 Cor. 3:18), but these writers are led by their belief in the internality of true virtue to exploit the figure also as a faithful image of conscience and the soul's state (cf. Jeremy Taylor, *Ductor Dubitantium,* in *Works,* ed. R. Heber [1822], 11.389; Arthur Dent, *The Plain Man's Pathway to Heaven* [1731], 60; Thomas Wilson, *A Complete Christian Dictionary* [1655], 237-38; Benjamin Keach, *Tropology: A Key to Open Scripture Metaphors* [1681], 570-72). Ultimately the tradition is best epitomized in the second part of *The Pilgrim's Progress,* when Mercy is given a looking glass by the Shepherds of the Delectable Mountains: the episode is loaded with all the associative significance of the *speculum sine macula* and mirrors Bunyan's own assessment of his allegory's didactic worth.

See also GLASS, MIRROR; MARY, MOTHER OF JESUS.

Bibliography. Forrest, J. F. "Mercy with Her Mirror." *PQ* 42 (1963), 121-26; Schwarz, H. "The Mirror in Art." *Art Quarterly* 15 (1952), 97-118.   JAMES F. FORREST

MISERERE, DOMINE The opening words of Ps. 51 (Ps. 50, Vg.) in Latin are *Miserere mei, Deus;* numerous Latin hymns on this theme, as well as both Latin and vernacular settings of the Psalm for liturgical use, are called by one or another form of the "Have mercy upon me, O Lord" appeal. *"O miserere, Domine"* is the refrain of Sir Walter Scott's poem "The Monks of Bangor's March," and *"Miserere, Domine"* is the refrain of Coleridge's "A Voice Sings."

MISHAEL *See* SHADRACH, MESHACH, AND ABEDNEGO.

MISHNAH *See* HALAKAH.

MIZPAH In the Hebrew *mispah* means "lookout" or "watchtower" and as such figures as a place name or in conjunction with place names (e.g., Mizpah of Gilead [Judg. 11:29]). The term is most frequently associated with Jacob's covenant with Laban just before crossing the Jabbok (Gen. 31:48-49). After setting up a cairn Laban said, "This heap is a witness between me and thee this day. Therefore was the name of it called Galeed; and Mizpah; for he said, The LORD watch between me and thee, when we are absent one from another." In the original context the expression signifies mistrust between the two parties, and functions as a kind of warning against breach of covenant. In the 19th cent., however, the expression became widely sentimentalized and rings inscribed "Mizpah" were exchanged or used as tokens of loyal affection by separated friends and lovers. The gap between a sentimental reading and one which remembers the biblical story is captured by Ernest Hemingway in *For Whom the Bell Tolls.* At the time of young Robert Jordan's departure for school, his father's over-emotional farewell in the railway station includes the commendation, "May the Lord watch between thee and me while we are absent one from another" — words which from the son's point of view actually reinforce the distance between them.

MOAB, MOABITE From ancient times (Lot's older daughter named her son Moab [LXX — "from my father"], Gen. 19:37), kinsmen, vassals, and enemies of Israel. Territorially associated with the southern portion of Trans-jordan, the Moabites were an agricultural people, mostly shepherds, who spoke a Northwest Semitic dialect similar to Hebrew. The Moabite Stone, a stele of black basalt found at Dhībān (OT Dibon), contains an account of the accomplishments of Mesha, king of Moab (9th cent. B.C.), and describes the conflict with Israel (cf. 2 Kings 3:4-27), in which, according to the Moabite record, seven thousand Israelite men and women were slain, having been "devoted. . . to the destruction of Ashtar-Chemoth," the Moabite fertility deities. Ruth (1:22; 2:2, etc.) was a Moabite, as were some of Solomon's wives (1 Kings 11:11).

See also ARIEL; LOT; RUTH.

MOLOCH Moloch, a Canaanite god to whom children were sacrificed by being burned alive, is first mentioned in Lev. 18:21, an injunction to the biblical people not to give their children to Moloch. The prohibition is repeated in Lev. 20:2-5, where stoning is prescribed as the penalty for this transgression. It is again stressed in Deut. 12:31 and 18:9-10. No son or daughter was to be "passed through the fire," an abomination of the Canaanites, who burned their children as sacrifices. Nevertheless, this prohibition was violated by Ahaz, king of Judah, who even sacrificed his own son (2 Kings 16:3). After the destruction of the kingdom of Israel in 722 B.C., the inhabitants of Judah were warned that a similar fate would overtake them if they caused their children to pass through the fire (2 Kings 17:17). This warning was heeded by King Hezekiah. However, Manasseh, who succeeded Hezekiah, restored the Moloch-abomination and offered his son to Moloch (2 Kings 21:6). His successor, Amon, tolerated the worship of Moloch, but King Josiah, in purifying the Jewish religion of alien excrescences, abolished the Moloch cult (23:10). The prophets Jeremiah and Ezekiel still spoke out against child sacrifice (Jer. 19:4-6; 32:35; Ezek. 20:31; 23:37, 39), but there is no evidence of its persistence among Jews thereafter. In Phoenicia and North Africa Moloch worship continued until the Romans destroyed Carthage in 146 B.C.

Some Jewish exegetes since Rashi have interpreted the passing of children through fire figuratively, as a rite of initiation into the religion of Moloch, of whom an image for worshipers was set up in Jerusalem at Tophet, overlooking the Valley (Heb. *Gay'*) of Hinnom. (From *Gē-Hinnom* is derived Gehenna, the Jewish hell.) Rashi's interpretation was challenged by Abraham ibn Ezra and Nachmanides (Ramban), who argued that the child was not passed merely symbolically by priests of Moloch between two fires but was really consumed by flames. Although the OT did not elaborate details of the Moloch cult, subsequent Midrashim, such as Ekha Rabbah, in commenting on Lam. 1:9, did so —probably following Greek sources such as Diodorus Siculus and Plutarch.

In English literature, Moloch occupied the imagination of John Milton far more than that of any other writer. In "On the Morning of Christ's Nativity," st. 23 describes sullen Moloch fleeing from the earth along with other heathen gods after the birth of Christ and leaving behind both his burning, blackened idol and his worshipers dancing dismally about his furnace.

In *Paradise Lost,* Moloch is the first of the vanquished angels to be roused from the pit of hell by Satan. He is identified as the future god of the Ammonites, who will be besmeared with blood of human sacrifices and with the tears of parents whose children pass through fire. Milton follows a tradition which equates Moloch with the god for whom Solomon built a temple at Gē-Hinnom, opposite the Temple of Israel's true God. Milton's Moloch is the fiercest of Satan's crew, the first to advocate immediate resumption of the war against the Lord of Heaven.

Abraham Cowley, in bk. 2 of his uncompleted sacred epic *Davideis* (1656), characterizes Moloch as "the bloody god who was fed in his seven chambers new, roasted babes, his dear, delicious meat." William Blake, profoundly influenced by Milton, includes Moloch among the Seven Eyes of God in his poetic allegory *Jerusalem.* The Seven Eyes signify the seven stages in man's spiritual ascent from Lucifer to Jesus. Moloch, who succeeds Lucifer and is the Second Eye, delights in human sacrifices, in orgies of warriors with the daughters of Albion, in offerings of the first-begotten male children (3.68). Coleridge, Blake's contemporary and, like him, an opponent of Albion-Britain's campaigns against the revolutionary French, lashes out in his "Religious Musings" (1794) against the warmongers and the Moloch priests who prefer the prayer of hate to that of love.

Robert Southey sees the spirit of Moloch reappearing in the "Satanic School" of the poets Byron, Shelley, and Leigh Hunt. In his elegy "A Vision of Judgment" (1821) he characterizes these poets as being inspired by the spirit of Belial in their lascivious verse and by the spirit of

Moloch in their loathsome images of atrocities and horrors. Tennyson begins "The Dawn" (1892) with reference to the worshipers of Moloch at the dawn of mankind and emphasizes the all-too-slow pace of progress since then. He concedes the inevitability of mankind's ascent but wonders how long it will take humanity to rid itself of the brute within. James Stephens recalls the pagan deity in a narrower context as he derides the killing of birds for trimming hats ("Hymn to Moloch").

The horrors of Moloch worship, at which English poets from Milton to D. H. Lawrence hinted, were elaborated with greater vividness in the German dramas of Christian Dietrich Grabbe and Friedrich Hebbel and in the novels of the French realist Gustave Flaubert. In *The Source* (1965), James Michener provides an imaginary history of the development of the Moloch cult in prepatriarchal centuries and the demise of this ritual horror when the Hebrews, in the name of the invisible Lord of the Universe, overthrew the abominable idol of the Canaanites. G. K. Chesterton treats the Canaanite gods of child sacrifice in *The Everlasting Man* (chap. 6). Francis Brett-Young's novel *The Crescent Moon* describes a revival of Moloch worship in Africa.

Bibliography. *EncJud* 12.280-83; Liptzin, S. *Biblical Themes in World Literature* (1985); "Moloch." *IDB* 3.422.

SOL LIPTZIN

MONARCHIANISM   *See* HERESY.

MONOPHYSITISM   *See* HERESY.

MONTANISM   *See* HERESY.

MORDECAI   Mordecai is a central figure in the book of Esther, a court official of King Ahasuerus of Persia (Shushan, or Susa). His cousin and adopted daughter Esther became, through his efforts, the king's concubine and queen after Vashti, and thus was positioned to intercede for him and for all the Jewish people against the evil machinations of Haman. Subsequently a heroic figure in Jewish legend, Mordecai is also remembered in the expression "a Mordecai at your gate," meaning an important person, for the way in which he persisted at the entrance to the harem to obtain news of Esther (2:11). "Mordecai bold and cringeless proud" figures in A. M. Klein's "Five Characters," a poetic commentary on the dramatis personae of the book of Esther, as in most treatments of its central character.

See also ESTHER.

MORNING STARS SANG TOGETHER   To Job's questioning of God's justice, the Lord replies out of the whirlwind in a series of his own questions, revealing the utter inadequacy of Job's perspective: "Where wast thou when I laid the foundations of the earth? . . . When the morning stars sang together, and all the sons of God shouted for joy?" (Job 38:4, 7).

Carlyle's Professor Teufelsdröckh, who seems not to have recollected Job's humbling, writes, "Is not Man's History, and Men's History, a perpetual Evangel? Listen, and for organ-music thou wilt ever, as of old, hear the Morning Stars sing together" (*Sartor Resartus,* 3.7). For Whittier, in "The Worship of Nature," the song likewise continues:

> The harp at Nature's advent strung
> Has never ceased to play;
> The song the stars of morning sang
> Has never died away.

In D. G. Rossetti's *The Blessed Damozel,* the allusion is somewhat better contextualized:

> Her gaze still strove
> Within the gulf to pierce
> Its path; and now she spoke as when
> The stars sang in their spheres.

MOSES   Moses is the chief prophet of Jewish tradition, the traditional author of the Pentateuch (also called "The Five Books of Moses"), leader of the exodus of Israel from Egypt, a miracle-worker, and the "lawgiver" who received from God the Ten Commandments. Although he was once credited with authorship of the book of Job, this ascription was subsequently rejected by both talmudic and patristic sources (e.g., B. Bat. 15a-15b contra Soṭa 5, 20c; St. Gregory the Great, *Moralia in Iob,* pref. contra St. Methodius, St. Ephraim Syrus, et al.). Moses may be regarded as the single most important personage in the Hebrew Scriptures and, after Jesus Christ and perhaps the Virgin Mary, the most important personage in the sacred text so far as Western art and literature are concerned. First among prophets and men of piety for the Jews, in the pre-modern Christian Church Moses was universally regarded as one of the signal OT types of Christ.

Several events in the life of Moses receive frequent attention in Western arts and letters. Best known, perhaps, is the infancy narrative (Exod. 1:1-11). In order to circumvent Pharaoh's decree of death for male Hebrew children, Moses was left by his mother in a floating basket in the river where he was by chance found by Pharaoh's daughter, who saved the child and eventually brought him to the Egyptian court. Subsequently, as a young man, Moses slew an Egyptian persecutor of the Hebrew slaves, an incident which, when discovered, forced him to flee from Egypt to the land of Midian. It was here, while Moses was tending sheep, that he saw the famous theophany of the burning bush; as he approached the bush which burned without being consumed, God spoke to him, announcing that he was to rescue the children of Israel from slavery in Egypt (Exod. 3). The ineffective embassy of Moses and his brother Aaron before Pharaoh (Exod. 5) was the occasion (or prolegomena) of the ten plagues. Acting under God's instructions, Moses and Aaron coerced Pharaoh into liberating the Hebrews by inflicting upon him a series of pestilences: blood in the waters of Egypt, an epidemic of frogs, then of lice and flies, a murrain upon the cattle, boils in people and beasts, hail, locusts, and darkness over the whole land, and finally the death of all the eldest Egyptian children, "from the firstborn of Pharaoh that sat on his throne unto the firstborn of the captive that was in the dungeon" (Exod. 7–11; 12:29-30). Moses then led the Hebrews out of Egypt, guided by a pillar of fire by night and a pillar of cloud by day (Exod. 13). Pursued by Pharaoh's army, he appealed to God, who miraculously parted the waters of the Red Sea to allow the children of Israel to pass through unharmed and drowned Pharaoh and his army when they tried to follow (Exod. 14). Moses was the instrument of various miracles of feeding in the wilderness, where the children of Israel sojourned for forty years (e.g., provision of quails and manna [Exod. 16] and of water miraculously springing from the hard rock [Exod. 17]). He received the Ten Commandments on Mt. Sinai (Exod. 20) and then, coming down from the mountain, was enraged to discover that the Israelites had fallen into idolatry during his brief absence; in his anger he smashed the tablets of the Law. Finally, Moses was allowed to see — but not to enter — the promised land of Canaan from atop Mt. Nebo, where he died at the age of 120, "his eye . . . not dim, nor his natural force abated" (Deut. 34). His body was hidden by God, and never found.

The dramatic richness of the narrative of Moses is exploited in the Haggadah and in such apocryphal texts as the Assumption of Moses. There is also in the history of the Exodus, however, a powerful literary delineation of character, and this aspect of the sacred text likewise inspired hagiographic veneration in many of its readers, even though Moses, biblically speaking, is not an unblemished hero. A murderer before he was called by God, he is presented as a reluctant savior, an impatient prophet, and at times a dangerously irascible overlord. The children of Israel, for their part, are frequently ungrateful and unfaithful; their usual response to the miracles worked through Moses on their behalf is indifference followed by grumbling.

In talmudic writings Moses not only excels all the other great and pious Hebrew heroes (cf. Josephus, *Ant.* 4.8.49; Philo, *De vita Mosis*, 1), but is a kind of *Übermensch* or demigod, "half terrestrial, half celestial" (Pesiq. R. 32.198b; Tehillim 90.388), not merely "a man of God" in the ordinary sense, but "master of the angels" (cf. Philo, *De mutatione nominum*, 3.22). Messianic activity in cooperation with Elijah or the Messiah is predicted for Moses "at the end of the days" (Tg. Yer. Deut. 33:21; Midr. Tannaim 219). An archetype of modesty, the meekest of men (Num. 12:3) sometimes uses his humility as an excuse for tardy obedience, and his stammering tongue and occasional temerity are also made to

be the concomitants of a scholarly temperament (Meg. 21a; Onkeneira, Ayyumah Kannidgalot 17a). Yet his scholarship is foundational; he is likened to a burning candle from which many other lights of wisdom are kindled (Num. 11:25; Sipre 3.252; Philo, *De gigantibus*, 6), an image which has as much currency among medieval rabbinic commentators as does "seeing further because we stand upon the shoulders of the giants who have gone before" (e.g., Bernard of Chartres) among their Christian counterparts (e.g., Tikkun Middot ha-Nefesh 5.2). Many a halakah was revealed to Moses on Sinai, but Philo (*De vita Mosis*, 1.5-7) makes him also a careful student of Greek and Egyptian wisdom as well as of the traditions of other lands. He is said to have given the Hebrews the art of writing, from whence the Phoenicians learned it and, later, the Greeks from the Phoenicians (Eupolemus, 431c). Artapanus (432) makes him the divine disciple of Orpheus, whom the Egyptians call Hermes. He is said to have expounded the Torah in seventy languages and prophesied in seventy-one; at the time of his death on Mt. Nebo (cf. *nabi'* "prophet"), he quickly wrote thirteen scrolls of the Torah, one for each of the twelve tribes of Israel and a control copy for deposit in the Ark of the Covenant. According to the Haggadah of R. Akiba (Alphabet 16), no less than "five thousand gates of wisdom," "eight thousand gates of understanding," and "eleven thousand gates of knowledge" were opened to him on Sinai — the numbers corresponding to the number of the books of the Hebrew Bible multiplied by a thousand: five books of Moses, eight of the prophets (Minor Prophets taken as one book) and twelve of the Hagiographa (Ezra and Nehemiah considered as one book) (Sanh. 93b).

In patristic commentary the Pentateuch is followed somewhat more closely, if selectively, than in the Talmud, yet the range and variety is still considerable. The most famous patristic essay on Moses, St. Gregory of Nyssa's *Vita Mosis*, takes the holy man of the Exodus to be the type of the ascetic life. Developing ideas current both in the Haggadah and in the Judaism of Alexandria, Gregory provides an essentially monastic portrait of Moses which greatly influenced medieval and Renaissance conceptions of him. Even in commentaries as late as those of Theodore Beza and Cornelius à Lapide (well known to Donne, Herbert, Andrews, and Browne), or William Warburton's *The Divine Legation of Moses* (1738) (known to Blake), Gregory was cited to support the idea of Moses as an ideal type of the contemplative, who goes into the desert to hear the voice of God (see also St. Gregory the Great, *Moralia in Iob*, 5.23.37). Moses' gentleness and meekness are stressed by Gregory the Great (*Moralia,* 5.27.17); St. Ambrose emphasizes the same qualities, observing in *De officiis ministrorum*, 2.7.31, that they "captivated the minds of all the people to such an extent that they loved him more for his gentleness than admired him for his deeds." Like John the Baptist he was not merely a "desert father," but a self-conscious forerunner and "friend of the

Bridegroom"; evoking the levirate custom familiar from the book of Ruth, Ambrose says, "Moses was not the Bridegroom, for to him comes the word, 'Loose thy shoe from off thy foot' (Exod. 3:5), that he might give place to the Lord" (*De fide*, 3.71). He is said to be, along with Samuel, a great exemplar of contemplative and intercessory prayer (cf. Jer. 7:16; 15:1), distinguished for praying for his enemies (Gregory, *Moralia*, 2.9.24) and for obtaining swift response from God. These ideas are still reflected in Richard Baxter's *Saints' Everlasting Rest* (1650), which concludes: "As Moses, before he died, went up into Mt. Nebo to take a survey of the land of Canaan; so the Christian ascends the mount of contemplation, and by faith surveys his rest."

The association of Moses with mountaintop experience, hence mystical vision and transfiguration, was complicated by one of the most celebrated aspects of his medieval iconography, his "horns." The depiction of the "horned Moses" was occasioned by a confusion in the Vg translation of the Hebrew expression used to convey the "rays of light" which shone from his forehead after his sojourn with the Almighty on Sinai (Exod. 34:29). The Latin word chosen was *cornu,* or "horn"; "Moses wist not that the skin of his face shone" (KJV) was thus rendered *ignorabat quod cornutaesset facies sua.* This confusion led to representations of Moses in prophetic or monastic dress with bovine horns protruding from just above his hairline. Notable examples are found in illustrations of the *Biblia Pauperum* and *Bible moralisée,* but the most famous is Michelangelo's statue of Moses (1513) for the tomb of Pope Julius III. In Guillaume de Guilville's *Pèlerinage de la vie humaine,* translated into English in the early 15th cent. by John Lydgate, Lady Reason counsels a character called Moses, who is sometimes represented with horns (Old Law), sometimes with a bishop's miter (New Law). Moses, who tonsures servants who come for ordination, imagines that he must have been given horns to butt his "sheep" into line; Reason urges that he temper this Old Law function with a New Law dispensation of humility and lovingkindness (MSS Douce 300 and Laud 740).

The other celebrated feature of Moses' iconography relates to the same biblical incident: when speaking to the people, Moses was obliged to shield his face so that their eyes might not be blinded by the reflected radiance of God's glory from whose presence he had come (Exod. 34:33-35). Gregory the Great offers the typical explanation for the "veiled Moses" when he observes that Moses did this "surely, in order to denote that the people of the Jews knew the words of the Law, but did not at all see the clearness of the Law" (*Moralia*, 4.18.60). "Veiled Moses" is thus a type of the Word yet to be fulfilled in Christ, the letter of the Law without its fullness and clarifying spirit, yet a type revealed in such terms as strongly preserves the sense of Moses' own integrity and stature as a mediator of the divine word to mankind (cf. 2 Cor. 3:12-18).

The rod Moses sometimes bears, along with the Decalogue (e.g., in the painting by Phillip de Champagne), is generally held to be a sign of the Incarnation. When Moses cast down his rod and it became a serpent which devoured the serpents of Egypt (Exod. 7:12), it signified, says Ambrose, "that the Word should become flesh to destroy the poison of the dread serpent [Satan] by the forgiveness and pardon of sins" (*De officiis*, 3.15.94). The tablets and the rod, when featured together, are thus images of the Old Covenant and of the New Covenant prefigured in it (cf. Picinelli, *Mundus Symbolicus,* 3.83.245-52, s.v. *"Moses . . . auxiliante Deo"*).

The 8th-cent. *Exodus* represents Moses as a wise leader, characterized by *sapientia et fortitudo* and a type of Christ. He is similarly cast in the medieval cycle dramas such as the York "Departure" and N-Town "Moses and the Two Tables." At the end of Chaucer's *Pardoner's Tale,* the Pardoner invites his fellow pilgrims to avail themselves of his highly dubious spiritual ministrations. Referring to his written warrant of authority from the Pope, he says: ". . . offer nobles or sterlinges, / Or elles silver brooches, spoones, ringes. / Boweth your heed under this holy bulle!" — an allusion to the story of the golden calf. In *Piers Plowman,* Will angrily tears a "pardon" to pieces in an action which imitates, physically and morally, Moses' angry destruction of the tables of the Law.

It was principally Moses' role as a lawgiver and prophet of the covenant which attracted attention in Reformation commentary and literature. Calvin sees the Mosaic miracles as "so many sanctions of the law delivered, and the doctrine propounded, by him," a clear witness of God to Moses' authority (*Inst.* 1.8.5-8). Milton concurs, finding Moses "the only lawgiver that we can believe to have been visibly taught of God" (*The Reason of Church Government,* pref.). In Bunyan's *Pilgrim's Progress* Moses is a stern fellow: Faith relates to Christian how after his nearly succumbing to the attempt by the Old Man, "Adam the first," to deflect him from his journey, he was chased and knocked to the ground by a man who refuses to stop hitting him, saying "I know not how to show mercy." The character was Moses, and only Jesus could dissuade him from punishing Faith for his weakness. It is within this same nonconformist tradition that Moses still appears, as a judge, in Thornton Wilders's *The Skin of Our Teeth* (1942). Predictably, Moses' typological connections with Christ are also emphasized by a writer like Milton, who, in *Paradise Regained,* draws the parallel between the forty-day fast of Moses in the desert and the temptation of Christ (346-56) and has Satan tempt Christ to take for himself the rabbinical eminence of Moses' wisdom, "on points and questions fitting Moses Chair."

In Dryden's *Absalom and Achitophel* Corah, rebel against David, is given "a Moses' face" (presumably shining), but in Longfellow's *Evangeline* the afterglow of the setting sun is described as Moses veiling his face on coming down from Sinai. Whittier has "Rabbi Ishmael" see the face of the Lord in the Holy of Holies and then, "Radiant as Moses from the Mount, he stood / And cried aloud unto the multitude: / 'O Israel, hear! The Lord our God is good!'" According to William Blake, Moses delivered Israel from Egyptian bondage only to impose a more severe bondage to Law, which he had actually borrowed from the Egyptians, "the forms of dark delusion" (*Africa*, 3.17) as Blake imagines, probably on the basis of reading Warburton. What happens in Blake's reworking of this idea in *Ahania* and "The Song of Los," where the bondage of Mosaic law becomes as sinister as the bondage in Egypt, is that Israel has effectively absorbed much of Egyptian culture. The first chapter of *Ahania* parallels the commissioning of Moses as prophet of righteousness; the second covers the events in Exodus from the defeat of Pharaoh to the arrival on Sinai; the third deals with the establishment of the Law from the mountain; the fourth concerns the forty years wandering in the wilderness; and the fifth the coming into Canaan, Moses' farewell speeches (or songs), and the lament after his death.

The death of Moses became a major theme in Romantic and post-Romantic literature. The haggadic legend of "Moses and the Worm," popularized by Johann Gottfried Herder in the 18th cent., is central to American poet Richard Henry Stoddard's "The Death of Moses," which ends with Moses reconciled to his demise, able to trust Israel's fortunes to his successor, Joshua. James Montgomery's "Death of Moses" is less optimistic, as Moses looks into the future from atop Mt. Nebo to find trans-Jordan bloodstained and abounding in pagan abominations. Thomas Moore's dirge on the death of Moses is also a less than hopeful lament. George Eliot's poetic narrative *The Death of Moses* is more elaborate, and based on haggadic Jewish sources. God himself comes to take Moses away, drawing forth his soul with a kiss and carrying it up to heaven (cf. B. Bat. 17a; Petirat Mosheh 129). Israel is comforted with the words: "He has no tomb. He dwells not with you dead, but lives as Law." Rilke's "Der Tod Moses" (1922) draws on some of the same sources, in which the angels of death prove unable to interrupt Moses in his mountain task of making the final thirteen copies of the Torah, and only God himself can with a kiss steal away the soul of Moses, burying his body in a cleft of the mountain, then closed over with the very hands which, as Moses himself had only just written, fashioned the creation *ex nihilo*. One of the last poems of Dietrich Bonhoeffer to be smuggled out of prison before his execution was "Der Tod des Mose," which takes its optimistic motto from Deut. 34:1: "And the LORD showed him all the land."

The strong influence of the character of Moses upon German literature, which in turn has strengthened his presence in English and American literature, owes at least

in part to Martin Luther, who once said that he "had endeavored to make Moses so German that no one would suspect he was a Jew." His vivid image of the prophetic individual, a leader of his people from bondage into freedom, is the antithesis of Blake's Fuzon-Moses. It corresponds, however, to the later typology of Moses in American literature. Such an image of Moses, which stresses the individual, the spiritual, and the psychological at the expense of the national and the political, finds an acculturated secular continental expression in Friedrich Schiller's essay *Die Sendung Moses* (1790) and in Sigmund Freud's celebrated and controversial *Moses and Monotheism* (1937-39), in both of which it is suggested that Moses was in fact not representative of his people but an Egyptian all along — an old idea (cf. George Herbert, "The Church Militant," 21-46), but one made yet more unsettling in its modern guise, even that of Karl Shapiro, "The Murder of Moses," which takes up from Freud the theory that he was murdered by Hebrews in the wilderness.

The image of Moses as a political leader has also had great influence in the 19th and 20th cents. The Jews' long experience of persecution has encouraged the parallel, common in all periods of Jewish messianic thought, between the historical Moses and the savior to come who has, indeed, on occasion been described as a *Moses redivivus*. Similar modes of thinking have characterized various oppressed or marginal groups within the Christian world, including the religious community of African-Americans, whose self-identification with the children of Israel suffering beneath Pharaoh's yoke is powerfully suggested in many spirituals, including the well-known "Go Down, Moses" (which was taken as the title of one of William Faulkner's novels). Many black American leaders of the 20th cent., especially Martin Luther King, have phrased their contemporary agenda for political action in the metaphoric vocabulary of the Exodus story. Precisely parallel is the phenomenon of Irish nationalist identification with Israel vis-à-vis the "Egypt" of imperial England recorded in the fictionalized version of an actual political speech in James Joyce's *Ulysses* ("Oxen of the Sun"). In Sholem Asch's postwar novel *Moses* (1951), allegorical connections are made throughout to the German persecutions and holocaust. Moses has in fact become the perennial symbol of the messianic leader who is despised in times of leisure and yearned for in times of crisis, as when H. G. Wells said of Europe after the war, "Never before were the nations so eager to follow a Moses who would take them to the long promised land where wars are prohibited and blockades unknown" (*Short History of the World*, "The Political and Social Reconstruction").

The Moses narrative, which has also inspired works as diverse as Handel's *Israel in Egypt* (1738), Alfred de Vigny's *Moïse* (1822), Chateaubriand's somewhat cumbersome tragedy of the same title (1836), Lytton

Strachey's *A Dialogue between Moses, Diogenes, and Mr. Locke* (1922), and Schoenberg's opera *Moses und Aron* (1930-32, unfinished), continues to be one of the most enduring sources for serious writers in English literary tradition. Howard Nemerov observes, however, that Moses is an awkward character from the point of view of modern literature because he cannot be dispensed with according to merely aesthetic categories. Reflecting on critical displeasure with an exhibition of simple but powerful paintings, he writes:

> When Moses in Horeb struck the rock,
> And water came forth out of the rock,
> Some of the people were annoyed with Moses
> And said he should have used a fancier stick. ("On Certain Wits")

In complementary fashion, George Steiner has suggested (*In Bluebeard's Castle*) that the rod of Moses, like his "pen," has always been a blunt instrument, culturally speaking. But it is there precisely, in its raw moral force, that its literary power also resides.

See also BRAZEN SERPENT; EXODUS; MANNA; PHARAOH; PISGAH SIGHT; SMITTEN ROCK; TEN COMMANDMENTS.

Bibliography. Daiches, D. *Moses: The Man and his Vision* (1975); Glasson, T. F. *Moses in the Fourth Gospel* (1963); Hanson, R. P. C. "Moses in the Typology of St. Paul." *Theology* 48 (1945), 174-77; Liptzin, S. *Biblical Themes in World Literature* (1985); Mellinkoff, R. *The Horned Moses in Medieval Thought and Art* (1970); Roshwald, M. and M. *Moses: Leader, Prophet, Man/The Story of Moses and his Image through the Ages* (1969).   DAVID L. JEFFREY
JOHN V. FLEMING

MOSES, SONG OF   Two OT passages have traditionally been identified as "songs" of Moses —Exod. 15:1-18 and Deut. 32:1-43. The Exodus passage celebrates God's triumph over the army of Pharaoh at the Red Sea and is today often called the "Song of the Sea." Although there appears to be a connection between this poem and Exod. 15:21, the "Song of Miriam," scholarship is divided over the historical issues involved (see Childs, 240-53).

Most frequently in modern study the title "Song of Moses" is given to the poetic passage in Deut. 32. It is one of two poetic texts occurring near the end of the book, the other being the so-called "Blessing of Moses" (33:1-29). In context, the "Song of Moses" is a covenant song taught by Moses to the assembled Israelites on the Plains of Moab for use in the Covenant Renewal Festival. There is debate as to the antiquity of the Song, some arguing that it is an example of archaic Hebrew poetry, others detecting in it the later characteristics of both prophetic and wisdom poetic style. The poem contains reflections on the nature of God, on the Israelites, their past failures and future prospects, and on the significance of the covenant in the context of the world's nations.

In the NT, Rev. 15:2-4 describes a scene beside the "sea of glass" where the new elect celebrate victory over "the beast," singing "the song of Moses . . . and the song of the Lamb" —in clear allusion to the Exod. 15 passage, with an echo also in v. 3b of Deut. 32:4.

The Exodus "song" was translated into English by Richard Rolle in the 14th cent., who regarded it as a mystic's lyrical outpouring of praise. Both "songs" attracted special interest and commentary during the first century of the English Reformation. Indeed, both were cited in defense of poetry and of liturgy.

Sidney, in his discussion of poetic "kinds," calls those poets "chief, both in antiquity and excellency" who "did imitate the inconceivable excellencies of God," including "Moses and Deborah in their Hymns" (*Apology*, 18). Hooker uses the first song of Moses to justify set forms of prayer: if prayers must be always new, "we cannot excuse Moses" for "not being contented to praise the name of almightie God according to the usuall naked simplicitie of Gods Spirit for that admerable victorie given them against Pharoa," since he thus left a precedent

> for the castinge of prayers into certaine poeticall mouldes . . . which might be repeated often although they never had againe the same occasions which brought them forth at the first. For that verie hymne of Moses grew afterwardes to be a parte of the ordinarie Jewish liturgie; nor onlie that, but sundrie other sithence invented. (*Lawes*, 5.26)

Both songs were among the "canonical hymns" included in collections of metrical Psalms such as George Wither's *Hymns and Songs of the Church*, set by Orlando Gibbons, and George Sandys's *Paraphrase* with Psalm settings by Henry Lawes. Wither's headnote to the first song of Moses explains that it should be sung

> both with respect to the historical and mystical senses thereof: Historically, in commemoration of that particular deliverance, which God had so long ago and so wondrously vouchsafed to his persecuted and afflicted church: Mystically, in acknowledgment of our own powerful deliverance from the bondage of those spiritual adversaries, wherof those were the types: for Pharoah (signifying *Vengeance*) typified our great enemy, who, with his host of temptations, afflictions, & c. pursueth us in our passage to the spiritual Canaan.

His explanation recommends both public and private use in Christian worship. Wither's note on the second song of Moses explains, "This Song was given by God himself. . . . For it appears the Divine Wisdom knew that when the Law would be lost or forgotten, a Song might be remembered to posterity."

Major poets took Moses as well as David as a model. Milton's invocation in *Paradise Lost* refers mainly to Moses' hexameron. But Donne explicitly refers to Moses as the first inspired song writer. In his poem on the Sidney Psalms he calls Philip and Mary "this *Moses* and this *Miriam*" (alluding to Exod. 15:1-21); and he ends *The First Anniversary*,

Vouchsafe to call to minde, that God did make
A last, and lastingst peece, a song. He spake
To *Moses* to deliver unto all
That song: because hee knew they would let fall
The Law, the Prophets, and the History,
But keepe the song still in their memory.
Such an opinion (in due measure) made
Me this great Office boldly to invade.

Verse hath a middle nature: heaven keepes soules,
The grave keeps bodies, verse the fame enroules.

See also MIRIAM.

Bibliography. Albright, W. "Some Remarks on the Song of Moses." *VT* 9 (1959), 339-46; Alter, R. *The Art of Biblical Poetry* (1985); Boston, J. "The Wisdom Influences of the Song of Moses." *JBL* 87 (1968), 166-78; Childs, B. *The Book of Exodus* (1974); Craigie, P. *The Book of Deuteronomy* (1976); Skeham, P. "The Structure of the Song of Moses in Deuteronomy." *CBQ* 13 (1951), 153-63.
DIANE MCCOLLEY
PETER C. CRAIGIE

MOTE AND BEAM   After his admonishment against unjust judgment, "Judge not that ye be not judged," Jesus adds the emphasis: "And why beholdest thou the mote that is in thy brother's eye, but considerest not the beam that is in thine own eye?" (Matt. 7:3). The person who is blind to his own vices Jesus calls a hypocrite. While to complain against sin is the duty of good and benevolent persons, says St. Augustine, "there is in fact a class of troublesome pretenders much to be guarded against, who even while motivated to complain against all manner of others' faults merely from hatred and spite, wish to present themselves as counsellors." Therefore, he observes, "if on reflection we find ourselves involved in the same fault as one whom we are beginning to censure we should neither censure nor rebuke but mourn deeply over the case, and rather than invite that person to obey us, rather urge them to join us in a common effort" (*De sermone Domini in Monte*, 2.19.64). "Rarely, therefore, and only in a case of great necessity, are rebukes to be administered," he concludes, "yet in such a way that even in these very rebukes we make it our earnest endeavor, not that we, but that God should be served." One's first task, in any case, is to remove from one's own eye "the beam of envy, malice, or pretence" (2.19.66). For Calvin, Christ's words suggest that "we should not be too eager or ill-natured or malicious, or even over-curious in judging those nearest to us" (*Comm.* sup. Matt. 7:1-3).

Chaucer's Reeve, insulted by *The Miller's Tale*, which lampoons an old carpenter whose life circumstances bear considerable relationship to his own, exclaims in the Preface to his own tale: "I pray to God his nekke mote to-breke; / He can wel in myn eye seen a stalke, / But in his owene he kan nat seen a balke" (*Canterbury Tales*, 1.3918-20). He then commences, predictably, to tell a tale about a miller. In Shakespeare's *Love's Labour's Lost*, Berowne reproves his three friends:

But are you not ashamed? Nay, are you not,
All three of you, to be thus much o'ershot?
You found his mote, the king your mote did see;
But I a beam do find in each of three. (4.3.156-59)

The saying is often paraphrased, as in John Newton's lines, "Ere you remark another's sin, / Bid your own conscience look within" *(Olney Hymns),* and frequently misapplied, as in Charles Lamb's definition of a poor relation as "a mote in your eye" ("Poor Relations"). A. M. Klein directs the saying against anti-Semitism in Germany in his poem "Johannus, Dei Monachus, Loquitur," in which the sinister narrator exclaims, "Before you cast the beam from Palestine / Pick out the mote from Mainz; perish the Jews!"

MOUNTAIN   "There was an idea of sanctity attached to rocky wilderness, because it had always been among hills that the Deity had manifested Himself most intimately to men, and to the hills that his saints had nearly always retired for meditation, for special communion with Him, and to prepare for death." Ruskin's comment (*Modern Painters,* 3.4.14) epitomizes the positive significance of biblical mountains. There are 21 narratively significant mountains mentioned in Scripture, among which Sinai-Horeb is prominent as the mountain of God (Exod. 3:1; 4:27; 18:5; 24:13; 1 Kings 19:8) and Zion is exalted not just as the holy seat of Jerusalem (Pss. 2:6; 3:4; 15:1; 43:3; Isa. 27:13; 56:7; 57:13, etc.), but also as the sacred abode in the messianic age to come (Isa. 2:2-3; Ezek. 40:2; Mic. 4:1-2). Other mountains of note include Ararat, where Moses' ark found repose (Gen. 8:4); Hor, where Aaron died (Num. 20:25, 27); Nebo (Pisgah), the site of Moses' death (Deut. 34:1); and Hermon, the mount, some think, of transfiguration (Matt. 17:1-2). If Hermon is not the place of transfiguration, then Mt. Tabor probably is. Etymologically, Tabor is related to *tabor* (Heb., "navel"). The mountain at the omphalos of the earth is a common archetype found in many religions; certainly several pre-Israelite cults worshiped mountains. The Babylonian ziggurat, in fact, was a sacred tower meant to resemble the cosmic mountain on which, according to the myth, the gods had been born.

Medieval tradition provides a variety of allegorizations: St. Gregory the Great in his *Moralia in Iob* (sup. 40:20 [Vg 40:15]) is representative:

By a mountain is expressed the covenant of God, as Habakkuk says, "God will come from Libanus, and the Holy One from the shady and thick mountain. . . ." And this covenant is well said to be a shady and thick mountain, because it is darkened by the thick obscurities of allegories. Again, by a mountain is designated the apostate angel, as is said of preachers concerning the ancient enemy under the character of the King of Babylon, "Lift ye up a banner upon the gloomy mountain." For holy preachers lift up a banner above the gloomy mountain, when they exalt the virtue of the cross against the pride of Satan, which is frequently concealed under the mist of hypocrisy.

Medieval texts sometimes view the universe as three tiered and, as in *Piers Plowman,* imagine the world of present existence as the "mountain called Middle Earth" (B.11.315).

As "sacred places," mountains in Scripture are the locations for theophanies of various sorts. So, too, in literature. Although Mt. Sinai is a threatening reminder of the Old Law in Bunyan's *Pilgrim's Progress,* God is the "lord of the hills," and Christian must win through to the vision of Jerusalem he attains from the "Delectable Mountains." This moment is akin to Moses' sighting of Canaan, the Promised Land, from atop Nebo (Deut. 34:1-4); it suggests, too, Rev. 21:10: "And he carried me away in the spirit to a great and high mountain, and shewed me that great city, the holy Jerusalem. . . ." Such a sight belongs, too, to the Redcrosse Knight from a peak which is a compound of Sinai, Olivet (Matt. 24:3), Parnassus, and the apocalyptic mount of Rev. 21 (Spenser, *Faerie Queene,* 1.10.53-58). Similarly, Michael leads Adam to a "Hill / Of Paradise the highest" to show him the panorama of history below (Milton, *Paradise Lost,* 11.366-428). Pisgah "sights" are an important feature in 19th-cent. literature.

Although echoes of such mountaintop experiences resonate throughout literature, two modern examples will serve as further illustrations. In James Baldwin's *Go Tell It on the Mountain* (1953), visionary experiences abound. Perhaps the most critical occurs when John goes to Central Park, to a hill in the center of the park (the navel?), and from the summit is afforded a prospect of the skyline of New York as a "shining city which his ancestors had seen with longing from far away." This vision of the New Jerusalem recedes, however, with the realization that the city is one of destruction, whose Broadway leads to perdition. In *The Mountain and the Valley* (1952), by Ernest Buckler, the hero, David Canaan, scales the mountain, experiences an epiphany, and dies because, unlike Redcrosse Knight, he is unwilling to descend from his mount of contemplation. David's struggle to ascend the mountain recaptures the notion of moral exertion associated with Bunyan's "Hill Difficulty" in *Pilgrim's Progress,* the mountainous terrain in Herbert's "The Pilgrimage," and Dante's Purgatorial climb (cf. Zech. 4:7).

A major exegetical crux results from biblical ambiguity about the creation of mountains. Some have supposed that the earth was flat before the Flood, since mountains are not mentioned until the ark comes to rest on Ararat (Gen. 8:4). In entertaining this idea, St. Augustine (PL 34.450), the Venerable Bede (PL 93.75, 85), and later Luther (*Luther on the Creation,* ed. Lencker, 1.164-65) lent credibility to the popular use of such epithets as "tumors," "wens," and "blisters" to describe the disfiguration of the earth by mountains as a consequence of sin and the Deluge. Some of the literary manifestations of this belief have been surveyed by Nicholson. An impressive example is Marvell's "Upon the Hill and Grove at Bill-borrow," which uses the contrast between well-proportioned hill and protuberant mountain as an epideictic device in honor of Lord Fairfax. That "every mountain and hill shall be made low" in the messianic age (Isa. 40:4) gives L. P. Hartley a pretext and a dominant image for his satirical novel on the democratic desire for equality, *Facial Justice* (1960). Although mountains sometimes connote pride — witness Thomalin's claims in "July" of Spenser's *The Shepherds' Calendar,* Mount Ambition in the 13th-cent. poem *Architrenius,* or Earl Birney's *David* — biblical tradition does not generally support this second pejorative sense for the image (though it condemns the idolatrous worship of Israel's neighbors and apostates in Canaanitic "high places" [e.g., 1 Kings 11:7ff.; 2 Kings 23]).

The first writer to consider the sublimity of mountains, according to Nicholson, was Thomas Burnet in *The Sacred Theory of the Earth,* a 17th-cent. work which much influenced the thinking of the Romantics. Wordsworth, Shelley, Coleridge, and Ruskin lifted their eyes to the hills to find not just everlastingness — mountains were among the "types and symbols of eternity" — but also an awful beauty and a stimulus to solitude and imaginative re-creation. The Mt. Snowdon episode in Wordsworth's *The Prelude* (bk. 14), Shelley's "Mount Blanc," and the comments scattered profusely through the works of Ruskin all revert to reverence for the mountain as a setting for the numinous. For Coleridge, climbing a mountain yields "allegoric lore" ("To a Young Friend" [1796]) which is reminiscent of Richard of St. Victor's 12th-cent. postulate: "Let the soul which strives to rise to the loftiness of knowledge take as its first and principal study to know itself. . . . A great and lofty mountain is the full understanding of a rational soul" (PL 196.54). Debunkers of Romantic fascination with mountains, such as Carlyle (*Sartor Resartus,* 2.6) or Samuel Butler (*The Way of All Flesh,* chap. 4) perhaps failed to realize that they were dealing not just with a new literary fad, but with a long-standing tendency to find sermons in stones.

See also FLOOD; PISGAH SIGHT; TEN COMMANDMENTS; TRANSFIGURATION.

Bibliography. Abrams, M. H. *Natural Supernaturalism: Tradition and Revolution in Romantic Literature* (1971); Albright, W. F. "The High Place in Ancient Palestine." *SVT* 4 (1957), 242-58; Clifford, R. J. *Cosmic Mountain in Canaan and the Old Testament* (1972); Hilton, N. "Blake and the Mountains of the Mind." *Blake: An Illustrated Quarterly* 14 (1981), 196-204; Landow, G. *Victorian Types, Victorian Shadows: Biblical Typology in Victorian Literature, Art and Thought* (1980); Nicholson, M. H. *Mountain Gloom and Mountain Glory: The Development of the Aesthetics of the Infinite* (1959); Piehler, P. *The Visionary Landscape: A Study in Medieval Allegory* (1971).   RONALD B. BOND

MULIER FORTIS Prov. 31:10-31, an acrostic poem in praise of female virtue, constitutes an extension of the sayings of Lemuel (perhaps an Arab king) which he attributes in vv. 1-9 to his mother. The passage may thus provide a rare instance of non-Hebrew and female authorship of Scripture. Rabbinic commentary prefers to see "Lemuel" (Heb. = "Belonging to God") as a nom de plume or attribute name for Solomon, and does not comment on the maternal source of the "wisdom" (Tg. Sheni 1.2.4; Shir ha Shirim Rabbah 1.1). The passage describes the "strong woman" (Vg *mulier fortis*) as of inestimable value to her husband and children; her price is "above rubies." She is a spinner of wool and flax, an effective and prosperous businesswoman, a benevolent force in society, and a disciple of wisdom.

Medieval commentary on this passage, along with an analogue in Ecclus. 26:1-24, is extensive. Among the most important elaborations are the *Liber Consolationis et Consilii* of Albert of Brescia, which Chaucer paraphrases closely in his characterization of Dame Prudence in *The Tale of Melibee* (*Canterbury Tales*, 7.1064ff.). The *mulier fortis* is here Lady Wisdom herself, a figure from the earlier chapters of Proverbs, the proper object of a young ruler's highest affection. Other commentators were to identify the *mulier fortis* allegorically with the Church (e.g., *Glossa Ordinaria* [PL 113.1114-16] or Bride of Christ in whom Christ may safely trust as both faithful and fruitful unto good works. Applied literally, the description becomes a kind of medieval stereotype for womanly virtue, as in John Gower's *Vox Clamantis*, where the text is invoked to explain how the character of good and bad women affects men (5.6). Chaucer appears to have drawn heavily on this passage for his sympathetic characterization of the wife in *The Shipman's Tale;* his Wife of Bath, also a spinner of flax and wool and a businesswoman of some enterprise, is a kind of parody of the *mulier fortis* (Prov. 31:10 is found as a gloss on line 689 of the Prologue to her tale in some MSS of *The Canterbury Tales*). Bunyan's portrait of Prudence and Christiana in pt. 2 of *Pilgrim's Progress* is indebted to Prov. 31. In Hardy's *Tess of the D'Urbervilles* (chap. 39), when Angel Clare returns home alone and without explanation three weeks after his ill-fated marriage to Tess, his father chooses to read "The words of King Lemuel" to honor the absent bride. Mrs. Clare's sense of the aptness of the passage in describing Tess underscores Angel's confusion and torment:

> The perfect woman, you see, was a working woman; not an idler; not a fine lady; but one who used her hands and her head and her heart for the good of others. "Her children arise up and call her blessed; her husband also, and he praiseth her. Many daughters have done virtuously, but she excelleth them all." Well, I wish I could have seen her, Angel. Since she is pure and chaste she would have been refined enough for me.

The passage is extensively cited throughout Mulock's *John Halifax,* where it is usually applied to the character of Mrs. Halifax (e.g., chaps. 22, 30). In Somerset Maugham's *The Mixture as Before,* "People envied Harenger the possession of her as they envied nothing else that he had. She was worth her weight in gold. Her price was above rubies. Richard Harenger beamed with self-complacency when they praised her" ("The Treasure"). One of the novels of Louis Bromfield, *The Good Woman* (1927), concerns the relationship between a dominated son and his missionary mother, and there are oblique references in Berthold Brecht's *Good Woman of Setzuan* and *Mother Courage* (1941).

See also WISDOM.

Bibliography. Boren, J. "Alysoun of Bath and the Vulgate 'Perfect Wife.'" *NM* 76 (1975), 247-56; Coletti, T. "Biblical Wisdom: Chaucer's Shipman's Tale and the *Mulier Fortis.*" *ChauR* 15 (1982), 236-49.

MUSIC AND MUSICAL INSTRUMENTS That music played a significant role among those peoples whose history is related in biblical literature is clear; further, it played a role similar to its function in the 20th cent., serving both secular and sacred functions. Song is the oldest of musical expressions, but instruments, of a sort, are likely to have played a supporting role very swiftly, e.g., the rhythmical banging of wood (solid or hollow) and stone. Biblical literature records more sophisticated developments beyond the merely percussive stage, and Jubal (a descendant of Cain) is credited with the invention of both the *kinnor* (called the harp in the KJV but more probably the lyre) and the *'ugab* (or organ, probably a joined set of mouth-blown pipes). There is a record of both string and wind instruments at a very early stage of biblical chronology, and the nature of these instruments presupposes a knowledge of the effect of the tension of the strings on pitch in one case and of the effect of pipe length and/or diameter on pitch in the other.

Thus, in coming to the later references (in Genesis and following books) an assumption can be made that melody was not haphazard but ordered and that it was often accompanied, even before any accompaniment is specifically noted. Song and song with rhythmical body movement (developing into patterned dance) had their place (Gen. 31:27; Exod. 15:20) even as purely social and pleasurable expressions; music was used in public celebrations by prophets (see again Exod. 15:20) and by rulers and priests (e.g., 1 Kings 1:40). Frequently instruments are specifically named (e.g., Isa. 5:12; 14:11; 2 Sam. 20:21; Dan. 3:5, 7, 10; and Amos 6:7 [which refers to those "That chant to the sound of the viol, *and* invent to themselves instruments of musick, like David"]). In Hab. 3:19 the reference is more general in simply referring to "stringed instruments," which may be harps, lyres, or guitars. Music was seen to give vent to and to affect the emotions: sound could be used for both inspiration (hence its employment by kings, priests, and prophets) and for healing (as in the case of David playing for Saul [1 Sam. 16:16-23] upon the *kinnor*). It was the common property of the individual and the group, of the king and the worker in the field. The Psalmist is, after all, a single singer, but his voice is no less beautiful and important than the raised chorus (e.g., 2 Chron. 29:25). Of all the OT musicians, the one most firmly before the mind is David, for he was aware of music's enormous power, its emotional capacity, and his use of it is to be found always in terms of fundamentally spiritual rather than physical associations (even in his musical therapy for Saul); he was the singer of the praises of God (2 Sam. 22:50), and his example and instruction (1 Chron. 15:16-29) were followed, in a public way, by Solomon (e.g., 2 Chron. 9:11), by Hezekiah (2 Chron. 29:25; 30:21), and by Josiah (2 Chron. 35:15).

Music, then, both vocal and instrumental, had an established and important place in Hebrew society, even as it did in that of the other peoples with whom the Hebrews came in contact. Dan. 3:5-10 records Nebuchadnezzar employing music in a symbolic way, and it is likely that the captive Hebrews derived musical influences, both melodic and technical, from their captors. Instruments clearly played an accompanying role in much vocal music, particularly in state panegyrics and religious observances (which were often, again, state occasions themselves).

In brief, biblical instruments fall into three obvious categories: (a) stringed, (b) wind, and (c) percussion. Of the stringed instruments, the *kinnor* (noted earlier) is the most significant; while described in the KJV as a harp, it was probably a lyre, or a small portable harp-type instrument; like the *nebel* (psaltery in the KJV and possibly, in some contexts, a harp) and the associated *'asor*, the *kinnor* had to be carried, as in the procession with the Ark of the Covenant (see 1 Chron. 15:28). (The *nebel* could refer to a variety of forms, including the large Egyptian harp.) The *sabbeka'* and *psanterin* are related instruments; all share the basic principle of stretched strings between frame members. The *makalat*, like the *gittit* and *minnim*, refer to stringed instruments generally and to strings generally. The dulcimer, as mentioned in 1 Chron. 15, was probably a kind of *nebel* or psaltery — possibly struck with mallets even at that time, just as the *kinnor* may have been played at times with a plectrum (see Josephus, *Ant.* 7.12.3). The wind instruments included the *qeren* (a ram's horn); the most celebrated example is found in the account of the fall of Jericho (Josh. 6:5, 8-9, 13, etc.). Other winds were the *shopar* (a trumpet, less curved than the *qeren*), the *hasoserah* (a straight trumpet), the *yobel* (a trumpet, possibly sharper-sounding, used to signify celebrations and emergencies), the *halil* (a bored pipe with holes to allow pitch variation — hence an early recorder or flute), the *mashroqita'* (a Chaldean two-reed flute), and the *'ugab* (a mouth-blown set of pipes, referred to above). The

percussion instruments included the *top* (tambourines and drums), the *pa'amon* (small bells attached to priests' robes), *selselim, mesillot,* and *mesiltayim* (cymbals, both large and small — i.e., hand and finger held — consider 1 Cor. 13:1), the *shalishim* (probably a triangle), and the *mena'an'im* (a sistrum or metal rattle).

Music, as documented in the Bible, is not regarded simply as the music of mankind; it is also — directly or in simile or metaphor — the music of heaven and of divine messengers, of the angelic chorus which glorifies God and proclaims this majesty to humans (Rev. 1:10; 4:1; 8:2, etc.; 14:2-3; 18:22; and see, e.g., Milton's *Paradise Lost,* 7.594-99). However, it is also used by persons antithetical to God, as has been noted in the case of Nebuchadnezzar, and by quasibiblical creations of that sort found in other literature: Milton's Satan in his construction of Pandemonium (see *PL* 1.709-12 and 786-87) involves music in an ironic and totally improper way — in the service of chaos rather than of order.

St. Augustine's *De musica* is the earliest of several influential medieval Christian treatises on music. Drawing on classical Greek as well as scriptural tradition, Augustine sees music not merely as a liberal art (one of the quadrivium, along with arithmetic, geometry, and astronomy), but as a spiritual *accessus* by which "the mind is raised from the consideration of changeable numbers in inferior things to unchangeable numbers in unchangeable truth itself" (PL 18.1170). Accordingly, in the last of the six books of his dialogue-treatise Augustine arrives at a reflection on metaphysics and epistemology. The proper study of music involves not only technical accomplishment, which reflects the senses and memory, but the theoretical knowledge of music — its *scientia* engaging the intellect. Supremely, however, the *sapientia* of music is a "wisdom" to which the commitment of the will is necessary if indeed a musician is to arrive at the highest goal of the art, a truer understanding of the glory of God. We know from Augustine's *Confessiones* that actual singing in church was introduced in Milan only in the time of St. Ambrose (7.7), in Carthage in his own generation (*Retractiones,* 2).

The *De Institutione Musica* of Boethius, though in some ways less scripturally integrated than Augustine's text, became the standard medieval authority, and remained a standard textbook at Oxford until the 18th cent. Boethius divides music into three kinds, each kind reflective of a complementary aspect of universal order in creation. *Musica mundana* is the music of the spheres, the rhythm of the season and harmonious combination of earth's elements; *musica humana* is the harmony of body and soul, and the accord of rational and suprarational attributes within the soul. *Musica in instrumentis constituta* is only the audible embodiment of these superior and essential harmonies. For Boethius, then, music is the one member of the quadrivium to engage moral and ethical matter intrinsically.

The emphasis in Western theory on harmony and number centers on the rational aspect of "creational" music. The stipulations of Pope Gregory I (A.D. 590-604) are for an integrity of word and intonation which stresses this *ratio;* the "purity" of Gregorian chant is a reflection of an ordinate, mathematical, and deliberated theory. Later the eight Church Modes (10th cent. ff.), or scale arrangements, were evidently deduced from vestiges of melodic formulas in Gregorian chant. The earliest recorded ME lyric captures the secular authority of England hearkening, as is reasonable for them, to such music:

Merie sungen ðe munaches binnen Ely
Ða Cnut ching reu ðer-by.
'Roweð, cnites, noer þe land,
And here we þes munaches saeng!'

[Merry sang the monks in Ely cathedral
When King Cnut rowed nearby.
'Row, knights, near the land,
And let us hear these monks' song!']

This emphasis on rationality in theory and in practice still anchors the defense of plainsong by Jacob de Liège (ca. 1330) in his *Speculum Musicae,* in which he attacks the 14th-cent. *ars nova* for its experiment with *musica mensurata,* a more extensive lyricism with binary rather than "rational" ternary rhythms. Jacob rebukes modernizers such as Philippe de Vitry (*Ars Nova,* ca. 1325) for departing from both reason and hallowed tradition: "Long ago," he writes, "venerable men (among them Tubal-Cain, before the Flood), wrote reasonably on plainsong: since that time many more . . . have done the same . . ." (bk. 7). The apprehension concerning nonrational music, figured in the later medieval and Renaissance retelling of the myth of the contest between Apollo and Marsyas (pictured graphically in the ceiling of the Vatican Stanza della Segnatura by Raphael), reflects a concern that in nonrational music carnal rather than spiritual passions might be aroused (cf. the version of the myth recounted by Diodorus Siculus, and later elaborated by the late 15th-cent. English poet John Skelton (EETS 233, 1.301-03). When earlier (13th-cent.) Franciscan friars had made popular or folk song (performed on simple instruments and sung at street corners) the basis for a kind of vernacular hymnody, they had attracted criticism for purveying music of the Marsyan kind. Their own *apologia* was derivatively Augustinian; the "old song" of cupiditous love and foolishness, they said, was being redeemed by them as "Egyptian gold," and made into scriptural "new song" (cf. Pss. 148–150) of God's love and the wisdom of faith (Jeffrey, *The Early English Lyric,* chap. 2).

St. Thomas Aquinas, himself a Dominican friar, raised the question of whether God should be praised in song at all, given the instability of music by its nature (*Summa Theol.* 22.1.q.39.8.31; 54.2.2.q.91.2). St. Jerome, he acknowledges, recommends singing to God with the heart more than the voice, but the praise of the heart is too easily distracted by praise of the voice: he worries that music in worship tends to the theatrical — especially polyphonic singing. The organ he allows as a stimulus to devotion, however.

In 1324-25 Pope John XXII issued a bull against the new polyphonic music. He quoted Boethius as support for his conviction that "a person who is intrinsically sensuous will delight in hearing these indecent melodies, and one who listens to them frequently will be weakened thereby and lose his virility of soul" (Woolridge 1.294-95). Pope John may have been aware from the writings of St. John Chrysostom that the heretic Arius had made considerable use of sensual music in the proclamation of his theological views, setting liturgical and polemical texts to sailors' songs and having singers parading through the streets of Constantinople at night, singing them. In any case, his warnings were akin to those of Chrysostom. These cautions notwithstanding, the Franciscans friars particularly, employing their music mostly outside the church, went on about their business of being *ioculatores Dei.* By the time of Chaucer the friars had helped to create a large repertoire of vernacular "evangelistic" or devotional songs, many of which are preserved in the annals of the ME lyrics. Chaucer, however, was skeptical about the compatibility of medium and message in persons such as his *Canterbury Tales* Friar, "a wantowne and a merye" songster of whom he observes: "And certeinly he hadde a murye note: / Wel koude he synge and pleyen on a rote" (*General Prologue,* 1.235-36). The concern that such music might better serve Mammon than God is persistent in Chaucer: he notes of his Pardoner that

. . . alderbest he song an offertorie;
For wel he wiste, whan that song was songe,
He moste preche and wel affile his tongue
To wynne silver, as he ful wel koude;
Therefore he song the muriely and loude. (*General Prologue,* 1.710-14)

The *Parliament of Fowls* ends on a more candidly secular note, and dancing and caroling have unambiguously carnal associations in *Romaunt of the Rose* (see, e.g., 801ff., 1149ff.). On the other hand, *The Second Nun's Tale* is a life of St. Cecilia; see, e.g., *CT* 8.134-35, in which the real "music" of St. Cecelia is the melody of saintliness, and a harmony engendered by multiplication of that melody in the community of faith. Virtue resides not in the capacity for literal music, but in its spiritual directedness. It is doubtless no accident that Chaucer gives to Chauntecleer a ". . . voys . . . murier than the murie orgon / On messe-days that in the chirche gon" (*Nun's Priest's Tale,* 7.2851-52). The singing of mass and other church music is well documented by English writers (see, e.g., chap. 10 of Malory's *Le Morte Darthur* and Spenser's music-filled *Epithalamion,* with its biblical precursor in the *Song of Solomon*):

Open the temple gates unto my love, . . .
And let the roring Organs loudly play
In praises of the Lord in liuely notes,
The whiles with hollow throates
The Choristers the ioyous Antheme sing,
That al the woods may answere and their eccho ring.
(204, 218-22)

In this context must also be mentioned Spenser's *Fowre Hymnes,* two, as he notes in the dedication, ". . . of earthly or naturall love and beautie, two others of heauenly and celestiall." *Prothalamion* is a song of a different character; the *Faerie Queene* contains significant musical references, such as that in bk. 1 (12.13) to "shaumes, . . . trompets, and . . . Clarions sweet . . ."; and pipes figure significantly in *The Shepheardes Calendar.*

The contrast between sacred and secular was not simply a literary concern; in the Renaissance musical world the Roman church found itself having to deal with increasingly secular trends, as tunes which had their origin and hence associations in the profane world tended, when liturgical texts were set to them, to carry their worldly suggestions into the houses of worship. Many masses, including two by Palestrina (e.g., *Missa Quarta,* 1582) (1582) and Josquin des Prez, were based upon the long-standingly popular song, "L'homme armé." Other persistently recognizable examples of the *cantus firmus* include a German love song "Mein G'mut is mir veswirret" ("My heart is all confused") through Paul Gerhardt's application to it of St. Bernard's hymn *"Salve Caput Cruentatum"* ("O Haupt, voll Blut und Wunden"), which became the chorale in Bach's *St. Matthew's Passion.* Luther, for whom music was the one appropriate art for the Church, had set the Reformation precedent in putting the words of hymns to popular tunes (e.g., his Christmas song "Vom Himmel hoch da Komm ich her" ["From Heaven Above to Earth I Come"]). Most of Luther's own 38 hymns then recur in some form in Bach's cantatas. Mendelssohn's *Fifth Symphony in D Major* ("The Reformation Symphony") is a fugue-like elaboration of Luther's chorale, "Ein feste Burg ist unser Gott" ("A Mighty Fortress Is Our God").

Calvin, by contrast, followed St. Jerome in asserting that singing is "not of the least consequence" unless it "proceeds from deep feelings in the heart." Indeed, if anything less prompts music it "provokes the anger of God" (*Inst.* 3.20.31). Calvin acknowledges that singing in churches is of ancient origin, citing 1 Cor. 14:15 and Col. 3:16 as exemplary, but suggests that there are nonetheless reasons to be cautious: "We must . . . carefully beware, lest our ears be more intent on the music than our minds on the spiritual meaning of the words" (3.20.32), and he restricts the use of musical settings to the Psalms. Successors in the Reformed tradition — including some of the English Puritans — hewed to the side of caution. In Catholic tradition attention was focused most particularly on the evident secularity of some tunes: if the

congregation actually sang — let alone thought of — the secular words, much of the point of a religious text was going to be missed. Hence, the problem of church music became, quite properly, one of the concerns of the Council of Trent; the result, finally, was the choice of Palestrina's music as the touchstone of Counter-Reformation style, and the influence of that choice on Byrd and his English successors (as well as upon nonmusicians who were exposed to it) was profound. Indeed, Byrd declared that the chief employment for the singing voice was the praise of God. But the struggle in English church music did not end; it went on through the 17th and 18th cents. (consider the Puritans' destruction of organs — despite the predilections of Cromwell and Milton) and is present in the 20th cent. in the controversy over the jazz mass and the introduction to church music of instruments (*Confiteor tibi in guituara*) normally associated with the dance hall or rock concert.

References to sacred music continued to abound in English literature. With Donne (as in "At the round earth's imagined corners blow / Your trumpets, angels") and Herbert (as in "Easter") the references are pointedly biblical. Writers like Pepys and Evelyn comment specifically on the issue of apparent secularity: Pepys, always ready for a good time and always unready to be bored by a sermon, welcomed the addition of stringed music to the services after the Restoration, while the more circumspect Evelyn thought such sounds more appropriate to a "tavern" or a "playhouse." Musical references are found frequently in Milton. In the third preparatory stanza in "On the Morning of Christ's Nativity" he asks, "Hast thou no verse, no hymn, or solemn strain / To welcome him to his new abode. . . ?" (see also "The Hymn," sts. 9-14). "L'Allegro" and "Il Penseroso" make reference to song and dance, while "At a Solemn Music," proclaiming the sisterhood of "Voice and Verse," speaks of a heavenly harmony, takes its imagery in part from Ezek. 1:26 and Rev. 14:3-4, and anticipates *Paradise Lost,* 7.594-99. Even Samson's "Acts" will be ". . . enroll'd / In copious Legend, or sweet Lyric Song" (*Samson Agonistes,* 1736-37). Music devoted to worship, when the nature of worship is not subverted, is in every way beneficial and proper; hence Milton would commend the practice of suitable music in "Of Education" (1644; 1673). (Like Calvin and the Council of Trent, he was prepared to admit that not all music is appropriate.)

Dryden, as a playwright, knew full well the importance of music on the stage, and he also produced two of the most important music poems in the language as contributions to the long tradition of occasional works (of both poetry and music) for St. Cecilia's Day — "A Song for ST. CECILIA'S Day, 1687" and "Alexander's Feast" (1697), the first with its references to Jubal, to the power of music, the qualities of various instruments, and the primacy of St. Cecilia as reputed inventor of the organ, and the second with its praise of music and the skill of

Timotheus (who can at least share the laurels with Cecilia) couched in the form of a pure music ode, a model of the enthusiastic display piece. And despite the currency of the Copernican worldview and the work of Newton, both "A Song" and "AN ODE, ON THE DEATH OF Mr. Henry Purcell" (1695) document the notion of the harmony of the spheres; in harmony was divine order and the universe was so managed and perfectly tuned, especially as represented in Ptolemaic thought:

So when the last and dreadful hour
This crumbling Pageant shall devour,
The TRUMPET shall be heard on high,
The Dead shall live, the Living die,
And MUSICK shall untune the Sky. ("A Song. . . ,"
59-63)

In the 18th cent., the Rev. Jonathan Swift certainly knew of biblical references to music, at least by virtue of his calling as a divine, and his casual dismissal of the subject in his flippant description of the second course of a dinner in the King's palace at Laputa (*Gulliver's Travels*, bk. 3) is presumably ironic; some of Dryden's precious instruments are reduced to ducks, sausages, puddings, and a breast of veal. Swift's friend Pope, however, followed the clear poetic lead of Dryden not only in style and technique but often in substance; he is prepared to state in *An Essay on Man* (Epistle 4.49) that "ORDER is Heaven's first law. . . ." Certainly, Pope, like Johnson, wanted to believe that — the alternative was chaos and loss of faith, a prospect which had visibly shaken the first part of the preceding century. But Newton had uttered his truths, and even if the earth was not at the center of the whirling planets, at least the universe and all things physical could be understood to be working according to definable or potentially definable laws. Thus he could also note, echoing Boethius rather than Dryden's scientific anachronisms (*Essay on Man*, 3.284, 289-96), that the

Follow'r of God or friend of human-kind,
. . .Taught Pow'r's due use to People and to Kings,
Taught nor to slack, nor to strain its tender strings,
The less, or greater, set so justly true,
That touching one must strike the other too [the
    principle of sympathetic vibration];
'Till jarring int'rests of themselves create
Th'according music of a well-mix'd State.
Such is the World's great harmony, that springs
From Order, Union, full Consent of things!

Pope was not venturing onto unfamiliar ground in using musical terms; indeed, his analogies, metaphors, and adjectival embellishments are frequent. Like Dryden, he wrote an ode for St. Cecilia's Day ("Ode for Musick" [ca. 1708, publ. 1715]); its classical and biblical heritage is clear, and its points about the power of music over human passions and the statement that "By Musick, Minds an equal Temper know" (22) (cf. Milton's "On

Education") are standard for Pope's era. (The poem, though, is not as successful as either of Dryden's, both of which were set by Handel.) One other example is appropriate: in "Moral Essays Epistle 4. To Richard Boyle, Earl of Burlington" (1731) Pope offers a satirical portrait of bad taste in his description of Timon's Villa, and includes, in his discussion of the chapel, the following:

And now the Chapel's silver bell you hear,
That summons you to all the Pride of Pray'r:
Light quirks of Musick, broken and uneven,
Make the soul dance upon a Jig to Heaven. (141-44)

In English Baptist and Independent congregations of Dryden's day, music was still largely restricted to the Psalms. By the time of Isaac Watts this pattern had begun to loosen, and Watts's *Hymns* (1707), richly commended by Samuel Johnson in his *Life* of Watts, were an almost immediate influence upon English religious verse and hymnody ("When I Survey the Wondrous Cross," "O God Our Help in Ages Past," etc.). His *Divine Songs* (1715), hymns for children, ran to more than 100 editions by the mid-19th cent., and established a tradition to which Christopher Smart's *Hymns for the Amusement of Children* (1772) and Blake's *Songs of Innocence* each in its own fashion owe a debt. In the climate of revival spirituality which flowered in the 18th cent. the separation between Greek and Hebrew, secular and sacred began to seem less important, and many English poets could affirm the sense of Smart's lines in *Jubilate Agno*:

For the story of Orpheus is of the truth.
For there was such a person a cunning player on the
    harp.
For he was a believer in the true God and assisted in
    the spirit.
For he playd upon the harp in the spirit by breathing
    upon the strings.
For this will affect every thing that is sustaind by the
    spirit, even everything in nature.

Charles Wesley is undoubtedly the greatest name in Christian hymnody in this period. His lyrics and musical settings include 6,500 hymns, about 500 of which are still in use in a variety of Christian denominations. In such hymns as "Love Divine, All Loves Excelling," "And Can It Be That I Should Gain," and "Jesus, Lover of My Soul," Wesley established, with the assistance of his Welsh contralto wife Sally Gwynne, a lasting influence of Welsh lyricism upon English hymnody. His hymns are mostly Christocentric, praises for redemption and atonement. John Newton ("Amazing Grace") and William Cowper jointly authored the *Olney Hymns* (1779), a series of biblical and doctrinal hymns more closely reflecting — especially Cowper's numbers — the Reformed theological tradition. Notable is their series on the names of God ("Jehovah-Jirah," "Jehovah-Nisi," etc.).

In the 18th and 19th cents. there were numerous other accomplished hymn writers and poets (some of whom were composers as well) whose linkage of voice and verse in the biblical tradition had far-reaching effects. Here, e.g., one finds Toplady, Bonar, Heber, Montgomery, Steele, Keble, Newman, Caswall, Faber, and Ingelow.

Blake, who denied the order and regulation which Pope and the earlier 18th cent. found not only comfortable but necessary, nevertheless welcomed with joyous, energetic, and individual lyricism in poetry (and in painting) the primacy of God and divine rule. Here, too, musical references abound — apt enough, given the nature and style of Blake's expression. In "Song,"

Like as an angel glittering in the sky
In times of innocence and holy joy,
The joyful shepherd stops his grateful song
To hear the music of an angel's tongue;

and in "Mad Song" the poet exclaims:

"Lo! to the vault
Of paved heaven,
With sorrow fraught
My notes are driven. . . ."

Blake's *Songs of Innocence* and *Songs of Experience* are like the Psalms, pure songs with a clear moral purpose, and the "Introduction" (one of the Blake texts most often set to music) to the former group involves the pastoral piper. In "Auguries of Innocence" he exclaims: "A skylark wounded in the wing, / A cherubim does cease to sing . . ." (15-16). Blake sees himself as a musical prophet, and musicality is implicit in his content and manner. Even *Jerusalem* (ca. 1815-20) is, after all, a *song*, to use Blake's own term.

Wordsworth, in "Mutability," "Prospectus" to *The Recluse* (33-35), *The Prelude* (14.98-99), and *Intimations of Immortality,* also offers examples of musical imagery in the biblical tradition, as do Coleridge (e.g., in *The Eolian Harp, Christobel,* and *Dejection: An Ode*) and Byron (e.g., in *The Vision of Judgment,* and *Hebrew Melodies,* in which several poems [e.g., "The Harp the Monarch Minstrel Swept," "My Soul Is Dark," "Song of Saul Before his Last Battle," "By the Rivers of Babylon We Sat Down and Wept"] are concerned with notable uses of music in the Bible). Echoes of biblical tradition are to be found also in Shelley (in "Ode to the West Wind," "To a Sky-Lark," and "Adonis") and Felicia Hemans (e.g., "Flowers and Music in a Room of Sickness" and "Cathedral Hymn").

Of the Victorians, Tennyson and Browning deserve particular mention. In Tennyson's works the reader will find not only musical allusions but ones which clearly are in the biblical and Christian tradition; hence one finds bugles, trumpets, and other forms of tonal expression, specifically, e.g., in "The Palace of Art." For Tennyson, poetry is song: he instances this conviction in his account of the sacrifice by Jephthah of his daughter (Judg. 11:30-40) in "A Dream of Fair Women" (189-200), the final stanza of "Sir Galahad,"

the opening stanzas of *In Memoriam* (25-29) and sects. 105 and 106 of the same elegy, and the bells of "Far-Far-Away" and "Crossing the Bar." Even more conspicuously musical in his references was Browning. It is Pippa who *sings,* "God's in his heaven — / All's right with the world!" (*Pippa Passes,* "Morning"); there is the procession in "Up at a Villa — Down in the City" (50-54), and the singing of Theocrite in "The Boy and the Angel." More extended treatment is to be found in "A Toccata of Galuppi's," "Abt Vogler," "Master Hugues of Saxe-Gotha," and "Saul." (With respect to the last poem see also 1 Sam. 16:14-23.) In "Abt Vogler" Browning urges the reader to consider the immeasurable power of music — beyond its healing capacity as reflected in "Saul" or its much discussed influence over the emotions as reflected in "Parleying with Charles Avison." Browning confesses that he knows not ". . . if, save in this, such gift be allowed to man, / That out of three sounds he frame, not a fourth sound, but a star" (51-52).

Arnold heard on earth the ring of ". . . a thousand discords" ("Quiet Work") and he wrote of the silent chapel (in "Stanzas from the Grande Chartreuse") ". . . where no organ's peal / Invests the stern and naked prayer . . ." (37-38). The Rossettis also employed significant musical references, as did Swinburne (see, e.g., "Mater Triumphalis"). In the poetry of post-Darwinian disillusion one finds the tradition countered; in Hardy's "The Darkling Thrush" ". . . tangled bine-stems scored the sky / Like strings from broken lyres . . ." (5-6), an apparently hostile and ironic setting for the ". . . full-hearted evensong . . ." (19) of the thrush. Hopkins, on the other hand, full of faith — musician and poet — left lyric works clearly in the biblical tradition. The social lot of humanity can provoke such work, as can his conflicts, as, e.g., in the case of Owen (see "Anthem for a Doomed Youth" [1920]). Eliot (who was actually opposed to his words being set to music) nevertheless provides an oblique example, even in the negative music of Chapel Perilous in *The Waste Land* (1922), as do Auden (who, like Edith Sitwell, could work closely with musicians) in the title and form of the implicitly musical but cynical "Fugal-Chorus from 'For the Time Being'" (1945) and Dylan Thomas in his depiction of nature's music of praise (e.g., in "Fern Hill" and "In Country Sleep").

The clearest echo in modern English poetry of the Augustinian view of music expressed by Christian antiquity, however, may be Hopkins's "On a Piece of Music," which includes the lines:

How all's to one thing wrought!
The members, how they sit!
O what a tune the thought
Must be that fancied it.

Nor angel insight can
Learn how the heart is hence:
Since all the make of man
Is law's indifference.

[Who shaped these walls has shewn
The music of his mind,
Made known, though thick through stone,
What beauty beat behind.]

What makes the man and what
The man within that makes:
Ask whom he serves or not
Serves and what side he takes. (sts. 1, 2, 3, 6)

Bibliography. Adey, L. *Class and Idol in the English Hymn* (1989); *Hymns and the Christian "Myth"* (1986); Bukofzer, M. "Speculative Thinking in Medieval Music." *Speculum* 17 (1942), 165-80; Flew, R. N. *The Hymns of Charles Wesley: A Study of their Structure* (1953); Hollander, J. *The Untuning of the Sky: Ideas of Music in English Poetry, 1500-1700* (1961); Jeffrey, D. L. *The Early English Lyric and Franciscan Spirituality* (1975); Pelikan, J. *Bach Among the Theologians* (1940); Smith, B. "The Contest of Apollo and Marsyas." In *By Things Seen: Reference and Recognition in Medieval Thought.* Ed. D. L. Jeffrey (1979); Stevens, J. *Music and Poetry in the Early Tudor Court* (1961).

                                                    BRYAN N. S. GOOCH

MUSTARD SEED   In one of his parables Jesus compared the kingdom of heaven to "a grain of mustard seed, which a man took, and sowed in his field: which indeed is the least of all seeds: but when it is grown, it is the greatest among herbs, and becometh a tree, so that the birds of the air come and lodge in the branches thereof " (Matt. 13:31-32; cf. Mark 4:32; Luke 13:19). The particular type of mustard intended may be the *sinapis nigra*, the cultivated black mustard (commonly 4 ft., but capable of reaching 15 ft.). The parable suggests, nonetheless, deliberate hyperbole: rabbinic commentary made reference to the mustard seed as an example of minuteness, a commonplace echoed in Jesus' observation that if the disciples had "faith as a grain of mustard seed" they would move mountains (Matt. 17:20; Luke 17:6).

Carlyle was fond of the mustard seed parable, using it in his essay "Boswell's Life of Johnson" to describe the fertility and power of Johnson's prose, and again in *Sartor Resartus* to describe the growth of an idea into an institution (2.10). Hardy, of whom Phelps in his *Essays on Modern Novelists* observes that "after a time he ceased to have even the faith of a grain of mustard seed," writes of another aspiration in *Far from the Madding Crowd:* "This fevered hope had grown up again like a grain of mustard seed during the quiet which followed the hasty conjecture that Troy was drowned" (chap. 49). And in another description of a writer's power Alexander Anderson echoes Carlyle as well as St. Matthew in his *Aldous Huxley,* "He has only to note an idea, and it proliferates rapidly into a vast foliage, like the Biblical seed of mustard sprouting into a lodging for the fowls of the air" (243).

MY BROTHER'S KEEPER   "Where is Abel thy brother?" asked God after Cain had murdered him. "I know not," Cain replied: "Am I my brother's keeper?" (Gen. 4:9). The disingenuousness of Cain's reply is typically highlighted in literary allusions, such as when Carlyle in *Past and Present* attributes it to mercenary sweatshop mill owners. Atypically, Somerset Maugham employs it as an expression of virtuous toleration: "I am not my brother's keeper. I cannot bring myself to judge my fellows; I am content to observe them" (*The Summing Up,* chap. 17).

See also ABEL; CAIN.

MY YOKE IS EASY   In Matt. 11:28-30 Jesus invites sin-weary hearers: "Come unto me, all ye that labor and are heavy laden, and I will give you rest. Take my yoke upon you, and learn of me, for I am meek and lowly in heart: and ye shall find rest unto your souls. For my yoke is easy, and my burden is light." This text was especially popular among preachers in the 18th-cent. Great Revival (e.g., John Newton, *Sermons in Olney* [1767], nos. 10, 11, 12, and 13), and on into the Victorian era. In Victorian times the "weary and heavy-laden" were identified typically with the poor (e.g., Carlyle, *Sartor Resartus,* 3.4; Thoreau, *Walden,* "Sounds"), though the original sense is reckoned with by Stephen in Joyce's *Portrait of the Artist* (chap. 4): "It was easy to be good. God's yoke was sweet and light. It was better never to have sinned."

MYSTIC ROSE   The *Rosa mystica* is an appellation for the Virgin Mary based upon a typologized reading of Song of Songs 2:1.

See also MARY, MOTHER OF JESUS.

N

NAAMAN Naaman was a Syrian military commander during the reign of Ben-hadad. When afflicted with leprosy he was urged by a Hebrew slave girl in his Damascus household to seek help of God's prophet, Elisha (2 Kings 5). When he arrived at the house of Elisha Naaman was instructed by the prophet to go to the river Jordan and there dip in its waters seven times (v. 10). Naaman was offended at what seemed summary treatment and at the notion that the tepid Jordan had cleansing powers: "Are not Abana and Pharpar, rivers of Damascus, better than all the waters of Israel? May I not wash in them and be clean? So he turned and went away in a rage" (v. 12). His servants, however, prevailed upon him to do the prophet's bidding. When he did, "his flesh came again like unto the flesh of a little child, and he was clean" (v. 14).

St. Ambrose comments that "being forthwith cleansed, he understood that it is not of the waters but of grace that a man is cleansed" (*De mysteriis*, 3.17). Both St. Irenaeus (*Fragments*, 34) and Tertullian (*Adv. Marc.* 9, 10) see the narrative as typifying the efficacy of baptism. A brief commentary in the *Glossa Ordinaria* characterizes Naaman as a figure for the conversion of the Gentiles, whose strength has been eroded by "the leprosy of an idolatrous faith" but who when cleansed by the gospel have their strength recovered to a higher purpose (PL 113.613-14). In the minimal haggadic discussion of the narrative, Naaman's leprosy is seen as a punishment for his pride (Num. Rab. 7.5); the story is important in demonstrating the great humility Naaman showed before the prophet (Haserot 35; cf. Sanh. 10.29b). (Another, unrelated Jewish tradition, recorded by Josephus among others, credits Naaman with killing the ungodly King Ahab by "drawing his bow at a venture" [1 Kings 22:34].) For Matthew Poole the prophet's instruction to dip in the Jordan was partly intended "to try Naaman's Faith and Obedience" (*Annotations*, sup. 2 Kings 5:10).

The story attracts little attention in literature until the 19th cent., when the narrative became popular in evangelical preaching such as that of Charles Spurgeon. Though Lamb's allusion, "The Cam and the Isis are to him better than all the waters of Damascus" is learned ("Oxford in the Vacation"), most later references tend to echo the homiletic tradition. Trollope writes in *Barchester Towers:*

> Then his faith was against him: he required to believe so much; panted so eagerly to give signs of his belief; deemed it so insufficient to wash himself simply in the waters of Jordan; that some great deed, such as that of forsaking everything for a true church, had for him allurements almost past withstanding. (Chap. 20)

In Butler's *The Way of All Flesh* the narrator, attending Theobald's old church, "felt as Naaman must have felt on certain occasions when he had to accompany his master on his return after having been cured of his leprosy," and Christina "was sure that she had grown in grace since she had left off eating things strangled and blood — this was as the washing in Jordan as against Abana and Pharpar, rivers of Damascus" (chap. 21).

See also AHAB; ELISHA.   DAVID W. BAKER

NABAL 1 Sam. 25:2-42 tells the story of churlish Nabal (Heb. *nabal,* "fool") who refused hospitality to David and his men, even though they had been protecting his flocks, meanwhile making a huge banquet for himself and his own men, thereby invoking David's wrath. As a "rebel" (Midr. Tehillim 53.287-88) and "man of Belial" (v. 25), Nabal attracts attention in patristic literature as a self-serving fool and, as the *Glossa Ordinaria* (PL 113.561) puts it, following Rabanus, *vir durus et pessimus,* an obstinate and pessimistic man. Jerome (*Ep.* 125.10) compares him to the man who dies in his riches without understanding, such as the rich man of the parable upon whom the judgment is pronounced, "Thou fool, this night thy soul shall be required of thee: then whose shall these things be which thou hast provided?" (Luke 12:20). Milton alludes to Nabal's churlishness in discussing uncivil debate in *Apology for Smectymnuus.*

See also ABIGAIL; BELIAL.

NABOTH'S VINEYARD When King Ahab wanted the vineyard of Naboth to add to his estates, the owner refused to part with it, even for a good price, because it was "the inheritance of [his] fathers" (1 Kings 21:3). When Ahab sulked and refused to eat on this account, his evil queen Jezebel had Naboth falsely accused of blasphemy and treason and executed so that she could seize the vineyard for Ahab.

"Naboth's vineyard" comes to signify any illicitly coveted possession. In patristic tradition Naboth himself is generally seen as an example of the innocent poor victimized by those in power (e.g., St. Ambrose, *De officiis ministrorum,* 2.5.17; 3.9.63-64), while in rabbinic commentary he is thought to have lied to save his property (Sanh. 89a; Shab. 102b; Tg. 1 Kings 22:21, 23) and so to have been denied "the abode of the pious" in the afterlife. In Trollope's *Framley Parsonage* the story of Naboth is grafted onto a vicar's sense of domestic territory. He would like to banish the cabbage patch of his neighbors, the Podgens: "For has not the small vineyard of Naboth been always an eyesore to neighboring potentates?" But "the potentate in this case had as little excuse as Ahab" (chap. 2).

See also AHAB; JEZEBEL.

NACHON'S THRESHING FLOOR *See* ARK OF THE COVENANT.

NAKED CAME I This phrase was uttered by Job in his first statement of acceptance of the great calamities which had fallen upon his household: "Naked came I out of my mother's womb, and naked shall I return thither:

the LORD gave, and the LORD hath taken away; blessed be the name of the LORD" (1:21). These words are typically coupled in Christian commentary with St. Paul's reminder that "We brought nothing into the world, and it is certain we can carry nothing out" (1 Tim. 6:7; cf. St. Jerome, *Ep.* 22.32). Among the Fathers of the Church the passage is consistently applied to an understanding of the problems of death and suffering; even in the midst of trouble one should not lose faith in the persistent goodness of God. In a letter of support for a widow, directed to her friend Marcello, Jerome writes,

> God is good, and all that he does must be good also. Does he decree that I must lose my husband? I mourn my loss, but because it is his will I bear it with resignation. Is an only son snatched from me? The blow is hard, yet it can be borne, for He who has taken away is He who gave. (*Ep.* 39.2; cf. *Ep.* 127.13-14)

Matthew Henry (*Comm.* 3.11-12) follows Calvin in observing the similarity of Job's and Paul's formulations to parallel statements in Seneca and Epictetus.

The normative application of the text leads in both Jewish and Christian tradition to its invocation in funeral litany and oration. The passage has also been connected (with reference to the image of the womb) to Nicodemus's question to Jesus: "How can a man be born when he is old? Can he enter the second time into his mother's womb, and be born?" (John 3:4).

Chaucer's patient Griselda, tested extravagantly by her husband, the marquis Walter, is at last sent by him back to her humble place of origin stripped of her royal clothing and wedding ring. She replies (*Clerk's Tale,* 4.865-72) with exemplary Christian resignation:

> "To yow broughte I nought elles, out of drede,
> But feith, and nakednesse, and maydenhede. . . .
> Naked out of my fadres hous," quod she,
> "I cam, and naked moot I turne agayn."

In Oliver Goldsmith's *The Vicar of Wakefield* the unfortunate and Job-like vicar, enraged over his daughter's seduction, is admonished by his son for cursing her kidnapper. Recomposing himself, he reflects that a "more than human benevolence has taught us to bless our enemies: Blessed be His holy name for all the good He hath given, and for all that He hath taken away" (chap. 17; cf. Matt. 5:44). In the Victorian *Framley Parsonage* by Anthony Trollope, the verse is more dubiously applied in an expression of gratitude or relief that calamity has fallen upon neighbors but spared the parsonage (chap. 48).

See also JOB.

NAME The name in the Bible is more than a means of identification: it is part of the bearer's personality, often expressing his role or character. "Thou shalt call his name Jesus," it was said of Mary's child, "for he shall save his people from their sins" (Matt. 1:21). Jesus, the Greek form of Joshua, contains the root of the Hebrew word meaning "save"; sometimes it is understood to mean "the LORD is salvation," Joshua being already a theophorous name.

An early naming story tells how the Creator brought the animals to Adam to see what he would call them. "Whatsoever Adam called every living creature, that was the name thereof" (Gen. 2:19). This was no haphazard exercise, for the Creator listened to see if any of the names indicated recognition of a suitable companion for Adam. Since no such recognition was indicated, the Creator formed a woman from Adam's body, and Adam greeted her as *'ishshah,* "woman," because she was taken out of *'ish,* "man" (Gen. 2:23). Later, after their sin and exile from Eden into a world of suffering and certain death, he called her Eve, "because she was the mother of all living" (Gen. 3:20). There is a plangent irony in this second naming, Eve being Heb. *ḥawwah,* from the verb meaning "live."

A change of name marked a change of role, character, or personality. Jacob ("he seizes by the heel") was renamed Israel ("God strives" or, as it is implied in Gen. 32:28, "he strives with God"). Changes in place names, familiar today for political reasons, were common in biblical times for other reasons. The Canaanite city of Luz was renamed Bethel ("house of God") after Jacob received his vision of God there (Gen. 28:19).

People might be renamed when they moved to a new environment: Joseph in Egypt received the name Zaphnath-paaneah, meaning perhaps "The god speaks; he lives" (Gen. 41:45), and the Babylonian king called Daniel Belteshazzar, "according to the name of my god" (Dan. 4:8) — probably *Bel-balaṭsu-uṣur* ("may Bel protect his life"). Daniel's Hebrew name, meaning "God is judge," is illustrated by the story of Susanna, originally prefaced to the Greek text of the book of Daniel, where Daniel as a youth showed the judicial wisdom which gave rise to the proverb "A Daniel come to judgment" (Shakespeare, *Merchant of Venice,* 4.1.223).

The name of the God of Israel was especially sacred. It was spelled with four consonants, YHWH, commonly pronounced Yahweh. The sanctions on misusing it were so severe that eventually it was deemed safest not to use it at all, except on the annual Day of Atonement, when the high priest uttered it in the Temple of Jerusalem.

In Deuteronomy and the historical books closely related to it, Israel's central sanctuary is described as the "place which the LORD your God shall choose to cause his name to dwell there" (Deut. 12:11, etc.). Solomon accordingly announces, at the dedication of his temple in Jerusalem, that he has "built an house for the name of the LORD God of Israel" (1 Kings 8:20).

A person's name might denote his authority. To call on the name of the Lord is literally to acknowledge his authority. His worshipers confess their exclusive allegiance to him in the words: "by thee only will we make mention of thy name" (Isa. 26:13).

The name of Jesus fills a unique role in the NT. Since in resurrection all power has been given to him (Matt. 28:18), to pray in his name is to invoke his power. To be baptized in his name is to place oneself under his lordship. In Acts especially his name conveys his power; it is active and irresistible. The name of Jesus, invoked by St. Peter and St. John, cures the cripple in the temple court (Acts 3:6, 16).

Knowledge of the name of a powerful being enabled one to control, or at least to share, that power. The stranger who wrestled all night with Jacob (Gen. 32:24-30) and the angel who appeared to Samson's parents and foretold the birth of their son (Judg. 13:7, 8) refused to divulge their names.

The man who expelled demons in Jesus' name, although he was not one of his followers, was probably encouraged to do so by seeing how powerful Jesus' name was when invoked by the disciples. Yet Jesus discerned that his motives were honest and forbade the disciples to stop him (Mark 9:38-40).

A more sinister use of Jesus' name is disclosed in the story of the seven sons of Sceva at Ephesus (Acts 19:13-16). Observing the effectiveness of Jesus' name on St. Paul's lips, they tried to practice exorcism in the name of "Jesus whom Paul preacheth," but they came to grief. Magical papyri which have come down from antiquity witness to this kind of activity. One of them contains the formula: "I adjure you by Jesus, the God of the Hebrews." This illustrates not only the recognition of the power of Jesus' name but also the conviction that, if only the secret name of the "God of the Hebrews" could be discovered, this would be an exceptional source of power. The magical papyri preserve several attempts to reproduce the correct pronunciation of that name. Since only one man had authority to pronounce it, Sceva gave himself out to be a Jewish high priest to impress people with his access to its hidden power (no such name as Sceva appears in the list of genuine high priests of Israel).

Frequently the name is synonymous with a person's reputation. When the Psalmist says to God, "they that know thy name will put their trust in thee" (Ps. 9:10), he means that God has established such a reputation for trustworthiness that his people instinctively turn to him as one on whom they can depend. In this sense "a good name is better than precious ointment" (Eccl. 7:1). This usage is not exclusively biblical. There is no necessary biblical background to Shakespeare's words:

Good name in man and woman, good my lord,
Is the immediate jewel of their souls. . . .
But he that filches from me my good name
Robs me of that which not enriches him
And makes me poor indeed. (*Othello,* 3.3.155-56, 159-61)

Closely allied to this sense is the sense of renown. When God says to Abraham, "I will . . . make thy name great" (Gen. 12:2), he means "I will make you very famous." On the other hand, when someone's name is blotted out (e.g., Deut. 29:20), his memory is forgotten. He has no descendants to perpetuate his name; it is as though he never existed. Similarly the name of a community or nation may be blotted out; in that sense it loses its corporate identity. The Israelites were charged to "blot out the remembrance [lit., the name] of Amalek from under heaven" (Deut. 25:19); by contrast, in a time of extreme national danger the Lord refused to "blot out the name Israel from under heaven" and brought about their deliverance (2 Kings 14:27).

The name is frequently used by metonymy for the person. When Christ says that Paul is going to suffer "great things . . . for my name's sake" (Acts 9:16), he means simply "for my sake"; when John tells his readers that he has written his Gospel "that ye might believe that Jesus is the Christ, the Son of God; and that believing ye might have life through his name" (John 20:31), "through his name" is equivalent to "through him."

In patristic writings considerable effort is made to etymologize biblical names. In St. Augustine's *De doctrina Christiana* he advises his students that one of the most useful clues to the meaning of an OT narrative may be the meaning of the Hebrew names. Though some of the meanings, he notes, are given in the biblical text, "we cannot doubt that . . . many Hebrew names which have not been interpreted by the writers of these books would, if any one could interpret them, be of great value and service in solving the enigmas of Scripture." He goes on to commend Hebraists who have clarified the meaning of names such as Adam, Eve, Moses, Jerusalem, Sion, Sinai, Lebanon, and Jordan, and observes that "when these names have been investigated and explained, many figurative expressions in Scripture become clear" (2.16.23). Unfortunately, not all those who in late antiquity or the Middle Ages offered etymologies of Hebrew and Greek names were well enough versed in the languages to do so aptly; indeed, some of the most persistent false etymologies acquiring traditional exegetical acceptance were created by Augustine himself. To obtain a prefigurative reading of the three sons of Noah, e.g., he says that Shem means "named," Japheth "enlargement," and Ham "hot":

> And what is of greater name than Christ, the fragrance of whose name is everywhere perceived, so that even prophecy sings of it beforehand, comparing it in the Song of Songs to ointment poured forth? Is it not also in the houses of Christ, that is, in the churches, that the "enlargement" of the nations dwells? For Japheth means "enlargement." And Ham (i.e., hot), who was the middle son of Noah, and, as it were, separated himself from both . . . what does he signify but the tribe of heretics, hot with the spirit, not of patience but impatience, with which the breasts of heretics are wont to blaze. . . . (*De civ. Dei* 16.2)

Each of these names acquires an ethnographic significance in later tradition, Shem taken to signify the Semitic-language peoples, Ham (Cham) the Egyptian and related languages; Japheth the "Japhitic" or Indo-European languages. In other cases, though Augustine may be wrong in a particular root or stem, he nonetheless captures the general etymological values surprisingly faithfully; e.g., he reads "Israel" (Gen. 32:28) as "seeing God, which will at last be the reward of all the saints" (*De civ. Dei* 16.39), and while, strictly speaking, his etymology is conjectural, in the conflation of sense with Peniel (Heb. *penu'el* ["face of God"]) it preserves at least the apparent broad intention in the name change of Jacob.

In Judaism names given to infants (males at circumcision, traditionally the 8th day) are often drawn upon biblical prototypes. As previously noted, the originals may have been theophorous, prophetic, or bearing an aetiological relationship to events in the narrative in which the named person prominently figured. In early Christian tradition the "Christian" name, strictly speaking, was that given at christening or baptism, paralleling the Jewish practice. While in the first three centuries after Christ new converts most frequently kept (as catacomb inscriptions and other records show) their pagan Roman names, from the 4th cent. there was a developing tendency to use names formed from Christian virtues (e.g., Agape, Fides, Irene), doctrine (Athanasius, Christophorus), and festivals (e.g., Epiphanius, Natalia). Use of names of NT saints or of the Virgin Mary is exceedingly rare until much later; the name *Mary* was almost never used in England until after the 12th cent. While adult converts had earlier occasionally taken a new name at baptism (cf. the Venerable Bede's account of King Caedwalla's baptismal christening [Peter] in Rome — *Hist. eccl.* 7.21), after infant baptism became normative this rarely happened. Exceptions might be made in cases where someone with an obscene family name asked to have it changed by the officiating priest; a rubric in the *Rituale Romanum* makes it a pastoral duty not to pass on in baptism names *"ne obscoena, fabulosa aut ridicula vel inanium."* Names with sexual or vulgar connotations might in such cases be replaced with names of national saints, martyrs, or apostles.

After the Reformation, however, and especially in the Puritan communities, the use of biblical names (esp. from the OT) and of names based upon doctrines or virtues (Faith, Hope, Charity, Grace, Patience, Prudence) begins to multiply rapidly. One reason for this was the Puritans' association of saints' names with Catholicism; another was widespread availability of the English Bible and hence its panoply of curious names in hitherto unknown passages. But covenant theology and its attendant typologies among the Puritans, and the seriousness with which they regarded OT law, are probably more important factors. In any event, after the late 16th cent., as one disenchanted observer notes, "such a locust swarm of new names burst upon the land that we may well style it the Hebrew invasion" (Bardsley, *Curiosities of Puritan Nomenclature,* 37). Infants began to appear on baptismal registers with names such as Melchizedek, Abimelech, Shadrach, Hezekiah, Zerubbabel, and even Pelatiah. "Cromwell," said Cleveland, "hath beat up his drums clean through the Old Testament; you may know the genealogy of our Saviour by the names of his regiment. The muster master hath no other list than the first chapter of Matthew" (quoted in Bowman, *The Story of Surnames* [1931], 93). With the advent of theological controversy parents began to declare their party more openly in their children's names: Faint-not Dighurst, Flie-fornication Andrews, Glory-be-to-God Penniman, Hew-Agag-in-Pieces Robinson, and Obadiah-bind-their-king-in-chains-and-their-nobles-in-arms Needham all bore witness to the fashion. The more celebrated Barebone family, remembered in connection with the so-called Barebones Parliament, included among its members Praise-God Barebone, Fear-God Barebone, Jesus-Christ-came-into-the-world-to-save-Barebone, and If-Christ-had-not-died-for-thee-thou-hadst-been-damned Barebone, commonly known simply as Dr. Damned Barebone. Among the Puritans who left for America similar names occurred, though most of the colonists were content with basic OT names for their offspring.

The doctrinal names and those suggesting Christian virtues enter into literature as part of an allegorical structure. Dante's Beatrice, Chaucer's Prudence (*The Tale of Melibee),* and Spenser's Una (*Faerie Queene)* are familiar examples — the first drawn with the Beatitudes in mind, the second with Lady Wisdom from OT wisdom literature (esp. Proverbs), and the last with the unity discourse of Christ concerning the Church (John 14–17). Thus, names such as Mercy, Faith, Joy, and Hope, familiar from late medieval morality plays (e.g., *Castle of Perseverance, Mankind*) recur with direct or ironic associations from Charity in Bunyan's *Pilgrim's Progress* to Chastity in Evelyn Waugh's *Vile Bodies* (1930). The medieval tendency to write elaborate (false) etymologies for Roman saints' names, familiar from Chaucer's prologue to his *Second Nun's Tale,* falls out of favor after the Renaissance, though names in the vices / virtues tradition remain popular for some time, as Lady Candour and Sir Benjamin Backbite from Sheridan's play *School for Scandal* (1777) illustrate. The Dickensian penchant for names suggestive of moral allegory (e.g., Lady Deadlock in *Bleak House,* Uriah Heep in *David Copperfield)* would seem to suggest a continuation, mediated in Dickens's own case by the popular influence of Bunyan. Names of personages from the Bible tend to occur, when not ironically invoked, in ways which conform to the function of the pertinent literary character in his or her narrative. Various attributes may be emphasized: Moses in Sheridan's *School for Scandal,* e.g., bears only the most general and clichéd relationship to his prototype, while Moses in Thornton

Wilder's *The Skin of Our Teeth* (1942) is, more proximately, a judge. Information about biblical names found reasonably frequently in English literature texts will be found under their respective entries.

See also NAMES OF GOD; NAMING OF THE ANIMALS.

Bibliography. Copeland, E. L. "Names as Medium of Revelation-Paralleling *Logos* in Ante-Nicene Christianity." *ST* 27 (1973), 51-61; Noth, M. *Die israelitischen Personennamen* (1928); Reaney, P. H. *A Dictionary of British Surnames.* 2nd rev. ed. (1976); Robinson, F. C. "The Significance of Names in OE Literature." *Anglia* 76 (1968), 14-58.

F. F. BRUCE

NAMES OF GOD The OT names of God (in addition to many descriptive epithets or appellatives) number roughly a dozen, the exact number varying with the interpretation of names which occur infrequently and in problematic passages. The common Semitic designation *'el,* which may have to do with the idea of power, has also a longer variant, *'eloah* or *'eloha,* whose grammatical plural, *'elohim,* was almost always understood as semantically singular when applied to the one God and so took a singular verb. *'el* frequently combines with other divine names, some of which can also stand alone — as do *'elyon,* "highest"; *shadday,* "might" or "mountain"; and *'olam,* "duration" — while others occur only in combination, such as *'el ro'i,* "God of vision," and *'el berit,* "God of covenant." God's proper and holiest name, *YHWH,* produces *Yah* by apocopation and also forms such combinations as *YHWH seba'ot,* "God of armies." *YHWH* and *'ehyeh* appear together in Exod. 3:13-16; the latter means "I am," and the former may be an early causative form of the same verb, thus indicating God's creativity.

From ancient times, the special status of *YHWH* resulted in bans on speaking this name aloud (cf. Lev. 24:11). These strictures led the devout to substitute *'adonay,* "my lord," for the unutterable Tetragrammaton when reading the text aloud. A Christian misunderstanding of orthographic conventions in the NT produced the corrupt form "Jehovah" in the early 16th cent., which appeared eventually in the KJV (e.g., Ps. 83:18). William Tyndale's Pentateuch of 1530 was the first English OT translation to use "Jehovah," e.g., at Exod. 6:3, where both the Vg and Wycliffe had incorporated the substitute *'adonay.*

On certain occasions in the OT God revealed himself by name and insisted on the special significance of *YHWH* (Exod. 3:13-16; 6:3; 33:17-19; 34:6-7). The commandments (Exod. 20:7; Deut. 5:11) forbade misusing the sacred names, which became clues to God's character through their association with divine attributes (Exod. 34:6-7) and activities (Amos 4:13; Jer. 33:1-4). Belief in the power of names lies behind the stories of the name changes of the patriarchs (Gen. 17:5, 15; 32:27-30; Num. 13:16) and helps account for the inquisitiveness of biblical characters about the names of God and his messengers

(Judg. 13:17-18). This belief also helped establish the great popularity of theophoric propositional names such as Elijah (*'eliyah,* "my God is Yah").

The Jewish fascination with divine names is directly reflected in the NT and early Christian literature: the hallowing of God's name in the Lord's Prayer (Matt. 6:9; Luke 11:2), e.g., has parallels both in the OT (Ezek. 36:23; Ps. 96:2) and in the *Qaddish* or rabbinic doxology. Christian baptizing, prophesying, healing, exorcising, and performing miracles were all "in the name of Jesus" (Matt. 28:19; Acts 4:7-10), and believers called on his name in prayer and repentance, for forgiveness and salvation (Luke 24:47; John 16:23-24). The Gk. *Iēsous* is also the LXX name for Joshua, which in Hebrew (*yehoshua'*) means "*YHWH* saves," or "*YHWH* is salvation," as reflected in Matt. 1:21. *Christos,* which translates *mashiah,* "anointed" ("Messiah") in the LXX, remains a title in some passages (Matt. 26:63), but in others (Acts 3:6) is used almost as a name for Jesus. Tradition eventually found as many as 200 names and titles for Jesus through the energetic application of OT prophetic and messianic terminology to him. In the NT itself Jesus has more than 40 names and titles.

The great force of the rules against pronouncing *YHWH* caused the rabbis to develop a rich and elaborate vocabulary of nearly 150 substitute names for God. Speculation on secret names of 12, 42, 45, and 72 letters was a favorite cabalist theme, and the relation between divine names and attributes became a regular problem for Jewish philosophers from Saadiah Gaon onward. Meanwhile, Origen and earlier exegetes had amalgamated Jewish and Christian onomastics by interpreting the "sign" (the Hebrew letter *tau,* whose primitive form was written like an "X") of Ezek. 9:4 (cf. Rev. 7:2; 14:1; 22:4) as the initial letter (*chi,* whose shape is also an "X") of *Christos* and as a cross. The chief transmitter to the Middle Ages of early Christian analysis of Hebrew divine names was St. Jerome in his *Hebraicae quaestiones in libro Geneseos* and related works, while the *Divine Names* of pseudo-Dionysius (commented on by numerous subsequent authorities such as Aquinas and used, e.g., by the English author of *The Cloud of Unknowing*) started an independent line of mystical philosophizing deeply influenced by Proclus and other Neoplatonists. Among medieval Jewish commentators, Maimonides insisted that all the names save *YHWH* were really veiled references to God's actions which revealed nothing of his essence. In the late 15th cent. Pico della Mirandola and Johann Reuchlin inaugurated a tradition of Christian Cabala, one of whose central preoccupations was to derive christological and Trinitarian meaning from the Hebrew names of God. Readers of Marlowe's *Tragicall Historie of Doctor Faustus* discover that part of the conjuration of the devil Mephistopheles by the apostate theologian Faustus is a degradation of the Tetragrammaton: Faustus makes his incantations, observing, "Within this circle is Jeho-

vah's name / Forward and backward anagrammatized, / The breviated names of holy saints . . ." (1.3.8-10).

The earliest recorded English poem, Caedmon's miraculous hymn of praise recorded by the Venerable Bede in his *Historia Ecclesiastica Gentis Anglorum,* is made up of a series of formulaic names of God. Later in the Anglo-Saxon period, in Cynewulf's *Christ II,* many lines consist of or contain epithets for God. Some of these expressions are borrowed out of pagan sources (e.g., þeoden, "chief") while others are specifically biblical names or epithets (e.g., Lamb, Physician, Teacher, Sun) or "christianisms" (e.g., *godbearn,* "God's Son"; *gaestsunu,* "Spiritual Sun").

An English law of 1605 banning profane use of divine names may account for substitutions of terms like "the High'st" for "God" or names of the Trinity in Shakespeare's plays (e.g., *All's Well That Ends Well,* 4.2.24); that some of these substitutions call to mind rabbinic usage is coincidental and entirely explainable in terms of ordinary Christian vocabulary. Milton, on the other hand, was a learned enough Hebraist to discuss the Hebrew names of God at length in *De Doctrina Christiana,* where he gave special attention to the plural *'elohim,* to "Jehovah" and its pronunciation, and to the application of divine names to the Son and other beings (*Complete Prose Works,* Yale ed. [1973], 138-39, 148-49, 226-33, 250-64, 697-98). Certain passages in *Paradise Lost* are explicable in terms of his learned interest in the divine names: in *PL* 8.349-451, after Adam has linked his knowledge of the animals with his having named them, he asks God, "by what name, for thou above all . . . Surpassest far my naming, how may I adore thee. . . ?" only to have his "presumptuous" question left unanswered (cf. Gen. 32:29; Judg. 13:17-18); and in *PL* 12.310-12, 457-58 "Joshua whom the Gentiles Jesus call" bears the "name and office" of him "who shall quell the adversary Serpent" and be "exalted high Above all names in heav'n" (cf. Phil. 2:9-11). William Cowper expresses his extensive interest in the Hebrew names of God in his contributions to the *Olney Hymns* written with his pastor, John Newton. Among these hymns, "Jehovah-Jireh, The Lord Will Provide — Gen. 22:14" (1.6), "Jehovah-Raphi, I Am the Lord That Healeth — Ex. 15" (1.14), "Jehovah-Nissi, the Lord My Banner — Ex. 17:15" (1.17), "Jehovah-Shalom, the Lord Send Peace — Jdg. 6:24" (1.22), "Jehovah-Shammah — Ezek. 38:35" (1.72), and "Jehovah-Jesus" (2.38) are Cowper's.

Blake, who lacked Milton's erudition yet managed to teach himself a little Hebrew, treated the divine names more idiosyncratically and bound them closer to the fabric of his thought. He knew and criticized the Jewish prohibition on pronouncing *YHWH* (*Milton,* 1.11.13-14); he recognized the problematic relationship between the divine names and God's attributes or perfections (*Four Zoas,* 7b.274; *A Descriptive Catalogue,* in *Complete Writings,* ed. G. Keynes [1957], 571); and he understood that

Shadday meant "almighty" and that *'elohim* was a plural which could refer to heathen gods (*Ghosts of Abel,* ed. Keynes [1957], 780-81). Four of the seven members of his "Seven Eyes of God," a theological progression loosely based on Zech. 4:10 and Rev. 5:6, bear divine names: Elohim, Shaddai, Jehovah, and Jesus. In *Finnegans Wake* Joyce's Shem has a name which means "name" and also reminds one of the Shema (Deut. 6:5), but Shem is "always blaspheming" like his creator, who played on the divine names throughout the *Wake:* "jehovial oyeglances"; "Weh is me, yeh is ye!"; ". . . yav hace not one pronouncable teerm that blows . . . to signify majestate."

See also NAME; *TAU.*

Bibliography. Chepin, A. "The Names of God in the Church Fathers and in Old English Poetry." *Studia Patristica* 9 (1966), 525-31; Copenhaver, B. P. "Lefèvre d'Etaples, Symphorien Champier, and the Secret Names of God." *JWCI* 40 (1977), 189-211; Hartmann, F., and L. I. Rabinowitz. "God, Names of." *EncJud* 7, 674-85; Lagarde, P. de. *Onomastica Sacra* (1887); Marmorstein, A. *The Old Rabbinic Doctrine of God:* I, *The Names and Attributes of God.* Jews' College Publications, no. 10 (1927); McVeigh, D. M. "Coleridge's Doctrine of the Imagination and the Enigmatic Name of God." *Religion and Literature* 17 (1985), 61-75; Summerfield, H. "Blake and the Names Divine." *Blake: An Illustrated Quarterly* 15 (1981), 14-22; Taylor, V. *The Names of Jesus* (1953).   BRIAN P. COPENHAVER

NAMING OF THE ANIMALS   In Gen. 2:19-20, God is described as forming the animals "out of the ground" and presenting them to Adam, who then named them. The immediate purpose of this narrative is to explain that among all the animals none was fit to become Adam's companion; the creation of Eve immediately followed. But this kernel of story early assumed independent life. Three interrelated but occasionally distinct implications have traditionally been drawn from the naming of the animals: the narrative has been taken to signify Adam's wisdom, his dominion, and more recently his oneness with the natural world.

Wisdom receives the greater emphasis in the tradition, especially among patristic and medieval writers. St. Augustine's scattered references to the incident point in this direction, as do the more detailed comments of Tertullian and St. Gregory of Nyssa. Gregory (in *Contra Eunomium*) argues that Adam's naming indicates the perfection of unfallen human intelligence: "we maintain that the intellectual faculty, made as it was originally by God, acts thenceforward by itself when it looks out upon realities and that there be no confusion in its knowledge, affixes some verbal note to each several thing as a stamp to indicate its meaning" (NPNF 5.290). St. Thomas likewise says that Adam's mind was such that it could move from physical objects to intellectual concepts instantly and that the naming is the clearest sign of this (*Summa Theol.* 1.94.2-4). A similar treatment may be seen in Jewish tradition: the Midr. Rabbah (1.135) records a rabbinic story that God had

first asked the angels to perform the naming, which they were unable to do; God then used the contrast between their ignorance and Adam's wisdom to teach them of the superiority of humanity.

In the Reformation Luther reiterates the "wisdom" emphasis, arguing (in his commentary on Genesis) that Adam by the accuracy of his naming proved himself to be the greatest of all philosophers and etymologists. Calvin's commentary, while recognizing Adam's wisdom —Adam "had imposed names on them, not rashly, but from certain knowledge" (1.131) —emphasizes his dominion: God "endued [the animals] with the disposition to obedience, so that they would voluntarily offer themselves to the man" (1.132). But after Adam's fall the animals would no longer be so disposed; sin necessarily involves the sacrifice of such dominion.

Most English commentators —especially in the 17th cent., during which period the subject achieves an unprecedented prominence —follow Luther's line. Milton, e.g., is impressed by the instantaneousness of Adam's act of naming: "Certainly without extraordinary wisdom he could not have given names to the whole animal creation with such sudden intelligence" (*De Doctrina Christiana,* 1.7). In *Paradise Lost,* Adam's description of his discovery of speech shares this emphasis: "to speak I tried, / and forthwith spake, / My tongue obeyed and readily could name / What e'er I saw" (8.271-73).

Many commentators attempt to specify the nature of the wisdom Adam exemplified in the naming, arguing that he perfectly united *verba* and *res,* word (or name) and thing. For Gregory of Nyssa, the names apparently were assigned arbitrarily by a profound intelligence intent upon "avoiding confusion." John Donne, following this tradition, says that

> Adam's first act was not an act of Pride, but an act of lawfull power and jurisdiction, in naming the Creatures; Adam was above them all, and he might have called them what he would; There had lyen no action, no appeale, if Adam had called a Lyon a Dog, or an Eagle an Owle. (*Sermons,* ed. Potter and Simpson, 2.294-95).

Tertullian, in contrast, argues that Adam named the creatures "on the ground of the present purpose which each particular nature served; [he] called [each creature] by that to which from the beginning it showed a propensity" (*De virginibus velandis* [ANF 4.30]). English post-Reformation commentators tend to follow Tertullian in their speculations upon an Adamic language able to make things fully present through perfect naming. Milton, in the *Tetrachordon,* suggests that "Adam . . . had the wisdom given him to know all creatures, and to name them according to their properties," a notion echoed in *Paradise Lost* in the description of the naming ritual: "I named them, as they passed, and understood / Their nature, with such knowledge God endued / My sudden apprehension" (8.352-54; cf. Raphael's words to Adam at 7.494: "And thou their natures know'st, and gavest them names"). John Webster, the Rosicrucian critic of British higher education, sums up this position in his *Academiarum Examen* of 1654:

> I cannot but conceive that Adam did understand both their [the animals'] internal and external signatures, and that the imposition of their names was adequately agreeing with their natures: otherwise it could not univocally and truly be said to be their names, whereby he distinguished them.

The naming of the animals is appropriated for their own uses by the proponents of what Donne called the "New Philosophy." Francis Bacon suggests that it may be possible, through the advancement of learning and experimental science, to recapture the Adamic wisdom: "Whensoever he [man] shall be able to call the creatures by their true names he shall again command them" (*Valerius Terminus to the Interpretation of Nature* [*Works*, 3.222]). John Locke later goes even further: "The same liberty also that Adam had of affixing any new name to any idea the same has anyone still" (*Essay Concerning Human Understanding*, 3.6.51).

George Fox, who, like John Webster, wrote within a tradition indebted to the German mystic Jakob Boehme, claims the power Bacon and Locke speak of, but through divine revelation rather than the progress of learning or innate natural intelligence:

> I knew nothing but pureness, and innocency, and righteousness, being renewed up into the image of God by Christ Jesus, so that I say I was come up to the state of Adam which he was in before he fell. The creation was opened to me, and it was showed me how all things had their names given them according to their nature and virtue. (*Journal*, 27)

Fox's understanding of the naming ritual focuses on the spiritual state, the oneness with the world, in which such naming is possible. Subsequent references to the naming of the animals become increasingly oblique and are regularly subordinated to a sense of Edenic unity which predates language or renders it unnecessary. Thomas Traherne, the English poet most obsessed with the Edenic state, alludes to the naming indirectly in his "Adam":

> He had an Angel's Ey to see the Price
> Of evry Creature; that made Paradise:
> He had a tongue, yea more, a Cherub's Sense
>   To feel its worth and Excellence. (27-30)

and elsewhere alludes to the mysterious potency in human speech:

>   And I being Dum
> (Nothing besides was dum;) All things did com
> With Voices and Instructions; but when I
> Had gained a Tongue, their power began to die.
> ("Dumnesse," 65-68)

Walt Whitman presents in "There Was a Child Went Forth" a pre-verbal Adam who need not name the things of the world because he can instantaneously become them or take them into his being —a power likewise attributed to Brahma in Emerson's poem of that name.

Although direct references in the modern period are frequently incidental (e.g., "Adam Pos'd" by Anne Finch, Countess of Winchelsea, which imagines Adam, fresh from the naming of the animals, as a brutish farmer "pos'd" — perplexed —by the appearance of a nymph), serious evocations of the story also occur. Christopher Smart, in his *Jubilate Agno*, written in the madhouse, consciously reenacts an Edenic naming ritual with reference to contemporary England (e.g., "Let Ross, house of Ross rejoice with the Great Flabber Dabber Flat Clapping Fish with Hands" [109]). When W. H. Auden takes up the subject in the 20th cent., in the third of his "Sonnets from China," he rearranges the biblical story to place the naming of the creatures after the Fall, conflating it with God's giving the animals to Noah's family for food (Gen. 9:2-3): Adam "by naming thought to make connection / Between himself as hunter and his food" (150). Recent poems by Francis Sparshott ("Naming of the Beasts"), A. D. Hope ("Imperial Adam"), and John Hollander ("Adam's Task") attest to the continuing vitality of the tradition.

See also ADAM.

Bibliography. Aarsleff, H. *From Locke to Saussure: Essays on the Study of Language and Intellectual History* (1982); Leonard, J. *Naming in Paradise: Milton and the Language of Adam and Eve* (1990); McCaffrey, I. *Paradise Lost as "Myth"* (1959); Williams, A. *The Common Expositor: An Account of the Commentaries on Genesis 1527-1633* (1948).   ALAN JACOBS

NAOMI   Mother-in-law of Ruth.
    See also RUTH.

NAPHTALI   One of the twelve sons of Jacob.
    See also AARON; JACOB; TRIBES OF ISRAEL.

NARROW (GATE) WAY   *See* STRAIT AND NARROW.

NATHAN   Nathan was the prophet who, after David's adultery with Bathsheba and murder of her husband Uriah the Hittite, told David a parable to confront him with his unconfessed sin. The parable concerned a rich man with many sheep who stole from a poor neighbor the "one little ewe lamb" in his possession. David, outraged at the thought of such radical injustice, exclaimed, "As the LORD liveth, the man that has done this thing shall surely die," to which the prophet responded, "Thou art the man" (2 Sam. 12:1-12).

Nathan's role in conveying God's judgment on the sin of David is largely bypassed in early commentary and literature in favor of allegorization or extenuation of the adultery, murder, and repentance. By the 19th cent., however, attention had shifted to the prophetic task of Nathan himself and to the crafty way in which he unmasked David by luring him into interpretation and self-condemnation. Ruskin notes, in *Modern Painters*, the particular aptness of such a narrative for a genteel reader: when David's own story "is told him under a disguise, though only a lamb is concerned, his passion about it leaves him no time for thought. 'The man shall die' — note the reason — 'because he had no pity.' A vulgar man would assuredly have been cautious and asked, 'Who was it?'"

The "one little ewe-lamb" became a figure for one's most cherished possession or pleasure, so that the unfortunate Diggery Venn in Hardy's *The Return of the Native,* after having lost his love Thomasin to Wildeve, nevertheless worked nearby "though he never intruded upon her who had attracted him thither. To be in Thomasin's heath, and near her, yet unseen, was the one ewe-lamb of pleasure left to him" (cf. *Far from the Madding Crowd,* chap. 26). In *The Mayor of Casterbridge* Hardy has Elizabeth-Jane, upon discovering that the wealthy Lucetta had stolen her lover, stutter "in Nathan tones, 'You-have-married Mr. Farfrae!'" In Brontë's *Wuthering Heights,* Lockwood dreams of challenging the Rev. Jabes Branderham for preaching a self-indulgent sermon on sin, only to have Jabes upstage him by "leaning over his cushion" and declaring, "Thou art the man!" This latter phrase, as well as the larger narrative, was used by Whitefield, Wesley, and other revivalists for just such sermons as gave rise to Brontë's parody and, as such, likely provided the immediate associations for an allusion in Twain's *Pudd'nhead Wilson:* "Once when Judge Driscoll said, 'What's the matter with you? You look as meek as a nigger,' he felt as secret murderers are said to feel when the accuser says, 'Thou art the man!'" (chap. 10).

See also BATHSHEBA; DAVID.

Bibliography. Frontain, R.-J., and J. Wojcik. *The David Myth in Western Literature* (1980).

NATHANAEL When Philip brought Nathanael to Jesus, Jesus saw him approach and said, "Behold, an Israelite, indeed, in whom is no guile" (John 1:47). St. Augustine and others relate him in this respect to "holy Jacob" (*Enarr. in Ps.* 88.1) and to the "true children of Israel," faithful and guileless followers of Christ (*Enarr. in Ps.* 103.12) — who are spiritually numbered among the "twelve tribes" (*Enarr. in Ps.* 122.8). Though evidently a disciple of Jesus and a man of considerable spiritual virtue, Nathanael was apparently not one of the twelve apostles. According to Augustine this was because he was "learned in the law"; the Lord rather "chose unlearned persons, that he might by them confound the world" (*In Joan. Ev.* 7.15-18). As an exemplar of the guileless soul Nathanael appears in one of the poems in Larry Woiwode's *Even Tide,* in which he is compared to a butterfly turning to the sun: "Or is he that form that follows in the / Shape of a shadow? Called Nathaniel, I'd / Fly to your realm and shield you from sight" (17).

NATIVITY The Nativity (birth) of Jesus Christ is chronicled in extensive narratives in the first and second chapters of both Matthew and Luke. Both versions emphasize the divine nature of Jesus' conception, his birth from a virgin, and his destiny as the Christ (Messiah) appointed to be the savior of Israel and the world.

Matthew and Luke agree that at the time of Jesus' conception, his mother Mary and his guardian Joseph are engaged but have not yet had sexual relations (Matt. 1:18; Luke 1:27, 34). Thus Jesus is identified as being a descendant of David's line, the "Son of David" through Joseph by adoption (Matt. 1:16, 20; Luke 1:27, 32; 2:4). In both Gospels an angelic announcement heralds Jesus' birth (Matt. 1:20-23; Luke 1:30-35), identifying "Jesus" as the child's name (Matt. 1:21; Luke 1:31) and proclaiming him as "Saviour" (Matt. 1:21; Luke 1:31). Both accounts name Bethlehem as Jesus' birthplace (Matt. 2:23; Luke 2:39). The birth is chronologically situated during Herod the Great's reign (Matt. 2:1; Luke 1:5).

The accounts of Matthew and Luke, however, differ significantly in their inclusion of different events and personae as well as in their decisions to focus attention on the Nativity from the perspectives of Joseph in Matthew and Mary in Luke.

Matthew begins with a genealogy of Jesus' Davidic descent through Joseph (1:17). From 1:18-25, Matthew reports on Joseph's reaction to the news that Mary has conceived a child "of the Holy Spirit" (1:20). "An angel of the Lord" (1:21) appears to Joseph in a dream to convince him of the veracity of the divine nature of Jesus' conception and proclaim him as the long-awaited "Emmanuel," the promised savior of Israel (1:21, 23).

In Matt. 2 the actual birth is recorded (2:1). The universal significance of the Nativity is communicated through the story of the Gentile Wise Men who travel in search of "the King of the Jews" guided by a star (2:2). They pay him homage with symbolic gifts referring to his kingship, royal priesthood, and future Passion and death: gold, frankincense, and myrrh (2:1). Herod's enmity toward the foretold Messiah and the consequent avoidance of him by the Magi (2:12), as well as the flight of Mary, Joseph, and Jesus into Egypt (2:13) and Herod's slaughter of Bethlehem's male children (2:16) foreshadow the future conflict between Jesus and political authority. Divinely initiated dreams (1:20; 2:12, 13) and quotations from OT prophecy (1:23; 2:6, 18) are important literary devices in Matthew.

Luke uses the narrative of John the Baptist's birth (1:5–2:25) to foreshadow Jesus' Nativity. The focus is on Mary's reaction to the angelic pronouncement of Jesus' birth and her acceptance of her role in the divine plan (1:38). Luke contextualizes the Nativity during the Roman census. Jesus' birth in lowly circumstances (the stable of an inn) contrasts with the accolades of the heavenly host (2:7, 14). Human recognition is afforded him by shepherds (2:15-17) and by the prophet Simeon and the prophetess Anna at the Temple (2:22-39). The Temple episode emphasizes Jesus' fulfillment of Jewish prophecy. Unique to Luke's account are the three canticles of praise recited by Mary (2:46-55), Zechariah (2:68-79), and Simeon (2:29-32).

Because the biblical Nativity narratives are so rich in dramatic events, there are stong literary traditions associated with each element and possible topic, including the Annunciation, the Incarnation, the Slaughter of the Innocents, John the Baptist, Mary, Joseph, Shepherds, Magi, Herod, Simeon, and Anna. The birth of Jesus itself, however, is central to a host of literary adaptations, most of which illustrate the remarkable warmth with which the event is annually recollected in Christian tradition. As the history of Christmas celebration shows, however, the subject was far less popular among the Fathers of the Church and early medieval Christians (e.g., Tertullian, Origen, St. Jerome), largely because of their desire to avoid any association with celebrations of the natal feast of Roman emperors and pagan deities. Thus, while St. Augustine was obliged to defend against gnostic and Manichean views of the Incarnation — Faustus had characterized the event as "the shameful birth of Jesus from a woman" (see *Contra Faustum,* 32.7; cf. 11.1) — and to stress the real humanity of Christ and the actuality of his physical birth, even he denied the Feast of the Nativity a place among signal celebrations of the Christian year. Although it gradually acquired such a place, exegetical commentary directed to the event itself is exceedingly spare until the late Middle Ages, and narrative or poetic adaptations even more rare. Two hymns by Prudentius in the 4th cent., one the still popular *"Corde natus ex parentis"* ("Of the Father's Love Begotten"), emphasizes not the event, but rather the significance of the Incarnation theologically:

> He is Alpha and Omega,
> He the Source, the Ending he,
> Of the things that are, that have been,
> And that future years shall see. . . .

Quem Quaeritis tropes in monastic liturgy of the 11th cent. emphasize the fact of the Incarnation and the joy of the *pastores'* discovery; the great 12th-cent. hymn *"Veni Emmanuel"* ("O Come, O Come, Emmanuel") anticipates the Second Coming rather than focusing on the Nativity. The subject goes virtually untreated in OE poetry, even in the *Advent Lyrics of the Exeter Book,* again in deference to the controlling theological concept of the Incarnation. Visual and plastic representation is correspondingly almost nonexistent during this period; when the Christ child is depicted with Mary before the 13th cent., he is shown as a *homunculus,* a miniature man, not as a realistic infant. This occurs not because medieval painters did not know how to paint real babies, but because their intent was to depict the idea of the Incarnation iconographically; Mary is not seated beside a manger, but typically enthroned in a "chair" which is at once a "tower of David" and "true

Jerusalem" — a castle, or the walled city of St. John's Revelation.

Nativity literature owes its sudden growth of popularity after the 13th cent. to the humanizing Christology and affective, emotional spirituality of the Franciscan revival. For St. Francis, the heart of the message of the Incarnation was that Christ from his splendor of divine majesty had condescended to identify with human nature — not with elevated rank or social position, but with the poorest and humblest of persons. Christ's birth in a crude cave-stable, his being laid in a manger and among the animals, and the revelation of the event first to poor people (Mary, Joseph, the shepherds) are all of crucial significance for Francis. Indeed, part of what requires radical identification with Christ in his singularly innocent suffering is that from the first he has radically identified with humanity in its universal condition of suffering in a sinful world. The first recorded Nativity pageant is in 1223, when Francis obtained ecclesiastical permission to set up a crèche and pageant in an Italian church, complete with live animals, straw, and an actual baby. Looking at the completed scene, he is said to have been so overcome with emotion that he leaped into the set, snatching up the baby into his arms and breaking out in songs of praise to God. The subsequent influence of Franciscan spirituality on expansionary retellings of the biblical narratives (e.g., the widely popular *Meditationes Vitae Christi* and its translations, including Nicholas Love's *Mirrour of the Blessed Lyf of Jesu Christ* [1400], upon the growth and development of Nativity plays, lyrics, carols, and graphic representation), has been widely studied (see Van Marle; Fleming; Jeffrey). These incorporate many elements from early (2nd-5th cent.) apocryphal narratives such as the Protevangelium of James, the pseudo-gospels of Matthew and Thomas, the so-called History of Joseph the Carpenter, and Gospel of the Infancy.

Among the best Nativity lyrics in English, none of which is earlier than the late 14th cent., is John Grimestone's "In bedlem is a child i-born" (ed. C. Brown, *Religious Lyrics of the XIVth Century,* no. 57). It encapsulates the entire narrative in eighty lines, stressing

> Wol loweliche þat lord gan lithte
> þou he were comen of kenne;
> In pouerte þat prince him pitthe
> to ben born in a bynne.
>
> þis ensample he hat vs brouth
> to liuen in lounesse,
> & pride to putten out of oure þouth,
> þat brout vs in bitternesse.

Grimestone, a Franciscan friar, wrote also "A Lullaby to Christ in the Cradle," "Christ weeps in the Cradle for the Sin of Mankind" (Brown, nos. 65, 59), and an effective imaginary dialogue between the newborn Jesus and his mother titled by its editor "The Christ Child Shivering with Cold" in which the Atonement is already anticipated as the reason for Christ's being born — hence the "cradle" makes Mary think of a bier, and the cave a grave (no. 75).

The 15th and 16th cents. witnessed a popular diffusion of carols, dance songs adapted to Christian worship which were often (though not exclusively) associated with the Nativity. Many of these celebrate not just the Bethlehem story but the entire plan of salvation. Exemplary is a 15th-cent. carol with the refrain "Now may we syngyn as it is, / *Quod puer natus est nobis*" (ed. R. Greene, *The Early English Carols,* no. 19); the first stanza is indicative:

> This babe to vs that now is bore,
> Wyndyrful werkys he hath iwrowt;
> He wil not lese that was ilore,
> But baldly ayen it bowth.
> And thus it is,
> Forsothe, iwys,
> He askyth nouth but that is hys.

Others recapitulate the basic Nativity narrative (e.g., Greene, no. 28), focus on one element (e.g., no. 32), or recount prophecies of the event (no. 68); still others are merely brief *lauda in exultatio,* like "Honnd by honnd we schalle ous take" (no. 12), probably intended to be danced as well as sung, or praise of the "gift" of the season itself such as the 16th-cent. carol "Marke we mery in hall and bowr; / Thys tyme was born owr Savyowr" (no. 27):

> In this tyme God hath sent
> Hys own Son to be present,
> To dwell with us in verament.
> God, that ys owr Savyowr.

William Dunbar's "Of the Nativitie of Christ" is an early 16th-cent. Scottish adaptation of the Latin hymn *"Hodie Puer Natus Est."* The late medieval Corpus Christi plays, with their recapitulation in dramatic form of biblical salvation history, offered the best English opportunity for presentation of the Nativity narrative, and rustic but effective reenactments are to be found in all the major cycles (York, Chester, N-Town, Towneley). The Towneley cycle's chief dramatist, the so-called Wakefield Master, produced two plays featuring the Nativity, his "First Shepherd's Play" and better-known comic "Second Shepherd's Play." While the latter closes with a vivid tableau (Joseph, Mary, the Child, and adoration of the shepherd), the first play is more fully responsive to the biblical narrative and presents a moving, even worshipful reenactment. The closing scene of the "Second Shepherd's Play" (746-49), however, poignantly captures the paradoxical double meaning of the moment — a joy already tinged with an incalculable sense of impending doom:

> *1 Pastor:* Fare well, lady, so fare to beholde,
>   With thy childe on thi kne.
> *2 Pastor:* Bot he lygys full cold!
>   Lord, well is me!

Reformation attitudes toward the celebration of Christmas were not always affirmative. Luther was one, however, whose celebration was vigorously and joyously medieval, and the carol he wrote on Luke 2:10 for his little son (1540) is of the angel's "glad tidings." "To you this night is born a child," it begins, then goes on to draw a lesson obverse to that heralded by the Franciscans — that the poverty into which Christ was born was God's way of declaring his scorn of "this world's honour, wealth and might." The carol then becomes a child's Christmas prayer:

> Ah, dearest Jesus, holy child,
> Make thee a bed, soft, undefiled,
> Within my heart, that it may be
> A quiet chamber kept for thee. (trans. C. Winkworth)

English poetry of the period holds many fine treatments of the subject, both Catholic and Protestant. Among Catholic poems Thomas Ford's "A Heavenly Visitor" is a sober querying of Puritan disregard for the Feast of Christ's Nativity, observing that though none would fail to do their utmost in regal preparation were Christ known to be coming to earth the next day, he is dishonored by contemporary neglect of his first coming:

> We wallow in our sin
> Christ cannot find a chamber in the inn.
> We entertain Him always like a stranger
> And as at first, still lodge Him in a manger.

The 16th-cent. Jesuit poet Robert Southwell wrote several Nativity poems, among them his visionary "The Burning Babe" as well as an incarnational meditation, "A Child my Choice" and the lovely carol, "Behold a silly [simple] tender Babe." Richard Crashaw (who converted to Catholicism after refusing to sign the Puritans' Covenant in 1644) wrote a complex antiphonal "Hymn of the Nativity" composed from the shepherds' point of view. It concludes with the "shepherds" singing in chorus:

> To thee, meek Majesty, soft King
> Of simple graces and sweet loves!
> Each of us his lamb will bring,
> Each his pair of silver doves!
> At last, in fire of thy fair eyes
> Ourselves become our own best sacrifice!

Francis Quarles's "The Child Jesus" is complemented in its sense of paradox by Giles Fletcher's section on the Nativity in his *Christs Victorie and Triumph in Heaven and Earth,* one stanza of which reads:

> A Child He was, and had not learn't to speake,
> That with His word the world before did make;
> His mother's armes Him bore, He was so weake,
> That with one hand the vaults of Heau'n could shake;
> See how small roome my infant Lord doth take,
> Whom all the world is not enough to hold!
> Who of His yeares, or of His age hath told?
> Neuer such age so young, neuer a child so old.

The playwright Ben Jonson composed a poem emphasizing the motif of Christ in the manger as the glowing fire or light of the world: "I sing the birth was born tonight, / The Author both of life and light." As in late Renaissance paintings of the Nativity scene, so in these two poems of Crashaw and Jonson the darkness of the stable is lit from within the manger by the Christ child himself.

In contrast, John Donne's "Nativitie" ("Holy Sonnet 3"), an address to the Virgin, reads like a précis of the biblical infancy narrative, and has little of the dramatic power of much 16th-cent. Nativity poetry. The first part of Henry Vaughan's "Christ's Nativity," a two-part lyric in his *Silex Scintillans* (1650), is in the form of a classic aspiration:

> I would I had in my best part
> Fit Roomes for thee! Or that my heart
> Were so clean as
> Thy manger was!
> But I am filth, and obscene,
> Yet, if thou wilt, thou canst make clean. (19-24)

Mid-17th-cent. literary adaptations of the Nativity story must have been severely restrained by rigid Puritan opposition to observance of the major Christian festivals. On June 8, 1647, the celebration of Christmas, Easter, Whitsun (Pentecost), and all saints' days "heretofore superstitiously used and observed" was abolished by an Act of Parliament. It is thus somewhat ironic that Milton, with his thoroughgoing Puritan sympathies, should have written the most important Nativity poem of the period, his ode "On the Morning of Christ's Nativity" (1629). Its theme, however, is the early Christian one of the triumph of the infant Christ over the pagan gods. The poem begins by celebrating the Christmas season as replacement for the pagan *Natalis invicta:*

> This is the Month, and this the happy morn
> Wherein the Son of Heav'n's eternal King,
> Of wedded Maid, and Virgin Mother born,
> Our great redemption from above did bring. . . .

Milton then moves on to characterize the birth as an act of battle with Satan as the adversary, concluding (after 244 lines) with an image of Mary, guarded by armored angels, leaning over the manger:

> Her sleeping Lord with Handmaid Lamp attending:
> And all about the Courtly Stable,
> Bright-harness'd Angels sit in order serviceable.

Milton's poem was to exercise a powerful influence on subsequent treatments of the subject, including those by Edward Caswall and Elizabeth Barrett Browning.

Eighteenth-cent. Nativity hymns by Isaac Watts ("Joy to the World" [1719]) and Charles Wesley ("Hark the Herald Angels Sing" [1739]), both of whom had inherited a strong Puritan sensibility, are among the most noteworthy from that period. But it is Hannah More, the noted evangelical feminist, who best calls up the old Franciscan

emphasis on the meaning of Christ's birth into poverty. In her "Oh, how wondrous is the story," she turns from the scene and its import of human salvation to her reading audience:

> Come, ye rich, survey the stable
> Where your infant Saviour lies;
> From your full, o'erflowing table
> Send the hungry good supplies.
>
> Boast not your ennobled stations;
> Boast not that you're highly fed;
> Jesus — hear it, all ye nations! —
> Had not where to lay his head.

But her insistence on the responsibility of the rich is then balanced by her assurance that there is something in Christ's poverty to encourage and comfort the poor:

> Come, ye poor, some comfort gather;
> Faint not in the race you run:
> Hard the lot your gracious Father
> Gave his dear, his only Son.

While none of this theme survives in E. B. Browning's "The Virgin Mary to the Child Jesus," Mary's extended soliloquy in this poem as she watches her baby sleep constitutes possibly the richest English meditation in the affective tradition since the late medieval period. In the fifth of its thirteen stanzas Mary muses over the events of the day:

> We sate among the stalls at Bethlehem.
> The dumb kine from their fodder turning them,
> Softened their horned faces
> To almost human gazes
> Towards the newly Born.
> The simple shepherds from the star-lit brooks
> Brought visionary looks,
> As yet in their astonished hearing rung
> The strange, sweet angel-tongue.
> The magi of the East, in sandals worn,
> Knelt reverent, sweeping round,
> With long pale beard their gifts upon the ground,
> The incense, myrrh, and gold,
> These baby hands were impotent to hold.
> So, let all earthlies and celestials wait
> Upon thy royal state!
> Sleep, sleep, my kingly One!

Other 19th-cent. Nativity meditations include Coleridge's "The Shepherds," Christina Rossetti's lyric "In the Bleak Midwinter," since set to music, Bliss Carman's "Christmas Song," and Thomas Hardy's "The Oxen."

Modern plays and pageants have been written by the score since the 19th cent.; relatively few have literary significance. Exceptions include Longfellow's *The Golden Legend* (1851), a true Nativity play, John Masefield's one-act *The Coming of Christ* (1928), Dorothy Sayers's *The Man Born to Be King* (1941-42), and a curious dramatic poem by Ezra Pound, *Christmas Prologue* (1910). In its Emmaus-like retrospect, one of the Magi converses about the Nativity with the shepherds. Of these Longfellow's play is the most erudite, drawing largely on pseudepigraphal and apocryphal texts — the Protevangelium, Arabic Gospel of the Infancy, Pseudo-Matthew, Gospel of Thomas, and the History of Joseph the Carpenter.

The turn of the century was notable for an outpouring of verse from Catholic poets, often relatively new converts: Francis Thompson's "Little Jesus," Alice Meynell's "Unto Us a Son is Given," and G. K. Chesterton's "A Christmas Carol" are examples. A generation later, in the United States, different influences prevailed: Sara Teasdale's "A Christmas Carol" is indebted to Christina Rossetti, and Edna St. Vincent Millay's "To Jesus on his Birthday" is more secular in its governing sensibility. William Faulkner's *A Fable* (1954) is a mythic invocation of biblical narrative in which the hero is born at Christmas in a Middle Eastern stable; his sister cannot remember whether they "were driven from the inn itself or just turned away." For most modern readers, however, it is probably T. S. Eliot's "Journey of the Magi" (1927) which most traditionally declares the paradoxical nature of the birth of Jesus, the poverty which proves richer than wealth, weakness stronger than imperial might, a birth whose purpose is death, that death may be conquered. Here it is one of the Wise Men who looks back on the Bethlehem event, his lingering question an acknowledgment that, as Alice Meynell ("No Sudden Thing of Glory" [1896]) and William Everson ("The Coming" [1962]) also suggest, simple adoration was not enough:

> . . . this Birth was
> Hard and bitter agony for us, like Death, our death.
> We returned to our places, these Kingdoms,
> But no longer at ease here, in the old dispensation,
> With an alien people clutching their gods.
> I should be glad of another death.

See also INCARNATION; JESUS CHRIST; JESUS CHRIST, CHILDHOOD OF; MAGI.

Bibliography. Brown, R. E. *The Birth of the Messiah* (1977); Campbell, T. P. "Eschatology and the Nativity in English Mystery Plays." *ABR* 27 (1976), 297-320; "The Nativity in the Medieval Liturgy and the Middle English Mystery Cycle." *DAI* 33 (1973), 2885A-86A; Chenu, M. D. "Nature and Man: The Renaissance of the Twelfth Century." In *Nature, Man, and Society in the Twelfth Century.* Eds. J. Taylor and G. K. Little (1968), 1-48; Fiore, P. A. "The Nativity Theme in Late Renaissance Minor Devotional Verse." *Wascana Review* 15 (1980), 3-19; Fleming, J. *From Bonaventure to Bellini* (1982); Furman, W. A. "The Augustinian Tradition in English Nativity Poetry." *DAI* 45 (1985), 2533A; Hagebusch, L. M. "Nativity Poetry in Seventeenth-Century England." *DAI* 41 (1981), 4719A; Hemingway, S. B. *English Nativity Plays* (1909; rpt. 1966); Jeffrey, D. L. *The Early English Lyric and Franciscan Spirituality* (1975); "James Ryman and the Fifteenth Century Carol." In *Fifteenth Century English Literature.* Ed. R. F. Yaeger (1984), 303-20; "Franciscan Spirituality and the Rise of the Early English

Drama." *Mosaic* 8 (1975), 17-46; Mâle, E. *L'Art religieux du XIIe siècle en France* (1931); Sledge, L. C. "The Nativity in English Poetry." *DAI* 37 (1976), 3652A; Van Marle, R. *The Development of the Italian Schools of Painting.* 19 vols. (1923-28); Wagenknecht, E. *The Story of Jesus in the World's Literature* (1946).
DAVID L. JEFFREY
LENORE GUSSIN

NAZARETH The relatively insignificant little town in which Jesus grew up is mentioned in numerous places in the NT in association with his name (Matt. 21:11; Mark 1:24; 10:47; Luke 4:34; 18:37; 24:19, etc.) but most memorably in the incredulous question put by Nathanael when Philip was urging him to meet Jesus: "Can there any good thing come out of Nazareth?" to which Philip replied, "Come and see" (John 1:46). The phrase becomes a tag, often implying the negative judgment which in the text itself is reversed. Thus in Hardy's *Tess of the D'Urbervilles,* "she had almost fancied that a good thing could come out of Nazareth — a charming woman out of Talbothay's Dairy" (chap. 29).

NAZARITE Nazarites (from Heb. *nazar,* "to separate" or "consecrate"), both male and female, were persons who vowed to "separate themselves unto the LORD," abstaining from strong drink and other forms of indulgence and allowing their hair to grow uncut (Num. 6:2-5). Samuel, according to Ecclus. 46:11, was a "Nazarite of God among the prophets." The most noteworthy OT Nazarite, however, was Samson, who informed Delilah that he had been "a Nazarite unto God from [his] mother's womb," and added, "If I be shaven, then my strength will go from me, and I shall become weak, and be like any other man" (Judg. 16:17-19; cf. 13:5-7). Samson's particular form of observance is discussed by various rabbinic commentaries, since he was evidently licentious in other respects (e.g., Nazir 1.3-4; Babli 4b; Shemuel 1.49-50; Tg. 1 Sam. 1:11). John the Baptist lived by Nazarite vows. Jesus was not a Nazarite, and contrasted himself with John the Baptist in this respect (Matt. 11:18ff.). St. Paul had evidently taken a Nazarite vow but formally terminated it in Cenchrea by cutting off his hair (Acts 18:18; cf. Acts 21:23ff.).

The term *Nazarite* has been frequently confused with *Nazarene,* signifying one who comes, as did Jesus, from Nazareth. English Bibles before the KJV did not distinguish the two terms. Hence in Shakespeare's *Merchant of Venice* Shylock refuses Bassanio's invitation to dinner by saying, "Yes to smell pork, to eat of the habitation which your prophet the Nazarite conjured the devil into . . ." (1.3.31-33). Milton has the reference right in *Samson Agonistes,* having benefited from both more accurate translation and Jewish commentary. Samson tells the Chorus (1354-60) that he will not go to the fateful temple of the Philistines without resistance, since he does not wish to stain his "vow of Nazarite." He then indicates something of his repentance and reformation:

> Shall I abuse this Consecrated gift
> Of strength, again returning with my hair
> After my great transgression. . . .
> A *Nazarite* in place abominable
> Vaunting my strength in honour to thir *Dagon?*

Oliver Goldsmith alludes to the Nazarite's long hair in poking fun of the cultivation of wiggery in the 18th cent.: "To make a fine gentleman several trades are required, but chiefly a barber. You have undoubtedly heard of the Jewish champion whose strength lay in his hair. One would think that the English were for placing all their wisdom there" ("The Citizen of the World"). Carlyle's Professor Teufelsdröckh has a different class of "dandies" in mind when he says that "they affect great purity and separatism; distinguish themselves by a particular costume . . . and on the whole strive to maintain a true Nazarene [*sic*] deportment, and keep themselves unspotted from the world" (*Sartor Resartus*, 3.10; cf. James 1:27).

See also DELILAH; JOHN THE BAPTIST; SAMSON.

NEBO   1. Isa. 46:1 refers to the Assyrian deity, son of Marduk, the god of writing who knew all things. A temple to him was discovered in the ruins of Nineveh (1904-05), and subsequently excavated. He is associated with the massive libraries of clay tablet texts collected by Ashurbanipal (669-633 B.C.), successor to Sennacherib, including the Gilgamesh Epic.

2. Name of the mountain from which Moses saw the Promised Land before he died there, associated in Deut. 34:1 with Pisgah.

See also PISGAH SIGHT.

NEBUCHADNEZZAR   Nebuchadnezzar (or Nebuchadrezzar; KJV Apoc. Nabuchodonosar), king of Babylon 605-562 B.C., is mentioned in 2 Kings 24–25 as responsible for the destruction of Jerusalem and the Babylonian exile of Judah (587-537 B.C.). Jeremiah regards Nebuchadnezzar as God's instrument for the punishment of Judah (e.g., Jer. 25), a theme also mentioned in Ezra 5:12. In the apocryphal book of Judith, Nebuchadnezzar appears unhistorically as king of Assyria. In Dan. 1–4 Nebuchadnezzar appears as Daniel's overlord and as the king responsible for the trial in the fiery furnace of Shadrach, Meshach, and Abednego.

The OE *Daniel* begins with an account of Nebuchadnezzar's sacking of the Jerusalem temple and deportation of the Israelites (1–79), while the remainder of the poem treats the events of Dan. 1–5, presenting them as a struggle of Daniel and his friends against Nebuchadnezzar and his line. Although the ME *Purity* or *Cleanness* deals mainly with Belshazzar's Feast, there is a long section devoted to Nebuchadnezzar's conquest of Jerusalem

(1157-1332), and the poet praises Nebuchadnezzar for his reverent treatment of the sacred vessels of the Temple (1309-20). Nebuchadnezzar's dream of the composite statue made of four metals, symbolizing four world empires, and Daniel's interpretation of that dream (Dan. 2) became part of the literary tradition which dealt with Daniel as an apocalyptic prophet. Nebuchadnezzar's condemnation of Shadrach, Meshach, and Abednego to the fiery furnace for their refusal to worship the golden statue which he had set up (Dan. 3) is referred to in Milton's "Eikonoklastes" (chap. 15, *Works* [1932], 5.215).

Nebuchadnezzar's importance in literary tradition, however, derives primarily from Dan. 4, which concerns Nebuchadnezzar's dream of a great tree reaching to heaven and a voice ordering it to be cut down (Dan. 4:10-17). Daniel interprets the dream as portending Nebuchadnezzar's fall from greatness and temporary exile to a beastlike existence (4:19-27), and the story concludes with the fulfillment of this prophecy.

In the biblical account the offense which apparently causes Nebuchadnezzar's fall is a boast about the great city which he has built (Dan. 4:30-31). In later tradition, however, his offense was often magnified into blasphemous emulation of God; in Jewish tradition, references are made to Nebuchadnezzar as a "hater and adversary of God" (Lam. Rab., pr. 23); he was also seen as proud (Exod. Rab. 30.1; Num. Rab. 9.24) and insolent (Lev. Rab. 7.6). Like the Roman emperors, he is accused of self-deification (Gen. Rab. 9.5; Exod. Rab. 8.2 on Isa. 14:14). Commentators came to associate other biblical texts with the Nebuchadnezzar of Dan. 4 — including Jdt. 6; Ezek. 28 and 31, and Isa. 14:12, the latter of which forms the basis of the identification of Nebuchadnezzar with the devil in several medieval commentators (cf. Doob, 58-64). Chaucer's Monk emphasizes Nebuchadnezzar's pride and presumptuous emulation of God (*Monk's Tale*, 7.2159-69; 2562-63), as does Gower (*Confessio Amantis*, 1.2785-809) and the ME *Miroure of Man's Salvacionne* (ed. H. Huth [1888], 128). Spenser likewise refers to Nebuchadnezzar's absurd pride: "There was that great proud king of Babylon, / That would compell all nations to adore, / And him as onely God to call vpon" (*Faerie Queene*, 1.5.47.1-3). Matthew Arnold cites Nebuchadnezzar's pride and fall as a political warning against excessive confidence in the British empire (*Complete Prose Works* [1973], 9.38), and Byron makes a similar application in his "Ode to Napoleon Buonaparte" (127-35).

On the other hand, Christian tradition has also emphasized Nebuchadnezzar's final redemption from his colossal pride through his humiliation and exile. The dew which fell on Nebuchadnezzar (Dan. 4:33) was often interpreted as divine grace, and Albert the Great links the "seven times" period of Nebuchadnezzar's exile (Dan. 4:23) to the seven parts of the Sacrament of Penance, thereby emphasizing the restorative aspect of the king's madness and exile (*Commentaria in Librum Danielis*, in *Opera Omnia* [1893], 18.515; cf. Doob, 71-72). In a similar way Chaucer's Parson compares penitence with a tree, its roots being contrition, its leaves confession, and its fruit satisfaction, and he then refers to Nebuchadnezzar's dream of the great tree (*Parson's Tale*, 10.112-25). Chaucer's Monk also stresses Nebuchadnezzar's penance and acknowledgment of God's power (*Monk's Tale*, 7.2177-82), as does a ME lyric "The Bird with Four Feathers" (C. Brown, *Religious Lyrics of the XIVth Century* [1924], nos. 121, 145-64). In the ME *Purity* Daniel tells Belshazzar about Nebuchadnezzar's degradation and suffering, which ultimately led to his self-understanding in relation to God (1669-1704). In the ME romance *Robert of Sicily*, the proud king Robert is punished by being made a king's fool dressed as an ape. The English version of this romance is unique in having Robert remember Nebuchadnezzar's similar plight and follow his example of prayer and humility (eds. French and Hale, *Middle English Metrical Romances* [1930], 325-76; cf. Lillian Hornstein in *PMLA* 79 [1964], 16). Anne Bradstreet's long historical poem *The Foure Monarchies* emphasizes the divine origin of Nebuchadnezzar's madness and his subsequent restoration to sanity and repentance (*Complete Works* [1981], 66).

Medieval descriptions of madness, whether actual or literary, often reflect the symptoms of Nebuchadnezzar's condition (cf. Doob, 31-33), and Nebuchadnezzar remains the archetypal madman in later literature as well. A character in Mark Twain's *Huckleberry Finn* remarks: "The nigger's crazy — crazy's Nebokoodnezzer" (chap. 41). In *Nature* Emerson bemoans the irrational separation of humanity from the natural world: "We are, like Nebuchadnezzar, dethroned, bereft of reason, and eating grass like an ox" (*Collected Works* [1971], 1.42). In an antislavery poem "The Panorama," Whittier compares the madness of slavery to Nebuchadnezzar's madness (253-57).

References to Nebuchadnezzar's eating grass like an ox (Dan. 4:32-33) are frequent in literature. A clown in Shakespeare's *All's Well That Ends Well* says: "I am no great Nebuchadnezzar, sir, I have not much skill in grass" ([Riverside ed.] 4.5.20-21), and the grotesque image of the great king grazing like a beast appealed to Donne ("The Liar," 3-4), Byron (*Don Juan*, 5.6.472-75), Hazlitt (*Complete Works* [1933], 17.270), and Ruskin (*Works* [1905], 19.62). Melville characterizes Omoo's diet as "the Nebuchadnezzar fare of the valley" (*Omoo* [1968], 7), and Keats's sonnet "Nebuchadnezzar's Dream" begins: "Before he went to feed with owls and bats / Nebuchadnezzar had an ugly dream" (1-2).

In the biblical narrative the mad Nebuchadnezzar resembles a beast in his diet and in letting his hair and nails grow, but he is apparently not actually transformed into a beast. Commentators such as St. Jerome and Peter Comestor emphasize that Nebuchadnezzar was not literally transformed (PL 25.517; 198.1452), and the author of *Purity*, although describing the fallen Nebuchadnezzar in vivid bestial terms, reminds the reader that the king did not literally become a beast but only thought himself so in his delusion (1681-85). Sir Thomas Browne also states that Nebuchadnezzar, unlike Lot's wife (cf. Gen. 19:26), was not literally metamorphosed (*Works* [1964], 1.48). In John Gower's romance-style retelling of the story, however, Nebuchadnezzar is actually transformed (*Confessio Amantis*, 1.2992-3039), and Gower emphasizes the pathos of the situation in his description of the king's restoration, for Nebuchadnezzar weeps as he becomes aware of his hairy coat,

> And thogh him lacke vois and speche,
> He gan up with his feet areche,
> And wailende in his bestly stevene
> He made his pleignte unto the heven.
> He kneleth in his wise and braieth. (3023-27)

before his human form is restored. Spenser, too, seems to regard Nebuchadnezzar's transformation into a beast as actual (*Faerie Queene*, 1.5.47.5), as do Charlotte Brontë (*Jane Eyre*, chap. 37) and Edwin Arlington Robinson ("The Man against the Sky," 45-46).

In Saul Bellow's novel *Henderson the Rain King*, Nebuchadnezzar's transformation into a beast functions as a major theme in the story of Henderson's search for identity. Henderson is obsessed with Daniel's prophecy that Nebuchadnezzar will be driven from the realm of mankind and will dwell with the beasts of the field (chap. 16), and under the instruction of an African chieftain the troubled Henderson achieves a healing psychological transformation into a beast (chap. 18).

See also DANIEL; MADNESS; SHADRACH, MESHACH, AND ABEDNEGO.

Bibliography. Doob, P. B. R. *Nebuchadnezzar's Children: Conventions of Madness in Middle English Literature* (1974); Ginsberg, H. L. "Daniel, Book of." *EncJud* (1971), 5.1277-89; Hartman, L. F., and Di Lella, A. A. *The Book of Daniel.* AB 23 (1978); Jerome. *Commentary on Daniel.* PL 25. Ed. F. Glorie in CChr 75A (1964). Trans. G. L. Archer, Jr. (1958); Moffatt, J. *Literary Illustrations of the Bible*, vol. 2, *The Book of Daniel* (1905); Montgomery, J. A. *A Critical and Exegetical Commentary on the Book of Daniel* (1950).

LAWRENCE T. MARTIN

NEHEMIAH Nehemiah was a postexilic governor of Judah (ca. 445 B.C.) whose chief importance lies in his role in organizing the rebuilding of the walls of Jerusalem with the permission of Artaxerxes, king of Persia, to whom he was cupbearer. As narrator of the biblical book which bears his name, he records how he obtained the respect and cooperation of those who might have opposed his building project and instituted a number of social and religious reforms, including observance of the Feast of Booths, renewal of instruction in the Torah, and strictures against intermarriage. His assistant in all these activities was Ezra, a priest. Nehemiah's Babylonian name, according to talmudic sources, was Zerubbabel, and he is so identified regularly in Jewish commentary on the book (e.g., Sanh. 38a; Alphabet R. Aleiba 27-28; cf. Neh. 7:7). As Zerubbabel he is a figure of signal eminence, one of those said to be born circumcised and destined to be a "messianic herald," at whose cry Michael and Gabriel will undertake a war of annihilation against the pagan world (cf. Kalir, in Lamentations; Pirqe Mashiah 75). He is chiefly identified in Christian commentary of the patristic period as one who "cleanses" the Temple and reconsecrates the sacrifice (e.g., St. Ambrose, *De officiis ministrorum*, 3.17.100-101).

As a builder of the walls of Jerusalem he is celebrated in post-Reformation Protestant exegesis as a type of the "restorer of the Church" (e.g., Matthew Poole, *Annotations*). It is this tradition which informs the vision of American Puritan Jonathan Mitchell's *Nehemiah on the Wall* (1671); a century later Thomas Frink can still say that Nehemiah's Jerusalem "does most graphically set forth in Figure this Wonderful Reformation of the World in these latter days" (*A Sermon Delivered at Stafford*, 1757). Thomas Tilston's *The Return from Captivity* (1793), a verse drama interspersed with songs and choruses, is based on Nehemiah, anticipating Eleanor Wood Whitman's *Nehemiah the Builder* (1926), a four-act American biblical drama with music (based on chaps. 1–7; 12:27-47; 13:4-31). One of the best-known American adaptations of Nehemiah as a type of the spiritual builder is Cotton Mather's "Nehemias Americanus," the appellation by which in *Magnalia Christi Americana* he salutes John Winthrop as one of the great builders of Christian civilization in the New World.

A. M. Klein's poem "Nehemiah" considers the Persian king: he has been so swayed by his cupbearer Nehemiah's appeal that "He dreams he sees dead streets and yawning jackals roam / Through the lone city" and, in a hint of his decree permitting Nehemiah to undertake the work, "The king will drink a tear-drop in his wine." For T. S. Eliot Nehemiah is a central figure in his choruses from *The Rock* (4-5), one who builds with "The trowel in the hand, and the gun rather loose in the holster" (5). In Margaret Avison's "The Earth That Falls Away," Roman soldiers in occupied Judea are restless on a watch:

But in that night in the courtyard
they hear the silence
(the ancient voices:
"Hide not thy face from me")
(the voice of Nehemiah:
"Let thine eyes now be open"). (*Winter Sun*, 131)

Bibliography. Bercovitch, S. *The American Jeremiad* (1978); Rowley, H. H. "Nehemiah's Mission and its Background." In *Men of God* (1963), 246-76.

NESTORIANISM *See* HERESY.

NEW BIRTH *See* CONVERSION.

NEW HEAVEN, NEW EARTH *See* APOCALYPSE.

NEW JERUSALEM The book of Revelation concludes with St. John's vision of the "holy city, new Jerusalem, coming down from God out of heaven, prepared as a bride adorned for her husband." A "great voice out of heaven" addressed John regarding the celestial city (Rev. 21:2-5):

Behold, the tabernacle of God is with men, and he will dwell with them, and they shall be his people, and God himself shall be with them, and be their God. And God shall wipe away all tears from their eyes; and there shall be no more death, neither sorrow, nor crying, neither shall there be any more pain: for the former things are passed away. And he that sat upon the throne said, Behold, I make all things new.

This passage, reminiscent of the vision of Ezekiel (Ezek. 40:1-4; 48:35) looks forward to a time when the fallen creation will be completely renewed. The holy city, descending from heaven, will be suspended over the earth and filled with such divine radiance that it has "no need of the sun, neither of the moon to shine in it" (v. 23). In the New Jerusalem the people of God are in unity at last (vv. 22, 24), having no need for a Temple because the "temple is the Lord God the Almighty and the Lamb" (v. 22). Familiar and even hallowed symbols have passed away as shadows, pale simulacra beside the glory of God's actual presence.

St. Augustine's famous commentary on this passage in *De civitate Dei* declares the basic understanding of the Church that this vision concerns not the historical "city set on a hill," but the future dwelling of the "immortality and eternity of the saints" following the Last Judgment. The celestial Jerusalem he calls the *visio pacis* of the Christian pilgrim, glimpsed only from afar in this life, but at last "to come down out of heaven, because the grace with which God formed it is of heaven" (*De civ. Dei* 20.19.17). Concerning the city's twelve gates of pearl, each named for one of the tribes of Israel (Rev. 21:12, 21), and the precious stones of which the walls are constructed (vv. 18-20), St. Ambrose elaborates a connection with the twelve stones of Aaron's breastplate (*De fide*, 2, pr. 1ff.).

In some strains of early Christian interpretation, despite the ordering of events in St. John's text, in which the descent of the New Jerusalem is posthistorical and following the millennium, the coming of the New Jerusalem is seen to represent the advent of a "third age" of the Spirit, following the OT "Age of the Father" and the NT "Age of the Son" (e.g., Montanus, Tertullian, St. Irenaeus, Joachim of Fiore). The principal commentators, however, regarded the New Jerusalem as the eternal and celestial city of the faithful elect, signaling the culmination of history and the commencement of the New Creation (e.g., Nicholas of Lyra, St. Thomas Aquinas).

Chaucer's Parson provides for pilgrims and readers of *The Canterbury Tales* an Augustinian analogy between the pilgrimage from Southwark to Canterbury and the spiritual journey from Babylon to "Jerusalem celestial," a "viage" through history and out of time to eternal felicity, "the endelees blisse of hevene":

there joye hath no contrarioustee of wo ne grevaunce; ther alle harmes been passed of this present lyf, ther as is the sikernesse fro the peyne of helle, ther as is the blisful compaignye that rejoysen hem everemo everich of otheres joye, / ther as the body of man that whilom was foul and derk is moore cleer than the sonne, ther as the body that whilom was syk, freele, and fieble, and mortal, is inmortal, and so strong and so hool that there may nothing apeyren it, / there as ne is neither hunger, thurst, ne coold, but every soule replenyssed with the sighte of the parfit knowynge of God. (*CT* 10.1076-79)

The vision of the celestial city set on a "cliff" afforded by the *Pearl* Poet begins with its physical characteristics —walls and gates of jewels and pearls (2.60ff.). Interpretation of these features from St. John's vision develops through the Pearl Maiden's Beatrice-like instruction concerning the state of the blessed, in which all the conditions described in Rev. 21 are detailed in turn (cf. Dante, *Paradiso*, 30.59-122). Such conventional descriptions, owing directly to the passage in Revelation, are frequently adumbrated by phrases from medieval Latin hymns on the celestial Jerusalem, including the anonymous *"Jerusalem Luminosa"* and *"Urbs Beata Jerusalem"* as well as the *"Ad Perennis Vitae Fontem"* of St. Peter Damian and *"De Contemptu Mundi"* of St. Bernard of Cluny, which concludes with a glorious vision of "Jerusalem the Golden." (The hymn of this title by the Scots writer David Dickson [1583-1663] is a kind of loose cento of these Latin hymns.)

The goal of "liberating" the literal Jerusalem (and establishing, perhaps, its celestial counterpart) was a preoccupation of some of the Crusades. The idealistic and millennialist aspect of medieval military expeditions still hovers in the background of Tasso's enormously influential 16th-cent. epic, *Gerusalemme Liberata* (1580; Eng. trans. by R. Carew [1594] and by E. Fairfax [1600]). In Spenser's contemporary English epic, Redcrosse Knight is led to "the highest Mount" and "a goodly City . . . whose wals and towres were builded high and strong / Of perle and precious stone"—a synthesis of Sinai, the Mount of Olives, and Parnassus which is nonetheless finally identified by the "godly aged Sire" as

The New Hierusalem, that God has built
For those to dwell in, that are chosen his,
His chosen people purg'd from sinful guilt
With pretious blood. (1.10.57-61)

In the Reformation period John's vision of the New Jerusalem is given extensive literal and spiritual interpretation. Various features of the historical Jerusalem — e.g., its being set on a hill (cliff, or tableland)—are blended with the details in Revelation in describing heaven or the millennial reign of Christ and his saints. John Bale's *A comedy concernynge thre lawes* projects that after the exhaustion of human moral suffering will come the new heaven of renewed faith and the new earth of mankind's understanding of that faith. Sir David Lindsay's poem *The Monarchie* (1553), possibly inspired by a sermon of John Knox, presents a "history" of the world from Creation to Last Judgment and imagines how "Heven renewit salbe, than / Rychtso, the erth, with devyse / Compair tyll hevinlye Paradyse" (6055-57), with the millennial kingdom passing in an hour, because in effect all those present for the Second Coming will be immortal and eternally preserved at the age of 33. Sir Walter Raleigh's *History of the World* (1614) similarly speaks of the descent of the New Jerusalem as the culmination of history.

The tracts and texts of political utopianism in the 17th cent. often envisioned temporally realized versions of the New Jerusalem —both in England and abroad. The dissenters who fled their homeland and settled the (apocalyptically named) New World also saw in John's Apocalypse a pertinent revelation of their own destiny, imagining, in the words of Johnson's *Wonder-Working Providence,* that "this is the place where the Lord will create a new Heaven and a new Earth in, new Churches, and a new Commonwealth together." John Cotton called his brethren to "Awake, awake, put on thy strength, O New English Zion and put on thy Beautiful Garments, O American Jerusalem." For Cotton Mather, "AMERICA is legible" in biblical promises of the New Jerusalem.

In devotional literature of the period, the New Jerusalem bespeaks a spiritual rather than a political realm. Jeremy Taylor's "A Meditation of Heaven" contemplates that city

Where the great King's transparent throne
Is of an entire jasper stone;
There the eye
O' the chrysolite,
And a sky
Of diamonds, rubies, chrysoprase,
And above all thy holy face
Makes an eternal clarity.

Among the best known of such meditations on the hereafter is Richard Baxter's *Saints' Everlasting Rest,* in the 16th and final chapter of which Rev. 21 provides the basis of a striking contrast between the "way of the wilderness . . . that howling desert" and

thy Father's glory . . . the glorious new Jerusalem, the gates of pearl, the foundation of pearl, the streets and pavement of transparent gold. That sun which lighteth all the world will be useless there; even thyself shall be as bright as yonder shining sun. God will be the sun, and Christ the light, and in his light thou shalt have light.

Baxter's vision is essentially that of Bunyan, whose *Pilgrim's Progress* has as its goal, at the culmination of a journey prompted by grace and carried out in perseverance, "the City [which] stood upon a mighty hill," "Mount Sion, the heavenly Jerusalem." Bunyan's pilgrim will there join "the innumerable company of Angels, and the Spirits of Just Men made perfect in the Paradise of God," his angel hosts tell him, where he shall "see the Tree of Life, and eat of the never-fading fruits thereof."

One of the best-known English hymns on the subject of the New Jerusalem is John Newton's "Glorious things of thee are spoken, / Zion, city of our God," based principally on Isa. 33:20-21. Blake's *Jerusalem: the Emanation of the Giant Albion* mixes biblical prophecy with social criticism, looking to the historical realization of the heavenly kingdom, in which the giant England will awake from its vegetable slumber to eternal life when at last "Jerusalem is called Liberty among the Children of Albion" (3.54.5). Similar sentiments are expressed in Blake's well-known prefatory poem to *Milton,* beginning, "And did those feet in ancient time / Walk upon England's mountains green?" and ending,

> I will not cease from Mental Fight
> Nor shall my Sword sleep in my hand
> Till we have built Jerusalem
> In England's green & pleasant Land.

It is not a utopian social vision but rather a yearning to be free of the world which prompts Anne Bradstreet's extensive quotation of Rev. 21 in "The Flesh and the Spirit," which begins, "The City which I hope to dwell / There's none on earth can parallel." Similarly, in Hawthorne's *The Scarlet Letter* Dimmesdale discourses of "saintly men, who walk with God on earth" and "would fain be away! To walk with him on the golden pavements of the New Jerusalem" (chap. 9; cf. Gen. 5:22). This passage is reminiscent of another homiletical invocation (here of Rev. 21:27) in Sir Walter Scott's *Kenilworth,* in which Foster discusses the exposition of Master Holdforth with Doctor Alasco, observing that "the Holy Writ says that the gold and precious stones are in no sort for those who work abominations, or who frame lies" (chap. 22). In Whittier's "The Pageant," winter's "wild work of frost and light" becomes a "foregleam of the Holy City / Like that to him on Patmos given, / The white bride coming down from heaven!"

Nineteenth-cent. references in English literature range from sentimentality to cynical debunking. Exemplary of the former is Sabine Baring-Gould's "The City God hath Made," which has its "foundation-stones" in "the beauteous fields of Eden" and in which the standard species of an English country garden somewhat overgrow the crystal river and golden pavements. Christina Rossetti wonders, "What will it be at last to see a 'holy' city! For

Londoners, for Parisians, for citizens of all cities upon earth, to see a holy city!" In Wilde's *De Profundis,* "Far off, like a perfect pearl, one can see the city of God. It is so wonderful that it seems as if a child could reach it in a summer's day." Tennyson's "Ode on the Death of . . . Wellington" talks about the warrior as a spiritual pilgrim who

> with toil of heart and knees and hands
> Thro' the long gorge to the far light has won
> His path upward, and prevail'd
> Shall find the toppling crags of Duty scaled
> Are close upon the shining table lands
> To which our God himself is moon and sun.

Hardy's narrator in *Jude the Obscure* recasts the vision somewhat:

> Through the solid barrier of cold cretaceous upland to the northward he was always beholding a gorgeous city — the fancied place he had likened to the New Jerusalem, though there was perhaps more of the painter's imagination and less of the diamond merchant's in his dreams thereof than in those of the Apocalyptic writer. (1.3)

See also EXILE AND PILGRIMAGE; HEAVEN; OLD AND NEW; SECOND COMING.

Bibliography. Bercovitch, S. *Puritan Origins of the American Self* (1975); Cohn, N. *The Pursuit of the Millennium* (1957); Damrosch, L. *Symbol and Truth in Blake's Myth* (1980); Firth, K. R. *The Apocalyptic Tradition in Reformation Britain, 1530-1645* (1979); Reeves, M. *The Influence of Prophecy in the Later Middle Ages* (1969); Ryken, L. *The Apocalyptic Vision in Paradise Lost* (1970); Tannenbaum, L. *Biblical Tradition in Blake's Early Prophecies* (1982).

NEW LAW   *See* COVENANT; GRACE, WORKS; OLD AND NEW.

NEW SONG   *See* OLD AND NEW.

NEW TIDINGS   *See* OLD AND NEW.

NEW WINE, OLD BOTTLES   *See* CANA WINE; OLD AND NEW.

NEW YEAR   *See* OLD AND NEW.

NICODEMUS   Nicodemus was a Pharisee and a member of the Sanhedrin, "a ruler of the Jews" whose profound if covert late-night conversation with Jesus is a key narrative in the Gospel of John (chap. 3). He also appears on two further occasions. When Jesus proclaimed himself in the Temple to be the source of "living water," Nicodemus intervened against those Pharisees who wished to censure him, and was rebuffed for doing so (John 7:50-52). He reenters the narrative at the burial of Jesus (John 19:38-42) when, with Joseph of Arimathea, another member of the Sanhedrin who had become a supporter of Jesus, he prepared the body for entombment in the sepulchre.

The first narrative represents the situation of thoughtful religious Jews, intent on the law but figuratively still "in the dark" concerning the nature of the spiritual "kingdom" spoken of by Jesus. Leaders such as Nicodemus yearned for a political messiah who would deliver their people from Roman oppression; to many, Jesus' teaching was therefore not only perplexing but suspect or even anathema. Nicodemus nonetheless honored Jesus with the title "Rabbi" and acknowledged him as a "teacher sent from God" (3:2), inviting further explanation of the "kingdom within." In his reply, Jesus spoke of the need for being "born again of water and the Spirit" (v. 5), suggesting the primary need for repentance and inward renewal. At first Nicodemus did not understand Jesus' figurative language: can one "enter the second time into his mother's womb, and be born?" he asks incredulously. After hearing Jesus speak of the difference between the invisible direction of God's Spirit and the carnal motivations of the flesh ("That which is born of the flesh is flesh; and that which is born of the spirit is spirit. Marvel not that I said unto thee, Ye must be born again" (vv. 6-7), Nicodemus exclaims in frustration: "How can these things be?" Jesus chides him gently for his literal-mindedness: "Art thou a master of Israel and knowest not these things?" (v. 10), thereby indicating the congruence of his message (and metaphor) with that of the "law and the prophets" in which Nicodemus was in some sense expert.

This passage has been enormously important in Christian tradition among commentators concerned with the essential continuity between the OT and NT as much as with those who have wished to emphasize the radical challenge of Jesus' teaching. St. Augustine relates Nicodemus's evening conversation with Jesus to the events of the previous chapter, counting Nicodemus among those who were impressed by the "signs" which Jesus did and therefore "believed in his Name." Such is the case of all catechumens, he suggests, people intent on coming to a knowledge of Christ but who have yet to pass through the complete process of repentance, baptism, and public identification with Christ. These become "children of the light" when, filled with the Spirit, they participate in the mysteries to which they give intellectual assent (*In Joan. Ev.* 11.1-4). Augustine then sets upon explaining how all of these sacramental steps are scripturally prefigured and anticipated in the OT history of the chosen people, developing at length the distinction between Jacob and Esau and between the offspring of Sarah and of Hagar, promised inheritance and offspring according to the flesh (cf. Gal. 4:22-27); the distinction Jesus draws for Nicodemus, he argues, is in fact at the heart of all that a faithful reader of the Jewish Scriptures knows: "Who are born after the flesh? Lovers of the world, lovers of this life. Who are born after the Spirit? Lovers of the kingdom of heaven, lovers of Christ, men that long for eternal life, that worship God freely" (11.12). Concerning Nicodemus's incredulous "How can these things be?" Augustine is sympathetic: "in fact, in the carnal sense he knew not how"; of Jesus' gentle rebuke he adds, "Oh brethren! what? do we think that the Lord meant to taunt scornfully this Jewish rabbi? Hardly. The Lord knew what he was doing; he wished the man to become born of the Spirit" (12.6). Augustine further celebrates Nicodemus's appeal to the Torah in defending Jesus (33.2; John 7:50-52), and his progress in faith (120.4).

The 4th-cent. *Acta Pilati* and the *Descensus Christi ad infernos* were foundational to the creation of the so-called Gospel of Nicodemus, widely popular by the 14th cent. for its narration of the Harrowing of Hell. The text is partially translated in the Eng. *Cursor Mundi* (ca. A.D. 1300), which refers to Nicodemus throughout the Gospel paraphrase as "Sire Nicodemus," the "frend" of Jesus and his "knight." Referring to the events in John 19:38-42, the text ascribes Nicodemus's "book" to his difficulty in persuading his fellow Jews of his own hard-won convictions about Jesus (3.17277-88). The apocryphal Gospel to which Nicodemus's name is attached had considerable influence upon English medieval literature, including, notably, the Towneley cycle play "The Deliverance of Souls" and the "harrowing" analogue in *Piers Plowman* (B.18.262, 316a-17).

If Nicodemus fared somewhat less well in English literature after the Reformation it may have been in large part due to the Reformation theologians' impatience with apocryphal texts. Another factor may have been Calvin's harsh and unsympathetic reading of Nicodemus's interview with Jesus (e.g., "Nicodemus rejects [Jesus' words] as a fable"; "Because Christ sees that He is wasting his time and energy in teaching this proud man, He now rebukes him" [*New Testament Comm.* 4.60-61, 69, 203-04]). Nevertheless, a more sympathetic view persists. John Donne's sermon on "John 22:21" accords with the ME *Ancrene Riwle* in seeing Nicodemus in John 19:39 as a dramatic symbol of penance, and Henry Vaughan's "The Night" reflects his reading of Augustine's commentary throughout:

> . . . Wise Nicodemus saw such light
> As made him know his God by night.
> Most blest believer he!
> Who in that land of darkness and blinde eyes
> Thy long expected healing wings could see,
> When thou didst rise,
> And what can never more be done,
> Did at mid-night speak with the Sun!

Matthew Henry (1728) departs markedly from Calvin in his commentary: "Not many mighty and noble are called; yet some are, and here was one . . . this was a man of the Pharisees, bred to learning, a scholar" (*Comm. on the Whole Bible,* 5.88); of the encounter Henry goes on to say: "These were *Noctes Christianae —Christian nights,* much more instructive than the *Noctes Atticae — Attic nights,"* and of Jesus' "answer" he draws a general application:

> This is a reproof (1) To those who undertake to teach others and yet are ignorant and unskillful in the word of righteousness themselves. (2) To those who spend their time in learning and teaching notions and ceremonies in religion, niceties and criticisms in the Scripture, and neglect that which is practical and tends to reform the heart and life. (885)

Henry defends Nicodemus against the blame of some Christian commentators (including Calvin) that Nicodemus yet "retained his place in the council and his vote among them," and observes rather that Christ "never said to him *Follow me* . . . therefore it seems rather to have been his *wisdom* not immediately to throw up his place." Most praiseworthy for Henry, however, is Nicodemus's later public defense of Jesus and equally visible participation in the burial of his body: "Let none justify the disguising of their faith by the example of Nicodemus, unless, like him, they be ready upon the first occasion openly to appear in the cause of Christ, though they stand alone in it; for so Nicodemus did here, and ch. xix.39" (5.978).

Matthew Henry notwithstanding, Nicodemus seems to have attracted little interest in 18th-cent. literature. In Dickens's *Our Mutual Friend* there may be a recollection when at the return of John Harmon from the "dead" Nicodemus Boffin wakes up and asks a series of apt questions. A spate of 20th-cent. dramatizations reflect the importance of John 3 in evangelical preaching, including Katherine Lee Bates's *Pharisees* (1926), in which Nicodemus and a rabbi are the chief characters; P. E. Osgood's *The Fears of Nicodemus* (1928), a dramatic sermon dialogue between Nicodemus and Joseph of Arimathea; and Perry J. Stackhouse's *The Disciple of the Night* (1926), also designed as an aid to preaching. The title poem of Edwin Arlington Robinson's collection *Nicodemus* (1932) features a dramatic dialogue between Nicodemus and Caiaphas, at whose bidding Nicodemus has evidently interviewed Jesus secretly. The poem is about fear of the unknown, and "flawed complacency." When Caiaphas finds that Nicodemus has been swayed by "the carpenter" he is gently — but also menacingly — reproving, refusing Nicodemus's request that he join his colleague, "but once, to see and hear him, Caiaphas." Sholem Asch's novel *The Nazarene* (1939) alternates between the 1st and 20th cents. in its view of the life of Yeshua; Nicodemon figures prominently as a faithful rabbi. Perhaps the most penetrating modern literary representation is that of the American poet Howard Nemerov, which amplifies the questions of Nicodemus artfully; in the final section of his poem "Nicodemus," Nemerov shows close familiarity with the exposition of St. Augustine to his catechumens (*In Joan. Ev.,* esp.

11.7-13) a millennium and a half earlier, but represents Nicodemus's final response to Jesus' invitation to the new birth in terms rather of a request to reiterate the exodus deliverance and the covenant promise to Abraham:

> Rabbi, let me go up from Egypt
> With Moses to the wilderness of Sinai
> And to the country of the old Canaan
> Where, sweeter than honey, Sarah's blood
> Darkens the cold cave in the field
> And the wild seed of Abraham is cold.

See also HARROWING OF HELL; PHARISEES; WIND BLOWETH WHERE IT LISTS.

NICODEMUS, GOSPEL OF   *See* APOCRYPHA AND PSEUDEPIGRAPHA; HARROWING OF HELL.

NIGHT COMETH, WHEN NO MAN CAN WORK
Jesus said, "I must work the works of him that sent me, while it is day: the night cometh when no man can work" (John 9:4). In *Jane Eyre* Charlotte Brontë affords the traditional application of this saying: "Repent — resolve, while yet there is time. Remember, we are bid to work while it is day — warned that 'the night cometh when no man shall work'" (chap. 35).

NIMROD   *See* BABEL.

NINEVEH   Nineveh was the last capital of Assyria, which was located on the Tigris River in northern Iraq opposite modern Mosul. Excavations show occupation from prehistoric times (ca. 4500 B.C.), and the OT names its founder as Nimrod (Gen. 10:11). Mentioned in Sumerian sources as early as the third millennium, it was a cultic and commercial center as well as a royal city from the time of Tiglath-pileser I (1114-1076 B.C.). At its height the inner city was enclosed by a wall of some 12 km. in length, so it was indeed a "great city" when Jonah preached repentance (Jonah 1:2; 3:2). The subsequent conversion (3:4-5) is not attested extrabiblically, but it is referred to by Jesus (Matt. 12:41; Luke 11:30) and rabbinical sources (Ta'an. 2.1; Midr. Jonah 100-102), though some of these saw the change as being only temporary (Ta'an. 2.1; Pirqe R. El. 43).

The repentance of Nineveh at Jonah's preaching is seen as an example by the rabbis (Exod. Rab. 45.1; Eccl. Rab. 5; 6.1) and the Church Fathers (*Constitutions of the Holy Apostles,* 3.22; Augustine, *Enarr. in Ps.* 50.11). Luther credits its building to Asshur, who could not bear to live with the ungodly Nimrod (*Works,* 2.214). Dante Gabriel Rossetti's "The Burden of Nineveh" ponders the arrival at the "Muslim galleries" of the British Museum of a "winged beast from Nineveh." The poem's speaker imagines the world of preconverted Nineveh, when the "Bull-god" statue may have been worshiped, and also

That day whereof we keep record,
When near thy city gates the Lord
Sheltered his Jonah with a gourd,
This sun (I said), here present, poured
Even this shadow that I see.

See also JONAH.
Bibliography. A. Parrot, *Nineveh and the Old Testament* (1955).   DAVID W. BAKER

NO RESPECTER OF PERSONS Among the ordinances for social justice laid down in Leviticus are several which have to do with impartiality in judgment. In one of these, "Ye shall do no unrighteousness in judgment: thou shalt not respect the person of the poor, nor honor the person of the mighty: but in righteousness shalt thou judge thy neighbor" (Lev. 19:15; cf. Deut. 1:17; 16:19; Num. 16:15; James 2:1-9). Judgment which is above influence is likewise said to be characteristic of God (e.g., 1 Sam. 14:14); according to St. Peter this is why the gospel is sent to all peoples, and not Israel only: "Of a truth I perceive that God is no respecter of persons: But in every nation he that feareth him, and worketh righteousness, is accepted with him" (Acts 10:34-35; cf. Luke 20:21). Chaucer's Parson in *The General Prologue* to *The Canterbury Tales* is praised as one who makes no distinction in his pastoral duty among his socially diverse parishioners, "what so he were, of heigh or lough estat" (1.522; cf. 1.516-28). The English tradition of common law, and its American stem enthrone this principle as fundamental to civil justice, and modern literary allusions typically reflect the legal context. Thus, a vigorously American frontier character in J. F. Cooper's *The Pioneers* says: "The law, gentlemen, is no respecter of persons in a free country. It is one of the greatest blessings that has been handed down to us from our ancestors, that all men are equal in the eye of the law as they are by nater" (chap. 13). J. S. Mill gives the term its more specifically legal bearing: "It is held that there should be no restraint not required by the general good, and that the law should be no respecter of persons, but should treat all alike" (*The Subjection of Women,* chap. 1). G. K. Chesterton fills out the concept with an explanation of the English usage reflected in the KJV formulation now grown archaic, however familiar. He writes: ". . . democracy is no respecter of persons. It is no respecter of them, either in the bad and servile or in the good and sympathetic sense" (*What I Saw in America,* "Facts and Opinions").

NOAH Noah is the central figure in two OT narratives. As a "just man" he, with his family, is preserved from annihilation in the Flood (Gen. 6:5–9:17). As a cultural hero who discovers the art of making wine, he is surprised drunk by his son Ham; Noah later curses Ham's son Canaan and blesses his own sons Shem and Japheth for respecting his shame (Gen. 9:25-27). Noah is the last of the antediluvian patriarchs and at the same time another Adam from whom mankind descends.

The meaning of the name *Noah* is not clear. In Gen. 5:29 the name is explained by a play on *naham* ("to comfort"), possibly a reference to the fact that the wine discovered by Noah was a source of consolation (Gen. 5:29). Some commentators and the LXX relate the name to the Hebrew word *nuah* ("to rest"). Noah is mentioned in the genealogies of 1 Chron. 1:4 and Luke 3:38; he is called a righteous man (Ezek. 14:14, 20) and a preacher of righteousness (2 Pet. 2:5), and he is cited as an example of faith (Heb. 11:7). Noah receives considerable attention in the Pseudepigrapha (see index in Charlesworth, *Old Testament Pseudepigrapha,* 2.980-81).

Early rabbinical commentators tend to downplay Noah's righteousness on the basis of the statement that he was "perfect in his generations" (Gen. 6:9) and are divided about how to evaluate Noah's drunkenness. They explain Ham's crime as an attempt to sexually abuse or emasculate his father. With Noah's curse, some claim, slavery entered the world. Philo equates the biblical Noah with Deucalion and allegorizes the Flood Story as a cleansing of the soul.

For early Christian commentators Noah is an example of obedience, a colonizer of the world, and a new Adam. Later exegetes emphasize his righteousness, viewing him chiefly as a type of Christ. Some of the Church Fathers condemn Noah's drunkenness, others such as Origen excuse it on the grounds of his inexperience, while still others allegorize the incident in connection with Christ's Passion (e.g., St. Augustine, *De civ. Dei* 16.2).

Noah's wife, scarcely mentioned in Scripture, is the leading character in the lost gnostic *Book of Noria.* She attempts to prevent the building of the ark and eventually resorts to burning it (cf. M. R. James, *The Lost Apocrypha of the Old Testament* [1936], 12-15). She is given continuing prominence in later redactions of the story. In medieval drama, especially in the Chester, York, and Towneley plays, Noah's wife is depicted as a shrewish gossip (cf. Prov. 7:10-12) who refuses to board the ark. In the Newcastle-on-Tyne version she serves as an agent of the devil. Noah himself, though henpecked, is represented as a good craftsman and dignified leader. (The ME poem *Cleanness,* by contrast, stays close to the OT and concentrates on the conventional theological implications of the story.)

A parodic Noah figure appears in Chaucer's *Miller's Tale* in the character of an Oxford carpenter who fears a second flood. Shakespeare's Sir Toby refers to Noah the sailor in a comic context (*Twelfth Night,* 3.2.18-19). Drayton's *Noah's Flood* shows the protagonist in the role of preacher, as does Milton (*Paradise Lost,* 11.719-26), who regards Noah as the antitype of Adam (12.6-7) and type of the Christ to come (11.808-09, 876-77). In "The Bunch of Grapes" George Herbert sees in Noah's vine a prefiguration of Christ "who of the Laws sowre juice sweet wine did make, / Ev'n God himself being pressed for my sake" (cf. John 15:1). Marvell compares Cromwell, who "planted the vine of liberty," to Noah and the Puritan opponents of Cromwell to Ham ("The First Anniversary of the Government"). For Dryden, Charles II rather than Cromwell is the Noah figure ("To His Sacred Majesty").

In the 17th-19th cents. Noah is still occasionally invoked as a type of Christ (e.g., Keble, *The Christian Year;* Isaac Williams, *The Cathedral;* Francis Thompson, "The Mistress of Vision"). More frequently, however, he is relegated to trivial or satiric contexts. Byron, who mentions Captain Noah and Captain Cook in one breath (*English Bards and Scotch Reviewers,* 356), characterizes Japheth first as a dutiful son, then as a disillusioned rebel who cannot understand why he should be spared when all else perishes ("Heaven and Earth"). In Emily Brontë's *Wuthering Heights* self-righteous Joseph, like the drunk Joseph Poorgrass in Hardy's *Far from the Madding Crowd,* invokes the memory of Noah. The patriarch as a discoverer of wine is referred to in Scott's *Anne of Geierstein,* Melville's *The Confidence-Man,* and Twain's *The Mysterious Stranger.* In Kipling's "Sappers" Noah appears as the builder of the first pontoon, one who would not have become drunk if he had trained with Her Majesty's Royal Engineers. Peepy in Dickens's *Bleak House* replays the drunkenness of Noah by dipping a toy figure of Noah "head first into the wine-glasses" (chap. 30). Daniel Webster is indirectly compared to Noah in Whittier's antislavery poem "Ichabod," the last stanza of which alludes to Gen. 9:23.

In the 20th cent. Noah appears in a variety of guises. While science-fiction writers such as G. P. Serviss *(The Second Deluge)* and A. C. Clarke *(The Song of Distant Earth)* turn him into a worldly scientist, C. Day Lewis transforms him into a bourgeois willing to join the rebellion of the proletariat *(Noah and the Waters).* In H. G. Wells's *All Aboard for Ararat* he becomes a utopian novelist, in Golding's *The Spire* an ambitious church builder, and in Burgess's *End of the World News* first the builder of a space ark, then a Nazi-like leader, and finally an imaginative science-fiction writer. In Malamud's *God's Grace,* Cohn, the sole human survivor of an atomic war, compares himself to Noah.

In Conelly's *Green Pastures* Noah is a black preacher. In Odets's *The Flowering Peach* he is a heavy drinker even before the Flood, a worried father, and a man who, however unhappy with God's commands, learns humility. He appears as a cruel brother in Robert Coover's story "The Brother," and as a stern patriarch married to a humane wife in David Garnett's novel *Two by Two.* Timothy Findley, in *Not Wanted on the Voyage,* sees Noah as an experimenter, a disciplinarian, and a pitiable man who, since God remains silent, has to seek refuge in cheap tricks.

The story of how Noah is discovered in his shame is the subject of Zora Neale Hurston's play "The First One," which stresses Ham's willingness to leave his family and accept his fate as a black man. James Joyce, in *Ulysses,* implicitly compares Bloom to the patriarch by describing Stephen as a Japheth in search of a father.

See also FLOOD; HAM.

Bibliography. Allen, D. C. *The Legend of Noah: Renaissance Rationalism in Art, Science, and Letters* (1949); James, M. R. *The Lost Apocrypha of the Old Testament* (1936); Lewis, J. P. *A Study of the Interpretation of Noah and the Flood in Jewish and Christian Literature* (1968); Marks, J. H. "Noah." *IDB* 3.554-56; Westermann, C. *BKAT Genesis* (1976).   PAUL GOETSCH

NOAH, SONS OF   In the Genesis account (Gen. 7:13; 9:18-19) three are identified as, with their wives, survivors of the Flood and progenitors of subsequent human life: Shem, Ham, and Japheth. The genealogy of each (Gen. 10) divides postdiluvian humanity into linguistically or onomastically recognizable traditions. The sons of Japheth (Gomer, Magog, Tubal, Meshech, et al.) are northern or European, the sons of Ham (Cush, Canaan, Sheba, et al.) are recognizably African and non-Semitic Middle Eastern peoples; the sons of Shem (father of "all the children of Eber," Elam, Asshur, Aram, et al.) are identified onomastically as the Semitic peoples.

See also FLOOD; HAM; NOAH; SHEM.

NOAH'S ARK   *See* FLOOD.

NOD, LAND OF   *See* EAST, EAST OF EDEN.

NO MAN CAN SERVE TWO MASTERS   *See* MAMMON.

NO NEW THING UNDER THE SUN   *See* VANITY OF VANITIES.

NOLI ME TANGERE   When Jesus appeared to Mary Magdalene in the garden after his resurrection (John 20) she did not at first recognize him, "supposing him to be the gardener." (This "error" has often been seen as typologically apt; in the Digby play *Mary Magdalen,* e.g., Jesus observes,

> So I am, for-sothe, mary:
> mannys hartt is my gardyn here;
> þer-In I sow sedys of vertu all þe ȝere;
> þe fowle wedes and wycys, I read vp be þe rote.
> whan þat gardyn is watteryd with terys clere,
> than spryng vertuus, and smell full sote. [2.1080-85].)

When Jesus addressed her, she acknowledged him instantly, saying "Rabboni" ("Master") and presumably, as in many artistic representations of the scene (e.g., Dürer, Titian), reached out to touch him. Jesus forbade her to do so, saying, "Touch me not, for I am not yet ascended unto my Father" (John 20:17; Vg *Dicit ei Jesus: Noli me tangere . . .*).

For St. Jerome, Jesus' words of restraint indicate that Mary was not worthy to touch the Master she supposed still in the tomb (*Ep.* 39.6). According to St. Augustine, since "she did not touch him while he stood on earth, how then could she touch him while ascending to the Father?" (*In Joan. Ev.* 26.3). In Walter Hilton's *Ladder of Perfection* Mary Magdalene is presented conventionally as a type of the contemplative life. Hilton observes that the exchange serves as a reminder of how Mary "loved our Lord ardently before his Passion, but her love was perhaps more directed to his physical nature and less to the spiritual. She knew well enough that he was God, but she concentrated little on that fact, for she was not able for it then" (2.31). Hilton goes on to read the passage as indicative of Jesus' preparation of Mary for growth toward perfection in the spiritual life.

In the ME Corpus Christi drama the incident is the basis of an important pageant. In the York play, the *noli me tangere* is amplified by charged repetition: in the second instance Jesus says: "negh me noght, my loue, latte be!" (39.82), as if to strengthen the sense of Mary's ardor, a tension tempered somewhat in the next line when he calls her "Marie, my doughtir swete." Mary's own language continues to be that of a lover, however: "Thi loue is swetter thanne þe mede" (89). N-Town's version of the same narrative chooses not to develop this potential characterization of the incident.

The suggestion of erotic tension magnified by late medieval and early Renaissance painting and dramatic treatment of the passage may have prompted the satiric edge in Wyatt's "Whoso List to Hunt," in which a female deer who bears the emblazoned *"noli me tangere"* undoubtedly refers to one of the unfortunate targets of Henry VIII's amorous forays, and hence *chasse gardé.* Smollett's *Humphry Clinker* flirts with the erotic ambivalence of the passage: "This precious aunt of yours is become insensibly a part of my constitution — Damn her! She's a *noli me tangere* in my flesh, which I cannot bear to be touched or tampered with." A more straightforward reading is implied in the climactic scene of Tennyson's *Becket*, where as the Archbishop holds off his murderers, he cries out, "Touch me not!" De Brito then says, with heavy sarcasm: "How the good priest gods himself! / He is not yet ascended to the Father." Wilde adapts the passage in treating the relationship between John the Baptist and Salome, in his play of that name; in the temptation scene, Jokanaan cries, "Back, daughter of Sodom! Touch me not. Profane not the temple of the Lord God." Her response compares him implicitly to the suffering rather than the resurrected Christ. And in Lawrence's *St. Mawr* the passage is quoted and commented upon by a woman who cannot bear the press of humanity, especially the touch of a man: "and marriage — oh no! *Noli me tangere, homine!* I am

not yet ascended to the Father. Oh leave me alone, leave me alone! That is all my cry to the world."

See also MARY MAGDALENE.

NON SERVIAM   "I will not serve," a sentiment attributed by Milton (*Paradise Lost,* 1.262-63) to Satan in his rejection of God and heaven, and echoed by Joyce's Stephen Dedalus in his reprise of Cranley in *Portrait of the Artist as a Young Man* (chap. 5) in the Latin form (cf. Josh. 24:15), is not canonically related to Satan, but to reprobate Judah in Jer. 2:20 (Vg and Douay — not KJV). It first occurs in Joyce's narrative in Fr. Arnall's sermon (chap. 3).

NOONDAY DEMON   The Vg translation of Ps. 90:5-6 (KJV Ps. 91:4-6) reads: *"Scuto circumdabit te veritas eius, non timebis a timore nocturno, a sagitta volante in die, a negotio perambulante in tenebris, ab incursu et daemonio meridiano."* The English Douay-Rheims, following the Latin, has: "His truth shall compass thee with a shield: thou shalt not be afraid of the terror of the night. Of the arrow that flieth in the day, of the business that walketh about in the dark: of invasion, or of the noonday devil." The passage has a colorful translation history: the Wycliffite version (1382) renders the Vg *daemonio* as "goblin"; in the 16th cent. the so-called "Bug Bible" (1551) memorably translates: "Thou shalt not nede to be afraied for eny bugges by nyghte" (*bug* meaning "bugbear" or "bogie" in Tudor English). The expression *noonday devil* or *noonday demon* survived in Compline or Night Prayers in the Roman Breviary until the Jesuit revision of the Psalter; cf. the KJV rendering, based on the Hebrew original: "the destruction that wasteth at noonday."

In the Middle Ages the phrase proves important to a number of literary works. Heurodis in the Orpheus legend as narrated by Pierre Bersuire *(Ovidus Moralizatus)* and as portrayed by the illustrators of the *Ovide moralisé* is carried off to Hades from under the "ympe" tree by the Noon-Day Demon; these sources have been linked by Dronke to the rapture of Eurydice (Heurodis) in the ME poem *Sir Orfeo.* Perhaps the most vivid extended use of the expression in English is by the Augustinian canon Walter Hilton, whose *Ladder of Perfection* (2.26) includes the warning to "beware of the Noonday Demon," which counterfeits light as if "straight from Jerusalem" but is in fact "nothing of the kind" (cf. St. Bernard of Clairvaux, *Cantica Canticorum* [PL 183.956]). Hilton goes on to explain the glossy luster of spiritual opportunists, self-righteous preachers, and would-be prophets. The noonday demon, he argues, superficially seems like a *bona fide* man of religion. However:

whatever light of knowledge or experience or fervor shines upon a soul, when it is accompanied by presumption, self-promotion, and disdain of one's fellow Christians at the same time, it is not a light of grace granted by the Holy Spirit. This is so even when the knowledge itself is of the truth. No, it is either of the devil if it comes suddenly, or of man's own wit if it comes by study.

The "demon" is elsewhere frequently understood in connection with the sin of sloth or *accidie*. The character Need in *Piers Plowman* (B.20.1-49) has been read as a manifestion of the noonday demon (R. Adams, "The Nature of Need in Piers Plowman BXX." *Traditio* 34 [1978], 273-301). St. Thomas More (*Dialogue of Comfort against Tribulation*, 2.12.1182A; cf. *Confutation of Tyndale's Answer*, 8.810B) takes the "noonday devil" in the manner of Bernard of Clairvaux, as the fourth of the four "vexations of the Church," each of which is assigned a specific "devil." The long note in the Douay lists the four devils as terrors, open persecution, circumvention, and long torments. More (*Comfort*, 2.16.1199A; 3.2.1216B; 16.1234H; 17.1236F; 21.1248G) is concerned enough about misconstrual that he glosses the expression again and again, even leaving it in its Latin original. The Eng. *The Ordinary of the Christian Man* (1502), translated from French, may have been influenced by Hilton; in it the noonday devil is glossed as vainglory: "The arrow or dart of the devil the which fleeth right perilously in the midday and at the hour of noon, that is vainglory."

Because of the determinant influence of the KJV after 1611, references to the noonday demon gradually disappear. An exception may be Alexander Pope, a Catholic familiar with both the Vg and the Douay translations, whose revision of Chaucer's *Merchant's Tale* refers to the third and fourth vexations, a "night-Invasion and a Midday-Devil." In continental literature, the phrase still occurs occasionally, as in Paul Bourget's *Le demon de midi* (1914), a modern chronicle of the temptations of middle age.

Bibliography. Dronke, P. "Eurydice, Heurodis, and the Noon-day Demon." *Speculum* 41 (1966), 22-29; *Orpheus in the Middle Ages* (1970), 175-94; Kuhn, R. *The Demon of Noontide* (1976); Marc'Hadour, G. *The Bible in the Works of Thomas More* (1969), 1.164-66; Wenzel, S. *The Sin of Sloth* (1960).   ERNEST N. KAULBACH

NORTH "How art thou fallen from heaven, O Lucifer ... for thou hast said ... I will sit upon the mount of the congregation of the north" (Isa. 14:13-14). Rabbinical and patristic commentary on these verses seems to be the chief source for the medieval and Renaissance commonplace that north is the home of the devil and the place of evil in general. But it seems both from this passage and from Ps. 48:2-3 that north was also seen as the seat of God's throne, which Lucifer tried to overthrow. In other parts of the OT the north carries negative connotations because invading armies often came through Syria, to the north of Israel (Isa. 14:31; Jer. 1:14; 4:6; 6:22; 10:22; 16:15; 25:9; Ezek. 26:7; see J. McKenzie, *Dictionary of the Bible* [1965], s.v. "North").

Jewish tradition is somewhat contradictory. On the one hand, north is a deliberately unfinished part of creation, a kind of chaos with hellfire, smoke, ice and darkness, and a variety of devils, a place from which all evil comes. On the other hand, Paradise lies to the north or northwest (L. Ginzberg, *LJ* 1.12; 3.160-61, 232-33).

St. Augustine consistently associates Satan with the north and dwells on the antithesis of north and south in Scripture, where, he says, north never signifies anything good (*Enarr. in Ps.* 47; *De gratia Novi Testamenti, seu epistola*, 140 [PL 33.561]; *Annotationum in Job. Liber Unus* [PL 34.876]).

In the early medieval period there may also have been some vestigial association with the Hel of Old Norse tradition, which was situated both northward and downward. As early as the OE *Genesis* (32-33, 275) and as late as Milton's *Paradise Lost* (5.688-89, 725-26, 755-60; 6.79-91) Satan is shown massing his legions in the north. In *Piers Plowman* Langland speculates on this association of Lucifer with the north (B.1.117; C.2.111ff.); in his note to this passage Skeat points out that in many of the medieval references which he cites there is an association of Lucifer with the north. In Chaucer's *Friar's Tale* (*Canterbury Tales*, 3.1413) the devil is from "fer in the north contree," and the medieval stage plan for the *Castle of Perseverance* shows the scaffold of Belial on the north side.

In medieval iconography north was also associated with Synagogue or the OT as contrasted with Holy Church or the NT. Hence a statue of Synagogue was often to be found on the north side of the church door or of the church itself; she wore a blindfold or carried some symbol of lost power such as a broken staff or a tumbling crown.

Bibliography. Kellog, A. *Chaucer, Langland, Arthur: Essays in Middle English* (1972); Murphy, M. "North: The Significance of a Compass Point in Medieval English Literature." *Lore and Language* 3 (1983), 65-76.   MICHAEL MURPHY

NOT PEACE BUT A SWORD In the context of Jesus' instruction to his disciples concerning the message of the kingdom of heaven which they were to profess, he said, "Think not that I am come to send peace on earth, but a sword" (Matt. 10:34; cf. Luke 12:51-53). He then went on to outline the uncompromising commitment and self-denial required of his followers, and the inevitable opposition they would face from even within their own households.

St. Augustine identifies the "sword" with Jesus' word, which some obey, some resist, and some resist others obeying (*Enarr. in Ps.* 45.10; 68.5): "the sword of his own word hath in salutary wise separated us from evil habits ... and separated every believer either from his father who believed not in Christ, or from his mother in like manner unbelieving; or at least, if we were born of Christian parents, from our ancestors ... among the heathen" (*Enarr. in Ps.* 97.7). This basic interpretation is followed by Calvin and other Reformation commentators, Calvin observing that from reading the Prophets the disciples might well have expected the reign of Christ to be one of peace. Such peace could only be realized, however, if "all the world were to subscribe to the authority of the Gospel. But as the majority is not only opposed, but actually in bitter conflict, we are not able to profess Christ without the strife and hatred of many" (*Harmony of the Gospels,* sup. Matt. 10:32-35).

In English literature, the phrase "not peace but a sword" is typically turned against its source, or at least its context. Swinburne's "Hymn of Man" champions the liberation of persons from religious orthodoxy, and addresses Jesus: "Ah, thou that darkenest heaven — ah thou that bringest a sword — / By the crimes of thine hands unforgiven, they beseech thee to hear them, O Lord." In Montague's *A Hind Let Loose,* "Thither, as a Christian publicist, each brought not peace but a sword, or, where a sword would not have been in place, a squirt of weed-killer" (chap. 1). Of a character in Somerset Maugham's *Catalina* it is observed that "the people approved his strictness . . . and did what was in their power to support him. There had been in consequence unfortunate occurences, and the authorities had been obliged to intervene. He had brought not peace to the city, but a sword" (chap. 34). Howard Nemerov, in his poem "Morning Sun," asks: "How many more this morning are there dead of / The peace I came to bring a sword instead of?" (*Gnomes and Occasions* [*Collected Poems,* 420]).

See also PEACE WHICH PASSETH UNDERSTANDING; PEACE, WHEN THERE IS NO PEACE.

NUMBER OF THE BEAST   *See* MARK OF THE BEAST.

NUMEROLOGY   Number symbolism has enjoyed a prominent role in the Judeo-Christian tradition, although its roots — whether primitive and elemental, astrological, Pythagorean, or Platonic — are essentially pagan. Its importance to the literary arts, especially in the medieval and Renaissance periods, is attributable to the Ptolemaic view of a symmetrical universe structured upon sympathetic correspondences syncretized with the Hebraic view that God created all things "in measure, and number, and weight" (Wisd. 11:21). In earliest Judaism one encounters primitive forms of numerology — two used to indicate a few, or three used as a sign of totality. Abraham goes three days into the wilderness to sacrifice Isaac (Gen. 22:4); God calls Samuel three times before Eli realizes that it is the Lord calling (1 Sam. 3:8-9); Elijah covers the dead child of the widow of Sarepta three times with his own body before the Lord restores it to life (1 Kings 17:21). In each instance three is the full measure necessary for the event to be perfected. Seven is also used in the Bible as a totality, and is often connected with divine actions and religious observance — the seven-day creation and the practice of Sabbath "rest." Ritual acts are frequently measured by seven, or seven times seven, or seventy, or seventy-seven (e.g., Matt. 18:21-22). Seven is a prominent number in the Revelation to St. John the Divine, a book addressed to the "seven churches which are in Asia" and which speaks of seven seals (Rev. 4:1–8:1), seven trumpets (8:2–11:19), seven vials (15:1–16:21), seven angels (Rev. 15:6, etc.), seven dooms (17:1–20:15), etc. The number twelve is often used as symbolic of Israel and the elect (hence the twelve tribes and twelve apostles) and is also an important apocalyptic number (see esp. the description of the New Jerusalem in Rev. 21). Forty as a period of denial or sojourn apart or in exile (cf. the forty days the Pleiades are obscured in the rainy season, thus prohibiting navigation, or the period of evil days, etc. which ancient *kalendaria* sometimes mention). The rains of the Flood fell for forty days and forty nights (Gen. 7:4, 12); Israel sojourned in the wilderness for forty years. Moses, Elijah, and Jesus all fasted for forty days (Exod. 34:28; 1 Kings 19:8; Matt. 4:2 and parallels). Forty days passed between the Resurrection and Ascension (Acts 1:3). The Church's Lenten observance is forty days.

Biblical numerology is intricately tied up with structural devices, rhetoric, and techniques of exegesis. Its compass includes not only specific number metaphors but also the study of parallel treatments and significant proportioning of material, what we would customarily think of as allegory, extended analogy, or "layers" of meaning. Thus, twenty-two becomes a significant number because of the number of letters in the Hebrew alphabet. Ps. 119, e.g., employs an alphabetic structure of twenty-two eight-line stanzas, each set off by a letter of the alphabet. A curious combination of sevens and twenty-twos may be seen in Lamentations, with its alphabetic chapters of 22, 22, 66, 22, and 22 verses, where the central chapter, the third, repeats the pattern three times over so that there are seven times twenty-two verses.

Numerology becomes increasingly important in the midrashic commentaries which were attached to scriptural texts in the 3rd and 2nd cents. B.C. The first truly distinguished product of the midrashic tradition is Philo Judaeus's monumental *De opificio mundi,* an extended commentary on the creation story in Genesis. An Alexandrian Jew (ca. 20 B.C.–A.D. 50), Philo brought hellenistic number theory to bear on the biblical text to reveal an intricate allegory, justifying his method on the grounds that Pythagoras and Plato derived their knowledge of the art of numbers from Moses and the Prophets. Philo's work provided a model for subsequent commentators, both Jewish and Christian. His influence is evident in the earliest of the great Christian commentators, St. Clement and his student Origen, at the Christian Catechetical School at Alexandria. Origen made a complete allegorical interpretation of the OT, working his method into an exact science, with threefold interpretation (literal, moral, and mystical, the latter two of which contain the significance; cf. *De principiis,* 1.16). Philo also remained a source for

Jewish commentaries, especially of a mystical kind, which culminated in the Cabala of the later Middle Ages. The NT writings themselves, especially the Gospels, reflect attitudes toward the Law and Prophets similar to those of Philo and Midrash. Regularly, the NT authors assert that the event being described occurred so that the older Scripture might be fulfilled. Jesus' very life becomes a reinterpretation of Scripture.

New Testament numerology thus has an added dimension: Jesus' forty-day sojourn in the wilderness (Luke 4:1-13; cf. Matt. 4:1-11 and Mark 1:12-13) reflects that of Elijah before him (1 Kings 19:8), which in turn reflects the wanderings of the children of Israel in the desert. But Jesus is not to be understood simply as one like Elijah; rather, he is the fulfiller of that pattern — one of whom Elijah and Moses were but prefigurations. Commentators on Luke point out that Elijah, who himself was translated bodily to heaven, as was Enoch before him (Jesus being the third, the fulfillment of that pattern), raised the widow's dead son through a triple ritual by stretching himself in the manner of death across the corpse; but Jesus, in his three-day sojourn with death, raised all the patriarchs. The widow, a figure of the Holy Church, prepared the meal for Elijah with two sticks (1 Kings 17:12); for Jesus the two sticks preparatory for the feast became the Cross (see the collection of glosses on Luke 4:24-26 in Aquinas's *Catena Aurea* and *Biblia Pauperum,* pl. 20).

For the Middle Ages the greatest proponent of numerological analysis of Scripture was St. Augustine, the former professor of rhetoric, whose commentaries on Psalms and the Gospels were regularly cited in the commentaries of the Venerable Bede and Rabanus Maurus and in collections of glosses such as the *Glossa Ordinaria* and Aquinas's *Catena Aurea.* Ignorance of numbers, he insists in *De doctrina Christiana,* 2.16.25, causes things figuratively and mystically expressed to be misunderstood. The science of numbers was not instituted by humans, but rather discovered and investigated by them (2.38.56). Much of the most useful learning on numerology is found in pagan sources, Augustine admits, but it should be regarded as Egyptian gold, to be taken and put to the service of God in unlocking Scripture's hidden secrets (2.42.63). St. Isidore of Seville, in his *Etymologiae,* draws heavily upon Augustine in discussing the importance of numerology: number offers "paths of intelligence" through the material and spiritual universe (3.23.2); without number, all things would perish (3.4.3). Other important texts which espouse Augustine's explication of the science of numerology are Rabanus Maurus, *De Universo* (composed in 22 books), and Hugh of St. Victor, *Exegetica de Scripturis.* The tradition culminated in Jewish and Christian cabalists in the 15th through the 17th cents.

Though Roger Bacon followed Aristotle in ridding scientific study of numerological analysis, wherever

Neoplatonic ideas were admired, so too was numerology. Even so, there is within the Pythagorean-Platonic tradition a kind of numerology devoted to the practical arts which differs from the more mystical number symbolism prominent in scriptural exegesis. Adjacent to St. Augustine, who stressed hidden doctrine in numerological riddles, was Boethius, whose music, arithmetic, and geometry texts and numerological metaphysics in *De Consolatione Philosophiae* ultimately had a far greater impact on European intellectual history than Augustine's theological exercises. Augustine's *De musica* dealt with sounding numbers, heard numbers, voiced numbers, remembered numbers, and discriminating numbers. Boethius's *De Musica* focused the topic more precisely on prosody; it remained a standard text on "music" into the 18th cent. Boethius's *De Arithmetica* studies number proportions, ratios, and sequences; it fastidiously avoids theological or mystical issues and leads toward Roger Bacon and the beginnings of pure mathematics. To the numerologist, however, his *De Consolatione* is the truly fascinating work. Boethius saw deeply into the relationship between arithmetical proportioning and geometric arrangements and human thought processes. Even more than Augustine's *Confessiones, De Consolatione* explores notions of mental health and illness through spatial metaphors and geometric figures pertaining to unity, duplicity, fragmentation, disintegration, sufficiency, potency, centrality, and tangents. Twentieth-century studies like George Poulet's *Metamorphosis of a Circle* or Gaston Bachelard's *Poetics of Space* suggest that this area of number symbolism is as alive today as it was in the 5th cent.

The relationship between biblical exegesis and secular literary and rhetorical theory in the Middle Ages has been well documented in widely divergent approaches by D. W. Robertson, Jr. (*Preface to Chaucer* [1962]), Peter Dronke (*Fabula* [1974]), and Frank Kermode (*Genesis of Secrecy* [1979]). The pagan techniques for unlocking hidden meanings in Scripture were borrowed back from the theologians for the making of secular poetry — Egyptian gold restored to Egypt. But the new poetry, like the *Roman de la Rose,* differed markedly from its classical ancestors, and the difference is largely attributable to delight in enigma and indirection, a delight originating in scriptural exegesis, with its advanced taste for numerology. The new mode tends to be allegorical, sometimes even layered with triple or fourfold perspectives, with abundant interlacement of parallel or analogous situations — all of which techniques are to be understood as forms of numbering. One dominant genre is dream vision, populated with courtly personae who bear strong likenesses to the populace of Boethian psychology. Another is romance, where journeys are measured by other journeys, both within the poem and within the culture. Usually the matter is developed by rhetorical devices such as digression and amplification; sometimes it is so craftily developed as to follow predetermined stanza and line count and in some instances even syllable count, rather than some more obvious Aristotelian principle of unity. The fruit of such an intricate poetic is works like Dante's *Divine Comedy,* Chaucer's *Troilus and Criseyde,* the ME *Pearl,* Spenser's *Epithalamion* and *Faerie Queene,* and Milton's *Paradise Lost,* all of which employ the various forms of numerology extensively.

See also CABALA; GEMATRIA; MARK OF THE BEAST.

Bibliography. Birch, B. C. "Number." *ISBE* 3.556-61; Butler, C. *Number Symbolism* (1970); *Essays on Dante.* Ed. M. Musa (1964); Farbridge, M. H. *Studies in Biblical and Semitic Symbolism* (1923); Fowler, A. *Spenser and the Numbers of Time* (1938); Hopper, V. *Medieval Number Symbolism* (1938); Peck, R. A. "Numerology and Chaucer's *Troilus and Criseyde.*" *Mosaic* 5 (1972), 1-29; "Number as Cosmic Language." In *Essays in the Numerical Criticism of Medieval Literature.* Ed. C. D. Eckhardt (1980), 15-64; Singleton, C. *Dante Studies.* 2 vols. (1954, 1958).   RUSSELL A. PECK

NUNC DIMITTIS *Nunc dimittis* (Luke 2:29-32), named from its first words in the Vg (*Nunc dimittis servum tuum, domine,* "Lord, now lettest thou thy servant depart"), is the canticle sung by Simeon when Mary and Joseph went to the Temple with the infant Jesus for the ritual purification of Mary required by Jewish law (Luke 2:22-24). Simeon, a "just and devout man," had waited for "the consolation of Israel" — a phrase which signifies the advent of Messiah — and the Holy Spirit had revealed to him that he would not die until he had seen "the Lord's Christ" (vv. 25-26). Simeon held the child in his arms and sang a canticle, after which he prophesied to Mary the trials and sorrows the future held for her and the child. An ancient prophetess, Anna, then thanked God in turn for the redemption of Israel (vv. 36-38).

Simeon's speech is the last of four canticles in the first two chapters of Luke's Gospel (1:46-55, 67-79; 2:13-14), and, like the others, it shows the influence of OT ideas and semiticized language. Used liturgically since very early times, it is associated with evening prayers in the Apostolic Constitutions of the 4th cent. and becomes a canticle for compline in the Roman breviary, and hence for Evensong (and Compline) in the *Book of Common Prayer,* where it is sung after the NT lesson. The four canticles form quite different responses to the Incarnation; Mary's *Magnificat* is a song of joy by the mother of Jesus, Zacharias's *Benedictus,* a triumphant paean of the Lord's justice, and the *Gloria* sung by the angels a celestial authentication of the birth of the Messiah. Simeon's song, coming after the Nativity narrative, is peaceful and resolute; it leaves no doubt that the ancient prophecies are fulfilled, and indeed the episode is often taken as fulfilling the prophecy of Malachi that "the LORD shall suddenly come to his temple" (3:1). There may also be an echo of Jacob's deathbed speech (esp. Gen. 49:18), but the strongest OT parallels are from Isaiah (40–55): like the *Magnificat,* the *Nunc dimittis* echoes the servant theology there.

Simeon has often been presumed to be a priest and to be of great age, though neither of these attributes is explicit in Luke's text. The suggestions arise partly from the presence of the 84-year-old widow Anna, and partly from Simeon's having waited so long for the consolation of Israel; that he takes the infant Jesus in his arms has been thought to imply a priestly function. A sermon attributed to St. Augustine calls Simeon "aged" and "long-lived"; Mirk (*De Purificacione Beati Marie, Festial*) calls him "a passyng old man"; and Keble writes (in *The Christian Year*) that Simeon is "by years bowed, / But erect in heart." Donne's Christmas sermon for 1626 says that the idea of Simeon's great age is received "by general tradition from all," and of his priesthood, "[we] have not this in the letter of the story, nor so constantly in the tradition . . . but it is rooted in antiquity, too." Simeon is thus often depicted in art both as old (as in Rembrandt's portrait of himself as Simeon) and as a priest (as by Bellini).

Early and late commentators speak of the spiritual nature of Simeon's vision. *The Myroure of Oure Ladye* says that he sees the infant with his physical eyes but his understanding of the child's significance is spiritual. Aelfric's sermon for the Feast of the Purification emphasizes this spiritual significance; Jesus appears as a child, he says, because he will raise "ða lytlan . . . up to his rice." Simeon's name, Luther notes, means "one who hears," and he associates him therefore with the prophets. Calvin says that the "Spirit of God illuminated" Simeon's eyes "by faith," and he adds that the infant Jesus, having provided such tranquillity to Simeon, should so much the more cause Christians joy, who have the full glory of the Gospels.

Simeon is also said to furnish an example of the proper Christian attitude toward death. St. Cyprian cites the canticle as evidence that death is not an occasion for sorrow (*De mortalitate,* 3.299, 2), and Lancelot Andrewes links this song with the *Benedictus* when he preaches that "Zacharies peace well followed will bring us Simeon's peace" (Christmas sermon, 1616). In this context the psalm is seen to contain two main spiritual themes. One takes its lead from Simeon's assumed age and imminent death, and the other from his joy at seeing "the Lord's Christ."

Simeon appears frequently in biblical poetry of the Middle Ages. In the *Ludus Coventriae* play of the Purification (19) he is called Symeon Justus and identifies himself as an old priest whose sight "begynne to fayle." An angel notes that "The dyrknes of orygynal synne / [Jesus] xal make lyght and clarefye." The canticle is sung in Latin, followed by a translation spoken by Simeon.

Milton presents the Simeon incident obliquely as Mary recalls the Nativity and presentation of the infant Jesus in the Temple (*Paradise Regained,* 1.255-58; 2.87-91). Milton may also have Simeon's words in mind when, at the end of *Samson Agonistes,* the chorus speaks of how God "His servants . . . / With peace and consolation hath dismist / And calm of mind. . . ." Shakespeare echoes the words of Simeon in the opening lines of the aged Bedford's death speech in *1 Henry 6*, 3.1.110-11: "Now quiet soul, depart when heaven please / For I have seen our enemies' overthrow." (There may be a comic parody of the Simeon episode in *2 Henry 6*, 2.1 in the false miraculous restoration of the sight of Simon Simpcox and his unpeaceful departure.) In Browning's *Jochanan Hakkadosh* (31.35) a group of Jewish scholars gather at the bedside of their dying colleague — a figure of great age and wisdom — and ask,

> Among the envious nations, Lamp us, pray,
> Thou the Enlightener! Partest hence in peace?
> Hailest without regret — much less, dismay —
>
> The hour of thine approximate release
> From fleshly bondage soul hath found obstruct?

Browning twice alludes to Simeon's Canticle in *The Ring and the Book* (1.536 and 2.127); in both cases old people are speaking and in both cases the release is ironic.

Simeon's joy is well represented by Robert Southwell's poem on the presentation in *Moeoniae* (1595): "Old *Simeon,* cheape penny worth and sweete / Obteind when thee in armes he did imbrace." This aspect of the *Nunc dimittis* is also present in an early and untitled poem by Gerard Manley Hopkins ("He hath abolished the old drouth"): "I shall live, I shall not die / But I shall when the shocks are stored / See the salvation of the Lord."

In T. S. Eliot's "A Song for Simeon," a companion piece to "The Journey of the Magi," the poet conjoins the *Nunc dimittis* and the *Agnus Dei* of the Mass. Simeon's ominous prophecies figure here more directly than the joy of his song: an ancient man, he meditates on the complexities intertwining his own death and those of his descendants with the birth and death of Christ and the salvation it offers.

Bibliography. Aytoun, R. "The Ten Lucan Hymns in their Original Language." *JTS* 18 (1917), 274-88; Brown, R. E. *The Birth of the Messiah* (1977); Jones, D. "The Background and Character of the Lukan Psalms." *JTS* n.s. 19 (1968), 19-55.   PHILLIP ROGERS

O

O VOS OMNES From the Vg, *O vos omnes qui transitis per viam* ("O you who pass by the way") is found in Lam. 1:12, and in context it represents the mourning of Jerusalem for her having been laid waste (cf. 1:1: "How doth the city sit solitary, that was once full of people!"). This passage became part of the medieval liturgy, and the speaker of it is understood typologically to be Christ or Mary: "Is it nothing to you, all ye that pass by? behold, and see if there be any sorrow like unto my sorrow . . ." (KJV). In various English liturgies it has been part of the liturgy for Holy Week; in the first and second Prayer Books of Edward VI the entire chapter was established as the lection for even-song of Maundy Thursday. The Franciscans, who emphasized spiritual identification with the Passion of Christ, wrote vernacularizations of this passage, especially in its liturgical rendering, and were fond of preaching on the theme, as many notes in the *Fasciculus Morum* attest. The 14th-cent. English Franciscan John Lathbury wrote a commentary on Lamentations sprinkled with verse and containing a discussion of Jeremiah's versification. Influenced also by the sermons of St. Anthony, *Domenica II in Quadragesima* (1.91a), he compares the mourning city to the *mater dolorosa* of the Crucifixion scene. English Friar John Grimestone offers a typical English versification, in which Christ speaks from the cross to "passers-by":

3e þat pasen by þe wey3e,
Abidet a litel stounde!

Be-holdet, al mi felawes,
3ef ani me lik is founde.
To þe tre with nailes þre
Wol fast i hange bounde,
With a spere al þoru mi side
To min herte is mad a wounde. (C. Brown, ed.
Religious Lyrics of the XIVth Century, no. 74)

OBEDIENCE In the OT, obedience (Heb. *shama'*, lit. "hear") describes the proper human response to God: God reveals himself through his "voice" and "word"; individuals must "hear and obey," a response which encompasses physical hearing, trusting receptivity, and obedient action. This is a prime requirement God makes of humans (Jer. 11:7), is better than sacrifice (1 Sam. 15:22), is the cause of Abraham's blessing (Gen. 22:18; 26:5), and is the condition of God's enduring covenant with Israel (Exod. 19:5). The NT interprets Jesus as the one person uniquely obedient (Rom. 5:18), even "unto death" (Phil. 2:8), who, through his own perfect obedience, becomes "author of eternal salvation unto all them that obey him" (Heb. 5:9). This obedience serves in turn as a model for all human relations: husband and wife, child and parent, master and servant (Eph. 5, 6).

The centrality of obedience is maintained and strengthened in the early Church Fathers and in monasticism but acquires new features as well. St. Augustine attributes the Fall to disobedience (*De civ. Dei* 13.1; 14.3;

cf. Rom. 5:18), the waywardness of the body, particularly sexual desire, remaining as "a proof and penalty of their rebellion against God" (14.17). Obedience, on the other hand, is the "mother of all virtues" (14.12), the response to authority which makes possible the "ordered harmony" of the City of God (19.16) and of the Christian life: "This, then, in this world, is the life of virtue. When God commands, man obeys; when the soul commands, the body obeys" (19.27). St. Jerome observes that "one act of obedience is more meritorious than all other virtuous acts put together" (*Hom.* 95) — because all of the others are susceptible to pride. St. Gregory, giving to obedience a role similar to that which Aristotle had assigned to courage, holds that it alone "introduces other virtues into the soul and safeguards their presence" (*Moralia*, 25.14). Monasticism attempts to "return to God by the labour of obedience" (*Rule of St. Benedict*, Prol.), mortifying the individual will, progressing from obedience in small things to obedience in great, from obedience to others to obedience to God. The monk vows poverty, chastity, and obedience — and the greatest of these is obedience (St. John Cassian, *Institutes*, 12; Sulpicius Severus, *Dialogues*, 17).

This integration of all aspects of obedience — personal, familial, social, political, ecclesiastical, and spiritual — and the placement of obedience at the center of the Christian life are in some measure challenged by Aquinas (*Summa Theol.* 2a.2ae.104), who, while defending the consonance of rational obedience with freedom ("to obey one's superior is a debt we owe in accordance with the divine order immanent in all things"), nonetheless insists that obedience is a moral rather than a theological virtue: thus the first sin was not disobedience per se but the pride which led to it; and the measure of faithfulness to God is not obedience per se but the charity which inspires it. As Chaucer's Parson observes, "Obedience is perfit, whan that a man dooth gladly and hastily, with good herte entierly, al that he sholde do" (*Parson's Tale*, 10.673-75).

To the 16th-cent. Reformers the issue was "true obedience," in the search for which they forcefully distinguished aspects of obedience previously yoked together: inner and outer, ecclesiastical and political, human and divine. Luther attacks the "artificial," "external" obedience of monasticism as mere "sacrifice" unless it is preceded by an inner command from God (*Lectures on Genesis*, sup. 12:4; 17:23-27); he frequently envisions that inner obedience as in conflict rather than in harmony with human (and particularly ecclesiastical) authority; one must maintain "obedience to Christ, though all the world crashes to the ground on this account, as it ultimately will" (*Lectures on Psalms*, sup. 110:2). Others distinguish the obedience variously owed to princes, especially when in conflict with God's commands (Wyclif, *English Tracts*, 11.1; Calvin, *Inst.* 4.20.26, 32); owed by princes to God and by subjects to the "godly" prince (Tyndale,

The Obedience of a Christian Man; cf. Luther's work of the same name); owed to princes when in conflict with the church (Gardiner, *Of True Obedience;* More, passim; *Homilies Appointed to Be Read in Churches* [1562], "An Exhortation to Obedience").

English literature of the 16th and 17th cents. frequently draws upon these and other conflicts of obedience, sometimes directly, as in Donne's "Satire 3" — "That thou mayest rightly obey power, her bounds know / Those past, her nature, and name is changed; to be / Then humble to her is idolatry" (100-102), or in Shakespeare's *Henry 5*, where an archbishop's confidence that the "natural" obedience of the honeybee may serve as pattern "to a peopled kingdom" (1.1.183-89) is sharply tested. Sometimes the subject is treated playfully, as in Shakespeare's exploration of authority and obedience between the sexes in *The Taming of the Shrew*. A poet like Spenser can express, almost in the same words, the old Augustinian orthodoxy ("in a body which doth freely yeeld / His partes to reasons rule obedient / And letteth her, that ought, the scepter weeld / All happy peace and goodly government / Is settled there in such establishment" [*Faerie Queene*, 2.9.2]) or the new Petrarchan uncertainty ("Whom then shall I, or heaven or her, obey?" [*Amoretti*, 46]). Others yearn for a "natural" obedience unavailable to mankind: "Oh that with thee [the sun] my Race I now could run / Oh that I could with thee obey / And oh that I did never stray!" (Traherne, "Fourth Day," 14-16).

But obedience is capable of corruption by hypocrisy. As Marlowe's Faustus observes, the devil himself comes "full of obedience and humility" (258). The resulting conflict between true and false, apparent and real, angelic and demonic obedience which figures significantly in Christian tradition is explored in Shakespeare's *Othello* and *King Lear*. In *Othello*, the sinister "obedience" of Iago counterpoints and undermines the perfect, suffering obedience of Desdemona ("Whate'er you [Othello] be, I am obedient" [3.3.89]), which Othello mocks in his furious blindness (4.1.266). Beginning with Cordelia's opening declaration to Lear that she does "Obey you, love you, and most honor you" (1.1.100), "true obedience" in *Lear* is continually in question and in danger of being misprized and lost, overcome by the false "obedience" of Goneril, Regan, and Edmund, reasserted and recovered by Kent and Cordelia — too late.

Milton's is the most extended treatment of the complex psychology of obedience, defined as "that virtue whereby we propose to ourselves the will of God as the paramount rule of our conduct and serve him alone" (*De Doctrina Christiana*, 17.69). In each of his major works the central problem is obedience, whether lost, maintained, or recovered. *Paradise Lost* focuses on disobedience, both that of the unredeemable Satan, "self-tempted, self-deprav'd" (3.130; see esp. his anguished soliloquy, 4.32-113) and that of the redeemable Adam and Eve. *Paradise Regained* demonstrates "one man's

[Jesus'] firm obedience fully tried" (1.4). *Samson Agonistes* portrays Samson's despair at a childlike obedience lost (633-51), and his recovery or achievement of a mature obedience ("If I obey . . . I do it freely" [1372-73]).

Between Milton and the Romantics the emphasis usually falls on the social and moral utility of rational obedience as the indispensable prop of personal, domestic, and political order — the medieval synthesis is secularized and domesticated. Thus Marvell on political authority: "How fit is he to sway / That can so well obey" ("Horatian Ode," 83-84), or Dryden on obedience (and love) according to reason: "Thus we love God, as author of our good / So subjects love just kings, or so they should" ("Eleanora," 180-81). John Wesley, as intent as the monastics on breaking the will by "proper discipline" so that it may be receptive to God's will, stresses obedience to parents (Sermon 96) and pastors (Sermon 97). For Samuel Johnson

> The first duty of subjects is obedience to the laws; such obedience . . . as arises from a conviction of the instability of human virtue, and of the necessity of some coercive power, which may restrain the exorbitancies of passion, and check the career of natural desires. (Sermon 24)

For Johnson, however, obedience is also crucial theologically: "Hope of salvation must be founded on . . . obedience; and where obedience has failed . . . repentance" (Boswell, *Life of Johnson*, 15 Apr. 1778; cf. Sermon 28).

With the Romantic poets, one finds a renewed sense of the possible conflicts between the obedience demanded by society and that owed to nature, to one's genius, or to oneself. Blake couples obedience with insincerity (*Four Zoas*, 3.118) and recognizes as necessary and healthy the disobedience of the infant America (*America*, pl. 11, 1.15). Wordsworth contrasts "a spirit thoroughly faithful to itself" with "society's unreasoning herd" which is "glad to be rocked on in safe obedience" (*Prelude*, 10.167-78; cf. *Excursion*, 9.113-28). Shelley takes the most extreme position, asserting that "The man / Of virtuous soul commands not, nor obeys" and describing obedience as the "Bane of all genius, virtue, freedom, truth" which "Makes slaves of men, and, of the human frame / A mechanized automaton" ("Queen Mab," 3.174-80).

The debate is joined by Victorian writers who, while in varying degrees sympathetic to the claims of the self and its needs, feel that these can or must be reconciled with some sort of obedience. Matthew Arnold observes that fate forces a person "to obey / Even in his own despite his being's law" ("The Buried Life," 36-37), counsels those who have abandoned theism to "More strictly, then, the inward judge obey" ("The Better Part"), and reserves highest praise for him "who dares / To self-selected good / Prefer obedience to the primal law" ("Antigone," 28-30). Carlyle concedes that obedience cannot be unquestioning, but insists that it is still essential to both individual and society: "Wise command, wise obedience: the capability of these two is the net measure of culture, and human virtue, in every man. . . . He is a good man that can command and obey; he that cannot is a bad" (*Latter-Day Pamphlets*, "New Downing Street").

Ruskin, believing that true liberty comes only through restraint, makes obedience the seventh of his lamps of architecture, "the crowning grace of all the rest; that principle . . . to which Polity owes its stability, Life its happiness, Faith its acceptance, Creation its continuity." Obedience, moreover, is the fundamental and sustaining virtue of the ideal society of *Fors Clavigera*: "The practice of faith and obedience to some of our fellow creatures is the alphabet by which we learn the higher obedience to heaven; and it is not only needful to the prosperity of all noble united action, but essential to the happiness of all living spirits" (6.67; cf. 4.37, 45). Hilaire Belloc's "Bad Child" books, "A Moral Alphabet," and especially "Cautionary Tales" illustrate the reaction to this strong Victorian emphasis on obedience.

Among the moderns, the treatment of obedience is diverse, not only because of its many ramifications — theological, political, social, and moral — but also in accord with inherited positions (the Catholic and Protestant, Romantic and Victorian debates are still, in various forms, alive), as well as individual interest and temperament. D. H. Lawrence tried several possibilities ranging from the Augustinian/Ruskinian ("Learn they must to obey, for all harmony is discipline / And only in harmony with others the single soul can be free" ["Discipline"]), to regretting, with Milton and Traherne, loss of the "glad freedom of obedience" ("Monologue of a Mother"), to Romantic impatience ("Louisa was angry to see him standing there, obedient and acquiescent. He ought to show himself a man" ["Daughters of the Vicar," 185]), and Romantic hope ("The few must look into the eyes of the gods, and obey the look / in the eyes of the gods / And the many must obey the few" ["False Democracy and Real"]).

Several aspects of the problem of obedience remain central. As ever, it is seen to be a specifically and characteristically human question: Yeats's swans, so much simpler than their observer, "cannot tell / What's good or bad, or what it is to triumph / At the perfection of one's own obedience" ("The Wild Swans at Coole," 107-09). As ever, there is a longing for an "unfallen" obedience: "Heyt envied the Chinaman's obedience to his instincts, the powerful simplicity of purpose which made his existence appear almost automatic in the mysterious precision of its facts" (Conrad, *Victory*). As ever, people suffer conflicting claims on their obedience, whatever the sources of those claims, God or others, society or self: Joyce's Stephen Daedalus, "when the moment had come for him to obey the call [to ordination] . . . had turned aside, obeying a wayward instinct"; the *Portrait* ends with the words *non serviam*. As ever, individuals search for a mature obedience, both faithful and free: Robert Frost wonders aloud "Why is his [mankind's] nature forever so hard to teach / That though there is no fixed line between wrong and right / There are roughly zones whose laws must be obeyed?" ("There Are Roughly Zones," 11-13).

    Bibliography. Cary-Elwes, C. *Law, Liberty, and Love: A Study in Christian Obedience, Foundation of European Civilization* (1951).   ROBERT WILTENBURG

OF MAKING MANY BOOKS   Included in the summary of vanities in Ecclesiastes is the vanity of summarizing: "And further, by these, my son, be admonished: of making many books there is no end; and much study is a weariness of the flesh" (12:12). The phrase has appealed to many a weary modern student, but in late antiquity and the Middle Ages when books were hand-copied, hence scarce and treasured, the verse was not so much commented upon as rationalized to these circumstances. Citing the passage, Hugh of St. Victor interprets the injunction as a commending restraint: concerning books other than Scripture, including commentary on Scripture, "it is necessary to use great discretion, lest what has been sought for our recovery may be found to stifle us. . . . The number of books is infinite; do not pursue infinity! When no end is in sight, there can be no rest. Where there is no rest, there is no peace. Where there is no peace, God cannot dwell" (*Didascalicon*, 5.7). Richard de Bury in his *Philobiblion* relates the verse to the necessity of manual copying and remanufacture of books made necessary by decay: "It is needful to replace the volumes that are worn out with age by fresh successors, that the perpetuity of which the individual is by nature incapable may be secured to the species; and hence it is that the Preacher says: *Of making many books there is no end*" (16.1). After the Reformation the observation of Matthew Henry that the Preacher implies that canonical Scripture "is as much as God saw fit to give us, saw fit for us, and saw us fit for," becomes a commonplace among Puritan and Separatist writers. "Let men write ever so many books for the conduct of human life, write till they have tired themselves with much study, they cannot give better instructions than those we have from the word of God" (*Comm. on the Whole Bible*, 4.1051).

    The reading suggested by Shakespeare in *Love's Labour's Lost* is prompted by a suspicion of excessive intellectualism, a suspicion voiced by Berowne in his springtime counsel to the king of Navarre:

> Why, all delights are vain, but that most vain
> Which, with pain purchased, doth inherit pain:
> As, painfully to pore upon a book,
> To seek the light of truth, while truth the while
> Doth falsely blind the eyesight of his look. (1.1.72-76)

Berowne's words represent an acknowledgment that everything is "fit in his place and time" (1.1.99; cf. Eccl. 3:1), as well as a plea for common sense. In his

Areopagitica Milton argues that one of the functions of God-given reason is to make a rational choice among available books: "Solomon informs us, that much reading is a weariness of the flesh; but neither he, nor other inspired author, tells us that such or such reading is unlawful; yet, certainly had God thought good to limit us herein, it had been much more expedient to have told us what was unlawful, than what was wearisome." Thomas Fuller in *The Holy and Profane State* begins his chapter "Of Books" by averring: "Solomon saith truly, 'Of making many books there is no end,' so insatiable is the thirst of men therein: as so endless is the desire of many in buying and reading them." Elizabeth Barrett Browning cites the phrase conventionally in the first chapter of her *Aurora Leigh;* numerous other 19th- and 20th-cent. authors allude to "a weariness of the flesh" — and not always in contexts which recall the first part of the verse. In this vein Hardy observes of one of his characters in *A Pair of Blue Eyes* that "he saw nothing outside himself tonight; and what he saw within was a weariness of the flesh" (chap. 10).

    See also VANITY OF VANITIES.

OFFERING   *See* ATONEMENT; ATONEMENT, DAY OF; EUCHARIST; PASSOVER; SUBSTITUTION; TEMPLE.

OG OF BASHAN   Og was the king of Bashan, the high fertile plain east of the Sea of Galilee, noted for its grain crops, good cattle, and strong men. Paralleling Amos's denigration of luxury-loving women as "ye kine of Bashan," its gigantic and typically ferocious men were called "bulls of Bashan." The most familiar of many OT references to Bashan is that found in Ps. 22:12, where the speaker in his extremity complains that "strong bulls of Bashan have beset me round," which is as much as to say, "I am oppressed by brutes on all sides" (cf. v. 13). Deut. 3:1-14 records a battle against Og and his forces by Moses and the Israelites (cf. Num. 21:33-36), adding that among the trophies recovered from the defeated army of Bashan was the iron bedstead of Og which measured nine by four cubits (about 13 × 16 ft.), an indication of his enormous physical stature. Og's lands were later apportioned by Moses to the tribe of Manasseh, the son of Joseph (Num. 32:33).

    In Shakespeare's *Antony and Cleopatra*, Mark Antony scolds Cleopatra for entertaining Thyreus's wooing on behalf of his master Caesar, bellowing: "O, that I were / Upon the hill of Basan, to outroar / The horned herd! For I have savage cause" (3.13.126-28). Dryden makes the apparently corpulent Thomas Shadwell play Og's part in *Absalom and Achitophel* (2.459-65):

> Og, from a Treason Tavern rowling home.
> Round as a Globe, and Liquor'd ev'ry chink,
> Goodly and Great he Sayls behind his Link.
> With all this Bulk there's nothing lost in Og,
> For ev'ry inch that is not Fool is Rogue:

A Monstrous mass of foul corrupted matter,
As all the Devils had spew'd to make the batter.

Oliver Wendell Holmes, in his *Autocrat of the Breakfast Table*, reports of his British hosts that they were exceedingly fond of puns, as when "Lord Bacon playfully declared himself a descendant of 'Og, the King of Bashan'" (chap. 1). In Scott's *Ivanhoe* "man and steed rushing on each other like wild bulls of Bashan!" illustrates the cliché of brute strength and ferocity, while in Butler's *The Way of All Flesh* "that bellowing bull of Bashan, the village blacksmith, strikes a sounder key of remembrance."

OHOLAH AND OHOLIBAH   See AHOLAH AND AHOLIBAH.

OIL OF MERCY   The 19th chap. of the apocryphal Gospel of Nicodemus (chap. 3 of the *Descensus Christi ad Infernos*) provides the source for the legend of the oil of mercy. When Seth returns to Eden to win it for his father, Adam, the angel guarding the entrance describes the tree of life at whose top is a baby, the "oil of mercy." In the late 13th-cent. *Cursor Mundi* (1355-62),

þis barn . . . þat þou has sene,
Is goddes sun wit-outen wene;
þi fader sin now wepes he
þat he sal clens sum time sal be,
Quen þe plenteȝ sal cum o time;
þis is þe oile þat was hight him;
Til him and til his progeni.

("This child that you have seen
is God's son without doubt.
Your father's sin he now weeps over.
The time shall come when he shall cleanse it:
(that is,) when the fullness of time shall come;
this is the oil which was promised to him,
to him and to his progeny.")

See also SETH.   ERNEST N. KAULBACH

OLD ADAM   See ADAM; OLD AND NEW.

OLD AND NEW   As a component of the dual biblical motif old/new, the image of "old" is relevant only in relation to the image of "new." Otherwise, oldness per se in the Hebrew canon applies primarily either to old age, concerning which the texts display a marked ambivalence (i.e., honor and reverence, fear of the attendant ills, and special repugnance at the idea of sinfulness associated with it), or to references to old and traditional ways. The attitude toward the latter, associated with the time of the patriarchs and of Moses, is of course wholly positive, and later biblical writers, contrasting those old ways with their own degenerate or decadent eras, call for renewal of those days of old (e.g., Lam. 5:21). In contrast, nothing is more

anathema to the upholders of the Hebrew faith in the Lord God than the introduction of "new gods" (Judg. 5:8).

Nevertheless, despite this veneration of ancient ways and the suspicion of novelty in the Hebrew scriptures, the idea of renewal in certain poetic and prophetic texts is so intense as to constitute a theme of newness. The frequent refrain in the Psalms of singing a "new song" unto the Lord (Pss. 33:3; 40:3; 96:1; 98:1; 144:9; 149:1) not only celebrates God's redemptive action but is intended to actualize it as a new experience of grace within the Temple liturgy; for Isaiah the "new song" is an eschatological hymn, an anticipation of the new Exodus out of exile and the inauguration of a messianic age (Isa. 42:10). In Isaiah God proclaims that "I will do a new thing" (Isa. 43:19; cf. 42:9; 48:6), and so overwhelming is the promised vision that, against the whole tenor of the theme of remembrance in the Hebrew scriptures, Israel is even enjoined, "Remember ye not the former things, neither consider the things of old" (Isa. 43:18). In this new age Israel will be given a new name (Isa. 62:12); more important, she will be given a new heart and a new spirit (Ezek. 11:9; 18:31; 36:26). Ezekiel sees this new age as a virtual re-creation of Paradise (Ezek. 47:12), and Isaiah envisions what Kosnetter (744) calls "an eschatological re-creation of the entire cosmos" in the ecstatic verse "For behold, I create new heavens and a new earth: and the former things shall not be remembered, nor come into mind" (Isa. 65:17; cf. 66:22). Finally, then, this newness can extend even to God's entering into a "new covenant" with Israel (Jer. 31:31).

This theme of radical renewal / newness occurs in certain texts of the OT apocrypha which envision a "new creation when heaven and earth and all that they contain will be renewed" (Jub. 1:29; cf. 4:26 and 1 Enoch 72:1; 91:16). The Qumran community viewed itself as called to a life of purification lived according to a new covenant imperfectly realized in this life but fulfilled at the end of time (see H. Kosmala, *Hebraer-Essener-Christen* [1959], 226ff.). As Hanson concludes (407), in apocalyptic eschatology *Endzeit* resembles and fulfills the paradisal *Urzeit* in the providential history of Israel.

Thus the background for the NT theme of "newness" and the new/old dichotomy is fully indicated within OT and Intertestamental literature, especially in the context of apocalyptic eschatology. Two words —*kainos* and *neos* —are used to convey the meaning for "new" in the NT, both being used to render Heb. *hadash* ("recent, fresh, unused," or "new, not yet in existence"). These terms incorporate both temporal and qualitative aspects. Qualitatively, the NT idea of newness implies at once elements of continuity, change, finality, and self-actualization, characteristics which are especially evident in the theme of newness in Revelation, whose roots are deeply planted in traditions of apocalyptic eschatology.

In Revelation, as Harrisville shows, continuity with OT eschatology is everywhere evident: the Spirit bestows a "new name" (Rev. 2:17; 3:13), and, upon the Lamb's opening of the seventh seal of the scroll, "the singing of the 'new song' in Rev. 5:9 implies that a totally new state in the unfolding of the divine purpose has been reached. . . . The song itself is a song of deliverance, sung on the basis of the redemption wrought by Christ." Moreover, the "new song" is an instance of performative or self-actualizing language: "the 'new song' does not merely imply, but actually leads to" the redemptive moment (Harrisville, 75). The culmination of the eschaton in Revelation is the concluding vision of the heavenly Jerusalem, ushered in with the opening words of the 21st chapter:

And I saw a new heaven and a new earth; for the first heaven and the first earth were passed away, and there was no more sea. And I John saw the holy city, new Jerusalem, coming down from God out of heaven, prepared as a bride adorned for her husband. And I heard a great voice out of heaven saying, Behold, the tabernacle of God is with men. And he will dwell with them, and they shall be his people, and God himself shall be with them, and be their God. And God will wipe away all tears from their eyes; and there shall be no more death, neither sorrow, nor crying, neither shall there be any more pain: for the former things have passed away. And he who sat upon the throne said, Behold, I make all things new. (Rev. 21:1-5)

(This "permanent renewal of the cosmic whole" shows that what Bultmann calls "the 'total otherness of the Christian situation' applies not just to men," but also to all of creation [Kosnetter, 748].)

Other NT reflections of OT prophetic and apocalyptic ideas are the bestowing of a new spirit in tongues of fire, which enabled the disciples to speak with new tongues (Acts 2:1-4; cf. Mark 16:17; Heb. 6:4-6), and the reformation of life according to a "new and living way" (Heb. 10:20), "the newness of spirit" (Rom. 7:6). But the NT also introduces the more graphic image of conversion, *metanoia,* and of a person's being "born again" (John 3:3; 1 Pet. 1:23). As explained by St. Paul, this new life is uniquely realized in the Christian initiate's participation in Christ's death and Resurrection:

What shall we say then? Shall we continue in sin, that grace my abound? God forbid. How shall we, that are dead to sin, live any longer therein? Know ye not, that so many of us as were baptized into Jesus Christ were baptized into his death? Therefore we are buried with him by baptism into death: that like as Christ was raised up from the dead by the glory of the Father, even so we also should walk in newness of life. (Rom. 6:1-4)

In this mystery, contrasted in Galatians with the old sign of circumcision, the disciple becomes a "new creature" (KJV; RSV: "new creation"; Gal. 6:15; cf. 2 Cor. 5:17; Eph. 2:14-15).

Consequently, a major Pauline theme becomes the purging of the "old" and its replacement by the "new,"

e.g., in 1 Cor. 5:7-8, where Paul allegorizes the Hebraic Passover practice of cleansing a household of all old leaven in preparation for the Feast of Unleavened Bread:

Purge out therefore the old leaven, that ye may be a new lump, as ye are unleavened. For even Christ our passover is sacrificed for us. Therefore let us keep the feast, not with old leaven, nor with the leaven of malice and wickedness; but with the unleavened bread of sincerity and truth.

Another key Pauline metaphor is the "old man," an image of the former life, dominated by the Law and by sin, in contrast to the new life in Christ: "Knowing this, that our old man is crucified with him. . . . Now if we be dead with Christ, we believe that we shall also live with him. . . . Likewise, reckon ye also yourselves to be dead indeed unto sin, but alive unto God through Jesus Christ our Lord" (Rom. 6:5-11). Similarly, Colossians and Ephesians admonish their hearers to "put off the old man with its deeds and . . . put on the new man, which is renewed in knowledge after the image of him that created him" (Col. 3:9-10; cf. Eph. 4:22-24), both in the context of sections developing the contrast between what Ephesians calls the former ways of "darkness" and the ways appropriate to "children of light" (Eph. 5:8).

It is evident that the theme of newness in the NT is distinctly bound up with complementary ideas about the supplanting of the old. Hence, a distinct keynote in the NT is the idea that Jesus' words represent a "new doctrine" (Mark 1:27) in terms both of content and of his presumption of divine authority, which were a scandal to the Pharisees. (By contrast, the Athenians were at first superficially attracted to the novelty of Paul's "new doctrine" [Acts 17:19-21].)

In the fourth Gospel Jesus says outright, "A new commandment I give to you, That ye love one another" (John 13:34) —which by the time of the Johannine epistles has become "no new commandment, but an old commandment" —yet always "new" in its renewed application (1 John 2:7-8; 2 John 5). And, of course, the tenor of the Matthean Sermon on the Mount and its parallels is Jesus' revisionist teaching formula: "Ye have heard it said. . . . But I say unto you . . ." (Matt 5:21-48), an attitude to the old laws and ordinances which Jesus describes as his coming "not to destroy but to fulfil" (Matt. 5:17).

The paradigm metaphor to express the early Church's understanding of the relation of Jesus' teachings to former traditions is embodied in Jesus' answer to the question about why his disciples did not fast as John the Baptist's disciples did:

No man putteth a piece of new cloth unto an old garment, for that which is put in to fill it up taketh from the garment, and the rent is made worse. Neither do men put new wine into old bottles; else the bottles break, and the wine runneth out, and the bottles perish: but they put new wine into new bottles, and both are preserved. (Matt. 9:16-17 and parallels)

Finally, the cornerstone of NT newness theology is, of course, the concept of the "new covenant" itself. (The familiar term *testament* derives from the Latin *testamentum,* adopted as the equivalent for the Greek word *diathēkē,* employed by the LXX to render the Heb. *berit,* "covenant.") This term, which has come to be most commonly associated with the collection of Christian canonical Scripture itself (a usage dating back to the 2nd or 3rd cents.), originally was associated with the words of Jesus at the Last Supper in the Synoptic Gospels and recalled also by Paul: "This cup is the new testament in my blood" (1 Cor. 11:25; cf. Matt. 26:28-29; Mark 14:24-25; Luke 22:20), alluding to the blood of the "old covenant" in Exod. 24:28. Paul's understanding of this "New Covenant" is that "the sacrificial principle has been perfected in Christ. The sacrificial system is ended, not because it is repudiated, but because it is perfected" (*Interpreter's Bible,* 10.683). Paul defines the contrast between the "old testament" (2 Cor. 3:14) and the new in terms of spirit and letter, for the new covenant is written "not in tables of stone, but in fleshly tables of the heart" (3:3), and "the letter killeth, but the spirit giveth life" (3:6). Moreover, as Paul argues in Romans, "now we are delivered from the law, that being dead wherein we were held; that we should serve in newness of spirit, and not in the oldness of the letter" (7:6; cf. Gal. 2:19).

The contrast between old and new dispensations is conveyed also in the allegory of the children of Hagar (children of slavery and the Law) and the children of Sarah (children of freedom and the promise) in Gal. 4:21-28. But it is developed most elaborately in the extended typological analysis of Hebrews, in the course of which it is explicitly explained that when Christ referred to a new covenant, "he hath made the first old [KJV; cf. RSV: 'obsolete']. Now that which decayeth and waxeth old is ready to vanish away" (Heb. 8:13). Throughout the Epistle to the Hebrews, "the relationship between the old and new is that of copy to pattern, shadow to substance. There is therefore a principle of continuity between them" (*IB* 11.684).

As the understanding of the relationship between two sets of historical realities, a prior reality (the old "type") whose full significance and realization are embodied in a succeeding reality (the new "antitype"), typology is indeed at the heart of biblical theology. Within the framework of the OT itself, as Daniélou has shown, "we see the Prophets proclaim a new Exodus of which the first was the type, as they also proclaimed a second cataclysm of which the Flood was the type" (154), but typological analysis, which viewed OT persons and events as being uniquely "fulfilled" by NT realities, became the hallmark of Christian exegesis. "Typology," as Northrop Frye puts it, "is a one-directional and irreversible conception of

history" (*The Great Code* [1982], 86). Daniélou explains, in typology

> There is no question of nostalgia for some remote ideal, as in the case of Greek descriptions of a Golden Age. The past is only recalled as a foundation for future hope. As God had set man in Paradise so must Israel wait to be brought into a New Paradise. This is precisely the essence of typology, which is to show how past events are a figure of events to come. (12)

Not intended to be a system of contrasting binary "opposites," typology was intended to present a harmonious but hierarchical relationship between "old" and "new." Emile Mâle offers extensive evidence of how the iconographic programs in 13th-cent. stained glass at Bourges, Chartres, Tours, Lyons, and Rouen all illustrate "the concordance of the two Testaments" in the systematic grouping of OT scenes around their NT "fulfillment" (140-51), a visual language common right up through the 15th cent. in printed block books such as the *Biblia Pauperum.* Nonetheless, in practice, it is difficult not to see this typological relationship between Old Law and New Law, Old Song and New Song, Synagogue and Church, as a set of oppositions. In medieval images of the Crucifixion, e.g., not only does one recognize how the Church, as a second Eve, is born in the blood and water flowing from the side of Christ, the second Adam, but one sees, as in a window at Bourges, how

> Jesus not only founded the Church, but abolished the authority of the Synagogue. . . . On the one side the Church, crowned and wearing a nimbus and with a triumphal standard in her hand, receives in a chalice the water and blood that flow from the Savior's side. On the other the Synagogue with blindfolded eyes, her crown falling from her head, still grasps in one hand the broken staff of her standard, and lets fall from the other the tables of the Law. (Mâle, 188-89; for discussion of similar images, see Robertson, 195, 303)

Mâle cites a single illustration of the Crucifixion from the *Hortus Deliciarum* as an epitome of the iconographic symbolism of old/new:

> To the right of the Cross are seen the centurion, the Virgin Mary, the penitent thief and lastly the Church, figured as a woman riding a hybrid animal in whose four heads the emblems of the evangelists can be recognized. To the left are the man with the sponge, St. John [a figure of the Old Law because he deferred to Peter in entering Christ's tomb], the impenitent thief and lastly the Synagogue mounted on an ass, that obstinate beast which when it should go forward draws back. The general meaning is given by the rent veil of the Temple placed at the top of the composition, clearly showing that the subject is the substitution of the New for the Old Law. (192-93)

The dangerously anti-Semitic tendency of this symbolism is evident; Mâle relates it to a desire to convince the Jews of the futility of their faith, or rather to reassure the faithful in the face of a proud and stiff-necked people who alone claimed to be able to expound the Scriptures. The great figures of the Church and of the Synagogue with veiled eyes on the facade of Notre Dame at Paris proclaimed to the Jew that the Bible had no longer any meaning for the Synagogue, and to the Christian that it held no riddle for the Church. (193)

Robertson offers an extensive analysis of old / new themes in medieval art and literature:

> In theological terms the melodies of love are the "New Song" of St. Paul's "New Man" and the "Old Song" of the "Old Man," who represents the inherited evil habit of the flesh. These songs, or melodies, are frequently illustrated in the visual arts of the Middle Ages. (127)

Robertson adduces a series of illustrative examples from 13th- and 14th-cent. psalters and books of hours in which sinners, devils, or grotesques playing drums or bagpipes in association with scenes of lechery or discord are contrasted with saintly or angelic figures singing or playing celestial harmonies on harps or lyres. Moreover, Robertson explains, "Either of the two 'songs' might be accompanied by a dance. . . . Variations on what might be thought of as a New Dance to accompany the New Song and what was actually called the 'Old Dance' were common in late medieval art," in which images of angelic dance (the best-known example of which is probably Botticelli's *Mystical Nativity*) are contrasted with images of lewd profane dancing; the latter

> may be compared with the usual illustrations of the dance of Deduit, which is certainly not the "New" dance, in the *Roman de la Rose*. . . . We are invited to this dance by Oiseuse, and the music provided, which here involves a bagpipe, leads us to the domination of Cupid and Venus. (127-30, figs. 29-42)

Chaucer, who translated the *Roman de la Rose*, reflects this symbology of old and new song and old and new dance (see *Roman de la Rose*, 4300: "For she knew all the olde daunce") in his own writings. The good Parson reminds his listeners, in the words of St. Augustine, that "But he be penytent for his olde synful lyf, he may nat bigynne the newe clene lif" (*Canterbury Tales*, 10.95-100). We do hear the celestial harmonies of the new song on occasion, as in the song to St. Valentine at the end of *The Parliament of Fowls*, the Prologue to the *Legend of Good Women*, the song St. Cecelia sings alone in her heart (*Second Nun's Tale*, 8.134-40), or that which the young boy sings with fatal consequences "thurghout the Juerie" in the *Prioress's Tale* (7.579-85).

More commonly, in Chaucer one encounters references to the old song. In the well-known description of the Wife of Bath it is said that "Of remedies of love she knew her chaunce, / For she koude of that art the olde daunce" (*General Prologue*, 1.475-76), and the worldly wise physician reminds governesses that they have been put in position either for their "honestee" or because, on the contrary, "ye han falle in freletee, / And knowen wel ynough the olde daunce" (*Physician's Tale*, 6.78-79). There are numerous more straightforward allusions in the *Tales*, especially by the Parson, to the "olde lawe" (*Parson's Tale*, 10.835-40, 885-90) and to "olde folies" (10.970-75) and the "old synful lyf" (10.95-100; cf. *Tale of Melibee*, 7.2650-55; *Miller's Tale*, 2.453). The Merchant's reference to the old song —"Swiche olde lewed words used he" (*Merchant's Tale*, 4.2149) —is unintentionally ironic in that old Januarie's call to dalliance is actually a paraphrase of the Song of Solomon, which in medieval exegesis was understood to refer to the spiritual marriage of Christ and the Church. Of course, Januarie, who is "oold and may nat see" (*Merchant's Tale*, 4.2168), is foremost among Chaucer's many allusions to the Pauline "old man" of sin, along with the Old Man of the *Pardoner's Tale*.

While Chaucer's use of the new / old theme is particularly rich, other examples also occur in medieval English literature. (There are, of course, references to relevant biblical texts in OE, e.g., to the "niwan lofsong" [Rev. 14:3] and "niwe heofon" [Rev. 21:1] in Aelfric's homilies [1.90, 618] or the reference to the "nywne lofsong" [Ps. 98:1] in *Harrowing of Hell*, 137.) References to the theme of the Old and the New Law are common in the medieval mystery plays, as in the words of the Fourth Burgess in the York Skynners' play:

> Oft in our Temple has he preached
> Against the people that lived wrong,
> And also new laws has he teached
> Against our laws we used so long,
> And said plainly,
> The old shall waste, the new shall gang —
> That we shall see. (25.143-46)

Later in the same play Zaccheus testifies how people flock to Jesus, "New laws to hear. / Our old laws outworn now they hate, / But hold his dear" (403-6). And in the York Baksteres' play, Jesus himself says at the Last Supper, "Of Moyses' law here make I an end"; and in place of the old paschal sacrifice, "In that stead shall be set / A new law us between," a new law which requires that "In heart they must be clean and chaste" (27.34-37; cf. Chester 15.1.73).

The theme of "tydings new" is central to all the Nativity plays (e.g., York 15.1.72), and that occasions a glad new song; as one of the shepherds says in the Towneley "Second Shepherd's Play," "Be mery and not sad; of myrth is our sang" (668). The motifs of new joy, new bliss, new love, and the new song are found throughout the medieval English lyric, especially in a Nativity context (see C. Brown, *Religious Lyrics of the XVth Century*, nos. 73-84, or R. Greene, *Early English Carols*, nos. 117-25, 180, 239, 256) or in the context of heavenly joy, as in relation to Mary's assumption (e.g., Brown, *XVth Century*, 36.54; 39.55), and these references are in counterpoint to the "old trespasse" (131.19), "oure mescheves old" (30.22), and the "olde serpent" (135.42, 56, 70).

"New Year" references abound in *Sir Gawain and the Green Knight,* both in terms of the seasonal time of the narrative and with reference to the poem's liturgical implications: January 1, the Feast of the Circumcision, is the day on which Sir Gawain receives his slight cut on the neck from the Green Knight, marking his spiritual renewal, the "new order" which will be symbolized by the Order of the Garter at Arthur's court. But among the works of the Pearl Poet, it is *Pearl* itself which most deeply expresses the theme of spiritual renewal. The narrator's "pearl," a spotless spouse of God, one of the "newe fryt to God ful due" (894), explains to him the vision of the New Jerusalem in terms of the Apocalypse: "þe olde Jerusalem to vnderstonde / For þere þe olde gulte wat, don to slake / Bot þe nwe þat lyȝt of Godeȝ sonde / þe apostel in Apocallypce in theme con take" (941-44; "In the old Jerusalem, understand, / The ancient sin He could forsake. / But the New ordained through God's command / The Apostle in Apocalypse could take / As theme" [trans. S. DeFord, 1967]). She rehearses for the narrator St. John's vision of "þe nwe cyte o Jerusalem" (792) and the new song which resounds therein (877-82; 985-88). The familiar counterpart in medieval continental literature is Dante's vision of the Earthly Paradise and the new song in *Purgatorio,* 29-33 and his vision of the Celestial Rose of the Heavenly City in *Paradiso,* 30.

In the English Renaissance, Jonson consoles himself for the death of *his* muse, Lady Venetia Digby, by envisioning her place among the angels

> That, planted round, there sing before the *Lamb,*
> A new Song to his praise, and great *I AM:*
> And she doth know, out of the shade of Death,
> What 't is t'enjoy, an everlasting breath! ("Eupheme 9. Elegie on my Muse," 89-92)

In a more philosophical vein, Donne deals with the theme in his spiritual meditation *An Anatomy of the World: The First Anniversary,* reflecting on how a new world is ever recycled from the decay of the old; Mistress Elizabeth Drury has died, but

> The twilight of her memory doth stay;
> Which from the carcasse of the old world, free
> Creates a new world, and new creatures bee
> Produce'd: the matter and the stuffe of this,
> Her vertue, and the forme our practice is. (74-78)

Spenser's Redcrosse Knight is offered a vision of the heavenly Jerusalem after being led to a high mount such as that on which Moses received the Old Law, "writ in stone / With bloudy letters by the hand of God, / The bitter doome of death and balefull mone," but here the site of the city of grace, "The new *Hierusalem,* that God has built / For those to dwell in that are chosen his" (*Faerie Queene,* 1.10.53-57). After receiving this vision, "The

knight with that old Dragon fights" (1.11 arg.). The polar opposition of the Lady of the New Jerusalem and the Old Dragon, derived from the Apocalypse, becomes one of the most familiar expressions of the new / old motif in Western literature.

Shakespeare's explicit use of the biblical old / new motif is best exemplified in his references to "old Adam," in particular, when the queen invokes a vernacular version of typology in her response to a gardener's report that Richard II has been deposed:

> Thou, old Adam's likeness,
> Set to dress this garden, how dares
> Thy harsh rude tongue sound this unpleasing news?
> What Eve, what serpent, hath suggested thee
> To make a second fall of cursed man? (*Richard 2,* 3.4.73-77)

As many critics have suggested, Falstaff is perhaps the most fully developed representation in English literature of the Pauline "Old Man" — "that old white-bearded Satan," as Prince Hal calls him (*2 Henry 4,* 2.4.463). And despite Falstaff's eloquent defense — "if to be old and merry be a sin . . . banish plump Jack, and banish all the world" — Hal vows that he will; at the end of *2 Henry 4,* Hal, now King Henry V, rebuffs Falstaff precisely as the Pauline "Old Man":

> I know thee not, old man. Fall to thy prayers.
> How ill white hairs become a fool and jester!
> I have long dreamt of such a kind of man,
> So surfeit-swell'd, so old, and so profane,
> But, being awak'd, I do despise my dream. (5.5.47-51)

Among other Shakespearean references to old, sinful ways is the famous comic line "a trick of the old rage" (*Much Ado About Nothing,* 5.2.417), and there are several proverbial sayings about making new garb out of an old garment (*Merry Wives of Windsor,* 1.3.17; *Antony and Cleopatra,* 1.2.168) and about the impropriety of mixing old and new clothes (*The Taming of the Shrew,* 3.2.43; *Romeo and Juliet,* 3.1.28) —which may reflect the Gospel saying about new wine in old bottles. Finally, there is Antony's profane echoing of the biblical vision of a new heaven and new earth in his protestation of love to Cleopatra (*Antony and Cleopatra,* 1.1.16-17):

> Cleo. I'll set a bourn how far to be belov'd.
> Ant. Then must thou needs find out new heaven, new
> earth.

Shakespeare's most memorable allusion to the theme of a new world is, however, Miranda's exclamation

> O, wonder!
> How many goodly creatures are there here!
> How beauteous mankind is! O brave new world,
> That has such people in 't! (*The Tempest,* 5.1.183-86).

The entire theme of *The Tempest* can be thought of as renewal, or redemptive transformation, emblematized in the miraculously renewed clothing of the shipwrecked sailors (2.1.71-74) and Ferdinand's declaration that he has received "a second life" (5.1.195).

Donne may be alluding to the Pauline idea of becoming a "new creature," in "Elegie 28: Loves Progress" ("But if I love it, 'tis because 'tis made / By our new nature" [15-16]) and in the "The Extasie" ("Wee then, who are this new soule, know / of what we are composed, and made" [45-46]).

Herbert makes conventional reference to our "old foes," Sin and Satan ("Decay," 13), and he trembles equally for "th' old sinnes and new doctrines of our land" ("The Priesthood," 33), elaborating on the theme in "The Church Militant":

As new and old *Rome* did one Empire twist;
So both together are one Antichrist, . . .
Thus Sinne triumphs in Western *Babylon,*
Yet not as Sinne, but as Religion. . . .
Old and new *Babylon* are to hell and night,
As is the moon and sunne to heav'n and light. (205-16)

In contrast, Jesus in his parables, says Herbert, put the old and the new in a proper, harmonious relation: with "Nature serving God . . . for he was the true householder, who bringeth out of his treasure things new and old; the old things of Philosophy, and the new of Grace; and maketh the one serve the other" (*A Priest to the Temple,* 23). The essence of repentance, for Herbert, lies in "renouncing sin, and turning unto God in truth of heart, and newnesse of life" (33). The fulfillment of a Christian life is a Christian death, "when souls shall wear their new aray, / And all thy bones with beautie shall be clad" ("Death," 19-20).

Similarly, Vaughan prays,

Day, and night, not once a day
I will blesse thee,
And my soul in new array
I will dresse thee. ("Praise," 13-16)

The soul must put off the old: "Who will ascend, must be undrest," Vaughan says in "Ascension-Hymn," continuing:

And yet some
That know to die
Before death come,
Walk to the skie.
Even in this life, but all such can
Leave behind them the old Man. (7-12)

No poet makes such reiterated use of the theme of spiritual newness as Vaughan, with such images as "new strength" ("Easter Hymn," 10) and "new lights" ("White Sunday," 9). A particularly eloquent prayer of renewal concludes the poem "The Book":

O knowing, glorious spirit! when
Thou shalt restore trees, beasts and men,
When thou shalt make all new again,

Destroying onely death and pain,
Give him amongst thy works a place,
Who in them lov'd and sought thy face! (25-30)

The collection *Silex Scintillans* in fact begins and ends with the theme: in the opening poem, "Regeneration," the poet records a paradisaic vision in which "all was chang'd, and a new spring / Did all my senses greet" (39-40); and the final poem, "L'Envoy," returns to the vision of "The new worlds new, quickening Sun" in whose spiritual light all God's creatures become "cloudless glass, / Transparent as the purest day" (1-13).

The theme of spiritual regeneration informs all of Milton's poetry. The new song, e.g., is not merely *referred to* in "On the Morning of Christ's Nativity" —rather, it is actually *re-created* in the "Hymn" within the Ode, which in itself constitutes the new song of the "new-enlight'n'd world" (82), particularly the "enrapturing harmony of the angelic choir" in sts. 9 to 15, which sweeps away the pagan order of "Th'old Dragon" in sts. 18 to 25. The eschatological extension of that motif is reiterated in *Paradise Lost* as the cleansing holocaust preparatory to the creation of a new heaven and new earth: in the court of heaven, God pronounces that "The World shall burn, and from her ashes spring / New Heav'n and Earth, wherein the just shall dwell" (3.334-35; cf. 10.647; 11.900). After the Fall, Michael reveals to Adam how Christ will come again and "raise, / From the conflagrant mass, purg'd and refin'd, / New Heav'ns, new Earth" (12.549-50). Milton's Puritan contemporary Bunyan wrote what perhaps for two centuries was the most widely read account or vision of the New Jerusalem in the concluding chapter (the Tenth Stage) of pt. 1 of *Pilgrim's Progress,* Pilgrim's arrival in the Land of Beulah and his welcome to the Celestial City, a passage woven out of imagery from Isaiah, the Song of Solomon, and Revelation. Meanwhile, in America, Anne Bradstreet in "The Flesh and the Spirit" offered a conventional poetic paraphrase of the New Jerusalem: "The City where I hope to dwell / There's none on earth can parallel. . . . A crystal river there doth run, / Which doth proceed from the Lamb's throne. . . ." Of course, the New World, from the time of its discovery and exploration by Europeans, had been mantled in the newness metaphor encoded in its very name, and there the Puritans and other reform and utopian groups were to view their "errand into the wilderness" as a quest to fulfill their vision of what Winthrop had called the "city on a hill."

Less well-known but more poetically intense and sustained visions of the New Jerusalem are found in the 17th-cent. prose meditations of Thomas Traherne or in such rapturous poems as his "Wonder," "Nature," "The City," and "Christendom." For Traherne, this glorious New Jerusalem is not a place or condition of the future or of an afterlife but rather the natural world as seen with virgin eyes or human society as it would be if lived according to the new dispensation (i.e., without walls, hedges, boundaries, shops, or money). This transformed vision of the world when seen "with New and Open Eys" ("The Approach," 25), recapturing the first, innocent vision of childhood, is conveyed in an ecstatic passage in the "Third Century" of *Meditations:*

> The Corn was Orient and immortal Wheat, which never could be reaped, nor was ever sown. I thought it had stood from Everlasting to Everlasting. The Dust and Stones of the Street were as Precious as GOLD. The Gates were at first the End of the World. The Green Trees when I saw them first through one of the Gates Transported and Ravished me; their Sweetness and unusual Beauty made my Heart to leap, and almost mad with Extasie. . . . Eternitie was manifest in the Light of the Day, and som thing infinit Behind evry thing appeared: which talked with my Expectation and moved my Desire. The Citie seemed to stand in Eden, or to be Built in Heaven. (111.3)

A comparable vision, using the same metaphor of seeing the world with virgin eyes, is used repeatedly by Nikos Kazantzakis, both with reference to his spiritual heroes St. Francis and Zorba and to his own experience, as recorded in *Report to Greco* (pp. 44-49, 376, 445; cf. *The Odyssey: A Modern Sequel,* bk. 16). William James records numerous instances of "new vision" in lectures 9 and 10 ("Conversion") of *Varieties of Religious Experience* (1961), e.g., the testimony of the illiterate English evangelist Billy Bray:

> In an instant the Lord made me so happy that I cannot express what I felt. I shouted for joy. I praised God with my whole heart. . . . I remember that everything looked new to me, the people the fields, the cattle, the trees. I was like a new man in a new world. (203)

The contemporary American writer Annie Dillard, who cites Billy Bray, recounts her striking vision of a "tree with lights in it," a kind of modern counterpart to the experience of Moses before the burning bush, in *Pilgrim at Tinker Creek* (1974):

> I stood on the grass with the lights in it, grass that was wholly fire, utterly focused and utterly dreamed. It was less like seeing than like being for the first time seen, knocked breathless by a powerful glance. . . . I had been my whole life a bell, and never knew it until at that moment I was lifted and struck. (33-34)

The major voice in mainstream English literature expressing this prophetic vision of newness is William Blake, in such works as *Milton* and *The Four Zoas.* In the Preface to *Milton,* Blake issues a clarion call for art that will be true to the imagination rather than to the hirelings of court and university: "Rouze up. O Young Men of the New Age! Set your foreheads against the ignorant Hirelings!" —following it with the New Age hymn to the building of the New Jerusalem:

> I will not cease from Mental Fight,
> Nor shall my Sword sleep in my hand,

> Till we have built Jerusalem
> In England's green & pleasant Land.

The Four Zoas represents Blake's epic of human regeneration and renewal, his mythopoetic re-creation of themes drawn from biblical prophecy, Gospel, Apocalypse, Dante, and Milton. After representations of the Fall, alienation, and disunity in Nights 1 through 6, we see Los (the fallen imagination), in Night the Seventh, begin the rebuilding of Jerusalem, opening up "new heavens & a new Earth" (7.380). The New Jerusalem, personified as a woman, is the Bride of the Lamb; as a city, it allegorically represents renewed human community. Ahania (the consort or Emanation of Urizen) in death becomes, Persephone-like, the promise of eternal renewal, patterned on the Bride of the Lamb, Jerusalem, "Which now descendeth out of heaven a City yet a Woman / Mother of myriads redeemed & Born in her spiritual palaces / By a New Spiritual birth Regenerated from Death" (9.222-24). In Night the Ninth, as Urizen is made whole with passion, so Vala is made whole with reason, and, in an ecstatic sequence drawing upon the rhetoric of the Song of Solomon, she sings out, "For in my bosom a new song arises to my Lord" (9.433). After the apocalyptic wine treading and winnowing, "Then All the Slaves from every Earth in the wide Universe / Sing a New Song drowning confusion in its happy notes" (9.682-83), heralding the birth of the image of the Eternal, "the New born Man" (9.643, 831).

The Romantic period — contemporary with the revolutionary decades from 1789 to 1848 — was indeed dominated by the theme of newness and renewal. To the liberal idealists it seemed the dawning of a new age; as Wordsworth said in *The Prelude,* "Europe at that time was thrilled with joy, / France standing on the top of golden hours, / And human nature seeming born again [6.339-41]. . . . Bliss was it in that dawn to be alive / But to be young was very Heaven! [11.108-09])." Throughout *The Prelude* Wordworth alludes to new life, new existence, "new-born Liberty" (6.442), and a new world — until disillusioned by violence and reaction. Still, in the tenth strophe of the "Intimations" ode, Wordworth can evoke the Psalmist's new song: "Then sing, ye Birds, sing, sing a joyous song! / And let the young Lambs bound / As to the tabor's sound!" (169-71). The works of Coleridge are also filled with references to new life, new hope, new joy (see, e.g., "Pantisocracy"); even in "Dejection: An Ode" the poet recalls how it is Joy which is

> the spirit and the power,
> which wedding Nature to us gives in dower
> A new Earth and new Heaven,
> Undreamt of by the sensual and the proud —. (67-70)

Ultimately, however, Coleridge too is disillusioned by events in France, so that references to "new freedom" and "new Crusade" become ironic (see, e.g., *Robespierre,* 1.197; 3.205).

The theme of newness in Wordsworth and Coleridge is tempered also by their fondness for the old and venerable (see, e.g., Wordsworth's "Michael" or "Resolution and Independence"). Such is not the case with Shelley, however, for whom the vision of newness is unalloyed, as, notably, in *Prometheus Unbound,* in which the Chorus of Spirits sings of

> A world for the Spirit of Wisdom to wield;
> We will take our plan
> From the new world of man,
> And our work shall be called the Promethean.
> (4.155-58)

and the Semichorus of Hours responds, "Ceaseless and rapid, and fierce, and free, / With the Spirits which build a new earth and sea, / And a heaven where yet heaven could never be" (163-65) —which is for Shelley the new song:

> New notes. . . .
> 'Tis the deep music of the rolling world
> Kindling within the strips for the waved air
> Aeolian modulation. (185-88)

Keats, too, is wholly committed to the theme of newness, even in the context of stasis, as in "Ode on a Grecian Urn": "And, happy melodist, unwearied, / For ever piping songs for ever new" (24). *Endymion* offers images of new life, new growth, and new delight (2.528; 3.239, 472, 993), but it is in *Hyperion* and *The Fall of Hyperion* that Keats expresses the theme of cosmic renewal most forcefully and in comparable scope to *Prometheus Unbound;* as Saturn says, with more truth than he realizes, " 'There must be Gods thrown down. . . . and there shall be / Beautiful things made new' " (*Hyperion,* 1.128-32).

Byron's treatment of the theme, by contrast, is comic and satiric, as in references to "new Utopias. . . . To teach man what he might be or he ought, / if that corrupted thing could ever such be taught" (*Childe Harold's Pilgrimage,* 2.36) and to "new creation" as perpetual diminishment, in a reference to Cuvier's theory of catastropic evolution (*Don Juan,* 9.38, 39). He also alludes to new wine in old bottles, as in his Dedication to *Don Juan* ("This old song and new simile holds good") or his mock sentimentalizing in Canto 1 ("Sweet is old wine in bottles, ale in barrels" [1.126]) —or the barb in Canto 10: "Old flames, new wives, become our bitterest foes —" (10.12).

With Tennyson, the theme of regeneration and renewal returns to high seriousness, notably in *Idylls of the King.* A simple image of the life cycle in nature becomes symbolically portentous, as expressed in the songs of Vivien ("The new leaf ever pushes off the old" ["Balin and Balan," 436]) and Dagonet ("New leaf, new life —the days of frost are o'er" ["The Last Tournament," 278-89]). A repeated refrain — "The old order changeth, yielding place to new" — becomes the opening and closing leitmotif of the Arthurian poems ("The Coming of Arthur," 509; "The Passing of Arthur," 408; cf. "Morte d'Arthur,"

240). Similarly, as the poet overcomes his dark night of the soul in mourning for Arthur Hallam, his reconciliation with loss and faith in renewal are expressed in the New Year strophe of *In Memoriam:*

> Ring out the old, ring in the new,
> Ring, happy bells, across the snow;
> The year is going, let him go;
> Ring out the false, ring in the true. (106.5-8)

One of the richest treatments of the old / new theme in English literature is to be found in the works of Robert Browning. He alludes to new wine in old bottles in "Jochanan Hakkadosh," when the rabbi says,

> What wouldst thou? Is it needful I discuss
> Wherefore new sweet wine, poured in bottles caked
> With old strong wine's deposit, offers us
> Spoilt liquor we recoil from, thirst-unslaked? (280-83)

Elsewhere he refers to poetry as the "new wine" (see "Aristophanes' Apology," 950; "Pacchiarotto," Epilogue). In the fifth section of "Paracelsus," the adept, facing death, declares,

> New being waits me; new perceptions must
> Be born in me before I plunge therein;
> Which last is Death's affair; and while I speak. . . .
> I turn new knowledge upon old events. (5.500-507)

Earlier in the poem he offered an ecstatic vision of the new age of truth embodied in his art (1.370-74) along with declarations of the necessity of the new supplanting the old (1.247), a leading motif in Browning generally. For example, the "primal thesis" of the speaker in "A Death in the Desert" is that

> Man is not God but hath God's ends to serve,
> A master to obey, a course to take,
> Somewhat to cast off, somewhat to become?
> Grant this, then man must pass from old to new,
> From vain to real, from mistake to fact. (542-46; cf.
> "Red Cotton Night-Cap Country," 3562; "Prince
> Hohensteil-Schwangau," 731; 2010; *The Ring and the
> Book,* 9.282)

The thought is given more conventional religious coloration by the speakers in "By the Fire-Side" ("Think, when our one soul understands / The great Word which makes all things new, / When earth breaks up and heaven expands. . . ." [131-33]) and "Any Wife to Any Husband" ("Vainly the flesh fades; soul makes all things new" [18]), as well as by the Pope in *The Ring and the Book,* who praises the suffering wife whose patience "couldst rise from law to law, / The old to the new, promoted at one cry / O' the trump of God to the new service" and be found sublime (10.1055-59).

The contrast between the old and new law is, not surprisingly, prominent in *The Ring and the Book,* especially in "The Pope" (see 10.1863-65, 1874-77; also 8.697-720 ["The Gospel checks the law which throws the stone"]), although Guido challenges Christendom's willingness to abide by the radical new law:

> "No," venerable sire, I hear you smirk,
> "No, for Christ's gospel changes names, not things,
> Renews the obsolete, does nothing more!
> Our fire-new gospel is retinkered law,
> Our mercy justice, —Jove's rechristened God, —
> Nay, whereas, in the popular conceit,
> 'Tis pity that old harsh Law somehow limps,
> Lingers on earth, although Law's day be done, —
> Else would benignant Gospel interpose,
> Not furtively as now, but bold and frank
> O'erflutter us with healing in her wings, —
> Law is all harshness, Gospel were all love! —
> We like to put it, on the contrary, —
> Gospel takes up the rod which Law lets fall. . . ."
> (11.362-75; cf. "Mr. Sludge, 'The Medium,' " 877-90)

Among the numerous references in Browning to newness or new life are some explicit biblical allusions, such as the Pauline image of dying into new life (*The Ring and the Book*, 3.1569) and the image of the Athenians reacting to Paul's "new thing" in Acts 17:19-21, alluded to ironically in "Mr. Sludge, 'the Medium' ": "Didn't Athens treat Saint Paul so? —at any rate, / it's 'a new thing' philosophy fumbles at" (744-45; cf. "Christmas-Eve," 687). Another explicit allusion is to the NT exhortation to become new leaven ("Prince Hohensteil-Schwangau," 323-28). Other noteworthy references are the weary narrator's description of St. Peter's as a new Jerusalem in "Christmas-Eve" (532); Mr. Sludge's confounding of "the Golden Age, old Paradise / Or new Eutopia!" ("Mr. Sludge, 'The Medium,' " 1431-32); the numerous references to "new life" in "Fifine at the Fair" (e.g., 838, 1640, 1676) and "Saul" (282, 312, 331), as well as the complementary theme that the old is ever new (see, e.g., "Christopher Smart," 53-59, 148; "Bishop Blougram's Apology," 186; "Red Cotton," 1231, 1795; and "Prince Hohensteil-Schwangau, 176-77: "old yet ever new / The process: 'tis the way of Deity").

Very different is the melancholic vision of Matthew Arnold. In the dream-vision of "Obermann Once More" the visionary Obermann urges the poet that even though "the world lies forlorn," for "the old is out of date" and the "new is not yet born," yet "Some new such hope must dawn at last, / Or man must toss in pain" (241-48). Calling attention to the sun —"He breaks the winter of the past; / A green, new earth appears" (285-86)—Obermann urges the poet, "though to the world's new hour / Thou come with aspect marr'd" and shorn of joy, to "yet tell / Hope to a world new-made!" (301-16). With deeper pessimism, Arnold's Empedocles concludes:

> We mortals are no kings
> For each of whom to sway
> A new-made world up-springs,
> Meant merely for his play;
> No, we are strangers here; the world is from of old. . . .

> The world is what it is, for all our dust and din.
> Born into life! —'tis we,
> And not the world, are new. . . . ("Empedocles on
> Etna," 1.2.179-200)

In light of Arnold's wistful attachment to the "immortal chants of old" ("Thyrsis," 181), his attitude toward the idea of a new age is, not surprisingly, ambivalent. In his ironic "Bacchanalia; or, The New Age,"

> Bards make new poems,
> thinkers new schools,
> Statesmen new systems,
> Critics new rules.
> All things begin again. . . . (84-92)

"Poet, what ails thee, then?" Arnold asks himself and instantly answers, "The world but feels the present's spell, / The poet feels the past as well." Thus Arnold's retelling of the Sermon on the Mount, in "Progress," has Jesus rebuke his eager disciples for their hasty conclusion — "The old law, they cried, 'is wholly come to nought, / Behold the new world rise!' " (3-4) —reminding them that the old law must be fulfilled before it can be superseded:

> So Christ said eighteen hundred years ago.
> And what then shall be said to those to-day,
> Who cry aloud to lay the old world low
> To clear the new world's way? . . .
> "Say ye: 'The spirit of man has found new roads,
> And we must leave the old faiths, and walk therein'? —
> Leave then the Cross as ye have left carved gods,
> But guard the fire within!" (13-16, 25-28)

More in the Romantic vein are Meredith's symbolic references to new life in nature —"New life when deathless Spring shall touch the hills" ("The Wild Rose and the Snowdrop," 30), when "Earth's mists did with the sweet new spirit wed" ("Song: Two Wedded Lovers," 12) —and to "worn Humanity['s] new youth" ("The Thrush in February," 96). The new life is the symbolic opposite of the "old sweat and anguish Adamite" ("Carlyle," 8) and of "the old revolt from Awe" ("Lucifer in Starlight," 10), although Meredith warns lest "the God of old time will act Satan of new, / If we keep him not straight at the higher God aimed" ("The Empty Purse," 417-18). Far more conventional are references in John Keble's *The Christian Year,* such as the expression in "Burial of the Dead" of Christian hope for a "new heaven, new earth . . . for their new immortal birth," so that every loss and grief will but breed "Hope of new spring" in every "new-brac'd heart" (48-60; cf. "Fourth Sunday after Trinity," 82). Other hymns speak of laying "New hearts before their Savior's feet" ("St. Barnabas," 33) and of the "new morning" of grace which comes with penitence ("Sixth Sunday After Trinity," 1-8; cf. "Third Sunday after Trinity," 27). The latter image of being reborn or reawakened into a new life of grace is a virtual monomyth of Christian literature, including such obvious examples as Dickens's *A*

Christmas Carol, Dostoyevsky's *Crime and Punishment*, Tolstoy's *Resurrection*, Lagerqvist's *Barabbas*, or Douglas's *The Robe*. A sustained poetic rendition is Masefield's "The Everlasting Mercy," in which the narrator, Saul Kane, gives rapturous testimony to the transformation of the world attendant upon a transformed heart:

> O glory of the lighted mind.
> How dead I'd been, how dumb, how blind.
> The station brook, to my new eyes,
> Was babbling out of Paradise,
> The waters rushing from the rain
> Were singing Christ has risen again.
> I thought all earthly creatures knelt
> From the rapture of the joy I felt. (Masefield, *Poems* [1971], 81)

To "look at the world with new eyes" in a more universalist sense is the theme of Emerson's "Nature" (*Works* [1903], 1.75). "The beauty of nature," Emerson says, "re-forms itself in the mind . . . for new creation" (1.23), and "every object rightly seen, unlocks a new faculty of the soul" (1.35). Throughout the essay, Emerson celebrates the way in which the Spirit "puts . . . [nature] forth through us, as the life of the tree puts forth new branches and leaves through the pores of the old" (1.64). Emerson's celebrated "The American Scholar" is an even more explicit paean to newness: "Who can doubt, that poetry will revive and lead in a new age. . . ?" (1.82). Not out of the exhausted systems and cultures of the Old World, he says, "comes the helpful giant to destroy the old or to build the new, but out of unhandselled savage nature" (1.99). Like Wordsworth in "The Prelude," Emerson rejoices at being alive at the prospective dawn of a new age:

> If there is any period one would desire to be born in, — is it not the age of Revolution; when the old and the new stand side by side, and admit of being compared: when the energies of all men are searched by fear and by hope; when the historic glories of the old can be compensated by the rich possibilities of the new era? (1.110)

Emerson's contempt for the intellectual cowardice of clinging to old formulations is even sharper in "Self-Reliance," whose clarion call is "Every new mind is a new classification" (11.79). "Whenever a mind is simple," Emerson says, "and receives a divine wisdom, then old things pass away —means, teachers, texts, temples fall. . . . When we have new perception, we shall gladly disburden the memory of its hoarded treasures as old rubbish" (11.66, 68).

Similar images occur in Emerson's poetry. For example, in "The World-Soul," the prophetic poet declares,

> When the old world is sterile,
> And the ages are effete,
> He will from wrecks and sediment
> The fairer world complete. . . .

> Spring still makes spring in the mind,
> When sixty years are told;
> Love wakes anew this throbbing heart,
> And we are never old. (97-108; cf. "Boston," 19, 92)

Elsewhere Emerson sings of the mind "New-born" out of contemplation of beauty ("Ode to Beauty," 19), paralleling the recurrent new birth in nature: "Life out of death, new out of old" ("May-Day," 27). His fellow Transcendentalist Thoreau returns the thought to a biblical context in *Walden*, warning,

> beware of all enterprises that require new clothes, and not rather a new wearer of clothes. . . . Perhaps we should never procure a new suit, however ragged or dirty the old, until we have . . . so enterprised or sailed in some way, that we feel like new men in the old, and that to retain it would be like keeping new wine in old bottles.

Images of the New Jerusalem are common in religious poetry of the New World, building on the Puritans' heavy emphasis on the theme; e.g., in "The Pageant," Whittier describes the beauty of a winter landscape as "The white bride coming down from heaven!" References to the New Jerusalem and the new song abound in African-American spirituals, such as "Great Gettin' Up Mornin' " and "I Got a Robe, You Got a Robe." But in Hawthorne's *The Scarlet Letter*, the reference takes on ironic overtones as Chillingworth twice reminds Dimmesdale that pure and saintly men are the golden coin of the New Jerusalem, prompting Dimmesdale's Election Day sermon on the "glorious destiny for the newly gathered people."

The theme of newness in modern poetry is too complex to permit useful generalization. The "orthodox" Christian tradition continues to be heard in Gerard Manley Hopkins's incarnational vision —"nature is never spent; / There lives the dearest freshness deep down things" ("God's Grandeur," 9-10) —and in Eliot's "Gerontion" ("in the juvescence of the year / Came Christ the tiger" [19-20]) and *Four Quartets*:

> Time present and time past
> Are both perhaps present in time future. . . .
> ("Burnt Norton," 1-2)
> . . . In my end is my beginning.
> ("East Coker," 211)
> What we call the beginning is often the end
> And to make an end is to make a beginning.
> ("Little Gidding," 216-17)

as well as in Auden's "For the Time Being" and bk. 7 ("Mabinog's Liturgy") of David Jones's *Anathemata*. The theme of *la vita nuova*, derived from Dante, is at the center of both the critical/philosophical and the literary work of Charles Williams, notably in his *Descent into Hell* and *All Hallows' Eve* (the first chapter of which is titled "The New Life").

The theme of newness is equally prominent among "unorthodox" modern poets. Yeats, in particular, is notable for his alternative vision of cycles of time, set forth in *A Vision* and reflected in poems such as "The Second Coming," in which the Christian eschaton is parodied. In a different vein, that of erotic mysticism, D. H. Lawrence offers a revisionist reading of the biblical image in "New Heaven and Earth," in which the poet emerges from a world-weary dark night of the soul, an extreme narcissism, and through touching "the flank of my wife," rediscovers self and other, "rising, new-awakened from the tomb!":

> I touched her flank and knew I was carried by the
>   current in death
> over to the new world, and was climbing out on the
>   shore,
> risen, not to the old world, the old, changeless I, the
>   old life,
> wakened not to the old knowledge
> but to a new earth, a new I, a new knowledge, a new
>   world of time. (Sect. 7)

Contemporary feminist literature, including such works as Adrienne Rich's "Diving into the Wreck" and Margaret Atwood's *Surfacing*, offers distinctive renditions of the theme of newness and regeneration, often in conscious reaction to traditional biblical notions of "conversion" and "renewal" (see Carol Christ, *Diving Deep and Surfacing: Women Writers on Spiritual Quest* [1980]). The mystical regeneration of the narrator in the latter work, in which she creatively "unnames" the creatures around her as a prelude to self-discovery, is a paradigm instance of what has been called the motif of "new naming" in women's spiritual-quest literature.

See also CONVERSION; NEW JERUSALEM; TYPOLOGY.

Bibliography. Daniélou, J. *From Shadows to Reality: Studies in the Biblical Typology of the Fathers.* Trans. W. Hibbard (1960); Hanson, P. *The Dawn of Apocalyptic: The Historical and Sociological Roots of Jewish Apocalyptic Eschatology* (1979); Harrisville, R. A. "The Concept of Newness in the New Testament." *JBL* 74 (1955), 69-79; Kosnetter, J. "Renewal (Newness)." In *Encyclopedia of Biblical Theology: The Complete "Sacramentum Verbi."* Ed. J. B. Bauer (1981), 743-48; Mâle, E. *The Gothic Image: Religious Art in France of the Thirteenth Century.* Trans. D. Nussey (1972); Nock, A. D. *Conversion: The Old and the New in Religion from Alexander the Great to Augustine of Hippo* (1933); Oates, J. C. *New Heaven, New Earth: The Visionary Experience in Literature* (1974); Robertson, D. W. *A Preface to Chaucer: Studies in Medieval Perspectives* (1962); Singleton, C. S. *An Essay on the* Vita Nuova (1977).

GEORGE L. SCHEPER

OLD MEN DREAM DREAMS "Your old men shall dream dreams, your young men shall see visions" (Joel 2:28) is part of an eschatological prophecy of the outpouring of the Spirit of God at some indefinite future time, and the mention of old men and young men functions as an indication that the spirit of prophecy will extend to all Israel. In his sermon in Acts 2:14-21, St. Peter quotes Joel 2:28-32, declaring that the prophecy has been fulfilled in Jesus' sending the Holy Spirit at Pentecost (2:16-18).

The phrase "to dream a dream" imitates Hebrew usage; the introduction of this construction into English was influenced by the Vg wording of Joel 2:28, *somnia somniabunt* (the usual construction in the Vg is *somnium videre,* "to see a dream"; *somnium somniare* occurs elsewhere only in Jer. 29:8). The phrase "to dream a dream" occurs in English at least as early as the ME *Story of Genesis and Exodus* (ca. 1250), in a passage where there is no warrant for the redundant construction in the Vg text being paraphrased (EETS o.s. 7 [1873], 2095). It occurs frequently throughout the history of English literature, and some writers, such as Shakespeare (*Richard 3,* 5.3.212; *Romeo and Juliet,* 1.4.50) and Eugene O'Neill, seem to be particularly fond of it. While not every occurrence of this phrase can be regarded as a conscious allusion to Joel 2:28, there is a variety of English literary allusions which clearly refer to the Joel verse as a whole.

The *Cursor Mundi* narrates the events of Acts 2, including Peter's quotation of the Joel prophecy: "ȝoure ȝonge men shul siȝtes se / ȝoure eldremen shul dremes dreme" (EETS o.s. 62 [1876], 18984-85 in the Trinity MS version). Francis Bacon, in his essay "Of Youth and Age," refers to a rabbinic opinion which from Joel 2:28 "inferreth that young men are admitted nearer to God than old, because vision is a clearer revelation than a dream" (*Essays* [1890], 300). Shakespeare possibly alludes to the Joel verse in *Troilus and Cressida* when he has Priam say: "Come, Hector, come, go back. / Thy wife hath dremt, thy mother hath had visions" (5.3.62-63).

In "Ivan Ivanovitch" Robert Browning has an ancient Russian priest quote Joel 2:28 as support for the divine authority of his judgment (316-21), and in another Browning poem, "Mr. Sludge, 'The Medium,' " Sludge pictures his patrons urging him to continue his spiritualism by saying: "There's no one doubts you, Sludge! / You dream the dreams, you see the spiritual sights" (412-13). Bernard Shaw uses the Joel verse to characterize utopian political thinking in the preface to *Geneva*, and in the preface to *Farfetched Fables* he concludes a list of great thinkers and artists of the past with this: "to say nothing of living seers of visions and dreamers of dreams." In *Man and Superman* Shaw has John Tanner say that a true artist knows that women "have the power to rouse his deepest creative energies, to rescue him from his cold reason, to make him see visions and dream dreams" (*Works* [1930], 10.24). In his "Laments for a Dying Language 3," Ogden Nash satirizes bureaucratic euphemisms:

> To the sociologist squeamish
> The words "Your old men shall dream dreams" are less
>   than beamish,
> so "Your senior citizens shall dream dreams" it shall
>   henceforth be,

Along with Hemingway's "The Senior Citizen and the Sea." (*I Wouldn't Have Missed It* [1975], 330.8-11)

See also DREAMS, VISIONS.

Bibliography. *Middle English Dictionary.* Ed. Hans Kurath (1952), 1297-1300; *A New English Dictionary on Historical Principles.* Ed. J. A. H. Murray (1887-1928), 3.655-56.   LAWRENCE T. MARTIN

OLIVET, MOUNT   A mountainous ridge east of Jerusalem, location of an olive grove; hence "Mount of Olives." Here David, in flight from Absalom, stopped to worship (1 Sam. 15:23-32); here Solomon in his dissipation built "high places" for Chemosh and Molech (1 Kings 11:7; 2 Kings 23:13); here Ezekiel saw in his vision the departing glory of God leave the Temple and alight (Ezek. 11:23; cf. 43:2-5); here, Zechariah (chap. 14) predicts, the Lord's feet shall alight in the apocalyptic Day of the Lord; here Lazarus was raised at Bethany; here Jesus gave the Olivet Discourse (Matt. 24; Mark 13) on the signs of the Last Days; here, in the Garden of Gethsemane, Jesus was apprehended by the soldiers and Judas (John 18; Matt. 26:47-57; Mark 14:43-50); here, forty days after his Resurrection, Jesus ascended into heaven.

OMNIPOTENCE   The term *omnipotent* occurs only once in the KJV, at Rev. 19:6 as a translation of the Vg *omnipotens* and the Gk. *pantokratōr.* The Latin poets (Ovid, *Metamorphoses,* 1.54) regularly use *omnipotens* as a divine epithet, and the LXX uses *pantokratōr* 168 times, usually to translate the divine names *ṣeba'ot* (Jer. 3:19; cf. 1 Sam. 3:4) or *shadday* (Job 5:17; cf. Ezek. 10:5). In the OT, KJV uses "Almighty" to translate *shadday* (except at Dan. 11:38, where it renders *ma'uzim*), an archaizing name found most frequently in Job. The NT "Almighty" of the KJV always represents *pantokratōr* and occurs only once outside Revelation at 2 Cor. 6:18. Other important Hebrew and Greek terms indicating God's power, might, and strength are *koah* (Jer. 10:12; LXX *ischys*), *'oz* (Ps. 62:11; LXX *kratos*), *geburah* (1 Chron. 29:12; LXX *dynasteia*), and *hazaq* (Exod. 6:10; LXX *krataios*). *Dynamis* and its derivatives become very important in the NT. *Dynamis* is a name for God at Matt. 26:64 and Mark 14:62 (cf. Luke 22:69); Christ possesses a divine *dynamis;* and Christ's miracles are *dynameis* or acts of power.

Creation was the original act of power (Isa. 40:12-13; Jer. 10:11-16), the immediate and unassisted work of a God whose very name (*'el;* cf. Akk. *ilu*) may mean "power" and who is called "the mighty One of Israel" (Isa. 1:24) and "God Almighty" (Exod. 6:3). Nothing is impossible to God: his power is without limit and beyond comparison (Gen. 18:14; Job 42:2; Jer. 10:6; 32:17; Dan. 4:35; Zech. 8:6); if his might is compared to that of creatures (Deut. 3:24), therefore, it must be in an absolute, not a relative sense. Yet the urge to compare God with other agents is a natural consequence of the personal

character of his power, for his mighty works (Deut. 11:2-7; Job 38; Pss. 65–66; Jer. 5:22) are not the manifestations of an impersonal force immanent in nature but of a personal and individual will active in history — a conception best expressed in the words of LXX Deut. 3:24 and by the deeds of the Exodus. In praise of such mighty acts, David's doxology in 1 Chron. 29:10-12 (cf. Ps. 62:11) recognizes power as a primary attribute of God, as does Christ's doxology of the Father found in some later NT MSS at Matt. 6:13.

The early rabbis also praised the divine power in the second of the Eighteen Benedictions, and several of the rabbinic names for God ("Might," "Strength of Israel," "King of All Kings") emphasize various aspects of God's power. At the same time, biblical confidence in unqualified divine power was attenuated as the rabbinic theology of prayer opened itself to philosophical or at least proto-philosophical questions. Does God alter his immutable decrees in order to answer prayer? Can God hear the prayers of all people? The historical catastrophes which culminated in the Roman destruction of Jerusalem likewise sharpened the debate on the limits of God's might. Early Christian theologians were troubled by the antinomy between two central doctrines: that humanity was created by an omnipotent and omniscient God and that God had endowed mankind with a free will; the controversy pitting the human will against God's power reached an early crisis with St. Augustine's attack on Pelagius in the 5th cent. Five centuries earlier, Philo had treated omnipotence under the rubric of divine attributes, a topic whose genuinely philosophical examination he inaugurated and passed on to medieval Jewish philosophy. Eventually Maimonides was to deny that our apprehension of the concept represented by *omnipotence* gives any clue to God's essence since any name applied to God is perfectly and only homonymous with the corresponding term of nondivine reference. The search for true descriptions of God had also been a major problem for Christian theologians since the time of pseudo-Dionysius, who nonetheless ascribed to God power (*The Divine Names,* 8.1-2) and other transcendent perfections possessed by creatures in less perfect form. St. Thomas Aquinas, basing his "analogy of attribution" on a prior "analogy of being" between Creator and created, was prepared to attribute power and other qualities to God in a much more positive way than Maimonides allowed. Aquinas concluded that "God is called omnipotent because he can do all things which are possible in an absolute sense" but that "the omnipotence of God does not exclude impossibility and necessity from things" (*Summa Theol.* 1.q.25.a.3.c.ad 4).

Since *omnipotence* and its derivatives are of such great theological significance, it is no surprise to find them occurring as designations for God in vernacular literature from the 14th cent. onward. Perhaps because *omnipotens* is more prominent in Latin poetry than are the corresponding terms in the NT of the Vg or KJV, *omnipotence* could be used in English literature without much theological weight (Chaucer, *The Wife of Bath's Prologue*, 3.423) or even in a distinctly non-Christian sense (Pope, *Odyssey*, 1.78, where it corresponds vaguely to *olympie* in the Greek). When Marlowe's Faustus promises himself "a world of . . . power, of honour, of omnipotence" (*Doctor Faustus*, 1.1.80-81), the term has been extended from the divine to the diabolical, yet one's appreciation of the magician's blasphemous megalomania depends on the traditional theological meaning of *omnipotence*, as does the humor in Shakespeare's *1 Henry 4*, 1.2.109, where Poins's blasphemy is less serious. In *Paradise Lost*, the theological and attributive force of the word remains especially clear and consistent. At *PL* 1.44-49 (". . . Him the Almighty Power / Hurled headlong flaming . . . / Who durst defy th'Omnipotent to arms"), Milton introduces a motif of creaturely strength pitched helplessly against divine might which runs throughout his epic (1.273; 4.86; 5.616; 6.136, 294; 7.136). Blake, less Latinate than Milton in his diction, follows the KJV in preferring "Almighty" to "Omnipotent" as a divine name, using it sometimes to allude to divine power (*Milton*, 1.4.1; 2.30.18), sometimes more loosely as a neutral appellative (*Four Zoas*, 1.554; *Jerusalem*, 1.10.56). Shelley's famous lines, "To know nor faith, nor love, nor law; to be / Omnipotent but friendless is to reign" (*Prometheus Unbound*, 2.4.47-48), express a pagan sentiment and hence demand a clearer memory of the opposing and traditional Christian doctrine than that required by the merely classicizing line of Pope's *Odyssey*.

See also THEODICY.

Bibliography. Bromiley, G. W. "Omnipotence: History of the Doctrine." *ISBE* 3.592-95; Danielson, D. *Milton's Good God* (1982); Oakley, F. *Omnipotence, Covenant and Order: An Excursion in the History of Ideas from Abelard to Leibniz* (1984). BRIAN P. COPENHAVER

OMNIPRESENCE The word *omnipresent* is not found in the KJV, and unlike *omnipotens* it is used neither in ancient Latin literature nor in the Vg. However, there is a biblical basis for the development in Jewish and Christian theologies of various doctrines of divine omnipresence. Because no creature can avoid the ubiquitous presence of God (Ps. 139:7; Prov. 15:3), God's knowledge of creatures is perfect and universal (Jer. 23:24), thus linking the two perfections of omnipresence and omniscience. God is said to fill the universe (Jer. 23:24) or other places symbolic of the universe (Isa. 6:1), but the deity's relation to cosmic space as a material and finite location was already recognized as problematic by some biblical authors (1 Kings 8:27), while others (Ps. 90:1) were content to suggest some relationship of similarity if not of identity between the Creator and the universe as dwelling place of creatures. To say that God *contains* all things is not equivalent to the pantheist claim that God *is*

all things, though pantheist influences from Stoicism and other hellenistic thought-systems were common enough by the time the author of Acts 17:28 recorded St. Paul's famous sermon on the God in whom "we live, and move, and have our being; as certain also of your own poets have said. . . ."

God's omnipresence was quite important in the theology of the early rabbis, many of whose substitute names for God have spatial or cosmological associations. Three were especially significant: *shamayim* ("heavens"), *shekinah* ("presence"), and *maqom* ("place"). Though the rabbis did not usually treat the biblical *maqom* as a divine name, they did allege certain occurrences of the word (Gen. 22:14; 28:16; Exod. 33:21; Ezek. 3:12) as evidence for their own use of *maqom* as a name of God. The most famous dictum on *maqom* is ascribed to R. Jose bar Halafta, a Tannaitic teacher of the 2nd cent. A.D.: ". . . the Lord is the place of His world, but His world is not His place" (Gen. Rab. 68.9). Echoes of Jewish speculations on God's presence can be heard in St. Cyprian of Carthage, St. Theophilus of Antioch, pseudo-Dionysius, and St. Gregory the Great, but it was Arnobius who presented the boldest patristic treatment of this topic, calling God "the place and true space, the foundation of all things that exist . . . in which the world that contains us . . . sits and turns" (*Adversus nationes*, 1.31; 2.58; cf. Lucretius, *De rerum naturae*, 1.471-72). Since a creative and provident God must stand apart from what he brings into being and yet abide with what he sustains, and because the closed world of premodern cosmology was too small a theater for an infinite God, the question of God's location became deeply controversial in medieval and early modern philosophy, receiving some of its subtlest treatments from Maimonides, Crescas, Spinoza, and other Jewish philosophers. St. Thomas Aquinas also took up this problem (*Summa Theol.* 1.q.8; cf. *Summa contra Gentiles*, 1.43), but he treated it under the heading of the adverb *ubique* ("everywhere") rather than the noun *omnipraesentia*. While certain themes of Zoharic Cabala (whose beginnings were roughly contemporary with Aquinas) are related to the topic of sacred or divine space, such ideas became central only in the new Cabala of Isaac Luria, who worked in the 16th cent. The Lurianic conception of *ṣimṣum*, the divine act of contraction which left space for the creation of the cosmos, first became widely available to Christians with the publication of Knorr von Rosenroth's *Kabbala Denudata* in 1677-84. In England the most influential recipient of Knorr's Cabala was Henry More, whose views on the divinity of space influenced not only the science of Isaac Newton but also the popular literary polemics of such figures as John Toland.

Milton (*Paradise Lost*, 7.588-90) uses the attribute of omnipresence to explain how on the seventh day God could rest from the work of creation and yet remain providentially present to what he had made. In *Religious Musings,* Coleridge made divine love both omnificent and omnipresent, but in a note on lines 31 to 33 of the poem,

> Manifest Godhead, melting into day
> What floating mists of dark idolatry
> Broke and misshaped the omnipresent fire,

he cites the Neoplatonist Damascius on the problem of representing God with positive attributes like omnipresence. Perhaps the finest expression in English poetry of the theophanies whereby the OT God manifested himself is to be found in Wordsworth's *Excursion* (4.649-59):

> . . . Man excaped the doom
> Of destitution; — solitude was not.
> Jehovah — shapeless Power above all Powers,
> Single and one, the omnipresent God,
> By vocal utterance, or blaze of light,
> Or cloud of darkness, localized in heaven;
> On earth, enshrined within the wandering ark;
> Or, out of Sion, thundering from his throne
> Between the Cherubim — on the chosen Race
> Showered miracles, and ceased not to dispense
> Judgments, that filled the land from age to age.

See also THEODICY.

Bibliography. Bromiley, G. W. "Omnipresence: History of the Doctrine." *ISBE* 3.595-98.   BRIAN P. COPENHAVER

OMNISCIENCE   Though *omniscience* does not occur in the KJV nor the scholastic Lat. *omniscientia* in the Vg, both the OT and NT insist on the perfect and absolute character of God's knowledge. God sees everywhere (Job 28:24), knows human thoughts (Ps. 139:2), and entirely understands mankind and all he does (Prov. 5:21; Isa. 37:28; Acts 1:24). Prov. 8 and Job 28 gave rise to theological speculations which ultimately hypostatized divine Wisdom. The NT particularly emphasizes the providential character of divine knowledge (Matt. 6:8; Luke 12:6), and Eph. 3:10 views "the manifold wisdom of God" in an eschatological context.

The rabbis, some of whose names for God allude to his wisdom, were aware that the attributes of omnipresence and omniscience were mutually implied by such OT passages as Job 28:24, which gives an extensional character to God's knowing. Jewish and Christian philosophers alike realized that the coupling of omnipotence with omniscient foreknowledge complicated the question of human freedom and responsibility. Levi ben Gerson's response to these problems was to suggest that God foreknows only the general order of determined events in the universe, not the particulars of each individual human act. In his critique of the Thomist view that the freedom of human will is itself determined by God, the Jesuit Luis de Molina proposed that God possesses a "middle knowledge," which is neither a simple comprehension of all possible events nor a case-by-case

knowledge of all that happens in past, present, and future. God knows precisely what a person will do in given circumstances, but such knowledge is not the cause of those circumstances.

For Milton, God's omniscience implies his infallibility (*Paradise Lost,* 6.430; 10.7) in the precise sense implied by the etymology from Lat. *fallor:* God's freedom from error means not only that he makes no mistakes but also that it is impossible to deceive him. The doctrine of God's omniscience also teaches that the knowledge of some things is reserved to divinity (*PL* 7.123).

Reflecting on the Creator's knowledge of the cosmos inevitably leads one to ask how the cosmos stands as an effect of divine causation, as Dryden understands when he associates "Omniscient Pow'r" (*Palamon and Arcite,* 3.1054) with the existence of due order in a universe regulated by an ultimately divine body of law. Coleridge handles the matter less optimistically:

> He knows (the Spirit that in secret sees,
> Of whose omniscient and all-spreading Love
> Aught to *implore* were impotence of mind)
> That my mute thoughts are sad before his throne, . . .
> ("To a friend," 26-29)

But in a note on these lines, Coleridge professes to "utterly recant the sentiment contained in [them]. . . , it being written in Scripture, 'Ask, and it shall be given you.' " Thus, in Luke 11:9 he discovers the "propriety of offering petitions as well as thanksgivings" to an omniscient God who knows every wish before it is consciously formulated.

See also THEODICY; WISDOM.

Bibliography. Bromiley, G. W. "Omniscience: History of the Doctrine." *ISBE* 3.600-603.   BRIAN P. COPENHAVER

ONAN   As Judah's second son (Gen. 38:4; 46:12; Num. 26:19; 1 Chron. 2:3), it was Onan's responsibility to enter into a levirate marriage with the childless widow of his older brother Er, in order for his name to be preserved. Onan sidestepped this obligation, bringing down God's anger and leading to his death (Gen. 38:8-10). The means which Onan used have been seen as masturbation (Nid. 13a), "unnatural intercourse" (Yeb. 34b), or, most probably, coitus interruptus (Gen. Rab. 85.5; Rashi on Gen. 38:9; Luther). Mark Twain, in *Letters from the Earth,* insincerely speculates that Moses may have killed the Midianites because of Onanism, and the incident is alluded to cryptically in the "Burnt Offering" breakfast passage of the "Ithica" chapter in Joyce's *Ulysses.* The Fifth Earl of Hauberk in Aldous Huxley's *After Many a Summer* alludes to the means by which the male carp fertilizes spawn as onanism.   DAVID W. BAKER

ONE THING IS NEEDFUL   Luke 10:42 excludes the reply of Jesus to Martha following her complaint that Mary sat listening to Jesus when she might have been helpful in preparing and serving the meal. Martha is "careful and troubled about many things"; while "But one thing is needful: and Mary hath chosen that good part, which shall not be taken away from her." Early medieval exegesis made the phrase *(Porro unum est necessarium)* indicative of the exalted character of a contemplative spiritual vocation. Reformed exegesis interpreted the "one thing" as a call to purity of heart focussing on the Word of God with undivided attention (e.g., Matthew Henry, *Comm.* 5.690-91). It is this latter emphasis which Matthew Arnold attacks in his chapter *("Porro Unum Est Necessarium")* in *Culture and Anarchy:* "The Puritan's great danger is that he imagines himself in possession of a rule telling him the *Unum necessarium,* or one thing needful, and that he then remains satisfied with a very crude conception of what this rule really is." Jeremy Taylor's *Unum Necessarium* (1655) is a Reformation version of the medieval penitential manual — an exposition of the NT doctrine as well as a guide to "a Strict, a Holy, and a Christian Life," grounded in a strong presupposition of the reality of "original sin."

See also MARTHA; MARY MAGDALENE.

OPHIR A region on the Red Sea in southwest Arabia, it was the place where Solomon acquired gold for the furnishings of the Temple, and also his throne. "Gold of Ophir" is as much as to say, "Gold of the finest quality." En route to the alchemists' house to fetch the philosopher's stone, Ben Jonson's Surly in *The Alchemist* tells Sir Epicure Mammon, plying his cupidity, that it will be as good as having "the golden mines, / Great Solomon's Ophir!"

ORIGINAL SIN The term *peccatum originale* is not found in the Bible, but first appears in the writings of St. Augustine, especially in the context of his debate with the Pelagians. (In the writings of Pelagius any notion of inherited sinfulness had been rejected.) Augustine draws on scriptural texts to make the point that "no one is clean, not even if his life be only for a day" (Job 14:4 [Vg]; KJV: "Who can bring a clean thing out of an unclean? Not one"). Essentially, his argument amplifies the words of the Psalmist (51:5), "Behold I was shapen in iniquity, and in sin did my mother conceive me" *(De peccatorum meritis et remissione,* 1.33). In *De gratia christi, et de peccato originali* he traces the taint of sin in mortal nature to Adam and Eve's sin in the garden. This taint is communicated to each new generation in the concupiscence or *libido* which in a fallen world, he argues, is intrinsic to every procreative act. *De traduce peccati,* the transmission of sin, is thus inescapably part of the human condition. All people partake of it "in Adam," in whose fall they effectually participate. It ought not to be thought, says Augustine, that original sin renders marriage evil (2.38-42); on the contrary, Christian marriage is a means of grace bringing into submission those impulses which

more readily than most exhibit humanity's inherently concupiscent nature. But he insists upon the necessity to children — even infants born to "regenerate parents" — of baptism as a means of remission of the penalty of original sin. (Pelagius on contrary grounds opposed infant baptism.) Augustine does not argue that willful sin does not then arise fairly early in such infants (e.g., *Conf.* 1.7.11-12) but rather that in their baptism they are "delivered from the bondage of the Devil through the grace of Christ" *(De gratia Christi,* 2.45). This is grace indeed, he argues, since one's parental "concupiscence of the flesh would be prejudicial *(obesset)* [i.e., to the child], just so far as it were present in us *(inesset)* if the remission of sins [i.e., in baptism] were not so beneficial *(prodesset)*" (2.44).

The views of St. Thomas Aquinas, in which Rom. 5:18 is a key verse, are similar to those of Augustine in most respects (e.g., Disputations, *De Malo,* 4.1; 1 ad 2, 3; *Summa Theol.* 1a-2ae.81.1). He speaks of it as "racial sin" — however, a function of nature — or analogously, as "a lack of original justice" *(Compendium Theologicae,* 196). "Augustine," he observes, "reads the symptom for the cause when he maintains that lust transmits sin" (Disp., *De Malo,* 46.16). In Thomas's view concupiscence is thus a "penalty, not a fault — except perhaps virtually, in that physical weakness may conduce to wrong." Applying Aristotelian causal analysis, he concludes, "The formal element in original sin is the lack of original justice, the material element is concupiscence. We may draw an analogy with actual and personal sin: there the turning away from God is formal, and the turning to creatures is material. Likewise original sin; it estranges us from God, and commits us to this world" *(De Malo,* 4.2). But for Thomas, as for certain other late medieval thinkers, this "turning away" is not a total corruption of the image of God in human nature. The "higher nature" represented by the soul and rational faculty is still capable of perceiving that one has turned away, and it still expresses something of "original justice" in its affirmation of what Aquinas calls "human virtue" *(Summa Theol.* 1a-2ae.71.2). As he puts it elsewhere, "The spark of reason cannot be extinguished so long as the light of mind remains; and sin can never make away with the mind" *(2 Sent.* 29.3.1); or again, "Sin is not pure hollowness, but an act showing a gap which ordered goodness should fill" (81.6).

The doctrine of original sin, already taught since the Council of Carthage (A.D. 418), was to be further refined by the Council of Trent (1545-63) and also by the Reformers. Most important among the Reformers on this subject is Calvin. Like Thomas, he strives to sharpen the distinction of Augustine, yet at the same time he separates himself even more sharply from Thomas and his successors. Calvin locates original sin not in concupiscence so much as in Adam and Eve's infidelity to God:

From infidelity . . . sprang ambition and pride, together with ingratitude; because Adam, by longing for more than was allotted him, manifested contempt for the great liberality with which God had enriched him. . . . In fine, infidelity opened the door to ambition, and ambition was the parent of rebellion, man casting off the fear of God and giving free vent to his lust.

Following St. Bernard of Clairvaux, he further says that whereas the door to damnation is opened by one's giving ear to Satan, the "door of salvation is opened to us when we receive the gospel with our ears." The requirement for regeneration stressed by Calvin is not baptism per se but obedience to the Word of God (*Inst.* 2.1.4-5). Calvin echoes Augustine and Aquinas in their notion of generational transmission; however, he significantly strengthens his formulation of the seriousness of the contagion. Like his predecessors he quotes Job 14:4, but in his rendering, "All, without exception, are originally depraved" (2.1.6). In his definition, contra Thomas:

Original sin . . . may be defined as an hereditary corruption and depravity of our nature, extending to *all parts of the soul,* which first makes us obnoxious to the wrath of God, and then produces in us works which in Scripture are termed works of the flesh . . . such as adultery, fornication, theft, hatred, murder, revellings. . . . (2.1.8; italics added)

The view of original sin typically expressed in medieval English texts, such as that found in Chaucer's *Canterbury Tales,* is Augustinian in its main outlines. Concupiscence, in all its manifestations, is the malady of original sin. The pattern of the Fall is seen to be inherent in all human sin, and, in a sense, repeated in each act of sin: "first, suggestion of the feend, as sheweth heere by the naddre; and afterward, the delit of the flessh, as sheweth heere by Eve; and after that, the consentynge of resoun, as sheweth heere by Adam" (*Parson's Tale,* 10.1.330-32). Concupiscence which is not "obeisaunt unto God," the Parson goes on to tell the pilgrims, is bound to lead to temptation and willful sin. This is to be understood as the perpetual struggle spoken of by St. Paul in which "The flessh coveiteth [KJV "lusteth"] agayn the spirit, and the spirit agayn the flessh; they been so contrarie and so stryven that a man may nat alway doon as he wolde" (342-43; see Gal. 5:17). In the person whose flesh is subordinate to reason and reason to the will of God, health *(sanitas)* prevails despite the presence of original and natural sin in the world; whenever an individual consents to concupiscent desire, or temptation, the internal hierarchy is overturned, thrown "up-so-doun" in the manner of our first parents' undoing:

For it is sooth that God, and resoun, and sensualitee, and the body of man been so ordeyned that everich of thise foure thynges sholde have lordshipe over that oother; as thus: God sholde have lordshipe over resoun, and resoun over sensualitee [affectual and emotional faculty] and sensualitee over the body of man. But soothly, whan man

synneth, al this ordre or ordinaunce is turned up-so-doun. (*ParsT* 10.261-63)

The disposition of original sin is thus to be resisted by active penitence and active virtue.

Milton's notion of original sin, especially as developed in *Paradise Lost,* is indebted to a Calvinist order of reasoning. The fall of Satan precipitates a cosmic Chaos (2.890-97). With the fall of Adam and Eve the sin "in power" in hell becomes "actual" in the world (10.585-89). By contrast God's creation, like his redemption or re-creation in Christ, is the establishment of Order. Adam's fall is utter, into "an Abyss of fears / And horrors . . . out of which," he cries, "I find no way, from deep to deeper plunged" (10.842-44). Not only condemned himself, he has learned that "all mankind" (10.822) will on his account participate in his condemnation: "But fromme what can proceed, / But all corrupt, both Mind and Will deprav'd, / Not to do only, but to will the same . . ." (824-26). The "original good" of Eden required obedience as an expression of love; obedience to the word of God and love for his ordinance are now required if humankind is to be redeemed.

In English literature of the Renaissance Calvinist views of original sin largely prevail; as in Marlowe's *The Tragicall Historie of Doctor Faustus* it is generally held that in the corruption of the will the corruption of the reason is contained, and Marlowe in fact seems to mock the sort of scholastic reasoning which might have it otherwise. In the 18th cent., however, with higher confidence in the rule of reason, a view of human nature derivatively Thomist yet more relaxed than Aquinas himself appears in the theodicy of Alexander Pope's *Essay on Man:* "Respecting Man, whatever wrong we call, / May, must be right, as relative to all" (1.51-52). When humanity understands its own instinct for reason and order, says Pope, then it will understand the order willed by God:

Then say not Man's imperfect, Heav'n in fault;
Say rather, Man's as perfect as he ought;
His knowledge measur'd to his state and place.
If to be perfect in a certain sphere,
What matter, soon or late, or here or there?
The blest today is as completely so,
As who began a thousand years ago. (69-75)

The gen'ral ORDER, since the whole began,
Is kept in Nature, and is kept in Man. (171-72)

Later in the century, William Cowper continues to exhibit a strongly Calvinist view of original sin, echoing also Milton's formulations (*The Task,* 6.348-70). Human wisdom, he says in "Charity," always resists admitting

That man, in nature's richest mantle clad,
And grac'd with all philosophy can add,
Though fair without, and luminous within,
Is still the progeny and heir of sin. (341-44)

His scarcely concealed allusion in these lines to the

"whited sepulchres" of Matt. 23:27 underscores his Calvinist sentiments more clearly still.

Original sin grew to be less popular a concern in 19th-cent. letters. As Wordsworth and Ruskin illustrate rather well, the essential benignity of human nature ascribed to an uncorrupted or "natural" state was imagined to be readily nurtured by a pastoral setting and art. The subject comes up for discussion in a strained Calvinistic fashion in texts such as Hogg's *Confessions of a Justified Sinner* and Scott's *Old Mortality,* while the doctrine is attacked as a form of guilt-enslavement and misanthropy by writers as diverse as Hawthorne, Melville, Emerson, Whitman, Arnold, and D. H. Lawrence. Literature since World War II has found new interest in the subject, with numerous writers more disposed to reconsider the biblical concept of original sin as part of the reality of human nature. Albert Camus, T. S. Eliot, Aldous Huxley, C. S. Lewis, J. R. R. Tolkien, Flannery O'Connor, and Walker Percy all explore its meaning in the persistence of the will to evil despite every apparent social advance of reason. In John Betjeman's "Original Sin on the Sussex Coast" (1954) the musing directs itself in painful whimsy to the violent behavior of well-cultured but bullying schoolboys; the theme is developed memorably by William Golding in his novel *Lord of the Flies* (1954). Theodore Roethke's examination of conscience in *Words for the Wind* (1958) turns the reflection selfward, in Augustinian existential fashion if not in Augustinian hope:

> Should every creature be as I have been,
> There would be reason for essential sin;
> I have myself an inner weight of woe
> That God himself can scarcely bear.

See also SEVEN DEADLY SINS.

Bibliography. Braswell, M. *The Medieval Sinner* (1983); Fish, S. E. *Surprised by Sin: The Reader in Paradise Lost* (1971); Grant, P. *The Transformation of Sin: Studies in Donne, Herbert, Vaughan, and Traherne* (1974); Marks, B. A. "The Origin of Original Sin in Hawthorne's Fiction." *Nineteenth Century Fiction* 14 (1960), 359-62; Marshall, W. H. "Thomas Traherne and the Doctrine of Original Sin." *MLN* 73 (1958), 161-65; Patrides, C. A. *Milton and the Christian Tradition* (1966); Pattison, R. B. "The Little Victims: The Child Figure and Original Sin in English Literature." *DA* 37 (1976), 3647A; Stewart, L. *American Literature and Christian Doctrine* (1958).

OUR DAILY BREAD *See* MANNA; *PATER NOSTER.*

OUT OF THE EATER Passing by the remains of a lion he had earlier killed with his bare hands (Judg. 14:6), Samson saw "a swarm of bees and honey in the carcass of the lion" (v. 8). At his wedding feast he then set a riddle for his Philistine neighbors: "Out of the eater came forth meat, and out of the strong came forth sweetness." If they should answer correctly, he would award a considerable prize (v. 12), but if not, they should pay him the same. Unable to expound the riddle, they convinced Samson's wife to entice the answer from him. When they produced it Samson was enraged, saying, "If ye had not plowed with my heifer, ye had not found out my riddle" (v. 18).

Patristic exegesis saw in the slaying of the lion "not only a prodigy of valor but also a mystery of wisdom, an utterance of prophecy," as St. Ambrose puts it — a foreshadowing of the Eucharist: "O manifest sacrament! we have escaped from the slayer, we have overcome the strong one. The food of life is now there, where before was the hunger of a miserable death. Dangers are changed into safety, bitterness into sweetness. Grace came forth from the offence, power from weakness, and life from death" (*De Spiritu Sancto,* 2, pr. 6, 8). In later tradition, Samson's riddle is seen as a preeminent example of biblical paradox. In Bunyan's *Grace Abounding to the Chief of Sinners,* "Temptations, when we meet them at first, are as the lion that roared upon Samson; but if we overcome them, the next time we see them, we shall find a nest of honey within them." Professor Teufelsdröckh in Carlyle's *Sartor Resartus* sees the incident as prefiguring a paradox of generation, of beauty from ugliness: "Thy own amber-locked, snow-and-rose bloom Maiden . . . has descended, like thyself, from that same hair-mantled, flint-hurling Aboriginal Anthropophagus! Out of the eater cometh forth meat; out of the strong cometh forth sweetness. What changes are wrought, not by Time, yet in Time!" (1.5). Later he apostrophizes, "Thrifty, unwearied Nature, ever out of our great waste educing some little profit of thy own, — how dost thou, from the very carcass of the killer, bring life for the living!" (2.8). In Pater's essay on "The Poetry of Michelangelo," in *The Renaissance,* he says that in the painter's mellowing "patriarchal age" the "sweetness it had taken so long to secrete in him was found at last. Out of the strong came forth sweetness, *ex forti dulcedo.*" R. L. Stevenson applies the phrase to his discovery of peace where he had not looked to find it, "in the bleak and gusty North" ("On the Enjoyment of Unpleasant Places"). Emerson, in his "Ode, Inscribed to W. H. Channing," applies the phrase in the same vein as Carlyle, but in the expression of an overtly racist notion of social engineering:

> He who exterminates
> Races by stronger races
> Black by white faces —
> Knows to bring honey
> Out of the lion;
> Grafts gentlest scion
> On pirate and Turk.

See also SAMSON.

OUT OF THE MOUTH OF BABES "Out of the mouth of babes and sucklings hast thou ordained strength . . . that thou mightest still the enemy and the avenger." The second verse of Ps. 8 associates the strength of God with the innocence of children. The verse has formed part of the liturgy of the Feast of Holy Innocents since as early as the 8th cent. and has been included in the collect for that feast day in the *Book of Common Prayer* since 1661. The phrase "out of the mouth of babes" has come to be popularly used of children or of innocents who speak the truth which adults or the more sophisticated either do not see or lack the candor to state. It is often set side by side with Matt. 11:25, where Jesus speaks of spiritual knowledge "hid . . . from the wise and prudent" but "revealed . . . unto babes." Although some modern translations of the Bible associate the first part of Ps. 8:2 with the second part of v. 1 (e.g., RSV, "Thou whose glory above the heavens is changed / by the mouth of babes and infants"; see also JB), the KJV and *Book of Common Prayer* retain the Vg reading, which is also reflected in the Matt. 21:16 quotation of the OT passage.

Midrashic commentary interpreted the babes and sucklings as new candidates for the rabbinate and the strength as Torah, but Christian commentary has usually concentrated on the alimentary suggestion of "sucklings" (Vg *lactentium*). Thus faith or doctrine affords the nourishment required to understand things spiritual and eternal, according to St. Augustine (who cites 1 Cor. 3:1-2 in support) and Cassiodorus (who cites 1 Pet. 2:2); Luther says that the sucklings seek no other food but the unadulterated word of the gospel. The psalm was one of three interpreted by Theodore of Mopsuestia (5th cent.) as prophetic of Christ, probably following the lead of Jesus himself, who quotes v. 2 to the priests and scribes in Jerusalem as a justifying explanation of the children's greeting him with cries of hosanna.

The psalm has been versified by numerous English poets, notably Sidney and Milton. Chaucer's Prioress, herself an innocent of sorts, paraphrases vv. 1-2 as the opening theme of her tale:

"O Lord, oure Lord, thy name how merveillous
Is in this large world ysprad," quod she;
"For noght oonly thy laude precious
Parfourned is by men of dignitee,
But by the mouth of children thy bountee
Parfourned is, for on the brest soukynge
Somtyme shewen they thyn heriynge."

She returns to the phrase later in her tale (*Canterbury Tales,* 7.607-08).

Shakespeare frequently assigns a witty wisdom to children — e.g., to Macduff's prattling son in *Macbeth* (4.2) and to the young Prince of York in *Richard 3* (3.1). Also his fools, such as Lear's fool and Lavatch in *All's Well,* are childlike adults who voice proverbial wisdom. (In Dostoyevsky's *The Idiot,* Prince Mysteru is likewise a strangely wise innocent.)

Ps. 8:2 fits neatly with Wordsworth's conception of the innocence of children and their closeness to God; he uses the phrase "babes and sucklings" in the sonnet "Young England," and the thought may lie behind his various attributions of wisdom or knowledge to children or childlike adults (see, e.g., *Prelude* [1850], 2.232-55; 13.183; "Immortality Ode"). Both Byron and Tennyson use the innocence of "babes and sucklings" ironically. Byron compares the distress of "ladies who cannot have their own way" with that of animals robbed of their "babes and sucklings" (*Don Juan,* 5.133), and Tennyson puts the phrase into the mouth of St. Thomas Becket, who derives great satisfaction from the praise accorded him by a crowd of people for confronting the secular powers (*Becket,* 2.2.158).

See also CHILDREN.

Bibliography. De Vreesse, R. *Le Commentaire de Theodore de Mopsueste sur les Psaumes (I-LXXX)* (1939); *Midrash on Psalms.* Trans. W. G. Braude (1959); Smith, H. "English Metrical Psalms in the Sixteenth Century and Their Literary Significance." *HLQ* 9 (1945-46), 249-71.

PHILLIP ROGERS

OUT-HERODS HEROD   This phrase, from Shakespeare's *Hamlet* (3.2.12-13), refers to Herod the Great, and occurs also in the title of a poem by Anthony Hecht, "It Out-herods Herod. Pray you, avoid it" (*The Hard Hours* [1968], 67-68). The allusion refers to Herod's characteristic hyperbole and threatening bluster followed by mean violence against the weak and defenseless (Matt. 2:1-8, 15-19).

See also HEROD THE GREAT.

OX AND ASS   *See* ASS.

OX KNOWS HIS OWNER   *See* ASS.

P

PALATIEL *See* ABNER.

PARABLE The biblical terms *mashal* (Heb.) and *parabolē* (Gk.) refer to a wide variety of utterances including proverbs, riddles, and wisdom sayings as well as the kind of brief narrative one normally thinks of as a parable. Modern scholarship typically employs the term to designate only the brief narratives —such as those recorded among the teachings of Jesus in the Gospels.

When Jesus preached in parables, he made use of a literary genre which had a long tradition in both the Semitic milieu (e.g., 2 Sam. 14:5-13; Isa. 5:1-7; Pirqe 'Abot 3.18) and the Greek and Roman world (cf. Aristotle, *Rhetoric,* 2; Quintilian, *Institutio oratoria,* 5). Many of the images used in Jesus' parables are also to be found in the writings of Hillel, Shammai, and other great rabbis (e.g., the parables of the pearl, workers in the vineyard, and wise and foolish virgins). All the Gospel parables appear in the Synoptics; there is no true parable in John.

Biblical parables take their true-to-life stories from nature or the human scene. They exhibit a variety of folktale characteristics, such as economy of presentation (only two or three main characters are generally involved); the treatment of groups as individuals; development by action and speech (and omission of feelings and motives); repetition; contrast; numerical patterning (e.g., use of the number three). Every parable is tropical—having a point or moral—and invokes comparison. Some parables are extended metaphors or similes ("the kingdom of heaven is like . . ." [e.g., Matt. 13:24]); others are extended synecdoches (the exemplary stories [e.g., the rich fool, Luke 12:16-21]). Biblical parables always have an ethical or religious meaning; they afford a lesson or teaching about God's character and actions and often challenge the behavior of their hearers. The parables are rhetorical (and heterotelic) devices, not poetic (or autotelic) as is sometimes imagined. Their purpose is to provoke a change of position in the hearer. The NT parables owe their persuasive power to an appeal to the common experience of their audience ("Which of you. . . ?") or to the unique authority of the teller ("I say to you . . .").

Scholars have long wrestled with the problem of how to explain the ancient view, expressed notably in Mark 4:10-12 and its parallels, that parables are mysterious speech. Jülicher's late-19th-cent. argument, now generally discounted, is that Jesus himself preached in straightforward extended similes which were clear enough for the simple in his audience to grasp but that Mark distorted them, presenting them rather as allegories, purposefully obscure "dark sayings." A more balanced explanation sees Mark's recounting of the parables, always tropical, as serving his overall theme of mystery — which, as elsewhere in Scripture (e.g., Isa. 29:9-16), is related not to intellectual obtuseness but to moral obduracy, the hearer's "hardness of heart." Because of their tropical and paradoxical elements, many of the parables can be grasped only "spiritually": on the surface they may be merely confounding. According to Kermode, to "confound" is in this sense one of the purposes of parable: appealing to Mark 4:10-12 (cf. Matt. 13:10-17) he describes it as a "genesis of secrecy," discourse which divides insiders from outsiders, both creating and separating the community of its hearers at the same time.

The major parables of Jesus include The Hidden Treasure and The Pearl (Matt. 13:44-46), The Lost Sheep, Lost Coin, and Lost (or Prodigal) Son (Luke 15:3-32); The Rich Man and Lazarus (Luke 16:19-31); The Ten Virgins (Matt. 25:1-13); The Two Builders (Matt. 7:24-27); The Wheat and Tares (Matt. 13:24-30); The Talents (Matt. 25:14-30; Luke 19:11-27); The Rich Fool (Luke 12:16-21); The Unjust Steward (Luke 16:1-9); The Workers in the Vineyard (Matt. 20:1-16); The Two Sons and the Vineyard (Matt. 21:28-32); The Pharisee and the Tax Collector (Luke 18:9-14); The Good Samaritan (Luke 10:29-37); The Unmerciful Servant (Matt. 18:23-35); The Tower Builder and the King Going to War (Luke 14:28-32); The Friend at Midnight (Luke 11:5-8); The Unjust Judge (Luke 18:1-8); The Great Supper (Matt. 22:1-14; Luke 14:16-24); The Leaven (Luke 13:20-21); The Mustard Seed (Mark 4:28-32); The Seed Growing Secretly (Mark 4:26-29); The Sower (Mark 4:3-8); and The Wicked Tenants (Mark 12:1-12). One may also read the account of Jesus' cursing of the fig tree as an enacted parable (similar to the various prophetic mimes of such prophets as Jeremiah or Hosea or the story of the wounded prophet in 1 Kings 20:35-43).

From the NT period to the Reformation, "allegorizing," i.e., either changing the original meaning or adding tropical meaning, usually by interpreting literal details as metaphors, was the primary method of reading the parables. Philo of Alexandria in the 1st cent. and Origen in the 3rd set a precedent by allegorizing even small details. In so doing, they were adopting a method of interpretation well established in the classical world (Homer having been the first author to receive such allegorical treatment) but also employed by NT writers themselves in interpreting the parables of the sower, the tares, and the net. St. Irenaeus and Tertullian, while trying to correct some of the fanciful allegorizing of the gnostic writers, nevertheless continued to interpret parables in the allegorical mode. St. Augustine in the 4th and 5th cents. often outdid Origen in ingenious application of the method, but the Antiochene Fathers in the same period set themselves against such allegorizing. St. John Chrysostom, e.g., set forth these principles in his *Homilies on Matthew*: "Interpret the elements in the parables that are urgent and essential . . . do not waste time on all the details. . . . Seek out the scope for which the parable was designed . . . and be not overbusy with the rest."

This view did not gain prominence in the West until the Reformation, when interpreters such as Luther de-

nounced allegorizers as "clerical jugglers performing monkey tricks." Nonetheless, Luther still allegorized certain elements in pressing his own emphases (e.g., his sermon on the good Samaritan), as have many subsequent Protestant commentators.

Contemporary studies have tended to stress the social and moral implications of the parables. Robert Funk discusses the way parables expose and frustrate the intentions of those who "insist on interpreting the word of grace rather than letting themselves be interpreted by it" (17). A story such as the great supper, he says, is "an offense to the religiously disposed (the Pharisees) but a joyous surprise to the religiously disinherited (tax collectors and sinners)." Crossan sees parable as a form which subverts cherished preconceptions and established value systems. Parable is, for him, "paradox formed into story" (93). The good Samaritan, the Pharisee and the tax collector, and the rich man and Lazarus subvert the taken-for-granted social, ethical, and economic standards of the day.

Literary use of parables is of two principal kinds: specific allusions to biblical parables and imitation of the parabolic form. The NT parables most commonly referred to in English literary tradition are the prodigal son, the good Samaritan, and Lazarus and Dives. Somewhat less frequently alluded to are the sower, the talents, the wise and foolish virgins, the laborers in the vineyard, and the wedding supper. The authors most indebted to biblical parables are Bunyan, Milton, and Shakespeare, but multiple instances of such use are also found in Carlyle, Tennyson, Ruskin, Browning, Whittier, Joyce, Hardy, Lawrence, and others.

The use of a biblically inspired parabolic mode is more difficult to appraise because of the uncertain boundaries between allegory and parable. Certain of the poems of George Herbert, e.g., employ the studied understatement, apparent simplicity, mystery veiled by familiarity, and homely language which one associates with Jesus' parables (e.g., "Time," "Redemption," "The Pulley"). In the Victorian age parable is perhaps best represented by such children's classics as Kingsley's *Water Babies* and George Macdonald's *The Princess and the Goblin*. Hawthorne's fiction has a parabolic character: the author starts with a dominant moral idea, for which a character or scene or whole narrative becomes an illustration. In Pearl of *The Scarlet Letter, e.g.,* one finds a specific echo of the NT pearl of great price; in "Rappaccini's Daughter" are seen more generally the consequences of science and pride, love and lust, and in "The Minister's Black Veil," the nature of human fallenness and mortality.

Parables are frequently embedded in a larger narrative, e.g., Stephen's parable of the plums in *Ulysses.* In exploring the use of parable in modern literature Louis MacNeice cites such works as Beckett's *Waiting for Godot,* Pinter's *The Caretaker,* Golding's *Pincher Martin,* and the poems of Edwin Muir. Bertolt Brecht wrote what he himself called parables for the theater. Kafka wrote fiction in parabolic form *(The Castle, The Trial)*, using a spare, even stark narrative to struggle with doubt, *angst* over the gulf between God and Man, and the moral complexities of the law. The contemporary parables of Latin-American writer Jorge Luis Borges have had a significant impact in North America and have been widely translated into English.

See also DIVES AND LAZARUS; GOOD SAMARITAN; LOST SHEEP, PARABLE OF; MARRIAGE FEAST, PARABLE OF; PRODIGAL SON; SOWER, PARABLE OF; WHEAT AND TARES; WISE AND FOOLISH BUILDERS; WISE AND FOOLISH VIRGINS.

Bibliography. Boucher, M. *The Mysterious Parable* (1977); Crossan, J. D. *Raid on the Articulate* (1976); Dodd, C. H. *The Parables of the Kingdom* (1961); Dupont, J. *Pourquoi des paraboles? La méthode parabolique de Jésus* (1977); Funk, R. *Language, Hermeneutics, and the Word of God* (1966); Jeremias, J. *The Parables of Jesus* (1970); Kermode, F. *The Genesis of Secrecy: On the Interpretation of Narrative* (1979); Kissinger, W. *The Parables of Jesus: A History of Interpretation and Bibliography* (1979); Lockyer, H. *All the Parables of the Bible* (1963); MacNeice, L. *Varieties of Parable* (1965); Perrin, H. *Jesus and the Language of the Kingdom* (1976); "Parable." In *Semeia* 1 (1974), 236-74; Via, D. *The Parables: Their Literary and Existential Dimension* (1967).
CORBIN S. CARNELL
MADELEINE BOUCHER

PARACLETE   The "Comforter" promised by Jesus in John 14:16.
See also HOLY SPIRIT.

PARADISE   *See* EDEN; FOUR RIVERS OF PARADISE; HEAVEN.

PAROUSIA   *See* SECOND COMING.

PARTING OF THE SEA   *See* BAPTISM; EXODUS.

PASSION, CROSS   *Passion,* an anglicized form of the late Lat. *passio,* is used by ecclesiastical writers to refer to the suffering and death of Jesus on the cross and to the narratives of these events in the Gospels (Matt. 26–27; Mark 14–16; Luke 22–23; John 18–19). The Latin term and its cognates translate the NT Greek word group "suffer" *(paschō, pathos, pathēma),* and in all but one instance (Heb. 2:9) the NT employs the plural of the noun *(pathēmata)* of the sufferings of Jesus (2 Cor. 1:5-6; Phil. 3:10; Heb. 2:10; 1 Pet. 4:13). By metonymy other more concrete terms are used for the Passion: (1) the cross *(stauros,* 1 Cor. 1:18); (2) death, understood as the saving event of the cross (Rom. 6:3; 1 Cor. 11:25; 15:3); (3) blood and the shedding of blood (Rom. 3:25; 5:9; 1 Cor. 10:16; 11:27; Eph. 1:7; 2:13; Heb. 9:14; 10:19; 1 Pet. 1:2; 1 John 1:7); (4) the handing over or betrayal of Jesus (Rom. 4:25; 1 Cor. 1:23); and (5), especially in the Gospel of John, the "lifting up" of Jesus on the cross (3:14; 12:32) with the nuance of exaltation and return to the Father (14:28; 16:16; cf. Luke 9:51; Acts 2:33).

The Hebrew Scriptures provide the major influence on the language of the Passion. Faced with the "offense" of the cross (Deut. 21:23; Gal. 5:11) and the absence of any OT expectation of a suffering Messiah who would be rejected by his own people, early Christian preachers turned to the OT as an authority shared with fellow Jews to argue that the Passion was "according to the Scriptures" (1 Cor. 15:3; cf. Mark 14:21). Among the major OT motifs and texts are: (1) Jesus as the Second or "last" Adam (1 Cor. 15:45) whose obedience unto death (Phil. 2:8) reversed the disobedience of the first Adam (Gen. 2:17; 3:17-19), himself described as "a figure *(typos)* of him who was to come" (Rom. 5:14); (2) Jesus' death as the Passover sacrifice (1 Cor. 5:7) and he himself as the Passover lamb (John 19:36; cf. 1:29, 36; Rev. 5:6, 12; 7:14; 12:11; 13:8); (3) the Suffering Servant of Isaiah 52:13–53:12; (4) Jesus as the High Priest "after the similitude" *(homoiotēta)* of Melchizedek (Heb. 7:15) who by his death offers the definitive sacrifice for sin (Heb. 5:1-10; 7:1-27; 9:1-28; 13:11-12, 20).

While these motifs are found mainly in the NT epistolary literature, the Passion narratives themselves reflect other OT (and some Intertestamental) motifs both for apologetic reasons and to illustrate details of the narrative. In Mark alone there are over 57 explicit quotations and 160 allusions. Chief among the OT influences are (1) lament psalms where a suffering and persecuted individual prays for deliverance (Pss. 31, 34, 69, 109, and esp. 22, which provides many pictorial details of the Crucifixion [Mark 15:24, 28, 34]); (2) the figure of "the suffering just one" who, though persecuted and mocked (cf. Mark 15:27-30), is vindicated by God (Wisd. 2:1-10; 5:1-12); (3) the Suffering Servant of Isaiah; (4) stories of martyred prophets (e.g., 2 Chron. 24:20-22; cf. Luke 13:33) and especially of the Maccabean martyrs (2 Macc. 6:18-31; 7:1-42); (5) texts from Daniel on the Son of man (Dan. 7:9-14, 18, 27; cf. 2 Esdr. 13; 1 Enoch 71:10-17; Mark 8:31; 9:31; 10:33-34; 13:26-27; 14:21, 62).

Typological interpretation of NT Passion narratives focuses naturally on the cross as their principal symbol. This begins with the earliest commentators. St. Justin refers to Noah's ark, the tree of life, and the rod of Moses as prefigurations of the cross *(Dial.* 86; 131.3; 138.2), and St. Clement of Alexandria interprets Isaac's carrying the wood for his sacrifice as a type of Christ's carrying the instrument of his death *(Paidagogos,* 1.5). In the writings of St. Irenaeus occurs one of the most influential expansions on Scripture: he interprets the mystery of which St. Paul speaks in Eph. 3:3 as referring to the cross and the "breadth and length, and depth and height" of Eph. 3:18 as uniting East, West, North, and South *(Epideixis,* 1.34). This cosmic interpretation of the cross continues among the post-Nicene Fathers (e.g., St. Cyril of Jerusalem, *Catechesis,* 13.28; St. Gregory of Nyssa, *Oratio cate-*

chetica, 32). St. John Chrysostom makes important contributions to the literature of the cross in his *Homilies* on Matthew, John, 1 Corinthians, and Philippians and in his *Against Marcionists and Manicheans*.

In the Western Church St. Augustine provides the fullest commentary on the Passion and Crucifixion. In his *Sermones* on the NT, letters, and *Confessiones* he quotes and elaborates most of the key passages, including Gal. 6:14. Preoccupied, as his predecessors had been, with the cross as a cosmic symbol, Augustine goes beyond them in identifying the dimensions of the cross with moral and spiritual values: the transverse beam represents the breadth of charity, the upright represents steadfastness; the headrest represents the hope of heavenly reward, and the part hidden in the ground, the mystery of grace. This moral symbolism of the cross recurs in several of his works and was to exert a strong influence throughout the Middle Ages *(De doctrina Christiana*, 2.41.62; *Sermones* [PL 38.371, 903]; *Ep.* 55, 140; *In Joan. Ev.* 118.5).

At approximately the same time, two significant events were being recorded: Constantine's vision of the cross, followed by his victory and conversion, and the discovery of the True Cross by his mother Helena (Eusebius, *Vita Constantini,* 1.28-32; 3.26; St. Ambrose, *Sermo in obitu Theodosii,* 40-48; Rufinus of Aquileia, *Hist. eccl.* 1.8 [PL 21.475-78]; St. Cyril of Jerusalem, *Ep. ad Constantium* 3; *Catecheses,* 4.10; 10.19; 13.4). With the triumph of Constantine, the cross was publicly proclaimed the emblem of victory. It was celebrated as the tree of life in the great Passion hymn of Fortunatus, *"Pange, Lingua Gloriosi,"* and in his *"Vexilla Regis"* the cross is a banner signifying the triumph of life over death and a gleaming tree from which the divine king reigns (F. J. E. Raby, ed., *The Oxford Book of Medieval Latin Verse* [1959], nos. 54, 55).

In OE, Cynewulf's *Elene* glorifies the cross through a recapitulation of the narrative of Constantine and Helena. In the *Dream of the Rood,* the dreamer first sees the cross adorned with jewels and reaching into the heavens, then as a blood-stained tree, and the cross itself speaks of its part in the Crucifixion. A vision of the cross at the Last Judgment appears at the end of *Christ,* where the radiant cross, red with the Savior's blood, towers over the universe, replacing the sun as the source of all light. The *Passione Sanctorum* of Aelfric is, as its title suggests, a martyrology; in it Aelfric is at pains to relate the virtue of the suffering of any individual saint to that of the cross of Christ; martyrdom is par excellence *imitatio Christi.* There are also, in OE as in Latin, legends connected with the wood of the cross. In the most important of these, the cross is made of a descendant of the tree of which Adam and Eve ate, thus connecting the suffering and ultimate triumph of Jesus to the original sin in the garden (*History of the Holy Rood Tree,* ed. A. S. Napier [EETS o.s. 103 (1894)]; *Legends of the Holy Rood,* ed. R. Morris [EETS

o.s. 46 (1871)]; *Cursor Mundi,* ed. R. Morris [EETS o.s. 57, 59, 62 (1874-78)]; E. Quinn, *The Quest of Seth* [1962], esp. 2, 9-12, 103-30).

Of the numerous medieval Latin hymns written in honor of the Passion and cross of Christ, the Victorine sequences *"Laudes Crucis"* and *"Salve, Crux"* represent ingenious reworkings of earlier traditions (*The Liturgical Poetry of Adam of St. Victor,* ed. D. S. Wrangham [1881], 2.46-83; 3.2-5). More fervid are the hymns of the Franciscans who create around their meditations on Christ's Passion a new literature of the cross. The purpose of meditation on the Crucifixion is, for the Franciscans, identification with the Passion of Christ, the most radical image of which in Franciscan spirituality is the stigmata which St. Francis received himself while so meditating on Mt. Verna. Among the most famous poetic renditions of such an affectual meditation on the Passion are Jacopone da Todi's poems *Stabat Mater* and *Donna de Paradiso* (Lauda 93), in the former of which the poet prays, *"Fac ut portem Christi mortem . . .* Make me to bear the death of Christ, his lot and Passion, and renew in me his injuries. Cause me to be wounded with the wounds, the Cross, and make me drunk *(inebriari)* with the love of your son." In St. Bonaventure's hymn *"Laudismus de Sancta Cruce"* the scriptural account of the Crucifixion is made vivid as Christ appeals directly to humanity from the cross, often in the words of Jeremiah (Lam. 1:12), *"O vos omnes qui transistis per viam. . . ."* In some Franciscan poetry the focus shifts to identification with the sorrow of Mary, as in the sequence *Stabat Mater Dolorosa.* This emphasis governs the Franciscan *Meditationes Vitae Christi,* translated into English by Nicholas Love (ca. 1400) as *the Mirrour of the Blessed Lyf of Jesu Christ* (ed. L. F. Powell [1908]).

The ME lyrics continue the tradition of the Franciscans: the cross is the center of intense personal devotion, and in some the focus shifts from Christ to Mary (e.g., "Nou goth sonne" and "Stond wel, moder, ounder rode," in C. Brown, *English Lyrics of the XIIIth Century*, nos. 1, 49), the latter of which is an adaptation of Jacopone da Todi's *Stabat Mater.* Among the 14th-cent. English lyrics on the cross, a free translation of Fortunatus's *"Vexilla Regis"* beginning "The kynges baneres beth forth y-lad / The rode tokne is nou to-sprad" is especially splendid (C. Brown, *Religious Lyrics of the XIVth Century,* no. 13). Of the many 15th-cent. Passion lyrics, the most interesting continue the tradition of representing Christ appealing directly to humanity, including "The Dollorous complant of oure lorde Apoune the croce Crucifyit" (C. Brown, *Religious Lyrics of the XVth Century,* no. 102).

The sufferings of Jesus provide the subject not only for medieval lyrics but for devotional prose as well, including the prayers addressed to the cross in the *Ancrene Riwle* (trans. M. B. Salu [1955], 1.7-8, 19-20; for the metaphor of the cross as shield, see 4.128-30; 7.173-74). Richard Rolle in his *Meditations on the Passion* addresses

Christ directly at each stage in the events leading to Calvary.

Among the major texts of the 14th cent. *Piers Plowman* provides the most imaginative and reverent passages relating to the Passion of Christ. The poet sees in his dream the Tree of Charity with its roots of Mercy and trunk of Pity (B.16.3-5); on Easter morning the poet calls his wife and daughter to honor God's Resurrection: they are to creep on their knees to the cross and kiss it, a reference to the adoration of the cross (18.428); the poet dreams that he sees Piers all stained with blood and bearing a cross, and Conscience explains that the figure is Christ (19.6-8); and finally, the dreamer sees Grace give Piers the cross with which to make Holy Church (19.321-22). For Langland the cross is also a talisman for warding off spiritual danger or evil: "And it afereth the fende for such is the my3te, / May no grysly gost glyde there it shadweth" (B.18.430-31). This persists as a perennial image in gothic and horror fiction.

There are numerous, generally less emotional, references to the Passion and cross in Chaucer: in his ABC addressed to the Virgin (60, 82, 162); at the conclusion of *Troilus and Criseyde* (5.1842-46); in *The Man of Law's Tale,* the prayer of Custance addressed to the cross (*Canterbury Tales,* 2.449-62); in *The Clerk's Tale,* Griselda's prayer (4.556, 558); and in *The Parson's Tale* (10.258, 271, 667, 819).

The dramatic enactment of the Crucifixion forms the central aspect of all four English Mystery cycles. In the York "Mortificacio Christi" Jesus' address from the cross is especially effective with its line, "On roode am I ragged and rente," twice repeated (36.120, 253, 304; cf. plays no. 34 and 35, as well as those in the Towneley, Coventry, and Chester cycles).

After the Reformation there is little innovation in the tradition of the Passion and Crucifixion. References occur throughout English literature, but most are conventional reflections, among the best known of which involves the characterization and narration of the pilgrimage of Spenser's Redcrosse Knight, champion of Christian holiness (*Faerie Queene,* 1.1.2). St. Thomas More's poem "Consider Well" is a traditional Catholic invitation to meditation on the Passion even in the midst of "our disport, our revel, and our play."

In Shakespeare, references occur chiefly in the history plays, as in *1 Henry 4* (1.1.20.27) where Henry refers both to the blessed cross and the bitter cross (cf. *Richard 2,* 4.1.94, 241; *3 Henry 6,* 4.4.21). Seventeenth-century poetry continues the tradition of meditation on the cross, as in John Davies's long poem *The Holy Roode or Christs Crosse.* Richard Crashaw maintains the traditions of Franciscan (Capuchin) meditation on the Passion in numerous vivid poems, including "O these wakeful wonds of Thine! / Are they mouths? or are they eyes?" ("On the Wounds of our Crucified Lord") and his highly charged poem "On the Bleeding Wounds of our Crucified Lord":

Jesu, no more, it is full tide;
  From Thy head and from Thy feet,
  From Thy hands and from Thy side,
All Thy purple rivers meet.

Crashaw's baroque litany of poems in his "The Office of the Holy Cross," with its sequence of poetic versicle, responsor, hymn, antiphon, versicle, responsor, and prayer for each of the eight canonical *horae* constitutes perhaps the richest of 17th-cent. English meditations on the Passion; it draws consciously on the 13th-cent. "Hours of the Passion" of William Shoreham.

John Donne's poetry combines most of the earlier traditions with ingenuity and strong personal feeling. Most remarkable is his 64-line poem entitled "The Crosse," in which he refers to the cross as an altar, speaks of stretching his arms to form his own cross, contrasts material and spiritual crosses, and ends with the "Crosse of Christ." Other meditations on the Passion include his "The Progresse of the Soul," "Hymn to God, my God, in my sicknesse," the sonnet "Crucifying," "Satyre 4," and "Goodfriday, 1613. Riding Westward." Herbert also represents a high point in 17th-cent. meditative poetry on the Passion. His "Sacrifice," a 252-line poem, belongs to the *O vos omnes* tradition of Christ's appeal from the cross (cf. John Grimestone's 14th-cent. "O Vos Omnes," ed. C. Brown, *Religious Lyrics of the XIVth Century,* no. 74). Related poems include "Easter," "Affliction," "Conscience," "The Crosse," "The Church Militant," and "L'Envoy." Sir Thomas Browne's *The Garden of Cyrus* includes numerous expressions of admiration for landscape design inviting of meditation because it incorporates the "metaphysical cross"; in his *Religio Medici,* though eschewing Capuchin-styled adoration of the cross, he confesses to its importance in his spiritual reflection: "At the sight of a Crosse or Crucifix I can dispence with my hat, but scarce with the thought and memory of my Saviour; I cannot laugh at but rather pity the fruitlesse journeys of Pilgrims, or contemne the miserable condition of Friers; for though misplaced in circumstance, there is something in it of devotion. . . " (1.3). Milton's "The Passion" is an early, unfinished poem; two other references to the cross in Milton's poetry prophesy its place in the scheme of salvation: in "Hymn on the Morning of Christ's Nativity," "The Babe lies yet in smiling Infancy / That on the bitter Cross / Must redeem our loss" (151-53), and in *Paradise Lost* Michael tells Adam that in future ages God's Son will be "nailed to the Cross" (12.413-17). In Bunyan's *Pilgrim's Progress* a vision of the cross causes Christian's burden to fall at last from his shoulders.

Despite the influence of the Wesleys and the "great revival" of the 18th cent., relatively few important cross poems were written and the Passion in general was eschewed as a subject for "polite" literature. William Cowper provides a notable exception, though his treatment tends to be abstract by comparison with his 17th-cent. forebears, as, e.g., in the closing lines of his "The Progress of Error," in which "the Cross, once seen is death to ev'ry vice: / Else he that hung there suffer'd all his pain, / Bled, groan'd, and agoniz'd, and died, in vain." On the other hand, like some of the Puritan and Reformed hymn writers before him, he uses the blood of Christ metonymically for the Passion and the cross in a fashion almost as vivid as the French Capuchins, the painter Matthias Grünewald, or Richard Crashaw. One of the most popular of his *Olney Hymns* (no. 15) begins:

There is a fountain fill'd with blood
Drawn from Emmanuel's veins;
And sinners, plung'd beneath that flood,
Lose all their guilty stains

and includes lines reminiscent of St. Bonaventure or Jacopone:

E'er since, by faith, I saw the stream
Thy flowing wounds supply;
Redeeming love has been my theme,
And shall be till I die.

Among the Romantic poets, the most important in relation to this subject is Blake, who alludes to the cross in *The Four Zoas,* Night the Eighth (ed. Keynes, 325, 331, 338, 593-95); *Milton* (5.3; 22.58); and *Jerusalem* (652, 688, 695). Especially interesting is Blake's continuation of the tradition of the vision of the cross at the Last Judgment (444; cf. *The Everlasting Gospel,* 749, 751, 759). In Wordsworth references to the cross are conventional: *The Prelude,* 6.484; *The White Doe of Rylstone* (124, 356, 663); *The Excursion,* 5.907; *Ecclesiastical Sonnets,* 3.40.9. In Coleridge, *Christabel* (389) and *The Rime of the Ancient Mariner* (141-42) are noteworthy. Shelley's references reflect his opposition to established Christianity: e.g., *Queen Mab* (7.138, 174, 219, 229) and *Hellas* (224, 501, 603, 638, 1018). In *Don Juan* Byron ironically echoes Col. 1:20: "the crimson cross . . . red with no redeeming gore" (8.972-74).

Among 19th-cent. novelists Scott refers to relics of the cross in novels set in the Middle Ages: *Ivanhoe,* chap. 5; *Quentin Durward,* chap. 33; *The Talisman,* chap. 4. A more imaginative use of this tradition appears at the end of Melville's *Billy Budd.* In later 19th-cent. poetry, Longfellow's sonnet "The Cross of Snow" and Sidney Lanier's "A Ballad of the Trees and the Master" are remarkably original and moving. The poetry of Tennyson contains a number of references to the cross: "Sea Dreams" (186); "Vastness" (15); "Happy" (3, 6, 12); and in *The Idylls of the King,* "The Coming of Arthur" (271-74), "Balin and Balan" (108, 451-53), and "The Last Tournament" (493). Christina Rossetti recollects the Passion in "What Is It Jesus Saith," "Tuesday Holy Week," "Good Friday Morning," and "General Assembly"; cf. E. A. Robinson's sonnet, "Calvary." In the poetry of Hop-

kins the image of Christ and his cross figures in "Rosa Mystica"; "The Wreck of the Deutschland," esp. st. 24, and "Pilate."

Yeats deals with the crucifixion in three verse dramas: *Land of the Heart's Desire, Calvary,* and *Resurrection.* Lawrence's poems, including "Reminder," "Meeting among the Mountains," and "The Cross," reveal his interest in the cross as an instrument of suffering and as a recurring form of life, as also does his "The Man who Died." Robert Frost in "The Peaceful Shepherd" projects an ironic view of "the Cross of Faith" in league with "the Crown of Rule," "the Scales of Trade," and "the Sword," and a cross substitute becomes a symbol of human suffering in Hemingway's *The Old Man and the Sea.* The most memorable reference to the cross in Joyce is the sermon in *A Portrait of the Artist,* chap. 3; it is the subject of frequent wordplay in *Finnegans Wake.*

In 20th-cent. fiction sermons on the cross appear not only in Joyce's *Portrait* but also in the conclusion of Faulkner's *The Sound and the Fury* and in Flannery O'Connor's *The Violent Bear It Away,* chap. 5. *Helena,* by Evelyn Waugh, is a fictional retelling of the story of the finding of the True Cross. Various modern "fifth gospels" offer revisionist versions of the Passion in which the hero suffers violent death at the hands of his adversaries (see T. Ziolkowski, *Fictional Transfigurations of Jesus* [1972], 290).

Twentieth-cent. poems on the Passion and cross include several by Joyce Kilmer, A. E. Housman's "Easter Hymn," Ezra Pound's "Ballad of the Goodly Fere," and Edith Sitwell's "Still Falls the Rain." Perhaps the best of the longer 20th-cent. cross poems are David Jones's *Anathemata* and "Tribune's Visitation," while Geoffrey Hill's "Canticle for Good Friday" and *"Lachrimae"* present more typical modern views.

See also ATONEMENT; GETHSEMANE; JESUS CHRIST.

Bibliography. Bentzinger, S. E. "Comic Structure and Perspective in Middle English Treatments of Christ's Passion." *DAI* 41 (1980), 2117A; Conzelmann, H. "History and Theology in the Synoptic Passion Narratives." *Int.* 24 (1970), 178-97; Dillistone, F. W. *The Novelist and the Passion Story* (1960); Donahue, J. R. "Passion Narrative." *IDBSup* (1976), 643-45; Fleming, J. V. " 'The Dream of the Rood' and Anglo-Saxon Monasticism." *Traditio* 22 (1966), 43-72; Frend, W. H. C. *Martyrdom and Persecution in the Early Church* (1965); Grant, P. "Augustinian Spirituality and the Holy Sonnets of John Donne." *ELH* 38 (1971), 542-61; *Images and Ideas in Literature of the English Renaissance* (1979); *Literature and the Discovery of Method in the English Renaissance* (1985); Gray, D. *Themes and Images in the Medieval English Religious Lyric* (1972); Jeffrey, D. L. *The Early English Lyric and Franciscan Spirituality* (1975); Kee, H. C. "The Function of Scriptural Quotations and Allusions in Mark 11–16." *In Jesus und Paulus: Festschrift für Werner Georg Kummel.* Eds. E. E. Ellis and E. Grasser (1975), 165-88; Ladner, G. B. "St. Gregory of Nyssa and St. Augustine on the Symbolism of the Cross." In *Late Classical and Medieval Studies in Honor of A. M. Friend.* Ed. K. Weitzmann

(1955), 88-95; Leon-Dufour, X. "Passion." *DBSup.* Eds. H. Cazelles and A. Feuillet (1928–), 6.1419-92; Lindars, B. *New Testament Apologetic: The Doctrinal Significance of Old Testament Quotations* (1961); Martz, L. L. *The Poetry of Meditation: A Study of English Religious Literature of the Seventeenth Century* (1954); Morris, L. *The Cross in the New Testament* (1965); Nesaule, V. "The Christ Figure and the Idea of Sacrifice in Herman Melville's *Billy Budd,* in Graham Greene's *The Potting Shed,* and in Fedor Dostoevsky's 'The Dream of a Ridiculous Man'." *DAI* 36 (1976), 5284A; Raby, F. J. E. *A History of Christian Latin Poetry.* 2nd ed. (1953); Rahner, H. *Greek Myths and Christian Mystery.* Trans. B. Battershaw (1963); Reijners, G. Q. *The Terminology of the Holy Cross in Early Christian Literature* (1965); Robinson, H. W. *The Cross in the Old Testament* (1955); Seymour, W. W. *The Cross in Tradition, History, and Art* (1898); Smith, J. J. "Donne and the Crucifixion." *MLR* 79 (1984), 513-25; Stevens, W. O. *The Cross in the Life and Literature of the Anglo-Saxons* (1904); Sullivan, J. *A Study of the Themes of the Passion in the Medieval Cycle Drama* (1943); Szöverffy, J. " 'Crux Fidelis' . . . Prolegomena to a History of the Holy Cross Hymns." *Traditio* 22 (1966), 1-41; Trocmé, E. *The Passion as Liturgy: A Study in the Origin of the Passion Narratives in the Four Gospels* (1983); Vanhoye, A. "Structur et théologie des récits de la Passion dans les évangiles synoptiques." *NRT* 99 (1967), 135-63; Woolf, R. *The English Religious Lyric in the Middle Ages* (1968).
ESTHER C. QUINN
JOHN R. DONAHUE

PASSOVER (Heb. *pesaḥ;* Gk. *pascha;* cf. Eng. "paschal") Passover, the most important festival of the Jewish year — the origins of which are recounted in Exod. 11–12 — is the first day of a week-long Feast of Unleavened Bread. It commemorates the night of the tenth plague in Egypt, in which the firstborn of every Egyptian household was slain by the angel of death, while the firstborn of their Israelite slaves, who had followed the divine instructions to sprinkle the blood of a sacrificial lamb on their doorposts and lintels, were "passed over" and spared. The importance of Passover in Jewish literature especially, both as setting and as symbolic structure, is considerable in relation to the role of the father as a source of teaching within the family. He (not a substitute) was to explain the meaning of the ceremony in response to his children's questions (Exod. 12:26ff.; 13:8, 14); in modern formula: "Why is this night different from all other nights?" In response, the father's "explanation" or "telling" (Heb. *haggadah*) gradually produced the traditional Passover *Haggadah,* the book which tells the meaning of the *pesaḥ* celebration. (Matt. 26:17 suggests that the Last Supper was a Passover meal.) The most famous medieval Passover Haggadah is that of Dom Abarbanel (15th cent.).

See EXODUS; HAGGADAH; MOSES; PLAGUES OF EGYPT.

Bibliography. Cohen, J. *The Sephardi Haggadah, and the Laws of Pesach and the Seder* (1978); Goldschmidt, D. *The Passover Haggadah: Its Sources and History* (1977); Goodman, P., ed. *The Passover Anthology* (1961); Jeremias, J. *"pascha." TDNT* 5.896-904; Kanof, A. "Passover." *EncJud* 13; Klein, M., ed. *Passover* (1973); Segal, J. *Hebrew Passover* (1963).

PATER NOSTER The *Pater Noster* ("Our Father") Prayer was taught by Christ to his disciples (Matt. 6:9-13; cf. Luke 11:2-4). From apostolic times it has been regarded as the most important "common" prayer for Christians. In the 2nd-cent. manual The Didache (8.2-3), the longer version of the prayer is prescribed for use thrice daily, and the importance of teaching the prayer to the laity was stressed uniformly by the Fathers and by successive church councils. The Lord's Prayer has a central place in Christian liturgies in Latin and in the vernaculars. There are about ten extant OE versions — both verse and prose — in translation, gloss, and paraphrase. ME versions and expositions are also very common, though there seems to have been no authorized English translation until 1541. One form of exposition for the laity was the Paternoster Play, of which there were versions (now lost) at Lincoln, Beverly, and York. The York play was performed as late as 1572, when the Protestant Archbishop Grindal confiscated the text.

One of the strangest commentaries on the Pater Noster is in OE, a poetic *Dialogue of Salomon and Saturn* together with a prose piece from the same MS (ed. by R. J. Menner [1941]), in which the Pater Noster is represented as a huge creature which fights the devil in various guises. In the poem, Salomon instructs Saturn on the powers of the Pater Noster and of every letter or rune in it. The characters (given in both Roman and runic) are personified as warriors who defeat the devil. Such letter mysticism was known among the Greeks and Hebrews, but the presence of the runes here suggests also the old pagan Germanic association of runes with magic. In fact, the Pater Noster was used in some periods as something of a magic formula in charms, medicine, and exorcism (cf. the "white paternoster" in Chaucer's *Miller's Tale,* 1.3485).

The seven petitions of the Lord's Prayer were regarded from patristic times as a compendium of the things for which the Christian should pray; to these petitions a good deal else in Christian doctrine could be and was related, frequently in parallel heptamerologies. St. Augustine associated the seven petitions with the seven gifts of the Holy Ghost and with seven of the eight Beatitudes. Later writers added the association with the seven deadly sins, seven virtues, seven works of mercy, etc. Recitation was thought, in the Middle Ages, to be sufficient for the daily remission of venial sins. Hugh Latimer, in a sermon preached in 1552, makes the Paternoster "a prayer above all prayers," to prayer in general what the "law of love" (Matt. 22:37) is to "all the laws of Moses" (ed. G. Corrie [1844], 327). Latimer's point is that the Paternoster is not only a model for every kind of prayer, but that it is the précis of a rounded, prayerful life. Hence it is to be taken most seriously, "for it is better once said deliberately with understanding, than a thousand times without understanding: which is in very deed but vain babbling, and so more a displeasure than pleasure unto God" (329).

The doxology "For thine is the kingdom, the power, and the glory for ever and ever" (based on 1 Chron. 29:11-12) was also in early liturgical use (with variations), although in the West its use has until recently been confined to Protestant churches. It has provided the title for several books, most notably Graham Greene's novel *The Power and the Glory.* References to the Lord's Prayer in English literature are, of course, numerous (e.g., Dickens, *Bleak House,* where Alan Woodcourt tries unsuccessfully to teach the prayer to Jo), as are parodic revisions, such as Steinbeck's in *Cannery Row* ("Our Father who art in nature, who has given the gift of survival to the coyote, the common brown rat, the English sparrow, the house fly and the moth . . .") and Hemingway's in "A Clean Well-Lighted Place" ("Our nada who art in nada, nada be thy name thy kingdom nada thy will be nada in nada as it is in nada"). The term *Pater Noster,* or its shorter form, *Pater,* is not in much use among writers of English after the Reformation except in sardonic or anti-Catholic contexts. Joyce plays with the Latin form of the word "Patrecknocksters" in *Finnegans Wake.*

See also PRAYER; SEVEN DEADLY SINS.

Bibliography. Aarts, F. "The Pater Noster in Medieval English Literature." *PLL* 5 (1969), 1-16; Albert, S. P. "The Lord's Prayer and *Major Barbara.*" *ShawR* 1 (1981), 107-28; Ayo, N., C.S.C. *The Lord's Prayer: A Survey Theological and Literary* (1991); Hussey, M. "The Petitions of the Pater Noster in Medieval English Literature." *MAE* 27 (1958), 8-16.

MICHAEL MURPHY

PATMOS A small Greek island in the Aegean Sea, it was one of the barren places where the Roman Empire banished exiles. In Rev. 1:9 St. John says he was exiled there "on account of the word of God and the testimony of Jesus." Associated thus with John's apocalyptic Revelation, its occurrences in literature are almost exclusively in connection with apocalyptic themes and prophetic vision.

See also APOCALYPSE; JOHN THE BELOVED DISCIPLE; REVELATION.

PAUL No single figure, except that of Christ himself, has more influenced the subsequent interpretation of Scripture and the formulation of biblical tradition: the writings of St. Paul not only interpreted the kerygma for Mediterranean communities of Gentile Christians but laid down (e.g., Gal. 4:22-27) principles for a typological interpretation of the Hebrew Scriptures which became foundational for Christian religion and culture.

In the West, the principal sources for Paul's life have been the account given in the Acts of the Apostles and autobiographical glimpses scattered throughout the thir-

teen letters traditionally ascribed to him (ten general letters to various churches and three pastoral letters, Titus and 1 and 2 Timothy). Although the early Church credited him with the Epistle to the Hebrews, by the later Middle Ages this attribution was already doubted; Hugh of St. Victor is typical in speculating that the author of Hebrews might rather have been Barnabas or even Clement (*Didascalicon,* 4.6). While St. Jerome apparently knew an *"Acta Pauli et Theclae"* (*De viris illustribus,* 7), this and two other fragments of apocryphal Acts of Paul have only reemerged in modern times (ed. Schmidt [1904, 1905]). In the Middle Ages a collection of fourteen spurious *Letters of Paul and Seneca* was widely popular, extant since at least the 4th cent.

Among the biographical elements recorded in the NT, those which, with the writings themselves, do most to characterize Paul include (1) his presence at the martyrdom of Stephen (Acts 8:1; 22:20); (2) his early persecution of the Christians (Acts 9:1-2); (3) his dramatic Damascus road conversion and temporary blinding (Acts 9:3-8); (4) his escape from Damascus in a basket let down from the walls (Acts 9:23-25); (5) his preaching in the agora of Athens (Acts 17:16-34); (6) his shipwreck (Acts 27); and (7) his notable confrontation with adverse political forces and imprisonments on his missionary travels. His martyrdom at the gates of Rome by decapitation with a sword in A.D. 65 is not recorded in the NT itself, but along with the other events listed yields a persistent aspect of Pauline iconography. Among these, in painting since the Middle Ages, the most frequently occurring identifiers have been the sword — for his martyrdom and his proclamation of the *miles Christi* (e.g., Dürer, van Dyck, Quartararo, Rembrandt) — and the book (Lorenzetti, Dürer, Van Leyden, Rembrandt, Lievens, etc.) — for his role as writer and expositor. These two dominant features of his pictorial iconography correspond respectively to the courage and wisdom (*fortitudo et sapientia*) for which he is typically remembered in later literature. Throughout the history of Western art he is usually represented as short (pseudo-Chrysostom calls him "the man of three cubits" [4'6"]), bald, bearded, and in Roman dress; occasionally he is shown in prison encumbered with chains.

Because of his trade as a tentmaker (Acts 18:3) and principal apostolic vocation, Catholic tradition has made him the patron saint of tentmakers, weavers, saddlers, and basket makers, as well as of journalists, theologians, and labor unions. These associations often provide a context for allusions to Paul in vernacular literature. Other attributes include his self-acknowledged lack of eloquence (1 Cor. 2:12) and his persistent "thorn in the flesh" (Phil. 4:3), identified as anything from congenital bowed legs (*Acts of St. Paul* [2nd cent.]) to a difficult wife (St. Clement of Alexandria) to epilepsy (Findlay, in Hastings's *Dictionary of the Bible*).

Perhaps the most controversial of Paul's legacies for both the early and modern Church — his counsels on marriage and virginity (1 Cor. 7:7; Eph. 5) — called forth an extensive debate among major 4th-cent. theologians. Notable here are Jerome's *Epistle* 70, *Adversus Jovinianum*, which was so hotly resented by Chaucer's Wife of Bath (*Canterbury Tales*, 3.674-75), and St. Augustine's *De virginitate, De bono conjugali,* and *De bono viduitatis.* Paul's Epistle to the Romans was the book St. Augustine found before him in the garden at the moment of his conversion (*Conf.,* bk. 8). Swiftly the writings of Paul demonstrated to the once proud teacher of rhetoric that wisdom was of more value than eloquence in a Christian teacher: Paul, Augustine comes to argue, avoids the "eloquent nonsense" of the rhetoricians (*De doctrina Christiana*, 7.11) and offers instead an example of "true eloquence," which, for the sake of wisdom, uses select devices of rhetoric (e.g., periodic sentences) as a natural effect of the progression of his thought, not merely for the sake of style or ornament. In these and important philosophical respects, such as the view of reality embodied in his doctrine of the Incarnation, Paul comes to supersede Plato for the sometime Platonist (*Conf.* 7.21.27). Augustine characterizes Paul as a man of plain speech, resisting the imaginations of those like Jerome who construe, e.g., his debate with St. Peter about "Judaizing" (Acts 15; Gal. 2) as rhetorical "stagecraft" to clarify doctrine (cf. Jerome, *Ep.* 56, and the pref. to his translation of Galatians).

The Paul of St. John Chrysostom is preeminently a heroic example of simple Christian life, an exemplar of voluntary poverty (*Hom. on 1 Corinthians,* 15.13), gentleness, and magnanimity (*Hom.* 50) and, despite his great zeal, humility and self-effacement (*On the Priesthood*, 3.7). Commenting on his "poverty of speech" and the relative paucity of miracles in his ministry, Chrysostom says of Paul that it is in his "life and conversation rather than his miracles" that the reader will find "this Christian athlete a conqueror" (*On the Priesthood*, 4.6; cf. *Hom. on 1 Corinthians,* 6; *Hom. on 2 Corinthians,* 1). In an interesting development of the accounts of Paul's execution Chrysostom also relates (*Hom. on Acts of the Apostles,* 46) that he had enraged Nero by converting both his favorite concubine and his "cupbearer" Narcissus (cf. Rom. 16:11).

Partly because of his own sudden and spectacular conversion and partly because of his travels converting others, Paul became a prototype for the hagiographers; numerous saints' lives come to imitate features of both his biblical and legendary biography. Among the more colorful extraneous contributions to the legendary lore is the *Visio Sancti Pauli,* a Latin translation of a 3rd-cent. Greek text which, despite the fact that Aldhelm and (three cents. later) Aelfric both called it a "fevered fantasy," had by the 11th cent. been translated also into OE. Opening with a quotation from 2 Cor. 12:2-4 in which Paul describes his rapture into the third heaven (a passage St. Bernard thought ironic), the narrator describes how the "text" was

found in a marble box under the foundation of Paul's house in Tarsus. The account is divided into four parts, concerning respectively (1) a cosmic tour by angel-guide (similar to the "spirits of Christmas" in Dickens's *A Christmas Carol*); (2) a Dantesque tour of the "places of the righteous" and (3) the dwellings of the wicked, an inferno with familiar Vergilian features; and (4) a visit to the Paradise of Eden. An interesting feature of his third stop is that Paul's visit is said to prompt a suspension of the torments of sinners, weekly, on Sundays.

Relating the story that, when on Malta Paul was bitten by a viper without effect (Acts 28:3-6), St. Hilary tells that no descendant of the Maltese man who gave the apostle hospitality was ever after susceptible to snakebite. Another story passed down in the legenda clearly has its basis in Acts 20:7-12, but in it the sleeper who falls from the window to his death is not Eutychus but one Patrochlus, an intimate of Nero. When resurrected he goes to Nero to report, and Nero, having heard of his death, is first astonished and then enraged at the young man's decision henceforth to serve Christ, the "true King of Kings." It is this threat to Nero's pride and insecurity which is said to prompt his beheading of Paul and burning of hundreds of Christians (cf. Caxton, *Golden Legend*). Later elements of the legenda include the nighttime disinterral of the bodies of Paul and Peter and reburial, according to the Chronicle of the World's Six Ages ascribed to Bede, on the Vatican Hill of Nero's old palace, in A.D. 256.

Later medieval spiritual writers develop the image of Paul as a "hero of faith." Among the Cistercians, e.g., he is above all the "clarion voice of the New Testament" (William of St. Thierry, *Meditationes*, 3.5), "whose faith is not grasped by a worldly person, nor his meaning explained better by the words of another than his own" (*Enigma Fidei;* cf. Hilary, *De Trinitate*, 9.10). For St. Aelred of Rievaulx (*De Jesu Puero Duodenni*, 19), he is the "vessel of election" (cf. Acts 19:15), yet most intensely *sympatico,* able to be "weak with the weak, on fire with the scandalized" (*De Amicitia Spirituali,* 2.50). Bernard of Clairvaux sees him not merely as a model of Christian wisdom but, in his writings, a superb ironist (*De consideratione ad Eugenium Papam*, 1.4; 1.10), highlighting a feature of his epistles to which writers in the later Middle Ages were on the whole more alert than those of subsequent periods.

Preeminently among ecclesiasts in the 13th cent., the events of Paul's life are less frequently highlighted than his influence upon hermeneutics. Paul becomes increasingly recognized, following the 12th-cent. Augustinian revival, as providing the key which unlocks neglected books of the OT, integrating them with the Gospels. Abbot Suger in his *De Administratione* describes how Paul is depicted in the "anagogical" window of St. Denis, turning a mill toward which the prophets carry sacks of grain. The inscription reads: "By working the mill, Paul, you drew the flour out of the bran; you make known the innermost meaning of the Law of Moses." In the same window Paul is shown removing a veil which covers Moses' face (E. Panofsky, *Abbot Suger on the Abbey Church of St. Denis* [1946], 74-75).

Appearances of Paul in OE and ME literature are nonetheless rare. Part of this may owe to the omission of the Acts of the Apostles and Pauline epistles from early programs of biblical translation: while surviving materials in OE include psalters, gospels, and a variety of OT paraphrase, the earliest systematic translation of Pauline material into English comes only in the 14th-cent., with Wyclif and his contemporaries. There are OE examples of comic misuse of Paul: his comparison of the body to a grain of wheat (1 Cor. 15:37) yields Riddle 28 in the Exeter Book, which describes the brewing process as the "death" of barley followed by its "resurrection" in the bodies of inebriates. Even in the ME period, with preaching focused on the Gospels rather than lections from the Epistles, Paul remains a somewhat undefined figure. In the *Castle of Perseverance* "Confessio" says of Paul that, like Peter, he has "powere to lese and bynde" (496). For all that he has no role in the major cycles of Corpus Christi plays, whose biblical material is tied fairly closely to the liturgical year, and although the Fleury Playbook has a modest trope *"conversio Beati Pauli apostoli"* for his feast day (Jan. 25), it is not until the time of Chaucer that he becomes a major figure as such in the literary imagination.

Chaucer's extensive use of quotation from Paul in *The Canterbury Tales* reflects a shift toward a renewal of appreciation of the Epistles. This is already apparent in St. Thomas Aquinas, who is said to have once had a vision of Paul while praying to be enlightened about a difficult passage in his writings. Aquinas apparently valued only the Gospels more highly, and expresses a deep commitment to the Pauline doctrine of justification by faith and gratuity of grace, as well as to his expectation that individuals will be finally judged by the works they have done (see his commentaries on 2 Cor. 5:10; 11:15; 2 Tim. 4:14; Rom. 2:6-9). But reflection on Paul's doctrine of grace began in the 14th cent. to take a more characteristically Augustinian direction. Archbishop Thomas Bradwardine (d. 1348), whom Chaucer mentions in *The Nun's Priest's Tale*, had observed in a personal comment on Rom. 9:6 (*De Causa Dei contra Pelagium*, 1.35.308C) that at one point whenever he heard Romans read in church, with its emphasis on grace and reservation concerning free will, he felt Paul must have been in error. Yet when he read Paul carefully, the statement in Rom. 9:16 ("So then, it is not of him that willeth, or of him that runneth, but of God that sheweth mercy") finally provided the insight he says was fundamental to his own *conversio* and afterward became the central text of his theological work. This emphasis on God's grace as the means of salvation takes on, following Bradwardine and Fitzralph as well as Augustine, a still larger importance in the

writings of Wyclif and the Wycliffites. It tends to be coupled with a critique of "self-help" merit-peddling in some of the friars, against whom, in general terms, Paul is seen as having proleptically "prechede to the peuple ofte" (*Piers Plowman*, C.16.72-75). In one tract, *The Leaven of the Pharisees,* the Wycliffite author charges friars with destroying the spirit of the text by burdensome legalisms, unlike the converted Pharisees Nicodemus and Paul, in whom a recognition of grace "brouȝte hem out of hir odris to fredom of þe gospel" (1.2). In a more traditional vein, John Mirk's sermon *De Conuercione Sancti Pauli,* after paraphrasing the account in Acts 9, an "ensampull of heȝ amending," offers a cautionary tale that "St. Austyn likeneþ him unto a unycorne," and the pure virgin maiden who tames his fierceness is "þe faythe of holy chyrch." Yet, he adds, "anon he fell don of his pryde, and was sympull, and meke, and soget to Crystys seruants" — the last phrase probably a reference to controversy over Paul's teaching on grace in Lollard times.

The penchant for doctrinal disputation in later scholastic theology may itself have increased Paul's stature in medieval eyes. If for Wyclif, as for Bradwardine, Paul became a hero of faith — "grettost clerk of þe apostles echone" *(South English Legendary)* — for his championing of God's grace against reliance on human effort, he was prototypically "Godes champion" in dispute against those who opposed or misread Scripture. The ideas of "reformation in sensibility" and "reformation through faith," familiar in Walter Hilton's *Ladder of Perfection,* are, when echoed at the conclusion of the 15th-cent. morality play *Wisdom,* firmly associated there with Paul:

> Now wyth Saint Powle we may say thus
> þat be reformyde thorow feyth in Jhesum:
> We haue peas and acorde betwyx God and ws,
> *Justificati ex fide pacem habemus ad Deum.* (1148-51)

Paul is more frequently cited in the late C-text of *Piers Plowman* (ca. 1390) than in its predecessors ("A" [1362]; "B" [1383]); the apostle is much admired by the author of "C" for his willingness to support himself: "Paul after his prechynge panyeres he made / And wan with hus hondes al that hym neodyde" (C.18.17-18).

At the very end of the Middle Ages, in the Digby saints' play *The Conversion of St. Paul* (ca. 1502), we have the first full characterization of the apostle in English literature since the apocryphal OE *Vision of St. Paul.* One of only two surviving full texts of medieval saints' plays, this play, like its counterpart in the Digby MS *Mary Magdalen,* probably owes its unusual preservation to the fact that it treats a biblical saint. The text makes repeated direct references to the Acts of the Apostles, encouraging its readers to "vnderstande þis matter wo lyst to rede / the holy bybyll for the better spede" (158-59; cf. 10-11, 352-59, 652), but concentrates on the psychology of conversion, the bringing of the human will into conformity with the will of God in response to an intervention of God's grace.

These themes, controversial in the 14th cent., were to gain much strength by the 16th-cent. John Colet, before he was made Dean of St. Paul's, lectured on the Pauline epistles at Oxford to large audiences (including those with Lollard sympathies) who were attracted to his refreshing direct textual study of the apostle. Among Colet's hearers was Erasmus, for whom the lectures were also a turning point. Erasmus's *Enchiridion Militis Christiani* (1504) takes its title from the arming of the Christian soldier (Eph. 6:14-17) and, indebted to his own commentary *In Epistolam Pauli ad Romanos* (inspired by Colet), recommends intensive direct reading of Paul (Caxton trans., 206.32-33). Renaissance English use and characterization of Paul tends to alternate between the views of Erasmus and Colet — in which Paul is, next to Christ, placed first in the *ad fontes* of a larger scriptural tradition — and the more extreme views represented by Luther, in which Paul *(sola scriptura)* is virtually set over and against that tradition. Luther, trained in scholastic theology, claims that from the scholastics he nonetheless learned "ignorance of . . . the entire Christian life" and that, indeed, he had "lost Christ there, but now found him again in St. Paul" (*WA* 2.414.22) — referring to his own pivotal lecture course (1515) on the text of Paul to the Romans.

English literary responses to Paul are in the Renaissance inclined, if not exclusively so, to the Erasmian perspective. Shakespeare, who makes most of his references to the apostle in *Richard 3,* creates in Paulina of *The Winter's Tale* a Pauline teacher for Leontes on the undeservedness of grace, the effect of which upon a repentant heart is a resurrection to new life. George Herbert finds Paul an indispensable guide to priestly vocation in *A Priest to the Temple,* whose life and letters demonstrate that "there is no greater sign of holinesse, than the procuring, and rejoycing in anothers good" (chap. 7); he is thus a model for Herbert's Parson (as Peter was for Chaucer's) in that "hee first preacheth to himselfe, and then to others" (chap. 33). Paul stands in a somewhat different fashion behind the character Interpreter in Bunyan's *Pilgrim's Progress.* The Puritans were committed to the emphasis of Luther and Calvin on Paul's teaching about election and grace, and made more use of Paul as typologist and perseverant *miles Christi* than as exemplar of conversion (cf. John Owen's *Grace and Duty; Of the Mortification of Sin in Believers* [1656], and *The Nature, Power, Deceit, and Prevalency of Indwelling Sin* [1667], all of which take their central texts from Romans). Restoration writers emphasized, for their own purposes, an apostle of resignation and humility; Isaac Barrow's notable Pauline sermons are *On Quietness, and Doing Our Own Business* (1 Thess. 4:11), *Of a Peaceable Nature and Carriage* (Rom. 12:18), and two on Phil. 4:11, "I have learned, in whatsoever state I am, therewith to be content" — ironically enough the very passage the unquiet Cromwell had read to him on his deathbed. For Jeremy Taylor, as for Barrow, Paul is also the apostle of

industry and charity (cf. Barrow, *Sermon 10* and *Sermon 18*); in a meditation on grace Taylor elevates love over knowledge, saying "as was rarely observed by St. Paul, *knowledge puffeth up, but Charity edifieth;* that is, Charity makes the best Scholars" (*Via Intelligentiae,* 31). Two decades later, in *The Worthy Communicant* (1683), Taylor's reflections on the vision or rapture of Paul led to the conclusion that "after all the fine things that he saw, we know only what we knew before" (394); Paul is less to be admired as a visionary or mystic than as a practical rationalist of sublunary experience. John Dryden's *Religio Laici* celebrates the "great Apostle" for his comments (Rom. 2:14-15) on the efficacy of natural revelation and, by extension, reason, concluding, in a curiously un-Pauline fashion:

> Then those who followed *Reasons* Dictates right;
> Liv'd up, and lifted high their *Natural Light;*
> With *Socrates* may see their Maker's Face,
> While Thousand *Rubrick-Martyrs* want a place.
> (199-202)

However sharply at variance the wisdom they read in Paul sometimes is, writers of the Enlightenment tend to agree in seeing him as an exemplary teacher and sage. "The great Christian convert and learned apostle," Shaftesbury writes in *Characteristics,* shows that the safest state is "the sceptical and modest" (6.2.3). According to Jonathan Edwards, the Apostle to the Gentiles is the first teacher of the typological interpretation fitted to all of God's works. In "Trees," from his *Images and Shadows of Divine Things* (no. 78), Edwards remembers Paul as the most fruitful and thrifty of the apostolic branches to shoot forth from the trunk of the risen Christ, "so that the bigger part of the future tree came from this branch." The Pauline practice of paradox as a logical response to the hidden unity of being is compellingly attractive to Pope. His "The Dying Christian to His Soul," an ode in imitation of Hadrian's sonnet to his departing spirit, speaks of "the bliss of dying," of "languish[ing] into life," and ends with 1 Cor. 15:55: "O Grave! where is thy Victory? / O Death! where is thy Sting?" For Johnson, the reasonableness of Paul's humility is not difficult to distinguish from the unreason of garrulous mystics. He responds with this irony to Boehme's claim of kinship with Paul in having seen "unutterable things": "[He] would have resembled St. Paul still more, by not attempting to utter them" (Boswell, *Life of Johnson,* ed. G. B. Hill [1934], 2.123). In the retrospective "Conclusion" of *Biographia Literaria,* Coleridge takes pains to locate his reading of Paul in the context of the Enlightenment. Having abridged the history of his mental life in the motto *"Credidi ideoque intellexi,"* he associates his own last thoughts in *Biographia* with the reflections ending Spinoza's *Ethics:* they are "thoroughly *Pauline . . .* compleatly accordant with the doctrines of the established Church." "The Scheme of Christianity . . . though not discoverable by human

Reason, is yet in accordance with it," Coleridge avers. Blake is of another mind, his heterodoxy almost complete. While he does follow "his master St. Paul" in distinguishing the "body-garment" from the "self" (cf. 2 Cor. 5:4), as Damrosch proposes (170), Blake's abiding conviction that poetic vision, cleansed of natural reason, "can attain a direct apprehension of truth" (23) seems as much un-Pauline as anti-Newtonian. The chastened later Wordsworth, by contrast, is surely unspeculative in his recollection of Pauline iconography: "and lo! with upright sword / Prefiguring his own impending doom, / The Apostle of the Gentiles" ("Musings near Aquapendente," 310-12).

Given the ideological temper of most Victorian literature, the conflicting responses to Paul in the protracted mêlée over the authorities of faith and reason during that period are not surprising. For Bentham, the Pauline scriptures lack a sound empirical foundation: "Whatever is in Paul, and not . . . in any of the four Gospels, is not Christianity, but Paulism" (*Not Paul*, 367). While Mill agrees in philosophical principle, he finds Paul's the least uncongenial writings in the NT: "St. Paul, the only known exception to the ignorance . . . of the first generation of Christians, attests to no miracle but that of his conversion, which of all the miracles of the New Testament is the one which admits of the easiest explanation from natural causes" ("Theism," pt. 4, in *Three Essays on Religion*). According to Hardy in *Tess of the D'Urbervilles*, the NT of the evangelical Mr. Clare "was less a Christiad than a Pauliad . . . — less an argument than an intoxication" (chap. 25). Unlike the disapproving Hardy, Emerson revels in the inebriating effect of his Paul: "the conversion of Paul; the aurora of Behmen; the convulsions of George Fox and his Quakers" — all illustrate that "openings of the religious sense" are often attended by "a certain tendency to insanity" ("The Over-Soul"). Tennyson, in one of the moments of undoubting faith which *In Memoriam* records, likens himself to Paul in his struggle with "Death" or a "Science" which reckons man merely a "greater ape" (canto 120). Melville is altogether independent, taking Paul for a subverter not only of reason but also of faith. "St. Paul . . . argues the doubts of Montaigne," he writes in *Mardi* (2.15). This anti-rational Paul is to be numbered among the "destroyers of confidence," according to the sentence of *The Confidence-Man* (chap. 9), since his paradoxy makes him a doubtful prophet or an unreliable guide to ethical praxis. For Arnold in *St. Paul and Protestantism*, Paul is an apostle of both culture and science. He is a cultivated rhetorician who "Orientalizes," while his Puritan commentators "Judaise" (pt. 1). Unlike Arnold's Paul, who comes to his religion "psychologically and from experience" which can be "scientifically verified," these philistines come to theirs "theologically and from authority" (pt. 2). Browning shows a more refined historical sense and surer rhetorical touch in "Cleon." A nostalgic old pagan answering a letter from

his king regrets that Zeus has not yet revealed some future state of felicity after death. But the accomplished Cleon is disturbed by the thought that his correspondent would for a moment consider that "one called Paulus," a "mere barbarian Jew" to whome King Protus has also written, could have "access to a secret shut" from the wisest and most cultivated of mortals (343-45). John A. Hall's *A Christian Home* emphasizes the unaristocratic character of Paul's work: "Paul was a tent-maker, and he was not ashamed of it" (87).

In the 20th cent., Conrad's *Victory*, though its title and theme refer to 1 Cor. 15:51-57, is anything but cheering. The "parody is savage" in this novel (D. Purdy, *Joseph Conrad's Bible* [1984], 122), the action of which ends in bloody mayhem, fire, and suicide, and the last word of which is "Nothing." If the book's title may be accepted as an "Omen" to an English public in the trammels of war, as Conrad suggests in his note to the first edition (1915), the augury *Victory* provides is clearly ambiguous. John Buchan's *Mr. Steadfast*, published four years later, is free of doubt. Peter Piennar, the humble pilot who gives up his life to stop the Boche in that spy-thriller, reckons in a letter that "the head man" at the job of "the big courage . . . the cold-blooded kind . . . 'Fortitude'" is "the Apostle Paul" (chap. 11). The hero of Sholem Asch's epic narrative *The Apostle* is "compounded of nothing but faith" (1.6). As Saul was before him, Paul is always true to the Torah. "Hear, O Israel, the Lord our God, the Lord is One" are his last words. George Bowering's poem "Grandfather" pays tribute to a long-suffering and much-traveled laborer, church builder, and preacher who takes for his ruling test "Saul on the road to Damascus" (9). The same test was used by thirteen-year-old Ernest Hemingway in his first and only formal sermon at a Chicago missionary convention. If Paul was to have only marginal impact on the later fiction of Hemingway, the apostle's notable attribute of raw courage seems to have had its enduring appeal. It appealed in a somewhat different way to Margaret Avison in "A Comment on Romans 1:10," where she says, speaking of Paul's full knowledge of the mortal risk he ran in going to Rome:

> Yet he urged it. He was
> glad these new Romans existed.
> His wisdom was enlisted as
> their ally, to find them his.
> It did not save his neck
> or probably theirs: he knew beforehand that when light
>   appears
> it must night split and earth quake. (*sunblue*, 55)

Bibliography. Andrews, E. *The Meaning of Christ for Paul* (1949); Bruce, F. F. *Paul: Apostle of the Heart Set Free* (1977); Chadwick, H. "All Things to All Men," *NTS* 1 (1954-55), 261-75; Damrosch, L., Jr. *Symbol and Truth in Blake's Myth* (1980); Daube, D. *The New Testament and Rabbinic Judaism* (1965); Ellis, E. E. *Paul's Use of the Old Testament* (1957); Fass, B. "Shelley and St. Paul." *CP* 4 (1971), 23-24;

Hassell, R. C., Jr. "Saint Paul and Shakespeare's Comedies." *Thought* 46 (1971), 371-88; Hooker, M., and S. Wilson, eds. *Paul and Paulinism* (1982); Lake, K. *Paul, His Heritage and Legacy* (1934); Metzger, B. M. *Index to Periodical Literature on the Apostle Paul* (1960); Moule, C. F. D. "St. Paul and Dualism: The Pauline Conception of Resurrection." *NTS* 12 (1965-66), 106-23; Peck, R. A. "St. Paul and the *Canterbury Tales*." *Mediaevalia* 7 (1981), 91-131; Robinson, A. W. *The Christianity of the Epistles* (1927); Robinson, J. A. T. *The Body: A Study in Pauline Theology* (1952); Sanders, E. P. *Paul and Palestinian Judaism* (1977); Schultze, J. *Paul: In Legend and Art* (1964); Scroggs, R. *The Last Adam: A Study in Pauline Anthropology* (1966); Zuntz, G. *The Text of the Epistles: A Disquisition on the Corpus Paulinum* (1953).

DAVID L. JEFFREY
CAMILLE R. LA BOSSIÈRE

PEACE WHICH PASSETH UNDERSTANDING

St. Paul exhorts the Philippians (4:6-7) not to be anxious about anything but to make all their concerns a subject of thankful prayer to God, promising that if they do so "the peace of God which passeth all understanding" will keep (lit. "stand guard over") their hearts and minds. The thought echoes Isa. 26:3: "Thou wilt keep him in perfect peace, whose mind is stayed on thee: because he trusteth in thee," and takes up Jesus' exhortation to have no concern over practical needs because "your heavenly Father knoweth that ye have need of all these things" (Matt. 6:24-34). The peace Paul speaks of passes all understanding both in the sense that it is inconceivably great, beyond human capacity to comprehend (cf. Eph. 3:19, 20), and also in that it is far better than any "peace" which human "understanding" could bring. Notably, it is a peace which is found in the midst of trouble, not by escaping from it.

Commenting on Job 9:4 (Vg) in which Job observes that God is "wise in heart and mighty in strength. Who has resisted him, and had peace?" Wyclif says that "we are to see by this description of peace that it is achieved by conformity of [one's] will to that of God." He goes on to say that peace is not, as one might expect, a matter of temporal quietude free from attack or hostility; rather, it is just when the battle is raging most fiercely that one is most likely to experience the benefits of being at peace with God (*Sermones*, 4.25). A later Wycliffite writer takes up the theme, "þer be trew pees and fals pees, and thai be ful diverse" — true peace being grounded in God, false peace grounded in "rest with our enemies" when "we assent to þem withoute aȝen-standyng" (Arnold, ed., *Selected English Works of John Wyclif* [1871], 1.321).

In George Herbert's "The Sacrifice" the *O Vos Omnes* hymn is developed with Christ drawing a contrast between himself and Barabbas: "And a seditious murderer he was: / But I the Prince of Peace; peace that doth passe / All understanding, more than heav'n doth glasse" (117-19; cf. Ruskin, *Unto This Last,* chap. 3). Herbert's poem "Peace" makes the point that the "Prince of Peace" himself had no peace: "He sweetly liv'd; yet sweetnesse did

not save / His life from foes" (25-26), and that he won peace for others at the expense of his own struggle and death (cf. *A Priest to the Temple,* chap. 34). In Vaughan's "Peace" the poet speaks of a peace which is not to be found in this life, but in "a Countrie / Far beyond the stars," sentiments echoed in an early 20th-cent. American sonnet by Joyce Kilmer, written while the author was soldiering in France during World War I ("The Peacemaker"). Aldous Huxley thinks hints of such peace can be derived from art: "Even from the perfection of minor masterpieces — certain sonnets of Mallarmé, for instance, certain Chinese ceramics — we can derive illuminating hints about the 'something far more deeply interfused,' about 'the peace of God that passeth understanding' " (*Ends and Means,* chap. 14; cf. Wordsworth, "Tintern Abbey," 96). In *Black Boy* Richard Wright tells of an unsuccessful application of the traditional interpretation in the home of his grandmother: "Granny bore the standard for God, but she was always fighting. The peace that passes understanding never dwelt with us." Recalling the prophetic promise that in the days of the Messiah peace shall flow "as a river" (Isa. 48:18; 53:5), Margaret Avison writes that "Word has arrived that / peace will brim up, will come / 'like a river and the / glory . . . like a flowing stream' " — an unprecedented, unimagined grace ("Stone's Secret," 20-22).

Bibliography. Eisenbeis, W. *Die Wurzel ŠLM im Altes Testament* (BZAW 113 [1969]); Hammer, P. L. *Shalom in the New Testament* (1973); Harris, D. J. *Shalom! The Biblical Concept of Peace* (1970); Macquarrie, John H. *The Concept of Peace* (1973); Montefiore, C. G., and H. Loewe, eds. *Rabbinic Anthology* (rpt. 1974), 530-38; White, H. C. *Shalom in the Old Testament* (1973); Wiseman, D. J. "Shalom." *VT* 32 (1982), 311-26.

R. T. FRANCE

PEACE, GOOD WILL TOWARD MEN

"On earth, peace, good will toward men" forms part of the angels' song of praise at the birth of Christ (Luke 2:14), the preceding phrase being "Glory to God in the highest." The two lines thus express respectively the heavenly and earthly results of the Incarnation.

The KJV here follows a reading of the later manuscripts (Textus Receptus) which has "good will" in the nominative (*eudokia*). Modern textual critics agree that the older reading *eudokias* (genitive) is to be preferred; hence the modern versions such as the RSV, "on earth peace among men with whom he is pleased." The second line of the song thus describes not the mutual relations of persons on earth but the "peace" or well-being which Christ's Incarnation brings to persons "of [God's] goodwill," i.e., those who are the objects of his favor.

St. Augustine relates the verse to the seventh Beatitude ("Blessed are the peacemakers: for they shall be called the children of God" [Matt. 5:9]), saying that the "peacemakers" are those whose own minds and hearts are reconciled to God. "And this is the peace which is given on earth to men of good will; this is the life of the fully developed and perfect wise man." He concludes, "When this peace has been inwardly established and confirmed, what ever persecutions . . . shall be stirred up from without . . . only increases the glory which is accorded to God" (*De sermone Domini in Monte,* 1.3.9). The phrase is memorable in the liturgy from its place in the *Gloria,* an evocation of the angels' song, and as such it enters into countless medieval hymns, vernacular lyrics, and carols.

The corrupt text followed by the KJV has been not a little responsible for shifting the focus of the Christmas message from divine grace to human camaraderie both in interpretative and literary contexts. In Tennyson's *In Memoriam* the poet hears at Christmastime "four voices of four hamlets round":

> Each voice four changes on the wind,
>   That now dilate, and now decrease,
>   Peace and goodwill, goodwill and peace,
> Peace and goodwill, to all mankind.

The association of the angels' song with human yearning for a peaceful world occurs also in Whittier's "The Peace convention at Brussels":

> Lend, once again, that holy song a tongue,
> Which the glad angels of the Advent sung,
> Their cradle-anthem for the Saviour's birth,
> Glory to God, and peace on earth.

Washington Irving writes in "The Pride of the Village" of a pastor "who was a lover of old customs, and one of those simple Christians who think their mission fulfilled by promoting joy on earth and good-will among mankind." This sentiment has readily been shaped toward millenarianism such as is captured by Trollope in *Barchester Towers,* where one of the clergymen surmises: " 'Peace on earth and good will among men, are like heaven, promises for the future,' said he, following rather his own thoughts than hers. 'When that prophecy is accomplished, there will no longer be any need for clergymen' " (chap. 21). On the eve of the Great War, Robert Bridges's "Noel: Christmas Eve 1913" offers a wistful reflection, aspiring to a *"pax hominibus bonae voluntatis"* even though he is not sure there is a will for peace.   R. T. FRANCE

PEACE, WHEN THERE IS NO PEACE This saying, part of Jeremiah's denunciation of the total corruption of the people of Judah (Jer. 6:14; 8:11), is echoed in a similar context in Ezek. 13:10. "Peace, peace" is the superficial response of priest and prophet (also scribe and wise man [Jer. 8:8-9]) to the incurable "hurt of the daughter of my people." J. Bright (*Jeremiah,* AB 45) captures the sense well: "They treat my people's fracture with nostrums, and cry 'It is well! It is well!' but it is not well!" Ezekiel adds the image of daubing a loosely constructed wall with whitewash (KJV "untempered

mortar" is inaccurate), as if that would protect it against storms.

False prophets who said what people wanted to hear and earned their living by so doing are frequently attacked in the OT (e.g., Jer. 23:16-22; Mic. 3:5). "Thus they degrade themselves into pledged supporters of every piece of wishful thinking" (W. Eichrodt, *Ezekiel* [1970], 168). In Jeremiah's day there was a rooted conviction that God was pledged to protect his people, come what may, and the false prophets played on this.

"Peace" in these passages, as always in the OT, does not signify merely absence of war, but total well-being. Henry Vaughan is concerned with the spiritual state of the believer's heart when in "The Check" he bemoans the lack of inner or outer peace; in "Affliction" he speaks of how, in the practical life of a follower of Christ, it may be that "Peace, peace; it is not so." The passage from Jeremiah is nevertheless often invoked in time of war, or a threat of war. Two such instances of renown are themselves the source of many subsequent allusions. One of Patrick Henry's most famous speeches (1775) includes the lines: "Gentlemen cry peace, peace, when there is no peace. I know not what course others may take; but as for me, give me liberty, or give me death!" Neville Chamberlain's ill-fated words of a century and a half later are recalled in their biblical (and liturgical) context, "Give us peace in our time, O Lord," by David Jones in his *Anathemata* (7.186).

See also PEACE WHICH PASSETH UNDERSTANDING.
                                                R. T. FRANCE

PEARL OF GREAT PRICE In one of his brief parables of the kingdom Jesus likened the kingdom of heaven to "a merchant man, seeking goodly pearls: who, when he had found one pearl of great price, went and sold all that he had, and bought it" (Matt. 13:45-46). The parable illustrates a theme common to the kingdom parables, that to gain the kingdom of God is worth almost any extravagance, breach of custom, or what might otherwise appear responsible management.

The pearl was considered by the ancient world to be a symbol of both mystery and perfection; St. Augustine compares the pearl of great price to Christ himself, who alone is able to satisfy the inner yearnings of the soul, and also to "the kingdom of God within" (*Quaestiones ex Matthaeum,* 13; *Conf.* 8.1.2), a comparison echoed by St. Jerome (*Ep.* 66.8) and subsequently by many others. Elsewhere Augustine calls the pearl charity (*In 1 Epistola Joannis,* 5.7). Jerome likens the pearl of great price for which all else is surrendered to the contemplative or monastic life (e.g., *Ep.* 54.11; 125.3-4), an interpretation which becomes influential in contemplative literature of the later Middle Ages; here, the "pearl" is often a figure for purity or chastity. Some of these associations characterize both allegory and dialectic in the ME *Pearl,* in which the focus falls on what may be necessary to "purchase" the kingdom, and the relationship of grace to all that the pearl may signify. The poet may have been influenced by the anti-Pelagian writings of Fitzralph, Bradwardine, and Wyclif, which are concerned to elicit a proper understanding of "purchasing" the kingdom of heaven. Calvin, in his *Harmony of the Gospels* (2.83), takes up this same theme in earnest, asserting that:

> by the word "bought" Christ does not mean that men bring any payment to purchase the heavenly life. For we know how the Lord invited his faithful in Isaiah: "Come and buy without money, etc." (Isa. 55:1). But although the heavenly life and everything pertaining to it is God's free gift, yet we are said to pay a price when we willingly deprive ourselves of carnal desires so that nothing may prevent us obtaining it.

George Herbert, in "The Pearl: Matt. 13.45," says he "knows the wayes of Learning," as of "Honour" and "Pleasure," yet what he loves is the Pearl of Great Price:

> And at what rate and price I have thy love;
> With all the circumstances that may me move:
> Yet through these labyrinths, not my grovelling wit,
> But thy silk twist let down from heav'n to me,
> Did both conduct and teach me, how by it
>   To climbe to thee.

His poem finds an echo in the commentary of Matthew Henry (1721), who observes:

> 1. All the children of men are busy *seeking goodly pearls:* one would be rich, another honorable, another would be learned; but the most are imposed upon, and take up with counterfeits for pearls. 2. Jesus Christ is a *Pearl of great price,* a Jewel of inestimable value, which will make those who have it rich, truly rich, rich toward God; in having him, we have enough to make us happy for ever. (*Comm.* 5.192)

William Cowper, for whom "wisdom is a pearl," asks in the third book of his long poem *The Task:*

> What pearl is it that rich men cannot buy,
> That learning is too proud to gather up;
> But which the poor, and the despis'd of all,
> Seek and obtain, and often find unsought?
> Tell me — and I will tell thee what is truth. ("The Garden," 285-89; cf. 381)

The association of the pearl of great price with chastity was strengthened in 18th- and 19th-cent. literature of manners and morals. There is thus bitterness as well as irony in the outcast Hester's christening of the little girl born of her adulterous relationship with Rev. Dimmesdale in Hawthorne's *The Scarlet Letter:* "She named the infant 'Pearl,' as being of great price, — purchased with all she had" (chap. 6). The irony is later reinforced when old Master Wilson tells little Pearl: "Thou must take heed to instruction, that so, in due season, thou mayest wear in thy bosom the pearl of great price" (chap. 8). The association persists, often with a suggestion of prudishness, into

20th-cent. literature. In Somerset Maugham's *Theatre* appears a somewhat precious and old-fashioned woman "who felt like a high-born damsel, with all the traditions of a great and ancient family to keep up; her purity was a pearl of great price; she also felt she was making a wonderfully good impression" (chap. 6). A comparable secularization is afforded in London's *In a Far Country,* in which "that pearl of great price [is] true comradeship."

Bibliography. Abel, D. "Hawthorne's Pearl: Symbol and Character." *ELH* 18 (1951), 50-66; Eisinger, C. E. "Pearl and the Puritan Heritage." *CE* 12 (1951), 323-29; Powers, L. H. "Hawthorne and Faulkner and the Pearl of Great Price." *Papers of the Michigan Academy of Science, Arts, and Letters* 52 (1967), 391-401; Robertson, D. W., Jr. "The Pearl as Symbol." *MLN* 65 (1950), 155-61.

PEARLS BEFORE SWINE   In the Sermon on the Mount Jesus admonishes his hearers: "Give not that which is holy unto the dogs, neither cast ye your pearls before swine, lest they trample them under their feet, and turn again and rend you" (Matt. 7:6). St. Augustine applies this verse to the study and teaching of Scripture and spiritual matters:

> By pearls . . . are meant whatever spiritual things we ought to set a high value upon, both because they lie hid in a secret place, as it were brought up out of the deep, and are found in wrappings of allegory, as it were in shells that have been opened.

He goes on to say that the "holy" understanding should not be offered to those spiritually unprepared to receive it, either assailants of the truth (dogs) or despisers of it (swine), both of which animals, he notes, are "unclean" (*De sermone Domini in Monte*, 2.20.68-69).

This application became standard not only for scriptural interpretation (e.g., John Scotus Erigena, *Expositiones super Ierarchiam Caelestem* [PL 122.151-52, 170]) but also for the high purposes of medieval secular poetry. The preface to the influential *Anticlaudianus* of Alain of Lille is representative:

> For in this work the sweetness of the literal sense will caress the puerile hearing, the moral instruction will fill the perfecting sense, and the sharper subtlety of the allegory will exercise the understanding nearing perfection. But may the approach to this work be barred to those who, following only the sensual motion, do not desire the truth of reason, lest a thing holy be defouled by being offered to dogs, or a pearl trampled by the feet of swine be lost, and the majesty of these things be revealed to the unworthy. (ed. Bossuat, 43; cf. *De Planctu Naturae* [PL 210.445])

This sentiment is echoed by Boccaccio in his *De Genealogia Deorum Gentilium.*

In his "Sonnet 12" Milton writes about hostile reaction to his liberal views on divorce: "But this is got by casting Pearl to Hoggs," a secularized employment of the phrase which was to become general in the century following.

The Gospel context is still in Cowper's mind, however, when he writes of those who "live in pleasure, dead ev'n while they live," that ". . . truth, propos'd to reasoners wise as they, / Is a pearl cast — completely cast away" ("Hope," 230, 258-59). In his poem "Sir John Oldcastle" Whittier imagines Wyclif defending his translation of the Bible by turning a charge of his attackers back on them: "The Gospel, the priest's pearl, flung down to swine — / The swine, laymen, lay-women, who will come, / God willing, to outlearn the filthy friar." In Sarah Orne Jewett's "The Dulham Ladies" Miss Dobbin prides herself on trying always "to elevate people's thoughts and direct them to higher channels." When it comes to "that Wolden woman," however, her principles fail her: "there is no use casting pearls before swine." In *Music at Night* Huxley adapts the phrase in judging that Lucretius's aim was to see that religion was "put underfoot and trampled on in return" ("And Wanton Optics Roll the Melting Eye").

PECULIAR PEOPLE The book of Deuteronomy describes Israel as chosen by God "to be a peculiar people unto himself, above all the nations that are upon the earth" (14:2; cf. 26:18). Other passages refer to Israel as chosen for a "peculiar treasure" (Exod. 19:5; Ps. 135:4). St. Paul applies the phrase to those who are redeemed in Christ: "Who gave himself for us, that he might redeem us from all iniquity, and purify unto himself a peculiar people, zealous of good works" (Titus 2:14), a formula echoed in 1 Pet. 2:9: "But ye are a chosen generation, a royal priesthood, an holy nation, a peculiar people; that ye should shew forth the praises of him who hath called you out of darkness into his marvellous light." The KJV's choice of the word "peculiar" to translate the Heb. *segullah* ("personal property" or "special possession") and Gk. *periousios* (lit. "rich," "special," "choice") depends upon derivation of the English word via the Lat. *peculium* ("private property"); in the 17th cent. the word meant primarily "belonging exclusively to one person or group." David Jones employs the more usual contemporary meaning of the word as well as 17th-cent. usage in his *Anathemata* in referring to "this peculiar people" — both chosen and countercultural (8.241).

PELAGIANISM See HERESY.

PENANCE See REPENTANCE.

PENINNAH One of the wives of Elkanah, who repeatedly taunted her long-barren rival Hannah.
See also HANNAH.

PENITENTIAL PSALMS In the medieval Church, seven "penitential" psalms were recited after lauds on Fridays during Lent. Many vernacular rhyming versions were made of these psalms (6, 32, 38, 51, 102, 130, 143), among which the Anglo-Norman series in Camb. MS

Univ. Lib. Gg. 1.1 (eds. Jeffrey and Levy, *Anglo-Norman Lyric* [1990]) is notable for its quality. For catechetical purposes the psalms were appropriate to the Seven Deadly Sins: six *contra iram,* wrath; 32 against pride; 38 against gluttony; 51 against lechery; 102 against avarice; 130 against envy; 143 against sloth. The *Book of Common Prayer* appointed these as Proper Psalms for Ash Wednesday: the first three at Matins, 51 at the Commination, and the last three at Evensong. They were also used in the Coronation service until 1603.
See also DE PROFUNDIS.

PENTATEUCH Gk. *penta* ("five") + *teuchos* ("book") signifies the first five books of the Bible, the "Books of Moses"; the term derives from LXX nomenclature through the Latin Vg translation. The Hebrew name is *Torah,* which derives from the verb *yarah* ("teach"); since it combines doctrinal teaching with historical narrative and saga history of the Jewish people, it is the most important unit in the Jewish canon. Jewish writers nevertheless also use the Greek term, as A. M. Klein illustrates in his "Psalm XV," where on the day of his "espousals" he celebrates an old rabbi "who solved each letter's mystic hook / Upon the parchment Pentateuch." The word does not occur in the KJV translation.

PENTECOST Gk. *pentēkostē* derives from the numeral *pentēkostos,* "fifty," and refers in Jewish and Christian texts to the fiftieth day after Passover (Macc. 12:32; Tob. 2:1; Philo, *De decalogo,* 160; *De specialibus legibus,* 2.176; Josephus, *Ant.* 3.252, 14.337, etc.). The feast is also called the *hag shabu'ot* or "feast of weeks," the second feast of the Jewish year and a harvest festival celebrated seven weeks after the beginning of the barley harvest (Exod. 23:16; 34:22; Lev. 23:15-21; Num. 28:26-31; Deut. 16:9-12). As the offering of a sheaf of barley marked the beginning of harvest, so the offering of loaves made from the new wheat marked its completion. The festival was hence sometimes called Azarta or closing festival, and in a very late Targum (2 Targum 3.8) it is said that celebrants climbed to the roofs of the synagogue and threw down apples, to be picked up by those below with the words, "As these apples are gathered up, so may we be gathered together from our dispersion among the heathen."

Jewish traditions about Pentecost predate the life of Jesus, by which time it had already begun to be celebrated as a feast of covenant renewal (Jub. 6:17-21) in communities such as that at Qumran. The book of Jubilees makes it an anniversary of God's covenant with Noah after the Flood, but, as was the case in the tradition of the Samaritans, it appears that a connection had also been established between Pentecost and the giving of the Law at Sinai. In writings of the later rabbis from the mid-2nd cent. A.D. this association is rendered explicit (S. 'Olam Rab. 5; Shab. 86a-88a; 'Arak. 1.9; Pesaḥ. 68b), with the most extensive early documentation being that of R. Johanan. In his elaboration of the Sinai revelation, "each word which proceeded from the mouth of the Almighty divided into seventy tongues [languages]" (Shab. 88b), subsequently connected in midrashic texts with the LXX and seen as harmonious with the "seven weeks" following barley harvest. Later, Pentecost is also said to be the day on which Enoch was translated (Tamid 28), the day on which Cain and Abel offered their diverse sacrifices (Tg. Yerushalmi Gen. 4:3), and the day on which Hannah prayed that she might be given a son (Shemuel 1.46).

The NT apostles gathered in Jerusalem were likely conscious of Pentecost as a feast of covenant renewal. And while the events described in Acts 2 invite comparison with rabbinic legends of Sinai, they were also markedly distinct from them. At Sinai one divine voice from the mountaintop was said to proclaim the Law in seventy languages; in Jerusalem 120 human voices were inspired by the Spirit to praise God in an unspecified number of languages.

For the earliest Christians Pentecost had eschatological meaning, signifying the outpouring of the Spirit promised for the end time (Joel 2:28; Acts 2:17ff.; Rom. 5:5; Titus 3:5-6). The first Christian Pentecost was an ecstatic prophetic experience involving "a sound from heaven as of a mighty rushing wind," "cloven tongues like as of fire" sitting upon each of the assembled, and an infilling of the Holy Spirit as a result of which they all "began to speak with other tongues, as the Spirit gave them utterance." These events, along with St. Peter's sermon, resulted in the conversion of about three thousand persons (Acts 2:2-4, 41) and constituted a new and enthusiastic community. Pentecost became thus a "birthday" for the Church, the people of the New Covenant (cf. St. Augustine, *Contra Faustum*, 2.12) just as the giving of the Law, the "Old Covenant," had signified the birth of community for the Hebrew pilgrims. The experience of Pentecost was early seen as an evident fulfillment of OT promises of a New Covenant, the law now "written upon the heart" (Deut. 30:6; Jer. 31:31-34; cf. Acts 2:38ff.; 3:25). It was also, in effect, a beginning for Christian missionary enterprise (Acts 1:8; 2:5, 9-11, 39), as well as confirmation that such a bearing of the "good news" would be continuous with the gospel proclaimed by Jesus, whose assistance was now present in the form of the Comforter he had promised (John 20:22; 14:16-24). Augustine (*Enarr. in Ps.* 67.9) develops the harvest festival connection to sum up these points:

The fruit of the earth was first in Jerusalem. For from there began the Church. There came the Holy Spirit and filled up the holy men gathered together in one place. Miracles were wrought, they spoke with the tongues of all mankind. They were filled full with the Spirit of God, the people were converted that were in that place. Fearing and yet receiving the divine outpouring, by confession they brought forth so much fruit that all their goods they brought together into a common stock, distributing out of

it to the poor, in order that no one might call anything his own, but that all things might be available to them in community, and that they might have one soul and one heart unto God.

The connection of the NT Pentecost with the giving of the Law at Sinai was a major theme in patristic writings. St. Jerome (*Ep.* 78.12), Augustine (*Contra Faustum*, 32.12; *De catechizandibus rudibus*, 23.41), and St. Leo the Great (*Sermo de Pentecoste*, 1) all comment on it, implying a typological connection, as does St. Gregory of Nazianzus: "The Jews keep the festival as well as we, but only in the letter. For while following after the bodily Law, such a one has not attained unto the spiritual Law" (Oration 31, "On Pentecost"). Augustine comments also on the relationship between the descent of the Holy Spirit as a dove upon Christ at his baptism and that of tongues of fire upon the apostles at Pentecost: "in the former simplicity is shown; in the latter, fervency" (*In Joan. Ev.* 6.3).

The typological connection of the *glossolalia* of Acts with the division of tongues at Babel (Gen. 11) causes St. Ambrose to observe that the condition prompting the antediluvian catastrophe was pride; that which opened the way for the Holy Spirit at Pentecost was humility (*Sermo*, 36.2). This point is later developed in reference to John 16:12-13 by St. Maximus of Tours in his classic series of sermons on Pentecost (*De Solemnitate Sanctae Pentecostes* [PL 17.371-80, 629-42]). Maximus observes that "the Holy Spirit . . . teaches simply this: what the Lord himself has already taught," observing that Pentecostal unity in the Church can only be preserved by persevering in Christ and his teaching (PL 17.377-78, 641).

The dramatic character of Pentecost, as well as its typological possibilities, produced a colorful *enchiridion symbolorum*. The tongues of fire were related by St. Cyprian to the smoke and fire on Sinai and to the burning bush (*Treatises*, 101.555). St. Cyril of Jerusalem comments that "a fiery sword barred of old the gates of Paradise; a fiery tongue, which brought salvation, restored the gift" (*Catechetical Lectures*, 17.15). The wind is conventionally related by Cyril to God's breath, or *pneuma*. Drawing on John 20:22 he observes: "This was the second time he breathed on mankind (his first breath having been stifled through wilful sins)" (17.12). He also likens the wind to a "heavenly trumpet" (15). The apostles' speaking in tongues confounds the hearers, he says, but as "a second confusion, replacing that first evil one at Babylon":

For in that confusion of tongues there was division of purpose, because their hearts were at enmity with God. Here minds were restored and united, because the object on which they focused was of God. The means of falling were the means of recovery. (17; cf. Gregory of Nazianzus, *Oratio*, 41.16).

Of the bystanders who said dismissively, "They are full of new wine," Cyril observes: "They spoke truly though in mockery. For in truth the wine was new, even the grace of the New Testament; but this new wine was from a spiritual Vine which had oftentimes ere this borne fruit in the Prophets, and had now blossomed in the New Testament" (18-19). These symbols — trumpet; breath; wind; tongues of fire; new wine — all become part of the iconography of Pentecost in the Middle Ages, where the color of priestly vestments for that Sunday was red (reflecting the "tongues of fire") even though the day itself was called "Whitsunday" in England for the white vestments worn by catechumens baptized during the vigil.

The office of Pentecost has only one Nocturn: at Terce the *"Veni Creator"* is sung instead of the usual hymn, because at the "third hour" or about nine in the morning the Holy Spirit descended. In Italy it was apparently customary to scatter rose petals from the ceilings of churches to recall the tongues of fire so that Pentecost there was often denominated *Pascha Rosatum* (cf. Chaucer's "Chaplet of roses of Whitsunday," in *Romaunt of the Rose,* 2275-79). In France trumpets were blown during the Mass of Pentecost to recall the sound of the mighty wind. In Eastern traditions Pentecost is closely associated with both the Resurrection (e.g., St. Basil, *On the Spirit,* chap. 27) and the Last Judgment. St. John Chrysostom's *Hom.* 4 on Acts 2:1-2 opens with the words: "Do you perceive the type? What is this Pentecost? The time when the sickle was to be put to the harvest, and the ingathering made." These associations are played upon throughout the centuries so that, e.g., the Pentecost sermons of Abelard begin by establishing the parallel to Sinai and those of Hugh of St. Victor move on to apply the notion of the multiple tongues to *"de multiplici operatione Spiritua sancti in nobis"* (PL 178.500-512, 183.330-32).

In bk. 19 of the "B" text of *Piers Plowman* there is a "Pentecost" in which the Holy Spirit descends, giving gifts to all Christians, and specially equipping Piers. The dreamer is advised by Conscience that the Paraclete is Christ's messenger called Grace, and is to be worshiped with the singing of the *"Veni, Creator Spiritus."* (The gifts distributed by the Paraclete here constitute an innovative list.) The Chester cycle of Corpus Christi plays, probably played at "Whitsuntide," has a notable Pentecost play ("The Fishemongers Playe," no. 21) which begins with the election of Matthias to replace Judas — implying the presence of the twelve only — but goes on to recognize the 120 present as specified in Acts 1:15. Peter reminds his brethren that Jesus has promised "a counselor, / his Ghoost, as he beheight" (11-12), and after the installation of Matthias the apostles all kneel and sing the *"Veni, Creator Spiritus"* (121ff., which is broken into eight stanzas, one to each apostle). At this point Christ intervenes with his Father in heaven and in a long speech the Father gives the practical reasons for sending the Holy Spirit:

Throughout the world they shall gonne,
my deeds to preach manye one.
Yett steadfastnes in them ys nonne
to suffer for me anoye.
Fletchinge yett they binne ichone.
But when my Ghoost ys them upon,
then shall they after be styffe as stonne
my deedes to certyfie.
Dreade of death ne no distres
shall lett them of stydfastnes. (207-16)

After the tongues of fire have descended, an angel tells the apostles the purpose of the glossolalia:

And through the Ghooste that I you bringe
yee shall have understandinge
of every lond speakinge,
whatsoever the saye. (247-50)

The disciples then severally discuss their gift of tongues: as Philip puts it in one of several parallel speeches:

And I that never could speake thinge
save Ebrewe as I learned yonge,
nowe I can speake at my likinge
all languages, both iowe and hye. (279-82)

Peter then calls upon them to join in a sequential proclamation of their faith in the form of the Apostles' Creed. The play thus succeeds in dramatizing Pentecost as the birth of the Church and relating the infilling of the Holy Spirit to clear teaching about Jesus.

Chaucer's *Summoner's Tale,* with its elaborate antifraternal satire in which the obtuse friar tries to divide a fart equally among his eleven confreres seems to be (as Levitan and Levy have argued) a parody of the "mighty wind" at Pentecost. But a more serious series of allusions is found in Malory, in whose *Le Morte Darthur* "at the feste of Pentecost alle manner of men assayed to pulle at the swerde that wold assay, but none myghte prevaille" (1.7). Numerous crucial feasts and tournaments are held at Pentecost (1.8; 3.15; 6.1), and it is the day of the commencement of the quest for the Holy Grail:

Than anone they harde crakynge and cryynge of thundir, that hem thoughte the paleys sholde all to-dryve. So in the myddys of the blast entyrde a sonnebeame, more clerer by seven tymys than ever they saw day, and all they were alyghted of the grace of the Holy Goste. Then began every knyght to beholde other, and eyther saw other, by their semyng, farer than ever they were before. (13.7; cf. 15.6)

Here, however, the knights do not break out into glossolalia, but are struck dumb.

Whitsun, or Whitsuntide, the time of a parish festival grown popular in the late 15th and 16th cents., featured merrymaking of various sorts, including plays and morris dances which have little to do with the biblical Pentecost but are frequently celebrated in literature (e.g., Robert Herrick's "The Country Life"). Sidney's Stephen prepares himself "with leavy twiggs of *Laurell* tree / A garland . . . /

. . . that *Whitsontide* to beare" ("Lamon"), and Julia in Shakespeare's *Two Gentlemen of Verona* recollects how "at Pentecost, / When all our pageants of delight were play'd, / Our youth got me to play the woman's part" (4.4.158-60). Recollections of another spirit likewise inform Perdita's dreams in *A Winter's Tale,* and her saying to Florizel, "Come, take your flowers: / Methinks I play as I have seen them do in Whitsun pastorals" (4.4.132-34). Pentecost was notably the season for weddings (cf. *Romeo and Juliet,* 1.5.36-39).

Francis Bacon's *New Atlantis* offers a more straightforward analogy, when the Governor tells how his thoroughly international colonists were by a miracle enabled to read the writings of St. Bartholemew, a miracle like that "in the original gift of tongues." George Herbert's "Whitsunday" is an invocation of the Holy Spirit for a renewal of Pentecost in the poet's own life and community: "Restore this day, for thy great name, / Unto his ancient and miraculous right." Henry Vaughan's mirroring "White Sunday" similarly prays for a renewal in "hearts dead and sinful cold" of "Those flames which on the Apostles rush'd," concluding: "O come! refine us with thy fire!" (cf. Mal. 3:2-3).

Reformation commentary produced little innovation in the interpretation of Pentecost, except in Calvin and his followers an atypically literalized reading of a spiritual event. Calvin curiously rejects Augustine's typologizing parallel of Pentecost with Sinai, only to take up the parallel with Babel:

> The diversity of tongues did hinder the gospel from being spread abroad any farther. . . . For whence came the diversity of tongues, save only that the wicked and ungodly counsels of men might be brought to nought? (Gen. 11:7). But God doth furnish the apostles with the diversity of tongues now, that he may bring and call home, into a blessed unity, men which wander here and there. These cloven tongues made all men to speak the language of Canaan, as Isaiah foretold. (Isa. 19:18)

By the tongues of fire the Lord shows preachers of this gospel "that their voice shall be fiery" — the emphasis falls upon preaching and evangelism. Milton's archangel Michael "predicts" more expansively to Adam in *Paradise Lost* that

> the Spirit
> Pour'd first on his Apostles, whom he sends
> To evangelize the Nations, then on all
> Baptiz'd, shall them with wondrous gifts endue
> To speak all Tongues, and do all Miracles
> As did thir Lord before them. (*PL* 12.497-502)

A similar emphasis occurs in Matthew Henry's *Comm. on the Whole Bible* (6.726), which identifies the "tongues" with the apostles' new capacity to overcome linguistic fragmentation and so better effect a program of worldwide evangelism. Henry follows Bishop Lightfoot in suggesting that as the division of tongues at Babel was

"the casting off of the heathen. . . , now, after above two thousand years, God, by another dividing of tongues, restores the knowledge of himself to the nations." Matthew Poole's reading of the glossolalia leans on the Babel typology even more heavily, making the speaking in tongues a sign rather than a recurrent gift: it was

> to signifie the varieties of Languages which the Apostles should be enabled to speak; to qualifie them to Preach the Gospel unto all Nations, and to remove the obstacle which the confusion of Tongues caus'd: and which represented (1) The light that the Apostles should impart. (2ndly). The fervent heat and zeal which they should be endued with. (3rdly). The Gospel's spreading in the World, and carrying all before it, prevailing over all errors. (4thly). The purity and holiness which they and all that Preach the Gospel ought to appear withal. [It] Remained, as far as was necessary for the founding of the Christian religion.

By this reading the gift of tongues, alone among the spiritual gifts, effectively becomes only a sign and foreshadowing of the evangelistic enterprise.

One of the most influential commentaries of the period (used extensively, e.g., by John Donne) is that by the Jesuit Cornelius à Lapide. Lapide takes up the notion that the glossolalia was provided so that the gospel might be made known in all languages, but says that the many languages signify also the multiplicity of the Spirit's gifts to the Church (connecting the narrative with 1 Cor. 12:4). Lapide emphasizes that actual working languages of the time were involved, that these were European, Middle Eastern, and African, and that one ought to see the miracle as having a practical, not merely ecstatic focus (*Comm. in Acta Apostolorum,* 2.80-81). He chides Theodore Beza, Calvin's disciple, for "ineptly and imperiously" insisting (contra Acts 1:14–2:1) that the Virgin Mary and "the other woman" were not present among the 120 gathered at Pentecost (77, 88). Following Augustine he sees the Holy Spirit at Pentecost and ever after as Christ's Vicar, and the descent of the Spirit and indwelling in human hearts as an analogy with the Incarnation: as the Word took on the substance of human flesh in Christ, so the Spirit inhabits human flesh in the gathered community of her apostles (84).

John Wesley moves away from Calvinist sources and the Babel typology in favor of the pre-Reformation connection to Sinai. In his *Explanatory Notes on the New Testament* (1754) he asserts:

> At the Pentecost of Sinai in the Old Testament, and the Pentecost of Jerusalem in the New, were the two grand manifestations of God, the legal and the evangelical; the one from the mountain, and the other from heaven; the terrible and the merciful one. *They were all with one accord in one place* —So here was a conjunction of company, minds, and place; the whole hundred and twenty being present.

He follows the tradition in interpreting the miracle as "an

earnest that the whole world should in due time praise God in various tongues," saying that "Moses, the type of the law, was of a slow tongue, but the gospel speaks with a fiery and flaming one" (2.1-4).

Eighteenth-cent. authors, generally averse to "enthusiastick utterance," had little affection for the story of Pentecost. Swift represents this aversion in his accusing some of the Puritans in their worship of establishing "a Fellowship of *Christ* with *Belial,*" adding, "such is the Analogy they make between 'cloven Tongues' and 'cloven Feet'" (*Mechanical Operation of the Spirit,* 2.1). He considers it an open question whether "our English Enthusiastick Preachers, were [cases of] *Possession* or *Inspiration*" — indicating his conviction that it is impiety for any contemporary preacher to associate his animus with that of the apostles at Pentecost.

Associating a pentecostal spirit with Lollard evangelism, Tennyson's "Sir John Oldcastle" praises the

> Heaven-sweet Evangel, ever-living word,
> Who whilom spakest to the South in Greek
> About the soft Mediterranean shores,
> And then in Latin to the Latin crowd,
> As good need was — thou hast come to talk to our isle.
> Hereafter thou, fulfilling Pentecost,
> Must learn to use the tongues of all the world. (28-34)

Elizabeth Barrett Browning, of nonconformist lineage, longs for a poet's "tongue of baptismal flame" ("The North and the South"; cf. "A Tale of Villafranca"). In Matthew Arnold's "Westminster Abbey" the "tongues of fire" are but flickering movements of stained-glass light playing on the interior surfaces of the "Nave, choir and transept glorified with light." In Hawthorne's *Scarlet Letter* the Puritan self-assurance which Swift abhorred comes to a fruition such as he feared. Of the solemn assembly of clergymen in consistory court Hawthorne writes:

> All that they lacked was the gift that descended upon the chosen disciples, at Pentecost, in 'tongues of flame', symbolizing, it would seem not the power of speech in foreign and unknown languages, but that of addressing the whole human brotherhood in the heart's native language. These fathers, otherwise so apostolic, lacked Heaven's last and rarest attestation of their office, the Tongue of Flame. (chap. 11)

Later, the corrupt and cowardly Rev. Dimmesdale seeks from his victim Hester sympathy for the growing burden of pretense his hypocrisy has created:

> Cans't thou deem it, Hester, a consolation, that I must stand up in my pulpit, and meet so many eyes turned upward to my face, as if the light of heaven were beaming from it! — must see my flock hungry for the truth, and listening to my words as if a tongue of Pentecost were speaking! — and then look inward and discern the black reality of what they idolize? (chap. 17)

Hawthorne's notion that the Pentecost gift of tongues is "that of addressing the whole human brotherhood in the heart's native language" finds a Transcendentalist counterpart in Emerson:

> The passive Master lent his hand
> To the vast soul that o'er him planned;
> And the same power that reared the shrine
> Bestrode the tribes that knelt within.
> Ever the fiery Pentecost
> Girds with one flame the countless host. ("The Problem," 47-52)

In "Woodnotes 2," the pine tree requests of the poet to adopt the language of Nature:

> The least breath my boughs which tossed
> Brings again the Pentecost;
> To every soul resounding clear
> In a voice of solemn cheer, —
> 'Am I not thine? Are not these thine?'
> And they reply, 'Forever mine!'
> My branches speak Italian,
> English, German, Basque, Castilian. . . . (133-55)

Whitman's "tongues of flame" is the spirit of humanity such as vivifies the American ethos ("By Blue Ontario's Shores"; "On, on the Same, Ye Jocund Twain") — a more clearly secularized version of Carlyle's notion that the Church arises out of society, manifesting itself in individuals self-actualizing "as with cloven tongues of fire" (*Sartor Resartus,* 3.2).

The tongues of flame with which Stephen Dedalus conjures are a source of terror and oppression; though the priest who uses the image in his sermon does not so intend it, it becomes a symbol of the vocation Stephen wants to evade, so that the tongues of flame are metamorphosed in his imagination into images of hellfire (chap. 3). Later he reflects on the "divine gloom and silence wherein dwelt the unseen Paraclete," a gloom unrelieved for him by the Mass at Pentecost in which the priests were "robed in the scarlet of the tongues of fire" (chap. 4). T. S. Eliot's "Little Gidding" (*Four Quartets,* 4), with its memorable "enfolding of fire and rose," is an intense, lyrical reflection on "pentecostal fire / In the dark time of the year" and of the heart. Eliot's fire is likewise terrifying, a "pyre," but a passage to redemption, a "refining fire" (cf. Mal. 3:2-3), so that the "flame of incandescent terror / Of which the tongues declare" offers a choice — "To be redeemed from fire by fire" (4.4). The tone of Francis Thompson's "The Poppy to Monica" is wistful, more subdued, an invitation rather than a confession:

> But you, who love nor know at all
> The diverse chambers in Love's guest hall
> Where some rise early, few sit long:
> In how differing accounts hear the throng
> His great Pentecostal tongue. (10)

Philip Larkin's *Whitsun Weddings* (1964) is a volume of verse about an outsider forever looking in on an epithalamion or dance he cannot quite bring himself to join. Richard Wilbur's "October Maples," by contrast, celebrates in community the fall of maple leaves: "A showered fire we thought forever lost / Redeems the air. Where friends in passing meet, / They parley in the tongues of Pentecost." The tantalizing allure of a pentecostal renewal is expressed by one of the characters in Rose Macaulay's *Told by an Idiot,* who muses, "Perhaps there really *is* a Holy Ghost. Perhaps my life will be made all new, with tongues of fire upon my head and me talking in strange languages the wonderful works of God" (3.7).

See also APOSTLE; BABEL; HOLY SPIRIT; TONGUES, GIFT OF.

Bibliography. Bruce, F. F. *The Book of Acts* (1954); Ceard, J. "De Babel à la Pentecôte: La transformation du mythe de la confusion des langues au XVIᵉ siècle." *Bibliothèque d'Humanisme et Renaissance* 42 (1980), 577-94; Dunn, J. *Baptism of the Holy Spirit* (1970); Goppelt, L. *Apostolic and Post-Apostolic Times* (trans. 1970); Levitan, A. "The Parody of Pentecost in Chaucer's *Summoner's Tale.*" *UTQ* 40 (1971) 236-46; Levy, B. S. "Biblical Parody in the Summoner's Tale." *TSLL* 11 (1966), 45-60.

PEREZ-UZZAH *See* ARK OF THE COVENANT.

PERFECTION In the OT terms associated with *perfection* pointed to humanity's kinship and fellowship with God. Those possessing sincerity, integrity, wholeness, goodness, and loyalty to God were "perfect" in contrast to their ungodly neighbors (Deut. 18:13). The adjective *tamim,* used to describe Noah's character (Gen. 6:9), refers in over one half of its occurrences to animals "without blemish" and therefore fit for sacrifice. When describing personal character, it is often translated "perfect," "upright," or "sincere" in righteousness. The adjective *tam,* meaning "sincerity," is translated "perfect" in various ascriptions to Job (1:8; 2:3; 8:20; 9:20-22; cf. Ps. 37:37). In Job one learns that suffering is one path to perfection (cf. Heb. 12:10).

The adjective *shalom* is translated "perfect" in parallel passages in Kings, Chronicles, and Isaiah. Typical is 1 Kings 8:61, "Let your heart . . . be perfect with the LORD" (cf. 1 Kings 11:4; 15:3, 14; 2 Kings 20:3; Isa. 38:3). The RSV uses "perfect" less often than the KJV, avoiding the absolute sense typically conveyed by the word in modern English. The RSV uses "perfect" to describe a human being only once in the OT, Job 36:4, where Elihu claims that he is "perfect *[tamim]* in knowledge" because divinely inspired.

Individual and corporate ideas of perfection are represented in the NT by *teleios* — completion, maturity (Eph. 4:13, 14) — and *katartizo* — make whole (1 Cor. 1:10; Eph. 4:12; Heb. 13:21). Usually the term refers to ethical and spiritual completeness and Godlikeness — to imparted rather than imputed righteousness. Jesus sets forth the great ideal in Matt. 5:48, which is a call to share in the full and undifferentiating love of God for every person, whether evil or good, just or unjust (44-47).

Christian perfection in the NT is often stated in terms of loving God with all the heart and soul and mind (Matt. 22:37-40; 1 Cor. 13; Col. 3:14; 1 John 4:12, 17). Faith in Christ is basic, yet it is dependent upon the cooperative efforts of individuals (2 Cor. 7:1; Phil 2:12; James 5:8; 1 John 2:5; 4:12). It must have pure intent, the single eye (Matt. 6:33). St. Paul claimed perfection of desire (Phil. 3:12-15) and motive (1 Thess. 2:10), but not "perfection" in an eschatological sense until death. James reiterates that sincerity and moral integrity are essential to the perfect man (4:8). Johannine literature includes purification (John 15:2; 1 John 3:3) and fellowship with God (1 John 1:7), culminating in unity within the community as well as union with the divine (John 17:23).

A kind of perfection is expected of each stage of the Christian life: (1) condition of discipleship (Matt. 19:21); (2) complete knowledge of divine things (1 Cor. 2:6); (3) the reward of discipline (Heb. 2:10; 5:9); (4) the culmination of redemption (1 Cor. 13:10; Phil. 3:12; Heb. 12:23). Two questions arise: Does Christian perfection imply a sinless state? 1 John 3:6, 9 seems to imply that, yet 1 John 1:8-10 seems to state the contrary. Is it attainable in this life? No single passage provides a definitive reply, but the obligation to seek perfection of desire as an attainable goal is stated in Matt. 5:43-48; 2 Cor. 7:1; Phil. 3:15; and Heb. 6:1.

In the first two centuries such Apostolic Fathers as St. Clement of Rome (*Epistola ad Corinthos,* 49), St. Ignatius, and St. Irenaeus held to the belief of perfection of love by grace through faith. They nevertheless recognized a certain paradoxical character in the notion of such perfection. While St. Clement of Alexandria under gnostic pressure took pains to state that human perfection was relative, he insisted, "The Father wishes us to be perfect by living blamelessly according to the obedience of the Gospel" (*Stromateis,* 7.14). Later St. Jerome and St. Augustine reflect reaction to the Pelagians who emphasized perfection by human effort; although Augustine approved of Christian perfection as a goal, he believed that sin persisted in the most perfect Christian to preserve true humility: "Perfection is a person's knowledge of his own imperfection" (*Sermo,* 170.8).

During the 3rd cent. the belief had emerged among ascetic communities that perfection was the fruit of vigilance and self-mortification, a view which was later to gain stature in Benedictine monasticism as well as in the Eastern Church. Stressing an intuitive approach to God, mystics of the Middle Ages sought perfection through three stages: purification, illumination, and union (see E. Underhill, *Mysticism;* W. R. Inge, *Christian Mysticism*). Some of the best known of these writers emphasizing such a growth in perfection are Meister Eckart, Thomas à Kempis, Richard Rolle, and Julian of Norwich, but Walter Hilton perhaps provides the most direct and coherent elaboration of the idea in his *Ladder of Perfection.* Hilton's text may be seen partly in the light of the spiritual biography of St. Francis, the 13th-cent. *Speculum Perfeccionis,* in which "perfection" of obedience is thematically linked to the closest possible imitation of the life of Christ. In Hilton's text the primary concern is with growth in spiritual maturity. Perfect correspondence to the love of Jesus may not be obtained before heaven, "when we shall see him as he is"; en route a continuous sharpening of one's vision of Jesus, contemplating him in every action and reflection of life, will give a progressively clearer image with which to identify. Hilton's conception is of a progress toward perfect love through a "reformation of faith," or conversion, followed by a "reformation of spiritual consciousness," the illuminative and unitive goals of high mystical contemplation. Following Christ "perfectly" for Hilton thus means what it did to earlier monastic and fraternal writers — *imitatio Christi,* with as little wasted motion as possible.

Related to this spiritual usage is Chaucer's description "he was a verray, parfit gentil knight" (*General Prologue* to *The Canterbury Tales,* 1.72); although at the literal level Chaucer is identifying comparative excellence, the fact that his Knight lives up to his paramonastic chivalric vows suggests that his "perfection" is analogous to that of a blameless devotee of a religious ideal. Echoing her patristic sources, notably St. Jerome, the Wife of Bath allows that "Virginitee is greet perfeccioun" but that "Crist . . . of perfeccioun is welle" (*Wife of Bath's Tale,* Prol. 3.105-07), thus explicating the comparative rather than the absolute sense in which the term is typically used. Later, Spenser's faithful knight "grew . . . to such perfection of all heavenly grace" (*Faerie Queene,* 1.10.21.3). Shakespeare's Gonzalo echoes this vocational ambition when he says to Sebastian, "I would with such perfection govern, sir, to excel the golden age" (*The Tempest,* 2.1.167).

According to Luther and Calvin perfection is never realized in the present life, nor is sin eradicated. Sin is defined in Pauline terms (Rom. 3:23) as any lack of conformity to the standard of absolute perfection. All persons are, therefore, sinners. Perfection is only to be had, as Calvin puts it, by the imputed righteousness of Christ in the covenant of grace (*Inst.* 3.22.2; 4.1.17). For Milton's Satan the perfection of Christ himself is in question: "What of perfection can in man be found, / Or human nature can receive," he taunts (*Paradise Regained,* 3.230-31).

The Renaissance produced a notion of perfection based upon the unfinished, continually self-renewing character of the created world. The 16th-cent. Italian writers J. J. Scaliger and Lucilio Vanini draw upon Empedocles to argue that if the world were perfect it could not improve, and this world not possess "true perfection," which (in their presupposition) depends upon progress. Thus, this world is not perfect in the sense of *teleos perfectus* (finished or flawless) but rather *perfectus propter imperfectionem* (perfect through its imperfection), a paradox similarly expressed by Descartes (*Meditation,* 4).

This notion is harmonized with the traditional goal of spiritual maturation in Donne's "Sappho" and reflected in his "Obsequies to the Lord Harrington," where he makes the analogy:

> Just as a perfect reader doth not dwell,
> On every syllable, nor stay to spell,
> Yet without doubt, hee doth distinctly see
> And lay together every A, and B;
> So, in short liv'd good men, is'not understood
> Each severall vertue, but the compound good;
> For, they all vertues paths in that pace tread,
> As Angells goe, and know, and as men read. (93-100)

In *The Second Anniversary* he returns to an Augustinian model of spiritual progress reminiscent of Hilton:

> She who in th'art of knowing Heaven, was growne
> Here upon earth, to such perfection,
> That she hath, ever since to Heaven she came,
> (In a far fairer print,) but read the same:
> Shee, shee not satisfied with all this waight,
> (For so much knowledge, as would over-fraight
> Another, did but ballast her) is gone
> As well t'enjoy, as get perfection. (311-18)

George Herbert emphasizes rather the contrast between human and divine perfection: "How shall infection / Presume upon thy perfection?" ("Miserie," 35-36; cf. "Obedience"). In his "Briefe Notes on Valdesso's Considerations," however, he also makes use of the relative sense of the word:

> The H. Scriptures (as I wrote before) have not only an Elementary use, but a use of perfection, neither can they ever be exhausted, (as Pictures may be by a plenarie circumspection) but still even to the most learned and perfect in them, there is somewhat to be learned more. . . . ("To the 32 Considerations")

The question of Christian perfection was taken up in earnest in the 18th cent. William Law's *A Practical Treatise upon Christian Perfection* (1726) hearkens back to the medieval ideal of *imitatio Christi;* its 13th chapter, titled "All Christians are required to imitate the life and example of Jesus Christ," succinctly states the theme of his work:

> When it is said that we are to imitate the life of Christ, it is not meant that we are called to the same manner of life, or the same sort of actions, for this cannot be, but it is certain that we are called to the same spirit and character which was the spirit and character of our Blessed Saviour's life and actions. We are to be like Him in heart and mind, to act by the same rule, to look towards the same end, and to govern our lives by the same spirit. . . . I am, said the Blessed Jesus, "The way, the truth, and the life, no man cometh unto the Father but by me." Christians often hear these words, and perhaps think that they have enough fullfilled them by believing in Jesus Christ. But they should consider that when Jesus Christ says He is the way, his meaning is that his way of life is to be the way in which all Christians are to live, and that it is by

living after the manner of his life that any man comes unto the Father. So that the doctrine of this passage is this, that however we may call ourselves Christians or disciples of Christ, yet we cannot come unto God the Father except by entering into the way of life which was the way of our Saviour's life.

In practical terms this means that the ideal of Christian perfection

> calls us to be born again of God, to live by the light of his Holy Spirit, to renounce the world and all worldly attitudes, to practise a constant, universal self-denial, to make daily war with the corruption and disorder of our nature, to prepare ourselves for divine grace by a purity and holiness of conversation, to avoid all pleasures and cares which grieve the Holy Spirit and separate Him from us, to live in a daily constant state of prayer and devotion.... (chap. 14)

The influence of Law's book upon George Whitefield, John and Charles Wesley, John Newton, and Hannah More, among others, helped to make Christian perfection a widely discussed topic in 18th- and 19th-cent. theology and literature. It is an item of concern, e.g., in Samuel Richardson's epistolary novel *Clarissa.* William Cowper offers a Calvinist rejoinder to one effect of the "doctrine of perfection" when he asks rhetorically if God enacts laws for a frail humanity "so strict, that less than perfect must despair? / Falsehood! which whoso but suspects of truth / Dishonours God, and makes a slave of man" (*The Task,* 5.641-43).

Expounding the Arminian doctrine begun in the teaching of the Remonstrant divines, John Wesley had argued that it was the privilege of every Christian believer to love God with all his heart, mind, soul, and strength. Wesley admits the difficulty of discriminating between sinless faults and willful transgressions (he defines sin as a voluntary transgression of a known law [*Works,* 11.396]). Although he believes perfection may be received instantaneously by faith (*Works,* 11.386, 428) and is therefore possible in this life (11.389, 393, 402), he also expresses the view that it is sometimes achieved at the time of one's death (11.429; cf. 373). Such perfection is not absolute; it does not make one infallible; it is perfection in love; its fruits are boundless joy, ceaseless prayer, and endless gratitude. It is improvable and it is capable of being lost. Wesley himself seems not to have professed reaching this state (cf. his *The Character of a Methodist* [1742]). Wesley's successor-to-be, John Fletcher of Madeley, wrote a somewhat more coherent "Essay on Christian Perfection," clarifying some of the obscurities of Wesley's own views of the subject — which proved occasionally problematic to adherents as well as opponents of his "doctrine of perfection."

In 19th-cent. American literature the residue of doctrinal controversy is reflected in fiction such as Hawthorne's *Blithedale Romance* and *Scarlet Letter,* and persists even into the 20th cent., where the sometime Wesleyan view of perfection as entire sanctification is applied to non-Christian pursuits of perfect sanctity. J. D. Salinger's chronicles of the Glass family in his novels and short stories, as well as the story of Holden Caulfield in *The Catcher in the Rye,* afford examples of such an adaptation of the theme, while William Golding's *Free Fall* gives an account of how a secular "consciousness of sin" may lead to a vision of sanctity.

Bibliography. Cox, L. G. *John Wesley's Concept of Perfection* (1964); Dussinger, J. A. "Conscience and the Pattern of Christian Perfection in *Clarissa.*" *PMLA* 81 (1966), 236-45; Fleming, J. V. "Gospel Asceticism: Some Chaucerian Images of Perfection." In *Chaucer and Scriptural Tradition.* Ed. D. L. Jeffrey (1984), 183-95; Flew, R. N. *The Idea of Perfection* (1934); Foss, M. *The Idea of Perfection in the Western World* (1946); Hansot, E. *Perfection and Progress* (1974); Johnson, C. D. "Hawthorne and Nineteenth-Century Perfectionism." *AL* 44 (1973), 585-95; La Rondelle, H. *Perfection and Perfectionism* (1971); Mahan, A. *Scripture Doctrine of Christian Perfection* (1918); Pauly, H. "Perfection." *Review of Religion* 11 (1947), 261-72; Perkins, H. W. *The Doctrine of Christian Perfection* (1927); Peters, J. L. *Christian Perfection and American Methodism* (1956); Sontag, F. *Divine Perfection* (1962); Tatarkiewicz, W. "Paradoxes of Perfection." *Dialectics and Humanism* 7 (1980), 77-80; Warfield, B. B. *Perfectionism* (1967); Watson, G. P. "Wesley and Luther on Christian Perfection." *Ecumenical Review* 15 (1963), 291-302.   ERWIN P. RUDOLPH

PESHER, PESHAT   Hebrew words implying the primary, plain, natural sense of the text; consistent with the medieval *sensus literalis* as developed by Nicholas of Lyra and St. Thomas Aquinas, "that which the author intends."

See also HERMENEUTICS.

PETER   St. Peter, foremost among the disciples and, with St. Paul, most prominent of the apostles after Pentecost, is one of the most colorful and complex of NT characters. He has traditionally been credited with two contributions to the NT canon, the Epistles of 1 and 2 Peter. Because he is so often a foil for Jesus, the signal events of his life closely parallel the main events in the ministry and proclamation of Jesus. After the Ascension, as leader of the young church in Jerusalem, later at Antioch, and then in Rome, he fulfilled the role assigned to him by Jesus as a foundation for the Church. Roman bishops have been chief among bishops in the Western church since Linus, Anencletus, and Clement I, Peter's first successors in Rome, although the title "Pope" (Gk. *pappas*; Lat. *papa*) did not come to be associated exclusively with the Roman bishop until after the 5th cent.

Born in Bethsaida (probably at the north end of Lake Gennesaret), the town also of St. Philip, Peter was a brother of St. Andrew. Their father's name was Jonah (Matt. 16:7; John 1:42) — the notion that Bar-Jona means "anarchist" or "zealot" is fictional. After Peter's marriage he settled in Capernaum, where he was living in the home of his mother-in-law (Matt. 8:14; Mark 1:30; Luke 4:38) at the beginning of the public ministry of Jesus. According to St. Clement of Alexandria (*Stromateis*, 3.6), he had children, and that his wife accompanied him on at least some of his missionary tours is suggested by the fact that she was known at Corinth (1 Cor. 9:5). Clement indicates that at some later point she, like her husband, suffered martyrdom (*Stromateis*, 7.9). While in Capernaum Peter plied his trade as a fisherman, and owned his own boat (Luke 5:1-11). He and Andrew had been attracted there to the penitential preaching of John the Baptist (John 1:40-42).

The statement in Acts 4:13 that Peter and John were "unlearned and ignorant men" probably ought not to be taken too extremely; the phrase may mean merely that they lacked recourse to rabbinical training in the Torah and its interpretation. On the other hand, Peter is always presented in the NT as rough and ready, earnest yet volatile, desirous of spiritual good yet neither disciplined in his thought nor meditative.

Several of the key narratives concerning Peter in all four Gospels underline Peter's human fallibility, but the most emphatic representation of his weaknesses comes in Mark's account (which has been thought to derive directly from Peter's own recollections as related to the author). Like John and the other Synoptics, Mark ranks Peter as first of the disciples and chief spokesperson for the Twelve, but he also singles him out for blame at critical points in the narrative. It is Peter who leads the group to Jesus and tries to press on him the role of popular teacher (1:35-37). At Caesarea Philippi (8:27-33) Jesus hears Peter's confession that he is the Messiah with some reserve, and when Peter rebukes Jesus for saying that "the Son of man must suffer many things, and be rejected . . . and be killed, and after three days rise again," Jesus reprimands Peter in turn, saying, "Get thee behind me, Satan: for thou savorest not the things that be of God, but the things that be of men" (8:33). At the Transfiguration Peter's suggestion that three "tabernacles" be set up to honor Moses, Elijah, and Jesus appears to have been an utterance of nervous foolishness, the narrative adding, "For he wist not what to say, for they were sore afraid" (9:6). He is singled out for reproach for falling asleep while he should be praying in Gethsemane (14:37), and his famous three denials of Jesus after the capture (14:66-72) are recounted in such a way as to create the suspicion that he may even have "cursed" his Lord (v. 71), a cardinal offense in the early Church (1 Cor. 12:3). Yet for all that, the resurrected Jesus sends with the angel at the tomb a special message to Peter (16:7).

The accounts of Matthew, Luke, and John in various ways soften the notice of these failings, balancing the frailty of Peter, as exhibited in his lapse of faith after his bold request to walk to Jesus on the water, with an emphasis on his learning to depend absolutely on his Lord rather than acting unreflectingly merely on his own strength (Matt. 14:23-33). Also, at the confession incident, Matthew includes Jesus' response to Peter's recognition of his Messiahship which, even as it points to Peter's mortal limitations, makes the famous pun on his name (Aram. *Kepha'* > *Kephas;* Gk. *Petros/Petra;* Lat. *Petrus/Petrum*) the introduction to an unmatched special calling of Peter to apostolic leadership in the church:

> Blessed art thou, Simon Bar-jona: for flesh and blood hath not revealed it to thee, but my father which is in heaven. And I say also unto thee, That thou art Peter, and upon this rock I will build my church; and the gates of hell shall not prevail against it. And I will give unto thee the keys of the kingdom of heaven: and whatsoever thou shalt bind on earth shall be bound in heaven: and whatsoever thou shalt loose on earth shall be loosed in heaven. (Matt. 16:17-19)

This call to apostleship was renewed following Peter's denials and the events surrounding Calvary and the tomb, when Jesus met Peter and some of the other disciples after they fished in vain all night. From the shore, unrecognized, Jesus urged Peter to cast his net again, and when he did, the catch was so great it could hardly be hauled in. The disciples (having experienced another such miraculous draught of fishes [Luke 5:4-11]) then recognized Jesus, and Peter leapt into the sea to get to shore, where Jesus already was cooking fish over a fire of charcoal. After the meal, Jesus asked Peter, "Simon, son of Jonas, lovest thou me?" and twice received the answer, "Yea, Lord, thou knowest that I love thee." When Jesus asked the third time, exasperated, Peter replied emphatically, "Lord, thou knowest all things; thou knowest that I love thee." Then, the threefold confession having reversed the earlier threefold denial, Peter received his commission, "Feed my sheep," along with a prophecy concerning his own martyrdom (John 21:16-19). Even on this occasion, however, Peter was chastened by Jesus for improper curiosity concerning the vocation of another of the disciples (vv. 21-24). Only John (18:10) among the four evangelists names Peter as the "one standing by" at the betrayal and arrest of Jesus who struck off the servant of the high priest's ear (and was reprimanded by Jesus for his action).

For all his shortcomings, Peter remained *primus inter pares* in the accounts of Matthew and Luke especially: he speaks for all on a number of occasions (e.g., Matt. 15:15; 19:27; Luke 12:41) and answers the Lord in their name (e.g., Matt. 16:16). In addition, there are numerous instances in which Jesus makes addresses to Peter (e.g., Matt. 26:40; Luke 22:31) or sends him on a special errand of instruction, e.g., when Peter is sent to catch the fish in whose mouth is found the coin necessary to pay the tribute money (Matt. 17:24-27).

After the Ascension, when the disciples and Jesus' mother Mary were met together at Pentecost, there to experience the descent of the Holy Spirit, Peter stood up to answer the mockers and, as spokesman for the community, preached a powerful sermon at which 3,000 people were converted. He was also the first to open up the Christian community to Gentile converts, in the conversion of Cornelius the Roman centurion (Acts 11:18). He became the evident leader of the Jerusalem community, in decision-making as well as in preaching (Acts 1:15-22; 2:14-40; 3:12-26). He was spokesperson before the Jewish leaders (4:5ff.). Within the fledgling Christian community he provided dynamic leadership (5:1-11), even performing miracles (5:15). His still headstrong character and tendency to focus on external matters caused him initially to insist upon Jewish observances for converts at Antioch, for which he was rebuked by Paul. (His first epistle is often adduced as evidence that he responded well to this admonishment.)

After a brief appearance at the Jerusalem Council (Acts 15:7-11) Peter vanishes from the NT record. It is in later sources, such as the Epistle of Clement to the Corinthians, St. Irenaeus (*Adv. haer.* 3.1.1), and Eusebius (*Hist. eccl.* 2.25.8; cf. 4.14.1), that one learns of Peter and Paul's joint labors in building the church at Rome and their martyrdom there. The apocryphal Acts of St. Peter and St. Paul as well as Acts of St. Peter adds details about Peter's crucifixion upside down, ca. 67, and the dates and other details accord well with Tacitus's description of Nero's pogrom against Roman Christians in 65-68 (*Annales*, 15.44). The statement in 1 Clem. 5–6 that both Peter and Paul were executed under Nero's rule has been generally accepted by historians. The feast of St. Peter and St. Paul was kept in Rome as early as the 3rd cent. on June 29.

The oldest extant representation in art of Peter is a bronze medallion showing the heads of the apostles (late 2nd or early 3rd cent.) in which Peter is depicted with a roundish head, prominent jaw, receding forehead, and thick curly hair and beard (Vatican Library, Christian Museum). This physiognomy recurs in two representations in the Catacomb of Peter and Marcellinus (3rd cent.). Peter appears in Christian art in various contexts: seated at one side of Christ (with Paul on the other); trying to walk on the water of Lake Gennesaret; submitting reluctantly to Jesus washing his feet at the Last Supper; raising Tabitha from the dead; denying his Lord; and suffering his own execution. Iconographic representations after the 6th cent. emphasize the keys, usually crossed, one each of silver and gold. He is sometimes shown with chains, referring to his imprisonment, a fish (symbolizing his trade and Jesus' invitation for him to become a "fisher of men" [Matt. 4:19; Mark 1:7]), or a rooster (reminiscent of his denial but also perhaps his priestly purpose as an "announcer of the resurrection of the Sun," an association made popular by St. Gregory the Great in his *Regulae pastoralis*).

Early patristic treatments of Peter (e.g., Irenaeus, Tertullian, Clement, Eusebius, St. Jerome) venerate him as *primus inter pares* (e.g., Irenaeus, *Adv. haer.* 3.3.1; Tertullian, *Adv. Marc.* 4.5.2) but do not elaborate his association with apostolic succession and the Roman See. St. Ambrose expresses concern for the attack of the Novatians on the "power of the keys" with respect to forgiveness of sins, and in so doing indicates that he acknowledges a spiritual lineage: "for they have not the succession of Peter, who hold not the chair of Peter, which they rend by wicked schism" (*Libri duo de poenitentia*, 1.7.33). His identification of the true Church with clear scriptural foundation and Peter with the original vicarship offers a more explicit formulation than can be found in many of his contemporaries. On the other hand, the commentary of the chief pupil of Ambrose may indicate that more explicit formulation of the idea of apostolic succession was becoming a sensitive issue. St. Augustine finds in Peter, in both his strengths and his weaknesses, a type for the Church. In two sermons on the walking on the water narrative (*Sermo,* 25; 26), he develops this theme: "Let us, looking at ourselves in this member of the Church, distinguish what is of God and what of ourselves" (*Sermo*, 26.4). Peter's naming by Jesus is taken by Augustine (*Sermo*, 26.1) in the following way:

> Now this name Peter was given him by the Lord, and that in a figure, that he should signify the Church. For seeing that Christ is the rock (Petra), Peter is the Christian people. For the rock (Petra) is the original name. Therefore is Peter so called from the rock; not the rock from Peter; as Christ is not called Christ from the Christian, but the Christian from Christ.

Augustine goes on to cite Paul (1 Cor. 1:12) regarding the misplaced sense of allegiance which may be engendered when "men who wish to be built upon men, said 'I am of Paul and I of Apollos; and I of Cephas,' who is Peter. But others who did not wish to be built upon Peter, but upon the Rock, said, 'But I am of Christ.' " Peter is the ideal figure for the Church, for Augustine, in his being both strong and weak at once: "now he trusts, and now he totters; now he confesses the Undying; now he fears lest he should die. Wherefore? Because the Church of Christ has both strong and weak persons, and simply cannot be any other way" (26.4). Augustine's rhetorical question concerning Peter as an exemplar of pastoral leadership seems to imply a caution to the growing organizational strength of the church: "Lo, what Peter was in the Lord; what was he in himself?" (26.8). After the 5th cent., especially as gnostic and other heresies were defined and distinguished from Roman orthodoxy, the idea of apostolic succession took on firmer institutional shape, and though it endured numerous challenges (e.g., the Schism, the Avignon Papacy and late 14th-cent. dual Papacy, the Reformation) it has continued to grow in strength and detail of theological articulation until the first full expression of the modern doctrine of the Roman Catholic Church, in art. 21 of the Second Vatican Council.

Representation of Peter in early English literature is, at least until the 14th cent., surprisingly marginal. Despite his dramatic life and prominence in the apostolic community, the most famous OE poem on the early missionary church is *Andreas*, concentrating almost exclusively, as its title suggests, on Peter's brother Andrew. *The Fates of the Apostles* merely notes, following the tradition, that Peter, like Paul, was among those who gave their lives in Rome through Nero's cruel cunning, and that "their apostleship is widely honored among the nations" (14-15). In his sermon *"Domenica VI post Pentecosten"* (Luke 5:1-11) Aelfric develops the narrative of the great draught of fishes and Peter's calling to be a "fisher of men" in such a way as to link his apostolic calling to the missionary effort by which England and northern Europe had been evangelized: "Petrus waes a fiscere, þe is apostol nu." The Lord's later pressing Peter's ship into service as a platform from which to preach to the crowds becomes a figure for the role of Peter in the apostolic ministry of the Church, yet an Augustinian context for the interpretation is afforded by the interposition (119) of a text (given in Latin and OE) from Ps. 127:1: "Except the LORD build the house, they labour in vain that build it." Another Aelfric sermon, *Domenica post Ascensionem Domini* (John 15:26–16:4), develops the sermon of Peter in Acts 10:34-43, that God is "no respecter of persons" (exemplified in the narrative in which, to the surprise of the Jews present, the Holy Spirit is poured out upon Gentiles as well [v. 45]), to ground his assertion that the Christian king ought to see himself as Christ's vicar. Such a king, he argues, should trust only in counselors who have clearly proven themselves by their actions to be faithful servants of God (20-63; 64-82), a view in which he may be following Sedulius Scotus's 9th-cent. *Liber de Rectoribus Christianis* (PL 103.291ff.).

Perhaps because he is regarded as sacrosanct (or in the 14th cent. by reason of the papal schism indirectly controversial) Peter receives little individual development in later medieval literature. The notable exception is Langland's allegorical treatment in *Piers Plowman*, where the name Piers or Peter implies that the idealized ploughman is a "Rock," in some sense a foundation or bedrock for whatever strength the Church in the world might have. He is in this poem the type of the good Christian layperson as well as priest: in bk. 15 (B-text) the dreamer is told that only Piers can show him Charity (cf. 1 Pet. 4:8) and here he is equated with Christ: *"Petrus, id est Christus."* Throughout the poem Piers represents the apostle's ministry, resembling at various points the patriarchs, prophets, Christ, disciples, apostles, and, of course, Peter (bk. 19). In terms of medieval fourfold allegory he may be seen literally as a ploughman; tropologically as the good Christian layperson; allegorically as Christ's temporal Church; anagogically as a figure, like Peter, for the ideal priesthood.

No saints' play of St. Peter has survived. However, he figures largely in the Corpus Christi drama's treatment of the life of Christ and the apostles, e.g., in York (nos. 29, 30, 42, 43, 49), and in the N-Town cycle he is given a full and vigorous representation. His biblical speeches are filled out with credal and evangelical expositions (e.g., N-Town "Passion," 1.222-53), though his Pentecost sermon is severely truncated (*Modo de die Pentecostes*, 26-39). Peter's role as *janitor coeli*, guarding the gates of heaven with keys in hand, is reflected in the Doomsday pageant of N-Town (53-65), where Peter greets the elect:

The ȝatys of hevyn I opyn this tyde
Now welcome dere bretheryn to hevyn i-wis
Com on and sytt on goddys ryght syde
Where myrthe and melody nevyr may mys.

On kne we crepe we gon we glyde
to wurchepp oure lorde þat mercyfful is
Ffor thorwe his woundys þat be so wyde
he hath brought us to his blys
holy lorde we wurcheppe þe.

In the York play (no. 45) on the death of Mary, Peter is rapt away from a sermon he is preaching in Judea to appear, somewhat bewildered, at the dying Virgin's bedside with James, John, Andrew, a devil, and the angel Gabriel. In this instance, however, as in the next play on the appearance of Mary after her death to doubting Thomas, Peter has little to say.

Reformation writers, because of their central dispute with papal authority and its appeal to foundation in the doctrine of apostolic succession, are inclined either to slight Peter somewhat, to attack the claim of Roman succession, or to try to undermine the readings typically given to certain biblical texts and especially to extra-canonical tradition. Calvin is conservative, explaining Matt. 16:18 ("Thou art Peter, and upon this rock . . .") in such a way that it not only refers admiringly to Peter but "extends to all believers, each of whom is a temple of God, and compact together by faith makes up one temple." But, he allows, "it also marks out Peter's preeminence, as each in his own order receives more or less according to the measure of the gift of Christ" (*Harmony of the Gospels*, 2.186). He connects the "keys" with Luke 11:52, where "Christ says . . . that the Scribes and Pharisees, as interpreters of the Law, likewise have the key of the kingdom of heaven. For we know that the gate of life is only opened to us by the Word of God." In polemic against Roman authority in the *Institutes*, however, he argues against Peter ever having been bishop of Rome (4.6.14-17) and asserts his conviction that the "ancient Church" did not recognize itself as unified in allegiance to Rome or to Peter, but rather to Christ (cf. 4.7.1-30). It is Calvin's position in the *Institutes* which tends to characterize Reformation and later Puritan views, so typically diminishing the prominence of Peter in literature written within a Protestant sphere of influence.

The renaming of Peter and the keys of the kingdom

passage (Matt. 16:17-19) are conspicuously absent from Spenser's *Faerie Queene,* as from most major English literary texts after the Reformation. The Jesuit poet Robert Southwell has, however, a remarkable long poem, *St. Peter's Complaint,* based on an Italian work by Luigi Tansillo. In it Peter describes his misery: "I that in vaunts displayed Pride's fairest flags / Disrobed of Grace, am wrapped in Adam's rags." The poem focuses on Peter's grief and sense of guilt after his denial of Jesus in order to develop his absolute dependence upon God's mercy, a mercy complete enough to extend even to one who has turned his back on Christ. Richard Crashaw, whose *"Umbra S. Petri Medetur Aegrotis"* is a brief meditation on Acts 5:15 in the light of apostolic succession, also wrote two similar quatrains in English *(Steps to the Temple).* The first, "On St. Peter Cutting off Malchus' Ear," addresses the apostle:

> Well, Peter, dost thou wield thy active sword;
> Well for thyself, I mean, not for thy Lord.
> To strike at ears is to take heed there be
> No witness, Peter, of thy perjury.

The second, which equally captures the apostle's sometimes self-contradictory character and the moral lesson he affords future Christians, is "On St. Peter Casting away his Nets at Our Saviour's Call":

> Thou hast the art on't, Peter, and canst tell
> To cast thy nets on all occasions well.
> When Christ calls, and thy nets would have thee stay,
> To cast them well's to cast them quite away.

In his notes on Valdesso's "Considerations," George Herbert, like Calvin, identifies Peter with the conveyance of Scripture. Referring to the conversion of Cornelius he writes: "There the case is plaine, *Cornelius* had revelation, yet Peter was to be sent for, and those that have inspirations still must use *Peter,* God's Word." In Milton's *Lycidas* Peter appears in traditional guise as a model for clerical vocation. He is "the Pilot of the *Galilean* lake. / Two massy keys he bore of metals twain, / (The Golden opes, the Iron shuts amain). / He shook his Mitred locks and stern bespake. . . ," and Milton has him declaim words pertinent to the office of those who would feed Christ's sheep (108-31). Bunyan, like Herbert and others, notes Peter's rebuke of Simon Magus (Acts 8:19-22), but like many of his Puritan contemporaries follows the line that Peter vacillated between boasting bravery and cowardice when the chips were down:

> He would swagger, Ay he would: He would, as his vain mind prompted him to say, do better, and stand more for his Master, then all men: But who so foiled, and run down with these Villains [Faint-heart, Mistrust, and Guilt] as he?

Writers in the 18th cent. continue to treat Peter circumspectly, if at all. Dryden, e.g., in his Catholic conversion poem *The Hind and the Panther,* avoids direct mention. Swift's ecclesiastical satire *The Tale of a Tub* pits three brothers against each other in contest for the cloak of the Church, Peter (Rome), Martin (Luther, and by extension, Anglicanism), and Jack (more extreme English dissenters); but it is not the biblical character one sees in this "Peter" so much as a caricature of the Catholic doctrines of apostolic succession and ecclesiastical authority.

Specific incidents in the life of Peter are, however, often parodied, as when in Byron's "The Vision of Judgment," "Saint Peter sat by the celestial gate: / His keys were rusty and the lock was dull" (1-2; cf. 121-22, 131-32, 151-52, 197, 825-27); he finds the keys all there is to hand now, since the sword with which he cut off the ear of Malchus has been lost (149-52). John Ruskin is much moved by the final narrative of Jesus' conversation and commissioning of Peter on the beach of Lake Galilee in *Modern Painters* (3.4.16), but imagines in "Arrows of the Chase" (2.209, 184) that the injunction to "Feed my sheep" is best understood by a clergyman of refinement most liberally: ". . . feeding either sheep or fowls, or unmuzzling the ox, or keeping the wrens alive in the snow, would be received by their Heavenly Feeder as the perfect fulfilment of His 'Feed my sheep' in the higher sense." In Tennyson's *Becket* Walter Map tells Herbert of Basham about King Henry's sumptuous banquet: "And as for the flesh at table, a whole Peter's sheet, with all manner of game, and four footed things, and fowls." Herbert, recognizing the allusion to Acts 10:9-8, asks, "And all manner of creeping things too?" In Thackeray's *The Newcomes* the words of Jesus to Peter, "Thou art Peter, and upon this rock . . ." (Matt. 16:18), are associated primarily with the Vatican church (chap. 35); and in De Quincey's "Levana and Our Lady of Sighs," the eldest sister "carries keys more than papal at her girdle, which open every cottage and every palace."

In other cases there is conflation of a biblical passage concerning Peter with a previous literary allusion to it, as when G. B. Shaw, in revising Matt. 16:18, speaks of "the rock on which Equality is built," or when Wilde seems to recollect Bunyan as well as Matt. 16:18 ("and the gates of hell shall not prevail against it") in his "The Canterville Ghost," in which the young adventurer is warned: "You will see fearful shapes in the darkness, and wicked voices will whisper in your ear, but they will not harm you, for against the purity of a little child the powers of hell cannot prevail" (5).

Direct portrayals of Peter, or adaptations from biblical and apocryphal texts, have become more prevalent in the 20th cent. Thornton Wilder's play *Now the Servant's Name was Malchus* (1928) and Henry Sienkewicz's novel *Quo Vadis?* (as well as the play based upon it by Marie Doran) were followed by Morris West's novel about the Papacy, *The Shoes of the Fisherman,* and Peter Marshall's *The Robe,* in both of which Peter is also given vivid treatment. Peter's irate slicing off of the ear of Malchus is one of the incidents most often alluded to, as in David Jones's *Anathemata* (153). His crucifixion upside down, recalled more rarely, is alluded to in Anthony Hecht's *A Summoning of Stones*:

> the Rock that bears the Church's weight,
> Crucified Peter, raised his eyes and yearned
> For final sight of heavenly estate,
> But saw ungainly huge above his head
> Our stony base to which the flesh is wed. ("A Roman Holiday")

The two epistles of Peter are frequently referred to, with 1 Pet. 4:8 ("For charity shall cover the multitude of sins") being among the most common recollections. Blake repeatedly alludes to this verse in *The Marriage of Heaven and Hell,* and it becomes a Puritan and Victorian commonplace. Gaskell cites it typically in respect to benevolence in "The Squire's Story," and in *Walden* Thoreau's benevolent person will exhibit goodness which "must not be a partial and transitory act, but a constant superfluity, which costs him nothing and of which he is unconscious. This is a charity which hides a multitude of sins" ("Economy"). In another of the familiar passages found in 1 Peter the writer exhorts the other elders to "Feed the flock of God which is among you, taking the oversight thereof, not by constraint, but willingly; not for filthy lucre, but of a ready mind. Neither as being lords over God's heritage, but being ensamples to the flock" (1 Pet. 5:1-3). Readers of Chaucer's *Canterbury Tales* will recognize that this passage (assisted with commentaries from St. Gregory the Great and probably Wyclif) found its way into the description of the good Parson: "Benygne he was, and wonder diligent, / and in adversitee ful pacient" (*General Prologue*, 1.483-84; cf. 518); "This nobel ensaumple to his shepe he yaf, / that first he wroghte, and afterward he taughte" (1.496-97); he demonstrated his belief that "Wel oghte a preest ensaumple for to yive, / By his clennesse, how that his sheep should lyve" (505-06);

> He waited after no pompe and reverence
> Ne maked him a spiced conscience,
> But Cristes lore and his apostles twelve
> He taughte, but first he folwed it hymselve. (525-28)

This way of viewing the relation of person and office in the clergy, urged by Peter (1 Pet. 5:3), is in English tradition supported vigorously in exegesis and commentary (e.g., Sedulius Scotus, Aelfric, Fitzralph, Wyclif, Langland, Chaucer) and may in some way account for the relative diminishment of Peter himself in English literature. The good pastor he became, despite his frailty, and which he calls for in this Epistle, became a literary type (Langland's Piers, Chaucer's Parson, Herbert's Parson, Fielding's Parson Adams, etc.) and at its best an "ensaumple" of something greater than Peter himself.

See also CLEAN AND UNCLEAN; GET THEE BEHIND ME; KEYS OF THE KINGDOM; MALCHUS; TRANSFIGURATION.

Bibliography. Brown, R. E., K. P. Donfried, and J. Reumann, eds. *Peter in the New Testament* (1973); Bruce, F. F. *Peter, Stephen, James, and John* (1979); Cullmann, O. *Peter: Disciple–Apostle–Martyr* (1962); Moule, C. F. D. "The Nature and Purpose of 1 Peter." *Essays in New Testament Interpretation* (1982), 133-45.

ST. PETER'S VISION OF THE SHEET   (Acts 10:9-18)

See also CLEAN AND UNCLEAN.

PHARAOH   The term *Pharaoh* originally came from Egyp. *pr-ʿ ʾ*, meaning "great house." By the 9th cent. B.C. the term was affixed to the royal name and thus became the title for the king of Egypt. The OT specifically names five pharaohs and mentions six others by title. Some English writers use the term to suggest simply the pomp of pagan antiquity (Byron, "The Age of Bronze," 142; Yeats, "Vacillation," 84; Dylan Thomas, "Altarwise by owl-light," 45, 123). Most references, though, deal with the pharaohs mentioned in Gen. 40–41 and Exod. 1–2 and 5–14. Allusions to the pharaoh of Genesis usually concern Joseph's interpretation of the king's dreams of the "lean and fat kine" and of the seven ears of wheat, which prompted his elevation to political prominence in Egypt (Chaucer, *The Nun's Priest's Tale*, 7.3130-35; Shakespeare, *1 Henry 4*, 2.4.526-28; Browning, "Christmas-Eve and Easter-Day," 232-39).

By far the greatest number of references in English literature, however, are to the "Pharaoh of the Oppression" who "knew not Joseph" and enslaved the Hebrew residents of his kingdom (Exod. 1–2) and the "Pharaoh of the Exodus" who, obdurate despite the embassy of Moses and Aaron and a subsequent series of divinely sent plagues, refused to liberate the Israelites (Exod. 5–14). These are often conflated into a single figure, invariably portrayed as a hard-hearted tyrant. Early Christian theologians — St. Ambrose, St. Augustine, Cassiodorus, St. Gregory the Great, St. Isidore of Seville, and the Venerable Bede among them — see Pharaoh as a type of devil; the Exodus becomes an allegory of the Christian's passing out of the power of the devil and sin into "the Promised Land" of eternal life, generally by means of baptism. Hence the OE *Exodus* refers to Pharaoh as *godes andsacan* (15) or "God's adversary," a phrase normally reserved for Satan. Medieval drama portrays the king as a ranting tyrant, much like the devil himself. Other writers who employ this typology include Aelfric (homily "For the Holy Day of Pentecost," *The Homilies of the Anglo-Saxon Church,* ed. Thorpe [1844], 1.312-13); St. Thomas More ("A Treatise upon the Passion"); and Edward Taylor (*Preparatory Meditations* [2nd ser.], no. 58). In *Paradise Lost,* Milton uses the same typology when he refers to the defeated Pharaoh as "the river-dragon tamed" (12.191) and earlier when he compares the defeated devils lying in the burning lake to "Busiris and his Memphian chivalry" (1.307) afloat in the

Red Sea. In a more recent setting, John Updike revives the concept of Pharaoh as God's adversary in his short story "From the Journal of a Leper," where the Satanic "healing" of the narrator's disease of "humiliation" is accomplished partly through "Pharaonic pills."

From at least the 17th cent. on, English authors use the figure of Pharaoh in political allegory and satire to represent an arrogant and oppressive monarch, often French. Milton compares Charles I's blindness in religious matters to Pharaoh's hard-heartedness ("Eikonoklastes," 5.231). Marvell uses him to represent Clarendon's greed and corruption ("Clarindon's House-Warming," 37-40) and elsewhere to suggest the corruption of the English court by the French ("Britannia and Rawleigh," 27-28). Dryden uses Pharaoh to represent the proud Louis XIV, whose oppression over his people is contrasted with the benevolence of David, i.e., Charles II (*Absalom and Achitophel,* 331-39; cf. *The Second Part of Absalom and Achitophel* [usually ascribed to Nahum Tate], 671-92). In *The Task,* Cowper sees the tyranny in France as deserving the punishment sent upon Egypt: "Her house of bondage worse than that of old / Which God avenged on Pharaoh — the Bastille" (5.382-83). Wordsworth compares Napoleon's defeat in Russia to Pharaoh's in the Red Sea ("By Moscow self-devoted to a blaze," 12-13), and elsewhere he rails against political tyranny in England: ". . . has she no wand / From this curst Pharaoh-plague to rid the land?" ("Imitation of Juvenal — Satire 8," 15-16). In "Red Leaves," Faulkner parallels the events of the Exodus by having the Indian chieftains, oppressive and decadent, enslave and harass their Negroes just as the pharaohs did the Hebrews.

Reflecting venerable Christian tradition (e.g., Adam the Scot, *Sermo 36, In Die Sanctorum Innocentium* [PL 198.332]), English writers frequently use the plagues visited on Egypt or the destruction of Pharaoh's army in the Red Sea as images of punishment for pride or the fall of prosperity and worldly glory (Herbert, "Praise," 3.17; Wordsworth, "To Enterprise," 104-18; Emily Dickinson, " 'Red Sea,' indeed! Talk not to me," 2; Tennyson, *Aylmer's Field,* 771).

See also EXODUS; JOSEPH; MOSES; POTIPHAR'S WIFE.

Bibliography. Cross, J., and S. Tucker. "Allegorical Tradition and the Old English Exodus." *Neophil* 44 (1960), 122-27; Lucas, P. J., ed. [The Old English] *Exodus* (1977); Meagher, P. K., T. C. O'Brien, and Sister C. M. Aherne, eds. *Encyclopedic Dictionary of Religion* (1979), 3.2762; *New Catholic Encyclopedia* (1967), 5.196-203; Wilson, J. A. "Pharaoh." *IDB* 3.373-74.　　　　　　　　KARL TAMBURR

PHARISEES Pharisees were religious observants (Heb. *perushim,* "set apart"; Gk. *pharisaioi*), members of a Jewish religious and political party active during the period of the Second Temple, and the one most frequently mentioned in the NT. They were an elite and scholarly brotherhood, many of them members of the school of

Hillel (and later Gamaliel). The (probably false) derivation of their name from Heb. *pesher,* "interpretation," may owe to their subtle and argumentative exegesis. Unlike the scribes, who were formally trained in rabbinic law, most Pharisees were laymen. Their concern was oral law, or Halakah, which they taught as a "tradition *(paradosis)* of the elders" (cf. Mark 7:1-13; Matt. 15:1-9) — handed down from Moses and of equal authority with the Torah. By elaboration and observance of oral law they strove to create a community committed to a "walk" *(halak; halakah)* of purity, fasting, prayer, tithing, and separation from the wider society of the "unclean," and in this way to fulfill the injunction of Lev. 11:44 and Exod. 19:6. Commentary on Lev. 11:44 reflects the Pharisees' sense of calling: "Be holy ones *(qadoshim)* for I am holy *(qadosh),* that is: 'As I am holy so you should be holy ones *(qadoshim);* as I am a separated one *(parush)* so should you be separated ones *(perushim)' "* (Sipra 39a; cf. Mek. Exod. 19:6). As distinct from the Sadducees, who were more strictly biblicist, the Pharisees admitted a process of development in their magisterial legal tradition, which eventually contained several hundred extracanonical prohibitions and commandments. The view of Josephus (*Vita* 2.10-12; *J.W.* 2.8.14; *Ant.* 18.1.3, etc.) is that they were the most powerful political force in Jewish society of the first century. In contrast to the Sadducees they were eschatologically oriented, believing not only in life after death and the resurrection of the body, but in the advent of the Messiah and the Day of Judgment. As a powerful and elitist party, the Pharisees attracted the criticism of other sects (including the community at Qumran), and indeed of their own rabbinic successors.

Though numerous early Christian converts were Pharisees (notably St. Paul and Nicodemus), the associations which continue from the NT, especially because of the words of Jesus recorded in the Gospels, are extremely negative. Pharisees are typically condemned for exalting the "letter of the law" while remaining obtuse to its "spirit" or intention (Matt. 3:7; 23:13-35; Luke 18:9-14). Jesus' characterization of them as "whited sepulchres" and a "generation of vipers" was influential enough that "Pharisee" has become in Western literature substantially synonymous with "self-righteous," "charlatan," "fundamentalist," "bigot," and "hypocrite."

Hypocrisy is the focus of many of Jesus' own comments. The parable of the Pharisee recorded in Luke 18:9-14, e.g., contrasts the religious disposition of two characters — a Pharisee and a publican. The Pharisee is confident that as a result of his good works he enjoys God's favor and can pray with special assurance of receiving divine blessing. The publican or tax collector, an outcast in Jewish society because of a deserved reputation for dishonesty and ungodliness, has no confidence in himself and, acknowledging his sin, merely casts himself on the mercy of God. Jesus' observation that "this man went down to his house justified rather than the other" was doubtless intended to shock his audience, although it reiterated a familiar biblical principle that self-exaltation (especially as indicated in contempt for others) leads to humiliation, and humility to exaltation.

The politics of religion have frequently occasioned literary reference to the Pharisees as exemplars of hypocrisy or false piety. Intersectarian quarrels in the Middle Ages, especially as reflected in the antifraternal and antimendicant satire of William of St. Amour, Jean de Meun's *Roman de la Rose,* Langland's *Piers Plowman* (B.15.100-112, in which Pharisees are called "a dunghill full of snakes"), and Chaucer's *Friar's Tale* and *Summoner's Tale,* frequently allude to Jesus' condemnations of the Pharisees. The widow-persecuting summoner of the *Friar's Tale* answers nicely to Bunyan's context in *Pilgrim's Progress,* where in response to religious trick questions concerning true piety by Mr. Hold-the-World, Christian answers: "The Hypocritical Pharisees were also of this Religion, long prayers were their pretence, but to get widows houses was their intent, and greater damnation from God was their Judgment, *Luke* 20.46, 47."

"Pharisaism" has, unsurprisingly, been a charge leveled by all manner of religious groups against perceived adversaries from the 14th cent. well into the modern period. The Wycliffite *Leaven of the Pharisees* is directed against friars; Tyndale's "Pharisees" of a century later are "papists" of any vocation; and those which appear in Dryden's *The Hind and the Panther* are illegitimate progeny of the Reformation. Concern for the "spirit" as distinct from the external "letter" of religion is evident in Donne's "Pharisaicall Dissemblers" who "feigne devotion" ("Holy Sonnet 8"), and for Herbert "things inwardly good to have an eye to the world may be pharisaicall" ("Reasons for Arthur Woodnoth's living . . ."). Carlyle, in his *Characteristics,* argues that "as soon as Prophecy among the Hebrews had ceased, then did the reign of Argumentation begin; and the ancient Theocracy, in its Sadduceeisms and Phariseeisms, and vain jangling of sects and doctors, give token that the *soul* of [religion] had fled." Melville in *Billy Budd* says of Claggart's hidden evil nature: "The Pharisee is the Guy Fawkes prowling in the hid chambers underlying some natures like Claggart's." Among the best known of modern novelists to draw on these allusions is François Mauriac, whose *Le noeud de vipeurs* and *La Pharisienne* are studies in contemporary perversion of the spirit of faith by "religious" manipulation and hypocrisy.

Bibliography. Avi-Yonah, M., and Z. Baros, eds. *Society and Religion in the Second Temple Period* (1977); Marshall, I. H. *The Gospel of Luke* (1978); Mason, S. N. *Flavius Josephus on the Pharisees* (1990); Neusner, J. *From Politics to Piety: The Emergence of Pharisaic Judaism* (1973); Sanders, E. P. *Paul and Palestinian Judaism* (1977); Smith, M. "Palestinian Judaism in the First Century." In M. Davis, ed. *Israel: Its Role in Civilization* (1956).   DAVID L. JEFFREY
I. HOWARD MARSHALL

PHILIP   Philip the apostle is chiefly remembered for his bringing Nathanael to Jesus (John 1:43-45), and later for his conversation with an Ethiopian eunuch concerning the passage in Isaiah he had been reading, which resulted in the eunuch's conversion and baptism (Acts 8:30-39). Because of his prominent role in the narrative of the feeding of the 5,000 (John 6:5) he is sometimes pictured in art with five loaves of bread. The disillusioned and unbelieving minister who is the protagonist of Sinclair Ross's *As for Me and My House* once had visions of being an evangelist like his namesake, but eventually identified himself according to a Greek etymology of his name as a "lover of horses," the shift suggesting his temptation to pleasures of the flesh.

See also EUNUCH.

PHILISTINE   Philistine (*pelishtim*) refers to someone or something of Philistia, the nation of Canaan along the coast between Joppa and the Wadi Ghazzeh, just south of Gaza, in OT times. The origin of the word, and the nation itself, is obscure. The people may have been from the Aegean or they may have been the Caphtorim from Caphtor (Crete) who expelled the Avim and took over their land (Deut. 2:23), although in Genesis they are associated with the (otherwise unknown) Casluhim (Gen. 10:14). Of their early history in Canaan not much is known. Their prominent deities were Dagon, Ashtoreth, and Baal-zebub (2 Kings 1:2-6). They became prosperous farmers and had a strong army, equipped with weapons from iron foundries and smiths (1 Sam. 13:20; 17:5-6). During the Judges period of Israel's history the Philistines formed a confederation of five major cities: Gaza, Ashkelon, and Ashdod on the coast, and Gath and Ekron inland. They also carried on guerilla warfare with Israel and at a later date sold captured Israelites as slaves (Joel 3:6; Amos 1:6). When the Israelites united under a king, they fought the Philistines more intensively until David defeated them around 965 B.C. Solomon included all of Philistia in his kingdom.

Following the division of the kingdom of Judah, the Philistines once again grew in power and waged continuous war with their neighbors, even through the Babylonian captivity of the Jews, after which the Philistines were defeated by Nebuchadnezzar and intermarried with the people of Israel (1 Sam. 8:20; 10:5; 31:1-7; 1 Kings 4:21-24; 2 Kings 12:17; 1 Chron. 28:1; 2 Chron. 9:26; 18:18; 26:6; Neh. 13:23-24; Isa. 9:11-12; Jer. 25:20; 47:1; Ezek. 25:15-17).

An early story of victory over the Philistines centers around the hero Samson, who was enticed by Delilah and betrayed to the Philistines (Judg. 16:17-30). Another famous victory over the Philistines was achieved by David when with a stone and sling he killed the huge Philistine soldier, Goliath (1 Sam. 17:1-51).

The Philistines are always represented in the OT as ungodly, uncovenanted, and uncircumcised. They do not listen to God, are carnally obsessed, and worship false gods. Hence they persist as aliens and adversaries in exegetical tradition. In English literature the "Philistine" appears most often as an enemy of the Jews, until the 17th cent. Milton's blind hero Samson Agonistes is an example of one fighting the enemy who are outside God's covenant. The meaning "enemy" later is broadened to refer not to a geographical nation, but to people from whom one must protect oneself: Dryden speaks of falling among the Philistines (*The Hind and the Panther*); Swift (*Polite Conversations*) says of one unfortunate that he went to court very drunk because he had been among Philistines; and Henry Fielding (*Amelia,* chap. 5) equates Philistines and bailiffs.

In the 19th cent. Carlyle uses the term *Philistines* to represent bores, dullards, and children of darkness (*Sterling*). The term thus enlarged came to mean a person who is so unenlightened that he thinks only the ordinary material things of life are of merit. Matthew Arnold gave the term general currency when speaking about the materialistic middle class, who are opposed to the enlightened and chosen few (e.g., in "Sweetness and Light," from *Culture and Anarchy*). His first use of the term in this way comes in his essay on "Heinrich Heine" (*Essays in Criticism,* 1), and conveys particularly Germanic overtones; "Philistine" was a term applied to hostile townsmen by German university students in "town/gown" controversy. The students Arnold took to be "children of the light" (cf. Luke 1:8). In his *On the Study of Celtic Literature* he writes: "We are imperilled by what I call the 'Philistinism' of our middle class. On the side of beauty and taste, vulgarity; on the side of morals and feelings, coarseness; on the side of mind and spirit, unintelligence, — this is Philistinism." For American essayist H. L. Mencken Mark Twain was a great artist unable to throw off his "native Philistinism," so that in American letters of the 19th cent. "the voice of Mark Twain was the voice of the Philistine." Via Arnold the anticultural Philistine soon became a commonplace, as in Gilbert's lyrics for *Patience:* "Though the Philistines may jostle, you will rank as an apostle / In the high aesthetic band."

See also ASHTORETH; DAGON; DAVID; GOLIATH; SAMSON.

Bibliography. Dahiyat, E. A. "The Portrait of the Philistines in John Milton's *Samson Agonistes.*" *Studia Anglica Posnaniensa* 14 (1982), 293-303; Greenfield, J. C. "Philistines." *IDB* 3.791-95.   LINDA BEAMER

PHOENIX The mythical phoenix (Gk. *phoinix*), a gorgeously plumed Arabian bird fabled to be unique in its kind, was said to travel at long intervals to Heliopolis where it died and was reborn. This bird formed the nucleus of a complex legend of immense popularity in the ancient world.

The phoenix may be a literary descendant of the *benu* or *bnw* of Egyptian solar myths, a sacred bird which, through association with the self-renewing deities Rē and

Osiris, became a symbol of renewal or rebirth (R. T. Rundle Clark). The bird makes its first appearance in the West under its Greek name in a cryptic fragment of Hesiod (*Fragmenta Hesiodea* [1967], frg. 304). The earliest account both of its appearance and its behavior occurs in Herodotus (*Persian Wars,* 2.73), where it is said to be an Arabian bird, eagle-like in appearance but with bright red and gold plumage. It is preeminently remarkable, reports the author (citing Egyptian priests), for the way in which it encases its dead parent in a ball of myrrh and then carries it for burial to the Temple of the Sun at Heliopolis.

Later classical authorities, attracted by the mystery of the bird's reputed ability to regenerate itself (a subject omitted by Herodotus), substantially embellished the story, adding many details and making the theme of rebirth the central aspect of the myth (e.g., Ovid, *Metamorphoses,* 15.391-407; Pliny, *Naturalis historia,* 10.2). Although many pagan writers (notably Pliny) remained decidedly sceptical about the bird's supposed powers of rejuvenation, the phoenix nonetheless became, in pre-Christian writings, an important symbol of metempsychosis and the rebirth of the soul.

There are no certain references to the phoenix in the Bible itself. Three texts, however, have sometimes been cited as possible references. The first is Ps. 92:12: "The righteous shall flourish like the palm tree" (LXX: *Dikaios hōs phoinix anthēsei*), where the confusing homonymy of the Greek noun *phoinix* — meaning both palm tree and phoenix — led some early exegetes (notably Tertullian, *De resurrectione mortuorum,* 13.3) to translate the phrase as "The righteous shall flourish like the phoenix." The second text is Job 29:18: "I shall die in my nest, and I shall multiply my days as the sand (*hol*)," where the word *hol* is sometimes translated "palm tree" (LXX: *stelechos phoinichos;* Vg. *palma*) and, in rabbinical tradition, is frequently glossed as "phoenix" (e.g., Midr. Gen. 19:5; and L. Ginzberg [5.51, n. 151]). The third reference is John 12:13, where J. S. Hill has argued that the awkward Johannine tautology *ta baïa tōn phoinikōn* ("the palm branches of the palm trees") functions as a proleptic allusion to the Resurrection by invoking the image of Christ as the true Phoenix (133-35).

While biblical references to the phoenix, if they exist at all, are few and lexically ambiguous, precisely the reverse is true in subsequent biblical tradition, both Jewish and Christian. The phoenix appears, e.g., in Jewish apocalyptic literature, most notably in chaps. 6-8 of the Greek Apocalypse of Baruch, where a cosmic phoenix, symbolizing God's mercy, spreads its protective wings to shield the earth from the sun's consuming fire, symbolizing God's just wrath. (See Sister M. F. McDonald.)

Among early Christian writers, beginning with St. Clement of Rome in chaps. 25-26 of *Epistola 1 ad Corinthios* (PG 1.261-66), the pagan myth of the death and rebirth of the phoenix was employed both as a symbol of human resurrection and as a proof of its possibility. Many patristic writers enthusiastically endorsed this analogy (e.g., St. Epiphanius, *Ancoratus,* 84; St. Cyril of Jerusalem, *Catecheses,* 18.8; St. Ambrose, *De excessu fratris sui Satyri,* 2.59). Tertullian may be said to speak for them all when, in *De resurrectione mortuorum* (13.4), he asserts: "God has declared that we are worth more than many sparrows: unless we are also worth more than many a phoenix, this is no great thing. And indeed, can it be that men will die once and for all, while Arabian birds are assured of a resurrection?"

Not surprisingly, early Christian writers construed the phoenix as a symbol not only of resurrection in general but also of Christ himself and his resurrection in particular. Thus, in the Greek *Physiologus,* the reborn phoenix arises from its predecessor's ashes only after three days have elapsed — a detail inserted in order to underscore the typological symbolism. Still another early Christian tradition, deriving from the insistence of classical authorities that the phoenix, being *singularis* and *unicus,* reproduced itself without sexual union, made the phoenix a symbol of the Virgin Mary and the virgin birth (see Rufinus, *Expositio symboli,* 9).

In both classical and Christian sources, where the death and rebirth of the phoenix become the focal point of its myth, there exist two separate versions of the bird's self-regeneration. In one version, represented by Pliny and Clement of Rome, the phoenix, having built itself a nest of aromatic twigs, simply dies; its decaying flesh produces a worm which grows into the new phoenix. In the second (and more popular) version, followed by most patristic writers and also by the pagan poet Claudian in his late 4th-cent. *Phoenix,* the phoenix nest is ignited by the sun's rays, and the bird, fanning the flames with its wings, is quickly consumed, the new phoenix arising miraculously from its ashes. Although a transitional wormlike larva is often retained, virtually all accounts after the 1st cent. adopt the immolation motif.

The earliest full-scale treatment of the myth in imaginative literature occurs in a 4th-cent. Latin poem, *Carmen de ave phoenice,* attributed to Lactantius. In 170 elegiac verses, the *Carmen* expands earlier versions of the myth in a profusion of descriptive detail, laying particular stress on the unique beauty of the phoenix, its exotic, almost "edenic" homeland, its elaborate preparations for death, and its wonderful rebirth after a fiery demise. Although not overtly Christian in tone or imagery, the Lactantian poem provided later Christian poets with an irresistible literary elaboration of the story. The fruits of this influence are evident in the OE *Phoenix.* Freely expanding and revising materials from Lactantius in the first half of his poem, the anonymous OE author imparts to his work a thoroughly Christian tone absent in his source; then, departing entirely from his Latin model in the second half of the *Phoenix,* he explicitly allegorizes the myth as a symbol of Christian

resurrection (387-92), and the phoenix itself as a type of Christ (637b-54).

Apart from the bestiaries and a 12th-cent. English sermon known as the Phoenix Homily (R. D. N. Warner, ed., 146-48), references to the phoenix in ME literature are scarce. Among major English poets, its appearance is confined to two brief allusions — both treating it as a symbol of virginal purity (Chaucer, *Book of the Duchess,* 981-84; *Pearl,* 429-32). In the *Inferno,* Dante describes the punishment of Vanni Fucci as perpetual phoenix-like immolation and restoration — a grotesque parody of the "everlasting life" enjoyed by the saints (24.97-108).

In Renaissance and 17th-cent. literature, the phoenix reappears in a flourish of allusions ranging all the way from Donne's witty phallic resurrections in "The Canonization" (23-27) to Crashaw's conventionally typological image of Christ as a phoenix in a 1648 Nativity hymn (*Poetical Works,* 2nd ed. [1957], p. 249, 46-49). Although Sir Thomas Browne devotes a portion of his *Pseudodoxia Epidemica* (1646) to whimsical speculation about the possibility of the phoenix's actual existence, English writers generally are content to treat the phoenix as purely mythical. Broadly speaking, Renaissance phoenixes come in four varieties. First, they appear as religious symbols of resurrection and immortality, as in meditative lyrics like Henry Vaughan's "Resurrection and Immortaility" or funeral elegies such as Jonson's "'Tis a Record in Heaven." The most powerful and complex use of traditional associations is Milton's extended prefigurative simile (Samson-phoenix-Christ) in *Samson Agonistes* (1699-1707). Second, the phoenix appears as a metaphor of the secular immortality to be gained through one's progeny: "My ashes, as the phoenix, may bring forth / A bird that will revenge upon you all" (Shakespeare, *3 Henry 6,* 1.4.35-36; see also *1 Henry 6,* 4.7.92-93; *Henry 8,* 5.4.19-22; and, further, Crashaw's panegyric "Upon the Duke of Yorke his Birth" and Herrick's religio-political "Another New-yeeres Gift, or Song for the Circumcision"). Third, the phoenix appears as a secularized symbol of unparalleled female beauty, virginal purity, and idealized passion, as in Ben Jonson's "The Phoenix Analysde" and Shakespeare's "The Phoenix and the Turtle" (in Robert Chester's *Love's Martyr* [1601]). Deriving from Petrarch's platonized love-phoenix, a favorite symbol of his beloved Laura in the *Rime sparse* (cf. lyrics 135, 185, 210, 321, and 323), the image of the phoenix as chaste, often remote, female beauty found its way into many Renaissance English lyrics (e.g., Sidney, *Astrophil and Stella,* sonnet 92; Donne, "Epithalamion on the Lady Elizabeth"; Herrick, "Love Perfumes All Parts." See also the Elizabethan poetic miscellany *The Phoenix Nest* [1593]). Last, the phoenix becomes a poetic synonym for a rarity, since it was itself reputedly unique. Thus, "she calls me proud, and that she could not love me, / Were man as rare as phoenix" (Shakespeare, *As You Like*

It, 4.3.17-18; cf. *All's Well That Ends Well,* 1.1.170; *The Tempest,* 3.3.21-24).

After the Renaissance, during which time the secularizing pressures of humanism had largely demoted the rich Christian phoenix symbolism of ancient and medieval Europe into something approaching incidental metaphor, the phoenix virtually disappears from English literature for a period of some two hundred years. Apart from Dryden, who favored phoenixes in his funeral poems ("Upon the Death of the Lord Hastings"; "Threnodia Augustalis"; "To the Pious Memory of Mrs. Anne Killigrew"), 18th-cent. English writers remained largely untouched by phoenix lore. There are no significant references in Romantic literature, although Keats briefly likens his Muse to a phoenix in his "King Lear" sonnet. And in Victorian poetry, although the idea of the reborn phoenix may occasionally be present under the surface (as in Hopkins), the bird itself is absent in all the major works, except for a handful of casual references in Browning (*Ring and the Book,* 3.335; 9.349). The fate of the phoenix, its decline from complex symbol to simple metaphor (= a paragon), is perhaps most clearly illustrated in Shaw's early novel, *Cashel Byron's Profession* (1901): "Her best course would be to marry another phoenix; but as she — poor girl! — cannot appreciate even her own phoenixity, much less that of another, she perversely prefers a mere mortal" (Constable ed. [1932], 221).

Early modern writers, however, rediscovered the Arabian bird and undertook to make it their own, primarily by fusing together the sacred and secular/erotic strands of traditional phoenix symbolism. D. H. Lawrence is particularly noteworthy, adopting the phoenix as his personal icon, and using the self-regenerating bird in his writings from 1915 onwards to symbolize his philosophy of dying into new life, especially through a new-Freudian reconsecration of sexual energies (see his "Phoenix" in *Last Poems* [1932], and Tennessee Williams's one-act dramatic tribute to Lawrence, *I Rise in Flames, Cried the Phoenix*).

For Yeats, who is more traditional and petrarchan than Lawrence, Maud Gonne is a phoenix ("The People"); in the mutability-conscious lyric "His Phoenix," where he mourns her lost youth and beauty, he nonetheless declares Maud Gonne an eternal paragon — still and always unique for him in the long catalogue of beauties from mythical Leda and Helen of Troy to modern young belles who walk and talk men wild: "I knew a phoenix in my youth, so let them have their day." Louis Untermeyer, in his witty "Appeal to the Phoenix," beseeches the bird, which here represents consuming sexual passion, to submit itself at last to mortality: "Turn to me at last with love, / Not with agonies . . . Come, and in this glowing nest, / Phoenix, learn to die."

G. K. Chesterton, after experiencing an epiphany at the famous Dublin Eucharistic Conference of 1932, revived the traditional symbolism of Christ as phoenix in "The Phoenix in Phoenix Park" (Essay 4, *Christendom in Dublin* [1932]). In Joyce's riddling allegory of the fall and resurrection of mankind, *Finnegans Wake,* the phoenix symbolizes every conceivable sort of death and rebirth (spiritual and/or erotic) and appears in an infinity of guises — from an early image of the fall, "O foenix culprit!" (uniting Adam's *felix culpa* with H. C. Earwicker's sin in Phoenix Park), to the paschal phoenix rising at the beginning of the novel's last section as dawn breaks over Dublin on Easter Sunday morning: "Array! Surrection! . . . Phlenxty, O rally! To what lifelike thyne of the bird can be." In Dylan Thomas's troubled and difficult epithalamion "Unluckily for a Death," an erotic yet spiritual phoenix becomes the central symbol of love in a connubial "ceremony of souls" in which the human and divine are inextricably united.

See also RESURRECTION.

Bibliography. Blake, N. F., ed. *The Phoenix* (1964); Clark, R. T. Rundle, "The Origin of the Phoenix." *University of Birmingham Historical Journal* 2 (1949-50), 1-29, 105-40; Dessen, A. C. "Middleton's *The Phoenix and the Allegorical Tradition." SEL* 6 (1965), 291-308; Hill, J. S. "*ta baïa tōn phoinikōn* (John 12:13): Pleonasm or Prolepsis?" *JBL* 101 (1982), 133-35; Hubaux, J., and M. Leroy. *Le mythe du Phénix dans les littératures grecque et latine* (1939); Kaplan, M. "The Phoenix in Elizabethan Poetry." *DA* 25 (1965), 5258-59; McDonald, Sister M. F. "Phoenix Redivivus." *The Phoenix* 14 (1960), 187-206; McMillan, D. "The Phoenix in the Western World from Herodotus to Shakespeare." *D. H. Lawrence Review* 5 (1972), 238-67; Montgomery, L. L. "The Phoenix: Its Use as Literary Device in English from the Seventeenth Century to the Twentieth Century." *D. H. Lawrence Review* 5 (1972), 268-323; Van den Broek, R. *The Myth of the Phoenix according to Classical and Early Christian Traditions* (1972); Warner, R. D. N., ed. *Early English Homilies from the Twelfth Century MS. Vesp. D. XIV.* EETS o.s. 152 (1917).   JOHN SPENCER HILL

PHOTINE Traditional name given to the Samaritan woman at the well with whom Jesus discoursed about the "water of life."

See also WOMAN AT THE WELL.

PHYLACTERY The word *phylactery* (Gk. *phylaktērion,* "safeguard") occurs only once in the Bible (Matt. 23:5). It is an amulet, a small box containing Scripture verses, one of which was bound by leather straps on the forehead and another on the left arm during prayer. Otherwise known as the *tefillin,* phylacteries were worn by every adult male Jew at daily worship except on the Sabbath and high festivals as "a sign upon thy hand, and for frontlets between thine eyes" (Exod. 13:16; cf. Orehot Hayyim 58d). Discoveries at Qumran and Murabba'at suggest that previous to the 2nd cent. A.D. the usual content was five Scriptures: the Decalogue (Deut. 5:1–6:3); Deut. 6:4-9; Deut. 10:12–11:21; Exod. 13:1-10; and Exod. 13:11-16 (Sanh. 11.3). Later mishnaic regulation (e.g., the Palestinian Talmud) removed the Ten Commandments (Bera. 3c, 12a), a practice still followed.

Even though she was, as a woman, exempted by the law, various Jewish sources say that Michal, the daughter of Saul and wife to David, wore phylacteries (Mek. Bo 17, 21; Bera. 2.4c). They are part of the emblematic attire worn by the Panther in Dryden's *The Hind and the Panther:*

> as the mistress of a monarch's bed,
> Her front erect with majesty she bore. . .
> And fathers, councils, church and churches head,
> Were on her reverend *Phylacteries* read. (1.393-99)

In A. M. Klein's poem "Sacred Enough You Are" he asks ironically:

> Why should I praise
> You, make you holier
> Than is the case?
> One does not wear
> Phylacteries
> On Sabbath days.

In Klein's novel *Second Scroll,* when Melech Davidson comes to reject his faith and make "a denial of the Name," joining the Russian cavalry, it is rumored among his shocked kin that he has gone so far as to make "his phylacteries part of his horse's harness" (chap. 1).

In Christian literature the word is sometimes used to describe the streamers bearing Scripture texts in medieval and Renaissance paintings.

PHYSICIAN In both the OT and NT disease is represented as being, in many instances, a result of individual or parental transgression against the will of God (Exod. 15:26; Deut. 32:39; John 9:2) or as the work of Satan (Job 2:7) or evil spirits (Mark 9:25). In this context the Lord in the OT and Christ in the NT are seen as healers or physicians. The Psalmist thus exclaims, "Bless the LORD, O my soul . . . who forgiveth all thine iniquities; who healeth all thy diseases" (Ps. 103:2-3). In both Testaments God is said to heal not only physical diseases (e.g., Gen. 20:17; Num. 12:13) but also broken hearts (Ps. 147:3), backsliding spirits (Jer. 3:22; Hos. 14:4), and a sinful land (2 Chron. 7:14). Jesus, who was a frequent healer of physical ailments (e.g., Matt. 17:14-17; Luke 8:43-56; 11:11-13; 14:2-4), also alleviated spiritual distress through forgiving sin; indeed, he often explicitly combined both ministries in a single encounter (e.g., Mark 2:1-12, where miraculous healing authenticates Jesus' authority to forgive sins). With reference to his earthly mission, Jesus explained that "They that are whole have no need of a physician, but they that are sick: I came not to call the righteous, but sinners to repentance" (Mark 2:17; cf. Matt. 9:12; Luke 5:31-32).

The apostle Luke, one of the four evangelists and author also of the Acts of the Apostles, is referred to by Paul as "the beloved physician" (Col. 4:14). Elsewhere in

Scripture, earthly doctors are typically contrasted with the divine physician, as when Asa, in his diseased state, "sought not to the LORD, but to the physicians" (2 Chron. 16:12; cf. Mark 5:15).

That Christ is the great Physician is a commonplace for the Church Fathers. St. Ambrose writes that Christ came "to heal our wounds. . . . He heals those that are willing and does not compel the unwilling" (*De interpellatione Job et David,* 3.2.4). St. Augustine, in his "Second Discourse on Psalm 33" *(Enarr. in Ps.),* writes that "He is a surgeon . . . and He will not withdraw his hand until He hath cut away as much as seems needful to Him . . . that He may heal and spare us for evermore." The Fathers typically offer a spiritual or allegorical reading of the healing narratives: Christ is "that Physician who heals our inward sight and enables us to behold that very light eternal which is himself" ("Second Discourse on Psalm 36"). Alluding to Luke 5:18-22, Augustine also identifies an "inward" as well as an outward palsy. St. John Chrysostom, in his *Hom. on Hebrews* (9.8), speaks of the medicine of repentance; it is in this sense of effecting repentance and a transformation of heart that Lady Philosophy calls herself Boethius's "physician" (in *De Consolatione Philosophiae,* 4, pr. 2).

In the Wakefield Cycle Noah calls the Lord a "Beyter of Baill" ("healer of sorrow"). The triple fountain in the shepherd's park at the end of the *Roman de la Rose,* identified with Christ, is said to be "health-giving"; those who drink of it "will live as they wish without sickness or death" (20369-479; cf. Rev. 22:1-2). In Chaucer's *Book of the Duchess* the narrator describes his initial state of sleepless disorder as a sorrowful *accidia,* a "sicknesse" for which "there is phisicien but oon / That may me hele; but that is don . . ." (39-40), a suggestion, apparently, that Christ has already provided the universal remedy for such a malady. In this poem it is only by engaging in "healing" the grieving Black Knight that the persona can himself find healing — an ironic and therapeutic application to the self, perhaps, of Luke 4:23 ("Physician, heal thyself"). As Christ is a healer, so also his Church is to be a source of healing; accordingly Romeo hopes for "holy physic" from the friar (*Romeo and Juliet,* 2.3.52). Spenser elaborates the allegorical device of spiritual healing in his *Faerie Queene* (1.10-11). Redcrosse Knight, physically and spiritually emaciated, enters the House of Holiness, where Fidelia (faith), Speranza (hope), Penance, Patience, and others minister to his needs. Once healed he is ready to fight the Satanic dragon — with healing respites in the Well of Life and at the base of the Tree of Life, both Well and Tree being allegorically related to Christ.

In light of these traditions Vaughan can say that "Sickness is wholsome," since it might be a part of God's chastising "physick" for humanity ("Affliction"; cf. Marvell's "A Dialogue between the Soul and the Body"). Donne, writing while he himself is gravely ill, makes the same point in his *Devotions* (4). He begins with a citation of Ecclus. 38:15:

> "He that hath sinned against his Maker, let him fall into the hands of the physician": and wilt thou afford me an understanding of those words? . . . Is not the curse rather in this, that only he falls in the hands of the physician . . . and neglects that spiritual physic which thou also hast instituted into thy church. So to fall into the hands of the physician is a sin, and a punishment of former sins; so, as Asa fell, who in his disease "sought not to the Lord, but to the physician."

Donne goes on to pray that the "universal" physician might assure his spiritual health and aid his earthly physicians.

Sir Thomas Browne's *Religio Medici* (1642) has much to say about the tensions Browne felt between a biblical and a scientific prospect on disease and the physician's art. In discussing biblical healing miracles "scientifically" he nonetheless concludes by affirming belief in them. George Herbert sees the priest, in his imitation of Christ, as an imperfect medic, whose human condition, "Though it be ill, makes him no ill Physician" ("Church Porch," 443-44; cf. "A Priest to the Temple," chaps. 23, 33). In "A Treatise of Temperance and Sobrietie," a prose tract on what today might be called holistic medicine, he also suggests that the relationship between physical and psychic or spiritual nature is such that "indeed, no man can be a perfect physician to another, but to himself onely." In his poem "The Sacrifice," adapted from the Latin hymn *"O Vos Omnes,"* Christ on the cross responds tellingly to the taunting cry of his tormentors (Luke 4:23):

> *Now heal thy self, Physician; now come down.*
> Alas! I did so, when I left my crown
> And fathers smile for you, to feel his frown:
> Was ever grief like mine? (221-24)

Preoccupation with the inadequacy of physicians is a minor theme in 18th-cent. literature (e.g., in Pope and Swift), but in a moving passage in his *Jubilate Agno* Christopher Smart, much injured by his almost savage medical attendants, prays to Christ the Physician principally on behalf of his fellow sufferers:

> For I pray to the Lord JESUS that cured the LUNATICK to
>> be merciful to all my brethren and sisters in these houses.
> For they work at me with their harping-irons, which is
>> a barbarous instrument, because I am more unguarded than others.

In Romantic and Victorian literature the association of Christ with the physician is less prominent. St. Luke is remembered sardonically by Byron in his "English Bards and Scots Reviewers" when he quips of Lewis and Scott that "If tales like thine may please, / St. Luke alone can vanquish the disease" (279-80). But in a 20th-cent.

American story, as in Herbert's treatise, the office of Christ the Physician and the priest as vicar of that office are memorably conjoined: Flannery O'Connor's "The Enduring Chill" is a masterful exposé of the spiritual root of a physical disease. Here, though the patient fancies a Kafkaesque death, his one-eyed, garrulous Southern priest sees through his facade and diagnoses his spiritual sickness suddenly, unceremoniously, and confoundingly, offering precisely the biblical cure his "patient" has been least disposed to inquire after.

See also BLINDNESS; DISEASE AND HEALING; LEPROSY; LUKE; *O VOS OMNES*.   H. DAVID BRUMBLE

PILATE *See* PONTIUS PILATE.

PILATE'S WIFE The only mention of the wife of Pontius Pilate in the NT consists of the few words in Matt. 27:19: "When he [Pilate] was set down on the judgment seat, his wife sent unto him, saying, Have thou nothing to do with that just man, for I have suffered many things this day in a dream because of him." Although unnamed in the NT, Pilate's wife is called Claudia Procla or Procula in extracanonical literature. There is a tradition that she may have been a secret follower of Jesus; Origen, St. John Chrysostom, and St. Hilary all affirm that she converted to Christianity. An apocryphal letter from Pilate to Herod refers to Procla going with Longinus, "the believing centurion," and some soldiers to the sepulcher of Jesus (M. R. James's *The Apocryphal New Testament* [rpt. 1966], 155). An appendix to the Acts of Pilate (the first part of the Gospel of Nicodemus) says that Pilate was beheaded by Albius at the order of Caesar, and that when an angel of the Lord received his head Procla was filled with joy and "straightway gave up the ghost and was buried with her husband." In one of the additions (manifestly of Christian origin) in the Slavonic version of Josephus's *Jewish Wars* (immediately after bk. 2, sect. 174), Jesus is said to have healed Pilate's wife when she was dying. According to the *Paradosis Pilati* both Pilate and his wife suffered martyrdom under Tiberius. They are regarded as saints in the Coptic Church (their feast day being June 25), although in the Greek Church only Pilate's wife is honored (on Oct. 27).

In the medieval Cornish *"Passio Christi"* (1907-68; 2193-2218), Lucifer, in an effort to thwart the plan of redemption, sends Beelzebub to speak to Pilate's wife in a dream, warning her that if her husband convicts Jesus both Pilate and her children will suffer. Claudia conveys the message to Pilate but his attempts to save Jesus are in vain (see also *Piers Plowman,* B.18.297-301).

Pilate's wife has a minor role in various modern "gospels," including Sholem Asch's *The Nazarene,* Robert Graves's *King Jesus,* and Anthony Burgess's *Man of Nazareth.*

See also PONTIUS PILATE.   RONALD M. MELDRUM

PILLAR OF CLOUD AND FIRE On their way out of Egypt toward the Red Sea crossing and freedom from bondage, Moses and the children of Israel were led by the Shekinah presence of the Lord, who "went before them by day in a pillar of a cloud, to lead them in the way; and by night in a pillar of fire, to give them light . . ." (Exod. 13:21). The pillar of cloud (Heb. *'ammud 'anan*) and pillar of fire (*'ammud 'esh*) indicated the constancy of the divine presence; when the people were at rest the pillar of cloud hung over the Tabernacle (Exod. 40:36; Num. 9:17; 14:14). When the Lord spoke to Moses, the pillar descended to the door of the tent (Exod. 33:9-11; Num. 12:5; Deut. 31:15).

St. Augustine regards the pillars of cloud and fire as exemplary of miraculous "signs," created to signify something, then to pass away when their purpose is served — likening them in this respect to the flame in the burning bush (*De Trin.* 8.6.11). Matthew Henry, in his *Commentary* (1.327), follows the general pattern of typological exegesis after Augustine in seeing the signified as "the eternal Word, which, in the fulness of time, was to be made flesh and dwell among us. Christ was with the church in the wilderness." John Donne's poem "The Annunciation and Passion" takes up the theme of the Incarnation, and describes the pilgrimage of the Church as one mapped between " 'the Angel's *Ave,* ' and *Consummatum est,*" with God himself going before: "His Spirit, as his fiery Pillar doth / Leade, and his Church, as cloud; to one end both."

In Sir Walter Scott's *Ivanhoe* "Rebecca's Hymn" celebrates the past —

When Israel of the Lord beloved,
  Out from the land of bondage came,
Her father's God before her moved,
  An awful guide in smoke and flame
By day, along the astonish'd lands
  The cloudy pillar glided slow;
By night, Arabia's crimson sands
  Return'd the fiery column's glow.

In *Sartor Resartus* Carlyle laments the passing of a Viking age of heroes: "Alas, where now are the Hengsts and Alaracs of our still growing, still expanding Europe; who, when their home is grown too narrow, will enlist, and, like Fire-pillars, guide onwards those superfluous masses of indomitable living Valour" (3.4). He further laments that in an age of modern materialism and loss of faith ". . . no Pillar of Cloud by day, and no Pillar of Fire by night, any longer guides the Pilgrim." Twain's narrator in *Roughing It* romanticizes the wilderness experience in American fashion:

I thought it just possible that its like had not been seen since the children of Israel wandered on their long march through the desert so many centuries ago over a path illuminated by the mysterious "pillar of fire." (2.33)

Some later 19th-cent. commentators strove for natu-

ralistic explanations of the phenomenon, as in his own way does Thomas Hardy, who describes in *Tess of the D'Urbervilles* how "when a fire glowed, banks of smoke, blown level along the ground, would themselves become illuminated to an opaque lustre, screening the workpeople from one another, and the meaning of the 'pillar of a cloud,' which was a wall by day and a light by night, could be understood." One of the best-known uses of the image is John Henry Newman's "The Pillar of Cloud," a hymn whose opening lines are "Lead, kindly Light, amid the encircling gloom; / Lead thou me on"; these lines are themselves bitterly recollected in Anthony Hecht's "More Light! More Light!," a poem relating religious persecution through the ages to the horrors of the Holocaust.

See also EXODUS.

PISGAH SIGHT Deut. 34:1-4 says that before Moses died, God commanded him to ascend Mt. Nebo (possibly related to *nabi',* "prophet"), "to the top of Pisgah," a peak whose name means "cleft" in Hebrew. There he granted him a view of the Promised Land. As the Lord explained to Moses in Deut. 32:51-52, he could not enter the Promised Land because he had disobeyed the divine command and, rather than pray, struck the rock to bring forth water in Kadesh (Num. 20:1-13). The Pisgah sight is thus a coming together, a confrontation, of human and divine, temporal and eternal, immediately before the death of the prophet who had given his life to serving God and his chosen people, and it therefore stands simultaneously as the culmination, reward, and punishment for the acts of that life. As such, it has become a topos for the temporal culmination of projects greater than one life can see through. Baikie, in his study *The English Bible*, uses it in this way: "One of the pathetic things about such great undertakings as the production of The Authorized Version is that so often the men who were responsible for the initiation of the work do not live to see its completion. Like Moses, they only get a Pisgah-sight of the godly land into which they are not permitted to enter" (chap. 22). This draws on a long exegetical tradition which from the Middle Ages saw Moses standing in the cleft of the mountain, replete with the experience of God's leading his people under the terms of the OT; now, though not in his flesh, about to enter into the promises of the New Covenant, he is able with the eyes of faith to "see afar off the advent of the Redeemer, who by his blood would obtain the ultimate liberation of his people" (*Glossa Ordinaria* [PL 113.504]). Pisgah enters thus naturally into reflections on the death of the faithful, looking forward to the consummation of the Divine Plan of history and the Resurrection, as in the conclusion of Richard Baxter's *The Saints' Everlasting Rest* (1650) and in funeral orations.

The history of the literary use of the Pisgah sight is complicated by the fact that it frequently blends with its secular analogue, the prospect. Moments of revelatory vision occur to Petrarch on Mt. Ventoux, to Dante on the mount of Purgatory, to Spenser's Redcrosse Knight on the mount of Contemplation, to Rousseau's St. Preux in the Valois, to Wordsworth on Mt. Snowdon, and to Coleridge, Shelley, and Ruskin in the Alps. Some of these visions refer to Moses' sight of Canaan explicitly.

By the late 18th cent. the Pisgah sight serves as a type of the deathbed of the true believer, who leaves this life confident in his faith. Moses' sight of Canaan prefigures the Christian's dying sight of his Savior or of heaven. Evangelical hymns made such readings of the Pisgah sight a commonplace. Thus the anonymous hymn "Jerusalem, My Happy Home" (1801) claims that the believer does not shrink from pain or death, because "I've Canaan's goodly land in view, / And realms of endless day." Isaac Watts's "There Is a Land of Pure Delight" (1709) similarly takes Canaan itself as a type of heaven. Augustus Montague Toplady's "Deathless Principle, Arise!" (1777) extends the original type, since he employs the secular analogue of the Pisgah sight, which is the prospect, rather than the literal vision from Mt. Pisgah. William Cowper, in his *Olney Hymn* (no. 52), says "I was a grovelling creature once," then tells how he obtains by grace "wings of joy and love": "With these to Pisgah's top I fly, / And there delighted stand." A similar extended vision appears in the closing pages of Charles Kingsley's *Alton Locke,* where it combines political and religious visions, for the dying workingman, surely no Moses, nonetheless has "come out of Egypt and the house of bondage." In Hardy's *The Return of the Native* the perspicacious Mrs. Yeobright is observed to have moments when "she seemed to be regarding issues from a Nebo denied to others around."

Paradoxically, much of the Pisgah sight's power and richness as an allusive device derives from the fact that it is so difficult to employ literally. The Pisgah scene comprises seven basic elements, each of which can be modified for literary effect: (1) the presence of God with the one who has the Pisgah sight; (2) the time in the viewer's life when such a sight occurs; (3) the physical position, usually a mountaintop or high place, from which the prophet gazes; (4) the removal from the viewed object, his separation from the promised land; (5) his isolation from other people; (6) the content of the vision; and (7) the relation of the viewed object to human time — whether, in other words, it is something to be obtained in time (in the future) or outside time (in eternity).

Although orthodox Pisgah sights claim the direct sanction and sponsorship of God, characteristically romantic and modern incidents seek the same education, solace, and reward in his absence. Nineteenth-cent. authors with relatively firm belief employ the orthodox and extended forms of the Pisgah sight to describe dying visions or to create images which act as windows into eternity; those without such belief employ the Pisgah sight for the ironies potential in the situation. Even

believers, such as Tennyson, will use Pisgah sights to dramatize troubled faith. For example, *The Idylls of the King* closes by granting Bedivere, the last of Arthur's knights, a consolatory vision which is yet tinged with irony, since it is riddled with doubt even as it consoles. Matthew Arnold's "Empedocles on Etna" (1852), which depicts its protagonist on a mountain height screened by fog and mist, might seem a parody of the Pisgah sight, but this form, too, turns out to be a commonplace of religious verse. James Montgomery's "For Ever with the Lord!" (1853), e.g., first presents glimpses of the "golden gates" in standard fashion but then admits that "clouds will intervene." Similarly, Toplady's "I Saw, and Lo! a Countless Throng" (1759-74) emphasizes how soon "clouds return" and "hide the hill of Sion." Or, as Robert Louis Stevenson puts it in a secular context, "Desire is a wonderful telescope, and Pisgah the best observatory" (*Memories and Portraits,* chap. 16).

Poets mine the situation for its inherent ironies. Robert Browning compares himself to Moses in "Pisgah Sights" to show that since the divinely inspired vision comes just before death, it comes too late to communicate. In contrast, Elizabeth Barrett Browning's *Aurora Leigh* (1856), which uses this commonplace to show the essential difficulty of communicating with the contemporary audience, asks if anyone "getting to the top of Pisgah-hill, / Can talk with one at bottom of the view, / To make it comprehensible?"

When telling the story of his own life in *Praeterita,* John Ruskin, who frequently felt himself painfully alienated from an uncomprehending public, employs another element in the Pisgah sight structure — the perceiver's frustrating separation from the land of promise. Newman, in "Day-Labourers" (1833), makes the orthodox use of this situation when he points out that even Moses "wearied on Nebo's height" and that only Christ can finish "the work of grace, which he began." In contrast, Ruskin, who arranges his autobiography in terms of a series of Paradises Lost and Pisgah visions, emphasizes the cost and incompleteness of his position.

See also MOSES.

Bibliography. Landow, G. P. *Victorian Types, Victorian Shadows: Biblical Typology in Victorian Literature, Art, and Thought* (1980), chap. 7.   GEORGE P. LANDOW

PITCHER BROKEN AT THE FOUNTAIN   *See* GOLDEN BOWL.

PLACEBO   Literary usage may relate less to direct biblical sources than liturgical mediation. *"Placebo"* is the first word of the first antiphon of Vespers in the Office of the Dead (*"Placebo Domino in regione vivorum"* ["I will walk before (strive to please) the LORD in the land of the living"]; from Ps. 116:9; Vg Ps. 114:9). *The Ancrene Riwle* places the *"Placebo"* after the hour of Evensong for certain solemnities and at its usual place, Vespers, in other solemnities of the dead. In this context *"Placebo"* means to sing Vespers of the Office of the Dead for the benefit of someone departed, as, e.g., in Langland, *Piers Plowman,* B.4.311-12:

> Preestes and persons wiþ *Placebo* to hunte,
> And dyngen vpon Dauid eche day til eue.
> ("Priests and parsons to hunt with
> *Placebo,* and make music upon
> David['s psalter] every day till eve.")

John Skelton's elegiac "Philip Sparowe" separates the syllables, apparently in imitation of the phrasing of the plainsong: *"Pla ce bo,* / Who is there, who?"

Chaucer uses the Latin meaning of the term ("I shall please") in both its liturgical context and in its more modern context, drawn from medicine. In *The Merchant's Tale* (*CT* 4.1476-1518) Placebo the courtier advises Januarie to follow his desires rather than his good sense (represented by Justinus). Placebo is politically a *placebo;* he pleases his aged lord, who barely remains in the land of the living but still wishes to marry a young bride. In *The Parson's Tale* the term suggests that flatterers are "lyk to Judas," betrayers or infernal chaplains who sing a Vespers of flattery for their departed: "Flatereres been the develes chapelleyns, that syngen evere *Placebo*" (10.616).   ERNEST N. KAULBACH

PLAGUES OF EGYPT After the unsuccessful attempt by Moses and Aaron to achieve the liberation of their people from slavery in Egypt, the Lord directed them to announce a series of plagues — each designed to induce Pharaoh's repentance and release of the people (Exod. 7:14–11:20). The ten plagues which ensued were: (1) the waters of the river turned to blood (7:14-24); (2) frogs (7:25–8:15); (3) lice (8:16-19); (4) flies (8:20-32); (5) murrain, an epidemic afflicting the Egyptians' livestock (9:1-7); (6) boils and blains (9:8-12); (7) hail (9:13-35); (8) locusts (10:1-20); (9) three days of palpable darkness (10:21-23); (10) slaying of the Egyptian firstborn (11:1–12:30). After each of the first nine plagues Pharaoh's heart was hardened, but in the wake of the tenth he granted the Israelite slaves their freedom. Almost immediately, however, he regretted his decision and pursued them into the wilderness where, with his entire army, he perished in the Red Sea.

Talmudic sources elaborate analogies for the ten plagues. They are likened to ten steps of ideal military strategy (Pesiq. Rab. Kah. 7.66b-67a) or seen as "measure for measure" retribution for specific wrongs perpetrated by the Egyptians against the children of Israel (Mek. Amalek 2.55a; Sipre Num. 106; Soṭa 1.7; cf. Sanh. 90a). Wisdom (chaps. 11–18) elaborates a parallel between the plagues and certain virtues and miracles accorded to Israel (cf. Mek. Beshallah 6.32; Soṭa 3.13). The Haggadah in Twelve Testaments, Benjamin 7.1-5, suggests that in Cain's long life each new era (generation or even century)

would have its own special plague (several of which are analogous with those in Exod. 7–12) until he should perish in the last, the Flood. (In a later recollection, perhaps, of such Jewish legends, Byron alludes to the first plague in the curses attaching to his Cain: "May the clear rivers 'turn to blood' as he / Stoops down to stain them with his raging lip!" [*Cain,* 3.1.432-33].)

Many early Christian commentators, like their Jewish counterparts, allegorize the plagues; indeed, St. Jerome mocks those who would suppose a literal reading of the narrative exhausts the full meaning of the account (*Ep.* 53.8). Some of the extremes of Origen's allegorizations vie with the later midrashim for incongruous novelty. A more conservative allegorical and moral exposition is reflected in the *Glossa Ordinaria,* which incorporates the commentary of Bede, Rabanus, and others. With reference to the water of the Nile River changing to blood (the Nile, according to talmudic sources, was often worshiped as a God by the Egyptians or seen as Pharaoh's creation), the *Glossa* offers a parallel with the first commandment:

> Water, from which all things are generated, signified the one God out of whom all things proceed; the blood stands for mere mortal flesh. The water is accordingly changed into blood, even as they [the Egyptians and in figura all sinners] "changed the incorruptible glory of God into an image made like to corruptible man" [Rom. 1:23], a characteristic transformation which is always going on in sinful hearts. (PL 113.205)

This relationship is worked out, in a manner somewhat reminiscent of the gnostic Manoimus (*Philosophoumena,* 8.7), for each of the ten plagues.

For St. Augustine (*De civ. Dei* 10.8-10), as for many subsequent Christian exegetes, the narrative of the plagues is a locus classicus for divine signs and wonders. Moses' confrontation with Pharaoh's magicians, whose conjuring "tricks" duplicate some of the visible marvels performed by Moses, demonstrates not only the sovereignty of the God of Abraham, Isaac, and Jacob over pagan deities, he says, but a qualitative distinction between godly miracles and the "fictions of deceiving demons" (10.10), the former being faithful testimonies of the divine character "wrought by simple faith and godly confidence, not by the incantations and charms composed under the influence of a criminal tampering with the unseen world" (10.9). Such views found vivid dramatic expression in several medieval biblical plays (e.g., York "Departure from Egypt," Wakefield "Pharaoh"). Protestant commentators such as Calvin, Beza, and Poole tend to follow Augustine in stressing the relationship between Egypt's punishments and Israel's blessings. Poole makes much of the fact that Pharaoh's magicians, while able to imitate Moses in creating some of the plague conditions ("it was not difficult for the Devil," he says, "to convey blood speedily"), were unable to remove the plagues (*Annotations,* sup. Exod. 7:21). He then turns to more oddly literalist conjectures: if all the water was already turned to blood, where did the clean water come from? — perhaps rain, he suggests. Matthew Henry observes concerning the plagues of frogs, lice, and flies, "little despicable animals [which] yet by their vast numbers rendered some plagues to the Egyptians," that "God could have plagued them with lions, or bears, or wolves, or with vultures or other birds of prey; but he chose to do so by these contemptible instruments" in order to "magnify his own power" and to "humble Pharaoh's pride, and chastise his insolence." "What a mortification must it needs be to this haughty monarch to see himself brought to his knees, and forced to submit, by such despicable means!" (*Comm.* 1.301).

In Milton's *Paradise Lost* Adam is given a vivid preview of the plagues to be visited upon "Pharaoh, the lawless Tyrant" who, as a type of the "River-dragon" or Leviathan opposing God, "must be compelled by Signes and Judgments dire" (12.170-92). William Cowper takes his cue from Calvin (and perhaps from Reformation hymnody):

> Let Egypt's plagues, and Canaan's woes proclaim
> The favours pour'd upon the Jewish name —
> Their freedom, purchased for them at the cost
> Of all their hard oppressors valued most;
> Their title to a country not their own
> Made sure by prodigies till then unknown.
> ("Expostulation," 169-74)

But Cowper also anticipates the proverbial and clichéd use of the story. In his "The Progress of Error" he chides the press for abusing its privileges, saying that because of its mendacity and flippancy in England "worse plagues than Pharaoh's land befel" (460-64). Charles Lamb in "Poor Relations" makes a trivializing allusion to "the most irrelevant thing in nature, — a lion in your path, — a frog in your chamber, — a fly in your ointment" (cf. Prov. 26:13; Eccl. 10:1). Similarly, in Arnold Bennett's *The Matador of the Five Towns,* "If you were a married man you'd know that the ten plagues of Egypts are simply nothing in comparison with your wife's relations" (chap. 1).

Some of the plagues have lent themselves to colorful invocation. Hardy is fond of the ninth plague, the "palpable darkness" as Milton phrases it, which can describe anything from arboreal gloom (*Far from the Madding Crowd,* chap. 24) to winter ombré: "On a moorland in wet weather it is thirty perceptible minutes to any fireside man, woman, or beast in Christendom — minutes that can be felt, like the Egyptian plague of darkness" (*The Hand of Ethelberta,* chap. 3). In Rose Macaulay's *Told by an Idiot,* "American merchant princesses are descending on the land like locusts" (1.10). Occasionally, however, some of the moral or spiritual force of earlier interpretation attaches itself deliberately to such allusions. Charlotte Brontë's *Jane Eyre* draws forcibly on the biblical

narrative in the memorable lines: "My hopes were all dead — struck with a subtle doom, such as, in one night, fell on all the first-born in the land of Egypt" (chap. 26). And a voice of the reprobate in Sinclair Lewis's *The God-Seekers* is heard to say: "My heart is literally harder than a millstone. My mind is as dark as the Egyptian darkness that could be felt. Can it be that Christ could die for one like me?" (chap. 34).

See also EXODUS; MOSES; PASSOVER; PHARAOH.

PLOWED WITH MY HEIFER   *See* OUT OF THE EATER.

PLOWMAN   The biblical image of the plowman is most firmly associated with Elisha. When the prophet Elijah had been assured by the Lord that there were yet "seven thousand in Israel" who had not "bowed unto Baal," he immediately came upon Elisha "plowing with twelve yoke of oxen before him" (1 Kings 19:19). As Elijah passed by he "cast his mantle upon him," indicating that Elisha was called to be his successor as prophet in Israel. The plowman is thus seen as a figure for the faithful servant of God in Israel, worthy to be ordained (much as in the NT some of the early disciples are called by Jesus from their own humble employment as fishermen). In Isaiah (28:24-29) the plowman is described as someone whose knowledge of his work and ability to make the earth fruitful is learned from God himself: "For God doth instruct him to discretion, and doth teach him" (v. 26). Hence in patristic commentary God himself is the archetypal plowman, and "it is the Church that is the Lord's land. It is her whom he, the Father, the tiller of it, waters and cultivates" (St. Augustine, *Enarr. in Ps.* 36.4 [37.4]). From this point of departure the plow is variously taken as a type of the Cross, or, in the interpretation of Thomas Brinton (*Sermo*, 20), of penance (cf. St. Gregory the Great, *Moralia in Iob*, 6.31). Plowmen thus become ready symbols for God's faithful stewards, especially priests and those in religious life. It is from this tradition that Langland derives his ideal faithful steward in *Piers Plowman,* and Chaucer, in a complementary fashion, describes the brother of his ideal Parson in *The Canterbury Tales* (*General Prologue*, 1.531-38):

> A trewe swynkere and a good was he,
> Lyvynge in pees and parfit charitee.
> God loved he best with al his hoole herte
> At alle tymes, thogh him gamed or smerte,
> And thanne his neighebor right as hymselve.
> He wolde thresshe, and therto dyke and delve,
> For Cristes sake, for every povre wight,
> Withouten hire, if it lay in his myght.

In a sermon on Rom. 15:4 preached at St. Paul's, London, Jan. 18, 1548 (one of a series of "Sermons on the Plough"), Bishop Hugh Latimer refers to "Christ's church and congregation" as "God's plough land" and sees the preacher as plowman, making connection to the parable of the sower in Luke 8:5 and Jesus' declaration in Luke 9:62 that "No man, having put his hand to the plow, and looking back, is fit for the kingdom of God." "Ever since the prelates were made lords and nobles," Latimer complains, "the plough standeth; there is no work done, the people starve." Then, in words reminiscent of Chaucer's description of his profane Monk (*CT* 1.165-207), he comments: "They hawk, they hunt, they card, they dice; they pastime in their prelacies with gallant gentlemen, with the dancing minions . . . so that preaching and ploughing is clean gone" (*Sermons* [ed. Corrie, 1844], 65-66).

By the 17th cent. Protestant pastors were applying the image to their task in much the same vein as George Herbert, for whom the good country parson "hath one Comment at least upon every book of Scripture, and ploughing with this, and his own meditations he enters into the secrets of God treasured in holy Scripture" (*A Priest to the Temple*, 4). Matthew Henry observes of the Elisha story that Elijah found his successor

> not in the schools of the prophets, but *in the field*, not reading, nor praying, nor sacrificing, but *ploughing*. . . . Though a great man (as appears by his feast . . . master of the ground, and oxen, and servants) yet he did not think it any disparagement to him to follow his business himself, and not only to inspect his servants, but himself to lay his hand to the plough. Idleness is no man's honour, nor is husbandry any man's disgrace. (*Comm.* 2.685)

Charles Spurgeon's *John Ploughman's Talk*, a series of vivid sermon illustrations which sold over 400,000 copies in his lifetime, and *John Ploughman's Pictures*, a sequel, give ample evidence of the continuing popularity of the figure in the Victorian era. It is Spurgeon's association of plowing with the preaching of salvation which lies behind John Masefield's poem "The Everlasting Mercy," in which a converted drunk, Saul Kane, is watching "Old Callow at his autumn ploughing" and longing that the hard ground of Callow's own soul might be tilled so as to accept the seed of the word. Here the "ploughman of the sinner's soul" is Jesus himself:

> O Christ who holds the open gate,
> O Christ who drives the furrow straight,
> O Christ, the plough, O Christ, the laughter
> Of holy white birds flying after,
> Lo, all my heart's field red and torn,
> And Thou wilt bring the young green corn,
> The young green corn divinely springing,
> The young green corn forever singing.

See also ELIJAH; ELISHA; HAND TO THE PLOW.

POMEGRANATE   The pomegranate, called in Hebrew *rimmon* (Akk. *armanna;* Arab. *rumman*), is mentioned in the OT in a variety of contexts. Among the extended praises of the beloved in the Song of Songs is the comparison, "thy temples are like a piece of pomegranate within thy locks" (4:3; repeated at 6:7). Elsewhere, the maiden in the Song declares, "I would cause thee to drink of spiced wine of the juice of my pomegranate" (8:2).

The pomegranate was not only a source of lyrical comparisons but an erotic symbol as well, as is clearly seen in the well-known *hortus conclusus* passage: "A garden inclosed is my sister, my spouse; a spring shut up, a fountain sealed. Thy plants are an orchard of pomegranates, with pleasant fruits; camphire, with spikenard" (Cant. 4:12-13). The pomegranate was traditionally a sign and symbol of fertility in the Near East, its budding presence a sign of a fertile land and the fruit itself, closely packed with seeds, a symbol of fertility, as in Cant. 6:11: "I went down into the garden of nuts, to see the fruits of the valley, to see whether the vine flourished, and the pomegranates budded" (cf. Cant. 7:12).

The pomegranate is an important element in the identification of the Promised Land (Deut. 8:8); indeed, the spies sent out to scout Canaan brought back with them as signs of the fertility and bounty of the land bunches of figs, grapes, and pomegranates (Num. 13:23). Conversely, the absence of pomegranates is a sign of the absence of God's favor (Num. 20:5; Joel 1:12; Hag. 2:19). This association accounts for the later legendary identification of the pomegranate with the tree of life, seen also in Christian iconography, as in the seventh tapestry in the series of Unicorn Tapestries at the Cloisters (New York).

The pomegranate is also used as a cultic/liturgical symbol in the OT. The hem of the robe of the high priest was to be decorated with an alternation of golden bells and pomegranates of blue, purple, and scarlet (Exod. 28:33-34; 39:24-25; Ecclus. 45:9). Exod. 28:35 implies that the sound the priest would make upon entering the sanctuary would be a kind of cultic warning, but some modern commentators have proposed that the "bells" were originally representations of pomegranate flowers, to alternate with images of the fruit. Similarly, the temple of Solomon included columns of brass whose capitals were carved with images of pomegranates (1 Kings 7:18, 20, 42; 2 Chron. 3:16; 4:13; also 2 Kings 25:17; Jer. 52:22).

In Jewish exegesis, the pomegranate is interpreted allegorically as symbolizing spiritual fertility, as in young scholars or rulers full of precepts or good works (Tg. Ketubim Cant. 4:3, 13; 6:11; 7:12; cf. Midr. Rab. on the same passages). The pomegranates budding are interpreted as "the children who are busy learning the Torah and sit in rows like pomegranate seeds" (Midr. Rab. Cant. 6:11), and the garden of pomegranates as an image of the messianic age (Midr. Rab. Cant. 4:13).

Christian allegorists, likewise, used the pomegranate to signify spiritual fruitfulness in the Church and the individual soul. The redness of the pomegranate rind and seeds was generally taken to refer to the Church's imitation of Christ's passion through actual martyrdom or the spiritual martyrdom of the austere monastic life, while the whiteness of the pith symbolized virginity or purity (see the commentators on Cant. 4:3, 13; 6:7, 11; 7:12; 8:2 cited in R. F. Littledale, *A Commentary on the Song of Songs* [1869]).

The OE word for pomegranate was *aeppel-cyrnel,* "kernel-apple," which became "appel-garnade" in ME, as in *Cleanness:* "þe fayrest fryt þat may on folde growe, / As orange . . . and apple garnade" (1043-44). The more familiar term *pome-sarnet-tys* occurs in Chaucer's translation, *The Romaunt of the Rose* (1355-58), as part of the description of the Garden of Love, a false "paradise" which parodies the spiritual garden of Christian exegesis.

There are several incidental allusions to the pomegranate in Shakespeare (*All's Well That Ends Well*, 2.3.276 and *1 Henry 4*, 2.4.42) and one reference (*Romeo and Juliet*, 3.5.1-7, 11) which strongly recalls its erotic — and thanatopic — associations. Keats may be echoing Shakespeare in his "Faery Song 1," where the pomegranate retains its age-old connotation as the paradisal tree of life:

Shed no tear — O shed no tear! . . .
For I was taught in Paradise
To ease my breast of melodies —
    Shed no tear.

Overhead — look overhead
'Mong the blossoms white and red —
Look up, look up — I flutter now
On this flush pomegranate bough — (1, 6-12)

In Canto 3 of *Don Juan* Byron uses the pomegranate image as part of the idyllic pastoral setting for the love of Juan and Haidee, "happy in the illicit / Indulgence of their innocent desires" (3.13.1-8; cf. 3.62.6-8; 3.33.1-6).

The Song of Songs, with its pomegranate image, is echoed also in Blake's prophetic poem *Ahania,* where Ahania, a personification of desire, longs for her lost mate, Urizen (reason or law):

    "And when he gave my happy soul
To the sons of eternal joy;
When he took the daughters of life
Into my chambers of love. . . .

    "Swell'd with ripeness & fat with fatness,
Bursting on winds, my odors,
My ripe figs and rich pomegranates
In infant joy at thy feet,
O Urizen, sported and sang.

    "Then thou with thy lap full of seed,
With thy hand full of generous fire,
Walked forth from the clouds of morning,
On the virgins of springing joy,
On the human soul to cast
The seed of eternal science. . . ." (5.9, 11-12)

In Joyce's *Ulysses,* Leopold Bloom cites Cant. 4:3 in his conversation with Stephen wherein "fragments of verse from the ancient Hebrew and ancient Irish languages were cited with modulations of voice and translation of texts by guest to host and by host to guest": *"Kifeloch harimon rakatejch m'baad l'zamatejch"* ("thy temple amid thy hair is as a slice of pomegranate"). Hopkins, in his *Meditations on 'Spiritual Exercises',* explicates the pomegranate as a symbol of the prelapsarian plenitude and wholeness of all creation and of each kind and individual:

    "Magnam capacitatem et ambitum mundi" — This suggests that "pomegranate," that *pomum possibilium.* The Trinity saw it whole and in every "cleave," the actual and the possible. We may consider that we are looking at it in all the actual cleaves, one after another. This sphere is set off against the sphere of the divine being, a steady "seat or throne" of majesty. Yet that too has its cleave to us, the entrance of Christ on the world. There is not only the pomegranate of the whole world but of each species in it, each race, each individual, and so on. Of human nature the whole pomegranate fell in Adam. (Aug. 26, 1885; *Sermons and Devotional Writings,* ed. Devlin [1959], 171)

No major poet seems to have been more fascinated by the pomegranate or to have made more persistent use of it than Robert Browning, for whom it was a powerful emblem of the loving heart. In *Sordello* (1840), Palma's lyric effusion in which she confesses her love for Sordello is filled with rich nature imagery, culminating with the pomegranate (3.344-59). In 1841, Browning inaugurated a series of pamphlets as the vehicle for the publication of his poetry, the general title of which was *Bells and Pomegranates.* The first number was *Pippa Passes,* and in the title work the pomegranate occurs again, somewhat obscurely, as an emblem of love and change of heart.

After six numbers of *Bells and Pomegranates* had been published, Elizabeth Barrett took public notice of Browning's poetry; in her poem "Lady Geraldine's Courtship," she pays tribute to Browning's poetry using the pomegranate image to compliment him. Browning himself used the pomegranate image again in *Bells and Pomegranates* no. 7, *Dramatic Romances and Lyrics* (Nov. 1845), in the poem "The Englishman in Italy."

The following year, after repeated requests, he reluctantly agreed to give a public explanation of the meaning of the title of his series. In the eighth and last number of *Bells and Pomegranates* (Apr. 1846), as a preface to *A Soul's Tragedy,* he wrote that

    I only meant by that title to indicate an endeavor towards something like an alternation, or mixture, of music with discoursing, sound with sense, poetry with thought; which looks too ambitious, thus expressed, so the symbol was preferred. It is little to the purpose that such is actually one of the most familiar of the many Rabbinical (and Patristic) acceptations of the phrase.

"Bells" was thus intended to convey the musical or sound

element of his poetry, while "pomegranates" represented the sense, what a medieval writer would call the "doctrine." That bells and pomegranates adorned the hem of the OT high priest was also suggestive for Browning, who, like many of his contemporaries, attributed a priestly function to poetry.

Bibliography. Berlin-Lieberman, J. *Robert Browning and Hebraism* (1934), chap. 2; Fairchild, H. N. "Browning's Pomegranate Heart." *MLN* 66 (1951), 265-66; Littledale, R. F. *A Commentary of the Song of Songs from Ancient and Medieval Sources* (1869); Pope, M. H. *Song of Songs / A New Translation with Introduction and Commentary.* AB (1977).

GEORGE L. SCHEPER

PONTIUS PILATE Pontius Pilate ruled from A.D. 26 to 36 as the fifth Roman governor of Judea, Samaria, and Idumaea.

His involvement in the Passion of Jesus Christ is recorded in the Gospels (Matt. 27; Mark 15; Luke 23; John 18:29–19:22, 31, 38), the Acts (3:13; 4:27; 13:28), and 1 Timothy (6:13). The evangelists (especially John and Luke) deemphasize Pilate's responsibility for Christ's death, instead stressing the involvement of the Jews and their leaders. Only Matthew mentions the dream of Pilate's wife and the handwashing scene (Matt. 27:19, 24). Luke writes that Pilate handed Jesus over to Herod, who sent him back (Luke 23:7-12). John reports Pilate's question "What is truth?" as well as the statements "Behold the man!" and "Behold your King!" (John 18:38; 19:5, 14). All four evangelists concur that Pilate originally intended to set Jesus free, but, prompted by the crowd, released Barabbas and had Jesus crucified.

Jewish historians treat Pilate unfavorably. Philo (quoting a letter of Agrippa I) calls him relentless and rapacious (*De legatione ad Gaium*, 38.301-02). Josephus records several instances of Pilate's anti-Jewish prejudice and brutality (*J.W.* 2.9.2-4; *Ant.* 18.3.1-2; cf. Luke 13:1). Yet Pilate co-operated with Caiaphas the high priest, whose position he regularly reaffirmed. Pilate was ultimately dismissed by Vitellius, the legate of Syria and his superior, because of his use of excessive violence (Josephus, *Ant.* 18.4.1-2). Before he arrived in Rome to defend himself, Tiberius had died.

Tacitus is the only classical Roman author to mention Pilate. He refers to him in connection with Nero's persecution of Christians: *"auctor nominis eius Christus Tiberio imperitante per procuratorem Pontium Pilatum supplicio affectus erat"* ("the creator of this name was Christ, who was put to death during the reign of Tiberius by the procurator Pontius Pilate") (*Annales*, 15.44).

There is extensive apocryphal literature on Pilate: the Acts of Pilate (the first part of the Gospel of Nicodemus, ed. H. C. Kim, chaps. 1–12); Letter of Pilate to Claudius (Kim, chap. 28); Letter of Pilate to Tiberius; Anaphora Pilati; Paradosis Pilati; Mors Pilati; Vindicta salvatoris; Cura sanitatis Tiberii (all of which are important for medieval English literature), and the Martyrium Pilati (in Arabic and Ethiopian). In these texts the characterization of Pilate varies greatly. The Greek Orthodox Church venerates his wife as a saint; both she and Pilate are saints in the Coptic Church, which remembers Pilate on June 25. The earliest reference to the Acts of Pilate is by St. Justin Martyr (*Apol.* 1.35). Tertullian makes Pilate *"iam pro sua conscientia Christianus"* (*Apologia,* 21.24). Eusebius tells of Pilate's forced suicide during the reign of Caligula and of forged Acts of Pilate under the emperor Maximin (ca. 311), who wanted to discredit Christianity (*Hist. eccl.* 2.7; 1.9).

Pilate has been extensively treated as a literary figure both in medieval and modern times. He appears in at least twenty-six European Passion plays, including all of the English cycles. The English often portray him as a braggart, whose pompous rhetoric produces a comical effect (see Stoephasius, 74; the best examples occur in the York cycle). In the Towneley cycle, however, Pilate is consistently depicted as a vicious tyrant. The Towneley "Play of the Talents" has Pilate gamble, along with Jesus' executioners, for his seamless garment. Although Pilate loses the game, he nevertheless acquires the robe through threats and manipulation. When performed, the role of Pilate was evidently spoken in a "loud magisterial voice" (*OED,* s.v. "Pilate") or a less than magisterial roar — as reflected in Chaucer's "in Pilates voys he gan to crie" (*Miller's Tale,* Prol. 1.3124).

The scene in which Pilate, in an act of self-vindication, "washes his hands" of responsibility for Jesus' fate (see Deut. 21:6-7; cf. Stoephasius, 8, n. 4) became a favorite literary motif. (There are also paintings by Duccio, Honthorst, Rembrandt, Turner, and others.) In his *Faerie Queene* (2.7.61-62) Spenser depicts Pilate as a wretch in Cocytus who washes his hands incessantly, trying in vain to rid himself of his guilt. Shakespeare uses the handwashing motif three times. In *Richard 2,* 4.1.239-42 the dethroned king condemns his adversaries, equating their sin to that of Pilate. In *Richard 3,* 1.4.270-71, the Second Murderer expresses his futile desire to wash the guilt from his hands. Likewise in *Macbeth,* 5.1.26-66, Lady Macbeth is unable to wash Duncan's blood from her hands. Similarly, in a modern context, Arthur Miller's *The Crucible* (1953) has John Proctor shout at the Reverend Hale: "Pontius Pilate! God will not let you wash your hands of this!"

Pilate's question about the nature of truth (John 18:38) has been echoed by English writers such as Francis Bacon, William Blake, and Aldous Huxley. Bacon begins his first essay, "Of Truth," with " 'What is Truth?' said jesting Pilate . . ." — words which become the motto for Huxley's *Jesting Pilate: The Diary of a Journey* (1928). Blake in his *Annotations to Bacon's Essays* (ca. 1798) comments: "Rational Truth is not the Truth of Christ, but of Pilate. It is the Tree of the Knowledge of Good & Evil" (397). In *The Task* (1785) William Cowper explains:

" 'twas Pilate's question, put / To Truth itself, that deign'd him no reply" (3.270-71). In his unfinished poem "Pilate" (1862-68) Hopkins presents a Pilate tortured by his conscience, who asks himself what he had asked Christ: "And what am I?" (118). In the end he seeks redemption by crucifying himself.

Other literary allusions to Pilate are frequent. In *Of Reformation* (47) Milton justifies separation of Church and State through Christ's remark to Pilate, "My kingdom is not of this world" (John 18:36). John Greenleaf Whittier refers to Luke 23:12 (where Pilate and Herod become friends) in his antislavery poem "Clerical Oppressors" (1836), identifying the pro-slavery Southern clergy with the high priests, who are the allies of the rulers. In his poem "St. Simeon Stylites" (1842) Tennyson links Pilate with Judas Iscariot (165). In Tennyson's play *Becket* (1884) the titular hero opposes the king, exclaiming: "The Lord be judged again by Pilate? No!" (1.3). George Meredith, in "The Song of Theodolinda," calls Pilate "Damned for ever for the deed!" (st. 11), but G. B. Shaw, in the preface to *Androcles and the Lion* (1916), supports Pilate the politician, who had to consider Jesus a threat to society (*Complete Prefaces* [1965], 547; see also "On the Rocks," 359-76). In Joseph Conrad's *The Rescue* (1920) "Pilate appears in the form of the chubby and pious Shaw" (D. Purdy, *Joseph Conrad's Bible* [1984], 103). James Joyce mentions Pilate in *Ulysses* and irreverently transforms his name to Pontius Pilax in *Finnegans Wake*. In Toni Morrison's novel *The Song of Solomon* (1977) Pilate Dead, whose first name has been randomly chosen from the Bible, is the major female character. In his poem "What I Have Written I Have Written" (1981) Peter Porter defends his work with Pilate's remark concerning the inscription on the cross (John 19:22).

Pilate is the titular figure in a host of 20th-cent. English works such as Hilary D. C. Pepler's modern Passion play *Pilate* (1928) and Carlo Maria Franzero's *The Memoirs of Pontius Pilate: From the Autobiography of G. Pontius Pilate* (1947), an amusing account of Pilate's life as a civil servant, written after his governorship in Judea. Paul Luther Maier's *Pontius Pilate: A Biographical Novel* (1968) combines historical facts and rich imagination. Warren Kiefer synthesizes the mystery of archeology with Jewish persecution in the thriller *The Pontius Pilate Papers* (1976). In the first of his *Rallying Cries: Three Plays* (1977) Eric Bentley draws a parallel between Pilate's examination of Christ and the interrogation of American writers (L. Stander, A. Miller) before the House Committee on Un-American Activities. He compares their refusal to disclose names with Christ's silence (65). The third of these plays, "From the Memoirs of Pontius Pilate," reveals a Pilate who wants to keep Jesus alive, although Jesus himself has "decided" to be crucified (179). In *The Pilate Tapes* (1986), a sequence of witty poems, New Zealand's Vincent O'Sullivan places Pilate and the various people associated with him in the modern world.

Pilate provides the title, as well, for a variety of non-English texts, including: *Pilatus* (a German poem of the 12th cent. with 621 rhymed lines); Anatole France, "Le procurateur de Judée" (with the surprising conclusion that Pilate is unable to recall Jesus); Luis Coloma, *Pilatillo* (1886); Mario Soldati, *Pilato: Tre atti* (1924); Heinrich Federer, *Pilatus* (1948); Franz Theodor Csokor, "Pilatus," in his *Olymp und Golgatha* (1954); Werner Koch, *Pilatus: Erinnerungen* (1959; trans. *Pontius Pilate Reflects,* 1962); Alexander Lernet-Holenia, *Pilatus: Ein Komplex* (1967); Carlos Heitor Cony, *Pilatos: Romancé* (1974); Roger Caillois, *Ponce Pilate: Récit* (1961; trans. Charles Markmann, 1963); Jean Grosjean, *Pilate: Récit* (1983).

Traditionally Pontius Pilate plays a significant role in literature about Jesus Christ. Indeed, in the encounter between Pilate and Christ, the chief representatives of secular and divine power confront each other. The trial, which has been described in literary criticism as a "discontinuous dialogue" (D. Jasper, *The New Testament and the Literary Imagination* [1987], 45), is full of dramatic irony and has served as an endless source of literary inspiration. Sholem Asch, in his play *The Nazarene* (1939), makes Pilate's wife Claudia the daughter of Tiberius Caesar. Pilate thereby becomes the son-in-law of the emperor, the world's ruler, and structurally mirrors Jesus, the Son of God. In his novel *King Jesus* (1946) Robert Graves represents Jesus as the grandson of Herod the Great and Pilate as a pragmatic politician. When Pilate learns that Jesus refuses his claim to the worldly throne and is thus useless to him, he takes a bribe from Herod Antipas and condemns Christ. Anthony Burgess, in his *Man of Nazareth* (1979), depicts Pilate as a mundane man, averse to the priests and weary of his tasks, who ultimately realizes his guilt and shows signs of repentance. In his much-acclaimed Russian novel *The Master and Margarita* (1938) Mikhail Bulgakov stresses Pilate's responsibility for Jesus's death in an original manner and has Herod send Jesus to Pilate, who lets Caiaphas decide between Christ and Barabbas.

Pilate lives on in various place names, often associated with his legendary burial ground. Both Ruskin and Turner produce drawings of a Mt. Pilate (*Pilatusberg*) near Lucerne, Switzerland (Library ed., vol. 38. Facing 274; 6.277). A nearby lake *(Pilatussee)* was considered to be the haunted final resting place of Pilate. Sir Walter Scott relates the tale of this mountain in *Anne of Geierstein* (chap. 1). A second Mt. Pilate is situated in the Rhaetian Alps, a third in the Apennines, and yet another in the Cévennes. (Etymologists contend that these names are corruptions of *pileatus,* meaning "cloud-capped.") Pilate is also thought to be buried in Vienne, in the Rhone valley.

Critical and literary representations of Pontius Pilate comprise the whole gamut of characterizations: he has been depicted as a sly and effective politician, a ruthless but reliable soldier, a skeptic and a cynic, an able yet corrupt administrator, a well-meaning but vacillating judge, both the adversary and an instrument of God, a devil and a saint — or simply an imperfect man. For Christians who profess the Creed, however, it matters only that Jesus Christ "suffered under Pontius Pilate."

See also CAIAPHAS AND ANNAS; *ECCE HOMO;* PILATE'S WIFE; SEAMLESS COAT.

Bibliography. Brandon, S. "Pontius Pilate in History and Legend." *History Today* 18 (1968), 523-30; Brawer, R. "The Characterization of Pilate in the York Cycle Play." *SP* 69 (1972), 289-303; Kim, H., ed. *The Gospel of Nicodemus* (1973); Maltman, Sister N. "Pilate —*os malleatoris."* *Speculum* 36 (1961), 308-11; Martin, H. "The Legend of Pontius Pilate." *Amsterdamer Beiträge zur älteren Germanistik* 5 (1973), 95-118; Stoephasius, R. von. *Die Gestalt des Pilatus in den mittelalterlichen Passionsspielen* (1938); Williams, A. *The Characterization of Pilate in the Towneley Plays* (1950).   PETER GROTH

POOR IN SPIRIT   See BEATITUDES.

POOR WITH YOU ALWAYS   In Matt. 26:6-14, after an unnamed woman (identified in John's account as Mary, sister of Martha and Lazarus [John 12:1-10]) had poured out a costly ointment, using it to anoint Jesus' head, the disciples rebuked her, saying that the ointment might have been sold and the money given to the poor (cf. Mark 14:3-10). Jesus defended her gesture, saying, "Why trouble ye the woman? For she hath wrought a good work upon me. For ye have the poor always with you; but me ye have not always. For in that she hath poured this ointment on my body, she did it for my burial. Verily I say unto you, Wheresoever this gospel shall be preached in the whole world, there shall also this, that this woman hath done, be told for a memorial of her." In both Matthew's and Mark's accounts, Judas's anger at this response prompted his going immediately to the chief priests to offer to betray Jesus.

In classical Greek two terms are used to designate the poor: *penēs,* the working poor who own little or no property, and *ptōchos,* the beggar or destitute who is totally dependent upon others for survival. While the LXX uses both terms to translate the various Hebrew words, the NT uses *ptōchos* in all but two instances (2 Cor. 9:9 uses *penēs* in a quotation of Ps. 112:9; and Luke 21:2 describes the poor widow who offered her "two mites" as *penichros).* In the NT the term *ptōchos* refers to both the person entrapped by the consequences of sin (Luke 4:18; 6:20; 7:22) and those who are the politically or economically downtrodden. In this latter broad sense, Jesus is said to be anointed by the Spirit "to preach good news to the poor" (Heb. 4:18), who are also the "captives," the "blind," and the "oppressed" (Luke 7:22; Matt. 11:15), recalling OT prophecies of messianic liberation (cf. Isa. 61:1ff.; Lev. 25; Deut. 15). Such expectations apparently contributed to Judas's growing anger as he realized the degree to which the "kingdom" announced by Jesus was to be, pro tem, a spiritual kingdom rather

than a political utopia. Care of the poor was a cardinal point in the ethics commanded in Mosaic law (Lev. 25:38, 42, 55; Deut. 25:18, 22). According to Ezekiel, Sodom was condemned not only for its sexual immorality but also because it "did not aid the poor and the needy" (16:49). By contrast, those who distribute freely and give to the poor will endure forever (Ps. 112:9; cf. Deut. 24:13).

What then does Jesus, who had earlier been at pains to encourage the rich young ruler to divest himself and distribute all to the poor (Luke 18:18-30), and who received as authentic the repentance of a tax collector who resolved to give half his goods to the poor (Luke 19:8), mean in this exchange? For most commentators, his phrase "the poor ye have always with you" should be seen in the light of firm Mosaic commitment to assist the poor, who are always to be found because of human sin. The ideal state, when "there shall be no poor among you" (Deut. 15:4), was to come to pass "only if thou hearken unto the voice of the LORD thy God, to observe to do all these commandments which I command thee this day" (v. 5). But as long as the people do not obey, "the poor shall never cease out of the land" (v. 11). Poverty is therefore a continuing axiomatic condition of the sinful world. And those who are obedient will always have ample opportunity to fulfill their obligations by ministering to the poor until poverty, like other products of sin, vanishes under God's judgment. Mary's action is thus seen as an extravagant exception which proves the rule: in a kind of celestial irony, she contributes to the preparation for Jesus' atoning death (Matt. 26:12; Mark 14:8), even as in diabolical irony Judas prepares for the triumph that death will achieve in making the ultimate kingdom possible.

The account in John, which identifies the woman as Mary, has her anointing Jesus' feet with her hair, and it undercuts any possible moral validity in Judas's reaction by pointing out that his motives, as treasurer, were in fact pecuniary and corrupt (v. 6). St. Augustine reconciles the accounts by seeing them as describing two separate incidents, since Judas is not in John's Gospel made to run out to the chief priests, but believes the woman was in both instances Mary (*De consensu evangelistarum,* 79.154-55). He sees her actions as exemplary of devotion, and while "good are the ministrations done to the poor, and especially the due services and the religious offices done to the saints of God" (*Sermo,* 103.5), he nevertheless inclines to an analogy suggested by the Martha/Mary incident in Luke 10, to aver that "Mary hath chosen that better part." This analogy has been reiterated by many later commentators.

Calvin observes that "Christ's defense of the anointing is not for our imitation but to teach us the reason for its earning favor." In a rejection of Catholic tendencies to see in Mary's extravagance a precedent for "incense, candles, splendour in vestment, and like ceremonial" (cf. *Glossa*

Ordinaria [PL 114.167]), he insists on the exceptional nature of the incident:

> Since he says the poor will always be in the world he is distinguishing between the daily services whose practice should flourish among the faithful, and the exceptional which ceased at his ascension into heaven. Do we want to lay out our money on true sacrifices? Let us expend it upon the poor: for Christ says that he is not with us, to receive the service of external ceremonies. (*Harmony of the Gospels*, 3.123)

Matthew Henry takes a strikingly different view, seeing the anointing "as an act of faith in our Lord Jesus, the Christ, the Messiah, the anointed," and her action as exemplary for all those who would make Christ King over their own hearts. "When there is true love in the heart to Jesus Christ, nothing will be thought too good, no, nor good enough, to bestow upon him." He cites Deut. 15:11 to observe that we cannot help but "see some in this world who call for our charitable assistance"; nevertheless, "sometimes special works of piety and devotion should take the place of common works of charity" (*Comm.* 5.385-86).

In English literature the passage generally excites less controversy than it does among the theologians; George Herbert refers matter-of-factly to the "poor box," a common feature of churches of the day ("Praise"; *A Priest to the Temple*) and, as in Cowper's "Charity," it is generally held by English poets that "to smite the poor is treason against God" (217). On the other hand, Jesus' words provide a caution for Cowper against misestimation of the high place of charity among Christian obligations:

> Some seek, when queasy conscience has its qualms,
> To lull the painful malady with alms;
> But charity, not feigned, intends alone
> Another's good — their centres in their own;
> And too short liv'd to reach the realms of peace,
> Must cease for ever when the poor shall cease.
> ("Charity," 447-52)

In *Walden* Thoreau observes that in America the tables have been turned and one of the burdens of his readers is that of owning superfluous property: "What mean ye by saying that the poor ye have always with you. . . ?" He then quotes Ezekiel (18:3) and alludes to Jeremiah (31:29) that "ye shall not have occasion any more to use this proverb in Israel." In Longfellow's *Evangeline,* however, the emphasis falls upon continuing obligation to the poor: the humble almshouse surrounded by the city's splendor has walls which "seem to echo / Softly the words of the Lord: — 'The / poor ye have always with you'" (2.5). The phrase, lifted out of context, as in a Depression era union song or the rhetoric of the Fabian socialists at the turn of the century (cf. G. B. Shaw's *Major Barbara*), becomes an attack on the instability of Christian commitment to really solving "once and for all" the "problem of poverty." Dickens anticipates this use of the phrase in *Our*

Mutual Friend. Podsnap, whose perversion of Christianity includes a red-letter edition of "the Gospel according to Podsnappery" (3.8), appropriates Jesus' words (1.11) to put down "the meek man" (i.e., citizen of the kingdom of heaven) who has dared to suggest that something may possibly be wrong with the economic system. When Podsnap insists that "Providence has declared," says Dickens's narrator, he is merely using an "absurd and irreverent conventional phrase," to declare what he himself means and wants.

See also SCRIP AND STAFF.

Bibliography. Larson, J. L. *Dickens and the Broken Scripture* (1985); Lynch, C. J., O.F.M., ed. *A Poor Man's Legacy: An Anthology of Franciscan Poverty* (1989).

POTIPHAR *See* ASENATH; JOSEPH THE PATRIARCH.

POTIPHAR'S WIFE The story of Joseph and Potiphar's wife is found in Gen. 39:7-20. Potiphar, an Egyptian official, bought Joseph from the Midianites to whom he had been sold by his brothers in a jealous rage (Gen. 37:28, 36). Potiphar made him an overseer of his house and finally left all he had in Joseph's hand (v. 6). When Potiphar's wife "cast her eyes upon" the young slave and tried to seduce him, he fled, leaving his garment in her hand. She then slandered him (claiming that he had tried to rape her), and consequently her husband cast Joseph into prison. This incident is alluded to in Jub. 39 and in the Testament of Joseph (in The Testaments of the Twelve Patriarchs), where it becomes the basis of an extended exhortation to chastity. These and other extracanonical Jewish sources provide elaborate embellishment of the temptation scene as well as dramatic heightening: Joseph is made to feel, if only fleetingly, a sinful passion for his mistress (see Ginzberg, *LJ* 2.53-54).

Tertullian, one of the earliest Christian commentators, mistakenly makes Potiphar's wife the queen of Egypt (*Ad nationes,* 1.8). St. Jerome, in *Ep.* 48.4, uses the incident to exemplify the truth of 1 Cor. 7:1 ("It is good for a man not to touch a woman") and repeatedly refers to Joseph's coat as symbolizing a possession which has to be left behind (e.g., *Ep.* 118.4). In distinguishing various kinds of temptation, St. Augustine says that Joseph "was tempted with the allurement of debauchery, but he was not brought into temptation" (*De sermone Domini in Monte,* 2.10.32). The Venerable Bede offers a typological interpretation which sees Joseph as a type of Christ and Potiphar's wife as a type of the Jewish Synagogue. Rather than relinquishing his claim to divinity and thus committing "adultery" with the doctrines of scribes and Pharisees, Christ left his life in their hands like a coat (*Comm. in Pentateuchum*). A return to a mainly ethical interpretation of the story can be found in Calvin, for whom it is both a warning against the "lust of the eyes" and a praise of a man's good conscience before God (*Comm. on Genesis*).

The story was included in the Koran (where in the 12th sura the woman's name is identified as "Suleika"), and has had a prominent place in world literature. It occurs, e.g., in Persian epos (Firdausi, *Yūsuf o Zuleichā* [1009]), Spanish drama (Lope de Vega, *Los trabajos de Jacob*), German novel (Philip von Zesen, *Assenat* [1670]), and German drama (Christian Weise, *Der keusche Joseph* [1690]). Goethe's *West-östlicher Divan* uses only the names of Jussuf and Suleika, but Hugo von Hofmannsthal (*Josephs Legende* [1914]) and Thomas Mann (*Joseph in Ägypten* [1943]) return to the story proper.

ME treatments of the Potiphar story tend both to alter and embroider it. The 13th-cent. poem *Iacob and Iosep,* e.g., repeats Tertullian's mistake: instead of Potiphar's wife, it is the Queen of Egypt who tries to seduce Joseph, while Pharaoh is hunting. Ranulph Higden's *Polychronicon* makes Potiphar a homosexual, while the 14th-cent. Northumbrian poem *Cursor Mundi* dwells primarily upon an aspect of the story deriving from extrabiblical legend: in a long passage (4265-4416), Potiphar's wife is made to illustrate the pains of love. Other variations can be found in versifications such as William Forrest's *The History of Joseph the Chaiste* (1569).

In the 17th cent. the story is frequently used as an illustration of the virtue of chastity. Bunyan, in *The Life and Death of Mr. Badman* (chap. 4), contrasts Joseph's behavior with that of Mr. Badman and his fellows. He goes on to state that many women are made "whores," like Potiphar's wife, "by the flatteries of Badman's fellows" and even by promises of marriage. In *Pilgrim's Progress,* Potiphar's wife turns up in the allegorical figure Wanton, who tries to seduce Christian's companion Faithful. He recognizes her hypocrisy in many who "cry out against sin in the Pulpit, . . . yet can abide it well enough in the heart, and house, and conversation." Christiana's son Joseph is exhorted to be like his OT namesake — "Chast, and one that flies from Temptation."

Laurence Sterne tells the story of the "shameless woman" in order to "recommend chastity as the noblest male qualification." ". . . the malice and falsehood of the disappointed woman naturally arose on that occasion, and there is but a short step from the practice of virtue, to the hatred of it" (*Guardian,* no. 45). Potiphar's wife turns up in Henry Fielding's *Joseph Andrews* (1.5), in the character of Lady Booby, who unsuccessfully attempts to seduce her young servant. Having proved himself to be a model of chastity, he is called Joseph, after his biblical namesake, throughout the remainder of the novel. Joseph's chastity is also alluded to by Surface in Sheridan's *School for Scandal,* when he tries to protect Lady Teazle (hidden behind a screen in his room) from her husband. He pretends that he is a rogue and the hidden person a French girl: ". . . tho' I hold a man of Intrigue to be a most despicable Character — yet you know it doesn't follow that one is to be an absolute Joseph either" (4.3). Byron refers to the story in a similarly piquant situation

of his *Don Juan* (1.186), and other allusions to "Dame Potiphar" are made in Sir Walter Scott's novel *Woodstock* (chap. 25), and in Anthony Trollope's *The Last Chronicle of Barset* (chap. 51). Keats calls Fame a "Gipsey" and a "Sister-in-law to jealous Potiphar," referring to her fickleness ("On Fame").

The garment left behind by Joseph plays both a real and a figurative role in a number of 19th-cent. works. William Blake repeatedly describes Joseph's many-colored coat as being stripped off by women, evidently in reminiscence of the incident with Potiphar's wife. Emerson admonishes his readers in his essay "Self-Reliance" not to rely on their memories but on the present: "Leave your theory, as Joseph his coat in the hand of the harlot, and flee." In "Hippolytus Veiled," Walter Pater echoes the biblical tale when he causes Hippolytus to flee from Phaedra's seductive advances, "his vesture remaining in her hands." When the husband returns suddenly, she tells him a false story "of violence to her bed," and he believes her.

In a passage of good-humored narrative irony in Herman Melville's *Redburn* (chap. 17) the pious black cook Thompson uses the story to admonish the ship's steward, a "sad profligate and gay deceiver ashore." In modern American literature Saul Bellow makes the account of Potiphar's wife the object of a Hebrew lesson in one of Moses Herzog's *heder* reminiscences (*Herzog,* Viking ed., 131).

See also ASENATH; JOSEPH THE PATRIARCH.

Bibliography. Damon, S. F. *A Blake Dictionary: The Ideas and Symbols of William Blake* (1965), 224; Frenzel, E. *Stoffe der Weltliteratur: Ein Lexikon dichtungsgeschichtlicher Längsschnitte,* 4th ed. (1976), 365-68; Yohannan, J. D., ed. *Joseph and Potiphar's Wife in World Literature* (1968).

MANFRED SIEBALD

POTTER'S FIELD *See* FIELD OF BLOOD.

POWER OF THE KEYS *See* CONFESSION; PETER.

PRAYER In the largest sense, to pray (Lat. *precari;* OF *preier,* "to request earnestly") is to address thoughts or words to God (e.g., Gen. 4:26). In the Bible prayer takes many forms: petition for one's own needs (e.g., 1 Kings 3:4-15), intercession for the needs of others (Exod. 32:11-14; John 17), confession and repentance (Ps. 51), vows (Gen. 28:20-22), thanksgiving and praise (2 Sam. 7:18-29; Pss. 104, 145), and thought or meditation, an application of the mind to the "things of God," carried on as if in his presence (Ps. 42). Even the "groans" of Christian believers are said to be accepted as prayers through the intercession of the Holy Spirit (Rom. 8:26-27). Doctrinal statements on prayer in its various biblical forms may be found in 1 Kings 8:27-53; Isa. 56:6-8; Matt. 6:5-15; 7:7-12; John 14:13-14; Eph. 6:18; Phil. 4:6-7. Examples of individual prayers occur in Gen. 24:12-15; 32:10-13;

Exod. 32:11-13; 1 Sam. 2:1-10; Pss. 17, 86, 90, and elsewhere in the Hebrew Scriptures.

Daniel prayed thrice daily (Dan. 6:10), apparently an ancient Jewish custom, as in the convention of the Second Temple Period in which the Great Assembly established morning recitation *(Shaharit),* afternoon *(Minah)* — corresponding to the time of daily sacrifice — and evening *(Ma'arib),* with an additional prayer *(Musap)* for Sabbaths and festivals normally requiring an additional sacrifice. The original version of daily prayer includes the Eighteen Benedictions *(Shemoneh 'Esreh).* Prayer substitutes for sacrifice since the destruction of the Temple, but includes always petitions for the rebuilding of the Temple and renewal of the daily sacrifice. From ancient times, therefore, the custom has been to turn toward Jerusalem while praying; in Jerusalem itself one turns toward the Temple mount. The *Shema* and its blessings are later additions to the three daily prayers, and also to the *al ha-mittah,* a personal prayer before falling asleep (Bera. 46). After the later Middle Ages the *Shema* came to form the conclusion of the Day of Atonement service. Contemporary books of prayer *(Siddur Tepillah)* vary slightly according to regional traditions (e.g., Ashkenazi, Sephardi), while in England and America Reformed (and some Conservative) prayer books include prayers in the vernacular. Recitation of certain prayers of the Siddur (e.g., Qedushah, after the third petition of the Eighteen Benedictions, and the Qaddish, the consecration doxology) may only be used in public worship, requiring a *minyan* (ten adult Jewish males) for congregational response.

In Christian tradition from earliest times there has been a similar allocation of prayers to public and private use, but no comparable minimum number required for recitation. Thus, an entire Eucharist may be celebrated with the celebrant (priest) alone present. Moreover, informal prayer receives proportionately greater emphasis. Discussion of prayer in the early Church evinces much concern for what might be termed the "ethics" of prayer, and distinctions between immature and mature prayer are a frequent preoccupation. Among the Fathers of the Church, prayer was considered to involve an intrinsic elevation of the mind in which state it becomes more clear what is proper to request and what is not (Origen, *On Prayer;* St. John of Damascus, *De fide,* 3.24 [PG 94.1090]). In a mature life of faith, prayer is communing or talking with God (St. Gregory of Nyssa, *On Praying to God* [PG 44.1125]; St. John Chrysostom, *Hom. on Genesis,* 30.5 [PG 53.280]), and perhaps the best-known book from the early Middle Ages, St. Augustine's *Confessiones,* is composed as such a conversational prayer, in which to Augustine's queries and requests the "answers" of God are in the form of quotations from Scripture (the *Proslogion* of St. Anselm is likewise written in the form of prayer). As Augustine's influential book makes clear, prayer by definition is an acknowledgment of the

petitioner's mortal neediness and dependency upon God, even for self-knowledge. By inference, those who believe themselves to be entirely self-sufficient do not pray. Yet prayer is not simply a mechanism, or reducible to technique: St. Ambrose observes that "although God is merciful, yet if he always responded completely, he would appear to act no longer of his own free will, but by a kind of necessity. In that case, since all ask for it, if he were to respond to everyone, no one would die" *(De excessu fratris Satyri,* 1.65).

From the establishment of the English church in the 6th cent. until the Protestant Reformation of the 16th cent. English devotional life was guided by the Roman liturgy read each day in the churches and monasteries and by two sorts of prayer books used in the home: Psalters and Books of Hours (or "primers"). Psalters typically contained biblical Psalms, the Lord's Prayer, and various traditional medieval prayers. Primers contained similar selections but added collections of prayers read at set hours in the monasteries, notably the Office of the Blessed Virgin and the Office of the Dead.

A rich and various theology of prayer was developed in monastic communities of the Middle Ages, and in the 12th cent. this is particularly evident in the writings of the Cistercians. According to the English Abbot, Aelred of Rievaulx (d. 1167), since persons can never find true happiness within themselves, prayer is ordained as a means of expressing desire for something better which can only come from without. Yet effective prayer can only proceed from a heart which lives in the righteousness of charity (cf. James 5:16). Charitable prayer requests only that which we are "permitted to have" *(Speculum Caritas,* 8.1), but since it is God's will that all our needs, which he knows best (and not necessarily our own less reliable desires), be met in an outpouring of his love, we may pray in confidence. In his litany "Pastoral Prayer," Aelred sees prayer, and exemplary encouragement in prayer, to be a foremost duty of a pastor toward his flock *(Oratio Pastoralis;* cf. Anselm's *Oratio,* on some of which Aelred has drawn). The 14th-cent. Augustinian canon Walter Hilton writes in his *Ladder of Perfection,* in much the same vein, that

> prayer is a most profitable and expedient means of obtaining purity of heart, the eradication of sin, and receptiveness to virtue. Not that you should imagine that the purpose of your prayer is to tell the Lord what you want, for He knows well enough what you need. Rather the purpose of prayer is to make you ready and able to receive as a clean vessel the grace that our Lord would freely give you. (bk. 1)

Hilton's treatise is practical, dividing prayer into "common" prayer, or the vocal, preestablished prayers of public and private worship; "personal" prayer, or spontaneous, vocal conversational prayer as prompted by the Spirit in private devotion; and silent personal prayer. Like

Aelred, Hilton relates the relative virtue of prayer to totality of commitment of the praying heart, in charity, to God. For Wycliffite writers of the late 14th and 15th cents. as for Franciscan and Dominican preachers after the 13th cent. (cf. *Speculum Christiani; Fasciculus Morum*), the Paternoster or Lord's Prayer illustrates in its various petitions the particular virtues which ought to pertain to any prayer, as well as the way in which prayer should relate to practical moral action (Jeffrey, 102-06). Prayer in ME literature shows the influence of such treatises on prayer directly. In Chaucer's *Knight's Tale,* part of the structure and thematic symmetry of the narrative is achieved by the reader's relating the spirit and formulation of prayers by Palamon (to Venus), Arcite (to Mars), and Emelye (to Diana) to each other and to their apparent answers. In Chaucer's *Second Nun's Tale,* the narrator begins with an *Invocatio ad Mariam,* which helps define for the reader the nun's charitable "entente" in her tale of St. Cecelia. The 14th-cent. alliterative poem *St. Erkenwald* is thematically devoted to the subject of prayer, demonstrating the efficacy of charitable prayer as a direct mediation of redeeming grace.

Until the later Middle Ages the need for prayer books was largely met by the Latin liturgy and by the vernacular Psalters and primers (e.g., Archbishop Thoresby's *Lay Folks' Mass Book* in the 14th cent.). When the English Reformation began during the reign of Henry VIII, however, liturgical and devotional works had to be made to conform to Protestant doctrine and changes in some aspects of worship. In general the Reformers' aim was to adhere to biblical models and teachings and to prune away what they saw as unscriptural material in the Roman Catholic prayer books. In particular, they abolished prayers to the saints, prayers for the dead, the use of Latin in the liturgy, and mystical forms of prayer favored in the monasteries. One of the longest chapters in Calvin's *Institutes* (3.20) concerns prayer, and while many traditional precepts are to be found in his discussion, a central section is devoted to his assertion that prayer may be legitimately offered in the name of Christ alone, and that intercession in the name of saints is impiety (17-27).

Prayers to the saints were rejected by Calvin, Tyndale, and even Erasmus on scriptural grounds. Catholic theologians argued that, although only God could answer prayers, petitions might be offered to the Virgin Mary or to other canonized saints, who could then intercede with God to grant the petitions (see the analogous case in 2 Macc. 15:12-14). Support for this view was found in Rev. 5:8 and 8:3-5 where "prayers of the saints" are described as "odors" which rise with incense before the throne of God. Protestants rejected such an interpretation, generally arguing that the word *saint* refers to any believer, not just to the saints of Catholic tradition, and that the Bible contains no precedent for prayers to persons other than God the Father and God the Son. According to Protestant theology, Christ is the only true mediator be-

tween God and humanity (see Heb. 7-9; Rom. 8:34; 1 John 2:1).

The English Protestants were also eager to eliminate prayers for the dead. According to Catholic doctrine, souls of the dead must pass through Purgatory if they die in the state of grace without having made full satisfaction for their sins. The intercessions of the living, however, avail with God to ease the painful process of purgation. Protestant theologians argued that biblical evidence for such prayers is weak (see 2 Macc. 12:44; 1 Cor. 15:29; 2 Tim. 1:18) and that the entire doctrine of Purgatory is unscriptural.

Besides such theological disputes, there were also controversies over practical matters of pastoral care and worship. Protestants argued that Roman prayer books did not fulfill Christ's command "Feed my sheep" or Paul's admonition that people pray with understanding (1 Cor. 14:15-19). The Latin liturgy was in fact inaccessible to most English-speaking laity, and the Books of Hours were better suited to monks than to ordinary working people, who found it difficult to pray at the appointed hours. It was also argued, less convincingly, that the otherworldly emphasis of many of the prayers in the primers went against the Protestant stress on temporal concerns and service in the world (see, e.g., Hugh Latimer's *On Prayer* [ca. 1530]). The result was a shift in perception or emphasis within a tradition in many other respects continuous.

Spenser's horatorical prayer in *Amoretti,* 68, e.g., is not merely for eternal life, but for the enabling gift of love: "So let us love, deare love, lyke as we ought, / Love is the lesson which the Lord us taught." Pre-fallen Adam's prayer in Milton's *Paradise Lost* praises God for his handiwork in creation and seeks to participate in creation's good in practical terms (5.153-208). Shakespeare's Portia in *The Merchant of Venice* says, "We do pray for mercy; / And that same prayer doth teach us all to render / The deeds of mercy" (4.1.200-202). Failure in prayer, because "words fly up" while "thoughts remain below," is dramatized in the attempt of Claudius to pray in *Hamlet* (3.3), a clear illustration of James 5:16 by its converse.

In 1549 Thomas Cranmer, Archbishop of Canterbury under Henry VIII and Edward VI, supervised the creation of a revised English liturgy. The work, entitled the *Book of Common Prayer,* was based on a version of the Roman liturgy, the Use of Sarum, but the English text was shortened and greatly simplified. It omitted all prayers to the saints and prayers for the dead; it left out several entire services (notably the consecration of church property and last rites for the dying); it greatly simplified symbolic ritual and changed key passages to accord with Reformed theology, especially the teachings on the Eucharist. The richly descriptive emotional style of many medieval prayers was set aside in favor of a resonant yet restrained style deemed more appropriate for the practical and sober form of worship approved by the Reformers. This is particularly evident in the 1552 revision.

Although the *Book of Common Prayer* soon gained popularity as a family prayer book as well as a national liturgy, it did not entirely satisfy the demand that every devotional books. The Protestants taught that every believer is a priest and the home a temple of worship, and, in consequence, family devotional manuals became exceptionally popular. More than eighty such works were published in the reign of Queen Elizabeth, and the demand remained strong until late in the 17th cent.

Early in Elizabeth's reign, there was also a vogue for collections of biblical prayers, especially new translations of the Psalms. In 1562 Thomas Sternhold and John Hopkins published a verse translation of the entire Psalter which was subsequently bound with the *Book of Common Prayer* and so attained wide and lasting influence. The best-known Psalms in the collection were set to simple tunes, and their success helped to encourage the production of other similar volumes. The most important example for students of literature is the verse Psalter of Sir Philip Sidney and his sister, the Countess of Pembroke.

Along with new translations of biblical prayers appeared a variety of devotional manuals which helped to reform the popular conception of prayer. Whereas medieval Catholic prayer books reflected the concerns of the *via contemplativa,* the new Protestant works concentrated upon involvement in the world; and whereas Catholic prayers tended to be universal, emphasizing concerns common to all Christians in all circumstances, Protestant prayers tended to be increasingly personal and occasional. For example, the volume *Foure Birds of Noahs Ark* (1609) by the playwright Thomas Dekker provides specific prayers for schoolboys, seamen, and even galley slaves.

Many of the most accomplished devotional writers of the English Renaissance wrote in the Protestant tradition, and their prayers reflect the Reformers' habitual reliance upon biblical authority. Richard Crashaw's *Sacred Poems,* however, offer in the work of a convert to Catholicism a reflection of both traditional and Counter-Reformation piety. His prayer-poems for "The Office of the Holy Cross" conclude each of the offices, from Matins to Compline, with a prayer, "O, my Lord Jesu Christ, Son of the living God! interpose I pray Thee, Thine own precious death, Thy Cross and Passion, betwixt my soul and Thy judgment, now and in the hour of my death. . . ." The influential prose writers Lancelot Andrewes and Jeremy Taylor were humanists who drew extensively from ancient and medieval sources, yet their principal text was the Bible. Andrewes, the chief translator of the Pentateuch in the Authorized Version, was one of the most learned biblical scholars of his age. His personal prayer book, *Preces Privatae* (trans. from Greek and Latin, 1675), begins with a list of biblical verses directing when, where, and how prayers are to be offered. The prayers themselves are interwoven with scriptural allusions and follow biblical forms: confession and penitence, supplication and intercession, thanksgiving and praise.

The prayers in Jeremy Taylor's books on Christian conduct likewise draw heavily upon scriptural texts. In fact, a number of them are simply medleys of verses from the Psalms. Taylor did not, however, confine himself to biblical forms. Several of the prayers in *Holy Living* (1650) follow the Protestant vogue for occasional prayers suited to people in various walks of life, e.g., "A Prayer to be said by merchants, tradesmen, and handicraftsmen." Those in *Holy Dying* (1651) follow a tradition of Protestant deathbed devotions which goes back to William Perkins's *Salve for a Sicke Man* (1585). Evident in his writings is a boundless confidence in the efficacy of prayer:

> Since prayer can obtain every thing, it can open the windows of heaven and shut the gates of hell; it can put a holy constraint upon God, and detain an Angel till he leave a blessing; it can open the treasures of rain, and soften the iron ribs of rocks, till they melt into tears and a flowing river; prayer can unclasp the girdles of the North, saying to a mountain of ice; be thou removed hence, and cast into the bottom of the Sea; it can arrest the Sun in the midst of his course, and send the swift winged winds upon our errand; and all those strange things and secret decrees and unrevealed transactions which are above the clouds and far beyond the regions of the starrs shall combine in ministery and advantages for the praying man: it cannot be but we should feel lesse evil, and much more good then we do, if our prayers were right. (*The Worthy Communicant* [1660], 160)

Prayers in the lyric poetry of the period also combine biblical materials with other influences, most notably the techniques of meditation developed by Catholic writers of the Counter-Reformation (see L. Martz, *The Poetry of Meditation* [1954]). For instance, the verse prayers of John Donne, George Herbert, and Henry Vaughan often take the form of a Catholic meditation, but they are typically Protestant in theology (Donne's "La Corona" may be an exception) and frequently biblical in inspiration. Donne's Holy Sonnets (1633) and prose *Devotions* (1624) deal with inner struggles against doubt and adversity reminiscent of many of the Psalms. Theologically, they explore Pauline doctrines central to Protestant piety: sin, the cross, election, faith, and the steps of salvation, though like his sermons they draw on commentary and exegesis as (apparently) diverse as that of the Jesuit Cornelius à Lapide and the Calvinist Theodore Beza.

George Herbert's *The Temple* (1633) and Henry Vaughan's *Silex Scintillans* (1650) frequently deal with these central doctrines, but they depend upon other biblical material as well. Herbert's central concern is with the Church as the body of Christ and the temple of the Holy Spirit. Accordingly, his verse prayers contain a good deal of biblical typology; i.e., they treat the life of the poet as a type of the life of Christ, and they present passages in the OT as foreshadowings of the NT revelations about Christ and the Church. A similar use of typology appears in Henry Vaughan's writing (e.g., "Ascension Day"), but there the emphasis is on the solitary relationship between the believer and God, not on the communion of believers in the Church.

Herbert's "Prayer (1)" is an apostrophe:

> Prayer the Churches banquet, Angels age,
>   Gods breath in man returning to his birth,
>   The soul in paraphrase, heart in pilgrimage,
> The Christian plummet sounding heav'n and earth;
> Engine against th'Almightie, sinners towre,
>   Reversed thunder, Christ-side-piercing spear,
>   The six-daies world transposing in an houre,
> A kinde of tune, which all things heare and fear;
> Softnesse, and peace, and joy, and love, and blisse,
>   Exalted Manna, gladnesse of the best,
>   Heaven in ordinarie, man well drest,
> The milkie way, the bird of Paradise,
>   Church-bels beyond the starres heard, the souls
>   bloud,
>   The land of spices; something understood.

In his "Prayer (2)" he reflects the sentiments of his countrymen Anselm and Aelred, that while God knows what we ask before we ask it, "We cannot ask the thing, which is not there, / Blaming the shallownesse of our request."

After the English Civil War, the vogue for devotional manuals waned and from the 18th through the 20th cents. fewer works of genuine literary importance appeared. Among the exceptions is Isaac Watts's *A Guide to Prayer* (1715), an eloquent treatment of the "gift" of prayer and a guide for those who would learn the disciplines of prayer. Prayer was a central theme in the Great Revival of the 18th cent., and some of the most enduring of English prayer-poems are hymns from the pens of Watts and Charles Wesley ("Jesu, lover of my soul," "Come, thou long expected Jesus," "Wrestling Jacob"). One of the most influential devotional manuals of the 18th cent., William Law's *A Serious Call to a Devout and Holy Life* (1728), begins by observing that:

> Devotion is neither private nor public prayer. Rather, prayers, whether private or public, are particular aspects or instances of devotion. Devotion signifies a life given, or devoted, to God.

Law also wrote *The Spirit of Prayer* (1749-50) and *The Spirit of Love* (1752-54). The fourteenth chapter of the former work is devoted to the disciplines of daily prayer. Samuel Johnson, both influenced and troubled by Law, wrote down his own *Prayers and Meditations* as an ongoing spiritual discipline of the sort Law recommended.

Among Catholic devotional manuals which had an impact in literary circles long after the English Reformation were St. John Fisher's *A Treatise on Prayer* (1640),

Richard Challoner's *Garden of the Soul* (1740), and John Henry Newman's *Meditations and Devotions* (1893). Some Protestant prayer books of the 17th cent. also retained their influence, as did the "Form of Prayer" for the Kirk in Scotland — satirized in Robert Burns's "Holy Willie's Prayer." In the 19th cent. Taylor's *Holy Living* and *Holy Dying* gained a wide audience, including literary figures such as Coleridge, Hazlitt, Lamb, Emerson, and Lowell (see *Holy Dying* [1952], ed. T. S. Kepler, xvii-xxii). Tennyson may have been thinking of Taylor's *Worthy Communicant* when he wrote the lines "More things are wrought by prayer than this world dreams of. . . ," and Law's *Spirit of Prayer* and *Spirit of Love,* read with keen interest by Coleridge, almost certainly are reflected in the suggestion at the end of *The Rime of the Ancient Mariner* that "He prayeth best who loveth best." John Henry Newman's translation of Part 1 of *Preces Privatae* helped to perpetuate the reputation of Andrewes, and the revival of metaphysical poetry early in the 20th cent. popularized once again the devotional works of Donne, Herbert, and Vaughan. These, in turn, have had their evident impact upon prayer-poems such as G. M. Hopkins's "Thee, God, I come from, to thee go" and "Thou art, indeed, just, Lord," and T. S. Eliot's *Ash-Wednesday* and Choruses from *The Rock* (though in the latter case biblical influence is more direct). Leonard Cohen's *A Book of Mercy* is a penitential cycle of Jewish prayer indebted not only to the *siddur* for Yom Kippur, but to Donne and Herbert.

Vigorous informal prayer is the basis of a sequence of A. M. Klein's *The Psalter of Avram Haktani,* while Klein's most striking formal prayer-poem is his "Stance of the Amidah," named for the first *tepillah* of the Eighteen Benedictions, prayed *amidah* ("standing"). Classic in its three-part movement from commemoration of the patriarchs and the might of God revealed in nature to praise of God for his holiness, it pleads for understanding, a penitent heart, forgiveness, redemption, healing, blessings of the harvest, ingathering of the exiles, and restoration of the judges. Klein omits the petition for sectaries, but includes those asking reward for "Thy saints Thy paupers," the rebuilding of Jerusalem, and restoration of the kingdom of David. The final movement includes a 19th petition from the Babylonian rite which becomes the priestly blessing (as at Yom Kippur) and spiritualizes the usual 17th petition for restoration of the Temple service, so that the last section (16-19) reads:

> Our prayers accept, but judge us not through our prayers: grant them with mercy.
> Make us of Thy love a sanctuary, an altar where the heart may cease from fear, and evil a burnt offering is consumed away, and good, like the fine dust of spices, an adulation of incense, rises up.
> Oh, accept, accept, accept our thanks for the day's three miracles, of dusk, of dawn, of noon, and of the years which with Thy presence are made felicitous.
> Grant us — our last petition — peace, Thine especial

blessing, which is of Thy grace and of the shining and the turning of Thy face.

Any number of examples of prayer with central thematic or structural significance in 18th- or 19th-cent. fiction could be cited, from Daniel Defoe *(Robinson Crusoe)* or Henry Fielding *(Tom Jones)* to several of the novels of Sir Walter Scott. One of the best examples of "prayer against prayer" in English fiction is afforded by Charlotte Brontë's *Jane Eyre,* where Jane, meeting the nerveless St. John Rivers after she has refused to marry him, suspects his surface piety and is confirmed by her experience in the wisdom of her decision. Gratefully, she says,

> I mounted to my chamber; locked myself in; fell on my knees; and prayed in my way — a different way to St. John's, but effective in its own fashion. I seemed to penetrate very near a Mighty Spirit; and my soul rushed out in gratitude at His feet. I rose from the thanksgiving — took a resolve — and lay down, unscared, enlightened, eager but for the daylight.

Prayer is sometimes a pivotal feature in modern narrative, as the sympathetic prayer of the Rev. Jenkins in Dylan Thomas's *Under Milk Wood* and the prayer in John Updike's "My Grandmother's Thimble" *(Pigeon Feathers)* attest. Hagar's inability to pray is a crucial moment in Margaret Laurence's *The Stone Angel,* as is Stephen's impasse in Joyce's *A Portrait of the Artist as a Young Man.*

Finally, the greatest of the Renaissance prayer books, the *Book of Common Prayer,* has, with some revision, endured as the liturgy of the Anglican and Episcopal churches and has added many familiar phrases to the English language. Until well into the 20th cent., English people in particular were expected to recognize phrases from its preface, prayers, collects, rubrics, and its (Coverdale) translation of the Psalms. Many phrases which have, indeed, a biblical "ring" to them derive from the *Book of Common Prayer.* Examples includes: "ashes to ashes, dust to dust" from the service for "Burial of the Dead" (quoted, e.g., in Irving's "The Pride of the Village" and Wolfe's *Look Homeward Angel* [chap. 37]) and "all the deceits of the world, the flesh, and the devil" from the "Litany" (quoted in C. Brontë, *Jane Eyre* [chap. 35]).

See also PATER NOSTER; SHEMA.

Bibliography. Bush, D. *English Literature in the Earlier Seventeenth Century, 1600-1660.* 2nd ed. (1962); Daniel, E. *The Prayer-Book: Its History, Language, and Contents* (26th ed. 1948); Davies, H. *Worship and Theology in England.* 5 vols. (1961-75); Jeffrey, D. L., ed. *The Law of Love: English Spirituality in the Age of Wyclif* (1988); Kelly, F. L. *Prayer in Seventeenth-Century England* (1966); Martz, L. L. *The Poetry of Meditation* (1954); Michell, G. A. *Landmarks in Liturgy* (1961); Munk, E. *The World of Prayer.* 2 vols. (1985); Warren, F. E. *Prayerbook Commentary with Complete Concordances* (1922); White, H. C. *The Tudor Books of Private Devotion* (1951).   DONALD V. STUMP

PREACHING   Preaching is not a dominant term in the OT. The Hebrew word *qarah* (Jonah 3:2) means "crier" or "herald." The other important OT term is *biśśar,* "to bring [good] news" (Ps. 40:9; Isa. 61:1), translated in the LXX as *euangelizō* ("preach" > *euangelion,* "gospel"). From the LXX translation of *qarah* as *keryssein,* "to proclaim," the NT derives another major term, "proclamation."

The most memorable preacher in the OT is Solomon's *Qohelet,* who has seemed to many readers to be primarily a bearer of bad news ("Vanity of vanities . . . all is vanity" [Eccl. 1:2]). The "preaching" of prophets such as Jeremiah and Amos often evokes a similar response. If the NT presents preaching as an important and largely positive activity, however, featuring not only major proclamations of Jesus (e.g., the Sermon on the Mount [Matt. 5–7]) but also the stirring sermons of St. Peter (Acts 2:14-40) and of St. Paul (e.g., Acts 28), it does not represent a radical departure from Jewish practice. Oral readings of Torah were central to Jewish worship. In every case for which records survive, as far back as the time of Ezra (400 B.C.), the oral text was immediately followed with an exposition of its meaning and significance: "And they read in the book, in the law of God, with interpretation," says the Hebrew text of Neh. 8:8, "and they gave the sense, so that those present understood the meaning." By the time of Jesus the Jewish community was long habituated to an order of service in which an audience for this activity was required in order for it to proceed: the Mishnah (A.D. 200) requires at least ten men as auditors. Jesus in the Temple at the age of 12, and Jesus in his first appearance in public life "preaching and teaching" (Matt. 4:17), was thus participating in a corporate rhetorical tradition with an extremely broad base — more representatively participatory than that "in any other community in the ancient world" (Murphy, *Rhetoric in the Middle Ages,* 273).

The noun *kēryx* ("herald," implying eloquence) is rare in the NT, appearing only three times. Nonetheless, the early Church increasingly revered the eloquence of various bishops whose charge it was to preach. St. Gregory the Great, St. Augustine, who in his *De doctrina Christiana* (A.D. 426) wrote the first of many *ars praedicandi,* and, most obviously, St. John of Constantinople, known as "Chrysostom" for his golden-tongued oratory, all established impressive reputations as preachers. St. Jerome deplored the adulation accorded heralds of God's word, lamenting, in the preface to his commentary on Galatians: "the simplicity and purity of apostolic language is neglected; we meet as if we were in the Athenaeum, or the lecture rooms, to kindle the applause of the bystanders; what is not required is a discourse painted and tricked out with spurious rhetorical skill . . . like a strumpet in the streets." Jerome's observation anticipates Protestant objections to the adoption of fables and unbiblical material by the preaching friars of the Middle Ages, as well as Donne's famous disclaimer, "Eloquence is not our net, only the Gospel is."

The eloquent homilies of the Fathers, especially those of Augustine and Gregory the Great, set such a high standard that for the early centuries they (and not original sermons) were read in religious communities. The Anglo-Saxon *Catholic Homilies* of Aelfric (ca. A.D. 1000), major texts in the history of English letters, were among the first of European sermons to innovate significantly for more than four hundred years. When an original preacher appeared, as in the case of St. Anselm of Canterbury, it thus created considerable excitement. Guibert of Nogent, a younger contemporary of Anselm, added to preaching theory a "Book on Making Sermons" (*Liber Quo Ordine Sermo Fieri Debeat* [PL 156.21-32]), in which he discusses the preacher's motives, principles, and spiritual attitude before preaching. The most influential development in the 12th cent. was Alain of Lille's *Ars Praedicandi* or *Art of Preaching* (ca. 1190). It heralded an explosion of manuals on preaching in the first quarter of the 13th cent.; literally hundreds of theoretical manuals appeared during the next three centuries. During this period proof of the ability to preach became a requirement for obtaining a university degree in theology, and the "university sermon" became a distinct literary genre.

Alain of Lille's text offers some useful definitions to the aspiring preacher:

> Preaching is an open and public instruction in faith and behavior, whose purpose is the forming of men; it derives from the path of reason and from the fountainhead of the 'authorities'. Preaching should be public, because it must be delivered openly. That is why Christ says: "What I say to you in your ear, preach upon the housetops." . . . Preaching is that instruction which is offered to many, in public, and for their edification. Teaching is that which is given to one or to many, to add to their knowledge. Prophecy gives warning of what is to come, through the revelation of future events. Public-speaking is the admonishing of the people to maintain the well-being of the community.

The good preacher, says Alain, will stick closely to his text, and he will avoid every temptation to indulge in mere entertainment:

> Preaching should not contain jesting words, or childish remarks, or that melodiousness and harmony which result from the use of rhythm or metrical lines; these are better fitted to delight the ear than to edify the soul. Such preaching is theatrical and full of buffoonery, and in every way to be condemned. Of such preaching the prophet says: "Your innkeepers mix water with the wine." (Trans. G. R. Evans [1981], 16-18)

Many of Alain's precepts can be found reflected in Chaucer's 14th-cent. characterization of the good Parson in his *Canterbury Tales*. Unlike the pompous Friar and huckstering Pardoner (whose texts and motives in each case are connected with money), the Parson "Christes

gospel trewely would preche" (*General Prologue,* 1.481); he eschews extraneous material: "Thou gettest fable noon ytold for me," he says, and he will not provide even the rhetorical pleasures of alliteration (*Parson's Tale,* Prologue, 10.31-44). Nor will he sow "chaff," but only wheat — his concern is with the "sentence" of his biblical text, in this case notably itself a command "to preach repentance" (Jer. 6:16). This ties the Parson's preaching, as Alain ties his guidelines, into the first "gospel" preaching of Jesus in Matt. 4:17 ("Repent, for the kingdom of heaven is at hand"): the preacher's "good news" is not pertinent unless the "bad news" which necessitates it is first clearly expressed and acknowledged. This relation of the Law's proclamation to its "hearing" or understanding and then willed obedience, the ground of all expository preaching from Ezra to the present, was thought by medieval commentators to be anticipated even in the Genesis narrative concerning Eden. Robert of Basevorn's 14th-cent. rhetorical manual *De Forma Praedicandi* observes that "after creating mankind, God preached (if we may extend our sense of the word) saying to Adam [Gen. 2:17], 'For in what day soever thou shalt eat of it, thou shalt die the death!' This was the first persuasion that we read of in Scripture."

For medieval teachers of homiletics and preachers alike, then, preaching was an activity closely circumscribed by the very texts of Scripture which commended the activity; Scripture provided the pertinent texts for exposition as well as the style of exposition, and Scripture afforded the means to judge the faithfulness of the preacher. For John Wyclif the "hermeneutic circle" in which the preacher finds himself is accordingly characterized by Scripture's distinctive grammar, logic, and rhetoric. The imposition of a rhetoric, logic, or grammar alien to the foundational text is doomed to confusion and will produce dangerous misreading. "From this," he says, seemingly echoing Chaucer's Parson, "we may infer that a Christian should speak Scripture's words on Scripture's authority in the form that Scripture itself displays" (*De Veritate Sacrae Scripturae,* 1.2; cf. his *De Officio Pastorali,* 24). The 14th-cent. English Augustinian Walter Hilton suggests that much the same test of preaching might be applied by the auditor, but adds a further litmus: some preachers, he notes, may seem to have the very words of God's truth but their extraneous, gratuitous remarks show up their preaching as "counterfeit light." "Presumption," he says, "or self-promotion, and disdain of one's fellow Christians at the same time" is clear evidence that the preaching, "even when the knowledge in itself is of the truth," is either "of the devil himself if it comes suddenly, or of the man's own wit if it comes by study" (*Ladder of Perfection,* pt. 2). The test of faithful preaching is conformity of the style of discourse to the proper subject of faithful preaching. Anything more is idolatry. Both Wyclif and Hilton were suspicious of the exalted characterization of the preacher as poet celebrated by Pierre Bersuire, in whose dictionary (*Opera Omnia,* 2.105b) the good preacher's rhetoric is characterized as like the "melodious notes of Orpheus." With Chaucer's Parson, they preferred the prose of plain speech.

Reformation preaching was rhetorically more self-conscious, and many of the issues of the later Middle Ages, including a concern that the subject of preaching remain the *euangelion,* became more controversial. The Reformers, however, were clearly possessed of explicit commitments in this regard. Luther, e.g., wrote his *The Freedom of a Christian* with an accompanying letter to Pope Leo X, and addressed the problem:

> I believe that it has now become clear that it is not enough or in any sense Christian to preach the works, life, and words of Christ as historical facts, as if the knowledge of these would suffice for the conduct of life; yet this is the fashion among those who must today be regarded as our best preachers. Far less is it sufficient for Christians to say nothing at all about Christ and to teach instead the laws of men and the decrees of the fathers. Now there are not a few who preach Christ and read about him that they may move men's affections to sympathy with Christ, to anger against the Jews, and such childish and effeminate nonsense. Rather ought Christ to be preached to the end that faith in him may be established that he may not only be Christ, but be Christ for you and me, and that what is said of him and is denoted in his name may be effectual in us. Such faith is produced and preserved in us by preaching why Christ came, what he brought and bestowed, what benefit it is to us to accept him.

Reformation preaching, often polemical and political, as well as Counter-Reformation preaching (on the Continent especially) became more and more a form of popular literature. Though Cranmer's *Homilies Appointed to Be Read in Churches* (1563) are in effect formal, catechetical treatises used in the manner early medieval churches used the homilies of Augustine, much fine, original preaching also ensued from the Reformation in England, both Anglican and Puritan. In some of this preaching eloquence could, and did, closely serve the scriptural text. For Hugh Latimer, this was especially true when a Pauline "boldness" rather than concern for "a fat benefice or bishopric" prompted the utterance: "for though a preacher be well learned, but yet lacketh that boldness, and is faint-hearted, truly he shall do but little good for all his learning. When he feareth men more than God, he is nothing to be regarded" (Sermon 27, ed. Corrie, 507; cf. Eph. 6:19-20).

Yet despite the popular preaching at Paul's Cross and the pulpit oratory of Hugh Latimer, John Donne, Lancelot Andrewes, Jeremy Taylor, or in America of Jonathan Edwards (e.g., "Sinners in the Hands of an Angry God"), preaching did not always succeed at "Informing and Inflaming," as George Herbert said it should (*A Priest to the Temple,* 257). Thus poetry, traditionally both *utile* and *dulce,* sometimes performed preaching's role: "A verse may finde him, who a sermon flies," states Herbert at the portals of *The Temple;* this line was often recalled during the 17th cent. as justification for evangelical poetry. A parallel impulse undergirds the important teaching role given to hymns in the evangelical revival of the 18th cent. Many of the great hymns of Isaac Watts, Charles Wesley, Augustus Toplady, and others are frankly catechetical, miniature sermons (which in their original versions were often of great length).

The sermons of John Wesley, Thomas Howeis, John Fletcher, and George Whitefield among the Methodists, and of Jonathan Swift, Bishop Butler, Laurence Sterne, and Archbishop Tillotson among the Anglicans, form an important part of 18th-cent. intellectual literature. John Newton's *Olney Sermons* (1767), many of which were heard and all read by William Cowper, and his two-volume series of fifty sermons, *Messiah: Or, the Scriptural Passages which Form the Subject of the Celebrated Oratorio of Handel* (1786), are typical of Newton's determination, as he says in the preface to the first volume, "to declare the whole counsel of God." Yet they were widely read and discussed as serious literature by persons who might not be expected to share Newton's enthusiasm. This pre-electronic age of powerful preaching (Whitefield could hold an open-air audience of 20,000) created for the next generation romantic stereotypes of the irresistible preacher. Some novelists cast the curate as an Orlando who, as George Eliot remarked in her comments upon the "white neckcloth" novel, enflamed the hearts of women "who can 'never forget *that* sermon'." On the other hand, Newman and Disraeli seconded the novel to a preaching function, in Newman's case on behalf of the Oxford movement, and perhaps unwittingly prompted the "liberal" fiction of Charles Kingsley.

Attitudes to preachers and preaching in literature run the gamut from Herbert's "The Windows" to Hardy's "In Church." The former insists on the reciprocity of the Word and the preacher by metaphorically equating him with stained glass, through which light must shine to be effective: "Doctrine and life, colours and light, in one / When they combine and mingle, bring / A strong regard and aw." Hardy's poem presents an adoring pupil's apprehension of her "idol" as he practices before his vestry mirror "Each pulpit gesture in deft dumb-show / That had moved the congregation so." Unreserved sympathy is rare in literary treatments of preachers and their art. Nonetheless, even as the Parson escapes Chaucer's customary irony, so Mr. Tryan, in "Janet's Repentance," one of George Eliot's *Scenes of Clerical Life,* succeeds in inspiring Janet Dempster's redemption with the evangelical fervor which the author herself repudiated. In *Adam Bede* there is a similarly positive portrait of the Methodist preacher Dinah Morris, who comforts her cousin Hetty in prison and eventually marries Adam. Ruskin, in one great breathless sentence, encourages genuine sympathy for the preacher and his legitimate task:

If once we begin to regard the preacher, whatever his faults, as a man sent with a message to us, which it is a matter of life or death whether we hear or refuse; if we look upon him as set in charge over many spirits in danger of ruin, and having allowed to him but an hour or two in the seven days to speak to them; if we make some endeavour to conceive how precious these hours ought to be to him, a small vantage on the side of God after his flock have been exposed for six days together to the full weight of the world's temptation, and he has been forced to watch the thorn and the thistle springing in their hearts, and to see what wheat had been scattered there snatched from the wayside by this wild bird and the other, and at last, when breathless and weary with the week's labour they give him this interval of imperfect and languid hearing, he has but thirty minutes to get at the separate hearts of a thousand men, to convince them of all their weaknesses, to shame them for all their sins, to warn them of all their dangers, to try by this way and that to stir the hard fastenings of those doors where the Master Himself has stood and knocked yet none opened, and to call at the openings of those dark streets where Wisdom herself hath stretched forth her hands and no man regarded, — thirty minutes to raise the dead in, — let us but once understand and feel this, and we shall look with changed eyes upon the frippery of gay furniture about the place from which the message of judgment must be delivered, which either breathes upon the dry bones that they may live, or, if ineffectual, remains recorded in condemnation, perhaps against the utterer and listener alike, but assuredly against one of them. (*Stones of Venice,* 2.2.14)

Sympathy, qualified by an acute awareness of mortal failing, emerges in Hawthorne's delineation of the Reverend Arthur Dimmesdale *(The Scarlet Letter)* who, though an eloquent preacher, is tormented by guilt for his concupiscence and hypocrisy. In a Canadian examination of the Puritan conscience, Sinclair Ross explores with muted irony the hypocrisy of Philip Bentley, an artist manqué and pharisaical philanderer whose most cherished sermon text (Josh. 24:15) is recalled in the novel's title, *As for Me and My House.*

Most depictions of sermons in literature verge on the sort of militant satire evident in Hardy's poem. The chicanery of Chaucer's Pardoner, Spenser's glance at the uneducated clergy in *Mother Hubberd's Tale,* and John Earle's character sketch of "A Young Raw Preacher" are cases in point. Like Owen Felltham's "Of Preaching," Earle's little essay, with its acerbic account of a sermon ("the labour of it is chiefly in his lungs; and the only thing he has made of it himself is the faces") helped to create the vogue for caricatured clergymen which one meets elsewhere in 17th- and 18th- cent. literature. Increasingly, the preacher becomes merely a mindless man of fashion, a medley, as Swift wrote of Dean Smedley, "Of Dullness, Pride, Conceit." Jane Austen's Collins *(Pride and Prejudice)* or Elton *(Emma)* may be the "vile creatures" Newman called them, but their preoccupation with social position and sartorial propriety is a literary commonplace.

The satirical tradition continues unabated through Browning, who sees in the "thump-thump, shriek-shriek" of the railway an analogue to the sermons of his "pastor vociferant" *(Christmas Eve,* 214-62), to Trollope's evangelical Mr. Everscreech and tractarian Dr. Middleage *(The New Zealander;* but cf. the more complex Rev. Slope in *Barchester Towers),* and to Shaw's characterization of the Reverend James Morrell as a "windbag" with "the gift of gab" *(Candida).* When preachers are not overtly cynical, as is Sinclair Lewis's Elmer Gantry, they are deluded fools like Faulkner's Hightower whose sermons are adulterated with allusions to the chivalric past *(Light in August)* or Evelyn Waugh's Mr. Tendril, who, returned from India, proffers not fear in a handful of dust, but rather a sermon quite irrelevant to his English congregation: " 'Instead of the placid ox and ass of Bethlehem . . . we have for companions the ravening tiger and the exotic camel, the furtive jackal and the ponderous elephant' " *(A Handful of Dust).*

Though satirists have derided pedantic or pointless preaching, sermons have served prominently as moral and doctrinal indices in literature. Chaucer's concluding Parson's sermon with its analysis of sin and penitence, justice and mercy, is a telling commentary on human pilgrimage, moving symbolically from the spiritual Babylon of the ale house to the figurative celestial Jerusalem of the blissful, holy martyr at Canterbury. Similarly, sect. 3 of T. S. Eliot's *The Waste Land* is "The Fire Sermon": the wisdom of Buddha, along with allusions to Ps. 137 and Augustine's *Confessiones,* furnishes an implicit assessment of the lives of those many whom death has undone. The Reverend Lawrence Sterne introduced his own sermons into *Tristram Shandy;* a signal example is the "Sermon on Good Conscience" read to Walter Shandy and Dr. Slop by Corporal Trim (2.17). In stressing the compatibility of reason and God's will, this sermon epitomizes the ethical concerns of the novel as a whole; in stressing, through the commentary on the audience, the effective import of Trim's delivery, it clarifies Sterne's general interest in the rhetorical power of the word to re-create and regenerate. Father Mapple's sermon in Melville's *Moby-Dick* has been called a "précis of the plot." Based on Jonah and Jeremiah, this sermon's prophetic conviction that necessity must be made a virtue stands at the helm of the book. The concluding consolation of Mapple's sermon dwells on "delight" and rejoicing in the midst of tragedy; so at the end of the novel the last ships sighted by the *Pequod* are significantly called *Delight* and *Rachel.* As contexts for the main action, the sermons included by Brontë in *Wuthering Heights* (Jabes Branderham's "Seventy Times Seven and the First of the Seventy-Seven") and by Joyce in *A Portrait of the Artist as a Young Man* (Father Dolan's sermon on the torments of hell) posit repressive standards against which occurs the romantic rebellion of lovers and artists, respectively.

While sermons in English literature usually tend to

enunciate a Christian position, a few writers use the device to advance philosophical propositions alien to most forms of traditional Christianity. In Yeats's play *Where There Is Nothing,* Paul Ruttledge preaches prophetically among those unready to receive him. His Blakean sermons herald the need for a wholly supernatural religion. Paul preaches on the biblical text "He ascended into heaven" and extrapolates from it a radically *contemptus mundi* exhortation: "destroy the World, and everything that has Law and Number, for where there is nothing, there is God" (4.2). This, the seminal assertion of the play, falls tragically on stony ground. Like Yeats, John Updike appropriates the sermon for his own purposes. In *A Month of Sundays,* four sermons provide the structural and conceptual substance of the novel and articulate a variety of eccentric interpretations of biblical texts which are crucial to the understanding of the novel and its protagonist's salvation. The first derives from John 8:11 ("Neither do I condemn thee") and argues sophistically that the Word, in overturning the Old Law, condones the rampant adultery which abounds in the narrative sections of the novel. The second is on miracles, and the third recognizes the presence of spiritual life even in the most depraved and desiccated of wastelands. The final sermon asserts the need not for the "antiquarian and elitist" faith of unbelieving or nominal Christianity, but rather for faith in the sanctity of the mundane and belief in the mysterious resurrection of the body. With Yeats and Updike, preaching ironically regains its original mandate of spreading "good news" to the unconverted (cf. Donald Davies, "The Evangelist," in *Brides of Reason*).

Updike's repertoire of fictional sermons also includes those of Eccles (an abbreviated form of Ecclesiastes) in *Rabbit, Run* and the Lutheran pastor's in *Of the Farm* (where it provides a key to the novel), as well as the "anti-sermon" preached by the Satan figure VanHorne in *The Witches of Eastwick.* Perhaps the most cynically telling portrait of modern American preaching, however, is Peter De Vries's *The Mackerel Plaza.* In the Rev. Mackerel's church — the first split-level church in America, called "People's Liberal" — one worships God free of the constraints of theology. Mackerel's favorite sermon proclaims that "it is the final proof of God's omnipotence that he need not exist in order to save us," a thesis which so delights his congregation that he is given "an immediate hike in pay and invited out to more dinners than he could possibly eat." Perhaps no more striking modern contrast could be imagined to the Christmas day sermon of Thomas à Becket in T. S. Eliot's *Murder in the Cathedral,* in which the beleaguered Archbishop declares to his flock that the "good news" of the gospel is inseparable from its antithesis, that which hates it in the world. Hence the joy of Christmas is juxtaposed by him with St. Stephen's martyrdom, soon to be celebrated more vividly than his congregation imagines. For Becket the power of the gospel "unto salvation" is made known in weakness, the "peace of God" in a time of crisis.

See also SERMON ON THE MOUNT.

Bibliography. Alain of Lille. *The Art of Preaching.* Trans. G. R. Evans (1981); Brown, R. M. "The Minister and Contemporary Literature." *USQR* 12 (1956), 9-20; Chapman, C. O. "Chaucer on Preachers and Preaching." *PMLA* 44 (1929), 178-85; Charland, Th.-M. *Artes Praedicandi* (1936); Daniel, W. C., ed. *Images of the Preacher in Afro-American Literature* (1981); Davies, H. *A Mirror of the Ministry in Modern Novels* (1959); Davy, M. M., ed. *Les sermons universitaires parisiens de 1230-31* (1931); Daw, M. E. "The Role of the Parson in the Literature of the Eighteenth Century." M.A. thesis, King's College, London, 1937; Gallick, S. "A Look at Chaucer and His Preachers." *Speculum* 50 (1975), 456-76; Grande, L. M. "Renegade Priests in Recent Fiction." *Catholic World* 32 (1961), 407-10; Jeager, H. "The Clergy in Modern Fiction." *CT* 4 (1960), 402-06; Keller, A. F., Jr. "The Clergyman in Recent Fiction." *Lutheran Church Quarterly* 20 (1947), 193-98; Oliver Lovesey, *The Clerical Character in George Eliot's Fiction*, English Literary Studies 53 (1991); McDonnell, L. V. "The Priest-Hero in the Modern Novel." *Catholic World* 196 (1963), 306-11; Magee, R. M. "Ambassador of God: The Preacher in Twentieth Century Southern Fiction." *DAI* 43 (1982), 1973A; Muehller, W. E. "Protestant Ministers in Modern American Novels, 1927-1958: The Search for a Role." *DA* 21 (1961), 3789; Murphy, J. J. *Rhetoric in the Middle Ages: A History of Rhetorical Theory from St. Augustine to the Renaissance* (1974), 269-356; Neider, C., ed. *Men of High Calling* (1954); Nelson, L. W. *Our Roving Bible: Tracking its Influence through English and American Life* (1945), 210-16; Nicholl, G. "The Image of the Protestant Minister in the Christian Social Novel." *CH* 37 (1968), 319-34; Packer, P. A. "The Portrayal of the Anglican Clergyman in Some Nineteenth-Century Fiction." Ph.D. diss., Durham, 1979; Pollard, A. H. *English Sermons* (1963); Smith, F. L. "Man and Minister in Recent American Fiction." *DA* 30 (1970), 1151A; Swadley, D. R. "Clerical Characters in Shakespeare's Plays." *DAI* 33 (1973), 2345A.

RONALD B. BOND
DAVID L. JEFFREY

PREDESTINATION The verb *predestine,* from which the noun is formed, comes from Lat. *praedestino,* the Vg rendering of *proorizō* (translated "predestine" in Rom. 8:29, 30; Eph. 1:5, 11, KJV; also in Acts 4:28, RSV). The thought each time is of God appointing a situation for a person, in advance. Other NT terms convey the idea of God preparing his plan of salvation: *proetoimazō,* "prepare beforehand" (Rom. 9:23; Eph. 2:10); *procheirizō,* "appoint beforehand" (Acts 3:20; 22:14); *procheirotoneō,* "choose beforehand" (Acts 10:41). *Problepō,* "foresee," signifies God foreordaining in Gal. 3:8; Heb. 11:40; so does *proginōskō,* "foreknow" (Rom. 8:29; 11:2; 1 Pet. 1:20). The same thought comes through when God is said to act in his world and fix human fortunes and destinies, according to his own "will" (nouns, *boulē,* Acts 2:23; 4:28; Eph. 1:11; Heb. 6:17; *boulēma,* Rom. 9:19; *thelēsis,* Heb. 2:4; *thelēma,* Eph. 1:5, 9, 11; verbs, *boulomai,* Heb. 6:17; James

1:18; 2 Pet. 3:9; *thelō,* Rom 9:18, 22; Col. 1:27), or his "good- pleasure" (noun, *eudokia,* Eph. 1:5, 9; Matt. 11:26; verb, *eudokeō,* Luke 12:32; 1 Cor. 1:21; Gal. 1:15; Col. 1:19).

This echoes, in soteriological connections, a basic OT conviction. The OT speaks constantly of God purposing particular things that only his power can bring to pass (cf. Ps. 139:16; Isa. 14:24-27; 19:17; 46:10-11; Jer. 49:20; Dan. 4:24-25), and emphasizes that as his power is unlimited, so his purposes are certain of fulfillment (Ps. 33:10-11; Isa. 43:13; Job 9:12; 23:13; Dan. 4:35). The Creator is Lord of every situation, directing everything toward the end for which he made it (Prov. 16:4), and determining every event, great or small, from the thoughts of kings (Prov. 21:1) and the premeditated words and deeds of all persons (Prov. 16:1, 9) to the seemingly random fall of a lot (Prov. 16:33). No task is too hard for him (Gen. 18:14; Jer. 32:17), and the idea that organized human opposition might be able to thwart him is simply absurd (Ps. 2:1-4). Isaiah, in particular, insists that God planned present and future events "long ago," "from the beginning" (Isa. 22:11, RSV; 37:26; 44:6-8; 46:10-11), and that, because it is he and no one else who rules the world, his predictions are sure to be realized (Isa. 14:24-27; 44:24–45:25). His power truly to predict seemingly incredible events proves his control of history, while the inability of the idols to foretell these things makes plain that they do not control it at all (Isa. 44:6-8; 45:21; 48:12-14).

That the Creator governs history teleologically, to fulfill a predestined plan for mankind's good, becomes clear in the OT as early as the protevangelium (Gen. 3:15) and the promise to Abraham (Gen. 12:3). The theme is pursued through prophetic pictures of messianic glory following judgment (Isa. 9:1-7; 11:1–12:6; Jer. 23:5-8; Ezek. 34:20-31; 36:22–37:28; Hos. 3:4-5; etc.), and reaches a climax in Daniel's vision of God overruling the rise and fall of pagan world-empires in order finally to establish the unending reign of the Son of Man (Dan. 7; cf. 2:31-45). The NT sees this kingdom as inaugurated (but not consummated) now, inasmuch as the risen Christ has all power at the Father's right hand (Matt. 28:18; 1 Cor. 15:25), and the book of Revelation pictures the world moving toward a day of final divine triumph, despite mounting opposition to Christ and his Church from both human and demonic sources (Rev. 18:1–22:5).

Biblically speaking, predestination refers to almighty God planning in eternity everything that he would bring about in historical time, particularly the salvation of sinners (Matt. 25:34; Eph. 1:4; 2 Tim. 1:9; 1 Pet. 1:20). The NT insists that all saving grace given to human beings in time (knowledge of the gospel, understanding of it and power to respond to it, preservation and final glory) flows from God's eternal predestination. Luke, e.g., in Acts bears striking witness to his belief, not merely that Christ

was foreordained to die, rise, and reign (Acts 2:23, 30-31; 4:27-28), but that salvation comes through prevenient grace (2:47; 11:18, 21-23; 14:25; 15:7-11; 16:14; 18:27) according to divine foreordination (13:48; 18:10).

John records Christ saying that he was sent to save all whom the Father had "given" him (John 6:37-39; 17:2, 6, 9, 24; 18:9). These are his "sheep," his "own" (John 10:14-16, 26-29; 13:1), for whom specifically he prayed (John 17:20). He undertakes to "draw" them to himself by his Spirit (John 12:32; cf. 6:44; 10:16, 27; 16:8-11); to give them eternal life in and through fellowship with himself and the Father (John 10:28; cf. 5:21; 6:40; 17:2-3; Matt. 11:27); to keep them, losing none (John 6:39; 10:28-29; cf. 17:11, 15; 18:9); to bring them to his glory (14:2-3; cf. 17:24), and raise them immortal (6:39-40; cf. 5:28-29; 11:23-26). Here it is implicit that those who enjoy salvation in Christ do so by virtue of divine grace.

St. Paul elaborates: from eternity God had a plan to save a church (Eph. 3:3-11). The plan was that lost sinners should be set right with God and adopted as his children and heirs through Christ, that they should further be renewed in his image (Eph. 1:3-6; Rom. 8:29), and that the whole company of those undergoing this renewal should grow to the fulness of Christ and eventually be made glorious as he is (Eph. 4:13; 5:25-27). Believers should rejoice in the certainty that as part of his plan God predestined them personally to share this destiny (Rom. 8:28-30; 2 Thess. 2:13; 2 Tim. 1:9), graciously choosing them with no regard for their desert and indeed in face of their foreseen ill-desert (Eph. 2:1-10). From God's sovereign predestinating choice of them flows, first, an effective calling, i.e., a summons to faith and repentance which elicits the response it seeks (cf. 1 Thess. 1:5; 2:13); then, through faith, justification, the gift of pardon and acceptance for Jesus' sake; then, the life of sanctification, which from Paul's perspective is glorification begun (2 Cor. 3:18; 2 Thess. 2:13-14); and thereafter glorification in its fulness (Rom. 8:30). Paul gives this teaching to Christians, persons who knew themselves "called," to assure them of present security and final salvation, and to make them realize the extent of their debt to God's mercy, and so lead them into great gratitude for great grace. That salvation is through predestination is thus basic to Paul's view of Christianity.

The biblical theme of predestination has, then, two focal centers. From one standpoint it belongs to the doctrine of God, affirming that whatever happens under God's sovereign providence was foreordained. In this respect it broaches problems such as the existence of evil and the suffering of the innocent. Varying conceptions of God's personhood, rationality, wisdom, goodness, freedom, foreknowledge, and power in relation to his world produce different understandings of foreordination, and issues of theodicy (is God arbitrary? is he the author of sin? are his ways justifiable?) press down on the whole discussion. Such issues are reflected in literature in a variety of ways. In *King Lear,* Gloucester argues that "As flies to wanton boys, are we to the gods; / They kill us for their sport" (4.1.38-39). *In Paradise Lost* (2.557-61), Milton writes of a group of devils who, sitting apart on a hill,

> reasoned high
> Of Providence, Foreknowledge, Will and Fate —
> Fixed fate, free will, foreknowledge absolute,
> And found no end, in wandering mazes lost.

This is satirical comment on academic discussion in Milton's own age, when, as in the later Middle Ages, much inconclusive speculation on these matters took place. In later years the doctrine of a sovereign, predestining God often yielded to angry renunciation, as, e.g., in Hardy's grim commentary at the conclusion to *Tess of the D'Urbervilles:* "Justice was done, and the President of the Immortals . . . had ended his sport with Tess."

From the other standpoint, however, biblical predestination belongs to the doctrine of grace, affirming that God saves some (not all) of a guilty, helpless, corrupt humanity, according to his own free and sovereign choice. In this context what may in one light have appeared disastrous (e.g., the Fall) can prove the necessary ground of future joy. So Milton writes of the *felix culpa:*

> O goodness infinite, goodness immense!
> That all this good of evil shall produce,
> And evil turn to good; more wonderful
> Than that by which creation first brought forth
> Light out of darkness! (*Paradise Lost,* 12.469-73)

This view raises moral and pastoral questions concerning the reality or otherwise of free will and responsibility, the causes of faith and unbelief, the importance or irrelevance of holy living and prayer, and the range and grounds of Christian assurance. Is there, as Hamlet concludes, "a divinity that shapes our ends, / Rough-hew them how we will" (5.2.10-11), or is it, as Herbert momentarily imagines in "The Collar," that "My lines and life are free; free as the road, / Loose as the wind, as large as store"?

Since both sets of questions bear on doxology and devotion together (do I honor or dishonor God by attributing everything to his predestination, including the salvation of those who are saved, myself included, and the damnation of those that are lost?), it is no wonder that they have been hotly discussed in most centuries since St. Augustine set the agenda of debate. Periodically the heat has been somewhat mitigated by voices like that of Boethius (*De Consolatione Philosophiae,* 2.m8; 3.m9; 4, pr. 6), who urged restraint of the impulse to rage against divine order, a nuancing of the Augustinian position not unlike that which appealed in the 18th cent. to Alexander Pope in his rational theodicy *An Essay on Man:*

> All Nature is but Art, unknown to thee;
> All Chance, Direction, which thou canst not see;
> All Discord, Harmony not understood;
> All partial Evil, universal Good. (1.289-92)

Pope's enlightenment naturalism, however, declared in the next couplet, reflects a very non-Boethian fatalism: "One truth is clear, 'What ever is, is RIGHT'." Such skepticism concerning rational argument on this issue is in its effect not unlike that of Milton (*PL* 8.167-84; *Samson Agonistes,* 300-323), but proceeds from a different premise. The lines of the chorus in *Samson Agonistes,* e.g., beg to be compared with the earlier lines of Samson himself, who, "eyeless in Gaza," self-remonstrates:

> Yet stay, let me not rashly call in doubt
> Divine Prediction; what if all foretold
> Had been fulfill'd but through mine own default,
> Whom have I to complain of but myself? (43-46)

Until Augustine debated the Pelagians (412-30), Christian teachers had in fact said little about predestination. Combating the fatalism of Gnostics and others, they stressed each person's free will, ability, and responsibility to do right, and the eternal significance of one's present decisions. No one disputed St. Clement of Alexandria's view of Rom. 8:29 as teaching that God's predestining of those whom he will glorify depends on his foreknowledge of what they will do. Augustine points out *(De fide et operibus)* that even Christians can be lost: the problem of predestination is here linked with the question of final perseverance (*De dono perservantiae* [PL 45.993-1027]). Augustine urged, however, that fallen human beings are morally and spiritually twisted by original sin in the direction of pride and self-assertion against God, so that they cannot choose to love, adore, and serve their Maker *(De praedestinatione sanctorum).* Therefore God must bestow the faith which issues in love, and the gift of perseverance, on anyone whom he is going to save. The foreknowledge spoken of in Rom. 8:29 is not passive precognizance but active predetermination: God in sovereign freedom, foreseeing all, chooses out of the corrupt mass of sinful humanity those whose hearts and wills he would change (*Enchiridion,* 107). Christ is central to this predestining purpose, for God first chose him to be Savior and Head and then chose particular sinners to trust in him and become his spiritual body, the flock of which he is Shepherd. Salvation, first to last, is thus the work of God, who gives to his elect what he requires of them, and knowing this is so will give proper shape to faith, love, and hope. Augustine's predestinarianism became thus a full-scale interpretation of Christian existence.

The reflections of some late medieval philosophers challenged this interpretation fundamentally enough to make it an issue of significant importance for secular literature in the 14th cent, bequeathing a legacy of both comic and serious speculation, yet defining the terms of the Reformation and modern debate. William of Occam, e.g., elaborated the basis for a distinction between absolute predestination and predestination as foreknowledge — i.e., whether predestination is an act of the will or of the intellect. Adoption of the latter view opens the way to a notion of "co-operation," by which God decides to elect because of the good works he foresees. In Occam's commentary on Lombard's *Sentences* (*1 Sent.* d.41.q.1G) he thus allows that God may require one to do one's very best to obtain saving grace. Reflecting on the conversion of St. Paul and the grace accorded the Virgin Mary (which he finds not to be on the basis of merit, though other cases for him do involve merit), Occam concludes that God predetermines some with cause and some without. Thomas Bradwardine, the 14th-cent. bishop (and, briefly, Archbishop of Canterbury) takes the strict form of the doctrine of absolute predestination *ante praevisa merita,* but like Albert the Great (*1 Sent.* d.40.a18), he attempts to safeguard the meaningfulness of human freedom by rejecting the *necessitas consequentis* which implies a compulsion of cause and effect and, like Duns Scotus, he feels that "it is obvious that a predestined person can be damned, because he has free will" (*1 Sent.* d.40.q.1a.1-3). Bradwardine's attack on Pelagian approaches to predestination seeks to counter Occam's emphasis on merit, as well as that of Occam's pupils such as Holcot and Woodham. His *De Causa Dei* elaborates thus a distinction between absolute and "conditional" necessity (lib. 3), upholding the spontaneity of the will; humans are not at the same level as animals, which have no free "volitio." As persons are moved by God, their responsibility is based upon the fact that they are not conscious of this and thus act freely.

It is this distinction which Chaucer has in mind in the beast fable told by his Nun's Priest. The tale is about the almost-successful capture of the rooster Chaunticleer by a devilish fox, a parable about the process and consequences of sin in one of the "elect" which comically engages the questions of reprobation, election, free will, and necessity. Blaming Chaunticleer for not heeding his prophetic dream of warning ("Thou were ful wel ywarned by thy dremes" [7.3232]), the Nun's Priest alludes to the huge body of scholastic discussion of "certein clerkis" (3234-39), allowing

> But I ne kan nat bulte it to the bren,
> As kan the hooly doctour Augustyn,
> Or Boece, or the bisshop Bradwardyn,
> Wheither that Goddes worthy forwityng
> Streyneth me nedely for to doon a thyng —
> "Nedely" clepe I symple necessitee —
> Or elles if free choys be graunted me
> To do that same thyng or do it noght
> Though God forwoot it er that it was wroght;
> Or if his wityng streyneth never a deel
> But by necessitee condicioneel. (7.3240-50)

The conclusion of his tale amplifies the question rather than delineating an answer. Similar concerns are taken up again in *Troilus and Criseyde* when the pagan lover, on realizing he has been jilted by Criseyde, "consoles" himself: "For al that cometh, cometh by necessitee: / Thus to

ben lorn, it is my destinee" (4.958-59). Troilus then goes on to rehearse the arguments concerning whether or not God's foreknowledge destroys "oure free chois every del" (1059) for more than 120 lines. Here, as in *The Nun's Priest's Tale,* however, the implication is that the "fre chois . . . yeven us everychon" (971) is, despite God's foreknowledge and predestination, inescapably bound up with human responsibility: it is that which makes for tragedy, as well as comedy. As Milton's God says in *Paradise Lost* (3.102-19):

> Freely they stood who stood, and fell who fell.
> Not free, what proof could they have giv'n sincere
> Of true allegiance, constant Faith or Love,
> Where only what they needs must do, appear'd,
> Not what they would? what praise could they receive?
> What pleasure I from such obedience paid,
> When Will and Reason (Reason also is choice)
> Useless and vain, of freedom both despoil'd,
> Made passive both, had serv'd necessity,
> Not mee. They therefore as to right belong'd,
> So were created, nor can justly accuse
> Thir maker, or thir making, or thir Fate;
> As if Predestination over-rul'd
> Thir will, dispos'd by absolute Decree
> Or high foreknowledge; they themselves decreed
> Thir own revolt, not I: if I foreknew,
> Foreknowledge had no influence on their fault,
> Which had no less prov'd certain unforeknown.

In the New England Puritanism of Cotton Mather's *Magnalia Christi Americana* (1702), on the other hand, history repeats eternal models precisely because it is predetermined by God from the beginning of time: this is what undergirds his view of the American settlers as the New Covenant elect.

Augustine's account of predestination has been a theological crux in biblical interpretation ever since his day. His thesis has been reaffirmed by some, including St. Thomas Aquinas, who, using his Aristotelian paradigm and treating the theme as part of the doctrine of providence, defined predestination as God's "set way *(ratio)* of directing a rational creature to eternal life as his end" (*Summa Theol.* 1.23.1). Luther, in *De Servo Arbitrio (The Bondage of the Will),* used Augustinianism polemically to subvert Erasmus's development of the notion of mankind's meritorious cooperation with enabling grace. Calvin, like Jansenius, defined predestination as a decision (*decretum* or "decree") which included, alongside the gracious choice of some sinners for salvation, the just reprobation of the rest. Calvin's doctrine, parodied by the drunken Cassio in Shakespeare's *Othello* —"Well, God's above all: and there be souls must be saved, / and there be souls must not be saved" (2.3.105-07) — involved a verbal (not substantial) change from that of Augustine, who had defined predestination as God's choice of sinners to save and had treated reprobation as a separate subject.

The Augustinian formulation favored by many Puritan

thinkers involved a view of both salvation and reprobation operating under the auspices of providence. Daniel Defoe's *Robinson Crusoe* reflects this more resigned view when he looks at his post-shipwreck situation in a positive light: "I then reflected that God, who was not only righteous but omnipotent, as He had thought fit thus to punish and afflict me, so He was able to deliver me; that if He did not think fit to do it, 'twas my unquestioned duty to resign myself absolutely and entirely to His will; and, on the other hand, it was my duty also to hope in Him, pray to Him, and quietly attend to the dictates and directions of His daily providence."

Thomas Hobbes presages a secular determinism which has affinities with this doctrine, showing in *Leviathan* that a strict determinist can easily concede human free will so long as he can maintain that individuals must always do what the strict chain of causes obliges them to, a position he concludes to be identical with much Reformation theology.

In the darker Calvinism of Herman Melville, *Moby-Dick* is an embittered debate over predestination and free will in which Ahab, the demonic hero, is fated or predestined, as Captain Peleg declares, to be a simulacrum of his biblical forerunner. *Pierre* also struggles with the insoluble conflict of predetermination and free will, reflecting the internal debate of an author who was nurtured on the formulations of the Synod of Dordrecht (1618-19), and whose very rebellion against Calvinism, ironically, is formulated in the vocabulary of Calvinism. (Ahab even considers the Manichean position, asking, "Be the white whale agent, or be the white whale principal . . . ?" but without resolution.)

A variety of theologians have chosen rather to modify than simply reaffirm Augustine's thesis. Semi-Pelagians, patristic (e.g., St. John Cassian), medieval (e.g., Gabriel Biel), and modern (e.g., Post-Tridentine Roman theologians such as Suarez and Bellarmine and Arminian Protestants such as Watts and Wesley) suspend salvation on a grace-aided human decision, or on a series of decisions which, though divinely foreseen, are not divinely determined. In the 20th cent. Karl Barth has reconstructed the doctrine in terms of mankind's solidarity in Jesus Christ: he represents Christ as mankind first reprobated on the cross and then elected in the Resurrection, and holds that the human race is now actually elect and redeemed in the Mediator. This position, perhaps anticipated to some degree by Aquinas (*Summa Theol.* 3.q.24.a.4), attempts to parry the accusation of divine arbitrariness and injustice; Barth in fact claims to turn predestination into good news by absorbing it into the gospel, rather than leaving it as a separate dark truth overshadowing the gospel. But the issue is one of theological exegesis: which construction flows naturally from the relevant texts? Does "predestiny," as the American poet Larry Woiwode puts it, continue to lie like "a cold spoon on the birthright of speech," or is it the basis

for a joyful affirmation of divine providence, such as leads the poet to conclude his volume, "I love our everlastingly interleaved / Lives predestined and reinstated by / The Word" (*Eventide*, 15.20; epilogue)? The debate continues.

See also ELECTION.

Bibliography. Buis, H. *Historic Protestantism and Predestination* (1957); Damrosch, L. *God's Plot and Man's Stories* (1985); "Hobbes as Reformation Theologian: Implications of the Free-Will Controversy." *JHI* 40 (1979), 339-52; Danielson, D. *Milton's Good God: A Study in Literary Theodicy* (1982); Hodge, C. *Systematic Theology* (1871-73); Oakley, F. *Omnipotence, Covenant and Order: An Excursion in the History of Ideas from Abelard to Leibniz* (1984); Oberman, H. *Thomas Bradwardine: A Fourteenth Century Augustinian* (1957); Parker, T. "Predestination." In *A Dictionary of Christian Theology.* Ed. A. Richardson (1969); Penny, D. A. *Freewill or Predestination? The battle over saving grace in mid-Tudor England* (1990); Rondet, H. "Predestination." In *The Concise "Sacramentum Mundi."* Ed. K. Rahner (1975); Warfield, B. "Predestination." In *Biblical and Theological Studies* (1952).   JAMES I. PACKER
DAVID L. JEFFREY

PRIMOGENITURE   *See* BIRTHRIGHT.

PRINCIPALITIES AND POWERS   "Principalities and powers" is a Pauline phrasing and concept referring to suprahuman, supernatural beings whose abode is "the heavenly places," a spiritual battleground mentioned in Eph. 6:11-18. Though the "principalities and powers" are creatures of God (Rom. 8:38; Col. 1:16), they are sometimes described as sinister, Satanic influences whose power to undermine the faith of believers has been diminished and conquered in the cross (Eph. 1:21; 6:12; Col. 2:10-15).

> It may be asked whether the powers mentioned in Eph. 6 are the same as the demons which according to the Gospels threaten, dominate and seek to destroy the life of individuals. An affirmative answer is suggested by the following observations: just like the powers in Eph. 6, so the demons mentioned in the Gospels are not of "blood and flesh"; both are specifically dangerous because of their "spiritual," seemingly intangible, unalterable and invincible character. The distinction between the demons and the powers, however, appears to be that the demons affect the individual incidentally, whereas the powers threaten all men at all times. (M. Barth, *Ephesians*, 801-02)

The early Church Fathers understood these principalities and powers as fallen angels, hostile demonic powers under the orders of Satan (St. John of Damascus, *Expositione fidei*, 2.21; St. Justin Martyr, *Apologia*, 2.5). Both St. John Chrysostom (*Hom. on Ephesians*, 125) and Origen (*Contra Celsum*, 5.234; 8.399) recognize these beings as evil and unredeemable. St. Thomas Aquinas distinguishes three classes of angelic beings: (a) cherubim, seraphim, archangels; (b) principalities and powers which may be good or bad; (c) the devil and the demons (Barth, *Ephesians,* 802 n. 235). It is the third category of Aquinas which clearly figures in the popular medieval legend about the pact of Theophilus with the devil, yet in Chaucer's similar *Friar's Tale* the self-blinding curiosity of the apostate Summoner prompts him to query his devilish bailif "out-ridere" as if he represented, in Aquinas's terms, morally ambivalent "principalities and powers," despite the fact that the "bailif" himself repeatedly makes clear that he is a devil from hell.

Spenser's *The Faerie Queene* has numerous references to the battle human beings must wage against "spirituall foes" (1.10.1.4; cf. 1.12.39.5; 2.8.2.5), but perhaps the most important demonic character in Renaissance literature is Christopher Marlowe's Mephistopheles in *The Tragical History of the Life and Death of Doctor Faustus.* This fallen angel promises Faustus, "And I wil be thy slave and wait on thee, / And give thee more than thou hast wit to aske" (478-79). Faustus trades his soul for the promise of wisdom which he cannot wrest from God. Directed by Mephistopheles, Faustus willfully miscontrues the meaning of biblical texts because he is "ravished with a desire for the intellectual power that can be his through making the spirits his subjects" (J. H. Sims, *Biblical Allusions in Marlowe and Shakespeare* [1966]).

That principalities and powers may subvert their victims' faith is also a theme in several of Shakespeare's plays. Antonio, in *The Merchant of Venice,* observes that "The devil can cite Scripture for his purpose"; likewise in *The Comedy of Errors,* Dromio, using biblical language to warn his master against the probability of venereal disease, describes the courtesan as if she were hell's emissary:

Ant. S.   Satan, avoid! I charge thee, tempt me not!
Dro. S.   Master, is this Mistress Satan?
Ant. S.   It is the devil.
Dro. S.   Nay, she is worse, she is the devil's dam, and here she comes in the habit of a light wench; and thereof comes that the wenches say, "God damn me"; and that's as much as to say, God make me a light wench. It is written, they appear to men like angels of light; light is an effect of fire, and fire will burn; *ergo,* light wenches will burn. Come not near her. (4.3.48-58)

Shakespeare's Juliet also fears demonic influence, wondering if her lover, Romeo, has, like Satan, been "transformed into an angel of light":

O nature, what hadst thou to do in hell,
When thou didst bower the spirit of a fiend
In mortal paradise of such sweet flesh? (3.2.80-82)

Carlyle's *Übermensch,* "while on the one hand, he trod the old rags of Matter, with their tinsels, into the mire, he on the other everywhere exalted Spirit above all earthly principalities and powers, and worshiped it" (*Sartor Resartus,* 3.1). Here the reference is divested of traditional Christian content, despite its "spiritual" vocabulary. Modern allusions are typically more straightforwardly secular, as the phrasing becomes more a metaphor for the absence of heavenly assistance than the danger of Satanic victory. A case in point is Anthony Burgess's *Earthly Powers* (1980), whose protagonist is an aging homosexual whose battle is against his fellow men, exemplified in his unsympathetic Catholic colleagues, and not against demonic forces.

See also ANGEL; DEMONS, DEMON POSSESSION; DEVIL.

Bibliography. MacGregor, G. H. C. "Principalities and Powers." *NTS* (1954), 19-28; Schlier, H. *Principalities and Powers in the New Testament* (1961); Wink, W. *Naming the Powers* (1984).   BRUCE L. EDWARDS

PROCULA   *See* PILATE'S WIFE.

PRODIGAL SON   One of Jesus' major parables, the story told in Luke 15:11-32 unfolds in three phases: the rebellion and subsequent repentance of the prodigal son who, having squandered his inheritance in "riotous living" in a far country, returns home in abject poverty; the unconditional forgiveness and welcome of the father; and the refusal, on the part of the elder and more "responsible" son, to participate in his brother's homecoming festivities.

In this context, the last phase of the story carries its central message; Jesus painted the satiric portrait of the elder brother as a rebuke to the Pharisees, who occasioned the parable by criticizing Jesus for his association with "sinners" (Luke 15:2). The most significant part of the story for most commentators, however, is the portrait of the forgiving father, which captures the gospel in miniature.

St. Ambrose sets the dominant tone of early exegesis in his treatise against the Novatian heresy, *De poenitentia,* where he argues from the example of the forgiving father that no one, on proof of authentic repentance, should be denied reconciliation:

Therefore most evidently are we bidden . . . to confer again the grace of the heavenly sacrament on those guilty even of the greatest sins, if they with open confession bear the penance due to their sin.

Chaucer's Parson uses the story in much the same way, to teach that no one should needlessly despair because of sin, but rather turn to God in penitence (*Parson's Tale,* 10.700). The narrative of the prodigal became, in fact, a staple of penitential teaching in the Middle Ages (cf. Bishop John Fisher's *Treatyse Concernynge the Seven Penytencyall Psalmes,* which contains both a paraphrase and exposition of the parable).

Although Calvin and other later commentators returned to a consideration of the older brother as an example of the "inhumanity [of] those who want maliciously to restrict God's grace, as if they grudged poor sinners their salvation" (Calvin, *Harmony of the Gospels*), exegetical and homiletical emphasis tended still to fall elsewhere. Ruskin, in his autobiographical *Praeterita* (3.1.16), complained that in a certain Puritan study group the parable was expounded to the utter exclusion of the elder son, since "the home-staying son was merely a picturesque figure introduced to fill the background of the parable agreeably, and contained no instruction or example for the well-disposed scriptural student. . . ."

Widespread literary interest in the story begins in the 16th cent., during which time a number of didactic continental plays were written on the subject — among them Burkart Waldis's German drama *De Parabell vam verlorn Szohn* (1527), Guilielmus Gnaphaeus's Latin *Acolastus* (1528; trans. into English by John Palsgrave in 1540), Georgius Macropedius's *Asotus* (1537), Jörg Wickram's *Schönes und evangelisches Spiel von dem verlorenen Sohn* (1540), and Lope de Vega's *El hijo pródigo* (1604).

In England, in the decades to follow, a multitude of plays, now commonly designated "Prodigal Son Plays," were fashioned. The tendency of these plays was to emphasize moral teaching and to portray the excesses of the prodigal's "riotous living." Among the better known of these dramas are the morality-like *Lusty Juventus* by R. Wever (ca. 1550), the anonymous *Nice Wanton* (ca. 1550), Thomas Ingeland's *The Disobedient Child* (ca. 1560), *Misogonus* (ca. 1570, of uncertain authorship), George Gascoigne's *The Glasse of Government* (1575), John Marston's *Histriomastix* (1599), the anonymous (Pseudo-Shakespearean) *The London Prodigal* (1604), Thomas Middleton's *A Mad World My Masters* (1606), and Francis Beaumont's *The Knight of the Burning Pestle* (1607).

Shakespeare alludes more often to this parable than to any other. There are references to the prodigal's departure from home and his loose living (*The Merchant of Venice,* 2.6.14-19), his waste of resources in trivial pursuits (*Love's Labour's Lost,* 5.2.64; *Twelfth Night,* 1.3.24) his prodigal spending (*Timon of Athens,* 4.3.278), his poverty and his swinekeeping (*As You Like It,* 1.1.38-42; *1 Henry 4,* 4.2.36-38; *King Lear,* 4.7.38-40), and his eventual return (*Comedy of Errors,* 4.3.18-19; *Winter's Tale,* 4.3.103). Pictorial renderings of the parable are mentioned in *Merry Wives of Windsor,* 4.5.8, and *2 Henry 4,* 2.1.56. There is clowning on its theme by Launce in *Two Gentlemen of Verona* (2.3.1-35): "I have receiv'd my proportion, like the Prodigious Son. . . ." The invention of such puns became a favorite pastime for later writers (e.g., Dickens: "a reg'lar prodigy son" [*Pickwick Papers,* chap. 43]; Maxwell Anderson: "I'd fiddle these prodigies back home to Sunday school" [*Winterset,* 1.2]).

Ben Jonson elaborates the plot in the career of Asotus (Latin for "prodigal") in *Cynthia's Revels, or The Fountain of Self-Love,* and later in the equally allegorical *The Staple of News* (cf. the allusions in 4.2.123; 5.6.18-19; 5.6.60-66); Jonson also uses the parable in a more specifically religious context in his poem "The Pleasures of

Heaven." Equally close to the original content of the text are Robert Southwell's poem "The prodigall childs soule wracke," describing the prodigal's career in terms first of a sea voyage and then of imprisonment, and William Drummond of Hawthornden's sonnet "For the Prodigal." George Herbert's poem "Love (3)" presents the thoughts and doubts of the homecoming prodigal and the father's (Love's) unperturbed words of welcome.

Robert Burton uses the first part of the parable to declare that times of sinful pleasure are frequently followed by a "cruel reckoning in the end, as bitter as wormwood" and the second part to show that repentance cures despair (*Anatomy of Melancholy,* 3.4.2.3-6). The prodigal's resolution to return is referred to in Francis Quarles's poem "The New Heart" and in Bunyan's *The Pilgrim's Progress.* When Christian is asked whether he is really determined to leave the City of Destruction, he answers, in the words of the prodigal, that where he goes there is "enough and to spare." Defoe's Robinson Crusoe, having acted against his father's counsel by going to sea, resolves during a terrible storm that he will "like a true repenting prodigal" go home to his father, who, being "an emblem of our blessed Saviour's parable had even killed the fatted calf for me." In the end, however, Robinson is ashamed to return.

When, in Fielding's *Joseph Andrews,* Parson Adams witnesses the encounter of Joseph and his father, he cries out, *"Hic est quem quaeris, inventus est etc."* (4.15). His combination of the angel's address to the two Marys at the empty grave (John 20:15) with the father's words in Luke 15:24 gives the reunion the quality of a resurrection. Goldsmith's *Vicar of Wakefield* echoes the situation and the atmosphere of the parable, when the vicar tries to reclaim "a lost child to virtue" (chaps. 17–18).

Alexander Pope's "Epistle to Richard Boyle, Earl of Burlington," aims at philistine prodigals in general. Before him, the older Samuel Butler had already satirized a prodigal as someone whose "Life begins with keeping of Whores, and ends with keeping of Hogs" (*Characters*). Laurence Sterne colorfully embroiders the parable in *The Sermons of Mr. Yorick* (20) only to launch into a discussion of young people's "love of variety."

In the sixth book of Wordsworth's *Excursion* (275-375), the priest tells the story of a Prodigal, a gifted young fortune-hunter, who returns home only to depart again after a while — a pattern which is repeated three times, until his parents witness his "last, repentant breath." In Byron's drama *Werner, or the Inheritance,* the impoverished protagonist, who is fighting incognito for his inheritance, is called

> A prodigal son, beneath his father's ban
> For the last twenty years: for whom his sire
> Refused to kill the fatted calf; and therefore,
> If living, he must chew the husks still. (2.1; cf. also 2.2)

When, in Dickens's *Martin Chuzzlewit* (chap. 6), Mr.

Pecksniff invites the protagonist to make himself at home in the Pecksniff house, he offers him "the fatted calf" — using it as a symbol of complete liberty; "but as no such animal chanced at that time to be grazing on Mr. Pecksniff's estate, this request must be considered rather as a polite compliment than a substantial hospitality." In *Dombey and Son* (chap. 22), Rob Toodle is several times called a "prodigal son." He prefers to be welcomed by his mother rather than his father, since "*she* always believes what's good. . . ." Miss Wren, in a "dire reversal of the places of parent and child," scolds her father and calls him a "prodigal old son" (*Our Mutual Friend*, 2.2).

Elizabeth Gaskell describes a prodigal's return that fails, when, in *Mary Barton* (chap. 10, "Return of the Prodigal"), John Barton flings the returning "long-lost Esther," his sister-in-law, away from him and refuses to forgive her for causing his wife's death. Charles Kingsley devotes chap. 27 ("The Prodigal's Return") of his novel *Hypatia* to Raphael Aben-Ezra's account of his conversion to Christianity after a long preoccupation with various philosophies. In Thackeray's novel *The Newcomes,* both Clive Newcome and Reverend Charles Honeyman are called prodigal sons — the latter because he has lived beyond his means and yet is to be treated kindly (chap. 26), the former on account of his thoughtless ingratitude toward his father, who "lay awake, and devised kindnesses, and gave his all for the love of his son; and the young man took, and spent, and slept, and made merry." The moral conclusion is that "Careless prodigals and anxious elders have been from the beginning: — and so may love, and repentance, and forgiveness endure even till the end" (chap. 20).

Little Maggie Tulliver, in George Eliot's *The Mill on the Floss,* encounters a remarkable series of pictures representing the Prodigal Son in the costume of Sir Charles Grandison. "In the Prison," chap. 45 of Eliot's early novel *Adam Bede,* shows Dinah Morris, the Methodist preacher, exhorting and comforting Hetty Sorrel, convicted of murdering her child. Dinah's fervent prayer for the Lord's mercy on Hetty, which culminates in the words ". . . make her cry with her whole soul, 'Father, I have sinned,'" leads to Hetty's confession of her past action (cf. George Macdonald's novel *Robert Falconer,* 2.3; 3.14).

John Ruskin offers a lengthy interpretation of the parable in *Time and Tide* (25.174-77), stressing its literal sense. His two main conclusions are that the love of money is the root of all evil, and that true repentance begins when a man "complains of nobody but himself." But in his second monologue, Robert Browning's Count Guido (*The Ring and the Book,* 11.760-63) tries to justify himself by pointing to the iniquities of others:

Each playing prodigal son of heavenly sire,
Turning his nose up at the fatted calf,

Fain to fill belly with the husks, we swine
Did eat by born depravity of taste!

While Christina Rossetti's poems (e.g., "I Will Arise," "A Prodigal Son") closely reflect the original intent of the parable, Rudyard Kipling's "The Prodigal Son (Western Version)" shows a basically unrepentant son who, disappointed by the moralism and narrowness of the home he has returned to, leaves again for the Yards. This prodigal foreshadows André Gide's narration "Le retour de l'Enfant prodigue," in which the returning son's younger brother leaves the father's house in order to attempt all the things the prodigal was not able to achieve. In Gide's wake, German poet Rainer Maria Rilke tells the story of a prodigal who leaves the parental home because he does not want to be loved (*Die Aufzeichnungen des Malte Laurids Brigge,* 938-46; cf. also his poem "Der Auszug des verlorenen Sohnes"). Other continental versions of the time are Franz Kafka's short prose piece "Heimkehr" and Swiss writer Robert Walser's "Die Geschichte vom verlorenen Sohn."

Thomas Hardy alludes to the parable in his tragic story "The Grave by the Handpost" (in *A Changed Man and Other Tales*), in which the protagonist has the words "I am not worthy to be called thy son" inscribed on his father's gravestone. Yeats, in "The Lake Isle of Innisfree," invests the speaker's choice of nature over civilization with moral depth by echoing the prodigal's moment of epiphany: "I will arise and go. . . ." In James Joyce's *Ulysses,* Stephen in a drunken mood echoes and at the same time significantly mutilates the same words when he says, "I will arise and go to my" — deliberately omitting the word "father."

There are several references to the parable in Alan Paton's *Cry, the Beloved Country,* most obviously in the conversation between Stephen and John Kumalo about Stephen's prodigal son Absalom, who has been found "not as he was found in the early teaching," but arrested for the murder of a white man (1.14; cf. also 1.2, 1.5, 2.12). Graham Greene's *Monsignor Quixote* offers a communist reading of the "pretty parable," presented by Mayor Enrique Zancas. In it, the prodigal feels stifled by his bourgeois surroundings, gets rid of his wealth in the quickest way possible ("perhaps he even gave it away"), and "in a Tolstoyian gesture" becomes a peasant. Another peasant tells him about the capitalist subjection of the working class and the class struggle, and when the young man returns home for a week, he is so disillusioned that he returns to the peasant, who offers a welcome similar to that of the father in vv. 20-21.

In America, the first literary treatments of the parable were imported from England or had English settings. Thus, an often-reprinted chapbook entitled *The Prodigal Daughter, or The Disobedient Lady Reclaimed* presents a cautionary tale about an English girl who tries to poison her parents, falls in a deathlike trance, but is reformed through a vision. In Washington Irving's tale "The Spectre Bridegroom" (from *The Sketch Book*), the "fatted calf" is killed for the wedding of the heroine and the fake bridegroom. After the couple has run away and returned, the bride's father, who has "lamented her as lost" and rejoices "to find her still alive," pardons them. Poe alludes to the prodigal's "riotous living" in his stories "Thou art the Man" and "Never Bet the Devil your Head." In Harriet Beecher Stowe's novel *Dred,* Nina Gordon's dying words are "Good-by! I will arise and go to my Father!" (chap. 36). Another prodigal comes home in Edward Eggleston's *The Circuit Rider,* chap. 18.

After having been "numbered with the dead," Herman Melville's Israel Potter is welcomed by his father like the prodigal son (*Israel Potter,* chap. 2), but he leaves his home again — this time for fifty years. During his years at sea, he works as one of the waisters, who are "sea-Pariahs, comprising all the lazy, all the inefficient, all the unfortunate and fated, all the melancholy, all the infirm, all the rheumatical scamps, scapegraces, ruined prodigal sons, sooty faces, and swineherds of the crew" (chap. 20). The Prodigal in Melville's *Clarel* (4.26) by his conduct represents an earlier stage of the biblical son's career: he is still occupied with amorous adventures and riotous living.

In his humorous sketch "The Scriptural Panoramist," Mark Twain describes a "moral-religious show" accompanied by a pianist's ill-matched playing. When a picture of the prodigal son's arrival at home is shown, the pianist plays, "Oh we'll all get blind drunk / When Johnny comes marching home." W. D. Howells refers to Luke 15:32 in a homecoming scene in *The Rise of Silas Lapham.* He identifies both Silas and young Tom Corey as prodigal sons — the one because in his youth he "cleared out West" and his return was a "Fatted-calf business," and the other because, upon returning from Texas, he has to learn that "the prodigal must take his chance if he comes back out of season."

When Stephen Crane's Maggie has left home, her mother anticipates triumphantly how "deh beast" will return. She corrects Maggie's brother when he talks of "dis prod'gal bus'ness": "It wa'n't no prod'gal daughter, yeh fool. . . . It was prod'gal son, anyhow" (chap. 13). Though her vocabulary is "derived from mission churches," her complaint, "Ah, what a ter'ble affliction is a disobed'ent chile" (chap. 19), only serves to illustrate Crane's insight into "the abandonment of Christian love by his culture" (Stein, "New Testament Inversion in Crane's *Maggie,*" 270).

Bret Harte's short story "Mr. Thompson's Prodigal" (a plot later expanded into the drama *The Two Men of Sandy Bar*) presents a well-to-do father in search of his runaway son, and an imposter who takes advantage of this situation. When the real son appears, he turns out to be a drunken tramp. Mary Hallock Foote's *The Prodigal* tells the story of the reformation of a rich man's son in San Francisco. In Jack London's "The Prodigal Father," Josiah Childs runs away to California from his domineering New England wife and when, upon returning after eleven years, he finds her unchanged, he persuades his son to run away with him again.

Eugene O'Neill alludes to the parable several times (e.g., *Dynamo,* 2.1; *Days Without End,* 1), usually with an ironic refraction of the parable's message. In *The Rope,* the returning son Luke is welcomed by a Scripture-chanting father who uses the exact words of vv. 22-24; but Luke soon turns out to be concerned only for the rest of his father's money. His unrepenting attitude is punished, however, by his niece's squandering the gold pieces before he can find them. In *Desire under the Elms* the role of the elder brother is given to Eben (3.1), but Eben is at the same time the real father of the son who has arrived.

Sinclair Lewis reverses the character constellation of the parable in his light-hearted novel *The Prodigal Parents,* in which parents refuse to be exploited by their greedy grown-up children and flee to Europe. In the end, the sobered daughter tries to comprehend the new distribution of roles, observing that her father is "Prodigal Son, obviously, with Mother as Assistant Prodigal, and I'm the forgiving parent and I'm afraid Howard is the swine, with Cal for husks, but who's the fatted calf, and who's the elder son that got sore?" (chap. 38).

The parable looms large in the works of Thomas Wolfe, as evidenced in such titles as *You Can't Go Home Again,* "The Lost Boy," "O Lost," and, most conspicuously, "The Return of the Prodigal." In his *Look Homeward, Angel,* Eugene is "not safe, not sound" (chap. 32), he is "like a man who had died, and had been re-born" (chap. 33), and he wants to pay his way to Harvard from his share in his father's estate (chap. 39).

In Morly Callaghan's *They Shall Inherit the Earth,* Michael Aikenhead, estranged from his father for ten years, hates being greeted upon his return by his half-brother Dave Choate, whom he later lets drown (chap. 4). Callaghan's *More Joy in Heaven* tells the story of a paroled criminal who is welcomed loudly by society, because "After all, they did a little feasting and celebrating for the prodigal son . . ." (chap. 5). The promise inherent in the parallel does not prove to be true: overburdened by society's expectations, the prodigal fails in his new life. Another returning prisoner is young Tom Joad, in Steinbeck's *The Grapes of Wrath.* His former preacher Jim Casy speculates that maybe old Tom Joad will "kill the fatted calf like for the prodigal in Scripture" (chap. 4).

Edwin Arlington Robinson's poem "The Prodigal Son" is a dramatic monologue spoken by the returned prodigal to his elder brother. It leaves out the forgiving father altogether and is not much more than a plea for human sympathy. Stephen Vincent Benét's "The Prodigal Children" describes the attitudes of the prodigal generation which left their ideals of peace behind and "got the world in a mess" — that of the Second World War. Elizabeth Bishop's poem "The Prodigal" evokes the sensations of the prodigal's degrading experience as an exile working among the swine and ends on the unspoken question of why it takes him so long to make up his mind to go home.

The 1970s saw the production of a number of "prodigal-son plays" revolving around the generation conflict and about particular problems of modern society. The troubles the prodigals of these plays run into are teenage pregnancy (J. E. Franklin and M. Grant, *The Prodigal Sister*), abortion (D. Turner, *The Prodigal Daughter*), and drugs and imprisonment (D. Evans, *The Prodigals*).

When in *The Fixer,* a novel by Bernard Malamud, protagonist Yakov Bok's wife Raisl is called "dead" by the rabbi because she has left her family, the saying reflects Jewish belief, particularly the ceremony of *ketsatsah,* which has been claimed to be the frame of v. 24 (cf. Rengstorf, *Die Re-Investitur des verlorenen Sohnes*). In Malamud's novel *God's Grace,* the gorilla George is an outsider who disrupts the seder celebration. The protagonist Calvin Cohn tries to assure him that he is forgiven by relating the story of the Prodigal Son. The gorilla listens "with tears flowing" (p. 124).

Bibliography. Beck, E. "Prodigal Son Comedy: The Continuity of a Paradigm in English Drama, 1500-1642." *DA* 33 (1973), 6339A; "Terence Improved: The Paradigm of the Prodigal Son in English Renaissance Comedy." *RenD* 6 (1973), 107-22; Brettschneider, W. *Die Parabel vom verlorenen Sohn* (1978); Ferrari, L. C. "The Theme of the Prodigal Son in Augustine's Confessions." *RechA* 12 (1977), 105-18; Helgerson, R. "The Prodigal Son in Elizabethan Fiction." *DA* 31 (1971), 3549A; *The Elizabethan Prodigals* (1976); Holstein, H. *Das Drama vom verlorenen Sohn* (1880); Luyben, H. L. "James Bridie and the Prodigal Son Story." *MD* 7 (1964), 35-45; Moseley, V. D. "Joyce's Exiles and the Prodigal Son." *MD* 1 (1959), 218-27; Robbins, J. *Prodigal Son/Elder Brother: Interpretation and Alterity in Augustine, Petrarch, Kafka and Levinas* (1991); Schweckendiek, A. *Bühnengeschichte des verlorenen Sons in Deutschland* (1930); Snyder, S. "King Lear and the Prodigal Son." *SQ* 17 (1966), 361-69; Young, A. R. *The English Prodigal Son Plays: A Theatrical Fashion of the Sixteenth and Seventeenth Centuries* (1979).   MANFRED SIEBALD
LELAND RYKEN

PROFANATION, PROFANITY   The act of profanation (Heb. *ḥll;* Gk. *bebēloō*) is a devaluation of the sacred or holy, treating it as if it were common or, worse, in an unclean or immoral way. Consecrated persons (e.g., priests, Lev. 21:4, 9), times (e.g., the Sabbath, Exod. 31:14), and objects (e.g., altars, Exod. 20:25) can all be profaned. Destruction or abuse of the Temple is termed profanation (Ps. 74:7; Dan. 11:31; 2 Macc. 8:2; 10:5). Legitimate "profanation" can also occur, as when a vineyard loses its consecrated status after its fourth year (cf. Lev. 19:24) and becomes eligible for common use

(Deut. 20:6, where KJV translates *ḥll* as "eat"; KJV also translates *ḥll* by "pollute, blaspheme," etc., while RSV uses "profane" more consistently).

The recurrent OT phrase "[to] profane the name of the LORD" has two complementary senses. First, it can designate an act of gross malfeasance against the Lord and all he stands for, such as sacrificing one's children to Moloch by fire (Lev. 18:21; 20:3). As with the name, "[t]he sphere of holiness is identified with God's presence on earth" (Milgrom), so that an affront to God by those to whom the sphere of holiness has been entrusted renders that sphere less powerful. The second sense refers more specifically to an act or condition of Israel which impugns the Lord's reputation among the nations (e.g., Isa. 52:5; Ezek. 20:5-24; 36:20-33; Amos 2:7). Paul's statement in Rom. 2:24, "the name of God is blasphemed among the Gentiles through you," is a reference to the aforementioned Isaiah text, and the petition "Hallowed be thy name" in the Lord's Prayer may be understood, at least in part, as an entreaty for the Christian community to avoid a similar fate.

Used as a noun or adjective, *profane* has slightly different connotations. In the OT, that which is designated profane (*ḥol*) is not unclean or immoral, but merely "common" as opposed to "holy." Sin is only involved when there is failure to distinguish between the common and the holy, especially by priests (Lev. 10:10; Ezek. 44:23). In the NT, this ritual sense of profane is not employed; instead, "profane" (*bebēlos*) has a function similar to words such as "lawless, disobedient, ungodly," etc. (1 Tim. 1:9). Esau becomes the type of the profane person who, in selling his birthright, shows himself to be spiritually insensitive and unreceptive to God (Heb. 12:16; cf. Gen. Rab. 63 on 25:29 and Philo's conception of a "profane disposition" in *De sacrificiis Abelis et Caini,* 138 and *De specialibus legibus,* 1.150). Gnostic speculation is termed "profane" in 1 Tim. 4:7; 6:20; 2 Tim. 2:16.

Profanity in the sense of irreverent, vulgar language is not directly addressed by any of the biblical texts employing *ḥll, bebēloō,* or any related terms. Indeed, unless one goes to the extremes of blasphemy or cursing, such speech, while perhaps offensive to religiously sensitive persons, is not in itself a concern of the biblical writers, nor indeed of Christian writers (e.g., Chaucer) until after the Reformation, especially after the Victorian period.

See also ABOMINATION OF DESOLATION; BLASPHEMY; CLEAN AND UNCLEAN.

Bibliography. Douglas, M. *Purity and Danger* (1966); Milgrom, J. "Desecration." *EncJud* (1972); Wenham, G. J. *The Book of Leviticus* (1979), 16-25.   WILLIAM M. SOLL

PROMISED LAND   *See* EXILE AND PILGRIMAGE; EXODUS; JOSHUA; LAND FLOWING WITH MILK AND HONEY.

PROPHET   Prophets in Israel went by a variety of names, the most common of which was *nabi'* (possibly deriving from a verbal root meaning "to call"). Prophecy was in the strictest sense of the word a "calling" or vocation: the prophet was not educated to be such nor, to be authentic, could he be self-appointed. He was called by God, and the people would wait to see evidence of his calling. Moses was in this sense the first *nabi'*; others included Jeremiah and Isaiah. Other terms such as *ro'eh* and *ḥozeh* ("seer") were used to speak in general terms of prophets, but these could be applied also to false prophets, as in the narrative of Elijah and the prophets of Baal or in the case of the raving 400 prophets who gave King Ahab the prognostication he wanted to hear (1 Kings 22). True prophets, such as Micaiah in that instance, more often told people what they did not wish to hear, and although their predictions came true (or perhaps because they did), most suffered dire consequences. Not always, however: in the case of Milton's preferred examples of the good and bad prophet, Moses and Balaam, almost the reverse is true (*Apology for Smectymnuus*, 1.363).

Association of honorable prophecy with the "good news" of the promised Messiah is fundamental to the long-term perspective of the reader of the Bible as a whole. Predictions unfulfilled in the time of the prophet, especially of the messianic type, have been the subject of intense and extensive discussion in both Jewish and Christian tradition. In the medieval Church the dramatic *ordo prophetarum* or "Procession of the Prophets" was presented as part of the Christmas liturgy. Its origins trace to a sermon attributed to St. Augustine, *"Contra Judaeos, Paganos, et Arianos sermo de symbolo"* (PL 42.1117ff.), which attempts to persuade Jews of Jesus' claim to be the foretold Messiah. The usual roster of prophets in the *ordo prophetarum* includes Moses, Isaiah, Jeremiah, Daniel, David, Habakkuk, Nebuchadnezzar, Balaam, Simeon, Elisabeth, and John the Baptist, as well as Virgil and Sybil (to whom were attributed inspired predictions concerning Christ). From a *lectio* for the Christmas season, in which the preacher summoned each of these prophetic witnesses by name and they proclaimed each of their messianic prophecies, to the Anglo-Norman *Jeu d'Adam* and the later Corpus Christi plays, this "procession" developed into an important part of the literary representation of the gospel, establishing Jesus' "genealogy" in the Scriptures (e.g., N-Town *"Ordo Prophetarum,"* 132). A 15th-cent. lyric by James Ryman, "This is the ston cut off the hill" (ed. J. Zupitza, no. 100), employs the *lectio* to create a Christmas carol.

In the OT, the Heb. term *naba'* is frequently associated not only with prediction but with speaking an important message, proclaiming, or "giving the word of the LORD" (Amos 3:1-8); hence the later identification of prophecy with "proclaiming the word" or preaching. Miriam, Moses' sister, is called a *nebi'ah*, "prophetess" (Exod. 15:20ff.), in a context which implies that the singing, music-making, and dancing in which she led the women after the defeat of Pharaoh's army was itself such a proclamation or "word from the LORD."

This sense of the musician or poet as prophet enters notably into early English literary tradition in *Piers Plowman,* whose author or authors see their task as analogous to that of the OT prophets. George Herbert's famous letter to his mother concerning his "calling" to the writing of poetry as part of his religious vocation expresses a quieter version of the perceived relationship. The connection of prophet with poet develops strongly through Milton, whose sense of his vocation is implicitly garnered on the biblical model in *The Reason of Church-Government* (*Works,* ed. Wolfe, 1.822), where he refers to himself as God's "Secretary," a topos at least as old for "prophetic" poetry as Dante, who frequently presents himself as writing at the behest of the Spirit as a scribe. When Milton invokes the "Heavenly Muse" at the outset of *Paradise Lost* he merely masks with a classical allusion this biblical image for his activity. William Blake, in a letter to Butts (25 Apr. 1803), also refers to himself as "Secretary" to "Authors . . . in Eternity" and speaks of himself as having been given a prophet's vision: "Now I a fourfold vision see / And a fourfold vision is given to me" (Poem to Butts, E693), and his "Prophecies" are perhaps the most characteristic expression of his art. Walt Whitman, in "A Backward Glance O'er Traveled Roads," discusses going "over thoroughly the Old and New Testaments" in preparation for writing *Leaves of Grass* and tells how he identified with the Hebrew prophets and saw the poet as a prophet in modern times. Referring to an older and speculative etymology (Heb. *naba'*, "bubble forth"), he writes:

> The word prophecy is much misused: it seems narrow'd to prediction merely. That is not the main sense of the Hebrew word translated "prophet"; it means one whose mind bubbles up and pours forth as a fountain, from inner, divine spontaneities revealing God. Prediction is a very minor part of prophecy. The great matter is to reveal and outpour the God-like suggestions pressing for birth in the soul.

In fact, according to Emerson, the very association of revelation with prophecy in the biblical sense becomes problematic for a modern theory of inspiration. The "Problem," expressed in the poem of that name (57-61), for the Transcendentalist poet is to get his reader to see that

> The word unto the prophet spoken
> Was writ on tablets yet unbroken;
> The word by seers or sibyls told,
> In groves of oak or panes of gold,
> Still floats upon the morning wind,
> Still whispers to the willing mind.

Celebration of the poet as prophet tends to subside after the Romantics; and in an age where the poet may more typically have the stance of a critic or skeptic, false prophets (or misled) come more often onto the stage. Howard Nemerov, in his poem "On Certain Wits," recalls

Elijah and the prophets of Baal satirically to call the critic's judgment itself into question:

> And when Elijah on Mount Carmel brought the rain,
> Where the prophets of Baal could not bring rain,
> Some of the people said that the rituals of the prophets
>   of Baal
> Were aesthetically significant, while Elijah's were very
>   plain.

Richard Wilbur's haunting "Advice to a Prophet" urges a prophet less on the model of a modern Amos than of Isaiah. Rather than coming "mad-eyed from stating the obvious," he asks the prophet to "Spare us all word of the weapons, their force and range, / The long numbers that rocket the mind" but "Speak of the world's own change," the crumbling of the biosphere in which we live and love. That our dark fate should be the axiom of a divinely established moral ecology is a proclamation from Isaiah; and in making this poem the title-piece of a volume of prophetic moral and ecological poems (1961), Wilbur continues the old topos.

See also INSPIRATION.

Bibliography. Bloomfield, M. *Piers Plowman as a Fourteenth Century Apocalypse* (1961); Brown, N. O. "The Prophetic Tradition." *Studies in Romanticism* 21 (1982), 367-86; Damrosch, L. *Symbol and Truth in Blake's Myth* (1980); Gallagher, S. "'The Sane Madness of Vital Truth': Prophets and Prophecy in the Fiction of Herman Melville." *DAI* 43 (1983), 3317A; Griffin, R. "Pope, the Prophets, and *The Dunciad.*" *Studies in English Literature, 1500-1900* 23 (1983), 435-46; Hill, J. S. *John Milton: Poet, Prophet, Priest* (1978); Kugel, J. L., ed. *Poetry and Prophecy: The Beginnings of a Literary Tradition* (1990); Laib, N. K. "Prophecy in the Victorian Novel." *DAI* 43 (1983), 2680A; Prickett, S. *Words and the Word: Language, Poetics, and Biblical Interpretation* (1986); Reeves, M. *The Influence of Prophecy in the Later Middle Ages* (1969); Wojcik, J., and R.-J. Frontain. *Poetic Prophecy in Western Literature* (1984).

PROPHET IS NOT WITHOUT HONOR   When Jesus returned to his own place of upbringing, and there "taught them in their synagogue," his former townspeople were put off by his "wisdom" and "mighty works," leading Jesus to observe that "a prophet is not without honor, save in his own country, and in his own house" (Matt. 13:57; John 4:44). This saying is modified in logion 6 of the 2nd-cent. Oxyrhynchus *Sayings of Our Lord* to read "A prophet is not acceptable in his own country, neither doth a physician work cures upon them that know him." Proverbial in status, by the 19th cent. this saying of Jesus was susceptible to inversion. Thus, Lytton Strachey says in his *Portraits in Miniature* of Carlyle's ambitions that "he had higher views: surely he would be remembered as a prophet. And no doubt he had many of the qualifications for that profession — a loud voice, a bold face, and a bad temper. But unfortunately there was one essential characteristic that he lacked — he was not dishonoured in his own country." In Butler's *The Way of All Flesh*, when

Ernest's father is irresponsible to his new commitment to the spiritual life, "He said to himself that a prophet was not without honour save in his own country, but he had been lately getting into an odious habit of turning proverbs upside down, and it occurred to him that a country is not without honour save for its own prophet" (chap. 40). John Dos Passos's celebration of an avant-garde architect, itself prophetic, is more straightforward: "His plans are coming to life. . . . His blueprints, as once Walt Whitman's words, stir the young men." Yet this architect-prophet Frank Lloyd Wright, "patriarch of the new building," is "not without honor except in his own country" (*The Big Money*, "The Architect").

PROVIDENCE   Lat. *providere*, "to foresee"; Gk. *pronoia*, "forethought." As typically used in the NT with reference to God, it signifies a provident action, preparation by God beforehand; closely related is the archaic KJV use of "prevention," or "going beforehand to prepare the way." In Christian doctrine, the term refers to God's general providence expressed in creation, but also to his special providence for his chosen people expressed in the covenant and in the Cross as final means of redemption.

See also ELECTION; SPARROW'S FALL.

Bibliography. James, M. H. "Pre-Chaucerian and Chaucerian Concern with Providence: The Question of Providence Examined in Representative Theologians and Poets . . ." *DA* 129 (1968), 604A.

PUBLICAN   "Publican" is the KJV translation of Gk. *telōnēs*, "tax collector." Matthew and Zacchaeus are notable NT examples of this despised element, antipathy to whom was elevated because of the Roman practice of letting tax agents work to a set figure, with anything they could collect above that amount being kept as their own profit. Abuse was notorious. The *telōnēs* is not to be confused with the British "publican" — the landlord of a pub — who in George Herbert's "Miserie" (earlier titled "The Publican") sings, "Man is but grasse, / He knows it, fill the glass."

See also PHARISEES.

PURE IN HEART   *See* BEATITUDES.

PURGATIO TEMPLI   *See* CLEANSING OF THE TEMPLE.

PURGATORY   In traditional Catholic theology, Purgatory is a state following death in which the souls of the faithful undergo purification before being admitted to the beatific vision. Unlike hell, Purgatory is temporal, and its punishments are not penal but purgative: following due expiation and expurgation of the residual effects of sin, souls admitted to this "Intermediate State" (a term favored by the 19th-cent. Tractarians) enjoy the fulness of eternal salvation.

The condition of the faithful between death and the

final resurrection is nowhere clearly defined in the Bible, though the doctrine of Purgatory has been inferred from certain scriptural passages. Most often cited is the apocryphal 2 Macc. 12:39-45, where Judas Maccabeus is reported to have "made a reconciliation for the dead, that they might be delivered from sin." In Matt. 12:31-32, Jesus speaks of a sin which will be forgiven "neither in this world, neither in the world to come," words which have been taken to imply that other sins *will* be forgiven after death. And in 1 Cor. 3:12-15, Paul speaks of everyone's work being tried or tested "as by fire" at the Day of Judgment, supplying the image which would dominate both theological and literary descriptions of the purgatorial state. Theological argument for the doctrine relies chiefly on the customary practice of praying for the dead and offering the eucharistic sacrifice on their behalf, a practice attested from the early Christian centuries (as in St. Cyril of Jerusalem's *Catechetical Lectures*, 5.9).

From the time of St. Clement of Alexandria and of Origen (who considers the doctrine in terms of his eschatological universalism), both Eastern and Western Fathers taught that sins not expiated in this life by penance can be purged by sufferings, particularly those inflicted by fire, in the next. St. Augustine, in *De civitate Dei* (21.13, 24, 26), writes that — in addition to salutary earthly sufferings — some who are predestined to salvation must undergo punishments between the time of physical death and the Day of Judgment. Augustine stresses that this process of suffering, which is aided by the prayers of the Church Militant (cf. *Conf.* 9.13), is one of discipline and correction for those who are saved, whereas those who are destined to damnation are consigned to the eternal fire which has no remedial effect. St. Gregory the Great added concrete detail to the geography of the afterlife, suggesting that purgatorial expiation might be associated with specific terrestrial locations, sites of sins formerly committed to which departed souls must return (*Moralia in Iob*, 12.13; 13.53; see also *Dialogues*, 4).

In his consideration of sin and of the condition of the human soul, Aquinas systematized Western teaching on Purgatory, distinguishing between the guilt *(culpa)* of venial sin, remitted at the time of death, and the punishment which "remains to be expiated" (*De Malo*, q.7, a.11 [trans. in Le Goff, 278]): in Purgatory, the stain of sinful habit is removed from the soul as it becomes perfectly united to God through the will (*Summa Theol.* 1.2ae, q.87, ad 7). The Councils of Lyons I (1254) and Florence (1439) affirmed both the existence of Purgatory as a place of expiation and the importance of offerings on behalf of the dead. In response to the Reformation, the Council of Trent (1545-63) reaffirmed the essence of the doctrine while refusing to make dogmatic pronouncement on details of purgatorial punishment, condemning vain, superstitious speculation and practice as well as financial exploitation of the doctrine.

Although the controversy was especially vigorous in England (Kreider, 93-153) and the Thirty-Nine Articles denounced the "Romish Doctrine concerning Purgatory," liturgical prayers for the faithful departed and the theological open-endedness of the *via media* have allowed latitude for Anglo-Catholic belief in Purgatory. A view of Purgatory as a positive continuation of the salvific process found strong advocacy in the Oxford Movement of the 19th cent. and has characterized sympathetic modern treatments.

Much of the actual description of Purgatory derives from visionary accounts of the afterlife which often draw on classical analogues, most notably Aeneas's descent into the underworld (*Aeneid*, 6). Numerous details were suggested by Jewish and Christian apocalyptic literature, especially the apocryphal Apocalypse of Paul, which distinguishes between two levels in which souls are classified and punished according to the nature of their sins: a lower hell of eternal duration and an upper hell from which souls will be delivered. In the anecdotal tradition of Gregory, the Venerable Bede recounts the Vision of Drycthelm (*History*, 5.12), describing in graphic detail the place where delayed penitents are punished by fire and ice until the Day of Judgment. The popular medieval view of Purgatory is summarized and illustrated in *The Golden Legend*'s entry for the Commemoration of Souls (Nov. 2).

The most elaborate and important literary treatment of Purgatory is in Dante's *Divine Comedy*, which depicts it as a seven-tiered mountain with each level designated for the punishment of one of the seven capital sins. As Dante's narrator is progressively purged of all stain of these sins, he ascends through the levels to the Earthly Paradise at the mountain's summit, and from thence to the celestial rose of heaven itself where he beholds the beatific vision.

In English literature Purgatory receives due though not ample notice. In *The Canterbury Tales,* Chaucer writes comically of the state of marriage as purgatorial, an association made by Augustine in his discussion of salvation "by fire" and its significance for carnal love (*De civ. Dei* 21.26). Thus in *The Merchant's Tale,* Justinus replies mockingly to Januarie's express desire that he should "have myn hevene in erth heere" in wedding May:

> Peraunter she may be youre purgatorie!
> She may be Goddes meene and Goddes whippe;
> Thanne shal youre soule up to hevene skippe
> Swifter than dooth an arwe out of a bowe. (4.1647,
> 1670-73; see also the Wife of Bath's comment,
> 3.489-90)

The Protestant playwrights Beaumont and Fletcher demythologize the doctrine with their own "There is no other purgatory but a woman" (*Scornful Lady*, 3.1). Shakespeare, however, draws on traditional views in portraying the Ghost of Hamlet's father as he reports on the "prison house" in which he dwells, there doomed to suffer "Till the foul crimes done in my days of nature / Are burnt and purged away" (*Hamlet*, 1.5.12-13).

In the 19th cent. Universalist Philip James Bailey, who rejected the conventional scheme of an afterlife and claimed that heaven is "no place" but rather a consciousness of the divine, writes in his poem *Festus* of those who experience purgatorial suffering: "It is a fire of soul in which they burn, / And by which they are purified from sin." More traditionally, Thomas Merton, in his autobiography *The Seven Storey Mountain*, draws on Dante to describe his personal and spiritual growth into the contemplative life of 20th-cent. monasticism.

Of Yeats's play *Purgatory*, T. S. Eliot, in his memorial lecture on Yeats, commented that he disliked the title because it offers "a Purgatory where there is no hint, or at least no emphasis, upon purgation." In his own *Four Quartets*, Eliot, like Merton, articulates the doctrine of Purgatory in modern terms. In "East Coker" Eliot introduces the traditional imagery into an extended 20th-cent. surgical metaphor, while in "Little Gidding" he interprets the World War II air raids on London in terms of the purgatorial process, reminding that the effect of all suffering depends on the inclination of the will. Echoing both Dante and the 14th-cent. mystic Julian of Norwich, Eliot concludes that whatever shape it takes, the tormenting fire is in fact the fire of divine love, the hope of which shall be fulfilled and revealed "When the tongues of flame are in-folded / Into the crowned knot of fire / And the fire and the rose are one."

Bibliography. Kreider, A. *English Chantries: The Road to Dissolution* (1979); Le Goff, J. *The Birth of Purgatory*. Trans. A. Goldhammer (1984); Sayers, D. L. Introduction. *The Comedy of Dante Alighieri the Florentine. Cantica II: Purgatory.* Trans. D. L. Sayers (1955).   ROBERT E. WRIGHT

PURIFICATION   Purification (Heb. *ṭiher*, "to purify") is the process by which someone or something which has suffered pollution is restored to purity. It generally requires both the lapse of time and ritual washing and in severe cases the offering of sacrifice to restore the situation. Purification is not a cure for the polluting condition, e.g., discharge or skin disease. Rather, when the person has recovered from the condition, then purification can take place to restore the person to ritual purity and the possibility of fellowship with God.

Minor pollutions, e.g., from touching a dead animal or from sexual intercourse (Lev. 11:39; 15:18) were treated simply by washing and waiting till nightfall. Longer-term discharges or serious skin diseases which warranted exclusion from the camp involved a seven-day waiting period and the offering of sacrifice (Lev. 14:1-32; 15:2-15). Contact with human corpses was treated by waiting seven days and receiving a double sprinkling with water containing the ashes of a heifer, i.e., an instant sin offering (Num. 19).

Polluted objects could be purified by washing, passing through fire, or in the worst cases smearing with blood (Lev. 16:19; Num 31:21-24).

These rites had a symbolic and didactic function. By constantly underlining the contrast between life and death, holiness and impurity, they emphasized that God, the source of life and perfection, may only be approached by those who enjoy wholeness of life.

Rites of purification prompt a variety of powerful tropes in English and American literature — one thinks of the ineradicable stains of blood in Shakespeare's *Macbeth* (5.1), and the repeated psychosomatic bathing of Blanche in Tennessee Williams's *A Streetcar Named Desire*, as well as the popular hymn refrain "What can wash away my sin? / Nothing but the blood of Jesus . . ." with its larger context of salvific redemption and atonement. Obsessive concern with ritual purity relating to the body is, in Christian literature, often associated with Protestants in general and the Puritan tradition in particular. Thus, the occasional satirizing of the Germanic maxim, "Cleanliness is next to Godliness" (i.e., soap and water, rather than personal holiness), and of Puritan doctrines of "separation from the world," as in Aldous Huxley's chapter "To the Puritan All Things are Impure" (*Music at Night*).

See also CLEAN AND UNCLEAN; PROFANATION, PROFANITY.

Bibliography. de Vaux, R. *Ancient Israel* (1961), 460-64; Wenham, G. J. *The Book of Leviticus* (1979), 206-38.

G. J. WENHAM

PURIM   The festival of Purim in the Jewish year celebrates the salvation of Persian Jews through the intermediation of Esther, whose appeal to King Ahasuerus prevented the villainous Haman from achieving his goal of exterminating the Jewish population. While the biblical account actually centers on Mordecai, Esther's uncle and mentor, who is in the end made by Ahasuerus a judge over the Jewish people, the festival focuses on Esther's mediation and the great deliverance. Because the date of the Jews' annihilation was fixed by "lots" (*purim*) for the month of Adar 13, Purim is observed on the following day, except in the old walled cities, where it is held on Adar 15.

The festival is accompanied by pageants and masquerades, and since the late Middle Ages has also incorporated plays based on the book of Esther; no English medieval text survives. A. M. Klein's "Five Characters," a five-part poem characterizing Mordecai, Esther, Vashti her arrogant and dispossessed predecessor, Ahasuerus, and Haman, is a modern evocation of the old Purim customs. In Mordecai Richler's novel *Joshua Then and Now*, some of the most significant events in the early life and memory of the protagonist occur during the observance of Purim.

See also ESTHER; HAMAN.

PUT OFF THY SHOES   *See* BURNING BUSH.

Q

QADDISH Heb. *qaddish,* or "consecration," is the name of the most illustrious doxology in Jewish liturgy. Used since the time of the Second Temple, its majestic refrain, "May his great Name be blessed for ever and for all time," is recited by the entire congregation after a haggadic exposition (Bera. 3a), before and after prayer or reading the Torah. The present version is still largely in Aramaic. Echoes of the *qaddish* are frequent in Jewish poetry. A. M. Klein invokes it in his "Signs and Wonders" and "Sword of the Righteous," as well as his "Psalm XXXIV: A Psalm of Abraham, to be Written Down and Left on the Tomb of Rashi," in the latter of which cases the reference is to a funeral *qaddish.* Another notable modern poem is the "Kaddish" by Allen Ginsberg.

See also PRAYER.

Bibliography. Scherman, N. *Kaddish* (1983).

QOHELETH The title of the book anciently ascribed to Solomon, Ecclesiastes, derives from St. Jerome's transliteration of the LXX Greek for *qohelet,* the Hebrew nom de plume of the author. The Hebrew term means "one who speaks in the assembly *(qahal)*" and is typically translated in English versions as "the Preacher." The most famous utterances of Qoheleth are "Vanity of vanities, all is vanity" (Eccl. 1:2, et passim) and "there is nothing new under the sun" (1:9). Hence G. B. Shaw's allusion (in *Man and Superman*): "You will discover the profound truth of the saying of my friend Koheleth, that there is nothing new under the sun, *Vanitas vanitatum.*" A. M. Klein's "Koheleth" is an evocation of Solomon, "on his damasked throne," wearily dictating the book: "Take your black quill, O Scribe, and write in wormwood and with gall. . . ."

See also SOLOMON; VANITY OF VANITIES.

Bibliography. Gordis, R. *Koheleth — the Man and his World* (1951).

QUEEN OF HEAVEN *See* MARY, MOTHER OF JESUS.

QUEM QUAERITIS One of the most popular and best developed of medieval Latin dramatic tropes is the liturgical *Item de Resurrectione Domine,* the earliest of which is found in a manuscript from the Monastery of St. Gall, in Switzerland. A précis of Luke 24:1-9 (cf. Matt. 28:1-8; Mark 16:1-8), it enacts, with clerics taking the part of the three Marys and the angel, the dialogue concerning their discovery of the empty tomb:

> *Interrogatio: Quem quaeritis in sepulchro, Christicolae?* (For whom are you looking in the tomb, you followers of Christ?)
>
> *Responsio: Iesum Nazarenum crucifixum, O caelicolae.* (Jesus of Nazareth who was crucified, O heavenly beings.)
>
> *Interrogatio: Non est hic, surrexit sicut predixerat; ite nuntiate quia surrexit de sepulchro.* (He is not here, but is risen as he foretold; go and tell the others that he has risen from the dead.)

The trope serves as an introit to the proper of the Mass. As liturgical drama developed, a Christmas trope was created along the same lines, presenting the visit of the Magi as narrated in Matt. 2:1-16, and another the visit of the shepherds (Luke 2:8-20): *"Quem quaeritis in praesepe, pastores, dicite?"* ("Whom are you seeking at the crib, O shepherds, tell us?")

QUIA AMORE LANGUEO These words form the refrain of two of the best-known and most beautiful of ME lyrics. They come from the Song of Songs (5:8 [Vg]), the KJV translation of which reads somewhat confusingly, "I charge you, O daughters of Jerusalem, if ye find my beloved, that ye tell him, that I am sick of love" (Vg "I languish with love").

In the allegorical interpretation of the earlier Middle Ages (as represented by Cassiodorus, Bede, and St. Gregory the Great), the love-longing is understood in connection with intercessory prayer or the promptings or conviction of the Spirit, and the speaker is seen as representing the human soul. In the writings of the Cistercians, especially St. Bernard of Clairvaux, the Bride-speaker is identified also with the Virgin Mary. Hence, one ME adaption, probably to be associated with the Feast of the Assumption of the Virgin (Aug. 15), begins:

> In a tabernacle of a toure,
> As I stode musyng on the mone,
> A crouned quene, most of honoure,
> Apered in gostly syght ful sone. (C. Brown, *Religious Lyrics of the XIVth Century,* no. 132)

The Virgin is interceding, languishing on account of the "loue of man my brother." She urges the reader to look upon her as a "sister and spouse":

> Thy syster ys a quene, þy broþer a kynge,
> Thys heritage ys tayled, sone come þer-to.
> Take me for þy wyfe and lerne to synge,
>   *Quia amore langueo.*

Another version (ed. Furnivall [EETS o.s. 15]) presents the speaker discovering "a man" (Christ) sitting under a tree upon a hill, wounded from head to foot, bleeding from the heart; the "sistyr" for whom he longs is "mannis soule." This faithful lover, Christ, is found by one seeking "in mounteyne and in mede, / Trustynge a trewe loue for to fynde." The poem combines features of the Passion lyrics with appeals drawn from the whole vocabulary of love in the Canticles.

An adaptation of Francis Quarles, more than a century later, concentrates on the "daughters of Jerusalem," which Quarles subtly identifies with the virgins of Jesus' parable about the coming of the Bridegroom (Matt. 25:1-13). The speaker gives voice to the soul convicted by the Spirit:

> Deep wounded with the flames that furnaced from His
>   eye.
> I charge you, virgins, as you hope to hear
> The heavenly music of your Lover's voice
> . .. tell him that a flaming dart
> Shot from his eye, hath pierced my bleeding heart,
> And I am sick of love, and languish in my smart.

See also SONG OF SONGS; WISE AND FOOLISH VIRGINS.

QUICK AND THE DEAD St. Peter declares in his Pentecost sermon (recorded in Acts 10:42) that it is Jesus who "was ordained of God to be the Judge of quick [living] and dead," a phrase he repeats in his First Epistle (1 Pet. 4:5) and which is found again in the Second Epistle of St. Paul to Timothy (2 Tim. 4:1). The force of these iterations is credal, and the phrase recurs in the Apostles', Athanasian, and Nicene Creeds as translated in the *Book of Common Prayer* of the Church of England. In *The English Mail-Coach* De Quincey describes a vision: "Lo, as I looked back for seventy leagues through the mighty cathedral, I saw the quick and the dead that sang together to God." The phrase most often, however, occurs in parodic contexts.

QUO VADIS? The 2nd-cent. apocryphal Acts of St. Peter includes a narrative in which Peter, having aroused the ire of some of the Romans by his preaching, is persuaded to flee Rome to avoid harm. As he leaves by the city gate Palmall he sees Christ entering and, surprised, asks him, *Domine, quo vadis?* ("Lord, where are you going?"). Jesus replies that he is going to Rome to be crucified afresh. Peter, chastened by the vision, returns to Rome to face his own martyrdom.

The legend was popular in the Middle Ages, giving rise to Latin lyrics, the ME poem "Nou wend we to þe Palmalle," and numerous representations in art, the best known of which is probably Annibale Carraci's 16th-cent. painting of the subject. The legend plays a small part in Henryk Sienkiewicz's popular novel about Rome in the time of Nero, *Quo Vadis?* (1895), which was subsequently adapted for the stage by Marie Doran (1928).

R

RABBI The title "Rabbi" (Heb. = "my teacher") came to be applied during the 1st cent. as a mode of address to the authoritative teachers who were members of the Sanhedrin. In the form "Rabboni" it is addressed in the NT on two occasions to Jesus (Mark 10:51; John 20:16); both Jesus (Matt. 26:25, 49; Mark 9:5; 11:21; 14:45) and John the Baptist (John 3:26) are called "Rabbi" by their disciples. In later Jewish tradition, notably in northern Europe, "rabbi" came to be a term properly reserved for those teachers of Jewish law who had received ordination, and so it remains in general use today.

Jesus was critical of teachers of the Law being anxious to be so addressed (Matt. 23:5ff.). This reservation lies behind the canting protest of the obsequious friar in Chaucer's *Summoner's Tale* (3.2185-88), who resists the term "master":

> "No maister, sire," quod he, "but servitour,
> Thogh I have had in scole that honour.
> God liketh nat that 'Raby' men us calle,
> Neither in market ne in youre large halle."

Characterizations of postbiblical rabbis frequently include biblical elements, as in Browning's "Rabbi Ben Ezra," or talmudic mashal, as in A. M. Klein's "Rev Levi Yitschok Talks to God." In some later 20th-cent. texts there has been a tendency to return to the literal "my teacher," as in the poems (and dedication) of Leonard Cohen's *Book of Mercy*.

RACHEL Rachel (*raḥel,* "ewe") was the younger daughter of Laban the Haranite, and the second wife of Jacob, even though she had been betrothed to him first (Gen. 29). She bore two sons: Joseph, who was later to save the twelve tribes of Israel from famine and through whom Rachel was later identified with the Northern Kingdom (Jer. 31:15), and Benjamin. Five specific associations with Rachel create literary allusions: (1) she was loved by Jacob, who served fourteen years for her; (2) she was barren while her sister bore children; (3) she bartered with Leah in order to win a night with Jacob; (4) she cleverly stole her father's *teraphim* or household gods; (5) she was identified with Israel as a mother weeping inconsolably for her children who "were not" (Jer. 31:15; Matt. 2:18).

Jacob encountered Rachel at a well, recalling his father Isaac's meeting with Rebekah at a well (Gen. 24). Later he contracted with Laban for Rachel as his wife, saying he would serve seven years for her: "and they seemed unto him but a few days, for the love he had to her" (Gen. 29:20), even though, "in the day drought consumed [him], and the frost by night" (Gen. 31:40). On Jacob's wedding night, however, Laban substituted the elder daughter Leah for Rachel. After Jacob discovered the deception, Laban convinced him to make Leah his wife since, he argued, it was customary that the younger should not marry before the elder. Midr. Genesis notes that this was a rebuke to Jacob, who as the younger son had put himself before his brother Esau to obtain the inheritance. Laban promised Jacob the hand of Rachel if he would complete another seven years of service, and Jacob agreed.

Leah, the "unloved," bore Jacob seven children, but Rachel was barren (Gen. 29:31), like Sarah before her and Hannah after her. She exchanged a mandrake, thought to promote conception, for a night with Jacob, yet Leah was the one who conceived. The ancient text known as The Testaments of the Twelve Patriarchs (T. Issachar 1.1-15) gives an expanded rendition of the discussion between Rachel and Leah concerning the mandrakes (described as "sweet-smelling apples"), portraying Rachel as a model of sexual continence (2:1-5) who sought sexual intercourse with Jacob solely for children "and not for pleasure."

St. Augustine, in his *Contra Faustum*, elaborates a detailed and influential typology:

> Two lives are held out to us . . . — the one temporal, in which we labour; the other eternal, in which we shall contemplate the delights of God. The names of Jacob's wives teach us to understand this. For it is said that Lia is interpreted "Labouring" and Rachel "the Beginning seen," or "the Word by which is seen the Beginning." Therefore the action of human and mortal life, in which we live by faith, doing many laborious works, is Lia. But the hope of the eternal contemplation of God, which has a sure and delightful understanding of the truth, is Rachel. (22.52)

This interpretation (paralleling that of the NT sisters Martha and Mary) is taken up, with certain modifications, by virtually all patristic and medieval commentators (cf. St. Gregory the Great, *Hom. in Ezechielem*, 2.2.10; St. Thomas Aquinas, *Summa Theol.*, "Of the Division of Life into Active and Contemplative"). It becomes a prevalent theme also in mystical writings, especially those of the Victorines — Richard of St. Victor's *Benjamin Minor* is a detailed allegorical exposition of the story of Jacob in which Leah and Rachel become "affection" and "reason" respectively, and their two handmaidens Zelfa and Bala (KJV Zilpah and Bilhah) represent "sensuality" and "imagination."

In English literature, Rachel the mourning mother is alluded to with considerable frequency. In Chaucer's *Prioress's Tale* (7.627), the slain boy's mother is a "newer Rachel" as she swoons by his bier. Melville's *Moby-Dick* describes the captain of the *Rachel* hunting for a lost son, weeping for children who are not. Charles Lamb ("In Praise of Chimney Sweepers") describes many noble Rachels weeping for their children, referring to the Victorian practice of abduction of boys for the sweep trade. In T. S. Eliot's *The Waste Land*, a "murmur of maternal lamentation" (367) recalls Rachel's inconsolable grief.

Associations with the Genesis narrative inform the characterization of Rachael in Dickens's *Hard Times*. Thirty-five, unmarried, and childless, Rachael is loved by

Stephen Blackpool, who wants to marry her even though he is already married to a drunkard; he must work (to afford a divorce) in order to marry Rachael. Rachel Ray in Trollope's novel of that name can be won only after service on the part of Luke; Angel Clare in Hardy's *Tess of the D'Urbervilles* has "three Leahs to get one Rachel" (chap. 23). Thackeray's novel *Henry Esmond* is the story of a man's service for Rachel, whom he loves but who spurns him, his subsequent labors for another woman, and his final marriage to Rachel. (The same theme is treated ironically by Thackeray in the sequel, *The Virginians*.) Rachel's barrenness is considered in the 20th-cent. novel by Margaret Laurence, *A Jest of God*. An unmarried, thirty-four-year-old younger sister, Rachel has an affair which she believes results in pregnancy but which in fact turns out to be a benign tumor which is surgically removed; bereft of both child and lover, she is left only with a childish old mother and the sense that God has somehow made a joke of her daring to sin.

See also JACOB; LEAH; MANDRAKE; RAMAH; SLAUGHTER OF THE INNOCENTS.

Bibliography. Temple, W. M. "The Weeping Rachel." *MAE* 28 (1959), 81-86; Young, K. *Ordo Rachelis* (1919).

LINDA BEAMER

RADIX MALORUM   In his First Epistle to Timothy, St. Paul warns of the perils to sound Christian living occasioned by the pursuit of wealth (1 Tim. 6:6-11), observing that "the love of money is the root of all evil" (v. 10). The Greek word is *philargyria,* and the Pauline statement resembles sentiments reflected by Greek writers such as Democritus, who described *philargyria* as the "mother city [*mētropolis*] of all evil" (see *Diogenes,* 6.50), as well as certain remarks of Jesus (e.g., Matt. 6:24; Luke 16:19-31) and injunctions recorded elsewhere in the NT (e.g., Heb. 13:5). St. Jerome translated this word with the Lat. *cupiditas* ("cupidity"), which can also have the broader meaning of selfishness.

Patristic and later exegetes find little to gloss in this verse, although Puritan and Reformed commentators of the 17th and 18th cents. occasionally try to blunt it with one version or another of Matthew Poole's words: "Money itself is not evil, but [only] the immoderate love of it" (*Annotations,* sup. 1 Tim. 6:10). Paul's warning (1 Tim. 3:3) that a bishop must be "no lover of money" (*aphilargyros*) is, however, the basis for numerous injunctions in patristic and medieval commentary to those with clerical obligations (e.g., St. Ambrose, *De officiis ministrorum,* 1.50.255; Wyclif, *De Officio Pastorali,* 1-10; cf. the ME translation of his *De Eucharistia et Poenitentia,* "Nota de Confessione," ed. Matthew [EETS o.s. 74, p. 331). It is this verse which also lies behind Chaucer's reference to the more familiar *radix malorum* passage in the Prologue to the *Pardoner's Tale* (6.424-28), where the reprobate Pardoner proudly announces:

I preche of no thyng but for coveityse
Therfore my theme is yet, and evere was,
Radix malorum est Cupiditas.
Thus kan I preche agayn that same vice
Which that I use, and that is avarice.

Melville's Ishmael in *Moby-Dick* observes cynically that "the urbane activity with which a man receives money is really marvellous, considering that we so earnestly believe money to be the root of all earthly ills. . . . Ah! how cheerfully we consign ourselves to perdition!" Miss Murdstone in Dickens's *David Copperfield* confuses or conflates the proverbial citation of St. Paul with another proverb ("The devil finds work for idle hands") to say, "The boy will be idle there . . . and idleness is the root of all evil." Although not cited directly, the text provides a theme in Conrad's *Nostromo,* where in Nostromo's death scene only Mrs. Gould realizes the degree to which inordinate appetite for silver has corrupted everyone, especially Nostromo himself.

See also CHARITY, CUPIDITY.

RAHAB   Josh. 2 recounts how two Israelite spies, sent to reconnoiter the hostile city of Jericho, took lodging with Rahab, a harlot. Rahab protected them from the enemy king by hiding them on her roof under stalks of flax, and then, declaring her conviction that the Lord had indeed given them the land, asked that her family be spared when the Israelites stormed the city. This promised, she let them down by a scarlet cord and was instructed to bind the cord to her window on the city wall. The blood oaths, sworn with ritual and ascribed great consequence, were fully honored when Jericho fell. Rahab and her family were taken to dwell in Israel (Josh. 6:22-25). The genealogy of Matt. 1 includes Rahab (Gk. *Rachab*) among the ancestors of David and therefore of Christ (v. 5). James 2:25 and Heb. 11:31 say respectively that Rahab (Gk. *Raab*) was justified by works *and* by faith.

According to the Talmud (Meg. 15a) Rahab became a proselyte and the wife of Joshua. (The Matthean account has her married to Salmon.) Rabbinic tradition further names Rahab as one of the four most beautiful women in the world; her name alone is said to have inspired lust. Some sources (e.g., Zebaḥ. 116ab) claim that in her forty years as a harlot there was no prince or ruler who had not possessed her. Later proponents of this tradition would insist on the depth of her conversion and on the possibility of forgiveness for even the greatest of sinners. Another tradition, however (see *EncJud*), argues that Rahab was an innkeeper, not a prostitute, a line followed by some Church Fathers.

St. Clement of Rome early finds in the Rahab story a type of Christ:

And they gave her a sign, that she should hang from her house something scarlet in color, clearly indicating

beforehand that through the blood of the Lord will redemption come to all who believe and hope in God. . . . Not only faith but also prophecy is found in this woman. (1 Clem. 12:7-8)

For St. Justin, Rahab's alien status and great sinfulness suggest the universality of the Christian message: "the red rope . . . was a symbol of the blood of Christ, by which those of every nationality who were once fornicators and sinful are redeemed" (*Dial.* 11.1). St. Augustine expounds on the practical consequences of her faith:

Because Rahab . . . received hospitably the men of God who were strangers, because she ran a risk in receiving them, because she believed in their God, because she hid them carefully where she could, because she gave them most reliable counsel about another way of going back . . . she may be praised and imitated even by the citizens of the heavenly Jerusalem. (*Contra mendacium,* 17)

St. Jerome expounds the range of typological meaning: Jericho, which collapsed in seven days, is a type of this world; Rahab, by taking in the messengers, is a type of the Church. The significance of her name (Heb. *raḥab* = "wide," "expansive") is elaborated: "She who was at one time the broad road to perdition, afterwards mounted upward into the memory of God" (*Hom.* 18). For Jerome the sinful but redeemable human soul is figured in Rahab: "Thus our soul, that Rahab, that meretrix, has the power to conceive and bring forth the saviour" (*Hom.* 91). St. Caesarius of Arles comments on the significance of a harlot's prefiguring the Church: "that harlot . . . prefigured the Church which was wont to commit fornication with many idols before the advent of Jesus. . . . A great miracle made her a virgin . . ." (*Sermo,* 116).

In Dante's *Paradiso* Rahab is found in the third heaven among the lovers and is said to be the first of the Hebrews to have been taken up to heaven. Milton in *Tetrachordon* (2.628 [Yale ed.]) uses her as an example of lawful marriage. In his *De Doctrina Christiana* she figures in various contexts as exemplary: of blind faith, unacceptable in itself but vindicated by coming to deeper foundation (1.20); of justifiable lying "because she deceived those whom God wished to be deceived . . . and saved those he wished to be saved, rightly preferring religious. to civil duty" (2.13); and of justification by faith "without the works of the law, but not without the works of faith; for a true and living faith cannot exist without works . . ." (1.22).

Etymologically unconnected with Rahab of Jericho is Rahab the monster, from a Hebrew root (not found outside the OT) meaning "to be proud or arrogant" or (from the Akk. *ra'abu*) "to rage or be agitated." This Rahab is one of the various names of a mythic water monster identified with the energies of primordial chaos and defeated by a creating God who thus brings the world into being. In Isa. 51:9-10 the breaking of Rahab into pieces parallels the stilling of the sea in the creation and also the Red Sea's parting in the Exodus. In this mythologizing of the division of the sea as a "new creation," the old and sterile Egypt is identified with the defeated sea: Isa. 30:7 (RSV) reads "Egypt's help is worthless and empty, therefore I have called her 'Rahab who sits still.' " (The same myth is at work in Ezek. 29:3, where Pharaoh, along with Egypt, is identified with "the great dragon that lieth in the midst of his rivers," and in Rev. 21:1, where the annihilation of the sea represents the end of tyranny and death.) Blake's application of the name Rahab to the Whore of Babylon (which is for him the seductive human form of nature) conflates the two Rahabs, harlot and monster. Blake's Rahab is natural religion, or (more precisely) nature as erroneously seen by it, the cruel indifference of the natural order to humanity. She is thus the killer of Jesus (*Four Zoas,* 8.341), the "female body of mystery which interposes itself between man and his divine apotheosis in the body of Jesus" (N. Frye, *Fearful Symmetry* [1947], 393).

See also LEVIATHAN.

Bibliography. Childs, B. S. *Myth and Reality in the Old Testament* (SBT 1/27 [1960]); Cohen, C. "Rahab." *EncJud* (1972); Cross, F. M. *Canaanite Myth and Hebrew Epic* (1973); Day, J. *God's Conflict with the Dragon and the Sea* (1985); Gunkel, H. *Schöpfung und Chaos in Urzeit und Endzeit* (1895).   RICHARD SCHELL

RAINBOW   After the Flood had subsided God established a covenant with Noah that he would never again send such a deluge upon the earth; in token he set a rainbow in the cloud as a continuing reminder after storms of the limit he set upon his own judgment (Gen. 9:8-17). The rainbow is given considerable attention in talmudic legend and commentary (see Ginzberg, *LJ* 1.83, 166), but has attracted surprisingly little attention in Jewish or Christian iconography. Bishop Hugh Latimer adds to the traditional view that the rainbow signifies that "God is true in his promise," the thought that

> when in the rainbow we see that it is of a fiery colour, and like unto fire, we may gather an example of the end of the world, that except we amend, the world shall at last be consumed with fire for sin; and to fear the judgement of God, after which they that are damned shall be burned in hell-fire. (*Sermons*, 14.2)

The rainbow thus rendered somewhat ambiguous as a sign of hope — by other Reformed preachers as well — fails to develop a strong literary tradition. Donne's application of God's "Rainbow" to Elizabeth Drury in *The First Anniversary* is not a very plausible allusion (347-52) to the relevant passage in Genesis. For Henry Vaughan, "The Rainbow" is still preeminently a sign of the covenant, "Bright pledge of peace and Sun-shine! the sure tye / Of thy Lord's hand," but he too appends a reference to its connection with judgement:

> For though some think, thou shin'st but to restrain
> Bold storms, and simply doest attend on rain,
> Yet I know well, and so our sins require
> Thou dost but Court cold rain, till *Rain* turns *Fire.*

Because of its special relevance in covenant theology the rainbow attracts attention not only from Milton (*Paradise Lost*, 11.883-97), but from New England preachers such as Jonathan Edwards and his poet grandson Timothy Dwight.

In Robert Browning's "Christmas Eve and Easter Day" (6), the sight of a second rainbow rising after a first anticipates the hope of final resurrection. But in most late 19th-cent. poetry the rainbow becomes at most a kind of silver lining in clouds of murkier sentiment, such as in S. T. Dobell's *The Roman*, which offers "Thoughts that shining through / Tomorrow's tears shall set in our worst cloud / The bow of promise." Ruskin aestheticizes the promise in *Stones of Venice:*

> In that heavenly circle which binds the statues of colour upon the front of the sky, when it became the sign of the covenant of peace, the pure hues of divided light were sanctified to the human heart for ever; nor this, it would seem, by mere arbitrary appointment, but in consequence of the fore-ordained and marvellous constitution of those hues into a seven-fold or, more strictly, threefold order, typical of the Divine nature itself. (2.5.32)

D. H. Lawrence's novel *The Rainbow* (1915) chronicles the childhood, family, and adult life of Ursula Brangwen through a series of tempestuous relationships and a particularly stormy romantic failure to an unresolved but somewhat hopeful conclusion in which she contemplates a rainbow arching symbolically over an ugly industrial city. James Baldwin's novel *Fire Next Time* takes its title from an African-American spiritual which remembers the promise to Noah and also portends coming judgment:

> God gave Noah de Rainbow sign,
> Don't you see?
> God gave Noah de Rainbow Sign,
> No more water but fire next time,
> Better get a home in dat rock,
> Don't you see?

See also FLOOD.

Bibliography. Lawrence, D. H. *Studies in Classic American Literature* (1923); Stein, S. "Jonathan Edwards and the Rainbow: Biblical Exegesis and Poetic Imagination." *NEQ* 47 (1974), 440-56.

RAMAH   The prophet Jeremiah, writing of the desolation and misery of scattered Israel, takes up a powerful image: "Thus saith the LORD; A voice was heard in Ramah, lamentation, and bitter weeping; Rachel weeping for her children refused to be comforted for her children, because they were not . . ." (31:15). The verse is quoted in the NT by Matthew's Gospel in reference to the Slaughter of the Innocents in Bethlehem by Herod the

Great, when he attempted to snuff out the life of the infant Jesus sought by the Magi (Matt. 2:18). Ramah is the name of several places in Palestine, and usually means "height" of land, though the Ramah (Ramathaim-zophim; 1 Sam. 1:1) cited as the birthplace and burial place of Samuel (1 Sam. 1:19; 2:11; 7:17; 25:1) is possibly to be identified with Arimathea, the hometown of the Joseph who obtained permission of Pilate to bury Jesus in his family tomb (Matt. 27:57-60; Mark 15:43-46; Luke 23:50-53; John 19:38). Ramah is also a short form for the name Ramoth-gilead (2 Kings 8:28ff.; cf. 1 Kings 22:3ff.), the site of King Ahab's last battle.

An allusion to the phrase from Jer. 31:15 and Matt. 2:18 is employed, ironically enough in historical perspective, in Chaucer's *Prioress's Tale* of the murdered boy Hugh of Lincoln, whose "mooder swownynge by his beere lay; / Unnethe myghte the peple that was theere / This newe Rachel brynge fro his beers" (7.625-27). Charles Lamb observes that some young London chimney sweeps were victims of abduction from "good families": "Many noble Rachels mourning for their children, even in our days, countenance the fact." In his "Levana and the Ladies of Sorrow," De Quincey applies the Jeremiah passage to "Our Lady of Tears," whereas Washington Irving makes a literal application to a mother's loss of her child "as a flower of the field cut down and withered in its sweetness; she was like Rachel, 'mourning over her children and would not be comforted'" ("The Pride of the Village"). The most famous literary allusion may be that found in Melville's *Moby-Dick,* when Captain Ahab refuses to stop to help the captain of the *Rachel,* who is hunting for his lost son, swept overboard: "But by her still halting course and winding, woeful way, you plainly saw that this ship that so wept with spray, still remained without comfort. She was Rachel, weeping for her children, because they were not." In O. Henry's "Compliments of the Season" the "Rachel" who "refused to be comforted" is herself a child.

Perhaps the most powerful use of the passage in contemporary literature is A. M. Klein's chilling "A Voice was Heard in Ramah," a dramatic monologue in the form of a quasi-legal deposition concerning the beating, arrest, and incarceration in Warsaw (1939) of a poor, demented (but exceedingly articulate) Jewish street beggar, "Solomon Warshawer." In a deliberate compounding of the poem's cold-blooded horror, the incident is said to take place on "Wodin's Day, sixth of December," also St. Nicholas' Day, commemorating the patron saint of children, especially of little boys.

See also RACHEL; SLAUGHTER OF THE INNOCENTS.

RAMOTH-GILEAD   *See* AHAB.

RAPE   *See* DINAH; TAMAR; VIRGINITY, CHASTITY.

RAPHAEL   The archangel Raphael ("God heals," "God is a healer," or "medicine of God") is "one of the seven holy angels" in the apocryphal book of Tobit which "present the prayers of the saints, and which go in and out before the glory of the Holy one" (Tob. 12:15). He appears, also, in numerous pseudepigrapha. In 1 Enoch, he is "set over all disease and every wound" (40:9); God sends him to bind the fallen angel Azazel, who had taught mankind the secrets of weapons and armor, vain adornment, alchemy, and "all forms of oppression upon the earth" (1:10; 9:6; cf. chaps. 29, 32, 54, 68, 71). In the Slavonic 3 Bar. 4:7 Raphael is the planter of the melon family in the Garden of Eden (whose relative the bottle gourd provides the water flask seen in representations of The Angel and Tobias). In the Testament of Solomon, which pits thwarting angels against specific demons, Raphael thwarts both Asmodeus, the enemy of marriage (5:7), and the female demon Obyzouth, who strangles newborn infants and causes pain, especially injuring eyes, mouths, and minds (13:1-7).

In the book of Tobit itself, Raphael, in answer to their prayers, brings God's providence to two faithful, much-tried Jewish families and joins them in marriage. Disguised as a young man named Azarias ("God helps"), Raphael accompanies Tobit's son Tobias on a dangerous journey to recover the family fortune, arranges his marriage, frees his bride from the demon Asmodeus, who has killed her first seven husbands before the marriage could be consummated, and teaches him how to cure his father's blindness.

In the 15th through 17th cents. the story was a frequent topic in the visual arts, used to represent the guardianship of angels over youths separated from their parents, the marriage contract, and the healing of blindness — a subject especially appealing to painters. Rembrandt illustrated the whole narrative in drawings and paintings, depicting the healing as cataract surgery. In many paintings Raphael and Tobias walk hand in hand, accompanied by the family dog and carrying the fish which will provide the demonifuge and eyesalve.

Raphael appears in the Digby Play *Mary Magdalen* as the angel sent to bid her become "an holy apostylesse" (pt. 2.33-34). Chaucer mentions him in connection with purity of motive in marriage (*The Parson's Tale,* 10.906). Milton makes him a major and glorious character in *Paradise Lost,* where he comes not disguised but in "his proper shape" in "colors dipt in Heav'n," a six-winged Seraph shaking "Heav'nly fragrance" from his plumes (5.276-87). The "sociable Spirit, that deign'd / To travel with *Tobias,* and secur'd / His marriage with the seven-times-wedded Maid" (5.221-23) narrates the war in heaven and the creation to Adam and Eve and converses with Adam "as friend with friend" (5.229) about divine, angelic, and human love, knowledge and nurture, growth through obedience, and marriage. Unlike the angel of Tobit, who says upon revealing himself "I did neither eat nor drinke, but you did see a vision," Milton's Raphael eats not "seemingly" but "with keen dispatch / Of real hunger" (5.434-36) and explains that angelkind and humankind are close kin, made "of one first matter all" (5.471). Raphael, a bard himself, is an appropriate choice for the blind poet much concerned with marriage, with the relationship of heaven and earth, and with the process of purging "with sovrain eyesalve that intellectual ray which *God* hath planted in us" (*Of Reformation Touching Church Discipline in England* [1641], 37).

Raphael receives brief mention from Smart (*Hymns and Spiritual Songs*, 24), Keats ("Addressed to the Same" [i.e., Haydon], 8), Melville (*Moby-Dick,* pref. to the preliminary Extracts), and Yeats (*Unicorn,* act 1). James Bridie's modern stage version of Tobit, *Tobias and the Angel,* went through thirty-eight printings between 1931 and 1961. Raphael figures, also, in the contemporary fantasy trilogy by R. A. MacAvoy, *Damiano, Damiano's Lute,* and *Rafael.*

See also ANGEL; ASMODEUS; TOBIT AND TOBIAS.

Bibliography. Hoenig, S. B. "Raphael." *IDB* 4.12; Rosenblatt, J. "Celestial Entertainment in Eden: Book V of *Paradise Lost.*" *HTR* 62 (1969), 411-27; Sherry, B. "Milton's Raphael and the Legend of Tobias." *JEGP* 78 (1979), 227-40; Swaim, K. M. *Before and After the Fall: Contrasting Modes in "Paradise Lost"* (1986). DIANE MCCOLLEY

REAL PRESENCE *See* EUCHARIST; TRANSUBSTANTIATION.

REBEKAH Daughter of Bethuel of Paddan-aram (Gen. 22:23) and sister of Laban (Gen. 24:29), Rebekah is principally noteworthy as the wife of Isaac (Gen. 24:1-67) and mother of Jacob and Esau (Gen. 25:21-26). Rebekah aided the younger son in obtaining Isaac's paternal blessing by deception (Gen. 27:1-45). She is mentioned by Paul (Rom. 9:10), along with Sarah, as one through whom God chose to fulfill the promise to Abraham. St. Clement *(Paedagogus)* and St. Ambrose *(De Abraham)* comment on her being adorned for marriage, not as a sign that brides should obtain material wealth, but that in her holy marriage she is adorned with heavenly virtues. As a bride adorned she is a figure of Holy Church, Isaac being a type of Christ. Rabanus Maurus likewise glosses Rebekah as *"sancta Ecclesia"* and comments extensively on her patience and virtue (PL 107.569-91). Her watering of the camels and Isaac's servant with her pitcher represents Ecclesia's dispensing of wisdom. In directing Isaac's blessing to Jacob she is a figure of the Holy Spirit guiding God the Father; Jacob represents humankind in the care of Ecclesia, while Esau is humankind in service to the devil (*Comm. in Genesim,* 3.4.13). In Albertano's *Liber Consolationis* Rebekah appears with Esther, Abigail, and Judith as an exemplary woman. In the marriage service she is cited as fit model for the bride, along with Sarah and Rachel — Rebekah

for *sapientia,* Sarah for *longaevitas et fidelitas,* and Rachel for *amabilitas.*

On the matter of the deception of Isaac by Jacob when coached by Rebekah, biblical commentators from early times through the 16th cent. tended to sanction Rebekah's conduct. For St. John Chrysostom, her act was praiseworthy because Rebekah did it "in obedience to the divine oracle" of 25:23. For Ambrose, "the mystery overweighed the tie of affection" in the mind of the pious mother; in "consecrating Jacob to be the firstborn" she was making a sacrifice which she knew would separate him from herself. St. John Cassian, who classifies the deception with Rahab's "lie" in reporting to the spies and Hushai's tricking of Absalom, says that Jacob received "gains of blessing and righteousness because he was not afraid to acquiesce in his mother's instigation" since the saints have sometimes with a right purpose used dissimulation as an allowable remedy for a deadly disease ("On Making Promises"). Cassian implies that the disease in Isaac's case was his shortsighted preference for a hunter's food. St. Augustine, however, argues that the deception was "not a lie," a view approved and repeated by St. Thomas Aquinas (*Summa Theol.* 2-2.110.3): "Jacob's assertion that he was Esau, Isaac's firstborn, was spoken in a mystical sense because, to wit, the latter's birthright was due to him by right: and he made use of this mode of speech being moved by the spirit of prophecy, in order to signify a mystery." Aquinas insists that "it is not a lie to do or say a thing figuratively."

Modern commentators are less sympathetic with the "figurative" approach. The phrase "stolen blessing" is often used. The annotator of *The Oxford Annotated Bible, RSV* (1962) gives Gen. 27 the headline "Jacob cheats Esau" and points to the "outright lying" in v. 20. Similarly, D. F. Payne (in *The New Layman's Bible Commentary* [1979]) writes: "Jacob's deceit was perhaps less blameworthy than his mother's, but he compounded a direct lie (v. 19) with the near-blasphemous 'The Lord your God helped me to find it' " (154). J. S. Ackerman, although observing that "Jacob is here acting to retain the birthright which had been forfeited to him," feels sympathy for "the two broken men who have been duped by a cruel ploy." Bruce Vawter, C.M., terms Rebekah a "possessive unscrupulous mother" and declares that "nothing can excuse the means" used by Jacob (*A Path Through Genesis* [1956], 194, 196). A particularly outspoken detractor of Rebekah is W. R. Bowie (*The Interpreter's Bible* [1952]), who argues: "Her love for Jacob was so fiercely jealous that it broke loose from any larger loyalty. . . . Blind to anything or anybody that might get hurt . . . she corrupted Jacob as she tried to cherish him" (1.668).

Popular tradition reflects a similarly mixed response to Rebekah's character and role in the OT. Because of her deception and willfulness, her name becomes synonymous with "shrew," with punning in French and English on a strident pear-shaped stringed instrument called a "rebekke." Yet the "rebekke" occasionally appears in illuminations of the Virgin Mary (Rebekah is a Mary-type), as a sign that she is God's instrument. Chaucer puns on "rebekke: shrew" and "rebekke: God's instrument" in his *Friar's Tale*. In *The Clerk's Tale* he develops an elaborate analogue to Rebekah in the character of Griselde, who patiently serves water from the well, becomes her lord's bride, and is adorned in her translation to a higher office. Analogies are sometimes drawn between Rebekah's serving at the well and the account in John 4 of the Woman of Samaria serving Jesus at the well of Jacob (Augustine, in his Homilies on the Gospel of John, suggests that Christ becomes her sixth husband, the perfect spiritual marriage after the sensual first five). Chaucer draws upon this conflation when he makes his "rebekke" Wife of Bath compare herself and her five husbands to the Woman of Samaria (though in her perceptions she is quite the opposite), then contrasts her to the Rebekah-like Griselde in *The Clerk's Tale*.

In the fragmentary play of Isaac in the Towneley cycle Rebekah appears as a wise counselor to Isaac, urging him to send Jacob to "Mesopotamea" that he might marry appropriately rather than take a heathen bride as Esau did. She is given the play's last words as she solicitously urges her departing son to "send me glad tythyngis." Rebekah enjoys an even more prominent role in the comic interlude *Jacob and Esau* (ca. 1557), where she argues (in asides) with Isaac, piously and cleverly convinces Jacob of his duty in stealing the birthright, then blunts Esau's anger after Jacob has duped him. The Prologue notes Paul's citation of Rebekah, as well as the Genesis account, as demonstration that God chooses whom he will.

In medieval art Rebekah is usually depicted as the exemplary bride at the well, serving the camels of Isaac's slave, as the crafty servant of God hiding in the background while Jacob obtains the blessing, or as the bride of Christ (Ecclesia) holding her pitcher or adorned with bracelets and earrings.

After the medieval period Rebekah virtually disappears as a reference or subject in English literature. She enjoys an attractive role in Henry Vaughan's "Isaac's Marriage" (ca. 1650), a poem in *Silex Scintillans* based on Gen. 24:63, where Isaac, at eventide, awaits the arrival of his bride — that "lovely object of thy thought," chaste, with virginal blushes and fears, bearing her pitcher, "O sweet, divine simplicity." But no mention of her is made in Spenser, Shakespeare, Milton, or the metaphysical poets of the 17th cent. She is given one line in Dryden's "To my Honour'd Kinsman, John Driden," where Driden, a second son, is likened to "Rebecca's Heir" (43). She is mentioned in Pope's paraphrase of Chaucer's *Merchant's Tale*, in a list of virtuous women based on Albertano, but credit for the reference there goes to Chaucer.

Matthew Arnold mentions her in "The Future," where her innocence is contrasted with the evils of industrial society —

> What girl
> Now reads in her bosom as clear
> As Rebekah read, when she sate
> At eve by the palm-shaded well?
> Who guards in her breast
> As deep, as pellucid a spring
> Of feeling, as tranquil, as sure?

But in the 19th cent. she mainly contributes a name, perhaps with erotic overtones, as in Coleridge's "Black ey'd Rebecca," the epitome of woman's wiles in "The Wills of the Wisp," and especially in Scott's *Ivanhoe,* with its beautiful Jewess heroine, burlesqued by Thackeray in *Rebecca and Rowena.* (She also appears as Pendennis's mare, in Thackeray's novel *Pendennis,* so named after the hero's favorite heroine in fiction!) Elsewhere Thackeray uses a pun which may reflect earlier literary associations of Rebekah and rebekke when his Becky Sharp assumes a more stylish name, Madame Rebecque, in *Vanity Fair.* Daphne du Maurier's *Rebecca,* from which Hitchcock made his haunting movie, derives its dark, romantic shades from Scott and the Gothic novel tradition.

See also ESAU; ISAAC; JACOB.   RUSSELL A. PECK

RECHABITES   The Rechabites were a pietistic group of Israelites, perhaps originally Kenite converts who joined Israel during the wilderness wanderings (1 Chron. 2:55; cf. Num. 10:29-32), and may have been, as their name suggests (*rakab* = "rider" or "charioteer"), horsemen. Jehonadab the Rechabite assisted Jehu in destroying King Ahab's Baal altars (2 Kings 10:15-23). In Jer. 35:2-18 the Rechabites are said to have remained faithful to vows to abstain from alcohol and not to own permanent dwellings. This covenantal obedience earned them Jeremiah's praise and his assurance that though Israel's disobedience would lead to exile, the Rechabites' fidelity would obtain future honors. Neh. 3:14 lists one Malchiah, the "son of Rechab," as a prominent returnee engaged in the rebuilding of Jerusalem.

The Rechabites' abstinence from alcohol is chief among their attributes for Dryden, in whose *Absalom and Achitophel* the scurrilous Shimei is spartan: "No *Rechabite* more shund the fumes of Wine" (617). Seventeenth-cent. Protestant commentaries (e.g., Matthew Poole) are evidently uncomfortable with the apparent commendation of total abstinence, a position not popular even among Puritans. Matthew Henry (1728) engages a careful accommodation of the Jeremiah text, recommending moderation (*Comm. on the Whole Bible,* 4.628-29). In Matthew Prior's *The Wandering Pilgrim* abstinence is a condition of lamentable penury: "A Rechabite poor Will must live / And drink of Adam's ale." Theobald, in Butler's *The Way of All Flesh,* reflects a later 19th-cent. emphasis on abstinence as a positive virtue in normative Christian life. He is fascinated with the tale of an "Eastern traveler" who claimed to have "come upon a hardy, sober, industrious little Christian community — all of them in the best of health — who turned out to be the actual living descendents of Jonadab, the son of Rechab" (chap. 20).

REDEEM THE TIME   In admonishing the Christians at Ephesus to pursue a wise and virtuous life in Christ, St. Paul writes: "See then that ye walk circumspectly, not as fools, but as wise. Redeeming the time, because the days are evil" (Eph. 5:15-16); the injunction is repeated in his Epistle to the Colossians (4:5). The concept is invoked in the context of conversion and the redemption of wasted years (cf. Joel 2:25) in St. Augustine's *Confessiones* but attracts only modest attention up to the medieval era (cf. *Glossa Ordinaria* [PL 114.598, 616]).

With the Reformation, however, this *desideratum* acquired the aspect of an urgent pragmatism. Calvin, in his *Commentary* on Eph. 5:16, observes:

> Since the age is so corrupt, the devil appears to have seized tyrannical power; so that time cannot be dedicated to God without being in some way redeemed. And what shall be the price of its redemption? To withdraw from the endless allurements which would so easily pervert us; to extricate ourselves from the cares and delights of his world; and, in a word, to renounce every hindrance. Let us be eager to recover the opportunity in every way; more, to let the numerous offences and arduous toil, which many are in the habit of alleging as an apology for indolence, rather sharpen our vigilance.

Calvin develops this logic in his comment on Col. 4:5 toward a doctrine of separation from the "social intercourse and general affairs" of the world "lest we are defiled by their pollutions and gradually become profane." Such sentiments proved attractive to many Puritan writers, from thence they entered the mainstream theology of work (*Sermons, or Homilies Appointed to Be Read in Churches,* "Against Idleness"), and eventually became an imperative in the ideas of self-help and Christian stewardship preached by John Wesley.

In Shakespeare's *1 Henry 4* Prince Hal announces his coming repentance and "putting off of the old man" symbolized by his mentor-in-mischief, Falstaff. Falstaff sets up the Pauline context of Hal's soliloquy by speaking, with quite other intentions, like a Puritan preacher, in allusion to Eph. 5:15:

> Well, God give thee a spirit of persuasion and him the ears of profiting, that what thou speakest may move and what he hears may be believed, that the true Prince may, for recreation sake, prove a false thief; for the poor abuses of the time want countenance. (1.2.169-75)

Hal, after the others have left, reveals that his time of "re-creation" indeed draws nigh, in which he must come to "imitate the sun," his "reformation" so thorough as to be set off by his sinful past: "I'll so offend to make offense a skill, / Redeeming time when men think least I will" (1.2.213-14).

William Cowper applies the phrase to conversion late in life in his "Retirement" (31-40), and caustically contrasts this "redemption" with another kind of pragmatism which strikes at youth (559-62):

> Anticipated rents, and bills unpaid,
> Force many a shining youth into the shade,
> Not to redeem his time, but his estate,
> And play the fool, but at a cheaper rate.

T. S. Eliot's "Ash Wednesday" speaks of the call of the soul to its elected peace as an injunction to restore "with a new verse the ancient rhyme. Redeem / the time. Redeem / The unread vision in the higher dream" (4.18-20; cf. 26-27). But in the opening lines of "Burnt Norton" *(Four Quartets),* reflecting, perhaps, on bk. 11 of Augustine's *Confessiones,* Eliot reconsiders the relation of time to eternity in which, "If all time is eternally present / All time is unredeemable."

Bibliography. Grant, P. "Redeeming the Time: the *Confessions* of St. Augustine." In *By Things Seen: Reference and Recognition in Medieval Thought.* Ed. D. L. Jeffrey (1979), 21-32; Jorgensen, P. A. " 'Redeeming Time' in Shakespeare's *Henry IV.*" *TSL* 5 (1960), 101-09.

REDEMPTION   The Greek word *lyō* was sometimes used in the sense "to loose," "to release." When this was done by payment of a ransom, the noun *lytron* was used for the price. From this there developed a new group of words such as *lytroō,* meaning "to release on payment of a price." Redemption, *lytrōsis,* thus indicates not simply deliverance, but deliverance effected, by payment of a price. It was used, e.g., of the ransoming of prisoners of war.

In the OT the word is used of redeeming people who had fallen into slavery (Lev. 25:47-49), or of the redemption of possessions sold off in time of need (Lev. 25:25-29). Firstborn males both of humans and of animals belonged to God (Exod. 13:12). Where the animal was a cow, sheep, or goat, redemption was not permitted; such an animal must be offered in sacrifice (Num. 18:17). But it was required that the firstborn of humans and that of animals forbidden to be used in sacrifice be redeemed (Exod. 13:13; 34:20; Num. 18:15-16).

Sometimes God is said to redeem his people (Exod. 6:6; Isa. 63:9). While it is unthinkable that God should pay anyone a price, in many passages there is the notion that salvation entails cost.

The NT applies the concept to the saving work of Christ, who "gave himself [as] a ransom for all" (1 Tim. 2:6; cf. Matt. 20:28; Mark 10:45). Believers have redemption "through his blood" (Eph. 1:7; Col. 1:14), a redemption which is "eternal" (Heb. 9:12). It is a redemption from the curse of the law by the bearing of that curse (Gal. 3:13). In one passage the body is said to be included in its scope (Rom. 8:23). This looks forward to the consummation of salvation in what is called "the day of redemption" (Eph. 4:30). There is a sense in which redemption was completed when Christ died: it is a past event (1 Pet. 1:18-19); in another sense it is yet future (Luke 21:28). Redemption comes through Christ alone; even the sins committed under the first covenant were redeemed by his death (Heb. 9:15). Nowhere in the NT is there any suggestion of a recipient of the price.

The meaning behind the redemption terminology is that people belong to God, who created them in his own image (Gen. 1:27) and put them in the garden "to dress it and to keep it" (Gen. 2:15). But instead of living in fellowship with God they sinned (Gen. 3), and in doing so they became the slaves of sin (John 8:34). When the NT writers use this terminology, they are saying that sinners are slaves, but that in his death Christ has paid the price which set them free (cf. 1 Cor. 6:19-20). Redemption means that salvation is costly, as the shocking reversal in George Herbert's poem "Redemption" suggests. Also, the redeemed are to live as free people (Gal. 5:1). C. S. Lewis's character Ransom in his science-fiction trilogy *(Perelandra; Out of the Silent Planet; That Hideous Strength)* provides a focus for the author's analysis of the relation between spiritual bondage and actual freedom of the will, which then ensues in social freedom. In neither its Jewish nor its Christian contexts, however, can redemption be properly understood without reference to the concept of Atonement.

See also ATONEMENT; ATONEMENT, DAY OF; EXODUS; FREEDOM, BONDAGE; PASSION, CROSS OF CHRIST.

LEON MORRIS

REFUGE OF SINNERS *See* MARY, MOTHER OF JESUS.

REMNANT The promise of Isaiah's fearful prophecy was that after her national destruction at the hands of Assyria, "the remnant shall return, even the remnant of Jacob, unto the mighty God" (Isa. 10:20-23). Matthew Arnold refers to this passage when, in his *Discourses in America,* he wishes to herald the intelligent minority who, in his view, would save the United States from "the unsound majority."

RENDER UNTO CAESAR Each of the Synoptic Gospels (Matt. 22:15-22; Mark 12:13-17; Luke 20:20-26) tells the story of Jesus' response to the messengers sent by the Pharisees and members of Herod's party to test him with a question concerning the lawfulness of paying taxes to the Roman emperor. A "yes" would find no favor with a people resentful of their subjugation to infidel Rome; a "no" would put him in defiance of the secular authority. Seeing through their flattery and dissimulation, Jesus turned the tables on his inquirers. "Whose is this image and superscription?" he asked them with reference to a silver piece, the coin of tribute. From their answer, "Caesar's," followed his own: "Render therefore unto Caesar the things which are Caesar's; and unto God the things that are God's" (Matt. 22:21).

Rom. 13:17 and 1 Pet. 2:13-17 require obedience to the civil authority as the securer and minister of mankind's temporal welfare, a position characteristic of early Christianity. This principle informs St. Augustine's *De civitate Dei,* where the task assigned to the state is the maintenance of that good order required by both the wicked and the just in this world, and it is reiterated in the political theory of St. Thomas Aquinas (Copleston, *A History of Philosophy* [1962], 2.2.132-42; cf. J. Maritain, *Man and the State* [1951], 108). The argument for ecclesiastical sovereignty in temporal matters such as Giles of Rome advances in his 13th-cent. *De Ecclesiastica Potestate* is exceptional, even in the late Middle Ages, and runs counter to the traditional teaching. It is in large measure the medieval effort to tease out a detailed legal code from Matt. 22:21 that led to the repeated conflicts between church and state which come to a head in the Reformation.

Langland's *Piers Plowman* is the first major work of English literature explicitly to take "Render unto Caesar . . ." as its ruling text. According to Lady Holy Church Christ's words are intended to warn against luxury or an inordinate love of "the money of this world" and to counsel thrift (B.1.50-55). The application of Matt. 22:21 in Shaftesbury's *Characteristics* conforms to the usage made traditional by three centuries of Reformation polemics, picturing the Church of Rome's hierarchy in embrace with the Caesars (2.6.2.3). Blake's application is more comprehensive. His vision of all the established churches as inimical to Christ and friendly to Caesar leads him to an ironic inversion in annotating Dr. Thornton's "New Translation of the Lord's Prayer": "God is only an Allegory of Kings." Thoreau's "Civil Disobedience" effectively responds to the affluent citizen who would be exempt from taxation: "If you use money which has the image of Caesar on it and which he has made current and valuable, that is, *if you are men of the State,* and gladly enjoy the advantages of Caesar's government, then pay him back some of his own when he demands it." In Joyce's *Ulysses,* the fact that "To Caesar what is Caesar's, to God what is God's" appears to Stephen "a riddling sentence" does not allow him clearly to distinguish between these authorities; nor does his perception of himself as "the servant of two masters . . . an English and an Italian" encourage him to prefer one to the other. The abbot who argues against euthanasia in Walter M. Miller, Jr.'s *A Canticle for Leibowitz* urges obedience to Caesar's law, but not when it contravenes God's (chap. 27).

CAMILLE R. LA BOSSIÈRE

REPENTANCE Biblically, *to repent* means "to change one's mind" (2 Chron. 6:37-42; Isa. 1:27; Jer. 5:3; Ezek. 14:6, etc.) or to turn back (Ps. 7:12), to learn one's lesson, to be filled with remorse (Matt. 21:29, 32; 27:3). The Greek root in most NT instances (e.g., 2 Tim. 2:25; Heb. 12:17) is the word *metanoia,* which implies a profound change of heart. The Hebrew word *naham* is onomatopoeic and implies difficulty in breathing — hence "pant," "sigh," or "groan" (e.g., 1 Kings 8:47-52) — and comes to signify also lament (Job 42:6).

In certain OT instances God is said to "repent" of a previously intended action such as punishment (Exod. 32:11-14) or blessing (1 Sam. 15:11, 39; Jer. 18:10). The most memorable incidents perhaps are God's "repenting" of his having made humankind and accordingly sending the Flood, and his "repenting" of his decision to destroy Nineveh because, in response to Jonah's preaching, the people had in fact "repented of their evil ways" (Jonah 3:9-10; cf. Matt. 12:41). There are other instances (e.g., Ezek. 24:14) where people persist so long without repentance that God is said to be past changing his mind. Speaking of God's actions in this way is nonetheless seen as actually a kind of anthropomorphic misrepresentation in various passages (e.g., Num. 23:19; 1 Sam. 15:29).

In the NT the words *metanoeō* and *metanoia* occur most frequently in Luke-Acts and Revelation, and only rarely in the Pauline epistles. The Vg translation *poenitentiam agere* ("to exercise penitence") is actually imprecise, since Lat. *poenitentia* etymologically signifies "pain, grief and distress" more akin to what is expressed in the idea of contrition, rather than what is central to the Gk. *metanoia*, a "fundamental change of outlook or purpose." In this instance a translator's choice has had significant implications for subsequent theology and spiritual tradition. In the Vg Jesus and the disciples call persons to "do penance" *(poenitentiam agite)* rather than, as in translations affected more directly by the Greek (KJV; RSV; JB), simply "to repentance" or "to repent" (e.g., Luke 13:3, 5). The Latinate phrase creates a difficulty which causes some later English translations from the Vg to drop the term altogether (e.g., Douay Matt. 9:13; Mark 2:17).

In his classic informal discussion of the process of repentance, his own, in *The Confessiones*, St. Augustine lays the emphasis on active repentance as *metanoia*, citing (after reference to Matt. 3:2 and allusions to Heb. 6:4 and Ps. 42:22) the injunction of St. Paul: "Be not conformed to this world, but be ye transformed by the renewing of your mind" (Rom. 12:2); this emphasis is consistent throughout his book (*Conf.* 13.12.13). St. Jerome lays a heavy stress, however, on the grief and lamentation involved in the repentance of one who already has a believer's vocation, referring to the prophets Jeremiah and Ezekiel as well as several of the more emotional psalms (6; 32; 51; 56) in an epistle of subsequent fame among those in contemplative life (*Ep.* 122).

The notion of a once-in-time repentance which is fundamental to conversion (the dominant NT usage), and of actions of penitence for sins committed *in lapsus* by the nominally faithful (more common in OT usage) came to characterize widely divergent ecclesiastical traditions. According to Rabbi Joseph B. Soloveitchick, Judaism keeps to an active practice of two such orders of repen-

tance, the "repentance of acquittal" and the "repentance of purification" (Peli, 49-66). In Western Christianity, as Church and society became less distinguished one from another and infant baptism more than adult conversion the means of entering the Church, the shift from repentance as *metanoia* to *poenitentiam agite* became pronounced. While not yet a sacrament, even in the time of Tertullian (*De poenitentia*, 10-12) the latter became an important feature of church discipline, the most serious breaches of which occasioned excommunication, temporary or permanent. In the patristic period, penalties (in the form of specific compensatory actions, performed especially during the Lenten period) began to be schematized (e.g., Innocent I, *Ep.* 1.7). Nonetheless, public excommunication with a once-only penance for reconciliation remained normative until the 8th cent. (Rahner, *"Sacramentum Mundi"*). The creation of lesser penances for less serious individual breaches of spiritual life seems to have originated in Irish and Anglo-Saxon monastic communities. In a considered departure from continental practice, these communities produced a system in which repeated absolution was given by the ordinary priest, no longer only solemnly by the bishop on Holy Thursday, but any day (see St. Columbanus, *Poenitentiale*). After the 12th cent., the period of the first Lateran Councils, and English Archbishop Pecham's Lambeth Constitutions (1273), intermittent penance and auricular confession became thoroughly established, although until the time of St. Thomas Aquinas it was still generally held (e.g., Hugh of St. Victor, *De Sacramentis*, 2.14.1) that contrition, not priestly absolution, achieves forgiveness of sins. Only with Scotus did absolution by itself become the sufficient means of grace and only in the 14th cent. in England did canonical schema for specific compensatory actions ("satisfaction") begin to gain importance. Robert Mannyng of Brunne could still say in his penitential manual *Handlyng Synne* (ca. 1300) that "wyþ sorow of herte and repentaunce þou mayst pay God wyþ lytyl penaunce" (5229).

Chaucer's Parson, whose tale is less a traditional sermon than a treatise on repentance, specifies the three aspects of the full penitential process as accepted in the later 14th cent. First he defines his subject:

> verray repentance of a man that halt hymself in sorwe and oother peyne for his giltes. And for he shal be verray penitent, he shal first biwaylen the synnes that he hath doon and stidefastly purposen in his herte to have shrift of mouthe and to doon satisfaccioun, and never to doon thyng for which hym oghte moore to biwayle or to compleyne, and continue in good werkes, or elles his repentance may nat availle. (*The Parson's Tale*, 10.86-89)

Contrition, confession (shrift of mouth) and satisfaction — compensatory or therapeutic actions designed to confirm resolve in the already baptized Christian — are all here. The Parson's sermon is as thorough and theologically informed a meditation on its subject as Chaucer's *Canterbury Tales,* with its framing Lenten pilgrimage to Canterbury undertaken as "satisfaccioun," is a psychologically and exegetically rich workshop on typical occasions of "synnes," "good werkes," and "fruits meet for repentance" (Matt. 3:8).

As is evident in morality plays such as *Everyman,* repentance was in the 15th cent. somewhat more strongly associated with an ultimate choice between salvation and damnation, and could have about it the force of a once-in-time penitence, as in deathbed conversion: the author of *Merlin* writes, "So fer haste thow gon that late it is to repente" (328). The same condition seems to apply to Shakespeare's Falstaff who, in contemplation of his faltering vigor, says, "Well, I'll repent, and that suddenly, while I am in some liking. I shall be out of heart shortly, and then I shall have no strength to repent" (*1 Henry 4,* 3.3.5-6); ironically, in finally putting off the influence of Falstaff, the "old man" who is "known as well as Paul's" (2.4.324, 575-76), it is actually Prince Hal who repents in the NT and Augustinian sense. The possibility of becoming so "hardened in heart" that the will cannot be broken is a terrifying prospect in Marlowe's *Doctor Faustus.*

With the Reformers' attempt to return to a biblical, especially NT, redefinition of major doctrines, and to simplify these wherever possible along lines suggested by the early Fathers, *poenitentiam agite* tends to fade away, replaced by a renewed concern with adult conversion and repentance as *metanoia.* This is the emphasis of Luther, who discovered from the Greek NT of Erasmus the misconstruction of the Vg *poenitentiam agite* in Matt. 4:17 and noted that the original sense was not that one should "do a penance" but rather "change one's mind." This led him to a view of repentance which may be as traumatic as a lightning stroke "if the old man is to be put off" — involving not specific actions but a wholesale transformation by faith (*Sermo de Poenitentia* [WA 1.317-24]. Luther nevertheless attributed some sacramental grace to penance, as a renewal of baptism. Calvin rejected the whole evolution of penitential doctrine, from the early Church ceremony of formal reconciliation by the bishop on Holy Thursday to an elaborate canonical system of offenses and penances (*Inst.* 4.19.14). He rejected also its sacramental status: "You will speak most correctly," he says, "if you call baptism the sacrament of penitence, seeing it is given to those who aim at repentance to confirm their faith and seal their confidence" (*Inst.* 4.19.17). Inasmuch as Calvin's point of view gained supporters within the Established Church as well as among Puritans, it is not difficult to find those like Sir Thomas Browne who came to wonder "What patience could be content to . . . accept of repentances which must have after penitences" (*Christian Morals,* 3.26).

The official Anglican position, as codified in the *Homilies Appointed to Be Read in Churches* (1562), attempted to deal with both the repentance "unto new life"

and the repentance of believers. The relevant homily avers that "no doctrine is so necessary in the church of God, as is the doctrine of repentance and amendment of life," which "true preachers of the Gospel, and of the glad and joyful tidings of salvation, have always . . . joined . . . together." But it also speaks of repentance as "return" in contexts which point to remedy for continuing sin. The fusion of the older Roman framework with a more Lutheran emphasis on *metanoia* leads the "Homily of Repentance" to declare "four parts of repentance": the first is "contrition of the heart" prompted specifically by reading the Scriptures and hearing them expounded; the second, "unfeigned confession and acknowledging of . . . sins unto God" as well as confession "one to another" (as enjoined in James 5:16). The "third part of repentance" (instead of penances, the traditional "satisfaction") "is faith, whereby we do apprehend and take hold upon the promises of God," and the fourth is "amendment of life, or a new life, in bringing forth fruits worthy of repentance. For they that do truly repent must be clean altered and changed, they must become new creatures, they must be no more the same as they were before" (2.456-61).

George Herbert's "Repentance" and especially his extended discussion of believers' repentance in *A Priest to the Temple* (chap. 33) stresses that "repentance is an act of the mind, not of the Body," and reiterates much of the content of the official Homily, concluding that "the essence of repentance . . . consisteth in a true detestation of the soul, abhorring, and renouncing sin, and turning to God in truth of heart, and newnesse of life" ("The Parson's Library"). For Jeremy Taylor repentance is not only the "one necessary thing" for salvation, but it has a particularly beautifying effect upon the human spirit, highlighting its best attributes: "it scatters its beams and holy influences" even as it "kills the lust of the eyes, and mortifies the pride of life; it crucifies the desires of the flesh and brings the understanding to obedience of Jesus" (*Unum Necessarium,* 668). Henry Vaughan's poem "Repentance" describes how, when he had resisted repentance in his unbelief, the counsel of a friend, the beauties of creation, and the narrative of Christ's Passion combined to make him feel his own impurity and need for God's mercy.

Puritans, including those who like Bunyan were driven out of the Established Church in part for placing too much emphasis on parts 3 and 4 of the official Homily's distinction, could be generally Calvinistic in their theology while retaining a strong commitment to repentance to "new life" (see *Grace Abounding to the Chief of Sinners* as well as *Pilgrim's Progress*). The fundamental association of repentance and conversion is apparent in Defoe's *Moll Flanders,* a tale long in sensational sin, and culminating in a lightning stroke of repentance, as well as in his *Robinson Crusoe,* which argues a general Puritan thesis that "None teach repentance like true penitents." Because of an almost exclusive focus on *metanoia,* in which repentance grows inseparable in discourse from regeneration or "the new birth," the Puritan emphasis reflected in Defoe contributed substantially to the rise of spiritual autobiography as a popular genre, and hence arguably to the rise of the novel (Starr; Damrosch).

John Wesley, although throughout his own life an Anglican, had strong roots in Puritan tradition, as is evident in his sermon on the "New Birth," in which he insists that "baptism is not the new birth," and in his *Earnest Appeal to Men of Reason and Religion* (1743), in which he defends his "encouragement" of sinners to repent; he argues as well for a necessary continuing repentance of believers in "The Repentance of Believers." Dr. Johnson, who knew and liked Wesley, shared the Methodist reformer's opinion that a repentant call for God's mercy even at the point of death by a "very wicked man" might prove efficacious for salvation, a conviction Boswell did not share (*Life,* 4.212; cf. Boswell's note). Johnson clearly worried, however, about whether a sufficient *metanoia* had been wrought in his own life, and as his *Prayers and Meditations* make clear, was often in terror of dying without effectual repentance. This fear was still more extravagantly visited upon William Cowper, in his case because of a keen Calvinist uncertainty about whether he was one of God's elect. Yet Cowper firmly believed in the possibility and necessity of a "national repentance" and in his poetry lamented "a nation scourged, yet tardy to repent" ("Expostulation," 723), intending by that a return to obedience of God's law such as "Bespeaks a land, once christian, fall'n and lost" ("Table Talk," 428; cf. 414-77).

Wordsworth senses with some perspicuity the 19th-cent. de-emphasis on repentance, personifying it as "a tender Sprite" (Prologue to "Peter Bell," 148). Romantic poetry can seem more often marked by "Bitterness of Soul, / Pining regrets, and vain repentances" (Shelley, "Queen Mab," 5.246). The term *repentance* is more often than before gently divested of its religious associations, as when in Thackeray's *Pendennis* it becomes a woman to "have checked herself repentantly, saying 'Well, we must not laugh at her' " (chap. 27). American literature in this period treats repentance somewhat more seriously, if only to subject it to critical examination, as in Hawthorne's *Scarlet Letter* (1850). With the increasing popularity of confessional literature in the later 19th and 20th cents., comes a renewed interest in the possibility, at least, of repentance and forgiveness. While on the Continent such repentance is actually achieved in the Jansenist vision of François Mauriac (*Le noeud de viperes* [1932]), repentance is more typically frustrated in English fiction in which, nevertheless, its possibility remains a crucial narrative element (e.g., Oscar Wilde's *The Picture of Dorian Gray* [1891]; Joyce's *Portrait of the Artist as a Young Man* [1916]; Joyce Cary's *Not Honour More* [1955]; Margaret Laurence's *The Stone Angel* [1969]). An exception to the pattern of frustrated or resisted repentance is Graham Greene's story of the renegade alcoholic

priest who, going back into a trap to hear the confession of a dying man, makes of his actions as well as words an expression of repentance (*The Power and the Glory*).

In the second half of the 20th cent. confession and repentance have become largely disjoined, in part as a result of the replacement of priest by psychiatrist in both literature and religious life. The influence of psychiatry favors comprehension and reintegration of the "old person" rather than repentance and "new birth." D. M. Thomas's *The White Hotel* offers an example of reintegration on Freudian lines; Morris West's *The World is Made of Glass* explores the Jungian model. This shift is sometimes reflected in religious rites themselves, which also downplay repentance, sometimes over the objections of literary scholars: M. Doody has quipped in reference to late 20th-cent. revisions of the *Book of Common Prayer* that "being loved by God [now] means never having to say you are sorry — almost" (Ricks and Michaels, 113). Yet some contemporary poets still write expressions of repentance: William Everson (Brother Antoninus) in his "Penitential Psalm" (cf. Ps. 51) begs for "the cleanly thing I could become!"; John Betjeman writes of his experience in "A Lincolnshire Church" in which "the Presence of God Incarnate" brought him to his knees to murmur "I acknowledge my transgressions . . . and my sin is ever before me" (*Collected Poems*, 164). In a Jewish book of repentance, Leonard Cohen expresses a sense of exhaustion with self-analysis: "We cry out for what we have lost. . . . We look for each other, and we cannot find us, and we remember you. . . . I'll do it myself, we said, as shame thickened the faculties of the heart. . . ." At last he sees "something shining, men of courage strengthening themselves to kindle the lights of repentance" (*Book of Mercy*, 32).

See also CONFESSION; CONTRITION; CONVERSION; EXILE AND PILGRIMAGE; SACRAMENT.

Bibliography. Brantley, R. *Locke, Wesley, and the Method of English Romanticism* (1984); Braswell, M. *The Medieval Sinner* (1983); Canfield, V. G. "From Parnassus Mount to Sion's Hill: Repentance and Conversion in English Non-Dramatic Poetry of the First Half of the Seventh Century." *Ohio State University Abstracts of Doctoral Dissertations* 60 (1948-49), 41-46; Damrosch, L., Jr. *God's Plot and Man's Stories* (1985); Peli, P. H. *Soloveitchick on Repentance* (1984); Rahner, K. *Concise "Sacramentum Mundi"* (1975); Ricks, C., and L. Michaels. *The State of the Language* (1980); Starr, G. *Defoe and Spiritual Autobiography* (1965).

RESURRECTION Belief in resurrection is at the core of Christian faith. It has as its foundation the death and rising again of Christ, proclaimed in the gospel as the promise of a future general resurrection when the dead will be raised for judgment and reward. The interdependence of the resurrection of Christ and that at the Last Judgment is succinctly articulated by St. Paul when he writes to the church at Corinth that "if there be no resurrection of the dead, then is Christ not risen: And if Christ be not risen, then is our preaching vain, and your faith is also vain" (1 Cor. 15:13-14). The NT typically does not so much reflect metaphysical speculation as express confidence in the ultimate defeat of death, the end of the curse resulting from the Fall (cf. Rom. 6:9-11; 1 Cor. 15:20-22).

The Christian doctrine of resurrection is distinguished from belief in reincarnation, which usually involves a series of rebirths from which the soul may seek release; nor is it the same as a doctrine of immortality, which concerns only the indestructibility of souls. Resurrection instead has primary reference to bodies. It is literally a "rising again" (the root meaning of the Gk. *anastasis* and the Lat. *resurrectio*), or a "rousing up" (*egeirō,* the Greek verb often used in the NT, means "to awaken" or "to arouse"). Since this raising up is to judgment and transformation in the life to come, resurrection is also distinguished from mere reanimation, a return to mortal life, which is subject again to death (as in the Lazarus story, John 11).

In spite of the KJV's now problematic translation of Job 19:25-27 (and Handel's compelling setting of it), little of resurrection may be discerned in the OT. Nevertheless there is a conviction that God's power extends even to Sheol (e.g., Ps. 49:15). The reanimation stories surrounding the prophets Elijah and Elisha (1 Kings 17:17-24; 2 Kings 4:18-37; 13:21), and prophetic visions such as Ezekiel's, with dry bones brought together and given life (37:1-14), further affirm God's dominion over death and power to raise to newness of life. Though the vision of dry bones refers to the nation Israel (as may Isaiah's words in 26:19; cf. vv. 14-15), the elements of a doctrine of individual resurrection are discernible in the later OT writings, and explicit in Dan. 12:1-3 where many who sleep in the dust of death awake, and the righteous shine as stars. Belief in resurrection to judgment, punishment, and reward is reflected in the story of the seven martyred brothers in 2 Macc. 7, as well as in other Intertestamental literature (see Nickelsburg). In Judaism around the time of Jesus there was no single view of life after death. The Wisdom of Solomon speaks of immortality but not resurrection (though it is immortality granted by God, rather than the inherent characteristic of souls, as in Greek metaphysics). And whereas the Pharisees believed in resurrection the Sadducees denied it (Mark 12:18; Acts 23:8; Josephus, *J.W.* 2.163-65).

During Jesus' own ministry he disputed sharply with the Sadducees about the dead (Mark 12:18-17) and demonstrated his power in restoring life on three occasions (Luke 7:11-17; 8:49-56; John 11). Such words and deeds, however, achieved their full significance only in the light of his own resurrection, when, on the "third day," he triumphed over death. The Gospel accounts struggle with the sameness and newness of Jesus' resurrected body: it is the same Jesus who asks to be handled and fed (Luke 24:39, 41), yet he is difficult to recognize (Luke 24:16; John 20:14), disappears or appears at will

(Luke 24:36; John 20:19), and finally ascends to heaven (Luke 24:51).

Among the evangelists, John emphasizes that Christ's resurrection life has already begun in believers (e.g., John 6), a process to be completed in resurrection at the end time (6:54; 11:23-26). Paul's message is essentially the same, though he expresses it in the symbolism of baptism; since those who are "in Christ" have new life here and now, their coming out of the burial waters of baptism is like a resurrection (Rom. 6). There is future promise as well: physical death is only a sleep (1 Cor. 15:51; cf. Matt. 9:24; John 11:11-13), from which believers shall be wakened at the summons of the trumpet (1 Cor. 15:52; 1 Thess. 4:16). The destiny of the believer remains Paul's chief concern, and his themes are sameness and transformation. In the simple image of seed and full-grown grain (1 Cor. 15; cf. John 12:24) he captures the persistence of the individual but also the radical difference in resurrection, in which one's lowly body will be changed to the likeness of the risen Christ's glorious body (Phil. 3:21).

The Church confessed its belief in the resurrection of the body in the earliest baptismal formulas and later in its creeds ("Christ is risen!" Resp. "He is risen indeed! Alleluia!"). At the end of the 1st cent., St. Clement of Rome used the pagan myth of the phoenix to illustrate God's promise of resurrection (*Epistola 1 ad Corinthios* [PG 1.261-66]). In the next two centuries, writers such as Athenagoras, St. Irenaeus, and Tertullian argued for a physical resurrection against gnostic spiritualizing. Origen, however, relied on the Pauline notion of the "spiritual body" in order to emphasize transformation and discontinuity in resurrection; he also held the controversial belief that all souls, including those of demons, would be redeemed in the life to come.

The Fathers wove together doctrines of immortality (as the postmortem persistence of the individual) and resurrection (as the eschatological reunion of soul with reconstituted body), finding it difficult to hold one without the other: unless the soul persists, there can be no beatific enjoyment of God in the life to come; but without the body the personality has no vehicle of expression, as the Incarnation itself attested. Exactly how the raised body could be the same and yet transformed remained a subject of debate. St. Augustine, in the closing chapters of *De civitate Dei* defends bodily resurrection against the objections of skeptics. At the same time, he recognizes that if resurrected eyes are to look upon the invisible God, some transformation of present capacities is required (22.11-29).

An Aristotelian understanding of psychophysical unity provided Aquinas a philosophical framework for the belief that the resurrection of the body (and not just the persistence of the soul) was the natural expectation for a future life — though supernatural power would be required to bring it about (*Summa Theol.* 3a, Supp. 75-86; *Contra Gentiles*, 4.79ff.). The 16th-cent. Reformers continued to emphasize the raising of Christ and the omnipotence of God, challenging only what they considered unwarranted additions to this belief. Resurrection was affirmed in the Lutheran Augsburg Confession, pt. 1, art. 17, and by Calvin, though he refused to explore the "corners" of heaven, calling this a "superfluous investigation of useless matters" (*Inst.* 3.25).

The earliest extended use of the resurrection theme in English literature is the OE *Phoenix*, which follows patristic precedent in treating the phoenix myth as an allegory of Christ and his followers: they, covered with the ground until the coming of the consuming and purifying fire, rise from ashes to the life of life. In the ME Corpus Christi plays, the Resurrection of Christ is portrayed as a triumph over the devil in the harrowing of hell; and the raising of the dead is central in the "last judgment" plays (see esp. the Chester, York, and Towneley cycles). The anonymous author of *St. Erkenwald* makes the miraculous reawakening of a righteous pagan long dead the occasion for his spiritual rebirth through Christian baptism; the latter miracle is seen to be of more importance than the revivification of his flesh.

Spenser uses a resurrection allegory in the Redcrosse Knight's battle with the dragon in *The Faerie Queene.* After a day of fighting the knight is knocked into the Well of Life, from which he rises "new born" (9.34.9), as in Christian baptism; the second night he receives from the Tree of Life a healing balm, the stream which can "rear again / The senseless corpse appointed for the grave" (9.48.7). Like Christ, he is victorious on the third day.

Shakespeare locates the theme of resurrection in plots which end in reconciliation and harmony. In *All's Well That Ends Well,* Helena is willing to embrace death to set Bertram free; she is indeed believed dead until her sudden reappearance exposes hidden truth and establishes a new beginning. The Christian understanding of resurrection is especially strong in the losses and recoveries of the late plays, though clothed in magic and in pagan classical garb. The threatening seas of *The Tempest* are merciful: lost Ferdinand is restored to Alonso, Milan's misfortune ends in Naples' blessing, and all find themselves "When no man was his own" (5.1.213). Likewise in *The Winter's Tale:* Paulina's dramatic "re-awakening" of the lifelike "statue" of Hermione serves to vindicate injured innocence and reward the "faith" of Leontes. Resurrection is central to John Milton's vision of the loss and regaining of Paradise, for unless death is ultimately defeated God's purposes will not be justified. Christ's victorious Resurrection is thus announced before the Fall in *Paradise Lost* (3.245-49) and is later foretold to the fallen but repentant Adam (12.431-35); God promises a second life for mankind in the "renovation of the just" along with a renewal of heaven and earth (11.61-66). At the end of *Samson Agonistes* Milton uses the phoenix as a simile of the resurgence of Samson's power, a pre-Christian harbinger of resurrection.

John Donne's verse provides a variety of resurrection images — from the commonplace pictures of death as "rest and sleep" from which one wakes to the death of Death ("Death, be not proud") to the alchemical conceit in which the gold of Christ's buried body rises "all tincture," able not only to change "leaden and iron wills" but also to transmute sinful bodies into his likeness ("Resurrection, Imperfect"). Elsewhere, the prospect of resurrection and final judgment moves the poet to repentance ("At the round earth's imagined corners"). For George Herbert resurrection becomes the ultimate answer to affliction, from which one will rise with Christ ("Easter Wings").

The poetry of the last two centuries has explored resurrection themes in a variety of ways. In Coleridge's *Rime of the Ancient Mariner* a "troop of spirits blessed" (349) enlivens the corpses of the mariner's shipmates, fallen through his wanton sin; this "rising" proves a means to his salvation. Like her American contemporary Emily Dickinson, Christina Rossetti befriends death (in "Life and Death") for its rest and relief. But while for Dickinson immortality and heaven lie in that rest, Rossetti confesses hope that from the husk will rise the sap of Spring, from fire will come a life remolded ("A Better Resurrection"). For Gerard Manley Hopkins, resurrection hope flashes unexpectedly in the darkness, and its transformation "at trumpet crash" brings radical discontinuity: without a hint of alchemical magic, this highly combustible "matchwood," man, is "immortal diamond" ("That Nature is a Heraclitean Fire and of the Comfort of the Resurrection"). In evident echoing of Paul (1 Cor. 15:13-14), John Updike challenges romanticized views of resurrection in "Seven Stanzas at Easter":

> Make no mistake: if He rose at all
> it was as His body;
> if the cells' dissolution did not reverse, the molecules
>   reknit, the amino acids rekindle,
> the Church will fall. . . . (*Telephone Poles and Other Poems,* 72)

Margaret Avison probes the fear that "light will burn / and wake the dead" in "Waking and Sleeping: Christmas" *(sunblue),* while in the title poem of Christopher Rush's *A Resurrection of a Kind* the dead rise delicately in the evanescence of memory alone.

Examples of resurrection in prose fiction are equally diverse. In Dickens's *A Tale of Two Cities,* Dr. Manette is "recalled to life" by the love of his daughter, and the self-sacrificing Sydney Carton anticipates as he mounts the scaffold resurrection and the redemption of his life in a new future; even Jerry Cruncher's work as "Resurrection-man" serves the theme as foil. A decidedly non-spiritual interpretation of the raising of the flesh is provided by D. H. Lawrence's *The Man Who Died,* a novel in which the symbolic bird is not the phoenix but the cock (cf. Lawrence's essay "The Risen Lord," which refashions resurrection into a new kind of life in the body). C. S. Lewis re-creates explicit Christian allegory in Aslan's return to life and his breathing on the stone statues at the castle of the White Witch (*The Lion, the Witch, and the Wardrobe*). In J. J. R. Tolkien's *Lord of the Rings* there are parallels with Christ's resurrection in Gandalf's death and return to life: he falls into an abyss in combat with an evil Balrog, and returns in shining clothes as Gandalf the White, though veiled and not immediately recognized by his followers. A much transmuted development of the theme comes in the early novel of John Gardner, *The Resurrection,* which plays off the philosophically refined thoughts of a professor dying in mid-career against the effects of his dying on himself and on those around him: the issue is not rebirth in an afterlife so much as the struggle of love toward resurrection in the present. In Jack Hodgins's *The Resurrection of Joseph Bourne,* a strange woman of compelling beauty but unknown origin arrives in a port town stinking of death after a deluge, and effects old Bourne's death and his return to life. The miracle leaves no one untouched, and other unexpected personal transformations force decisions about relationships and community — until in the final apocalyptic scene some are destroyed or excluded and the rest join in a dance of reconciled and resurrected life.

See also DEATH, WHERE IS THY STING?; HEAVEN; LAST JUDGMENT; PASSION, CROSS; PHOENIX.

Bibliography. Andreach, R. J. *The Slain and Resurrected God: Conrad, Ford and the Christian Myth* (1970); Barth, K. *Resurrection of the Dead* (Eng. trans. 1933); Charles, R. H. *Eschatology: the Doctrine of the Future Life in Israel, Judaism, and Christianity: A Critical History* (rpt. 1963); Cullmann, O. *Immortality of the Soul or Resurrection of the Dead?* (Eng. trans. 1958); Dewart, J. *Death and Resurrection* (1986); Gatch, M. M. *Death: Meaning and Mortality in Christian Thought and Contemporary Culture* (1969); Kremer, K. R. "The Imagination of the Resurrection: The Poetic Continuity and Conversion of a Religious Motif in Donne, Blake, and Yeats." *DAI* 31 (1971), 5366A; Nickelsburg, G. W. E., Jr. *Resurrection, Immortality, and Eternal Life in Intertestamental Judaism.* HTS 26 (1972); Rowland, C. *The Open Heaven: A Study of Apocalyptic in Judaism and Early Christianity* (1982); Stendahl, K., ed. *Immortality and Resurrection* (1965); Wheeler, M. *Death and the Future Life in Victorian Literature and Theology* (1990).   PAUL W. GOOCH

REUBEN   One of the twelve sons of Jacob.

See also AARON; JACOB; JOSEPH THE PATRIARCH; TRIBES OF ISRAEL.

REVELATION   The Revelation to John on Patmos, or the Apocalypse, is the last book of the NT. His ultimate vision is of a new creation, a perfected re-beginning, and as Genesis began with a week of creation, Revelation sets itself out as the "week" which ends the old and marks the advent of the new creation. Hence Genesis and Revelation bracket all sacred history and so constitute a unity with

one another which partakes of the identification of the Word with God. This is part of what is signified by the divine utterance twice stated near Revelation's beginning and twice near its end: "I am Alpha and Omega, the beginning and the end" (Rev. 1:8, 11; 22:13). In its elaborate patterning the work consists of seven sections of seven elements each. These together form a symbolic seven weeks of seven years with a concluding section, all shaping the Jubilee or fifty-year cycle of the Jewish calendar, here typifying the completion of an aeon or age (Austin Farrer, *A Rebirth of Images* [1949]).

It is necessary to emphasize the deliberate structure of Revelation, for this opaque and apparently bewildering work has a coherence unlike that of a narrative or story, mirroring linear time, but rather taking its meaning from its symbolic structures and the allegorical or typological correspondences within its intricate unity. The work is modeled on Jewish apocalyptic, drawing, e.g., on the sevenfold sequence of visions in Zech. 1:7–6:15. In keeping with the genre, it takes the form of a series of visions mediated to a visionary by a supernatural figure. It also adapts to its purposes the elements of address set by the genre of the Pauline apostolic letter, while in its progression it may make use of a quasi-dramatic form (Frank Bowman, *The Drama of the Book of Revelation* [1955]). John Milton seems to have thought so when he described Revelation as a literary "model for a high and stately Tragedy" (*The Reason of Church Government*). But there is a kind of narrative line in the visions which emerges not as a story but as a movement, through polarized conflicts, from the impure mixed nature of the actual world to the purified world at the end of time, when demonic evil is entirely separated from the divine goodness of the new creation.

The cryptic and evocative nature of Revelation's essentially poetic vision accounts for much of its extraordinary influence. The rest derives from the powerful expectation it generates of a universal destruction which will clear the way for a heaven on earth in which an elect remnant and the resurrected righteous dead will live beatifically. It has, however, four distinguishable literary aspects, and these characterize as well the types of influence it has exerted. The first is its very character as visionary revelation symbolically and allegorically expressed. Here Revelation has been a general influence on such English religious allegories as William Langland's *Piers Plowman,* John Bunyan's *The Pilgrim's Progress* and *The Holy War,* and more specifically Edmund Spenser's *The Faerie Queene,* especially its first book, the allegory of Holiness.

Closely related is Revelation's second aspect as a progressive visionary unfolding of sacred history. The most notable parallel in English is the Archangel Michael's revelation to Adam, in *Paradise Lost,* of all that will follow upon Adam's fall to the end of time, a revelation climaxing with Christ's Second Coming:

Last in the Clouds from Heav'n to be reveal'd
In glory of the Father, to dissolve
Satan with his perverted World; then raise
From the conflagrant mass, purg'd and refin'd,
New Heav'ns, new Earth, Ages of endless date
Founded in righteousness and peace and love,
To bring forth fruits Joy and eternal Bliss. (*PL*
12.545-51)

The third aspect of its literary influence is seen in the disposition of writers who, as they handled themes derived in part from the Apocalypse, used in some way or another its sevenfold form. There is first a generalized influence which is diffused through hexameral and heptameral literature, a tradition which blends the influence of Creation's first seven days and Revelation's last seven "days." It is exemplified in Renaissance Latin by Pico della Mirandola's *Heptaplus* (1489), after which Thomas Traherne modeled his sevenfold *Meditations on the Six Days of Creation.* But again, most notable is John Milton's cryptic use of the sevenfold Apocalyptic structure (and its thematic corollaries) as one of the underlying progressions in *Paradise Lost* (Michael Fixler, "The Apocalypse within *Paradise Lost,*" in *New Essays on "Paradise Lost,"* ed. T. Kranidas [1969], 131-78).

Most ubiquitous is the fourth category of Revelation's influence, through its themes, motifs, figures, imagery, and symbolism, which merit individual entries in the present volume. There is here an embarrassment of riches too great for citation. Milton's work is again the richest, with such an early work as *The Nativity Ode* anticipating the use of Revelation's themes, motifs, and imagery throughout the rest of his writing. William Blake's well-known poem, "And did those Feet in ancient time," setting Apocalyptic strife and renewal in "England's green and pleasant land," appropriately is part of the preface to his prophetic poem, *Milton* (ca. 1804-10). More recent writers seem less inclined to identify with a coming New Jerusalem than with the demonic and doomed city of Rev. 18:19, as in Pat Frank's *Alas Babylon* (1959).

Finally there is a fifth but distinct category of influence in English literature in the form of the literary commentary on Revelation whether as a work apart or as part of some other work. The first English commentary on Revelation was by the Tudor playwright and Bishop John Bale (in *Select Works of John Bale* [1849]); the last of any literary importance was D. H. Lawrence's *Apocalypse* (1931). Commentary on the Apocalypse also describes a powerful formative impulse in the works of Northrop Frye. Notably in his *Anatomy of Criticism* (1957), in *Fearful Symmetry* (1947), and very specifically in *The Great Code: The Bible and Literature* (1982), Revelation figures for Frye as a master paradigm of the creative imagination.

See also ALPHA AND OMEGA; APOCALYPSE; ARMAGEDDON; MARRIAGE FEAST, APOCALYPTIC; SECOND COMING; WHORE OF BABYLON; WOMAN CLOTHED WITH THE SUN.

Bibliography. Caird, G. B. *The Revelation of St. John the Divine* (1966); Farrar, A. *The Revelation of John the Divine* (1964); Fiorenza, E. S. "Revelation." *IDBSup* (1976); Kermode, F. *The Sense of an Ending* (1967); Patrides, C. A., and J. Wittreich, eds. *The Apocalypse in English Renaissance Thought and Literature: Patterns, Antecedents, and Repercussions* (1984); Wagar, W. W. *Terminal Visions: The Literature of Last Things* (1982).   MICHAEL FIXLER

RICH FOOL, PARABLE OF This parable, which appears in the noncanonical Gospel of Thomas as well as in Luke 12:16-21, forms part of Jesus' response to a man who asks him to become involved in the matter of a disputed inheritance. Jesus pointedly refuses to become "a judge or divider" (v. 14). He warns against "all covetousness" and admonishes the man that "a man's life consisteth not in the abundance of the things which he possesseth" (v. 15). The parable which follows illustrates these teachings.

Jesus speaks of a rich farmer whose all-consuming concern is preserving and enjoying his wealth. He contemplates a future time when his "ample goods" (v. 19) are securely stored and he will be free to "eat, drink, and be merry" (v. 19) with self-indulgent abandon.

Abruptly, God enters the scene to disrupt the wealthy man's plans. God addresses the farmer as "fool" (v. 20), a term applied to one who does not give God proper acknowledgment and reverence (Ps. 15:1). The fool is informed that his soul is at God's disposal; indeed, it is required by God "this night" (v. 20). God reminds the fool that at his death he will not even have the power to give away the goods he has worked to acquire and keep for himself: "Whose will they be?"

The parable ends with the warning that the rich fool's fate awaits all those who rely on material goods as their ultimate form of security instead of putting their lives and possessions at the disposal of God. "So is he that layeth up for himself and is not rich towards God."

Although it has lent itself to two modern books entitled *A Certain Rich Man,* one by W. Allen White (1909) and the other by Vincent Sheehan (1949), this parable is better recognized in literature for two of its sayings than for its use as a model for narrative. The rich fool's smug "eat, drink, and be merry" has become proverbial, and is applied trenchantly by William Hazlitt, e.g., in his "Merry England." G. K. Chesterton, in a similar context, his book on *George Bernard Shaw,* quips: "Let us endure all the pagan pleasures with a Christian patience. Let us eat, drink, and be serious" ("The Philosopher"). The divine response, "Thou fool, this night thy soul shall be required of thee" (v. 20), has also found its way into literary idiom, as in Butler's *The Way of All Flesh:* "And there is not one of us can tell but what this day his soul may be required of him" (chap. 49). The basic structure of the parable has been employed repeatedly in didactic literature, from the medieval play *Everyman* to a modern dramatization by

Mary Moncure Parker, *The Soul of the Rich Man: a morality play* (1908).   LENORE GUSSIN

RIMMON A Syrian god worshipped by Naaman before he was cured by Elisha of his leprosy. Milton makes Rimmon one of the fallen angels in *Paradise Lost* who "against the house of God was bold," a seducer of Ahaz (*PL* 1.467-75).

See also AHAZ; DAGON; ELISHA; NAAMAN.

RIVER OF LIFE In Rev. 22:1 the apostle John pictures a "pure river of the water of life, clear as crystal, proceeding out of the throne of God and of the Lamb." In the midst of it and on either side is the tree of life with its twelve fruits and healing leaves (Rev. 22:2). The water is freely available to whoever desires it (Rev. 22:17). The Lamb shall lead the martyrs to living fountains (Rev. 7:17). In the OT this river is associated with the Garden of Eden (Gen. 2:10), the Temple on Zion (Ezek. 47:1-12), and the City of God (Ps. 46:4; Zech. 14:8); it signifies fertility, rejuvenation, joy, and eternal life, all of which allusions are incorporated into St. John's vision.

In the Middle Ages knowledge of the image's significance was ensured by popular commentaries on the Apocalypse, the most influential being those of Beatus (late 9th cent.), Berengardus (ca. 1100), Rupert of Deutz (d. 1129), Joachim of Fiore (1130-1202), and Alexander of Bremen (ca. 1242). A remarkable outpouring of illustrated Apocalypse MSS, particularly in England between 1240 and 1350, provided visual complements to the texts. The seminal *Trinity Apocalypse* (ca. 1250; Cambridge, Trinity College, MS R.16.2.fol. 27) explains that the river means the glory of the saints; it has the brightness of crystal because it makes each of the righteous sparkle according to his works. By the two sides of the river are understood angels and mankind. The accompanying illustration, splendidly adorned with gold leaf, shows the City in projection enclosing Christ enthroned, the Lamb, and the river flowing from beneath Christ's feet and through the branched tree. Below, John and an Angel ascend a mountain to view the heavenly scene. St. Bonaventure's *Arbor Vitae* associates light and joy with the stream, attributes also of Dante's river of light in *Paradiso*, canto 30.

In English literature the most significant treatments occur in *Pearl* (ca. 1380) and in Bunyan's *Pilgrim's Progress,* pts. 1 (1678) and 2 (1684). The narrator of *Pearl,* having fallen asleep in a garden, finds himself in a brilliant paradise beside a stream gleaming with jewels. On the opposite bank he sees his lost "pearl," now a Bride of Christ. After instructing him about salvation, she directs him to a hill from which he can view the City, the wounded Lamb, the company of the blessed which includes the Pearl-Maiden, the tree of life, and the clear river, brighter than sun and moon. Despite a warning that death must precede the crossing of the river, the Dreamer

attempts to plunge in and his vision abruptly ends. Bunyan's river also represents death, its flavor bitter, its depth varying according to the pilgrim's faith: the mere crossing does not ensure entry into the City. On the near side is Beulah, a *locus amoenus* where the traveler awaits the Master's summons.

Spenser's Redcrosse Knight is saved from the dragon by the silver flood from the well of life (*Faerie Queene,* 1.11.29-30, 46-48). In Milton's *Lycidas,* the drowned hero's apotheosis carries apocalyptic associations of purifying and healing water. The anagogical river appears also in Blake's *Milton* and *Jerusalem* and in Christina Rossetti's *Whitsun Monday* and *Holy City.* It forms part of the Otherworld landscape in such Christian fantasies as George Macdonald's *Lilith* (1895) and C. S. Lewis's *The Last Battle* (1956). Hymnody has popularized the image and its associations with salvation, divine love, grace, fellowship, joy, and release from "sorrow, sin and death." Among the most familiar of such hymns are "O Mother dear, Jerusalem" (1580), John Newton's "Glorious Things of Thee are Spoken" (1779), the 18th-cent. Welsh hymn "Guide Me, O Thou Great Jehovah," and Robert Lowry's revivalist "Shall We Gather at the River" (1864).

See also LIVING WATER.

Bibliography. Brieger, Peter H., ed. *The Trinity Apocalypse* (1967); Kean, P. M. *The Pearl* (1967); Nolan, B. *The Gothic Visionary Perspective* (1977).   MURIEL WHITAKER

RIVERS OF BABYLON *Super flumina Babylonis* begins the Vg version of Ps. 137: "By the rivers of Babylon we sat down and wept: yea, we wept when we remembered Sion" (KJV). This lament out of the captivity of Israel, one of the most moving in the Bible, has produced many translations and adaptations. It is still sung by Jews in memory of the captivity, and from the time of the early Church it also became a familiar part of Christian hymnody. St. Augustine's sermon on Ps. 137 allegorizes the waters of Babylon as "all things which here are loved, and pass away" (*Enarr. in Ps.* 137.2).

Izaak Walton relates, in his *Life of Dr. John Donne,* how Donne grieved over his wife's death: "as the Israelites sate mourning by rivers of Babylon when they remembered Sion, so he gave some ease to his oppressed heart by thus venting his sorrow." Byron has two poems on the subject. In "By the Rivers of Babylon We Sat Down and Wept," the speaker is one of those who wept, "and thought of the day / When our foe, in the hue of his slaughterers, / Made Salem's high places his prey." In "Oh Weep for Those!" he invites his reader to identify compassionately with "those that wept by Babel's stream, / Whose shrines are desolate, whose land a dream." Swinburne's poem celebrating the resistance of Italy to Austrian tyranny, *Super flumina Babylonis,* identifies Italy with captive Israel, "that for ages of agony has endured, and slept. . . ." Hardy gives voice to his quarrel with the Bible he knows so well when, in *The Return of the Native*, he writes:

> Human beings, in their generous endeavour to construct a hypothesis that shall not degrade a First Cause, have always hesitated to conceive a dominant power of lower moral quality than their own; and, even while they sit down and weep by the waters of Babylon, invent excuses for the oppression which prompts their tears. (6.1)

A similar viewpoint is represented by Ruskin in his *Fors Clavigera* (Letter 91). The narrator of Eliot's *The Waste Land* describes his post-party emptiness with an allusion to the verse, replacing "Babylon" with "Leman," a ME word for "lover": "By the waters of Leman I sat down and wept." Elizabeth Smart's autobiographical *By Grand Central Station I Sat Down and Wept* recalls the verse in order to lend poignancy to her own often bitter recollections of an alienated and "exiled" life.

See also BABYLON; HARP.

RIZPAH   Rizpah was a concubine of King Saul. Ishbosheth, Saul's son, accused Abner of having relations with her (2 Sam. 3:7-11). Two of her sons were subsequently hanged by the Gibeonites (2 Sam. 21:8-11), along with five sons of Saul's daughter Michal; Rizpah kept watch over their bodies to prevent the birds and beasts from devouring them. The pathos of her story was popular with 19th-cent. preachers and is prominent in William Cullen Bryant's poem "Rizpah" as well as Tennyson's "Rizpah," both of which are dramatic monologues.

ROCK   Although there are exceptions, the Bible and ancient translations of it usually make a distinction between rock (*ṣur* or *selaʿ* in Hebrew; *petra* in Greek) which is part of a natural rock formation and stone (*ʾeben* in Hebrew; *lithos* in Greek) which is not part of a natural rock formation. Although "rock" and "stone" are used in similar ways as symbols of hardness or strength or were both used as altars or landmarks, the only place where they are used as parallels is in the expression "stone of stumbling and rock of offence."

The words for "rock" are often used to describe a place of refuge in the rocky hill-country of Palestine. From this developed the practice of referring to God as a "rock" (nearly always with the word *ṣur*). This OT title for God is most often found in prayers and poetry, and while other ideas may be included, the name conveys primarily that God saves and protects his people (e.g., Deut. 32:15, 18; Pss. 62:2; 71:3).

The best-known occurrence of "rock" in the Bible is probably that in Matt. 16:18 where there is a wordplay between the name *Peter* (the masculine Greek form *Petros*) and the rock (the feminine form *petra*) on which the Church was to be built. Roman Catholics have interpreted this verse to mean that St. Peter would be the foundation for the Church and have used the verse to justify the Papacy. Historically, Protestants have tended to interpret the rock as Peter's confession that Jesus was the Christ, the Son of the living God. In the modern period there is a tendency even by Protestants to recognize that this verse did point to Peter's foundational role in the origin of the Church, but without seeing this as a basis for the Roman Catholic Papacy.

The use of the word *rock* in 1 Cor. 10:4 is surprising, for it identifies Christ as the spiritual rock which followed the Israelites in their wilderness wanderings. This identification has its origin in the OT accounts of water being supplied to the Israelites from a rock (Exod. 17; Num. 20). That the rock followed the Israelites is not part of the OT text, but was adopted by Paul from Jewish tradition (see, e.g., the targums on Num. 21:16-20 or Midr. Num. 1.2 and 19.26). This text then assumes that the preexistent Christ ministered to the ancient Israelites and is used to substantiate a warning to the Corinthians. It is this passage which yields such allusions as characterize F. W. Faser's "The Shadow of the Rock," in which "The Rock moves ever at thy side, / pausing to welcome thee at eventide"; the metaphor is extended in Willa Cather's novel *Shadows on the Rock* (1931). Augustus Toplady's "Rock of Ages, Cleft for Me" (1775) identifies the smitten rock of Exod. 17 and Num. 20 with the cross, and is probably an influential mediation of such allusions in later literature. T. S. Eliot's fragmentary play *The Rock* derives most of its biblical information from imagery connected with Heb. *ʾeben* and Gk. *lithos,* "stone."

See also PETER; SMITTEN ROCK; STONE; STONES CRY OUT; TEMPLE.   KLYNE SNODGRASS

ROOT OF ALL EVIL   *See* MAMMON; *RADIX MALORUM.*

ROSA SINE SPINA   *See* MARY, MOTHER OF JESUS; ROSE WITHOUT A THORN.

ROSE OF SHARON   A reference to the bride of the Song of Songs (2:1), the rose of Sharon becomes part of medieval typology of the Virgin Mary (e.g., in St. Anthony of Padua and St. Bernard of Clairvaux). Jonathan Edwards, in his *Personal Narrative,* says that the words represent to him "the loveliness and beauty of Jesus Christ"; for Edward Taylor the phrase inspires a poem in his *Poems and Sacramental Meditations,* the "Reflexion" to his first meditation, which compares the perfume of the rose to the sweetness of Christ's sacrifice celebrated in the Eucharist. In Sir Walter Scott's *Ivanhoe,* Prior Aymer agrees with her temporary captor that Rebecca is as beautiful as "the very Bride of the Canticles," indeed "the Rose of Sharon and the Lily of the Valley," then counters his licentious intentions with the parry "but your Grace must remember that she is still but a Jewess" (chap. 7).

ROSE WITHOUT A THORN   From at least as early as St. Paul's reference to "the thorn in the flesh," the thorn comes to represent even more than the thousand natural ills and shocks to which humanity is heir: it stands as a generic term for the moral imperfection and all our woe which entered the world through the Fall. Reading the curse mentioned in Gen. 3:18 ("Thorns also and thistles shall it bring forth to thee") in this way, the Fathers infer a *rosa sine spina* of the lost Eden, creating the tradition to which Herrick refers ("Before Man's fall, the Rose was born / (*St. Ambrose* says) without the Thorn" ["The Rose" in *Noble Numbers*]), and thus establish one of the principal cultural utensils for Milton's poetic recapture of Paradise: "Flowers of all hue, and without thorn the rose" (*Paradise Lost*, 4.256).

Milton's image is not therefore, as was sometimes supposed by early commentators, an Italian conceit, but is well documented from patristic sources (e.g., St. Basil, *Hexameron*, 5.45 [PG 32.1211]; St. Ambrose, *Hexaemeron*, 3.2 [PL 14.188], cited in G. W. Whiting, "And Without Thorn the Rose," *RES* n.s. 10 [1959], 60-62). The tradition is glanced at in Marvell, who sees in the freshness of the nymph playing amid the flowers the possibility of removing Nature's blight by disarming "roses of their thorns" ("The Picture of Little T. C. in a Prospect of Flowers"), while a sentimental age later, in Burns's song "The Banks o' Doon," the lass separates the rose from its thorn to image the gulf, here sexual, between innocence and experience ("But my fause luver staw my rose, / And left the thorn wi' me").

Bibliography. Seward, B. *The Symbolic Rose* (1960).

JAMES F. FORREST

RUTH The OT story of Ruth the Moabitess is an idyllic romance built around the life of a domestic heroine. As a pastoral work, the story has a strong elemental quality in its references to home, family, religious devotion, earth, harvest, love, and nation.

The plot is a comic, U-shaped sequence. The four chapters are structured so as to accentuate the climactic nighttime meeting between Ruth and Boaz: (1) the tragic background of the story, (2) the early stages of the romance, (3) the encounter at midnight on the threshing floor, and (4) the denouement. Underlying the story is a quest for a home (Ruth 1:9; 3:1), and there is a continuous tension between emptiness and fullness which is resolved happily in the last chapter. The story is noteworthy for its careful ordering of events; its use of the archetypes of harvest and the stranger or exile; its drama; its dramatic irony (Ruth and Boaz are oblivious to the likelihood of marriage); its controlling metaphor of ingathering; the use of allusion to salvation history (the domestic world of an obscure woman becomes linked with the mainstream of OT history); and the intricate characterization of Ruth, Boaz, and Naomi.

Thematically the story celebrates the commonplace (nature, earth, harvest, family, home), domestic values, and wedded romantic love. It is also a story of divine providence. Late in the story (4:17) the writer suggests yet another interpretive framework when he places the child of Ruth in the Davidic/messianic line, thereby calling attention to the story as a chapter of salvation history. (The only other biblical reference to the story, Matt. 1:5, likewise places Obed and Boaz in the genealogy of Jesus.)

In midrashic commentary Ruth is praised for her extraordinary beauty (Ruth Rab. 2.4; cf. Shab. 113b; Peshitta Ruth 3.3), but also for her piety (Ruth Rab. 3.3; Pirqe R. El. 23.115b), and though she was by birth a Moabitess, by virtue of her acceptance by Boaz and his blessing she became for tradition one of "the mothers of Israel" (Pesiqta Rab. Kah. 16.124a). For St. Augustine she was a model widow and yet blessed in her second marriage because her motive was "having seed such as was at that time necessary in Israel" (*De bono viduitatis*, 10). In lines which anticipate the image of Keats, St. Jerome writes to a female Christian convert: "My soul rejoices, yet the very greatness of my joy makes me feel sad. Like Ruth, when I try to speak I burst into tears" (*Ep.* 71). Dante's Ruth is a model of modest faith, seated on a petal of the white rose with two other mothers of Israel, Sarah and Rebecca, representing "those who believe in Christ yet to come" (*Paradiso*, 32.10-24).

Poets' allusions to the story have covered its main phases. In Milton's Sonnet 9 ("Lady that in the prime of earliest youth") Ruth appears with Mary, sister of Martha, as a norm of true spiritual virtue, and if the speculation is accurate that the young woman of the sonnet is Milton's first wife Mary Powell, the allusion also includes Ruth's domestic identity as the idealized bride.

Blake, in *Jerusalem*, follows Dante, listing Ruth with Bathsheba and others as the "Material Line" culminating in Mary (62.11), so emphasizing her sexuality. In a series of popular early 19th-cent. graphic illustrations on the theme of Ruth, four of eleven plates deal with sexual iconography in the narrative — notably the paintings of Laurens, Rembrandt, Delacroix, and Poussin, in the latter of which a harvest scene provides relevant background. Another iconic representation frequent in the 19th cent. shows Ruth gleaning, as in "The Solitary Reaper."

Byron compares himself and his readers searching after truth to Ruth and Boaz gathering grain (*Don Juan*, 13.96). Whittier remembers Ruth at the feet of Boaz when he says regarding a mountain lake under the moon that it "Sleeps dreaming of the mountains, fair as Ruth / In the old Hebrew pastoral, at the feet / Of Boaz" ("Among the Hills").

Ruth the exile prompts the most evocative of all the allusions to the story. In his "Ode to a Nightingale," Keats elaborates his theme of the bird as a symbol of the immortality of nature by asserting that the song to which he is listening is "the selfsame song that found a path /

Through the sad heart of Ruth when, sick for home, / She stood in tears amid the alien corn" (65-67).

The book of Ruth has been the subject of a host of dramatic adaptations. While many of these have been intended for religious instruction, serious literary adaptations include *Ruth and Naomi* (1786) by the Comtesse de Genlis (Stephanie Felicite Ducrest du St. Aubin), Andrew Young's dramatic poem *Boaz and Ruth* (1920), and William Ford Manley's *Ruth* (1928).

Bibliography. Boattie, D. R. G. *Jewish Exegesis of the Book of Ruth* (1976); Rauber, D. F. "Literary Values in the Bible: The Book of Ruth." *JBL* 89 (1970), 27-37.   LELAND RYKEN

S

SABBATH REST   At the beginning of creation the Spirit of God was hovering over the watery chaos (Gen. 1:2) without apparent rest. After six days, however, God had made the universe according to his will and rested on the seventh (Sabbath) day (1:31–2:3; Heb. *shabbat,* "rested"). The earth reverted to chaos when God unleashed the Flood as a punishment for human sin, preserving only the family of Noah (one of the possible meanings of whose name is "rest"), whom alone God had found righteous in that generation (6:7-9; 7:1). After the Flood Noah released a dove from the ark, but the creature at first found no rest upon the waters and returned to Noah (8:9).

When the Israelites were in bondage in Egypt, they were permitted no rest, but after their liberation they were commanded both to rest on the Sabbath day and to give rest to their bondservants on that day (Deut. 5:14-15). In keeping the Sabbath they were to enter into God's creation rest (Exod. 20:8-11) and delight in God's works (Isa. 58:13-14). Furthermore, when they entered the Promised Land, they were to give the land sabbatical rest one year in seven (Lev. 25:1-7), lest they be chased out of the land, so as to give the land rest as it lay desolate (Lev. 26:33-35, 43), while Israel itself in such a situation would have no rest, but would pine in her iniquity (Lev. 26:36-39; Deut. 28:65-67). For the Israelites themselves, entering the Promised Land can be spoken of as entering God's rest (Deut. 12:9), though through unbelief the generation which left Egypt was divinely prevented from entering this rest (Ps. 95:7-11).

When Israel occupied the Promised Land, the people and the land enjoyed rest when their enemies were subdued (Josh. 1:13; 21:43-44; Judg. 5:31), and God himself was spoken of as resting after the wilderness journeys in the Temple at Jerusalem (1 Chron. 28:2; Ps. 132). Yet the true resting place of God is not a material structure but the hearts of the contrite (Isa. 66:1-2); and Israel, though in the Promised Land, was exhorted to rest in God and find strength (Isa. 30:15).

In Ecclus. 24:1-8 the Wisdom of God seeks rest in the watery chaos of the nations (cf. Gen. 1:2), but finds it only in Israel, while in the NT the Spirit of God rests upon Jesus Christ (as had been prophesied of the Messiah in Isa. 11:2) at his baptism (John 1:32; cf. Mark 1:9-10), a thought further emphasized in the apocryphal Gospel of the Hebrews (cited by St. Jerome in his commentary on Isa. 11:2). According to Matt. 11:29, humans can also rest in Jesus Christ, in contrast to Judaism, which had become a religion of heavy burdens.

Heb. 3:7–4:11 interprets Ps. 95:7-11, with its implied promise of rest for the people of God after Joshua's conquest, as referring to something which is available to Christian believers. This could be either rest from works (hence rest of conscience, 4:3, 10), or the coming heavenly rest (cf. Rev. 14:13).

In various Jewish and Christian apocalyptic writings, as well as in talmudic sources, the age to come is described as a perpetual Sabbath, and in Heb. 4:9 a similar

Sabbath "rest (*sabbatismos*) for the people of God" is mentioned. Here the concept of a temporal Sabbath observed by physical rest has been transformed into an eschatological rest, entered into by faith (Heb. 4:2ff.). Faith itself, on this construct, is in this life a rest from the need to work out the means of one's own redemption; the reward of faith is at last to be experienced as an eternal Sabbath respite from the bearing of one's cross while a pilgrim in the world. Observance of the Sabbath is thus, as rest, proleptic of the believer's ultimate reward.

The early Church observed the Sabbath with worship and rest, though without as many legal proscriptions as pertained in Judaism. However, because of Jesus' conflicts with the Pharisees concerning their Sabbath observance (Mark 1:23-38; cf. Matt. 12:1-8; Luke 6:1-5), his resurrection on "the first day of the week," and St. Paul's injunctions not to relegalize the Sabbath (Col. 2:16), historians have inclined to the belief that the movement in Christendom toward setting aside Sunday as the day of worship began in the 1st cent. In Acts 20:7 and 1 Cor. 16:2 the "breaking of bread" and collection "for the saints in Jerusalem" are associated with the first rather than the seventh day. Yet widespread Sunday observance was not in effect until the 2nd cent., and it was not until the 4th cent., when Constantine decreed that certain types of work should not be done on Sunday, that the day began to reacquire certain Sabbath characteristics.

St. Augustine largely allegorized the significance of the Sabbath, defining it in terms of "the peace of rest, the peace of the Sabbath, which has no evening" (*Conf.* 13.35.50, noting the absence of the refrain "and the evening and the morning . . ." after Gen. 1:31). The Sabbath is therefore figuratively "eternal life" (*Conf.* 13.36.51), anticipated here in those "reasonable creatures" who try to orient their lives toward "the perfectly ordered and harmonious enjoyment of God, and of one another in God" (*De civ. Dei* 19.17; cf. *De Genesi ad litteram,* 4.9). Augustine was on this model led to see world history as divided into six temporal ages, of which the last would be followed by the millennial reign of the faithful with Christ (Rev. 20:1-7; cf. 2 Pet. 3:8). Later commentators elaborated a schema in which human history was expected to last for 6,000 years before the millennial Sabbath began.

During this same period, there was debate within the Roman church concerning whether one ought to fast "on the Sabbath" — i.e., Sunday — "and to receive the eucharist daily" — i.e., not merely on Sunday (St. Jerome, *Ep.* 71.6). The tendency toward sabbatarianism increased over the next centuries until the Decretals of Gregory IX (1234) made it an ecclesiastical law that Sunday should be a day of rest.

Luther and other Reformers tended at first to reject the sabbatarian emphasis, following Augustine in spiritualizing the Sabbath commandment and arguing that any day might do for rest or worship. Calvin, however, emphasized the biblical precedent for worship and assembly "to hear the Law, and perform religious rites" as well as "rest . . . and the intermission of labor." Examining many passages in which "this adumbration of spiritual rest held a primary place in the Sabbath" (*Inst.* 2.8.28), he defends a more strict sabbatarian practice in his own time against some of the other Reformers who criticized this emphasis as a form of revived "Judaism" (2.8.32-33). In so doing, along with some 16th-cent. Anabaptists, he helped lay the foundation for the sabbatarianism of 17th-19th cent. biblical literalists, some of whom, like modern Seventh Day Adventists, eventually returned to a "seventh day" observance.

In medieval and Renaissance English literature, spiritual analogies are more prevalent than an emphasis on literal sabbath observance. In Spenser's *Faerie Queene* there is an implied analogy in the Redcrosse Knight's schedule of service — "six yeares in warlike wize" to "that great Faerie Queene," followed by a sabbatical (1.12.18). On the other hand, when severe Puritan enforcement of strict sabbatarianism a generation later provoked King James to issue *The Declaration of Sports* (1618), declaring morris dancing and the maypole as suitable entertainments for Sunday, it was sufficient offense to many that they emigrated, via Plymouth and the Mayflower, to Massachusetts in 1620. Hawthorne (in *The Scarlet Letter*) recalls their establishment of strict Sabbath observance in the New World. The relationship between sabbatarianism and millenarianism in American thought, from the chiliasm of Cotton and Increase Mather through Thomas Shephard's *Theses Sabbaticae* (1649) to Jonathan Edwards's *History of the Work of Redemption,* has been well documented. The eschatological dimension of the subject occupies the attention of Thomas Bromley in his *The Way to the Sabbath of Rest* (1759). The same connection is found vigorously argued in a different scheme by the Adventist William Miller in his *Evidence from Scripture History of the Second Coming of Christ, about the Year 1843, exhibited in a course of lectures* (1836).

By contrast, the English clergyman George Herbert's poem "Sunday" is a summation of the Augustinian tradition. His concession to Calvin is his focus on a specific day of worship and rest (which he presents as a metonym, "the fruit of this, the next world's bud"): his good country parson will keep himself and his parishioners informed "how *Sundayes, holy-days, and fasting days* are kept" (*A Priest to the Temple,* chap. 17). William Cowper provides an excellent example of the growth of sabbatarian rigor in later Calvinist and evangelical circles, typically contrasting the proper use of Sunday with prevalent abuse, even by "a pastor of renown":

> Love, joy, and peace, make harmony more meet
> For sabbath ev'nings, and perhaps as sweet.
>   Will not the sickliest sheep of every flock
> Resort to this example . . .
>   . . . and justify the foul abuse

Of sabbath hours with plausible excuse?
If apostolic gravity be free
To play the fool on Sundays, why not we?
If he the tinkling harpsichord regards
As inoffensive, what offense in cards? ("Progress of
Error," 140-49)

Elsewhere he speaks of "Sabbaths profaned without
remorse" ("Bill of Mortality, 1793") as the unmistakable
mark of a reprobate (cf. *The Task*, 4.650-58). Yet for the
elect:

The groans of nature in this nether world,
Which Heaven has heard for ages, have an end.
Foretold by prophets, and by poets sung,
Whose fire was kindled at the prophet's lamp,
The time of rest, the promised sabbath comes.
Six thousand years of sorrow have well-nigh
Fulfilled their tardy and disastrous course. (*The Task*,
6.729-35)

Among the strictest Sabbatarians in Britain were the
Scottish Covenanters, best known to readers of English
literature through Sir Walter Scott's *Old Mortality*. The
subject of Sabbath observance was highly sensitive in
Scotland. The preference of Robert Burns for "The
Cotter's Saturday Night" with its "ease and rest to
spend" in a simple family meal, hymn singing, and
conversation, after which "the priest-like father reads
the sacred page," instead of the "simmer Sunday morn"
in which "Orthodoxy raibles" ("The Holy Fair"), was
controversial.

In the 19th cent. generally liberalized views, sometimes supported by references to Jesus' admonitions
against the legalism of the Pharisees, became more
popular (e.g., Ruskin, *Fors Clavigera*, Letter 11). In the
20th cent. the opposite pole from sabbatarianism is
reached in the luxurious self-indulgence depicted in Wallace Stevens's "Sunday Morning" (to which A. M.
Klein's "Saturday Night" is a satiric answer). "Sunday,"
by Howard Nemerov, captures more traditional analogies
("He rested on the seventh day, and so . . .") in modern
guise, yet argues that

It's still a day to conjure with, if not
Against, the blessed seventh, when we get
A chance to feel whatever He must feel,
Looking us over, seeing that we are good.
The odds are six to one He's gone away;
It's why there's so much praying on this day.

See also TEN COMMANDMENTS.

Bibliography. Folliet, G. "La Typologie du Sabbat chez
S. Augustin." *REA* 11 (1956), 371-90; Goen, C. C. "Jonathan
Edwards: A New Departure in Eschatology." *CH* 27 (1959),
32ff.; Katz, D. S. *Sabbath and Sectarianism in Seventeenth-
Century England* (1988); Parker, K. L. *The English Sabbath:
A Study of Doctrine and Discipline from the Reformation to
the Civil War.*   DAVID L. JEFFREY
                                                    PAUL GARNET

SABBATH OF SABBATHS   *See* ATONEMENT, DAY OF.

SACKCLOTH AND ASHES   Sackcloth, usually made
of black goat hair, was used by the Israelites and their
neighbors in times of mourning or social protest. The
modern English word is ultimately derived from the Semitic (Akk. *šaqqu;* Heb. *śaq;* Gk. *sakkos;* Lat. *saccus;* OE
sacc), and the linguistic evidence suggests a widespread
practice of wearing it in mourning, perhaps especially when
the wearer wished to publicize his or her sorrow. Mordecai
wore sackcloth publicly in Shushan to protest the order to
kill all Jews (Esth. 4:1-4). But sackcloth could also be worn
to signify public repentance (e.g., Neh. 9:1). When Jonah
had finally fulfilled his charge to preach to the Ninevites,
the king of Nineveh "arose from his throne, and he laid his
robe from him, and covered him with sackcloth, and sat in
ashes," after which the whole nation followed suit (Jonah
3:5-8). A convention so universal was open to insincerity,
and Isaiah points out therefore that the repentance which
pleases God is more likely to be evidenced by active deeds
of justice than by the mere wearing of sackcloth and ashes
(58:5-9).

The wearing of sackcloth and ashes as a sign of public
penance was still common in the Roman church of the 4th
cent., as attested by St. Jerome (*Ep.* 77), but understood
as a preliminary to works of justice. In the *vitae* of St.
Benedict and St. Alexis, as well as other signal medieval
saints' lives, sackcloth takes the form of the "hair shirt"
worn under the outerclothes and against the body, where
it would produce a maximum of penitential discomfort.
Later in the Middle Ages, the hair shirt becomes a self-
imposed instrument of mortification (used, e.g., by St.
Catherine of Siena); it is for Roper, in his *Life* of St.
Thomas More, an index of More's sanctity that after his
execution his body was found to be garbed in a hair shirt.

In Shakespeare's *2 Henry 4*, Falstaff commiserates
with the Lord Chief Justice that Prince Hal has given him
a "box on the ear." "I have checked him for it, and the
young lion repents," he says, adding, "marry, not in ashes
and sackcloth, but in new silk and old sack" (1.2.197-
200). A scene reminiscent of that described by St. Jerome
occurs in Hawthorne's "The Gentle Boy," where the
young Quaker woman Catherine denounces the Puritans
in their own meetinghouse. Taking off her cloak and hood,
she exposes herself "in a most singular array. A shapeless
robe of sackcloth was girded about her waist with a
knotted cord; her raven hair fell down upon her shoulders,
and its blackness was defiled by pale streaks of ashes
which she had strewn upon her head."

See also DUST AND ASHES; REPENTANCE.

SACRAMENT   The word *sacrament* is not found in the
English Bible. Lat. *sacramentum* was used to translate
Gk. *mystērion*; it was also associated in Roman culture
with a pledge of allegiance, a meaning which strengthened the word's appeal to the early Church for use in

connection with recitations of the creed and liturgies of adult baptism. Gk. *mystērion* generally referred to "the unseen things of God" (Rom. 1:20); hence its general application to "signs" of grace — dreams, visions, miracles, the prophetic word, and ultimately the Incarnate Word, "God manifest in the flesh" (1 Tim. 3:16). In Jesus the kingdom of God is said to be actually present (Luke 17:21); this is the "mystery of the kingdom" (Mark 4:11; Matt. 13:11), which will only be generally made known in the final resurrection (1 Cor. 15:51ff.).

The connection with the Incarnation, "the Word made flesh," was basic to the idea of sacrament in the early Church. St. Augustine established much of the terminology by which *sacramentum* was to be explained. Like other Church Fathers, he gave the name *sacrament* or *mystery* to everything which signified one thing at the level of reason and observation and another at the level of faith. (When St. Cyprian speaks of the "sacrament" of the Lord's Prayer, he refers simply to the meaning in it which is hidden to anyone who is not a Christian.) Reflecting on verses such as Ps. 19:1 ("The heavens declare the glory of God; and the firmament sheweth his handiwork") and Rom. 1:20 ("For the invisible things of him from the creation of the world are clearly seen, being understood in the things that are made, even his eternal power and Godhead . . ."), Augustine saw the whole created order as a vast sacramental system. It is this sense which Aubrey de Vere invoked in his "The Sacraments of Nature" — a 19th-cent. response to the Augustinian idea and a reflection on natural revelation. Hopkins gives the same idea powerful expression in "God's Grandeur," a meditation on the whole Creation as a rich *enchiridion symbolorum* in which "The world is charged with the grandeur of God" essentially "because the Holy Ghost over the bent / World broods," making all things natural and human ("man's smudge . . . and smell") part of a divinely ordained text referring to the Creator.

Liturgical sacraments, necessary for salvation, are merely a special case of the general class — special because divinely instituted. Commenting on Jesus' words in John 15:3 ("Now are ye clean through the word which I have spoken unto you"), Augustine sees the word *clean* as a synecdoche for baptism; yet it is "the word that cleanseth. Take away the word, and the water is neither more or less than water. The word is added to the element, and there results the Sacrament, as if itself also a kind of visible word" (*In Joan Ev.* 80.3).

For Augustine, there were "sacraments of the Old Testament," such as circumcision, "celebrated in obedience to the law" as "types of Christ who was to come" (*Contra Faustum*, 19.13-18; cf. St. Thomas Aquinas, *Summa Theol.* 3.70.1-4), as well as sacraments of the NT, which "flowed from the side of Christ on the Cross" and were grounded in the Incarnation. The basic NT sacraments for Augustine, as for the early Church, were, following 1 Cor. 10:1-22, baptism and the Eucharist (*De*

peccatorum meritis et remissione, 1.34), which Augustine calls "the outward signs of inward and spiritual grace." This definition was later to be adopted by the Council of Trent (1547), which added the words "instituted by Christ for our sanctification" (2.4).

In the interval, however, a fundamental elaboration of sacramental thought was effected. In the 12th cent. Hugh of St. Victor made modest amendments to patristic definitions, designating only baptism and the Eucharist as sacraments necessary for salvation but adding a second class of rituals, such as the water of aspersion and imposition of ashes, which are "of benefit to sanctification," and a third class, which involves education or preparation for faith (*De Sacramentis*, 1.10.7). Hugh's contemporary, Peter Lombard, had a greater impact upon subsequent sacramental thinking, however, by introducing a new class of sacraments, which in their significance fell somewhere between "signs" in general, such as words or images, and baptism and the Eucharist, which he accepted as the preeminent signs. Lombard arrived at seven sacraments conveying salvific grace, the additional five being penance, confirmation, marriage, holy orders, and extreme unction. These were officially recognized by the Council of Trent (1546).

Confirmation does not attract much attention in English literature. Extreme unction, "anealing" (cf. *Hamlet*, 1.5.76-79), or "last rites" does, from *Everyman* to *Ulysses,* perhaps the best meditation upon it being Ernest Dawson's poem which begins "Upon the eyes, the lips, the feet, / On all the passages of sense, / The atoning oil is spread . . ." and ends,

> Yet, when the walls of flesh grow weak,
> In such an hour it well may be,
> Through mist and darkness, light will break,
> And each anointed sense will see. ("Extreme Unction")

Marriage, a rich and important subject in English literature, is only infrequently referred to as a sacrament. In one such example, in Shakespeare's *Twelfth Night* the priest refers to

> A contract of eternal bond of love,
> Confirm'd by mutual joinder of your hands,
> Attested by the close of holy lips,
> Strength'ned by interchangement of your rings;
> And all the ceremony of this compact
> Sealed in my function, by my testimony. (5.1.155-60)

(The other sacraments, more frequently alluded to as such, are considered elsewhere in this dictionary.)

Reformation theologians allowed that the word *sacrament* might have a general *sensus symbolum* but reserved a liturgical use of the term for baptism and the Lord's Supper only. Luther added an exception clause for penance, as a renewal of baptism. Most Protestant traditions have seen sacraments as witnesses to the covenant and to God's promises to his elect. The Anglican *Book of Common Prayer* includes "A Catechism," which defines sacrament in Augustinian terms, with emphasis falling upon the phrase "ordained by Christ himself." Baptists and the more radical reformers of the 16th cent. tended to reject the word *sacrament* altogether in favor of terms such as *ordinance* and *commemoration*; they nevertheless share with other Reformed groups the view that baptism and the Lord's Supper function also as pledges of Christian profession.

In England, art. 25 of the Established Church holds with the Reformers that a sacrament is a "witness" rather than a "cause" of divine grace and officially recognizes only "two sacraments of the Gospel," though it effectively tolerates practice of the additional five Catholic rites. In the 19th cent. the Oxford Movement (Pusey, Newman, Keble, et al.) began a trend in Anglican tradition toward reincorporating the remaining five sacraments and other Roman ordinances. In so doing, they helped to create a wing of the church which has come to be known as Anglo-Catholic and which later attracted writers such as T. S. Eliot and W. H. Auden. In its revival of interest in the medieval church, this movement also influenced Tennyson, William Morris, Christina Rossetti, and the Pre-Raphaelites.

"Sacramentalism" has in the modern period had considerable impact on aesthetic theory and literary criticism. Dorothy Sayers provides an informal elaboration of a sacramental theory of art in her *The Mind of the Maker* (1941). Drawing on Keble and Newman but reflecting also the general sacramental view of language and symbol found in the early Fathers, she develops an analogy between human creativity and divine creation. A more rigorously Thomistic sacramentalism infuses the aesthetic of Jacques Maritain and Etienne Gilson, in which the point that "Analogous concepts are predicated of God preeminently" (Maritain, *Art and Scholasticism*, 30) is pushed in the direction of a generalized sign and symbol theory. In this view, while "no fine art as such is sacred art" (Gilson, *Arts of the Beautiful*, 175), effective art is a sign-craft which has the potential (when form and matter are unified) to be a *lauda Sion*. These writers and others in their train have influenced authors as diverse as Charles Williams, Flannery O'Connor, and Walker Percy.

See also BAPTISM; BRIDE, BRIDEGROOM; EUCHARIST; REPENTANCE; VOCATION.

Bibliography. Denzinger, H., and A. Schönmetzer, *Enchiridion Symbolorum* (1965); Rahner, K. *The Concise "Sacramentum Mundi"* (1975); Wallace, R. S., and G. W. Bromiley, "Sacraments." *ISBE* 4.256-58.

SACRIFICE   Usually in the Bible this word refers to the atoning sacrifices of OT Judaism, in which a lamb, kid, or pair of doves might be sacrificed in an appeal for the propitiation of human guilt and sin. In the NT it is typically used of Christ's Passion, the ultimate atoning sacrifice in which the victim is God himself, taking the place not of the substitute lamb, but in effect of humanity.

Perhaps the best-known English poem on the NT theme is Herbert's "The Sacrifice."

See also ATONEMENT; ATONEMENT, DAY OF; EUCHARIST; ISAAC; LAMB OF GOD; LITURGY; MOLOCH; PASSOVER; REDEMPTION; SUBSTITUTION; TRANSUBSTANTIATION.

SADDUCEES   *See* PHARISEES.

SALEM   The royal city of Melchizedek, which was visited by Abram (Gen. 14:18; Heb. 7:1). At times the city is identified with Jerusalem (see the parallelism with "Zion" in Ps. 76:2; see Calvin, *Commentaries*, 1.388). A play on the meaning of the name, "peace," is picked up in Heb. 7:2. Other identifications have been made, including Adonai Jirah (Gen. 22:14 in Gen. Rab. 56.10), a village near Beth-shan (Eusebius, *Onomasticon*, 152; also, for a time, St. Jerome, *Ep.* 73.2), one near Shechem based on the Greek, Latin, and Syriac traditions behind the KJV in Gen. 33:18, and the village near which John baptized (John 3:23). Salem lends its name to the Puritan settlement in Massachusetts which gained notoriety for its witchcraft trials in the late 17th cent., and which was the setting, ironic in its biblical associations for Hawthorne, of his composition of *The Scarlet Letter.*

See also MELCHIZEDEK.   DAVID W. BAKER

SALOME   Salome was the daughter of Herodias and stepdaughter of Herod Antipas, Tetrarch of Galilee and Perea in the 1st cent. Her claim to notoriety derives from the dance she performed before Herod at his birthday feast, which led him to offer her anything she wished. At the instigation of her mother, she asked for the head of John the Baptist, who had been imprisoned for denouncing as unlawful (according to Lev. 18:16) the marriage of Herod and Herodias. The story of Salome's dance and the beheading of John the Baptist is related in Matt. 14:6-11 and Mark 6:21-28. Though not mentioned by name in the NT, the "daughter of Herodias" is identified as Salome by Josephus (*Ant.* 18.5.4).

The Gospels present Salome essentially as an instrument of her mother's political machinations. From the 4th cent., however, she became the object of pious denunciations by St. John Chrysostom and St. Jerome and an example of the evils to which dancing may lead.

She was adopted fairly widely as a subject of painting during the Middle Ages and early Renaissance (e.g., Gozzoli, Giotto, Donatello, Titian, Andrea del Sarto, and Fra Lippo Lippi) and as the subject of sporadic literary attention (e.g., Chaucer, *The Pardoner's Tale* [*CT* 6.488-91]).

Biblical plays of the early 16th cent. often took up the subject of Salome's dance. John Bale (1495-1563), an early Reformation playwright and probably the first Protestant writer of biblical plays, wrote *John Baptist's Preaching* and a lost life of the Baptist which presumably contained references to Salome. Nicolas Grimald's *Archipropheta* (1546-47), which draws on the Synoptic Gospels, Josephus, and to some extent on Jakob Schoepper's *Johannes Decollatus* (1546), includes Salome's dance in act 5. A romantic tragedy which deals with the impassioned relationship of Herod and Herodias, Grimald's play is, both in intention and effect, different from George Buchanan's static *Baptistes* and Bale's satirical and polemical *Preaching*. Sixty years before Shakespeare's tragedies, it attempts the creation of vital dramatic characters.

Clerical strictures against dancing which had been applied to Salome in the early Middle Ages persist in the Calvinist atmosphere of Scott's *Heart of Midlothian*. Old David Deans, overhearing his daughters talking about a dance, declares it to be "the readiest inlet to all sort of licentiousness." Denouncing the "profane pastime," he recalls "the unhappy lass wha danced aff the head of John the Baptist." Better, he says, to "hae been born a cripple . . . than to be a king's daughter, fiddling and flinging the gate she did" (chap. 10). Ruskin, commenting on the novel in *Fors Clavigera* (7.268), attacks the "Deadly Museless-ness" of those who "would read of the daughter of Herodias dancing before Herod, but never of the son of Jesse dancing before the Lord; and banished sackbut and psaltery, for signals in the service of Nebuchadnezzar, forgetting that the last law of Moses and the last prayer of David [i.e., Deut. 32; 2 Sam. 22:1–23:1] were written in song."

It was not until the 19th cent., however, that Salome emerged as a central and popular figure of the literary imagination. The prevailing climate of taste and opinion reflected in the French symbolist and the aesthetic movements found her a compelling subject. The dim figure of biblical anecdote was both re-created in the overheated atmosphere of late 19th-cent. "decadence" and transformed by it into an archetype of the femme fatale; in this context Salome bore strong affinities with Keats's "La Belle Dame sans Merci: A Ballad," Swinburne's *Laus Veneris*, and Pater's *La Giaconda* (see Praz [1933], passim).

The apogee of this response to Salome occurs in Huysmans's *A rebours*, whose central character, Des Esseintes, owns two pictures of Salome by Gustave Moreau in which he sees "realised at long last the weird and superhuman Salome of his dreams." She is not merely a dancing girl but the "symbolic incarnation" of lust and hysteria, an "accursed Beauty exalted above all other beauties . . . poisoning, like the Helen of ancient myth . . . everything that she touches" (chap. 5).

At his trial Oscar Wilde identified *A rebours* as the "yellow book" which Lord Henry gave to Dorian Gray in *The Picture of Dorian Gray*. Inspired by Huysmans's descriptions of Salome, Wilde also wrote his French play *Salome*. In this "tale spawned from the leprous literature of the French decadence," as the *Daily Chronicle* called it, Wilde set out to create, in his own words, "quelque chose de curieux et de sensuel." His Salome is a virgin consumed by "evil chastity," whose passion for Jokanaan is both erotic and thanatogenous.

Salome's general popularity through the 19th and early 20th cents. may be indicated by the fact that she appears in literary works by Flaubert, Heine, J. C. Heywood, Huysmans, Laforgue, Lorrain, Mallarmé, Renan, O'Shaughnessy, Schwob, Landau, Sudermann, Symons, Wilde, Sturge Moore, Stephen Phillips, and Wratislaw; she was painted by Mucha, Moreau, Matisse, Beardsley, and Klimpt, among others, and is the subject of musical composition by Strauss, Massenet, Granvell Bantock, and Hindemith.

In Browning's "Fra Lippo Lippi" Salome appears in the painting which shocks the learned priors who want an art which "instigates to prayer" rather than one which arouses the senses: "Oh, that white smallish female with the breasts, / She's just my niece . . . Herodias [*sic*], I would say — / Who went and danced and got men's heads cut off!" (195-97).

See also HEROD ANTIPAS; JOHN THE BAPTIST.

Bibliography. De Kornitz, B. *Salome: Virgin or Prostitute* (1953); Krishnayya, D. Radha. "Wilde's Salome: Deviations from the Biblical Episode." *ComQ* 2 (1978), 71-76; Praz, M. *The Romantic Agony* (1933); Psichari, J. "Salome et la décollation de saint Jean-Baptiste," *RHR* 72 (1915); Zagona, H. G. *The Legend of Salome and the Principle of Art for Art's Sake* (1960).   MICHAEL GOLDBERG

SALT OF THE EARTH In his Sermon on the Mount, Jesus calls his listeners the "salt of the earth" (Matt. 5:13) and adds, as a warning, that savorless salt is "good for nothing but to be cast out, and to be trodden under foot of men" (cf. parallels in Mark 9:50 and Luke 14:34-35).

While some modern scholars believe that Jesus' words about savorless salt originally referred to the "state of Judaism" in his time (Dodd, 111; cf. Hunter, 21), the Fathers took Jesus' exhortation and warning as addressed to the disciples (e.g., St. John Chrysostom, *Hom. on Matthew*, 15.10) and more especially the bishops, prelates, and preachers of the Word (e.g., St. Jerome, *Dialogus adversus Luciferianos*, 5; cf. St. Thomas Aquinas, *In Matthaeum*; St. Thomas More, *A Dialogue of Divers Matters*, 1.18). This interpretation was then reinforced by spiritualizing the theories of the origin of salt: its origin from the water of the ocean — tribulation — and the heat of the sun — love (Aquinas, *In Matt.*; cf. Wyclif, *In Omnes Novi Testamenti Libros*).

The function of salt as a preservative was emphasized by many of the Fathers (e.g., St. Augustine, *De sermone Domini in Monte*, 1.6). Its effect was said to be felt both in the Church and in the world, since "society is held together as long as the salt is uncorrupted" (Origen, *Contra Celsum*, 8.70). The importance of salt in healing, purifying, and seasoning was also stressed, as was the fact that salt makes the soil barren; hence the apostles' teaching suppresses carnal desires and vices in their listeners (Bede, *In Matthei Evangelium Expositio*; Aquinas, *In Matt.*). The loss of the salt's savor can, according to these same exegetes, be brought about by the fear of temporal persecutions, by wealth and worldly entanglements, or by deviation from the truth.

Following the application of Jesus' word to teachers of the gospel, the Reformers used the text to criticize the Pope, clergy, and monks. They read it as a serious warning for the Church not to become savorless (Calvin, *Harmony of the Gospels*), accusing monks of staying in their "dens" instead of "salting" their neighbors (Tyndale, *Exposition of Matthew*) and clergy of shying away from preaching the "biting" message that "everything born and living on the face of the earth is unworthy before God, rotten and corrupted" (Luther, *WA* 32.343-54). For John Wesley, Matt. 5:13 underscores the practical implications of the gospel, indicating that "Christianity is essentially a social religion" (*Standard Sermons*, 19.1).

ME literature follows the main line of interpretive tradition in identifying the salt as the clergy. Thus Anima in *Piers Plowman* (B.15.421-34) says that "we han so manye Maistres, / Prestes and prechoures and a pope aboue, / þat goddes salt shulde be to saue mannes soule." Similarly, Frère John, in Chaucer's *Summoner's Tale* (3.2196), is called (albeit ironically) "the salt of the erthe and the savour."

In the 19th cent., John Ruskin made ironic use of the metaphor in referring to the salt Swiss Catholics needed in the making of their cheeses, but which over-eager Protestants denied them in order to convert them (*Time and Tide*, 9.45). Equally ironic is Dickens's reference to the presumptuous mayor Thomas Sapsea: "Of such is the salt of the earth" (*The Mystery of Edwin Drood*, chap. 12). Gerard Manley Hopkins ("The Candle Indoors") makes a connection between the liar who is "cast by conscience out, spendsavour salt," and the "beam-blind" man of Matt. 7:1-5.

In Flannery O'Connor's short story "Good Country People," a fake Bible salesman calls himself a "country boy," and Mrs. Hopewell remarks that "good country people are the salt of the earth!" Her ignorance blinds her to the fact that he is an imposter and an atheist.

Having acquired proverbial status, the metaphor is frequently deprived of any spiritual content. The salt of Swinburne's poem "The Salt of the Earth," e.g., is childhood, without which "This were a drearier star than ever / Yet looked upon the sun." D. H. Lawrence's poem "Salt of the Earth" likewise secularizes the passage: "the wisdom of wise men, the gifts of the great" are salt of the earth which becomes salt of the ocean of the afterward. Yet the younger generations would be better without such "pickling." In *Ulysses*, James Joyce makes the salt an epithet of military efficiency when he calls the royal Dublins "the salt of the earth, known the world over."

Bibliography. Dodd, C. H. *The Parables of the Kingdom.* Rev. ed. (1936); Gundry, R. H. *Matthew: A Commentary on His Literary and Theological Art* (1982); Hunter, A. M. *The Parables Then and Now* (1971); Luz, U. *Das Evangelium nach Matthäus* (1985).   MANFRED SIEBALD

SAMARIA   A region in Palestine located between Galilee in the north and Judah (or Judea) in the south, and bounded by the Jordan River to the east and the coastal plain of Sharon to the west. It was a territory after the schism from Judah in the time after Solomon. Sometimes also called "Israel" (1 Kings 12:20), sometimes "Ephraim" (Hos. 5:3; 11:8; Mic. 1:1, 8), for the hill country of its central mountain ridge, in Isaiah the region in general is Ephraim and its capital, on the hill of Samaria, "Samaria" (7:9).

See also AHOLAH AND AHOLIBAH; GOOD SAMARITAN; WOMAN AT THE WELL.

SAMARITAN WOMAN   *See* WOMAN AT THE WELL.

SAMMAEL   *See* DEMONS, DEMON POSSESSION; DEVIL.

SAMSON   The Hebrew name *Shimshon* (LXX *Samsōn*) may derive from *shemesh*, "sun"; it has been suggested that the biblical stories associated with Samson may in fact have their origin in solar myth. The pericope of Samson in Judg. 13–16 appears to have developed from the tradition of oral poetic sagas common in premonarchic Israel and, specifically, from a series of popular stories preserving accounts of a local hero from the district of Mahaneh-dan. Dating (probably) from the 10th cent. B.C., the Samson saga was incorporated into the cyclic pattern of apostasy-faith-apostasy underpinning the Judges narrative (cf. Judg. 2:16-19). It appears that at this time significant portions of the localized Samson legend were tailored to fit the paradigm of the charismatic *shophet*, or "judge," who, impelled by God, delivered the errant Israelites from subjugation to political freedom by bringing them back to the faith of their fathers.

The story of Samson falls into three clearly defined sections: (a) the distinctively religious birth narrative (chap. 13), in which Samson's birth is supernaturally foretold to a previously childless Danite couple and in which Samson is dedicated from birth as a Nazarite (cf. Num. 6); (b) the essentially nonreligious heroic exploits of Samson (chaps. 14 and 15), in which the Danite strongman harasses the hostile Philistines by repeated attacks and stratagems; and (c) the religious conclusion (chap. 16), which moves from Samson's defeat and humiliation at the hands of Delilah to his final victory over the Philistines when he pulls down the pagan temple of Dagon on the heads of his enemies. The only other biblical reference to Samson occurs in Heb. 11:32, where he is included in the roster of those who subdued kingdoms "through faith."

The earliest extrabiblical treatment of the story — that in Josephus (*Ant.* 5.8.1-12) — attempts, by expanded characterization and the addition of human motivation for the characters, to make the story more plausible and to transform Samson from a brawling figure of legendary proportions into a noble and authentically historical

Hebrew hero. In an entirely original passage (*Ant.* 5.8.12), Josephus concludes his account by lauding Samson's heroic valor and excusing his weaknesses on the basis of generic human frailty — thus paving the way (as does the Heb. 11 reference) for later patristic and scholastic accounts of Samson as a historical personage of unquestioned sanctity.

In the mass of commentary which grew up around the Samson story during the first twelve centuries of the Christian era, F. M. Krouse has identified three main trends. In the literal tradition, descending from the Antiochan school of historico-grammatical exegesis, the story was merely retold without explicit interpretation, although it treated Samson as a saint and often made rhetorical use of his deception by Delilah in arguments in favor of chastity (e.g., St. Ambrose, *Ep.* 19 [PL 16.1026-36]). In the allegorical tradition, descending from the Alexandrian school of exegesis, Samson was seen as a prefiguration of Christ (e.g., St. Augustine, *Sermo de Samsone* [*Sermo*, 364 in PL 39.1639-45], and St. Isidore of Seville, *Mysticorum expositiones sacramentorum* [PL 83.389-90]). Finally, in late Graeco-Roman pagan mythology, as well as in some patristic sources, Samson was identified with the classical hero Hercules (e.g., St. Philaster, *Liber de haeresibus,* and Augustine, *De civ. Dei* 18.19).

During the scholastic period (8th-12th cents.), although the main lines of patristic exegesis still predominated, the emphasis shifted decidedly to the events at the end of Samson's career, especially his downfall and betrayal by Delilah. As a result, Delilah emerged as a prominent figure, and the dominant thematic interest of the story focused clearly on its antifeminist potential. Nowhere, perhaps, is this more apparent than in Peter Abelard's eighty-seven-line *Planctus Israel super Samson,* which presents Samson as a Judeo-Christian Hercules — duped and destroyed (like Adam before him) by a woman's perfidy — and concludes with a vituperative denunciation of Delilah and all her faithless sex: *"O semper fortium / Ruinam maximam, / Et in exitium / Creatam feminam!"* (54-57) ("O woman, always the greatest ruin of the strong! Woman, created only to destroy!").

In English literature, the story receives its earliest detailed retelling in the 14th-cent. *Cursor Mundi* (7083-7262), where Samson is depicted as a noble hero brought low by feminine deceit. The narrator seems to delight in Samson's eventual revenge, when he is made (in an original twist) to pull down the temple at the marriage-feast celebrating Delilah's marriage to one of her fellow Philistines. Both Chaucer (*Monk's Tale,* 7.3205-84) and Lydgate (*Fall of Princes,* 2.6336-6510) set Samson in the *De casibus virorum illustrium* tradition (cf. Boccaccio, *De Casibus,* 1.17), emphasizing the tragedy of his fall from high to low estate and treating his ill-fated liaison with Delilah as a moral exemplum of domestic treachery.

Gower (*Confessio Amantis,* 8.2703-04) also treats the Hebrew champion as a tragic lover, comparing him with Paris, Hercules, and Troilus. Typically, as these examples suggest, ME poets (unlike theologians) tended to eliminate — or at least downplay — the religious elements of the Samson story, preferring to shape it as a secular tragedy in which a noble hero, lacking discretion, was tumbled from high to low degree on Fortune's turning wheel because he fondly loved and foolishly confided in a treacherous woman.

In Renaissance literature, however, the spiritual significance of Samson's history re-emerges as a central preoccupation. Although the medieval view of Samson as a victim of unwise and ungoverned passion survived (e.g., Spenser, *Faerie Queene,* 5.8.2, and Shakespeare, *Love's Labour's Lost,* 1.2.70-88), Renaissance writers after 1600 almost invariably depicted him as a repentant sinner purified by trial and restored to God's favor. Francis Quarles devoted 3,468 lines of rhyming couplets in his *Historie of Sampson* (1631) to prolix retelling of the OT story, interspersed with twenty-three versified "meditations" explaining the prevailing theological interpretations of each episode. George Herbert, more economically, revived the allegorical interpretation of Samson as a prefiguration of Christ in his meditative lyric "Sunday" (47-49). Milton, in *Areopagitica* (1644), casts his vision of a regenerate England in the simile of a reviving Samson: "Methinks I see in my mind a noble and puissant nation rousing herself like a strong man after sleep, and shaking her invincible locks" (*Prose Works* [Yale ed.], 2.552-53).

This focus owes a good deal to a series of German and Dutch Samson dramas composed during the 16th and 17th cents. Basing their conception firmly on Heb. 11:32 and dealing freely with the materials of the Judges account, such continental playwrights as Hieronymus Zieglerus (*Samson, Tragoedia Nova* [Basel, 1547]), Marcus Andreas Wunstius (*Samson, Tragoedia Sacra* [Strassburg, ca. 1600]), and Joost van den Vondel (*Samson, of Heiligue Wraeck, Treurspel* [Amsterdam, 1660]) transformed Samson from a quasichivalric hero of brute physical endowments into a divinely led instrument of faith. They made him, progressively, an exemplum of *mentis caecitas* (spiritual blindness) rather than love-blindness and transferred the dramatic interest away from his superficial relationship with Delilah, fixing it instead on Samson's own inner anguish and conflicts. The process of Samson's spiritual regeneration and eventual restoration as God's faithful champion became, thus, the dominant thematic concern.

The crowning glory of this Renaissance reformulation comes in Milton's *Samson Agonistes* (1671), a poetic drama synthesizing all the major literary and theological traditions which had grown up around the story. Introducing a Samson already betrayed, blinded, and slaving at the Philistine mill, Milton limits the action to the last few hours of his hero's life and centers attention on the process by which Samson is led, through a series of temptations, to repentance and spiritual renovation. The movement of the drama is focused on Samson's transformation from a hubristic Hebrew Hercules to a humble and obedient servant of God who becomes, in the closing semichorus (1687-1707), a prefiguration of Christ. Physical actions are reported rather than played out before the audience, and the OT emphasis on Samson's strength and heroic exploits are largely parodied in the (nonbiblical) figure of Harapha, a vainglorious braggadocio who taunts Samson.

After *Samson Agonistes* there are no major treatments of the Samson saga in English literature. References after 1671 are confined largely to incidental allusions, and these — almost invariably miscellaneous metaphors of physical strength or of love betrayed — do nothing to enhance or develop the literary Samson tradition brought to a climax by Milton. Blake, e.g., has a fragment of a prose poem on Samson in his *Poetical Sketches,* and Browning includes an interesting typological exploration in bk. 8 of *The Ring and the Book* (632-49). The most original modern version of the story is D. H. Lawrence's short story "Samson and Delilah," which, in the encounter between a voluptuous innkeeper and her estranged husband, reflects Lawrence's own stormy and passionate relationship with his wife, Frieda.

See also DELILAH; PHILISTINE.

Bibliography. Gossman, A. "Samson, Job, and 'the Exercise of Saints'." *ES* 45 (1964), 212-24; Kirkconnell, W. *That Invincible Samson: The Theme of Samson Agonistes in World Literature with Translations of the Major Analogues* (1964); Krouse, F. *Milton's Samson and the Christian Tradition* (1949; 1974); Simon, U. "Samson and the Heroic." In *Ways of Reading the Bible.* Ed. M. Wadsworth (1981).

JOHN SPENCER HILL

SAMUEL The last of the OT judges and first of the prophets (after Moses), Samuel played a pivotal role in the establishment of kingship in Israel. He was born to Elkanah and Hannah, Elkanah's beloved but long-barren wife, after she vowed to consecrate to God any son he would give her. The etymology of his name, given in 1 Sam. 1:20 ("Because I have asked him of the LORD"), is based on puns on the verb *sha'al* (meaning both "request" and "dedicate"; cf. 1:28). Hannah was subsequently blessed with more children — three sons and two daughters — thus alleviating her misery at the hands of Peninnah, Elkanah's other wife, whose spitefulness and taunting had provoked her almost desperate plea for a child (1 Sam. 1:1-11).

As soon as he was weaned, Samuel was brought to the Temple at Shiloh by Hannah to serve Eli, the priest. As a boy he was called by God in the night, who revealed to him the imminent demise of the priestly line of Eli because of the wickedness of Eli's sons (1 Sam. 3). Samuel himself, it became clear, was to succeed Eli as priest.

In his role as priest and judge, Samuel was able both to rid Israel of the worship of Canaanite gods and to drive the Philistines out of Israel (1 Sam. 7:3-17). When his own sons, like those of Eli, proved faithless and unworthy to succeed him, the elders of Israel demanded "a king to judge us like all the nations" — thus rejecting not only the temporal authority of Samuel and his family but also the unique kingship of God himself over Israel (1 Sam. 8:7). Warning the people of the consequences of their rejection of theocracy, Samuel nevertheless, with God's assent, bowed to their demands and appointed Saul. Twice Samuel confronted Saul about his disobedience, and with his own hands he killed Agag, whom Saul had spared against God's explicit directive (13:8-15; 15:1-35). Samuel's last important act was the anointing of David — a man after God's own heart — to succeed Saul as king (16:1-13). He later sheltered David from Saul's wrath (19:8-24). His death is mentioned very briefly (25:1; 28:3). At the behest of Saul, the Woman of Endor called up Samuel's ghost, which again foretold Saul's doom (28:3-20). This posthumous prophecy has appealed more to writers than any other event in Samuel's career.

Samuel is among the "famous men" praised in the book of Ecclesiasticus, where his prophetic career is also rehearsed (46:13-20). Other biblical references to him are found in 2 Chron. 35:18; Ps. 99:6; Jer. 15:1; Acts 3:24; 13:20. The author of Hebrews includes him among the great heroes of the faith (Heb. 11:32).

Jewish sources speak of Elkanah as a "second Abraham," the only pious man of his generation, and credit both of Samuel's parents with prophetic gifts (Ginzberg, *LJ* 4.57). Samuel's own exemplary disinterestedness and incorruptibility as a judge are likened to those of Moses (Yelammedenu in Liqqutim 4.69; 5.90b-91a). Early Christian commentators emphasize Samuel's many roles — judge, prophet, priest — and in general terms consider him a forerunner of Christ. For St. Augustine, the most significant event of Samuel's career is his supplanting of the house of Eli, because it foreshadows the supplanting of the old Law by the new (*De civ. Dei* 17.4). Augustine interprets Saul's tearing of Samuel's mantle (1 Sam. 15:27-28) as signifying Israel's loss of the kingdom of God by its rejection of Christ; ultimately the torn mantle also signifies the radical division between the City of God and the earthly city (*De civ. Dei* 17.7).

Samuel's warning against the evils of kingship (8:10-18) became a key text in the constitutional controversies of the 17th cent. Divine-right monarchists interpreted it as a statement of the prerogative of kings, while constitutional monarchists and republicans thought it to be merely a description of the way kings usually behave, with no implication of divine approval. Each party weighted God's reluctant acceptance of kingship (see also 8:7-9; 12:13-15) to suit its interests (e.g., R. Filmer, *Patriarcha* [1680], sect. 23; Milton, *Defense of the English People,* chap. 2). In the following century Fielding accuses the

Jacobites of supporting precisely the kind of king Samuel describes (*Jacobite's Journal*, nos. 25 [21 May 1748] and 46 [15 Oct. 1748]). Thomas Paine and the young Coleridge cite this passage as displaying the inherent evil of kingship and God's unambiguous disapproval of it (*Common Sense*, "Of Monarchy and Hereditary Succession"; *Lectures on Revealed Religion*, 2).

In most of the many plays devoted to Saul and David and in Abraham Cowley's unfinished epic *Davideis* (1656), Samuel plays a minor role; indeed, he is often given less prominence than his ghost. D. H. Lawrence, however, gives him an eloquent and moving prayer in sc. 2 of his *David* drama.

As the main character of Laurence Housman's *Samuel the Kingmaker*, Samuel is a scheming politician who identifies his own will with God's, engineers all his miracles, falsifies the historical record, and undermines and destroys Saul in order to satisfy his own lust for power and revenge. As the narrator of Robert Penn Warren's long monologue "Saul at Gilboa," Samuel meditates on the meaning of Saul's tragic career. A vivid contemporary retelling of the story of Samuel's childhood call by God (1 Sam. 3) occurs in Rudy Wiebe's "The Vietnam Call of Samuel Reimer," chap. 12 of his *The Blue Mountains of China* (1970).

See also DAVID; HANNAH; SAUL; WITCH OF ENDOR.
WILLIAM KINSLEY

SANCTUM SANCTORUM *See* HOLY OF HOLIES.

SANHEDRIN Gk. *synedrion*, "place of those who sit together," becomes in postbiblical Hebrew *sanhedrin*. It refers to the Jewish court in Jerusalem, held by Jewish tradition to have been in continuous existence since the seventy elders appointed by Moses (Num. 11:16), though the earliest use of this term or its equivalent *gerousia* is ascribed by Josephus to the period of Antiochus Ephiphanes (223 B.C. – 187 B.C. [*Ant.* 12.3.3]). In the sense of "council" (Soṭa 9.11; Qidd. 4.5; Sanh. 4.3) it suggests a body of seventy religious and political leaders, mostly priests, who were at a peak of influence in the hellenistic era. Herod the Great killed forty-five members when they tried to restrain his power, and with the fall of Jerusalem (A.D. 70) shortly thereafter, it ceased to exist (but cf. Rosh Hash. 31a). Cf. Matt. 5:22; Acts 5:21.

SAPPHIRA *See* ANANIAS AND SAPPHIRA.

SARAH The first of the four OT matriarchs and the first of Abraham's two wives is introduced in Gen. 11:29-30 as Sarai (Heb. *śaray*, "princess"), an archaic form, which God changes to Sarah (Heb. *śarah*) in Gen. 17:15. Sarah dies in Hebron at age 127 and is buried in what becomes the ancestral burying ground, the cave of Machpelah (Gen. 23:1-20).

In Genesis Sarah is enigmatically old, barren, and strikingly beautiful. Her age — 65 when she enters the narrative, 90 at the birth of her son Isaac — and her long infertility test Abraham's faith in God's promises of numberless offspring (12:2; 13:16; 15:4-5; 17:2, 16-21; 18:10). Upon receiving a promise that Sarah will bear a son in her old age, Abraham smiles (17:17), but Sarah laughs incredulously (18:12); their reactions are ironic anticipations of Sarah's actual joy over the birth of Isaac (21:1-6), which is highlighted in his name (Heb. *Yiṣḥaq*, "Isaac," from the verb *ṣḥq*, "play, be amused; rejoice over, smile on [a newborn child]" [AB 1.125]).

Sarah's earlier frustration over her barrenness is recounted through the story of Hagar and Ishmael, told in Gen. 16 and 21. The first account reflects a conflict between, on the one hand, Sarah's wish to bear children, her jealousy over Hagar's fertility, and her offense at Hagar's presumption and, on the other hand, Hurrian family law, which required a barren wife to provide her husband with a concubine for the purpose of childbearing but which denied the wife the authority to remove the concubine. Sarah's only recourse was to harass Hagar into voluntary exile. In the second account (chap. 21) Sarah casts out Hagar and Ishmael when she sees Ishmael "playing with" (Heb. *ṣḥq*) Isaac (cf. Jub. 17:4-5 and Gen. 21:9 [Vg]); the KJV, assuming something less innocent, has Ishmael "mocking" Isaac, and in rabbinic commentary Sarah's anger is frequently justified by tales of Ishmael's wickedness (*Jewish Encyclopedia* [1907], 11.56).

Sarah's beauty is stressed in the *Genesis Apocryphon* 20.2-8 (ed. and trans. J. A. Fitzmyer [1971]) and in rabbinic sources (e.g. B. Bat. 58a, pt. 4, vol. 3). It is said to have aroused the erotic interest of the Egyptian pharaoh (Gen. 12:10-20) and King Abimelech of Gerar (Gen. 20:1-18). Abraham's passing off Sarah as his sister in these instances is at once both subterfuge and a reflection of the Hurrian custom of enhancing a wife's prestige by adopting her as a sister. Although these two episodes seem somewhat tangential to the main narratives of Abraham and Sarah, they demonstrate the matriarch's high social standing and give witness to the purity of the race.

Elsewhere in the Bible and in Christian tradition Sarah serves a variety of historical and symbolic functions. She is genetrix (Isa. 51:2), sign of God's truth and power (Rom. 9:9), allegory of life in the Spirit (Gal. 4:21-31), symbol of faith and obedience (Heb. 11:11; 1 Pet. 3:6). Her conception of Isaac when she is well past childbearing age is the first in a series of similar biblical miracles, including Hannah's conception of Samuel and Elisabeth's of John the Baptist. The motif of the paradoxical fruitfulness of the barren woman is, however, prevalent in Scripture (e.g., Ps. 113:9; Isa. 54:1; Gal. 4:27). Because of the miraculous nature of her child's conception, Sarah is sometimes regarded as a type of Mary (e.g., St. Ambrose, *Commentarius in epistolam ad Romanos*, 9 [PL 17.131]). Philo allegorizes Sarah as Virtue; her laughter at Isaac's birth is explained as Virtue giving birth to Happiness

(*Legum allegoriae*, 2.82). Dante, in *Paradiso*, 32.10, places Sarah one seat beneath Rachel in the amphitheater of the celestial rose, where she represents the classical virtue of Justice (G. Mazzotta, "Sara," *Enciclopedia Dantesca* [1970-78], 5.30).

The usual medieval view of Sarah's laugh, interpreted through Heb. 11:11 and reflected in such standard sources as the *Glossa Ordinaria,* is that, although Sarah initially lacked faith in the prophecy, faith awakes in her when she is rebuked. One legend holds that at the moment she conceived Isaac "she rejoiced in an heir and repented of her laughter" (Prudentius, *Psychomachia,* 45-49). With respect to the Hagar story, Gal. 4:21-31 provides a ready-made allegory of explanation; thus, Hagar and Sarah could represent for medieval commentators the Old and New Covenants, the Old and New Testaments, or Jews and Christians (*Glossa Ordinaria* on Gen. 16:4 and 21:9-12). While Protestant commentators tended to focus less on allegorical significance, they persisted in seeing the doubtful laugh and the Hagar episode as temporary lapses of faith from which Sarah recovered (e.g., Calvin, *Comm. on Genesis*, trans. J. King [1847], 1.430, 474; Richard Hooker, "Sermon on the Certainty and Perpetuity of Faith," *Works,* ed. J. Keble [1847], 3.447; Matthew Poole, *Synopsis Criticorum Aliorumque Sacrae Scripturae Interpretum* [1669-76], 1, on Gen. 16, 21).

In pre-Romantic English literature, Sarah is something of a stock figure. In the OE *Genesis* (1719-2767) she is the archetypal matriarch; in the ME *Genesis and Exodus* and *Metrical Paraphrase of the Old Testament* she is, additionally, the faithful Sarah of Heb. 11:11 superimposed on the narrative of Gen. 12–21. In *Cleanness* Sarah's obedience, faith, and fruitfulness are contrasted to the disobedience, impiety, and sterility of Lot's wife and of the Sodomites. In Chaucer's *Merchant's Tale* (*CT* 4.1703-05) Sarah is held up as an example of the perfect wife for youthful May to emulate. One literary remembrance of Sarah's feminine appeal is in Burns's song "Ken ye ought o' Captain Grose?," which asks, "Is he to Abram's bosom gane? / . . . Or haudin Sarah by the wame?" (13, 15).

Dramatic adaptations of Isaac's being sacrificed occasionally feature Sarah as a foil for Abraham. The Dublin Abraham play (*Non-Cyclic Plays and Fragments,* ed. N. Davis [1970]) is the first of these and the only English medieval drama which includes Sarah. Later adaptations tend to follow fairly consistent plot and theme; typically, Sarah's maternal attachment to Isaac causes her to oppose the journey to Moriah, but when Isaac returns unharmed, she praises God. There are, however, interesting variations. In the Dublin Abraham play, Abraham's fears that Sarah will not understand the purpose of his journey are a projection of his own doubts onto her. In Arthur Golding's translation of Theodore Beza's *Tragedie of Abraham's Sacrifice* (1577), a lively argument between Sarah and Abraham (386-421) develops the contrast between the "natural man" and the man of faith. In George Lesly's "Abraham's Faith" (*Divine Dialogues* [1678]), Sarah is uncharacteristically trusting, despite her dream of a heavenly bow which shoots Isaac; she nevertheless displays extravagant jealousy of Hagar. In *The Trial of Abraham* (1790) by a Mr. Farrer, Sarah's objections to Abraham's journey are so exaggerated that she outdoes Shakespeare's weeping queens. A recent play in this vein is Laurence Housman's *Abraham and Isaac,* which strips away the miraculous so that the characters must discover God within themselves; Housman's chief departure from his predecessors, however, is to deny Sarah the understanding of God which Abraham and Isaac ultimately achieve.

Apart from poetry and drama based specifically on Genesis, Sarah makes few appearances in English literature. J. Vogel, however, has observed that the many prominent Sarahs in Dickens, all "jealous, crabbed, reactionary, wizened, primitive-souled" (*Allegory in Dickens* [1977], 278), are based on the OT Sarah. One of the more remarkable Sarahs in recent literature is in Archibald MacLeish's drama *J.B.* (1956), an adaptation of the Job story set in modern America. MacLeish's Sarah is the wife of the successful, life-loving businessman J.B., with whom she shares the loss of her children — Rebecca, Ruth, David, Jonathan, and Mary. Although J.B. is Job-like throughout, Sarah falls from piety into despair before her faith is resurrected in the likeness of her husband's.

See also ABRAHAM; HAGAR; ISAAC; ISHMAEL.

Bibliography. Carmichael, C. M. *Women, Law, and the Genesis Traditions* (1979); Graves, R., and R. Patai, eds. and trans. *The Hebrew Myths: The Book of Genesis* (1963); Hirsch, E. D. "Sarah." In *Jewish Encyclopedia* (1907); Speiser, E. A. "The Wife-Sister Motif in the Patriarchal Narratives." *Biblical and Other Studies* (1963), 15-28.

M. W. TWOMEY

SATAN *See* BEELZEBUB; DEVIL.

SAUL Saul, the first king of Israel, is the principal figure of a considerable portion of the first book of Samuel (chaps. 9–31). A member of the tribe of Benjamin, he was anointed king by the prophet Samuel, performed deeds of valor, and rescued Israel from many enemies. However, when he disobeyed God's commandment to exterminate the Amalekites by sparing their king, Agag, he was disowned by Samuel in favor of David, a "man after God's own heart." In repeated efforts to capture and to kill his young rival, who had gained fame and popularity through his extraordinary defeat of the Philistine giant Goliath (1 Sam. 17), he failed and succumbed to depression. Recognizing that God had turned against him, he consulted a medium in order to seek counsel from the ghost of Samuel, only to have judgment pronounced upon him again. Finally, wounded on the battlefield while fighting against the Philistines, he took his own life. A period of national mourning was led by David, who succeeded him and ushered in Israel's Golden Age.

In many ancient Jewish sources Israel's first king is treated sympathetically — as "a hero and a saint" whose piety is unequaled even by that of David. Summarizing, Ginzberg comments that "compared with David's sins, Saul's were not sufficiently grievous to account for the withdrawal of the royal dignity from him and his family. The real reason was Saul's too great mildness, a drawback in a ruler. Moreover, his family was of such immaculate nobility that his descendents might have become too haughty . . ." (Ginzberg, *LJ* 4.68, 72; but cf. Soṭa 1.17b; Shemuel 13.85; and Num. Rab. 11.3, where Saul is said, like Absalom, to have possessed beauty of body but not of soul).

In the patristic era Saul is universally castigated for his disobedience. St. John Chrystostom (in his *Hom. on Matthew*) sees him as an example of those ruined by pride, rashness, and malice, lured by the devil from small sins into ever greater ones. St. Augustine, in *De civitate Dei*, speaks of the kingdom of Saul as a "shadow of a kingdom yet to come which should remain to eternity." "Therefore," he continues, "what it signified has stood and shall stand; but it shall not stand for this man [Saul], because he himself was not to reign for ever, nor his offspring." Samuel's prophecy of the "rending" of the kingdom from Saul (1 Sam. 15:26-29) is understood by Augustine to speak also of the division of the carnal Israel ("Israel pertaining to the bond woman") from spiritual Israel ("Israel pertaining to the free").

In the Reformation, Saul's despair and ultimate suicide receive prominent attention. For Luther, Saul's besetting sin, which lay at the root of his other crimes, is disobedience of God's word (*Comm. on Gen.* 6:22; 21:15-16). Calvin (in his *Comm. on Psalms*) speaks of Saul as an administrator who seriously hindered Israel's worship and was responsible for its spiritual decline. During Saul's reign, he observes, the Temple was profaned by "contemners of God," the role he sees the Catholics playing in his own day: "Saul and all his counselors were subverters of the Church," he argues, forerunners of the Pope and all his retinue, who usurp the title of the priesthood.

As a tragic figure Saul has fascinated painters from Rembrandt to Joseph Israels, musicians from Handel to Honneger, and international writers such as Jean de la Taille, Grimmelshausen, Pierre du Ryer, Voltaire, Lamartine, Friedrich Ruckert, Karl Gutzkow, Karl Beck, André Gide, Richard Beer-Hofmann, Max Zweig, David Pinski, R. M. Rilke, and Karl Wolfskehl.

Among English authors, Milton refers to Saul frequently in his prose works as a bad and treacherous king, an example of unregenerate humanity. He sees Charles I as following Saul's course in fearing the people more than God while, like Saul, insisting on the righteousness of his acts. Charles's court and prelates are likened to the cattle of Amalek. For Milton, Charles is more blameworthy than

Saul, however, because Saul "was at length convinc'd," whereas Charles remained "to the howr of death fix'd in his fals perswasion" (*Eikonoklastes,* 9). Saul plays a prominent role in Abraham Cowley's unfinished epic, *Davideis* (1656). In Dryden's political allegory *Absalom and Achitophel,* Saul is made to stand for Oliver Cromwell and Saul's son Ishbosheth for Cromwell's son Richard.

Byron devotes to Saul four of the twenty-three *Hebrew Melodies* (1816). In two of these lyrics the Romantic poet pours his own restless temperament into the soul of Israel's king; in a third he deals with Saul's invocation of the ghost of Samuel on the eve of battle; and in the fourth Saul sings his defiant song before entering into battle. For Byron, Saul represents the superior individual who walks to his doom with head unbowed before divine and human adversaries. Byron regarded Saul's encounter with the ghost of Samuel as the finest ghost scene ever written and refers to it in *Manfred,* 2.175-82, in the eleventh stanza of "Dedication to Don Juan," and in *The Age of Bronze,* 2.380-83.

Browning's *Saul,* published in fragmentary form in 1845 and in completed form two years later, is a dramatic monologue spoken and sung by David, who recalls the memorable hour when Abner first brought him, the young shepherd, to comfort with his music the stricken king. The aging monarch is gradually uplifted from despair by the talented harpist and singer. David, feeling love as well as sympathy for Saul, prophesies:

> O Saul, it shall be
> A Face like my face that receives thee; a Man like to me,
> Thou shalt love and be loved by, forever: a Hand like this hand
> Shall throw open the gates of new life to thee! See the Christ stand!

This promise of Saul's forgiveness and ultimate salvation provides a new sense of closure for the Saul story. Nevertheless, Saul himself remains silent. The political future belongs to David.

D. H. Lawrence's play *David* (1926) begins with the conflict between Saul and Samuel after the defeat of the Amalekites and ends with David's flight to escape death by the envious Saul. The sixteen scenes focus on the decay of Saul's personality under the influence of jealousy at David's ever increasing popularity. J. M. Barrie's play *The Boy David* (1936) introduces Saul as a noble figure about whom the clouds of despondency have begun to gather. Browning's poem and Rembrandt's painting were Barrie's models for his characterization of Saul. The play ends, as does the final scene of Lawrence's play, with the covenant between David and Jonathan.

See also DAVID; DESPAIR; SAMUEL; WITCH OF ENDOR.

Bibliography. Everett, G. "Typological Structures in Browning's 'Saul.' " *VP* 23 (1985), 267-79; Hellstrom, W.

"Time and Type in Browning's *Saul*." *ELH* 33 (1966), 370-89; Liptzin, S. *Biblical Themes in World Literature* (1985).

SOL LIPTZIN
JOSEPH MCCLATCHEY

SCALES In the ancient world virtually all commercial transactions involved the use of weights and balances. Thus it is not surprising that the Bible contains many injunctions concerning the need for fair practices: "You shall do no unrighteousness in judgment, in meteyard, in weight, or in measure. Just balances, just weights, a just ephah [a container for dry measure], and a just hin [jar for liquid measure], shall ye have" (Lev. 19:35-36; cf. Ezek. 45:10-11). According to Prov. 11:1, "a false balance is abomination to the LORD: but a just weight is his delight" (cf. Deut. 25:13-16; Prov. 20:10, 23; Hos. 12:7; Amos 8:5; Mic. 6:10-11).

In the OT God is often pictured as the just judge holding scales. Hannah, in her prayer of thanksgiving after the birth of Samuel, celebrates the justice of God: "the LORD is a God of knowledge, and by him actions are weighed." In Prov. 16:2 God is said to weigh the motives (KJV "spirits") of people, specifically the self-righteous, those who are "clean in their own eyes." When Job despairs of his misfortunes, he pleads to God for just measure: "Oh that my grief were thoroughly weighed, and my calamities laid in the balances together!" (Job 6:2). Belshazzar, by contrast, is an unwitting and terrified recipient of divine estimation when his blasphemous feast is interrupted by a divine hand writing on the wall: "TEKEL" — "Thou art weighed in the balance, and art found wanting" (Dan. 5:27).

The only explicit NT reference to scales is in Rev. 6:5, where the third of the four Apocalyptic horsemen (signifying famine) is said to carry a balance. The image of the scales is implicit, however, when Jesus enjoins his listeners to judge justly, applying a constant standard of measure to themselves and others: "with what measure ye mete, it shall be measured to you again" (Matt. 7:2; cf. Mark 4:24-25; Luke 7:34-38).

In early Christian exegesis, the cross is often likened to a balance with cross-beam and scape. Christ's sufferings are seen to offset the sins of mankind, engendering "justice" and justification. (The power of the image is strengthened by the possibility of wordplay on *pondere* ["to weigh"] and *pendere* ["to hang"].) The patristic background for this association, as sketched in part by F. Wormald, involves St. Augustine (PL 40.98), St. Gregory the Great (PL 75.767), and the *Glossa Ordinaria* (PL 113.772); the same tradition also informs Fortunatus's hymn *"Vexilla Regis Prodeunt."* Such passages characteristically assign the act of measuring or weighing to God the Father (cf. OE *metod,* an epithet for God, which means "measurer").

Literary use of these motifs flourishes in the Renaissance. Herbert's "Justice (2)" hinges on the contrast between "dreadful justice," whose scales appear to be "a torturing engine" (sts. 1-2), and benign mercy, inherent in Christ's cross and responsible for loading the pans so that "Against me there is none, but for me much" (sts. 3-4). Similarly, Donne, in the "Second Prebend Sermon," recalls the tradition by juxtaposing against numerous biblical passages which insist on the aggravation of human vanity the alleviating notion of *pondus gloriae* ("the weight of glory"): "For our light affliction, which is but for a moment, worketh for us a far more exceeding and eternal weight of glory" (2 Cor. 4:17). Although the image itself is not foregrounded, the scales give rise to frequent weighing metaphors in several of Shakespeare's plays, notably *Measure for Measure* and *The Merchant of Venice*.

Spenser imaginatively recollects many of the relevant OT passages in his account of the Giant who attempts to redo God's creative work by weighing in his balance the world and its elements (*Faerie Queene,* 5.2.30-50). Obsessed with absolute equality, the leveler is tutored in the ways of justice by Artegall, who demonstrates first that God had originally measured all things (cf. Wisd. 11:20) and then that no Aristotelian mean will suffice in a comparison of the true and false. Spenser asserts the importance of equity, not equality, in a manner consistent with the Christian revaluation of measure-for-measure justice.

Further potential for literary ingenuity is realized in the connection of the astrological sign Libra to biblical and exegetical commonplace. Pierre Bersuire suggests that when the Sun (Christ as *sol iustitiae*) ascends into Libra (the throne of judgment), he will make the equinox, i.e., he will weigh night and day, sin and righteousness, so as to arbitrate justly. Chaucer invokes this idea when he alludes to Libra at the "thropes ende" of *The Canterbury Tales* (*Parson's Tale,* Prol. 10.10-12). Glimpsed in Chaucer, this fusion of ideas becomes in bk. 4 of *Paradise Lost* the occasion for exuberant linguistic display. In writing this pivotal book about the "pendant world" poised between hell and heaven, Milton sets the action in an equinoctial twilight zone and puns on "evening," "eve," "level," "beam," "pendulous," and "ponder," all as prelude to God's hanging forth "in Heav'n his golden Scales" (997), "wherein all things created first he weigh'd" (999) and wherein, now, he weighs Satan and finds him wanting (1012). The moment Christianizes an epic motif found in Homer (*Iliad,* 8.69-77 and 22.209-13) and Virgil, *Aeneid,* 12.725-27).

The image of the divine scales is less prominent in post-Renaissance literature. Scales continue to signify justice, but as the understanding of justice becomes more secular the hieratic nuances of the image diminish. Shelley's *Queen Mab* suggests that the "good man's heart" approximates "the sum of human weal" in the "just and equal measure" in which "all is weighed" (5.235-37). The icon in this instance, as elsewhere in 19th- and 20th-cent. literature, is only remotely biblical.

See also HANDWRITING ON THE WALL; JUDGE NOT.

Bibliography. Parker, P. "Eve, Evening and the Labor of Reading in *Paradise Lost.*" *ELR* 9 (1979), 319-42; Wood, C. *Chaucer and the Country of the Stars: Poetic Uses of Astrological Imagery* (1970); Wormald, F. "The Crucifix and the Balance." *JWCI* (1937-38), 276-80.   RONALD B. BOND

SCALES FELL FROM HIS EYES   After the blindness incurred in his Damascus road experience, Saul was visited by Ananias, who laid hands on him, saying: "The Lord, even Jesus . . . hath sent me, that thou mightest receive thy sight, and be filled with the Holy Ghost. And immediately there fell from his eyes as it had been scales: and he received sight forthwith, and arose, and was baptized" (Acts 9:17-18). Most literary allusions in the modern period use the phrase to mean something like having been disabused of a cherished illusion. This is the force of Samuel Butler's observing that after their quarrel over money, Ernest sees Ellen in an entirely different light, "The scales fell from Ernest's eyes." Likewise, in Henry James's *The American,* Newman declares: "I congratulate you . . . upon the scales having fallen from your eyes. It's a great triumph; it ought to make you feel better" (chap. 17).

See also PAUL.

SCAPEGOAT   "And Aaron cast lottes ouer the .ii gootes: one lotte for the Lorde, and another for a scapegoote": thus Tyndale translates Lev. 16:8, coining a word to be adopted and given wide currency by the KJV. Like the Vg *caper emissarius,* Tyndale's *scapegoat* is evidently a mistranslation of *'aza'zel,* which the main body of scholarship takes here to name a demon who haunts the wilderness. *Scapegoat* does not appear in the RV of 1884. One lot "for the Lord" and another "for Azazel" is the more venerable (cf. Yoma 6.1) and now preferred rendering (cf. *New Bible Dictionary* [1984], 113-14). The identity of the demon in question, however, has remained obscure. In some extracanonical sources, Azazel is a leader of evil angels and seems to be identified with Satan (e.g., 1 Enoch 8–10; 54:5; 55:4; Apoc. Abr. 13–14; 23; 29; 31; see also Ginzberg, *LJ* 5.11). Milton, in *Paradise Lost* (1.534), makes him a cohort cherub of Satan.

The casting of lots over two goats forms part of the priestly ritual prescribed in Lev. 16:1-34 for the Day of Atonement. The goat on which the Lord's lot fell was to be sacrificed; the scapegoat, or goat for Azazel, was to be presented live before the Lord (16:9-10). With the blood of the first, the high priest was to sprinkle the altar and Tabernacle; he was then to place "both his hands upon the head of the live goat, and confess over him all the iniquities of the children of Israel, and all their transgressions in all their sins, putting them upon the head of the goat, and send him away by the hand of a fit man into the wilderness," there to be "let go" (16:21-22). The fat of the sacrificed goat was then to be burned on the altar, and its entire remains consumed in a fire outside the camp (16:25, 27). The lore of the Mishnah adds considerable detail to the rite, recalling, e.g., that the high priest in Jerusalem divided a thread of crimson in two, tying one half to a rock and the other between the scapegoat's horns, and that the goat was led into the wilderness not to be let go but to be pushed over a precipice to its death (Yoma 6.6; cf. the NEB rendering, "the goat . . . for the Precipice" [Lev. 16:8, 10, etc.]).

Hebrews 13:11-13 makes a connection between the sacrifice of animals on the Day of Atonement and the death of Christ "outside the gate" (of Jerusalem). The early Fathers variously took each of the two goats to represent Christ. Tertullian and the author of the Epistle of Barnabas (6:4-5) have the priests of the temple eat the innards of the goat-for-the-Lord, which action is said to signify Christ's offering his flesh for the sins of the people; both see figures of Christ's passion and crucifixion outside the walls of Jerusalem in the strips of scarlet cloth and the goat who bears them and is slain in the desert. For St. Cyril of Alexandria and Theodoret the goats are representative of Christ in his two natures: the first, his human nature — the Son of Man dying in the flesh — and the second (here the scapegoat is let go and not killed), his divine nature — the Son of God triumphing over death by his resurrection.

The history of the biblical scapegoat in English literature following Tyndale's translation is a virtually blank page. What direct references there are occur chiefly in nonfiction prose, as in "Of the Office of Our Blessed Saviour," chap. 41 of *Leviathan.* Ironically enough in view of the atheism it has been taken to advance, Hobbes's book, more than half of which concerns scriptural and religious matters, gives a standard Christian reading: the Savior was "both the sacrificed Goat, and the Scape Goat. . . ; sacrificed, in that he died; and escaping, in his Resurrection."

Notwithstanding William Holman Hunt's famous painting of the scapegoat expiring by the Dead Sea (1854), the scapegoat has almost entirely lost the force of biblical association by the Victorian period. In literature it tends merely to indicate a person, group, or thing that bears the blame for others. Charlotte Brontë, e.g., has the other servants in *Jane Eyre* make of her heroine "the scapegoat of the nursery" (chap. 2). "That huge scapegoat of the race" figures as Maud's brother in Tennyson's monodrama: the soliloquist's beloved, a lady in the house of his sworn enemy, is all virtuous, daughter of her mother alone; while the hated brother is all vicious, son of his father alone (*Maud*, 13.3). Early in Tennyson's play *Harold*, Aldwith resolves to offer herself to Harold as "a peace offering," to enter into "a scapegoat marriage"; by taking "all the sins of both / The houses" on her head in this way she would reconcile England with Wales (1.2). Browning is characteristically difficult and ironic in "Holy-Cross Day," where a Jew coerced into attending a

Christian sermon in Rome refers to those who leave the true flock as "scapegoats" (51). Near the end of the century with the publication of "Scapegoats" in Frazer's *The Golden Bough*, the Levitical rite of atonement was buried in a lavish array of ritual expulsions of evil as practiced by cultures widely separated in time, place, and religious belief. Taking its lead from Frazer's anthropological method, Arthur L. Madson's "The Scapegoat Story in the American Novel" (1966) has traced the general theme of the redeeming victim through such works as Cooper's *The Bravo,* Twain's *Personal Recollections of Joan of Arc,* and Melville's *Billy Budd.* Hall Caine's adaptation of the theme is no less broad in his late-Victorian novel *The Scapegoat.*

More recently, Sackville-West's *The Edwardians* makes a passing reference to Viola as a "scapegoat . . . a safety-valve" for her mother's ill humor (chap. 2). Joyce's *Finnegans Wake* plays with "Scape the Goat, that . . . ate the Suenders bible"; "the skoopgoods bloof"; and "the skipgod." Frost's "From Plane to Plane" ingeniously reckons Santa Claus "a scapegoat": someone was needed to take the credit for Christmas giving so that givers might be freed from the oppression of the grateful. In Shirley Jackson's chilling short story "The Lottery," Tessie Hutchinson is a reluctant scapegoat in a town's annual expiation ritual. The scapegoat plays a significant role in the development of Walter M. Miller, Jr.'s, main theme in *A Canticle for Leibowitz:* the goat, representative of the medieval church in its role as the preserver of ancient learning, is to be adorned with a crown of honor by the Renaissance scientist, then driven by him into the desert, bearing on its head a crown of thorns or the responsibility for the coming harvest of annihilation which secular science sows (chap. 20). In Colin McDougall's World War II novel *Execution,* the helpless, innocent Jonesy "is a scapegoat" (4.1) in two senses. His execution satisfies an administrator's need to revenge a murder and serves to heal the internal wounds suffered by a number of his fellow soldiers.

See also ATONEMENT, DAY OF.

Bibliography. Frazer, Sir J. *The New Golden Bough* (1961); Lesêtre, H. "Bouc émissaire." *Dictionnaire de la Bible* (1912), 1.1871-76; Madson, A. "The Scapegoat Story in the American Novel." *DA* 27 (1966), 1828A; Vickery, J. "The Scapegoat Story in Literature: Some Kinds of Uses." In *The Binding of Proteus: Perspectives on Myth in the Literary Process* (1979), 264-78.   CAMILLE R. LA BOSSIÈRE

SCARLET WOMAN   (Rev. 17:4-5)
See also APOCALYPSE; WHORE OF BABYLON.

SCRIP AND STAFF   In his commissioning of the disciples Jesus admonishes them, "Take nothing for your journey, neither staves, nor scrip, neither brand, neither money, neither have two coats apiece" (Luke 9:3). One of the basic texts on Christian poverty, this verse was frequently alluded to by early writers: St. Bonaventure is representative not only of the Franciscan but of the more general ascetic traditions in habitually referring to those who would become perfected in their Christian walk as *religio carentium loculis* or "them that bear no purse" (*Apologia Pauperum,* 10).

A staff by itself (cf. Mark 6:8) could be seen in the Middle Ages simply as the badge of the wayfaring pilgrim, an ordinary seeker after faithful repentance. But it was capable of suggesting perversion of the pilgrim vocation; Langland describes troops of phony hermits traipsing to Walsingham with wenches in tow and bearing "hoked staves" (*Piers Plowman,* B.Prol. 51) — alluding perhaps to the notorious Latin pun of *hamus/amus* (hook/love), since the hermits in question are evidently neither true pilgrims nor shepherds.

The dubious friar lampooned in Chaucer's *Summoner's Tale,* who "with scrippe and tipped staf, ytuckked hye, / In every hous he gan to poure and prye" (*Canterbury Tales,* 3.1737-38), evidences disobedience both to Christ's injunctions to an apostolic life of poverty and the codification of those injunctions in the Franciscan Rule. Possible sexual connotations of such anti-apostolic imagery are further exploited by Chaucer in his characterization of the Pardoner, whose "walet" brims with *bullae,* "comen from Rome al hoot" (*CT* 1.686-87); the double entendre underscores the preeminence of carnal rather than spiritual affections in a person with explicit religious vocation.

In the 19th cent. Carlyle damns his own "Scrip Age" in "Hudson's Statue" *(Latter Day Pamphlets),* in which the "Fathers of the Scrip-Church" — contractors and chairmen of boards — "piously" interpret the Bible to neophytes, adding new levels to the meaning of words like "Providence." The scrip and staff are more oddly charged with ambivalent meaning in Dante Gabriel Rossetti's allegorical "The Scrip and Staff" (1856), in which a Pilgrim knight leaves his scrip and staff with the Queen for whom he fights as champion and then dies in battle. She hangs the staff "carved lovely white and slim" above her bed until in death she will join him in "imperishable peace" in heaven. The ascetic and gospel ideal of apostolic obedience is recalled in Gerard Manley Hopkins's "The Habit of Perfection," in which the scrip and staff are stripped away so that Poverty may "be . . . the Bride" when the pilgrim journey is over.

Bibliography. Fleming, J. V. "Gospel Asceticism: Some Chaucerian Images of Perfection." In *Chaucer and Scriptural Tradition.* Ed. D. L. Jeffrey (1984), 183-95; Lynch, C. J., O.F.M., ed. *A Poor Man's Legacy: An Anthology of Franciscan Poverty* (1989); Miller, R. P. "Chaucer's Pardoner, the Scriptural Eunuch and the Pardoner's Tale." *Speculum* 30 (1955), 180-99; Szittya, P. R. "The Friar as False Apostle." *SP* 71 (1974), 19-46.

SCROLL   *See* BOOK.

SEAMLESS COAT   After the soldiers had divided Christ's garments at the foot of the cross, they cast lots for his "seamless coat" (John 19:23-24) "that the scripture might be fulfilled, which saith, 'They parted my raiment among them, and for my vesture they did cast lots'" (citing Ps. 22:18; the Synoptics do not mention the robe, recording simply that the soldiers divided the garments by casting lots).

Patristic and medieval commentators typically interpreted the division of the garments as a figure for the church spread to the four quarters of the world, whereas the *tunica inconsultis* signified the unity of the physically separated church through the bond of love, and its indivisibility as the mystical Body of Christ (Peter Lombard, *Comm. in Ps.* 21 [PL 191.235]; St. Bernard, *Ep.* 334 [PL 182.538-39]; *Glossa Ordinaria* [PL 113.875; 114.174, 238, 347, 421-22]). The seamless coat is identified by St. Thomas Aquinas with the physical body of Christ, *corpus Christi,* especially as revealed in the Eucharist: "The seamless garment denotes the body of Christ, which is woven from above: for the Holy Spirit came upon the Virgin, and the power of the highest overshadowed her. The holy body of Christ is then indivisible: for although it be distributed from everyone, sanctifying the soul and body of each one individually, yet it subsists in all wholly and indivisibly" (*Cantena Aurea,* sup. John 19:23-24; quoting Theophylact).

In the Towneley "Play of the Talents," which follows the "Crucifixion" and precedes "The Deliverance of Souls," the actual subject is the casting of lots for the seamless coat or "robe" of Christ. When the three torturers and Pilate try to find a seam along which they might cut the coat and so divide it (24.274-82), they are symbolically trying to divide what cannot be divided. Hildebert refers the biblical incident to the profanation of Scripture and sacraments by heretics which is nonetheless unable to sever the bond of charity in the Body of Christ (*Ad Manochos, "Hanc unitatem in corpore suo tunica sua designavit"* [PL 171.185]; cf. Lombard, *Comm. in Ps.* 21). The robe is further identified with the Incarnation as the flesh, or "garment," Mary gave Jesus when he was in her womb (*Stanzaic Life of Christ,* ed. Foster [EETS o.s. 166, 6697-6700; 6729-30]). In the Towneley "Crucifixion" play Mary laments at the foot of the cross:

> To deth my dere is dryffen
> His robe is all to-ryffen
> That of me was hym gyffen
> And shapen with my sydys. (23.386-89)

In the ME lyric *"Quis est iste qui uenit de Edom?"* (C. Brown, *Religious Lyrics of the XIVth Century,* no. 25), the Crucifixion and apocalyptic last battle are juxtaposed, following traditional exegesis of Isa. 63:1-7, so that Christ's garments are "by-spreynd wyth hoer blod ysome, / And al my robe y-uuled to hoere grete shome," spattered

and befouled not with his own blood but that of the enemy, and the robe notably not torn.

George Herbert contrasts the "seamlesse coat" of Christ's own teaching, "cleare as heav'n," with the "curious questions and divisions" of the theologians in "Divinitie." The incident at the cross, and its identification with the "Body of Christ" in various senses, comes up for a modern reappraisal in Lloyd Douglas's popular novel, *The Robe.*

Bibliography. Coletti, T. "Theology and Politics in the Towneley *Play of the Talents." M & H* 9 (1979), 111-26; Gibson, G. M. "Swaddling Cloth and Shroud: the Symbolic Garment of the Incarnation in Medieval Art and Literature." Unpubl. M.A. thesis, Duke University, 1972.

SECOND ADAM   In Rom. 5:12-21 and 1 Cor. 15:21-22, 45-49, St. Paul relates Christ to Adam, contrasting the life-giving effect of Christ's redemptive work to the baneful results of Adam's sin. In 1 Cor. 15:45, Christ is called "the last Adam" and in 15:47, "the second man." These passages stimulate a continuing theological and literary theme of Christ as "second Adam," who reverses the effects of Adam's failure and offers a new beginning for the human race.

The significance of the Adam-Christ typology is expounded by some of the most prominent theologians in Christian tradition, including St. Irenaeus, Tertullian, St. Ambrose, St. Jerome, St. Augustine, St. Gregory the Great, St. Isidore of Seville, Peter Lombard, St. Thomas Aquinas, Luther, Calvin, More, and John Wesley. Probably its most famous literary expression is found in Milton's invocation to *Paradise Lost:*

> Of man's first disobedience, and the fruit
> Of that forbidden tree, whose mortal taste
> Brought death into the world, and all our woe,
> With loss of Eden, till one greater man
> Restore us, and regain the blissful seat,
> Sing heavenly Muse. . . . (1.1-6; cf. 3.285-97)

The poet connects the fruit of the tree of knowledge with the redemptive firstfruits (1 Cor. 15:20, 23) of the "greater man," Christ.

Elaboration of Adam-Christ typology takes many forms in early Christian tradition. The cross or wood of salvation *(lignum salvationis)* upon which the second Adam is said to undo the ruin caused by the forbidden tree or wood of damnation *(lignum perditionis)* of which the first Adam tasted (e.g., Aelfric, *The Homilies of the Anglo-Saxon Church,* ed. Thorpe [1846], 2.240-41; Herbert, "The Sacrifice," 202-03). According to popular legend, the cross is not only made of the same wood as the tree of knowledge but is also raised on the same spot where the tree grew (e.g., *History of the Holy Rood-tree,* ed. Napier [EETS o.s. 103]; *Cursor Mundi,* ed. R. Morris [EETS o.s. 57, 1320-63; o.s. 62, 16939-48]; Caxton's translation of the *Golden Legend,* ed. F. S. Ellis [1900], 1.77). John Donne in his "Hymne to God my God, in my sicknesse," refers to the legend in order to make a Pauline application:

> We think that Paradise and Calvary,
> Christ's Cross, and Adam's tree, stood in one place;
> Look, Lord, and find both Adams met in me;
> As the first Adam's sweat surrounds my face,
> May the last Adam's blood my soul embrace. . . .
> (21-25; cf. "The Progresse of the Soule," 71-90)

Edward Taylor extends this idea to show that the Eden lost by Adam was restored by Christ in the Church and in the soul of the Christian believer (*Preparatory Meditations* [2nd ser.], no. 83, 1-6, 19-30).

Gregory the Great draws an analogy between the temptations to which Adam succumbed — gluttony, vainglory, and avarice, according to his reading — and those overcome by Christ during the temptation in the wilderness (Hom. 16, *Homiliarum in Evangelia* [PL 76.1136]). This interpretation is reiterated in medieval works such as the *Stanzaic Life of Christ* (ed. Foster [EETS o.s. 166, 5249-5332]), the Chester play of the Temptation, and the *Golden Legend* (1.77-78); it also lies behind the diatribe against gluttony by Chaucer's Pardoner (*The Pardoner's Tale*, 6.498-511). Milton draws on this tradition in *Paradise Lost* (11.377-84): the hill in Eden from which Adam has a vision of the future is the same one from which "our second Adam" is shown the kingdoms of the earth by Satan. This typology recurs in Milton's statement of theme and his conclusion for *Paradise Regained* (1.1-7; 4.606-15).

The redemption of the first by the second Adam is generally seen to be completed in the Crucifixion and harrowing of hell. Adam is sometimes depicted praying at the foot of the cross or being led by Christ out of hell. Literary examples of the tradition include OE and ME translations of the Gospel of Nicodemus, the OE *Christ and Satan* (398-511), Corpus Christi plays on the Descent, the *Metrical Life of Christ* (ed. Sauer [1977], 3408-17), *Piers Plowman* (B.18.210-23), and the *Golden Legend* (1.100). Humanity's new relationship to God after the redemption is expressed as a marriage between Christ and his Bride, the Church, the antetype of which is the marriage of Adam and Eve. Chaucer's Parson applies this Pauline connection to his discussion of marriage (*Canterbury Tales*, 10.926-28).

As the second Adam, Christ relieves the guilt of original sin — often expressed as sickness or wounds — for the individual sinner as well as for humanity as a whole. In this way each Christian will have "put off the old man with his doings" and "put on the new man that is being renewed unto knowledge after the image of him that created him" (Col. 3:9-10). In *De doctrina Christiana,* Augustine speaks of Christ as the Physician who heals the wounds of sin caused by the Fall (PL 34.24). In the *Cursor Mundi* (1387-1400; 17925-72) Christ is the oil of mercy, the "medicen" (1378) promised to the dying

Adam to cleanse his sin. The Pearl Maiden declares that water and blood spurted from Christ's side during the Crucifixion and symbolized baptism "þat washeȝ away þe gylteȝ felle / þat Adam wyth inne deth vus drounde" (655-56). These are later linked to the motif of the well of mercy (1057-60), an image occurring in *The Faerie Queene* when Redcrosse Knight reenacts the Fall and Resurrection: after being wounded by the Dragon, Redcrosse undergoes symbolic baptism at the well of life and partakes of the tree of life, becoming a second Adam and regaining the Paradise forfeited by his first parents.

Adamic typology has persisted into the modern period. Many references recall traditional Christian associations (Ruskin, *Modern Painters,* 2.3.1.14; Newman, "The Dream of Gerontius"; Emily Dickinson, "Paradise is of the option"; Hopkins, "The Blessed Virgin compared to the Air we Breathe," 66-72). Emerson ("Promise") and Whitman (*Song of Myself,* 33.790, 832, "To the Garden of the World"; "As Adam Early in the Morning") make use of Adamic typology in an optimistic but more secular way to suggest that humanity can achieve a prelapsarian state of innocence and perfection without a specifically Christian form of redemption. Other writers are more pessimistic. In *Moby-Dick,* Ahab sees himself as bearing hatred and suffering since Adam but fails to seek out the "new Adam" for any personal salvation. Billy Budd's adamic innocence is not able to exist in a fallen world, and so he undergoes a Christlike trial and death.

Twentieth-cent. authors employ, often ironically, the Adam-Christ parallel to suggest a new beginning, morally or spiritually. Joe Christmas in Faulkner's *Light in August* may embody this idea: his life follows — sometimes in an inverted way — that of Christ, and after death he achieves a kind of apotheosis by becoming "the man," i.e., "adam." In *The Player Queen,* Yeats has Septimus, a drunken poet, announce the beginning of a new age: "Man is nothing till he is united to an image. Now the Unicorn is both an image and beast; that is why he alone can be the new Adam" (420; cf. 416-17, 422-23).

See also ADAM; EVE; HARROWING OF HELL; TEMPTATION OF CHRIST; TREE OF KNOWLEDGE; TREE OF LIFE.

Bibliography. Barrett. C. K. *From First Adam to Last* (1962); Schneidau, H. "The Antinomian Strain." In *The Bible and American Arts and Letters.* Ed. Giles Gunn (1983), 18; Scroggs, R. *The Last Adam: A Study in Pauline Anthropology* (1966).   KARL TAMBURR

SECOND ADVENT   *See* SECOND COMING.

SECOND COMING   During his earthly ministry Jesus himself declared that although he was to face death, he would rise from the dead and one day "come again" (e.g., John 14:2-3), a message reiterated by angelic witnesses at the Ascension (Acts 1:11): "this same Jesus, which is taken up from you into heaven, shall so come in like manner as ye have seen him go into heaven." The fundamental relationship between the Ascension and the Second Coming is reflected in all the major creeds of the Church. In the words of the Apostles' Creed, "He ascended into heaven, And sitteth on the right hand of God the Father Almighty; From thence he shall come to judge the quick and the dead" *(Book of Common Prayer)*.

In Matt. 24, in response to a question from his disciples — "What shall be the sign of thy coming, and of the end of the world?" (v. 3) — Jesus describes at length the circumstances which portend his return. There will be a period of "great tribulation," and then,

> immediately shall the sun be darkened, and the moon shall not give her light, and the stars shall fall from heaven, and the powers of the heavens shall be shaken: And then shall appear the sign of the Son of man in heaven: and then shall all the tribes of the earth mourn, and they shall see the Son of man coming in the clouds of heaven with power and great glory. And he shall send his angels with a great sound of a trumpet, and they shall gather together his elect from the four winds, from one end of heaven to the other. (vv. 29-31)

Mirroring the expectations of the OT prophets, Jesus talks about a historical judgment to fall upon Jerusalem in the near future (vv. 1-2) and about that destruction as an anticipation of the sacrilege of the last days, the desolation and destruction of Antichrist. His description recalls the imminent "Day of the Lord" spoken of by Amos (5:18) and Isaiah (2:12ff.), as well as the ultimate "Day of the Lord" also referred to by the prophets (Joel 3:14-21; Zeph. 1:14-18). The phrase "day of the Lord" is used widely in the NT to indicate the day at which Christ will return to bring history to an end and inaugurate the age to come (e.g., 1 Thess. 5:2; 2 Thess. 2:2; 2 Pet. 3:10); sometimes the expression occurs in other forms (e.g., "the day of the Lord Jesus" [1 Cor. 5:5; 2 Cor. 1:14], "the day of Jesus Christ" [Phil. 1:6]; "the day of God" [2 Pet. 3:12]; "the last day" [1 Pet. 1:5]).

St. Paul uses three words to describe the return of Christ: (1) Gk. *parousia* ("presence," "arrival" — as in 1 Cor. 16:17; 2 Cor. 7:7), a word normally used to describe a visit of royalty or one of exalted rank, and here applied to Christ's personal return (Acts 1:11) at the end of the age (Matt. 24:3) in power and glory (24:30) to raise the dead (1 Cor. 15:23), gather his people to himself (2 Thess. 2:1), and destroy evil (1 Thess. 2:19; 3:13; 4:15; 5:13); (2) *apokalypsis* ("unveiling" or "disclosure"), in which his power as God, heretofore partially hidden, is disclosed to the world, which then will of necessity acknowledge his lordship (Phil. 2:10ff.); (3) *epiphaneia* ("appearing"), indicating that it is to be a visible return (2 Thess. 2:8); the term is used to designate the Incarnation as well, connecting these two events as chief elements in Christ's redemptive work.

John's Patmos vision of the conclusion of human history ends with the promise of "He which testifieth these things," saying, "Surely I come quickly," to which the evangelist responds, "Even so, come, Lord Jesus" (Rev. 22:20). That note of expectancy was prevalent among the early Christians, many of whom expected Christ's return within their own lifetime. When, especially following the destruction of Jerusalem, this did not happen they turned away from preoccupation with the date and manner of Christ's return, observing the words of Jesus that "of that day and hour knoweth no man, no, not the angels of heaven, but my Father only" (v. 36). Most writers in the period between Augustine and the end of the first millennium were content with the Bishop of Hippo's sentiments as expressed in his *De civitate Dei* (20.30), asserting the fact of the Last Judgment rather than speculating on the time of Christ's return to effect it:

> That the last judgment, then, shall be administered by Jesus Christ in the manner predicted in the sacred writings is denied or doubted by no one, unless by those who, through some incredible animosity or blindness, decline to believe these writings [the Scriptures], though already their truth is demonstrated to all the world. And at or in connection with that judgment the following events shall come to pass, as we have learned: Elias the Tisbite shall come; the Jews shall believe; Antichrist shall persecute; Christ shall judge; the dead shall rise; the good and the wicked shall be separated; the world shall be burned and renewed. All these things, we believe, shall come to pass; but how, or in what order, human understanding cannot perfectly teach us, but only the experience of the events themselves. My opinion, however, is that they will happen in the order in which I have related them.

As the year 1000 approached, the sabbatarian view of history which made the last age (like the others) to last a thousand years, prompted an expectation of the imminent Second Advent. Commentaries on the Apocalypse began to be written in earnest. The emphasis of vernacular British poems on the subject, like the commentaries themselves and the Latin poem *De Die Judicii* attributed to the Venerable Bede, is still upon the Last Judgment rather than the *parousia* itself: *Christ and Satan* and *Doomsday* III (or *Christ* III) of the Exeter Book, like *Ascension (Christ* II), emphasize that Christ's coming again will be in severity of judgment, and many will be punished (346b-57). The theme of Christ's Second Coming and prophecies related to it were developed strongly in lections for Advent; after the 12th cent., when St. Bernard of Clairvaux made the connection between Christ's first and second advent the theme of an important series of sermons, Advent became more widely seen as a season for the examination of Christian conscience preparatory not only for Christmas but for the "Last Day" or "Day of the Lord." Much the same sentiment is expressed in the hymn *"Dies Irae, Dies Illae"* of the Franciscan (contemporary and biographer of St. Francis) Thomas of Celano. It has often been translated; one of the most powerful versions in English is that by the 17th-cent. poet Richard Crashaw:

Oh, that Trump! whose blast shall run
An even round with th' circling sun,
And urge the murmuring graves to bring
Pale mankind forth to meet his King.

When the millennium passed without the Lord's return, 1260 was put forward as another date of the Parousia; it was calculated as concluding a period of 42 generations (× 30 years), according to an interpretation of the generations of Christ in Matthew's genealogy. Joachim of Fiore's apocalypticism made much of this date, but others were also put forward: 1233, 1300, 1333, and 1400 among them. Some commentators made their calculations on the basis of Dan. 9:24-27. As Morton Bloomfield has shown, *Piers Plowman* participates in the later phase of this apocalyptic expectation. The connection with judgment was emphasized in popular preaching during this period, and this in turn lies behind the ME "Doomsday" lyrics, which are immediately followed in two important MSS by "þene latemeste dai," poems on the *terminus* of mortal life and repentance (C. Brown, *English Lyrics of the XIIIth Century*, nos. 28a-b, 29a-b). Fourteenth-cent. lyrics, such as *"Quis Est Iste Qui Uenit de Edom?"* (Brown, *Religious Lyrics of the XIVth Century*, no. 25) and "How Christ shall Come," followed in the MS by a poem on the vision of the Four Horsemen of the Apocalypse (Rev. 6:1-8), suggest a heightened interest in the Parousia itself ca. 1325-30. But that Christ's return seemed (in view of many failed predictions) to be somehow far off in a longed-for future is evident in the transference of emphasis once again to *apokalypsis*, a future unveiling of peace and order which finds its poetic counterpart in the idea of a "once and future king." The Arthuriad which develops from Wace and Laȝamon through the alliterative *Morte Arthure* to Malory is "apocalyptic" romance, but in none of these poems is the "coming again" parallel sharply focused or clearly realized. The "Last Judgment" play of York refers to all men seeing Christ descending with his five wounds clearly visible (48.70-71) but offers no further image; N-Town's "Doomsday" has a stage direction suggesting that Jesus *descendente cum Michaele et Gabriele archangelis* at the outset of the pageant, but then plunges right into the Last Judgment, its principal subject.

With the Reformation new interest in eschatology was awakened, and some older interests downplayed. A late 16th-cent. hymn of Nikolai Philipp, a Lutheran pastor, "Wachet auf! ruft uns die Stimme" was composed in 1599 in Westphalia in the midst of a raging epidemic of plague; its great popularity may have led to the tune being adapted by Mendelssohn in his *Elijah*. Philipp's hymn, translated into English by Frances Elizabeth Cox, develops the theme of the sudden arrival of the Bridegroom (Matt. 25:1-13). Calvin, meanwhile, was exceedingly wary of apocalypticism, and studiously avoided making any commentary on Revelation, privately doubting its value to the

canon. He both dismissed the late medieval Catholic doctrine that the kingdom of Christ would be realized in an earthly millennium (*Harmony of the Gospels*, sup. Matt. 24:3) and strove to turn attention away from historical speculation about Christ's return by interpreting Matt. 24:29-31 *in figura*, to refer to the entire history of the Church in the world and awaiting the completion of its redemption:

> Not that the glory and majesty of Christ's kingdom will only appear at his final coming, but that the completion *(complementum)* is delayed till that point — the completion of those things that started at the resurrection.... By this way Christ keeps the minds of the faithful in suspense to the last day, in case they should think that there was nothing to the testimony of the prophets on the restoration to come; for it had lain hid for a long time under a dense cloud of troubles. ... In other words, as long as the Church's pilgrimage in this world lasts, the skies will be dark and cloudy, but as soon as the end of distress arrives, the daylight will break to show his shining majesty. (*Harmony*, sup. Matt. 24:29)

In English Reformation writers such as John Bale the Second Coming is an urgent subject (*The Image of Bothe Churches* [1545]) but, as in Tyndale, is connected with anti-Catholic polemic. John Knox expresses in his *History of the Reformation in Scotland* the more positive side of British Reformers' expectations of the Second Coming when he sees it as a time of cosmic restitution:

> We believe that the same Lord Jesus shall visibly return for this last Judgment as He was seen to ascend. And then, we firmly believe, the time of refreshing and restitution of all things shall come, so that those who from the beginning have suffered violence, injury, and wrong for righteousness' sake shall inherit that blessed immortality promised them from the beginning. (2.102-03)

Among the most extensive treatments of the Second Coming among English Reformation writers is that by Bishop Hugh Latimer, in his "Sermon for the Second Sunday in Advent," 1552. Working from his text in Luke 21:25-28, he develops a full biblical exposition on the subject, citing as well Fathers of the Church and dealing with the apocalyptic expectations of Reformers Luther and Bilney (his own mentor). For Latimer the right way to prepare for the "last day" is not by speculating about the day or the hour but, on the example of Christ, "by keeping ourselves from superfluous eating and drinking, and in watching and praying.... Therefore Christ addeth, saying, *Vigilate et orate*, 'Watch and pray' ...." (*Sermons*, 8).

Yet the instinct to look for a near date for Christ's return is very strong in English Reformation tradition. Even in the 17th cent., Henry Vaughan's "The Dawning" expands upon a hint in George Herbert's poem of the same title to pose a question increasingly upon the minds of English Protestant readers of the Bible: "Ah! what time wilt thou come? when shall that crie / The *Bridegroome's*

Comming! fil the sky?" Vaughan concludes, however, in a prayer which Latimer would have approved:

> when that day, and hour shal come
> In which thy self wil be the Sun,
> Thou'lt find me drest and on my way,
> Watching the Break of thy great day.

In America, the millenarian Sabbath-history of the Puritans developed dramatically, with writers of the stature of Cotton and Increase Mather anticipating the imminent return of Christ, especially to "His New English Israel" (Cotton Mather, *Wonders of the Invisible World* [1692]; cf. Increase Mather, *The Mystery of Israel's Salvation* [1699]). The eager anticipation expressed in Michael Wigglesworth's poem *The Day of Doom* (1662) is undiminished in the writings of Jonathan Edwards, who expected Christ's Second Coming to inaugurate the millennial kingdom in America, in all probability in New England, "the most likely of all the American colonies" (*Some Thoughts Concerning the Present Revival of Religion in New England* [1742]).

That the "day of the Lord" should be not principally thought of as a "Day of Wrath" but rather as a day of release and redemption is a strong theme in the preaching of the Wesleyan revival of the 18th cent. It finds expression in the well-known hymn of Cowper's cousin Martin Madan, a cento, in fact, of hymns by Charles Wesley (nos. 38 and 39 of his *Hymns of Intercession for all Mankind*), and one by John Cennick, the first stanza coming direct from Wesley:

> Lo! he comes, with clouds descending,
>   Once for favored sinners slain
> Thousand thousand saints attending
>   Swell the triumph of his train:
>   Hallelujah!
> God appears, on earth to reign!

The last stanza, also Wesley's, concludes with an allusion to Rev. 22:20, "O come quickly, / Everlasting God, come down!" hearkening back to the theme of the early Church. Another hymn of the Second Coming by an associate of the Wesleys and Whitefield, "The Alarum" by Richard Kempenfelt, contrasts the "shriek and despair" of those who have rejected God with the "glories benign" of the disclosed "incarnate God" of whom the redeemed sinner need have no further terror:

> O my approving God!
> Washed in thy precious blood,
>   Bold I advance;
> Fearless we range along
> Join the triumphant throng,
> Shout an ecstatic song
>   Through the expanse.

These hymns and poems contrast in their joyous expectation not only the dread anticipation of medieval works on the theme but also a milder and more self-conscious evocation of them in Joseph Addison's "How Shall I Appear" (*Spectator,* Oct. 18, 1712), to which Addison adds in a note that his concern for the moment when the last trumpet shall sound and the dead arise is with having "to appear naked and unbodied before Him who made him":

> When rising from the bed of death
>   O'erwhelmed with guilt and fear,
> I see my Maker face to face,
>   Oh, how shall I appear?

Thomas Moore's "Lord, Who Shall Bear That Day?" relates, in a similar vein, the moment when "The Saviour shall put forth his radiant head" only to reveal also the countenance of the "eternal Judge." Charles Kingsley's strident "The Day of the Lord at Hand" (1850) strikes a millennial theme, as he almost welcomes the "last battle" as an opportunity for setting the fallen and sinful world right; in its triumphalist apocalypticism it is reminiscent of Blake's "Jerusalem." An American version of some of the same sentiments appears in Julia Ward Howe's "Battle Hymn of the Republic" (1862), one of the most popular of American patriotic songs, which draws much of its imagery from biblical descriptions of the Second Coming:

> Mine eyes have seen the glory of the coming of the
>   Lord
> He is trampling out the vintage where the grapes of
>   wrath are stored!
> He hath loosed the fateful lightning of his terrible swift
>   sword,
> His truth is marching on.

After the second stanza, for which the variant refrain is "His day is marching on," the third reads:

> He has sounded forth the trumpet that shall never call
>   retreat;
> He is sifting out the hearts of men before his judgment
>   seat;
> Oh, be swift, my soul, to answer him! be jubilant, my
>   feet!
> Our God is marching on.

The final stanza, with its appeal — "As he died to make men holy, let us die to make men free" — is an evident recrudescence of the millennialist application of the Parousia. By contrast, John Keble's Advent poems in *The Christian Year* emphasize the age-old liturgical association of the Second Coming with the Advent, especially his poem for the Second Sunday in Advent, "Not till the freezing blast is still."

The theme of Christ's coming again occurs in late 19th- and 20th-cent. writers in a diversity of guises. The best-known modern evocation of "The Second Coming" is undoubtedly the poem of that title by Yeats. Here, in a realization that "things fall apart; the centre cannot hold; / Mere anarchy is loosed upon the world," the speaker reflects on the collapse of civilization and its hopes for rational and natural harmony, a reflection which turns to apocalyptic speculation:

> Surely some revelation is at hand;
> Surely the Second Coming is at hand.
> The Second Coming! Hardly are those words out
> When a vast image out of *Spiritus Mundi*
> Troubles my sight. . . .

The image is of the darker side of apocalypse, the "rough beast, its hour come round at last," which "slouches toward Bethlehem to be born" — conjuring up associations not with Christ but rather his great antagonist, not with redemption but with tribulation.

In some Catholic writers such as David Jones, the focus is more on "Sejunction Day," or "Day of Disjoining" as he calls it, the great "Uncover" *(apokalypsis)* to Judgment in which a true moral analysis of history will be rendered (*Anathemata*, 5.164; 8.236). Others such as J. R. R. Tolkien and C. S. Lewis have incorporated an eschatological vision of the Second Coming in children's or fantasy fiction (Lewis, *The Last Battle;* Tolkien, *The Return of the King*). *The Second Coming*, by American novelist Walker Percy, uses fundamentalist preaching of an imminent return of Christ to unsettle his protagonist's assurance that his version of the American dream is secure (recalling Yeats, he finds that "things fall apart"), but then shifts perspective on the title to make the "second birth" or spiritual regeneration of his anti-hero and anti-heroine the real subject of his story.

See also ADVENT; APOCALYPSE; LAST JUDGMENT; SABBATH REST; THIEF IN THE NIGHT.

Bibliography. Bloomfield, M. *Piers Plowman as a Fourteenth Century Apocalypse* (1961); Cohn, N. *The Pursuit of the Millennium* (1957); Cullmann, O. *Christ and Time* (trans. 1964); Firth, K. R. *The Apocalyptic Tradition in Reformation Britain: 1530-1645* (1979); Harrison, J. F. C. *The Second Coming: Popular Millenarianism, 1780-1850* (1979); Hoekema, A. *The Bible and the Future* (1979); Glasson, T. F. *Second Advent* (1945); Mowinckel, S. *He That Cometh* (trans. 1956); Ploger, O. *Theokratie und Eschatologie* (1959); Reeves, M. *The Influence of Prophecy in the Later Middle Ages: A Study in Joachimism* (1969); Robinson, J. A. T. *Jesus and His Coming* (1957).

SECOND DEATH   *See* LAKE OF FIRE AND BRIMSTONE.

SEEK AND YE SHALL FIND   Jesus' invitation to his hearers in the Sermon on the Mount is "Ask, and it shall be given to you; seek, and ye shall find; knock, and it shall be opened unto you: For every one that asketh receiveth; and he that seeketh findeth; and to him that knocketh it shall be opened" (Matt. 7:7-8). St. Augustine says that

> the asking refers to the obtaining by request soundness and strength of mind, so that we may be able to discharge those duties which are commanded; the seeking, on the other hand, refers to the finding of truth. For inasmuch as the blessed life is summed up in action and knowledge,

action wishes for itself a supply of strength, contemplation desires that matters should be made clear: of these therefore the first is to be asked, the second is to be sought; so that the one may be given, the other found.

He adds, "The possession itself . . . is opened to him that knocks" (*De sermone Domini in Monte*, 2.21.71), and concludes that "there is need of perseverance in order that we may receive what we ask, find what we seek, and that what we knock at may be opened" (2.21.73). Calvin follows Augustine in this emphasis. Bunyan, in *Pilgrim's Progress*, exhibits the faithful pilgrim Christian as an essay in perseverance; when Christian finally reaches the strait Gate he finds written over it "Knock and it shall be opened unto you." John Wesley follows the main lines of traditional exegesis, but understands "asking" to mean the study of Christian doctrine and "seeking" to be "searching the Scriptures" — hearing them expounded and participating in the Eucharist; "knocking" involves the disciplines of prayer (*Sermon* 30 [Sermon on the Mount, no. 10] [1747]). Christopher Smart's *A Song to David* gives Wesley's emphasis poetic form:

> But stronger still, in earth and air,
> And in the sea, the man of pray'r;
>   And far beneath the tide;
> And in the seat to faith assign'd
> Where ask is have, where seek is find,
>   Where knock is open wide.

SEILA   *See* JEPHTHAH AND HIS DAUGHTER.

SENNACHERIB   Sennacherib was son and successor of Sargon II as king of Babylon and Assyria (705-681 B.C.). His main campaigns were against Babylonia, but of biblical significance are those against Judah under Hezekiah, who sought to take advantage of Assyria's occupation in Babylonia to express his own independence (2 Kings 18:13–19:37). Sennacherib advanced to put down the unrest, taking Judah's fortified cities, including Lachish (2 Kings 18:13-14; see *ANET*, 287-88; *ANEP*, 372-73) but not Jerusalem, though Hezekiah did have to pay tribute, including the contents of the Temple treasury (2 Kings 18:15-16). Sennacherib was finally assassinated by his own family (A. K. Grayson, *Assyrian and Babylonian Chronicles* [1975], 81.34-35; 2 Kings 19:37).

Rabbinic tradition shows Sennacherib to be wicked (Gen. Rab. 89.6) and proud (Exod. Rab. 8.2; Num. Rab. 9.24). Even though he did not worship the Lord, he was blessed by him (Num. Rab. 21.23), so he only turned against Hezekiah after first conquering the rest of the world (Meg. 11b). When Sennacherib returned home it was to fulfill a vow to sacrifice his sons, if he were successful against Hezekiah, on a plank of Noah's ark which he had found. Hearing this, his sons assassinated him (Sanh. 96a).

The most famous appearance of Sennacherib in English literature is in Byron's "The Destruction of Sennacherib," once memorized by countless thousands of schoolchildren ("The Assyrian came down like the wolf on the fold, / And his cohorts were gleaming in purple and gold").   DAVID W. BAKER

SEPARATE SHEEP FROM GOATS In Matt. 25 Jesus describes to his disciples the scene to take place at the Last Judgment "when the Son of man shall come in his glory . . . And before him shall be gathered all nations: and he shall separate them one from another, as a shepherd divideth his sheep from the goats: And he shall set the sheep on his right hand, but the goats on the left" (vv. 31-33). The "goats," in this instance, are sent "into everlasting fire prepared for the devil and his angels" because of their lack of charity. "For I was an hungered, and ye gave me no meat: I was thirsty, and ye gave me no drink" (vv. 41-42). In Jesus' own exposition, distinguishing between those who have acted in unselfish charity toward the needy stranger and those who have not, the former are counted as having acted charitably toward Christ himself, albeit unwittingly, while the latter are seen to have deprived and neglected Christ himself.

Subsequent Western exegesis makes the sheep a figure of the faithful, the goats of schismatics (e.g., St. Augustine, *Sermo* 146, sup. John 21:16). St. John Chrysostom follows the text more closely, noting that while all are "mingled together" in the world, "the division then shall be made with all exactness," but on the basis not of doctrinal purity but of charity or lack of charity to those in need. Chrysostom observes that the poor are said by Jesus to be his "brethren" (v. 40), "because they are lowly, because they are poor, because they are outcast," and should be received by us as brethren too (*Hom.* 79.1, sup. Matt. 25:31-41). The principle is given memorable fictional form in Tolstoy's "What Men Live By" and is discussed in his book of essays *The Kingdom of God is Within You*.

Michael Wigglesworth's *The Day of Doom* (1662) commences with the midnight coming of Christ to a sinful world and the separation of goats, including people who have performed good works and lived moral lives, from the sheep, the repentant and humble sinners. Carlyle's *Inaugural Address,* "The Reading of Books," adapts the text to the purposes of his own judgment: "In short . . . I conceive that books are like men's souls — divided into sheep and goats." In *Culture and Anarchy* Arnold inveighs against the Victorian predilection for large families, sarcastically upbraiding the "British Philistine" who imagines that he "would have only to present himself before the Great Judge with his twelve children, in order to be received among the sheep as a matter of right!" ("Sweetness and Light"). In modern literature the phrase often appears in humorous contexts. P. G. Wodehouse's *Uncle Fred in the Springtime* offers an example: " 'I wish I had a brain like yours,' said Lord Ickenham. 'What an amazing thing. I suppose you could walk down a line of

people, giving each of them a quick glance, and separate the sheep from the goats like shelling peas' " (chap. 8).

See also LAST JUDGMENT.

SERAPH *Seraphim* (sing., *seraph*), from Heb. *śaraph* ("fiery"), appear in the Bible only in Isa. 6:1-7, where they are described as six-winged creatures standing above God's throne and repeating in loud voices the chant which has become known in Christian tradition as the "trisagion": "Holy, holy, holy, is the LORD of hosts: the whole earth is full of his glory" (v. 3; cf. the *Te Deum* canticle of Morning Prayer in the *Book of Common Prayer,* lines 3-5). Seraphim are not primarily "messengers" (angels) but are rather attendants on God and celebrants of his holiness and power. In Rev. 4:8, the four beasts of the Apocalypse have six wings and recite the trisagion, representing an apparent conflation of the creatures of Isa. 6 with those of Ezek. 1:5-14.

In Jewish lore seraphim function as angels: they are messengers between God and man in Paradise, perform the last rites on Adam, and intimidate evil spirits so that they fear to do harm to humankind. They are especially remarkable for their wings (often allegorized), their loud voices (lightning flashes and fiery darts issue from their mouths), and their prodigious size (it would take 500 years to traverse their length and breadth). The prince of the seraphim is variously given as Seraphiel, Metatron, Michael, Jaoel, and Satan (before his fall).

Early Christian exegetes, notably Pseudo-Dionysius (*De caelesti hierarchia,* 7), made the seraphim the highest of nine orders of angels — an eminence not seriously challenged in Christian angelology until the 16th cent. — and medieval poets followed patristic example (e.g., Dante, *Paradiso,* 27.98-126). The Protestant Reformers, however, regarded the Dionysian system as overly elaborate and a pious fraud: "If we would be duly wise," Calvin counsels (*Inst.* 1.14.4), "we must renounce those vain babblings of idle men, concerning the nature, ranks, and number of angels."

In Christian art, seraphim are usually red (denoting fire) and carry a *flabellum* (flaming sword) with the inscription "Holy, holy, holy."

Postmedieval references in English, given Protestant antipathy to the Dionysian system, tend to be brief, few in number, and rigidly scriptural in imagery: e.g., Spenser's "eternal burning *Seraphins*" ("An Hymne of Heavenly Beauty," 94) and Vaughan's "flaming ministrie" ("The Search," 60). An exception is Crashaw's baroque preconversion poem on St. Teresa, the full title of which is "The Flaming Heart vpon the Book and Picture of the seraphicall saint TERESA, (as she is vsvally expressed with a Seraphim biside her)." Milton, on the other hand, represents a more typical English attitude: the term *seraph* is used in *Paradise Lost* as a periphrasis for *angel* (e.g., 1.794; 7.198), and the prominent angels in the poem (Satan, Raphael, Michael) are archangels, not seraphim, although Raphael is once called a seraph and described as having six wings (5.277-85). There is an interesting invocation of Isa. 6:6-7 in the autobiographical Preface to bk. 2 of *Reason of Church Government* (1642), where Milton links his poetic vocation with the OT prophets' calling and asserts that God "sends out his Seraphim with the hallow'd fire of his Altar to touch and purify the lips of whom he pleases" (*Prose Works* [Yale ed.], 1.821).

Apart from Pope (*Essay on Man*, 1.110, 278; *Eloisa to Abelard*, 218, 320), few references appear in 18th-cent. literature. With the Romantics and Victorians, however, there is a resurgence of interest. Blake adopts seraphim as the spirits of love, whose symbol is fire (e.g., *Jerusalem*, 86.24-25) and makes Mne Seraphim (a version of *Bne Seraphim* = "the sons of the Seraphim") the parent of Thel and her sisters (*Thel*, 1.1). In *The Rime of the Ancient Mariner* Coleridge draws on the medieval symbology of seraphim as angels of love and light when the shining "seraph-band" enspirits the mariner's shipmates and brings the stricken ship to safe harbor (488-95). There is an allusion to "burning seraphs" in Wordsworth (*Prelude*, 10.522), and the traditional associations of Christian exegesis — seraphim as messengers of fire and love — are rehearsed in Byron's *Cain* (1.133, 418) and in Elizabeth Barrett Browning's 1051-line dramatic lyric "The Seraphim" (1838), which imagines the Crucifixion as seen through the eyes of two sentimental seraphim named Ador and Zerah. Byron (*Don Juan*, 3.258; 4.881) together with Keats (*Eve of St. Agnes*, 275-76) led the way in the secularization of seraph as a synonym either for "angelic" intellect (Tennyson, *Palace of Art*, 133; *In Memoriam*, 30.27; 109.5) or, more commonly, "angelic" female beauty (Browning, *The Ring and the Book*, 6.1492). In Dickens's "Mrs. Lirriper's Lodgings" (*Christmas Stories* [1871]), Seraphina, the heroine, is described as "the most beautiful creature that ever was seen, and she had brown eyes, and she had brown hair all curling beautifully, and she had a delicious voice, and she was delicious altogether." This creature, like Shaw's languid temptress Seraphita Lunn in *Overruled* (1912), is a long way from the winged guardians of God's throne in Isaiah's vision.

More interesting — and arresting — treatments, however, do occur. In Twain's *Huckleberry Finn* (chap. 17), Emmeline Grangerford's "greatest picture," unfinished at her death, depicts "a young woman in a long white gown . . . [who] had two arms folded across her breast, and two arms stretched out in front, and two more reaching up towards the moon — and the idea was, to see which pair would look best and then scratch out all the other arms."

In Rudy Wiebe's wry tale "The Angel of the Tar Sands," Alberta oil workers dig up a seraph who flexes its wings ("three sets of wings now sweeping back and forth as if loosening up in some seraphic 5BX plan") and roars at them in low German before flying off (*The Angel of the Tar Sands and Other Stories* [1982]).

See also ANGEL; FLAMING SWORD.

Bibliography. Davidson, G. *A Dictionary of Angels* (1967); Ward, T. *Men and Angels* (1969); West, R. *Milton and the Angels* (1955).   JOHN SPENCER HILL

SERMON ON THE MOUNT   The most frequently cited standard of the teaching of Jesus, this extended sermon is recorded in unusual detail by Matthew (5:1–7:29). It begins with the Beatitudes, proceeds through a reevaluation of the Law in terms of its "spirit" or intent rather than mere "letter," offers practical instruction in self-sacrificing moral behavior and spiritual humility and an entreaty to spiritual honesty, perseverance, and wisdom, and concludes with the parable about the wise and foolish house builders. Of the many special injunctions of Jesus recorded in the Sermon, numerous are treated separately in independent entries. Major exegetical commentaries include St. Augustine's *De sermone Domini in Monte*, Peter Lombard's 12th-cent. *Sentences*, Calvin's commentary in his *Harmony of the Gospels*, and John Wesley's series of thirteen sermons (*Sermons on Several Occasions* [1747]). Jorge Luis Borges's "Fragmentos de un Evangelio Apocrifo" is a more or less systematic modern recasting of the Sermon (*In Praise of Darkness*, 106-11).

See also BEATITUDES; GOLDEN RULE; JUDGE NOT; MOTE AND BEAM; *PATER NOSTER;* SALT OF THE EARTH; TREASURES UPON EARTH.

SERPENT   The first instances of the serpent in English literature are clearly derived from Gen. 3, where Satan takes the form of a "subtle" and beautiful creature to tempt Eve (3:1-6) and is then condemned by God to crawl upon the earth and live in enmity with "the seed" of the woman (vv. 14-15). In one of the most influential commentaries on this passage, St. Augustine allegorizes the story in such a way that the psychology of temptation is described: Adam stands for *sapientia*, Eve for *scientia*, and the serpent for sensuality, which, when it obtains mastery, subverts wisdom, confounds knowledge, and inverts their ordinate relationship (*De Trin.* 12.12.17; see also *De Genesi ad litteram*). References to the serpent in Exod. 4:3 (the rod of Moses, transformed by God in order that the Hebrews would "believe that the LORD God of their fathers, the God of Abraham, the God of Isaac, and the God of Jacob, hath appeared unto thee") and to the brazen serpent set up by Moses in the wilderness as a means of healing for those bitten by serpents (Num. 21:8-9; 2 Kings 18:4; cf. John 3:14) are also important. The most important NT citation is Christ's sending out of his apostles with the injunction that they be "wise as serpents, harmless as doves" (Matt. 10:16). In the book of Revelation (12:9; 20:2) Satan is referred to as both "dragon" and "serpent," designations which persist in subsequent literature (the celebrated and sinister dragon of the OE *Beowulf* is referred to throughout the poem as both *draca*, "dragon," and *wyrm*, "serpent").

Genesis B, a late OE poem with close Old High German and continental connections, affords a significant variation on the Genesis account: the serpent first approaches Adam, telling him that God wishes him to taste the fruit of the tree of knowledge. In the ME poem *Pricke of Conscience* the familiar connection between serpents and evil is maintained (6925-26). For the author of *Ancrene Riwle* the serpent is particularly associated with the sin of envy. Chaucer's Prioress, as part of her vicious anti-Semitic tale, alludes to "oure first foe, the serpent Sathanas, / That hath in Jewes herte his waspes nest" (*Canterbury Tales,* 7.558-61). In his *Man of Law's Tale* the narrator is only too happy to excoriate the wicked "Sowdenesse," mother-in-law of Custance, as

Virago, thou Semyrame the secounde!
O serpent under femynynytee
Lik to the serpent depe in helle ybounde! (2.358-61)

Here the association of serpentine antagonism to God and his chosen servants is magnified by the name Semiramis, a mythical Assyrian queen who murdered her husband and founded Babylon. Reminiscence of such legends, as well as of the dragon-serpent of Revelation, lies behind the depiction of Errour, "the vgly monster plaine, / Halfe like a serpent" in Spenser's *Faerie Queene* (1.1.14.6–16.8).

St. Thomas More takes up the Exodus passage referring to the rod-serpent several times in his writings and provides an interesting version of the image in *An Answer to the First Part of . . . The Supper of our Lord* (1.16). Here Christ's body is described as "that holy, wholesome serpent that devoureth all the possessed serpents of hell" (see Exod. 7:9-12). Marlowe (*The Jew of Malta,* 796-98) provides a double inversion of Matt. 10:16 when he has a Machiavellian character proclaim himself as "more of a serpent than the Dove; that is, more brave than foole."

The Genesis episode has a central place in Milton's *Paradise Lost* and *Paradise Regained,* where several departures from the biblical account invoke ancient associations of gnostic wisdom with the serpent. The most important of these is in bk. 9 of *Paradise Lost,* where Satan's approach to Eve, in the body of the Serpent, is filled with sinister allure:

. . . Oft he bow'd
His turret Crest, and sleek enamell'd Neck,
Fawning, and lick'd the ground whereon she trod.
His gentle dumb expression turn'd at length
The Eye of *Eve* to mark his play; he glad
Of her attention gain'd, with Serpent Tongue
Organic, or impulse of vocal Air,
His fraudulent temptation thus began. (*PL* 9.524-31)

Eve is surprised to hear the serpent speak: "Thee, Serpent, subtlest beast of all the field / I knew, but not with human voice endu'd" (9.560-61). Elsewhere in *Paradise Lost,* Sin, one of the two guardians (with Death) of the gates of Hell, is described as

Woman to the waist, and fair,
But ended foul in many a scaly fold
Voluminous and vast, a Serpent arm'd
With mortal sting. (2.650-53)

This description nicely conforms to Renaissance pictorial representations of the serpent about to tempt Eve in the garden (e.g., Cranach's "Temptation" or Bosch's "Haywain" triptych).

Blake develops a central place for the serpent in his own alternative mythology. Northrop Frye observes that "Orc, or human imagination trying to burst out of the body, is often described as a serpent bound on the tree of mystery, dependent upon it, yet struggling to get free" (*Fearful Symmetry,* 136). For Blake the serpent shedding its skin symbolizes immortality, and he is happy to conflate the brazen serpent with that in Eden, or with the dragon of the Apocalypse, as occasion permits (cf. Damrosch, 106-07, 204-09, 224-26, etc.). These conflations appear in simple lyrics such as his "Infant Sorrow," but enlarge and gain complexity in larger works such as *The Four Zoas.*

In Byron's *Cain* the serpent's insinuations are given new credibility:

The snake spoke truth; it was the tree of knowledge;
It was the tree of life: knowledge is good,
And life is good; and how can both be evil? (*Cain,* 1.36-38)

Tennyson and Browning employ the Genesis commonplace straightforwardly. The curse of the serpent is a popular motif in the writings of Swinburne, who manipulates it to serve secular, typically political ends ("The Armada," "A Song of Italy," "A Counsel"; see Landow, 153-54). Conrad makes complex symbolic use of the same motif in *Victory* and *The Secret Agent* (Purdy, 49-50, 50-51).

The serpent or snake, since the time of Augustine an image of sensuality, is in the modern period increasingly associated with sexuality and sexual license. D. H. Lawrence in *The Plumed Serpent* describes the fascination of Kate Leslie, a restless and unfulfilled Irish widow, with a revived Mexican serpent-cult, its dark and elemental rituals an explicit repudiation of Christianity. Joyce's Stephen calls the sexual organ to which he has become subservient "the serpent, the most subtle beast of the field" (*A Portrait of the Artist as a Young Man,* chap. 3).

A more complex evocation of the serpent of Genesis, and one of the central scenes in the Faulkner myth, is found in "The Bear" from *Go Down, Moses,* in which the snake is described as "the ancient and accursed about the earth, fatal and solitary":

he could smell it now: the thin smell of rotting cucumbers and something else which had no name, evocative of all knowledge and an old weariness and of pariah-hood and of death. At last it moved. Not the head. The elevation of the head did not change as it began to glide away from him, moving erect yet off the perpendicular as if the head and that elevated third were complete and all: an entity walking on two feet and free of all laws of mass and balance and should have been because even now he could not quite believe that all that shift and flow of shadow behind that walking head could have been one snake.

Mark Twain twists and even reverses the Genesis passage in his later writings, most particularly in his *Diary of Adam* and *Diary of Eve,* while in *Letters from the Earth* he gives Satan's point of view on the events of the Fall. Langston Hughes offers a tongue-in-cheek rejoinder to the whole tradition of the Fall as occasioned by the serpent in his "Temptation," where Simple points out to the supposedly more "learned" narrator:

> I am not talking about no symbol . . . I am talking about the day when Eve took the apple and Adam et. From then on the human race has been in trouble. There ain't a colored woman living what would take no apple from a snake — and she better not give no snake-apples to her husband.

See also BRAZEN SERPENT; BRUISE THY HEAD, BRUISE HIS HEEL; DRAGON OF THE APOCALYPSE; EVE; FALL; WISE AS SERPENTS.

Bibliography. Brown, D. *The Enduring Legacy: Biblical Dimensions in Modern Literature* (1975); Damrosch, L. *Symbol and Truth in Blake's Myth* (1980); Ensor, A. *Mark Twain and the Bible* (1969); Frye, N. *Fearful Symmetry* (1947); Joines, K. R. *Serpent Symbolism in the Old Testament* (1974); Landow, G. *Victorian Types, Victorian Shadows: Biblical Typology in Victorian Art, Literature, and Thought* (1980); Purdy, J. *Joseph Conrad's Bible* (1984).

ROBERT FARRELL
CATHERINE KARKOV

SERVANT OF THE LORD   *See* MAN OF SORROWS.

SETH   The chief biblical reference to Seth is Gen. 4:25. Seth is the third son of Adam and Eve and, according to Eve's explanation of his name, he is God's replacement for Abel, whom Cain slew. Further mention of him is made in Gen. 4:26; 5:3-8; 1 Chron. 1:1; and Ecclus. 49:6, which refers to Seth's glory among humans. In rabbinical tradition the name *Seth* is interpreted as meaning "foundation."

Luke 3:38 traces the genealogy of Jesus back through Seth to Adam, the son of God; the passage sets down the pattern of divine sonship, present from the beginning and fulfilled through the coming of Jesus.

Seth and his descendants are traditionally represented as righteous, in contrast to the impious Cainites. Josephus records a tradition which was drawn upon frequently in later centuries: Seth and his descendants were astronomers who inscribed their findings on two pillars, one of brick and one of stone, so that whether the world were destroyed by flood or fire, one of the pillars would endure (*Ant.* 1.2.3).

Evidence for the importance of Seth among the gnostic

sects can be found in the polemical antignostic works of early Christian commentators, including St. Irenaeus, St. Hippolytus, Origen, and St. Epiphanius; see, e.g., Hippolytus, *The Refutation of All Heresies,* 14-17. The ancient collection of writings found at Nag Hammadi now gives direct access to gnostic speculation about Seth, as illustrated in such texts as *The Three Steles of Seth* (see J. M. Robinson, *The Nag Hammadi Library: In English* [1977]).

St. Jerome interprets *Seth* to mean not only "seed" (as in the Genesis account) but "plant" and "resurrection" (Robinson, 30). St. Augustine likewise interprets Seth as signifying resurrection and refers to Seth and his sons as the founders of the heavenly city (in opposition to Cain, founder of the earthly city) (*De civ. Dei* 15.17).

Also current in the early Christian centuries was the apocryphal account of Seth's journey to Paradise in search of the oil of mercy for his dying father. Originally Jewish, the earliest extant versions are the Greek text sometimes called the Apocalypse of Moses and the Latin *Vita Adae et Evae* (see Ginzberg, *LJ* 1.93-101; J. H. Charlesworth, *The Old Testament Pseudepigrapha,* 2.249-95). The story of Seth's journey to Paradise entered Christian tradition in the apocryphal *Descensus ad Inferos,* which was incorporated with the *Acta Pilati* into the so-called Gospel of Nicodemus. Here Seth is represented as giving an account of his journey to the patriarchs who await Christ's coming to deliver them from the lower world (M. R. James, *The Apocryphal New Testament* [1924], 126-28). Seth's journey was also linked to the legends which traced the wood of the cross back to Paradise where an angel gave Seth seeds or a twig to plant on the grave of Adam. In the expanded version of Seth's journey, which appears in a number of works, Seth followed the dry footprints made by his father as he left Paradise and he was granted three visions: of a dry tree, a serpent in the tree, and a newborn baby in the topmost branches (see, e.g., *Cursor Mundi,* 1237-1432). Apart from Seth's being linked to legends of the cross there are relatively few indications in English literature of his importance in the early centuries. (See, however, the OE *Genesis,* 1104-1257.)

All four English mystery cycles contain Christ's *Descensus ad Inferos,* but the full version, including Seth's account of his journey to Paradise, appears only in the Chester cycle (no. 17, lines 65-80). The Towneley plays "Noah" and "Abraham" contain references to the "oyle of mercy," as does play no. 28 of the Coventry Cycle. The most fully developed dramatic version of the Seth legend extant is in the Cornish *Ordinalia.*

Seth's journey to Paradise is referred to in *Mandeville's Travels,* in Jacobus de Voragine's *Legenda Aurea,* and in William Caxton's *The Golden Legend.* A passage in *Piers Plowman* continues the traditional dichotomy between the descendants of Seth and those of Cain, although the angel who appears to warn Seth may be related to the angel in the apocryphal tradition who addresses him at the gates of Paradise (A.10.151-62).

After the medieval period, there are few references to Seth in English literature. In the 17th cent. both John Donne and Andrew Marvell echo the traditions found in Josephus: Donne, in "The Progresse of the Soule," refers to "a worke t-outweare Seth's pillars, brick and stone" (9) and later to "blest Seth" who "vext us with Astronomie" (516-17). Marvell, in "The Loyal Scot," also alludes to the brick and stone pillars of Seth (158). Among post-medieval writers it is perhaps William Blake who incorporated the biblical Seth into his imaginative vision most fully. In *Milton* (37.36) and *Jerusalem* (pl. 75) Seth is designated as one of twenty-seven "Heavens and their Churches," and in the *Vision of Judgment* Seth is placed among the persons who ascend to meet the Lord, above the head of Noah, "being nearer the state of Innocence."

See also HARROWING OF HELL; OIL OF MERCY; TREE.

Bibliography. Charlesworth, J. H. *The Old Testament Pseudepigrapha.* 2 vols. (1983-85); Klijn, A. F. J. *Seth in Jewish, Christian, and Gnostic Literature* (1977); Quinn, E. C. *The Penitence of Adam* (1980); *The Quest of Seth* (1962); Robinson, F. C. "The Significance of Names in Old English Literature." *Anglia* 86 (1968), 14-58.

ESTHER C. QUINN

SEVEN CHURCHES The letters to the seven churches (Rev. 2–3) are closely structured into the intricate literary unity of the book of Revelation. Most of the attributes of Christ from John's vision on Patmos (Rev. 1) recur in the titles introducing the seven repetitively formalized addresses to the "angels" of the churches. These letters in their turn introduce the series of sevenfold visions in the remaining chapters (Rev. 4–22).

The number seven is evidently symbolically meaningful, but the initial address to the churches in seven named cities anchors the book very precisely. Sir William Ramsay argued convincingly that these cities lay successively on the circular route of a messenger traveling from Ephesus (the landing point from Patmos) around the principal existing Christian centers in the Roman province of ("proconsular") Asia, in western Asia Minor. "*The* Seven Churches" may thus have been a group already recognized before the time of Domitian (A.D. 81-96), to whose latter years the Revelation is usually attributed. In Christian tradition this was a time of persecution: while this setting is sometimes questioned, there are convincing grounds for documenting the sufferings of the Asian churches under complex social pressures reinforced by imperial policy.

The symbolic imagery of the Revelation (or Apocalypse) as a whole relates it obviously to the Jewish genre of "apocalyptic." Yet while using apocalyptic imagery, it differs in spirit. The writer John repeatedly designates the book "prophecy" (1:3; 22:7, 10, 18, 19), and his deepest affinities are with the OT prophets. The imagery of the letters abounds in OT reminiscences but is pointedly applied to the needs of the individual churches, which are often closely identified with their cities.

The "angels" of the churches are not easily understood; they may be heavenly counterparts or guardians of the churches, virtually personifications. Many of the other symbols in the passage are concretely allusive. Ephesus was the "city of change," where the church had lost its "first love" (2:4): outward success and tenacity in doctrine were not enough. Smyrna was the "city of suffering," which had been destroyed and "lived again" after 300 years. The call to be "faithful unto death" brings the victor's "crown of life": Polycarp was to be its classic martyr. Pergamum was the religious capital, where emperor worship was enforced by the power of the sword. The "white stone" (2:17), an extraordinarily rich and suggestive image, may be a token of acquittal or a bond of relationship. Thyatira was a city of trade guilds, where the Christian was confronted with the compromises inherent in working life in a pagan society. Sardis, the city of Croesus, had vain confidence in its apparently impregnable strength, but had fallen for lack of vigilance. The church, too, seemed alive, but was dead at heart and unready for the coming of its Lord. Philadelphia was the "missionary city," where despite recurring earthquakes a community persisted, living when necessary outside the town. The faithfulness of a harassed church is fortified with the promise that the victor "shall no more go outside" (3:12). The letter to Laodicea is marked by a series of local allusions. References to gold, eyesalve, and white raiment reflect its wealth from banking, ophthalmic medicine, and black woolen clothing. Its water was literally lukewarm and impure, obtained through an aqueduct whose lime-choked pipes are preserved, an artificial supply in pointed contrast with the natural medicinal hot springs of its neighbor Hierapolis and the perennial cold stream of its neighbor, Colossae. "Lukewarmness" may originally have signified ineffectiveness rather than halfheartedness, human self-sufficiency against divine provision (see M. J. S. Rudwick and E. M. B. Green, "The Laodicean Lukewarmness," *ExpTim* 69 [1957-58], 176-78). The common sense of "lukewarmness," however, derives from traditional understanding of this passage.

Christian exegesis of the seven churches is not extensive and tends to give greater emphasis to the Laodiceans than to the other six churches (although the Philadelphians gained attention in the 19th cent.). The number seven is seen by St. Augustine, typically, as signifying "the perfection of the Universal Church"; he thus relates Rev. 2–3 to Prov. 9:1: "Wisdom hath builded her house, she hath strengthened her seven pillars" (*De civ. Dei* 17.4; cf. *Sermo*, 95.2).

Late medieval apocalypticism focused its interest elsewhere: even Joachim of Fiore expressed little interest in the seven churches, apart from reiterating Augustine's identification of the symbolic number with the Church universal. Some of those influenced by Joachim, however, such as the 14th-cent. English Franciscan Henry of Cossey, went further. In his commentary *Super Apocalypsim,* Cossey discussed the seven churches of Asia in terms of the seven ages of the Church. The church of Sardis he made to occupy the period between Charlemagne and Joachim himself, who was imagined to have inaugurated the next age. These historical periods were connected also to seven persecutions in the OT, said to have their counterparts in seven persecutions of the Church. The 14th-cent. Austin friar Agostino Trionfo, another follower of Joachim, elaborated a dispensationalist schema relating the seven churches, the seven ages of the Church, and Joachim's "seven orders" in the Church *(Dispositio Novi Ordinis).*

While Calvin eschewed any commentary on Revelation, other Reformation leaders were less cautious. In England, notably, Henry of Cossey had successors, among the most influential of these being John Foxe, author of the famous *Book of Martyrs.* Foxe's proccupation with persecution shaped his overall interpretation of the Apocalypse, which he begins to lay out in his *Actes and Monuments* (1583 ed.) and then, in a more orderly and systematic way, in his *Eicasmi* (1587), still incomplete at his death. Building a concordance of the number seven, a "universal number for the Church," he concluded that all biblical images employing the number seven properly pertained to the Church. Puritan John Brightman, in his *A Revelation of the Revelation* (1607), reacting in part to the less persecution-oriented commentaries of the Jesuits (e.g., Robert Bellarmine), applied the Apocalypse to the memorable past. In the letters to the seven churches he saw both "panes" and "counterpanes," not only the churches so named but periods of church history from the first century to the present. The church of Ephesus, e.g., has its "counterpane" in the apostolic Church up until the time of Constantine. Smyrna extended from Constantine to Gratian (382), Pergamum to the year 1300, a type of the "corrupt" Roman church. Thyatira was seen as the pre-Reformation church (1300-1520), Sardis represented the German Reformation under Luther, Philadelphia was the Genevan Reformation under Calvin, and Laodicea was the Church of England. The distances of the churches from Ephesus in Rev. 2–3 was taken to suggest the length of their respective ages; the geographic direction in which each lay, relative to Ephesus, was a guide to their relative purity in preserving the apostolic faith: northwest locations were in a process of corruption, southward the opposite. Philadelphia, parallel to Ephesus, was the new apostolic Church. Laodicea was "a peerless Paragon," the Church of Eden as she might become if her potential were realized.

In subsequent redactions, such as in Robert Pont's *A newe treatise of the right reckoning of the yeares . . .* (1599), this basic pattern was repeated, but specific assignations were in a continuous process of reorganization.

Patrick Forbes, *An exquisite commentarie . . .* (1613), allows Sardis to be the early Reformed Church, but in his view Philadelphia and Laodicea exemplified, respectively, keenness for reform and spiritual "lukewarmness" in the entire reformed community — a reading which was to prove more enduring than that of Brightman, reoccurring in popular pamphlets such as *The Bloody Almanack* (1643) by John Booker, Reader of Gresham College and "licenser of almanacs, prognostications, and mathematical works" (Firth, 230).

Matthew Henry's widely used commentary, while giving considerable attention to the epistles to the seven churches, nevertheless urged a moral and universal reading which ultimately came to predominate even in Reformed congregations. This part of the *Commentary,* completed by William Tony, concludes:

> What is contained in [these "epistles"] is not of private interpretation, not intended for the instruction, reproof and correction of these particular churches only, but of all churches in Christ in all ages and parts of the world; and as there will be a resemblance in all succeeding churches to these, both in their graces and sins, so they may expect God will deal with them as he dealt with these, which are patterns to all ages. (6.1137)

The tradition of historicist apocalypticism in exegesis of the seven churches continued in England down through the Plymouth Brethren and into the 20th cent. It has its diversified counterparts in America in New Light Calvinism after the Great Awakening and William Miller's adventism in the 19th cent., and is reflected also in the dispensationalism of Scofield's famous notes to the KJV Bible.

Six of the seven churches and their possible significances have held little interest for English and American authors; the seventh, that of the "lukewarm Laodiceans," has received more attention. John Ruskin, however, in his *Fors Clavigera,* offers an extended reflection on all seven, "churches that live no more — they having refused the word of His lips, and been consumed by the sword of His lips." Yet, following Henry, he takes the passage as of value for moral instruction of contemporary "churches." In his analysis, the address to each of the Seven Churches divides into four parts (attribute, declaration, judgment, promise), the first of which he emphasizes most strongly:

> Observe, first, they all begin with the same words, "I know thy works."
> Not even the maddest and blindest of Antinomian teachers could have eluded the weight of this fact, but that, in the following address to each Church, its "work" is spoken of as the state of its heart. Of which the interpretation is nevertheless quite simple, that the thing looked at by God first, in every Christian man, is his work; without that, there is no more talk or thought of him.

Ephesus, he says, has for its essential attribute "the spiritual power of Christ, in His people, — the 'lamp' of the virgins, the 'light of the world.'" Its fierceness against sin, he continues, "which we are so proud of being well quit of, is the very life of a Church; the toleration of sin is the dying of its lamp." Smyrna has the attribute of "Christ's endurance of death"; Pergamum the attribute of "Christ the Judge, visiting for sin" (he confesses he does not understand the metaphor of the stone, and the new name); Thyatira is the type of the practical Christian life, which enables a people "to rule the nations with a rod of iron"; Sardis is identified with the gifts and presence of the Holy Spirit; Philadelphia the attribute of the truly separated life; and Laodicea has as its attribute the faithful witness of the Word, while the judgment against it is that it lives in a complete confusion of values, "dross for gold — slime for mortar — nakedness for glory — pathless morass for path — and the proud blind for guides" (Letter 84).

See also LUKEWARM LAODICEA.

Bibliography. Firth, K. *The Apocalyptic Tradition in Reformation Britain: 1530-1645* (1979); Hemer, C. J. "Unto the Angels of the Churches." *Buried History* (Melbourne) 11 (1975), 4-27, 56-83, 110-35, 164-90; Ramsay, Sir W. M. *The Letters to the Seven Churches of Asia and Their Place in the Plan of the Apocalypse* (1904); Reeves, M. *The Influence of Prophecy in the Later Middle Ages: A Study in Joachimism* (1969).   COLIN HEMER

SEVEN DEADLY SINS The seven deadly sins are pride, envy, wrath, sloth, avarice, gluttony, and lechery, or, to use the Latin equivalents, *superbia, invidia, ira, acedia, avaritia, gula,* and *luxuria*. Strictly speaking, they are not "deadly" sins, for they are not necessarily "mortal," leading irrevocably to damnation. The term *deadly sins*, however, came into common usage, largely replacing the more accurate expression *capital* (or *cardinal*) sins, which makes clear that the seven vices are the principal sources, or "heads," of other sins.

While there are several noteworthy lists of sins in the Bible (e.g., Gal. 5:19-21) and while seven is a number of special biblical significance, the Bible is not the direct source of the traditional list of vices. The individual sins that compose the catalog of seven all occur in the Bible, however, and medieval exegetes found it relatively easy to provide scriptural warrant for the list. That pride, e.g., eventually asserted itself as the primary sin is related exegetically to Ecclus. 10:15 ("Pride is the beginning of all sin"; see St. Thomas Aquinas, *Summa Theol.* 1.2.q.84.art.2). And figurative interpretations of such passages as Luke 8:2, concerning the exorcism of seven devils from Mary Magdalene, were used to make the Bible support the seven-sin scheme (e.g., St. Gregory the Great [PL 76.1075]).

A precursor of the Christian classification of the sins appears in the pseudepigraphal Testament of the Twelve Patriarchs, but the first Christian writer to treat the concept directly is Evagrius of Pontus, who, in his treatise *On the Eight Evil Thoughts* (PG 40.1271-73), expresses a theme common in the 4th-cent. monastic communities of the Egyptian desert: the cardinal sins involve temptations that specifically beset the ascetic life. Evagrius notes eight sins. He may, nonetheless, have been influenced by Origen's view that Joshua's destruction of seven Canaanite nations (Deut. 7:1-2) is an allegory of the soul's effort to expel sins (PG 12.866).

At the source of Western Christianity's preoccupation with the vices is John Cassian. In his *Institutes of Cenobites* (bks. 5-12 [PL 49.201-476]), Cassian reveals his debt to Evagrius; he even uses Greek names for four of the eight temptations he discusses. Cassian inaugurates the practice of considering the progeny of each sin, and he regards the order in which he presents the sins as significant. Writing with a monastic in mind, he begins his list of temptations with assaults on the flesh, specifically with *gula,* the opposite of fasting, and continuing with lechery, covetousness, anger, melancholy (*tristitia*), sloth, vanity, and pride. The Cassianic order provides the basis for consideration of gluttony as the first sin of which Adam and Eve were guilty when they ate the apple, and it also justifies the prominence of the tavern as a setting for a range of sins in medieval literature.

A century and a half after Cassian's death, Gregory the Great wrote his influential commentary on Job. In the fourth part of this *Moralia* (PL 76.9-782), Gregory treats the vices, now numbering seven, in the sequence which was to become common. He inserts envy into the list, combines sloth and melancholy, and makes pride, as St. Thomas Aquinas was later to explain (*Summa Theol.* 2.2.q.162.art.8), both the genus of all sins and, in the form of vanity, the first species. Gregory's exposition, moreover, suggests that the sins are like links in a chain, proceeding from spiritual to carnal sins: "And so the first offspring of pride is vainglory, which now destroys the burdened mind and soon gives rise to envy. . . . Envy in turn produces anger . . ." etc. (PL 76.621). When in the 13th cent. Peter Lombard's *Sentences* affirmed the Gregorian scheme, its position as locus classicus for consideration of the sins was secured.

Aquinas does not give the seven deadly sins much prominence in the *Summa,* although he discusses them in four brief articles in 1.2.q.84 and develops their opposition to appropriate virtues throughout 2.2. Aquinas frames the former account in a way which reflects his concern over the lack of biblical provenance for the standard list and his desire to reconcile Ecclus. 10:15, which asserts pride as the beginning of all sin, and 1 Tim. 6:10, which speaks of cupidity as the root of all evil.

The fine distinctions of scholastic philosophy were to have little influence on the literary tradition. The introduction of the seven deadly sins to literature comes in the wake of a host of sermon books, penitential treatises, and confesssors' manuals resulting from the decrees promulgated by Innocent III at the Fourth Lateran Council

(1215). Chief among these is a work designed to inspire the examination of conscience, Guilelmus Peraldus's *Summa de Vitiis* (1236). Peraldus is a likely source for Chaucer's presentation of the sins in *The Parson's Tale* and a certain source for Dante's organization of the sins in *Purgatorio*, 9-28.

In the second book of *The Divine Comedy*, Dante describes the sinner's entry into Purgatory through Peter's Gate, which is approached by the three steps of penitence (contrition, confession, satisfaction). The sinner then traverses seven purgatorial terraces representing the seven sins; as the sinner leaves each terrace, a tutelary angel erases one of the seven *P*s (*peccata*, "sins") which he bears on his forehead. The process of erasing the sins completed, the pilgrim arrives at the Earthly Paradise, no longer needing Virgil as his guide. In canto 17, however, Virgil performs one of his last instructive acts for Dante by explaining the arrangement of the cornices on which they are traveling. Sin, says Virgil, following Peraldus, is misdirected love. Love can be directed toward an evil object, as in the case of pride, envy, and wrath, or it can be directed toward a good object, as in the cases of sloth (love defective) and of avarice, gluttony, and lust (love excessive). The seven sins are thus centrally defined as radical distortions of love.

Chaucer refers to the seven deadly sins at length in *The Parson's Tale*, elaborating a distinction between the fruitful tree of penitence —the root of which is contrition, branches and leaves are confession, and fruit is satisfaction —and the barren tree of sin —whose root is pride: "of this roote spryngen certein braunches" (the other deadly sins) and "everich of thise chief synnes hath his braunches and his twigges" (*Canterbury Tales*, 10.387-88).

John Gower twice employs the seven deadly sins as a major structural device. In the French *Miroir de l'omme* he treats at length both the seven children whom Death incestuously sires on Sin (Death's mother), and the thirty-five grandchildren produced when Time, the great polygamist, marries and impregnates all seven. Gower then goes on to suggest remedies for the seven protagonists as well as for each of the members of the second generation. In Gower's English *Confessio Amantis* the sins are taken up in the Gregorian order, illuminated by moral fables and historical exempla, which Genius uses to edify the catechumen, Amans.

Probably the most vigorous account of the sins in medieval English literature is found in *Piers Plowman*. Langland (in B.5.23) imagines Reason preaching to the people in an attempt to persuade them to come forward to make confession to Repentance. The seven sins comply. Langland uses deft description of physiognomy to help characterize the moral weakness of each character and hints at a typical societal milieu for some of the sins: Envy, e.g., has an emaciated yet swollen body (B.5.84) and snake-like tongue (B.5.87). According to B.5.129-30 (also C.7.95-96), Envy is at home in London among the merchants. When Repentance enjoins Envy to be sorry for sin, his reply involves a witty recollection of the Gregorian definition of his vice as sadness at another's fortune: "I am sori," quod that segge, "I am but selde other" (B.5.127).

The seven sins are regularly paralleled with opposing virtues in various medieval schemas. Gregory the Great had conceived of the vices as "leaders of wicked armies," and the sins were often pressed into service as Satan's lieutenants in psychomachian dramas. In this guise the sins are sometimes said to oppose such virtuous heptads as the seven petitions of the Lord's Prayer or the seven corporal works of mercy. The ingenuity evidenced in such writers as Hugh of St. Victor (PL 175.405-14) in elaborating such paradigms is reflected also in medieval lyrics. The catalog of sins turns up persistently even in apparently unlikely poems such as "Jesus Appeals to Man by the Wounds" (C. Brown, *Religious Lyrics of the XIVth Century*, no. 127), in which the five wounds neatly accommodate the seven sins. The proud should learn humility from the crown of thorns; the gluttonous should be instructed in abstinence from the bitter drinks proffered the thirsty Christ, etc.

In *The Castle of Perseverance*, seven evil characters bearing the names of the seven sins contend with seven virtuous characters for the soul of humanity. The sins are assigned to three evil powers, Belial, Caro, and Mundus, who represent the Devil (pride, envy, wrath), the Flesh (gluttony, lechery, sloth), and the World (avarice). In *Nature*, each vice has a speciously virtuous alter ego, so that Pride masquerades as Worship, Envy as Disdain, Wrath as Manhood, Sloth as Ease, Gluttony as Good Fellowship. The most inventive depiction of the sins in medieval drama, although also the most oblique, occurs in *Wisdom*, which affiliates them not with the World, the Flesh, and the Devil, but rather with depraved versions of the faculties of Understanding, Will, and Mind.

Because the list lacked specific biblical warrant, it was largely rejected by the Reformers. The conventional list is mentioned in Luther's works, but Luther generally avoids enumerating the vices —as if delineating all seven would smack of Roman Catholicism. In England, the two official collections of homilies authorized by Queen Elizabeth and then by King James include sermons on individual sins such as fornication, idleness, and gluttony, but do not deal with the seven vices as a group.

The traditional list of sins nevertheless continued to have literary currency even among Protestant writers. Thus Spenser enlists the seven sins when describing Redcrosse Knight's encounter with Lucifera in The House of Pride (*Faerie Queene*, 1.4.18-35), drawing on thoroughly traditional iconography to present each sin. The parading sins provide more of an entertainment than a genuine threat to Redcrosse, however; they have no power to detain him in his quest for Holiness. In the second act of Marlowe's *Doctor Faustus*, Lucifer presents Faustus with a tableau of the seven sins in order to confirm him in the pact he has made. When asked how he likes the spectacle, Faustus replies, "O how this sight doth delight my soul" (2.2.731). The pageant, having whetted his appetite for the pleasures of sin, prompts Faustus not to confession and penance but rather to *curiositas* and his own inexorable degradation. Milton, likewise, finds a place for the seven sins in both *Paradise Lost* and *Paradise Regained.*

The catalog of sins provides the framework also for several works of Elizabethan and Jacobean prose. The most accomplished of these is *Wits Miserie and the Worldes Madnesse* (1596), a moral essay in which Thomas Lodge exposes each of the sins in chapters named after the seven devils he uses to embody the normal Gregorian scheme: Leviathan, Beelzebub, Baalberith, Mammon, Ashtaroth, Asmodeus, and Beelphogor. Lodge's work has more subtlety and learning than Nashe's *Pierce Penniless* (1592), a journalistic squib which nonetheless expresses acute social observation under the rubric of the seven sins. By the time of Dekker's *The Seven Deadly Sinnes of London* (1606), the concept has been virtually emptied of theological substance. Sloth is one of the sins leading London to decay, but here it means merely indolence rather than spiritual lassitude. The other six sins do not appear by name; in their stead are political and economic practices of which Dekker disapproves: Politick Bankruptisme, Shaving (usury), Apishnesse (fashion-mongering), and the like.

The seven sins are referred to infrequently in 17th- and 18th-cent. literature. The most unusual return to the topic is in Pope's *Essay on Man,* the philosophy of which reflects both traditional religious concerns and contemporary interest in "natural" religion. In the Second Epistle (187-94), Pope strives to recharacterize the vices as veiled virtues:

> See anger, zeal and fortitude supply:
> Ev'n av'rice, prudence; sloth, philosophy;
> Lust, thro' some certain strainers well refin'd,
> Is gentle love, and charms all womankind:
> Envy, to which th'ignoble mind's a slave,
> Is emulation in the learn'd or brave:
> Nor Virtue, male or female, can we name,
> But what will grow on Pride, or grow on Shame.

Although gluttony is absent, this passage derives its force from Pope's revisionist approach to the old and still familiar classification of the seven sins.

The "seven damnable sciences," as they are called by Scott (*Kenilworth,* chap. 3), occupy a sanctified place in Blake's imagination. Blake's allusions to the sins, customarily termed by him the "diseases of the soul," are explicable in terms of his statement (to Crabb Robinson) that "what are called vices in the natural world are the highest sublimities in the spiritual world." Accordingly, before Urizen and the Fall, the sins were essentially innocent forces (*Book of Los,* 3.14-19):

> But Covet was poured full,
> Envy fed with fat of lambs,
> Wrath with lion's gore,
> Wantonness lull'd to sleep
> With the virgin's lute
> Or sated with her love.

Before the dissolution of harmony, "the pride of the peacock" was "the glory of God"; the "lust of the goat" was "the bounty of God"; "the wrath of the lion" was "the wisdom of God" (*Marriage of Heaven and Hell,* 8.2-4). But in the imperfect world where "incense is a cloudy pestilence of seven diseases" (*Jerusalem,* 79.56), only Jesus can restore health (*Jerusalem,* 77.24) and, by implication, convert the vices to the virtues they once were. Perhaps under a Blakean aegis, Swinburne imagines having seven towers in which he can participate in each of the deadly sins in weekly rotation.

Vestiges of the seven sins appear in a variety of 19th-cent. texts. A full-fledged continental use of the formula is found in Eugene Sue's *Les sept peches capitaux* (1847-49), a series of stories illustrating each of the sins in turn. And in England, Arthur Symons's "The Dance of the Seven Sins" has seven dancers utter lengthy monologues, each an ornate and sensuous explication of vice. The poem begins with lust and ends with lying, the latter of which confesses that "'Tis I who speak in each," an admission preceding Soul's rejection of mundane pleasures.

Although T. S. Eliot evokes the sins in *The Rock* in a doctrinally predictable way, 20th-cent. references are more typically parodic. For Shaw, who detests hell as "the home of honor, duty, justice, and the rest of the seven deadly virtues" (*Man and Superman,* 3), the seven millstones which only money can lift from a man's neck are "food, clothing, firing, rent, taxes, respectability, and children" (*Major Barbara*). Brecht's *The Seven Deadly Sins of the Petite Bourgeoisie* is a satire on the American Dream, depicting two women questing through seven cities for a cozy little house. In these successive cities they are forced to reject and sublimate all their natural inclinations (the sins) in order to satisfy their tawdry middle-class ambition. Auden's "Ode" (1931) introduces the sins as the battalion of Fear:

> There's Wrath, who has learnt every trick of guerrila
> warfare,
> The shamming dead, the night-raid, the feigned retreat;
> Envy, their brilliant pamphleteer, to lying
> As husband true,
> Expert impersonator and linguist, proud of his power
> To hoodwink sentries.

In the Circe episode of *Ulysses,* Joyce epitomizes Stephen's apostasy with a surrealistic fantasy in which he becomes Cardinal Dedalus attended by "seven dwarf simian acolytes" who giggle, nudge, and ogle each other when they are not peeping under his train. This vision is a far cry from the presentation of the sins in symbolic form during the "purgatorial" evening Gabriel endures in Joyce's short story "The Dead." It is, however, in keeping with the irreverent regard accorded the list in Flann O'Brien's *At-Swim-Two-Birds.* This novel's hero is dominated by Sloth, but his other vices are cataloged, alphabetically, as anthrax, boys, conversations (licentious), dirtiness, eclecticism (amorous). A more traditional rendering is afforded by American poet Anthony Hecht in his "The Seven Deadly Sins" sequence (*The Hard Hours* [1968], 49-55).

H. G. Wells considers the Gregorian list in *The Anatomy of Frustration* as a "map of the disputed territory, and a plan of the warfare between the life of the Greater Man in us fighting to save us from frustration, and the 'natural' individual life." Wells modernizes the sins by making gluttony the craving of the drug addict and envy the root of xenophobia and class hatred. Reducing the traditional seven sins to four, Wells eventually argues that pride is not a sin but rather the virtue of "intellectual integrity." Aldous Huxley, in *On the Margin,* provides a clever analysis of ennui in his essay on Accidie. And a 20th-cent. anthology entitled *The Seven Deadly Sins* brings together essays by such contributors as Edith Sitwell (pride), Angus Wilson (envy), Cyril Connolly (avarice), Evelyn Waugh (sloth), and W. H. Auden (anger). In these personal, often witty examinations of the vices, one sees the continuing pull the seven deadly sins have had on the literary imagination.

See also WORLD, FLESH, AND DEVIL.

Bibliography. Blythe, J. H. "Spenser and the Seven Deadly Sins: Book I, Cantos IV and V." *ELH* 39 (1972), 342-52; Bloomfield, M. W. *The Seven Deadly Sins: An Introduction to the History of a Religious Concept with Special Reference to Medieval English Literature* (1952); Braswell, M. F. *The Medieval Sinner* (1983); Chew, S. "Spenser's Pageant of the Deadly Sins." *Studies in Art and Literature for Belle da Costa Greene.* Ed. D. Miner (1954), 37-54; Fink, H. *Die Sieben Todsunden in der mittelenglischen erbaulichen Literatur* (1969); Fox, R. "The Seven Deadly Sins in *Paradise Lost.*" *DA* 17 (1957), 1328; Goldfarb, C., and R. Goldfarb, "The Seven Deadly Sins in *Doctor Faustus.*" *CLAJ* 13 (1970), 350-63; Holloway, J. "The Seven Deadly Sins in *The Faerie Queene.*" *RES* n.s. 3 (1952), 13-18; Lowes, J. L. "Chaucer and the Seven Deadly Sins." *PMLA* 30 (1915), 237-371; Orange, L. E. "The Role of the Deadly Sins in *Paradise Regained.*" *SoQ* 11 (1973), 190-201; Tupper, F. "Chaucer and the Seven Deadly Sins." *PMLA* 29 (1914), 93-128; Wenzel, S. "Dante's Rationale for the Seven Deadly Sins (*Purgatorio* XVII)." *MLR* 60 (1965), 529-33; Wilson, A., et al. *The Seven Deadly Sins* (1962).

RONALD B. BOND

SEVEN GIFTS   *See* GIFTS OF THE HOLY SPIRIT.

SEVEN LAST WORDS   Known also as the Passion Sayings, Words (Sayings, Seven Words) from the Cross, and the Last Words of the Redeemer, the Seven Last Words are the utterances of Christ on the cross, as reported in the four Gospels: (1) "Father, forgive them; for they know not what they do" (Luke 23:34); (2) "Verily I say unto thee, Today shalt thou be with me in paradise" (Luke 23:43); (3) "Woman, behold thy son! . . . Behold thy mother!" (John 19:26-27); (4) "Eli (Eloi), Eli, lama sabachthani? . . . My God, my God, why hast thou forsaken me?" (Matt. 27:46 and Mark 15:34); (5) "I thirst" (John 19:28); (6) "It is finished" (John 19:30); and (7) "Father, into thy hands I commend my spirit" (Luke 23:46). This harmonized arrangement, now almost universally the focus of Good Friday observances, is a recent development, although public reading during the Easter "octave" of the Gospel narratives concerning the sufferings of Christ began early.

The "Seven Last Words" are the subject of many noteworthy musical settings, including those of Graun (*Der Tod Jesus* [1755]), Haydn (*Seven Last Words,* first publ. in Vienna as *Seven Sonate* [ca. 1802]), Beethoven (*Mount of Olives* [1803]), Spohr (*Calvary* [1833]), Dubois (*The Seven Words of Christ* [1867]), Williams (*Gethsemane* [ca. 1880]), Gounod (*Redemption* [1882]), Stainer (*Crucifixion* [1887]), and Somervell (*The Passion of Christ* [1914]). Saverio Mercadante's oratorio *The Seven Last Words of Our Savior,* published the year of James Joyce's birth, 1882, achieved literary prominence by occurring several times in Leopold Bloom's stream of consciousness during *Ulysses.*

Probably because of the comparatively late focus on the Seven Last Words themselves, English writers turned for inspiration before the last century to the entire Passion, the Crucifixion, the cross itself, Good Friday, or to specific words — mainly the second, third, sixth, and seventh. One of the earliest extant uses of an individual word is a 10th-cent. frontispiece of an OE psalter MS, a drawing of Christ on the cross with his mother and John below (third word). Medieval poetry in general favored the potentially dramatic second and third words, the only two mentioned in Rolle's "Meditations on the Passion," but both the alliterative *Morte Arthure* and *Everyman* use the seventh word in Latin, *In manus tuus,* as the last words of their hero. The Crucifixion passage of *Piers Plowman* alludes to the sixth word but differs from most other medieval works in referring also to the fifth word ("I thirst"), the first to be self-directed and the one Clemence Dane said in *Will Shakespeare* (1922) caused Queen Elizabeth to exclaim, "This was a God for kings and queens of pride, and Him I follow." The Wakefield Mystery Cycle's inclusion of all but the second word, substituting torturers for thieves, is significant (cf. Masefield's *Good Friday* [1912], one of his five biblical plays modernizing the mystery plays). Marlowe's Faustus uses the sixth word blasphemously when signing away his soul, and Congreve's *Love for Love* employs it parodically to indicate the consummation of marriage.

Structural influences may appear in the seven-stress

line of Thomas Halles's "Passion of Our Lord," Milton's seven-line stanza in his unfinished ode on the Passion, and Coleridge's seven-part design in the *Rime of the Ancient Mariner.*

Since the Reformation and the Counter-Reformation it has been the spirit rather than the format of the Seven Last Words which has caused theological debate, a controversy whose influence can be traced not only in literature but also in church music, architecture, and decoration. The emphasis of the Church during the Middle Ages was increasingly on the desolation and darkness of the Words from the Cross, the first three being interpreted as petition, penitence, and piety, and the last four as desolation (although not despair). An atmosphere of mystery was provided by the medieval cathedral for the continual reenactment of the sacrifice of Christ's Passion in the Mass, and the power of the priest to effect transubstantiation of the bread and wine to absolve the meditating laity was stressed. But Luther, in an attempt to recapture aspects of primitive Christianity, opposed the "theology of the cross" to the established "theology of glory" (phrases he coined), arguing that the hiddenness of God lies in the reversal of values the cross revealed — life through death, light through darkness, power through weakness. Calvin thought the desolate cry of the fourth word, interpreted by the early Church as a meditation on Ps. 22, to be a cry of dereliction consistent with the sense of abandonment by God felt by one assuming the sins of the world.

The Reformers read the "Words from the Cross" as words of love summarizing the whole gospel, their sequence reflecting the gradual unfolding of God's will and purpose for the redemption of mankind in the seven stages of Jesus' life: Incarnation, Intercession, Blessing, Suffering, Thirsting, Reconciliation, and Triumph. Picturing Christ's life as "a continual Passion," Donne wrote in his last sermon (1630), entitled "Death's Duel or a Consolation to the Soule, against the Dying Life, and Living Death of the Body," "That which we call life is but *Hebdomada mortium,* a weeke of deaths, seaven dayes, seaven periods of our life spent in dying, a dying seaven times over."

Not until Good Friday observances instituted the harmonized arrangement of the Seven Last Words in the late 19th cent. does the direct influence of the whole sequence become noticeable again in English literature. During the 1880s Hopkins, by then a Jesuit priest, composed seven "terrible" sonnets, which plumb the emotional depths of each utterance. Soon after, the Jesuit-trained Joyce wrote *Stephen Hero,* an early version of *A Portrait of the Artist as a Young Man,* in which Stephen, after hearing the "Three Hours' Agony," a Good Friday liturgy in which the Seven Last Words figure prominently, wanders for three hours in agonized silence before deciding to "regard himself seriously as a literary artist" (cf. Alice Munro's "Age of Faith" episode in *Lives of Girls and Women*

[1971]). At the end of his career Joyce characterized the artist in *Finnegans Wake* as a "first to last alchemist . . . writing in seven divers stages of ink."

Dylan Thomas, in Sonnet 8 of his sequence on the artist, "Altarwise by Owl-light" (1953), paraphrases all the words (although not in order), beginning "This was the crucifixion on the mountain, / Time's nerve in vinegar" and ending with "Suffer the heaven's children through my heartbeat." Echoing Thomas's last line in his own ("the year packs up / Like a tatty fairground, / That came for the children"), Ted Hughes adds to the poignancy of his ostensibly secular picture of the "destructive reality we inhabit" in "The Seven Sorrows" (1976) with a dim recollection of the Seven Last Words in their traditional order. Geoffrey Hill's "LACHRIMAE or *Seven tears figured in seven passionate Pavans*" (*Tenebrae* [1978]) blends musical and literary tradition in a sonnet sequence: *"Lachrimae Verae," "The Masque of Blackness," "Martyrium," "Lachrimae Coactae," "Pavana Dolorosa," "Lachrimae Antiquae Novae," "Lachrima Amantis."*

Samuel Beckett seems indebted to the Seven Last Words in his insistence upon Good Friday as his birthday and his declaration that his "birthmark" is his "deathmark." In the "single sentence" of the spiritual biography gradually unfolding in his magnum opus, "flesh becomes word" only to degenerate through a series of "last words" into sound, "a stain upon the silence."

See also PASSION, CROSS.

Bibliography. Cuming, C. J. *History of the Anglican Liturgy* (1969); Davies, J. G., ed. *Dictionary of Liturgy and Worship* (1972); Hastings, J., et al., eds., *Encyclopaedia of Religion and Ethics* (1906; rpt. 1973); Jacobsen, J., and W. R. Mueller. *The Testament of Samuel Beckett* (1964); Pomeranz, V. "Meyerbeer and Mercadante." *JJQ* 9 (1972), 482-83; Thompson, V. *International Cyclopaedia of Music and Musicians* (1975); Thurston, H, S.J. *Lent and Holy Week* (1904).

VIRGINIA MOSELEY

SEVEN PILLARS OF WISDOM In his praise of Lady Wisdom and her benefits, the author of Proverbs writes, "Wisdom hath builded her house, she hath hewn out her seven pillars" (9:1). The seven pillars are identified in rabbinic commentary as the pillars on which the harmonious elements of earth rest (Midr. Tehillim 104.442; Seder Rabba di-Bereshit 11). Alphabeti 103 and the pseudo-Clementine writings identify the pillars with seven patriarchs: Adam, Enoch, Noah, Abraham, Isaac, Jacob, and Moses. St. Augustine sees the pillars as prefiguring the Seven Churches which make up the unity of the universal Church (*De civ. Dei* 17.4). Tennyson's *In Memoriam* propounds the optimistic view (unlike Proverbs) that Wisdom is universally loved:

Who loves not knowledge? Who shall rail
Against her beauty? May she mix
With men and prosper! Who shall fix
Her pillars? Let her work prevail. (cf. Prov. 31:31)

Ruskin seems to think the pillars imply a stable and ordered foundation for life (*Unto This Last,* chap. 4). T. E. Laurence's *The Seven Pillars of Wisdom* is a romantic account of the Arab revolt in World War I and of Laurence's own involvement, as "Lawrence of Arabia," in the conflict.

SEVEN SEALS   The book "written within and on the back, sealed with seven seals" (Rev. 5:1) is one of the central images in the Apocalypse. The meaning of these seven seals has occupied the Christian imagination in all periods. The author seems to echo Ezek. 2:9-10, where the Lord sends a scroll "written within and without," and Isa. 29:11-12, where "no one unlearned" can read the book. Thus the book in the Apocalypse is a scroll which cannot be fully read until all the seals are broken; only the Lion of the Tribe of Judah can do this. At the opening of the first four seals the four horsemen appear in succession on their white, red, black, and "pale" (or livid) horses, derived from Zech. 1:7-12. Although the first horseman has often been interpreted as Christ, the figure appears to belong to the well-known sequence of tribulations: conquest, slaughter, famine, and pestilence (or death). At the opening of the fifth seal the martyrs cry: "How long. . . ?"; at the sixth there is an earthquake and tempest; at the seventh there is "silence in heaven about the space of half an hour." Immediately after appear the seven angels with trumpets for the consuming of the world.

In general terms commentators have agreed that the meaning of this image concerns human destiny. The sacred number *seven* is the symbol of completeness or finality, and thus the seven seals contain the totality of God's plan for asserting sovereignty and judgment over a sinful world. But the sequence of the seals tempted more precise interpretations concerning human history. Interpreters divided into two categories: those who saw the history of the Church recapitulated in the successive visions of the Apocalypse and those who interpreted the Apocalypse as one continuous revelation of salvation history. For the first, the seven seals represented the entire history of the Church. Among early commentators this view is taken by Tyconius in the 4th cent. (P. E. B. Allo, *Saint Jean. L'Apocalypse* [1921], 222), by Primasius in the 6th cent. (PL 68.819-54), and by Andrew of Caesarea in the 6th-7th cent. (PL 93.146-54). But the danger of attempting precise historical applications was apparent, and certain commentators took a more general and moralistic line: the seven seals were images and experiences which repeated themselves in the world's history. St. Jerome emphasized the spiritual interpretation of the Apocalypse, and St. Augustine understood it as portraying the perpetual conflict between Church and World (Allo, *Saint Jean,* 223-24), rather than a sequence of historical events, while the moralistic style of interpretation was popularized by the influential commentary of Beatus of Liebana in the 8th cent. (*In Apocalypsim Libri*

Duodecim, ed. H. A. Sanders [1930], 335-406). In this tradition one finds Haymo of Auxerre (formerly known as Haymo of Halberstadt) in the 9th cent. interpreting the first horseman as Christ and the Church, the second as the Devil, the third as the Devil's followers, and the fourth as all the reprobate (PL 117.1024-27).

In the 12th cent. a new significance seems to attach to church history and therefore there appears to be a new interest in its periodization. For this writers turned to the seven seals. The time between the First and Second Advents was no longer seen as simply one of waiting and soul-winning but rather as stages in the working out of God's purpose through the Church. Thus Anselm of Havelberg interprets the seven seals as the seven *status* of the Church. The opening of the first seal represents the Church in its early purity, with Christ the rider on the white horse; the red and black horses of the second and third seals are the periods of persecuted martyrs and conflict with heretics; the fourth seal symbolizes the period of false brethren; the fifth, the continuing labours of the Church; the sixth, the final crisis of tribulation under Antichrist; and the seventh, the beatific silence after the consummation of history (PL 188.1149-60). (In the same period Eberwin of Steinfelden also divides the church's history into six periods, although the symbol he uses is that of the six jars at the marriage of Cana rather than the seals of the Apocalypse [PL 182.676-80].)

The decisive influence in establishing the seven seals as a revelation of the meaning of history was that of Joachim of Fiore in the second half of the 12th cent. Furthermore, he created a pattern of double sevens, i.e., seven divisions of OT history, represented by the seven seals, to be interpreted in concord with seven stages in post-Incarnational history, symbolized in the seven seal-openings. Each stage, except the seventh, is marked by a conflict between the chosen people and a power of evil. In order to make a pattern of seven conflicts, a double one is assigned to the sixth stage. Though there are variations in his works, the following gives a general outline of Joachim's pattern:

SEALS	CONFLICT WITH
1. Abraham — Moses / Joshua	Egyptians
2. Joshua — Samuel / David	Philistines, Canaanites, etc.
3. David — Elijah / Elisha	Syrians
4. Elisha — Isaiah / Hezekiah	Assyrians
5. Hezekiah — Babylonian Captivity	Chaldaeans
6. Ezekiel — Daniel	Double conflict: Assyrians, Persians
7. Malachi — Zacharias	Sabbath Age

SEAL OPENINGS	CONFLICT WITH
1. Apostolic Age	Jews
2. Apostles — Constantine	Gentiles (Pagans)

3. Constantine — Justinian	Arians and Barbarians
4. Justinian — Pope Zacharias	Saracens
5. Zacharias — Emperor	
Henry III, or present time	Germans
6. to come	Double conflict:
	mystic Antichrist
	great Antichrist
7. Sabbath Age	

Associated with the first four seals was the well-known sequence of order: Apostles, Martyrs, Doctors, Hermits and Virgins. Joachim expounded this pattern of history many times in his main works, in his *Liber Figurarum* and in a small separate tract, *De Septem Sigillis*.

In Joachim's dynamic theology of history the opening of the sixth seal would bring the climax in church history, marked by the double tribulation of Antichrist and the transition to the "silence" of the seventh seal, the blessed Sabbath Age which, according to Joachim, would fall within history. Because his calculations purported to show that the sixth seal-opening was imminent, Joachim's program gave a new impetus to the interpretation of the later seals in terms of contemporary and future history. Thus the Franciscan Salimbene includes in his chronicle a similar pattern up to his own day (*Cronica*, MGHS, 32.440). A notable symbolic identification was that of St. Francis as the angel of the sixth seal who ascends from the east bearing the sign of the living God (Rev. 7:2) and with power to "seal" the faithful before the onset of the greatest tribulation (S. Bihel, *Antonianum*, 2.59-90). He was also seen as already embodying the life of the seventh seal. Many Franciscans were inspired by this vision of church history and of Francis's place within it, including not only the so-called "Spiritual Franciscans" Angelo Clarendo, Peter John of Olivi, and Ubertino da Casale (see M. Reeves, *The Influence of Prophecy in the Later Middle Ages* [1969], 191, 196-200, 208-09), but also St. Bonaventure (see J. Ratzinger, trans. Z. Hayes, *The Theology of History in St. Bonaventure* [1971]), and, in the 14th cent., Bartholomew of Pisa (AF 4.40-42, 74-78), Pietro Aureoli (Reeves, *Influence of Prophecy*, 183-84), and Nicholas of Lyra, whose 14th-cent. scheme of church history in his *Liber Apocalipsis* (f.6ᵛ) runs thus:

1. time of apostles	persecution by Jews
2. time of martyrs	persecution by Romans
3. time of heretics	persecution by Arians etc.
4. time of hypocrites	persecution by hypocrites
5. time before Antichrist	persecution by false churchmen
6. time of Antichrist	greatest persecution of all time
7. time after Antichrist	no persecution

In the 15th cent. St. Bernardino of Siena actually used Joachim's tract on the seven seals — without apparently knowing its authorship — in working out his interpretation of history (Reeves, *Influence of Prophecy,* 230-33).

In the later Middle Ages the interpretation of the opening of the seals as periods in post-Incarnational history became general, with or without a Joachimist conclusion in a seventh age as a Sabbath Age on earth. There also developed, however, a wariness among some English theologians in particular about the potentially fractious and disruptive character of much apocalyptic speculation (e.g., Fitzralph, Wyclif); and among English poets, even in the "apocalyptic" 14th cent., the seven seals are treated with circumspect reserve. The poet of the *Pearl* is content merely to describe, in his vision of the celestial Jerusalem, the book of which "there seuen syngetteʒ wern sette inseme" (838), and *Piers Plowman* seems to offer only the slightest of allusions (Adams).

In the Renaissance and Reformation periods there is a continuing interest in the seals, especially the sixth and seventh. Petrus Galatinus, living in the brilliant Rome of the early 16th cent., sees the Church as now entering the time of the sixth seal which — rather unusually — he interprets at one point as the golden age of the Church — *foelicissimum tempus* — to be ended by the sharp tribulation of the last Antichrist and a brief seventh age (Reeves, *Influence of Prophecy,* 236-38). On the other hand, Damián Hortolá, Abbot of Ville-Bertrand, finds the climax of iniquity now at hand in the opening of the sixth seal and looks beyond it to the descent of the New Jerusalem at the seventh seal (*In Canticum Canticorum . . . Explanatio* [1585], 377-80), while Berthold Purstinger, Bishop of Chiemsee, sees its beginning in the fall of Constantinople, the Italian wars, and the Lutheran "locusts" who appear when the fifth angel trumpets (Rev. 9:3; Purstinger, *Onus Ecclesiae . . .* [1532], caps. 39-66). Two typical 16th-cent. commentators on the Apocalypse, Serafino da Fermo and Coelius Pannonius (alias F. Gregorio), give similar interpretations (*In Apocalipsim* [1570], 623-55; *Collectanea in Apocalypsim* [1571], Pref., 372-432).

In the period of the Reformation the explosive possibilities of such historicizing interpretations became apparent and there developed a school of commentators who sought to neutralize these dangers. This is well represented by the Spanish writers such as Alcazar, who accepted the interpretation of the first four seals as the first four ages of the Church but then placed the opening of the last three seals safely in a future known only to God (Allo, *Saint Jean,* 76). The great Jesuit commentator Francesco Ribeira interpreted the first five seals as relating to the period up to Trajan, while the sixth and seventh seals concerned Last Things (Allo, 76). But there was another school of thought among Jesuits of those who succumbed to the heady influence of Joachimism (Reeves, *Influence of Prophecy,* 274-86). These took the seals and other visions of the Apocalypse as providing clues leading right up to their own time, which they located at the end of the fifth or beginning of the sixth seal. This enabled them to interpret contemporary events in terms of the drama of history now mounting to its climax and to assign roles to themselves in this drama. Some Jesuits claimed to fulfill Joachim's prophecy, based on Rev. 14:14, of a new order of spiritual men to lead the Church into the Sabbath Age. Many more felt themselves involved in a final drama both of conflict (with the anti-Christian manifestation of Protestantism) and of renewal (in their missionary work).

Protestants reinterpreted the seven seals to suit their understanding of contemporary events as the enactment of the final stages of history. Servetus saw the six seal openings as the ages of labor and tribulation now ending, while the impending seventh would at last bring rest (*Christianismi Restitutio* [1553], 408-10). Thomas Müntzer believed that only the elect possessed the key of David to unlock the book with seven seals and that he himself must bring in this new age of spiritual understanding (G. Williams, *The Radical Reformation* [1962], 45-55). Giacopo Brocardo, a Venetian who fled north from the Inquisition, worked out a detailed interpretation of salvation history based on seven divisions of OT history (belonging to the Father), seven of the Church (belonging to the Son), and a further seven of the Spirit which he added (*Revelation of St. John reveled . . . Englished by J. Sanford* [1582], f.5r-v). The seventh opening of the Son "began to shyne as the mornynge doth" when Luther started to preach; after this Brocardo develops his third sequence of seven thus: the first from Luther's preaching to Zwingli, the second and third, the preaching in England and elsewhere, while the fourth "Cometh to the French troubles," the fifth "ran even unto the universall slaughter of the Gospellers," and now in the sixth he awaits Christ's judgment against the Papists.

Finally, in Britain, the sense of a dawning new age brought the interpretation of the Apocalypse and its seven seals into a new focus. John Bale's *Image of Bothe Churches* takes the seven seal openings for its framework and works up to the climax of the seventh opening when "in the tyme of this swete silence shall Israel be revived, the Jews shall be converted, the heathen shall come in again. Christ will seke up his lost shepe . . . that they may appere one flock, lyke as they have one shepherde" (M. Reeves, *Joachim of Fiore and the Prophetic Future,* 153-54). John Foxe, in his unfinished *Eicasmi seu Meditationes in Sacram Apocalypsim,* throws the first four seals back into the far past and concentrates on the last three. Under the fifth there have been ten persecutions from the time of Wyclif to that of Mary in England and Philip in Spain and Flanders. To the sixth belongs Divine Judgment and to the seventh the Sabbath Age (*Eicasmi . . .* [1587], 41-60). John Napier argued that, while the "historical" part of the seven seals had been opened by Christ and the apostles to the primitive Church and fulfilled in their day, the real mystery of the "booke within" had never been opened up until now "in this our seventh

age in which Christ opens all the propheticall mysteries thereof." "Then let the Pope and all earthlie Princes looke for no longer delay, but that in this seventh age, alreadie begun in the yeare of Christ 1541, the corner stone Jesus Christ shal become a mountaine and shal destroy all temporal kingdomes and raigne for ever" (*A Plaine Discovery of the whole Revelation of St. John . . .* [1539], 142-43). Although the influential commentator Thomas Brightman, treating the visions of the Apocalypse seriatim, places the opening of the seals far back in church history, he nevertheless periodizes the total progress of the Church in seven stages, leading, as always, to the climactic seventh age. After "this storme (of Antichrist) has blowne over there shall followe presently gawdy dayes" (*A Revelation of the Revelation* [1615], Pref.). "And indeed," he writes, "we waite now every daye, while the Antichrist of Rome and the Turks shal be utterly destroyed. Till this victory be obtained, the Church shal be still in her warfaring estate, she must keepe in Tents" (852). But when the seventh age has fully dawned "then shall be indeed that golden age and highest top of holy felicity and happiness which mortal men may expect or think of in this earthly and base habitation" (*A most Comfortable Exposition of . . . the Prophecie of Daniel* [1644], 966).

In English literature after the Middle Ages, references to the "book with seven seals" are infrequent. One of the most memorable allusions is that of Spenser in his *Faerie Queene,* in which the great book of Fidelia is described in language unmistakably drawn from Rev. 5. It is "A booke, that was both signd and seald with blood" (1.10.13.8) and "that none could read, except she did them teach" (1.10.19.2; cf. Rev. 5:9). Yet the seven seals themselves are almost pointedly eschewed here, and in this Spenser anticipates the pattern in much later literature. Too many conflicting historiographies (up to and including the dispensationalism of late 19th-cent. evangelical interpretation reflected in Scofield's notes to the KJV) seem to have disabled the image.

Patrick Forbes, in his *An exquisite commentarie upon the Revelation of St. John* ([1613], 39), offers the modern investigator a useful guide, at least, to the extremes in the post-Reformation spectrum of opinions:

> The first, is of these, who typing themselves to more strait rules of interpretation then the holy Spirite hath laid to them, wil needes have these seven Seales, as also the Trumpets & Vials to bee so many knots or periods of time exactlie cutted, within which, the accommodation of each is to be sought; whereas they are no knots of time but types of distinct matters; and the whole matter comprehended in seven Seales. . . . The other extremity, is of these, who well perceiving the absurdity of the first neglect ih [*sic*] the accommodation, all consideration of distinct time, so jumbling Seales, Trumpets and Vials, to the confusion of al order, and light of Story, which in this

Prophesie is most orderly set downe, with special relation to distinct events.

It may fairly be observed that, as far as English literature is concerned, the post-Reformation movement is irregular, but definitely toward the latter of Forbes's "extremities," to the almost total neglect of the image in Enlightenment and Victorian literature.

Ingmar Bergman's screenplay for his widely heralded *Seventh Seal* (1958) is undoubtedly the most effective modern use of the seven seals, perhaps in part because it eschews historiographic and eschatological speculation in favor of a simpler application of the text. When a wearily disillusioned crusader knight returns from Jerusalem to find his native Sweden ravaged by plague, he engages Death in a chess game for the lives of an "innocent" family, his friends, and wife. He loses, however, and as the group sits down to a last meal in the castle and the knight's wife commences to read from the book of Revelation, the figure of Death appears — in Bergman's view the ultimate significance of the seventh seal.

See also BOOK OF LIFE; MILLENNIUM; NUMEROLOGY.

Bibliography. Adams, R. "The Nature of Need in *Piers Plowman XX*." *Traditio* 34 (1978), 273-301; Bousset, W. *The Antichrist Legend*. Trans. A. H. Keane (1896); Caird, G. B. *A Commentary on the Revelation of St. John the Divine* (1966); Farrer, A. *A Rebirth of Images* (1949); *The Revelation of St. John the Divine* (1964); Kamlah, W. *Apokalypse und Geschichtstheologie* (1935); Luneau, A. *L'Histoire du Salut chez les Peres de l'Église* (1964); Patrides, C. A., and J. Wittreich, eds. *The Apocalypse in English Thought and Literature* (1984); Reeves, M. *The Influence of Prophecy in the Later Middle Ages* (1969); *Joachim of Fiore and the Prophetic Future* (1976).   MARJORIE REEVES

SEVEN YEARS OF PLENTY, FAMINE   *See* JOSEPH THE PATRIARCH.

SEVENTY TIMES SEVEN   When St. Peter asked Jesus about forgiveness, he tacitly proposed a high standard: "Lord, how oft shall my brother sin against me, and I forgive him? till seven times?" But Jesus answered, "I say not unto thee, Until seven times: but, Until seventy times seven" (Matt. 18:21-22). St. Augustine (who reads the number as seventy plus seven) takes Christ's answer as meaning "indefinitely," referring the matter to the conditional petition for forgiveness in the Lord's Prayer (Matt. 6:12, 14-15) and to Paul's injunctions to the same effect (*Sermo*, 83; cf. Col. 3:13; Eph. 4:32). A Christian soul whose patience has expired with a putatively exact calculation of offenses is portrayed in Nelly, the housekeeper in Emily Brontë's *Wuthering Heights*, who exclaims, "Sir . . . sitting here within these four walls . . . have I endured and forgiven the four hundred and ninety heads of your discourse. Seventy times seven have I plucked up my hat and been about to depart — Seventy times seven have

you preposterously forced me to resume my seat. The four hundred and ninety-first is too much" (chap. 3).

SHADRACH, MESHACH, AND ABEDNEGO
Shadrach, Meshach, and Abednego are the Babylonian names given to Hananiah, Mishael, and Azariah, the three companions of Daniel. They appear in Dan. 1, where they participate in Daniel's rejection of the king's food in favor of a simple diet of pulse and water, and they are the heroes in the story of the fiery furnace in chap. 3, in which Daniel himself does not appear. The story of the three young men in the fiery furnace belongs to the genre "romance of the successful courtier" (Hartman and Di Lella, AB 23, 55). The three youths' prestige at court is envied by their fellow courtiers, who turn the king against the heroes by taking advantage of their fidelity to the God of Israel. In the end, however, the youths are miraculously rescued from the furnace, and their faith is embraced by the king. The LXX version of the story, reflected also in the Latin Vg, contains several elements not found in the Hebrew text: (a) the song of Azariah (LXX 3:24-45), (b) a prose narrative which adds some details concerning happenings within the furnace (LXX 3:46-50), and (c) the song of the three young men, or "three holy children" (LXX 3:51-90).

In the OE *Daniel*, which deals with the episodes of Dan. 1–5, the section devoted to the story of the fiery furnace (168-451) is probably the most imaginative portion of the entire poem, emphasizing in particular the ironic reversal which has the Babylonian soldiers themselves perishing from the heat of the furnace (243-55, 265-68, 343-45). The poem includes compressed paraphrases of the songs of Azariah (279-332) and the song of the three young men (358-408). In the Exeter Book another OE poem, *Azarias,* provides a fuller treatment of these two songs, with considerable expansion upon the nature imagery found in the biblical version.

The Rouen version of the Latin *Procession of Prophets* includes a dramatization of the fiery furnace story (Karl Young, *Drama of the Medieval Church,* 2.164, 168). This episode does not appear in any of the ME cycle plays, but there is a late 16th- or early 17th-cent. play attributed to Joshua Sylvester, *Nebuchadnezzars Fiere Furnace* (ed. Rösler, *Materials for the Study of Old English Drama,* ser. 2, 12). Christopher Fry's *A Sleep of Prisoners,* in which British prisoners of war relive the experiences of various OT characters, concludes with the story of the three young men in the furnace (39-46).

The three young men are put forth as examples of courageous faith in 1 Macc. 2:59, a theme used also in Sulpicius Severus's letter on the death of St. Martin (PL 20.179 = CSEL 1.143-44), in Aelfric's sermon "On the Memory of the Saints" (EETS o.s. 82 [1885], 71-77), in one of Anne Bradstreet's *Meditations* (no. 75, *Complete Works* [1981], 208), and in one of Hazlitt's *Political Essays* (*Complete Works* [1932], 7.241). Similarly, a sermon of John Donne refers to the three youths as examples of confidence in God (ed. Carrithers, *Donne at Sermons*, 246). The youths' deliverance from the furnace functions as an illustration of God's power to save the persecuted in the ME *St. Juliana* (EETS o.s. 51 [1872], 32) and in *The Life of St. Katherine* (EETS o.s. 80 [1884], 1426-38), while the *Ayenbite of Inwit* connects their escape with their rejection of the king's fancy food in Dan. 1:11-15, for such food is said to nourish lechery as oil does fire (EETS o.s. 23 [1866], 205). The rescue of Quakers from Puritan persecution in Salem in 1658 is compared to the rescue of the three young men in Whittier's poem "Cassandra Southwick" (3-4, 147-48). In Tennyson's play *Queen Mary,* ironic reference to the escape of the youths from the fiery furnace is addressed to Cranmer as he is about to be burned (4.3.59-61).

Wordsworth describes a boy uncontaminated by the world as "Like one of those who walked with hair unsinged / Amid the fiery furnace" (*Prelude,* 7.369-70). A more jarring comparison to the rescue of the three youths is made in Melville's description of the processing of a captured whale in *Moby-Dick:* after the whale is cut into pieces, he is "condemned to the pots, and, like Shadrach, Meshach, and Abednego, his spermaceti, oil, and bone pass unscathed through the fire" (chap. 98). E. L. Doctorow's novel *The Book of Daniel* is introduced by a quotation from Dan. 3, and the protagonist, Daniel Lewin, reflects on the effect that the fiery furnace trial must have had on his biblical namesake, Daniel, whom he regards as the brother of the three young men in the furnace.

Nebuchadnezzar's setting up of the golden image to be adored (Dan. 3:1-6) represents the human tendency to make idols of material things and of wealth in Ben Jonson's *Bartholomew Fair* (3.6.49-53) and in Ruskin's *The Crown of Wild Olives* (*Works* [1905], 18.457-58). In Robert Frost's *Masque of Mercy,* a rather startling application of this story occurs:

> We have all the belief that is good for us.
> Too much all-fired belief and we'd be back
> Down burning skeptics in the cellar furnace
> Like Shadrach, Meshach, and Abednego. (*Complete Poems* [1964], 636)

A somewhat similar idea may lie behind a reference in Joyce's *Finnegans Wake* to "the fierifornax being thrust on him motophosically" — i.e., thrust on him metaphysically (cf. Roland McHugh, *Annotations to Finnegans Wake,* 319).

In *Paradise Lost* Milton alludes to Nebuchadnezzar's command that the fire be heated "seven times more than it was wont to be heated" (Dan. 3:19) in relation to God's creation of the fire of hell (2.170-72). Browning refers to this passage in the context of misused authority in *The Ring and the Book* ([1961], 989-93), and Longfellow uses it in *Giles Corey of the Salem Farms* in a ranting speech of Cotton Mather against witchcraft (1.2, *Works* [1886], 5.380). Hawthorne compares the heat of midsummer to

Nebuchadnezzar's seven-times heated furnace (*American Notebooks* [1932], 185), and Edwin Arlington Robinson makes a similar comparison in "The Man against the Sky" (41-46). In Tennyson's *The Holy Grail,* Lancelot is prevented from seeing the grail by a heat "as from a seven-times-heated furnace" (838-43). Shaw has Joan of Arc say that being "shut up from the sight of sky, fields, and flowers" is "worse than the furnace in the Bible that was heated seven times" (*St. Joan, Collected Works* [1930], 17.145).

The litany of musical instruments used to call the worshipers to Nebuchadnezzar's idol (Dan. 3:5) is used by Shakespeare in *Coriolanus,* 5.4, when the hero's mother, who has betrayed her son, is hailed by Rome as the city's patroness. The same passage is referred to in an attack on clergy who make music on the Sabbath in William Cowper's "The Progress of Error" (128-33). Ruskin mentions it in relation to the morality of dancing (*Works* [1907], 29.269), and Poe makes use of a very similar list of musical instruments in a call to prayer in "A Tale of Jerusalem" (*Complete Works* [1902], 2.219).

In the biblical narrative Nebuchadnezzar sees four men walking unhurt in the midst of the fiery furnace, and "the form of the fourth is like the Son of God" (Dan. 3:25). St. Jerome observes that most Christian commentators considered this fourth figure to be Christ, but he himself cannot see how "an ungodly king could have merited a vision of the Son of God," and he therefore considers the fourth figure an angel, although the typological significance is Christ (PL 25.511-12 = CChr 75A.807, 716-808). In the OE *Daniel,* similarly, it is an angel that Nebuchadnezzar sees (273). This detail of the narrative is the basis for Nebuchadnezzar's appearance in the Latin *Ordo Prophetarum* as one of the Gentile prophets of Christ. Here he is characterized as a proud king who has learned humility at the sight of Christ (Young, 2.136, 142, 149, 165). William Blake makes use of the same incident in a complex allegorical framework (cf. John Beer, *Blake's Visionary Universe,* 36, 50). Christina Rossetti's "Martyr's Song" offers the encouraging thought that in adversity, "Be it furnace-fire voluminous, / One like God's Son will walk with us" (5-6). In Whittier's narrative poem "Saint Gregory's Guest," which tells a legend of St. Gregory the Great's kindness to a poor man who turns out to be Christ himself, the experience is compared to the vision of the fourth man in the fiery furnace (27-28). Whittier refers to this passage again in his poem "Astrea at the Capital," which celebrates the abolition of slavery in the District of Columbia in 1862 (57-60). In the same vein, Newman's poem "Temptation" addresses God: "O Holy Lord, who with the Children Three / Didst walk the piercing flame" (1-2).

See also DANIEL; NEBUCHADNEZZAR.

Bibliography. Braverman, J. *Jerome's Commentary on Daniel: A Study of Comparative Jewish and Christian Interpretations of the Hebrew Bible* (1978); Ginsberg, H. L.

"Daniel, Book of." In *EncJud* (1971), 5.1277-89; Hartman, L. F., and A. A. di Lella. *The Book of Daniel.* AB 23 (1978); Jerome. *Commentary on Daniel.* PL 25 = CChr 75A (1964). Trans. G. L. Archer, Jr. (1958); Moffatt, J. *The Book of Daniel.* In *Literary Illustrations of the Bible.* Vol. 2 (1905); Montgomery, J. A. *A Critical and Exegetical Commentary on the Book of Daniel* (1950); Roston, M. *Biblical Drama in England: From the Middle Ages to the Present Day* (1968).

LAWRENCE T. MARTIN

SHALOM The Hebrew word for "peace" and the most important greeting among Jews, *shalom* is a root for the names Jerusalem and Solomon, among others. The biblical concept of peace is discussed in English literature typically in contexts which distinguish between inner peace and outer conflict.

See also PEACE, GOOD WILL TOWARD MEN; PEACE, WHEN THERE IS NO PEACE; PEACE WHICH PASSES UNDERSTANDING.

SHEBA, QUEEN OF Sheba (Heb. *Sheba';* LXX *Saba*) is a name which appears in both Semitic and Hamitic genealogies. In Gen. 10:7 Sheba is a descendant of Ham, while another Sheba is listed in Gen. 10:28 as descended from Shem. But the Queen of Sheba (1 Kings 10:1-10, 13; 2 Chron. 9:1-9, 12) is said to be a queen of the South (possibly modern Ethiopia and Yemen), who traveled to Jerusalem to visit King Solomon (cf. Matt. 12:42; Luke 11:31). She apparently came "to test him with hard questions" and to see if the reports of his wisdom and the splendor of his palaces were justified. The chronicler reports that "when the queen of Sheba had seen all of Solomon's wisdom, and the house that he had built . . . there was no more spirit in her" (1 Kings 10:4-5).

The first rabbinic account of a sexual liaison between Solomon and Sheba, the Alphabet of Ben Sira 21b, which suggests that Nebuchadnezzar was the offspring, is late. Some Islamic accounts follow Tg. Job 1:15, in which Sheba is discovered by Solomon to have hairy feet and to be the night demon Lilith. Ethiopian accounts make Menelik I the child of Solomon and Sheba, and so trace their religious and national claim to succeed the Jews as God's chosen people to the liaison. Medieval Christian exegesis simply allegorizes the event: Solomon is Christ, the report of whose miracles prompts the Church to come and sit at his feet in pursuit of his wisdom and glory, which are recorded in the "testimonies of Sacred Scripture" (*Glossa Ordinaria* [PL 113.601-02]). This interpretation tends to glorify representations of Sheba.

In Shakespeare's *Henry 8* Archbishop Cranmer is made to prophesy of the child Elizabeth that she will be

> a pattern to all princes living with her,
> And of all that shall succeed. Saba was never
> More covetous of wisdom and fair virtue
> Than this pure soul shall be. (5.5.22-25)

Milton makes a similar epic comparison in praising Queen Christine of Sweden as a "queen of the north . . .

worthy to appear in the court of the wise king of the Jews, or any king of equal wisdom" *(Second Defense).* Descending toward cliché, in Scott's *Kenilworth* Dame Amy is seen by Anthony to appear "as proud and as gay as if she were the Queen of Sheba" (chap. 5). The sagging spirit of the Queen of Sheba emerges as a counter-motif in modern literature, with Hardy offering a pertinent example. When Angel Clare asks Tess why she appears dejected, Tess answers that she feels her life is a litany of lost opportunities. "When I see what you know, what you have read, and seen, and thought, I feel what a nothing I am! I'm like the poor Queen of Sheba who lives in the Bible. There is no more spirit in me" (chap. 19). This last phrase has also become a tag (cf. Dorothy Sayers, *The Unpleasantness at the Bellona Club,* chap. 13; Rose Macaulay, *Told by an Idiot,* 2.15).

See also SOLOMON.

Bibliography. Liptzin, S. "Solomon and the Queen of Sheba." *Dor le Dor* 7 (1979), 172-86; Pritchard, J. B. *Solomon and Sheba* (1974).

SHECHEM *See* DINAH.

SHEEP There are over 500 references to sheep in the Bible. Surely it was the most important animal in an economic as well as symbolic sense in ancient Palestine. Sheep provided food to eat (1 Sam. 14:32), milk to drink (Isa. 7:21-22), wool for clothing (Lev. 13:47; Job 31:20), and covering for tents (Exod. 26:14). They also served as a medium of exchange (2 Kings 3:4). In pastoral symbolism, special attention is given to the ways of the animal itself, i.e., its gregariousness (the word comes from the Latin for "flock"), docility, tendency to wander or stray but also to be easily led, etc. Moreover, it is set in opposition to other animal symbols. Whereas the bull or calf suggests idolatry (the golden calf in Exod. 32, the bull-pillars of 1 Kings 12:28), and the horse stands for the delusive glories and mad frenzies of warfare (Job 39:19-25; Ps. 33:17; Hos. 1:7), sheep are metaphorically the humble, easily led, and easily victimized people — of Israel or of the world — while the lamb stands specifically for the sacrificial victim who dies so that the people may live.

In the Genesis account the lives of the patriarchs were closely related to those of their sheep. Abel's sacrifice of sheep was acceptable while Cain's harvest of the field was not (Gen. 4:3-5); Abraham and his descendants were great sheepherders (Gen. 21:27), and Jacob's skill as a breeder (Gen. 30) became proverbial (Shylock links it to usury, *Merchant of Venice,* 1.3.73-84). Fittingly it is Jacob who first calls God the "shepherd" of Israel (Gen. 49:24). Moses and David are among the prominent successors to these early herdsmen. The most unforgettable parable in the OT, perhaps in the whole Bible, is the prophet Nathan's tale of the poor man and his ewe lamb which was beloved as a household pet (2 Sam. 12:1-5); David condemns himself by his angry denunciation of the rich man who takes the poor man's lamb for a meal, failing to recognize that the story is really about his own theft of Bathsheba from her husband Uriah.

By NT times, the symbolism had been elaborately prepared by these texts and by prophecies such as Isaiah's Fourth "Servant Song" (53:6-7):

> All we like sheep have gone astray; we have turned every one to his own way; and the LORD hath laid on him the iniquity of us all. He was oppressed, and he was afflicted, yet he opened not his mouth: he is brought as a lamb to the slaughter, and as a sheep before her shearers is dumb, so he openeth not his mouth.

These lines were applied to the Crucifixion at a very early date (Acts 8:32; 1 Pet. 1:19), just as was the injunction that the bones of the Passover lamb should not be broken (John 19:36 and Exod. 12:3-6; cf. Ps. 34:20). Zech. 13:7 provided yet another pastoral analogy, cited in Matt. 26:31 and Mark 14:27: "I will smite the shepherd, and the sheep shall be scattered." Jesus is identified as the Lamb of God, who "taketh away the sin of the world" (John 1:29). The imagery is continued in the Lost Sheep and Good Shepherd discourses (see Matt. 18:12-13; Luke 15:3-7; John 10) and other sayings involving the "lost sheep" of Israel, the "sheep without a shepherd," and "sheep among wolves," and by the commandment to "feed my sheep" (see Matt. 15:24 and 10:6; Mark 6:34; Matt. 9:36 and 1 Pet. 2:25; Matt. 10:16; John 21:16, 17). The Lamb of Revelation (chap. 5 et passim) becomes himself the Shepherd in Rev. 7:17 (cf. Isa. 40:11). Such references from OT imagery, including the Psalms (e.g., 23; 74:1; 78:52; 79:13; 80:1; 95:7; and 100:3), treat people as God's flock, the sheep "of his pasture" or "of his hand." (For variations on the theme, see Num. 27:17; 2 Sam. 5:2; 1 Kings 22:17; Jer. 23; Ezek. 34; Mic. 7:14; and Zech. 11).

The literary tradition is made diffuse by cliché: many passages have become so proverbial that their source has been forgotten. Thus the "false prophets" in "sheep's clothing" of Matt. 7:15, which become the "ravening wolves" of the end of the verse, come to stand for any threatening form of hypocrisy or treacherous obsequiousness (note the biblical resonances of Dickens's Uriah Heep). While it would be difficult to argue that all "wolves in sheep's clothing" are derivatively biblical, a distant echo of the scriptural passage may often be detected. The same may be said of the many literary references to "lost" or "scattered" sheep or lambs (frequently sentimentalized in the 19th cent.) or to separating "sheep from goats" (see Matt. 25:32). In Twain's *Huckleberry Finn* (chap. 1), Huck recounts how "The widow she cried over me, and called me a poor lost lamb, and she called me a lot of other names too, but she never meant no harm by it." Twain undoubtedly knew the biblical source, but the allusion is indirect. Some direct allusions are tortuously entwined with irony and therefore problematic. At the moment of Billy Budd's execution "it chanced that the vapory fleece hanging low in the East was shot through with a soft glory as of the fleece of the Lamb of God seen in mystical vision." Whether this reference signals Melville's final peaceful acceptance of Christianity, or constitutes a bitter parody, is unclear, although the source is evidently scriptural. Whenever sheep are made to stand for persons, overtones of the biblical imagery may be present, but at widely differing degrees of proximity.

See also BLOOD OF THE LAMB; LAMB OF GOD; LOST SHEEP, PARABLE OF; SHEPHERD.   HERBERT SCHNEIDAU

SHEKINAH Hebrew word meaning "dwelling": this is a circumlocution used in rabbinic literature to signify God's presence. The word does not occur in the Bible, though its root *shkn* is found in *mishkan*, "dwelling place" or "Tabernacle."

See also ASCENSION; GLORY; TEMPLE; WHEELS WITHIN WHEELS.

SHEM Shem was the eldest of Noah's sons, brother to Ham and Japheth. In biblical tradition the post-Deluge world was said to be divided into three groups, each of which was descended from one of the sons. This crude distinction still has currency in the study of languages, where the term *Hamitic* refers to Egyptian and related tongues, *Japhetic* to Indo-European languages, and *Shemitic* (*Semitic*) to those of Palestine and the Middle East. As a result of Noah's cursing Ham for exposing his father's drunken nakedness, the blessings accorded to Shem and Japheth were intertwined; notably, Japheth would "dwell in the tents of Shem" (Gen. 9:27). For St. Augustine this story prefigures the collaboration in God's plan of salvation of Jews and Greeks, or "the circumcision and uncircumcision," the Synagogue and the Church (*De civ. Dei* 16.1-3). That Japheth should "dwell in the tents of Shem" is thus seen to be proleptic of the coinherence of Christian revelation within that given to the Jews (*Glossa Ordinaria* [PL 113.113]).

Washington Irving's Knickerbocker in *A History of New York* speculates that if Noah had had another son "he would doubtless have inherited America." De Quincey applies Gen. 9:27 in a curious way in "Levana and Our Ladies of Sorrow" (*Suspira de Profundis*) when he writes of his Our Lady of Sighs that "she also carries a key; but she needs it little. For her kingdom is chiefly among the tents of Shem, and the houseless vagrant of every clime." The narrator in Kipling's *The Long Trail* imagines the tents as luxurious homes: "Ha' done with the Tents of Shem, dear lass, / We've seen the seasons through, / And it's time to turn on the old trail."

See also HAM.

SHEMA Heb. *shema'* is the first word of Deut. 6:4: "Hear, O Israel, the LORD our God, the LORD is one" (*shema' yiśra'el yhwh 'elohenu yhwh 'eḥad*). These words, as well as those which immediately follow in v. 5 ("And thou shalt love the LORD thy God with all thine heart, and with all thy soul, and with all thy might"), are recited twice daily in contemporary Jewish worship, although modern use replaces *yhwh* with *'adonai.* The injunction to talk of these things "when thou liest down, and when thou risest up" (Deut. 6:7) is taken literally in the Talmud, where the Shema is especially recommended as a night prayer (Bera. 1.1, 4b). Technically it is not a prayer, but a confession of faith or creed. Women, children, and slaves were not required to recite it, but little boys were taught it as soon as they could speak (Sukk. 42a), and it became integral to deathbed confessions of faith and the dying utterance of martyrs. Jesus, when asked what was the "most important commandment" in the Law, replied by quoting the Shema (Matt. 23:34-40; Mark 12:28-34), extending the command to love God with an additional command (cf. Lev. 19:8) to love one's neighbor as oneself. A. M. Klein's "Stance of the Amidah" is an appeal to the God of Israel to reveal himself in power and mercy: "Thyself do utter the Shema! Sound the great horn of our freedom, and gather from the four corners of the earth . . . Thy people, Thy folk, rejected, Thine elect."

SHEOL (Heb. *she'ol*) This word generally signifies "grave" or "pit," but also can be found with the apparent meaning of "nether world" (cf. Ezek. 31–32), "death" (Job 17:13-16), "Hades" (the LXX regularly translates it thus — 1 Sam. 28:15; Eccl. 9:10; Ps. 6:5), and the notion of Hell-Mouth (Isa. 5:14). After the hellenistic era (333 B.C. and following) it is sometimes pictured as having compartments of varying degrees of comfort and torment (1 Enoch 22). NT use of Hades associates it exclusively with confinement for the unregenerate until their final destruction in Gehenna (Matt. 10:28; Rev. 20:13-15).

See also HELL.

SHEPHERD The shepherd is a key element in the pastoral complex of symbolism in the Bible, a complex which includes sheep, tents, wandering, flocks needing care and guidance, nourishing pastures and refreshing waters; unsurprisingly, the shepherd's crook becomes a badge of office in the Christian Church. This complex is pervasive, often used in the OT to stand for Israel as a flock under the care of God (Gen. 49:24; Pss. 23; 80:1; 100:3) or his appointed leaders. And although the NT almost never mentions actual shepherds, the "Good Shepherd" is one of the most important of Jesus' parables of self-explanation (John 10); it was for a long time the dominant mode of portraying Jesus in early Christian art.

The power of this symbolism is only partly explained by the fact, noted in most Bible commentaries, that "shepherd" was a common metaphor for rulers in the ancient Near East. Rather, as J. Jeremias observes, the term in biblical usage is "not just a formal oriental divine predication," but comprises "new and vivid developments of the metaphor of the Shepherd who goes before His flock, who guides it, who leads it to pastures and to places where it may rest by the waters, who protects it with His staff, who whistles to the dispersed and gathers them, who carries the lamb in His bosom and leads the mother-sheep" (G. Kittel and G. Friedrich, *TDNT,* trans. G. W. Bromiley [1964-73], 6.487; for these attributes see Pss. 23 and 68:7; Isa. 40:11; 49:10; and 56:8; Jer. 50:19; Zech. 10:8).

The shepherd, and associated pastoral imagery, forms something like a totemic badge for the Hebrew nation: sheep-herding was the patriarchs' way of life, and their self-identification as such kept them "separate" in Egypt, "for every shepherd is an abomination unto the Egyptians" (Gen. 46:34). Indeed, most biblical usage stresses this paradox of humility and lowliness combined with hidden favor, the quality of being chosen: Moses and David, the most famous shepherds, exemplify a pattern of emerging from obscurity to manifest God's choice of the unregarded or despised as appointed leaders. (Significantly, David's first great victory over Goliath was achieved with shepherds' weapons; he rejected armor just as he and Joshua — but not Solomon — rejected chariots.) This theme, that of the obscure but chosen instrument, links the shepherd to such motifs as the reluctant leader (e.g., Gideon, Saul, Jeremiah, and Moses) and the younger son (e.g., Jacob, Abel, Isaac, Joseph, Ephraim, David, and Solomon): the youngest of the family was often given the shepherd's duty, as in David's case (1 Sam. 16:11; 17:28-50). The implication is that such obscurity may be preparation for greatness.

By NT and rabbinic times, the same cultural evolution which had made shepherds almost outlaws in Mesopotamia earlier had occurred also in Israel. So shepherds were despised, and considered thieves, at the time of the famous annunciation to them (Luke 2) — part of a theme which links up with that of Jesus being sent to the "lost sheep" of Israel (Matt. 15:24), now defined as the poor, the harlots, and other "habitual sinners" in rabbinic eyes. There is thus all the more irony in the Midrash on Ps. 23: "Rabbi Jose bar Hanina taught: In the whole world you find no occupation more despised than the shepherd, who all his days walks about with his staff and his pouch. Yet David presumed to call the Holy One, blessed be he, a shepherd!" (*Midrash on Psalms* [trans. Braude]). Not all Jewish thought was so forgetful of the overwhelmingly positive OT associations. Philo used the shepherd as a figure for *nous* controlling the irrational powers, and called the *logos* the shepherd of mankind. The NT, however, does even more with the symbol, elaborating both the duties and virtues of the Good Shepherd — his watchfulness, even while others sleep; his concern for all, including the least member of the flock; and his willingness to risk his life against predators. All these qualities and more were used in Christian theology, and many were implicit in prophetic conceptions of God. The most idyllic of the "messianic" prophecies of Isaiah, e.g., is 11:1-9, where "a little child shall lead" all the world's creatures, lion and lamb together, in a flock. Even the Crucifixion is explained in Jesus' quotation of Zech. 13:7, "I will smite the shepherd, and the sheep shall be scattered" (Mark 14:27; cf. Matt. 26:31). And Jesus' post-resurrection address to Peter (John 21) charges him with specific pastoral responsibilities which are themselves subsequently reflected in Peter's own Epistles (e.g., 1 Pet. 5:2-4).

The literary adaptation of this symbolism ranges from simple and direct to tangential and convoluted. Direct examples occur in the *Roman de la Rose,* with its Shepherd's Park, and in Chaucer's portrait of the Parson in the *General Prologue* to his *Canterbury Tales,* which makes use of John 10 and NT corollaries (see, besides those already mentioned, Matt. 18:12 and 25:32-33; Heb. 13:20; 1 Pet. 2:25; Rev. 7:17). Noteworthy also are the medieval shepherds' plays; in the best-known, the *Secunda Pastorum* ("Second Shepherd's Play"), the sheep-thief Mak and his wife perform a parody of the Annunciation.

The "pastoral" genre which flowered in the Renaissance, although derivatively classical, was nonetheless infused with values and meanings from the Bible. In Spenser's *Shepheardes Calendar* some "shepherds" are identifiable as ecclesiastics known to Spenser; the work concerns religious issues throughout, and preaches the virtues of obscurity and retirement (classical *otium;* Bacon shows how the biblical and classical merge by glossing Cain and Abel as types of the active and contemplative lives [*Advancement of Learning,* 1.6.7]). Milton's *Lycidas,* the preeminent pastoral elegy in English, makes use of Ezekiel's denunciation of the "bad shepherds" of Israel (chap. 34), and many of Milton's other poems employ similar symbols. A famous passage in *Paradise Lost* compares Satan to the "hireling" of John 10 (*PL* 4.183-93; cf. King Henry's remark on the "reckless" shepherd in *3 Henry 6,* 5.6.7).

Even anti-Christian authors must evoke some of the associations. In E. M. Forster's *The Longest Journey* Stephen the shepherd is meant to revive Pan and paganism rather than Christ and the Bible. But biblical symbolism is present, if only by opposition, just as it is in the references to real shepherds in the fiction of Hardy or Lawrence, or, more explicitly, in John Barth's parodic rewriting of the gospel, *Giles Goat-Boy.*

See also LOST SHEEP, PARABLE OF.

Bibliography. Cooper, H. *Pastoral: Medieval into Renaissance* (1977); Empson, W. *Some Versions of Pastoral* (1935); Schneidau, H. N. "The Hebrews Against the High Cultures: Pastoral Motifs." In *Sacred Discontent: The Bible and Western Tradition* (1976). HERBERT SCHNEIDAU

SHIBBOLETH In the book of Judges (chap. 12) occurs the story of Jephthah and the Gileadites, who in trying to discern the escaping Ephraimites, similar in appearance and attire to themselves, tested suspected enemies they found trying to cross the Jordan by asking each, "Say now Shibboleth: and he said Sibboleth: for he could not frame to pronounce it right. Then they took him and slew him at the passages of Jordan: and there fell at that time . . . forty and two thousand."

Samson, in Milton's *Samson Agonistes,* recalls how Jephthah took revenge on those who betrayed him "Without reprieve . . . / For want of well pronouncing Shibboleth" (289-90). The idea of such a password, mispronounced by an enemy whose dialect differs, is familiar in modern English literature. Whittier's poem "Letter from a Missionary of the Methodist Episcopal Church South" relates how vigilantes in Kansas watched the river ferry to catch Yankees "(As they of old did watch the fords of Jordan,) / And cut off all whose Yankee tongues refuse the Shibboleth of the Nebraska bill." The term subsequently acquired the meaning of partisan code language or in-talk, as in Galsworthy's *The Patrician,* where the protagonist speaks of those whose "motions seemed a little meaningless to me so far removed from all the fetishes and shibboleths of Westminster" (2.6). Shaw uses the word with the same force in *Back to Methuselah,* where one of the men's club conversationalists retorts: "You have not offered me any principles. Your party shibboleths are not principles." "Supernaturalism of politics" is attacked by H. L. Mencken as a Puritan legacy in America, by which "the most successful American politicians" in his view "have been those most adept at twisting the ancient gauds and shibboleths of Puritanism to partisan uses" ("Puritanism as a Literary Force").

See also ALPHABET, HEBREW; JEPHTHAH AND HIS DAUGHTER.

SHIELD From very early times the shield served as a figure for God's protection and care. In Gen. 15:1 the Lord said to Abraham, "Fear not Abram: I am thy shield." The Psalms make especially heavy use of the figure: "But thou, O LORD, art a shield unto me" (3:3); "Thou hast also given me the shield of thy salvation" (18:35); "The LORD is my strength and my shield" (28:7); "For the LORD God is a sun and shield" (84:11); "his truth shall be thy shield and buckler" (91:4; see also 33:20; 35:2; 59:11; 84:9; 115:11; 144:2). The Lord "is a shield unto them that put their trust in him" (Prov. 30:5). The righteous will "take holiness for an invincible shield" (Wisd. 5:19). In the NT the shield is an important item in St. Paul's list of the Christian's armor: "Put on the whole armor of God . . . . above all, taking the shield of faith, wherewith ye shall be able to quench all the fiery darts of the wicked" (Eph. 6:11, 16).

Those who hid behind physical shields, rather than the shield which was the Lord, had no real safety: "In Salem also is his tabernacle, and his dwelling place in Zion. There he brake the arrows of the bow, the shield, and the sword, and the battle" (Ps. 76:3). And so the righteous can despise the seeming strength of the shields of their foes; David said to Goliath, "Thou comest to me with a sword, and with a spear, and with a shield: but I come to thee in the name of the LORD of Hosts" (1 Sam. 17:45). As St. Augustine says in his commentary on Ps. 76:3, "they that have rightly believed see that they ought not to rely upon themselves . . . and whatsoever [the wicked] seem of great virtue wherewith to protect themselves temporally . . . all these things He hath broken there" (NPNF 8.356).

As to the precise allegorical meaning of the spiritual shield, on the other hand, the Fathers are in some disagreement: for Aphrahat the shield is baptism (NPNF 13.363-64); for St. John Chrysostom, in his commentary on Eph. 6:16, the shield represents that species of faith "by which miracles are wrought" (*Hom. on Ephesians*). Augustine typically follows the Psalms directly rather than Paul, seeing the shield as God himself. But usually when the Fathers refer to the shield, as they frequently do in their discussions of Christian soldiering, they are referring directly to Eph. 6:16 (e.g., St. Jerome, *Ep.* 33).

In *Sir Gawain and the Green Knight* a pentangle is painted on Gawain's shield, "In Betoknyng of trawthe"; one of the senses in which one is to understand Gawain's "trawthe" is "his afyaunce" in Christ (626-43). To his grief, Gawain later trusts to the protection of the magical girdle rather than his shield of faith. The motif of unwisely casting aside one's shield is a commonplace in medieval and Renaissance literature. In John Harington's translation (1591) of the *Orlando Furioso,* despairing Orlando "casts away his curats and his shield. . . . He scatters all his armour in the field" (23.106), and in *The Faerie Queene* (3.11.8-10), Scudamour, also despairing, rages against God after casting away his shield and other armor. Arthur retains his own "sunshiny shield," and so when this "the Gyaunt spyde with staring eye, / He downe let fall his arme" (1.8.19-20; cf. 1.6.50; 1.7.33; 5.11.46). For William Dunbar in "The Goldyn Targe," the shield, or *targe,* is Reason, which protects against amorous advances. (Dunbar's *targe* and Arthur's brilliant shield owe at least as much to Goddess of Wisdom Minerva's crystal shield as to St. Paul; see Peele's *Araignment of Paris*, 981, and Milton's *Comus*, 450.) But the "shield of truth" in Cowper's *Task* (6.875) is clearly that of Eph. 6:16, able to defend the persevering Christian against the "bolts" of the "infidel."

See also ARMOR AND WEAPONS; *MILES CHRISTI;* SWORD OF THE SPIRIT. H. DAVID BRUMBLE

SHIELD OF FAITH *See* ARMOR AND WEAPONS; FAITH; *MILES CHRISTI.*

SHILOH After entering into the Promised Land under Joshua, the Israelites set up the Tabernacle and the Ark of the Covenant at Shiloh (Josh. 18:1). Shiloh remained the

worship center during the period of time covered by the books of Joshua and Judges. It was here that the tribal division of conquered lands was made (Josh. 18:8-10); and it was here, in the "Valley of Maidens," that at an annual feast in which young virgins danced in the vineyards the wifeless Benjamites could select brides.

The name has also been associated with the blessing of Jacob (Gen. 49:2-27). Gen. 49:10 includes the phrase translated "until Shiloh come," suggesting that Shiloh (viz., "rest") might be metonymic for the advent of the Messiah (Sanh. 98b), although the reading remains problematic. This, however, is the understanding of Bishop Latimer in his Lincolnshire Sermon for the "Third Sunday in Advent" (1552). In his *Magnalia Christi Americana* Cotton Mather blends biblical and classical allusion to describe the Puritans' victory over Indian King Philip: "'twas unto a Shilo, that the planters of New England have been making their progress, and King Philip is the Python that has been giving them obstruction, in a fatal enterprize [against] our Lord Jesus Christ, the great Phoebus [Apollo]" (ed. Robbins, 2.578-79); here the type is evidently the Shiloh of Josh. 18:1.

See also MESSIAH.

SHIMEI When King David was in flight from Absalom's rebellion, and vulnerable, a kinsman of Saul, Shimei son of Gera, cursed him, and threw stones and dust (2 Sam. 16:5-13). While David did not retaliate, and later forgave him, on his deathbed he asked Solomon to settle the score (2 Sam. 19:16-23; 1 Kings 2:8-9, 36-46). Dryden makes Shimei one of those who plot against David: "The wretch who heaven's anointed dared to curse. / . . . / Shimei was always in the midst. . . ."

See also ABSALOM; DAVID.

SHINAR *See* BABEL.

SHOFAR The shofar (Heb. *shopar*) was a simple trumpet made from the horn of a ram, or of any "clean" animal except a cow. It was to be blown to announce the New Year and Day of Atonement as well as to herald the "release" of the Year of Jubilee (Lev. 25:9). In later tradition it was sounded also on feast days, at the beginning of the Sabbath, and in times of famine or plague. Associated with battle (Judg. 9:8, 16-22; Jer. 4:19-21), it is to herald the Last Judgment (Zeph. 1:16) and the ultimate return to Zion (Isa. 28:13). The connection of the shofar with deliverance from persecution is reflected in A. M. Klein's "Ballad of Signs and Wonders," which concludes: "Israel, blow the *shofar;* Oyez! / Praise the Lord with hallelujahs!" In Howard Nemerov's autumnal recollections of the Day of Atonement, "When apples smell like goodness, cold in the cellar, / You hear the ram's horn sounded in the high / Mount of the Lord, and you lift up your eyes" ("Runes").

SHULAMITE, SHUNAMITE   In Song of Songs 6:13, the Shulamite was the beautiful woman brought to David (1 Kings 1:3). She became a figure for ideal beauty.

See also ABISHAG; SONG OF SONGS.

SIBYLLINE ORACLES   *See* FISH.

SIC TRANSIT GLORIA MUNDI   *See* GLORY.

SICKNESS   *See* DISEASE AND HEALING; PHYSICIAN.

SICKNESS UNTO DEATH   *See* HEZEKIAH.

SIGNS AND WONDERS   "Signs" (Heb. *'ot, 'otot*) and "wonders" (Heb. *mopet, umopetim*) occur together frequently in the OT; the expression "signs and wonders" is used notably in relation to the events of the plagues of Egypt and the Exodus (e.g., Exod. 7:3). This theme of the signaling of God's redemption of his people is central to Deuteronomy (e.g., Deut. 4:34; 6:22; 7:19; 26:8; 28:4) also, and it recurs in the prophets (Isa. 8:18; 10:3; Jer. 32:20). Because it is used so often in connection with memories of the Exodus, in Greek-speaking Judaism it became a byword for the days of deliverance, the Greek phrase as found in the LXX being *semeia kai terata*.

NT usage applies the phrase to the miracles of Jesus (e.g., Acts 2:22) and those associated with the establishment of the Church (e.g., Acts 2:19, 22, 43; 4:30; 5:12; 6:8; 7:36; 2 Thess. 2:9; Heb. 2:4). *Teras* suggests "unusual wonder," or "miracle"; and to the normal Greek locution St. Paul occasionally adds *dynameis*, "mighty works" (2 Cor. 12:12).

St. Augustine, in his debate with Neoplatonists who dabble in theurgy and the occult sciences, outlines what he takes to be a biblical distinction between godly and pagan "wonders" (*De civ. Dei*, esp. bk. 10). Moses' confrontation with Pharaoh and his magicians merits special consideration, since it depicts so dramatically the God of Abraham, Isaac, and Jacob sovereign over other gods, his wonders supreme over the sorcerers' arts. For Augustine such passages do more than demonstrate the supreme power of God, however. Not only might but truth, virtue, humility, and trust are vindicated in Moses' triumph:

> These miracles, and many others of the same nature, which it were tedious to mention, were wrought for the purpose of commending the worship of one true God, and prohibiting the worship of a multitude of false gods. Moreover, they were wrought by simple faith and godly confidence, not by the incantations and charms composed under the influence of a criminal tampering with the unseen world. (*De civ. Dei* 10.9)

The very fact that the Egyptian magi were able to duplicate certain of the visible and physical marvels performed by Moses illustrates the need for a qualitative rather than a merely descriptive differentiation between true and false

miracles: God's wonders are, for Augustine, always "signs" in the root sense; they have an interpretative function. Ultimately, all point to the incarnate wonder, Christ himself, the definitive sign of God's presence. While the devil and his ilk can counterfeit, feign, imitate, and thus occasionally deceive those who should know better, says Augustine, such ungodly wonders are mere spectacles and special effects — they mean nothing.

Augustine's discussion is foundational for the way "signs and wonders" are treated throughout the medieval period — from various renderings of biblical stories themselves to hagiography (e.g., *St. Erkenwald*) and even much secular literature. Ironically, it was with the recovery and dissemination of classical, especially Aristotelian, preoccupation with the marvelous as a form of aesthetic exaggeration that the "Christian marvelous" gradually waned in significance. Although lip-service was given to the Christian supernatural, in some instances for the sake of its power to compel religious awe and wonder, the sense of sublimity with which it came to be identified was little concerned with faith and frequently became "in substance a substitute for theology" (Hathaway, 68; Brown, 180-86).

The phrase "signs and wonders" is still a frequent literary occurrence and is sometimes suggestive of its complex biblical and traditional associations. A. M. Klein's "Ballad of Signs and Wonders" is a Passover poem about an apostate Jew who converts, hoping to marry the daughter of a Christian prince, but in his frustrated passion kills her instead. Just in time to save the whole Prague community from suffering the outrage of the prince, the dead girl rises from her grave to identify her slayer, so sparing the rest. John Betjeman uses the phrase in his poem "St. Saviour's, Aberdeen Park," in which he reflects on receiving the Eucharist in his parents' church, and on the "Wonder beyond Time's wonders, that Bread so white and small," the "Power" of which "Is God who created the present, the chain-smoking millions and me."

Bibliography. Blondel, J. "Le merveilleux dans le paradis Miltonien." *Foi et Vie* 66 (1967), 43-54; Brown, K. B. "Wonders as Signs: An Introduction to the Christian Marvellous in English Literature of the Middle Ages." M.A. thesis, Regent College, 1980; Hathaway, B. *Marvels and Commonplaces: Renaissance Literary Criticism* (1968); Quinn, D. "Donne and the Wane of Wonder." *ELH* 36 (1969), 626-47; McAlindon, T. "The Treatment of the Supernatural in Middle English Legend and Romance, 1200-1400." Ph.D. diss., Cambridge University, 1961; Semon, K. "Fantasy and Wonder in Shakespeare's Last Plays." *SQ* 25 (1974), 89-102; Tanner, T. *The Reign of Wonder: Naivety and Reality in American Literature* (1965).   KATHERINE B. JEFFREY

SIGNS OF THE TIMES   One of Jesus' reproaches of the Sadducees and Pharisees was their willed obtuseness to unfolding national and religious catastrophe: "can ye not discern the signs of the times?" (Matt. 16:3). Aldous

Huxley writes in this sense in *Chrome Yellow:* "It was not for these reasons that we regard this war as a true sign of the times, but because in its origin and progress it is marked by certain characteristics which seem to connect it almost beyond a doubt with the predictions in Christian prophecy relating to the Second Coming of the Lord" (chap. 9).

See also ESCHATOLOGY; SECOND COMING.

SILOAM, SHILOAH Isaiah's prophecy (Isa. 8:6-7) includes a metaphoric raison d'etre for God's coming judgment: "Forasmuch as this people refuseth the waters of Shiloah that go softly. . . . Now therefore, behold, the LORD bringeth up upon them the waters of the river, strong and many, even the king of Assyria, and all his glory." The softly flowing waters of Shiloah probably refer to the little brook which feeds the pool of Siloam in Jerusalem from the spring of Gihon, its source outside the walls (cf. Neh. 3:15).

Because the pool of Siloa(m) was where Jesus sent the blind man to wash off the clay and spittle from his eyes, so to discover the miracle of his healing (John 9:1-11), St. Augustine connects John's etymology for the name ("Sent" [v. 7]) with a commissioning to apostolic vocation. The one who accepts his apostolic commission, so to speak, is one who says, "once I was blind, but now I see" (*Sermo,* 135.1-2). This is the connection in Milton's mind when he invokes at the beginning of *Paradise Lost* the "Heavenly Muse" who inspired Moses on Sinai to receive the first covenant; wishing his readers to understand his desire for obedience to that Law, but also his claims upon the prophet's vocation, he adds:

> Or if Sion Hill
> Delight thee more, and Siloa's Brook that flowed
> Fair by the Oracle of God; I thence
> Invoke thy aid to my adventurous Song. (*PL* 1.10-13)

Carlyle's Professor Teufelsdröckh, not less desirous of an oracular voice, used to muse on how the little brook Kuhbach flowed in prehistoric days, "assiduous as Siloa was murmuring on across the wilderness, as yet unnamed, unseen" *(Sartor Resartus).* In American literature of the 19th cent., in the wake of popular hymns such as Bishop Heber's "By cool Siloam's shady rill" (1811), Siloam became associated with the peace and blessedness of heaven. Hence Whittier's lines:

> Gone to thy Heavenly Father's rest!
> The flowers of Eden round thee blowing,
> And on thine ear the murmurs blest
> Of Siloa's waters softly flowing. ("To the Memory of
> Thomas Shipley")

SILVER CORD *See* GOLDEN BOWL.

SIMEON One of the twelve sons of Jacob.

See also AARON; JACOB; JOSEPH THE PATRIARCH; TRIBES OF ISRAEL.

SIMEON THE JUST *See* MARY, MOTHER OF JESUS; *NUNC DIMITTIS.*

SIMON MAGUS Simon is first mentioned in Acts 8:9-24, where it is said that he "used sorcery, and bewitched the people of Samaria, giving out that himself was some great one"; the word *Magus* was attached to his name in subsequent tradition. According to the Acts narrative, Simon, converted and baptized under the ministry of Philip, was amazed by the miracles the apostles worked and, observing that the Holy Spirit was given through the laying on of their hands, offered them money for a share of the same power. He was so severely reprimanded for his presumption that he begged the apostle Peter to pray for his forgiveness.

Second-century sources indicate Simon's unrepentant persistence in magic, however, and ecclesiastical writers in the early Church represent him as the first heretic; St. Irenaeus, e.g., argues that Simon's faith was not genuine but feigned (*Adv. haer.* 1.23.1). In the writings of St. Justin Martyr and the Pseudo-Clementines (Recognitions 2.8-11; cf. *Hom.* 2.23-24), he acquires legendary status as a magician and opponent of the apostle Peter as well as of the family of Clement (the members of which all bear varieties of the name Faustus). Simon confronts Peter in Rome while accompanied by Simon's paramour, Helena of Tyre (later Troy), said by Simon to be the first emanation of the deity. In the apocryphal Acts of St. Peter, Simon's magical powers are further displayed when, to prove his power, he conjures before Nero and his court and ascends into the air, only to be caused by the prayers of Peter and Paul to fall and injure himself fatally. In the wake of these legends, Simon is typically identified as the father of Gnosticism (Irenaeus, *Adv. haer.* 1.23.2; St. Epiphanius, *Refutation of All the Heresies,* 21.7.2; 27.2.1) as well as a necromancer. There are thus two quite distinct traditions concerning Simon Magus: one develops from his attempt to purchase the privileges and status of religious office and pervert them to pecuniary ends; the other develops from the legends an emphasis on magic and heresy and offers the prototype of the fortunes and fate of the black magician in literature.

The word *simony* and its meaning derive from the Acts 8 narrative; as Chaucer points out in *The Parson's Tale,* "Certes symonye is cleped of Simon Magus, that wolde han boght for temporeel catel the yifte that God had yeven by the Hooly Goost" (*Canterbury Tales,* 10.783). Accordingly, Chaucer places Simon among those of infamous memory in *The House of Fame* (1274). John Donne considered simony the "worst of all spiritual vices" (*To the Countess of Bedford,* 2) and compared the abuses of poetry and the law to "Symonie and Sodomy in Churchmens lives" ("Satire 2," 75). Dryden employed the idea analogically to complain about the English stage of his time: "Witchcraft reigns there, and raises to Renown / *Macbeth,* the *Simon Magus* of the town" ("Epilogue to the University of Oxon. [1673]," 30). In a more literal application of the story, Christian in Bunyan's *The Pilgrim's Progress* attacks the religion of Mr. Money-love and Mr. Hold-the-world; "Simon the Witch was of this Religion too; for he would have had the Holy Ghost, that he might have got Money therewith, and sentence from Peter's mouth was according" (pt. I). Similarly, Swift attacked Dr. Rundle's appointment to the rich bishopric of Derry by comparing him to "Our Bishop's predecessor, Magus" (*Dr. Rundle,* 41).

More recently, simony appears as a theme in Joyce's *Dubliners,* where Father Flynn in "The Sisters" is called a "simoniac" because of some mysteriously related incident of a broken chalice. In the other stories of *Dubliners* as well as in *Stephen Hero* (esp. chap. 18), Joyce indicts the Irish clergy's use of the instruments of divine grace for worldly ends. In *A Portrait of the Artist as a Young Man* Stephen hears the priest's voice "offering him secret knowledge and secret power. He would know what was the sin of Simon Magus" (chap. 4). What also attracts Stephen to Simon Magus, however, is the fact that Magus was considered the first and arch-heretic. Joyce implies that young Irishmen were encouraged to seek the priesthood for the status and power it offered rather than as a spiritual calling. The characterization of Stephen Dedalus, consistent with this theme, represents, in part, a conflation of Faustus and Simon Magus, who, on the basis of his legendary "fall from the sky" as punishment for soaring ambitions, has often been compared to Icarus.

Charles Williams has written about Simon Magus in *Witchcraft,* and the legendary history of Simon seems to lurk behind the story of the magician Considine in his *Shadows of Ecstasy.* Simon Magus also figures prominently in Anita Mason's *The Illusionist* and in the Deptford trilogy of Robertson Davies —*Fifth Business, The Manticore,* and *World of Wonders* —with its master illusionist Magnus Eisengrim.

Bibliography. Aune, D. E. "Simon Magus." *ISBE* 4.516-18 (1988); Beyschlag, K. *Simon Magus und die christliche Gnosis* (1974); Brown, B. D. "Marlowe, Faustus, and Simon Magus." *PMLA* 54 (1939), 82-121; Butler, E. M. *The Myth of the Magus* (1948); Salles-Dabadie, J. M. A. *Recherches sur Simon le Mage.* Cahiers de la Revue biblique 10 (1969).

DOMINIC MANGANIELLO

SIMON THE ZEALOT *See* APOSTLE.

SIN AGAINST THE HOLY GHOST (SPIRIT) *See* HOLY SPIRIT; HOPE; UNPARDONABLE SIN.

SIN WILL FIND YOU OUT "Be sure your sin will find you out" is a warning by Moses to the children of Gad and Reuben who were balking at the divine com-

mand to cross over the Jordan (Num. 32:23). D. H. Lawrence opined in his *Studies in Classic American Literature* that the theme of Hawthorne's *The Scarlet Letter* is "Be good, and never sin! Be sure your sins will find you out."

SINAI *See* HOREB; MOSES; MOUNTAIN; TEN COMMANDMENTS.

SINS . . . AS SCARLET "Come now, and let us reason together, saith the LORD: though your sins be as scarlet, they shall be as white as snow; though they be red like crimson, they shall be as wool" (Isa. 1:18; cf. Ps. 51:7; Rev. 7:14). Scarlet was a deep and permanent dye, virtually impossible to wash out once set (cf. Isa. 63:2-3). Hence scarlet sins have the connotation either of such habitual character or public ill-repute as to prove ineradicable; the "scarlet woman" is beyond the pale of honorable restitution for the Puritan morality of Hawthorne's Pharisaical New England. Such allusions neglect the whole context, which focuses rather on the efficacy of forgiveness despite the gravity of human offense. Shelley, in his "A Defense of Poetry," makes the cleansing "mediator and redeemer, Time"; the scarlet offenses he has in mind are literary.

See also SINS OF THE FATHERS.

SINS OF THE FATHERS In the pronouncement of the second of the Ten Commandments, God observes to Moses: "I the LORD thy God am a jealous God, visiting the iniquity of the fathers upon the children unto the third and fourth generation of them that hate me" (Exod. 20:5). Rabbinic commentary tends to the view that, perhaps because of Moses' intercession, God abrogated the force of this law so that children should not be put to death for their fathers, nor indeed the reverse: "Every man shall be put to death for his own sin" (Deut. 24:16). This view, they note, is elaborated by the prophet Ezekiel in chap. 18, where God rejects a literal application of the proverb "The fathers have eaten sour grapes and the children's teeth are set on edge" (v. 2), saying simply, "the soul that sinneth, it shall die" (v. 4; cf. Sanh. 111a-111b; B. Qam. 50b; Num. Rab. 19.33).

In the view of St. Jerome the original passage helps to explain evil in the world, but not to answer doubts about the "injustice" one feels when "untutored youth and innocent childhood are cut down in the bud," or "children three years old, or two, and even unweaned infants, are possessed with devils, covered with leprosy, and eaten up with jaundice, while godless men and profane, adulterers, and murderers, have health and strength to blaspheme God." Nor does Ezek. 18 fully meet this concern. Like Job, one must bear in patience the will of God (*Ep.* 39.2). St. Augustine observes that God's judgment in Exod. 20:5 is lifted from the guilty by grace: "For upon him who has been changed in Christ they [the sins of his fathers] are not visited, since he has ceased to be a child of the wicked forebears by not further imitating their conduct." Augustine not only appeals to Ezek. 18 but observes also that the wording of Exod. 20:5 is "of them that *hate* me," while the following verse (v. 6) adds "And shewing mercy unto thousands of them that love me and keep my commandments"; the imitation of wicked forebears causes persons "to suffer not their own deservings only, but also those of the ones they have imitated," while "the effect of imitating the good is that even their own sins are blotted out" (*Enarr. in Ps.* 109.14).

Calvin, commenting in the *Institutes* (2.8.19-21), adduces related passages (Num. 14:18; Jer. 32:18) which echo Exod. 20:5, and concludes that what is represented is to be understood in a straightforward, deterministic sense:

> For the punishment denounced here and in similar passages is too great to be confined within the limits of the present life. We must therefore understand it to mean, that a curse from the Lord righteously falls not only on the head of the individual, but also on all his lineage. When it has fallen, what can be anticipated but that the father, being deprived of the Spirit of God, will live most flatigiously; that the son, being in like manner forsaken of the Lord, because of his father's iniquity, will then follow the same road to destruction; and be followed in his turn by succeeding generations, forming a seed of evil-doers?

Calvin rejects appeal to Ezek. 18, saying that the context is God's denial of an attempt by Ezekiel's contemporaries to evade moral responsibility for their own actions by blaming the sins of previous generations, when the punishments were clearly "for their own iniquity" (v. 20). Over and against this lineage of damnation, says Calvin, is

> the solemn covenant made with the Church — I will be "a God unto thee, and to thy seed after thee" [Gen. 17:7]. With reference to this Solomon says, "The just man walketh in his integrity: his children are blessed after him" [Prov. 20:7]; not only in consequence of a religious education [though this certainly is by no means unimportant], but in consequence of the blessing promised in the covenant — viz. that the divine favor will dwell forever in the families of the righteous. (v. 21)

Calvin's emphasis entered the Church of England via Cranmer, especially in the *Articles of Religion* (17, 27, 29), although in less rigid form. It is reflected in the accusing words of Lady Constance to Queen Elinor in Shakespeare's *King John* (2.1.179-82), in which she asserts that her son John has usurped the "royalties and rights" of Arthur, the son of Lady Constance:

> Thy sins are visited in this poor child;
> The canon of the law is laid on him,
> Being but the second generation
> Removed from thy sin-conceiving womb.

But Shakespeare seems to view this doctrine as a function of the human condition *sub specie legibus,* not *sub specie gratia.* In *The Merchant of Venice* Launcelot Gobbo teases Jessica about her father Shylock, saying, "Look you, the sins of the father are to be laid upon the children. . . . Therefore be o' good cheer, for truly I think you are damn'd. There is but one hope . . . that your father got you not. . . ." Jessica's pragmatic response underscores the willful determinism in Gobbo's jesting condemnation: "That were a kind of bastard hope indeed. So the sins of my mother should be visited upon me" — lines that may indicate Shakespeare's knowledge of Jewish views on the lineage of generations as well as Jessica's perception of the obvious moral corollary to Gobbo's insinuation (3.5.1-16).

John Donne's translation of "The Lamentations of Jeremy" formulates its source (Lam. 5:7-8) crisply:

> Our Fathers did these sins, and are no more,
> But we do beare the sins they did before.
> They are but servants, which do rule us thus,
> Yet from their hands none would deliver us.

William Cowper endeavors to analyze the bankruptcy of a covenantal tradition in which those who were once numbered among the "generations blessed by God" have become in practice something else; his target is the Church of England, but he frames his judgment by an appeal to the history of Israel: "They, and they only amongst all mankind, 'Receiv'd the transcript of th'eternal mind,' " yet in a demonstration that "grace abus'd brings forth the foulest deeds / . . . Cur'd of the golden calves, their fathers' sin, / They set up self, that idol god within" ("Expostulation," 197-99; 215-16). As a result, he says, "Thus fell the best instructed in her day, / And the most favour'd land, look where we may" (225-26); even "Thy Levites, once a consecrated host, / [are] No longer Levites, and their lineage lost" (263-64).

The Russian novelist Turgenev offers a powerful narrative essay on the near impossibility of sons escaping from the sins of their fathers in his *Fathers and Sons,* a story about the disintegration of Czarist Russian feudalism. In Trollope's *Framley Parsonage* the biblical idea has been watered down to something like a notion of the "burden of the past," a reflection of the de-emphasis of Calvinism in the 19th-cent. Church of England:

> The world, it is true, had pressed upon her sorely with all its weight of accumulated clerical wealth, but it had not utterly crushed her — not her, but her only child. For the sins of the father, are they not visited upon the third and fourth generation? (chap. 48)

But for Thomas Hardy, who was raised in a soberly religious family and once aspired to train as an Anglican clergyman, loss of faith at the age of 27 involved revulsion from a doctrine which seemed to him to justify — by "explaining" — the degradation and misery of many. In *Tess of the D'Urbervilles* his narrator says bluntly: "But though to visit the sins of the fathers upon the children may be a morality good enough for divinities, it is scorned by average human nature" (chap. 11). Sir Edmund Gosse, a close friend of Hardy's, criticizes the Calvinist formulation more gently in his novel *Father and Son* (1907), a narrative based upon his relations with his fundamentalist father, the eminent zoologist P. H. Gosse. And Samuel Butler, son of a clergyman and grandson of a bishop, had, like Hardy, plans to take holy orders and was so educated at Cambridge only to drop out because of religious doubts. His semi-autobiographical novel *The Way of All Flesh* (1903) presents a protagonist, Ernest, who in rebellion against his father and schoolmasters has turned inward in search of his "true self" (what Cowper had called "that idol God within"). It seems to say to him: "Obey me, your true self, and things will go tolerably well with you, but only listen to that outward and visible old husk of yours which is called your father, and I will rend you in pieces even unto the third and fourth generation as one who hated God; for I, Ernest, am the God who made you" (chap. 31). That these words seem to savor as much of Freud as of the Decalogue is, of course, no accident; both sources hover, less explicitly, over the dialogue in T. S. Eliot's play *The Family Reunion* (1939).

See also TEN COMMANDMENTS.

SISERA   A Canaanite military commander defeated by Deborah and Barak, Sisera was himself ignominiously murdered by a Kenite woman, Jael, wife of Heber (Judg. 4:4-24). Edwin Arlington Robinson's "Sisera" makes him the victim of a woman he knew and already was attracted to; the manner of his death is made the action of a psychologically complex femme fatale (*Nicodemus, A Book of Poems* [1932], 14-25).

See also AJALON, VALE OF; DEBORAH, SONG OF DEBORAH; JAEL.

SIX-HUNDRED AND SIXTY-SIX (666)   *See* DRAGON OF THE APOCALYPSE; MARK OF THE BEAST.

SLAUGHTER OF THE INNOCENTS   The tyrannical insecurity of King Herod the Great, "King of the Jews" under the Romans (37-4 B.C.), was great enough that when a group of oriental magi appeared at his court asking, "Where is he that is born King of the Jews?" (Matt. 2:2), he was put into fearful distress "and all Jerusalem with him" (v. 3). After taking advice from the "chief priests and scribes" about where, according to scriptural prophecies, the Messiah was to be born, and being told "in Bethlehem of Judaea," Herod endeavored to employ the Wise Men as agents to spy out this potential rival. The Magi, however, were warned in a dream that they should not return to Herod, and when they had found and worshiped the infant Jesus, they departed into their own country another way. Joseph, similarly warned, took Mary and the child and fled into Egypt just in time to

avoid Herod's troops, sent by the despot to massacre "all the [male] children that were in Bethlehem, and in all the coasts thereof, from two years old and under" (v. 16).

Events from the life of Moses (Exod. 1:15-22) and the flight from Egypt are counterpoised vividly in Matthew's narration of the events, although in Christian exegesis this connection is curiously undeveloped. The horror of the event itself, contrasting as it does with the angels' message of "Peace, good will toward men" (Luke 2:14) to the shepherds the night of Jesus' birth, helped to create the theme of the liturgy for Holy Innocents' Day (28 December), also called "Childermas" in the medieval Church. This liturgy includes the typological readings of commentators such as St. Augustine ("but as for Christ, even a Child, the children dying for him did he Crown" [*Enarr. in Ps.* 47.5]), and it connects the murdered children with the 144,000 redeemed virgins who form the procession of the Lamb in the Revelation of St. John the Divine (Rev. 14:1-4), the "first-fruits unto God and to the Lamb." In medieval tradition these children rather than St. Stephen are often regarded as the first martyrs of the Christian Church (*Glossa Ordinaria* [PL 114.76]). The narrative of the slaughter also produced a number of important Latin hymns, including the "*Salvete, Flores Martyrum*" of Prudentius, in which (in the 19th-cent. translation of John Chandler) the children "in fearless innocence . . . sported gayly with the murderous blade." Another is the "*Hymnum Canentes Martyrium,*" ascribed to the Venerable Bede, which begins, "The hymn for conquering martyrs raise: / The victor innocents we praise" (trans. John Mason Neale).

Although an insular writer in his *Commentary* on the Gospels (PL 68) attempts to demonstrate that the 144,000 spoken of in Rev. 14:1-4 should not be taken to be the literal number of the infants slain in Bethlehem, but rather as a symbolic number of infinitude (he argues that the number Herod slew was more likely closer to 2,000), the number of the virgins in John's vision is occasionally transposed onto readings of the Slaughter of the Innocents in the later Middle Ages (e.g., *Towneley Plays*, 16.487-88). In the ME *Pearl* the little maiden seen by the dreamer is presented at one level as a child who died in her innocence, going to heaven straightaway "Vnblemyst . . . wythouten blot"; she describes herself to the dreamer as one of "þe Lambes vyueȝ in blysse . . . / A hondred & forty thowsande flot / As in þe Apocalyppeȝ hit is sene" (785-87), invoking thus the traditional typological connection (although for whatever reasons she has the number slightly wrong).

Probably the first expansions of the Christmas cycle in Latin liturgical drama after the *Quem Quaeritis in Praesepe* were the *Stella* (Magi [Jan. 6]) and the *Slaughter of the Innocents,* the latter of which in the famous Fleury playbook is designated *Ordo Rachelis* (in reference to Jer. 31:15 and Matt. 2:17-18, both of which, along with Rev. 14:1-4, are lections for the feast). The narrative of the Innocents is included in the Laon *Officium Stellae,* beginning with a procession of children carrying a lamb and singing *Ecce Agnus Dei,* after which they are "slaughtered." Numerous vernacular plays on the subject survive, the most extensive treatment of which is the independent Digby *Killing of the Children* (ed. Furnivall [EETS e.s. 70 (1896)]), where the representation of the massacre is violent. It appears also in the Corpus Christi cycles, in Chester (no. 10) in a much more comic and macabre fashion, and in the York and N-Town cycles in a somewhat restrained version (Towneley, like Digby, is violent). It may also have been a part of St. Anne's Day plays, now lost: the Digby *Killing of the Children* is described in the MS as part of a St. Anne's Day pageant, although a later hand has written at the head of the text "candelmas day & the kylling of the children of Israell" (Candlemas, Feb. 2, celebrates the "Purification of Mary"). That the typological connection between the Slaughter of the Innocents and Pharaoh's slaying of the Hebrew children at the time of Moses is undeveloped in these plays seems all the more curious in the light of York's allusion to the earlier event (67-78) in its Exodus play and the prominence of the Flight into Egypt plays in all the cycles.

In Shakespeare's *Henry 5* King Henry demands the surrender of Harfleur, telling its defenders that if they do not yield, terrors will fall upon their civilian population:

> Your naked infants spitted upon pikes
> Whiles the mad mothers with their howls confused
> Do break the clouds, as did the wives of Jewry
> At Herods bloody-hunting slaughtermen. (3.3.38-41)

In later literature the horror of Herod's massacre is sometimes lost in comic allusion, as when in Mark Twain's *Tom Sawyer* Tom persuades Ben to whitewash the fence for him; then, while his victim "worked and sweated in the sun, the retired artist sat on a barrel in the shade close by, dangled his legs, munched his apple and planned the slaughter of more innocents." Hymns in the 19th cent. for the most part gloss over the gruesome character of the incident: John Keble's "The Innocents' Day" formulates the event (and a curious moral) with remarkable detachment:

> Bethlehem, of cities most forlorn,
> Where in the dust sad mothers mourn,
> Nor see the heavenly glory shed
> On each pale infant's martyred head.
>
> 'Tis ever thus: who Christ would win,
> Must in the school of woe begin. . . .

Anthony Hecht's "It Out-Herod's Herod: I pray you avoid it" is a "Childermas" poem for his children written after the Holocaust, and reflects rather on his own impotence to protect them from another such time of slaughter as that and Herod's tyranny bring to mind. And Margaret Avison, in "Waking and Sleeping: Christmas," reaching for ways to relate the inevitable juxtaposition of New Birth and Death (cf. T. S. Eliot's "Journey of the Magi"), appeals to an older paralleling of biblical stories:

> But hard on the manger vigil
> came Herod's massacre — like
> the Pharaoh's once — and Rachel's
> heart then broke.

See also HEROD THE GREAT; MAGI; RAMAH.
Bibliography. Young, K. *The Drama of the Medieval Church.* 2 vols. (1933; 1962).

SMITE THEM HIP AND THIGH   After the Philistines had killed his wife and father-in-law, Samson "smote them hip and thigh with a great slaughter" (Judg. 15:8). While it has been conjectured that the phrase signifies crippling or disabling rather than mortal wounds, the opposite is as likely the case; in any event, the idiom suggests a complete rout. Van Wyck Brooks commends Dr. Holmes for his leadership in transforming Boston into a center of culture, saying in Arnoldian fashion: "It was he who had smitten the Philistines hip and thigh" (*New England: Indian Summer,* chap. 1).

SMITTEN ROCK   When the Israelites were desperate from thirst during their desert wanderings, the Lord instructed Moses, "Behold, I will stand before thee there on the rock in Horeb; and thou shalt smite the rock, and there shall come water out of it, that the people may drink" (Exod. 17:6). As Num. 20:1-13 tells, the prophet brought forth water again when he struck a second rock, even though this time he had been instructed only to pray for water. Henry Melvill, the "Evangelical Chrysostom" who was the favorite preacher of Ruskin and Browning, gives the standard Victorian interpretation of the first incident when he holds that "this rock in Horeb was typical of Christ," and its yielding water when struck by Moses signifies "that the Mediator must receive the blows of the law, before he could be the source of salvation to a parched and perishing world." Melvill also cites the NT authentication of this type when he explains that "it is to this that St. Paul refers, when he says of the Jews, 'They did all drink of the same spiritual drink; for they drank of that spiritual rock that followed them, and that rock was Christ' (2 Cor. 10:4)."

Melvill's reading of the smitten rock is far from novel. Medieval commentary treats the incident as a prefiguration of the Atonement: The *Glossa Ordinaria* sees the rock as Christ, struck by his tormentors with the rod, obliquely signifying the cross, in *lignum passionis,* releasing the blood and water by which the faithful are redeemed (PL 113.242). The illustrated *Biblia Pauperum* depicts the incident not only with the Crucifixion but also with the creation of Eve from Adam's left *(sinistra)* ribs, and with Christ's being wounded by the spear of Longinus in the right *(dextra)* side, drawing thus on the First Adam/Second Adam typology as well as contrasting the old and new command of Moses and Christ (pl. 21). Similar typology is maintained in later Protestant commentators (e.g., Matthew Poole, *Annotations*, sup. 1 Cor. 10:4).

English literature alludes to the smitten rock in several chief ways, most obviously as the embodiment of God's sustaining the Israelites and all human beings. Less common in literature is St. Paul's use of the image as a type of baptism, although this interpretation occurs in the visual arts. The smitten rock appears most often as (1) a type of Christ himself, who when struck (crucified) produced waters of grace, or as (2) the stony heart of the believer that when struck by God or Christ produces waters of grace. Both these typological readings appear in secularized forms.

The reference to "stony heads suffered by grace," familiar from Dante's "Rime Pietrosa," is subverted in Donne's "Twicknam Garden," when the rejected lover, denied the "Paradise" of love, pleads to be returned to "a stone fountaine weeping out my yeare."

Other 17th-cent. poets make similarly ingenious variations on these typological applications. Reflecting perhaps on the context for Exod. 17 provided by its use as a reading for the third week of Lent, George Herbert presents the smitten rock in "The Sacrifice" as a type of the Savior's sufferings when Christ himself describes how his tormentors "strike my head, the rock from whence all store / Of heav'nly blessing issue evermore" (169-71). The same poet's "Love Unknown," on the other hand, invokes the second major intonation of this typological commonplace when it describes in visionary terms how a servant of his lord seized his heart "and threw it in a font, wherein did fall / A stream of bloud, which issu'd from the side / of a great rock" (12-15). This concatenation of biblical images, types, and emblems turns the waters of the OT scene into the blood of Christ's sacrifice, thus making explicit the prophetic blending of times and beings always potential in a type. In "Easter Day," Richard Crashaw makes the smitten rock a type of Christ's tomb, from which issue forth the risen Christ and immortality for all believers.

Eighteenth- and nineteenth-century hymns and devotional verse make extensive use of the smitten rock to generate a typological universe surrounding the reader. Like Gerard Manley Hopkins's dramatic monologue "Soliloquy of One of the Spies Left in the Wilderness" (ca. 1864), Isaac Watts's "Go, Worship at Immanuel's Feet" (1709), William Williams's "Guide Me, O Thou Great Jehovah!" (1774), and John Newton's "When Israel by Divine Command" (1799) make the general situation rather than the smitten rock itself a type and thus emphasize the contemporary believer's postfiguration of the sinful wandering Israelites. In contrast, John Newton's "That Rock Was Christ" (1772), Augustus Montague Toplady's "Rock of Ages" (1776), and Horatius Bonar's "The Cross" present the smitten rock simply as a type of the Crucifixion.

Another perhaps less strictly orthodox type occurs when poets use Moses' striking of the rock to prefigure Christ's bringing forth tears of repentance from the stony heart of the individual worshiper. This version of the type, which has had a long history in English verse, appears in the "author's emblem of himself," which opens the first part of Henry Vaughan's *Silex Scintillans* (1650), and in bk. 6 of *The Excursion* (1814), where Wordworth has Ellen explain that God "at whose command the parched rock / Was smitten, and poured forth a quenching stream" has softened her "hardness of heart" (6.920-21). This use of the smitten rock, which occurs again in John Ruskin's "The Broken Chain," John Keble's "Sixth Sunday after Trinity" and "Easter Eve," and Tennyson's "Supposed Confessions," provides the climax and poetic center of Tennyson's *In Memoriam* and of Christina Rossetti's "Good Friday."

Purely secular applications of the type — those which require the reader to perceive the existence of the Christian reading of the OT event as a prefiguration of Christ and his dispensation but that themselves have no religious theme — appear occasionally throughout the 19th cent. Robert Calder Campbell's untitled love sonnet, which appeared in the Pre-Raphaelite periodical *The Germ* (1850), tells the speaker's beloved that when she departs he has "no speech — no magic that beguiles / The stream of utterance from the harden'd rock," and Emily Dickinson's "A Wounded Deer — leaps highest" makes the "Smitten Rock that gushes" one of several instances of sharp reaction to a blow. In Matthew Arnold's "The Progress of Poesy,"

> Youth rambles on Life's arid mount,
> And strikes the rock, and finds the vein,
> And brings the water from the fount,
> The fount which shall not flow again.

These examples, like the following from Meredith's *The Egoist*, draw upon commonplace traditions of biblical exegesis primarily for emphasis: "We cannot quite preserve our dignity when we stoop to the work of calling forth tears. Moses had probably to take a nimble jump away from the rock after that venerable Law-giver had knocked the water out of it" (chap. 31). The allusion achieves its full effect only if one recognizes the traditional association of Christ's calling forth tears of repentance from the sinner. A more elaborate allusion to Moses' striking the rock appears in Robert Browning's "One Word More," which emphasizes that just as the ungrateful Jews failed to appreciate Moses' bringing forth water from the rock, so, too, the Victorian audience fails to appreciate what the poet produces on their behalf. A characteristically complex multiple use of the smitten rock appears in A. D. Hope's "An Epistle from Holofernes," when the ghost of Israel's enemy meditates upon myth, truth, and poetry; and a confused reference is found in O. Henry's "The Assesser of Success," where the pun-dit has his Bible wrong: "You are a fool, my friend. The world is a rock to you, no doubt, but you must be an Aaron [*sic*], and smite it with your rod. Then things better than water will gush out of it for you. That is what the world is for."

See also MOSES; PISGAH SIGHT; ROCK.

GEORGE P. LANDOW

SMOKING FLAX   *See* BRUISED (BROKEN) REED.

SNARE   *See* TRAP.

SODOM AND GOMORRAH   Sodom and Gomorrah were among the five "cities of the plain" (Gen. 14:2) in the Jordan River valley which God destroyed for their iniquity when not even ten righteous men could be found there (Gen. 18:16–19:29). Although to this day Sodom and Gomorrah together represent human depravity or divine judgment because they are thus linked in biblical prophetic warnings (Isa. 1:9; 13:19; Jer. 23:14; 49:18; Amos 4:11; Zeph. 2:9; Matt. 10:15; Rom. 9:29; Jude 7), the reputation is chiefly Sodom's: no legend of Gomorrah survives. Among the sins of Sodom are its lack of justice (Isa. 1:9-10; 3:9); backsliding into idolatry (Deut. 32:15-43; Isa. 1:10; expressed through the metaphor of adultery in Jer. 23:14); "pride, fulness of bread, and abundance of idleness," disregard for the poor, and whoring after false gods (Ezek. 16:49-50). In rabbinic literature, Sodom is known for greed and Procrustean inhospitality to strangers (Pirqe R. El. 25).

The homosexuality of the Sodomites (whence "sodomy") is referred to in Gen. 19:5, where the men of Sodom are said to congregate around Lot's house and demand that he send out two male houseguests, "that we may know them" (cf. Judg. 19:22-24). Lot, horrified by their wicked intentions (v. 7), offers his virgin daughters instead but is himself threatened with violence. The visitors, revealing themselves to Lot as angels, strike the men of Sodom with blindness and pronounce God's judgment upon the city.

The sexual sin of Sodom is spoken of in Jub. 16:5-6 and T. Naphtali 3:4-5, as well as in 2 Pet. 2:4, 6-8 and Jude 6-7. Philo condemns the sexual perversity of Sodom (e.g., *Quaestiones et solutiones in Genesim*, 4.37-38).

Sodom's homosexuality and inhospitality to strangers, the sins of Gen. 19:1-11, were seen by commentators to violate the most basic laws of God, nature, and humankind. Indeed, in Sodom, abusing strangers *was* the law (e.g., Seder Nezekin, Sanh. 4.6; St. Jerome, *Commentarium in Osee*, 3.11.8.9 [CCSL 76]; Bede, *Adnotationes in Genesim*, 4.19.4-5 [CCSL 118A]; *Cleanness*, 841-44).

The plain around the five cities was originally so fertile that it was "as the garden of the LORD" (Gen. 13:10); after the destruction it became the Dead Sea (or Salt Sea or Lake Asphaltites), a desolate region where nothing could grow except the apples of Sodom (or Dead

Sea fruit), which turned to ashes when touched. These details, together with the asphalt found floating on the waters and the pillar of salt believed to be Lot's wife, are typical in the Bible, in chronicles, and in descriptions of the Holy Land (e.g., Deut. 29:23; Isa. 1:7, 9; Jer. 49:17-18; 50:39-40; Wisd. of Sol. 10:7; Josephus, *J.W.* 4.8.4; Solinus, *Collectanea rerum memorabilium*, 47; *Mandeville's Travels,* chap. 12; James Ussher, *Annals of the World* [1658], 6; Jean Le Clerc, *Twelve Dissertations,* trans. Brown [1696], 227-29, 238-69; see further *Wisdom of Solomon* [AB 43.215-17]).

Medieval exegesis offers figurative views of Sodom. To Jerome, Sodom meant "a silent beast," or "yellowish, or sterile" (*Liber interpretationis Hebraicorum nominum* [CCSL 72.151]) — silent, explained the *Glossa Ordinaria* on Rev. 11:8, because Sodom has nothing spiritual to preach. Typologically, Sodom, like Babylon, is the earthly city at the Last Judgment (St. Augustine, *De civ. Dei* 16.30).

Renaissance commentators are mainly literal or polemical concerning Sodom and Gomorrah. Often they mention a Hebrew legend which maintained that the punishment of Lot's wife reflected her refusal to give the two angels salt (A. Williams, *The Common Expositor* [1948], 164; see also the 14th-cent. postil on Gen. 19:26 by Nicholas of Lyra in *Biblia Sacra cum Glossis* [1588], 1.73G, and O. Emerson, "A Note on the ME *Cleanness,*" *MLR* 10 [1915], 373-75). Predictably, Protestant polemicists liken the Roman Catholic Church to Sodom and Gomorrah (e.g., Hooker, "A Learned Discourse of Justification," in *Works* [1874], 3.496). Matthew Poole's commentary on Genesis in *Synopsis Criticorum Aliorumque Sacrae Scripturae Interpretum* (1669), 1, a collection of Renaissance opinion, is perhaps the most learned and evenhanded Renaissance treatment of Sodom and Gomorrah written in England, bringing together both literal and figurative interpretations. Post-Renaissance demythologizing led to criticism such as Jean Le Clerc's in *Twelve Dissertations,* which offers a naturalistic explanation of everything in the Sodom story (213-22, 236-69). Modern critics see the Sodom and Gomorrah story as background for the uncomplimentary narrative of the Moabites' and Ammonites' origin (Gen. 19:30-38; see *Genesis* [AB 1.142-46]).

In English literature there are many treatments of the Sodom and Gomorrah story, all of which, until the 20th cent., stay close to traditional lines. In addition, there are numerous allusions, though few in which "Sodom and Gomorrah" is anything more than a byword. The OE *Genesis* (1920-2162, 2399-2599) and the ME *Genesis and Exodus* (837-942, 1050-1122) both include Abraham's wars in defense of Sodom (Gen. 14) and the destruction; *Genesis and Exodus* also describes the Dead Sea region (1123-32). *Cursor Mundi* includes, in addition, a moralization (2491-2547, 2765-2912). A similar but much briefer account is in *A Middle English Metrical*

Paraphrase of the Old Testament (571-616; ed. H. Kalén, Göteborgs Högskolas Årsskrift, 28.5 [1922]). Langland's use of Sodom and Gomorrah as an example of luxury in Pacience's speech on charity and patient poverty (*Piers Plowman*, B.14.73-81; C.16.231-33) follows Ezek. 16:49; Chaucer's *The Parson's Tale*, 10.839, follows Gen. 19:5 and Jude 7. In *Cleanness* the literal and figurative sterility of Sodom's homosexuality and faithlessness is a chief instance of the uncleanness against which the poet preaches and is symbolized by the apples of Sodom (671-1048).

The broadside ballad "Of the Horrible and Woefull Destruction of Sodom and Gomorrah" (1570) describes the suffering of the Sodomites in the rain of fire and brimstone, then urges Englishmen to amend their lives lest they should suffer likewise. In George Lesley's verse drama "Fire and Brimstone" (*Divine Dialogues* [1678]), the Sodomites decide to beg the angels for mercy, but too late; they lament their sins as their city burns, and the play closes with a choral exhortation to avoid lust and gluttony. The hero of Marlowe's *Tamburlaine* climaxes his career as scourge of God by capturing Babylon and ordering the drowning of all its inhabitants in Lake Asphaltites (*2 Tamburlaine*, 5.1). In the peroration of "Reason of Church Government," Milton likens "prelaty" to Sodom and Gomorrah (*Complete Poems and Major Prose* [1957], 689). Milton assigns Belial, angel of lust and violence, to Sodom (*Paradise Lost*, 1.503-05) and has the devils, metamorphosed into snakes, eat of the apples of Sodom as punishment for tempting Adam and Eve (10.560-77). Following Milton, Blake makes Belial chief of Sodom and Gomorrah, one of the twelve synagogues of Satan, in *Milton*, 37.30-32. In *Jerusalem*, 67.40, Sodom and Gomorrah are among the many loci in the vessels of the circulatory system joined to the heart of the Polypus of Generation, the worldly society which is "the antithesis of the Brotherhood of Man" (S. F. Damon, *Blake Dictionary*, 33). For Byron's Childe Harold the thought that

> . . . life will suit
> Itself to Sorrow's most detested fruit,
> Like to the apples on the Dead Sea's shore,
> All ashes to the taste

arises from contemplating the return of spring at the Waterloo battlefield and the loss there of his friend Howard (*Childe Harold's Pilgrimage*, 3.34.4-7).

Melville alludes several times to Sodom and Gomorrah as a symbol of sexual depravity or of catastrophe (*White Jacket*, chap. 89; *Israel Potter*, chap. 19; *Redburn*, chap. 31); but in *Moby-Dick* the allusions portend the destruction of the *Pequod* and Ishmael's Lot-like escape (chaps. 2, 9, 117). Browning's vision of Christ "Like the smoke / Pillared o'er Sodom, when day broke," in *Easter-Day* (640-41) foreshadows his being sentenced to the world for eternity because all his life he chose the world. For Lord Lufton in Trollope's *Framley Parsonage*, mar-

riage to the girl Lucy will be like tasting the Dead Sea fruit because "the sweetest morsel of love's feast has been eaten . . . when the ceremony at the altar has been performed, and legal possession has been given" (chap. 48). In Twain's *Mysterious Stranger* (chap. 8), Satan's "history of the progress of the human race" includes Sodom and Gomorrah in its relentless series of murders and wars. The focus here is not the destruction of Sodom and Gomorrah but the "attempt to find two or three respectable persons there." In Lawrence's story "Things," Valerie and Erasmus Melville regard America as "the Sodom and Gomorrah of industrial materialism," but the image reflects back on them, since their European life is a Sodom and Gomorrah of cultural materialism.

Departing from tradition, Maria Ley-Piscator's novel *Lot's Wife* (1956) relates a fictional life of Lot and his wife, Ti-sar-ilani, which explains why she looks back at Sodom as it burns: in order to define herself existentially and participate in divine justice. Completely drained of biblical significance, Isaac Bashevis Singer's short story "The Interview" (*New Yorker*, 16 May 1983, 41-48) uses Sodom and Gomorrah as an image for the personal sexual unhappiness of one woman and for the general misery of Jewish history.

See also LOT; LOT'S WIFE.

Bibliography. Kay, R. "The Image of Sodom: Old Testament" and "The Image of Sodom: New Testament." In *Dante's Swift and Strong: Essays on Inferno XV* (1978), 209-89.
M. W. TWOMEY

SOLOMON Solomon was the third king of Israel (ca. 961-922 B.C.) and the second son of David (2 Sam. 12:18, 24). His kingdom, excluding Philistia and Phoenicia, stretched from Kadesh in the north to Eziongeber in the south (1 Kings 4:21). Largely free from external threat, Solomon built extensively in Jerusalem, his best-known structure being the Temple. He strategically established fortified cities throughout the empire and negotiated trade agreements with other nations. On the Gulf of Aqabah and from Phoenicia, he developed maritime trade (9:26-28; 10:11, 22-29). But his legendary, wealthy reign (v. 23) bled the nation's resources, requiring heavy taxation and forced corvées (4:7; 5:13-14; 9:21).

Unlike Chronicles, which omits a negative assessment, 1 Kings traces Solomon's decline largely to religious syncretism provoked by marriage to "many foreign women" (11:1-3, RSV). For these he built cultic sites and permitted worship of alien deities (vv. 7-8). The nation's strong unity faded under this influence (cf. Sir. 47:13-21).

Solomon's celebrated wisdom reportedly "excelled the wisdom" of "the east country, and all the wisdom of Egypt" (4:20-34). Notably illustrated in the episode with the two harlots (3:16-28) and the visit of the Queen of Sheba (10:1-29), this wisdom expressed itself in riddles and proverbs, as well as in extraordinary judicial acumen. Solomon's sagacity was sufficiently renowned that he was frequently credited with later canonical, apocryphal, and pseudepigraphal literature (e.g., the biblical "wisdom" books as well as Wisdom of Solomon, Psalms of Solomon, Odes of Solomon, and Testament of Solomon). In the NT, Jesus mentions both Solomon's splendor (Matt. 6:29; Luke 12:27) and his wisdom (Matt. 12:42; Luke 11:31).

Jewish tradition assigns Solomon extensive knowledge of many subjects (Wisd. of Sol. 7:17-22; Giṭ. 59a). He is said to have authored works on medicine, mineralogy, and magic. Legends of Solomon's liaison with the Queen of Sheba (Balkis), also known in Arabic and Ethiopian versions, tell how Solomon married Balkis and gained control of Sheba. Arabic lore makes Solomon a devout follower of Allah and prototype of Mohammed. With the winds and demons at his disposal (Koran, *Sura* 21:82), he visits the Valley of the Ants (*Sura* 27:16-17) and the Queen of Sheba (vv. 20-45). One legend, resembling the *Arabian Nights,* has the jinn weave an enormous carpet on which Solomon goes on a hajj to Mecca, where he prophesies the birth of Mohammed.

In both Judaism and Christianity, the association of Solomon with demonology and magic flourished during late antiquity. According to the Testament of Solomon, Solomon received a magic ring seal from the archangel Michael with which to subjugate the demons and set them to building (1.5-7); Josephus connects magical seal rings with Solomon in an account of exorcism (*Ant.* 8.42-49). Scores of Jewish and Christian amulets and talismans invoke his power over demons. One amulet declares, "Seal of Solomon, drive away all evil from him who wears [this]" (E. R. Goodenough, *Jewish Symbols* [1953-68], 2.238). This notion of Solomon's power gives rise to the legend of his conquest of Asmodeus, the prince of demons, and his acquisition of the stonecutting *shamir* (Giṭ. 68a-69b).

Patristic theology, on the other hand, focuses on Solomon's sagacity as a king and judge (cf. St. Ambrose, *De fide,* bk. 1, prol.) and often portrays him as a type of Christ (cf. Ambrose, *De interpellatione Iob et David,* 4.4.15). Debate among the Fathers concerning whether Solomon repented his fall into luxury constitutes a tacit criticism of his wisdom, as does the medieval tale of Solomon's besting by Marcolphus the dullard and Morolf the dwarf.

While interest in Solomon as magician is strong in the Middle Ages — many books of magic, including the *Clavicula Salomonis,* are ascribed to him — he is, above all else, seen as a great moral teacher and leader. *The Ancrene Riwle* invokes him as an author of wise sayings (Camden Society [1883], 64) who judges rightly (90). In Dante's *Paradiso,* the voice of St. Thomas Aquinas introduces Solomon as the brightest of the twelve lights of philosophy (10.109-14), then argues for him as the model of kingly prudence (13.94-108). The fate of Solomon is the subject of speculation in *Piers Plowman.* In the "C" text, Conscience uses the case of Solomon to argue that

God's blessings can be withdrawn if the recipient proves unworthy (C.4.326-34) and concludes that Solomon is now in hell (see also B.12.266-74). The presence of Solomon the magician can be detected in Chaucer's *Squire's Tale* (*CT* 5.248-51). The successor of David appears elsewhere in *The Canterbury Tales* as "he that so wel teche kan" (*Summoner's Tale,* 3.2085) and as "the wise man" (*Parson's Tale,* 10.664). He is cited extensively as an authority and fount of trustworthy counsel in *The Tale of Melibee.* For Luther, Solomon is the "Wise Man" (*Works* [1955-57], 45.306), a type of Christ (14.327), and a magus, having "secret knowledge of nature" (52.161).

Solomon appears principally as the great castigator of human folly and ignorance in Renaissance literature. As Rosalie L. Colie points out, satirists such as Brant and Erasmus unleash the wisdom of Ecclesiastes on all fools, themselves included (*Paradoxia Epidemica* [1966], 6-23, 458). If Tottel's *Miscellany* of 1557 takes Solomon for a "sober wit" (Arber ed. [1870], 168), Sir Thomas Browne is less restrained: his *Religio Medici* counsels its reader to follow Solomon's advice (Prov. 6:6) and go to insects for genuine wisdom (1.16). In Butler's *Hudibras,* a lady contrasts contemporary fools with the ancient Solomon (3.195). More directly constructive, Bacon's *New Atlantis* envisions a program of empirical sciences in the "House of Solomon." Bunyan works out a typology in *Solomon's Temple Spiritualized.* For the major neoclassical satirists from Dryden to Johnson, Horace or Juvenal rather than Solomon provides the exemplary analogue of the combatant against vanity, unreason, and the realm of dunces.

The Solomon of the 19th cent. comes in many guises. Walter Scott's *Anne of Geierstein* recalls the man of wit so unlike the fool (chap. 30); and Dickens refers to "sentiment . . . Solomonic" in *Little Dorrit* (1.13) and in *Dombey and Son* has his Captain Cuttle make a warmhearted philanthropist of Solomon, quick to share a good bottle with the less fortunate (chap. 15). By contrast, the last paragraph of Thackeray's *Vanity Fair* calls up the somber wisdom of Solomon's Ecclesiastes: "Ah! *Vanitas Vanitatum!*" In Browning's "Mr. Sludge, 'The Medium,'" the charlatan caught in a deception turns the moral indignation of his superficial Boston patron back on the accuser, pronouncing as the most hateful form of foolery that of "the social sage, Solomon of saloons / And philosophic diner-out" (773-74). A story of "Wisdom in the abstract facing Folly in the concrete" (chap. 13), Hardy's *Far from the Madding Crowd* alludes to Solomon as misogynist (chap. 22) and womanizer (chap. 7). "The Preacher" is enlisted as an ally of scientific and artistic culture in the "Conclusion" of Arnold's *Literature and Dogma:* the proposition that God "hath set the world" in the "heart" (Eccl. 3:11) advances the argument that the Bible is symbolic rather than dogmatic in design. In *King Solomon's Mines,* a popular romance of fabulous hidden wealth and exotic adventure, H. Rider Haggard exploits another memory of that monarch.

Melville centers his entire work after *Typee* and *Omoo* on Solomon's view of earthly wisdom as folly. "I read Solomon more & more, and every time see deeper & deeper and unspeakable meanings in him," he writes to Hawthorne (Leyda, *The Melville Log* [1951], 1.413). In *Moby-Dick,* the sceptical Ishmael invokes the "unchristian Solomon's wisdom" in confirmation of the nullity he perceives at the center of the entire creation: "the truest of all books is Solomon's, and Ecclesiastes is the fine hammered steel of woe. 'All is vanity.' ALL" (chap. 96). The blank, perfectly balanced stone signed "Solomon the Wise," which encapsulates Melville's theme in *Pierre, or The Ambiguities*, is a text devoid of all light: the reflexive logic of the sceptic's foolish wisdom is self-canceling. Such annihilating doubt is alien to Solomon Swap, Lot Sap Sago, and Jonathan Ploughboy, the shrewd, homely Yankee characters of the early 19th-cent. popular American stage who were derived from Solomon Gundy, the French Cockney of George Colman the Younger's *Who Wants a Guinea?* The stories of "ole King Sollermun" in Twain's *Huckleberry Finn* serve to poke fun at more than just the languor and unprofitableness of royalty. The "learned" Huck recalls that Solomon "had about a million wives," and the wise Jim, who understandably reckons Solomon a fool for having a "harem" of that size, foolishly misconstrues that king's most celebrated act of judicial wisdom (chap. 14).

In Conrad's *Typhoon,* a tale of wise ignorance or ignorant wisdom, the avuncular and enlightened chief engineer, Mr. Solomon Rout, "Old Sol," who rarely sees the light of day, writes entertaining letters filled with sagacious observations comically mistaken for his biblical namesake's. By tale's end, he finds that his obtuse captain, MacWhirr, who writes uninspired letters, is a rather wise and clever man. More recently, the Solomon of Langston Hughes's poem "Brass Spittoons" delights in wine cups, like the reveler of James Ball Naylor's *Ancient Authors:*

> King David and King Solomon
>   Led merry, merry lives,
> With many, many lady friends
>   And many, many wives.

See also FOOL, FOLLY; WISDOM.

Bibliography. Duling, D. C. "Testament of Solomon." In *The Old Testament Pseudepigrapha.* Ed. J. H. Charlesworth (1983), 1.935-87; Huntley, F. L. "King James as Solomon, the Book of Proverbs, and Hall's Characters." In *Essays in Persuasion: On Seventeenth-Century English Literature* (1981), 49-56; Myers, J. M. "Solomon." *IDB* 4.399-408; McCown, C. C. "The Christian Tradition as to the Magical Wisdom of Solomon." *JPOS* 2 (1922), 1-24; Seymour, J. D. *Tales of King Solomon* (1924); Weil, G. *The Bible, the Koran, and the Talmud; or, Biblical Legends of the Mussulmans Compiled from Arabic Sources, and Compared with Jewish Traditions* (1846).   CAMILLE R. LaBOSSIÈRE
                                                                      JERRY A. GLADSON

SON OF GOD   Although the plural form is often used in the OT to refer to angels and to Israel and in the NT with reference to the Church, the term in the singular appears in the OT only in Dan. 3:25 *(bar 'elohim),* where an angelic being seems intended by the original Aramaic. (The capitalization of the term in the KJV owes to the translators' importing into the passage a reference to the pre-incarnate Christ.) In some OT passages Israel is referred to collectively by God as "my son" (e.g., Exod. 4:22; Hos. 11:1) or "my firstborn" (e.g., Jer. 31:9), but this is simply a variation on the plural usage cited above.

Of more significance in interpreting the NT's frequent use of "Son of God" as a title for Jesus is the OT description of King David and his royal successors as God's "son." The key passages seem to be 2 Sam. 7:14; Pss. 2:7; 89:26-27, where many OT scholars find echoes of an ancient coronation ceremony and acclamation formula, the coronation of the king of Judah being described in these passages as a ceremony by which the king becomes God's son by adoption. As God's son, the king has authority, based on his intimacy with God as implied by the term *son.*

The most familiar use of the term "Son of God" is in the NT, where it is a major title for Jesus in the faith of the early Church (e.g., Matt. 16:16; Mark 1:1; John 1:49; Gal. 2:20; cf. "his Son," 1 John 1:3, 7; "his own Son," Rom. 8:3, etc.). Although there is a great deal of debate about the historical background of the title in the Greco-Roman period (see Hengel), in the context of the biblical tradition the term describes Jesus as enjoying a unique relationship with God, as the definite article connotes ("*the* Son of God"; cf., e.g., John 3:16, where the term "only begotten" has the same effect). This relationship bestows upon Jesus the status of final and fully authoritative revealer of God and executor of God's redemptive plan (see 1 Cor. 15:27-28).

Although in John 1:49 and Matt. 16:16 the title appears to have messianic connotation, in other NT passages a much deeper meaning seems intended, and certainly in Christian writings of the 2nd cent. and later the title came to designate Jesus' divine nature in the developing Christian doctrine of the two natures of Christ, "Son of Man" designating Christ's human nature.

The title "Son of God" (and variations of it) seems particularly important in the Gospel of Mark, where it introduces the book (1:1) and then is used again when Jesus is addressed by God or other supernatural beings (1:11; 5:7; 9:7; cf. 1:24, 34). Although many who come into contact with Jesus are unable to understand his true significance (e.g., 1:27; 2:7; 4:41), he is acclaimed as "the Son of God" at the Crucifixion by a Gentile soldier (15:39). All this is Mark's way of making the title a designation of Jesus' transcendent significance, which for Mark is most clearly revealed in Christ's atoning death.

In Paul's writings as well, the description of Jesus as God's Son seems to express most fully Jesus' true being (e.g., Gal. 1:16; 4:4; Rom. 1:4, 9; 5:10; 8:32), especially when referring to Jesus' redemptive self-sacrifice.

The term "Son of God" is discussed by patristic and later writers mostly in connection with the divinity of Christ, establishing his unity with God the Father (e.g., St. Ambrose, *De fide;* St. Augustine, *De symbolo ad catechumenos*). Elsewhere Augustine distinguishes between the unique sonship of Christ ("the only begotten Son of God") and the adoptive sonship of believers: "For there is but one Son of God by nature, who in his compassion became Son of Man for our sake, that we, by nature sons of men, might by grace become through him sons of God" (*De civ. Dei* 21.15). These same concerns are central for Calvin, who, in traditional fashion, relates the terms "Son of God" and "Son of Man" to the doctrine of the Incarnation (*Inst.* 2.14.6-7); in his *Harmony of the Gospels* he observes that Mark's emphasis on the Son of God in the first chapter of his Gospel (Mark 1:1, 11) balances and complements the emphasis on Jesus as Son of Man in the other Synoptic accounts.

In theologically self-conscious writing after the Reformation, the interrelationship of the terms "Son of God," "sons of God," "Son of Man," and "sons of men" is often invoked. John Donne explores the paradoxical nature of NT sonship and adoption in "Holy Sonnet 15":

> The Father having begot a Sonne most blest,
> And still begetting, (for he ne'r begonne)
> Hath deign'd to chuse thee by adoption,
> Coheire to his glory, and Sabbaths endlesse rest. . . .
> 'Twas much, that man was made like God before,
> But, that God should be made like man, much more.

For Milton, Jesus is "this man of men, attested Son of God" (*Paradise Regained,* 1.122); i.e., he obtains the title "Son of God" through obedience to his Father:

> . . . men hereafter may discern
> From what consummate virtue I have chose
> This perfect Man, by merit call'd my Son,
> To earn Salvation for the Sons of men. (*PR* 1.164-67)

Satan, in a subtle and disingenuous appeal to Jesus' sonship, tempts him to forfeit it through disobedience: "If thou be the Son of God, Command / That out of these hard stones be made thee bread" (1.342-43). The motivation of Milton's Satan is clearly envy of Jesus, whom he heard declared "the Son of God belov'd" at his baptism (4.513). Seeking to claim this coveted title for himself, he calculatedly mistakes the unique sonship of God's "only begotten," peevishly addressing him as "Son of *David,* Virgin-born" (since "Son of God to me is yet in doubt"):

> Thenceforth I thought thee worth my nearer view
> And narrower Scrutiny, that I might learn
> In what degree or meaning thou art call'd
> The Son of God, which bears no single sense;
> The Son of God I also am, or was,
> And if I was, I am; relation stands;

> All men are Sons of God; yet thee I thought
> In some respect far higher so declar'd. (4.514-21)

This declaration immediately precedes Satan's final temptation of Jesus —to abuse the privileges of sonship by "proving" them to his antagonist's satisfaction: "Cast thyself down; safely if Son of God. . . ."

Apart from religious verse and Christian hymnody (e.g., W. C. Bryant's "Thou Hast Put All Things under His Feet"), use of the term is intermittent after the 17th cent. Matthew Arnold, concerned to separate literature from dogma, psychologizes the term, engaging in his own form of redefinition: "Speaking as the Bible speaks, we say that Jesus is verifiably the Son of God. Speaking [in another manner] and calling God a natural law, we say that of this natural law Jesus is verifiably the offspring or outcome" ("The God of Experience," in *God and the Bible,* 3.8). Elsewhere he says that Jesus is "Christ the Son of God" in the sense that in his "admirable figure of the *two lives* of man, the real life and the seeming life, he connected this profound fact of experience with that attractive poetry of hopes and imaginings which possessed the minds of his countrymen." And in the preface to his *Last Essays on Church and Religion,* he outlines his "theology":

> Eternal life? Yes, the life in the higher and undying self of man. Judgment? Yes, the trying, in conscience, of the claims and instigations of the two lives, and the decision between them. Resurrection? Yet, the rising from bondage and transience with the lower life to victory and permanence with the higher. The kingdom of God? Yes, the reign amongst mankind of the higher life. The Christ the son of God? Yes, the bringer-in and founder of this reign of the higher life, this true kingdom of God.

Arnold's views are consistent with those of the rational and demythologizing school of contemporary continental biblical criticism, concerned to detach the "historical Jesus" from the Son of God of NT faith. Such interests found their popular counterpart in a spate of fictional biographies and "fifth gospels." One of the earliest and most influential of these, Ernest Renan's *Life of Jesus* (1863), concludes with a noteworthy affirmation that typifies the new dechristianized Jesus, whose "parentage" is strictly human: "All centuries shall proclaim that among the sons of men, there was none greater than Jesus."

See also SON OF MAN; SONS OF GOD.

Bibliography. Dickson, D. W. "Milton's 'Son of God': A Study in Imagery and Orthodoxy." *Papers of the Michigan Academy of Sciences, Arts, and Letters* 36 (1950), 275-81; Hengel, M. *The Son of God: The Origins of Christology and the History of Jewish-Hellenistic Religion* (1976); Johnson, S. E. "Son of God." *IDB* 4.408-13; Marshall, I. H. "The Divine Sonship of Jesus." *Int.* 21 (1967), 87-103; *The Origins of Christology* (1976); MacCallum, H. *Milton and the Sons of God: The Divine Image in Milton's Epic Poetry* (1986); Michel, O. "Son of God." *NIDNTT* 3.634-39; Ziolkowski, T. *Fictional Transfigurations of Jesus* (1972).
L. W. HURTADO
DAVID L. JEFFREY

SON OF MAN In the OT the expressions "son(s) of man (men)" mean "human being(s)," and most frequently translate the Hebrew phrases *ben(e) 'adam,* though one also finds the variations *bene 'ish* (Ps. 4:2), *bene ha 'adam* (Ps. 33:13; Eccl. 1:13; 2:3, 8; 3:10, 18, 19; 8:11; 9:3, 12), and the Aramaic equivalents *bene 'enashah* (Dan. 5:21) and *bar 'enosh* (Dan. 7:13). In some cases the plural Semitic phrases are translated "children of men" (11 times in Psalms; Ezek. 31:14; Dan. 2:38). There are other ways of referring to humans individually and corporately in Hebrew, e.g., "the man" (*ha 'adam,* Gen. 2:15 et al.), "men" (*'adam,* Ps. 82:7 et al.; *'anashim,* 2 Sam. 7:14), "man" (*'enosh,* Ps. 8:4 et al.), "a man" (*'ish,* Jer. 49:18 et al.), and it appears that "son(s) of man (men)" and "children of men" have a particular rhetorical quality, for the terms in both singular and plural forms appear only in poetical passages and/or passages of a solemn or ceremonial nature. Thus, the terms appear in Psalms often, and in prophetical oracles (Num. 23:19; 2 Sam. 7:14; Isa. 51:12; 52:14; 56:2; Jer. 32:19; 49:18, 33; 50:40; 51:43; Ezek. 31:14; Dan. 2:38; 5:21; Joel 1:12; Mic. 5:7), in Job 25:6, and in the visions of Dan. 7:13; 10:16.

In addition, the phrase "sons of men" appears nine times in Ecclesiastes (e.g., 1:13; 2:3), a book with many poetic passages and other indications of rhetorical concern. Some 92 times in Ezekiel the phrase "son of man" appears as the title by which God addresses the prophet (e.g., 2:1, 3, 6, 8), and there is an intimation of this usage in Dan. 8:17.

In several cases explicitly, and in the other cases implicitly, the terms connote human beings as mere mortals with creaturely limitations and faults. Thus, God is contrasted with "a son of man" (Num. 23:19), and humans are seen as puny in comparison with the larger cosmos (Job 25:6; Ps. 8:4; cf. Pss. 144:3; 146:3; Isa. 51:12). When God addresses Ezekiel as "son of man," this ceremoniously reflects the essence of the prophetic calling, that a mere man is called to speak for God. All these occurrences reflect the OT picture of humans as both weak and thoroughly creaturely, yet also as given dignity, nobility, and authority (esp. Ps. 8; cf. Gen. 1:27-28). This dialectical view of the human race is one of the major contributions of the Bible to thought on human self-understanding.

The vision figure in Dan. 7:13 ("one like the Son of man") became highly influential in subsequent Jewish and Christian thought, and this is one of the most frequently studied passages in biblical scholarship to this day. In the context of the vision and the interpretation (Dan. 7:15-28), the figure is contrasted with the four beasts (Dan. 7:1-12) who represent pagan kingdoms, and it seems to symbolize "the saints of the Most High" (7:27). The Aramaic paraphrases of the OT (Targums) used in ancient Jewish circles in the early centuries of the Christian era interpret this figure as the Messiah, and the same interpretation is reflected in the Talmud (G. Vermes,

Jesus the Jew [1973], 170-72), though the term "son of man" is never used in these writings as a title for the Messiah. Other terms are used by ancient Jews for this representation of the Messiah: "cloud man," "son of the cloud." (The Aramaic of Dan. 7:13 describes the figure as, literally, "one like a son of man," i.e., "one in human appearance.") The KJV translation, by capitalizing "son" and by attaching the definite article to the term, reflects the traditional Christian understanding of the figure as Jesus Christ.

In the NT "the Son of man" appears 80 times in the Gospels on the lips of Jesus as a self-designation, being by far the most frequent title attributed to him in these writings. This has aroused a most intense scholarly investigation and debate as to the meaning and origin of the term (see I. H. Marshall, *Origins of New Testament Christology* [1976], 63-82). The Synoptic Gospel uses of the term can be grouped into three categories: (a) references to Jesus' earthly life and ministry (e.g., Matt. 11:19; 12:32; Mark 2:10; Luke 9:58); (b) references to Jesus' Passion (e.g., Mark 8:31; 9:31; 10:33); and (c) references to Jesus' return in glory (e.g., Matt. 13:26; 14:62; 19:28). The distinguishing feature in all the Gospel uses of the term is that Jesus is called "the Son of man," giving the term a titular appearance and presenting Jesus in a certain representative meaning as "the Man" and / or, in at least the third category of sayings, identifying Jesus with the vision-figure of Dan. 7:13. As the Son of Man Jesus proclaims the kingdom of God in humble circumstances, is rejected and killed, but is vindicated by his resurrection, and is to be the eschatological judge at the last day. In this trajectory of obedience – humiliation – vindication is embodied the experience and piety of a great part of the OT, expressed in the Psalms (e.g., 10, 14, 17) and the servant passages of Isaiah (e.g., 52:13–53:12), to give but a few examples.

In John's Gospel "the Son of man" is thoroughly absorbed into the Johannine emphasis upon Jesus as the one who has come from heaven to bear witness for God and who ascends back, being vindicated against his accusers. Some of the Synoptic pattern of usage remains, but the title has received a distinctively Johannine stamp.

Outside the Gospels "Son of man" is used as a title only once in the NT, in Acts 7:56 by the martyr Stephen, where it seems merely to be an echo of the Synoptic usage. Stephen sees the "Son of man" standing at God's right hand in glory and ready to receive the martyr.

Though "Son of man" is not used as a title for Jesus elsewhere in the NT, there is evidence that Jesus was identified with certain OT passages where the term appears. In Heb. 2:5-9, the writer sees the fulfillment of Ps. 8:4-6 in the humiliation and exaltation of Jesus, meaning that Jesus is seen here as the prototype and promise of human salvation and exaltation precisely because he is a participant in human nature (Heb. 2:10-18). Also noteworthy is the description of Jesus as "the last Adam" and "the second man" (1 Cor. 15:20-28, 42-50), where St. Paul likens Jesus to Adam in his significance for human destiny. Here Jesus is the eschatological bringer of new life in contrast with Adam's failure and its consequence, death. In 1 Cor. 15:27 Paul alludes to Ps. 8:6, hinting that he, like the author of Hebrews, saw Jesus as "the Son of man" to whom all is to be subjected.

In Rev. 1:13 and 14:14 are recorded visions of a figure described after the fashion of the figure in Dan. 7:13, and probably the author indicates by this that the glorified Jesus (who is referred to in 1:12-18, and possibly in 14:14 also) is the glorious figure which was foreseen in the OT vision.

Jewish apocalyptic writings, now widely believed to have been produced in the late 1st cent. A.D., mention an eschatological figure resembling the vision-figure of Dan. 7:13. In 4 Ezra 13, a manlike figure appears who flies with the clouds of heaven and is explained as the Messiah preserved in heaven and to be revealed in the end time. A similar figure occurs in 1 Enoch 37–71, likewise modeled after the vision of Dan. 7. In this case, Enoch, to whom the vision is credited, is told that he is to be this messianic figure. In these writings one finds evidence of the influence of Dan. 7:13 upon ancient Jewish eschatological hopes, but, contrary to much earlier opinion, it is unlikely that these writings provide the origin of the Gospel usage of the term (Vermes, *Jesus*, 172-77).

In the Church Fathers the title "Son of Man" appears, but not frequently. Where it does appear, the term has been totally absorbed into the "two-nature" view of Christ of "orthodox" Christianity which predicated a human nature and a divine nature to Jesus. "Son of Man" is the title which reflects for the Church Fathers the humanity of Jesus, while "Son of God" reflects his divinity (see F. H. Borsch, *Christian and Gnostic Son of Man*, 36-57, for references and discussion). This usage has remained the traditional meaning of "Son of Man" in Christian writers down to modern times.

By contrast, in Christian gnostic writings of the early centuries the title "Son of Man" appears often, but there is still another meaning for the term. In gnostic circles either the high god or one of his chief emanations was often known as "Anthropos" (Man), who begot another who is known as "Son of Anthropos" or "Son of (the) First Man," and is the cosmogonic prototype of the elect. Here one encounters an almost totally different thought-world from that of the Gospel writers, and it seems that the use of the "Son of Man" term in gnostic circles is a radical departure from biblical usage, reflecting the gnostic pre-occupation with protological and cosmogonic questions and the characteristic myths of these groups.

In the best-known poem in English on the subject of the Son of Man, George Herbert develops to full advantage both the English pun on *sun/son* and the theological theme of the identification of God with mortal mankind which Jesus' title expresses:

Let forrain nations of their language boast,
What fine varietie each tongue affords:
I like our language, as our men and coast:
Who cannot dresse it well, want wit, not words.
How neatly doe we give one onely name
To parents issue and the sunnes bright starre!
A sonne is light and fruit; a fruitfull flame
Chasing the fathers dimnesse, carri'd farre
From the first man in th'East, to fresh and new
Western discov'ries of posteritie.
So in one word our Lords humilitie
We turn upon him in a sense most true:
    For what Christ once in humblenesse began,
    We him in glorie call, *The Sonne of Man*.

As might be expected, the term has complex associations (cf. Swedenborg) in the writings of William Blake. While Blake retains the story of the historical Jesus, he turns him into a function or principle rather than the unique Son of Christian tradition. Accordingly, in his *Milton* Jesus is an embodiment of prophetic principle, the culmination of prophetic tradition: "With one accord the Starry Eight became / One Man Jesus the Saviour, wonderful!" (42.10-15; cf. 21:58; 123:28).

In the 19th cent. the term tended for various religious reasons to become the preferred term of reference for Jesus, but gradually implying less of what the OT and NT mean by the title, and more of what Blake intended. Matthew Arnold, e.g., in *Literature and Dogma* and *God and the Bible* finds Jesus to be a "Son of Man" in the paradigmatic historical sense. In *St. Paul and Protestantism* Arnold argues that it is pointless to scrutinize the content in this or related terms; Jesus acquired them from sources such as Daniel and the book of Enoch, and was using them in a charged (but undefined) metaphoric sense, even (or especially) in passages such as Matt. 24:

> The practical lesson to be drawn . . . is, that we should avoid violent revolution in the words and externals of religion. Profound sentiments are connected with them; they are aimed at the highest good, however imperfectly apprehended. Their form often gives them beauty, the associations which cluster around them give them always pathos and solemnity. They are to be used as poetry; while at the same time to purge and raise our view of that ideal at which they are aimed, should be our incessant endeavour. Else the use of them is mere dilettantism. How freely Jesus used them, we see. ("A Psychological Parallel")

Arnold's desire for fundamental redefinition of the content of Christianity was not less ardent than his love of the "pathos and solemnity" he found in biblical language. In a poem first published as "Anti-Desperation" (1867), then two years later reprinted as "The Better Part," he attempts to resolve the debate between implications of a thoroughgoing naturalist and liberal fideist notion of what it might be for Christ to be Son of Man: " 'More strictly then, the inward judge obey! / Was Christ a man like us? Ah! let us try / If we then, too, can be such men as he!' "

While Arnold in this instance speaks for many modern writers, there are dissenting voices. Among the most perspicuous in their use of the term are David Jones *(Anathemata)* and T. S. Eliot, who alludes to Ezek. 2:1 at the beginning of *The Waste Land* to lament the dissipation of the power of tradition through an emptying out of its content:

What are the roots that clutch, what branches grow
Out of this stony rubbish? Son of man,
You cannot say, or guess, for you know only
A heap of broken images. . . . (19-22)

And in her poem "Christmas: Becoming," Margaret Avison writes of the meaning of Christmas as process, unfolding, in which the meaning in image and name might be given back:

A strange flesh
of only son of man
torn and emtombed, but raised
timeless, then
— the eyes turning to look up blur before him —
is still the Christmas presence
flower-frail, approachable:
the timeless Father does not leave
us broken, in our trouble.

See also SECOND ADAM; SON OF GOD.

Bibliography. Borsch, F. H. *The Son of Man in Myth and History* (1967); *The Christian and Gnostic Son of Man* (1970); Casey, M. *Son of Man: The Interpretation and Influence of Daniel 7* (1979); Cullmann, O. *The Christology of the New Testament.* Trans. S. C. Guthrie (1963); Hooker, M. D. *The Son of Man in Mark* (1967); Marshall, I. H. *The Origins of New Testament Christology* (1976); Martin, P. A. "'Son of Man' in the Book of Ezekiel and T. S. Eliot's *The Waste Land.*" *ArQ* 33 (1977), 197-215; Moloney, F. J. *The Johannine Son of Man* (1978); Mowinckel, S. *He That Cometh.* Trans. G. V. Anderson (1956); Todt, H. E. *The Son of Man in the Synoptic Tradition.* Trans. D. M. Barton (1965); Vermes, G. *Jesus the Jew* (1973); "The Use of *Bar Nash/Bar Nashah* in Jewish Aramaic." In *An Aramaic Approach to the Gospels and Acts.* Ed. M. Black (1967), 310-30.

LARRY W. HURTADO
DAVID L. JEFFREY

SON OF PERDITION *See* ANTICHRIST.

SONG OF SOLOMON *See* SONG OF SONGS.

SONG OF ASCENTS Psalms 120–134 are pilgrim songs meant to be sung, in a spiritual sense at least, while going up to the Temple to worship. (Male worshipers would climb up fifteen steps to the Court of Men.) Howard Nemerov's "A Song of Degrees" is a confession of "descents," composed of fifteen lines, leading not to worship at the Temple, but to "fiercely exult / in Zion everywhere."

See also EXILE AND PILGRIMAGE; PASSOVER.

SONG OF SONGS The Song of Songs (Song of Solomon, Canticles) is the fifth and final book in the wisdom literature of the OT and appears as the first of the five scrolls in the Hebrew Bible, where it is entitled *Shir ha-Shirim,* "the greatest of songs." A series or collection of richly detailed love songs involving at least one male and one female voice, it has consistently inspired controversy over its form and meaning. Much of the text consists of descriptions of physical beauty, but occasionally a narrative element is obviously present (3:1-4; 5:2-8). The book has been traditionally ascribed to Solomon in both Jewish and Christian tradition, and some recent scholarship has supported the view that it originated in that king's time, perhaps from within his court. Others have suggested a composition or redaction as late as the post-exilic period. The entire work is in verse, with much emblematic parallelism ("As the lily among thorns, so is my love among the daughters" [2:2]). Canticles uses many words found nowhere else in the OT and is "a curious mixture of pastoral, urban and royal allusions" (R. Alter, *The Art of Biblical Poetry* [1985], 186).

Throughout most of the Jewish and Christian traditions, the Song of Songs has been read allegorically, but whether its allegorization preceded or followed its entry into the canon is disputed. Early Jewish readings saw Canticles as a depiction of God's love for Israel, a reading not reflected in the LXX. Some challenges to the book's canonicity arose at the Council of Jamnia (ca. A.D. 90), to which R. Aqiba (Akiva) responded by describing it as "the Holy of Holies." His injunction against singing the Canticles in banquet houses suggests that there were tendencies to reduce it to secular song (Sanh. 12.10). Allegorical reading of the Song of Songs was supported by similar marital imagery in Hos. 2 and the comparison of Israel to a lily, dove, and bride in 4 Esdr. 5:24, 26; 7:26. This approach continues in the Talmud and Midr. Rabbah; in the Targum it is further developed as a historical narrative of Israel from the Exodus to the advent of the Messiah, with an emphasis on the oral Torah as the discourse between God and Israel. Medieval and Renaissance Jewish exegesis generally followed this line, except for such commentators as Moses Ibn Tibbon, for whom Canticles represented a dialogue between the active and passive intellects *(Comm. on the Song of Songs).* By the 8th cent. the Song was being read as part of the Passover liturgy.

Early and medieval Christian readings of Canticles follow three main lines: the lover is consistently interpreted as God or Christ, and the beloved is seen either as the Church, the individual soul, or the Virgin Mary. These readings were not mutually exclusive and frequently overlap in a particular commentary. St. Hippolytus of Rome (fl. A.D. 200) provides the earliest surviving Christian exegesis *(Fragmenta in Canticum Canticorum);* it influenced Origen's *Commentary,* an ecclesiological reading translated by Rufinus and propagated by St. Jerome and St. Augustine. Origen's work, along with St. Gregory of Nyssa's *Comm. in Canticum Canticorum,* which was incorporated into the *Glossa Ordinaria,* were the most influential early commentaries. Christian exegesis of Canticles found its fullest and most influential expression, however, in St. Bernard of Clairvaux's 86 *Sermones in Canticum,* where he equated the beloved with the individual soul seeking God and used the language and imagery of the Song to speak of the heart of the mystical life. The frequency with which commentaries on Canticles appear in monastic manuscript collections attests to its popularity. Many commentators, however, caution that the Song of Songs is the "bread" referred to in 1 Cor. 3:1-2, fit only for those mature in the faith (*Sermones in Canticum,* 1.1).

In spite of his important place in the development of the cult of the Virgin, Bernard's work made no use of the Marian interpretation of Canticles. This reading began in the linking of the verses *"veni de Libano sponsa"* (4:8) and *"surge amica mea speciosa mea et veni"* (2:13) with Christ's calling forth Mary from the grave in the Assumption, a connection made as early as the 4th cent. by St. Ambrose (*Comm. in Canticum Canticorum*) but not fully developed or widespread until Rupert of Deutz's *In Cantica Canticorum* (ca. 1120).

Bernard's sermons influenced meditative lyrics such as "In a Valey of þys Restless Mynde" (ed. Furnivall, *Political, Religious, and Love Poems* [1866]), which focus on Christ's Passion and the soul's painful yearning for unity with Christ. In that poem *"Quia amore langueo"* (Cant. 2:5; 5:8) recurs as a refrain. A similar allusion is found in the poetry and meditative prose of Richard Rolle and his followers (ca. 1350), and in some instances this searching desire for Christ is associated with Mary Magdalene's visit to the empty tomb (*"Dulcis Jesu Memoria,"* in A. Wilmart, ed., *Le "Jubilus" Dit de Saint Bernard* [1944]). Readings of the Song involving Mary Magdalene go back to at least St. Gregory the Great; Song of Sol. 3:1-4 (*"quaesivi quem diligit anima mea"*) was the lesson for the Mass on St. Mary Magdalene's Day. The Digby *Mary Magdalen* uses the setting of a garden for Mary's conversion to recall the allegorical rendering of the Song (D. Fowler, *The Bible in Middle English Literature* [1984], 109).

Of the three allegorical readings, the Marian had the greatest influence on medieval literature. Phrases from Canticles appear in the liturgy for the Assumption of Mary (Epistle in the *Sarum Missal); from* these, lyric poems such as *"Surge Mea Sponsa"* (C. Brown, *Religious Lyrics of the XIVth Century,* no. 37), "Annot and John," and "Nou shrinkeþ rose ant lylie-flour" (K. Böddeker, ed., *Altenglische Dichtungen des MS. Harl. 2253*) developed. Prominent in many such lyrics was the threefold injunction of Christ to Mary: *"Veni."* On a few occasions the language of Canticles was extended to describe other worthy women. Near the end of Dante's *Purgatorio* (30.11) the prophets call forth Beatrice with the words *"Veni, sponsa, de Libano"* (Cant. 4:8), repeated three times; a comparison to the Virgin (or a partaking in her perfect nature) at the Assumption is evidently suggested. The narrator in Chaucer's *Book of the Duchess* may be making a similar, but less obvious, analogy when he describes Blanche with such phrases as "hyr throte . . . semed a round tour of yvorye" (945-46). The goliardic poems of *Carmina Burana* (such as *"Si Linguis Angelicis"*) parody Canticles and the Marian lyrics based upon it. Similarly, in the English poem "The Clerk and the Husbandman" (Böddeker, *Altenglische Dichtungen*) the line *"Quia amore langueo"* (Cant. 5:8) is used to describe the clerk's love for a woman (cf. "Blow, northerne wynd" and "Wiþ longyng y am lad," also in Böddeker, *Altenglische Dichtungen*). Whether this use of divine imagery in secular lyrics involves an idealization of *cupiditas* remains in dispute. Some Provençal poetry and such 11th-cent. "Cambridge Songs" as *"Iam, Dulcis Amica, Venito"* and *"Levis Exsurgit Zephirus"* (F. Raby, ed., *Oxford Book of Medieval Latin Verse* [1959], nos. 122 and 123) are difficult to classify as secular, divine, or purposely enigmatic.

In Chaucer's *The Merchant's Tale* and *The Miller's Tale* two lecherous males, Januarie and Absolon, misuse the "olde lewed wordes" (*Merchant's Tale,* 4.2149) of the Song of Songs by applying it to disreputable women. Januarie addresses May with the verses associated with Mary's Assumption: "Rys up, my wyf, my love, my lady free! / The turtles voys is herd, my dowve sweete; / The wynter is goon with alle his reynes weete" (4.2138-40). Later in the tale it becomes clear that Januarie's garden is not the *"hortus conclusus"* usually associated with Mary's virginity. *The Miller's Tale* depends on phrases which echo Canticles but do not quote directly from it. In both cases biblical parody serves to emphasize the characters' substitution of *cupiditas* for *caritas.*

Although the Reformers rejected the increasingly elaborate fourfold allegorical readings of Song, they generally maintained that its single "literal" sense concerned God's love for his Church or elect and frequently cited the earlier allegorical readings of Origen and Bernard. As G. Scheper has noted, Protestant readings differed in allegorical explication of specific passages rather than in method. Luther read the text as an "encomium of the political order" (*Works,* 15.195) and recalled the Jewish exegetical tradition in equating the bride with the people of Israel. Sebastian Castellio argued that it was nothing more than a secular love song and should be excluded from the canon; the resulting dispute played a part in his break with Calvin, who suggested that it was an epithalamium similar to Ps. 45 (*Opera* [1863-1900], 674-76). Puritans especially tended to read Canticles as a historical or prophetic account of the development of the Church (e.g., John Cotton, *Brief Exposition of the Whole*

Book of Canticles [1642]; Thomas Brightman, *A Comm. on the Whole Book of Canticles, or Song of Solomon* [1614]).

William Baldwin's *The Canticles or Balades of Salomon* (1549) reflects the title given to the Song of Songs in the *Great Bible* ("Ballet of Balettes of Salomon") and was presented in the hope that it would drive "out of office the bawdy balades of lecherous love." It was the first of many English Protestant verse translations and paraphrases of varying fidelity to the original, including those by such notables as Drayton (*The Intercourse betwixt Christ . . . and his best beloved contracted Spouse* [1591]) and Quarles (*Sions Sonets* [1625]). Religious lyric poetry of the 17th cent. drew heavily upon commentaries on the Song of Songs. Lewalski has argued "that *Canticles* provides the framework for Herbert's use and transformation" of secular love poetry; the few direct echoes of Canticles in his work are in those poems where a sense of ecstasy is achieved. Herbert's "Paradise," Marvell's "The Garden," Joseph Beaumont's "The Gardin," and a number of the poems in Vaughan's *Silex Scintillans* echo the Song or make use of its imagery, with the result that the poet's spiritual growth is set in the context of the complex associations of the garden of Canticles and other biblical gardens (see Lewalski, *Protestant Poetics*, 323; Stewart, *The Enclosed Garden*). In the final two books of Quarles's *Emblems* nearly half the epigraphs are drawn from the Song of Songs, and although Traherne's "Thanksgivings for the Body" makes pervasive use of the Psalms, he ends with passages from the Song (4:9-11; 6:12-13; 8:1, 2). Edward Taylor uses Canticles extensively in his *Meditations* (2.115-53 are based on 5:10–7:6 consecutively), not by imitation or paraphrasing, but by meditating upon individual verses, frequently lamenting the poet's unworthiness to be the bride of Christ. Only in a few poems written after the *Meditations* does Taylor have the confidence to identify himself with the bride and use her language. The Marian reading continued its influence in the works of Crashaw ("On the Assumption"), and in Thomas Robinson's *Life and Death of Mary Magdalene* (ca. 1620, unpubl. until EETS e.s. 78 [1899]) the poetry of Canticles is used to describe Christ (935-50).

Spenser's verse translation of Canticles, referred to in Ponsonbie's preface to the *Complaints,* is lost, but the influence of the Song can be seen in the descriptions of a number of women in his poetry. Israel Baroway argues that "Epithalamium," 167-77 (which concludes "Her snowie necke lyke to a marble towre"), is dependent on the blazon of Canticles but, more importantly, in its comparison of body parts to things which they in no way resemble (cf. *Amoretti*, 15, 64, 76, and 77; the descriptions of Belphoebe and Mirabella in *The Faerie Queene*, 2.3.24 and 28; 6.8.42; and *Colin Clouts Come Home Again,* 596-609). All of these involve a nonallegorical use of Canticles to praise real or fictional women. Milton's

Adam uses the language of the song to call upon Eve, another ideal female type: "Awake / My fairest, my espous'd, my latest found" (*PL* 5.17-25; cf. Song of Songs 2:10, 13 and 7:12). Later in the same book Eve echoes the words of the beloved seeking her lover: "I rose as at thy call, but found thee not" (5.175; cf. Cant. 5:6). In *The Doctrine and Discipline of Divorce,* 1.4, Milton quotes, "many waters cannot quench it [love], neither can the floods drown it" (Cant. 8:7), and while attributing it to the "spouse of Christ," he uses the passage in arguing that conjugal love is a good thing (1.4).

In *The Reason of Church Government* Milton recognizes Canticles as a "divine pastoral drama" in form (bk. 2, pref.); increasingly in the later 17th and 18th cents. the dramatic reading increased in popularity as the allegorical came into question. Bossuet suggested that the book depicts the marriage of Solomon with the daughter of Pharaoh and corresponds to the week-long Hebrew wedding celebration (*Libri Salomonis: Canticum Canticorum* [1693]). This reconsideration found its most significant expression in Robert Lowth's lectures at Oxford (1741-51, publ. in Latin in 1753), in which he cautioned against both excessive allegorizing and attempts to make the Song fit classical models (*Lectures on the Sacred Poetry of the Hebrews* [1787], 30 and 31). His work influenced Thomas Percy's 1764 prose translation of Canticles, which attempted to reflect the parallelism of the Hebrew poetry. The German poet Herder celebrated the freeing of the Song from traditional allegorical frameworks (*Lebensbild* [1846], 1.464) and may have been the first to suggest that Canticles was a collection of separate songs celebrating human love, a view which became central in 19th- and 20th-cent. interpretations and is reflected in Sue Bridehead's anger at "such humbug as could attempt to plaster over with ecclesiastical abstractions such ecstatic, natural, human love as lies in that great and passionate song" (Hardy, *Jude the Obscure*). Many of the numerous 18th-cent. poetic renderings of the Song stress its voluptuous nature, and to a certain degree this attention was part of a growing interest in oriental literature. As part of the primitivist and Romantic movements it came to influence Byron's *Hebrew Melodies,* especially the opening poem, "She walks in beauty, like the night." Among theologians, both Catholic and Protestant, the allegorical reading remained firmly entrenched, but this reading played an increasingly small role in literature.

Throughout the 19th cent. the dramatic interpretation of Canticles vied with Herder's view that it was a collection of songs. Various suggestions were made about the number and identity of characters in the drama: generally it is seen as involving two figures (Solomon and a Shulamite maiden) or three (a Shulamite girl faithful to her shepherd lover in spite of the advances of Solomon). Both readings are reflected in the numerous late-19th-cent. dramatic renderings of the Song.

Early in this century T. J. Meek suggested that Canticles is a revised version of a liturgy from the cult of Tammuz-Adonis; this reading seems to be reflected in e. e. cummings's "lean candles hunger" in *Orientale;* other poems in that collection use sensual description which recalls that of Canticles in structure.

Some 20th-cent. works play upon the tension between the older, allegorical readings and contemporary, sexual ones. In Eugene O'Neill's *Desire Under the Elms* (2.1) Ephraim's praise of Abbie with the words from the Song of Songs is just one of a number of misuses of Scripture which underline that character's distortion of Christianity. As a cuckolded elderly lover, Ephraim behaves like Januarie in *The Merchant's Tale* (cf. Wilbur Daniel Steele's story "How Beautiful with Shoes"). The Cistercian novice Adso's invocation of the language of the Song of Songs lovingly to describe a peasant girl in Eco's *The Name of the Rose* owes more to contemporary than medieval readings of the text.

Other 20th-cent. writers have drawn upon Canticles to explore the connection between divine and sexual love. In Morley Callaghan's *Such Is My Beloved* (1934), an idealistic priest attempts to love and care for two prostitutes as an expression of the divine love found in the Song of Songs. In the process he questions whether the local church or the prostitutes are the true bride of Christ. At the end of Rudy Wiebe's *My Lovely Enemy* (1983) James Dyck calls his mother up from the grave with the words traditionally associated with the Assumption of the Virgin Mary: "Rise up, my love, my fair one, and come away," apparently to indicate that love, whether that of his mother, mistress, wife, or Christ, is "stronger than death."

Toni Morrison's *Song of Solomon* (1977) and *Beloved* (1987) both draw on the language and thematic interpretation of the Song of Songs. In the latter novel, which takes Rom. 9:25 (a quotation itself of Hosea) as epigraph, the protagonist, Sethe, and a woman named "Beloved" are escaped slaves after the Civil War whose reveries and haunted dreams are fraught with allusions to Canticles.

See also BRIDE, BRIDEGROOM.

Bibliography. Allingham, A. "The Song of Songs as Literary Influence in Selected Works of the English Renaissance." *DAI* 37 (1977), 5840A; Baroway, I. "The Bible as Poetry in the English Renaissance." *JEGP* 32 (1933), 447-80; "The Imagery of Spenser and the Song of Songs." *JEGP* 33 (1934), 23-45; Clark, R. "Herder, Percy, and the Song of Songs." *PMLA* 61 (1946), 1087-1100; Dronke, P. *Medieval Latin and the Rise of the European Love Lyric* (1968); Fisch, H. *Poetry with a Purpose* (1990), 80-103; Flinker, N. "Biblical Sexuality as Literary Convention: The Song of Songs in E. E. Cummings' 'Orientale'." *PLL* 16 (1980), 184-200; "Canticles and Juxtaposition of Holy and Sexual in Seventeenth-Century England." In D. Hirsch and N. Aschkenasy, *Biblical Patterns in Modern Literature* (1984); Fox, M. *The Song of Songs and Ancient Egyptian Love Poetry* (1985); Gordis, R. *The Song of Songs and Lamentations*; Hays, P. L. "Biblical Perversions in *Desire Under the Elms*." *MD* 11 (1969), 423-28; Kaske, R. E. "The *Canticum Canticorum* in the *Miller's Tale*." *SP* 59 (1962), 479-500; Landy, F. *Paradoxes of Paradise: Identity and Difference in the Song of Songs* (1983); Lewalski, B. *Protestant Poetics and the Seventeenth-Century Religious Lyric* (1979); Matter, E. A. *The Voice of My Beloved: The Song of Songs in Western Medieval Christianity* (1990); Meek, T. J. "Canticles and the Tammuz Cult." *AJSL* 39 (1922), 1-14; Ohly, F. *Hohelied-Studien: Grundzüge einer Geschichte der Hoheliedauslegung des Abendlandes bis um 1200* (1958); Pope, M. *Song of Songs.* AB (1977); Roston, M. *Prophet and Poet: The Bible and the Growth of Romanticism* (1965); Rowe K. E. "Sacred or Profane?: Edward Taylor's Meditations on Canticles." *MP* 72 (1974-75), 123-38; Rowley, H. H. "The Interpretation of the Song of Songs." In *The Servant of the Lord and Other Essays* (1952); Scheper, G. "Reformation Attitudes toward Allegory and the Song of Songs." *PMLA* 89 (1974), 551-62; "The Scriptural Marriage: The Exegetical History and Literary Impact of the Song of Songs in the Middle Ages." *DA* 32 (1972), 3963A; Stewart, S. *The Enclosed Garden: The Tradition and the Image in Seventeenth-Century Poetry* (1966); Wimsatt, J. "Chaucer and the Canticle of Canticles." In *Chaucer the Love Poet.* Eds. J. Mitchell and W. Provost (1972); "St. Bernard, the Canticle of Canticles, and Mystical Poetry." In *An Introduction to the Medieval Mystics of Europe.* Ed. P. Szarmach (1984); Wright, C. S. "The Influence of the Exegetical Tradition of the Song of Songs on the Secular and Religious English Love Lyrics of MS Harley 2253." *DA* 27 (1966), 754A; Wurtele, D. "The Blasphemy of Chaucer's Merchant." *AnM* 21 (1981), 91-110.

JAMES DOELMAN

SONS OF DARKNESS   *See* CHILDREN OF LIGHT.

SONS OF GOD   "Sons of God" (Heb. *bene ha'elohim;* Gk. *huioi theou*) is used in the OT to denote angels (e.g., Gen. 6:2, 4; Job 1:6; 2:1; 38:7), but, in keeping with the biblical picture of God, without implying that they are his offspring. Rather, the term refers to them as God's heavenly courtiers and servants, connoting great intimacy to God's purposes, and thus great honor as well.

From this, probably earlier, use, the term is extended to refer to the covenant nation, Israel (e.g., Isa. 4:3-6; Hos. 1:10; Wisd. of Sol. 18:13), as enjoying a special relationship with God. In other places, Israel collectively is called "my son, even my firstborn" by God (Exod. 4:22; Jer. 31:9, 20; Hos. 11:1; Ecclus. 36:12), with the same connotation. In the NT, the Church is incorporated into this honor by means of Jesus Christ (e.g., John 1:12; Gal. 4:5-6), and the future hope of the elect is their open vindication, expressed as "the manifestation of the sons of God" (Rom. 8:19; cf. 8:14). In all these cases where the human elect (Israel or the Church) are so described, the ancient significance of "son" as connoting intimate, household relationship and full rights of inheritance is to be kept in view. At the same time, the fact that God is totally separated from the gods of other nations, who are usually a personification of the forces of nature, especially procreative forces, means that the designation of humans as "sons of God" refers to them as "adopted" by God, by means of his gracious covenant election.

Interpretation of the "sons of God" referred to in Gen. 6:1 as marrying the "daughters of men" was not uniform in the patristic period. Many writers thought them to be angels, while others, like St. Jerome (*Ep.* 10), regarded them as giants. St. Augustine also rejects the notion that these beings could have been angels, doubting that "God's holy angels at that time could have so fallen" as to pursue sexual intercourse with humans. He considers the possibility that the reference might be to demonic spirits, *incubi,* sylvans, fauns, or "Duses," concluding at last (with an appeal to Gen. 6:4b) that they were probably men from the lineage of Seth. Their marriage to the "daughters of men" (understood as the lineage of Cain) is seen as a figure for the admixtured presence of the "two cities" in the world (*De civ. Dei* 15.22). Augustine treats NT passages concerning the "sons of God" (e.g., John 1:12; Rom. 8:14, 19) in a straightforward way to express the doctrine of the believer's adoption in Christ (21.5). This is the sense generally employed also by Aquinas, Calvin, and the English Reformers.

In *Paradise Lost,* Milton alludes to Gen. 6:2-4 in describing the glories of unfallen Eve:

> O innocence
> Deserving Paradise! if ever, then,
> Then had the Sons of God excuse to have been
> Enamour'd at that sight; but in those hearts
> Love unlibidinous reign'd. (5.445-49)

Later in the epic the sons of Seth, at first deservedly called "the sons of God," fall from grace and are lured from their mountain homes down onto the plains to marry and beget a giant race on the lascivious daughters of Cain — "a Bevy of fair Women," Milton calls them, "Bred only and completed to the taste / Of lustful appetence, to sing, to dance / To dress, and troll the Tongue, and roll the Eye" (11.582, 618-20; cf. *Paradise Regained*, 4.197-200). In Melville's *Moby-Dick,* Ishmael imagines Queequeg to be such a man as might spring from a union of this sort (chap. 50). By contrast, in D. H. Lawrence's *Women in Love,* the first blush of sexual attraction is described with an allusion to "the old magic of the Book of Genesis, where the sons of God saw the daughters of men, that they were fair. And he was one of these, one of these strange creatures from the beyond, looking down at her" (chap. 2).

The suggestion of lower and higher orders of being in the phrase "sons of God, daughters of men" prompted a memorable witticism in Samuel Johnson's preface to his *Dictionary of the English Language:* "I am not yet so lost in lexicography, as to forget that words are the daughters of the earth, and that things are the sons of heaven." In Tennyson's "Aylmer's Field," the poet describes a baronet bristling with horror because "he had heard his priest / Preach an inverted scripture, sons of men / Daughters of God."

William Cowper recalls another text, Job 38:7, in celebrating Creation,

> when ev'ry star in haste
> To gratulate the new-created earth,
> Sent forth a voice, and all the sons of God
> Shouted for joy

— by which he clearly understands the voices of angels (*The Task*, 5.819-22). Romantic writers adopted and adapted the term to refer to the angelic or godlike character of humankind. In *The Spirit of Modern Philosophy*, however, Josiah Royce recollects the traditional NT sense of "adopted sons": "We are thus not only the sons of God; so far as we are wise our lives are hid in God, we are in Him, of Him" (1.7).

See also ANGEL; GIANTS IN THE EARTH; SONS OF GOD.

Bibliography. Johnson, S. E. "Son of God." *IDB* 4.408-13; MacCallum, H. *Milton and the Sons of God* (1986); Michel, O. "Son." *NIDNTT.* Ed. C. Brown (1975-78), 4.634-39.

LARRY W. HURTADO
DAVID L. JEFFREY

SONS OF LIGHT   *See* CHILDREN OF LIGHT.

SONS OF THUNDER   In Mark's account of the renaming of Peter, Jesus is also said to rename James and John, the sons of Zebedee: "he surnamed them Boanerges, which is, The sons of thunder" (Mark 3:17). The Greek form "Boanerges" is a transliteration of the Aram. or Heb. *bene regesh,* and the name may allude to Greek mythology, suggesting that James and John are like sons of Zeus. St. Ambrose (*De Spiritu Sancto*, 2.6.55) relates James and John as "brothers of the Lord" to the "thundering" voice of God out of heaven during one of Jesus' discourses, in response to his prayer, "Father, glorify thy name" (John 12:28-30). St. Jerome calls the proclamation of John ("the beloved disciple") "the blast of that gospel trumpet, that son of thunder" (*Ep.* 96.1). Cotton Mather, in his *Magnalia Christi Americana,* relates the preaching of John Eliot against "Carnality" and "Indulgence in sensual Delights" to that of his biblical namesake: he was, Mather says, "a right Boanerges . . . he spoke as many *Thunderbolts* as *Words.*" Tennyson characterizes a rabid anti-Catholic preacher as "Our Boanerges with his threats of doom / And loud-lunged Antibabylonianism" ("Sea Dreams"), instancing thus a common 19th-cent. association with a certain type of pulpit-pounding. In a milder vein, David Jones reminds the reader of his *Anathemata* that the apostle James, with his emphasis (in his Epistle) on the practical virtues of Christian life, was "the other Son of Thunder" (1.53).

See also JOHN THE BELOVED DISCIPLE.

SOUNDING BRASS   In the best-known biblical essay on love, St. Paul commences by saying, "Though I speak with the tongues of men and of angels, and have not charity, I am become as sounding brass or a tinkling cymbal" (1 Cor. 13:1). St. Augustine, who knew better than most the rhetorician's temptations, comments on the passage: "He possesses all things to no useful purpose who does not have the one means by which he can use all things well. So then let us embrace charity. . . . Let not those seduce us who understand the Scriptures in a carnal manner" (*Sermo*, 88.21; cf. *Sermo*, 90.6; *Sermo*, 142.8-9).

In Bunyan's *Pilgrim's Progress* Christian expresses his wariness of Talkative's polished discourse: "Paul calleth some men, yea, and those great Talkers too, sounding Brass and tinckling Cymbals." Hazlitt, in "On Familiar Style," observes that it is the vulgar reader who most admires florid writing: "Keep to your sounding generalities, your tinkling phrases, and all will be well." In Thackeray's *Vanity Fair*, when Becky Sharp has attended the "private and select parties of Lord Steyne," Thackeray inquires sarcastically, "Ah, ladies! — ask the Reverend Mr. Thurifer if Belgravia is not a sounding brass, and Tyburnia a tinkling cymbal. These are vanities" (chap. 51). Like Thackeray, Robert Louis Stevenson applies the phrase not to rhetoric but to idle chitchat when, in *Virginibus Puerisque*, he avers that "it is more important that a person should be a good gossip, and talk pleasantly and smartly of common friends and the thousand and one nothings of the day and hour, than that she should speak with the tongues of men and angels" (chap. 1). Stevenson's ironic reversal of the passage, like Thackeray's application of it, is social criticism deriving from Paul's general emphasis, the emptiness of both conversation and society where selfless love, or charity, is missing.

See also CHARITY, CUPIDITY; GLASS, MIRROR.

SOUR GRAPES   Dependence upon God's promise to extend his covenant "from generation to generation" (*dor le dor*) seemed to produce in some periods of Israel's history a deterministic complacency about personal responsibility. In Jeremiah (31:29-30) and Ezekiel (18:2-3) this is strongly admonished: "In those days they shall say no more, The fathers have eaten a sour grape, and the children's teeth are set on edge. But every one shall die for his own iniquity: every man that eateth the sour grape, his [own] teeth shall be set on edge."

See also SINS OF THE FATHERS.

SOW THE WIND   God explains to Hosea the coming judgment upon Israel as consistent with the nature of Israel's offense: "For they have sown the wind, and they shall reap the whirlwind" (Hos. 8:7). The force of the image is not simply to say that one "reaps what one sows," but that the sinful seeding will yield a monstrous crop. In Puritan literature this verse is inevitably connected with Num. 32:23, "Be sure your sin will find you out" (cf. John

Owen, *Of the Mortification of Sin in Believers* [1656]), and the idea that the sins of one generation are visited upon another (see Calvin, *Inst.* 2.8.19-21). Hawthorne is reflecting this tradition when, in *The Scarlet Letter,* he says that Hester can see her own "wild, desperate, defiant mood" in her illegitimate daughter Pearl. The "very colored-shapes of gloom . . . were now illuminated by the morning radiance of a young child's disposition, but later in the day of earthly existence might be prolific of the storm and the whirlwind." Byron speaks in *Childe Harold* of "the fatal spell": "and still it draws us on, / 'Reaping the whirlwind' from 'the oft-sown winds' " (4.1104-05); in his *Don Juan,* where the allusion has a more trenchant pertinence, the quotation is parodic: speaking of the people he would "emancipate," the narrator says, "Whether they may sow scepticism to reap hell, / As is the Christian dogma rather rough, / I do not know" (9.197-99). The phrase is evoked in a context similar to Hawthorne's by Hardy in *Two on a Tower* (chap. 37).

See also SINS OF THE FATHERS.

SOWER, PARABLE OF   Jesus' parable of the sower is found in all three Synoptic Gospels (Matt. 13:3-8; Mark 4:3-8; Luke 8:5-8; cf. also Gos. Thom. 82:3-13), and each time it is followed by an allegorical interpretation. Using the sowing metaphor common in the OT prophets (e.g., Isa. 55:10), Jesus describes in three steps how portions of the seed cast by a sower fall into places (by the wayside, on rocky ground, among the thorns) where they cannot yield grain. A fourth portion, which falls into good soil, is divided into three categories, yielding a hundredfold, sixtyfold, and thirtyfold. (Mark has the reverse order; Luke, only the hundredfold.) The interpretation identifies the seed as the word of the kingdom, which is received in the world in four ways: some do not understand it, some are superficial in accepting it, some are too occupied by worries and material desires to accept it, and some, the fourth group, accept it and bear fruit.

That Jesus himself here uses a figurative device, so making the parable effectively the "literal" meaning of the text, seems to have made further allegorizations unnecessary to most Church Fathers — with the exception of the assignment of meaning to the various numbers given in Matt. 13:8 and 23. Numerous allegorical readings for the hundredfold, sixtyfold, and thirtyfold fruit appeared — e.g., perseverance, perfection of good works, and belief in the Trinity respectively (Bede, *In Matthaei Evangelium Expositio*); or life in quiet peace, victory over minor temptations, and strong resistance against strong temptations (St. Augustine, as cited in St. Thomas Aquinas, *Expositio in Evangelium S. Matthaei*). The most popular interpretations were those of St. Cyprian (who saw the hundredfold fruit realized in the martyrs and the sixtyfold in the virgins [*De habitu virginum,* 21] and St. Jerome (who attributed the hundredfold to virginity, the sixtyfold to widowhood, and the thirtyfold to matrimony [*Adv. Jov.* 1.3]). Jerome's view was adopted by many exegetes throughout the Middle Ages, and Wyclif still adhered to it (*In Omnes Novi Testamenti Libros,* 27d). Augustine, on the other hand, had his doubts (*Of Holy Virginity,* 46), and Martin Luther flatly called it "utterly unchristian" (*Fastenpostille,* 1525, WA 17.2, 154-61).

In his *Harmony of the Gospels,* Calvin warned against any contempt for the less excellent fruit — "since the Lord himself in his mercy praises the inferior ones as being good soil." Latimer used the parable to refute the Anabaptists (who denounced Anglican preaching as fruitless), explaining that "the word of God, though it be most sincerely and purely preached, yet it taketh little fruit; yea, scant the fourth part doth prosper and increase" (Sermon 44; cf. a similar emphasis on the loss of much of the seed in Thomas Shepard, *The Sincere Convert,* 5).

Treatment of the parable in English literature seems to begin with the ME dialogue *Vices and Virtues* (EETS o.s. 89, 69), which uses it to illustrate Mark 10:17-27. Other works, e.g., Dan Michel's *Ayenbite of Inwit* (EETS o.s. 23, 234), follow Jerome's allegorization. In Chaucer's *The Parson's Tale* Chaucer likewise refers to a girl's virginity as to "thilke precious fruyt that the book clepeth the hundred fruyt" (*Canterbury Tales,* 10.869).

A brief reference is found in Shakespeare's *King John* (4.3.141), where the Bastard thinks he loses his way "Among the thorns and dangers of this world." Milton's sonnet "On the Late Massacre in Piemont" commemorates the fate of the slain Waldenses by merging elements of the parable with Tertullian's image of the martyrs' blood being the seed of the Church (*Apology,* 50). He asks God to sow their blood and ashes over the Italy of the Pope (the "triple Tyrant"), "that from these may grow a hunder'd-fold. . . ." Thus he echoes Cyprian's interpretation.

John Bunyan's protagonist Christian, in *The Pilgrim's Progress,* elaborates, during a conversation with his companion Faithful, on the difference between talking and doing. Referring to the parable, he compares the sowing to the hearing of the gospel, which then has to result in fruit, not in talking only.

Jonathan Swift illustrates Matt. 13:22 by showing that a "Man of Business" cannot even be reached by telling him the words of the parable: "his Faculties are all gone off among Clients and Papers, thinking how to defend a bad Cause, or find Flaws in a good one; or, he weareth out the Time in drowsy Nods" (sermon "Upon Sleeping in Church"). There are rather remote echoes of the parable in *Robinson Crusoe* ("The Journal: I Throw Away the Husks of Corn") and in Keats's "Sleep and Poetry" (245, 255).

Washington Irving produced a secularized, Romantic version of the parable's action in his sketch "Roscoe," in which a writer of genius is depicted as one of Nature's chance productions: "She scatters the seeds of genius to the winds, and though some may perish among the stony places of the world, and some be choked by the thorns and brambles of early adversity, yet others will now and then strike root even in the clefts of the rock, struggle bravely up into sunshine, and spread over their sterile birthplace all the beauties of vegetation" (for other poetic twists of the parable cf. Byron, *Don Juan,* 16.6, and Ruskin, *The Bible of Amiens,* 1.30).

For Ruskin the good fruit is like charity which does not fail — after the blade of fresh religious feeling and the ear of well-formed purpose have passed away (*Letters,* 21 June 1861). Anthony Trollope, in *The New Zealander,* a book of social criticism, refers to the parable in suspecting that the seed sown in churches is one of religious hatred (chap. 6). When Donald Farfrae, in Hardy's *The Mayor of Casterbridge* (chap. 24), comments on a new seed drill, he contrasts this innovation with the traditional agricultural methods described in the parable: "No more sowers flinging their seed about broadcast, so that some falls by the wayside and some among thorns, and all that. Each grain will go straight to its intended place, and nowhere else whatever!"

In an early sonnet ("See how Spring opens with disabling cold") G. M. Hopkins uses the parable's imagery to lament the belatedness of his learning the truth. In "New Readings" (11-15) he leaves Christ's explanation of the parable aside and instead praises him by applying the rocks, thorns, and birds of the parable to episodes in Christ's life:

> From wastes of rock He brings
> Food for five thousand: on the thorns He shed
>   Grains from His drooping Head;
> And would not have that legion of winged things
>   Bear Him to heaven on easeful wings.

The song of the fairy people in Yeats's drama *The Land of Heart's Desire* describes how "the lonely of heart is withered away" — which reflects the futile attempts of father Hart to save Mary Bruin's soul. Gabriel in Baldwin's *Go Tell It on the Mountain* would have "fallen by the wayside" had it not been for the support of Deborah.

The parable furnishes the "central dramatic metaphor" in Flannery O'Connor's novel *The Violent Bear It Away* (J. May, *The Pruning Word,* 137). Protagonist Tarwater's granduncle has planted the seed of the word in his nephew Rayber and his grandnephew, neither of whom believes the granduncle has succeeded. The novel shows that Tarwater is not the "rock" he believes himself to be, nor is Rayber successful in keeping the seed "under control" (2.9). In John Updike's novel *Couples* (chap. 1), the seed fallen among the thorns — recognized by Piet Hanema in a freckle on Georgena's (his lover's) face — serves as an image of the fallen world of the town of Tarbox. The leader of the "post-pill Paradise" created by the couples is Freddy Thorne, whose name may allude both to the parable and to Gen. 3:18 ("Thorns also and thistles shall it bring forth to thee") — the world after Eden.

Bibliography. Dodd, C. H. *Parables of the Kingdom* (1935; 1961); Hunter, A. *The Parables Then and Now* (1971); May, J. *The Pruning Word: The Parables of Flannery O'Connor* (1976).   MANFRED SIEBALD

SPARE THE ROD   The biblical phrase is from Proverbs: "He that spareth his rod hateth his son: but he that loveth him chasteneth him betimes" (13:24). The more terse proverbial expression "Spare the rod and spoil the child" is from Butler's *Hudibras* (2.1.843). If Washington Irving's Ichabod Crane thought of Butler's locution as a "golden maxim" ("The Legend of Sleepy Hollow"), Mark Twain's Aunt Polly in *Tom Sawyer* repeats the popular assumption that it is itself a biblical text: "I ain't doing my duty by that boy," she says, "and that's the Lord's truth, goodness. Spare the rod and spile the child, as the Good Book says" (chap. 1). One senses that the favor accorded the first phrase of the verse from Proverbs in Calvinistic circles acquired for successive generations in the Puritan tradition a legendary reinforcement. Hawthorne writes in *The Scarlet Letter* of how

> the discipline of the family in those days was of a far more rigid kind than now. The frown, the harsh rebuke, the frequent application of the rod, enjoined by Scriptural authority, were used, not merely in the way of punishment for actual offenses, but as a wholesome regimen for the growth and promotion of all childish virtues. (chap. 6)

And the narrator of Samuel Butler's *The Way of All Flesh* (1903) likewise observes of an earlier day: "At that time it was universally admitted that to spare the rod was to spoil the child" (chap. 5).

SPARROW'S FALL   Jesus, warning his disciples that they, like himself, would be persecuted, encouraged them not to lose heart: "And fear not them which kill the body, but are not able to kill the soul: but rather fear him which is able to destroy both soul and body in hell. Are not two sparrows sold for a farthing? and one of them shall not fall on the ground without your Father. But the very hairs of your head are all numbered. Fear ye not therefore, ye are of more value than many sparrows" (Matt. 10:28-31).

In commentary by the early Fathers of the Church emphasis is placed upon the general injunction to trust in God's provident care. Calvin and other Reformation commentators pick up the image of the sparrow, Calvin adducing Luke's variant ("Are not five sparrows sold for two farthings?" [Luke 12:6]) to make the point that

> Christ asserts that each single creature is distinctly under God's hand and protection, that nothing may be left open to chance. For the will of God is opposed to contingency. . . . In the nature of things itself, I agree there is contingency, but I say that nothing occurs by the blind turn of fortune where God's will holds the cords. (*Harmony of the Gospels*, 1.307)

In Shakespeare's *Hamlet,* when Horatio suggests postponing the deal with Laertes because of evil omens, Hamlet overrules him: "Not a whit, we defy augury: there's a special providence in the fall of a sparrow. If it be now, 'tis not to come; if it be not to come, it will be now; if it be not now, yet it will come" (*Hamlet,* 5.2.221-24). This parody of Calvinist theological formulation on predestiny is prepared for earlier in the scene: "There's a divinity that shapes our ends, / Rough-hew them how we will" (5.2.10-11), and relates the scene to ongoing theological debate about the operations of Providence.

In Alexander Pope's *Essay on Man* a view more like that of St. Thomas Aquinas is reflected. According to Aquinas, "All events that take place in this world, even those apparently fortuitous or casual, are comprehended in the order of divine Providence, on which fate depends." To the question, "If divine Providence be the direct cause of everything that happens in the world, at least of the good things, does it not then seem that everything must come about because of necessity?" Aquinas answers in the negative: "The divine will cannot fail, but we cannot therefore ascribe necessity to all its effects" (Expositio, *Perihermenias,* 1.14). In Pope's theodicy:

> Heav'n from all creatures hides the book of Fate,
> All but the page prescrib'd, their present state;
> From brutes what men, from men what spirits know:
> Or who could suffer Being here below? . . .
> Oh blindness to the future! kindly giv'n,
> That each may fill the circle mark'd by Heav'n;
> Who sees with equal eye, as God of all,
> A hero perish, or a sparrow fall,
> Atoms or systems into ruin hurl'd,
> And now a bubble burst, and now a world. (*Essay on Man,* 1.3.77-80, 85-90)

In later tradition, as in Mark Twain's *The Mysterious Stranger,* the figure is usually employed in the context of special providence, personally conceived. When the poor old widow Ursula tells Satan that God will help her find the means to care for the stray kitten she wants to keep, Satan sarcastically asks, "What makes you think so?" Ursula retorts heatedly, "Because I know it. Not a sparrow falls to the ground without his seeing it." In one of Emily Dickinson's poems, "Mame never forgets her birds," her dead aunt is presented as an omniscient viewer of the mortal life of her children, noticing "with cunning care" (her ongoing maternal scrutiny) "if either of her 'sparrows fall.'" David Jones simply adduces the passage as an instance of God's compassion for his creatures: "They say he cared / when sparrows fall" (*Anathemata,* 8.240).

See also PREDESTINATION.

SPIRIT IS WILLING   *See* FLESH IS WEAK.

SPOIL THE EGYPTIANS   *See* EGYPTIAN GOLD.

STABAT MATER   The term comes from the phrase *stabat mater crucem* or *stabat mater dolorosa,* the latter of which is usually given as the title of the Latin hymn by the Italian Franciscan Jacopone da Todi, "The sorrowing mother stood in tears under the cross." It relates not to any specific verse in the Gospels but to the whole Passion scene. Jacopone's poem was translated into many vernaculars; notable ME variations include the "Stond wel, moder, vnder rode" (C. Brown, *English Lyrics of the XIIIth Century,* nos. 49a, 49b, 47; cf. 4). The original Latin hymn has frequently been set to music (e.g., Pergolesi) for liturgy connected with the Seven Sorrows of the Virgin and the Franciscan-inspired Stations of the Cross.

See also MARY, MOTHER OF JESUS; PASSION, CROSS.

STARS IN THEIR COURSES   "They fought from heaven," says the narrator of Judg. 5; "the stars in their courses fought against Sisera" (Judg. 5:20). Sisera has become typical of one who takes up arms against fate in a futile effort. Shakespeare, in *Romeo and Juliet,* suggests of his "star-crossed lovers" (prol. 6) that Romeo so opposes himself to Fate or Fortune, crying, "Then I defy you, stars!" (5.1.24). G. B. Shaw turns the allusion around in his preface to *Back to Methuselah* when he writes, "Thus the stars in their courses fought for Darwin. Every faction drew a moral from him; every catholic hater of faction founded a hope on him." H. G. Wells inverts in similar fashion: "The world is for man, the stars in their courses are for man — if only he will follow the God who calls to him and take the gift God offers" (*The Undying Fire,* chap. 5).

STELLA MARIS   *Stella maris,* or "star of the sea," is an exceedingly popular (false) etymology of the name Mary, and in reference to the mother of Jesus it dates to St. Jerome (*De nominibus Hebraicis* [PL 23.789, 842]), where he reads *stilla,* or "drop." Later copyists readily transferred the ligatures *e* and *i,* giving rise to *stella,* "star." Marian treatises of the Middle Ages, such as John Garland's 13th-cent. *Stella Maris,* amplified the tradition, and it became one of the most familiar names for Mary in the ME lyric and carol (e.g., Friar William Herebert's "Heyl, leuedy, se-stoerre bryht"; C. Brown, *Religious Lyrics of the XIVth Century,* no. 17; cf. nos. 41, 45). Alexander Barclay includes a dedication to Mary as *Stella maris* in his translation of Brant's *Narrenschiff* into English verse, *The Ship of Fools* (1509), and Dunbar opens his "Ane Ballat of Our Lady" with a similar invocation. Allusions in modern literature are more rare, although the Welsh poet David Jones's reference to the Blessed Virgin Mary as a "lode" star hearkens back to the tradition (*Anathemata,* 8.239).

See also MARY, MOTHER OF JESUS.

STEPHEN   Although the Slaughter of the Innocents (Matt. 2:16-18) was frequently adduced by the medieval Church as the first occasion of martyrdom for the sake of Christ, the early Church and Protestant tradition (e.g., Foxe's *Book of Martyrs*) have typically commenced their martyrologies with the execution of St. Stephen recorded in the book of Acts. The high priest and elders of the Sanhedrin, after hearing Stephen deliver a sermon concerning Jesus, caused him to be taken out and stoned. One of the witnesses was Saul (later St. Paul), who "consented to his death" and watched the cloaks of Stephen's executioners (Acts 6:8–8:1). The effect of Stephen's courageous witness, beatific vision (7:55-56), and patient death were widely felt in the early Church.

Stephen is recollected in every martyrology from the Hieronymian (5th cent.) to the *Legenda Aurea* of Jacobus de Voragine and Foxe's *Book of Martyrs,* and is celebrated in hymns such as the 18th-cent. St. Stephen's Day anthem (translated from Latin in 1861):

> First of martyrs, thou whose name
> Doth thy golden crown proclaim
> . . . First like him in dying hour
> Witness to almighty power;
> First to follow where he trod
> Through the deep Red Sea of blood;
> First, but in thy footsteps press
> Saints and martyrs numberless.

Like an ancient office hymn devoted to "Saint of God, elect and precious, Protomartyr Stephen, bright," it calls attention to Stephen's name (*stephanos* = "crown") to speak of his ultimate reward.

Stephen does not have a martyr's role in ME drama. Nor does he figure prominently in English literary tradition. St. Thomas More had a special reverence for him and mentions him frequently in his writings. Apart from religious works such as William Henry Temple's sacred drama *Saul and Stephen* (1921), Harry W. Githens's *The First Martyr* (1929), and Mary Whitney's *The Martyrdom of Stephen* (1927), however, he is the subject of only incidental literary allusion. He occasionally figures in art, usually dressed in a deacon's alb and dalmatic, praying as the stones hail down upon him.

Bibliography. Cavanaugh, J. R., C.S.B. "The Saint Stephen Motif in Saint Thomas More's Thought." *Moreana,* 8.59-66.

STEWARDSHIP   *See* ADAM; CHILDREN OF LIGHT; UNPROFITABLE SERVANT, PARABLE OF.

STIGMATA   The *stigmata* are the five wounds which Christ suffered in his Crucifixion and which he revealed to St. Thomas, the "doubting apostle," to prove definitively his Resurrection (John 20:25-29). The term is usually connected in hagiography with St. Francis of Assisi, who, in intense identification with the Passion of Christ, is said to have received the imprint of the five wounds on his hands, feet, and side during a vision on Mt. Alvernia (Mt. Verna) on 17 September 1224. St. Catherine of Siena and

St. Catherine of Genoa have also been associated with this sign of their fervent meditation on the Passion of Christ. The dreamer in Langland's *Piers Plowman,* falling asleep after Mass, dreams that he sees Piers with the stigmata; so like the wounded Savior does he appear that he asks Conscience whether indeed it is Piers or Christ that he sees (B.19.1-12ff.). Poems concerning Christ's own stigmata are numerous; one of the most concise is that of Richard Crashaw, "On the Still Surviving Marks of our Saviour's Wounds":

> Whatever story of their cruelty,
> Or nail, or thorn, or spearhead writ in Thee,
> Are in another sense
>   Still legible;
> Sweet is the difference:
>   Once I did spell
> Every red letter
>   A wound of Thine:
> Now what is better
>   Balsam for mine.

See also PASSION, CROSS.

STILL SMALL VOICE   Thoroughly discouraged despite his victory over the pagan prophets on Mt. Carmel, and afraid for his life at the hands of King Ahab and his wife Jezebel, Elijah fled and hid in a cave on Mt. Horeb. There he complained bitterly to the Lord, saying in effect that although he had done his best, Israel was in a state of utter rejection of God, martyring prophets and desecrating altars. "And I," he concluded, "even I only am left; and they seek my life, to take it away" (1 Kings 19:10). God responded with an object lesson, displaying his power to the prophet first in a mighty wind which "rent the mountains, and brake in pieces the rocks before the LORD . . . and after the wind an earthquake . . . and after the earthquake a fire." But "the LORD was not in" these phenomena (vv. 11-12). Only in the last manifestation — "a still small voice" — was God revealed.

Matthew Henry (like some rabbinic sources) contrasts this event with the encounter of Moses with God on Mt. Sinai. In that instance God was indeed revealed in a mighty rushing wind, earthquake, smoke, and fire (Exod. 19:16-19; cf. Heb. 12:18ff.). What Elijah experiences, says Henry, is a renewal of the Law, "especially the first two commandments," and the still small voice indicates to Elijah how he himself is to reflect this voice in his own proclamation (*Comm.* 2.683-84). The term came to be applied during the Great Awakening of the 18th cent. to the convicting voice of God's Holy Spirit or of conscience, prompting the sinner to repentance or the believer to specific vocation. For Jonathan Edwards in his *Treatise Concerning Religious Affections* (chap. 9), the still small voice is said to be characteristic of God's speaking to those faithful to him, "like a friend."

John Greenleaf Whittier contrasts the efforts of the ancients to stimulate religious feelings through drugs, drink, and dancing with the peacefulness and composure of Christian worship: "Let us be dumb, let flesh retire; / Speak through the earthquake, wind, and fire, / A still small voice of calm" ("The Brewing of Soma"; cf. the last stanza of the hymn "Dear Lord and Father of Mankind"). The hushed anticipation of a Quaker meeting is reflected in Whittier's "First-Day Thoughts," in which he prays: "There, syllabled by silence, let me hear / The still small voice which reached the prophet's ear." In Dickens's *The Old Curiosity Shop* the term is used to refer to a clear conscience when Brass exclaims of his own "honesty," "The still, small voice, Christopher . . . is a singing of cosmic songs within me, and all is happiness and joy!" (chap. 57). In Evelyn Waugh's *Decline and Fall,* the still small voice is a "whole code of ready-made honour that is . . . trained to command, of the Englishman all the world over" (3.4). For his part, said G. K. Chesterton, he had "always maintained, quite seriously, that the Lord is not in the wind or the thunder of the waste, but, if anywhere, in the still small voice of Fleet Street" ("The Surrender of a Cockney"). For A. M. Klein "The Still Small Voice" is heard in Passover seders around the world, crying out, "Jerusalem, next year! Next year, Jerusalem!" *(Hath Not a Jew. . .).*

See also ELIJAH.

Bibliography. Prickett, S. "Towards a Rediscovery of the Bible: The Problem of the Still Small Voice." In *Ways of Reading the Bible.* Ed. M. Wadsworth (1981), 105-17; *Words and the Word: Language, Poetics and Biblical Interpretation* (1986); Wiener, A. *The Prophet Elijah in the Development of Judaism* (1978).

STONE   A distinction was usually made in the Bible and its ancient translations between the words for "rock" (Heb. *ṣur, selaʿ;* Gk. *petra*), referring to matter which is part of a natural rock formation, and the words for "stone" (Heb. *ʾeben;* Gk. *lithos*), which is used of that which is not part of a natural rock formation.

Stones were used in ancient times for a variety of purposes: as weapons, boundary markers, "witnesses" (Josh. 24:27), measuring weights, in buildings, and as monuments. (Note that in 1 Sam. 7:12 a monument is named *Ebenezer,* which literally means "stone of help.") In one place God is referred to as the "Stone of Israel" (Gen. 49:24), though some scholars feel that there has been a corruption in the text.

The real importance of the word *stone* is its theological and symbolic use. In Isa. 8:14 God is viewed as a potential stone of stumbling and rock of offense for the nation of Israel. In Isa. 28:16 the author adapts the imagery to show that God has set a costly and choice foundation stone, a cornerstone, which will provide a place of refuge in the coming flood of destruction. What the stone refers to is debated, but the promise of God is probably the intention. In Ps. 118:22 reference is made to a "stone which the builders refused [rejected], which has become the head stone of the corner." Again the intention of the symbol is uncertain and depends on a reconstruction of the context of the psalm. The stone may refer to Israel and the builders to the other nations. More likely, however, the original context is the rebuilding of the Temple in 520 B.C.; the stone then refers to the foundation stone of the new temple. In this case "the builders" refers to the elders who had seen the greater glory of the first temple (cf. Ezra 3:12). The same focus on the foundation stone of the second temple appears in Zech. 3:9 and 4:7. In Dan. 2:34-35 and 45 God's ultimate kingdom is viewed as a stone which destroys the kingdoms of the world.

In pre-Christian Judaism some of these texts were understood of the end time or of the Messiah. The Essenes of Qumran interpreted Isa. 28:16 of their own end-time community. (See 1QS 8:5-7 as well as Tg. Isa. 28:16 and the LXX.) Ps. 118:22 was also interpreted of the end time. (See Midr. Ps. 118:22; Pesaḥ. 119a; and J. Jeremias, *The Eucharistic Words of Jesus* [1966], 256-57.)

The NT explicitly uses only Isa. 8:14; 28:16; and Ps. 118:22 in referring to the stone symbolism. Jesus used Ps. 118:22 as the conclusion to the parable of the wicked tenants (Matt. 21:42 and parallels), so indicating the meaning of the parable. A wordplay between the Hebrew words for "son" *(ben)* and "stone" *('eben),* which is also present in Matt. 3:9, is the basis of the use of Ps. 118:22. The builders, the Jewish leaders, have rejected the son of God, who is the most important part of God's purposes. Ps. 118:22 is also used in Acts 4:11 as a demonstration of the resurrection and in 1 Pet. 2:7 along with passages from Isa. 8:14 and 28:16. In 1 Pet. 2:4-8 these three OT texts are used for a variety of theological purposes: to indicate the importance of Christ and belief in him; to show the character of the Church; and to emphasize the failure of those who reject Christ. Similarly, in Rom. 9:32-33 the two Isaiah texts are conflated to show why Israel did not believe in Christ. The stone on which they stumbled was Christ.

Much discussion has been given to the location of the cornerstone in the building, with many arguing that the reference is to a stone at the top of the building, a keystone. However, the linguistic evidence for this is later than the NT, and almost certainly the reference is to a large foundation stone at the corner of the building.

In postapostolic Christianity OT passages referring to a stone were indiscriminately interpreted of Christ. For example, the stone cut out without hands (Dan. 2:34) was understood as a reference to the Virgin Birth (St. Justin, *Dial.* 70), and the stone upon which Jacob slept in Gen. 28:11 was viewed as a reference to Christ (St. Cyprian, *Testimonies against the Jews,* 2.16).

An effective literary development of the biblical witness-stone (Josh. 24:27) is Henry Vaughan's "The Stone," in which the stone which has "heard" the covenant agreement between God and his people is metonymic for the silent witness of all creation to human transgressions

against God's Law, once writ in stone. The same passage recurs, with a suggestion of Vaughan's influence, in T. S. Eliot's *The Rock,* where the Rock is personified as a blind prophet, Tiresias-like, "led by a boy." Speaking in the idiom of Qohelet, he also gives witness against human transgression and its consequences. He is called by the Chorus header "The Rock. . . . He who has seen what has happened / And who sees what is to happen. / The Witness" (pt. 1). In the next scene the crumbling civilization of England is compared to a spiritually arid Jerusalem, or its Temple, no longer "built upon the foundation / Of apostles and prophets, Christ Jesus himself the chief cornerstone." The Rock's question for modern culture is then drawn from Ps. 118:22 and its NT citations: "You, have you built well, have you forgotten the cornerstone? / Talking of right relations of men, but not of relations of men to GOD" (*Collected Poems, 1909-62,* 166).

Medieval treatments of Christ as the cornerstone often associate the messianic implications of Ps. 118:22 with the image in Dan. 2 of the stone cut out without hands which rolls down from the mountain to destroy the kingdoms of this world. Thus James Ryman's carol "The Sone of God in trone" (1492) concludes:

> Kutte of the hill withowte manys hond,
> Crist is the cornere stone,
> Born of a meyde, I vnderstond,
> To saue mankynde alone. (R. Greene, *The Early English Carols,* no. 63)

The identification of Christ with the rejected cornerstone (Ps. 118:22; cf. Dan. 2:34, 45) is often implicit even in modern allusions, as, e.g., in the "message" of Doming Perez delivered to Father Antonio in Somerset Maugham's *Catalina* (chap. 13). The identification of Christ as "unto the Jews a stumbling-block" (1 Cor. 1:23; cf. Rom. 9:32-33; Isa. 57:14) has become something of a cliché. In *The Crown of Wild Olive* Ruskin cites this passage to suggest that in architecture as well as theology, their worship of Wisdom made the "stumbling block" of the Jews seem "to the Greeks — Foolishness." A "stumbling block" thus becomes something over which one trips because it is alien to one's own "construction" of the world.

See also PETER; ROCK; SMITTEN ROCK; STONES CRY OUT.

DAVID L. JEFFREY
KLYNE SNODGRASS

STONE OF HELP   *See* EBENEZER.

STONES CRY OUT

When during Jesus' triumphal entry into Jerusalem the disciples spontaneously broke out into rejoicing and praising God for the "mighty works that they had seen," some of the Pharisees in the crowd enjoined Jesus to rebuke them. "He answered and said unto them, I tell you that, if these should hold their peace, the stones would immediately cry out" (Luke 19:37-40). St. Augustine, reflecting the Vg rendering of *pueri* ("children") for disciples in v. 37, allegorizes the passage in such a way as to make it prophetic: "Us he saw when he spoke these words. . . . Who are stones but they who worship stones? If the Jewish children shall hold their peace, the elder and the younger Gentiles shall cry out" (*Sermo,* 121.3).

George Herbert appeals to the passage in his shaped poem "The Altar," where he builds the altar out of contrition and the tears of a broken stony heart, so "That, if I chance to hold my peace / These stones to praise thee may not cease." Chesterton slightly misremembers the passage in *Tremendous Trifles,* saying, "When the street children shouted too loud, certain priggish disciples did begin to rebuke them in the name of good taste" ("The Tower"). The KJV rendering of Luke 19:39-40 is printed by Richard Wilbur as the rubric for his "A Christmas Hymn," in which the account of the Nativity in Luke 2 is joined with that of the Passion and Second Coming of Christ to undisputed praise and glory. In the meantime, Christmas, and by implication the world's rebuke of its praise of Christ, is metonymic of the whole plan of redemption:

> But now, as at the ending,
> The low is lifted high;
> The stars shall bend their voices,
> And every stone shall cry.
> And every stone shall cry
> In praises of the child
> By whose descent among us
> The worlds are reconciled.

The passage also provides a key motif for Margaret Avison's poem "Stone's Secret" (*sunblue,* 21).

STRAIT AND NARROW   Jesus indicated to his hearers in the Sermon on the Mount that the way of life he commanded was one of self-scrutiny and moral discernment: "Enter ye in at the strait gate: for wide is the gate, and broad is the way, that leadeth to destruction, and many there be which go in thereat. Because strait is the gate, and narrow is the way, which leadeth unto life, and few there be that find it" (Matt. 7:13-14). This portion of the Sermon on the Mount is among the best known in Christian literary tradition. Commentary upon it in the *Sayings of the Fathers* of the Egyptian desert (6.81) pertains to vocation as a solitary, but in other respects differs little from that of St. Benedict in his *Rule:*

> It is for the sake of obedience that they [i.e., those who love Christ] enter into the narrow way of life of which the Lord said: "Narrow is the way that leads unto life" (Mt. 7:14 [Vg]). The "narrowness" of the way is opposite to the broad way suggested by self-will and desire and pleasure: and they follow it by delighting to dwell in a community, to be subject to their abbot, and to follow the judgement of another. Such men live up to the practice of our Lord, who tells us: "I come not to do mine own will, but the will of him that sent me" (John 6:36). (*Regula Magistri,* 5)

While such words reflect the typical orientation of monastic interpretation, St. Augustine reads the passage with an eye to Christians in secular occupations, yet who desire spiritual progress in "searching for and possessing wisdom, which is a tree of life." In the contemplation of such wisdom the "eye is led through all that precedes to a point where there may now be seen the narrow way and strait gate." Augustine observes that Jesus does not say that "his yoke is rough or his burden heavy"; it is in fact because "few are willing to bring their own labors to an end," and instead spurn "this easy yoke and light burden," that they cannot squeeze through the "narrow way which leads to life and the strait gate by which it is entered upon" (*De sermone Domini in Monte*, 2.33.77). The appeal of the broad road, suggests Augustine, is the appeal of popular and conventional "wisdom."

Sir John Clanvowe, a friend of Chaucer and sympathizer with Wyclif, takes up this point in his spiritual treatise *The Two Ways,* which draws its title and first section from Matt. 7:13-14. The broad way is attractive to many, says Clanvowe, because it maintains the illusion that all those set upon the broad way are part of a grand consensus, even as it promotes a contradiction, that each person is a law unto himself. Clanvowe defines the "narghwe wey" as simply the keeping of God's commandments, "which is wisdom," and the "strait gate" which leads into this way as the fear of God, through which one is prompted to abandon sinful appetites and self-will. The broad way, conversely, is the breaking of God's laws, and leads to hell; the wide gate through which one enters it is a kind of studied carelessness about God's law in deference to self-will or pride (1-2).

In Shakespeare's *All's Well That Ends Well,* the clown Lavatch jokes about serving the "The Black Prince, sir, alias the Prince of Darkness, alias, the Devil," one who is "sure, Prince of the world." But he prefers another domicile: "Let his nobility remain in 's Court. I am for the house with the narrow gate, which I take to be too little for pomp to enter. Some that humble themselves may, but the many will be too chill and tender, and they'll be for the flowery way that leads to the broad gate and the great fire" (4.5.42-55). After the murder scene in *Macbeth,* a series of loud knocks at the gate of Macbeth's castle is responded to slowly by the thick-headed porter. Hearing the insistent knocking, he quips: "But this place is too cold for Hell. I'll devil-porter it no further. I had thought to have let in some of all professions that go the primrose way to th' everlasting bonfire" (2.3.15-20; hence the phrase "led down the primrose path").

Reformation writers tend to elaborate the main line of commentary but with particular emphasis falling on the carnal appetite and the emotions as they pertain to the "way that leads to destruction." Calvin, influenced by ascetic spiritual writers, finds that

Christ's teaching is at no point more opposed to the flesh; no-one ever makes any headway on this until he has learned to get a real grip on his emotions and on all his desires, so as to keep them in that narrow way which the heavenly Teacher prescribes for the restraint of our cravings. Men are so permissive toward themselves, so uncontrolled, and lax, that Christ here tells his disciples to get themselves onto the narrow and thorny road. . . . That we should not be trapped by the delights of a licentious and dissolute life, and drift along at the impulse of the desire of the flesh, he declares that men are rushing to their death, when they prefer to enter by the spacious way and broad gate, rather than negotiate the straits which lead to life. How is it that men knowingly and willingly rush on, carefree, except that they cannot believe that they are perishing, when the whole crowd goes down at the same time. Contrarily, the small numbers of the faithful make many cowards, for it is hard to induce us to renounce the world, and to pattern our life upon the ways of a few. We think it unnatural to be forced out of the generality, as if we were not part of the human race. (*Harmony of the Gospels*, sup. Matt. 7:13-14)

Calvin's exegesis offers a pertinent introduction to Bunyan's *Pilgrim's Progress*, in which, though almost dissuaded by Mr. Worldly Wiseman in the "Town of Carnal Policy," Christian arrives at last at the "Strait" or "Wicket-gate," over which is written: "Knock and it shall be opened unto you" (Matt. 7:8). Good-Will bids Christian enter, and because he is contrite for his sins, he is able to set upon the "narrow way . . . cast up by the Patriarchs, Prophets, Christ, and his Apostles, and . . . is as straight as a Rule can make it." He finds many temptations to leave this path for ways "Crooked, and Wide," but eventually arrives at the gate of his destination, that of the Celestial City, over which is written in gold letters "Blessed are they that do his commandments, that they may have right to the Tree of Life; and may enter in through the Gates into the City" (cf. Rev. 22:14).

Although George Herbert identifies "the narrow way and little gate" with his baptism as an infant ("H. Baptisme 2"), the typical usage of evangelical and Puritan writers is to identify the strait gate with adult conversion. For Matthew Henry, "Conversion and regeneration are *the gate*, by which we enter into this way, in which we begin a life of faith and serious godliness; out of a state of sin into a state of grace we must pass, by the new birth, John iii.3, 5. This is a strait gate, hard to find, and hard to get through; like a passage between two rocks, 1 Sam. xiv.4." Once through the gate and set upon the narrow way, Henry says, "we must be strict and circumspect in our conversation" and expect that "we must swim against the current," for "it is easier to set a man against all the world than against himself, yet this must be in conversion" (*Comm.* 5.92-93). This is the theme also of John Wesley's address on the passage (Sermon 31 in the [1747] *Sermons on Several Occasions*), in which he defines the "inseparable properties" of each way, underscoring the

need to strive for a "separated" life in pursuit of the narrow way.

Such striving itself could take on carnal forms, and in the 19th cent. Dickens indicates in *Little Dorrit* something of the abuse of the distinction which had come about in hypocritical and moralizing preaching, when Clennam proves to have profited little from the rigid reiterations of a woman ("strait," "narrow," "far straiter and narrower") who herself had been "brought up strictly, and straitly," on a Bible bound in the "straitest boards" (1.3.30; 2.30.753). It is this kind of exposition as much as Wesley's which Samuel Butler reflects when, in *The Way of All Flesh,* he has the Rev. Gideon Hawke preach to the followers of Charles Simeon at Cambridge: "My dear young friends, strait is the gate, and narrow is the way which leadeth to Eternal Life, and few there be that find it. Few, few, few, for he who will not give up ALL for Christ's sake, has given up nothing."

The phrase has become a cliché in modern literature and as such appears in diverse contexts. For Ruskin there is no value in "grumbling provided always you have entered in at the strait gate" (*Praeterita*, 3). Dean Inge says in "The Idea of Progress" — conversely to his source, one suspects — that "there will never be a crowd gathered round this gate; 'few there be that find it.'" Theodore Dreiser, on the other hand, offers self-conscious reflection on the theme in revivalist preaching in both *American Tragedy* and *The Financier;* the protagonist of the latter novel "in his younger gallivantings about places of ill repute, and his subsequent occasional variations from the straight and narrow path . . . has learned much of the curious resources of immorality" (chap. 20). In England, Aldous Huxley complains of a residue of Puritan morality associated with contemporary social values: "Today a man is free to have any or no religion; about the Established Church and its divinities he can say almost anything he likes. But woe to him if he deviates from the narrow path of sexual orthodoxy" (*Music at Night,* "To the Puritan All Things are Impure"). Upton Sinclair's *Wide is the Gate* (1943) is one of an eleven-volume series of novels warning of the drift of modern political ethics and destiny.

STRANGER IN A STRANGE LAND The first son born to Moses and Zipporah was called by his father Gershom: "for he said, I have been a stranger in a strange land" (Exod. 2:22). The name derives from Heb. *gur* — to "be a sojourner" — but it is the phrase which has become proverbial for exile or pilgrim status. Leacock's study *Mark Twain* refers to Samuel Clemens as uncomfortable in the deep South, "But he was equally far from being a 'Yankee.' His brief sojourn as a youth in New York and Philadelphia was that of a stranger in a strange land" (chap. 2).

STRANGER, AND YE TOOK ME IN   (Matt. 25:35)
See also SEPARATE SHEEP FROM GOATS.

STREETS OF GOLD   *See* HEAVEN.

STUBBORN AND STIFF-NECKED   Ps. 78:8 urges education of children in the mighty works of God so that in generations to come Israel will live in the knowledge of their redemptive history, obedient to God's Law: "And might not be as their fathers, a stubborn and rebellious generation. . . ." The phrase recollects Exod. 32:9, "a stiffnecked people" (cf. Exod. 33:3, 5; Deut. 9:6; 2 Chron. 30:8). Matthew Arnold in *Culture and Anarchy* says that "Philistine gives the notion of something particularly stiff-necked and perverse" ("Barbarians, Philistines, Populace"), and in Howard Nemerov's "Debate with the Rabbi," the persona resists taking up his faith to the point where the exasperated Rabbi cries out, "Stubborn and stiff-necked man!"

STUMBLING BLOCK   *See* STONE.

STUMBLING STONE   *See* ROCK.

SUBSTITUTION   The term *substitution* is not found in Scripture, but the idea is prevalent in Christian thought especially. Initially, it referred to the OT sacrificial system, where the worshiper offered an animal as an atonement for his sin. The animal took his place. Christ's atoning work is likewise seen as substitutionary by the NT writers. Jesus himself said that he came to give his life, "a ransom for many" (Mark 10:45; note the use of the substitutionary preposition *anti*). The same view is expressed in St. Paul's statement that God "made him [Jesus] to be sin for us" (2 Cor. 5:21), and his words about Christ's being made a curse for us (Gal. 3:13). It is there in Caiaphas's unconscious prophecy that Jesus would die for others (John 11:49-52). It is involved in Christ's bearing of people's sins (Heb. 9:28; 1 Pet. 2:24), and in his being "the propitiation for our sins" (1 John 2:2; 4:10).

This substitution is not, however, a mechanical, external thing. Christ is said to be one with the Father, the Judge (John 10:30), and one with sinners (Heb. 2:11, 14-17). And the saved are so changed that they are of one mind with Christ (Phil. 2:5). Nor is this the only NT way of looking at the death of Jesus. That death is an example (1 Pet. 2:21); it is a revelation of the love of God (John 3:16) and more. But much of the teaching of the NT depends on the assertion that when he died Jesus "took the place of" sinners.

Analogous "substitutions" in literature typically invoke the idea of substitutionary sacrifice. Such is the case, e.g., when in Dickens's *Tale of Two Cities* Sydney Carton conspires to effect the escape of his look-alike Charles Darnay from prison, replacing him on the guillotine scaffold so that Darnay can be reunited with his wife Lucie (with whom Carton is secretly in love). Elizabeth Barrett Browning's poem "Substitution" tells how in the absence of a loved one caused by death no present alternative can meet the emptiness; the only "substitute" is Christ, whose "presence" alone can "fill this pause." Charles Williams's Romantic Theology came to include the idea that "bearing one another's burdens" could extend to taking over another's emotional burdens, even his or her physical pain — a notion he may have found precedented in Kipling's story "The Wish House." He called this transference "Substitution."

See also ATONEMENT; LAMB OF GOD; SCAPEGOAT.

Bibliography. Carpenter, H. *The Inklings: C. S. Lewis, J. R. R. Tolkien, Charles Williams, and Their Friends* (1979); Williams, C. "The Way of Exchange." In *Selected Writings.* Ed. A. Ridler (1961), 122-31.   LEON MORRIS

SUFFER FOOLS GLADLY   In 2 Cor. 11:19 St. Paul commends the Corinthians, "For ye suffer fools gladly, seeing ye yourselves are wise." Paul's point, basic to the ironic remarks which follow, is that it is a mark of wisdom to bear with those who lack it. By suppression of the second phrase the point is often obscured or inverted in modern allusion.

See also FOOL, FOLLY; WISDOM.

SUFFER THE LITTLE CHILDREN   Once when Jesus was teaching the multitudes, several of his audience brought him little children to bless, asking that he "put his hands on them and pray." The disciples rebuked them for what they regarded as an intrusion, perhaps, as Calvin suggests, because they thought it was "beneath his dignity to receive children" (*Harmony of the Gospels*, 2.251). But Jesus intervened, saying, "Suffer the little children to come unto me, and forbid them not: for of such is the kingdom of God. Verily I say unto you, Whosoever shall not receive the kingdom of God as a little child, he shall not enter therein" (Mark 10:14-15; cf. Matt. 19:13-15; Luke 18:15-17).

Calvin saw the text as a ground for opposing the Anabaptists on the issue of infant baptism. Matthew Henry draws the inference that "little children may be brought to Christ as needing, and being capable of receiving, blessings from him, and having an interest in his intercession." "We cannot do better for our children," he adds, "than to commit them to the Lord Jesus, to be wrought upon, and prayed for, by him." Yet "we can but beg a blessing for them, it is Christ only that can command the blessing" (*Comm.* 5.271-72). Henry, while he does not mention baptism, sees in the narrative the basic principle of covenant theology: "The promise is to you and to your children. I will be a God to thee and thy seed." W. M. Hutchins's hymn (1850), "When mothers of Salem their children brought to Jesus," is a sentimentalized rendering of the passage, with "suffer little children to come unto me" as a recurrent refrain.

In his essay "Jonathan Edwards," Oliver Wendell Holmes represents Edwards as saying that children who are "out of Christ" are "young vipers." Holmes asks: "Is it possible that Edwards read the text mothers love so well, 'Suffer the little *vipers* to come unto me, and forbid them not, for of such is the kingdom of God'?" Swinburne's poem "Of Such is the Kingdom of Heaven" concludes sarcastically:

> Earth's creeds may be seventy times seven
> And blood have defiled each creed:
> If such be the kingdom of heaven,
> It must be heaven indeed.

In general the text has suffered more than been suffered by 20th-cent. writers. Aldous Huxley has little patience with the catechetical sensibility: "Dear priceless creatures! Of such is the kingdom of our anglican heaven" (*Music at Night,* "Foreheads Villainous Low"). In Joyce's *A Portrait of the Artist as a Young Man,* Stephen reflects in his temporary agony of conscience that "It was better never to have sinned, to have remained always a child, for God loved little children and suffered them to come to Him. It was a terrible and a sad thing to sin" (chap. 3). Later, however, when his sadness has been banished by other emotions and his choice, *"non serviam,"* declared, Stephen, Temple, and Cranly can only disdain the use of the passage by Glynn the teacher, who says, "I suffer little children to come unto me." Temple, recurring to the New Testament source of the phrase, retorts, "If Jesus suffered the children to come why does the church send them all to hell if they die unbaptized?" (chap. 5).

See also CHILDREN; MILLSTONE ABOUT HIS NECK.

SUFFERING SERVANT   *See* ECCE HOMO; LAMB OF GOD; MAN OF SORROWS; MESSIAH.

SUFFICIENT UNTO THE DAY   Jesus said in the Sermon on the Mount: "Seek ye first the kingdom of God, and his righteousness: and all these things shall be added unto you. Take therefore no thought for the morrow: for the morrow shall take thought for the things of itself. Sufficient unto the day is the evil thereof" (Matt. 6:33-34). Aldous Huxley turns this piece of evangelical wisdom on its head to say "Like Jesus' ideal personality, the total, unexpurgated, now canalized man is . . . like a little child, in his acceptance of the datum of experience for its own sake, in his refusal to take thought for the morrow, in his readiness to let the dead bury their dead" (*Eyeless in Gaza,* chap. 11; cf. Matt. 8:22).

See also LILIES OF THE FIELD.

SUICIDE   *See* DESPAIR.

SULEIKA   *See* POTIPHAR'S WIFE.

SUN OF RIGHTEOUSNESS   (Mal. 4:2; cf. Ps. 27:1; 1 John 1:5)

See also LIGHT.

SUN STOOD STILL   *See* AJALON, VALE OF; HEZEKIAH; JOSHUA.

SUSANNA   Susanna, wife of a Babylonian Jew, "a very fair woman, and one that feared the LORD" (Dan. 13:2, apoc.), refused to submit to the lustful advances of two elders who assailed her while she bathed in her garden. When the elders took vengeance by falsely accusing her of adultery, the young Daniel intervened to save her from stoning. Cleverly examining the elders separately, Daniel convicted them of "false witness by their own mouth" (61) so that not Susanna but the elders were executed.

This terse addition to the Daniel cycle, briefest of the books of the Apocrypha, has had an impact on Western culture out of all proportion to its size. Sixty-seven plays are based directly on the Susanna story, twenty-eight in German alone. The variety of genres in which variations of the story appear is even stronger evidence of its universal appeal. In addition to drama, Susanna appears in ME alliterative poetry (*The Pistil of Swete Susan*), American opera (Floyd's *Susannah*), Elizabethan ballad (Elderton's "The Constancy of Susanna"), French sculpture (*Portail St. Honore* at Amiens), German oratorio (Handel's *Susanna*), Roman cemetery fresco (Callistus's catacomb), Polish epic (Zochanowski's *Zusanna*), Greek poetry (Deprana's *Istoria tes Sosannes*), Flemish novel (Goris's *Het boek van Joachim van Babylon*), French chanson (di Lasso's "Susanne un jour"), Italian motet (Palestrina's *Susanna ab improbis*), English song (Byrd's "Susanna fayre sometimes assaulted was"), and German operetta (Gilpert's *Die keusche Susanne*).

"Thirty St. Susannahs," Alice Miskimin points out, "most of them martyrs to chastity, to be found in the Catholic encyclopedias, are further evidence of the continuity of the tradition" (*Susanna* [1969], 198). This motif of sexual virtue rewarded (cf. the story of Joseph and Potiphar's wife) is one of two main currents of Susanna allusion in English literary tradition. Most references to Susanna are variants of the "Genevieve tale," the story of patient feminine virtue ultimately prevailing over masculine perfidy. Constance in Chaucer's *Man of Law's Tale,* falsely accused of murder, appeals to that Genevieve tradition:

> She sette hire down on knees, and thus she sayde,
> "Immortal God, that savedest Susanne . . .
> If I be giltless of this felonye,
> My socour be, for ellis shal I dye!" (*Canterbury Tales,* 2.638-39, 643-44)

The apparently Wycliffite ME version (Yorkshire dialect; ed. R. A. Peck) emphasizes the heroic, saintly patience of the innocent Susan and of her husband, neither of whom, innocence notwithstanding, rail against the justice of the Law itself. Her deliverance, by grace (as much as by wisdom), is made to be some degree a reward for the consistency of her faithfulness under duress.

The other major motif derived from the Susanna story emphasizes Daniel as clever young judge. Helena alludes to that "wise youth" tradition in Shakespeare's *All's Well That Ends Well*: "So holy writ in babes hath judgement shown / When judges have been babes" (2.1.141-42). The quotation reflects the description of Daniel as a "young child" in the Geneva Bible translation of the Susanna story. In *The Merchant of Venice* "a Daniel come to judgment" (4.1.222) refers also to the story of Susanna.

Both of those allusive strains tend to make Susanna a prime biblical representative of the theme of vindication of the falsely accused. That emphasis often pairs Susanna with Lucrece, the classical prototype of chastity wrongly accused, as when Browning links "Lucretia and Susanna" in *The Ring and the Book* (4.887). As late as 1855 Thackeray can have Lord Kew in *The Newcomes* casually allude to the "innocence" of "Susanna between the two Elders" (287).

Recent literary allusions to Susanna frequently stray from these central motifs of virtue rewarded and wise innocence. Susanna has come to represent the apotheosis of beauty, a transcendent spiritual loveliness revealed through the graces of the flesh. As prominent a modern poet as Wallace Stevens invites his readers' blood to pulse "pizzicati of Hosanna" with the elders in his tribute to Susanna in "Peter Quince at the Claviar":

> Beauty is momentary in the mind —
> The fitful tracing of a portal;
> But in the flesh it is immortal. . . .
> Now, in its immortality, it plays
> On the clear viol of her memory,
> And makes a constant sacrament of praise.

See also DANIEL.

Bibliography. Baumgartner, W. "Susanna: Die Geschichte einer Legende." *ARW* 24 (1927), 259-80; Carroll, P. "Myth, Methodology, and Transformation in the Old Testament: The Stories of Esther, Judith, and Susanna." *SR* 12.3 (1983), 301-12; Kay, D. M. "Susanna." In *The Apocrypha and Pseudepigrapha of the Old Testament in English.* 2 vols. Ed. R. H. Charles (1913), 2.638-51; MacKenzie, R. A. F. "The Meaning of the Susanna Story." *CJT* 3.3 (July 1957), 211-18; Miskimin, A. *Susanna: An Alliterative Poem of the Fourteenth Century* (1969); Moore, C. A. *Daniel, Esther, and Jeremiah: The Additions.* AB 44 (1977); Peck, R. A. *Heroic Women from the Old Testament in ME Verse* (1991); Walker, S. *Seven Ways of Looking at Susanna* (1986).

STEVEN C. WALKER

SWEAT OF THY BROW Part of the curse upon Adam for his disobedience was hard farming: ". . . cursed is the ground for thy sake. . . . In the sweat of thy face shalt thou eat bread, till thou return unto the ground" (Gen. 3:17,

19). Matthew Henry's *Commentary* grinds in the point: "If Adam had not sinned, he had not sweated. . . . we are bound to work, not as creatures only, but as criminals; it is part of our sentence, which idleness daringly defies" (1.32). In his Preface to *Saint Joan*, G. B. Shaw writes that "To a professional critic . . . theatre-going is the curse of Adam. The play is the evil he is paid to endure in the sweat of his brow; and the sooner it is over, the better."

See also ADAM.

SWORD OF THE SPIRIT In St. Paul's closing instructions to the Christian community in Ephesus, the "sword of the Spirit, which is the word of God" (Eph. 6:17) is the only offensive weapon in the catalog of the spiritual armor needed by the Christian to stand firm against the powers of darkness (vv. 10-18). The sword is the *machaira*, the short, straight, double-edged blade of the Roman legionary, used in single combat, distinct from the *rhomphaia*, the large Thracian broadsword; in the NT *machaira* is the usual word, whereas *rhomphaia* occurs only in Rev. 1:16, 2:16, and 19:15 (the messianic sword of Christ's mouth) and in Luke 2:35 (the sword which is to pierce Mary's soul). *Machaira* is used more rarely to refer to the surgeon's knife or razor (as in the case of the penetrative dividing sword of the Word in Heb. 4:12) and to the stone knife used in circumcision.

The idea of spiritual armor has parallels in Egyptian and Persian traditions (M. Barth, *Ephesians*, 789) as well as in Greek writings. Aristotle's *Politics* (1.2.16) argues that individuals are born with native moral and intellectual armor. Philo describes *logos* (in the Greek sense of "rational speech" or "reason") as a weapon given by God (cited in Barth, 789n). In non-Christian writings spiritual armor is usually understood in the Stoic sense as virtues residing in man's highest nature, to be used in the inner battle of reason against passions. The sword of Eph. 6, however, is not a native spiritual quality but is extrinsic, a power furnished and authorized by the Holy Spirit. The idea of divinely given armor has many parallels in Qumran literature and Jewish apocalyptic literature (Barth, 788-90); indeed, the golden sword given Judas Maccabeus in a vision (2 Macc. 15:15-16) can be traced through literature in the Charlemagne tradition, where it is identified with the sword of Paul's *miles Christi*. A more specific traditional parallel for Eph. 6:17 can be found in the Babylonian Talmud (Bera. 5a), in which the faithful Jew who recites the Shema is like one who holds a two-edged sword in his hand.

The early Fathers emphasize particularly the dividing and penetrating function of the sword of the Word in conversion and in the trials following that commitment, in which adherence to the Word separates the convert from the "ungodly" among his friends and family (see esp. Tertullian [ANF 3.333]); the sword of the Word is associated with the divisive sword of Matt. 10:34 and with the sword of judgment proceeding from Christ's mouth in Revelation (e.g., Tertullian, ANF 3.333; St. Augustine, NPNF 8.245). In the Christian's inner battle, the Word acts as an inner judge identifiable with the logos of Heb. 4:12, both destructive and healing in cutting away fleshly desires. In the external battle, the sword of the Spirit refers to the right use of Scripture, sound teaching, and preaching of the gospel, all weapons to combat heresy, wrong teaching, and other works of the devil. Origen identifies the sword of the Spirit with the two-edged sword of Scripture, wielded by the inspiration of the Holy Spirit, held by constant prayer (Eph. 6:18) and ascetic discipline. St. Bonaventure provides a tripartite definition of the sword of the Spirit: the sword of true teaching to fight heresy; the sword of mortification of the flesh, to fight concupiscence; the sword of the way of charity, to fight violence inspired by the devil (*Opera Omnia*, 6.612).

There are a variety of interpretations for the two edges of the spiritual sword. Origen understands two areas of effectiveness: *inner* lusts and temptations insinuated by the Enemy and *outer* enemies of the faith (see Etcheverria, 367), whereas both Augustine and Tertullian interpret the two edges as the two testaments (NPNF 2.441; ANF 3.162); 19th-cent. exegetes suggest that the sword of the Word cuts both ways, piercing some souls "with conviction and conversion, and others with condemnation" (e.g., Jamieson, *Critical and Experimental Comm.* [1877], 6.423). By contrast, literary tradition plays on "two-edged" in the Delphic sense of "cutting both ways" — cutting the user as well as the object, susceptible to double meanings, able to be used for evil as well as good. Relevant examples can be found in Dryden, *The Hind and the Panther* (3.191-92), referring to the "Delphick sword" of the Hind's religious argument, and in Browning, *The Ring and the Book* (12.707-08), a satire on "two-edged" interpretation of Scripture: "I, it is, teach the monk what scripture means, / And that the tongue should prove a two-edged sword."

Wyclif and some Reformation commentators continued the general patristic line of interpretation, heightening the eschatological significance of the immediate conflict with great emphasis on the spoken word of preaching and on the Word in Scripture: believers are engaged in continuous spiritual battle, and their chief weapon is the Word of God — Scripture, preaching the gospel, sound doctrine — against the evil swords of heresy and wrong teaching which "pierce" pure souls (Luther, *Works* [trans. Bouman], 10.165) and against those who would leave Christians "swordless" by depriving them of the Bible (Calvin, *Comm.* [trans. T. H. L. Parker], 11.221). The Reformers further identified the sword of the Spirit with the spiritual authority of the Church in the form of preaching, excommunication, and prayers. The sword of the Spirit in this sense was contrasted with the physical sword of civil power, an issue of tremendous concern in both the 16th and 17th cents., as first the Reformers objected to church usurpation of tem-

poral power and then the Puritans objected to temporal usurpation of spiritual power in "matters of conscience." In fact, the Puritan "soldiers of God" ultimately gave the sword of the Spirit temporal authority in their political and military actions, adopting the sword and the Bible as their insignia and "the sword of the LORD and of Gideon" as their battle cry.

A major strand in interpretation from the Reformation through the Methodist and Evangelical movements of the 18th and 19th cents. is the role of the sword of the Spirit in conversion and in equipping ministers of the Word.

Literary tradition draws on Eph. 6:17 in two main ways: first, in various versions of the ongoing spiritual battle and, second (from the Restoration to the present), in the concept of the power of poetic perception and "word." The chivalric tradition of late medieval writing is founded largely in the NT *miles Christi,* which shapes the medieval ideal of knighthood. The monastic (Cistercian, Bernardine) idea of an inner spiritual battle to achieve Christian perfection equates the armor of God and sword of the Spirit with ascetic discipline and prayer, a "rule of life" which slays earthly lusts. This inner spiritual conflict governs Malory's Grail story in *Le Morte Darthur,* in which the Christian armor is regularly distinguished from the false armor of the world. In Malory the sword is the essence of knighthood; it is both given (usually by a quasi-divine or divine agent) and achieved and is endowed with magical or spiritual properties. "Holy" swords like Galahad's can be used only by the consecrated one, a fact which reflects contemporary theological emphasis on purity and worthiness to bear Christian armor: whoever takes it wrongfully is wounded by it through his own sinfulness. Galahad's sword also follows biblical interpretation in defeating figures representing false teaching, hypocrisy, mortal sin, and the Old Serpent.

In the *chansons de geste* tradition, the battle to recover the earthly Jerusalem from the heathen is seen both to reflect and to participate in the eschatological battle between God and his enemies. Physical swordsmanship is the essence of knightly skill, but victory is given only through grace; in general, however, the "holy war" motif and the central image of the sword of Charlemagne are more reminiscent of Judas Maccabeus and Jewish apocalyptic literature than of the NT.

The most significant extended literary development of Eph. 6:10-17 in English literature is in bk. 1 of *The Faerie Queene,* in which Spenser combines a specific allusion to Ephesians with chivalric traditions and the popular St. George legend. Redcrosse is a sort of knightly Christian Everyman, whose "godly armes" are those of each Christian; the battle takes place on different levels: an inward spiritual battle with Despair, Pride, and the "Sans" brothers; an outward battle with Errour, false teaching, and spiritual deception; and an eschatological battle with Antichrist and the Old Serpent, a battle which also reflects

Christ's redemption of mankind in slaying the dragon which holds Una's parents captive. Redcrosse has no strength of his own but is wholly dependent on his God-given arms to achieve "Holinesse"; Spenser's prefatory letter to Raleigh, alluding specifically to Eph. 6, emphasizes that "arms make the man." Thus, when overcome without his armor by Orgoglio, Redcrosse cannot wield "his bootlesse single blade" (5.11.6), an implicit contrast between the human word and the double-edged sword of the Spirit. Even after his rescue and healing, he cannot wound the dragon with the sword until he is renewed in the well of life and the sword becomes a "bright deaw-burning blade" (11.35.6). Thereafter, he slays the dragon through the mouth (11.53.5-9).

Early Tudor biblical plays follow Reformation issues closely: the Reformation "sword of the Spirit" lies behind Bale's *Three Laws,* a comic dramatization of Luther's admonition to use Scripture as a weapon against the false church; Foxe's *Christus Triumphans* emphasizes that prayers are more efficacious than spears in the spiritual battle. In the polemical writing of the 16th and 17th cents., the sword of the Spirit is often seen as a necessary weapon against corrupt ecclesiastical authority: Milton, e.g., declares that to extirpate "Popery and Prelacy . . . Heresy, Schism, and prophaneness" is "no work of the Civill sword, but of the spirituall which is the Word of God" ("Observations upon the Articles of Peace"). To the Puritan writers, the sword of the Spirit in this context meant the intrinsic power of truth in Scripture and the preaching of the gospel to work on consciences through the Holy Spirit.

The most significant development of the "sword of the Spirit" allusion in 17th-cent. Protestant literature is found in Bunyan's allegory of Christian life as a spiritual battle in *The Holy War* and in *Pilgrim's Progress.* Like Milton, Bunyan views the constant battle with temptation as salutary; the soul must be tested in order to grow strong in grace, and the armor of God is given for that purpose. In *Pilgrim's Progress,* almost immediately after he receives his armor in the Palace Beautiful, Christian encounters Apollyon in the Valley of Humiliation; Apollyon tempts him with accusations and despair, but Christian is saved in the battle by using the sword of the Spirit, making thrusts with it as he quotes Scripture. Bunyan evidently regards "All-prayer" (Eph. 6:18) as a weapon in itself, which helps him against the illusions of the Valley of the Shadow of Death, which "care nothing" for his sword; here Bunyan identifies the sword only with Scripture, and regards prayer as yet another weapon. After the battle with Apollyon, Christian proceeds with "his Sword drawn in his hand, for fear lest he should be assaulted." In *The Holy War* Diabolus arms the people of Mansoul with an infernal panoply ironically paralleling that of Ephesians: the "Sword is a *Tongue that is set on fire of Hell,* and that can bend itself to speak evil of *Shaddai,* his Son, his wayes, and people," all drawing on

the image that evil speaking is like a sword in Pss. 57:4 and 64:3 (as well as the description of the tongue in James 3) and reflecting the tradition that such evil speaking is a sword appropriately countered by the sword of the Spirit.

Restoration satire and raillery found little room for the direct scriptural approach of Bunyan; yet the frequent image of the "sword of wit" draws indirectly on the sword of the word by portraying the perceptions and words of the writer (particularly the satirist) as moral and spiritual weapons. In the frequent contrast between good satire and mere abuse, the former is seen as a sharp, discerning sword, the latter as a blunt weapon or dull razor "never so apt to cut those they are employed on, as when they lose their edge" (Swift, pref. to *Tale of a Tub*). Dryden uses the image in the context of religious controversy, referring to the sword of "satyr," which the Roman Catholic Church could use against the Anglican: the Hind "knew the virtue of her blade, nor won'd / Pollute her satyr with ignoble bloud: . . . And back she drew the shining weapon dry" (*The Hind and the Panther,* 3.263-66). And in the Preface to *Religio Laici* Dryden uses homiletical material as "weapons" in the same way Reformation writers used Scripture as the sword of the Word — "the weapons with which I combat irreligion, are already consecrated."

In Pope's *Epilogue to the Satires, Dialogue 1,* he exalts "Ridicule" itself to the stature of a prophetic denunciation of vice (cf. Isa. 49:2: "He hath made my mouth a sharp sword"):

> O sacred *Weapon!* left for Truth's defence,
> Sole dread of Folly, Vice, and Insolence!
> To all but Heav'n — directed hands deny'd,
> The Muse may give thee, but the Gods must guide.
> Rev'rent I touch thee! but with honest zeal,
> To rowze the Watchmen of the Publick Weal
> To Virtue's Work provoke the tardy Hall,
> And goad the Prelate slumb'ring in his Stall. (212-19)

The chief function of the sword of satiric wit is to penetrate the moral insensibility of the vicious and, more importantly, that of the officers of the Church and law, who have abdicated their moral and spiritual responsibility. In this epilogue and in Pope's later satire generally the sword of the satiric word also shares the discerning nature of the sword of God's judgment, separating truth from falsehood and unmasking vice from a pretense of virtue.

Later in the century, Cowper develops the sword of wit in a more specifically Christian context, echoing Pope's words in "Hope" (594-95): one who lives only for earthly pleasure "laughs, whatever weapons Truth may draw / And deems her sharp artillery mere straw"; Cowper goes on to associate those weapons with Scripture. In "Conversation" he draws on wit / sword imagery to support Christian wit and learning (608-09); elsewhere (*Task,*

2.808-11) he deplores the current decay of the Church's spiritual weapons.

In the Romantic period the poetic word is allied with the imaginative vision as a prophetic weapon in the struggle to bring about a new creation in mankind and society. The most significant Romantic exponent of Eph. 6:17 is Blake, who describes himself as "a soldier of Christ" at his "station" (letter to Butts [10 Jan. 1802]) and who takes Eph. 6:13 as his motto for *Four Zoas*. In Blake's interpretation, the battle is not with bodily desires but with the spiritual forces of negativism, mechanistic philosophy, a false vision of God based in "necessary" reasoning, and a limited material worldview. The "sword" of the well-known hymn "And Did Those Feet" ("Nor shall my sword sleep in my hand / Till we have built Jerusalem . . .") is an essential weapon in that "mental fight." In *Jerusalem* the "spiritual sword" is forged by Los (representing the Poet and Prophet in Man), in an echo of Heb. 4:12: the poetic vision, like the word of God, cuts through to the center of being and can make suffering redemptive:

> [I] took the sighs and tears and bitter groans,
> I lifted them into my Furnaces to form the spiritual
> sword
> That lays open the hidden heart. I drew forth the pang
> Of sorrow red hot . . . . (chap. 1, pl. 9, 17-20)

From the mid-19th cent. on, the sword of Eph. 6 appears in more varied contexts and different versions of the spiritual battle. Elizabeth Browning follows the traditional Christian interpretation in her early poem "The Appeal," concerning England's responsibility in the worldwide spreading of the gospel: The Spirit's sword is "sheathless" (as in *Pilgrim's Progress*) and is identified with the gospel preached in love. In her later work the sword of the Spirit is further identified with the prophetic word of the poet; there is a direct reference in "A Curse for a Nation," in which the poet greets the angelic command to "Write" (cf. Rev. 1–3; 10:11) with the same reluctance shown by various OT prophets: "I faltered, taking up the word: / 'Not so my lord!' " "The word" here appears to be a sword to be "taken up," as in Eph. 6:17, one which participates in God's word of judgment: "From the summits of love a curse is driven, / As lightning is from the tops of heaven."

The governing image of Robert Browning's *The Ring and the Book* is that of a spiritual battle of "peace and joy and light and life" (6.1527) against oppression and death; both Pompilia, the virtuous young wife who runs from her tyrannical and ultimately murderous husband, and Caponsacchi, the priest who helps her, are soldiers in the battle. Pompilia is imaged as an avenging angel who holds lightning for a sword (in effect, her sword is the word of judgment, for her evidence convicts Guido [7.1636-41]); Caponsacchi is repeatedly called "Saint George" and "soldier — saint." The thematic center of the book, the Pope's judgment in bk. 10, uses the imagery of Eph. 6 and

the monastic concept of the priest as a soldier of God to show that in his "irregular" aid of Pompilia, Caponsacchi is a far more effective soldier of Christ than the "laggards," the apathetic, cloistered, yet worldly priests who failed to rescue "the pure soul" or clear her name. The sword of Eph. 6 is also identified here with papal authority and God's judgment, as the Pope uses "Paul's sword" to enact judgment on Guido, doing so in defiance of the "new tribunal . . . Higher than God's — the educated man's!" (1975-76). Here Browning touches ironically on the contemporary theme of how the explosion of materialistic learning and "Science" are affecting religious and imaginative vision. The Pope addresses Pompilia,

> Everywhere
> I see in the world the intellect of Man,
> That sword, the energy his subtle spear,
> The knowledge which defends him like a shield
> Everywhere; but they make not up, I think,
> The marvel of a soul like thine, earth's flower
> She holds up to the softened gaze of God! (10.1012-18)

Francis Thompson typically refers to the sword of the Spirit in traditional Roman Catholic terms — the "unmortal sword" of ascetic discipline, "prayer, the very sword of saints." "In Darkest England" draws an extended comparison between the militarism of the Salvation Army and that of the Franciscan Tertiaries, in which the "sword" is the image for most aspects of the rule of life:

> What sword have they, but you have a keener? For blood and fire, gentle humility; for the joy of a religious alcoholism, the joy of the peace which passeth understanding; for the tumults, the depths of the spirit; for the discipline of trumpets, the discipline of the Sacraments . . . .

Shaw, by contrast, takes up the same subject in *Major Barbara*, which, like *Saint Joan*, deals directly with the theme of Christian warfare. *Major Barbara* keeps biblical reference well in Shaw's ironic hand in the counterpoint and parallel of the Salvation Army's spiritual weapons and Undershaft's cannons. St. Joan, on the other hand, whom Shaw himself calls "the most notable warrior saint in the Christian calendar," embodies a much more independent spiritual power, akin to the Shavian Life Force, even when speaking in medieval chivalric terms of "soldiers of God." Her sword has a spiritual and moral rather than a physical function — "My sword shall conquer yet: the sword that never struck a blow. Though man destroyed my body, yet in my soul I have seen God" (Epilogue).

In another kind of moral battle, D. H. Lawrence gives a kind of spiritual sword to "the one passionate principle of creative being, which recognizes the natural good, and has a sword for the swarms of evil" in the struggle to reject contemporary artifice and materialism — the "accumulation of life and things" which breeds "rottenness" — and to "adhere to that which is life itself, creatively destroying as it goes" (*St. Mawr*).

Some recent works make use of the medieval monastic

concept of the priest as a soldier of God, whose vestments are his armor and who fights the devil both in his monastic rule of life and in the task of the liturgy. D. H. Lawrence draws on this tradition (with an echo of Eph. 6:17) in "The Death of the Baron." The baron, a vicar, was once a Polish soldier and "was a soldier always" in the pulpit, "flash[ing] and trembl[ing] with the fire of his soul." He is a soldier in the struggle of passionate life against barren convention and artificiality, but his mission fails: "his passionate foreign breath / Refused to be molded in arrows of English words." Most striking, however, is Greene's *Monsignor Quixote,* which uses this tradition to deepen the chivalric Don Quixote parallel: the Monsignor's collar, *pechera,* and purple socks are his spear, sword, and armor, even if they are "as absurd as Mambrino's helmet." The climactic battle (taking on the local church "auction" of Our Lady) for which he dons his armor, though ludicrous, is a genuine spiritual struggle — an outward wrestling with certain "powers and principalities" at a cost as great as that of any such battle.

See also ARMOR AND WEAPONS; *MILES CHRISTI.*

Bibliography. Barth, M. *Ephesians: Translation and Commentary on Chapters 4-6.* AB 34a (1974); Etcheverria, R. M. *En Lucha contra Las Potestrades: Exegesis primitiva de Ef. 6,11-17 hasta Origenes. Victoriensa* 28 (1968); Horowitz, S. H. "The Sword Imagery in Beowulf: An Augustinian Interpretation." *DAI* 39 (1978), 2248A.

KATHERINE QUINSEY

SWORDS INTO PLOWSHARES "They shall beat their swords into plowshares," a generally recognized image for the cessation of war, occurs in Isa. 2:4 and Mic. 4:3 in similar descriptions of the universal peace of the messianic age, when Jerusalem is to be the spiritual center of the world and God the arbiter of disputes and judge of nations. The image is reversed in Joel 3:10 in an ironic challenge from God to the Gentile "men of war," as he calls those nations to judgment in "the valley of decision": "Beat your plowshares into swords and your pruning hooks into spears."

The sword is the usual OT *hereb,* usually a short, straight, two-edged blade for close fighting, generally associated in the OT and NT with violence, oppression, and God's vengeance. The plowshare (Heb. *'et,* also meaning "hoe," "mattock," or a "digging tool" in general) is simply the digging end of the primitive plow, the sharpened end of the handle-stick; by David's time most shares were sheathed in iron.

Swords and plowshares may well have been commonplace symbols of war and peace in the ancient world. In Virgil's *Georgics,* written specifically to promote the peaceful arts of agriculture after the ravages of civil war, imagery similar to that of Joel 3:10 is used to describe war prevailing over peace — *et curvae rigidem falces conflatur in ensem* — "And straight spears were forged from the curved sickle."

For some patristic and medieval commentators the conversion of swords to plowshares symbolizes a moral transformation by which fierce minds are changed to good and productive ones (Tertullian, ANF 3.346). Lapide provides an extensive commentary on this image as representing the new reign of Christ in the individual Christian: the bodily members and senses which were weapons of the devil are turned into plowshares tilling God's field of works of charity; however, the inner battle of fleshly desires against those of the Spirit continues; he cites Hugh of St. Victor's application of Joel 3:10 — the "plowshares" of mortified bodily members are converted to spiritual weapons to guard faith (*Comm.* 11.124; 13.521; see also St. Athanasius, *De incarnatione verbi Dei,* 52).

Plowing is also connected with the Word of God (Isa. 2:3; Mic. 4:2), imaged throughout the OT and NT as a "two-edged sword"; patristic commentators give the plowshare to Christ, in whose hands it penetrates the soul much as does the sword of the Word in Heb. 4:12. Thus St. Jerome in his commentary on Isa. 2:4 argues that "when all the hardness of our hearts has been broken by Christ's plow, and the thorny weeds of our vices have been eradicated, then the seeds of God's word can grow up in the furrows." Similarly, St. Bonaventure's discussion of the "plowshares" of the word of God, referring to the preaching of gospel truth (*Opera Omnia,* 9.565), draws on the NT use of plowing as an image for the apostolic mission (Luke 9:62; 1 Cor. 9:10).

References to swords and plowshares follow three main strands in English literary usage: (1) the NT and patristic concept of the preacher/apostle as plowman, (2) the straightforward image of a time of peace and its ironic reversal, and (3) the apocalyptic plowing under of the old creation so that the new can spring forth. *Piers Plowman* is most significant in establishing the tradition of the plowman as both visionary and righteous preacher, drawing from traditional symbolism which suggests that plowing prepares the heart to receive the word of truth and that the plowshare is the tongue (or word) of the preacher (see S. Barney, 276-77). Plowing also symbolizes the true priestly functions of preaching and praying: in the satire on clerical worldliness in Passus 15 of *Piers Plowman* the priest must replace his gilt-edged sword with the "plow" of the breviary (120-23). In the 18th cent., Cowper echoes the idea of the plowshare of Scripture in "Truth," 459-62:

> But the same word that, like the polished share,
> Ploughs up the roots of a believer's care,
> Kills the flowery weeds, where'er they grow,
> That bind the sinner's Bacchanalian brow.

And in the mid-19th cent. Browning's villainous Guido (*The Ring and the Book,* 11.1505-10), after vilifying the lust and greed of the clergy, draws ironically on the traditional spiritual interpretation of converting "members" to righteousness, which evidently formed part of church teaching and counseling:

> I, boast such passions? 'Twas, "Suppress them straight!
> Or stay, we'll pick and choose before destroy:
> Here's wrath in you, — a serviceable sword, —
> Beat it into a ploughshare! What's this long
> Lance-like ambition? Forge a pruning-hook,
> May be of service when our vines grow tall!"

Allusions to the swords/plowshares prophecies appear most frequently in the traditional war and peace context. Langland quotes Isa. 2:4 directly when describing the millennial reign of God's justice (*Piers Plowman*, B.3.295-326), adding to it an element of the judgment of Matt. 26:52: all who bear weapons will be condemned to death unless they forge them into sickles and scythes. The image became popular in the Romantic period as part of the vision of the new age which the power of imagination can help bring into being. It is used in Shelley's "The Witch of Atlas," where the witch writes dreams of the age to come on the brains of the dead who sleep and soldiers dream "that they [are] blacksmiths . . . Beating their swords to plowshares." Hardy uses the traditional interpretation of Isa. 2:4 to drive home the point that "the Christian era is *not* one of peace" ("Leipzig [1813]"):

> "O," the old folks said, "ye Preachers stern!"
> O so-called Christian time!
> When will men's swords to ploughshares turn?
> When come the promised prime?

In his well-known "In Time of 'The Breaking of Nations,'" however, Hardy draws on the allusion more indirectly, using the associations of plowing, a seemingly insignificant yet timeless activity, to make war seem ephemeral.

Allusions to Joel 3:10, where agricultural tools become weapons, are sprinkled throughout the literary canon; one notable instance is in Sidney's *Old Arcadia*, describing the riot in which the mob converts "husbandry to soldiery," making "things serviceable for the lives of men, to be the instruments of their deaths." Occasionally the images of sword and plowshare are conflated. In Marlowe's *Dido, Queen of Carthage*, Dido calls upon her descendant (Alexander) to avenge her on Aeneas by "ploughing up his countries with his sword" (5.1.308), and in Blake's version of the Samson story Manoa cries that "our country is plowed with swords, and reaped in blood!" D. H. Lawrence, in *The Man Who Died*, draws on the OT plow of devastation to underline the cyclical nature of earthly life, destroying as it goes:

> Let the earth remain earthy. . . . The ploughshare of devastation will be set in the soil of Judaea, and the life of

this peasant will be overturned like the sods of the field. No man can save the earth from tillage. It is tillage, not salvation.

In Christian eschatology, the destructive nature of plowing ultimately redeems the natural creation, as in Francis Thompson's "Song of the Hours":

> Through earth, sea, and Heaven a doom shall be driven,
>   And, sown in the furrows it plougheth,
> As fire bursts from stubble,
>   Shall spring the new wonders none troweth.

Blake is a significant later exponent of the swords and plowshares image: it runs throughout his writings in various applications, and the "Plow of Ages" and "starry harvest" of creation are dominant images of his apocalyptic vision. In a passage which appears both in *Four Zoas* ("Night the Seventh," 170-79) and *Jerusalem* (chap. 3, pl. 65), Blake uses the imagery of Joel 3:10 to embody his contention that materialistic reasoning and delight in machinery for its own sake lead inevitably to violence: the "sons of Urizen" (associated with the reasoning power in humans) leave "the plow & harrow" to forge the sword, chariot, and battle axe — "And all the arts of life they changed to arts of death." The sons contemn the hourglass and waterwheel as the simple workmanship of "the plowman" and "the shepherd." The end of earthly time, however, sees Urizen at his true work, tilling "the wide universal field" of the creation with "the Plow of Ages" and sowing "the seed" of human souls to await the final Resurrection (*Four Zoas*, "Night the Ninth," 335-38). In *Milton* that apocalyptic plowing causes the tribulations of the end time; but the violent role of the plow in that time is most vividly portrayed in the climactic scene in *Jerusalem* (chap. 3, pl. 56), where Albion (Mankind) falls under his plow. Having become subservient to his rational nature, . . . "Albion fled from the Divine Vision; with the Plow of Nations enflaming, / The Living Creatures madden'd, and Albion fell into the Furrow; and / the Plow went over him & the Living was Plowed in among the Dead." In Blake's eschatology, this plowing under of both the quick and the dead precedes the final Resurrection, a parallel further supported by Jesus' death and subsequent resurrection in 35-36: "Who fell beneath his instruments of husbandry & became Subservient to the clods of the furrow. . . ."

See also PLOWMAN; SWORD OF THE SPIRIT.

Bibliography. Barney, S. "The Plowshare of the Tongue: The Progress of a Symbol from the Bible to *Piers Plowman.*" *MS* 35 (1973), 260-93; Frye, N. *Fearful Symmetry* (1947); Paley, N. D. *The Continuing City: William Blake's Jerusalem* (1983); Robertson, D. W., Jr., and B. F. Huppé. *Piers Plowman and Scriptural Tradition* (1969).   KATHERINE QUINSEY

T

TABERNACLE Heb. *mishkan,* "dwelling place." The portable tent *('ohel)* sanctuary made at God's command during Israel's wilderness wanderings (Exod. 25–31, 35–40), it was eventually to be replaced by Solomon's Temple. Its construction details, adornment, and function are extensively allegorized by Bede, *De Tabernaculo ac Vasis et Vestibus Ejus.*

See also TEMPLE; TENT.

Bibliography. Halderman, I. M. *The Tabernacle, Priesthood and Offerings* (1925); Haran, M. *Temples and Temple Service in Ancient Israel* (1978); Meyers, C. L. *The Tabernacle Menorah* (1976); Morgenstern, J. *The Ark, the Ephod, and the "Tent of Meeting"* (1945); Nicholson, W. B. *The Hebrew Sanctuary: A Study in Typology* (1951); Rothenburg, B. *Timna* (1972), 125-207.

TAKE NO THOUGHT FOR THE MORROW *See* LILIES OF THE FIELD.

TALE THAT IS TOLD Ps. 90, which is called in the rubric of the KJV "A Prayer of Moses the man of God," compares the transience and impermanence of sinful human life to the majesty, righteousness, and eternality of God: "For all our days are passed away in thy wrath: we spend our years as a tale that is told" (v. 9; cf. Vg *anni nostri sicut aranea meditabuntur,* "our years shall be considered as a spider" — where the Hebrew has a word meaning "sigh," St. Jerome apparently confused it with

the Syriac word for spider, which had in fact already been brought into the LXX).

Shakespeare makes frequent allusions to the text, as when Friar Lawrence relates what has happened at the end of *Romeo and Juliet:* "I will be brief, for my short date of breath / Is not so long as is a tedious tale" (5.3.230-31). In *King John* the melancholy Dauphin of France complains, "Life is as tedious as a twice-told tale, / Vexing the ear of a drowsy man" (3.4.108-09), and Macbeth, hearing that Lady Macbeth is dead, speaks out of the nihilism which his own life has come to typify:

> Life's but a walking shadow. . . .
> It is a tale
> Told by an idiot, full of sound and fury,
> Signifying nothing. (*Macbeth,* 5.5.24-28)

This rendering provides, in turn, the title of Faulkner's *The Sound and the Fury* as well as Rose Macaulay's *Told by an Idiot.* Washington Irving recalls the biblical passage while touring the monuments in "Westminster Abbey" : "Thus man passes away; his name perishes from record and recollection; his history is as a tale that is told, and his very monument becomes a ruin." Because of the prominence accorded Ps. 90 in the liturgy of the *Book of Common Prayer* the verse is frequently quoted in 19th-cent. reflections on impermanence. In Dickens's *The Old Curiosity Shop,* a homecoming provokes a philosophical observation: "The old house had long ago been pulled down and a fine broad road was in its place. . . . So do things pass away, like a tale that is told!" (chap. 73). The phrase has ominous portent in Hardy's *Tess of the D'Urbervilles*, where the narrator describes "the new residents in the garden, taking as much interest in their own doings as if the homestead had never passed its primal time in conjunction with the histories of others, besides which the histories of these were but as a tale that is told" (chap. 54).

TALENTS, PARABLE OF   *See* UNPROFITABLE SERVANT, PARABLE OF.

TALMUD   See the bibliographical essay on "The History of Biblical Interpretation" (pp. 885ff. below).
See also MIDRASH, HALAKAH, HAGGADAH.

TAMAR   There are two Tamars of note in the Bible. The first was the daughter-in-law of Judah, by whom he had (through her successful ploy) twin sons; her pretended harlotry and sexual union with Judah actually allowed fulfillment of the laws of levirate marriage (Gen. 38:6-24; cf. Ruth 4:12). The other Tamar was a daughter of King David, sister to Absalom, who was raped by her half-brother Amnon (2 Sam. 13:1-32). This is the most notorious case of incest in the Bible, resulting in Absalom's tragic rebellion.
See also ABSALOM; INCEST.

TAMMUZ   *See* ADONIS.

TAU   *Tau (thau)* is the latinized name of the Hebrew letter *tau* (graphically represented as *x* in the ancient script), corresponding to the Gk. *tau (t)* and the Lat. *T.* In the ancient Greek language it was, as it remained in Hebrew, the final letter of the alphabet. The actual word appears only in the Vg and Douay-Rheims translations of Ezek. 9:4, 6, but its complex exegetical associations are discernible in a wide range of medieval Christian texts and artifacts. In Hebrew to "make a *tau*" was to make a sign or mark (as in English "X marks the spot"); and the context of Ezek. 9, where the sign has a prophylactic or redemptive function, inevitably brought the idea of the *tau* by implication to other similar passages. Hence in medieval art the mark made by Aaron on the houses to be spared by the destroying angel (Exod. 12:23), the standard on which the brazen serpent was lifted up (Num. 21:9; cf. John 3:14), and the sign to be written on the foreheads of the elect in the Apocalypse (Rev. 7:3) are usually assumed to be *tau*s. The fact that the form of the letter, the majuscule Roman T, was a form of the cross captured the attention of early Christian exegetes, who related it to the already profound christological associations of the Passover in the NT. There are numerous and diverse patristic explanations of the sign's power. The mystery of the T-shaped cross was enhanced by its

iconographic associations with St. Anthony (Abbot) of the Desert, one of the greatest of therapeutic saints in the later Middle Ages, and with the hospital work of the Antonine Order. Its connection with Anthony, an Egyptian saint, may involve the ancient syncretism attested to in early texts by which the sign *tau* was related to the Egyp. *ankh* (†), the hieroglyph for "life." As with a good deal of other cabbalistic lore of exegetical origin, the *tau* has both its learned and its popular traditions in the Middle Ages and the Renaissance. Carved, wrought, or painted *tau*s were commonly worn or carried as a protection against the plague and other diseases. In the 13th cent. St. Francis of Assisi adopted the *tau* as his special sign and signature. Its appearance in learned authors (Richard de Bury and, in a more complicated way, Rabelais) reflects a critical awareness of the sign's Franciscan associations.

   Bibliography. Daniélou, J. *Primitive Christian Symbols* (1964), 136-45; Fleming, J. V. "The Iconographic Unity of the Blessing for Brother Leo." *Franziskanische Studien* 63 (1981), 203-20; Rahner, H. *Symbole der Kirche* (1964), 406-31; Vorreux, D. *Un symbole françiscaine, le Tau* (1977).

TEARS   *See* VALE OF TEARS.

TEKOA   *See* AMOS.

TEMPLE   The Temple is a rich symbol in the OT, profoundly central to the Hebrews' consciousness of the Lord God and of their own identity as his people. *Temple* refers to Israel's places of worship — the Tabernacle for the Ark of the Covenant (Exod. 25–31) and the magnificent structure built (965-928 B.C.) by Solomon (1 Kings 5–8; 2 Chron. 1–6). Solomon's Temple housed the Ark of the Covenant, and was the seat of the divine presence. Writers of the Psalms express a longing for the "house" or "courts" of God because it is his dwelling place (Pss. 27:4; 84). The Temple was also an important sign of Israel's election from among the nations: the structure symbolizing his presence among his people is a tangible assurance to them of God's faithfulness and succor.

   Solomon's edifice, sacked at the Babylonian captivity, was partially restored by Zerubbabel ca. 500 B.C., while a Second Temple, erected by Herod I (73 B.C.–A.D. 4), was then demolished by the Romans in the destruction of Jerusalem. Ezekiel's vision (esp. chaps. 41–42) of a restored Temple in the messianic kingdom is sometimes referred to as the Third Temple.

   As the heir of OT concepts, the NT refers to the Temple in rich and varied contexts. The Temple is still the "house of God" (Matt. 12:4): Jesus was brought there to be circumcised, debated with the elders as a 12-year-old there, taught there, cleansed the court of the Gentiles, and also foretold the Temple's destruction (Luke 2:27-52; 19:45-47; 21:37; John 2:19). Yet he was at pains to declare to the Samaritan woman that as a place of worship it was of much less importance than the spirit of worship (John 4:19-25); indeed, he compared himself to the Temple in such a way as to suggest that its central importance had been eclipsed by his advent (John 2:19-21). At the moment of Christ's death, the Temple veil which hung over the Holy of Holies was rent from top to bottom (Matt. 27:51), signifying the beginning of a new covenant between God and humanity in which open access had been obtained by his sacrifice on the cross. Other NT references to the Temple speak of Christ as the cornerstone of his Church (Matt. 27:42; 1 Pet. 2:6), and of the Christian as a lively stone and member of a holy priesthood (1 Pet. 2:5). Paul writes of the Christian as a temple of the Holy Ghost (1 Cor. 6:19), a temple of the living God (2 Cor. 6:16), and a temple in which God's Spirit dwells (1 Cor. 3:16).

For St. Augustine the human heart, cleansed from unbelief, is the principal temple of God (*De fide et symbolo*, 7). The believer's body is also God's temple; referring to 1 Cor. 3:16-17 and 5:19, therefore, Augustine admonishes Christians to "take heed, then, what you do, take heed that you do not offend the Indweller of the temple, lest He forsake you, and you fall into ruins" (*Sermo*, 82.13). For Christians as well as Jews the Temple is not merely a part of spiritual history but also a feature of eschatological hope. Jews particularly, recognizing that the Second Temple built by Ezra was not the rebuilt Messianic Temple outlined by the prophet Ezekiel (chaps. 40–48), have looked forward to a Third Temple. But medieval Christian writers also reflected on these matters. The Venerable Bede's *Liber de Templo Solomonis* is an example of early Christian biblical scholarship which takes literally the relationship between Solomon's Temple and that prophesied by Ezekiel, down to close concern for exact dimensions and construction plans. Jewish scholars more especially — notably Rashi (11th cent.), David Kimchi (12th cent.), and Maimonides in his commentary on the Mishnah, tractate Middot (cf. his *The Book of Temple Service*) — actually tried to reconstruct something like a working blueprint. And Nicholas of Lyra, a 14th-cent. Franciscan whose upbringing was probably Jewish (and who wrote the most erudite Christian commentary on the Bible in the later Middle Ages), devoted extensive space to particulars of the Temple design, clearly sharing with Maimonides the conviction that such knowledge needed to be precise, since the Temple with its ritual was to be reconstructed exactly when the time of the Messiah's coming was at hand. Apocalyptic interest in the time of the Reformation led to renewed interest in the historical Temple and in Ezekiel's vision. Calvin first used the word to signify a Christian church, as part of his challenge to Rome and assertion of his own linkage in covenantal theology with the priesthood of Aaron. Detailed diagrams of the Solomonic Temple are provided in the Latin Estienne Bible (1540); Sir Isaac Newton later wrote *A Description of the Temple of Solomon* (1728) in which he analyzed its exact measurements.

There are thus two distinct applications of the biblical Temple available to writers aware of the tradition. In the first instance the Temple is the historical center of Jewish worship, the once-and-future high sanctuary of which all other synagogues (and churches) are thought to be but distant reflections. Second, there is the trope, the body, spirit, person, or Church which after Christ took on functions of the Temple. In English literary tradition, dominantly Christian, the tropic or spiritualized applications naturally dominate.

Both Chaucer and Spenser refer to temples which generally have a classical rather than a biblical context, but Chaucer (following Augustine) also writes of the body as a spiritual temple (*Parson's Tale*, 10.875-80). In *The House of Fame* one of the central symbols is Fame's temple, an image with double significance. The temple of Fame or Fortune is a classical image, and Chaucer has chosen to sharpen this reference through the ironic evocation of images of scriptural temples.

Although Milton, too, may use "temple" in a classical context, he also refers specifically to the Temple at Jerusalem as a place into which the triumphant Messiah rode (*Paradise Lost*, 6.890) and as a place where Christ went to talk with the learned rabbis (*Paradise Regained*, 4.217). In bk. 12 of *Paradise Lost* Milton recounts Israel's history and stresses the importance of the Temple as the fulfillment of God's covenant with his people. He writes of God's promise to Israel, and of the people's assurance that "The clouded ark of God 'till then in tents / Wandering, shall in glorious temple enshrine" (12.330ff.).

The Temple as metaphor undergoes diverse development in the 17th cent. Reflecting the notion that the king's body is a representative temple, Shakespeare declares that "sacrilegious murder hath broke ope the Lord's anointed Kingdom" (*Macbeth*, 2.3.373), suggesting that the sacred body of the king is not only God's temple but figuratively God's anointed kingdom. Thomas Adams insists on each individual's being a temple, and holds the Church to be God's great temple (*Works*, 981, 987). Through a series of analogies Daniel Featley contends that the inward temple, built and furnished by God, far surpasses the outward temple (*Clavis Mystica*, 581-82; cf. John Bunyan's *Solomon's Temple Spiritualized*). Joseph Hall thinks of the heart as the altar of the new temple made not by Solomon but by God (*Contemplations*). In "Holy Sonnet 2," John Donne struggles to resign himself fully to the God who has made and redeemed him, writing "I am . . . a temple of thy Spirit divine." For Thomas Vaughan nature itself is a spiritual temple (*Works*, 192).

Thomas Traherne suggests that various parts of the Temple have a moral or spiritual antitype (*Christian Ethicks*, 129). Thinking along such lines, some readers of George Herbert's collection of poems *The Temple* have attempted to make its three parts, "The Church-Porch,"

"The Church," and "Church Militant," concomitant with the three major divisions of the Solomonic Temple (the porticus, or *'ulam;* the house proper, or *hekal;* and the Holy of Holies, or *debir*). In the first two parts there is indeed a close affinity with the sections of the OT Temple, but it seems more accurate to hold that Herbert uses the temple as his unifying symbol to embrace precepts for the Christian's moral behavior, the essence of the Christian experience, and the troubles of the Church in the world. Certain poems focus on observances centered first in the Tabernacle and later in the Temple, followed by others which show the human heart as the center of praise and devotion ("The Altar," "Redemption," "Sepulchre").

In the late 18th cent., William Blake uses the Temple at Jerusalem as one of the central symbols in his poetic and philosophic system, defining "temple" in his own atypical way. For Blake, the Temple is always a negative symbol, precisely *because* it has been perceived as being the dwelling place of God. The very existence of a temple structure Blake regards as a denial of the immediacy of truth and vision, for temples attempt to hide God from the world behind a false veil of mystery. He describes the Temple as "Dividing & uniting at will in the Cruelties of Holiness / . . . then was hidden within / The bosom of Satan the false Female, as in an ark and veil / Which Christ must rend & her reveal" (*Four Zoas,* 8.279, 291-93). But the Temple has been seen as a negative image by writers much more orthodox than Blake. For example, in "The Crucifixion," John Greenleaf Whittier imagines the Temple, a symbol of the Old Covenant, growing cold and dim at the sight of Christ on the cross. He writes, "a curse is on its trembling walls, / Its mighty veil asunder falls!" For Whittier, the Temple is a potent symbol of an outworn order: the temple which concerns him most in the present is the one which Christ promised to "raise up again in three days."

References to the Temple abound in the 19th cent. Almost every reference by John Keats seems to exclude the biblical concept; a possible exception is his allusion to Milton as a "live temple" ("Milton," 12). Wordsworth seems to refer to the biblical metaphor in his allusion to "temples of their hearts" ("Ecclesiastical Sonnets," 2.30.12). Nature's "temple" also appears to be a focus of Wordsworth's usage (*Prelude,* 2.462; 7.256; "Yewtrees," 29; "Ossian," 14). In *The Excursion,* Wordsworth's consideration of the significance of the Temple is strangely similar to Milton's treatment of the same concept in bk. 12 of *Paradise Lost:* despite the Fall, God is still available to humanity, "enshrined within the wandering ark," finally coming to rest within the "inclusive walls and roofs of temples" (*Excursion,* 4.631ff.).

Coleridge thinks of the Temple as a "magnificent place" ("Fears in Solitude," 195, and "Catullian," 10), while Alfred Lord Tennyson invokes it both as ancient place (*Becket,* 1.3.61) and metaphorically as the human body ("Lover's Tale," 1.685). Only three references to

"temple" appear in Gerard Manley Hopkins's work (*Poems,* 1.7.1; 41.93; 144.13), and his statement "This was no classic temple order'd round" ("The Escorial") conveys his central argument.

A modern treatment of the scriptural concept of temple is T. S. Eliot's "Choruses from *The Rock,* " in which he draws together the notions of Temple and Church, and more obliquely the NT metaphor which compares the body with the Temple. In Eliot's poem, the Church and Temple are seen as a single symbol, for both represent "the body of Christ Incarnate." The Temple is both a symbol of human love and devotion for God and a sign of God's presence; therefore it is a potential source of meaning in a weary and vacant world. Eliot illustrates the emptiness of a world from which the Temple is absent, stressing that "where there is no temple there shall be no homes." Hope is to be found in "the lights that we have kindled / The light of altar and of sanctuary" which provide for mankind "the visible reminder of Invisible Light."

Another 20th-cent. use of Temple imagery is found in Flannery O'Connor's short story "A Temple of the Holy Ghost," which uses the Pauline notion of the body as the temple of the Holy Spirit ironically to suggest that purity comes from the intentions of the heart, not from an externally imposed orthodoxy. O'Connor may have imagined her title to call up the reader's memory of another Southern tale, William Faulkner's *Sanctuary* (1931), whose protagonist Temple Drake becomes a profaned and violated version of the temple/body metaphor. (The legal phrase *mulier est templum* may be one source for her name, but Faulkner evidently has the NT in mind as well.)

See also ECCLESIA, SYNAGOGA; HOLY OF HOLIES; TEMPLE OF THE HOLY GHOST.

Bibliography. Gaston, L. *No Stone on Another* (1970); Gutmann, J., ed. *The Temple of Solomon: Archaeological Fact and Medieval Tradition in Christian, Islamic, and Jewish Art* (1976); Rosenau, H. *Vision of the Temple: The Image of the Temple of Jerusalem in Judaism and Christianity* (1979); "The Architecture of Nicolaus de Lyra's Temple Illustrations and the Jewish Tradition." *JJS* 25 (1974), 294-304; Stinespring, W. F. "Temple, Jerusalem." *IDB* 4.534-60; Walker, J. D. "The Architectonics of George Herbert's *The Temple.*" *ELH* 29 (1962), 289-305.

E. BEATRICE BATSON

TEMPLE OF THE HOLY GHOST   In 1 Cor. 6:19, after a discussion of sins of concupiscence, St. Paul asks, "Know ye not that your body is the temple of the Holy Ghost which is in you, which ye have of God, and ye are not your own? For ye are bought with a price: therefore glorify God in your body, and in your spirit, which are God's" (cf. 1 Cor. 3:16). These verses have always been applied in Christian teaching to ethics and the disciplines of personal life (e.g., St. Augustine, *Sermo,* 82.12-13; 99:9), especially as an injunction against sexual impurity and drunkenness. The exemplary biblical "temple" of the

Holy Spirit is the Virgin Mary, "Temple of the Trynyte, most blessed & most benygne, / Where the hooly goste his gold dewe lyst down shed" (according to a 15th-cent. ME trans. of *Stella celi extirpavit*).

The image occurs frequently in the writings of John Donne, who speaks of "those Virgins, who thought, that almost / They made joyntenants with the Holy Ghost, / If they to any should his Temple give" ("Of the Progresse of the Soul," 353-55). In "Holy Sonnet 2" he speaks of himself as "a temple of Thy Spirit divine," and in "Holy Sonnet 15" ponders the meaning of such an indwelling:

> Wilt thou love God, as He thee? then digest,
> My soul, this wholesome meditation,
> How God the Spirit, by angels waited on
> In heaven, doth make his Temple in thy breast.

George Herbert's *The Temple,* the volume in which his poems were collected, refers at once to a church, to the Church or Body of Christ, and to himself as a temple of the Holy Spirit (cf. his *A Priest to the Temple,* chap. 21; Letter 11). The typological commentary in which Herbert engages, with Solomon's Temple, the temple yet to be built, the Church as a renewal of the Temple, and the individual Christian self as spiritual temple, is well exemplified in both Puritan and Anglican preaching of the 17th cent. Joseph Hall's *Contemplation upon the Principall Passages of the Holie Storie* (1642) is illustrative:

> Each renewed man [is] the individual temple of God....
> What is the Altar whereon our sacrifices of prayer and praise are offered to the Almighty, but a contrite heart?
> ... Behold, if Solomon built a Temple unto thee, thou hast built a temple unto thy selfe in us. We are not only through thy grace living stones in thy Temple, but living Temples in thy Sion. . . . Let the Altars of our cleane hearts send up ever to thee the sweetest perfumed smoake of our holy meditations, and faithful prayers, and cheerful thanks-givings. (1158-59)

In one of his "Choruses from *The Rock,*" T. S. Eliot pens a Pauline condemnation of an unfit church: "Your building not fitly framed together, you sit ashamed and wonder whether and how you may be builded together for a habitation of God in the Spirit, the Spirit which moved on the face of the waters" (cf. Ezra 5:8; Eph. 2:19-22). Flannery O'Connor's short story "A Temple of the Holy Ghost" concerns two pubescent convent schoolgirls who mock each other as "Temple One" and "Temple Two," deriving their nicknames from a nun's instructions concerning what to do if accosted by a young man in "an ungentlemanly manner in the back of an automobile" — which was to exclaim, "Stop sir! I am a Temple of the Holy Ghost!"

See also HOLY SPIRIT; TEMPLE.

TEMPTATION *See DELECTATIO MOROSA;* DEMONS, DEMON POSSESSION; DEVIL'S PACT; SEVEN DEADLY SINS; TEMPTATION OF CHRIST.

TEMPTATION OF CHRIST Matthew (4:1-11) and Luke (4:1-13) offer the fullest accounts of the temptation of Jesus during his fast in the desert. After a period of forty days without food, Satan came to him and tempted him in three ways. In the first instance, he taunted, "If thou be the Son of God, command this stone that it be made bread." Jesus answered him, saying, "It is written, That man shall not live by bread alone, but by every word of God." Next, according to St. Luke's account, the devil took Jesus up into a high mountain, showing him "all the kingdoms of the world in a moment of time" and proposing, "All this power will I give thee, and the glory of them: for that is delivered unto me; and to whomsoever I will I give it. If thou therefore wilt worship me, all shall be thine." Jesus, unmoved, rebuked him for his blasphemous presumption: "Get thee behind me, Satan: for it is written, Thou shalt worship the Lord thy God, and him only shalt thou serve." Satan then brought Jesus to a pinnacle of the Temple in Jerusalem and challenged him to cast himself down: if he were really the Son of God, he would surely be protected from harm by angels, Satan argued, citing Ps. 91:11-12. Jesus replied simply, "Thou shalt not tempt the LORD thy God," and the devil departed, at which point "angels came and ministered unto him." In the Matthean account the order of the last two temptations is inverted.

The forty days' fast of Jesus is seen by commentators from St. Augustine (e.g., *De consensu Evangelistarum,* 4.9) to Matthew Henry (*Comm.* 5.31) as paralleling those of Moses (Exod. 34:28) and Elijah (1 Kings 19:8); Henry imagines further that the temptation of Jesus accordingly occurred "probably in the great wilderness of Sinai."

Augustine, who established the main lines of medieval exegesis on the passage, describes the three temptations as "by food, that is, by the lust of the flesh . . . by vain boasting . . . and . . . by curiosity" (*Enarr. in Ps.* 9.13). Later commentators tended to view the three temptations as paralleling those by which Adam fell, described as gluttony, vainglory, and avarice. St. Gregory the Great, who follows this schema in one of his homilies, is quoted by Peter Lombard in his influential *Sententiae* (2.21.5):

> The Ancient Enemy raised himself in three temptations, against our first parents, for then he tempted them with gluttony, vainglory and avarice. And in tempting he was triumphant, for he made them subject to him through their consent. Indeed, he tempted them with gluttony, when he showed them the food of the forbidden tree and persuaded them to eat. He tempted them with vainglory when he said, "you shall be as Gods" [Gen. 3:5]. And having made progress to this point he tempted them through avarice when he spoke of "knowing good and evil." For avarice has as its object not only money, but loftiness of estate. The desire which seeks elation is rightly called avarice in this sense.

Lombard then draws the parallel:

> But in the same way that he [Satan] overcame the first man, he lay subdued before the Second. He tempted him

also with gluttony when he said, "Command that these stones be made bread" [Matt. 4:3]. He tempted him with vainglory when he said, "If thou be the Son of God cast thyself down." And with avarice for loftiness and power, he tempted him when he showed him all the world, saying, "All these things will I give thee if falling down thou wilt adore me."

The commentary of the Venerable Bede on Matthew's version of the temptation narrative (PL 92.19-20) offers an early English example of the established typology; in his comments on Luke's version Bede adds other biblical parallels, including the three excuses in the parable of the wedding feast (Luke 14:16ff.) and the temptation described in John's First Epistle as "the lust of the flesh, and the lust of the eyes, and the pride of life" (1 John 2:16). Later commentators elaborate the motif of the triple temptation with reference to the "three foes of man," the World, the Flesh, and the Devil.

The earliest English literary adaptation of the narrative of the temptation of Christ is in the OE *Christ and Satan* (665-710), in which the age-old struggle between Christ and Satan for the souls of men is summed up with an exemplary model for resistance to diabolical temptation. The 13th-cent. *Cursor Mundi* and 14th-cent. *Stanzaic Life of Christ* both treat the text in light of the parallels suggested in the commentaries. The temptation provides an important subject for the Corpus Christi drama, notably N-Town (22), York (22), and Chester (12), the latter of which pairs it with the narrative of the woman taken in adultery. In York the devil confides in the audience that he will "assaye" Christ with gluttony, vainglory, and "couetise." The text concludes in the manner of earlier vernacular treatments, with Jesus saying:

> For whan þe fende schall folk see,
> And salus þam in sere degre,
> þare myrroure may þei make of me
> for to stande still;
> For ouere-come schall þei noȝt be,
> bot yf þay will.

With the Reformation came a shift in typology and a replacement of medieval paradigms of moral theology with an emphasis on justifying faith. Calvin sees a typological parallel not with Eden but with Sinai: the fasting of Christ in preparation for his ministry is likened to Moses' being taken apart by God to receive the Law (*Harmony of the Gospels*, 1.134). Calvin rejects the medieval identification of the first temptation with gluttony, saying that "it is ridiculous to speak of the immoderate display of gluttony in the case of a hungry man seeking food to satisy his nature. . . . What kind of high living is there in bread? . . . So we gather that Satan had made a direct attack on Christ's faith, that by overcoming it he might drive Christ into illicit and corrupt ways of finding food" (1.137). The Son of God was tempted for the sake of mankind, says Calvin, "that by his victory he might win us the triumph" (1.135). It was also significant for our example: "The first thing worth noting is that Christ uses Scripture as a shield against [Satan], and this is the true way of fighting, if we wish to win a sure victory" (1.135).

John Bale's *A brief comedy or interlude concernynge the temptacyon of Our Lorde and Sauer Jesus Christ by Sathan in the desart* (1537) is a dramatic representation along largely medieval lines, despite its Reformation polemic, and adds as part of the temptation to kingdoms of this world an offer of "fayre women, of countenaunce ameable, / With all kyndes of meates, to the body delectable." In Giles Fletcher's *Christ's Victorie, and Triumph* (1610) Satan disguises himself as "A good old Hermit . . . / That for devotion had the world forsaken" (2.16, 20) — a stratagem which the author may have derived from the popular "Temptations of St. Anthony" (cf. Spenser, *Faerie Queene*, 1.1.29-35). Joseph Beaumont's *Psyche: Or Loves Mysterie in XX Cantos, Displaying the Intercourse betwixt Christ and the Soule* (1648) presents Satan as a wealthy monarch with a long train of servants offering food and aid to the hungry Christ if he will only consent to prove his divine entitlement by performing a miracle. When Christ rejects the offer, the entire pageant vanishes into thin air, leaving only "Ashes, which so strongly smelt / That other Stincks compar'd with this, might seem / Perfumes" (9.241).

Protestant writers frequently parallel the temptation of Christ to Satan's "tempting" of Job. Henry Oxenden's *Jobus Triumphans* (1656) concludes with such a comparison, and allusions to Job flavor Beaumont's *Psyche*. These texts, along with numerous other Protestant "Christiads" identify Rome (and by implication the Roman Church) as the principal kingdom offered to Christ.

The best-known English poem on the subject is Milton's *Paradise Regained* (1671), which he based on the Luke version because it suited his "grand design" to place the "temptation of the tower" last. Milton combines the older medieval motif — showing Christ's heroic resistance to Satan as redressing Adam's disobedience (2.129-39) — with Calvin's emphasis, that Satan, often abusing Scripture for his own purposes, can best be answered from out of a firm command of Scripture. Milton's Satan discovers that while "persuasive rhetoric" had been powerful enough to defeat Eve (4.1-9), the "It is written" of Scripture is more powerful still. Christ refutes Satan not with rational argument but with revelation (4.285ff.).

Carlyle's *Sartor Resartus* has Professor Teufelsdröckh exclaiming (at the beginning of "The Everlasting Yea"): "Temptations in the Wilderness! Have we not all to be tried with such?" In his contemporary reading "Our wilderness is the wide World in an Atheistic century; our Forty Days are long years of suffering and fasting: nevertheless, to these also comes an end." In Somerset Maugham's *Of Human Bondage* Philip, looking down from a hill in Heidelberg, "thought how the tempter had stood with Jesus on a high mountain and shown him the kingdoms of the earth. To Philip . . . it seemed that it was the whole world that was spread before him, and he was eager to step down and enjoy it. He was far from degrading fears and free from prejudice. . . . He was his own master at last. From old habit, unconsciously he thanked God that he no longer believed in him." A more traditional response is represented by T. S. Eliot in *Murder in the Cathedral.* Thomas is approached by a series of tempters whose seductions parallel those faced by Christ in the wilderness: the first tempts him to gratify bodily appetite; the second to seize power over "all the kingdoms of the earth"; and the third to misappropriate spiritual power. A final, unanticipated tempter ("I expected three visitors, not four," says Thomas [476-77]) tries to lure him into the sin of spiritual pride.

See also GET THEE BEHIND ME; SECOND ADAM; WORLD, FLESH, AND DEVIL.

Bibliography. Kermode, F. "Interpretive Continuities and the New Testament." *Rariton: A Quarterly Review* 1 (1982), 33-49; Lewalski, B. *Milton's Brief Epic: The Genre, Meaning, and Art of Paradise Regained* (1966); Pope, E. M. *"Paradise Regained": The Tradition and the Poem* (1947).

TEN COMMANDMENTS The Ten Commandments are presented initially in the OT as the basic law of the covenant community formed at Mt. Sinai (Exod. 20:2-17). Although the matter is debated, they would appear to date from the 13th cent. B.C., the earliest period of Israel's history. The commandments are repeated, with minor differences, in Deut. 5:6-21, in the context of an account of the renewal of Israel's covenant on the plains of Moab during the last days of Moses. In Hebrew, the commandments are called the "Ten Words," from which title (via the Greek translation) comes the term *Decalogue.*

In their original context the commandments were the criminal law (or state law) of ancient Israel, a central part of the constitution of the nascent theocratic state established at Sinai. They were strictly apodictic laws in ancient Israel and passed into the religious and moral realms only with the demise of the Hebrew kingdoms. The commandments are said to have been inscribed on two stone tablets (Deut. 5:22). Each tablet (contrary to later popular tradition) contained the full text of the commandments; one tablet belonged to each partner in the covenant relationship, symbolizing thereby the mutual recognition of responsibilities and authority. The first five commandments pertain primarily to the relationship between God and Israel and are thus essentially theological; the second five focus on interhuman relationships and regulate the social dimensions of life in the covenant community. According to many historians, the breach of any one of the commandments, upon a conviction being secured in the courts, could be followed by the sentence of death. In the reality of Israel's history, however, the command-

ments more often expressed the ideal of national life than the actuality. The fundamental presupposition of the commandments is *love,* God's electing love for Israel and the love required by God from Israel in return (Deut. 6:5).

There is variation between different religious traditions as to the sequence and numbering of the commandments; the most commonly accepted sequence is employed in the following summary of their substance:

(1) *The prohibition of gods other than the Lord of Israel* (Exod. 20:3). The first commandment secures the integrity of Israel's faith and requires of the people total commitment to the single God. (2) *The prohibition of images* (Exod. 20:4-6). Specifically, images of the God of Israel are prohibited. Thereby the idolatry common in the religious practices of Israel's neighbors is eliminated, and the transcendence of the deity is safeguarded. (3) *The prohibition of the improper use of the divine name* (Exod. 20:7). The Law was not concerned with blasphemy or bad language, but with the protection of the sanctity of God's personal name (JHWH) from abuse in such practices as magic and incantation. (4) *The observation of the Sabbath* (Exod. 20:8-11). This positive commandment preserved the sanctity of the seventh day in commemoration both of creation (Exod. 20:8-11) and of Israel's redemption from Egypt (Deut. 5:15). (5) *The honor of parents* (Exod. 20:12). While having general familial implications, the primary thrust is the honor bestowed on parents by the children's acceptance of parental instruction in the faith (Deut. 6:7). (6) *The prohibition of killing* (Exod. 20:13). The Law pertains specifically to culpable murder (other legislation deals with such matters as manslaughter and killing in warfare). (7) *The prohibition of adultery* (Exod. 20:14). (8) *The prohibition of theft* (Exod. 20:15). (9) *The prohibition of false witness* (Exod. 20:16). The Law specifically pertains to the giving of testimony in the courts of law, though it has general implications with respect to truthfulness. (10) *The prohibition of coveting* (Exod. 20:17). This is the most comprehensive of the commandments and is preventative in purpose, attempting to address those desires which might give rise to specific actions as anticipated in the first nine commandments. In his Sermon on the Mount Jesus develops the general principle of the tenth commandment in the understanding of such matters as murder (Matt. 5:21-23) and adultery (Matt. 5:27-28).

Philo *(De decalogo)* and Josephus *(Ant. 3.5.5)* divide the Decalogue somewhat differently than the rabbis (e.g., Tg. Yer. Exod. 20:1-17) and early Christian Fathers did; they count Exod. 20:2-3 as the first commandment, vv. 4-6 as the second, v. 7 as the third, vv. 8-11 as fourth, v. 12 as fifth, v. 13 as sixth, v. 14 as seventh, v. 15 as eighth, v. 16 as ninth, and v. 17 as tenth. Jewish commentary from the early targums through Philo to later medieval midrashim generally emphasizes the fundamental unity and interrelatedness of the Ten Commandments. Under the principle that the breaking of any one commandment leads to or involves the breaking of another, the first five commandments, said to be inscribed on one side of the sapphire tablets, were related symmetrically to the second five opposite them (cf. Mek. Bahodesh 8.706; Philo, *De decalogo*, 12). Each of the commandments in turn is related to one of the "ten words," or commands, God is said to have spoken at the Creation. (Thus, e.g., "I am the LORD thy God" is made to correspond to "Let there be light," etc. (Pesiq. R. 21, 108a; but cf. Tg. Lekah on Deut. 5:6 for a different organization of the material). Various suggestions concerning how the tablets were engraved, the arrangement of the commandments, and the number of times repeated (up to four) arise from a persistent emphasis on the unity of the Decalogue, expressed in its strongest form by Philo, who says that the Ten Commandments contain the kernel of the entire Torah (*De decalogo*, 29), a metonymic association that talmudic-midrashic sources normally reserve for the Shema itself (Deut. 6:4-5), although the same view is reflected elsewhere in the suggestion that the rest of the Law appeared "between the lines" of the Ten Commandments (e.g., Num. Rab 13.14-16). In an analogous fashion, the command forbidding Adam and Eve to eat the fruit of the tree of the knowledge of good and evil is sometimes said to contain the kernel of the Decalogue (Zohar 1.36a), a suggestion found also in the second book of Tertullian's *Adversus Judaeos*. An important emphasis in talmudic sources concerns the fact that the singular number is used ("I am the LORD *thy* God") in order that the individual hearer should recognize that "On my account the world was created, and on my account the law was given" and that obedience is personal; these sources often add that in the eyes of God the obedience of one person finally outweighs the disobedience of the whole world (Philo, *De decalogo*, 10; Sanh. 4:5). Another commentary reads that the singular number was used because in that day the entire nation was of one mind and therefore was addressed by God as one person (Zohar 3.84).

Among early Christian commentators, Origen divides the commandments four to the first table, six to the second (*Hom.* 8, on Exod. 20), a division followed in Protestant churches. St. Augustine's division is employed by Catholics (*In Exod.* q.71; *Contra duas epistolas Pelagianos*, 3.4; *Ep.* 119.11). Augustine is at pains to say that while mere observance of the Decalogue is insufficient for salvation (since after Christ that comes as a gift of grace), it remains nonetheless appropriate for Christians carefully to keep each of the commandments. If legalistic observance can make the Ten Commandments "the letter that kills" (*De spiritu et littera*, 23-24), nonetheless the "law of God was necessary not only for the people of that time but remains necessary now for the right ordering of our lives as well" (*Contra duas epistolas Pelagianos*, 3.10). The effect of grace upon those who approach the Decalogue in the spirit of the New Law in Christ, "they whom the Spirit quickens," is that they obey the precepts of the Law out of "faith which works by love in the hope of spiritual rather than material benefits" (*Contra duas Epistolas Pelagianos*, 3.11). To such observers the Ten Commandments are no longer "the letter that kills," or Old Law, but a means of "freely obeying" the Spirit. For Augustine one implication of this view is that Jewish observance of the Sabbath is related to the larger fabric of Judaic law and not held to be strictly binding upon Christians (*De spiritu*, 23). The commandments remain basic to moral law and a virtuous life, as illustrated by Christ's enjoinder of the rich young ruler (Matt. 19:17), but the New Law asks for a more radical spirit in their application: "If thou wilt be perfect, go and sell that thou hast, and give to the poor, and thou shalt have treasure in heaven: and come and follow me" (v. 21). This principle refers every commandment to its common source and purpose in bringing all persons to communion in Christ (*Hom.* 84; 85, sup. Matt. 19:17), a purpose made clear in the Great Commandment or "summary of the Law" in Deut. 6:5 and extensively reiterated by Jesus in the Sermon on the Mount (Matt. 5:3–7:29) as well as in response to a question from the Pharisees concerning the "greatest commandment" (Matt. 22:34-40; Mark 12:28-34).

The Ten Commandments were from the beginning foundational to English law: King Alfred prefixed the Decalogue to his own legal code, and in a time when moral and civil law were not yet distinct Aelfric, in his *Catholic Homilies* (2.12), as also in his sermon *De Populo Israhel* ([ed. Pope], 2.20), could apply the commandments readily to a civil context. Treatises on the Decalogue proliferated after the 13th cent., partly in response to Archbishop Pecham's insistence in his Lambeth Constitutions (1273) on expanded catechetical instruction, an encouragement which led to popular ME lyrics on the subject (e.g., C. Brown, *English Lyrics of the XIIIth Century*, nos. 23, 70) and verse sermons (e.g., Brown, *Religious Lyrics of the XIVth Century*, no. 102). In the seventh play of the Towneley cycle (as in the sixth play of the *Ludus Coventriae*, or N-Town Corpus Christi cycle), Moses proclaims in epitome a typical pulpit exposition of the Decalogue, which is anachronistically followed later by the corresponding ten plagues upon Pharaoh's Egypt, said to be "for brekinge of the X commaundementis." The biblical order is retained by George Herbert's "The Church Militant," where, in the redeemed life of God's chosen, "The Ten Commandments there did flourish more / than the ten bitter plagues had done before." A connection between transgression and natural judgment is reflected in hexaemeral literature from Bede to St. Bonaventure (e.g., the *De Legibus* of William of Auvergne and the *De Legibus et Consuetudinibus Angliae* of the great 13th-cent. English jurist Henri de Bracton (or "Bretton"). Matthew Tyndale's argument that the "lawe of the kynge is Gods lawe" (*Obedience of a Christian Man*, 79) accords with basic English tradition from Alfred through Bracton to Blackstone.

Commentary on the second commandment in the 14th and 15th cents. was controversial, since it reflected directly on the use of images in churches, especially the propriety of their relation to meditation and catechism and the possibility that excessive veneration might constitute idolatry. This issue was strongly contested by the Lollards, who opposed images (see Owst, 134-43), and by members of the regular clergy such as John Mirk (*Festial*, 171ff.), who argued, against the Lollards, that simple people are not really led to believe that Matthew, Mark, Luke, and John were animals or that Moses really had "two hornes" (261, 302); such images, they said, were not associated with the idolatry prohibited in the second commandment but were an invaluable instrument for teaching the gospel to illiterate or semiliterate persons: "I say boldly that ther ben many thousand of pepull that couth not ymagen in her hert how Crist was don on the rood, but as thei lerne hit by sy3t of ymages and payntours" (171).

Concerning the third commandment — which was thought to involve everything from blasphemous explication to false oath and perjury — there was less debate in the 14th cent. Lollards and regular clergy agreed that breach of the commandment was out of hand among laity and clergy, young and old, male and female alike. "Horible sweryinge, as the most parte of the pepull dose now-adaies" (MS Royal 18.B.23, fol. 86b) is a concern of many sermons, as it is in Chaucer's *Canterbury Tales,* whose Host is reproved for profanity and whose "coy" Prioress is said to swear by "St. Loy," the patron saint of cart drivers (*General Prologue*, 1.120). Chaucer's Parson takes up the matter in his discussion of the sin of wrath (*"Sequitur de Ira"*): "What seye we eke of hem that deliten hem in sweryng, and holden it a gentrie or a manly dede to swere grete othes, al be the caus not worth a straw? Certes, this is horrible synne" (*Parson's Tale*, 10.600-603). The early 15th-cent. dialogue sermon *Dives et Pauper* offers a dramatic exchange on the import of all the commandments, following typical patristic commentaries.

The Decalogue assumed fresh importance in the Reformation, in that many Reformers felt that a signal feature of corruption in the Church was a lax regard for rampant sin and insufficient attention to obedient living. Some of this laxity may have been occasioned theologically, arising from implications of the principle that "the Old Law was good but imperfect" and that the Law ought to be seen as a means subservient to the end of inward grace (e.g., St. Thomas Aquinas, *Summa Theol.* 1a-2ae.98.1; 106.1.2). For Matthew Tyndale, by contrast, though the Law is not our means of salvation, it is surely the standard of "perfeccion and the marke where at all we oughte to shote" (*Obedience of a Christian Man*, 127). Calvin follows the main patristic tradition in most respects but gives more space to analysis of the Decalogue as basic to the Law by which the life of Christians is proscribed; for him

a reading of the Decalogue is essential in regular worship, since it is effectively a statement of God's sovereign claim on the total obedience of his covenant people. "Hence," he says, "I make part of [worship] to consist in bringing our consciences into subjection to his Law." He adds, amplifying Augustine, "car c'est un hommage spirituel" (*Inst.* 2.8.13-59). Calvin departs from Augustine in enjoining strict observance of the fourth commandment, concerning the Sabbath, applying it to the Lord's Day, Sunday; in general he substantially elevates the role of the Decalogue in both liturgy and catechism. The official *Homilies Appointed to Be Read in Churches* (1562) in the time of Queen Elizabeth included homilies on the second (2.1.2), third (1.7), seventh (1.7), and eighth, ninth, and tenth commandments (1.12). Elizabeth also ordered that the Decalogue be painted over the communion table in English churches (over existing triptych altar paintings featuring the Crucifixion or Annunciation), or else on the tympanum. Later, under Archbishop Laud, much of the earlier type of painting and statuary was reintroduced, and some inscriptions of the Ten Commandments were then blotted out and replaced by crucifixes.

In England under the Puritans, differences of opinion concerning the degree to which Christians under the "dispensation of grace" were obliged to literal observance of all precepts of the Law led to disagreements between the Puritans, who in general took the strong view of Calvin, and most Roman and some Anglican theologians, who took a less rigorous view, not only with respect to the fourth commandment but also, it was sometimes argued, with respect to the third, *de facto* winking at parishioners "jurans par S. Jaques ou S. Antoine," as Calvin puts it (*Inst.* 2.8.25). The Puritans were strong on enforcement of the seventh comandment; their detractors wondered if in their mercantile practices they were as scrupulous concerning the eighth. In Shakespeare's *Measure for Measure,* in which excessive Puritan ardor in judgment concerning the seventh commandment is seen (in Angelo) as an index of spiritual pride, the devilish Lucio says to one of his bewildered interlocutors, "Thou concludest like the sanctimonious pirate that went to sea with the Ten Commandments, but scraped one out of the table." The gentleman replies, "Thou shalt not steal?" — to which Lucio responds in the affirmative. Another then observes, "Why, 'twas a commandment to command the captain and all the rest from their functions. They put forth to steal" (1.2.6-14).

In *King Lear*, when Edgar is feigning madness in the hut with Lear and Kent, he offers a crude summary of the commandments whose breach most affects the King's fortunes: "Take heed o' the foul fiend. Obey thy parents, keep thy word justly, swear not, commit not with man's sworn spouse, set not thy sweet heart on proud array. Tom's a-cold" (3.4.82-85): the commandments ignored, anarchic passions reign instead.

The representation in Bunyan is, by contrast, that of

the vindictive passion of the Mosaic law, when in *The Pilgrim's Progress* Moses overtakes Christian and trummels him, saying, "I know not how to show mercy" for his breaches of the Law.

For the Calvinist poet William Cowper the Decalogue is as uncompromising as the occasion of its transmission was terrifying. Echoing the opening sentiments of Milton's *Paradise Lost,* he writes how God

> Marshalling all his terrors as he came;
> Thunder, and earthquake, and devouring flame;
> From Sinai's top Jehovah gave the law —
> Life for obedience — death for ev'ry flaw.
> When the great Sov'rein would his will express,
> He gives a perfect rule; what can he less? ("Truth," 547-52)

For Cowper the alternative to God's order is chaos, as the sinful world "in scorn of God's commands" suggests, and inevitably judgment follows:

> Sad period to a pleasant course!
> Yet so will God repay
> Sabbaths profaned without remorse,
> And mercy cast away. ("Bill of Mortality, 1793")

The poems of Lord Byron, whose *Don Juan* ascribes to Malthus "the eleventh commandment / Which says, 'Thou shalt not marry,' unless 'well'" (15.297-99), are replete with rewritings of the Decalogue. In *The Deformed Transformed* the makings of Byron's demonic hero are already apparent: "And thank your meanness, other God have you none" (2.3.318); the curse for dishonoring parents is alluded to in *Werner; or the Inheritance* (1.1.92-98; 3.4.597); the commandment against blasphemy is parodied in "English Bards and Scotch Reviewers" (504-06), as also is the fourth commandment (320-21, 636-37), which is more gently treated in *Childe Harold* (1.684-97). " 'Thou shalt not bear false witness' like 'The Blues' " (*Don Juan,* 1.1643), rhyming with " 'Thou shalt not covet' Mr. Sotheby's Muse" (1641), introduces a pervasive theme in Byron's *Don Juan* (cf. 12.121-23) as in others of his poems ("Parisina," 65-66, 883). In his *Prophecy of Dante,* "They who kneel to idols so divine / Break no commandment" (4.31-32); in short, as a creature of secular grace, the Romantic poet enjoys unlimited freedom *contra legem.*

The tendency to disparage or rewrite the Ten Commandments is unsurprisingly a common theme in modern literature. The "eleventh commandment" of modern cynicism, as noted in the *Oxford English Dictionary,* is "Thou shalt not be found out," since, as Somerset Maugham puts it in *Mrs. Craddock,* "in real life everyone [is] very virtuous and very dull" where "the ten commandments" hedge one around "with the menace of hell fire and eternal damnation" (chap. 27).

In fact, Byronic parody, though it takes a variety of forms, is but one strategy for deflecting the burden of the Decalogue. In Hardy's *Tess of the D'Urbervilles* "to visit

the sins of the fathers upon the children may be a morality good enough for divinities, [but] it is scorned by average human nature" (chap. 11), a stance Hardy generalizes upon not only with his satire on the evangelistic sign painter in that novel (who goes about painting the precepts of the Decalogue) but also in *Far from the Madding Crowd* (chap. 26), "An Imaginative Woman," and elsewhere.

Thackeray finds little respect paid to the sixth and seventh commandments in French society, but rather the disavowal of them common among "the politest people in the world" (*The Newcomes,* chap. 37). Carlyle's Teufelsdröckh pontificates, " 'At a time when the Divine Commandment, Thou shalt not steal, wherein truly, if well understood, is comprised the whole Hebrew Decalogue . . . at a time, I say, when this Divine Commandment has all but faded away from the general remembrance; and, with a little disguise, a new opposite Commandment, Thou shalt steal, is everywhere promulgated — it perhaps behooves . . . the sound portion of mankind to bestir themselves and rally" (*Sartor Resartus,* 2.10). Some of the satire is more double-edged, such as Arthur Clough's "The Latest Decalogue," in which are found the lines "Thou shalt have but one God only; who / Would be at the expense of two," and "No graven image may be / Worship'd, except the currency." Carlyle's own position may be more clearly defined in his essay "Characteristics," where he takes the view that "The Duties of Man . . . to what is Highest in himself make but the First Table of the Law," a rationalization only too quickly seized upon by Sinclair Lewis's *Elmer Gantry* but bypassed in favor of gleeful antinomianism by Pilon in *Tortilla Flat:* " 'I have been bad,' Pilon continued ecstatically. He was enjoying himself thoroughly. 'I have lied and stolen. I have been lecherous. I have committed adultery and taken God's name in vain' " (chap. 8). This is a popular form of John Stuart Mill's argument that Christian morality as reflected in use of the Decalogue is negative and passive rather than positive and vigorous: "in its precepts 'thou shalt not' predominates unduly over 'thou shalt' ("On Liberty"). Christina Rossetti, however, seems to have thought otherwise: her *Letter and Spirit* examines the Ten Commandments positively, with a view to evincing their intention in constructive social terms. This was, however, even among Victorians, knowingly to go against the grain.

D. H. Lawrence regards American liberty as "a liberty of THOU SHALT NOT . . . [in] the land of THOU SHALT NOT" *(Studies in Classic American Literature),* whereas H. G. Wells, considering the opposite side of the coin, reflects that "there are two distinct and contrasting methods of limiting liberty; the first is Prohibition, 'thou shalt not,' and the second Command, 'thou shalt' " (*A Modern Utopia,* chap. 2).

As the need has arisen, modern writers have taken

renewed interest in at least one of the commandments, as James Russell Lowell illustrates:

> In vain we call old notions fudge
> And bend our conscience to our dealing;
> The Ten Commandments will not budge,
> And stealing will continue stealing. ("International Copyright")

See also GREAT COMMANDMENT; LETTER AND SPIRIT.

Bibliography. Harrelson, W. *The Ten Commandments and Human Rights* (1980); Nielson, E. *The Ten Commandments in New Perspective* (1968); Owst, G. R. *Literature and Pulpit in Medieval England* (1966); Phillips, A. *Ancient Israel's Criminal Law: A New Perspective* (1970); Phillips, J. *The Reformation of Images: Destruction of Art in England, 1535-1660* (1973); Stamm, J. J., and M. E. Andrew. *The Ten Commandments in Recent Research* (1967); Steinmetz, D. C. "The Reformation and the Ten Commandments." *Int.* 43.3 (1989), 256-66.
PETER C. CRAIGIE
DAVID L. JEFFREY

TENDER MERCIES In Scripture the "tender mercies of the Lord" are sometimes contrasted with the miseries which come upon those who pursue salvation by their own means (e.g., Ps. 77:9; James 5:1-11). Most often, however, the phrase is simply descriptive of the infinite patience and kindness of God toward his fallible people (Pss. 103:4; 119:156; 145:9). The Psalmist thus prays: "Remember, O LORD, thy tender mercies and thy lovingkindnesses; for they have been ever of old. Remember not the sins of my youth, nor my transgressions: according to thy mercy remember thou me for thy goodness' sake, O LORD" (Ps. 25:6-7; cf. 51:1ff.; 40:11; 79:8; 119:77). This application of the phrase is commonplace in English spiritual writing — particularly that of Puritan writers from Richard Baxter and John Bunyan in England to Jonathan Edwards and Cotton Mather in America.

Another instance of the phrase "tender mercies," unique in the Bible, forms an ironic contrast to normative usage: "A righteous man regardeth the life of his beast, but the tender mercies of the wicked are cruel" (Prov. 12:10). This verse had generated a common cliché which occasionally in modern parlance confuses the primary meaning. John Woolman, in his *Journal,* reflects on his life as a young Quaker and in a famous passage sets the two uses in their proper biblical relationship. He had idly thrown stones at a nesting robin and finally hit and killed it. "Seized with horror" at his exploit, "having killed an innocent creature while she was careful for her young," he climbed the tree where the nest was and put an end to the young birds,

> supposing that better than to leave them to pine away and die miserably; and believed, in this case, that Scripture proverb was fulfilled, "The tender mercies of the wicked are cruel." I then went on my errand, but, for some hours, could think of little else but the cruelties I had committed, and was much troubled. Thus He, whose tender mercies

are over all his works, hath placed that in the human mind, which incites to exercise goodness towards every living creature, and this being singly attended to, people become tender-hearted and sympathizing, but being totally rejected, the mind shuts itself up in a contrary disposition.

TENEBRAE *Tenebrae* (Lat., "darkness") is a popular designation for the special liturgy of Matins and Lauds now used in the last three days of Holy Week but historically observed during the entire week leading up to Easter. The term is not of biblical derivation, but refers to a ceremonial observance of the Middle Ages, an extinguishing of candles (usually fifteen by the altar) one by one following recitation of a Psalm until one only, hidden behind the altar, remained after the singing of Ps. 51 and the *benedictus.*

In his *Sermo Iste Debet Dici ad Tenebras,* 15th-cent. English preacher John Mirk explains the liturgy at length as a commemoration of the dark night of Jesus' prayers in Gethsemane, the betrayal after midnight by Judas, and the midday darkening of the sun at Christ's crucifixion when "þe sonne wythdroȝ hyr lyȝt and was darke þrogh þe world" (ed. T. Erbe, 27.117). Subsequent literary treatments tend to be associated with Holy Week liturgy, as is Oscar Wilde's *"E Tenebris"* (1881), an appeal for mercy out of personal spiritual darkness:

> Come down, O Christ, and help me! reach thy hand,
> For I am drowning in a stormier sea
> Than Simon on thy lake of Galilee:
> The wine of life is spilt upon the sand,
> My heart is as some famine-murdered land
> Whence all good things have perished utterly,
> And well I know my soul in Hell must lie
> If I this night before God's throne should stand.
> 'He sleeps perchance, or rideth to the chase,
> Like Baal, when his prophets howled that name
> From morn to noon on Carmel's smitten height.'
> Nay, peace, I shall behold, before the night,
> The feet of brass, the robe more white than flame,
> The wounded hands, the weary human face.

More recent references to this theme, as well as the liturgy, are found in David Jones's *Sleeping Lords* sequence (27) and in Geoffrey Hill's *Tenebrae* (1978).

TENT The importance of this term in the Bible is multifold. Literally, the tent is the setting of many of the most memorable of patriarchal stories: of Noah's drunken shame (Gen. 9), of the promise by the "three men" to Abraham and Sarah (Gen. 18), of the loot taken by Achan at Jericho (Josh. 7), of Jael slaying Sisera (Judg. 4, 5; cf. Judith and Holofernes [Jdt. 12–13]), and others. It also recurs incidentally in many early narratives as the dwelling of the seminomadic Hebrews. The term *tent* could mean "household," "family," "domain" (e.g., Israel "spread his tent" beyond Edar, Gen. 35:21), and such associations in turn are capable of metaphoric extension.

Tent imagery may also be understood as part of a pastoral, antiurban complex of symbolism. To live in tents was the key vow of the Rechabites even in the time of Jeremiah (Jer. 35). In this context the tent peg which Jael used to murder Sisera has been seen as "a fitting symbol of nomad opposition to sedentary culture" (M. Pope, "Rechabites," *IDB* 4.14-16).

The other main source of symbolic power for the tent is its association, sometimes identification, with the Tabernacle. God, through Nathan, tells David not to build him a "house" or temple since he has always "walked in a tent," i.e., preferred a movable sanctuary (2 Sam. 7:6). In the NT, Stephen recalls Solomon's construction of a "house" or temple for God, but intimates that this was inappropriate: "The Most High dwelleth not in temples made with hands" (Acts 7:48; cf. 2 Cor. 5:1). The Epistle to the Hebrews (chaps. 8 and 9) likewise regards the tent or tabernacle rather than the temple as the true sanctuary.

The placing of God himself in a tent, as in 2 Sam. 7:6, has corollary expressions in metaphors of the Psalms, Prophets, and other writings. The most famous of these is the exalted image of God spreading out the heavens "as a tent to dwell in," dwarfing the palaces of kings and all works of mankind (Isa. 40:22). Elsewhere God's desirable "courts" are contrasted in Ps. 84:10 to the "tents of wickedness," a famous image which is the basis of a long passage in Milton's *Paradise Lost* (11.557-607). Jacob's tents in Jer. 30:18 (cf. Mal. 2:12), as well as Judah's in Zech. 12:7, stand for the nation; in Jer. 4:20 the ruined tent seems to signify both the nation and the prophet's personal fortunes. In Isa. 13:20, a place where no Arab will pitch his tent is the nadir of desolation, while in Isa. 38:12 Hezekiah's image of the quickly removed tent signifies the fleetingness of life.

In the NT, one usage is crucial. In John 1:14, the Word made flesh is said to have "dwelt among us"; the verb literally means "pitched his tent." Thus Herbert's "Anagram" on Mary: "How well her name an *Army* doth present, / In whom the Lord of Hosts did pitch his tent!"

Literary allusions to biblical tents are fairly numerous, as in the incarnational imagery of Edward Taylor's *Preparatory Meditations* (2.24.10), in which he desires "to make my flesh thy Tent, and tent with in't" (see also, e.g., "Olofernes'" tent in Chaucer's *Man of Law's Tale,* 2.940, and *Monk's Tale,* 7.3759; Abel's tent in Donne's "Progresse of the Soule," 414, 439; etc.). In Blake's "Mock on, Mock on, Voltaire, Rousseau" the atoms and particles of science become "sands upon the Red Sea shore, / Where Israel's tents do shine so bright" (cf. the "golden tent" of God in his "Little Black Boy," and further uses in *Milton, The Four Zoas,* etc.). D. H. Lawrence uses the image in a number of poems: "My Way Is Not Thy Way" speaks of "the tent of cloven flame." The Isa. 40:22 image has been popular in modern American writing — as in Emily Dickinson's poem "I've known a heaven, like

a tent," and the ending of chap. 57 of Melville's *Moby-Dick,* referring to "the fabled heavens with all their countless tents."

See also RECHABITES; TEMPLE.　　HERBERT SCHNEIDAU

TETRAGRAMMATON　　*See* NAMES OF GOD.

THADDAEUS　　*See* APOSTLE.

THEOCRACY　　Josephus is credited with devising the term *theocracy* (from Gk. *theos,* "God," and *kratos,* "power") to denote a god-oriented government which functions by "placing all sovereignty and authority in the hands of God" (*Contra Apionem,* 2.165). The term may be applied to any nation or tribe which claims to be directed by a god or gods, as, e.g., in the days of the Judges. Premonarchic Israel was a society in which priests were the authorities; although they were primarily religious leaders, they functioned also at various periods as judges, prophets, military advisers and leaders, and educators. Josephus asks, "Could there be a finer or more equitable polity than one which sets God at the head of the universe, which assigned the administration of its highest affairs to the whole body of priests, and entrusts to the supreme high-priests the direction of other priests?" (*Contra Apionem,* 2.185; 1.367). Joshua and Judges describe in detail such a working theocracy.

When the governing authority passed from the priests to kings, the ideal of a theocracy was still a fundamental concept of government; the king was supposed to be the Lord's vice-regent. Despite his misgivings about kingship (1 Sam. 8:5-22), Samuel chose Saul to be the first king of Israel (1 Sam. 8:9-27; 10:24), but Saul did not fulfill Samuel's expectations and so he secretly anointed David (1 Sam. 16:13). Only a few of the kings of the Israelites proved to be worthy; in fact, the majority of them, like Saul, were miserable failures — doing what was "right in their own eyes" rather than acting in obedience to God's law.

Some Utopian literature is predicated on the principles of theocracy; examples include More's *Utopia* (1516) and Bacon's *New Atlantis* (1627). The religious utopias extol the theory that a successful society must be essentially theocratic; however, the bulk of utopian literature is based on the premise that great societies are to be achieved through economic, political, or technological innovations. There have been many attempts throughout history to implement theocratic societies, one of the more recent being Puritan governance in Massachusetts which required obedience to religious laws. A contemporary example of theocracy is Islam.

In *Absalom and Achitophel,* Dryden describes the plot to discredit Charles II and replace him with his son, the Duke of Monmouth. One of the arguments used by the plotters was that a return to theocracy was needed:

Hot *Levites* Headed these; who pul'd before
From th' *Ark,* which in the Judges days they bore,
Resum'd their Cant, and with a Zealous Cry,
Pursu'd their old belov'd Theocracy. (*The Poems of
John Dryden* [1958], 230.519-22)

In the 20th cent., Margaret Atwood's *The Handmaid's
Tale* (1985) concerns itself with life in an American fundamentalist dystopia where the old Puritan ideal of
theocracy is realized as a particularly perverse and vulgar
tyranny.

Bibliography. Bercovitch, S. *The American Jeremiad*
(1978); Frankfort, H. *Kingship and the Gods: A Study of
Ancient Near Eastern Religion as the Interpretation of
Society and Nature* (1948); Kantorowicz, E. H. *The King's
Two Bodies* (1957); Negley, G., and J. Patrick, eds. *The Quest
for Utopia: An Anthology of Imaginary Societies* (1952);
Rowley, H. H. *The Faith of Israel: Aspects of Old Testament
Thought* (1956); Smith, W. R. *Lectures on the Religion of the
Semites: The Fundamental Institutions* (1889; rpt. 1927);
Wach, J. *Sociology of Religion* (1944).
RONALD M. MELDRUM

THEODICY Theoretical attempts to reconcile the
existence of evil in the world with belief in an omnipotent,
omniscient, and good God are called theodicy. The syl-
logistic expression of apparent contradiction in such
propositions is best known from classical times in the
formulation of Epicurus (341-170 B.C.), quoted by Lactantius (A.D. 260-330) in his *Treatise on the Anger of God*
(chap. 13). Modern formulations typically cited are those
of Leibniz, who coined the term *theodicy* in his work so
titled (*Théodicée* [1710]), and of David Hume. The point
of literary theodicy, as of theological theodicy, is to assert
the essential justice of God despite the existence of evil.
The chief biblical text employed is the book of Job; the
chief commentary upon it in Christian tradition is the
Moralia by St. Gregory the Great. A NT passage sometimes adduced in connection with theodicy is Matt. 21:33-
46, the parable of the usurping husbandmen, upon which
the commentary tradition is less unequivocally defined.

While St. Augustine's attempt to counter the Manicheans (esp. in his *Contra Faustum*) provides a locus
classicus for one sort of argument — namely, that evil is
a privation of good (i.e., is thus "no-thing" in the metaphysical sense) — subsequent arguments have varied
widely in their strategy. The most famous literary
theodicy in English is undoubtedly Milton's neo-
Augustinian attempt "to justify the ways of God to man"
in *Paradise Lost.* Other examples, such as Chaucer's
elegiac *Book of the Duchess,* draw on Boethius's *De
Consolatione Philosophiae* as well. In the 18th cent.
Pope's *Essay on Man* offers a neo-Aristotelian or Leib-
nizian (compatablist) rationale, and in the 20th cent.
J. R. R. Tolkien makes an imaginative contribution in his
trilogy, *The Lord of the Rings.*

See also NAKED CAME I; OMNIPOTENCE; PREDESTINA-
TION.

Bibliography. Besserman, L. *The Legend of Job in the
Middle Ages* (1979); Danielson, D. *Milton's Good God: A
Study in Literary Theodicy* (1982); Dawson, P. M. S. "Blake
and Providence: The Theodicy of *The Four Zoas.*" *Blake: An
Illustrated Quarterly* 20 (1987), 134-43; Forrer, R. *Theodi-
cies in Conflict: A Dilemma in Puritan Ethics and
Nineteenth-century American Literature* (1986); Goodheart,
E. "Job and the Modern World." *Judaism* 10 (1961), 21-28;
Klause, J. *The Unfortunate Fall: Theodicy and the Moral
Imagination of Andrew Marvell* (1983).

THEOLOGICAL VIRTUES   St. Paul's famous passage on the nature and quality of love in 1 Cor. 13 concludes with these words: "And now abideth faith, hope,
charity, these three; but the greatest of these is charity"
(v. 13). "These three," commonly linked in the NT (cf.
1 Thess. 1:3; 5:8; Gal. 5:5-6; Col. 1:4-5; Heb. 10:22-24),
are called the "theological virtues" by the Fathers, as
distinct from acquired "moral" or classical virtues (prudence, temperance, fortitude, and justice), because their
formal object is God himself. As such, faith, hope, and
charity are the qualities of a perfected Christian moral life,
says St. Augustine (*Enchiridion de fide, spe, et caritate,*
3-4), proceeding from biblical wisdom and issuing in
worship. Personal realization of these virtues is, in effect,
an internalization of the Scriptures: "Thus a man supported by faith, hope, and charity, with an unshaken hold
upon them, does not need the Scriptures except for the
instruction of others. And many live by these three things
in solitude without books. . . . And when anyone shall
reach the eternal, two of these having fallen away, charity
will remain more certain and vigorous" (*De doctrina
Christiana,* 1.39.43).

During the reign of Hadrian, when Roman Christians
were as likely to name children for theological virtues as,
later, were 17th-cent. Puritans, a Roman matron named
Sophia (Wisdom) with her three young daughters Pistis,
Elpis, and Agape (Faith, Hope, and Charity) were martyred and interred on the Aurelian Way; their tomb (in the
crypt of St. Pancratius Church) was still being frequented
by pilgrims in the 7th cent. (The feast day of Saints Faith,
Hope, and Charity is celebrated on August 11, September
17 in the Eastern Church.) Apparently mirroring this incident sometime later, a woman named Sapientia and
three companions — Spes, Fides, and Caritas — experienced a similar fate and are reported to have been buried
in the Appian Way (*Acta Sanctorum,* 35.16). Although
artistic representations sometimes show the theological
virtues in the company of a personified Sapientia or
Sophia (St. Gregory the Great, in his *Moralia* [1.27],
makes them the three daughters of the wise man Job), they
are more frequently in the later Middle Ages found under
the matronly influence of *humilitas,* as in the 12th-cent.
De Fructibus Carnis et Spiritus attributed to Hugh of St.
Victor (PL 176.997ff.) and the *Book of the Gospels* of the
Abbess Hilda of Meschede (ca. 1030), where the theolog-

ical virtues appear together with Humilitas in an illumination at the beginning of the Gospel of John.

The Dobet section of *Piers Plowman* is concerned with the theological virtues in relation to Jesus himself. In Spenser's *Faerie Queene,* Fidelia, Speranza, and Charissa are daughters of Dame Coelia, a virtuous matron who lives in the House of Holiness. Although personification allegory diminishes after the 16th cent., Faithful and Hopeful are Christian's fellow pilgrims in Bunyan's *The Pilgrim's Progress,* with Charity appearing as one of the four virgins who arm him with his sword and shield of faith.

John Donne strikes a parody of the theological virtues in effecting amorous disengagement: "Though hope bred faith and love; thus taught, I shall / As nations do from Rome, from thy love fall" ("Elegie 6"), although the lines are tinctured also with religious controversy. George Herbert associates faith, hope, and charity, as did Augustine, with "fruits meet for repentance" (cf. Matt. 3:8; Acts 26:20); drawing upon Augustine (*Enchiridion,* 3–4), he observes that "The Country Parson's Library is a holy Life," and that Christian virtues such as faith and love which the Parson models in his own life of repentance become, themselves, a "sermon" for others to read (*A Priest to the Temple,* chap. 33). In his prayer-poem "Trinitie Sunday" Herbert asks: "Enrich my heart, mouth, hands in me, / With faith, with hope, with charitie; / That I may runne, rise, rest with thee."

Inversion (rather than parody) of the theological virtues is for Ben Jonson a trenchant means of characterizing vice. In his *The Alchemist,* Sir Epicure Mammon speaks to Subtle the alchemist, who is cheating him, about the skeptic Surly, saying, "I told you he had not faith." Surly interjects, "And little hope, sir. / But much less charity, should I gull myself" (2.3.126-29). Jonson's point is not unlike that of George Eliot in the 19th cent., one of whose polite skeptics says, "Still — if I have read religious history aright — faith, hope, and charity have not always been found in a direct ratio with a sensibility to the three concords" (*Adam Bede,* chap. 3). In *Vanity Fair* Thackeray says his characters will include "Such people [as] there are living and flourishing in the world — Faithless, Hopeless, Charityless; let us have at them, dear friends, with might and main."

From latitudinarian preachers like Tillotson in the 18th cent. forward through the 19th cent., as well as in Wesleyan preaching (e.g., Wesley's "The Scripture Way of Salvation," *Sermons,* 1.35-52), the last phrase of 1 Cor. 13 received redoubled stress: "but the greatest of these is Charity." Curate Crawley in Trollope's *Framley Parsonage* reflects this emphasis:

> To the mother of my children you have given life, and to me you have brought light, and comfort, and good words — making my spirit glad within me as it had not been glad before. All this hath come of charity, which vaunteth not itself and is not puffed up. Faith and hope are great and beautiful, but charity exceedeth them all. (chap. 46)

Ruskin leans on the same verse (1 Cor. 13:4) in his appeal to turn the courage of the young from "the toil of war to the toil of mercy," success in which, he believes, will usher in a utopian era characterized by all three of the theological virtues, but especially charity ("The Mystery of Life and Its Arts"). G. B. Shaw's Lilith in *Back to Methuselah* uses the theological virtues in a sinister and threatening fashion to describe the attitude she bears toward probationary mankind, "for from the moment, I, Lilith, lose hope and faith in them, they are doomed" (5.300). Shaw's preface to this play is entitled "The Greatest of These Is Self-Control." It may be Shaw rather than St. Paul that A. M. Klein has in mind in his cryptic and derogatory poem "Of Faith, Hope, and Charity":

> Beware, — spiritual humankind, —
> Faith, contraceptive of the mind;
> And hope, cheap aphrodisiac,
> Supplying potency its lack;
> And also that smug lechery
> Barren and sterile charity.

See also CHARITY, CUPIDITY; FAITH; HOPE.

THEOPHANY An appearance of God to the human mind. The word is not biblical, but derives from Gk. *theos,* "god," and *phainō,* "shine," or, in the passive, "be revealed." There are, however, numerous biblical examples.

See also ANGEL; BURNING BUSH; CAPTAIN OF THE LORD'S HOST; JESUS CHRIST; PAUL; WHEELS WITHIN WHEELS.

Bibliography. Barr, J. "Theophany and Anthropomorphism in the Old Testament," *SVT* 7 (1960), 31-38; Jeremias, J. *Theophanie* (1965); Terrien, S. *Elusive Presence* (1978).

THEY KNOW NOT WHAT THEY DO (Luke 23:34)
See also SEVEN LAST WORDS.

THIEF IN THE NIGHT This startling simile for the Second Coming appears four times in the NT. Paul uses it to exhort and compliment the Thessalonians, who, unlike others, "know perfectly well that the day of the Lord cometh as a thief in the night" (1 Thess. 5:2). The author of 2 Peter "stir[s] up [the] pure minds" of his readers with Paul's phrase (3:1, 10), and the simile appears twice in Revelation (3:3; 16:15).

These four passages are echoed at Matt. 24:43-44 and Luke 12:39-40, which construct an analogy between the righteous awaiting the Son of Man and a good householder unprepared for a thief. These passages may be the original source, although at least one commentator on Matt. 24:43-44 cites an "ancient rabbinical saying" which shares the essence of the simile: " 'Three things come unexpectedly, Messiah, the discovery of a treasure, and a scorpion' " (*The Interpreter's Bible* [1978], vol. 7).

In the Middle Ages, the sense of urgency associated

with the passage is a prominent theme: "sure end-day cometh, all swift as thief by night," says the medieval paraphrase in *Vices and Virtues* (5.5.16-17). Calvin, in his commentary on the Thessalonians passage, notes that the Lord's day "will come suddenly to unbelievers when it is least expected, to take them by surprise as though they were asleep." He then asks, "What is the source of this sleep?" and answers, "Surely a profound contempt of God" (*Comm.* 367).

English and American writers have used the simile in a wide variety of contexts. Chaucer, though certainly without intending a metaphorical link with Scripture, describes Tarquin's stalking "in the night ful thefly" (*Legend of Good Women,* 1.1781). Shelley has the devil (rather than the Son of Man) appear as "a thief, who cometh in the night, / With whole boots and net pantaloons" ("Peter Bell the Third," 2.3). In Poe's "The Masque of the Red Death" Death comes at last to the contemptuous Duke "like a thief in the night." G. K. Chesterton, with characteristic wit, makes the observation (see the chapter "The Philosopher" in his *George Bernard Shaw*) that "The Superman will certainly come like a thief in the night, and be shot at accordingly; but we cannot leave our property wholly undefended on that account." Conrad, in his late novel *The Rescue,* makes an ironic contrast by alluding to the thief. His protagonist, Tom Lingard, has lost all for a married woman's sake, and, reflecting on their relationship, he says to her, " 'It began by my coming to you at night — like a thief in the night.' " Conrad draws attention to the scriptural source when Lingard then muses, " 'Where the devil did I hear that?' " His innocent allusion reflects Lingard's own egoism.

See also SECOND COMING.   DWIGHT H. PURDY

THIEVES, CRUCIFIED   The Gospels record that when Jesus was crucified, two others ("thieves" or "malefactors" in the KJV) were crucified with him, "one on the right hand, and another on the left" (Matt. 27:38). For Mark (15:27-28), this recalls and fulfills the prophetic narrative of the "Suffering Servant" (Isa. 53:12) who is "numbered with the transgressors." When the crowd began to taunt Jesus, the thieves joined in. Luke's account, however (23:32-43), elaborates an exchange between Jesus and the thieves, one of whom "railed on him, saying, If thou be the Christ, save thyself and us." The other rebuked him for his impiety, observing that Jesus, unlike themselves, "hath done nothing amiss" and was suffering an unjust punishment; this second malefactor then appealed to Jesus, "Lord, remember me when thou comest into thy kingdom," and received the assurance, "Verily I say unto thee, Today shalt thou be with me in paradise" (vv. 39-43).

The passage is a locus classicus for both the either/or presented by Christ's atonement and for repentance and conversion *in extremis*. St. Augustine sets the tone in his

many references to the exchange: "The Lord was in the middle crucified; near him were two thieves: the one mocked, the other believed; the one was condemned, the other justified: the one had his punishment both in this world and that which shall be, but unto the other the Lord said, 'Verily I say unto thee, today you shall be with me in Paradise" (*Enarr. in Ps.* 33.23). Elsewhere Augustine cites St. Paul to amplify:

> "For the just shall live by faith," and "Christ justifieth the ungodly" [Rom. 1:17; 4:5]. But how justifieth he any except believing and confessing? 'For with the heart man believeth unto righteousness, and with the mouth confession is made unto salvation" [10:10]. Therefore also that thief, although from his theft led to the judge, and from the judge to the cross, yet on the very cross was justified: with his heart he believed, with his mouth he confessed. (*Enarr. in Ps.* 34.11; cf. 39.15)

Augustine also argues that the repentant thief perfectly illustrates both aspects of "confession," repentance and praise:

> for in that he accused himself, he praised God, and made his own life blessed. He looked in hope for this from the Lord, and said to him, "Lord remember me when thou comest into thy kingdom." For he considered his own deeds, and thought it much, if mercy should be shown him even at the last. But the Lord immediately after the thief said "Remember me . . ." said to him "Verily I say unto thee, today thou shalt be with me in paradise." Mercy offered at once, what misery had deferred. (*Sermo,* 62.7)

In Western Christian elaboration of the Passion narrative the two thieves are given names; usually, following the apocryphal Gospel of Nicodemus, Dismas is the repentant thief, Gestas (or Gesmas) the unrepentant. In the ME *Cursor Mundi* the narrator observes that they hung Jesus between two thieves "als qua sai, / air maister theif am i" (16679-80); the specifying of which malefactor hung on the left and which on the right had by the 13th cent. been well established — both by a literary precedent in the apocryphal Gospel of Nicodemus (7.3, 11) and because of moral associations with Lat. *sinistra* (left) and *dextra* (right):

> þis theif þat hang on his righthand,
>   Dismas to name he hight.
> Gesmas hight þat toþer theif
>   þat was all maledight. (1637-40)

The Corpus Christi drama of the 14th and 15th cents. treats the incident variously; in Chester and Towneley Luke's account is omitted. In N-Town the unrepentant thief is called Jestes, whereas in York he is simply *Latro a sinistra,* and his counterpart, *Latro a dextra* (36.196-208).

Calvin follows Augustine in seeing in the repentant thief "a singular picture of the unexpected and unbelievable grace of God." For he was "received into heaven before the Apostles as the firstfruits of the new Church." Calvin emphasizes, however, that "it was not by native instinct of the flesh that he changed his cruel brutality and proud contempt for God to any instant repentance, but by the leading of the hand of God. As all Scripture teaches, penitence is his work" (*Harmony of the Gospels*, 3.201). From the unrepentant thief, Calvin says, one ought to "take a useful lesson . . . that it is outright opposition to God not to be taught humility by punishment" (3.202). He observes further that "the promise to the [repentant] thief was not relief from his present distress, not reduction in any degree of the penalty for the body. We are here warned not to reckon God's grace with fleshly sense: it will often happen that God will allow great affliction to fall upon those to whom he has favor" (3.205).

Resistance to the apocryphal gospels among the Reformers and their successors meant that the thieves tended to go unnamed in Protestant texts. Accordingly, in William Cowper's hymn "Praise for the Fountain Opened" (*Olney Hymns*, 15):

> The dying thief rejoiced to see
> That fountain in his day:
> And there have I, as vile as he,
> Washed all my sins away.

Allusions to the incident in modern literature are seldom prominent and usually indirect, as is the case in Graham Greene's *The Power and the Glory*, where the priest, himself about to die, urges the outlaw James Calver to repent "like the thief." In an unusual recollection, the surreal "Journal of Ernst von Hemmingstein," part of the literary remains of Ernest Hemingway from his days in Paris, concerns itself with the writer's apparent obsession with Tintoretto's painting of the Crucifixion — particularly its depiction of the face of the unrepentant thief, with whom Hemingway felt himself to be identified.

THIRD HEAVEN   In 2 Cor. 12:2-4, in what appears to be ironic or self-deprecating language, St. Paul talks about an experience, possibly visionary, of being "caught up to the third heaven," there to hear "unspeakable" and unrepeatable words. The *third heaven* is sometimes associated with theophanies in mystical writings.

See also PAUL.

THIRST   That the land of the Hebrews was a "dry and thirsty land" (Ps. 63:1) accounts for much of the concrete background for related imagery in the Bible, especially where the typology of salvation and yearning for God is concerned. Just as God led his people through the wilderness, giving them water from the rock (Exod. 17:6; cf. Deut. 8:15; Pss. 78:15-16; 105:40-41; Isa. 43:20), protecting them from the perils of a barren land, so also he protects, refreshes, and saves the parched souls who thirst after spiritual salvation. In the analogy of the Psalmist, "as the hart pants after the water brooks, so pants my soul

after thee, O God. My soul thirsteth for God, for the living God: when shall I come and appear before God?" (Ps. 42:1-2). Hence in the NT "Blessed are they who hunger and thirst after righteousness, for they shall be filled" (Matt. 5:6); as the Exodus people "hungry and thirsty" were "delivered out of their distresses" by the Lord (Ps. 107:5), so "he that believeth on me shall never thirst" (John 6:35; cf. John 7:37; Rev. 7:16; 21:6-7). Invitations by God to "drink freely" are invitations to the fullness of life and salvation which comes in the context of a covenant relationship with God (Isa. 55:1-3), so that the rock from which flows living water is explicitly identified in NT typology with Christ: "And [our fathers] did all drink the same spiritual drink: for they drank of that spiritual Rock that followed them: and that Rock was Christ" (1 Cor. 10:4).

NT imagery of thirst is incomprehensible outside of patterns established in OT narrative and poetry, and the weight of these associations lends force to three subsequently influential NT pericopes. The most familiar is the incident recorded in John 4 of Jesus' conversation with the Samaritan woman by the well (a "hospitality test" scene recalling the covenant narratives of Rebekah and Rachel [Gen. 24:13-21; 19:1-15]) in which a gracious and prejudice-subverting request for a drink of water occasions the opportunity to speak of satisfying a deeper thirst. Had the woman known who he was, Jesus tells the Samaritan, she would have asked of him, and he would have given her living water (John 4:10). For "whosoever drinketh of this [well] water shall thirst again: but whosoever drinketh of the water that I shall give him shall never thirst" (John 4:13-14).

In John 7 Jesus is recorded as making the same claim in the Temple on the last day of the Feast of Tabernacles: "If any man thirst, let him come unto me and drink. He that believeth on me, as the scripture hath said, out of his belly shall flow rivers of living water" (vv. 37-38). What Jesus says here (and later in chap. 8) is best understood in terms of the celebration of the Feast of Tabernacles, a feast associated with the triumphant "day of the LORD" (Zech. 9–14), in which living waters will flow out from Jerusalem to assuage all thirst (14:8). According to rabbinic traditions of the Tosepta, the texts read in conjunction with the Feast of Tabernacles were those relating to the rock in the desert (Exod. 17; Deut. 8:15; Pss. 78:15-16; 105:40-41; 114:8; Isa. 43:20; 44:3; 48:21). Among the ceremonies associated with the feast are prayers for rain, and on each of the seven mornings of the feast a procession went down to the fountain of Gihon on the southeast side of the temple hill. There a priest filled a golden pitcher with water, as the choir chanted in repetition Isa. 12:3, "With joy you will draw up water from the wells of salvation." After the procession returned up to the Temple through the Water Gate, the water was poured through a silver funnel at the altar, running into the ground; on the seventh day, this occurred after the altar had been circumambulated seven times. It was at this solemn moment on the seventh day that Jesus stood up in the temple court to proclaim himself the source of "living water."

A third crucial narrative moment comes in John 19:28 where, among the last words of Jesus from the cross, is recorded his parched cry, "I thirst," reflecting the expiring thirst of the Suffering Servant voiced in the messianic Ps. 22. For St. Augustine, that he was given vinegar was emblematic of the degeneration of his people from "the wine of the patriarchs and prophets" (*In Joan. Ev.* 119.4).

Augustine largely establishes the traditions of medieval exegesis on the Samaritan narrative as well. He interprets the water from the well as "the pleasure of the world in its dark depth." It is drawn out, he says, "with the vessel of lusts," adding "When one has got at the pleasure of the world . . . can it be that he will not thirst again?" (*In Joan. Ev.* 15.16). In contrast to such water ("it is drink, it is a bath, a show, an amour"), Augustine continues, "how shall they thirst, who 'shall be drunk with the fulness of thy house'?" (cf. Ps. 65:4). St. Ambrose makes the same point in his commentary on Exod. 15:23-26, Moses' making sweet the waters of Marah: the bitter waters signify that "when you drink, you will thirst; when you take the sweetness of the drink, again you take the bitterness" (*De mysteriis,* 2.4). St. Thomas Aquinas, in his gloss on Ecclus. 24:29 ("They that drink me shall yet thirst"), speaks of a "good" thirst for spiritual wisdom: "In this life, a faint perception of divine knowledge affords us delight, and delight sets up a thirst for perfect knowledge" (*Summa Theol.* 1.2.33.2) In a eucharistic hymn once ascribed to Aquinas, the theme of Christ as "fount of living water" is again articulated (trans. Ray Palmer, 1858):

> O Water, life bestowing,
> From out the Saviour's heart,
> A fountain purely flowing,
> A fount of love thou art:
> Oh, let us, freely tasting,
> Our burning thirst assuage;
> Thy sweetness, never wasting,
> Avails from age to age.

This hymn echoes the famous lines of St. Bernard of Clairvaux (ca. 1140) known to modern readers in Palmer's translation as "Jesu, thou joy of loving hearts." Here the "Fount of Life" and "Light of men" are the goal of restless spirits who sing: "We drink of thee, the Fountain-head, / and thirst, our souls from thee to fill."

In medieval and Renaissance literature "thirst" is often a figure for carnal desire. Lovers like those in Deduit's garden drink from the fountain whose waters are "so sweet that there is no man who drinks of it who does not drink more than he should" even though "those who go on drinking more burn with thirst than before. . . . Lechery so stimulates them that they become hydroptic" (*Romance of the Rose* [trans. Dahlberg], 5979-98). "For

ay thurst I," says Troilus of love, "the more that ich it drynke" (Chaucer, *Troilus and Criseyde,* 1.406). In the same vein, the persona of Donne's "St. Lucy's Day" imagines the whole earth to be "hydroptic," so much does he long for his departed love.

Sometimes, however, the thirst may be the "new thirst" Dante feels as he ascends the mount of Purgatory (*Purgatorio,* 18.3), the "strong, sober thirst" Donne feels in "La Corona" (1.12), or the thirst of Adam for Raphael's divine instructions, which "bring to their sweetness no satiety" (Milton, *Paradise Lost,* 8.316).

In 18th- and 19th-cent. poetry the motif of spiritual thirst is commonplace: in the minor Victorian poet and Catholic convert Fredrick William Faber's "The Shadow of the Rock," a weary pilgrim is invited "Cool water to take / Thy thirst to slake" in clear reference to Exod. 17 and its attendant typologies. William Chatterton Dix's "I Thirst" is a synthesis of relevant typologies:

> Weary beside the well he sat;
> Oh, who can tell but Jesus knew the thirst
> Which yet intenser grew, when on the cross
> For him no kindly fountain burst?
>
> "I thirst," his spirit may have cried,
> Thus long before the Passion-hour drew nigh;
> Thirsting for souls who sought some cooling stream
> Yet passed the Living Water by. (sts. 1-2)

In modern poetry "dryness" or "thirst" has become attached to intellectual or imaginative stagnation. Nevertheless, it is also in the sense of a spiritual drought that T. S. Eliot employs the motif in his *The Waste Land,* where the "dry stone" with "no sound of water" (1.24) is unmistakably revealed as the Rock in pt. 5, "What the Thunder said." Thirst prompts the persona's utterance ("If there were water we should stop and drink" [5.335]), which is frustrated even as drawn onward by hope, the "sound of water over a rock" (5.355). Eliot's thirst was to be quenched, he suggests, only when he could make the "Journey of the Magi," eventually to discover "the source of the longest river / The voice of the hidden waterfall" ("Little Gidding," 5.248-49).

See also LIVING WATER; WATER; WOMAN AT THE WELL.

Bibliography. MacRae, G. W. "The Feast of the Tabernacles in John 7:37-39." *CBQ* 22 (1960), 251-76; Dickson, D. R. "The Typological Water-Cycle in the Poetry of Herbert, Vaughan, and Traherne." *DAI* 42 (1981), 2683A.

DAVID L. JEFFREY
H. DAVID BRUMBLE

THIRTY PIECES OF SILVER   "Thirty pieces of silver" was the bribe accepted by Judas to betray Jesus, according to Matt. 26:14-16. In Matt. 27:3-10 the evangelist records that after Jesus was led off to his execution Judas remorsefully returned the money to the priests, who refused to put it back into the temple treasury, calling it "blood money." Instead, the priests used the money to buy "the potter's field" in which to bury strangers. In Matthew these events are portrayed as prophetic fulfillment of Zech. 11:12-13 (a passage incorrectly attributed to Jeremiah in Matt. 27:9). The sum in question was not great. In Exod. 21–32 it is the amount to be paid for the accidental death of a slave, and in Matthew's time the sum was worth far less. Thus Judas, whose deal with the priests to betray Jesus for money is mentioned only briefly in Mark 14:10-11, is here portrayed as selling his master for a paltry sum.

The incident is frequently alluded to in ME drama and lyric, often in a straightforward retelling: "When that my swete Son was thirti wynter old, / Then the traytor Judas wexed very bold; / For thirti plates of money his master he had sold" (R. Greene, *The Early English Carols,* no. 163). In the ME "Bargain of Judas," however, the narrative is extended to account for Judas's treachery. Jesus entrusts to Judas thirty pieces of silver to buy bread, but the money is stolen by his sister (or possibly his mistress); he is thus readily tempted to accept the offered silver and make good his loss (C. Brown, *English Lyrics of the XIIIth Century,* no. 25).

Allusion to "thirty pieces" soon becomes shorthand for betrayal for venal purposes. Thus, Shakespeare in *2 Henry 4* has the mistress of treacherous Falstaff ask, "and didst thou not kiss me, and bid me fetch thee thirty shillings?" (2.1.102). Mention of the kiss reinforces the nature of the betrayal of which Falstaff is being accused. George Herbert in "The Sacrifice" takes his theme from the Gospel story, alluding both to Matt. 26:14-16 and to John 12:4-6: "For thirty pence he did my death devise / Who at three hundred did the ointment prize."

Robert Browning is probably thinking of the betrayal of Jesus in "The Lost Leader," a poem attacking Wordsworth for his supposed desertion of the liberal cause:

Just for a handful of silver he left us,
　　Just for a riband to stick on his coat — . . .
They, with the gold to give, doled him out silver
　　So much was theirs who so little allowed. (1-2; 5-6)

John Ruskin in *The Crown of Wild Olives* makes a tongue-in-cheek suggestion of an architectural ornament for the British Exchange: "a statue of Britannia in the Market . . . her corselet, of leather, folded over her heart in the shape of a purse, with thirty slits in it, for a piece of money to go into it, each day of the month." James Russell Lowell in his poem "The Present Crisis" is scathing about the American annexation of Texas as a state in which slavery is legal: "For humanity sweeps onward: where today the martyr stands / On the morrow crouches Judas with the silver in his hands." T. S. Eliot in his "Journey of the Magi" describes, with more than a hint of foreboding, "Six hands at an open window dicing for pieces of silver, / And feet kicking the empty wineskins" (26-27).

See also FIELD OF BLOOD; JUDAS ISCARIOT.

JOYCE G. BALDWIN

THOMAS, DOUBTING　St. Thomas, who was not present at Jesus' first post-Resurrection appearance to his gathered disciples, was incredulous at the claims of the others to have seen the risen Christ and protested, "Except I shall see in his hands the print of the nails, and put my finger into the print of the nails, and thrust my hand into his side, I will not believe" (John 20:19-25). Eight days later, as the disciples were assembled once again, Jesus suddenly "stood in their midst" and addressed Thomas: "Reach hither thy finger, and behold my hands; and reach hither thy hand, and thrust it into my side, and be not faithless, but believing" (vv. 26-27). Appalled and ashamed, Thomas uttered his acknowledgment: "My Lord and my God," to which Jesus replied, "Thomas, because thou hast seen me, thou hast believed: blessed are they that have not seen, and yet have believed" (vv. 28-29).

The Aramaic form of Thomas's Greek name is *te'oma',* "the twin," and the Greek name, "Didymus" ("twin"), is attached to him in several places (John 11:16; 20:24; 21:2). In Syriac and gnostic tradition Thomas is called Judas Thomas and identified with the "Judas (not Iscariot)" of John 14:22. He figures only in the fourth Gospel, though an apocryphal Gospel of Thomas (2nd cent.) concerning the infancy of Jesus and a late 2nd- or early 3rd-cent. Acts of St. Thomas (subsequently elaborated) describe his being sent to India as a missionary by the other apostles in Jerusalem. When he resisted, these legends relate, he was sold as a slave to the messenger of the Indian king and arrived thus at his destination (much in the manner of the reluctant prophet Jonah).

In India, Thomas is said to have performed startling miracles and enjoined asceticism and sexual abstinence on his converts. The incorporation into the Acts of Thomas of many gnostic elements, including a gnostic hymn of the Pearl, marks it as having a probable Syriac origin. This text makes Thomas the "twin" of Christ, Christ sometimes appearing in Thomas's likeness. The tradition of Thomas's residence in India, maintained among Indian Christian communities, is supported also by Eusebius, who says that his missionary journeys took him to Parthia (between the Tigris and Indus rivers) and possibly beyond into India. According to the legenda, Thomas there met his death by martyrdom, pierced by four spears. He is said to have been, like Jesus, a carpenter, and later became the patron saint of architects, masons, and stonecutters. Also ascribed to him are an apocryphal Apocalypse of St. Thomas, a Coptic Gospel of Thomas, a Book of Thomas the Contender (Athlete), and coauthorship of an apocryphal Epistle of the Apostles.

Of all these sources, John's Gospel and the apocryphal Acts of St. Thomas most directly influence his role in Christian tradition and literature. In patristic commentary it is the scene of Thomas's acknowledgment and confession of Jesus as Lord which is central: St. Augustine says of Thomas: "He saw and touched the man, and acknowledged the God whom he neither saw or touched; but by the means of what he saw and touched, he now put away from him every doubt, and believed the other . . ." (*In Joan. Ev.* 121.20.5). Jesus' invitation for Thomas to touch him is contrasted by Augustine with Jesus' restraint of Mary Magdalene (*Noli me tangere,* "touch me not"), which immediately precedes it in John's Gospel (20:11-18). He says that the incident with Mary "portends a mystery," suggesting that her instinct was still to reach out in love to Jesus as to a man: "For how could it be otherwise than carnally that she still believed on him whom she was weeping over as a man?" (121.20.3).

In the elaborate biblical paraphrase of the ME *Cursor Mundi,* the doubting Thomas narrative is immediately followed by the command (from Mark 16:15) to "go into all the world and preach the gospel." "He bad þan his discipilis preche / Oueral þis werld his trouthe to teche . . ." (18709-10). In the ME Corpus Christi plays, York's "Incredulity of Thomas" closely follows the Johannine narrative, while Towneley's "Thomas Indiae" elaborates it with extensive discussion among the disciples mounting to a dramatic concordance of prophecies of and evidences for the Resurrection. The Cornish *Resurrection of Our Lord* assigns Thomas a key role, dramatizing his stubborn refusal to believe a host of witnesses to the Resurrection, including the Emmaus pilgrims, whom he castigates as knaves spreading groundless palmers' tales. Cleopas, speaking for all the disciples, delivers a stern judgment upon his impiety and warns him that unless he forsakes his blasphemous defiance, he will be lost. When Thomas retorts with his bold condition, it is almost instantly met by Jesus, whose entrance effects Thomas's immediate conversion. N-Town's pageant concludes with a soliloquy by Thomas repenting of his "dredfful dowte," saying "I trustyd no tales þat were me tolde, / tyll þat myn hand . . ." and "The prechynge of petir myght not conuerte me, / tyll I felyd þe wounde" (369; 377ff.). York adds a second Thomas play based on the apocryphal legenda, "The Appearance of our Lady to Thomas," in which his doubtfulness is recapitulated as he wends his way to India, only to be interrupted by a vision in "the Vale of Josaphat" of Mary and the angels at her ascension and coronation. He is told by her to relate this to his brethren back in Jerusalem, which he does, his colleagues not believing till he shows them Mary's token (her girdle) and they discover her grave to be empty.

"Doubting Thomas" is remembered in incidental reference in a variety of English texts, such as H. G. Wells's *The Undying Fire,* in which the skeptical Dr. Barrack proclaims, "I want things I can feel and handle. I am an Agnostic by nature and habit and profession. A *Doubting Thomas,* born and bred." More substantial allusions are rare, and Thomas himself has a minimal role except in dramatic reenactments of the Passion and Resurrection, where his confession of faith, as well as his initial doubt, is recalled. In her play cycle *The Man Born to Be King* (1943), Dorothy Sayers calls attention to the signal

irony that "the one absolutely unequivocal statement, in the whole Gospel, of the Divinity of Jesus . . . come[s] from Doubting Thomas. It is the only place where the word 'God' is used of him without qualification of any kind, and in the most unambiguous form of words (not merely *theos* but *ho theos mou* with the definite article)."

See also NOLI ME TANGERE.

THORN IN THE FLESH   *See* PAUL.

THORNS, FELL AMONG   *See* SOWER, PARABLE OF.

THOU ART THE MAN   *See* DAVID; NATHAN.

THOUGH HE SLAY ME   In the first round of the conversations in which Job's friends Eliphaz, Bildad, and Zophar try to convince him that he deserves the calamities which have befallen him, Zophar speaks last (Job 11). He points out Job's limitations, God's infinity, and the necessity of repentance. In his reply (chaps. 12–14), Job surpasses Zophar in the depiction of God's grandeur and accuses his friends of presumptuous talk. His desire "to reason with God" (13:2) is so overwhelming that he claims, "Though he slay me, yet will I trust in him: but I will maintain mine own ways before him" (13:15). The rest of Job's speech is a direct address to God.

The Hebrew text of Job 13:15 poses several problems which have led to largely divergent translations. The KJV follows the Geneva, which in turn agrees with the Vg in giving the main clause a positive meaning. The RSV, however, translates, "Behold, he will slay me; I have no hope. Yet I will defend my ways to his face." Whether one rejects the KJV wording as a "sublime mistranslation" *(Interpreter's Bible)* or argues for its appropriateness, it has had by far the greatest influence on English literature.

For St. Gregory the Great *(Moralia in Iob)* the verse is a reminder that the virtue of patience is seldom found in the midst of prosperity: "Hereby the righteous mind is distinguished from the unrighteous — that even in the midst of adversity the former offers praise to omnipotent God." St. Bonaventure similarly stresses Job's expression of patience and confidence in God *(Expositio in Psalterium,* 119.109).

According to Calvin, the passage indicates that God "lets the believers fall in order to test and improve their faith." Moreover, death is "like a blunt sword," which cannot injure us *(Sermons on Job).* John Donne, preaching on this text, tries to solve the textual problem by reading, "Behold he will kill me, yet shall not I hope in him?" and goes on to assert that God's omnipotence can indeed mean destruction to humanity. Yet "though he end a weary life, with a painefull death, as there is no other hope, but in him, so there needs no other, for that alone is both abundant, and infallible in its selfe." In Thomas Hooker's words, the verse reads, "Thou makest me a butt to shoot at; yet I will trust in thee though thou kill me" — which for him illustrates the fact that "A man's faith may be somewhat strong when his feeling is nothing at all" ("The Poor Doubting Christian"). For John Henry Newman, in his sermon on "Peace and Joy Amid Chastisement," Job's words reflect "that state of mingled hope and fear, of peace and anxiety, of grace and insecurity" which people are in because "the sins which we commit here . . . are not put away absolutely and once for all, but are in one sense upon us till the Judgment." Burton places Job in the ranks of the martyrs who endured with patience and willingness "the utmost that human rage and fury could invent" (*Anatomy of Melancholy*, 2.3.3).

Carlyle secularizes the sentence and gives it an ironic twist when he complains about being the "doomed everlasting prey of the Quack" in his essay "The Gospel of Mammonism" (*Past and Present*, 3.2). He concludes, "Though he slay me, yet will I *not* trust in him." In a similar vein, Melville uses the verse as a motto for his poem "The Enthusiast," which depicts an attitude of defiance against life's adversities and against bourgeois superficiality.

Miss Jessie Brown in Elizabeth Gaskell's *Cranford* repeats Job's words as a statement of trust in God after the loss of her father and while her only sister is dying. (chap. 2). In "Later Life," Christina Rossetti first paraphrases the verse and then gives it an eschatological twist: "Yea, though He slay us we will vaunt his praise, / Serving and loving with the cherubim. . . ." In Whittier's "Barclay of Ury," Barclay expresses his spiritual resignation: "Passive to his holy will, / Trust I in my Master still, / Even though he slay me." Less resigned but echoing Job's words is Emily Dickinson's poem "Bind me — I still can sing."

In his preface to *St. Joan*, George Bernard Shaw puts special emphasis on the second part of the verse ("but I will maintain my own ways before him") to characterize his Joan. American novelist Theodore Dreiser uses Job's words to describe the Quakers' traditional attitude toward God (*The Bulwark*, "Introduction"). In Archibald MacLeish's Job drama, J.B. accentuates the difference between the first and the second parts of the statement by uttering the first part "violently" and, after some silence, the second part with dropped voice (*J.B.*, 9). Yakov Bok's father-in-law Shmuel, in Bernard Malamud's novel *The Fixer*, tries to convince the unjustly imprisoned Yakov of God's justice and the necessity to trust in him: "He invented light, He created the world. He made us both. The true miracle is belief. I believe in Him. Job said, 'Though he slay me, yet will I trust in Him.' " Freethinking Yakov, however, dismisses Job as an invention. In Malamud's *God's Grace*, God repeatedly announces that he will have to "slay" protagonist Calvin Cohn. Even though Cohn's death is postponed, he does not, however, trust in God.

See also JOB; JOB'S COMFORTERS.　　MANFRED SIEBALD

THREE FOES OF MAN　　*See* WORLD, FLESH, AND DEVIL.

THREESCORE YEARS AND TEN　　According to Ps. 90:10, "we spend our years as a tale that is told. The days of our years are threescore and ten; and if by reason of strength they be fourscore years, yet is their strength labor and sorrow; for it is soon cut off, and we fly away."

See also TALE THAT IS TOLD.

THRONE OF GRACE　　The writer of the Epistle to the Hebrews encourages his readers to come to Christ, the "great high priest, that has passed into the heavens," in supplicatory prayer: "Let us therefore come boldly unto the throne of grace, that we may obtain mercy, and find grace to help in time of need" (4:16). The more familiar association his immediate readers had of the throne of God with justice and judgment (Ps. 89:14) made this a particularly striking image. In Christian tradition the image in this text was presented in terms of God's offering, in Jesus, of a high priest who was himself also the sacrifice. In English medieval painting, relief carving, and ornamental brasses, the "throne of mercy" is represented with God as the Ancient of Days enthroned, holding the crucified Christ (a crucifix) on his knee facing the suppliant, with a dove of the Holy Spirit descending over the Cross (cf. Raphael's *Disputa del Sacramento*). This graphic symbolizing of the Trinity did not often survive the Reformation, but the phrase, more usually in Protestant writings, "the throne of grace," is common, as in William Cowper's observation concerning the politic society of his own time: "To men of pedigree, their noble race / Emulous always of the nearer place / To any throne except the throne of grace" ("Hope," 237-39).

THRONE OF SOLOMON　　*See* MARY, MOTHER OF JESUS.

TIMOR MORTIS CONTURBAT ME　　Not a biblical allusion as such, but a Latin ecclesiastical tag meaning "The fear of death disquiets me." It forms the refrain of a famous 1582 poem by William Dunbar, "Lament for the Makaris," effectively a verse sermon.

See also HOW ARE THE MIGHTY FALLEN!

TIMOTHY　　Protégé of St. Paul, he is literarily notable chiefly as an example of faith and diligence in the young, and for the two letters written by Paul to him which form part of the canonical NT.

TI-SAR-ILANI　　*See* LOT'S WIFE; SODOM AND GOMORRAH.

TISHBITE　　*See* ELIJAH.

TOBIT AND TOBIAS　　The story of Tobit and his son Tobias is told in the book of Tobit (Tobias in the Douay version), part of the Apocrypha, which was bound into English Bibles regularly until 1640 and optionally thereafter. It is included in the *Book of Common Prayer* lectionary (called "Toby" in early editions), excerpted in the English *Alternative Service Book 1980,* and represented in recent American editions by Tobit's prayer of rejoicing (1928) and by Tobias's wedding prayer in the marriage rite (1979).

Tobit is a comedic analogue of the book of Job: in it two exiled Jewish families, faithful in affliction, discover the unforeseeable mercies of God manifested through pain and healing. Tobit, obedient to the Law and bountiful in almsgiving although he belongs to an apostate tribe exiled in Nineveh, has lost his worldly goods and still risks his life by illegally burying his murdered fellow Jews. While sleeping outdoors after returning unclean from such an errand of mercy, he is blinded by sparrows' droppings, and his wife Anna undertakes the support of the family. When she returns with a kid given her by an employer, Tobit falsely accuses her of stealing it, and when she upbraids him, his miseries overwhelm him. Accepting responsibility for the sins of Israel, he prays to die. At the same moment, a distant kinswoman raises a similar prayer: she is Sara, the "seven-times-wedded Maid" (*Paradise Lost,* 5.223) whose bridegrooms have all been killed by the envious demon Asmodeus before the marriage could be consummated and whose maids accuse her of these crimes.

The prayers of Tobit and of Sara are heard by God. "And Raphael was sent to heale them both, that is, to scale away the whiteness of Tobit's eyes, and to give Sara the daughter of Raguel, for a wife to Tobias the sonne of Tobit, and to bind Asmodeus the evill spirit, because she belongeth to Tobias by right of inheritance" (Tob. 3:16-17 [KJV 1611]). The subsequent journey of Tobias and Raphael to recover the family fortune is a happy adventure which illustrates divine concern for human welfare; the advice of Tobit and Raphael to Tobias contains much moral wisdom; and the warm and humorous portrayal of the two families celebrates generosity, gratitude, marriage, and healing.

Visual depictions of the story — particularly of Raphael's journey with Tobias (and, often, his dog) — were extraordinarily popular in the Renaissance (e.g., Pollaiuolol, Perugino, Verrocchio, Savoldo, di Bicci, Elsheimer, Rembrandt, Seghers, and innumerable engravers). In the early 17th cent., the healing of Tobit's blindness is represented by Rembrandt, de Backer, and Strozzi; the quelling of Asmodeus by Steen; and the marriage of Tobias and Sara by Steen and Rembrandt. The windows of King's College Chapel, Cambridge, England, represent the marriage as a type of Espousals of the Virgin Mary, Tobias's journey as a type of the Road to Emmaus, Tobias's return to Anna as a type of the Resurrection of Christ, and Tobit's death as a type of the Death of the Virgin.

Literary allusions to the story occur in the medieval lyric "Mercyful quene, as ye best kan" (C. Brown, *Religious Lyrics of the XVth Century,* no. 131) and in Chaucer's *Parson's Tale* (10.905-10) and *Tale of Melibee* (7.1115-20), where Prudence advises her husband to ready himself for God's counsel and comfort "as taughte Thobie his son." The author of *Piers Plowman* makes familiarity with the book of Tobit a mark of the man who has a responsible knowledge of Scripture (B.10.33; cf. 85-87) and uses Tob. 2:13 to argue that holy church should not accept offerings from thieves (C.2.144; C.7.290-93; C.18.37-43). Milton makes use of the narrative both in his introduction of Raphael and in his description of the fiend's arrival on earth to trouble the primal marriage — better pleased with the sweet smells of Paradise than "*Asmodeus* with the fishie fume, / That drove him, though enamoured, from the Spouse / Of *Tobits* Son" (*Paradise Lost,* 4.169-71).

Dryden mentions Tobit in the Prologue to *The Pilgrim* with reference to neglect of the Apocrypha. Christopher Smart's Michaelmas hymn finds "Tobit's charitable soul a type of Jesus Christ to come," and he invokes Tobias and Anna in *Jubilate Agno:* "Let Tobias bless Charity with his Dog, who is faithful, vigilant, and a friend in poverty. / Let Anna bless God with the Cat, who is worthy to be presented before the throne of grace, when he has trampled upon the idol of his prank" (Frg. A, 55-56). In Byron's *The Deformed Transformed* Caesar as Asmodeus makes cynical comments on marriage (2.3.180-87).

Browning uses the story to illustrate the accommodation of language:

Heaven speaks first
To the angel, then the angel tames the word
Down to the ear of Tobit: he, in turn,
Diminishes the message to his dog. (*The Ring and the Book,* 8.1500-1504)

James Bridie's *Tobias and the Angel,* first performed in Cambridge in 1930, portrays the families with sympathetic humor. James Joyce — who was, like Milton, concerned with eyesight — makes a pun on Tobit and Tobias in *Finnegans Wake;* Adaline Glasheen's pithy explanation might also be applied to the legend's wide appeal to other writers and artists: "Tobit was blind and saw again."

See also ASMODEUS; RAPHAEL.

Bibliography. Gerould, G. *The Grateful Dead* (1908); Liljeblad, S. *Die Tobiasgeschichte und andere Märchen mit toten Helfern* (1927); Sherry, B. "Milton's Raphael and the Legend of Tobias." *JEGP* 78 (1979), 227-40; Thompson, S. *The Types of the Folktale* (1961), nos. 505-08; Traherne, J. B. "Joshua and Tobias in the Old English *Andreas.*" *SN* 42 (1970), 330-32; Wikgren, A. "Tobit." *IDB* 4.658-62.

DIANE MCCOLLEY

TO EVERY THING . . . A SEASON Qoheleth wrote that "To every thing there is a season, and a time to every purpose under the heaven: A time to be born, and a time to die; a time to plant and a time to pluck up . . ." (Eccl. 3:1-8). The phrase had bcome proverbial by Chaucer's era, as when Harry Bailey prods the quiescent Clerk into telling a tale:

I trowe ye studie som sophyme;
But Salomon seith, "every thing hath tyme."
For Goddes sake, as beth of bettre cheere! (4.5-7)

See also QOHOLETH; WISDOM.

TONGUES, GIFT OF The miraculous ability to speak in "tongues," understood as unlearned languages by the NT writers, is mentioned both in Acts (2:1-21; 10:44-48; 19:1-7) and in 1 Corinthians (12:8-11, 29-30; 13:1; 14:1-27). The term for the charism, *glossalalia*, derives from Gk. *glōssa*, "tongue," + *laleō*, "to speak" (the common verb *legō* is never used in conjunction with "speaking in tongues"). In several instances where the NT text has simply *glōssais* or *dialektos* ("tongues," "languages") the KJV translators add the interpretative adjective "unknown" to clarify the special character of the speaking (1 Cor. 14:2, 4, 13, 14, 19).

Especially from Paul's discussion of the phenomenon, it seems to have been a relatively familiar feature of worship life in early Christian communities. The most influential passages concerning this spiritual gift are the Pentecost episode (Acts 2:1-21) and Paul's teaching on the limited value of tongue-speaking in public assemblies of Christians (1 Cor. 12–14). In the Pentecost account, the tongue-speaking of the apostles is accompanied by the sound of a mighty wind and by a vision of "cloven tongues like as of fire," which appear to sit "upon each of them." In later literary appropriation of the incident, the imagery of these "tongues of fire" is as important as the phenomenon of speaking in tongues itself.

The Acts 2 story is unique in the NT in that the extraordinary tongue-speaking attracts and amazes outsiders, Jewish pilgrims from various lands (vv. 5-13), who by this means hear the disciples speaking "the wonderful works of God" each in his own language. On Paul's view, however, tongue-speaking typically cannot be understood, even by the speaker, without a special gift of "interpretation of tongues" (1 Cor. 12:10; 14:13-14). Like the writer of the Acts, Paul may have intended an allusion to the sin-wrought confusion of Babel (Gen. 11:1-9) to which Pentecost is a spiritual answer or remedy, here symbolizing an overcoming of the division of the nations in the proclamation of the gospel and the gift of the Spirit. (The Acts account seems connected allusively also to the giving of the Law on Sinai [Exod. 19; cf. Jub. 6:14-21; 15:1-24; 16:28-30; 1QS 1.1–1.26; Meg. 31a].) Paul's passing reference to "tongues of men and of angels" (1 Cor. 13:1) may be an indication that the gift was thought to involve occasionally some sort of heavenly language. If so, even such wondrous utterance, unless

accompanied by love, is a mere "sounding brass, or a tinkling cymbal."

Paul's exposition suggests that one who speaks in tongues is not entranced and can exercise considerable self-control — enough to arrange ahead of time for an interpreter. Otherwise the person is to remain silent in the assembly (1 Cor. 14:28). An alternative is to pray for the gift of interpretation (*hermēneia*, v. 13). Because such utterances were common in the Corinthian church, Paul suggested that not more than two or three, in ordered succession, be included in the worship; persons who failed to accept such regulation were to be refused opportunity to give utterance. But the accounts of the second "pentecost" experience at Ephesus (Acts 19:1-6) and of the speaking in tongues in the household of Cornelius the Roman centurion which followed upon their conversion (Acts 10:44-46) suggests that "tongues" could be a definite sign of the presence of the Holy Spirit where the gospel had been heard and affirmed even among the Gentiles.

In the first centuries of the Church the phenomenon was reported in some places, not in others. St. John Chrysostom claims never to have seen it (*Hom. on 1 Corinthians*, 12); St. Irenaeus (*Adv. haer.* 5.6.1) found it frequently among those who were strictly observant of the gospel. Tertullian (*Adv. Marc.* 5.18.12) saw it as one of the signs *(sēmeia)* confirming theological orthodoxy; Origen, on the basis of Acts 2, regarded tongues as a means for preaching in multicultural contexts (*Comm. on Romans*, 1.13; 7.6).

For Calvin, too, the manifestation of tongues in Acts 2 has a utilitarian function: the apostles "had the understanding of various tongues given to them so that they might speak to the Greeks in Greek, and to the Italians in Latin, and thereby have true communication with their hearers" (*New Testament Comms.* 6.52). Calvin believed that the gift of tongues was not a continuing phenomenon. Commenting on the conversion of Cornelius and his household, he warns: "Certainly the gift of tongues and other things of that kind have long since ceased in the Church but the Spirit of understanding and regeneration thrives and will always thrive" (6.317). Calvin's convictions were shared by his followers in the Anglican and Puritan traditions, and parallel those generally held by Counter-Reformation Catholics.

Manifestations of glossalalia continued to appear in Western Christendom, however. St. Francis Xavier is reported to have successfully preached in tongues unknown to him, and St. Vincent Ferrer, when preaching in his own vernacular, is said to have been comprehended perfectly by auditors with no knowledge of it. In 18th-cent. Britain speaking in tongues was a familiar occurrence during the revival meetings of John and Charles Wesley (particularly in Scotland and the border country), though in many cases the glossalalia was by no means always intelligible to other parties, or even to the speaker.

Tongue-speaking is still an important feature of contemporary worship in some Christian communities, both Protestant and Catholic.

In the B-text of *Piers Plowman* (19.195-201), the gift of tongues is described in a "pentecostal" context. Conscience tells the narrator to kneel at the foot of the cross, whereupon:

> . . . thanne come, me thou3te,
> One *spiritus paraclitus* . to Pieres and to his felawes;
> In lyknesse of a li3tnynge . he ly3te on hem alle,
> And made hem konne and knowe . alkyn langages.
> I wondred what that was . and wagged Conscience,
> And was afered of the ly3te . for in fyres lyknesse /
> *Spiritus paraclitus* . ouer-spradde hem alle.

The poet then quotes from 1 Cor. 12:4 (Vg: *"Divisiones vero gratiarum sunt"*), listing the diverse charisms of practical knowledge and skills (19.224ff.) which are the gifts of "Grace" (19.248-49).

John Donne adopts the Pentecostal conceit of "cloven tongues" in his laudatory verse "Upon the Translation of the Psalmes by Sir Philip Sidney, and the Countess of Pembroke, His sister": ". . . as thy blessed Spirit fell upon / These Psalmes first Author in cloven tongue . . . , / So hast thou cleft that spirit, to performe that worke againe" (8-13).

John Dryden's "Upon the Death of the Lord Hastings" (24) develops a traditional biblical exposition of the gift of tongues; his "The Office of the Holy Ghost at Mattins" (13-14, 19-20) is an English translation of a liturgical hymn (*"Nobis Sancti Spiritus"* [*Analecta Hymnica,* 30.15]):

> From God the sacred Spirit came
> At *Pentecost* in tongues of flame; . . .
> The sev'nfold Grace and gift of Speech
> The blest Apostles Tongues enrich.

In Hawthorne's *The Scarlet Letter,* Mr. Dimmesdale ministers with a "tongue of flame," an ability "to express the highest truths through the humblest medium of familiar words and images," as a result of the "gift that descended upon the chosen disciples, at Pentecost, in tongues of flame." Hawthorne calls this gift "the heart's native language" (chap. 11).

Whittier, in "Call of the Christian," contrasts the apostolic "rush of the wind" at Pentecost to the postapostolic call to faith:

> Not always as the whirlwind's rush
> On Horeb's mount of fear,
> Not always as the burning bush
> To Midian's shepherd seer,
> Nor as the awful voice which came
> To Israel's prophet bards,
> Nor as the tongues of cloven flame . . .

In *Redburn* Melville transfers the image to the many languages spoken in the great American melting pot, where, he prophesies, "there shall appear unto them cloven tongues as of fire." In *Clarel* he takes a more traditional approach to the image: "Anew 'tis like a tongue of flame." In *Moby-Dick* when Queequeg lies in his coffin and utters the word "Rarmai," the gift of tongues takes on an eerie aspect. Starbuck tries to explain the strange utterance rationally, saying: "I have heard . . . that in violent fevers, men, all ignorance, have talked in ancient tongues; and that when the mystery is probed, it turns out always that in their wholly forgotten childhood those ancient tongues had been really spoken in their hearing by some lofty scholars." Later, in a pyrotechnic display of St. Elmo's fire, the "tongues" strike the masts of the *Pequod* and "instantly from the three mast-heads three shrieks went up as if the tongues of fire had voiced it."

James Joyce speaks in his *Notebooks* of "Art" having "the gift of tongues," reflecting his view of the artist as prophet and priest of the imagination. In the "Oxen of the Sun" section of *Ulysses,* more parodically, there is a pub called "The Utterance of the Word," at which "utterance" the language becomes drunken and multilingual. There is a sense in which Joyce's linguistic technique approximates a self-induced glossolalia, making of the writer's utterance a kind of demonic speaking in tongues (cf. Eugene Jolas's comments concerning the attempts of Gertrude Stein to find a "mysticism of the word" [85]). T. S. Eliot also adapts the Pentecostal image to the gift of poetic utterance in "Little Gidding." The priestly prophecy in poetic expression joins beginnings with endings; a seasonal "pentecostal fire" in the January thaw (1.1-10) relates to "communication" from the dead "tongued with fire beyond the language of the living" (1.53). As he longs for final understanding the persona is told by a "dead master" about the unsettled fate of a "spirit between two worlds" trying to find "refining fire" (2.39). The "baptism of fire" is the longed-for release:

> The dove descending breaks the air
> With flame of incandescent terror
> Of which the tongues declare
> The one discharge from sin and error. (4.1-4)

See also BABEL; PENTECOST.

Bibliography. Andrews, E. "Tongues, Gift of." *IDB* 4.671-72; Hoekema, A. A. *Tongues and Spirit Baptism* (1981); Jolas, E. "The Revolution of Language and James Joyce." *Our Exagmination Round his Factification for Incamination of Work in Progress.* Eds. S. Beckett, W. C. Williams, et al. (1929), 77-92; Lombard, E. *De la Glossolalie* (1910); Mosiman, E. *Das Zungenreden* (1911); Reilly, T. a K. "The Gift of Tongues: What was it?" *American Ecclesiastical Review* 43 (1910), 3-25; Samarin, W. J. *Tongues of Men and Angels* (1972).   DAVID L. JEFFREY
ERNEST N. KAULBACH

TONGUES OF FIRE   *See* PENTECOST.

TOPHET   Tophet was a "high place" in the Valley of Hinnom (cf. Gk. *Gehenna*, "hell") where parents were induced to sacrifice their children to the god Moloch, a practice abolished by Josiah and bitterly opposed by Jeremiah and Ezekiel. In literary allusion it is generally another name for hell, or, as Milton says, it is "the type of Hell" (*Paradise Lost,* 1.405).

See also MOLOCH.

TORAH   In its strictest sense, Torah (Heb. "law," "teaching") is the "written law" or Pentateuch, including the Law given to Moses on Sinai together with its narrative context and oral exposition. More broadly, in Jewish tradition it can be used to mean also the entire Mishnah, as well as talmudic literature and commentaries. Gk. *nomos* and English "law" thus tend to translate the rabbinic use of *torah* too narrowly. If one imagines the scene as one of worship, the narrower sense may be reflected in A. M. Klein's poem "Dance Chassidic":

> You, Chassidim, lift your caftans, dance;
> Circle the Torah and rejoice the soul,
> Look Godwards and He will not look askance.

To "circle the Torah" can, however, suggest Ezra and the circumspective "fence around the Torah," or oral Torah and its tradition — a nice ambiguity. The wider sense may be intended in Leonard Cohen's *Book of Mercy* (5): "Immediately the Torah sang to him, and touched his hair, and for a moment, as a gift to serve his oldest memory, he wore his weightless crown, the crown that lifts the weight away, he wore it till his heart could say, 'How precious is the heritage!'"

See also PENTATEUCH.

TORMENT, TORMENTOR   KJV "torment" translates several Greek words in the NT, among them *basanismos,* which is frequently used with reference to the sufferings of hell (Rev. 14:11; 18:7, 10, 15). The cognate *basanistēs* (Matt. 18:34) in the parable of the debtor is rendered "tormentor"; it is a legal term for one who uses torture as a means of exacting a confession or evidence. In Luke 16:19-31 the rich man in Hades experiences "torments" (*basanos* [16:23, 28]) and is "tormented" (*odynomai* [16:24, 25]); in this instance the sufferings referred to appear to be psychological as well as physical. Other uses of "torment" occur in Matt. 4:24; 8:6, 29; Rev. 11:10; 20:10; Heb. 11:37, and elsewhere (e.g., 1 John 4:18, "fear hath torment" [*kolasis*]). The word *torment* as such does not appear in the OT (but cf. Wisd. of Sol. 3:1: *basanos;* 2 Macc. 7:8: *basanos*).

The tormentor par excellence in Scripture is Satan, the "adversary" of God and humanity who seeks to destroy the faithful (Luke 22:31; 1 Pet. 5:8). This vicious harrying of Satan and his demonic cohorts will continue in some measure until the last days, when they will be vanquished (1 Enoch 16:1; T. Levi 18:12; Jub. 10:8-9) and cast into the Lake of Fire, there to suffer perpetual torment (Rev. 20:10). When Jesus exorcised the Gadarene demoniacs, the demons, acknowledging his authority, asked if he had come "to torment us before the time" — i.e., before the final judgment (Matt. 8:29).

In the Bible, the torment of the saints by their enemies is often ineffective physically — as when Shadrach, Meshach, and Abednego are cast into the fiery furnace (Dan. 3) and Daniel into a den of lions (Dan. 6) — and always ineffective spiritually, as in the Crucifixion (cf. Wisd. of Sol. 3:1: "The souls of the righteous are in the hand of God, and there shall no torment touch them"). In striking contrast, sinful tormentors who seek to harm saints are often tormented by the very means they had used against the righteous; thus wicked Haman is hanged on the gallows he had erected for the execution of Mordecai (Esth. 7:10).

Many of these narratives influence hagiography, notably the fiery furnace episode of Dan. 3. Fire or fire-heated tortures frequently harm the torturers, not the saints, as in Cynewulf's *Juliana* (582-89) and the ME *þe Liflade of St. Juliana.* In the ME *Ywaine and Gawaine,* those who kindle a fire to execute an innocent woman are killed in it themselves, with the narrator noting, "Wha juges men with wrang, / The same jugement sal ai fang" ("Whoever judges men wrongly shall receive the same judgment" [3.2641]; cf. Chrétien de Troyes, *Yvain,* 4564-69). Related is the warning uttered by the Duke of Norfolk to the angry Duke of Buckingham in Shakespeare's *Henry 8:* "Heat not a furnace for your foe so hot / That it do singe yourself" (1.1.140-41).

Dramatic treatments of OT subjects often elaborate or emphasize the (appropriately) dire end of perpetrators of evil. Thus the *Ordo Prophetorum* and its successors, including two 12th-cent. plays, include scenes in which lions devour Daniel's detractors (cf. Dan. 6:24). Haman's ignominious death on the gallows of his own making is likewise highlighted in Renaissance plays such as "Queen Esther and Proud Haman" and "Godly Queen Hester," and in the 19th-cent. "The Death of Haman."

The general biblical motif of tormentors killed by their own weapons (e.g., Ps. 37:14-15) also becomes a literary commonplace. The *Old English Martyrology* uses this motif five times. In Marlowe's *The Massacre at Paris* a friar stabs the French king, who then kills his assassin with the same knife (23.34-35). In Shakespeare's *Hamlet,* Laertes and Claudius both succumb to wounds from the poisoned foil intended to murder Hamlet. (This play is also the source of the famous expression "hoist with his own petar" [3.4.208].) The topos has continued popular into the modern period. Both Smollett *(Roderick Random)* and Dickens *(Nicholas Nickleby),* e.g., have flogging schoolmasters flogged.

Internal or psychological torment of the tormentor has a rich literary history. Milton's Satan who carries hell within him is a classic example (cf. *PL* 2.60-64, where

Satan likens God to a torturer). Traherne asserts of humanity in *Christian Ethicks* (6.1.7): "They all torment themselves!" Coleridge dramatizes such suffering in his tragedy *Osorio*. After plotting his brother's death, the protagonist cries:

> Let the eternal Justice
> Prepare my punishment in the obscure world.
> I will not bear to live — to live! O agony!
> And be myself alone, my own sore torment. (5.263-66;
> cf. *Remorse*, 5.1.228)

Tennyson elaborates the idea that the sinner's conscience torments him: in "Sea Dreams," a wife reminds her wronged husband:

> . . . he that wrongs his friend
> Wrongs himself more, and ever bears about
> A silent court of justice in his breast;
> Himself the judge and jury, and himself
> The prisoner at the bar, ever condemned:
> And that drags down his life: then comes what comes
> hereafter. (172-78)

In Austen's *Mansfield Park* (1814), the selfish and adulterous pair of Maria Rushworth and Henry Crawford become "for a while each other's punishment" and then separate, Maria to live with her equally selfish Aunt Norris: "it may be reasonably supposed that their tempers became their usual punishment" (chap. 16). In Camus's *The Fall* the narrator Jean-Baptiste Clamence is tormented, like Marlowe's Faustus, by the forgiveness he sees will never descend on him. William Golding's *Pincher Martin* tells of a man who kills another to save his own life, then experiences, after death, spiritual death in torment. Tolkien's Gandalf sums up the theme succinctly with reference to the evil Saruman, "Often does hatred hurt itself" *(The Two Towers)*.

See also DANIEL; HAMAN; HE THAT DIGGETH A PIT; HELL; JUDGE NOT; SHADRACH, MESHACH, AND ABEDNEGO.

Bibliography. Blackburn, R. H. *Biblical Drama under the Tudors* (1971); Campbell, L. B. *Divine Poetry and Drama in 16th-Century England* (1959; rpt. 1972); Roston, M. *Biblical Drama in England* (1968); Tkacz, C. B. "The Topos of the Tormentor Tormented in Selected Works of Old English Hagiography." *DAI* 44 (1983), 749A.

CATHERINE BROWN TKACZ

TOWER OF BABEL *See* BABEL.

TOWER OF DAVID *See* MARY, MOTHER OF JESUS; NATIVITY.

TOWER OF IVORY In the wealth of oriental imagery which constitutes the praise of the beloved woman in the Song of Songs (Canticles) is included the simile, "Thy neck is as a tower of ivory" (Song 7:4; cf. 4:4). For many of the early Fathers of the Church (e.g., Cassiodorus, Philo of Carpasia), the tower represents the Church, and

the "ivory" by which it is fortified is the whiteness and purity of its priests. The tower is also sometimes said to be "the knowledge of Scripture" (Philo of Carpasia), or that obedience which fitly joins the mystical Body of Christ with its Head.

As part of a conventional biblical description of the beautiful woman, this phrase was frequently borrowed in medieval secular poetry. Chaucer's Black Knight describes his lost love to the Dreamer in imagery drawn from the Song of Songs: "Hyr throte, as I have now memoyre, / Semed a round tour of yvoyre, / Of good gretnesse, and noght to gret" (*Book of the Duchess*, 945-47). In a bizarre Renaissance adaptation, the "fair Serena" in bk. 6 of Spenser's *Faerie Queene* is stripped naked by cannibals, who then "with their eyes the daintiest morsels chose," including prominently "her yvorie neck; her alabaster brest" (6.8.39, 42).

In elaborate concordances of symbols for the Virgin Mary, such as that compiled by St. Anthony of Padua, the tower of ivory (Vg *turris eburnea*) is taken to signify the strength and purity of Mary's virginity (*In Annuntiatione Sanctae Mariae*, 3), following a tradition already established by St. Bernard of Clairvaux *(Corona Beatae Mariae Virginis)*. This kind of allegorizing of the Song of Songs to praise the Virgin was sharply rejected by several of the Reformers, and those parts of the Litany of the Virgin which included such references were dropped from Cranmer's *Book of Common Prayer*.

The phrase is often employed in modern literature in self-conscious reflection of late medieval tradition. In Oscar Wilde's *Salome*, the title character teases and taunts Jokanaan (John the Baptist) in his dungeon with variations of the oriental lover's vocabulary, underscoring Wilde's parodic intent: "It is thy mouth that I desire, Jokanaan. Thy mouth is like a band of scarlet on a tower of ivory." Swinburne's poem "Dolores," addressed to "Our Lady of Pain," is another sacral parody: "O garden where all men may dwell, / O tower not ivory, but builded / By hands that reach heaven from hell." At Christmas dinner Dante tells Joyce's Stephen (*A Portrait of the Artist as a Young Man*, chap. 1) not to play with Protestants, because they mock the litany of the Blessed Virgin: "*Tower of Ivory*, they used to say, *House of Gold!*" His comment causes Stephen to think of a Protestant girl, Eileen, with "long, thin, cool white hands . . . like ivory, only soft. That was the meaning of *Tower of Ivory* but Protestants could not understand it and made fun of it. . . . Her fair hair . . . gold in the sun. *Tower of Ivory, House of Gold*. By thinking of things you could understand them."

See also SONG OF SONGS.

TRANSFIGURATION The Transfiguration is described, with minor variations, in Matt. 17:1-13, Mark 9:2-13, and Luke 9:28-36. The fourth Gospel does not mention it. All three descriptions agree that Jesus, accompanied by Peter, James, and John, went up to a mountain (unnamed in the text but, according to tradition and the Geneva Bible, Mt. Tabor), where he and his garments were illuminated by a heavenly light and where he spoke with Moses and Elijah. The key verb in the narration (Gk. *metamorphoō*) is translated by almost all English versions as the exact Latin equivalent, "transfigured." The only other biblical reference to the event is in 2 Pet. 1:16-18.

A. M. Ramsey has shown that two themes run through the Fathers' treatment of the Transfiguration: the unity of the Scriptures and the future glory of Christ and his followers. The first emphasis may be seen in St. Jerome (*Hom.* 80, in *The Homilies of St. Jerome)* and St. Augustine (*Sermons in New Testament Lessons,* no. 28), but perhaps the most important figure here is Tertullian, who uses Jesus' conversation with Moses and Elijah to refute Marcion's claims that the OT and NT are incompatible (*Adv. Marc.* 4.22). For St. Basil, the apostles present "were considered worthy to perceive with their eyes the beginning of his glorious coming [i.e., the Parousia]" (*Hom.* 17, *St. Basil: Exegetic Homilies* [1961]), but most commentators —Origen, Jerome, and St. Gregory the Great —tend to look instead toward the Resurrection. The major text in the Fathers' treatment of the Transfiguration is beyond doubt the magisterial sermon of Leo the Great (Sermon 51, NPNF 12), which brings together all these themes and more.

Despite extensive patristic discussion of the narrative, the influence of the Transfiguration upon the English spiritual tradition has been negligible: the Western Church in general has given it little liturgical attention (in contrast to the Eastern churches, where it is exceeded in importance only by Easter), and only in modern times has the Anglican Church recognized it with a red-letter day; from 1549-61 it was altogether absent from the *Book of Common Prayer.* Nevertheless, there are some significant homiletical treatments, notable among them being the "Three Contemplations of the Transfiguration" by Bishop Joseph Hall (1574-1656). Hall imagines the words Moses and Elijah had for Jesus: "A strange opportunity . . . when his face shone like the sun, to tell him it must be blubbered and spat upon; . . . and whilst he was Transfigured on the Mount, to tell him how he must be Disfigured on the Cross!" (quoted in Ramsey, 140-41).

Specific and direct references in literature are likewise relatively rare. In Spenser's "Mutability Cantos," the poet finds himself unable to describe the magnificence of the Goddess Natura and makes this pointed comparison:

Her garment was so bright and wondrous sheene,
That my fraile wit cannot deuize to what
It to compare, nor finde like stuffe to that,
As those three sacred *Saints,* thou else most wise,
Yet on Mount *Thabor* quite their wits forgat,
When they their glorious Lord in strange disguise,
Transfigur'd sawe; his garments did so daze their eyes.
(7.7.7)

Far more common than such a direct comparison is the use of the word *transfigure* to suggest glorification or illumination, much like the Ger. *verklären.* In fact, the chief influence of the biblical passage may be to give depth and resonance to the term *transfigure* that *metamorphose,* the more direct borrowing, lacks. Thus, in Spenser's *Faerie Queene* Britomart has a dream in which she performs the rites of a priestess:

Her seem'd, as she was doing sacrifize
To *Isis,* deckt with Mitre on her hed,
And linen stole after those Priestes guize,
All sodainely she saw transfigured
Her linnen stole to robe of scarlet red,
And Moone-like Mitre to a Crowne of gold,
That euen she her selfe much wondered
At such a chaunge, and ioyed to behold
Her selfe, adorn'd with gems and iewels manifold.
(*FQ* 5.7.13)

Here the reference to the altered garments links the event quite clearly to the Transfiguration of Jesus; a linkage only slightly less direct appears in Emily Dickinson's "Taking up the fair Ideal," after the Ideal becomes "fractured":

Cherishing —our poor Ideal
Till in purer dress
We behold her —glorified —
Comforts —search —like this —
Till the broken creatures —
We adored —for whole —
Stains —all washed —
Transfigured —mended —
Meet us —with a smile —

This poem merges the Transfiguration with the biblical metaphor of blood-soaked garments made clean and pure —especially common in the Protestant hymns on which Dickinson drew so heavily.

When Coleridge takes up the word *transfigure,* he assumes its resonances without referring strictly to the biblical event: in "Religious Musings" (1794-96) he describes a soul at first besieged and terrified by the spiritual dangers of this world, then calmed and assured, "refresh'd from Heaven." Now,

. . . faith's whole armor glitters on his limbs!
And thus transfigured with a dreadless awe,
A solemn hush of soul, meek he beholds
All things of terrible seeming; . . .

Thus the notion of transfiguration is accommodated to the Romantic doctrine of the Sublime.

Of the few direct modern addresses to the subject, Edwin Muir's neglected poem "The Transfiguration" is noteworthy. Muir assumes the perspective of one of the apostles:

We would have thrown our clothes away for lightness,
But that even they, though sour and travel stained,
Seemed, like our flesh, made of immortal substance,

And the soiled flax and wool lay light upon us
Like friendly wonders, flower and flock entwined
As in a morning field. Was it a vision?
Or did we see that day the unseeable
One glory of the everlasting world
Perpetually at work, though never seen
Since Eden locked the gate that's everywhere
And nowhere?

Bibliography. Liefeld, W. L. "Theological Motifs in the Transfiguration Narrative." In *New Dimensions in New Testament Study.* Eds. R. N. Longenecker and M. C. Tenney (1974), 162-79; Ramsey, A. M. *The Glory of God and the Transfiguration of Christ* (1949); Reisenfeld, H. *Jésus transfiguré* (1947); Rudrum, A. W. "Henry Vaughan and the Theme of Transfiguration." *SoR* 1 (1963), 54-67.

ALAN JACOBS

TRANSUBSTANTIATION Although the term *transubstantiation* is neither biblical nor patristic, the concept it expresses traces to Christian revelation. Scriptural evidence (Matt. 26:26-28; Mark 14:22-24; Luke 22:19-20; John 6:50-67) has been taken to mean that in the eucharistic celebration bread and wine cease to exist and Christ's body and blood become present. Christ's words at the Last Supper, "This is my body . . . this is my blood," indicate, as summarized by St. Thomas Aquinas, that "The whole substance of the bread is changed into the whole substance of Christ's body, and the whole substance of the wine into the whole substance of Christ's blood" (*Summa Theol.,* 3a, 75.4).

Prior to Thomas's formulation, some of the Church Fathers had employed terms which lacked precision, such as *transformation* or *transmutation,* to describe what takes place at the consecration of the Mass. For Thomas, the idea of transubstantiation involves something more than mere change *(mutatio)* of form or a mere process of substitution as in sleight-of-hand performances. It is rather an ontological or

> a substantial conversion *(conversio substantialis),* inasmuch as one thing is *substantially* or *essentially* converted into another. Thus from the concept of transubstantiation is excluded every sort of merely accidental conversion, whether it be purely natural (e.g. the metamorphosis of insects) or supernatural (e.g. the transfiguration of Christ). (Rahner, *"Sacramentum Mundi"*)

In the medieval period, St. Berengar of Tours (d. 1086) denied the eucharistic conversion altogether and advocated a purely spiritual and symbolic presence of Christ. His denial of the Real Presence of Christ paved the way for further clarification of the doctrine. The neologism *transubstantiation* seems to have been first used by Hildebert of Tours (about 1079), and by the 12th cent. it rapidly gained currency and began to appear frequently in conciliar documents. The Fourth Lateran Council in 1215, the Second Council of Lyons in 1274, and the

Council of Florence in 1439 all used the term in expositions of the doctrine.

Despite these elucidations, a new opposition set in with the Reformation. Luther, while admitting the Real Presence, repudiated transubstantiation and coined the term *consubstantiation* to express his view that the bread and wine remain along with the body and blood of Christ after the consecration. Ideas such as these were challenged by the Sacramentarians, particularly Zwingli who regarded the sacrament as no more than a visible symbol, a figure or sign of Christ's presence. Zwingli concluded that the idea of transubstantiation made the Mass a cannibalistic rite and therefore "monstrous, unless perhaps one is living among the Anthropophagi" *(Commentary on True and False Religion).* John Calvin attacked both transubstantiation and consubstantiation and maintained instead that Christ's body and blood are present not physically but "virtually," i.e., by a power emanating from the Holy Spirit. Calvin's objections stemmed from a widespread Protestant apprehension about the popular use of hermetic magic. Calvin linked the spiritual power of the priest in transubstantiation to that of the magician in his manipulation of material nature. He consequently equated the words of consecration with "magic incantation" and argued that Catholics labored under "the error of a magical conception of the sacraments" (*Inst.* 4.17.15; 4.14.4). (It is noteworthy in this regard that in the 17th and 18th cents. the notion that "hocus-pocus" was a parody of the Latin words used by the priest during consecration, *hoc est corpus,* gained some currency.) Faced with such challenges, the Council of Trent in 1551 issued an authoritative statement and insisted again that after the substantial conversion only the species of bread and wine remain.

By the last quarter of the 12th cent. the doctrine of transubstantiation had become a favorite subject not only in sermons but also in art, in ritual, and in sacred poetry. At this time, too, the story of a miraculous vessel called the Grail became popular with romance writers, who combined the Celtic story of the quest for the Grail with the Christian legend of Joseph of Arimathea in successive retellings for a specific didactic purpose. In the Grail story any object used for the consecration of the eucharistic bread and wine — chalice, paten, ciborium, or altar stone — could represent the miracle of transubstantiation. In the change from a magic to a holy vessel, the Grail became a symbol of transubstantiation.

From the Renaissance onward, however, references and allusions to transubstantiation reflect Protestant polemic. Spenser presents the cannibal priests in bk. 6 of the *Faerie Queene* as celebrating a kind of Mass in which the table guest, Serena, becomes, as it were, the "host" — a degenerate version of the sacrament. In *Paradise Lost* Milton employs the notion of transubstantiation ironically to highlight his own view that angels engage in corporeal rather than spiritual manducation:

. . . So down they sat,
And to their viands fell, nor seemingly
The angel, nor in mist, the common gloss
Of theologians, but with keen despatch
Of real hunger, and concoctive heat
To transubstantiate; what redounds, transpires
Through spirits with ease; nor wonder; if by fire
Of sooty coal the empiric alchemist
Can turn, or holds it possible to turn
Metals of drossest ore to perfect gold. (5.433-42)

John Donne continues the alchemical metaphor in *The First Anniversarie,* where, speaking of the virtuous Elizabeth Drury, he says, "Though she could not transubstantiate / All states to gold, yet guilded every state, / So that some Princes have some temperance" (417-19). Similarly, in "To the Countesse of Huntingdon," Donne distinguishes between the superficiality of gilding or "informing" as compared with the thoroughness of complete transubstantiation: "She [virtue] guilded us: But you are gold, and Shee; / Us she inform'd, — but transubstantiates you" (25-26). In "Twicknam Garden" the poet mocks himself for indulging in sighs and tears. Although he retreats to the garden, he has brought, in his own words, the serpent with him to Paradise: "But O, selfe traytor, I do bring / The spider love which transubstantiates all, / And can convert Manna to gall" (5-7). Here the parallel seems closer to the Eucharist. Poisonous love converts manna (an OT prefiguration of the Eucharist) ironically to (the NT) gall or bitterness.

In the 18th cent., transubstantiation is employed for purposes of parody. In *Tristram Shandy* Sterne describes the Roman Catholic priest, Dr. Slop, as being "beluted and so transubstantiated" (2.9). In the mock-epic toilette/arming scene in Pope's *Rape of the Lock* a comic Ovidian metamorphosis replaces transubstantiation in Belinda's rite: "The Tortoise here and Elephant unite, / Transform'd to *Combs,* the speckled and the white" (1.135-36). This same parody of transubstantiation occurs in the final book of the *Dunciad,* where the priests of Dullness celebrate a black Mass:

On some, A Priest succinct in amice white
Attends; all flesh is nothing in his sight!
Beeves, at his touch, at once to jelly turn,
And the huge Boar is shrunk into an Urn:
The board with specious miracles he loads,
Turns Hares to Larks, and Pigeons into Toads.
Another (for in all what one can shine?)
Explains the *Sève* and *Verdeur* of the Vine
What cannot copious Sacrifice atone? (4.549-57)

Byron also used the concept ironically in *The Deformed Transformed* to describe the loss of faith: "what cold Sceptic hath appalled your faith / And transubstantiated to crumbs again / The *body* of your credence?" (3.113-15). Blake for his part denies the Real Presence by claiming that Christ's words at the Last Supper were "This the Wine and this the Bread" ("My Spectre around me

night and day," st. 14). In *The Four Zoas* Blake reflects the Zwinglian idea of transubstantiation as cannibalism in his description of the dreadful marriage feast of the fallen Los and Enitharmon, who partake of the sexual bread and wine of the body: "They eat the fleshly bread, they drank the nervous wine" (12.44).

D. H. Lawrence inherited this sacramentarian horror in the next century. In his essay on Melville's *Typee* he boldly declares that a cannibal feast seemed to him a more valid sacrament than the Eucharist ("Herman Melville's *Typee* and *Omoo,*" in *Studies in Classic American Literature*).

Yeats emphasized another aspect of the symbolic presence in his consideration of art and artist as Eucharist. He pointed out that Blake had learned from alchemist writers how the "imagination was the first emanation of divinity, 'the body of God.' " In "Michael Robartes and the Dancer" Yeats asks, "Did God in portioning wine and bread / Give man His thought or His mere body?" Like Christ, the artist, by a rather extravagant analogy, gives his own body, the imagination, to nourish and transform those who "communicate" and enter into a covenant with him. Or, in the words of Forgael in the play *The Shadowy Waters,* "I have but images, analogies / The mystic bread, the sacramental wine" (*Collected Plays,* p. 152), presumably because for Yeats the priest is merely the poet's "shadow" or unsubstantial image. The bread and wine have a "doom," as he says in "The Host of the Air." This strand of modernist belief in a theurgic sacramentalism and in the imagination as a means of grace akin to the Eucharist is shared by Yeats's compatriot James Joyce, in whose work, despite the Catholic scaffolding, can be found a compendium of agnostic views of transubstantiation. Joyce called his stories in *Dubliners* "epicleti," referring to the invocation (*epiklesis* in Eastern liturgies) to the Holy Ghost to change the bread and wine into the body and blood of Christ. For Joyce, the artist must translate the Eucharist "into common sense," as he says in *Stephen Hero* — i.e., the artist must detheologize it. Stephen's mission as "priest of eternal imagination" empowers him to "transmute the daily bread of experience into the radiant body of everliving life" in *A Portrait of the Artist as a Young Man.* Joyce takes his cue from Shelley's *Defence,* where poetry is said to "transmute" all that it touches by its secret alchemy. In the villanelle which Stephen calls a "eucharistic hymn" (perhaps a parody of the eucharistic hymns such as *"Adoro Te Devote"* of St. Thomas Aquinas), he describes a sexual rather than a spiritual communion. Stephen first cloisters his temptress-muse within the confines of his own being and then pays homage to her and to himself as eucharist before the altar of his imagination. In *Ulysses* Joyce associates cannibalism with the eating of Christ's body and vampirism with the drinking of his blood. In an irreverent discussion about the connection between the Incarnation and the Eucharist, Joyce has Stephen consider both transubstantiation and the Lutheran consubstantiation. In *Finnegans Wake* Shem, another type of the hieratic alchemist, practices "transaccidentation" (a word apparently first used by Duns Scotus to signify a change of accidents or appearances rather than of substance) whereby under the accidents of ink the artist becomes symbolically present to his readers.

For David Jones the sacred host is not a mere formal symbol as it is for Joyce, but a vital sign. With Jones one returns to a Thomist understanding of transubstantiation, and it is appropriate that he conceived of the artist's task as "lifting up valid signs," as "uncovering" or "recovering" (in Tolkien's sense), lost words and lost meaning. In *Anathemata* Jones re-presents the Mass as the focal point from which to view all history since it is, as he says, a "true *historia*." The poet like the priest is a celebrant in and of form, particularly of transubstantiation. The bread and wine offered in the recalling, the *anamnēsis*, of the Eucharist are not mere wheat and grapes but quasi-artifacts which have already passed under the jurisdiction of the muse. Consequently, Jones relates the transubstantiatory nature of art as revealed in the primitive limestone sculpture known as the *Venus of Willendorf* and the recently discovered Lascaux cave paintings:

> Then it is these abundant *ubera,* here, under the species of worked lime-rock, that gave suck to the lord? . . .
> And see how they run, the juxtaposed forms, brighting the vaults of Lascaux; how the linear is wedded to volume, how they do, within, in an unbloody manner, under the forms of brown haematite and black manganese on the graved lime-face, what is done, without. (p. 60)

The *Anathemata* also marks a return to the Grail story. Jones observes that the sacrament of the Eucharist had constituted the supersubstantial nourishment of the declining West: "Failing / (finished?) West / your food, once." Thirst is another symptom of the modern wasteland, which can only be regenerated by "One man, [who] by water, restores to us our state" (*Anathemata,* 238). By the chalice or Grail and by the "viatic bread," symbols of transubstantiation, he revives the inhabitants of Eliot's Waste Land.

See also EUCHARIST; HOLY GRAIL; JOSEPH OF ARIMATHEA.

Bibliography. Boyle, S. J. *James Joyce's Pauline Vision: A Catholic Exposition* (1978), 47-57; Fisher, L. *The Mystic Vision in the Grail Legend and in The Divine Comedy* (1917); Manganiello, D. "The Artist as Magician: Yeats, Joyce and Tolkien." *Mythlore* (1983), 13-15, 25; "The Earthbound Vision of *A Portrait of the Artist*." *Renascence* 35 (1983), 219-34; Stone, D. *A History of the Holy Eucharist* (1909), 2 vols.   DOMINIC MANGANIELLO

TRAP Animal and bird traps were of several kinds in biblical times. The KJV's "trap" refers to what would have been a wood frame covered with mesh, either manually or automatically sprung. Always in the KJV traps are mentioned in conjunction with snares. KJV's "snare" or "gin" usually refers to loops of rope or wire which, when sprung, fasten upon the leg or neck of the creature caught, but "snare" can also refer to a jawed trap or to a pit-and-net trap. Metaphorically, however, traps, gins, and snares seem to be synonymous in the Bible — and virtually every biblical reference to these is metaphorical. Traps, gins, and snares could suggest how the wicked are caught up, all unawares, by the consequences of their sins — traps, then, which the Lord sets and springs. Concerning the wicked the Lord says: "I will spread my net upon him, and he shall be taken in my snare" (Ezek. 17:20); and in his wrath the Lord said of the Moabites: "he that getteth up out of the pit shall be taken in the snare" (Jer. 49:43-44; see also Josh. 23:13; Job 18:8-10; Ps. 69:22-23; Isa. 8:14; Amos 3:5).

Traps are also laid by the evil one and his minions either in the hope of destroying the righteous — enemies "have digged a pit for my soul," complained Jeremiah (18:20) — or in the hope of catching the unwary with the bait of temptation. The Lord warns his people, e.g., that the pagan gods "shall be a snare unto you" (Judg. 2:3); and it is said that a naive young man succumbs to the harlot "as a bird hasteth to the snare" (Prov. 7:23); and "they that would be rich fall into temptation and a snare" (1 Tim. 6:9). Repentant sinners, on the other hand, "recover themselves out of the snare of the devil" (2 Tim. 2:26).

In the Fathers those traps which God sets are usually intended for the devil: St. Augustine's exposition of one form of this allegory was well known: "The devil exulted when Christ died, but by this very death of Christ the devil was vanquished, as if he had swallowed the bait in the mousetrap. . . . The cross of the Lord was the devil's mousetrap; the bait by which he was caught was the Lord's death" (*Sermo,* 263 [PL 38.1210]; see also *Sermo,* 130.726; 134.745; and Peter Lombard, *Sentences* [PL 192.796]). In the Middle Ages this allegory seems to lie behind the righthand panel of the Merode Altarpiece, where the carpenter Joseph is at work on a mousetrap. This allegorical tradition should probably also inform one's reading of Chaucer's Prioress, in the *Canterbury Tales,* who was "pitous / She wolde wepe, if that she saugh a mous / Kaught in a trappe" (*General Prologue,* 1.143-45). Hamlet's hope that the play will be the thing wherein he'll "catch the conscience of the king" may be a late reference to this same tradition.

More commonly, however, both in the Fathers and in the English tradition, traps are figures for temptations, and the devil is the setter of traps, the fowler. Augustine glosses Ps. 141:9-10: "In the trap was set the bait of the present life" (*Enarr. in Ps.* 144.12-13); and further: "the snare was the sweetness of the present life" (124.9; see also 91.4; and St. Ambrose, *Homilarium,* 68). Similar references abound in the English sermon literature (e.g., G. R. Owst, *Literature and the Pulpit* [1966], 400; Lancelot Andrews, *Ninety-Six Sermons,* 1.401; 4.228, 397; John Donne, *Sermons,* 2.292; 3.59, 191; 5.208). And so it is appropriate that in Jonson's *Bartholomew Fair* (3.4.91) Wasp should regard the Fair's booths as "springs," fowlers' nets.

In Henry Vaughan's "Repentance" the flesh tries to persuade the spirit of the persona that the "narrow way" leading to salvation is a fowler's trap:

> . . . That little gate
> And narrow way, by which to thee
> The Passage is, He term'd a grate
> And Entrance to Captivitie;
> Thy laws but nets, where some small birds
> (And those but seldome too) were caught. . . .

More generally, in secular literature traps and snares came to serve as standard metaphors for temptations, particularly sexual allurements. (This development is complicated, although not contradicted, by the largely synonymous classical traditions; see, e.g., Juvenal's connection of promiscuity with nets in *Satire,* 10.) In Chaucer's *Troilus and Criseyde* (1.663) Phebus is said to be "bounden in a snare" by love. Wyatt could write, "Tangled I was in love's snare" ("Tangled I was"). Shakespeare's Lucrece, before she was sullied by rape, was a "bird never lim'd" (86). And in Richardson's *Clarissa,* the incorrigible Lovelace writes, in his letter of April 24, "I have been at work . . . spreading my snares like an artful fowler."

See also HE THAT DIGGETH A PIT.

Bibliography. Brumble, H. D. *"General Prologue: Canterbury Tales," Expl* 37 (1978); 45; Koonce, B. G. "Satan the Fowler," *MS* 21 (1959), 176-84; Schapiro, M. " 'Muscipula Diaboli,' The Symbolism of the Merode Altarpiece." In *Late Antique, Early Christian and Medieval Art.* Ed. M. Schapiro (1979), 1-19.   H. DAVID BRUMBLE

TREASURES UPON EARTH The phrase "treasures upon earth" derives from Christ's Sermon on the Mount: "Lay not up for yourselves treasures upon earth, where moth and rust doth corrupt, and where thieves break through and steal" (Matt. 6:19). "Treasures upon earth" is often contrasted with the parallel phrase "treasures in heaven," which is somewhat more common in English. In addition to several direct allusions, many authors refer indirectly to "treasures upon earth" by citing the phrases following it — "where moth and rust doth corrupt" or "where thieves break through and steal."

St. Augustine, in his *Sermo,* 60.7, emphasizes that the passage affords counsel "for keeping, not for losing," and ensures "not a wasting, but a saving." He draws an analogy with prudent husbandry:

> Thou puttest wheat in the low ground; and thy friend comes, who knows the nature of the corn and the land, and instructs thy unskilfulness, and says to thee, "What hast thou done? Thou hast put the corn in the flat soil, in the lower land; the soil is moist; it will all rot, and thou wilt lose thy labour." Thou answerest, "What then must I

do?" "Remove it," he says, "into the higher ground." . . . Behold the Lord thy God when he giveth thee counsel touching thine heart. . . . Lift up, saith he, thine heart to heaven, that it rot not in the earth. It is his counsel, who wisheth to preserve thy heart, not to destroy it.

Although St. Thomas More mentions "treasures in earth" in *Dialogue of Comfort* (3.15.1232E), Spenser is the first English poet to refer frequently to the phrase. He writes in "An Hymne in Honour of Beautie" of "That wondrous paterne, wheresoere it bee, whether in earth layd up in secret store" (37) and refers indirectly to earthly treasure three times in *The Faerie Queene:*

> The second was as Almner of the place. . . .
> The grace of God he layd up still in store. . . .
> And had he lesse, yet some he would give to the pore.
> (1.10.38.1, 6, 9)

> What secret place (quoth he) can safely hold
> So huge a masse, and hide from heavens eye?
> Or where hast thou thy wonne [riches], that so much gold
> Thou canst preserve from wrong and robbery?
> (2.7.20.1-4)

> For feare least Force of Fraud should unaware
> Breake in, and spoile the treasure there in gard.
> (2.7.25.3-4)

Marlowe writes in *The Massacre at Paris* of "all the wealth and treasure of the world" (1163). Pericles in Shakespeare's play of that name contemplates his demise and bequeaths "My riches to the earth from whence they came" (1.1.52). Herbert hymns in his *Valdesso* the "word of God, as their Joy, and Crowne, and their Treasure on earth" (34). Milton, in *The Reason of Church Government,* writes of his determination to speak freely about his religious opinions: "For me, I have determined to lay up as the best treasure and solace of a good old age . . . the honest liberty of free speech from my youth" (1.804.9).

The 19th cent. saw several uses of the "treasures upon earth" theme. Blake asks in "Visions of the Daughters of Albion," "Does not the eagle scorn the earth and despise the treasures beneath?" (149). Wordsworth writes in "Ode 1815," "And well might it beseem that mighty Town/Into whose bosom earth's best treasures flow" (46-47).

The phrase has become common enough that a biblically oriented poet such as Christina Rossetti can allude to the passage in at least four places: "Three Nuns" begins by quoting the verse from Matthew, then laments that "With foolish riches of this world / I have bought treasure where / Nought perisheth." In "Testimony" Rossetti puts the verse in meter: "Our treasures moth and rust corrupt, / Or thieves break through and steal." "Days of Vanity" includes the lines

> A scanty measure,
> Rust-eaten treasure,
> Spending that nought buyeth,
> Moth on the wing,
> Toil unprofiting.

There is a further indirect reference in "Old and New" in the lines "Rust in thy gold, a moth is in thine array."

In America Thoreau focused the allusion on the burden of owning property. Those who devote their lives to acquiring wealth, he says, "are employed, as it says in an old book, laying up treasures which moth and rust will corrupt and thieves break through and steal" (*Walden,* 51). Melville's *Moby-Dick* includes a more extensive allusion which plays on the multiple meanings of one of the words in the biblical verse. Captain Bildad offers Ishmael a very small share of the whaling profits, called a "lay"; mumbling from his Bible, Bildad says, " 'Lay not up for yourselves treasures upon the earth, where moth . . . and rust do corrupt, but lay — ' Ishmael thinks to himself, 'Lay indeed . . . and such a lay! The seven hundred and seventy-seventh! Well, old Bildad, you are determined that I, for one, shall not lay up many lays, here below, where moth and rust do corrupt.' "

In the 20th cent., Shaw twists Matthew's verses ironically in his preface to *Major Barbara:* "Let the deserving lay up for himself, not treasures in heaven, but horrors in hell upon earth" (215). Father Arnall alludes to the earth-heaven contrast in a passage from his famous sermon in *A Portrait of the Artist as a Young Man:* "How they will rage and fume to think that they have lost the bliss of heaven for the dross of earth" (chap. 3).

STEVEN C. WALKER

TREE Used since early classical times to suggest genealogical relationships, the tree appears in Scripture to depict the destiny of an individual (e.g., Nebuchadnezzar in Dan. 4), to show the relationship between races (Rom. 11:17- 25), and to describe the progress of life (Ps. 1; Jer. 17:8). Wisdom, "the fruits of righteousness," "a desire fulfilled," and "a wholesome tongue" are all likened to a "tree of life" in the book of Proverbs (3:18; 11:30; 13:12; 15:4). Spiritual fruitfulness is compared to that of a tree which brings forth good fruit, but "every tree which bringeth not forth good fruit is hewn down, and cast into the fire" (Matt. 3:10; 7:19; 12:33; Luke 3:9; 6:44).

The image of the tree also unifies the events of salvation history in the Bible and helps to clarify the meaning of redemption. By willfully eating fruit from the tree of the knowledge of good and evil (Gen. 2:17; 3:3-7), humanity forfeited eternal bliss and the tree of life (Gen. 2:9; 3:22) and was banished by God from Eden into the wilderness of the world. Christ's condescension to suffer and die on the tree of the cross restored the possibility of attaining Paradise and the eternal fruit of the tree of life (Rev. 2:7; 22:2).

Early Christian writers commented extensively on the doctrinal meaning and theological relationships of these biblical trees, and extrapolated from them a composite symbolic tree which embodied the major Christian doctrines and mysteries. The 4th-cent. Christian poem *De pascha* (attributed to Tertullian [PL 2.1171-74]) depicts

in elaborate detail a cosmological tree which is simultaneously the cross, the Church, and the tree of life. Originating as a twig taken from the dry and barren tree defiled by Adam, the branch brings forth a fruit which ripens on the cross, falls to the earth, and grows into a great tree stretching to heaven, paralleling the Incarnation, Passion, Burial, Resurrection, and Ascension of Christ. Other similar trees occur in *Piers Plowman,* Deguilleville's *Pèlerinage de l'âme,* and the *Vision of Tundale.* Following the example set for them by patristic writers, medieval exegetes elaborated the significance of these symbolic trees, particularly the theological appropriateness of a branch of the tree of knowledge becoming the wood of the cross.

The tree also became an important feature of medieval allegory. The tree of Jesse (Isa. 11:1) not only makes obvious the genealogical relationships of the line of Christ but is often used to suggest the virginity of Mary, the typological relationship between the OT and the NT, and the history of salvation from beginning to end. More overtly allegorical are the many trees of virtues and vices by which the medieval layperson could easily see pride as the "root" of the other deadly sins. Related to these are the many allegorical trees of Joachim of Fiore (12th cent.) in which the branching structure of the tree serves both a schematic and chronological function to depict Christ's lineage, the unfolding of biblical prophecy, theological mysteries, and historical eschatology. Even more significant in their direct connection with Christ's redeeming work are the closely detailed *ligna vitae* of St. Bonaventure and others, in which the twelve branches of the tree all depict various scenes from the life and Passion of Christ. In the 14th-cent. *Desert of Religion,* a work on penance, fifteen distinct allegorical trees are described in detail.

Related to the allegorical trees are the green and dry trees described in Ezek. 17:22-24: "And all the trees of the field shall know that I the LORD have brought down the high tree, have exalted the low tree, have dried up the green tree, and have made the dry tree to flourish" (v. 24). Of all the images which have come to signify the virginity of Mary and her Immaculate Conception, the figure of the dry tree which becomes green has been one of the most widespread because of its close connection with both the sin of Eve and the redemption by Christ through Mary. Deguilleville's *Pèlerinage de l'âme* is the most detailed significant literary elaboration of this image, where Mary is the green and fruitful branch which knew no sin and which, when grafted, will make the dry tree burst into bloom. Other allusions occur in Dante's *Purgatorio* (32.43-63) and the third volume of Tolkien's *Lord of the Rings.*

In medieval literature and art, the image of a grafted tree is often used to emphasize or to explain an enigmatic relationship between two diverse elements *(Mum and the Sothsegger,* Dan Michel's *Ayenbit of Inwyt).* When the woods of three trees are grafted together, as they are in a number of medieval works (e.g., the vision of the tree with three branches in Lovelich's *Holy Grail* or the Tree of Charity in *Piers Plowman,* the image expands its possibilities to suggest the mysterious union of the Trinity, underscoring the diversity of the Godhead while affirming its unity. Implied in a passage from Rom. 11:17-24 is another characteristic often exploited by medieval writers: for the branches of one tree to be united with another, the special intervention of a grafting agent is required. As an attempt to manipulate in order to increase fertility and improve the stock, the act of grafting is artificial. But when God is the grafter, as in the Romans passage, the action is miraculous, providing a symbolic analogy for the Incarnation (e.g., Dante, *Purgatorio,* 32; Christine de Pisan, *L'Épitre d'Othéa*), the Immaculate Conception and the Virginity of Mary (Deguilleville's *Pèlerinage de l'âme* and the Frankfurt "Paradise Garden," painted by the unknown Master of the Middle Rhine).

The grafted tree is also directly linked to the Passion. A body of legends which flourished in the Middle Ages and which is narrated in detail in the *Cursor Mundi* traces the wood of the cross back to its origin in three seeds taken from the tree of knowledge which grow into three rods: a cedar, a cypress, and a pine. Moses discovers these healing rods, carries them throughout the wilderness wanderings, and buries them at his death; when King David comes to take them to Jerusalem, he finds that they have been mysteriously grafted together. After the reigns of David and Solomon, the tree rests in the Temple until the cross is fashioned from it at Christ's Crucifixion. With a range of possible meanings which extend from depicting a complex relationship or a diversity in unity to symbolizing the cross and the mystery of redemption, the grafted tree is a significant image in a number of important medieval works *(Sir Orfeo;* Chrétien's *Cligès);* the image of mending by grafting is used by Shakespeare in *The Winter's Tale* (4.4.91) but has little currency after the Renaissance. In the 20th cent. the traditional grafting motif has received new attention from David Jones in *Anathemata.*

Several species of tree possess special symbolic import (not always biblically derived) within Christian tradition. The apple tree is typically associated with the forbidden tree of knowledge — partly by virtue of an etymological connection between Vg *malum* (apple) with *malus* (evil). The oak tree signifies death (e.g., Chaucer's *The Pardoner's Tale*), the holly tree life and hope, as well as the Passion (e.g., *Sir Gawain and the Green Knight*), the pear tree carnal love (Chaucer's *The Merchant's Tale*), and the cherry tree the miraculous Incarnation of Christ (the Towneley "The Second Shepherd's Play"). Even modern authors (notably T. S. Eliot, Dylan Thomas, and J. R. R. Tolkien) make use of such associations: the juniper tree, associated with Elijah's depression and

God's compassionate ministry to him (1 Kings 19), recurs in T. S. Eliot's "Ash Wednesday."

See also APPLE; TREE OF JESSE; TREE OF KNOWLEDGE; TREE OF LIFE.

Bibliography. Childs, B. S. "Tree of Knowledge." *IDB* 4.695-97; Collette, C. P. " *'Ubi Peccaverant, Ibi Punirentur':* The Oak Tree and the Pardoner's Tale." *ChauR* 19 (1984), 39-45; Cook, R. *The Tree of Life: Image for the Cosmos* (1974); Coolidge, S. "The Grafted Tree in Literature: A Study in Medieval Iconography and Theology." *DAI* 38 (1977), 2107A; Greenhill, E. S. "The Child in the Tree: A Study of the Cosmological Tree in Christian Tradition." *Traditio* 10 (1954), 323-71; Katzenellenbogen, A. *Allegories of the Virtues and Vices in Mediaeval Art.* Trans. J. P. Crick (1939); Ladner, G. B. "Vegetation Symbolism and the Concept of Renaissance." *De Artibus Opuscula XL: Essays in Honor of Erwin Panofsky.* Ed. M. Meiss. 2 vols. (1961); Rowlette, R. "Mark Twain's Barren Tree in the Mysterious Stranger: Two Biblical Parallels." *MTJ* 16 (1972), 19-20; Watson, A. *The Early Iconography of the Tree of Jesse* (1934).

SHARON COOLIDGE

TREE OF JESSE According to Isaiah's prophecy of a messianic deliverer, "there shall come forth a rod out of the stem of Jesse, and a Branch shall grow out of his roots: And the spirit of the LORD shall rest upon him, the spirit of wisdom and understanding, the spirit of counsel and might, the spirit of knowledge and of the fear of the LORD" (Isa. 11:1-2). This "root of Jesse," the prophet adds, "shall stand for an ensign of the people; to it shall the Gentiles seek: and his rest shall be glorious" (v. 10).

St. Paul clearly identifies the "root of Jesse" with Jesus, whose life, death, and resurrection signal a new dispensation of grace to the Gentiles (Rom. 15:12). In subsequent commentary the "tree of Jesse" motif is elaborated with reference to the lineage of "Jesus Christ, the son of David" (Matt. 1:1). Numerous medieval representations — in miniatures, MSS illustrations, altarpieces, and stained glass ("Jesse windows") — show Jesse, father of David, lying on his back with a tree growing upward from his loins; in the branches are signified noteworthy representatives of the genealogy of Christ, who is himself topmost as "fruit" of the tree. In one example, in the *Speculum Virginum* (Cologne, later 12th cent.) of Conrad of Hirsau, seven leaves radiate from Christ, on which are inscribed the gifts of the Holy Spirit and their qualities (cf. Wisd. of Sol. 7:22); on another seven leaves are *incipits* to the Beatitudes, the petitions of the Lord's Prayer, the seven last words of Christ, the seven prophecies concerning the seven churches from Rev. 2-3, the articles of the Creed, and the seven virtues (cf. Hugh of St. Victor, *De Quinque Septenis seu Septenariis* [PL 175.405ff.]). The "rod of Jesse" gives rise also to the flowering rod of Joseph in the NT Apocrypha.

The phrase in the Vg, *Egredietur virga de Jesse* (Isa. 11:1), introduces the pun *virga/virgo* (rod/virgin); in the prophets' preparation in the Corpus Christi plays (e.g.,

York), one sees a typical development in iconography of the Virgin:

A wande sall brede of Jesse boure;
And of þis same also sais hee.
Vpponne þat wande sall springe a floure,
Wher-on þe haly gast sall be,
To governe it with grete honnoure.
That wande maynes vntil vs
þis mayden, even and morne,
And þe floure is Jesus,
þat of þat blyst bees borne. (12.75-84)

Medieval lyrics frequently incorporate the same motif in litanies of the Virgin, especially those which follow the iconography of St. Anthony of Padua. In James Ryman's *"Gaude Mater Gloriosa"* Mary is greeted, "Haile, Iesse roote full of vertue" (ed. Zupitza, 15; cf. 20), and in his *"Ecce, Quod Natura Mutat Sua Iura"* (no. 17):

A yerde shall goo oute of Iesse rote,
Whereof a floure shall ascende full soote:
The floure is Crist, oure helth and boote,
This yerde Mary, his boure.

Protestant exegesis did not abandon this motif, central as it was to the *historia humanae salvationis* and covenant theology, but rather developed it with reference to other prophetic texts. Thus, in the allusions of Spenser to the Virgin birth, Dan. 4:10-11 is invoked in applying the motif: "That Tree, / Whose big embodied braunches shall not lin, / Till they to hevens hight forth stretched bee" (*Faerie Queene*, 3.3.22).

Although the Tree of Jesse retains a place in hymnody and religious poetry (e.g., the carol "O Come, O Come, Emmanuel"), allusions in literature are infrequent after the Renaissance.

See also DAVID; JESUS CHRIST; MESSIAH.

Bibliography. Katzenellenbogen, A. *Allegories of the Virtues and Vices in Medieval Art* (1964); Watson, A. *The Early Iconography of the Tree of Jesse* (1934).

TREE OF KNOWLEDGE   The tree of the knowledge of good and evil, lit. "the tree of [the] knowing good and evil" (Heb. *'eṣ hadda'at ṭob wara'*; Gen. 2:9, 17) was planted, with the tree of life, in the midst of the Garden of Eden, and was uniquely prohibited: "But of the tree of the knowledge of good and evil, thou shalt not eat of it; for in the day that thou eatest thereof thou shalt surely die" (Gen. 2:17). Eve, tempted by the serpent, found the tree "good for food, and that it was pleasant to the eyes, and a tree to be desired to make one wise, [and] she took of the fruit thereof, and did eat; and gave also unto her husband with her, and he did eat" (Gen. 3:6). Having eaten, Adam and Eve were immediately ashamed of their nakedness (Gen. 3:7) and hid themselves from God (Gen. 3:8); God pronounced judgment on the serpent, the woman, and the man (Gen. 3:14-19) and, since mankind had "become as one of us, to know good and evil,"

banished them from the garden, lest they "take also of the tree of life, and eat, and live for ever" (Gen. 3:22-23).

From ancient times, interpretation of this powerful but ambiguous symbol has divided on fundamental questions: What does the tree represent? Does eating of it merely produce sinful alienation, or does it, as the Gnostics were later to imagine, involve some positive knowledge, and, if so, of what kind? The exact Hebrew phrase used in the Genesis account does not appear elsewhere in the OT. In other passages, however, "knowing" good and evil seems to imply a level of maturity (Deut. 1:39), and moral (or more general) discernment and judgment (2 Sam. 14:17; 19:35; 1 Kings 3:9; Heb. 5:14), but there is no necessary connection between these passages and the Genesis tree.

Patristic writers suggest a variety of interpretations. St. Gregory of Nyssa sees the tree of knowledge as "latent evil" "decked with good," the type of all delusive desire (*Making of Man,* 20). On the contrary, St. Gregory of Nazianzus describes it as an image of contemplation which is "only safe for those who have reached maturity of habit" and which would, therefore, "have been good if partaken of at the proper time" (*Theophany,* 12).

St. Augustine gave currency to the most influential interpretation, in which the tree represents allegorically "the free choice of our own will" (*De civ. Dei* 13.21) and in which its name signifies "what good [Adam and Eve] would experience if they kept the prohibition or what evil if they transgressed it" (*De peccatorum meritis et remissione,* 2.35; *De civ. Dei,* 14.17). This interpretation remained normative through the Reformation. Calvin similarly sees the tree as a "proof and exercise" of man's faith (*Inst.* 2.1.4); Luther speculates that it may well have been a grove, as a "temple of divine worship," in effect "Adam's church, altar, and pulpit," and the prohibition concerning it a pre-Fall ritual law enabling humanity to demonstrate its obedience (*Lectures on Genesis,* sup. Gen. 2:9, 17).

This tradition culminates memorably in Milton's *Paradise Lost.* For Milton, as for Augustine, the tree is potent not in itself but as the "sole pledge" of man's obedience (3.95; 8.325), and the knowledge gained from eating of it merely, as Adam bitterly complains, of "Good lost, and Evil got" (9.1072). Moreover, in describing the temptation and fall of Eve (9.568-838), Milton gathers and enhances traditional interpretive details concerning the tree: it is beautiful, attracting all the senses; it stimulates (with the prompting of Satan) Eve's impatient ambition to be like God; its fair appearance (together with Satan's plausible analogies) is deceptive — Eve's first act after eating is to worship the power which "dwelt within" the tree, not to worship God.

Prior to Milton the tree was used by Chaucer, whose Pardoner sees in Adam's sin only gluttony (*Pardoner's Tale,* 6.505-12) and whose Parson describes Eve's temptation in terms of "the beautee of the fruyt" (*Parson's*

Tale, 10.325-29). An analysis of the tree considered from the literal, allegorical, tropological, and anagogical perspectives of medieval fourfold exegesis occurs in *Piers Plowman* (B.16.1-89). But far more common is the legend identifying the tree with the holy rood. This connection originates in the patristic interpretation of Adam as a type of Christ and the tree as a type of the cross (St. John Chrysostom, *Hom. on Romans,* 10.13-14). According to the *Cursor Mundi*, Seth received from an angel three seeds from the tree, seeds of cedar, cypress, and palm (corresponding to Father, Son, and Holy Ghost). These were planted, and Adam was buried beneath the trees which grew from them; David later found them grown together into a single tree of miraculous power. This tree resisted cutting for Solomon's temple and was thrown into a pool which became a place of healing (cf. Exod. 15:25). Later, having been preserved in the Temple until Christ's coming, it was made into the cross. The identification of the tree with the cross is widespread in medieval lyrics, and still survives in Luther (*Lectures on Genesis,* 4:16) and Donne ("Hymn to God, My God, in My Sickness").

By the time Milton was producing the richest traditional consideration of the tree, others had began to disregard or demythologize it. Sir Thomas Browne (*Pseudodoxia Epidemica*, 1) mentions as an irresolvable talmudic speculation "whether the tree in the midst of the garden, were not that part in the center of the body, in which was afterward the appointment of circumcision in males." Dryden jokes that "had our grandsire [Adam] walk'd without his wife / He first had sought the better plant of life!" ("To My Honor'd Kinsman, John Driden," 98-99); and Marvell, with casual irony, wishes that a learned decadent had "on the Tree of Life once made a feast / As that of Knowledge" ("Upon the Death of Lord Hastings," 19-20). Similarly satirical is Cowper's analogy between the tree and the popular press: "Like Eden's dread probationary tree / Knowledge of good and evil is from thee" ("Progress of Error," 468-69).

The tree's symbolic power is rediscovered and reconfigured by the Romantics and their heirs, who tend to view it less as reflecting a choice humanity has made or makes than as a condition to which he is (tragically) subject. It is frequently associated by William Blake with mankind's fall from innocent appetite into a satanic state of obsession with the rational, legal, and moral. Thus in *Jerusalem* one finds (pl. 28, 1.15) the "deadly Tree" of Albion, "Moral Virtue and the Law," and in the marginalia on Bacon's "Of Truth," "Self Evident Truth is one Thing and Truth the result of Reasoning is another Thing. Rational Truth is not the Truth of Christ, but of Pilate. It is the Tree of the Knowledge of Good and Evil." In *The Four Zoas* (Nights 7-9) it becomes a "Tree of Mystery" with "shining globes" of various poisons, among them passionate love and sorrow, to which the lamb is later nailed (the medieval legend revived) and which is burned at the Last Judgment.

Shelley reduces the tree to a "tree of evil" planted for man's misery by a malicious creator ("Queen Mab," 8.108-14).

Perhaps the most influential modern use has been that of Byron, who, in his poetic dramas *Cain* and *Manfred,* draws upon it for a tragic image of humanity's mixed condition. Reflecting Milton's observation in *Areopagitica* that "It was from out the rind of one apple tasted, that the knowledge of good and evil, as two twins cleaving together, leaped forth into the world. And perhaps this is that doom which Adam fell into of knowing good and evil, that is to say, of knowing good by evil," Byron sees good and evil, life and grief, knowledge and sorrow as indissolubly bound together. In *Manfred:*

> grief should be the instructor of the wise
> Sorrow is knowledge: they who know the most
> Must mourn the deepest o'er the fatal truth
> The Tree of Knowledge is not that of Life. (1.1.9-12)

Later writers have treated this theme in several moods, from the stoic irony of Henry James's story "The Tree of Knowledge," in which an older man, in trying to preserve the innocence of a young friend, loses the sustaining illusion of his own life, to the comic, vitalist vehemence of Shaw, who declares that, in Adam's place, he would

> have swallowed every apple on the tree the moment the
> owner's back was turned . . . it is godlike to be wise . . .
> it is stupid, and indeed blasphemous and despairing, to
> hope that the thirst for knowledge will either diminish or
> consent to be subordinated to any other end whatsoever.
> (*Doctor's Dilemma*, pref.)

In the demotic prometheanism of Macleish's *Nobodaddy* or Louis Untermeyer's "Eve Speaks," eating of the tree is defended as necessary in order that "Adam should know his godhood; he should feel / The weariness of work, and pride of it / The agony of creation, and its reward."

The tree continues to suggest the mystery attending many kinds of innocence and experience, various Edens to be gained, maintained, or lost. Carlyle remarks that

> In every well-conditioned stripling, as I conjecture, there
> already blooms a certain prospective Paradise, cheered by
> some fairest Eve; nor, in the stately vistas, and flowery
> foliage of that Garden, is a Tree of Knowledge, beautiful
> and awful in the midst thereof, wanting. (*Sartor Resartus,*
> 2.5)

In *Where There Is Nothing,* Yeats comments (in a gnostic inversion of Paul) on the intimate connection between law and sin: "they thought it would be better to be safe than to be blessed, they made the Laws. The Laws were the first sin. They were the first mouthful of the apple, the moment man had made them he began to die" (299-303). In his poem "The Two Trees," biblical and Celtic associations are combined to produce two mysterious trees, the "holy" one of life and love and a "fatal" one, barren and demonic, through whose "broken branches, go / The ravens of unresting thought." T. S. Eliot's reflection on the "wrath-bearing Tree" in "Gerontion" is more particularly mindful of biblical tradition in the question it poses: "After such knowledge, what forgiveness?"

See also APPLE; FALL OF MAN; TREE.

Bibliography. Childs B. "Tree of Knowledge." In *IDB* 4.695-97; Gordis, R. "The Tree of Knowledge of Good and Evil in the Old Testament and the Qumran Scrolls." *JBL* 76 (1957), 123-38; Patrides, C. A. "The Tree of Knowledge in the Christian Tradition." *SN* 34 (1962), 239-42; Reicke, B. "The Knowledge Hidden in the Tree of Paradise." *JSS* 1 (1956), 193-201; Witke, J. "Blake's Tree of Knowledge Grows out of the Enlightenment." *EnlE* 3 (1972), 71-84.

ROBERT WILTENBURG

TREE OF LIFE Adam and Eve forever forfeited their access to the tree of life in the Garden of Eden by their eating of the forbidden fruit of the tree of the knowledge of good and evil (Gen. 1:29; 2:9; 3:22).

Planted in the midst of the garden, the tree of life was said in talmudic legend to have issued forth from its roots four streams pouring out honey, milk, oil, and wine. (Other commentaries, drawing on Gen. 2:10-14, make the four streams the Ganges, Nile, Tigris, and Euphrates [e.g., Josephus, *Ant.* 1.13; cf. Gen. Rab. 16.4; Philo, *Quaestiones*, sup. Gen. 1:12-13, followed in part by St. Jerome].) According to some sources, the leaves and branches of the tree of life were transparent, fiery gold, and crimson; it provided shade for the whole of Paradise and bore fruit of 15,000 varieties; over it hung seven clouds of glory, while underneath it sat scholars, explaining the Torah (Zohar 1.125a; 140a). Although the tree's fruit of immortality was denied to Adam after his fall, the Torah was given as a "tree of life" in its stead (*Vita Adae* 25.4; Apoc. Mos. 27–29). The branch of the tree which made the waters at Marah sweet (Exod. 15:23-25) is said in some Jewish sources to have been taken from the tree of life, and is allegorized as the Torah (Makiri, Prov. 3.4b; cf. Pseudo-Philo 13a).

In the OT Wisdom is said to be a "tree of life to them that lay hold upon her" (Prov. 3:18), and in Ecclus. 24:12-30 Wisdom describes herself with imagery drawn from the tree of life legenda, saying she will "take root in an honorable people." The first Psalm, "Blessed is the man. . . ," declares that one rooted in the Law shall be "like a tree planted by the rivers of water, that bringeth forth his fruit in his season; his leaf also shall not wither" (1:3); this verse is often cited in both Jewish and Christian commentary, identifying the tree of life with that wisdom which proceeds from the Torah, or Scripture. Apocalyptic texts both canonical and apocryphal suggest that the tree of life is preserved for the faithful in heaven (Enoch 25:4; 4 Ezra 7:52; Rev. 2:7; 22:14).

Patristic commentaries frequently allegorize the tree of life. For St. Augustine, e.g., the physical immortality it secured for Adam and Even in the garden until they sinned prefigures redeemed life and Paradise: "Other fruits were,

so to speak, their nourishment, but this was their sacrament. So that the tree of life would seem to have been in the terrestrial paradise what the wisdom of God is in the spiritual, of which it is written, 'She is a tree of life to them that lay hold upon her' " (*De civ. Dei* 13.20). Other commentators were quick to connect the tree of life typology extending from Gen. 2:9 through Prov. 3:18 and Ecclus. 24:12-30 to the NT, notably to Pauline passages describing the "fruits of the Spirit" (Gal. 5:22ff.). This tree was then contrasted with the unfruitful tree condemned by Christ (Matt. 7:17ff.), the moral "root" of which was said to be pride; these parallel "trees" often appear in medieval allegories of the virtues and vices (e.g., Rabanus Maurus, *De Institutione Clericorum*, 3 [PL 107.415ff.]).

In the later Middle Ages, the cross came to be represented as the tree of life par excellence, prompting a contrast between the tree of sin and the tree of the cross: the *Arbor Vitae Crucifixi Jesu* of Ubertino da Casale draws upon this tradition as well as upon exegetical commentary on Isa. 65:22 (cf. Augustine, *De civ. Dei* 20.16; also Calvin, *Comm. on Genesis*, 1.117; sup. 2:9). In the *Liber Floridus Lamberti*, an encyclopedia of the early 12th cent., the *arbor bona* becomes a symbol of the faithful church, standing on the right hand of God and exhibiting the fruits of the Spirit and offshoots, or shrubs, which are the trees associated with such virtues in Ecclus. 24. Here charity is the root, while cupidity is the root of the *arbor mala*, also named "Synagoga."

An extension of the legend of Seth in the Cornish *Ordinalia* has him go back to the gate of Paradise, where he sees the dead tree of life, in which a serpent is coiled. At the top, however, is a child wrapped in swaddling clothes. In the scene where the Redcrosse Knight combats the dragon in Spenser's *Faerie Queene,* he discovers the tree of life growing (1.11.46). Donne's parody in "Elegie 7" rather conflates the trees of knowledge and of life: "Thy graces and good words my creatures bee; / I planted knowledge and life's tree in thee, / Which Oh, shall strangers taste?" (25-27). In George Herbert's "The Sacrifice" Christ speaks from the cross, echoing the *O vos omnes* of Jeremiah (Lam. 1:12): "Man stole the fruit, but I must climbe the tree; / The tree of life to all, but onely me" (203-04). In the writing of early American Puritan Edward Taylor similar typology of the tree of life abounds, sometimes in connection with John 3:14, "As Moses lift up the Serpent in the Wilderness so must the Son of Man be lift up" ("Meditation 61"). Henry Vaughan's "The Palm-Tree" proves to be the "Tree, whose fruit is immortality," which, watered by the tears of the saints, is the sign of faith. Milton presents the tree of life in *Paradise Lost:* "High, eminent, blooming Ambrosial Fruit / Of vegetable Gold; and next to Life / Our Death the Tree of Knowledge grew fast by" (4.219-21; cf. 3.354ff.). It is in the branches of this tree that Satan, "artificer of fraud" (4.121), alights in preparation for his temptation of Adam and Eve:

So clome this first grand Thief into God's Fold:
So since into his Church lewd Hirelings climb.
Thence up he flew, and on the Tree of Life,
The middle Tree and highest there that grew,
Sat like a Cormorant; yet not true Life
Thereby regain'd, but sat devising Death
To them who liv'd; nor on the virtue thought
Of that life-giving Plant, but only us'd
For prospect, what well us'd had been the pledge
Of immortality. (4.192-201)

In his temptation of Christ in *Paradise Regained*, Satan spreads before him a "table of Celestial Food, Divine, / Ambrosial, Fruits fetched from the tree of life" (4.588-89). In William Blake's *Urizen* the function of the tree of life is given to the Eternals; in *Ahanie* the Tree of Mystery symbolizes rather the tree of knowledge and the tree upon which Christ was crucified.

See also APPLE; TREE; TREE OF KNOWLEDGE; WISDOM.

Bibliography. Brumm, U. "The 'Tree of Life' in Edward Taylor's Meditations." *EAL* 3 (1968), 72-87; Halbert, L. "Tree of Life Images in the Poetry of Edward Taylor." *AL* 38 (1966), 22-34; Steadman, J. M. "The Tree of Life Symbolism in *Paradise Regained*." *RES* 11 (1960), 384-91; Werge, T. "The Tree of Life in Edward Taylor's Poetry: The Sources of a Puritan Image." *EAL* 3 (1968), 199-204.

TRIBES OF ISRAEL The tradition of twelve tribes of Israel — Reuben, Simeon, Levi, Judah, Zebulun, Issachar, Dan, Gad, Asher, Naphtali, Joseph (later Ephraim and Manasseh, replacing Levi), and Benjamin — descended from the sons of Jacob (also named Israel), is central to the biblical schema of the Exodus and the conquest of Canaan, and to ancient Jewish identity. Distinctively, *Israel* early designates a people, not a district or country, "a group of migrating tribes loosely organized by a sense of relationship, a common past, and common destiny" (S. W. Baron, *A Social and Religious History of the Jews*, 1.41).

The biblical term *shebeṭ* (= tribe) is used of the twelve tribes of Israel, but not those of other nations, even though the latter may have had a similar tribal structure. Sometimes (e.g., Num. 4:18; Judg. 20:12; 1 Sam. 9:21) *shebeṭ* denotes a family, the subunit of a tribe.

References to the twelve tribes abound especially in the Pentateuch, but certain passages are crucial. Gen. 48:9-20; 49:1-28 gives the first tribal list on the occasion of Jacob's deathbed blessing of his own and Joseph's sons. In this instance, Judah and Joseph receive special favor. Extensive midrashic commentary elaborates the tribal blessings and prophecies, the significance of the tribal names, and the sons' deathbed prophecies of their descendants' fortunes (2.187-222; cf. L. Ginzberg, *LJ* 2.140-47). The twelvefold division of Israel is said to be reflected in the twelve stones of Moses' altar (Exod. 24:4; cf. Elijah's altar on Mt. Carmel [1 Kings 18:31]) and in the design of the breastplate and onyx epaulets for the high priest's sacred regalia (Ginzberg, *LJ* 3.219-24, 230-38; Exod. Rab. [Tetzaveh] 38.8-9).

A second tribal list (Num. 1:1-16) has the format of a divinely ordained census, omitting Levi (the priestly tribe) but including Ephraim and Manasseh as two "half-tribes." A more analytical revision of the census by "families" in Num. 26:5-51 follows the plague incident of Num. 25:9. Then Num. 26:53-56 begins tribal division of Canaanite land, effected for two-and-a-half tribes in Deut. 3:12-17, and completed, in the fourth tribal list passage (Josh. 13:7, 14 to 19:20), for the remaining nine-and-a-half. Like Jacob, Moses blesses each tribe before his death in another list, this time omitting Simeon (Deut. 33:6-25; cf. Ginzberg, *LJ* 3.452-62). The final OT crux is the dense genealogy comprising 1 Chron. 2–8, a kind of post-exilic Midrash on the historic materials of the Pentateuch. Careful study of these passages shows curious variations in the names and ordering of the twelve tribes.

Among NT references to the tribes of Israel, two are conspicuous. Heb. 7:5-17 argues for the supersession of the Levitical priesthood by Jesus, sprung from Judah. And in Rev. 7:3-8, before the opening of the seventh seal, "the servants of our God," the elect, are sealed "in their foreheads," 12,000 of each tribe, enumerated by tribes (omitting Dan and including Joseph), with Judah, the tribe of Jesus, coming first (cf. James 1:1; Rev. 21:12). This provides an early example of Christian symbolic use of the "twelve tribes" to represent the Christian redeemed.

Patristic commentary includes a retelling by Origen (*Hom. on Exodus*, 5.5) and Eusebius (*In Psalmos*, 77.13) of a Hebraic legend of separate paths cleft in the Red Sea for each of the twelve fleeing tribes (N. R. M. de Lange, *Origen and the Jews* [1976], 129-30). John Calvin's *Commentaries* on Gen. 48 and 49 emphasize the providential nature of Jacob's blessings and the role of his sons as patriarchs of the Church and state.

English literary uses of the tribes of Israel have been generally limited to genealogical identification and historical or quasihistorical reference. Shylock mentions "tribe" thrice during his exchange with Antonio in *The Merchant of Venice*, twice treating the term generically, as synonymous with the Jews ("Cursed be my tribe / If I forgive him!" [1.3.52-53] and "For sufferance is the badge of all our tribe" [1.3.111]). Only the reference to his friend "Tubal, a wealthy Hebrew of my tribe" (1.3.58) has any genealogical particularity, such as Marlowe's Barabas means when he speaks of "the Tribe that I descended of" (*The Jew of Malta*, 1.2.113) or declares "I am not of the Tribe of Levy" (2.3.18). Parody of identification by tribe forms the title of Jonson's "An Epistle Answering to One That Asked to be Sealed of the Tribe of Ben." (207-10).

Michael's panorama of the future in *Paradise Lost* declares the twelve tribes essential to the government and laws of the Israelites once they possess Canaan (12.224-26). The tragedy of Samson the Danite and in particular of his marriage to a woman from outside the tribal structure entails frequent mention of tribal self-identification in *Samson Agonistes,* such as Manoa's pledge to "live the poorest in my tribe" (1479) rather than leave Samson unredeemed in prison (cf. 217, 876, 1540). The sardonic reference to Corah's Tribe, the Levites, as "Godalmightys Gentlemen" in pt. 1 of Dryden's *Absalom and Achitophel* (644-45) suggests his satire: collectively, the tribes are Dryden's English contemporaries; tribes, however, are also factional interests in the political allegory (cf. Marvell's satirical allusion to the twelve tribes' wealth and dutiful generosity in "Clarindon's House-Warming").

In spiritual allegory, similar strategies of reference are practiced by Cowper, in his *Olney Hymn 12,* "Ephraim Repenting, Jer. xxxi 18-20" (cf. also "Expostulation," 211-12). Blake evolves an extended metaphor of Israelitic tribes and modern Englishmen, from the cosmogony of *Vala, or The Four Zoas,* Night the Eighth to the culmination in *Jerusalem* (pls. 16, 72, 79, 86). A more humorous version of such equivalence occurs in the "Cyclops" chapter of *Ulysses,* where Irish institutions are given a false tribal polish: "the high sinhedrim of the twelve tribes of Iar" (which, of course, never existed).

See also LOST TRIBES.

Bibliography. Baron, S. W. *A Social and Religious History of the Jews* (1937); Gottwald, N. K. *The Tribes of Yahweh* (1980); de Lange, N. R. M. *Origen and the Jews: Studies in Jewish-Christian Relations in Third-Century Palestine* (1976); Liver, J. "The Israelite Tribes." *The World History of the Jewish People.* Ed. B. Mazar (1971), 3.183-211; Sachar, A. L. *A History of the Jews* (1968).

MARK S. MADOFF

TRIBULATION   Along with KJV "affliction," "travail," and "suffering," *tribulation* translates Heb. *șar, șarah* (Deut. 4:30; 1 Sam. 26:24). The Great Tribulation, a specific period of almost unbearable suffering at the end of human history (cf. Dan. 12:1; Matt. 24:15-31; Mark 13:14-27), is one of the notable apocalyptic events prophesied in the Revelation to St. John on Patmos (Rev. 7:14).

See also APOCALYPSE.

TRINITY   According to orthodox Christian doctrine, God is one nature in three persons: Father, Son, and Holy Spirit. No one of them preceded or created the others or stands above them in power or dignity. In precise theological terms, they are one in substance (or essence), coeternal, and coequal.

The doctrine so stated does not appear in Scripture, yet many biblical passages have been adduced to support it. Especially important in the early Church were OT verses which imply conversation between two divine beings, such as Ps. 110, which begins, "The LORD said unto my Lord, Sit thou at my right hand . . ." (cited by Jesus in Matt. 22:41-46; see also Ps. 45:6-7; Heb. 1:4-14). The accounts of creation in Gen. 1:1-3 and Prov. 8:22-31

suggest the agency of three divine figures: God, divine Wisdom, and the Spirit of God. Also significant in ancient exegesis was Gen. 1:26: "Let us make man in our image." Some of these passages figured in Jewish speculation about God and other divine beings, especially the principal angels. Some interpreters argue that, in the OT, such personifications are simply poetic devices. But in the NT and even more in early Christian exegesis, they are treated as points of doctrine. For example, divine Wisdom is equated with Christ, who is the Word of God or Logos which brought the world into being (John 1:1-18; 17:24; 1 Cor. 1:24; 8:6; Heb. 1:1-3). Several other NT passages have been taken as portraying the Trinity united in action (e.g., Luke 1:34-35; 3:21-22; 2 Cor. 13:14); still others assert the unity and equality of the Father and the Son (John 10:30; 14:7-11; Phil. 2:5-11); and one, the traditional formula for baptism, unites the three persons under a single "name": "Go ye therefore, and teach all nations, baptizing them in the name of the Father, and of the Son, and of the Holy Ghost" (Matt. 28:19).

The orthodox doctrine of the Trinity was hammered out gradually over a period of three centuries or more. St. Theophilus, Bishop of Antioch, applied the term to the Godhead about A.D. 170. Late in the 2nd cent. Tertullian, who may have first coined Lat. *trinitas* in theological writing, taught in the Western Church that God is one divine "substance" in three "persons," as distinct from three deities or three manifestations of a single deity. (A similar view had been published by Origen a few years earlier in the East.) The earliest Latin theological treatise, Novatian's *De Trinitate* (ca. A.D. 250), was to chart the normative course for Trinitarian theology, though its author and his followers fell into political schism sometime after the book appeared. Unsurprisingly, perhaps, the coeternity and coequality of the divine persons remained a matter of theological dispute, and so are frequently discussed in the context of heresy. Early in the 4th cent. Arius took the position that the Son and the Spirit were created by the Father and so are not coeternal, coequal, or even consubstantial with him. In response to the growing popularity of this teaching, the bishops of the Church, led by St. Athanasius, convened in 325 at Nicea and denounced Arianism as heretical. (A chief *raison d'etre* of the so-called Athanasian Creed is its Trinitarian formula.) In 381 the bishops convened again at Constantinople and set forth the orthodox doctrine in its final form (see Kelly, 83-137, 223-79). The hymn ascribed to St. Patrick (A.D. 372-466), "Saint Patrick's Breastplate," is in effect a doctrinal summary:

> I bind unto myself today
> The strong name of the Trinity,
> Through invocation of the same,
> The Three in One, the One in Three. . . .

St. Augustine's 5th-cent. treatise *De Trinitate* became a standard text both for medieval Catholic theologians such as St. Thomas Aquinas and for Protestant theologians such as Calvin. One of the most influential aspects of Augustine's exposition for the Middle Ages was its psychological modeling: even as we see in ourselves three faculties of mind in one personality — memory, intellect, and will — so we may imagine three faculties or functions of that Being in whose image we are made (*De Trin.* 10.12; 11.1–12.25). Boethius also wrote an important treatise on the subject, *De Sancta Trinitate.*

The liturgical expression of the doctrine is to be found throughout the Mass, though a special festival seems to have been inaugurated by Pope Gregory IV (A.D. 834), probably to counter effects of the Arian heresy. Pope Alexander II (1061-73) subsequently discouraged the festival, arguing that the doctrine was sufficiently preserved in the *Gloria Patri.* The festival spread, however, and in 1162 Archbishop Thomas à Becket appointed the Sunday following his consecration (the Octave of Whitsunday) as Trinity Sunday. Pope John XXII (1334) was the first to enforce universal observance of the Sunday following Whitsunday (Pentecost) as Trinity Sunday. The emphasis in medieval presentation of the doctrine is on divine sovereignty; praise is directed, as the hymn *"Deus Immensa Trinitas"* borrowed from the mozarabic breviary puts it, to

> O Glorious Immensity
> And One eternal Trinity,
> Father and Comforter and Word,
> Of all that is, unconquered Lord.

The emphasis of early liturgical prayers for this Sunday (the Collect) is on worship of the three persons of God as being one in power and in majesty *(et in potentia Majestasis adorare Unitatem)* or, as a 14th-cent. English primer puts it, "And in the myght of mageste to worchipe thee in oonheede." In the epistle for this Sunday (Rev. 4:1) one hears of the vision of St. John in which the four beasts salute the deity, saying, "Holy, Holy, Holy, Lord God Almighty, which was, and is, and is to come"; in traditional commentary the threefold repetition is said to indicate address to the Holy Trinity.

In English literature, invocations or allusions to the persons of the Trinity are common, but treatments of Trinitarian theology are understandably more rare. In medieval literature, the mystery is explored at length in such works as the OE Advent Lyrics of *Christ I,* Aelfric's sermon in the *Lives of the Saints* entitled "The Nativity of Our Lord Jesus Christ," and Langland's *Piers Plowman.* Langland's discussion is especially interesting. Here the doctrine of the Trinity is employed for conflict resolution in what is really a discussion of the basis of Christian unity. Langland employs a series of ingenious analogies to explain the paradox of the "three in one." The Trinity is likened, e.g., to the fist, finger, and palm of a hand, which must work together to perform one action (B.17.199-202), and to the wax, wick, and flame of a

candle which together compose one source of light (B.17.203-50). Langland also employs the analogy of Adam, Eve, and their offspring, in which, analogously, "either is otheres Ioye. In thre sondry persones, And in heuene and here, one syngulere name." He sees the Trinity reflected also in the three stages of life — virginity, marriage, and widowhood — composing Christian community (B.16.181-224).

English vernacular hymns, lyrics, and carols dedicated to the Trinity are plentiful in the Middle Ages, though most of these poems are focused on the Incarnation, with a refrain relating it to the Trinity. In one such refrain the Trinity is described as knit together ("Off al the knottes that I se / I prese the knot in Trinite") with the seamless knot of the plan of redemption. The God who was, is, and is to come is to be revealed fully only on "domesday," when God shall say in one voice, " 'Lo, man, what knot I knyt for the' " (R. Greene, *Early English Carols,* no. 282). In another (15th-cent.) poem James Ryman expounds the relationship among persons in the Trinity in which the Father expresses the omnipotence of God revealed in creation, the Son is known as the "Wisdome" of God displayed in redemption, and the Holy Spirit is honored as the source of grace.

> Of iii persones in one vnite,
> Beyng but one God and one light,
> One is substance, essense, and myght,
> Honour to the alone. (Greene, no. 283)

Twenty-six of the 166 poems by Ryman preserved in MS Camb. Univ. Lib. Ee.I.12 are carols devoted to the subject of the Trinity; several of these are adaptations from Latin hymns, such as the *"Dulciter Pangamus"* and *"Te Deum Laudamus, Te Dominum Confitemur."* Ryman has another long carol on the theme of the hymn *"Te Patrem Nostrum Invocamus"* which stresses the belief that all three persons of the Trinity were involved in the creation, that it is in the three persons of God that the fullness of the Godhead is expressed; this completeness, figured poetically as a circle or "O," is reflected in the circumscribed fullness of creation as well as the uncircumscribable eternity of God (*"O Deus sine Termino"* [Greene, no. 284; cf. Greene, nos. 285-88]). It is to the indivisible "endless God of Majeste," the "Alpha et O" (cf. Rev. 1:1), that the threefold "Holy, Holy, Holy" is directed:

> Cherubym and seraphyn with loue ardent
> Euirmore crie with one assent,
> O Lord God Sabaoth Omnipotent,
> *Te Deum verum laudamus.* (Greene, no. 296)

Some of these same themes are reflected in the concluding lines of Chaucer's *Troilus and Criseyde,* which are in the form of a prayer of dedication:

> Thow oon and two and thre eterne on lyve,
> That regnest ay yn thre and two and oon,

Uncircumscript and al mayst circumscryve,
Us from visible and invysible foon
Defende, and to thy mercy everychon
So make us, Jesus, for thi mercy digne,
For love of mayde and moder thyn benigne. Amen.

Calvin treats the "orthodox doctrine of the Trinity" extensively in his *Institutes,* emphasizing the historical development of the doctrine as a check on heretical opinions, such as those of the Manicheans, whose dualism served, "assuredly . . . both to destroy [God's] unity and restrict his immensity" (1.13.1). Nonetheless, Calvin stresses the "mystery" of this doctrine, asserting that even analogies — especially anthropomorphic ones — break down, and that it would be better to follow the track of early Greek Fathers such as St. Gregory of Nazianzus in focusing primarily on the unity of God: "The words Father, Son, and Holy Spirit, certainly indicate a real distinction. . . . Still, they indicate distinction only, not division" (1.13.17). The analogy he finds most useful is the most simple: the Father initiates, the role of the Son is wisdom and counsel, and "the efficacy of the action is assigned to the Spirit" (1.13.18). Calvin draws heavily on Augustine and Tertullian, yet affirms the harmony of St. Irenaeus, St. Justin, St. Hilary, and others in creating the orthodox doctrine (1.13.28-29). In its essentials, then, Reformed teaching about the Trinity remains consistent with Catholic teaching.

John Donne's *The Litanie* (4) reflects both the traditional instinct for analogies and a desire to focus finally on the unity of God:

> O Blessed glorious Trinity,
> Bones to Philosophy, but milke to faith,
>   Which, as wise serpents, diversly
> Most slipperinesse, yet most entanglings hath,
>   As you distinguish'd undistinct
>   By power, love, knowledge bee,
> Give mee a such selfe different instinct
> Of these; let all mee elemented bee,
> Of power, to love, to know, you unnumbered three.

Herbert, who wrote two poems entitled "Trinity Sunday," dealt also with the doctrine in relation to the Incarnation in his poem "Ungratefulnesse." Here he sees God's mercy in providing mankind these "two rare cabinets full of treasure, / The *Trinitie,* and *Incarnation.* . . ." Of them,

> The statelier cabinet is the *Trinitie,*
>   Whose sparkling light accesse denies:
>   Therefore thou dost not show
>   This fully to us, till death blow
>   The dust into our eyes:
> For by that powder thou wilt make us see.

To mortal view, however, the Incarnation offers sufficient temporal declaration of God's nature; in Christ we see him declared in terms we can best understand, the corporeal: "Because this box we know; / For we have all of us just such another."

Also during the Reformation, the Arian heresy was revived in various Protestant sects, most notably among the Socinians. In England their views prompted, among other responses, a lengthy and thoughtful reply in Dryden's Catholic poem *The Hind and the Panther* (52-153). Milton has been thought to have held Arian views, but recent scholarship suggests that he was following the Cambridge Platonists of his own day in their return to the position of early Church Fathers such as Tertullian (see Danielson). In any case the notion that the Son and the Spirit are not coequal or coeternal with the Father is difficult to discern in *Paradise Lost* or in his other poetic works. Heterodox views find clear expression only in his theological treatise *De Doctrina Christiana* (see Hunter et al., 29-61).

From Socinian roots arose the sect best known for its renunciation of the orthodox doctrine of the Trinity: the Unitarians. They influenced several important figures in the world of letters, including Charles Lamb, the young Coleridge (before his conversion to Trinitarian orthodoxy), and Emerson. Yet such authors wrote little about the biblical doctrine of the Trinity; in fact, Emerson's chief contribution to the evolution of the Unitarian movement was a plea, in his 1838 Address to the Harvard Divinity College, that Unitarians abandon their traditional preoccupation with biblical authority.

The only major writer after Milton notable for his (divergent) views on the Trinity is William Blake, who adopted the teachings of Swedenborg, the Swedish speculative theologian. Since Blake thought it impossible to comprehend an invisible deity, he worshiped Jesus Christ as the only true God. This exaltation of the second person of the Trinity as the "Human God" did not lead to a rejection of the other two persons, however. According to Blake, Jesus manifests himself in three forms: Father, Son, and Holy Spirit. These are not persons in the orthodox sense but expressions of various attributes of Jesus. Moreover, the three are not eternal since, in Swedenborg's view, the Trinity first manifested itself at the Incarnation.

The bitter narrator in Browning's "Soliloquy of the Spanish Cloister," striving to outdo his rival, Brother Lawrence, is obsessed with the externalities of religious observance. He tries to demonstrate his superior sanctity by making every gesture an analogy of doctrine. In his watered-down efforts, he insists, he does battle with heresy:

> I the Trinity illustrate,
> Drinking watered orange-pulp —
> In three sips the Arian frustrate;
> While he drains his at one gulp.

In John Keble's *The Christian Year* (1827) the poem for Trinity Sunday suggests that the possibility of analogous understanding is still available, however, to a worshipful spirit. To such a person even the architecture of the

Cathedral is a reminder of the unity in harmony bespoken in the doctrine:

Three solemn parts together twine
In harmony's mysterious line;
Three solemn aisles approach the shrine:

Yet all are One — together all,
In thoughts that awe but not appal,
Teach the adoring heart to fall.

Within these walls each fluttering guest
Is gently lur'd to one safe nest —
Without, 'tis moaning and unrest.

For Keble, though the mystery still defies total comprehension, the basic scriptural model suggests that God's triune self-expression declares fully his love for humanity:

Eternal One, Almighty Trine!
Since Thou art ours, and we are Thine,
By all Thy love did once resign,

By all the grace Thy heavens still hide,
We pray Thee, keep us at Thy side,
Creator, Saviour, strengthening Guide!

See also CREED; HERESY; HOLY SPIRIT; THRONE OF GRACE.

Bibliography. Bieman, E. "Triads and Trinity in the Poetry of Robert Browning." *Cithara* 19 (1980), 20-39; Danielson, D. *Milton's Good God* (1982); Davies, J. G. *The Theology of William Blake* (1948); Hunter, W. B., C. A. Patrides, and J. H. Adamson. *Bright Essence: Studies in Milton's Theology* (1971); Kelly, J. N. D. *Early Christian Doctrines* (5th ed.; rev. 1977); Modiano, R. "Naturphilosophie and Christian Orthodoxy in Coleridge's View of the Trinity." *Pacific Coast Philology* 17 (1982), 59-68; Muir, L. "The Trinity in Medieval Drama." *CompD* 10 (1976), 116-29; Pasch, W. A. "Trinitarian Symbolism and Medieval English Drama." *DAI* 38 (1977), 2108A; Toon, P., and J. D. Spiceland, eds. *One God in Trinity* (1980); Wilbur, E. M. *A History of Unitarianism.* 2 vols. (1947-52).   DONALD V. STUMP
DAVID L. JEFFREY

TRISAGION A chant of praise, beginning "Holy, holy, holy," sung by the seraphim in Isa. 6:1-7.
See also SERAPH.

TRIUMPHAL ENTRY With a loud cry of "Hosanna!" as they cast palm branches in his path, the crowd acclaimed Jesus as Messiah during his entry into Jerusalem "riding on the foal of an ass" on the Sunday prior to his death (Matt. 21:9; Mark 11:9; John 12:13). The ass on which, according to St. Mark's account, "never man sat," walked in complete obedience despite the roaring crowd. The Gospel writers explicate the connection between Jesus' action and the advent of the king prophesied in Zech. 9:9: "Rejoice greatly, O daugher of Zion . . . behold, thy king cometh unto thee: he is just, and having salvation; lowly, and riding upon an ass and upon a colt the foal of an ass." The salutation of the multitude was based on Ps. 118:25, where the term occurs as an appeal for deliverance (albeit in a joyous and triumphal context), meaning "Do save [us]!" (Heb. *hoshi῾ a(-n)na'*, which became *hōsanna* in Greek transcription). The subsequent words of the crowd, "Blessed is he that cometh in the name of the Lord," derive from the same psalm. The term "Hosanna" (which is found in an early eucharistic liturgy [Did. 10:6]) has retained its place in Christian worship as an exclamation of praise to Christ.

The strewing of branches in Jesus' path signified his being hailed as a heroic deliverer. For many in the multitude messianic expectations were evidently coupled with political aspirations: Jesus' entry into the city was thought by Zealots and others to portend liberation from Roman oppression.

The disparity between the ringing acclamation of the Palm Sunday crowd and the demands for Jesus' crucifixion on Friday of the same week has been the subject of frequent commentary and allusion. The discrepancy between the political expectations of the crowd and the spiritual nature of Jesus' "deliverance" in the Atonement has been the subject of many dramatic reenactments. The medieval Corpus Christi drama, e.g., exploits the dramatic irony (the audience knows what the "crowd" does not — that Jesus' "triumph" is to come through the Cross) to good effect. York's version combines the triumphal entry with narratives of healing the halt and blind, as well as the story of Zaccheus (no. 25); in Chester (no. 14) the procession forms part of the pageant of "Christ's Visit to Simon the Leper," and Judas's ire at the anointing of Jesus with costly ointment is matched by the first grumblings of dissent. The N-Town play, placing the triumphal entry after a well-developed "conspiracy" involving the high priests Annas and Caiaphas, forcefully juxtaposes Christ's weeping over unrepentant Jerusalem with the songs of thronging children:

Thow sone of davyd þou be oure sypporte
At our last day whan we xal dye
Where-fore we Alle Atonys to þe exorte
Cryeng mercy mercy mercye. (288-93)

Henry Vaughan's "Palm Sunday" is an address to the citizens of Jerusalem to join the procession: "Come, drop your branches, strow the way. . . ," since "here comes he / Whose death will be / Man's life, and your full liberty." With a marginal note citing Zech. 9:9, he too develops the dramatic irony:

Hark! How the children shril and high
    Hosanna cry,
Their joys provoke the distant skie,
Where thrones and Seraphins reply,
And their own Angels shine and sing
    In a bright ring:
    Such yong, sweet mirth
    Makes heaven and earth
Joyn in a joyful Symphony,

The harmless, yong and happy Ass,
Seen long before this came to pass,
Is in these joys an high partaker
Ordain'd, and made to bear his Maker.

What the cheering children and compliant beast in their innocence do not fully grasp, the angels and readers do; as Vaughan says in the following poem ("Jesus weeping"), citing Luke 19:41: "Had not the Babes *Hosanna* cryed, / The stones had spoke, what you denyed."

The narrative of the triumphal entry has given rise to numerous hymns, including most notably Theodulphe of Orléans' processional "All Glory, Laud and Honour, To Thee, Redeemer King" (translated into ME in the early 14th cent. by William Herebert as "wele, heriȝyng, and worshype boe to crist þat doere ous bouhte / To wham gradden 'osanna!' chyldren clene of þoute" [C. Brown, *Religious Lyrics of the XIVth Century,* no. 14]). Dean Milman's "Ride On, Ride On in Majesty!" is a notable 19th-cent. example, while John Keble's Palm Sunday poem "Ye whose hearts are beating high / With the pulse of Poesy," taking its text from Luke 19:40, celebrates the acclamation of the children in a typically Victorian manner:

Childlike though the voices be,
And untunable the parts,
Thou wilt own the minstrelsy,
If it flow from childlike hearts. *(The Christian Year)*

In the 20th cent. Faulkner's fictional reworking of the Gospel narrative, *A Fable,* opens with a scene reminiscent of the triumphal entry, as the corporal and his twelve associates enter the city past throngs of people lining the streets.

See also ASS; STONES CRY OUT.   WILLIAM M. SOLL

TROUBLING THE WATERS   *See* BETHESDA.

TRUTH SHALL MAKE YOU FREE   In one of his discourses, Jesus said to those who sought to identify with him, "If ye continue in my word, then are ye my disciples indeed; And ye shall know the truth, and the truth shall make you free" (John 8:31-32). This verse, often connected with John 14:65 ("I am the way, the truth, and the life") in patristic and medieval exegesis, is typically applied by St. Augustine to perseverance in faith: "To be a disciple it is not enough to come, but to continue. . . . To continue in the word of God, is it toilsome, or is it not? If it be toilsome, look at the great reward; if it be not toilsome, thou receivest the reward for nought. Continue we then in him who continueth in us. We, if we continue not in him, fall. . . ." He goes on to say that not to be in such freedom is to be in bondage to the world, for "every one that commits sin is the servant of sin, and if men will but acknowledge their bondage, they will see from whence they may obtain their freedom" (*Sermo,* 134.1-3). In a passage inspirational to John Wyclif's *De Veritate Sacrae Scripturae,* Augustine discusses John 14:6: "John

is true, Christ is the Truth; John is true, but every true man is true from the Truth. . . . The Truth, then, could not speak contrary to the true man, or the true man contrary to the Truth" (*In Joan. Ev.* 5.1).

When Chaucer's friend Phillipe de la Vache, like himself, fell into political disfavor with the rise to power of Gloucester and the Lords Appelant, Chaucer admonished La Vache, who had Lollard sympathies, by appealing to his own principles. Each of the stanzas of his "Balade de Bon Conseil (Truth)" has the same last line; one may exemplify the rest:

That thee is sent, receyve in buxumnesse;
The wrastling for this world axeth a fal.
Her is non hoom, her nis but wildernesse:
Forth, pilgrim, forth! Forth, beste, out of thy stal!
Know thy contree, look up, thank God of al;
Hold the heye way and lat thy gost thee lede,
And trouthe thee shal delivere, it is no drede.

Milton's "Sonnet 12" counters hostile reactions to his liberal ideas on divorce as set forth in his *Tetrachordon;* he finds his detractors unthoughtful, their outcry like that of hogs "that bawl for freedom in their senceless mood, / And still revolt when truth would set them free."

TUBAL-CAIN   Gen. 4:22 tells how Zillah, one of the wives of Lamech, "bare Tubal-Cain, an instructor of every artificer in brass and iron." As a descendant of Cain, he shared with him a tainted history: according to rabbinic sources he was the first "to learn how to sharpen iron and copper," and so made the first weapons of war (Gen. Rab. 23.2.3; Yashar Bereshit 10b). Medieval encyclopedias, such as that of Bersuire, Vincent of Beauvais, and the "Third Vatican Mythographer," relate the offspring of Lamech to pagan deities. Sir Walter Raleigh's *History of the World* follows suit, observing that "Jubal, Tubal, and Tubal-Cain [were] inventors of pastorage [care of livestock], smith's-craft and music, the same which were called by the ancient profane writers, Mercurius, Vulcan, and Apollo." In Cowper's *The Task* Tubal himself is

The first artificer of death; the shrewd
Contriver who first sweated at the forge,
And forced the blunt and yet unbloodied steel
To a keen edge, and made it bright for war.
Him, Tubal nam'd, the Vulcan of old times. (5.213-17)

Swedenborg makes him rather "an instructor . . . in the doctrine of natural good and truth, 'brass' denoting natural good, and 'iron' natural truth." For most 19th- and 20th-cent. writers, Tubal-Cain is simply a progenitor, like his brother, of the laborer. "Visible Ploughmen and Hammermen there have been, ever from Cain and Tubal-Cain downwards," says Carlyle (*Sartor Resartus,* 2.8). For G. B. Shaw, Tubal was the inventor of the wheel (*Back to Methuselah,* 1.2).

See also CAIN; JUBAL.

TURN THE OTHER CHEEK In his Sermon on the Mount Jesus reminded his audience of the *lex talionis* provisions of Mosaic law — "an eye for an eye, and a tooth for a tooth" (Matt. 5:38), and then added,

> But I say unto you, That ye resist not evil: but whosoever shall smite thee on thy right cheek, turn to him the other also. And if any man will sue thee at the law, and take away thy coat, let him have thy cloak also. And whosoever shall compel thee to go a mile, go with him twain. Give to him that asketh thee, and from him that would borrow of thee turn not thou away. Ye have heard that it hath been said, Thou shalt love thy neighbour and hate thine enemy. But I say unto you, Love your enemies, bless them that curse you, do good to them that hate you, and pray for them which despitefully use you and persecute you. (vv. 39-44)

The basic precepts of Christian nonviolent resistance and "overcoming evil with good" are in this passage set over against not only Mosaic law but universal notions of revenge-justice.

St. Augustine observes that here the "incomplete but by no means severe, but rather comparatively merciful [Mosaic] justice is carried to perfection by him who came to fulfil the law, not to destroy it." He goes on to say that "there are still two intervening steps which he has left to be understood": the first of these would be a system of retribution in which the punishment was more modest than the crime, the second in which there would be no retribution at all. Not even the second of these, however, reaches the quality of mercy which Jesus teaches: "Therefore he does not say 'But I say unto you that you are not to return evil for evil,' though even that would be a great precept. Rather he says 'that ye resist not evil,' so that not only are you not to pay back what may have been inflicted on you, but you are not even to resist other inflictions" (*De sermone Domini in Monte*, 1.19.57). Similarly, to "go the second mile" is for Augustine a metaphor for bearing twice the weight of an imposition, and to bear the burden "with tranquil mind" (1.19.61).

All through the history of Christian literature these words have been found a "hard saying," obtaining evasive commentary from theologians and sometimes trivializing quotations from others. In the 14th cent., however, a brief anonymous epistle, paraphrased in Walter Hilton's *Ladder of Perfection* and possibly authored by him, reiterates the challenge of the passage straightforwardly, insisting that Jesus' standard for dealing with enemies is made most clear in his own relationship with Judas. Despite his knowledge that Judas would betray him, says the writer, Jesus loved him and privileged him as much as any of the other disciples (1.69); Christians ought to do likewise. In his version of "the Lamentations of Jeremy," Donne's free translation of Tremellius is "He gives his cheekes to whosoever will / Strike him, and so he is reproched still" (3.221-22); there is no guarantee of temporal reward for Christlike forbearance.

In later times it may be, as Thoreau suggests in *Walden*, that "the law to do as you would be done by [cf. Matt. 7:12] fell with less persuasiveness on the ears of these who, for their part, did not care how they were done by, who loved their enemies after a new fashion" ("Economy"). In his "Former Inhabitants" chapter the intrepid outdoorsman reduces the allusion to a quip: "When the frost had smitten me on the cheek, heathen as I was, I turned to it the other also." In Ambrose Bierce's *Can Such Things Be?* an entrepreneurial gambler recounts his victory over a "mulish" opponent: ". . . after turning the other cheek seventy and seven times [cf. Matt. 18:22] I doctored the dice so he didn't last forever" ("The Haunted Valley"). Goldsmith's observation that "it was more than human benevolence that first taught us to bless our enemies" (*The Vicar of Wakefield,* chap. 17) indicates something of the difficulty of authentic Christian behavior. "I know it is my duty 'to pray for them that despitefully use me,'" writes Twain with tongue-in-cheek in *The Innocents Abroad;* "and therefore, hard as it is, I shall still try to pray for those fumigating, macaroni-stuffing organ grinders" (chap. 20). The experience of a practical demonstration — even if fleeting — comes as a shock in Wells's *Tono-Bungay:*

> "You sneak!" I said, and smacked his face hard forthwith. "Now then," said I.
> He started back, astonished and alarmed. His eyes met mine, and I saw a sudden gleam of resolution. He turned his other cheek to me.
> "'It it," he said; "'it it. I'll forgive you." (1.2)

See also LEX TALIONIS.

THE TWELVE *See* APOSTLE.

TWINKLING OF AN EYE At the Last Judgment, says St. Paul (1 Cor. 15:51-52), a great mystery will unfold: "We shall not all sleep, but we shall all be changed, In a moment, in the twinkling of an eye, at the last trump. . . ." The phrase has been thoroughly secularized, and appears in modern literature almost exclusively without allusion to its biblical source. The apocalypse conjured with in De Quincey's *Confessions of an English Opium Eater,* e.g., is chemically induced: "But suddenly her countenance grew dim, and, turning to the mountains, I perceived vapours rolling between us; in a moment it had all vanished; thick darkness came on; and, in the twinkling of an eye, I was far away from mountains, and by lamp-light in Oxford Street, walking again with Ann" ("The Pains of Opium").

See also LAST JUDGMENT; LAST TRUMP; RESURRECTION; SECOND COMING.

TWO LOVES *See* CHARITY, CUPIDITY.

TWO WITNESSES According to Christian eschatology, the two witnesses will appear at the end of time as representatives of Christ in the final battle against the powers of evil. Rev. 11:3-13 draws heavily on OT imagery when it describes two prophets dressed in sackcloth and represented by two lamps and two olive trees (cf. Zech. 4:3) who preach against the beast which ascends from the bottomless pit. They are killed by the beast in the great city called Sodom and Egypt, lie unburied for three and a half days while many rejoice, and then are resurrected by a breath of life from God (cf. Ezek. 37:10) and taken to heaven. An earthquake then destroys a tenth of the city, killing 7,000, and the seventh trumpet, the Second Advent, follows (Rev. 11:15).

The witnesses are associated with Christ, who in Rev. 1:5 and 3:14 is called a *martys*, or witness, although the context of the passage, which follows the angel's instruction to John that he eat the book (Rev. 10:8-11; cf. Ezek. 3:1), suggests that the witnesses more generally represent the importance of the prophetic office in the Church in the last days. Their miraculous powers — they use fire against their enemies, prevent rain, turn water into blood, and call forth plagues — also associate them with Elijah (cf. 2 Kings 1:10-15; 1 Kings 17:1) and Moses (Exod. 8–12), both of whom, according to tradition, had been translated to heaven and had appeared together with Christ at the Transfiguration (Mark 9:4-5). The identification of one witness with Elijah is particularly strong, since he had been taken to heaven in a fiery chariot (2 Kings 2:11) and was expected to reappear (Mal. 4:5; Mark 9:11). As early as St. Justin Martyr and throughout most of the Middle Ages, however, the second witness was identified with Enoch, the patriarch who "walked with God" and was taken up to heaven (Gen. 5:22-24). According to medieval exegesis, these two OT figures were held in the earthly Paradise, awaiting the appearance of the Antichrist (the beast from the abyss). They were expected to preach against him, convert the Jews to Christianity, and be killed, resurrected, and taken to heaven shortly before Christ's Second Coming.

In medieval literature, therefore, the two witnesses most commonly appear in literary treatments of either the earthly Paradise or the Antichrist. The major narrative source for their dwelling in the earthly Paradise, what the *Parliament of Three Ages* calls "iles of the Oryent," is the apocryphal Gospel of Nicodemus. Describing the harrowing of hell, it explains how Adam and the others released by Christ from the confines of Satan interview Enoch and Elijah while passing through the earthly Paradise. Brief references to this expectation are common throughout medieval literature, from OE sermons to the *Cornish Ordinalia's* "Resurrection." The notion even serves the purposes of satire in the *Land of Cokaygne,* which compares the undisciplined monks of Cokaygne with Enoch and Elijah in Paradise. The first extensive narrative linking the witnesses with the life of the Antichrist is Adso's *Libellus de Antichristo,* which was subsequently trans-

lated into OE. The crucial role of the witnesses in the events of the last days is developed in the sermons of Aelfric and in several ME moral works such as the *Cursor Mundi* and the *Pricke of Conscience.* Enoch and Elias are particularly prominent in medieval dramatic treatments of the Antichrist (e.g., *Ludus de Antichristo*).

The Chester "Harrowing of Hell" and "Prophets of Antichrist" depict the two witnesses both in the earthly Paradise and confronting the Antichrist at the end of time. The most developed literary treatment of the two witnesses is the same cycle's "Coming of Antichrist," where as Enoch and Elias they engage in a 360-line debate with Antichrist and succeed in converting to Christianity the four kings previously deceived by Antichrist. At the play's turning point, Antichrist murders the witnesses. Michael the archangel then appears, kills Antichrist, and resurrects the two witnesses, whose rise to heaven foreshadows the general resurrection which follows in the cycle's concluding play, "Doomsday."

The two witnesses have frequently been identified with particular groups, orders, or even individuals within the Church. In the 12th cent., Bruno of Segni argued that they represent "all the doctors of the church"; Joachim of Fiore associated them with two orders of "spiritual men"; later authors often identified them with the fraternal orders, especially the Franciscans. In Reformation polemics the witnesses were identified by Luther with all those who through the perilous reign of the Antichrist preached the OT and NT in opposition to papal doctrine. In his *Christus Triumphans,* John Foxe mentions that Hierologus and Theosebes are imprisoned for opposition to Pseudammus (the papal Antichrist). These characters probably refer both to Latimer and Ridley — who were executed in Oxford — and to the two witnesses, who according to Foxe represent all the Reformers, from Wyclif to Luther, Melanchthon, and Zwingli. Tennyson later takes up the same designation in his "Sir John Old Castle":

> Burnt — good sir Roger Acton, my dear friend!
> Burnt, too, my faithful preacher, Beverley!
> Lord, give thou power to Thy two witnesses,
> Lest the false faith make merry over them!
> Two — say but thirty-nine have risen and stand,
> Dark with the smoke of human sacrifice,
> Before thy light, and cry continually.

The most important later references to the witnesses are in the works of William Blake, who drew heavily on Revelation for some of his imagery. In "A Vision of the Last Judgment," he portrays the two witnesses in a traditional form, as human figures associated with the Second Coming of Christ who battle against their enemies. His visionary works, however, provide a more dramatic transformation of the tradition. In *Milton,* Blake labels Rintrah and Palamabron as the two witnesses. They are in some ways identified with the biblical witnesses, since Palamabron is associated with codifiers of religion, specifically

Moses, and Rintrah is associated with prophets, specifically Elijah. The division in their roles momentarily sets them against each other, but together they "view the Human Harvest beneath," and, as in the Apocalypse and throughout tradition, both prepare the universe "To go forth to the Great Harvest & Vintage of the Nations" (43.1).

See also ANTICHRIST; ELIJAH; ENOCH; HARROWING OF HELL; MICHAEL; MOSES.

Bibliography. Emmerson, R. *Antichrist in the Middle Ages* (1981); "Enoch and Elias, Antichrist, and the Structure of the Chester Cycle." In *"Homo, Memento Finis": The Iconography of Just Judgment in Medieval Art and Drama* (1985); Emmerson, R., and R. B. Herzman. *The Apocalyptic Imagination in Medieval Literature* (1992).

RICHARD K. EMMERSON

TYPOLOGY Christian typology in its biblical and basic sense has been defined by Andreas Rivetus, a Protestant commentator on the Bible, as occurring when something done in the OT is brought to notice and is shown to have signified or adumbrated something done or about to be done in the NT (*"Praefatio ad Ps. 45 in Commentarius,"* in *Psalmorum Propheticorum de Mysteriis Evangelicis* [1626]). Typology essentially sets forth a metaphysical point of correspondence between type and antitype, although occasionally, as in the typological link between Adam and Christ in 1 Cor. 15:22, the connection is a point of contrast. The NT at times invites typological interpretation by employing the words "type" (e.g., 1 Cor. 10:6; KJV "example"), "antitype" (e.g., 1 Pet. 3:2; KJV "figure"), "shadow" (e.g., Heb. 10:1), "mystery" (e.g., Eph. 5:32), and "allegory" (Gal. 4:24). It adds typological formulas, namely "the true. . ." (John 6:32) and "as . . . so" (e.g., Matt. 12:40). These matters seem clear enough, but NT typology presents complications: e.g., Melchisedek in Heb. 5–7 is generally regarded as a type of Christ, but Hebrews does not state this in the usual terms, using rather "similitude" (7:15) and the recurrent saying that Jesus was "made an high priest for ever after the order of Melchisedek" (e.g., 5:6, 10; 6:20; 7:17, 21). Paul's quotation of Aratus and Cleanthes's "For we are also his offspring" (Acts 17:28 [KJV]) seems to license pagan-Christian typology, a prominent idea for those of Greek background like St. Clement of Alexandria; Christ describes in Matt. 24 the coming fall of Jerusalem as if it intimated types in the NT of the Second Coming. All these considerations exemplify historical typology, namely that requiring time between appearances of type and antitype (e.g., the brazen serpent, the type [Num. 21:8]; Christ on the cross, the antitype [John 3:14]). A largely unregarded kind is ontological typology in which type and antitype exist simultaneously (e.g., the Temple, the type; Christ's dwelling in heaven [Heb. 9:24], the antitype).

The Church Fathers and later writers further extended the range of typology. St. Jerome, e.g. (*Ep.* 122), with certain other Fathers set forth (without biblical warrant) the ark as a type of the Church (cf. 1 Pet. 3:20-21); and John Bale with other Reformation apocalyptists designated (likewise without biblical warrant) the seven churches of Asia (Rev. 2–3) as types of seven, chronologically defined, successive ages of the Church.

The historical consciousness of typology dictates that its pairings will almost invariably be construed as a relation of "old" and "new," "then" and "now." The most obvious evidence of this is the division of Christian Scriptures into OT and NT, which then are provided with marginal references connecting, passage by pasage, one with the other. From the earliest biblical commentaries in the patristic period to modern Protestant dispensationalism and Scofield's famous notes to the KJV, typological approaches have been habitual in Christian reading of the OT especially.

See also ALLEGORY; NUMEROLOGY; OLD AND NEW.

Bibliography. Auerbach, E. "Figura." *Scenes from the Drama of European Literature* (1959), 11-76; Bercovitch, S. "Selective Check-List on Typology." *EAL* 5 (1970); *Typology and Early American Literature* (1972); Berkeley, D. S. "Some Misapprehensions of Christian Typology in Recent Literary Scholarship." *Studies in Early Literature* 18 (1978), 3-12; Brumm, U. *American Thought and Religious Typology* (1970); Charity, A. C. *Events and their Afterlife: The Dialectics of Christian Typology in the Bible and Dante* (1966); Daniélou, J. *From Shadows to Reality: Studies in the Biblical Typology of the Fathers* (1961); Goppelt, L. *Typos: The Typological Interpretation of the Old Testament in the New.* Trans. D. H. Madvig (1982); Keenan, H. T. "A Check-List of Typology and English Medieval Literature Through 1972." *Studies in the Literary Imagination* 8 (1975), 159-66; Landow, G. P. *Victorian Types, Victorian Shadows* (1980); Miner, E., ed. *Literary Uses of Typology from the Late Middle Ages to the Present* (1977); Preus, J. S. *From Shadow to Promise: Old Testament Interpretation from Augustine to the Young Luther* (1969).

DAVID S. BERKELEY

TYRE Tyrus, an important Phoenician city (modern Sur), south of Sidon, built upon an island and fortified. Achitecture and crafts of Tyre were employed by Solomon in building the Temple (cf. 1 Kings 9:26-28; 10:11-22). Once confederate with Sidon and in the late 8th cent. a separate kingdom, it was by 572 taken by Nebuchadnezzar. Subsequently part of the Ptolemaic kingdom (3rd cent. B.C.), by 64 B.C. it had been annexed to the Roman province of Syria. But this settlement was on the mainland. The island city had already been demolished by Alexander the Great (ca. 332), in a siege referred to by the prophet Zechariah (9:1-4). Kipling's "The Merchantmen" refers to 1 Kings 9–10:

> King Solomon drew merchantmen
> Because of his desire
> For peacocks, apes and ivory,
> From Tarshish unto Tyre.

U

UBI SUNT? (Latin, "Where are they now?") A common theme in OE and ME poetry of an elegiac nature, teaching that earthly greatness is of little enduring value. A modern *ubi sunt* is James Clarence Mangan's "Gone in the Wind."

See also HOW ARE THE MIGHTY FALLEN!

UNDER THE FIFTH RIB *See* ABNER.

UNEQUALLY YOKED St. Paul warned the Corinthians: "Be ye not unequally yoked together with unbelievers: for what fellowship hath righteousness with unrighteousness?" (2 Cor. 6:14). Paul's exhortation is to "separation" from the *societas* of paganism in general (v. 17), though the warning (cf. Deut. 7:3-4) has often been applied to the case of marriage with unbelievers in particular. "An improper and ill-yoking couple," such as Milton describes in *On Divorce,* 1.13.21, gradually comes to include, as for Milton himself, spiritual asymmetry of various kinds. An ideal marriage is, conversely, one such as Portia anticipates in Shakespeare's *Merchant of Venice,* ". . . companions / . . . / Whose souls do bear an equal yoke of love, / There must be needs a like proportion / Of lineaments, of manners, and of spirit" (3.3.11-15).

UNFORGIVABLE SIN *See* UNPARDONABLE SIN.

UNICORN The unicorn has become part of the biblical tradition through a happenstance of translation; the LXX translators, guided perhaps by the vision of a one-horned beast in Dan. 8:3, chose to render Heb. *re'em* (a word signifying some powerful horned animal, possibly the wild ox, but whose precise referent remains unknown) with Gk. *monokeros,* which in turn became *unicornis* (and in some passages, *rhinoceros*) in the Vg, *Einhorn* in Luther's Bible, and unicorn in the KJV. While the unicorn thus does not have roots in the Hebrew OT, later Jewish commentary supports the LXX: the Talmud explains how the huge *re'em* survived the Flood by being tied to the outside of the ark (*Zebaḥ.* 113b); the scene is depicted in medieval manuscripts (see Einhorn, 397), and several midrashim refer to the legendary animosity of the lion and *re'em,* in one case actually referring to the latter as *ha-unicornis* (cited in Jung, 462-63).

The biblical passages referring to the *re'em*/unicorn all emphasize the strength and liveliness of the creature, usually as an expression of God's own ruling power: God's voice will make the cedars of Lebanon skip like unicorns (Ps. 29:6); God asks Job, "Will the unicorn be willing to serve thee, or abide by thy crib? Canst thou bind the unicorn. . . ?" (39:9-10); and God as deliverer of Israel is praised because "he hath as it were the strength of an unicorn" (Num. 23:22; cf. 24:8); God's "horns are like the horns of unicorns: with them he shall push the people together to the ends of the earth" (Deut. 33:17). The Psalmist prays, then, to be exalted among his enemies "like the horn of an unicorn" (92:10). On the other hand, God's avenging power is expressed in the image of Edom laid waste in blood, all the bulls and unicorns brought down (Isa. 34:7). Finally, the power of the unicorn is expressed in the fearful cry of Ps. 22:21: "Save me from the lion's mouth . . . from the horns of the unicorns."

From these seven passages, reinforced by extrabiblical sources, the unicorn became a fixture of biblical tradition, appearing in translations, paraphrases, glosses, commentaries, and illustrations, particularly of Ps. 22, which was one of the most frequently explicated and illustrated texts in the Middle Ages because of the Christian interpretation of it as a prophetic account of the Passion of Christ.

The subsequent elaboration of the "natural history" of the unicorn — its size, power, swiftness, fierce and proud nature, solitary habits, and the alexipharmic properties of its magnificent spiral horn — all derive more from the various classical "naturalists" (Ctesias, Aristotle, Megasthenes, Aelian, Pliny) than from anything biblical. But the single most important source for all subsequent unicorn lore is a curious work of Christianized natural history, the *Physiologus,* a work originally of the 2nd or 3rd cent., but ultimately known in a great variety of text traditions — Greek, Egyptian, Syriac, Latin, vernacular — all through the Middle Ages and Renaissance. The versions differ in detail, but in general a consistent composite image of the unicorn was handed down. The most important contribution of *Physiologus* to unicorn lore is the story of the virgin capture: "A virgin girl is led to where he lurks, and there she is sent off by herself into the wood. He soon leaps into her lap when he sees her, and embraces her, and hence he gets caught" (T. H. White, *The Bestiary* [1960], 21). The capture scene became critical to the explicit interpretation of the unicorn as a symbol of Christ.

A vast tradition of conventional medieval natural history about the unicorn grew out of this account, elaborated by such writers as St. Isidore of Seville, who informed a whole lineage of encyclopedists and natural philosophers (Alain of Lille, St. Albertus Magnus, St. Hildegard of Bingen, Vincent of Beauvais, Natalis Comes). Isidore's passage on the unicorn was followed, e.g., by Bartholomaeus Anglicus and his English translator John of Trevisa. The tradition was further enhanced by legendary travelers' tales such as the medieval romances of Alexander, one of which gives us the detail of the wondrous "carbuncle" at the root of the animal's horn (see Shepard, 81-82), a detail found also in Wolfram's *Parzival* as one of the medicines used to try to cure Amfortas's wound (9.483). The unicorn figures also in the spurious Letter of Prester John; the French version describes the lion's ruse of sidestepping a unicorn's charge after positioning itself in front of a tree, whereupon (in Edward Topsells's 17th-cent. rendition of the story) "the Unicorn in the swiftness of his course runneth against a tree, wherein his sharp horn sticketh fast" (Shepard, 241) — an image which became an emblem of rash-

ness in medieval and Renaissance iconography (see Beer, figs. 28, 29). The unicorn figures in the whole range of Renaissance and 18th-cent. travel literature, albeit as a controverted subject (one curiosity is an account out of Ethiopia by the 17th-cent. Jesuit Jeronimo Lobo, including a description of the unicorn, which was translated by Samuel Johnson as *A Voyage to Abyssinia* [1735]). Throughout the 17th and 18th cents. scholarly battle was waged over the existence of the unicorn and/or the healing properties of its horn. Sir Thomas Browne, e.g., takes an uncharacteristically skeptical and cautionary view of the latter in *Vulgar Errors,* and by the time of Hogarth's *Marriage à la Mode,* the image of a unicorn horn in his shop is sufficient to identify a doctor as a quack.

Another tradition altogether, growing specifically out of the biblical associations and noticed already in *Physiologus,* was the allegorization of the unicorn. Thus, commenting on Deut. 33:13, Tertullian says of Christ, "His glory is that of a bull, his horn that of a unicorn" (*Adv. Jud.* [PL 2.626]); the one horn signifies Christ's common power with the Father, according to St. Basil (Hathaway, 14), and is a type of the cross for St. Justin Martyr (*Dial.* [PG 6.691]). Nilus explains that the holy hermit is a unicorn, a creature on its own (*Vita* [PG 120.69]). On the other hand, influenced by Ps. 22, some Fathers took the unicorn as an image of heathenish or demonic force. St. Jerome and St. Gregory say the enemies of the Lord are overweening as unicorns — although in comparing Saul, as persecutor of the Church, to the unicorn, Gregory also restores the positive allegorization: God tethered him, fed him the fodder of Scripture, and harnessed him (see Beer, 24). The influential commentary on Basil's *Hexameron* attributed to Eustathius places the unicorn in the Garden of Eden. Thus the unicorn became a staple of medieval symbolism and iconography.

Most important was the allegorization of the maiden-capture story; as explained in a key text by Honorius of Autun, "Christ is represented by this animal, and his insuperable strength by its horn. He who lay down in the womb of the Virgin has been caught by the hunters; that is to say, he was found in human shape by those who loved him" (*Speculum* [PL 172.817]). This symbolism is especially prominent in devotional Marian and mystical literature of the late Middle Ages, in which Mary's virginity and chastity are said to "lure" Christ to become incarnate. As Suso put it in addressing the Virgin, "Whoever has caught the savage unicorn if not thyself?" (Beer, 193). Thus, in the Annunciation scene, Gabriel is imagined as blowing a huntsman's horn and in the inevitable sequel, the Christ/unicorn allows himself to be sacrificed. The allegory was especially popular in Germany and is found in numerous religious lyrics by such authors as Heinrich von Frauenlob, Konrad von Megensburg, Heinrich von Laufenburg, and many others (see Einhorn, 194-218). As a 14th-cent. ME hymn to Mary expresses it:

Ine þe hys god by-come a chyld,
Ine þe hys wreche by-come myld;
þat vnicorn þat was so wyld
  Aleyd hys of a cheaste:
þou hast y-tamed and i-styld
  Wyþ melke of þy breste. (C. Brown, *Religious Lyrics of the XIVth Century,* 32.61-66)

A "courtly love" version of the allegory also developed in numerous lays, courtly lyrics, and minne-songs and in the versified "bestiaries" of Philipe de Thaun, William of Normandy, and Richard de Fournival. In the latter's *Bestaire d'amour* the lover compares his fate to that of the unicorn, lured by the sweet odor of the maiden, enchanted, and slain: "Even so has Love dealt cruelly with me" (Shepard, 55). Similar imagery is found in such poets as Thibaut of Champagne, Burkhardt von Hohenfels, Guido Cavalcanti, and various anonymous *lieder,* but in the famous ballad "Le roman de la dame à la lycorne et du biau chevalier au lyon" ("The Romance of the Lady Unicorn, or the Fair Knight Lion"), the courtly lover is associated with the lion, and the lady with the unicorn (as in the Cluny tapestries), because of her purity and chastity.

The many depictions of the unicorn in medieval iconography follow the exegetical and literary patterns. The fierce, threatening unicorn is common in typological illustrations of Ps. 22, as in the Stuttgart and Utrecht Psalters (for others, see Einhorn, 82-83, 397-404). But far more common is the noble unicorn among the creatures of Paradise, as in an 11th-cent. tapestry in Gerona Cathedral or a Flemish tapestry in the Academy of Fine Arts in Florence or a 15th-cent. manuscript by Bartholomaeus Anglicus (see Einhorn, 111-18, 389-96), or present with Mary and Gabriel in the *hortus conclusus* in depictions of the Annunciation as the Mystical Hunt. This latter motif is found in Byzantine manuscripts (the Chludov Psalter), frescoes (Memmengen), altarpieces (Lübeck), altar cloths (Goss), stained glass, relief carvings, woodcuts — indeed, every art medium of the Middle Ages (Einhorn, 356-81). This scene, with its sequel, the slaying of the Christ/unicorn, is most common in the art of Thüringen and Lower Saxony and the Upper Rhine and Switzerland from the 14th through the 16th cents. After that time, attacked by Luther and implicitly renounced by Trent, the motif disappeared.

The most spectacular depiction of the Mystical Hunt, however, is the series of seven tapestries now at the Cloisters in New York. The seven tapestries sequentially depict the hunt conducted in full royal regalia — the discovery of the unicorn, the chase, the maiden-capture, the kill, and the bringing of the slain unicorn back to the castle. The seventh tapestry, however, shows the revitalized unicorn leashed to a pomegranate tree in an enclosed garden. This last beautiful but enigmatic image represents on one level the consummation of the holy marriage and on the mystical level the risen, eucharistic Christ present in the garden of the soul. The magnificent series, virtually

unknown until the 20th cent., has in turn inspired other art works, such as the poems "The Unicorn" by Ann Morrow Lindburgh and "Imagining a Unicorn" by Barry Spacks, which follows the sequence closely and suggests its christological import:

> For passion we seek you, goat-chinned horse,
> Lover and teacher, feral Christ. . . .
> *Noblesse oblige:* ready for death
> As her handmaiden waves the spearmen in.
> Called to his death, mysterious,
> By the horn of the hunter Gabriel. . . .
> See, he returns; his wounds are gone,
> Princely, forgiving, unendingly born,
> He marries the garden of the earth,
> Plenitude upon plenitude. ("Imagining a Unicorn" [1978], 59-63)

The other great series of unicorn tapestries, the Lady and the Unicorn series at the Cluny monastery in Paris, does not deal with the Mystic Hunt but instead depicts the courtly allegory of the lady, the unicorn, and the lion. In nonnarrative fashion, these six tapestries elaborate on the motif of the five senses, indicated emblematically in five of the hangings and culminating in a grand tableau in the sixth, in which the lady is flanked by the two rampant beasts and framed before an open tent surmounted by the courtly legend "A mon seul désir." This series, too, has inspired other art: a ballet on the theme of virginal purity by Jean Cocteau, allusions in George Sand and Marcel Proust, and an extended passage in Rilke's *Malte Laurids Brigge,* in which Brigge takes Abelone on an imaginary descriptive tour of the tapestries. He focuses on the lady's every gesture and on the unicorn, who is "beautiful" and who "understands." Rilke alludes to the tapestries also in one of his *Sonnets to Orpheus,* in honor of the creature which "never was" — yet, not knowing that, they loved it, fed it "with the possibility that it might be," so that "To a virgin it came hither white — / and was in the silver-mirror and in her" (2.4).

Renaissance iconography of the unicorn tends to move away from the mystical or biblical associations (except in depictions of Eden, such as Raphael's *Creation of the Animals* in the Vatican), becoming primarily a moral allegory of chastity, as in Giorgione's *Allegory of Chastity,* Moretto's *S. Justine,* Tintoretto's *San Rocco,* Raphael's *Lady and the Unicorn* — and, above all, in allegorical depictions of the chariot of Chastity drawn by unicorns in illustrations of the *Hypnerotomachia* (1499) and Petrarch's *Trionfi.* More rarely, the unicorn was an emblem of rampageous *in*continence, as in Bosch's *Garden of Earthly Delights,* Dürer's *Rape of Persephone,* or Rabelais's bawdy description of the "erection" of the unicorn.

The relatively few references in Renaissance literature tend to be conventionally folkloric and emblematic. In Honoré d'Urfé's pastoral romance *L'Astrée,* lions and unicorns guard the Magic Fountain of True Love, and it is the unicorns who protect true lovers who come to the spring, whereas in Ariosto's *Orlando Furioso,* two decep- tive ladies whom translator Harington regards as Ambi- tion and Desire-for-Advancement come to Rogero's aid riding on white unicorns (6.69). Sometimes the legendary fierceness of the unicorn is the point of an allusion, as in Chapman's comparison of the vindictive fury of Bussy d'Ambois to that of the unicorn (2.1.117-23).

Several writers allude to the legend of a lion's defeat- ing a unicorn's charge by sidestepping it, "the whiles that furious beast / His precious horne, sought of his enimis, / Strikes in the stocke, ne thence can be releast" (Spenser, *Faerie Queene,* 2.5.10); Shakespeare uses it as a moral emblem (*Timon of Athens,* 4.3.340-42; *Julius Caesar,* 2.1.204) and elsewhere simply alludes to the unicorn as proverbially wild (*The Rape of Lucrece,* 956) or, in Sebastian's famous line in *The Tempest,* fabulous: "Now I will believe / That there are unicorns" (3.3.21-22). Donne, in Elegie 6, "The Perfume," wittily compares a father's recognition of perfume as an unaccustomed scent in his house to the Englishman's regarding "pretious Unicorns" as "strange monsters" (49-50).

Little attention was paid the unicorn in the 18th cent., but, not surprisingly, interest in the romantic creature gradually returned in the 19th. Twelve unicorns are part of the Roman carnival procession in E. T. A. Hoffman's *Princess Brambilla,* and Keats makes the "spleenful unicorn" part of the Bacchic rout in *Endymion* (4.256). Conversely, Tennyson's Sir Percival describes Arthur's wasted city as "heaps of ruin, hornless unicorns" ("The Holy Grail," 717), just as for Oskar Loerke in "Der Sil- berdistelwald" no unicorn sets foot in the Kingdom of Death. Similarly, in Romantic art the unicorn reappears as an image of exotic and erotic loveliness, as in Gustave Moreau's "Ladies and Unicorns" or the American A. B. Davies's "Unicorns." Rather different is the "imaginative realism" of various unicorn paintings of Viennese painter Ernst Fuchs (see Beer, 194).

In modern English literature, the most important use of the unicorn symbol occurs in Yeats. He alludes to the unicorn casually in a few poems (e.g., "The Two Kings," 18-20; "Phantom Hatred," 17-25) but develops it as a major apocalyptic symbol in a series of related plays. In *Where There Is Nothing* (1902), Paul Ruttledge recalls a trance in which he had a vision of being tormented by various creatures who seemed to him to be like the part of mankind which is not human, which keeps the soul from God, and then in a bright light suddenly the beasts were gone, and "I saw a great many angels riding upon unicorns, white angels on white unicorns. They stood all round me, and they cried out, 'Brother Paul, go and preach. . . .' And then they laughed aloud, and the unicorns trampled the ground as though the world were already falling in pieces" (4.2.175-80). A few years later Yeats, along with Lady Gregory, redesigned what he felt was a more sympathetic play with a similar revolutionary theme, *The Unicorn from the Stars* (1908), the name taken

from the title of one of the ranks (*monoceros de astris*) bestowed in the rituals of the Order of the Golden Dawn. In this play the visionary Martin describes a shamanistic experience in which he seemed to be carried away on a horse to a heavenly garden surrounded by wheat fields and vineyards — when suddenly the horses were trans- formed into unicorns which began trampling the wheat and grapes, until everything seemed to tremble and change, and then a great shining vessel was dropped, broken, and trampled by the unicorns: "They were break- ing the world to pieces — when I saw the cracks coming I shouted for joy! And I heard the command, 'Destroy, destroy, destruction is the life-giver! destroy!'" (1.557- 60). To Martin, it was exhilarating, "something that would make my whole life strong and beautiful like the rushing of the unicorns" (506-08). Father John responds, looking for the meaning, and remembers that a French monk had once explained that unicorns meant strength, "virginal strength, a rushing, lasting, tireless strength" (335-37). Later Martin makes a banner for a league of the dispos- sessed, the League of the Unicorns, which portrays the triumph of the unicorn over the lion (England): "We will go out against the world and break it and unmake it. We are the army of the Unicorn from the Stars! We will trample it to pieces. — We will consume the world, we will burn it away" (2.369-72).

Finally, in *The Player Queen* (1922), Yeats combines the theme of the search for the "antithetical Self" with the apocalyptic unicorn symbolism of the prior plays. Here a group of rude townspeople plot to overthrow their reclusive queen because a goatboy has reported that he once spied in a castle window and "saw her coupling with a great white unicorn." In their rude imaginations, the goatboy and townspeople have converted the medieval icon of the lady with the unicorn in her lap into a las- civious image. Only the drunken poet Septimus rises to the unicorn's defense: "Did I hear somebody say that the Unicorn is not chaste? It is a most noble beast, a most religious beast. . . . It is written in 'The Great Beastery of Paris' that it is chaste, that it is the most chaste of all the beasts in the world" (1.249-57; cf. 264-72). Indeed, it is later revealed that the queen's patron saint is a Saint Octema, who, like the saints in Renaissance paintings, was associated with the unicorn, an emblem of purity. As the rebellion grows, Septimus speaks prophetically of a coming new age which only the unicorn, being both ideal image and beast (2.479-81), can usher in: "I announce the end of the Christian Era, the coming of a New Dispensa- tion, that of the New Adam, that of the Unicorn; but alas, he is chaste, he hesitates" (2.381-84). Ironically, it is the very chastity of the unicorn which impedes his engender- ing the god of the new age. "The Unicorn will be terrible when it loves" (509) — if only it will!

The other most prominent use of the unicorn image in modern literature occurs in Tennessee Williams's *The Glass Menagerie* (1945). When Laura, the shy, lonely, and slightly crippled heroine, shows her rare gentleman caller her collection of glass animals, the parallel between the vulnerable girl and her favorite, the unicorn, is clear: "Poor little fellow," Jim says, "he must feel sort of lonesome." Later, when Jim waltzes Laura around the room, the unicorn is knocked to the floor, and its horn broken off. And when he takes his leave after announcing his engagement to another woman, Laura gives him the broken unicorn, emblematically, "for remembrance."

Among the many modern poets who have written of the unicorn, W. H. Auden in *New Year Letter* preserves the religious associations in his address to Christ as a unicorn:

O unicorn among the cedars
To whom no magic charm can lead us,
White childhood moving like a sigh
Through the green woods unharmed in thy
Sophisticated innocence
To call thy true love to the dance....

William Carlos Williams, in *Paterson*, makes the romantic association between the unicorn, the artist, and Death:

The Unicorn
has no match
    or mate • the artist
        has no peer •
Death
    has no peer.

Among other poets, André Lorde, in "The Black Unicorn," makes a connection between the chained, fenced unicorn and a sense of loss of freedom; more radically, Dudley Randall, in "The White Unicorn," questions the meaningfulness of the "universal" archetype: "A white unicorn? Does it believe in integration?" Shel Silverstein playfully adverts to the old rabbinical question of whether unicorns survived the Flood, in his popular song lyric "The Unicorn." For Jean Rubin in "The Unicorn Participates" it is one's openness to "something unaccounted for / And unaccountable" — which "may be summarized / As a unicorn lurking just out of sight" — that constitutes "what we are, beyond what we seem, / What we feel, beyond what we can say." In short, "One may attribute much / To the promptings of the unicorn" (*AAUP Bulletin,* Spring 1984, 8-12).

The unicorn figures in the titles or as an allusion in a number of modern novels, notably Iris Murdoch's *The Unicorn* (1963), Martin Walser's *Das Einhorn* (1966), and Günter Grass's *The Tin Drum,* in which Matzerath compares himself to the unicorn in relation to the gang moll Lucie. It also appears in the fanciful *The Unicorn, the Gorgon, and the Manticore* by Gian Carlo Menotti, in which the monsters represent the misunderstood writer's ideas and are the only ones to attend him on his deathbed; all are endangered — the writer must warn the unicorn against the virgin-decoy....

The unicorn has come to play an increasingly prominent role in children's literature and fantasy writing. The well-known tale of "The Brave Little Tailor" in the Grimm collection includes an episode in which the tailor uses the familiar method of sidestepping a unicorn's charge and capturing it when it impales itself in a tree. The Mother Goose collection includes the well-known

The Lion and the Unicorn
Fighting for the Crown,
The Lion beat the Unicorn,
All about the Town,

commonly thought to allude to the political troubles between England (the lion) and Scotland (the unicorn). Lewis Carroll incorporates the rhyme and brings the principals to life in *Through the Looking-Glass* (7); it has been suggested that Carroll's dialogue and Tenniel's drawings of the lion and unicorn were intended as caricatures of Gladstone and Disraeli, respectively. Other popular unicorns for young readers appear in L. Leslie Brooke's *Ring o' Roses,* Thurber's whimsical illustrated story "The Unicorn in the Garden," Madeleine L'Engle's *A Swiftly Tilting Planet,* C. S. Lewis's *The Last Battle* (final volume of the *Narnia Chronicles*), and T. H. White's *The Once and Future King.* In this narrative (2.7), young Gawain and his three brothers embark on a unicorn hunt. With the advice of a hermit, who instructs them out of an old bestiary, and using a rather unwilling girl from the scullery as bait, the boys unexpectedly succeed. In a suddenly lyrical passage, a unicorn appears, glorious and lovely, and, full of reverence, rests himself in the girl's lap. The episode turns to horror as the boys fall upon and slay the unicorn; in lurid detail White describes the clumsy and awful "gralloch," or butchery of the unicorn, "and, in proportion as they became responsible for spoiling its beauty, so they began to hate it for their guilt." Finally, what they bring back to the castle is only the remains of the head, "with eyes ruined, flesh bruised and separating from the bones," a "muddy, bloody, heather-mangled exhibit" — like some crucifixion by Grünewald.

The most sustained treatment of the unicorn in modern fantasy literature is the ethereal solitary unicorn of Peter Beagle's *The Last Unicorn* (1968), who, for part of the romance, becomes the beautiful and enigmatic Lady Amalthea. Beagle alludes to much of the traditional unicorn lore in conversation between a pair of hunters in his opening chapter. The unicorn of the title has found herself in a debased world where unicorns are not merely hated or forgotten but where humans have become incapable of seeing them (or perhaps anything else, including each other) for what they really are. She wonders if any other unicorns exist anywhere. What she learns is that a great cosmic adversary, the Red Bull, "has majesty, and his horns are the horns of a wild ox. With them he shall push the peoples, all of them, to the ends of the earth" (a curious reworking of the unicorn reference in Deut.

33:17) — and has indeed pushed all the other unicorns into the sea. The romance involves her quest to free them; when she and her friends succeed and the unicorn passes over the formerly smitten wasteland, wherever she touches, vitality returns as people learn again how to take joy in things "for no reason" — the gift of the unicorn.

Bibliography. Beer, R. *Unicorn: Myth and Reality.* Trans. Charles M. Stern (1977); Bradford, C. B., ed. *W. B. Yeats: The Writing of "The Player Queen"* (1977); Einhorn, J. *Spiritualis Unicornis: Das Einhorn als Bedeutungsträger in Literatur und Kunst des Mittelalters* (1976); Freeman, M. *The Unicorn Tapestries* (1976); Hathaway, N. *The Unicorn* (1980); Jung, C. *Psychology and Alchemy.* Trans. R. F. C. Hull (1968). See esp. "The Paradigm of the Unicorn," pp. 435ff.; Ley, W. *The Lungfish, the Dodo, and the Unicorn* (1948); Shepard, O. *The Lore of the Unicorn* (1979).

GEORGE L. SCHEPER

UNJUST STEWARD, PARABLE OF   *See* CHILDREN OF LIGHT.

UNKNOWN GOD   In his speech to Epicurean and Stoic philosophers at the Areopagus in Athens, St. Paul commented on a catchall altar with the inscription, "TO THE UNKNOWN GOD," saying "Whom therefore ye ignorantly worship, him declare I unto you" (Acts 17:23). Shelley responds obliquely to this narrative in *Hellas:*

> In sacred Athens, near the fane
>   Of Wisdom, Pity's altar stood:
> Serve not the unknown God in vain. (735-37)

The Unknown God is a volume of poems by A. E. (G. W. Russell), while John Middleton Murry's mystical *To the Unknown God* (1924) appropriates the phrase, as also does John Steinbeck's *To a God Unknown* (1933), a mystical and pantheistic narrative which has as its principal theme the relationship of man to the land.

UNPARDONABLE SIN   Of the three Gospel texts which speak of the unpardonable sin — Matt. 12:31-32; Mark 3:28-29; Luke 12:10 — the first has been the focus of most exegetical and literary commentary:

> Wherefore I say unto you, All manner of sin and blasphemy shall be forgiven unto men: but the blasphemy against the Holy Ghost shall not be forgiven unto men. And whosoever speaketh a word against the Son of man, it shall be forgiven him: but whosoever speaketh against the Holy Ghost, it shall not be forgiven him, neither in this world, neither in the world to come.

This hardest of Christ's sayings is directed at the Pharisees, who have ascribed to Beelzebub's power Jesus' healing of a dumb and blind demoniac. Pictured as perversely engaged in internecine war (see Fitzmyer, *The Gospel According to Luke, X-XV*, 921), the Pharisees, who call good evil, "gouge out their own eyes" and so commit the unpardonable folly of "moral suicide" (*IB* 7.400). The idea of an unforgivable sin appears also in

Heb. 6:4-8; 10:28-31 (where it seems to be apostasy from the Christian faith) and possibly in 1 John 5:16-17, which refers to a "sin unto death."

The early Fathers vary considerably in their interpretations of blasphemy against the Holy Ghost. St. Thomas Aquinas (*Summa Theol.* 2-2a, q.14, a.1) provides a useful summary of readings in his review of the three meanings traditionally assigned to the nature of this sin. The first, with which the body of patristic commentary generally agrees, distinguishes between sin against the Son of Man, or Christ in his human nature, and blasphemy against the Son of God, or Christ in his divine nature. As an act of deliberately willed unbelief in the one empowered to forgive, the sin is by its very nature unpardonable. The second meaning, advanced principally by St. Augustine, is of final impenitence or despair as a result of contempt, obstinacy, and pride (Augustine, *De correctione donatistarum*, 11.48-50). The sin is unforgivable because it is not repented of. A third interpretation takes blasphemy against the Holy Ghost to mean a considered rejection of the goodness appropriated to that person of the Trinity (cf. Augustine, *Contra litteras Petiliani Donatistae,* 2.62.139-40). Aquinas pictures this sinner as suffering from an incurable illness yet rejecting the very food and medicine necessary for healing. Fundamental to all three interpretations — and here Aquinas follows St. Albert the Great — is the notion that "to sin against the Holy Ghost is to take pleasure in the malice of sin for its own sake."

Although reference to the unpardonable sin is not prominent in the medieval literary tradition, a remarkable discussion of the subject occurs in *Piers Plowman* (B.17.135-50), where the dreamer is instructed by Charity about the nature of the Trinity. Father, Son, and Holy Spirit are likened to the fist, fingers, and palm of a hand. "He who blasphemes against the Holy Ghost pricks God as it were in the palm; so whoever sins against the Holy Ghost injures God in the place where he grips and deliberately murders his grace." Among the specific sins by which the Holy Spirit is blasphemed, says Charity, the most heinous is "murder of a good man": "this is the worst — to destroy deliberately . . . that which Christ bought so dearly" (Goodridge trans.).

Literary interest in the unpardonable sin increased dramatically in the Reformation period. The reprobate who has sinned against the Holy Spirit is a frequent figure in Puritan literature. Often implied in Renaissance drama (notably Marlowe's *Doctor Faustus*), the question of the blasphemy against the Holy Ghost is addressed directly and at length in John Bunyan's *Grace Abounding to the Chief of Sinners,* where the autobiographer's tormented cogitations regarding the nature of the mysterious offense and his guilt or innocence come to rest in his faith. In *Pilgrim's Progress,* Christian encounters, in Interpreter's House, a Man of Despair locked in an iron cage — past hope of repentance because of willful blasphemy against the Holy Ghost: "I have grieved the Spirit, and he is gone. . . ; I have provoked God to anger, and he has left me; I have so hardened my heart, that I *cannot* repent."

In the latter part of the 18th cent., both Christopher Smart and William Cowper explicitly refer to the sin against the Holy Ghost. In the eyes of the former, it is "INGRATITUDE" (*Jubilate Agno*, B.2.306). For Cowper, the nature of the blasphemy eludes definition: tortured by a sense of indefinable guilt, he sees in Milton's Satan a reflection of himself (J. Quinlan, *William Cowper: A Critical Life* [1953; rpt. 1970], 181), and his final poem, "The Castaway," ends on a note of despair. Ann Radcliffe's *The Mysteries of Udolpho* seems specific in taking the unpardonable sin to mean "the habit of gaming": the unfeeling and unrepentant arch-villain Montoni, kin to the diabolic schemers of Renaissance drama, treats people as pawns, taking pleasure in wrecking the lives of others (2.3). But this pseudomedieval fiction also appears to consider unforgivable a long and deeply repented premeditated murder (4.15).

Black magic, fratricide, incest, matricide, and malicious cunning in general are some of the unpardonable sins in Matthew Gregory Lewis's *The Monk,* where, in an ending fraught with allusions to Prometheus and Marlowe's Faustus, the proud and luxurious Ambrosio dies defying the heavens.

For all his vagaries regarding his incurable disease, Byron more clearly articulates "the Fatal Man of the Romantics" (see M. Praz, *The Romantic Agony* [1933; rpt. 1956], 61). Sick with "some strange perversity of thought," the Byronic solitary confounds "good and ill" (*Lara,* 1.18.340, 335) and repeats with Milton's Satan that the self-sufficient mind "would make a hell of heaven" (*Manfred,* 4.1.73). He is bound, out of pride, to slay "that which he loved" and die "unpardon'd" (*Manfred,* 2.2185-86). By contrast, George Borrow's popular tale of a Methodist preacher in Wales who repents, having committed what he believes is "pechod Ysprydd Glan," deliberately avoids probing into the nature of that sin (*Lavengro,* chaps. 74–79).

In 19th-cent. American literature, Hawthorne provides the fullest gallery of unpardonable sinners. Chillingworth in *The Scarlet Letter,* Dr. Giacomo Rappacini in "Rappacini's Daughter," the title character of "Ethan Brand" (initially published as "The Unpardonable Sin"), and Digby in "The Man of Adamant: An Apologue" are among Hawthorne's characters suffering from a "separation of the intellect from the heart" (*The American Notebooks of Nathaniel Hawthorne,* ed. R. Stewart [1932], 106), or "the self-destruction of the heart" (S. Dwight, "Hawthorne and the Unpardonable Sin," in *Studies in the Novel* 2 [1970], 455). They sin by treating others merely as objects of aesthetic amusement or scientific inquiry. Chillingworth, e.g., sifts Dimmesdale's soul "for the art's sake" (*The Scarlet Letter,* chap. 10). James E. Miller, Jr., takes Hawthorne's conception of the unpardonable sin to embrace narcissists and promethean intellectuals in general and reckons Melville's Ahab such a blasphemer ("Hawthorne and Melville: The Unpardonable Sin," *PMLA* 70 [1955], 91-114). John Greenleaf Whittier's "The Answer" summarizes the plight of the moral suicide in words which recall Bunyan's "iron cage":

> What if thine eye refuse to see,
>   Thine ear of Heaven's free welcome fail,
> And thou a willing captive be,
>   Thyself thine own dark jail? (st. 15)

Like Hawthorne's unpardonable sinners, Dr. Sloper of Henry James's *Washington Square* uses people as objects for play and experimentation. His creed: knowledge for its own sake, art for art's sake. D. H. Lawrence's reading of the unpardonable sin invites broad comparison with Hawthorne's: the abstracting intellect's want of reverence for the life of the flesh or instinctive consciousness, "the most essential self in us," constitutes "sinning against the Holy Ghost" ("God and the Holy Ghost").

See also BLASPHEMY; DESPAIR; HOLY SPIRIT.

Bibliography. Baym, N. "The Head, the Heart, and the Unpardonable Sin." *NEQ* 40 (1967), 31-47; Brennan, J. X., and S. L. Gross. "The Origin of Hawthorne's Unpardonable Sin." *Boston University Studies in English* 3 (1957), 123-29; Lemonney, A. "Blasphème contre le Saint-Esprit." In *Supplément au Dictionnaire de la Bible.* Ed. Louis Pirot (1928), 1.982-99; McCullen, T., and J. Guilds. "The Unpardonable Sin in Hawthorne: A Re-examination." *NCF* 15 (1960-61), 221-37; Miller, P. *The New England Mind: The Seventeenth Century* (1939); Quinlan, M. J. "William Cowper and the Unpardonable Sin." *JR* 23 (1943), 110-16; Schechter, H. "The Unpardonable Sin in 'Washington Square'." *SSF* 10 (1973), 137-42.   CAMILLE R. LA BOSSIÈRE

UNPROFITABLE SERVANT, PARABLE OF THE

The parable of the unprofitable servant is found in Matt. 25:14-30, with a variant version in Luke 19:12-27. Before traveling into a far country, a wealthy man distributes his money among his servants. In the Matthew version he gives five talents ("a large sum of money" [*IDB*]) to the first, two talents to the second, and one to the third. After his return he finds that by shrewd investment the first two servants have doubled the sums entrusted to them. He praises each of them for his stewardship ("Well done, good and faithful servant") and promises to reward them: "Enter thou into the joy of thy lord." The third servant, who has hidden his talent in the earth, is called wicked and slothful and is scolded for not having at least put the money out on interest. His talent is given to the first servant — "For unto every one that hath shall be given; and he shall have abundance" (v. 29) — and the "unprofitable servant" is cast "into outer darkness," where "there shall be weeping and gnashing of teeth" (v. 30).

The Matthean context suggests that the lord is Christ and the reckoning is the Last Judgment, the emphasis being on the obligation to be active during the time of Christ's absence.

The Fathers interpreted the money as the "office of the Episcopate." St. Augustine admonished spiritual leaders to "look after the salvation of all your household with all vigilance" (*Sermones*, 44; cf. his *De doctrina Christiana*, "Preface," 8). It could also be seen as the teaching of the gospel (e.g., St. Jerome, *In Evangelium Matthaei*) or as the faculty to understand the various meanings of Scripture (e.g., Origen, *Tractate 33* on the Gospel of Matthew). By analogy the five talents came also to mean the five human senses or "each person's ability, whether in the way of protection, or in money, or in teaching, or in what thing soever of the kind" (St. John Chrysostom, *Hom. on Matthew*, 78.3). The enhancement of the talents consequently meant a deeper understanding of the Scriptures (Jerome) or the teaching of them by word and deed (St. Gregory, *Hom. in Matthaeum*, 9), the "profit" (v. 27) of which was the good works of the hearers.

The burying of the one talent was seen by Gregory as the misappropriation of a heavenly gift for earthly purposes — a dictum which was later applied by Wyclif to corrupt spiritual leaders of his times, who worked for their own "honor, advantage, and profit" (*In Omnes Novi Testamenti Libros*, 47b). The thought that God receives his own with usury was taken to be a sign of God's incomprehensible grandeur (Augustine, in *Conf.* 1.4, calls him "never greedy, yet still demanding profit on his loans") and provoked explanations by later exegetes such as St. Thomas Aquinas, who stated that God only demands that good of people which he himself has sown in them (*Summa Theol.* 2-2, q. 62.4 ad 3). The hardness of the lord has usually been seen as irrelevant to the central message (see Calvin, *Harmony of the Gospels*).

Calvin opposed what he called a Roman Catholic teaching — that the unequal distribution of gifts is a matter of personal merit. Later exegetes used the parable to teach the acceptance of God's will and of one's station in life (e.g., Samuel Clarke, *Sermons*, 6). The narrative was also used by English churchmen to denounce the Puritan emigrants as unprofitable servants and America as the "outer darkness" — a thought which Cotton Mather, in *Magnalia Christi Americana* (Intro., sect. 3), sharply rejects.

The ME dialogue *Vices and Virtues* (EETS o.s. 89, 17) follows Gregory in likening the talents (*besantes*) to the five bodily senses: God expects humans to put them to use (cf. a similar use in a sermon collected in EETS o.s. 209, 39-40). Dan Michel's *Ayenbite of Inwit* expresses a thought also found in Thomas's *Summa* (2-2, q.28.3): God's joy is too great to be contained by a mortal person: "guo into þe blisse of þyne lhorde. Naȝt þe blisse of þine lhorde / guo in to þe" (EETS o.s. 23, 269). In *Piers Plowman* (C.9.247-59) Hunger paraphrases the parable of the "wrecche," illustrating to Piers his contention that the Bible reproves idleness. In another place, Imaginatif quotes vv. 21 and 23 to prove that God will not always reject unbaptized people but that he rewards those who are true beyond what he promises (C. 15.214).

St. Thomas More uses the slothful servant's fear as an example of pusillanimity and concludes that "all this fear commeth by the devilles dryft, wherin he taketh occasion of the fayntnes of our good & sure trust in god" (*Dialogue of Comfort against Tribulation*, 2.13). In Shakespeare's *Twelfth Night*, the Clown playfully refers to v. 29 and wishes that "God give them wisdom that have it: and those that are fools, let them use their talents" (1.5.14-16). The Duke's opening speech in *Measure for Measure* (1.1.29-40) echoes the parable and, indeed, the play's basic dramatic situation resembles that of the parable.

George Herbert's poem "Redemption" refers to Luke's version of the parable but reverses the part which speaks of Christ's going to heaven and returning to earth (Luke 19:12). He pictures Christ as a "rich Lord" who has left heaven to go "About some land, which he had dearly bought / Long since on earth, to take possession." Milton's famous "Sonnet 19" sees the exercise of the poet's "one Talent which is death to hide" as impeded by his blindness. But he arrives at the assurance that the will to serve his Maker may be enough: "They also serve who only stand and waite." John Bunyan uses the parable to account for his call to the ministry (*Grace Abounding*, sect. 270), and Dryden sees it fulfilled in the charitable life of the Countess of Abingdon: "Of her five talents, other five she made; / Heav'n, that had largely giv'n, was largely paid" ("Eleonora," 24-25; for further laudatory uses see Samuel Johnson's "On the Death of Dr. Robert Levet" and Robert Southey's "A Vision of Judgment," 7).

Fielding twice alludes to the parable in *Joseph Andrews* (1.3 and 2.8), suggesting that one should not "lament his Condition in this World" but rather endeavor "to improve his Talent, which was all required of him." Swift's sermon "On Mutual Subjection" stresses that "No Man is without his Talent" and ironically observes that worldly kings "have often most abominable Ministers and Stewards, and those generally the vilest, to whom they entrust the most Talents." Cowper considers the question of whether life is "an intrusted talent, or a toy" to be one of the marks distinguishing humans from animals ("Retirement," 650). In "Table Talk" (546) he warns against the preoccupation with "subjects mean and low," since "Neglected talents rust into decay" (cf. his allusion to the parable in "The Task," 2.725, and his ironic reference in "Conversation," 425).

The Romantic theory of art is evidenced in Blake's *Jerusalem* (pl. 77), where the poet equates the talent "which it is a curse to hide" with "Mental Studies and Performances"; elsewhere the talent represents his artistic gifts ("Letter to Thomas Butts," Aug. 16, 1803). Shelley's allusion to Matt. 25:24 in "Song: To the Men of England" is to alert the poor laborers of England to their unjust social situation: "The seed ye sow, another reaps; . . . Sow seed, — but let no tyrant reap; . . ." (for other social applications of the parable cf. Ruskin, "A Joy For Ever," 2.115-20; *Fors Clavigera*, 5.53.8 and 6.68.2, where he clearly distinguishes between God and the image of the "hard man" in v. 24).

When Carlyle's narrator in *Sartor Resartus* (2.7) establishes a solidarity of sinners by calling all people unprofitable servants, he does so in order to exculpate Professor Teufelsdröckh from being a wicked infidel. In Charlotte Brontë's *Shirley* (chap. 23), Rose Yorke has a discussion with Caroline Helstone about whether change is necessary to happiness. She insists, "Better to try all things and find all empty than to try nothing and leave your life a blank. To do this is to commit the sin of him who buried his talent in a napkin — despicable sluggard!"

Dickens refers to the parable in *David Copperfield*, chap. 9, where David calls his nurse Peggotty "that good and faithful servant . . . unto whom my childish heart is certain that the Lord will one day say: 'Well done.' " In similar fashion Abel Magwitch, the escaped convict in *Great Expectations*, thanks his protégé "Pip" for helping him to leave England: "Faithful dear boy, well done. Thankye, thankye!" (chap. 54). Further allusions can be found in Joyce's *Ulysses* (Vintage [1961], 421) and Beckett's *Waiting for Godot* (Faber, 33).

In early American literature Michael Wigglesworth's *The Day of Doom* (st. 60) makes use of the parable's eschatological implications. Another Puritan divine, Edward Taylor, made v. 21 the motto of three of his *Preparatory Meditations* (1.47-49), in which he promises God to use and to improve his poetic and musical gifts.

In his essay "Spiritual Laws" R. W. Emerson (who also alludes to the parable in "Prudence" and "Address to Kossuth") uses "gnashing of the teeth" as a synonym for self-inflicted intellectual and moral complications in a person's life (for a similarly hyperbolical use of this expression, cf. Stephen Crane's poem "I weep and I gnash," in *War Is Kind*, 97).

Melville's narrator in *Pierre* scorns the "downright matter-of-fact" world which does not recognize the spiritual meaning of v. 29 but follows the passage in a rather materialistic manner by "giving unto him who already hath more than enough, still more of the superfluous article, and taking away from him who hath nothing at all, even that which he hath. . . ." In his usual ambiguous way he goes on to suggest that if God really meant this, "then is the truest book in the world a lie" (18.2). When Elmer Gantry, Sinclair Lewis's infamous evangelist, alludes to the parable in one of his sermons, it is to convince businessmen of the "cash value of Christianity" (*Elmer Gantry*, 11.6). In Faulkner's *As I Lay Dying*, on the other hand, Anse Bundren reverses v. 29, claiming that in heaven God will create equality among people by giving to them who have not and taking from them who have.

Harry, the dying protagonist of Hemingway's "The Snows of Kilimanjaro," accuses himself of destroying his writing talent "by not using it, . . . by laziness, by sloth, and by snobbery. . . ." Randall Jarrell says of the American conquerors of the Pacific islands that they, who "hid their single talent in Chicago, / Des Moines, Cheyenne, are buried with it here," apparently equating "talent" with life in general ("The Dead in Melanesia").

The question of God-given talents has an important place at the beginning of John Updike's *Rabbit, Run*. There, in a children's television program, the way to happiness is described as learning to understand one's talents, something which is quite out of keeping with the small-town world in which "Rabbit" Angstrom lives. The parable figures even more largely in Updike's *The Centaur*. There George Caldwell, the frustrated science teacher, believes that he has no talents, but as the man with two talents, who "didn't get sore at the man with five," he comforts himself by saying, "Some have it and some don't. But everybody has something, even if it's just being alive" (chap. 4). According to his family's sardonic comment, his one talent is "to think up some new way of getting sympathy" (chap. 8).

Bibliography. Benrath, G. A. *Wyclifs Bibelkommentar* (1966); Clarke, S. "Of Resignation to the Divine Will in Affliction." *Sermons*, 2nd ed. Ed. John Clarke (1730); Dodd, C. H. *Parables of the Kingdom* (1935; rpt. 1961), 108-14; Jeremias, J. *Die Gleichnisse Jesu: Einführung und Auslegung*, 3rd ed. (1964); Kolve, V. A. "Everyman and the Parable of the Talents." In *The Medieval Drama*. Ed. S. Sticca (1972), 69-98.   MANFRED SIEBALD

UNTO THE PURE   St. Paul's letter to Titus observes that "Unto the pure all things are pure: but unto them that are defiled and unbelieving is nothing pure; but even the mind and conscience is defiled" (1:15). The passage has traditionally been taken, as by St. Augustine, to distinguish between outer and inner cleanness, or "cleanness of manner and purity of heart." Alluding to Christ's condemnation of the Pharisees for their failure to choose the latter (Luke 11:37-41), Augustine says that

> all are unclean who are not made clean by the faith of Christ, according to the expression, "purifying their hearts by faith" [Acts 15:9]; and . . . "Unto them that are defiled and unbelieving is nothing pure; but even their mind and conscience is defiled" [Titus 1:15]. . . . How, then, could all things be clean to the Pharisees, even though they gave alms, if they were not believers? And how could they be believers if they were not willing to have faith in Christ, and be born again of his grace? (*Enchiridion*, 75)

Calvin's commentary develops another line of Augustine's thought (e.g., *De sermone Domini in Monte*, sup. Matt. 5:28), that the internal component in sin is the commitment of the will, or intention, and that a genuinely charitable intention forestalls sinful misappropriation. Hence, as in his commentary on other Pauline passages (e.g., those concerning food laws), Calvin follows Augustine in saying that the verse "asserts our Christian freedom, declaring that nothing is unclean to believers," and stresses that "Christians are pure quite apart from legal ceremonies." He notes, further, that the passage specifically teaches that defiled intentions pollute things which in themselves are pure (*Comm.* sup. Titus 1:15).

Literary allusion seldom takes the text at face value and often, in fact, turns its meaning on its head. Milton merely adapts a Calvinist and Augustinian line of reasoning to support his argument against the censorship of books in *Areopagitica.* But D. H. Lawrence is entirely cynical; deriding the "spiritual love" of Dimmesdale in Hawthorne's *The Scarlet Letter,* he writes *(Studies in Classic American Literature)* of Hawthorne's American Pharisee that his purity "was a lie. . . . We are so pure in spirit. Hi-tiddly-i-ty! Till she tickled him in the right place and he fell. Flop. Flop goes spiritual love. But keep up the game. Keep up appearances. Pure are the pure. To the pure all things, etc." Aldous Huxley, in a chapter entitled "To the Puritan All Things are Impure" *(Music at Night),* expresses similar contempt for what he regards as preposterous contemporary hypocrisy concerning sexual morality.

See also CLEAN, UNCLEAN.

UPRIGHT The Hebrew words *yashar* (e.g., Job 1:1, 8), *yosher* (Ps. 119:7), and in the plural *mesharim yashar* (Ps. 58:1) are found, along with *ṣaddiq* ("righteous"; e.g., Hos. 14:9), indicating the person of scrupulous moral integrity. KJV "upright" (cf. Gk. *dikaios*) has nothing to do with physical erectness, but is an ethical term closely allied to the basic sense of *yashar* ("straight," "level"), the most common Hebrew term so translated. In the self-consciously democratic idiom of American English, "on the level" reasonably captures the moral sense of *yashar.* Indeed, since *yashar* is preeminently a quality of God himself (Pss. 25:8; 84:11) shared by those men and women who live "upright" in God's presence (Ps. 11:7), it is a quality humanly most evident in those who "fear the LORD" (Job 1:1, 8; 2:3; Ps. 112:1-4), and who are most likely to symbolize that reverence by humbling themselves "prostrate" before him. Yet it follows that God's "words do good to him that walketh uprightly" (1 Macc. 2:7), to those who already are striving to live ("walk") in accordance with his Law. The term is found especially in the Psalms, Proverbs, and other wisdom texts of Scripture, and subsequent borrowings usually have one or more texts from these books in mind.

In the writings of the medieval theologians such St. Anselm and St. Bonaventure, rectitude of the will *(rectitudo voluntatis)* is the object of moral philosophy, recognized "in the light of Sacred Scripture." To be "upright," for Bonaventure, is perspectival: one takes one's bearings from God's revelation of himself in Scripture and in Christ as Mediator, strives for ethical conformity to the "rule of life" or the "divine law," and, finally, elevates one's thought to focus on higher spiritual nature (*De*

Reductione Artium in Theologiam, 23-25). A person who possesses such coherence, consistency, and elevated thought is a worthy pilgrim, able to withstand the humbling vicissitudes of temporal fortune because, as Francis Bacon's poem "The Upright Man" (1630) suggests, his life is in consequence "on the level" emotionally as well:

> The man of life upright, whose guiltless heart is free
> From all dishonest deeds and thoughts of vanity:
> The man whose silent days in harmless joys are spent,
> Whom hopes cannot delude, nor fortune discontent;
> That man needs neither towers nor armor for defence,
> Nor secret vaults to fly from thunder's violence:
> He only can behold with unaffrighted eyes
> The horrors of the deep and terrors of the skies;
> Thus scorning all the care that fate or fortune brings,
> He makes the heaven his book, his wisdom heavenly things;
> Good thoughts his only friends, his wealth a well-spent age,
> The earth his sober inn and quiet pilgrimage.

Bibliography. Patrides, C. A. "The Upright Form of Man." *In Premises and Motifs in Renaissance Thought and Literature* (1982).

UR Ur was a city on the Euphrates River in southern Mesopotamia from which Abram originated (Gen. 11:28; 15:7; Neh. 9:7). It has a long and rich history as a temple city as well as a commercial and political center of the great Third Dynasty of Ur (ca. 2100-2000 B.C.). Royal tombs have yielded evidence of a high civilization centuries before Abram's time.

Calvin and Luther interpreted the city as a place of idolatrous worship of the sacred fire or the sun, based on Heb. *'ur,* "fire" (Calvin, *Comms.* 1.337; Luther, *Works,* 2.242).

DAVID W. BAKER

URIAH THE HITTITE Husband of Bathsheba, and faithful soldier of King David, Uriah was murdered by David in order to protect his adultery with Bathsheba (2 Sam. 11; 1 Kings 15:5). Moshe Samir's novel *Kivsat harash* (4th ed. 1959) retells the Bathsheba narrative from Uriah's point of view.

See also BATHSHEBA; DAVID; NATHAN.

URIM AND THUMMIM The terms *Urim* and *Thummim* are transliterations of Hebrew words of uncertain meaning; the terms occur together in five biblical texts (Exod. 28:30; Lev. 8:8; Deut. 33:8; Ezra 2:63; Neh. 7:65), and occasionally Urim stands alone (Num. 27:21; 1 Sam. 28:6). Some versions of the Bible have translated the terms (LXX, "the Manifestation and the Truth" [*tēn dēlōsin kai tēn alētheian*]; Vg *"doctrina et veritas";* Luther, "Licht und Recht"), but the translations have not found wide acceptance, and the etymology of the terms remains unclear. The fact that the words begin with the first and last letters of the Hebrew alphabet *(aleph* and *tau)* may be significant.

The Urim and Thummim were part of the high priest's equipment in ancient Israel, kept in a pocket or bag integral to the priestly ephod. They may have been two stones or sticks; they were used in divinatory practices for determining God's will. Usage is indicated by 1 Sam. 14:41 (LXX); the casting of the lots could give a "yes," "no," or "no answer" response. After David's establishment of a permanent sanctuary in Jerusalem, divination by Urim and Thummim disappears from the OT narrative. There are no references to them in the NT.

In rabbinical tradition, the most popular explanation (e.g., Yoma 73b) identifies Urim and Thummim with the twelve stones on the high priest's breastplate, each engraved with the name of a tribe of Israel (Exod. 28:17-21), and claims oracles were given by illumination, individual stones or letters glowing to reveal their answer. According to Josephus *(Ant.* 3.8.9), oracles were given by the flashing either of the sardonyxes on the high priest's shoulders or the twelve stones stitched into his breastplate — although (he adds) these lights had ceased to shine "two hundred years" before his time.

References to Urim and Thummim in English literature are few in number and restricted to incidental allusion. There are passing references in Donne, "Satyre 5" (83); Elizabeth Barrett Browning, *Casa Guidi Windows* (2.491); and Joyce, *Ulysses* ("Ithaca" episode). In more sustained fashion, George Herbert in "Aaron" weaves the imagery of the high priest's vestments (Exod. 28), including Urim and Thummim ("Light and perfections on the breast") into a meditation on Christ as the priestly archetype who makes even a humble parish priest like Herbert a new Aaron. In Milton's *Paradise Lost,* when Christ rides out to vanquish the rebel angels, he is armed with "radiant *Urim,* work divinely wrought" (6.761; cf. 3.596-601), symbolic of his role as Judge and Light incarnate. Elsewhere Milton refers to the oracular power of Urim in *Reason of Church Government* (1.5) and again in *Paradise Regained* (3.13-15) to "the Oracle/*Urim* and *Thummim,* those oraculous gems / On *Aaron's* breast."

See also AARON.

Bibliography. Robertson, E. "The *Urim* and *Tummim:* What Were They?" *VT* 14 (1964), 67-74; Lindblom, J. "Lot-casting in the Old Testament." *VT* 12 (1962), 164-78; Van Dam, C. "Urim and Thummim." *ISBE* 4.957-59.

PETER C. CRAIGIE
JOHN SPENCER HILL

UZZAH AND AHIO Sons of Abinadab who brought the Ark of the Covenant from Kirjath-jearim to Jerusalem. When Uzzah reached out to steady the Ark as the oxen's unsteady progress shook it, he was struck dead (2 Sam. 6).

See also ARK OF THE COVENANT.

V

VALE OF TEARS The Bible conveys such a strong sense of *lachrymae rerum* that St. Jerome was able to say that "the first man . . . was cast down from paradise into this vale of tears" (NPNF 6.26). The phrase "vale of tears," which is ubiquitous in English literature, derives from the LXX translation of Ps. 84:5-6, where the Hebrew phrase "valley of Baca" was confused with Heb. *bakah,* "weeping," and rendered "valley of weeping," thus entering into Western tradition through the Vg translation, *"in valle lacrymarum"* (Ps. 83:7). The idea of earthly existence as a vale of tears owes also to the biblical promise that God's final salvation will include the wiping away of all tears (Isa. 25:8; Rev. 7:17; 21:4). This same promise is reflected in the beatitude, "Blessed are ye that weep now: for ye shall laugh" (Luke 6:21; cf. Matt. 5:4). St. Augustine explicitly ties the beatitude to Jesus' weeping (NPNF 3.427), and other commentators explain the tears of the Man of Sorrows as a sign of his condescension to humanity (St. John Chrysostom [NPNF 14.232, 242]; St. Cyril [FC 47.121, 123]; St. Athanasius [FC 19.476-78]; St. Hilary of Poitiers [FC 23.442-45]; Calvin, *Harmony of the Gospels,* 2.295). Christ's tears are the basis for Vaughan's "Jesus weeping (1 and 2)" and are alluded to in Nashe's *Christ's Tears over Jerusalem* and in Joyce's *Ulysses.*

Weeping in the Scriptures is frequently the external manifestation of penitence (Ezra 10:1; Neh. 1:4; Joel 2:12-17; Matt. 26:75; Luke 23:28) and is regarded as a prime evidence of contrition by many exegetes. As type of the Church, St. Peter, according to St. Gregory (*Moralia in Iob,* 3.119), "strengthened the root of faith which was . . . withering away, by watering it with his tears." The "voice of weeping and lament" which characterizes the Church in an age of of persecution is the theme of a hymn by the Venerable Bede, but it is to the time when "every tear is wiped away" that the "little flock and blest" ought to turn its expectation (*Hymnum Canentes Martyrum,* trans. J. M. Neale). The tears of repentance are alluded to in Chaucer's *Parson's Tale* (*Canterbury Tales,*10.993-94) and in *The Tale of Melibee,* though in the latter Prudence commends the patience of Job in distinguishing for the weeper "attempree weeping" from "outrageous weeping." Milton ends bk. 10 of his *Paradise Lost* with Adam and Eve shedding tears of contrition; when Michael reveals the history of humanity in the following book, they realize that "the world erelong a world of tears must weep" (11.627), but when they leave Eden their realization of the *felix culpa* wipes away their "natural tears" (12.645; cf. Rev. 7:17; 21:4). Herbert's "Altar" is "Made of a heart and cemented with tears" (2) and, after sin has stained the marble of the "Church-floore," "all is cleansed when the marble weeps" (15). Drowning in tears is linked to the Flood by Milton (*PL* 11.754-58) and by Donne ("Holy Sonnet 5"; cf. Lam. 2:19), who elsewhere makes tears a type of baptism (*Sermons,* 9.290-91). Tears are regarded as God-sends by

Cowper in "To a Protestant Lady" (47-50) and by Blake in "The Grey Monk," where they are "intellectual" (i.e., imaginative) things. Elizabeth Barrett Browning's poem "Tears" is effectively a meditation on the beatitude, "Blessed are they who mourn, for they shall be comforted." For Hopkins, tears are a "melting," a "madrigal" (*Wreck of the Deutschland,* st. 18); for Auden, a "healing fountain" in the "deserts of the heart" ("In Memory of W. B. Yeats"). Dew is an emblem for tears in Marvell's "On a Drop of Dew" and in Herrick's "To Primroses filled with Morning-dew," a poem whose "lecture" confirms the perception that "we came crying hither" (*King Lear,* 4.6.175). The tears in "Jesus weeping [1]," and elsewhere in Vaughan, are compared to "soul-quickning rain" (10) and "live dew" (14). In the Cowper poem, tears find an analogue in the dew on Gideon's fleece (Judg. 6:36-40). The bottle of tears connected with the penance of Spenser's Mirabella (*Faerie Queene,* 6.8.24) and mentioned in Herbert's "Praise [III]" and Vaughan's "The seed growing secretly" is an image doubly related to Ps. 56:8 and the story of Ishmael (Gen. 21:14-19). The impenitent Ahab in Melville's *Moby-Dick* can muster only a single tear, but even it is redeemed by an "allusive comparison" to the widow's mite of Mark 12:41-44 (see H. T. Walter, *Moby Dick and Calvinism* [1977], 148).

Perhaps the most compelling of OT treatments of tears is Ps. 137, which begins "By the rivers of Babylon, there we sat down, yea, we wept, when we remembered Zion." In the ensuing verses, the Israelites' refusal to compromise their faith by singing songs of mirth is a witness to the fact that the "very praise of the Psalms is mourning" (Paschasius of Dumium [FC 62.159]). Versions of this psalm were written not only by authors such as the Countess of Pembroke, Campion, Bacon, Crashaw, Carew, and Denham, but also by Byron, Swinburne, and C. Rossetti. Burns puts it to humorous use in "The Ordination," and T. S. Eliot refers to it ironically in *The Waste Land* (182), where tears become part of the poem's water imagery.

The principal focus of "the literature of tears," as Martz terms a subgenre of Counter-Reformation poetry (*The Poetry of Meditation* [1962], 199-203), is Mary Magdalene, identified by medieval and some Renaissance commentators on three occasions in the Bible as weeping (Luke 7:38; John 11:33; 20:11): from the English pronunciation of her name we have the word *maudlin.* The fullest elaboration on the weeping Mary, who was often identified with the sister of Martha and Lazarus (Luke 10:42; John 12:3), is Crashaw's "The Weeper," a baroque poem whose biblical and exegetical roots have been established by Manning in "The Meaning of 'The Weeper' " (*ELH* 22 [1955], 34-47). Mary Magdalene also figures in medieval mystery plays, such as the Cornwall, Towneley, Chester, York, and Digby cycles. Chaucer, who knew some of these plays and the pseudo-Origen *De Maria Magdalena,* may be alluding to the biblical character ironically when he describes the Wife of Bath's sorrow for her fourth

husband (*CT* 3.587-92; see *ChauR* 12 [1977], 218-33). Among modern examples of the literature of tears the *"Lachrimae"* sequence from Geoffrey Hill's *Tenebrae* (1978) is noteworthy.

See also MAN OF SORROWS; MARY MAGDALENE; RACHEL; RAMAH; RIVERS OF BABYLON. RONALD B. BOND

VALLEY OF THE SHADOW OF DEATH There are many OT instances of the phrase "shadow of death" (Heb. *salmawet*) in the KJV (e.g., Job 3:5; 10:21, 22; 24:17; 34:22; 38:17; Amos 5:8; Jer. 2:6; 13:16), but the most influential uses of the phrase are in Ps. 107:10, Isa. 9:2, and, of course, Ps. 23:4, with its "valley of the shadow of death."

A rabbinic midrash on this latter passage identifies the valley as an allusion "to chastisement in Gehenna, whose fire God will cool for me." St. Irenaeus, in his *Against All the Heresies,* likewise alludes to the valley of the shadow with reference to hell, in this case harrowed by the resurrected Christ: "The Lord 'went away in the midst of the shadow of death' where the souls of the dead were." Luther, in his commentary on Ps. 23, makes a more specific address to the context of the phrase, using the image of the valley as an occasion to offer practical advice for life before the grave:

> Those who are the Lord's sheep are surrounded by much danger and misfortune. . . . Here you must not be guarded by your eyes or follow your reason as the world does. The world cannot see this rich, splendid comfort of the Christians, that they want nothing. . . . Listen to your shepherd.

Calvin, in his *Commentaries,* is similarly concerned with the temporal trials of this life: "The faithful . . . are nevertheless exposed to many perils. . . . When a sheep is walking in a dark valley, only the shepherd's presence keeps it safe from the attacks of wild beasts or from other accidents" (cf. *Inst.* 1.17.11; 3.2.21; 3.2.28; 3.13.5).

Marginal notes to the Geneva Bible refer to one who is "in danger of death as ye shepe that wandreth in the darke valley without his shepherd" — perhaps providing a hint for Bunyan's most famous use of the image. Of Bunyan's Valley of the Shadow in pt. 2 of *Pilgrim's Progress,* certain travelers who have abandoned their pilgrimage report that

> the Valley it self . . . is as dark as pitch: we also saw there Hobgoblins, Satyrs, and Dragons of the Pit: We heard also in that Valley a continual howling and yelling, as of a People under unutterable misery; who there sat bound in affliction and Irons: and over that Valley hangs the discouraging cloud of confusion, death also doth always spread his wings over it: in a word, it is every wit dreadful, being utterly without Order.

Christian, hearing of such horrors, prudently puts up his sword and turns to "All-Prayer." The moral drawn from Job 12:22 stresses in paradoxical terms the victory of Providence over the threat posed by the Valley of the

Shadow: "He discovereth deep things out of darkness, and bringeth out to light the shadow of death."

Notable among other literary allusions is the recollection of Chaucer's Parson (*CT* 10.177) of Job's apprehension of the afterlife — "the lond of mysese and of derknesse, where as is the shadwe of deeth, where as ther is noon ordre or ordinaunce, but grisly drede that evere shal laste." The dying Bosola in Webster's *Duchess of Malfi,* thinking rather of life as a kind of living hell, adds a level of angst (and misogyny) to the reference: "O, this gloomy world! / In what a shadow, or deep pit of darkness, / Doth womanish and fearful mankind live!"

The valley of the shadow has an important place in Poe's *Eldorado,* an evocative poem about the universality of death. And Shaw's Major Barbara, abandoning her Salvationist creed, pronounces a secularized version of Bunyan's paradoxes: the way to life, she says, lies "through the raising of hell to heaven and of man to God, through the unveiling of the eternal light in the Valley of the Shadow."

See also DEATH.   RICHARD SCHELL

VANITY OF VANITIES "Vanity of vanities, saith the Preacher, vanity of vanities; all is vanity" (Eccl. 1:2; Vg *"Vanitas vanitatem . . ."*). This most famous saying of the dyspeptic Qoheleth, commonly identified with Solomon, has become a tag or cliché in literature. It is the refrain, e.g., in William Dunbar's "Of the World is Vanitie," a 15th-cent. Scottish lyricist's denigration of "this vaill of trubbil": *"Vanitas Vanitatum, et omnia Vanitas."* Browning's corrupt bishop in "The Bishop Orders his Tomb at St. Praxed's Church" commences his deathbed request for an absurdly ornate and fabulously expensive tomb inscribed with "Vanity, saith the preacher, vanity" — ironically an epitaph all too suitable. The concluding paragraph of Thackeray's *Vanity Fair,* appropriately enough, cites the "Preacher": "Ah, Vanitas vanitatem!" Melville writes in *Moby-Dick* that "the truest of all books is Solomon's, and Ecclesiastes is the fine hammered steel of woe. 'All is vanity.' ALL. This wilful world hath not got hold of unchristian Solomon's wisdom yet" (chap. 96).

The view that Solomon's book was a source of "unchristian wisdom," echoed in the late 19th cent. by scholars who detected (and admired) "Hellenism" in it, as well as Stoic and Epicurean ideas (e.g., T. Tyler, *Ecclesiastes* [1874]; F. H. Plumptre, *Comm. on Ecclesiastes* [1881]), has since been largely discarded. It was, however, known and approved by Shaw (e.g., in *Man and Superman*), who liked to quote the phrase *vanitas vanitatem* from the author he called "my friend Koheleth." In his own *George Bernard Shaw,* Chesterton comments in response to his friend and rival: "That all is vanity, that life is dust and love is ashes, these are frivolities, these are jokes that a Catholic can afford to utter" ("The Critic").

See also QOHELETH; SOLOMON.

Bibliography. Ginsberg, H. L. *Studies in Koheleth* (1950); Gordis, R. *The Wisdom of Ecclesiastes* (1945); Wright, C. H. H. *Ecclesiastes in Relation to Modern Criticism and Pessimism* (1883).

VASHTI Vashti was the first queen of King Ahasuerus, the Persian Xerxes I (486-485 B.C.). The Hebrew form of her name given in Esth. 1:9-22 suggests that it means "most desired" (>*vahishta*). When she refused to appear at the king's command, after consulting with his court advisers he dismissed her, and from the "fair young virgins" had a replacement sought. Mordecai, a Jew, who had reared his young cousin Hadassah (Esther) as his own adopted daughter, sent her up to the king's house, where she "obtained favor in the sight of all them that looked upon her." Ahasuerus himself "loved Esther above all the women" and selected her to replace Vashti (2:1-17).

Vashti's refusal to obey her husband is granted extenuating circumstances in Jewish commentary, which suggests that his demand was for her to appear before his guests at a banquet naked, so that he could display her superior beauty (Meg. 12b; 'Aggadat Esth. 13; 1 and 2 Tg. Esth. 1:12). In Jewish legend she is sometimes said to have resisted appearing because the angel Gabriel, to effect the salvation of the Jews, had afflicted her with leprosy (Meg. 12b; cf. Midr. Tannaim 174). She is nevertheless often represented as a calculating and somewhat unsavory character.

In the extensive allegorizing of the book of Esther in Christian tradition, Vashti acquires significance only in connection with the elaboration of Esther as a type of the Virgin Mary. This occurred especially in the elaborate interpretation of the Esther/Ahasuerus story as a prefiguration for the relationship of Christ and Mary, where Vashti becomes a symbol for *Synagoga* or the hardened heart (St. Anthony of Padua, *In Annuntiatione Sanctae Mariae,* 3.836b; *In Assumptione Sanctae Mariae Virginiae,* 3.732). Antonian iconography lies directly behind the 15th-cent. lyric by James Ryman (ed. J. Zupitza, no. 20), in which, accordingly, the sexual imagery is imperfectly sublimated:

> King Assuere was wroth, i-wis,
> Whenne quene Vasti had done amys,
> And of her crowne priuat she is;
> But, when Hester his yerde did kis,
> By hir mekenes
> She chaunged his moode into softnes.
>
> King Assuere is god almyght,
> And quene Vasty synagoge hight,
> But when Vasty had lost his lyght,
> Quene Hester thanne did shyne full bright,
> For she forth brought
> The sonne of god, that alle hath wrought.

Plays on the theme, focusing principally upon Esther but highlighting Vashti as a foil, were popular after the Reformation. Here, as in the anonymous *Godly Queene*

Hester (1561), the allegorical possibilities often imply Catholic and Protestant Churches. The same may have been true of *Hester and Ahasuerus* (1594), the text of which is now lost. Domestic farce is the concern of Robert Cox's *King Ahasuerus and Queen Esther* (1673), while Racine's three-act play (1715), widely translated and performed in English, had as its theme "faith triumphant." Lascelles Abercrombi's *Vashti* is a dramatic poem (1912); John Masefield's *Esther* (1922) is an adaptation from Racine. Someone writing under the pseudonym Zeto published a five-act tragedy, *Vashti*, in *Vashti and Other Poems* (1897). A. M. Klein's poem "Five Characters" gives an account of Vashti's refusal which is likewise conversant with the account in Meg. 12b:

> The chamberlain burst on the royal feast
>   Of Vashti, and he caught the women flushed
>   With wine and maiden pleasure. They all blushed.
> But Vashti did not blush, not in the least.
> The chamberlain, as solemn as a priest,
>   Delivered the King's oracle, and hushed
>   The hall. Then Vashti's blood boiled, rushed
> Into her face, but she was pale as East
>   Before the worshippers may praise the dawn,
>   As pale as Shushan-lilies in moonlight
> "The King shall not see me, a naked swan . . ."
> She faltered, weeping almost, but not quite.
>   The chamberlain looked closer; deathly wan
> She was, not pale. No. She was leprous, white.

See also ESTHER.

VEIL The KJV uses the word *veil* (or *vail*) to translate six different Hebrew words, of which five occur only occasionally and refer to garments of various kinds: the most significant of the five is *masweh*, used in Exod. 34:33-35 of the veil worn by Moses to cover his face when it shone with reflected glory after his encounter with God. This story is taken up and allegorized by St. Paul in 2 Cor. 3:13-16, who explains that the glory which attached to the Mosaic covenant was only temporary compared with the lasting glory which shines without hindrance from Christ's face. Paul argues that the veil (Gk. *kalymma* —used by the LXX in Exod. 34) worn by Moses hid this truth from Israel and continues to cover Jewish hearts, but it is removed from all who turn to Christ. In Christ, Paul adds, "great plainness of speech" may replace the "veiled" language of the Law (2 Cor. 3:12).

The sixth Hebrew word is *paroket*, used exclusively of the curtain which divided the Holy Place from the inner sanctum, the Holy of Holies. This curtain, referred to chiefly in Exodus and Leviticus (e.g., Exod. 26:31-35; 40:21-22; Lev. 16:2, 12, 15), screened the Ark of the Covenant from view, and, according to Num. 4:5, was used to cover the ark itself on the journeys through the wilderness. Only the high priest was permitted to pass through the veil of the Temple and then only once a year, on the Day of Atonement. Josephus describes this veil and

another which hung at the entrance to the sanctuary (*Ant.* 3.125-33) and provides considerable information on the Jerusalem Temple of Jesus' time.

The evangelists report that at the moment Jesus died the Temple veil *(katapetasma)* was torn in two from top to bottom (Matt. 27:51; Mark 15:38; Luke 23:45). The KJV understands the veil in Heb. 10:19-22 as being Jesus' "flesh," his crucified body, allowing Christians free access to God. The Gospel story of the torn veil may likewise allude to Jesus' death as giving new access to God but probably was also intended as signifying divine judgment upon the Temple and its claims to exclusive significance as the place where God is to be approached.

In the apocryphal Protevangelium of James and Gospel of Pseudo-Matthew, Mary is said to have been among the undefiled virgins called upon to spin the linen for the Temple veil; little in these stories indicates the significance of the rending of the veil. Among early Christian liturgies appears a "Prayer of the Veil," which identifies the tearing of the veil (Christ's flesh) with immediate access to the holy (ANF 7.543). St. John Chrysostom elaborates the veil-flesh identification in one of his homilies (NPNF 14.438).

With the Reformation, the tearing of the veil came to be seen as a sign of the abolition of the official priesthood; it was sometimes advanced as an argument for plain style rather than elaborate rhetoric or allegory (cf. Heb. 6:9; 9:13). Calvin, in his commentary on Hebrews, sees in the Jewish "cult of the law" material signs of the "Spirit and truth" which "were covered over and hidden. Now that the veil of the Temple is torn, nothing is hidden or obscure." Milton argues with some wit that "the title of Clergy St. Peter gave to all Gods people till Pope Higinus and the succeeding Prelates took it from them . . . as if they had meant to sew up that Jewish vail which Christ by his death on the Cross rent in sunder" (*Reason of Church Government*, chap. 3).

Romantic poetry seizes on the torn veil image as a symbol of an increasingly personal and secular uncovering of truth. Blake's mythic character Vala embodies the veil image complex. Vala's veil is the flesh, covering the human spirit; it is the Mundane Shell, or body of the world, covering all reality; it is the code of moral law. All these things are to be stripped away. In *Jerusalem* (69.43-46) Blake associates the veil with repression and sublimation of sexuality:

> Hence the Infernal Veil grown in the disobedient
>   Female
> Which Jesus rends the whole Druid Law removes
>   away . . .
> Embraces are Cominglings from the Head even to the
>   Feet,
> And not a pompous High Priest entering by a Secret
>   Place.

Wordsworth alludes to the veil in speaking of brief

moments of personal revelation when the eternal shines through ordinary experience. In the "Prospectus" to *The Recluse,* the poet explains how, in his epic of the mind, he "must sink / Deep, and, aloft ascending, breathe in worlds / To which the heaven of heavens is but a veil." In such lines Wordsworth invites his reader to interpret the Miltonic heaven in much the same way as the writer to the Hebrews does the Holy of Holies: "For Christ is not entered into the holy places made with hands, which are the figures of the true; but into heaven itself" (Heb. 9:24).

Like Blake, Shelley associates the veil with repression and the rending of the veil with liberty. Thus, in *The Revolt of Islam,* "with strong speech I tore the veil that hid Nature, and Truth, and Liberty, and Love" (2523-24). In *Prometheus Unbound* life is said to be a veil (3.3.113) which must be torn to free humanity from its self-willed tyranny: "Free from guilt or pain / Which were, for his will made or suffered them" (3.4.198-99).

For subsequent poets the torn veil becomes a common image for revelation (e.g., Tennyson's "The Two Voices," 7-12; "The Holy Grail," 512-28; "The Ring," 35-39; *In Memoriam A. H. H.,* 61.25-28). For Robert Browning the image of the torn veil is used somewhat more casually to indicate clarity or enlightenment (*King Charles,* 1.136; *Sordello,* 4.337-38; 6.612-21; "Balaustion's Adventure," 712-14). Joyce's use of the image is more obviously Romantic if not downright Blakean. In the Proteus chapter of *Ulysses* "the good bishop of cloyne took the veil of the temple out of his shovel hat: veil of space with colored emblems hatched on its field." For Stephen Dedalus the veil is "the ineluctable modality of the inelectable visuality."

Byron is perhaps first to use the allusion to the veil with satiric intent. In *Don Juan* a young Moslem dying in battle is described as having a vision of Paradise:

> With all its veil of mystery drawn apart, . . .
> With Prophets, houris, angels, saints descried
> In one voluptuous blaze, — and then he died.
> But with a heavenly rapture on his face. . . .

Eugene O'Neill strikes a similarly ironic vein in *The Hairy Ape.* The social elite are overheard proposing a church bazaar: "We can devote the procéeds to rehabilitating the veil of the temple. / But that has been done so many times." G. B. Shaw uses the torn veil image complex with a similar mixture of social commentary and irony. In *The Simpleton of the Unexpected Isles,* the English clergyman is seduced into polygamy: "Maya, Maya is my name. I am the veil of the temple. Rend me in twain." The clergyman, a simpleton, learns nothing from his experience.

D. H. Lawrence uses the tearing of the veil as an image of moments of profound sexual experience (see "Passing Visit to Helen" and "Eloi, Eloi, Lama Sabachthani?"). In "Tortoise Shout" the tearing of the veil symbolizes the violation which coition reeks on the individual's solitude:

"Why was the veil torn? / The silken shriek of the soul's torn Membrane?" The poem ends with "That which is whole, torn asunder, / That which is in part, finding its whole again throughout the universe." In the last two lines of W. B. Yeats's "Crazy Jane Talks with the Bishop," "Nothing can be sole or whole / That has not been rent." Yeats's play on the homonyms of "sole" and "whole" suggests the union of the earthy and sublime, the earthly and the spiritual.

See also HOLY OF HOLIES; TEMPLE.

Bibliography. Murrin, M. *The Veil of Allegory* (1969).

WM. DENNIS HORN
MORNA D. HOOKER

VENGEANCE IS MINE St. Paul writes to the Romans concerning the New Law: "Dearly beloved, avenge not yourself, but rather give place unto wrath: for it is written, Vengeance is mine; I will repay, saith the Lord" (Rom. 12:19; cf. Deut. 32:35). Speaking of the biblical writers, Chesterton says, "But they treated vengeance as something too great for man. 'Vengeance is mine, saith the Lord; I will repay.' By contrast Shaw treats vengeance as something too small for man" (*George Bernard Shaw,* "The Dramatist").

See also CHARITY, CUPIDITY; MEEK SHALL INHERIT THE EARTH; TURN THE OTHER CHEEK.

VENI CREATOR SPIRITUS A hymn to the Holy Spirit of the 9th cent. attributed to Rabanus Maurus, and familiar to Western Christendom after the 10th cent. as the Vesper's Hymn of Whitsuntide, as well as at the ordination of priests and bishops. The English translation of Bishop John Cosin was included in the 1662 prayerbook ("Come, Holy Ghost, our souls inspire"), though the version of John Dryden *("Veni Creator Spiritus")* is also worthy of note:

> Creator Spirit, by whose aid
> The world's foundations first were laid,
> Come visit every pious mind. . .

The hymn is rich in biblical allusion, though tracing to no single source.

See also HOLY SPIRIT.

VENI, SANCTE SPIRITUS The Sequence for Whitsunday, once attributed to Pope Innocent III, but more likely the work of Stephen Langton. Translated into English by J. M. Neale ("Come, Thou Holy Paraclete") and E. Caswall ("Holy Spirit, Lord of Light"), it is sometimes confused in allusion with the *Veni Creator Spiritus*. A notable ME version is that by Franciscan William Herebert, edited by C. Brown, *Religious Lyrics of the XIVth Century,* no. 18.

VESSEL Earthen vessels, made of cheap pottery, might contain objects of great value or might perform useful services, as when an oil lamp costing a couple of copper coins gave light to a whole room. In Lam. 4:2 the poet laments that, in the overthrow of Jerusalem, "the precious sons of Zion, comparable to fine gold," have come to be "esteemed as earthen pitchers, the work of the hands of the potter!"

But the text about earthen vessels which is most frequently quoted is 2 Cor. 4:7, "We have this treasure in earthen vessels, that the excellency of the power may be of God, and not of us" — a passage which associates the image firmly with the doctrines of election and predestination (cf. St. Augustine, *De gestis Pelagii*, 7). The "earthen vessels" are the apostles and their associates; the treasure is the gospel entrusted to them, "the glorious gospel of Christ," as it is called in 2 Cor. 4:4. The preachers are expendable; the gospel is precious and durable. If the earthen vessel is broken, it is easily replaced; the gospel is irreplaceable. If success follows the preaching, that is due to no wisdom or skill on the preacher's part but to "the excellency of the power . . . of God."

St. Paul at his conversion is described by the risen Christ as "a chosen vessel unto me" (Acts 9:15); from the Vg *vas electionis* here comes Dante's *vas d'elezione* (*Inferno*, 2.28); cf. *il gran vasello dello Spirito santo* (*Paradiso*, 21.127-28).

As earthen vessels are to the potter, so human beings are to God. A potter's control over the vessels which he molds on his wheel illustrates the Creator's sovereignty over that which he has made, whether nations — as in the visit to the potter described in Jer. 18:1-12, which taught the prophet lessons about God's dealings with Israel and her neighbors — or individuals — as in Paul's discussion of divine election in Rom. 9:19-24. There vessels for honorable and dishonorable use, "vessels of wrath" (or "perdition") and "vessels of mercy," are both made from the same clay; in 2 Tim. 2:20-21 earthen vessels are for ignoble use, but Christians are called to be vessels of precious metal, "meet for the Master's use."

Chaucer's Wife of Bath misquotes the commentary on Rom. 9:21 of one of her patristic adversaries, St. Jerome, when she says in defense of her promiscuity, "For wel ye knowe, a lord in his houshold, / He nath nat every vessel al of gold; / Somme been of tree, and doon hir lord servyse" (3.99-101). Jerome's own argument is that just as in human terms different vessels have different purposes and that which is perfect in one situation is nonetheless imperfect in another, so also there are, in spiritual terms, vessels of gold, silver, brass, and "tree" (wood), and one should accept the lot which has been accorded one (*Adversus Pelagianos*, 1.16). The "Wyf" humorously indicates her own propensity to be a "vessel of wrath" by her learned allusion to a "thunder-mug," the usual wooden vessel in medieval households. Kipling alludes in an antifeminist way to the Colonel's wife in "Watches of the Night" as a "vessel of wrath appointed for destruc-

tion." H. G. Wells plays with the figure differently when he complains that "Gold is abused and made into vessels of dishonour, and abolished from ideal society as though it were the cause instead of the instrument of human baseness" (*A Modern Utopia,* chap. 3). The "vessel unto dishonor" had become associated in patristic exegesis with those whose "hearts have been hardened" (e.g., St. Augustine, *Enchiridion*, 99), an association still reflected in the scene of Rebecca's near-execution in Scott's *Ivanhoe,* where "Each eye wept that looked upon her, and the most hardened bigot regretted the fate that had converted a creature so goodly into a vessel of wrath, and a waged slave of the devil" (chap. 43; cf. Rom. 9:22).

The association of the metaphor with predestination converts in some modern texts into an association with determinism. Hence, one of the scientists in Wells's *The Undying Fire* says of the "grimmer" views of Dr. Barrack, "You say that this Process is utterly beyond knowledge and control. We cannot alter or appease it. It makes some of us vessels of honour and others vessels of dishonour" (chap. 5; cf. 2 Tim. 2:21). Similarly, in the moralizing of Carlyle, the destiny of the idle person was to be "a mere enamelled vessel of dishonour" (*Past and Present*, 3.11). Charlotte Brontë's *Jane Eyre* reflects an almost Arminian restraint on the traditional association: "My Master was long-suffering: so will I be. I cannot give you up to perdition as a vessel of wrath: repent — resolve, while there is yet time" (chap. 35).

Browning's "Rabbi Ben Ezra" affords a memorable allusion to Jer. 18:1-2, when the rabbi says, "Ay, note that Potter's wheel, / That metaphor! And feel / Why time spins fast, why passive lies our clay," concluding that the height of human fulfillment is to accept the employment for which one has been fashioned:

> Earth changes, but thy soul and God stand sure:
> What entered into thee,
> *That* was, is, and shall be:
> Time's wheel runs back or stops: Potter and clay
>   endure. (st. 27)

Bibliography. Morse, C. C. "The Image of the Vessel in Cleanness." *UTQ* 40 (1971), 202-16.   F. F. BRUCE

VEXILLA REGIS "The royal banners forward go," a translation of the 6th-cent. hymn of this title (ascribed to Venantius Fortunatus) by J. M. Neale, is preceded in English literature by the effective rendering of Friar William Herebert (ed. C. Brown, *Religious Lyrics of the XIVth Century,* no. 13). The image alludes to Ps. 20:5 and Song of Songs 6:4.

VIALS OF WRATH In St. John's vision of "final things" seven angels are given, by one of the beasts, seven vials "full of the wrath of God" (Rev. 15:7) which the "great voice" from the temple then commands to be poured out upon the world as seven last plagues (16:1–

17:1). Charlotte Brontë applies the image to Napoleon's final campaign of 1812 in Russia (*Shirley,* chap. 37). Conrad uses the image to describe the coming of a great storm in *Typhoon* (chap. 3).

See also APOCALYPSE; ARMAGEDDON; SEVEN SEALS.

VINE, VINEYARD The vine (Heb. *gepen;* Gk. *ampelos*) and vineyard (Heb. *kerem;* Gk. *ampelōn;* Lat. *vinea*) are central images in all Mediterranean cultures but in no Mediterranean literature are they more richly developed than in the Bible. One of the most memorable passages to make use of the image in the OT is Isaiah's "Song of the Vineyard" (5:1-7), a parable which likens Israel to a vineyard with the "choicest vine, and . . . a tower in the midst of it" (v. 2), which despite its careful tending has produced only wild grapes and is to be "laid waste": "For the vineyard of the LORD of hosts is the house of Israel, and the men of Judah his pleasant plant: and he looked for judgment, but behold oppression; for righteousness, but behold a cry" (v. 7). In the NT the figure is continued, notably in the parables of the vineyard in Matt. 20:1-16 and 21:33-43, where the vineyard is explicitly "the kingdom of God," and which is at last to be taken away from the false husbandmen who have abused it "and given to a nation bringing forth the fruits thereof" (43). (In one of the vagaries of Bible printing, the account of this parable in Luke 20:9-16 was titled the "Parable of the Vinegar," causing the version of royal printer John Baskett [1717] to become known as the "vinegar Bible.")

Central to NT use of the imagery of Isa. 5:1-7 is Jesus' application of it to himself ("I am the vine, ye are the branches") in a parable which has been taken to exhibit the relationship of Christ to the Church, and both to God the Father (John 15:1-10, 16). The fruitfulness of the branches is again stressed, a fruitfulness which can only be assured if the branches remain tightly grafted into the main stock of the vine (vv. 6-7). Since the images in the text are here given their significance, their exegesis in the Fathers is straightforward (e.g., St. Augustine, *In Joan. Ev.* 80, 81, 82), and is not much more prolix in commentaries after the Reformation (e.g., Calvin, Matthew Henry), although in Henry's commentary a concordance of vineyard / husbandry images of the OT and the NT is used to emphasize the theme of the fruit of the Spirit (*Comm. on the Whole Bible,* 5.1122-25).

George Herbert alludes to Isa. 5:1-7 in his "The Sacrifice" (161-63), where Jesus says from the cross: "Then on my head a crown of thorns I wear: / For these are all the grapes *Sion* doth bear, / Though I my vine planted and watred there." John 15:1-10 and the figure of Christ as the Vine (and its vintage) informs Herbert's "Bunch of Grapes" (cf. "Love-Joy") as well as "Good Friday" — "Or can not leaves, but fruit, be signe / Of the true vine?" Isa. 5:4, understood typologically in association with John 15, provides the vineyard as a figure for the Church in Herbert's "The Church Militant."

The notion of a pressing out of the final vintage, rooted in both Isaiah and Matt. 21:33-43, is expressed in relation to the Second Coming and Last Judgment in Rev. 14:18-20. The "grapes . . . of the wrath of God" provide a memorable image in Julia Ward Howe's "Battle Hymn of the Republic" and the title for John Steinbeck's best-known novel, *The Grapes of Wrath.*

See also LABORERS IN THE VINEYARD.

VIOLENT BEAR IT AWAY   See WRESTLING JACOB.

VIRGINITY, CHASTITY In the OT, two words are translated as "virgin." The word commonly used for a woman who has never had sexual intercourse is *betulah* (Gen. 24:16; Lev. 21:3, 14; Deut. 22:19, 23, 28; 2 Sam. 13:2; 1 Kings 1:2; Esth. 2:2; Isa. 62:5). The word is sometimes used metaphorically of a vulnerable city or country, seen as a "virgin" too weak and defenseless to avert the lust and conquering destruction to come upon her (2 Kings 19:21; Isa. 23:12; 37:22; 47:1; Jer. 14:17; 18:13; Amos 5:2).

The word *'almah* refers to a woman who is "ripe sexually," a maid or newly married woman. This word occurs seven times in the OT. It is rendered "maid" in Exod. 2:8 and Prov. 30:19; "damsels" renders the plural in Ps. 68:25. In Gen. 24:43; Cant. 1:3; 6:8; and Isa. 7:14, it is translated "virgin" (KJV). Since early Christian times, Isa. 7:14 has been regarded as a prophecy of the Virgin Birth because of the LXX Greek translation of *parthenos* ("virgin," perhaps implying a virgin dedicated to religious life) for *'almah* (cf. Matt. 1:23). In Gen. 24:16 and 43 Rebekah is called both *betulah* and *'almah,* though technically *'almah* need not always signify a virgin.

In the Jewish culture of the OT, a permanent state of virginity was not thought to be desirable (Gen. 2:18) or a good in itself. To deny marriage could be considered a denial of the image of God, which is viewed as being the marriage of male and female. Numerous biblical texts, notably Prov. 5–7, encourage chastity in the young man, as part of general spiritual purity and also as practical wisdom. Although virginity was the esteemed state for a young unwed woman and was in fact required for a valid marriage (Exod. 22:15; Lev. 21:14; Deut. 22:13-21), to remain unmarried or to be childless was a reproach difficult to bear. In Judg. 11:37 the daughter of Jephthah and her virgin companions bewailed her virginity. That is, they mourned because she was to die before the fulfillment of her life in marriage and childbearing.

In the NT the word *virgin (parthenos)* is used both of women (Matt. 1:23; 25:1, 7, 11; Luke 1:27; Acts 21:9) and men (Rev. 14:4). In 2 Cor. 11:2, it is used metaphorically of the church at Corinth, including males and females, as espoused to one husband, Christ. In 1 Cor. 7:25-38, St. Paul discusses the situation "concerning virgins" at Corinth, indicating his own preference for the unmarried state, especially for those in active ministry.

Some think that the "virgins" of 1 Cor. 7:15 are women only (e.g., KJV, Alford, Morris, Parry); others think that both men and women are under consideration (e.g., Barrett, Bruce, Moffatt); there is also the possibility that only male virgins are addressed (M. Black, *The Scrolls and Christian Origins,* 84-85; cf. J. F. Bound, 13-18, 89-100).

Whatever the case, in the first centuries of the Church, virginity became a Christian ideal for both men and women. A desire to imitate Christ, based on such passages as Matt. 19:12, Luke 18:28-30, and 1 Cor. 7, and the influence of Gnosticism and other asceticisms, caused virginity to be regarded as superior to marriage and on a level of excellence with the sacrifice of martyrs for the faith. Sexuality and marriage were on this view regarded as unfortunate consequences of the Fall and to be avoided by those who would aspire to the perfect life. Most Church Fathers speculated that originally humanity, like the angels, was created virginal and asexual (J. Bugge, *Virginitas,* 2-21). Origen, taking an allegorical approach, saw original human nature as purely spiritual, incapable of possessing sexuality in the sense of fallen humanity (*De principiis,* 2.8.3). St. Clement of Alexandria, however, considered the Fall to be a result of the sexual sin of Adam and Eve in intercourse (*Stromateis,* 3.17 [PG 8.1206). In St. Jerome's *Adversus Helvidium,* on the perpetual virginity of the Virgin Mary, and in his *Adversus Jovinianum,* a vigorous defense of the supremacy of virginity to married life drawn in large part on his interpretation of Paul in 1 Cor. 7:25-40, as well as in his *Ep.* 22 (to Eustochium), he becomes the Western champion of virginity as part of perfection in the spiritual life. Virgins are like "flowers of gold," Jerome writes, but the loss of virginity is an irreparable fall from the possibility of such perfection: "though God is almighty he cannot restore a virginity that has been lost" (*Ep.* 22.5). Celibacy within or after a marriage is much to be preferred to the *status conjugatorum,* or married state, but it remains inferior to original virginity, which for Jerome is the closest mortal flesh can approach the purity of the angels (22.40).

Consequently male and female virgins were described as becoming like the angels, and virginity symbolized the image of purity and innocence. Virgins were referred to as married to Christ and thought to have a special knowledge and direct communion with him. Their love and service were praised as being based upon total devotion and unselfishness which gained God's special favor, protection, and strength against attacks of evil. St. Thomas Aquinas maintains that perpetual chastity produces a special likeness to Christ, entitling those who achieve it to a special *aureola,* or crown (*Summa Theol.,* supp. q.96). Virginity was viewed as a seal of God's special grace for his chosen ones, with assurances of a special salvation for virgins. In fact, virginity was sometimes referred to as a badge of immortality, and for some even as a prerequisite for it.

St. Augustine had expressed a more conservative view of Paul's injunctions, which led him to take a high view of virginity, but also to see marriage as an ordinate good for Christians, even a means of grace (*De bono conjugali).* He argues, contra Origen and others, that the prelapsarian relationship of Adam and Eve was evidently a sexual and matrimonial union and obviously blessed by God: "it is quite clear that they were created male and female, with bodies of different sexes, for the very purpose of begetting offspring, and so increasing, multiplying, and replenishing the earth; and it is great folly to oppose so plain a fact" (*De civ. Dei* 14.22; cf. 14.23-26). As to the question of chastity itself, he maintains that it may not be spiritually violated without consent of the will. Opponents of Christianity, he notes, have mocked at the loss of chastity when in the barbarian rape and pillage of Rome "not only wives and unmarried maidens, but consecrated virgins were violated" (*De civ. Dei* 1.16). Augustine objects, saying that "the virtue which makes the life good has its throne in the soul; . . . the members of the body [become] holy in virtue of the sanctity of the will." While the will remains "firm and unshaken, nothing that another person does with the body, or upon the body, is any fault of the person who suffers it, so long as he [or she] cannot escape from it without sin." Some of the raped virgins, he allows, tragically killed themselves in an effort to avoid disgrace. Of these, he says, "who that has any human feeling would refuse to forgive them?" (1.17). He further condemns anyone who charges survivors with some complicity of will in that they survived. It ought to be evident, he says, that the lust of another person will not pollute an innocent victim (18). He therefore defends the chastity of Lucretia, the "noble matron of ancient Rome," after her rape by the son of Tarquin, commending the saying, "there were two, and only one committed adultery." He condemns, moreover, the failure of Roman justice to execute the young profligate for the crime (he was merely banished). Lucretia herself suffered "the extreme penalty," he observes, committing suicide because there was no way in Roman society to escape her shame: "she could not exhibit to men her conscience, but she judged that her self-inflicted punishment would testify to her state of mind." Here, Augustine concludes, is one of the clear advantages of a Christian spiritual perspective on the true seat of virtue. The raped Christian virgins "who suffered as she did and yet survive . . . declined to avenge upon themselves the guilt of others, and so add crimes of their own to those crimes in which they had no share." Within their own souls, Augustine says, they continue to "enjoy the glory of chastity." In God's eyes they are pure, and ought to be so in the eyes of their contemporaries and of posterity (19). This famous discussion lies behind and conditions numerous medieval and Renaissance treatments of the difference between pagan and Christian location of the virtue of virginity, examples of which include Chaucer's *Franklin's Tale* and *Physician's Tale,* as well as Shakespeare's *Rape of Lucrece.*

Initially the Church as the Bride of Christ was understood to refer to all Christian believers, whether male or female (2 Cor. 11:2). By the 4th cent., however, some writers were arguing that only consecrated virgin women were considered to be Christ's Bride (Schillebeeckx, *Celibacy*, 30; Bugge, *Virginitas*, 59-74). By the Middle Ages the literature expresses an increased emphasis upon the feminine role of virginity. The female virgin was encouraged to be submissive to Christ, and to draw upon her distinctly female resources to woo and hold his love. Thus the movement was away from the asexual ideal of virginity toward one expressed in distinctly (female) sexual imagery. In some quarters the effect of such tendencies was to disqualify the ideal of male monasticism from the fullest measure of Christ's love (Bugge, 106-10). But two complementary figurations of chaste love emerged. In the first of these male writers characterize their own "voice" in meditational literature as though they themselves were female — a common late medieval phenomenon (e.g., Richard Rolle). Alternatively, following St. Bernard of Clairvaux and increasingly from the 13th to 15th cents. the male monastic writer might represent himself as a chaste love-servant of the Virgin Mary.

The Reformation revolted against the monastic ideal of virginity, criticizing views of justification based upon sacerdotalism and ascetic celibacy (Lea, *Sacerdotal Celibacy*, 353-428). Arguing for a return to the Scriptures, Protestants emphasized justification by faith alone, and again referred to the Bride of Christ as including all Christian believers, whether male or female, married or single. Partly in response, the Council of Trent (24.10) reaffirmed Catholic views that virginity or celibacy was preferable to the state of marriage, and pronounced an anathema on opposing doctrine.

As a literary topic or motif, virginity appears in medieval contexts most frequently in relation to the Virgin Mary, Mother of Jesus, where vernacular literature became an important means of teaching her virginity as an exemplary spiritual value as well as theologically defending the doctrine of the Incarnation. It is also an important motif in poems like the ME *Pearl* (cf. Rev. 4:14), where virginity is a condition of spiritual innocence and figures membership in the 144,000 "Brides of the Lamb" in the New Jerusalem. Its notorious absence may be a condition for a story of conversion, such as in the Digby saints' play *Mary Magdalen*, or a means of characterizing persistent carnality and antagonism to conversion, as in Chaucer's presentation of the Wife of Bath. Dame Alice, as Chaucer calls her, takes the position of Jovinian against Jerome in its most vigorous form, citing from Jerome's summation of Jovinian, and perverting Jerome's text to make her contrary assertions:

Virginitee is greet perfeccioun,
And continence eek with devocioun,
But Crist, that of perfeccioun is welle,

Bad nat every wight he sholde go selle
Al that he hadde and gyve it to the poore,
And in swich wise folwe hym and his foore.
He spak to hem that wolde lyve parfitly;
And lordynges, by youre leve, that am nat I.
I wol bistowe the flour of al myn age
In the actes and in fruyt of mariage. (*CT* 3.105-14; cf. 59-104)

In Sir Thomas Malory's *Morte Darthur*, where the vow of chastity taken by knights is a leitmotif, knights who have kept this vow appear on Pentecost at Arthur's court for a tournament in honor of the Holy Grail: "And they with the coverynge of whyght betokenyth virginite, and they that hath chosyn chastite" (15.6.21).

Though Luther, Calvin, and most of the Reformers viewed marriage as a normative creational good and even, on biblical precedent, as a condition of representative leadership in the community of faith (e.g., Calvin, *Inst.* 4.12.23), Protestant poetry of the Reformation period could and did celebrate virginity as a spiritual ideal. The third book of Spenser's *The Faerie Queene* provides an extended example (though in this case the celebration also involves political homage to Elizabeth I, the "Virgin Queen").

Sometimes, as in Shakespeare's *The Tempest* or *Measure for Measure*, virginity is set in tension with the commerce of worldliness, or with another Christian virtue: Angelo's attempts to force Isabella to choose between charity and chastity (*caritas / castitas*) expresses a contrivance, or social "dilemma," familiar from the Middle Ages (e.g., Chaucer's *Franklin's Tale*), which itself becomes a theme in Renaissance literature (see E. Wynd, *Pagan Mysteries of the Renaissance*). Milton's *Comus, A Masque* (1634) is a defense of chastity in which the Puritan poet allows to Comus (the classical spirit of revelry) an extended speech in which he pleads that the Lady's chastity blasphemes Nature — an old and familiar line, celebrated and parodied alike by 17th-cent. poets (Donne, Herrick, Marvell) in *carpe diem* addresses to putatively virginal ladies. For Milton the Lady's temptation is a parallel to the seduction of Eve by Satan in *Paradise Lost* — virginity (or chastity) is to be a tested virtue (cf. William D'Avenant's *The Fair Favorite*, a Neoplatonic etherealizing of virginity).

Anglican bishop Jeremy Taylor's *Holy Living* (1650) characterizes virginity in relation to chastity, continence, and marriage in terms which seem drawn almost directly from Jerome:

Chastity is either *abstinence* or *continence*. *Abstinence* is that of Virgins or Widows: *Continence* of married persons. *Chaste marriages* are honorable and pleasing to God: *Widowhood* is pitiable in its solitariness and losse, but amiable and comely when it is adorned with gravity and purity, and not sullied with remembrances of the passed license, nor with present desires of returning to a second bed. But *Virginity* is a life of Angels, the enamel of the soul, the huge advantage of religion, the great opportunity for the retirements of devotion: and being empty of cares, it is full of prayers: being unmingled with the World, it is apt to converse with God: and by not feeling the warmth of a too forward and indulgent nature, flames out with holy fires, till it be burning like the Cherubim and the most ecstasied order of holy and un-polluted Spirits.

Nicholas Ferrar's community of Anglican Faithful at *Little Gidding* included his nieces, Mary Collett and her sister Anna, who took vows of perpetual virginity despite the opposition of their local bishop. This helped occasion a virulent Puritan attack upon the community in a pamphlet entitled *The Arminian Nunnery* (1641), which denounced Little Gidding as an attempt to reintroduce "Papism" into England. (The community was broken up and dispersed by the Puritans in 1646.)

In the 18th cent. latitudinarian loosening and "naturalizing" of biblical sexual standards in general helped to promote the kind of satirizing of virginity and chastity (among males in particular) that Henry Fielding presents in his novels *Joseph Andrews* (1742) and *Tom Jones* (1749), each of whom is described in such matters as "no better than he should be." Sexual double standards, by which ironically virginity becomes a commodity with a calculable market value, are the basis for novels such as Samuel Richardson's *Pamela* (1740) and *Clarissa* (1747-48), which are ostensibly concerned with the vulnerability of virginity as a spiritual and moral quality. Among the Romantics virginity is alternatively condemned as false virtue (e.g., Blake's "pale virgin shrouded in snow") or its virtues attributed to gross carnality, as in the pagan ideal of vestal virgin or "Virgin Whore" (e.g., Swinburne). Baudelaire's "Whore with a heart of gold" is expressive of antinomian revivals of the "courtly" heroine of unattainable love in the poetry of France as well as England. Rimbaud's poet "Savant" is one whose *gnosis* includes the revelation of sexual novelty — he debauches himself to make himself a *voyant,* a seer (*Oeuvres Complètes,* 270-71; cf. 268). Byron championed this view in both life and art *(Don Juan)*. Such ideas acquire a religious-erotic force as early as Keats and become a major feature of poetry in the Pre-Raphaelite movement and notably in Swinburne. The inversion dominates in much of the poetry of Oscar Wilde, in whose *Flowers of Gold* the flowering is a deflowering, and the aureola crowns a phallic "spear of the lily" ("In the Gold Room").

See also ADULTERY; BRIDE, BRIDEGROOM; CHARITY, CUPIDITY; JEPHTHAH AND HIS DAUGHTER; MARY, MOTHER OF JESUS.

Bibliography. Auer, A. "The Meaning of Celibacy." In *Celibacy and Virginity* (1968); Black, M. *The Scrolls and Christian Origins: Studies in the Jewish Background of the New Testament* (1961); Bloomfield, M. "Three Grades of Chastity: Tradition in the Middle Ages." *Anglia* 76 (1958), 227-53; Bound, J. F. "Paul's View of Celibacy as Presented in I Corinthians 7:25-40." M.A. thesis, University of Mon-

treal, 1979; Brill, L. W. "Chastity as Ideal Sexuality in the Third Book of *The Faerie Queene.*" *SEL* 11 (1971), 15-26; Bugge, J. *Virginitas: An Essay in the History of a Medieval Ideal* (1975); Camelot, O. P. *Virgines Christi: La Virginité aux premiers siècles de l'église* (1944); Hunt, I. "Celibacy in Scripture." In *Celibacy: The Necessary Option.* Ed. G. H. Brein (1968), 123-37; Lea, H. C. *The History of Sacerdotal Celibacy in the Christian Church* (1957); Moonan, J. T., Jr. "Celibacy in the Fathers of the Church: The Problematic and Some Problems." *Celibacy: The Necessary Option.* Ed. G. H. Brein (1968), 138-51; Plumptre, E. H. "Celibacy." *A Dictionary of Christian Antiquities,* vol. 1. Eds. W. Smith and S. Cheetham (1968); Relle, E. G. "Studies in the Presentation of Chastity Chiefly in the Post-Reformation English Literature, with Particular Reference to Its Ecclesiastical and Political Connotations and to Milton's Treatment of the Theme in *Comus.*" Ph.D. diss., Cambridge, 1969; Schillebeeckx, E. *Celibacy.* Trans. C. A. L. Jarrott (1968); Unrue, J. C. "*Hali Meidenhad* and other Virginity Treatises." *DAI* 31 (1971), 5378A.
                                                                                JAMES F. BOUND

VOCATION   The term *vocation,* like its cognate *calling,* commands a wide variety of meaning in the Bible. In Prov. 1–9, e.g., divine Wisdom is described as a street preacher who "calls" to "the sons of men" (8:4), entreating them to forsake folly and follow her. The call can also be a divine summons to a special function, such as that of prophet in Deutero-Isaiah (51:2), or, complementarily, a peculiar mark of gracious condescension (Amos 5:14-15). In general terms, while the calling out, or election, of individuals such as Abraham, Moses, Ezekiel, or even Cyrus is featured in OT narrative, the OT gives preeminent emphasis to national calling — to Israel's election as a "kingdom of priests and an holy nation" (Exod. 19:6).

In the NT, on the other hand, the emphasis on vocation is primarily personal. The individual is called to faith and salvation (Matt. 22:14; Rom. 11:29; Eph. 1:18, 4:4; Phil. 3:14; 2 Thess. 1:11; 2 Tim. 1:9; Heb. 3:1; 2 Pet. 1:10), good works being the seal and pledge of that calling (Matt. 5:16). In the Gospels the personal call is to leave everything and follow Jesus (Mark 10:28). Those who are "sent out" for the first time with a specific vocation in his service (Matt. 10:5; Mark 6:7; Luke 9:1) are named "apostles."

In early Christian tradition the form in which the question of vocation typically arose was the call to monastic life. Athanasius's life of St. Anthony (ca. A.D. 357) introduced the monastic ideal to the West. St. John Cassian elaborated different types of such vocation (PL 49.560-64), one of which, favored also by St. Benedict, was the presentation of young children to a monastic order by their parents — an option which persisted into and beyond the 11th cent. Other patristic writings on religious vocation include the discourse by St. Ephraim Syrus on the greatness of the priesthood, St. Jerome's commentary on the Epistle to the Galatians, and, especially, St. Gregory the Great's *Regulae pastoralis,* a manual on sacerdotal perfection. Among treatments by doctors of the Church, three works on the theology of vocation by St. Thomas Aquinas are noteworthy: *Contra Impugnantes Religionem, De Perfectione Vitae Spiritualis,* and *Contra Retrahentes ab Ingressu in Religionem.*

For medieval Christianity *vocation* continued to mean primarily "religious vocation" and was thus associated directly with the sacrament of holy orders. An individual was called out of the world to exercise a special function as priest, nun, friar, or monk. Chaucer's *Canterbury Tales* depicts a variety of characters who claim formal religious calling — some of whom serve with faithful *entente* and others of whom are characterized by radical infidelity or hypocrisy. Antifraternal and anticlerical satire in this period (reflected also, e.g., in *Piers Plowman*) often calls those of professed religious vocation to account before the creeds and vows upon which the legitimacy of their calling depends. Thus, Chaucer's *Summoner's Tale* presents a friar who in almost every respect betrays the Franciscan Rule; knowledge of the standard to which he is called permits Chaucer's readers to enjoy an intensely satiric characterization of his "vocation."

In the Reformation period, the idea that temporal and spiritual vocation are intimately connected gained emphasis. Luther, e.g., taught that all lawful occupations were divine callings, citing 1 Cor. 7:20, among other passages, as supporting evidence. Calvin shared this conviction, which became a staple of English Puritanism and found acceptance also with Anglicans. This secular yet divine calling required the individual to seek sanctification by engaging in the trade or profession assigned to him by God, best captured in the phrase *laborare est orare.* The form this sense of "Christian Calling" took in the writing of American Puritans, as exemplified in John Cotton's essay of that name, required an acute sense of balance between management of worldly affairs and mindfulness of spiritual affections (ed. P. Miller, 171-81). The idea of the sanctification of ordinary work had precedents in the writings of the Fathers, such as St. Clement of Alexandria's "Since we are convinced that God is to be found everywhere, we plough our fields praising the Lord, we sail the seas and ply all our other trades singing his mercies" (*Stromateis,* 7.7 [PG 9.45]). In the 14th cent. this concept was well developed in Walter Hilton's *Epistle on the Mixed Life,* in which ordinary labor is made prerequisite to spiritual labor, and a balance between them is seen as forming a distinctive variety of lay vocation. The doctrine in its distinctive Protestant guise was familiar enough in 16th- and 17th-cent. England to make it a ready subject for parody, so that Falstaff in *1 Henry 4* could invoke it to justify his addiction to larceny:

> *Prince*   I see a good amendment of life in thee — from praying to purse-taking.
>
> *Falstaff*   Why, Hal, 'tis my vocation, Hal. 'Tis no sin for a man to labour in his vocation. (1.2.103-06)

Similarly, in the 18th cent., Swift could write ironically, "a Whore in her vocation / Keeps punctual to an assignation" ("To Stella, Visiting Me in My Sickness").

Another important aspect of the understanding of vocation in Reformed thought relates to the distinction between *vocatio universalis* and *vocatio specialis.* In *De Doctrina Christiana* Milton argues that

> It is by *general* vocation that God invites all men to a knowledge of his true godhead. He does this in various ways, but all of them are sufficient to his purpose. . . . *Special* vocation means that God, whenever he chooses, invites certain selected individuals, either from the so-called elect or from the reprobate, more clearly and insistently than is normal. (*Complete Prose Works,* ed. Wolfe, 6.455; italics added)

Milton's God makes the same distinction in *Paradise Lost:*

> Some I have chosen of peculiar grace
> Elect above the rest; so is my will:
> The rest shall hear me call, and oft be warned
> Their sinful state, and to appease betimes
> The incensed Deity, while offered grace
> Invites; for I will clear their senses dark,
> What may suffice, and soften stony hearts
> To pray, repent, and bring obedience due. (3.183-90)

During the Counter-Reformation, the idea of vocation also occupied a central place in *The Spiritual Exercises* of St. Ignatius of Loyola, who counseled the faithful to seek God's will in three states of life: marriage, the priesthood, or the religious life. *The Spiritual Exercises* were a clear influence on John Donne's *Holy Sonnets,* and it has been suggested that these poems were the outgrowth of the poet's struggles with the problems of "election" or, in his case, a vocation to the priesthood in the Anglican Church. The difficulties of a priestly vocation are perhaps nowhere more dramatically presented than in George Herbert's "The Collar" (with its pun on "Caller"). At the climax of the poem the speaker's rebellion is overcome by a spirit of obedience to his call:

> But as I rav'd and grew more fierce and wilde
> At every word,
> Methoughts I heard one calling, *Child!*
> And I reply'd, *My Lord.*

In *A Priest to the Temple; or, the Country Parson* (32.15-18) and elsewhere, Herbert constantly praises vocation, work as opposed to idleness. This value set the stage for Carlyle's denunciation of the aristocracy's idleness and his cries of "Work! Work! Work!" in the 19th cent. Carlyle's lectures *On Heroes, Hero-Worship, and the Heroic in History,* which presented the Calvinist notion that a saint is a person who is called by an external agency to undertake some great worldly task, brought the idea of vocation once again into the foreground.

The Puritan view of profession, coupled with the economic ideology which Weber labeled the Protestant work ethic, provided a theological and thematic center of the 19th-cent. "novel of vocation." In chap. 15 of *Middlemarch,* e.g., George Eliot reflects that "in the multitude of middle-aged men who go about their vocation in a daily course determined for them in much the same way as the tie of their cravats, there is always a good number who once meant to shape their own deeds and alter the world a little." Eliot underlines a shift in vocational destiny — from man's relation to woman to his relation to the world. The writer's subjects, she claims, must now be the central experiences of the new age: work, vocation, and the passion to improve the world. It is interesting in this connection that the pastoral teaching "The labourer is worthy of his hire" (Luke 10:7) makes what is apparently its first and only English literary appearance in the work of Robert Browning ("With George Bulib Dodington," 16). Ben Jonson's cry "What several wayes men to their calling have!" ("On a Reformed Gam'ster," 7) still reverberates in the Victorian era. The search for an appropriate secular vocation is a characteristic feature of Dickens's novels, especially *Great Expectations* and *David Copperfield,* as it is of Hardy's *Jude the Obscure* and the literary locus classicus of the work ethic, Defoe's *Robinson Crusoe.* Wordsworth speaks of the "shepherd's calling" ("Michael," 46), of the "fine vocation of the sword and lance," i.e., knighthood (*Excursion,* 8.40), Coleridge of an apothecary's vocation ("The Devil's Thoughts," 18), and Byron of the singer's vocation (*Don Juan,* 4.80.6). Tennyson's St. Telemachus, who accepts martyrdom in the Colosseum as he repeats to himself "the call of God" ("St. Telemachus," 27, 42), is a notable exception to this secularized application.

In the 20th cent. James Joyce transfers this idea of the call to martyrdom from the religious to the aesthetic realm. His hero, Stephen Dedalus, imagines himself to be a martyr like his prototype, St. Stephen — but for his art rather than for God. At the end of chap. 4 of *A Portrait of the Artist as a Young Man,* the director of the Jesuit college asks Stephen, "Have you ever felt you had a vocation?" "To receive that call," he continues, "is the greatest honor the Almighty God can bestow on a man"; no one else on earth has the priest's "secret power" given by God to "bind and loose from sin," to transubstantiate. Dedalus, however, refuses the divine call, choosing rather to create proudly out of the freedom and power of his soul — transmuting the daily bread of experience into art. Stephen's vocation has all the traditional trappings of the sacred, but it is art, or the worship of art's devotées, not God, which calls him.

In American poetry, Robert Frost offers to redress the balance between art and religion in "Two Tramps in Mud Time" (66-72):

> My object in living is to unite
> My avocation and my vocation
> As my two eyes make me one in sight.
> Only where love and need are one,
> And the work is play for mortal stakes,
> Is the deed ever really done
> For Heaven and the future's sake.

See also APOSTLE.

Bibliography. Denzinger, H., and A. Schönmetzer. *Enchiridion Symbolorum* (1965); Douglas, R. M. "Talent and Vocation in Humanist and Protestant Thought." In *Action and Conviction in Early Modern Europe: Essays in Memory of E. H. Harbison.* Ed. T. K. Rabb and J. E. Siegel (1969); Michaelson, R. S. "Changes in the Puritan Concept of Calling or Vocation." *NEQ* 26 (1953), 315-36; Milward, P. *Christian Themes in English Literature* (1967).

DOMINIC MANGANIELLO

VOICE FROM THE WHIRLWIND   *See* JOB.

VOICE OF THE TURTLE   Actually, the turtledove, or mourning dove (Song of Songs 2:12); its call to love is parodied by Chaucer in his *Merchant's Tale,* where old Januarie beckons his young wife out into his enclosed garden with lines more familiar to medieval readers for their allegorical association with the Bridegroom and his eternal Bride:

> Rys up, my wyf, my love, my lady free!
> The turtles voyse is herd, my dowve sweete;
> The wynter is goon with alle his reynes weete.
> (4.2138-40)

See also SONG OF SONGS.

VOICE THAT CRIETH IN THE WILDERNESS   *See* JOHN THE BAPTIST.

VOX CLAMANTIS   John the Baptist responded to the Pharisees' questions concerning his identity and mission by making analogy with the prophet Isaiah: "I am the voice of one crying (Vg *vox clamantis*) in the wilderness, Make straight the way of the Lord, as said the prophet Esaias" (John 1:23). The notion of an unpopular call to repentance — especially national repentance — in Isaiah and John makes the phrase an ideal title for John Gower's late medieval poem of the same purpose.

See also JOHN THE BAPTIST.

W

WAGES OF SIN In his Epistle to the Romans St. Paul writes, "For the wages of sin is death, but the gift of God is eternal life through Jesus Christ our Lord" (6:23). This verse was particularly important to Reformation commentators, with their strong emphasis on "justification by faith." Calvin understands it to say, "As the cause of death is sin, so righteousness, which is Christ's gift to us, restores eternal life to us" (*Comm.* sup. Rom. 6:2; cf. Matthew Tyndale, *Parable of the Wicked Mammon* [ed. Russell], 1.110). For Tyndale, the "wages of the devil" are "the pleasures of this world, which are the earnest of everlasting damnation" (*Obedience of a Christian Man,* pref. 1.177).

In Marlowe's *Tragical Historie of Doctor Faustus,* one of the early clues to the audience that Faustus's impending damnation is self-willed is his perverse half-reading of crucial scriptural texts; for a professor of theology at Wittenberg his misconstrual of Rom. 6:23 is particularly telling of his rejection of grace:

> *Ieromes* Bible *Faustus,* view it well:
> *Stipendium peccati, mors est: ha, stipendium,* &c.
> The reward of sin is death? that's hard:
> *Si peccasse, negamus, fallimur, & julla est in nobis*
>   *veritas*:
> If we say that we haue no sinne
> We deceiue our selues, and there is no truth in vs.
> Why then belike we must sinne,
> And so consequently die,
> I, we must die, an euerlasting death. (1.1.65-73)

The supplementary verse (1 John 1:8) is likewise a half-quotation; Faustus omits v. 9: "If we confess our sins, he is faithful and just to forgive us our sins, and to cleanse us from all unrighteousness."

In Bunyan's *Pilgrim's Progress,* Apollyon confronts Christian as he traverses the Valley of Humiliation, claiming him as one of his subjects. Christian replies, "I was born indeed in your dominions, but your service was hard, and your wages such as a man could not live on, for the Wages of Sin is death." Tennyson incorporates the text in his poem "Wages," as does Carlyle to more dramatic effect in *The French Revolution* (2.6). In a commentary on the American "success Gospel," Richard Wright reminisces in *Black Boy* how when he came home from a road trip with a salesman-evangelist, his Granny was hopeful that some of his sins might have been remitted, "for she felt that success spelled the renewal of righteousness and that failure was the wages of sin."

WALK ON WATER *See* PETER.

WALK WITH GOD *See* ENOCH.

WANDERING JEW The legend of the Wandering Jew is not biblical, but probably of medieval folk origin. It has its first recorded appearance in the *Flores Historiarum* (1228) of Roger of Wendover, an English monk of St. Albans, who tells how a visiting Armenian

817

archbishop told of entertaining the Wandering Jew, who represented himself as originally one Cartaphilus, a doorkeeper to Pontius Pilate, who had personally struck Jesus while he was laboring to bear his cross to the place of crucifixion. He has also occasionally been identified with the officer of the high priest who struck Jesus at his trial (John 18:22). Cartaphilus apparently taunted Jesus, saying, according to the legend, "Go faster! Why linger about?" to which Jesus is said to have replied: "I indeed am going, but you shall tarry until I come." After a time, the man converted and was renamed Joseph. Matthew Paris expanded the story in his *Chronica Majora* (1259), a likely source for the brief cameo in the alliterative *Morte Arthure*. Versions of this tale surface in the 13th cent. in the Lowlands (Chronicles of Phillipe Mousket of Tournai) in 14th-cent. Italy, where the Wandering Jew is called Giovanni Buttadeo (Strikegod), and by the late 16th cent. in Germany Paulus von Eitzen, Lutheran bishop of Hamburg, claimed to have met this person in 1542, but on this occasion he was called Ahasuerus and had never converted. A pamphlet recounting the German version was published at Leyden in 1602.

The German tradition has received most literary attention. Goethe apparently contemplated (but did not compose) a poem fictionalizing a meeting between "Ahasuerus" and Spinoza. C. F. D. Schubert (1739-91) wrote a romantic version in which the wanderer represents discordant nature; the narrative is picked up in M. G. Lewis's *The Monk* (1796) and C. R. Maturin's *Melmoth the Wanderer* (1820), both of the "Gothic horror" school of fiction, and it forms the basis of a ballad in Percy's *Reliques of Ancient English Poetry* (1765). George Croly's speculative "historical" romance *Salathiel* (1828) grants the wanderer heroic pathos, preparing the way for Eugene Sue's *Le Juif errant* (1844-45). Here the protagonist is named Samuel, and has to endure his extended mortality with Herodias, wife of Herod Antipas, but the narrative is polemically anti-Jesuit.

See also MALCHUS.

Bibliography. Anderson, G. K. *The Legend of the Wandering Jew* (1965); Briggs, K. M. "The Legends of Lilith and of the Wandering Jew in Nineteenth-Century Literature." *Folklore* 92 (1981), 132-40; Fulmer, O. B. "The Wandering Jew in English Romantic Poetry." *DA* 27 (1967), 455A-456A; Leschitzer, A. F. "Reflections on Medieval Anti-Judaism, 5: The Wandering Jew. The Alienation of the Jewish Image in Christian Consciousness." In L. White, ed. *Viator: Medieval and Renaissance Studies* 2 (1971), 391-96.

WAR IN HEAVEN   Among the terrible events seen by St. John the Divine in his Revelation was a "war in heaven" in which "Michael and his angels fought against the dragon; and the dragon fought and his angels, And prevailed not; neither was their place found any more in heaven. And the great dragon was cast out, that old ser-

pent, called the Devil, and Satan, which deceiveth the whole world; he was cast out" (Rev. 12:7-9).

A large variety of interpretations attend this passage. Within the English commentary tradition, that of Thomas Brightman, in *A Revelation of the Revelation* (1615), is noteworthy: it takes the passage as predictive of an apocalyptic last battle on earth, in which the Jews would defeat the "dragon Turk," and the Western Protestants defeat the Roman Antichrist (836-38). These temporal forces would be led by "some excellent man, in whose person he may present a visible Michael" (see also his *A Most Comfortable Exposition of the last and most difficult parts of the Prophecie of Daniel* [1644], 937). The general outlines of this reading follow from the annotations of Franciscus Junius, incorporated into the 1602 Annotated Geneva New Testament.

Milton applies the motif rather to the rebellion of Lucifer and his cohorts, who are contested by Michael and Gabriel but finally defeated when Christ himself, as champion, throws the rebels out of heaven: "Nine days they fell; confounded Chaos roared . . ." (*Paradise Lost*, 1.34-49, 100-105; 6.1-912). In Milton, then, "War in Heaven / Among th' Angelic Powers" is what sets the stage for the Fall of mankind on earth. In Matthew Henry's *Commentary* the dragon is Satan, while his opponent, figuratively the Woman, is the Church in the world, struggling for victory in Christ: the account is "not a prediction of things to come, but rather a recapitulation and representation of things past, which, as God would have the apostle to foresee while future, he would have him to review now that they were past, that he might have a more perfect idea of them in his mind" (*Comm.* 6.1159-60). In Blake's mythic appropriation, "the apocalypse, like the Incarnation and Crucifixion, must be inseparable from the fallen body" (Damrosch, 34). The image is therefore redirected: "This Wine-press is called War on Earth, it is the Printing Press / of Los; and here he lays his words in order above the mortal brain / As cogs are form'd in a wheel" (*Milton*, 29.8-10). Charles Williams's novel *War in Heaven* (1930) is a modern treatment of the Grail legend, in which the Grail is discovered in a country church, then stolen by a black magician, who battles the Archdeacon and a Roman Catholic Duke who attempt to rescue it. Gradually, the quasi-realist narrative becomes a story of titanic apocalyptic struggle between forces of good and evil.

See also DRAGON OF THE APOCALYPSE; MICHAEL; SECOND COMING.

Bibliography. Damrosch, L., Jr. *Symbol and Truth in Blake's Myth* (1980).

WATER   Conflicting connotations of biblical waters flow from OT creation traditions and from both life-giving and destructive aspects of water itself. In Gen. 1:6-8 God divided the waters of chaos above and below the firmament (heaven); over the lower waters he stretched dry land (Gen.

1:9-10; Pss. 24:2; 136:6). Mythological overtones associated the subterranean "deep" with forces opposed to God. Origen, e.g., described these waters as the "abyss," the abode of the "adversary" and his angels (PG 12.148). 1 Enoch describes the valley of rebellious angels, where fumes arose amid a "convulsion of waters" and "fiery molten metal" (67:5-7). NT traditions link Christ's postresurrection descent into Hades with the "deep" (Rom. 10:7; 1 Pet. 3:19-21), and baptismal exorcisms reflect belief in evil spirits inhabiting waters. These waters were, however, controlled by the Lord, before whom "the waters . . . were afraid" and "the deep trembled" (Ps. 77:16; cf. 33:7; 104:9).

Viewed favorably, water is a means of cleansing (Lev. 14:50-52; Isa. 1:16; Ezek. 36:25), of quenching thirst (Ps. 42:1-2; Isa. 12:3; 55:1), of making land fertile (Job 5:10; Pss. 65:9-10; 104:10-13; 147:18; Isa. 55:10). Patristic exegesis frequently interpreted God's gift of water as the preaching of his word (St. Gregory on Isa. 41:18-20 in *Homilarium in evangelia*, 1.20 [PL 76.1166]; St. Jerome, *Comm. in Isa.*, CChr 73A, 473-75; cf. Amos 8:11) or as baptism (St. Cyprian on Isa. 48:21, *Ep.* 63.8 [PL 4.390-91]). Drought was often God's way of punishing the sins of the Israelites (Isa. 3:1) or their enemies (Isa. 19:5-8). When the Israelites complained about their lack of water, God sweetened the bitter waters at Marah and sent forth fountains from rocks at Horeb and Meribah. The NT writers saw in the desert rock a figure of Christ, source of living water. "Living water" flows, too, in eschatological imagery of the "river of the water of life . . . flowing from the throne of God and of the Lamb" (Rev. 22:1; cf. 7:17; 21:6; 22:17) and healing waters from the sanctuary in Ezek. 47:1-12 (cf. Zech. 14:8). Water symbolism is prominent in the narrative of John's Gospel.

Early literary allusions to biblical waters often resembled the almost-paraphrase account of creation in the OE *Genesis* (103-68). The more imaginative OE *Andreas* highlighted both beneficent and destructive attributes of the flood called forth from a rock, which destroyed the worst of the Mermedonians, taking them into the "grund" (the "abyss"; 1585-1600), and brought baptismal regeneration to the repentant. The cosmogony placing hell beneath the waters deepens the somberness of Byron's "white and sulphury" mists rising "Like foam from the roused ocean of deep Hell" (*Manfred*, 1.2.85-88). Gen. 2:6 underlies Tennyson's calmer description of eyes moistened not by tears but by "a happy mist / Like that which kept the heart of Eden green / Before the useful trouble of the rain" ("Geraint and Enid," 768-70). In Dryden's "Annus mirabilis" (1121-24) the waters above the firmament filled the "hollow chrystal Pyramid" with which God extinguished the London fire of 1666.

The ambivalence of water as a means of death and of regeneration provides a central theme in Flannery O'Connor's *The Violent Bear It Away* (1960) and "The River" (in *A Good Man Is Hard to Find* [1955]). In both

works a child's drowning brings spiritual rebirth at the moment of physical death. In "The River" the final scene also alludes to hostile powers in water: as the "waiting current" catches the child, his would-be rescuer, an elderly nonbeliever, rises out of the water "like some ancient water monster." A much earlier allusion to the "river of the water of life" (Rev. 22:1) in *The Pearl* describes the "water fre" that the "gemme clene" tells the dreamer he can cross only after death (299-324). The blending of Rev. 22:1 and John 4:10-14 produced the healing well of life in Spenser's *Faerie Queene*, a well capable of restoring life, cleansing sin, and enabling a "new-borne knight to battell new" to rise (1.11.30, 34). The rebirth of 14-year-old John in James Baldwin's *Go Tell It on the Mountain* (1953) involves two visions of water: the healing river that his people wait to cross to reach paradise and the "perpetual desert" where "they smote the rock, forever; and the waters sprang, perpetually." In contrast, Eliot's *Waste Land* remains a place with "no water but only rock" (331). (A section of this poem, "Death by Water," most probably owes to nonbiblical sources, likely including the I-Ching.) In "I Know where Wells Grow — Droughtless Wells" Emily Dickinson looks to eternity where "People 'thirst no more' " and no longer "remember Parching"; in "Thirst" she writes of the "adequate supply" of "that Great Water in the West— / Termed Immortality" (6-8).

See also BAPTISM; DEEP CALLETH UNTO DEEP; FLOOD; LIVING WATER; MARAH.

Bibliography. Bernard, J. H. "The Descent into Hades and Christian Baptism." *The Expositor* 8.11 (1916), 241-74; Daniélou, J. *Primitive Christian Symbols* (1964); Dickson, D. R. "The Typological Water-Cycle in the Poetry of Herbert, Vaughan, and Traherne." *DAI* 42 (1981), 2683A; Milward, P., S.J. "Biblical Imagery of Water in 'The Wreck of the Deutschland'." *HQ* 1 (1974), 115-20; Walsh, M. "The Baptismal Flood in the Old English 'Andreas': Liturgical and Typological Depths." *Traditio* 33 (1977), 137-58; Whitaker, E. C. *Documents of the Baptismal Liturgy.* 2nd ed. (1970).

MARIE MICHELLE WALSH

WATER INTO WINE   *See* CANA WINE.

WAY OF TRANSGRESSORS   Prov. 13:15 contrasts wisdom and waywardness: "Good understanding giveth favour: but the way of transgressors is hard." Thoreau draws the point admirably in his essay "Life without Principle," where he notes a resemblance betwen golddiggers and gamblers, saying: "It is not enough to tell me that you worked hard to get your gold. So does the Devil work hard. The way of the transgressors may be hard in many respects."

WEAKER VESSEL   The phrase "weaker vessel" comes from the injunction of St. Peter to married men that husbands are to "dwell with them [their wives] according to knowledge, giving honour unto the wife, as unto the weaker vessel, and as being heirs together of the grace of life; that your prayers be not hindered" (1 Pet. 3:7). This admonition is one of several in the NT (cf. Gal. 3:28; Eph. 5:25-31; 1 Cor. 7:4ff.) which considerably temper the normative Mediterranean relegation of women to a subordinate status in which they did not for practical purposes have either psychological or spiritual partnership with their spouses. Peter, like St. Paul, insists on respect for spiritual partnership in marriage, and enjoins sensitivity to the emotional needs of the wife and a serious attempt at personal understanding.

The Fathers, with their often intense commitment to celibacy, did not always do well by this passage. St. Jerome argues that the way to achieve appropriate relationship as coheirs is to persuade the wife, by degrees, to agree to a covenant of sexual abstinence (*Ep.* 48.4-7), believing that what Peter and Paul (e.g., 1 Cor. 7:5) both intend is that effectual prayer is impossible while cohabitation continues (*Ep.* 48.15; cf. *Ep.* 128.3; *Adv. Jov.* 1.7). Chaucer's Wife of Bath, who explicitly wars against Jerome's *Adversus Jovinianum* in her Prologue, is willing to acknowledge herself a "weaker vessel" (3.100-101, 440-42), only to demonstrate the opposite.

By the Reformation, following a more straightforward exegesis and the late medieval acceptance of marriage as a sacrament conveying grace, Calvin can say that the point of Peter's remarks is principally to induce respect, "for nothing destroys the fellowship of life more than contempt, and we cannot really love any but those whom we esteem, so that love must be connected with respect." He sees Peter as employing a

> two-fold argument, to persuade husbands to treat their wives honorably and kindly. The first is derived from the [physical] weakness of the sex; the other from the honor with which God favors them. These things seem in a way to be contrary, that honor ought to be given to wives because they are weak, and because they excel, but where love abounds, these things well agree together. (*Comm.* sup. 1 Pet. 3:7)

In Shakespeare's *Love's Labour's Lost* Don Adriano in a letter reports to the king that Costard, "a shallow vassal," has unlawfully "sorted and consorted" with Jaquenetta: "so is the weaker vessel called which I apprehended with the aforesaid swain" (1.1.266-67). Plucky Rosalind, disguised as Ganymede, is determined to "play the man" in adverse circumstances, weary and frightened though she is: "I could find in my heart to disgrace my man's apparel and to cry like a woman. But I must comfort the weaker vessel, as doublet and hose ought to show itself courageous to petticoat" (*As You Like It*, 2.4.4-9). The injunctions of Paul as well as Peter are wittily parodied in the decidedly .nonmarital relationship of Falstaff and Doll in *2 Henry 4* (2.4.60-66), while in *Othello* the Moor is a gross violator of his wife Desdemona's legitimate expectations: when he accuses her of infidelity she cries,

> No, as I am a Christian,
> If to preserve this vessel for my lord
> From any other foul unlawful touch
> Be not to be a strumpet, I am none. (4.2.82-85)

Lyly, in *Euphues,* expresses sympathy for the plight of women so abused: "Men are always laying baytes for women, which are the weaker vessels." Hardy's female characters are often similarly victimized. When in *Far from the Madding Crowd* Bathsheba's first marriage destructs and her life is in disarray, she "in spite of her mettle, began to feel unmistakable signs that she was inherently the weaker vessel" (chap. 31). A parody of Pauline and Petrine texts as well as Jerome's commentary is provided by Oscar Wilde in *The Importance of Being Ernest.* In act 2, Miss Prism says sententiously to Chausible, "And you do not seem to realize, dear Doctor, that by persistently remaining single, a man converts himself into a permanent public temptation. Men should be more careful; this very celibacy leads weaker vessels astray." Chausible replies, "But is a man not equally attractive when married?" to which Miss Prism counters, "No married man is ever attractive except to his wife."

See also BRIDE, BRIDEGROOM; VESSEL.

WEEDS *See* EDEN; FALL; WHEAT AND TARES.

WEEPING, WAILING, GNASHING In several of Jesus' descriptions of the punishments of hell after the Last Judgment he refers to the plight of the damned in terms of extreme torment: "But the children of the kingdom shall be cast into outer darkness: there shall be weeping and gnashing of teeth" (Matt. 8:12; cf. 22:13; 24:51; 25:30; Luke 13:28). In his parable of the wheat and tares Jesus describes the fate of those who are "tares" as being "cast . . . into a furnace of fire: there shall be wailing and gnashing of teeth" (Matt. 13:42). The phrase has been associated in literature with a certain kind of "fire and brimstone" preaching as well as with the unhappy lot of sufferers of all kinds. Melville exemplifies the former in *Moby-Dick* when Ishmael enters a black church in New Bedford and finds the preacher in full cry, "beating a book" in his pulpit and holding forth on a text (presumably from Matthew) about "the blackness of darkness, and the weeping and wailing of teeth gnashing there." The second kind of allusion can be found in Mark Twain's *Life on the Mississippi*, where the non-union river pilots and crew fired by captains of the steamboats are envisioned in their outcast state: "There was weeping and wailing and gnashing of teeth" (chap. 15). Dickens ominously describes revelers in the Reign of Terror as dancing "to the popular Revolution song, keeping a ferocious time that was like a gnashing of teeth in unison" (*A Tale of Two Cities*, 3.5). Aldous Huxley recalls the words of Jesus in a more innocuous context, arguing that in the modern era feelings themselves "have been exiled into an outer darkness apart from and below the personality co-ordinated by the principle of success" (*Proper Studies,* "Personality and Discontinuity of Mind").

See also LAST JUDGMENT; UNPROFITABLE SERVANT, PARABLE OF; WHEAT AND TARES.

WEIGHED IN THE BALANCES *See* BELSHAZZAR; DANIEL; HANDWRITING ON THE WALL.

WEIGHTS AND MEASURES *See* SCALES.

WELL DONE, GOOD AND FAITHFUL In Jesus' parable of the talents (Matt. 25:14-30), the two productive servants were praised on their master's return for their industry and fruitfulness: "Well done, good and faithful servant. . . . Enter thou into the joy of thy lord" (vv. 21, 23). In Christian commentary from early patristic writers to the present these words have been taken as the *desideratum non plus ultra* for a Christian meeting Christ's final evaluation. Often the commendation is associated with successful realization of the goal set for himself by St. Paul: "I have fought a good fight, I have finished my course, I have kept the faith" (2 Tim. 4:7).

Enriched by this connection and by the commentary of St. Augustine, Calvin, and other exegetes, the phrase has entered widely into English literature both in specific allusion to its primary context and in derivative and secularized parallels. In Milton's *Paradise Lost,* God says to Abdiel by way of congratulation for his faithfulness: "Servant of God, well done, well hast thou fought / The better fight" (6.29-30). Robert Southey's *A Vision of Judgment* pictures King George III appealing to God for pardon, and records the divine response: " 'Well done, / Good and faithful servant!' then said a voice from the Brightness; / 'Enter into the joy of thy Lord.' " The "profitable" as distinct from the "unprofitable" servant was a homiletical commonplace in preaching of the 18th and 19th cents.; Carlyle echoes it when, in *Sartor Resartus,* he commends his readers not to judge Professor Teufelsdröckh's quandary of religious doubt too harshly: "Unprofitable servants, as we all are, perhaps at no era of his life was he more decisively the Servant of God." In the "Oxen of the Sun" chapter of *Ulysses,* Joyce blends allusions to 2 Tim. 4:9 with the words of the master in Matt. 25:23 in the encomium for "dear old Doady" of the many, many children, a devotee of "the Sacred Book."

See also UNPROFITABLE SERVANT, PARABLE OF.

WHAT IS TRUTH? When Pilate finally obtained a response from Jesus at his trial, Jesus said to him: "To this end was I born, and for this cause came I into the world, that I should bear witness unto the truth. Every one that is of the truth heareth my voice." Pilate responded by asking, "What is truth?" (John 18:37-38). This question, for Western traditions of commentary an opposing of jaded relativism to serene confidence in transcendent

verity, came to be regarded as the essential rhetorical question posed by interlocutors of Jesus in any era (see, e.g., St. Thomas Aquinas, *De Veritate;* Wyclif, *De Veritate Sacrae Scripturae*).

Francis Bacon's essay "Of Truth" includes a memorable conjecture concerning Pilate's tone: " 'What is truth' said jesting Pilate, and would not stay for an answer." Recalling Bacon's essay in his "Boswell's Life of Johnson," Carlyle suggests that 18th-cent. English culture and even Johnson himself were "confused" about truth: " 'What is truth?' said jesting Pilate. What is Truth? might earnest Johnson much more emphatically say." Archibald MacLeish ("The Irresponsibles") accuses the modern scholar with being "as indifferent to values, as careless of significance, as bored with meanings" as certain narrowly focused scientists, along with whom "he has taught himself to say . . . — and with some others whom history remembers — 'What is truth?' "

See also ECCE HOMO; PONTIUS PILATE.

WHATSOEVER THY HAND FINDETH TO DO It is a maxim of Qoheleth that "Whatsoever thy hand findeth to do, do it with thy might; for there is no work, nor device, nor knowledge, nor wisdom, in the grave, whither thou goest" (Eccl. 9:10). Christian exegesis, particularly after Calvin and among the Puritans, makes this an injunction to Christian stewardship. Carlyle concludes "The Everlasting Yea" section of his *Sartor Resartus* by saying: "Produce! Produce! Were it but the pitifullest, infinitesimal fraction of a product, produce it, in God's name! . . . Up, Up! 'Whatsoever thy hand findeth to do, do it with thy whole might' " (2.9).

WHEAT AND CHAFF *See* LETTER AND SPIRIT.

WHEAT AND TARES Jesus' parable of the wheat and the tares (Matt. 13:24-30) concerns a man who sows wheat in his field. When all are asleep, his enemy sows tares (*lolium temulentum,* "noxious weeds"), which grow up among the wheat. When the proprietor's servants recognize this and want to pull out the tares, he determines to let both grow together until the harvest, when his reapers will gather and burn the tares and save the wheat. Jesus later explains the parable to his disciples (Matt. 13:36-43), identifying the field as the world, the good seed as the children of the kingdom, and the tares as the children of the wicked one. The enemy is the devil, the harvest is the end of the world, and the reapers are the angels. The explanation ends in a description of Christ's judgment, which will separate the righteous from the wicked, among whom "there shall be wailing and gnashing of teeth" (v. 42).

Christ's explanation made the allegorical implications of the parable so clear that the Fathers added little. For Origen (*In Matthaeum,* 10.2) the tares signify "evil words" and "bad opinions," and for Bede the sleeping men (v. 25) are the teachers of the Church (*In Matthaei Evangelium Expositio*; cf. also Latimer, Sermon 42). A notable variation occurs in the pseudo-Clementine literature of the 3rd-4th cent., where the "enemy" is St. Paul, who supposedly sowed the tares of antinomianism among the good seed of the gospel (*Letter of Peter to James*, 2; cf. *Clementine Recognitions*, 1.70-71).

The parable has been frequently quoted — usually by the advocates of moderation — in controversies over broad or narrow concepts of Church. Among these are the conflict between St. Callistus and St. Hippolytus (Hippolytus, *Philosophoumena*, 9.12), the Donatist schism (St. Augustine, *Sermons on New Testament Lessons*, 38.21), the Protestant Reformation (Luther, *WA* 52.835-36), and the controversy over the admission to the Lord's Supper in Puritan America (Jonathan Edwards, *Humble Inquiry*, 3.6).

Many exegetes have seen the parable as warning against the use of violence against even the wicked or heretics within the visible church. They offer three main arguments: (a) the distinction between wheat and tares is difficult because of the possible coexistence of both within the human judge himself (Augustine, *Sermons on New Testament Lessons*, 23.4; Thielicke, *Das Bilderbuch Gottes*, 88-89; Hunter, *The Parables Then and Now*, 48); (b) the wicked should not be denied the chance to repent, "for it is possible for them even to become wheat" (St. John Chrysostom, *Hom. on Matthew*, 46; cf. also Luther, *WA* 38.560-61; St. Thomas More, *Confutation of Tyndale's Answer*, 8.2; Thielicke, *Das Bilderbuch Gottes*, 89-93); (c) to destroy heresies does not necessarily imply "rooting up" (Chrysostom, *Hom. on Matthew*; Calvin, *Harmony of the Gospels*).

In ME literature the parable's description of Judgment and hell turns up in "þar is wop and woninge" of *Vices and Virtues* (EETS o.s. 89, 17; similar references appear regularly in later literature as well, e.g., Michael Wigglesworth, *The Day of Doom*, sts. 193, 207). Shakespeare's use of the Geneva Bible (which in v. 29 reads "plucke" instead of the KJV "gather up") is reflected in *2 Henry 4*, when the Archbishop sees the King's foes "so enrooted with his friends / That, plucking to unfix an enemy, / He doth unfasten so and shake a friend" (4.1.207-09).

In his defense of unlicensed printing in the final section of *Areopagitica*, Milton uses the parable to argue that within the Church it is not possible "to sever the wheat from the tares. . . ; that must be the angels' ministry at the end of mortal things." As a consequence he suggests "that many be tolerated, rather then [*sic*] all compell'd." Sir Thomas Browne speaks of his view of the soul being "not wrung from speculations and subtilties, but from common sense and observation; not pickt from the leaves of any author, but bred amongst the weeds and tares of mine own brain" (*Religio Medici*, 1.36) — an interesting use of the parable to defend private judgment. Jonathan Swift accuses the "Dissenting Teachers" of his day of sowing tares

among the wheat and of being more successful financially than "Men of a liberal Education" (*Examiner*, 42; cf. also "Some Remarks upon a Pamphlet").

Blake's allusion ("My crop of corn is but a field of tares") in *An Island in the Moon* suggests that the field is life and the harvest is death. In Shelley's "The Mask of Anarchy," people are summoned

> From the haunts of daily life
> Where there is waged the daily strife
> With common wants and common cares
> Which sows the human heart with tares — (283-86).

A similar application of the parable is found in Byron's *Childe Harold* (4.119-20), and in *Don Juan* (13.25) the poet guards himself against "censorious" men who "sow an author's wheat with tares," i.e., "Reaping allusions private and inglorious, / Where none were dreamt of . . ." (cf. John Donne, "To Mr. Rowland Woodward," 5-6; John Ruskin, *Fors Clavigera*, 8.88.6).

In *The Stones of Venice* (3.4.2.94) Ruskin interprets the Reformation (which he calls a reanimation) in the light of this parable, concluding that for the Reformers "there was no hope of ever ridding the wheat itself from the tares." George Eliot entitled the fifth book of *The Mill on the Floss* "Wheat and Tares," which hints at the experiences endangering Maggie Tulliver's religious resolutions.

Thomas Hardy makes figurative use of the parable in *The Dynasts* (1.2.5), where the "Phantoms of Rumour" are suspected of sowing tares — false tidings — to coax the population into a fancied safety. Hardy's poem "On the Portrait of a Woman about to Be Hanged" arrives at the question of theodicy: Why has the condemned murderer's Causer "Sowed a tare / In a field so fair"? — implicitly equating the "enemy" with God himself.

See also SOWER, PARABLE OF.

Bibliography. Dodd, C. *Parables of the Kingdom* (1935; rpt. 1961), 137-40; Hunter, A. *The Parables Then and Now* (1971); Jeremias, J. *The Parables of Jesus*. Trans. S. Hooke (1954), 64-68.   MANFRED SIEBALD

WHEELS WITHIN WHEELS   The author of the book of Ezekiel describes his vision of four tetramorphs, each of which had "the likeness of a man":

> And every one had four faces, and every one had four wings. And their feet were straight feet; and the sole of their feet was like the sole of a calf's foot: and they sparkled like the color of burnished brass. And they had the hands of a man under their wings on their four sides. . . . Their wings were joined one to another; they turned not when they went; they went every one straight forward. As for the likeness of their faces, they four had the face of a man, and the face of a lion, on the right side: and they four had the face of an ox on the left side; they four also had the face of an eagle. . . . As for the likeness of the living creatures, their appearance was like burning coals of fire, and like the appearance of lamps. . . . (1:5-13)

The creatures are seen to be mysteriously connected to wheels: "The appearance of the wheels and their work was like unto the color of a beryl: and they four had one likeness: and their appearance and their work was as it were a wheel in the middle of a wheel" (v. 16). The passage goes on in a highly charged metaphorical way to describe the luminous and lightning operation of this "chariot" *(merkabah),* which undergirded a throne extending up into the firmament, upon which was "the likeness as the appearance of a man" (v. 26), radiant in intense light, clearly representing the *shekinah* glory of God. The vision is repeated in chap. 10 and recurs, with modest variation, in Rev. 4.

Ezekiel's claim to have witnessed this unprecedented vision of the throne of God caused his book to be suspect, and the Council of Jamnia (A.D. 90) nearly rejected it. Reading of the first chapter was denied by R. Aqiba and other rabbinic authorities to all but mature readers (cf. Hag. 11b). The passage nonetheless gave rise to a tradition known as "Merkabah mysticism." In the commentary of Philo it is associated with the mysterious coinherence of the fourfold senses in exegesis.

Ezekiel's "wheels within wheels" are allegorized by St. Ambrose in his treatise on the Holy Spirit as referring

not to any appearance to the bodily perception but to the grace of each Testament. For the life of the saints is polished, and so consistent with itself that later portions agree with the former. The wheel then, within a wheel, is life under the Law, life under grace; inasmuch as Jews are within the Church, the Law is included in grace. (*De Spiritu Sancto,* 3.21.162)

The four "beast" faces were associated in early Christian interpretation (Origen, St. Irenaeus) with the four evangelists, Irenaeus identifying the man with St. Matthew, the lion with St. John, the ox with St. Luke, and the eagle with St. Mark. St. Jerome, Ambrose (in his Prologue to the *Expositio Evangelii secundum Lucam*), and St. Gregory (*In Ezechielem,* Hom. 4) contribute to the more popular identification in which Mark is the lion and John the eagle. The suggestion that not only the wheels but the creatures too were "full of eyes," symbolizing omniscient intelligence (Ezek. 10:12), is taken up by Dante (*Purgatorio,* 29.94) and Milton (*Paradise Lost,* 11.129ff.). In the biblical passage, all these features frame a climactic vision of the "form of one like a man" on the throne, who, although his exact description is unutterable, is evidently the sovereign deity —"Royal his shape majestic," as Keats puts it in *Hyperion,* "a vast shade / In midst of his own brightness." St. Gregory's commentary *(In Ezechielem)* follows Rev. 4 in identifying the one who sits upon the throne as Christ, the Lamb of God, a reading shared by most subsequent commentaries.

Among early English literary texts which make reference to the vision, Chaucer's *House of Fame* owes a debt to both the Ezekiel text and John's version in Rev.

4. Chaucer's loquacious eagle guide gently mocks any apocalyptic triumphalism of the visionary, yet the poem takes seriously the poet's calling, a theme rooted in Ezekiel rather than Revelation. The December 10 date of the poet's dream may also derive from a passage in Ezekiel (40:1-2), in which the prophet has a vision of the man measuring for the construction of the new Temple. Chaucer's playful handling of Ezekiel's images, such as the "gret swogh" or noise of wind, is unusual in English literature, but his use of the biblical prophet in connection with imagination and making of poems sets the stage for Milton, Blake, and Yeats, as well as Thomas Gray, whose image in "The Bard" (1757) of the prophetic poet is derived from the human form of the Supreme Being in Raphael's version of the *Vision of Ezekiel.*

Passing allusions to the vision in the 19th and 20th cents. focus principally on the strangeness of the "living creatures" and eyed wings. Launcelot, at the climax of his speech to Arthur in Tennyson's *The Holy Grail* (1869), relates his dream of entering the fires of a furnace and perhaps seeing the Holy Grail, which appears as "Great angels, awful shapes, and wings and eyes." Similarly, Tennyson's contemporary, Isaac Williams, in his poem "Ezekiel," characterizes the appearance of Christ to Ezekiel as "Dread speaking faces, peopling all the gloom; . . . / Their wheeling wings, and fiery shapes pass." Jean Valentine makes this strangely appealing and threatening vision the heart of the title poem of her book *The Messenger* (1980), whose opening section ends, "I hear the horses the fire the wheel bone wings / your voice."

Ezekiel's principal heirs, however —Milton, Blake, and Yeats —subordinate the strangeness of the vision to its power. Milton's early conception of the cherubim as a symbol of ecstatic transport in "The Passion" (1630) and "Il Penseroso" (ca. 1631) gives way in his later work to a theological representation of it as a symbol of the triumph of God's truth over Satan's lie. Milton's version of the cherubim in *Paradise Lost* is a war chariot with "burning wheels," whose rider, mounted on a throne in the divine chariot, is Christ himself. In his structural revision of his epic he moves this symbol of God's power to the end of bk. 6 (827-92), the literal center of the poem, and makes it a pivotal foreshadowing of the Son's ultimate victory. His identification of the chariot's rider as Christ may owe an immediate debt to Henry More, who interpreted the throne-chariot of cabalistic Merkabah mysticism as the "Heavenly Humanity of the Son of God," but Milton's utilitarian reworking of Ezekiel's vision as a war chariot shooting fire and lightning at Satan's legions is counter to any mystical tradition. And it is this fiery central image radiating throughout the epic (1.386-87; 7.585-87; 11.128-30) that assures readers of the triumph of truth in its battle with falsehood.

In contrast to Milton, Blake internalizes Ezekiel's vision, attributing to it psychological rather than historical power. Whereas Milton emphasizes obedience to the enthroned rider, Christ, and distinguishes him sharply from his chariot, Blake emphasizes imaginative liberty and cosmic warfare, insisting on the unity not only of the vehicle and its rider but also of both within the visionary, of whom Jesus is the archetype. In *Milton* Blake explicitly identifies Ezekiel's cherubim with the "Human Form Divine" and "holy Brotherhood" (32.13-15), and in his *Descriptive Catalogue* he merges this moral notion with an aesthetic one, calling the cherubim the "wonderful originals" of all art. This view culminates in the last plates of *Jerusalem* (1820), where he makes clear that the "Four Living Creatures" (98.24, 42) — the cherubim, or "visionary forms dramatic" — are embodied by his poem itself.

Jerusalem, an epic dedicated to imaginative liberty and the brotherhood of mankind, consists of a series of transformations of Blake's version of Ezekiel's vision — a furnace at the center of wheels. In each transformation of the poem he varies the relationship between these images and their landscape —a rock beside a river in a temple-city (a conflation of the scenes in Ezek. 1 and 10), which is ultimately the body of "Albion," or Everyman. Interaction between Albion and his lost soul, "Jerusalem" or imaginative liberty, symbolized by the furnace and wheels, provides the poem's dramatic form. In Blake's final transformation of the vision (94.1–99.5), Albion finds his soul, once again enthroning imagination in his body: the psychologically self-divided man is restored to unity as the drama of the furnace and wheels of his imaginative life is reunited with its true scene, the temple-city of his body.

Under the influence of Milton's vision and prophetic fervor, John Greenleaf Whittier and Vachel Lindsay in America also looked to Ezekiel's cherubim as the touchstone of their art, as well as a symbol of their calling. In his poem "Ezekiel" Whittier identifies with the prophet who sees the war chariot which enthrones the "flame-like form of One" and which makes all succeeding poetry seem "a trick of art." Moreover, the conceit at the heart of his elegy "Lucy Hooper" is that a child's life has given everything else life, just as did the "gorgeous vision rolled" on "Chebar's banks of old." Lindsay, who wrote "The Ezekiel Chant" while still in college, uses the wings and wheels for purposes of social criticism.

Blake's use of Ezekiel's vision as a symbol of the human imagination is paralleled in the prose of Coleridge and Ruskin. Distinguishing in *The Statesman's Manual* (1816) between imagination and reason, Coleridge defines imagination as a "reconciling and mediatory power" which "gives birth to a system of symbols, harmonious in themselves, and consubstantial with the truths, of which they are conductors." These "conductors" are the "Wheels which Ezekiel beheld," and the "truths and the symbols that represent them move in conjunction and form the living chariot which bears up (for us) the throne of the Divine Humanity" (*Bollingen Works,* 6.29).

Similarly, Ruskin asserts in *Ad Valorem* that of "all true work the Ezekiel vision is true," having an imaginative "check" on reason. And his meditation on the "use of Ezekiel's vision" in his description of the Altar-vault in *St. Mark's Rest* implies that it serves as an archetypal symbol of imaginative wholeness (cf. *Unto This Last,* chap. 4).

For Yeats, too, the cherubim are a manifestation of imaginative power, providing the necessary mythic basis for his art. His mystical reworking of the cherubim in *A Vision* (1925) provides the philosophical and imagistic foundation of *The Tower* (1928) and *The Winding Stair* (1933). Yeats had come under the influence of Ezekiel's cherubim early, for part of his initiation into the Rosicrucian order was an explanation of the "Kerubim," and at the climax of his instruction a paraphrase of Ezek. 1:4-5 was recited. Out of this experience, shaped in part by Blake's psychologizing of the narrative, came the "Great Wheel" of Yeats's *A Vision,* which, like Ezekiel's, is fourfold, contains and is contained by the "Spirit," burns with "alternations of passion," carries the hero at its center, and ultimately "draws" the visionary himself "up into the symbol." Yeats's possession of this symbol in *A Vision* makes possible, as Cleanth Brooks observes, the richness and precision of the Byzantium poems, as well as the structure of their respective books. In Yeats's expression of his desire for vision in "Sailing to Byzantium," the opening poem of *The Tower,* it is the whirling "holy fire" borrowed from Ezekiel's vision that transports him "out of nature" into the "artifice of eternity." Furthermore, in the vision itself in "Byzantium," the earlier poem's companion in *The Winding Stair,* the central image is that of "flames begotten of flame," the "fire infolding itself" of the cherubim. Yeats achieves ecstatic transport, as does the visionary in the book of Enoch, by means of this spiritual "flame that cannot singe a sleeve." For Hopkins, the "mystery of those things / . . . Shewn to Ezekiel's open'd sight / On Chebar's banks" is what still transports, "and why they went / Unswerving through the firmament; / Whose ken through amber of dark eyes / Went forth to compass mysteries" ("Il Mystico," 47-52).

See also CHARIOT OF FIRE; EZEKIEL.

Bibliography. Helms, R. "Ezekiel and Blake's Jerusalem." *Studies in Romanticism* 13 (1974), 127-40; Herrstrom, D. "Blake's Transformations of Ezekiel's Cherubim Vision in *Jerusalem*." *Blake Quarterly* 15 (1981), 64-77; Prickett, S. *Words and the Word: Language, Poetics and Biblical Interpretaion* (1986); Van Gemeren, W. "The Exegesis of Ezekiel's 'Chariot' Chapters in Twelfth Century Hebrew Commentaries." *DAI* 35 (1974), 3115A.

DAVID STEN HERRSTROM

WHERE TWO OR THREE ARE GATHERED

Knowing his disciples were to become outcasts from regular communion and worship in Israel, Jesus comforted them by saying, "For where two or three are gathered together in my name, there am I in the midst of them" (Matt. 18:20). In the anti-institutionalism of some 19th-cent. Christian writers — e.g., Carlyle in his essay "Characteristics" — the verse was gladly seized upon as supportive of spiritual individualism. Whittier describes the Quaker perspective in his poem "The Meeting":

> God should be most where man is least:
> So, where there is neither church nor priest . . .
> "Where, in my name, meet two or three,"
> Our Lord hath said, "I there will be!"

See also PRAYER.

WHITED SEPULCHRE   A metaphoric designation for the hypocrite, *whited sepulchre* originates from the sixth of the seven woes pronounced by Christ in Matt. 23:27-28: "Woe unto you, scribes and Pharisees, hypocrites! for ye are like unto whited sepulchres, which indeed appear beautiful outward, but are within full of dead men's bones, and of all uncleanness. Even so ye also outwardly appear righteous unto men, but ye are full of hypocrisy and iniquity." (Cf. St. Paul's denunciation of Ananias as a "whited wall" in Acts 23:3.) The actual image comes from the ancient Jewish practice of whitewashing the outside of tombs before the feast of Passover to make them more visible and thus to help prevent Jews from becoming ritually unclean by accidentally touching them.

Hypocrites here transliterates Gk. *hypokritai* (sing. *hypokritēs*), which, from the 2nd cent. forward, signifies actors or role players. As St. Augustine, following Origen's lead, comments, the kind of dissembling which is called hypocrisy is a pretense of sanctity by those who have no genuine desire for the reality they mimic. St. Isidore of Seville reckons the hypocrite a wearer of masks and creator of illusions, like the stage actors of antiquity. The NT meaning of *hypocritical* may be closer to "hypercritical" in the sense of "hairsplitting legal scrupulosity," which brings the Law into desuetude.

The denunciation of hypocrisy is a standard feature in the literature of moral reform, especially of protestation against ecclesiastical corruption; in such literature the "whited sepulchre" image occurs frequently. In *Piers Plowman* (B.15.113), Langland's "Prologue to Do-Better" combines the whited wall from Acts 23:3 with a dunghill shrouded with snow, to picture the teachers and churchmen who falsify true learning and the laws of God: they are dissemblers, "whitewashed with fair words and surplices of linen." In Shakespeare's *Merchant of Venice*, a play concerned very much about hypocrisy, a golden casket is discovered to be full of dead men's bones, "gilded [like 'whited'] tombs, do worms infold" (2.7.69). Milton, in *Tetrachordon*, reckons of a hypocrite that "the whole neighbourhood / Sees his foule inside through his whited skin" (1.16.40). In Blake, the call for reform is apocalyptic: "Wo Wo Wo to you Hypocrites!" he warns

"the Modern Church" or those who, "having no Passions of their own because No Intellect, Have spent their lives in Curbing & Governing other People's" *(A Vision of the Last Judgment)*.

Though the phrase "whited sepulchre" has currency in the literature of 19th-cent. Britain — e.g., Walter Scott, *Quentin Durward* (chap. 28); Charles Kingsley, *Alton Locke* (chap. 4); Hall Caine, *Manxman* (428) — the figure has by this time considerably diminished in its power to shape a moral critique. Not so in America. In the "Appendix" to his *Narrative of an American Slave,* Frederick Douglass likens "the Christianity of America" to the double-dealing of the Pharisees and scribes, citing Matt. 23:4-28 in its entirety. Hawthorne's *The Scarlet Letter* is ironic in its probing and articulation of the duplicity inherent in hypocrisy. In chap. 10, after evoking Christian's meeting with Hypocrisy and Formalism in *The Pilgrim's Progress,* the author likens Chillingworth to "a sexton digging into a grave" to retrieve a precious gem: the man of law and learning will discover if Dimmesdale, "looking pure as new-fallen snow," has an interior to match. In the second part of Melville's *The Paradise of Bachelors and the Tartarus of Maids,* the "large whitewashed building" of "a paper-mill" is likened to "some great whited sepulchre." In Eugene O'Neill's *Mourning Becomes Electra,* Christine, decking her house with flowers, comments, "I felt our tomb needed a little brightening. Each time I come back after being away it appears more like a sepulchre! The 'whited' one of the Bible — pagan temple front stuck like a mask on Puritan gray ugliness!"

With Conrad, the whited sepulchre returns to British literature with renewed force. Marlow of *Heart of Darkness* recalls a European capital which always makes him "think of a whited sepulchre" (pt. 1); however, as the lie to the intended and the pervasive gloom of the final pages insinuate, neither Conrad's narrator nor London is spared participation in hypocrisy. In *Chance* (1.2), the moralist and social reformer Mrs. Fyne is likened to the Pharisees, which comparison, as Purdy suggests (85-88), applies to Marlow as well. The final chapter of *Victory* makes frequent reference to Matt. 23 (see Purdy, 84-85), e.g., in the description of the dead outlaw Jones as "a heap of bones in a blue silk bag." D. H. Lawrence's "How Beastly the Bourgeois Is" follows in the tradition of Blake, though on a more domestic prophetic plane: "the fresh clean Englishman, outside" is "all wormy inside."

Bibliography. Albright, W., and C. Mann. *Matthew.* AB (1971); Purdy, D. *Joseph Conrad's Bible* (1984); Renard, P. "Hypocrisie." *Dictionnaire de spiritualité,* 7.1212-16; Young, F. W. "Hypocrisy, Hypocrite." *IDB* 2.668-69.

CAMILLE R. LA BOSSIÈRE

WHITSUNDAY   The English name for the Christian feast of Pentecost, occurring fifty days after Easter.

See also GIFT OF TONGUES; HOLY SPIRIT; PENTECOST.

WHOLE ARMOR OF GOD *See* ARMOR AND WEAPONS; *MILES CHRISTI.*

WHOLE CREATION GROANETH, THE St. Paul wrote to the Romans, "For we know that the whole creation groaneth and travaileth in pain until now" (Rom. 8:22). Matthew Henry (1727) offers the usual interpretation, which is that creation also, and not only humankind, lies "under the bondage of corruption" because of the consequences of sin: "there is an impurity, deformity, and infirmity, which the creature has contracted by the fall of man," hence also "there is a general outcry of the whole creation against the sin of man" (*Comm. on the Whole Bible*, 6.420). In *The Return of the Native* Hardy reflects this perspective: "I get up every morning and see the whole creation groaning and travailing in pain, as St. Paul says, and yet there am I, trafficking in glittering splendours with wealthy women and titled libertines, and pandering to the meanest vanities" (3.2).

WHOLE DUTY OF MAN At the end of his book, Qoheleth ("the Preacher") sums up his counsel: "Let us hear the conclusion of the whole matter: Fear God and keep his commandments: for this is the whole duty of man" (Eccl. 12:13). St. Augustine observes of this passage (in which the Vg reads only *hoc est enim omnis homo;* KJV adds "duty") that "whosoever has real existence is this, a keeper of God's commandments; and he who is not this, is nothing" (*De civ. Dei* 20.3). Matthew Henry call this verse "the summary of religion," adding, "In vain do we pretend to fear God if we do not make a conscience of our duty to him" (*Comm.* 4.1052).

This emphasis on "obedience," "conscience," and "duty" as the epitome of true religion finds an enormously popular expression in *The Whole Duty of Man* (1658), an anonymous work (possibly by Richard Allestree) which for more than a century had an undisputed place alongside the Prayer Book as a practical church guide to social conduct and responsibility. Although largely conventional in its religious precepts, this work was directed against nonconformity as well as the aspirations of those in the lower and middle classes — teaching that ordinary persons, like children, should "order themselves lowely and reverently to all their betters" (293). Prior to his conversion John Wesley held this work in high esteem; after it, in light of his concerns for the social outworking of the gospel, he publicly rejected it in terms akin to those of William Cowper, who described it as "a repository of self-righteousness and pharisaical lumber." It is often this book rather than the passage in Ecclesiastes which is alluded to by English writers, as is the case with Carlyle in *Sartor Resartus,* where Professor Teufelsdröckh wants to argue the "Everlasting Yea": "If Fichte's *Wissenschaftslehre* be, 'to a certain extent, Applied Christianity,' surely to a still greater extent, so is this. We have not a

Whole Duty of Man, yet a Half Duty, namely the Passive half: could we but do it, as we can demonstrate it!" (2.9).

WHORE OF BABYLON In the course of John's apocalyptic vision, an angel announces that "Babylon is fallen, is fallen, that great city, because she made all nations drink of the wine of the wrath of her fornication" (Rev. 14:8). Chaps. 17 and 18 elaborate: the whore of Babylon sits on many waters (17:1) and on "a scarlet coloured beast, full of names of blasphemy, having seven heads and ten horns" (17:3); dressed in purple and scarlet, decked with precious jewels and holding a golden cup, she commits fornication with the kings of the earth (17:2 and 4). John marvels at the beast and the woman, whose forehead bears the inscription "Mystery," and the angel then offers to explain the symbolism to him (17:6-18). The whore shall be stripped and burned (17:16); the city will collapse (chap. 18). Unfaithful Babylon contrasts with the New Jerusalem, the holy city prepared as a bride for Christ (21:2, 9-10), the woman clothed with the sun (12:1).

The basic image and many of the details found in Revelation derive from the OT prophets, who frequently depict Jerusalem or Israel as an adulteress to the Lord, her true husband. (See Hos. 1–3; Isa. 1:21; 57:7-13; Jer. 3:1–4:4; and esp. Ezek. 16 and 23.) The destruction of Babylon is foretold in Jer. 50–51, which draws on Isa. 3:17-24. Since cultic prostitution was a part of Canaanite religious practice, the metaphor of Judah's hankering after strange gods has particular point. That Babylon is the city or state primarily associated with false and idolatrous belief stems from two considerations. First, the Hebrew name for Babylon, *babel,* recalls the story of the infamous Tower of Babel, destroyed by God as a judgment on the impiety of its builders (Gen. 11). Second, the deportation of the Jews to Babylon, the Babylonian captivity of 604-562 B.C. (2 Kings 24–25), made Babylon the epitome of the kingdom hostile to true religion.

As a city, whorish Babylon is related to other apostate kingdoms, especially Tyre (Isa. 23:15-18) and Nineveh (Nah. 3:4-6). St. Victorinus's *Comm. on the Apocalypse* remarks that the Babylon of Isaiah and Revelation and the Sodom of Ezekiel "are all one," and this sort of typological conflation of evil cities influences D. G. Rossetti's "The Burden of Nineveh," a poem which alludes to both Rome and Babylon as types of the "delicate harlot," Nineveh, before assimilating London to the same scheme. As whore, Babylon is related principally to Jezebel (1 Kings 18:19–19:3), Ahab's queen, who adulterated the faith of Israel (2 Kings 9:1-37). This identification (which Bullinger, e.g., uses in *A Hundred Sermons upon the Apocalypse* [trans. 1561]) was promoted by Rev. 2:20, which refers to a prophetess named Jezebel who "seduces my servants to commit fornication."

Although evidence from the Qumran scrolls has been used to identify the whore of Babylon with unfaithful Jerusalem (*Revelation* [AB], 282-88), Rome, the city of seven hills, is usually thought to be figured in the harlot's seven-headed beast (Rev. 17:3). In ancient Judaism it was common to speak of Rome as Babylon *redivivus* (2 Apoc. Bar. 11:1; Sib. Or. 5:143, 158-59; 4 Ezra 2:36-40; cf. 1 Pet. 5:13). This interpretation is confirmed, among the Ante-Nicene Fathers, by Tertullian, St. Hippolytus, St. Irenaeus, and Victorinus. Although St. Augustine neglects the whore of Babylon per se, he adopts the distinction between Jerusalem (peace) and Babylon (confusion) and equates the latter with Rome (*De civ. Dei* 18.2, 22, 27). Rabanus Maurus says that Babylon is allegorically the church of the Gentiles; anagogically, hell; tropologically, the corrupted soul (PL 112.872). Bishop Haymo argues that Babylon is the house built on sand; Jerusalem the house built on a firm rock (PL 117.1139; cf. Matt. 7:24-27).

In the late medieval prophetic tradition, it was common to see the Papacy as the "ghost of the deceased Roman Empire sitting crowned on the grave thereof" (Hobbes, *Leviathan*, 4.47). In his *Postilla super Apocalipsim,* Peter Olivi branded the Papacy as the whore because of its cupidity and carnality, and Bernard Gui's *Inquisitor's Manual* (1324) inquires into the errors of the Beguins, a Franciscan order which taught that "at the end of the sixth era of the Church, the era in which they say we now are, which began with St. Francis, the carnal Church, Babylon, the great harlot, shall be rejected by Christ" (McGinn, *Visions of the End,* 219). In England, Wyclif sustains this Franciscan interpretation (*Tractatus de Ecclesia,* 5.356-57). It was the "Babylonian captivity" of the Avignonese papacy in particular which inspired this denigration, as is seen in Petrarch's sonnet 137, which presents a Babylon dominated by Venus and Bacchus, and in Dante's *Purgatorio,* where the harlot of false religion nestles into the arms of Philip the Fair.

In Reformation polemics, the decrying of the Papacy as the whore became ubiquitous and shrill. Luther's way of imagining the Reformation as a release from Babylonian captivity is typical: "We too were formerly stuck in the behind of this hellish whore, this new church of the Pope. We supported it in all earnestness, so that we regret having spent so much time and energy in that vile hole. But God be thanked that he rescued us from the scarlet whore" ("Against Hanswurst"). John Bale contrasts "the poore persecuted church of Christ or immaculate spouse of the lamb" with "the proude paynted churche of the Pope, or sinfull Synagogue" and applies this contrast to current affairs by associating Winchester, Bonner, and the "Romish" bishops with the whore and Cranmer and the Protestants with the pure spouse (*The Image of Bothe Churches* [ca. 1548]). Bale, like Milton later (in his *Means to Remove Hirelings* and *Of Reformation*), dates the establishment of the meretricious church with the Donation of Constantine, even though that document purporting to give the church temporal power had been exposed as fraudulent during the 15th cent. The Geneva Bible's gloss

on 2 Thess. 2:3-4 links the strumpet with the "man of sin" (Antichrist) there described, and this link occurs frequently during the 17th cent. when almost any political power could expect to be traduced in this way. As D. H. Lawrence points out in his idiosyncratic commentary on Revelation, inveighing against the whore has continued to be popular among the evangelically persuaded (*Apocalypse* [1932], 11-13).

Literary appropriations of Rev. 17–18 and the commentaries on it are many and varied. In *Piers Plowman* (B Version), Langland gives his dreamer a vision of two women, Holy Church and Lady Meed. The daughter of False, Meed is a sinister woman who lives in the Pope's palace (2.23) and who is as common "as a cartway" (3.131). The description of her accoutrements (2.8.18) makes clear that she is understood to be the Whore of Babylon. In Passus 3 and 4, she tries to deceive the King and corrupts the court. The King eventually spurns Meed's blandishments with the help of Reason and Conscience. Although papal corruption is attacked by Langland, the allegory is predominantly moral, not historical.

In bk. 1 of *The Faerie Queene* Spenser introduces Una and Duessa, who represent true and false religion respectively. Duessa, who wears the triple crown of the Papacy, is a "scarlet whore" (8.29) dressed in the manner described in Revelation (4.29). Duessa's Circean golden cup (Rev. 17:4) contrasts with Fidelia's (8.14.25; 10.13.19), so that there may be, as Waters has proposed, direct satire against the Mass, as in the Mistress Missa tradition. Duessa is stripped of her finery (8.46) in a passage which recalls Rev. 17:16 and Isa. 47:1, 3, 9 and 12 and 3:17, 24. On the historical plane Una is Elizabeth I, whose motto was *semper eadem* ("always constant"), and Duessa is Mary Stuart. Lucifera, the Queen of Pride, is a female version of Nebuchadnezzar, king of Babylon, who is called Lucifer in Isa. 14:12. On her chariot drawn by seven bestial sins (1.4), she resembles the whore on her seven-headed dragon. This image is explicit in Dekker's *The Seven Deadly Sins of London.*

In *The Whore of Babylon,* Dekker deals with a political contest between a loose Roman empress, whose triple crown represents Spain, France, and Italy; Titania, the fairy queen, is Elizabeth. In "Tropicall and shadowed collours," the "Drammatical Poem" sets forth thinly disguised traitors such as Edmund Campion and Dr. Parry; it climaxes with the defeat of the Armada. An inventive twist is the appearance of the "Truth, the Daughter of Time" motif, frequently attached elsewhere to Elizabeth:

> *Truth:* Besides I am not gorgious in attire,
> But simple, plain and homely; in mine eyes,
> Doves sit, not Sparrowes; on my modest
> cheekes,
> No witching smiles doe dwell; vpon my
> tongue
> No vnchast language lies; my Skins not
> spotted

With foule disease, as is that common harlot,
That baseborne truth, that lies in Babylon.
(3.3.6-12)

Like Dekker, Donne uses clothing as a way of differentiating two ecclesiastical polities, but he audaciously complicates the conventional responses. After pondering whether Christ's true spouse is "richly painted" or "rob'd and tore" as in England and Germany, he concludes that she is "most trew, and pleasing to thee, then / When she is embrac'd and open to most men" ("Holy Sonnet 18"). In *Bartholomew Fair* Jonson satirizes Zeal-of-the-Land Busy's puritanical strictures against the Whore and Antichrist.

For Blake, the Whore of Babylon is a major archetype. Albion is captivated not by Jerusalem, but by Vala, the Babylon which symbolizes Moral Virtue, Natural Religion, and Deism. This city-state's name is "Vala in Eternity: in Time her name is Rahab" (*Jerusalem*, 70.17). As the creator of Voltaire and rationalism (*Milton*, 22.41), Rahab is a whore of Babylon (*Four Zoas*, 8.277-82) who seduces mankind "to destroy Imagination" (*Jerusalem*, 70.17). After she kills Jesus (*Four Zoas*, 3.341), her foulness is revealed. She is burned, as in Revelation, but from the ashes springs anew the form of Natural Religion (*Four Zoas*, 8.618-20). Her daughter is Tirzah, the Prude, and they weave the Natural, as opposed to the Spiritual Body (*Four Zoas*, 8.201, 220). Since both Rahab and Tirzah are associated with the number three, their product is the "ninefold darkness" of Urizen (see Frye, *Fearful Symmetry* [1947], 301). Elsewhere Blake associates Rahab with the covering cherub of Ezek. 28:13-19, who frustrates mankind's attempt to return to Paradise (*Jerusalem*, 89.52-53). In *Blake's Apocalypse* (1963), Bloom comments on the name Blake gives the Whore of Babylon. Blake transforms the redeemed harlot Rahab (Josh. 2), the ancestress of Jesus (Matt. 1:5-6), whom exegetes read as a type of the Church, into a demonic figure. "For him Rahab is indeed the Church, all the Churches, but she is unceasing in her whoredoms, and no one is to be saved through her. Blake identifies the Rahab of Jericho with the other Rahab of the Old Testament, the sea monster associated with Egypt and Babylon in the Psalms [87:4] and Isaiah [51:9], and therefore a type of Job's Leviathan" (259-60).

Although the other Romantic poets were deeply indebted to Revelation (Abrams, *Natural Supernaturalism* [1971], 41-46), they treated the Whore of Babylon in relatively conventional ways. In the dramatic fragment *Charles the First,* Shelley has the citizens of London comment on Archbishop Laud, whose "London will soon be his Rome" (1.58), and on Henrietta Maria, the "Babylonian woman" and "Canaanitish Jezebel" (1.62, 69). Similar slurs are cast on the Roman Catholic Lady Castlewood in Thackeray's *Henry Esmond,* and similar antipapism occurs in Byron's *Childe Harold* (1.29).

Coleridge, in his *Religious Musings* (320-34), evokes the whore as "mitred Atheism," and in a footnote explains that Babylon does not refer to Rome exclusively, but "to the union of Religion with Power and Wealth, wherever it is found." In "Characteristics," Carlyle stigmatizes advertising as the Whore of Babylon. The *femme fatale* tradition overlays images from Revelation in Christina Rossetti's "The World-Self-Destruction," when Babylon the Great appears as a harlot intent upon enmeshing her denizens "in her wanton hair" and as a Salome-like dancer who "turns giddy the fixed gazer."

In Hawthorne's *The Scarlet Letter,* Hester is spoken of as "a scarlet woman, and a worthy type of her of Babylon." Yet Hawthorne says that were there a papist among the Puritans, he "might have seen in this beautiful woman, so picturesque in her attire and mien, and with the infant at her bosom, an object to remind him of the image of Divine Maternity." Robert Lowell includes a poem on "The Fall of Babylon" in *Land of Unlikeness,* but his most interesting effort in this vein is in "As a Plane Tree by the Water," where the Virgin goes almost unrecognized as "Our Lady of Babylon" through the streets of a city which is a composite of Babylon, Babel, and Boston. Joyce, though sometimes given to direct allusions to the Whore of Babylon, often subtly confuses the virgin with the whore. In *Ulysses,* in the encounter of Bloom with Gerty MacDowell, the colors of rose and scarlet symbolize Dante's Celestial Rose and the scarlet woman respectively: "He was eyeing her as a snake eyes its prey. Her woman's instinct told her that she had raised the devil in him and at the thought a burning scarlet swept from throat to brow till the lovely colour of her face became a glorious rose."

See also BABEL; BABYLON; JEZEBEL; RAHAB; WOMAN CLOTHED WITH THE SUN.

Bibliography. Bloom, H. *Blake's Apocalypse* (1963); Damon, S. F. *A Blake Dictionary* (1965); Haller, R. S. "The Old Whore in Medieval Thought: Variations on a Convention." *DA* 22 (1961), 564-65; Hankins, J. E. *Source and Meaning in Spenser's Allegory* (1971); McGinn, B. *Visions of the End: Apocalyptic Traditions in the Middle Ages* (1979); Pineas, R. "Biblical Allusion in [Dekker's] *The Whore of Babylon.*" *ANQ* 11 (1972), 22-24; Robertson, D. W., Jr., and B. F. Huppé. *'Piers Plowman' and Scriptural Tradition* (1951); Watters, D. D. *Duessa as Theological Satire* (1970).
RONALD B. BOND

WHOSOEVER HATH   After his parable of the sower, Jesus' disciples asked him why he spoke in parables, rather than discursively. He answered, "Because it is given unto you to know the mysteries of the kingdom of heaven, but to them it is not given. For whosoever hath, to him shall be given, and he shall have more abundance: but whosoever hath not; from him shall be taken away even that he hath. Therefore speak I to them in parables: because they seeing see not, and hearing they hear not, neither do they understand." Jesus then links the obtuseness of some hearers to that lamented by Isaiah (Isa.

6:9-10) — a carnality of motivation which occludes the spiritual meaning of the word — and commends the disciples for their own desire to understand, explaining the allegory of the parable in detail (Matt. 13:10-23; cf. Matt. 25:29; Mark 4:25; Luke 8:18; 19:26).

This *logion* of Jesus, one of his "hard sayings," has always been applied by biblical commentators to its context of rectitude in interpretation. It figures repeatedly in discusssion of biblical hermeneutic: in the 14th cent., e.g., John Wyclif sees it as instancing the principle that what makes any given passage of Scripture more or less intelligible is the degree to which the reader is able to refer it to the *totum integrum* of Scripture as one, unified "law of God" *(lex Dei* or *lex Christi)*. But this principle has its precise equivalent in the exegetical theories of R. Ishmael, R. Solomon, or Nicholas of Lyra among Wyclif's predecessors, and is still being reflected in Matthew Henry's 18th-cent. *Comm. on the Whole Bible.* Positively stated, says Henry, "The nearer we draw to Christ, and the more we converse with him, the better acquainted we shall be with gospel mysteries." But it is an axiom of God's graciousness, he says, that he "bestows [his gifts] on those who improve them, but takes them away from those who bury them." Hence, the negative clause implies that one who "has no desire of grace, that makes no right use of the gifts and graces he has: has no root, no solid principle," and so, inevitably, "from him shall be taken away that which he has or seems to have" (5.181-82).

The verse has suffered much misconstrual by being taken out of context. Robert Herrick, e.g., uses it in a poem beginning with the line, "Once poore, still penurious":

> Goes the world now, it will with thee goe hard.
> The fattest Hogs we grease the more with Lard.
> To him that has, there shall be added more;
> Who is penurious, he shall still be poore.

John Stuart Mill applies the verse as curiously in his "Three Essays on Religion," where he observes that "good and evil naturally tend to fructify, each in its own kind, good producing good and evil, evil. It is one of Nature's general rules . . . that 'to him that hath shall be given, but from him that hath not, shall be taken even that which he hath'." George Gissing, in *New Grub Street,* applies the text to monetary matters again: "And to those who have shall be given. When I have a decent income of my own, I shall marry a woman with an income somewhat larger" (chap. 1).

See also PARABLE.

WHOSOEVER WILL SAVE HIS LIFE

On a variety of occasions Jesus said to his disciples in some fashion what is reported in Matt. 16:24-25: "If any man will come after me, let him deny himself, and take up his cross, and follow me. For whosoever will save his life shall lose it: and whosoever will lose his life for my sake shall find it" (cf. Mark 8:35; Luke 9:24; 17:33; John 12:24-26). This type of statement, according to John Wyclif (*De Veritate Sacrae Scripturae*), illustrates that in the intrinsic logic of the Bible, the Aristotelian logic of noncontradiction is sometimes confuted: death *may* be life. The principle as well as the phrase is variously echoed in literature, but Thoreau's *Civil Disobedience* offers a classic allusion. Opposing Paley's "Duty of Submission to Civil Government" Thoreau writes: "If I have unjustly wrested a plank from a drowning man, I must restore it to him though I drown myself. This, according to Paley, would be inconvenient. But he that would save his life, in such a case, shall lose it. America must cease to hold slaves, and to make war on Mexico, though it cost them their existence as a people."

WIDOW'S CRUSE   *See* CRUSE OF OIL; ELIJAH.

WIDOW'S MITE

Jesus, observing wealthy Jews ostentatiously casting money into the Temple treasury box, noticed "a certain poor widow" who threw in "two mites" (Mark 12:42; Luke 21:2). Jesus told his disciples that "this poor widow hath cast more in, than all they which have cast into the treasury: For all they did cast in of their abundance; but she of her want did cast in all that she had, even all her living" (Mark 12:43-44; cf. Luke 21:3-4).

The Fathers treat the passage as indicative of the "mathematics of the kingdom," in which material quantity and spiritual quality are regularly distinguished: "little" can be all; "much" can be inadequate. St. John Chrysostom (*Hom.* 52, on the Gospel of Matthew) mentions the widow's mite in the context of his discussion of almsgiving:

> For though thou be exceedingly poor, and of them that beg, if thou cast in two mites, thou hast effected all; though thou give but a barley cake, having only this, thou art arrived at the end of the art.

Allusions to "the widow's mite," frequent in English literature, begin as direct references to the biblical widow singled out by Christ. Later references branch out into a broader sense identified by the *Oxford English Dictionary:* "with allusion to Mark 12:43, one's mite is often used for the small sum which is all that one can afford to give to some charitable or public object." The phrase has tended to become even more figurative over time, so that it can now be "applied to an immaterial contribution (insignificant in amount, but the best one can do) to some object or cause."

The earliest allusions to the widow's mite are the most direct, referring specifically to the biblical woman. She is mentioned in *The Ayenbite of Inwyt* (12.42-43), Langland's *Piers Plowman* (13.196), and Goodwine's dedication to *Blanchardine.* St. Thomas More in his *Confutation* stresses the biblical background of the phrase:

> Christ blamed not those that offered into the treasury of the temple, nor said that they offered too much; but

rather, by praising of the poor widow that offered somewhat of her poverty, rebuked the rich folk for offering too little, albeit that, as the Gospel saith, many offered much. (7.674 B)

Later allusions to the verse in Mark suggest the broader sense of "mite" as the pittance which is all a donor can afford to contribute to a social cause. Dryden writes in 1687, "Are you defrauded, when he feeds the poor? Our mite decreases nothing of your store" (*The Hind and the Panther,* 3.113). Swift asks a similar question about public charity: "Did I e'er my Mite withhold? / From the Impotent and Old?" ("Epistle to a Lady," 71-72).

As a result of a kind of metaphoric inflation, the biblical mite tends to become ever less substantive in English literary allusion —as its use expands it tends to devalue. Swift by 1709 pays his mite not in currency but in counsel: "I hope I may be allowed among so many far more learned men to offer my mite" (*Critical Essays,* 2.1.140). And Berkeley offers in 1747 to "contribute my mite of advice" ("Tar-water in Plague," 3.479). This nonmonetary use of the term made its way to America as well, where Franklin says in his 1784 *Autobiography* that his "mite for such purpose was never refused" (103).

References to "the widow's mite" proliferate in the 19th cent. Byron seems particularly enamored of widows' mites. In *Don Juan,* possessing "no great plenty," he gives up for love all that he had —his heart: " 'T was the boys' 'mite,' and, like the 'widow's,' may / Perhaps be weigh'd hereafter, if not now" (6.41). "Let each," he admonishes, "give his mite!" ("The Irish Avatar," 173). Jane Austen ("very glad that she had contributed her mite") alludes twice to the widow's mite in *Mansfield Park.* Herman Melville refers to the "widow's last mite" in *Moby-Dick.*

In the 20th cent., references are often parodic. George Bernard Shaw alludes to the phrase ironically in *Major Barbara:* "The odd twopence, Barbara? The millionaire's mite, eh?" (2.297). In Joyce's *Ulysses,* Bloom ponders "That widow on Monday was it outside Cramer's that looked at me. Buried the poor husband but progressing favorably on the premium. Her widow's mite." Joyce's allusion to the biblical phrase in *Finnegans Wake* is twisted by punning: "which I'm sorry, my precious, is allathome I with grief can call my own but all the same, listen, Jaunick, accept this witwee's mite."

STEVEN C. WALKER

WILD ASS   *See* ASS; ISHMAEL.

WIND BLOWETH WHERE IT LISTS   In the searching nocturnal dialogue between Jesus and Nicodemus, a Pharisee, Jesus instructed Nicodemus, "Except a man be born again, he cannot see the kingdom of God" (John 3:3). Confused, Nicodemus asked how such a thing was possible. Jesus replied with an injunction to consider the matter of regeneration not in physical but spiritual terms:

"That which is born of the flesh is flesh; and that which is born of the Spirit is spirit. Marvel not that I said unto thee, Ye must be born again. The wind bloweth where it listeth, and thou hearest the sound thereof, but canst not tell whence it cometh, and whither it goeth: so is every one that is born of the Spirit" (vv. 6-8). The intent of Jesus' remarks depends on the identity in Greek between the word for "spirit" and "wind" *(pneuma).*

The passage is treated by St. Augustine in relation to the operations of grace: "The Holy Spirit 'bloweth where he listeth,' not following men's merits, but even producing those very merits himself " (*De gratia Christi, et de peccato originali,* 2.28; cf. *Contra duas epistolas Pelagianorum,* 4.14; *De peccatorum meritis et remissione,* 1.32). This is the application made also by subsequent commentators such as St. Thomas Aquinas, Calvin, and Matthew Henry: Calvin observes that "Christ means that the movement of God's Spirit is no less perceptible in the renewal of man than the movement of the air in this earthly and outward life, but its mode is hidden" (*Comm.* sup. John 3:8).

The phrase is used straightforwardly in literature to the time of the Puritans to indicate the operations of the Holy Spirit or of grace. By the Romantic period, however, it often attaches to more secular subjects, often a great human mind or spirit. Charles Lamb, in his essay "On the Tragedies of Shakespeare," expresses the view that *King Lear* cannot be acted, and that only when read does it reveal "a mighty irregular power of reasoning . . . exerting its powers, as the wind blows where it listeth, at will upon the corruptions and abuses of mankind." Byron, in *Childe Harold's Pilgrimage,* observes that Voltaire's chief talent "breathed most in ridicule — which, as the wind / Blew where it listed, laying all things prone, — / Now to o'erthrow a fool, and now to shake a throne" (3.992-94).

The phrase came to be applied also to the *spiritus mundi,* or *Zeitgeist,* as in Trevelyan's *History of England,* which speaks of the notorious success of the Viking invasions of Europe as less attributable to retrospectively adduced causes than to "the wind [that] bloweth where it listeth. . . . There is an element of chance in the rise and decline of great movements" (1.5). Oliver Wendell Holmes speaks of human creativity in a similar fashion: "The creative action is not voluntary at all, but automatic; we can only put the mind into the proper attitude, and wait for the wind, that blows where it listeth, to breathe over it" (*The Autocrat of the Breakfast Table,* chap. 8). Trollope turns the biblical passage inside out in applying it mockingly to "ministers . . . [who] are not only as empty as the wind, but resemble it in other particulars; for they blow where they list, and no man knoweth whence they come, nor whither they go" (*Domestic Manners of the Americans,* chap. 12). G. K. Chesterton's "The Wind and the Trees" chapter in *Tremendous Trifles* makes an observation more consistent with the context in John 3:1-8, suggesting that "the material things of this world . . . are blown where the spirit lists."

WINGS LIKE A DOVE   The Hebrew poet yearning to escape oppression cries "Oh that I had wings like a dove! For then I would fly away and be at rest" (Pss. 55:6; 68:13). This aspiration, popularized in the American popular hymn with that title, is secularized in the title of Henry James's novel, *The Wings of a Dove* (1902).

WINGS OF THE MORNING   The Psalmist exclaims upon the persistence of God's love: "If I take the wings of the morning, and dwell in the uttermost parts of the sea; Even there shall thy hand lead me, and thy right hand comfort me" (Ps. 139:9-10). The "wings of the morning" suggest the goddess of the dawn, which in all Mediterranean cultures arises out of the eastern ocean to be pursued by the sun god (Phoebus, Apollo) across the sky. In Roman myth the winged dawn is Aurora, and the "hours" of the day are "airie angels" who surround the chariot of the sun as all follow her across sea and sky (a scene depicted in Guido Reni's fresco *Aurora*). The allusion in Nathaniel Hawthorne's *The House of Seven Gables* (chap. 14) is complex, referring both to the biblical phrase and to depictions of the Roman version of the myth:

> Thus parted the old man and the rosy girl; and Phoebe took the wings of the morning, and was soon flitting almost as rapidly away as if endowed with the aerial locomotion of the angels to whom Uncle Venner had so graciously compared her.

WISDOM   Wisdom (Heb. *ḥokmah;* Gk. *sophia*) is one of the most important topics in biblical literature, where it may be subject, theme, motif, or genre. Because of this wide range of application, as well as progressive historical incorporation of hellenistic characterizations of *sophia* into the original Hebrew concept, the content of biblical "wisdom" reflected in literature can vary somewhat according to historical period and literary context. In the OT, *ḥokmah* implies an educated discipline of mind coupled with skillful practice in mundane affairs — it involves what the Greeks would have termed both *theoria* and *praktika,* and is never purely one or the other (Exod. 28:3; 31:1-5; 35:26; Deut. 34:9; Prov. 1:2-7; Isa. 10:13). By the post-exilic period Wisdom was readily personified; since the word is feminine, she became "Dame" or Lady Wisdom (see, e.g., Prov. 8; cf. Job 28:23-28; Prov. 3:13-18). She is presented in Prov. 8 as a companion of God in creation, elsewhere frequently as an itinerant female teacher who offers, at the gates of the city, knowledge, discipline, and the secrets of success, happiness, and wealth to those who seek her (Prov. 1:20-33; 8:1-22; 9:1ff.). Her opposite in Proverbs is the "foolish woman," who came to be known as Lady Foolishness or Dame Folly in later tradition (cf. Prov. 9:13-18), and is sometimes depicted as a whore who lures men to hell (Prov. 7).

Wisdom concerns all that area of possible human knowing up to but not exceeding its terrestrial limits, at which point revelation takes over. Thus, in the earliest period of Jewish interpretation, "Wisdom" is idiomatic for a kind of religious writing comparable to the Torah and the Prophets. As Moses was identified with the literary genesis of the Torah, so Solomon was linked to the canonical wisdom books, Proverbs, Ecclesiastes, and Canticles (Song of Songs). His special divine gift, which he already had the insight to ask for, was wisdom (1 Kings 3:12ff.); and he is seen as the preeminent human sage (1 Kings 4:29-34; 10:23), a maker and solver of riddles (1 Kings 10:1-3; Prov. 1:6), a man commonly referred to in the Middle Ages as "The Wise Man." Yet his wisdom is not independent of the Torah; indeed, it must be accompanied by obedience to it (1 Kings 3:14). Rabbinic tradition called each of the three "Solomonic" books *ḥokmah,* and sometimes referred to the three collectively as *ḥokmah,* resulting in a threefold division of Scripture into Torah, Prophets, and Wisdom (cf. Yalqut Shimeoni Tehillim 702). Later rabbinic tradition made Song of Songs a poem of Solomon's youth, Proverbs the aphorisms of his maturity, Ecclesiastes the cynical reflections of his old age (Midr. Cant. Rab. 1.1.10).

In later Judaism there seems to have grown up a specifically Jewish equivalent of the international scribe school or "wisdom school," associated in the 2nd cent. B.C. with Ben Sira (Jesus ben Sirach, the author of The Wisdom of Jeshua ben Eleazer ben Sira, or Ecclesiasticus, the preeminent wisdom book of the Apocrypha). In this tradition wisdom is recommended as a chief means of studying "the law of the most high" (Ecclus. 39:1ff.). In Ben Sira's school most of the OT was received as authoritative Scripture, then interpreted by means of a combination of citations and allusions to comparative biblical text. The Wisdom of Solomon was another late apocryphal wisdom text of significant influence down to the medieval period in the Christian West; Job, one of the earliest of biblical texts, has also been seen (despite the dramatic character of its narrative) as wisdom literature (e.g., chap. 28; cf. St. Gregory the Great, *Moralia*). Sapiential rhetoric occurs elsewhere in the Bible, as, e.g., in many of the speeches of Amos (who was from Tekoa, home of the "wise woman" consulted by King David, at Joab's behest, in attempting to exonerate Absalom — 2 Sam. 14:2). King David's adviser Ahithophel had a reputation as a wisdom figure (2 Sam. 16:23), as did Daniel (1:17), who trained for such an office in a Babylonian school.

Between the Testaments, Jewish interpretation increasingly identified Wisdom with Torah, seeing the wisdom books as Torah commentary (cf. Pirqe 'Abot 6.10). Jesus appeared on the scene as a wisdom teacher in the style of Ben Sira (esp. in the Sermon on the Mount); his conflict with the Pharisees stems in part from his not reading Wisdom as a commentary on the Torah but, in a sense, the reverse; Wisdom is expounded in much the same vein by St. Paul in his Epistles (e.g., 1 Cor. 1:10–

4:21, which parallels Bar. 3:9–4:4; cf. Colossians, Ephesians). The Epistle of St. James bears more relationship to the OT genre, in that it refers to Christ directly only twice and is composed of a series of detachable aphorisms. Like Paul, who was suspicious of the "worldly wisdom" of the Greeks (where *sophia* is taken to mean philosophy generally), James distinguishes between a wisdom "from above" and a wisdom which is "earthly, unspiritual, devilish" (3:15). The Epistle of James is like the Solomonic books in its eschewing of claims to revelation and like Ecclesiasticus in that it interprets select passages of Scripture in order to explicate religious wisdom, while avoiding direct reference to the Torah. As the Solomonic books obtained canonicity in the Christian Church only slowly because of their lack of claim to direct revelation, so also with James; Martin Luther was among the last to want to reject it on these grounds.

The Didache of the 1st cent. A.D. is a Christianized version of a Jewish wisdom text; the apocryphal Gospel of Thomas shows a similar influence. St. Irenaeus proposed a division of the NT, echoing the genre distribution of the Jewish Scriptures, into Gospel, Epistles of Paul, and "Sayings of the Lord," a collection from apocryphal works of aphorisms ascribed to him. As patristic tradition developed in the East (e.g., following Origen, St. Gregory of Nyssa, and others) wisdom took on a strong philosophical component as *sophia*. In the West, from St. Clement of Alexandria to St. Augustine, more of the Jewish content remains. (The genre as represented by "The Sentences of Sextus" [2nd cent.] persisted even in the 5th cent. to influence Boethius's *De Consolatione Philosophiae*. As the Solomonic books lack explicit citation of the Torah, so these wisdom books of the Christian era lack explicit citation of the Gospels — though the tacit relation in both cases is self-evident.)

Meanwhile, after the destruction of the Second Temple (A.D. 70) the Pharisees emerged as chief guardians of Jewish tradition. They focused on midrashic commentary and talmudic deliberation rather than on traditional, aphoristic wisdom literature; Solomon was obliged to share pride of place with the sages in the tradition of the Tannaim, including Hillel the Elder, Eliezer ben Hyrcanus, Joshua ben Hananiah, R. Meir, and R. Aqiba. Turning away from apocalypticism and moral or philosophical matters, they collected and emphasized the "tradition of the elders."

The most important biblical books in the Wisdom collection to influence English literature are those linked to Solomon and Ben Sira. Of these, Proverbs provides the key for development of the wisdom topos — especially its personification — in the West. Its precept that "the fear of the LORD is the beginning of knowledge; but fools despise wisdom and instruction" (1:7) is the basis for the antithesis afforded by Wisdom and Folly in its own pages and afterward. Moreover, its quotability ensured countless reiterations. In Prov. 8, personified Wisdom herself

speaks and identifies herself with God (22-31), so that to oppose her would seem folly indeed. Yet her posture is as a suppliant, not a judge. She "cries out" at the gates, entreating the simple to "understand wisdom" (Prov. 8:1-6). She pleads with her hearers to receive her instruction rather than pursue wealth (vv. 10-11), for it is by such nobler means that "kings reign, and princes decree justice" (vv. 13-16). Her qualities are eternal, established by God from the beginning, where she was with him before the creation, "by him, as one brought up with him: and I was daily his delight, rejoicing always before him" (v. 30). She concludes, "For whoso findeth me findeth life, and shall obtain favour of the LORD. But he that sinneth against me wrongeth his own soul: all they that hate me love death" (vv. 35-36). This unreferenced echo of the Torah (cf. Deut. 30:19) unmistakably identifies Wisdom and Torah in purpose.

The aphoristic qualities of Ecclesiastes, Ecclesiasticus, and the Epistle of James make them the next most pervasive source of literary allusions, with the *De Consolatione Philosophiae* of Boethius a strong third influence in subsequent tradition. Chaucer, e.g., quotes more from Proverbs than from *any* other biblical book, but makes extensive use also of Sirach and James; he made his own translation of Boethius and quotes him extensively as well. For the Middle Ages, in fact, Boethius provided a lively, almost dramatic extension of the Wisdom figure from Prov. 8. In his *Consolatio* she appears as Lady Philosophy, and her instruction of a fictionally obtuse Boethius concerning true wisdom (which is to distinguish between tangible and intelligible good and choose always the latter) bears the character of biblical as well as classical tradition. Her robe, rent by detractors, is emblazoned with θ and π, *theoretika* and *praktika*, wisdom and understanding; she woos her student away from "strumpet muses" similar to the harlot of Prov. 7:4-27, here symbolized as Lady Fortune, a personification of temporal prosperity. A powerful exposition of Christian moral philosophy, this text nonetheless never mentions Christ, and stands in relation to the patristic theology of Augustine in much the same way as James and the Solomonic books stand in relation to the Gospels and the Torah respectively. Boethius's Lady Philosophy is so powerful a personification that she "becomes" Dame Wisdom to the Christian West, standing behind such figures as Alain of Lille's Lady Nature in *De Planctu Naturae,* Dame Reason in Jean de Meun's *Roman de la Rose,* Dante's Lady Philosophy in the *Convivio* —and, to a degree, Beatrice in the *Commedia.* Translations of Boethius's *De Philosophiae Consolatione* were frequent if variously nuanced; among the most prominent translators were King Alfred, Jean de Meun, Chaucer, King James of Scotland *(The Kingis Quair),* and Queen Elizabeth I.

In strictly theological writing such as exegesis and commentaries Wisdom tended to be defined in predictably more abstract or specifically doctrinal fashion. A considerable catalogue of medieval writers developed a theology of wisdom; in this brief guide, two voices only, perhaps the most eloquent and the most cogent, must speak for all. The former, as a voice of late Roman antiquity and a contemporary of Boethius, is acutely conscious of two wisdom traditions, one classical and one biblical. Augustine typically speaks of moving away from classical pagan wisdom to the wisdom of Christ. Yet the term he uses, "philosophy" (lit. "the love of wisdom") (*Conf.* 3.5.8), had already begun to edge out *sapientia,* the pre-Ciceronian term, in Latin usage, and indicates something of the blending of hellenic ideas with hebraic wisdom which had already taken place. Augustine's famous *Soliloquies* commence with a dialogue between "Augustine" and "Reason," in which the whole question of wisdom's value is assessed in the light of human suffering — instanced here by an excruciating toothache pain which hampers "Augustine" from following the dialogue with "Reason." The resemblance of parts of the discourse to Job, and of the role of "Reason" to that of Boethius's Lady Philosophy is not accidental: the work is psychopharmical, a wisdom dialogue dealing with issues of theodicy in much the same fashion as the *Consolatio.* But the resolution of this dialogue accordingly commences when "Augustine" can acknowledge as true what Reason teaches, that the Wisdom Augustine seeks is also Christ himself, and that "He whom I burn to see himself knows when I am in health; let him do what pleases him; when it pleases him let him show himself; for now I commit myself completely to his mercy and care" (26). Consistently with ancient Near Eastern tradition, Wisdom is nonetheless portrayed by "Reason" as a beautiful woman whom, as she recognizes, "Augustine" wants "to behold with most chaste view and embrace, and to grasp her unveiled charms in such wise as she affords herself to no one, except to her few and choicest votaries" (*Soliloquies,* 1.22; cf. Prov. 3:18). In his *De doctrina Christiana* Augustine treats Wisdom more abstractly as a concept, as the goal of life, and also in terms of its ultimate personification in the Second Person of the Trinity (cf. *Sermo,* 117.3). Wisdom is here still the unchangeable good of Plato and of Solomon (*De doctrina Christiana,* 1.8.8), though in our changeful state we could not hope to recognize it "had not Wisdom condescended to adapt himself to our weakness and to show us a pattern of holy life in the form of our own humanity." Yet

> while we, when we come to him, do wisely, he when he came to us was considered by proud men to have done very foolishly. And while we when we come to him become strong, he when he came to us was regarded as weak. But "the foolishness of God is wiser than men; and the weakness of God is stronger than men" [1 Cor. 1:25]. And thus, though Wisdom was himself our home, he made himself also the way by which we should reach our home. (1.11.11)

The binary rhetoric is part of Augustine's psychopharmicon: even as, "in the wisdom of God, the world by

wisdom knew not God" (1 Cor. 1:21), so in the wisdom of God foolishness is cured; the pride by which we fall into sinful stupidity is redeemed by the obedient wisdom of humility, our vices are cured by the example of his virtues; as "we were ensnared by the wisdom of the serpent, we are set free by the 'foolishness' of God" (1.14.13).

Finally, for Augustine, wisdom is of far greater importance than eloquence to the Christian teacher. (The tendency was for eloquence to predominate in classical education.) For this reason, the Bible is foundational for the education of a Christian: "One speaks with more or less wisdom to the degree he has made more or less progress in the knowledge of the Scriptures; neither do I mean simply by reading them often and committing them to memory, but by understanding them aright and carefully searching their meaning" (4.5.7). The highest attainment, he adds, nonetheless, is to both memorize the Scriptures and "correctly apprehend their meaning." For Augustine then, and for the Augustinian tradition after him, all of the Bible becomes wisdom literature in the broadest sense.

Augustine's choice of the Platonic dialogue as an ideal form for generic wisdom writing (*De magistro, De ordine, De beata vita contra academicos, De libero arbitrio*) was to exert a great influence upon writing in the wisdom tradition. Alcuin's *De Grammatica* commences with a *disputatio de vera philosophia* which recalls Augustine's *De magistro;* the strategy becomes commonplace in medieval philosophical texts and even texts about spiritual wisdom, such as Aelred of Riveaulx's *De Amicitia Spirituali.* The other forms of fictional discourse discussed frequently in medieval theory, parable and proverb (cf. Heb. *mashal*), are generally seen as variants of a common form. The Venerable Bede notes that where one might expect the word *parabolis* the Vg has "*paroemia,* that is, *proverbia*" (*Super Parabolas Salomonis Allegorica Expositio* [PL 91.937]), a conflation occasioned by the fact that each uses "obscure" or indirect language to "clarify" wisdom. Such obscurity enhances the development of interpretative skills, so that one reads the text *non juxta litteram,* but with discernment of the higher purpose, its "wisdom." This relation of instruction in wisdom to instruction in right reading is also basic to medieval reflections on biblical wisdom literature. Solomon's proverbs, according to Bede, are directed toward five representative goals of biblical wisdom teaching: how to believe rightly, how to live properly, how to perceive others truthfully, how to give sound direction to the intentions of one's own heart, and how to define proper objectives for one's own stewardship or work (ibid.).

St. Thomas Aquinas takes up from Augustine the central aspects of his thought on wisdom, except that where the hellenic component in the former development of biblical wisdom is Platonic (or Neoplatonic), in Thomas it becomes Aristotelian reasoning, especially pertaining to the First Cause. Yet the doctrine of Aquinas is centered, if anything, more squarely on the fact of the Incarnation as the foundation of Christian wisdom. Not the Solomonic books, but rather Ben Sira is his preferred pre-Christian text, and rather than personified wisdom (*philosophia* or *sapientia*) he stresses the coinherence of wisdom in the individual Christian with that Wisdom which proceeds from God in Christ as a gift of the Holy Spirit. Wisdom is thus "the gift of the Holy Spirit, descending from above [cf. Jas. 3:14], and differs from the wisdom which is an intellectual virtue and is acquired by human study. Because it appreciates divine things it also differs from faith, which simply assents to their truth" (*Summa Theol.* 2a-2ae.40.1, ad 2). One's experience of Christ is the supreme gift of the Holy Spirit, a gift figured already in Ecclesiasticus ("I, wisdom, have poured out rivers . . ." [24:40]). For Aquinas, the sphere of wisdom is, essentially, Christology:

> Among the diversity of doctrines proclaimed by various sages about where wisdom may be found, the position of St. Paul stands out firm and strong: *Christ is the power of God and the wisdom of God, who of God is made unto us wisdom* [1 Cor. 1:24, 30]. This does not mean that wisdom is uniquely the Son's, for he is one by wisdom, as he is one by nature, with the Father and the Holy Ghost, but that wisdom is attributed to him in a special manner because his character so well shows it forth. For this is what the highest wisdom does: it manifests the hidden truths of divinity [cf. John 1:18]; it produces the works of creation [cf. Prov. 8:22-31], and furthermore restores them at need; it brings them to the completion of achieving their own proper and perfect purpose [cf. Col. 1:16-20].

One cannot know the mind of God except by the wisdom of Christ (cf. Matt. 9:27), and "therefore is wisdom personified in the Son, of whom it is written, *I, wisdom, have poured out rivers.*" These rivers he interprets as meaning "the ineffable flow . . . of Son from Father, and Holy Spirit from them both." These streams flow out into the world, and "now that the Son has come he has brought good tidings and opened their courses to us," so that wisdom is made available through evangelization and baptism — the "hidden truths of divinity" or revelation (1 *Sententiae,* Prol.).

The creational function of wisdom follows:

> God's wisdom is that of an artist, whose knowledge of what he makes is practical as well as theoretical: *thou hast made all things in wisdom* [Ps. 104:24]. It is Wisdom in person who speaks: *I was with him in forming all things* [Prov. 8:30]. . . . And Aristotle declares that the original which comes first is the cause of its copies that come after.

Moreover,

> He who makes a thing is he who can repair it, and so the restoration of creation is the third function of wisdom: *by wisdom were they healed* [Wisd. 9:19]. This especially was the work of the Son, who was made man in order to

change the very state of our nature and restore everything human: *Through him reconciling all things to himself, both as to things that are on earth and the things that are in heaven* [Col. 1:20].

The final function of wisdom, "fostering of things to their fulfillment and purpose," is likewise the work of Christ: "the fruits which wisdom has abundantly watered are the harvest. It is Christ who brings us to glory, Christ who brings to birth the Church's faithful . . . and the fruits are his saints in glory" (1 *Sententiae,* Prol.). Summing this up, Aquinas suggests that the Christian really professes "two wisdoms in Christ, the uncreated wisdom of God and the created wisdom of man" (*Compendium Theologiae,* 21b). When one comes to Christ by grace one is transformed by that wisdom of Christ in God, but then imitates, by human effort, the wisdom of his human example. When this happens, the pragmatic wisdom of Christ will reveal itself in a tranquility with respect to the world. Questions of theodicy will have a communal, social aspect, and will be best met within concrete action rather than abstract speculation. Referring to the Beatitudes Thomas says that

> peacemaking, which brings peace to oneself and others, is the merit of Wisdom. It is the result of setting values in their proper order, for peace, says Augustine, is the tranquility of order [*De civ. Dei* 19.13]. To set things in order is wisdom's office; its role is eirenical. The "children of God" — here the reward of Wisdom is touched on. For we are called God's children by taking on the likeness of his nature and only-begotten Son: *predestinate to be conformed to the image of his Son* [Rom. 8:29] who is begotten Wisdom. (*Summa Theol.* 2a-2ae.40.6)

For Aquinas, then, it is the wisdom of *imitatio Christi* alone which can confront the folly and evil of the world.

Christian wisdom at the end of the Middle Ages is accordingly a sapience reflective of biblical, rabbinic, and patristic models. The tradition of Boethius is the most "Solomonic" perhaps, working toward achievement of an inner peace based upon a lifelong pattern of choices for intelligible rather than tangible goods, choices for Wisdom herself rather than for Fame or Fortune. The tradition represented by Augustine's *De doctrina Christiana,* as even its title suggests, draws on St. Paul and the Gospels to emphasize the wisdom of the Word, the Scriptures, as a rule and pattern for personal life and spiritual growth. Aquinas follows Augustine, adding Ben Sira, and makes Wisdom preeminently christological, an imitation of Christ's life on earth the model fusion of *theoria* and *praktika* for the life of Christians in community, transmitting "streams of wisdom" into the world. (Dominican commentaries after Thomas, such as that on Wisdom by the 14th-cent. English Dominican Robert Holcott, tend to reflect these emphases.) Where Boethius is a-theological, Augustine contrasts Christian wisdom with pagan substitutes, denigrating the latter. Aquinas borrows less grudgingly, especially from Aristotle, to make reason (logic) more integral to the ordering of a praxis which must follow from the example of Christ. All three emphases continue to influence subsequent tradition.

There is a sense, of course, in which so much of English literature is plausibly "wisdom literature" that an attempt even to catalogue it would prove foolish. It is possible, however, to indicate at least a proportion of the better-known texts which imitate biblical sources in genre and preponderant theme. In the OE period, the dialogues of *Solomon and Saturn* are a notable early variant on the doctrinal manifestation, in the second part of which Solomon, personifying Jewish and Christian wisdom, engages in a riddling contest with Saturn, who personifies pagan wisdom (including that of Woden). The poems of the Exeter Book include a collection of "wisdom books." *The Seafarer* and *The Wanderer* are wisdom allegories, the latter making few if any direct biblical references; the "Riming Poem," like Ecclesiastes, stresses the vanity of worldly achievement, a theme which the previous two poems echo. Anglo-Saxon homiletical writers (e.g., Wulfstan, Aelfric) see wisdom as opposing pagan false wisdom, or idolatry, and in the OE *Daniel* Nebuchadnezzar's frustrated desire to be wise (*"syntro on sefan"* [84a]) is a condition of his idolatrous pride, while his restoration to sanity is represented as the progress through humility and repentance to divine Wisdom. The OE "A Father's Teachings" is much in the vein of Proverbs, even as "Lar: or, an exhortation to Christian Living" (ed. Krapp-Dobbie, 6.67) bears a resemblance to the Epistle of James.

The great wisdom writer in early English literature is surely Chaucer, who not only translated Boethius *(Boece)* with some of the interlinear commentaries, but assimilated much of the *Consolatio* in his *The Knight's Tale, The Book of the Duchess,* and *Troilus and Criseyde* — works particularly designed as advice to rulers. It has been argued that *The Canterbury Tales* is also a work of covert counsel; if so, then Chaucer's own overtly synecdochic *Tale of Melibee* with its personification of wisdom in Dame Prudence and considerable reliance upon quotations from Proverbs and other "Solomonic" wisdom books, is an indicative autograph to the wisdom he has generally chosen to espouse. Dame Prudence begins with a quotation from Seneca and ends with one from the Epistle of James (allusions to James are heavily featured also in *The Clerk's Tale* and *The Parson's Tale*). Yet though "Salamoun" is meticulously quoted in *Melibee,* urging a counsel of reason, the soft answer which turns away wrath (Prov. 15:1), and the peaceableness which follows from self-possession and forgiveness (*CT* 7.1674-75, 1713-15), the central purpose of this borrowed tale is the teaching of sound exegesis. In his pilgrim guise Chaucer makes the classic *apologia* for wisdom literature, the according of its purpose with that of the primary narrative (and presumably with its theological conclusion

in the Parson's sermon), saying that much as is the case for the minor variances in the four Gospels, so,

> though that I telle somwhat moore
> Of proverbes than ye han herd bifoore
> Comprehended in this litel tretys heere
> ... as in my sentence,
> Shul ye nowhere fynden difference
> Fro the sentence of this tretys lyte
> After the which this murye tale I write,
> And therefore herkneth what that I shall seye. (*CT* 7.954-66)

The *Orologium Sapientiae* of the mystic Henry Suso was translated into ME in the first decade after Chaucer's death. It and Walter Hilton's *Ladder of Perfection* and *Epistle on the Mixed Life* combined their influence with writings of St. Bernard and extensive quotations from the Wisdom of Solomon, Song of Songs, Proverbs, Ecclesiasticus, Ephesians, Colossians, and Romans to shape the Macro morality play *Wisdom.* Here Wisdom, dressed as Christ the King, contests with Lucifer in providing counsel to Anima (Soul). In James Ryman's lyric later in the century, Dame Wisdom of Prov. 8 returns directly — indeed, the text of Prov. 8:10 (*"Accipite disciplinam meam . . ."*) is cited as an epigraph. She comes, she says, to teach her "lordes preciptes iuste and right," and offers a paraphrase of several verses of Prov. 8:

> My children dere, now be ye here
> Blessed be they, that truly kepe
> My wayes true both farre and nere
> And my doctrine profunde and depe. . . .
>
> I loue alle them, that loueth me.
> They, that wake tymely, shall me fyende.
> With me, truly, alle richesse be,
> Ioye, plentie and right of kyende.
>
> Both equite, witte, myght and maigne
> Counceill also in euery case
> Of me be had, and princes raigne
> By me iustely in euery place.

The poem proceeds to counsel all those whose responsibility it is to provide for the worship life of Christians, making it clear that Dame Wisdom in this poem is the voice of Mother Church. Like her counterpart in Proverbs, however, she is not without cheer: "When ye wolde laugh, lest that ye wepe, / Serue god and pley, when ye haue done."

Among Reformation commentators noncanonical books fared badly. Only slightly less admired were the books associated with Solomon, chiefly for their lack of claim to direct revelation and apparent lack of at least a typological christocentricity. Calvin, for whom wisdom consists of "knowledge of God and of ourselves" (*Inst.* 1.1.1; cf. Vives, *Introduction to Wisdome,* trans. Morison [1575]), emphasizes above all the Law, and the fulfillment of the Law in the Gospels. For Luther, who scarcely quotes biblical wisdom books, and doubted that James ought to be canonical, wisdom was identified with Christology — in a narrower sense than intended by Aquinas.

In 16th-cent. English literature, the "sapience" of Spenser, variously drawn on passages from Proverbs, Job, Wisdom, Ecclesiasticus, and Baruch, is similarly a thinner conception than that propounded by Dame Wisdom in late medieval texts, and he scarcely uses the relevant biblical books in an otherwise biblically rich *Faerie Queene*. But the extension of wisdom literature into the Renaissance was nonetheless pervasive. Erasmus's *Praise of Folly* depends for its rhetorical strategy on the opposition of the wise and foolish women of Proverbs. Books about the education of princes, such as Elyot's *the Governour* (1531), are also in the "wisdom" genre; although Platonic wisdom plays a large role in this and in Elyot's *Of the Knowlege Which Maketh a Wise Man* (1533), the Solomonic tradition also declares itself. Elyot's *Pasquil the Plain* is a wisdom dialogue in which one of the characters, Gnatho, enters the discussion with a copy of the New Testament in his hand and one of Chaucer's *Troilus and Criseyde* in his pocket. The *Bankette of Sapience* (1539) is a collection of wise and moral sayings; *A Treatise of Moral Philosophy, Containing the Sayings of the Wise* (1548), by William Baldwin, is a compendium more of hellenic than hebraic wisdom. John Heywood's *Epigrams upon Proverbs* mines folklore as well as Solomon and the Greeks, anticipating another work in the same genre by the 17th-cent. religious poet George Herbert, his *Outlandish Proverbs* (1640), which is heavily indebted to biblical wisdom literature and begins, "Man proposeth, God disposeth" (cf. Prov. 16:33). Shakespeare's late romance, *The Winter's Tale,* is heavily imbued with Pauline wisdom, the teacher in which is Paulina, whose counsel to the person who has yet to learn is that "he that is slow to anger is better than the mighty; and he that ruleth his spirit than he that taketh a city" (Prov. 16:32). Leontes is "redeless" ("Our perogative calls not your counsels" [2.2.163-64]), hence his beloved daughter Perdita (cf. Sophie in Chaucer's *Tale of Melibee* [*CT* 7.967]) is "lost to him." The wisdom he must receive is to "do as the Heavens have done, forget your evil, / With them forgive yourself?" (5.1.4-6), be restored to the wife of his youth (cf. Prov. 5:18), and see the ultimate power of Wisdom as that of transformation from death to life.

Milton's Christ in *Paradise Regained* assumes a radical distinction between knowledge *(scientia)* which derives from a study of tangible matters of this world, and *sapientia* — that wisdom which, as in the saying of St. James, comes only from above. The distinction is Augustinian (*De sermone Domini in Monte,* 2.23; *De Trin.* 12.14.22), though pervasive after the 12th cent., and draws upon Job 28:12-28 to differentiate between that wisdom which humans can hope to acquire and that which is divine and must be revealed. The distinction is often called upon, as Christ does in Milton's poem, to disparage

classical learning in respect of the Bible (cf. Luther, *Colloquia Mensalia,* 501, and Theodore Beza's *Job Expounded* [1589]). When Satan offers Christ human knowledge, terming it wisdom, he has offered knowledge of this world in place of that "which is from above." Christ's disparagement of classical poetry and the "many books / Wise men have said are wearisome" (*PR* 4.321-22) is thus to be read partly in the context of Eccl. 12:12 ("Of making many books there is no end . . .") and partly in the light of the antithesis of classical and biblical wisdom which had begun to emerge in Renaissance, especially Protestant, commentators.

The Enlightenment swung the balance in favor of classical wisdom — so much so that Cowper was to ask:

> Is Christ the abler teacher, or the schools?
> If Christ, then why resort at ev'ry turn
> To Athens or to Rome, for wisdom short
> Of man's occasions, when in him reside
> Grace, knowledge, comfort — an unfathom'd store?
> How oft, when Paul has served us with a text,
> Has Epictetus, Plato, Tully, preached! (*The Task,*
> 2.534-40)

Cowper also wrote a hymn entitled "Wisdom — Prov. 8:22-31" (*Olney Hymns,* 1.52), a free translation of the appeal of Dame Wisdom to mankind. Pope, who wrote a youthful poem after *"Boetius, de cons. Philos"* and included Solomonic dicta in his *Essay on Man,* nevertheless is more indebted, as in his extensive "Imitations of Horace," to Roman sources. Henry Fielding's Parson Adams, in *Joseph Andrews,* and the old man on the hill in *Tom Jones* are echoes in their counsel of biblical wisdom, notably that of Proverbs, Ecclesiastes, and James, but the passage of archetypes of wisdom from old man (or prophet) to anima figure (as in Dante's *Commedia*) is signaled in *Tom Jones* by the symbolically named Sophia Western, "Western Philosophy," which for Fielding is a blend of classical and biblical truths. Samuel Johnson's *Rasselas* recollects biblical tradition, even in its genre, and of all the great 18th-cent. essayists Johnson (e.g., *Rambler,* nos. 111, 114, 135, 178, 183-85) is most notably indebted to biblical wisdom literature.

If the Romantic poets tended to favor prophetic books and the Psalms (e.g., Blake, Byron, and Wordsworth), Coleridge's religious and philosophical treatise, the *Aids to Reflection* (1825), a collection of commentaries and aphorisms intended as a guide to young men, is indebted in genre as well as content to the biblical wisdom tradition. But the influence sours somewhat in the 19th cent. Melville and Emerson are fond of Ben Sira's Ecclesiasticus. The 19th-cent. theme of the *fol sage,* influenced by the interaction of biblical and classical wisdom literature in the writings of Montaigne, lies behind some of the Transcendentalist essays of the "sage of Concord" (as Emerson was called). Melville's *Mardi* engages questions of a moral and ethical nature, sin and guilt, innocence and experience. Beginning as a narrative in which various personages set out in the search for absolute truth, it ends in allegory and uncertainty, with many allusions to the perceived cynicism of Ecclesiastes. *Vanitas vanitatum* becomes in fact a principal Melville theme.

The 20th cent. seems to have done little to put the genre back on stage (though works of modern theodicy such as Archibald MacLeish's *J.B.,* an analogue to Job, may lay some claim in that direction). "Our Lady of the Torah" in Leonard Cohen's *Book of Mercy* is a kind of Dame Wisdom, discovered after much embracing of her opposite, and Walker Percy's *Lost in the Cosmos* is indicative of a tendency in late 20th-cent. writers to turn to work of a more reflective and "sage" character: Percy's book is set out in the form of elaborate riddles which point the way — often quite directly — to biblical wisdom. Yet the deeper questions and counsel of biblical wisdom have for the most part disappeared from all but fantasy literature (e.g., the elaborate parable of Tolkien's *Lord of the Rings*).

See also FOOL, FOLLY; JOB; QOHELETH; SOLOMON; VANITY OF VANITIES.

Bibliography. Beal, R. S. "The Medieval Tradition of the *Libri Salomonis* in Dante's *Commedia* and Chaucer's *Troilus and Criseyde.*" *DAI* 48 (1988), 2621A; Bloomfield, M. W. "The Tradition and Style of Biblical Wisdom Literature." In *Biblical Patterns in Modern Literature.* Eds. D. H. Hirsch and N. Aschkenasy (1984); Conway, M. D. *Solomon and Solomonic Literature* (1912; rpt. 1973); Gammie, J. G. *Israelite Wisdom* (1978); Gilson, E. *The Christian Philosophy of Saint Augustine* (1960); Glatzer, N. *Biblical Humanism* (1968); Gordis, R. *Koheleth: The Man and His World* (1968); Hirsch, S. R. *From the Wisdom of Mishlé.* Trans. K. Paritzky (1983); Jaeger, H. "The Patristic Conception of Wisdom in the Light of Biblical and Rabbinic Research." *Studia Patristica* 4 (1961), 90-106; La Bossière, C. R. *The Victorian Fol Sage* (1988); Leclercq, J. *The Love of Learning and the Desire for God: A Study of Monastic Culture* (1961); Lerer, S. *Boethius and Dialogue: Literary Method in the "Consolation of Philosophy"* (1985); Payne, A. *Alfred and Boethius* (1968); Rankin, O. S. *Israel's Wisdom Literature* (1936; 1969); Rice, E. *The Renaissance Idea of Wisdom* (1958); Scott, R. B. Y. *The Way of Wisdom in the Old Testament* (1971); Shippey, T. A. *Poems of Wisdom and Learning in Old English* (1976); Smalley, B. *Medieval Exegesis of Wisdom Literature* (1986); Urbach, E. E. *The Sages: Their Concepts and Beliefs.* 2 vols. (1979); Von Rad, G. *Wisdom in Israel* (Eng. trans. 1972).

WISE AND FOOLISH BUILDERS In Matt. 7:24-27, as he ends his Sermon on the Mount, Jesus compares those who hear his words and do them to a wise man who builds his house upon a rock, where rain, floods, and winds cannot shake it. On the other hand, those who hear Jesus' words without acting upon them are compared to a man building on sand. His house falls down from the force of the elements. A parallel in Luke 6:47-49 stresses the building process ("digged deep and laid the founda-

tion upon a rock") and mentions only one of the elements ("flood" or "stream").

Along with other "rock" metaphors in the NT, the rock of vv. 24 and 25 has often been identified allegorically with Christ (because of 1 Cor. 10:4; cf. St. Augustine, *De sermone Domini in Monte,* 2.25.87; Bede, *In Matthaei Evangelium Expositio;* St. Thomas Aquinas, *Expositio in Evangelium S. Matthaei;* Luther, *WA* 32.532-35; Richard Hooker, Sermon 6), with the Church (because of Matt. 16:18; cf. Augustine, *In Joan. Ev.* 124.7.14; Jonathan Edwards, *Humble Inquiry,* 2.6), and with the steadfastness of doctrine (St. John Chrysostom, *Hom. on Matthew,* 24.3; Hooker, Sermon 6).

If Christ is considered the builder, he can be said to build the Church upon himself, according to St. Thomas. But the house of the parable was also taken by some (e.g., Chrysostom) to be the soul, or the two houses seen as being Jerusalem and Babylon (e.g., Haymo, *Expositio in Apocalypsin* [PL 117.1139]).

Rain, floods, and winds were interpreted by various writers as "things present," such as temptations, superstitions, rumors, carnal lusts, the devil, Antichrist, and evil spirits. Occasionally they were taken to represent the Last Judgment (e.g., Bede; Hooker; Josef Schmid, *Das Evangelium nach Matthäus,* 153).

The common interpretation of the early Church that "without works nothing is sufficient" did not remain undisputed. Rejecting any justification by works, some Reformation exegetes warned against acting from the wrong motives. Calvin concludes from the text that "genuine piety can be distinguished from imitated piety only when put to the test" (*Harmony of the Gospels*), and Luther accuses the Catholic clergy and the monks of building "on the shifting sand of their own foolish conceitedness" and "their own holiness." Modern exegetes again put the emphasis on the "doing" of Christ's words and read the parable as a "call to Christian action" (Hunter, *The Parables Then and Now,* 86).

In English literature, Spenser's *Faerie Queene* (1.4.5.5) offers an early reference: Lucifera's House of Pride is built "on a sandie hill." George Herbert's poem "Giddinesse" complains of man's fickleness by alluding to the parable:

He builds a house, which quickly down must go,
 As if a whirlwinde blew
And crusht the building: and it's partly true,
 His minde is so.

Charles Dickens in *David Copperfield* furnishes an example of the secularization of the parable. The protagonist says, when talking about his new wife, Agnes, that his love of her is founded on a rock (chap. 62; a similar allusion is found in chap. 45, "Annie and the Doctor"). Christina Rossetti's poem "A Testimony" uses the second builder as an illustration of the vanity she discovers everywhere.

Referring to bourgeois and bohemian life-styles, Edna St. Vincent Millay's poem "Second Fig" (in *A Few Figs from Thistles*) reverses the order of values: "Safe upon the solid rock the ugly houses stand: / Come and see my shining palace built upon the sand!" William Faulkner makes a brief reference to the parable in his first novel, *Soldiers' Pay*, 317). In *Absalom, Absalom!* he puts the elements of the story in a secular context: the South has erected its economic system "not on the rock of stern morality but on the shifting sands of opportunism and moral brigandage" (260).

In black poet Countee Cullen's "Lines to my Father," the Methodist minister is depicted as one whose dreams have come true because they were built on rock. Finally, in James Baldwin's *Go Tell It on the Mountain* (77), a flashback depicts Florence's life on a Southern plantation. She and her fellow slaves know that the "house of pride" where the white folks live will come down, because it has not "so sure a foundation" as Florence's. The reference to the Word of God provides both comfort and hope to the slaves.

See also PETER; ROCK.

Bibliography. Davies, W. *The Setting of the Sermon on the Mount* (1964); Findlay, J. *Jesus and the Parables* (1950), 95-98; Hunter, A. *The Parables Then and Now* (1971).

MANFRED SIEBALD

WISE AND FOOLISH VIRGINS One of several parables on preparedness in Matt. 24 and 25, the parable (Matt. 25:1-13) tells of ten bridesmaids who are to meet the bridegroom and accompany him to the wedding. At midnight, when the bridegroom arrives late, five of them turn out to be short of oil for their lamps. Since the others do not have oil to spare, the foolish ones have to go to buy oil — only to find on their return that, being late, they are not admitted to the bridegroom's house. He answers them, "I do not know you" (v. 12). The parable closes with a call for watchfulness which is a repetition of Matt. 24:42.

In classical Christian tradition the parable is interpreted allegorically, and most exegetes have agreed on the basic points of comparison. Following v. 13, they take the bridegroom to be Christ (Origen's allegorical interpretation draws a further parallel to the bridegroom in Canticles [*Song of Songs*, 3.11]) and the feast to be the Second Coming. The virgins are usually seen as representing the whole Church, the number five being derived from the five human senses, and virginity signifying abstention from evil (St. Augustine, *Sermones*, 43.2) or from possessions (St. John Chrysostom, *Hom. on Matthew*, 78.2). The bridegroom's tarrying leads "His disciples away from the expectation that His kingdom was quite immediately to appear," according to Chrysostom; the virgins' sleep, according to Augustine, means death. For most Fathers, the oil which the foolish maids lack represents almsgiving and good works (e.g., St. Jerome, *Ep.* 125; Bede, *In*

Matthaei Evangelium Expositio). Consequently, according to St. Chrysostom, the merchants to whom the foolish ones are sent are the poor. Since their service is of no avail, however, Augustine believes them to be the worldly flatterers.

This emphasis on good works was, of course, contradicted by the Reformers and subsequent Protestant exegetes. Wyclif, who interprets the virgins as those with a calling to the contemplative life, still clings to the traditional reading but stresses the possibility of having wrong motives in doing good works (*In Omnes Novi Testamentum Libros*). For St. Thomas More the lamps mean faith and the oil, goodness (*Confutation*, 9.824). For Luther the virgins' lamps signify charity, and the oil represents faith (Sermon of Oct. 21, 1522). Calvin (in his commentary on Matthew) holds that the virgins' being directed to the merchants is not a command but a reproach, since the gifts of grace cannot be purchased but only accepted by faith. Puritans, both in England and America, used the parable for exposing hypocrisy. Bunyan considers the foolish maids "visible saints," who are yet cast away on account of their "secret sins" (*The Holy City*, 4.5), and Thomas Shepard, in his lengthy treatise on the parable, calls them "gospel hypocrites" (*Parable of the Ten Virgins*, 1.14.1; cf. also Jonathan Edwards, *Humble Inquiry*, 2.2).

Modern commentaries have dealt with the question of whether or not the parable is an allegory proclaiming Jesus' Parousia (e.g., Michaelis, *Gleichnisse*, 92-94; Jeremias, *The Parables of Jesus*, 51-53). Linnemann echoes Chrysostom in asserting that it teaches how foolish it is for the Church not to expect a long postponement of the Second Coming (*Gleichnisse Jesu*, 125-27), and for Christian socialist Leonhard Ragaz the parable warns against several wrong kinds of waiting: against the attitudes of liberalism, servilism, and Christian fatalism (*Gleichnisse Jesu*, 189-98).

The parable provides the dominant motif for the 12th-cent. Latin-French play *Sponsus* (in effect a Last Judgment play); a German "Zehnjungfrauenspiel" followed in the 14th cent. Both of them modify the parable by suggesting that only the foolish virgins have fallen asleep. Dan Michel's *Ayenbite of Inwyt* (EETS [1866], 189, 218, 232), however, follows the traditional interpretation faithfully. Langland, in *Piers Plowman,* directs the Vg version of v. 12 (*Amen dico vobis, nescio vos*) against wrongdoing clergy, the king, and the lawyers (B.5.56; cf. also B.9.65). John Donne creates a bold metaphor when he makes the blood of the martyrs of the Christian Church "Oyle to th' Apostles Lamps, dew to their seed" (*The Second Anniversary*, 352).

The girl addressed in Milton's ninth sonnet is credited with an exemplary way of living and is hailed as one of the parable's virgins, who fills her "odorous Lamp with deeds of light." Milton takes the identification so far as to predict,

Therefore be sure
Thou, when the Bridegroom with his feastful friends
Passes to bliss at the mid hour of night,
Has gain'd thy entrance, Virgin wise and pure.

In similar fashion, Marvell's "Upon Appleton House" (62) compares the Cistercian nuns to the wise virgins, who trim their "chast Lamps" hourly, "Lest the great Bridegroom find them dim"; and Henry Vaughan ("The Dawning") and Michael Wigglesworth *(The Day of Doom)* open their poems, respectively, on the Second Coming and the Judgment, by evoking the parable's nocturnal atmosphere.

The scientific mind of Sir Thomas Browne connects the number of the wise and foolish virgins with Antiquity's (esp. Plutarch's) belief that five was the "Conjugall or wedding number," consisting of "two and three, the first parity and imparity, the active and passive digits, the materiall and formall principles in generative Societies" *(Garden of Cyrus,* chap. 5). A passage in William Cowper's poem "Retirement" skillfully exploits the double meaning of "midnight oil." The poet favors the minds occupied with the Last Judgment over those "that give the midnight oil to learned cares or philosophic toil" (661-62). William Blake, on the other hand, says in a letter (no. 21) that those "who are fond of Literature & Humane & polite accomplishments" are they that "have their lamps burning." (He also alludes to the parable in *Four Zoas,* 8.541.)

John Ruskin makes a humorous allusion to the virgins' oil in *Fors Clavigera,* 4.45.19. Elsewhere he puts the parable in a social context by turning it against those who distribute only their "inestimable wisdom" to the poor, but not their "estimable rubies." The ironical justification given for the latter is v. 9. Melville's Wellingborough Redburn laments the fate of small ships which are run down by larger ones because of "their own remissness in keeping a good look-out by day, and not having their lamps trimmed, like the wise virgins, by night" *(Redburn,* chap. 20). Melville refers to the parable again in chap. 81 of *Moby-Dick,* "The *Pequod* Meets the Virgin." The German whaler *Jungfrau (Virgin)*, which has not yet captured one whale, has run out of lamp oil. The fact that the captain has to borrow oil from Ahab indicates an inexperience borne out by the *Jungfrau's* defeat in the race after a sperm whale.

Harriet Beecher Stowe's Uncle Tom, in his simple mysticism, associates Eva St. Clare's impending death with the midnight hour of the parable *(Uncle Tom's Cabin,* chap. 26). The theme of belatedness is dealt with in Tennyson's *Idylls of the King* ("Guinevere") when a young girl in a convent sings "Too late, too late! ye cannot enter now. / No light had we: for that we do repent" — verses which illustrate Queen Guinevere's fate.

The renderings of the parable by Christina Rossetti are rather straightforward ("Advent Sunday," "Easter Tues-

day," "I know you not"), but Thomas Hardy only lends some biblical overtones to his depiction of the thoughts of an English country bride by entitling his poem "The Tarrying Bridegroom."

In *Ulysses* James Joyce makes two references to the wise virgins which serve as ironic foils to an environment of prostitution. Faulkner follows the same line when, in *Requiem for a Nun* (2.1), he has Temple Drake call herself "the foolish virgin," because she stays in a brothel voluntarily.

The title of Eugene O'Neill's play *The Iceman Cometh* is obviously modeled after v. 6, and there are a number of parallels between the drama and the parable. The main difference, however, is to be found in the character of Hickey, the "Iceman of Death." With O'Neill, eschatology is narrowed down to the imminence of death for everybody.

See also SECOND COMING.

Bibliography. Bruce, F. F. *The Hard Sayings of Jesus* (1983), 233-35; Hill, D. *The Gospel of Matthew,* NCB (1972), 326ff.; Jeremias, J. *The Parables of Jesus* (1963), 51-53; Lang, G. H. *Pictures and Parables* (1955), 314-20.

MANFRED SIEBALD

WISE AS SERPENTS Commissioning his disciples for their difficult and dangerous task of announcing the kingdom, Jesus warned them: "Behold, I send you forth as sheep in the midst of wolves: be ye therefore wise as serpents, and harmless as doves" (Matt. 10:16). In his sermon on the text, St. Augustine describes it as indicating "how our Lord Jesus Christ strengthened his martyrs by his teaching." Noting how apparently absurd it is to send a few sheep in among many wolves, he then reflects on the advice of Jesus, "who has promised the crown, but first appointed the combat." Whoever really understands Jesus' words and holds to them, he adds, "may die secure in the knowledge that he will not really die" *(Sermo,* 44.1-2). He then considers the oxymoron, offering exegetical reflections which incorporate contemporary animal lore:

Now if the simplicity of doves be enjoined us, what has the wisdom of the serpent to do with that? What I love in the dove is that she is without gall; what I fear in the serpent is his poison. But do not fear the serpent altogether for he has . . . something for you to imitate. For when the serpent is weighed down with age and feeling the burden of his many years he contracts and forces himself into a hole, and casts off his old coat of skin that he may spring forth into new life. . . . And the Apostle Paul says to you also, "Put ye off the old man with his deeds, and put ye on the new man" [Col. 3:9; Eph. 4:22-24]. So you do have something in the serpent to imitate. Die not for the "old man," but for the truth. Whoever dies for any temporal good dies for the "old man."

Augustine observes, further, how the adder strives to protect its head when attacked; so also should the Christian, whose head and life is Christ (44.3). The simplicity of the dove is then to be imitated without the caution occasioned by the serpent's poison:

> Mark how the doves rejoice in society; they fly and feed together always; they do not love to be alone, they delight in communion, they preserve affection; their cooings are the plaintive cries of love; with kissings they beget their young. Even when doves dispute about their nesting places, it is a peaceful sort of strife — how different from the strife of wolves! Do they separate because of contention? No, still they fly and feed together, and any strife is very peaceful. (44.4)

Calvin follows Augustine's commentary on the first half of the verse but reduces the elaborate exposition on the second half, reading it rather as a pragmatic warning for Christians in a hostile world: "Briefly, discretion is to be so tempered with caution, that they are not to be excessively timid, nor yet over slow in their work." Calvin says the "double simile" serves to condemn too much "prudence of the flesh" on the part of those who "do not want to take any risks, and so . . . renounce the call of Christ" (*Harmony of the Gospels,* sup. Matt. 10:16).

The phrase gained wide currency in English literature of the 19th cent. Melville employs it in its Calvinist sense of prudential wisdom when speaking of Billy Budd: "With little or no sharpness of faculty, or any trace of the wisdom of the serpent, nor yet quite of a dove, he possessed that kind and degree of intelligence which goes along with the unconventional rectitude of a sound human creature" (chap. 2). The prudential theme is engrafted into discussions of ethical pragmatism in numerous 19th-cent. texts. Ruskin speaks in *Modern Painters* of the character which he imagines ought to pertain to a gentleman, saying that there is a "difference between honorable and base lying. . . . 'Be ye wise as serpents, harmless as doves' is the ultimate expression of this principle." Once so construed, the phrase readily admits of parody and inversion, often by or in reference to those less circumspect than Ruskin's ideal. Such a one is Aunt Althea Pontifex in Butler's *The Way of All Flesh,* one of whose "wicked sayings about Dr. Skinner" is that "he had the harmlessness of the serpent and the wisdom of the dove" (chap. 28). In Dorothy Sayers's *Unnatural Death* it is said of Dr. Edward Carr that he is "conscientious but a little lackin' in worldly wisdom — not serpentine at all, as the Bible advises, but far otherwise" (chap. 4). The backhanded compliment of the narrator hidden in this remark is missing in Somerset Maugham's *Then and Now,* where a similar character is described: "He is goodness itself, but it cannot be denied that he is a little simple. He does not combine the innocence of the dove with the craftiness of the serpent" (chap. 18). Aldous Huxley seems to have captured well the development of Jesus' injunction as a proverb of secular wisdom:

Men of good will have always had to combine the virtues of the serpent with those of the dove. This serpentine wisdom is more than ever necessary to-day, when the official resistance to men of good will is greater and better organized than at any previous period. (*Ends and Means,* chap. 10)

WISE MAN, THE   In medieval and Renaissance texts (e.g., Chaucer's *Tale of Melibee* in *The Canterbury Tales*), "the wys man seith" often refers to Solomon, or the books then most thought to have been written by Solomon (Proverbs, Ecclesiastes, and Song of Songs in particular).

See also SOLOMON.

WISE MEN   *See* MAGI.

WITCH OF ENDOR   The witch of Endor is a figure in the history of King Saul who received this designation in the chapter heading of early printings of the KJV; in the KJV text itself (1 Sam. 28) she is referred to as "a woman [at Endor] that hath a familiar spirit." On the eve of his final battle against the Philistines at Mt. Gilboa, Saul was anxious and fearful. Since the Lord had refused to resolve his doubts by dreams, by lot, or by prophets, and in spite of his earlier banishment of mediums and wizards, he came in disguise to consult the woman of Endor and asked her to call up Samuel. Afraid of being denounced by Saul, she at first refused, but after being reassured, she agreed. Samuel's ghost offered Saul no more comfort than the living Samuel had done; he repeated his earlier declaration (15:27-28) that the Lord had stripped the kingdom from Saul and predicted that Saul and his sons would die in battle the next day. At these words Saul collapsed.

1 Chron. 10:13 stresses Saul's sinfulness in consulting a medium; in 1 Samuel the emphasis is rather on the horrifying effect of Samuel's message. With its nocturnal setting, its elements of disguise and recognition, "gods ascending out of the earth," Samuel in his mantle, and Saul's abrupt collapse, the episode forms a vivid and arresting narrative. Lord Byron called it "the finest and most finished witch-scene that ever was written or conceived. . . . It beats all the ghost scenes I ever read" (quoted in Ashton, 174).

From a theological point of view the text has been a focus of considerable controversy. Early Christian exegetes were, like their Jewish counterparts, much concerned with the nature of the apparition. Was it really Samuel's spirit which appeared? If so, how could it have been raised by a witch? If it was a devil in disguise, how could it have delivered a true prophecy? (St. Augustine, *De octo Dulcitii quaestionibus* [PL 40.162-65; FC 16.452-58]; Tertullian, *De anima,* chap. 57). Smelik provides a thorough survey of these arguments, as well as of their rabbinic counterparts, up to A.D. 800, when they are reflected in Aelfric's treatment of the Witch of Endor passage in *De Auguriis*, and they continue to appear in Simon Patrick's *Comm. upon the Historical Books of the Old Testament* (4th ed., 1732), in Coleridge's *Notebooks* (ed. Kathleen Coburn, vol. 3, no. 3753), and in 19th-cent. commentaries. Literary echoes of the same questions occur in Chaucer's *Friar's Tale*, 1506-12, and in Abraham Cowley's "Reason: The Use of It in Divine Matters" (st. 3). The episode continued to have an important role in 17th-cent. controversies about the reality of witchcraft (see Stock). Thomas Henry Huxley saw it as a kind of theological fossil, revealing a primitive stage of Hebrew religion ("The Evolution of Theology" [1886]; *Science and Hebrew Tradition*, vol. 4 of *Collected Essays* [1900], 290-307).

Byron's "Saul," in *Hebrew Melodies*, retells the story, and it is alluded to briefly in *Manfred* (2.2.180-82). Twice Byron invokes the ghost of Samuel with the wish that modern monarchs could be as terrified as Saul was (*Don Juan*, "Dedication," st. 11, and *The Age of Bronze*, 380-82). An illustration of the witch and the ghost obsessed the young Charles Lamb ("Witches, and Other Night-Fears," *Essays of Elia*). Browning's "Mr. Sludge, 'the Medium'" cites the story in defense of his own trade (843-47). Kipling's powerful "En-Dor, 1914-19 — ?" depicts hordes of war widows and orphans seeking the perilous consolation of communion with their dead. Like Byron, Hardy alludes repeatedly to the witch. Perhaps most notably, in chap. 26 of *The Mayor of Casterbridge* a weather prophet plays her role as part of the parallel with Saul and David which permeates the novel (see Moynahan, 126-27). In Robert Frost's *Masque of Reason*, Job's wife claims the witch as a friend.

Saul's visit to the woman of Endor forms the climax of many of the plays devoted to him. In the prologue to Arthur Russel Thorndike's *Saul: A Historical Tragedy in Five Acts* (1906), she is shown writing mysterious words in the dust (an allusion to Jesus' act in John 8:6-8). She has an expanded role as a prophet of truth in opposition to the conniving Samuel in Laurence Housman's play *Samuel the Kingmaker* (1944), but in Howard Nemerov's powerful one-act play *Endor* she is central, the unwilling agent of a divine predestination she can no more control than Samuel can when she calls up to say as much. She then echoes his words: "I do nothing. And yet there is nothing which is not done." The opening lines of A. M. Klein's *The Psalter of Avram Haktani* lament the loss of such vision as even the witch of Endor represented:

> Since prophecy has vanished out of Israel,
> And since the open vision is no more
> Neither a word on the high places, nor the *Urim* and
>   Thummim
> Nor even a witch, foretelling, at En-dor, —
> Where in these dubious days shall I take counsel?

The polyglot pun on En-dor (*dor*, "generation") heightens

the modern Abraham's sense of religious and cultural exhaustion.

See also SAMUEL; SAUL; WITCHCRAFT.

Bibliography. Ashton, T., ed. *Byron's Hebrew Melodies* (1972); Moynahan, J. "The Mayor of Casterbridge and the Old Testament's First Book of Samuel: A Study of Some Literary Relations." *PMLA* 71 (1956), 118-30; Robbins, R. H. "Endor Witch." In *The Encyclopedia of Witchcraft and Demonology* (1959), 159-60; Smelik, K. "The Witch of Endor: 1 Samuel 28 in Rabbinic and Christian Exegesis till 800 A.D." *VigC* 33 (1979), 160-79; Stock, R. *The Holy and the Daemonic from Sir Thomas Browne to William Blake* (1982), 69, 87-94; Taylor, D. *Hardy's Poetry, 1860-1928* (1981), 135-37, 187n.   WILLIAM KINSLEY

WITCHCRAFT In OT prohibitions against magical arts, a wide variety of Hebrew terms are used, and their precise meaning is not always clear. The forbidden practitioners include necromancers, astrologers, diviners, charmers, enchanters, and several others. For example, in Deut. 18:9-14 there is a list of such figures whose practices are described as an "abomination to the LORD." Such persons appear in Exod. 7:11; 22:18; Lev. 19:31; 20:6; 1 Sam. 15:23, 28; 2 Kings 9:22; 21:6; 23:24; 2 Chron. 33:6; Isa. 8:19; 19:3; 47:9-12; 57:3; Jer. 27:9; Dan. 2:2; Mic. 5:12; Mal. 3:5, their functions being varied and undifferentiated. The most influential passages historically were Exod. 22:18, "Thou shalt not suffer a witch to live," frequently quoted during the 17th cent. as grounds for executing witches, and 2 Sam. 28, which relates the story of "the witch of Endor," although she is named in the text as one having a "familiar spirit" (i.e., a medium), but not as a witch. Magic and sorcery are less frequently mentioned in the NT, but are still rejected as evils and as incompatible with faith in Christ. In Gal. 5:20 and Rev. 9:21; 18:23; 21:8; and 22:15, the Gk. *pharmakeia* and its derivatives are translated indifferently as referring to "witchcraft" and "sorcery." There is also a reference in Acts 19:17-20 to Christian converts in Ephesus who turn from their former religious practices, which included "curious arts," probably magical arts.

Etymologically the term *witch* comes from OE *wicca*, from the Indo-European root *weik*, relating to religion and the sacred, which also produced OE *wiglera*, "sorcerer." The first attested use of the term is in the form *wic-cecraeft*, in the early 10th-cent. Laws of Aethelstan (B. Thorpe, *Ancient Laws and Institutes of England* [1840], 86). OE homilies such as those of Aelfric (ca. 955-1020) mention both *wiccan* and *wigleras*, and a charter of ca. 970 (D. Whitelock, ed., *English Historical Documents*, 2nd ed. [1979], 1.562-63) mentions a woman who was drowned and whose son was outlawed because of her practice of malevolent sorcery by sticking images with pins. OE usage, like the Bible's, made no clear distinction between witches, sorcerers, wizards, poisoners, or other such malefactors: all were deemed to be practicing simple sorcery, usually for evil purposes.

Historically, the term *witchcraft* has had three quite distinct meanings. First, it refers to various kinds of folk magic, sorcery, and other occult arts: this is the sense which the biblical and OE terms originally carried. Second, it refers to the supposed worshipers of the devil during the witch craze of the 15th to 18th cents. Third, since the 1940s certain neopagan groups have called themselves "witches." The concept shades into hags, lamias, succubi, and other creatures more or less supernatural. The witch is usually, though not always, presumed to be female.

The witchcraft in ME literature, like that in OE, was simple sorcery of a vague nature, as in Malory's *Le Morte Darthur,* which refers (2.3.79) to "enchauntement and sorssery"; Chaucer may not have intended much more in his reference to the "malefice of sorcerie" in *The Parson's Tale* (10.340). The Faust legend, which reached England in the late 16th cent., conjoins "high" Neoplatonic magic with popular conjuring and sorcery. In Marlowe's version, Faustus's ambition for magical and occult powers prompts his pact with the devil and leads inexorably to his own damnation. The villains of Spenser's *Faerie Queene* are sorcerers and enchanters of various kinds; the only witch per se, however, is the hag of bk. 3 (7-8), who is said to practice "divilish arts." Although skepticism concerning the reality of witchcraft was widespread in the Renaissance (see, e.g., Reginald Scot's *Discourse of Witchcraft* [1584]), interest and credulity persisted, even in high places. James I expressed his belief in and apprehension concerning diabolical witchcraft in his *Daemonologie* (1597) and in his English statute of 1604. Shakespeare's *Macbeth,* the most famous literary evocation of witchcraft in this period, was evidently intended to flatter James's interest in the subject (see also *Hamlet,* 1.1.163; 3.2.398; *1 Henry 6,* 1.5.5-6; 2.1.18). Thomas Middleton's play *The Witch* (1627; publ. 1778) includes a character called Hecate who has been compared with the witches of *Macbeth.*

Thomas Fuller took the "character" of a witch seriously in his *Profane State* (1642), but Thomas Dekker's *Witch of Edmonton* (1623; publ. 1658), written with John Ford and William Rowley, was more typical in its comic and skeptical treatment. Matthew Hopkins's *Discoverie of Witches* (1647) was a self-serving defense of witch hunting, and Joseph Glanvill's *Sadducismus Triumphatus* (1681) was an earnest intellectual defense of belief in the existence of witches. The future, however, belonged to the skeptics. John Webster's skeptical *Displaying of Supposed Witchcraft* (1677), reflected in Thomas Shadwell's *Lancashire Witches* (1682), was followed by Francis Hutchinson's *Historical Essay concerning Witchcraft* (1718), all of which texts largely dissuaded belief among the educated in diabolical witchcraft.

The Salem witch trials of 1692 produced a fascination with witchcraft in America, beginning with Cotton Mather's *Wonders of the Invisible World* (1693), warning that the witches were true followers of Satan. Later writers have often viewed the witches as victims of those who tried them. Cornelius Mathews's *Witchcraft* (1852), Henry Wadsworth Longfellow's *The New England Tragedies* (1868), and Arthur Miller's *The Crucible* (1953) are all sympathetic considerations of supposed "witches," the latter finding in Salem a metaphor of modern political persecution. Witchcraft serves an important symbolic function in Nathaniel Hawthorne's "Young Goodman Brown" (1846).

The 18th cent. was characterized by rationalist skepticism about witchcraft and the devil, and the gothic novels at the end of the century reinforced that skepticism by mingling witches, demons, ghosts, corpses, and specters indiscriminately in order to produce horror and special effects. Walter Scott, whose skepticism was matched only by his use of the supernatural to titillate, carried this tendency into the 19th cent. (see his *Letters on Demonology and Witchcraft* [1830]). The Romantics exploited the plasticity of the concept in order to create a positive image of the witch, as in Shelley's "Witch of Atlas" (1820). The Romantics viewed belief in witchcraft as absurd, but reconstructed the image of the witch as a positive symbol of the revolt against oppressive tradition and authority.

The image of the diabolical witch continues to appear in popular literature such as Ira Levin's *Rosemary's Baby* (1967). John Updike's *The Witches of Eastwick* is a serious modern treatment of the nature of evil, using the revived cult of witchcraft to show how the decay of faith coincides with the revival of ancient superstition. Witchcraft has begun to take on new importance in revisionist feminist literature, in which female sorcery and magic — emblematic of female power — have been reinvested with positive associations.

See also DEVIL; WITCH OF ENDOR.

Bibliography. Cohn, N. *Europe's Inner Demons* (1975); Klaits, J. *Servants of Satan* (1985); Mendelsohn, I. "Magic, Magician." *IDB* 3.223-25; Peters, E. *The Magician, the Witch and the Law* (1978); Russell, J. B. *A History of Witchcraft: Sorcerers, Heretics, and Pagans* (1980).

JEFFREY BURTON RUSSELL

WITNESS   In the KJV the word *witness* is used to translate the Hebrew nouns *'ed, 'edah,* and *'edut,* the Hebrew verb *'anah,* and the Greek word *martys* with all its derivative forms and cognates.

The main use of the word is forensic, and from this use all other applications are derived. A witness is one who can testify about what he has seen and heard. The Bible stresses the role of witnesses. Important legal agreements required the presence of attesting witnesses (Ruth 4:1-11; Jer. 32:10, 12). At least two witnesses were necessary to establish any charge (Num. 35:30; Deut. 17:6; 19:15). Unjust or deceitful witness was common, and false witness was criticized (Exod. 23:1; Ps. 27:12; Prov. 6:19; 19:5, 9) and prohibited by the Decalogue (Exod. 20:16).

The Talmud regarded it as sinful for a single person to come forward to accuse anyone (Pesaḥ. 113b; cf. Sanh. 9b). On the other hand, refusal to come forward as a witness when solemnly adjured to do so was sinful (Lev. 5:1). Certain people could not serve as witnesses: close relatives, minors, women, usurers, tax collectors, and slaves (Sanh. 3.3, 4; Rosh Hash. 1.7; B. Qam. 88a; cf. Josephus, *Ant.* 4.8.15).

Witnesses were required to participate in the execution of persons convicted by their evidence (Deut. 17:7; cf. Acts 7:58). If a person was found guilty of false witness, then he suffered the penalty which he meant to inflict upon the accused (Deut. 19:16-21). Despite the prohibitions, false witnessing was common in both the OT and NT (Ps. 35:11; Prov. 12:17; 24:28; Matt. 26:60; Acts 6:13).

The story of Susanna shows the need for scrupulous care in the examination of witnesses lest an innocent person be convicted. Nonhuman objects could also serve as witnesses, such as a pile of stones (Gen. 31:44-54; Josh. 24:27) or animals presented in concluding a covenant (Gen. 21:30). Sometimes God was invoked as a witness in an oath of affirmation or agreement (1 Sam. 20:23; 12:5-6; cf. Matt. 26:63, 72, 74).

In the NT *witness* is used both in a legal sense and in an extended sense. This is very clear in the Lukan writings, where the apostles function both as witnesses to facts *and* witnesses to convictions (Luke 24:47; Acts 1:8, 22; 5:32; 10:39-43; 13:31). The idea of witness is also prominent in the Fourth Gospel, where witness is primarily given to the truth of the Christian message rather than to facts. Thus John the Baptist (John 1:7-8, 15), the Scriptures (John 5:31-39), the "works" of Christ (John 10:25), and the Holy Spirit (John 15:26) all serve to bear witness to Jesus.

The ultimate test of a person's commitment to truth is willingness to lay down his life for it (Rev. 2:13; 17:6). In these instances, the witness *(martys)* becomes the martyr. The supreme inspiration for all true Christian witness is Jesus Christ, who himself is "the faithful and true witness" (Rev. 3:14).

Patristic commentators such as St. Jerome and their medieval successors make much of the association *martys / martyr,* and the enormous space given in medieval Christian libraries to martyrology, chiefly saints' lives, amply demonstrates the conviction that no more authentic witness to faith in Christ is possible. St. Augustine, taking up the enigmatic statement of Jesus about the value of his bearing witness to himself (John 5:31), argues that Jesus is speaking rhetorically to meet the unbelief of his hearers, and that the provision of a forerunner, John the Baptist, as a witness (cf. John 1:7-8) was designed to fulfill a basic OT requirement of the law (*Sermo,* 128.1-2). By the same token, he adds, those who follow Christ are called upon to bear him witness by their faithful obedience to his Word. Scripture and the life of the Church thus continue

as witness to God's redemption and fulfillment of his covenant promise in Christ.

For George Herbert, both Law and Grace bear continual witness to divine truth: the Jews, who "have their Law and Language bearing witnesse to them," are themselves "God's proof, and witnesses; as he calls them, *Isaiah* 43.12." Likewise, there has been a "continual succession (since the Gospell) of holy men, who have been witness to the truth" (*A Priest to the Temple,* chap. 34). Henry Vaughan develops another aspect of the notion of witness in his poem "The Stone," which he indicates is drawn on Joshua's declaration that a nearby stone has "heard" and bears witness to the covenant reestablished between God and his people Israel (Josh. 24:27). The poem includes an apocalyptic warning against transgression:

> Hence sand and dust
> Are shak'd for witnesses, and stones
> Which some think dead, shall all at once
> With one attesting voice detect
> Those secret sins we least suspect.
> For know, wilde men, that when you erre
> Each thing turns Scribe and Register,
> And in obedience to his Lord,
> Doth your most private sins record.

Although the reader is directed to the passage in Joshua, the poem also invokes by contrastive association a NT passage, in which Jesus says of his disciples' bearing witness to him, "If these should hold their peace, the stones would immediately cry out" (Luke 19:40).

Another NT passage frequently recollected in literature is that in Hebrews in which the writer admonishes his fellow Christians, "Wherefore, seeing we also are compassed about with so great a cloud of witnesses, let us lay aside every weight, and the sin which doth so easily beset us, and let us run with patience the race that is set before us" (12:1). Matthew Henry is typical of Christian commentators in interpreting the "cloud of witnesses" as "the word of God and the faithful servants of God" ("Scripture" and "tradition" for medieval exegetes). It is this witness of Scripture and the faithful throughout history which William Cowper also has in mind in his conclusion to bk. 5 of *The Task:*

> They are thy witnesses, who speak thy pow'r
> And goodness infinite, but speak in ears
> That hear not, or receive not their report.
> In vain thy creatures testify of thee
> Till thou proclaim thyself.... (853-57)

Hebrews 12 also provides the source for one of John Keble's best-known poems on the witness of Scripture and the Church, "Who Runs May Read."

See also CLOUD OF WITNESSES; MARTYR; STONES CRY OUT; SUSANNA; TWO WITNESSES. .   A. A. TRITES

WOLF SHALL DWELL WITH THE LAMB *See* LION LIES DOWN WITH THE LAMB.

WOLVES IN SHEEP'S CLOTHING In his Sermon on the Mount, after Jesus has distinguished between the narrow way leading to life and the broad way leading to destruction, he warns his hearers to "beware of false prophets, which come to you in sheep's clothing, but inwardly they are ravening wolves" (Matt. 7:15). Early commentaries readily associated these "wolves" with heresy, hypocrisy, and misuses of priestly office (e.g., St. Augustine, *Sermo*, 137.12; *De sermone Domini in Monte*, 2.24.80; cf. St. Ambrose, *De Spiritu Sancto*, 2.10.108-09; St. Jerome, *Ep.* 22.38; 147.11).

English literature likewise reserves the appellation almost exclusively for false or corrupted members of the clergy. Chaucer provides vivid portraits of such characters in his Friar, Summoner, and Pardoner, all of whom are "false prophets" in this sense; Langland quotes Jesus' words to denounce hypocrisy — "a braunche of pruyde" for which he says the clergy are notorious: "Ruȝt so many preestes prechours and prelates, / That beth enblaunched with *bel paroles* and with *bele* clothes; / And as lambes thei loken and lyuen as wolues" (*Piers Plowman,* C.17.268-70). In Shakespeare's *1 Henry 6* Gloucester is angered by the Bishop of Winchester's betrayals, concluding that Winchester is less an ally than a "wolf in sheep's array" (1.3.55). Thoreau, arguing that some members of the clergy played a deceptively ambiguous role in the slavery issue, uses the words of Jesus to condemn them in "A Plea for Captain John Brown." The "wolf in sheep's clothing, a bloodthirsty hypocrite, wearing the garb of innocence" in Thackeray's *The Newcomes*, is one among the "farrago of old fables" with which the novel begins, setting the theme which the author's stage "critics" deride. In Samuel Butler's *The Way of All Flesh* Ernest's considered opinion of the clergy of the Church of England is that most of them fall into this category; the narrator says "now that he had seen them more closely, he knows better the nature of these wolves in sheep's clothing, who are thirsting for the blood of their victim."

WOMAN AT THE WELL The story of Jesus' encounter with the Samaritan Woman at the Well and his offering her a "well of water springing up into everlasting life" (John 4:4-42) is one of the more complex narratives in the ministry sections of the Gospels. It involves cultural conflict (Samaritans vs. Jews), sex role issues (a woman married five times who meets and recognizes Jesus), an episode in the education of the disciples, and highly symbolic language ("water of life" and the end of "spiritual thirst"). The story bears a typological relationship with several Genesis narratives and constitutes one of the famous dialogues in John's Gospel (e.g., 3:1-5 [Nicodemus]; 6:25-59; 8:12-59 [crowds]; 11:17-44 [Martha and Mary]). Narratively, the story functions to show Jesus as

the promised Messiah, who fulfills Jewish hopes of redemption and who also comes to bring redemption to all peoples.

The setting of the conversation is reminiscent of betrothal stories which occur at wells — stories of Rebekah (Gen. 24:10-14), Rachel (Gen. 29:1-12), and the daughters of the priest of Midian (Exod. 2:15-21). "Living waters" (a wordplay on a Semitic expression for flowing water) has a rich OT background as a symbol for divine, life-giving activity (e.g., Jer. 2:13; Ezek. 47:9; Zech. 14:8). Water is such a symbol elsewhere in John also (e.g., 7:37; 19:34). In medieval and Renaissance exegetical writing the typology of the waters of life (v. 14) is linked to the fountain of Eden (Gen. 2:10-14), the crossing of the Red Sea (Exod. 14:21-29), the rock of Horeb (Exod. 17:6), and the sealed fountain (Cant. 4:12). In sacramental terms it is associated with the grace of the baptismal waters and, in conjunction with the rock of Horeb, it is also associated with the blood which flowed from Christ's side. In eschatological terms it prefigures the pure river of water (Rev. 22:1).

Extracanonical legends give the Samaritan woman the name St. Photine and record that she preached the gospel, was imprisoned for three years, and died for her faith in Carthage. In another apocryphal narrative she is said to have been martyred in Rome after converting the daughter of Nero and 100 of her retinue. Her feast day is March 20.

Origen interpreted the story of the woman at the well as an allegorical representation of the soul coming to spiritual understanding of the gospel. He saw the woman as a heretic lost to the world of the senses. Her five husbands represent the five senses, and the sixth man, to whom she is not married, represents false doctrines. She comes to spiritual understanding when she tastes of the living water and is released from the concerns of the flesh and the power of the Law (*Hom. on Genesis and Exodus,* trans. Heine [1982], 132-35). St. John Chrysostom (*Comm. on St. John*) presents an admiring portrayal of the Samaritan woman, who "of her own accord did the work of an evangelist with excited elation." She called a whole city to Christ and is thereby seen as superior to the apostles. She is characterized as wise, discerning, open, and kindly in crossing social barriers to speak with Jesus, a Jew. For Chrysostom the woman's disgraceful past makes her ultimate interest in sublime matters all the more remarkable: "Let us then be ashamed and let us now blush. A woman who had had five husbands and was a Samaritan manifested such deep interest in doctrine."

St. Augustine's interpretation of the Samaritan woman emphasizes the symbolic features of her story. The five husbands are analogous to the five books of Moses adhered to by the Samaritans and signifying the Old Law. Augustine assumes that the Torah "contains" Christ and provides the basis for her realization of the New Law of grace incarnate before her in the sixth "husband," to whom she is not yet married because she does not yet believe. Like Origen he also identifies the five husbands with the five senses. The sixth husband is the sixth sense, which enables spiritual understanding. Augustine allies this detail with the "sixth hour" setting of the scene (the sixth age of mankind) and with the six verbal responses which the woman makes to Christ, the sixth being her statement of spiritual recognition (*De diversus questionibus LXXXIII,* trans. Mosher [1981], 127-35).

"The Woman of Samaria," a scriptural paraphrase of seventy-seven rhymed couplets, is included in *An Old English Miscellany* (EETS o.s. 49). It follows the Gospel account closely but truncates the role of the disciples (vv. 27-38) and emphasizes the transformation and redemption of the woman, whose reluctance to give Christ water shows that "heo wes of wytte poure." *Jacob's Well,* a series of homilies from the 15th cent. (EETS o.s. 115), attaches to the image of the Samaritan woman, who, having received the gifts of the Holy Spirit, must shut five water gates — the five senses — to defend against sin. Only then will the well provide the refreshment of the water of grace.

Many medieval legends associated with Mary Magdalene include an episode in which she recognizes Christ at a well. The identification of the woman of Samaria with Mary Magdalene is based upon a common history of promiscuity and a conversion experience from which follows a career as a disciple of Jesus. The 15th-cent. Digby play *Mary Magdalen* incorporates several details from the story of the Samaritan woman into the Mary Magdalene narrative (see Fowler, 106-18).

Though the meditative writers and poets of the 13th-15th cents. paid much less attention to the stories of the ministry of Jesus than to the Nativity and Passion, the influential pseudo-Bonaventuran *Meditationes Vitae Christi* includes a meditation on this text. The woman, named Lucy, provides the focus for a meditation on the poverty and humility of Jesus, who speaks to this lowly and sinful woman as an equal. In his English translation and paraphrase of *Meditationes,* Nicholas Love adds that Christ favored her and "ignored the towns and the established and learned men" (*The Mirrour of the Blessed Lyf of Jesu Christ*).

Perhaps the best-known use of the story in medieval literature is the reference made to the Samaritan woman by the Wife of Bath in the prologue to her tale. She justifies her own robust sexuality by boasting that she, too, has had five husbands. She claims not to know what Jesus meant by the remark that the "sixth man" she has now is not her husband. D. W. Robertson has argued that the Samaritan woman, who achieves sublime wisdom, provides an ironic contrast with the Wife, who cannot understand Christ's words and is therefore a "literary personification of rampant 'femininity' or carnality, and her exegesis is, in consequence, rigorously carnal and literal" (318-22). She pretentiously challenges Christ's teaching of the spirit, favoring the Old Law, where "God

bad us for to wexe and multiplye; / That gentil text kan I wel understonde" (*Canterbury Tales,* 3.28-29).

The typological reading of the well in Samaria as the well of life and a symbol of baptism and regeneration was popular through the 16th and 17th cents. Edmund Spenser uses the well of life with its rejuvenative connotations in *The Faerie Queene* (1.2.43 and 1.11.29). Among the metaphysical poets, Herbert, Vaughan, and Traherne employed the imagery of redeeming waters. Vaughan makes explicit reference to the Samaritan woman's visit to Jacob's Well in "The Search," but unlike her he does not find his answers in experience. In "Religion," in which Vaughan employs the typology of the closed fountain of Cant. 4:12, he describes religion as a "tainted sink . . . like that Samaritans dead well" (*Silex Scintillans*).

Edward Taylor's meditations bring together his desire for spiritual awareness with his preparations for the Lord's Supper. He joins the Samaritan's experience at the well with the typology from Genesis, "the Well of Living Water and Tree of Life," to which he adds the sacramental dimension, "Lord bath mee in this Well of Life" (*Preparatory Meditations,* 2.47). Christopher Smart includes the story in his verse paraphrases, *The Parables of Our Lord and Saviour Jesus Christ* (1768). He adheres closely to the biblical account, emphasizing Christ's knowledge of the woman's marital history and her astonishment at his prophetic vision. He draws no conclusions about her past life, the immorality of successive marriages, and the problem of her current status but rather uses the episode to reveal Christ's marvelous omniscience. In Emily Dickinson's "I know where Wells grow — " the poet grapples with the idea of spiritual thirst: "I read in an Old fashioned Book / That People 'thirst no more' — " But she finds that her thirst is better satisfied by "a little Well — like Mine — / Dearer to understand — "

Edmond Rostand's biblical drama *The Woman of Samaria,* first performed in 1897, reflects on the ancient significance of the well and the Jewish-Samaritan conflict as it opens with the phantoms of Abraham, Isaac, and Jacob. The revolutionary rhetoric of a young Samaritan sustains the political concerns of the story. Photine, Rostand's heroine, approaches Christ at the well, singing songs of love from the Canticles. These songs continue through the play, though they gain symbolic meaning as her own awareness deepens from carnal to spiritual knowledge. Rostand makes little of Photine's moral history, though he does add the character of Azriel, Photine's sixth man, who is astonished when this illiterate woman learns to expound Scripture like an ecstatic preacher. The play includes pageantry and Photine's exuberant singing. Even the otherwise crusty disciples eventually join in the celebration of love.

See also LIVING WATER.

Bibliography. Dickson, D. R. *The Fountains of Living Waters: The Typology of the Water of Life in Herbert,*

Vaughan, and Traherne (1987); Fowler, D. *The Bible in Middle English Literature* (1984); Robertson, D. W., Jr. *A Preface to Chaucer* (1962).   FAYE PAULI WHITAKER

WOMAN CLOTHED WITH THE SUN   Rev. 12:1-6 describes as a great sign in heaven a woman clothed with the sun, standing on the moon, and wearing a crown of twelve stars. Pregnant and in pain to deliver a son who is destined to rule the nations, she is harassed by a great red dragon. This seven-headed creature awaits to devour the baby, but the baby is snatched away to God, and the woman flees to the desert, where she is nourished for 1,260 days.

Although the astrological language used to describe the woman has led scholars to associate her with a sun goddess and various Near Eastern myths, she is in the biblical context more likely a figure of the righteous community (cf. the representation of Israel [Isa. 66:7-11; Ezek. 16:8] and the Church [2 Cor. 11:2; Eph. 5:23-27; Rev. 21:2] as women). The woman in Revelation is associated with the Lamb (Rev. 19:7-8); together they symbolize the community of the righteous and its messianic deliverer in opposition to the whore of Babylon (Rev. 17) and the dragon. The sharp birth pangs suggest the persecution of the remnant awaiting its deliverance, a concept important to the Qumran community and developed in the Psalms of Thanksgiving (1QH 3). In Christian tradition exegetes have generally considered the woman to be a symbol of the community of the persecuted faithful, specifically the Christian Ecclesia embattled by the forces of the devil. To many medieval and later Christian commentators, the persecution of the woman became the central image of Revelation, which was understood as a whole to be essentially a prophecy of the trials of the holy Church.

According to R. H. Charles, the disappearance of the Messiah from birth until he is anointed "was an idea familiar to Judaism, but impossible as a purely Christian concept" (*Revelation,* 308, n. 1). The biblical text makes no allusion either to the woman's virginity or to the child being her firstborn. Nevertheless, because the pregnant, embattled woman is reminiscent of the woman whose seed will destroy the serpent in the Protoevangelium (Gen. 3:15) and because the scene parallels the sign given to Ahaz that a woman will bear a son named Immanuel (Isa. 7:10-17), exegetes as early as St. Irenaeus (*Adv. haer.* 3.22.7) argued for the association with Mary. Often, as in Paschasius Radbertus (*Comm. in Matthaei Libri XII,* 2.1) and Thomas à Kempis (*Prayers on the Life of Christ,* 1.2.25), the imagery has been applied both specifically to Mary and generally to Ecclesia. After the Reformation and in contrast to the Protestant emphasis on the ecclesial interpretation, Catholic exegetes identified the cosmically arrayed woman with the Virgin and developed the apocalyptic language to describe her Assumption and role as Queen of Heaven and to symbolize the Immaculate Conception. This imagery informs the work of great Spanish

and Italian Baroque painters (such as Murillo) and the introit in the Catholic Mass of the Assumption.

The woman's retreat to the desert was frequently identified with the withdrawal of the embattled Christian soul from the everyday world into contemplation. St. Bonaventure develops this imagery in his *Collationes,* where the vision of the woman not only represents "the splendor of the contemplatives, for they possess the sun, the moon and the stars" (20.28), but is also associated with the Church Militant (22.2) and the Christian soul seeking union with God (22.39). The image of the woman as soul is also important in mystical literature, where, as in the work of Mechthild of Magdeburg (*The Flowing Light of the Godhead,* 1.22), the soul is identified with Mary.

Dante describes the Virgin Mary in *Paradiso* (31.118-29) as a queen who, like the sun, outshines all others. Medieval literature not only specifically identifies the woman with Mary (as, e.g., in the ME lyric *"Quia Amore Langueo"*; cf. also T. Coletti, "Devotional Iconography in the N-Town Marian Plays," *CompD* 11 [1977], 22-44) but also more generally associates the woman with the Church and the individual soul. An ecclesial interpretation of the woman seems to lie behind portrayal of Lady Holy Church in *Piers Plowman,* since she is intended to contrast with Lady Mead, a type of the whore of Babylon; the woman's association with the soul probably informs the portrait of the maiden in *Pearl,* a 14th-cent. poem heavily dependent on apocalyptic imagery.

Later English literature associates the woman with the true, spiritual Church, often in contrast with the carnal church. This opposition is reflected in the first book of Spenser's *Faerie Queene.* Una, like the woman, is associated with the lamb and has an ancient royal lineage (1.1.5). Furthermore, her parents' kingdom has been besieged for years by the "huge great Dragon horrible in sight" (1.7.44), who elsewhere, like the apocalyptic dragon, is associated with Duessa, the harlot false church. Blake expands the traditional interpretation of the woman clothed with the sun, for she represents not only the Christian but also the universal Church, "composed of the Innocent civilized Heathen & the Uncivilized Savage, who, having not the Law, do by Nature the things contain'd in the Law. This State appears like a Female crown'd with stars, driven into the Wilderness: she has the Moon under her feet" (*Vision of the Last Judgment,* 609-10). Developing the image of the woman harassed by the dragon for polemical purposes in *Examiner,* no. 21, Swift identifies the Dissenters attempting to disestablish the Church of England with the seven-headed dragon attacking the woman, who by implication is given a double identity — the Anglican Church and Queen Anne.

More recently, Robertson Davies develops an interesting fictional allusion to the woman. In *Fifth Business* (2.2), the young hero, who especially enjoys reading Revelation, sees in a sudden flash just before sinking into a coma the woman harassed by the dragon. Although he later realizes that the "vision" was actually a sculpture representing the Immaculate Conception, he initially takes it to be a salvific omen; his subsequent search for the image dominates his life.

See also MARY, MOTHER OF JESUS; WHORE OF BABYLON.

Bibliography. Charles, R. H. *A Critical and Exegetical Commentary on the Revelation of St. John* (1920; rpt. 1956); Emmerson, R., and B. McGinn. *The Apocalypse in the Middle Ages* (1992); Fitts, W. D. "Cymbeline and the Woman in the Wilderness: The Twelfth Chapter of the Apocalypse as Source Study." *DAI* 46 (1986), 3039A; Hoagwood, T. A. "Pictorial Apocalypse: Blake's 'Great Red Dragon and the Woman Clothed with the Sun'." *Colby Library Quarterly* 2 (1985), 11-21; Le Frois, B. *The Woman Clothed with the Sun (Apoc. 12): Individual or Collective?* (1954); Paley, M. D. "William Blake, the Prince of the Hebrews, and the Woman Clothed with the Sun." In *William Blake: Essays in Honour of Sir Geoffrey Keynes.* Ed. M. D. Paley and M. Phillips (1973), 260-93; Prigent, P. *Apocalypse 12: Histoire de l'exégèse.* Beiträge zur Geschichte der biblischen Exegese, vol. 2 (1959).   RICHARD K. EMMERSON

WOMAN OF SAMARIA   *See* WOMAN AT THE WELL.

WOMAN TAKEN IN ADULTERY   When the scribes and Pharisees wished to entrap Jesus concerning his regard for the Mosaic law, they apprehended a woman in the act of adultery and brought her to him, saying,

> Now Moses in the law commanded us, that such should be stoned: but what sayest thou? This they said, tempting him, that they might have [something with which] to accuse him. But Jesus stooped down, and with his finger wrote on the ground, as though he heard them not. So when they continued asking him, he lifted up himself, and said unto them, He that is without sin among you, let him [be the] first [to] cast a stone at her. And again he stooped down, and wrote on the ground. (John 8:5-8)

At this the accusers of the woman withdrew, one by one, until Jesus was left alone with her. He then asked her, "Woman, where are those thine accusers? hath no man condemned thee? She said, No man, Lord. And Jesus said unto her, Neither do I condemn thee: go, and sin no more" (vv. 9-12).

Interpretation of this passage in the patristic period emphasizes the culpability of every sinner before the Law. What Jesus is saying to the accusers, according to St. Augustine, is effectively: "Let each of you consider himself, let him enter into himself, ascend the judgment seat in his own mind, place himself at the bar of his own conscience, oblige himself to confess. . . . Hence, either let this woman go, or together with her receive the penalty of the law." When Jesus says, "he that is without sin. . . ," says Augustine, one hears

> the voice of justice: Let her, the sinner, be punished, but not by sinners; let the law be fulfilled, but not by transgressors of the law. This certainly is the voice of justice: by which justice those men, pierced through as if by a

dart, looking into themselves and finding themselves guilty, one after another all withdrew. The two were left alone, the wretched woman and Mercy. . . . I suppose that the woman was the more terrified when she heard it said by the Lord, "He that is without sin." . . . She expected to be punished by him in whom sin was not to be found.

In his release of the woman to "go and sin no more," says Augustine, the Lord "condemned sins, not mankind." He did not say, "Go, live as you please . . . however much you sin I will deliver you even from the punishment of hell" (*In Joan. Ev.* 33.5-6). Other early exegetes follow the principal lines of Augustine's commentary, with minor variations. St. Jerome speculates (*Adversus Pelagianos,* 2.17) that what Jesus wrote on the ground was the names of the accusers; St. Ambrose makes a similar suggestion.

When Chaucer has Alisoun of *The Miller's Tale* put off Absolon the amorous deacon while she commits adultery with Nicholas the student, he gives her the words "Go forth thy wey, or I wol caste a ston" (1.3712), a transparent and crude reversal of Christ's words to the adulterous woman which underscores Alisoun's willful culpability. Chaucer's Parson in his sermon is unstinting in his condemnation of "Avowtrie," which he says is set between theft and homicide in the Decalogue, "for it is the gretteste theft that may be, for it is thefte of body and of soule. / And it is lyk to homycide, for it kerveth atwo and breketh atwo hem that first were maked o flessh. And therfore, by the olde lawe of God, they sholde be slayn." But, he adds,

> natheles, by the lawe of Jhesu Crist, that is lawe of pitee, when he seyde to the womman that was founden in avowtrie, and sholde han been slayn with stones. . . . "Go," quod Jhesu Crist, "and have namoore wyl to do synne." . . . Soothly the vengeaunce of Avowtrie is awarded to the peynes of helle, but if so be that it be destourbed [prevented] by penitence. (886-90)

The Corpus Christi plays offer dramatizations of the episode: York's, which is defective (missing a leaf), clearly underscores the hypocrisy of the "double standard" (24.9-10). The N-Town pageant begins with a speech by Jesus which roughly translates the absolution from the liturgy; indeed, a rubric in Latin has been added to the MS: "*Nolo mortem peccatoris*" (in the *Book of Common Prayer* rendering: "who desireth not the death of a sinner"). Jesus says:

> Man for þi synne take repentaunce
> If þou amende þat is amys
> Than hevyn xal be þin herytaunce. . . .
> Thow þat ȝour synns by nevyr so grett
> Ffor hem, be sad and aske mercy. (1-3; 9-10)

In this play the "Phariseus," "Scriba," and "Accusator" take pleasure in setting the trap both for the woman and for Jesus, each in his own way illustrating St. Paul's observation (Rom. 5:20; 9:31-32) that the Law's strength is diagnostic; it defines sin and judges it. These spokesmen for Law are concerned to oppose Jesus' preaching of "grace and mercy" (89ff.); when the frightened woman cries out for mercy, Accusator's reply (157-60) is:

> Aske us no mercy it xal not be
> We xul so ordeyn ffor þi lott
> þat þou xalt dye for þin Advowtrye
> þerfore com forth þou stynkynge stott.

The Pharisee adds (217-20):

> Ageyn þe lawe þou dedyst offens
> þerfore of grace speke þou no more
> As moyses gevith in law sentens
> þou xalt be stonyd to deth therfore.

When Jesus writes on the ground in this play, each of the accusers sees in turn "all myn synnys evyn propyrly namyd" (as in the narrative of Jesus' encounter with the Samaritan woman by the well [John 4:5-29]). After Jesus dismisses the woman with the admonition (277-80) to sin no more, she promises not only repentance but conversion: "all my lewde lyff I xal doun lete / and ffonde to be goddys trewe servaunt" (283-84).

Calvin establishes quite a different tone in his reading of the narrative. First, he points out that according to the Law (Deut. 17:7) "God commanded that the witnesses should put malefactors and evildoers to death with their own hands, so that very great scrupulousness might be shown in bearing witness." Calvin is troubled, however, lest it should be imagined that Jesus "seems to be driving all witnesses away from the witness box and all judges from the bench," and asserts that "this is not an absolute and simple prohibition, in which Christ forbids sinners to do their duty in correcting the sins of others. Rather, by this word, he only reproves hypocrites who gently flatter themselves and their own vices, but are excessively severe and even savage judges of others. None, then, must let his own sins stop him correcting the sins of others and even punishing them when necessary" (*Comm.* sup. John 8:8). When Jesus says "Neither do I condemn thee," one should not imagine, says Calvin, "that Christ simply absolved the woman," but rather that he let her go, because more than that "did not belong to his office." Moreover,

> those who deduce from this [event] that adultery should not be punished by death must, on the same reasoning, admit that inheritances should not be divided, since Christ refused to arbitrate between two brothers. Indeed, every crime will be exempt from the penalties of the law if the punishment of adultery is remitted, for the door will then be thrown open to any kind of treachery. (sup. v. 11)

Whether or not Shakespeare has Calvin's commentary in mind, the Calvinist emphasis in the views of his Puritan contemporaries provides a backdrop for *Measure for Measure,* in which a man is "taken in adultery" — actually fornication — and by the Puritan "protector" Angelo condemned to death despite his sister's pleas for mercy, so as not to "make a scarecrow of the law" (2.1.1). In Angelo's words (2.1.27-31):

> You may not so extenuate his offense
> For I have had such faults; but rather tell me,
> When I, that censure him, do so offend,
> Let mine own judgment pattern out my death,
> And nothing come in partial. Sir, he must die.

When Isabella's pleas for mercy for her brother result only in Angelo's lustful proposition that she trade her honor for her brother's life, and that villainy in turn is, with other breaches, uncovered, the accuser here too is robbed of his appeal to justice and must depend upon mercy. Because "grace is grace, despite of all controversy" (1.2.25-27), he too then receives mercy when the lesson is learned and repentance ensues.

Matthew Henry's *Commentary* (1721) emphasizes the need for the virtue of toleration borne of recognition of one's own sinful nature and propensities: "*Aut sumus, aut fuimus, vel possumus esse quod hic est* — We either are, or have been, or may be, what he is. Let this restrain us from throwing stones at our brethren and proclaiming their faults. *Let him that is without sin* begin such discourse as this," says Henry, observing that in another point of Mosaic law (Num. 5:15) it was stated that "if the husband who brought his wife to that trial had himself been at any time guilty of adultery," the penalty would not apply (6.982). Christ's refusal to condemn, he observes, is in fact a form of absolution (6.984).

In literature since the 18th cent. there has been a tendency to apply the text as an appeal for toleration as much as for mercy. In his preface to *Adonaïs* Shelley compares the accusers in the narrative to the critics he feels have hastened Keats to an early grave: "Against what woman taken in adultery dares the foremost of these literary prostitutes to cast his opprobrious stone? Miserable man! You, one of the meanest, have wantonly defaced one of the noblest specimens of the workmanship of God." William Morris, in *News from Nowhere*, takes this application one step further, claiming that in Utopia legal penalties are bound to be mild: "Paying a severe legal penalty, the wrongdoer can 'go and sin again' with comfort. . . . Remember Jesus had got the legal penalty remitted before he said 'Go and sin no more.' " When Miss Prism's erstwhile maternity (hence adultery) is revealed to her in the third act of Oscar Wilde's *The Importance of Being Earnest*, she recoils "in indignant astonishment": "Mr. Worthing! I am unmarried!" to which Jack replies, "Unmarried! I do not deny that is a serious blow. But after all, who has the right to cast a stone against the one who has suffered? Cannot repentance wipe out the act of folly? Why should there be one law for men, and another for women?"

WORD MADE FLESH   *See* INCARNATION.

WORD OF GOD   Different writings within the OT emphasize different aspects of the word of God. In the prophetic tradition a prophet can speak authentically only if he mediates God's word as a message from God to his people. Often some such title-phrase as "the word of the LORD that come to . . ." begins a prophecy (e.g., Jer. 1:2; Hos. 1:1; Jonah 1:1; Zech. 1:1). In the canonical prophets this divine word, however, is mediated through consciously reflective and responsible human agencies. Amos conveys a message which is also "the words of Amos" (1:1), and Jeremiah struggles with, even struggles against, the word which God has "put into" his mouth (1:9; 15:18; 20:7-9; 47:6, 7). Sometimes God's word can take the form of visionary or visual experience, but probably partly because of the divine prohibition against images of God the prophets are more at ease with the aural model of communication and disclosure.

In Deuteronomy and a number of Psalms the word of God takes the form of law. But since this word embodies God's directives for his people's highest good, the law of God is seen as a source of life and of delight rather than as primarily restrictive (Ps. 119:43-48, 50, 97-112, 139-44). In the wisdom literature the writers make little or no appeal to the authority of the divine word, but there is a parallel between the creative role of God's wisdom and the creative power of his word in Gen. 1 and Isa. 55:10-11. God's word is effective and powerful, and changes situations. Many scholars have tried to account for this emphasis on the basis of a dynamic view of words prevalent in the ancient Near East (e.g., L. Dürr). But the OT writers ascribe the power of God's word not to some supposed property of language as such, but to God's sovereign and gracious promise to perform it.

Jewish thought between the two Testaments tended to hypostatize the word of God as a quasi-independent divine attribute which, alongside wisdom, preexisted the world. Word and wisdom mediated God's Being and will to his creation. Hellenistic Judaism combined these ideas with Stoic and other Greek speculation about the divine word or *logos* as the rational principle which made things intelligible. In Philo, the word of God *(logos)* becomes a mediator almost occupying the place ascribed by the Church to Christ.

At least three distinct senses of the term occur in the NT. First in theological importance, Christ himself is the word of God enfleshed in personal life (John 1:1-18; cf. Heb. 1:1-2). In the Person of Christ God's word is both spoken and lived out. There is also an implicit claim in parts of the NT that Christ occupies the mediatorial place ascribed to word and wisdom in Jewish theology. Second, the OT is seen as the authoritative Scripture of the Church, not least because it remains the word of God to Christians. Third, God's word is heard in the present in the preaching of the gospel and in Christian edification (Acts 13:46; Phil. 1:14). This is synonymous with the "word of truth" (Eph. 1:13).

All three major NT uses have prevailed in the history of Christian thought. St. Athanasius *(Incarnation of the Word of God),* St. Augustine *(In Joannis evangelium; De Genesi*

ad litteram), St. Ambrose *(De Incarnationis dominicae sacramento),* and St. Gregory the Great *(Moralia in Iob)* are among the major writers who codify the theology. Later medieval theologians such as Peter Lombard *(Sententiae)* and John Wyclif *(De Benedicta Incarnatione)* for the most part merely clarify and restate the three NT senses. The Reformers stressed the complementary relation between gospel words and gospel sacraments as aural and visible words of God. After the 17th cent. the claim that the Bible as an anthology or "Book" is the word of God became increasingly controversial and polemical, serving to exclude any notion that the Bible could be viewed as no more than a record of Hebrew-Christian religious experience. Theologically this position embodies the claim that God reveals his will in Christ and in Scripture, and that through these means he addresses Christians in a way which invites obedient response.

John Donne's Holy Sonnet "Temple" is uncontroversial in its presentation of this idea. Jesus discussing and expounding the Scriptures in the Temple as a boy of 12 evokes Donne's sympathy with Joseph and Mary's awe: "the Word but lately could not speake, and loe, / It sodenly speakes wonders. . . ." In his remarks on "Valdesso's *Considerations. . .* ," George Herbert warns against a talismanic use of Scripture, observing that faith in the Word and in the Person who authored it are inseparable:

> All the Saints of God may be said in some sense to have put confidence in Scripture, but not as a naked Word severed from God, but as the Word of God: And in so doing they doe not sever their trust from God. But by trusting in the word of God they trust in God. Hee that trusts in the Kings word for any thing trusts in the King.

He goes on to criticize unreflective literalism by referring to the Davidic model of the Word of God inscribed in one's heart:

> Indeed he that shall so attend to the bark of the letter, as to neglect the Consideration of Gods Worke in his heart through the Word, doth amisse; both are to be done, the Scriptures still used, and Gods worke within us still observed, who workes by his Word, and ever in the reading of it.

By the 18th cent. the "Word of God" frequently appears as a synonym for the Bible, though the content given to that understanding of the term varies in accordance to belief. For Cowper, one may move from bark to sap, as it were, by responding to the spirit of the text inwardly:

> God's holy word, once trivial in his view
> Now by the voice of his experience true,
> Seems, as it is, the fountain whence alone
> Must spring that hope he pants to make his own.
> ("Hope," 706-9)

Ruskin's "Word of God" *(Fors Clavigera,* "Letter 36") is thoroughly internalized, but its relation to scriptural revelation is more elastic and capable of being construed as anything from *Zeitgeist* to the "great tradition" to a kind of educated conscience:

> By that Word, or Voice, or Breath, or Spirit, the heavens and earth, and all the host of them, were made; and in it they exist. It is your life; and speaks to you always, so long as you live nobly; — dies out of you as you refuse to obey it; leaves you to hear, and be slain by, the word of an evil spirit, instead of it. It may come to you in books, — come to you in clouds, — come to you in the voices of men, — come to you in the stillness of deserts. You must be strong in evil, if you have quenched it wholly; very desolate in this Christian land, if you have never heard it at all.

Overtones of a similar Romantic subjectivity tint the relatively orthodox content of John Greenleaf Whittier's poem "The Word." The 20th-cent. poet Margaret Avison attempts to wrestle back into this loosened metaphor something of the power of juxtaposition found in Donne and Herbert. In her "The Bible to be Believed,"

> The word read by the living Word
> sculptured its shaper's form.
> What happens, means. The meanings are not blurred
> by Flood — or fiery atom.

For Avison Jesus in the Temple is the "living word," the spirit opening the protective barrier, the "fence around the Torah":

> The Word dwells on this word
> honing His heart's sword,
> ready at knife-edge to declare
> holiness, and come clear.

And if the cross was a silencing, the Resurrection proclaims the Word of God in an unsilenceable register:

> His final silencing endured
> has sealed the living word:
> now therefore He is voiceful, to be heard,
> free, and of all opening-out the Lord.

See also LOGOS.

Bibliography. Ackroyd, P. R. "The Vitality of the Word of God in the Old Testament." *ASTI* 1 (1962), 7-23; Barr, J. *The Bible in the Modern World* (1973), 18-23; Barth, K. *Church Dogmatics: I, The Doctrine of the Word of God.* 2nd ed. (1975); Brown, R. E. *The Gospel according to St. John.* AB (1966), 519-24; Dürr, L. *Die Wertung des göttlichen Wortes im Alten Testament und im antiken Orient* (1938); Klappert, B. "Word." *NIDNTT* 3 (1978), 1087-1117; Rahner, K. *Theological Investigations,* 4 (1966), 253-86; Ringgren, H. *Word and Wisdom* (1947); Scheffczyk, L. "Word of God." *Sacramentum Mundi* 6 (1970), 362-68; Schmidt, W. H. *"dabar."* *TDOT* 3 (1978), 84-125; Thiselton, A. C. "The Supposed Power of Words in the Biblical Writings." *JTS* n.s. 25 (1974), 283-99; Wallace, R. S. *Calvin's Doctrine of Word and Sacrament* (1953); Zimmerli, W. "Wort Gottes." *RGG* 6 (1962), 1810-22.

ANTHONY C. THISELTON
DAVID L. JEFFREY

WORLD, FLESH, AND DEVIL The "three foes of man," as they were called in the catechism of the medieval Church, are the World, the Flesh, and the Devil —mortal enemies of the faithful, seeking ever to entice and lead them astray. The identification of this "unholy trinity" derives in part from a passage in the First Epistle of John which warns against excess affection for material things:

> Love not the world, neither the things that are in the world. If any man love the world, the love of the Father is not in him. For all that is in the world, the lust of the flesh, the lust of the eyes and the pride of life, is not of the Father, but is of the world. And the world passeth away, and the lust thereof: but he that doeth the will of God abideth forever. (1 John 2:15-17)

The three foes became linked with the three temptations of Christ by Satan in the wilderness —bread (flesh), kingdoms (world), and supererogatory power (devil) —and with the process of temptation and sin (corruption of the senses, intellect, and will) discussed by St. Augustine in his analysis of the Fall (*De sermo Domini in Monte,* 12.34). Chaucer's *Parson's Tale* (10.330-36) provides typical homiletical elaboration of the theme, as does the 13th-cent. ME lyric "Man must fight three foes" (C. Brown, *English Lyrics of the XIIIth Century,* no. 75). Occasionally a fourth foe is added —death —who capitalizes on the other three (C. Brown, *Religious Lyrics of the XIVth Century,* no. 27). In Chaucer's *Tale of Melibee* Melibee is informed by Dame Prudence that his calamity has been occasioned by his immoderate and conspicuous self-indulgence:

> "Thou hast doon synne agayn oure Lord Crist; / for certes, the three enemys of mankynde, that is to seyn, the flessh, the feend, and the world, thou hast suffred hem entre in to thyn herte wilfully by the wyndowes of thy body, / and hast nat defended thyself suffisantly agayns hire assautes and hire temptaciouns." (*Canterbury Tales,* 7.1412-22)

In medieval drama such as the morality play *The Castle of Perseverance* and the Digby play *Mary Magdalen,* the "kyng of the World" (Mundus), the "Kyng of the Flesch," and the "Dyfle" play out their part as allegories of the classic temptations.

After the Reformation this motif waned somewhat in importance, although the *Book of Common Prayer* retains, in its baptismal liturgy, an injunction to renounce "the devil and all his works, the vain pomp and glory of the world . . . and the sinful desires of the flesh." Henry Vaughan's poem "The World" is a meditation on the theme which concludes in a citation of 1 John 2:16-17. By the 19th cent. one finds rather straightforward allusions to 1 John 2:16 without the overlay of "psychomachic" elaboration. George Eliot has the narrator of *Adam Bede* observe that "Mr. Roe . . . had included Mr. Irwine in a general statement concerning the Church clergy in the surrounding district, whom he described as men giving up to the lusts of the flesh and pride of life" (chap. 5). In Pater's "The Child in the House" a "more than customary sensuousness" is earnestly commended, " 'the lust of the eye' as the Preacher says, which might lead him, one day, how far!"

See also TEMPTATION OF CHRIST.

Bibliography. Cullen, P. *Infernal Triad: The Flesh, the World and the Devil in Spenser and Milton* (1974); Howard, D. *The Three Temptations: Medieval Man in Search of the World* (1966).

WORLD WITHOUT END This phrase comes not from the Bible itself but from one of the oldest hymns of the Church, the *Gloria Patri* ("Glory be to the Father, and to the Son, and to the Holy Ghost. As it was in the beginning, is now, and ever shall be, world without end. Amen"). The Latin form of the phrase as sung in the Mass is *"saecula saeculorum"* ("through endless ages"). Joyce, in *Ulysses,* couples the phrase with the opening words of John's Gospel: "In the beginning was the word, in the end the World without end." John Betjeman's poem "N.W.5 & N.6" captures what must be a common reflection on the English phrase, here expressing a childhood conjuring with death:

> "World without end." What fearsome words to pray.
> . . . I caught them too,
> Hating to think of sphere succeeding sphere
> Into eternity and God's dread will.

WORM THAT DIETH NOT One of the attributes of hell spoken of by Jesus is that it is a place where for the damned "their worm dieth not, and the fire is not quenched" (Mark 9:44, 46, 48; cf. Isa. 66:24). The image gives rise to grotesque imaginings in *memento mori* literature of the late Middle Ages such as John Lydgate's *Dance of Death,* and, in the graphic arts, numerous vivid paintings of the tortures of the damned, especially among Flemish artists such as Hieronymus Bosch. "Gnawing of the worm" became a circumlocution for the operations of the conscience in medieval morality plays (e.g., *Everyman*). For De Quincey, in "The Affliction of Childhood," the phrase reflected rather the unrelieved grief experienced for years after the death of his sister, an association echoed in Poe's "Morella" and "Ulalume" in more grotesque fashion. In a lighter, if satiric vein, Aldous Huxley describes the inextinguishable Puritan Mrs. Grundy as resembling "the King and that infernal worm of the Bible — she cannot die" (*Music at Night,* "To the Puritan All Things are Impure").

WORMWOOD AND GALL *See* LAMENTATIONS.

WORSHIP In common with that of all other ancient Middle Eastern peoples, Israelite worship centered in sacrifice. The offering of animals, birds, and crops was primitively understood to be a presentation of gifts to the deity either to nourish him or to seek his aid (Gen. 8:21). Later the peace-offering (Lev. 7:11ff.) was believed to be the medium for the maintenance of harmonious relations with God, while the sin-offering (Lev. 4) was to remove any barrier between him and his worshipers. This latter sacrifice required the slaughter of a bull, goat, or lamb, after the offerer had identified himself with the victim by laying his hands upon its head; the blood, which is the life (Lev. 17:11), was then daubed on the horns of altar, symbolizing the divine presence, and God and man were thereby united. The entire sacrificial system, as it is presented in the OT, is comprised within the covenant between the Lord and his people; God has taken the initiative, having both prescribed and provided the means of access to himself. Worship was thus Israel's response to the covenant relationship and the means of ensuring its continuance. Its major festivals — many of them agricultural in origin — were therefore given a historical reference to the liberation from Egypt: the Passover recalling the Exodus and being the medium through which the chosen people annually re-engaged in the covenant, and Pentecost commemorating the giving of the Law.

In the premonarchic period worship could take place anywhere, and anyone could offer sacrifice (Judg. 17:5). There were local shrines, but none had a preeminence until Solomon built his temple. Henceforth a centralizing tendency asserted itself so that the ministry of sacrifice was restricted to the tribe of Levi and in the late 7th cent. B.C. Jerusalem was recognized as the sole sanctuary (Deut. 12:1-7).

Although some of the major prophets criticized the cultus as a vain activity unless it were accompanied by moral resolve and integrated with everyday life (Isa. 1:11-17), the temple worship of the postexilic era was highly elaborated. The regular round of sacrifices was accompanied by psalms and prayers, expressing adoration (Ps. 99:5) and thanksgiving (Ps. 107:8), and seeking forgiveness (Ps. 51) and help (Ps. 35:17). A trained choir was in attendance, and numerous musical instruments were in use (Ps. 68:25). Processions and dancing were also features of worship (Ps. 150:4), and indeed the Israelite emphasis upon the unity of spirit and matter is very evident in the Hebrew and Greek words used for worship since these all stress bodily movements. To worship is to lift up the hands toward heaven (Ps. 28:2); it is to bow down to the ground (Gen. 24:52), to kneel (1 Kings 8:54), to prostrate oneself (Ps. 97:7) in order to honor God and acknowledge his sovereignty.

The employment of material media for worship was continued in NT times — water in baptism and bread and wine in the Eucharist or Lord's Supper. Jesus himself attended the Temple and was a regular worshiper in the synagogue — a new institution developed in the Intertestamental period, its nonsacrificial worship centering in the reading and exposition of the Law and the Prophets. The first Christians continued to join in Jewish worship (Acts 2:46), both in temple and synagogue, until the former was destroyed and they were excluded from the latter, but they added a specifically Christian observance, namely the "breaking of bread." This last would appear to have been initially a repetition of the Last Supper *in toto,* i.e., the consumption of blessed bread, followed by a meal, and concluding with the partaking of a cup (1 Cor. 11:23-26). Eventually the meal was removed to become a separate *agapē* or love-feast, and the bread and wine were brought together to provide the structure of the Church's communion service. This communion service was understood to be a recalling of Christ's redemptive action — recalling not in the sense of a pious mental recollection but of the making present of a past event through its effects. Precisely because the Eucharist is a reactualization of Christ's saving work, it was invested with a multiplicity of meanings: it unites the worshiper with Christ in his death and resurrection; it conveys remission of sins; it nourishes the individual and builds up the Body of Christ (the Church) in unity; it re-engages the Christian community in the New Covenant; it anticipates the joy of the kingdom of God which is still to be established in its fullness. In view of this latter interpretation it is not surprising that worship is treated as a symbol of heavenly bliss (Rev. 4) or that it is an occasion for rejoicing and singing (1 Cor. 14), great stress being laid on the sense of fellowship, with the dining room of the private house being the regular place of gathering.

In the 4th cent. a considerable transformation took place with the conversion of Constantine and the recognition of Christianity as the religion of the empire. Acts of worship ceased to be domestic in character, being transferred to large public buildings where informality was out of place. The Church took over the function, previously executed by the pagan religions, of maintaining a public cultus for the well-being of the state. A priestly hierarchy developed, much influenced by OT models; noncommunicating attendance became the norm; the ministry of the word, adopted from the synagogue, tended to be irregularly emphasized until with the Reformation and Counter-Reformation the restoration of more primitive patterns was sought by Protestants and, notably among Catholic orders, the Jesuits. The Liturgical Movement of the 19th and 20th cents. has once more placed worship at the center of Christian devotion, and ecumenical approaches have led to a greater consensus as to its most appropriate forms and meaning. A poem of John Greenleaf Whittier, "Worship," is in effect an essay on James 1:27. Tracing the development of the worship impulse from "Pagan myths through marble lips" to the "pomp and rituals" of OT syncretism, challenging these with the requirements of God as suggested in the opening chapter of Isaiah and the actions of Jesus, Whittier concludes that true worship is the transformation of prayer to action, "Each loving life a psalm of gratitude."

See also ECCLESIA, SYNAGOGA; EUCHARIST; LITURGY; MUSIC AND MUSICAL INSTRUMENTS; PRAYER; PREACHING; QADDISH; SACRAMENT; TEMPLE.

Bibliography. Eaton, J. *Vision in Worship* (1981); Gibson, G. M. *The Story of the Christian Year* (1945); Hall, S. G. *Doctrine and Practice in the Early Church* (1991); Hurlbut, S. A. *The Liturgy of the Church of England Before and After the Reformation* (1941); Jones, C., G. Wainwright, and E. Yarnold, eds. *The Study of Liturgy* (1978); Marshall, I. H. *Last Supper and Lord's Supper* (1981); Martin, R. *Worship in the Early Church* (1964); Michell, G. A. *Landmarks in Liturgy: The Primitive Rite, A Medieval Mass, The English Rite to 1662* (1961); Moule, C. F. D. *Worship in the New Testament* (1961); Rowley, H. H. *Worship in Ancient Israel* (1967); Zundel, M. *The Splendour of the Liturgy* (Eng. trans. 1939).

J. G. DAVIES

WRESTLING JACOB The account of Jacob wrestling with the angel at the ford of the Jabbok River is replete with Hebrew puns (Gen. 32:24-32). Several of these relate to the root of Jacob's name, *'qb* ("heel"), and its compound standing as a West Semitic diminutive of "The LORD will pursue" or "The LORD preserves." At the river Jabbok ("twisting," which contains the root *'bq* ["to wrestle"] but also an audible reverse pun with *'qb*) Jacob confronted a great question: Would he cross back over as he came the first time, on the strength of his own staff (32:10)? Or would he, as John Donne puts it in a sermon (ed. Potter and Simpson, 1.7), learn to proceed in the strength of God's elective will for him? Apprehensive about the reception he was to receive from his wronged brother Esau, he sent a conciliatory message and a lavish present ahead and waited alone at the ford of the river, where "there wrestled a man with him until the breaking of the day."

When Jacob's opponent "saw that he prevailed not against him, he touched the hollow of his thigh . . . and he said, Let me go, for the day breaketh." The man who had more or less lived by "blows below the belt" now received one. Yet Jacob, who had wrestled also with his twin in the womb and for whom striving was characteristic, persevered, saying, "I will not let thee go, except thou bless me." The angel insisted on a condition: "What is thy name?" Jacob was forced to answer, *Ya'aqob,* perhaps mirroring the name of the river, *Yabbok,* but meaning "crooked" (Nahmanides, Deut. 2:10 of Jeshurun, gives this etymology for Jacob, "one who walks crookedly"; after the thigh wound delivered by the angel, Jacob literally "halted upon his thigh" [v. 31]). Although the mysterious opponent did not comply with Jacob's request that he reveal his name (v. 29), Jacob obtained the coveted blessing, which was confirmed in a transformation of his own name: "Thy name shall be called no more Jacob ("crooked") but Israel" (poss. *yashar-'el,* "God is reliable"). Jacob then named the place Peniel ("appearance of God" or "face of God"), "for he said, I have seen God face to face *(panim 'el-panim),* and my life is preserved" (v. 30).

Various haggadic sources make the "man" with whom Jacob wrestles the angel Metatron or Michael (Zerubbabel 5.5; cf. Abkir in Yalqut 1.132). Christian commentators uniformly accord with Jacob's own view that the wrestler is divine; St. Augustine sometimes identifies him as God the Father (*Sermo*, 122; cf. *Enarr. in Ps.* 147.28). The eventually dominant view, however (e.g., St. Clement of Alexandria, *Instructor*, 1.7), identifies him with Christ. Thus, "When the conqueror was blessed by the Conquered, Christ was figured. So then that angel, who is understood to be the Lord Jesus, said to Jacob, 'Thou shalt not any more be called Jacob, but Israel shall thy name be,' it is by interpretation 'seeing God'" (Augustine, *Sermo*, 122.3). (This etymology is probably transposed from Philo, for whom the "man who saw God" is identified with the Logos [*De confusione linguarum*, 16.20; cf. St. Justin Martyr, *Dial.* 75].)

Certain confusions accrue to patristic commentary on the passage, since the tendency to see Jacob as a type of Christ must in this instance be reconciled both with the fact of his being "bested" by his mysterious antagonist and with the commonplace identification of the "angel" as Christ. Hence, for Augustine, the irony of Jacob's "victory" can be said to mirror the irony of Christ's victory for the salvation of humankind: "Jacob blessed and Jacob lame" inverts to Christ "wounded by our transgressions" and "victorious over sin and death." Elsewhere, however, Augustine asks, "How did he [Jacob] understand with Whom he had wrestled, whom he had held? And for what reason did he wrestle violently and hold him? Because 'the kingdom of heaven suffers violence, and the violent bear it away' [Vg Matt. 11:12]" (*Enarr. in Ps.* 147.28; cf. Flannery O'Connor's title, *The Violent Bear It Away*).

For St. Hilary of Poitiers, building upon this complex of analogies, God's coming to Jacob "in human shape" prefigures the Incarnation (*De Trinitate*, 12), yet Christ is addressed in prayer through his antetype: "When you were wrestling you were Jacob; you are Israel now, through faith in the blessing which you claimed" (*De Trinitate*, 5.19).

Luther's commentary stresses that Jacob's opponent "was not an angel but our Lord Jesus Christ, eternal God and future Man" (*Lectures on Genesis*, 32.29-31 [Werke, 44.107-08]). Calvin sees the narrative as representing "all the servants of God in this world as wrestlers; because the Lord exercises them with various kinds of conflicts," and that in it one learns that faith is tried by God himself, that "whenever we are tempted, our business is truly with him, not only because we fight under his auspices, but because he, as an antagonist, descends into the arena to try our strength." This sort of reading is reflected in Izaak Walton's *Life of Dr. John Donne*, when he describes Donne's having gravely doubted his qualifications for ordination: "But God who is able to prevail wrestled with him, as the angel did with Jacob, and marked him . . . for his own . . . with a blessing of obedience to the motions of his blessed Spirit." Calvin is aware of the connection of Jacob's name to his birth (*'qb*), but reads the new name, Israel, from the following phrase (v. 28) as "Prince of God" (*Comm.* sup. Gen. 28:24-29).

The notion of Swedenborg that the "thigh" injury is a euphemism for a blow to the sexuality of Jacob recurs from time to time in interpretation of the phrase. In Swedenborg's formulation, the "hollow of the thigh" signifies "where celestial-spiritual good is conjoined with the natural good signified by 'Jacob' . . . evident from the signification of the 'thigh' as being conjugal love, and hence all celestial and spiritual love" (*Arcana Coelestia*, 6.4277). Swedenborg goes on to suggest that the nature of the injury indicates that Jacob and his descendants would henceforth be less than potent interpreters of the Word, a foundation for the bias against Jacob and for Esau, or "Edom," in which he is followed by Blake in *The Marriage of Heaven and Hell*.

The most famous poem of Charles Wesley, admired by Isaac Watts and others as one of the great achievements of religious verse in its time, is his "Wrestling Jacob." Combining insights from Luther and Augustine, Wesley concentrates on the "confession" of Jacob to the angel and his conversion to "Israel." The transformation models that of any Christian pilgrim coming to grips with the divine antagonist who, though perhaps at first seeming merely a mysterious stranger or a "Traveller unknown," reveals himself at last as "Jesus, the feeble sinner's friend." Wesley juxtaposes the Genesis text with a citation from Hos. 12:4, as if applied to the daybreak revelation after a long, dark night of the soul:

> The Sun of Righteousness on me
>   Hath rose with healing in his wings:
> Withered my nature's strength; from thee
>   My soul its life and succor brings.
> My help is all laid up above:
> Thy nature and thy name is Love.
>
> Contented now, upon my thigh
>   I halt, till life's short journey end;
> All helplessness, all weakness, I
>   On thee alone for strength depend. . . .

Christina Rossetti interpolates a reference to the Song of Songs (2:10) in her treatment of the passage:

> Weeping we hold him fast to-night;
> We will not let Him go
> Till daybreak smite our wearied sight
> And summer smile the snow.
> Then figs shall bud, and dove with dove
> Shall coo the livelong day;
> Then He shall say "Arise, My love,
> My fair one, come away." (cf. Matt. 24:30-32)

In Aubray de Vere's "Jerusalem," it is the City of David which bears the eponymous character of the event, as Israel before a God who looks upon that history and "knows that thou, obscured and dim, / Thus wrestling all night long with him, / Shalt victor rise at last."

In American literature many references are secularized and imprecise. The angel figures as Art, and the artist has "Jacob's mystic heart" in Melville's *Timoleon;* Emily Dickinson has the wrestling match take place "A little over Jordan," and whimsically notes:

> The Angel begged permission
> To breakfast and return.
>
> "Not so," quoth wily Jacob,
> And girt his loins anew,
> "Until thou bless me, stranger!"
> The which acceded to:
>
> Light swung the silver fleeces
> Peniel hills among
> And the astonished Wrestler
> Found he had worsted God!

The narrator in Hawthorne's *The House of Seven Gables* observes that "a recluse, like Hepzibah, usually displays remarkable frankness, and at least temporary affability, on being absolutely cornered and brought to the point of personal intercourse; — like the angel whom Jacob wrestled with, she is ready to bless you, when once overcome." In Longfellow's *Evangeline* "wild with the winds of September / Wrestled the trees of the forest, as Jacob / of old with the angel" (1.2). Whittier, in *My Soul and I,* advises:

> The Present, the Present is all thou hast
> For thy sure possessing;
> Like the patriarch's angel hold it fast
> Till it gives its blessing.

The wrestling can also become a figure for a modern "dark night of the soul," as in Howells's *The Rise of Silas Lapham:*

> He went in and shut the door, and by and by his wife heard him begin walking up and down. But when the first light whitened the window, the words of the Scripture came into her mind: "And there wrestled a man with him until the breaking of the day. . . . And he said, Let me go, for the day breaketh. And he said, I will not let thee go, except thou bless me." (chap. 25)

Similarly, Doña Maria "wrestled with the ghost of her temptation and was worsted on every occasion" in Thornton Wilder's *The Bridge of San Luis Rey* (chap. 2), and both psychological torment and sexual implications may lie behind Hemingway's use of "Jacob" as his struggling protagonist in *The Sun Also Rises*. It is a sexual analogy exclusively which prompts Pat Lowther's "Wrestling":

> Lover I must
> approach you as Jacob
> to his angel
> rough with that need.
> Yes I will
> pin you down,
> force answers from you. (*A Stone Diary* [1977], 47)

A more generic development of the allusion occurs in Margaret Laurence's *Stone Angel,* in which the toppled marble angel marking her mother's grave is righted with difficulty by Hagar Shipley's son John; looking on, she wishes in vain he "could have looked like Jacob then, wrestling with the angel and besting it, wringing a blessing from it with his might. But no" (chap. 6). Hagar's other son, Marvin, more faithful but less loved, comes to her on her deathbed, pleading for acknowledgment, and she reflects, "Now it seems to me he is truly Jacob, gripping with all his strength and bargaining. I will not let thee go except thou bless me." Hagar, who through a bitter life has herself become a "stone angel," ponders: "And I see I am thus strangely cast, and perhaps have been so from the beginning, and can only release myself by releasing him" (chap. 10).

See also JACOB.

X, Y, Z

XERXES   *See* ESTHER.

YHWH   *See* NAMES OF GOD.

YOKE   *See* MY YOKE IS EASY.

YOM KIPPUR   *See* ATONEMENT, DAY OF.

ZACCHAEUS   Zacchaeus was the chief tax collector whose encounter with Jesus in Jericho transformed his life (Luke 19:1-10). His name is associated with Heb. *zakkay* ("the righteous one"; cf. Ezra 2:9; Neh. 7:14). Wishing to see the passing Jesus, but unable to because of a crowd, the diminutive Zacchaeus hurried on ahead and climbed a sycamore (fig-mulberry). He was just as quick joyously to accept the invitation from Jesus ("Zacchaeus, make haste, and come down; for today I must dine at thy house") and to respond to this initiative and the murmurs of the crowd (he is "a sinner") with humility and repentance: he vowed to give half his goods to the poor and make fourfold restitution to anyone he had cheated. Jesus then proclaimed, "This day is salvation come to this house, forasmuch as he also is a son of Abraham."

The theological import of the Zacchaeus narrative has been summarized in this way: "tax collector though he is, Zacchaeus is entitled to salvation, for he too is a Jew, a member of the people to whom salvation was promised by God in the coming of the Messiah. But salvation comes even to Jews only when Jesus comes after them and brings them home" (Marshall, 694-95). The story of Zacchaeus, coming as it does at the end of Luke's long account of Jesus on his journey to Jerusalem, occupies an important place in that Gospel's plotting of salvation history.

The appearances of Zacchaeus in patristic literature are largely limited to sermons on the dangers of cupidity. The generosity of his repentance is applauded by Maximus of Turin; and in "De Zachaeo," which includes a typological reading of the enabling sycamore, Peter Chrysologus holds him up as a model of Christian charity (PL 57.731; 52.350-51). St. Augustine emphasizes the enormity of the chief publican's avarice and the importance of the fourfold restitution: Zacchaeus merits forgiveness not by returning what he has stolen from the poor, but by giving amply of his legitimately acquired wealth (*Sermons on New Testament Lessons*, 63.3). He is, Augustine frequently repeats, a model for the proud rich to emulate. According to the Clementine Homilies, Zacchaeus later traveled with Peter, who appointed him Bishop of Caesarea (3.63). The legend of Zacchaeus's journey to Gaul has led to a special veneration for him at the 17th-cent. pilgrimage church of Rocamadour (Lot), where he is featured in two bas-reliefs, which depict him in a palm tree and at home with Jesus.

The Zacchaeus episode does not have as wide a currency in English literature as that enjoyed by the other Lukan narratives. Even William Langland's homely *Piers*

Plowman, with its ruling theme of the dangers of cupidity, affords Zacchaeus but a small and relatively unattractive place: Did not Mary Magdalene gain more "for a box of salve" than Zacchaeus did for giving half his goods to the poor? (B.13.194-95). Langland simultaneously diminishes the monetary value of the "alabaster box of ointment of spikenard most precious" (Mark 14:3) and the spiritual value of the publican's humble generosity. Zacchaeus does figure prominently, though, in "The Entry into Jerusalem," from the York play of the Skinners: the "low" prince of publicans, baffled by the great new prophet's miracles and the fidelity of his enormous following ("Our people . . . / Our old laws as now they hate / And his keep yare"), blesses the "noble tree" which gives him sight and acknowledges Jesus as the true Lord. He is saved by the "clear confession" that he has cheated many.

Subsequent references to Zacchaeus tend to have a more personal character. Herbert's colloquy *In Christum Crucem Ascensurum* (*Passio* 12) is at once intimate in tone and intellectual in figuration: "*Zacchaeus, ut te cernat, arborem scandit*" (1). In the 20th cent., Lloyd C. Douglas's "The Mirror" has the publican account for his response to the gentle carpenter: "Good Master — I saw — mirrored in your eyes — the face of the Zacchaeus I was meant to be!" Robert Frost's "Sycamore," a transcription from *The New England Primer* — "Zaccheus he / Did climb the tree / Our Lord to see" — seems less instructive than evocative, its own moral purpose up in the air.

Bibliography. Loewe, W. P. "Towards an Interpretation of Luke 19:1-10." *CBQ* 36 (1974), 321-31; Marshall, I. H. *The Gospel of Luke* (1978); Réau, L. *Iconographie de l'art chrétien.* 3 vols. (1959).   CAMILLE R. LA BOSSIÈRE

ZACHARIAS   Zacharias was the husband of Elisabeth and father of John the Baptist (Luke 1:5, 12ff.). When he asked for a sign to confirm the authenticity of an angelic promise that he and his aged spouse were to have a child divinely appointed to prepare the way of the Messiah, Zacharias was struck dumb. This condition persisted until, at the circumcision and naming ceremony of his son, "his mouth was opened and his tongue loosed," and he became an eloquent witness to the dawning of the messianic era (Luke 1:67-79). This role is captured poetically in Margaret Avison's "Christmas: Anticipation":

> The patient years in the appointed place
> brought Zacharias, dumb with unbelieving,
> flame touched, to front
> the new sky,
> the ancient desert ways
> rustling with grasshoppers' thighs, yielding
> from dry, spiky places,
> wild honey, and a brook starting.

According to the apocryphal Protevangelium of James (23-24) Zacharias was murdered in the forecourt of the Temple by Herod's men, a conflation of the NT Zacharias in Luke 1 with a reference in Luke 11:51 to a prophet of the time of King Joash.

See also ELISABETH; JOHN THE BAPTIST.

ZEBULUN   One of the twelve sons of Jacob.
See also AARON; JACOB; TRIBES OF ISRAEL.

ZILLAH   Wife of Lamech, and mother to Tubal-cain.
See also TUBAL-CAIN.

ZILPAH   Handmaiden to Leah, one of the wives of Jacob.
See also LEAH; RACHEL.

ZION   *See* AT EASE IN ZION; NEW JERUSALEM.

ZOPHAR   *See* JOB'S COMFORTERS.

Bibliographies

BIBLICAL STUDIES

A Guide to Biblical Studies
for the Student of Literature

As is true of so many fields in modern scholarship, biblical studies today is characterized by complexity and an immense volume of published work. It is not the purpose of the present bibliography to give a complete list of published works available for use in biblical studies, but rather to offer a selection of important publications, arranged under major categories, primarily to meet the needs of the person who is not a specialist in biblical studies. A great deal of the scholarly literature in biblical studies is in German, and material of some importance is published in other languages such as French, Swedish, Dutch, Spanish, Italian, and Hebrew. For the purposes of this bibliography, however, primary attention will be given to works in English, although foreign language publications of special significance will be mentioned as well.

The categories chosen here likewise were selected with the needs of the projected primary users of this volume in mind. Thus, e.g., studies of biblical theology, a category of literature more appropriate for biblical scholars and theologians, have not been included. For the same reason, certain kinds of works dealing with the historical setting of the biblical writings have not been mentioned, e.g., discussions of religions of the ancient Near East or of the Greco-Roman world. On the other hand, there are sections devoted to ancient Jewish materials because these works are relevant in tracing the influence and interpretation of the biblical writings.

The order of categories moves from general introductory and reference works on to studies dealing with particular aspects of biblical studies. Commentaries are given late in the list because they draw on the sort of information provided in the categories of works which precede them here. Following this essay, the subject of literary studies of the Bible is taken up by J. H. Gottcent, in his "Studies of the Bible as Literature: A Select List."

BIBLIOGRAPHIES

The following items are a selection of major bibliographical sources for scholarly material in the field of biblical studies. Items are listed alphabetically. Those addressing the whole of the Bible are listed first, followed by those dealing with the OT, and then those covering the NT. The works mentioned here include periodical indexes as well as book lists. Some of the following works explain how to use the items to which they refer and are therefore especially valuable to the person beginning serious study of the Bible.

Danker, F. W. *Multipurpose Tools for Bible Study* (3rd ed.; St. Louis: Concordia Publishing House, 1970). Danker lists and tells how to use a selection of tools: concordances, critical editions of the Greek NT, Hebrew OT and Septuagint (Greek OT), Hebrew and Greek grammars and lexica, Bible dictionaries, ancient Bible versions, English versions, Judaica, archeology, the Dead Sea Scrolls, and commentaries. Now slightly dated, it is intended primarily for theological students and pastors, but is a full description (almost 300 pp.) of the sorts of items mentioned.

Fitzmyer, J. A. *An Introductory Bibliography for the Study of Scripture* (Subsidia Biblica 3, 3rd rev. ed.; Rome: Biblical Institute Press, 1991). This is a full and useful annotated bibliography of material on biblical studies by a major figure in the field, intended clearly for those who are or intend to become specialists in the "historical-critical" approach to the Bible.

Gottcent, J. H. *The Bible as Literature: A Selective Bibliography* (Boston: G. K. Hall, 1979). Particularly valuable for those from a literary-critical background who wish to approach the Bible from this standpoint. See his (updated) bibliography immediately following in this volume.

Nober, P. *Elenchus bibliographicus biblicus* (Rome: Biblical Institute Press, 1968–). Originally an annual part of the journal *Biblica,* this extremely valuable list took on independent existence as of 1968 and has continued to appear yearly since. No annotations are included, but there are very detailed indexes, and nearly anything of importance in biblical studies, periodical literature or books, is listed, covering all the major languages of scholarship.

Stier, F. (ed.). *Internationale Zeitschriftenschau für Bibelwissenschaft und Grenzgebiete* (Düsseldorf: Patmos). Appearing annually since 1951, this list abstracts periodical articles on the Bible and related areas.

Childs, B. S. *Old Testament Books for Pastor and Teacher* (Philadelphia: Westminster, 1977). The recommendations cover the texts of the OT, translations and introduction, its history and its theology, and include an evaluation of commentaries from various periods.

Longman, T. *Old Testament Commentary Survey* (Grand Rapids: MI: Baker Book House, 1991). Evaluations of commentaries on OT books.

Old Testament Abstracts (Washington, D.C.: Catholic Biblical Association). Published thrice yearly since 1978, this is a reasonably full list of abstracts of major periodical literature on the OT. It is topically arranged for ease of consultation and is patterned after *New Testament Abstracts* (see below).

Stuart, D. *Old Testament Exegesis: A Primer for Students and Pastors* (Philadelphia: Westminster, 1980). The first 78 pages explain how to do exegesis of the OT, with a view primarily to the needs of the preacher with scholarly leanings. The remaining 65 pages list and explain a large number of English-language works covering many aspects of OT study.

Aune, D. E. *Jesus and the Synoptic Gospels: An Introductory Bibliographical Study Guide and Syllabus* (Madison, WI: Theological Students Fellowship, 1980). The first of a series of such guides, this excellent tool discusses works relevant to Jesus and the Synoptics under the following headings: reference tools, literary criticism, tradition criticism, historical criticism, and theological studies.

France, R. T. *A Bibliographical Guide to New Testament Research* (Sheffield: JSOT Press, 1979). Intended primarily for graduate students, the guide gives annotations for a wide assortment of materials involved in the professional study of the field.

Mattill, A. J., Jr., and M. B. Mattill (eds.). *A Classified Bibliography of Literature on the Acts of the Apostles* (Leiden: Brill; Grand Rapids, MI: Eerdmans, 1966). Providing over 6,000 items from 180 periodicals, as well as books, book reviews, and dictionary articles, this list covers relevant items from the Church Fathers to 1960.

Metzger, B. M. (ed.). *Index to Periodical Literature on Christ and the Gospels* (Leiden: Brill, 1966). With over 10,000 entries from over 160 periodicals from their inception through 1961, and carefully organized under numerous headings, including the influence and interpretation of Jesus and the Gospels in worship, the fine arts, and general culture, this is an invaluable tool.

Metzger, B. M. (ed.). *Index to Periodical Literature on the Apostle Paul* (Leiden: Brill; Grand Rapids, MI: Eerdmans, 1960). A list of 2,987 articles in 114 periodicals from their inception through 1957 and grouped under headings.

New Testament Abstracts (Cambridge, MA: Weston School of Theology). Published since 1956, this work abstracts all periodical literature on the NT and its historical background, and lists almost all significant publications in the field.

Scholer, D. M. *A Basic Bibliographic Guide for New Testament Exegesis* (2nd ed.; Grand Rapids, MI: Eerdmans, 1973). A good discussion of the many categories of works used by NT scholars.

Carson, D. A. *New Testament Commentary Survey* (3rd ed.; Grand Rapids, MI: Baker Book House, 1986). A brief description and evaluation of commentaries arranged according to the order of books in the NT.

INTRODUCTIONS

As traditionally used in biblical studies, the term *introduction* means a study of the biblical books as historical documents: authorship, occasion, date, provenance, sources and literary integrity, basic structure and contents. Some are written to serve as basic texts for serious students and as reference volumes for the scholar, and are therefore usually rich in bibliographical aids. Others are less technical and are intended for use in undergraduate courses in colleges and universities. Some of the more recent volumes in the following list reflect the growing interest in approaching the Bible as literature and may therefore be of special interest to the reader who shares this interest. As in the previous category, items dealing with the whole Bible are listed first, followed by OT studies, then those pertaining exclusively to the NT, alphabetically arranged by authors' last name within each subcategory.

Harris, Stephen L. *Understanding the Bible: A Reader's Introduction* (2nd ed.; Mountain View, CA: Mayfield Publishing Company, 1985). A useful college/university textbook pleasingly arranged, with charts, maps, a glossary of biblical characters, terms and concepts, and numerous bibliographies.

Hauer, Christian E., and William A. Young. *An Introduction to the Bible: A Journey into Three Worlds* (2nd ed.; Englewood Cliffs, NJ: Prentice-Hall, 1990). Intended for undergraduate-level courses, the text approaches the Bible from historical, literary, and "contemporary" (i.e., religious meaning) perspectives.

Selby, D. J., and J. K. West. *Introduction to the Bible* (New York: Macmillan, 1978). This is a combination of earlier (1971) separate volumes by the two authors on the NT and OT respectively, and is one of the few works available which address the whole of the Bible. It is a competent (though now dated) treatment of standard matters in a format usable in university courses in religious studies.

Skehan, P. W., et al. (eds.). *Interpreting the Scriptures* (New York: Desclée, 1969); *Introduction to the New Testament* (New York: Desclée, 1968); also available in paperback in two volumes (New York: Doubleday, 1970). These volumes are well-informed discussions intended for the general reader, and are the English rendition of a two-volume French work edited by A. Robert and A. Feuillet. The latter work is now appearing in an expanded and thoroughly revised form as *Introduction à la Bible: Edition nouvelle* (4 vols.; Paris: Desclée, 1973–), with multiple parts by various French Catholic biblical scholars, and is an excellent recommendation for those with reading facility in French.

Thompson, L. L. *Introducing Biblical Literature: A More Fantastic Country* (Englewood Cliffs, NJ: Prentice-Hall, 1978). This volume focuses on the themes, language, and symbolism of the Bible, the author addressing himself especially to students of literature and the arts.

Anderson, B. W. *Understanding the Old Testament* (3rd ed.; Englewood Cliffs, NJ: Prentice-Hall, 1975). A widely used textbook for many years, this volume views the biblical writings against their historical background and incorporates archeological data and important secondary literature.

Childs, B. S. *Introduction to the Old Testament as Scripture* (Philadelphia: Fortress, 1979). The author makes use of standard, historical-critical study of the OT, but adds to it an approach which takes the literature seriously as part of Christian Scripture.

Eissfeldt, O. *The Old Testament: An Introduction Including the Apocrypha and Pseudepigrapha, and also the Works of Similar Type from Qumran* (trans. P. R. Ackroyd; New York: Harper & Row, 1965). Probably the most respected OT introduction among biblical scholars, this work gives detailed discussion of the OT books and their "preliterary" stages and forms (German original, 3rd ed., 1964).

Fohrer, G. *Introduction to the Old Testament* (trans. D. E. Green: Nashville: Abingdon, 1968). Somewhat comparable in technical erudition to Eissfeldt's work above, this discussion is limited to the books of the Hebrew canon.

Harrington, D. J. *Interpreting the Old Testament* (Wil-

mington, DE: Michael Glazier, 1981). This volume is intended for the beginning student and gives concise explanations of the critical approaches and questions involved in academic study of the Bible.

Soggin, J. A. *Introduction to the Old Testament: From Its Origins to the Closing of the Alexandrian Canon* (trans. J. Bowden; Philadelphia: Westminster, 1976). A learned and highly praised study translated from the 1974 Italian version.

Aune, D. E. *The New Testament in Its Literary Environment* (Philadelphia: Westminster Press, 1987). An excellent study which shows the relationship of the NT writings to literary genres of the Greco-Roman era.

Guthrie, D. *New Testament Introduction* (3rd ed.; Downers Grove, IL: Inter-Varsity, 1970). An erudite discussion of the standard questions of date, authorship, etc., from a conservative Protestant point of view.

Harrington, D. J. *Interpreting the new Testament: A Practical Guide* (Wilmington, DE: Michael Glazier, 1979). See Harrington, D. J., above.

Koester, H. *Introduction to the New Testament* (2 vols.; Philadelphia: Fortress, 1982). This massive set is a translation of the 1980 German version. Vol. 1 is entitled *History, Culture, and Religion of the Hellenistic Age,* and is a thorough introduction to the whole period out of which the NT grew. Vol. 2, *History and Literature of Early Christianity,* treats the NT writings and Christian apocryphal literature of the first few centuries. The work reflects a highly historicist approach toward the NT, with little attention to the NT as literature.

Kümmel, W. G. *Introduction to the New Testament* (rev. ed., trans. by H. C. Kee; Nashville: Abingdon, 1975). Translated from the 17th German edition, this is now the standard introduction to the NT for serious students in the discipline. It is rich (though now a bit dated) in bibliographical references, and handles the standard questions with thoroughness.

McKnight, E. *Postmodern Use of the Bible: the emergence of reader-oriented criticism* (Nashville: Abingdon, 1988). Overview of the evolution of biblical scholarship to the late 20th cent.

DICTIONARIES

Under this heading are listed general biblical dictionaries, which have alphabetically arranged articles dealing with the books of the Bible, persons mentioned in the Bible, biblical ideas or concepts, customs, sites, archeological backgrounds, and related topics. Under the next heading are listed "lexica," i.e., dictionaries of the biblical languages, including multi-author works, which have full descriptive articles dealing with important biblical vocabulary.

Bromiley, G. W. (ed.). *The International Standard Bible Encyclopedia (Revised)* (4 vols.; Grand Rapids, MI: Eerdmans, 1979-87). This is the most recent major reference set on all matters pertaining to the Bible.

Buttrick, G. A. (ed.). *The Interpreter's Dictionary of the Bible: An Illustrated Encyclopedia Identifying and Explaining all Proper Names and Significant Terms and Subjects in the Holy Scriptures, Including the Apocrypha, with Attention to Archaeological Discoveries and Researches into the Life and Faith of Ancient Times* (4 vols.; Nashville: Abingdon, 1962). The title says virtually all that needs to be said about its contents. The *Supplementary Volume* (ed. K. Crim; Nashville: Abingdon, 1976) updates many earlier entries and adds numerous new ones. This work is universally recognized as a "must" for any serious study of the Bible.

Cazelles, H., and A. Feuillet (eds.). *Supplément au Dictionnaire de la Bible* (Paris: Letouzey et Ané, 1928–). Eight volumes have appeared so far, containing articles as long as monographs in some cases. Though some of the earlier articles are now quite dated, this is still an important work of French scholarship.

LEXICA AND PHILOLOGICAL DICTIONARIES

The works listed below include both standard dictionaries of the relevant biblical languages and works which discuss biblical vocabulary at some length. The latter kind of "dictionary" is usually a selection of major terms of theological significance. As will be noted, several of the important items below require a reading knowledge of German. As in the earlier categories, OT works are listed first and then those dealing with NT vocabulary.

Baumgartner, W. (ed.). *Hebräisches und aramäisches Lexikon zum Alten Testament* (3 vols.; Leiden: Brill, 1967–). The third edition of the lexicon listed under Koehler and Baumgartner below, this is the best work available today for study of biblical Hebrew.

Botterweck, J., and H. Ringgren (eds.). *Theological Dictionary of the Old Testament* (Grand Rapids, MI: Eerdmans, 1977–). This is the English translation of the German original, which began appearing in 1970 and is not yet complete. Several volumes of the English version have appeared. The set corresponds to the Kittel-Friedrich set listed below, and like the latter it is an essay-format treatment of major biblical terms and associated concepts. It is a "must" for serious exegetes.

Brown, F., S. R. Driver, and C. A. Briggs. *A Hebrew and English Lexicon of the Old Testament* (corrected impression; Oxford: Clarendon, 1952). Includes both Hebrew and Aramaic words; the arrangement is not alphabetical but according to stems, and the etymologies involved are now often questionable. Somewhat dated, it is still a valuable lexicon.

Holladay, W. L. *A Concise Hebrew and Aramaic Lexicon of the Old Testament, Based upon the Lexical Work of L. Koehler & W. Baumgartner* (Leiden: Brill, 1971). This is an excellent tool for those beginning study of biblical Hebrew and Aramaic.

Koehler, L., and W. Baumgartner. *Lexicon in Veteris Testamenti Libros* (2nd ed.; Leiden: Brill, 1958). Hebrew and Aramaic words are listed in alphabetical order, with meanings and discussions given in German and English, the latter sometimes in need of correction.

Bauer, W., F. W. Gingrich, and F. W. Danker. *A Greek-English Lexicon of the New Testament and Other Early Christian Literature* (2nd ed.; Chicago/London: University of Chicago, 1979). An updated version of the 1957 translation of Bauer's great work (5th German ed., 1958), this is the best English-language lexicon to the NT.

Balz, H., and G. Schneider (eds.). *Exegetical Dictionary of the New Testament* (3 vols.; Grand Rapids: Eerdmans, 1990-92). In some ways the successor of the *Theological Dictionary of the New Testament*, though more focussed on the NT itself, briefer, and covering every word which appears in the NT.

Brown, C. (ed.). *The New International Dictionary of New Testament Theology* (3 vols.; Grand Rapids, MI: Zondervan, 1975-78). A thoroughly revised and translated version of a German set, the articles carry rich bibliographies and escape some of the criticisms directed against the Kittel-Friedrich set listed below. The present work is also less technical, and the entries are arranged alphabetically according to their common English translations.

Kittel, G., and G. Friedrich (eds.). *Theological Dictionary of the New Testament* (10 vols.; trans. G. W. Bromiley; Grand Rapids, MI: Eerdmans, 1964-76). A highly regarded translation of the monumental German set which is a required source for serious exegesis of the NT. Several of the early volumes were complete decades ago (1933–), and especially in these are articles based on outdated semantic theory and much in need of updating. Entries are listed alphabetically according to the Greek word, and provide information on the classical Greek background and the Hebrew OT equivalents of the words discussed.

Lampe, G. W. H. (ed.). *A Patristic Greek Lexicon* (Oxford: Clarendon, 1961). An excellent lexicon for the Greek Church Fathers which supplements Liddell-Scott for this literature (see below).

Liddell, H. G., and R. Scott. *A Greek-English Lexicon: A New Edition Revised and Augmented throughout by H. S. Jones, assisted by R. McKenzie* (9th ed.; 2 vols. [later bound in one]; Oxford: Clarendon, 1925-40, rpt. 1966). This lexicon is mainly devoted to classical

Greek but includes limited references to the NT and the Greek OT. The user should be aware of *A Supplement,* by E. A. Barber et al. (Oxford: Clarendon, 1968), a 153-page compilation of material giving more recent information on many words, and R. Renehan, *Greek Lexicographical Notes: A Critical Supplement to the Greek-English Lexicon of Liddell-Scott-Jones* (Hypomnemata 45; Göttingen: Vandenhoeck & Ruprecht, 1975).

Moulton, J. H., and G. Milligan. *The Vocabulary of the Greek Testament Illustrated from the Papyri and Other Non-Literary Sources* (2nd ed.; London: Hodder and Stoughton, 1957). This work lists a selection of NT vocabulary found in nonliterary sources of the ancient world, thus illustrating the extrabiblical usage of these words. Begun in 1914, it is now somewhat dated, though still worth consulting.

CONCORDANCES

Concordances are used for a variety of purposes, including the simple task of finding a particular statement in the biblical text when one knows a word in the statement, finding all references to a term in the Bible for making a topical study, checking frequency of occurrence of terms for study of authors' writing styles, and (especially by means of "original language" concordances) making investigations of word meanings and usage. Concordances come in three basic types: those based on a particular translation (e.g., the King James Version or the Vulgate), then concordances to the Hebrew and Greek OT texts, and finally concordances to the Greek NT.

Cruden, A. *Cruden's Complete Concordance* (Grand Rapids, MI: Zondervan, 1949, many reprints). Originally published in 1737, this is a widely known concordance to the KJV. Originally it covered the Apocrypha as well, but later reprints often omit this material.

Ellison, J. W. *Nelson's Complete Concordance of the Revised Standard Version Bible* (New York: Nelson, 1957; 2nd rev. ed. 1972).

Elder, E. *Concordance to the New English Bible: New Testament* (Grand Rapids, MI: Zondervan, 1964).

Kohlenberger, John R., III. *The NRSV Concordance Unabridged, Including the Apocryphal/Deuterocanonical Books* (Grand Rapids: Zondervan, 1991). The New Revised Standard Version translation is the official updating and replacement for the Revised Standard Version, and this concordance is now a must for readers of the NRSV.

Morrison, C. *An Analytical Concordance to the Revised Standard Version of the New Testament* (Philadelphia: Westminster, 1979).

Strong, J. *The Exhaustive Concordance of the Bible* (New York: Hunt Easton, 1894; often reprinted by various publishers). This concordance, together with the one by Young listed below, are the two best for study using the KJV. The system of arrangement is different, but either will serve well.

Young, R. *Analytical Concordance to the Bible* (22nd American ed. rev. by W. B. Stevenson; rpt. Grand Rapids, MI: Eerdmans, 1955). Under each main entry in this concordance to the KJV there are subdivisions of occurrences for each Hebrew or Greek word being translated.

Dutripon, F. P. *Concordantiae bibliorum sacrorum vulgatae editionis* (Paris: E. Belin, 1853; 8th ed.; Paris: Bloud et Barral, 1880; rpt. 1976). The best one-volume concordance to the Vg.

Fischer, B. *Novae concordantiae bibliorum sacrorum iuxta Vulgatam versionem critice editam* (5 vols.; Stuttgart/Bad Cannstatt: Frommann-Holzboog, 1977). A computer-generated concordance based on the Stuttgart critical edition of the Vg edited by R. Weber et al.

Mandelkern, S. *Veteris Testamenti concordantiae hebraicae atque chaldaicae* (2nd ed.; Berlin: Margolin, 1925; rpt. Berlin: Schocken, 1937; Graz: Akademischer Druck, 1955). A third, corrected and supplemented edition was released by M. H. Gottstein (Jerusalem/Tel Aviv: Schocken, 1959), and an edition reduced in size appeared in 1971 (9th ed.; Jerusalem/Tel Aviv: Schocken). This is the best such tool for the Hebrew and Aramaic text of the OT.

Hatch, E., and H. A. Redpath. *A Concordance to the Septuagint and Other Greek Versions of the Old Testament (Including the Apocryphal Books)* (2 vols.; Oxford: Clarendon, 1897; vol. 3 [Supplement], 1906; rpt. in 2 vols., Graz: Akademischer Druck, 1954; and Grand Rapids, MI: Baker Book House, 1983). Indispensable for study of the Bible, the work is, however, based on a few manuscripts of the Septuagint, and should be checked against critical editions.

Aland, K. *Vollständige Konkordanz zum griechischen Neuen Testament: Unter Zugrundelegung aller kritischen Textausgaben und des Textus Receptus* (Berlin/New York: Walter de Gruyter, 1975-83). A computer-generated work listing all variants in all the major critical editions of the Greek NT, it is so expensive that only institutional libraries can purchase it. For individual purchase and use, see the next item.

Computer Concordance to the Novum Testamentum Graece of Nestle-Aland, 26th Edition, and to the Greek New Testament, 3rd Edition. Institute for New Testament Textual Research. Berlin/New York: Walter de Gruyter, 1985. This is the best full, desk-reference concordance for the major modern critical editions of the Greek NT.

Moulton, W. F., and A. S. Geden. *A Concordance to the Greek Testament according to the Texts of Westcott and Hort, Tischendorf and the English Revisers* (5th ed., rev. H. K. Moulton; Edinburgh: Clark, 1978). A relatively modest price and the fact that this is a one-volume tool make this the most widely used concordance to the Greek NT. This edition has a supplement of 76 pages supplying references to seven words omitted in the original edition. It is, however, based on pre-20th-cent. critical editions of the NT, and so its references must always be checked in more recent critical editions.

PERIODICALS

Of the many periodicals relevant to biblical studies, only a small selection of the major ones are listed here, together with their abbreviations.

Biblica (Rome, 1920–). Published quarterly by the Pontifical Biblical Institute, with articles, reviews, and notes in English, French, German, Italian, Latin, and Spanish. *(Bib).*

Biblische Zeitschrift (Freiburg, 1903-39; Paderhorn, 1957-77). The leading Roman Catholic biblical journal in the German-speaking world. Languages: German, English, French. *(BZ).*

The Catholic Biblical Quarterly (Washington, D.C., 1939–). Published by the Catholic Biblical Association of America. Languages: English, occasionally French. *(CBQ).*

Interpretation: A Journal of Bible and Theology (Richmond, VA, 1947–). Exegetical, theological, and homiletical articles, often grouped around one subject, and often invited submissions. Language: English. *(Int).*

Journal of Biblical Literature (Philadelphia, 1881-1980; Atlanta, 1980–). Published for the Society of Biblical Literature by Scholars Press, it is probably the premier biblical journal in North America. It has a supplementary monograph series. Language: English, but occasionally French or German articles. *(JBL).*

Journal for the Study of the New Testament (Sheffield, UK, 1978–). Articles and reviews. Language: English. *(JSNT).*

Journal for the Study of the Old Testament (Sheffield, UK, 1976–). Articles and reviews. Language: English. *(JSOT).*

New Testament Studies (Cambridge, UK, 1954–). The official organ of the Studiorum Novi Testamenti Societas, it carries articles, short studies, and news of the society. Languages: English, French, German. *(NTS).*

Novum Testamentum (Leiden, 1956–). Articles and occasional reviews. Languages: English, French, German. *(NovT).*

Revue biblique (Paris, 1892). One of the most important journals in the field of biblical studies. Languages: French, occasionally English. *(RB).*

Semeia: An Experimental Journal for Biblical Criticism (Chico/Atlanta, 1974–). Published at somewhat irregular intervals, the journal features new approaches and hermeneutical points of view, often grouped around a given topic. Language: English. *(Sem).*

Vetus Testamentum (Leiden, 1951–). Published quarterly by the International Organization for the Study of the Old Testament. Languages: English, French, German. *(VT).*

Zeitschrift für die alttestamentliche Wissenschaft (Giessen, Berlin, 1881–). Published semiannually, it is the most important journal in OT studies. Languages: German, English, occasionally French, often with summaries of articles in the other two languages. *(ZAW).*

Zeitschrift für die neutestamentliche Wissenschaft und die Kunde des Urchristentums (Giessen, Berlin, 1900–). Published quarterly, it is the best German Protestant journal in NT studies. Languages: German, occasionally English. *(ZNW).*

BIBLICAL TEXTS

The texts given below are a selection of critical editions of the Hebrew OT, the Greek OT (usually called the "Septuagint," including the apocryphal or "deutero-canonical" OT writings), and the Greek NT, listed in this order.

Elliger, K., and W. Rudoph (eds.). *Biblia hebraica stuttgartensia* (Stuttgart: Deutsche Bibelstiftung, 1967-77). Now regarded as the best critical edition of the Hebrew OT, this work is based on a collation of major Hebrew and Aramaic manuscripts.

Kittel, R. (ed.). *Biblia hebraica* (7th ed.; Stuttgart: Würtembergische bibelanstalt, 1951). Inferior to the edition by Elliger and Rudoph, this is serviceable for basic reading, but has serious shortcomings for text-critical questions.

Brooke, A. E., N. McLean, and H. St.-J. Thackeray. *The Old Testament in Greek* (3 vols.; Cambridge: University Press, 1906-40). This gives the text of Codex B with supplements from other major manuscripts, together with an extensive critical apparatus containing variants of other manuscripts and some ancient versions. As portions of the Göttingen edition appear (see below), this edition is being superseded.

Rahlfs, A. *Septuaginta* (8th ed., 2 vols.; Stuttgart: Würtembergische bibelanstalt, 1965). Intended mainly for use as a handy manual edition for students and clergy, it serves this purpose well, but has an insufficient critical apparatus for text-critical matters.

Septuaginta: Vetus Testamentum graece auctoritate

Societatis Goettingensis editum (Göttingen: Vanden-hoeck & Ruprecht, 1931–). Eventually to comprise sixteen volumes, this will be the definitive critical edition when complete. Some thirty OT writings have appeared so far.

Aland, K., M. Black, C. M. Martini, B. M. Metzger, and A. Wikgren (eds.). *The Greek New Testament* (3rd ed.; New York/London/Edinburgh/Amsterdam/Stuttgart: United Bible Societies, 1975). A widely used edition, the text of the *GNT* is the same as the 26th edition of Nestle-Aland (see below), but its apparatus is designed differently and offers a more restricted selection of variants than the latter edition. There is a companion volume, which comments on the text-critical decisions made by the editors, B. M. Metzger, *A Textual Commentary on the Greek New Testament* (London/New York: United Bible Societies, 1971).

Nestle-Aland. *Novum Testamentum graece* (Stuttgart: Deutsche Bibelstiftung, 1979). This is the 26th edition of the work begin by E. Nestle in 1898, now edited by K. Aland with the collaboration of those who prepared the *GNT* listed directly above. In comparison with the *GNT,* Nestle-Aland has a more sophisticated apparatus and more detailed introduction and appendices; it is the NT scholar's preferred edition of the Greek NT.

INTRODUCTIONS TO THE BIBLICAL TEXTS

Provided here are a selection of works which discuss the textual history of the Hebrew OT, the Septuagint, and the Greek NT.

The Cambridge History of the Bible (3 vols.; Cambridge: University Press, 1963-70). This comprehensive and collaborative work discusses all sorts of matters dealing with the transmission of the Bible down to modern times.

Würthwein, E., *The Text of the Old Testament: An Introduction to the Biblia Hebraica* (trans. E. F. Rhodes; Grand Rapids: Eerdmans, 1979). An eminently suitable introduction to the Kittel edition of the Hebrew Bible and a criticism of its shortcomings.

Jellicoe, S. *The Septuagint and Modern Study* (New York/London: Oxford University, 1968; rpt. Ann Arbor, MI: Eisenbrauns, 1978). A major discussion of the origins and history of the Septuagint and its modern critical editions.

Aland, Kurt, and Barbara Aland. *The Text of the New Testament* (rev. ed., trans. E. F. Rhodes; Grand Rapids: Eerdmans; Leiden: E. J. Brill, 1990). Designed for the novice, it is a good introduction to textual criticism of the NT and to the use of modern critical editions of the Greek NT.

Metzger, B. M. *The Text of the New Testament: Its Trans-*mission, Corruption, and Restoration* (3rd ed.; New York/London: Oxford University, 1991). An excellent introduction to the history of the NT text and the field of NT textual criticism.

Metzger, B. M. *The Early Versions of the New Testament: Their Origin, Transmission, and Limitations* (Oxford: Clarendon, 1977). A valuable discussion of all the ancient versions, e.g., the Old Latin and the Vg.

GRAMMARS

Following is a short list of major reference grammars intended for the person with a basic knowledge of the languages in question. These grammars are intended to assist in exegesis of the biblical texts by offering more detailed discussion of finer points of usage and grammar, and complement the lexica listed above for making a study of the biblical texts in the original languages.

Gesenius, W., and E. Kautzsch. *Gesenius' Hebrew Grammar* (trans. A. E. Cowley; 2nd ed.; Oxford: Clarendon, 1910, and reprinted often). The best biblical Hebrew reference of grammar in English, but at times quite dated.

Jouon, P. *Grammaire de l'hébreu biblique* (2nd ed.; Rome: Biblical Institute, 1947; rpt. 1965). A widely respected reference grammar, especially strong in its treatment of Hebrew syntax.

Meyer, R. *Hebräische Grammatik* (4 vols.; Berlin: de Gruyter, 1966-72). A compact reference grammar with some account taken of data from the texts from Ugarit and Qumran.

Bauer, H., and P. Leander. *Grammatik des Biblische-Aramäischen* (1927; rpt. Hildesheim/New York: Olms, 1962). Though dated, it remains the best reference grammar for Aramaic.

Blass, F., and A. Debrunner. *A Greek Grammar of the New Testament and Other Early Christian Literature* (trans. and ed. R. W. Funk; Chicago: University of Chicago, 1961). This is the most widely used reference grammar for NT Greek.

Moulton, J. H., F. W. Howard, and N. Turner. *A Grammar of New Testament Greek* (4 vols.; Edinburgh: Clark, 1929-76). Though parts of this work are dated, it is still an authoritative work.

BIBLICAL HISTORY AND GEOGRAPHY

There is a great deal of technical literature in this area, but I list below a selection of general works which will be of help to the person desiring a basic familiarity with the time and the lands of the Bible.

Aharoni, Y. *The Land of the Bible: A Historical Geog-*

raphy (rev. ed.; Philadelphia: Westminster, 1980). An excellent and detailed discussion, but it goes no later than the Persian period.

Aharoni, Y., and M. Avi-Yonah. *The Macmillan Bible Atlas* (rev. ed.; New York: Macmillan, 1977). This is an extremely well-illustrated atlas whose maps are closely linked with particular biblical narratives.

Grollenberg, L. H. *Atlas of the Bible* (London: Nelson, 1956). A highly recommended atlas with over 400 pictures and illustrations.

Wright, G. E., and F. V. Filson. *The Westminster Historical Atlas to the Bible* (rev. ed.; Philadelphia: Westminster, 1956).

LITERATURE OF THE INTERTESTAMENTAL PERIOD

Although the term *Intertestamental* is a bit awkward in critical circles (presupposing a Christian Bible), it continues to be used to refer to Jewish literature of the approximate period 200 B.C. to A.D. 100 which is not included in the Hebrew OT or the "deuterocanonical" (apocryphal) books of the Christian tradition. In this category are listed (in this order) bibliographies, texts, translations, and studies of the Pseudepigrapha (Jewish religious writings often claiming to be written by OT figures; the term is becoming used to designate Jewish religious writings not included in any OT canon or otherwise classified), Philo of Alexandria, Flavius Josephus, and the Qumran finds (often referred to as the Dead Sea Scrolls). These materials are all valuable in understanding the nature of Jewish life and thought of the time, and, for the purposes of this essay, are important indications of the influence and interpretation of the OT and its themes among ancient Jews. The pseudepigraphal literature not only invokes OT characters as authors but also often reinterprets and expands upon OT narratives and themes. Philo was a Jewish leader of Alexandria who wrote extensively on the OT, trying to combine traditionally Jewish teachings with Greek learning. Josephus, made a well-cared-for captive of the Roman Emperor, wrote full histories of his people in which appear his views of the OT writings and the events they describe. The Qumran finds include our earliest copies of the OT books as well as a number of writings originating from the community itself. Among these are included commentaries on certain OT books, and these provide direct evidence of the way the community read their Bible.

Charlesworth, J. H. *The Pseudepigrapha and Modern Research, with a Supplement* (Chico, CA: Scholars, 1981). This valuable bibliography covers the period since 1970 and includes an essay discussing recent work.

Delling, G. *Bibliographie zur jüdisch-hellenistischen und intertestamentarischen Literatur: 1900-1970* (2nd ed.; Berlin: Akademie, 1975). The period covered makes this a good complement to Charlesworth's bibliography listed above.

Feldman, L. H. *Studies in Judaica: Scholarship on Philo and Josephus (1937-1962)* (New York: Yeshiva University, 1963).

Fitzmyer, J. A. *The Dead Sea Scrolls: Major Publications and Tools for Study* (rev. ed.; Atlanta: Scholars Press, 1990). The indispensable guide to literature on the Qumran writings.

Forestell, J. T. *Targumic Traditions and the New Testament: An Annotated Bibliography with a New Testament Index* (Chico, CA: Scholars, 1979). An invaluable guide to literature on the ancient Aramaic translations of the OT books called "targums." The highly paraphrastic character of these translations makes them valuable in revealing the way the OT writings were interpreted. (It must be noted that the specialists disagree about the date of the targums and their exact value in reconstructing Judaism of the period in question here.)

Schreckenberg, H. *Bibliographie zu Flavius Josephus* (Leiden: Brill, 1968). A *Supplementband mit Gesamtregister* has now appeared (Leiden: Brill, 1979).

Colson, F. H., and G. H. Whitaker. *Philo with an English Translation* (10 vols., with two supplementary vols.; Cambridge, MA: Harvard University, 1929-62). R. Marcus prepared the supplementary volumes. Here one has the Greek text of Philo, English translation, and brief notes.

Lohse, E. *Die Texte aus Qumran: Hebräisch und Deutsch* (2nd ed.; Darmstadt: Wissenschaftliche Buchgesellschaft, 1971; rpt. Munich: Koesel-Verlag, 1981). This is a handy edition of the major Qumran writings in pointed Hebrew with a facing German translation and brief notes.

R. A. Kraft (ed.). *Society of Biblical Literature Texts and Translations, Pseudepigrapha Series* (Atlanta: Scholars Press, 1972–). Volumes in this series each have their own editors and present the texts and English translations.

Thackeray, H. St.-J., et al. *Josephus with an English Translation* (9 vols.; Cambridge, MA: Harvard University, 1926-65). This set gives a good Greek text of Josephus, a translation, and brief notes.

Charles, R. H. (ed.). *The Apocrypha and Pseudepigrapha of the Old Testament* (2 vols.; Oxford: Clarendon, 1913). A collaborative work by various scholars, with English translations, introductions, notes, and a topical index. Widely used, though dated, the set edited by Charlesworth (see below) supersedes its second volume.

Charlesworth, J. H. (ed.). *The Old Testament Pseudepigrapha* (2 vols.; Garden City, NY: Doubleday, 1982, 1985). This collaborative work of many scholars gives

English translations, introductions, and brief notes to 53 texts, and is now the standard English source for these writings.

Dupont-Sommer, A. *The Essene Writings from Qumran* (Oxford: Blackwell, 1961; rpt. Gloucester/Magnola, MA: P. Smith, 1973). A somewhat idiosyncratic translation at various points, it is nevertheless valuable because it supplies column and line numbers so that one can find the text in the original language editions.

Gaster, T. H. *The Dead Sea Scriptures in English Translation with Introduction and Notes* (3rd ed.; Garden City, NY: Doubleday, 1976). This translation, together with Vermes's listed below, is a widely read translation. Both are by major scholars.

Nickelsburg, G. W. E., and M. E. Stone. *Faith and Piety in Early Judaism: Texts and Documents* (Philadelphia: Fortress, 1983). A useful anthology of translated texts from ancient Judaism illustrating the religious life of the time.

H. F. D. Sparks (ed.). *The Apocryphal Old Testament* (Oxford: Clarendon, 1984). A handy collection of translations of the major pseudepigraphal texts, somewhat comparable to the Charlesworth set but more limited in scope.

Vermes, G. *The Dead Sea Scrolls in English* (Baltimore: Penguin, 1968). A good English translation of major texts.

Cross, F. M. *The Ancient Library of Qumran* (rev. ed.; Garden City, NY: Doubleday, 1961). A standard introduction to the Qumran community and its literature.

McNamara, M. *Palestinian Judaism and the New Testament* (Wilmington, DE: Michael Glazier, 1983). A popular-level introduction to the various Jewish literature of the early Christian period.

———. *Targum and Testament* (Shannon: Irish University, 1972). A handy introduction to the targums and their possible bearing on the illumination of the use of the OT in the NT.

Nickelsburg, G. W. E. *Jewish Literature Between the Bible and the Mishnah: A Historical and Literary Introduction* (Philadelphia: Fortress, 1981). A discussion in chronological order of the Jewish literature from approximately 400 B.C. to A.D. 140.

Patte, D. *Early Jewish Hermeneutic in Palestine* (Missoula, MT: Scholars, 1975). The author concentrates on "early Judaism's attitude toward Scripture" as evidenced in sources from "classical Judaism" (targums, rabbinic sources) and from "sectarian Judaism" (apocalyptic literature, Qumran).

Sandmel, S. *Philo of Alexandria: An Introduction* (New York: Oxford University, 1979). This is probably the place to begin the study of Philo. The writer introduces Philo and those major scholars who have written about him.

THE LITERATURE OF RABBINIC JUDAISM

In addition to the literature referred to in the immediately preceding category, the literature of the rabbinic period is an important body of material for following the interpretation of the OT in ancient Judaism, as well as for obtaining a general familiarity with the nature of ancient Judaism as a whole. Listed here is a limited selection of items from a great body of studies in a very intricate field into which all but specialists must tread with caution. The actual literature of rabbinic Judaism (the form of Judaism which survived to dominate Jewish life after the Jewish revolt of A.D. 66-72) dates from no earlier than the second century of the Christian era, but some of the ideas and views expressed in the literature probably reflect forms of Judaism of earlier decades (although it is very difficult to determine how much of the tradition is earlier than the period of the composition of the literature). In the following list a selection of texts and English translations is given, alphabetically by author/editor, followed by a select number of major tools and studies of rabbinics. The reader unfamiliar with the literature should probably begin with a reading of H. L. Strack and G. Stemberger, *Introduction to the Talmud and Midrash* (trans. M. Bockmuehl; Edinburgh: T. & T. Clark, 1991).

Danby, H. *The Mishnah, Translated from the Hebrew with Introduction and Brief Explanatory Notes* (Oxford: Clarendon, 1933). The most widely used English translation of the Mishnah.

Epstein, I. (ed.). *The Babylonian Talmud* (35 vols.; London: Soncino, 1935-52). An English translation of the complete Talmud.

Freedman, H., and M. Simon (eds.). *Midrash Rabbah* (10 vols.; London-Bournemouth: Soncino, 1951). Vols. 1-9 are an English translation of the great Midrash on Genesis, Exodus, Leviticus, Numbers, Deuteronomy, and Lamentations, Ruth, and Ecclesiastes. Vol. 10 contains a glossary and indexes.

Goldschmidt, L. *Der babylonische Talmud* (9 vols., sometimes reprinted in 13 vols.; Berlin: Calvary, 1897-1935). The Hebrew text and German translation. There is a concordance to this edition: L. Goldschmidt, *'znym ltwrh: Subject Concordance to the Babylonian Talmud* (ed. R. Edelman; Copenhagen: Muncksgaard, 1959).

Lauterbach, J. Z. *Mkylt' drby Yšm' 'l: Mekilta de-Rabbi Ishmael: A Critical Edition on the Basis of the Manuscripts and Early Editions with an English Translation, Introduction, and Notes* (3 vols.; Philadelphia: Jewish Publication Society of America, 1933-35; rpt. 1949). A handy edition of an important midrash on Exod. 12:1ff.

Liebermann, S. *The Tosefta according to Codex Vienna, with Variants from Codex Efurt, Genizah Mss., and editio princeps (Venice 1521): Together with References to Parallel Passages in Talmudic Literature and a Brief Commentary* (2 vols.; New York: Jewish Theological Seminary, 1955, 1962). The Hebrew text with brief commentary. The author also published a more extensive commentary on the Tosefta: *Tosefta kifshutah: A Comprehensive Commentary on the Tosefta* (5 vols.; New York: Jewish Theological Seminary, 1955-62).

Neusner, J. *The Talmud of Israel: A Preliminary Translation and Explanation* (Chicago: University of Chicago, 1983–). A new translation of the Jerusalem Talmud by a most important Judaica scholar.

Rengstorf, K. H., and L. Rost (eds.). *Die Mischna: Text, Überstetzung und ausführliche Erklärung* (Berlin: Töpelmann, 1910–). The vocalized text of Mishnaic tractates, a German translation, and a commentary.

Albeck, C. *Einführung in die Mischna* (Berlin/New York: de Gruyter, 1971). A valuable guide to understanding the Mishnah, explaining many features of this early rabbinic collection.

Bonsirven, J. *Textes rabbiniques des deux premier siècles chrétiens pour servir à l'intelligence du Nouveau Testament* (Rome: Biblical Institute, 1955). A selection of passages from the Mishnah, Midrashes, Talmuds, and Tosefta, arranged according to the rabbinic tractates, with indexes of themes, OT and NT passages; only a few of the texts listed, however, come from the period mentioned in the title.

Montefiore, C. G., and H. Loewe. *A Rabbinic Anthology, Selected and Arranged with Comments and Introduction* (Cleveland/New York: World Publishing Co.; Philadelphia: Jewish Publication Society of America, 1960). This is an interesting collection of translated passages from talmudic and midrashic literature, with comments by former leaders of Reform and Orthodox Jewish groups, and with excellent indexes to topics, OT passages, and rabbinic passages, and a glossary.

Moore, G. F. *Judaism in the First Centuries of the Christian Era: The Age of the Tannaim* (3 vols.; Cambridge, MA: Harvard University, 1927-30; rpt., 2 vols.; New York: Schocken, 1971). A classic description of rabbinic Judaism, still of great value, but in need of correction and supplementation in the light of more recent finds and studies.

CHRISTIAN APOCRYPHAL AND HETERODOX LITERATURE

Although this category properly belongs to the field of the history of Christian thought, it may be appropriate to indicate some basic items which pertain especially to the field of biblical studies. Listed here are works having to do with what is called "New Testament Apocrypha," literature clearly indebted to the NT writings and claiming to be apostolic in authorship and authority, and books treating Christian Gnosticism. The study of Gnosticism is a complex and burgeoning field and the following list contains only a few of the major studies of the topic and other publications which focus on the gnostic interpretation of the Bible.

Bianchi, U. (ed.). *Le origini dello gnosticismo: Colloquio di Messina* (Leiden: Brill, 1967). A collection of articles, in English, French, German, and Italian, from a colloquium on Gnosticism held in 1966.

The Facsimile Edition of the Nag Hammadi Codices (12 vols.; Leiden: Brill, 1971–). Twelve volumes contain photographic reproductions of the various writings from the find, to be accompanied by an eleven-volume Coptic Gnostic Library series of translations and studies of the materials. For a good introduction to the Nag Hammadi codices, see J. M. Robinson, "The Coptic Gnostic Library Today," *New Testament Studies* 14 (1967-68): 356-401.

Foerster, W. (ed.). *Gnosis: A Selection of Gnostic Texts* (2 vols.; trans. R. M. Wilson; Oxford: Clarendon, 1972, 1974). Vol. 1 is a collection of patristic references to gnostics, and Vol. 2, a selection of Coptic and Mandean texts, all in English translation.

Pagels, E. *The Johannine Gospel in Gnostic Exegesis: Heracleon's Commentary on John* (Missoula: Scholars, 1973). An interesting study of gnostic biblical exegesis.

———. *The Gnostic Paul* (Philadelphia: Fortress, 1975). A study of gnostic exegesis of the letters of the apostle Paul.

Perkins, P. *The Gnostic Dialogue: The Early Church and the Crisis of Gnosticism* (New York: Paulist, 1980). A good student-level introduction to Gnosticism.

Robinson, J. M. (gen. ed.). *The Nag Hammadi Library in English: Translated and Introduced by Members of the Coptic Gnostic Library Project of the Institute for Antiquity and Christianity, Claremont, California* (3rd rev. ed.; Leiden: Brill, 1988). A translation of the entire body of forty-seven writings found in 1945 at Nag Hammadi, Egypt, this accessible and helpful volume makes the major gnostic sources readily available.

Rudolph, K. *Gnosis: The Nature and History of Gnosticism* (trans. and ed. R. M. Wilson; San Francisco: Harper & Row/Edinburgh: T. & T. Clark, 1983). From an internationally respected authority, this book is a major treatment of the whole field of Gnosticism, though some of the positions taken are hotly debated.

Santos Otero, A. de. *Los evangelios apócrifos: Colección de textos griegos y latinos, versión crítica, estudios introductorios, comentarios e ilustraciones* (3rd ed.; Madrid: Edica, 1975). Not only a Spanish translation, but also the original Greek and Latin texts (something not found in Schneemelcher and Hennecke below).

Schneemelcher, W. (ed.). *New Testament Apocrypha,*

Volume One: Gospels and Related Writings (Revised) (Philadelphia: Westminster/John Knox, 1991); and E. Hennecke, *New Testament Apocrypha, Volume Two: Writings Relating to the Apostles: Apocalypses and Related Subjects* (ed. W. Schneemelcher; trans. R. M. Wilson; Philadelphia: Westminster/John Knox, 1965). English translations, valuable introductory essays and bibliographies, these works include attention to the Nag Hammadi texts (on which see J. M. Robinson, below).

Scholer, D. M. *Nag Hammadi Bibliography 1948-1969* (Leiden: Brill, 1971). An invaluable key to studies on Gnosticism in general and the Nag Hammadi writings in particular, it has been updated annually in the journal *Novum Testamentum,* beginning with 1970.

COMMENTARIES

The commentary is a well-established genre in biblical studies, although the varying readerships for which commentaries are written mean that they differ, often markedly, from one another, both in contents and format. Regardless of the readers for whom they are prepared, commentaries usually introduce the biblical book being commented on, giving what is known (or the opinions held) on authorship, date, destination, purpose, major emphases, linguistic and literary characteristics, etc. Then there is a discussion of the actual text in question, passage by passage (in briefer treatments for more popular reading), or verse by verse, the detail and technical intricacy varying according to the intended readers. Commentaries range from one-volume treatments of the whole Bible to multi-volume sets (usually by teams of scholars), in which each volume deals in greater detail with one or more biblical book(s). In a few cases we have examples of commentaries of several volumes devoted to one or another biblical book that may be large (e.g., Psalms) or simply of special importance in the history of Christianity (e.g., the Gospel of John, Romans). It would make this essay unmanageably long to try to list all the important commentaries on particular books of the Bible. The reader is referred to the works by B. S. Childs, F. W. Danker, D. M. Scholer, and D. A. Carson listed under the "Bibliographies" category earlier in this essay, and to J. Goldingay, *Old Testament Commentary Survey* (London: Theological Students Fellowship, 1975) for descriptions and evaluations of particular volumes. (For an introduction to important historical commentaries which have had an influence on English literature, see the bibliography by D. L. Jeffrey later in this volume.) The present list is limited to a description of some important one-volume Bible commentaries and some major English-language commentary series. (Commentary series in other languages are found in J. A. Fitzmyer's bibliography listed above under the "Bibliographies" category.)

The Anchor Bible (Garden City, NY: Doubleday, 1964–). A multi-volume series on the OT, Apocrypha, and NT; the format and quality of the volumes vary considerably. Contributors include Jews, Protestants, and Roman Catholics.

Black, M., and H. H. Rowley (eds.). *Peake's Commentary on the Bible* (London: Nelson, 1962). Though retaining the name of the one-volume commentary published in 1919 by A. S. Peake, this is a completely new and highly regarded work, prepared by British and American scholars.

Black's New Testament Commentaries (London: A. and C. Black, 1957–). The American edition is known as *Harper's New Testament Commentaries* (published by Harper & Row and more recently by Hendrickson). Many contributors are well-known British and American biblical scholars, and the series is written for the general reader.

Brown, R. E., J. A. Fitzmyer, and R. E. Murphy (eds.). *The New Jerome Biblical Commentary* (Englewood Cliffs, NJ: Prentice-Hall, 1990). Comparable to *Peake's Commentary on the Bible* listed above, but written by a team of Roman Catholic scholars.

Cambridge Greek Testament Commentary (Cambridge: University Press, 1955–). C. F. D. Moule is general editor, and the series emphasizes both philological/historical matters and theological themes. Knowledge of Greek is presupposed. Only volumes on Mark, Colossians, and Philemon have appeared so far.

New International Biblical Commentary (Peabody, MA: Hendrickson, 1988–). The NT volumes are edited by W. W. Gasque. The text commented on is the New International Version translation published by the New York Bible Society, and the series is aimed at the general reader.

Hermeneia: A Critical and Historical Commentary on the Bible (Philadelphia: Fortress, 1971–). A modern series directed to scholars, based on the Hebrew or Greek text, with original translations, copious citation of secondary literature, and emphasizing the historical-critical questions of modern biblical scholars. Early volumes were translations of famous German commentaries, but these will be replaced by fresh treatments of the biblical books commissioned for the series.

The Interpreter's Bible (Nashville: Abingdon). Begun in 1952 with G. A. Buttrick as editor, the series comprises twelve volumes and is now quite dated. The format includes a homiletic exposition of each passage, but these sections have been criticized heavily. Intended mainly for pastors and theological students, the texts of the AV and RSV are printed in parallel columns. Vols. 1 and 7 are devoted to essays on OT and NT backgrounds.

The International Critical Commentary (Edinburgh: T. & T. Clark, 1895–). Intended as an English-

869

language counterpart to German technical commentary series, the original Hebrew or Greek texts are commented on, with detailed philological and critical discussions. The volumes are now quite dated, though some are still of value. Replacement volumes, edited by J. A. Emerton and C. E. B. Cranfield, are to appear, though so far only the commentary on Romans and two of three volumes on Matthew have been released.

New Century Bible: Based on the Revised Standard Version (R. E. Clements and M. Black, eds.; London: Oliphants; Grand Rapids: Eerdmans, 1966–). The series is intended for general readers, avoiding foreign words and explaining the Hebrew, Aramaic, or Greek text for nonspecialists.

The New International Commentary on the New Testament (Grand Rapids, MI: Eerdmans, 1952–). The contributors represent a learned, somewhat conservative Protestant viewpoint, and the series is intended for pastors and other serious students of the Bible.

The New International Commentary on the Old Testament (Grand Rapids, MI: Eerdmans, 1965–). The companion series to the immediately preceding item.

New International Greek Testament Commentary (Grand Rapids, MI: Eerdmans, 1978–). A series of scholarly and detailed commentaries, generally conservative, on the Greek text.

Old Testament Library (Philadelphia: Westminster, 1962–). A noteworthy collection of commentaries on OT books and monographs on topics connected with the OT (history, theology). Many of the series volumes are translations of German commentaries by important scholars.

Pelican New Testament Commentaries (London/Baltimore: Penguin). Written by major British scholars, the series appears in paperback and is intended for the general reader.

Torch Bible Commentaries (London: SCM; New York: Macmillan, 1951–). Brief but informed volumes emphasizing the religious significance of the biblical text discussed, the series is written for pastors and general readers.

Tyndale New Testament Commentaries (London: Tyndale; Grand Rapids, MI: Eerdmans, 1956–). Conservative in approach, with somewhat detailed introductions and an emphasis upon theological interpretation of the text. Over the last several years, every volume in the series has been either revised or replaced.

Tyndale Old Testament Commentaries (London: Tyndale; Downers Grove, IL: Inter-Varsity, 1964–). A companion series to the immediately preceding item, some twelve volumes have been published to date.

Word Biblical Commentary. Gen. eds. D. A. Hubbard and G. W. Barker (Waco, TX: Word Books, 1983–). A multi-volume series to cover all books of the Bible. Each volume is a detailed scholarly work from a traditional Protestant Christian perspective.

LARRY W. HURTADO

Studies of the Bible as Literature:
A Select List

Strictly speaking, the concern of *A Dictionary of Biblical Tradition in English Literature* is with the Bible *in* literature. Yet it will be evident in terms both of history and critical practice that the foundational character of the Bible for English (and other vernacular) literature has led to considerable overlap with what is usually described as the study of the Bible *as* literature. At least since the time of Matthew Arnold, this has been an important sphere for literary criticism and scholarship.

In its simplest sense, "the Bible as literature" describes an approach using the methods and terminology of conventional literary analysis. To move beyond this basic definition, we must note that the term *literary criticism* carries at least two distinct meanings. For traditional biblical scholars it usually means source analysis; for secular literary critics it describes analysis of established texts. We are concerned here only with the latter; using the term *literary analysis* to designate it may minimize the confusion.

Such literary analysis can be distinguished from two traditional approaches to the Bible: theological and scholarly. The theologian is interested in how a text supports a doctrinal point or elucidates a religious problem; for him, the Garden of Eden narrative in Gen. 3 may establish the doctrine of original sin or warn readers to be wary of temptation. The scholar's interests are historical; he or she wants to identify the various redactions which have contributed to the present text, or to compare the serpent with similar figures in other ancient stories. The literary analyst, in contrast, usually works with the final text and draws conclusions about the human experience based on its plot, characterization, and imagery. In short, he does to the Eden narrative what he might do to a short story or chapter from a novel.

In approaching the Bible this way, the literary analyst *generally* makes assumptions such as the following:

1. *Individual literary units can be extracted from the Bible and analyzed separately.* While analysts differ on the question of overall unity in the Bible, most feel justified in performing rather isolated analyses of units ranging in length from, say, an individual Psalm to the entire cycle of Abraham stories.

2. *The primary focus is on literary, not historical, reality.* Literary analysis sidesteps the question of the historicity of Adam and Eve, Moses, or Jesus, and treats these figures as literary characters.

3. *Later interpretations cannot be superimposed on earlier material.* In analyzing Gen. 3, literary people will not assume the serpent to be Satan, even though later hints in Revelation suggest that view. (This does not mean that allusion is not dealt with, as long as the references are clearly indicated in the text under consideration; e.g., Rev. 12:9 may allude to Gen. 3, but not vice versa.)

4. *The same methods and terminology used to study other literature can justifiably be used with the Bible.* If one can speak of narrative point of view in a novel, one can do so with the David story; if one can study reader response to "A Modest Proposal," one can do so with the book of Jonah; if one can deconstruct a fairy tale, one can deconstruct a Gospel.

Although several modern writers declare literary analysis of the Bible a recent phenomenon, in the broadest sense this is not true. The Bible as literature enjoys a long, if sketchy, history.

To be sure, earlier literary comments were often brief observations about the power of the Bible's style. The tradition may have begun with Longinus who — in one sentence — praised the style of the Genesis creation narrative. It continued in the Renaissance in scattered observations by writers like Sidney and Milton, and even into the last century, as evidenced by Walt Whitman's comment epitomizing the attitude: "Even to our Nineteenth Century here are the fountain heads of song."

Early literary analysis can also be seen in the traditional medieval approach to the Bible as allegory. Spearheaded by Origen and then St. Augustine, this attitude derived in part from the Bible itself, where St. Paul reads OT incidents as allegory (e.g., Gal. 4:22-31). Augustine noted Paul's distinction between "letter" and "spirit" (2 Cor. 3:6) and argued that the literal level of Scripture should be pierced to reveal the spiritual truth inside — the method of allegory.

However, the first extended studies of the Bible as an aesthetic object only emerged in the 18th century. In Germany, Johann Gottfried von Herder, in *The Spirit of Hebrew Poetry*, argued extensively for reading the OT as poetry. In England, Bishop Robert Lowth (*Lectures on the Sacred Poetry of the Hebrews*) first drew attention to parallelism as a characteristic of Hebrew poetry, and commented on everything from short biblical odes to the drama of Job.

The rise of "higher criticism" in the 19th cent. diverted some attention from the holistic approach of literary study to the segmentation and historical interests of the newer biblical scholars. However, the turn of the 20th cent. saw a renewed interest in genre studies as many literary analysts tried to categorize biblical writing as narrative, lyric, epic, drama, or folklore; a prime example is in the pioneering work of Richard Moulton (*The Literary Study of the Bible*, 1895). This movement helped pave the way for the intense interest in literary analysis which has emerged since 1970.

Contemporary literary study of the Bible employs various approaches. One is the *Formalist* approach of the New Criticism. An important forerunner was Erich Auerbach, who in the 1940s included studies of Abraham's dilemma of faith and Peter's denial of Jesus in his *Mimesis*, an anthology of insightful essays on Western literature. More recent Formalist studies have been undertaken by literary critics like Kenneth Gros Louis, biblical scholars like Edwin Good, and specialists in both fields, like David Robertson and Robert Alter.

A second approach is the *Archetypal*; it sees many of the characters and incidents in the Bible as reflections of the same universal patterns surfacing in other mythologies. Heavily influenced by mythology and psychoanalysis (esp. Carl Jung), its leading literary spokesperson is Northrop Frye, who has argued repeatedly that the Bible provides a central mythological framework for Western culture.

A good deal of work has been done on *Structuralist* analyses of biblical texts. This approach, derived from recent interest in language and semiology, attempts to decode such literary objects as the parables of Jesus to uncover deep structures reflected in the text itself. With obvious connections to literature, the method has been featured in the work of such biblical scholars as John Dominic Crossan.

Two newer literary schools are now also making their mark on biblical studies. *Deconstructionists*, under the influence of Jacques Derrida, look for loose threads they claim cause texts to unravel themselves. *Reader-response* (or *subjectivist*) critics encounter between reader and text the process of reading itself.

Among other perspectives now being studied is a *Feminist* approach reconsidering women's roles in the Bible; important contributors include Phyllis Trible, Meike Bal, and Regina Schwartz. *Evangelical* Christians have turned their attention to the aesthetic qualities of the Bible, sensing no conflict between this and their belief in a divinely inspired Scripture; among their leading literary analysts is Leland Ryken. Other *eclectic* critics are attempting to reconcile literary analysis with traditional biblical scholarship; e.g., Norman Petersen has called for a literary study of the Bible which will complement the historical-critical method. Still others, like Amos Wilder and Michael Fishbane, are attempting literary analyses in the context of traditional religious appreciation.

BIBLIOGRAPHY

(Some items adapted from John H. Gottcent, *The Bible as Literature: A Selective Bibliography*. Boston: G. K. Hall, 1979)

Alter, Robert. *The Art of Biblical Narrative* (New York: Basic Books, 1981). Alter defines and defends a literary approach to the Hebrew Bible, and presents readings of selected passages (mainly from Genesis and Samuel/Kings) studying such literary techniques as type-scenes, repetition, dialogue, narrative reticence, and characterization.

———. *The Art of Biblical Poetry* (New York: Basic Books, 1985). A companion volume to the above, using an analogous approach to the Hebrew Bible's poetry.

———, and Frank Kermode (eds.). *The Literary Guide to the Bible* (Cambridge: Harvard University Press, 1987). An anthology of essays by a wide variety of scholars and critics.

Auerbach, Erich. *Mimesis: The Representation of Reality in Western Literature*. Trans. Willard R. Trask (Princeton: Princeton University Press, 1953). Two essays in this collection represent older, but still valuable, examples of a New Critical approach to the Bible. In "Odysseus's Scar" Auerbach contrasts the literary styles of Homer and the OT writers, focusing on the binding of Isaac (Gen. 22). In "Fortunata" he discusses Mark's account of Peter's denial of Jesus.

Bal, Mieke. *Lethal Love: Literary Feminist Interpretations of Biblical Love-Stories* (Bloomington: Indiana University Press, 1987).

———. *Death and Dissymmetry: The Politics of Coherence in the Book of Judges* (Chicago: University of Chicago Press, 1989). Bal's studies combine post-structuralist techniques of literary criticism and feminist analysis to reinterpret both OT narrative in itself and its reception and understanding in Western culture.

Beardslee, William. *Literary Criticism of the New Testament* (Philadelphia: Fortress, 1970). A literary-critical analysis of relationships among the Gospels and Epistles.

Crossan, John Dominic. *In Parables: The Challenge of the Historical Jesus* (New York: Harper and Row, 1973). A commentary on the parables, acknowledging their literary nature. Emphasizes a structuralist approach.

Detweiler, Robert (ed.). "Derrida and Biblical Studies." *Semeia* 23 (1982). Four essays — one by Derrida himself — on the challenge of deconstruction to traditional biblical scholarship.

Fischer, James A. *How to Read the Bible* (Englewood Cliffs, N.J.: Prentice-Hall, 1982). Argues the contemporary need to read the Bible as literature, and offers practical suggestions for reading various biblical genres, including narratives, laws, reflective passages, the prophets, and prayers.

Fishbane, Michael. *Text and Texture: Close Readings of Selected Biblical Texts* (New York: Schocken Books, 1979). "The author has been particularly concerned with showing how literary analysis can mediate a new sense of the Bible as a complex of religious teachings." Sections focus on narratives, direct speech (including prayer and sermon forms), and selected motifs such as Creation, Eden, and Exodus. An important literary examination of different genres from the Hebrew Bible.

Frye, Northrop. *The Great Code: The Bible and Literature* (New York: Harcourt Brace Jovanovich, 1982). A culmination of Frye's oft-repeated assumption that the Bible provides the mythological framework for Western culture. Given its impact on imaginative literature, the Bible must be an imaginative work itself. The Christian Bible is considered as a unified whole in the light of language, myth, metaphor, and typology. Frye's sequel volume, *Words with Power* (New York: Harcourt Brace Jovanovich, 1990), comments more specifically on the text of the Bible itself.

Good, Edwin M. *Irony in the Old Testament* (2nd ed.; Sheffield, Eng.: Almond Press, 1981). A literary analysis focusing on irony in selected OT books. Sandwiched between an introductory chapter and an epilogue are essays on Jonah, Saul, Genesis, Isaiah, Qoheleth, and Job. "I am inclined to think that the presence of irony in the Old Testament casts a new light on the theological task of interpretation."

Gottcent, John H. *The Bible: A Literary Study* (Boston: Twayne Publishers, 1986). A brief introduction to the field. Following opening sections on historical background, the importance of the Bible, and the history of its literary study are chapters analyzing selections from both the OT and NT. Uses an eclectic methodology relating the text to human experience.

—————. *The Bible as Literature: A Selective Bibliography* (Boston: G. K. Hall, 1979). An annotated bibliography of books and articles useful in pursuing literary analysis of the Bible. Includes editions and translations, general reference works, and scholarly and critical material on the whole Bible, its major components (including the Apocrypha), and the individual books.

Grant, Patrick. *Reading the New Testament* (London: Macmillan; Grand Rapids: Eerdmans, 1989). Shows how the literary character of the Gospels and of Paul's letters to the Corinthians, Hebrews, and Revelation is in each case the instrument by which the primary goal is pursued, assent in the belief that the crucified Jesus is God. Grant's thesis is that the rich narrative and symbolic devices of the NT are consumed in an analysis which is finally intolerant of the fictive imagination.

Gros, Louis, and R. R. Kenneth, with James S. Ackerman and Thayer S. Warshaw. *Literary Interpretations of Biblical Narratives*. 2 vols. (Nashville: Abingdon Press, 1974, 1982). Collections of essays on literary analysis, most emphasizing a New Critical approach (although in Vol. 2 some attention is paid to structuralism and pedagogical matters). A wider variety of contributors is represented in the second volume, which is divided into sections on Methodology, Genesis, and Literary Approaches to Selected Biblical Narratives.

Jaspers, David. *The New Testament and the Literary Imagination* (Atlantic Highlands: Humanities Press, 1987).

Josopovici, Gabriel. *The Book of God: A Response to the Bible* (New Haven and London: Yale University Press, 1988). This work, by the author of *The World and the Book* (1971), examines the differing conceptions of unity underlying the Hebrew and Christian scriptures. Josopovici's analysis focuses on three "defining characteristics" of biblical literature: its rhythm (or reiteration), its attitude to language, and its conception of character.

Kermode, Frank. *The Genesis of Secrecy: On the Interpretation of Narrative* (Cambridge: Harvard University Press, 1979). A reading of the Gospels (esp. Mark), with frequent comparative references to modern literature. Demonstrates the close relationships between biblical hermeneutics and "secular" literary criticism.

Kort, Wesley A. *Story, Text, and Scripture: Literary Interests in Biblical Narrative* (University Park: Penn State Press, 1988). Explains and illustrates how four major literary methodologies have been applied to biblical narratives by contemporary practitioners.

Kugel, James L. *The Idea of Biblical Poetry: Parallelism and Its History* (New Haven: Yale University Press, 1981). An attempt to "arrive at some comprehensive notion of biblical parallelism," a stylistic feature usually perceived in biblical poetry, and to trace its history from antiquity to the present. Concludes that distinctions between biblical poetry and prose are often artificial and questions the validity of modern literary readings of the Bible.

Lowry, Shirley Park. *Familiar Mysteries: The Truth in Myth* (New York: Oxford University Press, 1982). An archetypal attempt to define what myth is and what it does. Cites many examples from the Bible, as well as from other mythologies and folklore. Sections include: The Symbolic Language of Myths, The Hero, The Compleat Home and the Monster at the Door, and Conquering Death.

Maier, John, and Vincent Tollers (eds). *The Bible in its Literary Milieu: Contemporary Essays* (Grand Rapids: Eerdmans, 1979).

————. *Literary Approaches to the Hebrew Bible* (Lewisburg: Bucknell University Press, 1990). Two valuable collections of essays by established scholars from both biblical and secular literary disciplines.

McConnell, Frank (ed.). *The Bible and the Narrative Tradition* (New York: Oxford University Press, 1986). An anthology of six essays by prominent scholars and critics on the study of biblical story.

Petersen, Norman R. *Literary Criticism for New Testament Critics.* Guides to Biblical Scholarship, New Testament Series (Philadelphia: Fortress Press, 1978). Argues for a literary analysis of the Bible which will complement the historical-critical approach. Discusses literary problems in the historical-critical paradigm and proposes a literary-critical model for historical criticism. Presents case studies of Mark (story time and plotted time in the narrative) and Luke-Acts (narrative world and real world).

Robertson, David. *The Old Testament and the Literary Critic.* Guides to Biblical Scholarship, Old Testament Series (Philadelphia: Fortress Press, 1977). Essays by a scholar trained in both biblical studies and contemporary literary criticism. An introductory chapter on the nature of a literary study of the Bible is followed by specific treatments of Exodus, Job, Ps. 90, and the Prophets.

Ryken, Leland. *How to Read the Bible as Literature* (Grand Rapids: Academie Books, 1984). An introduction to literary methodology by an evangelical Christian and professor of English. Chapters cover such literary types as story, poetry, proverb, gospel, parable, epistle, satire, and visionary writing.

Schwartz, Regina. *The Book and the Text: The Bible and Literary Theory* (Oxford: Blackwell, 1990). A strong collection of essays by notable scholars (including Alter, Bal, Bruns, Eagleton, Ricoeur, and Tolbert), exemplifying the impact of poststructuralist critical method upon the literary study of the Bible.

Sternberg, Meir. *The Poetics of Biblical Narrative: Ideological Literature and the Drama of Reading* (Bloomington: Indiana University Press, 1985). A sophisticated survey of literary methodology as applied to biblical texts, with particular emphasis on ambiguities, discontinuities, and "gaps" in the reading.

Trible, Phyllis. *God and the Rhetoric of Sexuality.* Overtures to Biblical Theology Series (Philadelphia: Fortress Press, 1978). A study of female imagery and motifs in the Bible. Traces implications of the metaphor in Gen. 1:27 in which the image of God is seen as both male and female. Special attention is paid to "the tragedy of disobedience in Genesis 2-3, the poetry of eroticism in the Song of Songs, and the struggles of daily existence in the story of Ruth."

————. *Texts of Terror: Literary-Feminist Readings of Biblical Narratives* (Philadelphia: Fortress Press, 1984). A second series of feminist readings, focusing this time on such often-overlooked women as Hagar, Tamar, and Jephthah's daughter.

Wilder, Amos N. *Early Christian Rhetoric: The Language of the Gospel* (Cambridge: Harvard University Press, 1971). The Introduction surveys the history of the Bible as literature and defends a modern posture which sees literary and theological approaches intertwined. Chapters focus on NT language in terms of modes and genres, dialogue, story, parable, poem, image, symbol, and myth.   JOHN H. GOTTCENT

The English Bible:
A Brief History of Translation

So far as anyone knows, the Bible first touched English soil near the end of the sixth century A.D. when a missionary, St. Augustine, carried one across the Channel. Of course, this was not yet an English version, but the Latin Vg of St. Jerome. For centuries, it would be virtually the only written Bible in Britain.

How, then, did ordinary folk — mostly illiterate — obtain their biblical knowledge? Essentially, from a variety of oral and visual sources. Preachers delivering sermons would preface their homilies with paraphrases of relevant texts. Art work on church windows and walls might depict the expulsion of Adam and Eve from the Garden, or Jesus' temptation in the wilderness. Later, the mystery play helped communicate the stories of Abraham and Isaac, Noah, the Christmas shepherds, and, indeed, the entire cycle of biblical narrative from Genesis to Revelation.

To be sure, from the 7th cent. on, a series of Anglo-Saxon versions of *parts* of the Bible emerged. Credit for the first usually goes to Caedmon, whose "Hymn" (ca. 670) paraphrased the Genesis creation story in verse form. Around 700, Aldhelm translated the Psalms, and several years later Bede himself may have translated at least the Gospel of John (ca. 735), though his work has not survived. In the 9th cent., King Alfred rendered portions of Exodus, Psalms, and Acts into Old English. From the 10th cent. on, there appeared a series of Anglo-Saxon gospels, including the famous Lindisfarne Gospels (actually an earlier Latin MS with an interlinear Anglo-Saxon translation added).

Credit for the first complete English translation of the Bible goes to John Wyclif, who rendered the Vg into Middle English in the 14th cent. Two versions of the *Wyclif Bible* appeared between 1380 and 1397, of which ca. 180 MSS survive. (While Wyclif clearly inspired both, the actual translators were probably Nicholas Hereford for the first, and John Purvey for the second.) Used by the Lollards as they crisscrossed England preaching Wyclif's doctrines, this version helped spread the influence of the Midland dialect, leading to Modern English.

Wyclif's translation suffered from one unfortunate circumstance, however; it appeared before the printing press, and hence could only be reproduced by hand. The development of the Gutenberg Press (1455), its introduction into England by Caxton (1475), and the onset of the Protestant Reformation paved the way for the flurry of new translations which appeared in the 16th cent. The first was the work of William Tyndale, whose NT (ca. 1525) was the first part of the Bible *printed* in the English language. Tyndale (whose place in this story has given him the name "Father of the English Bible") was the first to go beyond the Vg to a Greek text for his NT, and a Hebrew text for the portion of the OT he completed. Unfortunately, his work stirred up such English concern over possible "heresy" that it had to be published in Germany. Tyndale himself was burned at the stake in 1536.

The first complete Bible printed in English was the work of Miles Coverdale (1535). It was based on the Vg, Tyndale, and Luther's German translation. Two years later, it in turn became a source for *Matthew's Bible* (1537) — actually a combination of Tyndale and Coverdale by John Rogers (who used the pseudonym "Thomas Matthew"). This and the second edition of Coverdale (also 1537) were the first English Bibles to receive the approval of the king for publication. *The Great Bible* appeared in 1539 — requested by Henry VIII, commissioned by Thomas Cromwell, and translated by Coverdale. It was the first "authorized version," containing the line "This is the Byble apoynted to the use of the churches."

For the next product of this prolific century we turn to Geneva, Switzerland. There a group of English Puritans sought refuge from the persecutions of their Catholic monarch, Mary Tudor. And there they produced one of the most influential translations of all times: the *Geneva Bible* (1560). It was the first English version to number the verses throughout. It was the first to use italics for words not in the MSS but added by the translators (a tradition adopted in the King James and many later Bibles). Moreover, its Roman type and handy quarto size helped make it extremely popular. Sometimes called "the Bible of Shakespeare," it continued in popularity well into the 17th cent.

This Puritan version represented such a threat to mainline English Protestantism that the Anglican Church soon authorized its own revision of the Great Bible. The resulting *Bishops' Bible* (1568) became the official version in England.

As Puritans had fled Queen Mary in mid-century, Roman Catholics were to flee the Protestant Elizabeth I a generation later. Many found safety in France where, in 1582, they produced an English NT at Rheims. Work on the OT was completed at Douay in 1609. Based on the Vg, the *Rheims-Douay Bible* was translated by William Allen and Gregory Martin, and revised several times (mid-18th cent.) by Bishop Challoner. Well into the 20th cent., it remained the basis for most Catholic editions of the Bible in English.

By the end of the 16th cent., then, the English Bible had experienced a complete flip-flop. Whereas earlier there had been essentially no English translations (save Wyclif), now there was a confusing array. A fortunate event at the beginning of the new century helped minimize the confusion. In 1604 James I called a conference at Hampton Court to settle disputes between his High Church and the English Puritans. While in general the conference failed (its failure would lead to revolution in the next generation), it produced one happy result. Dr. John Reynolds, Puritan president of Corpus Christi College, proposed a new authorized translation to appear without marginal notes. James appointed a board of 54 scholars from Oxford, Cambridge, and Westminster. (The king himself, contrary to popular opinion, did *not* translate.) They began work in 1607 and, four years later, produced perhaps the most well-known and influential version of the Bible in any language. The *Authorized Version* of 1611 — also, though not officially, known as the King James Version — was technically a revision of the Bishops' Bible. It was not so much a new translation as a culminating synthesis of the English versions of the previous century ("translated out of the original tongues and with the former translations diligently compared and revised").

Ironically, the new "Authorized Version" was never officially sanctioned by law. It carried the phrase "Appointed to be read in Churches," but that was a holdover from the Bishops' Bible. Nonetheless, the AV (or KJV, as it is designated in the entries of this volume) had a number

of undeniable merits, and its importance justifies our briefly noting them there. First, it was highly accurate for its time — based on the best available early texts and, as we have seen, on previous English translations (particularly Tyndale). Second, it was stylistically beautiful, its language often still unsurpassed. (In part, this is because it was designed for public reading, making the translators acutely conscious of the *sound* of their language.) Finally, it was to become extremely influential, producing innumerable literary allusions and quotations (though some of its most widely used phrases were actually taken over from earlier translations). The extent of its cultural impact is illustrated in the way it has permeated everyday speech: "apple of his eye," "skin of my teeth," "salt of the earth," "millstone about the neck."

From a contemporary perspective, however, the AV has a number of undeniable weaknesses, too. For one thing, it is sometimes inaccurate by modern standards. For example, scholars do not think its rendering of Luke 2:14 ("Glory to God in the highest, and on earth peace, good will toward men") captures the sense of the original (cf. the RSV: "Glory to God in the highest, and on earth peace among men with whom he is pleased"). Moreover, as a translation designed for another time and place, it has become obscure for modern readers, especially in its prose passages. Perhaps most important, it has too often been considered *THE* Bible, instead of simply one translation.

Nonetheless, the AV succeeded in stopping the hectic translating pace of the 16th cent. While a number of translations were attempted over the 250 years following its appearance, none successfully replaced it. The most noteworthy episodes in Bible translating during this period were the changes in spellings and renderings in the AV itself, which continued well into the 19th cent., making modern editions of this Bible somewhat different from the 1611 printing. Some of these changes produced unintended horror, and then humor: e.g., a 17th-cent. edition inadvertently omitted "not" from Exod. 20:14, rendering that commandment "Thou shalt commit adultery." But the position of the KJV as the "Authorized Version" of the English Bible went unchallenged.

The first serious attempt to change that began in 1870 when an interdenominational committee appointed by the Church of England set about updating the AV with reference to more recently established texts and to changes in the English language itself. The result was the *Revised Version* (1885), and it was just that — not a new translation, but an attempt to bring the AV in line with recent scholarship and usage. The revisers were extremely literal, producing an awkward rendering which never supplants the 1611 version. But they did usher in another century of frenetic Bible translating, not to be completed without the appearance of the *New King James* (1979) and the *New Revised Standard Version* (1989). The latter, under the general editorship of Bruce Metzger, in addition to general philological and textual updating, has the added feature of inclusive language "as far as this can be done without altering passages that reflect the historical situation of ancient patriarchal culture."

Some of this new work involved revisions of the King James Bible. The 20th cent. brought about the *American Standard Version* (1901), an Americanization of the Revised Version (one of its noteworthy features was the use of "Jehovah" for "Lord"). More recently, a further updating of the ASV has appeared: the *New American Standard Bible* (1971). It is basically conservative, though it does not retain the word-for-word literalness of its predecessor.

The most significant modern attempt to continue the AV tradition began after World War II when a committee headed by Dean Luther Weigle of Yale Divinity School undertook the *Revised Standard Version* (1952; 2nd ed. of the NT, 1971). Prepared under the auspices of the American National Council of Churches (with most Protestant denominations authorizing its use), the original RSV is probably the most widely used English version today. Many scholars also consider it the most accurate (e.g., it follows modern consensus in translating Heb. *'almah* as "young woman" in Isa. 7:14, instead of the traditional "virgin"). In 1973, an ecumenical edition of the RSV (including the Apocrypha) was approved by both Protestant and Roman Catholic hierarchies. Called "The Common Bible," it superseded separate Protestant and Catholic versions of this translation and helped usher in an era when denominational distinctions among Bibles are diminishing.

Other 20th-cent. English Bibles are "fresh" translations — not revisions of the AV but new works of scholarship, based on the best texts now available. Early in this century, the Jewish Publication Society of America set about producing a standard English translation of the Hebrew Scriptures; in 1917, they published *The Holy Scriptures According to the Masoretic Text*. A half century later, the JPSA began updating their work and published the results in three sections: Torah (1963), Prophets (1978), and Writings (1982). Coordinated by novelist Chaim Potok, this standard version of Scripture for American English-speaking Jews is now available in a single volume: *Tanakh: A New Translation of the Holy Scriptures* (1985).

Fresh translations have also been produced in the Roman Catholic tradition. An important instance is the *New American Bible*, begun in the 1940s and completed in 1970. Called the "confraternity version" while in progress, this translation was prepared by the Catholic Biblical Association of America and was one of the first Catholic versions based on Hebrew and Greek texts instead of the Vg. As in most Catholic editions, the Apocrypha are interspersed among the OT books. Also in this tradition is the *Jerusalem Bible* (1966), prepared by Catholic scholars under the British priest Alexander Jones. Named because its annotations were translated from a French version prepared at the Dominican l'Ecole Biblique of Jerusalem, it is heavily influenced by its French predecessor, though also based on early Hebrew and Greek texts. Notably, it uses "Yahweh" instead of "Lord."

In the Protestant tradition, an important fresh translation is the *New English Bible,* prepared by British scholars (1961-71). Designed not to replace the AV but to be used alongside it for clarification, this is a relatively free translation in a modern vernacular (though it does retain the traditional "thee/thou" for the Deity). Another recent effort in this tradition is the *Good News Bible,* published by the American Bible Society (1976). Also known as *Today's English Version,* this colloquial translation is generally respected for its accuracy. (An earlier edition of the NT only, by Robert Bratcher, was called *Good News for Modern Man.*) In 1978, the New York Bible Society published the *New International Version,* an evangelical, interdenominational effort generally conservative in its approach.

Finally, the 20th cent. has produced other Bible translations, neither in the King James tradition nor easily classified as fresh translations with denominational origins. Some are ecumenical; the *Anchor Bible,* for instance, is a series of volumes by different scholars published since 1964, each including a new translation of biblical material. Other versions are "private" translations — the work of individuals rather than committees. The Scottish scholar *James Moffatt* produced his own NT in 1913, his OT in 1924. The American *Edgar Goodspeed* published a NT in 1923; it was later combined with the OT by J. M. Powis Smith et al. (1927) and published as *The Bible: An American Translation* (1935). In the same category, British scholar J. B. Phillips has produced *The New Testament in Modern English* (latest revision, 1973). Still other recent versions are paraphrases more than strict translations. Clarence Jordan's *Cottonpatch Versions* (1968 and thereafter) rendered selected NT books into the vernacular of the rural American South. Perhaps the most influential recent paraphrase is *The Living Bible* (1971), by Kenneth Taylor.

For comparison, here is the shorter Lord's Prayer (Luke 11:2-4) as presented in some of the more important English versions:

WEST SAXON GOSPELS, ca. 1000

Faeder ure thu the eart on heofonum, si thin nama gehalgod; to-becume thin rice; gewurthe thin willa on eorthan swa saw on heofonum; urne gedaeghwamlican hlaf syle us to daeg; and forgyf us ure gyltas swa saw we forgyfath urum gyltendum; and ne galaed thu us on costnunge, ac alys us of yfele, sothlice.

WYCLIFFITE BIBLE, ca. 1384

Fadir, halewid be thi name. Thi kyngdom come to the. ȝyue to vs to day oure eche dayes breed. And forȝyue to vs oure synnes, as and we forȝyen to ech owynge to vs. And lede not vs in to temptacioun.

TYNDALE NEW TESTAMENT, 1525

Oure father which arte in heve, halowed be thy name. Lett thy kyngdo come. They will be fulfillet, even in erth as it is in heven. Oure dayly bred geve us this daye. And forgeve us oure synnes: For even we forgeve every man that traspaseth us; and ledde us not into temptacio, Butt deliver vs from evyll Amen.

COVERDALE BIBLE, 1535

O oure father which art in heauen, halowed be thy name. Thy kyngdome come. Thy wil be fulfilled upon earth, as it is in heauen. Geue vs this daye oure daylie bred. And forgeue vs oure synnes, for we also forgeue all them that are detters unto vs. And lede vs not in to temptacion, but delyuer vs from euell.

MATTHEW'S BIBLE, 1537

O oure father which arte in heauen, halowed be thy name. Thy kyngdome come. Thy will be fulfylied, euen in erth as it is in heauen. Oure dayly breed geue vs euermore. And forgeue vs our synnes: For euen we forgeue euery man y' treaspaseth vs. And leade vs not into temptacion. But delyuer vs from euyll.

GREAT BIBLE, 1539

O oure father which art I heauen, halowed be thy name. Thy kyngdome come. Thy will be fulfylied, eue in erth also as it is in heaue. Oure dayly breed geue vs thys daye. And forgeue vs our synnes: For eue we forgeue euery man that treaspaseth vs. And Leade vs not ito temptacyon. But delyuer vs from euyll.

GENEVA BIBLE, 1560

2 Our Father, we art in heaue, halowed be thy Name: Thy kingdome come: Let thy will be done eue in earth, as it is in heauen:
3 Our daily bread giue vs for the day:
4 And forgiue vs our sinnes: for euen we forgiue euerie

man that is indetted to vs: And lead vs not into temptation: but deliuer vs from euil.

BISHOPS' BIBLE, 1568

2 O our father which art in heauen, halowed be thy name, thy kyngdome come, thy wyll be fulfylied, euen in earth also, as it is in heauen.
3 Our dayly breade geue vs this day.
4 And forgeue vs our synnes: For euen we forgeue euery man that trespasseth vs. And leade vs not into temptation, but delyuer vs from euyil.

KING JAMES BIBLE, 1611

2 Our Father which art in heauen, Halowed be thy Name, Thy kingdome come, Thy will be done as in heauen, so in earth.
3 Giue vs day by day our dayly bread.
4 And forgiue vs our sinnes: for wee also forgiue euery one that is indebted to vs. And lead vs not into temptation, but deliuer vs from euill.

ENGLISH REVISED NT, 1881, AND AMERICAN STANDARD EDITION, 1901

3 Father, Hallowed be thy name. Thy kingdom come. Give us day by day our
4 daily bread. And forgive us our sins; for we ourselves also forgive every one that is indebted to us. And bring us not into temptation.

THE NEW ENGLISH BIBLE NT, 1961

"Father, thy name be hallowed;
  Thy kingdom come.
3 Give us each day our daily bread.
4 And forgive us our sins,
  For we too forgive all who have done us wrong.
  And do not bring us to the test."

JERUSALEM BIBLE, 1968

2 'Father, may your name be held holy,
  Your kingdom come;
3 give us each day our daily bread,
  and forgive us our sins,
4 for we ourselves forgive each one who is in debt to us.
  And do not put us to the test.'

REVISED STANDARD VERSION, NT, 1971

2 "Father, hallowed be thy name. Thy kingdom come.

3 Give us each day our daily bread;

4 and forgive us our sins, for we ourselves forgive every one who is indebted to us; and lead us not into temptation."

GOOD NEWS BIBLE, 1976

2 'Father:

May your holy name be honored;

May your Kingdom come.

3 Give us day by day the food we need.

4 Forgive us our sins, for we forgive everyone who does us wrong.

And do not bring us to hard testing.'

NEW REVISED STANDARD VERSION, 1989

2 "Father, hallowed be your name.

Your kingdom come.

3 Give us each day our daily bread.

4 And forgive us our sins, for we ourselves forgive everyone indebted to us.

And do not bring us to the time of trial.

ANNOTATED BIBLIOGRAPHY

Excerpted from John H. Gottcent, *The Bible as Literature: A Selective Bibliography* (Boston: G. K. Hall, 1979), pp. 13-20.

Bruce, F. F. *History of the Bible in English: From the Earliest Versions* (3rd ed.; New York: Oxford University Press, 1978). Formerly entitled *The English Bible.* "Traces the history of the English Bible from its first beginnings in the seventh century up to the present time."

Butterworth, Charles C. *The Literary Lineage of the King James Bible, 1340-1611* (Philadelphia: University of Pennsylvania Press, 1941). The classic study of the development of the literary style of the King James Bible. Surveys earlier English translations and their influence on the King James. Bibliography. Rpt. New York: Octagon Books, 1971.

The Cambridge History of the Bible. Ed. P. R. Ackroyd and C. F. Evans (vol. 1), G. W. H. Lampe (vol. 2), and S. L. Greenslade (vol. 3) (Cambridge, Eng.: Cambridge University Press, 1963-70). Articles by different scholars covering the history of the Bible from the beginnings to the present day. Volume 1 carries the story up to Jerome, vol. 2 from the Fathers to the Reformation, and vol. 3 from the Reformation to the present. "We have tried to give . . . an account of the text and versions of the Bible used in the West, of its multiplication in manuscript and print, and its circulation; of attitudes toward its authority and exegesis; and of its place in the life of the Western Church." Bibliographies.

Daiches, David. *The King James Version of the English Bible: An Account of the Development and Sources of the English Bible of 1611 with Special Reference to the Hebrew Tradition* (Chicago: University of Chicago Press, 1941). A brief history of the English Bible from 1523 to 1611 is followed by studies of "the sources, equipment, and methods of the translators."

Deanesly, Margaret. *The Lollard Bible and Other Medieval Versions.* Cambridge Studies in Medieval Life and Thought, vol. 1 (Cambridge: University Press, 1920). Studies "the history of medieval translations of the Vulgate, their place in the social history of the time, and the attitude of authority towards them."

Grant, Frederick Clifton. *Translating the Bible* (Greenwich, CT: The Seabury Press, 1961). Covers the story of translating from the development of the Hebrew Bible, through the Greek and Latin versions, down to the NEB. A concluding chapter covers principles and problems of translation. Bibliography.

Herbert, A. S. *Historical Catalogue of Printed Editions of the English Bible 1525-1961* (New York: American Bible Society, 1968). "Revised and Expanded from the Edition of T. H. Darlow and H. F. Moule, 1903." A descriptive list of printed English Bibles, from Tyndale's NT (1525) to the New English Bible NT (1961). Appendices cover commentaries with new translations and versions in English provincial dialects. Selected Bibliography.

Hills, Margaret T. *The English Bible in America: A Bibliography of Editions of the Bible and the New Testament Published in America 1777-1957* (New York: American Bible Society and The New York Public Library, 1961). A descriptive bibliography of English Bibles published in America, including their locations. Includes an introductory essay on the history of the English Bible in this country. Bibliography.

Lupton, Lewis. *A History of the Geneva Bible* (8 vols.; London: The Fauconberg Press, 1966-76). The story behind the 16th-cent. Puritan translation. Illustrations.

MacGregor, Geddes. *A Literary History of the Bible: From the Middle Ages to the Present Day* (Nashville: Abingdon Press, 1968). The history and nature of the major versions of the Bible (mostly in English), starting with the early Middle Ages, through the important translations of the 16th and 17th cents. and down to the NEB (New Testament). "Designed for the intelligent general reader, including the college undergraduate."

Partridge, A. C. *English Biblical Translation.* The Language Library (London: Andre Deutsch, 1973). Surveys English versions of the Bible from Anglo-Saxon times to the era of the NEB and the JB. Of particular interest is the unusual attention given to translations before the 16th cent. and between King James and the late 19th cent. Bibliography.

Pollard, Alfred W., ed. *Records of the English Bible: The Documents Relating to the Translation and Publication of the Bible in English, 1525-1611* (Dawsons of Pall Mall, 1974). Rpt. of a 1911 work. An introduction surveying the Bibles of the period is followed by an extensive collection of documents relating to the production of English versions from Tyndale to King James. Includes the seldom re-printed preface to the KJV ("The Translators to the Reader," 340-77).

Reumann, John. *Four Centuries of the English Bible* (Philadelphia: Muhlenberg Press, 1961). A brief history of the English Bible, emphasizing the significant translations from Wyclif to the NEB.

Wegener, G. S. *6000 Years of the Bible.* Trans. Margaret Shenfield (New York: Harper and Row, 1963). Begins with a brief survey of historical backgrounds of early biblical times, and traces the origin and development of the Bible from its earliest stories, through the many translations from ancient to modern times, to the Dead Sea Scrolls in the 20th cent. For the general reader. Illustrations.   JOHN H. GOTTCENT

THE HISTORY OF BIBLICAL INTERPRETATION

Introduction

The history of biblical interpretation, even merely as it proves pertinent to use of the Bible by English authors, is far richer and more complex than any work of practical scope can adequately reveal. In a dictionary such as this, it will be seen, the necessarily more modest goal is representative characterization, a tracing of select but indicative lineaments of relevant tradition.

Century by century since the Christianization of England in the 7th cent., the available work of commentators was employed both directly and, as often, indirectly. To give a famous example, though St. Jerome may properly characterize the pejorative comparisons of marriage to celibacy attacked by Chaucer's Wife of Bath, it is by no means certain that Chaucer would need to have read the whole of Jerome's *Adversus Jovinianum* itself to "borrow" the 4th-cent. theologian's interpretation of St. Paul. Numerous more recent compendia, nameless anthologies with additional commentaries such as the one from which Dame Alice's fifth husband so irritatingly reads, were more accessible immediate sources. So too, for a 14th-cent. author, would be marginal biblical glosses, recent topical reflections, and contemporary exegesis.

John Donne further illustrates the point. As his sermons attest, he made use of the commentaries of the Jesuit Cornelius à Lapide (1567-1637), which he took the trouble to obtain as soon as they were published. Like the Calvinist Theodore Beza (1519-1605), whom Donne also used, Lapide collected the views of patristic, medieval, and more recent commentators conveniently. But Donne also went back to earlier sources, sometimes for confirmation or for further information.

Donne's way of going about things underlines a practical need which came to be felt early on, and which has been met in every age of Western biblical study by aids of various sorts. Jerome (ca. 342-420), translator of the Vg and one of the most influential of the Fathers in the Latin West throughout the Middle Ages, argues that the proper procedure for a commentator is to read as many opinions as he can and then give a fair account of differing views, with the proofs which have been offered for each and the arguments advanced in support of it (*Apol.* 1.16). Scholars in more of a hurry, without access to a well-stocked library, or put off by the lack of indexes and finding-systems in manuscripts before the 12th cent., were glad to make use of ready-made collections of excerpts from earlier commentators. Such an *Expositor* was available from at least Carolingian times. In the late 11th and 12th cents. something needed to be done to remedy deficiencies (the Psalms and the Pauline Epistles, e.g., were far more frequently commented on than other books, and some books had as yet almost no body of commentary at all). It was for this reason that the *Glossa Ordinaria* came into being. The names of some of those who helped create it are known — Lanfranc of Bec, Anselm of Laon, Gilbert of Poitiers — but it seems to have developed piecemeal, by a loose form of combined effort, over several scholarly generations. One of those involved, Peter Lombard (ca. 1100-1160), published a differently conceived collection under the title of *Sentences,* in which the material is arranged under the topic headings of systematic theology. This became the standard textbook of theology throughout the Middle Ages, lectured upon by every young master in the schools as part of his apprenticeship. The collecting of materials for commentary went on. St. Thomas Aquinas (ca. 1225-74) brought together a "golden chain" *(Catena Aurea)* in which Chrysostom (ca. 4347-4407) features largely alongside the Fathers of the West more commonly found in earlier collections (St. Ambrose [339-397], Jerome, St. Augustine [354-430], St. Gregory the Great [ca. 540-604], Bede [ca. 673-735]). Continuing this tradition, Cornelius à Lapide's commentaries, comprising twenty-four volumes, were widely used by Protestant as well as Roman Catholic readers and reprinted from the 17th to the 19th cent. This custom of using reference books encouraged the borrowing of standard interpretations and themes and images not only among commentators but also in literary and other contexts and help to account for the considerable coherence in traditions of biblical tradition over the centuries.

AUTHORITY AND CONFORMITY

It was never argued that "authorities," the Fathers or the later commentators, were as authoritative as Scripture. They had a place in a hierarchy of quotable authors between Holy Scripture itself and classical authors (Cicero, Aristotle, et al.). But throughout the Middle Ages and beyond, the Fathers were regarded as having sufficient authority to prove a point or settle a dispute.

The perennial need for authoritative interpretation introduces questions which can only be hinted at here. A thumbnail sketch of interpretative tradition bearing upon literature in English would, nonetheless, trace its roots to the Hebrew Scriptures themselves. In OT times a class of professional exegetes grew up among the priests and Levites. *Mishnah* (Heb., "repetition") was a practice of reiteration, amplification, and explication, the foundational Jewish method of scriptural exegesis by which various collections of mishnaic commentaries were gradually brought together in the authoritative synthesis of R. Judah ha-Nasi (ca. A.D. 135-220). Except for the Pirqe 'Abot, its predominantly halakic character formed the basis for the further commentary and response organized as the Palestinian and Babylonian Talmud. The latter contains an important set of Additional and Minor Tractates which, although of small consequence in early centuries of English biblical tradition, contain material important for Jewish literature in English (and Yiddish) of the 19th and 20th cents. But, as with Christian exegesis of Scripture, some of the most important developments in Jewish exegesis were of a theoretical or hermeneutical character. Some of these, via Rashi, Nicholas of Lyra, and Wyclif, among others, were to filter into Christian exegesis as well. For example, rabbinic exegesis from late antiquity on through the Middle Ages gave rise to a set of rules of interpretation. The reader was to look for analogies; he was to feel free to treat a group of related passages in such a way that a feature peculiar to one of them might be taken to apply to them all; he was to draw conclusions from the general to the particular, or vice versa; he was to use a similar passage elsewhere as a basis of inference in his reasoning about the passage in question; he was to interpret according to the context. All these rules depend upon the assumption that the Bible's teachings are all fundamentally in harmony. It is also a first principle of this approach that every detail of the text is significant and of divine origin. The Midrash, a method of exegesis which sought meanings which lay deeper than the literal sense apparent on first reading, made use of this belief and contributed to the rise of the allegorical pattern of interpretation in Christian exegesis. This was already well established in the early Christian centuries. Although the earliest surviving collection of midrashim dates from the 2nd cent. A.D., much of the content is a great deal older, and when Origen sought for spiritual senses in Scripture he was, to a considerable degree, drawing upon a Jewish tradition of some antiquity.

In Christian exegesis, individuals have, from the first, been free to put forward their own views, but not all those who published their opinions were accepted as sound by their own or subsequent generations. Origen (ca. 186-254), in whose hands Christian exegesis reached its first maturity, is a case in point; his understanding of the text came to seem dangerously unorthodox in parts and he was treated with both respect and caution in the Middle Ages. The test of reliability has been, for interpretation as for doctrine, a conformity with the rules of St. Vincent of Lérins's dictum: what has been accepted by all Christians at all times and in all places. In other words, the tradition of the Church under the direction of the Holy Spirit has been of consistent importance in forming the corpus of Christian exegesis. During the Middle Ages, that meant in practice that the clergy (who alone had access to academic education for many centuries) came to be regarded as having exclusive authority to comment on Scripture or to preach. The right to teach or preach was granted by ecclesiastical license. It was against this state of affairs that an articulate urban laity began to murmur from as early as the 12th cent. The Poor Men of Lyons (Waldensians, or Vaudois), e.g., astonished their clerical detractors by their command of the Bible and their ability to meet quotation with quotation in argument. One hears much more of this in English Lollard texts of the 15th cent.: claims that any good Christian man or woman is as fit an interpreter as any priest and ought to have freedom to preach, that every Christian may and should read the Bible for himself or herself. The notion that freedom of individual response to the Bible is irreconcilable with the Church's insistence upon control of teaching authority became one of the principal grounds of division between Catholic and Protestant in the 16th cent. It was in this way that "Scripture" and "tradition" came to be polarized, after this point, even artificially opposed conceptions, despite the inseparability of tradition from the process of forming the canon. This pattern of development of teaching and preaching within the Church is important because it encouraged an attitude of respect for past work and a tendency to conform to traditional interpretations. And conversely, toward the end of the Middle Ages, it spurred some to call for a return to "Scripture alone" *(sola scriptura)* and an abandonment of the whole apparatus in favor of a fresh personal response to Scripture by the individual. This, too, has its literary repercussions, not least the paradoxical one that Reformers tend to conceive their ideas by reaction against existing practices, and therefore act in some respects as a mirror image of those practices. Play on old and new ideas, a conscious comparing, goes on not only in Luther and Calvin but also in contemporary literature.

The Preaching of the Word: The Use of Stock Examples

The reading of Scripture in early Christian worship created a place for expository preaching as part of the ministry of the Word. Preaching was the natural vehicle of exegesis in the patristic period, as is suggested by the models of Augustine and Gregory the Great. Augustine attracted and moved large audiences; Gregory's explanations of the book of Job were so highly valued by the monks of his community that he was pressed to make a permanent record of them. During the Middle Ages there was little new preaching until the 11th or 12th cents. (Monastic communities were in the habit of having portions of the Fathers' homilies read to them.) In the early 13th cent. Stephen Langton, archbishop of Canterbury, expressed a conception of the preacher's function as minister of the Word. "Because the preacher's words are God's, whatever the failings of the preacher himself, we believe that our words will please your ears and your heart."

Although some Carolingian sermons survive, there is not much evidence that ordinary people often heard sermons before the 12th cent. The talks of St. Anselm of Canterbury and of St. Bernard of Clairvaux on the readings for the liturgical year, and especially the series on the Song of Songs unfinished at his death in 1153, set a new fashion in the late 11th and early 12th cent. Bernard preached in Latin, normally to a monastic audience, but he sometimes spoke to popular audiences. We have a report that he could move people more by his tone and gesture, even when they did not understand what he was saying, than a translator could do when he told the audience in their own language what Bernard had said. The story is in keeping with the evidence that popular preachers were able to attract large audiences in the 12th cent. It is also true that they sometimes led them into heresy. It was this latter development which made it necessary for the Church to produce preachers who could win back stray sheep. The first to take up the challenge were the next generation of Bernard's Cistercians, preaching to the heretics in southern France, then Dominicans, from the beginning of the 13th cent. The Franciscans, whose inspiration was simply the example of the apostles who went about preaching the kingdom of heaven, began their own preaching work at about the same time. The two orders of friars became the professional preachers of the later Middle Ages. They attracted able young men, and the friars soon began to win chairs in the universities in competition with the traditional masters. The emphasis of the Dominicans from the beginning, and soon of the Franciscans too, was upon a high level of academic excellence in the training of preachers. University sermons developed alongside and as a foundation for the preaching of popular sermons. An early preaching handbook by Alain of Lille dates from the end of the 12th cent., but the bulk of the surviving manuals seem to have been produced from about 1230. They set out a method of expounding a chosen scriptural text by dividing up its implications (usually into threes) and exploring them one by one. Stephen Langton, Archbishop of Canterbury under King John, had earlier been an outstanding master at the University of Paris. In a sermon on a text from the Song of Songs *("Sub umbra illius quem desideraveram sedi")* given in 1220 he promises, "We shall expound these words in three ways in order, first as they apply to the martyr whose Feast Day it is (Thomas à Becket); secondly as they apply to the soul or the Church on the birthday of our Lord; thirdly as they apply to this congregation."

The friars' working manuals of preachers' aids (such as the *Speculum Laicorum*) were stocks of images and examples. They collected these *exempla* on the model of the commonplaces or topoi of ancient rhetoric. Theirs was the only medieval rhetorical art which involved public speaking, and therefore necessitated acquiring some skill in thinking on one's feet. The Cistercian abbot John of Ford makes use of yet another practical aid developed from the late 12th cent., the dictionary of biblical terms. "My soul disturbed me on account of the chariots of Aminadab," says the bride of the Song of Songs (6:11): John of Ford is easily able to assemble a series of passages in which "wheels" are mentioned (Dan. 7:9; Isa. 5:28; Ps. 77:18; Ezek. 1:15-16, and Zech. 6:1, 8) because he can look them up in such a dictionary. Common associations are strengthened in this way.

The Principle of the Harmony of Scripture

But deeper reasons than the practical underlie the constant reuse of standard themes and images. As was already beginning to be apparent in the OT exegetical procedure of using proof-texts to bring one passage to bear upon the interpretation of another or to take the context as a test of correct interpretation of a difficult word or phrase, interpreters assumed the unity of Scripture, its fundamental harmony. Origen established the principle clearly for Christian exegesis. In later periods the views of the Fathers were thought to share that fundamental harmony, not as equally authoritative, but as agreeing with scriptural truth. Thus, where there is *convenientia,* "appropriateness," there is a form of proof accepted as forceful by the majority of patristic and medieval scholars. Here again we have a pattern which encouraged a certain sameness in adducing examples and in the interpretations put upon things.

The expectation that the text of Scripture will be found to be a unity existed side by side with the principle found in both later OT and early Christian exegesis, that every text can properly be taken in isolation from its context and treated independently. Because of the underlying harmony of everything Scripture says, it cannot be misleading to take even a single word or phrase in interpretation. No human interpreter can read into Scripture a meaning which is in accordance with true faith which the Holy Spirit has not already put there. The influential Bernard of Clairvaux (d. 1153) makes full use of the freedom this confidence gives him. In his description of the just man, e.g. (*On Loving God,* 7.21), he allows one text to suggest another, so that his argument unfolds by association of ideas. Those who remain inside the circle (Ps. 30:14) remind him of those who follow the wide road which leads to death (Matt. 7:13); the just man prefers the royal road which does not turn to right or left (Num. 20:17; 21:22); Isa. speaks, too, of the straightness of the path of the just (Isa. 26:7). They take a shortcut to salvation and avoid the dangerous roundabout way which does not bring them to their destination. They choose the shortened and shortening Word *(verbum abbreviatum)* of Rom. 9:28, and so on. He does not ask whether the human authors of these books of Scripture intended these cross-references; it is enough that the Holy Spirit has put them there to delight the reader who discovers them. Such noting of echoes and parallels was one of the rewards of "holy reading," the *lectio divina* of monastic life, with its emphasis on slow, reflective "chewing" and "savoring" of the text. Bernard himself is perhaps the supreme example of the way in which this filled the mind with the words of Scripture so that it became natural to speak in its words and to have close references always at the back of one's mind, images from Scripture underpinning one's illustrations.

I. THE NEED FOR INTERPRETATION: OBSCURITIES AND CONTRADICTIONS

The need for interpretation had always arisen (1) where a word was unclear in context, (2) where the text was compressed and needed to be unfolded, (3) where there seemed to be contradiction with other texts, and (4) where the obvious meaning was unacceptable. These four fundamental types of difficulty determined the direction of biblical exegesis until the 16th cent. and beyond, wherever the text of Scripture has been regarded as literally inspired and the possibility of errors arising in transmission and translation has not been systematically considered, or considered at all.

The attempt to resolve the first two difficulties remains an important exegetical task today. Where the meaning of a word is unclear and where a text is too compressed to be readily intelligible, the function of the ancient, medieval, or modern exegete is much the same (although they may not all furnish the same explanations). The aim is to make what is being said perfectly plain to the reader.

To take a case familiar from the KJV, we find in the opening of John's Gospel: "and the darkness comprehended it not." To a modern reader that appears at first glance to mean that the darkness did not understand. In 1611 English usage was closer to its Latin origins here and "comprehended" meant "enfolded" or "swallowed up." It was necessary for such shifts of meaning through changes of usage to be clarified in the Greek or Hebrew or Latin Vg text in every century. The concept of growth and change in usage came late. There is some notion of it in Peter Abelard in the 12th cent. He collected, as a school exercise for his pupils, a large number of apparently contradictory statements from the Fathers and set the reader the task of reconciling them. The prologue of this *Sic et Non* explores with a daring unparalleled in its time the possibility that the language of Scripture and the Fathers had changed, that words now did not mean what they meant in the past, that there had been errors in copying over the centuries which had resulted in mistakes even in the text of Scripture in present editions. But the conception was not fully developed until the 16th and 17th cents., when the study of Greek and Hebrew made it plain that languages evolve. (The apparatus provided by the 17th-cent. scholar Brian Walton [ca. 1600-1661] to the Polyglot Bible brings together several earlier treatises on such questions.)

The second two fundamental difficulties which underlie the majority of patristic and medieval exegetical endeavors are cases where the obvious meaning is unacceptable and cases where one passage seems to contradict another. The option of going back to the manuscripts — or to the Greek — to see whether there was any corruption of the text was not open to most medieval scholars, and in any case in the West the text of Jerome's Vg was in practice regarded as itself literally the Scripture, every jot and tittle. Its actual status as a translation had dropped out of sight. The exegetical task was to make sense of Jerome's text as it stood.

Origen suggested that one reason for the oddities of expression which appear in Scripture was the kindness of God in coming down to our level and speaking to us as clearly as it was possible to do in our limited human language. This idea was taken up by Gregory the Great and became a foundation-principle of medieval exegesis. The exegete must try to understand what the oddity was pointing to, the reason why it was there. The most convenient explanation was that, in the case of a word whose obvious meaning seems misplaced, a figurative meaning is intended, and in the case of apparently contradictory statements, one or both is to be taken figuratively.

This notion of the figurative involved a shifting *(translatio)* of meaning from the literal to the analogical. To call Christ a lion is to make a comparison between Christ and a lion in which some of the characteristics of the creature are singled out to illustrate. Christ is compared with things we can understand from our own experience. Christ used some of these metaphors of himself and could therefore clearly be seen to endorse the use of the method and to point the way the interpreter should go. It is against this background above all that the use of stock themes and images needs to be considered.

II. OLD TESTAMENT AND NEW: TYPES

Within the general assumption that Scripture is a unity is a further assumption that the OT looks forward to the NT. For the Jewish interpreters the task was to discover the fulfilment of Scripture in present history, a fulfilment which would indicate the beginning of the end. The Qumran community (1st cent.) — probably a group of Essenes — left materials which show them to have been sure that God's purposes were being fulfilled in their own day. The early Church saw OT prophecy in the same way, and it was natural for the NT authors to use OT phrases and references in their writing. They often did so, in the same way as medieval or post-Reformation Puritan authors, without indicating that they were quoting. (A familiarity with Scripture so thorough that its words became a natural vehicle for the expression of one's thoughts is — to a varying degree — a mark of most ancient and medieval Christian writing.) Sometimes there is acknowledgment (e.g., Rom. 10:11; Mark 12:36; Luke 20:42). This habit of looking for parallels between old and new life under God encouraged a concentration not on the Law (the natural focus of OT exegesis) but on the Prophets and the Psalms. The Psalms were understood to be conversations between Christ and the Church, sometimes with other participants. The main concern of Clement of Rome at the end of the 1st cent. and of Melito and St. Justin Martyr at the end of the 2nd cent. is to show how the Law and the Prophets are fulfilled in Christ. Melito and Justin worked out a pattern of "types" linking OT figures with Christ and with NT events (Adam, e.g., is a type of Christ because he represents all humanity, Isaac because he was offered as a sacrifice, and so on). These identifications made up a typology which gradually became standardized and which persisted well into the 17th cent. Dr. John Cosin, preaching to the Protestant members of the exiled English Queen's household in Paris on 16 April 1651, on John 20:9, provided a typological exegesis of Abraham's willingness to sacrifice Isaac at God's command as a foretelling of the Passion and Resurrection of Christ. He notes seven parallels between Isaac and Jesus. Both are their father's only and beloved sons; both accept death obediently; both are bound for the sacrifice, and the wood is laid on their shoulders; both are led to a mount; the thornbush in which the ram is caught parallels the crown of thorns; both were released within three days (*The Works of John Cosin, 1, Sermons,* 255).

III. ALLEGORIES AND OTHER FIGURES

By the end of the 2nd cent. the NT was recognized as having equal authority with the OT. That made it possible for the search for types to be enlarged into a system of allegory. Not all early interpreters accepted the value of this development. Theodore of Mopsuestia and the school of 4th-cent. Antioch preferred literal-historical interpretation, and their point of view had a continuing influence. But the majority of patristic and medieval interpreters made the most of the possibilities of the figurative interpretation. Philo of Alexandria (ca. 20 B.C.–ca. A.D. 50) had applied allegorical methods of exegesis to the OT, but the chief spur to Christian allegorical exegesis seems to have been the abuse of the allegorical method by dualist heretics. Tertullian (ca. 160-220) and St. Irenaeus (ca. 130-200) both remark on this practice among the Gnostics, and they themselves cautiously explored allegory as a way of refuting the conclusions the Gnostics were drawing.

The first full-scale development of the possibilities of allegorical interpretation is to be found in Origen. He took the view that Scripture has a deeper meaning than appears on the surface. Some passages have no literal meaning at all (those which, taken at face value, are unattractive or erroneous). God comes down to our level to speak to us in ways we can understand and by using this device of speaking figuratively he is able to speak to people at many different stages of spiritual growth and to say more than one thing in one passage. He identified three "spiritual" senses: that which is "allegorical" in the strict sense of comparing creature with Creator (transferring the usage of a word from its ordinary sense, as when Christ is called a lion); anagogical, where the language looks forward prophetically or speaks of heaven itself; and moral or tropological, where it has something to say about our living of a good and holy life.

Augustine made use of figurative and spiritual interpretations, but he had limited direct access to the Greek Fathers, and he does not adopt Origen's exact scheme. That was popularized by Gregory the Great, who made it the standard system in use in the medieval West. His *Moralia in Iob* and his *Cura Pastoralis* with their pastoral and practical emphasis were very widely read. Endless variations were played in the Middle Ages upon the theme of the three "higher" or "deeper" senses. The literal sense was seen as foundation of rough-cut stone, solid, but of no beauty to lift the soul. Upon it were erected constructions of soaring beauty, whose stones were cut as required and which leveled out the roughnesses of the foundation by being cut to fit into it. This architectural image of the senses of Scripture was much used by medieval authors;

it stressed the intimate relationship between the parts of the structure. No interpretation could be out of keeping with another or with the harmony of the whole edifice. It was possible for the interpreter to enjoy great freedom within this system provided he kept to significations which were in accordance with orthodox faith. Nothing he could think of was truly an innovation, because the Holy Spirit had certainly thought of it first and put the meaning there to be found. The controlling factors were the indwelling of the Holy Spirit guiding the reader and the unity of Scripture.

Two developments of the later Middle Ages are noteworthy here. From the time of Thomas Aquinas a movement which had begun a century or so earlier took a definitive form. Twelfth-century scholars had begun to work more seriously upon the literal sense, looking into the Hebrew (e.g., Andrew of St. Victor) and suggesting that its foundational purpose was in fact an important one; respect for the literal sense increased when it was suggested that it ought really to be understood as the sense the text primarily intended. That would mean that in, e.g., the parables of Jesus, where the intended sense is figurative, the figurative is in fact the literal sense. As Nicholas of Lyra explains in the prologue to his postils, giving a by now more or less standard account of the discussion of the 13th cent., this shift toward considering the author's intention extended in time to the human authors of Scripture, and encouraged the kind of reflection we find in the Reformers of the 16th cent. about the mind of Paul.

The second development was a distaste for the excesses of figurative interpretation. One hears more about that from the Reformers than from others, but the debate was a general one. A plain person's plain reading under the guidance of the Holy Spirit seemed to many the right thing to aim for. Meditation upon Scripture should lead not to the elaboration of interpretative castles in the air but to strong simple faith. The realities of keeping to plain interpretation did not, however, prove so straightforward. Luther and Calvin both make use of figurative interpretation while criticizing its overuse.

Literary use of figurative interpretations throughout the Middle Ages and well beyond, in Reformation and Counter-Reformation authors alike, is only to be expected. Imagery is the writer's stock-in-trade. The four-fold system was certainly alive for Donne. In more than one of his sermons he begins by explaining that he is going to take the passage on which he is preaching one sense at a time. On Ps. 38:3, e.g., he says that the words are to be considered first "as they are historically, and literally to be understood of *David;* And secondly, in their *retrospect,* as they look back upon the first *Adam,* and so concern *Mankind collectively,* and so *you,* and *I,* and all have our portion in these calamities; And thirdly, we shall consider them in their *prospect,* and their future relation to the *second* Adam, in Christ Jesus" (ed. Potter and Simpson, 2.75; cf. 3.353).

For all these reasons, then, one can expect to find a long, rich, and often complex history of borrowing behind the use of biblical themes and images in literature. One of the purposes of this dictionary is to suggest avenues of approach to that history, as well as to give a modest hint, in the entries, of the potential value in its recovery.

GILLIAN R. EVANS

* * *

The bibliography which follows is divided into three parts. The first offers a selection of general studies on the history of biblical interpretation which can provide further guidance to the student of literature or of exegetical history. The second is a checklist of commentaries on specific biblical books, organized according to popularity or accessibility to English readers for each principal period after the Christianization of England. The third bibliography is a chronological checklist of bibliographies of patristic, medieval, and Renaissance scriptural commentaries. This checklist offers the advanced student a guide to more intensive, detailed investigation into the foundational and most prolific periods of Christian exegetical writing.

Historical Studies in Biblical Hermeneutics

The following checklist identifies selected works which influenced the interpretation of the Bible generally. Most of these, but not all, are period studies in hermeneutics and theory of biblical interpretation. A supplementary checklist of useful modern studies is provided for each period, after the primary works.

BEGINNINGS TO 1066

Primary Works

Philo Judaeus. *Legum allegoriae* (ca. A.D. 42). A Jewish exegete and theorist, Philo developed an allegorical interpretation of Scripture indebted to hellenic Greek models. This departure from typical Jewish historical interpretation had a great impact upon the Alexandrian Christian theologians, notably St. Clement and Origen, and through them upon St. Ambrose and the Latin Fathers generally. His Logos doctrine is parallel to that of the Fourth Gospel in some respects, but no longer thought to be an influence.

Augustine, St. *De doctrina Christiana* (A.D. 427). *On Christian Doctrine,* as Augustine's introduction to interpretation and explanation of the Bible, became the foundational work in early Western hermeneutics. Here Augustine elaborates the principle of charity, or charitable intention and, accordingly, reference for understanding, and with it an allegorical approach to the OT based on the pattern suggested in Gal. 4:22-27 and Matt. 22:43-44.

Isidore of Seville, St. *Quaestiones in Vetus Testamentum* (ca. A.D. 620). Also found as *Mysticorum expositiones sacramentorum* (PL 83.207-424), this work treats nearly all the historical books of the Bible, drawing on the examples of Augustine and St. Gregory in allegorical exegesis.

————. *Quaestiones de Veteri et Novo Testamento.* Com-

pares the two testaments, demonstrating their unity and establishing elements of typology.

Origen. *De principiis.* Koetchan's text, the standard, is translated by G. W. Butterworth and introduced by Henri de Lubac (New York: Harper, 1966). Section 4 (of 4) is devoted to principles and methods of interpretation.

Secondary Works

Allenbach, J. et al., eds. *Biblia patristica: Index des citations et allusions bibliques dans la littérature patristique* (2 vols.; Paris: Centre national de la recherche scientifique, 1975-77). Produced by computer, this index covers patristic literature through the 3rd cent. (except Origen).

Altaner, B. *Patrology* (London, Edinburgh: Nelson, 1960). A valuable introduction to patristic literature.

Bonner, Gerald. "Augustine as Biblical Scholar." In *The Cambridge History of the Bible,* vol. 1, *From the Beginnings to Jerome,* ed. P. R. Ackroyd and C. F. Evans (Cambridge: Cambridge University Press, 1970).

Bonsirven, J. *Exégèse rabbinique et exégèse paulienne* (London: Tyndale, 1960).

Bowker, John. *The Targums and Rabbinic Literature: An Introduction to Jewish Interpretations of Scripture* (Cambridge: Cambridge University Press, 1969).

Bruce, F. F., and E. G. Rupp. *Holy Book and Holy Tradition* (Manchester: Manchester University Press, 1968). Valuable essays on oral Torah, Scripture, and tradition in the NT, the ancient Church and rabbinical tradition, etc.

Burghardt, Walter J. "On Early Christian Exegesis." *Theological Studies* 11 (1950), 78-116.

Daniélou, Jean. "The Conception of History in the Christian Tradition." *Journal of Religion* 30 (1950), 171-79.

————. *From Shadows to Reality: Studies in the Typol-*

ogy of the Fathers, trans. W. Hibberd (London: Burns and Oates, 1960). Analysis of 2nd- to 4th-cent. exegesis of the Hexateuch, with special attention to Exodus.

———. Primitive Christian Symbols, trans. D. Attwater (Baltimore: Helicon Press, 1964).

Daube, David. "Alexandrian Methods of Interpretation and Hellenistic Rhetoric." In Festschrift Hans Lewald (Basel: Helbing and Lichtenbahn, 1953).

Frankel, Israel. Peshat in Talmudic and Midrashic Literature (Toronto: LaSalle, 1956).

Goodspeed, E. J. Index Patristicus sive Clavis Patrum Apostolicorum (Leipzig: Hinrichs, 1907; rev. ed. Naperville, IL: Allenson, 1960). A concordance to the Apostolic Fathers which, used with Goodspeed's Index Apologeticum sive Clavis Justini Martyris Operum Aliorumque Apologetarum Pristinorum (Leipzig: Hinrichs, 1912), enables one to study how the early Fathers used biblical Greek terms.

Gorday, Peter. Principles of Patristic Exegesis: Romans 9–11 in Origen, John Chrysostom, and Augustine (New York: Edwin Mellen, 1983).

Hanson, Richard P. C. Allegory and Event: A Study in the Sources and Significance of Origen's Interpretation of Scripture (Richmond, VA and London: SCM Press, 1959). Traces the relationship of early Christian typology to its roots in Jewish liturgy.

Heinisch, Paul. Der Einfluss Philos auf die älteste christliche Exegese (Münster: Aschendorff, 1908). Authors shown to have been influenced by Philo include Barnabas, St. Justin Martyr, and St. Clement of Alexandria.

Hopper, Vincent. Medieval Number Symbolism (New York: Cooper Square, 1938). Traces number symbolism as found in the scriptural exegesis of the Fathers and later medieval writers to Pythagorean and cabalistic origins.

Jacobs, Louis. Jewish Biblical Exegesis (New York: Behrman House, 1973).

Jenkins, Claude. "Bede as Exegete and Theologian." In Bede, His Life, Times and Writing, ed. A. H. Hamilton (New York: Russell and Russell, 1966).

Kasher, Menachem Mendel, trans. Encyclopedia of Biblical Interpretation: a millennial anthology, ed. Harry Freedman (New York: American Biblical Encyclopedia Society, 1953-67). Translation of part of the Torah Shelemah (35 vols.) which contains all extant Jewish commentary from the 6th to 16th cents.

Kugel, James L. "Early Interpretation: the Common Background of Later Forms of Biblical Exegesis." In Early Biblical Interpretation, ed. James L. Kugel and R. A. Greer (Philadelphia: Westminster, 1986).

Laistner, M. L. W. "Antiochene Exegesis in Western Europe." Harvard Theological Review 11 (1947), 19-32).

Loewe, R. "The Jewish Midrashim and Patristic and Scholastic Exegesis of the Bible." Studia Patristica 1 (1957), 504-21.

———. "The 'Plain' Meaning of Scripture in Early Jewish Exegesis." Papers of the Institute of Jewish Studies, ed. J. G. Weiss (Jerusalem: Hebrew University Press, 1964), 1.140-85.

Lubac, Henri de. Histoire et esprit: L'intelligence de l'Écriture d'après Origène (Paris: Aubier, 1950). Good, detailed study of the influence of Origen and Philo.

———. "'Typologie' et 'allegorisme.'" Recherches de science religieuse 34 (1947), 180-226.

Malden, R. H. "St. Ambrose as an Interpreter of Scripture." Journal of Theological Studies 16 (1915), 509-22. Describes the role of Ambrose in helping to establish allegorical rather than historical interpretation of the biblical text.

de Margerie, Bertrand, S.J. Introduction à l'histoire de l'exégèse (3 vols.; Paris: Editions du Cerf, 1980). A study of the method of the Greek Fathers, earliest Latin exegetes, and St. Augustine.

Morrell, Minnie Cate. A Manual of Old English Biblical Materials (Knoxville: University of Tennessee Press, 1965). A thorough survey of Anglo-Saxon paraphrase and translation of OT, Psalms, and Gospels, with discussion of the miscellaneous glosses.

Pepin, Jean. Mythe et allégorie (Paris: Editions Montaigne, 1958). Traces the relationship of Heraclitian allegory through hellenistic Jewish exegesis, including that of Philo, to patristic allegory.

Pontet, Maurice. L'exégèse de Saint Augustine predicateur (Paris: Aubier, 1947).

Quasten, J. Patrology (4 vols.; Westminster, Maryland: Newman; Utrecht and Brussels: Spectrum, 1950-60). An important survey of patristic literature, including heterodox literature.

Rahner, Hugo. Symbole der Kirche. Die Ecclesiologie der Vater (Salzburg, 1964).

Sandmel, Samuel. Judaism and Christian Beginnings (New York: Oxford University Press, 1978). Landmark general study by an outstanding scholar.

Schneemelcher, W., ed. Bibliographia Patristica: Internationale Patristische Bibliographie (Berlin, New York: de Gruyter, 1959–). Produced by a team of patristic scholars, so far 17 volumes have appeared. An invaluable bibliographical source for any patristic topic.

Simonson, Solomon. "The Idea of Interpretation in Hebrew Thought." Journal of the History of Ideas 8 (1947), 467-74.

Tigay, Jeffrey H. "An Early Technique of Aggadic Exegesis." In History, Historiography and Interpretation: Studies in Biblical and Cuneiform Literatures, ed. H. Tadmor and M. Weinfeld (Jerusalem: Magnes; Leiden: Brill, 1984), 169-89.

Voegelin, Erich. Israel and Revelation (Baton Rouge:

University of Louisiana Press, 1956). This study of the relationship between biblical typology and historiography appeared as the first volume of his *Order and History*.

Wasselnyck, R. "L'Influence de l'exégèse de saint Gregoire le Grand sur les commentaires bibliques medievaux (VIIe–XIIe siècles)." *Recherches de théologie ancienne et médiévale* 32 (1965), 183-92.

Wiles, M. *The Spiritual Gospel* (Cambridge: Cambridge University Press, 1960). A study of the interpretation of the Gospel of John in early Christian Greek commentaries.

Wilken, Robert L. *The Divine Apostle: The Interpretation of St. Paul's Epistles in the Early Church* (Cambridge: Cambridge University Press, 1967). Considers both Greek and Latin commentaries of the early Church.

———. *Judaism and the Early Christian Mind: A Study of Cyril of Alexandria's Exegesis and Theology* (New Haven: Yale University Press, 1971).

Woollcombe, Kenneth J. "Le sens de 'type' chez les Peres." *La vie spirituelle* 84 (1951), 84-100.

———. "The Biblical Origins and Patristic Development of Typology." In *Essays on Typology,* ed. G. W. H. Lampe and K. J. Woollcombe (Naperville, IL and London: SCM Press, 1957). Lucid general introduction.

1067-1400

Primary Works

Alain of Lille (Alanus). *Distinctiones Dictionum Theologicarum* (ca. 1190). This theological dictionary by the Cistercian poet of the *Anticlaudianus* and *De Planctu Naturae* encodes many normative 12th-cent. doctrinal derivations from biblical tradition and exegesis, with illuminating citations.

Alexander of Hales. *Summa Theologica* (ca. 1240). Sometimes found as *Glossa in Quatuor Libros Sententiarum Petri Lombardi*. This pioneer Franciscan academic theologian made numerous biblical commentaries, now lost, but his hermeneutic principles articulated in the *Summa* influenced exegetes in both Franciscan and Dominican orders.

Anselm of Canterbury, St. *De Incarnatione Verbi* (ca. 1095); *Cur Deus Homo* (ca. 1098). While not a biblical expositor as such, in these two works, among others, Anselm established theological principles which were to have a great impact upon later hermeneutic and exegesis. *Cur Deus Homo* is the greatest medieval contribution to the Christian doctrine of the atonement.

Aquinas, St. Thomas. *Scriptum super Libros Sententiarum* (4 vols.; Paris, ca. 1252-56). Not, strictly speaking, a "commentary" on Lombard, as its title suggests, this

work elaborates the gospel text in the form of questions, and discusses themes arising from the texts. This work by the greatest Dominican and scholastic was widely influential in its method. On finishing it Aquinas preached and published two sermons, the *Commendatio Sacrae Scripturae* (1256), which set forth a practical division of all the books of the Bible, based on the example of Bar. 4:1, "Hic est liber mandatorum." Aquinas's work directly influenced Nicholas of Lyra, Calvin, Beza, and Lapide.

Bernard of Clairvaux, St. *Super Cantica Canticorum* (ca. 1135-51). This collection of 84 sermons on the Song of Songs is the great Cistercian abbot's chief legacy to medieval and Renaissance traditions of scriptural exegesis. His method is allegorical, his reading finally mystical.

Bonaventure, St. *Collationes in Hexaemeron* (ca. 1273). *De Reductione Artium ad Theologiam* (ca. 1250); *Glossa in Quatuor Libros Sententiarum Petri Lombardi* (ca. 1256). Bonaventure, greatest of the Franciscan scholastics, is interested in the growth of all three spiritual senses from the literal level, and in Neoplatonist fashion sees all created things, including words on the scriptural page, as *vestigia,* traces leading toward the Divine Wisdom. His work had a profound effect upon Wyclif, and through him upon Hus.

Hugh of St. Victor. *Didascalicon* (ca. 1128). Hugh's book on the study of reading applies to educational theory many principles derived, in a manner reminiscent of Augustine's *De doctrina,* from biblical exegesis. This work became an important influence on late medieval hermeneutics.

———. *De Sacramentis Christianae Fidei* (ca. 1130). This work of dogmatic theology by the great Victorine consists of an introduction to Scripture, written for ordinands about to commence upon allegorical interpretation, having already mastered historical interpretation. Its theoretical focus is a theology of the Incarnation.

Wyclif, John. *De Veritate Sacrae Scripturae,* ed. Rudolf Buddensieg (3 vols.; London: Wyclif Society, 1905; rpt. New York: Johnson Reprints, 1966). This important work, as yet untranslated, articulates Wyclif's theory of scriptural exegesis. Indebted to Augustine, Bonaventure, Chrysostom, Duns Scotus, and Fitzralph theoretically, it is an innovative traditionalist response to the impoverishment of biblical study at Oxford in the mid-14th cent.

Secondary Works

Bacher, Wilhelm. "Die Bibelexegese. Vom Angfange des 10. bis zum Ende des 15 Jahrhunderts." In *Die jüdische Literatur seit Abschluss des Kanons* 11 (1984), ed. J. Winter and A. Wunsche.

———. *Die Bibelexegese der jüdischen Religions-*

philosophers des Mittelalters vor Maimuni Budapest 1892 und Die Bibelexegese Moses Maimunis Budapest 1896 (Hantz: Gregg, 1973).

Baranski, Zygmunt G. "La lezione esegetica di Inferno I: Allegoria, storia e letteratura nella *Commedia.*" In *Dante e le forme dell'allegoresi,* ed. Michelangelo Picone (Ravenna: Longo, 1987), 74-97.

Berlin, Adele. *Biblical Poetry Through Medieval Jewish Eyes* (Bloomington: Indiana University Press, 1991). Excerpts from 17 Judeo-Arabic and Hebrew texts which comment on biblical poetry from the 9th to the 17th cent.; includes Judah Halevi, Moshe Ibn Ezra, Don Isaac Abravanel, and Azariah de Rossi.

Bloomfield, Morton W. "Allegory as Interpretation." *New Literary History* 3 (1972), 301-18.

———. "Symbolism in Medieval Literature." *Modern Philology* 56 (1958), 73-81.

Brandmuller, Walter. "*Traditio Scripturae Interpres:* The Teaching of the Councils on the Right Interpretation of Scripture up to the Council of Trent." *Catholic Historical Review* 73 (1987), 523-40.

Caplan, Harry. "The Four Senses of Scriptural Interpretation and the Medieval Theory of Preaching." *Speculum* 4 (1929), 282-90.

Charity, Alan C. *Events and their Afterlife: the Dialectics of Christian Typology in the Bible and Dante* (Cambridge: Cambridge University Press, 1966). Inter alia, an excellent introduction to medieval biblical hermeneutics.

Courtenay, William J. "The Bible in the Fourteenth Century: Some Observations." *Church History* 54 (1985), 176-87.

Grabois, Aryeh. "The *Hebraica Veritas* and Jewish-Christian Relations in the Twelfth Century." *Speculum* 50 (1975), 613-34. Discusses interlocutions of Stephen Harding, Hugh and Andrew of St. Victor, Rashi, Joseph Bekhor Schor, Peter Comestor, and Herbert of Bosham.

Gribomont, J. "Le lieu des Deux Testaments selon la theologie de S. Thomas. Notes sur le sens spirituel et implicite des Saintes Écritures." *Ephemerides theologicae lovaniensis* 22 (1946), 70-89.

Hailperin, H. *Rashi and the Christian Scholars* (Pittsburgh: Pittsburgh University Press, 1963). Groundbreaking and still invaluable study.

Hargreaves, Henry. "From Bede to Wyclif: Medieval English Bible Translations." *Bulletin of the John Rylands Library* 48 (1965-1966), 118-40.

———. "From Bede to Wyclif: Medieval English Bible Translations." *Bulletin of the John Rylands Library* 48 (1965-66), 118-40.

Harris, Victor. "Allegory to Analogy in the Interpretation of Scriptures." *Philological Quarterly* 45 (1966), 1-23.

Hurley, Michael. "'Scriptura sola': Wyclif and his Critics." *Traditio* 16 (1960), 275-352.

Husik, Isaac. "Maimonides and Spinoza on the Interpreta-

tion of the Bible." *Supplement to the Journal of the American Oriental Society* 55 (1935), 22-40.

Jeffrey, David L. "John Wyclif and the Hermeneutics of Reader Response." *Interpretation* 39 (1985), 272-87. Examination of the exegetical principles propounded by Wyclif in his *De Veritate Sacrae Scripturae.*

Kaske, R. E., with Arthur Groos and Michael W. Twomey. *Medieval Christian Literary Imagery: A Guide to Interpretation.* Toronto Medieval Bibliographies 11 (Toronto: University of Toronto Press, 1988). This invaluable general research tool contains chapters on liturgy, sermon literature, mythography, and the visual arts, but commences with an excellent annotated checklist of general and individual commentaries.

Katz, Jacob. "Rabbinical Authority and Authorization in the Middle Ages." In *Studies in Medieval Jewish History and Literature,* ed. Isadore Twersky (Cambridge, Mass.: Harvard University Press, 1979).

Kehoe, Richard. "The Spiritual Sense of Scripture." *Blackfriars* 27 (1946), 246-51. Offers a useful brief summary, ideal for a beginning student.

Kiecker, James G. "The Hermeneutical Principles and Exegetical Methods of Nicholas of Lyra, O.F.M. (ca. 1270-1349)." *DAI* 39 (1978), 3653A. Provides texts with translations of prefaces to Commentary on the Song of Songs in an appendix.

Klauck, H. C. "Theorie der Exegese bei Bonaventura." *Theologica* 4 (1974), 71-128.

Lapide, Pinchas. *Hebrew in the Church: The Foundations of Jewish-Christian Dialogue* (Grand Rapids: Eerdmans, 1984). The first two chapters, on "Medieval Christian Hebraica" and "Medieval Jewish New Testament Hebraica," are especially useful.

Loewe, R. "The Medieval Hebraists of England. The *Superscriptio Lincolniensis.*" *Hebrew Union College Annual* 28 (1957), 205-52.

Lordaux, W., and D. Verhelst, eds. *The Bible and Medieval Culture* (Louvain: Leuven University Press, 1979). Valuable essays on the effect of vernacularization of text and commentary both on the Continent and in England.

de Lubac, Henri. *Exégèse mediévále: Les quatre sens de l'Écriture* (4 vols.; Paris: Aubier, 1959-64). This magisterial survey from the beginnings of Christian exegesis in the West to Erasmus and the development of literary method among Renaissance Christian humanists is still authoritative and indispensable.

Mailhiot, M. D. "La pensée de S. Thomas sur le sens spirituel." *Revue Thomiste* 59 (1959), 613-63.

McNally, Robert E. *The Bible in the Middle Ages* (Atlanta: Scholars Press, 1959).

Meyer, Heinz. "Der Psalter als Gattung in der Sicht der mittelalterlichen Bibelexegese." *Frühmittelalterliche Studien* 20 (1986), 1-24.

Minnis, A. J. "Discussions of 'Authorial Role' and

'Literary Form' in Late Medieval Scriptural Exegesis." *Beiträge zur Geschichte der deutschen Sprach und Literatur* 101 (1979), 383-421.

————, and A. B. Scott, eds. *Medieval Literary Theory and Criticism c. 1100–c. 1375: The Commentary Tradition* (Oxford: Oxford University Press, 1987).

Nemetz, Anthony. "Literalness and the *Sensus Literalis.*" *Speculum* 34 (1959), 76-89.

Reau, Louis. *Iconographie de l'art chrétien* (6 vols.; Paris: Presses Universitaires de France, 1955-59). Useful for establishing the relationship between exegetical tradition and artistic representation, arranged historically.

Rosenthal, E. I. J. "The Study of the Bible in Medieval Judaism." *Cambridge History of the Bible* 2 (1969), 252-79.

————. "Medieval Jewish Exegesis: its Character and Significance." *Journal of Semitic Studies* 9 (1964), 265-81.

————. "Rashi and the English Bible." *Studia Semitica* 1 (1970), 56-85.

Shereshevsky, E. "Hebrew Traditions in Peter Comestor's *Historia Scholastica.*" *Jewish Quarterly Review* 59 (1968/69), 268-89. Compares Comestor and contemporary Jewish commentators on Genesis.

Smalley, Beryl. "A Commentary on the *Hebraica* by Herbert of Bosham." *Recherches de théologie ancienne et médiévalé* 18 (1951), 29-65.

————. "John Wyclif's Postilla *super Totam Bibliam.*" *The Bodleian Library Record* 4 (1953), 186-205.

————. *The Gospels in Schools ca. 1100-1280* (London: Hambledon, 1985).

————. *Medieval Exegesis of Wisdom Literature: Essays by Beryl Smalley,* ed. R. E. Murphy (Atlanta: Scholars Press, 1986). Four important essays, covering Alexander Nequam, St. Bonaventure, William of Tournai, John of Varzy, and Nicholas Gorran, among others.

————. *The Study of the Bible in the Middle Ages* (Oxford: Oxford University Press, 1941). This penetrating overview and analysis has a particularly valuable discussion of exegetical practice among the Victorines, notably of the influence of his rabbinic interlocutors on Andrew of St. Victor.

————. "Use of the 'spiritual' sense of scripture in persuasion and argument by scholars in the Middle Ages." *Recherches de théologie ancienne et médiévale* 52 (1985), 44-63.

————. "Wyclif's *Postilla* on the Old Testament and his *Principium.*" In *Oxford Studies presented to Daniel Callue* (Oxford: Oxford Historical Society, 1964).

Spicq, P. Ceslaus. *Esquisse d'une histoire de l'exégèse latine au Moyen Âge* (Paris: Libraire Philosophique J. Vrin, 1944). This survey is especially useful for the 12th to 14th cents., and is an invaluable reference guide to important late medieval commentaries, many still unedited as well as those better known.

Stegmuller, Friedrich. *Repertorium Biblicum Medii Aevi* (9 vols.; Madrid: Consejo Superior de Investigaciones cientificas, 1950-61). Vols. 2-5 inclusive contain as close to a complete list of medieval authors of biblical commentary, with identification of books commented upon, as yet exists. For sources of this bibliography, and analogues, see "A Checklist of Bibliographies of Patristic, Medieval, and Renaissance Scriptural Commentaries" (below).

Timmer, David E. "Biblical Exegesis and the Jewish-Christian Controversy in the Early Twelfth Century." *Church History* 58 (1989), 309-21.

Tobi, Y. "Saadia's Biblical Exegesis and his Poetic Practice." *Hebrew Annual Review* 8 (1984), 241-57.

Walsh, Katherine, and Diana Wood, eds. *The Bible in the Medieval World: Essays in Memory of Beryl Smalley* (Oxford: Blackwell, 1985). Important essays on Bede, Innocent III and vernacular versions of the Bible, Hugh of St. Cher, Richard Fitzralph, and Wyclif's exegesis.

Wilmart, Andre. "Les allegories sur l'Écriture attribuées a Raban Maur." *Revue Benedictine* 32 (1920), 47-56.

Wilpert, Paul, ed. *Judentum im Mittelalter: Beiträge zum Christich-Judischen Gesprach* (Berlin, 1966). An important collection of essays on typology, Jewish-Christian interchange, and exegetical influences. Appears as Band 4 of *Miscellanea Medievale: Veröffentlichungen des Thomas-Instituts an der Universität Köln.*

Wolfson, Harry A. "Maimonides on the Internal Senses." *Jewish Quarterly Review* n.s. 25 (1935), 441-67.

Wright, A. G. *The Literary Genre Midrash* (Staten Island: Alba House, 1968).

1401-1660

Primary Works

Biblia Pauperum, ed. Frank Cornell (Stockholm, 1925). Also Elizabeth Soltesz, *Biblia Pauperum, The Estergom Blockbook of Forty Leaves* (Budapest: Corvina, 1967). This "picture-Bible" of the 15th cent., influenced heavily by Franciscan traditions of iconography, is useful for establishing popular appreciation of the basic typologies of salvation in the later Middle Ages.

Broughton, Hugh. *A concent of scripture* (London, 1590).

————. *A defence of the booke entitled a concent of Scripture* (Middleburg, 1609).

Cartwright, Christopher. *Electa Thargumico-Rabbinica: sive Adnotationes in Genesin, Extriplici Targum; seu Chaldaica Paraphrasi, atque ex Interpretibus Ebraeis Una cum Animadversionibus* (London, 1648).

Chappuys, Gabriel. *Figures de la Bible* (Lyons, 1592).

Eliot, John. *Harmony of the Gospels* (1678).

Escalante, Ferdinand de. *Clypeus Concionatorum Verbi Dei, in Quo Sunt Sculptae Omni Visiones Symbolicae et Signa Reala Veteris Testamenti* (Hispalian, 1611). This exposition of Counter-Reformation period Catholic hermeneutics is a good general guide to the main lineaments of Roman method in the 16th and 17th cents.

Featley, Daniel. *Clavis Mystica: A Key Opening Divers Difficult and Mysterious Texts of Holy Scripture* (London, 1636).

Gerhard, Johann. *De Interpretatione Scripturae* (Geneva, 1610).

Gibbens, Nicholas. *Questions and disputations concerning the Holy Scripture, wherein are contained, briefe, faithfull and sound expositions of the most difficult and hardest places* (London, 1602).

Guild, William. *Moses Vnuailed: Or, Those Figures Which Served vnto the Patterne and Shaddow of Heauenly Things* (London, 1620). A vernacular layperson's handbook of biblical typology.

———. *Harmony of all the Prophets* (London, 1626). Typological study.

Knell, Paul. *Israel and England Paralleled* (London, 1648).

Lightfoot, John. *Horae Hebraicæ et Talmudicae* (6 vols.; London, 1658-78). Puritan, master of Catherine Hall, Cambridge, and biblical and rabbinic studies scholar, Lightfoot in this classic and in some ways still essential work characterizes the bearing of Judaic tradition on interpretation of the NT. An English translation appeared in a two-vol. edition of Lightfoot's works in 1684 and was reprinted in 1825, 1859, and again in 20th-cent. facsimile in 4 vols. (Peabody, Mass.: Hendrickson, 1989).

Mather, Samuel. *The Figures or Types of the Old Testament* (Dublin, 1683). This major treatise was seminal for the 18th-cent. tradition in colonial America, but retained its influence on both sides of the Atlantic well into the 19th cent. It was abridged and restructured by Caroline Fry Wilson as *The Gospel of the Old Testament* (London, 1834).

Owen, John. *Of the Divine originall, authority, self-evidencing light, and power of the Scriptures* (Oxford, 1659). Puritan divine, Dean of Christ Church, Oxford, during the Interregnum, Owen offers a representative example of Puritan erudition and Puritan biblicism.

Taylor, Thomas. *Christ Revealed, or the Old Testament Explained* (London, 1635). A major typological study which establishes many normative conventions for Protestant typology in the 17th cent. It also appeared in 1653 as *Moses and Aaron; of the Types and Shadows of the Old Testament Opened and Explained*.

Whitaker, William. *A Disputation Concerning Scripture, Against the Papists* (London, 1588). This Reformationist hermeneutic was popular also for apologetic reasons, and reprinted. In 1849 it was edited and reissued by William Fitzgerald at Cambridge.

Secondary Works

Aldridge, John W. *The Hermeneutic of Erasmus* (Richmond, VA: John Knox, 1966). Helpful in understanding Erasmus as a bridge between medieval and Reformation exegetical method.

Bercovitch, Sacvan. "New England Epic: Cotton Mather's *Magnalia Christi Americana.*" *English Literary History* 33 (1966), 337-51.

———. "Typology in Puritan New England: The Williams-Cotton Controversy Reassessed." *American Quarterly* 19 (1967), 166-91.

———, ed. *Typology and Early American Literature* (Boston: University of Massachusetts Press, 1972). Landmark and still indispensable guide to the field, with superb bibliographies.

———. *The American Jeremiad* (Madison: University of Wisconsin Press, 1978).

Bland, Kalman P. "Issues in Sixteenth-Century Jewish Exegesis." In D. C. Steinmetz, ed. *The Bible in the Sixteenth Century* (Durham and London: Duke University Press, 1990), 50-68.

Booty, John E., ed. *The Godly Kingdom of Tudor England: Great Books of the English Reformation* (Wilton, CT: Morehouse-Barlow, 1981).

Bornkamm, Heinrich. *Luther und das Alte Testament* (Tübingen, 1948). Analysis of Luther's typology.

Brumm, Ursula. *American Thought and Religious Typology,* trans. John Hoaglund (New Brunswick, NJ: Rutgers University Press, 1970). Although less tightly focussed than that of Bercovitch, Brumm's work is a useful complement to his.

Coles, Robert. "The Bible and the Puritans." In *In Praise of What Persists,* ed. Stephen Berg (New York: Harper, 1983), 45-55.

Dickson, Donald R. "The Complexities of Biblical Typology in the Seventeenth Century." *Renaissance and Reformation/Renaissance et Réforme* 11 (1987), 253-72.

Ebeling, Gerhard. "The New Hermeneutics of the Young Luther." *Theology Today* 21 (1964-65), 34-46.

Fatio, Olivier, and Pierre Fraenkel, eds. *Histoire de l'exégèse au XVIe siècle* (Geneva: Droz, 1978). This collection includes useful essays on rabbinic exegesis, Erasmus's exegesis of the Psalms, Bucer on Ps. 22, Calvin on the Second Commandment, and the Annotationes of Lorenzo Valla.

Hyma, Albert. *Renaissance to Reformation* (Grand Rapids: Eerdmans, 1951).

Jones, G. Lloyd. *The Discovery of Hebrew in Tudor England: A Third Language* (Manchester: Manchester University Press, 1983).

Knott, John R., Jr. *The Sword of the Spirit: Puritan Responses to the Bible* (Chicago: Chicago University

Press, 1980). Examines the influence of such commentators as Gerard Winstanley, Richard Sibbes, and Richard Baxter upon two major writers of the 17th cent., John Milton and John Bunyan.

Lowance, Mason I., Jr. "Images and Shadows of Divine Things: Puritan Typology in New England from 1660 to 1750." Ph.D. dissertation, Emory, 1967.

Preuss, James Samuel. *From Shadows to Promise: Old Testament Interpretation from Augustine to the Young Luther* (Cambridge, MA: Harvard University Press, 1969). An invaluable introduction, especially helpful in distinguishing Reformation from medieval Catholic typology.

Quinn, Dennis B. "John Donne's Principles of Biblical Exegesis." *Journal of English and Germanic Philology* 61 (1962), 313-29.

Reinitz, Richard. "Symbolism and Freedom: The Use of Biblical Typology as an Argument for Religious Toleration in Seventeenth-Century England and America." Ph.D. dissertation, Rochester, 1967.

Schwartz, Karl Adolph V. *Die theologische Hermeneutik des Matthias Flacius Illyricus* (München, 1933).

Steinmetz, David C., ed. *The Bible in the Sixteenth Century* (Durham and London: Duke University Press, 1990). An important collection of essays on issues in Reformation era exegesis both Jewish and Christian.

Strauch, Carl F. "Typology and the American Renaissance." *Early American Literature* 6 (1971), 167-78.

Torrance, T. F. *The Hermeneutics of John Calvin* (Edinburgh: Academic Press, 1988).

Williams, Arnold. *The Common Expositor: An Account of the Commentaries on Genesis, 1527-1633* (Chapel Hill: University of North Carolina Press, 1948).

1661-1800

Primary Works

Bunyan, John. *Divine Emblems, or, Temporal Things Spiritualized* (London, 1724). Originally published in 1686 as *A Book for Boys and Girls: or Country Rhimes for Children,* by J. B., this work helped to popularize many standard Puritan interpretations.

Butler, Joseph. *The Analogy of Religion Natural and Revealed, to the Constitution and Course of Nature* (London, 1736). Son of Presbyterian parents and student at a Dissenting Academy, Butler moved to the Church of England and became Bishop of Durham. This was the greatest 18th-cent. work of natural theology, directed against deistic anti-revelationism. In its second part it argues for a rationalist adequation of revelation — in effect a natural supernaturalism.

Collins, Anthony. *The Scheme of Literal Prophecy Considered* (London, 1727). Written to refute Edward

Chandler's *A Defense of Christianity from Prophecies of the Old Testament* (London, 1725).

————. *A Discourse of the Grounds and Reasons of Christian Religion* (London, 1737). Collins was a Deist, greatly influenced by Locke, whose principal work, *A Discourse of Freethinking* (1713), was roundly attacked by Bentley, Hoadly, Whiston, and Jonathan Swift. This work (1737) denies the canonicity of the NT, and that the OT contains any prophecies of Christ.

Daubuz, Charles. *A Perpetual Commentary on the Revelation of St. John* (London, 1720). This compendious and influential work was abridged in the 19th cent. as *A Symbolical Dictionary in which the general significance of all the prophetic symbols . . . is laid down* (London, 1842).

Edwards, Jonathan. *Images or Shadows of Divine Things* (New Haven: Yale University Press, 1948). This important work of the great American intellectual and religious leader was not edited for publication until this modern edition of Perry Miller.

Ernesti, Johann August. *Institutio Interpretis Novi Testamenti* (Leipzig, 1761). Lutheran classicist turned theologian, Ernesti attempted to reconcile traditional Reformation theology with historical criticism, emphasizing in his commentary the central role of philological and grammatical considerations in the establishment of meaning.

Francke, August Hermann. *Praelectiones Hermeneuticae* (Halle, 1723).

————. *Christus Sacrae Scripturae Nucleus,* trans. into English as *Christ the sum and substance of the Holy Scriptures in the Old and New Testament* (London, 1732). A leading German pietist, Francke had a notable influence on Cotton Mather and Jonathan Edwards in America as well as on some of the Wesleyan writers in England.

Hare, Francis. *The Difficulties and Discouragements which attend the Study of the Scriptures* (London, 1714).

Herder, Johann Gottfried von. *Briefe, das Studium der Theologie Betreffend* (Weimar, 1780). Herder's work, influential through the Romantic period, applies biblical typology to nature.

————. *The Spirit of Hebrew Poetry,* trans. James Marsh (Burlington, VT, 1833).

Holly, Israel. *The New Testament Interpretation of the Old* (London, 1771).

Jones, William. *A Course of Lectures on the Figurative Language of the Holy Scripture* (London, 1787).

Leonard, Abbe Martin-Augustin. *Traite du sens littéral et du sens mystique des Saintes Écritures* (Paris, 1727).

Mather, Cotton. *Psalterium Americanum* (Boston, 1718). The annotations to Mather's translation of the Psalms reveal learned indebtedness to rabbinical commentaries, Augustine, Bellarmine, Lapide, Beza, as well as

English commentaries such as those of Samuel Smith (1614) and William Bradshaw (1621).

McEwen, William. *Grace and Truth; or the Glory and Fulness of the Redeemer Displayed in an Attempt to Explain the Most Remarkable Types, Figures, and Allegories of the Old Testament* (Edinburgh, 1763). This popular work obtained more than twenty editions in England and America over the next century.

Newton, Thomas. *Dissertations on the Prophecies* (London, 1754; rpt. Northampton, Mass., 1796). This is by the editor and annotator of Milton's *Paradise Lost* (London, 1749) and *Paradise Regained* (1752). A widely popular 18th-cent. commentary by the Bishop of Bristol.

Priestley, Joseph. "Observations on the Prophets of the Old Testament." In his *Theological Repository* 4 (1794), 97-122.

———. *Harmony of the Evangelists* (London, 1777).

———. *History of Early Opinions concerning Jesus Christ* (London, 1786). Educated in Doddridge's Dissenting Academy at Northampton, Priestley later trained for the Presbyterian ministry, was ordained, then gradually shifted in the direction of the Unitarian Society, of which he was a founder (1791). His *History of Early Opinions . . .* provoked violent controversy, and was opposed by many orthodox theologians, notably Samuel Horsley.

Saurin, Jacques. *Dissertations . . . on the Most Memorable Events of the Old and New Testaments,* trans. I. Chamberlayne (London, 1773). This work was influential in both England and America, and is useful for an understanding of peculiarly 18th-cent. uses of typology.

Sherlock, Thomas. *Trial of the Witnesses* (London, 1729). A defense of the reliability of the Gospels in their account of the miracles, answering Woolston.

Warburton, William. *The Divine Legation of Moses Demonstrated* (2 vols.; London, 1737-41). This work is by the flamboyant Bishop of Goucester, who also edited Shakespeare and was a close friend of Alexander Pope. His unusual argument supporting the divine origin of Mosaic law was directed against the Deists. He also virulently opposed "enthusiasm" and published *The Doctrine of Grace* (1762) as an attack on John Wesley.

Watts, Isaac. *A Short View of the Whole Scripture History* (London, 1732).

———. *The Holiness of Times, Places, and People under the Jewish and Christian Dispensations* (London, 1738). Watts's work was influential among Independent, Presbyterian, and Evangelical circles in England and America.

Winchester, Elhanan. *Four Discourses, Entitled, The Face of Moses Unveiled by the Gospel* (Philadelphia, 1784). Popular American example of conventional 18th-cent. Protestant typological reading.

Woolston, Thomas. *Six Discourses on the Miracles of Our Saviour* (London, 1727-30). Woolston inaugurated a fierce argument over the credibility of NT miracles by entirely allegorizing them.

Secondary Works

Armogathe, Jean-Robert. *Le grand siècle et la Bible.* Bible de tous les temps, no. 6 (Paris: Beauchesne, 1989). One of the most useful volumes in this valuable series, containing essays on 17th-cent. Jewish exegesis, on Ralph Cudworth, Hugo Grotius, a review of prominent Christian Hebraists of the period, on Richard Simon, Descartes, St. Francis de Sales, Hobbes, Pascal, Racine, Malebranche, and Bunyan on the Bible, and a study of Sir Isaac Newton's interpretation of Daniel.

Brosseau, M. "Au sujet de quelques versions et commentaires de la Bible populaires en Angleterre au XVIIIe siècle." In *Aspects de la littérature populaire (XVIIe– XXe siècle)* (Pau: Université de Pau, 1977).

Davies, Horton. *Worship and Theology in England from Watts and Wesley to Maurice, 1690-1850* (Princeton: Princeton University Press, 1961). Useful for locating broader exegetical and hermeneutic controversy in the context of practical religious observance and divergent ecclesiastical traditions.

Frei, Hans W. *The Eclipse of Biblical Narrative: A Study in Eighteenth and Nineteenth Century Hermeneutics* (New Haven: Yale University Press, 1974). Excellent study of the interaction of literary culture and theology, influenced by Auerbach, Barth, and Gilbert Ryle. Has special value for history-of-narrative interpretation from Anthony Collins to Herder and Strauss.

Korshin, Paul J. "The Development of Abstracted Typology in England, 1650-1820." In *Literary Uses of Typology,* ed. Earl Miner (Princeton: Princeton University Press, 1977), 147-203. For a full range of studies devoted to the literary adaptation of biblical typology, see the bibliography "The Influence of the Bible on English Literature: Selected General Studies" (below).

Kraeling, Emil G. H. *The Old Testament Since the Reformation* (London, 1955). Valuable for its study of the political uses of biblical typology and interpretation.

Manning, Stephen. "Scriptural Exegesis and the Literary Critic." In *Typology and Early American Literature,* ed. Sacvan Bercovitch (Amherst: University of Massachusetts Press, 1972).

Reventlow, Henning Graf. *The Authority of the Bible and the Rise of the Modern World,* trans. John Bowden (London: SCM, 1984). Beginning with backgrounding in Wyclif, Erasmus, and Bucer, it assesses the crisis over authority of the Bible in the Puritan age in England, the reactions of Lord Herbert of Cherbury (Deism), Hobbes (Rationalism), and Locke and the

Latitudinarians. Especially thorough on Deism and rationalist apologetics (Toland, Tindal, Newton, Clarke, Butler, Swift, Collins, Whiston, Woolston).

1801-1900

Primary Works

Arnold, Matthew. *St. Paul and Protestantism* (London, 1870).

————. *Literature and Dogma* (London, 1973).

————. *God and the Bible* (London, 1875). Arnold's reconstruction of St. Paul as a genteel Victorian rationalist and his attempted demonstration that "God" was to be understood as a "stream of tendency" which "makes for righteousness" was opposed from both pietist and agnostic quarters in his own lifetime. His "literary" Bible, however, in which the text of Scripture is seen as an indispensable cultural foundation even though fundamentalist "bibliolatry" and its literal doctrinal interpretations are to be rejected as "unscientific," has proved more enduring. Among those whose approach to the Bible has been influenced by Arnold are R. G. Moulton, Frank Kermode, and Northrop Frye.

Bauer, G. L. *Hebraische Mythologie des Alten und Neuen Testamentes* (Köln, 1802). An attempt to do for the Bible what classical and pagan mythologists had done for their sources.

Baur, Ferdinand Christian. *Untersuchungen über die sog. Pastoralebriefe des Apostels Paulus* (Tübingen, 1835).

————. *Paulus, der Apostel Jesu Christi* (Eng. trans. London, 1873-75). Founder of the Tübingen School and disciple of Schleiermacher in his early years, Baur developed his revisionist canon and doctrines under the influence of Hegel's conception of history. His influence extends well into the 20th cent.

Bush, George, ed. *The Hierophant; or, Monthly Journal of Sacred Symbols and Prophecy* (New York: June 1842 to May 1843). This journal, by a man who also commented upon Leviticus, Numbers, Joshua, Judges, and Daniel, applied biblical typology to American history and culture. The journal ran for 12 numbers.

Chevallier, Temple. *On the Historical Types Contained in the Old Testament* (2 vols.; Cambridge, 1826). These were the Hulsean Lectures for 1826.

Cheyne, Thomas Kelly, and J. Sutherland Black, eds. *Encyclopaedia Biblica* (4 vols.; London, 1899-1903). Cheyne was Oriell Professor of the Interpretation of Scripture at Oxford from 1885 to 1908.

Conybeare, John J. *Bampton Lectures for the Year MDCCCXXIV. Being an Attempt to Trace the . . . Secondary and Spiritual Interpretation of the Scripture* (Oxford, 1824). Influenced by Marsh and Michaelis.

Denzinger, Henricus. *Enchiridion Symbolorum* (Wirceburgi, 1856). This enormously popular symbol dictionary offers access to 19th-cent. traditions of typological exegesis. It was published in a 33rd ed. in Freiburg, 1965.

Dods, Marcus. *An Introduction to the New Testament*, 8th ed. (London, 1898).

Drury, John, ed. *Critics of the Bible, 1724-1873* (Cambridge: Cambridge University Press, 1989). Important period essays by Anthony Collins, Thomas Sherlock, Blake, Coleridge, Thomas Arnold, Benjamin Jewett, and Matthew Arnold.

Edersheim, Alfred. *Prophecy and History in Relation to the Messiah* (London, 1885).

————. *The Life and Times of Jesus the Messiah* (2 vols.; London, 1833). This erudite but accessible work by a Jewish convert to Christianity was widely popular at the end of the century.

Fairbairn, Patrick. *The Typology of Scripture* (2 vols.; Edinburgh, 1845-47). Useful for assessing some aspects of Covenanter typology, this work came to have a much wider audience in England and America, and is a classic 19th-cent. study.

Farrar, Frederic William, *History of Interpretation* (London, 1886). A defense of Reformationist exegesis.

Feuerbach, Ludwig. *Wesen des Christentums* (1941). Appeared as *The Essence of Christianity* (London, 1854), in a translation by George Eliot, the novelist. Feuerbach's recasting of Hegel in rejection of Christian belief in transcendence influenced not only English literary figures like Eliot, but also continental philosophers such as Nietzsche, Marx, and later Communist theorists in Germany.

Horne, Thomas Hartwell. *An Introduction to the Critical Study and Knowledge of the Holy Scriptures* (London, 1818; 1821). This became the standard text for Scripture study employed in English colleges and universities until 1860; hence it went through a large number of editions. Coleridge was Horne's fellow student at Christ's Hospital. Although for many years a Wesleyan Methodist, he eventually was ordained an Anglican priest.

————. *A Compendious Introduction to the Study of the Bible* (London, 1827).

Kitto, John. *The Cyclopaedia of Biblical Literature* (Edinburgh, 1848; abridged by J. Taylor, Edinburgh, 1862). Widely used 19th-cent. state-of-the-art reference work, also distributed for home use in the abridged version (800 pp.). "Learned" backgrounding of biblical subjects by Victorian writers was often aided by Kitto.

Marsh, Herbert. *Lectures on the Criticism and Interpretation of the Bible* (Cambridge, 1828). Marsh was a student of J. D. Michaelis and English translator of his

Introduction to the New Testament (1793-1801). An anti-Calvinist and anti-Evangelical, who later as Bishop of Llandaff and Peterborough in succession refused to license Calvinist or Evangelical ordinands, he was among the first to popularize German critical methods in England. He held the Lady Margaret Professorship of Divinity at Cambridge from 1807 until his death in 1839, and was the most influential bishop and biblical scholar of this period.

Maurice, Frederick Denison. *The Kingdom of Christ; or, Hints to a Quaker concerning the Principle, Constitution and Ordinances of the Catholic Church* (2 vols.; London, 1838). Maurice considered himself a "Coleridgean," and was intimately concerned with the imaginative integration of revelation in literature. Like Coleridge, he was first a Unitarian, then gradually turned toward Anglican trinitarianism.

Meyer, Gottlob Wilhelm. *Geschichte der Schrifterklarung seit der Wiederherstellung der Wissenschaften* (Leipzig, 1802-09). Standard early 19th-cent. review of the history of biblical interpretation.

Moulton, Richard G. *The Literary Study of the Bible: An Account of the Leading Forms of Literature Represented in the Sacred Writings, Intended for English Readers* (Chicago, 1895; London, 1896). Pioneer in literary approach to the biblical text, laying aside preoccupations of "higher criticism" for stylistic, genre, and philological analysis of the translated text. Intended as a text for courses in colleges and universities, it had considerable if short-lived success.

Newman, John Henry. *Essay on the Development of Christian Doctrine* (London, 1845). This work by the great tractarian leader expressed his rationale for moving to a Catholic view of the relation of revelation to ecclesiastical tradition, and shortly preceded his Roman ordination in 1849.

Paley, William. *Horae Paulinae* (London, 1790). An influential attempt to establish the historicity of the NT by comparative analysis of the Epistles and Acts.

———. *A View of the Evidences of Christianity* (London, 1794).

———. *Natural Theology* (London, 1802). *Evidences* was an extremely popular work of apologetics throughout the 19th cent., expressing a traditional, supernaturalist view of revelation, a view restated in *Natural Theology*.

Sanday, William. *Inspiration: Eight Lectures on the Early History and Origin of the Doctrine of Biblical Inspiration* (London, 1893). Includes reflection on typology, notably of Jonah.

Schleiermacher, Friedrich D. E. *Hermeneutik* (Berlin, 1819), ed. Heinz Kimmerle (Heidelberg, 1959). Drawing on Ernesti and Semler, Schleiermacher's watershed work develops a general hermeneutic systematically from the analysis of understanding. Its impact upon Protestant thought was enormous, bringing Romantic idealism and intuitionism into the main-stream by influencing such figures as Ritschl, Harnack, and Troeltsch. Schleiermacher was a Reformed theologian who moved toward Romantic Pietism.

Scott, Caroline L. *Exposition of the Types and Antitypes of the Old and New Testament* (London, 1856).

Silver, Abiel. *Lectures on the Symbolic Character of the Sacred Scriptures* (New York, 1863).

Smith, Ethan. *A Key to the Figurative Language Found in the Sacred Scriptures* (Exeter, 1824).

Smith, Hannah. *Bible Readings on the Progressive Development of Truth and Experience in the Book of the Old Testament* (Boston, 1881).

Spurgeon, Charles Haddon. *Types and Emblems* (London, 1875; New York, 1876). Spurgeon was a Baptist preacher, Calvinist in doctrine and literalist/typologist in exegesis. Enormously popular in England and America, his sermons are also of value for the student of popular applications of biblical tradition in the 19th cent.

———. *Commenting and Commentaries* (London, 1876). This volume contains a list of commentaries of which Spurgeon approved (see "A Checklist of Bibliographies of Patristic, Medieval, and Renaissance Scriptural Commentaries" below for further details).

Strauss, David Friedrich. *Das Leben Jesu* (2 vols.; Bonn, 1835). (Landmark excursus into the question of the historical Jesus which ends by distinguishing this issue from the question of meaning in the Gospels.)

Steinschneider, Moritz. *Jewish Literature from the Eighth to the Eighteenth Century,* trans. William Spottiswoode (London, 1857; rpt. New York, 1970). This anthology made select talmudica, biblical commentary, and moral philosophy from Jewish tradition accessible to British readers on a wide scale and was frequently consulted and referred to by non-Jewish writers of the period, although not always with acknowledgment.

Van Mildert, William. *An Inquiry into the General Principles of Scripture Interpretation* (Oxford, 1815). These Bampton Lectures for 1814 by the Bishop of Llandaff and Durham bear comparison with the work of his successor, Herbert Marsh, of 1828.

Westcott, Brooke Foss. *History of the English Bible* (London, 1868). Representative of mainstream British academic historical criticism in the Victorian era.

Whitaker, William. *A Disputation on Holy Scripture against the Papists, especially Bellarmine and Stapleton,* trans. Fitzgerald (Cambridge, 1849).

Secondary Works

Abrams, M. H. *Natural Supernaturalism: Tradition and Revolution in Romantic Literature* (New York: Norton, 1973). Seminal study, which engages *inter alia* responses to issues in biblical hermeneutic among the Romantic poets and their peers.

Altmann, Alexander. *Biblica Motifs: Origins and Trans-*

formations (Cambridge, MA: Harvard University Press, 1966).

Brantley, Richard E. *Locke, Wesley, and the Method of English Romanticism* (Gainesville: University of Florida Press, 1984).

Brown, Jerry W. *The Rise of Biblical Criticism in America, 1800-1870* (Middletown: University of Connecticut Press, 1969).

Bruns, Gerald L. *Inventions, Writing, Textuality, and Understanding in Literary History* (New Haven: Yale University Press, 1982). Offers a history of interpretation among the Ancients, Romantics, and Moderns; considers rabbinical, traditional, and Romantic hermeneutics.

Cellier, Leon. *Fabre d'Olivet: Contribution a l'étude des aspects religieux du Romanticisme* (Paris: Nizet, 1953). Antoine Fabre d'Olivet's famous work, available to 19th-cent. readers only in French, was translated by N. L. Redfield as *The Hebraic Tongue Restored: and the Meaning of the Hebrew Words Re-established and Proved by their Radical Analysis* (New York: Putnam, 1921).

Frei, Hans W. *The Eclipse of Biblical Narrative: A Study in Eighteenth and Nineteenth Century Hermeneutics* (New Haven: Yale University Press, 1974). See 18th-cent. listing, above, for details.

Gasque, W. Ward. "Nineteenth Century Roots of Contemporary New Testament Criticism." In *Scripture, Tradition, and Interpretation,* ed. W. Ward Gasque and William Sanford LaSor (Grand Rapids: Eerdmans, 1978), 146-56.

Grusin, R. A. *Transcendentalist Hermeneutics: Institutional Authority and the Higher Criticism of the Bible* (Duke: Duke University Press, 1991).

Jasper, David, ed. *The Interpretation of Belief: Coleridge, Schleiermacher and Romanticism* (London: Macmillan, 1986).

Prickett, Stephen. *Words and the Word: Language, Poetics, and Biblical Interpretation* (Cambridge: Cambridge University Press, 1986). Discusses the late 18th-cent. divergence of biblical hermeneutics and literary criticism, which helped create a crisis in method for biblical interpretation in the 19th cent., and a crisis in meaning for literary theory lasting well into the 20th cent.

Shaffer, Elinor S. "The 'Great Code' Deciphered: Literary and Biblical Hermeneutics." *Comparative Criticism: A Yearbook* 5 (1983), xi-xxiv.

20TH CENTURY

The following brief list provides a selective introduction to recent questions and issues in the study of biblical hermeneutics but is necessarily selective and aimed only at the general or introductory student. Readers will want to consult the bibliographies "Studies of the Bible as Literature: A Select List," "A Checklist of Biblical Commentaries Available to English Authors," and "The Influence of the Bible on English Literature: Selected General Studies" for further relevant citations.

Barr, James. *The Bible in the Modern World* (New York: Harper & Row, 1973). An excellent popular-level discussion of the effect of modernity on study of the Bible.

Boone, Kathleen Confer. "Rightly Dividing the Word: The Discourse of Protestant Fundamentalism." *DAI* 48/5 (1987), 1201A.

Boyarin, Daniel. *Intertextuality and the Reading of Midrash* (Bloomington: Indiana University Press, 1990). Representation of midrash as a series of species of "strong reading" of Torah which nonetheless holds a high view of the original text. Argues that the mashal is prototype for all midrashic narrative interpretation.

Brown, Raymond E. *The Sensus Plenior of Sacred Scripture* (Baltimore: Catholic University of America Press, 1955). Magisterial synthesis by a renowned Jesuit biblical scholar and theologian.

Bruns, Gerald L. "The Hermeneutics of Midrash." In Regina Schwartz, ed. *The Book and the Text: The Bible and Literary Theory* (1990), 189-213. See also his related article in Robert Alter and Frank Kermode, *The Literary Guide to the Bible* (1989).

―――. *Hermeneutics Ancient and Modern* (New Haven: Yale University Press, 1992). An important historical contextualization for modern literary theory, locating its frequent scholasticism and rhythms of rhetorical reprise in an alternating love-hate relationship with biblical hermeneutics.

Clements, R. E. *One Hundred Years of Old Testament Interpretation* (Philadelphia: Westminster, 1976). A brief survey, concentrating on a few scholars whose work has been especially influential, emphasizing questions of methodology.

Cohn, Robert L. "Reading in Three Dimensions: the Imperative of Biblical Narrative." *Religion and the Intellectual Life* 6.3-4 (1989), 161-72.

Daniélou, Jean. "The Problem of Symbolism." *Thought* 25 (1900), 432-40.

Fackenheim, Emil L. *The Jewish Bible after the Holocaust: A Re-reading* (Bloomington: Indiana University Press, 1990). Important for post–World War II Jewish response to biblical tradition.

Farrer, Austin. *A Rebirth of Images* (London: Dacre Press, 1944).

Fisch, Harold. *Poetry with a Purpose: Biblical Poetics and Interpretation* (Bloomington: Indiana University Press, 1988). Taking up the question of whether biblical texts work in the same way as other texts, Fisch argues that biblical poetics bears an unusual tension between aesthetic and nonaesthetic modes of discourse.

Fishbane, Michael. "The Teacher and the Hermeneutical

Task: A Reinterpretation of Medieval Exegesis." *Journal of the American Academy of Religion* 43 (1975), 709-21.

Grant, Robert M. *The Bible in the Church: A Short History of Interpretation* (New York: Macmillan, 1948). Reprinted as *A Short History of the Interpretation of the Bible* (New York: Macmillan, 1972). A brief but valuable discussion, especially for beginning students.

Green, William Scott. "Romancing the Tome: Rabbinic Hermeneutics and the Theory of Literature." *Semeia* 40 (1987), 147-68.

Grusin, Richard A. *Transcendentalist Hermeneutics: Institutional Authority and Higher Criticism of the Bible* (Durham: Duke University Press, 1991). Useful revisionist exploration of hermeneutic principles shared by Emerson, Thoreau, and Theodore Parker.

Handelman, Susan Ann. *Slayers of Moses: The Emergence of Rabbinic Interpretation in Modern Literary Theory* (Albany: SUNY Press, 1982). Stimulating study, nearly indispensable for students of the influence of biblical tradition on modern literary theory. See also her dissertation "On Interpreting Sacred and Secular Scripture: The Relation of Biblical Exegesis to Literary Criticism." *DAI* 40 (1980), 5452A, and her *Fragments of Redemption: Jewish Thought and Literary Theory in Benjamin, Scholem, and Levinas* (Bloomington: Indiana University Press, 1991).

Hartman, Geoffrey H., and Sanford Budick. *Midrash and Literature* (New Haven: Yale, 1986). An important if eclectic volume by leading modern scholars covering the period from biblical to modern times.

Hauerwas, Stanley, and Steve Long. "Interpreting the Bible as a Political Act." *Religion and the Intellectual Life* 6.3-4 (1989), 134-42.

Johnston, Robert K. "Interpreting Scripture: Literary Criticism and Evangelical Hermeneutics." *Christianity and Literature* 32 (1982), 33-47.

Kümmel, W. G. *The New Testament: The History of the Investigation of Its Problems* (Nashville: Abingdon, 1972). An important survey of German Protestant scholarship; little attention is given to British, French, or American work.

Lampe, Geoffrey W. H. "Typological Exegesis." *Theology* 56 (1953), 201-8.

McNight, E. V. *Meaning in Texts: The Historical Shaping of a Narrative Hermeneutics* (Philadelphia: Fortress, 1978). Good treatment of recent attempts to develop a new hermeneutics for interpreting the Bible; discusses Heidegger, Dilthey, Gadamer, and others.

Neill, S., and N. T. Wright. *The Interpretation of the New Testament: 1861-1986* (Oxford, New York: Oxford University Press, 1987). An informed and highly readable discussion which complements Kümmel's book listed above by emphasizing British scholars.

Noll, Mark. "Bible Scholarship and the Evangelicals." *Religion and the Intellectual Life* 6.3-4 (1989), 110-24.

Osick, Carolyn. "The Feminist and the Bible: Hermeneutical Alternatives." *Religion and the Intellectual Life* 6.3-4 (1989), 96-109.

Scholem, Gershom Gerhard. *On the Kabbalah and Its Symbolism,* trans. Ralph Manheim (New York: Schocken, 1965).

Schneidau, Herbert N. *Sacred Discontent: The Bible and Western Tradition* (New Orleans: Louisiana State University Press, 1976; rpt. Berkeley: University of California Press, 1977). An eclectic work developing the thesis that the Bible is the foundational book for Western culture, it presents the cultural challenge of the Bible in terms of its "demythologizing" consciousness. Early deconstructionist approach.

————. "The Bible Under Attack." *Religion and the Intellectual Life* 6 (1989), 193-206.

Steiner, George. "The Good Books." *New Yorker,* Jan. 11, 1988. Reprinted in *Religion and the Intellectual Life* 6.3-4 (1989), 9-16. Magisterial review and reflection on Alter and Kermode, *The Literary Guide to the Bible,* opening up several key late 20th-cent. hermeneutical questions.

Thiselton, A. C. *The Two Horizons: New Testament Hermeneutics and Philosophical Description with Special Reference to Heidegger, Bultmann, Gadamer, and Wittgenstein* (Grand Rapids: Eerdmans, 1980). Valuable and thorough introduction.

DAVID LYLE JEFFREY

A Checklist of Biblical Commentaries
Available to English Authors

The purpose of this checklist is limited: to provide the student of biblical interpretation with a quick guide to popular commentaries pertinent to each of the major periods of English literary tradition. For each of five periods (roughly 597-1066; 1067-1400; 1401-1660; 1661-1800; 1801-1900) influential general commentaries are listed, with titles reflecting their original language of issue. (Representative commentaries since 1900 will be found listed in the bibliography above, "A Guide to Biblical Studies" [pp. 869-70]). Virtually all of the formative patristic commentators, some of the more central medieval commentators, and most foundational commentaries after 1500 are available in translation. English translations of Latin works are not normally listed here; this information is readily available in any good library, and new translations are currently appearing at such a welcome pace as would render any such list swiftly out of date. For each period represented the commentaries listed are known to have existed in English libraries during that period or in some other evident fashion to have been available to English writers of the time.

The medieval list is augmented with notable commentaries specific to individual biblical books. Throughout the medieval period commentary tradition was more fragmentary than in later periods, with some works on individual books (e.g., Robert Holcot's 14th-cent. commentary on Wisdom) enjoying popularity far eclipsing that of the general commentaries *in totam bibliam*. (Several important single-book commentaries are also included in the 19th-cent. list.)

It should be noted that this checklist can take no account of several kinds of general works which make a significant historical contribution to biblical exegesis. The reader will find a detailed account of such books in the bibliography "Historical Studies in Biblical Hermeneutics" (above), but for quick contextualization, influential materials which are not biblical commentary as such include the following: (1) sermon collections which, from the patristic and medieval periods (e.g., St. Augustine, St. Caesarius of Arles) to Anglo-Saxon times (e.g., Wulfstan, Aelfric), through the 18th cent. (e.g., Tillotson, Butler, Wesley, Newton) to the modern period (e.g., F. D. Maurice, J. H. Newman, C. H. Spurgeon), are nevertheless an indispensable supplementary guide to popular exegetical practice; (2) general expositions of a biblical or theological worldview, such as the *Jewish Antiquities* of Josephus (well known to Bede and ever after), Augustine's *City of God, Confessions, On the Trinity, On Christian Doctrine,* the Epistles of St. Jerome, the *Pastoral Care* of St. Gregory the Great, or Calvin's *Institutes:* these works often formulate a decisive reading of a particular passage, and it is usual that such readings will enter into the most popular specific commentaries; (3) versified biblical paraphrases incorporating glosses and commentary, such as the *Aurora,* or *Biblia Versificata* of Peter Riga, the various ME versions of the *Cursor Mundi,* or du Bartas's *Divine Weekes and Workes* in the 1633 translation of T. Sylvester, each of which was itself a compilation of secondary and derivative exegesis and had significant impact upon literary adaptation of the Bible; and finally (4) patristic and medieval treatments of biblical language, especially figurative language (e.g., Augustine, *De fide et symbolo;* Bede, *De schematibus et tropis*), which are occasionally foundational for certain allegorical or spiritual readings of a given passage.

The works included here are suggestive of the dominant traditions of biblical commentary as represented in English libraries (later also American, Canadian, and Commonwealth libraries). Asterisked items tend to lose popularity after the period in which they are listed; conversely, remaining items continue to be sources of reference down to the modern (post-Victorian) period, even if only as assimilated into more recent works of exegesis.

For the periods after 1500 when, with the advent of printing, commentary literature proliferates, only dominant commentaries in general use are listed.

THE MEDIEVAL PERIOD

General Commentaries on the Whole Bible

Pre-1066

During this period the extensive (though not complete) commentaries of St. Ambrose, St. Augustine, St. Jerome, and St. Gregory I are the dominant influence. However, the *Allegoriae in Universam S. Scriptorum* attributed to Rabanus Maurus (mid-9th cent. A.D.), along with the contextualizing influence of the same writer's *De Clericorum Institutione,* came to have a central influence in synthesizing the allegorical elements in patristic exegesis.

1067-1400

Rashi (R. Solomon ben Isaac). *Perush 'al ha-Torah (Commentary on the Pentateuch).* The work of the great 11th-cent. rabbi of Troyes was consulted and used by Andrew of St. Victor and Nicholas of Lyra. Translated into Latin in the 17th and 18th cents. (ed. F. Breithaupt, 1710-14), it influenced late Puritan as well as Jewish exegesis. It has been edited with English translation and notes in 5 vols. by M. Rosenbaum and A. M. Silberman (London, 1929-34).

Anselm of Laon et al. *Glossa Ordinaria* (vols. 113-14, J.-P. Migne, ed. *Patrologia Latina*). This collaborative effort of many 11th- and 12th-cent. scholars to establish a better Latin text of the Bible and to provide with it running marginal commentary for the use of scholars and clerics is eclectic to some degree. Its advantages are concision and partial synthesis; its disadvantages are the same, and, at least for the purposes of establishing "normative" medieval readings, it must accordingly be used with caution. Emphasis in the *Glossa Ordinaria* falls on the spiritual (e.g., moral, allegorical, and, less frequently, anagogical) senses.

Pierre Bersuire. *Reductorium Morale Veteris et Novi Testamenti.* Also found as *Reductorium Morale super Tota Biblia* and *Liber Bibliae Moralis Expositionum Interpretationumque Historiarum ac Figurarum Veteris Novique Testamenti,* this commentary by the early 14th-cent. Franciscan (later turned Benedictine), a close friend and correspondent of Petrarch, is especially valuable for its tropology and its treatment of figurative language in the Bible.

Rupert of Deutz. *De Sancta Trinitate et Operibus Eius.* A treatise on salvation history in forty-two books, this work is organized as an integrative commentary on the historical books of the Bible. *De Victoria Verbi Dei.* A

commentary on the twelve minor prophets. Rupert, a Benedictine monk of the late 11th and early 12th cents., wrote also a commentary on the Gospel of John having evident connection to this work, and a commentary on the Song of Songs in which the bride is interpreted to be the Blessed Virgin Mary.

Hugh of St. Cher. *Postillae in Universa Biblia Secundum Quadruplicem Sensum.* This traditional commentary by the French Dominican gives literal, allegorical, moral, and anagogical senses for each passage. The traditional senses are presented as modes, so that in effect there remain two senses, the literal and the spiritual, the latter of which has three expressions.

Nicholas of Lyra. *Postillae super Totam Bibliam (Postillae Perpetuae, seu Brevia Commentaria in Universa Biblia Libris LXXXV);* also his *Postillae Majores, seu Enarrationes in Epistolas et Evangelia Dominicalia Totius Anni.* Nicholas of Lyra was an early 14th-cent. Franciscan biblical scholar, possibly though not certainly of Jewish origin. In any event he knew Hebrew, and consulted the text of the Hebrew Scriptures as well as talmudic and rabbinic commentary, to which he (like Andrew of St. Victor and others in this period) came to be considerably indebted. Nicholas, also a close reader of St. Thomas Aquinas, makes provision for each of the usual four medieval senses of the text (literal or historical, allegorical, tropological or moral, and anagogical). His emphasis, however, falls markedly upon the *sensus literalis.* Without a sound historical reading, he argues, development of the other senses is gratuitous and often nugatory. He had a significant influence upon Wyclif and other late 14th-cent. commentators, to whom he was the refreshing *Doctor planus et utilis,* and his importance for Reformation commentators, including Luther, is considerable. His main commentary was published in a printed edition as *Postillae in Bibliam, cum Additionibus Pauli Burgensis, ac Replicis Matthiae Dorinck* (Venice, 1482), and in this form was widely consulted in the 16th cent.

Genesis

Pre-1066

Philo Judaeus. *Quaestiones et solutiones in Genesim et Exodum.*

Origen. *Hom. 2 in Genesim* (used by Bede and Alcuin); *Hom. 4 in Genesim; Hom. 17 in Genesim*

Ambrose, St. *De Abraham; De Noe et arca; Hexaemeron*

Augustine, St. *De Genesi ad litteram; In Genesi contra Manichaeos; Quaestiones in Genesi*

Jerome, St. *Quaestiones Hebraicae in Genesin*

Basil, St. *Hexaemeron.*

Bede. *In Genesim; De Temporum Ratione*

Alcuin. *Interrogationes in Genesin**

[Old Saxon] *Genesis* (influential on the OE *Genesis B*)*

1067-1400

Guibert of Nogent. *Moralium Geneseos**
Hugh of St. Victor. *De Arca Noe Morali*
Nicholas of Tournai. *In Genesim (Moralia)**
Nicholas Trevet. *In Genesim**
Peter Damian. *Expositio Mystica Libri Geneseos*
Peter-John Olivi. *In Genesim*
Nicholas of Cusa. *De Genesi*

Exodus

Pre-1066

Philo Judaeus. *De vita Mosis*
Pseudo-Bede. *Quaestiones super Exodum*
Isidore of Seville, St. *Quaestiones in Vetus Testamentum*

1067-1400

Nicholas of Tournai. *In Exodam**
Peter Damian. *De Decem AEgpti Plagis et Decalogo*

Leviticus

Pre-1066

Rabanus Maurus. *Comm. in Leviticam*

1067-1400

Nicholas Trevet. *In Leviticam**

Numbers

Origen. *Homiliae in Librum Numerorum*

Deuteronomy

Rabanus Maurus. *In Deuteronomium Libri IV*

Joshua

Isidore of Seville, St. *Commentaria in libros historicos Veteris Testamenti*

Judges

Pre-1066

Rabanus Maurus. *In Librum Judicum libri II*

1067-1400

Hugh of St. Victor. *Adnotationes Elucidatoriae in Librum Judicum, in Ruth, in Libros Regum*

Ruth

Pre-1066

Rabanus Maurus. *In Librum Ruth Liber Unus*

1067-1400

Hugh of St. Victor. *Adnotationes Elucidatoriae in Librum Judicum, in Ruth, in Libros Regum*

1 and 2 Samuel

Pre-1066

Origen. *Hom. 1 in Regem*
Ambrose, St. *Apologia Prophetae David*
Jerome, St. *Praefatio in Samuel et Malachim*
Bede. *In Samuelem Prophetam Allegorica Expositio*

1 and 2 Kings

Note: In the medieval period 1 and 2 Kings are found listed as "3 et 4 Regem," 3rd and 4th Kings being grouped with 1 and 2 Samuel ("1 et 2 Regem").

Pre-1066

Rabanus Maurus. *In Quatuor Libros Regum Libri IV*

1067-1400

Hugh of St. Victor. *Adnotationes Elucidatoriae in Librum Judicum, Ruth, in Libros Regum*

1 and 2 Chronicles

Jerome, St. *In Paralipomenon*
Rabanus Maurus. *In Duos Libros Paralipomenam*

Tobias

Bede. *Explanationes in Esdram, Tobiam, Job, Proverbia et Cantica*

Judith

Pre-1066

Rabanus Maurus. *In Librum Judith Liber Unus*

1067-1400

Hugh of St. Victor. *Annotationes Elucidatoriae Allegoriarum in Totum Testamentum Vetus* [except prophets and wisdom books]

1 and 2 Maccabees

Pre-1066

Rabanus Maurus. *In Macchabaeorum Libros Duos Commentarius ad Ludovicum regem*

1067-1400

Andrew of St. Victor. *In Macchabaeorum (ad Litteram)*

Ezra and Nehemiah

Bede. *In Esdram et Nehemiam Prophetas Allegorica Expositio*

Esther

Rabanus Maurus. *Super Judith et Hester*

Job

Pre-1066

Augustine, St. *Annotationes in Job*
Jerome, St. *Praefatio ad Job*
Gregory I, St. *Moralia in Iob* (not a commentary on Job alone, but a wide-ranging commentary upon Scripture which takes the text of Job as its starting place)
Ishodadh de Haditha. *In Job* (An introduction to this important but not very accessible work may be found in J. Schliebitz, "Isodadh's Kommentar zum Buche Hiob," in *Beihefte zur Zeitschrift für die alttestamentliche Wissenschaft* 11 [1907].)
Phillipus Presbyter. *Expositio interlinearis in Job*

1067-1400

Albert the Great, St. *In Job*
Thomas Aquinas, St. *Expositio in Job ad Litteram*
Peter of Blois. *Compendium in Job*
Thomas Walleys. *In Job*
Levi ben Gerson (Gershon, or Gersonides). *Super Job*
Ranulf Higden. *Expositionem super Job*

Psalms

Pre-1066

Ambrose, St. *De Psalmo CXVIII [119] Expositio*
Augustine, St. *Enarrationes in Psalmos*
Jerome, St. *Commentarioli in Psalmos*
Pseudo-Jerome. *Breviarum in Psalmos* (used heavily by Alcuin)
Pseudo-Bede. *In Psalmorum Librum Exegesis* (influenced by Theodore of Mopsuestia)
Prosper of Aquitaine. *Expositio Psalmorum* (Pss. 101–150 only)

1067-1400

Bruno, St. *Expositio in Psalmos*
Honorius of Autun. *Selectorum Psalmorum Expositio*
Peter Lombard. *In Psalmos Davidicos Commentarii (Glossae Psalterii)*
Richard of St. Victor. *Mysticae Adnotationes in Psalmos*
Innocent III. *Commentarium in Septem Psalmos Poenitentiales*
Robert Grosseteste. *Commentarius in Psalmos I–C*
Bonaventure, St. *Expositio Psalmorum*
Francis Petrarch. *Psalmi Poenitentiales VII*

Proverbs

Pre-1066

Isidore of Seville, St. *De libris Salomonis*
Bede. *Super Parabolas Salomonis Allegorica Expositio*
Rabanus Maurus. *In Proverbia Salomonis Libri III*

1067-1400

Honorius of Autun. *Quaestiones et ad Easdem Responsiones in Proberbia et Ecclesiasten*
Robert Holcot. *In Parabolas Salomonis*

Ecclesiastes

Pre-1066

Jerome, St. *In Ecclesiasten*
Alcuin. *Commentaria in Ecclesiasten*

1067-1400

Honorius of Autun. *Quaestiones et ad Easdem Responsiones in Proberbia et Ecclesiasten*
Hugh of St. Victor. *Salomonis Ecclesiasten* (systematic exposition in 29 homilies)
Bonaventure, St. *Commentarium in Ecclesiasten*
Robert Holcot. *In Ecclesiasten*
Thomas of Wales. *In Ecclesiasten*

Ecclesiasticus (Sirach)

Pre-1066

Rabanus Maurus. *In Ecclesiasticum*

1067-1400

Robert Holcot. *In Ecclesiasticus*
Robert Grosseteste. *Prohemium et Glose in Libros Sapiencie et Ecclesiastici*

Wisdom

Pre-1066

Rabanus Maurus. *In Librum Sapientiae Libri III*

1067-1400

Robert Grosseteste. *Prohemium et Glose in Libros Sapiencie et Ecclesiastici*
Bonaventure, St. *Expositio in Sapientiam*
Robert Holcot. *In Sapientiam*

Song of Songs (Canticles)

Pre-1066

Origen. *Commentarius in Cantica Canticorum*
Gregory I, St. *Expositio super Cantica Canticorum*
Bede. *In Cantica Canticorum Allegoria Expositio*
Alcuin. *In Cantica Canticorum* (Compendium)

1067-1400

Honorius of Autun. *Expositio in Cantica Canticorum*
Anselm of Laon. *Enarrationes in Cantica Canticorum*
Alan of Lille. *In Cantica Canticorum Elucidatio*
Bernard of Clairvaux, St. *Expositio super Cantica Canticorum* (in 24 systematic homilies)
William of St. Thierry. *Expositio Altera super Cantica Canticorum*
Richard of St. Victor. *Cantica Canticorum Explicatio*
John Peckham. *In Cantica Canticorum*

Isaiah

Pre-1066

Origen. *Hom. 5 in Isaiam; Hom. 7 in Isaiam*
Jerome, St. *In Isaiam*

1067-1400

Peter Lombard. *In Isaiam*
Andrew of St. Victor. *In Isaiam* (showing indebtedness to Jewish interpretation, especially of Isa. 7:14-15)
Richard of St. Victor. *De Emmanuele*
Thomas Aquinas, St. *In Isaiam Prophetam Expositio*

Jeremiah

Pre-1066

Origen. *Commentarii xiv in Hieremiam*
Jerome, St. *In Hieremiam*

1067-1400

Guibert of Nogent. *Tropologiae in Prophetas Osee et Amos ac Lamentationes Jeremiae**
Thomas Aquinas, St. *Postilla super Jeremiam*

Lamentations

Guibert of Nogent. *Tropologiae in Prophetas Osee et Amos ac Lamentationes Jeremiae**

Hugh of St. Victor. *Adnotationes Elucidatoriae in Threnos Jeremiae*
Albert the Great, St. *In Threnos Jeremiae Commentarii*
John Peckham. *In Lamentationes* (once attributed to Bonaventure)
Gilbert Crispin. *In Lamentationes Jeremiae*
Thomas Aquinas, St. *Postilla super Threnos*

Baruch

Albert the Great, St. *Commentarii in Librum Baruch*
Thomas Chabham. *In Baruch**

Ezekiel

Pre-1066

Gregory I, St. *Homiliae in Ezechielem*

1067-1400

John Peckham. *In Ezekielem**

Daniel

Pre-1066

Jerome, St. *In Danielem; Prefatio ad Versionem Danihelis*

1067-1400

Albert the Great, St. *Commentarii in Librum Danielis*

Minor Prophets

Pre-1066

Ambrose, St. *In Iohel et Amos*
Jerome, St. *In Amos; In Habacuc; In Jonam; In Oseam; In Prophetas Minores; In Zechariam*

1067-1400

Guibert of Nogent. *Tropologiae in Prophetas Osee et Amos ac Lamentationes Jeremiae**
Hugh of St. Victor. *Adnotationes in Joelem Prophetam; Expositio Moralis in Abdiam* (Obadiah)

Synoptic Gospels

Pre-1066

Origen. *Homiliae in Lucam; Homiliae XXVI in Jesum Nave*
Chrysostom, John, St. *Homilia in Nativitatem*
Ambrose, St. *In Lucam*
Augustine, St. *De concensu Evangelistarum; De sermone Domini in Monte; Enchiridion; Quaestiones Evangelicae*
Jerome, St. *Homiliae de Nativitate; In Matthaeum*

Pseudo-Jerome. *In Marcum*; In Quattuor Evangelia**
Bede. *Commentaria in Quatuor Evangelia et Acta Apostolorum*
Rabanus Maurus. *In Matthaeum*

1067-1500 (including some general four-Gospel commentaries)

John Duns Scotus (pseud.). *Notae super Evangelium Matthaei*
Anselm of Laon. *Enarrationes in Evangelium Matthaei*
Hugh of St. Victor. *Annotationes Elucidatoriae Allegoriarum in Quatuor Evangelia*
Joachim of Fiore. *Super Quatuor Evangelia (Concordia Evangeliorum)*
Peter Lombard. *Sententiarum Libri Quatuor*
Alexander of Hales. *Glossa in Quatuor Libros Sententiarum Petri Lombardi*
Thomas Aquinas, St. *Cantena Aurea: Glossa Continua super Evangelia*
Robert de Melun. *Quaestiones de Divina Pagina* (mostly on Matthew)*
Bonaventure, St. *Commentarium in Evangelium S. Lucae*
Nicholas of Tournai. *In Lucam**

Gospel of John

Pre-1066

Athanasius, St. *De Incarnatione Dei Verbi (passim)*
Augustine, St. *Enchiridion; De concensu Evangelistarum; In Johannis Evangelium*
John Scot Erigena. *In Johannis Evangelium Prohem* (on John 1:1-14).

1067-1400

Bonaventure, St. *In Joannis Evangelium*
Thomas Aquinas, St. *Lectura super Johannem Reportatio*

Acts

Ambrose, St. *De Spiritu Sancto*
Bede. *Super Acta Apostolorum Expositio*

"Pauline" Epistles

Pre-1066

Origen. *In Epp. Pauli*
Augustine, St. *In Epistolas S. Pauli*
Jerome, St. *In Epistolam Pauli ad Ephesos; In Galatianos; In Philemonem; In Titum*
Alcuin. *In Philemonem*; In Titum*
Rabanus Maurus. *Super Epistolas Pauli*

1067-1400

Hugh of St. Victor (pseud.). *Quaestiones et Decisiones in Epistolas D. Pauli*

Thomas Aquinas, St. *Expositio et Lectura super Epistolas Pauli Apostoli*
Peter Abelard. *Commentariorum super S. Pauli Epistolam ad Romanos Libri Quinque*
Robert Grosseteste. *Commentarius in Epistolam Pauli ad Romanos V-XVI; Commentarius in Epistolam Pauli ad Galathas*

Hebrews

Pre-1066

Chrysostom, John, St. *In Epistolam ad Hebraeos*
Alcuin. *Commentarius ad Hebraeos**

1067-1400

John Peckham. *In Epistolam ad Hebraeos*

Catholic Epistles

Augustine, St. *In Epistolam Johannis ad Parthos.*
Bede. *Commentaria in Epistolas Catholicas et Apocalypsin*

Revelation (Apocalypse)

Pre-1066

Cyprian. *In Apocalypsin*
Pseudo-Jerome. *Super Apocalypsim*
Bede. *Commentaria in Epistolas Catholicas et Apocalypsin*
Ambrosius Autpertus. *In Apocalypsim* (known and used extensively by Alcuin in his own commentary on the Apocalypse)
Alcuin. *Commentaria in Apocalypsin*
Haymo. *Expositio in Apocalypsin**

1067-1400

Anselm of Laon. *Enarrationes in Apocalypsin*
Bruno of Asti. *Expositio in Apocalypsim*
William of Auvergne. *In Apocalypsin**
Joachim of Fiore. *Expositio in Apocalypsim (Apocalypsis Nova)*
Peter-John Olivi. *Lectura super Apocalypsim*
Arnold of Villanova. *Expositio super Apocalypsim*; De Adventu Antichristi*

1401-1660

While certain books (notably of the Pauline corpus and Revelation in the NT) obtained a great deal of (often polemical) commentary during this period, the most influential commentators, broadly speaking, wrote larger running expositions of the Gospels, NT, or entire Bible. Of these, the ones most likely to prove useful to an analysis of biblical tradition in an English-speaking context are here arranged in chronological order of appearance.

Among commentaries on individual books of the Bible many, impossible to list even representatively here, are of genuine interest to the student of English or American literature. Such a list would include, e.g., William Tyndale's *A Prologue . . . on Romans* (1526), Pico della Mirandola's *Heptaplus* on the creation narrative (notable for its use of Cabala), which influenced John Colet; Colet's own landmark lectures on Romans, 1 Corinthians, and the creation narrative (ca. 1497); Andrew Willet's *Hexapla in Genesin* (1605) and *Hexapla in Exodum* (1608), works widely cited in New England, and Joseph Caryl's twelve-volume *An Exposition . . . upon the Book of Job* (1644-69). For the almost innumerable commentaries on Revelation, one should consult critical studies such as, e.g., Katherine Firth's *The Apocalyptic Tradition in Reformation Britain, 1530-1645*.

Jean Charlier de Gerson. *De Sensu Litterali Sacrae Scripturae* (1415). Conveniently edited as the third volume in his *Oeuvres Complètes* by P. Glorieux (Paris, 1962), this exposition by the notable conciliarist is influenced by Aquinas and Nicholas of Lyra, and in turn influenced later Renaissance exposition by both Catholics and (some) Protestants.

Lorenzo Valla. *Annotationes in Novum Testamentum* (Paris, 1505; Basel, 1541; Amsterdam, 1631). Valla also compiled a *Collatio Novi Testamenti* (1444), comparing the Vg and Greek texts. In his annotations he offered numerous novel interpretations of tropic and historical character. His influence was marked on both Renaissance humanists and Reformers, notably among the latter Martin Luther.

Don Isaac Abravanel. *Perush nabi'im 'aharonim V'terey* (Pesaro, 1520). This work has been republished as a *Commentary on the Later Prophets* (Jerusalem, 1963). A modern edition of this commentary on the Pentateuch, *Perush ha' Torah* (Venice, 1579), has been published (Jerusalem, 1955). Abravanel was a strong messianist, and his interlocution with Christian as well as Jewish interpretation caused him to have considerable influence on Renaissance biblical exegesis generally.

Martin Luther. *In Vetus Testamentum* (Wittenburg, 1524); *Annotationes in Aliquot Capita Matthae* (1528; rev. 1538); *Praefatio Methodica Totius Scripturae in Epistolam ad Romanos,* etc. Collected with others of his works in Tomes III-VII of the *Opera* (collected Latin works) published at Wittenberg 1542-80. The modern Weimar edition of Luther's collected works includes 12 volumes (i.e. *Die Deutsche Bibel*) in which Luther's commentaries are represented. Numerous translations of individual commentaries into English are available, notably the 55-volume edition produced jointly by the Muhlenberg Press and Concordia Publishing House, edited by Jaroslav J. Pelikan and Helmut T. Lehmann (St. Louis, 1955-71).

For Luther, Scripture was significant because it gave witness to Christ. In this role, it was the agent through which an encounter with the living God revealed in Jesus became accessible. Accordingly, all Scripture was to be interpreted in the light of Christ — referred to Christ for significance. In cases where such reference did not seem to work naturally, the biblical book in question was of questionable value. This is one reason Luther did not do a systematic commentary *in totam bibliam.* The books on which he did write include Genesis, Exodus *(Brevis Expositio Decalogi),* Deuteronomy, Psalms, Ecclesiastes, Song of Songs, Isaiah, Ezekiel, Daniel, all the minor prophets, Matthew (including three works on the Sermon on the Mount), Romans, Corinthians, Galatians, Epistles of Peter, and Jude. In addition he made several briefer expositions, and a more extensive commentary on Ps. 119 (Vg 118).

Luther was an Augustinian monastic before his schism, and his exegetical insights are in fact quite conservatively Augustinian for the most part. While he became one of the most important channels for neo-Augustinian exegesis in the 16th cent., his direct influence upon English interpretation was blunted somewhat until the 17th cent. by his less than diplomatic rejoinder to Henry VIII's *Defense of the Seven Sacraments,* in *Contra Henricum Regem Anglicum* (1522). Of all his biblical commentaries, that on Romans is of greatest hermeneutical significance.

Martin Bucer (Butzer). *Enarrationes in Sacra Quattuor Evangelia (Evangelienkommentar)* (Leipzig, 1530). A Dominican friar who began serious correspondence with Luther ca. 1518, Bucer was destined to have, in some respects, a more profound impact upon 16th-cent. England. Made Regius Professor of Divinity at Cambridge in 1549, he directly influenced Thomas Cranmer's *Homilies Appointed to be Read in Churches* and the 16th-cent. Anglican Ordinal.

Bucer rejects the Lutheran formula "Law and Gospel" as sophistical; the whole of Scripture is *lex* or, more precisely, *torah,* which he calls *doctrina et vitae institutio,* and in this sense (cf. Erasmus's *lex spiritualis* and Wyclif's *lex Christi*) the whole of Scripture is "teaching." The text of Scripture becomes much more an "objective revelation" than is the case with Luther. Tropological exegesis, akin to that of Gerson and à Kempis, and inculcation of an Erasmian *imitatio Christi,* accordingly, dominate the commentary.

Philipp Melanchthon. *Annotationes in Vetus Testamentum; Annotationes in Novum Testamentum* (Wittenberg, 1526; 1528). Melanchthon was an associate of Luther and protégé of Erasmus whose professorship in Greek at Wittenberg allowed him to have an important role in making more logical and temperate the Reformer's teaching. A Christian humanist, he discarded the medieval "four senses" and approached the text of the NT in much the same way he taught the Greek classics, combining literary analysis, historical contextualization, and archeological corroboration, with a view to recovering the *sensus literalis.* His most influential commentaries were those on Romans and Colossians.

John Calvin. *Commentaria in . . . Pentateuchos; . . . Josue; . . . Psalmos; . . . I Samuelem; . . . Job; . . . Prophetarum Majorem et Minorem; Commentarii in Novum Testamentum,* incl. *Harmonia ex Tribus Evangelista Composita;* etc. (Geneva, 1542-63). Calvin's NT commentaries, conveniently collected, edited, and translated by D. W. Torrance and T. F. Torrance (1972; 1980) are the most important of his exegetical writings, along with his exposition of the Pentateuch, for their influence upon subsequent commentary tradition in England and America, especially though not exclusively among Puritans. He wrote some of his commentaries in Latin, others (e.g., Jude) in French.

Matthais Flacius (Illyricus). *Clavis Scripturae Sacrae seu de Sermone Sacrarum Literarum* (Jena, 1567; rpt. 1674); *Glossa Compendaria in Novum Testamentum* (1570). Flacius was a Lutheran professor of Hebrew and an anti-humanist, whose NT commentary was enhanced in its influence by his *Clavis,* an important Protestant hermeneutical dictionary.

Theodore Beza. *Jesu Christi Domini Nostri Novum Testamentum . . . ejusdem Theod. Bezae Annotationes . . .* (Geneva, 1582). This second edition of Beza's first critical (variorum) edition of the Greek NT is printed with the Vg Latin text on one side, and Beza's improved Latin translation on the other. More compendious is the surrounding commentary, the "Codex Bezae," the Peshitta, a compendium of commentary from patristic and medieval sources, and cross references to contemporary writers such as Erasmus as well as comparative observations linking rhetorical figures, etc., to classical Roman authors such as Cicero and Seneca. Beza was a Calvinist and successor to Calvin at Geneva, yet one of his closest friends was St. Francis of Sales. In 1584 and 1598 editions of this work appeared in London with prefatory dedication to Queen Elizabeth I; the work was published several times in the 17th cent., including a corrected edition at Cambridge in 1642, so that it influenced the sermons of Anglican divines like John Donne and the commentary of Puritan apologists like Thomas Brightman, John Owen, and Richard Baxter alike. Beza was a prolific humanist writer; among his works is a biblical play, *Abraham Sacrifiant* (1550), one of the most popular of all 16th-cent. dramas.

Cornelius Lapide. *Commentaria in Omnes Divi Pauli Epistolas* (Antwerp, 1614); *Commentaria in Scripturam Sacram: Pentateuchos* (1617); *Jeremias, Baruch et Lamentationes* (1621); *Ezechiel* (1621); *Daniel* (1621); *Quattuor Maiores Prophetae* (1622); *Duodecim Minores Prophetae* (1625); *Actus Apostolorum; Epistolae Canonicae, Apocalypsis* (1627); *Ecclesiasticus* (1633-34); *Proverbia Salomonis* (1635). Lapide was a Flemish Jesuit, professor of exegesis at Louvain from 1596 to 1616. After that he worked at the Institute in Rome, commenting eventually on all canonical books except Job and the Psalms, and on Tobias and 1 and 2 Maccabees. His commentaries on the Wisdom books, Gospels, and historical books of the OT appeared posthumously from 1638 to 1645. He was a good Hebraist.

Lapide has had a great and abiding interest for both Catholic and Protestant readers. Among those who make regular use of his early commentaries are John Donne in his sermons, Jeremy Taylor in his meditations, and John Wesley in his tractates. In England and America he was used respectfully by a number of Puritan divines.

Henry Ainsworth. *Annotations Upon the Five Bookes of Moses; The Book of the Psalmes, and the Song of Songs, or Canticles* (London, 1627). An important and widely used dissenting commentary which made extensive use of Jewish commentaries.

Joseph Hall. *Plain and Familiar Explication by way of Paraphrase of All the Hard Texts of the Whole Divine Scriptures of the Old and New Testaments* (London, 1638). Hall was a Calvinist Anglican, who nonetheless lost his episcopacy and was sent to the Tower in 1641. John Wesley made use of this commentary, as did Puritan writers.

Hugo Grotius. *Annotationes in Vetus et Novum Testamentum* (Amsterdam, 1642; rpt. London, 1660). This commentary by the great Dutch jurist and theologian constitutes an important development in biblical hermeneutics. Discarding conventional notions of biblical inspiration, Grotius opted for philological criticism. Sympathetic to the Catholics and resistant to extreme Calvinism, he had political difficulties with both. Yet the erudition of his *Annotationes* made them an object of study by both parties. Grotius stresses the impossibility of balanced interpretation without recourse to tradition as well as the text. He holds that tradition bears the same relationship to Scripture as conventions of interpretation bear to the written law in jurisprudence.

John Diodati. *Pious and Learned Annotations upon the Holy Bible* (London, 1648). A popular commentary among Dissenters, Diodati's innovations include an interesting integration of cabalistic material with classic early Christian typology.

John Trapp. *A Clavis to the Bible, or a New Comment*

upon the Pentateuch, or Five Books of Moses (London, 1650); *Annotations upon the Old and New Testament* (London, 1654-62), 5 vols.

Henry Hammond. *A Paraphrase and Annotations Upon All the Books of the New Testament* (London, 1653). This staunch Church of England divine assisted Brian Walton in compilation of the latter's *Polyglot* (1657), and his commentary exhibits a considerable degree of text-critical and linguistic expertise.

1661-1800

While not as rich in clearly formative biblical commentary as previous periods, the Restoration and 18th cent. in England and America produced — perhaps especially in the Puritan, Independent, and Reformed communities — a group of commentaries which had in some respects a more far-reaching impact upon popular literary adaptation of biblical narrative. It should be noted that the selection listed here omits of necessity influential studies with a narrower focus or a more general theoretical character. Examples would include John Locke's posthumously published *A Paraphrase and Notes on the Epistles of St. Paul* (1705-07), Thomas Newton's *Dissertations on the Prophecies* (1754), or Robert Lowth's *De Sacra Poesi Hebraeorum Praelectiones Academicae* (1753), an excursus into the distinctive poetics of the Psalms which, along with his critically innovative commentary on Isaiah (1788), exerted a powerful influence on Christopher Smart, William Blake, and several Romantic poets. Some amateur contributions, such as Sir Isaac Newton's numerological and mathematically informed *Observations on the Prophecies of Daniel and the Apocalypse of St. John* (posthumous, 1733), continued to be taken seriously through the 19th cent. Such works may be identified through judicious use of the bibliography "Historical Studies in Biblical Hermeneutics" (above).

Cornelius Jansen. *Pentateuchus: sive Commentarius in Quinque Libros Moysis* (Paris, 1661).

Benedictus Pererius. *Primus Tomus Disputationum in Sacram Scripturam* (Lugduni, 1662). A Jesuit commentary used widely by Protestant as well as Catholic writers.

Matthew Poole. *Synopsis Criticorum Aliorumque Sacrae Scripturae Interpretum* (4 vols.; London, 1669-76). Issued in English as the two-volume *A Commentary on the Holy Bible* (London, 1685). Poole was one of the Presbyterian Nonconformists ejected from the Church of England for not swearing to the Act of Uniformity and its revised *Book of Common Prayer* (1662). His commentary is one of the most learned in the Dissenting tradition, but not without traces of invective. The edition of 1696 was edited, corrected, and further annotated by Samuel Clarke, who also provided a Concordance.

Richard Simon. *Histoire critique du Vieux Testament* (Paris, 1678), published in England in translation as *A critical history of the Old Testament in three books* (London, 1682). Fr. Simon, a member of the Oratory and an orientalist, was led by his stylistic analysis to doubt that Moses was author of the Pentateuch. His proto-modernist exegetical method earned him expulsion from his order, though his intent was in fact orthodox apologetics directed against the view of the Bible promulgated by Spinoza. Less a traditional commentary than an excursus in exegetical method, this work had a dramatic impact upon those approaches to the Bible which had assumed its textual stability, causing some former *sola Scriptura* Nonconformists to seek authority alternatively in magisterial tradition, and hence, as notably in John Dryden's case, to convert to the Catholic faith.

Richard Baxter. *A Paraphrase on the New Testament* (London, 1685). Though he was a Puritan within the Church of England, Baxter's formative education was a rigorously self-administered study of the medieval scholastics. His commentary quite improbably incurred his persecution at the hands of the notorious Judge Jeffreys, who sensed in it "Jesuitical" method and charged it with having "libelled" the Church of England. Actually, Baxter was ecumenist and a moderate, and his balanced commentary found favor during the next century among Anglicans as well as Dissenters.

Peter Allix. *Reflexions upon the Books of the Holy Scripture, to establish the Truth of Christian Religion* (London, 1688). Reprinted in *A Collection of Theological Tracts*, ed. Richard Watson (London, 1791).

Louis Capell and J. Cappel. *Commentarii et Notae Criticae in Vetus Testamentum* (Amsterdam, 1689).

Samuel Clarke. *The Old and New Testaments, with annotations and parallel scriptures* (London, 1690). Dissenting tradition commentary, revising and updating Poole.

Salmonis Glassus. *Philologia Sacra, Quae Totius Sacrosanctae Veteris et Novi Testamenti Scripturae Tum Stilus et Litteratura; Tum Sensus et Genuinae Interpretationis Ratio et Doctrina Libris Quinque Expenditur* (Frankfurt and Leipzig, 1691).

Simon Patrick. *A Commentary upon the Old Testament* (London, 1695-1710). 10 vols., covering Genesis to the Song of Songs.

———, W. Lowth, R. Arnold, and Daniel Whitby. *A Commentary upon the Old and New Testaments, with the Apocrypha* (London, 1727-60). 7 vols., rpt. (1809) with Moses Lowman's commentary on Revelation. Though Patrick was ordained a Presbyterian, the influence of Henry Hammond helped move him to the Church of England. Ordained by Bishop Joseph Hall, he later became Bishop of Ely. A Latitudinarian, he also published an allegory similar to that of Bunyan, *The Parable of the Pilgrim* (1664). A good example of Latitudinarian exegetical style and interpretation.

Matthew Henry. *Exposition of the Old and New Testaments* (6 vols.; London, 1706-10). This is perhaps the most widely known and used of all English commentaries on the Bible during the 18th and 19th cents., often reprinted as *Matthew Henry's Commentary on the Whole Bible.* Henry was a Presbyterian minister at Chester, and the commentary is conceived from a pastoral and practical pedagogical point of view. Critically balanced and often elegantly written, it achieved its wide appeal in part also because of its devotional tone.

Dom Augustine Calmet. *Commentaire littéral sur tous les livres de l'Ancien et du Nouveau Testament* (9 vols.; Paris, 1719-26). An integrative magisterial commentary with extensive critical apparatus, it was praised in its time (by Adam Clarke) as "the best comment on the Sacred Writings ever published either by Catholics or Protestants." Lapide was a formative influence, while Calmet in turn directly helped shape the work of William Dodd and Thomas Coke. Voltaire used Calmet as a representative summary in his attempt to refute the entire corpus of Christian exegetical tradition.

Samuel Humphreys. *The Sacred Books of the Old and New Testament . . . with Critical and Explanatory Annotations, Carefully Compiled from the Commentaries and Other Writings of Grotius, Lightfoot, Poole, Calmet, Patrick, Le Clerc, Lock, Burkitt, Henry, Pearce* (3 vols.; London, 1735-39). An attempt to out-Calmet Calmet, in a more salable English recension.

Johannes Albrecht Bengel. *Gnomon Novi Testamenti* (Ulmae, 1742, 1763). A pietist Lutheran NT scholar, Bengel is considered one of the pioneers of scientific textual criticism as a basis for exposition. His work was much praised by John Wesley and abridged in Wesley's *Explanatory Notes Upon the New Testament.* Its continuing influence into the 19th cent. was assisted by the translation of Charlton T. Lewis and Marvin R. Vincent, *Gnomon of the New Testament* (Philadelphia and New York, 1864). 2 vols.

John Wesley. *Explanatory Notes Upon the New Testament* (London, 1764; rpt. in 2 vols., New York, 1801, 1806); *Notes on the Old and New Testaments* (London, 1764). 4 vols. The Methodist leader's synthesis of previous commentaries, both continental and English, had a widespread influence in Methodist and Independent circles in England and America.

Philip Doddridge. *The Family Expositor: or, A Paraphrase and Version of the New Testament* (6 vols.; London, 1739-56). Influenced by Samuel Clarke, Doddridge became a leading Independent minister and devotional writer. His popular *Expositor* was intended for home use by the laity, and went through

many editions. One of these, published in London in 1792, was widely distributed in America. The commentary is nonpartisan; Bishop Barrington of Durham called it "an impartial interpreter and faithful monitor." The Baptist William Carey relied on this work in making his famous Bengali paraphrase-translation of the NT.

Gilbert Tennent. *The Substance and Scope of Both Testaments* (Philadelphia, 1749). Tennent was a New Jersey Presbyterian divine, supporter of George Whitefield's revivalist preaching in Boston in 1740, and author of such influential works as *Twenty-Three Sermons upon the Chief End of Man,* and *The Divine Authority of the Sacred Scriptures* (Philadelphia, 1743).

John Gill. *An Exposition of the Old Testament* (6 vols.; London, 1748-63; rpt. Philadelphia, 1818).

William Dodd. *A Commentary on the Books of the Old and New Testaments* (3 vols.; London, 1770).

Johann Gottfried Eichhorn. *Einleitung in das Alte Testament* (3 vols.; Leipzig, 1780-83); *Einleitung in das Neues Testament* (2 vols.; Leipzig, 1804-12). One of the earliest of form critics, Eichhorn exhibited many inaccuracies but was widely influential in stimulating biblical criticism, especially in his Introduction to the Old Testament.

Johann David Michaelis. *Einleitung in das Neues Testament* (Leipzig, 1750). Michaelis was a skilled orientalist who worked on the Peshitta, and from 1769 to 1791 published also an annotated translation of the OT in 13 volumes. In his famous six-volume *Mosaisches Recht* (1770-75; Eng. trans. 1840, 4 vols.) he regarded the Mosaic legislation anthropologically as a human cultural achievement. A formative voice in the development of rationalist German biblical criticism, his work was influential in the English-speaking world right through the 19th cent. This was made possible in part through the translation, with added notes, of his *Introduction to the New Testament* by Herbert Marsh (1793).

1801-1900

It should be noted that many of the most important commentaries in the 19th cent. were those first published in the 18th cent. The influence of German biblical criticism, with delayed translations, partly accounts for this. In part also more of the energy among 19th-cent. theologians was devoted to critical theory and hermeneutics. Listed here is a selection of the most visible commentaries in English.

Thomas A. Coke. *A Commentary on the Holy Bible* (6 vols.; London, 1801-03). This commentary is heavily dependent upon Doddridge's *Family Expositor,* of which it is an updating and modification. Coke was a Methodist bishop who traveled nine times to America; his commentary was widely used in Methodist circles on both sides of the Atlantic.

Samuel Horsley. *Biblical Criticism on the First Fourteen Historical Books of the Old Testament. Also on the First Nine Prophetical Books* (2 vols.; London, 2nd ed. 1844); *The Book of Psalms, Translated from the Hebrew, with Notes Explanatory and Critical* (London, 1815). Famous for his controversy with Joseph Priestley over the doctrine of the Trinity and Christ's divinity, Horsley was a scientist and Fellow of the Royal Society.

F. D. Maurice. *The Epistle to the Hebrews* (London, 1846). Given as the Warburton Lectures after Maurice had become Professor of English Literature and History at King's College in the University of London, this work contains Maurice's reply to J. H. Newman's *Theory of Development*. He also published *The Epistles of St. John* (London, 1852); *The Gospel of St. John* (London, 1857); and *The Unity of the New Testament* (London, 1854). A Coleridgean, Maurice after 1853 had become a "Christian Socialist" and opposed, among other things, the doctrine of eternal damnation.

Christian D. Ginsburg. *The Song of Songs and Koheleth.* First published separately in 1857, these works have now been reprinted in a single volume (New York, 1970).

John William Colenso. *Commentary on Romans* (London, 1861); *Introduction to the Pentateuch and the Book of Joshua* (London, 1862). Colenso was a Cambridge mathematician and in his second work used mathematical analysis reminiscent of Isaac Newton on Daniel, which in Colenso's case drove him to conclude that many of the early books of the OT could not be regarded as historically accurate. He was excommunicated in 1866, but his books caused a stir among academic expositors especially.

Joseph Barber Lightfoot. *A Fresh Revision of the New Testament* (London, 1871); *A Commentary on the Fourth Gospel* (London, 1861); *St. Paul's Epistle to the Galatians* (London, 1865); *St. Paul's Epistle to the Philippians* (London, 1868); *St. Paul's Epistle to the Colossians with Ephesians* (London, 1875). Bishop of Durham, Lightfoot was a superb classicist whose work on the NT and the Fathers of the Church drew admiration from all quarters for excellent nonpartisan scholarship.

Charles Haddon Spurgeon. *The Treasury of David, Con-taining an Original Exposition of the Book of Psalms* (7 vols.; London, 1860-67); *The Golden Alphabet . . . being a Devotional Commentary upon the One Hundred and Nineteenth Psalm* (London, 1887). Spurgeon also published an important and widely distributed three-volume work entitled *My Sermon Notes: A Selection from Outlines of Discourses delivered at the Metropolitan Tabernacle,* including studies seriatim from Genesis to Acts. Spurgeon, perhaps the single most popular preacher in Victorian England, was an English Baptist who regularly preached to crowds of more than 6,000 at the Metropolitan Bible Church in London.

Brooke Foss Westcott. *Introduction to the Study of the Gospels* (London, 1860); *Commentary on St. John's Gospel* (Cambridge, 1881); *Commentary on the Epistles of St. John* (Cambridge, 1883); *Commentary on the Epistle to the Hebrews* (Cambridge, 1889). Together with F. J. A. Hort, Westcott prepared the celebrated critical edition of the NT, with annotations (Cambridge, 1881). Westcott's criticism is of the British historical tradition, centrist, and it was widely praised. Regius Professor of Divinity for many years, he became Bishop of Durham.

F. C. Cook. *The Speaker's Commentary on the Whole Bible* (10 vols.; London, 1871-81). Prepared at the insistence of J. E. Denison, Speaker of the English House of Commons (1857-72), to defend a conservative view of Scripture against the liberalism of *Essays and Reviews* (1860).

Samuel Rolles Driver. *Isaiah: his Life and Times, with Commentary* (London, 1888); *A Commentary on Deuteronomy* (London, 1895); *A Commentary upon Joel and Amos* (London, 1897); *A Commentary upon Daniel* (London, 1900). Driver was the successor of Pusey as Canon of Christ Church, Oxford, where he was also Regius Professor of Hebrew. Before his death he completed commentaries on about half of the OT.

John Peter Lange, et al. *A Commentary on the Holy Scriptures: critical, doctrinal and homiletical. . .* Trans. and ed. Philip Schaff (5 vols.; Edinburgh, 1868-1880).

W. R. Churton, W. W. How, J. Wordsworth, et al. *Commentary on the Bible* (7 vols.; Oxford: Oxford University Press; London: SPCK, 1885-1901). Approved Anglican commentary for pulpit and lay use, with five volumes on the OT and two on the NT.

DAVID LYLE JEFFREY

A Checklist of Bibliographies of Patristic, Medieval, and Renaissance Scriptural Commentaries

This checklist is intended as a preliminary tool for students and scholars in religion, literature, art history, and other fields where a knowledge of the tradition of biblical commentary may be pertinent. The list is intended specifically to be of service to researchers who find themselves asking such questions as: what writers have commented on this particular biblical book or verse? what Fathers, or scholastics, or reformers, or rabbis have commented on this text? have the Cistercians, or the Jesuits, commented on it? who has preached sermons on a given text? how commonly, or rarely, was a given text explicated? at what period was greatest, or least, interest shown in it? These and a host of similar questions often confront those who wish to consider seriously the exegetic tradition involving a particular biblical text — but unfortunately there has been no systematic and comprehensive way of going about answering them.

Scholars using this checklist and interested in the tradition of biblical exegesis will still have to do with card catalogues, the published catalogues of major libraries, general and specialized encyclopedias, histories of exegesis, universal and national bibliographies, and whatever other bibliographical resources one may encounter in the course of a particular investigation. The fact is that there is no standard, comprehensive bibliography of biblical commentaries. There *are*, however, a number of bibliographical works in which such information is contained and which, when used in conjunction with each other, enable one to compile a reasonably complete if not exhaustive list of patristic, medieval, and renaissance commentaries on a given biblical text. (For the "modern" period, beginning roughly in the 18th century, quite different bibliographical resources are involved, such as annual bibliographies, the inclusion of which would have

vastly expanded and complicated the present checklist and given it quite a different character. Nonetheless, no cumulative bibliography of scriptural commentaries has been deliberately excluded, so the present checklist should be of some use to persons interested in 18th- and even 19th-cent. commentaries as well.)

Many of the items listed are relatively obscure works. Although accessible in major research libraries, they have never been listed together as they are here and the fact that they contain bibliographical information on scriptural commentaries is often not apparent either from the titles of the works or their library classification. Moreover, while most of the titles can be found somewhere in Besterman's *World Bibliography of Bibliographies* or Barrow's *Bibliography of Bibliographies in Religion*[1] (see list of resources at the end of this introduction), in both of these comprehensive works the relevant items are scattered under several headings and usually incorporated within larger categories encompassing, e.g., bibliographies of editions or translations of the Bible, or of general writings about the Bible. This checklist, by comparison, is intended to lead the researcher directly to works which list commentaries specifically and list them analytically, i.e., according to biblical book commented upon.

The following entries include works which constitute or contain bibliographies of scriptural commentaries listed analytically; works giving solely alphabetical or

---

1. Theodore Besterman, *A World Bibliography of Bibliographies* (4th ed.; Lausanne: Societas Bibliographica, 1965); John G. Barrow, *A Bibliography of Bibliographies in Religion* (Ann Arbor, 1955).

chronological listings of ecclesiastical writers or commentators are therefore not included.[2] The checklist, moreover, is limited to works which are what Besterman denominates "true bibliographies": works separately published which have as a primary purpose "the list[ing] of books arranged according to some permanent principle" (I, 25/26). Thus, this portion of the bibliographical apparatus does not include works primarily expository or narrative and which contain bibliographical information only in passing — unless such works happen to contain substantially complete indices of commentaries according to biblical book.[3] Nor, with a few exceptions made because of their particular usefulness, does it include catalogues of public or private collections or sale catalogues or catalogues of exhibitions, nor works that are primarily intended as pastoral or academic "study aids."[4] Similarly omitted are the major encyclopedias, although they often contain excellent bibliographies.[5] Finally, except for a few separately published monographs, bibliographies of commentaries on only a single biblical book[6] are not included.

Works are listed in chronological order, according to first edition; subsequent editions of each work are subentries to the main entry and as such are indented; supplementary volumes or specific references to a particular volume of an edition are also indented. Titles are given in full for the first reference and in short form for subsequent editions unless the titles substantially differ. In all cases spelling and punctuation follows the original, except that

capitalization is confined to beginnings of sentences and proper names. Sources are indicated, including in most cases the column number in Besterman, the page number in Barrow, and the National Union Catalogue entry number[7] (e.g., for Crowe's *Elenchus scriptorum in sacram scripturam*, 1672: Best 754, Bar 130, and NC 0809538). Editions personally examined are marked with a dagger †. Works I have been unable to examine in any edition but which the sources indicate belong in the checklist have been placed entirely in brackets.

Following is a list of the works used in compiling the checklist and which themselves contain some sort of bibliography of bibliographies of scriptural commentaries:

Besterman, Theodore. *A World Bibliography of Bibliographies and of bibliographical catalogues, calendars, abstracts, digests, indexes, and the like. Fourth Edition/revised and greatly enlarged throughout* (Lausanne: Societas Bibliographica, 1965).

Barrow, John G. *A Bibliography of Bibliographies in Religion* (Ann Arbor, 1955).

Shunami, Shlomo. *Bibliography of Jewish Bibliographies* (2nd ed.; Jerusalem: Magnes Press, Hebrew University, 1965).

and the following older works:

Crowe, William. *Elenchus scriptorum in sacram scripturam.* London, 1672. *See* "Indiculus authorum quibus usus sum in isto Elencho," pp. A7[subscript on 7]–A8[subscript on 8].

Dagens, Jean. *Bibliographie chronologique de la littérature de spiritualité et de ses sources* (1501-1610). Paris: Desclée de Brouwer, 1952. *See* VI "Répertoires de la littérature de spiritualité" and VIII. "Bibliographie des ordres religieux" (pp. 18f.).

Darling, James. *Cyclopaedia bibliographica: a library manual of theological and general literature. . . . Subjects. Holy Scriptures.* London, 1859. *See* "Commentaries, lectures, sermons, etc.": "Bibliography," pp. 114f.

Habersaat, Karl. *Materialien zur bibliographie des Hohenliedes.* Freiburg im Breisgau, 1945. See "Bibliographie," p. 3.

Horne, Thomas Hartwell. *An introduction to the critical study and knowledge of the Holy Scriptures.* 8th ed.

---

2. Works such as St. Jerome's *De viris illustribus* or St. Isidore of Seville's *De scriptoribus ecclesiasticis.* A major collection of such works is J. A. Fabricius, *Bibliotheca ecclesiastica* (Hamburg, 1718).

3. Thus, works such as D. G. Rosenmüller's *Historia interpretationis librorum sacrorum* (5 vols.; Lipsiae, 1795-1814) or Henri de Lubac's *Exégèse mediévale* (2 parts in 4 vols.; Aubier, 1959-64) are not included, while Spicq's *Esquisse d'une histoire de l'exégèse latine au Moyen Âge* (Paris, 1944), with its "Table des commentaires bibliques," is included.

4. Works such as E. Bickersteth, *The Christian Student* (London, 1829), or Philip Schaff, *Theological Propaedeutic* (New York, 1907).

5. Attention is called especially to encyclopedias of religion, such as: *Dictionnaire de la Bible,* ed. F. Vigouroux (5 vols.; Paris, 1895-1912) and Supplement, ed. L. Pirot (1928–); *Dictionnaire de spiritualité et mystique,* ed. M. Viller, F. Cavallera, and J. de Guibert (Paris, 1937–); *Dictionnaire de théologie Catholique,* ed. A. Vacant and E. Mangenot (Paris, 1903-50); *Realenzyklopaedie für Protestantische Theologie und Kirche* (3rd ed., 24 vols.; Herzog and Hauck, 1896-1913).

6. Naturally the researcher will want to supplement the comprehensive bibliographies in this checklist with information pertaining to individual books of the Bible, such as can often be found in detailed studies such as the Anchor Bible volume on the Song of Songs: Marvin H. Pope, *Song of Songs / A New Translation with Introduction and Commentary* (Garden City, NY: Doubleday, 1977) — see Bibliographies II and III (commentaries), pp. 236-88.

---

7. *The National Union Catalog Pre-1956 Imprints / a cumulative author list representing Library of Congress printed cards and titles reported by other American libraries.* Compiled and edited with the cooperation of the Library of Congress and the National Union Catalog Subcommittee of the Resources Committee of the Resources and Technical Services Division, American Library Association (Mansell, 1968–1980). 685 vols. to date (A-Seville).

Edinburgh & Dublin, 1839. *See vol. 2, pt. II:* Bibliographical Appendix, Introduction: "General bibliographical works," pp. 1-3.

Kihn, Heinrich. *Theologische bibliothek/encyklopädie und methodologie der theologie.* Freiburg im Breisgau, 1892. *See* "Literatur," pp. 204-5.

Mayer, Jo. Frid. *Bibliotheca biblica, sive dissertationvm de notitia auctorum, pontificiorum, reformatorum & lutheranorum, immo & judeorum, qui in sacram scripturam commentarios scripserunt.* Francofvrti & Lipsiae, 1709. *See* diss. 1–diss. 3, pp. 1-46.

Mursinna, Samuel. *Primae lineae encyclopaediae theologicae in vsvm praelectionvm dvctae.* Halae Magdeburgicae, 1784. *See* "Bibliothecas exegeticas," pp. 341-42.

Petzholdt, Julius. *Bibliotheca bibliographica.* Leipzig, 1866. *See* pp. 499-507, "Bibelliteratur."

Pfaffius, Christoph. *Introductio in historiam theologiae literariam.* Tubingae, 1724. *See* Liber primus: De theologia exegetica; sect. xi (pp. 140-45).

Rivius, Albinus. *De optimis interpretibus divinorum librorum praelectiones biblicae quatuor. Coloniae Munatianae, 1783. See* "Auctores qui symbolum huc contulerunt," pp. 1-10.

Schwindel, Georg Jacob. *Bibliotheca exegetico-biblica.* Francofurti, 1734. *See* "Prolegomenon II: de notitia commentt. bibliocorvm in genere," pp. 11-19.

[Smith, Wilbur M. *A list of bibliographies of theological and biblical literature published in Great Britain and America, 1595-1931.* Coatesville, PA, 1931].

Walch, Johann Georg. *Bibliotheca theologica selecta.* 4 vols. Jenae, 1757-65. *See* Cap. octavi: "De scriptis theologiae exegeticae. Sectio vii. De interpretibus scripturae sacrae," pp. 369-76.

THE CHECKLIST

1545-55. GESNER, CONRAD. Bibliotheca vniuersalis, siue catalogus omnium scriptorum locupletissimus, in tribus linguis, latina, graeca, & hebraica: extantium & non extantiū, ueterum & recentiorum in hunc usqȝ diem, doctorum & indoctorum publicatorum & in bibliothecis latentium. Opus nouum, & nō bibliothecis tantum publicis priuatisue instituendis necessarium, sed studiosis omnibus cuisuscunqȝ artis aut scientiae ad studia melius formanda utilissimum: authore Conrado Gesnero Tigurino doctore medico. Tigvri apvd Christophervm Froschouerum mense Septembri, anno M.D.XLV.

v. 2: Pandectarvm sive partitionum uniuersalium Conradi Gesneri Tigurini, medici & philosophiae professoris, libri XXI. Tigvri, M.D.XLVIII.

v. 4: Appendix Bibliothecae Conradi Gesneri. Tigvri, M.D.LV. *Bound with this is:* v. 3 Partitiones theologicae, pandectarum vniuersalium Conradi Gesneri liber ultimus. . . . Accedit index alphabeticus praesenti libro &

superioribus XIX. communis, qui tertii tomi olim promissi uicem explebit. Tiguri, M.D.XLIX. *See* Titulus II: "Continet Biblica, ad sacram scripturam et utrumque." † Best 803 Bar 1 NG 0178685-91

See supplements:

Elenchvs scriptorvm omnivm. . . . per Conradvm Lycosthenem. Basileae, 1551. Best 803 NG 0178736

Epitome Bibliothecae Conradi Gesneri . . . per Iosiam Simlerum Tigvrinvm. Tiguri, 1555. Best 803 NG 0178681

Bibliotheca institvta et collecta primvm a Conrado Gesnero . . . per Iosiam Simlerum. Tigvri, 1574. Best 803 NG 0178679

Bibliotheca institvta. . . . per Iohannen Iacobum Frisium. Tigvri, 1583. Best 803 NG 0178681

Svpplementvm epitomes bibliothecae Gesnerianae . . . . Antonio Verderio. Lvgdvni, 1585. Best 804 ND 0466204

1558. [[[Witzel, Georg]] Elenchvs theologorvm in tota sacra biblia. Coloniae, apud Maternum Cholinum, 1558.] Bar 1

1564. THEOPHILUS, G. Catalogus avtorvm omnivm qvotqvot in sacros biblicos libros aliquid commenti aut elucubrati sunt: nec ueterum tantùm, sed & recentiorum, quum typis euulgatorum, tum in priuatis bibliothecis latitantium, nunc denuō auctus & editus per G. Theophilum italum. Argentorati, ex Iosiae Rihelij officina, anno 1564. Best 771 Bar 127 NT 0142274

[another edition] Catalogus avthorum omnivm qvi in sacros biblicos libros Veteris & Noui Testamenti scripserunt: iam iterum, post G. Theophili itali aeditionem . . . auctus. Argentorati, 1572. Best 771 NT 0142270-71

[another edition] Catalogvs avthorvm qvi in sacros biblicos libros Veteris & Noui Testamenti scripserunt . . . . VVitebergae, 1575. NT 0142272

[another edition] Catalogvs avthorvm qvi in sacros biblicos libros Veteris et Noui Testamenti scripserunt: iam iterum, post G. Theophili itali aeditionem, ex varijs bibliothecis collectus, & plus quadringentis authoribus, recentioribus maximè, auctus, atqȝ in commune Christianorum commodum diuulgatus. B. Hieronymvs. . . . V-Vitebergae anno M.D.LXXVIII. † Best 771 Bar 128 NT 0142273

1566. SIXTUS SENENSIS [Sisto da Siena]. Bibliotheca sancta a F. Sixto Senensi . . . ex praecipuis catholicae ecclesiae authoribus, & in octo libros digesta. . . . Venetiis, apud Franciscum Franciscium Senensen, 1566. *2 vols.* NS 0586125

Other editions as follows:

. . . . Bibliotheca sancta. . . . Venetiis, apud Franciscum Franciscium, M.D.LXXIIII. NS 0586126

. . . . Bibliotheca sancta a F. Sixto Senensi, Ordinis praedicatorum, ex praecipuis catholicae ecclesiae autoribus collecta, & in octo libros digesta; quorum inscriptiones equens pagina indicabit. Adiectus est rerum notatu dignissimarum index locupletissimus, triplici ordine distinctus. Ad sanctiss. Pium V. Opt. Max. Tomus primvs [-secvndvs]. Lugdvni, apvd Carolvm Pesnot. M.D.LXXV. *2 vols. See v. 1:* Liber quartus, "De catholicis divinorum voluminum expositoribus." Bar 127 NS 0586128

. . . . Francofvrti, 1575. NS 0586127

. . . . Venetiis, 1575. NS 0586129

. . . . Secvnda editio. Coloniae, M.D.LXXVI. *See* "Index locorvm divinae Scripturae, quos diversi autores ob varias occasiones, sive obiter, sive ex professo, tractarvnt." Bar 127 NS 0586130

. . . . Editio tertia. Coloniae, 1586. Bar 128 NS 0586131

. . . . Nunc verò à Ioanne Hayo, Scoto, Societatis Iesv, plurimis in locis à mendis expurgata, atque scholiis illustrata. Lvgdvni, M.D.XCI. Bar 128 NS 0586132

. . . . Lvgdvni, 1592. NS 0586134

. . . . Lvgdvni, M.D.XCIII. Bar 128 NS 0586135

. . . . Paris, 1610. NS 0586136

. . . . Postmodvm a reverendo Societ. Isv Patre Ionne Haymo Scoto, revisa, scholiisqve illvstrata. Vltima demvm hac editione avctorvm recentiorvm accessione locupletata, plurimisq3 in locis tam hebraicis quam Graecis a mendis expurgata. Coloniae Agrippinae, ex officina Choliniana, sumptibus Petri Cholini. Anno M.DC.XXVI † Bar 128 NS 0586137

. . . . Fr. Sixti Senensis. . . Bibliotheca sancta criticis, ac theologicis animadversionibus, nec non duplici adjecto Sacrorum Scriptorum elencho adsucta et inlustrata a Fr. Pio-Thoma Milante. Neapoli, ex typ. Mutiana, 1742. NS 0586138

1591. [ZANACH, JAKOB. Bibliotheca theologica, siue catalogvs tam avtorvm, qvi in sacros biblicos libros veteris et noui testamenti in hunc usq3 annum scripserunt, quam materiarum, quarum auctores non extant, non solum ex Bibliotheca Gesneriana, quae anno 1583, prodijt. Mvlhvsii, 1591.] Best 771 Bar 128

[another edition: Elenchus alphabeticus. Avtorvm et scriptorvm, qvi in sacro sanctos libros biblicos, uvque in hunc annum commentati sunt. Servestae, 1606.] Bar 128

[another edition: . . . . Zerbst, 1608.] Bar 128

1595. MAUNSELL, ANDREW. The first part of the catalogue of English printed bookes: which concerneth such matters of diuinitie, as haue bin either written in our owne tongue, or translated out of anie other language: and haue bin published, to the glory of God, and edification of the Church of Christ in England. Gathered into alphabet, and such method as it is, by Andrew Maunsell, bookseller. London, printed by Iohn VVindet for Andrew Maunsell. 1595 † Best 2006 Bar 2 NM 0350504-08

1608. [BESODNERUS, PETRUS. Bibliotheca theologica, hoc est, index bibliorum praecipuorum, eorundemq3 interpretum, hebraeorum, graecorum, et latinorum, tam veterum, qvam recentiorum. Francofurti Marchionum, [[1608]] .] Best 771 Bar 3 NB 0388540

1608. [RIVADENEIRA, PEDRO DE. Illustrium scriptorum religionis Societatis Iesv catalogus. Antverpiae, 1608. Best 3260 Bar 249 NR 0304077

[another edition] Illustrium scriptorum. . . . secunda editione. Lvgdvni, 1609. Best 3261 Bar 249 NR 0304078

[another edition] Catalogvs scriptorvm religionis Societatis Iesv. . . . Secvnda editio, plurimorum scriptorum accessione locupletior. Antverpiae, 1613. Best 3261 Bar 249 NR 0304034

[another edition] Bibliotheca scriptorvm Societatis Iesv, post excusum anno M.DC.VIII. Catalogum R. P. Ribadeneirae societatis eivsdem theologi; nunc hoc nouo apparatu librorum ad annum reparatae salutis M.DC.XLII. editorum concinnata, & illustrium virorum elogiis adornata, a Philippo Alegambe Brvxellensi ex eadem societate Iesv. Accedit catalogus religiosorum Societatis Iesu, qui hactenus pro Catholicâ fide & pietate in variis mundi plagis interempti sunt. Antverpiae apud Ioannem Mevrsivm. Anno M.DC.XLIII. *See* "Index materiarvm. I. Sacra Scriptura," pp. 483f. † Best 3261 Bar 249 NR 0304028-30

[another edition] Bibliotheca scriptorvm Societatis Iesv. . . . Continvatvm a R. P. Philippo Alegambe ex eadem societate, vsque ad annum 1642. Recognitum, & productum ad annum Iubiliae M.DC.LXXV. a Nathanaele Sotvello. Romae, 1676. Best 3261 Bar 249 NR 0304031-32

1612. JUSTINIANUS, FABIANUS. Index vniversalis alphabeticvs materias in omni facultate consulto pertractas, earumq3; scriptores, & locos designans, appendice perampla locupletatus. Elenchus item avtorvm qvi in Sacra Biblia vel vniuerse, vel singulatim, etiam in versiculos, data opera, scripserunt. Romae, 1612. Best 771 NJ 0203268-69

[another edition] De Sacra Scriptura eivsque vsv, ac interpretibus commentarivs. In quo non solum ad sacrorum Bibliorum studium, et sacras conciones formandas institutio traditur: sed etiam selectorum librorum in vniuersam theologiam speculatiuā, practicam, et positiuam, singularis; et in tota sacram scriptura vniuersalis notifia perhibetur. Romae, 1614. † NJ 0203267

1613. BELLARMINO, S. ROBERTO. De scriptoribvs ecclesiasticis liber vnus. Cvm adivnctis indicibvs vndecim, & breui chronologia ab orbe condito vsque ad annum M.DC.XII. Romae, 1613. Best 6082 Bar 3 NB 0283692-94

Other editions as follows:

. . . . Coloniae Agrippinae, 1613. Bar 3 NB 0283689
. . . . Editio recognita, & ab autore ipso auctior facta. Lugduni, 1613. Best 6082 Bar 3 NB 0283690
. . . . Editio noua ab auctore aucta & recognita. Lvtetiae Parisiorvm, 1617. Best 6082 Bar 3 NB 0283695
. . . . Coloniae Agrippinae, 1622. NB 0283696
. . . . Parisiis, 1630. NB 0283697
. . . . Ultimo editio, ab auctore aucta & recognita. Lvtetiae Parisiorvm, 1631. † Best 6082 Bar 4 NB 0283699. *Also* Coloniae Agrippinae, 1631. NB 0283698
. . . . Vltima editio ab auctore aucta & recognita. Lvtetiae Parisiorvm, 1644. Best 6082 Bar 4
. . . . Coloniae Agrippinae, 1645. NB 0283700
. . . . Coloniae Agrippinae, 1657. Best 6082 NB 0283702
. . . . Vltima editio à mendis praecedentium sedulò ac diligenter expurgata. Cum appendice philologica & chronologica R. P. Philippi Labbe. Parisiis, 1658. Best 6082 Bar 5 NB 0283703
. . . . Parisiis, 1660. Best 6082
. . . . Editio ultima. Lugduni, 1663. Best 6082 Bar 5 NB 0283704
[supplement] Insignis libri de scriptoribus ecclesiasticis, eminentissimi Cardinalis Bellarmini continuatio, ab anno 1500, in quo desinit, ad annum 1600, quo incipit sequentis saeculi exordium. Auctore Andrea Du Saussay. Tulli Leucorum, 1665. Bar 6 ND 0458557
. . . . Editio ultima. Lvgdvni, 1675. Bar 6 NB 0283705
. . . . Editio sexta. Lovanii, 1678. Best 6082 Bar 6
. . . . Coloniae, 1684. Best 6082 Bar 7 NB 0283707
[supplement] Supplementum de scriptoribus vel scriptis ecclesiasticis a Bellarmino omissis, ad annum 1460. . . . Collectore F. Casimiro Ovdin. Parisiis, 1686. Bar 7 NO 0168375
. . . . Venetiis, 1697. NB 0283709
. . . . Editio novissima prioribus emendatior & plurimus scriptoribus, juxta exempla ab ipso auctore quondam recognitum, auctior, ac ampliatione chronologiae usque ad annum M.DCC.XVIII. Bruxellis, 1719. Best 6082 Bar 17 NB 0283710
. . . . Venetiis, 1728. NB 0283711

1614. [BOLDUANUS, PAULUS. Bibliotheca theologica, sive: elenchus scriptorum ecclesiasticorum illustrium, rabinorum, patrum, protestantium, Calvinianorum, & pontificiorum qui in sacros biblicos libros. . . commentati sunt, secundum seriem & ordinem librorum sacrorum. Lipsiae & Jenae, 1614.] Best 6083 Bar 3 NB 0608507
[another edition: . . . . Lipsiae, 1622.] Best 6083

1618. MOLANUS, JOHANNES. Bibliotheca materiarvm qvae a qvibvs avctoribvs, cvm antiquis, tum recentioribus sint pertractatae. Docentibus, concionantibus, ac scriptoribus pernecessaria. Accedunt catologi dvo: I. Catholicorvm S. Scriptvrae interpretum; biblicorum librorum ordine. II. Scholasticorvm theologorvm in Diui Thomae Aquinatis Summam. Coloniae Agrippinae apud Ioannem Kinchivm sub Monocerote. Anno M.DC.XVIII. *See the catalogue by Andreas Schott:* Catalogvs Catholicorvm S. Scripturae interpretvm, serie librorvm biblicorvm, studio Andreae Schotti. Coloniae Agrippinae, M.DC.XVIII. † Best 772 Bar 4 NM 0681565

1635. OXFORD UNIVERSITY. BODLEIAN LIBRARY. Catalogvs interpretvm S. Scripturae, ivxta nvmerorvm ordinem, qvo extant in Bibliotheca Bodleiana olim a D. Iamesio in vsum theologorum concinnatus, nunc vero altera fere parte auctior redditus. Accessit elenchus authorum, tam recentium quam antiquorum, qui in quatuor libros sententiarum & Th. Aquinatis Summas, item in Euangelia Dominicalia totius anni, & de casibus conscientiae; nec non in orationem Dominicam, Symbolum Apostolorum, & Decalogum scripserunt. Editio correcta, diu multumq͗ desiderata. Oxoniae, excudebat Iohannes Lichfield, Academiae Typographus. A° Dom. 1635. [*Based on pp. 163-79 of Thomas James's Bodleian Catalogus, Oxford, 1605, by Jean Verneuil.*] † Best 772 Bar 129

1637. VERNEUIL, JEAN. A nomenclator of such tracts and sermons as have beene printed or translated into English upon any place of holy scripture. Oxford, 1637. Best 5706 NV 0117442-43
[another edition] A nomenclator of such tracts and sermons as have beene printed, or translated into English upon any place or booke of Holy Scripture. Now to be had in the most famous and publique library of Sr. Thomas Bodley in Oxford. Operâ, studio, & impensis Ioh. Vernulii, A.M. Editio secunda correctior, & duplo auctior. Oxford, printed by Henry Hall. 1642. † Best 5706 Bar 129 NV 0117445-46

1646. WILKENS, JOHN. Ecclesiastes; or, a discourse concerning the gift of preaching, as it falls under the rules of art. London, 1646. Bar 4 NW 0309927

Other editions as follows:

.... The second edition. London, 1647. *See* subject lists, pp. 65f. Bar 4 NW 0309928-30

.... The third edition. London, 1651. *See* "The table," pp. 134f. Bar 4 NW 2309931

.... The fourth edition. London, 1653. *See* "Commentators upon the books of Scripture," pp. 43-63. † Bar 4 NW 0309933

.... The fifth edition. London, 1656. NW 0309935

.... London, 1659. Bar 5 NW 0309937

.... The fifth impression, corrected and enlarged. London, 1669. Bar 6 NW 0309938

.... The sixth impression, corrected and enlarged. London, 1675. Bar 6 NW 0309939

.... London, 1679. NW 0309940

.... The seventh edition, corrected and much enlarged. London, 1693. Bar 12 NW 0309941

.... The eighth edition, corrected and much enlarged. London, 1704. Bar 14 NW 0309942

.... The ninth edition, corrected and much enlarged. London, 1718. Bar 17 NW 0309944

[German translation]. Ecclesiastes; oder, Discurs von der gube zu predigen &c. darinnen überhaupt die englische predigermethode und gantze theologie, nebst denen berichten von dennen uebersetzungen, concordentzen, auslegern &c. der Bibel grundlich vergetragen wird; nach der letzen englischen aufl. ins Teutsche übersetzet und ... versehen von Heinrich Ittershagen. Leipzig, Martini, 1718. NW 0309943

1650. WADDING, LUKE. Scriptores ordinis minorvm. Qvibvs accessit syllabvs illorvm, qui ex eodem ordine pro fide Christi fortiter occubuerunt. Priores atramento, posteriores sangvine Christianam religionem asseruerunt. Recenvit Fr. Lvcas VVaddingvs, eiusdem instituti theologus. Romae, M.DC.L. *See* "Index materiarum. In Biblia." Best 2320 Bar 246 NW 0005221-22

[another edition] Scriptores ordinis minorum. Romae, 1806. Best 2320 Bar 247 NW 0005223

[another edition] .... Editio novissima. Romae, 1906. Best 2320 Bar 247 NW 0005217-25

Supplements published 1806 and 1908-36. Best 2320 Bar 247 NW 0005223, -25, -26

1663. CROWE, WILLIAM. An exact collection or catalogue of our English writers on the Old and New Testament, either in whole, or in part: whether commentators, elucidators, adnotators, or expositors, at large or in single sermons. Very useful for anyone's information as to what hath been writ upon any part of the Holy Scriptures. London, printed by R. Davenport for John Williams, 1663. Best l772 Bar 129 NC 0809539

[another edition] The catalogue of our English writers on the Old and New Testament .... Corrected and enlarged with three or four thousand additionals. The second impression. London, printed by E. Cotes for Thomas Williams, 1668. † Best 772 Bar 129 NC 0809537

1664. HOTTINGER, JOHANN HEINRICH. Bibliothecarivs quadripartitvs. I. pars, quae prolegomenis absolvitur, agit de officio bibliothecarij, bibliothecis, *c. II. De theologia biblica. III. De theologia patristica. .... IV. De theologia topica; symbolica, & systematica; tam universali, quam particulari. Tiguri, M DC LXIV. *See* Partis II. caput vi: "De exegetica reali, sive theologica." † Best 6084 Bar 5 NH 0540697

1671. [SPRINGINSGUTH, DANIEL. Aurifodina biblica, exhibens catalogum locupletissimum auctorum, qui ab ipsis inde ecclesiae incunabulis Sacrae Scripturae editiones ejusque expositiones procurarunt, itemque consilia varia de studio exegetico. Stralsund, 1671.] Bar 129

1672. CROWE, WILLIAM. Elenchus scriptorum in sacram scripturam tam graecorum, quam latinorum, &c. In quo exhibentur eorum gens, patria, professio religio: librorum tituli, volumina, editiones variae. Quo tempore claruerint vel obierint. Elogia item aliquot virorum clarissimorum. Quibus omnibus praemissa sunt S. Biblia, partesque Bibliorvm, variis linguis, variis vocibus edita. Opera & industria Guil. Crowaei. Londini, 1672. *See* "Cognominum scriptorum. Index," pp. 344ff. Best 754 Bar 130 NC 0809538

1674. [DORSCH, JOHANN GEORG. Biblia numerata seu index specialis, in omnes Veteris et Novi Testamenti libros. Ad singula omnium librorum capita & commata. Francofurti, 1674. *2 vols.*] ND 0342697

1677. [KEMPE, MARTIN VON. Charismatum sacrorum trias, sive, bibliotheca anglorum theologica. .... Regiomonti, impensis Martini Hallervordii, 1677.] NK 0088631

1680. DIONIGI DA GENOVA. Bibliotheca scriptorvm ordinis minorum S. Francisci Capvccinorvm a fratre Dionysio Genvensi eiusdem ordinis professore contexta. Illustriorumque virorum elogiis adornata. Cum indice materiarum, quas ijdem Capuccini scriptores illustrarunt, cui accedit cathalogus omnium provinciarum, conventuum, missionum, ac religiosorum, qui sunt in vnaquaque provincia; prout numerabantur anno 1678. Ad reverendiss. patrem Bernardvm à Portv Mavritio totius ordinis S. Francisci Capuccinorum ministrum generalem. Genvae, ex typographia Antonij Georgij Franchelli, de superiorum consensu, 1680. Bar 242 ND 0279183

[another edition] Bibliotheca scriptorum ordinis minorum S. francisci Capucinorum. .... In hac secunda editione accuratius coordinata, & ultra decentorum scriptorum elucu brationibus locupletata, & aucta. . . . ad 1685. Ad illustriss.^{um} ac reverendiss.^{vm} D. D. Io. Hieronymum de Avria episcopum Nebiensem. Genevae, ex typographia Ioannis baptistae Scionici. Superiorum permissu. 1691. Best 1135 Bar 242 ND 0279184

[revised edition] Bibliotheca scriptorum ordinis minorum S. francisci Capuccinorum retexta & extensa a F. Bernardo a Bononia ibidem sac. theologiae lectore Capuccino: quae prius fuerat a P. Dionysio Genuensi eiusdem ordinis concionatore contexta. Ad sanctissimum Patrem Benedictum XIV. pontificem optimum maximum. Venetiis. MDCCXLVII. Apud Sebastianum Coleti superiorum permissu ac privilegio. *See* "Index omnium materierum, de quibus hujus bibliotheca scriptores agunt. . . In S. Scripturam." † Best 1135 Bar 242 ND 0279185-87

[supplement] Catalogus scriptorum Ordinis minorum S. Francisci Cappuccinorum ab anno 1747 usque ad annum 1852. Romae, 1852. Best 1135 Bar 242

1682. WITTE, HENNING. Reportorium biblicum. Frankfort, 1682. Bar 130

[another edition]: Repertorium biblicum in qvo ex variis tam orthodoxorum qvam aliarum qvoqve religionum ac nationum scriptis vernacula in primis nostra extantibus materiae qvaecunqve maxime morales & practicae juxta capita & versus biblicos ubertim indicantur & recensentur. Editio secunda. Rigae, 1689. Bar 130

1686-91. DUPIN, LOUIS ELLIES. Nouvelle bibliothèque des auteurs ecclésiastiques. Contenant l'histoire de leur vie, le catalogue, la critique, et la chronologie de leurs ouvrages. Le sommaire de ce qu'ils continiennent. Un jugement sur leur stile, et sur leur doctrine. Et le dénombrement des differentes éditions de leurs ouvrages. Paris, 1686-91. *5 vols. bound as 6: fully indexed.* Bar 7

Note: "Most sets of Dupin found today are made up of various editions of the different volumes: and some libraries have the whole series of related works together as one set" (Barrow, p. 7).

Other editions and sets as follows:

. . . . Seconde édition revve, corrigé. Paris, 1688-91. *5 vols. bound as 6: only vols. 1-4 are 2nd edition.* Bar 8

. . . . Seconde édition. Paris, 1688-98. *12 vols. in 15.* ND 0444178

. . . . Seconde [dernière] édition reveue & corrigée. Paris/Mons/Amsterdam, 1690-1715. *19 vols., variously bound.* Bar 9 ND 0444180-82

. . . . Troisième édition revue & corrigée. Paris, 1693-

1715. *19 vols., most volumes same as preceding.* Bar 9 ND 0444185

[Latin translation] Nova bibliotheca auctorum ecclesiasticorum. Paris and Cologne, 1692-93. *3 vols. bound as one.* Bar 10 ND 0444189

[English translation] A new history of ecclesiastical writers: containing an account of the authors of the several books of the Old and New Testament; of the lives and writings of the primitive fathers; an abridgment and catalogue of their works; their various editions and censures, determining the genuine and spurious. Together with a judgment upon their style and doctrine. Also a compendious history of the councils; with chronological tables of the whole. [Translated by W. Wotton]. The second edition, corrected. London, 1693-95. 7 vols. ND 0444153

[another edition of the English translation] . . . . London, 1696. *8 vols.* ND 0444154

[another edition of the English translation] . . . . The third edition, corrected. London, 1693-99. *13 vols., bound as 5: v. 1 is 1696. Fully indexed, e.g., v. 1:* "A table of all the genuine extant writings of the ecclesiastical authors, according to the order of their arguments, that are mentioned in this volume. . . . Commentaries and discourses upon the Holy Scripture." † Bar 10 ND 0444175

[supplementary series, 16th cent.] Histoire de l'église et des auteurs ecclésiastiques du seiziè'me siècle. Paris, 1701-03. *5 vols.* Bar 13 ND 0444140

[another edition of the English translation] . . . . London, 1695-1703. *14 vols. bound as 4: tome 15 also separately published:*

A new ecclesiastical history of the 16th cent. London, 1703, 1706. 2 vols. † Bar 14 ND 0444173

[another edition of the English translation] . . . . The third edition, corrected. Dublin, 1723-24. *3 vols.* † ND 0444177

[epitome] Table universelle des auteurs ecclésiastiques, disposez par ordre chronologique, et de leurs ouvrages veritable ou supposez. Paris, 1704. *5 vols.: see v. 5:* "Table des principaux ouvrages des auteurs ecclésiastiques, disposez par ordre des matères." Bar 14

[supplementary volumes, 17th cent.] Bibliothèque des auteurs ecclésiastiques du dix-septiè'me siècle. Paris, 1708. *7 vols.* Bar 15 ND 0444113

[supplementary volumes, 18th century] Bibliothèque des auteurs ecclésiastiques du dix-huitiè'me siècle. Paris, 1711. *2 vols.* Bar 15 ND 0444114

[supplementary volumes] Bibliothèque des auteurs séparez de la communion de l'Église Romaine, du XVI. et du XVII. siècle. Paris, 1718-19. *2 vols., bound as 4.* Bar 16 ND 0444116

[another edition of 17th-cent. series] Histoire ecclési-

astique du dix-septième siècle. Paris, 1714. *4 vols.*
Bar 16 ND 0444151

[English translation of 17th-cent. series] A new ecclesiastical history of the seventeenth century; containing an account of the controversies in religion; the lives and writings of ecclesiastical authors, an abridgment of their works, and a judgment on their style and doctrine; also a compendious history of all affairs transacted in the church. . . . Translated and illustrated with additional annotations, by Digby Cotes. Oxford, 1725. Bar 18 ND 0444171

[another edition of 17th-cent. series] Histoire ecclésiastique du dix-septième siècle. Paris, 1727. *4 vols.* Bar 18

[another edition of the whole] Bibliothèque des auteurs ecclésiastiques. Paris, 1730. ND 0444115

[another edition] Nouvelle bibliotheque. Utrecht, 1731. ND 0444187

[supplement to 18th-cent. series] Bibliothèque des auteurs ecclésiastiques du dix-huitiè'me siècle. Pour servir de continuation a celle de M. Du-Pin. Par M. l'Abbe Goujet. Paris, 1736. Bar 20

1691. MABILLION, JEAN. Traite des études monastiques, divise en trois parties; avec une liste des principales difficultéz qui se recontrent en chaque siècle dans la lecture des originaux, & un catalogue de livres choisis pour composer une bibiotèque ecclesiastique. Paris, 1691. *See* "Catalogue des meilleurs livres avec les meileures éditions, pour composer une bibliothèque ecclésiastique," pp. 425-76. Bar 10 NM 0006467

[another edition] . . . . Seconde édition revue & corigée. Paris and Bruxelles, 1692. Bar 10 NM 0006468-69

[Latin translation] Tractatus de studiis monasticis. . . . Nunc autem in Latinam linguam translatus a R. P. Udalrico Staudigl. . . . Juxta secundam editionem revisam & correctam. Campoduni, 1702. *See* "Catalogus librorum, cum melioris notae, tum meliorum editionum ad instruendam rite bibliothecam ecclesiasticum." Bar 14 NM 0006457

Other editions of the Latin as follows:

. . . . Latine versus a P. D. Josepho Porta, Astensi. Venitiis, 1705. 2 vols. bound as one. See "Catalogus," pp. 547-630. Bar 14 NM 0006458

. . . . Editio secunda. Venitiis, 1729-32. *3 cols.: see v. 1:* "Bibliotheca ecclesiastica Mabillonica," pp. 295-353. Bar 19 NM 0006459-461

. . . . Editio altera. Venetiis, 1745. *3 vols.: see v. 1:* "Bibliotheca ecclesiastica Mabillonica," pp. 295-348. † Bar 21 NM 0006464

. . . . Venetiis, 1765. *2 vols. in one.* NM 0006465

. . . . Editio tertia veneta. Venetiis, 1770. *3 vols. in one.* Bar 23 NM 0006466

[Spanish translation] Tratado de los estudios monasticos. . . . Y traducido en Castellano de Valladolid. Madrid, 1779.

1709. LE LONG, JACQUES. Bibliotheca sacra sev syllabvs omnivm ferme sacrae scriptvrae editionvm ac versionvm secundum seriem linguarum quibus vulgate sunt notis historicis et criticis illvstratvs adiunctis praestantissimis codd. msc. Labore & industria Jacobi Le Long, Parisini, congregationis oratorii. . . .Totum opus cum additamentis, suo loco in nova hac editione collocatis, recesuit & castigavit, novis praeterea editionibus, versionibus, codd. mss. notisque auxit Christianvs Fridericvs Boernervs. . . . Antverpiae sumptibus Joh. Lvov. Gleditschii et Mavr. Georg. Weidmanni. M.DCC.IX. *Also Lipsiae; title page varies slightly, 2 vols., sometimes bound as one.* † Best 755 Bar 130 NL 0237697

[another edition] Bibliotheca sacra in binos syllabos distincta, quorum prior qui jam tertio auctior prodit, omnes sive textus sacri sive versionum ejusdem quâvis linguâ expressarum editiones; nec non praestantiores mss. codices, cum notis historicis & criticis exhibet. Posterior vero continet omnia eorum opera quovis idiomate conscripta, qui huc usque in sacram scripturam quidpiam ediderunt, simul collecta tum ordine auctorum alphabetico disposita; tum serie sacrorum librorum. Huic corondis loco subjiciuntur grammaticae et lexica linguarum, praesertim orientalium, quae ad illustrandas sacras paginas aliquid adjumenti conferre possunt. . . . Tomus primus [-secundus]. ·Parisiis, apud F. Montalant. . . . M.DCC.XXIII. *2 vols. bound as one: see* "Bibliothecae sacrae posterioris syllabi. Pars secunda," pp. 1029f. † Best 755 Bar 131 NL 0237695

[another edition] Bibliotheca sacra, post cl. cl. vv. Jacobi Le Long et C. F. Boerneri iteratis cvras ordine disposita, emendata, svppleta continvata ab Andrea Gottlieb Masch. . . . Halae. 1778-90. *5 vols., bound as 3.* Best 755 Bar 134 NL 0237696

1711. [COMPENDIEVSE priester-bibliothec, worinnen . . . die meisten alten und neuen commentarii . . . nach denen religionen . . . richtig recensiret werden. Jena, 1711.] Best 772 NC 0599499

1714-21. CARPZOV, JOHANN GOTTLOB. Introductio ad libros biblicos veteris testamenti omnes, praecognita critica et historica, ac avtoritatis vindicias exponens. Lipsiae, 1721. *3 vols. bound as one: pt. 1:* Introductio ad libros historicos, 1714. † NC 0155856-57

[another edition] Introductio ad libros canonicos bibliorum veteris testamenti omnes. . . . . Editio secunda. Lipsiae, 1727-31. *3 vols. bound as one.* † NC 0155858

[another edition] Introductio ad libros canonicos

bibliorum veteris testamentis omnes. Lipsiae, 1741. NC 0155859

[another edition] Introductio ad libros canonicos bibliorum veteris testamenti omnes. . . . Editio quarta. Lipsiae, 1757. NC 0155860

1721. [WENDLER, JOHANN CHRISTOPH. Prodromvs bibliothecae biblicae perfectioris, exhibens historiam criticam commentatorvm in Epistolas Pavlinas. . . . Jenae, 1721.] Best 780 Bar 156

1719-21. QUÉTIF, JACQUES. Scriptores ordinis praedicatorum recensiti, notisque historicis et criticis illustrati, opus quo singulorum vita, praeclareque gesta referuntur, chronologia insuper, seu tempus quo quisque floruit certo statuitur: fabulae exploduntur: scripta genuina, dubia, supposititia expenduntur: recentiorum de iis judicium aut probatur, aut emendatur: codices manuscripti, variaeque e typis editiones, & ubi habeantur, indicantur: alumni dominicani, quos alieni rapuerant, vindicantur, dubii, & extranei, falseque ascripti ad cujusque seculi finem rejiciuntur, & suis restituuntur: praemittitur in prolegomenis notitia ordinis qualis fuit ab initio ad an. MD. Tum series capitulorum generalium iis annis habitorum, denique index eorum qui ad ecclesiasticas dignitates promoti fuerunt, vel in hoc tomo laudatorum, vel alias ab aliis omissorum. inchoavit R. P. F. Jacobus Quetif S. T. P. absolvit R. P. F. Jacobus Echard ambo conventus SS. Annunciationis Parisiensis ejusdem ordinis alumni. Tomus primus [secundus]. Lutetiae Parisiorum, apud J-B-Christophorum Ballard. . . . M.DCC.XIX [-M.DCC.XXI]. See "Index materiarum quos ordinis praedicatorum scriptores illustrarunt. Sacra Scriptura. Qui in sacra biblia commentarios scripserunt," pp. 942-48. Best 1653 Bar 244 NQ 0016550-53

>   [facsimile edition] Scriptores ordinis praedicatorum. . . . Burt Franklin Bibliographical and Reference Series #16. New York: Burt Franklin, 1959. 2 vols. bound as 4. †
>   [another edition] Scriptores ordinis praedicatorum. . . . Editio altera emendata, plurimis accessionibus aucta, et ad hanc nostram aetatem perducta cruis et labore Fr. Thomae Bonnet. . . . Lugduni, excudebat Xaverius Jevain, typographus. 1885. Best 1654 Bar 245
>   [supplement] Scriptores ordinis praedicatorum. . . . Curis et labore Fr. Remigii Coulon. . . . Parisiis, apud Alphonsum Picard. . . . MCMX [-MCMXXXIV]. 12 fascicles. Best 1654 Bar 245 NQ 0016555

1723. [DORN, JOHANN CHRISTOPH. Bibliothecae theologicae criticae pars secvnda, qvam secvndvm singvlas divinioris scientiae partes disposavit atqve instrvxit. Francofvrti et Lipsiae, 1723.] Best 6121 Bar 17 ND 0340817

1724. LANGE, JOACHIM. Instituvtiones studii theologici litterariae: quibvs, methodologia de stvdiorvm sacrorum ordine, svbsidiis ac impedimentis praemissa, et monitis ac consiliis litterariis passim inspersis, notitia librorvm, praecipve selectorvm, in singvlis theologiae partibvs exhibetvr. Halae Magdebvrgicae, 1724. See: "Sectio qvinta. De bibliognosia stvdii exegetici," pp. 381f. † Bar 18 Best 6088 NL 0078833

1725. [ALARD, NICOLAUS. Bibliotheca harmonicobiblica, quae praeter historiam harmonicam tradit notitiam scriptorum harmonicorum cujuscunque aetatis et religionis, tam perpetuorum quam singularium. Hamburgi, 1725.] Best 772 Bar 131

1722-28. CALMET, AUGUSTIN. Dictionnaire historique, critique, chronologique, géographique et littéral de la Bible. Paris, 1722-28. 4 vols. See v.1, i-cviii: "Bibliothèque sacrée." NC 0053489

Other editions as follows:

>   2e édition. Geneve, 1730. *4 vols. bound in 2.* NC 0053490
>   . . . . Nouvelle édition. Paris, 1730. 4 vols. NC 0053491
>   . . . .4e édition. Paris, 1845-46. NC 00553492
>   . . . . Dixième édition. Paris, 1863. NC 0053493
>   [Latin translation] Dictionarium historicum criticum, chronologicum, geographicum, et literale sacrae scripturae; e gallico in latinum translatum. Lucae, 1725. 2 vols. NC 0053457

Other editions of the Latin translation as follows:

>   . . . .Venetiis, 1726. Petzholdt
>   . . . Lucensi, 1729-36. *4 vols. bound as 2. See v. 1, pp. 1-68:* "Bibliotheca sacra, sive catalogus optimorum librorum studio Sacrae Scripturae servientium." † NC 0053459
>   . . . .Venetiis, 1734. NC 0053460
>   . . . Augustae Vindelicorum, 1738. NC 0053461
>   . . . .Venetiis, 1747. NC 0053462
>   . . . .Venetiis, 1756. NC 0053463
>   . . . Augustae Vindelicorum, 1759. Petzholdt
>   . . . .Venetiis, 1766. NC 0053464
>   . . . Augustae Vindelicorum, 1776. NC 0053465
>   . . . Augustae Vindelicorum, 1790. Petzholdt
>   English translation *Dictionary of the Holy Bible.* Trans. John Colson and Samuel d'Oyley. London, 1732. *3 vols.*
>   another English translation *Calmet's Dictionary of the Holy Bible.* Trans. C. Taylor. London, 1797-1801. NC 0053467
>   *Numerous subsequent English and American editions of the English translation of Calmet's Dictionary*

(see NC 0053468-486); *but the English translation does not include the "Bibliotheca sacra." Petzholdt records a Dutch translation* (Leyden, 1725) *and a German translation* (Liegnitz, 1751-54 *and* Hanover, 1779-81).

1727. BUDDEUS, JOHANN FRANZ. Isagoge historico-theologica ad theologiam vniversam singvlasqve eivs partes. Lipsiae, 1727. NB 0922928-929

[another edition] . . . . novis svpplementis avctior. Lipsiae, 1730. *See* "Libri posterioris capvt octavvm de theologia exegetica," pp. 1240f. and "Index II. Rervm." *2 vols.* † NB 0922930

1715-33. WOLF, JOHANN CHRISTOPH. Bibliotheca hebraea, sive notitia tvm avctorvm hebr. cvjvscvnqve aetatis, tvm scriptorvm, qvae vel hebraice primvm exarata vel ab aliis conversa svnt, ad nostram aetatem, dedvcta. Accedit in calce Jacobi Gaffarelli index codicum cabbalistic. mss. quibus Jo. Picus, mirandulanus comes, usus est. Hamburgi & Lipsiae, 1715-33. *4 vols. (title page varies): see v. 4:* "Index II. Rervm in toto opere potiorvm." † Best 2825 Bar 107 NW 0409271

[supplement by HERMAN FRIEDRICH KOECHER] Nova bibliotheca hebraica secvndvm ordinem Bibliothecae hebraicae b. Io. Christoph. Wolfi disposita, analecta literaria hvivs operis sistens. Iena, 1783-84. *2 vols.* Best 2826 Bar 107 NK 0222319

1734. SCHWINDEL, GEORG JACOB. Bibliotheca exegetico-biblica, in qua, secundum seriem librorum capitumque biblicorum, libri & dissertationes eo pertinentes, cuiuscunque sint idiomatis, Lutheranorum, Catholicorum & Reformatorum, recensentur, diiudicantur, variisque observationibus literariis illustrantur. Accedit index autorum alphabeticus. Francofurti, 1734. † Bar 131

1734. [[[LETSOME, SAMPSON]] An index to the sermons published since the Restoration. Pointing out the texts in the order they lie in the Bible, shewing the occasion on which they were preached, and directing to the volume and page where they occur. London, 1734.] Best 5706 Bar 310 NL 0290504-506

Other editions as follows:

[. . . . London, 1738-39. *2 vols.*] Best 5706 Bar 310 NL 0290507
[. . . . London, 1751.] Best 5706 Bar 311 NL 0290508
[The preacher's assistant, in two parts. Part I. a series of the texts of all the sermons & discourses preached upon, and published from the restoration, to the present time. Part II. An historical register of all the authors in the series. London, 1753.] Bar 311 NL 0290509-511

1737. [NOORDBEEK, GERRIT and MOURIK, BERNARDUS. Naam-rol der godgeleerde schryvers, welke over den geheele Bybel, ofte byzondere boeken, capitelen en versen uyt dezelve in 't Nederduits geschreeve hebben zynde een handleyding voor predikanten, proponenten, studenten, en alle liefhebbers der godgeleerdheid. Amsterdam, 1737.] Bar 131

Other editions as follows:

[. . . . Amsterdam, 1738.] Bar 132
[. . . . Amsterdam, 1744.] Bar 132
[Naam-rol der godgeleerde schryvers, welcke over het Nieuwe Testament. . . geschreeven hebben. Amsterdam [[1750]].] Best 781
[. . . . Amsterdam, 1752.] NN 0292129
[. . . Amsterdam, 1781.] Bar 134
[De weg tot Bybelkennis gemaklyk gemaakt, door aanwyzing van alle de voornaamste nederduitsche schryvern, die de boeken van het Oude en Nieuwe Testament . . . verklaard of uitgebreid hebben. Nieuwe uitgave. 1794.] Best 756
[Naam-rol . . . . Vierde druk. Amsterdam, 1838.] NN 0292130

1757-65. WALCH, JOHANN GEORG. Bibliotheca theologica selecta litterariis adnotationibvs instrvcta. Tomvs primvs [-qvartvs isqve vltimvs]. Ienae svmtv vidvae Croeckerianae MDCCLVII [-MDCCLXV]. *4 vols.: see vol. 4, pp. 369-931:* "Capitis octavi. De scriptis theologiae exegeticae. Sectio VII. De interpretibvs scriptvrae sacrae." † Best 6091 Bar 22 NW 0026772

1729-63; 1782. CEILLIER, REMY. Histoire générale des auteurs sacrés et ecclésiastiques, qui continient leur vie, le catalogue, la critique, le jugement, la chronologie, l'analyse & le dénombrement des différentes éditions de leurs ouvrages; ce qu'ils renferment de plus interessant sur le dogme, sur la morale & sur la discipline de l'église; l'histoire des conciles tant generaux que particuliers, & les actes choisis des martyrs. 23 vols. Paris, 1729-63. *See:*

[index volumes] Table générale des matières contenues dans les XXIII volumes de l'Histoire générale des auteurs sacrés et ecclésiastiques. . . . Cette table a été redigée par Laur. Et. Rondet. . . . Paris, chez Nicolas Crapart. . . . M.DCC.LXXXII. 2 vols. † Best 6088 Bar 19 NC 0246903-905
[another edition] Histoire générale. . . . Nouvelle édition soigneusement revue, corrigée, complètes et terminée par une table générale des matières, par un directeur de Grand Séminaire [Louis Marie F. Bauzon]. 14 vols. Paris, 1858-63. *See:*
[index volume] Table générale. . . . revue corigée et augmentée par M. l'Abbe Bauzon, ancien directeur de Grand Séminaire, auteur de la nouvelle édition

de Dom Ceillier. 2 vols. Paris, 1868-69. † Best
6089 Bar 30 NC 0246907-910
[another edition] Paris, 1882. 14 vols. NC 0246912

1783. COOKE, JOHN. The preacher's assistant (after the
manner of Mr. Letsome), containing a series of the texts
of sermons and discourses published either singly, or in
volumes, by divines of the Church of England, and by the
dissenting clergy, since the restoration to the present time,
specifying also the several authors alphabetically arranged under each text — with the size, date, occasion, or
subject-matter of each sermon or discourse, by John
Cooke, M.A. . . . . MDCCLXXXIII. *2 vols.; vol. 1 follows order of biblical books.* † Bar 311 NC 0669693

1783. RIVIUS ALBINUS. De optimis interpretibus
divinorum librorum praelectiones biblicae quatuor, extra
ordi nes scripturae divinitus inspiratae stuidum opes,
gloriam, imperium, ac denique res eas omnes, quas mor-
tales amplecti solent, antecellit. S. Joannes Damas-
cenus praefatione in parallela sua, ipso initio. Coloniae Munatianae. Sumptibus Emanuelis Thurneysen.
MDCCLXXXIII. † Bar 134 NR 0310053

1791 [OELRICHS, JOHANN GEORG ARNOLD. Commentarii de scriptoribus ecclesiae latinae priorum VI
saeculorum ad Bibliothecam Fabricii latinam ac-
comodati. . . . Editionem curavit A. H. L. Heeren. Lipsiae,
1791.] Best 6094 NO 0026804

See Fabricius, Johann Albert. Bibliotheca ecclesiastica, in qua continentur de scriptoribus ecclesiasticis S. Hieronymus cum veteri versione graeca
quam vocant Sophronii, et nunc primum vulgatis
editoris notis, Hieronymum cum Eusebio accurate
conferentibus: adjunctis praeterea castigationibus
Suffridi Petri et Jo. Marcianaei, nec non integris
Erasmi, Mariani Victorii, Henr. Gravii, Aub.
Miraei, Wilh. Ernesti Tentzelii et Ern. Salomonis
Cypriani annotationibus. Appendix de vitis evangelistarum et apostolorum, graece et latine. Appendix altera, quae fertur jam sub titulo Hieronymi De
duodecim doctoribus, jam sub nomine Bedae De
luminaribus ecclesiae. Gennadius massiliensis, an-
notatis lectionibus condicis antiquiss. corbejensis,
et subjunctis variorum notis, Suffridi Petri, Aub.
Miraei, e Sal. Cypriani. S. Isodorus Hispalensis.
Idelfonsus Toletanus. Honorius Augustodunensis.
Sigebertus Gemblacensis, appendices Juliani ac
Felicis Toletani et tertia anonymi ad Isodorum et
Idelfonsum. Henricus Gandavensis. Anonymus
Mellicensis a R. P. Bernardo Pez nuper vulgatus.
Petrus Casinensis De viris illustribus monasterii
Casinensis, cum supplemento Placidi Romani et
Jo. Baptistae Mari annotationibus. Jo. Trithemii
abbatis Spanhemensis Liber de s. e. cum notis
editoris. Aub. Miraei auctarium de s. e. et a tem-

pore, quo desinit Trithemius, De scribtoribus
saeculi XVI. et XVII. libri duo. Curante Jo. Alberto
Fabricio. . . . Hamburgi apud Christian. Liebezeit
& Theodor. Christoph. Felginer. A.C. MDCCXIII
[1718]. † Best 6083 Bar 16 NF 0006613
*The earlier edition, by Aubert le Mire, was published
in 1639, with a supplemental second volume in
1649.* Best 6083 Bar 4

1803. [BECK, CHRISTIAN DANIEL. Monogrammata
hermenevtices librorum Novi Foederis. . . . Pars prima.
Hermenevtice N. T. vniversa. Lipsiae, 1803. *No more
published.*] Best 781 Bar 156 NB 0234894

1812. ROSSI, GIOVANNI BERNARDO DE. Libri stam-
pati di letteratura sacra ebraica ed orientale della biblioteca del dottore G. Bernardo de-Rossi. . . . Parma, dalla
stamperia imperiale, 1812. † Best 2826 Bar 135 NR
0442945

1816-18. [AANWIJZING van uitlegkundige schriften,
zoo over den geheelen Bijbel, als over bijzondere gedeel-
ten van denzelven. Amsterdam, 1816-18. *4 vols.*] Bar 135
NA 0006026

1821. WINER, GEORG BENEDIKT. Handbuch der
theologischen literatur, hauptsachlich des protestant-
ischen Deutschlands; nebst kurzen biographischen
notizen über die theologischen scriftsteller; von Dr.
George Benedict Winer. . . . Leipzig, Carl Heinrich
Reclam. 1821. Bar 26 NW 0365678-79
[another edition] Handbuch der theologischen
literatur. . . . Zweite sehr verbesserte und erweiterte auflage. Leipzig, Carl Heinrich Reclam,
1826. Best 5234 Bar 26 NW 0365680
[another edition] Handbuch der theologischen literatur. . . . Dritte sehr erweiterte auflage. Leipzig, bei
Carl Heinrich Reclam, 1838 [-1840]. *2 vols.: see
siebenter abschnitt: "Biblische Exegese," cols.
162-279.* † Bar 28 Best 5234 NW 0365681
supplement published 1842. Bar 28 Best 5234 NW
0365682

1818-21. HORNE, THOMAS HARTWELL. An introduction to the critical study and knowledge of the Holy
Scriptures. London, 1818-21. NH 0526715

Other editions as follows:

. . . . 2nd edition. London, 1821. NH 0526716
. . . . 3rd edition. Edinburgh, 1822. NH 0526717
. . . . 4th edition. London, 1823. NH 0526718
. . . Philadelphia, 1825. NH 0526719
. . . . 5th edition. London, 1825. NH 0526720
. . . . 3rd American edition. Philadelphia, 1827. NH
0526721

. . . . 6th edition. London, 1828. NH 0526722

. . . . 4th edition. Philadelphia, 1831. NH 0526723

. . . . 5th American edition. Philadelphia, 1833. NH 0526724

. . . . 7th edition. London, 1834. NH 0526725

. . . . New York, 1835. NH 0526726

. . . . New edition, from the 7th London. Philadelphia, 1835. NH 0526727

. . . . Philadelphia, 1836. NH 0526728

. . . . 8th edition. London, 1839. *4 vols. bound as 5: see v. 2. part 2:* Bibliographical appendix, chap. V: "Commentators, interpreters, and paraphrasts on the scriptures," pp. 223-364. † NH 0526729

[Bibliographical index separately published:] A manual of biblical bibliography; comprising a catalogue, methodically arranged, of the principal editions and versions of the Holy Scriptures; together with notices of the principal philologers, critics, and interpreters of the Bible. London, 1839. Best 757 Bar 136 NH 052678

. . . . New edition, from the 8th London. Philadelphia, 1840.

. . . . Philadelphia, 1841. NH 0526731

. . . . New York, 1844. NH 0526732

. . . . New York and Pittsburgh, 1846. NH 0526733

. . . . 9th edition. London, 1846. NH 0526734

. . . . New edition, from the 8th London. New York, 1847. NH 0526735

. . . . New York, 1848. NH 0526736

. . . . New York, 1849. NH 0526737

. . . . New York, 1850. NH 0526738

. . . . New York, 1851. NH 0526739

. . . . New York, 1852. NH 0526740

. . . . New York, 1853. NH 0526741

. . . . New York, 1854. NH 0526742

. . . . 10th edition, revised, corrected, and brought down to the present time. London, 1856. NH 0526744

. . . . London, 1856-1859. NH 0526745

. . . . 11th edition. London, 1860. NH 0526746

. . . . New York, 1860. NH 0526747

. . . . London, 1863. NH 0526748

. . . . New York, 1863. NH 0526749

. . . . New York, 1864. NH 0526750

. . . . Boston, 1868. NH 0526751

. . . . 12th edition. London, 1869. NH 0526752

. . . . 13th edition. London, 1872. NH 0526753

. . . . New York, 1872. *2 vols. See v. 2:* Appendix IV. Bibliographical appendix. . . . chap. V: "Commentators, interpreters, and paraphrasts on the scriptures," pp. 97f. † NH 0526754

. . . . 14th edition. London, 1877. NH 0526755

. . . . New York,, 1882. NH 0526756

1824. ORME, WILLIAM. Bibliotheca biblica: a select list of books on sacred literature; with notices, biographi-

cal, critical, and bibliographical. Edinburgh, 1824. † Best 757 Bar 135 NO 0132703

[another edition] Bibliotheca biblica. London, 1834. Bar 136

1824. WATT, ROBERT. Bibliotheca Britannica: or a general index to British and foreign literature. Edinburgh, 1824. *2 parts in 4 vols.: see IV. Subjects and entries for individual biblical books.* † Best 806 Bar 402

1835. [[[BROOKS, JOSHUA WILLIAM]] A dictionary of writers on the prophecies, with the titles and occasional descriptions of their works. Also an appendix, containing lists of commentators, annotations, &c. on the holy scriptures. London, 1835.] Best 773 Bar 381 NW 0118200

1839-42. LOWNDES, WILLIAM THOMAS. Lowndes's British librarian, or book-collector's guide to the formation of a library in all branches of literature, science, and art, arranged in classes, with prices, critical notes, references, and an index of authors and subjects. Class I. — Religion and its history. London, 1839. *Bound with Parts II-XI. 1839-42. See:* I. Holy Scripture. . . . 9. "Commentaries, interpretations, paraphrases," cols. 112-298. † Best 6097 Bar 28

[another edition] The British librarian, or handbook for students in divinity, a guide to the knowledge of theological works in English, and in the learned and other foreign languages, classified under heads; to these are added critical notes, extracted from authors in the highest repute, together with indications as to the best, or more correct editions, their peculiarities, and their usual prices. London, [1844? 1848?]. Best 6098 Bar 28 NL 0526122

1840. [FORSTER, JOHN. The churchman's guide; a copious index of sermons and other works, by eminent Church of England divines: digested and arranged according to their subjects. London, 1840.] Best 5706 Bar 311 NF 0249481-483

1844. [MURRAY, DAVID] The biblical student's assistant; containing references to works on doctrinal and practical theology, with occasional notes: together with an index to four thousand texts of sermons by eminent divines. By Clericus. Edinburgh, 1844. *See* "Index to . . . sermons." † Bar 136 NM 0897277

1849. STEWART, C. J., *booksellers.* A catalogue of Bibles and biblical literature, containing the best works, ancient and modern, on the criticism, interpretation, and illustration of Holy Scripture, and including such of the fathers and later ecclesiastical writers as have treated on these subjects: classified, with an analytical table of contents, and alphabetical indexes of subjects and authors. Also a select list of extensive and important works in other classes. On sale at the prices affixed, by C. J. Stewart, 11 King William Street, West Strand, London. MDCCCXLIX. Bar 136 NS 0934250

[another edition] . . . Bibles and biblical literature, including the best works, ancient and modern, on the criticism, interpretation, and illustration of Holy Scripture, being a very complete and extensive collection of Bibles in all languages, biblical commentators and critics of all ages, sects, and languages, Jewish and rabbinical authors, the most important works in every department of sacred philology, history, and antiquities, and other subjects by which the Bible is illustrated, with a collection of Samaritan manuscripts, including three very ancient Pentateuchs, to which are appended a minutely classified index of authors, and alphabetical index of subjects. On sale, at the prices affixed, by C. J. Stewart. . . London [1868?]. At p. [305]: "Supplement to C. J. Stewart's catalogue of Bibles and biblical literature. . . ." † Bar 136 NS 0934246

[another edition?] . . . Bibles and biblical literature. . . . London [1872?]. Bar 137 NS 0934247-48

1852-58. PITRA, J. B. Specilegium solesmense complectens sanctorum patrum scriptorumque ecclesiasticorum anecdota hactenus opera, selecta e graecis orientalibusque et latinis codicibus, publici juris facta curante Domino J. B. Pitra O.S.B. monacho e congregatione gallica, nonnullus ex abbatia solesmensi opem conferentibus. Tomus primus [-quartus] . . . . Parisiis, prostat apud Firmin Didot fratres, instituti Franciae typographos. MDCCCLII [-MDCCCLVIII]. In each vol. see "Index locorum sacrae scripturae" and see esp. vol. 3, cap. X, "De hominibus. . . ." † NP 0391466

[facsimile edition] Spicilegium solesmense. . . . Tomus primus [-quartus]. Graz: Akademische Druck -u. Verlagsanstalt. 1962 [-63]. †

1854, 1859. DARLING, JAMES. Cyclopaedia bibliographica: a library manual of theological and general literature, and guide to books for authors, preachers, students, and literary men. Analytical, bibliographical, and biographical. By James Darling. A-H [I-Z]. London: James Darling, 81 Great Queen Street, Lincoln's Inn Fields. 1854. See supplementary volume:

Cyclopaedia bibliographica: a library manual of theological and general literature, and guide to books for authors, preachers, students, and literary men. . . . Subjects. Holy Scriptures. London: James Darling, 22 & 23 Little Queen Street, and 81 Great Queen Street, Lincoln's Inn Fields. 1859. See "Commentaries, &c. on the Old and New Testament," cols. 123f. † Best 6099 Bar 29 ND 0045713

1852-60. STEINSCHNEIDER, MORITZ. Catalogus librorum hebraeorum in bibliotheca Bodleiana jussu curatorum digessit et notis instruxit M. Steinschneider. Berolini, 1852-60. See Index II. "Consepctus bibliorum eorumque partium," pp. lxxix f. Best 2826 Bar 109 NO 0185929

[facsimile edition] . . . . Berlin: Welt-verlag, 1931. NO 0185930

[revised edition by A. E. COWLEY] A concise catalogue of the Hebrew printed books in the Bodleian library. Oxford, at the Clarendon Press, 1929. See pp. 73-121. Best 2829 Bar 119 NO 0185952

1844-65. MIGNE, JACQUES-PAUL, editor. Patrologiae cursus completus; sive, Bibliotheca universalis, integra, uniformis, commoda, oeconomica, omnium ss. patrum doctorum scriptorumque ecclesiasticorum qui ab aevo apostolico ad usque Innocentii III tempora floruerant; recusio chronologica omnium quae existitere monumentorum catholicae traditionis per duodecim priora ecclesiae saecula, juxta editiones accuratissimas, inter se cumque nonnullis codicibus manuscriptis collatas, perquam diligenter castigata. Indicibus donata. Series prima in qua prodeunt patres, doctores scriptoresque ecclesiae latinae, a Tertulliano ad Gregorium Magnum. Parisiis, 1844-65. 221 vols.: title pages vary. See vols. 218-21, Indices, esp. XLIII: "Index generalis commentariorum in scripturas, secundum ordinem sacrorum librorum dispositus, a Genesi ad Apocalypsim" (v. 219, cols. 101-14), XLIV: "Index sacrae scripturae capitum et locorum notabilium quae commentariis et explanationibus ss. patres eluciderunt" (v. 219, cols. 113-22) and CXC: "Index homiliarum omnium de scripturis" (v. 221, cols. 39-42). Bar 201 NM 05667074-077 (and NM 0567101 — Indices)

Various volumes of PL reissued subsequently: for typical sets see NM 0567079-95 and other editions of the Indices as follows:
. . . . Paris, 1863-79 (v. 2 is 1879) NM 0567100
. . . . Paris, 1879-91 NM 0567086
. . . . Paris, 1887-90. †

1868. MALCOM, HOWARD. Theological index. References to the principal works in every department of religious literature. Embracing nearly seventy thousand citations, alphabetically arranged under two thousand heads. By Howard Malcom, D.D., LL.D. . . . Boston: Gould and Lincoln. . . London: Elliot, Stork & Co. . . . 1868. See "Commentators." † Best 6099 Bar 31 NM 0144637

[another edition] An index to the principal works in every department of religious literature. . . . Second edition, with addenda. . . . Philadelphia, J. B. Lippincott & Co., 1870. Best 6099 Bar 31 NM 0144638

1876. SPURGEON, CHARLES HADDON. Comment-

ing & commentaries: two lectures addressed to the students of the Pastors' College, Metropolitan tabernacle, together with a catalogue of biblical commentaries and expositions. By C. H. Spurgeon, president. London: Passmore & Alabaster, Paternoster buildings. 1876. †
Best 773 Bar 137 NS 0837059

[New York edition] Commenting on commentaries. . . . with a list of the best biblical commentaries and expositions. . . . New York: Sheldon & Co., no. 8 Murray Street, 1876. *See* "List of biblical commentaries and expositions," pp. [63]-281. Bar 137 NS 0837060

[another edition] . . . . London, 1890. NS 0837061

[another edition] . . . . London, 1893. NS 0837062

[another edition] Commenting & commentaries; comments on over 1400 commentaries and expositions, lectures on commenting and commentaries, textual index of Metropolitan Tabernacle sermons. Rev. ed. Grand Rapids: Kregel Publications, 1954. NS 0837063

1878. [PETTINGELL, JOHN HANCOCK. Homiletical index: a handbook of texts, themes, and authors, for the use of preachers and Bible scholars generally. Embracing twenty thousand citations of Scripture texts, and of discourses, founded thereon, under a twofold arrangement: I. Textual. In which all the principal texts of Scripture, together with the various themes they have suggested, are quoted and set forth in the order of the Sacred Canon, from Genesis to Revelation; to which is added a list of passages cited from the Old Testament in the New. II. Topical. In which Bible themes, with reference to texts and authors, are classified and arranged in alphabetical order, forming at once a key to homiletical literature in general, and a complete topical index to the Scriptures on new plan. . . . New York: D. Appleton and Co., 1878.] Best 2904 NP 0291063

1883. HURST, JOHN FLETCHER. Bibliotheca theologica: a select and classified bibliography of theology and general religious literature, by John F. Hurst, LL.D. New York: Charles Scribner's Sons, 1883. *See* Part II. "Exegetical theology. . . . Commentaries," pp. 45-75. †
Best 6 104 Bar 32 NH 0631877

[another edition] Literature of theology: a classified bibliography of theological and general religious literature, by John Fletcher Hurst. New York: Hunt & Eaton; Cincinnati: Cranston & Curts, 1896. Best 6 107 Bar 34 NH 0631906 & NH 0631876

1886. [PALM, AUGUST. Die Qohelet-litteratur. Ein Beitrag zur Geschichte der Exegese des Alten Testaments. Mannheim, 1886.] Best 778 Bar 154 NP 0038130

1895. [[[CHASTAND, GEDEON]] Répertoire de la predication protestante au XIXᵉ siècle précédé d'un index

bibliographique de tous les sermonnaires français parus jusqu'a ce jour. Vals, 1895.] Best 5705 Bar 312

[*another edition, by* Jean Ganguin, Paris, 1924. *See* "Repertoire des textes auxquels se rapportent les sermons," pp. 137-521.] Bar 312 NC 0323202

1895. [BIBLIOTHECA NACIONAL, *Rio de Janeiro.* [[Jose Alexandre Teixeira de Mello]], Catalogo por ordem chronologica das Biblias, corpos de Biblia, concordancias e commentarios existentes na Bibliotheca nacional. Bibliotheca nacional: Annaes, XVII, no. 1. Rio de Janeiro, 1895.] Best 759 NR 0289243

1909. [McFADYEN, JOHN E. Best books for OT and NT study, especially the best commentaries. Nashville & Dallas, 1909.] Bar 141

1890-1909. DE BACKER, AUGUSTIN and SOMMER-VOGEL, CARLOS. Bibliothèque de la Compagnie de Jésus. Première partie: bibliographie par les pères Augustin et Aloys de Backer. Seconde partie: histoire par le père Auguste Carayon. Nouvelle édition par Carlos Sommervogel, S. J. Strasbourgeois; publiée par la province de Belgique. Paris and Bruxelles, 1890-1909. *11 vols. arranged as follows:* vol. 1-vol. 8, Bibliographie, 1890-98; vol. 9, Supplement, 1900; vol. 10, Tables, 1909 [vol. 11, Histoire (par Pierre Bliard), 1932]. *See vol. 10:*

Bibliothèque. . . . Tome X. Tables de la première partie par Pierre Bliard. Paris, 1909. † Best 3261 Bar 251 NB 0018726-728

(*Earlier editions of De Backer's Bibliothèque —* 1855-61, *in* 7 vols. *and* 1869-76, *in* 3 vols. *— do not have Bliard's Tables.*)

[supplement] Corrections et additions a la Bibliotheque de la Compagnie de Jésus, supplement au "De Backer-Sommervogel" par Ernest M. Riviere, S. I. Toulouse, 1911-30. *5 fascicles.* Best 3262 Bar 252

1857-66; 1912. MIGNE, JACQUES-PAUL, *editor.* Patrologiae cursus completus, seu Bibliotheca universalis, integra, uniformis, commoda, oeconomica, omnium ss. patrum, doctorum scriptorumque ecclesiasticorum, sive latinorum, sive graecorum. . . . series graeca. Parisiis, 1857-66. *162 vols.* NM 0567057-059

[another edition] . . . . Parisiis, 1857-87. † NM 0567060-61

[index] Patrologiae cursus completus accurante J.-P. Migne. Series graeca. Indices digessit Ferdinandus Cavallera. Parisiis, 1912. *See* Index methodicus. IV. "Scriptura sacra," pp. 143f. † Bar 206 NM 0567062-064

[index] Theodore Hopner. Index locupletissimus tam in opera omnium auctorum veterum. . . . Paris, 1934, 1945. *2 vols. See* Tom. II. "Index methodicus. . . III. Scriptura sacra," 879-80. † NM 0567065-068

1928. [VACCARI, ALBERTO. Historiae exegeseos compendium. Pars I. Historia exegeseos aetate patrum. Romae, 1928. *No more published.*] Best 774 NV 0002080

1928-31. FRIEDBERG, BERNHARD. . . . Bet eked sepharim. Lexique bibliographique de tous les ouvrages de la littérature hebraique et judeo-allemande, y compris les ouvrages arabes, grecs, italiens, espagnols-portugais, persans, samaritains et tartares en caracteres hebraiques, imprimes et publies de 1475 a 1900. Avec table des matières et registre des auteurs. Antwerp, 1928-31. *2 vols.* Best 2829 Bar 119 NF 0383726-728

    [another edition]: Bet eked sepharim. Bibliographical lexicon. . . . 1474-1950. Tel Aviv, 1951-56. Best 2829 NF 0383730

1933-34. GLORIEUX, PALÉMON. Répertoire des maîtres en théologie de Paris au XIIIᵉ siècles. Paris: Librarie philosophie J. Vrin, 1933-34. *2 vols. See:* v. 2, table II: "Table idéologique. . . . Écriture sainte," pp. 367-68. † Best 84 Bar 40 NG 0256771

1944. SPICQ, P. C. Esquisse d'une histoire de l'exégèse latine au Moyen Âge. Paris: Bibliothèque Thomiste,

XXVI, 1944. *See:* "Table des commentaires biblique," pp. 395f. † NS 0816258-60

1945. HABERSAAT, KARL. Materialien zur Bibliographie des Hohenliedes. Freiburg im Breisgau, 1945. † Best 779.

1950-61. STEGMÜLLER, FRIEDRICH. Repertorium biblicum medii aevi collegit disposuit edidit Fridericus Stegmuller. . . . Tomus I-Tomus VII. Matriti: Consejo superior de investigaciones cientificos: Instituto Francisco Suarez. MCMXL [*sic.* 1950]. *7 vols. 1950-61. No index.* † Best 774 NS 0891492

1965-66. BRITISH MUSEUM. General catalogue of printed books. Photolithographic edition to 1955. London, 1965-66. *263 vols. See:* v. 19: Bible appendix — index. †
    For earlier editions of the British Museum catalogue, without a separately published Bible appendix. see: Catalogue of printed books (1892-99) *and* General catalogue of printed books, vols. XVI-XVIII (1936-37). Best 759

GEORGE L. SCHEPER

BIBLICAL TRADITION
IN ENGLISH LITERATURE

This Bibliography of Biblical Tradition in English Literature has been divided into three parts. The first is concerned with works devoted to the influence of the Bible on English literature (i.e., literature written in the English language) in general or on some aspect of English literature — e.g., literature of the 19th cent., American literature. An exemplary title is: *Biblical Patterns in Modern Literature*. The second part is concerned with works devoted to the influence of the Bible upon (or use of the Bible by) one or more specific named authors in English literary tradition. An exemplary title is: *Spelling the Word: George Herbert and the Bible*. Parts I and II follow here. Where titles are not self-explanatory, brief descriptive annotation is generally provided.

A third part of the bibliography is concerned with works devoted to the literary use of a particular biblical image, character, or theme. An exemplary title is: "The Prodigal Son in Elizabethan Fiction." Bibliographical items of this kind appear, in abbreviated form, within the select bibliographies accompanying entries in the *Dictionary* proper. Thus, the title just cited appears under the PRODIGAL SON entry in this volume. These items are not annotated; most often, their content will be reflected within the articles to which they are appended.

In all three listings, dissertation titles are, wherever possible, accompanied by their *DA/DAI* citation, to allow ready access to fuller abstracts. British theses and disser-

tations, and North American Masters' theses, where relevant, are generally listed by place and date. Collections of essays which are entirely devoted to the subject of biblical influence on literature are listed by main title only, although some annotation concerning individual chapter contents is generally given; where a single essay devoted to this subject occurs in a collection with another focus, only the relevant chapter is listed here.

"Biblical influence" is understood as incorporating, at times, the more specific influence of biblical theology, doctrine, or typology; thus, titles such as "Theological Bearings in Modern Literature" and *Typology and Early American Literature* have been included here, although similarly titled works which treat the Bible only incidentally have generally been excluded. It should be noted that this bibliography is principally concerned with biblical *influence upon* rather than biblical (or Christian or Jewish) *approaches to* literature, which is another subject altogether. Relevant titles in the latter category would include, e.g., T. S. Eliot's "Religion and Literature," in *Essays Ancient and Modern* (New York: Harcourt, Brace, 1932) and many of the works of Nathan Scott, Jr. (e.g., *The Broken Center: Studies in the Theological Horizon of Modern Literature* (New Haven: Yale University Press, 1966). (Works concerning the "Bible *as* literature" or "literary approaches to the Bible" appear in the preceding "Biblical Studies" bibliography.)

The Influence of the Bible on English Literature: Selected General Studies

Anderson, Duncan. *The Bible in Seventeenth Century Scottish Life and Literature* (London: Allenson and Co., 1936). Chapters 9 and 10 consider the "Influence [of the Bible] on the Literature of the Century."

Anderson, Katherine Anne Thomen. "Christian Concepts and Doctrine in Selected Works of Science Fiction." *DAI* 42/11 (1982), 4829A. Concentrates on Walter Miller's *A Canticle for Leibowitz,* Frank Herbert's *Dune* trilogy, and C. S. Lewis's space trilogy *(Out of the Silent Planet, Perelandra,* and *That Hideous Strength).*

Archibald, W. S. "Religion in Some Contemporary Poets." *Harvard Theological Review* 7 (1914), 47-71. Discusses the poetry of Kipling, William Vaughn Moody, and others in terms of general biblical influence.

Avni, Abraham. "The Influence of the Bible on American Literature: A Review of Research from 1955 to 1965." *Bulletin of Bibliography* 27 (1970), 101-06. A bibliographical essay, surveying a decade of scholarship. See also his "The Influence of the Bible on European Literature: A Review of Research from 1955-65." *Yearbook of Comparative and General Literature* (Bloomington: Indiana University Press, 1970-74) and his *The Bible and Romanticism: The Old Testament in German and French Poetry* (The Hague, Paris: Mouton, 1969).

Ayo, Nicolas. "A Checklist of the Principal Book-Length Studies in the Field of English and American Literature Devoted to a Single Author's Use of the Bible." *Bulletin of Bibliography* 25 (1966), 7-8. Brief but useful listing; includes theses and dissertations.

Bailey, Elmer James. *Religious Thought in the Greater American Poets* (1922; rpt. Freeport, NY, 1968). Considers Longfellow, Whitman, Emerson, Poe, and others. General discussion, with few specific biblical references.

Bailey, Samuel W., comp. *Homage of Eminent Persons to the Book* (New York, 1871). Testimonials by English writers and other "eminent persons" concerning the value and influence of the Bible. Sources of quotations are not always provided.

——. *Nahbion: The Bible and the Poets* (Cambridge: J. Wilson and Son, 1874). "Many of the choicest gems from about three hundred and fifty . . . poets" are cited, along with the biblical passages which influenced them.

Baker, Carlos. "The Place of the Bible in American Fiction." *Theology Today* 17 (1960), 53-76. The same article is reprinted in *Religious Perspectives in American Culture,* the second volume of James W. Smith and A. L. Jamison, eds., *Religion in American Life* (Princeton: Princeton University Press, 1961). Discusses, in brief, the stylistic and material influence of the KJV on American fiction.

Bartel, Roland, James S. Ackerman, and Thayer S. Warshaw. *Biblical Images in Literature* (Nashville: Abingdon, 1975). Collection of essays dealing with selected authors' use of Scripture. Intended for classroom use at the high school level. Index of biblical texts.

Beary, Thomas J. "Religion and the Modern Novel." *Catholic World* 166 (1947), 203-11. General discussion; no specific biblical allusions or references.

Beebe, H. Keith. "Biblical Adventures in an American Novel." *Journal of Bible and Religion* 27 (1959), 133-38. Discussion of biblical influence, with special attention to Bellow's *The Adventures of Augie March.*

Bercovitch, Sacvan, ed. *Typology and Early American Literature* (Amherst: University of Massachusetts Press, 1972). Collection of essays, followed by indispensable bibliographical essay which covers a great deal more than "early American" typology. First published in *Early American Literature* 5 (1970); subsequently modified and enlarged.

Berger, Thomas L., and William C. Bradford, Jr. *Index of Characters in English Printed Drama to the Restoration* (Denver: Microcard Editions, 1975). Includes many biblical characters and characters with biblically derived names.

Blackburn, Ruth. *Biblical Drama under the Tudors* (The Hague: Mouton, 1971). Attempts "to discern the phases of development through which the Biblical drama passed, and its relationship to the fortunes of the Reformation." Biblical sources given in notes. Index includes biblical characters and motifs. See also her Columbia dissertation, "Tudor Biblical Drama." *DA* 17/08 (1957), 1746.

Bludworth, Rosa Lyon. "A Study of the Biblical Novel in America, 1940-49, with a Survey of the Biblical Novel in General in the Nineteenth and Twentieth Centuries." Unpubl. diss., University of Texas, 1955.

Bracher, Peter. "The Bible and Literature." *English Journal* 61 (1972), 1170-75. Wide-ranging discussion of how to teach a course on the Bible and Literature; some specific references to biblical influences in 19th- and 20th-cent. literature.

Braden, Charles S. "The Bible in Contemporary Literature." *Literature in Life* 9 (1940), 113-27.

———. "The Bible in Contemporary Poetry." *Religion in Life* 19 (1949/50), 92-105.

Broadbent, John. "The Poets' Bible." In John Broadbent, ed. *John Milton: Introductions* (Cambridge: Cambridge University Press, 1973), 145-61. Brief history of use of the KJV by writers in the English language.

Brown, Douglas C. *The Enduring Legacy: Biblical Dimensions in Modern Literature* (New York: Charles Scribner's Sons, 1975).

Brumm, Ursula. *American Thought and Religious Typology* (New Brunswick, NJ: Rutgers University Press, 1970). First published as *Die Religiöse Typologie im Amerikanischen Denken. Ihre Bedeutung für die Amerikanische Literatur und Geistesgeschichte* (Leiden, 1963).

Buell, Lawrence. "Literature and Scripture in New England Between the Revolution and the Civil War." *Notre Dame English Journal* 15 (1983), 1-28. Traces the changing use of scriptural narrative in New England literature from literal to metaphorical/symbolic.

Burr, Nelson R. "Religion and Literature." In James Ward Smith and A. Leland Jamison, eds. *Religion in American Life*, vol. 4: *A Critical Bibliography of Religion in America* (Princeton: Princeton University Press, 1961), 847-942. An extensive and very well-annotated bibliographical essay, which includes a variety of subdivisions, including "Religion and Modern Literature: General"; "Literature and Religious Belief"; "Literature and Theology"; "Religion and American Literature: General"; "The Bible in Literature"; "Puritanism and Literature"; "Some Denominational Aspects"; "Religious Historical Novels"; and "The Religious Best Seller."

———. "New Eden and New Babylon: Religious Thoughts of American Authors: A Bibliography." *Historical Magazine of the Protestant Episcopal Church* 54 (1985), 7-37, 151-85.

———. "A Plea for Christian Culture." *Historical Magazine of the Protestant Episcopal Church* 53 (1984), 313-19. Appendix: "Religious Ideas of American Authors: A Bibliography."

Busailah, Rejae. "Christian Themes in the Formulaic Tradition of Old English Poetry." *DA* 33/2 (1972), 720A. Treats themes of creation, rebellion, fall of man, advent, passion, harrowing of hell, ascension, vision. Appendix A lists all occurrences of each of the themes in question in the *Anglo-Saxon Poetic Records*.

Bush, C. W. "The Treatment of Religion and Religious Character in the Nineteenth Century American Novel Through Selected Fiction by Cooper, Hawthorne, Melville, Harriet Beecher Stowe, Oliver Wendell Holmes and Mark Twain." Unpubl. M.Phil. thesis, King's College, London, 1967.

Cady, Chauncey Marvin. "The English Bible and English Writers." *The Biblical World* 9 (1897), 185-93. Emphasizes the importance of recognizing biblical reference and influence in literature, with reference to specific English authors.

Calvocoressi, Peter. *Who's Who in the Bible* (London: Viking, 1987). A selective list of persons in the biblical text, along with "the facts stated in the Bible about each of the persons listed" and the author's appraisal of their character and role. Attention is also devoted to how these figures have appeared in later tradition.

Campbell, Lily B. *Divine Poetry and Drama in Sixteenth-Century England* (1959; rpt. New York: Gordian Press, 1972). Traces the movement of the Bible from the confines of religious authority to literary expression in English poetry and drama. Index of works and authors.

Chapman, Edward Mortimer. *English Literature in Account with Religion 1800-1900* (Boston and New York: Houghton Mifflin, 1910). The impact of Christianity and biblical tradition upon English 19th-cent. authors.

Charity, A. C. *Events and Their Afterlife: The Dialectics of Christian Typology in the Bible and Dante* (Cambridge: Cambridge University Press, 1966). Valuable discussion of typology in the OT and NT and in *The Divine Comedy*. Extensive bibliography and index both of scriptural references and names and subjects.

Christianity and Literature. An interdisciplinary journal published quarterly by the Conference on Christianity and Literature. Articles, reviews, annotated bibliography.

Coleman, Edward D., comp. *The Bible in English Drama: An Annotated List of Plays . . . to 1931* (New York: New York Public Library, 1968). Indispensable reference guide, arranged according to biblical chronology. Provides index of authors, index to plays, index to special topics, and index to English translations of foreign plays.

Copland, James Alexander. "The Influence of Old Testament Versification on English Poetry after 1750." *DAI* 43/12 (1983), 3918A. Examines impact of "rhythms of the King James Bible" and the underlying parallelism of biblical Hebrew prosody on Smart's *Jubilate Agno,* Macpherson's *Poems of Ossian,* Blake's three major prophecies, and Whitman's *Leaves of Grass.*

Cook, Albert S. *The Authorized Version of the Bible and Its Influence* (Folcroft: Folcroft, 1910). Literary and stylistic comparison of various English biblical translations up to the 1611 version, along with general observations about the influence on Shakespeare, Milton, Swift, Scott, Wordsworth, and Ruskin, at the level of verbal allusion.

———. *The Bible and English Prose Style: Selections and Comments* (Boston: D. C. Heath, 1908). Considers the influence of Scripture on specific writers; cites the views of various writers concerning the importance of the Bible.

———. *Biblical Quotations in Old English Prose Writers* (New York: Macmillan, 1898). Index of biblical quotations is provided.

Craig, Hardin. *English Religious Drama of the Middle Ages* (Oxford: Clarendon, 1968). Biblical characters and subjects noted in index.

Craig, Raymond Allen. "The Stamp of the Word: The Poetics of Biblical Allusion in American Puritan Poetry." Unpubl. diss., University of California, Davis, 1989.

Crook, Margaret B., and Other Members of the Faculty of Smith College. *The Bible and Its Literary Associations* (New York: Abingdon, 1937). Chapters on "The influence of the Bible upon selected phases of Scottish and English literature" — including "Milton and the Bible"; "The Bible in the Hands of Richard Baxter, John Bunyan, and George Fox"; "The Biblical Drama in England"; "The King James Version in the Work of Two Masters of Nineteenth-Century Prose."

Dale, John Franklin. *The Dramatist's Use of Biblical Material.* Unpubl. diss., Iliff School of Theology, 1965.

Davies, T. H. *Spiritual Voices in Modern Literature* (New York: Doran, 1919). Discusses the expression of Christian imperatives in Ibsen, Francis Thompson, and Browning, among others. Not all biblical references are documented.

Dean, Ruth. "The Bible in Early English Drama: An Annotated Bibliography of Scholarship, 1955-1985." Unpubl. M.A. thesis, University of Akron, 1987. Includes bibliographical essay, followed by annotated bibliography organized around the play cycles — beginning with studies concerning the mystery plays in general and then moving specifically to Chester, N-Town, Towneley, and York; chapters on saints' plays and Tudor drama follow.

Detweiler, Robert, ed. *Art/Literature/Religion: Life on the Borders* (Chico: Scholars Press, 1983). Collection of essays. See especially John Shea, "Religious Imaginative Encounters with Scriptural Stories," and Theodore Ziolkowski's "Literature and the Bible: A Comparatist's Approach."

Dixon, Melvin. "Singing Swords: The Literary Legacy of Slavery." The *Slaves Narrative,* eds. C. T. Davis and H. L. Gates, Jr. (Oxford: Oxford University Press, 1985), 298-317. Biblical sources.

Donnelly, W. J. "Religion and the Poetic Imagination: A Study of the Relationships Between Religious Vision and Poetic Expression in Scotland from the Fifteenth Century to the Present." Unpubl. diss., Edinburgh, 1981.

Driver, Tom. "Religion and Literature." *Union Seminary Quarterly Review* 15 (1960), 142-50. Bibliography.

Ehlert, Arnold D. *The Biblical Novel: A Checklist with an Introductory Essay* (Anaheim, CA: BCH Publications, 1960). "Seeks to include all genuine Biblical novels (as distinguished from the merely religious)," excluding juvenile works. Organized alphabetically, according to biblical subject.

Fairchild, Hoxie Neale. *Religious Trends in English Poetry* (6 vols.; New York: Columbia University Press, 1939-68). Volumes are chronologically arranged: *1700-1740, Protestantism and the Cult of Sentiment; 1740-80, Religious Sentimentalism in the Age of Johnson; 1780-1830, Romantic Faith; 1830-80, Christianity and Romanticism in the Victorian Era; 1880-1920, Gods of a Changing Poetry; 1920-65, Valley of Dry Bones.* Each volume contains a bibliography of primary and secondary sources as well as indices both of names and topics.

Fairman, Marion A. *Biblical Patterns in Modern Literature* (Cleveland: Dillon/Liederbach, 1972). Albee, Pinter, Golding, Camus, Ionesco, and Faulkner are discussed.

Favre, Betty Atkinson. "Apple Blossoms: Bible Values in Secular Literature." *DAI* 44/8 (1984), 2463A. Concerned with the impact of "Bible values" — literal and moral — on secular literature. Focuses on Chaucer, Milton, Yeats, and Hemingway, among others.

Finch, H. A. "Biblical Typology in Late Sixteenth and Seventeenth Century English Poetry." Unpubl. M.A. thesis, Exeter, 1975.

Fisch, Harold. *Jerusalem and Albion: The Hebraic Factor in Seventeenth Century Literature* (New York: Schocken Books, 1964). Influence of the OT on Milton and others.

Flood, Ethelbert. "Christian Language in Modern Literature." *Culture* 22 (1961), 28-42. Traces some biblical echoes in modern literature.

Fowler, David C. *The Bible in Early English Literature* (Seattle: University of Washington Press, 1976). Chapters on medieval exegesis, OE and ME translations and paraphrases, the metrical Bible, and universal histories, followed by a useful bibliographical essay. Index lists biblical characters and subjects.

————. *The Bible in Middle English Literature* (Seattle: University of Washington Press, 1984). A companion volume to the above, with a similar format. Topics covered include medieval drama, medieval lyrics, Chaucer's *Parliament of Fowls,* the Pearl poet, and *Piers the Plowman.* Bibliographical essay and index.

Fox, John. "The Influence of the English Bible on English Literature." *The Princeton Theological Review* 9 (1911), 387-401. General discussion, with few specific examples.

Fulghum, W. B., Jr. *A Dictionary of Biblical Allusions in English Literature* (New York: Holt, Rinehart and Winston, 1965). Organized alphabetically according to selected biblical quotations, allusions, persons, etc. with brief listing of some literary occurrences.

Gaer, Joseph, and Ben Siegel. "American Literature and the Religious Tradition." *The Puritan Heritage: America's Roots in the Bible* (New York: New American Library, 1964).

Galdon, Joseph A., S.J. *Typology and Seventeenth-Century Literature* (The Hague, Paris: Mouton, 1975). Based on the author's Columbia dissertation (1965) of the same title. Includes chapters on "The Second Adam," "Eve and the Garden," "Exodus Typology," and "Noah and Temple Typology," as well as more general topics. Bibliography and Index.

Gardner, Helen. *Religion and Literature* (London: Faber and Faber, 1971). Two sets of essays: "Religion and Tragedy" and "Religious Poetry," which have a typological rather than biblical focus. No bibliography or index.

Goldman, Solomon. *The Book of Books: An Introduction* (2 vols.; New York: Harper and Brothers, 1948). *Vol. 1, chap. 4 includes a section entitled "Echoes and Allusions," for which a detailed bibliography is provided.*

Guberlet, Muriel Lewin. "The Classics and the Modern Magazine." *School and Society* 34 (1931), 599-605. Discusses the influence of the Bible on writers of popular literature.

Gunn, Giles B., ed. *Literature and Religion* (London: SCM Press, 1971). Collection of essays on various aspects of the interplay between religious thought and poetic expression. Not primarily biblical in emphasis or orientation.

————, ed. *The Bible and American Arts and Letters* (Philadelphia: Fortress, 1983). Part 3 of the Bible in American Culture series. Collection of essays discuss-

ing biblical influence on poetry, the novel, fiction, drama, architecture, music, painting, and folk arts. "Uniting all the essays is the paradoxical theme of the Bible as a source of both inspiration and dissatisfaction in the American experience."

Hahn, Friederich. *Bibel und Moderne Literatur* (Stuttgart: Quell-Verlag, 1966).

Hamilton, Kenneth M. "Theological Bearings in Modern Literature." *Dalhousie Review* 32 (1952), 121-30. Evaluates, in general terms, the influence of the Christian Bible on 20th-cent. fiction.

Hardison, O. B., Jr. *Christian Rite and Christian Drama in the Middle Ages: Essays in the Origin and Early History of Modern Drama* (Baltimore: Johns Hopkins Press, 1965). Examines biblical and liturgical influence on drama as it develops in the Middle Ages; specific scriptural sources are noted. Index lists biblical characters and events.

Harkness, David James. "The Bible in Fiction and Drama: A Bibliography with Notes." *The University of Tennessee News Letter* 35 (1956), 7-15. Lists novels and plays which make reference to biblical characters and "biblical times."

Henn, T. R. "The Bible in Relation to the Study of English Literature Today." *Hermathena* 100 (1965), 29-43.

Hert, M. P. *The Influence of the Bible on Contemporary American Poetry.* Unpubl. M.A. thesis, University of Redlands, 1939.

Hill, M. T. "The English Bible in America." *Bulletin of New York Public Library* 65 (1961), 277-88.

Hirsch, David H., and Nehama Aschkenasy. *Biblical Patterns in Modern Literature* (Chico, CA: Scholars Press, 1984). Series of essays concerning the use of the Hebrew Scriptures by various authors, not only English. The term *modern* here takes in Chaucer, Shakespeare, and Marvell, as well as more recent writers.

Holland, Harold E. "Fiction Titles from the Bible." *Oklahoma Librarian* 15 (1965), 116-22.

Horder, W. Garrett, *The Poet's Bible* (London: Isbister, 1883). Chronologically arranged, with list of authors and index of first lines.

Howard, Douglas Turner, Jr. "The Literary Uses of Religious Images and References in the Middle English Metrical Romances of the Fourteenth Century." *DAI* 39 (1979), 3567A.

Ichikawa, Sanki, Masami Nishikawa, and Mamoru Shimizu, eds. *The Kenkyusha Dictionary of English Quotations, with Examples of Their Use by Modern Authors* (Tokyo: Kenkyusha, 1952). Pp. 1-388 provide an ad hoc listing of quotations of the English Bible by "modern authors," not all of whom are literary figures per se. Organized by biblical text, verse by verse from Genesis through Revelation. The section immediately following, pp. 388-98, is devoted to quotations of the *Book of Common Prayer.*

Jennings, Elizabeth. *Christianity and Poetry* (London: Burns and Oates; New York: Hawthorn Books, 1965). A brief study of Christian poetry (mostly English) from the Anglo-Saxon period to the present. Allusions to the Bible but no references given.

Jones, Howard Mumford. *Belief and Disbelief in American Literature* (Chicago: University of Chicago Press, 1967). Some biblical references.

Jones, P. R. "The Treatment of Old Testament Characters and Incidents in Old and Middle English Poetry and Drama." Unpubl. M.A. thesis, University of Wales, 1959.

Joseph, Oscar Loos. *The Influence of The English Bible upon the English Language and upon English and American Literature* (New York: American Bible Society, 1936). A commemorative tract recognizing 400 years of the printed English Bible and celebrating its impact on English and American poets (from Langland to Edwin Arlington Robinson) and prose writers (from Francis Bacon to James Fenimore Cooper).

Joshi, Krishna Nand. *A Dictionary of Mythological and Biblical Allusions in Literature* (India: Prakash Book Depot, 1979). Student reference guide; entries arranged alphabetically.

Kahoe, Walter, comp. *Book Titles from the Bible* (Moylan, PA: The Rose Valley Press, 1946). A personal and somewhat random sampling of books (almost exclusively 20th cent.) using precise King James wording for their titles. In each instance, the biblical source text is cited.

Kohut, George Alexander, ed. *A Hebrew Anthology; a collection of poems and dramas inspired by the Old Testament and post Biblical tradition gathered from writings of English poets, from the Elizabethan period and earlier to the present day* (2 vols.; Cincinnati: S. Bacharach, 1913). Vol. 1 devoted to poetry, including lyrical narratives, vol. 2 to drama. Indices of titles, first lines, and authors.

Korshin, Paul J. *Typologies in England, 1650-1820* (Princeton: Princeton University Press, 1982). Both classical and biblical typologies are discussed.

Landow, George P. *Victorian Types, Victorian Shadows: Biblical Typology in Victorian Literature, Art, and Thought* (Boston, London and Henley: Routledge & Kegan Paul, 1980). Includes chapters on "The Smitten Rock" and "The Pisgah Sight" as well as more general topics. Index lists specific biblical texts which are discussed.

Lake, James Hammond, Jr. "The Influence of the Old Testament Upon the Early Drama of the English Renaissance." *DA* 30/04 (1969), 1530A. Discusses *Godly Queene Hester, King Darius, Jacob and Esau, Godlye Susanna, A Looking Glass for London and England,* and *David and Bethsabe.*

Lass, Abraham H., David Kiremidjian, and Ruth Goldstein. *Dictionary of Classical, Biblical, and Literary Allusions* (Oxford: Facts on File, 1988).

Lewis, C. S. *The Literary Impact of the Authorized Version* (London: Athlone Press, 1950). General discussion.

Liptzin, Sol. *Biblical Themes in World Literature* (Hoboken, NJ: Ktav, 1985). Organized according to stories and characters from the Hebrew Scriptures; richly illustrated with literary examples, though not exclusively (or in some instances even principally) English.

Lloyd, I. M. "The Influence of the Bible in English Literature of the Nineteenth Century." Unpubl. M.A. thesis, Wales, 1920.

Lloyd, Roger B. *The Borderland: An Exploration of Theology in English Literature* (London: Allen and Unwin, 1960). Lectures concerning the relationship between Christian theology and certain selected authors. No index or bibliography.

Long, Mason, comp. *The Bible and English Literature* (State College, Pennsylvania, 1935). Lists, in chronological order, English and American works of literature perceived to be significantly indebted to Scripture.

Los Reyes, Marie Philomene. *The Biblical Theme in Modern Drama* (Quezon City: University of the Philippines, 1978). Discusses the influence of biblical subject matter and motifs on "dramatists of note after 1920."

Lowell, Virginia M. *English Metrical Paraphrases of the Bible, 1549-1696* (Urbana: University of Illinois, 1947).

Lucock, H. E. *Contemporary American Literature and Religion* (New York: Willett, Clark, and Co., 1934). Treats the influence of Christianity on early 20th-cent. American literature; occasional biblical references.

Macaulay, Rose. *Some Religious Elements in English Literature* (London: Hogarth Press, 1931). A meandering survey of English religious literature. No biblical emphasis, nor systematic treatment of biblical themes etc. Index of names only.

McAfee, Cleland B. *The Greatest English Classic: A Study of the King James Version of the Bible and Its Influence on Life and Literature* (New York: Harper and Brothers, 1912). See especially pp. 130-94, which discuss biblical influence on a variety of English and American authors.

McAleer, John J. "Biblical Symbols in American Literature: A Utilitarian Design." *English Studies* 46 (1965), 310-22. Special emphasis on the "Mosaic myth."

McCasland, Vernon. "The Bible in Our Literature." In his *The Bible in Our American Life* (Bridgewater, VA: Virginia Council of Religious Education, 1942).

McClure, J. T. "The Bible in English Life and Letters." *Old and New Testament Student* (1891), 221-24, 278-281, 349-52.

McGlinn, Jeanne Blain. "The Bible in Modern American

Drama." *DAI* 40/5 (1979), 2684A. Establishes the continuing presence of biblical subject matter on the modern stage and explores reasons.

Marsicano, Vincent Anthony. "Medieval Old Testament Drama as Biblical Exegesis." *DAI* 41/1 (1980), 237A. Discusses plays about OT subjects written in Latin, French, German, Italian, and English.

Martin, Lawrence T., and Ruth Dean. "A Bibliography of Secondary Sources on the Influence of the Bible on English and American Literature." University of Akron, 1985. Unpublished.

Metford, J. C. J. *Dictionary of Christian Lore and Legend* (New York: Thames and Hudson, 1983). A popular handbook devoted to "the essentials of Christian tradition in the arts, music, and literature."

Miller, Edwin S. "Medieval Biblical and Ritualistic Elements in English Drama, 1476-1562." *University of North Carolina Record* 429 (1946), 143-44.

Miller, Perry. "The Garden of Eden and the Deacon's Meadow." *American Heritage* 7 (1955), 54-61. Discusses the importance of the Bible in American thought.

Milward, Peter. *Christian Themes in English Literature* (Tokyo: Kenkyusha, 1967). Organized thematically and includes: Belief in God; Providence, Fate and Free Will; Christian Humanism; Destiny of Man; Sin and Suffering; Incarnation and Redemption; Our Lady; Holy Spirit; Sacramental Symbolism. Index, principally of names.

————. *Shinaku Seisho to Eibungaku* (Tokyo: Chuo Shuppansha, 1971). The NT and English literature, in Japanese.

Miner, Earl, ed. *Literary Uses of Typology from the Late Middle Ages to the Present* (Princeton: Princeton University Press, 1977). Eleven essays ranging from "some medieval problems and examples" to "some features of religious figuralism in twentieth-century literature." A great deal of useful information concerning biblical types throughout, though it is not indexed, since "the Bible, its books, and its personages are to be assumed present passim."

Moffatt, James. *Literary Illustrations of the Bible* (8 vols.; New York: Armstrong; London: Hodder & Stoughton, 1905-06). A series of small-format volumes — on Ecclesiastes, Judges and Ruth, Daniel, Mark, Luke, Romans, James, and Revelation — citing examples from literature (as well as historical and biographical writing) in which "the Bible has been used or applied in what appears to be a forcible or notable manner." Arrangement is by chapter and verse of the biblical book in question.

————. *The Expositor's Dictionary of Poetical Quotations* (London: Hodder and Stoughton, 1913). Index of authors and of subjects.

————. *The Bible in Scots Literature* (London: Hodder & Stoughton, 1924). The impact of Scripture on Scottish verse and prose. Index of authors and subjects, as well as of biblical passages.

Morgan, K. E. "Christian Themes in English Poetry of the Twentieth Century." Unpubl. diss., Liverpool, 1964.

Murdock, Kenneth. *Literature and Theology in Colonial New England* (Cambridge, Mass.: Harvard University Press, 1949). "Attempts to outline the relation between the New England Puritans' fundamental theological ideas and their literary theory and practice." Bible mentioned incidentally.

Nakasawa, Junj. *Seisho to Eibungaku* (Tokyo: Daito Shuppan Centre, 1971). The Bible and English literature, in Japanese.

Nelson, Lawrence E. *Our Roving Bible: Tracking Its Influence Through English and American Life* (New York, Nashville: Abingdon-Cokesbury Press, 1945). An entertaining ramble through English and American literature in search of biblical influence. Extensive notes and index.

Nichols, Francis W. "Biblical Themes and Modern Literature." *Horizons* 8 (1981), 109-13. Discusses possible approaches to teaching biblical themes in modern literature. Considers significant Bible passages in conjunction with Camus, Beckett, Greene, and others.

Nunn, T. R., and F. D. Curtis. "Biblical References, Quotations, and Allusions in Popular Magazines." *School Review* 52 (1944), 239-44.

Owst, G. R. *Literature and Pulpit in Medieval England* (Oxford: Basil Blackwell, 1961). Index lists biblical characters and subjects.

Patrides, C. A. *Premises and Motifs in Renaissance Thought and Literature* (Princeton: Princeton University Press, 1982). Index of names and subjects, as well as extensive bibliographical footnotes.

Patterson, F. A. "English Prose Writers and the English Bible." *The Southern Workman* (1935), 345-49.

Pattison, Robert B. "Bible Words as Book Titles." *Religion in Life* 7 (1938), 439-50. A brief essay, followed by a list of "modern novels and plays with biblical titles" arranged according to the order of biblical books.

Pearlman, E. "Typological Autobiography in Seventeenth-Century England." *Biography* 8/2 (1985), 95-118.

Perry, William Gilmer. "English Literature's Debt to the Bible." *North American Review* 198 (1913), 227-39. An appreciation of the Bible as "the source of truest and most enduring literary inspiration" for English authors from Caedmon to Tennyson and Browning. Few specific allusions or examples.

Phy, Allene Stuart, ed. *The Bible and Popular Culture in America* (Philadelphia: Fortress; Chico: Scholars Press, 1985). Traces the influence and use of the Bible in American fiction and children's literature.

Rees, Robert A. "Toward a Bibliography of the Bible in

American Literature." *Bulletin of Bibliography* 29 (1972), 101-08. "An attempt to list those books, doctoral dissertations, master's theses, articles, chapters, bibliographies, and notes dealing with the influence of the Bible in American literature."

Reiter, Robert. "On Biblical Typology and the Interpretation of Literature." *College English* 30 (1969), 562-71. Literary examples confined to the 19th cent.

Religion and Literature. Formerly *Notre Dame English Journal.* Published three times a year at the University of Notre Dame. Articles and reviews.

Reynolds, David W. *Faith in Fiction: The Emergence of Religious Literature in America* (Cambridge and London: Harvard University Press, 1981). One chapter devoted to "biblical fiction." Index of authors and subjects.

Rollinson, Philip B. "The Influence of Christian Doctrine and Exegesis on Old English Poetry: An Estimate of the Current State of Scholarship." *Anglo-Saxon England* 2 (1973), 271-84.

Ross-Bryant, Lynn. *Imagination and the Life of the Spirit: An Introduction to the Study of Religion and Literature* (Ann Arbor: Scholars Press, 1982). Useful bibliographical notes.

Roston, Murray. *Biblical Drama in England from the Middle Ages to the Present Day* (Evanston: Northwestern University Press, 1968) An evaluative and interpretative study. Index lists biblical characters. See also his University of London dissertation, "The Use in English Drama of Themes from the Old Testament and Its Apocrypha" (1961).

————. *Prophet and Poet: The Bible and the Growth of Romanticism* (London: Faber and Faber, 1965). Argues that the Bible presented the Romantic poets with an alternative to the classical Augustan model of poetry. Special attention to Isaiah.

Sampson, Ashley. "Religion in Modern Literature." *Contemporary Review* 147 (1935), 462-70. General discussion, not specifically biblical.

Schneidau, Herbert N. *Sacred Discontent: The Bible and Western Tradition* (Baton Rouge: Louisiana State University Press, 1976). Discussion of the "underlying habits of thought" derived from the Bible upon which Western literature is based.

Scott, Nathan A., Jr. *The Climate of Faith in Modern Literature* (New York: Seabury, 1964). An anthology of critical essays studying the "transaction between the Christian faith and the world of modern literature." Focus not essentially biblical.

Seiss, J. A. "The Influence of the Bible on Literature." *The Evangelical Review* 5/17 (1853), 1-17. General discussion, with few specific illustrations.

Selby, Thomas G. *The Theology of Modern Fiction* (London: Charles H. Kelly, 1896). Study of George Eliot, Hawthorne, Hardy, George Macdonald, Mark Rutherford. No index.

Shaffer, E. S. *"Kubla Khan" and the Fall of Jerusalem: The Mythological School in Biblical Criticism and Secular Literature 1770-1800* (London: Cambridge University Press, 1975). See especially chap. 2, "The Visionary Character: Revelation and the Lyrical Ballad," and chap. 5, "Browning's St. John: The Casuistry of the Higher Criticism."

Shepard, O. "The English Bible and American Men of Letters." *Southern Workman* 64 (1935).

Siegel, Ben. "The Biblical Novel, 1900-1959: A Preliminary Checklist." *Bulletin of Bibliography* 23 (1961), 88-90. Lists titles of nonliterary biblical tales intended for a quasi-religious market as well as volumes of genuine literary merit.

Sivan, Gabriel. *The Bible and Civilization* (New York: Quadrangle / New York Times, 1973). Limited to the OT, but see pt. 4, "Biblical Themes and Echoes in World Literature."

Smith, Fred. "Fictionalizing the Bible." *Homiletic Review* 98 (1929), 118-90.

Smith, Wilbur M. "A Bibliography of the Influence of the Bible on English Literature (And in part on the Fine Arts)." *Fuller Library Bulletin* 9/10 (1951), 2-15.

Smyth, Mary Winslow. *Biblical Quotations in Middle English Literature before 1350* (Folcroft: Folcroft Library Editions, 1974 [rpt. of 1911 ed., *Yale Studies in English,* no. 41]). Includes bibliographical references and index. A continuation of the collection begun in Cook's *Biblical Quotations in Old English Prose Writers.*

Spanos, William Vaios. "Modern British Verse Drama and the Christian Tradition: The Strategy of Sacramental Transfiguration." *DA* 24/09 (1964), 03769. Focusses on Eliot, Williams, Sayers, and Masefield, among others.

Stephenson, William E. "Religious Drama in the Restoration." *Philological Quarterly* 50 (1971), 599-609. Discusses, among other things, the representation and misrepresentation of Scripture on the Restoration stage.

Stevens, James S. *The English Bible* (New York: Abingdon, 1921). Chaps. 14–16 discuss the Bible in English and American poetry; chap. 19, the Bible in the novel.

Stevenson, J. C. "The Influence of the Bible on English Literature of the Seventeenth Century." Unpubl. M.A. thesis, Birmingham, 1919.

Stewart, Randall. *American Literature and Christian Doctrine* (Baton Rouge: Louisiana State University Press, 1958). Doctrine of original sin is used as criterion for assessing Christian influence.

Stoddart, Jane T. *The New Testament in Life and Literature* (London: Hodder & Stoughton, 1914). A popular rather than scholarly anthology of quotations. No real principle of selection — includes periodicals, sermon literature, etc. as well as literary references. Has indices of scriptural references.

————. *The Old Testament in Life and Literature* (London: Hodder & Stoughton, 1913). Volume is similarly arranged to that cited above.

Suderman, Elmer F. "Religion in the American Novel: 1870-1900." *DA* 22/7 (1962), 2387.

Sutcliffe, Denham. "Christian Themes in American Fiction." *Christian Scholar* 64 (1961), 297-311.

Sypherd, W. O. *The Literature of the English Bible* (Oxford: Oxford University Press, 1938). See Appendix H, "Biblical Themes in Literature."

The Temple Bible. Ed. by various hands (London: J. M. Dent; Philadelphia: Lippincott, 1902). Each volume concludes with an appendix entitled "Biblical References in English Literature."

Tennyson, G. B. " 'So Careful of the Type?' Victorian Biblical Typology: Sources and Applications." *Essays & Studies* 37 (1984), 31-45.

Thorp, Willard. "The Religious Novel as Best Seller in America." In James Ward Smith and A. Leland Jamison, eds. *Religion in American Life,* vol. 2: *Religious Perspectives in American Culture,* 195-242 (Princeton: Princeton University Press, 1961). Discussion of Christian popular novels. Few scriptural references.

Tichy, Henrietta. *Biblical Influence in English Literature: A Survey of Studies* (Ann Arbor, MI: Edwards Brothers, 1953). Attempts comprehensive survey, but focusses primarily on English authors; coverage of American writers is slight. Annotated.

Tiplady, Thomas. *The Influence of the Bible on History, Literature and Oratory* (New York: Fleming H. Revell, 1924). General discussion of biblical influence on a variety of English writers.

Tkacz, Catherine Brown. "The Bible in Medieval Literature: A Bibliographic Essay on Basic and New Sources." *Religion and Literature* 19 (1987), 63-76. Intended as an aid to scholarship for "those whose literary research brings them to address the role of the Bible in medieval texts."

Toews, Aganetha Wall. " 'The Great Code' in Six Twentieth-Century European Novels." *DAI* 45/08 (1985), 2519A. Considers Evelyn Waugh's *Vile Bodies* and Joseph Conrad's *Heart of Darkness,* among other novels.

Turnell, Martin. *Modern Literature and Christian Faith* (London: Darton, Longman, and Todd, 1961). Brief study concerned principally with Lawrence, Forster, Woolf, Claudel, Mauriac, and Greene.

Urdang, Laurence, and Frederick G. Ruffner, Jr. *Allusions —Cultural, Literary, Biblical, and Historical: A Thematic Dictionary* (Detroit: Gale Research Co., 1981). Thematic arrangement of categories, under which allusions (including some biblical) are listed. Bibliography and Index of Allusions follow.

Van Dyke, Henry. "The Influence of the Bible in Literature." *Century Magazine* 80 (1910), 888-95. General discussion; few specific examples.

Weales, Gerald. *Religion in Modern English Drama* (Philadelphia: University of Pennsylvania Press, 1961). Chapters include "Sentimental Supernaturalism" and "Doctrine of Substitution." Authors discussed include Housman, Masefield, Charles Williams, Dorothy Sayers, Christopher Fry, and T. S. Eliot.

Webb, Eugene. *The Dark Dove: The Sacred and Secular in Modern Literature* (Seattle: University of Washington Press, 1975). Exploration of the sacred and secular in Yeats, Rilke, Joyce, and others. Establishes biblical context with specific references.

Wheeler, B. M. "Religious Themes in Contemporary Literature." *Journal of the Bible and Religion* 27 (1959), 50-56. Divided into four sections: Poetry, Drama, Prose Fiction, and Criticism.

Wilder, Amos. "American Literature and Its Religious Archetypes." *Festschrift zum 75 Geburtstag von Theodor Spira,* ed. Helmut Viebrock and Willi Erzgraeber (Heidelberg, 1961), 252-59. Explores the way the Bible is used in American letters.

————. *Modern Poetry and Christian Tradition: A Study in the Relation of Christianity and Culture* (New York: Charles Scribner's Sons, 1952). Broad-ranging discussion of the influence of various Christian denominations on various authors (Thomas, Eliot, Hopkins, etc.).

————. *Theology and Modern Literature* (Cambridge: Harvard University Press, 1958). General study ranging from "religious dimensions of modern literature" to "theology and aesthetic judgment."

Williams, Edwin W. "The Disappearance of God in American Literature." *Duke Divinity Review* 42 (1977), 165-74.

Wilson, A. N. "Christianity and the Novelists." *King's Theological Review* 6 (1983), 29-31.

Wilson, James Harrison. "Christian Theology and Old English Poetry." *DA* 27/02 (1966), 490. Patristic and theological background; some biblical references.

Woolf, Rosemary. *The English Mystery Plays* (Berkeley and Los Angeles: University of California Press, 1972). Chapters are arranged topically according to biblical/theological content of the plays. Index.

Work, Edgar Whittaker. *The Bible in English Literature* (New York: Fleming H. Revell, 1917).

Wright, L. B. "The Scriptures and the Elizabethan Stage." *Modern Philology* 26 (1928), 47-56.

Zemka, Sue. "Victorian Testaments: The Uses and Abuses of the Bible in Early Nineteenth Century British Literature." Unpubl. diss., Stanford, 1989.

KATHERINE B. JEFFREY

Use of the Bible by a Single Author or Group of Authors

The following list includes titles concerned with use of the Bible by individual named authors or groups of authors in English literary tradition. It is organized alphabetically by the last name of authors. Titles which include references to several authors are listed in full only under the first mentioned name; cross-reference listings appear under the names of the other authors.

Titles which contain reference to use of specific allusion by an author (e.g., "Tree of Life Imagery in the Poetry of Edward Taylor" or "Faith, Hope and Charity in Swift's Poems") are generally not included here but in the brief bibliographies accompanying relevant entries in the *Dictionary*. As such, many scholarly "notes" which identify a single allusion or specific biblical source-text for a work of English literature are similarly relegated to entry bibliographies.

ANDERSON, MAXWELL

Kliger, Samuel. "Hebraic Lore in Maxwell Anderson's *Winterset*." *American Letters* 18 (1946), 219-32. Use of the OT.

Pearce, Howard. "Job in Anderson's *Winterset*." *Modern Drama* 6 (1963), 32-41. Allusions to the book of Job.

ARNOLD, MATTHEW

Korinko, Stephen J. "Matthew Arnold and Biblical Higher Criticism." *DAI* 31/8 (1971), 4124A.

Savory, Jerold J. "The Gospel According to Arnold: Literature and Dogma and God and the Bible." *The Arnoldian* 5 (1978), 16-22.

———. "Matthew Arnold and 'The Author of Supernatural Religion': The Background to God and the Bible." *Studies in English Literature* 16 (1976), 677-91.

———. "Matthew Arnold and the Higher Criticism of the Bible: A Study of God and the Bible and the Last Essays on Church and Religion." *DAI* 3/32 (1971), 1528A.

ASCH, SHOLEM

George, Ralph W. "Sholem Asch — Man of Letters and Prophet." *Religion in Life* 20 (1950/51), 106-13. Discusses Asch's use of biblical material.

AUSTEN, JANE

Koppel, Gene. *The Religious Dimension of Jane Austen's Novels* (Ann Arbor: UMI Research, 1988).

BACON, FRANCIS

Hall, Joan Wylie. "'Salomon Saith': Bacon's Use of Solomon in the 1625 Essays." *University of Dayton Review* 15 (1982), 83-88. Biblical backgrounds to *The Essays or Counsels, Civill and Morall* (1597, 1612, 1625).

Whitney, Charles. "Bacon's Antithetical Prophecy." *Mosaic* 15 (1982), 63-77. Relation to biblical notions of prophecy.

BECKETT, SAMUEL

Baldwin, Helene L. "The Theme of the Pilgrim in the Works of Samuel Beckett." *Christian Scholar's Review* 8 (1978), 217-28. Discusses structural links of *Godot* with the parables of Jesus; Beckett's use of acrostics and name variations to evoke biblical characters.

Hutchings, William. "'The Unintelligible Terms of an Incomprehensible Damnation': Samuel Beckett's The Unnamable, Shelo, and St. Erkenwald." *Twentieth Century Literature* 27 (1981), 97-112. Discusses OT sources.

Jones, L. "Narrative Salvation in *Waiting for Godot*."

Modern Drama 17 (1974), 179-88. Christian influence; no specific biblical references.

Morrison, Kristin. "Neglected Biblical Allusions in Beckett's Plays: 'Mother Pegg' Once More." In Beja, Morris, with S. E. Gontarski, and Pierre Astier, eds. *Samuel Beckett: Humanist Perspectives* (Columbus: Ohio State University Press, 1983), 91-98.

Nykrog, Per. "In the Ruins of the Past: Reading Samuel Beckett Intertextually." *Christianity and Literature* 36 (1984), 289-311. Relationship to Matthew's Gospel.

O'Brien, William J. "To Hell with Samuel Beckett." In Apczynski, John, ed., *Foundations of Religious Literacy* (Chico: Scholars Press, 1983), 165-74. Sources in the Bible.

BELLOW, SAUL

Brophy, R. J. "Biblical Parallels in Bellow's *Henderson the Rain King.*" *Christianity and Literature* 23 (1974), 27-30.

Stout, Janet. "Biblical Allusion in *Henderson the Rain King.*" *South Central Bulletin* 40 (1980), 165-67.

BLAKE, WILLIAM

Barr, D. J. "William Blake's Use of the Bible." *Notes and Queries* 9 (1960), 312. Blake's use and misuse of Exod. 4:6 and Rev. 11:4.

Beer, John. *Blake's Visionary Universe* (Manchester: Manchester University Press, 1969). See especially "The Visionary's Bible," 30-38.

Curtis, F. B. "The Geddes Bible and the Tent of the Eternal in *The Book of Urizen.*" *Blake Newsletter* 6 (1973), 93-94.

Davis, Patricia Elizabeth. "William Blake's New Typology and the Revaluation of Prophecy in the 18th Century." *DAI* 40/12 (1980), 6288A.

Erdman, David V. "A Book to Eat." *Blake: An Illustrated Quarterly* 15 (1982), 170-75. Connections with book of Ezekiel.

Ferguson, J. B. "A Study of William Blake's *Jerusalem* with Special Reference to the Book of Ezekiel." Unpubl. diss., University of Edinburgh, 1975.

Grant, John E. "Apocalypse in Blake's 'Auguries of Innocence.'" *Texas Studies in Literature and Language* 5 (1964), 489-508. Discusses a variety of biblical texts, not specifically Revelation.

Helms, Randal. "Blake's Use of the Bible in 'A Song of Liberty.'" *English Language Notes* 16 (1979), 287-91.

Helmstadter, Thomas H. "Blake and Religion: Iconographical Themes in the *Night Thoughts.*" *Studies in Romanticism* 10 (1971), 199-212. Discusses biblical texts in Jude, Judges.

Holmes, John R. "William Blake's Place in the Mystical Tradition." *DAI* 47/1 (1986), 188A. See especially the chapter on Christ-like "self-annihilation."

Mewton, Robert. "Biblical Prophet or Deluded Vision-

ary? William Blake and a Double Error." *L'erreur dans la littérature et la pensée anglaises.* Actes du Centre Aixois de Recherches Anglaises (Aix-en-Provence: University de Provence, 1980), 107-26.

Miner, P. "Aspects of Blake's Biblical Symbolism." *William Blake: Essays for S. Foster Damon,* ed. Alvin H. Rosenfeld (Providence: Brown University Press, 1969).

Noll, Jacqueline Ann. "Old Testament Prophecy in Blake's Lambeth Poems." *DAI* 38/9 (1978), 5500A.

Rix, Donna Standfier. "The Function of Biblical Sources in the Structure and Meaning of Blake's *Milton.*" *DAI* 38/12 (1978), 7349A.

Roth, James Peter. "The Bible of Hell: William Blake's Lambeth Books." *DAI* 40/10 (1980), 5454A. Blake's use of Revelation.

Rose, Edward J. "Blake's Jerusalem, St. Paul, and Biblical Prophecy." *English Studies in Canada* 11 (1985), 396-412.

Smith, Mark Trevor. "William Blake's Transfiguration of the Bible in 'Jerusalem.'" *DAI* 43/8 (1983), 2685A.

Spicer, Harold Otis. "The Chariot of Fire: A Study of William Blake's Use of Biblical Typology in the Minor Prophecies." *DA* 23/6 (1962), 2141.

Tannenbaum, Leslie. *Biblical Tradition in Blake's Early Prophecies: The Great Code of Art* (Princeton: Princeton University Press, 1982). Analysis of six prophetic books of Blake's Lambeth period with reference to the Bible and contemporary biblical scholarship.

Tolley, M. J. "William Blake's Use of the Bible." Unpubl. diss., London, 1975.

Tolley, Michael J. "William Blake's Use of the Bible in a Section of 'The Everlasting Gospel.'" *Notes and Queries* 9 (1962), 171-76.

Van Schaik, Pamela. "Blake's Vision of the Fall and Redemption of Man: A Reading Based on the Contrary Images of Innocence and Experience." Unpubl. diss., University of South Africa, 1983.

See also Leslie Tannenbaum under BYRON; S. B. Fishman under SPENSER.

BRADSTREET, ANNE

McElrath, Joseph R., Jr., and Allan P. Robb, eds. *The Complete Works of Anne Bradstreet* (Boston: Twayne, 1981). Notes list biblical references.

Rosenmaier, Rosamond R. "The Wounds upon Bathsheba: Anne Bradstreet's Prophetic Art." *Puritan Poets and Poetics: Seventeenth-Century American Poetry in Theory and Practice,* ed. Peter White and Harrison T. Meserole (University Park: Pennsylvania State University Press, 1985), 129-46. Relates Bradstreet's fiction to a biblical tradition of prophecy in the Puritan context.

BRONTËS

Bluche, François. "Le Dieu De Monte Christo et De Jane

Eyre: Un Christianisme Romantique sans Christ?" *Revue d'histoire et de philosophie religieuses* 59 (1979), 161-86. The place of Christ, the Gospels, and the OT in *Jane Eyre.*

Dale, Peter Allan. "Heretical Narration: Charlotte Brontë's Search for Endlessness." *Religion and Literature* 16 (1984), 1-24. Sources in the Bible.

Hudson, Aida Regina. "The Religious Temper of Charlotte Brontë's Novels." *DAI* 42/9 (1982), 4006A. A theological, rather than strictly biblical, consideration.

BROWNING, ROBERT

Berlin-Lieberman, Judith. *Robert Browning and Hebraism: A Study of the Poems of Browning which are Based on Rabbinical Writings and Other Sources in Jewish Literature* (Jerusalem: Azriel Printing, 1934).

Charlton, H. B. *Browning as Poet of Religion* (Philadelphia: Richard West, 1978).

Cheskin, Arnold Ford. "Robert Browning and Hebraic Tradition." *DAI* 42/4 (1981), 1643A. A study of Browning's works which are grounded in Hebraic (primarily midrashic and rabbinical) materials.

Cook, A. K. *A Commentary Upon Browning's The Ring and the Book* (Hamden, CT: Archon Books, 1966). Biblical references are included in line-by-line commentary.

De Laura, David J. "The Religious Imagery in Browning's 'The Patriot.'" *Victorian Newsletter* 21 (1962), 16-18.

Harper, James Winthrop. "Browning and the Evangelical Tradition." *DA* 21 (1961), 3089-90. Theological rather than biblical focus.

Hassett, Constance W. "Browning's Caponsacchi: Convert and Apocalyptist." *Philological Quarterly* 60 (1981), 487-500. NT references, especially the book of Revelation.

Hellstrom, Ward. "Time and Type in Browning's *Saul.*" *English Literary History* 33 (1966), 370-89. Posits David and Saul as types of Christ.

Lawson, E. Leroy. *Very Sure of God: Religious Language in the Poetry of Robert Browning* (Nashville: Vanderbilt University Press, 1974). Based on dissertation of the same title (Vanderbilt, 1971). Theological emphasis.

Machen, Minnie (Gresham). *The Bible in Browning with Particular Reference to* The Ring and the Book (New York: Macmillan, 1903). Though dated, still a useful study.

McClatchey, Joe. "Interpreting 'Karshish.'" *Browning Society Notes* 13 (1983), 3-16. NT connections.

Melchiori, Barbara. "Browning and the Bible: An Examination of 'Holy Cross Day.'" *Review of English Literature* 7 (1966), 20-42.

Passarella, Lee. "A Biblical Allusion in *Fifine at the Fair.*" *Studies in Browning and His Circle* 7 (1979), 84-85.

Peterson, Linda Haenlein. "Biblical Typology and the Poetry of Robert Browning." *DAI* 39 (1979), 6147A-48A.

———. "Biblical Typology and the Self-Portrait of the Poet in Robert Browning." *Approaches to Victorian Autobiography,* ed. George P. Landow (Athens, OH: Ohio University Press, 1979), 235-68.

See also E. S. Shaffer in the bibliography "The Influence of the Bible on English Literature" (above).

BUNYAN, JOHN

Beal, Rebecca S. *"Grace Abounding to the Chief of Sinners:* John Bunyan's Pauline Epistle." *Studies in English Literature* 21 (1981), 147-60.

Blondel, Jacques. "Bunyan et la Bible dans *The Pilgrim's Progress.*" *Les Langues Modernes* 67 (1973), 57-66.

Bowman, Derek. "The Path of Life: Attitudes to the Bible in Some Autobiographies of the Seventeenth and Eighteenth Centuries." *Essays in German and Dutch Literature,* ed. W. D. Robson-Scott (London: Institute of Germanic Studies, 1973).

Bunyan, John. *The Pilgrim's Progress from this World to That which is to Come.* Ed. James Blanton Wharey. 2nd ed. rev. by Roger Sharrock (Oxford: Clarendon Press, 1960). Biblical references noted in the margins of the text.

Johnson, Clifford. "A Biblical Source for Bunyan's 'Wide Field Full of Dark Mountains.'" *Notes and Queries* 21 (1974), 413-14.

Jones, C. J. A. "Christian and his World: The Presentation of Some Areas of Religious Experience in the Writings of John Bunyan." Unpubl. diss., Oxford, 1976.

Stranahan, Brainerd P. "Bunyan and the Epistle to the Hebrews: His Source for the Idea of Pilgrimage in *The Pilgrim's Progress.*" *Studies in Philology* 79 (1982), 179-296.

———. "Bunyan's Special Talent: Biblical Texts as 'Events' in *Grace Abounding* and *The Pilgrim's Progress.*" *English Literary Renaissance* 11 (1981), 329-43.

BUTLER, SAMUEL

Freeman, Joanna M. "Biblical Allusions as a Rhetorical Device in *The Way of All Flesh.*" *DAI* 34/7 (1974), 4198A-99A.

Shaheen, Naseeb. "Butler's Use of Scripture in *The Way of All Flesh.*" *Essays in Literature* 5 (1978), 39-51.

BYRON, GEORGE GORDON, LORD

Cantor, Paul A. "Byron's *Cain:* A Romantic Version of the Fall." *Kenyon Review* 2 (1980), 50-71.

Eisl, Maria Emanuela. "Lord Byron and His Religous Pronouncements in *Cain, Don Juan,* and *A Vision of Judgment.*" Pp. 26-62 in James Hogg, ed. *Studies in Nineteenth Century Literature* (Salzburg: Institut für Anglistik & Amerikanistik, 1981). Discusses biblical sources.

Looper, Travis. *Byron and the Bible: A Compendium of Biblical Usage in the Poetry of Lord Byron* (Metuchen, NJ: Scarecrow Press, 1978). Based on the author's Baylor dissertation (1977). Very thorough and useful. There is a table of biblical references.

Marjarum, Edward N. *Byron as Skeptic and Believer.* Princeton Studies in English 16 (Princeton: Princeton University Press, 1938).

Minor, Mark. "Clare, Byron, and the Bible: Additional Evidence from the Asylum Manuscripts." *Bulletin of Research in the Humanities* 85 (1982), 104-26.

Ponitz, Arthur. "Byron und die Bibel." Unpubl. diss., University of Leipzig, 1906.

Stavrou, C. N. "Religion in Byron's *Don Juan.*" *Studies in English Literature* 3 (1963), 567-94. Theological approach.

Stevens, Harold Ray. "Byron and the Bible: A Study of Poetic and Philosophic Development." *DA* 25/9 (1965), 5286-87.

———. "Theme and Structure in Byron's *Manfred*: The Biblical Basis." *Unisa English Studies* (Pretoria, South Africa) 11 (1973), 15-22.

Tannenbaum, Leslie. "Lord Byron in the Wilderness: Biblical Tradition in Byron's *Cain* and Blake's *The Ghost of Abel.*" *Modern Philology* 72 (1975), 350-64.

Thompson, Leslie M. "Biblical Influence in 'Childe Roland to the Dark Tower Came.'" *Papers on Language and Literature* 3 (1967), 339-53.

CABLE, GEORGE W.

Morehead, Martha Hines. "George W. Cable's Use of the Bible in His Fiction and Major Polemical Essays." *DAI* 41/4 (1980), 1597A-98A.

CARLYLE, THOMAS

Sigman, Joseph. "Adam-Kadmon, Nifl, Muspel, and the Biblical Symbolism of *Sartor Resartus.*" *English Literary History* 41 (1974), 233-56.

CATHER, WILLA

Fetty, Audrey M. S. "Biblical Allusions in the Fiction of Willa Cather." *DAI* 34/5 (1973), 2621A-22A.

CHAPMAN, GEORGE

Bennett, F. J. "The Use of the Bible in the Dramatic Works of George Chapman, Thomas Dekker, John Marston, and John Webster." *DA* 25/2 (1964), 1187-88.

CHAUCER, GEOFFREY

Ames, Ruth M. "Prototype and Parody in Chaucerian Exegesis." *The Fourteenth Century,* ed. Paul E. Szarmach and Bernard S. Levy (Binghamton: Centre for Medieval & Early Renaissance Studies, SUNY Binghamton, 1978), 87-105. Chaucer's treatment of the OT.

Andrew, Malcolm. "Chaucer's 'General Prologue' to the Canterbury Tales." *Explicator* 43 (1984), 5-6. Notes, biblical sources, and allusions.

Besserman, L[awrence] L. "Chaucer and the Bible: The Case of the Merchant's Tale." *Hebrew University Studies in Literature* 6 (1978), 10-31.

———. "Chaucer and the Bible: Parody and Authority in the Pardoner's Tale." *Biblical Patterns in Modern Literature,* ed. David H. Hirsch and Nehama Aschkenasy (Chico: Scholars Press, 1984), 35-50. See also his essay in the Jeffrey anthology, cited above.

———. *Chaucer and the Bible: An Introduction, Critical Review of Research, Indexes, and Bibliography* (New York: Garland, 1988).

Black, Robert. "Chaucer's Allusion to the 'Sermon on the Mount' in the 'Miller's Tale.'" *Revue de l'Université d'Ottawa/University of Ottawa Quarterly* 55 (1985), 23-32.

Black, Robert Ray. "Sacral and Biblical Parody in Chaucer's *Canterbury Tales.*" *DAI* 35/9 (1975), 6090A.

Brown, Emerson, Jr. "Biblical Women in the Merchant's Tale: Feminism, Antifeminism, and Beyond." *Viator* 5 (1974), 387-412.

Buermann, Theodore Barry. "Chaucer's 'Book of Genesis' in *The Canterbury Tales:* The Biblical Schema of the First Fragment." *DAI* 28/12 (1968), 5009.

Bugge, John. "Tell-tale Context: Two Notes on Biblical Quotation in *The Canterbury Tales.*" *American Notes and Queries* 14 (1976), 82-85.

Cook, Robert. "Another Biblical Echo in the Wife of Bath's Prologue?" *English Studies* 59 (1978), 390-94. Possible reference to the book of 2 Kings.

Delaney, Sheila. "Doer of the Word: The Epistle of St. James as a Source for Chaucer's Manciple's Tale." *Chaucer Review* 17 (1983), 250-54.

Hermann, John P., and John J. Burke, Jr., eds. *Signs and Symbols in Chaucer's Poetry* (University, AL: University of Alabama Press, 1981). See "Bible" in index for reference to discussion of Chaucer's use of biblical texts.

Jacobs, Edward Craney. "Further Biblical Allusions for Chaucer's Prioress." *Chaucer Review* 15 (1980), 151-54.

Jeffrey, David Lyle, ed. *Chaucer and Scriptural Tradition* (Ottawa: University of Ottawa Press, 1984). Also published as vol. 53 of *Revue de l'Universite d'Ottawa/University of Ottawa Quarterly* (1983). Series of essays on various aspects of Chaucer's debt to Scripture.

Johnson, Dudley R. "The Biblical Characters of Chaucer's Monk." *Publications of the Modern Language Association of America* 66 (1951), 827-43.

———. "Chaucer and the Bible." *DAI* 31/7 (1971), 3506A. Argues an acquisition of biblical knowledge by Chaucer through secondary sources rather than direct familiarity with the Vg.

Jordan, Tracey. "Fairy Tale and Fabliau: Chaucer's *The Miller's Tale.*" *Studies in Short Fiction* 21 (1984), 87-93. Discusses OT sources.

Kaske, R. E. "The Canticum Canticorum in the *Miller's Tale.*" *Studies in Philology* 59 (1962), 479-500. Allusions to the Song of Songs.

Lancashire, Ian. "Moses, Elijah, and the Back Parts of God: Satiric Scatology in Chaucer's *Summoner's Tale.*" *Mosaic* 14/30 (1981), 17-30.

Landrum, Grace W. "Chaucer's Use of the Vulgate." *Publications of the Modern Language Association of America* 39 (1924), 75-100. Argues an extensive and direct knowledge of the Vg on Chaucer's part.

Levy, Bernard S. "Biblical Parody in the Summoner's Tale." *Tennessee Studies in Literature* 11 (1966), 45-60.

McNamara, John. "Chaucer's Use of the Epistle of St. James in the Clerk's Tale." *Chaucer Review* 7/3 (1973), 184-93.

Mendelson, Anne. "Some Uses of the Bible and Biblical Authority in the Wife of Bath's Prologue and Tale." *DAI* 39/4 (1978), 2295A.

Peck, Russell A. "St. Paul and the Canterbury Tales." *Mediaevalia* 7 (1981), 91-131.

Robertson, D. W., Jr. *A Preface to Chaucer* (Princeton: Princeton University Press, 1962). Foundational discussion of impact of exegetical tradition on Chaucer; references to biblical topics throughout.

Rudat, Wolfgang E. H. "Heresy and Springtime Ritual: Biblical and Classical Allusions in the *Canterbury Tales.*" *Revue Belge de Philologie et d'Histoire* 54/3 (1976), 823-36.

Thompson, Charlotte Barclay. "The Old Testament of Babylon: A Rereading of Chaucer's Knight's Tale." *DAI* 40/8 (1980), 4612A-13A. Views the *Knight's Tale* as a pagan analogue to the OT.

Turner, W. Arthur. "Biblical Women in the *Merchant's Tale* and the *Tale of Melibee.*" *English Language Notes* 3 (1965), 92-95.

Weever, Jacqueline de. *A Chaucer Name Dictionary: Guide to Astrological, Biblical, Historical, Literary, and Mythological Names in the Works of Geoffrey Chaucer* (New York: Garland, 1988). All biblical names which appear anywhere in Chaucer are listed, with some historical and literary background.

CHESTERTON, G. K.

Boyd, Ian. "Chesterton and the Bible." *Chesterton Review* 11/1 (1985), 21-33.

————. " 'The Ballad of the Battle of Gibeon.' " *Chesterton Review* 8 (1982), 95-100. Editor's notes specify some biblical allusions.

CLARE, JOHN

See Mark Minor under BYRON.

CLAUDEL, PAUL

See Jerry R. Talley under SHAW.

COLERIDGE, SAMUEL TAYLOR

Avni, Abraham. "Coleridge and Ecclesiastes: A Wary Response." *The Wordsworth Circle* 12 (1981), 127-29.

Barth, J. Robert, S.J. *Coleridge and Christian Doctrine* (Cambridge, Mass.: Harvard University Press, 1969). Includes chapters on "Nature and Role of Scripture," "One and Triune God," "Creation and Sinful Man," "The Redeemer, Redemption and Justification," "Last Things." Index to subjects and names.

Boulger, James D. *Coleridge as Religious Thinker* (New Haven: Yale University Press, 1961). Theological rather than specifically biblical focus. Subject index.

Brisman, Leslie. "Coleridge and the Supernatural." *Studies in Romanticism* 21 (1982), 123-59. Discusses NT sources.

Hall, William Thomas. "Coleridge's Religious Doctrines and Significant Parallels in Calvinism." *DA* 23/1 (1962), 224-25.

Harding, Anthony John. *Coleridge and the Inspired Word* (Kingston: McGill-Queen's University Press, 1985). Special emphasis on Coleridge's views of inspiration, both biblical and poetic.

Kaufman, Andrew. "Authority and Vision: William Blake's Use of the Gospels." *University of Toronto Quarterly* 57/3 (1988), 389-403.

Pater, Walter. "Coleridge as Theologian." *Sketches and Reviews* (New York: Boni and Liveright, 1919), 87-115. Concludes with discussion of Coleridge's view of the Bible.

Piper, H. W. " 'The Ancient Mariner': Biblical Allegory, Poetic Symbolism and Religious Crisis." *Southern Review* (Australia) 10 (1977), 232-42. Influence of biblical apocalyptic literature.

Prickett, Stephen. "Towards a Rediscovery of the Bible: The Problem of the Still Small Voice." *Ways of Reading the Bible,* ed. Michael Wadsworth (Brighton: Harvester; Totowa, NJ: Barnes and Noble, 1981).

Pym, David. *The Religious Thought of Samuel Taylor Coleridge* (Gerrards Cross: Colin Smythe, 1978). Two final chapters on Coleridge's concept of Scripture.

See also E. S. Shaffer in the bibliography "The Influence of the Bible on English Literature" (above).

CONRAD, JOSEPH

Messenger, Ann P., and William E. Messenger. " 'One of Us' : A Biblical Allusion in Conrad's *Lord Jim.*" *English Language Notes* 9/2 (1971), 129-32.

Purdy, Dwight H. "Conrad's Bible." *Philological Quarterly* 60/2 (1981), 225-38. Scriptural allusions.

————. *Joseph Conrad's Bible* (Norman: University of Oklahoma Press, 1984). The nature and range of Conrad's biblical allusions. Useful index.

————. "The Manuscript of *Victory* and the Problem of

Conrad's Intentions." *Journal of Modern Literature* 10/1 (1983), 91-108. Discusses biblical allusions.

———. "'Peace that Passeth Understanding': The Professor's English Bible in *Under Western Eyes*." *Conradiana: A Journal of Joseph Conrad* 13/2 (1981), 83-93.

———. "Paul and the Pardoner in Conrad's *Victory*." *Texas Studies in Literature and Language* 23/2 (1981), 197-213. Discusses NT sources, and Chaucer.

Steiner, Joan E. "Modern Pharisees and False Apostles: Ironic New Testament Parallels in Conrad's 'Heart of Darkness.'" *Nineteenth Century Fiction* 37/1 (1982), 75-96.

Thomas, Lloyd S. "Conrad's 'Jury Rig' Use of the Bible in 'Youth.'" *Studies in Short Fiction* 17/1 (1980), 79-82.

Williams, Porter, Jr. "The Brand of Cain in *The Secret Sharer*." *Modern Fiction Studies* 10/1 (1964), 27-30.

COOPER, JAMES FENIMORE

Jones, Daryl E. "Temple in the Promised Land: Old Testament Parallel in Cooper's *The Pioneers*." *American Literature* 57 (1985), 68-78.

McAleer, John J. "Biblical Analogy in the Leatherstocking Tales." *Nineteenth Century Fiction* 17 (1962), 217-35.

COTTON, JOHN

Rosenmeier, Jesper. "The Image of Christ: The Typology of John Cotton." *American Doctoral Dissertations* (1966), 131.

Steiner, Prudence L. "A Garden of Spices in New England: John Cotton's and Edward Taylor's Use of the Song of Songs." *Allegory, Myth and Symbol*, ed. Morton W. Bloomfield (Cambridge: Harvard University Press, 1981), 227-43.

COWPER, WILLIAM

Dilworth, Thomas. "Cowper's 'Lines Written During a Period of Insanity.'" *Explicator* 42/2 (1984), 7-10. Biblical allusion.

Quinlan, Maurice J. "Cowper's [Biblical] Imagery." *Journal of English and Germanic Philology* 47 (1948), 276-85.

Shields, K. D. "William Cowper (1731-1800): Studies in the Poetry of an Evangelical." Unpubl. diss., University of Edinburgh, 1965.

CRANE, STEPHEN

Johnson, Clarence Oliver. "'A Methodist Clergyman — of the old Ambling-Nag, Saddle-Bag, Exhorting King': Stephen Crane and his Methodist Heritage." *DAI* 43/10 (1983), 3318A.

Knapp, Daniel. "Son of Thunder: Stephen Crane and the Fourth Evangelist." *Nineteenth Century Fiction* 24 (1969), 253-91.

Monteiro, George. "Shilomville as Judah: Crane's 'A Little Pilgrimage.'" *Renascence* 19 (1967), 184-89. Crane's use of Jeremiah.

Stein, W. B. "New Testament Inversions in Crane's *Maggie*." *Modern Language Notes* 73 (1958), 268-72.

See also E. J. McGregor under DICKINSON.

CRASHAW, RICHARD

Williams, George Walton. *Image and Symbol in the Sacred Poetry of Richard Crashaw* (Columbia: University of South Carolina Press, 1963).

———, ed. *The Complete Poetry of Richard Crashaw* (New York: New York University Press, 1972). Provides list of biblical references.

DEFOE, DANIEL

Backscheider, Paula R. "Personality and Biblical Allusion in Defoe's Letters." *South Atlantic Review* 47/1 (1982), 1-20.

Moffatt, James. "The Religion of Robinson Crusoe." *The Contemporary Review* 115 (1919), 664-69. General discussion; brief mention of the Bible.

DEKKER, THOMAS

Pineas, Rainer. "Biblical Allusion in *The Whore of Babylon*." *American Notes and Queries* 11 (1972), 22-24.

See F. J. Bennett under CHAPMAN.

DE VRIES, PETER

See R. C. Wood under O'CONNOR.

DICKENS, CHARLES

Axton, William F. "Religious and Scientific Imagery in *Bleak House*." *Nineteenth Century Fiction* 22 (1968), 349-59. OT allusions.

Bowkett, C. E. V. "The Place of Religion in Some of the Major Novels of Charles Dickens." Unpubl. M.A. thesis, Durham, 1968.

Egan, Madonna, C.S.J. "Telling 'The Blessed History': Charles Dickens's *The Life of Our Lord* (Volumes I and II)." *DAI* 44/03 (1984), 758A. Dickens's religious beliefs as demonstrated in *The Life of Our Lord*.

Fleissner, Robert F. "Dickens' *Little Testament*: Spiritual Quest or Humanistic Document." *Research Studies* 49/1 (1981), 35-45. Discusses NT sources.

Hodge, Jan Douglas. "The Gospel Influence on Dickens' Art." *DAI* 38/2 (1977), 805A.

Hornback, Bert G. *Noah's Arkitecture: A Study of Dickens's Mythology* (Athens: Ohio University Press, 1972). Discusses aspects of a "Genesis mythology" whose recurring symbols — flood, ark, Eden, Tower of Babel — unify many of Dickens's novels.

Kent, William R. *Dickens and Religion* (London: Watts and Company, 1930).

Kubota, Melvin Yoshio. "The Legacy of Babel: The

Theme of Language and Imagination in Charles Dickens's Late Novels." *DAI* 44/6 (1983), 1800A.

Larson, Janet L. "The Battle of Biblical Books in Esther's Narrative." *Nineteenth Century Fiction* 38/2 (1983), 131-60. On *Bleak House.*

————. "Biblical Reading in the Later Dickens: The Book of Job according to *Bleak House.*" *Dickens Studies Annual* 13 (1984), 35-83.

————. *Dickens and the Broken Scripture* (Athens: The University of Georgia Press, 1985). A study which intends "to weigh Dickens' biblical allusions in their fictional and historical contexts." Chapters on *Oliver Twist, Dombay and Son, Bleak House, Little Dorritt, Our Mutual Friend.* Extensive notes; index includes biblical references and characters.

Nelson, Harland Stanley. "Evangelicalism in the Novels of Charles Dickens." *DA* 20/6 (1959), 2295-96. Some discussion of biblical influence.

Stevens, James S. *Quotations and References in Charles Dickens* (Boston: Christopher, 1929).

Vogel, Jane. *Allegory in Dickens* (University of Alabama Press, 1977). Narrative and allegorical correspondence between Dickens's novels and the Bible. Useful index.

Walder, D. J. "Dickens and Religion." Unpubl. M.Litt. thesis, University of Edinburgh, 1969.

————. "Religious Aspects of Charles Dickens' Novels." Unpubl. diss., University of Edinburgh, 1979.

Walder, Dennis. *Dickens and Religion* (Boston: George Allen and Unwin, 1981). General discussion.

DICKINSON, EMILY

Anderson, Peggy. "ED's Least Favorite Biblical Book?" *Dickinson Studies* 46 (1983), 27-28.

Anderson, Vincent. "Emily Dickinson and the Disappearance of God." *Christian Scholar's Review* 11/1 (1981), 3-17. Jesus Christ in the poems of Dickinson.

Anthony, Mother Mary. "Emily Dickinson's Scriptural Echoes." *Massachusetts Review* 2/3 (1961), 557-61. Principally OT prophetic books and Revelation.

Capps, Jack L. "The King James Version." In his *Emily Dickinson's Reading, 1836-1886* (Cambridge: Harvard University Press, 1966). Appendix A lists biblical allusions in the poems; Appendix C provides a numerical listing.

Doriani, Beth Maclay. "Emily Dickinson: Daughter of Prophecy." Unpubl. diss., Notre Dame, 1990.

Herndon, Jerry A. "A Note on Emily Dickinson and Job." *Christianity and Literature* 30/3 (1981), 45-52.

Johnson, Thomas H. *Emily Dickinson: An Interpretive Biography.* (Cambridge: Belknap Press of Harvard University, 1955). Role of the Bible in Dickinson's work, 151ff.

McGregor, Elizabeth Johnson. "The Poet's Bible: Biblical Elements in the Poetry of Emily Dickinson, Stephen

Crane, Edwin Arlington Robinson, and Robert Frost." *DAI* 39/10 (1979), 6133A.

Reed, E. C. "Emily Dickinson's Treasury of Images: The Book of Revelation." *Emily Dickinson Bulletin* 23 (1973), 156-60.

St. Armand, Barton Levi. "Dickenson's 'Red Sea.'" *Explicator* 43/3 (1985), 17-20.

DONNE, JOHN

Bond, Ronald B. "John Donne and the Problem of 'Knowing Faith.'" *Mosaic* 14/1 (1981), 25-35. Biblical background.

Bosanich, Robert. "Donne and Ecclesiastes." *Publications of the Modern Language Association of America* 90/2 (1975), 270-76.

Duncan, Joseph E. "Donne's 'Hymne to God my God, in my sicknesse' and Iconographic Tradition." *John Donne Journal* 3/2 (1984), 157-80. Tree of knowledge and the cross; sweat of brow and Christ's blood.

Frontain, Raymond-Jean. "Donne's Biblical Figures: The Integrity of 'To Mr. George Herbert. . .'" *Modern Philology* 81/3 (1984), 285-89.

————. "John Donne's Poetic Uses of the Bible." *DAI* 44/2 (1984), 3693A-94A.

Hamilton, Carl H. "A Study of Imagery in John Donne's Sermons." *DA* 29/1 (1968), 262A-63A. Includes a catalogue of images in the main text and a second image catalogue in Appendix A.

Lewalski, Barbara K. *Donne's Anniversaries and the Poetry of Praise: The Creation of a Symbolic Mode* (Princeton: Princeton University Press, 1973). See especially the section on "theological contexts," 73-215.

Manley, Frank, ed. *John Donne: The Anniversaries* (Baltimore: Johns Hopkins Press, 1963). Index lists biblical books. Discusses biblical echoes, influences, and allusions.

Quinn, Dennis B. "John Donne's Sermons on the Psalms and the Tradition of Biblical Exegesis." *DAI* 8/6 (1958), 2131.

————. "John Donne's Principles of Biblical Exegesis." *Journal of English and Germanic Philology* 61 (1962), 313-29.

Schleiner, Winfried. *The Imagery of John Donne's Sermons* (Providence: Brown University Press, 1970). Includes biblical imagery.

The Complete Poetry of John Donne, ed. John T. Shawcross (Garden City: Doubleday Anchor, 1967). Biblical allusions pointed out in Notes.

Stringer, Gary. "The Biblical Element in Donne's Poems of Sacred and Profane Love." *DAI* 30/11 (1970), 4957A.

————. "Learning 'Hard and Deepe': Biblical Allusion in Donne's 'A Valediction: Of My Name, in the Window.'" *South Central Bulletin* 33 (1973), 227-31.

DRYDEN, JOHN

Dicks, George W. "Dryden's Use of Scripture in his Non-Dramatic Poetry." *DA* 30/10 (1970), 4405A.

Kinsley, William. "John Dryden's Use of the Bible." *The Bible Today* 62 (1972), 914-21; 63 (1973), 1315-25.

Lewalski, Barbara K. "The Scope and Function of Biblical Allusion in *Absalom and Achitophel.*" *English Language Notes* 3 (1965), 29-35.

Tierney, James E. "Biblical Allusion as Character Technique in Dryden's *All For Love.*" *English Studies* 58 (1977), 312-18.

Zwicker, Steven N. "The King and Christ: Figural Imagery in Dryden's Restoration Panegyrics." *Philological Quarterly* 50/4 (1971), 582-98. Typology and allusion in *Astraea Redux* and *To His Sacred Majesty.*

———. "Dryden and the Sacred History of the English People: A Study of Typological Imagery in Dryden's Political Poetry: 1660-1688." *DAI* 33/2 (1972), 737A.

———. *Dryden's Political Poetry: The Typology of King and Nation* (Providence: Brown University Press, 1972). OT models.

EDWARDS, JONATHAN

Batschelet, Margaret Susan. "Jonathan Edwards' Use of Typology: A Historical and Theological Approach." *DAI* 38/6 (1977), 3493A.

Cady, Edwin H. "The Artistry of Jonathan Edwards." *New England Quarterly* 22 (1949), 61-72. Use of the Bible in "Sinners in the Hands of an Angry God."

Kolodny, Annette. "Imagery in the Sermons of Jonathan Edwards." *Early American Literature* 7/2 (1972), 172-82.

Lowance, M. I. "Images or Shadows of Divine Things: The Typology of Jonathan Edwards." *Early American Literature* 5/1 (1970), 141-81.

Stein, Stephen J. "A Notebook on the Apocalypse by Jonathan Edwards." *William and Mary Quarterly* 29, ser. 3 (1972), 623-34.

ELIOT, GEORGE

Baker, William. *George Eliot and Judaism.* No. 45 in *Romantic Reassessment* series, ed. James Hogg (Salzburg: Universität Salzburg, 1975). Influence of Judaism in general, including cabalistic influences.

Bonaparte, Felicia. *The Triptych and the Cross: The Central Myths of George Eliot's Imagination* (New York: New York University Press, 1979). Some biblical characters, symbols, and rites discussed.

Budgen, V. J. "The Influence of Evangelicalism on George Eliot's Life and Work." Unpubl. M.A. thesis, Manchester, 1964.

Carpenter, Mary Wilson. "The Apocalypse of the Old Testament: *Daniel Deronda* and the Interpretation of Interpretation." *Publications of the Modern Language Association of America* 99/1 (1984), 56-71. Argues significant dependence on the book of Daniel.

Jones, Jesse C. "The Use of the Bible in George Eliot's Fiction." *DAI* 36 (1975), 2846A.

Kowalski, Elizabeth Anne. "The Dark Night of Her Soul: The Effects of Anglican Evangelicalism on the Careers of Charlotte Elizabeth Tonna and George Eliot." *DAI* 44/9 (1984), 2773A. Some reference to biblical influence.

Sheets, Robin. "*Felix Holt:* Language, the Bible, and the Problematic of Meaning." *Nineteenth Century Fiction* 37/2 (1982), 146-69.

Szirotny, June M. "The Religious Background of George Eliot's Novels." *DA* 27/8 (1967), 2547A.

ELIOT, T. S.

Gow, H. B. "Religion, Literature, and T. S. Eliot." *Western World Review* 8 (1973-74), 19-26.

Jones, Florence. "T. S. Eliot Among the Prophets." *American Literature* 38 (1966), 286-302. Connections with OT prophecy.

Rexine, J. E. "Classical and Christian Foundations of T. S. Eliot's *Cocktail Party.*" *Books Abroad* 39 (1965), 21-26.

See also J. B. Talley under SHAW.

EMERSON, RALPH WALDO

Hall, Gary Richard. "Emerson and the Bible: Transcendentalism as Scriptural Interpretation and Revision." Unpubl. diss., U.C.L.A., 1989.

Loewenberg, Robert J. "Emerson's Platonism and 'The terrific Jewish Idea.'" *Mosaic* 15/2 (1982), 93-108. Influence of the Mosaic books, especially Exodus.

Zink, Harriet Rodgers. *Emerson's Use of the Bible.* University of Nebraska Studies in Language and Criticism 14 (Lincoln: University of Nebraska Press, 1935). Valuable, though dated, study.

FAULKNER, WILLIAM

Barth, J. Robert, ed. *Religious Perspectives in Faulkner's Fiction: Yoknapatawpha and Beyond* (Notre Dame: University of Notre Dame Press, 1972). Theological rather than biblical focus, but see the chapter by Philip C. Rule and J. Robert Barth, "The Old Testament Vision in *As I Lay Dying,*" 107-18.

Barth, J. R. "Faulkner and the Calvinist Tradition." *Thought* 52 (1964), 100-120.

Betland, Alwyn. "*Light in August:* The Calvinism of William Faulkner." *Modern Fiction Studies* 8 (1962), 159-70. Passing reference to OT influences.

Bjork, Lennart. "Ancient Myth and the Moral Framework of Faulkner's *Absalom, Absalom!*" *American Literature* 35 (1963), 196-204. Influence of biblical narrative.

Blake, Nancy. "Creation and Procreation: The Voice and the Name, or Biblical Intertextuality in *Absalom, Absalom!*" Pp. 128-43 in Michel Gresset and Noel Polk, eds. *Intertextuality in Faulkner* (Jackson: University Press of Mississippi, 1985).

Clark, Winifred. "The Religious Symbolism of Faulkner's Novels." *DAI* 32/3 (1971), 1506A.

Coffee, Jessie McGuire. *Faulkner's Un-Christlike Christians: Biblical Allusions in the Novels* (Ann Arbor, MI: UMI Research Press, 1983). Based on the author's 1971 dissertation (Nevada) of the same title. Classifies verses or combinations of verses from the KJV and explicates each in the context of the novel in question. Useful appendices.

Cottrell, Beekman W. "Christian Symbols in 'Light in August.'" *Modern Fiction Studies* 2/3 (1956), 207-13. NT imagery and allusions.

Elkin, Stanley Lawrence. "Religious Themes and Symbolism in the Novels of William Faulkner." *DA* 22/10 (1962), 3659-60. Principally concerned with themes and imagery associated with Job and Jesus.

Hagopian, John V. "The Biblical Background of Faulkner's *Absalom, Absalom!*" *College English Association Critic* 36/2 (1974), 22-24.

Hartt, Julian. "Some Reflections on Faulkner's Fable." *Religion in Life* 24 (1955), 601-07. Gospel parallels.

Hlavsa, Virginia Victoria James. "*Light in August:* Biblical Form and Mythic Function." *DAI* 39/10 (1979), 6130A.

―――. "St. John and Fraser in *Light in August:* Biblical Form and Mythic Function." *Bulletin of Research in the Humanities* 83 (1980), 9-26.

Hodges, Elizabeth L. "The Bible as Novel: A Comparative Study of Two Modernized Versions of Biblical Stories, Zola's *La Faute de L'abbe Mouret* and Faulkner's *A Fable.*" *DAI* 30/12 (1970), 5447.

Kunkel, F. L. "Christ Symbolism in Faulkner: Prevalence of the Human." *Renascence* 17 (1965), 148-56.

Lowe, John Wharton. "The Biblical Imagination and American Genius: Repetitive Patterns of Hebraic Myth in Faulkner's *Light in August.*" *DAI* 42/9 (1982), 4001A.

Malin, Irving. *William Faulkner: An Interpretation* (Stanford: Stanford University Press, 1957). See "Faulkner and the Bible," pp. 65-78.

Mellard, J. M. "The Biblical Rhythms of *Go Down, Moses.*" *Mississippi Quarterly* 20 (1967), 135-47.

Miner, Ward L. "Faulkner and Christ's Crucifixion." *Neuphilologische Mitteilungen* 57 (1956), 260-69. Considers crucifixion imagery in *Light in August, Sound and Fury,* and *A Fable.*

Phillips, K. J. "Faulkner in The Garden of Eden." *Southern Humanities Review* 19/1 (1985), 1-19.

Rose, Maxine. "Echoes of the King James Bible in the Prose Style of *Absalom, Absalom!*" *Arizona Quarterly* 37/2 (1981), 137-48.

―――. "From Genesis to Revelation: The Grand Design of Faulkner's *Absalom, Absalom!*" *DAI* 34/10 (1974), 6656A.

Smart, George K. *Religious Elements in Faulkner's Early Novels: A Selective Concordance.* University of Miama Publications in English and American Literature, no. 8 (Miami: University of Miami Press, 1965). Lists biblical quotations, stories, and characters.

Smith, Gary. "William Faulkner and the Adamic Myth." *DAI* 42/8 (1982), 3603A.

Simpson, Lewis P. "Sex and History: Origins of Faulkner's Apocrypha." Pp. 43-70 in Evans Harrington and Ann J. Abadie, eds. *The Maker and the Myth: Faulkner and Yoknapatawpha* (Jackson: University Press of Mississippi, 1978). Brief reference to the Fall, "Hebraic-Christian" sexuality, etc.

Spivey, Herman E. "Faulkner and the Adamic Myth: Faulkner's Moral Vision." *Modern Fiction Studies* 19/4 (1973-74), 497-505.

Urie, Margaret Ann. "The Problem of Evil: The Myth of Man's Fall and Redemption in the Works of William Faulkner." *DAI* 39/8 (1979), 4943A.

Walhout, Clarence. "The Earth is the Lord's: Religion in Faulkner." *Christian Scholar's Review* 4 (1974), 26-35.

Young, Thomas Daniel. "Religion, the Bible Belt, and the Modern South." Pp. 110-17 in Louis D. Rubin, Jr., ed. *The American South: Portrait of a Culture* (Baton Rouge: Louisiana State University Press, 1980). Faulkner and O'Connor discussed at some length.

See also Philip Eugene Williams under HAWTHORNE.

FIELDING, HENRY

Fisch, Harold. "Biblical 'Imitation' in *Joseph Andrews.*" *Biblical Patterns in Modern Literature,* ed. David H. Hirsch and Nehama Aschkenasy (Chico: Scholars Press, 1984), 31-42. Principally concerned with the Joseph/Potiphar's wife incident.

Preston, Thomas R. "Biblical Criticism, Literature, and the Eighteenth-Century Reader." In *Books and Their Readers in Eighteenth-Century England,* ed. Isabel Rivers (Leicester: Leicester University Press; New York: St. Martin's, 1982), 97-126.

FOWLES, JOHN

Runyon, Randolph. *Fowles/Irving/Barthes: Canonical Variations on an Apocryphal Theme* (Columbus: Ohio State University Press for Miami University, 1981). Connections principally with the apocryphal book of Tobit.

FROST, ROBERT

Borkat, Roberta F. "The Bleak Landscape of Robert Frost." *Midwest Quarterly* 16/4 (1975), 453-67. *Masque of Reason* reflects book of Job; *Masque of Mercy,* Jonah.

Borroff, Marie. "Robert Frost's New Testament: Language and the Poem." *Modern Philology* 69/1 (1971), 36-56.

Edwards, C. Hines, Jr. "Frost's 'Once by the Pacific.'" *Explicator* 39/4 (1981), 28-29. OT sources.

Hall, Dorothy Judd. "An Old Testament Christian." *Frost: Centennial Essays* III, ed. Jac Tharpe (Jackson: University Press of Mississippi, 1978), 316-49. Frost's view of the Bible; the Bible in Frost's poetry.

Marks, Herbert. "The Counter-Intelligence of Robert Frost." *Yale Review* 71/4 (1982), 554-78. Sources in the Bible, specifically Revelation.

Schneidau, Herbert. "The Antinomian Strain: The Bible and American Poetry." *The Bible in American Arts and Letters,* ed. Giles Gunn (Philadelphia: Fortress, 1983), 12-32.

See also E. J. McGregor under DICKINSON.

FULLER, THOMAS

Resnick, Robert B. "The Wit of Biblical Allusion and Imagery in Thomas Fuller." *Greyfriar* 10 (1968), 16-24.

GASKELL, ELIZABETH

Wheeler, Michael D. "The Sinner as Heroine: A Study of Mrs. Gaskell's *Ruth* and the Bible." *Durham University Journal* 37 (1976), 148-61.

GOLDING, WILLIAM

Clews, Hetty, "Darkness Visible: William Golding's *Parousia.*" *English Studies in Canada* 10/3 (1984), 317-29. OT and NT sources, primarily apocalyptic.

Crompton, Donald W. "Biblical and Classical Metaphor in *Darkness Visible.*" *Twentieth Century Literature* 28/2 (1982), 195-215.

Lachance, Paul R. "Man and Religion in the Novels of William Golding and Graham Greene." *DAI* 31/11 (1971), 6062A. Theological focus.

Thomas, Sue. "Some Religious Icons and Biblical Allusions in William Golding's *The Spire.*" *Journal of the Australasian Universities Language and Literature Association* 64 (1985), 190-97.

GRAY, THOMAS

Reed, Amy Louise. *The Background of Gray's Elegy: A Study in the Taste for Melancholy Poetry, 1700-1757* (New York: Columbia University Press, 1924). Biblical references listed in index.

GREENE, GRAHAM

See P. R. Lachance under GOLDING; J. M. Gallagher under O'CONNOR.

GREENE, ROBERT

Law, Robert Adger. "A Looking Glasse and the Scriptures." *Studies in English,* no. 3926 (Austin: University of Texas Press, 1939), 31-41.

HARDY, THOMAS

Anonby, John A. "Hardy's Handling of Biblical Allusions in his Portrayal of Tess in *Tess of the d'Urbervilles.*" *Christianity and Literature* 30/3 (1981), 13-26.

Meusel, Magdalene. *Thomas Hardy und die Bibel* (Kiel: Christian-Alberts University, 1937). Studies the influence of the Bible on Hardy, as well as biblical allusions in Hardy's works.

Moynahan, Julian. "The Mayor of Casterbridge and the Old Testament's First Book of Samuel: A Study in Some Literary Relationships." *Publications of the Modern Language Association of America* 71 (1956), 118-30.

Murray, Michael H. "The Pattern of Biblical and Classical Myth in the Novels of Thomas Hardy." *DAI* 33/11 (1973), 6320A-21A.

Springer, Marlene. *Hardy's Use of Allusion* (London: Macmillan; Lawrence: University Press of Kansas, 1983). Index has extensive listing of biblical texts, characters, and places.

Tuttleton, June Martin. "Thomas Hardy and the Christian Religion." *DA* 26/3 (1965), 1637.

Weatherby, H. L. "Of Water and the Spirit: Hardy's 'The Voice.'" *The Southern Review* 19/2 (1983), 302-08. Hardy's knowledge of the Greek NT.

HAWTHORNE, NATHANIEL

Benoit, Raymond. "Theology and Literature: *The Scarlet Letter.*" *Bucknell Review* 20/1 (1972), 83-92.

Bercovitch, Sacvan. "Endicott's Breastplate: Symbolism and Typology in Hawthorne's 'Endicott and the Red Cross.'" *Studies in Short Fiction* 4/4 (1967), 289-99.

Cameron, Kenneth Walter. *Hawthorne Index to Themes, Motifs, Topics, Archetypes, Sources and Key Works Dealt with in Recent Criticism* (Hartford: Transcendental Books, 1968). Useful access to relevant scholarship.

Clark, Marsden J. "The Wages of Sin in Hawthorne." *Brigham Young University Studies* 1 (1959), 21-36.

Dauphin, V. A. "Religious Content in Hawthorne's Works." *Southern University Bulletin* 46 (1959), 115-23.

Fairbanks, Henry G. "Hawthorne and the Catholic Church." *Boston University Studies in English* 1/3 (1955), 148-65.

————. "Sin, Free Will, and 'Pessimism' in Hawthorne." *Publications of the Modern Language Assocation of America* 71 (1956), 975-89.

Geraldi, Robert. "Biblical and Religious Sources and Parallels in *The Scarlet Letter.*" *Language Quarterly* 15/1-2 (1976), 31-34.

Magretta, Joan. "The Coverdale Translation: *Blithedale* and the Bible." *Nathaniel Hawthorne Journal* (1974), 250-56. Concerned principally with the NT.

Marks, Barry A. "The Origins of Original Sin in

Hawthorne's Fiction." *Nineteenth Century Fiction* 14/4 (1960), 359-62.

Reeve, Clayton C. "Hawthorne's Dilemma: The Confrontation Between Christian and Romantic Thinking in the Tales and Novels." *DAI* 31/5 (1970), 2397A.

Stock, Ely. "The Biblical Context of 'Ethan Brand.'" *American Literature* 37 (1965), 115-34.

———. "History and the Bible in Hawthorne's 'Roger Malvin's Burial.'" *Essex Institute Historical Collections* 100/4 (1964), 279-96.

———. "Studies in Hawthorne's Use of the Bible." *DA* 28/2 (1968), 645A-46A.

Thompson, W. R. "The Biblical Sources of Hawthorne's 'Roger Malvin's Burial.'" *Publications of the Modern Language Association of America* 77 (1962), 92-96.

———. "Theme and Method in Hawthorne's 'The Great Carbuncle.'" *South Central Bulletin* 21 (1962), 3-10. Biblical analogues.

———. "Patterns of Biblical Allusions in Hawthorne's 'The Gentle Boy.'" *South Central Bulletin* 22/4 (1962), 3-10.

Williams, Philip Eugene. "The Biblical View of History: Hawthorne, Mark Twain, Faulkner, and Eliot." *DA* 25/7 (1965), 4159-60. Doctrinal focus.

HEMINGWAY, ERNEST

Backman, Melvin. "Hemingway, the Matador and the Crucified." *Modern Fiction Studies* 1/3 (1955), 2-11.

Cheney, Patrick. "Hemingway and Christian Epic: The Bible in *For Whom the Bell Tolls.*" *Papers on Language and Literature* 21/2 (1985), 170-91.

Cowan, S. A. "Robert Cohn, the Fool of Ecclesiastes in *The Sun Also Rises.*" *Dalhousie Review* 63/1 (1983), 98-106.

Dring, John R. "The Religious Element in Ernest Hemingway's Novels." *Delta Epsilon Sigma Bulletin* 7 (1962), 63-71.

Flora, Joseph M. "Biblical Allusion in 'The Old Man and the Sea.'" *Studies in Short Fiction* 10/2 (1973), 143-47.

HERBERT, GEORGE

Bloch, Chana. "George Herbert and the Bible: A Reading of 'Love (III).'" *English Literary Renaissance* 8/3 (1978), 329-40.

———. "Spelling the Word: Herbert's Reading of the Bible." *"Too rich to clothe the Sunne": Essays on George Herbert*, ed. Claude J. Summers and Ted-Larry Pebworth (Pittsburgh: University of Pittsburgh Press, 1980), 15-31.

———. *Spelling the Word: George Herbert and the Bible* (Berkeley: University of California Press, 1985). Study is appended by index of biblical references.

Cohen, Herbert Joseph. " 'Lesse Then the Least of God's Mercies': Significant Hebraic Motifs in the Poetry of George Herbert." *DAI* 45/3 (1984), 848A.

The English Works of George Herbert, ed. G. H. Palmer

(Boston and New York: Houghton Mifflin, 1905). 3 vols. Biblical index to all three volumes in vol. 1.

Hunter, Jeanne Clayton. "*Mine-Thine* in Herbert's *The Temple* and St. John's Gospel." *Notes and Queries* 29/5 (227) (1982), 492-93.

Kinnamon, Noel. "Notes on the Psalms in Herbert's *The Temple.*" *George Herbert Journal* 4/2 (1981), 10-29.

Moore, C. M. "Faith and Language in the Poetry of George Herbert." Unpubl. diss., Cambridge, 1983.

Nuttall, A. D. "Gospel Truth." *Ways of Reading the Bible,* ed. Michael Wadsworth (Brighton, Eng.; Totowa, NJ: Harvester; Barnes and Noble, 1981), 41-54. NT sources of Herbert's poetry.

Shafer, Ronald Gene. "The Poetry of George Herbert and the Epistles of St. Paul: A Study of Thematic and Imagistic Similarities." *DAI* 36/8 (1976), 5327A-28A.

Stokes, Penelope J. "A Biblical Handbook to *The Temple.*" *DAI* 39/3 (1978), 1603A.

Tuve, Rosemund. *A Reading of George Herbert* (Chicago: University of Chicago Press, 1952). Extensive and valuable commentary on typology.

HODGINS, JACK

Horner, Jan C. "Irish and Biblical Myth in Jack Hodgins' 'The Invention of the World.'" *Canadian Literature* 99 (1983), 6-18.

HOGG, JAMES

Campbell, Ian, "James Hogg and the Bible." *Scottish Literary Journal* 10/1 (1983), 14-29.

HOPKINS, GERARD MANLEY

Byrne, Virginia C. "The Creator and the Maker in the Aesthetics of Gerard Manley Hopkins." *McNeese Review* 19 (1963), 60-73.

Cotter, James Finn. *Inscape: The Christology and Poetry of Gerard Manley Hopkins* (Pittsburgh: University of Pittsburgh Press, 1972). Useful index includes biblical books and characters. NT emphasis.

———. "Inscape, Once Again." *America* 150/1 (1984), 31-33.

George, A. C. "Nature as Poetic Theme in Gerard Manley Hopkins, and the Influence of the Bible on his Nature Lyrics." *The Literary Criterion* (India) 9/3 (1970), 14-26.

Jolliffe, David A. "The Tall Nun in 'The Wreck of the Deutschland': A Lioness in Her Own Right." *Victorian Poetry* 21/1 (1983), 79-84. OT sources.

Milward, Peter, S.J. "Biblical Imagery of Water in 'The Wreck of the Deutschland.'" *Hopkins Quarterly* 1 (1974), 115-20. Sources in Genesis, Psalms, Gospel of Matthew.

Swinford, A. P. "A Study of the Scriptural Influence in the Poetry of Gerard Manley Hopkins: Songs in the House of Pilgrimage." Unpubl. M.A. thesis, Birmingham, 1982-83.

HOUSMAN, A. E.

Freimarck, Vincent. "Further Notes on Housman's Use of the Bible." *Modern Language Notes* 67/8 (1952), 548-50.

Harding, David P. "A Note on Housman's Use of the Bible." *Modern Language Notes* 65/3 (1950), 205-07.

Watanabe, Kiyoko. "A. E. Housman no Shi ni Mirareru Seisho no Eikyo." In *A. E. Housman Kenkyu II* (Tokyo: Aratake, 1982). Biblical sources.

HUGHES, TED

Hahn, Claire. "*Crow* and the Biblical Creation Narratives." *Critical Quarterly* 19/1 (1977), 43-52.

IRVING, JOHN

O'Sullivan, Maurice J., Jr. "Garp Unparadised: Biblical Echoes in John Irving's *The World According to Garp*." *Notes on Modern American Literature* 7/2 (1983), no. 11.

See also R. Runyon under FOWLES.

JAMES, HENRY

Bellman, Samuel. "Henry James' 'The Tree of Knowledge': A Biblical Parallel." *Studies of Short Fiction* 1/3 (1964), 226-28.

Gale, Robert L. "Religion Imagery in Henry James's Fiction." *Modern Fiction Studies* 3 (1957), 64-72. Refers to James's use of biblical characters.

Salmon, Rachel. "Naming and Knowing in Henry James's 'The Beast in the Jungle': The Hermeneutics of a Sacred Text." *Orbis Litterarum: International Review of Literary Studies* (Denmark) 36/4 (1981), 302-22. Biblical concept of naming; discusses Genesis and other OT texts.

JEFFERS, ROBINSON

Bluestone, Stephen. "Robinson Jeffers and the Prophets: On *The Book of Jeremiah* and 'The Inhumanist.'" *Notes on Contemporary Literature* 5/4 (1975), 2-3.

Brophy, Robert J. "Biblical Resonances in Jeffers' 'Signpost.'" *Robinson Jeffers Newsletter* 39 (1974), 10-12.

————. *Robinson Jeffers: Myth, Ritual, and Symbol in His Narrative Poems* (Cleveland, London: Case Western University Press, 1973). Index lists biblical references in each poem discussed.

Turlish, Molly S. B. "Story Patterns from Greek and Biblical Sources in the Poetry of Robinson Jeffers." *DAI* 32/11 (1972), 6458A-59A.

JEWETT, SARAH ORNE

Mack, Tom. "A Note on Biblical Analogues in Sarah Orne Jewett's 'Miss Tempy's Watchers.'" *American Literary Realism* 17/2 (1984), 225-27.

JONES, DAVID

Cook, D. D. "Poetry and Religion in the Major Writings of David Jones." Unpubl. diss., East Anglia, 1981.

Stoneburner, Tony. "Notes on Prophecy and Apocalypse in a Time of Anarchy and Revolution: A Trying Out." *TriQuarterly* 23-24 (1972), 246-82.

JOYCE, JAMES

Aschkenasy, Nehama. "Biblical Females in a Joycean Episode: The 'Strange Woman' Scene in James Joyce's *A Portrait of the Artist as a Young Man*." *Modern Language Studies* 15/4 (1985), 28-39. OT sources.

Benstock, Shari, and Bernard Benstock. *Who's He When He's at Home: A James Joyce Directory* (Urbana: University of Illinois Press, 1980). Directory of names, including biblical names, in Joyce's works.

Bonheim, Helmut. "God and the gods in *Finnegans Wake*." *Studia Neophilologica* 34 (1962), 294-314.

Broes, Arthur T. "The Bible in *Finnegans Wake*." *A Wake Newsletter* n.s. 2/6 (1965), 3-11. See also 3/5 (1966), 102-05.

Callaghan, B. M. "Religious Imagery and Symbolism in Joyce's *Dubliners*." Unpubl. M.A. thesis, Bangor, Wales, 1973.

Damrosch, David Norman. "Scripture and Fiction: Egypt, The Midrash, *Finnegans Wake*." *DAI* 41/6 (1980), 2591A.

Gifford, Don, and Robert Seidman. *Notes for Joyce: An Annotation of James Joyce's Ulysses* (New York: E. P. Dutton, 1974).

Glasheen, Adaline. *A Census of Finnegans Wake* (Evanston: Northwestern University Press, 1956). Biblical names and characters listed. See also *A Second Census of Finnegans Wake* (1963) and *A Third Census of Finnegans Wake* (1977).

Hondebine, Jean-Louis. "De nouveau sur Joyce: 'Littérature' et 'religion.'" *Tel quel* 89 (1981), 41-73.

Lane, Gary. *A Word Index to James Joyce's Dubliners* (New York: Haskell House, 1972).

Lang, Frederick Karel. "The Joycean Liturgy: Religious Symbolism and Ritual from *Dubliners* through *Ulysses*." *DAI* 42/09 (1982), 4007A.

Manglaviti, Leo M. J. "Joyce and St. John." *James Joyce Quarterly* 9/1 (1971), 152-56. Focusses on the opening lines of the Gospel.

McHugh, Roland. *Annotations to Finnegans Wake* (Baltimore: Johns Hopkins University Press, 1980).

Moseley, Virginia. "Joyce and the Bible: The External Evidence." *Ulysses: Cinquante ans après,* ed. Louis Bonnerot (Paris: Didier, 1974), 99-110. Discusses biographical evidence that Joyce knew the Bible.

————. *Joyce and the Bible* (De Kalb: Northern Illinois University Press, 1967). General study of Joyce's use of the KJV.

Sohn, Naomi Elizabeth Hahn. "Allusive Methods: A

Comparative Study of Biblical Elements of Joyce's *Ulysses* and Doblin's *Berlin Alexanderplatz*." *DAI* 44/4 (1983), 1081A.

Thornton, Weldon. *Allusions in Ulysses: An Annotated List* (Chapel Hill: University of North Carolina Press, 1968).

Tolomeo, Diane. "Biblical and Spiritual Themes in James Joyce's *Ulysses:* An Interpretive Study." *DAI* 35/9 (1975), 6164A-65A.

Wilson, Gary. "The Old Testament Design of the Flood Episode." *A Wake Newsletter: Studies in James Joyce* (Switzerland) n.s. 11/2 (1974), 48-52.

KEATS, JOHN

Jeffrey, Lloyd N. "Keats and the Bible." *Keats-Shelley Journal* 10 (1961), 59-70. Statistical survey of biblical allusions, followed by brief critical discussion.

Maxwell, J. C. "Keats and the Bible." *Keats-Shelley Journal* 11 (1962), 15-16. Two short additions to Jeffrey's list (see above).

Ryan, Robert M. *Keats: The Religious Sense* (Princeton: Princeton University Press, 1976). See "Bible" listings in index.

KEROUAC, JACK

Walsh, Joy. "*Ecclesiastes* and the Duluoz Legend of Jack Kerouac." *Notes on Modern American Literature* 3/4 (1979), no. 27.

KIPLING, RUDYARD

Clark, Charles Gordon. "Christianity in Kipling's Verse." *Theology* 85 (1982), 27-37. Kipling's use of biblical stories; OT and NT allusions and themes.

LANGLAND, WILLIAM

Adams, M. Ray. "The Use of the Vulgate in *Piers Plowman*." *Studies in Philology* 24 (1927), 556-66. A census of biblical quotations, with critical discussion of their use.

Aers, David. *Piers Plowman and Christian Allegory* (London: E. Arnold, 1975).

Alford, John A. "*Piers Plowman* and the Tradition of Biblical *Imitatio*." *DAI* 317 (1971), 3536A-37A.

Ames, Ruth M. *The Fulfillment of the Scriptures: Abraham, Moses and Piers* (Evanston: Northwestern University Press, 1970).

Barney, Stephen A. "The Plowshare of the Tongue: The Progress of a Symbol from the Bible to *Piers Plowman*." *Mediaeval Studies* 35 (1973), 261-93. Biblical agricultural symbols and their use in *Piers Plowman*.

Eliason, Eric Jon. " 'Vanitas Vanitatum': *Piers Plowman*, Ecclesiastes, and Contempt of the World." Unpubl. diss., Virginia, 1989.

Quick, Anne Wenley. "Langland's Learning: The Direct Sources of *Piers Plowman*." *DAI* 43/12 (1983), 3905A.

Robertson, D. W., Jr., and B. F. Huppe. *Piers Plowman and Scriptural Tradition* (Princeton: Princeton University Press, 1951). Ground-breaking study of Langland's use of the Bible.

Smith, Ben H. *Traditional Imagery of Charity in "Piers Plowman"* (The Hague: Mouton and Co., 1966). Based on the author's North Carolina dissertation (1963). See especially the chapter on "The Good Samaritan."

LAURENCE, MARGARET

Koster, Patricia. "Hagar 'the Egyptian': Allusions and Illusions in *The Stone Angel*." *Ariel: A Review of International English Literature* 16/3 (1985), 41-52. Laurence's use of the book of Genesis.

LAWRENCE, D. H.

Bachmann, Susan M. "Narrative Strategy in the Book of Revelation and D. H. Lawrence's *Apocalypse*." *DAI* 45/9 (1985), 2870A.

Kennedy, Andrew. "After Not So Strange Gods in *The Rainbow*." *English Studies* 63/3 (1982), 220-30. Biblical language and echoes.

Manicom, David. "An Approach to the Imagery: A Study of Selected Biblical Analogues in D. H. Lawrence's *The Rainbow*." *English Studies in Canada* 11/4 (1985), 474-83. Apocalyptic and Edenic imagery.

Paniches, George A. "D. H. Lawrence's Biblical Play *David*." *Modern Drama* 6 (1963), 164-76. Lawrence's response to the biblical King David as evidenced in his play.

Urang, Susan Catherine. "Kindled in the Flame: The Apocalyptic Scene in D. H. Lawrence." *DAI* 41/7 (1981), 3103A. Connections with the book of Revelation.

Walker, Grady J. "The Influence of the Bible on D. H. Lawrence as Seen in his Novels." *DAI* 32/10 (1972), 5810A.

LONGFELLOW, HENRY WADSWORTH

Boggess, Arthur C. "The Old Testament in Longfellow's Poems." *Methodist Review* 103 (1920), 263-71. Quotations and allusions.

Schulze, Bernhard. *Das Religiöse bei Henry Wadsworth Longfellow und dessen Stehlung zur Bibel* (Leipzig, 1913).

LOWELL, JAMES RUSSELL

De Saegher, William James. "James Russell Lowell and the Bible." *DA* 25/6 (1964), 3551.

MACAULAY, THOMAS BABINGTON

Mallary, R. DeWitt. "Macaulay's Use of Scripture in His Essays." *Old Testament Studies* 7 (1888), 212-16, 246-49. Biblical references are given in notes.

MACLEISH, ARCHIBALD

Bieman, Elizabeth. "Faithful to the Bible in Its Fashion: MacLeish's *J.B.*" *Studies in Religion* 4 (1974), 25-30. Connections with the book of Job.

Bond, Charles M. "J.B. is not Job." *Bucknell Review* 9 (1961), 272-80.

Campbell, Colin C. "The Transformation of Biblical Myth: MacLeish's Use of the Adam and Job Stories." *Myth and Symbol: Critical Approaches and Applications,* ed. Bernice Slote (Lincoln: University of Nebraska Press, 1963), 79-88.

Christensen, Parley A. "J.B., the Critics and Me." *Western Humanities Review* 15/1 (1961), 111-26.

Hamilton, Kenneth. "The Patience of J.B." *Dalhousie Review* 41 (1961), 32-39.

Terrien, Samuel L. "J.B. and Job." *Christian Century* 76/1 (1959), 9-11.

MALAMUD, BERNARD

Sheres, Ita. "The Alienated Sufferer: Malamud's Novels from the Perspective of Old Testament and Jewish Mystical Thought." *Studies in American Jewish Literature* 4/1 (1978), 68-76.

MARLOWE, CHRISTOPHER

Barnes, Celia. "Matthew Parker's Pastoral Training and Marlowe's *Doctor Faustus.*" *Comparative Drama* 15/3 (1981), 258-67. Echoes from the Bishops' and Geneva Bibles.

Cornelius, Richard M. *Christopher Marlowe's Use of the Bible* (New York: Peter Lang, 1984). Based on the author's Tennessee dissertation (1971). Includes chapters on "Sources of Marlowe's knowledge of biblical materials"; "Marlowe's stylistic use of the Bible"; "Repeated biblical themes, concepts, and phrases"; and a summary. Appendix, pp. 129-290, lists biblical references as they occur chronologically through the Marlowe canon. Contains notes, bibliography, and index (principally of names).

Deats, Sara Munson. "Ironic Biblical Allusion in Marlowe's *Doctor Faustus.*" *Medievalia et Humanistica* 10 (1981), 203-16.

Hankins, John E. "Biblical Echoes in the Final Scene of *Doctor Faustus.*" *Studies in English in Honor of Raphael Dorman O'Leary and Seldon Lincoln Whitcomb* (Lawrence: University of Kansas, 1940), 3-7.

Hargrove, Anne. " 'Lucifer Prince of the East' and the Fall of Marlowe's Dr. Faustus." *Neuphilologische Mitteilungen* (Finland) 84/2 (1983), 206-13.

Hawkins, Sherman. "The Education of Faustus." *Studies in English Literature, 1500-1900* 6 (1966), 193-209. Brief reference to Scripture.

Hunter, G. K. "The Theology of Marlowe's *The Jew of Malta.*" *Journal of the Warburg and Courtauld Institutes* 27 (1964), 211-40. Influence of the Bible, principally NT.

O'Brien, Margaret Ann. "Christian Belief in *Doctor Faustus.*" *English Literary History* 37 (1970), 1-11. Scriptural and patristic influence.

Reno, Raymond Howard. "The Theological Background of Christopher Marlowe's *The Tragical History of Doctor Faustus.*" Unpubl. diss., George Washington University, 1958.

Sims, J. H. *Dramatic Uses of Biblical Allusions in Marlowe and Shakespeare* (Gainesville: University of Florida Press, 1966). Important and learned study.

Takemoto, Yukihiro. "The Jew of Malta and the Book of Job." *Shiron* 20 (1981), 23-41.

MARSTON, JOHN

See F. J. Bennett under CHAPMAN.

MARVELL, ANDREW

Buttrey, T. V., and Ruth Smith. "World and Time in Marvell's 'To His Coy Mistress.'" *Anglia* 103/3-4 (1985), 401-05. Identifies OT sources.

Hardman, C. B. "Marvell's 'Bermudas' and Sandys's *Psalms.*" *Review of English Studies* 32/125 (1981), 64-67.

Klause, John. *The Unfortunate Fall: Theodicy and the Moral Imagination of Andrew Marvell* (New York: Archon Books, 1983). See "Bible" in Index.

Rosenberg, John D. "Marvell and the Christian Idiom." *Boston University Studies in English* 4/3 (1960), 152-61.

MELVILLE, HERMAN

Anderson, Walter E. "Form and Meaning in 'Bartleby the Scrivener.'" *Studies in Short Fiction* 18/4 (1981), 383-93. Discusses OT sources.

Braswell, William. *Melville's Religious Thought: An Essay in Interpretation* (New York: Pageant Books, 1959). Brief reference to biblical influence.

Campbell, H. M. "The Hanging Scene in Melville's *Billy Budd:* A Reply to Mr. Giovannini." *Modern Language Notes* 70 (1955), 497-500. A reply to G. Giovannini's "The Hanging Scene in Melville's Billy Budd." *Modern Language Notes* 70 (1955), 491-97. Discusses Melville's nonironic references to the Bible.

Evans, Lyone, Jr. " 'Too Good to Be True': Subverting Christian Hope in *Billy Budd.*" *The New England Quarterly* 55/3 (1982), 323-53.

Gallagher, Susan van Zanten. " 'The Sane Madness of Vital Truth': Prophets and Prophecy in the Fiction of Herman Melville." *DAI* 43/10 (1983), 3317A.

Heflin, Wilson. "A Biblical Source for 'The Whale Watch' in *Moby-Dick.*" *Extracts* 23 (1975), 13. Echo of Job 7:12-15.

Heidmann, Mark. "Melville and the Bible: Leading Themes in the Marginalia and Major Fiction, 1850-1856." *DAI* 42/4 (1981), 1635A.

Holman, C. Hugh. "The Reconciliation of Ishmael:

Moby-Dick and the Book of Job." *South Atlantic Quarterly* 57 (1958), 477-90.

Holstein, Jay A. "The 'Inside' Role of Biblical Allusions in Melville's *Billy Budd* (an Inside Narrative)." *Rendezvous* 15/2 (1980), 35-46.

———. "Melville's Inversion of Jonah in *Moby-Dick*." *The Iliff Review* 42/1 (1985), 13-20.

———. "Melville's Ironic Treatment of Biblical Salvation Motifs." *The Iliff Review* 38/2 (1981), 15-27.

Hoffman, Daniel G. "Moby-Dick: Jonah's Whale or Job's?" *Sewanee Review* 69/8 (1961), 205-24.

Jeffrey, Lloyd N. "A Concordance to the Biblical Allusions in *Moby Dick*." *Bulletin of Bibliography* 21 (1956), 223-29.

Joseph, Vasanth. "Some Biblical Nuances in *Moby-Dick*." *Osmania Journal of English Studies* (India) 8/2 (1971), 69-77.

Kirby, Robert Kenneth. "Melville's Attitude Toward the Historicity and Interpretation of the Bible." *DAI* 44/10 (1984), 3066A.

Lackey, Kris. "Additional Biblical Allusions in *Moby-Dick*." *Melville Society Extracts* 54 (1983), 12.

Little, Thomas Alexander. "Literary Allusions in the Writings of Herman Melville." Unpubl. diss., Nebraska, 1950. Includes catalogue of biblical allusions.

Mansfield, Luther Stearns. "Symbolism and Biblical Allusion in *Moby-Dick*." *Emerson Society Quarterly* 28 (1962), 20-23.

Moorman, Charles. "Melville's *Pierre* and the Fortunate Fall." *American Literature* 25 (1953-54), 13-30. Melville's reworking of the Genesis account of the Fall.

Nelson, James Andrew. "Herman Melville's Use of the Bible in *Billy Budd*." *DAI* 39 (1979), 4987A-88A.

Rosen, Roma. "Melville's Use of Shakespeare's Plays." *DA* 23/9 (1963), 3356. See section on "Melville and the Bible, Milton, and Shakespeare."

Rosenfeld, William. "Uncertain Faith: Queequeg's Coffin and Melville's Use of the Bible." *Texas Studies in Literature and Language* 7 (1966), 317-27.

Rowland, Beryl. "Melville Answers the Theologians: The Ladder of Charity in 'The Two Temples.'" *Mosaic* 7/4 (1974), 1-13. Discusses Sermon on the Mount, Pauline Epistles, Jacob's ladder.

Sachs, Viola. *La Contre-Bible de Melville: Moby-Dick dechiffre* (The Hague: Mouton, 1975). Valuable study with excellent index.

Scherting, Jack. "The Chaldee Allusion in *Moby-Dick*: Its Antecedent and Its Implicit Scepticism." *Melville Society Extracts* 49 (1982), 14-15.

Stout, Janis, "Melville's Use of the Book of Job." *Nineteenth Century Fiction* 25 (1970), 69-83.

Thompson, Lawrence Roger. *Melville's Quarrel with God* (Princeton: Princeton University Press, 1952). Biblical quotations and allusions are discussed and indexed.

Timmerman, John. "Typology and Biblical Consistency in *Billy Budd*." *Religion and Literature* 15/1 (1983), 23-50.

Werge, Thomas. "*Moby-Dick* and the Calvinist Tradition." *StN* 1 (1969), 484-506.

Wright, Nathalia. "Biblical Allusion in Melville's Prose." *American Literature* 12 (1940), 185-99. Allusions, imagery, characterization, tone.

———. *Melville's Use of the Bible* (Durham: Duke University Press, 1949 [rpt. 1969]). Detailed, valuable study.

———. "*Moby-Dick*: Jonah's or Job's Whale?" *American Literature* 37 (1965), 190-95.

MILL, JOHN STUART

Aiken, Susan Hardy. "Scripture and Poetic Discourse in *The Subjection of Women*." *Publications of the Modern Language Association of America* 98/3 (1983), 353-71. Mill's use of biblical allusions, motifs, and prophetic poses.

MILTON, JOHN

Baldwin, Edward Chauncey. "Milton and the Psalms." *Modern Philology* 17 (1919), 457-63. Milton's knowledge of Hebrew and his translation of various Psalms.

Bargo, Martha Ellen Watson. "Milton's Biblical Concept of Women." *DAI* 46/2 (1985), 428A.

Blondel, Jacques. "Milton poète de la Bible dans le *Paradis Perdu*." *Archives des lettres modernes* 21-22 (1959). A series of small, individually bound volumes; scriptural themes and allusions noted.

Broadbent, John. *John Milton: Introductions* (Cambridge: Cambridge University Press, 1973), 145-61. Chapter entitled "The Poet's Bible" cites texts of the Bible used by Milton.

Daniel, Nathaniel Venable, Jr. "Biblical Proof Texts and Their Epic Contexts in *Paradise Lost*." *DAI* 40 (1980), 4050A. An attempt to explain the seeming theological anomalies of *Paradise Lost*.

Danielson, Dennis Richard. *Milton's Good God: A Study in Literary Theodicy* (Cambridge: Cambridge University Press, 1982). Biblical and theological underpinnings.

Dobbins, Austin C. *Milton and the Book of Revelation: The Heavenly Cycle* (University of Alabama Press, 1975). The biblical background to the war in heaven motif.

Elliott, Emory. "Milton's Biblical Style in *Paradise Regained*." *Milton Studies* 6 (1975), 227-41. Discusses use of biblical allusions.

Evans, J. M. *Paradise Lost and the Genesis Tradition* (Oxford: Clarendon, 1968).

Fixler, Michael. *Milton and the Kingdom of God* (Evanston: Northwestern University Press, 1964). NT background.

Fleck, Jade Carlson. "Eschatological Poetics in *Paradise*

Lost, Two Seventeenth Century Commentaries on Revelation, and Selected Sermons." Unpubl. diss., University of California, Berkeley, 1990.

———. "Milton and Rashi." *Journal of English and Germanic Philology* 27 (1928), 300-317. The influence of Buxtorf's *Biblia Hebraica Rabbinorum* on Milton's use of biblical material.

———. *Milton's Rabbinical Readings* (Urbana: University of Illinois Press, 1930). Index of biblical citations and quotations.

———. *Milton's Semitic Studies, and Some Manifestations of Them in his Poetry* (Chicago: University of Chicago Press, 1926). A consideration of the various versions of Scripture which influenced Milton, and which he used in his own writing.

———. "Milton's Use of Biblical Quotations." *Journal of English and Germanic Philology* 26 (1927), 145-65. A study of Milton's use and adaptations of a wide variety of biblical versions.

———. *The Use of the Bible in Milton's Prose* (Urbana: University of Illinois Press, 1929). Indices of biblical quotations and citations are arranged chronologically (1) in order of Milton's prose works and (2) in order of biblical books.

Forsyth, Neil. "Having Done all to Stand: Biblical and Classical Allusion in *Paradise Regained*." *Milton Studies* 21 (1985), 199-214.

Fresch, Cheryl H. " 'As the Rabbines Expound': Milton, Genesis, and the Rabbis." *Milton Studies* 15 (1981), 59-79.

Frye, Northrop. "The Typology of *Paradise Regained*." *Modern Philology* 53 (1956), 227-38.

Fulton, Pauline Robinson. "Milton's Use of the Book of Job in *Paradise Regained* and *Samson Agonistes*." *DAI* 44/4 (1983), 1092A.

Furman, Wendy. "*Samson Agonistes* as Christian Tragedy: A Corrective View." *Philological Quarterly* 60/2 (1981), 169-81. "Corrective" of the view that sees *Samson Agonistes* as a classical (Aeschylian) style of tragedy.

Goodman, Ellen. "The Design of Milton's World: Nature and the Fall in Christian Genesis commentary and *Paradise Lost*." *DAI* 38/1 (1977), 278A-79A.

Jacobson, Howard. "Some Unnoticed Echoes and Allusions in Milton's *Samson Agonistes*." *Notes and Queries* n.s. 29/6 [vol. 227 of cont. series] (1982), 501-02.

Kermode, Frank. "Interpretive Continuities and the New Testament." *Raritan: A Quarterly Review* 1/4 (1982), 33-49. On the temptation of Christ and *Paradise Regained*.

Knott, John R., Jr. "The Biblical Matrix of Milton's 'On the Late Massacre in Piemont.'" *Philological Quarterly* 62/2 (1983), 259-63. Patterns of submerged allusion.

Krouse, F. Michael. *Milton's Samson and Christian Tradition* (Princeton: Princeton University Press, 1949). Influence of biblical commentaries on *Samson Agonistes*. Useful index.

Kurth, Burton O. *Milton and Christian Heroism: Biblical Epic Themes and Forms in Seventeenth-Century England* (Berkeley: University of California Press, 1959 [rpt. 1966]). Chapters devoted to OT heroic poetry and NT narratives.

Lewalski, Barbara K. *Milton's Brief Epic* (Providence: Brown University Press; London: Methuen, 1966). Important study which includes detailed discussion of exegetical tradition and biblical typology. Valuable index and notes.

MacCallum, H. R. "Milton and Figurative Interpretation of the Bible." *University of Toronto Quarterly* 31/4 (1962), 397-415. Pauline and Augustinian letter/spirit distinction.

Madsen, William G. "Earth the Shadow of Heaven: Typological Symbolism in *Paradise Lost*." *Publications of the Modern Language Association of America* 75/5 (1960), 519-26.

———. *From Shadowy Types to Truth: Studies in Milton's Symbolism* (New Haven: Yale University Press, 1968).

Maurer, Iris Sue. "Allusions to the Epistle to the Romans in *Paradise Lost:* A Comparison of Their Contexts in the Light of Reformation Theology." *DAI* 42/2 (1981), 713A-14A.

McCarty, Willard Lee. "Biblical Language and Structure in *Paradise Lost*." *DAI* 46/5 (1985), 1287A.

Mollenkott, Virginia Ramey. "Milton and the Apocrypha." *DA* 27/1 (1967), 212A-13A.

———. "The Pervasive Influence of the Apocrypha in Milton's Thought and Art." *Milton and the Art of Sacred Song*, ed. J. Max Patrick and Roger H. Sundell (Madison: University of Wisconsin Press, 1979), 23-43.

Muskin, Miriam. "Milton's Understanding of Hebraism and *Samson Agonistes*." *DAI* 38/3 (1977), 1414A.

O'Keeffe, Timothy J. *Milton and the Pauline Tradition: A Study of Theme and Symbolism* (Washington: University Press of America, 1982). Chapters on Pauline themes — "the flesh"; "the law and the letter"; "foolishness of wisdom and strength of weakness," etc. Index has biblical references and characters.

Paskus, John Martin. "Not Less But More Heroic: A Treatment of Myth and the Bible in the Poetry of John Milton." *DAI* 34/10 (1973), 6600A-6601A.

Patrides, C. A. *Milton and the Christian Tradition* (Oxford: Clarendon Press, 1966). Chapters include: "Doctrine of the Godhead"; "Doctrine of Creation"; "Fall of Angels and Man"; "Christian Idea of Love"; "Christian View of History." Useful subject index as well as index of names.

———. " 'Something Like Prophetic Strain': Apocalyptic Configurations in Milton." *English Language Notes* 19/3 (1982), 193-207. A study of *Paradise Lost.*

Pecheux, Mother Mary Christopher, O.S.U. "Sin in *Paradise Regained:* The Biblical Background." *Calm of Mind: Tercentenary Essays on Paradise Regained and Samson Agonistes in Honor of John S. Diekhoff,* ed. Joseph A. Wittreich, Jr. (Cleveland: Case Western Reserve University Press, 1971), 49-65.

Radzinowicz, Mary Ann. *Milton's Epics and The Book of Psalms* (Princeton: Princeton University Press, 1989). Wide-ranging study. Excellent index and bibliography.

Shapiro, Marta Berl. "*Samson Agonistes* and the Hebraic Tradition." *DAI* 36/8 (1975-76), 5328A.

Shawcross, John T. "The Etymological Significance of Biblical Names in *Paradise Regain'd.*" *Literary Onomastics Studies* 2 (1975), 34-57.

Simon, Ulrich. "Samson and the Heroic." *Ways of Reading the Bible,* ed. Michael Wadsworth (Brighton: Harvester; Totowa: Barnes & Noble, 1981), 154-67.

Sims, James H. *The Bible in Milton's Epics* (Gainesville: University of Florida Press, 1962). Index of biblical references as well as of biblical subjects.

———. "Milton, Literature as a Bible, and the Bible as Literature." *Milton and the Art of Sacred Song,* ed. J. Max Patrick and Robert H. Sundell (Madison: University of Wisconsin Press, 1979), 3-21.

———, and Leland Ryken, eds. *Milton and Scriptural Tradition: The Bible Into Poetry* (Columbia: University of Missouri Press, 1984). A collection of essays, including "The Gospel of John and Paradise Regained: Jesus as 'True Light' "; "The Miltonic Narrator and Scriptural Tradition"; *Paradise Lost* and its Biblical Epic Models." Index.

Smith, Samuel Oswald. "Milton and the Book of Revelation: Attaining the 'Prophetic Strain' in *Paradise Regained.*" Unpubl. diss., Delaware, 1989.

Steadman, John M. *Milton's Biblical and Classical Imagery* (Pittsburgh: Duquesne University Press, 1984). Chapters arranged thematically, from "Sion and Helicon" to "*Paradise Lost* and the Apotheosis Tradition." Has index of names and extensive notes.

Sternheim, Arnold Ephraim. "Time and Narrative Construction." *DAI* 41/9 (1981), 4027A. Considers Exodus, Gospel of Mark, *Paradise Regained,* and other works.

Sumers-Ingraham, Alinda. "John Milton's *Paradise Regained* and the Genre of the Puritan Spiritual Biography." *DAI* 45/1 (1984), 193A. Influence of the book of Job.

Ulreich, John C. "Typological Symbolism in Milton's Sonnet XXIII." *Milton Quarterly* 8/1 (1974), 7-10.

Wall, John N., Jr. "The Contrarious Hand of God: *Samson Agonistes* and the Biblical Lament." *Milton Studies* 12 (1978), 117-39.

Walker, Fred B. "Milton's Use of the Bible in His Shorter English Poems." Unpubl. M.A. thesis, University of Florida, 1947.

Werman, Golda Spiera. "Paradise Lost and Midrash." *DAI* 43/8 (1982), 2686A.

Wittreich, Joseph Anthony. *Visionary Poetics: Milton's Tradition and His Legacy* (San Marino: Huntington Library, 1979). Contains a useful index, with extensive listing of biblical allusions.

Wollaeger, Mark A. "Apocryphal Narration: Milton, Raphael, and the Book of Tobit." *Milton Studies* 21 (1985), 137-56.

See also S. B. Fishman under SPENSER; R. A. L. Burnet, "Some Echoes . . ." and "Two Further Echoes," under SHAKESPEARE.

MORE, THOMAS

Allen, Ward. "More and the Bible." *Moreana* 30 (1971), 45-46. Versions of the Bible used by More.

———. "More, Shakespeare and the Bible." *Moreana* 27-28 (1970), 24. Use of 1 Corinthians.

Marc'hadour, Germaine. *The Bible in the Works of Thomas More* (Nieuwkoop: B. de Graaf, 1969-72). 5 vols. Catalogue of biblical quotations and references, with some critical comments. Several indices.

———. "Thomas More et la Bible: Mise au point." *Moreana* 7/25 (1970), 57-65.

———. "Thomas More et la Bible: un nouvel addendum." *Moreana* 7/26 (1970), 66-68.

———. "Thomas More et la Bible: Troisième mise au point." *Moreana* 8/29 (1971), 55-56.

Massaut, Jean-Pierre. "L'humanisme chrétien et la Bible: le cas de Thomas More." *Revue d'histoire ecclesiastique* 67 (1972), 92-112.

MUIR, EDWIN

Livingston, Travis L. "The Symbolic Use of Greek Myth and Biblical Saga in the Poetry of Edwin Muir." *DAI* 39/1 (1978), 281A.

OATES, JOYCE CAROL

Robson, Mark. "Oates's 'Where Are You Going, Where Have You Been?' " *Explicator* 40/4 (1982), 59-60. OT source — Judg. 19.

O'CONNOR, FLANNERY

Barnes, Linda Adams. "Faith and Narrative: Flannery O'Connor and the New Testament." Unpubl. diss., Vanderbilt, 1989.

Bowen, Rose. "Christology in the Works of Flannery O'Connor." *DAI* 45/9 (1984), 2874A.

Bryant, Hallman B. "Reading the Map in 'A Good Man Is Hard to Find.' " *Studies in Short Fiction* 18/3 (1981), 301-07. NT sources.

Eggenschwiler, David. *The Christian Humanism of Flannery O'Connor* (Detroit: Wayne State University Press, 1972).

Gallagher, Janet M. "Telling Stories about God: Narrative Voice and Epistemology in the Hebrew Bible and in the Fiction of Flannery O'Connor, Graham Greene, and Cynthia Ozick." Unpubl. diss., Fordham, 1990.

Linehan, Thomas M. "Anagogical Realism in Flannery O'Connor." *Renascence* 37/2 (1985), 80-95.

Wood, Ralph C. *The Comedy of Redemption: Christian Faith and Comic Vision in Four American Novelists* (Notre Dame: University of Notre Dame Press, 1991). Discusses O'Connor, Walker Percy, John Updike, and Peter De Vries.

See also T. D. Young under FAULKNER.

O'NEILL, EUGENE

Bowles, Patrick. "Another Biblical Parallel in *Desire under the Elms.*" *The Eugene O'Neill Newsletter* 2/3 (1979), 10-12. OT book of 1 Kings.

Hughes, Ann D. "Biblical Allusions in *The Hairy Ape.*" *The Eugene O'Neill Newsletter* 1/3 (1978), 7-9. OT and NT allusions.

McAleer, John J. "Christ Symbolism in *Anna Christi.*" *Modern Drama* 4/4 (1962), 389-96.

Shurr, William H. "American Drama and the Bible: The Case of Eugene O'Neill's *Lazarus Laughed.*" *The Bible and American Arts and Letters,* ed. Giles Gunn (Philadelphia: Fortress, 1983), 83-103. NT sources.

Tornqvist, Egil. "Jesus and Judas: On Biblical Allusions in O'Neill's Plays." *Etudes Anglaises* 24 (1971), 41-49. Fairly wide-ranging discussion of biblical echoes and allusions.

OWEN, WILFRED

Bartel, Roland. "Teaching Wilfred Owen's War Poems and the Bible." *English Journal* 61 (1972), 36-42. Specific reference to Gen. 22 and the Gospel of John.

Bouyssou, Roland. "Wilfred Owen's War Poetry and the Bible." *Caliban* (France) 19 (1982), 45-57. Influence of biblical apocalyptic literature.

Sinfield, Mark. "Wilfred Owen's 'Mental Cases': Source and Structure." *Notes and Queries* 29/4 (1982), 339-41.

OZICK, CYNTHIA

See J. M. Gallagher under O'CONNOR.

PERCY, WALKER

See R. C. Wood under O'CONNOR.

POE, EDGAR ALLAN

Campbell, Killis. "Poe's Knowledge of the Bible." *Studies in Philology* 27/3 (1930), 546-51.

Cheney, Patrick. "Poe's Use of *The Tempest* and the Bible in 'The Masque of the Red Death.'" *English Language Notes* 20/3-4 (1983), 31-39.

Forrest, William Mentzel. *Biblical Allusions in Poe* (New York: Macmillan, 1928). Series of appendices and indices provide helpful keys to allusions and references.

Smith, C. A. "Poe and the Bible." *Davidson College Magazine* 36 (1920), 1-4.

———. "Poe and the Bible." *Biblical Review* 5 (1920), 354-65.

Tucker, D. "'The Tell-Tale Heart and the 'Evil Eye.'" *Southern Literary Journal* 13/2 (1981), 92-98. Source in Gen. 18.

Zanger, Jules. "'The Pit and the Pendulum' and American Revivalism." *Religion in Life* 49/1 (1980), 96-105.

POPE, ALEXANDER

Bedford, Emmett G. "Biblical Typology and Related Forms of Christian Symbolism in the Poetry of Alexander Pope." *DAI* 31/7 (1970), 3495A. Typology, Christian symbolism, and structure.

Griffin, Robert. "Pope, the Prophets, and *The Dunciad.*" *Studies in English Literature* 23/3 (1983), 435-46.

Knuth, Deborah Jane. "*The Dunciad* and the Old Testament." *DAI* 41/11 (1980) 4721A. Importance of OT allusions.

Tichy, Henrietta. *The Bible in the Poetry of Pope and Swift* (New York: New York University, 1947). Examples and illustrations of biblical influence in both writers, with a consideration of the nature of that influence.

Zomberg, P. G. "The Biblical Source for Pope's Messiah." *Notes and Queries* 20/1 (1973), 4-7.

PYNCHON, THOMAS

Price, Ruby Victoria. "Christian Allusions in the Novels of Thomas Pynchon." *DAI* 40/3 (1979), 1472A. Pynchon's use of biblical and Christian allusion in *V* and *Gravity's Rainbow.*

Simons, John. "Third Story Man: Biblical Irony in Thomas Pynchon's 'Entropy.'" *Studies in Short Fiction* 14 (1977), 88-93. Ironic use of Acts 20.

QUARLES, FRANCIS

Taylor, Kenneth Lee. "Francis Quarles and the Renaissance Heroic-Biblical Poem: A Study of *A Feast for Wormes, Hadassa, Iob Militant,* and *The Historie of Samson.*" *DAI* 32/4 (1971), 2070A-71A.

RICHARDSON, SAMUEL

Wooten, Elizabeth Harper. "Biblical Allusion in the Novels of Richardson." *DAI* 34/8 (1973), 5130A.

ROBINSON, EDWIN ARLINGTON

Ayo, Nicholas. "Robinson and the Bible." *DA* 27/2 (1966), 469A-70A.

Fussell, Edwin S. *Edwin Arlington Robinson: The Literary Background of a Traditional Poet* (Berkeley: University of California Press, 1954). See "The English Bible," pp. 155-70.

Satterfield, Leon. "Robinson's 'An Evangelist's Wife.'" *Explicator* 41/3 (1983), 36-37. Connections with David and Michal story in 2 Samuel.

See also E. J. McGregor under DICKINSON.

ROSSETTI, CHRISTINA

Breme, M. Ignatia. *Christina Rossetti und der Einfluss der Bibel auf ihre Dichtung* (Münster: H. Schöningh, 1907). Rich selection of quotations and allusions throughout, especially in sections entitled "Die religiöse Dichtung Christina Rossettis in ihrem inneren Verhaltnis zur Bibel" and "Der stilistische Einfluss der Bibel auf Christina Rossetti."

Jimenez, Nilda, comp. *The Bible and the Poetry of Christina Rossetti: A Concordance* (Westport: Greenwood Press, 1979). Based on the author's 1977 dissertation [S.U.N.Y., Albany].

Wenger, Helen H. "The Influence of the Bible in Christina Rossetti's *Monna Innominata*." *Christian Scholar's Review* 3/1 (1973), 15-24. OT and NT sources.

ROSSETTI, DANTE GABRIEL

Bentley, D. M. "Religious Themes and Images in the Work of D. G. Rossetti." Unpubl. diss., King's College, London, 1975.

ROWLANDSON, MARY

Downing, David. "'Streams of Scripture Comfort': Mary Rowlandson's Typological Use of the Bible." *Early American Literature* 15 (1980-81), 252-59. Useful notes, including tables of scriptural allusions and echoes.

RUSKIN, JOHN

Arrowsmith, William. "Ruskin's Fireflies." *The Ruskin Polygon: Essays on the Imagination of John Ruskin*, ed. John Dixon Hunt and Faith M. Holland (Manchester: Manchester University Press, 1982), 198-235. Discusses biblical sources.

Burgess, William. *The Religion of Ruskin* (New York: Fleming H. Revell, 1907). Index lists biblical references.

Cook, E. T., and Alexander Wedderburn, eds. *The Works of John Ruskin* (London: George Allen; New York: Longmans, 1903-12), vol. 39. An extensive listing of biblical references in the index.

Gibbs, Mary, and Ellen Gibbs. *The Bible References of John Ruskin* (New York: Henry Frowde, 1898 [rpt. Folcroft, 1977]). References are listed according to biblical subject, alphabetically.

SALINGER, J. D.

Hamilton, Kenneth. "One Way to Use the Bible: The Example of J. D. Salinger." *Christian Scholar* 47 (1964), 243-51.

SANDBURG, CARL

Kolbe, Henry E. "Christ and Carl Sandburg." *Religion in Life* 28 (1959), 248-61.

Spitz, Leon. "Carl Sandburg's Bible Texts." *The American Hebrew* 158 (1948), 8, 13.

SCOTT, SIR WALTER

Dickson, Nicholas. *The Bible in Waverley, or Sir Walter Scott's Use of the Sacred Scriptures* (Edinburgh: Adam and Charles Black, 1884 [rpt. Folcroft, 1979]).

SHAKESPEARE, WILLIAM

Ackerman, Carl. *The Bible in Shakespeare* (Folcroft: Folcroft Library Editions, 1971). Biblical language, allusions, parallels.

Anderson, Douglas. "The Old Testament Presence in *The Merchant of Venice*." *English Literary History* 52/1 (1985), 119-32.

Battenhouse, Roy. "Shakespeare and the Bible." *Gordon Review* 8 (1964), 18-24.

Boose, Lynda E. "Othello's 'Chrysolite' and the Song of Songs Tradition." *Philological Quarterly* 60/4 (1981), 427-37.

Burgess, William. *The Bible in Shakespeare: A Study of the Relation of the Works of William Shakespeare to the Bible: With Numerous Parallel Passages, Quotations, References, Phrases and Allusions* (New York: Fleming H. Revell, 1903 [rpt. Haskell House, 1968]).

Burnet, R. A. L. "Shakespeare and the First Seven Chapters of the Genevan Job." *Notes and Queries* 29/2 (1982), 127-28. Echoes of Job in *Othello, Two Gentlemen of Verona, As You Like It,* and *Hamlet.*

————. "Shakespeare and the Marginalia of the Geneva Bible." *Notes and Queries* 26/2 (1979), 113-14. *Hamlet, Coriolanus, Cymbeline,* and *The Winter's Tale.*

————. "Some Echoes of the Genevan Bible in Shakespeare and Milton." *Notes and Queries* 27/2 (1980), 179-81. *Julius Caesar, Macbeth, Hamlet, Anthony and Cleopatra,* and *Paradise Lost.*

————. "Two Further Echoes of the Genevan Bible in Shakespeare and Milton." *Notes and Queries* 28/2 (1981), 129. *Hamlet* and *Samson Agonistes.*

Bryant, J. A. *Hippolyta's View: Some Christian Aspects of Shakespeare's Plays* (Lexington: University of Kentucky Press, 1961). Index lists biblical characters and books.

Bullock, Charles. *Shakespeare's Debt to the Bible* (Folcroft: Folcroft Editions, 1970). See especially "Shakespeare's biblical allusions . . ." and "Direct quotations of the leading truths of revelation."

Carter, Thomas. *Shakespeare and Holy Scripture* (New York: E. P. Dutton and Co., 1905).

Colie, Rosalie L. "The Energies of Endurance: Biblical Echo in *King Lear*." *Some Facets of King Lear: Essays in Prismatic Criticism,* ed. Rosalie L. Colie and F. T.

Flahiff (Toronto: University of Toronto Press, 1974), 117-44.

Cosgrove, Mark Francis. "Biblical, Liturgical, and Classical Allusions in *The Merchant of Venice*." *DAI* 31/7 (1971), 3498A.

Crannell, Philip W. "The Bible in Shakespeare." *Princeton Theological Review* 19/2 (1921), 309-30.

Eaton, Thomas Roy. *Shakespeare and the Bible: Showing How Much the Great Dramatist Was Indebted to Holy Writ for His Profound Knowledge of Human Nature* (London: James Blackwood, 1858).

Frye, Roland Mushat. *Shakespeare and Christian Doctrine* (Princeton: Princeton University Press, 1963).

Hassel, R. Chris, Jr. "Saint Paul and Shakespeare's Romantic Comedies." *Thought* 46 (1971), 371-88. Pauline allusions.

Knight, G. Wilson. *Shakespeare and Religion: Essays of Forty Years* (London: Routledge and Kegan Paul, 1967).

Landon, Antony. "Icon, Word and Paradox in *King Lear* and *Macbeth*." *Papers from the First Nordic Conference for English Studies, Oslo, 17-19 September, 1980,* ed. Stig Johansson and Byorn Tysdahl (Oslo: Institute for English Studies, University of Oslo, 1981), 109-33. Discusses biblical sources.

Lewalski, Barbara K. "Biblical Allusion and Allegory in *The Merchant of Venice*." *Shakespeare Quarterly* 13 (1962), 327-43. OT and NT.

McCombie, Frank. "*Measure for Measure* and the Epistle to the Romans." *New Blackfriars* 61 (1980), 276-85.

Matthews, Honor. *Character and Symbol in Shakespeare's Plays: A Study of Certain Christian and Pre-Christian Elements in their Structure and Imagery* (Cambridge: Cambridge University Press, 1962). Biblical names and motifs/events listed in index.

Milward, Peter. *Biblical Influences in Shakespeare's Great Tragedies* (Tokyo: Renaissance Institute, 1985 [rpt. Indiana University Press, 1987]). Catalogue of echoes, some critical discussion.

———. *Biblical Themes in Shakespeare — Centering on King Lear* (Tokyo: The Renaissance Institute, 1975). Thematic chapters include: "The heart of the mystery"; "In the beginning"; "The General Curse"; "Return of the Prodigal," etc.

———. *Shakespeare's Religious Background* (London: Sidgwick and Jackson; Bloomington: Indiana University Press, 1973). A biographical study intended "to ascertain precisely how far Shakespeare is influenced by Christian doctrine, and in what ways his dramatic and other work reflects the religious currents of his time. General index contains listing of biblical texts and figures.

Morris, Ivor. *Shakespeare's God: The Role of Religion in the Tragedies* (New York: St. Martin's, 1972).

Negata, Yoshiko. *Shakespeare's Underthought in the Later Plays* (Tokyo: Renaissance Institute, 1977). Discusses biblical and theological background.

Noble, Richmond. *Shakespeare's Biblical Knowledge and Use of the Book of Common Prayer* (London: S.P.C.K.; New York: Macmillan, 1935). Authoritative study; extensive and valuable indexes.

Roston, Murray. "Shakespeare and the Biblical Drama." *Iowa English Yearbook* 9 (1964), 36-43.

Schleiner, Louise. "Providential Improvisation in *Measure for Measure*." *Publications of the Modern Language Association of America* 97/2 (1982), 227-36. Biblical and theological background to the character of the Duke.

Shaheen, Naseeb. *Biblical References in Shakespeare's Tragedies* (London and Toronto: Associated University Presses, 1987). Contains indexes to Shakespeare's biblical references, references to the *Book of Common Prayer,* and references to the Official Homilies.

Sims, James H. "Some Biblical Light on Shakespeare's *Hamlet*." *Costerus* 6 (1972), 155-61.

Smith, Jonathan Clark. "Destiny Reversed: A Study of Biblical and Classical Allusion Patterns in Shakespeare's *Henry VI*." *DAI* 35/4 (1974), 2242A-43A.

Thompson, Stephen Paul. "Shakespeare and the Elizabethan St. Paul." Unpubl. diss., University of Iowa, 1990.

Westhoven, Morris. "Biblical Material in Shakespeare's Great Tragedies." *DAI* 31/11 (1970), 6026A-27A.

Wood, James O. "Shakespeare, *Pericles,* and the Genevan Bible." *Pacific Coast Philology* 12 (1977), 82-89.

See also J. H. Sims under MARLOWE.

SHAW, GEORGE BERNARD

Berst, Charles A. "In the Beginning: The Poetic Genesis of Shaw's God." *Shaw and Religion* 1. *Annual of Bernard Shaw Studies* (1981), 5-41. On biblical sources.

Carpenter, Charles A. "Shaw and Religion/Philosophy: A Working Bibliography." *Shaw and Religion* 1 (1981), 225-46.

Hoeveler, Diane Long. "Shaw's Vision of God in *Major Barbara*." *Independent Shavian* 17/1, 2 (1979), 16-18.

Nelson, Raymond S. "*Back to Methuselah:* Shaw's Modern Bible." *Costerus* 5 (1972), 117-23.

Stone, Susan C. "Biblical Myth Shavianized." *Modern Drama* 18 (1975), 153-63.

Talley, Jerry B. "Religious Themes in the Dramatic Works of George Bernard Shaw, T. S. Eliot, and Paul Claudel." *DA* 25/6 (1964), 3750.

SHELLEY, PERCY BYSSHE

Brisman, Leslie. "Mysterious Tongue: Shelley and the Language of Christianity." *Texas Studies in Language and Literature* 23/3 (1981), 389-417. NT parallels.

Fass, Barbara. "Shelley and St. Paul." *Concerning Poetry* 4/1 (1971), 23-24.

Shelley, Bryan Keith. "The Interpreting Angel: Shelley and Scripture." Unpubl. diss., University of Oxford, 1986.

Weaver, Bennett. *Toward the Understanding of Shelley* (New York: Octagon, 1966). Discussion of Shelley's views of the Bible, his biblical reading, and the influence of the Bible on his writing.

SIDNEY, PHILIP

Ray, Robert H. "Sidney's Astrophel and Stella." *Explicator* 41/3 (1983), 7-9. Biblical sources.

SINGER, ISAAC BASHEVIS

Hennings, Thomas. "Singer's 'Gimpel the Fool' and the Book of Hosea." *Journal of Narrative Technique* 13/1 (1983), 11-19.

Lee, Grace Farrell. "Isaac Bashevis Singer: Mediating Between the Biblical and the Modern." *Modern Language Studies* 15/4 (1985), 117-23.

Reyer, W. R. "Biblical Figures in Selected Short Fiction of Isaac Bashevis Singer." Unpubl. diss., Bowling Green State University, 1988.

SMART, CHRISTOPHER

Parish, Charles. "Christopher Smart's Knowledge of Hebrew." *Studies in Philology* 58 (1961), 516-32. Examines puns on names, biblical allusions, etc.

Strong, Hilda Gladys. "Christopher Smart's *Jubilate AGNO:* A Doomsday Poem." *DAI* 41/1 (1980), 265A. Argues that the A fragment is a nonchronological survey of the Bible, including the Apocrypha.

SPENSER, EDMUND

Baroway, Israel. "The Imagery of Spenser and the Song of Songs." *Journal of English and Germanic Philology* 33 (1934), 23-45.

Bulger, Thomas F. "Classical Vision and Christian Revelation: Spenser's Use of Mythology in Book I of *The Faerie Queene.*" *Greyfriar* 23 (1982), 5-25.

Farukhl, Suraiya. "Pagan-Christian Typology in Spenser's *Faerie Queene.*" *DAI* 36 (1975), 6700A.

Fishman, Sylvia Barack. "The Watered Garden and the Bride of God: Patterns of Biblical Imagery in Poems of Spenser, Milton, and Blake." *DAI* 41/3 (1980), 1063A.

Guy, William Harvey. "Spenser's Use of the Bible in Books One and Two of *The Faerie Queene.*" *DAI* 37/11 (1977), 7141A-42A.

Hankins, John E. "Spenser and the Revelation of St. John." *Publications of the Modern Language Association of America* 60 (1945), 364-81.

Landrum, Grace Warren. "Spenser's Use of the Bible and his Alleged Puritanism." *Publications of the Modern Language Association of America* 41 (1926), 517-44.

Appendix lists Spenser's biblical references and allusions.

Maltby, J. E. *Spenser's Use of the Bible in the Faerie Queene, Books I and II* (Seattle: University of Washington Press, 1926).

Russell, I. Willis. "Biblical Echoes in [Spenser's] Mother Hubberd's Tale." *Modern Language Notes* 44/3 (1929), 162-64.

Shaheen, Naseeb. *Biblical References in The Faerie Queene* (Memphis: Memphis State University Press, 1976).

————. "Spenser and the New Testament." *American Notes and Queries* 10/1 (1971), 4-5. Discusses the version used by Spenser.

STEINBECK, JOHN

Brasch, James D. "The Grapes of Wrath and Old Testament Scepticism." *San Jose Studies* 3/2 (1977), 16-27.

Cannon, Gerard. "The Pauline Apostleship of Tom Joad." *College English* 24/3 (1962), 222-24.

Carlson, Eric W. "Symbolism in *The Grapes of Wrath.*" *College English* 19/4 (1958), 172-75. Discusses biblical analogues.

Crockett, H. Kelly. "The Bible and *The Grapes of Wrath.*" *College English* 24/3 (1962), 193-99. Biblical parallels.

————. "The Other Cheek." *College English* 24/7 (1963), 567. A response to Dunn, below.

Dunn, Thomas F. "The Grapes of Wrath." *College English* 24/7 (1963), 566-67. Discusses OT analogues.

Hamby, James A. "Steinbeck's Biblical Vision: 'Breakfast' and the Nobel Acceptance Speech." *Western Review* 10/1 (1973), 57-59. OT and NT.

Lisca, Peter. *The Wide World of John Steinbeck* (New Brunswick, NJ: Rutgers University Press, 1958). Includes a chapter on biblical background to *The Grapes of Wrath.*

McDaniel, Barbara. "Alienation in *East of Eden:* The 'Chart of the Soul.'" *Steinbeck Quarterly* 14 (1981), 32-39. Discusses biblical sources.

Proctor-Murphy, Jeffrey Michael. "John Steinbeck's Use of Biblical Imagery in *The Grapes of Wrath:* American Dreams and Realities Examined." Unpubl. diss., School of Theology at Claremont, 1989.

Shockley, Martin. "Christian Symbolism in *The Grapes of Wrath.*" *College English* 18/2 (1956), 87-90.

Slade, Leonard A., Jr. "The Use of Biblical Allusions in *The Grapes of Wrath.*" *College Language Association Journal* 11/3 (1968), 241-47.

STERNE, LAWRENCE

Harries, Elizabeth W. "Sterne's Novels: Gathering Up the Fragments." *Journal of English Language History* 49/1 (1982), 35-49. NT background.

STEVENS, WALLACE

Ingalls, Jeremy. "The Poetry of Wallace Stevens: Christian Context." *Religion in Life* 31 (1961), 118-30.

STEVENSON, ROBERT LOUIS

Kelman, John. *The Faith of Robert Louis Stevenson* (Edinburgh and London: Oliphant, Anderson, and Ferrier, 1912).

STOWE, HARRIET BEECHER

Miller, Eleanor Aileen. "The Christian Philosophy in the New England Novels of Harriet Beecher Stowe." *DAI* 32/1 (1971), 445A.

Smylie, James H. "*Uncle Tom's Cabin* Revisited: The Bible, the Romantic Imagination, and the Sympathies of Christ." *Interpretation* 27/1 (1973), 67-85.

STYRON, WILLIAM

Cash, Jean W. "Styron's Use of the Bible in *The Confessions of Nat Turner.*" *Resources for American Literary Study* 12/2 (1982), 134-42.

SWIFT, JONATHAN

Beaumont, Charles Allen. *Swift's Use of the Bible: A Documentation and a Study in Allusion* (Athens: University of Georgia Press, 1965). Important early study.

Daw, C. P. "Swift's Favorite Books of the Bible." *Huntington Library Quarterly* 43/3 (1980), 201-12.

Jacobs, Edward C. "Echoes of Micah in Swift's *Modest Proposal.*" *Eire-Ireland* 13/3 (1978), 49-53.

Jacobson, Richard. "A Biblical Allusion in *Gulliver's Travels.*" *Notes and Queries* 17/8 (1970), 286-87.

Korshin, Paul J. "Swift and Typological Narrative in *A Tale of a Tub.*" *The Interpretation of Narrative: Theory and Practice,* ed. Morton W. Bloomfield (Cambridge: Harvard University Press, 1970), 67-91.

———. "Swift and Satirical Typology in *A Tale of a Tub.*" *Studies in the Eighteenth Century,* ed. F. Brissenden (Toronto: University of Toronto Press, 1973), 2.279-302.

Morrissey, L. J. *Gulliver's Progress* (Hamden: Archon Books, 1978). An examination of the relationship between the dates in *Gulliver's Travels* and the appropriate prayers and scriptural readings from the *Book of Common Prayer.*

See also H. Tichy under POPE.

TAYLOR, EDWARD

Benton, Robert M. "Edward Taylor's Use of his Text." *American Literature* 39/1 (1967), 31-41.

Davis, Thomas M. "Edward Taylor and the Traditions of Puritan Typology." *Early American Literature* 4/3 (1970), 27-47.

Hammond, Jeffrey A. "A Puritan *Ars Moriendi:* Edward Taylor's Late Meditations on the Song of Songs." *Early American Literature* 17/3 (1982-83), 191-214. Valuable notes.

———. "Reading Taylor Exegetically: The *Preparatory Meditations* and the Commentary Tradition." *Texas Studies in Language and Literature* 24/4 (1982), 347-71.

Keller, Karl. " 'The World Slickt Up in Types': Edward Taylor as a Version of Emerson." *Early American Literature* 5/1 (1970), pt. 1, 124-40.

Reiter, Robert E. "Poetry and Typology: Edward Taylor's *Preparatory Meditations,* Second Series, Nos. 1-30." *Early American Literature* 5/1 (1970), pt. 1, 111-23.

Rowe, Karen E. "A Biblical Illumination of Taylorian Art." *American Literature* 40/3 (1968), 370-74.

St. John, Raymond Alvin. "Biblical Quotation in Edward Taylor's *Preparatory Meditations.*" *DAI* 36/10 (1975), 6690A.

Stanford, Donald E. "Edward Taylor" (Minneapolis: University of Minnesota Press, 1965). Essay pamphlet, discusses biblical influence on Taylor's poems, 22-25.

Wiley, Elizabeth. "Sources of Imagery in the Poetry of Edward Taylor." *DAI* 23/6 (1962), 2122A-23A. See especially chap. 5, on the Bible.

See also P. L. Steiner under COTTON.

TAYLOR, JEREMY

Herndon, Sarah. *The Use of the Bible in Jeremy Taylor's Works* (New York: New York University Press, 1949).

TENNYSON, ALFRED LORD

Burton, Thomas Glen. "Tennyson's Use of Biblical Allusions." *DA* 27/3 (1966), 742A.

Robinson, Edna Moore. *Tennyson's Use of the Bible* (Baltimore: J. H. Furst Co., 1917 [rpt. 1968]). Tennyson's use of Scripture is seen to reflect "the successive and orderly stages of his artistic and poetic development."

Van Dyke, Henry. *The Poetry of Tennyson* (New York: Scribner's, 1911). Appendix gives biblical references and allusions.

———. *Studies in Tennyson* (New York: Charles Scribner's Sons, 1920). See pp. 187-213, "The Bible in Tennyson."

THOMAS, DYLAN

Kidder, Rushworth Moulton. "Religious Imagery in the Poetry of Dylan Thomas." *DAI* 33/1 (1969), 316A. Brief reference to biblical allusions.

Lander, Clara. "With Welsh and Reverent Rook: The Biblical Element in Dylan Thomas." *Queen's Quarterly* 65/3 (1958), 437-47. The Welsh Bible and the Writings of Thomas.

THOREAU, HENRY DAVID

Burns, John Robert. "Thoreau's Use of the Bible." *DA*

27/11 (1966), 3864A. Thoreau's biblical allusions and references listed, 82-226.

Ensor, Allison. "Thoreau and the Bible — Preliminary Considerations." *Emerson Society Quarterly* 33/4 (1963), 65-70.

Harding, Walter, and Michael Meyer. *The New Thoreau Handbook* (New York: New York University Press, 1980). The influence of the Bible on Thoreau, 100, 117.

Jacobs, Edward C. "The Bible in *Walden:* Further Additions." *Studies in the American Renaissance* (1983), 297-302. Addenda to item below.

Long, Larry R. "The Bible and the Composition of *Walden.*" *Studies in the American Renaissance* (1979), 309-53. Useful indexes.

———. "Thoreau's Portmanteau Biblical Allusions." *Thoreau Journal Quarterly* 11/3-4 (1979), 49-53.

———. "*Walden* and the Bible: A Study in Influence and Composition." *DAI* 37/11 (1977), 7130A. Comprehensive list of biblical quotations, allusions, and echoes.

Miller, Perry. "Thoreau in the Context of International Romanticism." *Nature's Nation* (Cambridge: Harvard University Press, 1967), 175-83. Discusses influence of typology and hermeneutics.

TREVISA, JOHN

Fowler, David C. "John Trevisa and the English Bible." *Modern Philology* 58 (1960), 81-98.

TWAIN, MARK

Brodwin, Stanley. "The Theology of Mark Twain: Banished Adam and the Bible." *Mississippi Quarterly* 29/2 (1976), 167-89.

Cracroft, Richard H. "The Gentle Blasphemer: Mark Twain, Holy Scripture, and the Book of Mormon." *Brigham Young University Studies* 11/2 (1971), 119-40.

Ensor, Allison. *Mark Twain and the Bible* (Lexington: University of Kentucky Press, 1969). Based on the author's Indiana dissertation, 1965.

McCullough, Joseph B. "Uses of the Bible in *Huckleberry Finn.*" *Mark Twain Journal* 19/3 (1979), 2-3. OT and NT.

McDermott, J. F. "Mark Twain and the Bible." *Papers on Language and Literature* 4/2 (1968), 195-98. Biographical emphasis.

Millichap, J. F. "Calvinistic Attitudes and Pauline Imagery in *The Adventures of Huckleberry Finn.*" *Mark Twain Journal* 16 (1971-72), 8-10.

Pochman, Henry August. "The Mind of Mark Twain." Unpubl. M.A. thesis, University of Texas, 1924. Provides a list of allusions, including biblical, in Twain's works.

Rees, Robert A. "Mark Twain and the Bible: Characters Who Use the Bible and Biblical Characters." *DA* 28/2 (1966), 692A.

Reimer, Earl A. "Mark Twain and the Bible: An Inductive Study." *DAI* 31/7 (1970), 3560A. Includes a concordance of over 3,000 biblical allusions.

UPDIKE, JOHN

See R. C. Wood under O'CONNOR.

VAUGHAN, HENRY

Dale, James. "Biblical Allusion in Vaughan's 'The World.'" *English Studies* 51/4 (1970), 336-39. Epistle of 1 John and Revelation.

Duvall, Robert. "The Biblical Character of Henry Vaughan's *Silex Scintillans.*" *Pacific Coast Philology* 6 (1971), 13-19. Biblical allusion as integral part of Vaughan's poetics.

Gregory, E. R. "A Grove of Stately Height Undescryed: The Bible and Henry Vaughan's 'Regeneration.'" *Christianity and Literature* 30/4 (1981), 63-74.

WEBSTER, JOHN

See F. J. Bennett under CHAPMAN.

WARREN, ROBERT PENN

Beebe, Keith. "Biblical Motifs in *All the King's Men.*" *Journal of Bible and Religion* 30/2 (1962), 123-30. OT allusions.

Watkins, Floyd C. "The Ungodly in Robert Penn Warren's Biblical Poems." *Southern Literary Journal* 15/3 (1983), 34-46.

WHITMAN, WALT

Allen, Gay Wilson. "Biblical Echoes in Whitman's Works." *American Literature* 6/3 (1934), 302-15. Detailed examination of biblical echoes.

Bergquist, Bruce Allen. "Walt Whitman and the Bible: Language Echoes, Images, Allusions, and Ideas." *DAI* 40/6 (1979), 3296A.

Engel, Wilson F., III. "Two Biblical Echoes in 'Crossing Brooklyn Ferry.'" *Walt Whitman Review* 23 (1977), 88-90. Proverbs 27, 1 Corinthians 13.

Gohdes, Clarence. "A Note on Whitman's Use of the Bible as Model." *Modern Language Quarterly* 2 (1941), 105-08.

Hays, Will. "The Birth of a Bible." *Texas Review* 8 (1923), 21-31. The influence of the Bible on Whitman's works.

Posey, Meredith N. "Whitman's Debt to the Bible, with Special Reference to the Origins of his Rhythm." Unpubl. diss., University of Texas at Austin, 1938.

Spitz, Leon. "Walt Whitman and Judaism." *Chicago Jewish Forum* 13 (1955), 174-77.

Steadman, John M. "Whitman and the King James Bible." *Notes and Queries* 3/12 (1956), 538-39. Whitman's use of the Dedicatory Epistle to the KJV.

WHITTIER, JAMES GREENLEAF

Jackson, S. Trevena. "Whittier's Use of the Bible." *Christian Advocate* 82 (1907), 1963-2015.

Stevens, James Stacy. *Whittier's Use of the Bible* (Orono: Maine University Press, 1930). Valuable introduction, with table of biblical allusions. Index of passages and of poems.

WORDSWORTH, WILLIAM

Avni, Abraham. "Overlooked Biblical Allusions in Wordsworth." *Notes and Queries* 20/2 (1973), 43-44. Allusions in "It is a Beauteous Evening."

———. "Wordsworth and Ecclesiastes: A 'Skeptical' Affinity." *Research Studies* 49/1 (1981), 66-71. OT sources for 'An Evening Walk.'

Barth, J. Robert. "A Moment on a Mountaintop." *Literature and Belief* 2 (1982), 51-53. NT sources of "Lines Composed a Few Miles Above Tintern Abbey."

Brown, Edith M. "The Influence of the Bible on Wordsworth's Diction." Unpubl. diss., Cornell, 1934.

Levinson, Marjorie. "Spiritual Economics: A Reading of Wordsworth's 'Michael.'" *English Literary History* 52/3 (1985), 707-31. "The function of the poem's sustained biblical allusion" — the Abraham and Isaac story. KATHERINE B. JEFFREY